Biographical Dictionary *of* Central *and* Eastern Europe *in the* Twentieth Century

Biographical Dictionary *of* Central *and* Eastern Europe *in the* Twentieth Century

Edited by

Wojciech Roszkowski
and Jan Kofman

M.E.Sharpe
Armonk, New York
London, England

The EuroSlavic fonts used to create this work are © 1986–2002 Payne Loving Trust.
EuroSlavic is available from Linguist's Software, Inc.,
www.linguistsoftware.com, P.O. Box 580, Edmonds, WA 98020-0580 USA
tel (425) 775-1130.

Library of Congress Cataloging-in-Publication Data

Slownik biograficzny Europy Srodkowo-Wschodniej XX wieku. English.
  Biographical dictionary of Central and Eastern Europe in the twentieth century / edited by
Wojciech Roszkowski and Jan Kofman.
     p. cm.
  Includes bibliographical references and index.
  ISBN 978-0-7656-1027-0 (cloth : alk. paper)
  1. Europe, Eastern—Biography—Dictionaries. I. Title: Biographical dictionary of Central
and Eastern Europe in the 20th century. II. Roszkowski, Wojciech. III. Kofman, Jan. IV. Title.

CT765.S59 2006
920.0409171′70904—dc22   2005031305

Printed in the United States of America

IBT (c)   10   9   8   7   6   5   4   3   2   1

Contents

Preface

This biographical dictionary has its own history. I started working on it nearly two decades ago, when the collapse of the communist empire in Central and Eastern Europe appeared imminent. The idea was born out of my reflection on the poor knowledge of the history and culture of Poland's neighbors in the "Lands Between"—the name given to the region between the uniting Europe and the Russian core of the Soviet empire by British historian Alan Parker. At that time, ignorance of the history of Central and Eastern Europe was evident not only in the West but perhaps even more so in the nations of the region, which were neighbors and belonged to one political bloc but were nonetheless isolated from one another. The thought of an increasingly likely political reorganization of the Lands Between occurred to me as early as the 1980s, partly under the influence of interwar "Promethean" ideas (decay of the Soviet Union into nation-states) and partly as a result of my observations of the deepening crisis of the Soviet empire. I believed that this kind of dictionary might play an important role in filling the information gaps and providing the knowledge necessary to build bridges between these nations—and between them and the rest of the world—in the future.

As the pace of history accelerated in the late 1980s and the early 1990s, I had many other things to keep me busy. Nevertheless, in the mid-1990s I decided to fulfill my original plan to make the twentieth-century history of the region more accessible to people through biographical notes on its key figures, because what interests me most in history, even in macro-scale history, is the fate of individuals. I was assisted in my work by the Central and Eastern Europe Department (*Zakład Europy rodkowej i Wschodniej*) of the Institute of Political Studies of the Polish Academy of Sciences (*Instytut Studiów Politycznych Polskiej Akademii Nauk* [ISP PAN]) and some of its other staff. We gradually secured the cooperation of additional authors from outside the Institute, and even outside Poland. Their names are given in alphabetical order, regardless of how many entries they wrote—some contributed over a hundred entries, and others wrote only one or two.

It was a great challenge to form a team of competent authors who would abide by the formal requirements and keep the deadlines. Editing the texts was another challenge. It is well known that the quality of dictionaries and encyclopedias to a large extent depends on careful attention to detail in terms of content and form. In the case of such a complicated matter as the modern history of a dozen or so nations using well over dozen languages, it was a very difficult task indeed. I had the first go at editing and was aware that I needed assistance in finding errors and mistakes in terms of substance, style, and form. Despite initial hesitation because of the size of the dictionary and numerous traps in the submitted texts, Professor Jan Kofman, Ph.D., known for his thoroughness and conscientiousness as well as for his excellent eye for linguistic abuse, finally agreed to be the second editor. The scale of Professor Kofman's editorial contribution to the final shape of the texts led me to persuade him to accept the role of co-editor of the whole dictionary.

We initially planned to establish a network of authors and editors from all the countries of the region, but that proved impractical; therefore, with some noteworthy exceptions, this dictionary was compiled and written mainly by Polish authors. Of course, the Polish perspective might seem one-sided, particularly in the case of countries that are Poland's neighbors. Therefore, objective presentation of the history of particular nations was another great challenge to the authors and editors of this dictionary. We might not have reached the ideal but it is worth keeping in mind how difficult the task was. We may not have satisfied proponents of radical views, but we believe that extreme views in historiography sow discord and are dangerous.

Preparing the list of entries was yet another challenge. There are numerous biographical dictionaries for particular countries of the region, varying in size and the degree of detail, so it was difficult to follow any particular model. We decided to focus on politicians, but we could not omit the main representatives of culture, because the social role of eminent artists or clergymen often surpassed that of politicians. However, we did not include sport or pop culture celebrities, except for representatives of art cinema. The reason for this was that we could not just add only a few representative figures of this kind from each country, and if we had included them all, the dictionary would have become even vaster.

Proportionate coverage of various countries was another question. We agreed that the larger countries should have more entries; however, irrespective of their population, we adopted a certain minimum for nations with their own statehood, even if only transitional. Some characters were linked with more than one country: the dictionary includes Hungarians from Transylvania and Slovakia, Ukrainians from Galicia, Albanians from Kosovo, and Jews from various countries and of varying degrees of assimilation. The size of each biographical entry depends on the importance of the person, but we often allowed some adjustments, taking into account the span of their life or the availability of biographical sources.

The term "Central and Eastern Europe" must be explained. It has been and still is interpreted in various ways. In fact there is no consensus as to its geographical or political extent, and the understanding of this notion has also changed quite a bit over time. In this dictionary we adopted the broadest definition, the concept of the "Lands Between," which generally corresponds to the European territory under communist rule after 1945. We excluded Germany, Austria, Russia, Finland, and Greece; we included the European countries that after World War II became satellites of the Soviet Union, as well as the European Soviet republics, which, in our opinion, differ from Russia culturally. The region covered in the dictionary is thus immensely varied historically, socially, economically, ethnically, and religiously; yet, it is precisely this diversity that defines the specific character of the area.

In this dictionary we tried to minimize evaluations. Nonetheless, the reader will certainly notice our critical attitude toward authoritarian, and particularly totalitarian, regimes. The authors and editors of this work cherish the rule of law, human rights, and the rights of national minorities, and value consistency of words and deeds. We also appreciate justified national interests. However, this biographical dictionary is neither a critical study nor a polemic; what the reader will find here is a reference work.

It is difficult to discuss in this short preface all the editorial principles adopted for the entries. The formal principles need no explanation. However, the use of some terms should be explained. For example, the reader may notice that the term "politician" is used for political figures in pluralist, or even authoritarian, systems, whereas in the case of communist regimes we generally use the term "political activist." We believe that the great majority of such persons served as functionaries of the system rather than as independent politicians. The term "post-communist" is to be understood as denoting affiliation with a movement or party that historically is rooted in a communist party and chose to preserve most of its communist legacy in the new situation after 1989.

Work on this dictionary lasted about five years. It could never have been completed without the support of the ISP PAN. In its research plans, the ISP PAN always provided funds for salaries and small fees for the authors, and the directors of the ISP PAN were invariably supportive of our work. Thus, credit for the completion of the dictionary in large part goes to the ISP PAN. However, I should also mention my two years with the Chair of Polish Studies at the University of Virginia in Charlottesville (2000–2002), where I compiled much material for the dictionary and wrote and edited a few hundred entries. Our thanks also go to Ms. Jolanta Kowalczuk, the Polish editor of the dictionary; to Rytm, the Warsaw-based publishers that took up the difficult task of publishing the work in Poland; to Ms. Marzena Zamłyńska, who translated most of the biographical entries into English; and to Dr. Marek Chodakiewicz, who is a contributor to the dictionary and assisted me in my work while I was in the United States. Our special thanks go to Professor Aleksander Manterys for his help with the East European type fonts used in the dictionary.

Wojciech Roszkowski

About the Editors

Wojciech Roszkowski is Full Professor of History at the Institute of Political Studies, Polish Academy of Sciences (IPS PAS), and the Warsaw School of Economics. He is also a Lecturer at the Collegium Civitas in Warsaw. He earlier served as Prorector of the Warsaw School of Economics (1990–93), Director of IPS PAS (1994–2000), a Wilson Center Fellow (1988), Visiting Professor at the University of Maryland, College Park (1989), and Kościuszko Chair of Polish Studies at the University of Virginia (2000–2). He is a specialist on the recent history of Poland and East Central Europe. Among his publications are *Landowners in Poland 1918–39* (East European Monographs/Columbia University Press, 1991), *Contemporary History of Poland 1914–1993* (in Polish; PWN, 1995; first published underground 1982–86), and (with Jan Kofman) *Transformation and Post-Communism* (in Polish; IPS PAS, 1999). Since 2004 he has been a member of the European Parliament.

Jan Kofman is Full Professor of History at the Institute of Political Studies, Polish Academy of Sciences, and the Uniwersytet Podlaski in Białystok. He is also a Lecturer at the Collegium Civitas in Warsaw. Dr. Kofman was Editor-in-Chief of the underground quarterly *Krytyka* (1982–94) and a participant in the Round-Table Talks in 1989. He served as Editor-in-Chief (1990–99) and Director (1998–99) of the Wydawnictwo Naukowe PWN Press in Warsaw. A specialist on the contemporary history of Poland and East Central Europe, he is the author of *Economic Nationalism and Development. Central and Eastern Europe between the Two World Wars* (Westview, 1997) and coauthor (with Wojciech Roszkowski) of *Transformation and Post-Communism* (in Polish; IPS PAS, 1999).

List of Contributors

Signed entries were authored by the following contibutors:

AB	Adam Burakowski, M.A., IPS PAS
AF	Andrzej Friszke, Professor, IPS PAS
AG	Aleksander Gubrynowicz, Ph.D., IPS PAS
AGr	Andrzej Grajewski, Ph.D., Institute of National Remembrance, Warsaw
AO	Agnieszka Orzelska, Ph.D., IPS PAS
AP	Andrzej Paczkowski, Professor, IPS PAS
AS	Alena Stryalkova, M.A., Belarus
ASK	Alicja Sowińska-Krupka, Ph.D., IPS PAS
AW	Artur Wołek, Ph.D., IPS PAS
BB	Bogusława Berdychowska, M.A., Centre for Eastern Studies, Warsaw
DP	Duncan M. Perry, Ph.D., University of Scranton, PA
DT	Dariusz Tołczyk, Professor, University of Virginia, Charlottesville, VA
EJ	Eriks Jekabsons, Ph.D., Riga, Latvia
EM	Eugeniusz Mironowicz, Professor, University of Podlasie, Białystok
FA	Florin Anghel, Ph,D, Bucharest, Romania
GG	Grzegorz Gromadzki, M.A., Centre for Eastern Studies, Warsaw
GM	Grzegorz Motyka, Ph.D., IPS PAS
IS	Inka Słodkowska, Ph. D., IPS PAS
JD	Józef Darski, Ph.D., Warsaw
JH	Joanna Hyndle, M.A., Centre for Eastern Studies, Warsaw
JJ	Jerzy Jackowicz, Professor, IPS PAS
JK	Jan Kofman, Professor, IPS PAS
JS	Jerzy Stańczyk, Ph.D., IPS PAS
JT	Janós Tischler, Ph.D. former Director, Hungarian Institute in Warsaw
JW	Yordan Vasiliev, Professor emeritus, Sofia, Bulgaria
LW	Lech Wojciechowski, M.A., IPS PAS
MC	Marek Chodkiewicz, Professor, Institute of World Politics, Washington, D.C.
MG	Mateusz Gniazdowski, Ph.D., Ministry of Foreign Affairs, Warsaw
MK	Miryna Kutysz, M.A., Centre for Eastern Studies, Warsaw
MS	Maciej Szymanowski, Ph.D., Director of Polish Institute, Budapest, Hungary
PC	Paulina Codogni, M.A., IPS PAS
PK	Paweł Kowal, M.A., IPS PAS
PU	Paweł Ukielski, M.A., IPS PAS
SA	Siarhiy Ausiannik, M.A., Belarus
TC	Tadeusz Czekalski, Ph.D., Jagiellonian University, Cracow
TD	Tadeusz Dubicki, Professor, University of Łódź
TS	Tomasz Stryjek, Ph.D., IPS PAS
TSt	Tomasz Strzembosz, late Professor, IPS PAS
WD	Waldemar Dziak, Professor, IPS PAS
WDj	Vera Deyanova, Lecturer, University of Sofia, Bulgaria
WR	Wojciech Roszkowski, Professor, IPS PAS
ZS	Zbigniew Stawrowski, Ph.D., IPS PAS

Institutional Abbreviations

ASSR	Antonomous Soviet Socialist Republic
CC	Central Committee
Cheka	Extraordinary Commission for Combating Counterrevolution and Sabotage
CMEA	Council for Mutual Economic Assistance
CPSU	Communist Party of the Soviet Union
CSCE	Conference on Security and Cooperation in Europe
DEMOS	Democratic Opposition of Slovenia
GRU	Main Intelligence Administration (Military)
KGB	Committee for State Security (from 1954)
MGB	Ministry for State Security (from 1946)
MVD	Ministry of Internal Affairs (from 1946)
NATO	North Atlantic Treaty Organization
NKGB	People's Commissariat for State Security (3 February 1941–20 July 1941; and 1943–1946)
NKVD	People's Commissariat of Internal Affairs (1934–1946)
NSZZ	Self-Governing Trade Union (Solidarity)
OGPU	Unified State Political Directorate
OSCE	Organization for Security and Cooperation in Europe
PRL	People's Republic of Poland
RKP(b)	Russian Communist Party (Bolshevik)
RSDWP	Russian Social Democratic Workers' Party
RSFSR	Russian Soviet Federative Socialist Republic
SSR	Soviet Socialist Republic
UN	United Nations
USSR	Union of Soviet Socialist Republics
VKP(b)	All-Union Communist Party (Bolshevik)

Source Abbreviations

Annuario Pontificio	*Annuario pontificio per l'anno (Pontificial yearbook).* Rome: Tipografia poliglotta vaticana.
Biographisches Lexikon	*Biographisches Lexikon zur Geschichte Südosteuropas,* eds. Mathias Bernath and Felix v. Schroeder, vols. 1–4. Munich: Oldenbourg, 1976–1981.
Bugajski	Janusz Bugajski, *Political Parties of Eastern Europe. A Guide to Politics in the Post-Communist Era.* Armonk, N.Y.: M.E. Sharpe, 2002.
ČBS	*Český biografický slovník XX století,* Encyklopedicky institut CSAV. Prague: Akademia, 1999.
EL	*Encyclopedia Lituanica,* vols. 1–4, Boston: J.Kapočius, 1970–1978.
Kunert	Andrzej Krzysztof Kunert, ed., *Słownik biograficzny konspiracji warszawskiej 1939–1944,* vols. 1–3. Warsaw: PAX, 1987–1991.
Lazitch	Branko Lazitch, ed., *Biographical Dictionary of the Comintern,* Stanford: Hoover Institution Press, 1973.
MERSH	Joseph L. Wieczynski, ed., *Modern Encyclopedia of Russian and Soviet History,* vols. 1–59. Gulf Breeze, Fla.: Academic International Press, 1976–1996.
Mołdawa	Tadeusz Mołdawa, *Ludzie władzy 1944–1991.* Warsaw: Wydawnictwo Naukowe PWN, 1991.
Polacy w historii . . .	*Polacy w historii i kulturze krajów Europy Zachodniej. Słownik biograficzny.* Poznań: Instytut Zachodni, 1981.
Posłowie . . .	*Posłowie i senatorowie Rzeczypospolitej Polski 1919–1939. Słownik biograficzny,* vol. I, Warsaw: Wydawnictwo Sejmowe, 1998.
PSB	*Polski Słownik Biograficzny.*
SBS	Vladimír Mináč et al., eds., *Slovenský Biografický Slovník: Od roku 833 do roku 1990.* Martin: Matica Slovenska, 1986–1994.

Note: Names mentioned in boldface type have their own entries in the dictionary.

Biographical Dictionary *of* Central *and* Eastern Europe *in the* Twentieth Century

A

ABAKANOWICZ Magdalena (20 June 1930, Falenty, near Warsaw), Polish artist. Abakanowicz studied in Gdańsk and Warsaw, where she graduated from the Academy of Fine Arts in 1954. She took part in the First Tapestry Biennial in Lausanne, Switzerland, in 1963, which helped her get a scholarship from the French government. While in France she studied the traditional art of weaving in the Gobelin style. After returning to Poland she started to create and exhibit original spatial tapestries, soon called the *abakans*. A gold medal at the Second Tapestry Biennial in Lausanne and a grand prix at the São Paolo Biennale in Brazil in 1965 opened the way to an international career. From the late 1960s Abakanowicz exhibited in the most prestigious galleries throughout the world, from Amsterdam and Stockholm to Venice and New York. In the early 1970s she concentrated on sculpting human figures ("Heads," 1973, and "Alterations," 1974), in the 1980s she partly returned to traditional sculpting ("War Games," 1987), and in the 1990s she developed the idea of "arboreal art," aiming at a transformation of the human habitat. In 1999 she received the prestigious Leonardo da Vinci Award, granted by the World Cultural Council. (WR)

Sources: *Wielka encyklopedia powszechna (PWN)*, vol. 1 (Warsaw, 2001); *Contemporary Artists* (Chicago and London, 1987); *The Dictionary of Art*, vol. 1 (London, 1996); Barbara Rose, *Magdalena Abakanowicz* (New York, 1994); *Magdalena Abakanowicz* (Warsaw, 1995).

ABDIĆ Fikret (29 September 1939, Dolni Vidovec, Bosnia), Bosnian political and economic activist. Born into a Muslim family, Abdić made a career in the Communist Party. In the mid-1980s he was involved in a huge financial scandal, when it appeared that Agrokomerc, the company of which he was the director, had drafted unprotected bills of exchange. The collapse of "Agrokomerc" cost the Yugoslav economy the equivalent of about half a billion dollars. Arrested and sentenced to a lengthy imprisonment, Abdić was released in 1990, and owing to his old connections and accumulated wealth, he became an influential politician. In the first presidential election in Bosnia in 1990 he gained most of the votes (868,000) but ceded the presidency to **Alija Izetbegović** in exchange for the position of minister of interior. In 1993, during the war among the Serbs, Croats, and Muslims and after prolonged discord with Izetbegović Abdić established the Autonomous Province of Western Bosnia in the region of Bihać. This led to further fighting against Muslim forces loyal to Izetbegović. In August 1994 Abdić's troops were defeated and retreated from the Bihać pocket, but returned there in November 1994 thanks to the support of the army of the Serb Republic of Kraina and the Bosnian Serbs. NATO air raids on Bosnia forced Abdić to flee to Croatia in August 1995. Considered by many Bosnian Muslims to be a traitor, Abdić did not return to the political arena of Bosnia-Herzegovina after losing in the first postwar parliamentary election of 1996. Accused by the Hague Tribunal of war crimes in the former Yugoslavia, he went into hiding, where he remains. (WR)

Sources: K. W. Banta, "Financial Scandal Turns into Political Bombshell," *Time*, 28 September 1987; Hrvoje Sosić, *Treće pokriće "Agrokomerca,"* (Zagreb, 1989); Ante Čuvalo, *Historical Dictionary of Bosnia and Herzegovina* (Lanham, Md., 1997); Željan E. Šuster, *Historical Dictionary of the Federal Republic of Yugoslavia* (Lanham, Md., 1999); Bugajski; www.rulers.org.

ABETSEDARSKY Laurentsi (12 July 1916, Gorki–6 July 1975, Minsk), Belorussian Soviet historian. In 1946 Abetsedarsky graduated from the Belorussian State University in Minsk, where he began his scholarly and pedagogical career. He was head of the Department of Soviet History between 1950 and 1958. For the following ten years he headed the Department of History of the Belorussian SSR. In 1966 he became a full professor of history. Abetsedarsky treated the history of Belarus strictly as a part of the history of Russia. According to him, the peasant movements in Belarus in the middle of the seventeenth century were a manifestation of the Belorussian peasants' aspirations to incorporate a part of the territory of the Grand Duchy of Lithuania into the Muscovite state. He described the mass displacements of the population of eastern Belarus to the territories beyond the Urals in 1654–55 as actions corresponding to the will of those people, and resulting from their desire to escape the reign of the Polish nobility. He considered the unification of the eastern Slavic lands under Moscow's dominance as a natural process that served the vital interests of the populations of Belarus and the Ukraine. He emphasized the right of tsarist Russia to possess these lands. He considered the Grand Duchy of Lithuania an alien state structure imposed on the Belorussian people by external forces. He considered the twentieth-century Belorussian national movement a nationalist degeneration. Abetsedarsky authored many supplementary materials for teaching the history of Belarus in the secondary schools; they were published in thirteen editions (1960–74). He also wrote a textbook that was reissued eleven times (1975–87). He was one of the authors of a five-volume official history of the Belorussian SSR. His works contributed to the Sovietization and Russification of the Belorussian intelligentsia. (EM)

Sources: "L. S. Abetsedarski: Niekroloh," *Viesnik BDU*, 1975, no. 2; *Entsyklapiedyia historyi Bielarusi*, vol. 1 (Minsk, 1993); *Bielaruskaia entsyklapiedyia*, vol. 1 (Minsk, 1996); Rainer Lindner, *Historiker und Herrschaft. Nationsbildung und Geschichtspolitik in Weissrussland im 19. und 20. Jahrhundert* (Munich, 1999).

ABRAMCHIK Mikalay (16 August 1903, Sychaviche, county of Vileika–29 May 1970, Paris), Belorussian émigré pro-independence activist, publicist. In 1920 Abramchik graduated from a Belorussian high school in Radoszkowicze. In 1924 he won a scholarship from the Czechoslovak government and the opportunity to study in Prague. (Such scholarships were funded to assist Belorussian youth and the Ukrainian citizens of Poland.) When the headquarters of the Belorussian People's Republic was moved from Berlin to Prague in 1925, Abramchik became a close associate of the leaders of the Belorussian government-in-exile, **Vasil Zakharka** and **Pyotr Krecheuski**. At the beginning of the 1930s Abramchik went to France to organize Belorussian groups that were dispersed there. However, the Union of Belorussian Working Émigrés, which Abramchik established, did not play any major role. The day before the outbreak of World War II he left for Berlin, obtaining the consent of the government of the Third Reich to publish *Ranitsa*, a weekly in the Belorussian language. Initially addressed to Belorussian émigré circles, the weekly was later distributed in all the countries subjugated by Germany. As the editor of the weekly between 1939 and 1944, Abramchik promoted the idea of building a Belorussian state allied with Germany. In 1940 he established Belorussian committees in the Third Reich, Bohemia, and occupied Poland. The committees were to be rudiments of the Belorussian government if Germany was victorious in the expected war against the USSR. In mid-1944, in the face of the defeat of the German armed forces, he left Berlin for Paris. In 1945 he became involved in organizing help for Belorussians who had worked as forced laborers in Germany or who had been released from concentration camps and for refugees from the USSR. At a conference in Paris on 28 November 1947 Abramchik was elected president of the Council of the Belorussian People's Republic, an émigré government that was in conflict with the Belorussian Central Council of **Radaslau Astrouski**. He held the position until the end of his life. In 1950 he published a brochure *I Accuse the Kremlin of the Genocide of My Nation*. In the 1950s and 1960s he also presided over the League for the Liberation of the Peoples of the USSR. (EM)

Sources: *Entsyklapiedyia historyi Bielarusi, vol. 1* (Minsk, 1993); *Bielaruskaia entsyklapiedyia*, vol. 1 (Minsk, 1996); Nicholas P. Vakar, *Belorussia: The Making of a Nation* (Cambridge, Mass., 1956); Jan Zaprudnik, *Historical Dictionary of Belarus* (Lanham, Md., 1998).

ABRAMOWSKI Edward (17 August 1868, Stefanin, near Vasilkov, Ukraine–21 July 1918, Warsaw), Polish philosopher and social activist. Abramowski was born into a landowner's family. After his mother died the family moved to Warsaw where he had private tutors; one of them was the famous poet Maria Konopnicka. At fifteen Abramowski published his first article in *Zorza*. In 1885 he began natural science studies in Kraków, and in 1886–89 he continued his studies in Geneva. There he became active in the Socialist movement, co-founding the Library of a Polish Socialist. At the beginning of 1889 Abramowski returned to Kraków, from where he went to Warsaw. In Warsaw, he was a co-founder of the Second Proletariat Party. In 1891 he established the Workers' Union (Zjednoczenie Robotnicze), promoting Socialist ideology among workers. He wrote a series of brochures, such as *Rewolucja robotnicza* (The workers' revolution; 1892), and an extensive sociological study, *Społeczeństwo rodowe* (Ancestral society; 1890). After the death of his new wife, Stanisława, in 1892 Abramowski suffered a nervous breakdown and returned to Geneva, where he took part in the formation of the Polish Socialist Party (Polska Partia Socjalistyczna [PPS]) and joined the party central (Centralizacja). He was the author of a proposed PPS program that set the independence of Poland through class struggle as a party goal. At that time, however, this program was not accepted.

Abramowski settled in Paris, but at the request of the Russian police he was expelled from France in January 1893. He went to London, and then to Zurich, where he wrote a brochure *Wszystkim robotnikom i górnikom polskim na dzień 1 maja–socjaliści polscy* (For all Polish workers and miners on May 1st Day—From Polish Socialists). Socialists-Internationalists held back the distribution of the brochure because of the independence aims it outlined. In 1894 Abramowski moved to Geneva, where he conducted sociological and psychological research. He worked out his own concept of Marxism, linked with sociological phenomenalism. In *Pierwiastki indywidualne w socjologii* (Individual elements in sociology; 1899) and *Zagadnienia socjalizmu* (Issues of socialism; 1899) he called for a revolutionary dictatorship of the proletariat, and stateless socialism based on a "moral revolution."

In 1897 Abramowski returned to Warsaw and began to establish "spiritual societies." Many radical intellectuals, including **Stefan Żeromski**, were influenced by these societies. In 1905 from the underground, Abramowski published *Zmowa powszechna przeciw rządowi* (General conspiracy against the government), where he proposed a general boycott as a way to struggle against tsarism. After the revolution of 1905 Abramowski exerted important influence on the development of the Polish cooperative movement and ideology. In 1906 he organized the Cooperative Society (Towarzystwo Kooperatystów). In his works *Nasza Polityka* (Our policy; 1906) and *Idee społeczne kooperatyzmu* (Social ideas of cooperativism; 1906), he presented the theory of the movement. Between 1908 and 1910 he worked on the theory of memory in Brussels and Paris. It was then that he joined a Masonic lodge called Wielki Wschód (Great East). After his return to Warsaw in 1910 he organized the Psychological Institute, conducting practical experiments. In 1915 he was appointed professor of psychology at the revived University of Warsaw, where he lectured on "experimental metaphysics." The results of his work were: *Badania doświadczalne nad pamięcią* (An experimental study of memory, 3 vols.; 1910–12) and *Źródła podświadomości i jej przejawy* (Sources of the subconscious and its aspects; 1914). Because of deteriorating health, Abramowski was not politically active during World War I. However, he supported the policy of **Józef Piłsudski** and the Polish Military Organization (Polska Organizacja Wojskowa). (WR)

Sources: Andrzej Walicki, "Stanisław Brzozowski i Edward Abramowski," *Studia Filozoficzne* 1975, no. 5; Maria Dąbrowska, *Życie i dzieło Edwarda Abramowskiego* (Warsaw, 1925); Kazimierz Krzeczkowski, *Dzieje życia i twórczości Edwarda Abramowskiego* (Warsaw, 1933); Oskar Lange, *Socjologia i idee społeczne Edwarda Abramowskiego* (Kraków, 1928); Bohdan Cywiński, "Myśl polityczna Edwarda Abramowskiego," in: *Polska myśl polityczna XIX i XX,* vol. 2 (Wrocław 1978).

ABRANTOWICZ Fabian (14 September 1884, Novogrudok [Navahrudak]–1940?), Belorussian priest and social worker. Abrantowicz was educated in Novogrudok and graduated from the Catholic Theological Academy in St. Petersburg. Ordained in November 1908, in 1910–12 he studied at the Catholic University in Louvain, Belgium, where he received a Ph.D. in philosophy in 1912. From 1914 to 1918 he lectured in philosophy at the St. Petersburg Theological Academy. In May 1918 he co-founded the Belorussian Christian Democratic Union in Petrograd and co-initiated a congress of Belorussian Catholic clergy in Minsk. In 1918 he became rector of the theological seminary in Minsk and, along with Bishop Zygmunt Łoziński, he offered the first Catholic Holy Mass in Belorussian. In 1921–26 Abrantowicz was prelate of the Pinsk chapter of the Roman Catholic Church. In 1926 he moved to a monastery of the Marist order in Druya, where a number of Belorussian Catholic priests had gathered to support lay Catholic publishing activity. Abrantowicz published a lot, demanding a wider use of Belorussian in the Novogrudok (Nowogródek) region and Polesie. In June 1928 he was sent by the Vatican to Harbin to carry on missionary activities among Russian émigrés. In the fall of 1939 he returned to the Soviet-occupied area of prewar Poland, but he was arrested by the NKVD. For a few months he was kept in the Lwów (Lviv) prison. Later Abrantowicz was deported deep into Russia, where he disappeared. (EM)

Sources: *Entsyklopedya katolicka,* vol. 1 (Lublin, 1973); *Entsyklapedyia historyi Belarusi,* vol. 1 (Minsk, 1993); *Bielaruskaya entsyklapedyia,* vol. 1 (Minsk, 1996); Vitaut Kipel and Zora Kipel eds., *Byelorussian Statehood* (New York, 1988); *Skazani jako "szpiedzy Watykanu"* (Ząbki, 1998).

ÁCHIM András Liker (15 March 1871, Békéscsaba–15 May 1911 Békéscsaba), Hungarian politician. Born into a rich peasant family in the region that became the cradle of the radical peasant movement, Áchim graduated from high school; from 1894 he managed a five-hundred-acre farm. A member of the county council in Békéscsaba and of the provincial assembly, in August 1904 he became a member of the Reformed Social Democratic Party and headed its local organization. In March 1906 he founded the Independent Socialist Peasant Union, which attracted farm workers, and became its leader. At the same time he became editor-in-chief of the party weekly, *Paraszt Újság.* Áchim was elected to the parliament three times (1905, 1906, and 1910–11), but in 1906 the electoral court annulled his mandate on account of electoral abuse (voters had been bought off with food and alcohol). Áchim advocated protection of the village poor, state redemption of entailed estates and church property and their lease to the peasants, abolishment of the upper house of parliament (House of Lords), free education for country folk, and electoral laws for secret ballots. Beginning in 1906 Áchim presided over the All-National Trade Union of Farmers, Smallholders, and Lifters. More than six hundred delegates from four hundred villages took part in its congress in June 1908. In April and May 1911, in gatherings and in his writings Áchim vigorously attacked local politicians, mainly his chief opponent, Endre Zsilinszky. On 14 May 1911, a quarrel with Zsilinszky's sons, **Endre** (**Bajcsy-Zsilinszky** as of 1925) and Gábor, in Áchim's home turned into a fight. Áchim was shot and died the next day. The case was widely publicized, but a few months later the court in Budapest acquitted both brothers, stating they had acted in self-defense. (JT)

Sources: *Biographisches Lexikon,* vol. 1; Magyar *Nagylexikon,* vol. 1 (Budapest, 1993); *Új Magyar Életrajzi Lexikon,* vol. 1 (Budapest 2001); János Tibori, *Az Áchim L. András-féle békéscsabai parasztmozgalom*

(Budapest, 1958); József Domokos, *Áchim L. András* (Budapest, 1971); Joseph Held, ed., *The Modernization of Agriculture: Rural Transformation in Hungary 1848–1975* (Boulder, Colo., 1980).

ACZÉL György (31 August 1917, Budapest–6 December 1991, Budapest), Hungarian Communist activist. After the death of his father Aczél was brought up in an orphanage. While still at school he began to work in construction. He took part in the youth Zionist movement called Somér. In 1935 he joined the illegal Communist Party. In 1936 he studied in a theater academy for half a year and later performed as an amateur actor. At the beginning of 1942 he was arrested and incorporated into work service, but he managed to quit. Under the German occupation (after March 1944) and the rule of the Arrow Cross Party (after October 1944) Aczél was active in the resistance, saving several hundred Jews. After the war he worked in the Budapest organization of the Hungarian Communist Party (HCP). From August 1946 he was the secretary of the party of Komitat Zémplen and from May 1948, of Komitat Baranya. In 1947–49 he was a deputy to the National Assembly. He was a member of the Central Committee (CC) of the Hungarian Workers' Party (HWP), which was formed at the "unification congress" of two workers' parties in June 1948. In June 1949 he was arrested and sentenced to life imprisonment in one of the trials accompanying the fake proceedings against **László Rajk**. Released in August 1954, he was rehabilitated a few weeks later. In the fall of 1954 he became the director of a building company.

On 3 November 1956 Aczél became a district organizational secretary of the Hungarian Socialist Workers' Party (HSWP), which was founded after the dissolution of the HWP. On 4 November he joined **János Kádár**. On 11 November, at a meeting of the executive of the HSWP, Aczél opted for a Yugoslav-style neutrality and insisted on the continuation of talks with **Imre Nagy**. During a debate on the resolution of the "four causes of the counterrevolution," which went on at the beginning of December, Aczél represented the "softer line"; therefore in February 1957 he had to carry out a self-criticism. Between April 1957 and February 1958 he was a vice-minister of culture and then until April 1967 the first vice-minister of culture. He had a much greater influence on Hungarian cultural policy than his formal powers would suggest. He owed this to his frequent personal contacts with Kádár. Aczél was the creator of the guidelines for the cultural policy, which were later referred to as "the three Ts" (*támogatás*—support; *türés*—tolerance; *tiltás*—forbidding). He had direct influence upon most decisions concerning cultural life, behaving like a one-man state patronage. The majority

of society and the elite approved, while outstanding writers and poets dedicated their works to him.

At the Ninth Congress of the HSWP in 1966 Aczél joined the Department of Agitation and Propaganda of the CC, and in April 1967 he was elected secretary of the CC, supervising the work of the Department of Science, Education, and Culture. In March 1969 he became the director of the Department of Agitation and Propaganda of the CC. At the Tenth Congress of the party in November 1970 he joined the Politburo. From 1971 he was a member of parliament again. In April of the same year Aczél became the president of the Working Group for Cultural Policy Affairs, which was created at that time within the CC. He held the post until 1975. In 1968 he began to take part in the implementation of "the new economic mechanism," and when the process was stopped in 1974, he was dismissed from his post in the CC. However, he retained his membership in the Politburo and became deputy prime minister and president of the State Educational Council. He held that post until 1976 and in 1980–82. In 1975 his book-interview, *Entretiens avec György Aczél,* was published in French and then in many other languages. In it, he argued with the French rightist politician Alain Peyrefitte. In 1979 Aczél submitted a resolution to the Politburo of the HSWP, denouncing the Hungarian signatories of Charter 77. At the beginning of the 1980s his heated discussions with the minister of culture, **Imre Pozsgay**, led to the resignation of both. In June 1982 Aczél ceased to be vice-premier and again became the secretary of the CC for cultural affairs. At the Thirteenth Congress of the HSWP in 1985 he was dismissed from most of his posts and then was appointed director of the Institute of Social Sciences of the CC. Between 1985 and 1990 he was again an MP. At the national conference of the HSWP in 1988 he did not run for the Politburo but retained his membership in the CC. At the meeting of the CC in June 1989 Aczél played a major role in the overthrow of **Károly Grósz** and the exchange of one-man leadership for a four-person executive board. (JT)

Sources: Bennet Kovrig, *Communism in Hungary from Kun to Kádár* (Stanford, 1979); Miklós Molnár, *From Béla Kun to János Kádár: Seventy Years of Hungarian Communism* (New York, 1990); *Magyar Nagylexikon* (Budapest, 1993), vol. 1; Sándor Révész, *Aczél és korunk* (Budapest, 1997); *A magyar forradalom és szabadságharc enciklopédiája,* CD-ROM (Budapest, 1999).

ADAMEC Ladislav (10 September 1926, Frenštát, near Radhošt), Czech Communist activist. The graduate of a trade academy, Adamec joined the Czechoslovak Communist Party (CPC) in 1946, and in the 1950s he worked in the political and economic apparatus in his hometown.

Between 1960 and 1962 he was deputy chairman of the Provincial National Council in Ostrava. In 1961 he graduated from a higher political school of the CPC Central Committee (CC), and in 1967 he received a Ph.D. from the Higher Economic School in Prague. From 1963 to 1969 Adamec was chairman of the CPC CC Industry Commission, from 1963 to 1971 member of its Economic Commission, and from 1966 member of the CPC CC. During the Prague Spring of 1968 he stood aside. From 1969 to 1990 he was a member of the Czech National Council and from 1969 to 1987 deputy prime minister of the Czech government. He reached the top rungs of Communist power when communism began to erode. In 1987 Adamec became a member of the Presidium of the CPC CC, then prime minister of the Czech Republic, and from March 1987 to October 1988 he was deputy prime minister of the federal government. After the resignation of **Lubomir Štrougal,** on 12 October 1988 Adamec became prime minister of Czechoslovakia. Despite the growing social tensions, he stubbornly resisted reforms. It was only after 17 November 1989 that he tried to save the system by reaching a compromise with the democratic opposition, and he entered into talks with the Civic Forum (Občanské Forum [CF]). At first, the CF delegation, as well as its Slovak equivalent, Public against Violence (Verejnost' Proti Násiliu), offered Adamec the position of president, but the evolution of a new system accelerated. On 24 November 1989 Adamec was dismissed from the CPC CC Presidium, and on 7 December, from the position of prime minister. From 21 December 1989 to 1 September 1990 he presided over the CPC, and in the first free elections in June 1990 he won a mandate in the Federal Assembly. After his term was over in June 1992, he retired. (PU)

Sources: *ČBS; Kdo byl kdo v našich dějinach ve 20. stoleti,* vol. 1 (Prague, 1998); *Československí politici 1918/1991* (Prague, 1991); *Who's Who in the Socialist Countries of Europe,* vol. 1 (Munich, London, and Paris, 1989).

ADAMKUS Valdas [originally Adamkavičius] (3 November 1926, Kaunas), engineer and politician, president of Lithuania. Born into a white-collar family, Adamkus started high school but had to quit owing to the Soviet invasion of 1940 and the German invasion of 1941. During the German occupation he published and distributed an underground periodical, *Jaunime, budek!* In July 1944 along with his family he left for Germany. In the fall of 1944 he returned to join anti-Soviet guerrillas. He took part in a battle against the NKVD troops at Seda, but seeing the hopelessness of the situation, he came back to Germany. He graduated from high school in Munich and entered university there. He worked at the YMCA, organizing sports events for dis-

placed persons from various countries. He was an athlete himself and won several gold medals at the Olympics of Captive Nations in 1948. In 1949 his family, along with the family of former president **Kazys Grinius,** left for the United States. Adamkus worked as a blue-collar laborer in an automobile factory in Chicago and as a draftsman in an engineering company, and he organized cultural events for Lithuanian émigrés. Among other things, he presided over the Lithuanian Student Center, Santara. In 1960 he graduated in engineering from the Illinois Institute of Technology. From 1958 to 1965 he was deputy chairman and from 1967 chairman of the Lithuanian cultural and political federation Santara-Sviesa, and he organized protests against the Soviet occupation of Lithuania. For instance, he handed a petition on this matter to U.S. President John F. Kennedy and to the UN secretary general.

In the 1970s Adamkus worked for the U.S. Environmental Protection Agency (EPA), among other positions as head of the EPA Great Lakes ecological project. He was also active in the Republican Party. Starting in 1972 he visited Soviet Lithuania within the framework of ecological cooperation. He supported the construction of waste treatment plants and the development of environmental monitoring, making contacts with opposition circles and bringing émigré literature. He helped Lithuanian specialists come to study in the United States, cooperating with Vilnius University, especially during the *perestroika* period. In 1988 he received an international ecological award and in 1989, an honorary doctorate from Vilnius University. In 1991 he supported efforts for the international recognition of Lithuania's independence, and after the fall of the USSR and reconstruction of a sovereign Lithuanian state, he increasingly was engaged in its public life. In the presidential campaign of 1993 he supported Stasys Lozoraitis Jr., who nevertheless lost. In 1996 Adamkus participated in the parliamentary campaign of the Lithuanian Center Union (Lietuvos Centro Sąjunga). In 1997 he became a member of the city council of Šiauliai.

In the first round of the presidential elections on 21 December 1997, Adamkus came in second, but in the second round (4 January 1998), thanks to the support of **Vytautas Landsbergis,** he won by a narrow margin of fourteen thousand votes (50.4 percent). He was sworn in on 26 February 1998. He gave up his U.S. citizenship, but making use of his American contacts (in 1993 President Bill Clinton personally thanked him for his work in the EPA), he promoted pro-Western policies in Lithuania, striving for its entry into NATO and the European Union. He supported settling accounts with the Soviet and German past, establishing a special commission for the investigation of Nazi and Communist crimes in 1940–91. He developed contacts with Scandinavian countries and European Union members; he normalized relations with Russia and Poland. In January 2003 he ran for re-election but lost to **Rolandas Paksas**. After Paksas was impeached, Adamkus was again elected president on 27 June 2004. (WR)

Sources: *Wielka encyklopedia PWN*, vol. 1 (Warsaw, 2001); *Lietuva, Žengiantiį XXI amžių. Valdo Adamkaus rinkimų programa* (Vilnius, 1997); *Eastern Europe and the Commonwealth of Independent States 1999* (London, 1999); Bugajski; Piotr Łossowski, *Litwa* (Warsaw, 2001); www.presisident.lt; www.rulers.org

ADAMOVICH Ales (3 September 1927, Kaniukhy, near Kopylsk–26 January 1994, Moscow), Belorussian writer and literary critic. Between 1943 and 1944 Adamovich was active in the Soviet underground in the region of Bobruysk. After the war he studied at the metallurgical technical college in Leninogorsk in the Altai *krai* (region); between 1945 and 1950 he studied in the Philology Department of the Belorussian State University in Minsk, and then in 1954–62 and 1967–83 he worked at the Institute of Literature of the Academy of Sciences of the Belorussian SSR. Between 1964 and 1966 he lectured on Belorussian literature at Lomonosov University in Moscow. In 1987 he became director of the Cinematography Institute in Moscow. He was a deputy to the Supreme Soviet of the USSR and from 1989 a member of the Belorussian PEN club. He began his literary activities as a critic. His theoretical considerations of literature and his analyses of the literary works of the main representatives of Belorussian literature appeared in Belorussian and in Russian. He authored such works as *Kultura tvarchosti* (The culture of creation; 1959), *Haryzonty bialoruskoi prozy* (Horizons of Belorussian prose; 1974) and *Vaina i vioska u suchasnai literatury* (War and the countryside in contemporary literature; 1982). He made his debut as a writer with a two-volume novel, *Partizany* (Partisans; 1960–63), which was devoted to the Soviet resistance movement in Belorussia. In all his works, fitted into the official current of Soviet culture, he dealt with war issues. His greatest fame came from his works *Khatynskaia apoviests* (Khatyn story; 1972) (from which the script of the film *Idi i smatri* [Come and see; 1985], by Elem Klimov, was based) and *Vybiery zhyttsio* (Choose life; 1986), which warned against the destruction of civilization. (EM)

Sources: *Wielka encyklopedia powszechna*, vol. 1 (Warsaw, 2001); *Bielaruskiya pismienniki 1917–1990* (Minsk, 1994); *Bielaruskiya pismienniki: Biiabibliahrafichny slounik*, vol. 1 (Minsk, 1995); *Bielaruskaia entsyklapiedyia*, vol. 1 (Minsk, 1994); *New York Times*, 31 January 1994.

ADAMOVICH Anton, pseudonyms "Birych" and "Zabransky" (26 June 1909, Minsk–12 June 1998, New York),

Belorussian émigré historian and theorist of literature. Adamovich studied at the Belorussian Pedagogical and Technical Institute in Minsk and, beginning in 1928, at the Belorussian State University. Arrested in 1930 for being a member of a nonexistent organization, the Union of Liberation of Belorussia, he was held in Glazov and in Viatka. In 1938 he was allowed to return to Minsk, where he completed his university studies. During the German occupation he took part in the formation of the structures of the Belorussian administration. In 1941–43 he was a member of the leadership of the Belorussian People's Mutual Aid, and then he joined the Belorussian Central Council, which was created in December 1943 and aspired to be a state government allied with Germany. Adamovich was active in the Belorussian Scientific Society and cooperated with the editorial offices of the newspapers *Mienskaia Hazieta, Bielaruskaia Hazieta,* and *Ranitsa* (Berlin). After the war he was in West Germany, where he edited the magazines *Viedamki, Batskaushchina, Sakavik,* and *Konadni* for émigrés from Belorussia. He was co-founder of the Munich Institute for Research on Problems of the USSR and first director of the Belorussian section of Radio Svaboda. In 1960 he emigrated to the United States. In his historical works, *Balshavism na shliakhakh stanauliennia kantrolu nad Belarussiu* (Bolshevism on the way to establishing control over Belarus; 1954) and *Balshavism u revalutsyinym rukhu na Belarusi* (Bolshevism in the Belorussian revolutionary movement; 1956), Adamovich demonstrated that the Bolshevik ideology did not have any traditions in Belorussia and was alien to the inhabitants of the Belorussian land and that Communist rule had been brought on the bayonets of the Red Army soldiers. In America, Adamovich was involved in analyzing the literary works of such Belorussian poets and writers as **Natalya Arsenneva, Maxim Bahdanovich, Ales Harun,** and **Yakub Kolas.** He wrote prefaces to anthologies of their works. Adamovich was the author of *Opposition to Sovietization in Belorussian Literature 1917–1957* (1958). (EM)

Sources: *Entsyklapiedyia historyi Bielarusi*, vol. 1 (Minsk, 1993); *Bielaruskaia entsyklapiedyia*, vol. 1 (Minsk, 1996).

ADAMOVICH Yazep (7 January 1897, Borisov–22 April 1937, Minsk), Belorussian Communist activist. Adamovich came from a working-class background. At ten he began to work in factories in Borisov, Minsk, and Tiflis. Drafted into the tsarist army in 1914, he fought on the southwestern front and on the Romanian front. In 1916 he joined the Russian Social Democratic Workers' Party, and he agitated among soldiers. After the February 1917 revolution he worked in the staff of the Red Guards in

Smolensk. In July 1918 he became head of the Smolensk garrison of the Red Guards and also a Bolshevik commissar of the *guberniya* (province) of Smolensk. He led the struggle against anti-Bolshevik groupings in Smolensk, Vitebsk, and Homel Provinces. In September 1920 he was appointed commissar for military affairs of the Belorussian SSR, and in 1921 he assumed the post of commissar of the interior and deputy president of the Council of People's Commissars of the Belorussian SSR. He was responsible for the persecution of the opponents of Bolshevism. As a representative of the Communist Party (Bolsheviks) of Belorussia, he took part in the formation of the USSR. In 1924 he became president of the Council of People's Commissars of the Belorussian SSR. He participated in the policy of Beloruthenization of public life, which was conducted on a large scale. Educational and cultural institutions, the press, the administration, and party structures were obliged to use the Belorussian language only. However, as 1927 saw the gradual abandonment of the nationalist policy, Adamovich was removed from his post. Another reason for his removal was his support for the New Economic Policy (NEP). Adamovich was initially transferred to work in the Soviet central administration, and he served, for example, as head of the USSR sugar industry department. In 1932 he was sent to Kamchatka, where he organized the fisheries. With the wave of persecutions of the nationalist elite of the Soviet republics, he was accused of Belorussian nationalism and of supporting the kulaks when he was head of the administration in Belarus. According to official information, Adamovich committed suicide. (EM)

Sources: *MERSH*, vol. 1; S. Shamardzin, "Staronki z biiahrafii Yazepa Adamovicha," *Polymia*, 1966, no. 4; Ivan S. Lubachko, *Belorussia under Soviet Rule, 1917–1957* (Lexington, KY 1972); *Entsyklapiedyia historyi Belarusi*, vol. 1 (Minsk, 1994).

ADAMSKI Stanisław (12 April 1875, Zielona Góra, near Szamotuły–12 November 1967, Katowice), Polish Catholic bishop. One of seven children of a trackwalker, in 1896 Adamski graduated from high school. He studied at a theological seminary in Poznań and Gniezno, and in November 1899 he was ordained. He worked as a curate in Gniezno. Politically active, from 1904 to 1910 Adamski was secretary general of the diocesan Union of Catholic Societies of Polish Workers (Związek Katolickich Towarzystw Robotników Polskich). He established educational, cultural, and mutual aid societies in the dioceses of Gniezno and Poznań. He founded and edited the weekly *Robotnik* (The worker). Adamski worked together with cooperative activists rallied around Reverend Piotr Wawrzyniak. In 1906 he became a member of the board of the Association of Commercial Cooperatives (Związek Spółek Zarobkowych i Gospodarczych) as a member of the patronage and in 1910 as the patron of the association. From 1906 he worked at the St. Wojciech Printing House and Bookstore (Drukarnia i Księgarnia św. Wojciecha); in 1911 he became its general manager and in 1923 president of its supervisory board. In 1919 he was a founding member of Poznań University, and he lectured on the cooperative movement at the Department of Law and Economics.

After the outbreak of World War I Adamski became involved in pro-independence activities. In 1916 he became head of a secret organization that was preparing for the revival of Polish statehood in Poznania. In 1918–19 he was a member of the commissariat of the National People's Council (Naczelna Rada Ludowa). From April 1918 he belonged to the National Workers' Party (Narodowe Stronnictwo Robotników [NSR]), and as a representative of the party he entered the Constituent Sejm (1919–22). When in 1919 the NSR split, Adamski became head of the Polish Christian Democratic Party (Polskie Stronnictwo Chrześcijańskiej Demokracji [PSChD]). Between 1922 and 1927 he was senator. After the coup of May 1926, disappointed with the rule of the *sanacja* regime, he withdrew from active politics. In 1930 he became the first general manager of the Institute of Catholic Action. On 2 September 1930 he was appointed ordinary bishop of Katowice. Co-founder of the statute of Catholic Action, in 1932 he became president of the executive committee of the Press Committee of the Polish Episcopate. He contributed greatly to promoting the use of the mass media in evangelical work.

Under strong pressure from Nazi authorities after 1939, Adamski was an advocate of hiding one's true national convictions from these authorities. He sent two lengthy memorials on this issue to the Holy See and to the Polish government in France. The government of General **Władysław Sikorski** initially accepted such activities with reservation but finally rejected them. In the fall of 1939 Adamski privately advised Silesian believers that they should submit declarations "leaning toward the German identity"; Adamski, however, declared himself Polish. He developed charity activities with the assistance of Caritas, which existed officially, and he also developed unofficial actions of sending parcels to internment and concentration camps. He informed the Holy See about the persecutions of the clergy of the Katowice diocese. In June 1940, because of blackmail by German gangs, Adamski instructed priests to restrict the use of the Polish language in pastoral work, with the exception of the confession box. He repeatedly intervened with the German authorities on behalf of imprisoned priests. Recognized as an enemy of the Third

Reich, in February 1941 Adamski was displaced from the Katowice diocese to the General Gouvernment (the official name of a Nazi-occupied area in central Poland). He arrived in Warsaw, where he lived with his family. He got involved in underground activities—for example, he became honorary president of the Civic Council of the Western Territories, which was established by the West Office of the Delegation of the Polish Government-in-Exile for the Homeland. During the Warsaw Uprising he was the only bishop to perform pastoral services. After the fall of the rising he went for a short time to Jasna Góra, and then in February 1945 he returned to Katowice.

In the fall of 1945 Adamski allowed clergymen whom he had chosen to work in the national councils at different levels. He intervened with local and central authorities against the abuses that took place during the response to the results of the so-called *Volksliste* (German national list) in Upper Silesia. His argument—expounded, for example, in his work *Pogląd na rozwój sprawy narodowościowej w Województwie Śląskim w czasie okupacji niemieckiej* (A view on the development of the nationalist issue in the Silesian Province during the German occupation)—was adopted by the governor (*wojewoda*) of Dąbrowa Silesia, Aleksander Zawadzki, who was able to convince the central authorities to moderate their restrictive policy toward the Polish-speaking natives of Upper Silesia. Adamski was involved in restoring a ministry in the Wrocław diocese; for example, he proposed the creation of a separate vicariate-general for Opole Silesia (Śląsk Opolski). From 1947 he repeatedly campaigned for the freedom to teach religion, which had been reduced by the authorities. In October 1952 he called on Catholics in the Katowice diocese to collect signatures for a petition to the Council of State demanding the restoration of religion classes in schools. Around seventy thousand signatures were collected. Communist authorities considered this action as anti-state. It demanded that the Episcopate condemn Adamski's activities. Since the Episcopate refused to do so, on 7 November 1952, under a decree by the Special Committee for Struggle against Fraud and Economic Sabotage, Adamski was expelled from the diocese for five years. He went to an Ursuline convent in Lipnica near Otorowo, county of Szamotuły. He was under constant surveillance by the secret police there. He returned to Katowice on 5 November 1956. He published over three hundred works. (AGr)

Sources: *Wielkopolski słownik biograficzny* (Warsaw and Poznań, 1981); K. Szaraniec, *Ks. Stanisław Adamski*, parts 1–3 (Katowice, 1990–91); *Księża społecznicy w Wielkopolsce 1894–1919. Słownik biograficzny*, vol. 1 (Gniezno, 1992); Andrzej Grajewski, *Wygnanie* (Katowice, 1995); *Słownik biograficzny Katolickiego Duchowieństwa Śląskiego XIX i XX wieku* (Katowice, 1996).

ADY Endre (22 November 1877, Érmindszent, Transylvania–27 January 1919, Budapest), Hungarian poet. Ady came from an impoverished Calvinist gentry family. He started writing as a student at a Calvinist high school in Zilah (1892–96). During his law studies in Debrecen and Budapest, which he failed to complete, he mixed the writing of poems with that of columns and articles for the local press. In 1903 he met Adél Brüll, the wife of a wealthy merchant. His passionate love for her made a strong impact on his future life. In 1904 he followed her to Paris and to Bavaria and Italy, where, among other things, he studied the poetry of Charles Baudelaire and Paul Verlaine. Enchanted by their poetry, he translated it into Hungarian. In 1906 Ady published his first volume, *Új versek* (New poems), which was a breakthrough in his career and made him one of the champions of Hungarian literary life. Apart from passionate love poems, the volume included a poetic vision of the Hungarian past and present. Ady also expressed his prophetic fears of turmoil and defeats that Hungary was soon to experience. After returning home, he settled in Budapest, where in 1907–12 he published five other volumes: *Vér és arany* (Gold and blood); *Az Illés szekerény* (Chariots of Elijah); *Szeretném, ha szeretnének* (I would like to if they wanted); *A minden titkok versei* (Poems of all secrets); and *Menekülö élet* (Passing life). Apart from developing earlier motifs, including fears of a revolution, these volumes recorded the existential struggles of the author and his longing for a wider presence of God in the world. At this time Ady drew closer to the literary vanguard centered on the periodical *Nyugat* (1908–41).

In 1912 Ady became a member of a Masonic lodge in Martinovics. He broke off his romance with Brüll, entering into correspondence and then marrying a landowner's daughter, Berta Boncza. His subsequent volumes—*A magunk szerelme* (Our own love; 1913), *Ki látott engem?* (Who saw me? 1914), *A halottak élén* (In the van of the dead; 1918), and the posthumous *Az utolsó hajók* (Last ships; 1919)—reflected the perplexities of a man torn apart by a growing fear of death (he suffered from advanced syphilis) and a declining enthusiasm concerning his own future and that of his country, a man fearfully watching the development of the war and the emerging European order. In November 1918 he took part in the parliamentary session, at which the Hungarian Republic was proclaimed. He became chairman of the literary association Vörösmarty Akadémia. His funeral turned into a large patriotic manifestation by the residents of Budapest. His literary greatness consisted in the symbolism and personal nature of his lyrics. At the same time he largely influenced the Hungarian national consciousness by mythologizing its past problems and by preaching the hopelessness of individual struggle against the Hungarian "wasteland" and the fragility of independence aspirations of the small Central European nations. (MS)

Sources: *Biographisches Lexikon,* vol. 1; Aladár Schöpflin, *Ady Endre* (Budapest, 1934); Watson Kirkconell, *The Poetry of Ady* (Budapest, 1937); Guglielmo Capacchi, *La poesie di Andrea Ady in una nuova traduzione* (Bologna, 1957); Mary Gluck, *Endre Ady: An East European Response to the Cultural Crisis of the Fin de Siecle* (New York, 1977).

AFTENIE Vasile (14 July 1899, Londroman–10 May 1950, Bucharest), Romanian Greek Catholic bishop, martyr for faith. Aftenie graduated from high school in 1918. In 1917 he was drafted into the army and spent a couple months on the front, mainly in Italy. In 1919 he started theological studies in Blaj and continued them in Rome, where he received a Ph.D. in philosophy and theology in 1925. After returning home, in January 1926 he was ordained, and the following month he became professor at the Theological Academy in Blaj. In 1939 he was appointed rector of this school, and in 1940 he was nominated auxiliary bishop of the Greek Catholic metropolis of Blaj (diocese of Alba Iulia-Făgăraş) and vicar general of Bucharest. After the war, the Communist authorities began the persecution of Greek Catholics and their priests and bishops; on 28 October 1948 Aftenie was arrested along with all five other Greek Catholic bishops and about six hundred priests. The official reason for his arrest was the possession of a letter from **Iuliu Maniu.** Together with the other bishops, Aftenie was imprisoned in a monastery in Dragoslavele, a summer residence of the Orthodox patriarch of Romania converted into a prison. On 1 December 1948 the Greek Catholic church was banned, and its structure was integrated into the Romanian Ortho- dox Church. At the end of February 1949 all the bishops were moved to the Căldăruşani Monastery near Bucharest. Aftenie was accused of maintaining contacts with parti- sans resisting the Communist power in the Transylvanian mountains. Interrogated many times in the Ministry of Interior headquarters in Bucharest, he was put in a villa in Sinaia, where **Gheorghiu Gheorghiu-Dej** and Patriarch **Justinian** tried to make him agree to join the Orthodox Church and offered him the position of Metropolitan of Iaşi. When Aftenie refused, he was put in the Jilava prison. At the beginning of 1950 he was again interrogated and tortured in the Ministry of Interior headquarters. Moved to Văcăreşti Prison in Bucharest, he was murdered there particularly brutally on the orders of General **Alexandru Nicolschi**, and he was buried in the Catholic Bellu Cem- etery in Bucharest. (LW)

Sources: Józef Darski, *Rumunia: Historia, współczesność, konflikty narodowe* (Warsaw, 1995); Paul Caravia, Virgiliu Constantinescu, and Flori Stănescu, *The Imprisoned Church of Romania, 1944–1989* (Bucharest, 1999); Denis Deletant, *Communist Terror in Romania: Gheorghiu-Dej and the Police State, 1948–1965* (New York, 1999); www.bru.ro.

AKEL Fredrich Karl (5 September 1871, Kaubi, near Pär- nu–3 July 1941, Tallinn), Estonian politician and doctor. Born into the family of a rich stockbreeder, Akel could af- ford medical studies at the University of Dorpat (Tartu) in 1892–97. Afterwards he worked in its hospital (1897–99). After a short practice in Ujazdów, near Warsaw, he con- tinued his studies in Berlin, Prague, and Leipzig (1901). For a short time he worked in an ophthalmological clinic in Riga, and then he continued his own practice in Tallinn (1902–4 and 1905–12). During the Russo-Japanese War he served in the tsarist army. In 1912 he founded his own ophthalmological clinic. Respect and popularity, which he had gained as a doctor, helped him win election to the Tallinn City Council. For many years he was also a justice of the peace in Tallinn-Haapsalu. In 1920–22 he was a lay deputy chairman of the consistory of the Estonian Luther- an Church and one of the leaders of the Christian People's Party (Kristlik Rahvaerakond [CPP]). On its behalf he won mandates in the second and third parliamentary terms. Despite moderate support (8–10 percent of the vote), the CPP, in which the Protestant clergy played an important role, had a significant influence in the fragmented Estonian parliament. In 1922–23 Akel was ambassador to Finland and then foreign minister (1923–24). From 26 March to 16 December 1924 he was the head of state (*riigivanem*). His was a minority government, which nevertheless tried to deal with inflation and problems with foreign payments (among other things) caused by the collapse and closing of the Russian market. Reforms carried out by the minister of finance, **Otto Strandmann**, though temporarily painful, were successful in the log run and helped to accelerate economic development in the late 1920s.

At first a supporter of parliamentary democracy, Akel gradually accepted authoritarian rule. In 1926–27 he was foreign minister again, and later he served as ambas- sador to Sweden (1928–34); after the **Konstantin Päts** coup he became ambassador to Germany (1934–36) and a member of the Upper House of parliament (1938–40). In 1936 he became head of diplomacy again, developing a pro-German line in which he saw a chance to maintain independence in case of Soviet aggression. He also con- tinued rapprochement with Sweden but failed to gain its engagement in the defense of Estonia. He supported the idea of an alliance of the Baltic states with Poland and pressed Lithuania to improve its relations with Poland.

During the Lithuanian-Polish crisis of March 1938 he called on President **Antanas Smetona,** supporting Polish postulates of normalization, and he helped in bilateral negotiations that were mostly held in Tallinn. Akel sat on the boards of the Northern Baltic Association of Doctors, the Tallinn Society of Folk Education, the Tallinn Loan and Insurance Company, and the Kreditpank. He also presided over the Society for Construction of the Estonia Theater and the Estonia Society in Tallinn. From 1907 he was chairman of the sports association Kalev in Tallinn, and he was the first chairman of the Estonian Olympic Committee (1923–31). In 1927–32 he was the Estonian representative to the International Olympics Committee. Arrested by the NKVD on 17 October 1940, Akel was shot. (AG)

Sources: Evald Uustalu, *The History of Estonian People* (London, 1952); Tõnu Parming, *The Collapse of Liberal Democracy and the Rise of Authoritarianism in Estonia* (London, 1975); Piotr Łossowski, *Stosunki polsko–estońskie 1918–1939* (Gdańsk, 1992); Matti Laur, Tõnis Lukas, Ain Mäesalu, and Ago Pajur Tõnu Tannberg, *History of Estonia* (Tallinn, 2000); www.eok.ee/olympialiikumine.php?view; www.president.ee/eng/riigipead/FriedrichAkel.

AKINCHITS Fabiyan (20 January 1886, Akinchitse, near Stolbtsy [Stołpce]–7 March 1943, Minsk), Belorussian politician. Between 1906 and 1913 Akinchits studied law at St. Petersburg University. In 1906 he became a member of the Russian Socialist Revolutionary Party. Having completed his studies, he worked as a defense attorney. In 1917 he joined the Bolsheviks. In 1923 he returned to his native land, which at that time was incorporated within Poland. He started working as a teacher in Zasulye, and he opened an office providing services in application writing and legal advice. In 1926 he allied himself with the Belorussian Peasant and Worker Hromada, and he became a member of the party executive. As defense attorney, he represented Hromada activists during political trials, and he coordinated the work of Hromada's parliamentary club. In November 1926 he became president of the Vilnius branch of the party, and he was the leader of the so-called nationalist current, which vied with the pro-Soviet and Communist current for influence in the organization. In January 1927 Polish authorities arrested Hromada leaders on charges of conducting activities aimed at separating the Eastern Borderland (Kresy) from Poland. The Vilnius court sentenced Akinchits to eight years in prison.

In July 1930 Akinchits was the last member of the Hromada leadership to leave prison, and he refused at the same time to go to the USSR. He joined the Central Council of Belorussian Cultural and Economic Organizations (Centrsayuz), a movement led by **Anton Lutskievich.** As a rival organization to the Communist movement, it was supported by the Polish government. Akinchits became a member of the leadership of the movement and he edited its newspapers, *Napierad* and *Bielaruski zvon.* In 1931 he published *Chamu tak stalasia? (Why did it happen?),* in which he proved that the Communist ideology was disastrous to the Belorussian movement. Soon he left the ranks of Centrsayuz, accusing Lutskievich of leftist leanings. In May 1931 he created the Vilnius Belorussian group called Revival, with a pro-Polish orientation. In 1933, along with Władyslaw Kozłowski, he began to publish the magazine *Novy shlakh,* which initiated the consolidation of the Belorussian nationalist movement. In 1937 he formed the Belorussian National Socialist Party (BNSP). The party, whose ideas bordered on German fascism, was banned by the Polish authorities. In June 1939 the congress of the BNSP was held in Gdańsk. At the congress it was decided that the future of independent Belorussia would be built in alliance with the Germans. From June 1939 Akinchits worked in the Belorussian Bureau of the Ministry of Propaganda of the Third Reich. At the beginning of 1940, within the framework of the Reich Ministry for the Occupied Eastern Territories, he became president of the Belorussian Committee in Warsaw, and a year later he was appointed head of a Belorussian school for propaganda workers near Berlin. He was assassinated during one of his visits to Minsk; the assassination was probably inspired by a rival group of Belorussian activists who collaborated with the Germans. His death was later announced as a success of the Soviet underground in the struggle against collaborators. (EM)

Sources: *Entsyklapiedyia historyi Belarusi,* vol. 1 (Minsk, 1994); *Wielka Encyklopedia PWN,* vol. 1 (Warsaw, 2001); Nicholas P. Vakar, *Belorussia: The Making of a Nation* (Cambridge, Mass., 1956); Y. Vapa, "Fabiyan Akinchits i iahony chas," *Niva,* 1993, nos. 38–41.

AKSYONAU [Aksyonov] Aleksandr (9 October 1924, Kuntarovka, near Homyel), Soviet party and state activist in Belorussia. In 1941–42 Aksyonau worked in a *kolkhoz.* In 1941 he graduated from the Higher Pedagogical School in Homyel, and in 1942–43 he served in the Red Army. From 1944 he worked in the apparatus of the Lenin Association of Communist Youth of Belorussia in Orenburg, Baranavichy, and Hrodna. From 1945 a member of the CPSU and from 1956 a member of the Central Committee (CC) of the Communist Party of Belorussia (CPB), in 1957 he became first secretary of the Komsomol in Belorussia and a member of the CPB Politburo, and he graduated from the Higher Party School in Moscow. In 1959 he became deputy chairman of the KGB of the Belorussian SSR, and from 1960 to 1965 he was minister of interior of the Belorussian republic, supervising repression against people not loyal enough to the Soviet system. In 1965 he became first secretary of the CPB District Committee in Vitebsk and in 1971, secretary of the CPB CC. From 1978 to 1983 he was prime minister of the Belorussian republican government and from 1983 to 1985 Soviet ambassador to Poland. In 1985 he became chairman of the Soviet State Television and Radio Committee, and in 1989 he retired. (EM)

Sources: *Belaruskaya SRR. Kratkaya entsyklopediya,* vol. 5 (Minsk, 1982); *Entsyklapedyia historyi Belarusi,* vol. 1 (Minsk, 1994); Borys Lewytzkyj, ed., *Who's Who in the Soviet Union* (Munich, 1984); Leonard Geron and Alex Pravda, eds., *Who's Who in Russia and the New States* (London, 1993).

ALAPY Gyula [originally Alapi] (18 December 1911, Komárom–18 February 1982, Fonyód), Hungarian Communist activist. Alapy was the son of the chief archivist of Komárom and of an heiress of the Frank-Kiss family, which owned many factories in town and in the neighborhood. After the Treaty of Trianon (1920) the family stayed in Czechoslovakia. In 1930 Alapy joined the Social Democratic Party and took part in leftist student group activities. He graduated in law from Brno University in 1934, and then he worked as an defense attorney in Érsekújvár (Nové Zámky). During World War II Catholic priests saved him and his Jewish mother from deportation and death. In 1945 he moved to Hungary, where from mid-1948 he belonged to the Hungarian Social Democratic Party, then to the (Communist) Hungarian Workers' Party, and from 1956 to the Hungarian Socialist Workers' Party (HSWP). In 1945–46 Alapy worked in the public prosecutor's office in Győr, and from 1946 to 1948 he was its chairman. From July 1948 to February 1949 he was a member of the Chief Prosecutor's Office (CPO) in Budapest, and in January 1949 he was the chief plaintiff in the trial of Cardinal **József Mindszenty.** For his role in the trial he was nominated CPO chairman. He was a ruthless tool of the **Mátyás Rákosi** dictatorship, passing numerous death sentences, and he frequently repeated that "there is only one way to get rid of mad dogs—they must be killed." He was the chief plaintiff in many political show trials, such as those of **László Rajk, József Kóvágó,** police and army officers, and many others. All together he passed about twenty death sentences in political trials. In 1956 he was dismissed and left for the USSR. He returned to Hungary in March 1958 and worked at the Institute of Law of the Hungarian Academy of Sciences. Later he worked as a legal adviser in a power and gas meter enterprise. In 1972 he retired. The only punishment he suffered was expulsion from the HSWP for the abuse of "socialist law and order" in 1962. In a state of depression he probably committed suicide. (JT)

Sources: *Új Magyar Életrajzi Lexikon,* vol. 1 (Budapest, 2001); *Magyarország 1944–1956,* CD-ROM (Budapest, 2001).

ALDEA Aurel (28 March 1887, Slatina–17 October 1949, Aiud), Romanian general. After graduating from the War College in Bucharest, Aldea steadily rose in the ranks of the army. As one of the closest advisers to King **Michael,** in May 1944 he took part in the first meeting of the king with representatives of the opposition to Marshal **Ion Antonescu;** the purpose of the meeting was to effect the withdrawal of Romania from an alliance with the Germans. He also took part in a crucial meeting of the king with Antonescu on 23 August 1944, during which the dictator was removed from power and arrested. Aldea became minister of the interior in the government of General **Constantin Sănătescu,** which was established after the coup, and he held the post until the beginning of November. Next, he was commander of territorial defense until 24 March 1945. Removed from this position, in the summer of that year he started to cooperate with the anti-Communist underground, and he soon became head of the National Resistance Movement (Mişcarea Naţională de Rezistenţă), which included such armed groups as the Haiduks of Avram Iancu (Haiducii lui Avram Iancu) and the Grey Greatcoats (Graiul Sangelui). In May 1946 Aldea was arrested on the grounds of plotting to "destroy the unity of the Romanian state." He was accused of directing the anti-Communist resistance movement and was also falsely charged with supporting Hungarian separatism in Transylvania. On 18 November 1946 he was sentenced to hard labor for life. He died of heart disease in prison. (WR)

Sources: Ivor Porter, *Operation Autonomous: With S.O.E. in Wartime Romania* (London, 1989); Dennis Deletant, *Communist Terror in Romania: Gheorghiu-Dej and the Police State, 1948–1965* (New York, 1999).

ALEKSA Jonas (25 December 1879, Kumetiškiai, Samogetia–20 April 1955, Tomsk), Lithuanian politician. Aleksa studied sociology and the natural sciences at Moscow University (1900–1907) and agronomy at the Agricultural Academy in Warsaw (1914–15). In 1902 he was temporarily arrested for anti-tsarist activities. During World War I he worked in Voronezh and was co-founder of the Populist Democratic National League of Freedom (Demokratine Tautos Laisves Santara), in brief called Santara. In 1918 he returned to Lithuania and became head of a department in the Ministry of Agriculture. From June 1920 to February 1922 and from February to June 1923 he was minister of agriculture. In 1925, along with **Petras Leonas** and **Vaclovas Sidzikauskas,** he was a founder of the Lithuanian Peasant Party (Lietuvos Ūkininkų Partija [LPP]). From 1925 he lectured in agrarian economics at Kaunas University. After the Nationalist coup of December 1926 the LPP supported the new government of **Augustinas Voldemaras**, and Aleksa became the minister of agriculture again. When the Nationalists dissolved the parliament in 1927, the LPP withdrew its support for the regime, but Aleksa stayed in the government as head of a new group called Peasant Unity, which enjoyed the support of rich peasants from southern Lithuania. As a result of the Great Depression, in September 1935 the group stopped supporting the government, so Aleksa gave up his position. He became chairman of the Agricultural Chamber and director of a cooperative bank.

After the Soviet invasion of June 1940 Aleksa was arrested, and his family was deported to Siberia. He was released after the German invasion in June 1941. Together with former president **Kazys Grinius** and former minister of agriculture Reverend **Mykolas Krupavičius**, he signed a memorandum to the German authorities protesting the expropriation of Lithuanians and the extermination of Jews. In the fall of 1942 he was arrested by the Gestapo and deported to Germany. After the end of the war he returned to Lithuania to reunite with his family, but in 1948 he was arrested and sentenced to forced labor in a camp near Krasnoyarsk. In 1952 he was allowed to reunite with his family in Tomsk, but he soon died. He authored the following among other works: *Lietuvių tautos likimo klausimo* (On the fate of the Lithuanian nation; 1925); *Ūkininkai ir jų jėga* (Peasants and their strength; 1929); *Mūsų žemės ūkio reikalu* (On our agricultural situation; 1930); and *Lietuviškųjų gyvenimo kelių beieškant* (In search of a Lithuanian way of life; 1933). (WR)

Sources: *EL,* vols. 1 and 6; Piotr Łossowski, *Kraje bałtyckie na drodze od demokracji parlamentarnej do dyktatury 1918–1934* (Wrocław, 1972); Wojciech Roszkowski, "Litewskie partie chłopskie (1905–1970), in Krzysztof Jasiewicz, ed., *Europa nieprowincjonalna* (Warsaw, 1999).

ALEKSA-ANGARIETIS Zigmas (25 June 1882, Obelutsiai, near Vilkaviškis–22 June 1940, Moscow), Lithuanian Communist activist. Born into a peasant family, after finishing secondary school, Aleksa-Angarietis enrolled in the Warsaw Veterinary Institute, and he took up revolutionary activities. In 1904 he was expelled from the institute and arrested. Released in 1905, he joined the Social Democratic Party of Lithuania. Between 1908 and 1909 he published the newspaper *Darbininku zodis.* Arrested in Marijampole in 1909, he was held in prison for two years, and then he was sentenced to deportation to the region of the Angara River in Siberia. After the February 1917

revolution he arrived in Petrograd and joined the leadership of the Lithuanian Bolsheviks. He also published the newspaper *Tiesa.* He took an active part in the Bolshevik coup in November 1917, and he started working in the Commissariat of Nationalities of the Council of People's Commissars. In November 1918 he arrived in Vilnius to conduct underground Communist activity. After the invasion by the Red Army at the beginning of 1919, he was appointed commissar of the interior of the Lithuanian-Belorussian SSR. He became notorious for his atrocities against "the enemies of the people." After the collapse of the Lithuanian-Belorussian SSR he worked in Smolensk, writing articles and brochures. In 1921 in Smolensk he published, for example, *Lietuvos revoliucinio judéimo ir darbininkų kovos istorija* (History of the revolutionary movement and of the workers' struggle in Lithuania, 2 vols.). From 1920 he was secretary of the Foreign Office of the Communist Party of Lithuania Central Committee, and from 1924 he was a member of the Politburo of the party. He also represented Lithuania in the Communist International. In the 1920s he supported Stalin in his struggle against Leon Trotsky. Between 1926 and 1935 he was secretary of the International Control Committee of the Comintern. Arrested by the NKVD in Moscow on 17 March 1938, he was held on remand for over two years, and then he was executed by firing squad. (WR)

Sources: *EL*, vol. 1; *MERSH*, vol. 1; Lazitch; Saulius Sužiedelis, *Historical Dictionary of Lithuania* (Lanham, Md., 1997); R. Šarmaitis, "Zigmas Angarietis," *Kommunist*, no. 7 (Vilnius, 1956); Alfred E. Senn, *The Emergence of Modern Lithuania* (New York, 1959).

ALEKSANDROV Todor (14 February 1881, Štip–31 August 1924, near Melnik), Macedonian revolutionary and politician. Very early on Aleksandrov got involved in the Macedonian revolutionary and nationalist movement, and he was one of the leaders of the Internal Macedonian Revolutionary Organization (Vnatrešna Makedonska Revolucionerna Organizacija [IMRO]). At first he opposed Turkish rule, and during the Balkan Wars (1912–13) he represented a pro-Bulgarian option. After the defeat of Turkey he opposed Greek and Serb interests in Macedonia. After World War I, in opposition to the leftist federalists in the IMRO, who wanted to associate the organization with the Kingdom of Serbs, Croats, and Slovenes (SHS), he suggested an autonomous Macedonia with Salonika as its capital. Tensions between the IMRO factions led to sharp conflict and a split in the organization. Along with General **Alexander Protogerov**, Aleksandrov assumed command of the right wing of the IMRO (the so-called autonomists), also in opposition to the Bulgarian Populist government of **Aleksandur Stamboliyski.** Aleksandrov's troops controlled Pirin Macedonia and organized attacks into Vardar Macedonia, inside the SHS Kingdom. In 1922 the Bulgarian authorities arrested him temporarily for his actions against the Stamboliyski regime. Aleksandrov took part in the coup that overthrew and killed Stamboliyski in June 1923. The new Bulgarian prime minister, **Aleksandur Tsankov,** supported Aleksandrov and his autonomists. As he failed to accomplish his goals, Aleksandrov began to cooperate with Croat nationalists and with the Young Turks who ruled in Istanbul. Finally he drew closer to the Communist International. In May 1924 he signed an agreement of cooperation with the leftist faction of IMRO federalists, but in practice he remained mistrustful of them. He also got involved in a conflict concerning the cooperation of the IMRO with the Soviet Union. As a result of this conflict, his comrades murdered him. There are several theories concerning his death. In 1994 his *Dnevnik i korespondencija ot prvata svecka vojna, 1915–1918 g.* (Diary and correspondence from World War I, 1915–1918) was published. (MC)

Sources: *Biographisches Lexikon,* vol. 1; Mercia MacDermott, *For Freedom and Perfection: The Life of Yané Sandansky* (London and Nyack, N.Y., 1988); *Zagovorut protiv Todor Aleksandrov po danni na Vutreshnata makedonska revoliutsionna organizatsiia* (Sofia, 1991); *Todor Aleksandrov. Zhivot-legenda: Avtobiogr., spomeni, interviuta i dr. materiali: Biblioteka Arkhiv* (Sofia, 1991); Decho Dobrinov, *Posledn'i'at 't'sar na planinite: Biografichen ocherk za Todor Aleksandrov, 1881–1924* (Sofia, 1992); Irena Stawowy-Kawka, *Historia Macedonii* (Wrocław, 2000).

ALEKSIYEVICH Svyatlana (31 May 1948, Ivano-Frankovsk), Belorussian journalist and writer. After graduating from high school in Kopytkovichy in Polesie in 1965, Aleksiyevich worked as a tutor in a boarding school, a teacher of history and German, and a journalist for the local press in Naroulja and Byaroza. In 1972 she graduated in journalism at the Belorussian State University in Minsk. She worked at *Syelskaya gazeta* (1972–73) and at a literary monthly, *Nioman* (1973–84). She made her literary debut in 1975. In 1985 she published her first novel, *U vayny nye zhenskoye litso* (War has no female face), which garnered a lot of criticism for downplaying the heroic image of Soviet women during World War II, for "nihilism," and for spreading "pacifist" views, but as a result of *perestroika,* about 2 million sold copies made her famous in Soviet literary circles. She won more fame and international recognition for another novel, *Tsynkovye malchiki* (Tin boys; 1989), which described the cruelty of the Afghan war, but Aleksiyevich was sued for slandering the honor of Soviet officers and soldiers. Her next book, *Chernobylskaya molitva* (The Prayer of Chernobyl; 1997),

showed a world endangered by the accumulation of the technical means of extermination. Her books have been published in nineteen countries, and she has received a number of prestigious national and international awards. Since 1989 Aleksiyevich has been a member of the Belorussian PEN club. (EM)

Sources: *Bielaruskiya pismienniki. Biyabibliyahraficzny slounik,* vol. 1 (Minsk, 1992); *Bielaruskiya pismienniki 1917–1990* (Minsk, 1994); *Kto iest kto w Respublike Belarus* (Minsk, 1999).

ALEXANDER I Karadjordjević (16 December 1888, Cetinje, Montenegro–9 October 1934, Marseilles, France), king of the Kingdom of Serbs, Croats, and Slovenes and king of the Kingdom of Yugoslavia. Alexander I spent his youth in Geneva and St. Petersburg. In 1903, after the overthrow of the Obrenović dynasty, his father, Peter I Karadjordjević, became king. In 1909, when his elder brother renounced his right of succession, Alexander came back to Serbia. A successful commander in the Balkan Wars of 1912–13, he was appointed regent on 24 June 1914. During World War I he served as commander-in-chief of Serbia's armed forces. On 31 October 1918 he triumphantly entered Belgrade, and on 1 December, as prince regent, he proclaimed the creation of the Kingdom of Serbs, Croats, and Slovenes. On 28 June 1921 there was an unsuccessful attempt on his life. On 16 June 1921 he succeeded his father as king. As the main representative of the Greater Serbia orientation, he belonged to the opponents of federalism.

The main sources of conflict in the Kingdom of Serbs, Croats, and Slovenes were the issues of a centralist versus a federal model of state and ethnic strife. On 20 June 1928 a Radical Party deputy shot dead two Croat Peasant Party deputies in the parliament and injured three others, among them **Stjepan Radić,** who soon died. This caused a very serious national crisis. On 6 January 1929 Alexander dissolved the parliament, abolished the centralist constitution of 1921, rendered all political parties illegal, dismissed communal self-government, introduced censorship, and established a royal dictatorship. On 3 October 1929, by decree, he changed the previous name of the country to the Kingdom of Yugoslavia. He also introduced an administrative reform, replacing the former thirty-three departments with nine *banovine.* They were headed by a *ban* nominated by the king. Alexander's intention was to put an end to the historical division into nations and create a unified Yugoslav state, which, he believed, would help suppress the constant ethnic conflicts. The Great Depression of the 1930s added to the domestic problems, and social discontent increased. On 9 September 1931 Alexander promulgated a new constitution that sanctioned dictatorship. However, neither the opening of the new parliament nor frequent government changes by Alexander helped to relieve the tensions in Yugoslavia. The Croatian Peasant Party insisted on the reorganization of the state on the basis of the equal rights of the nations. Also, the Slovene People's Party joined in criticizing the existing form of government. The authorities responded by repressing the politicians of the opposition parties. In December 1933 the Croatian Ustaše carried out an unsuccessful attempt on Alexander's life.

In foreign policy Alexander opted for maintaining the Versailles order. An alliance with France was of primary importance. Part of the pro-French policy was to include Yugoslavia in the Little Entente, created in 1920–22, whose members were also Czechoslovakia and Romania. Alexander engaged his country in the Balkan Entente (comprised of Greece, Turkey, and Romania), formed in February 1934, and he managed to improve relations with Bulgaria. During a visit to Marseilles, Alexander and the French foreign minister, Louis Barthou, were shot dead by Vlada Makedonski vel Velicko Georgijev-Kerin, a Macedonian linked with the Croatian Ustaše who was lynched on the spot by the crowd. (AO)

Sources: *Biographisches Lexikon,* vol. 1; Wacław Felczak and Tadeusz Wasilewski, *Historia Jugosławii* (Wrocław, 1985); Barbara Jelavich, *History of the Balkans, Twentieth Century,* vol. 2 (Cambridge, 1983); Mark Biondich, *Stjepan Radić, the Croat Peasant Party, and the Politics of Mass Mobilization, 1904–1928* (Toronto, 2000).

ALEXANDER Obrenović (14 August 1876, Belgrade–11 June 1903, Belgrade), king of Serbia, son of Milan and Natalie, née Keško. After his father's abdication, on 6 March 1889 Alexander ascended the throne, although the real power was exercised by three regents: Jovan Ristić, Kosta Protić, and Jovan Beli-Marković. In April 1893 Alexander declared himself of age and, against the terms of the constitution, he began to reign. In January 1894 his father returned to Belgrade to prevent anarchy and to support Alexander in his struggle against Radical Party leaders. The latter represented peasants and part of the lower middle class, and at that time they showed a sympathy toward socialism. In May 1894 Alexander suspended the relatively liberal constitution of 1888 and restored the conservative constitution of 1869. Inter-party strife intensified in the country. The splits were deepened by a conflict between Milan and his wife, Queen Natalie, who was backed by the Radicals. Alexander sometimes obeyed his father and sometimes followed his mother's advice. In 1899, after an unsuccessful assassination attempt on Milan, a state of emergency was declared, and radical

leaders were arrested. In 1900 Alexander caused a scandal by marrying Draga Mašin, the widow of a Czech engineer and a former lady-in-waiting to Queen Natalie, and by rejecting proposals to marry the Princess of Montenegro. This led to a conflict between Alexander and his father, who soon broke off relations with his son, left Serbia, and died in Vienna in February 1901.

On 19 April 1900 Alexander accepted a new constitution, which slightly increased the importance of the parliament (Skupština). Some Radicals became reconciled with the king, but not for long. He introduced an absolutist reign. In March 1903 he again suspended the constitution. As a result, an anti-royalist demonstration took place in Belgrade, organized by Dimitr Tucivić, the founder of the Social Democratic Party. During the demonstration several people were killed. Alexander restored the constitution, but he soon dissolved the parliament and ordered new elections. On the night of 10–11 June 1903 a group of officers staged a coup, killing Alexander, his wife Draga, her two brothers, and three ministers. The next day the army proclaimed the accession to the throne of Peter Karadjordjević. Such was the end of the Obrenović dynasty, which had ruled in Serbia from 1815. Simultaneously, there ended a period of subordination of Serb interests to the interests of Austria-Hungary, and the balance of power in the Balkans changed substantially. (AO)

Sources: *Biographisches Lexikon,* vol. 1; Vladan Georgevitch, *Das Ende der Obrenovitch: Beiträge zur Geschichte Serbiens 1897 bis 1900* (Leipzig, 1905); Chedomille Mijatovitc, *A Royal Tragedy* (London, 1906); Slobodan Jovanović, *Vlada Aleksandra Obrenovicia,* vols. 1–3 (Belgrade 1934/36); Wayne S. Vucinich, *Serbia between East and West: The Events of 1903–1908* (Stanford, 1954); Michael B.Petrovich, *A History of Modern Serbia 1804–1918,* vols. 1–2 (New York, 1976); Wacław Felczak and Tadeusz Wasilewski, *Historia Jugosławii* (Wrocław, 1985).

ALIA Ramiz (18 October 1925, Shkodër), Communist leader of Albania. Alia came from a poor Muslim family. Between 1939 and 1940 he belonged to a Fascist organization, the Albanian Lictorian Youth, and in 1942 he joined the Union of Communist Youth. In April 1943 he joined the Albanian Communist Party and became the leader of a party unit in Berat. After the collapse of the Italian occupation he joined the National Liberation Army, serving as political commissar in the Seventh Partisan Brigade and at the end of the war in the Fifth Division. Under the patronage of **Enver Hoxha** he rose rapidly in the government hierarchy. From 1944 to 1948 he was secretary general of the Communist youth organization, the Union of Working Youth of Albania. He completed shortened studies in a party school in Moscow, becoming a Stalinist apparatchik.

Beginning in February 1948 Alia worked in the Office

of Propaganda and Agitation of the Communist Party's Central Committee, and from September 1948 he was a member of the CC. From 1950 he was a deputy to the People's Assembly. Between 1955 and 1958 he was minister of education; in 1958 he was again a deputy to the People's Assembly, and in 1961 he became a member of the Politburo of the CC of the Party of Labor of Albania (PLA). From 1960 he was also a member of the Secretariat of the CC. In 1965 he headed the Albanian delegation at the congress of the Communist Party of China in Beijing. As chair of the Commission for Foreign Affairs of the People's Assembly, Alia followed the pro-Chinese policy of Hoxha. After breaking away from Beijing and after the removal of Prime Minister **Mehmet Shehu**, in November 1982 he became president of the Assembly, thus the titular head of state. In fact Alia advanced to the second-highest position in the government hierarchy and was jointly responsible for the policy of terror in the country. After Hoxha's death, on 13 April 1985 Alia took over the post of first secretary of the CC of the PLA. In November 1986 the Ninth Congress of the party decided to maintain the "revolutionary legacy" of Hoxha, realized by Alia. In 1990 he was also appointed president of the republic.

When the Communist government in Albania collapsed in February 1991, Alia began to clear the vestiges of Hoxha's rule and tried to anticipate events by making personnel changes at the highest levels. These were meant to ease mounting social tensions but proved ineffective. Yielding to opposition pressures, on 21 December 1991 Alia fixed a date for by-elections, which were held in March 1992 and brought victory to the opposition Democratic Party of Albania. On 3 April 1992 he resigned as president. Soon after the delegalization of the Communist Party he was arrested and sentenced to ten years' imprisonment for embezzlement and corruption. In July 1995 he was released under amnesty, but in February 1996 he was arrested again. After one year of preventive arrest he stood trial. He was accused, among other things, of sending thousands of people to forced labor camps and of giving orders to shoot people who had illegally tried to cross the border. When the Communists came to power in 1998, Alia was released from prison. (WD, WR)

Sources: *Alia Ramiz: Ditari i burgut* (Athens, n.d.); *Unë, Ramiz Alia: Dëshmoj për historinë* (Tirana, 1993); *Who's Who in the Socialist Countries of Europe* (Munich, London, and Paris, 1989); Stavro Skendi, *Albania* (New York, 1956); Jerzy Hauziński and Jan Leśny, *Historia Albanii* (Wrocław, 1992); www.rulers.org

ALIJAGIĆ Alija (20 November 1895, Bijeljina–8 March 1922, Zagreb), Bosnian Communist. Born into an impoverished Bosnian Muslim family, Alijagić worked as a carpenter's apprentice in Sarajevo, where he joined a trade union in 1912. Mobilized into the Austro-Hungarian army, he was temporarily arrested for disloyalty. In 1919 he joined the Socialist Workers' Party of Yugoslavia (from June 1920 the Communist Party of Yugoslavia) and in March 1921, the organization Red Truth (Crvena Pravda), which organized terrorist attacks against the authorities of the Kingdom of Serbs, Croats, and Slovenes. On 21 June 1921 he murdered Minister of interior Milorad Drašković, who, in reply to Communist terrorist attacks, had dissolved Communist organizations and banned revolutionary propaganda. Alijagić was captured and tried. Despite the efforts of his defense team, which argued that he had acted for political reasons, he was sentenced to death in October 1921 and executed. In Communist Yugoslavia he was remembered as a revolutionary hero. (WR)

Sources: *Enciklopedija Jugoslavije,* vol. 1 (Zagreb, 1955); *Hrvatski biografski leksikon,* vol. 1 (Zagreb, 1983); Ivo Politeo, *Politički delikt* (Zagreb, 1921).

ALITI Abdurahman (1945, Zhelino, near Tetovo), Macedonian Albanian politician. Aliti graduated in law from Ss. Cyril and Methodius University in Skopje in 1969. From 1970 he worked in the City Council of Tetovo. In 1990 he was elected a delegate of ethnic Albanians to the government of the Socialist Republic of Macedonia. From the first free elections of November 1990, he served as MP. He was also head of the Party for Democratic Prosperity (Partija za Demokratski Prosperitet/Partia ë prosperiteti demokratike [PDP]), founded in 1991. Aliti was presiding over the party when, in 1994, Arben Xhaferi broke away with a faction. Vice-president of the Macedonian parliament (Sobranie) from 1994 to 1998, Aliti has been a centrist and has supported integration but not assimilation. He has been active in the pursuit of equal rights for Albanians in Macedonia. Owing to the vagaries of Albanian politics in Macedonia, he was eclipsed and replaced by Imer Imeri in the mid-1990s. In 2000, he stood against **Stojan Andov** for Speaker of the Parliament but lost. Imeri resigned in 2002, and Aliti once more became head of the PDP, albeit in a controversial election. (DP)

Sources: Duncan Perry, "Republic of Macedonia: On the Road to Stability or Destruction?" *Transition,* 25 August 1995; Valentina Georgieva and Sasha Konechni, *Historical Dictionary of the Republic of Macedonia* (Lanham, Md., 1998).

ALIZOTI bey Fejzi (September 1874, Gjirokastra–March 1945, Tirana), Albanian politician. Alizoti studied administration and finance at university in Istanbul. From being an Ottoman official in Lebanon, he advanced to the position of governor (*mutesarrif*) of Libya and Anatolia. In 1904 he returned to Albania, becoming prefect of Korça.

For his contacts with the Albanian national movements he was removed to Kurdistan, and during the Italian-Turkish war he was interned for a few months. After release in 1911, he became governor of Prizren. In 1912 in Vlorë he signed the Albanian declaration of independence and became minister of the interior in the government of **Ismail Kemali.** When Prince **Wilhelm von Wied** came to Albania, Alizoti became secretary general in the Ministry of Interior. When in July 1915 Montenegrin troops entered Shkodër, he was arrested, but during the Austro-Hungarian occupation of Shkoder he helped to create an Albanian administration and became prefect of the town. When in 1918 a pro-Italian government was established in Durrës, he became its minister of finance. His pro-Italian sympathies were the reason for his arrest by the authorities of the Albanian state during the aggravation of a conflict over the control of Vlorë with Italy in 1920. Aliti returned to public life at a time of renewed Albanian-Italian cooperation. In 1926 he was on the board of directors of the National Bank of Albania, and in 1927 he became minister of finance. He was the author of spare budgets in the early 1930s. He wrote economic articles for leading government periodicals. It was then that he began to be accused of taking payoffs from the Italians. After the Italian invasion of April 1939 he was among the highest-ranking politicians who cooperated with the Italians. He was ranked among the "professionals of Gjirokaster"—that is, those experienced in state administration. A member of the Albanian Fascist Party, he also edited its organ, *Fashizmi.* In the first collaboration government of Shefqet bey Vërlaci (12 April 1939–3 December 1941) Aliti was minister of finance. In August 1941 he was appointed civil commissioner of New Albania (Kosovo). Captured by the Communist partisans and tried as the main defendant in a show trial in Tirana, on 1 March 1945 Aliti was sentenced to death and soon executed. (TC)

Sources: Jacomoni di San Savino Francesco, *La politica dell'Italia in Albania* (Rocca San Casciano, 1965); Pepa Pjeter, *Dosja e diktaturës* (Tirana, 1995); Gaçe Bardhosh, *Ata që shpallën Pavarësinë Kombëtare* (Tirana, 1997); Bernd Fischer, *Albania at War 1939–1945* (London, 1999).

ALLIK Hendrik (15 March 1901, Abja–8 May 1989, Tallinn), Estonian Communist activist. From 1916 Allik worked in a textile factory in Tallinn and was active in the trade unions. In 1917 he joined the Bolshevik party. In 1923 he was coopted to the Central Committee (CC) of the Communist Party of Estonia (CPE) and to the CC of the Estonian Komsomol. For participation in the December 1924 Communist rebellion he was sentenced to twenty-five years in prison. Released due to an amnesty

in 1938, he became a member of the CPE Politburo. After the incorporation of Estonia into the USSR, from mid-1940 to mid-1941 he was the Soviet commissioner for industry. In 1942–43 he served on the front as political commissar, and then he was deputy prime minister of the Estonian SSR. After the restoration of Soviet control, in 1945–46 he was also minister of agriculture. In 1948 he graduated in economics from the Tallinn Polytechnic Institute. From 1947 he was a member of the Supreme Council of the Estonian SSR. At this time he married the widow of the former prime minister of the Estonian SSR, **Olga Johannes Lauristin.** In 1950 Allik was accused of "bourgeois nationalism" and sentenced to twenty-five years in prison. Released in 1956, he was reinstated in his previous positions. In 1961–73 he was head of the Planning Commission of the Estonian SSR; from 1958 to 1976 he was a member of the CPE CC; from 1966 to 1970, a member of the Supreme Council of the USSR; and from 1959 to 1967 and from 1971 to 1975, a member of the Supreme Council of the Estonian SSR. His son, Jaan, rejected his father's Communist stance and sympathized with the democratic opposition. (AG)

Sources: *Eesti Entsuklopeedia,* vol. 14 (Tallinn, 2000); Rein Taagepera, *Estonia: Return to Independence* (Boulder, Colo., 1993); Romuald J.Misiunas and Rein Taagepera, *The Baltic States: Years of Dependence 1940–1990* (Berkeley, 1993).

ALLIKSAAR Artur (15 April 1923, Tartu–12 August 1966, Tartu), Estonian poet and playwright. In 1942 Alliksaar graduated from high school. During the "thaw" after Stalin's death he wrote poems combining irony and the surrealistic grotesque with reflections on contemporary life in a world of coercion. It was only in 1966 that his play *Anonüümne saar* (Island with no name) was published; in it reality was absurd, and absurdity became reality. Although known only to a narrow artistic circle, Alliksaar became a champion of nonconformism in the Estonian culture under Communist rule. From a formal point of view his works were characterized by a flexible and musical style, as well as by semantic experiments. He also translated into Estonian the works of Reiner Maria Rilke and Sergey Yesenin. Alliksaar died prematurely of cancer. Two of his major collections were published posthumously: *Olematus võiks ju ka olemata olla* (Nonexistence cannot exist; 1968) and *Luule* (Poems; 1976). His works had a very strong influence on Estonian literature in the last stages of communism. (WR)

Sources: *Eesti Noukogude Entsuklopeedia,* vol. 1 (Tallinn, 1985); *Wielka encyklopedia powszechna,* vol. 1 (Warsaw, 2001); Romuald Misiunas and Rein Taagepera, *The Baltic States: Years of Dependence 1940–1980* (Berkeley, 1983).

ALSHEUSKI Anatol [originally Yurka Pruzhynski] (4 July 1904, Bereza Kartuska [Byaroza]–1937, USSR), Belorussian Communist activist. In 1919 Alsheuski volunteered for the Red Army. In 1920 he began to study at Sverdlov Memorial Communist University in Moscow, and then he worked in the Bolshevik party apparatus in Ryazan and Nizhny Novgorod. In 1925 he was sent to work in Poland. He was (among other things) secretary of the Communist Youth Association of Western Belorussia, a member of the Central Committee (CC) of the Communist Youth Association of Poland, a member of the CC of the Communist Party of Western Belorussia (CPWB), and editor-in-chief of its press organs, *Balshavik* and *Chyrvony stsiah.* Arrested by the Polish authorities, he was kept in a Warsaw prison, and in 1929 he was exchanged for Soviet political prisoners. He returned to Belorussia and worked as the CPWB representative at the headquarters of the Communist Party (Bolshevik) of Belorussia in Minsk. He published a lot in the Soviet press, mostly propaganda articles on the situation of the "working classes" in Poland. In 1937 he was arrested on the grounds of alleged spying for Poland and was executed by firing squad. (EM)

Sources: U. Kalesnik, *Paslanyets Prameteya: Dakumentalnaya apovests* (Minsk, 1984); *Entsyklapedyia historyi Belarusi,* vol. 1 (Minsk, 1993).

ALTER Wiktor (7 February 1890, Mława–4 December 1941, Kuibyshev), Polish-Jewish Socialist politician. Alter was the son of a rich merchant. While at Wojciech Górski High School in Warsaw, he was arrested by the Russian police for organizing a school strike in 1905. At that time he started secret work for the Bund. From 1906 to 1910 he studied in Liege, Belgium, where he qualified as an engineer. In 1912 he returned to Warsaw but was arrested and deported to Narym, in Siberia, in April 1913. He managed to escape and spent 1914–17 in Belgium and Great Britain, where he belonged to the British Labour Party. In March 1917 he returned to Russia. After the Bolshevik revolution he was elected to the Central Committee of the Bund. In late 1918 he returned to Poland to represent the Bund in the Warsaw Council of Workers' Delegates. He urged the stop of Polish military operations in the east and called for a strike in Polish military works. Nevertheless, during the First Congress of the Polish Bund in Kraków in April 1920, he opposed the party's access to the Comintern. In mid-1921 he was sent to Moscow to negotiate the Bund's cooperation with the Comintern but was arrested by the Cheka for contacts with the Social Revolutionaries. Soon released, he returned to Warsaw, where he even more vigorously opposed the

Bund's cooperation with the Comintern. For some time he favored the Vienna International, but in 1930 he moved a resolution in favor of the Bund's access to the Second International. Along with **Henryk Erlich,** Alter represented the Bund in it. From 1934 he favored a united front of Communists and Socialists in Poland. He represented Jewish unions in the Central Committee of Trade Unions (Komisja Centralna Związków Zawodowych). In 1937 he was in Spain. He published many articles in the Bund press—for example, "Folks-Tsaytung," "Nowe pismo," and "Myśl socjalistyczna."

When the Third Reich invaded Poland in September 1939, Alter went eastward. Arrested by the NKVD in Kowel, he was released and agreed to organize an international Jewish anti-Fascist committee in Great Britain and the United States. After the Polish-Soviet agreement of July 1941 he got in touch with the Polish Embassy in Kuibyshev and was appointed the embassy's delegate to Sverdlovsk. During the recruitment of Polish citizens to the army of General **Władysław Anders,** he opposed Jewish nationalists who wanted separate Jewish troops. On 4 December 1941 he was arrested by the NKVD, along with Erlich, on the grounds of alleged cooperation with Nazi Germany. Both men were soon killed by the Soviets despite the energetic protests of the Polish embassy and the Allied governments. The accusations were absurd, and the whole Alter-Erlich affair remains a political enigma. Alter's sister, Estera Iwińska, was a Polish lawyer, and his brother, Issak Arens, was a Soviet diplomat. Alter authored several works, including *Socjalizm walczący* (Militant socialism; 1926), *Tsu der Yidnfrage in Poiln* (The Jewish question in Poland; 1927), *Antysemityzm gospodarczy w świetle cyfr* (Economic anti-Semitism in the light of data; 1937), and *Hiszpania w ogniu* (Spain on fire; 1937). (WR)

Sources: *Encyclopedia Judaica,* vol. 1; *Słownik biograficzny działaczy polskiego ruchu robotniczego,* vol. 1 (Warsaw, 1979); *Henryk Erlich i Wiktor Alter* (New York, 1951); *The Case of Henryk Erlich and Wiktor Alter* (London, 1943).

AMBRAZEVIČIUS-BRAZAITIS Juozas [originally Ambrazevičius] (9 December 1903, Trakišliai, near Marijampolė–28 October 1974, New York), Lithuanian historian of literature and politician. After graduating from high school in Marijampolė, in 1922–27 Ambrazevčius-Brazaitis studied literature at Kaunas University, and then he started working as a teacher in a high school for girls in Kaunas. In 1931–32 he studied in Bonn, and after returning to Lithuania, he taught in the same high school. In 1934 he began lecturing in Lithuanian literature and folk culture at Kaunas University. He authored several textbooks on the theory of literature and on the history of Lithuanian and world literature. He worked in the Catholic cultural movement, editing the dailies *Lietuva* and *XX Amžius*. During the first Soviet occupation (1940–41) he kept his job and engaged in underground activities. After the German invasion, on 23 June 1941 he headed the Provisional Lithuanian Government and was its minister of education. For six weeks he tried to win German acceptance but in vain. His government issued about one hundred decrees regulating property rights, administration, and education. On 5 August 1941 he finally gave up his mission but continued to work as head of the political commission of the secret Chief Committee of Lithuanian Liberation (Vyriausias Lietuvos Islaisvinimo Komitetas [CCLL]) and editor of its underground periodical *Į laisvę*. In the summer of 1944 he left for Germany, and in 1948 for the United States, where he edited a Catholic daily, *Darbininkas*, and continued his work in the CCLL in exile. He published a number of leaflets illustrating German and Soviet crimes in Lithuania and the Lithuanian resistance—for example, *In the Name of the Lithuanian People* (1946) and *Appeal to the United Nations on Genocide* (1951). In 1964 he published *Allein, ganz allein* (Alone, all alone) about the Lithuanian armed resistance. The Kremlin actively opposed his activities. In the 1970s he became a subject of interest for the Soviet media and American hunters of Nazi collaborators, who accused him of having worked for the Third Reich. In reply, he published an extensive dossier of his World War II activities. (WR)

Sources: *EL*, vol. 1; Saulius Sužiedelis, *Historical Dictionary of Lithuania* (Lanham, Md., 1997); Algirdas Budreckis, *The Lithuanian National Revolt of 1941* (Boston, 1968).

ANDERS Władysław (11 August 1892, Błoń, near Kutno–12 May 1970, London), Polish general and politician. Anders studied at the Polytechnic College in Riga, where he belonged to a student organization called Arkonia. During World War I he was drafted as a reserve officer in the Russian army, and in 1914–17 he served as a cavalry lieutenant. In 1917 he completed studies at the Academy of the General Staff in St. Petersburg, gaining first place, for which he received a golden sword from Tsar Nicholas II. Anders took part in the formation of the First Polish Corps, which was created by General **Józef Dowbór-Muśnicki** in Russia in 1917, and he served in the first regiment of the Krechowce *uhlans* (cavalrymen) of this corps. After its dissolution Anders returned to Warsaw. He took part in the disarmament of Germans in Poland. In 1918 he served in the Polish Army. He participated in the Great Poland (Wielkopolska) Uprising (1918–19). In 1919 he was the chief of staff of the Operational Unit of the command-in-chief of the armed forces in the former Prussian sector of partitioned Poland (Wielkopolska army in Poznań). He fought in the Polish-Bolshevik war (1919–21), commanding a regiment. In 1921 he left for Paris, where he graduated from the War College (École Supérieure de Guerre) in 1923. In 1924 he returned to Poland as a colonel and started work as director of a course for higher commanders. Later, he worked in the staff of the inspector general of the cavalry. During the coup of May 1926 he became the chief of staff of the government forces. However, after the coup he remained in the army. From 1928 to 1937 he commanded two cavalry brigades. In 1937 he became the commander of the Nowogródzka Cavalry Brigade within the "Modlin" Army of General Emil Przedrzymirski.

Anders commanded this brigade during the war with Germany until 12 September 1939. He then took command of the Cavalry Operational Group, fighting against German and Soviet forces. After the seizure of the Polish Eastern Borderland by the Soviets, the Polish authorities, which had evacuated to Romania, ordered Anders to get to Romania or Hungary. After severe battles, during which he was seriously injured, Anders was taken captive by the Soviets near Turka. For twenty-two months he was held by the NKVD in various prisons, including the ill-famed Lubyanka Prison. After the German attack on the USSR and the signing of the Polish-Soviet treaty on 30 July 1941, Anders was released. He assumed command of the Polish Army, which was forming in the USSR among Poles deported from the territories seized by the USSR. When in 1942, as a result of a British-Soviet agreement, this army had to leave the USSR and move to Iran, Anders became the commander of the Polish Army in the East (1942–43). From 1943 to 1946 he was in command of the Second Polish Corps within the Polish Armed Forces in the West (Polskie Siły Zbrojne na Zachodzie). This corps, consisting of two infantry divisions, one armored brigade, and an artillery group, took part in the battle of Monte Cassino, finally capturing the monastery in May 1944. This success opened the way to Rome for the Allies. At the end of the war the Second Corps also fought in the battle of Ancona, on the "Gothic line," at Bologna, and in the Apennines. In February 1945 Anders took a critical stand on the Yalta decisions. While General Tadeusz Bór-Komorowski was being held in captivity, from February to May 1945 Anders served as the commander-in-chief and inspector general of the Polish Armed Forces in the West.

Next, Anders assumed command of the Second Polish Corps, which after the end of the war was around 110,000-strong, posing a serious political problem to the Allies in the face of the Sovietization of Poland. The soldiers and officers of the corps, as well as their adored general Anders, wanted to maintain the corps as an independent military unit, capable of supporting the Polish cause after the war. However, in March 1946 the efforts of the British led to the dissolution of the Polish Armed Forces, including the Second Corps, and their integration into the Polish Adaptation and Resettlement Corps (Polski Korpus Przysposobienia i Rozmieszczenia). Anders left for London, where he continued to play a major political role. On 26 September 1946 the Communist government in Warsaw deprived him of his Polish citizenship, which was restored to him posthumously by the government of the Third Republic of Poland. From 1946 to 1954 Anders held the titular post of commander-in-chief and inspector general of the Polish Armed Forces in the West. He co-organized the National Treasury and from 1949 was its president. On 8 August 1954 he joined the Council of the Three, a substitute head of state in exile. In 1954 he became lieutenant general. He authored *Bez ostatniego rozdziału* (Army in exile; 1949), in which he depicted the fate of the Poles in the USSR in 1939–41. The work was translated into nine languages. He also wrote *Klęska Hitlera w Rosji, 1941–1945* (Hitler's defeat in Russia, 1941–45; 1952). In accord with his last will, he was buried at the Polish war cemetery in Monte Cassino. For thousands of Polish soldiers who had been saved from the USSR, Anders was the symbol of a common fate and patriotism. He was a kind of savior because of the protection he gave not only to his subordinates, but also to their families and to Polish orphans, who were evacuated along with them. (JS)

Sources: Marian Hemar, ed., *Generał Anders: życie i chwała* (London, 1970); Zdzisław Stahl, *Generał Anders i 2 Korpus* (London, 1989); Juliusz L. Englert and Krzysztof Barbarski, *Generał Anders* (London, 1990); Ewa Berberyusz, *Anders spieszony: "Aneks"* (London, 1992); Krzysztof Szmagier, *Generał Anders i jego żołnierze* (Warsaw, 1993); Piotr Stawecki, *Słownik biograficzny generałów Wojska Polskiego, 1918–1939* (Warsaw, 1994); Piotr Zaroń, *Armia Andersa* (Toruń, 1996); Henryk Piotr Kosk, *Generalicja polska: Popularny słownik biograficzny,* vol. 1 (Pruszków, 1998).

ANDOV Stojan (30 November 1935, Kavadarci, Macedonia), Macedonian politician, former Communist. Andov graduated in economics from Ss. Cyril and Methodius University in Skopje and the University of Belgrade. In the 1970s he supported market reforms in Yugoslavia. He served as the Federal Republic of Yugoslavia's ambassador to Iraq in the 1980s and spent much of his career in Belgrade and abroad. A member of the Federal Executive Council of Yugoslavia in the 1980s, he served for a time as the vice-president of the Yugoslav Federal Assembly. In November 1990 he was elected to the Macedonian

National Assembly (Sobranie), becoming its speaker in January 1991. He headed the Liberal Party, founded in 1993 as a coalition between the Alliance of Reformist Forces of Macedonia and the Young Democratic Progressive Party. Its members have been overwhelmingly ethnic Macedonians who support a free market economy. From October 1995 to the beginning of 1996 Andov acted as the president of Macedonia following an assassination attempt on **Kiro Gligorov**. Andov resigned the parliamentary speaker's post in 1996, joining the opposition when Prime Minister **Branko Crvenkovski** reshuffled the cabinet and dismissed members of the Liberal Party in a dispute involving industrial privatization. Andov ran unsuccessfully for president of the republic in October 1999. He regained the parliamentary speakership in November 2000 and held it until October 2002. He has opposed reforms meant to accord ethnic Albanians greater rights but is believed to be a staunch supporter of Macedonia's good relations with the United States and the European Union. Andov joined a coalition including the Internal Macedonian Revolutionary Organization-Democratic Party for Macedonian National Unity and the New Democracy Party in the September 2002 elections. (DP)

Sources: Valentina Georgieva and Sasha Konechni, *Historical Dictionary of the Republic of Macedonia* (Lanham, Md., 1998); James Pfeiffer, ed., *The New Macedonian Question* (London, 1999); *RFE/RL Newsline;* Bugajski; *OMRI Daily Digest;* www. rulers.org

ANDRÁSSY Gyula, Jr. (30 June 1860, Tőketerebes [Trebišov, near Košice, Slovakia]–11 June 1929, Budapest), Hungarian politician. The son of Prime Minister Gyula Andrássy, Andrássy began his career as a royal minister and MP on behalf of the Liberal Party (Szabadelvű Párt). In 1892 he became undersecretary of state in the Ministry of Interior, and in 1894–95 he was minister at the imperial court in Vienna. He supported the Austro-Hungarian compromise of 1867, but he increasingly competed with the leader of his party, **István Tisza**. During the parliamentary debate on the budget and military draft in February 1904, Andrássy belonged to the opposition against Prime Minister Tisza. The parliamentary conflict resulted in a new election. Under social pressures the right to vote was extended, so the Liberal Party lost. In 1905 Andrássy founded the Constitutional Party (Alkotmánypárt), which also supported the Austro-Hungarian compromise, and entered a new government coalition. In the **Sándor Wekerle** government Andrássy was Hungarian minister of interior from April 1906 to January 1910. He elaborated on a draft of the new electoral law, including universal but not fully equal voting rights in Hungary. Owing to the opposition of the left, the law did not come into force. He advocated a sharpening of the Magyarization policy and restrictions on the use of native languages in public life, elaborated by the minister of education and religious denominations, **Albert Apponyi** ("lex Apponyi"). Andrássy was an excellent parliamentary orator. During World War I he fully supported Hungary's engagement but remained in opposition to the subsequent government of Tisza (1913–17). In late October 1918 he was appointed foreign minister of Austria-Hungary, with the task of engaging in the peace talks with the Entente. On 3 November 1918 he concluded the armistice with the victorious coalition on its terms.

During the Hungarian Soviet Republic in 1919 Andrássy was one of the key organizers of the Anti-Bolshevik Committee in Vienna. In 1920 he was elected to the parliament again. In 1921 he presided over the Christian National Union. As a convinced legitimist and conservative, in October 1921 he took part in a futile attempt to enthrone Charles IV as King of Hungary and offered to become his foreign minister, for which he was arrested for a couple of weeks. After his release, he was one of the main opponents of the policy of national consolidation of Prime Minister **István Bethlen,** and until the end of his life he preached Austro-Hungarian legitimism. From 1904 Andrássy was a member of the Hungarian Academy of Sciences. He authored many articles and books, including *Az 1867-es kiegyezésről* (On the Compromise of 1867; 1896), *A magyar állam fönnmaradásának és alkotmányos szabadságának okai* (Constitutional freedoms of the Hungarian state, 3 vols.; 1901–11), *A királykérdés jogi szempontból Budapest* (Legal grounds of royal power in Hungary; 1920), and *A világháború előzményei* (Circumstances of the outbreak of World War II, 2 vols.; 1925–26). (MS)

Sources: *Biographisches Lexikon,* vol. 1; Steven Béla Várga, *Historical Dictionary of Hungary* (Lanham, Md., 1997); Paul Count Teleki, *The Evolution of Hungary and Its Place in European History* (New York, 1923); Sándor Pethő, *Andrássy Gyula és ellenfelei* (Budapest, 1924); Albert Apponyi, *Andrássy Gyula emlékezete. MTA Emlékbeszédek* (Budapest, 1930); Nicholas Horthy, *Memoirs* (Paris, 1954); Michael Karolyi, *Faith without Illusion* (London, 1956); Paul Ignotus, *Hungary* (London, 1972); István Diósegi, *A magyar külpolitika útjai: tanulmányok* (Budapest, 1984); Jerzy Kochanowski, *Węgry* (Warsaw, 1997).

ANDREESCU Gabriel (8 April 1952, Buzau), Romanian dissident. In 1976 Andreescu graduated in physics from Bucharest University. He taught physics in Buzau, and in 1980–89 he worked at the Meteorological and Hydrological Institute in Bucharest. In 1982, through a school friend living in the United States, he issued a couple of letters criticizing the rule of **Nicolae Ceauşescu** and his clan. In 1984 Radio Free Europe began to broadcast excerpts from his diary. In December 1987 he was arrested and accused

of high treason. Despite brutal interrogation, he did not disclose his collaborators, and he was released in accord with the amnesty of January 1988. Soon, Andreescu, **Doina Cornea,** and **Mircea Dinescu** sent a letter to the participants of the International Conference on Human Rights in Kraków, Poland, in which they delineated the violations of human rights in Romania and appealed to the Romanian society not to collaborate with the regime. In June 1989 they led a several-week-long hunger strike in defense of human rights in Romania. Andreescu's letter to the subsequent conference on human rights in Paris in 1989 raised a debate about Western interference in the internal affairs of Communist countries. Despite constant surveillance by the political police, Securitate, Andreescu gave a couple of interviews to the Western media. Starting in October 1989 he was in house arrest. He was imprisoned on 22 December 1989 but released the next day owing to the fall of the Ceauşescu regime. From January to May 1990 Andreescu belonged to the Council of the National Salvation Front, and then he worked with the Group in Favor of Social Dialogue (Grupul pentru Dialog Social). He is a leader of the Romanian Association for the Defense of Human Rights. (WR)

Sources: "Curriculum vitae Gabriel Andreescu" and Radoslav Doru, "Gabriel Andreescu"; manuscripts in the archives of the Karta Center in Warsaw.

ANDREI Stefan (29 March 1931, Podari-Livezi, Oltenia), Romanian Communist activist. In 1956 Andrei graduated in engineering from the Higher School of Building in Bucharest. From 1960 to 1963 he belonged to the Executive Committee of the Union of Student Associations, and in 1962–65 he was a member of the Central Committee (CC) of the Union of Working Youth. In both organizations he was responsible for foreign relations. From October 1965 he was deputy head of the Department for Relations with Socialist Countries of the CC of the Romanian Communist Party (RCP), and in April 1972 he became CC secretary for foreign affairs. From November 1974 he belonged to the Standing Presidium of the RCP CC Political Executive Committee, the highest party organ. In February 1978, during a conference of party secretaries of Communist parties in Budapest, Andrei held talks with the leaders of the Hungarian party on the burning issue of the Hungarian minority in Transylvania. He was one of the chief executors of **Nicolae Ceauşescu**'s foreign policy decisions. Andrei was famous for a pompous way of life and corruption. From March 1978 he was foreign minister. He accompanied Ceauşescu on many foreign trips. During visits to Budapest (March 1983) and Bonn (March 1984) he discussed the problem of national minorities in Romania. During the Thirteenth RCP Congress in November 1984 he was dismissed from the Standing Presidium. Ceausescu charged him with the special protection of his youngest son, Nicu. In theory Andrei was to prepare Nicu for future rule; in practice Andrei tolerated his scandalous conduct. At the end of 1985 Andrei left the Foreign Ministry and became RCP CC secretary, this time responsible for the ailing economy. The end of the Ceauşescu regime was also the end of his career. (PC)

Sources: Juliusz Stroynowski, ed., *Who's Who in the Socialist Countries of Europe* (Munich, London, and Paris, 1989); Robert King, *History of the Romanian Communist Party* (Stanford, 1980); Martin McCauley and Stephen Carter, *Leadership and Succession in the Soviet Union, Eastern Europe and China* (New York, 1985); Ion M. Pacepa, *Red Horizons* (New York, 1987).

ANDRESEN Nigol (2 October 1899, Vanamoisa, near Haljala–24 February 1985, Tartu), was an Estonian writer and Communist activist. In 1918 Andresen graduated from a training school in Rakvere, and then he worked as a teacher. In 1928 he was elected MP on behalf of the Estonian Socialist Labor Party but he left it, recognizing its program as too moderate. He founded the Marxist Union of Working People (MUWP); the group was attracted to the Communist International, which was seeking a chance to restore influence in Estonia after the Communist Party of Estonia had failed to overthrow the democratic government in 1924. In 1935 Comintern representatives signed an agreement of cooperation with the MUWP in the struggle against "fascism"—i.e., the **Konstantin Päts** regime.

At the time of the Soviet invasion in June 1940, Andresen belonged to a group of most trusted aides of the Communists. In the **Johannes Vares** government (June–July 1940) he became commissar of foreign affairs, and in the **Johannes Lauristin** government he was appointed deputy chairman (deputy prime minister) of the Council of People's Commissars of the Estonian SSR and commissar of education (1940–44). Supervising the transformation of the Estonian Foreign Ministry into the People's Commissariat of the Estonian SSR, he was responsible for personnel purges and the promotion of Soviet activists. However, there is evidence that he hoped to maintain remnants of the former diplomatic apparatus. As commissar for education, he implemented Soviet instructions, which meant the transformation of the education system along Soviet lines, the introduction of Marxism-Leninism into schools, purges among teachers, and the abolition of teacher and student organizations and their replacement by the Soviet Komsomol and pioneer organizations. He was also responsible for censorship in 1940–41 and 1944–46. After the restoration of Soviet power in 1944, Andresen was acting chairman of the Council of Ministers

of the Estonian SSR (1946–47) and deputy chairman of the republican Supreme Council (1946–49). In 1947 he graduated from a party school at the Central Committee of the Soviet party, and in 1948, from Estonian studies at the University of Tartu. In 1940–49 he was a member of the Supreme Council of the Estonian SSR, and in 1940–46, a member of the Supreme Council of the USSR. With the wave of purges that affected the Estonian party in 1950, Andresen was accused of "bourgeois nationalism" and deported to Siberia. After his return he withdrew from political life and worked as a teacher. He published biographies of *Friedebert Tuglas* (1968) and *Paul Kuusberg* (1976). He also translated works by Maksxim Gorky, Ilya Ehrenburg, and Arnold Zweig, as well as *Das Kapital*, by Karl Marx, and the *Communist Manifesto*. (AG)

Sources: *Eesti Entsuklopeedia*, vol. 14 (Tallinn, 2000); *Pravda*, 13 May 1950; Erik Nørgaard, *Mändene fra Estland* (Copenhagen, 1990); Toivo U. Raun, *Estonia and the Estonians* (Stanford, 1991); Matti Laur, Tõnis Lukas, Ain Mäesalu, Ago Pajur, and Tõnu Tannberg, *History of Estonia* (Tallinn, 2000); www.okupatsioon. ee/english/overviews/index.html; Mike Jones, "How Estonia Became Part of the USSR and" "Revolutionary History"; www. revolutionary-history.co.uk.

ANDRIĆ Ivo (10 October 1892, Dolac, near Travnik, Bosnia–13 March 1975, Belgrade), Yugoslav writer and diplomat. Andrić was born into a Catholic family in Bosnia. His father died when he was two years old. Andrić spent his childhood in the Bosnian town of Višegrad on the Drina River. In 1910 he began his education at the Great Gymnasium in Sarajevo. He was active in Mlada Bosna (Young Bosnia), a revolutionary youth movement that aimed at the unification of the south Slavic nations into one state and that was in opposition to Austria-Hungary. With the radicalization of Mlada Bosna, Andrić started to distance himself from this movement. In the fall of 1912 he began studies in philosophy in Zagreb. After one year he moved to Vienna, but for health reasons he left for Kraków, where in 1914 he studied at the Jagiellonian University. After the assassination of Archduke Francis Ferdinand (June 1914) by **Gavrilo Princip**, a member of Mlada Bosna, Andrić arrived in Split, where in July of the same year he was arrested. He was held in prison until mid-1917. After the end of World War I he got a job at the Ministry for Religious Affairs in the newly created Kingdom of Serbs, Croats, and Slovenes. In 1920 he entered the Yugoslav diplomatic service. In 1924 he completed his studies and obtained a Ph.D. from the university in Graz, Austria. He then continued his work in the diplomatic service. He served at diplomatic missions in Rome, Bucharest, Marseilles, Paris, Madrid, Brussels, and Geneva. In 1939 he was appointed ambassador to Berlin, where he stayed until April 1941, when the Third Reich invaded Yugoslavia. After World War II he joined the Communist Party. He also became president of the Yugoslav Writers' Union and deputy president of the Society for Cultural Cooperation of Yugoslavia with the USSR. In 1949, as a representative of Bosnia and Herzegovina, he was elected to the Yugoslav Federal Assembly.

Andrić was a representative of the so-called great generation, an avant-garde movement after World War I. His literary output belongs to three literatures: Croatian, Serbian, and Bosnian. He published his first literary work in 1910, under the title *U sumrak* (At twilight). In 1914 he issued a collection of poems, *Hrvatska mlada liryka* (Croatian young lyric poetry). He was an editor of the literary magazines *Književni Jug* and *Yugoslavenska njiva*. During his studies in Vienna he became acquainted with the literary works of the Danish philosopher Søren Kierkegaard; these exerted an influence on his writing that could be seen, for example, in his volumes of lyrical prose, *Ex ponto* (1918) and *Nemiri* (Unrest; 1920). In 1924, 1931, and 1936 collections of his short stories were published; each collection was entitled *Pripovetke* (Short stories). In 1925 he received an award from the Serbian Royal Academy for the first of these collections, and in 1938 he was honored with the Order of St. Sava. During the German occupation (1941–45) he lived in Belgrade, and he wrote three novels; these were published in 1945 and are considered his most important works. In 1961 these novels won him the Nobel Prize for Literature. In the first novel, *Na Drini ćuprija* (The Bridge on the Drina; 1959), Andrić presented the history of the small town Višegrad, which was created at the beginning of the sixteenth century, after the building of a great stone bridge. The bridge symbolized union and durability. His next novel, *Travnička hronika* (Bosnian story, 1959; also translated as Bosnian chronicle, 1963, and as Days of the consuls, 1992), was strongly set in the historical reality of 1807–14. Consul Daville, presented in the book as the personification of the civilized West, is helpless in his efforts to understand "wild," multinational, and multicultural Bosnia, ruled by laws that are beyond his comprehension. The third novel is titled *Gospodjica* (The woman from Sarajevo; 1965). Andrić's most important works also include *Nove pripovetke* (New stories, 1948), *Prokleta avlija* (The damned yard; 1954), *Zapisi o Goji* (Conversations with Goya; 1960) and *Omerpaša Latas* (Omer Pasha Latas; 1976). (AO)

Sources: *Biographisches Lexikon,* vol. 1; *Wielka encyklopedia PWN,* vol. 2 (Warsaw, 2001); Marek Klecel, ed., *Ivo Andrić: W dziesiątą rocznicę śmierci (1975–1985). Materiały sesji Zakładu Jugoslawistyki Instytutu Filologii Słowiańskiej Uniwersytetu Warszawskiego* (Warsaw, 1988); Celia Hawkesworth, *Ivo Andrić: Bridge between East and West* (London, 1984); Radovan Popović, *Ivo Andrić: Život* (Belgrade, 1988); Jan Wierzbicki, *Ivo Andrić* (Warsaw, 1965); Kazimierz Żórawski, *Ivo Andrić* (Warsaw, 1988).

ANDRZEJEWSKI Jerzy (19 August 1909, Warsaw–19 April 1983, Warsaw), Polish writer. In 1931 Andrzejewski graduated in Polish philology from Warsaw University. He made his debut in the Warsaw daily *ABC* in 1932. In 1935–37 he wrote for the weekly *Prosto z mostu,* where he edited a literary column. His first novel, *Ład serca* (Order of the heart; 1938), whose hero, a priest, finds a moral grounding in faith, won him wide recognition. In 1939 Andrzejewski won the Award of the Young of the Polish Academy of Literature. During the German occupation he was active in the underground cultural life of Warsaw. He presented his wartime experience in the collection of short stories *Noc* (The night; 1945). In 1946–47 he was chairman of the Kraków branch of the Trade Union of Polish Writers. In 1948 he published *Popiół i diament* (Ash and diamond), in which he presented postwar reality in a way acceptable to the Communists. The book, which was compulsory reading in the schools, became a part of the literary founding myth of communism in Poland and was made into a film by **Andrzej Wajda.**

In the early 1950s Andrzejewski declared himself a Marxist. This was, among other things, expressed in his collection *Partia i tworczość pisarza* (The Party and the work of a writer; 1952). In 1950–52 he was deputy chairman of the Association of Polish Writers and chairman of its Szczecin branch. In 1952–54 he edited *Przegląd kulturalny*; from 1955, the weekly *Twórczość*; and later, the weekly *Literatura.* From 1952 to 1957 he was MP. During the "thaw," starting in 1955, he was increasingly critical of the regime, for which **Stefan Żółkiewski** and **Jakub Berman** attacked him. His new approach was expressed in *Ciemności kryją ziemię* (Darkness covering the earth; 1956). In 1956–57 he co-authored the idea of a literary periodical, *Europa,* but the Communist authorities disapproved of it. In November 1957 he left he Communist Party, as a result of which his works were temporarily banned. This happened again in 1964 after he co-initiated and signed the "Letter of 34" intellectuals to the prime minister criticizing censorship and government cultural policies. In March 1968 he spoke up in defense of protesting students, and in August 1968, against the Polish participation in the Warsaw Pact invasion of Czechoslovakia. As a result, he was refused a passport, and his works were banned again. His accounts of communism are in the novel *Bramy raju* (Gates of paradise; 1960) and a pamphlet on contemporary culture, *Idzie skacząc po górach* (He comes jumping over the mountains; 1963).

Andrzejewski published in *Twórczość*, but in 1972 his novel *Miazga* (Pulp) was withdrawn from publication. As a signatory of the "Letter of 101" in January 1976, he protested against amendments to the constitution regarding mono-party rule and Poland's dependence on the Soviet Union. In 1976 he sent a letter to those persecuted after worker riots in Radom. He co-founded the Committee for the Defense of Workers (Komitet Obrony Robotników) and let the speaker of the parliament know about its creation in October 1976. As a result, his works were banned again, and he became the subject of a hostile press campaign and false accusations. He began to publish in underground periodicals and became a member of the editorial staff of *Zapis*. His *Miazga* appeared in an uncensored publication in 1979. Seriously ill, he took part in the First Congress of Solidarity in September 1981. (PK)

Sources: *Literatura polska. Przewodnik encyklopedyczny*, vol. 1 (Warsaw, 2000); *Opozycja w PRL. Słownik biograficzny 1956–1989*, vol. 1 (Warsaw, 2000); Maria Bursztyn, Katarzyna Rodymińska and Jerzy Eisler, *List 34* (Warsaw, 1993); Tadeusz Drewnowski, *Próba scalenia* (Warsaw, 1997).

ANGYAL István [originally Engel] (14 October 1928, Magyarbánhegyes–1 December 1958 Budapest), one of the leaders of the Hungarian revolution of 1956. During the war Angyal finished high school, but because of his Jewish origins, he was not allowed to take the final exams. In the summer of 1944, along with his mother and one of his sisters, he was deported to the Nazi concentration camp in Auschwitz-Birkenau, from which he returned alone. The Nazis shot his sister in his presence. After the war he was accepted into the Department of Humanities of Budapest University. In 1949 he spoke up in defense of **György Lukács**, for which he was fired from the university. He worked as a mechanic, and in 1951–55 he participated in the construction of the new town of Sztálinváros on the Danube; later he worked in a construction company in Budapest. On 23 October 1956 he took part in a demonstration at the József Bem monument, at the parliament building, and in the storming of the radio headquarters. On 25 October he joined a demonstration against Soviet intervention. On his initiative the demands of the demonstrators were proclaimed in front of the embassies of "people's democracies" and not in front of the U.S. Embassy. The next day he took over lead of the insurgents in Tűzoltó Street and took part in the defense of the Ninth Quarter of Budapest. On 29 and 30 October he negotiated conditions of armistice with Prime Minister **Imre Nagy.** When these were implemented, Angyal maintained peace and order and defended the idealized vision of a "Socialist society" against Stalinist restoration

and "capitalism." After the second Soviet intervention on 4 November he continued the armed struggle. He also wrote and distributed leaflets and proclamations. He tried to get in touch with the new government of **János Kádár,** but in vain. Angyal was encouraged to leave Hungary but refused. Arrested on 16 November 1956, on 17 April 1958 he was sentenced to death on the grounds of initiating and leading a plot against "the power of the people." On 27 November 1958 the Supreme Court upheld the sentence, and he was executed. (JT)

Sources: *Magyar Nagylexikon,* vol. 2 (Budapest, 1994); *A magyar forradalom és szabadságharc enciklopédiája,* CD-ROM (Budapest, 1999); *Új Magyar Életrajzi Lexikon,* vol. 1 (Budapest, 2001); András Lukácsy, *Felismerem-e Angyal István. Lelevek fiának* (Budapest, 1990); György Litván, ed., *Rewolucja węgierska 1956 roku* (Warsaw, 1996).

ANIELEWICZ Mordecai, pseudonyms "Aniołek" (Little Angel) and "Malachi," (1919, Wyszków, Poland–8 May 1943, Warsaw), activist of the Zionist left in Poland. Anielewicz came from a Jewish lower-middle-class family. He attended a Hebrew secondary school, where he established ties with Betar, a youth organization of a radical faction of Zionists-Revisionists. The outbreak of World War II caused an ideological breakthrough in his life. In September 1939 he found himself under Soviet occupation. While trying to cross the border into Romania, he was arrested by the NKVD but was released. He returned to German-occupied Warsaw, and then he went to Wilno (Vilnius), which was under Lithuanian rule. In January 1940 he came back to Warsaw and joined a leftist youth organization, Hashomer Hatzair (Young Guard), derived from a revolutionary wing of the Poale Zion Left. The Zionist program of the party was anti-German and pro-Soviet. The party was in favor of a Jewish kibbutz state in Palestine and recognized the annexation of the Polish Eastern Borderland by the USSR. Such an orientation was represented by *Neged Hazerem,* an underground newspaper founded by Anielewicz, who was also its editor-in-chief. Anielewicz was also involved in clandestine teaching and in party propaganda.

In March or April 1942 Anielewicz co-established the Anti-Fascist Bloc, an alliance of leftist Zionists and Communists. He traveled secretly throughout German-occupied Poland, organizing units of the bloc. He was away from Warsaw at the time of mass deportations from the ghetto in the summer of 1942, when over 250,000 Jews were transported to the extermination camp in Treblinka. After his return, in November of that year he co-founded the Jewish Fighting Organization (Żydowska Organizacja Bojowa [ŻOB]), which aimed at armed resistance to the

Germans. The ŻOB was a union of units of the Socialist Bund, leftist Zionists, and Communists from the Polish Workers' Party (Polska Partia Robotnicza [PPR]). He soon became commander-in-chief of the ŻOB. He managed to obtain some help from the Home Army (Armia Krajowa [AK]): weapons, ammunition, and instructions on how to fight. The first ŻOB action against the Germans took place on 18 January 1943 and lasted four days. The ŻOB resistance successfully prevented a German-planned deportation to Treblinka. The actual uprising in the ghetto began on 19 April and lasted until 16 May 1943. During the fighting, Anielewicz commanded the ŻOB but also tried to coordinate resistance by the rightist Jewish Military Union (Żydowski Związek Bojowy [ŻZB]) and the so-called wild insurrectionists. After two weeks of fighting, encircled by the SS in a bunker in Miła Street, Anielewicz, along with other leaders of the uprising, committed suicide. After the war a kibbutz named after him was created in Israel, Yad Mordecai, and one of the main streets of the former Jewish district in Warsaw was named Anielewicz Street. (MC)

Sources: Kunert, vol. 1; *Wielka encyklopedia PWN,* vol. 2 (Warsaw, 2001); Emanuel Ringelblum, *Kronika getta warszawskiego* (Warsaw, 1983); Tomasz Szarota ed., *The Warsaw Ghetto: The 45th Anniversary of the Uprising* (Warsaw, 1988); Hanna Krall, *Shielding the Flame: Intimate Conversations with Marek Edelman* (New York, 1986); Yitzhak Zuckerman, *A Surplus of Memory: Chronicle of the Warsaw Ghetto Uprising* (Berkeley, 1993); Marek Jan Chodakiewicz, *Żydzi i Polacy, 1918–1955: Współistnienie, Zagłada, Komunizm* (Warsaw, 2000).

ANTALL József, Jr. (8 April 1932, Pestújhely–12 December 1993, Budapest), Hungarian politician. In 1950 Antall graduated from a Piarist high school in Budapest. He was interested in politics and gained wide knowledge in this field. He graduated in history and Hungarian studies (1954) and in archive, library, and museum studies (1962) from the University of Budapest. In 1968 he earned a Ph.D. in history. From 1954 he taught in the József Eötvös High School in Budapest. During the 1956 revolution he chaired a revolutionary committee in this school, organized passive resistance against the **János Kádár** government, and reorganized the Independent Smallholders Party (ISP). After the revolution he was temporarily arrested and interrogated. Reprimanded and released, he was moved to another school. Owing to his political stance, in 1959 he was banned from teaching. In 1960–62 he worked as a librarian. In 1964 he got a job in the Ignaz Semmelweis Memorial Museum of the History of Medicine. First he was its deputy director (1964–74), then acting director (1974–84), and finally director (1984–91), upgrading the role of this institution.

In the 1970s and 1980s Antall worked as a scholar.

Among other things, he was deputy chairman of the International Association of the History of Medicine (1968–90) and chairman of the Hungarian Association of the History of Medicine (1982–90). In 1988 he entered the political scene. For family reasons he initially considered joining one of the historic parties: the ISP or the Christian Democratic People's Party (CDPP). Realizing that these parties would not take a leading role in systemic transformation, in the fall of 1988 he joined the Hungarian Democratic Forum (Magyar Demokrata Forum [HDF]). In the spring of 1989 he took part in the Round Table Talks of the Hungarian opposition, and in mid-June 1989 he became the HDF delegate to the Triangle Table Talks with the Communist leadership, aiming at a peaceful transition of power. During the talks (June–September 1989), Antall became one of the leaders of the opposition, gaining authority thanks to his knowledge of constitutional law and to his negotiating skills. In October 1989 he was almost unanimously elected chairman of the HDF and transformed it into a party that won the first free election in March and April 1990, gaining 42.5 percent of the vote and 165 out of 368 seats in the parliament.

Antall concluded a coalition of the HDF with the ISP and CDPP, and on 23 May 1990 he became prime minister. He strove for a stable parliamentary majority, which was all the more important as a result of the Triangle Table agreements, by which the range of laws requiring a two-thirds parliamentary majority was widened. This is why Antall also reached a compromise with the Alliance of Free Democrats (AFD). As a result, the parliament elected the AFD candidate, **Árpád Göncz,** president. Antall enjoyed substantial respect in the West and kept Hungary out of the Balkan conflicts. During his term Hungary was accepted into the Council of Europe as the first country from the former Soviet bloc (October 1990). He initiated cooperation with Czechoslovakia (later the Czech Republic and Slovakia) and Poland with the Visegrad Triangle (February 1991). At this time Soviet troops were evacuated from Hungary (June 1991), the Warsaw Pact was dissolved (July 1991), and Hungary signed an association agreement with the European Community (December 1991). Antall also initiated steps toward Hungary's entry into NATO. In the fall of 1990 it turned out that he was seriously ill. From that point he struggled with time, directing government work with great determination. He was, nevertheless, unable to resolve conflicts in his own party, although in 1993 he excluded from it the radical nationalist faction of **István Csurka.** With the maintenance of social order in mind, Antall advocated gradual transformation and abstained from more radical economic reforms. He was not a particularly skilled orator and the social costs of transformation eroded his initial popularity, but his death moved the whole country, and his funeral was attended by hundreds of thousands of people. (JT)

Sources: *Magyar Nagylexikon,* vol. 2 (Budapest, 1994); *Nagy Képes Milleniumi Arcképcsarnok* (Budapest, 1999); *Új Magyar Életrajzi Lexikon,* vol. 1 (Budapest, 2001); *Europa Środkowa i Wschodnia,* 1991, 1992, and 1993; Steven Béla Várga, *Historical Dictionary of Hungary* (Lanham, Md., 1997); Jerzy Kochanowski, *Wegry* (Warsaw, 1997); Rudolf L. Tőkes, "Party Politics and Political Participation in Postcommunist Hungary," in Karen Dawisha and Bruce Parrott, eds., *The Consolidation of Democracy in East-Central Europe* (Cambridge, 1997).

ANTALL József, Sr. (28 March 1896, Oroszi–24 July 1974, Budapest), Hungarian politician. Antall came from a middle-class family with patriotic traditions. During World War I he was a POW in Russia (1915–18). After returning home, in 1923 he graduated in law from Budapest University. Later he worked in the Ministry of Finance (1928–32), the Ministry of Labor, and the Ministry of Interior (1932–44). In 1931 he joined the Independent Smallholders Party (ISP) and was close to the so-called folk writers who opposed social and national values in favor of Socialist internationalism. From 1939, as head of the Department of Social Affairs of the Ministry of Interior, Antall coordinated Hungarian aid to war refugees. Along with his collaborators, he provided accommodations, supplies, and safety to thousands of Poles; to Allied soldiers (French, British, and Soviet) who escaped from POW camps; to persecuted Jews and Yugoslavs; and, in the course of the westward movement of the eastern front, to refugees from Transylvania and Bukovina, as well as to those from bombed German towns. He saved thousands of lives. He collaborated with the Hungarian and Polish resistance, personifying these circles, which opposed Hungarian engagement on the side of the Axis. After the Third Reich occupied Hungary, on 19 March 1944 he resigned, was arrested, and spent half a year in prison.

From May 1945 Antall was undersecretary of state in the Ministry of Reconstruction, and from November 1945 to July 1946 he was minister of reconstruction in the governments of **Zoltán Tildy** and **Ferenc Nagy.** In March and April 1946 he was temporarily minister of finance. In the parliamentary elections of November 1945 he won a seat on behalf of the ISP. In 1946–48 he chaired the Hungarian Red Cross, in the summer of 1947 he headed the ISP electoral commission, and in August 1947 he won a parliamentary seat again. In the elections of May 1949, when only one list from the Hungarian People's Independence Front was submitted, he won a seat again but was soon forced to give it up. At the end of 1949 he withdrew from

public life. During the revolution, on 30 October 1956 he returned to the ISP's top leadership. After the revolution was suppressed, he was interrogated as a witness. He was awarded the Great Cross of the Order of Merit of the Hungarian Republic (1947) and the Polish Commander's Order of Polonia Restituta, as well as French, Israeli, and British orders. In 1981 a street in Warsaw was given his name. His memoirs, *Menekultek menedéke: Emlékek és iratok* (Refugee camp: Memoirs and documents; 1997), were published posthumously. His son, **József Antall,** Jr. (1932–1993), was a Hungarian prime minister. (MS/JT)

Sources: *Magyar Nagylexikon,* vol. 2 (Budapest, 1994); *Új Magyar Életrajzi Lexikon,* vol. 1 (Budapest, 2001); *Magyarország 1944–1956,* CD-ROM (Budapest, 2001); Endre Várkonyi, "Antall József," *Magyarország,* 1974, no. 36; Ágnes Godó, *Magyar-lengyel kapcsolatok a második világháborúban* (Budapest, 1976); Helena and Tibor Csorba, *Ziemia węgierska azylem Polaków 1939–1945* (Warsaw, 1985).

ANTANOVICH Ivan (3 April 1937, Domashe, near Lyahavitsi), Belorussian Communist activist. Antanovich graduated from the Pedagogical Institute of Foreign Languages in Minsk in 1960. He worked in the Institute of Philosophy and Law of the Belorussian Academy of Sciences, publishing typical propaganda works such as *Amerikanskaia burzhuaznaia aksiologia na sluzhbe imperializma* (American bourgeois axiology in the service of imperialism; 1967) and two volumes on "bourgeois sociological theories" (1981–82). In 1977 he became professor. He was one of the authors of the *Belorussian Soviet Encyclopedia.* In the early 1970s he was the Belorussian representative to UNESCO. In 1977 he was sent to the party apparatus. From 1979 to 1987 he was secretary for culture of the Central Committee (CC) of the Communist Party of Belorussia (CPB); from 1987 to 1990, deputy rector of the Academy of Social Sciences at the CPB CC; and in 1990–91, secretary and Politburo member of the CC of the Communist Party of the Russian Federal SSR. As late as 1990 he published *Sovremennyi kapitalizm: Sotsy-dinamika vlasti* (Contemporary capitalism: Social dynamics of power). After the fall of the USSR he returned to Belorussia. From 1993 to 1995 he was director of the Belorussian Research Institute of Information and Forecasting; in 1995–97, deputy minister; and in 1997–98, minister of foreign affairs. He made futile attempts to lead Belorussia out of international isolation that had been caused by the policies of President **Alyaksandr Lukashenka.** (EM)

Sources: Jan Zaprudnik, *Historical Dictionary of Belarus* (Lanham, Md., 1998); *Kto iest kto v Respublike Belarus* (Minsk, 1999).

ANTCZAK Antoni (15 May 1890, Wolenice–31 July 1952, Wronki), Polish politician. The son of a laborer, Antczak completed four grades of a country grammar school and supplemented his knowledge through self-education. In 1914 he began political activity in the Polish Trade Union (Zjednoczenie Zawodowe Polskie [ZZP]), a Christian organization in Westphalia, Germany. In 1918 he joined the National Workers' Association (Narodowe Stronnictwo Robotnicze [NSR]) in Poland, and in 1921 he became a member of the Supreme Council of the National Workers' Party (Narodowa Partia Robotnicza [NPR]). In 1923–27 he was president of the Pomeranian board of the NPR; from 1929 to 1930 he was MP on behalf of the NPR. In 1937 he became a member of the board of the Labor Party (Stronnictwo Pracy [SP]). After the German aggression in 1939, he served as the government delegate to Pomerania. Fearing arrest, in July 1941 he moved to Warsaw, where he continued his activities as government delegate. Deported to Germany after the Warsaw Uprising, in March 1945, he returned to Poland and presided over the underground SP until the return of **Karol Popiel.** From November 1945, Antczak was treasurer of the party's Executive Committee and one of Popiel's trusted co-workers. In December 1945 Antczak became a deputy to the Communist-controlled National Home Council (Krajowa Rada Narodowa [KRN]). After an upheaval within the SP, caused by the pro-Communist activists of Zryw, Antczak, along with six associates, gave up their KRN seats in September 1946. Antczak cooperated with *Tygodnik Warszawski* (Warsaw Weekly) and unsuccessfully attempted to legalize the Christian Labor Party. Arrested by the secret police in August 1948 and sentenced to fifteen years in a rigged political trial on 6 April 1951, he died in prison. (WR)

Sources: Posłowie..., vol. 1; *Dzieje Zjednoczenia Zawodowego Polskiego 1889–1939* (Katowice, 1939); *Słownik biograficzny działaczy polskiego ruchu robotniczego,* vol. 1 (Warsaw, 1979); Karol Popiel, *Na mogiłach przyjaciół* (London, 1966).

ANTONCHIK Siarhey (1 April 1956, Pleshchenitsi, near Lahoysk), Belorussian trade and political activist. After high school Antonchik was a blue-collar worker in a Minsk tool factory, Belvar. In the late 1980s he was associated with the opposition Belorussian Popular Front (Belaruski Narodni Front [BNF]) and established structures of independent trade unions. In 1990 he was elected deputy to the Supreme Council on behalf of the BNF. As a member of the parliamentary anti-corruption commission, during the Supreme Council session of December 1994, he accused the **Alyaksandr Lukashenka** group of corruption, causing the first political crisis after the presidential elections.

His report, titled *Krainay kiruyus mafyoznyia klany* (The country is run by Mafia clans), pointed to corruption at the top echelons of Belorussian power. It was published in the paper *Svaboda,* thus becoming known to wider social circles. Antonchik was one of the deputies who went on a hunger strike in April 1995 to protest a referendum to change the state symbols initiated by the Lukashenka regime. In 1997 Antonchik established the Fund to Support the Unemployed, gathering funds for people fired for political reasons. (EM)

Sources: *Narodnyia deputaty Respubliki Belarus: Dwanattsataye sklikannie* (Minsk, 1992); Siergiej Owsiannik and Jelena Striełkowa, *Władza i społeczeństwo: Białoruś 1991–1998* (Warsaw, 1998).

ANTONESCU Ion (14 June 1882, Piteşti–1 June 1946, near Jilava), Romanian marshal and dictator. Antonescu graduated from the military academy and soon afterwards took part in the suppression of the Moldavian rebellion of 1907. During World War I he was first the operations chief of the Northern Army, then chief of the operations office of the general staff, and he planned the resistance of the Romanian army against the Germans. In 1922–27 he served as military attaché in Paris, Brussels, and London. In 1933–34 he was chief of the general staff, and in December 1937 he became defense minister in the government of **Octavian Goga.** The cabinet failed to reduce tensions in the country and suppress disturbances caused (among other things) by anti-Semitism. In February 1938 King Charles II removed the ruling coalition and established a "government of national unity" with Patriarch **Miron Cristea** as its head. In fact this was a royal coup d'état that destroyed the appearance of democracy. In March 1938 Antonescu resigned his post in protest at the use of the army for domestic repression. He found himself in opposition to the king and became involved with the Fascist Iron Guard, supported by the Third Reich.

After the USSR annexed Bessarabia and northern Bukovina from Romania in June 1940 and Hungary took a part of Transylvania as a result of the Viennese arbitration of 30 August 1940, and also since Bulgaria claimed southern Dobrudja, King Charles had to resign. After a failed attempt by the Iron Guard to seize power on 4 September 1940, Antonescu established a dictatorship with the help of the armed forces. As premier of a "National Legionary State," he began a complicated game with the Third Reich and the Iron Guard. Under German pressure, the leader of the Iron Guard, **Horia Sima,** became deputy prime minister. On 6 September, Antonescu reached an agreement with liberals and royalists and forced the abdication of Charles in favor of his son, Michael I. Once in power, one of Antonescu's first acts had to be the recognition of the Viennese arbitration by which Hungary gained a part of Transylvania and of the annexation of Bessarabia and northern Bukovina. The guardsmen unleashed a wave of terror and in November 1940 murdered the former premier, **Nicolae Iorga**, and an outstanding economist, **Virgil Madgearu**. This was followed by an attempted coup, to which Antonescu responded with force. Despite German support for the Iron Guard, the army suppressed the incidents and pogroms instigated on 21–23 January 1941 in the streets of Bucharest, and Antonescu forced Sima and other leaders of the Iron Guard to leave for Germany. Although the head of state was formally King Michael, henceforth Antonescu governed Romania integrally as premier, marshal, and commander (*conducatorul*) of the nation. However, the reward for the suppression of the "fifth column" by the Germans was concessions toward Hitler. In the fall of 1940 German troops came to the country under the guise of "protectors" of the Romanian petroleum fields and the country's industrial centers.

The treaty of 4 December 1940 with Germany subordinated the Romanian economy to the Third Reich, even though it temporarily promised favorable conditions. On 23 October 1940 Antonescu signed the anti-Comintern Pact, but in April 1941 he refused to take part in the war against Yugoslavia, with whom Romania had traditionally had good relations. Instead, in order to gain back Bessarabia and Bukovina, he ordered thirty Romanian divisions to support the German invasion of the USSR in June 1941. After his aim had been achieved, which added greatly to his popularity, he submitted to German pressure on 14 August 1941 and sent his troops beyond Dniester. This drew Romania into war against the Allies for good. Antonescu found himself under pressure from public opinion, which mistakenly expected that German support would help to regain the rest of Transylvania. Despite German pressure, he did not agree to the mass extermination of the Jewish population of the Old Kingdom and southern Transylvania, whereas in Bessarabia and Bukovina the authorities organized deportations and the annihilation of Jews accused of supporting the Soviet regime in 1940–41.

The collaboration policies of Antonescu depended upon two factors—the current power of the Third Reich and calculations as to who was going to win the war eventually. Under the influence of Foreign Minister **Mihai Antonescu**, Antonescu tried to enter into closer relations with Italy; by improving cooperation among the Romance-language countries—Romania, Italy, France, Spain, and Portugal—he intended to bring about a joint withdrawal from the war against the Western powers. These plans failed. Despite many indirect contacts, the Allies did not agree to a separate peace treaty with the German satellite governments without the consent of the USSR. In February 1944 Antonescu sent a special emissary, Prince **Barbu Ştirbei**, on a mission to prepare the capitulation of Romania to the Allies, but the Kremlin, which wanted to enter the defeated country, blocked even this attempt.

The Romanian army suffered heavy losses in the USSR in 1944. Antonescu failed to side with the Big Three. It was only King Michael who was able to take the initiative in the overthrow of the dictatorship (23 August 1944), when the Red Army stood at the borders of Romania. Antonescu was arrested by Michael during his visit to the royal palace. He was interrogated for a long time, and, after the events of February 1945, he was handed over to the Russian Communists and the Soviet authorities. During his trial, which began in May 1946, the history of an extremely difficult political situation in Romania in 1940–44 came to light. German witnesses confirmed the caution with which Antonescu had acted toward Hitler. To the end Antonescu maintained that he had tried to prevent the subjugation of Romania by the USSR. During the trial even the leader of the peasant opposition, **Iuliu Maniu**, did not hesitate to shake hands with him. Antonescu was sentenced to death and executed. (WR)

Sources: *Biographisches Lexikon,* vol. 1; Andreas Hillgruber, *Hitler, König Carol und Marschall Antonescu* (Wiesbaden, 1954); Andrzej Koryn, *Rumunia w polityce wielkich mocarstw 1944–1947* (Wrocław, 1983); Jipa Rotaru, Octavian Buran, and Vladimir Zodian, *Maresalul Ion Antonescu: Am facut "razboiul sfânt" Împotriva bolsevismului: Campania anului 1941* (Oradea, 1991); Gheorghe Barbul, *Memorial Antonescu: Al treilea om al Axei* (Iaşi, 1992); Ioan Dan, *"Prosesul" Maresalului Ion Antonescu* (Bucharest, 1993); Keith Hitchins, *Rumania 1866–1947* (Oxford, 1994); Iosif C. Dragan, *Antonescu: Marshal and Ruler of Romania, 1940–1944* (Bucharest, 1995); Gh. Buzatu, ed., *Maresalul Antonescu În fata istoriei, Documente, marturii si comentarii,* vols. 1–4 (Iaşi, 1990–1995); Denis Deletant, *Communist Terror in Romania: Gheorghiu-Dej and the Police State, 1948–1965* (New York, 1999).

ANTONESCU Mihai (18 November 1904, Nucet–1 June 1946, Jilava), Romanian lawyer and politician. Antonescu studied law at Bucharest University (1922–26). In 1927 he successfully defended a Ph.D. in law, and in 1931 he achieved the rank of assistant professor. In 1940 he defended General **Ion Antonescu**, who, on the orders of King **Charles II**, was being held prisoner at the Bistriţa monastery. It was then that Antonescu first established contact with Ion Antonescu, with whom he had no family ties. After the takeover of power by Ion Antonescu, from November 1940 to January 1941 he served as justice minister in the government formed in coalition with the Iron Guard. When, after an unsuccessful coup by the Guardists, Ion Antonescu liquidated the Iron Guard and became head of the government (27 January 1941), Antonescu was appointed deputy prime minister and minister of foreign affairs. After the attack against the USSR in June 1941 he acted as premier on several occasions, replacing Ion Antonescu, who was on the eastern front. Antonescu was also responsible for foreign policy, except for relations with the Third Reich, which were handled by Ion Antonescu himself. Antonescu had a positive attitude toward Polish refugees in Romania, and despite pressures he protected them from Germans. The Polish government in exile, acting within the framework of the so-called Tripod Action, got in touch both with Antonescu and with the Romanian dictator in order to withdraw the country from its alliance with Germany. This initiated Romanian involvement in secret negotiations with the Allies; between 1942 and 1943 these were held in Cairo, Ankara, Stockholm, Madrid, Lisbon, Geneva, and the Holy See. A separate secret initiative of Antonescu was to maintain contacts with Italy, Vichy France, Spain, and Portugal in order to establish a "Latin Axis," directed against the USSR and Hungary. Another goal that Antonescu pursued between 1941 and 1943 was to create a new "Little Entente" of Romania, Croatia, and Slovakia, which would be directed against Hungary.

In 1943 these activities, conducted with the knowledge of Ion Antonescu, were discovered by German intelligence in Turkey; as a result, Hitler demanded the dismissal of Antonescu. However, Marshal Antonescu did not agree to that. Antonescu continued his efforts to come to an agreement with the Allied countries through the diplomatic missions of neutral countries in Bucharest, especially through a Swiss envoy, Maurice de Weck, but in the face of a Soviet veto his attempts came to nothing. On the morning of 23 August 1944 Marshal Antonescu sent a wire to the diplomatic mission in Stockholm, trying to conclude peace with the USSR. The same day, however, a coup was staged, and Antonescu was arrested, along with the head of state. At the end of August they were both handed over to the Soviets and taken to Moscow, where they stayed until April 1946. Some sources state that they rejected a Soviet proposal to reassume power in Romania in exchange for close cooperation. In May 1946 their trial was held in Bucharest. At the trial, an amnesty proposed by King **Michael** was rejected, and the terms of the 1923 constitution and the Romanian penal code, which did not provide for the death penalty, were disregarded. Antonescu was executed by firing squad in the garden of the Jilava prison, along with Marshal Antonescu and two generals. Antonescu was the author of, among other works, *Organizarea păcii şi a Societaţii Naţiunilor* (The establishment of a peaceful order and the League of Nations; 1929) and *La Roumanie* (1933). (FA/TD)

Sources: *Biographisches Lexikon,* vol. 1; Gheorghe Buzatu, ed., *Mareşalul Antonescu în faţa istoriei,* vols. 1–4 (Iaşi, 1990); Gheorghe Barbul, *Mamorial Antonescu: Al treilea om al Axei* (Iaşi, 1992); Andreas Hillgruber, *Hitler, Regele Carol şi Mareşalul Antonescu: Relaţiile româno-germane in 1940–1944* (Bucharest, 1994); General Ion Gheorghe, *Un dictator nefericit: Mareşalul Antonescu. Calea României spre Statul satelit* (Bucharest, 1996); Ion Calafeteanu, "Mihai Antonescu şi ideea "Axei latine," in *România şi politica de alianţe: Istorie şi actualitate* (Bucharest, 1993); Florin Anghel, "O alternativă de colaborare în ineriorul Axei: Spre o nouă Mică Înţelegere, 1941–1944," in *Revista Istorica,* 1996, nos. 3/4.

ANTONESCU Victor (3 September 1871, Antoneşti–24 September 1947, Bucharest), Romanian lawyer, diplomat, and politician. Before the agrarian reform of 1921 Antonescu was a large landowner. He had no family ties with General **Ion Antonescu.** He studied law at the university in Bucharest (1888–91) and at the College of Political Sciences in Paris (1891–94), where in 1895 he defended his Ph.D. in law. Between 1897 and 1900 he was a professor at the College of Political Sciences in Bucharest. From 1900 until his death he was a member of the National Liberal Party (PNL). In 1901 he was elected to parliament. He held various diplomatic posts—for example, he was minister of the legation in Paris (1917–20) and a member of the Romanian delegation to the Paris Peace Conference (1919–20), where he played an important role in advancing the stance of Romania. In 1922–26 he represented Romania at the League of Nations in Geneva. On behalf of the PNL he served as justice minister in 1914–16 and 1933–35, finance minister in 1916–17 and 1935–36, and minister of foreign affairs between August 1936 and 1937. His efforts led to a rapprochement with Poland; as a result the diplomatic missions of both countries were elevated to the ranks of embassies (June 1936). He adopted a conciliatory stance toward the policy of Charles II. He authored, for example, *Economie politique* (Political economy; 1895). (FA/TD)

Sources: Şerban N. Ionescu, *Who Was Who in Twentieth Century Romania* (Boulder, Colo., 1994); Dov. B. Lungu, *Romania and the Great Powers 1933–1940* (Durham, N.C., 1989); *Historia dyplomacji polskiej,* Piotr Łossowski, ed., vol. 4 (Warsaw, 1995).

ANTONIADE Constantin (16 August 1880, Bucharest–1954, Sighet), Romanian diplomat. In 1902 Antoniade graduated in law from Bucharest University, and in 1907 he received a Ph.D. in philology there. From 1919 to 1921 he worked as secretary of the Romanian delegation to the peace talks with the Central Powers, and from 1922 to 1927 he served as a judge at the League of Nations Court in Geneva. In 1928–29 he worked as a representative to the League of Nations, and then until 1933, as a member of the League of Nations committee preparing an international conference on security and disarmament. From 1936 to 1939 he was minister plenipotentiary in the Romanian Embassy in Switzerland. After the takeover of power by General **Ion Antonescu** in 1940, Antoniade went into opposition against the regime and its foreign policy. He was a sophisticated intellectual, and he authored *Les ambassadeurs de Venise du XVIème siècle* (Ambassadors of Venice in the sixteenth century; 1934), as well as essays on Henri Bergson, Thomas Carlyle, and Niccolo Machiavelli. Arrested by the Communists in 1950, he died in prison. (FA/WR)

Sources: Şerban N. Ionescu, *Who Was Who in Twentieth Century Romania* (Boulder, Colo., 1994).

ANTONOV-OVSEYENKO Volodymyr [originally Ovseyenko] (21 March 1883, Czernichów–8 February 1938, Moscow), Bolshevik officer and diplomat. Antonov-Ovseyenko came from the family of an officer of the tsarist army. Although from the end of 1902 he was a member of the Russian Social Democratic Workers' Party, in 1904 he graduated as a second lieutenant from a Vladimir infantry school in St. Petersburg. At the turn of 1904/1905 he was assigned to military service in Warsaw and took part in the preparations for a military insurrection in the Kingdom of Poland. In the spring of 1905, after receiving a disciplinary transfer to the Far East to fight in the war against Japan, he left the army to continue revolutionary activities. Having allied himself with the Mensheviks, he was active in (among other places) St. Petersburg, Moscow, and Sevastopol, where he was captured and sentenced to death in 1907. The sentence was commuted to twenty years of penal servitude. He escaped soon after the sentence was passed and continued his activities. In 1909 he emigrated to France, where he assumed the name of Antonov. From 1910 he resided in Paris, and from 1914 he co-edited the magazine *Golos.* After the outbreak of World War I, in 1915 he expressed his support for the internationalist stance adopted by Lenin. At the end of 1915 he broke off with the Mensheviks and in May 1917 returned to Russia.

Antonov-Ovseyenko aligned himself with the Bolsheviks and conducted revolutionary agitation in Finland and Latvia, and in 1917 he became a member of the Military Revolutionary Committee in Petrograd. He took part in the Bolshevik coup in the capital, and at the All-Russian Congress of Soviets (8–9 November 1917) he was elected a member of the Council of People's Commissars for war and sea affairs. On 8 December 1917 he became commander of the armed forces for the struggle against counterrevolution in southern Russia (the Don, the Ukraine, and the Caucasus). Between December 1917 and February 1918 his units, attacking from the northeast, conquered the entire left bank of the Dnieper River in the Ukraine as far as Kiev. In March 1918 the Ukraine passed into the hands of the Germans, so between May and November 1918 he held various command posts in central Russia. In November 1918, with the collapse of the German occupation, he was appointed commander of the armed forces of the Kursk section (the so-called Ukrainian Front). From early December 1918 to early February 1919 he again seized the left bank of the Ukraine, including Kiev, this time pushing out the armed forces of the directorate of the Ukrainian People's Republic from this territory.

In the summer of 1919 the Ukraine passed into the hands of General Anton Denikin. Antonov-Ovseyenko was transferred to administrative work in the *guberniya* (province) of Povolzhye (middle and lower Volga region), which was suffering from famine and peasant insurrections. He was active there between 1921 and 1922. From 1917 he was a co-worker of the people's commissar for defense, Leon Trotsky, and between 1922 and 1924 he held the post of head of the Political Executive of the Revolutionary Military Council of Russia (Revvoiensoviet). As a Trotskyite, he was removed from his executive posts by Stalin. He was assigned to diplomatic work and headed a special negotiation mission to Canton (February–April 1924); he was subsequently a Soviet envoy to Czechoslovakia (1924–28), Lithuania (1928–30), and Poland (1930–34). In June 1934 he was suddenly recalled from his post and was appointed prosecutor of the RSFSR, but in July 1936 he was sent to Barcelona as consul general of the USSR. He was again recalled in September 1937 in relation to preparations for the trials of the Trotskyist opposition. On 12 October 1937 he was arrested and on 8 February 1938 sentenced to ten years in prison. According to recent findings, he was murdered in Lubyanka Prison the same day his sentence was rendered. He was rehabilitated at the Twentieth Congress of the CPSU in 1956. Between 1924 and 1933 four volumes of his memoirs of 1914–19, *Zapiski o grazhdanskoi voine* (Notes on the civil war), were published. They remain a valuable source of information on the course of revolution in Russia, although they are not free from propaganda, which gave prominence to the role of Stalin and diminished the role of Trotsky. (TS)

Sources: *MERSH,* vol. 2; A. V. Rakitin and Robert V. Daniels, *Red October: The Bolshevik Revolution of 1917* (New York, 1967); *Władimir A. Antonov-Owseienko: Istoriko-biograficheskii ocherk* (Moscow, 1989); V. A. Antonov-Ovsieienko, *V semnadtsatom godu* (Kiev, 1991).

ANVELT Jaan (18 April 1884, Võisiku–11 December 1937, USSR), Estonian Communist activist. Born into a peasant family, in 1907 Anvelt joined the Bolshevik party. He graduated in law from St. Petersburg University in 1912 and edited the Bolshevik magazine *Kiir.* During the February 1917 revolution he was head of a revolutionary committee and the head of the soviet in Narva. After the October 1917 revolution he was president of the Bolshevik Executive Council for Estonia. He came to Petrograd at the beginning of 1918, and at the end of the same year he returned to Estonia as head of the Council of People's Commissars and commissar for military affairs. After the failure of the revolution and after Estonia gained independence, he fought as the commander of the Red Army on different fronts of the Russian civil war. In 1921 he returned to Estonia and headed underground activities. On 1 December 1924 he led an unsuccessful Communist coup in Tallinn. After his return to the USSR he became commissar of a military academy in Moscow; between 1929 and 1935 he was head of the Central Council of Civil Aviation of the USSR, and later, a Comintern worker. Under the pen name "Aadu Eessaare" he published a number of works. Arrested during the Great Purge, he died in prison. In the 1980s some of his works and letters were published in Estonia. (WR)

Sources: MERSH, vol. 2; *Eesti Nõukogude Entsüklopedia,* vol. 1 (Tallinn, 1985); Jaan Anvelt, *Valitud teosed* (Tallinn, 1982); *Jaan Anveldi kirjavahetusi aastaist 1904–1914* (Tallinn, 1984).

APOR Vilmos (29 February 1892, Segesvár [now Sigişoara, Romania]–2 April 1945, Győr), Hungarian bishop, victim of Communist terror. The sixth child of a noble family, Apor was deprived of his father at a young age and was brought up by his mother. He completed theological studies at a Jesuit university in Innsbruck, where he received a doctorate. Ordained in August 1915 in Nagyvárad (now Oradea, Romania), Apor worked as a priest and lecturer in theology. For a short time he served as a chaplain in the army. From 1916 he was chaplain and in 1937–41 parish priest in Gyula. As he was especially devoted to the poor, Apor was called the "presbyter of the poor," and on 21 January 1941 Pope Pius XII consecrated him bishop of Győr. In October 1944, along with other Hungarian bishops, Apor appealed to Ferenc Szálasi to withdraw Hungary from the war in order to prevent a national catastrophe. In December 1944 he personally intervened on the issue with the head of the Hungarian Nazis, protesting against the deportation and extermination of Hungarian Jews. After the invasion of the Red Army many women took refuge in his residence, fearing rape by Soviet soldiers. Apor, who came to the defense of three girls, was seriously wounded, and he died in hospital. In May 1986 he was buried in a basilica in Győr, where his grave was a place of pilgrimage and prayer of the faithful. On 9 November 1997 he was beatified by Pope John Paul II as a martyr. (WR)

Sources: *Magyar Életrajzi Lexikon* (Budapest, 1967), vol. 1; *Fifth Interim Report of Hearings before the Subcommittee on Hungary of the House of Representatives Select Committee on Communist Aggression* (Washington, D.C., 1954); *Osservatore Romano* (Polish edition), 1998, no. 1.

APOSTOL Gheorghe (17 May 1913, Tudor Vladimirescu, near Tecuci), Romanian Communist activist. The son of a railway worker, after primary school Apostol attended a railway trade school, and then he worked as a switchman. In 1930 he joined the Communist Party of Romania (CPR), participating in its youth organization. In 1936 he was arrested for Communist activities and sentenced to a lengthy imprisonment. He was released only after the coup of 23 August 1944. As the Communist dictatorship consolidated, he advanced in the trade union apparatus. In 1944 he became secretary of the General Confederation of Labor, and from 1945 to 1952 he was its chairman. From 1945 he was a member of the Central Committee (CC) of the Romanian Communist Party (RCP; renamed in 1943); from 1948 to 1969 he was a member of the Politburo of the CC of the Romanian Workers' Party (RWP; its name in 1948–65), and then a member of the RCP again. From 1946 to 1974 he was MP. In 1948, 1950–51, and 1952 he was the parliament speaker. From May 1952 to January 1953 he was third deputy prime minister, and then until April 1954, deputy prime minister. From October 1953 to April 1954 he was also minister of agriculture and forestry.

Apostol was closely connected with the first secretary of the Communist Party, **Gheorghe Gheorghiu-Dej.** After Stalin's death, as a result of Soviet pressures to introduce "collective leadership," on 20 April 1954 Gheorghiu-Dej gave up the party leadership to Apostol and took the helm of the government. Having realized that this may deprive him of control over the state, on 30 September 1955 he dismissed Apostol from the position of first secretary. In 1955–61 Apostol was chairman of the Central Council of Trade Unions (CCTU), and from March 1961 to January 1967, first deputy prime minister. From 1965 to 1969 he was a member of the Presidium and of the Executive Committee of the RCP, and in 1967–69, chairman of the CCTU again. In 1968–70 he was a member of the National Council of the Front of Socialist Unity. As he consolidated control over the party and state by removing the clients of Gheorghiu-Dej, in 1969 **Nicolae Ceauşescu** dismissed Apostol from all these positions. From 1969 to 1975 he was director general of the State Reserve Fund, and from

1975 to 1977 he was sales director of the Semanatoarea enterprise in Bucharest. From 1977 to 1983 he was ambassador to Argentina, and in 1983–89, to Brazil. Probably from the early 1980s he stayed in touch with party leaders who had been fired by Ceauşescu. In 1989 Apostol was among six signatories of a letter criticizing Ceauşescu of the violation of human rights; the letter was broadcast on Radio Free Europe. According to one theory, this was a step toward toppling the dictator, which came to an end on 22 December 1989. Later on Apostol played no significant role in public life. (LW)

Sources: Klaus-Detlev Grothusen, ed., *Rumänien* (Göttingen, 1977); *Who's Who in the Socialist Countries of Europe* (Munich, London, and Paris, 1989); Ionescu Ghiţă, *Comunismul în România* (Bucharest, 1994); Józef Darski, *Rumunia: Historia, współczesność, konflikty narodowe* (Warsaw, 1995); Ion Alexandrescu, Ion Bulei, Ion Mamina, and Ioan Scurtu, *Enciclopedia de istorie României* (Bucharest, 2000).

APPONYI Albert (29 May 1846, Vienna–7 February 1933, Geneva), Hungarian politician and diplomat. Apponyi started his political career in 1872, when, after graduating from law studies at the universities in Pest and Vienna, he became an MP. Except for the years 1875–1877 and 1918–20, he remained in the parliament, representing various conservative and nationalist parties until the end of his life. Without denying the necessity to conclude the Austro-Hungarian compromise of 1867, he strove to extend Hungarian autonomy. From October 1901 to November 1903 he was the speaker of the Hungarian parliament. From April 1906 to January 1910 he was minister of education and religions in the second government of **Sándor Wekerle**, authoring a controversial law demanding instruction in Hungarian in all primary schools in Hungary (the so-called *lex Apponyi* of 1907) and a 1909 decree on the compulsory teaching of religion in Hungarian. After the fall of the Wekerle government Apponyi was one of the most radical leaders of the opposition to the governments of **István Tisza**. From August 1917 to October 1918 Apponyi was minister of education in the third cabinet of Wekerle.

After World War I Apponyi presided over the Hungarian delegation to the peace talks; on 16 January 1920 in the Trianon Palace in Versailles, the delegation was informed about the results of the peace conference, which deprived Hungary of the bulk of its prewar territory. In protest Apponyi resigned. In the spring of 1920 he was suggested as a possible regent of Hungary, but he failed to gain wider support. He changed his political orientation and became one of the top leaders of the revisionist movement and of the Hungarian legitimists, who demanded the return of the Habsburgs. From 1925 to 1933 he was representative to the League of Nations. He was the author of several books on the interdependence of Hungarian domestic and foreign policy, including the following: *A magyar nemzet természetszerű elhelyezkedése a világpolitikában* (The objective situation of the Hungarian nation in world politics; 1915); *The American Peace and Hungary* (1919); *Hungarian Foreign Policy* (1921); *Emlékirataim* (Memoirs, 2 vols.; 1922–34); and *Élmények és emlékek* (Experience and reflections; 1933). (MS)

Sources: *Biographisches Lexikon*, vol. 1; Steven Béla Várga, *Historical Dictionary of Hungary* (Lanham, Md., 1997); *Apponyi emlékkönyv* (Budapest, 1926); Imre Jósika–Herczeg, *Apponyi és Amerika* (New York, 1926); Sándor Pethő, *Gróf Apponyi Albert* (Budapest, 1926); József Kerekesházy, *Apponyi* (Budapest, 1943); Nicholas Horthy, *Memoirs* (Paris, 1954); Harold Steinacker, *Austro-Hungarica* (Munich, 1963).

APRÓ Antal [originally Klein] (8 February 1913, Szeged–9 December 1994, Budapest), Hungarian Communist activist. Brought up in an orphanage, after primary school Apró worked as a house painter in Makó and Budapest. In 1930 he joined the All-National Union of Hungarian Construction Workers (AUHCW), and a year later, the illegal Hungarian Communist Party (HCP). In 1935 he co-organized a strike of construction workers and was active in the United Trade Union Opposition. In 1936–44 he was arrested seven times. Elected to the national leadership of the AUHCW in 1938, in September 1944 he became a member of the Central Committee (CC) of the Party of Peace, founded in June 1943 by **János Kádár** as a cover for the Communist Party. From 1945 Apró was a member of the HCP CC; from 1948, a member of the CC of the Hungarian Workers' Party (HWP); and from 1956, a member of the CC of the Hungarian Socialist Workers' Party (HSWP).

For more than thirty years Apró stayed in the top leadership of the Communist Party and the state. From May to October 1946 he was a deputy member and then until June 1948 a member of the HCP CC Politburo; until 1956 he was a member of the HWP CC Politburo (except for the period from June to October 1953), and until 1980 he was a member of the HSWP CC Politburo. In 1946–52 he worked in the Organization Department of the HCP and HWP CC. In 1948 he was a member of the joint Organization Committee of the HCP and the Social Democratic Party; the committee's aim was to merge both parties under the control of the Communists. From 1945 to 1989 he was MP; from August 1948, secretary general of the National Council of Trade Unions; from August 1949 to January 1952 and from July to November 1953, a member of the Presidential Council; from the beginning of 1952 to July

1953, minister of the Ministry of Building Materials, and then deputy minister of building. In November 1953 he returned to the party Politburo and became deputy prime minister (until 31 October 1956) and permanent delegate to Comecon (until 1971). From the end of 1954 he belonged to the CC commission for the rehabilitation of unjustly sentenced party members, and in June 1956 he was elected chairman of the National Council of the Patriotic Front. On 6 October 1956 he made a speech during the funeral of **László Rajk** and his comrades.

Close to Kádár, Apró represented his political position. At the beginning of the revolution, on the night of 23 October 1956, he was elected to the CC Military Commission. From 26 October he was deputy prime minister and minister of building in the government of **Imre Nagy**. On 28 October he was co-opted to the HWP CC Politburo. On 1 November he turned up at the Soviet command in Tököl, near Budapest, and on 4 November he entered the Revolutionary Workers' and Peasants' Government of Kádár as minister of heavy industry. In December 1956 he became head of the Economic Commission of the HSWP CC. From May 1957 he was deputy prime minister, and from 1961 he headed the government's International Relations Committee. In May 1971 he was relieved of these duties and became speaker of parliament until December 1984. From 1976 to 1989 he was chairman of the Association of Hungarian-Soviet Friendship. In 1980 he was dismissed from the Politburo and in 1988 from the HSWP. In May 1989 he gave up his parliamentary mandate and retired. (JT)

Sources: *Magyar Nagylexikon,* vol. 2 (Budapest, 1994); *A magyar forradalom és szabadságharc enciklopédiája,* CD-ROM (Budapest, 1999); *Új Magyar Életrajzi Lexikon,* vol. 1 (Budapest, 2001); Bennet Kovrig, *Communism in Hungary from Kun to Kádár* (Stanford, 1979); Klaus-Detlev Grothusen, ed., *Ungarn* (Göttingen, 1987); Miklós Molnár, *From Béla Kun to János Kádár: Seventy Years of Hungarian Communism* (New York, 1990).

ARBNORI Pjetër (18 January 1935, Durrës), Albanian writer, political prisoner, and politician. Born into the family of a Catholic prewar gendarme killed by the partisans during the war, Arbnori attended school in Shkodër. In 1949 he joined a secret youth organization that distributed anti-Communist leaflets. He graduated from high school with distinction but because of his family background he could not study abroad (there were no universities in Albania at that time). He worked as a teacher in a small school in the mountains. After military service, he worked as a farmhand in Xhafzotaj near Durrës. When the University of Tirana was established, thanks to false documents, Arbnori managed to start philological studies. In 1960 he entered into contact with a small secret Social Democratic organization in Durrës, and he was the author of its program. Arrested in 1961, he was sentenced to death. His sentenced was commuted to twenty-five years in prison and in fact spent twenty-nine years in prison.

Released in August 1989, in January 1990 Arbnori joined the opposition against the Communist Party. He co-organized the Albanian Democratic Party (Partia Demokratike e Shqipërisë), and he became its first chairman in the Shkodër region, from where he won mandates in subsequent parliamentary elections. In 1992 and 1996 he was elected speaker of the parliament. An officer of the Security Service (Segurimi), identified Arbnori as an agent of the Segurimi who supposedly used the pseudonym Koromanja although these allegations were never confirmed by actual documentation. The only document that was preserved was Arbnori's agreement to cooperate with the Segurimi, and it is believed by his followers to be forged. Nevertheless, the case deeply divided former political prisoners. In August 1997 Arbnori went on a hunger strike to protest attempts by the ruling Socialists to block access of the opposition to public media. The independent Albanian press called him "an Albanian Mandela." As a result the parliament amended the constitution on this matter in 1998. Arbnori continued to work in the parliamentary human rights commission. He is the author of popular novels, including *Kur dynden Vikingjët* (When the vikings come; 1992), *Mugujt e mesjetës* (The darkness of the Middle Ages; 1993), and *E bardha dhe e zeza* (The black and the white; 1996). He has also translated French historical works. (TC)

Sources: B. Hamilton, *Albania—Who Cares* (Grantham, 1992); Elez Biberaj, *Shqipëria ne tranzicion: Rruga e vështrise drejt Demokracisë* (Tirana, 2001).

ARCISZEWSKI Tomasz (14 November 1877, Sierzchowy–20 November 1955, London), Polish Socialist politician. The son of a participant in the January Insurrection (1863), after his father's premature death Arciszewski was brought up in poverty. He completed a primary education and a course for locksmiths, and from 1887 he was a laborer. In 1896 he joined the Polish Socialist Party (Polska Partia Socjalityczna [PPS]). Fearing arrest, he left for England but in 1900 returned to Sosnowiec, where he rebuilt a Socialist unit. Temporarily arrested in August 1900, Arciszewski resumed his underground political activities. During the 1905 revolution he was a member of a Socialist council in Józefów and co-organized the PPS Fighting Organization. Later, he carried on underground Socialist agitation in Siedlce, Białystok, and Kraków, where he trained members of the PPS Fighting

Organization. When the party split in 1906, Arciszewski sided with the PPS Revolutionary Faction. Hunted by the police, he constantly had to change his place of residence. In September 1908 he was one of the organizers of an expropriation action at Bezdany.

In August 1914 Arciszewski joined the Polish Legions, and in 1915 **Józef Piłsudski** sent him to the German-occupied territories of the former Kingdom of Poland. There he was active in the Polish Military Organization, organizing its units in Warsaw, Łódź, and Lublin. He directed the trade union of metal workers, and when the occupation ended, he organized the Central Committee of Trade Unions in resurrected Poland. On 7 November 1918 he became minister of labor and social welfare in the government of **Ignacy Daszyński**, and on 17 November of the same year, minister of post and telegraph in the government of **Jędrzej Moraczewski**. In January 1919 he was elected an MP to the Constituent Assembly. During the Polish-Soviet war he organized the workers' Committee for the Defense of Independence (Komitet Obrony Niepodległości). In independent Poland he was uninterruptedly a member of the Chief Council of the PPS and of its Central Executive Committee. He was elected an MP representing the PPS in 1922, 1928, and 1939 and was active in the parliamentary committee for social issues. After the May 1926 coup, he joined the opposition against the Piłsudski regime, and in 1930 he co-organized the center-left opposition (Centrolew). As a member of the right wing of the party, in the mid-1930s he opposed its "united front" tactics and closer links with the Communists.

After the defeat of September 1939 Arciszewski was one of the leading organizers of the underground Polish Socialist Party-Freedom, Equality, Independence (PPS-WRN), and from the beginning of 1944 he represented the party in the Council of National Unity (Rada Jedności Narodowej). At the end of July 1944 he was secretly taken to London by plane. He opposed compromise with the USSR. After the resignation of **Stanisław Mikołajczyk**, on 29 November 1944 Arciszewski became prime minister of the Polish government in exile. In that capacity, in February 1945 he submitted a protest of the Polish government against the Yalta decisions of the Big Three concerning the Polish question. President **Władysław Raczkiewicz** appointed Arciszewski his successor but later changed his mind in favor of **August Zaleski**. In June 1947 Arciszewski resigned as prime minister in protest. From December 1949 he directed the works of the Political Council, which competed with Zaleski. Arciszewski became a member of the Provisional Council of National Unity, which was formed in July 1954, and along with General **Władysław Anders** and Ambassador

Edward Raczyński he joined the Council of the Three, which from 1956 served as the presidency of the Republic of Poland. At the same time, until his death, Arciszewski held the post of president of the Central Foreign Committee of the PPS. (WR)

Sources: *The International Who's Who 1950* (London, 1950); *Posłowie i senatorowie RP,* vol. 1; *Encyklopedia historii Drugiej Rzeczypospolitej* (Warsaw,1999); Zygmunt Zaremba, *Wojna i konspiracja* (London, 1957); Adam Ciołkosz, "Tomasz Arciszewski," *Kultura,* 1956, no. 1.

AREKHVA Mikalay, pseudonyms "Pyotr," "Klyshka-Malinouski," "Mikulich," and "Barysevich" [in Poland known as Orechwa] (24 November 1902, Boruny, near Oshmiany [Oszmiana]–16 July 1990, Minsk), Belorussian Communist activist. Having joined the Red Army in 1919, Arekhva fought against White Russian forces and against the Polish army. Between 1920 and 1924 he was in the Komsomol apparatus. From 1924 he served as the first secretary of the Central Committee (CC) of the Union of Communist Youth of Belorussia, and in January 1925 he was assigned to work in the northeastern territories of the Second Republic of Poland. He served as secretary of the Vilnius district of the Communist Party of Western Belorussia (CPWB). Arrested in 1926, he spent more than five years in a Polish prison. In 1934 he became head of the State Secretariat of the CPWB, and from 1936 he was a representative of the CC of the CPWB to the CC of the Communist Party of Poland (Komunistyczna Partia Polski). In 1939–44 he was in the USSR. In 1944 he was seconded to the Polish Army and then, on behalf of the Kremlin, he co-organized the Polish security apparatus. From July 1944 he was head of the Personnel Section, between March 1946 and December 1954 he served as director of the Personnel Department of the Ministry of Public Security of the Polish People's Republic, and between January and May 1955 he was director of the Personnel Department of the Committee for Public Security. As he flaunted his superiority as a Soviet officer, he was generally hated, even among the employees of the Polish security apparatus. In 1956 he left for the USSR. Between 1956 and 1984 he worked at the Party History Institute of the CC of the Communist Party of Belorussia. He was mainly involved in propagating the party's successes in the "struggle for the social and national liberation of Belorussians in Western Belorussia." He was the author of propaganda books—for example, *Revalutsyiny rukh u Zakhadniai Bielarusi u hady bielpolskai akupatsyii* (The revolutionary movement in Western Belorussia during the years of White Polish occupation; 1958) and *D'ela i ludi KPZB: Vospominaniia* (Issues and People in the CPWB: Memoirs; 1983). (EM)

Sources: *Entsyklapedyia historyi Belarusi*, vol. 1 (Minsk, 1993); Edward Jan Nalepa, *Oficerowie Armii Radzieckiej w Wojsku Polskim, 1943–1968* (Warsaw, 1995); *Bielaruskaia entsyklapiedyia*, vol. 1 (Minsk, 1996); Mirosław Piotrowski, *Ludzie bezpieki* (Lublin, 2000).

ARGETOIANU Constantin (3 March 1871, Craiova–1950, Sighet), Romanian politician and lawyer. The son of a general, Argetoianu studied law in Paris between 1888 and 1892, and in 1899 he received a Ph.D. in physics at the Paris Polytechnic. From 1898 to 1913 he worked in the diplomatic service, as secretary of the legation and as attaché. In 1914 he was appointed senator, representing the Conservative Party. He frequently changed his political orientation; for example, he was a member of the National Liberal Party and the National Democratic Party. Between January and March 1918 he was minister of justice in the government of General **Alexandru Avarescu**. In this capacity, in Buftea Argetoianu signed peace preliminaries unfavorable to Romania with the Central Powers; this led to the resignation of the cabinet and to the government of **Alexandru Marghiloman**. From March to June 1920 Argetoianu was finance minister, and then he served as minister of interior until December 1921. Between June and November 1927 he held the post of minister of agriculture. He had a good relationship with King **Charles II** from the moment of the king's accession in 1930. In the government of **Nicolae Iorga** (April 1931–June 1932) Argetoianu served as both minister of agriculture and minister of interior; in fact he was in charge of the work of the cabinet. At that time he tried to implement legislation that would cancel the debts of the peasants. However, the legislation did not come into force. After the introduction of the royal dictatorship in February 1938 and the dissolution of political parties, he was one of the first politicians to support the king, and he became a member of the Government of National Unity of Patriarch **Miron Cristea**. Until March 1938 Argetoianu served as minister of industry and trade, and then he was one of the leaders of the Front of National Rebirth, which was established in December 1938.

After the assassination of Prime Minister **Armand Călinescu**, on 28 September 1939 Argetoianu became the head of government and held the office until 28 November 1939. After the abdication of Charles II in September 1940, he went into political exile in Switzerland, where he remained until 1944. After the coup of 23 August 1944 he returned to Romania and formed a new political party, the Labor Party, which was supposed to take part in the elections of November 1946 but did not. Arrested by the Communist authorities in 1948, Argetoianu died in prison. He was the author of, among other works,

Problema constituţională (Constitutional problem; 1923); *Naţionalism şi internaţionalism* (Nationalism and internationalism; 1929); *Statul agrar* (The Agrarian state; 1933); and a famous diary, titled *Pe urmele trecutului: Memorii* (Tracing the past: Memoirs; 1938), it was published in part in the 1930s, and the entire work appeared in the 1990s as *Amintiri de azi pentru azi de mâine* (Memoirs from today to tomorrow; 1990–92). (FA/TD)

Sources: *Biographisches Lexikon*, vol. 1; Juliusz Demel, *Historia Rumunii* (Wrocław, 1986); Larry L. Watts, *Romanian Cassandra: Ion Antonescu and the Struggle for Reform 1916–1941* (Boulder, Colo., 1993).

ARGHEZI Tudor [originally Ion Theodorescu] (21 May 1880, Bucharest–14 July 1967, Bucharest), Romanian writer. Arghezi came from a peasant family that moved to Bucharest. In 1896 he graduated from high school and made his debut with a series of poems in the periodical *Liga ortodoxă*. Then he published his poems and prose in the periodicals *Revista modernă* and *Viaţa nouă*. In 1899 he entered the Cernică Monastery. A year later he became a deacon and soon secretary of the Bucharest metropolitan. He edited the periodicals *Revista de idei* and *Linia dreaptă*, but fearing church sanctions, he used his friend's name, Vasile Demetrius, as a pseudonym. In 1904 he left for Fribourg, Switzerland, to study, and in 1906 he broke with the church, moved to Geneva, and started studying in an evening school of handicrafts. He also worked in a watchmaker's shop. In 1910 he returned to Bucharest, doing both literary work and journalism in the daily *Viitorul* and in the periodicals *Viaţa sociala, Facla,* and *Rampa*. In 1913 he became editor-in-chief of the daily *Seară,* where he published political columns, articles, and reviews.

During World War I Arghezi lived in Bucharest. After the war he was accused of writing for the pro-German press and imprisoned with eleven other writers in the Văcăreşti Monastery. After his release, in 1920–27 he wrote for various periodicals, editing *Cugetul românesc* and, from 1927, the weekly *Naţiunea*. In 1928 he founded the periodical *Bilete de papagal,* which introduced a sort of allegorical pamphlet into Romanian literature, the so-called tablet. He published his first volume of poems, *Cuvînte potrivite* (Selected words), in 1927. His lyrics, combining tradition and modernist tendencies, garnered mixed feelings. His next volume, *Icoane de lemn* (Wooden icons; 1929), had anti-clerical overtones. In *Poarta neagră* (The black gate; 1930) he presented his memoirs from the Văcăreşti prison, and in *Tablete din Ţara Kuty* (Tablets from the Land of Kuty; 1933) he criticized Romanian society and its political elite in a grotesque way. He also published a volume of poems, *Cărticica de seară* (The evening booklet; 1935), and the novel *Cimitirul de Bună-Vestire* (The Annunciation Cemetery; 1936). He was critical of the **Ion Antonescu** regime. For a pamphlet on the German ambassador—*Baronul* (Baron)—in 1943 he was sent to the Tîrgu Jiu camp, where he wrote an anti-Fascist comedy *Seringa* (Syringe).

After his release in August 1944 Arghezi published pamphlets on collaborators of the regime, memoirs, and a new volume of "tablets," *Manual de morala practică* (Handbook of practical morality; 1945). On the fiftieth anniversary of his literary work in 1946, he received a state award. During the peak of Stalinism he chose to keep silent. In 1954 he resumed work with the daily and literary press. He published a volume of poems, *Prisaca* (Apiary), and a cycle of poems about the peasant rebellion, *1907*. In 1955 he became a member of the Romanian Academy and an MP. In 1956 he wrote a philosophical poem, *Cîntare omului* (Human song), and then new volumes of poems, including *Frunze* (Leaves; 1961). On his eighty-fifth birthday he received the title of Hero of Socialist Labor, and the University of Vienna gave him the prestigious Herder Award. (ASK)

Sources: *Wielka encyklopedia PWN,* vol. 2 (Warsaw, 2001); Halina Mirska-Lasota, *Mały słownik pisarzy rumuńskich* (Warsaw, 1975); Dumitru Micu, *Tudor Arghezi* (Bucharest, 1965); Serban Cioculescu, *Tudor Arghezi* (Bucharest, 1971); Nicolae Balota, *Opera lui Tudor Arghezi* (Bucharest, 1997); Pavel Tugui, *Arghezi necocoscut* (Bucharest, 1998).

ARLOU Uladzimir (25 August 1953, Polotsk), Belorussian writer. Arlou studied history at the Belorussian State University in Minsk. In 1975–76 he worked as a teacher of history in Novopolotsk and then as a journalist and deputy editor-in-chief of the regional daily *Khimik.* In 1988 he became an editor in Mastatskaya Literatura Press, and in 1989, deputy chairman of the Belorussian PEN club. He made his debut as a poet in 1973. In the late 1980s he published collections of short stories: *Dobry dzyen, maya Shipshina* (Good morning, my Shipshina) and *Dzyen, kali upala strala* (The day the arrow fell). He won wide recognition for his short stories, essays, and historical novels: *Poka nye pogasla svyecha* (Until the candle dies down; 1990); *Milast' knyazya Hyeranima* (The Love of Prince Hieronymus; 1993); *Tayamnitsy polatskay historyi* (Secrets of the history of Polotsk; 1994); and *Adkul nash rod* (From where our clan comes; 1996). He co-authored *Dzyesiats' vyakou belaruskay historyi* (Ten centuries of Belorussian history; 1999). In 1998 he published a collection of short stories, *Rekvyem dla byenzapily* (Requiem for a motor saw), a psychological portrait of Soviet Belorussian society of the 1970s and 1980s. His works have been translated in many European countries, and he has received many prestigious Belorussian awards. (EM)

Sources: *Bielaruskiya pismienniki: Biyabibliahrafichny slounik,* vol. 1 (Minsk, 1992); *Bielaruskiya pismienniki 1917–1990: Davyednik* (Minsk, 1994); *Belarus: Entsyklapedychny davyednik* (Minsk, 1995); *Kto jest kim w Białorusi* (Białystok, 2000).

ARSENNEVA Natalya [also spelled Arsen'neva Natal'lia] (20 September 1903, Baku–25 July 1997, Rochester, N.Y.), Belorussian poet. Arsenneva spent her childhood and youth in Vilnius. In 1921 she graduated from a Belorussian gymnasium in Vilnius, and she completed a course for teachers. Between 1921 and 1922 she studied in the Art Department of Stefan Batory University in Vilnius. In 1922 she married Franciszek Kuszal, a Belorussian activist and an officer in the Polish Army. Until September 1939 she lived in Słonim and in Chełmno. In the autumn of 1939, as a Polish officer's wife, she was arrested, along with her two sons, and she was deported to Kazakhstan. Released from exile thanks to the endeavors of **Janka Kupała**, she settled in Minsk. During the German occupation she worked in the editorial offices of the *Belaruskaya gazeta.* Her husband was a commander in an officers' school that was preparing cadres for the Belorussian military formations fighting on the side of Germany. In 1944 she and her family left for Germany, and in 1950, for the United States. She worked in the editorial offices of the émigré newspaper *Byelarus,* Radio Svaboda, and the Belorussian Institute of Literature and Arts in New York. In 1920 she made her debut with the poem "Nasha Dumka," published in a Vilnius newspaper. The first collection of her poems, *Pod sinim nebam* (Beneath the blue sky), appeared in Vilnius in 1927; the second, *Siahodnia* (Today), in Minsk in 1944. She wrote love poems and lyric poetry inspired by Belorussian nature. The war left a deep mark on her writing. The motives of people who were destroying the world were beyond her comprehension. She wrote patriotic poems for which music was composed. In 1979 an anthology of her émigré writings, *Mizh berahami* (Between the banks), appeared in the United States. Its recurrent motifs are the idea of freedom and a nostalgia for Belorussia. She also wrote stage works such as *Svaty* (1955) and librettos for operas by Mykola Kulikovich, *Lasnoie Oziero* (Forest Lake) and *Usiaslau Charadzei*. She translated librettos for operas by Wolfgang Amadeus Mozart, Georges Bizet, Johann Strauss, and Pyotr Tchaikovsky into Belorussian. (EM)

Sources: B. Sachanka, *S'niatstsaa sny ab Bielarusi . . .* (Minsk, 1990); *Bielaruskiya pis'mienniki 1917–1990: Daviednik* (Minsk, 1994); *Entsyklapiedyia historyi Bielarusi,* vol. 1 (Minsk, 1993); Jan Zaprudnik, *Historical Dictionary of Belarus* (Lanham, Md., 1998).

ARTUKOVIĆ Andrija (29 November 1899, Klobuk, near Ljubuska–16 January 1988, Zagreb), Croatian nationalist activist. Born into a peasant family in Bosnia Herzegovina, Artuković graduated from a French gymnasium in Široki Brijeg (Lištica) and in law from the university in Zagreb in 1924. While a student, he began to associate with Croatian extremist nationalists. After the royal coup of 1929 he joined the Ustaša movement. He took part in an assassination attempt at the gendarmerie post in Brušane in the mountains of Velebit in 1932, and then he fled from Yugoslavia. In Italy he was one of the closest associates of **Ante Pavelić** in the preparations for the assassination of King **Alexander Karadjordjević** in Marseilles (1934). The French extradited Artuković to Yugoslavia on condition that he would not be interrogated about all the details of his activities. In April 1935 he was convicted on a trivial offense. Released in 1936, he went to Austria and then to Berlin, where the Ustaša general headquarters was moved in 1937. On 15 April 1941 he returned to Croatia as minister of interior of the Ustaša government. In that capacity he organized concentration camps and the mass killing of Serbs and Jews. At that time he became notorious for issuing a law forbidding "Serbs, Jews, Gypsies, and dogs" to enter public places. From the beginning of October 1942 he was minister of justice and religious affairs, and from April 1943 he again served as minister of interior. When **Nikola Mandić** became prime minister, Artuković was transferred to the less important post of chancellor of the seal (*državni prabilježnik*).

After the war Artuković managed to escape from Yugoslavia. For a short time he stayed in France, then in Switzerland and Ireland, and in 1948 he arrived in the United States and settled in Seal Beach, California. In August 1945 a Communist Yugoslav court declared him a war criminal; however, the American authorities considered him a political exile. In 1981 the Yugoslav authorities demanded his extradition as a war criminal. He was arrested but was soon released under pressure from Croatian organizations in the United States. After a long effort, in February 1986 he was finally handed over to Yugoslavia, and after a one-month trial, at which he denied accusations of having taken part in genocide, he was sentenced to death. The execution was postponed due to his ill health. He died in prison. (WR)

Sources: *Hrvatski biografski leksikon,* vol. 1 (Zagreb, 1983); L. Hory and M. Broszat, *Der Kroatische Ustascha-Staat 1941–1945* (Stuttgart, 1964); Ivo Omrčanin, *Dramatis personae and finis of the Independent State of Croatia in British and American Documents* (Bryn Mawr, 1983); Bogdan Krizman, *Ustaše i Treći Reich* (Zagreb, 1983), vols. 1–2; Bogdan Krizman, *Ante Pavelić i Ustaše* (Zagreb, 1983); Djordje Ličina, *Dossier Artuković* (Zagreb, 1986); Jovo Popović, *Sudenje Andriji Artukovicia i sto nije receno* (Zagreb, 1986); *New York Times,* 19 January 1988.

ASKENAZY Szymon (23 December 1865, Zawichost–22 June 1935, Warsaw), Polish historian, politician, and diplomat. Askenazy came from an intellectual Jewish family. He favored assimilation and was a Polish patriot, advocating the independence of Poland. In about 1888 he became affiliated with Warsaw Freemason circles. He was not a formal member of any lodge but enjoyed the support of several Freemasons. Having graduated in historical studies, in 1902 he became a lecturer and then a professor at the University of Lwów (Lviv). From 1907 he was a member of the Academy of Arts and Sciences. He represented a neo-Romantic trend in Polish historiography, a reaction to the dominant conservative Kraków school. He was particularly interested in the partitions of Poland and with Napoleonic times. He argued with the theory of Polish guilt for the partitions at the end of the eighteenth century, and he glorified Polish armed struggles for independence. He placed the Polish cause in the European context—for instance, in *Przymierze polsko-pruskie* (The Polish-Prussian Alliance; 1900) and *Rosya-Polska* (Russia-Poland; 1907). In *Książę Józef Poniatowski, 1763–1813* (Prince Józef Poniatowski; 1905) and *Łukasiński* (2 vols.; 1908) he restored the myth of these heroes of the struggle for freedom, and in *Napoleon a Polska* (Napoleon and Poland, 3 vols.; 1918–19) he popularized the Napoleonic legend. Among his other works should be mentioned *Gdańsk a Polska* (Danzig and Poland; 1923) and *Rękopisy Napoleona w Polsce 1793–1795* (Napoleon's manuscripts in Poland, 1793–1795; 1929). Askenazy created his own historical school, and his best-known students were Władysław Konopczyński, **Marian Kukiel**, Henryk Mościcki, and Adam Próchnik.

During World War I Askenazy went abroad and was allied with the so-called activists, supporting the Central Powers. Despite his support for the pro-Austrian Chief National Committee, he collaborated with representatives of the opposite orientation. Along with **Henryk Sienkiewicz**, he established in Switzerland the Committee for Aid to War Victims in Poland. After Poland regained independence, he served as the first minister plenipotentiary at the League of Nations (1920–23). He gave up this post as a result of his conflict with Foreign Minister **Roman Dmowski.** Until the end of his life Askenazy was subjected to attacks from the nationalist right on account of his sympathies for freemasonry and his alleged anti-Polish activities. Owing to the anti-Semitic attitude of a part of the academic community, he did not return to Lwów University, and, despite efforts, he failed to gain a chair at

Warsaw University. In 1928 he received only an honorary professorship at Warsaw University. (MC)

Sources: *Wielka Encyklopedia PWN,* vol. 2 (Warsaw, 2001); Józef Dutkiewicz, *Szymon Askenazy i jego szkoła* (Warsaw, 1958); *Historycy warszawscy ostatnich dwóch stuleci,* eds. Aleksander Gieysztor, Jerzy Maternicki and Henryk Samsonowicz (Warsaw, 1986); Ludwik Hass, "W ujarzmionej stolicy—bez loży (1831–1905)," www.arsregia.home.pl; "Szymon Askenazy," www.arsregia. home.pl; *Słownik biograficzny szachistów polskich,* Part 1, www. dig.com.pl/pdf/Szachy.pdf.

ASPĀZIJA [pseudonym of Elza Pliekšāne, née Rozenberga] (16 March 1865, Zaļenieku, Courland–5 November 1943, Riga), Latvian poet and playwright. Aspāzija came from a rich peasant family. In 1884 she graduated from a high school for girls in Riga. In 1879 she wrote her first poem in German, and in 1888 her first drama, *Atrabēja* (Avengeress). Her works, reflecting social conflicts at the turn of twentieth century, were not welcomed by the conservative element of the Latvian intelligentsia but brought her recognition in modernist and leftist circles. From 1891 she worked as a private teacher, and in 1893–95, in a Latvian theater in Riga. Later she joined the movement for women's rights. After her first marriage ended, she made friends with and in 1897 married the poet **Jānis Rainis.** From 1897 to 1903 she voluntarily joined him in exile in Russia. She also periodically lived in Riga, where she worked at the daily *Dienas Lapa.* It was then that she wrote her best-known plays, *Zaudētās Tiesības* (Lost rights; 1894) and *Sidraba Šķidrauts* (Silver veil; 1905). In 1905 she took part in the revolution, and after its suppression she emigrated with her husband to Switzerland and continued her literary work. In April 1920 via Poland she returned with Rainis to Latvia, where they received an enthusiastic welcome. In 1920–22 she was a deputy to the Latvian Constituent Assembly on behalf of the Social Democratic Party. After her husband's death in 1929 she continued her literary work, becoming a leading figure in Latvian cultural life. She continued to write and publish plays and collections of poems, in which she frequently referred to her memories from childhood, as well as to Latvian history and mythology. She also translated *Quo Vadis,* by **Henryk Sienkiewicz,** into Latvian. She survived the fall of independent Latvia and the Soviet occupation and died after the German invasion. She is buried in Riga. (EJ)

Sources: *Raiņa un Aspazijas gadagrāmata 1968. gadam* (Vesterosa, 1967); Saulcerīte Viese, *Aspazija* (Riga, 1975); B. Amoliņa, *Aspazija—spēks un daiļums, un mūžam nerimstošais gars* (Riga, 1990); *Raiņa un Aspazijas gadagrāmata* (Riga, 1990); Saulcerīte Viese, *Gājēji uz Mēnesdārzu* (Riga, 1990); M. Butevica, *Aspazija* (Riga, 1993); Andrejs Plakans, *Historical Dictionary of Latvia* (Lanham, Md., 1997).

ASTRA Gunārs (22 October 1931, Riga–6 April 1988, Leningrad), Latvian dissident, victim of communism. Astra graduated from a technical high school and then studied Latvian philology. Afterwards he worked as a technician in the VEF factory in Riga. In 1961 he was arrested and sentenced to fifteen years in a labor camp for "anti-Soviet activities" since he had taken pictures of bridges and other facilities recognized by the authorities as secret. He was imprisoned in the Mordovian camps. Released in 1976, he became a blue-collar worker in Riga. In 1983 he was arrested again, this time for possession of the uncensored (illegal) novel *Piecas dienas* (Five days), which described everyday life in Soviet Latvia; for distributing copies of works by George Orwell and Aleksandr Solzhenitsyn; and for possessing recordings of Western broadcasts. Sentenced to seven years in prison and five years of forced settlement, Astra, in his last words before the court, openly criticized Russification policies and Russian colonization in Latvia. The text of his speech was widely distributed in Latvia and abroad in secret. He was imprisoned in the labor camps of the Perm region. Released on the basis of an amnesty in December 1988, he died in hospital after an operation. (EJ)

Sources: *Biographical Dictionary of Dissidents in the Soviet Union, 1956–1978* (The Hague, 1982); *Wielka Encyklopedia PWN,* vol. 1 (Warsaw, 2001); Māris Ruks, *Gunārs Astra* (Riga, 1998); Biruta Eglīte, *Kas jūs bijāt, Gunār Astra?* (Riga, 1998); *Policy of Occupation Powers in Latvia, 1939–1991,* ed. Elma Pelkhaus (Riga, 1999).

ASTROUSKI Radaslau (6 November 1887, Zapole, near Slutsk–17 October 1976, Benton Harbor, Michigan), Belorussian social activist and politician. Astrouski took part in anti-tsarist demonstrations during the revolution of 1905. Between 1908 and 1913 he studied mathematics at St. Petersburg University. Arrested in 1911 for his activities in the Russian revolutionary movement, he completed his studies at the University of Dorpat (Tartu). In 1914 he taught mathematics at a gymnasium in Częstochowa, and in 1915–17, at the Minsk Teachers' Institute. After the February 1917 revolution he was appointed commissar of Slutsk county and headmaster of a gymnasium in Slutsk. He introduced the use of the Belorussian language in the schools. In June 1917 he joined the Central Committee of the Belorussian Socialist Hromada, the most influential Belorussian party. After the Bolshevik revolution he opposed recognition of the new Russian government and advocated the establishment of Belorussian state authorities. In December 1917 he was a delegate to the All-Belorussian Congress, which passed a resolution to establish national state authorities. He fought in the army of General Anton Denikin against the Bolsheviks, and in November 1920 he took part in the Slutsk uprising. After the war he settled in Wilno (Vilnius), where he was one of the key Belorussian figures, serving as headmaster of a Belorussian gymnasium (1924–36), president of the Belorussian School Society (1924–25), and headmaster of the Belorussian Cooperative Bank (1925–26).

In 1926 Astrouski became deputy president of the Central Committee of the Belorussian Peasants' and Workers' Hromada and a member of the Communist Party of Western Belorussia. Arrested in January 1927, he denied any ties with the Communists. From 1928 he promoted cooperation with the Polish government. In 1930 he co-founded the Central Union of Belorussian Cultural and Economic Organizations (Centrsayuz). Politically and socially ostracized by Vilnius Belorussian organizations, he left for Łódź, where he taught mathematics at a local school. In 1940 he became president of the Belorussian Committee in Łódź, and he established close cooperation with the Germans. Between the fall of 1941 and the fall of 1943, on behalf of the Germans, he served as mayor of Smolensk, Brańsk, and Mahilyow (Mogilev) successively. In December 1943 the Germans promoted him to the post of president of the Belorussian Central Council (BCC). The council aspired to be the Belorussian government in exile. In June 1944 the council, under Astrouski's leadership, convened the Second All-Belorussian Congress in Minsk, which, in agreement with the Germans, proclaimed the creation of the Belorussian state. A few days later the Red Army seized Minsk. Astrouski left for Germany, where on 25 March 1948 he formally reestablished the BCC as an émigré government of Belorussia. However, his opponents in exile claimed that the only legal Belorussian representation was the government of the Belorussian People's Republic, which had existed since 1918. Astrouski continued his political activities in the United States, where he arrived in 1956. He gathered some war émigrés who supported the legality of the BCC as the only representation of the Belorussian nation. (EM)

Sources: *Bielaruskaia Sovietskaia Entsiklopediia,* vol. 1, 1969; *Entsyklapiedyia historyi Bielarusi,* vol. 1 (Minsk, 1994); Nicholas P. Vakar, *Belorussia: The Making of a Nation* (Cambridge, Mass., 1956); V. Kalush, *In the Service of the People for a Free Byelorussia: Biographical Notes on Professor Radaslau Ostrowski* (London, 1964); Vitaut Kipel and Zora Kipel, eds., *Byelorussian Statehood* (New York, 1988); Jerzy Turonek, *Białoruś pod okupacją niemiecką* (Warsaw, 1993); Jan Zaprudnik, *Historical Dictionary of Belarus* (Lanham, Md., 1998).

ATANASOV Georgi (25 July 1933, Pravoslaven, Plovdiv district), Bulgarian Communist activist. Atanasov gradu-

ated in history from Sofia University. In 1956 he joined the Bulgarian Communist Party (BCP). From 1958 he was active in the youth movement, participating in various functions in the Dimitrov Communist Youth League (DCYL) and attaining the post of first secretary of the DCYL Central Committee (1965–68). At the same time, he rose in the party hierarchy. He began as a member of the BCP Town Committee in Sofia. Next, he served as candidate member and then member of the CC of the BCP (1966–90), head of the Department of Science and Education of the CC of the BCP (1968–76), head of the Administrative Department of the CC of the BCP (1976–78), secretary of the CC of the BCP (1977–86), candidate member of the Politburo of the CC of the BCP, head of the Organization Department of the CC of the BCP (1984–86), and member of the Politburo of the CC of the BCP (March 1986–February 1990). He also occupied high posts in the government administration. He was the first deputy of the president of the State Planning Committee (1980–81), president of the State Control Committee and the People's Control Committee, and deputy president of the State Council (1981–84). From 1966 to 1990 he was MP and served (among other capacities) as a member of the committee established in August 1987 to prepare changes in the constitution. Furthermore, he served as a member of the National Council of the Patriotic Front. From 21 March 1986 he was prime minister. Under the pressure of demonstrations, in mid-December 1989 he agreed to roundtable talks with the opposition. On 3 February 1990 he stepped down as a result of criticism at the Extraordinary Fourteenth Congress of the BCP. After the fall of the regime, in April 1992 he was arrested, and on 3 November 1992 the Supreme Court sentenced him to ten years in prison for the embezzlement of 200,000 leva from a fund for orphans. After 333 days in prison he was released owing to ill health. (JJ)

Sources: *Koy koy e v Bulgariya* (Sofia, 1998); *Entsiklopediya Bulgariya* (Sofia, 1978); James F. Brown, *Bulgaria under Communist Rule* (New York, 1970).

ATANASOV Nedyalko [originally Mochurov] (8 July 1881, Slomer, near Turnovo [now Veliko Turnovo]–12 February 1960, Sofia), Bulgarian peasant politician and teacher. Having graduated from a gymnasium in Shumen in 1899, Atanasov worked as a teacher for fourteen years. From 1908 he was a member of the Bulgarian Agrarian National Union (BANU), and from 1911 he was an MP representing this party. He was also an MP in 1914–17, 1919–20, and 1920–23. In the government of **Aleksandur Stamboliyski**, he served as minister of construction, roads, and spatial management (February–May 1920);

minister of trade, industry, and labor (April–May 1920); and minister of post and telegraph (May 1920–June 1921 and March–June 1923). After the military coup of June 1923 he was arrested, tried, and acquitted in April 1924. He emigrated to Yugoslavia, where between 1924 and 1925 he was a member of the foreign representation of the BANU. After a split in the leadership of the peasant movement in exile he joined the leadership of its moderate, centrist wing. Atanasov was also one of the leaders of a group called Tselski Glas (Voice of the Village) and editor of a newspaper of the same name. From 1935 to 1944 he had an ambivalent attitude toward the tsarist Bulgarian regime, holding a parliamentary seat in 1938–39. After the Communist coup of 9 September 1944 he was one of the leaders of the BANU opposition led by **Nikola Petkov** (1945–47), and he was an MP on behalf of this party. Because of his opposition activities, in 1949 he was imprisoned in a concentration camp in Belene, where he was a "dean" of the so-called brigade of deputies, which consisted of deputies to the Sixth Grand National Assembly. Released in 1955, Atanasov joined the Fatherland Front. He was the author of the following works: *Tsanko Tserkovski: Lichni spomeni* (Tsanko Tserkovski: Personal diaries; 1921); *Zemedelski besedi* (Village talks; 1930); and *Po trudnija pyt: BZNS na vlast* (On a tough path: The BANU in power; 1931). (JJ)

Sources: *Entsiklopediya Bulgariya*, vol. 1 (Sofia, 1978); Zygmunt Hemmerling, *Ruch ludowy w Polsce, Bułgarii i Czechosłowacji 1893–1930* (Warsaw, 1987); Tasho V. Tashev, *Ministrite na Bylgariia 1879–1999* (Sofia, 1999).

AVAKUMOVIĆ Jovan (1 January 1841, Belgrade–11 August 1928, Belgrade), Serbian lawyer and politician. Avakumović graduated in law in Germany and France, and then he practiced as a defense attorney and was active in the Liberal Party. In 1880 he was minister of justice, and from August 1892 to April 1893 he was Serbian prime minister and minister of foreign affairs. From the end of the nineteenth century he, along with other liberals, remained in opposition to King **Alexander Obrenović**, demanding a universal voting franchise, a territorial self-government, and more independence from Austria-Hungary. After King Alexander was assassinated, on 11 June 1903 Avakumović resumed the position of prime minister until 4 October 1903. A leading expert in penal law, he authored the first Serbian handbook on the subject: *Teorija kaznenog prava* (Theory of penal law; 1877); he also wrote *Sticaj zločina* (Circumstances of a crime; 1883) and *Pokusaj* (Attempt at murder; 1884).

Sources: *Biographisches Lexikon*, vol. 1; *Enciklopedija Jugoslavije*, vol. 1 (Zagreb, 1955); Chedomille Mijatovitc, *A Royal Tragedy* (London, 1906); Michael B. Petrovich, *A History of Modern Serbia 1804–1918*, vol. 2 (New York, 1976); Željan E. Šuster, *Historical Dictionary of the Federal Republic of Yugoslavia* (Lanham, Md., 1999).

AVERESCU Alexandru (9 March 1859, Ismail, Bessarabia–3 October 1938, Bucharest), Romanian marshal and politician. After finishing high school, between 1878 and 1881 Averescu studied at a military school in Mănăstirea Dealu, and between 1882 and 1886 he attended the Military College in Turin, Italy. In 1894–95 he was a commander of the Military College in Bucharest, and from 1895 to 1898 he served as military attaché in Berlin. In 1907 he became a general, and between March 1907 and March 1909 he was minister of war in the government of **Dimitrie Sturdza**. In that capacity he commanded military units that suppressed a peasant revolt in Moldavia, Muntenia, and Oltenia. This claimed the lives of over ten thousand peasants.

During the Second Balkan War (1913) Averescu commanded the Romanian Army in Bulgaria. From Romania's entry into World War I until 1918, he commanded the Second Army and consolidated the defenses in Moldavia. During the heaviest battles, between late 1916 and August 1917, the lines of defense successfully resisted the attacks of the Central Powers. For example, Averescu won a victory over the Germans at Mărăşti in July 1917. Between 29 January and 5 March 1918 Averescu served as premier and minister of foreign affairs. He negotiated peace with the Central Powers on behalf of the royal court and the National Liberal Party (NPL). On 7 May 1918 a peace treaty was concluded in Bucharest, but the treaty was humiliating for Romania, which lost much territory, including southern Dobrudja and the Carpathian passes. Disagreements about political events led to mutual accusations between Averescu and the royal court; the latter accused him of "republicanism," while he accused his predecessor, Premier **Ion I. C. Brătianu**, of implementing a policy that proved disastrous for Romania. In 1918 in Iaşi Averescu set up his own People's Party (Partidul Poporului [PP]), in opposition to the ruling NPL. He was head of the PP until his death. In December 1919 he temporarily served as minister of the interior, and between 13 March 1920 and 17 December 1921 he was prime minister and minister of the interior, simultaneously serving as minister of industry and trade from November 1920. During his rule important social and political reforms were introduced—an agrarian reform (1921) and a social security reform (1920–21). The centralization of the government and the unification of the country was also carried out. Romania joined the Little Entente and signed an alliance treaty with Poland on 3 March

1921. In 1920 Averescu gained international recognition for the incorporation of Bessarabia into Romania. Averescu was fascinated with the experiment of Benito Mussolini in Italy.

On 30 March 1926 Averescu again became premier. He strengthened Romania's international position, concluding alliance treaties with France and Italy (1926). However, he was still perceived as a "republican" by the royal court and had bad relations with Ion I.C. Brătianu. Shortly before the death of King **Ferdinand**, on 7 June 1927, Averescu resigned as premier. In 1930 he was appointed marshal, but the same year he came into conflict with the new king, **Charles II**. However, in 1938 he became his adviser, supporting a royal dictatorship. In February and March 1938 he served as minister of state in the Government of National Unity of Patriarch **Miron Cristea**. Averescu authored (among other works) *Răspunderile* (Responsibility; 1918), *Cauza politică* (Political issue; 1927), and a book of memoirs, *Notiţe zilnice de război* (Daily notes from the war; 1937). (FA/TD)

Sources: David Mitrany, *The Land and the Peasant in Rumania* (New Haven, 1930); R.W. Seton-Watson, *A History of the Roumanians* (Archon Books, 1963); Holger H. Herwig and Neil M. Heyman, *Biographical Dictionary of World War I* (Westport, Conn., 1982); Juliusz Demel, *Historia Rumunii* (Wrocław, 1986); Constantin Kiriţescu, *Istoria războiului pentru întregirea României 1916–1919*, 2 vols. (Bucharest, 1989); Andrea Schmidt-Rösler, *Rumänien nach dem Ersten Weltkrieg* (Frankfurt am Main, 1994); Keith Hitchins, *Rumania 1866–1947* (Oxford, 1994); Vasile Alexandrescu, Costică Prodan and Dumitru Preda, *În apărarea României Mari: Campania Armatei Române 1918–1919* (Bucharest, 1995).

B

BABIĆ Milan (26 February 1956, Kukor, near Knin—5 March 2006, The Hague), leader of Serb separatists in Croatian Krajina. A dentist by profession, Babić had an office in Knin. Active in the Communist Party, in the late 1980s he became the mayor of Knin. In 1989 he co-founded the Serbian Democratic Party (Srpska Demokratska Stranka [SDP]), which in the first free elections of April–June 1990 won five mandates in the Croatian parliament. From early 1990 Babić strove for Serb autonomy in Croatia, but until the summer of 1990 he was in the shadow of the SDP leader, Jovan Rašković, who was ready to make a compromise with the Zagreb authorities. The radicalization of the Serbs and the creation in June 1990 of a Community of Serb-Administered Areas without consent from Zagreb, strengthened Babić's position. In July 1990 he became chairman of the Serbian National Council (SNC), a quasi-parliament of Serbs from Krajina that in December 1990 proclaimed secession from Croatia (it introduced the Cyrillic script, gave up paying taxes to Zagreb, and armed a local militia). In February 1991 Krajina proclaimed independence from Croatia, confirmed in a referendum among Serbs in the spring of 1991. When in June 1991 Croatia proclaimed independence, Serbs from Krajina, supported by the federal army, took a quarter of Croatian territory by force and proclaimed the Republic of Serbian Krajina, including other areas inhabited by a Serb majority—Slavonia, Baranya, and Srem.

This was a pyrrhic victory for Babić. Striving for the rapid unification of Krajina with the rest of Serb territories within a new Yugoslav federation, or Greater Serbia, he stood in the way of different plans proposed by **Slobodan Milošević**. In February 1992 Babić was removed from the SNC leadership and replaced by Goran Hadžić, who accepted UN peacekeeping forces in Krajina (the Cyrus Vance Plan). Babić tried to regain power in the presidential elections of December 1993, but he lost to the commander of the Krajina militia, Milan Martić, who was supported by Belgrade. For a few weeks, during the Croatian offensive in the summer of 1995, Babić was prime minister of the Republic of Serbian Krajina, but he failed to prevent the defeat and emigration of most of the Krajina Serbs from Croatia (he too emigrated). In January 2004 the Trial Chamber of the International Tribunal for War Crimes in Former Yugoslavia found him guilty of crimes against humanity during the Serbian offensive of 1991. He was found dead in his prison cell. (AW)

Sources: Robert Stallaerts and Jeannine Laurens, *Historical Dictionary of the Republic of Croatia* (Metuchen and London, 1995); Karen Dawisha and Bruce Parrot, eds., *Politics, Power and the Struggle for Democracy in South-East Europe* (Cambridge, 1997); Leszek Podhorodecki, *Jugosławia: Dzieje narodów, państw i rozpad federacji* (Warsaw, 2000); *Eastern Europe and the Commonwealth of Independent States 1992* (London, 1992); Bugajski.

BABITS Mihály (26 November 1883, Szekszárd–4 August 1941, Budapest), Hungarian writer, translator, and historian of literature. Born into a family with roots in the gentry, from his early years Babits was fascinated by ancient cultures and native literature. After graduating from high school in Pécs in 1901, he studied Hungarian and classical philology at the University of Budapest (1901–5). He wrote poems and other short pieces from an early age and published them in literary magazines. His first collections, *Levelek Irisz koszorújából* (Leaves from the wreath of Iris; 1909) and *Herceg, hátha megjön a tél is?* (My prince, and if winter comes as well?; 1911), already showed his formal mastery and intellectual depth. Babits considered art a phenomenon free from social implications. After his studies, he started working as a teacher, and he became the editor (from 1939 editor-in-chief) of the biweekly *Nyugat*, the leading literary magazine of interwar Hungary. He translated a lot from Dante Alighieri, William Shakespeare, Johann Wolfgang Goethe, and Charles Baudelaire. He also wrote novels, such as *A gólya kalifa* (The stork caliph; 1916), in which he applied the theories of Sigmund Freud; *Kártyavár* (House of cards; 1923), a satire on contemporary Hungary written from the point of view of a small town; and *Halál fiai* (Convicts; 1927), which was a family saga set against the background of social and cultural change at the turn of the twentieth century.

Babits was involved in the republican revolution of late 1918 and then, as a member of the Directorate of Writers, in the Hungarian Soviet Republic. After its fall he denied any connections with communism but nevertheless was forced to leave the University of Budapest, where he taught contemporary literature. From the late 1920s he was seriously ill with throat cancer. Losing his voice, he continued to write, publishing, among other things, a futurist novel on the coming destruction of humanity, *Elza pilóta vagy a tökéletes társadalom* (Woman pilot Elza, or the perfect society; 1933), and a two-volume collection of essays, *Az európai irodalom történelem* (History of European literature; 1934–35). His intellectual poetry and prose, as well as his translations, made him one of the outstanding Hungarian writers of the interwar period. (MS)

Sources: Aurél Kárpáti, *B. M. életműve* (Budapest, 1941); *Babits Emlékkönyv* (Budapest, 1941); Paul Ignotus, *Hungary* (London, 1972); *Mały słownik pisarzy węgierskich* (Warsaw, 1977); Tibor Hajdu, *The Hungarian Soviet Republic* (Budapest, 1979); *Mint különös hírmondó: Tanulmányok éd dokumentumok* (Budapest, 1983).

BABIUCH Edward (28 December 1927, Grabocin), Polish Communist activist. The son of a miner, Babiuch graduated from the Higher Party School at the Central Committee (CC) of the Polish United Workers' Party (Polska Zjednoczona Partia Robotnicza [PUWP]) and from the Central School of Planning and Statistics in Warsaw. In 1946 he joined he Polish Workers' Party, and in 1948, the PUWP. In 1949–55 he worked in the apparatus of the Polish Youth Union and from 1955 to 1959 in the CC apparatus; in 1959–63 he was secretary of the Warsaw Provincial Committee of the PUWP; from 1963 to 1965 he was deputy head of the CC Organization Department and editor of the party periodical, *Życie Partii.* Between 1965 and 1970 he was head of the CC Organization Department and from 1964, a member of the PUWP CC. After the fall of **Władysław Gomułka**, in December 1970 he entered the CC Secretariat and Politburo as one of the closest associates of **Edward Gierek**, but he preferred to remain in the shadows. From 1969 he was an MP; from 1972, a member of the Council of State; and from 1976 to February 1980 he was deputy chairman of the latter body. After the fall of **Piotr Jaroszewicz**, on 18 February 1980 Babiuch was made prime minister. He could not prevent the deepening social and economic crisis and the wave of summer strikes. His clumsy response to the Baltic Coast strikes, feeble authority, and badly received speech of mid-August led to his dismissal on 24 August 1980. He also gave up his position in the State Council. In October 1980 he was dismissed from the PUWP CC, and in December 1980 he gave up his parliamentary seat. In a resolution of the Eleventh PUWP Extraordinary Congress in July 1981, Babiuch was deemed in part responsible for the state and party crisis. On the basis of a decision of the Military Council of National Salvation, on 13 December 1981, Babiuch, along with a group of higher officials of the Gierek regime, was interned for propaganda reasons. Released after a few months, he retired from public life. (PK)

Sources: Mołdawa; *Słownik polityków polskich XX w.* (Poznań, 1998); Michał Czajka and Marcin Kamler, *Leksykon historii Polski* (Warsaw, 1995).

BACHYNSKYI Lev (14 February 1872, Serafinsti, near Horodenka–4 October 1930, Heilenstadt Grimmenstein, Austria), Ukrainian politician and lawyer. Bachynskyi came from a teacher's family. He graduated from high school in Kolomyia and in law in Tschernowitz (Chernivtsi). In 1897 he was arrested for taking part in an anti-Austrian demonstration. After his release he started practicing law in Stanisławów (Ivano-Frankivsk). As a representative of the Ukrainian Radical Party (URP), from 1907 to 1918 he was a member of the Chamber of Deputies of the Council of State in Vienna, where he represented the Pokutye region of the Hutsul people. Engaged in the struggle of Ukrainian students against the Polish authorities of Lwów (Lviv) University, he advocated Ukrainization of this university. On 16 December 1907, protesting the refusal of the chamber presidium to present a resolution of Ukrainian deputies concerning recent incidents at the university, he threw his reading desk at the speaker but hit and wounded someone else. In 1915–16 he was deputy chairman of the General Ukrainian Council in Vienna, and in 1918–19, deputy chairman of the Council (Rada) of the Western Ukrainian National Republic (WUNR). He prepared two laws passed by this Ukrainian parliament: one concerned the unification of the WUNR with the Kiev Ukrainian National Republic (3 January 1919), and the other concerned land reform. From 1918 until his death he was the leader of the URP (later the Ukrainian Social Radical Party) in Galicia. In 1928–30 he was MP of the Polish parliament. He advocated seeking support for the Ukrainian left in the Second International. (TS)

Sources: *Encyclopedia of Ukraine,* vol. 1 (Toronto, 1985); Czesław Partacz, *Od Badeniego do Potockiego: Stosunki polsko-ukraińskie w Galicji w latach 1888–1908* (Toruń, 1996); *Posłowie i senatorowie Rzeczypospolitej Polskiej 1919–1939. Słownik biograficzny* (Warsaw, 1998).

BACHYNSKYI Yulian (1870, Lviv–1940, USSR), Ukrainian politician and journalist, victim of Stalinist persecution. The son of a Greek Catholic clergyman, at the beginning of the 1890s Bachynskyi joined the Galician Ruthenian-Ukrainian Radical Party, which was formed in 1890. He became involved with the so-called young faction (of Viacheslav Budzynovskyi, Mykola Hankevych, and Volodymir Okhrymovich), which, unlike the moderates, the so-called old faction (of **Ivan Franko** and Mikhailo Pavlyk), evolved toward Marxism. In 1895 Bachynskyi published his famous book, *Ukraiina irredenta,* in which, for the first time in the modern history of the Ukraine, an independent and unified Ukrainian state was postulated. In 1914 he published *Ukraiinska emihratsia v Ziedynenykh Derzhavakh Ameryky* (Ukrainian emigration in the United States of America), which was the fruit of his stay overseas in 1905–6.

In the fall of 1918 Bachynskyi joined the Ukrainian National Council in Lviv (Lwów), taking part in a proclamation of the Western Ukrainian People's Republic (WUPR) in Eastern Galicia on 9 November 1918. After the unification of both Ukrainian states in January 1919, he headed the Ukrainian mission in Washington. In May 1921 he returned to Europe and became allied with the followers of **Yevhen Petrushevych**, the former dictator of the WUPR and prime minister of its government-in-exile. In this group he represented pro-Soviet views, favoring the agreement with the Kremlin; therefore in 1933 the Soviet authorities allowed him to come to the USSR. Traveling through Polish territory, he was arrested and held in prison for one year. After his arrival in Kharkiv in the summer of 1934 he worked in the editorial offices of the *Ukrainian Soviet Encyclopedia*. On 4 November 1934 he was arrested during a wave of persecutions of Ukrainian intellectuals. He was tried, along with **Antin Krushelnytsky**, and on 28 March 1935 he was sentenced to ten years in prison. He died in a labor camp. His publications include *Podil Ukrainy* (The division of the Ukraine; 1897) and *Bolshevytska revolutsiia i Ukraiintsi* (The Bolshevik Revolution and the Ukrainians; 1928). (TS)

Sources: *Encyclopedia of Ukraine*, vol. 1 (Toronto, 1984); Yaroslav Hrytsak, 'Molodi' radykaly v suspilno-politychnomu zhytti Halychyny," *Zapysky naukovoho tovarystva im. Shevchenka*, vol. 222 (Lviv, 1991); John-Paul Himka, "Young Radicals and Independent Statehood: The Idea of a Ukrainian Nation-State, 1890–1905," *Slavic Review*, vol. 41 (Summer 1982).

BACILEK Karel (12 October 1896, Chotiansky, near Poděbrady–19 March 1974, Bratislava), Czechoslovak Communist activist. The son of a Slovak bricklayer, in his youth Bacilek worked as a blacksmith and railroader. In 1915–18 he served in the Austrian army and between the end of 1918 and December 1919, in the Czechoslovak army. In 1921 he joined the Communist Party of Czechoslovakia (CPC). He was swiftly promoted, becoming the organizational secretary of the party in Slovakia (1930) and joining the CPC Central Committee (CC) in 1931. Sent to the USSR, he completed studies at a Comintern school in 1935. After the German invasion of March 1939 he left for Moscow. From December 1940 to March 1941 he stayed in Slovakia, organizing the Communist underground. After his return to the USSR he was attacked for his inability to win over Slovak comrades to the Kremlin's policies. He was arrested and sent to a labor camp in the Mordovian ASSR. Released in April 1943, he started working for Soviet intelligence. Dropped beyond the front lines near Warsaw, he managed to get to Slovakia. In August 1944, as secretary of the party, he organized the Slovak national uprising in Banská Bystrica. After the failure of the uprising he commanded a guerrilla unit.

After the Communist coup in February 1948 Bacilek was quickly promoted. In 1949 he joined the Secretariat of the CC of the Communist Party of Slovakia, and in 1950 he became the Slovak prime minister. In September 1951 he was appointed minister of state control. From January 1952 to September 1953 he headed the Ministry of State Security of Czechoslovakia, playing an important role in a purge related to the case of **Rudolf Slansky** and the Slovak activists led by **Gustav Husak**. In January 1953 he was appointed deputy prime minister of Czechoslovakia. He was also promoted to general, and in September 1953 he became secretary general of the Communist Party of Slovakia. In this capacity he counteracted attempts at a "thaw." On 4 April 1963 he was ousted from the party executive. This was related to the rehabilitation of the imprisoned Slovak activists. Since it was impossible to uncover all Communist crimes, Bacilek served as a political scapegoat. Even the reasons for his withdrawal were not officially explained. In 1966 he left the CC, and in 1968 he was finally expelled from the party. However, he was never brought before a court for his crimes. His publications include *Poučenie z procesu z vedenim protištatneho špionažneho a sprisahaneckého centra na čele s Rudolfom Slánskym* (Lessons from the trial of the anti-state, spy, and conspiracy center headed by Rudolf Slansky; 1953) and *Leninské učenie: Kompas na naše ceste k socialismu* (Lenin's teachings: A compass on our road to socialism; 1954). (WR)

Sources: Lazitch; *SBS*, vol. 1; Edward Taborsky, *Communism in Czechoslovakia 1948–1960* (Princeton, 1961); Eugen Loebl, *Stalinism in Prague* (New York, 1969); Jiří Pelikán, *The Czechoslovak Political Trials 1950–1954* (Stanford, 1971).

BAČKIS Audrys (1 February 1937, Kaunas), Archbishop of Vilnius (Wilno). From early childhood Bačkis lived abroad, where his father worked in the diplomatic corps, first in Paris, then in Washington, D.C. He studied theology in St. Sulpice Seminary in Paris in 1954–57, in St. Casimir College in Rome in 1957–61, and in the Ponitificia Academia Ecclesiastica in Rome in 1961–64. In March 1961 he was ordained, and in 1964 he received a Ph.D. in canon law at the Lateran University in Rome. In 1964 he also assumed the position of attaché in the papal nuncio's Office in Manila, the Philippines, and in 1965 he was consecrated titular bishop of Meta and appointed secretary of the papal nunciature in San Jose, Costa Rica. From 1968 he held the same office in Ankara, Turkey, and from 1970 in Nigeria. After his return from Africa, from 1973 he worked as auditor of nunciatures at the Secretary of State of the Council for Public Affairs of the Holy See. In 1979 he became undersecretary of state in this council, and in 1988, as archbishop, he assumed the position of papal nuncio in the Netherlands. On 24 December 1991 Pope John Paul II appointed him archbishop of the newly established Vilnius province, and in 1995–96 he presided over the Conference of the Lithuanian Episcopate. He moderated nationalistic tendencies among the clergy and encouraged the Lithuanian Christian Democrats to adopt a more open attitude toward neighboring countries. On 21 February 2001 he was elevated to the rank of cardinal. (WR)

Sources: *EL,* vols. 1 and 6; Algimantas P. Taškūnas, ed., *Lithuania in 1991* (Sandy Bay, Tasmania, 1992); Anatol Lieven, *The Baltic Revolution* (New Haven, 1993); *Annuario Pontificio,* 2001.

BACZYŃSKI Krzysztof Kamil, pseudonym "Jan Bugaj" (4 August 1921, Warsaw–4 August 1944, Warsaw), Polish poet. Baczyński, whose family was from the intelligentsia, wrote his first poems while at the Stefan Batory Gymnasium in Warsaw, where he passed his final exams in 1939. During the Nazi occupation he was connected with a leftist youth conspiracy. From 1943 he attended secret Polish studies at the university level and joined the Scouting Shock Troops, which were organized into the Home Army battalion Zośka. He graduated from an underground reserve cadet school, Agrykola. He took part in the Warsaw Uprising and was killed in the first days of fighting in Warsaw Theater Square. His wife, Barbara, whom he married in 1942, was killed at the same time elsewhere in Warsaw. Baczyński's poetic creativity developed fully during the occupation, which became the background of most of his poems, even love lyrics devoted to his wife. He published two collections secretly: *Wiersze wybrane* (Selected poems; 1942) and *Arkusz poetycki* (Poetic sheet; 1943). His whole output, five hundred poems and prose pieces, was preserved in manuscript and was published for the first time after the war in 1962 as *Utwory zebrane* (Collected works; 1962). Full of intense feelings of the moment and of symbolic visions, his poems combine reflections on the fate of the nation and personal responsibility with intimations of terror and threats to the sense of life. During the occupation critics already appreciated his poems. In the course of time he was recognized as the most outstanding poet of the war generation and was compared to Juliusz Słowacki. He even became the object of a cult of the generation coming of age in the 1960s and 1970s. His great talent and his tragic fate prompted one of his first critics, Kazimierz Wyka, to state that it was the fate of the Poles "to shoot at the enemy with diamonds." (WR)

Sources: *Literatura polska: Przewodnik encyklopedyczny,* vol. 1 (Warsaw, 1984); Zygmunt Wasilewski, ed., *Żołnierz, poeta, czasu kurz . . . Wspomnienia o Krzysztofie Kamilu Baczyńskim* (Kraków, 1979); Kazimierz Wyka, *Baczyński i Różewicz* (Kraków, 1994); Stefan Zabierowski, *Krzysztof Kamil Baczyński: Biografia i legenda* (Wrocław, 1990).

BADZIO Yuriy (24 April 1936, Kopynivka, near Mukachevo), Ukrainian specialist in literary theory and dissident. Badzio came from a large peasant family. In 1958 he graduated in Ukrainian philology at Uzhgorod University, and then he worked as a teacher and school director in the Transcarpathian countryside. Beginning in 1961 he worked at the Institute of Literature of the Academy of Sciences of the Ukrainian SSR in Kiev, and in 1961–64 he participated in the Council of Creative Youth Club, one of the first informal organizations of the generation of the 1960s (*shestidesiatniki*). In September 1965 he took part in a protest against the arrests of intellectuals. Removed from the Communist Party and fired from his job, he also was not allowed to publish. In 1971 he wrote a letter to the Sixth Congress of the Association of Ukrainian Writers, criticizing the uneven treatment of Ukrainian culture in the Ukrainian SSR. In 1972 he started working on a huge project demystifying Soviet totalitarianism—*Pravo zhyty* (The right to live). As a result of KGB searches, he twice (in 1977 and 1979) lost big portions of the manuscript. In April 1979 he was arrested, and in December 1979 he was sentenced to seven years in a special severe labor camp and to five years of exile. In March 1980 he was imprisoned in a Mordovian camp, where he protested against the Soviet invasion of Afghanistan and against the holding of the Olympics in Moscow. His wife and son were also subject to repression. From 1986 Badzio lived in exile in the village of Khandyga in Yakutia. He refused to ask for an earlier release. Freed in December 1988, he joined in the creation of an independent Ukraine. In May 1990 he wrote a manifesto for the Democratic Party of Ukraine, and in December 1990 he was elected its leader. Soon he withdrew from political life and returned to research at the Institute of Philosophy in Kiev. In 1996 he published *Pravo zhyty,* based on the manuscript that he was given back. He authored many works on contemporary Ukrainian politics, including *Vlada—opozytsiya—derzhava v Ukraini syohodni* (Power—opposition—state in contemporary Ukraine; 1994) and *Natsionalna ideya i natsionalne pytannia* (The national idea and the national question; 2000). (TS)

Sources: Kharkiv Group for the Defense of Human Rights; *Visnyk represiy v Ukraini* (New York), 1981, nos. 5 and 8; 1984, nos. 2, 9, and 10; Volodymir Baran, *Ukraina pislya Stalina: Naris istoryi 1953–1985 rr.* (Lviv, 1992); Heorhiy Kasyanov, *Nezhodni: Ukrainska intelihentsiya v rusi oporu 1960–80 rokiv* (Kiev, 1995); Anatoli Rusnachenko, *Natsionalno-vyzvolnyi rukh v Ukraini* (Kiev, 1998).

BAGIŃSKI Kazimierz (15 March 1890, Warsaw–27 July 1966, Phoenix, Arizona), Polish peasant politician. Having graduated from high school in Warsaw, Bagiński studied at the Polytechnic College in Lwów (Lviv) (1911–14). From 1914 he was active in the Polish Socialist Party (PPS), and he commanded a unit of the Polish Military Organization (Polska Organizacja Wojskowa) in the Lublin region. In 1915 he co-organized the Polish Peasant Party, Liberation (PSL Wyzwolenie), and from February 1919 he was a member of the Executive Board of the party. He served as a volunteer in the Polish-Soviet war. From March 1921 he was secretary of the Executive Board of the PSL Wyzwolenie; from March 1923, its vice president; and from 1925 to 1929, secretary general of the party. In 1919–28 he was an MP, representing the PSL Wyzwolenie. Co-organizer of the center-left opposition (Centrolew), in September 1903 he was arrested and imprisoned in the Brześć fortress. Released on bail, he co-organized a unified peasant movement in the form of the Peasant Party (Stronnictwo Ludowe [SL]), founded in 1931. From March 1931 he was a member of the Chief Council of the party and secretary of its Chief Executive Committee (CEC). On 15 January 1932 he was sentenced in a trial in Brześć to two years' imprisonment. After the validation of the verdict, at the end of September 1933 he left for Czechoslovakia, where he maintained contact with (among others) **Wincenty Witos** and the Czech Agrarians. Following the partition of Czechoslovakia in March 1939, Bagiński returned to Poland and was imprisoned in Płock. Released on 8 April 1939, in May 1939 he assumed the post of secretary of the CEC of the SL.

After the German invasion of Poland in September 1939 Bagiński went to Volhynia. In mid-1942 he returned to Warsaw and was active in an underground peasant movement called Roch. In 1943 he was editor-in-chief of its newspaper, *Wieś*. He represented the SL Roch in the Council of National Unity (Rada Jedności Narodowej [RNJ]), and from March 1944 he was director of the Interior Department of the Government Delegation for the Homeland. At that time he used a pseudonym, "Dąbrowski." In September 1944 he became deputy president of the RJN. During the Warsaw Uprising he was temporarily president of the Central Committee of the Peasant Movement. After the capitulation of the rising, Bagiński left Warsaw with the whole civilian population[Arrested on 28 March 1945 by the NKVD, he was taken to Moscow, and on 21 June 1945 he was sentenced to one year in prison in the Trial of the Sixteen. Released in November 1945, he returned to Poland and became one of the leaders of the Polish Peasant Party (Polskie Stronnictwo Ludowe [PSL]), organized by **Stanisław Mikołajczyk**. A member of the CEC and of the Chief Council of the PSL, as well as head of the Press and Propaganda Department of the party,

on 11 October 1946 Bagiński was arrested and in April 1947 sentenced to eight years by a military court in Warsaw. In July 1947 he was released under an amnesty agreement. Fearing another arrest, in October 1947 he secretly went with Mikołajczyk to the United States, where they initially cooperated, but in 1949 their paths parted. Bagiński stood on the side of the Political Council (Rada Polityczna), and along with **Stefan Korboński** he set up the PSL National Unity Faction (PSL Odłam Jedności Narodowej), in which he was active until his death. (WR)

Sources: Kunert, vol. 1; Bogdan Czaykowski, Bolesław Sulik, *Polacy w Wielkiej Brytanii* (Paris, 1961); Wincenty Witos, *Moje wspomnienia*, vols. 1–3 (Paris, 1964–65); *Tygodnik Powszechny,* 1966, no. 10; *Roczniki Dziejów Ruchu Ludowego,* 1966, vol. 8; Stefan Korboński, "Wspomnienie o Kazimierzu Bagińskim," *Wiadomości,* 1967, no. 19.

BAGRIANOV Ivan (27 November 1891, Voden–1 February 1945, Sofia), Bulgarian politician. In 1912 Bagrianov graduated from a military academy in Sofia. In the Balkan Wars and during World War I he served as an officer of artillery. After the war he completed law studies in Sofia and agriculture studies in Leipzig and Vienna. He was a member of the Agrarian Party and was in the close circle of political friends of Tsar **Boris III**. From 1938 Bagrianov was an MP, and from November 1938 to February 1941, minister of agriculture and of state property. He was considered a supporter of an agreement with Great Britain and resigned in disapproval of Bulgaria's adhesion to the Axis powers. When the regents attempted to unite Bulgaria with the Allies after the tsar's death, Bagrianov became prime minister on 1 June 1944. Tolerated by the Germans, he yielded to their pressure regarding anti-Jewish legislation, but in June 1944 he agreed to the opening of the Soviet consulate in Varna. On 17 August 1944 he announced a break with the "previous policy of chauvinism and war" and proclaimed the neutrality of Bulgaria. As a result of the uncompromising attitude of the USSR, which rejected this declaration, he failed to advance negotiations with the Allies, and on 1 September 1944 he resigned from his post. After the coup of 9 September 1944 he was arrested and, in accord with the directives of the Communist leadership, sentenced to death for "anti-national policies" in a major trial of the leaders of tsarist Bulgaria. He was immediately executed. (WR)

Sources: *Entsiklopediya Bulgariya,* vol. 1 (Sofia, 1978); Ilcho Dimitrov, "Vnyshnata politika na pravitelstvoto na Ivan Bagrianov, 1 juni–1 septemvri 1944 g.," *Godishnik na Sofiiskiia Universitet. Filozofsko-Istoricheski Fakultet,* 1967, vol. 61; Marshall Lee Miller, *Bulgaria during the Second World War* (Stanford, 1975); Jerzy Jackowicz, *Partie opozycyjne w Bułgarii 1944–1948* (Warsaw, 1997).

BAHDANKEVICH Stanislau (1 January 1937, Shapovaly, near Valozhyn), Belorussian economist and politician. In 1964 Bahdankevich graduated from the All-Union Financial and Economic Institute in Moscow. From 1956 he worked in the Soviet State Bank in Belorussia, gradually advancing in its management. In 1981 he took a chair in the Belorussian Institute of the National Economy, and in 1991 he became a professor of economics. In 1994 he assumed the position of deputy chairman of the International Eurasian Academy of Sciences. From 1991 to 1995 he was chairman of the National Bank of Belorussia. He was dismissed by President **Alyaksandr Lukashenka** for his opposition to a plan for the unification of the financial systems of Belorussia and Russia. From 1995 he was deputy to the Supreme Council, which was outlawed by Lukashenka in 1996 but was recognized by European countries as the only legal parliamentary assembly in Belorussia. In 1995–2000 Bahdankevich was chairman of the United Civic Party of Belorussia (Abjadnanaja Hramadzianskaja Partija Bielarusi), which was liberal in character. From 1998 he presided over the Commission for Economic Policy of the opposition National Executive Committee, which served as a shadow cabinet. (EM)

Sources: *Bielaruskaia entsyklapiedyia*, vol. 11 (Minsk, 1996); Jan Zaprudnik, *Historical Dictionary of Belarus* (Lanham, Md., 1998); *Kto iest kto w Respublike Belarus* (Minsk, 1999); David R. Marples, *Belarus: A Denationalization of a Nation* (Amsterdam, 1999).

BAHDANOVICH Maxim (9 December 1891, Minsk–25 May 1917, Yalta), Belorussian poet, critic, and translator. Bahdanovich's first work, an allegorical parable, *Muzika* (Music), was published in 1907. In 1908 he fell ill with tuberculosis. At that time he was living in Yaroslavl in Russia; from there he sent his works to the newspaper *Nasha niva*. Despite his illness, optimistic notes prevailed in his poetry. He completed high school in Yaroslavl, and in the fall of 1916 arrived in Minsk, where he worked as a secretary for a food committee of the *guberniya* (province). Seriously ill, in February 1917 he went for treatment to the Crimea. He died and was buried there. His collection of poems, *Vianok* (The garland; 1913), the only work published in his lifetime, has been considered a paradigm of classical poetics in Belorussian. Bahdanovich was a pioneer in writing about the history of Belorussian literature; he was the author of *Karotkaia historyia bielaruskai pismiennastsi da XVI staletsia* (Short history of Belorussian literature until the sixteenth century) and *Novy peryod u historyi bielaruskai litaratury* (A new period in the history of Belorussian literature). He was also a translator of poetry, especially Slavic poetry. He also translated the works of Heinrich Heine, Friedrich Schiller, Horace, Paul Verlaine, and poems from various nations of the world. Central in his works were social and national ideals, the concepts of equality and brotherhood among people, and a poetic vision of nature. He also originated Belorussian lyrical love poetry. At the end of the twentieth century many patriotic demonstrations were organized near his monuments. A complete collection of his works was published in 1991–95 under the title *Bahdanovich Maksim Adamovich, 1891–1917: Pouny zbor tvorau* (Bahdanovich Maksim Adamovich, 1891–1917: A complete collection of works). (AS/SA)

Sources: *Belarus: Entsyklapedychny daviednik* (Minsk, 1995); *Arhiunyia materyaly da zyttsia i tvorchastsi Maksima Bahdanovicha* (Minsk, 1996–97); *Batskaushchyna: Zbornik histarychnai litaratury* (Minsk, 1992); *Belarusian Children's Publications* (Minsk, 1993–95); A.V. Maldzis, ed., *Bielaruskiya pismienniki: Bibliahrafichny slounik* (Minsk, 1993–95); Jan Zaprudnik, *Historical Dictionary of Belarus* (Lanham, Md., 1998).

BAJCSY-ZSILINSZKY Endre (6 June 1886, Szarvas–24 December 1944, Sopronkőhida), Hungarian politician. Bajcsy-Szilinszky's ancestors were Slovak peasants. In 1904 he graduated from a Calvinist high school in Békéscsaba and in 1908 from law studies at the University of Kolozsvár (Cluj). From 1910 he practiced as a defense attorney. In May 1911, he and his brother sued a Socialist Agrarian politician, **András Áchim**, for slandering their father. During a fight, Áchim was badly wounded and died. A Budapest court acquitted the Zsilinszky brothers, stating that they had acted in self-defense. During World War I, Bajcsy-Zsilinszky fought as an officer on the Serbian and Russian fronts; in 1916 he was seriously wounded, and in 1917 he returned to the Russian front. From November 1918 he was back in Hungary, supporting the nationalist right and co-founding the Hungarian National Defense Association and the Hungarian Race Research Society. In 1919 he fought against the Hungarian Soviet Republic, and after its fall he cooperated with **Gyula Gömbös** as editor (1919–22) and later editor-in-chief (1922–26) of an anti-Semitic daily, *Szózat*. In 1922 he was elected to the parliament on behalf of the government Party of Unity. In view of the growing conflict between Prime Minister **István Bethlen** and the nationalists, in 1923 Bajcsy-Zsilinszky left the party and co-founded (with Gömbös, among others) the Hungarian National Independence Party (HNIP). In 1925 he received the prestigious title of "hero" (*vitéz*) and changed his name to Bajcsy-Zsilinszky by adding his mother's maiden name.

After the lost election of 1926, Bajcsy-Zsilinszky

parted company with Gömbös, and in the fall of 1927 he left the HNIP. From 1928 to 1932 he edited the periodical *Előörs*. After the elections of 1929, when, owing to electoral fraud by the authorities Bajcsy-Zsilinszky was defeated, he became increasingly critical of the political system and of the German threat. In 1930 he founded the opposition National Radical Party, and in 1931 he won a mandate on its behalf. After Hitler's takeover in Germany, he warned against the Nazi threat and attacked the Gömbös government for its pro-German policy. He favored a pro-French orientation and recommended reconciliation with Yugoslavia. In 1935 the authorities prevented him from winning a parliamentary seat. In response he gave up the title of "hero," and in 1936 he led his party into the Independent Smallholders' Party (ISP). Elected to the parliament again in 1939, he edited an anti-German weekly, *Független Magyarország* (1939–41), and the periodical *Szabad Szó* (1941–44), which condemned laws of 1938, 1939, and 1941 that limited the citizenship rights of Jews.

When in June 1941 Hungary went to war against the USSR and in December 1941 against Great Britain and the United States, Bajcsy-Zsilinszky sharply criticized Prime Minister **László Bárdossy**. In the parliament and in letters to Regent **Miklós Horthy** he demanded Hungary's withdrawal from its alliance with Germany. He protested the Hungarian murders of Serbs in Voivodina in January 1942, demanding a severe punishment for those responsible. After the fall of the Mussolini regime in 1943 he, along with ISP leader **Zoltán Tildy**, sent a memorandum to Prime Minister **Miklós Kállay** in which they demanded Hungary's withdrawal from the war, a proclamation of neutrality, and the rescinding of anti-Jewish legislation; they encouraged reconciliation with neighbors and called for resistance to the potential German occupation of Hungary. Bajcsy-Zsilinszky was known for his support for Poland. On 19 March 1944, SS soldiers raided his apartment, badly wounded him, and took him prisoner. He tried to commit suicide in prison. In October 1944 he was transferred to the Hungarian authorities, which set him free during an attempt by Regent Horthy to withdraw from the war. When the Arrow Cross Party took over power, Bajcsy-Zsilinszky went into hiding. On 5 November 1944 he became leader of the Hungarian National Insurgent and Liberation Committee, composed of a coalition of opposition parties. Because of a betrayal, on 23 November he was arrested. On 6 December 1944 he was put on trial before military court in Budapest. Because Soviet troops were advancing, he was transferred to Sopronkőhida, sentenced to death by an Arrow Cross court, and executed. (JT)

Sources: *Biographisches Lexikon,* vol. 1; *Magyar Nagylexikon,* vol. 3 (Budapest, 1994); *Nagy Képes Milleniumi Arcképcsarnok* (Budapest, 1999); *Új Magyar Életrajzi Lexikon,* vol. 1 (Budapest, 2001); *Magyarország 1944–1956,* CD-ROM (Budapest, 2001); Paul Ignotus, *Hungary* (London, 1972); Sándor Tidrenczel, *Bajcsy-Zsilinszky Endre és politikai pátriája* (Nyiregyhaza, 1986); Károlyi Vigh, *Bajcsy-Zsilinszky Endre, 1886–1944: A küldetéses ember* (Budapest, 1992).

BAJRAKTARI Muharrem (1 May 1896, Domaj–21 January 1989, Brussels), Albanian politician. Bajraktari was from Kosovo. He graduated from a high school in Kolesjan, and in 1917–18 he studied in a military academy in Vienna. In March 1920 he was one of the leaders of an anti-Serb uprising in the region of Stiqnit. Back in Albania in 1921, he served as an officer in the military police in Krume. In 1924 he supported **Ahmet Zogu**, as a result of which he was promoted to the rank of major. He worked in the military court in Shkodër and then as a commander of the military police in the Dibra region in Peshkopi. In December 1926 he led a punitive expedition suppressing rebellion in the region of Dukagjini. Accused of an abuse of power, he was transferred to Tirana. In 1929 he took over command of the military police in the capital, in 1931 he became an aide-de-camp to Zogu, and then he was transferred to control the region of Lumë. Suspected of an anti-government plot, in 1935 he was called to the capital. Fearing for his life, he escaped to Yugoslavia and from there to France, where he joined the National Union (Bashkimi Kombëtar) and remained in opposition to the king. In 1939 he moved to Italy, where he was offered a ministry in the collaboration government or leadership of the Albanian Fascist Militia, but he declined. He returned to Albania and, along with Gani Kryeziu, he led preparations for an anti-Italian uprising in northern Albania organized by British intelligence. The plan was abolished in December 1940.

During the German invasion of Yugoslavia in April 1941, Yugoslav officers wanted to gain Bajraktari's cooperation, but the rapid fall of Yugoslavia put an end to these plans. The region of Lumë remained under the control of Bajraktari's troops until March 1942, when an Italian operation, supported by Catholic Mirdytes, dispersed these troops. In the spring of 1943 major resistance groups negotiated with Bajraktari, who promised support but refused to subordinate his troops to any larger group. He opposed the armed resistance of the Communist guerrillas, which led to an intensification of repression. In 1944 he participated in talks with partisans from the Communist Fifth Brigade of the National Liberation Army, but at the end of 1944 open conflict erupted between them. After the Communist takeover, Bajraktari became affiliated with royalist troops operating between Peshkopi and Kukës, but he acted on his own, controlling the region of Lumë and exercising his own notions of justice. In September 1946 he was forced to flee to Greece with a small group of his followers. In exile he co-initiated the Committee of Free Albania, created in Paris in August 1949, and worked for it until its end in 1953. In 1994 President **Sali Berisha** posthumously awarded him with the order of Për veprimtari patriotike (For Patriotic Activity). (TC)

Sources: Çejku Lufti, *Luma neper sfidat e historisë–gjakfolurit e varrhumburit (7 prill 1939–10 gusht 1988)* (Prizren, 1997); Bernd J. Fischer, *King Zog and the Struggle for Stability in Albania* (New York, 1984); Pallushi Petrit, *Muharrem Bajraktari ne vitet 1945–1946* (Tirana, 1998); Sh. Hoxha, *Muharrem Bajraktari gjatë pushtimit italian (1939–shtator 1943)* (Tirana, 2001).

BAKARIĆ Vladimir (8 March 1912, Velika Gorica, near Zagreb–16 January 1983, Zagreb), Yugoslav Communist activist of Croatian nationality. After graduating from high school and law studies in Zagreb in 1935, in 1937 Bakarić received a Ph.D. In 1933 he joined the then illegal Communist Party of Yugoslavia. From 1936 to 1941 he worked as a defense attorney in Zagreb, contributing to the legal periodicals *Izraz* and *Naše novine*. Arrested three times, from 1937 he was head of the Department of Agitation and Propaganda of the Central Committee (CC) of the Communist Party of Croatia (CPC), and from 1940 he was a member of the CPC CC. From the end of 1941 he cooperated with the partisans of **Josip Broz Tito**, directing their operations in Croatia. He became a member of the Anti-Fascist Council of the National Liberation of Yugoslavia (Antifašističko Vijeće Narodnog Oslobodenja Jugoslavije [AVNOJ]), founded in November 1942. Political commissar of the general staff of the National Liberation Army, from October 1944 he was secretary of the CPC.

In April 1945 Bakarić became prime minister of the Croatian republic, supervising the repression of Ustasha activists and of people accused of collaborating with them. In 1946 he was a member of the Yugoslav delegation to the Paris Peace Conference. In January 1948 he took part in Moscow talks with the Soviet leadership, which did not ease the conflict between Tito and Stalin. After the Information Bureau of the Communist and Workers' Parties condemned Yugoslavia in June 1948, Bakarić gave Tito strong support, and after the dismissal of **Andrija Hebrang** he took over the leadership of the Croatian party. From 1950 he supported the new economic policy, including decollectivization and a system of self-government in ownership and management in industry. He also helped in the purge of opponents of this policy. He headed the Croatian government until 6 February 1953, and on 18 December 1953 he became speaker of the Croatian parlia-

ment. At the Fifth Congress of the Communist Party of Yugoslavia (CPY) in 1948 Bakarić became a member of its CC, and from the Sixth Congress he was a member of the Executive Committee of the Union of Yugoslav Communists. In the 1960s he showed some understanding of Croatian national feelings, but in 1971–72 he supported Tito in his purges of Croatian Communists accused of nationalism and counterrevolution. In 1974 he was the co-author of a new constitution that decentralized power in the Yugoslav federation. After Tito's death he became a member of the collective leadership of Yugoslavia. Bakarić was a theoretician of the Yugoslav model and authored several works in this field, including *O poljoprivredi i problemima sela* (On agriculture and problems of the countryside; 1960), *Socijalistički samoupravni sistem i društvena reprodukcija* (The Socialist system of self-management and social reproduction; 1974), and dozens of articles on ideological and constitutional issues. He was a member of the Yugoslav Academy of Arts and Sciences. (WR)

Sources: *Enciklopedija Jugoslavije*, vol. 1 (Zagreb, 1955); *Hrvatski biografski leksikon*, vol. 1 (Zagreb, 1983); Vladimir Dedijer, *The Battle Stalin Lost* (New York, 1970); Stephen Clissold, ed., *Yugoslavia and the Soviet Union, 1939–1973* (Oxford, 1975); *Vladimir Bakarić, 1912–1983* (Zagreb, 1983); Miko Tripalo, *Hrvatsko proljeće* (Zagreb, 1989); www.rulers.org.

BALABANOV Aleksandur (18 January 1879, Štip–30 November 1955, Sofia), Bulgarian philologist and journalist. The son of a merchant, Balabanov studied classical philology in Leipzig, and then he received a Ph.D. in Erlangen, Germany. He already distinguished himself during his studies, mastering all the major European languages and Latin. In 1904–12 he taught in a high school in Sofia and lectured at Sofia University, where he established the chair of classical philology. In 1908 he became associate professor and in 1917, full professor. He authored a handbook of classical literature (1914) and translated *Faust*, by Johann Wolfgang Goethe, and a whole series of classical Greek works. Co-founder of the periodicals *Hudozhnik* and *Razvigor*, contributor to the daily *Vreme*, and friend and adviser to Tsar **Boris III**, Balabanov included the classical work of Bulgarian literature, *Zapiski po bulgarskite vystanniya* (Notes from Bulgarian uprisings), by Zakhari Stoyanov, in the compulsory school reading list. Balabanov was the author of *Lyubov i poeziya* (Love and poetry; 1939), the memoirs *I az na tozi swiat* (I am in this world as well; 1955), and many other works. After the Communist takeover, he was pushed into oblivion and isolated in his attempts to maintain links with European culture. It was with humor that he suffered the fate of a "bourgeois scholar," as he was described by the official propaganda. (JW)

Sources: *Entsiklopediya Bulgariya*, vol. 1 (Sofia, 1976); *Aleksandur Balabanov i Simeon Radev v spomenite na suvremennitsite si* (Sofia, 1986).

BĂLAN Ioan (11 February 1880, Teiuş–4 August 1959, Bucharest), Romanian Greek Catholic bishop. After graduating from the theological seminar in Blaj, Bălan studied theology in Budapest and Vienna. In 1903 he was ordained in Blaj and returned to Vienna to continue studies. In 1906 he received a Ph.D. in theology there. In 1906 he started his ministry in Bucharest. From 1909 to 1920 he was vicar general of Bucharest, and in 1919 he moved to Blaj, where he was appointed metropolitan canon and (in 1921) rector of the Blaj Greek Catholic Theological Academy. In 1927–29, appointed by Pope Pius XI, he was a member of a special commission to elaborate canon law for the eastern churches. In 1936 he was consecrated Bishop of Blaj. After the Communist takeover and the formal liquidation of the Greek Catholic Church, Bălan refused to join the Orthodox Church. Arrested on 28 October 1948 along with five other Romanian Greek Catholic bishops, he was placed in the Dragoslavele Monastery, the summer residence of Romanian Orthodox patriarchs, now converted into a prison. In early 1949 he was moved to the prison in the Căldăruşani Monastery, and in 1950 to Sighet Marmaţiei Prison. He was kept there without trial until 1955, when, on the orders of **Gheorghe Gheorghiu-Dej**, he was released with two other (still living) bishops, **Iuliu Hossu** and **Alexandru Rusu**. He was put under house arrest in the Curtea de Argeş Monastery, which soon became a place of Greek Catholic pilgrimages. Communist Speaker of the Parliament **Petru Groza** visited the bishops and tried to convince them that their church did not exist in Romania, but in 1956 they sent a memorandum to the government demanding the reconstruction of the Greek Catholic Church. The memorandum was signed by many people, so the authorities separated the bishops to reduce their influence. Bălan was placed in the Ciorogârla Monastery, where he lived in isolation. Seriously ill, in 1959 he was put in a Bucharest hospital, where he soon died. He was buried in the Catholic Bellu Cemetery in Bucharest. His beatification is under way. (LW)

Sources: Józef Darski, *Rumunia: Historia, współczesność, konflikty narodowe* (Warsaw, 1995); Paul Caravia, Virgiliu Constantinescu, and Flori Stănescu, *The Imprisoned Church of Romania, 1944–1989* (Bucharest, 1999); Dennis Deletant, *Communist Terror in Romania* (New York, 1999); www.bru.ro.

BALANTIĆ France (21 November 1921, Kamnik–24 November 1944, Grahovo), Slovenian poet. After high school Balantić studied linguistics in Ljubljana. In 1941 he was arrested by the Italian occupation authorities. Sent to a concentration camp in Gonars, after his release he joined the anti-Communist Countryside Guard and in 1943, the nationalist Homeland Guard, which cooperated with the Italians. He was killed in a Communist guerrilla attack on Grahovo. Balantić was influenced by the traditions of Slovene Social Catholicism, and he combined formal expressionism with a metaphysical message. He wrote his first collection, *Sonetni venec* (Wreath of Sonnets), in 1940. *V ognju grozy plapolam* (I Struggle through the fire of terror) was published after his death in 1944. Despite his great talent, his works were totally ignored in Communist Yugoslavia for political reasons. A major collection of his poems, *Izbrano delo* (Selected works), was published in Buenos Aires in 1976. In Yugoslavia, a volume of his poems that was ready for print in 1964 could not appear until 1984, when there was a relative easing of censorship. It was only after Slovenia gained independence that Balantić's poetic mastery was acknowledged. (WR)

Sources: *Enciklopedija Slovenije*, vol. 1 (Ljubljana, 1987); F. Pibernik, "Zgodnij Balantić," *Nova Revija*, 1986, no 5; Leopoldina Plut-Pregelj and Carole Rogel, *Historical Dictionary of Slovenia* (Lanham, Md., 1996).

BALCEROWICZ Leszek (19 January 1947, Lipno), Polish economist and politician. In 1970 Balcerowicz graduated from the Foreign Trade Department of the Central School of Planning and Statistics in Warsaw (CSPS; now the Warsaw School of Economics—Szkoła Główna Handlowa [WSE]), and in 1974 he received an MBA from St. John's University in New York. From 1969 to 1981 he belonged to the Polish United Workers' Party (PUWP). In 1970–80 he was a researcher at the CSPS Institute of International Economics, and from 1978 to 1980, at the Economic Policy Department of the Institute of Basic Problems of Marxism-Leninism at the PUWP Central Committee. In 1975 he received a Ph.D. at the CSPS. From 1980 he was research secretary at the CSPS Institute of Economic Development, and in 1981 he was an expert at the Sieć (Network) community in Solidarity, elaborating systemic reforms. During the period of martial law he led an independent seminar on economic systems at the CSPS. In 1989–90 he was a member of the Civic Committee of the chairman of Solidarity.

From September 1989 to December 1991 Balcerowicz was deputy prime minister and minister of finance in the government of **Tadeusz Mazowiecki** and chairman of its Economic Committee. He elaborated and implemented a plan for the rapid stabilization and transformation of the Polish economy, which was in deep structural crisis.

The plan consisted of the removal of all price and wage controls, the introduction of a single rate of exchange for the Polish złoty, an economic opening to the West, and the curbing of high inflation by a special tax on excessive wage increases. During the first three months of 1990 the monthly rate of inflation fell from 76 percent to 6 percent, but the reform deepened the recession, and hidden unemployment surfaced. Balcerowicz's "shock therapy" became a point of reference for all economic reforms in post-Communist countries. Thanks to this policy, Poland was the first post-Communist country to overcome the recession during transition. In 1990 Balcerowicz received a postdoctral degree and in 1992 he assumed a professorship at the WSE and was a visiting professor to many foreign universities. Among other works, he authored *The Soviet Type of Economic System and Innovativness* (1988); *Systemy gospodarcze: Elementy analizy porównawczej* (Economic systems: Elements of comparative analysis; 1989); *800 dni: Szok kontrolowany* (800 Days: A shock under control; 1992); *Macropolicies in Transition to a Market Economy: A Three Year Perspective* (1995); *Socialism, Capitalism, Transformation* (1995); *Wolność i rozwój: Ekonomia wolnego rynku* (Freedom and development: Free market economics; 1995); and *Państwo w przebudowie* (The state under reconstruction; 1999). He has received many honorary doctorates and other awards.

From 1992 to 2000 Balcerowicz presided over the Board and Research Council of the Center for Social and Economic Research (CASE). From April 1995 to December 2000 he was chairman of the Union of Freedom (Unia Wolności [UF]). In the parliamentary elections of September 1997 he gained the best results in the Silesian region of Katowice. From October 1997 to June 2000 he was deputy prime minister, minister of finance, and head of the Economic Committee of the government of **Jerzy Buzek**. He resigned in when the UF left the ruling coalition. From December 2000 he was chairman of the National Bank of Poland (Narodowy Bank Polski). His top priority was curbing inflation. (IS WR)

Sources: *Wielka encyklopedia PWN,* vol. 3 (Warsaw, 2001); *Kto jest kim w Polsce* (Warsaw, 2001); Janusz A. Majcherek, *Pierwsza dekada III Rzeczypospolitej* (Warsaw, 1999); Antoni Dudek, *Pierwsze lata III Rzeczyspospolitej 1989–2001* (Kraków, 2002); Wojciech Roszkowski, *Historia Polski 1914–2001* (Warsaw, 2002).

BALICKI Zygmunt (30 December 1858, Lublin–12 September 1916, Petrograd), Polish publicist and nationalist politician. Balicki graduated from high school in Lublin. While a student in St. Petersburg, he joined the Commune of Polish Socialists. In 1880 he arrived in Warsaw, but, fearing arrest, he moved to Lwów (Lviv), where along with **Bolesław Limanowski** he founded a Socialist association called Lud Polski (Polish People). In 1881 the association issued a manifesto with a program of independence—the first such program since the failure of the January uprising of 1863. Balicki was arrested by the Austrian authorities. Facing the threat of extradition to Russia, in 1883 he went to Switzerland. He acquired Swiss citizenship and did his military service there. In 1886 he secretly returned to Warsaw. After talks with the supporters of the national movement, in January 1887 he left for Kraków, where he set up the Union of Polish Youth, popularly called Zet. In January 1888 this organization became subordinated to the Polish League (Liga Polska). Acting with the Polish League, in 1889 Balicki founded the Association of Polish Emigration (Związek Wychodźstwa Polskiego). In 1890 he began a cooperation with **Roman Dmowski**, as a result of which the National League (Liga Narodowa) was founded in 1893. Although for two years Balicki was formally still a member of the Foreign Union of Polish Socialists, in fact he had already rejected socialism in favor of nationalism. In 1896 in Geneva he earned a doctorate in law. At the National League Congress in Budapest in 1896 he was elected a member of the league's Central Committee. From 1898 he lived in Kraków, founding units of the league in Upper Silesia and in Greater Poland. He was also active in the Society of People's Schools and in the Gymnastic Society Sokół (Falcon). In 1902 he published *Egoizm narodowy wobec etyki* (National egoism against ethics), in which he justified Polish nationalism and outlined a program of national education. Balicki favored the ethics of the nation to individual ethics and considered the rights of the nation as natural rights.

In 1905, along with Dmowski and Jan Ludwik Popławski, Balicki moved to Warsaw. He backed the pro-Russian shift in Dmowski's orientation; as a result the National League broke off ties with the Union of Polish Youth. Between 1908 and 1914 Balicki edited *Przegląd narodowy,* explaining the objectives of the anti-German and pro-Russian policy of the league. He was sentenced to one year's imprisonment for the publication of the article "Program Szymona Konarskiego" (The program of Szymon Konarski; 1908). He served his sentence in Włocławek and was released in June 1910. Two years later he published *Psychologia społeczna* (Social psychology), a work he had begun in prison. His lively attitude and didactic talents won him great popularity and affection among the young. After the outbreak of World War I Balicki became a member of the Polish National Committee (Komitet Narodowy Polski [KNP]) in Warsaw, and in 1915 he moved along with the KNP to Petrograd.

There he became involved in organizing the Polish Legion. It was to fight on the side of the Russian army in counterbalance to the Polish Legions (Legiony Polskie) of **Józef Piłsudski**, which were fighting on the side of Austria-Hungary. Balicki was buried in St. Catherine's Church. In 1918 the Bolsheviks removed his body and buried it in a common grave. (WR)

Sources: *PSB,* vol. 1; Stanisław Bukowiecki, "Zygmunt Balicki," *Kurier Warszawski,* 1916, no. 271; Marian Seyda, *Polska na przełomie dziejów* (Poznań, 1927); Władysław Pobóg-Malinowski, *Narodowa Demokracja 1887—1918* (Warsaw, 1933); Roman Wapiński, *Narodowa Demokracja 1893—1939* (Wrocław, 1980); Bogumił Grott, *Zygmunt Balicki: Ideolog Narodowej Demokracji* (Kraków, 1995).

BALITSKY Anton (17 September 1891, Baliche, near Hrodna [Grodno]–31 October 1937?), Belorussian politician. In 1913 Balitsky graduated from a teachers' seminary in Svisloch. For a short time he worked as a teacher. He began to study at the Vitebsk Teachers' Institute but was mobilized into the army. During the February 1917 revolution he was in St. Petersburg, where he joined the Bolsheviks. Until 1919 he fought with the Red Army on the southern front. In November 1919 he became a member of the Bolshevik party. He took part in the formation of the Soviet government in Odessa. In 1921–26 he was deputy commissar and then (1926–29) commissar for education of the Belorussian SSR. His name is associated with the process of the Beloruthenization of education in the Belorussian SSR. In 1929, as the struggle against so-called national democratism intensified, Balitsky was strongly suspected of Belorussian nationalism. In 1930 he was accused of being a member of a conspiratorial (in fact nonexistent) organization called the Belorussian Liberation Union. In March 1931 he was sentenced to ten years in labor camps. As a result of a retrial in 1937 his sentence was changed to death, and he was executed. (EM)

Sources: Ivan S. Lubachko, *Belorussia under Soviet Rule, 1917–1957* (Lexington, Kentucky, 1972); Vitaut Kipel and Zora Kipel, eds., *Byelorussian Statehood* (New York, 1988); *Entsyklapiedyia historyi Bielarusi,* vol. 1 (Minsk, 1993); N. Vasilieuskaia, *Abvinavachvaietstsa u natsionaldemakratyzmie* (Minsk, 1995).

BALLUKU Beqir (14 February 1917, Tirana–1975 Tirana?), Albanian Communist activist. Balluku was born into a poor Muslim family. After graduating from a technical school in Tirana, in 1935–39 he worked in a metal factory in Tirana. He took part in anti-Italian demonstrations in April 1939, and from 1940 to 1942 he served in the army. In the Shkodër garrison he entered into contact with a radical group of youth. Demobilized in 1942, he joined the Communist resistance. He co-initiated the formation of local cells of the Communist Party and assumed the position of political commissar of the Third Brigade of the **Enver Hoxha** guerrillas. At the end of the war he was political commissar of the First Corps. As a member of a special people's tribunal to try "war criminals and enemies of the people," he was responsible for the prosecution of political opponents. From 1945 he was deputy chairman of the Democratic Front, and in 1947 he became commander of an infantry division with the rank of colonel. In February 1948 he was promoted to general, and until 1953 he was chief of staff of the army. A member of the Central Committee and Politburo of the Albanian Labor Party and MP from 1948, in 1952–53 he studied at the Voroshilov Military Academy in Moscow.

In 1953–74 Balluku was minister of defense and from 1954, also one of the deputy prime ministers, responsible for the control and indoctrination of the populace. In the 1950s he became famous for saying proudly that the Albanian army had in fact become a part of the Soviet army. In accordance with the Hoxha line, in September 1960 he nevertheless sharply criticized Soviet policy at the congress of the North Vietnamese party in Hanoi. In March 1961 in Warsaw he represented Hoxha at the last meeting of the Warsaw Pact in which the Albanian delegation participated. After the breach with the USSR, he became an equally zealous supporter of the Chinese line. In September and October 1968 he gained Mao Zedong's assurance that China would defend Albania in the case of a threat to its sovereignty. In July 1974 Balluku was dismissed under mysterious circumstances. Officially he was accused of neglect in the armed forces and of attempted rebellion. According to one source, he is believed to have opposed Hoxha's idea of defending Albania by means of thousands of bunkers. According to another source, he was to write a report, which Hoxha called the "black thesis," on the disastrous situation in the army. It is also possible that Balluku had simply become too strong a rival of the dictator. At first Balluku was interned at Roskovec, near Fieri, and then he was imprisoned, sentenced to death, and executed. (TC)

Sources: Stavro Skendi, *Albania* (New York, 1956); William E. Griffith, *Albania and the Sino-Soviet Rift* (Cambridge, Mass., 1963); Peter R. Prifti, *Socialist Albania since 1944: Domestic and Foreign Developments* (Cambridge, Mass., 1978); Arshi Pipa, *Albanian Stalinism: Ideo-Political Aspects* (New York, 1990); Gjergji Titani and Hasani Proleter, *Personalitete ushtarake shqiptare në vite 1912–1997,* vol. 1 (Tirana, 1997); Bardho Hysen, *Beteja dhe duele: Esse dhe kujtime* (Athens, 2000).

BALODIS Janis (20 February 1881, Trikatas–8 August 1965, Saulkrasti), Latvian general and politician. In 1898 Balodis joined the Russian army, and in 1902 he graduated from the military academy in Vilnius (Wilno). He was decorated for his service in the Russo-Japanese War (1904–5). Balodis was wounded during World War I in East Prussia and taken captive by the Germans. In November 1918 he returned to Latvia, and he joined the Latvian army in the making as a captain. He was soon promoted, at first to command a battalion, next a brigade, and then a division. After the death of Colonel Oskar Kolpaks, from March to June 1919 Balodis commanded the Latvian army fighting the Bolsheviks, the White Russians, and the Germans in southern Latvia. On 16 October 1919 he was officially appointed commander-in-chief of the Latvian Army. On 30 December 1919 he signed a treaty of military cooperation with Poland in the liberation of Latgalia. The operation began on 3 January 1920 with an attack by the Polish-Latvian group under the command of General **Edward Rydz-Śmigły**. In January 1920 Balodis was appointed general. In July 1921 he went into the reserves. From 1925 he was an MP associated with the Peasant Union of **Kārlis Ulmanis**, and from 1931 he served as defense minister. In this role he significantly advanced preparations for the coup d'état of 15–16 May 1934. The army's commander-in-chief, General Martins Penikis, was not informed of the plot, and Balodis neutralized the army. The most significant role in the coup was played by Aizsargs, a paramilitary organization of the Peasant Union. On 16 May, together with Ulmanis, Balodis signed a program manifesto for the new government. In it, they presented evidence that the country was on the verge of ruin as a result of widespread corruption, unstable government, and the imminent threat of civil war because of the activities of the radical right and left wings. From 1936 Balodis served as vice president and defense minister. Although he was ready to accept Ulmanis's dictatorial methods of government and even his cult status as "the leader of the nation," Ulmanis dismissed him on 5 April 1934 because he had demanded that Ulmanis fulfill a promise made in 1934 to convene the parliament and pass a new constitution.

After the Red Army entered Latvia in July 1940, together with a group of independence activists, Balodis attempted to put forward a list of non-Communist candidates in the elections to the National Assembly, but he was prevented from doing so by a special deputy from the Kremlin, Andrei Wyshynsky. Balodis was then arrested by the NKVD, and after many years in prisons and forced labor camps, he returned to Latvia, where he died. He was decorated with many Latvian orders and with the Polish Virtuti Militari Cross. (WR/EJ)

Sources: Arnolds Spekke, *History of Latvia* (Stockholm, 1951); Adolf Blodnieks, *The Undefeated Nation* (New York, 1960); Piotr Łossowski, *Kraje bałtyckie na drodze od demokracji parlamentarnej do dyktatury (1918–1934)* (Wrocław, 1972); Adolfs Šilde, *Latvijas Vēsture* (Stockholm, 1976); Visvaldis Mangulis, *Latvia in the Wars of the 20th Century* (Princeton Junction, N.J., 1983).

BALOGH István (30 March 1894, Stájerlak [now in Romania]–21 July 1976, Budapest), Hungarian Catholic priest and political activist. After high school Balogh graduated from a theological seminar in Temesvár (Timişoara) and was ordained in 1918. In 1921–25 he studied philosophy at the universities in Budapest and Szeged, and in 1929 he received a Ph.D. in philosophy. From 1926 to 1946 he was vicar in Szeged. He co-initiated summer festivals in this town, and in 1934 he was elected to the local government on behalf of the government Party of Unity. He founded and edited the *Szegedi Katolikus Tudósító* (1927–35) and a periodical for country folk, *Tanyai Újság* (1936–38). In 1930–32 he edited the daily *Szegedi Hírlap,* and from 1938 to 1944 he was co-owner of a liberal daily, *Délmagyarország,* and two presses.

In November 1944 Balogh took over the leadership of the Independent Smallholders' Party (ISP) organization in Szeged, although he had not belonged to this party. In December 1944 he took part in the creation of the Hungarian National Independence Front (HNIF), which included the ISP, Communists, Social Democrats, and the National Peasant Party. Until May 1945 he presided over the HNIF cell in Szeged and belonged to the preparatory commission of the Provisional National Assembly. From December 1944 to May 1947 he was secretary of state for political affairs in the government, and until the summer of 1945 he headed the government Press Bureau. He was a signatory to the Hungarian-Soviet armistice of 20 January 1945. In 1945–46 he was a government commissioner of abandoned property. From August 1945 he was a member of the ISP national leadership. After the arrest of **Béla Kovács**, in February 1947 Balogh was elected secretary general of the party. After the ISP prime minister, **Ferenc Nagy**, was forced to resign, Balogh also gave up his ministerial position, and in early June 1947 he left the ISP. With Communist support, a month later he founded the Independent Hungarian Democratic Party, which gained 5.2 percent of the vote and eighteen parliamentary seats in the elections of 31 August 1947. From 1947 he was a member of the Hungarian-Soviet Cultural and Educational Society. As a result of his political involvement, in September 1948 Balogh was suspended as a Catholic priest. In February 1949 he led his party into the Communist-controlled Hungarian Independence People's Front and soon was elected to the presidium of its national board. From August 1949 to December 1951 he was a member of the Presidential

Council of the Hungarian Republic. In 1950 he co-initiated a "peace movement" of the Catholic clergy, and later he became a member of the National Peace Council and the National Council of the Popular Patriotic Front. In 1951 he moved out of Budapest but returned in 1953. Later, until his death, Balogh was allowed to work in Budapest as a priest and from 1968, as a titular abbot. (JT)

Sources: *Magyar Életrajzi Lexikon,* vol. 3 (Budapest, 1981); *Magyar Nagylexikon,* vol. 3 (Budapest, 1994); *Magyarország 1944–1956,* CD-ROM, 1956-os Intézet (Budapest, 2001); *Új Magyar Életrajzi Lexikon,* vol. 1 (Budapest, 2001).

BANACH Kazimierz (4 March 1904, Korytkowo, near Opoczno–29 August 1985, Warsaw), Polish political activist. Banach graduated from the Free Polish University (1932). From 1922 he belonged to the Polish Peasant Party Liberation (Polskie Stronnictwo Ludowe Wyzwolenie) and from 1931, to the Peasant Party (Stronnictwo Ludowe [SL]). Active in the peasant youth movement, chairman of the Academic Union of Peasant Youth (1929–30), chairman of the Central Board of the Peasant Youth Association Wici (1931–32), and a member of the presidium of the Slavonic Union of Peasant Youth, in 1935–39 Banach was active in the Wici organization in Volhynia. In March 1940 he co-organized the underground peasant movement SL Roch and was chief of staff of the Supreme Command of the Peasant Battalions (Bataliony Chłopskie); then he edited peasant underground periodicals and served as a delegate of the Polish government in exile in Volhynia. In 1944 he took part in the Warsaw Uprising. In 1945 he joined the Polish Peasant Party (Polskie Stronnictwo Ludowe [PSL]) of **Stanisław Mikołajczyk.** At first a member of the PSL Chief Executive Committee and Supreme Board, he represented the party in the Communist-controlled Home National Council (Krajowa Rada Narodowa). He advocated a conciliatory attitude toward the Communists. In the parliamentary elections of January 1947 he won a seat, having organized a splinter group called PSL-Left. Excluded from the PSL in April 1947, after the escape of Mikołajczyk in the fall 1947, he took part in the takeover of the party by a pro-Communist faction and its merger with the Communist-controlled Peasant Party into the United Peasant Party (Zjednoczone Stronnictwo Ludowe [ZSL]) in November 1949. In 1950–55 he was marginalized and worked in the cooperative movement. From 1956 he became one of the ZSL leaders. He was a member of the Chief Committee, editor of ZSL periodicals, chairman of the People's Press Cooperative (1951–71), MP (until 1972), a member of the Council of State (until 1971), deputy chairman of the Communist war veterans' Union of Fighters for Freedom and Democracy (1956–74), and

a long-time member of the Communist-controlled International Federation of Resistance Movements. (AP)

Sources: Mołdawa; *Słownik Biograficzny Działaczy Ruchu Ludowego* (Warsaw, 1989); Roman Buczek, *Stronnictwo Ludowe w latach 1939–1945* (London, 1975); Krystyna Kersten, *Narodziny systemu władzy: Polska 1943–1948* (Poznań, 1990); Andrzej Paczkowski, *Stanisław Mikołajczyk, czyli klęska realisty* (Warsaw, 1991).

BANACH Stefan (30 March 1892, Kraków–31 August 1945, Lwów [Lviv]), Polish mathematician. In 1910–14 Banach studied at the Lwów Polytechnic, but with the outbreak of World War I he had to break off his studies. In 1919 he, along with **Hugo Steinhaus**, published his first scholarly work. From 1920 he worked at the Lwów Polytechnic as an assistant professor. In the same year he received a Ph.D.; in 1922 he received a postdoctoral degree, and he became full professor. From 1924 he was a member of the Polish Academy of Arts and Sciences. In the mid-1920s he already had international standing as a mathematician; he co-established the Lwów school of mathematics and was the discoverer of a new branch of mathematics: functional analysis, known at that time as the theory of linear operations. In 1929, along with Steinhaus, he founded the periodical *Studia Mathematica,* which in a short time won worldwide recognition. In 1932 he published his major work, *Théorie des opérations linéaires* (Theory of linear operations), which was the first handbook of functional analysis. In it he introduced the concept of the "Banach space." Along with Alfred Tarski, he also presented the theorem of the paradoxical factoring of a sphere. In 1939 he was elected chairman of the Polish Mathematical Association. The outbreak of World War II found him in Lwów, which was taken by the Red Army. In 1940–41 he was dean of the Soviet-controlled University of Lwów. After the seizure of the city by the Germans, he lost his job and worked as a feeder of lice in an institute producing anti-typhoid vaccine. When the Soviet army returned in the summer of 1944, Banach returned to scholarly work at the university. He intended to move to Kraków, but he died before he could. His main works were published in *Oeuvres avec des commentaires* (Works with commentary, 2 vols.; 1967–79). (WR)

Sources: Hugo Steinhaus, "Stefan Banach," *Studia Mathematica,* 1963, no 1; *Polacy w historii i kulturze krajów Europy Zachodniej,* ed. Krzysztof Kwaśniewski and Lech Trzeciakowski (Poznań, 1981); Roman Kałuża, *Stefan Banach* (Warsaw, 1992); S. Wagon, *The Banach-Tarski Paradox* (Cambridge, 1993); Roman, Kałuża *Throught a Reporter's Eye: The Life of Stefan Banach* (Boston, 1996); J. Kozielecki, *Banach-geniusz ze Lwowa* (Warsaw, 1999).

BAŃCZYK Stanisław (25 October 1903, Lubiszów, near Opoczno–16 April 1988, Washington, D.C.), Polish peasant politician. Bańczyk graduated from a training school in Sieradz. From 1919 he belonged to the Polish Peasant Party Wyzwolenie (Polskie Stronnictwo Ludowe Wyzwolenie), and from 1931 to the Peasant Party (Stronnictwo Ludowe [SL]). He was one of the top leaders of the Peasant Youth Association Wici, and he co-organized the peasant strike of 1937. He favored cooperation with the Polish Socialist Party and supported a united front of the left with the Communists; he was arrested several times. During the German occupation he was a member of the underground SL Roch, and then he co-organized the SL Wola Ludu (Will of the People), on whose behalf he became a member of the Communist-controlled Home National Council (Krajowa Rada Narodowa). In 1945 he was chairman of the Chief Executive Committee of the pro-Communist SL, but he advocated its autonomy and cooperation with the Polish Peasant Party (Polskie Stronnictwo Ludowe [PSL]) of **Stanisław Mikołajczyk**. In November 1945, with a group of followers, Bańczyk moved to the PSL, where he became deputy chairman of its Chief Executive Committee. He won a parliamentary seat in the fraudulent elections of January 1947. He supported Mikołajczyk's policies, and after Mikołajczyk's escape he resigned and secretly left Poland as well. One of the top PSL leaders in exile, in 1954 Bańczyk opposed Mikołajczyk and, along with Stanisław Wójcik, he took the lead of a separate PSL. Later he resigned from it, since one of his chief aides proved to be an agent of Communist intelligence. In 1964 he joined the **Kazimierz Bagiński** group, and in 1968–75 he was the head of the PSL in exile, after most splinters groups were again reunited. The party split again in 1975, and Bańczyk ceased to play a significant role in the political life of Polish émigrés. (AP)

Sources: Mołdawa; *Słownik Biograficzny Działaczy Ruchu Ludowego* (Warsaw, 1989); Roman Buczek, *Stronnictwo Ludowe w latach 1939–1945* (London, 1975); Krystyna Kersten, *Narodziny systemu władzy: Polska 1943–1948* (Poznań, 1990); Andrzej Paczkowski, *Stanisław Mikołajczyk, czyli klęska realisty* (Warsaw, 1991).

BANDERA Stepan (1 January 1909, Uhryniv Staryi, near Kalush–15 October 1959, Munich), Ukrainian nationalist politician. The son of a Greek Catholic priest, Bandera graduated from high school in Stryi. As a student of agronomy at the Lwów (Lviv) Polytechnic, in 1927 he joined the Ukrainian Military Organization (Ukrajinska viiskova orhanizatsiia [UVO]). He also belonged to the Union of Nationalist Ukrainian Youth (Soyuz Ukraiinskoii Natsionalistychnoi Molodi). From 1929 he was a member of the Organization of Ukrainian Nationalists (Orhanizatsiia Ukraiinskykh Natsionalistiv [OUN]), and from 1931 he was head of the propaganda section of the OUN Executive Department. With the support of the young, radically anti-Polish members at the OUN leadership (*provid*) meeting in Prague on 6 June 1933, he was appointed the OUN leader (*providnyk*). On his recommendation the OUN continued terrorist actions against Polish authorities—for example, the assassination of the minister of interior, **Bronisław Pieracki**. Arrested on 14 June 1934, in January 1936 Bandera was sentenced to death. The sentence was then commuted to life imprisonment. He was held in the Święty Krzyż, Rawicz, Wronki, and Bereza Kartuska prisons.

Released in early September 1939 along with a group of young nationalists, Bandera attempted to resume power in the OUN. In view of the resistance of the followers of **Andriy Melnyk**, on 10 February 1940 the organization split. Bandera took over the leadership of the revolutionary OUN faction, named the Bandera faction after him (OUN-B); it took over most of the organizational network in the Ukraine and acted mostly against Soviet power. Counting on a German-Soviet war, the OUN-B formed military units cooperating with the German Wehrmacht and special troops aimed at taking over power in the territory taken by the Germans. On 30 June 1941 in German-controlled Lviv, Bandera's followers announced the creation of an independent Ukraine with a government headed by **Yaroslav Stetsko**. Bandera was probably to become the head of state. The Germans refused to recognize the Stesko government and demanded a withdrawal of the declaration of independence. When the OUN-B refused, its activists were arrested. Bandera was placed in the Sachsenhausen-Zellenbau concentration camp as a special prisoner. He made contact with the commander-in-chief of the Polish Home Army, General **Stefan Grot-Rowecki**, also kept there, but no details of these contacts are known.

Changes in the German policy toward the Ukraine led to Bandera's release in mid-September 1944. His position toward the Third Reich in the last months of the war is not clear. Probably he gradually distanced himself from the German authorities. After the war he remained in the Western occupation zones of Germany, heading Foreign OUN Groups (Zakordonnyie Chastyny OUN [ZCh OUN]). Differences grew between Bandera and OUN activists connected with the Ukrainian Insurgent Army (Ukrainska Povstanska Armia [UPA]) and its political superstructure, the Ukrainian Supreme Liberation Council. In particular Bandera questioned a resolution of the Third OUN Congress that rejected democratization of the organization. He also refused to recognize the council's leadership in exile.

He supported a continuation of the UPA armed struggle, leaving the choice of methods to its commander-in-chief, **Roman Shukhevych**. Discrepancies within the ZCh OUN led to a split in the organization in 1948. Activists connected with the council questioned Bandera's power and established the so-called OUN-Z, led by **Lev Rebet** and Zinoviy Matla. Attempts by Shukhevych to ease the tension between the factions failed. Representatives of both factions sent to the Ukraine were caught by the Soviets. Bandera's representative, the head of the ZCh OUN Security Service, Myron Matviyenko, disclosed important secrets of the organization to the Soviets. His arrest, as well as the creation of an OUN network controlled by the Polish Communist security apparatus, further weakened Bandera's position. Nevertheless, as a long-term prisoner, for many Ukrainians he was still a symbol of the national struggle for independence. For this reason the head of the Soviet KGB, Aleksander Shelepin, ordered his assassination. On 15 October 1959 Bandera was murdered by a KGB agent, Bohdan Stashynskyi. Bandera was buried in Munich. In 1978 a collection of his works, *Perspektyvy ukraiinskoy revolutsii* (Prospects of the Ukrainian revolution), appeared in Munich. (GM)

Sources: *Encyclopedia of Ukraine,* vol. 1 (Toronto, 1984); Petro Mirczuk, *Bandera: Symvol revolutsionnoy bezkompromisovnosti* (New York and Toronto, 1961); *Murdered by Moscow: Petlura, Konovalets, Bandera: Three Leaders of the Ukrainian Liberation Movement* (London, 1962); Karl Anders, *Mord auf Befehl- der Fall Staschynskyj* (Tübingen, 1963); *Moskovsky vbivtsy Bandery pered sudom* (Monachium, 1965); Ryszard Torzecki, *Polacy i Ukraińcy: Sprawa ukraińska w czasie II wojny światowej na terenie II Rzeczypospolitej* (Warsaw, 1993); *Ubiistvo Stepana Bandery* (Lviv, 1993); Wasyl Kuk, *Stepan Bandera 1909–1999* (Ivano-Frankovsk, 1999).

BÁNFFY Dezső (28 October 1843, Kolozsvár [Cluj]–24 May 1911, Budapest), Hungarian politician. After graduating from law and administration studies in Cluj, Berlin, and Vienna, Bánffy was governor of Szolnok-Doboka Province (1876–90) and then of Beszterce-Naszód Province (1890–92). He was a conservative of a peremptory nature. Speaker of the parliament on behalf of the Liberal Party (1892–95), from January 1895 to February 1899 he was prime minister at the time of the culmination of the Hungarian nationalist offensive, the so-called struggle for culture. Bánffy's personal engagement and his skillful policies helped his government to force a modernization of the civil law. He also made a number of decisions to consolidate a strong national state. For instance, the celebration of the millennium of Hungarian statehood in 1896 strengthened national consciousness and pride among Hungarians and transformed Budapest into a modern European capital. Bánffy's nationalist policies led

to a long-term crisis of the Dual Monarchy. In 1904 he returned to politics, becoming an MP and chairman of the conservative New Party (Új párt), which, however, failed to play a significant role. He was the author of *Magyar nemzetiségi politika* (Hungarian national policy; 1902) and *A horvát kérdésről* (On the Croatian question; 1907), in which he presented an uncompromising attitude toward national minorities (MS)

Sources: *Bánffy Dezső nemzetiségi politikája* (Budapest, 1899); Lajos Bíró, "Bánffy Dezső," *Huszadik Század,* 1912, no. 23; Steven Béla Várga, *Historical Dictionary of Hungary* (Lanham, Md., 1997).

BANGERSKIS Rūdolfs (21 July 1878, Taurupe, Livonia–25 February 1958, Oldenburg, Germany), Latvian general. After high school Bangerskis served in the Russian army from 1895. In 1901 he graduated from the infantry cadet school in Petersburg and served as an officer in the Ninety-Third, Ninety-Sixth, and Thirty-Sixth Regiments. He took part in the Russo-Japanese War of 1904. In 1912–14 he studied in the Academy of the General Staff but broke off his studies at the outbreak of World War I. In December 1916 he was a colonel in the staff of the Fourteenth Corps and later of the Thirty-First Corps; from January 1917 he commanded the Seventeenth Regiment of Siberian Riflemen. Demobilized in March 1918, he went to Yekaterinburg, where he joined the anti-Bolshevik Siberian Army of General Aleksander Kolchak. Chief of staff of a division and later commander of a division, he was promoted to lieutenant-general. From October 1919 he commanded a corps and then a group of armies. In December 1920 he returned to Latvia. From 1924 he was commander of a division of the Latvian Army and headed higher military courses. From December 1924 to December 1925 and from December 1926 to January 1928 he was minister of war. In 1925 he was confirmed as general, and in 1936 he retired. After the Soviet invasion of 1940 he avoided arrest, although he was listed for deportation. During the German occupation, in 1942–43 he worked in the General Juridical Administration of the Latvian government. From April 1943 a general inspector of the Latvian Legion in the rank of Gruppenführer SS, he withdrew with the German army to the west and was elected chairman of the Latvian National Committee in Potsdam in February 1945. From June 1945 he was in a British POW camp. Released in December 1946, he settled in Oldenburg. He wrote a four-volume memoir, *Mana mūža atmiņas* (Memoirs of my life; 1958–60). He was killed in a car crash. (EJ)

Sources: *Es viņu pazīstu* (Riga, 1939); Adolfs Blodnieks, *The Undefeated Nation* (New York, 1960); Ēriks Jēkabsons and U. Neiburgs,

"Ģenerālis Rūdolfs Bangerskis," *Vīri*, 1995, no. 4; Andrejs Plakans, *Historical Dictionary of Latvia* (Lanham, Md., 1997); *Latvijas armijas augstākie virsnieki: Biogrāfiska vārdnīca* (Riga, 1998).

BANUSHI Ireneo Ilia (18 August 1906, Shkodër–25 November 1973, Lushnjë), Albanian Orthodox bishop. In 1925 Banushi graduated from Iliricum, a Franciscan high school in Shkodër and in 1931, from the Orthodox theological seminary in Cetinje. In 1938 he graduated in theological studies in Belgrade. After returning to Albania, he lectured in a theological seminary, and he taught Latin and history in a high school in Tirana. During the Italian occupation he was imprisoned in Shkodër as a "political suspect" and was later interned near Mantua in Italy. Released in June 1940, he returned to Tirana. From October 1941 to January 1942 he again taught in a high school. In January 1942 he was appointed archimandrite of Shen Naum Monastery, and the following month he was consecrated bishop. In June 1942 the Holy Synod reorganized the church administration, taking into consideration territories included in Italian-occupied Albania. Banushi took over the Struga-Prespa diocese. He sympathized with the Communist guerrillas but remained passive.

At the end of World War II Banushi dedicated himself to writing pastoral works. In July 1945 he became ordinary bishop of the Gjirokaster diocese, but he resided in Tirana because the Communists prevented him from coming to Gjirokaster, wishing to place one of their priests there. On 28 October 1946 Banushi was arrested, and in April 1947 he was sentenced to five years for "collaboration with the occupiers." Released owing to an amnesty on 28 April 1949, he recovered from tuberculosis, which he had acquired in prison. Interned in the Shen Vlashi Monastery in Durrës, he took part in the Third Congress of the Albanian Orthodox Church in February 1950. He was pressed to give up his consecration as bishop. Since he refused, on 22 August 1952 he was arrested again, and on 9 April 1953 he was sentenced to five years in prison. After his release, in 1958 he was interned in the Ardenice Monastery near Lushnjë. In 1967, when all religious practice was prohibited by Albanian law, he was allowed to settle and work as a blue-collar laborer in Lushnjë. He worked in railway construction, as a storekeeper, and as an accountant. He died of tuberculosis. (TC)

Sources: Beduli Dhimiter, *Kisha orthodokse autoqefale e Shqipërise gjer në vitin 1944* (Tirana, 1992); Beduli Kristofor, *Episkop Irine Banushi: Martir i Kishës Orthodhokse Autoqefale te Shqipërise* (Tirana, 2000).

BARADULIN Ryhor (24 February 1935, Verasovka, Vitebsk region), Belorussian poet, critic, and translator. From 1954 to 1959 Baradulin studied philology at the Belorussian State University in Minsk. Later he worked for the periodicals *Sovetskaya Byelorussiya, Byarozka, Belarus*, and *Polymya*. In 1996 he became editor-in-chief of the monthly *Mastatskaya literatura*. In 1990–99 he was chairman of the Belorussian PEN club, and in 1995–97, a member of the board of the Belorussian Soros Foundation. He made his literary debut in 1953. The major collections of his poems include the following: *Meladzik nad stepami* (New moon over the steppes; 1959); *Adam i Yeva* (Adam and Eve; 1968); *Vyartannie u pyershy snieh* (Return to the first snow; 1972); *Absiah* (The range; 1978); *Amplituda smielastsi* (The amplitude of braveness; 1983); *Mauchannie pieruna* (The silence of thunder; 1986); and *Samota palomnitstwa* (The solitude of pilgrimage; 1990). His poems have been translated into eleven languages. Baradulin also translated the works by García Lorca, Aleksandr Voznesenksiy, Omar Chajjam, Pablo Neruda, William Shakespeare, George Byron, Adam Mickiewicz, and Władysław Broniewski into Belorussian. It is believed that he authored the anonymous poems *Raskaz pra Lysuyu Haru* (The tale of Bald Mountain) and *Luka Mudishchau*, the former being a satire of the Soviet system and the latter of President **Alyaksandr Lukashenka**. Baradulin won numerous national and international awards. (EM)

Sources: *Entsyklapedyia litaratury i mastatstva Belarusi*, vol. 1 (Minsk, 1984); *Bielaruskiya pismienniki: Biyabibliagrafichny slounik*, vol. 1 (Minsk, 1992); Jan Zaprudnik, *Belarus: At a Crossroads in History* (Boulder, Colo., 1993); *Bielaruskiya pismienniki 1917–1990: Davednik* (Minsk, 1994); Jan Zaprudnik, *Historical Dictionary of Belarus* (Lanham, Md., 1998); *Kto iest kto w Respublike Belarus* (Minsk, 1999).

BARÁK Rudolf (11 May 1915, Blansko–12 August 1995, Prague), Czech Communist activist. Between 1930 and 1945 Barák was a laborer in his home, Blansko. In 1945 he joined the Communist Party of Czechoslovakia (CPC), and as an obedient executor of orders, he was soon promoted in the party hierarchy. He advanced from membership on a factory committee to the party secretariat in the district of Blansko, and after the coup in February 1948 he became the chair of the Regional National Committee in Blansko. Owing to the support of the equally swiftly promoted **Antonín Novotný**, in October 1950 Barák was appointed head of the CPC in Brno and in December 1952 deputy member, and soon thereafter member, of the CPC Central Committee. At the beginning of 1953 he was briefly deputy prime minister, and in September 1953 he assumed the post of interior minister. In this role he headed the state terror. Over a hundred Czechoslovak concentration camps fell within his power. From June 1954 he was a member of the Politburo of the CC and chaired a special committee for investigating the political trials of 1948–53; the committee was created after Stalin's death in the first stages of collective leadership in Czechoslovakia. The committee covered up most of the Stalinist crimes, and its report was never made public. However, Barák collected a great deal of evidence incriminating his political rivals. Along with Novotný, he played a major role in holding back de-Stalinization and prevented its spread to Czechoslovakia from neighboring countries. He directed the program Return, in which postwar emigrants were encouraged to return to Czechoslovakia. From 1959 he was deputy prime minister and enjoyed great popularity among the party masses, especially after the amnesty of 9 May 1960, through which many political prisoners were released.

When unrest connected with a bad economic situation and Khrushchev's "second thaw" in the USSR began in 1961, Barák was most frequently mentioned as Novotný's successor. Alarmed by the independence of Barák's policies and by the fact that Barák knew about Novotný's role in the trial of **Rudolf Slánsky**, Novotný counterattacked. In June 1961 Barák was dismissed from the Ministry of Interior and was assigned a marginal post as plenipotentiary for a local administration a month later. On the night of 23–24 January 1962 President Novotný, Prime Minister **Viliam Široký**, and Minister of Interior **Lubomir Štrougal** personally arrested Barák under the pretext of his having embezzled $1,000. On Novotný's motion the CC Plenum of 6–7 February 1962 denounced Barák for his activities in the ministry and his "manipulations of state property." On 20 June 1962 he was sentenced to fifteen years of prison. Released and rehabilitated by the Supreme Court during the Prague Spring in May 1968, he did not return to political life. (WR)

Sources: *ČBS*; *Who's Who in the Socialist Countries* (New York, 1978); William E. Griffith, ed., *Communism in Europe*, vol. 2 (Cambridge, Mass., 1966); Edward Taborsky, *Communism in Czechoslovakia 1948–1960* (Princeton, 1961); Eugen Loebl, *Stalinism in Prague* (New York, 1969); Jiří Pelikán, *The Czechoslovak Political Trials 1950–1954* (Stanford, 1971).

BARANIAK Antoni (1 January 1904, Sebastianów, near Śrem–18 August 1977, Poznań). Polish archbishop. Born into a peasant family, after primary school in Sebastianów Baraniak studied in schools run by the Order of St. Francis Salesius in Oświęcim and Kraków, where he passed his graduation exams and took vows in May 1924. In August 1930 he was ordained. From 1927 to 1933 he studied in Warsaw and at the Gregorian University in Rome, where he received a Ph.D. in canon law. From 1933 he was per-

sonal secretary to the Primate of Poland, **August Hlond**, and later to Primate **Stefan Wyszyński.** On 26 April 1951 he was appointed auxiliary bishop of the Gniezno bishopric and was consecrated on 8 July 1951. He kept working in the secretariat of the Primate of Poland, acting as bishop in western and northern dioceses, where the Communist authorities had removed the apostolic administrators.

As Baraniak was a close aide to Primate Wyszyński, on 25 September 1953 Communist security officers arrested him in Warsaw. He was tortured physically and mentally in a Warsaw prison. (For instance, he was kept naked in a wet and cold cell.) His forced confessions were to serve as a foundation for the trial of Primate Wyszyński, but he refused to testify against the primate. On 21 December 1955 Baraniak was released and transferred to a Salesian convent in Marszałki, near Ostrzeszów, where he was kept in strict isolation. He was set free in October 1956. Imprisonment had ruined his health. On 30 May 1957 Pope Pius XII appointed him archbishop of Poznań, which was perceived as a sign of solidarity between the Pope and the persecuted bishop. Baraniak took over the Poznań archbishopric on 2 July 1957. He established a number of new parishes and reactivated the collegiate church in Środa; he participated in the Second Vatican Council and in the synods of bishops in 1969 and 1971. In 1968 he also organized a diocesan synod. Thanks to his endeavors, the Papal Theological Department was created in Poznań. Baraniak was known as an outstanding preacher; he frequently spoke in defense of the rights of believers and priests harassed for building churches without special permission from the Communist authorities. (AGr)

Sources: Piotr Nitecki, *Biskupi Kościoła w Polsce: Słownik biograficzny* (Warsaw, 1992); *Leksykon duchowieństwa represjonowanego w PRL w latach 1945–1989*, vol. 1 (Warsaw, 2002); Marian Przykucki, "Z kalendarium życia i pracy ks. arcybiskupa Antoniego Baraniaka metropolity poznańskiego," in *W służbie Kościoła Poznańskiego* (Poznań, 1974); Andrzej Micewski, *Kardynał Wyszyński: Prymas i mąż stanu* (Paris, 1982); Antoni Dudek, *Państwo i Kościół w Polsce w latach 1945–1970* (Kraków, 1995); Jan Żaryn, *Stolica Apostolska wobec Polski i Polaków w latach 1944–1958* (Warsaw, 1998).

BARANKOVICS István (13 December 1906, Polgár–13 March 1974, New York), Hungarian Christian Democratic politician. Barankovics was born into a teacher's family. In 1925 he passed his high school final examinations at the Cistercian Gymnasium in Eger, and then he entered the law department of the university in Budapest. He interrupted his studies in order to concentrate on journalism. It was only in 1944 that he obtained his degree in political science. In 1928 he was elected secretary general of the National Union of Hungarian Catholic College Students.

A committed Christian sensitive to social problems, Barankovics found an ally in the person of Count Gyula Dessewffy, the president of the Ferenc Deák Society. In 1937 Dessewffy founded a political periodical, *Az Ország útja*, and asked Barankovics to join him as co-editor. In 1943 the magazine ceased publication, and Barankovics became editor-in-chief of the nationwide daily *Magyar Nemzet*. In it, he outlined his political program in the spirit of Christian Democracy. After the German occupation of Hungary (March 1944), *Magyar Nemzet* was suspended.

When the Arrow Cross Party took over power in October 1944, Barankovics went into the underground and was active as secretary general of the Christian Democratic People's Party of Count József Pálffy. In April 1945 the party officially appeared as the Democratic People's Party (DPP). Barankovics wanted to transform the party into a modern Christian Democratic party with a program based on papal social encyclicals. He recognized the republican state, and in the face of the postwar situation, he considered it necessary to maintain good relations with the USSR. Because of this he came into conflict with Cardinal **József Mindszenty** and also with Count Palffy, who enjoyed the support of the cardinal. In the summer of 1945 the party split in two. In the elections of November 1945 Barankovics's wing gained two seats under an electoral agreement with the Smallholders' Party (SP). Despite electoral fraud, in the elections of 1947 Barankovics entered parliament, and the DPP obtained sixty seats, becoming the second largest faction. After the split, the SP became a base for middle-class forces. Although he was ready for compromise, Barankovics could not lead the opposition for long. In his last parliamentary speech in December 1948, he sharply criticized the concentration of power and the government policies of economic planning and collectivization. Under political pressure, on 2 February 1949 Barankovics issued a statement in which he announced the dissolution of the party, and then he fled the country. At first he lived in Austria, where he was head of the office for the affairs of refugees in Salzburg. In 1951 he settled in the United States. In 1954, together with a group of his supporters, he revived the DPP. From 1958 he was a member of the Hungarian Committee and president of the Christian Democratic Union of Eastern Europe in New York. (JT)

Sources: Ferenc Nagy, *The Struggle behind the Iron Curtain* (New York, 1948); *Prominent Hungarians Home and Abroad* (Munich, 1966); Imre Kovacs, ed., *Facts about Hungary: The Fight for Freedom* (New York, 1966); *Magyar Nagylexikon*, vol. 3 (Budapest, 1994); *A magyar forradalom és szabadságharc enciklopédiája*, CD-ROM, 1956-os Intézet (Budapest, 1999).

BARCIKOWSKI Kazimierz (22 March 1927, Zglechów, near Mińsk Mazowiecki), Polish Communist activist. Born into a peasant family, Barcikowski was active in the Peasant Youth Association Wici during his studies. In 1950 he graduated from the Central School of Farming in Łódź. In 1953 he joined the Polish United Workers' Party (Polska Zjednoczona Partia Robotnicza [PZPR]). In 1954–56 he was deputy editor-in-chief of the state publishing house Iskry; in 1956 he became secretary of the Supreme Board of the Polish Youth Association, and from 1957 to 1960 he was vice president of the Supreme Board of the Peasant Youth Association (Związek Młodzieży Wiejskiej [PYA]). In 1960–62 he studied at the Higher School of Social Sciences at the PUWP Central Committee (CC), where he received a Ph.D. in 1962. From 1963 to 1965 he presided over the PYA Supreme Board; from 1965 to 1968 he was deputy head of the Organization Department of the PUWP CC and editor-in-chief of the party organ, *Życie Partii*. From 1964 a deputy member and from 1968 to 1990 a member of the PUWP CC, in 1965–89 he was MP. From 1968 to 1970 he was first secretary of the PUWP Provincial Committee in Poznań, and from December 1970 to February 1974, he was CC secretary for agriculture and contacts with the parliament. From 1971 he was a deputy member of the party Politburo. From February 1974 to December 1977 he was minister of agriculture, and later, until February 1980, he was first secretary of the PUWP Provincial Committee in Kraków. After that he returned to the government, assuming the position of deputy prime minister (February–October 1980). Then, until November 1985, he was PUWP CC secretary again.

During the Baltic coast strikes of August 1980, Barcikowski headed a government commission to negotiate with the Inter-Factory Strike Committee in Szczecin headed by **Marian Jurczyk**. On 30 August 1980, without full coordination with the party leadership, Barcikowski signed an agreement with the committee. A few days later, after **Edward Gierek** was toppled, Barcikowski became a member of the Politburo and remained in this position until July 1989. In September 1980 he became a member of the newly founded Joint Commission of the Government and Episcopate. Co-chairman of the commission from 1980 to 1989 and co-author of legislation regulating relations between the state and the church, he was the CC secretary responsible for the control of the church and of satellite parties. He played a significant role in the introduction of martial law, and on 14 December 1981 he joined the so-called directorate, an informal political team to rule Poland. In 1980–85 he was the head of the PUWP parliamentary caucus. From 1980 to 1989 he was a member of the Council of State, and in 1985–89 he was its deputy chairman. From 1989 chairman of the Chief Cooperative Council, Barcikowski published the memoirs *Na szczytach władzy* (At the top of power; 1998). (PK)

Sources: Mołdawa; Włodzimierz Janowski and Aleksander Kochański, *Informator o strukturze i obsadzie personalnej centralnego aparatu PZPR 1948–1990* (Warsaw, 2000); Antoni Czubiński, *Dzieje najnowsze Polski 1944–1989* (Poznań, 1992); Andrzej Paczkowski, *Droga do "mniejszego zła." Strategia i taktyka obozu władzy, lipiec 1980–styczeń 1982* (Kraków, 2002).

BÁRDOSSY László (10 December 1890, Szombathely–10 January 1946, Budapest), Hungarian politician. The son of a white-collar worker, in 1912 Bárdossy graduated in law from the University of Budapest. In 1913 he chose an administrative career, taking a job in the Ministry of Religious Denominations and National Education. He was promoted when he moved to the Ministry of Foreign Affairs in 1922. He became deputy head and (in 1927) head of the Press Department of the Foreign Ministry. From 1930 he was a councillor in the embassy in London, and in 1934–41, ambassador in Bucharest. After the sudden death of István Csáky, in February 1941 Bárdossy was appointed minister of foreign affairs, and after Prime Minister **Pál Teleki** committed suicide, on 3 April 1941 Bárdossy became prime minister, retaining the position of head of diplomacy.

Bárdossy believed in the victory of the Third Reich, and driven by a desire to recover Voivodina for Hungary, he agreed to the movement of German troops through Hungarian territory after Hitler decided to attack Yugoslavia. After the proclamation of "independent" Croatia—in agreement with Regent **Miklos Hórthy**—on 11 April 1941 Bárdossy decided to join in the German attack. As a result, the Hungarian army took Voivodina. After the German invasion of the USSR on 22 June 1941, Bárdossy broke off relations with the Soviet Union. Four days later, he submitted to the government Horthy's decision to join the war against the USSR, and the next day he announced this decision in the parliament without asking it for consent. Under German and Italian pressure, in the absence of Horthy and without the consent of the cabinet, after the Japanese attack on Pearl Harbor, on 11 December 1941 Bárdossy announced that Hungary was also at war with Great Britain and the United States. In domestic policy Bárdossy represented the extreme right. In 1941 the so-called third anti-Jewish law was passed, which prohibited marriages between Jews and gentiles and declared sexual relations between them a race crime. In January 1942 Bárdossy contributed to the creation and shipment of the Second Army, numbering some two hundred thousand soldiers, to the eastern front, and he allowed the recruitment of about twenty thousand Hungarian Germans to the Waffen-SS. In 1943 the Second Army suffered heavy losses on the Don River. One out of four soldiers was killed, and some twenty-eight thousand were taken by the Soviets. Bárdossy's submission to the Germans eroded his position and that of his government, while pro-Western conservatives demanded his dismissal. His position was additionally weakened by his conflict with Horthy, who wanted to create the position of deputy to the regent and saw his son as a candidate. Bárdossy was opposed, but the regent achieved his goal in February 1942.

On 7 March 1942 Bárdossy was forced to resign, but he remained one of the key leaders of the extreme right. In 1943 he took over the lead of the radical United Christian National League. In 1944 he became MP. After the Arrow Cross took power in October 1944, Bárdossy remained MP. At the end of the war he escaped to Bavaria. Arrested by the Americans, in October 1945 he was handed over to Budapest. A month later, the People's Court in Budapest sentenced him to death for war crimes, and he was soon executed. (JT)

Sources: *Biographisches Lexikon,* vol. 1; *Magyar Nagylexikon,* vol. 3 (Budapest, 1994); *Nagy Képes Milleniumi Arcképcsarnok* (Budapest, 1999); *Új Magyar Életrajzi Lexikon,* vol. 1 (Budapest, 2001); *Magyarország 1944–1956,* CD-ROM (Budapest, 2001); John F. Montgomery, *Hungary: The Unwilling Satellite* (New York, 1947); Nicholas Horthy, *Memoirs* (Paris, 1954); *Bűnös volt-e Bárdossy László* (Budapest, 1996); Steven Béla Várdy, *Historical Dictionary of Hungary* (Lanham, Md., 1997); Pál Pritz, *A Bárdossy-per* (N.p., 2001).

BARKAUSKAS Antanas (20 January 1917, Paparchiai), Lithuanian Communist activist. After the Soviet invasion of Lithuania in June 1940 Barkauskas joined the Communist youth organization Komjaunimas and took a job in the Soviet administration in Kaunas. When the Third Reich attacked the USSR, in June 1941 he joined the Red Army and in 1942, the Soviet Communist Party. After the war he resumed his work in the administration of the Lithuanian SSR, supporting Sovietization and Stalinist policies. He graduated from a higher party school in Moscow. From 1950 he was a functionary of the Vilnius committee of the Communist Party of Lithuania (CPL), supporting collectivization and the extermination of the remaining freedom fighters. In 1953–55 he lectured at the Polytechnic Institute in Kaunas, and from 1959 he was head of a department of the CPL Central Committee (CC). From 1961 to 1975 he was a member of the CC Secretariat, and from 1962 to 1966, of the CPL CC Politburo. During the administration of Leonid Brezhnev Barkauskas became one of the leading supporters of the Kremlin policy of Sovietization. In 1982 he published a Soviet version of Lithuanian history, *Lithuania: Years and Deeds.* From 1975 to 1985 and from 1988 to the beginning of 1990 he was chairman of the Supreme Council of the Lithuanian SSR, ineffectively trying to prevent *perestroika* and *glasnost.* (WR)

Sources: *The International Who's Who 1984/85* (Europa 1985); Romuald J. Misiunas and Rein Taagepera, *The Baltic States: Years of Dependence 1940—1990* (Berkeley, 1993).

BÂRLĂDEANU Alexandru (25 January 1911, Comrat, Moldavia–13 October 1997, Bucharest), Romanian Communist activist. In 1936 Bârlădeanu joined the Communist Party of Romania (Partidul Comunist din România [CPR]). In 1937 he graduated in law from the university in Iaşi. In 1937–40 he was assistant professor and held the chair of political economy at this university, and in 1940 he received a Ph.D. in economics there. From 1940 to 1946 he worked at a research institute in Chişinău, the capital of the Moldavian SSR since 1940, created from the formerly Romanian Bessarabia. In 1946 he moved to Romania, already under Communist control. From 1946 to 1947 he was an economic expert of the Romanian delegation to the Paris Peace Conference. From 1946 to 1951 he held a chair in the Institute of Economics. Appointed professor in 1949, he was deputy minister of the national economy in 1946–48 and minister of foreign trade from 1948 to 1954. In 1955–56 he was deputy chairman and then chairman of the State Planning Commission. He implemented the Stalinist economic concepts of **Gheorghe Gheorghiu-Dej**—for instance, he supervised the construction of a metallurgical plant in Galaţi. From 1955 he was a member of the Central Committee (CC) of the Romanian Workers' Party (as of 1965 the Romanian Communist Party [RCP]). In 1955 he became a deputy to the National Assembly; in 1962–65 he was a deputy member and in 1965–68 a member of the RCP CC Politburo. From 1955 to 1965 (with a break in 1956) he was deputy prime minister for economic affairs, and then until 1967, first deputy prime minister. At a Comecon meeting on 15 February 1963 he protested the imposition of Comecon plans on Romania.

After the takeover of power by **Nicolae Ceauşescu** in 1965, as a close aide of Gheorghiu-Dej, Bârlădeanu was gradually moved to the shadows. In 1968 he was forced to give up all his posts, excluded from the RCP, and placed under house arrest, in which he stayed until the fall of Ceauşescu in December 1989. From the mid-1980s he is believed to have been in touch with other high RCP officials who had been removed by Ceauşescu and who were considering a return to power with Soviet support. On 10 March 1989 the BBC broadcast a letter signed by Bârlădeanu and five other former Gheorghiu-Dej aides protesting the Ceauşescu dictatorship and its economic policies. After the fall of the dictator Bârlădeanu belonged to a close circle of leaders constituting the provisional government of the National Salvation Front (Frontul Sălvari Naţionale [NSF]). After the parliamentary elections of May 1990 he was the speaker of the Senate until 1992, and in 1990–91 he co-chaired the National Assembly. In 1992 he was dismissed from the NSF in view of his unreformed Communist views on the economy, and he joined the extreme nationalist Greater Romania Party (Partidul România Mare), attracting many former Communists. From 1955 he was a member of the Romanian Academy of Sciences, and from 1990 to 1994 he was its deputy chairman. (LW)

Sources: *Dictionar Enciclopedic,* vol. 1 (Bucharest, 1993); Ghita Ionescu, *Communism in Romania 1944—1962* (London, 1964); Ion Raţiu, *Contemporary Romania* (Richmond, 1975); Juliusz Stroynowski, ed., *Who's Who in the Socialist Countries of Europe* (Munich, London, and Paris, 1989); Józef Darski, *Rumunia: Historia, współczesność, konflikty narodowe* (Warsaw, 1995); Dorina N. Rusu, *Membrii Academiei Române 1866–1999* (Bucharest, 1999); Ion Alexandrescu, Ion Bulei, Ion Mamina, and Iona Scurtu, *Enciclopedia de istorie României* (Bucharest, 2000).

BARLICKI Norbert, pseudonyms "Grzela," "Betani," and others (6 June 1880, Sieciechów, near Kozienice–27 September 1941, Auschwitz), Polish Socialist politician, lawyer, and journalist. Barlicki initially was an adherent of **Józef Piłsudski**; in 1902–6 he was a member of the Polish Socialist Party (PPS), then the PPS-Left (1906–14), and then the PPS-Revolutionary Faction. Between 1917 and 1918 he was a member of the Central Workers' Committee and the Peasant Union, and in 1919 he returned to the PPS. Between 1919 and 1939 he was a member of the Chief Council of the PPS and in 1920–26, a member of the Central Executive Committee (CEC); between 1926 and 1931 he served as president of the CEC. From November 1918 to January 1919 he was deputy minister of interior in the government of **Jędrzej Moraczewski**. In 1919–33 he was an MP, and between 1920 and 1926 he served as president of the Union of Polish Socialist Deputies (Związek Polskich Posłów Socjalistycznych). In 1920 he was a member of the State Defense Council. From February to April 1926 he was minister of public works. After the coup of May 1926 he joined the opposition to the *sanacja* regime. Co-organizer of the center-left opposition (Centrolew), in 1930 Barlicki was arrested and imprisoned in the Brześć fortress. In January 1932 he was sentenced to two and one-half years' imprisonment. After his release in 1933 he became quite radicalized, favoring cooperation between the PPS and the Communist Party of Poland (KPP). From 1936 to 1937 he was editor-in-chief of *Dziennik popularny.* In his political journalism Barlicki propagated the ideas of a united people's front. In 1937 he was elected mayor of Łódź, but he was not approved by the state authorities. From 1939 to 1940 he co-organized leftist Socialist groups. In 1940 he edited an underground newspaper, *Chłop i robotnik*. Arrested in 1940 by the Germans, he perished in the Auschwitz concentration camp. He authored *Aleksander Dębski: Życie i działalność, 1857–1935* (Aleksander Dębski: Life and activity, 1857–1935; 1937) and *Proletariat* (1947). (JS)

Sources: *Słownik polityków polskich XX wieku* (Poznań, 1998); Jan Tomicki, ed., *Norbert Barlicki: Wybór przemówień i artykułów z lat 1918–1939* (Warsaw, 1964); Jan Tomicki, *Norbert Barlicki, 1880–1941: Działalność polityczna* (Warsaw, 1968); Norbert Barlicki, *Muszą zamilknąć spory na lewicy: Wybór pism* (Warsaw, 1980); Marian Leczyk, ed., *Sprawa brzeska* (Warsaw, 1987).

BARONS Krišjānis (31 October 1835, Strutele, Courland–8 March 1923, Riga), Latvian folklorist, journalist, and writer; one of the originators of the Latvian national awakening. Barons was the son of a provincial official. In 1855 he graduated from a gymnasium in Mitava (Jeglava), and in 1856–60 he studied mathematics and astronomy at the university in Dorpat (Tartu), where he took part in the social life of Latvian students. In 1856 he published his first story and soon after a geography textbook. In 1862 he moved to Petersburg, where until 1865 he co-edited the magazine *Pēterburgas avīzes* (from 1862 he was its editor-in-chief). Later, he worked as a translator in the Russian Ministry of Education. He was the author of the first Latvian bibliography. He wrote articles on social and political issues, stories, and poems. From 1867 he worked as a private tutor and later as a German teacher in Moscow. He was affiliated with the Moscow Society of Friends of the Natural Sciences, Anthropology, and Ethnography. In 1893 he returned to Riga and continued working on a compilation and scholarly edition of Latvian folk song texts, a project that began in 1878. He was a precursor of the Latvian science of folklore. Between 1894 and 1915, 217,996 folk songs edited by Barons were published in eight volumes. In independent Latvia Barons enjoyed great respect as one of the main developers of Latvian cultural life. (EJ)

Sources: A. Baumanis, *Krišjānis Barons* (Riga, 1935); *Krišjāņa Barona piemiņai* (Riga, 1962); K. Arājs, *Krišjānis Barons un latvju dainas* (Riga, 1985); *Atmiņas: Stāsta K. Barons un laikabiedri* (Riga, 1985); R. Pussars, *Pie dižozola saknēm* (Riga, 1985); S. Viese, *Mūža raksts* (Riga, 1985); *Krišjānis Barons: Bibliogrāfiskais rādītājs* (Riga, 1990).

BARTEL Kazimierz (3 March 1882, Lemberg [Lwów, Lviv])–26 July 1941, Lwów), Polish politician and mathematician. The son of a railway worker, Bartel was trained as a metalworker, and in 1901 he graduated from high school in Lwów. From 1902 to 1907 he studied machine construction at the Lwów Polytechnic and until 1909, philosophy and mathematics at Lwów University. Then he continued studies at the university in Munich. After returning home, he started working at the Lwów Polytechnic, where he got a chair in descriptive geometry in 1913. In 1917 he became professor. During World War I he served in the Austrian army, and in November 1918 he organized a Polish railway regiment to fight against the Ukrainians in Lwów. In 1919 he took command of the railway troops, and then he took part in the Polish-Soviet war. In December 1919 he became minister of railways in the government of **Leopold Skulski.** He continued to serve in this capacity in the subsequent government until December 1920. In 1922 he won a parliamentary seat on behalf of the Polish Peasant Party Liberation (Polskie Stronnictwo Ludowe Wyzwolenie), but in 1925, in protest against its plans to expropriate large estates without compensation to their owners, he withdrew from the party and founded the Club of Labor, supporting **Józef Piłsudski.**

After the coup of May 1926, Bartel was prime minister five times (15 May–4 June 1926, 8 June–24 September 1926, 27–30 September 1926, 27 June 1928–13 April 1929, and 29 December 1929–29 March 1930) and deputy prime minister once (2 October 1926–27 June 1928). Until January 1927 he was also minister of religious denominations and public education. His major task as head of government after the coup was to stabilize the country and gain social support. The state of emergency was abolished, construction of the port of Gdynia was accelerated, and food prices were regulated. After **Ignacy Mościcki** was elected president, Bartel created a new cabinet, which prepared an amendment to the constitution strengthening the role of the president, and introduced personnel changes in the state administration. As a result of a parliamentary crisis, in September 1926 his government had to resign, but he was given the task of creating another cabinet. Since its composition was exactly the same as that of the preceding cabinet, relations between the ruling circle and the parliament grew tense. When Piłsudski became prime minister, Bartel was practically the acting head of government and mediated between Piłsudski and the parliament. When the conflict with the parliament became aggravated and Piłsudski resigned, Bartel created another government. Seen as Piłsudski's moderate follower, he also faced strong opposition in the government, where advocates of a hard line criticized him for liberalism and subjection to the parliament. In April he resigned, but he soon became head of government again. During his fifth term he got involved in a sharp conflict with the parliament, which passed a vote of no confidence on several of his ministers. As a result Bartel himself resigned. The Piłsudski tactics of manipulating Bartel were known as "Bartelling," since despite his formally high position Bartel did not belong to the inner circle of Piłsudski aides.

Leaving the political scene, Bartel gave up his parliamentary mandate and returned to the Lwów Polytechnic. In 1930 he became its rector. As an opponent of confrontation with the opposition, in the Brześć trial he testified as a witness for the defense. In 1937 President Mościcki appointed him senator, but Bartel did not return to politics. In 1926–38 he belonged to the Great National Lodge. After the outbreak of World War II and the entry of the Soviet army, he worked at the Lwów Polytechnic, adopting a submissive attitude toward the Soviets. When the Germans entered the city, on 21 July 1941 he was arrested and soon shot. He was the author of (among other works) *Geometria wykreślna* (Descriptive geometry; 1919); *Perspektywa malarska* (Perspectives in painting, 2 vols.; 1928–58); and *Mowy parlamentarne* (Parliamentary speeches; 1928). (PU)

Sources: Adam Próchnik, *Pierwsze piętnastolecie Polski niepodległej* (Warsaw, 1983); Władysław T. Kulesza, *Koncepcje ideowo-polityczne obozu rządzącego w Polsce w latach 1926–1935* (Wrocław, 1985); *Prezydenci i premierzy Drugiej Rzeczypospolitej* (Warsaw, 1992); *Kto był kim w Drugiej Rzeczypospolitej* (Warsaw, 1994); Ludwik Malinowski, *Politycy II Rzeczypospolitej,* vol. 2 (Toruń, 1995); *Encyklopedia historii Drugiej Rzeczypospolitej* (Warsaw, 1999).

BARTÓK Béla (25 March 1881, Nagyszentmiklós [Sinnicolau Mare]–26 September 1945, New York), Hungarian composer, pianist, and ethnographer. Bartók inherited his musical interest and talent from his mother, the pianist Paula Voit. In 1892–96 he studied with László Erkel in Pozsony (Bratislava), and from 1899 he studied piano at the Musical Academy in Budapest, from which he graduated in 1903 and where he worked from 1907. In 1903 he made his first tour as a pianist (Vienna, Berlin, Pozsony). His first compositions (the symphonic poem *Kossuth* in 1903 and a suite for orchestra in 1905–7) bear the marks of inspiration from the works of Johannes Brahms and Richard Strauss. Influenced by his friendship with **Zoltan Kodály**, Bartók was increasingly interested in folklore (not only Hungarian folklore), and he collected it as he traveled through the Carpathian region, the Balkans, and North Africa. Drawing from the motifs, rhythms, and harmonies of folk music, as well as from Kodály's works, Bartók created his own Hungarian style. Initially Hungarian audiences received his works with reserve. As a result he went through a crisis and withdrew from public life for a couple of years.

Despite the crisis Bartók worked uninterruptedly, and he wrote music for three stage works—an opera, *A*

kékszakállú herceg vára (Bluebeard's castle; 1911), and the ballets *A fából faragott királyfi* (The wooden prince; 1914–16) and *A csodálatos mandarin* (The miraculous Mandarin; 1919). During the Soviet Hungarian Republic (1919) Bartók joined the Directorate of Musicians, so after the counterrevolution he was not allowed to teach for a year. In 1923 he divorced his wife, Marta Ziegler, and married a student, Ditta Pásztory. In the 1920s he toured Germany, Great Britain, France, the Netherlands, and Italy. In 1928 he went to the United States and the Soviet Union. His growing foreign reputation increased his popularity in Hungary and resulted in a commission in 1923 to compose a suite commemorating the five hundredth anniversary of the establishment of Budapest. Because of Bartók's unwillingness to publicly support Hungarian claims to territories lost as a result of World War I, there was antipathy against him among nationalist circles. Preaching international reconciliation, he composed the *Cantata Profana* (1930). In 1934 he left the Musical Academy in Budapest to focus on the source materials he had gathered. This resulted in the work *Népzenénk és a szomszéd népek népzenéje* (Our folk music and our neighbors'; 1934). In 1936 he made his last ethnographic trip, this time to Turkey.

Bartók was at the height of his creativity in 1926–39. His formal discipline and great taste in combining elements of classical music with stylized folk motifs resulted in such works as his first and second piano concertos (1926, 1930–31), the *Sonata for Two Pianos and Percussion* (1937), and the *Second Violin Concerto* (1937–38). In reaction to the ban on his music in the Third Reich and Italy and fearing the growing influence of the Fascists in Hungary, in 1940 Bartók emigrated with his family to the United States, where he taught as visiting professor at Columbia University in New York. It was then that he composed the *Concerto for Orchestra* (1943) and—upon the request of Yehudi Menuhin—the *Sonata for Violin* (1944). He died of leukemia a few months after World War II. His ashes were brought to Hungary in 1988. After the war, both under communism and later, he was recognized as the most outstanding Hungarian pianist and composer, as well as an untiring seeker of a synthesis in music of East and West. His work as a musical ethnographer, as well as his creative talent, contributed greatly to the survival and popularization of the most typical features and motifs of East and Central European musical cultures. At the same time he was one of the pioneers of modern art of the early twentieth century. (MS)

Sources: János Deményi, *Bartók élete és művei* (Budapest, 1948); Witold Rudziński, *Warsztat kopozytorski Beli Bartoka* (Kraków,

1964); *Béla Bartók Letters* (London, 1971); Tedd Crow, ed., *Bartok Studies* (Detroit, 1976); *Béla Bartók: Mit Selbstzeugnissen und Bilddokumenten* (Hamburg, 1977); Malcolm Gillies, *Béla Batók Essays* (Lincoln, Neb., 1993); *Bartok Remembered* (London, 1991); *Béla Bartók, 1881–1945* (Paris, 1993); Benjamin Suchoff, ed., *Így látták Bartókot* (Budapest, 1995); Peter Laki, ed., *Bartok and His World* (Princeton, 1995); Ernő Lendvai, *Bartók és Kodály harmóniavilága* (Budapest, 1997).

BARTOSZEWSKI Władysław (19 February 1922, Warsaw), Polish historian, diplomat, and social and political activist. During the Nazi occupation Bartoszewski was imprisoned in the Auschwitz concentration camp (1940–41). From 1941 to 1944 he studied Polish philology at the underground Warsaw University, and he graduated in 1949. He worked for the Front of Polish Renaissance, a secret Catholic organization, and from 1942, in the Office of Information and Propaganda (Biuro Informacji i Propagandy [BIP]) of the High Command of the Home Army (Komenda Główna Armii Krajowej [KG AK]). Engaged in saving the Jews, from 1942 he belonged to the Provisional Committee of Assistance to Jews, Żegota. From 1943 he was deputy head of the Jewish section of the Department of Interior of the Homeland Delegation of the Government-in-Exile. He took part in the Warsaw Uprising of 1944, and in 1945 he was secretary of the BIP KG AK *Biuletyn Informacyjny*. He belonged to the underground organization Nie and worked in the Homeland Delegation of Armed Forces.

In 1945 Bartoszewski started working in the Chief Commission to Investigate German Crimes in Poland. In 1946–82 he belonged to the Association of Polish Journalists. In 1946 he joined the Polish Peasant Party (Polskie Stronnictwo Ludowe [PSL]) of **Stanisław Mikołajczyk** and worked in the editorial staff of *Gazeta Ludowa*. Arrested during the repression of the PSL, he spent 1946–48 and 1949–54 in prison. Rehabilitated in 1955, he worked for the Association of Polish Librarians and from 1957 to 1960, at the weekly *Stolica*. From 1957 he wrote for the *Tygodnik Powszechny*, and in 1961–62 he was active in the political discussion group, the Crooked Circle Club. From 1963 he was a secret correspondent for Radio Free Europe (RFE). In 1966 he received the medal of Righteous among Nations. In 1970 he was repressed (his home was searched, he was investigated, and a few years' ban was placed on his publications) for his work for RFE and for opposition activities (for example, the preparation of the "Letter of 34," from intellectuals to the prime minister concerning censorship). From 1972 to 1984 he was secretary general of the Polish PEN club; from 1973 to 1985 he lectured at the Catholic University of Lublin, and in 1974–75 he held a secret seminar in

Warsaw on the recent history of Poland. A participant in the Polish Independence Agreement, in 1978 he co-founded the Society of Scientific Courses and lectured there on World War II history and Polish-Jewish relations. He appealed many times to the Communist authorities to respect human rights, arguing, for example, for a pardon for **Andrzej** and Benedykt **Czuma** in 1974 and the limitation of censorship in 1978. In the summer of 1980 he supported striking workers.

Bartoszewski was engaged in the creation of the free trade union Solidarity. Interned during the period of martial law from December 1981 to April 1982, he was released under pressure from international public opinion. Active in underground publishing activities, in 1983–90 he also lectured in Germany. In 1986 he received the prestigious Peace Award of German Booksellers. In 1987 he was invited by Lech Wałęsa to participate with a group of intellectuals to sign a declaration of goals for the Polish opposition. President of the International Council of the State Museum in Oświęcim (Auschwitz) from 1990, in 1991 Bartoszewski received honorary citizenship from the State of Israel. In 1995 he received the Order of the White Eagle. In 1990–95 he was ambassador to Austria; from March 1995 to December 1996 and from July 2000 to October 2001 he was minister of foreign affairs. Senator from 1997 to 2001, he played an important role in the improvement of Polish-German and Polish-Jewish relations. In 2003 he criticized German plans to erect a Center of the Expelled (Vetriebene) in Berlin, arguing against a selective interpretation of the fate of war victims. An honorary doctor at several universities, he authored *Prawda o von dem Bachu* (The truth about von dem Bach; 1962); *Ten jest z ojczyzny mojej: Polacy z pomocą Żydom 1939–1945* (Righteous among nations: How Poles helped the Jews, 1939–1945, co-authored with Zofia Lewinówna; 1967); *Warszawski pierścień śmierci* (Warsaw death ring; 1967), *Palmiry* (1969); *1859 dni Warszawy* (1859 Days of Warsaw; 1974), *Polskie państwo podziemne* (The Polish underground state; 1979); *Die Warszchauer Ghetto: Wie es wirklich war* (The Warsaw ghetto: How it really was; 1983); the memoirs *Warto być przyzwoitym* (It is worth being an honest person; 1990); *The Convent of Auschwitz* (1991); and the collections of speeches and interviews *Above Divisions* (2001) and *Common European Responsibility* (2001). (PK)

Sources: *Kto jest kim w Polsce: Informator biograficzny* (Warsaw, 1984); *Opozycja w PRL: Słownik biograficzny 1956–1989* (Warsaw, 2000); *Władysław Bartoszewski: Życie i twórczość* (Warsaw, 1999); *Prawda i Pojednanie. W 80. Rocznicę urodzin Władysława Bartoszewskiego* (Warsaw, 2002); Roman Kuźniar and Krzysztof Szczepanik, eds., *Polityka zagraniczna RP 1989–2002* (Warsaw, 2002).

BAŠAGIĆ-REDŽEPASIĆ Safetbeg (6 May 1870, Nevesinje, Herzegovina–9 April 1934, Sarajevo), Bosnian poet, historian of literature, and politician. Born into a Muslim family belonging to the Ottoman elite, Bašagíc-Redžepasić was the son of a poet writing in Turkish. After moving to Sarajevo, he went to a local high school (1885–95). In 1899 he graduated from Oriental studies at Vienna University. In 1910 he received a Ph.D.; his thesis was, *Die Bosniaken und Herzegovcen auf dem Gebiete der islamischen Literatur* (Bosnians and Herzegovinians in Islamic literature). He taught Arabic in a high school in Sarajevo (1900–1906) and established a number of cultural and social organizations, including Gayret, El-Kame, and a Muslim club (1903–7). Elected to the Bosnian Assembly, after the death of Ali Hodzha bey Firdus in 1910 he became its speaker. He supported both the Habsburgs and broad autonomy for Bosnians in the Austro-Hungarian Empire. He also cooperated with conservative Hungarian politicians. He wrote for such periodicals as *Behar* and *Ogledalo*, and he published many works on the history of Bosnia and Herzegovina, as well as on the history of literature. He translated classical Arabic works and published a couple of collections of his own poems. After World War I he withdrew from politics. From 1919 he worked as a custodian in a museum in Sarajevo. He amassed a significant collection of books in the field of Oriental studies. At the end of his life he advocated a rapprochement of Bosnians with Croats, which was reflected in his work *Znameniti Hrvati, Bosnjaci i Hercegovci u Turskoj carevini* (Outstanding Croats, Bosnians, and Herzegovinians in the Turkish state; 1931). In 1971 his *Izabrana djela* (Selected works) were published in Sarajevo. (MC)

Sources: *Biographisches Lexikon,* vol. 1; Ante Čuvalo, *Historical Dictionary of Bosnia and Herzegovina* (Lanham, Md., 1987); "Safvet Beg Basagic-Redzepasic," bosna.com/basagic.html; "Safetbeg Basagic-Redzepasic," uni/koeln.de/phil/fak/soeg/ethnos/inhalte/inhalte2dzaja.htm.

BASANAVIČIUS Jonas (23 November 1851, Ožkabaliai, near Vilkaviškis–16 February 1927, Wilno [Vilnius]), Lithuanian doctor, ethnographer, and politician. The son of a peasant, in 1873 Basanavčius started to study history at the University of Moscow, but after a year he moved to its medical department. He graduated in 1878, and two years later he left for Bulgaria, where he practiced as a doctor and directed a hospital in Lom Polanka. In 1891 he adopted Bulgarian citizenship. In 1892 he assumed the position of director of a hospital ward in Varna, and in 1894 he became the personal physician of Prince Ferdinand. At that time he was a member of the Bulgarian Democratic Party, but he was always interested in his homeland. During his many trips to Germany and Austria he studied source materials concerning Lithuanian history. He also collected folktales and folk songs, which he published in *Mitteilungen der Litauischen Literarischen Gesselschaft* (1880–85), edited in Tilsit in so-called Lithuania Minor, belonging to Germany. In 1883 he was co-founder of the first periodical in Lithuanian, *Aušra*. He edited a number of collections of legends, tales, and folk songs, including *Ožkabalių dainos* (Songs from Ožkabaliai, 2 vols.; 1902); *Lietuviškos pasakos* (Lithuanian tales, 2 vols.; 1898–1902); *Iš gyvenimo lietuviškų vėlių ir velnių* (From the life of Lithuanian devil spirits; 1903); and *Lietuviškos pasakos ivarios* (Various Lithuanian tales, 4 vols.; 1903–5). All together he published about 1,000 stories and 300 folk songs, as well as a description of about 280 plants typical of the Lithuanian flora. Historical works in which he tried to prove a Tracian-Phrygian origin of the Lithuanians were of less importance.

When Basanavičius reached retirement age in January 1905, he asked the Russian Ministry of Interior for consent to return to Lithuania. He could not wait to receive a reply, and in April 1905 he secretly crossed the Russian border and came to Vilnius at a time of growing revolutionary tensions. On 29 October 1905 he appealed in *Vilniaus Žinios* for the convention of an all-Lithuanian congress in Vilnius. During the Great Assembly in Vilnius (4–5 December 1905) he called for unity among all political groups in the struggle for freedom, demanding an autonomous Lithuania with a parliament in Vilnius and the introduction of Lithuanian in the schools, churches, and offices. A major problem was that Lithuanians were a minority in the Vilnius area. After the suppression of the revolution the Russian authorities eased their policies toward the Lithuanians, so in February 1907 Basanavičius established the Lithuanian Research Society (LRS) in Vilnius and presented it with his own huge collections. He also edited the periodical *Lietuvių Tauta*. He represented a conciliatory attitude toward Russia and an increasingly confrontational attitude toward the Poles. On his initiative, in 1912 Lithuanian priests sent a letter to the Holy See demanding the elimination of Polish from the church ministry in Lithuania. In 1913, along with **Martynas Yčas**, he went to the United States, where he collected funds for the construction of LRS headquarters. The outbreak of World War I made such construction impossible, while the donated funds soon lost their value.

Basanavičius spent World War I years in Vilnius. In July 1917 he gained German consent for the organization of a conference of Lithuanian delegates on local self-government. When on 22 September 1917 the Lithuanian Council was created, he, as its senior member, was the first to sign the declaration of Lithuanian independence on 16 February 1918. He stayed in Vilnius during Bolshevik rule at the turn of 1919, as well as after the town was taken over by the Poles, first in April 1919 and then in October 1920. In the Lithuanian elections of June 1920 he ran on the list of the (nationalist) Party of National Progress, but he lost. Until the end of his life he demanded the incorporation of the Vilnius area to Lithuania. He also continued with his ethnographic explorations and journalism. He authored memoirs titled *Autobiografija*, published in *Lietuvių Tauta* in 1928. (WR)

Sources: *EL*, vol. 1; Saulius Sužiedelis, *Historical Dictionary of Lithuania* (Lanham, Md., 1997); R. Mackevičius, *Jonas Basanavičius* (Vilnius, 1930); Jerzy Ochmański, *Litewski ruch narodowo-kulturalny w XIX wieku* (Białystok, 1965); Alfred E. Senn, *Jonas Basanavičius: The Patriarch of the Lithuanian National Renaissance* (Newtonville, Mass., 1980); Adolfas Nezabitauskas, *Jonas Basanavičius* (Vilnius, 1990); Henryk Wisner, *Litwa: Dzieje państwa i narodu* (Warsaw, 1999).

BATA István (5 March 1910, Tura–17 August 1982, Budapest), Hungarian Communist activist. Bata graduated from primary school, and in 1935–38 he worked as a tramway conductor in Budapest. In 1930 he joined the Social Democratic Party. From 1939 he was a member of the leadership of the Trade Union of Tramway Workers. In 1942 he was briefly arrested and later kept under police surveillance. From 1945 he was a member of the leadership of the Trade Union of State Workers and a member of the Hungarian Communist Party (HCP). From 1947 to 1949 he was HCP secretary of the Third Quarter of Budapest. In 1949 he was accepted into the army as a colonel, and then he was sent for training to the Military Academy in Moscow. After his graduation, in 1950 he became commander of the National Air Defense with the rank of general. In October 1950 he was appointed Chief of the General Staff (until August 1953). In 1951–53 he was a deputy member of the Central Committee (CC) of the Hungarian Workers' Party (HWP), and in June 1953 he became a CC member and a deputy member of the HWP Politburo. In July 1953, after the dismissal of **Mihály Farkas**, he was appointed minister of national defense, and in 1954 he was promoted to the rank of general of the army. In May 1955 he belonged to the Hungarian delegation that signed the Warsaw Pact. At the HWP CC meeting on the night of 23– 24 October 1956 he was dismissed from all his posts. Four days later he left for Moscow. On 4 November, the day of the second Soviet invasion, he returned to Hungary, but the Kádár government did not accept his return, and in February 1957 the CC of the new Hungarian Socialist Workers' Party (HSWP) extended the term of his exile. In September 1958 he was allowed to return. Excluded from the HSWP and deprived of his military

rank in February 1959, he returned to his early trade. He became director of a tramway depot, and later he worked as head of the Department of Traffic Safety in the Budapest Transportation Company. In 1972 he retired. (JT)

Sources: *Magyar Életrajzi Lexikon (1978–1991)* (Budapest, 1994); *Magyar Nagylexikon*, vol. 3 (Budapest, 1994); *Magyarország 1944–1956*, CD-ROM, 1956-os Intézet (Budapest, 2001); *Új Magyar Életrajzi Lexikon*, vol. 1 (Budapest, 2001).

BAT'A Tomáš (3 April 1876, Zlín–12 July 1932, Otrokovice), Czech entrepreneur. Bat'a was apprenticed to his father, a shoemaker. At the age of eighteen, along with his brother Antonín and his sister Anna, he founded his own shoe company, which was bequeathed to Antonín. The firm expanded thanks to its introduction of light and cheap footwear to the market. In 1904 Bat'a began the machine production of shoes, founding the first factory of this kind in Austria-Hungary. To gain experience, he left for the United States, where he got a job with Ford, the first company to introduce assembly-line production methods. In the 1920s, thanks to the introduction of similar innovations in his factories and to a reduction in the cost of raw materials, Bat'a became a monopolist in the domestic market (he controlled 80 percent of the production of footwear), while Czechoslovakia became the world leader in footwear production in 1928. In order to avoid the high duties imposed on the import of his products in other countries, from 1929 to 1931 Bat'a founded branches in Germany, Switzerland, Poland, and India. At the beginning of the 1930s he was the largest entrepreneur in light industry in Czechoslovakia, employing sixteen thousand workers in thirty-two factories. He introduced modern methods of management and organization, as well as an innovative system, called *batismus*, that motivated workers. In 1931 his industrial plants were transformed into a joint-stock company, and after World War II they were nationalized by the Communist authorities. Bat'a was killed in an air accident. In 1942 his memoirs, *How I Began*, were published; in 1986 came *Úvahy a projevy* (Comments and speeches), and in 1992, *Knowledge in Action: The Bata System of Management*. (PU)

Sources: *ČBS*; J. T. Pagač, *Bat'a a 30 let jeho podnikatelské práce* (N.p., 1926); A. Cekota, *Bat'a-Myšlenky, činy, život, práce* (N.p., 1929); *Kto bol kto za I. ČSR* (Bratislava, 1993); *Politická elita meziválečného Československa 1918–1938: Kdo byl kdo za první republiky* (Prague, 1998).

BATTĚK Rudolf (2 November 1924, Bratislava), Czech sociologist and political activist. At the end of World War II Battěk took part in the resistance movement, and in 1952 he graduated from the Higher Political and Social School in Prague. In 1951–61 he worked as an economist in the communal administration; from 1961 to 1965, in the railways; and in 1965–69, in the Sociological Institute of the Czechoslovak Academy of Sciences. During the Prague Spring of 1968 he co-founded the Club of Engaged Non-Party Members (Klub Angažovaných Nestraníků). From July 1968 to November 1969 he was a deputy to the Czech National Council. In the spring and summer of 1969 he opposed the so-called normalization, demanding a debate on the political situation in the council. In September 1969 he was stripped of immunity and arrested, and two months later he was deprived of the parliamentary mandate. In 1969–70 he was in prison, accused of an attempt to overthrow the republic. After his release he worked as a doorkeeper in the State Statistical Office. In 1971 he was arrested again, accused of distributing leaflets before an election, and sentenced to three and a half years in prison. After his release in 1974 he took a job as a turner, and then as a shop window cleaner. In 1977 he signed Charter 77, and in 1978 he co-founded the Committee for the Defense of the Unjustly Prosecuted (Výbor na Obranu Nespravedlivě Stíhaných [VONS]). In 1980 he became the spokesman for Charter 77. Arrested for the third time and falsely accused of assault on a social worker and in 1981 additionally of an "attempt to overthrow the republic," he was sentenced to five and a half years in prison. He was released in 1985. From 1983 he was an honorary member of the Executive Committee of the Czechoslovak Social Democracy in exile in Zurich.

In 1988 Battěk belonged to the founders of the Movement for Civic Freedom (Hnutí za Občanskou Svobodu), and in November 1989 he took part in the creation of the Civic Forum (Občanské Fórum [OF]). From January 1990 to June 1992 he was a deputy in the House of Commons of the Federal Assembly and from June 1990, its speaker and deputy speaker of the Federal Assembly. In 1989–90 he was deputy chairman of the preparatory committee of the Czechoslovak Social Democratic Party (Československá Sociální Demokracie [ČSSD]), but before the elections of June 1990 he organized the Social Democratic Club within the OF and was excluded from the ČSSD. In 1992 he founded the movement Democrats 92, whose aim was to defend the Czechoslovak state, but in the elections of June 1992 he lost and retired from political life. He devoted himself to journalism. In 1994 he became chairman of the European Movement in the Czech Republic, and in 1996 he lost in the election to the senate, running as an independent candidate. (PU)

Sources: *ČBS*; *Československí politici: 1918–1991* (Prague, 1991); *Kdo byl kdo v našich dějinach ve 20. stoleti,* vol. 1 (Prague, 1998); *Who's Who in the Socialist Countries of Europe,* vol. 1 (Munich, 1989); *Kdo je kdo 91/92 Česká Republika: Federální orgány ČSFR,* vol. 1 (Prague, 1991).

BAZHAN Mykola (9 October 1904, Kam'yanets Podilskyy [Kamieniec Podolski]–23 November 1983, Kiev), Ukrainian poet, translator, and Soviet activist. Born into a military family, Bazhan was brought up in Uman. In 1921 he began to study at the Institute of Foreign Affairs in Kiev, but he did not complete his studies. In the 1920s he was involved in cinematography and edited the magazine *Kino.* In 1925 he made his literary debut with a futurist poem, *Aeromarch.* He was one of the co-founders of the Free Academy of Proletarian Literature (Vaplite). He also was affiliated with a group called Nova Heneratsiia (New Generation) and with the magazine *Literaturnyi iarmarok.* Abandoning the futurism and constructivism in the collection *17-i patrul* (Seventeenth patrol; 1926), he became a romantic expressionist in his collections *Budivli* (Buildings; 1929) and *Chyslo* (Number; 1931). A leading figure in the cultural revival of the Ukraine in the 1920s, Bazhan created his own style, marked by a dynamic imagination; monumentalism; and a richness of language, metaphors, and rhymes. In the collection *Rozmova serdets* (Conversation of hearts) he criticized the traditions of Russia. The above-mentioned volumes, as well as his subsequent collections, *Doroha* (Path; 1930), *Poezii* (Poems; 1930), and *Sliptsi* (The blind; 1933), served as grounds to accuse him of "detachment from Socialist reality," abstractionism, idealism, and Ukrainian nationalism.

Bazhan gained official recognition at a time of mounting Stalinist terror. Between 1935 and 1937 he published a trilogy, *Bezsmertia* (Immortality), dedicated to Sergey Kirov; he also translated from the Georgian the poem *Shota Rustavele Vitiaz' v tigrovii shkuri* (Knight in tiger's skin; 1937), and he published the collections *Bat'ky i syny* (Fathers and sons; 1938) and *Iamby* (Iambs; 1940), which were written in the spirit of Stalinist patriotism. From 1943 to 1948, within the framework of Stalin's policy of winning over the Ukrainians, Bazhan served as deputy president of the USSR Council of Ministers. He was a long-term member of the CC of the Communist Party of the Ukraine (Bolshevik) and of the Supreme Soviets of the Ukrainian SSR and the USSR. In 1941–45 he wrote works on war themes. He received a Stalinist award for the collection *Kliatva* (Oath; 1941). After the war he published several works of propaganda. After Stalin's death he remained in the public realm: he presided over the Union of Ukrainian Writers (1953–59); from 1951 he was a full member of the USSR Academy of Sciences, and from 1958 he was head of the publishing house Ukrains'ka Radians'ka Entsyklopedia. He wrote a series of verses and poems in which he more extensively drew on the European cultural heritage. These works include the poems *Mitskevych v Odesi: 1825 rik* (Mickiewicz in

Odessa: The year 1825; 1957); *Italiis'ky zustrichi* (Italian meetings; 1961); *Bohy Hretsii* (Gods of Greece; 1968); and translations of the poetry of Cyprian Kamil Norwid. Bazhan received the Shevchenko Award for *Polit kriz' buriu* (Flight in the storm), and he based the philosophical volume of lyrical poetry *Chotyry opovidannia pro nadiiu* (Four stories of hope; 1967) on the motifs in the poetry of Rainer Maria Rilke. The last volumes he wrote also received wide recognition: *Umans'ki spohady* (Memoirs from Uman; 1970) and *Nichni rozdumy staroho maistra* (Night reflections of an old master; 1974). (TS)

Sources: *Encyclopedia of Ukraine,* vol. 1 (Toronto, 1984); *Rozstrilane vidrodzhennia,* ed. Yurii Lavrinenko (Paris, 1959); Y. Adelgeim, *Mikola Bazhan* (Moscow, 1970); Y. Surovtsev, *Poeziia Mikoly Bazhana: Kriticheskii ocherk* (Moscow, 1970); N. Kostenko, *Poetyka Mykoly Bazhana 1923–40 rr.* (Kiev, 1971); N. Kostenko, *Poetyka Mykoly Bazhana 1941–1977* (Kiev, 1978).

BEBLER Aleš (8 June 1907, Idria–12 August 1981, Ljubljana), Slovene Communist activist and diplomat. Bebler studied law in Ljubljana and from 1927 in Paris, where he received a Ph.D. in 1930. In 1927 he joined the Association of Yugoslav Communist Youth (Savez Komunističke Omladine Jugoslavije [SKOJ]), and in 1929, the Communist Party of Yugoslavia. He was also secretary of the International Organization of Assistance to the Revolutionaries, organizing legal and financial aid to political prisoners and striking workers. While in Paris, he edited the newspapers *Plamen* and *Delo*. In 1933 he went to Moscow for an annual party training program. He took part in the Spanish Civil War as captain of the Fifteenth International Brigade. He was twice wounded and went to France for treatment. When in 1939 he came to Yugoslavia, he was arrested and sentenced to one year in prison. After his release he became deputy head of the Commission for Agitation and Propaganda of the Central Committee (CC) of the Communist Party of Slovenia (CPS) and was active in the Association of Friends of the USSR.

During World War II Bebler organized Communist guerrillas in Slovenia. In 1942–44 he operated in the Primorski krai. He was a member of the regional CPS committee and of the regional council of the Slovene Liberation Front (SLF). From June to November 1944 he was a member of the CPS committee in Steiermark. In September 1944 he became a member of the SLF executive committee, and in May 1945, minister of finance of the Slovene republic. In August 1945 he assumed the position of deputy minister of foreign affairs of Yugoslavia. He belonged to the Yugoslav delegation during the first six sessions of the UN General Assembly, and in 1950–51 he was Yugoslav representative to the United Nations. He

closely followed the line of **Josip Broz Tito**. After the Cominform condemned Yugoslavia in June 1948, Bebler implemented Tito's opening to the West. Between 1948 and 1954 he belonged to the CC of the CPS (as of 1952, the Union of Slovene Communists) and to the CC of the CPY (as of 1952, the Union of Yugoslav Communists). In 1955–57 he was ambassador to France, then chairman of the parliamentary foreign affairs commission, and afterwards ambassador to Indonesia. In 1963 he was appointed judge of the Constitutional Tribunal of Yugoslavia. He published (among other works) the following: *Za pravedne granice nove Jugoslavije* (For just frontiers of the new Yugoslavia; 1949); *Potovanje po sončnih deželah* (Journeys in sunny lands; 1956); *Otroci zemlje in morja* (Children of earth and sea; 1966); and *Čez drn in strn* (Across country; 1981). (AO)

Sources: *Enciklopedija Jugoslavije,* vol. 1 (Zagreb, 1955); Lazitch; Edvard Kardelj, *Reminiscences* (London, 1982); Milovan Džilas, *Rise and Fall* (San Diego, 1985); *Enciklopedija Slovenije,* vol. 1 (Ljubljana, 1987); Beatrice Heuser, *Western "Containment" Policies in the Cold War: The Yugoslav Case, 1948–53* (London, 1989).

BECHYNĚ Rudolf (6 April 1881, Nymburk–1 January 1948, Prague), Czech Social Democratic politician and journalist. Becjumě was a locksmith by profession. From 1905 he worked in the Social Democratic press (*Právo lidu* and *Rovnost*), and in 1909 he became the editor-in-chief of *Hlas Lidu,* which was published in Prostějov. At that time he established contacts with **Vlastimil Tusar**, who encouraged him to become a parliamentary correspondent from Vienna. From 1911 to 1918 he was an MP representing Social Democracy to the Austrian parliament. In 1915 he was arrested on the charge of treason and was sent to the eastern front with a rank or private. He returned from the front in January 1917, with his health seriously undermined. He resumed his activities in the Social Democratic Party, in which he represented a socially moderate wing. In the fall of 1917 an article of his was published in *Právo Lidu.* In it, Bechyně insisted that Social Democratic policy should become anti-Habsburg, and he demanded changes in the party executive ranks. When the postulated changes took place in 1918, he found himself in the party executive.

During the formation of the Czechoslovak state in the fall of 1918 Bechyně represented Social Democracy in the National Committee, and then he was an MP in parliament for twenty years (1918–38). Along with Tusar he formed the anti-Communist wing of Social Democracy. After the collapse of the Tusar government and the appointment of the nonparty cabinet of **Jan Černý** in 1920 Bechyně was a representative of his party in the Five, a non-parliamentary body consisting of the representatives of the five major parties in Czechoslovakia. This body was to ensure the stability of the country. Under the "red and green" government, based on a coalition of the Social Democrats and the Agrarians, Bechyně held many ministerial posts. He was minister of education between 1922 and 1924, minister of railways and deputy prime minister in 1925–26, minister of supplies between 1929 and 1932, and again minister of railways in 1932–38. He never accepted the Pact of Munich. In July 1939 he emigrated to Great Britain via Poland. In Great Britain, between 1940 and 1945 he was a member of the Czechoslovak National Council (Státní rada Československa) in London, and in 1940–41 he was the first president of the council. After the end of the war he returned to Czechoslovakia but not to political life, although he received offers to join the government. He was the author of the essay *Pero mi zustalo* (I have only my pen left; 1948). His daughter, Jarmila, was a well-known actress. (PU)

Sources: *ČBS*; *Kto bol kto za I. ČSR* (Bratislava, 1993); *Politická elita meziválečného Československa 1918–1938: Kdo byl kdo za prvni republiky* (Prague, 1998).

BECK Józef (4 October 1894, Warsaw–5 June 1944, Stanesti, Romania), Polish politician and diplomat. Beck came from a family of a labor, cooperative, and self-government activists. He grew up in Galicia and studied at the Polytechnic College in Lwów and the Export Academy in Vienna. He interrupted his education during World War I and was assigned to the artillery of the First Brigade of the Polish Legions. He fought on the Russian front—for example, at Kostiuchnówka, where he became famous for his courage on the battlefield. On behalf of the Polish Military Organization Beck went on a secret mission to the Ukraine. From 1918 he was in the Polish Army and took part in the Polish-Soviet war. Because of Beck's diplomatic skills, **Józef Piłsudski** often sent him on secret missions. In 1922–23 Beck was a military attaché in Paris and Brussels. In 1925 he graduated, with the rank of lieutenant colonel of artillery, from the Higher Military School in Warsaw. He was active in the coup of May 1926, being the chief of staff of Piłsudski's main armed forces. From 1926 to 1930 he was the chief of staff of the minister for military affairs; between the end of August 1930 and December 1930 he was deputy prime minister and minister without portfolio in Piłsudski's government. From 6 December 1930 he was vice minister, and from 2 November 1932, minister of foreign affairs. From 1935 he was a senator representing Warsaw.

Considered one of Piłsudski's most trusted confidants, Beck was chosen by Piłsudski to realize his vision of Polish foreign policy. Taking into account that the international balance in Europe was disturbed and that collective security on the continent was undermined, Piłsudski recommended that Beck concentrate on strengthening Polish foreign policy. After Piłsudski's death in May 1935, Beck tried to continue his policy, which consisted of maintaining an equal distance to both the Soviet Union and Germany. His efforts led to the signing of a non-aggression treaty with the USSR on 25 July 1932 and a non-aggression declaration with the Third Reich on 26 January 1934. On 5 May 1934 he extended the Polish-Soviet non-aggression treaty for ten years. He also sought the greater independence of Poland from France. He opposed Polish participation in collective agreements, fearing the violation of Polish interests by foreign powers. The policy of balancing between France and Germany, as well as between Germany and the USSR; Beck's decisive attitude toward Lithuania in March 1938; his forcing Czechoslovakia to cede Zaolzie to Poland in October 1938; and lingering (though unjust) imputations of Beck's having spied during his diplomatic mission in France—all these factors led to Beck's unpopularity in the European capitals. At first Beck thought that Germany did not pose a great threat to Poland. However, in 1938 and 1939 he rejected German demands from Poland (the incorporation of Gdańsk to the Third Reich, the extraterritorial corridor, and accession to the Anti-Comintern Pact). After the annexation of Czechoslovakia by Germany Beck accepted the security guarantees given to Poland by Great Britain on 31 March 1939, and he signed an alliance with Great Britain based on the treaties of 6 April 1939 and 25 August 1939.

After the renunciation of the Polish-German declaration of non-aggression by Hitler in April, on 5 May 1939 Beck gave a now famous address in the Sejm. In it, he reacted to Hitler's speech and to his demand for *Lebensraum* (living space) for the Germans. His words ("In Poland, we do not know the notion of peace at all cost. There is only one thing in the life of people, nations, and states that is invaluable. That thing is honor") brought him temporary popularity in Poland. During the British-French-Soviet talks in Moscow in the summer of 1939 Beck consequently rejected Moscow's demands for the right of the Red Army to march into Polish territory as an ally, because he feared that they would never leave Poland. The declaration of war on Germany by Great Britain and France on 3 September 1939 has been considered as Beck's diplomatic success. Nonetheless, Poland did not receive the help of the two powers. Along with the entire government Beck crossed the border into Romania on the night of 17–18 September

1939. He was interned in Romania. His attempt to escape failed. He spent the rest of his life in exile. After 1939, his policy was the subject of criticism from various sides in Poland and was often presented in an unfavorable light in the Western countries and the USSR, where Polish raison d'état was generally not taken into consideration. The question of whether his policy had any alternative remains open. In exile Beck wrote *Ostatni raport* (The last report; 1946), in which he explained his policy. (PK)

Sources: *Czy wiesz, kto to jest?* (Warsaw, 1937); Stanisław Mackiewicz, *Polityka Becka* (Paris, 1964); Doman Rogoyski, "Pułk. Józef Beck więźniem w Rumunii," *Zeszyty Historyczne,* 1970, no. 18; P. Starzeński, *Trzy lata z Beckiem* (London, 1972); Olgierd Terlecki, *Pułkownik Beck* (Kraków, 1985); Andrzej Albert (Wojciech Roszkowski), *Najnowsza historia Polski 1914–1993,* vol. 1 (Warsaw, 1995); *Słownik polityków polskich XX w.* (Poznań, 1998).

BEDNORZ Herbert (22 September 1908, Gliwice–12 April 1989, Katowice), Polish bishop. The son of a metalworker and Polish independence activist, after the division of Upper Silesia in 1922 Bendorz, along with his family, had to move to Katowice, where he graduated from high school. He studied at the Theological Department of the Jagiellonian University and at the Theological Seminary in Kraków. In June 1932 he was ordained and left for Louvain and Paris, where he received a Ph.D. He specialized in Catholic social teachings and canon law. After his return in 1937, he became secretary general of the Catholic Youth Association. During the German occupation he worked in the Brzeziny parish. From March 1946 he headed the ministry department of the Katowice curia. On 24 December he was consecrated auxiliary bishop of the Katowice diocese. On 4 November 1952 he was arrested for preparing an appeal to restore religious instruction in the schools and forced to move out of his diocese. He settled in Poznań, maintaining contacts with priests loyal to the purged bishops. In November 1956 he returned to Katowice, and after the death of Bishop **Stanisław Adamski**, on 12 November 1967 he became ordinary bishop of the Katowice diocese. Pope John XIII appointed him one of the consultants responsible for preparing the Second Vatican Council. He cooperated with the commission for the laity and mass media. He took part in four sessions of the council and served as the spokesman of the Polish Episcopate. He gave special attention to the ministry of workers and chaired the Commission for Ministry to Workers of the Conference of the Polish Episcopate. He strove to obtain Communist permission to build new churches, especially in new housing areas of big towns. In 1972–75 he organized the first synod of the Katowice diocese attracting the participation of lay believers.

Bednorz was a spokesman for the religious and cultural rights of Silesians. He encouraged pilgrimages of various social groups to Piekary, which shaped the social, religious, and political formation of Upper Silesian workers. For more than a dozen years the main preacher in Piekary was the Kraków cardinal Karol Wojtyła, later Pope **John Paul II**. Bednorz protested against the four-brigade system of work in Silesian mining, which was introduced in the 1970s and deprived miners of free Sundays. During the summer 1980 strikes, his call for free Sundays became one of the main demands of the striking workers and was agreed to by the authorities in the Jastrzębie agreement. Bednorz supported ministry to the strikers and endeavors to unite Solidarity structures in Upper Silesia and the Dąbrowskie region. During the period of martial law he repeatedly appealed to the authorities to free Solidarity activists. In March 1982 he established the Episcopal Committee of Relief to the Imprisoned and Interned. He also defended the cross, placed in front of the so-called Wujek mine, where riot police shot several miners in December 1981 and which was devastated by the security police. Caring for the formation of clerics, Bednorz, as the only bishop in Poland, sent them to a yearly training session in factories. In June 1983 he welcomed Pope John Paul II at Muchowiec Airfield, near Katowice, in the name of half a million believers. When Bednorz turned seventy-five, he offered his resignation and retired after the appointment of his successor in June 1985. (AGr)

Sources: *Słownik Biograficzny Katolickiego Duchowieństwa Śląskiego XIX i XX wieku* (Katowice, 1996); *Leksykon duchowieństwa represjonowanego w PRL w latach 1945–1989,* vol. 1 (Warsaw, 2002); Jerzy Myszor, *Historia diecezji katowickiej* (Katowice, 1996); Jerzy Myszor, "Życie i działalność ks. biskupa Herberta Bednorza (1908–1989): Szkic biograficzny," *Śląskie Studia Historyczno-Teologiczne,* 1989, vol. 22; Andrzej Grajewski, *Wygnanie, Diecezja katowicka w czasach stalinowskich* (Katowice, 2003).

BEGMA Vasyl (1 January 1906, Odessa–12 August 1965, Kiev), Soviet Communist activist in the Ukraine. In 1927 Begma joined the Communist Party, and from 1928 he held executive posts in the Komsomol, in trade unions, and in the Communist Party apparatus in the Kherson, Dnepropetrovsk, and Kharkiv regions. In 1938 he became secretary of the regional committee of the Communist Party (Bolshevik) of the Ukraine (CP[B]U) in Kiev. After the Polish Eastern Borderland was incorporated into the USSR, in 1939–41 Begma was first secretary of the regional party committee in Równe, supervising Soviet deportations. From 1940 he was a member of the Central Committee (CC) of the CP(B)U. In 1941–42 he belonged to the War Council of the Twelfth Army. In 1942–44 he was secretary of a secret CP(B)U committee in Równe, head of the regional partisan staff, and commander of a guerrilla detachment that operated against the Germans and against the Polish underground army. As a reward he was promoted to the rank of major general. From 1944 to 1949 he was first secretary of the regional party committee in Równe again, and in 1950–59 he was head of the party committee in Khmelnytskyi. From 1959 he was head of a CP(B)U CC department. He was also a deputy to the Supreme Council of the USSR and the Ukrainian SSR. (GM)

Sources: *Ukraiinska Radianska Encyklopediya*, vol. 1 (Kiev, 1977); Mieczysław Juchniewicz, *Polacy w radzieckim ruchu partyzanckim 1941–1945* (Warsaw, 1975).

BELISHOVA Liri (14 October 1926, Belishovë, near Ballsh), Albanian Communist activist. Born into a Muslim white-collar family, Belishova studied in Berat and in a training school for girls in Tirana. Attracted by the aims of **Liri Gega**, from 1940 she was affiliated with a Communist group in Shkodër. In February 1943 she joined the Communist Party and then became a member of the leadership of a Communist youth organization in Tirana. Suspended from school for taking part in an anti-Italian demonstration in July 1943, in which she lost an eye, in October 1944 she returned to Albania after an operation in a British hospital. She became a member of the secretariat of the Albanian Anti-Fascist Youth and of the Central Committee (CC) of the Communist Party of Albania (CPA), and from 1945 she was a member of the General Council of the Communist-controlled Democratic Front. She was in favor of the CPA's independence from the Yugoslav party and was in opposition to the **Koçi Xoxe** faction. After the death of her husband, **Nako Spiru**, who allegedly committed suicide in 1947, Belishova was dismissed from the CC and the Communist youth organization, and she headed a social service department in the government.

At the First CPA Congress in November 1948, when the name of the party was changed to the Albanian Party of Labor and when Xoxe was dismissed, Belishova, at the age of twenty-two, became a member of the Politburo. From 1948 she was a deputy to the Popular Assembly (Kuvendi Popullor) and from 1950, secretary of the parliament presidium. From 1951 to 1954 she studied, along with **Ramiz Alia**, at the Institute of Marxism-Leninism in Moscow. She was a member of the Albanian delegation to Stalin's funeral in March 1953. Later she dealt with propaganda. She was dismissed from the party leadership in June 1960 in connection with her visit to the (Communist) World Council of Trade Unions, where she openly supported the Soviet standpoint and then reported to the Soviets about Chinese intentions and suspended a publication praising Stalin and criticizing resolutions of the Twentieth Congress of the Soviet party. In September 1960 she became head of a primary school in Tirana and then a teacher in Goranzi, near Gjirokaster. When her second husband was dismissed from a ministerial position, she was deprived of work. In May 1961 she was removed from the party and interned with her family, first in Kuç, near Vlory; then in Progonat; and finally in Cerrik, near Elbasan. Released in May 1991, she first lived in Cerrik, and then she returned to Tirana. She attracted public attention again on 12 June 1991 when, in an interview for *Rilindja Demokratike*, she accused **Enver Hoxha** of assassinating Spiru. (TC)

Sources: Raymond Hutchings, *Historical Dictionary of Albania* (Lanham, Md., 1996); William Griffith, *Albania and the Sino-Soviet Rift* (Cambridge, 1963); Henry Hamm, *Albania: China's Beachhead in Europe* (London, 1963); interview with Liri Belishova by Tadeusz Czekalski, 10 February 2002, Tirana.

BELŠEVICA Vizma [originally Elsberga] (30 May 1931, Riga), Latvian poet. Belševica graduated from a trade school (1948), a technical school for cultural workers (1955), and the Maksim Gorky Literary Institute in Moscow (1961). For many years she worked as a journalist for the periodical *Pionieris* in Riga. She made her literary debut in 1947. From 1958 she was a member of the Association of Latvian Writers. In the poems published in the collections *Visu ziemu šogad pavasaris* (This year it is spring all through the wintertime; 1955) and *Zemes siltums* (The warmth of the earth; 1959) she dealt with the relationship between an individual and society, with human dignity, and with the persistence of the national consciousness despite totalitarian pressures. In 1959 she published a poem, *Piezīmes uz Livonijas Indriķa hronikas malām* (Notes in the margins of the chronicle of Henry of Livonia), in which she alluded to the enslavement of the Latvian nation by the Soviets. Despite her rich vocabulary and style, she often used simple expressions. On the wave of the cultural revival in the early 1960s she published the collections *Jūra deg* (The sea aflame; 1966) and *Gadu gredzeni* (Rings of years; 1969), which were seriously attacked by the party leadership. In 1970–74 her works were banned from publication. In 1987 she published *Dzeltu laiks* (The leaves of time grow yellow). She also authored a novel, *Ķikuraga stāsti* (Kikuraga tales; 1965), and numerous short stories, collected in *Nelaime mājās* (Misfortune at home; 1979); she also translated from English and Russian. In 1988–90 she was the head of the Latvian PEN club. Decorated with the Order of the Three Stars of Latvia, she is an honorary member of the Latvian Academy of Sciences. (EJ)

Sources: *Latviešu rakstniecība biogrāfijās* (Riga, 1992); *Who Is Who in Latvia* (Riga, 1996); *Wielka encyklopedia PWN*, vol. 3 (Warsaw, 2001); R. Ādmīdiņš, "'Pārsāpētās dzejaas' dzimšana un atdzimšana," *Karogs*, 1981, no. 5; Andrejs Plakans, *Historial Dictionary of Latvia* (Lanham, Md., 1997).

BENEŠ Edvard (28 May 1884, Kožlany, near Plzneň–3 September 1948, Sezimovo Ústí near Tábor), Czech diplomat and politician. Beneš graduated from a Vinohrady high school in Prague in 1904, and then he studied philology, philosophy, and sociology at the Department of Philosophy of Charles University in Prague. It was there that he met his mentor and future friend, **Tomáš Garrigue Masaryk**. In 1905 Beneš left for France, where he studied sociology and political science at the Sorbonne and the École Libre des Sciences Politiques, as well as law at he University of Dijon, where he received a Ph.D. in 1908. In 1906 he also studied in London, and in 1907–8, in Berlin. In 1909 he returned to Prague, where he received a Ph.D. in philosophy. From 1909 to 1915 he lectured at a trade school; from 1912 he was associate professor at Prague University and, from 1913, also at the Prague Polytechnic. In 1921 he became professor of sociology at Charles University. Initially he was close to Social Democracy, and while abroad he wrote for its organ, *Právo lidu*. Later he turned to the Czech Progressive Party (Česká Strana Pokroková) of Masaryk. Before World War I he, like Masaryk, thought the best solution for the Czechs would be to convert the Habsburg monarchy into a federation.

After the outbreak of World War I Beneš co-founded an anti-Habsburg independence movement led by an informal group called Mafia (Maffie). On 3 September 1915 he went to Paris, from where, along with Masaryk and **Milan R. Štefánik**, he guided Czechoslovak policies in exile. In 1916–18 he was secretary general of the Czechoslovak National Council in Paris, trying to attract Western powers to the idea of an independent Czechoslovak state. He established close contacts with French freemasonry. He was the right-hand man of Masaryk, and during the latter's trip to Russia and the United States from May 1917 to the end of the war Beneš was actually in charge of the movement abroad. In February 1918 he signed an agreement on the creation of a Czechoslovak army in France. On 14 October 1918 he established a provisional government in Paris and took over its foreign and interior ministries. In late October 1918 he took part in the Geneva talks between the foreign and domestic centers of the independence movement on the shape of the future Czechoslovak state.

Thanks to the unlimited trust of President Masaryk, from November 1918 to December 1935 Beneš was foreign minister. His affiliation to freemasonry was also helpful. From 20 September 1921 to 8 October 1922 he was also prime minister. He had an overwhelming influence on the Czechoslovak foreign policy of the 1920s and 1930s. It was based on cooperation with France (a mutual aid treaty of 25 January 1924) and within the Little Entente (Czechoslovakia, Romania, and Yugoslavia). He was co-founder of the League of Nations, in which he held important positions. In 1920 he was its vice-president; in 1923–27 he was a member of its council, and in 1935, president. In 1919–20, along with Prime Minister **Karel Kramař**, he took part in the Paris Peace Conference and succeeded in achieving most of the Czechoslovak territorial demands. In view of the growing German danger, on 16 May 1935 he signed an alliance with the USSR.

In domestic policy Beneš belonged to the inner circle of Masaryk's Castle group (Hrad), from 1923 to 1933 he was one of the leaders of the Czechoslovak Socialist Nationalist Party, and in 1919–26 and 1929–35 he was MP on its behalf. After President Masaryk resigned in 1935, Beneš was his candidate to succeed him, and, after overcoming resistance from the rightist MPs, on 18 December 1935 he was elected president. He assumed this position in an increasingly aggravated international situation. Initially his priority was a peaceful solution to nationality problems (especially coming to terms with the Sudeten Germans) in the face of growing pressure from the Third Reich. He counted on the cooperation of Western democracies and the USSR. In late 1936 he passed information to the Kremlin on alleged contacts of high Soviet officers with Germany, which indirectly contributed to a bloody purge in the Red Army. His policies failed. Pressed by Great Britain and France, in September 1938 he had to accept the Pact of Munich and cede the Sudetenland to Germany. On 5 October 1938 he resigned and left for London. In February 1939 he went to the United States and lectured at the University of Chicago. In July 1939 he returned to England.

After the outbreak of World War II, Beneš returned to active politics. Despite problems with his earlier resignation, he managed to resume rule as Czechoslovak president-in-exile and to establish a government in exile in London in July 1940. He strove for the restoration of Czechoslovakia's prewar borders and for the resettlement of the German population. He won recognition of his government from Western allies. Realizing the inevitability of postwar Soviet domination in Central Europe and not trusting the Western powers after the Pact of Munich, Beneš wanted to establish good relations with the USSR. This policy resulted in a new Czechoslovak-Soviet alliance, signed on 12 December 1943. Beneš's compliance toward Stalin is sometimes explained by the suspicion, based on quite credible sources, that he might have collaborated with Soviet intelligence.

In April 1945 Beneš appointed the first government

of postwar Czechoslovakia, the so-called Košice government, which included Communist ministers. On 16 May 1945 he triumphantly returned to Prague as president of the new state. In June 1945 he passed decrees on the punishment of Hitlerite war criminals and traitors, as well as on the resettlement and expropriation of Sudeten Germans. From 1945 to 1948 he seemed a symbol of continuity of democratic Czechoslovakia, but he failed to oppose Communist strategies of takeover, and during the coup of February 1948, under pressure from **Klement Gottwald**, he accepted the resignation of democratic ministers; this was a forewarning of full Communist control. In May 1948 he refused to sign a new, Stalinist constitution. On 7 June 1948 he resigned, and soon he died.

Beneš was the author of a number of works in sociology and political science, including the following: *Le problème autrichien et la question tchèque* (The Austrian problem and the Czech question; 1908); *Otázka národnostní* (The question of nationality; 1909); *Stručný nástin vývoje moderního socialismu* (Outline of development of modern socialism, 4 vols.; 1910–11); *Stranictví* (Party membership; 1912); *Democracy Today and Tomorrow* (1939); and *Úvahy o slovanství* (Slav character; 1944). He also published the memoirs *Světová válka a naše revoluce* (My war memoirs, 1928; 1927–28); *Paměti: Od Mnichova k nové válce a novému vítězství* (1947; *From Munich to New War and New Victory*, 1954); and *Mnichovské dny* (Munich days; 1968). He also published numerous collections of speeches, some of them in English. (PU)

Sources: *ČBS; Kdo byl kdo v našich dějinach ve 20. stoleti,* vol. 1 (Prague 1998); *Politická elita meziválečného Československa 1918–1938. Kdo byl kdo za prvni republiky* (Prague 1998); *Kto bol kto za I. ČSR* (Bratislava, 1993); Ferdinand Peroutka, *Był Edvard Beneš vinen?* (Paris, 1950); R.W. Seton-Watson, *A History of the Czechs and Slovaks* (Hamden, Conn., 1965); Ludwik Hass, *Ambicje, rachuby, rzeczywistość: Wolnomularstwo w Europie Środkowo-Wschodniej 1905–1928* (Warsaw, 1984); František Havlíček, *Eduard Beneš–člověk, sociolog, politik* (Prague, 1991); Karel Kaplan, *Poslední rok presidenta: Edvard Beneš v roce 1948* (Prague, 1993); Eduard Táborský, *President Beneš mezi Západem a Východem* (Prague, 1993); Josef Hanzal, *Edvard Beneš* (Prague, 1994); Igor Lukes, *Czechoslovakia between Stalin and Hitler: The Diplomacy of Edvard Beneš in the 1930s* (Oxford, 1996); Antonín Klimek, Zbyněk Zeman, *The Life of Edvard Beneš: Czechoslovakia in Peace and War* (Oxford, 1997); Nigel West, *Venona: The Greatest Secret of the Cold War* (London, 1999); Piotr Majewski, *Edvard Beneš i kwestia niemiecka w Czechach* (Warsaw, 2001).

BENKE Valéria (26 June 1920, Gyönk), Hungarian Communist activist. The daughter of a watchmaker, after high school Benke started to study pedagogy, but she broke off her studies because of World War II. In 1941 she joined the Social Democratic Party, and in 1944, the Hungarian Communist Party (HCP). From 1943 she worked as a country teacher in southern Hungary. When in March 1944 Hungary was occupied by Germany, she helped to hide worker activists from Szeged. In the spring of 1945 she graduated from an HCP school in Debrecen and became lecturer of the central party school. From the summer of 1946 she worked in the HCP committee in the Tenth Quarter of Budapest and later in the Budapest city party committee. From July 1947 she worked in the HCP Central Committee (CC) Secretariat for Women, from 1948 to the end of 1950 she was secretary of the Budapest committee of the (Communist) Democratic Union of Hungarian Women, and from 1949 to 1971 she was an MP. In 1951–54 she was secretary of the All-National Peace Council. At the same time she was a deputy member, and until October 1956 a member, of the CC of the (Communist) Hungarian Workers' Party. Chairman of Hungarian Radio from 1954, on 23 October 1956 she refused to allow Budapest demonstrators to present their demands on the air. A week later she was dismissed, but on 6 November 1956 the new government of **János Kádár** appointed her a special radio commissar. In February 1957 she was coopted to the CC of the Hungarian Socialist Workers' Party (HSWP). From January 1957 she was deputy chairman, and from August 1957 chairman, of Hungarian Radio and Television. In 1957 she finally graduated from Budapest University, although her intellectual capabilities were the subject of many jokes. From January 1958 to September 1961 she was minister of culture and education. From 1961 she was editor-in-chief, and from 1966 to 1988 chairman, of the editorial board of the monthly *Társadalmi Szemle,* a theoretical organ of the Communist Party. In 1967–71 she belonged to the Presidential Council. From 1970 to 1985 a member of the HSWP CC Politburo, in 1970–75 she was responsible for agitation and propaganda. In December 1988 she retired. (JT)

Sources: *Magyar Nagylexikon,* vol. 3 (Budapest, 1994); *A magyar forradalom és szabadságharc enciklopédiája,* CD-ROM, 1956-os Intézet (Budapest, 1999); *Ki kicsoda 2000* (Budapest, 2001).

BERAN Josef (29 December 1888, Plzeň–17 May 1969, Rome), Czech cardinal, Primate of Bohemia. The son of a teacher, in 1907–11 Beran studied at the Papal University in Rome, where he was ordained in 1911. After returning to Bohemia, he defended a Ph.D. in theology. In 1912–17 he worked in the parish of Chyši and then in Prague. From 1917 to 1928 he was a teacher and then director of St. Ann Training School for Girls in Prague. From 1929 he lectured in theology in the Prague metropolitan seminary, and in 1932 he became rector of this seminary. He also lectured in pedagogy at the Theological Faculty of Charles University in Prague. During the Nazi occupation he maintained contacts with the Czech resistance. After the assassination of Reich Protector Reinhard Heydrich, in May 1942 Beran was taken hostage by the Gestapo and sent to the Terezin concentration camp in July 1942. In 1943 he was moved to the camp in Dachau, where he met some of the Czech Communist activists.

On 25 May 1945 Beran returned to the Prague seminary. From 1941, when Cardinal **Karel Kašpar** died, the Prague metropolis had no bishop. Because of Beran's good contacts with the ruling circles and his moral authority, Pope Pius XII appointed him the Prague metropolitan and then the Primate of Bohemia on 4 November 1946. Beran took over the Prague archbishopric a week later, and he started efforts to reconstruct the church organization, increase priestly vocations, and revitalize popular piety. He paid special attention to the all-Czech celebrations of St. Adalbert (Vojtech), which attracted thousands of believers throughout the country. At the same time he protested steps by the authorities to limit religious freedom that threatened the unity of the Catholic Church. As head of the Conference of the Czech Episcopate, he opposed attempts by the state to organize so-called patriotic priests in the Catholic Action. During the Communist coup of February 1948, he issued a pastoral letter, *Nemič arcibiskupe! Nesmiš mlčet!* (Do not remain silent, Archbishop! You must not remain silent!), in which he condemned the totalitarian actions of the Communist Party of Czechoslovakia. In a series of articles in the daily *Lidova demorace* he pointed to the democratic mechanisms of interwar Czechoslovakia as a pattern to follow. He agreed to celebrate a solemn service in St. Vitus Cathedral in Prague on the occasion of **Klement Gottwald**'s becoming president, but on 15 June 1948 he issued a letter to believers presenting the authorities with six major demands of religious freedom.

On 19 June 1949 the Communists provoked unrest during the Corpus Christi celebrations in Prague. The militia intervened, beating and arresting many participants, while Beran was interned in the archbishop's palace. Not willing to risk an international scandal, the Communists did not give him a show trial, but they kept him in prison without trial in various places until 1963, when he was released thanks to a temporary "thaw." He was not allowed to return to Prague and was forced to stay in a home for the aged, first in Mukařov and later in Radvanov in southern Bohemia. On 22 February 1965 Pope Paul VI appointed him cardinal. A few days earlier a special Vatican envoy, Archbishop Agostino Casaroli, had met with him and had presented to him the conditions agreed upon with the Communist authorities: Beran was to leave Czechoslovakia, and in exchange the Prague archbishopric would get an apostolic administrator in the person of Bishop **František Tomašek**. Beran agreed, and on 19 February 1965 he left for Rome. In exile he continued to be involved in the church affairs of Czechoslovakia. He often spoke in defense of religious freedom and visited Czech communities in Western Europe and America. During the Second Vatican Council he delivered a homily on tolerance, *O svobode svědomi* (On the liberty of conscience), in which, among other things, he appealed for the church rehabilitation of Jan Hus. He welcomed the Prague Spring of 1968 and began preparations to come back to Prague. A serious illness forced him to change these plans, and the Warsaw Pact invasion of August 1968 made them impossible. After the suicide of **Jan Palach**, he appealed for respect for the sovereignty of the nation and paid homage to Palach. Procedures toward his beatification started in Prague in 1990. Beran was the author of many works in theology and the history of the church, including *Blahoslavená Anežka Česká* (Blessed Agnes of Bohemia; 1974) and an autobiographical volume, *Velká mše* (The Great Holy Mass). (AGr)

Sources: *ČBS*; Josef Tomeš et al., *Česky Biografický Slovnik XX. Stoleti* (Prague, 1999); Maria Teresa Carloni, *Il cardinale scomodo: Il Card. Giuseppe Beran, arcivescovo di Praga* (Urbania, 1972); Bohdan Cywiński, *I was prześladować będą* (Lublin and Rome, 1990); Václav Vaško, *Neumlčená: Kronika Katolickè Cirkve v Československu po druhé svétové válce* (Prague, 1990); Karel Kaplan, *Stát a Cirkev v Československu 1948–1953* (Brno, 1993); Hansjakob Stehle, *Eastern Politics of the Vatican 1917–1979* (Athens, Ohio, 1981); Cardinal Agostino Casaroli, *Il martirio della pazienza: La Stante Sede e i paesi comunisti 1963–1989* (Turin, 2000).

BERAN Rudolf (28 December 1887, Pracejovice–28 February 1954, Leopoldov), Czech Agrarian politician. Beran came from a family of smallholders. In 1905 he graduated from an agricultural vocational school in Strahonice, and he began his political activities, taking up work in the secretariat of the Czech Agrarian Party (Česká Strana Agrární) in Prague. In 1909 he became secretary of the Union of Agrarian Youth. He became known as one of the main organizers of the Agrarian Party and of the agricultural cooperative movement in south Bohemia. Thanks to his organizational skills, he became an important figure among Agrarians and a close associate of **Antonín Švehla**. After the formation of Czechoslovakia he held the post of secretary general of the Agrarian Party for fifteen years; as of 1922 the party was known as the Republican Party of Peasants and Smallholders (Republikánská Strana Zemědělského a Malorolnického Lidu). He took an active role in shaping the local organs of the party; as a result, in the first elections in April 1920, the Agrarians gained forty-two parliamentary seats and nineteen senatorial seats. Throughout the interwar period he sat in the National Assembly and was president of the parliamentary club of the Agrarians.

Beran had strong influence within the party, and after Švehla's withdrawal from political life in 1927, his role became even more important. In 1933 he was incumbent vice-president of the party, and in 1935 he was unanimously elected its president. In his view, he was a representative of the right wing of the Agrarians. He was in favor of strong-handed rule, and in foreign policy he advocated cooperation with Germany. This led to conflict with **Edvard Beneš**, the main architect of Czechoslovak foreign policy. In 1935 Beran tried to form a bloc in parliament in order to prevent the election of Beneš as president of Czechoslovakia and to push the candidacy of Bohumil Němec. After his attempts failed, Beran began to lean toward cooperation with the Sudeten German Party (Sudetendeutsche Partei [SdP]), with the Slovak People's Party of Reverend **Andrij Hlinka**, and with the Czech Fascist parties.

After the Munich dictate Beran became president of the Party of National Unity (Strana Národní Jednoty), which was subservient to Germany, and between 1 December 1938 and 15 March 1939 he was simultaneously prime minister of the Second Czechoslovak Republic. At that time he had to deal with many social and economic problems linked to the mass influx of refugees from the territories occupied by the Third Reich and from Slovakia. After the German invasion, as head of the government of the German Protectorate of Bohemia and Moravia (16 March–27 April 1939), he received Hitler and Reich Protector Konstantin von Neurath in Prague. After resigning, Beran maintained contacts with the resistance movement, mainly with the Defense of the Nation (Obrana Národa), a national organization that he supported financially. Arrested by the Gestapo in June 1942, he was sentenced to ten years. Released in 1943, he was held under house arrest until the liberation in 1945. However, he was soon imprisoned again, and in April 1947 he was sentenced to twenty years and his property was confiscated because of his collaboration with the Third Reich. He died in prison. (PU)

Sources: *ČBS*; Vojtech Masny, *The Czechs under Nazi Rule* (New York and London, 1971); *Kto bol kto za I. ČSR* (Bratislava, 1993); Libor Vukoupil, *Slovník českých dějin* (Brno, 2000); *Českoslovenští politici: 1918–1991* (Prague, 1991); *Politická elita meziválečného Československa 1918–1938: Kdo byl kdo za první republiky* (Prague, 1998); *Kdo byl kdo v našich dějinách ve 20. stoleti*, vol. 1 (Prague, 1998).

BERDNYK Oleksandr (Oles') (25 November 1927, Vavilovo, near Mikolaiiv), Ukrainian writer and dissident. From 1943 to 1945 Berdnyk fought on the front lines. After high school, in 1949 he graduated in theater studies at the Ivan Franko Memorial Dramatic Theater in Kiev, where he also worked as an actor. In 1950 he was sentenced to ten years in a labor camp for protesting the denunciation and propagandistic treatment of classical literature. He was imprisoned in the northern Russian camps and in Kazakhstan. Released owing to an amnesty in 1955, he returned to Kiev, joined the Association of Ukrainian Writers (AUW), and started writing. He won recognition as an author of science fiction. Among other things, he published two collections of short stories, *Poza chasom i prostorom* (Beyond time and space; 1957) and *Marsiians'ki zaitsi* (Hares of Mars; 1962), and the following novels: *Liudyna bez sertsia* (A man without a heart [with Yuri Bedzyk]; 1958); *Shliakhy tytaniv* (Paths of titans; 1959); *Dity bezmezhzhia* (Children of infinity; 1964); *Khto ty?* (Who are you? 1966); *Chasha Amrity* (Amrita's cup; 1971); and *Zoryanyi korsar* (Star pirate; 1971).

Berdnyk lived in **Mykola Rudenko**'s house. In April 1972 during a search there the Soviet police confiscated a work by **Ivan Dziuba**, *Internatsionalizm chy rusyfikatsiya?* (Internationalism or Russification?), and typewriters. Berdnyk's response, a sixteen-day hunger strike, led to a meeting with the first secretary of the Communist Party of the Ukraine (CPU), **Petro Shelest**, and to the return of the confiscated items, but Berdnyk's works were subjected to ideological criticism for their futuristic ideas and defense of religion. In May 1973 he was dismissed from the CPU, in 1974 he was denied permission to leave the USSR, and in 1976 his books were removed from libraries. On 9 November 1976 he, along with Rudenko, Oksana Meshko, and **Levko Lukyanenko**, founded the Ukrainian Helsinki Group (UHG). In 1976 and 1979 Berdnyk signed memoranda to the Soviet authorities and to international public opinion in defense of the persecuted. In November 1977 he authored the Manifesto of the Ukrainian Movement for the Defense of Human Rights, and in May 1978, an open letter to the UN Human Rights Commission. He went on a hunger strike again, demanding the release of Rudenko. Arrested in March 1979, in December 1979 Berdnyk was sentenced to six years of labor camp and three years of exile. He spent 1980–81 in a camp in Kuchino, near Perm. Amnestied in March 1984, he distanced himself from other dissidents. In 1987 he founded the Noospheric Front, whose aim was to defend the values accumulated through centuries of "cosmohistory" against contemporary "pseudocivilization." From December 1989 he presided over an association called the Spiritual Republic of Ukraine and edited the periodicals

Svyata Ukraiina and *Zhoda.* In 1991 he ran for the Ukrainian presidency but lost. Four collections of his uncensored works were published in the West: *Zoloti vorota* (The golden gate; 1975); *Blakytnyi koval* (Blue smith; 1975); *Ukraiina Sichi Vohnyanoii* (Ukraine of the Burning Sich; 1977); and *Svyata Ukraiina* (Holy Ukraine; 1980). These were also published in the Ukraine after 1990. (TS)

Sources: *Encyclopedia of Ukraine,* vol. 1 (Toronto, 1984); *Informatsiini byuleteni Ukraiinskoii hromadskoii hrupy spryiannja vykonanniu Helsinkskykh ugod* (Baltimore and Toronto, 1981); *Ukraiinska Helsinska Hrupa 1978–1982* (Toronto and Baltimore, 1983); Ludmila Aleksieyeva, *Istorija inakomyslja v SSSR* (Vilnius and Moscow, 1992); Hrihoriy Kasyanov, *Nezhodni: Ukraiinska intelihentsiia w rusi oporu 1960–80 rokiv* (Kiev, 1995); Anatoliy Rusnachenko, *Natsionalno-vyzvolnyi rukh w Ukraiini* (Kiev, 1998); Bohdan Nahaylo, *The Ukrainian Resurgence* (Toronto, 1999).

BERECZ János (18 September 1930, Ibrány), Hungarian Communist activist. Berecz joined the Hungarian Workers' Party (HWP) in 1951. In 1955 he graduated from the Lenin Memorial Institute, and in 1966 from the Academy of Social Sciences of the Central Committee (CC) of the Communist Party of the Soviet Union in Moscow. Gradually advancing in the ranks of the Communist youth organization, in 1966 he became secretary of the Hungarian Socialist Workers' Party (HSWP) committee in the Ministry of Foreign Affairs. From 1972 he was deputy head, and from 1974 head, of the Foreign Affairs Department of the HSWP CC. In 1982–85 he was editor-in-chief of the party daily, *Népszabadság*, and from 1985 to 1989 he was HSWP CC secretary for ideology and propaganda. From 1980 he was member of the CC, and from 1987, of the CC Politburo. From 1985 to 1990 he was MP and head of the parliamentary commission of foreign affairs. In the 1980s he belonged to the top party leadership, and he had substantial influence on cultural policies. He authored many articles and several books, trying to legitimize communism in Hungary. His work *Ellenforradalom tollal és fegyverrel 1956* (Counterrevolution by pen and arms, 1956; 1969) was an official version of the history of the 1950s and of the revolution of 1956, and it was read both at home and, thanks to numerous translations, in other Communist countries. Soon after the HSWP was transformed into the Hungarian Socialist Party in 1989, Berecz reestablished an orthodox Communist HSWP and belonged to its top leadership until 1991. Later he gave up politics but always defended communism and HSWP policies. (MS)

Sources: *Politikus pályák* (Budapest, 1984); Klaus-Detlev Grothusen, ed., *Ungarn* (Göttingen, 1987); Miklós Molnár, *From Béla Kun to János Kádár: Seventy Years of Hungarian Communism* (New York, 1990); *Ki Kicsoda 2002* (Budapest, 2001).

BERISHA Sali Ram (15 October 1944, Tropoje), Albanian politician and doctor. Born into a Muslim peasant family, in 1967 Berisha graduated from the medical school of the university in Tirana. Later he lectured there. At the same time he worked as a cardiologist in a hospital, where he headed the Albanian Labor Party (ALP) cell. In the 1970s he went abroad several times, which was only possible among the ruling elite. He continued specialized studies in cardiology in France on a UNESCO scholarship. He authored several articles in cardiology that were published in European periodicals. In 1986 he was elected a member of the European Commission of Doctors in Copenhagen. In 1988 he received a Ph.D., and in 1989 he became a full professor. Enjoying relative freedom, even during the rule of **Enver Hoxha** Berisha could read his favorite French authors, Jean-Paul Sartre and Albert Camus, unavailable to most Albanians. For many years he was the personal doctor of **Hysni Kapo**, but he also treated other members of the leadership, including Hoxha.

In April 1990 Berisha left the ALP, and then he published a number of articles pointing to the necessity of introducing democracy into Albania. These articles were published with the silent consent of the party leadership, which in this way helped him become a political figure. In December 1990 Berisha co-organized student demonstrations and the Democratic Student Movement. On 12 December 1990 he was co-founder of the Party of Youth and Intellectuals, which after a couple of days took the name of the Albanian Democratic Party (Partia Demokratike e Shqipërisë [ADP]) and was the first legal opposition party since World War II. In March 1991 Berisha was elected MP in the National Assembly. In the next parliamentary elections, in March 1992, he gained 98 percent of the vote in the Kavaje district. On 8 April 1992 the National Assembly chose him as president.

Initially Berisha enjoyed Western support, since he was recognized as one of the most credible Balkan politicians and was praised for his support for market reforms. His collaborators from the ADP were of a different opinion, accusing him of autocratic tendencies. He was re-elected president on 3 March 1997, under increasing political crisis and an opposition boycott. Faced with the possible collapse of the state administration, caused, among other things, by the collapse of financial pyramids, Berisha agreed to a coalition government and earlier elections, but he refused to step down. As a result, on 4 June 1997 he barely escaped an attempt on his life in the south of Albania. Under pressure from the Organization for Security and Cooperation in Europe and after his party lost the election to the post-Communist Albanian Socialist Party, on 23 July 1997 Berisha finally resigned. In January 1998, not willing to accept the results of the election, he demanded the dissolution of the parliament and new elections. After the assassination of **Azem Hajdari**, in September 1998 the post-Communists accused Berisha of an attempted coup. He was stripped of immunity but not arrested. Despite another election loss and a split in the ADP, in 2001 Berisha was elected its chairman. (TC)

Sources: "Sali Berisha," *Rilindja Demokratike,* 15 October 1994; Raymond Hutchings, *Historical Dictionary of Albania* (Lanham, Md., 1996); Elez Biberaj, *Shqipëria ne tranzicion: Rruga e vështrisë drejt Demokracisë* (Tirana, 2001); Miranda Vickers and James Pettifier, *Albania: From Anarchy to a Balkan Identity* (New York, 1997); Bugajski; www.rulers.org.

BERĶIS Krišjānis (26 April 1884, Īslīces, Courland– December 1941, concentration camp near Perm), Latvian general. Berķis came from a peasant family. After completing a municipal school in Bauska, he joined the Russian Army. In 1906 he graduated from the Junker School in Vilnius (Wilno) and served as officer in the second regiment of Finnish riflemen in Helsingfors. During World War I he was commander of a company and then a battalion, and in 1917 he was transferred to the sixth regiment of the Latvian Riflemen. He rose to the rank of lieutenant colonel. Demobilized in December 1917, he stayed in Finland until the spring of 1919, when he returned to Latvia. In March 1919 he joined the Latvian Army. He was commander of a regiment, and from August 1919, of the Latgalian division. In 1925 he was appointed general. Between 1933 and 1934 he worked in the general staff of the army. From April 1934 he was commander of the Livonian division and chief of the Riga garrison. He took part in the coup of **Kārlis Ulmanis** of 15 May 1934. From November 1934 he was the commander-in-chief of the Latvian Army. On 5 April 1940 he was appointed minister of war. After the seizure of Latvia by the USSR, on 20 June 1940 Berķķis was dismissed from his post and transferred to the reserves. Soon after, while attempting to leave for Finland, he was arrested in Tallinn and was deported to Russia, where he died. (EJ)

Sources: A. Berķis, *Ģenerālis Krišjānis Berķis* (Riga, 1995); *Latvijas armijas augstākie virsnieki 1918–1940: Biogrāfiska vārdnīca* (Riga, 1998).

BERKLAVS Eduārds (15 June 1914, Kuldīgas, Courland), Latvian Communist activist and dissident. After primary school Berklavs worked as a blue-collar laborer in Kuldīga and (from 1935) in Riga. He belonged to an illegal Communist youth organization, for which he was imprisoned in 1936–39. In 1939–40 he was a leader of the Union of Working Youth of Latvia. After the Soviet invasion of June 1940, he took an active part in the incorporation of Latvia into the USSR. From February 1941 he was second secretary of the Riga regional committee of the Communist Party of Latvia (CPL), and from 1941 to 1944 he served as an officer in the Red Army, advancing to the rank of major. Demobilized in 1946, he worked as first secretary of the Komsomol in Latvia. In 1951 he graduated form the Higher Party School in Moscow, and then he was active as secretary of the Riga party committee. From 1954 to 1956 and from 1958 to 1959 Berklavs was deputy chairman of the Council of Ministers of the Latvian SSR, and in 1957–58, first secretary of the Riga party committee.

Berklavs belonged to the leadership of a "national" wing of the party, which opposed the inflow of Russians into Latvia and strove for wider cultural autonomy in the Latvian SSR. At a meeting of the CPL Central Committee in early July 1959 Berklavs criticized the Russification policies of the Kremlin. Despite gaining some support in the CPL leadership, on 15 July 1959 he was dismissed from his position. **Jānis Kalnbērzinš** and **Vilis Lacis**, veterans of Soviet power in Latvia, were also dismissed for their defense of Berklavs, while the new CPL leader, **Arvids Pelše**, carried out a purge of the supporters of autonomy. Berklavs was soon sent to Vladimir, where he worked in the economic administration. In 1968 he returned to Latvia and worked as a white-collar and then a blue-collar worker in a Riga factory. In 1971 he signed a "Letter of 17 Latvian Communists" in protest against Russian colonization and the cultural Russification of Latvia. The letter was published in the West. Removed from the party, Berklavs was harassed by the KGB. On 18 June 1988 he signed the founding declaration of the Latvian National Independence Movement (Latvijas Nacionālas Neatkarības Kustība [LNIM]) and became one of its leaders. In November 1988 he represented Latvia at the conference of Baltic activists for the withdrawal of the Soviet Army from Estonia, Latvia, and Lithuania. In 1988–91 he was a member of the Council of the Latvian Popular Front, and from 1990 he was MP of the Supreme Council of the Latvian SSR. After Latvia regained independence, in 1993–95 Berklavs was MP on behalf of the LNIM. His memoirs, *Zināt un neaizmirst* (To know and not to forget), were published in 1998. (EJ)

Sources: Romuald J. Misiunas and Rein Taagepera, *The Baltic States: Years of Dependence 1940–1990* (Berkeley, 1993); Andrejs Plakans, *The Latvians: A Short History* (Stanford, 1995); *Who Is Who in Latvia 1996: Biographical Dictionary* (Riga, 1996); Jurijs Dreifelds, *Latvia in Transition* (Cambridge, 1996); Andrejs Plakans, *Historical Dictionary of Latvia* (Lanham, Md., 1997); *Policy of Occupation Powers in Latvia, 1939–1991* (Riga, 1999); Bugajski.

BERLING Zygmunt (27 April 1896, Limanowa–11 July 1980, Warsaw), Polish officer, appointed general by Stalin. From 1912 Berling was a member of the Riflemen Society. From 1914 to 1918 he was in the Polish Legions and in the Polish Auxiliary Corps, and from the end of 1918 he served in the Polish Army. Between 1918 and 1919 he took part in the Polish-Ukrainian war and then, as a battalion commander, in the Polish-Soviet war. He was decorated with the Order of Virtuti Militari. In 1925 he graduated from the Military College in Warsaw. From 1925 to 1927 he was chief of staff of the Fifteenth Infantry Division, and in 1930–32 he served as chief of staff of the command of the district of the Fifth Corps in Kraków. From 1935 to 1937 he commanded an infantry regiment of the First Infantry Division of the Legions. After a conflict with General Stefan Dąb-Biernacki Berling was transferred to the command of an infantry regiment of the Second Infantry Division of the Legions. He squandered the property of his wife and then divorced her, leaving her and their children without means of support. Because of that, in July 1939 he was dismissed from service.

During the September campaign of 1939 he was in Wilno (Vilnius). After the Soviet invasion he was interned in the Starobielsk camp. He escaped the fate of the majority of Starobielsk prisoners—that is, transport to Kharkiv and death at the hands of the NKVD—and he was relocated in the Gryazovets camp. There he expressed a wish to cooperate with the USSR authorities without any political conditions. In November 1940 he was transferred to Malakhovka (the "villa of happiness"), where along with a couple of Polish officers he embarked on a project to organize a Polish division. After the signing of the Polish-Soviet treaty of July 1941 he became chief of staff of the Fifth Infantry Division of the Polish Army, commanded by General **Władysław Anders**, and later commander of the evacuation base in Krasnovodsk. In September 1942, after the evacuation of the army, Berling willingly stayed in the USSR, and until May 1943 he was at the disposal of the Soviet authorities. He was co-founder and activist of the Union of Polish Patriots (Związek Patriotów Polskich). From May 1943 he was an organizer and commander (until November 1943) of the First Tadeusz Kościuszko Infantry Division, which he commanded during the battle at Lenino. In August 1943 he was appointed general by the Kremlin, and he commanded the First Corps of the Polish Military Forces in the USSR. From May to July 1944 he was commander-in-chief and from July to October 1944 deputy commander-in-chief of the Polish Army in the USSR, commanding the First Polish Army both in the battles at Dęblin and Puławy, at Magnuszew bridgehead, and in the fights for Warsaw bridgeheads. Because of his attempt to come to the aid of the insurgents in Warsaw, Berling was dismissed from his position by the Soviet command and transferred to the post of deputy head of the defense department of the Polish Committee of National Liberation (PKWN).

In 1944–47 Berling was MP to the National Home Council (Krajowa Rada Narodowa [KRN]). After a conflict with leaders of the Polish Workers' Party (PPR) and the PKWN, whom he denounced to the Kremlin as "Trotskyists," he was permanently dismissed from command of the troops. From January 1945 to February 1947 he studied at the Kliment Voroshilov Academy of the General Staff in Moscow. In 1947–48 he was a co-organizer, and from 1948 to 1953 commander, of the Academy of the General Staff at Rembertów. He retired in 1953. Between 1953 and 1956 he was undersecretary of state in the Ministry of State Farms and then in the Ministry of Agriculture in 1956–57. From 1957 to 1970 he was inspector general of hunting, and from 1963, a member of the Polish United Workers' Party (Polska Zjednoczona Partia Robotnicza [PUWP]). He was the author of the three-volume *Wspomnienia* (Memoirs; 1990–91). He was considered a hero by former soldiers of the Polish Army in the USSR while regarded a traitor by other soldiers. (WD)

Sources: Jan Nowak, "Sprawa Generała Berlinga," *Zeszyty Historyczne*, 1976, no. 37; A. Topol, *Zygmunt Henryk Berling 1896–1980* (Katowice, 1990); Stanisław Jaczyński, *Zygmunt Berling* (Warsaw, 1993); Daniel Bargiełowski, *Konterfekt renegata* (Warsaw, 1996); *Wielka Internetowa Encyklopedia Multimedialna wiem.onet.pl*; Stanisław Dronicz, *Wojsko i politycy* (Warsaw, 2001).

BERMAN Jakub (23 October 1901, Warsaw–10 April 1984, Łomża), Polish Communist activist. Born into a Jewish middle-class family, in 1925 Berman graduated in law from Warsaw University. In 1924 he became a member of the Communist Union of Youth, and in 1928 he joined the Communist Party of Poland (Komunistyczna Partia Polski [KPP]). In 1938 the KPP was dissolved by the Comintern and its leaders in the USSR were killed on the pretext of having succumbed to the influence of Polish intelligence. The same year Berman, on behalf of the Comintern, took part, along with **Stanisław Radkiewicz**, in the liquidation of KPP units in Poland. In September 1939 Berman headed east. In spring 1941 he edited an organ of the Communist Party in Belorussia, and between November 1941 and May 1943 he ran a Polish course in a Comintern school in Kushnarenkovo, where he educated cadres for the Polish Workers' Party (PPR). From December 1943 he was secretary of the Home Department of the Union of Polish Patriots (Związek Patriotów Polskich). He co-founded the Central Bureau of Polish Communists in the USSR. As he enjoyed the trust of the Kremlin, Berman became a member of the top leadership of the bureau and was responsible for contact with Communists in occupied Poland, as well as for preparing members of the initiative groups of the PPR that were deployed in occupied Poland.

From August 1944 Berman was formally in the PPR, and from the start he was made a member of the Central Committee (CC) and the Politburo of the party. In the party leadership he represented a strict pro-Moscow "internationalist" wing. From 1944 to 1945 he was deputy head of the foreign department of the Polish Committee of National Liberation (Polski Komitet Wyzwolenia Narodowego [PKWN]) and deputy minister of foreign affairs of the provisional government. From 1945 to 1952 he was undersecretary of state in the Presidium of the Council of Ministers and a member of the Presidium of the Government. He played a key role in government structures, but he was not formally appointed deputy prime minister until 1954. From 1944 to 1946 he was a member of the National Home Council (Krajowa Rada Narodowa [KRN]) and from 1947, an MP. From December 1948 he was a member of the CC of the Polish United Workers' Party (Polska Zjednoczona Partia Robotnicza [PUWP]) and its Politburo. In 1948–54 he was a member of the CC Secretariat, and between February 1949 and 1954 he was a member of the Public Security Commission of the Politburo.

Along with **Bolesław Bierut**, **Hilary Minc**, and **Roman Zambrowski**, Berman belonged to the top leadership of Stalinist Poland. He was in charge of public security, foreign policy, education, ideology, propaganda, and culture. On behalf of the party he monitored the security apparatus, and because of his position, he was co-responsible for its crimes. In accord with a decision of the Politburo in August 1945 he organized a series of show trials of pro-independence activists. Many of these trials ended in death sentences, as it was alleged, according to Berman's horrendous testimony, that the Home Army (Armia Krajowa [AK]) had collaborated with the Gestapo during the Nazi occupation. Berman considered propaganda and culture important parts of the arsenal of "class struggle." For example, in 1947 he held a special conference with intellectuals who were linked to the PPR. At the conference he outlined the propaganda tasks for scholars and artists. He took an active part in the suppression of the Polish Peasant Party (Polskie Stronnictwo Ludowe [PSL]) between 1945 and 1947. At the Sixth Plenum of the CC of the PPR in August and September 1948 he was one of the main architects of the dismissal of **Władysław Gomułka** from the party leadership. Along with Bierut and Minc, he initiated investigations that were aimed at bringing about

the trial of Gomułka. As a result of these activities, the Ministry of Public Security and the Information Service of the Polish Army arrested and tortured hundreds of people, and a dozen or so were sentenced to death.

Berman's position weakened at the beginning of the 1950s as an anti-Semitic wave began to spread in the USSR. In May 1956 he was forced to resign from the Politburo, and at the Seventh Plenum of the CC of the PUWP in July 1956 he was sharply attacked by (among others) **Mieczysław Moczar**. Although at the Eighth Plenum of the CC of the PUWP on 21 October 1956 he undertook a self-criticism, he was dismissed from the CC, and in 1957 he was expelled from the PUWP for "lack of alertness." The Ninth Plenum of the CC of the PUWP issued a resolution on the party responsibility of functionaries of the Ministry of Public Security. In this resolution, Berman was stigmatized, along with Radkiewicz, but the main burden of blame was shifted to lower-level functionaries. Despite the attempts of Public Prosecutor General Andrzej Burda in 1957, the Politburo did not agree to prosecute Berman for his crimes in the Stalinist period. Until 1968 Berman worked in the publishing house Książka i Wiedza, and then he retired. During martial law Berman came back into the public light, and in December 1983 he was decorated with the medal of the KRN. He left memoirs that are kept in the Archive of New Records (Archiwum Akt Nowych) in Warsaw. (PK)

Sources: Mołdawa; *Słownik polityków polskich XX w.* (Poznań, 1998); Zbigniew Błażyński, *Mówi Józef Światło: Za kulisami bezpieki i partii* (London, 1985); Marek Łatyński, *Nie paść na kolana: Szkice o opozycji lat czterdziestych* (Warsaw, 1987); Krystyna Kersten, *Narodziny systemu władzy: Polska 1943–1948* (Poznań, 1990); Stanisław Marat and Jacek Snopkiewicz, *Ludzie bezpieki* (Warsaw, 1990); Teresa Torańska, *Oni* (Warsaw, 1990); Jerzy Poksiński, *"TUN"—Tatar-Utnik-Nowicki: Represje wobec oficerów Wojska Polskiego w latach 1949–1956* (Warsaw, 1992); Andrzej Werblan, *Stalinizm w Polsce* (Warsaw, 1993).

BERON Petyr (14 March 1940, Sofia), Bulgarian politician. The grandson of one of the nineteenth-century pioneers of the Bulgarian national revival, Beron studied biology at the University of Sofia. After studies in France, he returned to Bulgaria and received a Ph.D. in 1975. Later he worked in the Institute of Biology of the Bulgarian Academy of Sciences and was director of the Museum of Natural Sciences in Sofia. In April 1989 he joined Ekoglasnost, and on behalf of this organization he became secretary of the Union of Democratic Forces (Sayuz na Demokratichnite Sili [UDF]). During round-table talks in 1990 he decided to support the reformation government of **Andrey Lukanov** as a "lesser evil." Beron was perceived as a representative of the nationalist faction of the UDF and one of the key persons responsible for rejecting a motion to accept the (Muslim) Movement for Rights and Freedoms of **Ahmed Dogan** into the UDF. After the parliamentary elections of June 1990, Beron won a seat in the Grand National Assembly, where he headed the UDF club. When **Zhelyu Zhelev** was elected president in August 1990, Beron became UDF chairman. In this capacity he negotiated with the post-Communist Bulgarian Socialist Party (BSP) on the formation of a coalition cabinet dominated by the UDF, but these talks failed. After Lukanov resigned, Beron was considered a candidate for prime minister, but the BSP objected. At this time it was revealed that Beron had been a collaborator in the Communist Ministry of Interior for twenty-one years. As a result he had to give up his position as UDF chairman and head of its parliamentary club in December 1990. In April 1991, after a split in the UDF owing to a conflict on de-communization and dates for elections, Beron, along with some radical activists, left the UDF and founded a rightist bloc. In 1992 he ran for vice-president. When he lost, he returned to his job in the Museum of Natural Sciences in Sofia. (AG)

Sources: *Koy koy e v Bulgariya* (Sofia, 1998); Raymond Detrez, *Historical Dictionary of Bulgaria* (Lanham, Md., 1997); Jerzy Jackowicz, *Bułgaria od rządów komunistycznych do demokracji parlamentarnej 1988–1991* (Warsaw, 1999); www.omda.bg/engl/personalia/beron_engl.htm.

BEROV Luben (6 October 1925, Sofia), Bulgarian historian and politician. Berov graduated in economics at the University of Sofia in 1949. From 1950 to 1962 he worked as an assistant professor at the Higher Institute of Economics (HIE) in Sofia. Gradually advancing, he received a Ph.D.; in 1971 he became professor, and in 1976 he was given a postdoctoral degree in economics. He held a chair in economic history and was deputy dean and dean in the HIE and professor in the Institute of Balkan Studies of the Bulgarian Academy of Sciences. In 1990–92 he was adviser to President **Zhelyu Zhelev** on economic affairs. From 30 December 1992 to 17 October 1994 Berov was prime minister and (until June 1993) minister of foreign affairs. His government, composed of experts, faced great difficulties without a stable parliamentary majority, but it functioned thanks to the support of the (Turkish) Movement for Rights and Freedoms and the post-Communist Bulgarian Socialist Party (BSP). The government was opposed by the Union of Democratic Forces faction of **Filip Dimitrov** and, at the end, by President Zhelev. The opposition accused the Berov government of hampering institutional reforms and personnel changes. The state administration malfunctioned; there was growing crime,

financial pyramids, and a banking crisis. In March 1994 Berov had a heart attack and was hospitalized for a month. When he lost the support of the BSP, on 2 September 1994 his government resigned but continued operation until a new one was formed. In 1995 Berov became chairman of the Agricultural Credit Center and a member of the Presidium of the Open Society Foundation. He authored many works, including the following: *Ikonomicheskoto razvitye na Bulgariya prez vekovete* (Economic development of Bulgaria through the centuries; 1974); *Dvizhenye na tsenite na Balkanite prez XVI–XIX v.* (Price changes in the Balkans in the sixteenth to nineteenth centuries; 1976); *Razvityeto na industriyata w Bulgariya 1884–1947 g.* (Development of industry in Bulgaria, 1884–1947; 1989); *Stopanska istorija* (Economic history; 1994); and *Istoriya na sveta* (World history; 1996). (JJ)

Sources: *Entsiklopediya Bulgariya,* vol. 7 (Sofia, 1996); Raymond Detrez, *Historical Dictionary of Bulgaria* (Lanham, Md., 1997); *Koi koi e v Bulgariya* (Sofia, 1998); Tasho Tashev, *Ministrite na Bulgariya 1879–1999: Entsiklopedichen spravochnik* (Sofia, 1999); Evgeniya Kalinova and Iskra Baeva, *Bulgarskite prekhodi 1944–1999* (Sofia, 2000); Angel Tsyrakov, *Entsiklopediya. Pravitelstvata na Bulgariya. Khronologiya na politicheskiya zhivot 1879–2001* (Sofia, 2001).

BĒRZIŅŠ Alfreds (21 October 1899, Jeri, Livonia–30 November 1977, New York), Latvian politician. Bērziņš was educated in a city school in Valka. Arrested by the Bolsheviks in 1918, in 1919 he escaped from prison and volunteered for the Latvian Army. In 1919–20 he went through an officer training course in a military academy, and in 1920–21 he served as a lieutenant of infantry. Demobilized, he graduated from an evening high school and studied in the Trade Institute in Riga. He published a lot and was active in youth organizations. From 1926 he was a member of the Agrarian paramilitary organization Aizsargi, and later he was its instructor and head of a department in its headquarters. In 1931 he was elected MP on behalf of the Latvian Agrarian Union (Latviešu Zamnieku Sanienība [LAU]). Along with **Kārlis Ulmanis** and **Janis Balodis**, he belonged to a close circle of organizers of the coup of 15 May 1934, after which he became deputy minister of interior and, from April 1937, minister of social affairs. After the Soviet invasion of June 1940 he was the only member of the government who managed to escape through Estonia and Finland to Sweden, while the NKVD deported his whole family. In exile he resumed activities aimed at restoring the independence of Latvia. Arrested by the Gestapo in Berlin in early 1941 while returning to Sweden from Switzerland, where he had conferred with Latvian ambassadors and ministers, he was sent to the Sachsenhausen concentration camp. Released in November 1943, he was forced to stay in Berlin under police surveillance. At the end of the war he was released from a displaced persons camp, and he worked in Latvian émigré organizations and published a lot.

In 1950 Bērziņš he left for the United States. He settled in New York, where he took an active part in émigré organizations. He edited the periodicals *Latvijas Brīvībai* (1952–60), *The Baltic Review* (1953–61), *La Revue Baltique* (1954–61), *Zemnieku Vienība* (1954–62) and *Revista Baltica* (1957–67). He published (among other works) *Atmiņas par Kārli Ulmani* (Memoirs on Kārlis Ulmanis; 1947); *I Saw Vishinsky Bolshevize Latvia* (1948); *Kārlis Ulmanis* (1952); *Labie gadi* (Good years; 1963); *The Unpunished Crime* (1963); *The Two Faces of Coexistence* (1967); *Tāls ir ceļš atpakaļ uz mājām* (It is a long way back home; 1971); *Kārlis Ulmanis: Cilvēks un valstsvīrs* (Kārlis Ulmanis: A man and a statesman; 1973); *1939* (1976); and several concise works on independent Latvia and Soviet occupation published in English, French, Spanish, Arabic, and Armenian. (EJ)

Sources: *Es viņu pazīstu* (Riga, 1939); *Kadets,* 1939, no. 1; *Latvju encklopēdija,* vol. 1; *Enciklopēdiskā vārdnīca,* vol. 1 (Riga, 1991); Andrejs Plakans, *Historical Dictionary of Latvia* (Lanham, Md., 1997).

BĒRZIŅŠ Jānis [originally Peteris Kiusis] (13 November 1889, Jaunpils–29 July 1938, Moscow), Latvian Communist activist in the USSR. The son of a landless peasant, Bērziņš studied in a theological seminary, but in 1905 he joined the revolution. For some time he even fought in a detachment of "forest partisans" against the tsarist army. He was caught and sentenced to death in 1907, but owing to his young age the sentence was commuted, and after two years he was released. In 1911 he was arrested again for his revolutionary activities, and he was sent to Siberia. He escaped from exile and returned to Latvia in 1914. In 1915 he was recruited to the Russian Army and took part in the February 1917 revolution. In November 1917, during the Bolshevik coup, he commanded the Kremlin Guard in its attack on the Winter Palace in Petrograd. In 1918 he took the leadership of the People's Commissariat of Interior of the Bolshevik government of Latvia. After the collapse of the Latvian revolution, he returned to Petrograd and served in the Red Army. In November 1920 he was appointed head of the Cheka special section in the Fifth Army, and in December 1920 he started his career in military intelligence. For his role in the suppression of the Kronstadt Revolt, in April 1921 he was promoted to director of the Third Bureau of the Chief Intelligence Administration (Gławnoje Razwiediwatielnoje Uprawlienie [GRU]). In March 1924 he became head of intelligence of the Red Army, with the rank of general. He supervised many intelligence operations against true and alleged enemies of the USSR. Frequently these were liquidation operations. In October 1935 he decided to resign and became deputy commander of the Far East Army. From 1936, as "General Grishin," he headed a Soviet mission supervising the International Brigades during the Spanish Civil War. In June 1937 he returned to the Soviet Union and resumed the position of head of Red Army intelligence. Accused by his superior, Kliment Voroshilov, of espionage for the Third Reich, he was arrested at the end of 1937, sentenced to death, and executed. (WR)

Sources: *MERSH,* vol. 4; *Latvijas PSR Maza Enciklopedija,* vol. 1 (Riga, 1967); D. J. Dallin, *Soviet Espionage* (New Haven, 1955); Robert Conquest, *The Great Terror* (New York, 1968); Boris Levytskyj, *The Stalinist Terror in the Thirties* (Stanford, 1974); Burnett Bolloten, *The Spanish Revolution* (Chapel Hill, N.C., 1979); Pierre de Villemarest, *GRU: Le plus secret des services soviétiques, 1918–1988* (Paris, 1988).

BETHLEN István (8 October 1874, Gernyeszeg, Transylvania–5 October 1946, Moscow), Hungarian politician. Bethlen graduated in law from Budapest University. From 1901 to 1939, with a short break in 1919–20, he was MP. He represented a traditional conservatism, opposing all kinds of extremism. During World War I he served in the army. Realizing the inevitability of national separatisms in the Kingdom of Hungary, at the end of the war he began to be inclined toward the **Oszkár Jászi** idea of a federal system based on the equal rights of all the nationalities of the Habsburg monarchy. In the fall of 1918 he sharply criticized the liberal republican government of **Mihály Károly,** mostly for its plans for land reform and for its foreign policy.

After the proclamation of the Hungarian Soviet Republic (HSR), in April 1919 Bethlen was one of the key organizers of the Anti-Bolshevik Committee in Vienna, uniting conservative and Christian National politicians with Admiral **Miklós Horthy,** **Pál Teleki,** and **Gyula Gömbös.** After the collapse of the HSR in August 1919 Bethlen opposed both a military dictatorship and a restoration of Habsburg rule. He saw the best chance for political consolidation in Hungary in a provisional system of a kingdom without a king, with Regent Horthy at the helm. Bethlen won wide support for this idea, including the support of most Hungarian Jews, which was particularly important in view of nationalist accusations that the Jews had supported the HSR. Bethlen was most instrumental in consolidating Hungary after the shock of the revolution and the Treaty of Trianon, to which he was a signatory on 4 June 1920 and by which Hungary lost two-thirds of its prewar territory, while every third Hungarian was left outside the new state. In the elections of January 1920 the Christian National Unity Party (Keresztény Nemzeti Egyesülés Partja [KNEP]), led by Bethlen, won 35 percent of the vote and was runner-up to the Smallholders and Agrarian Laborers' Party (Országos Kisgazda és Föld-müves Párt [OKFP]), which won 40 percent of the vote.

On 14 April 1921 Bethlen became prime minister. He strove for domestic consolidation and the strengthening of the Christian National government. In October 1921, during a second attempt by Charles IV Habsburg to recover the throne of Hungary, Bethlen fiercely opposed him, and, although he was a royalist, on 6 November 1921 he forced through a law dethroning the Habsburgs. In December 1921 he reached a secret agreement with the Social Democratic leader **Károly Peyer** that led to the legalization of the Social Democratic Party as an opposition, though loyal, party. On 22 February 1922 Bethlen renewed and extended an agreement between the KNEP and the OKFP that led to their merger into the government Unity Party (Egységes Párt). The agreement included the consent of the conservatives to a land reform and of the populists to limit voting rights. In March 1922 Bethlen changed the electoral law and—with the exception of Budapest and a few large towns—he restored open elections, which helped the government party win a parliamentary majority in subsequent elections. In 1923 he dismissed a group of Gömbös nationalists from the ruling party. In 1926 he promoted the creation of the Upper House, which replaced the House of Lords, abolished in 1918.

In domestic policy Bethlen tried to maintain a balance between the restriction and the neutralization of opposition groups. He made a concession to the extreme right and the populists when he decided to retain the *numerus clausus* principle in relation to Jewish students (1920–28). In the mid-1920s his government achieved economic stability. In 1924 he managed to obtain a significant loan from the League of Nations. Through a tax increase he managed to balance the budget, and in 1927 he introduced a new currency, the pengő. In foreign policy he strove for the revision of the Treaty of Trianon, the restoration of a modernized but historical Kingdom of Hungary, and a reduction in the German and Soviet danger. In 1927 he weakened the encirclement of Hungary by the Little Entente by means of a treaty of friendship with Italy. He understood that to revise the Treaty of Trianon Hungary would need German support, but he first tried to improve relations with Western powers such as Great Britain. He was temporarily minister of treasury (1921), foreign affairs (1924), agriculture (1924), and justice (1924 and 1929). Ten years of his government strengthened the authoritarian nature of the political system, with elements of democracy, such as a relatively free press and trade unions and with an elected parliament. This system was also against extreme nationalism.

Owing to a political crisis caused by the Great Depression, on 19 August 1931 Bethlen resigned. As one of the most influential aides of Regent Horthy and until 1935 leader of the government party, he still played a key political role. In 1935 he left the Unity Party in protest against the pro-Fascist policy of Prime Minister Gömbös, and until 1945 he was the leader of the so-called defense of the constitution, opposing extremist tendencies. He was also the leader of a pro-British group of Hungarian politicians. In February 1939 he contributed to the resignation of a pro-German prime minister, **Béla Imrédy**, and supported the foreign policy of the Teleki government. He did not run in the elections of 1939, but in May 1939 Horthy appointed him a member of the Upper House for life.

In April 1941, during the German invasion of Yugoslavia, Bethlen appealed to the government of **László Bárdossy** to stay out of the conflict. He did not agree to a one-sided pro-German orientation and was against breaking off contacts with the Western powers. He thought it a grave mistake for Hungary to declare war on the USSR, Great Britain, and the United States and tried to convince Horthy to change this line. In 1943–44 he attempted to reconcile with the Anglo-Saxon powers and to conclude a separate peace treaty with them. In order to unite anti-German forces, in 1943 he founded the Hungarian National Circle. He also condemned anti-Jewish legislation. When Germany occupied Hungary on 19 March 1944, he went into hiding in the countryside. Despite Gestapo efforts to arrest him, he maintained contact with Regent Horthy. In June 1944 he appealed to Horthy to appoint a government that could restore Hungary's sovereignty. He urged the establishment of contacts with the USSR and the conclusion of an armistice. In his plans for an armistice and for the creation of a provisional government, Horthy saw a leading role for Bethlen. Nevertheless, when the Arrow Cross took over power in October 1944, Bethlen had to go into hiding again. In early December 1944 he reported to one of the Soviet commanders, counting on an agreement with the Kremlin. He was first kept under house arrest, but when he refused to cooperate with the Communists, in April 1945 he was transferred to Moscow, where he died in the Butyrki Prison hospital. In June 1994 his ashes were returned to Hungary. (JT)

Sources: *Biographisches Lexikon*, vol. 1; *Magyar Nagylexikon*, vol. 3 (Budapest, 1994); *Nagy Képes Milleniumi Arcképcsarnok* (Budapest, 1999); *Új Magyar Életrajzi Lexikon*, vol. 1 (Budapest, 2001); *Magyarország 1944–1956,* CD-ROM (Budapest, 2001);

Bethlen István beszédei és írásai, vols. 1–2 (Budapest, 1933); C. A. Macartney, *October Fifteenth: A History of Modern Hungary,* vols. 1–2 (Edinburgh, 1957–1961); William M. Batkay, *Authoritarian Politics in a Transitional State: Istvan Bethlen and the United Party in Hungary, 1919–1926* (Boulder, Colo., 1982); Ignac Romcics, *Bethlen István: Politikai életrajz* (Budapest, 1991); Steven Béla Várga, *Historical Dictionary of Hungary* (Lanham, Md., 1997).

BIADULA Zmitrok [originally Samuil Plaunik] (23 November 1886, Posadets, near Vileika–3 November 1941, Uralsk), Belorussian writer. The son of a Jewish leaseholder (*arendar*), Biadula was educated at a rabbinical school, and then he worked as a tutor. In 1912 he moved to Wilno (Vilnius), where he established ties with Belorussian activists. He worked in the editorial offices of *Nasha Niva,* where he published poems, feature articles, and short literary essays. He also contributed to the conservative magazine *Byelarus.* The first collection of his lyrical miniatures written in prose, *Abrazki* (Pictures), appeared in 1913 from the St. Petersburg Belorussian publishing house Zahlanie Sontsa i u Nashava Kontsa (The Sun Will Also Shine in Our Window). In this collection, nature and peasants were the main motifs. In his stories he idealized the peasant community, depicting its ethical values, inborn sense of justice, and capacity for deep spirituality. Against this background he presented the picture of a degenerate nobility and middle-class society. In 1915 he went to Minsk, where he participated in the work of the Belorussian Relief Committee for War Victims. In 1917 he took part in all the most significant events that led to the creation of the Belorussian People's Republic. He attended the First All-Belorussian Congress and participated in the work of the Belorussian Military Committee. In 1919 he accepted the idea of Belorussian Soviet statehood. He appealed to Belorussian Jews to join in the work for the economic and political revival of Belorussia. In 1919 he published *Zhydy na Bielarusi* (Jews in Belorussia). He was one of the most widely read writers in the Belorussian SSR, but he became popular only after his death in the postwar period, when his works were published in large print runs. His most important works include *Pad rodnym niebam* (Under our native sky; 1922); *Deliehatka* (Woman delegate; 1928); *Salaviei* (Nightingale; 1928); *Try paltsy* (Three fingers; 1930); *Yazep Krushynski* (1929–1932); *Niezvychainyia historyi* (Not ordinary stories; 1931); and *Na pradoptanykh stsezhkakh* (On trodden paths; 1940). In 1985 *Zbor tvorau u piatsi tamakh* (Collected works in five volumes) was published. (EM)

Sources: *Bielaruskiya pis'mienniki (1917–1990): Daviednik* (Minsk, 1994); I. Navumienka, *Zmitrok Biadula* (Minsk, 1995); Jan Zaprudnik, *Historical Dictionary of Belarus* (Lanham, Md., 1998); *Wielka Encyklopedia PWN,* vol. 2 (Warsaw, 2001).

BIBÓ István (7 August 1911, Budapest–10 May 1979, Budapest), Hungarian politician, lawyer, and political scientist. The son of an ethnologist and director of the University Library in Szeged, Bibó attended the local Piarist gymnasium and from 1929 studied law at the university in Szeged. He established close contacts with **Ferenc Erdei,** one of the outstanding representatives of peasant writers. In 1933–35 he was on state scholarships in Vienna and Geneva. From November 1938 he worked in the Ministry of Justice. In 1937 he was the co-author of a programmatic declaration of the March Front, which aimed at the development of the Hungarian countryside. In the summer of 1944 he formulated the Peace Proposal (Békeajánlat) between the working class and the middle class. During the German occupation Bibó used his post in the ministry to save many Jews by issuing safe conduct permits for them. Because of this, on 16 October 1944 he was arrested by the Arrow Cross Party. After a few days he was released and went into opposition.

In February 1945, at Erdei's request, Bibó started working in the Ministry of Interior under the Provisional National Government. Between March 1945 and July 1946 he directed the administrative department of the Ministry of Interior and worked on the reform of the county (*comitat*) system. Between July 1945 and October 1946 he represented the National Peasant Party in the Committee on Legal Reform, where he helped to prepare changes in the electoral law. In October 1945 his article, "A magyar demokrácia válsága" (The crisis of Hungarian democracy), was published, stimulating much debate. The next year his analytical studies were issued—for example, *A kelet-európai kisállamok nyomorúsága* (The misery of small East European nations; 1946) and *Zsidókérdés Magyarországon 1944 után* (The Jewish question in Hungary after 1944.). From 1946 to 1950 Bibó was a professor at Szeged University, and from July 1946, a member of the Hungarian Academy of Sciences; between 1946 and 1949 he was professor at the East European Research Institute, and then he became the director of the institute. In 1950 he was removed from all his posts and went to work as a librarian at the University Library in Budapest.

During the revolution of 1956 Bibó took part in the reorganization of the National Peasant Party, which on 3 November appointed him minister without portfolio in the coalition government of **Imre Nagy.** On 4 November, along with **Zoltán Tildy,** Bibó conducted talks with the commander of the Soviet units, which had seized the parliament building. After that he formulated a manifesto to the people. On 6 November he published the text, "Tervezet a magyar kérdés megoldására" (The project of a compromise solution to the Hungarian question), and then he left the parliament. On 12 November he was officially dismissed from his post by the head of the Presidential Council, **István Dobi**. At the beginning of 1957 Bibó wrote a study, *Magyarország és a világhelyzet* (Hungary and the world situation), which was sent abroad and published in London. In May 1957 he was arrested, and on 2 August 1958 the Supreme Court sentenced him to life imprisonment. Released under an amnesty in 1963, Bibó worked in the library of the Central Statistical Office in Budapest until 1971. During his retirement he edited his works, undertook translations, and published minor works. In 1976 in London, without the assent of the Hungarian authorities, his work *Paralysis of International Institutions and the Remedies* was published in English. Bibó's funeral became an opportunity for the first open appearance of various currents of the opposition to the **János Kádár** regime. (JT)

Sources: *Magyar Nagylexikon* (Budapest, 1994), vol. 3; *A magyar forradalom és szabadságharc enciklopédiája,* CD-ROM (Budapest, 1999); *Nagy Képes Milleniumi Arcképcsarnok* (Budapest, 1999).

BIELECKI Jan Krzysztof (3 May 1951, Bydgoszcz), Polish economist and politician. Bielecki graduated from the Higher School of Economics in Sopot in 1973, where he later worked as an assistant professor. From 1975 to 1982 he worked in the Center for Training for Managers of the Ministry of Metallurgy and the Machine-Building Industry in Gdańsk. From 1980 he belonged to Solidarity, and worked in the Social and Professional Center for the Dansk region. From the end of 1981 he was its director. Removed from there in 1982, he ran a handicraft workshop and later was co-owner and driver of a truck. In 1985–89 he was co-founder and worker in a cooperative, Doradca (Adviser), employing several dozen experts deprived of jobs during martial law. From the end of 1981 he was active in the Solidarity underground in Gdańsk; from 1984 he was a liaison of the Gdańsk regional management with the Provisional Coordinating Commission. In 1988 he co-founded the Liberal Congress in Gdańsk. In the elections of June 1989 he won a parliamentary seat, and he joined the Civic Parliamentary Club. From February 1990 he was a member of the Presidium of the Liberal-Democratic Congress (Kongres Liberalno-Demokratyczn [KLD]), and he co-organized the presidential campaign of **Lech Wałęsa**. After Wałęsa's victory, from 4 January 1990 to 5 December 1991 Bielecki was prime minister. He continued the policies of his predecessor, **Tadeusz Mazowiecki**, paying special attention to the economic transformation and rapprochement of Poland with the West. In 1991–93 he presided over the KLD Political Council, and from March

to September 1992, over the KLD parliamentary club; from November 1993 to April 1994 he was vice-president of the KLD National Board. After the merger of the KLD with the Democratic Union, he was a member of the Union of Freedom (Unia Wolności) until 2001. In the government of **Hanna Suchocka** he was minister responsible for contacts with the European Economic Community from July 1992 to October 1993. From December 1993 he was Polish representative to the European Bank of Reconstruction and Development, and from 2003, chairman of one of the largest Polish banks, the PeKaO SA. (AF)

Sources: *Nasi w Sejmie i Senacie* (Warsaw, 1990); Teresa Torańska, *My* (Warsaw, 1994); Janusz A. Majcherek, *Pierwsza dekada III Rzeczpospolitej 1989–1999* (Warsaw, 1999); Antoni Dudek, *Pierwsze lata III Rzeczypospolitej 1989–2001* (Kraków, 2002).

BIELECKI Tadeusz (30 January 1901, Słupia, near Kielce–5 February 1982, London), Polish politician and lawyer. Bielecki graduated from the Department of Philosophy of the Jagiellonian University in Kraków and received a Ph.D. there. He subsequently belonged to various organizations of the National Democratic movement. In 1924–27 he belonged to the National League, then to the Camp of Great Poland (Obóz Wielkiej Polski [OWP]) and the National Party (Stronnictwo Narodowe [SN]). For some time he was the personal secretary of **Roman Dmowski**, and, having gained his trust, after the dissolution of the OWP in 1933 he became head of the SN Department of Organization and one of the leaders of the so-called faction of the young in the party's leadership. From 1928 he was secretary of the headquarters of the secret National Guard and member of the SN informal leaderships, the so-called seven and nine. From 1935 he was vice-president of the SN Supreme Board for organization, and, in view of the ailing health of Dmowski, he gradually took over the party leadership. After Dmowski's death, in June 1939 Bielecki became president of the SN Supreme Board. In 1930–35 he was MP, and in 1938–39, a member of the Warsaw City Council.

After the September 1939 disaster, Bielecki escaped to France and later to Great Britain, where he was active as chairman of the SN Political Committee, chairman of the National Democratic Foreign Committee (1942–45), and (until 1968) chairman of the SN Executive Committee. He belonged to the émigré National Council of the Polish Republic, and he was its vice-president from 1940–41. He remained in opposition to the governments of General **Władysław Sikorski** and **Stanisław Mikołajczyk**. He was particularly critical of concessions concerning Poland's eastern frontiers and the provisions of the Yalta Conference on Poland. In 1947 he supported the takeover by President **August Zaleski**, but afterwards he went into opposition against his rule. He belonged to the founders of the Political Council, an union of parties opposing Zaleski, and he belonged to the council until 1954. An active participant in the talks held by General **Kazimierz Sosnkowski** on the unification of political émigrés, on 14 March 1954 Bielecki was among the signatories of the Unification Act, which, however, was rejected by the followers of Zaleski. From 1954 to 1971 Bielecki was chairman of the Provisional Council of National Unity and then of the Council of National Unity. From 1979 to 1981 he chaired the Council of the Roman Dmowski Institute in London. In 1984 he published *W szkole Dmowskiego: Szkice i wspomnienia* (In Roman Dmowski's school: Essays and memoirs; 1968). (PK)

Sources: Roman Wapiński, *Narodowa Demokracja 1893–1939* (Wrocław, 1980); *Kto był kim w Drugiej Rzeczpospolitej* (Warsaw, 1994); Andrzej Albert [Wojciech Roszkowski], *Najnowsza historia Polski 1914–1993,* vol. 2 (Warsaw, 1995); Andrzej Friszke, *Życie polityczne emigracji* (Warsaw, 1999); Stanisław Kilian, *Myśl społeczno-polityczna Tadeusza Bieleckiego* (Kraków, 2000).

BIELINIS Jurgis (16 March 1846, Purviškiai–18 January 1918, Vilnius [Wilno]), Lithuanian independence activist, famous smuggler of books. Born into a peasant family, Bielinis graduated from a German primary school in Riga. From 1873 he took part in secret anti-tsarist activities. When in 1864 Russian authorities banned the publication of Lithuanian in Latin characters, many Lithuanian activists antedated their publications or published them in so-called Little Lithuania in German East Prussia. Then these books and leaflets were smuggled across the Russian border into Lithuania. Bielinis was one of the main organizers of the network of smugglers (*knygnešiai,* or book carriers), first in cooperation with the Samogetian bishop Motiejus Valančius and then on his own. The center of these operations was in the village of Garšviai in Panevežys county. Bielinis once said that he would not die until "the Muscovites got out of Lithuania." In fact he died soon after the Germans occupied Lithuania and a month before the Lithuanian declaration of independence. (WR)

Sources: *EL,* vol. 1; Petras Ruseckas, *Knygnešys,* vols. 1–2 (Kaunas, 1925–1928); Jerzy Ochmański, *Litewski ruch narodowo-kulturalny w XIX wieku* (Białystok, 1965).

BIEŃ Adam, pseudonyms "Alfa," "Witold Bronowski," and "Walkowicz" (14 December 1899, Ossala, near Połaniec on the Vistula–4 March 1998, Warsaw), Polish politician, lawyer, and journalist. From 1914 to 1917 Bień was a member of secret scouts in Sandomierz. He took part in the liberation of Sandomierz from the Austrians. From 1919 he was a member of the Central Union of Rural Youth (Centralny Związek Młodzieży Wiejskiej [CZMW]). After high school, he fought as a volunteer in the Polish-Soviet war. In 1925 he graduated in law from Warsaw University. Next, he underwent a two-year legal training and worked in the judiciary. In 1925–35 he was president of the Mazovian Association of Folk Theaters and co-author of the book *Teatry ludowe w Polsce* (Folk theaters in Poland; 1928). He also co-founded the Institute of Folk Theaters. In 1928 he co-organized the Union of Rural Youth of the Republic of Poland, called Wici (Związek Młodzieży Wiejskiej Rzeczypospolitej Polskiej Wici). At first he was vice-president, and in 1929–31, president of its Main Board. He exerted a decisive influence on the elaboration of the ideological principles of Wici. In 1921–31 he was a member of the Polish Peasant Party Liberation (Polskie Stronnictwo Ludowe Wyzwolenie). He began underground activities during World War II in an attack on a train near Staszów that had been organized by partisans from a group called Jędrusie. In the spring of 1940 he joined the underground Peasant Party Roch (SL Roch). From 1941 to 1943 he presided over the Legal Commission of the Central Leadership of the Peasant Movement. From May 1944 he was minister of justice and member of the Home Council of Ministers of the Polish Government in London. He also served as first deputy to Vice-Premier **Jan Stanisław Jankowski**. Bień belonged to the civil command of the Warsaw Uprising, and after its fall, to an underground military and political organization called Niepodległość (Independence [NIE]). He contributed to underground newspapers of the peasant movement.

On 28 March 1945 Bień was arrested by the NKVD, and in June of that year, following the Trial of the Sixteen in Moscow, he was sentenced to five years. He served most of his sentence in Lubyanka Prison. After his return to Poland in 1949 he was not allowed to work as a judge until 1953; instead he translated Russian literature for the People's Publishing Cooperative. In 1953–73 he worked as defense attorney in Przasnysz. In 1974 he retired and settled in his native Ossala. He was the author of the memoirs *Więźniowie Moskwy* (Prisoners of Moscow; 1987); *Wyprawa moskiewska* (Moscow expedition; 1989); *Bóg wyżej—dom dalej, 1939–1949* (God higher, home further, 1939–1949; 1991); and *Listy z Łubianki* (Letters from Lubyanka; 1997), for which he received many awards. He was also involved in political journalism, articles of which appeared in uncensored publications in Poland and abroad. In 1987 he was signatory to the founding document of the Independent Peasant Movement Solidarity (Niezależny Ruch Ludowy Solidarność). In 1990 he was one of the authors of an appeal to the Sejm (National Assembly) of the Republic of Poland for the establishment of the Institute of National Remembrance (Instytut Pamięci Narodowej [IPN]), and for the passing of a law condemning Stalinist crimes in Poland. The appeal was published in *Tygodnik Solidarność*. In 1994 Bień was decorated with the Order of the White Eagle. In 1995 he questioned the ethical grounds of **Aleksander Kwaśniewski**'s accession to the presidency because Kwaśniewski had made false claims in the presidential campaign that he had a university degree. According to his will, Bień was buried at a village cemetery in Niekrasów. After his death, his memoirs were published: *Bóg wysoko—dom daleko: Obrazy przeszłości 1900–1920* (God high, home far away: Pictures of the past 1900–1920; 1999). (JS)

Sources: Waldemar Grabowski, *Delegatura Rządu Rzeczypospolitej Polskiej na Kraj* (Warsaw, 1995); *Proces szesnastu: Dokumenty NKWD* (Warsaw, 1995); Hanna and Stanisław Bielscy, eds., *Adam Bień, Bóg dał, Bóg wziął: Dokumenty i teksty z lat 1920–1995* (Warsaw, 1997); Jacek Chrobaczyński, *Ostatni z szesnastu: Biografia polityczna Adama Bienia, 1899–1998* (Warsaw, 2000).

BIENERT Richard (5 September 1881, Prague–3 February 1949, Prague), Czech politician and police officer. From 1906 Bienert served in the Austrian police in Prague. During World War I he cooperated with the national independence movement, which was rallied around a secret committee formed by a group of famous political activists (e.g., **Karel Kramář** and **Alois Rašin**), the so-called Mafia (Maffie). In the interwar period, as the head of the Prague police, he carried out its reorganization so as to adapt it to the new political and legal situation. From 1924 to 1939 he was the vice-head and then the head of the territorial political executive in Bohemia. At the beginning of 1942 he held the portfolio of the interior minister of the Protectorate of Bohemia and Moravia, and from 19 January 1945 to 5 May 1945 he was its last prime minister. At the same time he frequently replaced the ailing president, **Emil Hácha**. In May 1945 Bienert was arrested and on 31 July 1946 sentenced by the Supreme Court to three years of prison. (PU)

Sources: *ČBS*; *Kdo byl kdo v našich dějinách ve 20. století*, vol. 1 (Prague, 1998); Vojtech Masny, *The Czechs under Nazi Rule* (New York and London, 1971).

BIENIASHEVICH Uladzimir (21 August 1874, Druja–27 January 1938?), Belorussian historian and paleographer. In 1897 Bieniashevich graduated in law from Petersburg University. In 1897–1900 he studied in Berlin and Heidelberg. Until 1905 he worked in West European archives and museums, analyzing Roman and Byzantine manuscripts. In 1909 he became professor at Petersburg University. His two-volume work, *Ahliad prats pa slavianaznavstvu* (Overview of Slavic studies), was the first bibliography of Belorussian history, ethnography, literature, and language studies in Belorussia. In the 1920s he was director of the manuscript section of the Leningrad Library. In 1929 he was arrested and accused of counterrevolutionary activities. Imprisoned until 1933, when he was released as a result of the intervention of such outstanding scholars as Albert Einstein, in 1937 he was arrested again and soon shot, along with his two sons and his brother. His major works include the following: *Opisannie grecheskikh rukopisei monastyria sv. Yekateriny na Sinaie* (Description of Greek manuscripts of St. Catherine Monastery in the Sinai, 3 vols.; 1912–1915); *Ocherki po istorii Vizantii* (Outline of Byzantine history, 4 vols.; 1912–1915); *Sinagoga v 50 titulov i drugie iuridicheskiie sborniki Joana Skholastika* (Synagogue in 50 titles and other collections of law by Joannes Scholasticus; 1914); *Sbornik pamiatnikov po istorii tserkovnogo prava, preimushchestvo russkoi tserkvi do epokhi Petra Velikogo* (Collection of relics of legal history writing in the Russian Orthodox Church prior to Peter the Great, 2 vols.; 1914–1915). (EM)

Sources: *Entsyklapedyia historyi Belarusi*, vol. 2 (Minsk, 1994).

BIEŃKOWSKI Władysław (17 March 1906, Łódź–15 April 1991, Warsaw), Polish Communist activist, sociologist, and journalist. The son of a laborer, in 1934 Bieńkowski graduated in philosophy from Warsaw University, and then he worked as a teacher in Lwów (Lviv). During the German occupation he took part in a Communist conspiracy. From 1942 he belonged to the Polish Workers' Party (Polska Partia Robotnicza [PPR]), and he closely cooperated with **Władysław Gomułka**. In December 1943 he was co-founder of the Home National Council (Krajowa Rada Narodowa). From February 1945 to September 1946 he was deputy minister of education, and then, until February 1947, head of the Department of Propaganda of the PPR Central Committee (CC), playing an important role in shaping education and cultural policies. As the result of a fraudulent election in January 1947 he became MP in the Constituent Assembly on behalf of the PPR. From September 1946 to March 1947 and from January to October 1948 he was secretary of the PWP CC, but with the decline of Gomułka's position, Bieńkowski lost importance as well. In December 1948 he joined the Polish United Workers' Party (Polska Zjednoczona Partia Robotnicza [PUWP]), but he was dropped from the party's CC. At the end of 1948 he was appointed director of the National Library and held this position until November 1956.

Bieńkowski returned to politics in 1956, siding with Gomułka. In Gomułka's name he talked to the imprisoned primate, Cardinal **Stefan Wyszyński**, about the latter's release. From November 1956 to October 1959 he was minister of education, and in 1957–69 he was an MP again. He took an active part in the proceedings of the political discussion group, the Crooked Circle Club. Dismissed by Gomułka along with a group of party liberals, he gradually shifted toward the opposition. The publication of his works by the émigré Literary Institute in Paris was a political sensation: *Motory i hamulce socjalizmu* (Stimulators and brakes of socialism; 1969); *Drogi wyjścia* (Ways out; 1971); and *Socjologia klęski. Dramat gomułkowskiego czternastolecia* (The sociology of defeat: The drama of Gomułka's fourteen years in power; 1971). These works kept within the limits of Marxism, but Bieńkowski advocated increased powers for the parliament, limitations on censorship, and a reduction of the state bureaucracy. In May 1970 he was expelled from the PUWP. In 1976, simultaneously with the "Letter of 101" (men of culture protesting against amendment of the constitution), Bieńkowski sent his own "Open Letter on Polish-Soviet Relations." In 1977, along with Andrzej Kijowski and **Stefan Kisielewski**, he took part in a citizens' commission auditing the Committee for the Defense of Workers (Komitet Obrony Robotników [KOR]). In a special statement of September 1977 the commission issued a positive opinion on KOR activities. In 1978 Bieńkowski co-founded the independent Society of Scholarly Courses and took an active part in its activity. In 1981 he published *Theory and Reality: The Development of the Soviet System*, and in 1988 he broke with Marxist ideology in the work *Zrozumieć społeczeństwo* (To understand the society), published in Paris. (PK)

Sources: Mołdawa; Krystyna Kersten, *Narodziny systemu władzy* (Warsaw, 1990); Andrzej Friszke, *Opozycja polityczna w PRL 1945–1980* (London, 1994); Marek Łatyński, *Nie paść na kolana: Szkice o polskiej polityce lat powojennych* (Wrocław, 2002); *Opozycja w PRL: Słownik biograficzny,* vol. 2 (Warsaw, 2002).

BIERUT Bolesław (18 April 1892, Rury Jezuickie, near Lublin–12 March 1956, Moscow), Polish Communist leader. Born into a Catholic peasant family, Bierut completed five grades of primary school. He started working at fourteen, at first in construction and then as a typesetter. In 1910 he met a radical cooperative activist, Jan Hempel. Under his influence, Bierut severed his ties with religion and became close to the revolutionary left. In 1912 he joined the Polish Socialist Party-Left (Polska Partia Socjalistyczna-Lewica). After the outbreak of World War I he went into hiding in Warsaw and Lublin to avoid being drafted by the army and to continue his revolutionary activities. In December 1918 he joined the Communist Workers' Party of Poland (KPRP; as of 1925 the Communist Party of Poland [KPP]). In the fall of 1919 he left the KPRP and, along with Hempel, joined the extremely leftist Union of Workers' Consumer Associations (Związek Robotniczych Stowarzyszeń Spożywczych). In 1921 Bierut returned to the KPRP. From 1923 he was active in the party apparatus in Zagłębie Dabrowskie, in the cooperative movement, and in the Polish Freethinkers' Society. In 1924 he was arrested for his Communist activities. Acquitted and released, he became a full-time party functionary. From May 1925 to May 1926, under the pseudonym "Jan Iwaniuk," Bierut studied at a party school in Moscow, where he underwent training in intelligence and sabotage work and where he met the majority of the KPP leadership. From 1925 to 1927 he was a member of the KPP Central Committee (CC); in 1926–27 he was head of the party's Central Technical Department, and from May 1927 he was a member of its Provisional National Secretariat. Temporarily arrested, in November 1927 Bierut again went to the USSR, where he attended the International Lenin School. Although from 1918 he was married to Janina Górzyńska, with whom he had two children, Bierut entered into a relationship with Małgorzata Fornalska and had a daughter with her.

In the faction struggle within the KPP Bierut supported the anti-Stalinist "majority," so he was "transferred" from the KPP to the All-Union Communist Party (Bolsheviks), and from 1930 he was active as an instructor in the Balkan Secretariat of the Executive Committee of the Comintern. As a Comintern agent and member of the CC of the Bulgarian party, Bierut, under the pseudonym "Mikołaj," often went to Austria, Czechoslovakia, and Bulgaria. In July 1932 he returned to Poland, taking over the secretariat of the KPP committee in Łódź. From 1933 he served as secretary of the CC of the International Organization for Aid to Revolutionaries in Poland. He also started working in the KPP Military Department, which cooperated with Soviet intelligence. On 11 December 1933 he was arrested and sentenced to seven years for his activities against the Polish state. In December 1938 he was released under an amnesty. In 1936 the KPP CC commission for the verification of the party's top members expelled him from the party for "behavior unbecoming of a Communist" during an investigation and trial. However, while Bierut served out his sentence, the Comintern dissolved the KPP, and the majority of its leaders were exterminated in the USSR. After his release Bierut worked in the cooperative movement.

In September 1939 Bierut went to the Polish Eastern Borderlands, which were occupied by the Red Army. From October 1939 he worked in Kowel, and between November 1939 and June 1941, at a construction project conducted by the USSR Commissariat of Transportation. In July 1940 the Control Commission of the Communist International quashed the charges that had been leveled against him by the KPP CC commission. The period between 1939 and 1943 in Bierut's life remains shrouded in mystery. Most probably, having regained the trust of the Kremlin, Bierut must have entered into closer contact with the Soviet intelligence service because after the Germans entered Minsk in June 1941, he assumed the post of deputy head of the economic and supplies department of the city board. At that time he moved in with Anastasia Kolesnikova, who bore him a daughter.

In July 1943 Bierut returned to occupied Poland. He started working in the editorial offices of *Trybuna Wolności*, an organ of the Polish Workers' Party (Polska Partia Robotnicza [PPR]), and, under the pseudonym "Bolesław Birkowski," he joined the CC of the PPR. He also often used the pseudonym "Tomasz." After the arrest of Fornalska and **Paweł Finder**, in December 1943 Bierut became secretary of the CC of the PPR, and at the founding congress of the National Home Council (Krajowa rada Narodowa [KRN]) on 1 January 1944, he was made its president. Already a conflict between Bierut and **Władysław Gomułka**, head of the PPR, was emerging. Gomułka wanted to formally broaden the political base of future Communist authority by including, for example, members of the Central People's Committee (Centralny Komitet Ludowy), while Bierut counted mainly on the backing of the Red Army and Soviet services. On 10 June 1944 he sent a letter to Georgi Dimitrov, head of the Comintern, accusing Gomułka of "sectarian" and "opportunist" tendencies and suggesting a change at the head of the party. This clash allowed the Kremlin to even more tightly control the leadership of the PPR.

At the end of July 1944 PPR and KRN leaders, including Bierut, arrived in Lublin, where the Polish Committee of National Liberation (Polski Komitet Wyzwolenia Narodowego [PKWN]) was installed. In addition to Gomułka, **Jakub Berman**, **Hilary Minc**, and **Aleksander Zawadzki**, Bierut became a member of the newly founded Politburo of the party. Along with the last three mentioned above, Bierut represented an extreme pro-Moscow tendency. Information about his membership in the PPR lead-

ership was not announced; he was presented as a nonparty head of the KRN. On 5 August 1944 in the Kremlin Bierut participated in talks with the prime minister of the Polish government-in-exile, **Stanisław Mikołajczyk**. Bierut pretended then that he did not know anything about the outbreak of the Warsaw Uprising; in this way he wanted to make it more difficult for Mikołajczyk to use the uprising as an argument in support of the Polish cause. In the autumn of 1944 Bierut was instrumental in introducing harsher repressive measures against pro-independence forces in the territory of "Lublin Poland." These measures were employed by USSR intelligence, the NKVD, and the newly forming apparatus of the security department of the PKWN.

The day after the Red Army took the ruins of Warsaw, Bierut arrived in the capital, where on 19 January 1945, on behalf of the KRN, he received a military parade of the units of the new Polish Army. On his return from Yalta, Stalin called Bierut to Moscow and informed him about the decisions made there. Bierut became involved in propagating the Yalta agreements as the basis of the new Poland. On 21 April 1945 he was in Moscow again, where the Polish-Soviet treaty of friendship, mutual assistance and cooperation was signed. From 16 to 21 June he participated in Moscow talks that ended up in the formation of the Provisional Government of National Unity. The announcement of the creation of this government coincided with the announcement of sentences in the trials of the leaders of Underground Poland. Although Mikołajczyk joined the Provisional Government of National Unity and accepted the Yalta agreements, Bierut played a key role in the struggle to crush the Polish Peasant Party (Polskie Stronnictwo Ludowe), which enjoyed the support of the majority of Poles.

After the Communists stole the elections in January, on 5 February 1947 the Constituent Assembly elected Bierut president of Poland. In the summer of 1948 there emerged a sharp conflict in the PPR leadership. While Gomułka opposed the acceleration of collectivization and sanctions against the Yugoslav party, Bierut supported Stalin's line all the way. During his visit to the Kremlin on 15 August 1948 Bierut obtained Stalin's consent for the removal of Gomułka. At the PPR CC plenum, which started on 31 August, Bierut delivered the main speech, attacking Gomułka and bringing about his resignation. Subsequently, Bierut himself became secretary general of the PPR. After the PPR absorbed the already dependent Polish Socialist Party to form the Polish United Workers' Party (Polska Zjednoczona Partia Robotnicza [PUWP]) in December 1948, Bierut assumed the post of first secretary of the CC of the PUWP. He led the purge in the party apparatus and consolidated the party's strictly Stalinist leadership. He increased the number of Soviet advisers in the police and military. From May 1950 to March 1954 he was president of the Secretariat of the Organizational Bureau of the CC and then the first secretary of the CC of the PUWP. From May 1950 he was the actual head of the Presidium of the Council of Ministers, and between November 1952 and March 1954, prime minister. From 1949 until his death Bierut presided over the Public Security Commission of the PUWP CC Politburo. In this role he was directly responsible for the persecution of Polish pro-independence activists. He personally supervised investigations against officers and soldiers of the Home Army and the Polish Army and against some activists of the PPR and the wartime People's Army, including Gomułka. Bierut accepted cruel methods of extorting testimony. He also led the struggle against the Catholic Church, which culminated in the arrest of Primate Stefan Wyszyński in September 1953. Bierut supported the policy of collectivization and accelerated industrialization, which brought about a sharp supply crisis in 1954–56. Between May 1951 and July 1952 Bierut presided over the Constitutional Commission. As head of state, Bierut did not use his right to grant pardons in the cases of hundreds of people unjustly sentenced to death.

Bierut built a personality cult around himself modeled on that of Stalin. After Stalin's death in March 1953 Bierut opposed changes in the government system of Poland. However, under pressure from the Kremlin's "collective leadership" and because of ferment in the PUWP linked to the revelations of Józef Światło (a high-ranking security functionary who had fled to the West), Bierut resigned as prime minister in March 1954. Then, in December of the same year, he agreed that the Ministry of Public Security be replaced with the Public Security Committee. Formally supporting the "thaw," Bierut did all he could to deter the thaw process in Poland. In February 1956 he went to the Twentieth Congress of the CPSU in Moscow. During the debates he developed influenza, and after the congress his health deteriorated further. While Bierut was in Moscow, the PUWP's "active core" (i.e., the most active comrades) held a conference in Warsaw. At the meeting, the party leadership was subjected to much criticism. A few days later Bierut died in a Moscow hospital. (WR)

Sources: Mołdawa; Zbigniew Błażyński, *Mówi Józef Światło: Za kulisami bezpieki i partii* (London, 1985); Marek Łatyński, *Nie paść na kolana: Szkice o opozycji lat czterdziestych* (Warsaw, 1987); Jan Nowak, *O proces Bolesława Bieruta* (Warsaw, 1989); Krystyna Kersten, *Narodziny systemu władzy: Polska 1943–1948* (Poznań, 1990); Czesław Kozłowski, *Namiestnik Stalina* (Warsaw, 1993); Andrzej Werblan, *Stalinizm w Polsce* (Warsaw, 1993); Andrzej Garlicki, *Bolesław Bierut* (Warsaw, 1994); *Polska-ZSRR. Struktury podległości. Dokumenty WKP(b), 1944–1948* (Warsaw, 1995); Piotr Lipiński, *Bolesław Niejasny* (Warsaw, 2001).

BIJEDIĆ Džemal (22 April 1917, Mostar–18 January 1977, Inač kod Kreševa), Bosnian Communist activist. Born into a Muslim family, Bijedić graduated from high school in Mostar and studied law at the University of Belgrade. In 1938 he joined the Union of Yugoslav Communist Youth (UYCY), and in 1939, the Communist Party of Yugoslavia (CPY). In 1940–41 he was secretary of the UYCY committee in Herzegovina. From the end of 1941 he fought with the Communist guerrillas of **Josip Broz Tito**. He was secretary of local CPY organizations in Mostar, Sarajevo, and Tuzla. From the founding congress of the Communist Party of Bosnia and Herzegovina in 1948 he was a member of its Central Committee. In 1970 he was elected speaker of the federal National Assembly. From 30 June 1971 until his death he was president of the Federal Executive Council (government) of Yugoslavia. In this capacity he advocated rapprochement between Yugoslavia and the Arab countries, which caused tension in the southern republics of the Yugoslav federation. Bijedić was killed in a plane crash. There were unconfirmed rumors that the accident could have been the work of anti-Muslim forces in Bosnia and Herzegovina. (WR)

Sources: *Enciklopedija Jugoslavije,* vol. 1 (Zagreb, 1980); Ante Čuvalo, *Historical Dictionary of Croatia* (Lanham, Md., 1997).

BIL'AK Vasil (11 August 1917, Krajná Bystrá, near Svidník), Slovak Communist activist of Ukrainian descent. Bil'ak worked as a tailor until 1949. From 1945 he belonged to the Communist Party of Czechoslovakia (CPC), and during the period of accelerated advancement of workers after 1948 he joined the party apparatus and was a Central Committee (CC) member from 1954. In 1955–68 he was secretary and member of the CC Presidium of the Communist Party of Slovakia (CPS), and from January to August 1968 he was first secretary of the CPS CC. From December 1958 to February 1963 he was plenipotentiary for education (the equivalent of minister in the Slovak government). From July 1960 to January 1963 he was also minister of education in the Czechoslovak government. In 1960–63 he was deputy chairman of the Slovak National Council. From 1960 to 1969 he was MP to the National Assembly, and from 1969 to 1989 he was deputy to the House of Commons of the Federal Assembly.

In April 1968 during the "Prague Spring," Bil'ak was elected as a representative of the party hardliners, to the Presidium of the CPC CC. A staunch opponent of democratic change, in August 1968, along with other dogmatics, such as **Alois Indra** and Antonín Kapek, he signed a letter to the Soviet leadership asking for intervention in the defense of "socialism." In August 1968 he took part in Moscow talks between Czechoslovak and Soviet leaders, openly supporting the Soviet point of view. In November 1968 he became secretary of the CPC CC responsible for foreign policy and ideology. In the 1970s and 1980s he belonged to the chief engineers of "normalization," and, among other things, he was responsible for the purges of intellectuals. Trusted by Leonid Brezhnev, he had significant influence in the CPC apparatus and shaped the neo-Stalinist line of the party. After 1985 he was a fierce opponent of *perestroika.* In December 1989, as one of the most compromised functionaries of the regime, he was deprived of all positions. Removed from the CPC, he retired to Bratislava. From June 1990 there was an investigation into his role in the preparation of the Warsaw Pact invasion of August 1968, but in 2002 he was acquitted of high treason. Despite his protests, in 1991 his unauthorized memoirs, *Míľniky môjho života* (Milestones of my life), were published. (PU)

Sources: *ČBS*; *Kdo byl kdo v našich dějinách ve 20. století*, vol. 1 (Prague, 1998); *Who's Who in the Socialist Countries of Europe*, vol. 2 (Munich, London, and Paris, 1989); *Českoslovenští politici: 1918–1991* (Prague, 1991); Gordon H. Skilling, *Czechoslovakia's Interrupted Revolution* (Princeton, 1976); Vladimir V. Kusin, *From Dubcek to Charter 77: A Study of "Normalization" in Czechoslovakia 1968–1978* (New York, 1978); Zdenek Mlynař, *Nightfrost in Prague: The End of Humane Socialism* (New York, 1980); Alexander Dubcek, *Hope Dies Last* (New York, 1993).

BILCZEWSKI Józef (26 April 1860, Wilamowice, near Kęty–20 March 1923, Lwów), Roman Catholic archbishop of Lwów. Bilczewski came from a peasant family and was one of nine children. After finishing high school, he worked in Mogiła, near Kraków, and then he went to study archeology and theology in Vienna, Rome, and Paris. Ordained in July 1884, in 1890 he defended a postdoctoral degree thesis in archeology at the Jagiellonian University, where he started working the following year. In 1893 he received the title of professor of archeology. From 1900 he was a member of the Polish Academy of Arts and Sciences (Akademia Umiejętności), and in 1900–1 he was rector of the Jagiellonian University. On 17 December 1900 he was appointed archbishop of Lwów in the Latin rite. He followed the program of social Catholicism in the spirit of the teachings of Pope Leo XIII. For example, he founded many professional, educational, economic, and charity organizations. In 1906 he was one of the co-founders of the Catholic Social Union. He was also a patron of Catholic trade unions in Galicia; these were coming into existence

at that time. Bilczewski used his income to found schools, shelters for orphans and poor children, libraries, and reading rooms. He was the author of (among other works) textbooks on archeology and catechism and volumes of *Listy pasterskie* (Pastoral letters; 1922–24), which were translated into several foreign languages. During World War I he defended its victims regardless of whether they were Poles, Ukrainians, or Jews. In November 1918, along with **Andrey Sheptytsky**, Bilczewski tried in vain to prevent the outbreak of Polish-Ukrainian fighting, and when the struggle took place (1918–19), he was able to maintain good relations with the Greek Catholic hierarchy. On 26 June 2001 Pope John Paul II beatified Bilczewski during ceremonies in Lviv. (WR)

Sources: *Encyklopedia historii Drugiej Rzeczyspospolitej* (Warsaw, 1999); *Osservatore Romano* (weekly edition in English), 2001, nos. 25 and 27.

BILIŃSKI Leon (15 June 1846, Zaleszczyki–6 June 1923, Vienna), Polish economist and politician. Biliński graduated in law from the University of Lviv (Lwów). In 1867 he earned a doctorate there, and a year later, a postdoctoral degree. In 1879 he was elected rector of this academy, as a result of which he entered the State Diet in Lviv. In 1883 he was elected to the Austrian Council of State, where he attracted attention with his speeches on taxation and the budget. In 1892 he became the president of the General Management of State Railways, and between 1895 and 1897 he was minister of finance in the government of Kazimierz Badeni. Next he assumed the post of governor of the Austro-Hungarian Bank, in which he served until 1909. From 1909 to 1911 he was again minister of finance of Austria, and from 1912 to 1915, minister of finance of Austria-Hungary. In July 1914 Biliński was one of four ministers who supported a moderation of the demands of an ultimatum presented to Serbia so that its government could accept them. After the end of the war he moved to Warsaw, where from August 1919 he served as minister of finance in the Polish government headed by **Ignacy Paderewski**. He attempted to balance the budget and to control inflation by floating an internal loan. His criticism of uncoordinated government expenses led to a serious clash between him and Paderewski, and in November 1919 Biliński resigned. In 1920 he returned to Vienna, where he assumed the presidency of the Polish-Austrian Bank. He was also a member of the liquidation committee of the Austro-Hungarian Bank and the author of many scholarly works—for example, *Wykłady ekonomii społecznej* (Lectures on social economics; 1873–74) and *System nauki skarbowej* (System of financial science; 1876). He represented theoretical views similar to those of the historic school. He published *Wspomnienia i dokumenty* (Memoirs and documents, 2 vols.; 1924–25). (WR)

Sources: *Polacy w historii*; *Encyklopedia historii Drugiej Rzeczypospolitej* (Warsaw, 1999).

BĪLMANIS Alfreds (2 February 1887, Riga–26 July 1948, Rehoboth Beach, Delaware), Latvian diplomat. After graduating from high school in 1905, Bīlmanis studied in the Department of History of Moscow University. He graduated in 1910, and later he received a Ph.D. at the University of Vilnius (Wilno). In 1910–11 he served in the army, and between 1912 and 1914 he worked as a teacher and director of a high school in Yerevan and Volhynia. Mobilized into the army as a reserve officer in July 1917, he served on the staffs of various armies and edited military periodicals. He was moved to the reserves in April 1918 and returned to his job as a teacher and social worker in Równe. After returning to Latvia in 1920, he was secretary and then head of the Press Department of the Foreign Ministry. From June 1932 to October 1935 he was ambassador to the USSR and then to the United States. After Latvia was occupied by the Red Army and incorporated into the USSR, in July 1940 Bīlmanis was dismissed by the new authorities, but he continued his mission as Latvian ambassador to the United States until his death. In this capacity he was deputy to the ambassador to Great Britain, **Kārlis Zariņš**, whom the last independent Latvian government had appointed an extraordinary minister plenipotentiary to direct diplomatic services and to represent the state in case its legal authorities would not be able to. Bīlmanis authored and edited a number of historical works illustrating the Latvian right to independence, including *Latvia in the Making* (1928); *Latvia in the Present World Crisis* (1941); *Three Stars between the Anvil and Hammer* (1942); *Baltic States and the Problem of Freedom of the Baltic Sea* (1943); *Latvian-Russian Relations* (1945); and *The Church in Latvia* (1945). His *History of Latvia* was published posthumously in 1951. (EJ)

Sources: *Latvijas darbinieku galerija* (Riga, 1928); *Es viņu pazīstu* (Riga, 1939); *Latvia in 1939–1942* (Washington, D.C., 1942); J. Feldmans, "Alfreds Bīlmanis," *Tēvzeme,* 14 August 1948; A. B., "Dr. A. Bīlmanis un viņa mūža darbs," *Latvija Amerikā,* 20 October 1951; A. Dzirkale, "Alfrēda Bīlmaña piemiņai," *Latvija Amerikā,* 2–6 February 1952; P. Priedītis, "Dr. Alfreds Bīlmanis diplomāts un tiesību cīnītājs," *Universitas,* 1974, no. 33.

BIRK Aadu (Ado) (14 November 1883, Tarvastu–2 February 1942, Sosva, Sverdlovsk region), Estonian politician and economic activist. Birk studied at the Orthodox theological seminar in Riga and later at the Theological Academy in Petersburg. Afterward he studied law at the universities in Dorpat (Tartu), Petersburg (1908–11), and Leipzig (1911). In 1911 he became head of the Statistical Office in Tallinn, where he was noticed by one of the city's most prominent lawyers, **Jaan Poska**, mayor of Tallinn from 1912. In 1912–17 Birk was Poska's assistant, and he advanced with the increasing influence of his boss. In 1917 he became secretary of the Estonian Provincial Assembly (Eesti Maanõukogu [EPA]). After Estonia was occupied by Germany in 1918, Birk went to Helsinki, where he tried to get local politicians involved in the Estonian cause. After the liberation of Estonia, in 1918–19 he was EPA president and chaired a committee preparing elections to the Estonian Constituent Assembly (Eesti Asutav Kogu). Later he became its deputy speaker. In 1919–20 he was twice minister of foreign affairs. From 28 to 30 July 1920 he was briefly prime minister and then ambassador to Moscow until 1925.

In 1925 Birk was appointed foreign minister again. He tried to avoid frictions with the USSR. When at the end of 1925 the Ministry of Foreign Affairs was taken over by the pro-Polish **Ants Piip**, Birk was sent as ambassador to Moscow again. The Kremlin tried to win over Estonia through trade contracts, but differences in perceiving the long-term benefits of such cooperation became a source of problems for Birk, who was recalled home in 1926. He refused to return and stayed in the USSR, where he fell victim to a GPU (gosudarstvennoe politicheskoe upravlenie) provocation and was arrested. In 1927 he managed to return to Estonia, where he was arrested on account of spying for the Soviet Union. His case became one of the most publicized political trials in the country, and prominent lawyers were engaged in his defense, including the Social Democratic leader **August Rei**. The accusation against him was not proved, and in November 1927 Birk was released. The question of whether he was or was not a Soviet agent remains open. Until 1940 he was involved in business and social work, with, among others, the Estonian Rifle Association and the Estonian Apostolic Orthodox Church. After the Soviet invasion, on 14 June 1941 he was arrested and transferred to the Sosva labor camp, where he was sentenced to death. He died a few days before execution. (AG)

Sources: Piotr Łossowski, *Stosunki polsko-estońskie 1918–1939* (Gdańsk, 1992); www.president.ee/eng/riigipead/AaduBirk.html; Pekka Erelt, "Eesti Diplomat GPU Võrgus," *Eesti Ekspress,* 3 June 1999, www.ekspress.ee/Arhiiv/1999/22/Aosa/Elu.html, www.orthodoxa.org/estonie/histoireeaoc/thesegb.htm.

BIRKAVS Valdis (28 July 1942, Riga), Latvian politician. Birkavs graduated from the Department of Law of the Latvian State University (LSU) in Riga in 1969. In

1968–86 he worked as an expert, head of section, and director of a criminological laboratory, and from 1986 he lectured at the LSU in Riga, where he received a Ph.D. A member of the Communist Party of Latvia, in 1988 he was co-founder and chairman of the Association of Latvian Lawyers. In 1990–93 he was deputy to the Supreme Council of the Latvian SSR, and after restoration of independence, of the Supreme Council of Latvia. He represented the Latvian National Front and was deputy chairman of its parliamentary club. In 1993 he was elected to the parliament (Saeima) on behalf of the Latvian Way (Latvijas Ceļš) as one of its leaders and was chairman from 1997. From 8 July 1993 to 15 September 1994 he was prime minister. He resigned as the result of a split in the ruling coalition of his party and the Latvian Agrarian Union. The collapse of the coalition resulted from different approaches to tariff policies and to the disclosure in the parliament that two members of the cabinet—Foreign Minister Georgs Andrejevs and minister without portfolio Edvins Inkers—had been KGB agents. In 1994–98 Birkavs was minister of foreign affairs; from September 1994 to November 1995 he was deputy prime minister, and from July 1999 to May 2000, minister of justice. He played an important role in Latvia's endeavors to integrate with European and Atlantic security structures. In October 2000 he was reelected to the parliament. (EJ)

Sources: *Who Is Who in Latvia 1996: Biographical Dictionary* (Riga, 1996); *Wielka Encyklopedia PWN*, vol. 4 (Warsaw, 2001); Andrejs Plakans, *The Latvians: A Short History* (Stanford, 1995); Jurijs Dreifelds, *Latvia in Transition* (Cambridge, 1996); *Kas ir kas Latvijâ* (Riga, 1999); www.rulers.org.

BIRŽIŠKA Mykolas (12 August 1882, Viekšniai–24 August 1962, Los Angeles, Ca.), Lithuanian historian of literature and politician. The son of a doctor, in 1907 Biržiška graduated in law from Moscow University and settled in Vilnius (Wilno). In 1910–11 he edited the periodical *Visuomenė* and took part in the activities of the Lithuanian Research Society and the Social Democratic Party. After Vilnius was occupied by the Germans in 1915, he stayed and worked for the Lithuanian Committee of Aid to War Victims. He also directed the first Lithuanian high school in Vilnius. He wrote several textbooks on the Lithuanian language and the history of literature, and he lectured at the Higher School of Humanities. During a September 1917 conference he joined the Lithuanian Council (Lietuvos Taryba), and on 16 February 1918 he co-signed the declaration of Lithuanian independence. From December 1918 to March 1919 he was minister of education. When Vilnius came under Polish self-government, representing the Polish majority of the city, on 2 January 1919 Biržiška published a protest, and after the city was seized by the Bolsheviks, he was temporarily arrested. When the Polish Army took the city in April 1919, he was elected chairman of the Lithuanian Committee. He took part in talks held with the Poles in Suwałki; these were concluded on 7 October 1920 with an agreement on the separation of Polish and Lithuanian troops, leaving Vilnius on the Lithuanian side. After the violation of this agreement and seizure of the city by the Polish troops under General **Lucjan Żeligowski**, Biržiška secretly published papers and leaflets criticizing Polish activities. Arrested by the Polish authorities, in February 1922 he was released on the condition that he leave for Lithuania.

Biržiška settled in Kaunas, where he directed a high school and lectured in the history of Lithuanian literature at the newly founded Vytautas Magnus University. In 1925 he published his main work, *Mūsų raštų istorija* (History of our literature). In 1922–25 he was dean, and in 1926–27 rector, of the Kaunas university. He belonged to the editorial board of the Lithuanian encyclopedia (1932–44), and from 1940 to 1944 he was a member of the Lithuanian Academy of Literature. He was engaged in publicizing true or alleged Polish wrongdoings to the Lithuanians—for instance, in the Union of Liberation of Vilnius (Vilniui Vaduoti Sąjunga). He published a chronicle, *Vilniaus Golgota* (The Golgota of Vilnius; 1930), exaggerating Polish repression. In 1931 he visited the United States, promoting the Lithuanian vision of the historical and contemporary reality of Vilnius. He published *Iš mūsų kultūros ir literatūros istorijos* (From the history of our culture and literature, 2 vols.; 1931–38). When Lithuania got the Vilnius region from the Soviets, Biržiška became rector of Vilnius University, purged the Polish teachers, and published his version of its history as *Senasis Vilniaus Universitetas* (The old Vilnius University; 1940). He remained the rector under the German occupation. In April 1943 he chaired a meeting of Lithuanian politicians who supported the creation of Lithuanian troops to fight against the Soviets and published a proclamation on the subject that was censored by the Germans. Biržiška signed the document. Before the return of the Red Army in the summer of 1944, Biržiška left for Germany, where he was professor of the Baltic University in Hamburg and then in Pinneberg until 1949, when he settled in the United States. He also published a collection of documents in Polish, *Na posterunku wileńskim* (On the Vilnius outpost, 4 vols.; 1920–36). In exile he published *Lietuvių tautos keliais* (The way of the Lithuanian nation, 2 vols.; 1952–53) and two volumes of memoirs, *Dėl mūsų sostinės* (For our capital; 1960–62). (WR)

Sources: *EL*, vol. 1; V. Maciunas, "Mykolas Biržiška," *Aidai* (Brooklyn), 1952, no. 7; Alfred E. Senn, *The Emergence of Modern Lithuania* (New York, 1959); Piotr Łossowski, *Litwa a sprawy polskie 1939–1940* (Warsaw, 1982); Alfonsas Eidintas and Vytautas Žalys, *Lithuania in European Politics: The Years of the First Republic, 1918–1940* (New York, 1997).

BISTRAS Leonas (20 October 1890, Liepaja–18 October 1971, Kaunas), Lithuanian politician. In 1911–14 Bistras studied medicine in Geneva and Dorpat (Tartu), as well as philosophy in Fribourg, Switzerland, where he received a Ph.D. in 1921. From 1910 he wrote for a Catholic periodical, *Ateitis*, and he belonged to the Christian Democratic Party. For some time he was its chairman, and for many years he belonged to its leadership. Three times elected to the parliament, in 1922–23 he was its speaker. From 25 September 1925 to 15 June 1926 he was prime minister and minister of defense. For some time he also directed the Ministry of Foreign Affairs. His government failed to convince the Holy See about its vision for the Lithuanian province, including Vilnius (Wilno). When in April 1926 Pope Pius XI attached the Vilnius metropolis to the Polish church organization, the Lithuanian Christian Democrats suffered a defeat in prestige. Bistras resigned as a result of the May 1926 elections lost by the right. After the Nationalist coup of December 1926, he returned to the government as minister of education and held this office until May 1927, when the Christian Democrats withdrew from the government. During the regime of **Antanas Smetona** he remained in opposition until March 1939, when the Nationalists attempted to widen the political foundation of their government and offered him the portfolio of education again. He held this office until November 1939. From 1922 to 1940 he lectured in philosophy at Kaunas University. In 1929–36 he was editor-in-chief of the Catholic daily, *Rytas*, critical of the Nationalist dictatorship to the extent that was allowed by censorship, and from 1936 he contributed to the periodical *XX Amžius*. He translated the papal encyclicals *Rerum navarum*, *Graves de communi*, and *Quadragesimo anno* into Lithuanian. After Lithuania was occupied by the Red Army, on 11 February 1940 Bistras was arrested and then deported to Siberia. He spent sixteen years in the Gulag and in forced settlement. In 1956 he was allowed to return to Kaunas. (WR)

Sources: *EL*, vol. 1; Alfonsas Eidintas and Vytautas Žalys, *Lithuania in European Politics: The Years of the First Republic, 1918–1940* (New York, 1997).

BISZKU Béla (13 September 1921, Márokpapi), Hungarian Communist activist. Biszku was born into a peasant family that moved to Budapest in 1929. He qualified as a metalworker and started working in a crane and machinery factory in 1937. In 1943 he joined the Metalworkers' Trade Union, and in 1944, the illegal Hungarian Communist Party (HCP). Between 1944 and 1945 he was one of the leaders of armed resistance in the Thirteenth Quarter of Budapest, Angyalföld. After the war he organized the HCP structures there. From 1946 he worked in the Budapest committee of the party, and in June 1949 he became head of its personnel department. In 1951 he was appointed secretary of the Tenth Quarter (Kőbánya) committee of the Hungarian Workers' Party (HWP), and in September 1953 he started studying in the HWP Higher Political School. From the spring of 1955 he was secretary of the Angyalföld HWP committee. In the first days of the 1956 revolution he organized armed groups of party members and workers in order to suppress the insurgency.

After the revolution was suppressed, Biszku became a member of the Central Committee (CC) and Politburo of the new Hungarian Socialist Workers' Party (HSWP). On 8 December 1956 he became first secretary of the Budapest party committee, and in February 1957, minister of interior in the government of **János Kádár**. Biszku bears the responsibility for the repression against the insurgents of 1956. He played a key role in preparing the trial of **Imre Nagy** and his aides. In August 1957 in Moscow he discussed the general idea of the trial, the indictment, and possible sentences. In 1958–71 and 1975–85 Biszku was MP, and in September 1961 he was promoted to the post of deputy prime minister. In November 1962, at the eighth party congress, he was elected the CC secretary for administration. At the same time he left his government post. From December 1963 he was the CC secretary for organization, and from 1966, for both administration and organization. He represented the extreme dogmatic wing of the party leadership, in opposition to the economic mechanism launched in 1968, and largely contributed to its failure. In the fall of 1972, enjoying the support of the Kremlin, Biszku tried to force a more conservative line, challenging Kádár. In January 1973 he was appointed head of the Commission for Physical Education and Sports. In 1980 he was dismissed from the Politburo and in 1985 from the HSWP CC. (JT)

Sources: *Magyar Nagylexikon*, vol. 4 (Budapest, 1995); *A magyar forradalom és szabadságharc enciklopédiája*, CD-ROM (Budapest, 1999); *Ki kicsoda 2000* (Budapest, 2001); Bennet Kovrig, *Communism in Hungary from Kun to Kádár* (Stanford, 1979); Miklós Molnár, *From Béla Kun to János Kádár: Seventy Years of Hungarian Communism* (New York, 1990).

BIZAUSKAS Kazimieras (2 February 1893, Pavilosta–26 June 1941, near Minsk), Lithuanian Christian Democratic politician. Bizauskas studied law in Moscow, and after that he worked as a teacher. Elected to the Lithuanian Council (Tarybe) in 1917, he signed the declaration of independence of Lithuania of 16 February 1918. From 1920 he was an MP representing Christian Democracy. He negotiated the Soviet-Lithuanian peace treaty of 12 July 1920. In 1922 he was a Lithuanian representative to the Vatican, and from 1923 he was at missions in the United States, Latvia, Great Britain, and the Netherlands. From 28 March 1939 to 17 April 1940 he was deputy prime minister in the government of **Antanas Merkys**. In September 1939 he opposed an alliance of Lithuania with Germany against Poland that was proposed by some members of the government. After the fall of Poland he was summoned to Moscow, and on 10 October 1939 he signed a treaty of mutual assistance with the USSR providing the incorporation of the district of Vilnius (Wilno) to Lithuania. In November 1939 he assumed the post of government plenipotentiary in that region. In relations with the local Polish committee he remained moderate, although he opposed the patriotic gestures of the Polish clergy. At the time of the invasion of the Soviet forces, on 15 June 1940, he represented the Lithuanian authorities to the special representative of the USSR, Vladimir Diekanozov. After the "elections" to the new National Assembly he was arrested in November 1940. After the outbreak of the German-Soviet war in June 1941 he was evacuated from prison in a death march and was shot by the NKVD somewhere around Minsk. (WR)

Sources: *EL*, vol. 1; Piotr Łossowski, *Litwa a sprawy polskie 1939–1940* (Warsaw, 1982).

BLACHNICKI Franciszek Karol (24 March 1921, Rybnik–27 February 1987, Carlsberg), Polish Catholic priest and social activist. In 1939 Blachnicki graduated from high school in Tarnowskie Góry. He fought in the Polish-German war of September 1939 and then worked in the underground. Arrested in the spring of 1940 and deported to the concentration camp in Auschwitz (identification number 1201), he was held there until September 1941. In March 1942 he was sentenced to death, but owing to the efforts of his family, his sentence was commuted to ten years' imprisonment. Released by the American Army in April 1945, Blachnicki returned to Poland and entered the Silesian Theological Seminary in Kraków. Ordained in June 1950, he worked as a curate in the parishes of Upper Silesia (1950–56). In 1957 he founded a sobriety movement called the Temperance Crusade. In August 1960 the Polish Communist authorities liquidated the headquarters of the movement in Katowice. In response, he sent out a number of memorials. Arrested in March 1961 and sen-

tenced to nine months, after his release he pursued further studies and scholarly work at the Catholic University of Lublin. In 1965 he defended his doctoral thesis, and in 1977 he received a postdoctoral degree. He published around one hundred scholarly and popular works. Between 1964 and 1980 he worked for the postconciliar renewal of the liturgy in Poland.

In 1963 Blachnicki began to conduct retreats that evolved into the "oasis" movement. From 1969 this movement was called the Living Church Movement, and from 1976, the Light and Life Movement. His initiative was accepted in hundreds of Polish parishes, becoming the basis for great educational work among the youth, as well as among the elderly, and in 1973 Blachnicki began to create the Home Church Movement for the renewal of family life in Poland. In 1981 in Lublin he established the Independent Christian Social Service, whose aim was to prepare staff for social and political work. On 9 December 1981 he left Poland and went to Rome. He was there when martial law was declared in Poland. He settled in Marianum, a Polish center in Carlsberg in Germany. There he established the International Evangelization Center, Life and Light. In June 1982 Blachnicki founded the Christian Service for the Liberation of Nations, which propagated the ideals of nonviolent resistance in Eastern Europe. He also initiated the establishment of consecrated life communities: a women's Institute of the Immaculate Mother of the Church and the Community of Priests of Christ the Servant. In February 1994 he was posthumously decorated with the Commander's Cross of the Order of Polonia Restituta. In November 2001 the diocesan phase of his beatification process was completed. Blachnicki published, for example, *Dziesięć kroków ku dojrzałości chrześcijańskiej* (Ten steps toward Christian maturity; 1977) and *Prawda–Krzyż–Wyzwolenie: Ku polskiej teologii wyzwolenia* (Truth–Cross–Liberation: Toward a Polish theology of liberation; 1985). (AGr)

Sources: *Słownik biograficzny katolickiego duchowieństwa śląskiego XIX i XX wieku* (Katowice, 1996); M. Paluch, *Zarys historii Ruchu Światło-Życie* (Lublin and Kraków, 1998); J. Mikulski, *Polska teologia wyzwolenia: Teologia wyzwolenia człowieka w ujęciu ks. Franciszka Blachnickiego*; an extensive bibliography included (Tarnów, 2000).

BLAGA Lucian (5 May 1895, Lancrâu, Transylvania–6 May 1961, Cluj), Romanian diplomat, poet, and philosopher. The son of an Orthodox priest, Blaga initially studied in a theological seminary in Sibiu (Hermannstadt) and then at Vienna University (1916–20), where he received a Ph.D. on the basis of his work *Kultur und Erkenntnis* (Culture and knowledge). Later he wrote poems and was engaged in journalism. For many years he contributed to a traditionalist periodical, *Gladirea* (1921–41). He was in large part influenced by Friedrich Nietzsche and Oswald Spengler, and he glorified nature and the national mystique. He used elements of Dionysian expressionism, both in his philosophical works and in his poems and plays. He combined his reflections on the mystical ethos of the Romanian peasantry ("Mioritic space," from the folk ballad "Miorița") with the intuitive German philosophy of his time. He also opposed French influence on Romanian culture and advocated replacing it with German influence.

This philosophical stance was instrumental in Blaga's political activity. From 1926 he worked in diplomacy, advancing from attaché in Warsaw to counselor of the embassy in Switzerland (1928–32) and Vienna (1932–37) and ambassador in Lisbon (1938–39). His diplomatic career came to an end with the development of the royal dictatorship of Charles II. His Germanophilic and mystical philosophy was unacceptable to the regime, since it was too close to the extreme nationalism of the Iron Guard. In 1937 Blaga became a member of the Romanian Academy of Sciences, and in 1939 he was appointed professor of the philosophy of culture at Cluj University (1939–49). After the Communist takeover he was deprived of the right to teach, although he formally remained a "scholarly worker" of the university. He was ostracized, kept under police surveillance, and died in oblivion. In 1966 his memoirs, *Hronicul și cînterul vîrstelor* (Chronicle and song of life) were published. In the 1980s some aspects of his intellectual output were rehabilitated by the Communist regime, and since its collapse his thought has revived. In 1989 a large collection of his poems was published in the United States as *At the Court of Yearning: Poems*. In 1990 his autobiographical novel, *Luntrea lui Caron* (Charon's boat), was published, in which he presented the tragic fate of the Romanian intelligentsia and nation after World War II. (MC)

Sources: *Biographisches Lexikon,* vol. 1; Kurt W. Treptow and Marcel Popa, *Historical Dictionary of Romania* (Lanham, Md., 1996); Dimitrie Vatamaniuc, *Lucian Blaga, 1885–1961: Biobibliografie* (Bucharest, 1977); I. Oprìşan, *Lucian Blaga printer contemporani: Dialoguri adnotate* (Bucharest, 1987); Corin Braga, *Lucian Blaga: Geneza lumilor imaginare* (Iaşi, 1998); Dorli Blaga, *Blaga supravegheat de Securitate* (Cluj, 1999); Mircea Muthu, *Lucian Blaga: Dimensiuni rasaritene* (Piteşti, 2000); R. T. Allen, "The English Language Web Site for Lucian Blaga (1895–1961)," htttp://homepage.ntlworld.com/rt.allen/blagaindex.html.

BLAGOYEV Dimiter (14 June 1856, Zagorichane, Aegean Macedonia [now in Greece]–7 May 1924, Sofia), Bulgarian theorist of Marxism and revolutionary activist. Blagoyev came from a poor peasant family. From 1870 to 1877 he was educated in Istanbul, Adrianople, Gabrovo, and Stara Zagora, and in 1878 he went for further education to Russia. During his natural science and law studies in Petersburg he became involved in the Russian revolutionary movement. In 1883 he created the first Social Democratic organization in Russia, from where he was expelled in 1885 because of his revolutionary activities. After his return to Bulgaria he propagated Socialist ideas in the *Syvremennyi pokazatel* newspaper and in *Den* magazine. On his initiative the Bulgarian Social Democratic Party was created at a congress in Buzludzha in 1891. In his first original Bulgarian work on Marxism, *Shto e sotsializym i ima li toi pochva u nas?* (What is socialism and does it have roots in our country? 1891), he argued with the proponents of socialism who pursued limited, mainly economic, aims without forming a strong party of the working class. After the unification of the Socialist organizations in 1894 Blagoyev became the leader of the Marxist current within the Bulgarian Workers' Social Democratic Party (BWSDP). He expressed his views in *Novo Vreme* magazine, which he edited. There he also published many articles including "Marksizym ili bernshtainianstvo?" (Marxism or revisionism? 1901), and "Opportunizym ili sotsializym?" (Opportunism or socialism? 1902). He also published articles in the Leninist *Iskra*.

In 1903 Blagoyev, along with Gavrilo Georgiev and Georgi Kirkov, caused a split in the BWSDP into "broad" and "narrow" Socialists, and he became the leader of the latter (Tesnyaks). With his direct involvement, the General Workers' Syndicate Union was created in 1904, the organization that led a wave of strikes in 1906–9. Blagoyev laid the foundations for Marxist philosophical and economic thought in Bulgaria. He was also the author of works on the history of the workers' movement in Bulgaria, esthetics, and the theory of literature. He wrote (for example) *Dialektychen materializym i teoriia na poznanieto* (Dialectical materialism and the theory of cognition; 1903–4) and *Prinos kym istoriiata na sotsializma v Bylgariia* (Contribution to the history of socialism in Bulgaria; 1906). During the Balkan Wars (1912–13) and World War I (1914–18) the BWSDP (Tesnyaks) under his leadership struggled against "militarism" and "Greater Bulgarian chauvinism," putting forward slogans of peace and cooperation among the Balkan nations for the sake of the revolution. Blagoyev attended two Balkan Socialist conferences and the congress of the Second International in Copenhagen (1910) as the chairman of the Tesnyak delegation. In 1902–19 he was elected to the parliament three times, and he presided over the parliamentary group of Tesnyaks; between 1911 and 1915 he was also a councillor in the Sofia commune.

There, especially after 1914, he spoke against granting credits for war purposes. It was with satisfaction that he welcomed the Bolshevik Revolution in Russia. He was a co-organizer of the Communist International. The party he led evolved in 1919 into the Bulgarian Communist Party and passed a programmatic declaration in the Leninist spirit. Blagoyev published (mainly in the *Rabotnicheski vestnik* newspaper) articles denouncing imperialism and criticizing the views of Karl Kautsky, who spoke against the principle of the dictatorship of the proletariat. In the spring of 1923 Blagoyev withdrew from active political life due to ill health. (JJ)

Sources: *Entsiklopediya Bulgariya*, vol. 1 (Sofia, 1978); *Dimiter Blagoev 1856–1966*, eds., Ruben Avramov and Maria Chervendineva (Sofia, 1970); *Letopis za zhivota i deynostta na Dimiter Blagoev 1856–1924*, vols. 1–2 (Sofia, 1974–1975); Kiryl Vasiliev, *Dimiter Blagoev: A Biography* (Sofia, 1977); Tadeusz Wasilewski, *Historia Bułgarii* (Wrocław, 1988).

BLAHO Pavel (25 March 1867, Skalica–29 November 1927, Bratislava), Slovak Agrarian politician and cultural and educational activist. Blaho came from a peasant Catholic family. In 1898 he completed medical studies in Vienna, where he was a leader of the Slovak academic youth, and then he worked as a doctor in Skalica. From 1903 to 1914 and in 1918 he also worked seasonally at the health resort of Luhačovice in Moravia. Along with **Vavro Šrobár** he founded and edited the magazine *Hlas* (1898–1904), which provided a platform for young Slovak intellectuals who opposed conservatism, Russophilia, and the policy of passive resistance of the Slovak National Party (Slovenská Národná Strana) leadership. From 1906 to 1918 he was a member of the Hungarian parliament. Along with **Milan Hodža** he was one of the main proponents of the agricultural cooperative movement. He conducted extensive educational work in the Slovak countryside, established libraries and temperance societies, and organized education for the youth in Czech schools. He advocated cooperation with the Czechs and initiated the so-called Luhačovice conferences (1908–14), at which the representatives of the Slovak and Czech national independence movements met. He organized training trips for Slovak farmers to farms in Bohemia and Moravia. From 1912 to 1913 he traveled throughout the United States, giving lectures that contributed to the political activation of Slovak émigrés.

At the end of 1918 Blaho participated in the organization of the Czechoslovak state administration in Slovakia, and he joined the Slovak Club in the National Assembly in Prague. The assembly was convened under the provisional constitution that was passed by the Czechoslovak National Committee. In 1919 he became president of the National Republican Peasant Party (Národná a Republikanská Strana Rol′nícka), later renamed the Slovak Agrarian Party (Slovenská Národná a Rol′nícka Strana), which in 1922 merged with the Czech Agrarians into a nationwide party, the Republican Party of Farmers and Peasants (Republikánská Strana Zemědělského a Malorolnického Lidu). In 1920–27 Blaho was member of the National Assembly and deputy president of the Agrarian parliamentary club. In 1921 he became president of the Agricultural Council in Bratislava. (MG)

Sources: *SBS; Reprezentačný–biografický lexikón Slovenska* (Martin, 1999); *Politická elita meziválečného Československa 1918–1938: Kdo byl Kdo* (Prague, 1998); Štefan Janšák, *Život Dr. Pavla Blahu*, vols. 1–2 (Trnava, 1947); Włodzimierz Wincławski, *Lud, naród, socjologia: Studium o genezie socjologii słowackiej* (Toruń, 1991).

BLAKYTNYI Vasyl [originally Ellanskyi], pseudonyms "Markiz Popelastyi," "Vasyl Ellan," and others (12 January 1894, Kozel, Chernikhiv region—4 December 1925, Kharkiv), Ukrainian writer and Communist activist. Blakytnyi graduated from the Chernikhiv theological seminary, and in 1912–15 he studied in the Trade Institute in Kiev, where he was active in illegal student revolutionary groups. In 1917 he joined the Ukrainian Party of Socialist Revolutionaries (Ukraiinska Partiia Sotsialistiv-Revolutsioneriv), becoming a leader of its leftist wing, which became the Ukrainian Communist Party. The left wing group was the so-called Borotbists, named after their periodical, *Borot'ba*, meaning Struggle. Blakytnyi was also editor of this periodical and of the research and literary biweekly *Zshytky borotby*. One of the initiators of the merger of the Borotbists with the Communist Party (Bolsheviks) of Ukraine (Komunistyczna Partia [Bilszowykiw] Ukrajiny [CP(B)U]), from 1920 Blakytnyi was a member of the CP(B)U, and from 1920 to his death, of its Central Committee. In 1920–21 he was director of the Ukrainian State Publishing House, and from 1921 to his death, editor-in-chief of the newspaper *Visti VUTsVK*. He started his literary career in 1912, but he published his first works in 1918. He was one of the pioneers of Ukrainian Soviet literature, editor of and contributor to many periodicals (such as *Shlakhy mystetstva*, *Vsesvit*, and *Chervonyi perets*), and co-founder (1923) and leader of Hart, the Association of Proletarian Writers. In 1920 he published a volume of proletarian lyrics, *Udary molota i sertsia* (Hammer strokes and heartbeats). He also wrote political satire. In 1924 he published *Notatky olivtsem* (Pencil notes) and *Radyanska hirchytsia* (Soviet charlock), and in 1925,

Derzhavnyi rozum (State reason). In the 1930s Stalinist authorities found nationalistic elements in his writings, so his works were confiscated, and his statue in Kharkiv was demolished. The most complete edition of his works is *Tvory* (Works, 2 vols.; 1958). (BB)

Sources: *Encyclopedia of Ukraine*, vol. 1, (Toronto, 1984); *Ukraiinska Literaturna Entsyklopediia*, vol. 1 (Kiev, 1988); *Malyi Slovnyk Istorii Ukraiiny* (Kiev, 1997); *Dovidnyk z Istorii Ukraiiny* (Kiev, 2001).

BLANDIANA Ana [originally Otilia Coman] (6 February 1942, Timişoara), Romanian poet and dissident. Blandiana's father spent fourteen years in a Communist prison, which strongly influenced her childhood and youth. She made her literary debut in 1959, and in 1967 she graduated in philology from the university in Cluj. In 1968–84 she edited a student periodical, *Amfiteatrul*, and from 1968 she wrote columns for *Contemporanul* and *România Libera*, critical of Stalinist schemes. In her collections of poems and essays, such as *A tria taina* (Third secret; 1969); *Cinzece de poeme* (Fifty poems; 1970); *Cele patru anotimpurii* (Four seasons; 1977); *Întîmplări din gredina mea* (Events from my garden; 1980); and *Stea de pruda* (Rapacious star; 1985), she was not only innovative, but also intellectual and sensible. In 1968 she won an award from the Association of Romanian Writers, in 1974 an award from the Romanian Academy, and in 1982 the Herder Award. In view of the repression of the freedom of creativity and the violation of human rights of the **Nicolae Ceauşescu** regime, Blandiana spoke up against it. In 1984 she wrote *Questionarul pentru Ana Blandiana* (A questionnaire for Ana Blandiana), in which she protested against artistic conformism. She also wrote a series of poems, *Analogica*, in which she warned against the demographic policy of the regime, which forbade abortion so as to increase the population but caused such ills as poverty and depersonalization. Publication of this collection was banned and *Amfiteatrul* was closed down, but her poems circulated in *samizdat*. In 1988 Blandiana was punished again with the ban on the publication of a collection of verses for children, *Întîmplării de pe strada mea* (Events in my street), whose hero, a cat by the name of Arpagic, was a parody of the dictator. On 3 March 1989 she wrote an open letter to Ceauşescu protesting censorship and stressing that her poems could have been published in the USSR and East Germany: and not in Romania.

After the revolution of December 1989, Blandiana was included in the Council of the National Salvation Front (Frontului de Salvare Naţional). Soon, however, she resigned in protest against post-Communist manipulation,

which deprived the council of a democratic character. In 1991 she published *100 poeme* (100 Poems). She co-organized the Civic Alliance (Alianca Civica [CA]) and joined its leadership. The organization declined to seek power but aimed at a critical analysis of systemic transformation and democratic development. The CA became one of the foundations of the Democratic Convention of Romania (Convenţia Democrată Română [RKD]). After the convention took over power in 1997, the CA left it in 1999, criticizing its anti-democratic policies and excessive submission to the post-Communist Democratic Party, its coalition partner. Blandiana was in favor of this secession, expressing her attachment to democracy. In 1990 a collection of her poems was published in London as *The Hour of Sand*. From 1994 she was director of the Museum of Remembrance of the Victims of Communism. (ASK)

Sources: Andrei Codrescu, *The Hole in the Flag* (New York, 1991); Daniel N. Nelson, ed., *Romania after Tyranny* (Boulder, Colo., 1992); Şerban N. Ionescu, *Who Was Who in Twentieth Century Romania* (Boulder, Colo., 1994); www.memorialsighet.ro.

BLAUMANIS Rūdolfs (1 January 1863, Ērgļu, Livonia–4 September 1908, Takaharju, Finland), Latvian writer and poet. Blaumanis's father worked as a cook at an estate. In 1881 Blaumanis graduated from a German trade school in Riga. He lived in his rural district, and for some time he was a scribe at the estate in Koknese. He published his first novel, written in German, in 1882. In 1887–93 he wrote reviews in a German newspaper in Riga. Later, in Riga and in Ērgļu, he concentrated entirely on writing. Between 1898 and 1903 he contributed to Latvian newspapers in Riga and St. Petersburg, and from 1906 he edited a newspaper, *Latvija*. He wrote poems, stories, and stage plays. Latvian peasants, estate workers, and fishermen were predominant in his works; they were representatives of the life he knew from experience. He used humor extensively. Among other works, he was the author of *Skroderdienas Silmačos* (Tailors' days in Silmaci; 1902), the most often produced Latvian stage play, and a comedy, *Uguni* (Fires; 1906). He also wrote patriotic poetry about the heroism of Latvian soldiers in the fight against the Teutonic knights in the thirteenth century: *Tālavas taurētājs* (Trumpeter from Tālava). Blaumanis died of tuberculosis and was buried in Ērgļi. (EJ)

Sources: P. Zālīte, *Rūdolfs Blaumanis: Viņa darbi un nozīme literatūrā* (Riga, 1923); Antons Birkerts, *Rūdolfs Blaumanis dzīvē un darbā* (Riga, 1930); Alfons Vilsons, *Latviešu literatūras klasiķis Rūdolfs Blaumanis* (Riga, 1956); *Rūdolfs Blaumanis laika biedru atmiņās* (Riga, 1962); Lutsia Volkova, *Tapšana* (Riga, 1988); Andrejs Plakans, *Historical Dictionary of Latvia* (Lanham, Md., 1997).

BŁODNIEKS Ādolfs (24 July 1889, Tukums, Courland–21 March 1962, Brooklyn, N.Y.), Latvian politician. Born into a peasant family, Błodnieks was educated in a trade school in Tukums. In 1905 he took part in the revolution and was seriously injured. Later he graduated from a high school oriented toward the natural sciences and mathematics in Kursk, and from 1910 he studied at the Riga Polytechnic Institute. During World War I he volunteered for the Russian Army and served in the air force. In 1917 he was elected a member of the Soviet of Workers' and Soldiers' Deputies in Petrograd. Later, however, he was a co-founder of the Latvian Party of National Democrats and was active in the Union for the Defense of the Fatherland and Freedom, an anti-Bolshevik organization under the leadership of Boris Savinkov. In 1919 he returned to Latvia and became head of a department in the Ministry of Finance. He was a member of the Latvian Provisional National Council and then a deputy to the Constituent Assembly and the parliaments (Saeima) of subsequent terms. He was one of the founders of the new Farmers' and Smallholders' Party (Jaunsaimnieku un Sīkgruntnieku Partija), and from 1921 he was editor of the party newspaper, *Latvija*. From 23 March 1933 to 17 March 1934 he was prime minister. After the occupation of Latvia by the Red Army in 1940 he avoided deportation, and in 1944 he went into exile. In 1960 in New York he published *The Undefeated Nation*. (EJ)

Sources: *Latvijas darbinieku galerija* (Riga, 1928); *Latvijas vadošie darbinieki* (Riga, 1935); *Es viņu pazīstu* (Riga, 1939); Piotr Łossowski, *Kraje bałtyckie od demokracji parlamentarnej do dyktatury (1918–1934)* (Wrocław, 1972); Andrejs Plakans, *Historical Dictionary of Latvia* (Lanham, Md., 1997).

BNIŃSKI Adolf (21 August 1884, Kossowo, near Gostyń–7/8 July 1942, near Poznań), Polish politician and social worker. Bniński graduated from high school in Inowrocław in 1905, and then he studied at the Jagiellonian University in Kraków and later in Munich and Halle in Germany. He was active in laying the foundations of the Polish administration in Greater Poland (Poznania) and Central Poland; he was government commissioner in Łódź (1918–19) and head of the county administration (*starosta*) in Środa Wielkopolska (1919–20). In 1923–28 he was provincial governor (*wojewoda*) of Greater Poland. He sympathized with National Democracy, and with its support he ran in the 1926 presidential election, but he lost to **Ignacy Mościcki**. Apart from his political activities, Bniński ran family estates in Gułtowy and Biskupice in Greater Poland and took part or presided over many social and economic organizations, such as the Greater Polish Agricultural Chamber (1920–22), Catholic Action, and the

Supreme Council of Landowners' Organizations (1937). He was also one of the chairmen of the Chief Administration of Popular Reading Rooms. After the May coup of 1926 he approached the ruling group of **Józef Piłsudski**, and as a result he was appointed senator. In the 1930s he tried to stimulate conservative circles, creating the Conservative Party (Stronnictwo Zachowawcze) in 1938, but to no major avail. After the German invasion of 1939 he joined in underground activities under the pseudonym "Białoń," de facto holding the position of delegate of the government-in-exile for the territories incorporated into Germany from 3 May 1940. Prime Minister General **Władysław Sikorski** confirmed him formally in this position on 4 December 1940. At the end of July 1941 Bniński was arrested by the Gestapo in Poznań, imprisoned in Fort VII, sentenced to death, and shot (probably with seven aides) in a forest near Poznań. (AG)

Sources: *Kto był kim w Drugiej Rzeczypospolitej* (Warsaw, 1994); S. Dworacki, ed., *Wojewoda Adolf hr. Bniński (1884–1942): Materiały do sesji okolicznościowej w Gułtowach* (Poznań, 1997); Andrzej Kwilecki, *Ziemiaństwo wielkopolskie* (Poznań, 1998); Krzysztof Jasiewicz, *Lista strat ziemiaństwa polskiego 1939–1956* (Warsaw, 1995); Waldemar Grabowski, *Delegatura Rządu Rzeczypospolitej na Kraj* (Warsaw, 1995).

BOBAN Mate (1940, Sović, near Grude–7 July 1997, Mostar), Croatian leader from Bosnia. In 1958 Boban joined the League of Communists of Yugoslavia (LCY). For more than twenty years he was its local functionary. A turning point in his career came in 1990, when he founded the Democratic Union of Herzegovina and soon merged it into the Croatian Democratic Union of Bosnia-Herzegovina (CDUBH). On behalf of this party he won a parliamentary seat. Soon he became the CDUBH deputy chairman and later chairman. He took over from the previous party leader, Stjepan Kljujić, who had lost the support of the Croatian president, **Franjo Tudjman**. On 3 July 1992 Boban took the lead of Herceg-Bosnia, thought to be a Croatian state within Bosnia-Herzegovina and supported militarily by Croatia. For about a year heavy fighting took place in the Lašvanska Valley between the Croats and Muslims, and about thirty thousand people perished. Boban initially took part in international negotiations and accepted the Cyrus Vance and David Owen Plan of 1992–93. Boban's idea of resettling Bosnian Croats to parts of Bosnia-Herzegovina where they were in the majority, thought to be coordinated with the Roman Catholic Church, in fact led to a conflict between Boban and Archbishop **Vinko Puljić**. In view of growing international criticism of the Bosnian Croats—it was connected to information about the torture of Muslims in concentration camps—Tudjman called upon Boban to respect international law. Finally, accused of ethnic cleansing, Boban was dismissed as a result of international pressure. (AO)

Sources: Laura Silber and Allan Little, *The Death of Yugoslavia* (London, 1995); David Owen, *Balkan Odyssey* (New York, San Diego, and London, 1995); Norman Cigar, *Genocide in Bosnia* (Texas A&M University Press, 1995); Susan L. Woodward, *Balkan Tragedy* (Washington, D.C., 1995); Ante Čuvalo, *Historical Dictionary of Bosnia and Herzegovina* (Lanham, Md., 1997); www.rferl.org; www.bosnet.org.

BOBOSHEVSKI Tsvetko (8 August 1884, Vratsa–21 December 1952, Sofia), Bulgarian politician and lawyer. In 1906 Boboshevski completed law studies in Paris. He returned to Bulgaria and became a lawyer in Vratsa. He joined the National Party, and after it merged with the Progressive Liberal Party, he joined the United National Progressive Party, in which he served as secretary from November 1920. Having joined the oppositional Constitutional Bloc in 1922, he participated in the preparations for the military coup of 9 June 1923, in which he took an active part. After the coup he joined the People's Alliance. In the government of **Aleksandur Tsankov** he served as minister of trade, industry, and labor (June 1923–November 1924) and as minister of justice (November 1924–January 1926). In the cabinet of **Andrei Liapchev** he again assumed the position of minister of trade, industry, and labor (January 1926–May 1930). In the 1930s he joined a political group centered around the magazine *Mir.* He supported the coup of 19 May 1934. In 1934–36 he was president of the Bulgarian Mortgage Bank. During World War II he maintained an anti-Fascist and anti-German stance, but he refused to cooperate with the Communists. He was also against organizing a guerrilla movement. In March 1943 he was involved in a movement to save the Bulgarian Jews. He was a supporter of the pro-English and pro-French lines in foreign policy. However, he joined the Fatherland Front as an independent intellectual. The Communists rewarded him for that, appointing him, along with **Venelin Ganev** and **Todor Pavlov**, one of the three regents of Bulgaria. Boboshevski took an ambiguous stance on various issues; sometimes his attitude was even favorable to the opposition. He held the post of regent from 9 September 1944 until 8 September 1946, when Bulgaria was proclaimed a republic. (JJ)

Sources: *Entsiklopediya Bulgariya*, vol. 1 (Sofia, 1978); Tasho V. Tashev, *Ministrite na Bylgariia 1879–1999* (Sofia, 1999).

BOBROWSKI Czesław (17 February 1904, Sarny–17 May 1996, Warsaw), Polish economist and politician. In 1925 Bobrowski graduated from Warsaw University and in 1927, from the Ecole des Sciences Politiques in Paris. In 1925–26 he worked in the Polish General Consulate in Prague; from 1931 to 1932 he was director of a Polish-Soviet trade company, Sovpoltorg, in Moscow; and in 1936–39 he was director of a department in the Ministry of Agriculture and Land Reforms. In 1931 and 1933–36 he edited the biweekly *Gospodarka Narodowa.* During World War II he lived in the West, where he co-authored the "plan for the first six months" of Polish economic policy after the war. He came back to Poland in August 1945. A deputy to the Communist-controlled Home National Council (1945–47) and to the Constituent Assembly (1947–51), from August 1946 to December 1948 he was a member of the Supreme Board of the Polish Socialist Party (Polska Partia Socjalistyczna [PPS]), and from November 1945 to March 1948 he chaired the Central Planning Office (Centralny Urząd Planowania [CUP]) and was deputy chairman of the Economic Committee of the Council of Ministers. He co-authored the Three-Year Plan for Economic Reconstruction, passed in September 1946 and based on a well-balanced concept of an even rate of growth in all branches of the economy. He distanced himself from the Soviet model of planning and from the "battle for trade" policy of the (Communist) Polish Workers' Party (Polska Partia Robotnicza [PPR]), which meant complete nationalization. At a joint meeting of PPS and PPR leaders on 18–19 February 1948 **Hilary Minc** (PPR) attacked the CUP for favoring consumption and not production, for deviation from Marxist "science," and for mixing up planning and forecasting. The resignation of Bobrowski and liquidation of the CUP are thought to be the beginnings of Stalinization in the Polish economy.

In 1948–50 Bobrowski was an ambassador to Sweden, and then he remained abroad. In 1952–56 he worked in the Centre Nationale de la Recherche Scientifique in Paris. On 30 October 1951 he was stripped of his parliamentary mandate. He returned to Poland during the "thaw." From 1956 he worked at Warsaw University, where in 1959 he became a full professor. In 1957–63 he was deputy chairman of the Economic Council of the government and favored the decentralization of economic management and a more flexible, indicative planning. From 1964 to 1968 he was president of the Main Board of the Popular Knowledge Society. In the 1960s and 1970s he worked for various international organizations. He was UN planning adviser for the governments of Algeria, Ghana, and Syria. He also taught in France and Italy. As dean of the Department of Economics, on 8 March 1968 he intervened with the authorities on behalf of repressed students. After the introduction of martial law in December 1981, he took the position of chairman of the Consultative Economic

Council, authenticating party and government policies. From 6 December 1986 to 17 July 1989 he belonged to the Consultative Council for the Chairman of the Council of State, General **Wojciech Jaruzelski**. Bobrowski authored numerous works, including *U źródeł planowania gospodarczego* (At the roots of economic planning; 1956), and *Wspomnienia ze stulecia* (Memoirs of one hundred years; 1983). (PK)

Sources: Mołdawa; *Wielka Encyklopedia Powszechna*, vol. 4 (Warsaw, 2001); Jan Drewnowski, "Proces Centralnego Urzędu Planowania," *Zeszyty Historyczne*, 1974, no. 28; Krystyna Kersten, *Narodziny systemu władzy* (Poznań, 1990).

BOBRZYŃSKI Michał (30 September 1849, Kraków–3 July 1935, Poznań), Polish historian of law and politician. After graduating from St. Ann High School in Kraków, Bobrzyński studied law at the Jagiellonian University in Kraków. In 1872 he received a Ph.D. there. He mainly dealt with the history of Polish and German law. From 1879 he was a full professor at the Kraków university. In 1878 he became a member of the Academy of Arts and Sciences. In the next dozen years he published several works, including *Dzieje Polski w zarysie* (Outline of Polish history; 1879), revised and reedited many times. He was of the opinion that Old Poland's problems were a result of a weak state authority and not the greed of its neighbors. This view stimulated fierce debates among historians and politicians. One of the founders of the so-called Kraków historical school, in 1885 Bobrzyński was elected to the Galician Land Parliament (Sejm) and to the parliament in Vienna, where he sat until 1908 (with a break in 1900–1903). He was one of the leaders of the Kraków Conservatives, the so-called Stańczyk group, advocating "organic work" and not armed insurrections as the best national policy. He thought Galician Poles should support the Habsburgs in exchange for guarantees of national development. In 1891–1901 Bobrzyński was vice-president of the Land School Council in Lwów (Lviv) and contributed to the extension of the school network and the upgrading of Galician education.

When Governor Andrzej Potocki was assassinated by a Ukrainian in April 1908, Bobrzyński became his successor. In the five years of his term his main goals were the easing of Polish-Ukrainian tensions and a reform of the Galician electoral law. He thought it in the interest of Poland to support Ukrainians against Russia, which he perceived as the main threat to Poland. On both issues he faced strong opposition from the National Democrats, and when both projects failed, he resigned in May 1913. After the outbreak of World War I he tried to push through a plan for the unification of the Russian-controlled former Kingdom of Poland with Austria. In 1916–17 he was Austrian minister for Galicia, focusing his efforts on a draft law separating Galicia and making it easier for its future merger with the rest of Polish territories. After Poland regained independence, Bobrzyński retired from political life. In 1919 he settled on the Poznanian estate of Graby and returned to scholarly work. In 1919 he chaired the Inquiry (Ankieta), a group of experts evaluating various projects of the constitution. In 1922 he co-authored a proposal for the autonomy of Lwów (Lviv), Stanisławów (Ivano-Frankivsk), and Tarnopol (Ternopil) Provinces, and in 1926 he took part in the Commission of Three to prepare a reform of the administration. He was also the author of *Wskrzeszenie państwa polskiego* (Revival of the Polish state, 2 vols.; 1920–25) and the memoirs *Z moich pamiętników* (From my diary, 2 vols.; 1957). (PU)

Sources: *PSB*, vol. 2; *Encyklopedia historii Drugiej Rzeczypospolitej* (Warsaw, 1999); Waldemar Łazuga, *Michał Bobrzyński: Myśl historyczna a działalność polityczna* (Warsaw, 1982); Henryk Wereszycki, *Historia polityczna Polski 1864–1918* (Wrocław, 1990); Wojciech Kaute, *Synteza dziejów Polski Michała Bobrzyńskiego* (Katowice, 1993); Józef Buszko, *Polacy w parlamencie wiedeńskim 1848–1918;* (Warsaw, 1996); Piotr Majewski, ed., *Michał Bobrzyński o potrzebie "silnego rządu" w Polsce* (Warsaw, 2001).

BOCHEŃSKI Józef [monastic name Innocenty] (30 August 1902, Czuszów, near Kraków–8 February 1995, Fribourg, Switzerland), Polish logician and philosopher. Born into a landowner's family, in 1920 Bocheński took part in the Polish-Soviet war. Later he studied economics in Poznań (with, among others, with **Florian Znaniecki**), philosophy in Fribourg, and theology in Rome. At first he considered being an agnostic; in 1926, however, he entered a theological seminary in Rome, and in 1932 he was ordained in the Dominican Order. In 1931 he received a Ph.D. in philosophy, and in 1934, in theology. Afterward he lectured at the Collegium Angelicum in Rome and at the Jagiellonian University in Kraków. He took part in the Polish-German war of 1939, and as chaplain of the Polish Army in the Italian campaign, he was at the Battle of Monte Cassino (May 1944). From 1945 he was a professor at Fribourg University, where he lectured in the history of twentieth-century philosophy. In 1950–51 he was dean of the Philosophical Department and from 1964 to 1966, rector of this university. He also taught at the University of Notre Dame (1955–56), UCLA (1958–59), the University of Kansas (1960), the University of Pittsburgh (1968), and the Canadian University of Alberta in Edmonton (1971). In 1972 he retired but continued intensive scholarly activities.

As a philosopher Bocheński firmly opposed relativism

and skepticism. He was of the opinion that the world is a logic structure, recognizable through experience and common sense. In numerous works and public presentations he criticized nationalism, racism, pacifism, feminism, and anarchism as contrary to the rudiments of European culture. He also opposed a liberal interpretation of humanism and democracy and argued that they stemmed from Christianity. His main philosophical interest was in liberty and authority. The most important of his early works include the following: *De cognitione existentia Dei* (On the recognition of the existence of God; 1936); *Elementa Logicae Grecae* (Elements of Greek logic; 1937); *Europäische Philosophie der Gegenwart* (Contemporary European philosophy; 1947); *The Ancient Formal Logic* (1951); *Formale Logik* (Formal logic; 1956); and *The Logic of Religion* (1965). Until 1994 he was president of the World Council of Societies of Logic and Methodology of Science.

Bocheński was a pioneer of Sovietology. He founded the Institute of Eastern Europe in Fribourg and was its first director. He advised the governments of West Germany (the Konrad Adenauer cabinet), the United States, Argentina, and Switzerland. He considered Marxism as a set of false enunciations and stressed the contradictions between communism and the European tradition. He edited *Studies in Soviet Thought* and the series Sovietica. He authored dozens of books, including *Handbuch des Weltkommunismus* (Handbook of world communism; 1958); *Der sowjetrussische dialektische Materialismus (Diamat)* (Soviet dialectics of materialism [Diamat]; 1962), and *Sto zabobonów: Krótki filozoficzny słownik zabobonów* (One hundred superstitions: A short philosophical dictionary of superstitions; 1987). He held numerous honorary doctorates, from Polish, U.S., Latin American, and African universities. He founded the Polish Catholic Mission in Switzerland and was its first rector. From 1945 to 1989 his works were banned in Poland, but after the fall of communism he was reappeared in the Polish media and publications. (PK)

Sources: *International Who's Who 1983/84*; Ks. D. Gabler, "Józef Maria Bocheński: Logik, filozof, mędrzec," *Tygodnik Powszechny,* 25 October 1987; Aleksander Bocheński, *Materiały do kroniki rodzinnej Bocheńskich* (Fribourg, 1981); *Słownik historii doktryn politycznych,* vol. 1 (Warsaw, 1997); E. Morscher and O. Neumaier, *Joseph Maria Bocheńskis Leben und Werk* (Salzburg, 1988); *Między Logiką a Wiarą. Z Józefem M. Bocheńskim rozmawia Jan Parys* (Warsaw, 1998).

BODNARAŞ Emil (10 February 1904, Kolomyia–24 January 1976, Vienna), Romanian Communist activist. Bodnaraş' father was Ukrainian, and his mother was German. After graduating from high school he studied law at the university in Iaşi. However, he did not complete his studies, and he switched to the Officers' Academy in Timişoara, from which he graduated in 1927. Next, he began his military service, first in Craiova and then in Sadagura, close to the Soviet border. From there, as an agent of Romanian intelligence, he managed to get to the USSR in 1931. Captured, he agreed to switch loyalties; he underwent training in the OGPU (Obedinennoe gosudarstvennoe politicheskoe upravlenie) center in Astrakhan and started working in the foreign intelligence of the NKVD. As an NKVD agent, Bodnaraş, who was fluent in German, went on many spy missions to Poland and the Baltic states. On his way to Bulgaria in 1934 he was recognized at a station in Bucharest, and he was arrested. Condemned to death for desertion and for crimes against the security of Romania, he had his sentence commuted to ten years' imprisonment. He served his sentence in prisons in Doftana, Aiud, Galaţi (Galatz), Braşov, and Caransebeş, where he met the leadership of the Romanian Communist Party (RCP), became close to **Gheorghe Gheorghiu-Dej,** and formally entered the RCP.

Released on 7 November 1942, Bodnaraş settled in Brăila, where, under the pseudonym "Engineer Ceauşu," he continued to spy for the USSR despite the fact that he was under police surveillance. The most mysterious period in his life was between 1942 and 1944. In those years he visited Tîrgu-Jiu Prison and met the RCP leaders who were being held there. This must have taken place with the full knowledge of Siguranţa, the security police of Marshal **Ion Antonescu,** who probably hoped that Bodnaraş might become a willing tool in his hands when Romania joined the side of the Allies. However, Bodnaraş was a key figure chosen by the Kremlin not only to direct the Communist takeover, but also to remove unwanted persons from the Communist leadership. As early as April 1944 he dismissed the formal head of the party, **Ştefan Foriş.** As a result, the leadership of the RCP was assumed by a group that arrived from the USSR and by Gheorghiu-Dej. Bodnaraş represented the RCP in the group of politicians who were preparing Romania's shift to the side of the Allies. In May 1944 he attended a meeting with King **Michael** at which the overthrow of Antonescu was mentioned for the first time. During the coup in August 1944 Bodnaraş commanded the Patriotic Guard, a unit of which imprisoned Antonescu and then handed him over to the Soviets. The Patriotic Guard was the germ of the Communist political police, to which Bodnaraş recruited not only Soviet agents, but also criminals and members of the Fascist Iron Guard who wanted to avoid responsibility. On 15 January 1945 the prime minister, General **Nicolae Rădescu,** called for the dissolution of the Patriotic Guard, but Bodnaraş ignored this order.

In February 1945 Bodnaraş was instrumental in overthrowing the government of Rădescu. In the cabinet of **Petru Groza**, Bodnaraş served as undersecretary of state in the Prime Minister's Office, and in fact he controlled Groza's moves. In April 1945 Groza formally appointed him head of the government political information service. In this capacity, until 1947 Bodnaraş was in charge of the cruel suppression of opposition leaders. In December 1947 he became defense minister and was promoted to general. He monitored the army's behavior toward the Communist-imposed abdication of King Michael, and then he conducted a purge of the army. As a member of the party Politburo, Bodnaraş often acted as a mediator between fractious factions. He was also responsible for brutal persecutions in the Greek Catholic Church, the Roman Catholic Church, and the Orthodox Church, as well as for collectivization, during which many resisting peasants were killed and tens of thousands were sent to forced labor camps—for example, along the Danube-Black Sea Canal.

Bodnaraş supported Gheorghiu-Dej in his efforts to eliminate the group of **Ana Pauker**, **Vasile Luca**, and **Teohari Georgescu** in 1952 and to dismiss and then murder **Lucreţiu Pătrăşcanu** (1948–54). Bodnaraş gradually removed direct Soviet executors from the security apparatus and from the army and replaced them with similar Romanian elements. During the Hungarian Revolution of 1956, when the leadership was afraid that the unrest might spread to Romania, Bodnaraş became head of the government's special military and police command. This command pressured the Kremlin to launch a military intervention in Budapest. When the Communists arrested **Imre Nagy** and took him to Bucharest, Bodnaraş also had an opportunity to interrogate him. At the end of November 1956 he arrived in Budapest to help **János Kádár** rebuild the political police, with the assistance of Hungarian agents from Transylvania.

Bodnaraş supported Gheorghiu-Dej in his struggle against **Miron Constantinescu** and **Iosif Chişinevschi** in 1957. From 1956 to 1959 Bodnaraş was formally only a minister of transport, and his position in the party leadership was due to his position in the KGB. From the end of the 1950s he closely cooperated with Gheorghiu-Dej in his efforts to carve out a more independent foreign policy for the RCP. However, the degree of the Kremlin's tolerance for this policy, as well as Bodnaraş's true motives in this matter, are controversial. As early as 1955, Gheorghiu-Dej and Bodnaraş were intending to demand the withdrawal of Soviet troops from Romania, and they achieved this goal in May 1958. In February 1964 Bodnaraş was a member of the Romanian delegation sent to Moscow and Beijing in an attempt to ease the conflict between China and the USSR. He was closely connected with **Nicolae Ceauşescu** from the time the latter was his subordinate as chief political commissar of the army. After Gheorghiu-Dej's death, in March 1965 Bodnaraş supported Ceauşescu's candidacy as Gheorghiu Dej's successor. At the Ninth Congress of the RCP in July 1965 Bodnaraş joined the new seven-member Standing Presidium of the CC. He remained a member of this presidium until the end of his life, probably to make credible the RCP's "independent line" toward the Kremlin. Although in 1954 he voted in favor of the execution of Pătrăşcanu, after Pătrăşcanu's rehabilitation in 1968 Bodnaraş published an article mourning the death of a "great personality" and a "good friend." Bodnaraş supported the consolidation of Ceauşescu's power, delivering, for example, the main speech on amendments to the constitution in 1974. (WR)

Sources: Michael Shaffir, *Romania: Politics, Economics and Society* (Boulder, Colo., 1985); Victor Frunză, *Istoria stalinismului în România* (Bucharest, 1990); Edward Behr, *Kiss the Hand You Cannot Bite: The Rise and Fall of the Ceauşescus* (New York, 1991); Şerban N. Ionescu, *Who Was Who in Twentieth Century Romania* (Boulder, Colo., 1994); G. Iavorschi, "Pentru cine a lucrat 'inginerul Ceauşu?" *Magazin Istoric*, 1994, no. 9; Dennis Deletant, *Communist Terror in Romania: Gheorghiu-Dej and the Police State, 1948–1965* (New York, 1999).

BŐHM Vilmos (6 January 1880, Budapest–28 October 1949, Stockholm), Hungarian politician and trade union activist. A mechanic by trade, Bőhm started his political career in the Hungarian Social Democratic Party (HSDP) with trade union activity. In 1912 he was elected to the HSDP leadership and soon became secretary of the National Union of Iron and Nonferrous Metal Workers. During the republican revolution of late 1918, he was secretary of state in the Ministry of Defense and chairman of the committee for demobilization. From January 1919 he was minister of defense in the government of Dénes Berinkey. After the proclamation of the Hungarian Soviet Republic (HSR) in March 1919 he continued directing this ministry and took over the high command of the Hungarian Red Army fighting in Slovakia. In the spring of 1919 he favored armistice with the Entente and opposed the Soviet-type rule of "the dictatorship of the proletariat." In March and April 1919 he was also people's commissar for nationalization. He was proud that nationalization in Hungary went further than in Soviet Russia.

From July 1919 Bőhm was minister plenipotentiary in Vienna, where he held talks with the representatives of the Entente on the international recognition of the HSR. After the fall of Soviet rule in Hungary he stayed in Vienna, where he worked as a senior salesman in a department store. At the same time he wrote memoirs and articles on the Hungarian revolution, including *A Magyar Tanácsköztársaság keletkezése és összeomlása* (The rise and fall of the Hungarian Soviet Republic; 1920) and *Két forradalom tüzében* (In the flames of two revolutions; 1923). From 1934 he lived in Czechoslovakia and then in Sweden, where he was active in the Hungarian Social Democracy movement abroad. Among other things, during World War II he was a go-between in the talks between the Hungarian government and the anti-German coalition. In 1945 he returned to Hungary, taking the lead of the right wing of the Social Democratic Party, unwilling to merge with the Communists. From 1946 he was ambassador to Sweden. In 1948 he resigned and refused to go back to Hungary. In Communist historiography he is shown as a representative of the conservative, or even treacherous, attitude of the Social Democrats. (MS)

Sources: *Magyar Nagylexikon*, vol. 3 (Budapest, 1994); *Nagy Képes Milleniumi Arcképcsarnok* (Budapest, 1999); *Új Magyar Életrajzi Lexikon*, vol. 1 (Budapest, 2001); Rudolf L. Tőkes, *Béla Kun: The Man and the Revolutionary* (New York, 1966); Éva Szabó, "Adalékok Bőhm Vilmos politikai élatrajzához," *Történeti Szemle*, 1980, no 1; László Havanyecz, "Egy elsőgenerációs hazafi," *Népszabadság*, 1997, no. 107.

BOJKO Jakub (7 July 1857, Gręboszów, near Dąbrowa Tarnowska–7 April 1943, Gręboszów), Polish peasant politician. Bojko did not finish school but was an autodidact. He worked on his family farm and was also a peasant teacher, a communal writer, and an administrative head of the Gręboszów rural district. He published articles in *Wieniec* and *Pszczółka* and then in *Przyjaciel Ludu* and *Piast*. From the beginning of the 1890s he was active in the peasant movement. He was a co-founder of the Peasant Party (Stronnictwo Ludowe [SL]) and a member of the party's top executive body. He was the SL deputy to the Galician Diet (1895–1914) and to the Austrian Reichsrat (1897–1918). After the split in the SL he joined the Polish Peasant Party Piast (Polskie Stronnictwo Ludowe Piast), and in 1914–18 he was president of the party. In independent Poland Bojko was a member of the Main Board (1918–20) and of the Chief Council (1919–27) of the PSL Piast. On behalf of this party he was elected to the Constituent Assembly and served as deputy speaker. From 1922 to 1927 he was senator and deputy Senate speaker. He backed the coup of May 1926; therefore in 1927 he left the PSL Piast and founded Peasant Unification (Zjednoczenie Ludu), a party that supported the new regime. However, his new party did not gain any significant support among the peasants, so he was reelected to the Assembly in 1928 on behalf of the Nonparty Bloc of Cooperation with the Government (Bezpartyjny Blok Współpracy z Rządem [BBWR]). In 1930 he became a BBWR senator. However, owing to his age and health he was less and less active, and he focused mainly on writing his memoirs. In his village, Bojko was a well-known storyteller, and his articles, stories, and poems were very popular. It was his book *Dwie dusze* (Two souls; 1904) that brought him the greatest fame. He also authored *Ze wspomnień* (From the memoirs; 1959). (WR)

Sources: *Kto był kim w Drugiej Rzeczypospolitej* (Warsaw, 1994); Wilhelm Feldman, *Stronnictwa i programy polityczne w Galicji 1846–1906* (Kraków, 1907); Zygmunt Lasocki, *Polskie Stronnictwo Ludowe w czasie wojny* (Kraków, 1935); Andrzej Zakrzewski, *Wincenty Witos* (Warsaw, 1978).

BOLETINI Isa (15 January 1864, Boletin, near Mitrovica–23 January 1916, Podgorica), Albanian independence activist. Boletini came from a rich family from Kosovo. From 1878 he participated in the League of Prizren, which was instrumental in the Albanian national awakening. He took part in the last battle of the league's supporters with the Turkish troops at Slivove (22 April 1881). After the fall of the league, with his detachment Boletini continued operations in the neighborhood of Sokolica, avoiding Turkish pacification in 1884–85. During the Greek-Turkish war of 1897 he cooperated with the Greeks. As a representative of the Mitrovica region, he took part in the congress of Albanian delegates in Peje (Peć) in 1899. In 1899–1900 he was aligned with **Bajram Curri** and with the Beselidhja Shqiptare society in Peje. In 1902 he went to Istanbul, trying to organize support for the Albanian cause in Turkey, but he was interned. He returned to political activity in 1908, after the Young Turk revolution. In 1910–12 he was one of the most influential leaders of the anti-Turkish uprising in northern Albania. His troops controlled the area between Mitrovica and Prishtina. During the First Balkan War, in October 1912 he fought against Serbian troops that entered this territory. He took part in the Congress of Vlorë, which proclaimed Albanian independence on 28 November 1912. In 1913, along with **Ismail Kemali**, Boletini represented Albania at a conference of major European powers in London and tried to counteract a division of the territories inhabited by Albanians. Then he returned to Kosovo, where he organized an anti-Serb uprising. In 1914 his troops supported Prince **Wilhelm von Wied** against separatists operating in the region of Shijak. Boletini was killed in an ambush organized by a Montenegrin detachment. (TC)

Sources: *Fjalori Enciklopedik Shqiptar* (Tirana, 1995); Bardhosh Gaçe, *Ata që shpallën Pavarësinë Kombëtare* (Tirana, 1997).

BONDARCHUK Sergei (29 September 1920, Bilozerka, near Kherson—October 20, 1994, Moscow), Soviet actor and movie director of Ukrainian descent. Before World War II Bondarchuk studied at the Theater School in Rostov. After the German invasion in 1941 he played in various front-line theaters, and in 1945–48 he studied at the All-Union Institute of Cinematography in Moscow. He made his stage debut in 1948 in the play *Molodaia Gvardiia* (Young Guard), based on a novel by Aleksandr Fadyeev. His movie directing debut was *Fate of a Man* (1959), based on a story by Mikhail Sholokhov, for which he received the top award at the film festival in Moscow. In it Bondarchuk played the lead role of Andrey Sokolov, a Soviet soldier and prisoner of war who fulfilled his duties to the fatherland but lost out in his private life. The movie was thought to be a metaphor for the Soviet man. Bondarchuk was the first Soviet actor who after the war played in a Western movie—*Era notte a Roma* (There was a night in Rome; 1960). In 1966–67 Bondarchuk directed the Russian national saga *War and Peace*, based on the novel by Leo Tolstoy; in it he played Pyotr Bezukhov. He also directed an Italian-Soviet-British production of *Waterloo* (1970), one of the best battle films in history. He strengthened his international reputation with subsequent movies: *Oni srazhalis za rodinu* (They fought for the fatherland; 1975); a Yugoslav film, *The Peaks of Zelenogore* (1976); and *Step* (Steppe; 1978). Ukrainians—also the Ukrainian émigré community—applauded his leading role in the biographical films *Taras Shevchenko* (1951) and *Ivan Franko* (1956). (TS)

Sources: *Encyclopedia of Ukraine*, vol. 1 (Toronto, 1985); Jurij Chanjutin, *Sergei Bondarchuk* (Moscow, 1962); Nina Tolczenowa, *Mera krasoty: Kino Sergeia Bondarchuka* (Moscow, 1974); Vyacheslav Podvig and A. Chernenko, *Masterskaia Sergeia Bondarchuka* (Moscow, 1985); Yuri Tiurin, *Serguéi Bondartchouk* (Moscow, 1988).

BOREJSZA Jerzy [originally Beniamin Goldberg] (14 July 1905, Warsaw–15 January 1952, Warsaw), Polish Communist activist. The son of the editor-in-chief of the Jewish newspaper *Haint*, Borejsza was the half-brother of **Józef Różański**. The name Borejsza was a literary pseudonym. Borejsza attended high school in Warsaw, where he was active in a radical youth organization called Hashomer Hatzair. In 1924 he went to Germany. He was expelled from high school for smuggling revolutionary books. Between 1924 and 1925 he studied at the Polytechnic College in Toulouse, and then he moved to Paris, where he worked as a laborer and also studied Romance philology, especially Spanish literature, at the Sorbonne. In 1926 he took part in the preparations for the Catalonian revolt and became editor of the Spanish magazine *Acción*. At the end of 1927 he returned to Poland. Drafted into the army, Borejsza served in an infantry regiment in Grodno and Sokółka, and then he worked as a printer and proofreader in Warsaw. In 1929 he joined the Communist Party of Poland (Komunistyczna Partia Polski [KPP]). He worked as secretary for agitation and propaganda of the KPP Warsaw committee. Arrested several times for his Communist activities, he was always released after a few months. He was secretary of the Trade Union Central Department (Centralny Wydział Zawodowy) and the KPP CC and its instructor in Upper Silesia, where he edited *Tygodnik Robotniczy*. From 1936 he wrote for the official newspapers—for example, *Lewar*, *Dziennik Popularny*, *Sygnały*, *Wiadomości Literackie*, and *Skamander*. With the consent of the KPP, Borejsza entered into cooperation with the *Czarno na Białem* and with *Dziennik Poranny*, the organ of the Polish Teachers' Union. In 1937 he co-organized a sit-in strike of this newspaper. He gained publicity after a series of articles in defense of the Spanish Republic for the *Wiadomości Literackie* and a book on the subject, *Hiszpania (1873–1936)* (Spain, 1873–1936; 1937). After the dissolution of the KPP, in 1938–39 he contributed to *Robotnik*.

At the end of 1939 Borejsza managed to get to Lwów (Lviv), where he worked as a director of Ossolineum (a museum and archive). From 1940 he belonged to the Soviet Writers' Union. The outbreak of the German-Soviet war in June 1941 found him in Kiev. Next, he went in Moscow and Kuibyshev. Owing to the support of Georgi Dimitrov, Borejsza was admitted to the Red Army as a volunteer, and he fought as a captain on the front. In 1943 he took an active part in organizing the Union of Polish Patriots (Związek Patriotów Polskich [ZPP]) and the First Tadeusz Kościuszko Infantry Division. In 1943–44 he contributed to *Nowe Widnokręgi*, the organ of the ZPP, and was editor-in-chief of *Wolna Polska*. He also served as a major in the First Polish Army, publishing a series of battlefront reports.

From 1944 Borejsza was an activist in the Polish Workers' Party (Polska Partia Robotnicza [PPR]). Thanks to his efforts, a part of the Ossolineum collections was brought to Wrocław after the war. In April 1947 he was appointed a deputy member of the CC, and on 1 October 1948, deputy head of the Department of Propaganda, Culture, and Education of the PPR CC. From May 1945 he was a deputy to the National Home Council (Krajowa Rada Narodowa [KRN]). Borejsza was the first editor-in-chief of *Rzeczpospolita*, the organ of the Polish Committee of National Liberation (Polski Komitet Wyzwolenia Narodowego [PKWN]). He organized and was president of the publishing cooperative Czytelnik (1945–48) and was editor-in-chief of the social and literary magazine *Odrodzenie* (1948–50). He also initiated the construction of the publishing house Dom Słowa Polskiego. At the Unification Congress of the PPR and the Polish Socialist Party in December 1948 Borejsza was appointed a deputy member of the CC of the Polish United Workers' Party (Polska Zjednoczona Partia Robotnicza [PUWP]) and deputy head of the Department of Culture, Education, and Science of the PUWP CC. Borejsza was a co-organizer and secretary general of the World Congress of Intellectuals for Peace, initiated for Soviet propaganda purposes and held in Wrocław in 1948. In January 1949 a serious car accident drastically reduced his political activity. His books include *Rewolucja łagodna* (Mild revolution; 1945); *Ostrożnie z bombą atomową* (Careful with the atomic bomb; 1945); and *Na rogatkach kultury polskiej* (On the turnpike of Polish culture; 1947). (WD)

Sources: *Słownik Pracowników Książki Polskiej*; CA KC PZPR, zespół Jerzego Borejszy, 257 BSK PZPR 237/XXIII, personal file no. 15; *10 lat książki "Czytelnika"* (Warsaw, 1954); K. Małłek, *Z Mazur do podziemia* (Warsaw, 1970); Zofia Nałkowska, *Dzienniki czasu wojny* (Warsaw, 1970); *Organizacja i działalności bojowe LWP 1943–1945*, vol. 4 (Warsaw, 1963); Edmund Osmańczyk, *Był rok 1945* (Warsaw, 1970).

BORETSKY Mykola (19 December 1879, Sarny–1936, Leningrad?), Metropolitan bishop of the Ukrainian Orthodox Church, victim of Communist persecution. In 1901 Boretsky graduated from the theological seminary in Kiev. Ordained in 1904, in 1921 he joined the Ukrainian Autocephalous Orthodox Church, established by Archbishop **Vasyl Lipkivsky**. From 1922 he was bishop of Haysyn. When the Soviet authorities removed Lipkivsky, on 17 October 1927 the Second Ecumenical Council chose Boretsky as the metropolitan bishop and the head of the Ukrainian autocephalia, composed of around three thousand parishes. As a conciliatory hierarch, he was able to organize ecclesiastical conferences and edit *Tserkva i Zhyzn* magazine for some time. Despite his efforts to maintain correct relations with the authorities, he was ordered in 1930 to liquidate the autocephalia. As a result of his refusal he was arrested by the authorities and sent to a camp in Medvezhegorsk and then to the Solovets Islands, where he is believed to have turned insane as a result of the appalling living conditions. His later life is unknown. According to one version, he died in prison in Leningrad. (WR)

Sources: *Encyclopedia of Ukraine* (Toronto, 1984); *Russian Oppression in Ukraine* (London, 1962).

BORILĂ Petru (13 February 1905, Silistra–?), Romanian Communist activist. From the early 1920s Borilă was active in Communist youth organizations, and from 1924, in the Communist Party of Romania (CPR). He took part in the Tatar-Bunar uprising in 1924. Serving in the army, he escaped to the USSR and was tried in Romania for desertion. He graduated from the Leninist School of the Comintern and the Mikhail Frunze Memorial Military Academy, and in the late 1930s he fought in the International Brigades in the Spanish Civil War. He commanded a battalion and was wounded. After returning to the USSR, he co-organized and was one of the commanders of the Tudor Vladimirescu Division within the Red Army, to which former Romanian POWs were recruited. In August 1944 he came back to Romania, where he joined the Central Committee of the Communist Party. From April 1947 he was secretary of the party organization in Bucharest. In 1948 he was appointed political commissar of the Romanian Army and advanced to general. From February 1949 to March 1950 he was deputy minister of defense and chief of the Political Directorate of the army. From March 1950 to March 1951 he was minister of construction and then chief of the state control commission. After the purge of **Ana Pauker**, **Vasile Luca**, and **Teohari Georgescu** in 1952, Borilă joined the Politburo of the CC of the Romanian Workers' Party (RWP), and from October 1953 to October 1955 he was deputy prime minister. In April 1954 he extensively and falsely testified against **Lucrețiu Pătrășcanu**. Closely connected with **Gheorghe Gheorgiu-Dej**, Borilă was RWP delegate to the Twentieth Congress of the Soviet party in February 1956 and to the Moscow conference of Communist parties in 1960. From March 1961 to March 1965 he was deputy prime minister again. In the course of the elimination of Gheorgiu-Dej's followers by **Nicolae Ceaușescu**, Borilă was dismissed from the Politburo in December 1968; his daughter, Ioana, was married to Ceaușescu's son, Valentin. (WR)

Sources: Lazitch; Stephen Fischer-Galati, ed., *Romania* (New York, 1957); Dennis Deletant, *Communist Terror in Romania: Gheorghiu-Dej and the Police State, 1948–1965* (New York, 1999); Ion Alexandrescu, Ion Bulei, Ion Mamina, and Ioan Scurtu, *Enciclopedia de istorie României* (Bucharest, 2000); Thomas Kunze, *Nicolae Ceaușescu: O biografie* (Bucharest, 2002).

BORIS III Sachsen-Coburg-Gotha (30 January 1894, Sofia–28 August 1943, Sofia), Tsar of Bulgaria. Boris was the son of **Ferdinand** and Maria-Louisa Bourbon-Parma. After his father's abdication he succeeded him on 3 October 1918. The change in sovereigns was, along with territorial concessions and war reparations, one of the conditions of armistice and later of the peace treaty signed by the victorious coalition with Bulgaria in Neuilly on 27 November 1919. From 1918 to 1923 Boris played a strictly titular role. On **Aleksandur Stamboliyski**'s demand, he dissolved the National Assembly in February 1920, which led to early elections and the assumption of dictatorial power by the Bulgarian Agrarian National Union. However, Boris's importance as an agent uniting the divided political scene grew steadily. He backed **Aleksandur Tsankov**'s rightist coup of 9 June 1923 and resisted a Communist upheaval in September 1923. In April 1925 on two occasions he avoided being killed by the Communists. They organized an unsuccessful attack on him in the Arabakonak Pass, and two days they later blew up the Orthodox church of Holy Sunday in Sofia. One hundred and fifty people were killed then, and five hundred were injured. Along with his government Boris was late for the mass and therefore survived. After the attack, the Communist Party of Bulgaria was delegalized, and its leaders were arrested. The repressive measures alarmed the more moderate political forces, which wanted a return to democracy, so Boris persuaded Tsankov to resign.

Between 1926 and 1934 Boris supported democratic governments, but they were unstable. There was an increase in radical nationalist attitudes, on the one hand, and on the other hand, an increase in the influence of the republican military group Zveno. Boris, in turn, steadily expanded his own political base. The military coup of 19 May 1934, staged by the Zveno officers, threatened not only democracy, but monarchy as well. Prime Minister **Kimon Georgiev** announced radical reforms and established relations with the USSR. All this induced Boris to reach for a full control of power. With the help of some of the officer corps faithful to him, Boris forced the government of Georgiev to resign, purged the army of the opponents of the monarchy, and, in November 1935, appointed the cabinet of **Georgi Kioseivanov**, who proved a useful instrument of the tsarist government. The manipulated elections of 1938 gave Boris full control over the parliament. In foreign policy he chose a pro-German course, hoping for the backing of the Third Reich in the precarious surroundings of the Balkan Entente (Yugoslavia, Greece, and Romania) and for support for Bulgarian territorial claims against its neighbors in the future. The increase in trade with Germany temporarily brought prosperity to Bulgaria but subordinated its economy to the Third Reich. However, the support of Germany helped in the signing of an agreement with the Balkan Entente states in which the signatories renounced the use of force and agreed to remove the restrictions on the number of soldiers in the Bulgarian Army.

After the outbreak of the Polish-German war in 1939 Bulgaria proclaimed neutrality. The Molotov-Ribbentrop Pact of August 1939 gave Bulgaria a sense of stability, but in 1940 Boris became involved in the rivalry between Berlin and Moscow for influence in the Balkans. Owing to the support of Berlin, in August 1940 Bulgaria gained southern Dobrudja, which was annexed from Romania. This intensified pressure from the USSR, which sought a treaty of mutual assistance with Bulgaria. This pressure induced Boris to seek further rapprochement with Germany. On 1 March 1941 he decided Bulgaria would join the anti-Comintern Pact. The German Army used the Bulgarian territory for an attack on Yugoslavia and Greece, and in April 1941 the Bulgarian Army occupied Macedonia, which was annexed from Yugoslavia. Despite the deterioration of Bulgarian-Soviet relations after June 1941, Boris opposed the involvement of Bulgaria in the war against the USSR. This was easier especially because Hitler no longer had much to offer Bulgaria. The declaration of war against England and the United States was of a symbolic nature, but it made Bulgaria's situation difficult at the end of the war. Temporarily, Boris's effective tactics won him great popularity. German pressure increased after the defeat at Stalingrad. In March 1943 the government in Sofia disenfranchised and expropriated the Bulgarian Jews, but Boris did not agree to their deportation to the Nazi extermination camps.

Noticing a breakthrough on the Eastern Front, in the summer of 1943 Boris started secret negotiations with England; the agreement aimed at an offensive on the Balkans, and Boris also more and more seriously considered joining the side of the Allies. On 14 August 1943 Boris arrived, at Hitler's invitation, at his headquarters in Rastenburg (Kętrzyn). Hitler demanded that two Bulgarian divisions be put at his disposal, but Boris refused. Soon after his return to the country, during a stay in a mountain health resort, Tsarska Bistritsa, on 23 August Boris suddenly fell ill, and he died after five days. There is a theory that he was poisoned because Hitler was alarmed by his attitude toward the Allies. According to the doctors who examined his heart, the cause of death was an extensive infarction. (WR)

Sources: *Biographisches Lexikon,* vol. 1; *Entsiklopediya Bulgariya,* vol. 1; Hans-Joachim Hoppe, *Bulgarien–Hitlers eigenwilliger Verbündeter* (Stuttgart, 1979); Stefane Groueff, *Crown of Thorns: The Reign of King Boris III of Bulgaria, 1918–1943* (Lanham, Md., 1987); Marshall Lee Miller, *Bulgaria during the Second World War* (Stanford, 1975); *Duma,* 12 November 1991.

BORISEVIČIUS Vincentas (23 November 1887, Bebrininkai, near Vilkaviškis–November 1946, Vilnius), Lithuanian bishop, victim of communism. Born into a peasant family, Borisevičius studied theology and philosophy in the theological seminary in Sejny and at the University of Fribourg, Switzerland. In 1910 he was ordained and started his ministry in the Samogetian parishes. In 1916–17 he was chaplain of the Tenth Russian Army in Minsk. After returning to Lithuania, he worked as a school chaplain in Marijampolė; in 1922–26 he lectured in theology in the Gižai theological seminary, and then he was chancellor of the Telšiai diocese. From 1927 to 1935 he was professor and rector of the Telšiai theological seminary. In 1940 he was consecrated bishop and appointed auxiliary bishop of the Telšiai diocese, and in 1941 he took it over as an ordinary bishop. After the Red Army returned to Lithuania in the summer of 1944, the Soviet authorities demanded that the bishops condemn the anti-Communist guerrillas. Since Borisevičius refused, he was arrested in 1946 and shot in prison. (WR)

Sources: *EL*, vols. 1 and 6; Andrius Baltinis, *Vyskupo Vincento Borisevičaus gyvenimas ir darbai* (Rome, 1975); Constantine R. Jurgėla, *Lithuania: The Outpost of Freedom* (St. Petersburg, Fla., 1976); Irena Mikłaszewicz, *Polityka sowiecka wobec Kościoła katolickiego na Litwie 1944–1965* (Warsaw, 2001).

BOROVETS Taras, pseudonym "Bulba" (9 March 1908, Bystrzyce, near Równe–15 May 1981, New York), Ukrainian social and political activist. In the Second Republic of Poland Borovets was the owner of masonry works in Volhynia. He made a plaque for the grave of the mother (and the heart) of Marshal **Jozef Piłsudski** at the Rossa cemetery in Vilnius. For his activities in the Ukrainian nationalist underground he was imprisoned in the Bereza Kartuska camp. In 1940–41, on the recommendation of the president of the Ukrainian National Republic, **Andrei Livytsky**, Borovets organized an armed underground in Polesie. After the outbreak of the German-Russian war in 1941, he formed the Polesian Sich, which fought against the remnants of the Red Army. When the Germans demanded the disarmament of his troops, he withdrew to the forests near Olevsko. There he formed the first Ukrainian Insurgent Army (Ukrainska Povstanska Armiia [UPA]), which fought against the Germans and Communists. He disagreed with the unification of his formation with the UPA composed of the **Stepan Bandera** faction of the Organization of Ukrainian Nationalists (OUN-B). He also did not support the anti-Polish actions carried out by the Bandera movement, which led to mass killings in the Polish population in Volhynia in 1943. In the summer of 1943 the majority of Borovets's people were incorporated by force into the Bandera faction of the UPA. Borovets changed the name of his divisions to the Ukrainian National Revolutionary Army (UNRA) in order to distinguish them from those of his political rivals. In the autumn of 1943 he entered into negotiations with the Germans. Arrested and sent to the Sachsenhausen concentration camp in November 1943, he was released in 1944. In 1946 he was arrested by the British and charged with the murder of Poles, but he was released. He did not play a major role while in exile in Germany, Canada, and the United States. In West Germany he was involved in various activities, including the organization of the Ukrainian National Guard and the editing of the magazine *Mech i Volia* (1951–53). He later went to the United States. Borovets authored the memoirs *Armiia bez derzhavy* (An army without a state; 1981). (GM)

Sources: *Encyclopedia of Ukraine*, vol. 1 (Toronto, 1984); Baley Petro, *Fronda Stepana Bandery v OUN 1940 r.* (Las Vegas, 1997); *Entsyklopediia Ukraiinoznavstva,* vol. 1 (Kiev, 1993); Torzecki Ryszard, *Polacy i Ukraińcy: Sprawa ukraińska w czasie II wojny światowej na terenie II Rzeczypospolitej* (Warsaw, 1993).

BOROWSKI Tadeusz (12 November 1922, Zhytomyr–3 July 1951, Warsaw), Polish writer. Borowski spent his childhood in the Soviet Ukraine. After coming to Poland, his family settled in Warsaw in 1932, and his father worked as a blue-collar laborer. During the German occupation Borowski graduated from an underground high school and started Polish studies at the underground Warsaw University. He was also active in the cultural life of the leftist youth. In February 1943 he was arrested by the Gestapo and sent to the Auschwitz concentration camp in Oświęcim. From August 1944 he was in the Natzweiler-Dautmergen and Dachau camps. Liberated by the American Army in May 1945, he stayed in a displaced persons' (DP) camp on the outskirts of Munich. In 1946 he returned to Poland, where he graduated in Polish studies. In 1948 he joined the Polish Workers' Party (as of December 1948, the Polish United Workers' Party [Polska Zjednoczona Partia Robotnicza]) and wrote for the Communist press—in, among other publications, the daily *Rzeczpospolita* and the weekly *Nowa Kultura*. He made his debut as a poet during the occupation and while in the DP camp, describing the degradation of humanity under totalitarian Nazi rule. In his most popular series of short stories, *Pożegnanie z Marią* (Farewell to Maria; 1948) and *Kamienny świat* (World of stone; 1948), he dispassionately elaborated on the mechanism of moral depravation in the system of mass murder. Borowski initially interpreted totalitarianism as the result of social engineering experiments. In his later works he gave over his talent to Communist propaganda and promoted Socialist Realism. He committed suicide. A collection of his short stories was published in New York as *This Way for the Gas, Ladies and Gentlemen* in 1967. (WR)

Sources: *Literatura polska XX wieku: Przewodnik encyklopedyczny,* vol. 1 (Warsaw, 2000); Czesław Miłosz, *Captive Mind* (New York, 1953); Tadeusz Drewnowski, *Ucieczka z kamiennego świata* (Warsaw, 1978); Joanna Szczęsna, *Tadeusz Borowski-poeta* (Poznań, 2000).

BORUSEWICZ Bogdan (11 January 1949, Lidzbark Warmiński), Polish social and political activist. In 1968, as a student at an artistic high school in Gdyna, Borusewicz was arrested for producing and distributing leaflets calling for the defense of repressed university students, but he escaped. In 1969 he was sentenced to three years in prison, but he was released after a year and a half. In 1970–75 he studied history at the Catholic University of Lublin. From June 1976 he helped workers persecuted after the Radom riots, and from November 1976 he was a member of the Committee for the Defense of Workers (Komitet Obrony Robotników [KOR]). He also organized self-education activities on the Baltic Coast. In 1978 he was co-founder of the Free Trade Unions of the Baltic Coast. He edited the uncensored trade newspapers *Robotnik* and *Robotnik Wybrzeża*. In the 1970s he was arrested many times but usually for short periods of time. In 1979 he co-authored and signed a "Charter of Workers' Rights," which was the program of a trade union movement independent of Communist authorities. He also maintained contact with the underground Young Poland Movement (Ruch Młodej Polski). In 1980 he was one of the main leaders of the August strikes on the Baltic Coast, but he did not join the Inter-Factory Strike Committee in Gdańsk. In 1980–93 he was a member of Solidarity, and in 1980–81, a member of its Inter-Factory Founding Committee in Gdańsk. He criticized the style of **Lech Wałęsa** and cooperated with the leader of the inter-union opposition, Andrzej Gwiazda. After the introduction of martial law in December 1981 Borusewicz went into hiding as a member of the Solidarity Regional Coordinating Commission in Gdańsk. From 1984 he was a member of the national Provisional Coordinating Commission. In January 1986 he was caught by the security service and kept in prison until the amnesty of July 1986.

In 1989 Borusewicz belonged to the opponents of the Round Table Talks. From 1990 he chaired Solidarity's Gdańsk Region and belonged to the Presidium of the National Commission of Solidarity. From 1991 he was deputy chairman of the union. In the parliamentary elections of October 1991 he won a seat on behalf of Solidarity. He chaired its parliamentary club and the Extraordinary Commission to Investigate the Effects of Martial Law. In the 1993 and 1997 elections he won seats on behalf of the Democratic Union (Unia Demokratyczna; as of April 1994, Unia Wolności [Freedom Union]). From 1993 to 1997 he chaired the parliamentary commission of special services. From 1991 he was deputy chairman, and from 1993 to 1997 chairman, of the Polish-Ukrainian Inter-Parliamentary Group. In 1997–2000 he was deputy minister of interior and administration. From 2000 he was a member of the board and deputy speaker of the Pomeranian Provincial Diet. In 2002 he was reelected to this position. (PK)

Sources: *Wielka encyklopedia PWN,* vol. 4 (Warsaw, 2001); Jerzy Holzer, *Solidarność* (Warsaw, 1983); Andrzej Friszke, *Opozycja polityczna w PRL 1945–1980* (London, 1994); *Opozycja w PRL: Słownik Biograficzny 1956–1989,* vol. 2 (Warsaw, 2002); Antoni Dudek, *Pierwsze lata III Rzeczypospolitej 1989–2001* (Kraków, 2002).

BORUTA-SPIECHOWICZ Mieczysław (20 February 1894, Rzeszów–13 October 1985, Zakopane), Polish general. Already in high school Boruta-Spiechowicz joined the Rifle Association (Związek Strzelecki). In 1914–18 he fought in the Polish Legions and in the Second Polish Corps in the East and was active in the Polish Military Organization in the Ukraine. At the end of 1918 and 1919 he commanded a sector of the defense of Lwów (Lviv). Next he left for France, where he commanded the regiment of riflemen in the army of General **Józef Haller**. After his return to Poland, in 1921 he graduated from the School of the General Staff and also completed studies at the university in Antwerp. Then he held various command and staff posts. From 1934 he was the commander of a division, and in 1936 he was appointed brigadier general. In the Polish-German war of 1939 he commanded the Operational Group (OG) Bielsko and then the OG Boruta in the Kraków army. After the end of the military operations, in November 1939 he was arrested by the Soviets. In August 1941 he was released from prison under the Sikorski-Majski agreement, and he commanded the Fifth Infantry Division, which was beginning to form at that time. Next he was in command of Polish troops that were being evacuated from the USSR to Iran. After his arrival in Great Britain, from February 1943 he was the commander of the First Corps in Scotland. In December 1945 he returned to Poland and entered the "people's" Polish Army, but in mid-1946 he retired and settled in Zakopane. At the end of the 1970s he joined the ranks of the democratic opposition, and in 1977 he was one of the co-founders of the Human and Civil Rights Defense Movement (Ruch Obrony Praw Człowieka i Obywatela). In September 1981 he was an honorary guest of the First Congress of the Independent Self-Governing Trade Union Solidarity. (WR)

Sources: K. Kryska-Karski and S. Żurakowski, *Generałowie Polski* Niepodległej (London, 1976); *Nowy Dziennik,* 1 November 1985; Piotr Stawecki, *Słownik biograficzny generałów Wojska*

Polskiego, 1918–1939 (Warsaw, 1994); Andrzej Friszke, *Opozycja polityczna w PRL 1945–1980* (London, 1994); *Generał Ludwik Mieczysław Boruta-Spiechowicz* (Szczecin, 1997).

BOSILKOV Evgeni [originally Vikenti] (16 November 1900, Belene on the Danube–12 November 1952, Sofia), Bulgarian Roman Catholic bishop, martyr for the faith. Born into a peasant family, at eleven Bosilkov entered a lower theological seminary in Oresh; in 1913 he moved to the seminary in Ruse and later to a high school in Kortrijk, Belgium. In 1919 he entered the novitiate of the Passionist Order in Ere, Belgium, adopting the monastic name of Eugene of the Most Holy Heart of Jesus. He completed theological studies in Ruse, where he was ordained in July 1925. Soon he left for further studies in Rome. In the Papal Institute for Oriental Studies he received a Ph.D. for his thesis on the union of the Bulgarian church with the Roman church in the thirteenth century. After returning to Bulgaria in 1932, he became parish priest of Ruse Cathedral and secretary to the local bishop and then parish priest in Bardarski Geran, where he stayed until 1947. He won great popularity among the faithful owing to his active ministry, organizational activities, and care for the poor.

In 1946 Pope Pius XII appointed Bosilkov apostolic vicar of the Nikopoli diocese, and on 27 October 1947 he was consecrated as bishop of this diocese with the seat in Ruse. In 1948 he managed to go to the Netherlands and to Rome for a short time, where he sought material aid for his faithful. Although his superiors wanted to keep him abroad, he decided to go back to Bulgaria, knowing he was risking repression, especially after the Communist authorities broke off relations with the Holy See in 1949. Repression affected Catholics both of the Eastern rite (for example, the arrest of exarch **Kiry Kurtev**) and of the Latin rite. On 16 July 1952 Bosilkov was arrested along with twenty-seven priests, monks, lay believers, and a group of Orthodox who had cooperated with them. Communist interrogators tried to make Bosilkov break off relations with Rome and create a Bulgarian national church. When he refused, he was accused of founding a Vatican spy ring. Proofs for this were items collected from an exposition of Bulgarian World War I effects—a few old arms, a typewriter, and a radio. All the convicted were brutally tortured. On 3 October 1952 Bosilkov was sentenced to death. The execution was held secretly at night at the Sofia prison. Three other martyr monks were executed with Bosilkov: Pavel Dzhidzhov, Jozafat Shishkov, and Kamen Vichev. For years the fate of Bosilkov was unknown. It was not until 1975, during an audience with Pope Paul VI, that the head of the Bulgarian Communist Party, **Todor Zhivkov**, confirmed his death. On 15 March 1998 Pope John Paul II declared Bosilkov blessed. He was the first Bulgarian Roman Catholic to be beatified. In May 2002 John Paul II blessed the three other Bulgarian martyrs as well. (AGr)

Sources: Hansjakob Stehle, *Tajna dyplomacja Watykanu: Papiestwo wobec komunizmu (1917–1991)* (Warsaw, 1993); Desmond O'Grady, *Punkt zwrotny: Chrześcijaństwo przed i po obaleniu Muru Berlińskiego* (London, 1997); "Bł. Wincenty Eugeniusz Bosiłkow," *L 'Osservatore Romano* (Polish edition), 1998, nos. 5/6; Fernando Taccone, *Evgeni Bosilkov: Bolgarski episkop i muchenik* (Ruse, 1998); Todor Gospodinov, *Blazheniyat Episkop Evgeni Bosilkov-rozhba na khiliadeletnata istoriya na Belene* (Swisztow, 1999).

BOZANIĆ Josip (20 March 1949, Rijeka), Archbishop of Zagreb. Born into a peasant family, after primary school in Vrbnik on the island of Krk, Bozanić graduated from high school in Pazin. Then he studied theology in Rijeka and at the Pontificia Universita Gregoriana in Rome. In June 1975 he was ordained. He received his licentiate at the Lateran University in Rome. After returning to Croatia, he worked in the curia of the Krk diocese, where he was vicar general from 1987. On 10 May 1989 he was consecrated. For a couple of months he was auxiliary bishop and then ordinary bishop of the Krk diocese. He took part in the synods of European bishops in 1991 and 1999. From 5 June to 22 November 1996 he was apostolic administrator of the Rijeka-Senje metropolis. On 5 July 1997 he was appointed the successor of Cardinal **Franjo Kuharić** as Archbishop of Zagreb. From this time he was also chairman of the Conference of Croatian Bishops and co-president of the commission for state-church relations. He was in charge of the preparations for two pilgrimages by Pope **John Paul II** to Croatia (in 1998 and 2003). On 21 October 2003 Bozanić was included in the College of Cardinals. He often spoke up in defense of the poor, who suffered most from the systemic transformations. He also criticized manifestations of nationalism and intolerance. He developed charity organizations and supported the development of Catholic schools. On his initiative the dialogue with representatives of the Serbian Orthodox Church in Croatia, broken off as a result of the war in the former Yugoslavia, was resumed. (AGr)

Sources: *Glas Koncila*, 2003, no. 40; *Annuario Pontificio*, 2003; www.Hrvatska Biskupska Konferencija, www.catholic-hierarchy.org.

BOZHILOV Dobri (13 June 1884, Kotel–1 February 1945, Sofia), Bulgarian financier and politician and high-rank Mason. From 1922 to 1935 Bozhilov was vice-president, and in 1935–38 president, of the National Bank of Bulgaria. In November 1938 he assumed the post of minister of finance in the government of **Georgi Kioseivanov**, and then held the post in the cabinet of **Bogdan Filov** until September 1943. After the death of Tsar **Boris III**, when Filov became one of the regents, on 14 September 1943, Bozhilov assumed the post of head of the government, while retaining the Ministry of Finance. He no longer believed in the victory of Bulgaria's German ally but remained Filov's loyal co-worker. In October he announced a broad amnesty to the opponents of the regime. After the Allied air raids on Sofia in November 1943 the government's popularity declined considerably, and Bozhilov did not manage to resolve the impasse in the country. He failed to move forward the matter of Bulgaria's withdrawal from the war or the matter of an agreement with the Allies, especially an agreement that the Allies abandon their plans to invade the Balkans. On 18 May 1944 he resigned as head of the government. This was to signify a change in Bulgarian policy. After the overthrow of the Regency Council in September 1944 Bozhilov was arrested. Along with about a hundred leading politicians of the regime he was sentenced to death and executed. (WR)

Sources: *Entsiklopediya Bulgariya*, vol. 1 (Sofia, 1978); Marshall Lee Miller, *Bulgaria during the Second World War* (Stanford, 1975); Hans-Joachim Hoppe, *Bulgarien: Hitlers eigenwilliger Verbündeter* (Stuttgart, 1979); Tasho Tashev, *Ministrite na Bylgariia 1897–1999* (Sofia, 1999).

BRÂNCUŞI Constantin (21 February 1876, Peştişani Gorj, near Tîrgu Jiu–16 March 1957, Paris), Romanian sculptor. Brâncuşi came from a large family of poor peasants. At the age of eleven he was admitted to the Craiova School of Arts and Crafts. After graduating from this school, he began to study at the Sculpture Department of the Bucharest School of Fine Arts. In 1901, after completing his studies, he set off to continue his education. Having no money, he set out for Paris on foot. He went through Budapest, Vienna, Zurich, and Munich, and after two years he arrived in Paris. In 1904 he settled in Paris for good. He studied at the Ecole des Beaux Arts. He began to exhibit in Paris and was very successful. Impressed with his works, Auguste Rodin invited him to join his atelier, but Brâncuşi decided to create independently, breaking away from idealized naturalism and academicism. He made a breakthrough in twentieth-century art, as he carved directly in stone and abandoned a modeling of the initial maquettes. His first sculptures of that period, *The Kiss*, *The Wisdom of the Earth*, and *The Prayer*, were done in 1907, and they bore the features of naturalism. However, in the same year he created the first sculpture in the famous series called *Maiastra*, and it was a breakthrough in the

art of sculpture. In 1913 he began to exhibit in New York, London, Prague, and his own country. In 1920 in Paris, he exhibited *Princess X* (1916), but the work was denounced as indecent even by the Salon des Indépendants.

Recognition for Brâncuşi came in 1922, when statuettes from the Paleolithic era, the most primitive and pure works of art, were found in French caves. These statuettes looked as if they had been made by Brâncuşi. At the invitation of the Romanian minister of foreign affairs, **Nicolae Titulescu**, in 1935 Brâncuşi began to create the biggest collection of monumental open-air sculptures in the world in Tîrgu Jiu, not far from his native village. He created the following: a thirty-three-meter-high *Endless Column*, as well as *Gate of Kiss*, *Table of Silence* (also called *Table of Dacians*), and *Alley of Chairs*. During his lifetime, Brâncuşi won his greatest fame in the United States. It was there that the majority of his most precious sculptures were bought. In all his works, a fascination with the primordial "powers of the universe" and with form can be observed. The subjects of his works stemmed from myths and legends. His artistic output includes over 750 sculptures, which are dedicated to various themes—for example, the origin of the world, love, the myth of dreams and death, and a nostalgia for infinity. On the occasion of the 125th anniversary of his birth, UNESCO declared the year 2001 as the International Year of Constantin Brâncuşi. Museums in Philadelphia and New York have the greatest number of his works. (LW)

Sources: *Dictionar Enciclopedic*, vol. 1 (Bucharest, 1993); *The Dictionary of Art*, vol. 4 (London, 1996); Carola Giedion-Welcher, *Constantin Brâncuşi* (Neuchâtel, 1959); Petru Comarescu, Mircea Eliade, and Ionel Jianu, *Témoignages sur Brâncuşi* (Paris, 1967); Petru Comarescu, *Brâncuşi* (Bucharest, 1972); Miro de Michelli, *Brâncuşi* (Milan, 1966); Geist Sydney, *Brâncuşi: The Sculpture and Drawings* (New York, 1975).

BRĂȚIANU Constantin I. C. (Dinu) (11 February 1866, Florica–1950, Sighet), Romanian economist, engineer, and politician. Brățianu was the son of the head of the Liberal Party and premier Ion Brățianu (1821–1891) and the brother of **Ion I. C. Brățianu** and **Vintilă Brățianu**. He studied at the Ecole des Mines in Paris from 1884 to 1888, specializing in the petroleum industry, railways, and finance. From 1890 to 1930 he directed petroleum companies and railway construction projects, and for over thirty years he administered credit companies that provided services for the rural sector. For over thirteen years he was director of the Letea paper factory. Along with his brother Vintilă he reformed banks he administered: the Banca Muscel, Banca Românesca, and Creditul Agricol. He aimed at the modernization of agriculture, and he promoted the principles of protectionism. In 1895, as a representative of the National Liberal Party (Partidul Național Liberal [NLP]), he was elected to the parliament. As a government expert, he negotiated trade agreements with other countries in 1896–1907. He was also a budget specialist. During the premierships of both of his brothers (1922–26 and 1927–28) he refused to participate in their cabinets. He opposed the return of **Charles II** to Romania in 1930. Between 1933 and 1934 he was minister of finance in the governments of the so-called young liberals, **Ion Duca** and **Gheorghe Tătărescu**. Later, he was in conflict with Tătărescu. In 1934–47 BrăȚianu was head of the NLP. From 1934 to 1940, especially at the time of the royal dictatorship (1938–40), he was in opposition to King Charles. In August 1940, along with **Iuliu Maniu**, he supported the abdication of the king and the transfer of power to General **Ion Antonescu**. After Romania recovered Bessarabia and northern Bukovina from the USSR in June and July 1941, he turned against Antonescu and his pro-German policy in particular. At that time he came into contact with the representatives of Polish diplomacy in exile, especially within the framework of the Tripod Action (Akcja Trójnóg), prepared in Lisbon by the Polish diplomats in exile and aimed at the withdrawal of Romania, Italy, and Hungary from the Axis.

In June 1944 BrăȚianu co-founded the National Democratic Front, which included the Socialists, the National Peasant Party, the NLP, and the Communists. He took an active part in the preparation of the coup d'état against Antonescu. After the coup, from August 1944 to October 1944, he was minister of state. He also presided over the Romanian National Bank. In 1944–47 he tried to reorganize the NLP, opposing the Tătărescu faction. From the formation of the Petru Groza government in March 1945, until his arrest, BrăȚianu, along with Maniu, led the political resistance to the Communist regime. In the elections of November 1946 his party, cooperating with Mainu's National Peasant Party, obtained around 80 percent of the vote, but the election results were falsified. In July 1947 BrăȚianu was arrested along with other leaders of the opposition. Despite his advanced age, he was sentenced to life imprisonment, and he died in the Sighet prison. He was the author of, among other works, *Agricultura în România* (Agriculture in Romania; 1919) and *La situation economique de la Roumanie*. In 1992 his *Amintiri, documente, corespondență* (Memoirs, documents, correspondence) was published. (FA/TD)

Sources: *Biographisches Lexikon,* vol. 1; C. I. C. BrăȚianu and I. G. Duca, *Partidul Național Liberal* (Bucharest, 1932); Ghita Ionescu, *Communism in Rumania 1944–1962* (London and New York, 1964); Mareşal Ion Antonescu, *Epistolarul Infernului* (Bucharest, 1993); Józef Darski, *Rumunia: Historia, współczesność, konflikty narodowe* (N.p., n.d.); J. Kurcyusz, *Na przedpolu Jałty: Wspomnienia z tajnej służby w dyplomacji* (Katowice, 1995); Denis Deletant, *Communist Terror in Romania: Gheorghiu-Dej and the Police State, 1948–1965* (New York, 1999).

BRĂȚIANU Gheorghe I. (12 February 1898, Ruginoasa–23, 26, or 27 April 1953, Sighet), Romanian politician. BrăȚianu was the son of **Ion I. C. BrăȚianu** and Princess Maria Moruzi-Cuza. Between 1919 and 1922 he studied at the Sorbonne, at the Ecole Pratique des Hautes Études in Paris, and at the École des Chartes in Paris. In 1923 he earned a Ph.D. in history from the university in Chernivtsi. In 1922 he also completed law studies. From 1923 he was professor of medieval history at the university in Iaşi, where he worked with **Nicolae Iorga**. From 1928 he was a member of the Romanian Academy of Sciences. In 1929 he lectured at the Sorbonne. In 1940 he was a professor at the University of Bucharest. From 1941 to 1947 he was director of the N. Iorga Institute of History in Bucharest. In his works, he dealt with the social and economic history of the decline of the Roman Empire and the Middle Ages, paying special attention to the Danube Basin.

BrăȚianu was politically active from 1926, when he joined the National Liberal Party (Partidul Național Liberal [NLP]). He was an MP in 1927–28, 1931–32, and 1933–37. In June 1930 he brought about a split in the NLP. A group of his adherents, the so-called Georgists, who supported Charles II, the soon-to-be king of Romania, emerged from the NLP. In January 1938 his group returned to the NLP. In January 1941 he refused to accept a ministerial post in the government of General **Ion Antonescu**. From June to October 1941 he served in the army, fighting against the USSR. He then returned to his scholarly work, and in 1943 he received an honorary doctorate from the University of Bonn. In August 1944 he mediated in talks on setting terms with the Allies. The talks were held between Marshal Antonescu and the leader of the National Peasant Party (NPP), **Iuliu Maniu**. On 23 August 1944, speaking on behalf of his own party as well as the NPP and the Socialists, BrăȚianu planned to convince Antonescu about the necessity of concluding an immediate truce. Negotiations on the issue were interrupted by a coup that took place on the afternoon of the same day. In February 1947 BrăȚianu protested against the Paris Peace Conference decisions on Romania (the loss of northern Bukovina and Bessarabia). In 1947–50 he was under house arrest. In May 1950 he was arrested. He probably committed suicide in the Sighet prison. The place of his burial is unknown.

BrăȚianu published (among other works) *Le problème des frontiers russo-roumaines* (The question of Russo-

Romanian borders; 1922); *Problemele politicii noastre de stat* (Problems of our state policy; 1937); *Acțiunea politică și militară a României în lumina corespondenței diplomatice a lui Ion I. C. Brătianu* (Romania's political and military activities in light of the diplomatic correspondence of Ion I. C. Brătianu; 1939–40); *Către români: Zece conferințe și prelegezi* (To the Romanians: Ten conferences and lectures; 1942); *Une énigme et un miracle historique: Le people roumain* (Enigma and a miracle of history: The Romanian people; 1942); *Tradiția istorică despre întemeierea statelor românești* (Historical tradition about the creation of the Romanian states; 1945); *Formules d'organisation de la paix dans l'histoire universelle* (Forms of peace organization in world history; 1945); he also authored the memoirs *File rupte din Cartea Războiului* (Pages torn from the book of war). (FA/TD)

Sources: *Biographisches Lexikon*, vol. 1; R.W. Seton-Watson, *A History of the Roumanians* (Hamden, CT 1963); Andrzej Koryn, *Rumunia w polityce wielkich mocarstw 1944–1947* (Wrocław, 1983); Șerban Papacostea, "Gheorghe I. Brătianu: Istoricul și omul politic," *Revista Istorica*, 1993, nos. 1–2; M. Brătianu, *Gheorghe Brătianu–enigma morții sale* (Bucharest, 1997).

BRĂȚIANU Ion I. C. (20 August 1864, Florica–24 September 1927, Bucharest), Romanian liberal politician. Brătianu was the son of Ion Brătianu, called the elder, one of the leaders of the Romanian independence movement. He attended Sfântul-Sava High School in Bucharest, and later he graduated from the École Polytechnique in Paris (1889). He worked on the construction of the bridge over the Danube near Černavoda and then in the construction of the railway line between Bacău and Piatra Neamț. In 1889 he joined the National Liberal Party (NLP). Elected to parliament for the first time in 1895, he was named minister of foreign affairs in 1897. In 1901 he was appointed head of diplomacy in the government of **Dimitrie Sturdza**. In March 1907 Brătianu joined the next government of Sturdza, becoming minister of interior. In this capacity, he was in charge of the pacification of the peasant uprising in Moldova that claimed eleven thousand lives. From 9 January 1909 and 11 January 1911 he served as prime minister for the first time. The two Balkan Wars enhanced the prestige of the Conservative Party; therefore the NLP, which was led by Brătianu from 1909, could resume power only by promoting a bolder program of social reforms. The program included, for example, the promise of agricultural reform and universal suffrage.

On 17 January 1914 Brătianu was appointed prime minister for the second time. In parliament, he proposed amendments to the constitution toward democratic reforms, which had been promised earlier. In foreign policy he cautiously supported the Entente countries. When the war broke out, he was able to restrain the pro-German sympathies of King **Charles I**, hoping that if the Central Powers lost the war, Romania would get the territories that were inhabited mostly or partly by Romanians and that belonged to the Habsburg monarchy. However, Brătianu's government did not formally express itself in favor of any side, playing on the needs of both sides. On 2 October 1914 Russia agreed to Romania's conditions, but the successes of Germany and Austria-Hungary on the Eastern Front inhibited Brătianu from bringing Romania into the war on the side of the Entente. It was only the Russian summer offensive of 1916 and the impatience of England and France, as well as their support for the territorial claims of Romania, that prompted the government to declare war against the Central Powers on 27 August 1916. Under Brătianu's influence King **Ferdinand** also eventually decided to cast his lot with the Allies. Almost immediately the Romanian Army suffered a series of defeats, and Brătianu's government had to withdraw from Bucharest to Iași. The defeat of Russia in 1917 and the Brest-Litovsk Peace Treaty of March 1918 led Romania to the verge of catastrophe. Brătianu again used his diplomatic skills, beginning peace negotiations with the Germans. However, as the German conditions were unacceptable, on 8 February 1918 he resigned from the premiership. He was succeeded by General **Alexandru Averescu** and then by a pro-German conservative, **Alexandru Marghiloman**. The decision on the change of government was reached between Brătianu and Marghiloman in the form of a gentlemen's agreement. The impossibility of implementing peace, which was signed with the Central Powers in Bucharest in May 1918, created a situation in which Brătianu could maintain, not very truthfully, that Romania had never renounced the Entente.

On 12 December 1918 Brătianu again became head of the government. He represented Romania at the Paris Peace Conference, demanding that the victorious Entente keep its territorial promise of 1916. His stance would probably have been disregarded had it not been for the fact that the Romanian troops seized Transylvania, Bessarabia, and Bukovina. This convinced Italy at first, and then France, to back the Romanian demands. However, the formation of the Hungarian Soviet Republic, to which Romania was an important barrier, had a decisive impact on the situation. The Romanian troops even entered Budapest. Peace treaties signed with Bulgaria at Neuilly and with Hungary at Trianon granted the Romanians the territories they claimed. On 27 September 1919 Brătianu resigned as prime minister. He was recalled to office on 19 January 1922, becoming head of a government dominated by the liberals. He consolidated social and political reforms introduced by his predecessors. The constitution of 28 March 1923 included a provision that the agrarian reform was a part of the constitution. As a result of his efforts, voting rights were extended under a law of 1926. He also brought about the "act of 4 January 1926," by which Prince Charles, who had a relationship with his mistress, **Magda Lupescu**, was formally excluded from the royal succession and the succession went to Prince **Michael**. On 30 March 1926 Brătianu finally resigned as head of the government because of ill health. In 1927, after the death of King Ferdinand, he appointed a Regency Council. Brătianu was the author of (among other works) *România şi Peninsula Balcanică* (Romania and the Balkan Peninsula; 1913) and *Le rayonnement de génie latin* (Radiance of the Latin genius; 1919). (FA/AD/WR)

Sources: *Biographisches Lexikon*, vol. 1; Sabina Cantacuzino, *Din viaţa familiei I. C. Braţianu* (Bucharest, 1933); Georghe Brătianu, *Acţiunea politică şi militară a României în 1919 în lumina corespondenţei diplomatice a lui I. I. C. Brătianu* (Bucharest, 1939); David Sherman Spector, *Rumania at the Paris Peace Conference: A Study of Diplomacy of I. C. Braţianu* (New York, 1962); Holger H. Herwig and Neil M. Heyman, *Biographical Dictionary of World War I* (Westport, Conn., 19820); Vasile Alexandrescu, *Romania in World War I* (Bucharest, 1985); Mircea Muşat and Ion Ardeleanu, *România dupa Marea Unire*, vols. 1–2 (Bucharest, 1986); Glenn Torrey, *General Henri Bertholet and Romania, 1916–1919* (Boulder, Colo., 1987); Emile Turdeanu, *Modern Romania: The Achievement of National Unity, 1914–1920* (Los Angeles, 1988); Ioan Scurtu, *I. I. C. Brătianu: Activitatea politică* (Bucharest, 1992).

BRĂTIANU Vintilă I. C. (28 September 1867, Florica–22 December 1930, Bucharest), Romanian politician and economist. Brătianu was the son of the leader of the Liberal Party and premier, Ion Brătianu (1821–1891) and the brother of **Ion I. C. Brătianu**. From 1897 he was an active member of the National Liberal Party (NLP). He studied at the École Polytechnique in Paris from 1885 to 1889. In 1895 he became a member of the construction management of the railway bridge over the Danube between Černavoda and Feteşti. Later, he held many administrative and government positions. For example, he was president of the State Monopoly (1899–1901) and secretary general in the Ministry of Finance (1901–4). In 1903 he was elected to the parliament for the first time, and in 1907 he took up the post of mayor of Bucharest. From 1910 he headed the Romanian National Bank. During World War I he served as war minister (August 1916–August 1917). After the end of the war he was finance minister (January 1922–March 1926), and after his brother's death he simultaneously served as prime minister and minister of finance (24 November 1927–16 November 1928). From 16 November 1927 until his death he was head of the NLP.

An expert in the field of public finance, he contributed to the stabilization of the Romanian leu after World War I. He also initiated the policy of Romania's economic self-sufficiency (Prin Noi Înşine [By Ourselves]). In November 1928 he helped **Iuliu Maniu**, head of the National Peasant Party, to assume the post of prime minister. He was the author of (among other works) *Interesele României in actualul război* (Romania's interests in the present war; 1914); *Petrolul şi politica de stat* (Petroleum and state policy; 1919); *Consolidarea finanţelor României* (Financial stabilization of Romania; 1922); and *Politica financiară* (Financial policy; 1927). (FA/TD)

Sources: *Biographisches Lexikon*, vol. 1; R.W. Seton-Watson, *A History of the Roumanians* (Hamden, CT, 1963); Şerban N. Ionescu, *Who Was Who in Twentieth Century Romania* (Boulder, Colo., 1994); Keith Hitchins, *Rumania 1866–1947* (Oxford, 1994).

BRATKOWSKI Stefan (22 November 1934, Wrocław), Polish journalist. Bratkowski graduated in law from the Jagiellonian University in Kraków in 1955 and worked there as an assistant professor for a year. In 1949–56 he belonged to the Polish Youth Union, and in 1956 he joined the student movement demanding de-Stalinization. Then he worked as a journalist for the weekly *Po prostu*. In 1956–57 he was a member of the Central Committee of the Socialist Youth Union. From 1954 to 1981 he belonged to the Polish United Workers' Party (PUWP). From 1971 to 1974 he edited a weekly supplement to the daily *Życia Warszawy* entitled *Życie i Nowoczesność*, which promoted innovations and reforms in the command economy. In 1978 he co-initiated the Discussion Forum Experience and Future (Konwersatorium Doświadczenie i Przyszłość [DiP]) and co-authored a "Report on the State of the Republic and the Means to Improve It," including an analysis of the crisis and suggested reforms within the ideological framework of the Communist system. He continued these analyses in subsequent reports of the Discussion Forum. In 1980–81 he was editor of *Życie i Nowoczesność* again, and on 30 October 1980 he was elected president of the Association of Polish Journalists (Stowarzyszenie Dziennikarzy Polskich [SDP]). He belonged to the reform movement in the Communist Party aiming at cooperation with Solidarity. In October 1981 he was removed from the PUWP. During martial law, after the suspension and then the dissolution of the SDP, he wrote for the underground press. From 1983 to 1988 he authored twenty issues of *Gazeta Dźwiękowa*, recorded on tape. From December 1988 he was a member of the Civic Committee of the Chairman of Solidarity, and from February to April 1989 he took part in the Round Table Talks. In 1989–90 he was president of the restored SDP and then its honorary president. In 1991–92 he chaired the publishing cooperative Czytelnik. He wrote for *Gazeta Bankowa, Gazeta Wyborcza, Rzeczpospolita,* and other dailies and periodicals. He authored many popular books in economics, social affairs, and history, such as *Księga wróżb prawdziwych* (A book of true prophecies; 1969); *Skąd przychodzimy?* (Where do we come from? 1975); *Z czym do nieśmiertelności* (on Tadeusz Kościuszko) (With what to immortality? 1977); *Wiosna Europy: Mnisi, królowie, wizjonerzy* (The spring of Europe: Monks, kings, visionaries; 1997); *Pan Nowogród Wielki* (Mister Novgorod the Great; 1999); and *Podróż do nowej przyszłości* (A trip to a new future; 2000). (AF)

Sources: *Wielka encyklopedia PWN,* vol. 4 (Warsaw, 2001); Jerzy Holzer, *Solidarność* (Warsaw, 1983); Dariusz Fikus, *Foksal '81* (Poznań, 1989).

BRAUN Jerzy (1 September 1901, Dąbrowa Tarnowska–17 October 1975, Rome), Polish writer, philosopher, and politician. The son of a notary, already as a student in high school Braun became involved in scouting. In 1919 he became a scoutmaster in Tarnów, where he edited the Scout monthly *Czuwaj.* In November 1918 he wrote the text and music to a popular scout song, *Płonie ognisko i szumią knieje* (The glowing campfire). In 1919 entered the Jagiellonian University, but he interrupted his studies in 1920 to take part in the Polish-Soviet war, for which he was decorated with the Cross of Valor. He graduated in Polish philology at the Jagiellonian University in 1923, and then he developed literary activities. He published poetry volumes (including collections of scout songs) and wrote novels, stage plays (e.g., *Europa,* staged in Warsaw's Atheneum Theater by Stefan Jaracz), and film scripts. From 1926 to 1928 he edited the *Gazeta Literacka,* which he founded in Kraków. After moving to Warsaw in 1929, Braun came into contact with the Messianism of Józef Maria Hoene-Wroński and with the Messianic Institute. Soon he became an expert in this philosophy, as well as its popularizer. In 1932 he began to publish the biweekly *Zet,* where he propagated the ideas of Hoene-Wroński. However, he attributed a world-saving mission not to Poland but to Christianity and to a revived church. Among other works he wrote *Zagadka dziejowa Polski* (The Polish historic puzzle; 1938).

In September 1939 Braun fought in the defense of Warsaw. Wanted by the Gestapo, he left for Krosno, where he joined the then-forming underground organization called Nowa Polska and became its leader. He returned to Warsaw in the spring 1940 to preside over a Catholic underground organization called Unia, and he was the author of its ideological declaration. After the incorporation of Unia into the Labor Party (Stronictwo Pracy [SP]) in

March 1942, Braun became a member of the party's Main Board and vice-president of its Program Council. He was also active in the Chief Commission of the Directorate of Civil Resistance. In 1943, under the pseudonym "Inżynier Z.," he published *Marksizm, kapitalizm, a gospodarka dynamiczna* (Marxism, capitalism, and a dynamic economy). From 1944 to 1945 he represented the SP in the Council of National Unity (Rada Jedności Narodu [RJN]). He fought in the Warsaw Uprising. From March to July 1945, under the pseudonym "Rogowski," he was president of the RJN and signed its last manifesto on 1 July 1945.

After the RJN as well as the Delegation of the Polish Government-in-Exile were dissolved, Braun cooperated with the group of **Karol Popiel** in the SP. In November 1945 he was arrested along with his wife on the charge of illegally attempting to cross the border in Cieszyn. Released in March 1946, both returned to Warsaw, where between February 1947 and September 1948 Braun co-edited the *Tygodnik Warszawski.* In January 1948 he graduated in philosophy at the Catholic University of Lublin. On 3 September 1948 he was arrested along with his wife for his wartime underground activities. On 19 April 1951 he was sentenced to life imprisonment. He served his sentence in Warsaw and Wronki. Under an amnesty, in April 1956 his sentence was commuted to twelve years, and then it was suspended due to his ill health. In May 1958 he was rehabilitated. He returned to his literary, journalistic, and social work. Active in the Club of Catholic Intellectuals in Warsaw, he served as vice-president of the Warsaw branch of the Polish Writers' Union. He was also involved in the preconciliar work of the Polish laity and ecumenical movement, cooperating with Primate Stefan Wyszyński. From 1966 he lived in Rome. He attended the fourth session of the Second Vatican Council and worked with Radio Vatican and *Osservatore Romano.* He is buried at the Powązki Cemetery in Warsaw. He left his memoirs, *Czasy i ludzie* (Times and people), and co-authored memoirs about Jan Hoppe, *Człowiek ze spiżu* (Man of bronze; 1981). (JS)

Sources: Kunert, vol. 1; *Encyklopedia katolicka,* vol. 2 (Lublin, 1976); Jacek Bartyzel, "Jerzy Braun: Człowiek i dzieło," *Tygodnik Powszechny,* 1985, no. 42; Maria Żychowska, *Jerzy Braun, 1901–1975: Harcerz, poeta, filozof, publicysta, mąż stanu* (Tarnów, 1986); *Muza poezji w celi Jerzego Brauna* (Kraków, 1997); Janusz Zabłocki, *Chrześcijańska Demokracja w kraju i na emigracji 1947–1970* (Lublin, 1999); www.biblioteka.tarman. pl/patroni/braun2.html.

BRAZAUSKAS Algirdas Mykolas (22 September 1932, Rokiškis), Lithuanian Communist activist and post-Communist politician, president of Lithuania. After graduating from high school in 1951, Brazauskas completed engineering studies at the Kaunas Polytechnic in 1956.

During studies he belonged to the Komsomol, and in 1959 he joined the Communist Party of the Soviet Union. In 1958 he became chief engineer of Energostroy, which constructed the Kaunas Hydropower Plant, and then, until 1962, he directed a power engineering company. In 1962–65 he was head of the department of building materials in the Economic Council of the Lithuanian SSR, and from 1965 he was minister of the building materials industry. In 1966 he became a deputy member of the Central Committee (CC) of the Communist Party of Lithuania (CPL) and deputy chairman of the State Planning Commission of the government of the Lithuanian SRR. From 1967 he was a deputy to the republican Supreme Council. In 1974 he received a Ph.D. in economics, and in 1977 he became secretary for economic affairs and a member of the CPL CC Politburo. Although he began his career during the reign of Leonid Brezhnev and was a loyal executor of Soviet policies, he became known for his administrative skills and openness to *perestroika*.

When the Lithuanian Movement for Perestroika (Lietuvos Persitvarkymo Sąjūdis) was created in June 1988, Brazauskas realized that the Communist Party would no longer be able to suppress Lithuanian aspirations for freedom and that he should join the movement. The first member of the top Communist leadership to take part in the mass gatherings of the movement, he won wide support and sympathy in the society. His viewpoint prevailed in the CPL CC, which, after a brutal police crackdown on a commemoration of the anniversary of the Molotov-Ribbentrop Pact on 23 August 1988, decided to dismiss the previous first secretary, Ringaudas Songaila, and entrusted Brazauskas with this position. Brazauskas' first decision, which gained him even more sympathy, was to give back Vilnius Cathedral to the Roman Catholic Church. As head of the CPL, he was in favor of the political and economic autonomy of Lithuania but was more cautious than the Estonian leadership. In October 1988 in the Supreme Council Brazauskas blocked a declaration of Lithuanian independence similar to the Estonian declaration. The council adopted the declaration on 18 May 1989, when the downfall of the Soviet Union seemed closer. Following Brazauskas, most of the Lithuanian Communists left the Soviet party in December 1989, founding an independent CPL. From January to March 1990 Brazauskas was chairman of the Supreme Council. Despite the victory of the Lithuanian Movement for Perestroika in the elections to the Supreme Council in February and March 1990 and Brazauskas's departure from the chairmanship of the council, which had declared the full independence of Lithuania, Brazauskas became deputy prime minister in the government of **Kazimiera Prunskiene**. He held this position from April 1990 to early January 1991. In December 1990 he became chairman of the Lithuanian Democratic Labor Party (Lietuvos Demokratinė Darbo Partija [LDPP]), created by former CPL activists.

During the crisis that followed the declaration of Lithuanian independence, Brazauskas was increasingly criticized for his cautious policies and his Communist past, but he managed to maintain a good reputation in the society. After the elections of October 1992 he became the speaker of the parliament, and, after withdrawing from the LDPP, on 14 February 1993 he won the presidential election. He effectively continued the pro-independence and pro-democracy line of Lithuanian politics. At the end of August 1993 the last Soviet troops left Lithuania, and at the beginning of September 1993 Brazauskas welcomed Pope John Paul II. This was the first papal pilgrimage to any former Soviet republic. As the first president of any post-Soviet country, on 4 January 1994 Brazauskas officially stated that membership in NATO was a strategic goal for Lithuania. During his term as president, he signed a border agreement with Russia and a breakthrough treaty of friendly relations and neighborly cooperation with Poland (26 April 1994). In June 1995 Lithuania signed an association treaty with the European Union, and in December 1995 it officially submitted its candidature for union membership. Despite his continued popularity, Brazauskas did not run for reelection in December 1998. He organized the Social Democratic Coalition including the LDPP, the Lithuanian Social Democratic Party, the New Democracy, and the Union of Russians in Lithuania; it won the parliamentary elections of October 2000. In January 2001 both leftist parties merged into the Social Democratic Party of Lithuania. On 3 July 2001 Brazauskas assumed the post of prime minister and played an important role in the accession of Lithuania into the European Union, decided by national referendum in the spring of 2003. (MK)

Sources: Saulius Suziedelis, *Historical Dictionary of Lithuania* (Lanham, Md., 1997); *Kas yra kas Lietuvoje 95/96*; Alexander Rahr, ed., *A Biographical Directory of 100 Leading Soviet Officials* (Boulder, Colo., 1990); Alfred E. Senn, *Lithuania Awakening* (Berkeley, 1990); Anatol Lieven, *The Baltic Revolution* (New Haven, 1993); Romuald J. Misiunas and Rein Taagepera, *The Baltic States: Years of Dependence, 1940–1990* (Berkeley, 1993); V. Stanley Vardys and Judith B. Sedaitis, *Lithuania: The Rebel Nation* (Boulder, Colo., 1997); Piotr Łossowski, *Litwa* (Warsaw, 2001).

BŘEZINA Otokar [originally Václav Jebavý] (13 September 1868, Počátky, near Pelhřimov–25 March 1929, Jaroměřice nad Rokytną, near Třebič), Czech writer. After graduating from high school in 1887, Březina started working as a teacher and led a solitary life. He read a lot and wrote many letters, acquiring a vast literary and philosophical knowledge. In 1913 he became a corresponding member, and in 1923 a full member, of the Czech Academy of Science and Art. In 1919 he received an honorary doctorate from Charles University in Prague, and in 1923 he rejected an offer to assume a chair of philosophy at Brno University. He was twice a candidate for the Nobel Prize in literature (1921 and 1928). He made his literary debut in the spirit of positivism in 1886, but from 1892 he was closer to symbolism and soon became one of the major exponents of Czech modernism. His first volume, *Tajemné dálky* (Secret distances; 1895), was mostly pessimistic and elegiac. In two subsequent volumes—*Svítání na západě* (Dawn in the West; 1896) and *Větry od pólů* (Winds from the poles; 1897)—he presented hymns that showed the human experience as a means to better recognize the Absolute. In his next collections—*Stavitelé chrámu* (Builders of the temple; 1899) and *Ruce* (Hands; 1901)—he argued that love was the major uniting force and the ultimate goal of life. After the latter collection, in which people appeared as brothers and sisters working together to improve the world, he found that he had no more to say and ended his poetic career. He started writing essays. In the volume *Hudba pramenů* (Music of the roots; 1903) he considered the mysteries of art, beauty, and world order. In 1908 he gave up active literary work, apart from essays that he never completed and that were published in 1970 as *Skryté dějiny* (Hidden histories), in which the incomplete works were reconstructed by Otokar Fiala. (PU)

Sources: *ČBS*; *Slovník českých filozofů* (Brno, 1998); Miloš Marten, *Otokar Březina* (Prague, 1903); Miloš Dvořak, *Tradice díla Otokara Březiny* (Prague, 1928); Antonín Veselý, *Otokar Březina: Osobnost a dílo* (Brno, 1928); Emanuel Chalupný, *Dopisy a výroky Otokara Březiny* (Prague, 1931); Jakub Deml, *Mé svědectví o Otokaru Březinovi* (Prague, 1931); Oldřich Králík, *Otokar Březina* (Prague, 1948); Józef Zarek, *Eseistyka Otokara Březiny: W kręgu dylematów symbolisty* (Wrocław, 1979).

BRIEDIS Fridrihs (24 June 1888, county of Polotsk–28 August 1918, Moscow), Latvian officer in the Russian Army. Born into a peasant family, Briedis attended school in Dvinsk (Daugavpils, Dünaburg). In 1906 he entered the Junker school in St. Petersburg, from which he graduated in 1909. Next, he served as an officer in the Ninety-ninth Infantry Regiment in Dvinsk. From 1914 he took part in the fighting in Prussia and in Poland. In 1915 he was transferred, at his own request, to the units of Latvian Riflemen on the Riga front. He was one of the more outstanding combat officers and was wounded many times. In 1917 he was promoted to colonel and was appointed commanding officer of the First Regiment of Latvian Riflemen. Arrested by the Bolsheviks in October 1917,

he managed to escape. He went to Vitebsk and then to Petrograd and Moscow. In January 1918, along with other Latvian officers, he joined the Union for the Defense of the Fatherland and Freedom, an anti-Bolshevik organization led by Boris Savinkov. Under Briedis's pressure, the leadership of the union planned to demand autonomy for Latvia, within the framework of democratic Russia. In July 1918 Briedis was one of the leaders of the anti-Bolshevik uprising in Rybinsk and Yaroslavl. On 7 August 1918 he was arrested in Moscow, and then he was executed by a firing squad in Lubyanka Prison. (EJ)

Sources: *Pulkvedis F. Briedis* (Riga, 1921); Edvins Mednis, *Pulkvedis Briedis* (Riga, 1934); P. Dardzāns, "Pulkvedis F. Briedis cīņās un dzīvē," *Latviešu Strēlnieki*, 1938, no. 25; M. Akmenājs, *Briedis* (Stockholm, 1963); V. Stinkulis, *Pulkvedis Fridrihs Briedis* (Riga, 1992); Andrejs Plakans, *Historical Dictionary of Latvia* (Lanham, Md., 1997).

BRONIEWSKI Stanisław, pseudonym "Orsza" (29 December 1915, Warsaw–30 December 2000, Warsaw), Polish scouting activist. From 1928 Broniewski was a member of the Polish Scouting Association (Związek Harcerstwa Polskiego [ZHP]). He graduated from the Law and Economics Department of Poznań University. In September 1939 he co-organized the Scouting Emergency Organization (Pogotowie Harcerzy) in Warsaw. During the German occupation he commanded the Warsaw troop of the Gray Ranks (Szare Szeregi; the underground ZHP), and then its Shock Troops. In March 1943 he commanded the famous Warsaw Arsenal operation in which several Pawiak prisoners, including Jan "Rudy" Bytnar, were rescued from German hands. From May 1943 he was head of the Gray Ranks. He fought in the Warsaw Uprising, and after its failure he was imprisoned in the POW camp in Bergen-Belsen. In 1945 he took over the command of Polish scouting in Germany. In 1946 he decided to return to Poland. From 1946 to 1948 he worked in the Central Planning Office, and in 1948–53, in the Union of Consumer Cooperatives Społem. Contrary to Communist endeavors to take over total control of Polish scouting, Broniewski embodied the tradition of the Gray Ranks and set a pattern for three generations of Polish scouts. After October 1956 he initiated an organizational committee aiming at the renewal of Polish scouting after Stalinism. He joined the ZHP Central Headquarters, but he was purged from it by the Communists in 1958. From 1957 to 1963 he worked in the Economic Council of the Council of Ministers and then in the Institute of Environmental Protection. After receiving a Ph.D. and a postdoctoral degree, he also lectured at the University of Łódź. In 1989 he presided over the National Committee for ZHP Renewal. He authored numerous works on town planning and economics; memoirs, *Całym życiem: Szare Szeregi w relacji naczelnika* (With all my life: The Gray Ranks story told by its head; 1983); and a biography, *Florian Marciniak: Naczelnik Szarych Szeregów* (Florian Marciniak: Head of the Gray Ranks; 1988). (WR)

Sources: Kunert, vols. 1–3; *Wielka Encyklopedia Powszechna*, vol. 4 (Warsaw, 2001); Jerzy Jabrzemski, ed., *Szare Szeregi: Harcerze 1939–1945*, vols. 1–3 (Warsaw, 1988); *Więź*, 2001, no. 3.

BRONIEWSKI Władysław (17 December 1897, Płock–10 February 1962, Warsaw), Polish poet. In 1915–17 Broniewski served in the Polish Legions on the side of the Austro-Hungarian Army. After refusing to swear an oath of loyalty to the Central Powers, he was interned in the Szczypiorno camp. In 1919–21 he served in the Polish Army; he took part in the Polish-Soviet war and was decorated with the Order of Virtuti Militari for bravery on the battlefield. From 1921 to 1924 he studied philosophy at Warsaw University, but he did not graduate. At this time he drew closer to the extreme left and worked with periodicals inspired by the Communist Party of Poland. Temporarily arrested, after release he was secretary of the editorial board of *Wiadomości Literackie*. In 1939 he was in Lwów (Lviv), where, after the Soviet invasion, he was arrested and deported to the Gulag. As a result of the Polish-Soviet agreement of July 1941, he was released. He joined the Polish Army in the USSR and was evacuated with it to Iran and the Middle East in 1942. In 1945 he returned to Poland. In his poetry he combined patriotic emotions and revolutionary pathos and agitation with lyrical exaltation. He alluded to Polish Romantic poetry but also to contemporary poetics, using a simple or even colloquial language. In the volumes *Wiatraki* (Windmills; 1925) and *Dymy nad miastem* (Smoke over the city; 1929) and in the poem *Komuna Paryska* (The Paris Commune; 1929) he expressed the revolutionary mood, and in the collection *Krzyk ostateczny* (Ultimate shout; 1938), a presentiment of the coming disaster of war. In April 1939 he wrote his most popular poem, *Bagnet na broń* (Bayonets ready!), in which he called people to arms in defense of Polish independence. After World War II he became a leading poet of the Communist regime, creating political and propaganda works, such as the poem *Słowo o Stalinie* (A word on Stalin; 1949), but also personal and landscape lyrics (WR)

Sources: *Literatura polska XX wieku: Przewodnik encyklopedyczny*, vol. 1 (Warsaw, 2000); *Wielka encyklopedia PWN*, vol. 4 (Warsaw, 2001); Jan Zygmunt Jakubowski, *Władysław Broniewski* (Warsaw, 1975); Feliksa Lichodziejewska, *Broniewski bez cenzury 1939–1945* (Warsaw, 1992).

BRUCAN Silviu (18 January 1916, Bucharest), Romanian Communist and post-Communist activist. Before World War II Brucan graduated in political science and worked as a journalist. During the war he was active in the Communist underground but hiding because of his Jewish descent. After the coup of August 1944, he became one of the leaders of the Romanian Communist Party (Partidul Comunist Român [RCP]). Until 1956 he was editor-in-chief of the main party daily, *Scânteia*, helping to carry into effect numerous Stalinist propaganda campaigns. In 1944–56 he was in Moscow many times. From 1956 to 1963 he was ambassador to the United States and to the United Nations and was engaged in acquiring American high technologies. After his return, in 1963 he became head of state television. Soon after the takeover of power by **Nicolae Ceauşescu** in 1965, as a member of the **Gheorghe Gheorghiu-Dej** group, Brucan was dismissed from this position. He worked at Bucharest University and was deputy director of the Association of International Studies.

In the 1980s Brucan was a member of a group of Communist functionaries supported by the Kremlin and ready to take over power in case the Soviet leadership determined that Ceauşescu was no longer acceptable. The political police, Securitate, knew of his affiliation but did nothing. In 1987, after the army bloodily suppressed a workers' rebellion in Braşov, Brucan gave interviews to Western journalists criticizing the use of force. In 1988 he was allowed to go to the United States, where he met the head of the East European desk of the State Department. He also visited London, Vienna, and Moscow, where he met Mikhail Gorbachev, who probably promised his support for an alternative Romanian government. After Brucan returned to Romania, on 10 March 1989 the BBC broadcast the "Letter of Six," written by former high Communist functionaries protesting the violation of human rights and the economic policy of the Ceauşescu regime. Brucan was briefly arrested. After the fall of Ceauşescu on 22 December 1989, Brucan became one of the leaders of the National Salvation Front (Frontul Sălvari Naţionale), which took over power. Brucan was against the withdrawal of Romania from the Warsaw Pact, political pluralism, and appropriation of the peasants. When **Ion Iliescu** was elected president in May 1990, Brucan became one of his closest advisers. Nevertheless, at the end of 1990 he was marginalized by Iliescu, as he was thought to be too conservative a Communist. Brucan authored (among other works) the following: *Originele politici americane* (The roots of American policy; 1968); *Dialectic of World Politics* (1978); *Post-Brezhnev Era: An Insider's View* (1983); *Stâlpii noii puteri în România* (Foundations of new power in Romania; 1996); *Social Change in*

Russia and Eastern Europe: From Party Hacks to Nouveaux Riches (1998); and the memoirs *Generaţia irosita: Memorii* (Wasted generation; 1993). (LW)

Sources: Ion Raţiu, *Contemporary Romania* (Richmond, 1975); Józef Darski, *Rumunia: Historia, współczesność, konflikty narodowe* (Warsaw, 1995); Ion Alexandrescu, Ion Bulei, Ion Mamina, and Ioan Scurtu, *Enciclopedia de istorie României* (Bucharest, 2000); www.wyborcza.pl; www.abcnet.com.pl; www.diploweb.com; www.loc.gov.

BRUSZNYAI Árpád (27 June 1924, Derekegyháza–9 January 1958, Budapest), one of the leaders of the Hungarian Revolution of 1956. In 1949 Brusznyai graduated *cum laude* in classical philology and history, and in 1950 he received a Ph.D. It was predicted that he would have a brilliant scholarly career. In 1949–50 he worked in the Institute of Classical Philology of Budapest University. In 1951 his father was imprisoned for political reasons; his brother, a Roman Catholic priest, was interned in Kistarcsa; and Brusznyai himself was fired from work. First he worked as an organ player in the Vác basilica, where he also taught Old Greek, Latin, and music in the local theological seminary. In 1952 he got a teaching job at László Lovassy High School in Veszprém. After the outbreak of the revolution, on 26 October 1956 he was elected to the Revolutionary Council of Veszprém County; on 31 October he became its deputy chairman, and on 1 November, chairman. The council urged the government of **Imre Nagy** to start negotiations on the withdrawal of Soviet troops from Hungary, to announce free parliamentary elections, and to "build socialism" with respect to the national tradition. Enjoying substantial authority, Brusznyai vetoed lynchings and prevented bloodshed. He issued a decree on the partial dissolution of collective farms and on the takeover of Communist Party property by the council. He made sure that all the Communist security functionaries gave up their arms and handed them over to the council members. On 2 November he agreed in Budapest that the military commander of Veszprém should transfer arms to the newly formed detachments of the Revolutionary National Guard, and he helped to organize its units with respect to discipline and order. A day after the second Soviet intervention, on 5 November 1956 he was arrested and transferred to the USSR. Six weeks later he returned to Hungary, but on 25 April 1957 he was arrested again by the Hungarian authorities, and on 19 October 1957 he was sentenced by a military court in Győr to life imprisonment for "leading a plot against the power of the people." On 7 January 1958 the Supreme Military Court changed this verdict to a death sentence, and two days later he was executed. (JT)

Sources: Attila Szakolczay, *Az 1956-os forradalom és szabadságharc* (Budapest, 2001); *Új Magyar Életrajzi Lexikon*, vol. 1 (Budapest, 2001); György Litván, ed., *Rewolucja węgierska 1956 roku* (Warsaw, 1996).

BRYJA Wincenty (16 June 1897, Morawczyn, near Nowy Targ–27 January 1973, Morawczyn), Polish Peasant Party politician. Bryja completed secondary school in Nowy Targ. From 1917 he served in the Austrian Army, and from 1918 to 1921, in the Polish Army. In 1925 he graduated in law from the Jagiellonian University. A member of the Polish Peasant Party Piast (Polskie Stronnictwo Ludowe Piast) from 1924, he worked in a bank. Between 1935 and 1938 Bryja was head of the Union of Peasant Intelligentsia and edited its periodical, *Zagon*. During the Nazi occupation he revived the organization in the underground under the code name "Orka," in close union with the secret Peasant Party. From October 1942 he was head of the Department of Finance of the Delegation of the Polish Government-in-Exile for the Homeland (Delegatura Rządu na Kraj) in Warsaw. Seriously wounded during the Warsaw Uprising, Bryja was forced out of the city along with the civilian population of the capital. He later worked as a treasurer of the peasant movement called Roch and managed the finances of the Delegation. From July 1945 he co-organized the structures of the Polish Peasant Party (Polskie Stronnictwo Ludowe [PSL]) in the capacity of (for example) treasurer of its Chief Executive Committee and member of its Supreme Council. In December 1945 Bryja was coopted to the National Home Council (Krajowa Rada Narodowa) as a PSL representative. In fake elections in January 1947 he gained a seat in the Constituent Assembly. Fearing arrest, he attempted to cross the border but was caught by the Czechoslovak police and delivered to the Communist authorities in Poland. After his arrest, on 15 November 1947, the Constituent Assembly canceled his parliamentary immunity. He was kept in prison for four years without a trial, and on 8 October 1951 he was sentenced to ten years. Released in 1954, until his death he worked on his own farm. (WR)

Sources: Kunert, vol. 2; Stanisław Łach, *Polskie Stronnictwo Ludowe w latach 1945–1947* (Gdańsk, 1995).

BRYSTYGIEROWA Julia, pseudonym "Luna," (25 November 1902, Stryj–9 October 1975, Warsaw), Polish Communist activist. The daughter of a Jewish druggist, Brystygierowa attended high school in Lwów (Lviv) and then studied history at Jan Kazimierz University in Lwów. After receiving a Ph.D. from this university in 1926, she studied in Paris and Lwów. She earned her living giving private classes and also worked as a teacher in Vilnius but was dismissed for her participation in a strike. Linked with the Communist movement from 1927, in 1931 she began to edit *Przegląd Współczesny* in Lwów, for which she was arrested. In 1931 she joined the Communist Party of Western Ukraine (Komunistyczna Partia Zachodniej Ukrainy [KPZU]), where she was involved in agitation and propaganda. Imprisoned between 1932 and 1933 after a conflict with party authorities, in 1936 Brystygierowa again joined the leadership of the KPZU and was a secretary of the CC of the International Organization for Aid to Revolutionaries of Western Ukraine. As a representative of the KPZU CC, she took part in negotiations on the establishment of a people's front. She wrote for the press and acted in legal pro-Communist organizations. In May 1936 she co-organized the Congress of Culture Workers in Lwów. Arrested and convicted in April 1937, she was released in April 1939. From the fall of 1939 she lived in Lwów and worked as a secretary in the District Committee of the International Organization for Aid to Revolutionaries. She also had contacts with *Nowe Widnokręgi* and probably with the NKVD. After the outbreak of the German-Soviet war in June 1941 she went to Kharkiv and then to Samarkand. At the First Congress of the Union of Polish Patriots (Związek Patriotów Polskich [ZPP]) in Moscow (9–10 June 1943), she joined the Main Board of the ZPP. Later, she served as secretary of the Presidium of the Main Board of the ZPP and as head of its personnel and organizational department.

In September 1944 Brystygierowa arrived in Lublin and took up a seat in the National Home Council (Krajowa Rada Narodowa [KRN]). She was a member of the Polish Workers' Party (Polska Partia Robotnicza [PPR]) from October 1944. She took part in the First and the Second Congresses of the PPR and in the Unification Congress of the Polish United Workers' Party (Polska Zjednoczona Partia Robotnicza [PUWP]). Until 1954 she was a member of the Central Commission of Party Control. On 20 December 1944 she became head of a section in the Investigation Bureau of the Public Security Department of the Polish Committee of National Liberation (Polski Komitet Wyzwolenia Narodowego [PKWN]), and then she quickly rose in the Communist hierarchy. From January 1945 she was head of the Third Department ("for the struggle against political banditry") of the Ministry for Public Security. In October 1945 she became acting director of the Fifth (Political) Department, and between January 1950 and July 1954 she served as director of this department. In this capacity she controlled political parties, cultural institutions, and religious organizations. She contributed significantly to the establishment of the group centered around *Dziś i jutro*, the weekly of **Bolesław Piasecki**.

Her role in the government structures was greater than her official position would suggest, because she attended the plenums of the PUWP CC and prepared many key decisions of the party leadership. She supervised electoral fraud during the referendum of June 1946 and the parliamentary elections of January 1947. She also played a key role in the struggle against the Catholic Church. In 1949 she co-organized the Committee of Priests in the Association of Fighters for Freedom and Democracy as an opposition group to church authorities. Her efforts, which won her the nickname of "bloody Luna," led to many arrests, including those of around nine hundred priests, several bishops, and Primate Stefan Cardinal Wyszyński. After the escape of Józef Światło to the West, in August 1954 she became head of the Third Department (for the struggle against the underground) of the Ministry of Public Security. In December 1954 the Third Department was transferred to the Committee for Public Security. During the thaw Brystygierowa supported the pro-liberal course of the Puławska group, and she began to criticize abuses committed by the security apparatus. In March 1955 she inspired the creation of the Club of the Crooked Circle in Warsaw, but she simultaneously continued the firm policy of struggle against the church. After the liquidation of the Committee for Public Security, in November 1956 she left the security services. In May 1958 she retired and devoted herself to literary work, publishing (for example), under her maiden name, Julia Prajs, the novel *Krzywe litery* (Crooked letters; 1960). At the end of her life Brystygierowa, who was losing her sight, found care at the Laski Institute for the Blind, run by nuns, where she converted to Catholicism. (PK)

Sources: *Trybuna Ludu*, 13 October 1975; Andrzej Micewski, *Współrządzić czy nie kłamać: PAX i Znak w Polsce 1945–1976* (Paris, 1978); *Słownik biograficzny działaczy polskiego ruchu robotniczego*, vol. 2 (Warsaw, 1987); Antoni Dudek and Grzegorz Pytel, *Bolesław Piasecki: Próba biografii politycznej* (London, 1990); Michał Czajka and Marcin Kamler, *Leksykon Historii Polski* (Warsaw, 1995); Leszek Żebrowski, "Brystygierowa Julia," *Encyklopedia "białych plam,"* vol. 3 (Radom, 2000).

BRZEZINSKI Zbigniew (28 March 1928, Warsaw), American political scientist and politician of Polish descent. The son of a Polish diplomat, from 1938 Brzezinski lived with his parents in Canada. After World War II they remained abroad. After graduating from Columbia University, in 1953 he received a Ph.D. at Harvard University. He specialized in international relations and in the Communist system in particular. In 1956, along with Carl Friedrich, he published a classic work, *Totalitarian Dictatorship and Autocracy*, which included a typology of nondemocratic systems. His subsequent works—*The Soviet Bloc: Unity and Conflict* (1960) and *Ideology and Power in Soviet Politics* (1962)—strengthened his position among American experts on totalitarianism and Soviet policy. In 1966–68 he was a member of the Council of Policy Planning of the U.S. State Department, and from 1973 to 1977, director of the Tripartite Commission for American-European-Japanese Cooperation. An adviser to Jimmy Carter during his presidential campaign in 1976, from January 1977 Brzezinski was head of the National Security Council. Under his influence, the Carter administration followed events in Poland very closely, particularly in the context of human rights and the developing democratic opposition. At the end of December 1977, along with Carter, Brzezinski visited Poland, meeting, among others, Primate **Stefan Wyszyński**. In December 1980 he warned the Kremlin that a planned invasion aimed at the suppresion of the Solidarity movement could bring fatal consequences for international relations. He also maintained a close contact on this matter with Pope John Paul II.

After leaving the administration, Brzezinski returned to scholarly work at Columbia University and as an adviser to the Center for International Studies at Georgetown University in Washington, D.C. In 1988 he joined an interparty group of advisers on international security. As an expert in this field, he supported a hard line toward the Soviet Union. His support for systemic transformation in Poland and other East Central European countries was always taken into consideration. He advocated an American mission as a superpower to stabilize international relations, and he supported the extension of NATO into Poland and other well-prepared East Central European countries. He frequently visited Poland. In *The Grand Failure* (1989; Polish edition: *Wielkie bankructwo*; 1990) he analyzed the historic importance of the fall of Soviet communism, and in *The Grand Chessboard* (1997; Polish edition: *Wielka szachownica*; 1997) he presented his vision of the post-Communist world order. Among other works, he also published memoirs: *Power and Principle* (1985; Polish edition: *Cztery lata w Białym Domu*; 1990). In 1981 he was awarded the Presidential Medal of Freedom, and in 1995, the Polish Order of the White Eagle. From 1991 he was a member of the Polish Academy of Arts and Sciences. (WR)

Sources: *The International Who's Who* (1991); *Wielka encyklopedia PWN,* vol. 4 (Warsaw, 2001); Christine E. Thompson, *The Works of Zbigniew Kazimierz Brzezinski* (Monticello, Ill., 1985); Gerry Argyris Andrianopoulos, *Kissinger and Brzezinski: The NSC Struggle for Control of US National Security Policy* (New York, 1991); Józef Frankiewicz, *Zbigniew Brzeziński i jego związki z Przemyślem* (Przemyśl, 1999).

BRZOZOWSKI Stanisław, pseudonym "Adam Czepiel" (28 June 1878, Maziarnia, near Chełm–30 April 1911, Florence, Italy), Polish writer and philosopher. Brzozowski started studies in natural science at Warsaw University, but in 1897 he was dismissed from the university for having organized an anti-Russian demonstration. In September 1898 he was arrested and imprisoned in the Warsaw Citadel, where he gave extensive testimony. In prison he fell ill with tuberculosis, which overshadowed the rest of his life. He made his literary debut in 1900 in *Przegląd Filozoficzny*, and then he contributed to *Przegląd Społeczny, Krytyka,* and *Głos*. His novels, *Pod ciężarem Boga* (Under the burden of God; 1901) and *Wiry* (Whirls; 1904–5), were written in the spirit of modernism. His biting journalism started two important debates of the early twentieth century, and they were frequently referred to later. In an extensive article published in *Głos* in 1903 Brzozowski attacked **Henryk Sienkiewicz** for supporting the myth of a noble conservatism and for promoting a vision of Polish history so that Poles would not lose heart. In 1904 he criticized Zenon Przesmycki "Miriam" for launching the motto "art for art's sake." At this time Brzozowski favored a "philosophy of the deed," based on his interpretation of Friedrich Nietzsche, and in his critiques he stressed the moral and social aspects of a literary work. For him the ultimate measure of an idea was the "quality and quantity of deeds born of it." Thence his critical attitude toward the Polish insurgent tradition and his apotheosis of labor. He was not uncritical of scienticism, positivism, or Marxism, though, and he rejected social determinism.

In 1905 Brzozowski drew closer to Socialist ideology but never joined the Polish Socialist Party. He gathered his essays on the main intellectual trends of his time in *Kultura i życie* (Culture and life; 1907). He condemned the decadence of contemporary elites—for instance, in *Legenda Młodej Polski* (The legend of Young Poland; 1909). As a great polemicist, he exerted significant influence on students; thus in order to compromise him the followers of National Democracy published a booklet with his testimonies of 1898. For health reasons Brzozowski settled in Zakopane, and in 1907 he moved to Florence. In 1908 he was accused of collaborating with the Russian political police, Okhrana. He vigorously denied the charges and demanded an independent civil investigation, but in 1910 nothing was proved. Increasingly isolated and bitter, under the influence of the writings of John H. Newman, he turned to religion and died a Roman Catholic. His works had an enormous influence on Polish social and artistic thought in the twentieth century. His *Dzieła* (Works) were published in four volumes in 1973–90. (WR)

Sources: *PSB*, vol. 3; *Literatura polska XX wieku: Przewodnik encyklopedyczny*, vol. 1 (Warsaw, 2000); Marian Zdziechowski, *Gloryfikacja pracy: Myśli z pism i o pismach Stanisława Brzozowskiego* (Petrograd, 1916); Bohdan Suchodolski, *Stanisław Brzozowski: Rozwój ideologii* (Warsaw, 1933); Andrzej Stawar, *O Brzozowskim* (Warsaw, 1961); Czesław Miłosz, *Człowiek wśród skorpionów: Studium o Stanisławie Brzozowskim* (Paris, 1962); Andrzej Walicki, *Stanisław Brzozowski: Drogi myśli* (Warsaw, 1977).

BUČAR France (2 February 1923, Bohinjska Bistrica), Slovene lawyer and politician. At the end of 1941 Bučar joined the anti-Italian guerrillas. Caught in 1942, he spent almost two years in the camps of Gonars and Novara. After the capitulation of Italy, he was transported to a camp in Germany, but he escaped on the way and returned to Slovenia to resume guerrilla activities. In 1944 he joined the Communist Party. After the war, he graduated in law from the University of Ljubljana, and in 1956 he received a Ph.D. in law there. In 1963 he became secretary of the Republican Chamber of the Assembly of the Slovene republic and began lecturing at the Department of Public Administration of the University of Ljubljana. In view of his criticism of Yugoslav politics, expressed in his book *Podjete in družba* (Entrepreneurship and society; 1972), and for his activity in the radical Marxist group Praxis, in 1976 he was banned from lecturing and forced into early retirement. He still wrote in the spirit of the revision of communism. In 1986 he published *Resničnost in utvara* (Reality and myth), and in 1988, *Usodne odločtive* (Fateful decisions), becoming one of the key opponents of the system in the 1980s. He was one of the leaders of the opposition coalition DEMOS, and as a result of the first free elections of April 1990 he won a parliamentary seat and was elected speaker of the National Assembly. It was during his term that Slovenia declared independence on 25 June 1991. In December 1992 he was elected MP again, but in 1994 he lost in the elections for the mayor of Ljubljana. (WR)

Sources: *Enciklopedija Slovenije*, vol. 1 (Ljubljana, 1987); Leopoldina Plut-Pregelj and Carole Rogel, *Historical Dictionary of Slovenia* (Lanham, Md., 1996).

BUCHKO Ivan (1 October 1891, Hermaniv, near Lviv [Lwów]–21 September 1974, Rome), Ukrainian Greek Catholic bishop and social activist. Buchko graduated from the Academic High School in Lviv, and in 1911–15 he studied theology in Rome. In 1915 he was ordained, and in 1922 he received a Ph.D. in theology. In the 1920s he was rector of the Minor Seminary and professor at the Greek Catholic Theological Seminary in Lviv. From 1929, as auxiliary bishop of the Lviv archbishopric, in cooperation with Metropolitan Andriy Sheptytskyi, he helped to develop various institutions to stimulate Ukrainian religious life, such as the Ukrainian Youth for Christ (Ukrajinśka Mołod' Chrystowi) and Catholic Action (Katołyćka Akcija). He also began defending Ukrainian social initiatives before the Polish authorities. In 1939 he visited Ukrainian communities in South America, and from 1940 he was bishop of the Philadelphia exarchate and Greek Catholic minister of New York. From 1942 until his death he resided in the St. Josaphat College in Rome, a Basilian seminary training Greek Catholic priests. In 1946 he became apostolic visitator of Ukrainians in Western Europe. He maintained contacts with the underground Greek Catholic Church in the Soviet Ukraine. In 1953 he became titular archbishop of Leucadia, and in 1958 he became a consultant of the Congregation of Eastern Churches, a member of the Vatican Commission of Eastern Churches of the Second Vatican Council, and vice-president of the Conference of the Ukrainian Episcopate. He was active in the social, scholarly, and religious life of the Ukrainian diaspora, an honorary member of the Taras Shevchenko Scientific Society, and an honorary doctor of the Free Ukrainian University and the Ukrainian Technical and Economic Institute in Munich, Germany. (TS)

Sources: *Encyclopedia of Ukraine*, vol. 1 (Toronto, 1985); *Annuario Pontificio, 1974*.

BUDAJ Ján (10 February 1952, Bratislava), Slovak politician. Budaj started studies in mathematics and physics but did not complete them. In the 1970s and 1980s he was repressed for opposition activities, and from 1976 to 1989 he worked as a stoker. He cooperated with the Czech Charter 77 and Polish Solidarity, among other things as editor and author of political and cultural periodicals published without censorship. In November 1989 he was active in Bratislava protests, moderated meetings of the Velvet Revolution, and co-organized the Public against Violence movement (Verejnost proti násiliu [VPN]) in Slovakia. He was the first VPN chairman, and during the reconstruction of the parliament in 1990 he was coopted to the Slovak National Council. He became its speaker and largely contributed to the victory of the opposition in the first free elections in Czechoslovakia in June 1990. After the split of the VPN, in the spring of 1991 he withdrew from politics and turned to journalism. After the creation of independent Slovakia, in 1993, along with **Milan Kňažko**, Budaj founded a liberal-democratic party, the Alliance of Democrats (Aliancia Demokratov). When the group of **Jozef Moravčik** left the **Vladimir Mečiar** movement and founded the Democratic Union of Slovakia

(Demokratická Únia Slovenska [DUS]), the Alliance of Democrats joined it. In March 1997 Budaj was elected the DUS deputy chairman. Before the elections of 1998, along with other DUS candidates, he joined the Slovak Democratic Coalition (Slovenská Demokratická Koalicie [SDK]), co-authoring its program and winning a parliamentary seat on its behalf. He opposed the transformation of the coalition into one party, as well as unification of the DUS with the Slovak Democratic and Christian Union (Slovenská Demokratická Krest'anská Únie [SDKÚ]), founded by **Mikulaš Dzurinda** in 2000. When Budaj lost the struggle for party leadership and when the DUS joined the SDKÚ, in November 2000 he founded the Liberal Democratic Union, which returned to the name DUS in 2002. (PU)

Sources: *Kto je kto na Slovensku 1991* (Bratislava, 1991); *Slovensko 1996: Súhrnná správa o stave spoločnosti* (Bratislava, 1997); *Slovensko 1997: Súhrnná správa o stave spoločnosti* (Bratislava, 1998); *Slovensko 1998–1999: Súhrnná správa o stave spoločnosti* (Bratislava, 1999); *Slovensko 2000: Súhrnná správa o stave spoločnosti* (Bratislava, 2000); http://www.du.sk.

BUDAK Mile (30 August 1889, Gračac, Bosnia–7 June 1945, Zagreb), Croatian journalist, poet, and nationalist politician. From 1907 Budak contributed to Bosnian Croat magazines. He obtained a Ph.D. in law from the university in Zagreb (1920). In the 1920s and 1930s he was active in the Croat nationalist opposition to the dictatorship of King **Alexander Karadjordjević**, and he belonged to the Croatian Party of Rights (Hrvatska Stranka Prava). He also published many stories and novels—for example, *Pod gorom* (Under the mountain; 1930) and *Ognijšte* (A hearth; 1938). He was a proponent of the theory that the Croats were not Slavs but the descendants of Goths; therefore they were a Germanic people. In his books he glorified violence and ethnic hatred. In 1932 he was seriously injured as a result of a Serb police action. After his recovery he went to Italy and then to Germany, where he became one of the closest associates of **Ante Pavelić**. He returned to Yugoslavia in 1939 and took part in a bomb attack on the Yugoslav authorities. He was taken into custody, and at the same time his wife committed suicide.

After the creation of the Independent Croatian State in April 1941 Budak became its education minister. In this role, he actively supported the mass killing of Serbs and Jews. At the same time he attracted the cooperation of Bosnian Muslims; as a result Djafer bey Kulenović was appointed as the Ustaša deputy prime minister. In October 1941 Budak became ambassador of Croatia to Berlin. In April 1943 he assumed the portfolio of foreign affairs, but he resigned soon after the creation of the

government of **Nikola Mandić** in October 1943. During the war he published books in which he presented extremely nationalist views—for example, *Ratno roblje* (Prisoners of war; 1941); *Na vulkanima* (On the volcano; 1941); and *Kresojića soj* (The Kresojić clan; 1944). As was discovered later, his wife had cooperated with Communist intelligence. On 6 May 1945 he fled from Zagreb but was captured by the British and handed over to the Communists on 18 May. He was sentenced to death and executed by a firing squad. In the independent Croatia of **Franjo Tudjman** the legacy of Budak became the subject of sharp political disputes when streets began to be named after him and when some of his works were being revived, such as *Ognijšte* and *Ratno roblje*. (WR)

Sources: *Enciklopedija Jugoslavija*, vol. 2 (Zagreb, 1982); Ivo Omrčanin, *Dramatis presonae and finis of the Independent State of Croatia in British and American Documents* (Bryn Mawr, Pa. 1983); Bogdan Krizman, *Ustaše i Treći Reich* (Zagreb, 1983), vols. 1–2; Bogdan Krizman, *Ante Pavelić i Ustaše* (Zagreb, 1983); Ivan Gabelica and Ivan Pandzić, eds., *Nad Velebitom sviće: Zbornik o Mili Budaku* (Zagreb, 1995); Marcus Tanner, *Croatia: A Nation Forged in War* (New Haven, 1997).

BUDIŠA Dražen (27 July 1948, Drniš), Croatian politician. The son of a white-collar worker, in 1967 Budiša started philosophical and sociological studies at the University of Zagreb. During the Croatian Spring of 1971 he took part in the independent student movement, for which he was arrested and sentenced to four years of hard labor. After his release in 1975, he continued his studies and graduated in 1976. In 1977 he started working in the National Library and then in the library of the University of Zagreb. After some time he became the head of its special collection. He also published. In the 1980s he was active in the anti-Communist opposition, and in 1990 he was co-founder of the first opposition party—the Croatian Social Liberal Party (Hrvatska Socijalno Liberalna Stranka [HSLS]). In 1996–97 he was chairman of the HSLS Supreme Board, and then he became the HSLS president. On its behalf he was elected to the parliament in 1992, and from July 1991 to April 1992 he was minister without portfolio in the government of Franjo Greguriæ.

In the presidential elections of August 1992 Budiša came in second (22 percent of the vote), and as a result of simultaneous parliamentary elections, the HSLS became the strongest faction opposing the ruling Croatian Democratic Union of President **Franjo Tudjman**. After the elections of October 1995 Budiša became deputy speaker of the House of Representatives. In 1995 the opposition won the local elections in Zagreb, and Budiša was elected mayor of the capital, but Tudjman refused to accept this result and finally nominated a government commissioner to rule the city. In 1998 the HSLS entered into a coalition with the post-Communists of **Ivica Račan**. Together they won forty-seven seats in the parliament in the elections of January 2000. According to an agreement, Račan became prime minister of a wide center-left coalition, and Budiša its candidate for president. Nevertheless, in February 2000 he unexpectedly lost to **Stipe Mesić**, coming in second (27 percent of the vote in the first round and 44 percent in the second round). As a result, he resigned as the HSLS president, but in 2002 he was reelected to this position. After the government crisis of March 2002 he became deputy prime minister in the reconstructed government of Račan, but in July 2002 his party left the coalition and Budiša resigned. Budiša authored more than forty books and articles on the history of Croatian literature and culture, including *Počeci tiskarstva u evropskih naroda* (Beginnings of printing in European countries; 1984); *Hrvatske knjige tiskane u Mlečima od XV. do XVIII stoljeca* (Croatian books printed in Venice from the fifteenth to the eighteenth centuries; 1990); and *Razgovori o hrvatskoj državi* (Debates on Croatian statehood; 2001). (AW)

Sources: *Tko je tko u Hrvatskoj* (Zagreb, 1993); Vít Hloušek, "Stranický systém Chorvatska: Nedokoněená transformace," in M. Strimiska, ed., *Postkomunistické stranické sostavy a politická pluralita* (Brno, 1999); Alex J. Bellamy, "Croatia after Tudjman: The 2000 Parliamentary and Presidential Elections," *Problems of Post-Communism*, 2001, no. 5; Karen Dawisha and Bruce Parrot, eds., *Politics, Power and the Struggle for Democracy in South-East Europe* (Cambridge, 1997); Zoran Kusovac, "The Prospects for Change in Post-Tudjman Croatia," *East European Constitutional Review*, 2000, no. 2; *Europa Środkowo-Wschodnia 1991–1998* (Warsaw, 1992–2000); www.hsls.hr/cv.htm.

BUDKA Mykyta (7 September 1877, Dobromirka, near Zbaraż [Zbarazh]–1 October 1949, Karaganda), bishop of the Greek Catholic Church, martyr for the faith. After theological studies at a Jesuit university in Innsbruck, in October 1905 Budka was ordained a priest, and then he continued his studies in Vienna, earning a Ph.D. in 1909. Later, he worked at a theological seminary in Lwów (Lviv) and performed pastoral duties for the Ukrainian émigrés. He also edited the magazine *Emigrant*. On 15 July 1912 he was consecrated bishop. Next, the Pope appointed him apostolic exarch in Canada. He remained in Canada until 1927. In 1928, after a short stay in Rome, he was appointed vicar general of the Lwów chapter and auxiliary bishop of Lwów. As the Soviet authorities were withdrawing from Lwów in June 1941, the NKVD was threatening him with execution. On 11 April 1945 he was arrested, along with Archbishop **Yosyf Slipyi**, and taken to a prison in Kiev. He was accused of treason, and on 3 June 1946 the military

court sentenced him to five years in a labor camp. He died there. On 27 June 2001 Pope John Paul II beatified him at a solemn Holy Mass in Lviv. (WR)

Sources: *Encyclopedia of Ukraine*, vol. 1 (Toronto 1984); *Martirolohia ukrain's'kikh tserkov u chetyriokh tomakh,* vol. 2 (Toronto, 1985); Bohdan R. Botsiurkiv, *The Ukrainian Greek-Catholic Church and the Soviet State (1939–1950)* (Edmonton, 1996); *Osservatore Romano* (weekly edition in English), 2001, nos. 25 and 27.

BUGAJ Ryszard (22 February 1944, Gawłowo, near Skierniewice), Polish economist and politician. As a student at the Department of Economics of Warsaw University Bugaj took part in the student protests of March 1968. Dismissed from the university, he worked as a blue-collar laborer. After graduating from the Central School of Planning and Statistics in 1970, he worked in the Institute of Building and in the Planning Commission of the Council of Ministers, and from 1982, in the Institute of Economics of the Polish Academy of Sciences. In 1976–80 he was affiliated with the Committee for the Defense of Workers (Komitet Obrony Robotników [KOR]) and published in the uncensored press. In 1980–81 he was a member of the board of the Mazowsze region of Solidarity and one of the chief economic advisers in the National Coordination Commission of Solidarity. He represented the union in the Commission for Economic Reform. In 1981 he became deputy head of the Center for Social and Professional Studies of the Solidarity National Commission, and he co-authored the union's economic program. After the introduction of martial law in December 1981, he was interned. After his release in 1982, he cooperated with the underground leadership of Solidarity. He published in uncensored periodicals and in *Tygodnik Powszechny*. In 1987 he initiated the Society for Reform and Democracy, in which proposals for state reform were discussed. From 1988 he was a member of the Civic Committee of the Chairman of Solidarity. He took part in the Round Table Talks (February–April 1989).

With the elections of June 1989 Bugaj was an MP on behalf of the Civic Parliamentary Club (Obywatelski Klub Parlamentarny [OKP]), and he chaired the parliamentary commission on economic policy, the budget, and finance. Critical of the reforms of Deputy Prime Minister **Leszek Balcerowicz**, as early as November 1989 Bugaj co-founded the Group for the Defense of Labor within the OKP. In 1990–92 he chaired the Solidarity of Labor and its parliamentary club; then he co-founded, and from January 1993 he chaired, the National Council of the Union of Labor (Unia Pracy [UP]) and its parliamentary club. He advocated market reforms with strong social shields and a strict control of privatization. He opposed grassroots privatization and favored government intervention to prevent an excessive stratification of income. An advocate of the separation of church and state, Bugaj opposed cooperation with the post-Communists. After the electoral defeat of the UP in September 1997 and the party's evolution toward cooperation with the post-Communists, he left the UP in 1998. (AF)

Sources: *Nasi w Sejmie i Senacie* (Warsaw, 1990); Jan Skórzyński, *Ugoda i rewolucja: Władza i opozycja 1985–1989* (Warsaw, 1995); Janusz A. Majcherek, *Pierwsza dekada III Rzeczpospolitej 1989–1999* (Warsaw, 1999); *Opozycja w PRL: Słownik biograficzny 1956–89*, vol. 1 (Warsaw, 2000); Antoni Dudek, *Pierwsze lata III Rzeczpospolitej 1989–2001* (Kraków, 2002).

BUGÁR Béla (7 July 1958, Bratislava), Hungarian politician in Slovakia. Bugár graduated in mechanics from the Bratislava Polytechnic in 1982, and later he worked as an engineer in a heavy mechanical equipment factory in Bratislava. After the Velvet Revolution of 1989 he was one of the founders of the Hungarian Christian Democratic Movement (HCDM), registered in March 1990. In the first free elections, in June 1990, Bugár was elected to the Federal Assembly of Czechoslovakia, and in 1991 he took the lead of the HCDM. In the elections of June 1992 he won a seat in the Slovak National Council, which after the split of Czechoslovakia in January 1993 was renamed the National Council of the Slovak Republic. Bugár sat in the Slovak parliament after the elections of 1994, 1998, and 2002. He played a significant role in the unification of all Hungarian parties into the Party of the Hungarian Coalition (Magyar Koalíció Pártja, Strana Maďarskej Koalicie [PHC]) before the parliamentary elections of September 1998. At the PHC founding congress on 21 June 1998 he was elected its chairman and maintained this position at subsequent PHC congresses in 1999 and 2001. Under his leadership in 1998 the PHC won about 9 percent of the vote and entered the government coalition. This led to an improvement in the relationship between the Hungarian minority and the Slovak government, while Hungarians gained some influence on government decisions. As a result of this electoral success, Bugár assumed the position of deputy speaker of the parliament, while the PHC won three portfolios in the government of **Mikulaš Dzurinda**. In the subsequent election, in September 2002, the PHC further improved its standing, gaining more than 11 percent of the vote, entering into the same coalition, and maintaining three portfolios in the second Dzurinda cabinet. (PU)

Sources: *Slovensko 1996: Súhrnná správa o stave spoločnosti* (Bratislava, 1997); *Slovensko 1997: Súhrnná správa o stave spoločnosti* (Bratislava, 1998); *Slovensko 1998–1999: Súhrnná správa o stave spoločnosti* (Bratislava, 1999); *Slovensko 2000: Súhrnná správa o stave spoločnosti* (Bratislava, 2000); mesto.sk/samorin/?ID=1335; www.nevyberjusmev.sk/lidri-smk-bugar.php.

BUJAK Zbigniew (29 November 1954, Łopuszno), Polish trade union activist and politician. From 1974 Bujak worked in Ursus, a mechanical equipment factory; in 1974–76 he served in the Sixth Pomeranian Airborne Division, and in 1977 he graduated from an evening electrical-technical school. From 1978 he was engaged in distributing materials from the uncensored press. In July 1980 he co-organized a strike in Ursus, and in August 1980 he co-founded the Workers' Committee in Solidarity with the Striking Baltic Coast Workers. From September 1980 he presided over the Mazowsze region of Solidarity, and from February 1981 he belonged to the Presidium of the National Coordinating Commission of Solidarity and took part in a number of negotiations with the authorities. On the night martial law was introduced, 13 December 1981, Bujak avoided arrest and went into hiding, organizing underground structures of Solidarity. In 1982–86 he was chairman of the Regional Executive Committee of Solidarity and a member of the All-Polish Provisional Coordination Commission of the union. Arrested on 31 May 1986, he was amnestied in September 1986. He joined the Solidarity Provisional Council and, in 1987, the National Executive Commission of the union. From December 1988 he belonged to the Civic Committee of the Chairman of Solidarity, and from February to April 1989 he took part in the Round Table Talks.

In 1990, during a growing conflict with **Lech Wałęsa** on the role of the Civic Committee, Bujak supported **Tadeusz Mazowiecki**. He left Solidarity in June 1990, joining the Civic Movement-Democratic Action (Ruch Obywatelski-Akcja Demokratyczna [ROAD]). One of its plenipotentiaries until January 1991, he opposed unification of the ROAD with other groups supporting Mazowiecki and wanted to transform it into a Social Democratic party. After these groups merged into the Democratic Union, on 20 April 1991 Bujak co-founded the Democratic Social Movement, on whose behalf he was elected to the Assembly in the fall of 1991. In June 1992, the movement merged with the Solidarity of Labor group into the Union of Labor (Unia Pracy [UP]). From January 1993 he was its deputy chairman. He actively supported the freedom of abortion, and in 1992 he presided over a committee demanding a referendum on this matter. From September 1993 he was MP on behalf of the UP. After the electoral defeat of the UP in September 1997 and after it evolved toward cooperation with the post-Communists, in February 1998 Bujak left it, joined the Union of Freedom, and became a member of its leadership. In 1998 he graduated from the Department of Journalism and Political Science of Warsaw University. From May 1999 to the beginning of 2002 he was chairman of the Chief Office of Tariffs. He authored an interview considered controversial by most Solidarity members: *Przepraszam za "Solidarność"* (I am sorry for Solidarity; 1991). (AF)

Sources: *Wielka encyklopedia PWN*, vol. 5 (Warsaw, 2001); *Opozycja w PRL: Słownik biograficzny 1956–89*, vol. 1 (Warsaw, 2000); Jan Skórzyński, *Ugoda i rewolucja: Władza i opozycja 1985–1989* (Warsaw, 1995); Antoni Dudek, *Pierwsze lata III Rzeczypospolitej 1989–2001* (Kraków, 2002).

BULAK-BALAKHOVICH Stanislau (10 February 1883, Meyszty, near Brasław [Braslau]–10 May 1940, Warsaw), Belorussian general and politician of Polish descent. Bulak-Balakhovich stemmed from a landowner's family and was brought up in the Polish tradition, but because of his Populist convictions, he drew closer to the Belorussians. He graduated from an agricultural school, and in 1905 he took part in the organization of peasant riots in the Brasław region. It was then that he was nicknamed "Bats'ka." In August 1914 he volunteered for the Russian Army and fought on the southwestern front. Promoted to the rank of colonel, he commanded troops thrown behind the front line to disorganize the subsidiaries of the German army. In 1917 he commanded a cavalry division near Riga. In the spring of 1918 he joined the Red Army, but in November 1918 he attached his regiment to the White Guard Voluntary Corps operating in the Pskov area. After the seizure of Pskov he was promoted to major general. In August 1919 General Nikolai Yudenich appointed him commander of the Northwestern Army Corps. Since Bulak-Balakhovich was a Socialist revolutionary, he soon left the White Russian Army.

In early 1920 Bulak-Balakhovich entered into contact with the military mission of the Belorussian National Republic (BNR) and subordinated his 1,200-man detachment to the BNR authorities. Belorussians accounted for 75 percent of the soldiers. As a result of an agreement of the Belorussian military envoy to Riga and Tallinn, **Kanstantsin Yezavitau**, with **Józef Piłsudski,** in June 1920 the Bulak-Balakhovich detachment was transferred to Polesie. Developed into a corps of a few thousand men called the Belorussian National Army, it disrupted the Bolsheviks heading for the Vistula River. After Poland signed an armistice with the Bolsheviks, in October 1920 Bulak-Balakhovich made an agreement with the Belorussian Political Committee in Warsaw, headed by Pavel Aleksyuk. On the committee's behalf Bulak-Balakhovich continued operations against the Bolsheviks, and he captured Pinsk

and Mozyr. In Mozyr he announced that the BNR had authority over the liberated areas and presented himself as the head of state. His offensive of November 1920 was stopped before he could seize Minsk. A part of his troops stayed in Soviet Belorussia and fought as guerrillas until 1922, while others, including Bulak-Balakhovich, withdrew to Poland and were interned. In September 1921, the Belorussian Socialists who met in Prague accused him of the usurpation of power and war atrocities.

In Poland Bulak-Balakhovich became a brigadier general and was active in the pro-government Federation of Polish Associations of Homeland Defenders. In 1929 he co-initiated the Central Committee of the Collection of Funds for Combating Espionage. He wrote strongly anti-German articles. In 1937–39 he was a member of the Polish military mission sent to General Francisco Franco, but he remained without a formal assignment to the army. In September 1939 he commanded a group of volunteers in the defense of Warsaw. At the beginning of the German occupation he organized a secret National Volunteer Army, also called the Military Confederation. He was killed in unclear circumstances during an attempted arrest by the Gestapo in the Warsaw quarter of Saska Kępa. Bulak-Balakhovich authored a few volumes of poetry and two books: *Wojna będzie czy nie będzie?* (Will there be war or not? 1931) and *Precz z Hitlerem czy niech żyje Hitler* (Down with Hitler or long live Hitler; 1933). (EM)

Sources: Marek Cabanowski, *Zapomniany bohater: Generał Stanisław Bułak-Bałachowicz* (Warsaw, 1993); Oleg Łatyszonek, *Białoruskie formacje wojskowe 1917–1923* (Białystok, 1995); Andrzej Nowak, *Polska i trzy Rosje: Studium polityki wschodniej Józefa Piłsudskiego (do kwietnia 1920 roku)* (Kraków, 2001).

BULATOVIĆ Momir (21 September 1956, Belgrade), Communist and post-Communist activist, president of Montenegro. Bulatović graduated in economics and worked as an assistant professor at the Department of Economics at the university in the Montenegrin capital of Titograd (now Podgorica). In 1974 he joined the League of Communists of Montenegro (LCM). In January 1989 he headed a demonstration that led to a change in the Montenegrin republican authorities. As a result he assumed the position of chairman of the LCM Central Committee. In 1988–90 he favored maintaining the Yugoslav federation even by force. It was his position (among other things) that made the Slovene, Croatian, and Bosnian delegations leave the Fourteenth Extraordinary Congress of the League of Communists of Yugoslavia in the spring of 1990. As a result the party split. From December 1990 Bulatović was chairman of the Presidium of the Montenegrin republic, and in January 1993 he was elected its president. After the LCM was renamed the Democratic Party of Socialists (Demokratska Partija Socijalista) he was its head until July 1997, when it split. In October 1997 presidential elections were held that would determine whether Montenegro would continue its pro-Serb policy and remain in the Yugoslav Federation or would choose more autonomy. As an advocate of the former option, Bulatović lost, and in January 1998 **Milo Djukanović** assumed the post of president. Owing to the support of **Slobodan Milošević**, in May 1998 Bulatović became prime minister of the federal Yugoslav government. He served in this capacity until November 2000. From March 1998 to January 2001 he also headed the Socialist People's Party (Socijalistička Narodna Partija [SNP]). The end of his political career was connected with the fall of the Milošević regime. (AO)

Sources: *Noty biograficzne*, Polish Press Agency, June 2001; Laura Silber and Allan Little, *The Death of Yugoslavia* (London, 1995); Bugajski; www.rferl.org/newsline.

BULIĆ Frane (4 October 1846, Vranjic, near Split–29 July 1934, Zagreb), Croatian Catholic priest, archaeologist, and historian. Born into a peasant family, Bulić graduated from high school in Split and from a theological seminary in Zadar (1869). Later he studied philosophy and archaeology at the University of Vienna (1869–78). He also specialized in the history of the Dalmatian Catholic Church. He worked as a teacher, schoolmaster, and superintendent of the Split region (1873–96); director of the Archaeological Museum in Split (1883–1923); and conservator of Dalmatian monuments. He described his explorations mostly in the periodical *Vjesnik za arheologiju i historiju dalmatinsku*, which he co-founded and headed for forty years (1888–1928). He also published in Austrian, Vatican, and Serbian scholarly periodicals. Among other things, he published *Hrvatski spomenici u kninskoj okolini* (Croatian monuments from the Knin region; 1885) and *Car Dioklecjan* (Caesar Diocletian; 1916). He combined the work of a Dalmatian regionalist with the promotion of Croatian culture. In 1923 he published *Stopama hrvatskih narodnih vladara* (Following the footsteps of Croatian rulers). He was engaged in founding Croatian schools in Dalmatia; he struggled to make Croatian the official language, and he tried to unite Dalmatia (under Austrian jurisdiction) with most of the old Kingdom of Croatia (within the Kingdom of Hungary). He was elected to the local diet in Split and then twice to the parliament in Vienna (1887 and 1907). He was a member of the Serbian Academy of Sciences and then of the Yugoslav Academy of Science and Arts (from 1922). He endowed his property to the students of archaeology and art history. (MC)

Sources: *Biographisches Lexikon*, vol. 1; *Enciklopedija Jugoslavije*, vol. 2 (Zagreb, 1956); *Hrvatski biografski leksikon*, vol. 2 (Zagreb, 1989); Stjepan Antoljak, *Hrvatska historiografija do 1918*, vols. 1–2 (Zagreb, 1992); Nenad Cambi, "Predgovor: Frane Bulić život i djelo," in Frane Bulić, *Izabrani spisi* (Split, 1984); Darko Zubrinic, "History of Croatian Science," www.hr/darko/etf/et22.html#buli.

BUMBAROV Boris (29 March 1996, Izvor, near Radomir–28 June 1959, Virshets), Bulgarian leftist politician. After graduating from high school in Kiustendil (1914), Bumbarov worked as a teacher in the village of Kosharite (1915–16) and then as a telegraph worker at the Sofia Central Telegraph Station (1916–19). In 1920 he joined the Bulgarian Agrarian National Union (BANU). During the rule of Aleksandur Stamboliyski he served successively as personal secretary to the president of the National Assembly; secretary in the Ministry of Railways, Post, and Telegraphs; and administrative director of the Pernik mine. After the military coup of June 1923 he was arrested and detained for several months in Sofia. After his release he emigrated to the Kingdom of Serbs, Croats, and Slovenes, from where he controlled the trafficking channel Sofia-Istanbul and maintained contacts with the illegal leadership of the BANU and of the Bulgarian Communist Party. In 1926 the Sofia Regional Court sentenced him to death in absentia for his activities in exile, which aimed at the creation of a united front of the left. Additionally, he was convicted to fifteen years for illegally crossing the border and for weapons smuggling. After an amnesty he decided to return to Bulgaria in February 1933 but was arrested at the border, and then he spent several months in prison in Sofia. Released in July 1933, he returned to political life in the BANU faction called Pladne.

During World War II, as a dangerous enemy of the system, Bumbarov was removed first to Ardino (1939) and then to a concentration camp in Gonda Voda (1941–42). After his release he was under close police surveillance in Krumovgrad (1942). In 1943–44 he was again in prison. After release, he participated in the creation of the illegal Fatherland Front. After the coup of 9 September 1944 he was elected a member of the BANU Chief Committee and was appointed minister of public works, roads, and spatial planning in the government of **Kimon Georgiev**. As he did not accept the totalitarian methods of government, in July 1945 along with several other ministers (e.g., **Grigor Cheshmedzhiev, Petko Stainov, Asen Pavlov,** and **Nikola Petkov**) Bumbarov left the cabinet subordinated to the Communists. He became one of the leaders of the opposition BANU that was created by Petkov and a member of the editorial board of the party's press organ, *Narodno zemedelsko zname*. As a representative of the

BANU led by Petkov, from 1946 to 1947 Bumbarov was a deputy to the Sixth Grand National Assembly (Constituent Assembly), where he sharply criticized the policy of the Communist government. In 1949 he was arrested and sentenced to twenty years' imprisonment. Released under an amnesty in 1956, he died three years later. In 1990 he was posthumously rehabilitated. (JJ)

Sources: J. F. Brown, *Bulgaria under Communist Rule* (New York, 1970); John D. Bell, *Peasants in Power: Alexander Stamboliski and the Bulgarian Agrarian National Union, 1899–1923* (Princeton, 1977); Tasho V. Tashev, *Ministrite na Bylgariia 1879–1999* (Sofia, 1999).

BUMÇI Luigji (7 November 1872, Shkodër–1 March 1945, Lezhë), Albanian Roman Catholic bishop and diplomat. The son of a merchant, Bumçi studied in Shkodër and then in Italy. He was ordained and then in 1912 he was consecrated ordinary bishop of the Lezhë diocese. In July 1911, on behalf of the metropolian of Shkodër, he tried to mobilize Albanians of the Cetinje region against plans to divide territories inhabited by Albanians. In July 1919 he intervened with Pope Benedict XV against the Italian-Greek agreement sanctioning the division of these territories. He headed the Albanian delegation to the Paris Peace Conference and took part in the talks held in Belgium and Great Britain aimed at improving the image of Albania in Europe. In December 1919 he went to Rome, where he asked the Pope for support for the Albanian argument in the conflict with Greece over the Korçë and Gjirokastër area. He represented Roman Catholics in the Supreme Council, which held the regency of Albania. He held the position in the Supreme Council until December 1921. He also gathered representatives of the four major religions of Albania to an All-Albanian Congress in January 1921. He favored a wider engagement of the Catholic Church in the formation of a democratic society, including a promotion of the parliamentary system among the faithful. In 1921 he also mediated during the rebellion of the Catholic Mirdyte tribe against the central power. As a result of his conflict with the papal nuncio, in 1922 he was forced to go to Fiume (Rijeka), where he worked for two years. Owing to the appeals of his faithful, he was allowed to return to Albania. Because of the political tension preceding the revolution of 1924, he was temporarily deprived of the freedom to move around but was later allowed to function normally. When at the end of 1944 the Lezhë diocese was brought under Communist control, he was put in house arrest, where he died. (TC)

Sources: Vllamasi Sejfi, *Ballafaqime politike ne Shqiperi (1897–1942)* (Tirana, 1995); Tadeusz Czekalski, *Zarys dziejów chrześcijaństwa albańskiego w latach 1912–1993* (Kraków, 1996); Gurakuqi Romeo, "Aspekte të qëndrimit të klerit katolik Shqiptar," in *Krishtërimi ndër shqiptarë: Simpozium Ndërkombëtar* (Shkodër, 2000).

BUROV Atanas (30 January 1875, Gorna Oriakhovitsa–15 May 1954, Pazardzhik), Bulgarian politician and banker. Burov's father was a tradesman, a banker, and on several occasions a deputy to the parliament. Expelled from high school in Gabrovo for organizing a student strike, Burov completed law and economic studies in Paris. After his return to Bulgaria he directed the construction of the Sofia-Kiustendil railway line. He also began his political activity in the National Party. From 1911 to 1913 he was vice-president of Fifteenth National Assembly. This post did not pose an obstacle for him to take part as an officer in the Balkan Wars (1912–13). He was minister of trade in the cabinet of **Stoian Danev** (June–July 1913) and in the coalition government of **Aleksandur Stamboliyski** (October 1919–March 1920). After the military coup of 9 June 1923 he was one of the founders of Democratic Concord. Between 1926 and 1931 Burov held the portfolio of foreign minister in the cabinet of **Andrei Lapchev**, implementing a policy of rapprochement with France. After the fall of the Democratic Concord government he was active in the opposition against successive governments whose policy was rapprochement with Nazi Germany. In March 1941 he decisively opposed Bulgaria's adhesion to the Tripartite Pact and the subordination of the country to Germany. For a short time he served as minister without portfolio in the government of **Konstantin Muraviev** (2–8 September 1944), which broke off the alliance with Germany.

After the assumption of power by the Communists, Burov was subjected to repressive measures. From 10 September 1944 he was under house arrest and was later put in prison in one cell with **Dimiter Gichev**, **Nikola Mushanov**, **Konstantin Muraviev**, and Vergil Dimov. On 1 February 1945 the "people's court" sentenced him to one year of prison and two years of deprivation of public rights. At the beginning of September 1945 he was released on a pardon. On 14 May 1948 Burov, along with his wife, was removed to Drianovo, where he had to report to the police station twice a day. In 1950 he spent a month in a forced labor camp, Dulovo, in Dobrudja, and then he returned to Drianovo owing to the intervention of **Todor Pavlov**. On 21 April 1951 he was arrested and on 13 November 1952 sentenced in a fake trial to twenty years of prison for "activities against the people." At first he served the sentence in Shumen and then in Pazardzhik, where he died. (JJ)

Sources: *Kratka bulgarska entsiklopediya*, vol. 1 (Sofia, 1964); Marshall Lee Miller, *Bulgaria during the Second World War* (Stanford, 1975); Zh. Tsvetkov, *Atanas Burov: Zhivot za Bulgaria* (Sofia, 1992).

BURSCHE Juliusz (19 September 1862, Kalisz–20 February 1942, Sachsenhausen-Oranienburg), Polish pastor, victim of Nazism. Bursche graduated from high school in Warsaw and from the Department of Evangelical Theology at the university in Dorpat (Tartu). In 1884 he started working as a curate in Warsaw, where in December 1904 he was appointed superintendent of the Evangelical Church of the Augsburg Confession in the Polish lands annexed by Russia. Removed by the Russian authorities to Orenburg in 1915, after the February 1917 revolution Bursche left for Stockholm, from where he returned to the Congress Kingdom of Poland, which was occupied by the Germans. In 1918 he became a member of the Provisional Council of State, and he was also appointed head of the Calvinist Church in Cieszyn Silesia. In 1919 he was an expert of the Polish government in the treaty commission at the Paris Peace Conference. Next, he directed a plebiscite action in Mazuria. In March 1920 he became superintendent of the Evangelical Church of the Augsburg Confession in Poland. In 1928 he assumed the post of president of the Council of Evangelical Churches in Poland, and on 3 July 1937 he was appointed bishop. Soon after the outbreak of World War II he went to Lublin, where he was arrested by the Gestapo and transported to a prison in Berlin. Since he refused to collaborate, he was sent to the camp in Sachsenhausen-Oranienburg, where he died a martyr's death. According to another version, he perished in Berlin's Moabit Prison. Bursche was a doctor of theology and the author of many dissertations on the history of the Reformed churches. He was also the founder and editor of the periodicals *Zwiastun Ewangeliczny* (1898–1914) and *Gazeta Mazurska* (1922–39). (WR)

Sources: *Wielka encyklopedia PWN*, vol. 5 (Warsaw, 2001); *Kto był kim w Drugiej Rzeczypospolitej* (Warsaw, 1994); D. Staemmler, *Der Protestantismus in Polen* (Posen, 1925); Waldemar Gastpary, *Biskup Bursche i sprawa* polska (Warsaw, 1972); Krzysztof Krasowski, *Związki wyznaniowe w II Rzeczpospolitej* (Warsaw, 1988).

BUZALKA Michal (18 September 1885, Svätý Anton–7 December 1961, Tábor), Slovak Roman Catholic bishop. Buzalka graduated in theological studies in Vienna and was ordained there in 1908. Later he worked as a teacher of religion in a high school in Banska Štiavnica and chaplain in St. Stephan Hospital in Budapest. In 1912 he received a Ph.D. in theology in Vienna. In the first years of independent Czechoslovakia Buzalka took part in the formation of the autonomous Slovak movement. In 1922–23 he edited the daily of the Slovak People's Party (Slovenská Ľudová Strana [SĽS]), *Slovák*, but he did not join the party. From 1922 to 1924 he was lecturer and from 1931 rector of the theological seminary in Trnava, and from 1936, rector of the Bratislava seminary. In 1938 he was consecrated and appointed auxiliary bishop of Trnava. From 1939 he directed Catholic Action and the Association of Catholic Youth. In 1940–45 he edited the daily *Katolícke noviny*. From 1941 he was field vicar of the Slovak Army. During the war he was not engaged in politics but rather opposed the participation of priests in the power structures of the Slovak state. He helped the repressed Jews, and through the papal nuncio he informed the Vatican about German war crimes on the eastern front. In 1945 he was imprisoned by the new Czechoslovak authorities for a few months. In 1950, along with two other bishops—**Jan Vojtaššák** and **Pavel Gojdič**—he was arrested by the Communist secret police. Tortured during interrogation, in January 1951 he was sentenced in a show trial to life imprisonment for "high treason" and "espionage for the Vatican." Released conditionally for health reasons in 1956, he was forbidden to return to Slovakia. Forced to settle in a home for the aged in Děčín and in Tábor, he died of a heart attack. In 2002 his beatification process was started. (MG)

Sources: Augustín Matovčik et al., *Reprezentačný biografický lexikón Slovenska* (Martin, 1999); Jozef A. Mikuš, *The Three Slovak Bishops: Their Struggle for God and Slovakia until Their Condemnation by the Communists in 1951* (n.p. 1951); Róbert Letz, "Boži sluha Michal Buzalka, pomocný biskup trnavskej apoštolskej administratúry," in *Boli solou a svetlom* (Trnava, 2001); *Boli traja* (Bratislava, 2001).

BUZEK Jerzy (3 July 1940, Śmiłowice, Teschen Silesia), Polish politician. Buzek graduated in power engineering from the Silesian Polytechnic in 1963 and then worked in the Institute of Chemical Engineering of the Polish Academy of Sciences in Gliwice. In 1969 he received a Ph.D. and in 1979 a postdoctoral degree. From 1997 he was a professor of technical sciences and the author of several dozen works on mathematical modeling and chemical processes. From 1980 he belonged to Solidarity and its regional and national authorities. One of the key organizers of Solidarity in Upper Silesia and the Dąbrowskie Industrial Region, in September 1981 Buzek presided over the proceedings of the First Congress of Solidarity in Gdańsk. After the introduction of martial law, in 1981–89 he was active in the underground structures of Solidarity (for example, in the Silesian Regional Executive Commission), working with **Marian Krzaklewski**. In 1996 he was an expert in Solidarity's Electoral Action (Akcja Wyborcza Solidarność [AWS]) and co-author of its economic program. After the electoral victory of the AWS in September, on 31 October 1997 Buzek became prime minister of a coalition government based on the AWS and the Freedom Union (Unia Wolności [UW]), and he held this position until 4 October 2001. After the UW withdrew from the coalition in June 2000, Buzek's was a minority government. It prepared and implemented reforms of the administration, social security, education, and health service. Some of these reforms created confusion, which, given the aggressive rhetoric of the post-Communist opposition, led to a serious decline of approval ratings for the cabinet and for Buzek himself. Buzek succeeded in finalizing talks concerning Poland's entry into NATO; these ended with a ceremonial delivery of ratification acts for new members on 12 March 1999. As a new NATO member, Poland supported the NATO air raids on Yugoslavia. Buzek played an indirect role in gaining a positive solution for Poland on some questions during the Nice summit of the European Union in December 2000. From January 1999 he presided over the AWS Social Movement, which aimed at becoming a political party, and he was the AWS leader from October 2001. After the election of September 2001 was lost, Buzek resigned from these positions. From 2002 he was chairman of the Pro Publico Bono Civic Society Institute and professor and deputy rector of the Polonia Academy in Częstochowa. (IS)

Sources: *Kto jest kim w Polsce* (Warsaw, 2001); *Wielka Encyklopedia PWN*, vol. 5 (Warsaw, 2001); Antoni Dudek, *Pierwsze lata III Rzeczypospolitej 1989–2001* (Kraków, 2002); Wojciech Roszkowski, *Historia Polski 1914–2001* (Warsaw, 2002).

BYKAU Vasil (19 May 1924, Bychki, Vitebsk region–22 June 2003, Minsk), Belorussian writer. In 1939–40 Bykau studied sculpture at the Vitebsk School of Fine Arts. In 1942 he was recruited to the Red Army and graduated from an officer training school in Saratov; from 1943 he fought on the front in the Ukraine, Romania, Bulgaria, Yugoslavia, Hungary, and Austria. Demobilized in 1947, he worked in artistic workshops in Hrodna (Grodno) and on the editorial staff of the local daily. In 1949–55 he served in the army again. Moved to the reserves, he returned to journalism. In 1978 he moved to Minsk. In 1978–80 he was a deputy to the Supreme Council of the Belorussian SSR, and in 1989–91, to the Supreme Council of the USSR. From 1989 he was connected with the opposition Belorussian National Front. In 1990–93 he presided over Homeland, the World Belorussian Union. In 1998 he emigrated to Finland. He later lived in Germany. In 2000 he returned to Belorussia and lived there under very difficult conditions. Later he moved to the Czech Republic but returned to Belorussia before his death.

Most of Bykau's novels and short stories allude to the fate of the Red Army soldiers during World War II. Because he presented wartime events in a realistic way, based on his own experience, he was frequently accused of slandering the Soviet state and its army. He became famous for the novels *Żurauliny kryk* (Crane's cry; 1960); *Zdrada* (Betrayal; 1961); *Tretsyaya rakyeta* (1962; *Third Flare*, 1963); *Pastka* (Trap; 1964); and particularly *Myortvym nie balits* (The dead do not hurt; 1965). These books were usually published after long and stormy debates of Soviet writers with the Communist ideologists. Bykau's subsequent novels—*Kruhlyanski most* (Kruhlany Bridge; 1969); *Sotnikov* (1970); *Abyelisk* (Obelisk; 1971); *Dazhyts da svitannya* (1974; *Alpine Ballad: Hold Out Till Dawn*, 1989); and *Yaho batalyon* (1975; *His Battallion*, 1981)—were published for broad circulation and in Russian. Twelve of his novels and short stories were filmed, including *Ascension*. In the last years of his life Bykau increasingly dealt with the Soviet past, but under the regime of **Alyaksandr Lukashenka** his stories and novels could be published only in literary periodicals. His collection of stories, *Stsyana* (Wall), was published in Minsk in 1997 in a print run of 750 copies thanks to reader subscriptions. The work included a shocking image of the history of Soviet Belorussia. (EM)

Sources: V. Buran, *Vasil Bykau: Narys tworchastsi* (Minsk, 1976); I. Dyedkov, *Vasil Bykov: Ocherk tvorchestva* (Moscow, 1980); *Entsyklapiedyia litaratury i mastatstva Belarusi*, vol. 1 (Minsk, 1984); *Belaruskiya pismenniki: Biyabibliahrafichny slounik*, vol. 1 (Minsk, 1992); *Belaruskiya pismienniki 1917–1990: Davednik* (Minsk, 1994); Jan Zaprudnik, *Belarus: At a Crossroads in History* (Boulder, Colo., 1993); Jan Zaprudnik, *Historical Dictionary of Belarus* (Lanham, Md., 1998); David R. Marples, *Belarus: A Denationalization of a Nation* (Amsterdam, 1999).

C

ČAKSTE Jānis (14 September 1859, Lielsesavas, Courland–14 March 1927, Riga), Latvian lawyer and politician. Born into a peasant family, Čakste graduated from a German gymnasium in Jelgava (Mitava). Next, he studied law at Moscow University, and he was in charge of the Society of Latvian Students in Moscow. His early views were influenced to a great extent by Krišjānis Valdemārs, the revival movement activist who worked in Moscow. After graduating from university in 1886, Čakste worked as a lawyer in Jelgava. He was also one of the leaders of the Latvian social movement there. From 1888 he published and edited the newspaper *Tēvija*, which he used to fight against the influences of the German landed gentry. During the revolution of 1905 he was one of the authors of a proposal for autonomy for Latvia within the framework of Russia. In 1906 he was elected deputy to the Duma, where he actively participated in the discussions on land ownership. After the First Duma was suspended in 1908, he signed the so-called Viborg Protest, and consequently he was held in prison for three months.

From 1915 Čakste was in charge of Latvian organizations that provided relief for war refugees in Jelgava and then in Dorpat (Tartu). In 1916 in Stockholm he published *Die Letten und ihr Lettland* (The Letts and their Latvia). Elected commissar (governor) of Courland in April 1917, he held his office in Dorpat and from October 1917, in Kazan and St. Petersburg. He took part in the work of the Latvian Provisional National Council, defending the idea of full independence for Latvia. Soon he returned to Latvia, and on 17 November 1918 he was elected president of the Latvian Provisional National Council in Riga. In January 1919, as a plenipotentiary of the council abroad, he arrived in London, and from March 1919 he was involved in the work of the Latvian delegation to the Paris Peace Conference. In July 1919 he returned to Latvia. From April 1920 he served as president of the Constituent Assembly, and he simultaneously lectured as professor at the University in Riga. He was connected with the Democratic Center Party. In November 1922 the Saeima (Parliament) elected him president of the Republic of Latvia. In this role, he strove to tighten Latvia's contacts with other Baltic states; for example, he made visits to Estonia (February 1925) and Finland (May 1926). He was buried in Riga. (EJ)

Sources: Emile Doumergue, *La Lettonie et la Baltique* (Paris, 1919); *Jānis Čakste: Ilustrēts piemiņas rakstu krājums* (Riga, 1928); R. Legzdiņš, *Pirmais latvijas Valsts prezidents Jānis Čakst* (Riga,

1978); Andrejs Plakans, *Historical Dictionary of Latvia* (Lanham, Md., 1997); *Čakste J. taisnība vienmēr uzvarēs: Atziņas, runas, dokumenti, raksti, vēstules* (Riga, 1999).

ČALFA Marián (7 May 1946, Trebišov), Czechoslovak lawyer and politician. In 1964 Čalfa joined the Communist Party of Czechoslovakia (CPC), and in 1970 he graduated in law from Charles University in Prague. Later he worked as a lawyer in the Czechoslovak Press Agency. In 1972–87 he worked in and later presided over the legislative committee of the Office of the Czechoslovak Prime Minister. From 1987 to 1988 he was deputy director of this office. From April 1988 to December 1989 he was minister without portfolio in the governments of **Lubomir Štrougal** and **Ladislav Adamec**. At the same time he presided over the government Legislative Council. In 1989 he supervised the preparation of a new constitution for Czechoslovakia and the Czech and Slovak Republics. During the Velvet Revolution he took part in the negotiations with the opposition and contributed greatly to the agreement that was reached. For one week Čalfa was first deputy prime minister, and from 9 December 1989, prime minister of the "government of national reconciliation." He remained prime minister after the first free elections of June 1990. In January 1990 he left the CPC and joined the movement Public against Violence (Verejnost' proti Nasiliu). After this movement split, in 1991 he became vice-president of a liberal party, Civic Democratic Union–Public against Violence (Občianská Demokratická Únia–Verejnost' proti Nasiliu). From June 1990 to June 1992 he was a deputy to the Chamber of Nations of the Federal Assembly.

Čalfa headed the government in the first stages of systemic transformation. His cabinet led Czechoslovakia from communism to democracy and began the creation of a market economy based on privatization. He tried to resolve the question of Czechoslovak relations in the light of state law and took part in all rounds of negotiations, firmly defending the federation. Despite his Communist past, he quickly turned into a liberal democrat and aligned himself with the ideas of President **Václav Havel**. He became a close aide to Havel, supporting his candidacy for president from his first days in power as prime minister. After the electoral defeat of his party, on 26 June 1992 Čalfa resigned, remaining an unofficial adviser to Havel. After the split of Czech-Slovakia he adopted Czech citizenship. From 1993 to 1995 he was editor-in-chief of the monthly *Právní rádce*. He is co-owner of the consulting firm CTL Consulting and a legal adviser of Chemapol. From 1997 he has been chairman of the board of the IC Bank, in which he has shares. (PU)

Sources: *ČBS*; *Českoslovenští politici: 1918–1991* (Prague, 1991); *Kdo byl kdo v našich dějinach ve 20. stoleti*, vol. 1 (Prague,

1998); Timothy Garton Ash, *We the People* (Cambridge, 1990); Eric Stein, *Czecho/Slovakia: Ethnic Conflict, Constitutional Fissure, Negotiated Breakup* (Ann Arbor, 1997); Jan Rychlík, *Rozpad Československa: Česko-slovenské vztahy 1989–1992* (Bratislava, 2002); http://wtd.vlada.cz/scripts.

CĂLINESCU Armand (4 June 1893, Piteşti–21 September 1939, Bucharest), Romanian politician. Călinescu studied law and philosophy at the university in Bucharest and received a Ph.D. in economics in Paris (1919). He began his political career by joining the Peasant Party of **Ion Mihalache**. He served as president of this party in Argeş County. In 1926 Mihalache's party merged with the National Party of Transylvania to form the National Peasant Party (Partidul Naţional Ţărănesc [NPP]), led by **Iuliu Maniu**. From 1926 Călinescu was an MP. Between 1928 and 1930 he served as deputy minister of agriculture, and at the beginning of 1930 he assumed the post of deputy minister of interior. After the accession to the throne of **Charles II** in June 1930, two factions formed within the NPP, one against Charles (including Maniu, Mihalache, and **Alexandru Vaida-Voievod**) and the other supporting him (including **Grigore Gafencu** and **Nicolae Titulescu**). Călinescu supported the latter group. He remained in the NPP until 1937.

Between December 1937 and February 1938 Călinescu was the minister of interior in the government of **Octavian Goga**. After the royal coup d'état of 10 February 1938, Călinescu remained in his post in the government of "national unity," which was headed by Patriarch **Miron Cristea**. After Cristea's death, Călinescu took over the responsibilities of prime minister on 7 March 1939. In foreign policy he represented an anti-German line. Following the orders of King Charles II, he brought about the suppression of the Iron Guard (fourteen leaders of the Iron Guard, including **Corneliu Zelea-Codreanu**, were liquidated on 29 November 1938). In September 1939 Călinescu implemented a policy of formal neutrality toward the Polish-German war, although he actually favored Poland. Călinescu was assassinated by a fighting squad of the Iron Guard on 21 September 1939 in Bucharest. This assassination was considered to be retaliation for his involvement in the suppression of the Iron Guard. In his memoirs René de Weck, the Swiss minister to Romania, presented a version of Călinescu's plans that had heretofore not been known; according to Weck, Călinescu had tried to persuade King Charles II to declare war on the USSR and on Germany. Călinescu was the author of *Discursuri parlamentare 1926–1933* (Parliamentary speeches 1926–33; 1938) and other works. In 1990 his *Insemnări politice 1926–1939* (Political notes) were published in Bucharest. (FA/TD)

Sources: *Biographisches Lexikon,* vol. 1; T. Dubicki and K. Dach, *Żelazny Legion Michała Archanioła* (Warsaw, 1996); A. Hillgruber, *Hitler, Koenig Carol und Marschall Antonescu: Die Deutsch-Rumaenischen Beziehnugen 1938–1944* (Wiesbaden, 1954); Al. Gh. Savu, *Dictatura regala 1938–1940* (Bucharest, 1970); Rene de Weck, *Jurnalul unu diplomat elvetian in România 1939–1945* (Bucharest, 2000).

CÂMPEANU Radu (28 February 1922, Bucharest), Romanian politician. In 1947 Câmpeanu graduated from the Department of Economics and Law of the University of Bucharest. During his studies, in 1944–47, he was president of the youth organization of the National Liberal Party (Partidul Naţional Liberal [NLP]). After the Communist takeover, he was imprisoned for this activity in 1947–56. Afterward he was kept under house arrest in Bărăgan. He worked as a blue-collar laborer, technician, and head of construction work. In 1973 Communist authorities allowed him to leave for France, where he received political asylum. In 1977 in Paris he founded the Association of Former Romanian Political Prisoners (Asociaţia Foştilor Deţinuţi Politici din România). In 1979 he co-founded the Committee of the Union of Organizations of Refugees from the East (Comitetul de Legătură a Organizaţiilor de Refugiaţi din Est) and became its deputy chairman. From 1983 to 1990 he was director of the daily *Bire* for Romanian émigrés. In 1985 he founded the Club of Liberal Thought.

On 5 January 1990, two weeks after the fall of **Nicolae Ceauşescu,** Câmpeanu returned to Romania and took the lead of the reborn NLP. From February to May 1990 he was vice-president of the Provisional Council of National Unity (Conciliul Provizoriu Uniuni Naţionale), including representatives of the post-Communists and from democratic parties. In the presidential elections of May 1990 he came in second (after **Ion Iliescu**), gaining 10.6 percent of the vote. In 1990–92 he was senator and then deputy speaker of the Senate on behalf of the NLP, which was the third largest parliamentary faction. In 1991 his party joined the Democratic Convention of Romania (Convenţia Democrată Română [DCR]), which included parties opposing the anti-democratic rule of the post-Communist National Salvation Front (Frontul Sălvari Naţionale) and of President Iliescu. Despite the convention's stance, without the knowledge of his partners from the DCR, Câmpeanu negotiated with the post-Communists, and in 1991 the NLP entered the ruling coalition. Before the parliamentary elections of September 1992 the NLP broke off with the DCR and failed to get into the parliament. In 1993 Câmpeanu was dismissed from the NLP leadership, but he remained its vice-president. Aiming at overthrowing the new party leader, **Mircea Ionescu-Quintus,** in 1994

Câmpeanu convened an alternative NLP congress, which deemed the new authorities illegal. Since the Ionescu-Quintus leadership was acknowledged by a court verdict, in 1995 Câmpeanu founded a new liberal party, which failed altogether in the elections of November 1996. In the presidential elections Câmpeanu gained 0.35 percent of the vote and disappeared from the political scene. (LW)

Sources: *Dictionar Enciclopedic,* vol. 1 (Bucharest, 1993); *Personalități politice, publice* (Bucharest, 1994); Józef Darski, *Rumunia: Historia, współczesność, konflikty narodowe* (Warsaw, 1995); *Europa Środkowo-Wschodnia 1994–1995* (Warsaw, 1997); Ion Alexandrescu, Ion Bulei, Ion Mamina, and Ioan Scurtu, *Enciclopedia de istorie României* (Bucharest, 2000); Bugajski; www.nordest.ro.

CANKAR Ivan (10 May 1876, Vrhnika–11 December 1918, Ljubljana), Slovene writer, poet, and playwright. The eighth child of a tailor and a peasant woman, Cankar spent his childhood in poverty. His love for his mother was reflected in his writing. He attended high school in Ljubljana, and it was there that his talent was discovered by a teacher of Slovene. After graduating from high school in 1896, Cankar took up studies at the polytechnic in Vienna, where he got to know working-class life. He did not complete his studies because he devoted himself to literary work. In 1907 he returned from Vienna to Slovenia. He made his literary debut as a poet, but he later dedicated himself to prose and drama; he was one of the leading representatives of the Slovene modernists. His only volume of poetry, *Erotika* (Erotica; 1899), was denounced in Catholic circles as immoral, and the first edition was almost entirely bought up and burned by the bishop of Ljubljana. In 1897 Cankar debuted as a playwright with *Romantične duše* (Romantic souls). His next play, *Jakob Ruda* (1900), showed obvious influences of Henrik Ibsen. Cankar's views came close to those of the Socialists, which he explained in his sketch *Kako sem postal socialist* (How I became a Socialist; 1913). In 1907 he ran unsuccessfully in parliamentary elections. In 1913 in his lecture *Slovenci in Jugoslovani* (Slovenes in Yugoslavia) he formulated a program of unification of the Slovenes, Croats, and Serbs within a federal state while the national, cultural, and linguistic identity of the three nations was maintained.

After the outbreak of World War I Cankar was interned in Ljubljana, and then he was inducted into the army. Released owing to illness, he published short stories in which he depicted the war suffering of individuals and of the nation. In 1917 he published his works under the title *Podobe iz sanj* (Pictures from dreams). He exerted a great influence on the development of the Slovene national culture and social thought. A masterful prose stylist, Cankar is best known for his short stories and novels. His major works include the following: *Na klancu* (On the slope; 1902); *Hiša Marije Pomočnice* (The ward of Our Lady of Mercy; 1904); *Martin Kačur* (1906); *Za križem* (Following the cross; 1909); *Moje življenje* (My life; 1913); and *Grešnik Lenart* (Sinner Lenart; 1921). Cankar won international fame with *Hlapec Jernej in njegova pravica* (The bailiff Jernej and his rights; 1930; or Jernej's justice; 1926), the story of a man who sought justice in vain. The most complete collection of his works can be found in *Zbrano delo* (Collected works, 30 vols.; 1967–1976). English publications of his works include *My Life and Other Sketches* (1978). (AO)

Sources: *Enciklopedija Jugoslavije,* vol. 2 (Zagreb, 1966); *Enciklopedija Slovenije,* vol. 1 (Ljubljana, 1987); *Spominu Ivana Cankara 1876–1918* (Ljubljana, 1919); *Cankarjev zbornik* (Ljubljana, 1921); J. Matl, "Ivan Cankar und die heutige slowenische Lyrik," *Jahrbücher für Kultur und Geschichte der Slaven* (Breslau, 1932); Janko Lavrin, *The Conscience of a Small Nation: On Ivan Cankar* (London, 1935); B. Vodušek, *Ivan Cankar* (Ljubljana, 1937); *100 Sto let Ivana Cankarja* (Ljubljana, 1976).

CANTACUZINO Gheorghe Grigore (16 September 1837, Bucharest–24 March 1913, Bucharest), Romanian politician. Cantacuzino came from a family of Moldavian *hospodars* (political rulers from a few families) of Greek origin. A lawyer and a conservative politician, owing to his wealth he was called "Nabob." Between 1855 and 1859 he studied in Paris, where in 1861 he earned a Ph.D. in law. He was a political opponent of Alexandru Ion Cuza, Prince of Romania. In 1866 Cantacuzino was a member of the Constituent Assembly and of the commission on the passage of a new constitution for the Principality of Romania. He began his political activity in 1867, joining the Conservative Party (CP). On behalf of the party in 1869 he was elected an MP, and in 1869–70 he simultaneously served as mayor of Bucharest. Moreover, in the conservative governments he held the posts of minister of justice (January–February 1870), minister of public works (April–December 1870 and December 1873–January 1875), and minister of finance (January 1875–January 1876). In 1889–91 and 1900–1901 he presided over the Chamber of Deputies. Between 1892 and 1895 and in 1913 he served as president of the Senate. In 1899–1913 he was the leader of the CP. From April 1899 to July 1900 he was prime minister. In 1905 he issued *Programul Partidului Conservator* (The program of the Conservative Party). On 4 January 1905 he again assumed the premiership, but on 25 March 1907 he resigned as a result of a great peasant revolt in Moldova for which his government was totally unprepared. (FA/TD)

Sources: *Chronological History of Romania* (Bucharest, 1972); Ion Bulei, *Sistemul politic al: României moderne. Partidul Conservator* (Bucharest, 1987); Ion Bulei, *Atunci cândveacul se naştea* (Bucharest, 1990); Keith Hitchins, *Rumania 1866–1947* (Oxford, 1994).

ČAPEK Karel (9 January 1890, Malé Svatoňovice, near Trutnov–25 December 1938, Prague), Czech writer. After graduating from high school in 1909 Čapek studied philosophy at Charles University in Prague, then in Berlin and Paris (1910–11), and he graduated in Prague. In 1915 he received a Ph.D. in philosophy. He joined the followers of modern art and philosophy, becoming a member of the Group of Visual Artists. In 1917–21 he edited the periodical *Národní listý*, but he left it because of its political line, contrary to that of **Tomáš Garrigue Masaryk**, with whom Čapek had made friends. Until his death he wrote for *Lidové noviny*. He also contributed to other periodicals, such as *Umělecký měsíčník, Přítomnost, Nebojsa,* and *Volne směry*. In 1921–23 he wrote plays for the Prague Theater on Vinohrady. With his brother, Josef, he organized meetings of the Prague intellectual elite with politicians from Masaryk's circle, known as the Caste (Hrad). Čapek seriously contributed to the creation of the Masaryk legend, both through his journalism and through his three-volume *Hovory s T. G. Masarykem* (1928–35; English selections: *President Masaryk Tells His Story,* 1935; *Masaryk on Thought and Life,* 1971; *Talks with Tomaš G. Masaryk,* 1995) and *Mlčení s T. G. Masarykem* (Silence with T. G. Masaryk; 1935). One of the key spokesman of Czechoslovak democracy, Čapek was on friendly terms with several outstanding European writers, such as George Bernard Shaw, H. G. Wells, G. K. Chesterton, and Thomas Mann. In the 1930s he engaged in the struggle against Nazism. The disaster of the Pact of Munich (September 1938) was a serious blow for him as it represented the destruction of values in which he had believed. His death from pneumonia symbolically coincided with the end of the Czechoslovak democratic republic.

Čapek made his literary debut with two volumes of short stories, *Zářivé hlubiny a jiné prózy* (Shining depths and other stories; 1916) and *Krakonošova zahrada* (The Garden of Karkonoš; 1918), written with his brother Josef and dominated by the issues that would be crucial in his future works: the question of understanding the world and the catastrophic prospects of civilization. In his own volumes of prose, *Boží muka* (God's suffering; 1917) and *Trapné povídky* (Embarassing tales; 1921), he contemplated the complexity of human nature and the contradictions between objective and subjective truth. Čapek raised similar issues in plays, both in those written with his brother, such as *Ze života hmyzu* (From the life of insects; 1921), and in those he wrote alone, such as *Loupežník* (Brigand; 1920) and *R.U.R.* (RUR: Rossum's Universal Robots; 1921), in which he moved the Prague legend of Golem into the present. With the latter play he became famous for inventing the term "robot," adopted later into many languages. In the novel *Krakatit* (1924; An *atomic phantasy,* 1931) he showed the tragic effects of the development of a technical civilization.

Čapek's literary interests changed with the development of fascism in Europe. He gave up his relativist ideas of truth and began to defend democracy and humanism. It was then that he wrote three novels thought to be crucial in his output: *Hordubal* (1933), *Povětroň* (1934; *Meteor,* 1934), and *Obyčejný život* (1934; *Ordinary Life,* 1936); they advocated equality and the brotherhood of men. Čapek was increasingly anxious about the growing wave of fascism and expressed his fears in a grotesque novel, *Válka s mloky* (1936; *War with the Newts,* 1937), in which, with a variety of styles and measures of expression, he envisioned a world dominated by totalitarianism. With the approaching danger of war he even gave up his pacifism. In a scene in his play *Matka* (1938; *Mother,* 1939), the heroine hands a gun to her youngest son and sends him off to fight. Čapek has also left a rich journalistic output. In his columns he discussed various topics connected with the theater, journeys, literature, politics, journalism, and the delights of home. He also wrote a popular book for children, *Dášeňka čili Život štěněte* (1932; *I Had a Dog and a Cat,* 1940). He received frequent awards and was very popular abroad. His works were translated into many languages, and his plays were performed all over Europe, the United States, and Japan. Many of his works were filmed. In 1938 a group of French writers nominated him for the Nobel Prize in Literature, but to no avail. (PU)

Sources: *ČBS; Kdo byl kdo v našich dějinach ve 20. stoleti,* vol. 2 (Prague, 1998); *Politická elita meziválečného Československa 1918–1938: Kdo byl kdo za první republiky* (Prague, 1998); Halina Janaszek-Ivančikova, *Karel Čapek czyli poszukiwanie prawdy* (Warsaw, 1985); Václav Černý, *Karel Čapek* (Prague, 1936); Ivan Klíma, *Karel Čapek* (Prague, 1962); Miroslav Halík, *Karel Čapek Život a dílo v datech* (Prague, 1984); František Buriánek, *Karel Čapek* (Prague, 1988); Lászlo Dobossy, *Karel Čapek* (Budapest, 1961); William E. Harkins, *Karel Čapek* (New York, 1962); Sergey Nikolsky, *Karel Čapek* (Moscow, 1952); Bohuslava R. Bradbrook, *Karel Čapek: In Pursuit of Truth, Tolerance, and Trust* (Sussex, 1998).

CAR Stanisław (26 April 1882, Warsaw–18 June 1938, Warsaw), Polish lawyer and politician. After high school Car started law studies at Warsaw University but because of his participation in the student strike of 1905, he had to leave Warsaw and graduated in Odessa in 1907. For three years he did his apprenticeship, and in 1911 he opened his own law office. In June 1914 he was a delegate to the congress of Polish lawyers in Lwów (Lviv), and from 1915 he was a judge in Warsaw. From December 1918 to December 1922 he was director of the Civil Chancellery of the head of state, **Józef Piłsudski**, becoming the latter's trusted aide. Later he was director of the Civil Chancellery of Presidents **Gabriel Narutowicz** and **Stanisław Wojciechowski**. He resigned in 1923 and practiced for two years. In 1924–26 he was editor-in-chief of the monthly *Palestra*, and in May 1925 he became prosecutor of the Supreme Court. He returned to politics after the coup of May 1926, assuming the position of director of the Civil Chancellery of President **Ignacy Mościcki**. In November 1926 he became deputy minister of justice, and in 1927–28 he was general electoral commissioner. From December 1928 to December 1929 and from March to December 1930 he was minister of justice, drawing close to the *sanacja* group of "colonels," hardliners among the followers of Piłsudski. Car favored the strengthening of presidential power. After the elections of November 1930 he became MP on behalf of the Nonparty Bloc of Cooperation with the Government (Bezpartyjny Blok Współpracy z Rządem [BBWR]) and deputy speaker of the Lower House (Sejm). From August 1931 he was deputy chairman of the BBWR parliamentary club, and after the elections of 1935 he became speaker of the Sejm. Chairman and general reporter of the parliamentary constitutional commission, he contributed greatly to the passing of the new authoritarian constitution of April 1935. He was the author of *Z zagadnień konstytucyjnych Polski: Istota i zakres władzy Prezydenta Rzeczpospolitej Polski* (The constitutional questions of Poland: The essence and range of presidential power; 1924), *Zarys historii adwokatury w Polsce* (Outline history of the Polish bar; 1925), and other works. (PU)

Sources: *Posłowie i senatorowie Rzeczpospolitej Polski 1919–1939: Słownik biograficzny*, vol. 1 (Warsaw, 1998); *Encyklopedia historii Drugiej Rzeczypospolitej* (Warsaw, 1999); Andrzej Ajnenkiel, *Historia sejmu polskiego*, vol. 2, part 2 (Warsaw, 1989); *Słownik biograficzny adwokatów polskich*, vol. 2 (Warsaw, 1988); Jacek Majchrowski, ed., *Stanisław Car: Polska koncepcja autorytaryzmu* (Warsaw, 1996); Krzysztof Pol, *Poczet prawników polskich* (Warsaw, 2000).

ÇARÇANI Adil (5 May 1922, Fushë Bardhë, near Gjirokaster–12 October 1997, Tirana), Albanian Communist activist. Born into a Muslim family, in 1942 Çarçani joined the Communist Party of Albania. In 1943 he assumed the position of political commissar of a battalion, and in 1944, of the Seventh Brigade of the National Liberation Army. After a reorganization of the guerrilla units he was transferred to the Fourth Division. After the war he was party secretary in Durrës and then in Shkodër (1946). From 1948 he worked in the Ministry of Trade. In 1950 he was elected MP from Gjirokaster. From July 1954 he was minister of industry; from April 1952 he was a deputy member, and from June 1956 to June 1991 a member, of the Politburo of the Central Committee of the Albanian Party of Labor (APL). From June 1958 he was minister of industry and mining. Deputy prime minister from 28 December 1965 to 15 January 1982, after the death of **Mehmet Shehu**, Çarçani became prime minister. Always loyal to the party line, he endorsed the proclamation of Albania as the first fully atheist state (1967), a break with China, and the succession of **Ramiz Alia** as head of the APL after the death of **Enver Hoxha** (1985). In 1966–1971 Çarçani was chairman of the Commission for Complete Electrification. In 1967 he was elected a member of the Supreme Council of the Democratic Front, and in 1990–91 he was its chairman. He headed the Albanian delegations signing credit agreements with China in 1968 and 1975. In 1975 he was a member of the commission preparing changes in the constitution. In the early 1990s he was ranked among the party conservatives. His departure from the post of prime minister on 22 February 1991 and the succession of **Fatos Nano** were aimed at showing Communist moderation but did not prevent the collapse of the Communist regime. In 1991 Çarçani was elected to the parliament on behalf of the post-Communist Albanian Socialist Party and made an inaugural speech there, but on 3 December 1991 he was deprived of immunity, tried, and in 1994 sentenced to five years for the abuse of power and fraud. The sentence was changed to house arrest. (TC)

Sources: *Fjalori Enciklopedik Shqiptar* (Tirana, 1985); Klaus-Detlev Grothusen, ed., *Albanien* (Göttingen, 1993); Elez Biberaj, *Shqipëria ne tranzicion: Rruga e veshtrise drejt Demokracisë* (Tirana, 2001); www.rulers.org.

ČARNOGURSKÝ Ján (1 January 1944, Bratislava), Slovak lawyer and politician. The son of **Pavol Čarnogurský**, in 1969 Čarnogurský graduated in law from Komensky University in Bratislava, and in 1971 he received a Ph.D. From 1970 he worked as a lawyer. He was counsel for the defense in many trials of political dissidents, for which he was removed from the bar in 1981. He worked as a driver and briefly as a lawyer, but in 1987–89 he was unemployed. From 1988 he edited an uncensored periodical, *Bratislavské listy*. He was active in the democratic opposition, representing Christian Democratic ideas. In August 1989 he was arrested and accused of "an attempt to overthrow the republic." He was released as a result of an amnesty on 25 November 1989.

During the Velvet Revolution Čarnogurský took an active

part in the negotiations between the opposition and the Communist authorities. In the government of **Marian Čalfa** he became first deputy prime minister (10 December 1989–27 April 1990). Until the end of 1989 he was co-responsible for the Ministry of Interior and then for the legislation that introduced the democratic rule of law in Czechoslovakia. He initiated the creation of the Christian Democratic Movement (Krest'ansko-Demokratické Hnutie [KDH]), in Slovakia and from its founding congress in February 1990 he was its chairman. In the first free elections in June 1990 he gained a seat in the Chamber of the People of the Federal Assembly, and he became the first deputy prime minister in the Slovak government of **Vladimír Mečiar**. He held this position until the the Mečiar government fell as a result of the conflict in the association Public against Violence (Verejnost' proti Nasiliu [VPN]). On 23 April 1991 Čarnogurský became prime minister of the Slovak Republic and held this position until 24 June 1992, when he resigned as a result of the election. He greatly influenced the Czecho-Slovak talks on the shape of the future state, which he wanted to maintain as a union but on the condition of wide autonomy for Slovakia. At that time he planned a division of Czechoslovakia only after its entry into the European Union.

From June 1992 to September 1998 Čarnogurský was an MP of the Slovak National Council (renamed the National Council after the separation of the sovereign Slovak Republic in January 1993). From 1993 to 1994 he was vice-president of the Parliamentary Assembly of the Conference of Security and Cooperation in Europe (CSCE), and from 1994 to 1998 he was a member of the Slovak delegation to the CSCE and the Organization for European Security and Cooperation. One of the key opponents of the Mečiar regime, in order to remove him from power, in 1997 Čarnogurský introduced the KDH into the Slovak Democratic Coalition (Slovenská Demokratická Koalícia [SDK]), led by **Mikulaš Dzurinda**. After the SDK electoral victory in September 1998, Čarnogurský became minister of justice, but he soon entered into conflict with Dzurinda, who planned to transform the SDK into one party. Čarnogurský remained minister of justice until the elections of September 2002. Meanwhile the KDH split on account of a conflict between the so-called conservatives who, like Čarnogurský, wanted to retain it, and reformers who wanted to join the Slovak Christian Democratic Union (Slovenská Demokratická Krest'anská Únie [SDKÚ]) of Dzurinda. In 2000 Čarnogurský gave up the KDH leadership. His articles and speeches of the 1980s and early 1990s were published as *Videné od Dunaja* (As seen from the Danube; 1997). (PU)

Sources: *ČBS*; *Kdo byl kdo v našich dìjinach ve 20. stoleti*, vol. 1 (Prague, 1998); *Českoslovenští politici: 1918–1991* (Prague, 1991); Jan Rychlík, *Rozpad Československa: Česko-slovenské vz-*

tahy 1989–1992 (Bratislava, 2002); Eric Stein, *Czecho/Slovakia: Ethnic Conflict, Constitutional Fissure, Negotiated Breakup* (Ann Arbor, 1997); *Slovensko 1996: Súhrnná správa o stave spoloènosti* (Bratislava, 1997); *Slovensko 1997: Súhrnná správa o stave spoločnosti* (Bratislava, 1998); *Slovensko 1998–1999: Súhrnná správa o stave spoločnosti* (Bratislava, 1999); *Slovensko 2000: Súhrnná správa o stave spoločnosti* (Bratislava, 2000); www.kdh.sk/tvare/zivot_carnogursky.htm#.

ČARNOGURSKÝ Pavol (21 January 1908, Malá Franková, Spiš–27 December 1992, Bratislava), Slovak politician and journalist, father of **Jan Čarnogurský**. Čarnogurský graduated from the training school in Spišska Kapitula. He started law studies in Prague, but in 1930 he had to break them off for political reasons, and he finally graduated in Bratislava. From the late 1920s he was active in the Slovak People's Party of Reverend **Andrej Hlinka** (Hlinkova Slovenská L'udová strana [HSL'S]). He worked as a teacher in Vajnory and wrote for the daily *Slovák*; from 1935 he was secretary general of the Association of Catholic Youth. He belonged to the Polonophile wing of the HSL'S, headed by his close aide, **Karol Sidor**. In 1938–44 he was deputy to the Slovak parliament in Bratislava; in 1939–40 he organized Slovak radio and the Slovak press agency. He opposed the pro-German policy of the Slovak government and cooperated with the domestic resistance, helping persecuted Jews and intervening in the defense of imprisoned politicians, including, among others, **Gustav Husák** and **Ján Ursíny**. Along with other Slovak diplomats in Budapest, he supported activists of the Camp of Fighting Poland. After Germany occupied Hungary in March 1944, he helped in the evacuation of Polish freedom fighters into Slovakia and contributed to the establishment in Bratislava of a transfer center of the Polish government-in-exile.

In June 1944 Čarnogurský was deprived of his parliamentary seat. Along with General Augustín Malár, he was preparing two Slovak divisions to pass over to the side of the Red Army, and after the outbreak of the Slovak National Uprising in August 1944 he cooperated with the insurgents. Then he returned to his home village, where he helped the guerrillas and gave shelter to Jews who were in hiding and to the former Polish minister of labor, General Stefan Hubicki. From February to May 1945 he was an officer of the Czechoslovak army in Košice; after the war he edited the daily *Katolícke noviny*. He took part in the negotiations between former HSL'S activists with the Democratic Party and in failed attempts to create a Christian Republican Party. He was imprisoned in 1945, 1947–48, 1951–52, and 1976. The Communist secret service confiscated his extensive archives. Until 1977 he worked as a blue-collar laborer and was active in anti-

Communist activities and in the underground structures of the Roman Catholic Church. He maintained contacts with Slovak émigré communities. He authored memoirs that are an important source for the recent history of Slovakia. (MG)

Sources: *ČBS*; Jozef Jablonický, *Z ilegality do povstania: Kapitoly z občianskeho odboja* (Bratislava, 1969); Ján Korček, *Slovenská republika 1943–1945* (Bratislava, 1999); J. Berghauzen, "Ze wspomnień o stosunkach polsko-słowackich," *Dzieje Najnowsze*, 1977, no. 4; "Z memoárových statí Pal'a Čarnogurského," *Slovanský přehled*, 1968, no. 6.

CARP Petre (29 June 1837, Iaşi–18 August 1918, Bucharest), Romanian politician and writer. Carp graduated from high school in Berlin and completed his law studies in Bonn (1860). He represented a strong pro-German attitude, but that did not mean he was uncritical of the policy pursued by King Charles I. Carp's saying, "It's impossible, Your Majesty!," became proverbial in Romania. He was also active in the field of culture; along with **Titu Maiorescu**, Ioan Negruzzi, Vasile Pogor, and Theodor Rosetti, he was co-founder of the literary circle Junimea (Youth). From 1867 this group edited the literary review *Convorbiri Literare*. Carp was a long-term activist of the Conservative Party (Partidul Conservator) and its president between 1907 and 1914. His political views were close to those of Maiorescu and **Alexandru Marghiloman**, who promoted social elitism and opposed democracy as a system unsuited to Romanian conditions. Carp held numerous posts; for example, he was head of the Ministry of Foreign Affairs (1870), and then, with the rank of minister, he was on diplomatic missions to Vienna, Berlin, St. Petersburg (1871–75), and again Vienna (1880–85). In Vienna he brought about a meeting between Premier **Ioan C. Brătianu** and Chancellor Otto von Bismarck. He also significantly contributed to reaching a secret alliance between Romania and the Central Powers (1883). In 1876 he was minister of education, and in 1888–89, again minister of foreign affairs. Between 1891 and 1895, as minister of public property, Carp prepared the mining and forest law. Moreover, as a result of his efforts, the National Bank of Romania issued bonds payable in gold.

While serving as premier between 19 July 1900 and 26 February 1901, Carp introduced taxes on alcohol and tobacco. He resumed the premiership on 11 January 1910, but this time he again made unpopular economic decisions—for example, nationalizing tramway enterprises. He resigned on 10 April 1912, the day before the outbreak of the Balkan War. He opposed a Crown Council decision of 3 August 1914 that declared the neutrality of Romania, and he advocated that a secret alliance with Germany be enforced. After Romania entered the war on the side of the Allies in August 1916, he maintained that for Romania even a military defeat would be better than a victory by Russia and its allies. He remained in German-occupied Bucharest, where he died. He published (among other works) *Era nouă* (New era; 1888); *Discursuri* (Speeches; 1907); *România şi războiul european* (Romania and the European war; 1915); *Politica externă a României* (Foreign policy of Romania; 1915); and *Auswaertige Politik und Agrarreform* (Foreign policy and land reform; 1917). (FA/TD)

Sources: *Biographisches Lexikon*, vol. 1; Radu Budişteanu, *Petre P. Carp* (Bucharest, 1933); Constantine Gane, *P. P. Carp şi locul său în istoria politică a ţarii*, vols. I–II (Bucharest, 1936); George Taşcă, *Politica economico—sociala a lui P. P. Carp* (Bucharest, 1938); Titu Maiorescu, *Inseminări zilnice* (Bucharest, 1939–1940); R. W. Seton-Watson, *A History of the Roumanians* (Hamden, CT, 1963); Zigu Ornea, *Junimea şi junimismul* (Bucharest, 1978); Ion Bulei, *Sistemul politic al. României moderne: Partidul Conservator* (Bucharest, 1987); Ion Bulei, *Atunci când veacul se năştea . . .* (Bucharest, 1990); Dumitru Vitcu, *Diplomats of the Union* (Bucharest, 1989).

ČATLOŠ Ferdinand (7 October 1895, Liptovský Hrádok, near Liptovský Mikuláš–16 October 1972, Martin), Slovak general. Čatloš graduated from a high trade school. In September 1915, as a cadet of the Austro-Hungarian army, he was taken prisoner of war by the Russians. In 1917 he joined the Czechoslovak Legion in Russia, in which he commanded a battalion. After returning to Czechoslovakia, in 1925–26 he worked in the Ministry of National Defense in Prague, and then he was deputy military attaché in Budapest for one year. In the late 1920s he studied at the Higher Military School in Paris. After returning home, he was chief of staff of a division in Hranice in Moravia (1935–38) and commander of the military chancellery of the Slovak autonomous government (1938–39). Promoted to the rank of general in 1939, he became minister of national defense of the Slovak Republic, whose government facilitated the German invasion of Poland and then declared war on Poland. At first he supported the radical faction of **Vojtech Tuka**; later, however, he took a more moderate attitude and sided with President **Jozef Tiso**. In view of the approaching German defeat, he tried to establish contact with the Slovak resistance, and in the summer of 1944 he elaborated a plan called the "Čatloš Memorandum," in which he offered the Soviet command the cooperation of Slovak troops in opening the way to the west. The regular Slovak Army was to overthrow the pro-German government and establish a military dictatorship. The Kremlin did not even respond to this offer. After the outbreak of the Slovak National Uprising Čatloš at first opposed it, but on 2 September 1944 he broke through to the territory conquered by the insurgents, where he was interned and temporarily deported to the USSR. In 1947 he was tried in Czechoslovakia and sentenced to five years in prison but released after one year. From 1948 he was a white-collar worker in Martin. (PU)

Sources: *ČBS*; *SBS*, vol. 1; *Kdo byl kdo v našich dějinach ve 20. stoleti*, vol. 1 (Prague, 1998); *Reprezentačný biografický lexikón Slovenska* (Martin, 1999); Valerián Bystrický and Štefan Fano, eds., *Slovensko na konci druhej svetovej vojny* (Bratislava, 1994); Václav Štefanský, *Generál Ferdinand Čatloš* (Bratislava, 1998).

CEAUŞESCU Elena [née Petrescu] (7 January 1919, Petreşti–25 December 1989, Tîrgovişte), wife of **Nicolae Ceauşescu**. Born into a peasant family, Ceauşescu completed a few grades of primary school. From 1937 she belonged to the Communist Party of Romania. At the beginning of World War II she worked in a textile factory in Bucharest. From 1944 she was a member of the Central Committee (CC) of the Union of Communist Youth, and from 1965, a member of the CC of the Romanian Workers' Party. In 1973 she became a member of the Political Executive Committee of the CC of the Romanian Communist Party (RCP, renamed so in 1965); in 1974 she became a member of the Standing Political Bureau of the Executive Committee of the RCP CC, and from 1975 she was a deputy to the Grand National Assembly. She had an extensive and destructive influence on Romanian politics. She even usurped titles and degrees in chemistry. From 1964 to 1975 she was director of the Institute of Chemistry, and from 1965 to 1989, general director of the Central Chemical Research Institute. In 1979–89 she presided over the National Council of Science and Technology. From 1980 she was first deputy prime minister. In 1981 she became chairperson of the National Committee of People of Science and Peace. From 1984 to 1989 she presided over the central Council of Classification, Standardization, and Quality, and in 1985 she became a member of the Romanian Academy of Sciences. She was a member of many scholarly societies and received many national and foreign awards, both in Western democracies and in Third World countries. In 1970 she became an honorary member of the International Association of Industrial Chemistry in France; in 1973, a member of the New York Academy of Sciences; in 1974, an honorary doctor of the University of Buenos Aires in Argentina; and in 1975, an honorary doctor of universities in Manila and Tehran. She published a few works in chemistry, probably not her own. Her formal position in science was one of the worst scandals in this field. Because of her appetite for luxury, her haughtiness, and her malicious nature,

she was hated by even her closest aides. As a result of the coup in December 1989, she was arrested along with her husband, hastily tried, sentenced to death, and shot in the Tîrgovişte military barracks. (LW)

Sources: *Persolanităţi româneşti ale ştinţelor naturii şi technicii* (Bucharest, 1982); *Dictionar Enciclopedic* (Bucharest, 1993); Ion Raţiu, *Contemporary Romania* (Richmond, 1975); Vlad Georgescu, *Istoria Românilor de la origini pînă în zilele noastre* (Oakland, 1984); Juliusz Stroynowski, ed., *Who's Who in the Socialist Countries of Europe* (Munich, London, and Paris, 1989); Edward Behr, *Kiss the Hand You Cannot Bite* (New York, 1991); Ion Alexandrescu, Ion Bulei, Ion Mamina, and Ioan Scurtu, *Enciclopedia de istorie României* (Bucharest, 2000).

CEAUŞESCU Nicolae (26 January 1918, Scorniceşti–25 December 1989, Tîrgovişte), Romanian Communist leader. Born into a large peasant family from Oltenia, Ceauşescu completed four grades of primary school. From 1932 he worked as a tailor's apprentice. In 1933 he joined the illegal Union of Communist Youth (UCY) and the Communist Party of Romania (Partidul Comunist din România [CPR]). In 1936 he became secretary of the regional CPR committee in Prahova. According to the instructions of the Comintern, the CPR, which included mostly non-Romanians, advocated the secession of post-World War I Romanian acquisitions in Bessarabia, Bukovina, Transylvania, and Dobrudja. In 1936 Ceauşescu was arrested for anti-state activities and sentenced to two and a half years, which he spent in the Braşov and Doftana prisons. In 1939 he was imprisoned again and sentenced to three years with suspended execution, but since he continued his activities, in 1940 he was put in jail. He was imprisoned in the Jilava and Caransebeş prisons, and in 1943 he was moved to the Tîrgu Jiu camp, where he met the leadership of the Communist Party of Romania and became a protégé of **Gheorghe Gheorghiu-Dej**.

Released after the coup of 23 August 1944, Ceauşescu became the head of the UCY and was promoted to the rank of colonel, although he had no formal military education. It was then that he married Elena Petrescu, who remained with him until death. In November 1946 he became regional RCP secretary in Oltenia and was responsible for rigging the parliamentary elections. During the pre-election campaign he became famous for brutality. At least one of his murders was documented. In 1945–48 he was a member of the RCP Central Committee (CC), and from February 1948, a member of the CC of the newly established Romanian Workers' Party (Partidul Muncitoresc Român [RWP]). In 1946 he became a deputy to the Grand National Assembly. From 1948 to 1950 he was deputy minister of agriculture, brutally forcing peasants into *kolkhozes*. From 1950 to 1954 he was head of the

Political Administration of the army and deputy minister of national defense. After the party purge of 1952, directed against the followers of **Ana Pauker** and **Vasile Luca**, Ceauşescu advanced to the position of the head of the RWP CC Organization Bureau and CC secretary, and in 1955 he became a member of the CC Politburo, responsible for personnel policy. In November 1956 he monitored the influence of the Hungarian Revolution on the Hungarian minority in Romania. For some time **Imre Nagy** was held in Romania. Along with **Emil Bodnaraş**, Ceauşescu sent specially trained security officers of Hungarian nationality from Transylvania to Hungary to help **János Kádár** reconstruct the political police in Hungary.

On 22 March 1965, three days after the death of Gheorghiu-Dej, thanks to the support of the nationalist faction in the RWP leadership and to his own influence in the army and in the party apparatus, Ceauşescu was appointed first secretary of the RWP CC. In July 1965 he changed the name of the party to the Romanian Communist Party (RCP), and in August 1965 he introduced a new constitution and changed the name of the country to the Socialist Republic of Romania. He also changed his title to secretary general of the RCP CC. In 1967–74 he was also chairman of the State Council. In 1974 he introduced the title of president and assumed this position for life. By 1969 he had consolidated his position by gathering all the reins of power into his hands. Skillfully fanning rivalries among the highest officials of the system, he got rid of his major rival, Minister of Interior **Alexandru Draghici**. He also fired most of the so-called old Communists and rehabilitated those murdered on the orders of Gheorghiu-Dej, including **Lucreţiu Pătrăşcanu** and **Ştefan Foriş**, as well as some of the political prisoners of the years 1951–58. Promoting his protégés, in 1969 he expanded the CC and secured total control over the party.

Ceauşescu continued the foreign policy of his predecessor, based on nationalism and hidden anti-Russian emotions. In some respects he distanced himself even further from Moscow. In 1965 he opposed the subordination of Romania to the economic plans of the Comecon. He initially slowed down the pace of industrialization, and in 1968 he refused to send Romanian troops to Czechoslovakia. Romania was the only Warsaw Pact country that did not condemn American air raids on Vietnam and that maintained diplomatic relations with Israel after the Six-Day War in 1967. Theses policies gained Ceauşescu some trust in the West and at home. Democratic countries extended Romania credit, counting on a widening gap between Bucharest and Moscow, and they closed their eyes to the totalitarian rule, terror, and violation of human rights by the Ceauşescu regime. Credit and technologies from the West were nevertheless transferred through Romania to the USSR, as Ceauşescu did not move far from the Soviet bloc. In 1971 he accelerated the pace of industrialization again. Investment funds came from huge concessions from the society and from West German and Israeli payments for Romania's consent to allow Romanian Germans and Jews to emigrate. Actual Romanian-Soviet relations were much closer than the officially declared sovereignty of Romania, especially in the field of intelligence and in economic and military contacts. Nonetheless, Ceauşescu was accepted and honored as a politician almost independent of the Kremlin. For instance, in 1975 he received members of the British nobility. He made numerous foreign trips, achieving significant personal gains. He mediated between the USSR and Israel, but he also maintained close relations with Palestinian terrorists. In 1977 he contributed to the establishment of contact between Egypt and Israel and to the visit of the president of Egypt, Anwar Sadat, to Jerusalem.

At the same time Ceauşescu extended neo-Stalinist policies and strengthened his own personality cult. He also introduced a "dynastic socialism," since he filled the top positions in the state and party apparatus with members of his own family. In 1972 he promoted his wife to the Politburo of the RCP CC. One of his brothers, Nicolae Andruţa, was a Securitate general and deputy minister of interior; another, Ilie, was deputy minister of national defense; a third, Ioan, was deputy chairman of the State Planning Commission; a fourth, Florea, was editor of the party daily, *Scintea*; a fifth, Marin, was head of an economic agency in Vienna that arranged family business; his sister Maria was deputy chairman of the Red Cross; another sister, Elena, was married to Vasile Barbulescu, the CC secretary for agriculture; his son Nicu was provincial party secretary in Sibiu; and his brother-in-law, Gheorghe Petrescu, was deputy head of the trade unions. The spouses of some of these relatives also held high positions. In 1971 Ceauşescu initiated a mini-cultural revolution that led to a total subordination of the whole society to the party and security apparatus and ultimately to Ceauşescu himself.

With the help of the political police, Securitate, which applied the harshest methods of terror, blackmail, treacherous killings, and forced placements in psychiatric wards, Ceauşescu forced the absolute obedience of the society. Workers' protests were bloodily suppressed in the Jiu region in 1977, in Motru in 1981, and in Braşov in 1987. At the same time the Ceauşescu clan surrounded itself with ostentation, building palaces at a time when most of the population was suffering from growing shortages. The cult of Ceauşescu and his wife took grotesque forms. He was called the "Father of the Romanians" and the "Carpathian

Genius," while she was celebrated as a scholar despite her incomplete primary education. The low cultural level of the Ceauşescu clan went hand in hand with displays of its power. The first breach in the monolith of Ceauşescu power was achieved by **Ion Pacepa**, deputy head of intelligence, who escaped to the West at the end of 1978 and shook the credibility of the Ceauşescu system. Pacepa's revelations made it clear that the Ceauşescu dictatorship was primitive and ruthless, with Securitate agents not hesitating to murder Romanian émigré activists.

The intensive industrialization of the 1980s, as well as Ceauşescu's ambition to discharge foreign debts (Ceauşescu had noted the fall of the Polish regime of **Edward Gierek** because of its foreign debts), dramatically worsened the economic situation in Romania. Nonetheless, the regime continued its bombastic projects, such as the construction of a Palace of the Republic at the cost of the demolition of old buildings in downtown Bucharest and the plan of "systemization," aiming at the elimination of traditional village communities. Another serious challenge to the regime came with the Soviet *perestroika*. In view of the reforms advocated by Mikhail Gorbachev, the ideological orthodoxy of Ceauşescu began to be a burden for both the Soviets and the West. The new Soviet policy raised the hopes of the functionaries who had been fired by Ceauşescu and who were now ready to return at his expense. Some of them must have had contacts with the Soviet KGB. In March 1989 six of these functionaries sent a letter to Ceauşescu criticizing his thoughtless economic and social policies and the atmosphere of terror that he had created.

As late as November 1989, Ceauşescu managed to orchestrate the Sixteenth RCP Congress in the spirit of his apotheosis. After the riots in Timişoara, where the militia tried to evict Pastor **László Tőkés** but where the local community stood up in his defense, Ceauşescu ordered the use of guns to suppress demonstrations. On 20 December the protests took on massive proportions. The next day a meeting in Bucharest, organized in order to support the leader and at which Ceauşescu spoke, changed into an anti-government demonstration. In view of the immediate danger Ceauşescu fled by helicopter. On the night of 21–22 December a part of the army crossed over to the side of the demonstrators. New Communist leaders emerged in control of some units. Ceauşescu was arrested while escaping from the capital. He was brought, along with his wife, to the military barracks in Tîrgovişte, where they were hastily "tried," sentenced to death, and executed, most probably on 25 December 1989. (LW)

Sources: *Dictionar Enciclopedic*, vol. 1 (Bucharest, 1993); Ion Raţiu, *Contemporary Romania* (Richmond, 1975); Vlad Georgescu, *Istoria Românilor de la origini pînă în zilele noastre* (Oakland, 1984); Juliusz Stroynowski, ed., *Who's Who in the Socialist Countries of Europe* (Munich, London, and Paris, 1989); Mark Almond, *The Rise and Fall of Nicolae and Elena Ceauşescu* (London, 1992); Silviu Brucan, *The Wasted Generation* (Boulder, Colo., 1993); Józef Darski, *Rumunia: Historia, współczesność, konflikty narodowe* (Warsaw, 1995); Denis Deletant, *Ceauşescu and the Securitate: Coercion and Dissent in Romania, 1965–1989* (New York, 1995); Costin Scorpan, *Istoria Romaniei: Enciclopedie* (Bucharest, 1997); Ion Alexandrescu, Ion Bulei, Ion Mamina, and Ioan Scurtu, *Enciclopedia de istorie Românei* (Bucharest, 2000).

CELMIŅŠ Gustavs Adolfs (1 April 1899, Riga–10 April 1968 San Antonio, Texas), Latvian politician. In 1917 Celmiņš graduated from a trade school in Moscow and started studies at the Riga Polytechnic Institute, which had been relocated outside the city. In the spring of 1918 he returned to Riga, and in December 1918 he joined the Latvian Army. For bravery in Courland he was awarded the Order of Lāčplēsis, and in July 1919 he was promoted to the rank of lieutenant. From January 1920 he was deputy military attaché in Poland. During the Battle of Warsaw (August 1920) he stayed at his outpost, reporting to the Latvian government. In 1924 he retired. From 1925 to 1927 he was a white-collar worker, but he was dismissed for his rightist ideas. From 1927 he belonged to the Latvian National Union (Latviešu Nacionālā Apvienība) and directed its academic section. In 1929 he graduated in philology and philosophy from the University of Latvia in Riga. In 1930–32 he worked in the Ministry of Finance and was dismissed for political reasons again. From 1932 he presided over the Union of the Latvian Nation, Ugunskrusts (Fire Cross), and after its outlawing in 1933 he was the head of a Fascist organization, the Cross of Perkun (Pērkonkrusts). Dressed in gray shirts and black berets, members of the organization propagated extreme nationalism, anti-Communism, and anti-Semitism. Arrested after the **Kārlis Ulmanis** coup in 1934, in August 1935 Celmiņš was sentenced to three years in prison. After his release in 1937, he was banned from Latvian territory, and he lived in Italy, Poland, Hungary, Romania, Yugoslavia, Turkey, and Germany. From December 1939 to March 1940 he was aide-de-camp of the commander of the "Sisu" Legion fighting against the USSR in Finland.

After the Finnish-Soviet war, Celmiņš lived in the Third Reich, and in 1941 he returned to Latvia, which was occupied by the German Army. He strove to form a Latvian division in exchange for a German declaration of the restoration of Latvian statehood. He directed the Committee of Latvian Volunteer Organizations. In view of the failure of his plans, in 1943–44 he secretly edited the periodical *Brīvā Latvija*, in which he advocated the reconstruction of the Latvian state against the will of the German authorities. Arrested by the Germans in March 1944, he was sent to the Flossenburg camp and then to Dachau. In 1945, along with other prisoners, he was moved to Italy, where he was liberated by the American Army. In 1945–49 he lived in Italy and from 1949 in the United States. In 1950–52 he was a military instructor at the University of Syracuse, and then he was active as an industrialist in Mexico. In 1956 he became librarian at Trinity College in San Antonio, Texas, and from 1959 he lectured in Sovietology at St. Mary University there. He authored, among other things, the memoirs *Eiropa krustcelēs* (Europe at the crossroads; 1947) and *Sauli Latvijai: Latvijas atbrīvošanas ierindas spēku organizācijas mērķi, uzdevumi un darbības veidi jautājumos un atbildēs* (Goals, tasks, and measures of Latvian liberation organizations in questions and answers; 1948). (EJ)

Sources: Philip Rees, *Biographical Dictionary of the Extreme Right since 1890* (New York, 1990); *Lāčplēša Kara ordeņa kavalieri: Biogrāfiska vārdnīca* (Riga, 1995); Piotr Łossowski, *Kraje bałtyckie na drodze od demokracji parlamentarnej do dyktatury 1918–1934* (Wrocław, 1974); H. Biezais, "Gustava Celmiņa Pērkoņkrusts dokumentu gaismā," *Latvijas Zinātņu Akadēmijas Vēstis,* 1992, nos. 1–4; Latvijas Valsts vēstures arhīvs (State Historical Archives of Latvia).

CELMIŅŠ Hugo (30 July 1877, Lubanas–30 July 1941, Moscow), Latvian Peasant party politician. Celmiņš graduated in agronomy at the Riga Polytechnic in 1903. He later also studied in Bern. In 1907–13 he was editor of the *Baltijas Lauksaimnieks* magazine in Riga. Between 1904 and 1905 and then from 1914 he served as an officer in the Russian Army, and in 1915 he was taken prisoner by the Germans. At the end of 1918 he returned to Latvia and fought for its independence, attaining the rank of captain. From 1919 he was in the National Council and from 1920 a deputy to the Constituent Assembly, where he represented the Peasant Union of **Kārlis Ulmanis**. Between 1920 and 1921 he was minister of agriculture and from 1923–24, minister of education. He served as prime minister from 19 December 1924 to 23 December 1925 and then from 1 December 1928 to 26 March 1931. In 1925 he was also minister for foreign affairs. From 1931 he was mayor of Riga. After the coup d'état staged by Ulmanis in 1934, he continued to work at his post to 1935, and between 1935 and 1938 he was ambassador to Germany, Austria, and the Netherlands. After the invasion of Latvia by the Red Army in July 1940 he attempted to run for the People's Assembly, but the list was rendered null. He was arrested by the NKVD in October 1940, sentenced to death, and executed in the Lubyanka Prison in Moscow. (WR, EJ)

Sources: Alfreds Bilmanis, *Latvia as an Independent State* (Washington, D.C., 1947); Arnolds Svabe, ed., *Latviju enciklope-

dija (Stockholm, 1950–51); Piotr Łossowski, *Kraje bałtyckie na drodze od demokracji parlamentarnej do dyktatury (1918–1934)* (Wrocław, 1972).

ČEPIČKA Alexej (18 August 1910, Kroměříž–30 September 1990, Dobříš), Czechoslovak Communist activist. The son of a postman, Čepička graduated in law from Charles University in Prague, and in 1935 he earned a Ph.D. there. Member of a Communist youth organization between 1932 and 1935, in 1938 he joined the Communist Party of Czechoslovakia (CPC). From 1939 to 1942 he was active in the Communist underground in the Protectorate of Bohemia and Moravia. In 1942 he was arrested by the Gestapo and put in the Buchenwald camp. After his release in May 1945 he returned to his work in the apparatus of the CPC. Elected an MP on behalf of the party in 1946, in 1947 he became minister of domestic trade, and after the Communist coup in February 1948, minister of justice. His marriage to the daughter of **Klement Gottwald** in July 1948 rapidly enhanced his position in the party leadership. In May 1949 he joined the Central Committee (CC), and in October 1949 he became head of the State Council for Church Affairs. He supervised, for example, the suppression of the Catholic Church. He actually dictated many verdicts in the political trials of opposition leaders, the clergy, and high-ranking army officers.

In April 1950 Čepička was appointed minister of national defense and was promoted to general. In September 1951 he also joined the Secretariat and the Presidium of the CPC CC. Sent to the Kremlin by Gottwald in July 1951, he attended the meeting of the CPSU CC Politburo. At this meeting, it was affirmed that charges against **Rudolf Slanský** had not been sufficiently proven; nevertheless, it was determined that Slanský had made too many mistakes in personnel policy to remain secretary general of the party. In the fall of 1952 Čepička took part in the party committee that prepared the indictment against Slanský. He was also responsible for many other political cases in the 1950s. In 1953 he became deputy prime minister, and in April 1954, a member of the CPC CC Politburo. After Gottwald's death and especially after the Twentieth Congress of the CPSU in the spring of 1956, his influence began to decline. The leadership of the party, and particularly the first secretary of the CPC CC, Antonín Novotný, decided to make him a scapegoat for Stalinism in Czechoslovakia. Čepička's resignation was to show that the "errors and distortions" had been overcome. On 26 April 1956 he was dismissed from all posts. He assumed a minor position as director of the Bureau for Invention and Standardization, and in 1959 he retired. In April 1963 he was expelled from the party for his role in staging the political trials. However, he was never brought to justice for his judicial crimes. (WR)

Sources: *ČBS*; *Who's Who in the Socialist Countries of Europe* (Munich, London, and Paris, 1989); Edward Taborsky, *Communism in Czechoslovakia, 1948–1960* (Princeton, 1961); William. E. Griffith, ed., *Communism in Europe*, vol. 2 (Cambridge, Mass., 1966); Jiří Pelikán, *The Czechoslovak Political Trials, 1950–1954* (Stanford, 1971).

ČERNÍK Oldřich (27 October 1921, Ostrava–19 October 1994, Prague), Czech Communist activist. A metalworker by trade, Černík joined the Communist Party of Czechoslovakia (CPC) in 1945. In 1964 he graduated from the Higher School of Mining and Metallurgy in Ostrava as an extramural student. He belonged to one of the action committees (*akční výbor*), carrying out political purges after the February 1948 Communist coup. In 1949–52 he was a worker and secretary of the provincial CPC committee in Ostrava, then secretary general of the provincial CPC committee in Opava, and from 1954 to 1956 he was chairman of the Provincial National Council in Ostrava. In 1956–60 he was secretary of the CPC Central Committee (CC) and then until 1963 minister of fuels and power, deputy prime minister of Czechoslovakia, and head of the State Planning Commission. A member of the CPC CC from 1958 and of its Presidium from 1966, in 1960–69 he was a deputy to the National Assembly, and in 1969–70, to the Chamber of the People of the Federal Assembly.

In the second half of the 1960s Černík was one of the key party reformers. He was a pragmatist, and he was concerned mostly with the economy. During the Prague Spring, on 8 April 1968 he became prime minister of the Czechoslovak government. After the invasion of the Warsaw Pact troops in August 1968, along with other Czechoslovak leaders, he was sent to Moscow for talks with the Kremlin leadership. After three days of negotiations he signed the so-called Moscow Protocol, endorsing the invasion and obliging the CPC to "normalize" the situation. Černík wanted to keep his party and government position at all costs, so he supported the "normalization" line. In August 1969 he ordered the termination of a demonstration on the first anniversary of the invasion, and at a CC meeting in September he revoked his support for the 1968 reforms. Despite all this, his power gradually declined, and on 28 January 1970 he was dismissed from the position of prime minister. For some time he was minister-head of the Federal Committee for Technical and Investment Development. In June 1970 he was deprived of all posts and in 1971 expelled from the CPC. He was one of the directors of a standardization institute in Prague. After the fall of the Communist system, in 1990–91 he chaired the Council of the Union of Towns and Communes. (PU)

Sources: *ČBS*; *Českoslovenští politici: 1918–1991* (Prague, 1991); *Kdo byl kdo v našich dějinach ve 20. stoleti*, vol. 1 (Prague, 1998); Vladimir V. Kusin, *The Intellectual Origins of the Prague Spring: The Development of Reformist Ideas in Czechoslovakia 1958–1967* (Cambridge, 1971); Gordon H. Skilling, *Czechoslovakia's Interrupted Revolution* (Princeton, 1976); *Zaciskanie pętli: Tajne dokumenty dotyczące Czechosłowacji 1968 r.* (Warsaw, 1995).

ČERNIUS Jonas (6 January 1898, Kupiškis, near Panevežys–3 July 1977, Claremont, California), Lithuanian general and politician. At the end of World War I Černius joined the Lithuanian army-in-the-making. In July 1919 he was one of the first graduates of the War Academy in Kaunas. He also took part in operations on the front. He supplemented his engineering and military education in Brussels (1929) and Paris (1932). After returning to Lithuania, he was promoted to lieutenant colonel and became head of the technical section of the General Staff. In 1934 he was promoted to colonel and made head of the operations section of the General Staff. He also commanded the War Academy. In 1935–39 he was chief of the General Staff, and afterwards he was promoted to general. From 30 March to 22 November 1939 he was prime minister of the government that took a neutral attitude toward the German invasion of Poland in September 1939, but in October 1939 he accepted a Soviet ultimatum: he agreed to allow Soviet troops into Lithuania in exchange for the incorporation of the Wilno (Vilnius) area into Lithuania. After the Soviet occupation of Lithuania in June 1940 he avoided deportation, and during the German occupation (1941–44) he remained passive. Before the return of the Red Army in the summer of 1944 he left for Germany and later to Great Britain. In 1948 he settled in the United States. (WR)

Sources: *EL*, vol. 1; Saulius Sužiedelis, *Historical Dictionary of Lithuania* (Lanham, Md., 1997).

ČERNÝ Jan (4 March 1874, Uherský Ostroh, near Uherské Hradiště–10 April 1959, Uherský Ostroh), Czech politician. Černý graduated in law from the Czech university in Prague in 1898, and in 1899–1908 he worked for the district authorities in Hodonín. From 1908 to 1910 he worked in the Ministry of Social Affairs in Vienna, and then for two years he was head of the Prostějov district. From 1912 to 1918 he was head of the Moravian province in Brno, and from 1920 to 1928, chairman of the *land* political authority of Moravia. After the administrative reforms and until World War II he was president of the Moravian-Silesian Land. From 15 September 1920 to 26 September 1921 and from 18 March to 12 October 1926 he was prime minister of a clerical government, created in view of problems with the formation of a ruling coalition. Four times—in 1920–22, 1926–29, 1932–34, and in late 1938—he was minister of interior. As prime minister he tried to increase the efficacy of the police and military. His was to become an "iron rod" government, aiming at strengthening the foundations of democracy. With the formation of his first cabinet, representatives of the five strongest parties created a group of "Five" (Pětka), designed to be a body that would formally mediate between the government and the parliament, but it was one that actually made the key decisions. As minister of interior, Černý largely contributed to easing the social tensions and preventing social radicalism in the first years of independent Czechoslovakia and to the introduction of the administrative reform of 1928. In 1939 he retired. (PU)

Sources: *ČBS*; *Československí politici: 1918–1991* (Prague, 1991); *Politická elita meziválečného Československa 1918–1938: Kdo byl kdo za první republiky* (Prague, 1998); *Kdo byl kdo v našich dějinach ve 20. stoleti*, vol. 1 (Prague, 1998).

ČERNÝ Václav (26 March 1905, Jizbice, near Náchod–2 July 1987, Prague), Czech historian and theoretician of literature. After graduating from high school in Nachod and the Carnot Lycée in Dijon, France, in 1928 Černý graduated in Romance and Czech studies in the Philosophy Department of Charles University in Prague. In 1929–30 he taught in a high school in Brno, and then for four years he was secretary of the Institute of Slavic Studies in Geneva. It was there that he received his postdoctoral degree in 1931. From 1934 he lectured at the University of Geneva. After returning home, he taught in a high school in Prague, and until 1939 he was associate professor of Romance literature at Charles University. In 1938–39 he was also professor at Masaryk University in Brno. After all the universities were closed down by the German occupation authorities, from 1939 to 1944 Černý taught in a Prague high school, and (with a break in 1942–45) he edited the monthly *Kritický měsíčník*. During the Nazi occupation he took part in the domestic resistance, and in 1941–42 he belonged to the National Revolutionary Intelligentsia Committee (Národně Revoluční Výbor Inteligence). From January to May 1945 he was imprisoned by the Germans. From 8 to 11 May 1945 he belonged to the Czech National Council (Česka Národní Rada). From 1945 he was professor of the history of literature at Charles University.

After World War II Černý was active in cultural organizations. He criticized Marxist dogmatism and the abuses of Communist rule, preaching democracy and human rights. After the Communist coup of February 1948 he suffered from various forms of repression. In 1951 he was forced to leave the university, and from September 1952 to April 1953 he was imprisoned without trial. After his release until 1961, he worked in the Institute of Contemporary Philology of the Czechoslovak Academy of Sciences and then until 1968 in its manuscript section. During the Prague Spring he returned to public life, resuming his lectures and advocating reforms and democratization. During the "normalization" he was fired from the university and brutally attacked by propaganda. He cooperated with dissident organizations, and he wrote in *samizdat* publications and abroad. On 1 January 1977 he was one of the first 242 signatories of Charter 77.

Černý dealt with Czech and European literature. Among other things, he discovered manuscripts of two plays by Luís Calderón in the library of the Mlada Vožica castle. He did research on existentialism and the influence of Henri Bergson's philosophy on contemporary literature. He authored the following monographs: *Ideové kořeny současného umění: Bergson a ideologie současného romantismu* (Intellectual roots of contemporary art: Bergson and the ideology of contemporary Romanticism; 1927); *První sešit o existencialismu* (First notebook on existentialism; 1948); and *Druhý sešit o existencialismu* (Second notebook on existentialism; 1992); he also wrote *Co je kritika, co není a k čemu je na světě* (What criticism is, what it is not, and what it is for in this world; 1968). He translated French writers (including Bergson), Spanish writers (Miguel de Cervantes, José Ortega y Gasset), and Italian writers. He published three volumes of important memoirs, *Paměti* (Toronto, 1977–83; Brno, 1992–94). (PU)

Sources: *ČBS*; *Kdo byl kdo v našich dějinach ve 20. stoleti*, vol. 1 (Prague, 1998); *Slovník českých filozofů* (Brno, 1998); Julius Vanovič, *Osobnost Václava Černého: Personalistický portrét* (Bratislava, 1999).

CHACIŃSKI Józef (13 March 1889, Warsaw–6 May 1954, Góra Kalwaria), Polish Christian Democratic politician. While in a trade school, Chaciński joined the National Youth Organization (Organizacja Młodzieży Narodowej) and a self-education group rallied around the Catholic magazine *Prąd*. Arrested in 1909 at a secret youth congress, he spent four months in the Warsaw citadel. Released, he began to study in Switzerland but had to interrupt his studies owing to a lack of funds. From 1912 he worked for the editorial office of *Prąd* and was active in the Christian Workers' Association (Stowarzyszenie Robotników Chrześcijańskich [SRCh]). In the same year he graduated from high school in Libawa (Liepaja), and then until 1918 he studied law in Kiev. After his return to Poland he worked in the State Property Board, and in 1920 he served in the Polish Army as a volunteer. A secretary general of the SRCh from 1919, between 1920 and 1922 he co-organized the Christian National Labor Party, which as of 1925 was called the Polish Christian Democratic Party (Polskie Stronnictwo Chrześcijańskiej Demokracji). Between 1927 and 1928 Chaciński was leader of this party. In 1922–30 he was an MP and president of the Christian Democratic parliamentary club. At the beginning of May 1926 he was a candidate for the office of prime minister, but he failed to come to an agreement with President **Stanisław Wojciechowski** on the appointment of the minister of interior. After the coup of May 1926 he was in opposition, and in 1930 he co-organized the Centrolew opposition bloc. In the 1930s he was mainly involved in running a law firm.

During the Nazi occupation Chaciński was arrested (July 1940) and deported to the concentration camp in Auschwitz. Released at the beginning of 1942, he returned to Warsaw, where, as president of the program commission, he was active in the underground Labor Party (Stronnictwo Pracy [SP]). From the spring of 1943 he was a member of the Program Council of the Christian Democratic Unia. From the beginning of August 1944 he served as president of the SP Executive Committee. He firmly opposed the outbreak of the Warsaw Uprising. After its defeat he left the capital along with the civilian population. Arrested by the NKVD on 28 March 1945 in Pruszków, he was taken to the Lubyanka Prison in Moscow and was sentenced in the Trial of the Sixteen to four months. After returning to Poland, he continued his activities in the SP, but after the party was taken over by pro-Communist splinter groups, he abandoned political activity and worked as a legal adviser in the Governing Board of the City of Warsaw. (WR)

Sources: Kunert, vol. 1; Stanisław Łoza, *Parlament Rzeczypospolitej Polskiej 1919–1927* (Warsaw, 1928); Karol Popiel, *Na mogiłach przyjaciół* (London, 1966); *Encyklopedia Katolicka*, vol. 3 (Lublin, 1979); Jacek Majchrowski, "Stronnictwo Pracy: Działalność polityczna i koncepcje programowe 1937–1945," *Zeszyty Naukowe UJ*, 1979, no. 88; *Proces szesnastu: Dokumenty NKWD* (Warsaw, 1995).

CHAJĘCKI Bronisław, pseudonym "Boryna" (15 December 1902, Warsaw–5 or 20 December 1953, Warsaw), Polish officer and politician, victim of communism. The son of a railwayman, in 1920, while in high school, Chajęcki fought as a volunteer in the Polish-Soviet war. After graduating from high school in Warsaw and from the Reserve Officers' School in Ostrów Mazowiecka in 1927, he worked as a teacher. He was also active in scouting and became a scoutmaster. During the defense of Warsaw in September 1939 he was deputy to the civil commissioner,

Stefan Starzyński, and he was in charge of the municipal administration in the Warsaw suburb of Praga. Next, he began conspiratorial activities. On behalf of the Christian Democratic organization called Unia, he joined the State Security Corps (Państwowy Korpus Bezpieczeństwa [PKB])—that is, the underground military police—and from August 1942 he was its commander for Warsaw. Taken captive at the end of the uprising, he managed to escape during transport, and he joined the Home Army Kampinos group. In March 1945 he joined the "people's" Polish Army, and in September 1946 he was demobilized in the rank of captain. He worked in administration and taught in a vocational school in Pruszków. On 11 November 1948 he was arrested by the State Security Office (Urząd Bezpieczeństwa [UB]). After a long and brutal investigation he was sentenced to death on trumped-up charges of cooperation with the Germans. On 20 October 1952 the Supreme Court affirmed the judgment. President **Bolesław Bierut** did not exercise his right to grant a pardon; therefore Chajęcki was executed. The sentence was quashed in 1958, and Chajęcki was posthumously rehabilitated. (WR)

Sources: Kunert, vol. 1; Centralne Archiwum KC PZPR, 202/II/33, k. 40; *Cywilna obrona Warszawy we wrześniu 1939 r.* (Warsaw, 1965); Jan Hoppe, "Fragmenty wspomnień," *Więź* 1969, no. 4.

CHAJN Leon (3 March 1910, Warsaw–1 March 1983, Warsaw), Polish Communist activist. Chajn was born into a white-collar family. In 1931 he graduated from the Higher School of Journalism, and in 1933, from the Law Department of Warsaw University. Then he worked as a lawyer. From 1932 he belonged to the Communist Party of Poland, and in the late 1930s also to the so-called democratic clubs connected with the extreme left. During World War II he lived in the USSR. In 1941–42 he served in the Red Army, and from 1943 he was active in the (Communist) Union of Polish Patriots (Związek Patriotów Polskich). In the summer of 1944 he was briefly a political officer in the First Polish Army in the USSR. In August 1944 he became deputy head of the Department of Justice of the Polish Committee of National Liberation and then deputy minister of justice of the Communist-controlled Provisional Government (January–June 1945), the Provisional Government of National Unity (June 1945–February 1947), and later in the government of **Józef Cyrankiewicz**. He was one of the chief organizers of the Stalinist judiciary in Poland. Delegated to the Democratic Party (Stronnictwo Demokratyczne), from March 1945 to July 1961 he was secretary general of its Central Committee, supervising its cooperation with the (Communist) Polish Workers' Party and from 1948 with the

Polish United Workers' Party. In 1944–69 he was a deputy to the Home National Council and to the parliament (Sejm). From March 1949 to November 1952 he was deputy chairman of the Supreme Chamber of Control and later deputy minister of labor and social welfare. From February 1957 to June 1965 he was a member of the Council of State and then, until retirement in March 1976, director of the Supreme Directorate of State Archives. In 1964 he published his memoirs, *Kiedy Lublin był Warszawą* (When Lublin was the capital), and in 1975, a history of Polish freemasonry, *Polskie wolnomularstwo 1920–1938* (Polish freemasonry, 1920–1938). (WR)

Sources: Mołdawa; Marek Łatyński, *Nie paść na kolana: Szkice o opozycji lat czterdziestych* (Warsaw, 1987); Wacław Barcikowski, *W kręgu prawa i polityki* (Warsaw, 1988); Krystyna Kersten, *Narodziny systemu władzy: Polska 1943–1948* (Poznań, 1990); Andrzej Rzepliński, *Sądownictwo w PRL* (London, 1990).

CHARLES I Hohenzollern-Sigmaringen (20 April 1839, Sigmaringen–27 September 1914, Sinaia), Prince (10 May 1866–10 May 1881) and King (10 May 1881–27 September 1914) of Romania. Charles was the second son of Prince Karl Anton of the cadet branch of the Hohenzollern-Sigmaringen family and of Josephine Beauharnais of Baden. He received a thorough education at home. In 1857 he began his military career, rising to the rank of lieutenant in the Prussian Royal Guard in 1863. Subsequently, he began historical studies at the university in Bonn, and in his free time he traveled throughout France, Spain, and Africa. He fought in the war against Denmark in 1864, rising to the rank of captain. In 1866 he accepted the offer of the Romanian throne. In a referendum held in April 1866 in Romania 685,000 voters were in favor of his candidacy as prince while 224,000 voted against him. Opting for a foreign ruler, Romania's political elites wanted to avoid domestic conflicts; consolidate the position of the state, which was in the process of liberating itself from Turkish supremacy; and gain full independence. The prestige and support of the royal families to whom the future sovereign was related were also important factors.

Charles fulfilled the requirements. On 30 June 1866 he swore an oath to uphold the new constitution, one of the most liberal in Europe at that time. According to the principle of the three-way division of power, adopted to balance the possible dominance of one institution, the prince shared legislative power with the parliament and executive power with the government. A curial electoral law with property qualifications for members of parliament was introduced. This constitution lasted unchanged for over half a century. In 1869 Charles married Princess Elizabeth of Wied, and, together with his wife, he joined the Orthodox faith. The only child from this marriage, a daughter, Maria, born in 1870, died at the age of four. A dynastic-family agreement signed in 1881 designated Ferdinand, a nephew of Charles, as his successor. As a new figure among the Romanian political elite, Charles was guided by a feeling of duty toward Romania. His rule brought political stability, economic development, and independence to the country. He had good relations with the Romanian political elite, although some politicians accused him of dictatorial leanings. It was only in 1870, during the Franco-Prussian War, that the radical wing of the Liberal Party mobilized the pro-French Romanian public opinion against the prince, who was emotionally linked to Prussia. Under such pressure, he was going to abdicate, but the conservative government did not let this happen. Charles broadened Romania's contacts with other countries. He opened diplomatic missions in Vienna, Berlin, St. Petersburg, and Rome. He brought about a postal convention between Romania and its neighboring countries, and in 1875 his efforts led to the conclusion of a commercial convention with Austria-Hungary. In order to entirely free itself from subordination to Turkey, in 1877, during the Russo-Turkish war, Romania took the side of Russia, turning this war into a struggle for its own independence. After the recognition of Romanian independence by the Berlin Congress in 1878, Charles was crowned king on 10 May 1881.

With Europe about to split into two opposing camps, Charles signed a treaty of alliance with Austria-Hungary, thus placing Romania in the camp of the Central Powers. On the same day, 18 October 1883, this treaty was also signed by Germany. Because this alliance blocked the reincorporation of Transylvania from Hungary, Charles managed to keep it secret, and only a small group of people knew about it. With the outbreak of World War I, unlike most members of the Royal Council, who opted for neutrality, Charles advocated Romanian support for the Central Powers. He encouraged the representatives of the Romanian ethnic minority in Transylvania to remain faithful to Austria-Hungary during the war and to join the Austro-Hungarian Army. Charles died at the beginning of World War I. Soon after his death the leaders of the National Liberal Party called for an alliance with the Entente. (ASK)

Sources: *Biographisches Lexikon*, vol. 2; Dimitrie A. Sturdza, *Charles I, roi de Roumanie: Chroniques, actes, documents*, vols. 1–2 (Bucharest, 1899–1904); Paul Lindenberg, *König Karl von Rumänien*, vols. 1–2 (Berlin, 1923); Marie, Queen of Romania, *The Story of My Life* (New York, 1934); Joseph Roucek, *Contemporary Romania and Her Problems* (Stanford, 1932); Michel Sturdza, *The Suicide of Europe* (Belmond, Mass., 1968); Titu Maiorescu, *România regilor*, vol. 1 (Bucharest, 1996); Ion Bulei, *Scurta istoriea Românilor* (Bucharest, 1996).

CHARLES II Hohenzollern-Sigmaringen (15 October 1893, Sinaia–3 April 1953, Lisbon), King of Romania. Charles's father, King **Ferdinand**, was of German origin, and his mother, Marie, was English. After completing a military high school in Iaşi, Charles studied history at the university in Bucharest. In the military, he rose to commander of a mountain rifle unit and became the general inspector of the Romanian Navy and Air Force (1920). Intelligent but hot-headed, he was often a victim of his impetuousness and ran into problems in public life. In August 1918 he escaped from the front in Moldavia to Odessa and renounced his rights to the throne to marry Valentina (Zizi) Lambrino, the daughter of a Romanian general. As a successor to the throne, he did not have the right to marry a Romanian. Thus, the marriage to Zizi was a morganatic one, and the son born of this union, Paul, did not have a right to the throne. Under pressure from his parents, Charles agreed to the annulment of his marriage, which was declared null and void by the Supreme Court of Appeals on 8 January 1919. However, in August 1919 he again stated that he was Zizi's husband and the father of her son, and he renounced the throne. In order to break up this marriage, Charles's family sent him to the front at Tisza to fight against the Hungarian Soviet Republic, and later he was sent on a long journey across Europe and then on to Egypt, India, and Japan. Upon his return, he agreed to divorce Zizi, and on 23 March 1921 he married Helen, daughter of King Constantine and Queen Sophie of Greece. From this union his second son, **Michael**, the future king of Romania, was born (7 November 1921).

However, serious disagreements soon erupted between Charles and his wife, as well as between Charles and his father. Charles wanted to have a greater part in governing the country, and, against his father's will, he tried to remove **Ion I. C. Brătianu**, who was the head of the National Liberal Party (Partidul Naţional Liberal [NLP]), from any influence on the institution of the monarchy. Then Charles began to publicly flaunt his relationship with **Magda Elene Lupescu**, a divorcee whom he had met in 1924. Because of strong anti-Jewish attitudes in the country, the Jewish origins of his mistress turned the relationship into a public scandal. On 28 December 1925 Charles sent yet another declaration in which he renounced his rights to the throne, and this time it was accepted by King Ferdinand and the parliament. Charles was excluded from the royal family, and, under the name Carol Caraiman, he settled with Lupescu in Paris. In 1928 he obtained a divorce from Queen Helen. After the death of Ferdinand in 1927, a regency led by Patriarch **Miron Cristea** was established since Michael was under age.

Taking advantage of the weak authority of the regency,

as well as the conflict between the major Romanian political parties, the National Peasant Party (Partidul Naţional Ţărănesc [NPP]) and the NLP, Charles succeeded in his efforts to gain the throne. In June 1930 he unexpectedly arrived in Romania. He was supported by many prominent politicians, including General **Alexandru Avarescu, Constantin Argetoianu, Gheorghe Brătianu**, and **Nicolae Iorga**. He was also supported by some members of the Peasant Party and their leader, **Ion Mihalache**, and even by the Iron Guard. Charles brought about the resignation of the regency and he got the support of most political circles, which allowed him to become king as Charles II, on condition that he abide by the constitutional system and that he break up with Lupescu. He did not keep any of these promises. He began to establish a dictatorial regime and surrounded himself with the court camarilla, which consisted of favored entrepreneurs and society people. Acting behind the scenes, this group became a new power center. Members of this group had to be accepted by Lupescu. Because of this, Charles alienated members of the NPP and a great part of public opinion. Charles used the tactics of dividing and breaking up political parties and choosing factions and activists, such as **Armand Călinescu** and **Alexandru Vaida-Voievod** from the NPP, **Ion Duca** from the NPL, and the so-called young liberals with their leader, **Gheorghe Tătărescu**. Initially, Charles favored the Iron Guard because he wanted to discredit the democratic government. However, when it became clear that the Iron Guard was going to implement its totalitarian program, which was in competition with the king's, Charles began to suppress this organization. At the end of 1933 the Iron Guard was outlawed. After the retaliatory assassination of the interior minister and Premier Duca by the Guardists on 29 December 1933, Charles ordered the arrest of many members of the Iron Guard.

On 10 February 1938 Charles staged a coup d'état and introduced an authoritarian regime. He declared a state of emergency and appointed a new cabinet, called the government of national unity, which was led by Patriarch Cristea and which consisted of politicians faithful to Charles. On 10 March 1938 the parliament passed a new constitution, which proclaimed Charles the head of state. The king was to exercise legislative power through the National Representation and executive power through the government. The government was to be appointed by the king and was to report to him. The new constitution sanctioned broad prerogatives of the sovereign in foreign policy, in which Charles had taken a leading role as early as 1936, following the dismissal of **Nicolae Titulescu**, the minister for foreign affairs. Charles established the Royal Council, which served as an advisory organ and consisted of politicians who supported him. All political parties and trade unions were disbanded, and civil liberties were greatly restricted. Boys aged 7–18 and girls aged 7–21 had to be members of the Homeland Guard, a youth organization established under the command of the king as early as 1934. To secure a social and political base for his regime, Charles established the Front of National Rebirth (FNR), the sole political party, with himself as head.

In foreign policy Charles favored France and Great Britain, recognizing them as guarantors of the Versailles order that had brought Romania great territorial gains. In 1934, he signed the Balkan Entente with Yugoslavia, Greece, and Turkey, a pact added to the anti-Hungarian alliance of the Little Entente. The Balkan Entente was directed against Bulgarian revisionism. Charles based the security of Romania on treaties, since he had no funds with which to strengthen the army. The change of power structures in Europe in the second half of the 1930s forced Charles to improve relations with Germany through the economic treaties of 1936 and 1938 and particularly through the treaty of March 1939, which subordinated the Romanian economy to the Third Reich. Germany insisted that the Fascist Iron Guard join the government, but Charles disposed of his rivals by ordering the liquidation of Iron Guard leaders. Three hundred Guardists, including their leader, **Corneliu Zelea-Codreanu**, were killed in November and December 1938.

To counter the growing threat to Romania from the USSR and Germany and also from Hungarian and Bulgarian revisionism, Charles decided to reconcile with the political parties and he proposed to include the representatives of the opposition groups into the FNR and the government. However, the NPP and the NLP rejected that proposal. Only the Iron Guard accepted it. Charles ordered a mass release of Guardists from prisons and internment camps. The Guardists signed declarations of loyalty to the royal regime. The FNR was transformed into a uniform Party of the Nation, and all public functionaries, trade union leaders, and company directors were obliged to join it. On 22 June 1940 a decree was issued that provided severe penalties for propaganda and conspiratorial activities aimed at changing the political organization of the state. On 4 July 1940 Charles appointed **Ion Gigurtu**, a Germanophile, as premier, and he brought **Horia Sima**, the new leader of the Iron Guard, into the cabinet. On 8 August 1940 anti-Jewish legislation was introduced.

Any attempts at gaining Germany as an ally were shattered by the Molotov-Ribbentrop Pact of 23 August 1939, which isolated Romania in the international arena. The partition of Romania was a consequence of this pact. This partition began with the annexation of Bessarabia and northern Bukovina by the USSR in June 1940, followed by the incorporation of northern Transylvania by Hungary in August and the incorporation of southern Dobruja by Bulgaria in September of that year. This meant bankruptcy and a discredit of Charles' policy, and it gave rise to unrest. The Iron Guard attempted a military coup d'état. Germany insisted on Charles's resignation. In those circumstances, on 6 September 1940, Charles abdicated in favor of his son Michael. However, it was General **Ion Antonescu** who took power. Soon afterward, along with Lupescu, Charles left Romania. He went to Spain, then on to Cuba in 1941. In 1942 he moved to Mexico. In 1943 he settled in Lisbon, where he died. (ASK)

Sources: *Dictionar Enciclopedic*, vol. 1 (Bucharest, 1999); *The Times*, 6 April 1953; Marie, Queen of Romania, *The Story of My Life* (New York, 1934); Alexander L. Easterman, *King Carol, Hitler, and Lupescu* (London, 1942); Arthur Gould Lee, *Helen, Queen Mother of Romania* (London, 1956); Andreas Hillgruber, *Hitler, König Carol und Marschall Antonescu* (Wiesbaden, 1965); Ghislain de Diesbach, *La princesse Bibesco* (Paris, 1986); *Carol al. II-lea regele României: Însemnări zilnice*, vol. 1 (Bucharest, 1995); Ion Bulei, *Scurtă istorie a Românilor* (Bucharest, 1996).

CHARNETSKYI Mykola (14 December 1884, Semakivci, near Stanisławów [Ivano-Frankovsk]–2 April 1959, Lviv), Greek Catholic bishop. Charnetskyi studied theology in Stanisławów and then in Rome, where in 1909 he earned a Ph.D. He was ordained in October 1909, and in 1919 he joined the religious order of Redemptorists in Zboiska. He lectured at a Stanisławów seminary, and in 1926–31 he worked in various parishes of Volhynia. He also founded a monastery in Kostopol. In 1931 he was appointed apostolic visitor to Catholics of the Byzantine rite in Poland. On 2 February 1931 he was ordained bishop. On 9 October 1939 Archbishop Andrii Sheptytsky appointed him exarch of Volhynia, Podlasie, and Polesie. Until September 1940 he also served as exarch of Belorussia. During the Soviet occupation (1939–41) and the German occupation (after 1941) he was not allowed to go to Belorussia; therefore he served in Lviv. He lectured in philosophy, psychology, and moral theology at a local seminary. On 11 April 1945 he was arrested by the NKVD and was accused of collaboration with the Germans. During the liquidation of the Greek Catholic Church by the authorities of the USSR, on 3 June 1946 the military court sentenced Charnetskyi to five years of labor camp and three years of exile for "the betrayal of the homeland." He was held in (among other places) Kemerovo, Dubrovlag in the Mordovian ASSR, and Inta. Shortly before the end of his sentence in 1950 he was sentenced to a further ten years of labor camp. In 1956 he was allowed to return to Lviv, where he soon died. On 27 June 2001 Pope John Paul II beatified him at a solemn Holy Mass in Lviv. (WR)

Sources: *Encyclopedia of Ukraine,* vol. 1 (Toronto, 1984); *Martirologia ukrainskikh cerkov u chetyriokh tomakh,* vol. 2 (Toronto, 1985); Bohdan R. Bociurkiv, *The Ukrainian Greek-Catholic Church and the Soviet State (1939–1950)* (Edmonton, 1996); *Osservatore Romano* (weekly edition in English), 2001, nos. 25 and 27.

CHEKHIVSKY Volodymyr (19 July 1876, Horokhuvatka, near Kiev–after 1936, USSR), Ukrainian politician and religious activist. Chekhivsky graduated from the Kiev Orthodox Theological Academy, and in 1901–5 he was an inspector of a theological seminary in Kam'yanets Podilsky. In 1906 he was elected to the first State Duma in St. Petersburg. Before World War I he was arrested and spent one year in exile in Vologda. Next, he settled in Odessa and was active in the Ukrainian Hromada and in the Prosvita Society. From 1917 he was editor of *Ukrainsko Slovo.* He was a member of the Central Committee of the Ukrainian Social Democratic Workers' Party. In 1918 he became president of the Ukrainian Military Revolutionary Committee, which planned to overthrow the regime of Hetman **Pavlo Skoropadsky**. After the capture of Kiev by the troops created by the supporters of the former Ukrainian Central Rada of the Directorate and after Skoropadsky's flight, between 26 December 1918 and 11 February 1919 Chekhivsky headed the Directorate. He also served as prime minister of the government of the Directorate and as minister of foreign affairs. Under his leadership, on 1 January 1919 the government of the Ukrainian National Republic passed the autocephalia of the Ukrainian Orthodox Church. On 8 January 1919 the nationalization of land was also ordered; however, it was forbidden to divide the land into plots without permission of the authorities. In the face of a very difficult situation on the front, a compromise was sought with the command of the French landing troops, and the Socialist cabinet of Chekhivsky was replaced with a more moderate government. From 1921 he was a member of the Council of the All-Ukrainian Orthodox Church. After the Bolsheviks took power in central Ukraine, he withdrew from political life. On 29 July 1929 he was arrested by the OGPU in connection with the show trial of the Union for the Liberation of Ukraine. On 19 April 1930 he was given a death sentence, which was later commuted to ten years of prison. He served his sentence in Kharkiv and Yaroslavl. In 1933 he was deported to the Solovets Islands, where in 1936 his sentence was prolonged by an additional twenty years of labor camp. He was then transported to camps in the Far East, where he perished. He was the author of theological articles published in the magazine *Tserkva i zhyttia,* and of the pamphlet *Za Tserkvu, Khrystovu hromadu, proty tsarstvu t'my* (For the Church, Christ's community, and against the kingdom of darkness). (WR)

Sources: *Encyclopedia of Ukraine,* vol. 1 (Toronto, 1984); Orest Subtelny, *Ukraine: A History* (Toronto, 2000); Jan Jacek Bruski, *Petlurowcy: Centrum państwowe Ukraińskiej Republiki Ludowej na wychodźstwie 1919–1924* (Kraków, 2000).

CHERVENKOV Vulko (6 September 1900, Zlatitsa–21 October 1980, Sofia), Bulgarian Communist leader. Chervenkov was the son of a noncommissioned officer in the Bulgarian Army. After graduating from a gymnasium in Sofia in 1919, he joined the Communist Party. From 1921 to 1923 he edited the magazine *Mladezh*. He took part in an unsuccessful Communist uprising in 1923. In 1924–25 he was a member of the Central Committee (CC) of the League of Communist Youth of Bulgaria and was its representative in the military structure of the Bulgarian Communist Party (BCP). After the delegalization of the party in connection with an attempt on the life of Tsar **Boris III** in 1925, Chervenkov escaped from the country, where he was sentenced in absentia to death. In Moscow he studied at the International Leninist School, from which he graduated in 1928. Between 1928 and 1937 he lectured at the Communist University for National Minorities from the West, and between 1937 and 1938 he was the director of the school. From 1934 to 1935 he worked in the Balkan Secretariat of the Comintern. In 1938–41 he was director of the schools for foreigners of the Comintern's Executive Committee. During World War II he edited the "Khristo Botev" broadcasts of Radio Moscow in the Bulgarian language. In 1937, thanks to his marriage to the sister of **Georgi Dimitrov**, he joined the inner circle of the Bulgarian Communists in the USSR, and between 1941 and 1944 he belonged to the Foreign Office of the CC of the BCP.

Chervenkov returned to Bulgaria in September 1944 as a member of the Politburo and the secretary of the CC, also becoming minister of culture and science in the government already dominated by the Communists. Between December 1947 and August 1948 he was president of the Committee for Science, Culture, and Art. In 1948 he became secretary general of the Fatherland Front, and on 20 July 1949, deputy prime minister. In this capacity he played a key role in the overthrow and execution of **Traicho Kostov**. Although he was little known in Bulgaria, Chervenkov enjoyed the strong support of Stalin; therefore after the death of Dimitrov in July 1949 and the death of **Vasyl Kolarov** in January 1950, he subsequently assumed the highest posts, becoming prime minister on 3 February 1950, president of the Fatherland Front on 3 March, and secretary general of the party on 11 November 1950. He became famous for his swift seizure of power in the Stalinist style and for his brutal methods of government. He dismissed nationalist activists, surrounded himself with newcomers from Moscow, and promoted the younger generation. He supervised the state terror against opponents of the regime and purges in the government apparatus. He was also responsible for the terror accompanying the beginning of the collectivization of Bulgarian agriculture. In a short time he created the cult of his own personality.

After Stalin's death in 1953 Chervenkov announced changes in agricultural policy, though he never carried out his promises. This failure was connected with mounting tension in the countryside, as well as with the fact that Bulgaria had modeled its domestic policies on those of the Soviet Union. At the Sixth Congress of the party in March 1954 the "nationals" gained the majority in the CC, and Chervenkov was induced by the Kremlin to share power according to the principle of "collective leadership." He yielded his post as party leader to **Todor Zhivkov**, retaining the post of prime minister. However, Zhivkov, his former protégé, quickly built his own political base. The personality cult of Chervenkov was soon abandoned, and in the summer of 1955, when he became ill, rumors of his resignation began to spread. The Twentieth Congress of the CPSU heralded the end of his rule. In the spring of 1956 his opponents in the party executive received the strong support of Nikita Khrushchev; therefore on 17 April 1956 he lost his post as prime minister in favor of **Anton Yugov**. He resigned in an atmosphere of criticism of the "personality cult." However, he remained in the government as deputy prime minister and minister of education. He also retained his membership in the Politburo of the CC. In the fall of 1958 he headed a Bulgarian delegation to China. While some activists joined in the idea of a Great Leap Forward, in January 1959 Chervenkov criticized the ideological pretensions of the Chinese.

Despite everything Chervenkov remained an orthodox Stalinist. At the Twenty-second Congress of the CPSU he opposed Khrushchev's new "thaw." Khrushchev's personal dislike of Chervenkov brought about his final downfall. In November 1962, at the Plenum of the CC, he was removed from the Politburo and from the CC, and soon also from the party, for his "errors" and for "putting himself above the party." He was especially sharply attacked by Zhivkov. For some time he lived in complete isolation, but in 1969 his party membership was reinstated. However, he did not hold any executive posts. (WR)

Sources: *Entsiklopediya Bulgariya*, vol. 7; *Annual Obituary* (New Haven, CT, 1980); *Vylko Chervenkov* (Sofia, 1950); J. F. Brown, *Bulgaria under Communist Rule* (New York, 1970); L. A. D. Dellin, *Bulgaria* (New York, 1957); Tasho Tashev, *Ministrite na Bylgariia 1897–1999* (Sofia, 1999).

CHERVIAKOU Alyaksandr (8 March 1892, Dukarka, near Minsk–16 June 1937, Minsk), Belorussian Com-munist activist. In 1915 Cherviakou graduated from the Teachers' Training Institute in Wilno (Vilnius). Recruited into the Russian Army in 1916, in 1917 he was one of the organizers of the Belorussian Social Democratic Party. In December 1917 he took part in the First All-Belorussian Congress in Minsk. From 1918 he sided with the Bolsheviks and assumed the position of a political commissar on the southern front. He was commissar for education in the first government of the Lithuanian-Belorussian Soviet Socialist Republic, which emerged in January 1919. In 1920 he presided over the Military-Revolutionary Committee in Minsk and was responsible for the Bolshevik terror in the Minsk region. In 1920–24 he was chairman of the Belorussian Council of People's Commissars (government) and Central Executive Committee, as well as a member of the Central Committee of the Communist Party (Bolsheviks) of Belorussia. He negotiated the peace treaty with Poland in Riga. From 1922 to 1937 he was a member of the Central Executive Council of the USSR. He was engaged in the Beloruthenization of public life in the Belorussian SSR. Belorussian became the only official language in the state and party administration, schools, and cultural and research institutions. During the Great Purge in 1937 he was accused of anti-Soviet and counterrevolutionary activities, and he committed suicide. (EM)

Sources: *MERSH*, vol. 7; *Belarus: Entsyklapedychny davednik* (Minsk, 1995); Ivan S. Lubachko, *Belorussia under Soviet Rule, 1917–1957* (Lexington, KY, 1972); Vitaut Kipel and Zora Kipel, eds., *Byelorussian Statehood* (New York, 1988); H. Głogowska, *Białoruś 1914–1929: Kultura pod presją polityki* (Białystok, 1996); Jan Zaprudnik, *Historical Dictionary of Belarus* (Lanham, Md., 1998).

CHESHMEDZHIEV Grigor (4 March 1879, Peshtera–16 September 1945, Sofia), Bulgarian Socialist activist, advocate, and writer. In 1903 Cheshmedzhiev graduated in law from the Sofia Higher Institute (now Sofia University). He co-founded a Socialist organization in Peshtera in 1899. After the split in the Bulgarian Social Democratic Workers' Party (BSDWP) in 1903, he joined the faction of "broad Socialists." In 1907–8 he was a member of the Executive Committee of the Bulgarian Teachers' Union, and then he worked as a defense attorney in Sofia. As a reserve officer, he took part in the Balkan Wars and in World War I. After the war, he was a member of the top leadership of the BSDWP (united), and until 1934 he belonged to its Central Committee. He represented the right wing of the party, opposing communism and the government of **Aleksandur Stamboliyski** (1920–23). He supported the coup of June 1923. He was a deputy to the National Assembly from 1919 to 1934. After the coup of May 1934 he backed the policy of the Bulgarian Communist Party, which aimed at creating a united front of the left. He edited the newspaper *Tribuna*, which promoted this idea, and he insisted on amnesty for political prisoners. He was a member of the leadership of the Civic Committee for the Defense of Political Prisoners and Amnesty (1936–37) and remained in close touch with some Communist leaders.

After the outbreak of World War II Cheshmedzhiev supported the idea of concluding a pact of friendship between Bulgaria and the USSR, and he campaigned in defense of Bulgaria's neutrality. He opposed Bulgaria's accession to the Tripartite Pact. He condemned the passage of the anti-democratic Law for the Protection of the Nation by the National Assembly, and he campaigned in defense of Jews in Bulgaria. In 1940 he initiated an appeal to Prime Minister **Bogdan Filov**, protesting the sanctions against Bulgarian Jews that were being prepared by the government. The appeal was signed by twenty-one Bulgarian writers. He pleaded the cases of Communists and other people accused under the Law for the Protection of the Nation—for example, in the trial of the "parachutists" (Bulgarian Communists dropped onto Bulgarian territory by USSR planes in 1942). From September 1943 he represented the BSDWP in the illegal National Committee of the Fatherland Front.

After the coup of 9 September 1944 Cheshmedzhiev became minister of social policy in the government of **Kimon Georgiev**. From November 1944 he was a member of the BSDWP CC. After crypto-Communists took over the leadership of the party in May 1945, he became head of the party that was independent from them—the BSDWP (united). In July 1945 he asked the leader of the British Socialists and Prime Minister Clement Atlee to support the postponement of elections, and he also insisted that the elections be held under international control. In protest against the policies of the government of the Fatherland Front, which was dominated by Communists, on 17 August 1945 Cheshmedzhiev resigned. He began to edit the newspaper *Svoboden narod*. A month later he died. He authored novels, dramas, and short stories, among them the following: *Sinovete na Balkana* (The sons of the Balkans; 1926); *Moisei: Drama* (1939); *Politicheski spomeni* (Political memoirs; 1988); and *Izbrani sychineniia* (Selected works, 7 vols.; 1938–41); he also edited many newspapers and magazines. He was also one of the founders of the Union of Bulgarian Writers and was a member of its leadership until his death. (JJ)

Sources: *Entsiklopediya Bulgariya*, vol. 7 (Sofia, 1996); J. F. Brown, *Bulgaria under Communist Rule* (New York, 1970); Marshall Lee Miller, *Bulgaria during the Second World War* (Stanford, 1975); *Rechnik na bylgarskata literatura*, vol. 3 (Sofia, 1982); Tasho V. Tashev, *Ministrite na Bylgariia 1879–1999* (Sofia, 1999).

CHINEZU Tit Liviu (22 November 1904, Huduc [now Maioreşti]–15 January 1955, Sighet Marmaţiei), Romanian Greek Catholic bishop, martyr for the faith. Chinezu studied in Reghin, and he graduated from high school in Blaj. In 1925 he went to study at St. Athanasiu College in Rome, where most Romanian Greek Catholic bishops studied. In 1930 he received a Ph.D. in theology and philosophy, and he was ordained. In 1931 he returned to Blaj, where he taught at a high school for boys. In 1937–46 he lectured at the Blaj Theological Academy. In 1947 he was sent to Bucharest, where he became a parish priest. On 28 October 1947, along with most of the Romanian Greek Catholic clergy, he was arrested by the Communist authorities. He was placed in the Neamţ Monastery along with twenty-five priests. In 1949 he was moved to the Căldăruşani Monastery, converted into a prison, where all the Romanian bishops were held. On 3 December 1949 Bishop **Valeriu Traian Frenţiu** secretly consecrated him there as the bishop of Bucharest. The Communist security service found out about it, and he was falsely accused of collaborating with the anti-Communist guerrillas operating in the Transylvanian mountains. On 24 May 1950, along with other bishops, he was transferred to Sighet Prison in Marmureş. He was held there in extremely harsh conditions. In January 1955 he fell ill. Put in an unheated cell without windowpanes, in two days he died. He was buried secretly at night in an unmarked grave in Săracilor Cemetery. He was never formally tried or sentenced. His beatification case is under way. (LW)

Sources: Józef Darski, *Rumunia: Historia, współczesność, konflikty narodowe* (Warsaw, 1995); Paul Caravia, Virgiliu Constantinescu, and Flori Stănescu, *The Imprisoned Church of Romania, 1944–1989* (Bucharest, 1999); Dennis Deletant, *Communist Terror in Romania* (New York, 1999); www.bru.ro.

CHIŞINEVSCHI Iosif [originally Ion Roitman] (1905, Bălţi–23 September 1964, Bucharest), Romanian Communist activist. Born into a Jewish family from Bessarabia, Chişinevschi graduated from primary school. In 1928 he joined the Communist Party of Romania (CPR), which advocated the secession of Bessarabia from Romania. Imprisoned in Doftana in 1928–30, after his release he went to the USSR, where in 1931, thanks to the support of **Béla Kun** and **Dmytro Manuilskyi**, he became a member of the CPR Central Committee (CC). From 1931 he also worked for the NKVD and was considered one of the highest-ranking Soviet Romanian agents. In 1931–33 he studied in the Leninist School in Moscow, also improving his knowledge of the Romanian language. Transferred to Romania in 1933, he reorganized the CPR Propaganda Bureau. From 1933 to 1936 he was imprisoned in Doftana again. Between 1936 and 1940 he was a member of the CPR CC Secretariat and head of the Bucharest committee of the party. In 1941–44 he was imprisoned in Caransebeş and in the Tîrgu Jiu camp, with, among others, **Gheorghe Gheorghiu-Dej** and **Teohari Georgescu**. In this way he became a member of the new "prison" leadership of the CPR. Released after the coup of 23 August 1944, from September 1944 he was also a member of the CPR CC Politburo.

As head of the Communist propaganda apparatus, in 1944–57 Chişinevschi directed the Stalinization of Romanian culture and supervised the mass media. From 1952 he was also head of the Department of Foreign Relations of the CC of the Romanian Workers' Party. He took part in the founding conference of the Information Bureau of Communist and Workers' Parties (Cominform) in Szklarska Poręba in September 1947. He was so trusted by the Soviets that he took part in the meetings of the Soviet delegation. He co-organized the propaganda campaign against **Josip Broz Tito** and supervised the operations of the political police, Securitate. In May 1951, along with Gheorhiu-Dej and **Miron Constantinescu**, he discussed the elimination of the group of **Ana Pauker**, **Vasile Luca**, and Georgescu in Moscow, and then he implemented this purge along with Soviet advisers in 1952. He also had a key part in the staging of the trial of **Lucreţiu Patraşcanu** in 1954. After the Twentieth Congress of the Soviet party in February 1956, in which he participated as a member of the Romanian delegation, Chişinevschi tried to make use of the new trend. At a Politburo meeting in early April 1956 he, along with Constantinescu, attacked Gheorghiu-Dej for resisting de-Stalinization. Gheorghiu-Dej's counterattack resulted in the purge of both from the party leadership on 3 July 1957. By 1961 Chişinevschi had lost all his party positions. From 1962 he worked as director of the Scânteia Press. After **Nicolae Ceauşescu** took over power in 1965, Chişinevschi was posthumously rehabilitated. (FA/TD/WR)

Sources: Ghita Ionescu, *Communism in Rumania 1944–1962* (Oxford, 1964); Vladimir Tismăneanu, *Arheologia terrori* (Bucharest, 1992); Lavinia Betea, *Maurer şi lumea de ieri: Mărturii despre stalinizarea României* (Arad, 1995); Stelian Tănase, *Elite şi societate în timpul lui Gheorghiu Dej* (Bucharest, 1999); Denis Deletant, *Communist Terror in Romania: Gheorghiu-Dej and the Police State, 1948–1965* (New York, 1999); Robert Levy, *Ana Pauker: The Rise and Fall of a Jewish Communist* (Berkeley, 2000).

CHMIELOWSKI Albert [original name Adam] (20 August 1846, Igołomia, near Kraków–25 December 1916, Kraków), Polish painter and monk, saint of the Roman Catholic Church. After graduating from high school, Chmielowski started studies at the Agricultural Institute in Puławy, from where he joined the anti-Russian January Uprising of 1863. He fought in the Stanisław Frankowski unit, was wounded, and lost a leg. In 1865–66 he studied drawing at the Wojciech Gerson School in Warsaw and then painting in Paris and Munich (1869–74). He made friends with the painter Maksymilian Gierymski, **Henryk Sienkiewicz**, and the actress Helena Modrzejewska (Modjeska). He painted poetic, religious, and symbolic compositions, as well as portraits. His pictures *Death of a Suicide*, *A Dream*, and *Ecce Homo* in particular won him wide recognition. Giving up a promising artistic career, in September 1880 Chmielowski entered the novitiate of the Jesuit Order in Stara Wieś. Because of disease and a mental crisis, in April 1881 he gave up the idea of entering the order. After he recovered, in 1884 he came to Kraków, where he continued painting and cared for homeless beggars. After long hesitation, in 1888 he took vows and the monastic name of Albert. He established a tertiary congregation of Albertine brothers and in 1890 of Albertine sisters. For the next twenty-eight years he worked in the congregation in Galicia, personally involved in nursing the sick and poor in (among other places) a "nestling home" (*przytulisko*) in the Kraków quarter of Kazimierz, where he died. He was particularly remembered in the Kraków church. He became the hero of a drama by Bishop Karol Wojtyła (later Pope **John Paul II**), *Brat naszego Boga* (Brother of our God). He was canonized by John Paul II in 1989. (WR)

Sources: *PSB*, vol. 3; Czesław Lewandowski, C.M., *Brat Albert* (Kraków, 1927); Ks. Andrzej Szeptycki, *Ze wspomnień o bracie Albercie* (Kraków, 1934); Maria Morstin-Górska, "Adam Chmielowski, brat Albert: Szkic życiorysu," *Verbum*, 1936; Konstanty Michalski, *Brat Albert: Życie i dzieło* (Warsaw, 1978); Alicja Okońska, *Adam Chmielowski: Brat Albert* (Warsaw, 1999).

CHŇOUPEK Bohuslav (10 August 1925, Bratislava-Petržalka–28 May 2004, Prague), Slovak journalist and Communist politician. Chňoupek graduated in economics in Bratislava in 1950, and then he worked as a Communist Party journalist, first on the daily *Smena* and from 1958 on the Bratislava daily *Pravda*, whose Moscow correspondent he was from 1960 to 1965. In 1965–67 he was editor-in-chief of the periodical *Predvoj*, and in 1967–68 he was deputy minister of culture and information. He published collections of his reporting, written in the spirit of Socialist realism. He made his literary debut in 1957 with *Dunaj sa končí pri Izmaile* (The Danube ends at Izmail). Then he published *Komunismus sa začína už dnes* (Communism begins today; 1962); *Generál s levom* (General with a lion; 1974); and *Mil'niky* (Milestones; 1975). In late 1968 he began to advance rapidly in the party and state structures, in part as a result of his full support for the Warsaw Pact intervention in Czechoslovakia. In 1969 he became a member of the Central Committee (CC) of the Communist Party of Czechoslovakia (CPC), and he was head of central radio broadcasting for a year. In 1970–71 he was ambassador to the USSR, and after his return he was made minister of foreign affairs. He was one of the leaders of the CPC "normalization" policy. In the late 1980s, however, he became an adherent of the Soviet perestroika and its application in Czechoslovakia. Because of his too open support for perestroika, he was dismissed in October 1988. After the Velvet Revolution he retired from political life, and in March 1990 he was excluded from the CPC. Later he published a monograph on Andy Warhol (*Andy*; 1993) and memoirs, *Memoáre in claris* (Memoirs Claris; 1998). (PU)

Sources: *ČBS*; *Československtí politici: 1918–1991* (Prague, 1991); *Who's Who in the Socialist Countries of Europe*, vol. 1 (Munich, London, and Paris, 1989).

CHOJECKI Mirosław (1 September 1949, Warsaw), Polish dissident and editor. Born into a family with a patriotic tradition—his mother was a Home Army soldier—from 1967 Chojecki studied at the Warsaw Polytechnic and in 1968–73, at Warsaw University. In 1974–76 and 1980–81 he worked at the Institute of Nuclear Research in Warsaw. Engaged in opposition activities, in 1968 he took an active part in the student strike at the Warsaw Polytechnic, and in 1975 he gathered signatures for a petition against the amendment of the constitution that stipulated the "leading role" of the Communist Party and the "alliance" with the USSR. After the June 1976 riots he was involved in organizing help for the repressed workers of Ursus and Radom, and then he became a founding member of the Committee for the Defense of Workers (Komitet Obrony Robotników [KOR]). Several times beaten by the police, Chojecki took an active part in the development of underground publishing, mimeographing several publications, including *Komunikat* and *Biuletyn Informacyjny KOR*. In 1977, after the demonstrations connected with the murder of Stanisław Pyjas, a student cooperating with the KOR, Chojecki was imprisoned for a few months. In 1977–80 he was head of the independent printing house NOWa, the largest secret press in Poland and in the Soviet bloc. Kept under police surveillance and arrested dozens of times for forty-eight hours, in June 1980 he was falsely accused and sentenced to a year and a half with suspended execution. During the summer 1980 strike in the Gdańsk shipyard Chojecki co-organized independent printing. He became an adviser to Solidarity's Mazowsze region, where he

dealt with publications. In 1981–90 he was abroad, as of 1982 in Paris, where he published the monthly *Kontakt* and directed a film-making company, Video-Kontakt. From 1991 he was head and owner of the film-making group Kontakt. His attempts to establish Independent Polish Television (Niezależna Telewizja Polska) and New Warsaw Television (Nowa Telewizja Warszawa) were in vain. In 1999–2000 Chojecki was adviser to the minister of culture and national heritage. (PK)

Sources: Andrzej Friszke, *Opozycja polityczna w PRL 1945–1980* (London, 1994); *Opozycja w PRL: Słownik Biograficzny 1956–1989*, vol. 1 (Warsaw, 2000).

CHORNOVIL Viacheslav (1 January 1938, district of Kiev–26 March 1999, Kiev), Ukrainian dissident and politician. Chornovil belonged to the so-called *shestidesiatniki*, the main group in which ideas of opposition to communism originated between 1960 and 1990 in the Ukraine. A member of the Komsomol, he worked at many Komsomol construction sites. After graduating from the university in Kiev, he started working in Kiev radio and television. He was sent to a trial of cultural activists that was held in 1966 in Lviv, and he began to protest the sentences that were pronounced. On 22 May 1966 he wrote a protest letter to the Central Committee of the Communist Party of the USSR. He refused to testify as a witness at a secret trial of opposition activists. After he lost his job as a journalist, he started working in the Lviv branch of the League for the Preservation of Nature. On 3 August 1967 he was arrested for the preparation and publication of *Lykho z rozumu* (Woe to the clever), a documentary on the persecutions in the Ukraine, and on 15 November he was sentenced to three years of prison. After his release he did not stop his opposition activities, co-editing *Ukrains'kyi Visnyk*. After the arrest of **Nina Strokata-Karavanska** he joined a civic committee for her defense. He was arrested again in 1972 and was sentenced to six years of labor camp and three years of exile. In the labor camp he initiated a struggle for the introduction of the status of political prisoner. In 1979, while in exile, he acceded to the Ukrainian Helsinki Group (UHG), which was demanding a respect for human rights in the USSR.

On the wave of glasnost in the summer of 1987 Chornovil again began to publish *Ukraiins'kyi Visnyk*. He was also active in the reactivated UHG, which was soon transformed into the Ukrainian Helsinki Union. In November 1987 he wrote an open letter to Mikhail Gorbachev in which, appealing to "Leninist principles," he called for a verification of the national policy that was implemented in the USSR. He was active in the Ukrainian Popular Movement (Rukh). At the Rukh congress in 1989 he was one of the first to speak in support of independence and sovereignty for the Ukraine. In 1990 he became president of the Lviv City Council. Thanks to him, agrarian reform and freedom of speech were introduced. In March 1990 he became a deputy to the Supreme Council of the USSR. In 1991 he spoke in support of the independence of the Ukraine. He ran in the first presidential elections in the Ukraine (1 December 1991), winning 7.4 million votes (23.3 percent) and was runner-up to **Leonid Kravchuk**. After the elections he advocated that Rukh remain in opposition to President Kravchuk. In December 1992 he became the president of Rukh and led it to transform into a political party. He was elected deputy to the Ukrainian parliament in the elections of 1994 and 1998. Under his leadership Rukh became the most powerful party of the opposition, but its political influence gradually declined. At the turn of 1998/99 a conflict broke out between Chornovil and a group of Rukh activists under the leadership of Yuri Kostenko. The conflict was about tactics for the presidential election in 1999. The party split into two branches: Chornovil's faction and Kostenko's faction. Chornovil was killed in a car crash in the suburbs of Kiev, and the circumstances of the accident are the subject of much speculation. (GM)

Sources: Volodymyr Baran, *Ukraiina 1950–1960-kh rr: Evoliutsiia totalitarnoi systemy* (Lviv, 1996); Jaroslaw Hrycak, *Historia Ukrainy 1772–1999* (Lublin, 2000); Gorgii Kasianov, *Nezhodni: Ukrains'ka intelihentsiia v rusi oporu 1960–1980-kh rokiv* (Kiev, 1995); *Istoriia Ukraiiny* (Lviv, 1998).

CHRUŚCIEL Antoni, pseudonym "Monter" (16 June 1895, Gniewczyna Łańcucka. near Przeworsk–30 November 1960, Washington, D.C.), Polish general. From 1909 Chruściel was active in scouting, and after graduating from high school, in September 1914 he was recruited into the Austro-Hungarian Army. He graduated from a noncommissioned officers' school and, in 1915, from a school for reserve officers. From December 1918 he served in the Polish Army. He took part in the fighting on the Polish-Ukrainian front and during the Polish-Soviet war. Afterward he studied law at the University of Lwów (Lviv). In 1929–31 he studied at the Higher Academy of War, and then he was a lecturer there. In April 1932 he became head of the military training course at the Center of Infantry Training in Rembertów, and in 1934–36 he headed a course in the Higher Academy of War. In January 1937 he was appointed deputy commander of an infantry regiment in Lwów, and from March 1938 he commanded a rifle regiment in Brześć (Brest). During the Polish-German campaign of September 1939 he fought in the Piotrków Operation Group within the "Łódź" Army.

After the capitulation of the Modlin fortress he was taken prisoner of war.

At the end of October 1939 Chruściel escaped from a POW camp in Działdowo and returned to Warsaw, where from March 1940 he participated in the clandestine activities of the Union for Armed Struggle (as of 1942, the Home Army—Armia Krajowa [AK]); he was head of its Third Department of Tactics and Training. In October 1940 he became chief of staff and deputy commander and in May 1941 commander of the Warsaw city district. In 1942 he was promoted to the rank of colonel. On the orders of General **Stefan Rowecki**, the AK commander-in-chief, at the end of 1942 Chruściel made contact with Jewish fighters in the Warsaw Ghetto. He was co-responsible for the decision to start the Warsaw Uprising on 1 August 1944. During the fighting, on 14 September, he was appointed brigadier general and on 20 September, commander of the Warsaw AK corps. In view of the illness of General **Tadeusz Komorowski**, he was the de facto commander of the uprising. After its fall he was taken prisoner of war and deported to Germany. After the liberation by the American troops, in 1945 Chruściel went to London, where from July to September 1945 he was second deputy chief of staff of the Polish Armed Forces (Polskie Siły Zbrojne [PSZ]) in the West; then until November 1947 he was deputy chief of staff and chief of the Main PSZ Liquidation Commission. After demobilization Chruściel was active in war veteran organizations. In 1955–56 he planned to return to Poland, but he could not, since the Communist authorities had deprived him of Polish citizenship in 1946. He settled in Washington, D.C., where he died. He was buried in the Polish cemetery in Doylestown, Pennsylvania. He authored *Powstanie Warszawskie* (The Warsaw Uprising; 1948). (JS)

Sources: Kunert, vol. 1; Zbigniew Mierzwiński, *Generałowie II Rzeczypospolitej* (Warsaw, 1990); Tadeusz Kryska-Karski and Stanisław Żurakowski, *Generałowie Polski Niepodległej* (London, 1976); Henryk Piotr Kosk, *Generalicja polska: Popularny słownik biograficzny*, vol. 1 (Pruszków, 1998); *Koniec polskiego państwa podziemnego* (Łódź, 1987); Marek Łatyński, *Nie paść na kolana: Szkice o opozycji lat czterdziestych* (London, 1985); Marek Ney-Krawicz, *Komendanci Armii Krajowej* (Warsaw, 1992).

CHRZANOWSKI Wiesław (20 December 1923, Warsaw), Polish lawyer and politician. During the German occupation, from 1940 Chrzanowski was active in the Youth of Great Poland and from 1942, in the National Party (Stronnictwo Narodowe). He was a soldier of the National Military Organization and of the Home Army (Armia Krajowa), and he fought in the Warsaw Uprising of 1944. He studied at the secret School of Law of Warsaw University and graduated from the Jagiellonian

University in Kraków in 1945. In 1945–46 he belonged to the (Christian Democratic) Labor Party (Stronnictwo Pracy), and from 1945 he worked as an assistant professor at Warsaw University and at the Warsaw School of Economics (Szkoła Główna Handlowa). In 1946 he became chairman of the Odnowa (Revival) Christian Youth Union. In 1947–48 he edited the weekly *Tygodnik Warszawski*. Arrested by the Communist authorities in 1948, he was sentenced to eight years in prison. Released in 1954, in 1956 he was rehabilitated. In 1957 he co-founded Start, the Young Intelligentsia Club, which was not registered by the authorities. From 1957 to 1960 he completed the requisites to become a lawyer but was denied bar registration. From 1960 he was a legal adviser to the Warsaw consumer cooperative Mokotów, and from 1972 he worked in the Cooperative Research Institute. After receiving his postdoctoral degree, from 1980 to 1988 he was associate professor and from 1988 full professor. From 1982 he lectured at the Catholic University of Lublin, where he also held the chair of civil law, and in 1987–90 he was deputy dean of the Department of Canon and Lay Law.

In 1965–81 Chrzanowski belonged to an informal group of advisers to the Primate of Poland, and in the second half of the 1970s he was active in the democratic opposition, mostly with the Young Poland Movement (Ruch Młodej Polski). A member of Solidarity from 1980 and the union's plenipotentiary in the registration procedures before the Provincial and Supreme Courts, he was adviser to the National Commission of Solidarity. In 1981 he became deputy chairman of the Program Board of the Center for Social and Professional Work of the Solidarity National Commission. From 1981 to 1984 he was a member of the Social Board of the Primate of Poland and his representative in the negotiations with the authorities on the establishment of the Church Agricultural Foundation. In 1982 he co-authored *Tezy Prymasowskiej Rady Społecznej w sprawie ugody społecznej* (Theses of the Social Board of the Primate of Poland on the social agreement). He cooperated with the Catholic press. In December 1988 he refused to join the Civic Committee of the chairman of Solidarity, **Lech Wałęsa**. He joined it in 1990, after its leadership changed, and in October 1990 he became its treasurer and member of the Presidium. In October 1989 he was co-founder and became chairman of the Main Board of the Christian National Union (Zjednoczenie Chrześcijańsko-Narodowe [ZChN]). From January to November 1991 Chrzanowski was minister of justice and prosecutor general in the government of **Jan Krzysztof Bielecki**. In 1991–93 he was MP and speaker of the Lower House (Sejm). From 1994 he was chairman of the ZChN Supreme Council. He authored many books and articles, mostly abroad and in the uncensored press, such as *Rzecz o obronie czynnej* (On active defense; 1977) and *Więźniowie polityczni w Polsce w latach 1945–56* (Political prisoners in Poland, 1945–56; 1983), as well as several works in law. In 1997 he published an extensive interview book *Pół wieku polityki, czyli rzecz o obronie czynnej* (Half a century of politics, or on active defense). (AF)

Sources: *Kto jest kim w Polsce* (Warsaw, 2001); *Opozycja w PRL: Słownik biograficzny 1956–89,* vol. 1 (Warsaw, 2000); Antoni Dudek, *Pierwsze lata III Rzeczypospolitej 1989–2001* (Kraków, 2002).

CHUBAR Vlas (22 February 1891, Fedorivka, Yekaterynoslav district–26 February 1939, Kiev?), Ukrainian Communist activist. In 1911 Chubar graduated from a technical high school. He took part in the 1905 revolution, and in 1907 he joined the Russian Social Democratic Workers' Party. He worked in factories in Kramatorsk, Maryupol, Kharkiv, Petrograd, and Moscow. During the Bolshevik Revolution in 1917 he was commissar of the revolutionary committee (*revkom*) of the Chief Command of Artillery in Petrograd. In 1918–19 he chaired the management of engineering factories and was a member of the Supreme Council of the National Economy. From December 1919 he was active in the Ukraine, organizing reconstruction of local industry. At the end of 1920 he became chairman of the Ukrainian Supreme Council of the National Economy (Wyshcha Rada Narodonoho Hospodarstva), and from December 1921 he presided over the Chief Administration of the Coal Industry of the Donbas Region. After the dismissal of **Khristyan Rakovski** in July 1923, Chubar became chairman of the Council of People's Commissars of the Ukrainian SSR. He proclaimed himself to be against spokesmen of Ukrainian "national communism," such as **Oleksandr Shumskiy**, **Mykola Khvylovyi**, and **Mykola Skrypnyk**. Chubar introduced the Stalinist line of accelerated industrialization, but he resisted an accelerated collectivization of agriculture and the imposition of overly high grain quotas on the Ukrainian republic. As a result, in 1934 he was dismissed and appointed deputy chairman of the Council of People's Commissars of the Soviet Union. He was the first Ukrainian included in the Politburo of the Central Committee of the All-Russian Communist Party (Bolsheviks). In 1937 he became minister of finance but later in the same year was arrested, and two years later he was shot without a trial. (BB)

Sources: *Encyclopedia of Ukraine*, vol. 1 (Toronto, 1984); *Dovidnyk z Istoriyi Ukraiiny* (Kiev, 2001); *Malyi Slovnyk Istoriyi Ukrajiny* (Kiev, 1997); Hryhory Kostiuk, *Stalinist Rule in the Ukraine* (New York, 1960); Trokhim M. Kolyak, *Vlas Yakovlevich Chubar: Zhizn i dyeyatelnost* (Kiev, 1981).

CHVALKOVSKÝ František (30 July 1885, Jílové, near Prague–25 February 1945, Berlin), Czech politician and diplomat. Chvalkovský studied law at the Czech university in Prague (1903–8) and then in Berlin and London. In 1911–13 he was director of the legal department at the Kraków branch of the Živnostenska Banka. He later worked as a lawyer. From 1918 to 1920 he was personal secretary to the interior minister, **Antonín Švehla**, and until 1921 he served as head of the political department in the Ministry of Foreign Affairs. He took part in the peace negotiations with the Hungarians in Trianon. In 1921 he became ambassador to Japan and later to the United States. Between 1925 and 1927 he was the Agrarian Party deputy to the National Assembly. He resigned his seat after he was appointed ambassador to Germany. He stayed at the diplomatic mission in Germany for five years, and then he served as ambassador to Italy until 1938.

In post-Munich Czecho-Slovakia, Chvalkovský assumed the post of minister of foreign affairs and was an advocate of cooperation with Germany and Italy. He participated in the so-called Vienna Award of 2 November 1938, by which the foreign ministers of Germany and Italy granted a part of the Slovak lands and a part of Subcarpathian Ruthenia to Hungary. He hoped for a compromise with Germany. He considered the reports that warned about Hitler's plans against Czechoslovakia, supplied by František Moravec, the head of special services, as "figments of the imagination." His hopes of maintaining good relations with Germany fell apart when, on 21 January 1939, during his talks with Ribbentrop and Hitler, he heard a series of accusations against Czechoslovakia and demands placed on it. However, in an attempt to maintain the existence of his country, on 22 February 1939 he sent a letter asking for a guarantee that the borders of post-Munich Czecho-Slovakia would remain. This guarantee would be an implementation of the Munich agreement. However, as a result of Hitler's objections, Chvalkovský's attempts were in vain. On the night of 14–15 March 1939, along with President **Emil Hácha**, Chvalkovský participated in the negotiations with Hitler and Ribbentropp in Berlin, where, under brutal pressure, both he and Hácha signed the act that "put the fate of the Czech nation and the Czech people into the hands of the Führer of the German Reich." Chvalkovský informed Prime Minister **Rudolf Beran** by phone about the German plans to march into the territory of the republic, insisting that the Czecho-Slovak troops offer no resistance. During World War II Chvalkovský represented the Protectorate of Bohemia and Moravia in Berlin. He was killed during the American air raid of Berlin. (PU)

Sources: *ČBS*; *The International Who's Who* (London, 1935); Vojtech Masny, *The Czechs under Nazi Rule* (New York and London, 1971); *Českoslovenští politici: 1918–1991* (Prague, 1991); *Politická elita meziválečného Československa 1918–1938: Kdo byl kdo za první republiky* (Prague, 1998); *Kdo byl kdo v našich dějinách ve 20. století*, vol. 1 (Prague, 1998).

CHYHIR Mikhail (24 May 1948, Usovo, near Kopylsk), Belorussian politician. In 1970 Chyhir graduated from the Belorussian State Institute of National Economy and in 1982 from the Moscow Financial Institute. In 1982–86 he was director of the Minsk branch of the National Bank of the USSR, and between 1988 and 1994 he held various managerial positions in Belorussian republican banks. For instance, he was chairman of Belagroprombank. On 21 July 1994 he was asked by the newly elected president, **Alyaksandr Lukashenka**, to become prime minister. At the end of 1994 Chyhir was accused by MP **Sergey Antonchyk** of corruption, but he continued as head of government until 18 November 1996, when he resigned in protest against a referendum that was aimed at strengthening the position of President Lukashenka. In 1998–99 Chyhir was managing director of the European CEA concern in Moscow. He ran as a candidate for president in the May 1999 elections announced by the Supreme Council, which was no longer recognized by Lukashenka. During the campaign, at the end of March 1999, he was arrested and accused of embezzlement during his term as prime minister, and on 19 May 2002 he was sentenced to three years in prison. In 2001 he tried to run for president, but he lacked the one hundred thousand signatures required by electoral law. (EM)

Sources: Jan Zaprudnik, *Historical Dictionary of Belarus* (Lanham, Md., 1998); Siergiej Owsiannik and Jelena Striełkowa, *Władza i społeczeństwo: Białoruś 1991–1998* (Warsaw, 1998).

CHYKALENKO Yevhen (9 December 1861, Pereshory, Kherson Province–20 June 1929, Prague), Ukrainian social worker and politician. Born into a rich landowner's family, during his studies in natural science at Kharkiv University Chykalenko belonged to the radical followers of Mykhailo Drahomanov. In 1884 he was arrested and spent the next five years under police surveillance on the family estate in Pereshory. Management of the estate gave him broad agricultural experience. It was then that he wrote a five-volume handbook in agronomy, *Rozmovy pro selske khozyaystvo* (Discourse on agrarian economy; 1897). From 1900 he lived in Kiev, where he financially supported Ukrainian cultural initiatives. He was probably the richest Ukrainophile in the Russian Ukraine before World War I. He sponsored the publication of a Russian-Ukrainian dictionary (1893–98) and an award for the best history of Ukraine, and he offered pay to writers publishing in the periodical *Kiyevskaya starina*. He also supported the aid fund for writers of the Taras Shevchenko Scholarly Society and a dormitory for Ukrainian students studying in Lemberg (Lviv, Lwów). Although he was not a man of the left, he also helped the radical Lviv periodical *Selnanyn*. He took part in various Ukrainian political initiatives—for instance, the so-called Old Hromada (from 1900) and the Ukrainian Democratic Radical Party (from 1905). He was de facto president of the Association of Ukrainian Progressives (Tovarystvo Ukraiinskych Postupovtsiv). He was the first publisher of Ukrainian dailies in the Russian part of the Ukraine—*Hromadskyi Holos* (1906) and *Rada* (1906–14). For fear of arrest, during World War I he stayed in Finland, Petrograd, and Moscow, far from the front lines. When he came to East Galicia in January 1919, he was interned by the Polish authorities. From 1920 he lived in Rabenstein, Austria. He belonged to the founders and lecturers of the Ukrainian Economic Academy in Podiebrady, Czechoslovakia. He published his memoirs, *Spohady* (Memoirs, 3 vols.; 1925–26), and *Szczodennyk 1907–1917* (Diary 1907–1917; 1931). His daughter, Hanna Chykalenko-Keller, and son, Levko Chykalenko, were active participants in the Ukrainian revolution in 1917–20 and then organizers of the Ukrainian émigré community in Germany. (TS)

Sources: *Encyclopedia of Ukraine*, vol. 1 (Toronto, 1985); Dmytro Doroshenko, *Yevhen Chykalenko: Yoho zhyttia i hromadska diyalnist* (Prague, 1934).

CHYTILOVÁ Věra (2 February 1929, Ostrava), Czech film director. In the late 1940s Chytilová studied architecture for two years, and then she worked as a draftswoman and laboratory assistant in, among other places, the Barrandov film studios. In 1962 she graduated from the Film and TV Department of the Academy of Musical Arts in Prague. During her studies she had already attracted attention with her medium-feature films *Zelená ulice* (Green Street; 1960) and *Strop* (Ceiling; 1961). In the 1960s she was one of the main representatives of the Czechoslovak "new wave" of filmmakers who rejected Socialist realism and sought new means of expression. She made her feature film debut with *O něčem jiném* (On something else; 1963), a semi-documentary on two entirely different contemporary women; in it she introduced a feminine perception of the world into Czechoslovak filmmaking. In her movie *Sedmikrásky* (Daisies; 1966), which brought her international renown, she showed, in a grotesque way, two girl heroines living empty and artificial lives. In the 1970s and 1980s she made satirical films presenting society and

politics in the period of "normalization." As an artist of the "new wave" she faced serious problems in realizing these projects. Her best movies of this period include the following: *Ovoce stromů rajských jime* (Fruit of paradise; 1970); *Panelstory* (1979); *Kalamita* (Calamity; 1981); *Faunovo velmi pozdní odpoledne* (Very late afternoon of a faun; 1983); and *Kopytem sem, kopytem tam* (With a hoof here, with a hoof there; 1988). After the fall of communism Chytilová directed *Dědictví aneb Kurvahošigutntag* (The inheritance or fuckoffguysgoodbye; 1992) and *Pasti, pasti, pastičky* (Traps, traps, little traps; 1998). She also made outstanding documentaries, such as *Praha, neklidné srdce Evropy* (Prague, the anxious heart of Europe; 1984) and *TGM, Osvoboditel* (Tomaš Garrigue Masaryk, the Liberator; 1990). In 1994–98 she was a member of the Prague City Council. (PU)

Sources: *ČBS*; *Kdo byl kdo v našich dějinach ve 20. století*, vol. 1 (Prague, 1998); Šárka Bartošková and Luboš Bartošek, *Filmové profily* (Prague, 1986); Jerzy Płażewski, *Historia filmu 1895–2000* (Warsaw, 2001); *International Dictionary of Films and Filmmakers*, vol. 2 (Chicago and London, 1991); Geoffrey Nowell-Smith, *The Oxford History of World Cinema* (Oxford, 1996); Jean Loup Passek, ed., *Dictionnaire du cinéma* (Paris, 1991); www.hollywood.com/celebs/bio/celeb/1677987.

CHYZHEVSKYI Dmytro (4 April 1894, Oleksandria, near Kherson–18 April 1977, Heidelberg), Ukrainian philosopher and theorist of literature. Born into a poor family of landowners of Cossack descent, in 1911 Chyzhevskyi enrolled at St. Petersburg University, intending to complete mathematical and astronomical studies. Having attended the lectures of the outstanding Russian philosophers Alexandr Vvedensky and Nikolai Lossky, he changed course, and from 1913 to 1919 he continued philosophical and philological studies in Kiev. At that time he was already an avowed Marxist. In 1916 he was arrested for his affiliation with the Social Democratic faction of the Mensheviks, but thanks to the February 1917 revolution, he regained his freedom. In 1917 he was elected to the Ukrainian Central Council (Rada, UCR). On 22 January 1918, at the forum of the UCR, he voted against the independence of the Ukrainian People's Republic. After the failure of the Kiev campaign in 1920 Chyzhevskyi stayed for a short time in Poland. At the beginning of 1921 he became assistant professor in the Philosophy Department at Kiev University. However, in the summer of the same year he left the Ukraine to continue his studies in Germany.

During the next few years Chyzhevskyi attended the lectures of (among others) Karl Jaspers, Martin Heidegger, Edmund Husserl, and Heinrich Rickert.

From 1924 he was a lecturer and then a professor at the Ukrainian Higher Pedagogical Institute; from 1929 he also worked at the Ukrainian Free University in Prague, and from 1930, at the Ukrainian Scientific Institute in Berlin. From 1932 he lectured on literature and Slavonic languages at the university in Halle, and from 1935 he also gave lectures at the university in Jena. He maintained intensive contacts with Russian émigré intellectuals. He opposed the Nazi government. He spent the war in Halle, not allowed to leave the town. In 1945 he started to teach courses in Slavic philosophy in Marburg. However, in 1949 he went to the United States at the invitation of Harvard University. Disappointed with the possibilities for further scholarly development overseas, he returned to Germany in 1956 and became chair of Slavic studies at the University of Heidelberg. There he directed the Slavic Institute, one of the major centers for Slavic studies research in Western Europe. He continued his work in the institutions of the Ukrainian diaspora: the Ukrainian Free University in Munich (1945–49, 1956–63) and the Orthodox pedagogical academy (1945–49). He also organized a Ukrainian free academy of sciences in Augsburg. He was a full member of the Heidelberg Academy of Sciences and the Croatian Academy of Sciences in Zagreb, and he belonged to the Hegelian society and the Kantian society.

Chyzhevskyi's publications include over nine hundred items in the history of literature, literary criticism, philology, philosophy, and esthetics. His particular research interests were Ukrainian philosophy and literature (especially of the Middle Ages and the Baroque), literature, and the comparative intellectual history of the Slavs. He derived the specificity of Ukrainian philosophy from Ukrainian emotionality, sentimentality, and lyricism; a tendency toward spiritual solitude; harmony between the external and internal worlds; a desire for order and peace; and tolerance in the sphere of ethics. Chyzhevskyi was discoverer of many of the manuscripts of Jan Ámos Komenský. He left the following works (among others): *Logika* (Logic; 1924); *Filosofiia na Ukraiini* (Philosophy in the Ukraine; 1926); *Narysy z istorii filosofii na Ukraiini* (An outline of the history of Ukrainian philosophy; 1931); *Ukraiins'kyi literaturnyi barok* (The Baroque in Ukrainian literature, 3 vols.; 1941–44); *Istoria ukraiins'koi literatury: Vid pochatkiv do doby realizmu* (History of Ukrainian literature: From the beginning to the end of realism; 1956); *History of Russian Literature from the Eleventh Century to the End of the Baroque* (1960); *Comparative History of Slavic Literatures* (1971); *Skoworoda: Dichter, Denker, Mystiker* (Skorowoda: Poet, thinker, and mystic; 1974); and *A History of Ukrainian Literature* (1975). (TS)

Sources: *Encyclopedia of Ukraine,* vol. 1 (Toronto, 1984); I. V. Ohorodnyk and V. V. Ohorodnyk, *Istoriia filosofs'koii dumky v Ukraiini* (Kiev, 1999).

ČIČ Milan (2 January 1932, Zákamenné, Dolný Kubín district), Slovak post-Communist lawyer and politician. In 1961 Čič graduated in law from the university in Bratislava, and then he worked there as assistant professor in 1961–64 and 1967–72, as associate professor in 1972–79, and later as full professor. From 1977 to 1987 he was chair of criminal law. From 1987 he was a member of the Slovak Academy of Sciences and director of its Institute of State and Law. In 1989–92 he worked in the Czechoslovak Academy of Sciences, dealing with criminal law and criminology. He published, among other things, *Československé trestné právo ako súčast' trestnej politiky* (Czechoslovak criminal law as a part of penal policy; 1976); *Teoretické otázky československého trestného práva* (Theoretical problems of Czechoslovak criminal law; 1982); and academic textbooks. In 1961–90 he belonged to the Communist Party of Czechoslovakia. From 1964 he worked in the Slovak Secretariat of Justice, and after the federalization and formation of the Slovak government, he was deputy minister of justice (1969–70) and minister of justice (1988–89) of the Slovak Socialist Republic.

After the Velvet Revolution, in December 1989 Čič became prime minister of the Slovak government and deputy prime minister of the Czechoslovak government. He held these positions until the first free parliamentary elections of June 1990, in which he ran on behalf of the movement Public against Violence (Verejnost' proti Nasiliu [VPN]) and won a seat in the Chamber of the People of the Federal Assembly. After the VPN split in the spring of 1991, he joined the (Populist) Movement for a Democratic Slovakia (Hnutie za demokratické Slovensko [HZDS]) of **Vladimir Mečiar**. With the elections of 1992 Čič was a deputy in the Chamber of Nations, deputy prime minister, and minister-chairman of the Federal Office for Competition in the government that was to dissolve the Czechoslovak federation. After the formation of sovereign Slovakia in January 1993, he formally left the HZDS, and in March 1993 he became chairman of the Slovak Constitutional Tribunal. From 2000 he was deputy chairman of the small Party of the Democratic Center (Strana Demokratického Středu). In December 2001 he ran for head of Bratislava Province in the first Slovak local elections, but he lost. (PU)

Sources: *ČBS*; *Kdo byl kdo v našich dějinách ve 20. stoleti,* vol. 1 (Prague, 1998); Jan Rychlík, *Rozpad Československa: Česko-slovenské vztahy 1989–1992* (Bratislava, 2002); Eric Stein, *Czecho/Slovakia: Ethnic Conflict, Constitutional Fissure, Negotiated Breakup* (Ann Arbor, 1997); wtd.vlada.cz/scripts/detail.php?id=588.

CIEPLAK Jan (17 August 1857, Dąbrowa Górnicza–17 February 1926, Passaic), Polish Catholic archbishop. The son of a miner, Cieplak attended high school and seminary in Kielce, and then he studied at the Theological Seminary in St. Petersburg (1878–82). Ordained in July 1881, he began to work at this academy, lecturing in biblical archaeology, liturgy, and moral theology. In 1901 he earned a Ph.D. in theology. He contributed to the *Encyklopedia Kościelna* (Church encyclopedia). In 1900 he was appointed honorary canon and then regular canon of the chapter in Kielce. In June 1908 he was consecrated auxiliary bishop of the Mahilyow (Mogilev) diocese, the largest in the world, comprising the majority of Russia's territory. Substituting for Metropolitan Apolinary Wnukowski, who was ill, between April and September 1909 Cieplak made a great visitation to Siberia. He got as far as Sakhalin, baptizing and confirming thousands of people from Catholics communities. In June 1910, on the orders of the new metropolitan, Archbishop Wincenty Kluczyński, Cieplak visited the diocese of Minsk, and in September 1911, that of central Russia. His homilies aroused Catholic spirit and patriotism among Poles. Therefore, as a result of denunciations accusing Cieplak of acting against the Orthodox Church, the Russian government dismissed him from all government-related posts and deprived him of a government-funded salary. The authorities also opposed the appointment of Cieplak to the post of rector of the Theological Academy in St. Petersburg. After the resignation of Archbishop Kluczyński, on 6 August 1914 Cieplak was made apostolic administrator of the Mahilyow archdiocese. When in December 1917 the Pope appointed **Edward Ropp** as archbishop, Cieplak delegated his powers to Ropp.

Under the religious freedom that followed the February 1917 revolution, Cieplak not only provided pastoral and charity services to the faithful, but he also worked for the Liquidation Commission (Komisja Likwidacyjna) for the Congress Kingdom of Poland (Królestwo Polskie), and he published a lot. When the Bolshevik authorities arrested Archbisho Ropp and then forced him to leave for Poland, Cieplak resumed the post of apostolic administrator of the Mahilyow diocese. In April 1919, in recognition of his merits, the Holy See granted him the title of titular archbishop of Achrida. Cieplak was harassed by the Bolsheviks and not allowed to pursue his pastoral duties. He was arrested on Good Thursday 1920 but was soon released. In view of Soviets decrees ordering the nationalization of churches and the confiscation of valuables, as well as cult objects, and forbidding the teaching of religion to children and youth, Cieplak delegated Prelate Konstanty Budkiewicz to Moscow to conduct talks with the authorities. In June 1922 both were arrested, and along with a dozen or so other priests they were tried in an ill-famed Moscow trial on 21–25 March 1923. Cieplak and Budkiewicz were sentenced to death. Owing to the publicity the case received all over the world, Cieplak's sentence was commuted to ten years. However, Cieplak was not informed about it; instead he was taken to Lubyanka, where he expected execution. Budkiewicz was executed by firing squad. Without being informed about anything, Cieplak was transported to the Latvian border and was left there. In April 1924 he left Riga and arrived in Warsaw. Then he went to Rome, where he informed Pope Pius XI about the situation of the church in Russia. In October 1925 Cieplak visited Polish parishes in the United States. In December of that year he learned about his appointment to the post of metropolitan of Vilnius. However, he did not live to assume the post because he died of pneumonia in the United Sates. (WR)

Sources: *PSB*, vol. 4; Francis McCullagh, *Bolshevik Persecution of Christianity* (London, 1924); Franciszek ks. Rutkowski, *Arcybiskup Jan Cieplak* (Warsaw, 1934).

CIMOSZEWICZ Włodzimierz (13 September 1950, Warsaw), Polish post-Communist politician. The son of a Communist intelligence officer, in 1972 Cimoszewicz graduated in law from Warsaw University, where he also received a Ph.D. in international law in 1977 and later worked as assistant professor. During his studies he was active in the Union of Socialist Youth, and in 1973 he became head of the Warsaw University organization of the Association of Polish Students. From 1971 to 1990 he belonged to the Polish United Workers' Party (Polska Zjednoczona Partia Robotnicza [PZPR]). In 1980–81 he worked as a Fulbright scholar in the United States. In view of his independent views, in 1985 he entered into conflict with the authorities of the PZPR Warsaw Provincial Committee and moved to Kalinówka Kościelna, near Białystok, where he ran a farm.

In June 1989 Cimoszewicz was elected to the Lower House (Sejm) on behalf of the PZPR. After its dissolution in January 1990, he presided over the post-Communist Parliamentary Club of the Democratic Left, although he formally stayed out of the Social Democracy of the Polish Republic (Socjaldemokracja Rzeczpospolitej Polskiej [SdRP]). It was only in 1999 that he joined the Democratic Left Alliance (Sojusz Lewicy Demokratycznej [SLD]). In the presidential elections of 1990 he ran as a candidate of the post-Communist camp but gained only 9.2 percent of the vote. After the parliamentary elections of October 1991 he refused to preside over the SLD club in protest against the presence of **Leszek Miller**, who was accused of illegal operations connected with the so-called Moscow loan for the SdRP. In 1992 Cimoszewicz was included in the so-called **Antoni Macierewicz** list as an agent of Communist military intelligence, but he was cleared by the Lustration Court in 2001. As an MP, he accused the Roman Catholic Church of attempts to clericalize Polish politics. He also criticized limitations on the right to abortion. Having gained wide popularity in post-Communist circles, after the elections of September 1993 Cimoszewicz became deputy prime minister and minister of justice. In this capacity he issued a list of politicians who had violated anti-corruption legislation, including some post-Communists. From February 1995 to February 1996 he was deputy speaker of the Sejm. Before the presidential elections of November 1995 he discouraged **Aleksander Kwaśniewski** from running, but in the end he supported Kwaśniewski as head of his electoral staff. After Kwaśniewski won, Cimoszewicz took over the presidency of the constitutional commission of the parliament.

On 7 February 1996 Cimoszewicz became prime minister of the government, based on a coalition of the SLD and the Polish Peasant Party. During his term the coalition suffered from serious tensions. In view of a conflict over agricultural policy, in August 1996 the Peasant Party suggested recalling Cimoszewicz as head of government, but later it withdrew the motion. The Cimoszewicz government introduced a reform of the administration and, as a result of the May 1997 referendum, a new constitution. Cimoszewicz's accusation of neglect, aimed at peasants who had failed to insure their farms, destroyed by a huge flood, was widely publicized and became one of the reasons for the relative failure of the ruling post-Communists in the elections of September 1997 and the resignation of his cabinet in October 1997. Until 2001 Cimoszewicz was an MP on behalf of the SLD, and after the victorious elections of September 2001 he became minister of foreign affairs in the Miller government. Cimoszewicz played an important role in the negotiations on the Polish entry into the European Union and in the elaboration of a strongly pro-American stance after the terrorist attacks of 11 September 2001 and the participation of Polish troops in the war in Iraq in 2003. (AG)

Sources: *Wielka encyklopedia PWN*, vol. 6 (Warsaw, 2002); Janusz A. Majcherek, *Pierwsza dekada III Rzeczpospolitej 1989–1999* (Warsaw, 1999); Antoni Dudek, *Pierwsze lata III Rzeczypospolitej 1989–2001* (Kraków, 2002); Wojciech Roszkowski, *Historia Polski 1914–2001* (Warsaw, 2002); Bugajski; www.msz.gov.pl/, info.onet.pl/1064428,artykul.html, euro.pap.com.pl/cgi-bin/ludzie.pl?ID=154.

CINCAR-MARKOVIĆ Aleksandar (1889, Belgrade–1952), Serbian diplomat. The son of a general and Serbian prime minister, Cincar-Marković graduated from high school in Belgrade, and in 1911 he graduated in law in Freiburg and Berlin. Later he received a Ph.D. in France. From 1918 he worked as a secretary in the Foreign Ministry. As personal secretary to **Nikola Pašić**, he took part in the Paris Peace Conference in 1919. He was also secretary general of the delegation to the Rapallo conference, where the Kingdom of Serbs, Croats, and Slovenes (SHS) signed the peace treaty with Italy in 1920. From June 1921 he was the SHS consul in Zadar (then Italian), and from July 1921, in Trieste. He was the first secretary and then councillor of the legation to Albania (July 1923–May 1925); he headed the Balkan section of the Foreign Ministry (1925–26); then he was chargé d'affaires in Budapest (from June 1926), councillor of the legation in Paris (until the fall of 1926), in Sofia (from May 1927), in Vienna (from August 1928), and again in Paris (from 1930). In 1934–35 he was the SHS legate to Bulgaria and then to Germany (1935–39).

In February 1939 Cincar-Marković became minister of foreign affairs in the government of **Dragiša Cvetković**. On 5 September 1939 Yugoslavia declared neutrality, but Cincar-Marković did not hide his sympathy for Poland and France. Until February 1941 the Cvetković government was reluctant to join the Tripartite Pact, but in view of growing German pressure, it succumbed. Cincar-Marković held talks on this matter. He obtained positive German answers to the questions of whether Yugoslav territorial integrity would be respected, whether Yugoslavia would be free from pressure to allow German or Italian troops to enter it, and whether Yugoslavia could count on support for its claims to the port of Salonika. Despite street demonstrations under the slogan "Better death than the pact," on 25 March 1941 in Vienna Cvetković and Cincar-Marković, in Hitler's presence, signed the Tripartite Pact. The Yugoslav government thought it had saved the country from war, but on the night of 26–27 March it was toppled by a bloodless coup led by **Dušan Simović**. On 6 April Germany attacked Yugoslavia. On 17 April, Cincar-Marković, as a representative of the Yugoslav General Staff, signed an armistice, meaning capitulation. During the war and under Communist rule he remained in Yugoslavia but played no role. (AO)

Sources: Jacob B. Hoptner, *Yugoslavia in Crisis, 1934–1941* (New York, 1962); Dragiša N. Ristić, *Yugoslavia's Revolution of 1941* (Stanford, 1966); Johann Wuescht, *Jugoslawien und das Dritte Reich* (Stuttgart, 1969); Michał J. Zacharias, *Jugosławia w polityce Wielkiej Brytanii 1940–1945* (Wrocław, 1987); www.mfa.gov.yu/history/Ministri/ACincarmarkovic_s.html.

CIOŁKOSZ Adam (5 January 1901, Kraków–1 October 1978, London), Polish Socialist politician, journalist, and historian. From 1911 Ciołkosz was a scout activist; between 1918 and 1920 he was a soldier in the Polish Army, and in 1921 he took part in the Third Silesian Uprising. He graduated in law from the Jagiellonian University and completed the School of Political Sciences in Kraków (1923). In 1921–24 he was an initiator and theoretician of the leftist Free Scouts. From 1921 he belonged to the Polish Socialist Party (Polska Partia Socjalistyczna [PPS]), and in 1928 he was elected to the parliament. In 1930 he was one of the activists of the center-left opposition (Centrolew) who were imprisoned in the fortress of Brześć. In 1933 he was sentenced to three years in prison, of which he served one year. From 1931 he was a member of the Chief Council of the PSP; in 1931–33 and from 1937 he was a member of its Central Executive Committee. From 1936 Ciołkosz was also head of the PPS unit in Lesser Poland (Małopolska). An opponent of collaboration with the Communists, he advocated cooperation with the Socialist parties of the national minorities, especially with the Bund.

After the September defeat of 1939 Ciołkosz fled from occupied Poland to France. He joined the Foreign Committee of the PPS, and until 1945 he belonged to the National Council of the Polish Government-in-Exile. In 1941–42 he was a member of the Committee of Ministers for Home Affairs and maintained radio communication with the leadership of the underground Polish Socialist Party–Freedom, Equality, Independence at home. He cooperated with the leadership of the Labor Party, published on Polish issues in the party's periodicals, and belonged to the committee preparing reconstruction of the Socialist International. Ciołkosz criticized the governments of General **Władysław Sikorski** and **Stanisław Mikołajczyk** for insufficiently clear programs for social change after the war and for too compliant a policy toward the USSR. He was active in publicizing information about Nazi crimes in Poland to the Anglo-Saxon world, including information about the extermination of Jews.

In 1945 Ciołkosz condemned the Yalta decisions and remained in Great Britain. He was one of the main leaders of the PPS in exile and of the Polish émigré community. In 1946–57 he was president of the PPS in Great Britain; from 1946 to 1959 he was editor-in-chief of the monthly *Robotnik Polski*, and in 1957–59 he was president of the Central Council of the PPS. From 1949 he took part in the works of the Socialist International and was a member of the committee preparing its Frankfurt program in 1951. From 1949 he was in the Political Council, one of the three main centers of Polish emigration, and he directed its Department of Foreign Affairs. After the unification action of Polish political émigrés in 1954, at the beginning of 1956 Ciołkosz became the head of the Executive of National Unity (ENU), which served as the government-in-exile. In that capacity he conducted talks in the U.S. Department of State in 1956 and set forth a program for the neutralization of Central Europe. He backed projects of extensive economic assistance for Poland. He firmly defended the inviolability of the border along the Oder and Neisse Rivers. Skeptical toward the prospects of thaw in the Polish People's Republic, he fell into conflict with the majority of the PPS in exile and was removed from the party in 1960. He reconstructed an alternative organization of the PPS, was its head until 1977, and represented it in inter-party bodies of the Polish émigré community. In 1963–66 he was again the president of the ENU.

Ciołkosz was the author of several books, a dozen or so brochures, hundreds of articles, and radio programs broadcast on Radio Free Europe. His work *Zarys dziejów socjalizmu polskiego* (An outline of the history of Polish socialism, 3 vols.), which he wrote with his wife Lidia, has been one of the most important achievements of emigration historiography. His publications were characterized by his attachment to the principles of socialism, in opposition to communism; the recognition of democracy as a condition for Socialist transformation; an emphasis on the traditions of the PPS; opposition to conciliatory tendencies toward the Communist authorities in Poland, as well as toward Soviet imperialism; distrust of the German; and a struggle against nationalism. Ciołkosz was involved in attempts at Polish-Jewish dialogue and cooperated with magazines published by the Bund. He frequently referred to his extensive historical knowledge. (AF)

Sources: *Słownik biograficzny działaczy polskiego ruchu robotniczego*, vol. 1 (Warsaw, 1978); *Posłowie i senatorowie*, vol. 1; D. Urzyńska, *Polski ruch socjalistyczny na obczyźnie w latach 1939–1945* (Poznań, 2000); Andrzej Friszke, Paweł Machcewicz, and Rafał Habielski, *Druga wielka emigracja 1945–1990*, vol. 3 (Warsaw, 1999).

CIORAN Emil (8 April 1911, Rășinari, Transylvania–20 June 1995, Paris), French writer and philosopher of Romanian descent. Cioran was of the opinion that it was best for an intellectual to have no national affiliation. In 1921 he went to high school in Sibiu, and in 1928–32 he studied at the Department of Philosophy and Literature of the University of Bucharest. In 1933 he made his literary debut with *Pe culmile disperarii* (On the heights of despair; 1992), which earned him an award for young writers from the Royal Academy in 1934. In the 1930s he sympathized with the (Fascist) Legion of the Archangel Michael, which later became the Iron Guard. In 1933–35 he worked as a Humboldt Fellow at the University of Berlin. After returning to Romania, in 1936–37 he taught philosophy at a high school in Braşov. In 1937 he was sent by the French Institute in Bucharest to France to continue his doctoral studies. He enrolled in the Sorbonne in Paris, but for the next ten years he traveled throughout France without a clear purpose. In 1940 he was a cultural attaché at the Romanian Embassy in Paris. After World War II and the Communist takeover in Romania, he decided to stay in France for good.

In 1949 Cioran published his first work in French, *Précis de décomposition* (Short history of decay; 1975). As a result, he was proclaimed one of the leading prose writers and thinkers in France. Later he published fifteen books in French in various styles—usually collections of essays, short texts, and aphorisms. His most important works include the following: *Syllogisme de l'amertume* (Syllogism of bitterness; 1952); *La Tentation d'exister* (1956; *Temptation to Exist*, 1968); *Historie et Utopie* (1960; *History and Utopia*, 1987); *La Chute dans le temps* (1964; *Fall into Time*, 1970); *Le Mauvais Demiurg* (The evil demiurge; 1969); and *L'inconvénient d'être né* (1973; *Trouble with Being*, 1976). His "philosophy of despair" resulted from his dissent with Christianity. In masterful style he combined existentialism with atheism. From this point of view he analyzed the problem of evil, human nature, and the lack of sense in history. Many times he refused to accept awards. At the end of his life he ceased to write, arguing that he had always thought creativity a kind of therapy that liberated one from anxiety and emotions. After the fall of the **Nicolae Ceauşescu** regime in Romania (December 1989) Cioran was elected (along with **Eugene Ionesco**) honorary member of the Association of Romanian Writers. His books began to appear in Romania in the 1990s, but he never returned there. (LW)

Sources: *Dictionar Enciclopedic* (Bucharest, 1993); *Wielka encyklopedia PWN*, vol. 6 (Warsaw, 2002); Georgescu Vlad, *Istoria Românilor de la origini pînă în zilele noastre* (Oakland, 1984); Sylvie Jaudeau, *Cioran ou le dernier homme* (Paris, 1990); *The Temptations of Emile Cioran* (New York, 1997); Patrice Bollon, *Cioran, l'hérétique* (Paris, 1997); Simion Ghinea, *Mircea Eliade si Emil Cioran în tinerete* (Bucharest, 1998); Aleksandra Gurzinska, ed., *Essays on E. M. Cioran* (Costa Mesa, Ca., 1999).

CIORBEA Victor (26 October 1954, Ponor), Romanian politician and trade union activist. Ciorbea graduated in law from Cluj University in 1979. In 1979–84 he worked as a judge in Bucharest, specializing in civil cases. From 1981 to 1989 he belonged to the Romanian Communist Party but held no positions in it. In 1984–88 he was civil prosecutor in the General Prosecutor's Office. From 1984 to 1990 he was assistant professor and then lecturer at the School of Law of the University of Bucharest, and he received a Ph.D. in civil and commercial law. After the fall of the **Nicolae Ceauşescu** regime in December 1989 Ciorbea engaged in trade union activities. From 1990 to 1996 he was chairman of the Federation of Free Trade Unions of Teachers, and in 1990–96, chairman of the National Confederation of Free Trade Unions of Romania (Confederaţia Naţionala Sindicatlor Libere din România [CNSLR]), in opposition to the ruling post-Communists. In 1992 he studied management at Case Western Reserve University in Cleveland, Ohio. From 1993 to 1996 he was a member of the Executive Committee of the International Confederation of Free Trade Unions, and in 1990–96 he represented Romanian trade unions in the International Labour Organization.

In 1996 Ciorbea ran for mayor of Bucharest on behalf of the Christian Democratic National Peasant Party (Partidul Naţional Ţărănesc–Creştin Democrat [CDNPP]), a part of the Democratic Convention of Romania (Convenţia Democratică din România [DCR]), and he won. Also in 1996 he joined the CDNPP, and after the DCR won the parliamentary elections, on 12 December 1996 Ciorbea became prime minister of a government based on a coalition of the DCR, the Social Democrats, and the Hungarian minority. In 1997 he was elected deputy chairman of the CDNPP. Thanks to a high level of social confidence, he could start economic reforms, but after a year he lost the support of the Social Democrats. As a result of a conflict within the CDNPP, Ciorbea left it, lost the support of the DCR, and had to resign on 30 March 1998. At the same time he gave up the position of mayor of Bucharest. In 1999–2000 he headed the small National Christian Democratic Alliance (Alianţa Naţională Creştin Democrată [NCDA]). In 2000 his party joined the restored Democratic Convention of Romania 2000, including the center and right-wing parties, but the coalition failed to reach the required threshold to get into the parliament. In 2001 the NCDA joined the CDNPP, and Ciorbea was elected its chairman. (LW)

Sources: Józef Darski, *Rumunia: Historia, współczesność, konflikty narodowe* (Warsaw, 1995); Ion Alexandrescu, Ion Bulei, Ion Mamina, and Ioan Scurtu, *Enciclopedia de istorie României* (Bucharest, 2000); Duncan Light and David Phinnemore, *Post-Communist Romania* (New York, 2001), Bugajski; www.rulers.org; www.ijs.si.

CIOSEK Stanisław (2 May 1939, Pawłowice, near Radom), Polish Communist and post-Communist activist. Born into a white-collar family, in 1959 Ciosek joined the Polish United Workers' Party (Polska Zjednoczona Partia Robotnicza [PZPR]), and in 1961 he graduated from the Higher Economic School in Sopot. From 1960 he was active in the Association of Polish Students (Zrzeszenie Studentów Polskich [ZSP]). In 1963–66 he was secretary of the Executive Committee; from 1966 to 1969 he was vice-president, and in 1969–73, president of the ZSP Main Board. At the same time he advanced in the party apparatus. From 1971 he was a deputy member of the PZPR Central Committee (CC), and in 1972–85 he was an MP. From 1973 to 1975 he was president of the Main Board of the Federation of Socialist Unions of Polish Youth. In 1975–80 he was first secretary of the provincial PZPR committee in Jelenia Góra, and in February 1980 he became a member of the PZPR CC. At the Ninth Extraordinary PZPR Congress in July 1981 he was dropped from the CC. From November 1980 to November 1985 he was minister for contacts with trade unions, and he took part in several negotiations with the leaders of Solidarity (1980–81). From March 1983 to May 1984 he was minister of labor, wages, and social affairs; in 1985–86 he was head of the Social and Legal Department of the PZPR CC, and from 1986 to 1989 he was head of the Commission for Law, Order, and Moral Health of the PZPR CC. A close aide of General **Wojciech Jaruzelski**, on the latter's request in 1987–88 Ciosek, along with **Jerzy Urban** and General Władysław Pożoga from the Ministry of Interior, prepared special confidential assessments of the political situation and stressed the necessity of far-reaching systemic reforms. In 1988 Ciosek belonged to the key PZPR negotiators with the Catholic Church and the opposition. He took part in confidential talks in Magdalenka, near Warsaw, which led to the roundtable agreements. From 1986 Ciosek was again a member of the PZPR CC, and in 1986–89 (with a short break in 1988) he was secretary of the PZPR CC. In 1988 he was a deputy member and then a member of the PZPR CC Politburo until January 1990, when the party was dissolved. In 1989–90 he headed the Commission of Law and Order and the Commission of Information Policy of the PZPR CC. From 1990 to 1995 he was ambassador to the USSR (from 1991 to Russia). From 1997 he was foreign policy adviser to President **Aleksander Kwaśniewski**. (PK)

Sources: Mołdawa; Andrzej Paczkowski, "Nastroje przed bitwą," *Zeszyty Historyczne*, 1992, no. 100; Jan Skórzyński, *Ugoda i rewolucja: Władza i opozycja 1985–1989* (Warsaw, 1995); *Polska 1986–1989: Koniec systemu*, vols. 1–3 (Warsaw, 2002).

ČIURLIONIS Mikolajus Konstantinas (22 September 1875, Varéna–10 April 1911, Pustelnik, near Warsaw), Lithuanian composer and painter. The son of an organist from Druskininkai, Čiurlionis learned to play many instruments in his childhood, showing great talent. From 1882 to 1893 he attended the school of Prince Michał Ogiński in Plungé, and then he left for Warsaw, where he studied at the conservatory under the direction of (among others) Adolf Sygietyński and Zygmunt Noskowski. He was also interested in nature, in the history of literature, and in art. During his studies he composed the cantata *De Profundis*, two sonatas, and short pieces for the piano. After graduating from the conservatory, he decided to earn a living by giving private lessons and to continue his creative endeavors. In 1901 his symphonic poem *In the Forest* won a prize in a competition organized by the Zamoyski family. Thanks to the financial support of Prince Ogiński, Čiurlionis studied at the Leipzig Conservatory (1901–2) and also at the Academy of Fine Arts in Warsaw (1904–6). After the Russian revolution of 1905 he returned to Lithuania and devoted himself to his creative work. From 1906 to 1907 an exhibition of his works was held in Vilnius, where he was a member of the Lithuanian Art Society and a conductor of the Rūta Choir. This exhibition made a great impression. Transformed folk motifs were the substance of his second exhibition in Vilnius (Wilno) in March 1908. In the fall of 1908 Čiurlionis left for St. Petersburg, where he joined a circle of artists known as Mir Isskustva (World of Art). He enjoyed the recognition of critics but lived in poverty, and as a result of overwork he developed a mental illness. He was treated in a sanatorium near Warsaw, where he died. He was buried at Rossa Cemetery in Vilnius.

Despite his short life, Čiurlionis left a vast legacy, considered neo-Romantic. Many of his 250 compositions are assessed today as pioneering contributions to Lithuanian symphonic music. His most famous works include a string quartet (1902); a symphonic poem and piano series under the same title, *The Sea* (1907 and 1908); and numerous collections of songs and miniatures based on folk motifs. He also left around three hundred paintings from the series *The Creation of the World*, *The Deluge*, *Silence*, *Music of the Forest*, *The Funeral*, and several others. His works also include engravings, sketches, and book covers. His paintings, deeply rooted in his experience of his native landscape, were characterized by a transition from realistic symbolism to mystical symbolism. In independent Lithuania, between 1924 and 1925 a special gallery was built in Kaunas, where his works were exhibited. Later, his works were moved to Vytautas the Great Museum of Culture, which became the State Museum of Arts during the Soviet period. In 1913 Georgy I. Sedov, a polar explorer, named the mountains on the coast of Franz Joseph Land after Čiurlionis. (WR)

Sources: *EL*, vol. 1; *The Dictionary of Art*, J.Turner ed., vol. 7 (London, 1996); P. Galauné, ed., *M. K. Čiurlionis* (Kaunas, 1938); N. Vorobiev, *M. K. Čiurlionis: Der litauische Maler und Musiker* (Kaunas, 1938); A. Rannit, "M. K. Čiurlionis: The First Abstract

Painter of Modern Times," *Lituanus,* 1957, no. 3; Alfred E. Senn, *Mikalojus Konstantinas Čiurlionis: Music of the Spheres* (Newtonville, Mass., 1986); Vytautas Landsbergis, *Zodzio kūryba: Mikalojus Konstantinas Ciurlionis* (Vilnius, 1997).

CLEMENTIS Vladimir (20 September 1902, Tisovec, Slovakia–3 December 1952, Prague), Czechoslovak Communist activist. After completing a gymnasium in Skalica, Clementis studied in Germany and France; then he graduated from Charles University in Prague, where he obtained a Ph.D. in law. In 1925 he joined the Communist Party of Czechoslovakia (CPC). In 1927 he became head of a society that sought rapprochement with the USSR. In the 1930s he ran a law practice in Bratislava and organized Communist cells in Slovakia. In 1935–38 he was an MP representing the CPC in the parliament. In May 1939 he went via Poland to Paris. In the fall of 1939 he criticized the Molotov-Ribbentrop Pact, so he was expelled from the party for his "incomprehension of the situation" in Europe. In the summer of 1940 he left for London, where after 1941 he wrote pro-Soviet articles under the pseudonym of "Peter Hron."

At the beginning of 1945 Clementis returned to Czechoslovakia, was again admitted to the party, and soon became a member of its Central Committee. In April 1945 he assumed the post of deputy prime minister in the Košice government, and after the Communist coup in February 1948 he became minister for foreign affairs. On 29 June 1945 in Moscow he signed a treaty under which Subcarpathian Ruthenia was ceded to the USSR. After the elections of May 1946, when the Communists strengthened their position in the coalition government of **Klement Gottwald**, Clementis supported the Kremlin's standpoint regarding the rejection of the Marshall Plan by Czechoslovakia in July 1947. He also opted for the incorporation of the area west of the Olza River (Zaolzie) and the Kłodzko Valley into Czechoslovakia, and this led to a conflict with Poland. On the wave of anti-Titoist and anti-Semitic purges, in March 1950 Clementis was deprived of his post, and in January 1951 he was arrested. Tortured during investigations, in November 1951 he was sentenced to death in the trial of **Rudolf Slansky** and comrades and was executed. In 1963 he was rehabilitated, and his membership in the party was restored to him posthumously. His publications include *Usmerňované Slovensko* (Slovakia on the right track; 1942); *Medzi nami a Mad'arami* (The Czechoslovak-Hungarian relationship; 1943); *Odkazy z Londyna* (The legacy of London; 1947); *Naše zahranični politika* (Our foreign policy; 1947); and letters from prison published in *Daleko od Teba* (Far away from you; 1964). (WR)

Sources: *SBS,* vol. 1; Artur London, *The Confession* (New York, 1970); Artur London, *On Trial* (London, 1970); Zdenka Halotíková and Viliam Plevza, *Vladimir Clementis* (Bratislava, 1968); Jiří Pelikán, *The Czechoslovak Political Trials, 1950–1954* (Stanford, 1971); Stefan Drug, *Vladimir Clementis: Život a dielo v dokumentoch* (Martin, 1993).

COANDĂ Constantin (5 March 1857, Craiova–4 April 1932, Bucharest), Romanian general and politician. After graduating from high school, Coandă studied at the Paris Polytechnic. He graduated from it in 1877 and from the Saint-Cyr Military Academy in Fontainebleau in 1891. He fought in both Balkan Wars (1912–13). In 1913–16 he was chief inspector of the Romanian Army and then briefly its commander-in-chief. Later he was a representative of the Romanian Army to the Russian high command. In May 1918 he was a member of the delegation for talks on a separate peace treaty with the Central Powers in Bucharest. On 6 November 1918 he became prime minister at a turning point when, because of the decay of the Habsburg monarchy and the weakening of Germany, the government of **Alexandru Marghiloman**, supported by the Central Powers, resigned. The Coandă cabinet declared war on Austria-Hungary and Germany, so German troops started withdrawing from Romania. On 28 November Romanians from Bukovina resolved to join the Old Kingdom and were followed by the Romanians gathering in Transylvania on 1 December. After the return of King Ferdinand I and his court from Iaşi to Bucharest, on 14 December 1918 Coandă resigned. In 1919 he joined the People's Party (Partidul Poporului) of General **Alexandru Avarescu**. In 1919–20 he a member of the Romanian delegation to the Paris Peace Conference and to the negotiations that led to the signing of the peace treaty with Hungary in Trianon. On 9 November 1919 in Paris he signed the minority treaty of the League of Nations, which allowed for the Entente's final acceptance of Romanian territorial acquisitions. From March to July 1926 he was minister of industry, and from August 1926 to June 1927, minister without portfolio in the Averescu government. In 1920–21 and 1926–27 he was speaker of the Senate. His son, Henri Coandă, designed the Concorde aircraft in France. (FA/WR)

Sources: R. W. Seton-Watson, *A History of the Roumanians* (Hamden, CT, 1963); Şerban N. Ionescu, *Who Was Who in Twentieth Century Romania* (Boulder, Colo., 1994); Keith Hitchins, *Rumania 1866–1947* (Oxford, 1994).

ÇOBA Ernesto M. (16 February 1913, Shkodër–8 January 1980, Tirana), Albanian Catholic archbishop, Jesuit, victim of communism. Çoba studied at the theological seminary in Shkodër, and then he studied theology in Tirana and Rome. In February 1936 he was ordained, and then he taught religion in the seminary and in Catholic schools in

Shkodër. After the arrest of Reverend **Mikel Koliqi**, Çoba was the local parish priest. Consecrated on 20 April 1952 as a bishop and the apostolic administrator of the Shkodër diocese, after the death of Bishop **Bernardin Shllaku** in 1956, Çoba became ordinary archbishop of Shkodër. In 1951, as secretary of the episcopate, he negotiated a new legal status of the Catholic Church in Albania with the Communist authorities. As the new archbishop of Shkodër, he became, according to tradition, the head of the Albanian church. Contrary to Communist policy, he maintained contacts with the Holy See through the Italian legation in Tirana. His term in office coincided with the harshest period of the "cultural revolution" of the 1960s. In view of an intensifying anti-religious campaign, Çoba could not protect church property from nationalization. In 1965 he was summoned by the local structures of the Democratic Front several time and learned about the takeover of other churches, which were then turned into youth clubs. He was also informed about a ban against the use of bells during religious celebrations and about a limitation on baptisms to be performed only in the area of archbishops residence. When in 1967 all religious institutions were finally outlawed, Çoba tried to intervene with the local authorities and with the Office of the Council of Ministers, but in vain. When all churches in Shkodër were closed down, he celebrated the Holy Mass in private homes. During one of these celebrations he was seriously beaten by the political police. Arrested on 3 April 1976, he was sentenced to twenty-five years in prison for maintaining contacts with a foreign country (the Vatican), and he died in the prison hospital. Before 1990 it was thought that he had been killed in Ballsh Prison after celebrating the Holy Mass. (TC)

Sources: State Archives in Tirana, Durrës Archdiocese Collection; Brian Curdy and Lulash Dajçi, "Bishop Ernest Coba, Father of the Poor: The 10th Anniversary of Martyrdom," *Albanian Catholic Bulletin*, 1989; Nogaj Ndoc Dom, *Kisha Katolike Shqiptare 1944 nentor 1990: Humbje dhe fitore* (Shkodër, 1999); Simoni Zef, "Përsekutimi i kishës katolike në Shqipni nga 1944–1990," in *Krishtërimi ndër shqiptarë: Simpozium Ndërkombëtar* (Shkodër, 2000).

CODREANU-ZELEA Corneliu (13 September 1899, Iaşi–30 November 1938, Bucharest), leader of the Romanian Fascists. Codreanu-Zelea's mother was of German origin and his father of Polish origin. He was brought up and educated in Iaşi, a town with a Jewish majority and where anti-Semitic attitudes were strong. From his youth he remained under the influence of the nationalistic theories of Alexandru Cuza. Codreanu-Zelea studied law at the university in Iaşi and then in France and Germany. He began his political career at the University of Iaşi, gaining popularity with his radical anti-Bolshevik and anti-Semitic slogans in 1919. He declared absolute loyalty toward the Orthodox Church, condemned the corruption of the administration, and expressed a dislike of capitalism and a mystical faith in the peasantry. In 1924 he shot the prefect of Iaşi, who had tried to suppress the activities of nationalistic fighting squads. Released after a short imprisonment, he became convinced that "the atrocities of the Jewish-Bolshevik revolution" should be answered by similar methods—that is, the use of terror. He maintained that in prison he had had a vision: the Archangel Michael had instructed him to revive the Romanian nation. Therefore in 1927 he organized the Legion of the Archangel Michael, which became the Iron Guard in 1930.

The Guardists, who planned to gain absolute power, used nationalistic, anti-Semitic, and mystical-religious slogans. They conducted pogroms in Cluj, Oradeia, Hunedoar, and other towns. Liberal and peasant governments unsuccessfully attempted to prevent the development of the movement, which, especially during the Great Depression, became very influential. At the beginning of December 1933 the authorities outlawed the activities of the Iron Guard, and on 29 December the Guardists murdered Premier **Ion Duca**. King **Charles II** used the Iron Guard as an instrument in his fight for full power, although he did not trust it. In 1934 Codreanu-Zelea introduced the slogan "All for the fatherland." His fighting squads, wearing green shirts and carrying small bags of Romanian soil, began to terrorize the streets. On 20 March 1935 Codreanu-Zelea officially registered a new party, called All for the Fatherland, and made General Gheorge (Zizi) its leader. Under that new name the Iron Guard continued its activities even after it had been declared illegal. The All for the Fatherland Party was successful in the elections of December 1937, gaining over 15 percent of the vote. In 1938 Codreanu-Zelea stated, "Let us destroy the Jews before they are able to destroy us." Charles II felt threatened by the Iron Guard, and on 15 April 1938 he imprisoned its leaders, including Codreanu-Zelea, who was sentenced to ten years in prison. On the night of 29–30 November Codreanu-Zelea, along with twelve other prisoners, was murdered; according to the official explanation, "they were shot while trying to escape." That incident worsened relations between Romania and the Third Reich, which supported the Iron Guard. Codreanu-Zelea was the author of *Die Eiserne Garde* (The Iron Guard; 1939) and other works. (WR)

Sources: *Biographisches Lexikon*, vol. 1; Eugen Weber, "The Men of Archangel," *Contemporary History*, 1966, no. 1; Nicholas M. Nagy-Talavera, *The Green Shirts and the Others: A History of Fascism in Hungary and Romania* (Stanford, 1970); Alexander E. Ronnett, *Romanian Nationalism: The Legionary Movement* (Chicago, 1974); Tadeusz Dubicki and Krzysztof Dach, *Żelazny Legion*

Michała Archanioła (Warsaw, 1996); Zigu Ornea, *The Romanian Extreme Right* (Boulder, Colo., 1999).

ČOLAKOVIĆ Radoljub (7 June 1900, Bijeljina–1983?), Yugoslav Communist activist from Bosnia. Čolaković graduated from high school in Sarajevo. During trade studies in Zagreb, he joined the Communist Party of Yugoslavia (CPY). In 1921 he was sentenced to twelve years in prison for taking part in the assassination of the minister of interior, Milorad Drašković. While in prison, he translated *Capital* by Karl Marx. Released in 1932, he left for the USSR, where in 1933–35 he studied at the Lenin School of the Comintern. Sent to Vienna, he worked there in the CPY émigré headquarters under the pseudonym "Rudi." In April 1936 he became a member of the CPY Politburo under the pseudonym "P. Vuković" and was active in Paris and Prague, where the CPY headquarter was moved. During a purge within the CPY, in 1937 Čolaković was dismissed from the Politburo, and his book, *ABC Leninizma* (The ABCs of Leninism), was condemned by the Comintern. Sent to Spain, in 1936–39 he fought in the International Brigades under the pseudonym "Ivan Pavlović." In 1939 he returned to Yugoslavia, where he spent half a year in prison. When in June 1941 the CPY took an anti-German attitude, he joined the Communist guerrillas in Serbia and then in Bosnia. In November 1943 he became a member and secretary of the Anti-Fascist Council of National Liberation of Yugoslavia (Antifašističko Vijeće Narodnog Oslobodenja Jugoslavije). After the war, between April 1945 and September 1949 Čolaković was head of the republican government of Bosnia and Herzegovina and then federal minister and member of the Central Committee of the League of Yugoslav Communists (LYC). In 1945–48 he was also chairman of the Yugoslav Association for Cultural Cooperation with the USSR, and, after the Soviet-Yugoslav split in 1948, he was chairman of the Council of Culture and Science. After the constitutional reform of 1953, he joined the Union Executive Council (government), and then he became its deputy chairman. In 1955 he was responsible for the reform of education. At the Ninth LYC Congress in 1969 he made the inaugural speech but was dropped from the party leadership. In 1977 he published *Zapisi iz oslobodilakog rata* (Records from the war of liberation), and in 1978, *Govori, članci, polemika* (Speeches, articles, polemics). (WR)

Sources: Lazitch; Enciklopedija Jugoslavije, vol. 2 (Zagreb, 1966); Denison Rusinow, *The Yugoslav Experiment, 1948–1974* (Berkeley, 1974); Kritićari o djelu Radoljuba Čolakovića (Sarajevo, 1983).

COLOTKA Peter (10 January 1925, Sedliacka Dubová, Dolný Kubín district), Slovak Communist activist and lawyer. In 1947 Colotka joined the Communist Party of Czechoslovakia (CPC). In 1950 he graduated in law from Comenius University in Bratislava, and he worked there as associate professor from 1956 and as professor from 1964. In 1956–57 he was deputy dean, in 1957–58 dean of the School of Law, and in 1958–61 deputy rector of this university. A member of the International Tribunal in the Hague from 1962 to 1970, in 1963–68 he was a member of the Slovak National Council and its secretary of justice. In 1966–89 he was a member of the Central Committee (CC) of the Communist Party of Slovakia (CPS) and of the CPC, and from 1968 to 1988 (with a break from January to September 1969) he was deputy prime minister of Czechoslovakia. At the same time he was head of the government of the Slovak Socialist Republic from May 1969 to October 1988. From December 1968 to February 1989 he was an MP to the Federal Assembly, and from January to April 1969 he was its speaker. In April 1969 he became a member of the CPC CC Presidium, and in May 1969, a member of the CPS CC Presidium. He sat in these bodies until October 1988. At the end of his career as a colorless party apparatchik of "normalization," from January 1989 to January 1990 he was ambassador to France. For his activities in the 1970s and 1980s Colotka was ousted from the party in February 1990, and in June 1990 he was accused of embezzlement. In 1994 he was cleared of these accusations. (PU)

Sources: ČBS; *Českoslovenští politici: 1918–1991* (Prague, 1991); *Who's Who in the Socialist Countries of Europe,* vol. 1 (Munich, London, and Paris, 1989).

CONSTANTINESCU Alexandru (9 March 1873–1949, Bucharest?), Romanian Communist activist. An upholsterer by trade, Constantinescu was one of the pioneers of the Socialist movement in Romania, representing its left wing. He first became known in 1907, making radical speeches to Bucharest workers in which he supported the peasant rebellion in Moldavia, which was soon bloodily suppressed by the army. In 1907 he was a Romanian representative to the Congress of the Second International in Stuttgart. During World War I he remained in Bucharest, where, after Romania acceded to the Entente in 1916, he established the Committee for the Struggle against War. In 1917 he organized the first Communist underground cells, active in the German-occupied part of Romania. Many members of these groups were sent to Russia after the war. In 1921 Constantinescu played an important role in the creation of the Socialist-Communist Party, which took the name of the Communist Party of Romania (Partidul Comunist din România) in 1922. In 1919–23 he published in the periodical *Lupta de clasă*, supporting Communist tendencies in the Second International and later the Third International (Comintern). In 1923, probably in connection with the growing repression against the Communist Party, he moved to France and then to the USSR, where he was active in the Bolshevik party. In 1937 he secretly moved to Romania, where he was soon removed from the party owing to the Stalinist purge. He died in oblivion after World War II. (LW)

Sources: Ion Raţiu, *Contemporary Romania* (Richmond, 1975); Grothusen Klaus-Detlev, *Südosteuropa-Handbuch: Rumänien* (Göttingen, 1977); Vlad Georgescu, *Istoria Românilor de la origini pînă în zilele noastre* (Oakland, 1984); Ghiţă Ionescu, *Comunismul în România* (Bucharest, 1994); Ion Alexandrescu, Ion Bulei, Ion Mamina, and Ioan Scurtu, *Enciclopedia de istorie României* (Bucharest, 2000).

CONSTANTINESCU Emil (19 November 1939, Tighina), Romanian politician, lawyer, geologist, and president of Romania. In 1960 Constantinescu graduated in law from the University of Bucharest. In 1960–61 he worked as a judge in Piteşti, but then he undertook geological studies at the same university and graduated in 1966. He stayed at the university, where he received a Ph.D. in geology in 1979 and became professor in 1990. From 1990 to 1992 he was deputy rector of the University of Bucharest. In 1991–92 he lectured at Duke University in Durham, N.C. In 1990 he co-founded University Solidarity (Solidarităţi Universitare) and became its head. The organization attracted university teachers, scholars, and students striving to democratize Romania. In 1990 he also co-founded the Civic Alliance (Alianţa Civica), an anti-Communist party aiming at the development of a civil society. In 1991 he became its deputy chairman and head of the Anti-Totalitarian Forum (Forumului Antitotalitar) and Civic Academy (Academia Civice), opposing the post-Communist rule of **Ion Iliescu**. In 1992, thanks to the support of **Corneliu Coposu**, Constantinescu became chairman of the Democratic Convention of Romania (Convenţia Democratica din România [DCR]), a coalition of democratic and anti-Communist groups, and its candidate for president. In the elections of October 1992 he was runner-up to Iliescu, with 38.6 percent of the vote. From 1992 to 1996 Constantinescu was rector of the University of Bucharest and chairman of the National Council of Romanian Rectors. Between 1994 and 1998 he was a member of the International Union of Rectors. In 1995 he was reelected chairman of the DCR.

In October 1996 the DCR won the parliamentary elections, and on 17 November 1996 Constantinescu won the presidential election. During his term, which lasted until December 2000, he supported steps toward the accession of Romania into the European Union and NATO. He gave his backing to the NATO intervention in Kosovo. He tried to introduce structural reforms leading to the strengthening of the market economy and the civil society. Nevertheless, he failed to lead the country out of economic recession. In the presidential elections of 2000 he backed Prime Minister **Mugur Isărescu**, who nevertheless lost. In 2001 Constantinescu returned to the University of Bucharest. He continued lecturing as a visiting professor of mineralogy and crystallography in many countries and received honorary doctorates from universities in Ankara, Athens, Paris, Beijing, and Montreal. He published twelve scholarly books and several dozen articles in geology. (LW)

Sources: Józef Darski, *Rumunia: Historia, współczesność, konflikty narodowe* (Warsaw, 1993); *Personalităţi politice, publice* (Bucharest, 1994); Tom Gallagher, *Romania after Ceausescu* (Edinburgh, 1995); Costin Scorpan, *Istoria României: Enciclopedie* (Bucharest, 1997); Ion Alexandrescu, Ion Bulei, Ion Mamina, and Ioan Scurtu, *Enciclopedia de istorie României* (Bucharest, 2000); Bugajski.

CONSTANTINESCU Miron (13 December 1917, Chişinău [Kishinev]–18 July 1974, Bucharest), Romanian Communist activist. Constantinescu graduated from high school in Arad in Transylvania and studied philosophy at the University of Bucharest in 1935–39. In 1935 he joined a Communist youth organization. During his studies he contributed to the leftist periodicals *Cadran*, *Cuvântul liber*, and *Era nouă*. In 1939 he became secretary general of the Communist youth organization. Arrested for Communist activities, until the coup of August 1944 he was detained in the Galaţi, Caransebeş, and Lugoj prisons with a group of activists who, under the leadership of **Gheorghe Gheorghiu-Dej**, soon took over control of the Communist Party. After his release Constantinescu was editor-in-chief of the central party daily *Scânteia*. In 1946 he became a member of the Central Committee (CC) of the Romanian Communist Party (Partidul Comunist Român), and from 1948 he was a member of the CC Politburo of the Romanian Workers' Party (RWP). In 1947–48 he was deputy minister of national education; in 1948–49, minister of mining and oil industry; and from 1948, a lecturer at the University of Bucharest. In the late 1940s he supported **Ana Pauker** in her endeavors to make the RWP a mass party, even by including repentant members of the (Fascist) Iron Guard. In 1949–55 Constantinescu was head of the State Planning Commission and from August 1954 to July 1957, deputy prime minister. He supported Gheorghiu-Dej in his struggle against the Ana Pauker-**Vasile Luca-**

Teohari Georgescu faction, consulting on this matter in Moscow in September 1951. In January 1954 he also consulted with the Kremlin regarding the death sentence in the trial of **Lucreţiu Patraşcanu**.

After Stalin's death in March 1953, Constantinescu oriented himself toward the Kremlin reformers of Georgy Malenkov and then toward **Nikita Khrushchev**. Constantinescu was a member of the Romanian delegation at the Twentieth Congress of the Soviet party, but contrary to Gheorghiu-Dej, he chose de-Stalinization. This led to his dismissal from top party and government positions in 1957. In 1957–58 he was director of the Institute of Economic Research, and in 1959–65 he directed a department in the Nicolae Iorga Institute of History. After **Nicolae Ceauşescu** took over power, Constantinescu returned to politics. From August 1969 to February 1970 he was minister of education, and in November 1972 he became deputy chairman of the Council of State. He also presided over the Economic Council, and from March 1974, shortly before his death, over the National Assembly. In 1974 he also became a member of the Romanian Academy of Sciences. He published a number of books presenting the Communist vision of history, sociology, and economics. (LW)

Sources: *Dictionar Enciclopedic*, vol. 1 (Bucharest, 1993); Ion Raţiu, *Contemporary Romania* (Richmond, 1975); Klaus-Detlev Grothusen, ed., *Rumänien* (Göttingen, 1977); Ghiţă Ionescu, *Comunismul în România* (Bucharest, 1994); Kurt W. Treptow and Marcel Popa, *Historical Dictionary of Romania* (Lanham, Md., 1996); Dorina N. Rusu, *Membrii Academiei Române 1866–1999* (Bucharest, 1999); Dennis Deletant, *Communist Terror in Romania: Gheorghiu-Dej and the Police State, 1948–1965* (New York, 1999); Ion Alexandrescu, Ion Bulei, Ion Mamina, and Ioan Scurtu, *Enciclopedia de istorie României* (Bucharest, 2000).

COPOSU Corneliu (16 September 1916, Bobota–9 November 1995, Bucharest), Romanian lawyer, journalist, and politician. From 1933 to 1937 Coposu studied law at the university in Cluj. He published in the press organs of the National Peasant Party (NPP) that were issued in Cluj: *România Nouă* and *Patria* (1935–40). During the Hungarian occupation of Transylvania (30 August 1940–25 October 1944), Coposu remained in Bucharest, where he wrote for the magazine *Ardealul* and also edited broadcasts on Romanian radio. From 1936 to 1946 he was the political secretary of **Iuliu Maniu**, and he took part in the organization of a coup on 23 August 1944. In 1943–44 he maintained close contacts with leaders of other parties and also with the Romanian Ministry of Foreign Affairs. He participated in the talks between Romania and the Allies that were held in Cairo. After the war he played a major role in the NPP, holding (among other positions) the post of

deputy secretary general. On 14 July 1947 he was arrested and then sentenced in a rigged trial to life imprisonment for "sabotage" and "anti-state activities."

Until 1964 Coposu was a political prisoner and spent seven years in complete isolation. Later he attempted to reorganize his party, both at home and among emigrants in Western Europe and the United States. In 1987 he introduced the illegal NPP into the European Union and affiliated it with the Christian Democrats. Soon after the overthrow of the regime of **Nicolae Ceauşescu** (22 December 1989) the Christian and Democratic National Peasants' Party was created, and Coposu became its leader. Between 1992 and 1995 he was president of the opposition Democratic Convention, which was formed together with (among others) the National Liberal Party and the Romanian Social Democratic Party. In 1992–95 Coposu served as senator. As an influential Romanian politician, he proposed **Emil Constantinescu** for the post of president of Romania. Being a monarchist, Coposu opted for the return of King **Michael I** and suggested calling a referendum on that issue. An avowed opponent of Russia, he initiated détente with the Hungarians. In October 1995 he was decorated with the French Legion of Honor. He was the author of several works, including *Ungaria ne cere pământul* (The Hungarians claim our land; 1940); *Ţara Sălajului* (The land of Sălajului; 1944); *Armistiţiul din 1944 şi împlicaţile lui* (The armistice of 1944 and its implications; 1988); and *Retrospetive asupra istorici contemporane* (A look at contemporary historians; 1990). (FA/TD)

Sources: V. C. Arachelian, *Corneliu Coposu: Dialoguri* (Bucharest, 1992); *Corneliu Coposu in faţa istoriei* (Bucharest, 1996); Józef Darski, *Rumunia: Historia, współczesność, konflikty narodowe* (N.p., n.d.); R. Wyborski and Tadeusz Dubicki, "Rumunia przed i po listopadzie 1996," in M. Wilk, ed., *Nowa Europa 1989–2000: Fakty i prognozy* (Łódź, 1998).

CORNEA Doina (30 May 1929, Braşov), Romanian dissident. In 1952 Cornea graduated in French studies from Babeş-Bolyai University in Cluj-Napoca. From 1952 to 1958 she taught at a high school in Zalău, and from 1959 she held the chair of French Language and Literature at the Cluj-Napoca university. In 1980 in the uncensored press she published her first book, *Încercarea labirintului* (Attempt at a labyrinth), and four translated texts. In 1983 she was fired from the university. In 1982 her daughter smuggled her first open letter against the **Nicolae Ceauşescu** regime to France: *Scrisoare către cei care n-au încetat să gândească* (Letters by those still remembered) was presented on Radio Free Europe. From 1982 to 1989 Cornea published thirty-one literary texts and political protests in France. In 1983 her activities became the subject of investigation; she was repeatedly interrogated and beaten. In the late 1980s she continued her activities together with her son, Leontin Iuhas. After the workers' riots in Braşov in November 1987 Cornea distributed manifestos of solidarity with the workers. Arrested again, along with her son, she was kept in prison until 21 December 1989, when she took part in a street demonstration demanding the resignation of Ceauşescu and the establishment of a democratic government.

On 22 December 1989, soon after the overthrow of the Ceauşescu dictatorship by a group of Communist activists, Cornea, without her knowledge, was included in the Supreme Council of the National Salvation Front (Frontul Sălvari Naţionale [NSF]), which took over power. At the very end of 1989 she was among the fifty intellectuals who established the Group for Social Dialogue (Grupul pentru Dialog Social). In January 1990 she left the NSF because its program was to reform the system and not abolish it and because of how the Front's leaders treated her. Later in 1990 Cornea was co-founder of the Anti-Totalitarian Forum, which failed to unite the anti-Communist opposition, and then she co-founded the Civic Alliance (Alianţa Civica), which strove to develop civil society. After 1989 she published more than one hundred articles in defense of human rights and democracy in Romania. In 1991 she was one of the co-founders of the Democratic Convention of Romania (Convenţia Democratica din România [DCR]), a coalition of anti-Communist and democratic parties and groups, but she abstained from direct participation in DCR activities. She authored many books, including *Liberté?* (Freedom? 1990); *Scrisori deschise şi alte texte* (1991; Open letters and other texts; 1991); and *Faţa nevazută a lucrurilor* (The invisible side of things; 1999). In 2000 she was honored with the French Legion of Honor and the Romanian Order of the Star with the Great Cross. (LW)

Sources: *Dictionar Enciclopedic*, vol. 1 (Bucharest, 1993); Darski Józef, *Rumunia: Historia, współczesność, konflikty narodowe* (Warsaw, 1995); Scorpan Costin, *Istoria Romaniei: Enciclopedie* (Bucharest, 1997); Ion Alexandrescu, Ion Bulei, Ion Mamina, and Ioan Scurtu, *Enciclopedia de istorie României* (Bucharest, 2000); *Who's Who in Romania 2002* (Bucharest, 2002); www.aliantacivica.ro.

ĆOSIĆ Dobrica (29 December 1921, Velika Drenova), Serbian writer and Communist activist. Born into a peasant family, Ćosić was expelled from high school for his activity in the Union of Communist Youth. He joined the Communist Party of Yugoslavia. During World War II he was a political commissar of a guerrilla battalion. After the war, he graduated from the Higher Party School. In 1951 he published his first novel, *Daleko je sunce* (The sun is

far away), and in 1954, *Koreni* (Roots), for which he received the highest Yugoslav literary critics' award. In 1961 he met **Josip Broz Tito**, he gained his trust, and accompanied him on his many foreign trips. In 1965–68 Ćosić was a member of the Central Committee of the League of Serbian Communists and a deputy to the Federal Assembly. He demanded a revision of the nationality policy (mostly in Kosovo), so in 1968 he was expelled from the party on account of trying to fuel Serbian nationalism. In subsequent years he was active in the opposition and wrote books. He is thought to have been the initiator of a 1986 memorandum, signed by sixteen members of the Serbian Academy of Sciences and Arts, that referred to Serbian nationalism. Ćosić has been called the "spiritual father" of **Slobodan Milošević** and even "father of the Serbian nation." An advocate for an "ethnically pure" Great Serbia, Ćosić favored the unification of all Serbs in one country. In June 1992 Ćosić became the first president of the new Federal Republic of Yugoslavia, founded in April 1992. At this time he distanced himself from Milošević, and in the presidential campaign in Serbia in December 1992 he supported his rival, the moderate **Milan Panić**. In June 1993 the parliament dismissed Ćosić from the presidency. His major works include the following: *Deobe* (Divisions; 1961); *Vreme smrti* (Time of Death; 1972–75); and a trilogy on a Communist revolting against Stalinism, *Vreme zla* (Time of Evil), comprised of the novels *Gresnjik* (Sinner; 1985), *Otpadnik* (Renegade; 1986), and *Viernik* (Believer; 1991). (AO)

Sources: *Enciklopedija Jugoslavije*, vol. 2 (Zagreb, 1956); Sabrina P. Ramet, *Nationalism and Federalism in Yugoslavia, 1962–1991* (Bloomington, 1992); Nebojša Popov, *Serbski dramat: Od faszystowskiego populizmu do Miloševicia* (Łódź, 1994); Laura Silber and Allan Little, *The Death of Yugoslavia* (London, 1995); David Owen, *Balkan Odyssey* (New York, 1995); John Lampe, *Yugoslavia as History* (Cambridge, 1996); Bugajski.

COSTINESCU Emil (12 March 1844, Iaşi–6 July 1921, Bucharest), Romanian economist, financier, and politician. In 1862 Costinescu completed his studies in Iaşi. He belonged to the Liberal Party since its creation in 1875, and then he was a member of its successor, the National Liberal Party (NLP). At the end of the nineteenth century he was one of the leading Romanian financiers. A co-founder of the National Bank of Romania in 1880, he was later president of one of the largest Romanian banks. He edited the magazine *Românul*. When **Ion I. C. Brătianu** became head of the NLP, he on many occasions appointed Costinescu as minister of finance. Costinescu was in charge of the finance ministry in 1902–4, 1907–10, and 1914–16. Additionally, between 1916 and 1917 he served as minister without portfolio. At the end of World War I, as a financial expert, Costinescu became a member of the Romanian delegation to the Paris Peace Conference. His works include *Le tarif des douames* (Customs tarrifs; 1904) and *Incurajea industrei naţionale* (Stimulating the national economy; 1912). (FA)

Sources: Ion Gheorghe Duca, *Memorii*, vols. 2–3 (Bucharest, 1992).

CRISTEA Miron [original name Ilie] (18 July 1868, Toplicza [now Topliţa, Transylvania]–6 March 1939, Cannes), patriarch of the Romanian Orthodox Church, premier of Romania. The son of a Transylvanian peasant, Cristea attended a German gymnasium in Bistritz (Bistriţa) and a Romanian gymnasium in Năsâud, where he was president of a society called Virtus Romana Rediviva. He was educated at the Theological Institute in Hermannstadt (Sibiu, 1887–90), and he graduated in philosophy and philology from Budapest University in 1894. He earned a Ph.D. on the basis of his dissertation about Mihaiu Eminescu; it was written in Hungarian. From 1901 Cristea belonged to the Romanian Cultural Union in Transylvania (RCUT). After graduation he decided to pursue an ecclesiastic career. From 1895 he was secretary of the consistory in Sibiu. In June 1902 he took on the name Miron and entered the monastery in Hodos-Bodrog. In 1905 he became director of the RCUT. On 21 November 1909 the consistory elected him bishop of Caransebeş. He took holy orders in May 1910 in Sibiu.

Cristea played an important role in organizing the National Assembly in Alba Iulia, the historic capital of Transylvania. On 1 December 1918 the assembly passed a resolution on unification with the Old Kingdom. Cristea served as a member of the presidium of this assembly, and he was a member of the delegation of Transylvanian Romanians who submitted the Act of Unification to King **Ferdinand**. On 31 December 1919 an overwhelming majority elected Cristea archbishop of Bucharest and metropolitan of the principality of Walachia. From 1920 to 1925 he also served as "the first metropolitan" of Romania, contributing to the unification of the Romanian Orthodox Church in Transylvania, the Old Kingdom, and Bessarabia. When on 12 February 1925 the Romanian parliament changed the metropolis of Bucharest into a patriarchate, Cristea became the patriarch of Romania. He enjoyed great respect; therefore between July 1927 and June 1930 he was a member of the Regency Council, created after the election of Prince **Michael**, who was under age, as king. However, Cristea recognized the return of Michael's father, **Charles II**, to the throne, and on 10 February 1938, after

Charles had introduced a royal dictatorship, Cristea took over the premiership of the new government. He remained in office until his death. He approved of the execution of the Iron Guard leaders, including **Corneliu Zelea-Codreanu**, the Guard's founder, in November 1938. Cristea died suddenly while on a journey to France. He was the author of (among other works) *România şi Vatican* (Romania and the Vatican; 1921); *Adevăruri istorice asupra întegirii neamului* (Historical truth about national integration; 1929); and *Inseminaryii de faimă: Jurnal* (Notes of Fame: Diary; 1997). (FA/TD)

Sources: *Biographisches Lexikon*, vol. 1; Ion Rusu Abredeanu, *Patriarhul României Dr. Miron Cristea* (Bucharest, 1929); Prinţul *Nicolae al României: In umbra coroanei României* (Iaşi, 1991); *Regele Carol al. II-lea al. Romaniei, Inseminaryi zilnice*, vols. 1–2 (Bucharest, 1995); Armand Calinescu, *Inseminaryi politice* (Bucharest, 1990).

CRISTESCU Eugen (3 April 1895, Grozaveşti–12 June 1950, Vacareşti), Romanian politician. The oldest of ten children of a teacher, after graduating from a theological seminary, Cristescu started law studies in Iaşi but discontinued them because of the outbreak of World War I. He took part in the fall campaign of 1916. He graduated in 1920, and in 1926 he received a Ph.D. in law. From 1920 he worked in the central police headquarters. In 1927 he became its deputy director, and in 1929, director. He represented Romania in the International Police Commission in the Hague. He co-initiated and was the first head of the police trade union. An opponent of political extremism, be it Communist or Fascist, Cristescu elaborated a report on the revolutionary Communist movement in Romania in 1918–26 and on its connections with the Communist International; he handed the report to the U.S. legation in Bucharest. He created a special section to survey and combat Communist activities. He prevented riots planned by the Iron Guard in 1933, for which the Guard issued him a death sentence. In 1934 he resigned, but he maintained a high rank in the Ministry of Interior. In 1937 he was appointed its delegate to a special requisition commission, subordinated to the General Staff, where he met the top military, including General **Ion Antonescu**.

After Antonescu took power, on 15 November 1940 Cristescu was appointed head of the Special Information Service (Serviciu Special de Informaţii [SSI]), which played a key role in preventing the Iron Guard coup against Antonescu. Cristescu reorganized the SSI, making it an efficient tool of dictatorial power. He personally had no Fascist inclinations, but he cooperated with the German Abwehr and Gestapo, trying to maintain some independence for the Romanian service. The SSI both did surveillance on and protected democratic politicians from the Germans and mediated in the contacts between **Iuliu Maniu** and Antonescu. At the same time Cristescu initiated the creation of ghettos and internment camps, taking part in decisions on the political arrest and expulsion of foreigners. At the end of 1942, on orders from Antonescu, Cristescu entered into contact with U.S. intelligence, sending his brother on a mission to Turkey. He intercepted the British mission parachuted into Romania in December 1943 and controlled talks held by Maniu and **Barbu Ştirbei** with the Allied command in Cairo about the conditions of armistice. He informed Antonescu on the preparations for a coup by King Michael, in cooperation with the Communists, but the dictator did not believe him. During the coup of 23 August 1944 Cristescu went into hiding, but on 24 September he was arrested by the Communists. Taken by the Soviet mission on 14 October, he was transported to Moscow, detained in Lubyanka Prison, and interrogated for sixteen months. As a result he agreed to cooperate with the Soviet services. In April 1946 he returned to Bucharest, where he was sued, along with other key figures of the Antonescu regime, for "national treason and disaster." Sentenced to death, he was pardoned by King Michael on the motion of the Communist minister of justice, **Lucreţiu Patraşcanu**. His sentence was changed to hard labor for life. He was imprisoned in the Dumbraveni, Aiud, and Vacareşti prisons. From November 1949 to April 1950 he underwent a new investigation by the political police, Securitate, and he died in prison. (ASK)

Sources: Haralamb Zinca, *Spion. Prin. Arhiwele secrete* (Bucharest, 1993); Larry L. Watts, *Romanian Cassandra: Ion Antonescu and the Struggle for Reform, 1916–1941* (Boulder, Colo., 1993); Cristian Troncota, *Eugen Cristescu asul servicilor secrete romanesti: Memorii, marturi, documente 1916–1944* (Bucharest, 1994).

CRISTESCU Gheorghe (19 May 1882, Copaciu–23 July 1973, Iaşi), Romanian Communist activist. Cristescu was a quilt maker; thence his party pseudonym, "Plăpamarul." He belonged to the revolutionary wing of the Romanian Social Democratic Party, which decided to affiliate itself with the Communist International. On 8 May 1921 Cristescu was co-founder of the Romanian Socialist Communist Party in Bucharest. The founding congress of the Communist Party of Romania (Partidul Comunist din România [CPR]) met in Ploieşti in October 1922, and Cristescu was elected secretary general. The Comintern insisted that the CPR support the dismemberment of Romania, with Bessarabia and Northern Bukovina ceded to the Soviet Ukraine and Transylvania and Dobrudja recognized as separate states. This line was supported by non-Romanians in the party, but it was hard for the Romanians to accept. Against this background, in 1923 the party was divided by a conflict in which Cristescu represented the Romanian point of view. During a visit by Cristescu to Moscow in September 1923, the CPR delegation was forced to accept the Comintern standpoint, and Cristescu was dismissed from the leadership at the Third CPR Congress in Vienna in August 1924. In the 1920s he was still a party member, for which he spent several years in prison. Disillusioned with communism, in 1928 he joined the United Socialist Party (Partidul Socialist Unitar), and in 1938 he withdrew from politics altogether. When the Communists took power in Romania after World War II, Cristescu was arrested in 1948 and imprisoned for "rightist deviation." Among other places, he worked in a labor camp, Capul Midia, at the construction of the Danube-Black Sea Canal. He was released in 1968. (WR)

Sources: Lazitch; Şerban N. Ionescu, *Who Was Who in Twentieth Century Romania* (Boulder, Colo., 1994); Dennis Deletant, *Communist Terror in Romania: Gheorghiu-Dej and the Police State, 1948–1965* (New York, 1999).

CRNJANSKI Miloš (26 October 1893, Csongrád, Hungary–30 November 1977, Belgrade), Serbian poet and writer. After studying the history of art in Rijeka, Vienna, and Paris, Crnjanski graduated in philosophy from the University of Belgrade. Later he worked as a high school teacher and journalist. He made his literary debut in 1908. During World War I he fought on the Galician front. In 1921 he was co-founder of a literary group, Alpha. In 1928–29 and 1935–41 he worked as a cultural attaché in Berlin, Rome, and Lisbon, and in 1941–65 he lived in London. His first works, included in the collection of poems *Lirika Itake* (Lyrics from Ithaca; 1919) and the prose work *Priče o muškom* (Tales of a boy; 1920), as well as the novel *Dnevnik o Černojeviću* (Notes of Černojević; 1921), reflected his perception of the crisis of civilization and being lost amid the absurd. He proclaimed the unity of the real and created reality. He was influenced by expressionism, often using free versification. In a two-volume novel, *Seoba* (1929; *Migrations*, 1994) and *Druga knjiga seoba* (The second book of migrations; 1962), he combined images from Serbian history with his poetic vision of human fate, full of suffering and a lack of fulfillment. He also authored the dramas *Maska* (Mask; 1919), *Konak* (Staying overnight; 1965), and *Tesla* (Hoe; 1966); a longer poem, *Lament nad Beogradom* (Lament over Belgrade; 1962); the novel *Roman o Londonu* (The London story; 1971); memoirs and essays collected in *Ljubav u Toskani* (Love in Tuscany; 1930), *Knjiga o Nemačkoj* (The book of Germany; 1931), and *Kod Hiperborejaca* (The Hyperborean wheel; 1966); a diary, *Embahade* (1983);

and a monograph, *Mikelandjelo* (Michalangelo; 1982). In 1983 his *Izbrana dela Miloša Crnjanskog* (Collected works of Miloš Crnjanski) were published in twenty-six volumes. (WR)

Sources: *Wielka encyklopedia PWN*, vol. 6 (Warsaw, 2002); Petar Džadžić, *Prostori sreće u delu Miloša Crnjanskog* (Belgrade, 1976); *Milos Crnjavski and Modern Serbian Literature* (Nottingham, England, 1988); ed. David Norris, N. Petrovoić, *Lirika Milosa Crnjanskog* (Belgrade, 1994).

CRVENKOVSKI Branko (12 October 1962, Sarajevo), Macedonian politician. The son of a Yugoslav military officer, Crvenkovski graduated from the School of Mechanical Engineering, Computer Science, and Automation in Skopje in 1988. Upon graduation, he worked in Semos-Skopje as a chief of department before entering politics. A former Communist, he became an MP in 1990, the same year that he became a member of the presidency of the Social Democratic League of Macedonia (Socijaldemokratski Sojuz na Makedinija [SSM]). He became its president in 1991. Crvenkovski served as president of the Commission for Foreign Political Affairs and Relations and was elected prime minister on 17 August 1992, heading a four-party coalition that included ministers from two Albanian parities. A cornerstone of this government's platform was the creation of inter-ethnic harmony. Between 1992 and 1995, Crvenkovski guided Macedonia through two harmful Greek economic boycotts. During this same period, most countries recognized the sovereignty of the nascent Macedonian state (if not its name—it was the Former Yugoslav Republic of Macedonia). Crvenkovski's government was responsible for initiating the 1993 privatization program, an ineffective but long-heralded attempt to bring greater economic stability. Crvenkovski remained in power into 1994, when he received a second mandate to become prime minister. He formed another coalition government that included representatives of Albanian parties. During this administration, he made an effort to reach out to the opposition in order to maintain political stability. With his popularity plummeting in response to deteriorating economic conditions, Crvenkovski reorganized the government in 1996. The Social Democratic Union of Macedonia was upended in the 1998 fall elections by the Internal Macedonian Revolutionary Organization–Democratic Party for Macedonian National Unity. After stepping down on 30 November 1998, Crvenkovski moved into the opposition and remained the head of the SSM. In the elections of September 2002 the majority of seats was won by a coalition, Alliance for Macedonia (Makedonija so Razum), in which Crvenkovski's Social Democrats played a leading role. On 7 October 2002 he became

prime minister again. After the death of President **Boris Trajkovski**, on 28 April 2004 Crvenkovski was elected Macedonia's president. (DP)

Sources: Duncan Perry, "Republic of Macedonia: On the Road to Stability or Destruction?" *Transition*, 25 August 1995; Duncan Perry, "Destiny on Hold: Macedonia and the Dangers of Ethnic Discord," *Current History*, March 1998; Valentina Georgieva and Sasha Konechni, *Historical Dictionary of the Republic of Macedonia* (Lanham, Md., 1998); Bugajski; *RFE/RL Newsline*; *OMRI Daily Reports*; www.rulers.org.

CSÁKY Pál (21 March 1956, Šahy, Levice district), Hungarian politician in Slovakia. After graduating from high school in 1975 Csáky studied at the Higher Chemical Technological School in Pardubice, where he graduated as a chemical engineer in 1980. For ten years he worked as a technologist in the Levitex Levice Company. After the Czechoslovak Velvet Revolution, in March 1990 he was co-founder of the Hungarian Christian Democratic Movement (HCDM), and he won a parliamentary seat in the Slovak National Council in the first free elections in June 1990. Later he was elected to the Slovak parliament in 1992 and 1994. From 1992 to 1998 he was HCDM deputy chairman, exerting a strong influence on the unification of all Hungarian parties into the Party of the Hungarian Coalition (Magyar Koalíció Pártja; Strana Maďarskej Koalicie [PHC]). At the PHC's founding congress, on 21 June 1998 Csáky was elected its deputy chairman. In the parliamentary elections of September 1998 the PHC won more than 9 percent of the vote and entered the ruling coalition, which was to lead Slovakia out of isolation and stagnation after the regime of **Vladimír Mečiar**. In the **Mikuláš Dzurinda** government, sworn in on 30 October 1998, Csáky became deputy prime minister for human rights and minorities. Thanks to the PHC's entry into the ruling coalition, relations between the Slovak government and the Hungarian minority improved a great deal. In the elections of September 2002 the PHC won more than 11 percent of the vote, staying in the government, and Csáky remained deputy prime minister. (PU)

Sources: *Slovensko 1996: Súhrnná správa o stave spoločnosti* (Bratislava, 1997); *Slovensko 1997: Súhrnná správa o stave spoločnosti* (Bratislava, 1998); *Slovensko 1998–1999: Súhrnná správa o stave spoločnosti* (Bratislava, 1999); www.vlada.gov.sk/csaky/podpredseda_pal_csaky.html; www.nevyberajusmev.sk/lidri-smk-csaky.php.

CSERNOCH János (18 June 1852, Szakolca [Skalica, now in Slovakia]–25 July 1927, Esztergom), cardinal, Primate of Hungary. Born into a poor Slovak peasant family, Csernoch maintained his peasant accent all his life.

After theological studies in Pazmaneumin in Vienna, in November 1874 he was ordained. He continued his studies at the Augustineum in Vienna, where he received a Ph.D. in theology in 1876. From 1877 he worked as a chaplain in Budapest; from 1879, as a lecturer in theology in the Esztergom seminary; and from 1882, as secretary to the Primate of Hungary and papal chamberlain. In 1888 he was appointed canon, and in 1893, vicar of the Esztergom basilica, the main headquarters of the Catholic Church in Hungary. From 1896 Csernoch was diocese censor and from 1898, archdeacon of Nógrád; in 1901–10 he was MP on behalf of the Popular Catholic Party, which supported the agreement with Austria of 1867 but opposed the separation of church and state. One of the restorers of political Catholicism, Csernoch played an important role in the organization of the Christian Social movement, including both Catholics and Protestants. He published a lot in *Magyar Korona* and *Religio*.

In 1905 Csernoch was appointed archdeacon of the Esztergom basilica, and on 16 February 1908, bishop of Csanád. He was consecrated on 10 May 1908. On 20 April 1911 he became archbishop of Kalocsa, and on 13 December 1912, archbishop of Esztergom and prince primate of Hungary. On 25 May 1914 he was elevated to the rank of cardinal and proved to be the last Hungarian primate to crown the king of Hungary (Charles IV Habsburg in 1916). A close friend of Prime Minister **István Tisza**, after the outbreak of World War I Csernoch supported the war tactics of his government, but from 1916 his stance evolved toward pacifism. In the fall of 1918, in the name of the episcopate, he supported the republican government of sovereign Hungary headed by **Mihály Károlyi**. During the Hungarian Soviet Republic he remained passive. Afterwards, as a moderate legitimist, he tried to mediate between Charles IV and Regent **Miklós Horthy**. After some time he found that the return of the Habsburgs would be impossible, and he supported the policy of consolidation of Prime Minister **István Bethlen**. In 1908–18 he was a member of the House of Lords, and from 1927, a member of the Upper House of the Hungarian parliament. From 1915 he was a member of the Hungarian Academy of Sciences. (JT)

Sources: *Magyar Életrajzi Lexikon*, vol. 1 (Budapest, 1967); *Magyar Nagylexikon*, vol. 6 (Budapest, 1998); *Új Magyar Életrajzi Lexikon*, vol. 1 (Budapest, 2001); Nicholas Horthy, *Memoirs* (Paris, 1954); Ferenc Reisner, *Csernoch János, hercegprímás és a katolikus egyház szerepe IV. Károly monarchiamegmentési kísérleteiben* (Budapest, 1991).

CSOÓRI Sándor (3 February 1930, Zámoly), Hungarian writer. Csoóri graduated from the Calvinist high school in Pápa (1950) and studied Russian language and literature at the University of Budapest in 1951–52. In contrast to other writers of his generation, he made his literary debut in 1953 with a poem free of Socialist realism. His first volume, *Felröppen a madár* (A bird flying up; 1954), written under Romantic and symbolist influences, became a harbinger of the "thaw." In 1953–54 he edited the literary biweekly *Irodalmi Újság* and in 1955–56, a poetic column in the literary monthly *Új Hang*. He fully supported the revolution of 1956. After its suppression, he had no steady job for years but remained true to his poetic vocation. He also wrote press reports and prose dealing with social problems. His breakthrough volume was *Második születésem* (My second birth; 1967). Since its publication he has been considered one of Hungary's leading contemporary poets. Subsequent volumes—*Szép versek* (Beautiful poems; 1970) and *Párbeszéd a sötétben* (Dialogue in the dark; 1973)—established his position as a master of simple versification but visionary poetry, full of national symbols and existential motifs.

From 1968 Csoóri has worked with the Hungarian film studio Mafilm, writing screenplays for historical and documentary movies, mostly directed by Sándor Sára and Ferenc Kósa—for example, *Tízezer nap* (Ten thousand days; 1967); *Földobott kő* (A stone going up; 1989); *Itélet* (Sentence; 1970); *80 huszár* (80 Hussars; 1978); and *Pergőtűz* (Spitfire; 1982). From the late 1970s he returned to poetry and published several new volumes, such as *A tizedek este* (Tenth evening; 1980) and *A világ emlékművei* (Monuments of the world; 1989). Full of elegiac symbolism but clearly alluding to the Communist reality, these poems made Csoóri one of the informal leaders of the nation. He also published a number of collections of essays, such as *Nomád napló* (Nomadic diary; 1978) and *Készülődés a számadásra* (Getting ready to settle accounts; 1987). As a person of unquestionable authority, in 1988 Csoóri became editor-in-chief of the first official non-Communist periodical, *Hitel*. In 1989 he became co-founder and member of the first non-Communist political party, the Hungarian Democratic Forum (Magyar Demokrata Fórum). From 1991 he was chairman and then honorary chairman of the World Association of Hungarians. He strongly influenced the literary and political life of Hungary at the end of the twentieth century. Many of his works celebrated Hungarian aspirations for freedom, becoming literary expressions of the views and feelings of a society enslaved by communism. In his opposition to the internationalist, urban intelligentsia, Csoóri aligned himself with the tradition of populist writers. (MS)

Sources: *Mały słownik pisarzy węgierskich* (Warsaw, 1977); Ferenc Kiss, *Csoóri Sándor* (Budapest, 1990); Steven Béla Várdy,

Historical Dictionary of Hungary (Lanham, Md., 1997); *A lélek senki földjén: Csoóri Sándor köszöntése* (Budapest, 1992); Géza Vasy, *A nemzet rebellise* (Budapest, 2000).

CSURKA István (27 March 1934, Budapest), Hungarian writer and politician. The son of a writer, in 1957 Csurka graduated from the Higher School of Theater and Film Arts. His first volume of short stories was published in 1956. During the 1956 revolution he was elected head of the National Guard at his school, and in March 1957 he was arrested for half a year. During interrogations he promised to cooperate with the security service, but in fact he failed to report. After his release he lived from author's fees. He authored more than twenty dramas. With irony and a grotesque style he described the decline of moral values in the society. In the 1980s Csurka was one of the leaders of the emerging populist and nationalist opposition, which had roots in the tradition of the 1930s. He considered the countryside the "true root" of the nation, rather than the liberal and urban (mostly Budapest) intelligentsia. In 1985 he co-organized the only meeting of the entire Hungarian opposition, at which he criticized the inertia of the Hungarians after the suppressed 1956 revolution ("a nation of waiters" was his term), and he argued that without a reconstruction of the moral health, the nation faced disaster. In his opinion, it was only the consciousness of national goals and values, as well as entrepreneurship in a "truly Hungarian" sense, that could prevent this disaster.

In September 1987 Csurka co-founded the Hungarian Democratic Forum (Magyar Demokrata Forum [HDF]), the first official opposition party. Elected to its National Presidium (1988–93), in 1991–92 he was its deputy chairman. From 1990 he was MP on behalf of the HDF, the largest parliamentary faction. In August 1992 he stated that there had been no real systemic change in Hungary, that there was only an agreement of elites, and that key political figures—including President **Árpád Göncz**—were only figureheads implementing the orders of Israel and the United States. He also sharply criticized Prime Minister **József Antall**, head of the HDF. Csurka announced a radical program of the Hungarian right and created the Movement of the Hungarian Way (Magyar Út Mozgalom). In 1993 he was excluded from the HDF. On the basis of his movement and of the weekly *Magyar Fórum*, whose editor-in-chief he was from 1989, in 1993 he founded the Hungarian Justice and Life Party (Magyar Igazság és Élet Pártja [HJLP]), an extreme rightist and anti-Semitic group demanding, among other things, a return to the so-called historical Greater Hungary, meaning a revision of the Treaty of Trianon of 1920. In the elections of 1998 the

HJLP won 5.5 percent of the vote and fourteen mandates. In the elections of 2002 it won 4.3 percent of the vote and stayed out of the parliament. Csurka authored several dramas, including *Ki lesz a bálanya* (Who builds now; 1970); *Házmestersirato* (Bitter sorrows in the watchman lodge; 1978); and *Eredeti helyszín* (On Location; 1979), as well as novels. (JT)

Sources: *Magyar Nagylexikon*, vol. 6 (Budapest, 1998); *A magyar forradalom és szabadságharc enciklopédiája*, CD-ROM (Budapest, 1999); Steven Béla Várga, *Historical Dictionary of Hungary* (Lanham, Md., 1997); *Mały słownik pisarzy węgierskich* (Warsaw, 1977); Bugajski.

CUNESCU Sergiu (16 March 1923, Bucharest), Romanian politician. From the late 1930s Cunescu belonged to the Social Democratic Party of Romania (Partidul Social-Democrat din România [SDPR]). Soon after World War II he graduated from the Polytechnic Institute in Bucharest. After the split in the SDPR in 1946 he joined the Independent Social Democratic Party (Partidul Social-Democrat Independent [ISDP]), which included opponents of cooperation with the Communists. After the ISDP was outlawed in 1948 and its leaders were arrested, Cunescu abandoned political activity. He worked as a teacher in the Polytechnic Institute and as a machine engineer. Two days after the **Nicolae Ceauşescu** regime was toppled, on 24 December 1989 Cunescu joined a group that reactivated the ISDP as the Romanian Social Democratic Party (Partidul Social-Democrat Român [RSDP]). In early 1990 Cunescu became one of its leaders, and in 1991, its formal chairman. For a short time, the RSDP was a part of the National Salvation Front, but in January it left the front along with other historical parties because it was controlled by the post-Communists. In 1990–2000 Cunescu was an MP on behalf of the RSDP. In late 1990 the party joined other anti-Communist groups in the National Convention for the Establishment of Democracy, and in 1991, the Democratic Convention of Romania (Convenţia Democrată Română [DCR]). In view of his party's weak position in the DCR, in 1995 Cunescu led the RSDP out of the convention and into a coalition with the Social Democratic Union (Uniunea Social Democrat [SDU]), strongly influenced by the post-Communists. In the parliamentary elections of November 1996 the coalition won 13 percent of the vote and entered the ruling coalition with the DCR. In 1999 Cunescu broke off the coalition with the SDU and resigned from chairing his party, but he stayed its honorary chairman. Before the November 2000 elections the RSDP entered into a coalition with the post-Communist Party of Social Democracy in Romania (Partidul Democraţiei Sociale din România), and with the end of the parliamentary term in 2000, Cunescu withdrew from political life. (LW)

Sources: Ion Alexandrescu, Ion Bulei, Ion Mamina, and Ioan Scurtu, *Enciclopedia de istorie României* (Bucharest, 2000); Józef Darski, *Rumunia: Historia, współczesność, konflikty narodowe* (Warsaw, 1995); romania-on-line.net; www.cdep.ro.

CURRI Bajram bej (1862, Gjakove–29 March 1925, Gryka e Matines), Albanian independence activist. Curri started his public career as one of the organizers of the Albanian League in Peje (Peč) in 1899. In 1908 he joined a political club, Bashkimi (Union), in Skopje, and in 1912 he was one of the commanders of the anti-Turkish uprising in Kosovo. When in 1913 the Conference of Ambassadors excluded Kosovo from the area that was allocated to Albania, Curri's units took up arms against the Serbian Army. Counting on a political solution to the Kosovo problem, in 1918 Curri joined the Committee for the Defense of Kosovo, which delegated him to the Paris Peace Conference. In January 1920 he became minister without portfolio in the government of **Suleyman Pasha Delvina** and a member of the Senate. He was no diplomat, though, so he returned to the battlefield to fight for the region of Vlorë against the Italians. Authorized by the minister of war to suppress the rebellion of the followers of **Esad Pasha Toptani**, he gathered a few hundred soldiers and cleared the north of Albania, and then he controlled the borderland with the Kingdom of Serbs, Croats, and Slovenes (SHS).

The abandonment of the Kosovo question by the Albanian government made Curri start anti-government activities. After taking part in the negotiations that were aimed at the formation of a new cabinet in 1921, he began to actively support the **Hasan Prishtina** rebellion. The reason he gave was the lack of adequate representation for the Albanian north in the parliament. In February 1922 his units numbered about two thousand men. He was able to maintain his bases thanks to a decision by the Conference of Ambassadors at the turn of 1923 on the creation of a neutral zone along the frontier between Albania and the SHS. In early 1923 the Albanian Ministry of Interior attempted to get rid of his bases in cooperation with the SHS Army, but in vain. Opponents of the minister, **Ahmed Zogu**, sought Curri's support for a coup. The question of "Kosovo separatists" led to a deterioration of relations between Albania and the SHS in the spring of 1924. During the 1924 revolution it was Curri who gave the signal to attack the troops of the government of Shefqet bey Vërlaci, and the Curri units were the backbone of the troops supporting **Fan Noli**. From June to December 1924 Curri was minister of war in the government of Noli.

After the defeat of the Noli revolution, Curri was one of its few leaders who stayed in Albania, becoming a target of the Zogu gendarmerie. Along with a group of his closest aides he went to the region of Krasniqë. In 1925 he was encircled by the gendarmerie near Theth. According to various sources, Curri was either killed or committed suicide in Dragobi Cave. A town in northeastern Albania bears his name. (TC)

Sources: *Biographisches Lexikon*, vol. 1; Stefanaq Pollo and Arben Puto, *The History of Albania from Its Origins to the Present Day* (London, 1981); *Bajram Curri (trajtësa e dokumente)* (Tirana, 1982); Drini Skendër, *Bajram Curri* (Tirana, 1984); Sejfi Vllamasi, *Ballafaqime politike në Shqipëri (1897–1942)* (Tirana, 1995); Raymond Hitchings, *Historical Dictionary of Albania* (Lanham, Md., 1996); Neol Malcolm, *Kosovo: A Short History* (New York, 1998).

CUVAJ Slavko (26 February 1851, Bjelovar–31 January 1931, Vienna), conservative Croatian politician. As an official and later chief of the Osijek and Požega district (1885–1905) and Lika district (1905–6), Cuvaj represented loyalism to the Hungarian authorities. During the rule of **Pavao Rauch**, the governor (*ban*) of Croatia (1908–10), Cuvaj was mayor of Zagreb. As a result of the elections to the parliament (Sabor) in Zagreb in 1911, he lost to the Croatian-Serbian Coalition, which was increasingly critical of the dictatorial rule of the Austro-Hungarian *bans*. Despite this, on 20 January 1912 Cuvaj assumed the position of the *ban* of Croatia. He believed the conflict could be resolved by the use of force. On 27 January he dissolved the Sabor. As a result of mass student demonstrations and a school strike, the Austro-Hungarian authorities called a state of emergency, and Cuvaj was appointed a special commissioner. In June and October 1912 he twice avoided attempts on his life organized by the terrorists connected with Young Bosnia (Mlada Bosna). Hated by the Croats, in late 1912 Cuvaj was granted a leave of absence, and in the fall of 1913 he formally resigned. His rule only aggravated the ethnic tensions among the Habsburg Slavs. Awarded the title of baron by the Habsburgs, Cuvaj later lived in Austria. (WR)

Sources: *Enciklopedija Jugoslavije*, vol. 2 (Zagreb, 1956); *Hrvatski bografksi leksikon*, vol. 2 (Zagreb, 1989); *R. W. Seton-Watson and the Yugoslavs: Correspondence*, vol. 1, *1906–1918*; vol. 2, *1918–1941* (London and Zagreb, 1976); Nicholas J. Miller, *Between Nation and State: Serbian Politics in Croatia before the First World War* (Pittsburgh, 1997).

CUZA Aleksandru C. (8 November 1857, Iaşi–4 November 1947, Sibiu), Romanian politician and ideologist. Cuza studied in Dresden and Brussels. Initially connected with the Socialist movement, in 1883 he co-edited the influential émigré periodical *Dacia*, in which nationalist and Socialist viewpoints were mixed. He also published in the Socialist periodical *Contemporanul* and in the literary magazines *Convorbiri Literare*, *Unirea*, and *Neamul Romanesc*. In 1899 he was given a prestigious award by the Romanian Academy, and he became a member. From 1901 he worked as a professor at the University of Iaşi. It was then that he began to promote integral nationalism, based on the French model of Charles Maurras and the theories of Herbert Spencer. Cuza proclaimed himself in favor of authoritarian power and the domination of the Romanian majority defined by ethnic and religious categories. In his opinion "race and blood" were also key factors in art. His ideology was also strongly anti-Semitic, as he thought that Jews were not only alien, but also harmful to Romania.

In 1909 Cuza co-organized, with (among others) **Nicolae Iorga**, the National Democratic Party. In 1918 he created the National Christian Union, which became the League of National Christian Defense in March 1923. The league cooperated with another radical nationalist, **Corneliu Zelea-Codreanu**. On behalf of the league Cuza was elected to the parliament in 1926. Although both Cuza and Codreanu agreed on the necessity of the close cooperation of Romania with Fascist Italy and Nazi Germany, their ways parted mostly because Cuza resisted the totalitarian mobilization of the society suggested by Codreanu. In 1935 Cuza created the Popular National Bloc. Although he won a parliamentary seat again in 1936, he played no significant role, as he was neutralized by the royal dictatorship of King **Charles II**. In June 1938 his party merged with the Popular Party of General **Alexandru Avarescu** into the National Christian Popular Party, but it gained little support. Disappointed by politics, Cuza retired, remaining a symbol and intellectual inspiration for the new generation of radical Romanian nationalists. The circumstances of his death are not clear. Cuza authored (among other works) *Generaţia de la 1848 şi era nouă* (The 1848 generation and the new era; 1889) and *Naţionalitatea in artă* (Nationality in art; 1910). (MC)

Sources: *Biographisches Lexikon*, vol. 1; Pamfil Seicaru, *Un junimist antisemit A. C. Cuza* (Madrid, 1956); Nicholas Nagy-Talavera, *The Green Shirts and Others* (Stanford, 1970); Radu Ioanid, *The Sword of the Archangel* (Boulder, Colo., 1990); Leon Volovici, *Nationalist Ideology and Antisemitism: The Case of Romanian Intellectuals in the 1930s* (Oxford, 1991); Randolph L. Braham, *The Destruction of Romanian and Ukrainian Jews during the Antonescu Era* (Boulder, Colo., 1997); motic.wiesenthal.com/text/x05/x0567.html.

CVETKOVIĆ Dragiša (15 January 1893, Niš–18 February 1969, Paris), Yugoslav politician. Cvetković studied law in Subotica. A member of the Serbian Radical Party, he began his political activity in the 1920s as a local government activist in Niš. Elected to the parliament (Skupstina) in 1927, he became minister of religious affairs a year later. After the royal coup d'état of 6 January 1929 and the assumption of dictatorial power by King **Alexander Karajordjević**, Cvetković joined the United Opposition a group of politicians of various parties that were in opposition to the monarch. After the king was assassinated in 1934, Cvetković linked up with the rightist Yugoslav Radical Union of **Milan Stojadinović**. As a result, in 1935 he was reelected to the Skupstina and joined the new government as minister of health and social policy. In the face of mounting political crisis, caused by ethnic conflicts and resistance to the authoritarian and pro-Fascist government of Stojadinović—this resistance was manifested in the elections of December 1938—Cvetković entered into an agreement with the regent, Prince **Paul Karadjordjević**, and **Anton Korošec**, leader of the Slovenes, and he contributed to the fall of the government on 3 February 1939. A quick political about-face and the trust of the real ruler (Prince Paul) of Yugoslavia helped Cvetković win the post of prime minister, which he assumed on 5 February 1939.

Cvetković's government attempted to abandon authoritarianism. In domestic policy, his most important step was an agreement (*sporazum*) signed with the Peasant Democratic Coalition of **Vladko Maček** on 26 August 1939, by which the existence of the Croatian nation was de facto recognized, Zagreb was formally granted broad autonomy (the so-called Croatian Banovina), and Maček joined the government as deputy prime minister. The agreement, which was to open the way to equal rights for Croats in Yugoslavia, turned out to be a tactical "cease-fire" between the two nations, and actually many provisions of this agreement were not enforced. In foreign policy, Cvetković tried to loosen ties with Germany, and, by declaring strict neutrality (also in the war that began with the German aggression against Poland), he sought rapprochement with Great Britain and France. However, relations with the Allies did not progress beyond the stage of contacts of the general staffs of both countries, nor beyond the stage of talks on the possible involvement of Yugoslavia in the war on the side of the Western countries. The Cvetković government was under strong pressure from Germany. This could be observed in a politically motivated increase in trade and the inflow of German capital; in the granting of preferences to the German minority; and in the adoption of anti-Jewish legislation. As the allies of the Third Reich surrounded Yugoslavia, Italy made territorial claims to Dalmatia, and actions were taken by Croatian separatists, Cvetković decided to officially declare strict neutrality in the ongoing war but also to accede to the Tripartite Pact. By signing the pact on 25 March 1941, the Axis states agreed to respect Yugoslav claims to Greek Salonika, and they exempted the Yugoslavs from the military provisions of the pact. However, these terms were not publicly announced.

The signing of the Tripartite Pact, to which Cvetković agreed reluctantly and after long pressure from Germany (Hitler had even threatened Yugoslavia with war), caused serious protests in Yugoslavia and created a breeding ground for a coup, which was staged two days later by a group of officers led by General **Dušan Simović**, who removed Prince Paul and Cvetković from power. As a result of the coup, at the beginning of April 1941 Yugoslavia was invaded and broken up by the Axis powers and neighboring countries. Cvetković remained in occupied Yugoslavia until 1943, and then he went into exile. In 1951–57 he published ten volumes of *Dokumenti o Jugoslaviji* (Documents about Yugoslavia). (AG)

Sources: *Biographisches Lexikon*, vol. 1; *Enciklopedija Jugoslavije*, vol. 2 (Zagreb, 1956); Jacob B. Hoptner, *Yugoslavia in Crisis, 1934–1941* (New York, 1962); Ljubo Boban, *Sporazum Cvetković-Maček* (Belgrade, 1965); Dragiša N. Ristić, *Yugoslavia's Revolution of 1941* (Stanford, 1966); Johann Wuescht, *Jugoslawien und das Dritte Reich* (Stuttgart, 1969); Wacław Felczak and Tadeusz Wasilewski, *Historia Jugosławii* (Wrocław, 1985); Michał J. Zacharias, *Jugosławia w polityce Wielkiej Brytanii 1940–1945* (Wrocław, 1987).

CVIJIĆ Džuro (25 October 1896, Zagreb–1937, USSR), Croatian Communist activist. The son of an accountant, Cvijić became active in the revolutionary movement in his youth. In 1912 he was sentenced to three years' imprisonment for his involvement in the preparation of the assassination of **Slavko Cuvaj**, the *ban* of Croatia. Released in 1914, he worked as a journalist. From 1917 to 1918 he served in the Austro-Hungarian Army, and after demobilization he was active in the Croatian Socialist Party and in the trade unions. At the founding congress of the Communist Party of Yugoslavia (CPY) in 1919 he became a member of its Central Committee and was head of the Croatian section. After the delegalization of the party in 1921 he went to Vienna, where he got in touch with the Comintern. Using the pseudonyms "Krešić" and "Kirsch," Cvijić traveled between Vienna and Zagreb, and he secretly edited the party's newspaper, *Borba*. In June 1923, as "Vladetić," he attended the Third Plenum of the Comintern's Executive Committee. When in April 1925 the Comintern dismissed the leadership of the CPY, he was appointed interim secretary of the party. In 1926 he opened the Third Congress of the party in Vienna, and in April 1928, after the ouster of **Sima Marković**, he became

secretary general of the CPY. However, in October of that year, as a result of factious strife, the Comintern removed Cvijić as well. After his return to Zagreb he was arrested, and he spent two and a half years in prison. In 1932 he went to Vienna, where he edited the newspaper *The Balkan Federation*, and he worked for TASS, the Soviet news agency. In 1933 he spoke at the Reichstag fire trial, which was simultaneously held in London and Dresden and was organized by the Comintern. At the trial, Cvijić defended the Communist cause. In 1934 he was summoned to the USSR, where he worked at the Institute of Agriculture in Moscow. During the Great Purge in 1937 he was arrested and then executed. (WR)

Sources: Lazitch; *Enciklopedija Jugoslavije*, vol. 2 (Zagreb, 1966); *Enciklopedija Leksigrafskog Zavoda*, vol. 1 (Zagreb, 1966).

CYRANKIEWICZ Józef (23 April 1911, Tarnów–20 January 1989, Warsaw), Polish Socialist and Communist politician. Born into a white-collar family, Cyrankiewicz studied law at the Jagiellonian University in Kraków but did not graduate. From 1931 he belonged to the Polish Socialist Party (Polska Partia Socjalistyczna [PPS]), and from 1935 he was head of the PPS organization in Kraków. During World War II he was active in the underground PPS Freedom-Equality-Independence (Wolność, Równość, Niepodległość [PPS-WRN]) and in the inter-party political committee in Kraków. He was PPS-WRN candidate for deputy homeland delegate of the government-in-exile. In April 1941 he was arrested by the Nazis, detained in Montelupi Prison in Kraków, and then sent to concentration camps in Auschwitz and Mauthausen, where he co-organized clandestine structures. After his release, in the spring of 1945 Cyrankiewicz joined the leadership of the PPS, now under Communist control. He became a member of the PPS Supreme Board, and from July 1945 to December 1948 he was secretary general of its Central Executive Committee. Broken by the concentration camp experience and by the fatal evolution of the Polish cause at the end of World War II, he was among those Polish Socialists who chose close cooperation with the (Communist) Polish Workers' Party (Polska Partia Robotnicza [PPR]). From 1945 he supported crypto-Communists in the PPS leadership. In November 1946 he became minister without portfolio in the government of **Edward Osóbka-Morawski**.

After the elections to the Constituent Assembly (Sejm), tampered with by the Communists, on 5 February 1947 Cyrankiewicz became prime minister of the government dominated by the PPR. His candidature was approved in Moscow, and he followed the Moscow line—for instance, he gave up Polish participation in the Marshall Plan in July

1947. Many times he attacked Socialist leaders, such as **Zygmunt Żuławski**, who defended the integrity of the PPS. In 1948 Cyrankiewicz strove to merge the party with the PPR. During the "unification" congress in December 1948, he was elected to the Central Committee (CC) of the Polish United Workers' Party (Polska Zjednoczona Partia Robotnicza [PUWP]). He also became a member of the PUWP CC Secretariat and Organization Bureau, and from March 1954 he was a member of the PUWP CC Politburo. From 1952 to 1955 he presided over the Main Board of the Society of Polish-Soviet Friendship, and from 1952 to 1956 he was a member of the Presidium of the All-Polish Committee of the National Front.

After the new constitution was passed in July 1952 and the head of the PUWP, **Bolesław Bierut**, took over the position of prime minister on 21 November 1952, Cyrankiewicz remained deputy prime minister, but as a result of the redistribution of power within the "collective leadership" promoted by the Kremlin after Stalin's death, on 18 March 1954 he resumed the position of prime minister. He was active in anti-church actions, both in the early 1950s and in the 1960s, particularly during the celebration of the Millennium of Christianity in Poland in 1966. In June 1956 he sharply attacked workers demonstrating in Poznań, threatening them with "chopping off hands." Apart from this, Cyrankiewicz was thought a cynical pragmatist and was not engaged in the struggle between the Puławska and Natolin factions. After October 1956 he closely co-operated with **Władysław Gomułka**. In March 1968 he sharply attacked demonstrating students. Replying to the parliamentary interpellation of Znak, a Catholic club, on this matter, on 10 April 1968 he made a long and demagogical speech supporting the official line.

In December 1970 Cyrankiewicz participated in a top emergency party task force to deal with the crisis connected with the protests of workers on the Baltic Coast. As prime minister, he accepted the decision made by the party leader, Gomułka, to shoot at the workers, and he implemented the decision through the police and military apparatus. Thus he was co-responsible for the massacre on the Baltic Coast. As a result of the dismissal of Gomułka's ruling group, on 23 December 1970 Cyrankiewicz gave up the position of prime minister, but he was "kicked up" to the position of chairman of the Council of State. He held this position until 27 March 1972. In 1949–72 he was also chairman of the Supreme Council of the Union of Fighters for Freedom and Democracy, a Communist war veterans' organization. In 1972 he was dropped from the list of candidates to the Sejm, and in December 1975, from the PUWP CC. From March 1973 to April 1986 he remained head of the All-Polish Peace Committee, and

until July 1983 he was a member of the Presidium of the All-Polish Committee of the National Unity Front; the position really had a symbolic meaning: subsequent ruling groups were in fact recognizing his contribution to the introduction and strengthening of the Communist system in Poland. (PK)

Sources: Mołdawa; Eleonora and Bogusław Syzdkowie, *Nim będzie zapomniany* (Warsaw, 1986); Krystyna Kersten, *Narodziny systemu władzy* (Poznań, 1990); Paweł Machcewicz, *Polski rok 1956* (Warsaw, 1993); Andrzej Albert [Wojciech Roszkowski], *Najnowsza historia Polski 1914–1993*, vol. 2 (Warsaw, 1995); *Słownik Polityków Polskich XX w.* (Poznań, 1998); Jerzy Eisler, *Grudzień 1970* (Warsaw, 2000); Dariusz Stola, *Kampania antysyjonistyczna w Polsce 1967–1968* (Warsaw, 2000).

CYWIŃSKI Bohdan (19 July 1939, Milanówek, near Warsaw), Polish historian and social activist. After attending Tadeusz Reytan High School in Warsaw, in 1961 Cywiński graduated in Polish studies from Warsaw University and in philosophy from the Catholic University of Lublin (Katolicki Uniwersytet Lubelski [KUL]). From 1960 he was active in the Catholic Intelligentsia Club in Warsaw. In 1962–65 he worked in the National Library; from 1966 he worked at the Catholic monthly, *Znak*, and in 1973–77 he was its editor-in-chief. He lectured at the Academy of Catholic Theology in Warsaw, at the KUL, and at the Pauline Higher Theological Seminar in Kraków. In 1971 he published *Rodowody niepokornych* (Genealogy of the unvanquished), which greatly stimulated and consolidated the Catholic and lay opposition to the Communist regime. Cywiński analyzed the formation of the Polish intelligentsia at the turn of the twentieth century, showing that Polish Catholicism included strong social, and even progressive, undercurrents, while lay Socialists were the leading patriotic force. Remembering the values of the "unvanquished" Polish Catholics, Socialists, and liberals was an important incentive for the Poles disappointed or frustrated by communism in the 1970s.

In 1976 Cywiński took part in protests against amendments to the Communist constitution that would include articles on the "leading role" of the Communist Party and the "alliance" with the USSR. In 1977 he co-organized a hunger strike in defense of imprisoned workers and members of the Committee for the Defense of Workers. In 1977–80 he belonged to the organizers of the Society of Scholarly Courses and lectured at the "Flying University," which, despite assaults by Communist gangs, broke the state monopoly on education. He was arrested several times, and his apartment was frequently searched. In 1979 he protested before the chairman of the Council of State against the persecution of the free trade unions. In August 1980 he joined the Commission of Experts of the

Inter-Factory Strike Committee in the Gdańsk shipyard, and in the spring of 1981 he became deputy editor-in-chief of the Solidarity weekly *Tygodnik Solidarność*. After the introduction of martial law Cywiński lived in Switzerland. He lectured in Geneva and Fribourg, and he edited the periodical *Widnokrąg*. After his return to Poland in 1991 he strove to unite the transformation efforts of the East Central European countries. In 1992–94 he lectured in Belorussia and Ukraine, and in 1995–98, at the University of Vilnius (Wilno). In 1995 he received a postdoctoral degree from the KUL. From 1999 he was a professor of contemporary history at the Warsaw Academy of Catholic Theology (now the Cardinal **Stefan Wyszyński** University). He also authored a collection of essays, *Zatruta humanistyka* (Contaminated humanities; 1979); *Potęgą jest i basta* (It is mighty, period; 1981); and a history of Communist oppression of Catholic churches in East Central Europe, *Ogniem próbowane* (Ordeal by fire, 2 vols.; 1982–90) (AG)

Sources: *Wielka encyklopedia PWN*, vol. 6 (Warsaw, 2002); Andrzej Friszke, *Opozycja polityczna w PRL 1945–1980* (London, 1994); wiem.onet.pl/wiem/00e4bd.html; www.uksw.edu.pl/wydzialy/wnhis/politol/struktura/biogramy/bohdan_cywinski.html.

CZAPIK Gyula [originally Géza Czékus] (3 December 1887, Szeged–25 April 1956, Budapest), Hungarian bishop. Born into a printer's family, after high school Czapik entered the theological seminary in Temesvár (Timişoara), and then he studied at the Pazmaneum in Vienna. Ordained in 1910, in 1911 he received a Ph.D. in theology at the Augustineum in Vienna. Later he worked as a tutor for the children of Regent **Miklós Horthy**, as a parish priest, and as a lecturer in the theological seminary in Szeged. From 1913 he was a professor of theology at the Higher Theological Academy in Temesvár. In 1918 he was appointed diocese prosecutor, and in 1919, deputy director of the theological seminary. When the Romanian troops entered Temesvár in 1919, he moved to Budapest. From 1922 he was papal chamberlain, from 1929 canon, from 1935 prelate, and from 1938 apostolic protonotary. In 1913–14 he edited the monthly *Havi Közlöny*; in 1917–18, *Temesvarer Neuer Post*; and in 1920–39, *Egyházi Lapok*, *Magyar Kultúra*, and *Utunk*. In 1929 he founded, and from 1950 he directed, the Korda Press, which played an important role in Catholic publishing. He authored and translated a number of books and theological articles.

In July 1939 Czapik was appointed bishop of Veszprém. As a result he became a member of the Upper House. From May 1943 he was archbishop of Eger. Trying to adapt the Catholic Church to the new political circumstances, he played an important role in the preparation and signing of a compromise agreement with the Communist state in 1950. He took note of the dissolution of religious orders but tried his best to help the ousted monks and nuns. After the arrest of Archbishop **József Grősz** in May 1951, he became president of the Hungarian Episcopate. Two months later, the entire Hungarian hierarchy still at large, except for one auxiliary bishop, swore an oath of loyalty to the new constitution. Czapik tried to save what remained of church activity, but the price was his acceptance of Stalinist lawlessness and his participation in the international peace movement. For instance, in 1955 he spoke at a meeting of the World Council of Peace in Helsinki. He also endorsed the peace movement of Catholic priests, thus serving the interests of Communist propaganda. From 1954 until his death he was a member of the All-National Council of Peace and of the Presidium of the National Council of the Patriotic People's Front. (JT)

Sources: *Magyar Életrajzi Lexikon*, vol. 1 (Budapest, 1967); *Magyar Nagylexikon*, vol. 6 (Budapest, 1998); *Magyarország 1944–1956*, CD-ROM, 1956-os Intézet (Budapest, 2001); *Új Magyar Életrajzi Lexikon*, vol. 1 (Budapest, 2001).

CZAPIŃSKI Kazimierz (18 November 1882, Minsk–July 1941 Oświęcim [Auschwitz]), Polish Socialist politician. From 1900 to 1910 Czapiński was a member of the Russian Social Democratic Workers' Party and of the Social Democracy of the Kingdom of Poland and Lithuania. He studied law at the University of St. Petersburg but was expelled for agitating among workers. Repeatedly arrested, he remained under police surveillance, was later deported, and lived in forced exile. In 1904 in Geneva he met Vladimir Lenin. In 1907 Czapiński arrived in Kraków, where in 1909 he resumed legal studies at the Jagiellonian University. Expelled in 1911 for organizing student demonstrations, he lectured at people's universities. He also conducted lectures in philosophy and literature at the Kraków College of Academic Lectures. Although he moved away from the extreme revolutionary left, in 1914 he participated in causes supporting Lenin's release from jail. In 1910–19 Czapiński was a member of the Polish Social Democratic Party. From 1919 he belonged to the Polish Socialist Party (Polska Partia Socjalistyczna [PPS]). From 1920 to 1939 he was a member of the Chief Council of the PPS, and in 1921–39, of its Central Executive Committee. From 1919 to 1935 he was an MP and secretary of the Union of Polish Socialist Deputies. In February 1921 he was a delegate of the PPS to the founding congress of the Working Union of Socialist Parties (also known as the Vienna Union) in Vienna. He opposed the conclusion of the concordat and insisted on the separation of church and state. He advocated that schools and education be secular.

Czapiński was against the cooperation of the PPS with the Communists.

A devoted educator, in 1923 Czapiński co-founded the Workers' University Society. From 1924 to 1934 he was vice-president of this society, and in 1934–39 he was president of its Main Board. In 1937 he co-founded the Warsaw Democratic Club. He was involved in journalism and commented on international issues. From 1907 to 1914 he co-edited the periodical *Przedświt*. In 1914–19 he was editor of the magazine *Naprzód*. For many years he contributed to the newspaper *Robotnik*, and in 1935–39 he was its deputy editor-in-chief. On the eve of World War II Czapiński advocated the cooperation of Poland with the USSR and with the Little Entente. Arrested by the Germans in September 1940 and imprisoned in Pawiak Prison, on 6 February 1941 he was sent to the concentration camp in Auschwitz, where he died. He authored many works, including the following: *Bankructwo bolszewizmu* (Bankruptcy of Bolshevism; 1921); *Czy socjaliści mogą walczyć razem z komunistami? Kwestia międzynarodówki i "jednego frontu" proletariatu* (Can Socialists fight together with Communists? The question of the international and of the "united front" of the proletariat; 1922); *Czarna ofensywa: Drogi i cele wojującego klerykalizmu* (The black offensive: Ways and aims of militant clericalism; 1922); *Socjalizm czy komunizm?* (Socialism or communism? 1924); *Państwo a Kościół: Konkordat Polski z Rzymem* (The state and the Church: The Concordat between Poland and Rome; 1925); *Faszyzm współczesny* (Contemporary fascism; 1932); *Świat na wulkanie: Krótki zarys sytuacji międzynarodowej* (The world on the volcano: A short outline of the international situation; 1938). (JS)

Sources: *Słownik Biograficzny Działaczy Polskiego Ruchu Robotniczego*, vol. 1 (Warsaw, 1978); *Encyklopedia Historii Drugiej Rzeczypospolitej* (Warsaw, 1999); Michał Czajka, Marcin Kamler, and Witold Sienkiewicz, *Leksykon Historii Polski* (Warsaw, 1995); Jerzy Holzer, *Polska Partia Socjalistyczna w latach 1917–1919* (Warsaw, 1962); Jan Tomicki, *Norbert Barlicki, 1880–1941: Działalność polityczna* (Warsaw, 1968); Aleksandra Tymieniecka, *Polityka Polskiej Partii Socjalistycznej w latach 1924–1928* (Warsaw, 1969).

CZAPSKI Józef (3 April 1896, Prague–12 January 1993, Maisons-Lafitte, near Paris), Polish painter and art critic. Born into an aristocratic family from the Minsk area, in 1916 Czapski graduated from a high school in Petersburg and started law studies there. In 1917 he served in the Krechowce Uhlan Regiment. In October 1918 he entered the School of Fine Arts in Warsaw, Poland. At the turn of 1919 he went to Petrograd with a mission to find Polish officers captured by the Bolsheviks. In 1920 he took part in the Polish-Soviet war, and he was awarded the Order of Virtuti Militari. In 1924 he graduated from the Academy of Fine Arts in Kraków and became a co-founder of the artistic Paris Committee. Then Czapski left for France, where he studied at the Académie Rancon in Paris, met the leading French artists of that time, and organized many exhibitions. In 1931 he returned to Poland and published in the weekly *Wiadomości Literackie*, painted in the Colorist style, and exhibited in Poland and abroad. During the September 1939 campaign he fought as an officer. Captured by the Red Army, he was imprisoned in the Starobelsk, Pavlishchev Bor, and Gryazovets camps. After the signing of the Polish-Soviet agreement of July 1941, he was released, and on the orders of General **Władysław Anders** he searched for Polish officers who had been imprisoned in the Soviet camps of Kozelsk, Starobelsk, and Ostashkov but had disappeared. Since the Soviet authorities could not explain what had happened to them, his mission failed. It was later disclosed that these officers had met a tragic fate, murdered by the NKVD on the orders of the Soviet Politburo in March and April 1940. Evacuated with the army of General Anders via Iran and Iraq, Czapski got to Palestine, and then, along with the Polish Second Corps, he took part in the Italian campaign. After the war he settled in France, where he co-founded and (along with his sister Maria) edited the monthly *Kultura* in Paris. Continuing to adhere to Colorism and presenting simple themes (mostly landscapes and still lifes), Czapski painted a lot and took part in many exhibitions, mostly in France, Italy, Great Britain, Canada, and the United States. He published important memoirs of his experience in the USSR, *Wspomnienia starobielskie* (Starobelsk memoirs; 1944), and *Na nieludzkiej ziemi* (1949; *Inhuman Land*, 1951), as well as collections of essays: *Oko* (The eye; 1960); *Tumult i widma* (Turmoil and specters; 1981); *Czytając* (Reading; 1990); and *Dzienniki* (Diaries; 1986). (WR)

Sources: *Wielka encyklopedia PWN*, vol. 6 (Warsaw, 2002); Murielle Werner-Gagnebin, *Czapski: La main et l'espace* (Lausanne, 1974); Joanna Pollakówna, *Czapski* (Warsaw, 1994); Wojciech Karpiński, *Portret Czapskiego* (Wrocław, 1996); Jan Zieliński, *Józef Czapski: Krótki przewodnik po długim życiu* (Warsaw, 1997).

CZERNIAKÓW Adam (30 November 1880, Warsaw–23 July 1942, Warsaw), Jewish social activist in Poland. Born into a family with assimilation tendencies, in 1908 Czerniaków graduated in chemistry from the Warsaw Polytechnic and in 1912 in industrial engineering in Dresden. He also studied at the Higher Trade School in Warsaw. Then he worked as a teacher. In 1909 he was briefly arrested by the Russian authorities for his part in the Polish independence conspiracy. In 1919–21 he was head of a section in the Ministry of Public Works; from 1927 to 1934 he was a member of the Warsaw City Council; and in 1931 he was appointed senator on behalf of the ruling Nonparty Bloc of Cooperation with the Government. He failed to take the oath, so he never took a senator's seat. He was active in education and published in *Izraelita*, *Nasze Życie*, and *Handwerker Tsaytung*. In 1938 he joined the commissionaire board of the Jewish Commune, imposed by the Polish authorities after the 1938 strikes; it antagonized both the Jewish left and the extreme right against him.

After the German invasion and in view of the departure of the Jewish Commune leaders, on 23 September 1939 Czerniaków was appointed by the president of Warsaw, **Stefan Starzyński**, as chairman of the Jewish Council (Judenrat). In this role he was recognized by the Nazi authorities. He turned down an offer to leave Poland. His activities aroused extreme feelings among the survivors of the Warsaw Ghetto. Czerniaków was perceived as someone who was assimilated in the Polish society and lacked a political background in the Jewish community, so his position was shaky. His main target was to secure the survival of the Jewish community, assuming a short duration of the war. He tried to make the Warsaw Ghetto institutions function, paid a lot of attention to maintaining Jewish education, and organized charity work—for instance, giving out food to the starving and homeless.

Czerniaków's activity had a price. Becoming a "transmission belt" for German decisions, he was hated by much of the Warsaw Ghetto community. With his consent the Jewish Council employed opportunists and careerists, including Gestapo agents. Some of his decisions were perceived as particularly traumatic. Quotas of slave workers supplied by the Warsaw Ghetto added to his troubles. He was also accused of inefficient intervention with the German authorities and of avoiding contacts with underground organizations. On the other hand, while the civic authorities of the German General Gouvernement tolerated him, the Nazi security apparatus treated him as a dangerous enemy. Unlike some other leaders of ghettos in the Polish territories, Czerniaków never tried to reap personal benefits from his activities, and when the Germans did not approve of the steps he had taken, he was seriously beaten several times. Until the end he was attached to the idea of Polish statehood, and despite German threats, he kept a portrait of **Józef Piłsudski** in his office. In July 1942 the German authorities demanded his cooperation in organizing deportations from the ghetto. Realizing that this most likely meant death for the deportees, Czerniaków chose to commit suicide. (AG)

Sources: *Encyclopedia of the Holocaust*, vol. 1 (New York, 1990); Roman Zimand, *W nocy od 12 do 5 rano nie spałem* (Paris, 1979); *Adama Czerniakowa dziennik getta warszawskiego 6 IX 1939–23 VII 1942* (Warsaw, 1983); *The Warsaw Diary of Adam Czerniakow: Prelude to Doom* (Chicago, 1999); Jerzy Tomaszewski and Andrzej Żbikowski, eds., *Żydzi w Polsce: Leksykon* (Warsaw, 2001).

CZERNIN Ottokar, Count (Graf) von und zu Chudenitz (26 September 1872, Dimokur [now Dymokury]–4 April 1932, Vienna), head of Austro-Hungarian diplomacy. Czernin came from a family of the old Czech aristocracy that was loyal to the Habsburgs. After graduating from the German university in Prague, he entered the diplomatic service and was assigned to Paris and later to The Hague. His career was temporarily interrupted by a lung disease. From 1903 he sat in parliament, and from 1912, also in the Czech senate, where he was the backbone of conservatism and monarchism. He strongly opposed the introduction of universal suffrage. He considered the aristocracy as the pillar of the throne and of the empire. He was closely connected with Charles, the heir to the throne, and with Archduke Francis Ferdinand, thanks to whom he returned to the diplomatic service, this time as minister to Romania (1913–16). On 22 December 1916 Charles, as the new emperor, appointed him foreign minister for Austria-Hungary. Initially, Czernin yielded to the persuasion of the German ally and recognized the necessity of an unlimited sea war, with the use of (among other things) submarines. However, seeing the weakness of Austria-Hungary, he tried to induce Charles and the German command to sign a peace with the Entente, even at the price of Germany's returning Alsace and Lorraine to France. Czernin was hoping for territorial gains from Russia—for example, from Polish lands. He also planned to draw Serbia and Romania into a Danube federation in which Austria-Hungary would play a key role. In April 1917 he warned that if a peace was not concluded, the empire might not survive the following winter. His signing, on behalf of Austria-Hungary, of peace treaties with the Ukraine (9 February 1918), Bolshevik Russia (3 March 1918), and Romania (14 April 1918) was the culmination of his career. The terms of these treaties were advantageous to Austria-Hungary. On 16 April 1918 Czernin resigned, paying the political price for secret attempts by Charles and Sixtus of Bourbon-Parma, Charles's brother-in-law, to negotiate a separate peace with France. The disclosure of the secret correspondence by Georges Clemenceau, who aimed at the unconditional defeat of the Central Powers, discredited Czernin in the eyes of the Germans.

After the defeat of Austria-Hungary, Czernin settled in the imperial estates in Salzkammergut, Austria. He attempted to maintain his estates in Bohemia, but when they were lost as a result of Czechoslovak agrarian reforms, he settled permanently in Austria. Between 1920 and 1923 he served as a deputy of the Civic Labor Party (Bürgerliche Arbeitspartei) in the Austrian parliament, and then he went into political retirement. He was the author of several books, including *Österreichs Wahlrecht und Parlament* (Austrian electoral law and the parliament; 1905); *Politische Betrachtungen* (Political studies; 1908); and *Im Weltkriege* (In the world war; 1919). (WR)

Sources: *Biographisches Lexikon*, vol. 1; *Neue Deutsche Biographie*, vol. Brațianu (New York, 1956); Holger H. Herwig and Neil M. Heyman, *Biographical Dictionary of World War I* (Westport, Conn., 1982); Ladislau Singer, *Ottokar Graf Czernin* (Graz, 1965); Robert A. Kann, *Die Sixtusaffäre und die geheime Friedensverhandlungen Österreich-Ungarns im Ersten Weltkrieg* (Vienna, 1966); Ingeborg Meckling, *Die Aussenpolitik des Grafen Czernin* (Munich, 1969); August Demblin, *Minister gegen Kaiser* (Vienna, 1997).

CZESZEJKO-SOCHACKI Jerzy (29 November 1892, Nieżyn, near Chernihov–4 September 1933, Moscow), Polish Socialist and Communist activist. Born into a white-collar family, after high school in Dzvinsk (Dyneburg, Daugavpils), from 1911 Czeszejko-Sochacki studied at the School of Law at Petersburg University, but he failed to graduate. He worked as a teacher in Wilno (Vilnius), Warsaw, and Syennitsa, near Minsk. In 1915 he joined the Polish Socialist Party (Polska Partia Socjalistyczna [PPS]), and in 1917, the Lithuanian Social Democratic Party. He worked on the editorial boards of *Przegląd Wileński* and *Jedność Robotnicza*. From 1919 he was secretary general and member of the Supreme Board and Central Executive Committee of the PPS. He was particularly concerned with education and belonged to the Main Board of the Union of Workers' Cooperatives. He represented a pro-Communist line in the party. In 1921 he was arrested and imprisoned for a few months in Warsaw. Suspended as a PPS member, he left the party, and in December 1921, with a group of followers, he joined the Communist Workers' Party of Poland (as of 1925 the Communist Party of Poland, Komunistyczna Partia Polski [KPP]). In 1921–25 he was a member of the illegal Communist Party Central Committee (CC), and in 1922 he was a co-founder and leader of the legal Union of Urban and Rural Proletariat. In 1925 he took part in the International Conference of Communists in Brussels.

In 1926–28 Czeszejko-Sochacki was an MP, filling the gap after another Communist deputy, Stanisław Łańcucki, had given up his mandate. He was also secretary of the Communist parliamentary club. In 1928 he was one of the key organizers of the electoral bloc Workers' and Peasants' Unity and was elected to the parliament from Będzin. In 1928 he escaped from Poland and was deprived of the mandate. He joined the CC of the Communist Party of Western Ukraine. From 1929 he was a member of the KPP CC; from 1930 he was its representative in the Executive Committee of the Communist International (Comintern) in Moscow, where he lived under the pseudonym "Jerzy Bratkowski." From 1931 a deputy member of the Presidium and Political Secretariat of the Comintern, in 1932 Czeszejko-Sochacki was dismissed from the KPP leadership because of his alleged role as a PPS provocateur. On 15 August 1933 he was arrested by the Soviet political police. He committed suicide. He was posthumously excluded from the KPP, but rehabilitated in 1956. (PK)

Sources: *Parlament Rzeczypospolitej Polskiej 1919–1927* (Warsaw, 1928); *Posłowie i senatorowie Rzeczypospolitej Polskiej 1919–1939: Słownik biograficzny* (Warsaw, 1998); Jerzy Holzer, *Polska Partia Socjalistyczna w latach 1917–1919* (Warsaw, 1962).

CZINEGE Lajos (26 March 1924, Karcag–10 May 1998, Leányfalu), Hungarian Communist activist. Czinege's father was a farm worker and then a postman. After primary school Czinege trained to become a blacksmith. In the fall of 1944 he joined the Metalworkers' Trade Union and in early 1945, the Hungarian Communist Party (HCP). As a well-known athlete, he became secretary of a local branch of the Hungarian Democratic Youth Union, controlled by the Communists. In 1946 he volunteered for the army, and in 1947 he was appointed HCP secretary in Karcag and sent to a two-month party school in Budapest. In 1948–51 he headed a section in the Hungarian Workers' Party (HWP) committee in Szolnok County and then in the Ministry of National Defense, where, without professional qualifications, he served as inspector in the Political Department and deputy commander of artillery for political affairs. At this time he graduated from the Military Political Academy. In 1954 he was made deputy head of the Administration Department of the HWP Central Committee (CC), and in 1955 he became its head.

At the beginning of the revolution, on 23 October 1956 Czinege became a member of the CC Military Commission and took part in the elaboration of a plan for a military crackdown on demonstrators. After the second Soviet intervention of 4 November 1956, he was appointed head of the Administration Department of the CC of the Hungarian Socialist Workers' Party (HSWP), and the next day he was put in charge of the special forces of the Ministry of Defense and Ministry of Interior. From January 1957 he organized the Workers' Guard. In 1957–60 he was first secretary of the HSWP Provincial Committee in Szolnok County. From 1958 to 1967 he was an MP, and from 1959 to 1988, a member of the HSWP CC. From May 1960 to December 1984 he was minister of national defense. In 1961 he also became head of the National Defense Commission of the party CC. In 1960 he was promoted to general of a division, in 1962 to general of arms, and in 1979 to general of the army. He supervised the participation of the Hungarian Army in the Warsaw Pact intervention in Czechoslovakia in August 1968. In 1961–70 he was a deputy member of the party Politburo; it was a rather low rank, considering that other ministers of defense of the Warsaw Pact countries were usually full Politburo members. From December 1984 to June 1987 Czinege was deputy prime minister, and then he retired. In November 1989, when various embezzlement scandals were revealed in the army, he gave up his military rank. (JT)

Sources: *Magyar Nagylexikon*, vol. 6 (Budapest, 1998); *A magyar forradalom és szabadságharc enciklopédiája,* CD-ROM (Budapest, 1999); *Új Magyar Életrajzi Lexikon*, vol. 1 (Budapest, 2001); Bennet Kovrig, *Communism in Hungary from Kun to Kádár* (Stanford, 1979); Klaus-Detlev Grothusen, ed., *Ungarn* (Göttingen, 1987); Miklós Molnár, *From Béla Kun to János Kádár: Seventy Years of Hungarian Communism* (New York, 1990).

CZUMA Andrzej (17 December 1938, Lublin), Polish activist of the democratic opposition. Born into an intelligentsia family of patriotic traditions, in 1963 Czuma graduated in law and administration from Warsaw University. At the same time he studied history at the Catholic University of Lublin. He worked as a legal adviser in the Ministry of Transportation and in the District Administration of the Polish State Railways in Warsaw. In 1965 he co-founded a pioneer secret opposition organization, Ruch (Movement). In June 1970 he was arrested for preparations to set fire to the Lenin Museum in Poronin. He refused to testify, although he was threatened with a death sentence. In the Ruch trial in October 1971 he received the longest sentence: seven years in prison. Released owing to an amnesty in September 1974, he favored the continuation of the secret activities. In March 1977 he co-founded the secret Independence Stream, and he also co-organized an open Movement for the Defense of Human and Civil Rights (Ruch Obrony Praw Człowieka i Obywatela [ROPCiO]). He co-edited the ROPCiO periodical, *Opinia*. In October he took part in a hunger strike at Holy Cross Church in Warsaw in protest against the arrest of the Czechoslovak organizers of Charter 77. He was arrested several dozen times, but owing to the détente policies of the **Edward Gierek** regime, for short periods only. In March 1981 he became an adviser to the Inter-Factory Founding Committee of Solidarity in Katowice. He also edited the daily *Wiadomości Katowickie* of the Solidarity Regional Board in Silesia. In mid-1981 Czuma tried to organize the Movement for Independence (Ruch Niepodległościowy) as a political party, but he failed. Interned after the introduction of martial law in December 1981, he was released in December 1982, and he cooperated with the underground Solidarity structures. In 1985 he left for the United States, where he became co-owner of a radio station in Chicago and (in 1988) owner of an information radio program, the Czuma Radio Show. (WR)

Sources: *Opozycja w PRL: Słownik biograficzny 1956–89* (Warsaw, 2000); *Wielka encyklopedia PWN*, vol. 6 (Warsaw, 2002).

D

DĄBAL Tomasz (29 December 1890, Sobów, near Tarnobrzeg–21 August 1937, Moscow), Polish Communist and Peasant Party activist. From 1909 to 1911 Dąbal studied law in Vienna and medicine in Kraków. From 1909 he was active in the Polish Peasant Party in Galicia, and in 1913 he joined the Polish Peasant Party–Piast. During World War I he served in the Austro-Hungarian Army and in the Polish Legions. In November 1918, he attempted to instigate a peasant revolution, and with a priest, Eugeniusz Okoń, he founded the Tarnobrzeg Republic. As a gifted speaker Dąbal became an MP of the Polish Peasant Party-Left in the elections of 1919. However, he soon left the party, became involved with the Communists, and joined the Communist Polish Workers' Party. In 1920 he was the only MP to support the Soviets in the Polish Seym. In July 1921 Dąbal, along with Stanisław Łańcucki, founded the parliamentary club of the Communists. In November 1921 he was deprived of his immunity and arrested for anti-state agitation. Sentenced to six years in July 1922, in 1923 he was exchanged for Polish prisoners in the USSR, and he left for Russia. He worked in the Executive Committee of the Third International as a secretary for agriculture, and in October 1923 he became vice-president of the Peasant International (Krestintern). After Stalin's victory over his rivals in the Bolshevik party, Dąbal went to Minsk, where he started his academic career in the Belorussian Academy of Sciences. In 1932 he was appointed its vice-president. In 1932–37 he was also a member of the Central Committee of the Belorussian Communist Party (Bolshevik). During the purge of Polish Communists in the USSR in December 1936, Dąbal was arrested, sentenced to death on 31 July 1937, and executed. His wife spent eight years in prisons and forced labor camps, one of his two sons died of hunger in an orphanage, and the other survived and returned to Poland with his mother in 1957. Dąbal's publications include *Powstanie krakowskie* (The Kraków uprising; 1926); *Polacy Związku Radzieckiego* (The Poles in the Soviet Union; 1926); and *Zametki o kriestianskom dvizhenii v Ievrope* (Notes on the peasant movement in Europe; 1927). (WR)

Sources: *Posłowie . . .*, vol. 1; J. D. Jackson, *Comintern and Peasant in East Europe,1919–1930* (New York, 1966); Henryk Cimek, *Tomasz Dąbal 1890–1937* (Rzeszów, 1993).

DABČEVIĆ-KUČAR Savka (6 December 1923, Korčula), Croatian Communist activist and economist. Dabčević-Kučar came from a family with a rich civic tradition going back to the Habsburg monarchy. During World War II she took part in an anti-German conspiracy. After the war she studied economics at the universities in Leningrad and Zagreb, where she received a Ph.D. In 1951–71 she worked at the Department of Economics of Zagreb University, gradually advancing to professor. Connected very early on with the Communist movement, from 1961 to 1966 she was a deputy to the republican parliament and a member of the Yugoslav delegation to the UN General Assembly. In 1967–68 she headed the Croatian republican government, and in 1969 she became chairman of the Central Committee of the League of Communists of Croatia. She supported the movement for the wider autonomy of the Croatian republic within the Yugoslav federation, called the Croatian Spring. After **Josip Broz Tito** condemned "Croatian nationalism" at a meeting of the Presidium of the League of Yugoslav Communists in Karadjordjevo in December 1971, Dabčević-Kučar was dismissed from all her party and state positions, as well as from the university. A far-reaching purge in the Croatian party followed.

Dabčević-Kučar returned to public life in the spring of 1990, when in the first free elections she ran on behalf of the Coalition of National Understanding, which included the Social Democrats, liberals, and Greens. The coalition won 9.4 percent of the vote and 3.8 percent of the mandates. In the fall of 1990, the leaders of the Croatian Spring founded the Croatian National Party (Hrvatska Narodna Stranka [HNS]). Dabčević-Kučar became the chairperson of the party, whose name alluded to the first modern Croatian party, established in the nineteenth century. The HNS was meant as a nationalist alternative to the ruling Croatian Democratic Union and a leftist alternative to the post-Communists, but it failed. In the elections of 1992 it gained 6.6 percent of the vote, and in the presidential election Dabčević-Kučar won 6.0 percent of the vote. The HNS entered various center-right coalitions, which helped it to survive in the parliament. After the elections of 1995 a coalition of five parties, including the HNS, won 20 mandates, and Dabčević-Kučar resigned from the HNS leadership. She authored, among other works, the following: *Politička ekonomija* (Political economy; 1954); *John Maynard Keynes: Teoretičar državnog kapitalizma* (John Maynard Keynes: Theoretician of state capitalism; 1957); *Osnovne zakonitosti u proizvodnji, razmjeni, raspodjeli i potrošnji u socijalizmu* (Basic rules of production, exchange, distribution, and consumption under socialism; 1960); *SKH u političkoj akciji* (The League of Communists of Croatia in political action; 1971); and *'71: Hrvatski snovi i stvarnost* ('71: Croatian dreams and reality; 1997). (AW)

Sources: *Tko je tko u Hrvatskoj* (Zagreb, 1993); Robert Stallaerts and Jeannine Laurens, *Historical Dictionary of the Republic of Croatia* (London, 1995); Klaus-Detlev Grothausen, ed., *Südosteuropa Handbuch, Band I–Jugoslawien* (Göttingen, 1975); Ante Čuvalo, *The Croatian National Movement, 1966–1972* (Boulder, Colo., 1990); Karen Dawisha and Bruce Parrot, eds., *Politics, Power and the Struggle for Democracy in South-East Europe* (Cambridge, 1997).

DĄBROWSKA Maria (6 October 1889, Russów, near Kalisz–19 May 1965, Warsaw), Polish writer, translator, and social activist. Dąbrowska came from an impoverished noble family. From 1901 to 1906 she studied at girls' boarding schools in Kalisz and Warsaw. She studied the natural sciences at the University of Lausanne and at the Université Libre in Brussels, where she obtained the degree of Candidate of Natural Sciences in 1912. She simultaneously studied social science and philosophy and worked for the Joachim Lelewel Polish Association, a patriotic organization in exile. She also maintained contacts with Polish workers employed in Belgian mines. In 1910 she started writing for *Zaranie, Społem, Gazeta Kaliska, Przedświt*, and *Gazeta Robotnicza*. In 1911 she married Marian Dąbrowski, a Socialist activist. She made her literary debut in 1913. Between 1913 and 1914 she was in London on a scholarship funded by the Society of Supporters of the Cooperative Movement (Towarzystwo Kooperatystów); she herself was involved in the cooperative movement. In July 1914 she returned to Poland. She lived in Piotrków and Lublin and from 1917 in Warsaw, where she aligned herself with the independence movement. She also was affiliated with a radical faction of the peasant movement and co-edited the magazines *Chłopska Sprawa* and *Polska Ludowa* and the youth magazine *W słońcu*.

From 1918 to 1924 Dąbrowska worked for the government as head of a department in the Ministry of Agriculture and State Property and in the Ministry of Agrarian Reforms, where she was in charge of the library and the press and editorial department. From 1924 she dedicated herself only to writing. She was involved politically in 1926, taking part in protest actions organized by the League for the Defense of Human and Citizen Rights. From 1926 she was in a relationship with Stanisław Stempowski, a Freemason and liberal journalist. From 1930 she was a member of the Polish PEN club. In 1935 she refused to accept the Golden Laurel Award from the Polish Academy of Literature because she considered the academy too closely linked with the *sanacja* government. From 1936 she worked for the Central Cooperative Union (Centralny Związek Spółdzielczy). From 1938 she belonged to the board of the Warsaw branch of the Polish Writers' Trade Union.

After September 1939, along with Stempowski, Dąbrowska lived in the Eastern Borderland occupied by the USSR. She lived in Łuck and Lwów (Lviv), and in 1941 she returned to Warsaw. She was active in the underground cultural movement. During the Warsaw Uprising she was in Warsaw, and after the end of the fighting she left the capital. From 1947 to 1962 she was vice-president of the Main Board of the Polish PEN club. In 1948 she joined the Organizational Committee of the World Congress of Intellectuals for Peace in Wrocław. She took part in the work of the Polish Writers' Union, and from 1956 she was a member of the board of the union. In 1955 she received a First Degree State Award for her literary work. In 1956 she was a member of the Polish delegation to the International Congress of PEN Clubs in London. In 1957 she was awarded an honorary doctorate from Warsaw University. In 1964 she was one of the signatories of the "Letter of 34," which was seen as the first protest since October 1956 of writers and scholars against Communist cultural policies.

Dąbrowska's writing evolved from positivism to modernist realism. Her most important works include the stories *Ludzie stamtąd* (Folks from over yonder; 1926) and *Marcin Kozera: Opowiadania* (Marcin Kozera: Stories; 1927); the monumental novel that was an apotheosis of her work, *Noce i dnie* (Nights and days; 1932–37); a collection of war stories, *Gwiazda zaranna* (The morning star; 1955); a second monumental novel, *Przygody człowieka myślącego* (Adventures of a thinker; 1970); and the dramas *Geniusz sierocy* (Genius of an orphan; 1939) and *Stanisław i Bogumił* (1945–46). She also authored numerous essays and translations, as well as works on the cooperative movement and on economics—for example, *Życie i dzieło Edwarda Abramowskiego* (The life and work of **Edward Abramowski**; 1925) and *Ręce w uścisku: Rzecz o spółdzielczości* (Hands in a shake: On the cooperative movement; 1938). Throughout her life Dąbrowska wrote her *Dzienniki* (Diaries). The first five-volume edition of the diaries, abridged by censorship, appeared in 1988, and in 1998–99 it was supplemented by another three volumes. (PK)

Sources: Andrzej Kijowski, *Maria Dąbrowska* (Warsaw, 1964); Ewa Korzeniewska, *Maria Dąbrowska: Poradnik bibliograficzny* (Warsaw, 1969); Ewa Korzeniewska, *Maria Dąbrowska: Kronika życia* (Warsaw, 1971); *Współcześni polscy pisarze i badacze literatury: Słownik bibliograficzny*, vol.2 (Warsaw, 1994); Grażyna Borkowska, *Maria Dąbrowska i Stanisław Stempowski* (Kraków, 1999); *Literatura polska XX wieku: Przewodnik encyklopedyczny* (Warsaw, 2000).

DĄBROWSKI Bronisław (2 November 1917, Grodziec, near Konin–25 December 1997, Warsaw), archbishop, secretary of the Polish Episcopate. Dąbrowski came from an artisan family. His father perished in the Polish-Soviet war. In 1935 Dąbrowski entered the Orionist Order of the Roman Catholic Church. At first he studied in the order's seminary in Zduńska Wola and then in Rome. After the German invasion of Poland in 1939, he returned to Poland, where he continued his studies and worked in the Orionist Order in Warsaw. He also studied at the clandestine Pedagogical Department of Warsaw University. He graduated in 1943, and then he managed an Orionist dormitory for boys in Warsaw. He survived the Warsaw Uprising; after its failure he was placed in an internment camp in Bitinheim, near Dachau, Germany. Upon his return to Poland, in June 1945 Dąbrowski was ordained. He worked among youngsters in Warsaw, and in 1948 he started working at the Secretariat of the Polish Episcopate, where he was entrusted with the Department of Orders of the Secretariat of the Primate of Poland. He held this post until 1992. It was thanks to his endeavors (among those of others) that despite threats and repression under Stalinism, religious orders in Poland were not liquidated and stayed united with the diocese hierarchy. Dąbrowski was later a member of the Vatican Congregation for Institutes of Consecrated Life and Societies of Apostolic Life, as well as chairman of the Commission for Religious Orders of the Polish Episcopate. On 16 November 1961 Pope John XXIII nominated him auxiliary bishop of Warsaw. On 25 March 1962 he was consecrated by Primate **Stefan Wyszyński**.

In 1969–92 Dąbrowski was secretary of the Polish Episcopate, working closely with Primate Wyszyński and Primate **Józef Glemp**. On 8 June 1982 Pope **John Paul II** elevated him to archbishop. Dąbrowski was a member of the Joint Commission of the Polish Government and Episcopate. He took part in all the major talks of the Polish bishops with the Communist authorities. In 1972 he played an important role in the negotiations of the Polish Communist government with Pope Paul VI on the creation of new church structures in the new Polish territories in the north and west. From 1979 he co-organized five pilgrimages of Pope John Paul II to Poland. In talks with the Communist authorities he was also an advocate of all-national and social questions. In February 1981 in Bielsko-Biała he took part in talks that led to the termination of a long strike in the Beskidy region and to the resolution of a sharp conflict between the Communist authorities and Solidarity. During the period of martial law he demanded the release of all political prisoners. On behalf of the Episcopate he took part in the negotiations that brought about a political breakthrough and led to the Round Table Talks and the June 1989 elections, won by the opposition. A record of his meetings with the Polish Communist authorities was published as *Rozmowy z władzami PRL: Arcybiskup*

Dąbrowski w służbie Kościoła i narodu (Negotiations with the authorities of Communist Poland: Archbishop Dąbrowski in the service of the Church and the nation; 1995). In 1990 the Catholic University of Lublin granted him an honorary doctorate, and in 1993 President **Lech Wałęsa** awarded him the Commander's Cross with Star of the Polonia Restituta Order. (AGr)

Sources: Peter Raina, *Rozmowy z władzami PRL: Arcybiskup Dąbrowski w służbie Kościoła i narodu*, vols. 1–2 (Warsaw, 1995); Peter Raina, *Kościół w PRL: Kościół katolicki a państwo w świetle dokumentów 1945–1989*, vols. 1–3 (Poznań, 1994–95); Pelplin 1996; *Biuletyn Prasowy Katolickiej Agencji Informacyjnej*, 30 December 1997; Peter Raina, *Arcybiskup Dąbrowski–rozmowy watykańskie* (Warsaw, 2001); Henryk Łechtański, "Abp Bronisław Dąbrowski," *Gazeta Wyborcza*, 24–26 December 2002.

DĄBSKI Jan (10 April 1880, Kukizów, near Lwów [Lviv]–5 June 1931, Warsaw), Polish Peasant Party politician. The son of a peasant, after graduating from a high school in Lwów in 1900, Dąbski studied law for a year, and then he graduated in chemistry from the University of Lwów (1906). During his studies he was active in the Society of Popular Schools and served in the Austrian Army. In 1905 he joined the Polish Peasant Party (Polskie Stronnictwo Ludowe [PSL]), and in 1906 he was elected to its Supreme Council. After he brought about a split in the party in 1908, he founded the Independent Peasant Party. From 1911 he was active in the Polish Riflemen Teams, and in 1912–13 he belonged to the Provisional Commission of Confederated Independence Parties (Tymczasowa Komisja Skonfederowanych Stronnictw Niepodległościowych). In 1914 Dąbski joined the PSL Piast. He was a member of the pro-Austrian Supreme National Committee. He served in the Polish Legions. In 1917–18 he was active in the Popular Union (Zjednoczenie Ludowe), and then, in 1918, he attracted a part of its membership to the PSL Piast. He was deputy chairman of its Main Board, and from 1920, also of its Supreme Council.

In January 1919 Dąbski was elected to the Constituent Assembly on behalf of the PSL Piast, and from March 1920 to October 1921 he was deputy minister of foreign affairs. He headed the Polish delegation to the peace talks with Soviet Russia, and on 18 March 1921 he signed the Polish-Soviet Peace Treaty of Riga. From mid-May to mid-June 1921 he directed the Foreign Ministry. He opposed the formation of a center-right government (the so-called Chjeno-Piast government of **Wincenty Witos**), and in 1923 he left the PSL to establish the PSL-Peasant Unity, which, along with the PSL-Liberation faction, joined the Union of Polish Peasant Parties. In 1923–25 Dąbski was its deputy chairman. Elected to the parliament in 1922, 1928, and 1930, he played an important role in the elaboration of the land reform of 1925. In 1926 he was co-founder of the Peasant Party (Stronnictwo Chłopskie), then he became a member of its Main Board, and in 1929–30 he was chairman of its Chief Executive Committee. At first he supported the May coup d'état of 1926, but in 1927 he joined the opposition. From 1928 the deputy speaker of the Lower House, in 1929 Dąbski co-organized the Centrolew, a coalition of center and leftist parties against the ruling *sanacja*. After the unification of the peasant movement in 1931, he was active in the Peasant Party (Stronnictwo Ludowe). He was the first chairman of the Union of Polish Journalists, chairman of the Union of Legionnaires, and a member of the Executive Department of the International Union of Radical Parties in Paris. He took part in the proceedings of the Green International of Peasants. He published in many newspapers, including *Kurier Lwowski* (1919–23 editor-in-chief), *Przyjaciel Ludu, Gazeta Ludowa* (1908–13 and 1915–26 editor-in-chief), *Gazeta Chłopska*, and *Polityka*. He also authored the following books: *Walka o Sejm Ludowy* (Struggle for a popular parliament; 1919); *Pokój ryski: Wspomnienia, pPertraktacje, tajne układy z Joffem, listy* (Peace Treaty of Riga: Negotiations, secret agreements with Joffe, letters; 1931); and *Wojna i ludzie: Wspomnienia z lat 1914–1915* (War and people: Memoirs of 1914–1915; 1969). (JS)

Sources: *PSB*, vol. 5; *Posłowie i senatorowie Rzeczypospolitej Polskiej, 1919–1939: Słownik biograficzny*, vol. 1 (Warsaw, 1998); *Słownik biograficzny działaczy ruchu ludowego* (Warsaw, 1989); *Kto był kim w Drugiej Rzeczypospolitej*, vol. 1 (Warsaw, 1994); *Przywódcy ruchu ludowego: Szkice biograficzne* (Warsaw, 1968); Stanisław Giza, *Jan Dąbski: Całe życie dla ludu* (Warsaw, 1979); Bernard Singer, *Od Witosa do Sławka* (Warsaw, 1990).

DALBOR Edmund (30 October 1869, Ostrów Wielkopolski–13 February 1926, Poznań), cardinal, Primate of Poland. Dalbor graduated from high school in Ostrów, and then he studied theology in Münster; in 1892–94 he studied canon law at the Gregorianum in Rome, where he received a Ph.D. Ordained on 26 February 1893, in 1894–99 he worked in the Poznań curia, and then he taught canon law in the theological seminary in Gniezno. In 1901 he became canon metropolitan in Poznań and in 1909 vicar general; on 30 June 1915 he was appointed archbishop of Poznań and Gniezno. He assumed the office under complicated circumstances, when the German Army was occupying the former (Russian) Kingdom of Poland and taking control of most of the Polish territory. The German authorities hoped for a friendly attitude on the part of the Poles, but the ingress of Dalbor in September 1915 and

his first announcements were not to their liking. On the other hand, Dalbor's grateful letter to Emperor William II on the occasion of the Act of 5 November 1916 was unwelcome among the Poles. Dalbor organized charity and ministry for the Polish prisoners of war and refugees, and in 1918 he protested to the German authorities against the assaults of German soldiers and functionaries on churches. In December 1918 he became a member of the Provincial Parliament in Poznań and allowed the Polish clergy to take part in the Greater Polish Uprising and in plebiscite propaganda in Upper Silesia, Ermland, and Mazuria. At the end of 1918 he organized the first conference of Polish bishops; it passed a resolution in which they appealed to the clergy and believers to unite for the reinstitution of Polish statehood. Soon Dalbor established the Primate's Chancellery in Warsaw, which later turned into the Office of the Polish Episcopate. As a metropolitan of the oldest Polish archdiocese, Dalbor actually became the primate of united Poland. On 18 December 1919 he was appointed cardinal. In July 1920 he co-authored a letter of the Polish Episcopate appealing for a defense of the nation against the Bolshevik invasion. He organized ministry for the Poles living in France and Germany. He strove to regulate the legal status of the Catholic Church in Poland, and his efforts were noticeable in the March 1921 constitution and in the concordat of 10 February 1925. From 1922 his health was poor, and he was less and less active. (WR)

Sources: *PSB*, vol. 4; *Encyklopedia katolicka*, vol. 3 (Lublin, 1979); Ks. Józef Glemp, "Ksiądz prymas kardynał Edmund Dalbor," *Prawo kanoniczne* 1974, nos. 3–4; Feliks Lenort, ed., *Na stolicy prymasowskiej w Gnieźnie i Poznaniu* (Poznań, 1982).

DAMIANOV Georgi (23 September 1892, Lopushna, near Montana–27 November 1958, Sofia), Bulgarian Communist activist. In 1911 Damianov graduated from high school in Vratsa, and he became a village teacher. From 1912 he belonged to the faction of "close Socialists" (*Tesnyaki*) of the Bulgarian Social Democratic Party cooperating with the Russian Bolsheviks. After graduating from a school for reserve officers in 1915, he took part in World War I operations, conducting antiwar agitation. From 1919 he was a member of the Vratsa district committee of the Bulgarian Communist Part (BCP). One of the leaders of the September 1923 uprising in the Vratsa region, after its failure he escaped to the Kingdom of Serbs, Croats, and Slovenes. In Bulgarian he was sentenced to death in absentia. In exile he cooperated with the BCP Foreign Committee. At the end of 1925 he left for the USSR. After graduating from the Frunze Military Academy in 1929, he served as an officer of the Red Army, and then he taught tactics and chemistry in this academy (1932–34). On the orders of **Georgi Dimitrov**, in 1934 Damianov was sent to work in the Personnel Department of the Communist International (Comintern). In 1935 he became a member of the BCP Central Committee (CC). He illegally returned to Bulgaria, where he was a member of a three-man commission to " free" the party of "sectarian elements." In February 1936, when the BCP CC adopted the tactics of the Popular Front, Damianov became a member of the CC Politburo. In 1937 he left for the USSR again, where he was a member of the BCP Foreign Committee and head of the Personnel Department of the Comintern. He was a political inspector of the International Brigades during the Spanish Civil War, and he adopted Soviet citizenship.

During World War II Damianov served in the Red Army, preparing Communist cadres to take over power in Bulgaria. In October 1944 he returned to Bulgaria to direct the Military Department of the Communist Party. At the Eighth Plenum of CC in 1945 he returned to its Politburo and in 1946 joined its Secretariat. In 1945 he became a major general and in 1947 a lieutenant general. From November 1946 to May 1950 he was minister of defense (until December 1947, the title was minister of war) in the governments of Georgi Dimitrov, **Vasyl Kolarov**, and **Vulko Chervenkov**. In this capacity he was responsible for a bloody purge in the army. His strong position in the power structure was due to his long-term and wide contacts in the Soviet General Staff. From 1945 until his death he was an MP to the National Assembly, and from 1950 until his death he was chairman of the parliamentary Presidium. (JJ)

Sources: Lazitch; *Entsiklopediya Bulgariya*, vol. 2 (Sofia, 1981); J. F. Brown, *Bulgaria under Communist Rule* (New York, 1970); Tosho Tashev, *Ministrite na Bulgariya 1879–1999: Entsiklopedichen Spravochnik* (Sofia, 1999); Evgenia Kalinova and Iskra Baeva, *Bulgarskite prekhodi 1944–1999* (Sofia, 2000); Angel Tsurakov, *Entsiklopediya: Pravitelstvata na Bulgariya: Khronologiya na politicheskiya zhivot 1879–2001* (Sofia, 2001).

DANEV Stoyan (7 February 1858, Shumen–29 July 1949, Sofia), Bulgarian politician and scholar. As a high school student in Shumen, in 1876 Danev joined a revolutionary circle and had to leave the country. In 1878 he graduated from high school in Prague, and then he studied law in Zurich and Heidelberg, where he received a Ph.D. in 1881. Later he also studied law and political science in London and at the Sorbonne. From 1884 he had a law practice in Sofia and lectured at Sofia University (1894–98). He also published in the periodicals *Sredets, Svetlina*, and *Bulgariya*. At first he was connected with the Liberal Party, and from 1889 he headed the Progressive Liberal Party. He was a radical Russophile and called for the territorial

expansion of Bulgaria. He strove for the annexation of Turkish Macedonia together with Serbia. He thought the best solution for the Balkans would be a Bulgarian-Serbian federation at the expense of the Ottoman Empire.

From March 1901 to January 1902 Danev was minister of foreign and religious affairs in the government of **Petko Karavelov**, and from 4 January 1902 to 19 May 1903 he was prime minister. He closely cooperated with Russian diplomacy and gained its support in economic negotiations in Paris, but he failed to solve the Macedonian question. Acting under pressure from the great powers, he entered into a conflict with the Internal Macedonian Revolutionary Organization and dissolved its structures in 1903. Russian pressure made him appoint a Serbian metropolitan alongside the Bulgarian metropolitan, which led to the fall of his cabinet. In 1911 he was elected speaker of the Great National Assembly. During the Balkan Wars he was foreign minister again, and from 14 June to 17 July 1913, prime minister. He took part in the negotiations that followed the First Balkan War in 1912. He did not support the policy of Tsar Ferdinand, which led to the outbreak of the Second Balkan War. Danev disagreed with a sudden Bulgarian attack on Greece and Serbia in order to recover Macedonia. He was right, since the Bulgarian offensive was stopped, Greece and Serbia were supported by Romania and Turkey, and Bulgaria was defeated. As a result he resigned.

For several years Danev stayed in the opposition. He returned to the University of Sofia, where he became professor of law (1916–34). In 1931 he published *Ocherk na diplomaticheskata istoriya na balkanskita dyrzhavi* (Outline of diplomatic history of the Balkan states). An opponent of Bulgaria's entry into World War I, he was minister of finance in the governments of **Todor Todorov** and **Aleksandur Stamboliyski** (1919–20). Later he joined the United National Progressive Party within the Constitutional Bloc. After the Stamboliyski regime was toppled in June 1923, Danev was elected to the parliament and advocated rapprochement with the Kingdom of Serbs, Croats, and Slovenes; with Czechoslovakia; and, despite his anti-Communist attitude, with Soviet Russia. He published memoirs and contributions to the diplomatic history of the Balkan Wars. After retirement he was active in the Bulgarian Red Cross. In 1992 his *Memoari* (Memoirs) were published. (MC)

Sources: *Biographisches Lexikon*, vol. 1; *Entsiklopediya Bulgariya*, vol. 2 (Sofia, 1981); Stephen Constant, *Foxy Ferdinand, 1861–1948, Tsar of Bulgaria* (London, 1979); Richard J. Crompton, *Bulgaria 1878–1983: A History* (Boulder, Colo., 1983); Richard C. Hall, *Bulgaria's Road to the First World War* (Boulder, Colo., 1996); Tasho Tashev, *Ministrite na Bulgariya 1879–1999: Entsi-*

klopedichen spravochnik (Sofia; 1999); www.minfin.government. bg/en/index.html.

DANI Riza (1884, Shkoder–October 1949?), Albanian politician. Born into a Muslim family, Dani studied in a madrassa, and then he graduated from higher studies in Istanbul. In 1908–11 he was active in patriotic clubs, affiliated with the outstanding artists and cultural activists **Gjergji Fishta** and **Luigji Gurakuqi**. During World War I he was active in the National Faction (Krahu Kombëtar) in Shkodër, which he left in 1919, becoming its active adversary. In 1924 he was elected to the parliament. During the 1924 revolution he supported **Fan Noli** and directed the Durrës prefecture. After the failure of the revolution he emigrated and was sentenced to death in absentia. He lived in Italy, Austria, and Yugoslavia. He returned to Albania in 1939, and he worked as a merchant in Shkodër. In 1945 he was elected chairman of the National Council in Shkodër, and then he became an MP. In view of the lack of a political alternative to the Communists, Dani became the leader of the parliamentary opposition. During the election of the parliamentary Presidium he opposed the submission of candidates by the Communists only and suggested other candidates. He also opposed a resolution suggested by **Koçi Xoxe** and **Sejfulla Malëshova** that was aimed at making it impossible for the parliament to criticize the government. Along with three other deputies, on 23 December 1946 Dani was deprived of immunity and soon arrested. His followers, called the "group of deputies" were accused by the Communists of founding an independent political party and of plotting in connection with the "Postryba movement" (anti-Communist riots in Postryba on 9 September 1946). Dani was tried in a show trial, and on 31 December 1947 he was sentenced to death. The exact date of the execution is not known. (TC)

Sources: *Bashkimi*, 25 November 1945; Demir Dyrmishi, "Krijimi i organizatës opozitare nacjonaldemokratike dhe veprimtaria e saj ne asamblene kushtetuese (1944–mars 1946)," *Studime Historike*, 1995; Pjeter Pepa, *Dosja e diktatures* (Tirana, 1995); Sejfi Vllamasi, *Ballafaqime politike ne Shqipëri (1897–1942)* (Tirana, 1995).

DANKERS Oskars (26 March 1883, Lielauces, Courland–11 April 1965, Grand Rapids, Michigan), Latvian general. Dankers graduated from high school in Jelgava. From 1902 he served in the Russian Army; in 1906 he graduated form a military school in Wilno (Vilnius), and then he served as an officer in the Sveaborg fortress. During World War I he commanded a company and a battalion. In early 1916 he was advanced to lieutenant-colonel, and he was wounded several times. In June 1916 he was taken prisoner of war by the Austrians. After his release in December 1918, he served as an officer in the German expeditionary corps of General Rüdiger von der Goltz in Finland. After returning to Latvia, in May 1919 he joined the Latvian Army. He was commander of a regiment, and from August 1919, head of the military district of Lejaskurzeme (Lower Courland), in command of the struggle against the German and White Russian army of Pavel Bermondt-Avalov near Liepāja. In December 1919 he was promoted to he rank of colonel and appointed commander of the Semigalian Division. From 1920 this division was stationed in Daugavpils (Dyneburg, Dünaburg). In 1925 Dankers was appointed general, and in 1933, commander of the Courland Division. In January 1940 he retired. After the Soviet invasion of Latvia, on 19 June 1940 he managed to escape to Germany. He returned to Latvia after the establishment of the German occupation. In 1941–45 he was director general for the interior (actually head) of the Latvian self-government. Before the second Soviet invasion, in mid-1944 he left for Germany again. In 1945–46 he was interned by the Western allies in Germany and then released. In 1957 he left for the United States, where he lived until his death. He was the author of *Lai vēsture spriež tiesu* (Let history pass a verdict; 1965) and of the memoirs *No atmiņu pūra* (From the corners of memory; 1973). (EJ)

Sources: I. Dankere, *Maz tu man solīji* (N.p., 1982); H. Biezais, *Latvija kāškrusta varā: Sveši kungi—pašu ļaudis* (N.p., 1992); Andrejs Plakans, *Historical Dictionary of Latvia* (Lanham, Md., 1997).

DARÁNYI Kálmán (22 March 1886, Budapest–1 November 1939, Budapest), Hungarian politician. After graduating in law from the University of Budapest in 1909, Darányi worked in the state administration. In 1910–17 he was secretary of Fogaras County and then governor of Zólyom, Győr-Komárom, and Moson Counties. From 1927 he was an MP. In 1928–35 he was secretary of state in the Office of the Prime Minister, and in April 1935 he became minister of agriculture in the government of **Gyula Gömbös**. Due to the illness of the prime minister, from early May 1936 Darányi was actually in charge of the government until 10 October 1936, when he formally became prime minister. He continued efforts toward rapprochement with the Third Reich and Italy, but at the same time he wanted to maintain good relations with France and Great Britain. At home he was rather inefficient in his attempts to contain the influence of the (Fascist) Arrow Cross Party. He intensified police and administrative measures against its leaders and tried to ease social tensions (e.g., by introducing a minimum wage and a forty-eight-hour work week), but such measures did not prevent the popularity of the extreme right. Darányi also strove to strengthen executive power at the expense of the legislature. His government made the parliament pass a plan of intense armament (the so-called Györ Program of 1938), as well as the first so-called anti-Jewish law of 1938, limiting the chances of people of Jewish descent from working as free professional and white-collar employees. In reaction to his attempt at a more pro-German policy, caused by the incorporation of Austria by the Third Reich, on 14 May 1938 Darányi was dismissed by Regent **Miklós Horthy**. At the end of 1938 Darányi was elected speaker of the parliament, but he soon died. (MS)

Sources: *20. századi magyar történelem 1900–1994* (Budapest, 1997); *Magyar életrajzi lexikon*, CD-ROM 2000; C. A. Macartney, *October Fifteenth: A History of Modern Hungary*, vols. 1–2 (Edinburgh, 1957–1961); Paul Ignotus, *Hungary* (London, 1972); Steven Béla Várga, *Historical Dictionary of Hungary* (Lanham, Md., 1997).

DARVAS József [originally Dumitras] (10 February 1912, Orosháza–3 December 1973, Budapest), Hungarian Communist activist and writer. Born into a poor peasant family and orphaned early by the death of his father in World War I, after attending a training school, Darvas could not find a job, so he left for Budapest, where he was both a blue- and white-collar worker. In 1932 he joined the illegal Communist Party; in 1933 he was arrested and put on police surveillance for five years. He published poems and short stories in leftist periodicals. From 1936 to 1937 he worked as an editor of a Communist periodical, *Gondalat*. He also collaborated with the left wing of the Populist writers and with their periodicals, *Szabad Szó* and *Kis Újság*. He authored several historical and sociological novels on the so-called class struggle in the countryside. His sociographic image of his home village, *A legnagyobb magyar falu* (The largest village in Hungary; 1937), won him wide popularity. During World War II he was active in the leftist antiwar movement and wrote a lot. After the war he was formally a member of the National Peasant Party, but actually he collaborated with the Communists. In 1945–73 he was an MP. From 1945 to 1947 he edited the leftist daily *Szabad Szó*, and then he was minister of building (1947–50), education (1950–53), and culture (1953–56). During the "thaw" after Stalin's death and during the 1956 revolution he sided with the party conservatives, unwilling to reform the totalitarian system. From 1957 he was director of the Hunnia Filmstúdió. He authored several screenplays, novels, and dramas presenting the collectivization of agriculture and the 1956 revolution from the Communist perspective. These works included *Hajnali tűz* (Fire at dawn; 1961) and *Részeg eső* (Drunken rain; 1963). In 1951–53 and 1959–73 he presided over the

Association of Hungarian Writers, and from 1960 he was also vice-president of a façade group, the Patriotic People's Front. A member of the Presidential Council from 1972, at the end of his life Darvas began to distance himself from communism, returning to the ideology of the Populist writers, stressing folk and national values. (MS)

Sources: Gábor Garai, "Emlékezés Darvas Józsefre," *Élet és Irodalom*, 1977, no. 8; Szilveszter Ördögh, "Darvas és az örökösök," *Napjaink*, 1977, no. 4; Zoltán Biró, *Vállamások és kételyek* (Budapest, 1987); Klaus-Detlev Grothusen, ed., *Ungarn* (Göttingen, 1987); *Új magyar irodalmi lexikon* (Budapest, 1994); Steven Béla Várga, *Historical Dictionary of Hungary* (Lanham, Md., 1997).

DASKALOV Rayko (8 December 1886, Byala Cherkva–26 August 1923, Prague), Bulgarian politician. Born into a peasant family, after attending a trade high school in Svishtov, Daskalov studied finance at the University of Berlin (1903–8). From his youth he was connected with the Agrarians and was a neighbor and close aide to Tsanko Tserkovski, a co-founder of the Bulgarian Agrarian National Union (Bulgarski Zemedelski Naroden Soyuz [BANU]). From 1914 he published in the BANU periodical *Zemedelsko zname*. He opposed Bulgaria's entry into World War I. Along with other leftist politicians, including **Aleksandur Stamboliyski**, he was involved in the "Declosier Affair," in which the French politician Declosier tried to prevent a German-Bulgarian alliance. As a result, Daskalov was arrested and was kept in prison until the defeat of Bulgaria. Released on 25 September 1918, in the town of Radomir, along with Stamboliyski, he proclaimed the Bulgarian Republic, and he became the commander-in-chief of its revolutionary armed forces. They were defeated on 29–30 September near the village of Vladaya (near Sofia) by Bulgarian royalists allied with Macedonian and German troops. Daskalov took shelter among the Entente units, where he stayed until the royal amnesty of December 1918.

Daskalov soon returned to politics. In 1919–23 he was an MP to the National Assembly. In the government of Stamboliyski he was minister of agriculture and state property; minister of trade, industry and labor; minister of foreign affairs; minister of health; and minister of finance. In December 1922 he survived an attempt on his life by members of the Internal Macedonian Revolutionary Organization. In May 1923 he became an envoy to Czechoslovakia. He entered into contact with the Communist International in Moscow and tried to establish military cooperation between the BANU and the Bulgarian Communist Party. Despite this, during the coup of June 1923 the Communists stayed neutral, and they soon attempted to seize power themselves, but in vain. Daskalov remained in Prague, where he was shot by a Macedonian terrorist. In 1986 his two-volume *Izbrani proizvedeniya* (Selected works) were published. (MC)

Sources: *Biographisches Lexikon*, vol. 1; John D. Bell, *Peasants in Power: Alexander Stamboliski and the Bulgarian Agrarian National Union, 1899–1923* (Princeton, 1978); Paun Genov, *Rayko Daskalov: Istoria na edni kratyk, no s buri izpylenen zhivot* (Sofia, 1978); Dimityr Tishev, *Rayko Daskalov: Zhizen put i obshtestvena deynost* (Sofia, 1988); Dobrin Michev, Dimityr Tishev, and Bonka Chavdarova, eds., *Dr. Rayko Daskalov: Politicheska i dyrzhavna deynost* (Sofia, 1988).

DASZYŃSKI Ignacy (26 October 1866, Zbaraż [now Zbarazh, Ukraine]–31 October 1936, Bystra, near Cieszyn), Polish Socialist politician. The son of a clerk, Daszyński was orphaned at the age of nine and brought up in poverty. While in high school in Stanisławów, he came in contact with a Socialist youth circle. Expelled from school for a patriotic speech in 1883, he did odd jobs and studied on his own. In 1887 in Kraków he passed his high school final examinations (*matura*) extramurally and took up studies in philosophy at the Jagiellonian University. He was working as a tutor near Łomża during his holidays in 1889, when he was arrested by the Russian police, who mistook him for his brother Feliks, at that time already a well-known Socialist activist. After a six-month investigation Daszyński was expelled to Galicia. This experience strengthened his radical anti-tsarist views. After his brother's death, he intended to go to America, but after a short stay in Switzerland he returned to Galicia. In 1890 in Lwów (Lviv) he organized the Workers' Party. When the Polish Social Democratic Party of Galicia and Silesia (Polska Partia Socjal-Demokratyczna Galicji i Śląska [PPSD]) was created in 1892, Daszyński joined it. He represented the party at the rallies of the Austrian Social Democrats and at the congresses of the Socialist International. He organized demonstrations, made speeches, and wrote articles and brochures. From 1893 he was editor-in-chief of the PPSD newspaper, *Naprzód*. In March 1897 he was elected by an overwhelming majority of the Kraków constituency to the Austrian Reichsrat (parliament) and was a member until 1918, winning fame as an orator. He also cooperated with the Socialists from the Russian partition of Poland—for example, with **Józef Piłsudski**. During the 1905 revolution the PPSD lent its firm support to the Polish Socialists who fought against tsarism. Nevertheless, Daszyński published an "Open Letter to the Central Workers' Committee of the Polish Socialist Party (CKR PPS)," in which he criticized the PPSD for too close contacts with Russian revolutionaries and for the excessive use of strikes for political purposes. When the PPS split in November 1906 Daszyński supported the moderate PPS-Revolutionary Faction against the radical PPS-Left.

From 1912 to 1914 Daszyński was one of the leaders of the Galician Provisional Commission of Confederated Independence Parties (Tymczasowa Komisja Skonfederowanych Stronnictw Niepodległościowych). After the outbreak of World War I, in August 1914 he took part in the cadre company of Piłsudski, who appointed him war commissar of the county of Miechów. The action was aimed at inciting an anti-Russian uprising there, but it failed. Daszyński co-founded the Supreme National Committee (Naczelny Komitet Narodowy), and he supported the struggle against Russia alongside Austria-Hungary. Initially, he proposed the transformation of Galicia into a separate part of the Habsburg monarchy, equal in rights with Austria and Hungary (the "trialist" concept). At the end of the war he adopted a definitely pro-independence stance. In January 1918 he spoke in the Reichsrat, demanding the convocation of the Polish Sejm and insisting on the participation of Polish delegates from all three sections of partitioned Poland in the Brest-Litovsk peace negotiations. He also urged the conclusion of a peace treaty with Russia and the creation of a unified Polish state.

During the disarmament of the Austro-Hungarian Army in Galicia, on 28 October 1918 Daszyński became vice-president of the Polish Liquidation Commission (Polska Komisja Likwidacyjna [PKL]) in Kraków. On 7 November 1918 he became head of the Provisional People's Government of the Republic of Poland in Lublin. He promoted a program of radical social reforms, including land reform and the nationalization of some branches of industry. When on 10 November Piłsudski returned from Magdeburg Prison to Warsaw, Daszyński agreed to hand over power to the central Socialist-People's government of **Jędrzej Moraczewski**, and this was done on 17 November. Elected an MP on behalf of the PPSD in January 1919, Daszyński contributed to the swift unification of the PPSD with the Socialist parties from other parts of partitioned Poland into a united Polish Socialist Party (Polska Partia Socjalistyczna [PPS]) in April 1919. From July 1920 to January 1921 he served as deputy prime minister of the coalition government of **Wincenty Witos**. At that time he very vigorously promoted the Polish cause among Western Socialists, showing discrepancies between Bolshevism and Democratic Socialism. In 1921–28 he was president of the Chief Council of the PPS, and between 1922 and 1923, also president of the PPS Central Executive Committee. He represented the moderate wing of the party, and he often criticized Bolshevik policies in Russia. Elected to the Sejm on behalf of the PPS in 1922, he served as deputy speaker of the parliament from 1922 to 1927. After president **Gabriel Narutowicz** was murdered in December 1922, Daszyński firmly opposed leftist plans of a coup d'état. From 1923 he was a long-standing president of the Workers' University Society.

In May 1926 Daszyński supported the coup d'état staged by Piłsudski, trying to prevent a split among the Socialists. After the elections of 1928 he became speaker of the Sejm, and he temporarily resigned his party positions. He opposed the abuse of power by the *sanacja* regime. However, in the face of the looming economic crisis and of the danger of conflicts between the *sanacja* regime and the opposition, on 24 June 1929 he suggested to Piłsudski that a coalition be formed between the PPS, the Nonparty Bloc of Cooperation with the Government (BBWR), and the Polish Peasant Party–Liberation (Polskie Stronnictwo Ludowe–Wyzwolenie). After Piłsudski rejected this suggestion, relations between Daszyński and Piłsudski definitely deteriorated, and Daszyński began to sharply criticize the ruling group. In October 1929 he refused to open the Sejm session in the presence of armed officers in the parliamentary hall. In 1930, as the Sejm speaker in office, he sent a solidarity telegram to the congress of the center-left opposition (Centrolew), held in Kraków. In 1930 he again won a parliamentary seat, and after the elections he protested the abuse of power by the *sanacja* regime. In 1931 he was reelected president of the Chief Council of the PPS. However, owing to deteriorating health, he gradually retired from public life, and in 1934 he resigned his post. Daszyński's works include *O formach rządu* (About forms of government; 1902); *Wielki człowiek w Polsce* (Great man in Poland; 1925); *Sejm, rząd, król, dyktator* (The Sejm, the government, the king, the dictator; 1926); and the two-volume *Pamiętniki* (Diaries; 1926). (WR)

Sources: *PSB*, vol. 4; *Encyklopedia historii Drugiej Rzeczypospolitej* (Warsaw, 1999); Adam Próchnik, *Ignacy Daszyński: Życie, praca, walka* (Warsaw, 1946); Jerzy Holzer, *Polska Paria Socjalistyczna w latach 1917–1919* (Warsaw, 1962); Aleksandra Tymieniecka, *Polityka Polskiej Partii Socjalistycznej w latach 1924–1928* (Warsaw, 1969); Andrzej Ajnenkiel, *Od rządów ludowych do przewrotu majowego* (Warsaw, 1978); Stanisław Grau and Ignacy Wilczek [Jerzy Holzer], "Ignacy Daszyński," *PPN*, 1980, no. 42; Adam Próchnik, *Pierwsze piętnastolecie Polski niepodległej* (Warsaw, 1983); Jan Tomicki, *Polska Partia Socjalistyczna 1892–1948* (Warsaw, 1983); Walentyna Najdus, *Ignacy Daszyński 1866–1936* (Warsaw, 1988).

DAVID Josef (Jóža) (17 February 1884, Kylešovice, Opava—21 April 1968, Prague), Czech journalist and politician. Before World War I David worked as a journalist and social activist in Silesia. In 1903 in Opava he founded his first Socialist-Nationalist organization. From 1905 to 1907 he wrote for *Pokrok*, a magazine of Socialist-Nationalist orientation that came out in Brno. Next, David founded and edited the periodical *Stráž českého severu* in the town of Most. He was in favor of universal suffrage and of the creation of a second Czech university in Brno. After the outbreak of World War I David fought on the eastern front, but in 1915 he was taken captive by the Russians. After the February 1917 revolution he co-organized the Czechoslovak Legion in Russia and was a representative of the Czechoslovak National Council in Russia. In December 1917 he also started working at *Československý deník*, the press organ of the legion. In December 1918 he was sent with a military delegation to Czechoslovakia, and in June 1919 he returned to Siberia with the mission of the Czechoslovak government. In May 1920 he finally returned to Czechoslovakia. From 1921 to 1939 David served as executive secretary of the Czechoslovak Legionnaire Community and as deputy to the National Assembly on behalf of the Socialist-Nationalist Party. In parliament, he was mainly involved with military and defense affairs, and from 1929 he was president of the parliamentary commission for defense. He was a member of the left wing of the party. From the beginning of the 1920s he urged the recognition of Soviet Russia.

In September 1938 David advocated the rejection of the Pact of Munich. At the beginning of the German occupation he tried to form a resistance movement. In October 1939 he went via Slovakia and Hungary to Belgrade, where he was active as a representative of the Czechoslovak resistance movement. His main task was to organize secret transport for Czechoslovak citizens to the West. He left Yugoslavia soon before the German invasion in April 1941. After the German attack against the USSR, he advocated cooperation among Slavs against the German threat. From the end of 1941 he was in London, where he became a member of the Czechoslovak National Council (Státní Rada Československá) and president of the Union of Czechoslovak Legionnaires (Svaz Československých Legionářů) in England. In March 1945 David participated in Moscow talks on the program and composition of a National Front government. Between 1945 and 1948 he was a member of the leadership of the Socialist-Nationalist Party, an MP, and president of the Legionnaire Community. Between April and October 1945 he served as deputy prime minister. Then he was president of the Provisional National Assembly, and from June 1946, president of the Constitutional National Assembly. He was passive during the coup of February 1948. After the elections of May 1948 David left political life entirely. (PU)

Sources: *ČBS*; Josef Korbel, *The Communist Subversion of Czechoslovakia, 1948–1960* (Princeton, 1959); Karel Kaplan, *The Short March: The Communist Takeover in Czechoslovakia, 1945–*

1948 (London, 1981); *Kdo byl kdo v našich dějinach ve 20. století*, vol. 1 (Prague, 1998); *Biografický slovník Slezska a Severní Moravy*, vol. 6 (Ostrava, 1996); *Českoslovenští politici: 1918–1991* (Prague, 1991); *Politická elita meziválečného Československa 1918–1938: Kdo byl kdo za první republiky* (Prague, 1998).

DAVIDOVIĆ Ljubomir (24 December 1863 Vlaška, Serbia–19 February 1940, Belgrade), Serb politician; prime minister of the Kingdom of Serbs, Croats, and Slovenes (SHS). Davidović was one of the co-founders of the National Radical Party. In 1912 he was elected president of the party. In 1914–18 he served as minister of education. From 1919 until his death he was the leader of the newly created Serbian Democratic Party. From 16 August 1919 to 19 February 1920 he was prime minister of the government created by a democratic-Socialist coalition. The normalization of the domestic situation in the country, which had been severely affected by war, was among the priorities of this cabinet. Davidović's government brought about the introduction of an eight-hour workday and the legalization of the social and trade organizations of workers, but it failed to bring down inflation. On 28 July 1924, after the fall of the cabinet of **Nikola Pašić**, Davidović again became the head of the government. He dismissed the charges against **Stjepan Radić**, the leader of the Croatian Peasant Party, thus allowing Radić to return to the SHS. Davidović resigned on 6 November 1924. The new elections in 1927 consolidated the Serbian nationalist parties. The Serbian Democratic Party split, and Davidović's faction went into the opposition. Under the dictatorship of King Alexander, Davidović opposed the nationalist policy of the government. In October 1937 Davidović, on behalf of his party, signed a settlement with the Croatian Peasant Party, and this paved the way to a broader Serbian-Croatian agreement of August 1939. (AO)

Sources: *Biographisches Lexikon*, vol. 1; Radoje Knažević, *Ljubomir Davidović 1863–1940* (Belgrade, 1940); Wacław Felczak and Tadeusz Wasilewski, *Historia Jugosławii* (Wrocław, 1985); Mark Biondich, *Stjepan Radić, the Croat Peasant Party, and the Politics of Mass Mobilization, 1904–1928* (Toronto, 2000).

DELCHEV Georgi Nikolov (Goce) (23 January 1872, Kukuš [now Kilkis, Greece]–4 May 1903, Banitsa), Macedonian revolutionary. After graduating from high school in Sofia in 1891, Delchev studied at the Sofia Military Academy, from which he was ousted in 1894 for Socialist activities. He worked as a teacher in Štip, where he met **Dame Gruev** and entered the leadership of the Internal Macedonian Revolutionary Organization (Vnatrešna Makedonska Revolucionerna Organizacija). He organized its cells, aiming at the liberation of Macedonia and the Adrianople region from the Turks. In 1896 he co-authored the program of the Secret Macedonian-Adrianople Revolutionary Organization (Tajna Makedonsko-Odrinska Revolucionerna Organizacija [SMARO]), which started military operations in 1899. In 1902 he revised the SMARO program, trying to attract all the ethnic groups living in the Adrianople area by emphasizing the quest for the region's autonomy. In his absence, in January 1903 the SMARO leaders made the decision to start an anti-Turkish uprising. Although Delchev thought it premature, he joined in the preparations. During a march of his *cheta* (unit) he was killed in a Turkish attack. (WR)

Sources: *Entsiklopediya Bulgariya*, vol. 2 (Sofia, 1981); Hristo Andonov-Poljanski, *Goce Delcev: His Life and Times* (Skopje, 1973); Marcie MacDermott, *Freedom or Death: The Life of Goce Delcev* (London, 1978); Duncan M. Perry, *The Politics of Terror: The Macedonian Liberation Movements, 1893–1903* (Durham, N.C., 1988); Raymond Detrez, *Historical Dictionary of Bulgaria* (Lanham, Md., 1997).

DELVINA Suleyman Pasha (1884, Delvinë–1 August 1932, Vlorë), Albanian politician and diplomat. Born into an aristocratic family, Delvina graduated from Zosimea High School in Janina and in law in Istanbul. Then he worked as a teacher in an Istanbul high school. In 1901 he returned to his hometown, Delvinë. In 1905 he went back to Istanbul. He taught in Galatasaray High School, and then he worked as a ministerial official of a lower rank. He joined in the activities of the Albanian national club Bashkimi (Unity) in Istanbul. In July 1911 he organized a student demonstration, demanding the right to use the Albanian alphabet in Turkey. In April 1919 the Albanian diaspora in Turkey delegated him to the Paris Peace Conference. As a result of the Congress of Lushnjë of 21 January 1920, in March 1920 Delvina was appointed the first prime minister of an independent Albanian government. Among other things, he concluded a treaty with Italy, which gave up its claims to a protectorate over Albania. Since Delvina proclaimed his desire to realize the "will of the people," he got into trouble with the conservatives and had to resign on 14 November 1920. In the subsequent government of Ilias bey Vrioni, until October 1921 he was minister of interior. In 1924 he won a parliamentary seat from Vlorë. During the revolution he supported **Fan Noli**, heading his ministry of foreign affairs from June to December 1924. Delvina was attributed with the idea of establishing diplomatic relations with the Soviet Union. After the failure of the revolution he went into exile. He was active in the leftist National Revolutionary Committee (Komiteti Nacional Revolucionar [KONARE]). Seriously ill, he took advantage of an amnesty to return to Albania. Since he was banned from living in Tirana, he settled in Vlorë, where he soon died. (TC)

Sources: Stefanaq Pollo and Arben Puto, *The History of Albania from Its Origins to the Present Day* (London, 1981); *Tre luftëtarë të çështjes kombëtare* (Tirana, 1983); F. Vejzi, *Qeveria e Kongresit te Lushnjes dhe veprimtaria e saj. (1918–1920)* (Tirana, 1987); Arben Puto, *Demokracia e rrethuar: Qeveria e Fan Nolit ne marredheniet e jashtme qershor–dhjetor 1924* (Tirana, 1990); Tadeusz Czekalski, *Albania 1920–1924: Aparat państwowy i jego funkcjonowanie* (Katowice, 1998).

DEMÉNY Pál (29 August 1901, Budapest–14 January 1991, Budapest), Hungarian Communist activist. Demény was born into a middle-class family. In 1918 he passed high school examinations and became a founding member of the so-called independent group of young workers. In February 1919 he joined the Hungarian Communist Party (HCP). During the Hungarian Soviet Republic (HSR) Demény was the leader of young workers in Budapest's Seventh District. He also joined the Hungarian Red Army, where he served as an artillerist. In August 1919, after the fall of the HSR, he organized the Communist Union of Young Workers. He also edited two illegal newspapers of the organization: *Értesítő* and *Örök forradalom*. Arrested in the fall of 1919, Demény was released after two months. In December of that year he started working in the Richter Chemical Plants. Between 1920 and 1921 he was an extramural student of chemistry at the Technische Hohschule in Vienna, but in August 1921 he was re-arrested for his revolutionary activities in Hungary. Demény rejected the chance to emigrate, which was part of the Soviet-Hungarian agreement on the exchange of POWs, and he spent 1921–24 in prison.

After his release, Demény and his supporters began to abandon the Comintern line. In 1925 Demény joined the Hungarian Social Democratic Party (HSDP) but was expelled for his revolutionary views. Later, he organized various workers' anti-alcohol, tourist, and sports associations. He was also busy with writing and publishing books. In 1938 he was tried for distributing anti-war leaflets. Sentenced to a two-year imprisonment, Demény served his sentence in Szeged, where he met **Mátyás Rákosi**. In November 1940 he was released. During the war, members of the movement (a circle of social democrats) rallied around Demény helped to hide people and to obtain false documents for them. Between September and December 1944 his faction was active under the name of the Communist Party of Hungary (the previous party, under the same name, had been dissolved by **János Kádár** in 1943). In November 1944 Demény came to an agreement with the Communists, represented by **László Rajk** and **Gábor Péter**, on the unification of two national groups. At that time, Demény was recognized as a member of the Central Committee (CC). On 13 February 1945, the day when the siege of Budapest ended, Demény was arrested by Péter, who by then was head of interior security services. In July 1946 the People's Court in Budapest accused Demény of "activities against the people" and sentenced him to four and a half years of forced labor. In 1950 he was interned in Kistarcsa, where in 1953 he was sentenced to a further ten years.

Demény was released on 13 October 1956. At the beginning of 1957 the Supreme Court quashed his last sentence, but Demény was not finally vindicated until 1989. After 1956 he worked in the National Bureau of Translators, and in 1967 he retired. He then began to work on his memoirs. In the autumn of 1989 he joined the Hungarian Socialist Party (HSP), which was founded in the place of the Hungarian Socialist Workers' Party (HSWP). In the first free parliamentary elections in 1990 Demény was elected to parliament from the national list of the HSP. His memoirs, titled *A párt foglya voltam* (I was a prisoner of the party), appeared in 1988. (JT)

Sources: *Magyar Nagylexikon*, vol. 6 (Budapest 1998); *A magyar forradalom és szabadságharc enciklopédiája* (Budapest, 1999).

DÉRÉR Ivan (2 March 1884, Malacky–10 March 1973, Prague), Slovak lawyer and politician. Dérér graduated in law from the university in Budapest, where in 1907 he obtained a Ph.D., and then he worked as a barrister. In his youth he aligned himself with groups linked to the magazine *Hlas*. In 1918 he was a co-author of the declaration of Turčiansky Sv. Martin. In 1920 he was elected to parliament in Prague from the Social Democratic list of candidates from Slovakia. He was an advocate of a close union of the Czechs and the Slovaks. From 1921 to 1922 he served as minister for unification and worked on the harmonization of law for the former Austrian and Hungarian lands of the Czechoslovak republic. In 1926 he was the author of the law on minorities, called the "lex Dérér." From February 1934 to the end of 1938 he was the minister of justice, and from 1933 he also served as vice-president of the Social Democratic Party. He represented the party at the Socialist International congresses. After the partition of Czechoslovakia in March 1939 Dérér did not support the Slovak state, which was created with the assistance of the Third Reich. He was active in the Social Democratic conspiracy in Prague, and in 1944–45 he was held prisoner in a Nazi camp in Terezín.

After the war Dérér criticized the takeover of the party by crypto-Communists, with **Zdenek Fierlinger** at the head, and at the congress of the Social Democrats in Brno in 1947 he openly came out against Fierlinger. In 1946 he became president of the Supreme Court, trying to maintain the principles of law and order that were being undermined by the Communists. For example, he criticized the wavering attitude of President **Edvard Beneš**, who did not with consult him about the death sentence of Reverend **Jozef Tiso**. Dérér was against this sentence. After the coup of February 1948 Dérér resigned from his post. In 1950 he was arrested without reason and sentenced to three and a half years of prison. After his release he did not hold any posts. Rehabilitated during the Prague Spring in 1968, he returned for a short time to the political scene and even received the Order of the Republic. During the "normalization" he was again placed in the shadows. He wrote (among other works) the following: *Ustawa o organizace Československe Republiky* (The act on the organization of the Czechoslovak Republic; 1922); *Slovensko v prevrate i po ňom* (Slovakia during the coup and after; 1924); *Katechizmus pozemkove reformy* (Catechism of the agrarian reform; 1925); *Prečo sme proti autonomii?* (Why are we against autonomy? 1934); *Česi a Slovacy ve strednej Evrope* (The Czechs and the Slovaks in Central Europe; 1938); *The Unity of Czechs and Slovaks* (1938); and "Anti-Fierlinger" (1952–61; manuscript). (WR)

Sources: *East Central Europe*, 1985, vol. 12, part 1; *SBS*, vol. 1; B. Koloušek, *Dr Ivan Dérér a národné školstvo na Slovensku* (Bratislava, 1935).

DERTLIEV Petyr (7 April 1916, ?–5 November 2000, Sofia), Bulgarian doctor and Social Democratic politician. Dertliev was born into a teacher's family. Before the war he was active in the Socialist Youth Union, for which he was imprisoned. Between November 1936 and March 1937 he was in the USSR. During World War II he opposed the pro-German policy of subsequent Bulgarian governments. After the seizure of power by the Communists he spoke against totalitarianism, defending Social Democratic ideas. From 1945 he was secretary of a youth organization of the unified Bulgarian Social Democratic Workers' Party. Because of his activities he was placed in the Rositsa concentration camp in May 1946. He was released as a candidate for the parliament five days before the elections to the Grand National Assembly of 27 October 1946. In parliament, he was a member of the health commission, and he also spoke in defense of democratic freedoms. On 1 July 1948 he was arrested, and in mid-November, after a rigged trial, he was sentenced to ten years of prison. He served the sentence in several labor camps and penal institutes. In 1957 he was released.

After the overthrow of the totalitarian government Dertliev became president of the Bulgarian Social Democratic Party (BSDP), which was reactivated on 26 November 1989, and director of the newspaper *Svoboden narod*, which came out as of January 1990. He was one of the founders of the Union of Democratic Forces (UDF). At the end of July 1990 he was a candidate for president, but because of the opposition of the Bulgarian Socialist Party deputies, he withdrew his candidacy. At that time the UDF elected **Zheliu Zhelev** president. In 1990–91 Dertliev was a deputy to the Seventh Constituent Assembly; from January 1991 he was co-president, and from May 1991 president, of the UDF parliamentary group. He took an active role in the preparation of the constitution of 12 July 1991, which he signed in opposition to the boycott against it by thirty-nine deputies of the UDF right. Since his party, the BSDP, failed to enter parliament in the subsequent elections of 1991, 1994, and 1995, the Dertliev's role diminished. He published two volumes of memoirs, *Den pyrvi, den posleden* (Day first, day last; 1996) and *Po zharavata* (On Tenterhooks; 1998), depicting his life and political activity, as well as his experience in the labor camps and prisons. (JJ)

Sources: Jerzy Jackowicz, *Bułgaria od rządów komunistycznych do demokracji parlamentarnej 1988–1991* (Warsaw, 1992); Petyr Dertliew, *Dosieto na dr Petyr Dertliew: Spomeni, dokumenti* (Sofia, 1994); Raymond Detrez, *Historical Dictionary of Bulgaria* (Lanham, Md., 1997).

DÉRY Tibor (18 October 1894, Budapest–18 August 1977, Budapest), Hungarian writer. Born into a rich family of Jewish descent, in his youth Déry suffered from bone tuberculosis, underwent several operations, and spent years in bed. After graduating from a trade high school, he worked in the timber processing factories of his mother's family, first in Galócás, Transylvania, and then in Budapest. He made his literary debut with the novel *Lia* (1917), rich in erotic scenes, for which he was sued for offending public morality. In 1917–19 he published several poems and short stories in the leading literary periodical, *Nyugat*. In 1919 he joined the Hungarian Communist Party, and during the Hungarian Soviet Republic (HSR) he became a member of the Writers' Directorate. At this time he lost his father, who committed suicide in reaction to the nationalization of his estate.

After the fall of the HSR in August 1919, Déry left Hungary, publishing surrealist and expressionist poems in the émigré press. In 1926 he returned to Hungary, but he kept traveling and living abroad from time to time, mostly in Western Europe and Scandinavia. His best works of this time include novels and short stories: *A két növér* (Two sisters; 1921); *A két hangú kiáltás* (A shout in two parts; 1922); *Ébredjetek fel!* (Awake! 1929); *Az éneklő szikla* (A singing rock; 1930); *Országuton* (On the road; 1932); he also wrote novels on the German workers' movement that were published after World War II: *Szemtől szembe* (Eye to eye; 1945) and *A befejezetlen mondat* (Unfinished sentence; 1947). The latter, about a rich burgher who broke off ties with his family and became a Communist, was based on his own experience. In 1934 Déry took part in the Schutzbund uprising in Vienna as a collaborator of the Rote Hilfe, and then he left for Spain for a year. In 1938 he translated *Retour de l'URSS*, by André Gide, for which he was arrested for two months, and he was banned from publishing. He spent the World War II years in Hungary and made his living by translating. During the German occupation he went into hiding.

After the Communist takeover, Déry returned to public life, holding high positions in the Association of Hungarian Writers and editing the monthly *Csillag*, which mostly published translations from Russian. Déry was one of the most often published writers of that time, and his plays—such as *Tükör* (Mirror; 1947), *Itthon* (Home; 1948), and *A tanúk* (Witnesses; 1948)—were always playing in the National Theater. This changed after Déry published the novel *Felelet* (Reply; 1950), announced as the first "truly Socialist realist" work. The extensive novel, dealing with the history of the interwar Hungarian workers' movement, was not well received by the authorities. Two years later, the second volume of the novel was given an even worse treatment, and Déry got into trouble for refusing a self-criticism. He was marginalized, but soon he joined the supporters of the "thaw." His collection of short stories *A ló meg az öregasszony* (The horse and the old woman; 1955) and his novella *Niki* were indirect criticisms of postwar Hungarian reality. In the summer of 1956 Déry was excluded from the Communist Party, and in 1957 he was sentenced to nine years in prison for expressing his negative attitude to the government of **János Kádár**. In prison he wrote one of his best novels, *A. úr X-ben* (Mr. A. G. in X; 1964), a political fiction of a future totalitarian system in which anarchy is law and any useful activity is outlawed. In a novel that he wrote after leaving prison in 1960—*A kiközösítő* (Throwing anathemas; 1966)—Déry also alluded to the dangers of the Communist social order. In 1969 he published his memoirs, *Ítélet nincs* (Lack of verdict), and two years later, the novel *Képzelt riport egy amerikai pop-fesztiválról* (Imaginative coverage of an American pop festival), later adapted as a theater play, in which the Woodstock festival was a pretext for reflections on modern civilization. Later works by Déry were full of irony and skepticism. Even during his lifetime he was considered one of the leading Hungarian writers of the twentieth century. (MS)

Sources: József Révai, *Kulturális forradalmunk kérdései* (Budapest, 1952); *Tibor Déry: Eingeleitet von Georg Lukacs und Tamas Ungvari* (Hamburg, 1969); Mario Szenessy, *Tibor Déry* (Stuttgart, 1970); Tamás Ungvári, *Déry Tibor alkotásai és vallomásai tükrében* (Budapest, 1973); Béla Pomogáts, *Déry Tibor* (Budapest, 1974); William Shawcross, *Crime and Compromise: Janos Kadar and the Politics of Hungary since Revolution* (New York, 1974); *Mały słownik pisarzy węgierskich* (Warsaw, 1977); *"D.T. úr X-ben." Tanulmányok és dokumentumok Déryról* (Budapest, 1995).

DEVA Xhafer (21 February 1904, Mitrovica–25 May 1978, Palo Alto, California), Albanian politician and economist. Deva studied in Salonika and then at Robert College in Istanbul. Later he worked in banks in Egypt and Britain. In 1941 he became the head of administration in Kosovo Mitrovica under German occupation. He was active in the (pro-Western) National Front (Balli Kombëtar), and on 16 September 1943 he co-founded the Second Prizren League, which coordinated Albanian political and cultural organizations and strove for the unification of Albanian territories, including those under Bulgarian occupation. Deva conceived the tactical idea of creating Albanian volunteer brigades armed by the Germans but thought to be the nucleus of a future Albanian army. In late 1944 he left for Vienna and from there for Syria, becoming one of the leaders of the Albanian diaspora, directing the Prizren League in exile, and advocating the formation of a Great Albania. After the death of **Midhat Frashëri**, Deva was forced by King **Zog** to be the political leader of all the Albanian diaspora. He took part in the military training of Albanian refugees and later parachuted into Albania during the "Valuable" operation (1951). Disappointed by the operation's failure, he moved to Rome, where he worked with the Polish Office of Aid to Emigrants, raising funds for Albanians escaping to the West. In 1956, along with his family, he left for the United States, where he lectured at Stanford University until 1971. He initiated the move of the Prizren League headquarters to New York. At a conference in Madrid in 1972, King **Leka I** described Deva as head of a "united front against the Albanian Communists," but despite the support of Leka, Deva failed to unite all the quarreling factions of the Albanian diaspora. (TC)

Sources: William Bland and Ian Price, *A Tangled Web: A History of Anglo-American Relations with Albania (1912–1955)* (London, 1986); Bernd Fischer, *Albania at War, 1939–1945* (London, 1999); *Xhafer Deva: Jeta dhe veprimtaria* (New York, n.d.).

DIENSTBIER Jiří (20 April 1937, Kladno), Czech journalist, politician, and diplomat. In 1960 Dienstbier graduated in journalism from Charles University in Prague. In 1958–69 he worked in the foreign language section of Czechoslovak Radio; in 1964–67 he was a correspondent in the Far East, and in 1968–69, in the United States. From 1958 he belonged to the Communist Party of Czechoslovakia (CPC). In 1968 he was one of most active advocates of democratization, and after the Warsaw Pact invasion in August 1968 he co-edited the anti-occupation broadcasts of Czechoslovak Radio. In 1970 he was expelled from the CPC, fired from work, and subjected to a complete ban of publication. He worked as a blue-collar laborer. In the 1970s and 1980s he belonged to the leaders of the democratic opposition. In 1977 he was one of the first signatories of Charter 77, and in 1979 and 1985, its spokesman. In 1978 he co-founded the Committee for the Defense of the Unjustly Prosecuted (Výbor na Obranu Nespravedlivě Stíhaných) and contributed to many uncensored periodicals. In 1979–82 he was imprisoned for "an attempt to overthrow the republic." In 1988–89 he took part in a number of opposition activities and was a member of the editorial board of the uncensored periodical *Lidové noviny*.

During the Velvet Revolution, in November 1989 Dienstbier co-founded the Civic Forum (Občanské Fórum [OF]) and was briefly its spokesman. In the first government that included non-Communists, headed by **Marián Čalfa**, Dienstbier was minister of foreign affairs from December 1989 and deputy prime minister from 9 April 1990. He resumed the same position after the first free elections of June 1990. He was the architect and realizer of the new Czechoslovak foreign policy. Under the new geopolitical circumstances he aimed to change it into a pro-Western direction. He also supported Central European cooperation. From June 1990 he was an MP to the Chamber of the People of the Federal Assembly, initially on behalf of the OF and after its split, on behalf of the Civic Movement (Občanské Hnutí [OH]), which he chaired. As a result of the electoral defeat of his party, which failed to get into the parliament, on 26 June Dienstbier resigned from his government posts. In 1991–93 he chaired the OH and cooperated with other liberal parties of limited influence. In 1993–95 he presided over the Free Democrats (Svobodní Demokraté), and in 1995–96 he co-presided over the Free Democrats-Liberal National Socialist Party (Svobodní Demokraté-Liberální Strana Národně Sociální). In the parliamentary elections of June 1996 his party lost, and when in the fall of 1996 Dienstbier lost the election to the Senate, he gave up party leadership. In 1997 he toured U.S. universities, giving a number of lectures, and in 1998 he became a special UN reporter on the violation of human rights in the former Yugoslavia. He was also a Czech ambassador for special missions.

Apart from his work in journalism, Dienstbier authored a book on the military coup in Indonesia in September 1965, *Noc nastala ve tři ráno* (The night came at 3 a.m.; 1967); essays on the new political order in Europe, *Sněni o Evropě* (Dreams of Europe; uncensored edition, 1986;

official version, 1990); and a couple of plays published in *samizdat* in the 1980s. Along with Karel Lánsky, he published a book on Czechoslovak Radio during the Soviet occupation, *Rozhlas proti tankům* (Radio against tanks; uncensored edition, 1986; official version, 1990). (PU)

Sources: *ČBS*; *Českoslovenští politici: 1918–1991* (Prague, 1991); *Kdo byl kdo v našich dějinach ve 20. století*, vol. 1 (Prague, 1998); *Kdo je kdo v České Republice na přelomu 20. století* (Prague, 1998); www.dienstbier.cz.

DIMITRIEV Radko (24 September 1859, Gradets–18 October 1918, Pyatigorsk), Bulgarian and Russian general. A soldier from his youth, Dimitriev was initially connected with the Bulgarian anti-Turkish conspiracy, and then he fought against the Turks in the Russian Army (1877–78). He graduated from a cadet school in Sofia, and later he studied at the Nicholas Academy of the General Staff in Petersburg. He distinguished himself in the Battle of Slivitsa against the Serbs (1885). After the victorious termination of this campaign, the Bulgarian prince, Alexander, abandoned the country's pro-Russian orientation. A Russophile and Panslavist, Dimitriev entered into a conflict with the ruler. He plotted against Alexander, and he took part in a failed attempt on his life in August 1886. As a result he had to emigrate to Romania, where he tried to organize a mutiny of Bulgarian officers in 1887. Then he served in the Russian Army in the Caucasus. After Bulgarian-Russian relations were stabilized, Dimitriev returned to Bulgaria and joined the Bulgarian Army in 1898. Thanks to Russian backing, in 1903 he became chief of the general staff. Under his command the Bulgarian Army proved victorious over Turkey in the First Balkan War (1912–13). He failed to repeat this success in the Second Balkan War, when the Bulgarian offensive was resisted by Serbia, Greece, and Romania. After this defeat Dimitriev opposed the pro-German line of Tsar **Ferdinand** and became Bulgarian envoy to Russia. When World War I broke out, he returned to the Russian Army. He commanded the Third Army at Przemyśl and during the Carpathian offensive of 1914–15. Forced to retreat, he managed to prevent panic. When Bulgaria entered the war on the side of the Central Powers, he was deprived of the command of the Third Army. The February 1917 revolution saw him as commander of the Eleventh Army in the Baltic area. As a result of a compromise with the Council of Soldiers' Deputies, Dimitriev managed to maintain discipline, and his units continued the struggle against Germany. Arrested by the Bolsheviks in Pyatigorsk, he was soon executed. (MC)

Sources: *Biographisches Lexikon*, vol. 1; Svetlozar Nedev, *Komandvaneto na bulgarskata voyska prez voynite za natsionalno obedinenie, 1885, 1912, 1913, 1915, 1918* (Sofia, 1993); Kristofor

Chesapchev, *Sluzhba na Bulgariia w chuzhbina: Voennodiplomaticheski spomeni, 1899–1914 g.* (Sofia, 1993); Richard C. Hall, *Bulgaria's Road to the First World War* (Boulder, Colo., 1996); Richard C. Hall, *The Balkan Wars, 1912–1913: Prelude to the First World War* (London and New York, 2000); "Enemy·Portrait: General Radko Ruskov Dmitriev," www.geocities.com/veldes1/boroevic.html.

DIMITRIJE Pavlović (15 October 1846, Požarevac–6 April 1930, Belgrade), patriarch of Serbia. In 1868 Dimitrije graduated from a seminary in Belgrade, and then he worked as a teacher. In 1870 he took holy orders and then studied at the Philology Department of the Higher School in Belgrade. After graduation he worked as a teacher at a theological seminary in Belgrade. Soon he entered the monastery, retaining his baptismal name. When King Milan Obrenović ousted Metropolitan Mihailo and appointed Mihailo's successor, Teodosije Mraović, in October 1884 Dimitrije was nominated bishop of Niš. After the abdication of King Milan, Mihailo returned as metropolitan and dismissed bishops appointed by Mraović. Dimitrije left for Paris, where he took up Slavic studies at the Sorbonne (1890–92), and then studied agriculture at the university in Montpellier. After his return to Serbia in 1894 he was sent to Athos, where he managed to ease the conflict between monks of Serbian and Bulgarian origin in the Serbian Hilandar Monastery. Owing to his scholarly works, as well as to the experience he had gained abroad, his role again grew in importance, both on the political and on the church scene. In 1895 he was elected to the State Council, and after the death of Metropolitan Mihailo in 1898, the new metropolitan, Inokentije, put Dimitrije in charge of the Šabac diocese. Dimitrije held the post until 19 August 1905, when he was elected metropolitan of Belgrade and of all of Serbia.

Following the annexation of Bosnia and Herzegovina by Austria-Hungary in 1908, Dimitrije began an energetic diplomatic campaign, sending information about the situation of the Serbian people to all Orthodox monasteries and to Russian authorities. After the end of the Balkan Wars, in 1913 he managed to extend the authority of the Serbian Orthodox Church to dioceses that until then had been under the jurisdiction of ecumenical patriarchs. After Serbia's defeat in World War I, along with the government, Dimitrije went to Corfu via Albania. Thanks to contacts that he established at that time with Anglican theologians, young Serbian priests were given a chance to study in England. After the end of World War I this group of priests played an important role in the life of the Serbian Orthodox Church. Having returned to the Kingdom of Serbs, Croats, and Slovenes in 1920, Dimitrije undertook effective actions aiming at the unification of all Serbian Orthodox churches. On 12 November 1920 he was elected patriarch of the United Serbian Orthodox Church. He remained in office until his death, contributing to the establishment of an excellent Theological Department in Belgrade and a professional journal, *Bogoslovije*. He also helped create the Theological Department in Zagreb. (AG)

Sources: *Biographisches Lexikon*, vol. 1; Djoko Slijepčević, *Istorija srpske pravoslavne crkve*, vol. 2 (Munich, 1966).

DIMITRIJEVIĆ Dragutin (byname Apis) (17 August 1876, Belgrade–26 June 1917, Salonika), chief of Serbian intelligence, leader of a terrorist secret society known as the Black Hand. The son of a craftsman, Dimitrijević completed a gymnasium in Niš and Belgrade and then graduated from the Belgrade Military Academy. He was one of the leaders of a plot to overthrow the autocratic rule of **Alexander Obrenović**. The first attempt to kill King Alexander and his wife failed in 1901. Dimitrijević was involved in the second attempt, which was successfully carried out on 28–29 May 1903. He was wounded during the shooting. After the accession to the throne of **Peter I Karadjordjević**, Dimitrijević continued his career in the army. In 1910–14 he was a lecturer in tactics at the Belgrade Military Academy, and from 1910 to 1912 he also held the post of chief of staff of a cavalry brigade in Belgrade. His posts allowed him to exert great influence on his students, as well as on members of the officer corps. In May 1911 he was one of the founders, and soon became the leader, of a secret nationalist society called Ujedinjenje ili Smrt (Union or Death), known as Cerna Ruka (Black Hand). The members of this society were active in the territories that they recognized as Serb, and they sought to create a Greater Serbia. Acting as a conspiracy and using brutal methods to punish disloyalty, the society organized attempts on Austro-Hungarian officials. Its sign, the imprint of a black hand, aroused fear and increased the nationalistic mood in Serbia. As early as 1911 Dimitrijević planned the assassination of Emperor Francis Joseph but was unsuccessful. In 1913 he became the chief of Serbian military intelligence.

Dimitrijević's responsibility for the attempt on the life of Archduke Francis Ferdinand in Sarajevo (28 July 1914) has not been quite explained, although the assassin, **Gavrilo Princip**, belonged to the Black Hand. After Serbia's defeat and the evacuation of the government from Belgrade, Dimitrijević rose to the rank of colonel in 1916. The Black Hand became so influential in the army and in the administration that Regent **Alexander Karadjordjević**, along with Prime Minister **Nikola Pašić**, decided to liquidate it. In October 1916 Dimitrijević lost his post of chief of the intelligence department and was assigned to the army staff on the Salonika front. On 28 December 1916 he was arrested and brought to trial under trumped-up charges of high treason and attempts on the life of the heir to the throne. After the so-called Salonika Trial he was sentenced to death on 5 June 1917, and despite the protests of Serbia's allies, Russia and Great Britain, he was executed. In 1953 he was rehabilitated by the courts of Communist Yugoslavia. (AO)

Sources: *Biographisches Lexikon*, vol. 1; M. Boghitchevitch, *Le process de Salonique, juin 1917* (Paris, 1927); M. Boghitchevitch, *Le colonel Dragoutine Dimitrievitch Apis* (Paris, 1928); Borivoje Nešković, *Istina o Solunskom procesu* (Belgrade, 1953); Vladimir Dedijer, *The Road to Sarajevo* (New York, 1966); *Spy-Counterspy: An Encyclopedia of Espionage* (New York, 1982).

DIMITROV Filip (31 March 1955, Sofia), Bulgarian lawyer and politician. Dimitrov graduated from a high school in which English was the language of instruction and from the Law Department of the University of Sofia (1977). Until 1989 he worked as a barrister. After **Todor Zhivkov** was removed from power in November 1989, Dimitrov took part in the creation of democratic structures. He initiated the Independent Bar Association and was co-founder of the Bulgarian Green Party. From 6 July 1990 he was deputy chairman, and from December 1990 to December 1991 chairman, of the National Coordination Board of the Union of Democratic Forces (Sayuz na Demokratichnite Sili [SDS]). He also established a monarchist society demanding the return of the king but to no avail. From January to March 1990 he participated in the Round Table Talks on behalf of the SDS, and from May 1991 he presided over the SDS central electoral committee. In the elections of October 1991 he won a parliamentary seat. When it proved possible to create a government majority of the SDS and the (Turkish) Movement for Rights and Freedoms (MRF), on 8 December 1991 Dimitrov became prime minister of this government. He tried to implement economic reforms, but their first social effects undermined his position. He faced growing social discontent, connected with deteriorating living conditions and with the reaction of the Turks to discrimination in their access to privatized state farms. He also faced internal tensions within the SDS on account of the attitude toward the Orthodox Church, the restoration of the monarchy, the pace of reforms, and President **Zhelyu Zhelev**. When the MRF supported a vote of nonconfidence, on 28 October 1992 Dimitrov had to resign as prime minister. After his resignation his position within the SDS weakened. In November 1992 he demanded UN intervention in the former Yugoslavia. After 1997 he was Bulgarian envoy to the United Nations. An amateur of psychoanalysis, a polyglot, and a writer, he authored *Ibo*

żiwjacha, Gospodi (Since they lived, My Lord; 1991) and *Istinskata istorija za ricarite na krygłata masa* (True knights of the Round Table; 1992). (JJ)

Sources: *Koy koy e v Bulgariya* (Sofia, 1998); *Europa Środkowo-Wschodnia 1991–1992* (Warsaw, 1992–94); Raymond Detrez, *Historical Dictionary of Bulgaria* (Lanham, Md., 1997); Bugajski.

DIMITROV Georgi "Gemeto" (15 April 1903, Eni Chyftlik, near Odrinsko–29 November 1972, Washington, D.C.), Bulgarian Peasant Party politician. Dimitrov was born into a peasant family. After high school he completed medical studies in Zagreb, where he earned a Ph.D. in 1929. From 1922 he was a member of the Bulgarian Agrarian National Union (Bylgarski Narodny Zemedelski Sojuz), and he practiced as a doctor in Dovientsa and Sofia. He was temporarily arrested during the coup in 1923 and after an attempt on the life of Tsar **Boris III** in 1925. However, he had nothing to do with the attempt. In 1928 Dimitrov became secretary of the party youth unit and founded the Agrarian Union of Academic Youth. In the 1930s he was at the head of the leftist faction of Agrarians, which was linked with the magazine *Pladne*. In 1931 he was elected MP. Although he criticized the Stalinist regime in the USSR, Dimitrov defended the Communists attacked in parliament and financially supported the mother of **Georgi Dimitrov**. After the royal coup of 1934 he criticized the autocratic government of the tsar and his policy of rapprochement with the Axis states. Because of this he was temporarily arrested in 1935.

After Bulgaria's accession to the anti-Comintern Pact Dimitrov was threatened with imprisonment. Therefore in February 1941 he secretly left for England, where he founded the Bulgarian National Committee, which favored the Allies. Later, he lived in the Middle East. When the Pladne faction joined an agreement with the Communists within the framework of the Fatherland Front in the country, after the coup of 9 September 1944 Dimitrov returned to Bulgaria, becoming the head of the Agrarians and of the non-Communist part of the ruling coalition. At first, the Communists considered appointing him prime minister, but after realizing that he was extremely popular and uncompromising in the defense of democracy, they decided to get rid of him. When he rejected a diplomatic post in England, the Communists attempted to remove him from the leadership of the party. The Agrarians rallied around him, so the Communists and their protector, the commander of the Soviet troops in Bulgaria, General Sergei Biryuzov, restricted his freedom of movement. On 21 January 1945 the police did not allow him to speak at a rally in Pleven and imposed house arrest on him. Despite his ill health, Dimitrov fearlessly stood up to the Communists, so they arrested him in April. After his release, which was conditioned on his resignation as head of the party, he remained the target of a mounting campaign of threats and blackmail. Fearing another arrest Dimitrov, who was suffering from pneumonia, took refuge in the American Embassy in May, and on 5 September 1945 an American military plane took him out of Bulgaria.

Dimitrov established contacts with other Bulgarian emigrant politicians who represented democratic views, and in June 1947 he established the National Bulgarian Committee in Washington. In the following years he was one of the leading activists of the Assembly of Captive European Nations (ACEN). In 1943 Dimitrov wrote *Bylgarskata tragedia* (Bulgarian tragedy); in 1952 he published his memoirs of **Nikola Petkov** (*Nicola Petkov: In Memoriam*); and in 1957 he published an analysis of the Hungarian uprising, *Inferences from the Hungarian Revolution*. In 1993 his *Spomeni* (Memoirs) were published in Sofia. (WR)

Sources: *Entsiklopediya Bulgariya*, vol. 2; Charles A. Moser, *Dimitrov of Bulgaria: A Political Biography of Dr. Georgi M. Dimitrov* (Ottawa, 1979); Dr. Georgi M. Dimitrov, *Lebenslauf und politische Tätigkeit: 15 April 1903–29 November 1972* (Munich, 1982); Jerzy Jackowicz, *Partie opozycyjne w Bułgarii 1944–1948* (Warsaw, 1997).

DIMITROV Georgi [originally Mikhailov] (18 June 1882, Kovachevtsi, near Radomir–2 July 1949, Moscow), Bulgarian Communist leader. The son of a laborer, Dimitrov left school at twelve and started working in a printing house. In 1900 he joined a trade union organization, and in 1902 he entered the Bulgarian Social Democratic Workers' Party. After the split in the leadership of the party, he backed its Bolshevik wing, the Tesnyaki, and in 1909 he became a member of the Central Committee (CC) of this faction. The same year he was elected secretary of a federation of revolutionary trade unions. In 1913 he was elected to parliament. He was arrested for anti-war and anti-state agitation in 1918 but was soon released in the face of Bulgaria's defeat in the war. After the Bulgarian Communist Party (BCP) was formed in April 1919, Dimitrov became a member of its CC. Arrested by the Romanian police on his way to Russia to the Second Congress of the Comintern in 1920, he arrived in Moscow in 1921. It was then that he met Lenin. At the founding congress of the Communist international trade union organization (Profintern), Dimitrov was a delegate representing Bulgaria and the Balkans. After returning to Bulgaria, he took part in the preparation of a Communist uprising in September 1923, and after its failure he fled to the USSR. The Bulgarian court sentenced him to death in absentia.

During his stay in the USSR Dimitrov quickly rose in the hierarchy of the Communist International (Comintern). He headed the Balkan Communist Federation. At that time he opted for a federation of Balkan states in which ethnic tensions could be avoided. For example, he saw Macedonia, a bone of contention between the Serbs and the Bulgarians, as an autonomous part of such a federation. In 1924 he attended the Fifth Congress of the Comintern. During Stalin's struggle against Leon Trotsky he supported the former; consequently he was promoted to the Executive Committee (EC) of the International. At the EC Plenum in 1926 Dimitrov was elected a deputy member of the Secretariat of the Comintern. Assigned to the secret apparatus of the International in 1929, he settled in Berlin, where, as "Doctor Hediger," he headed the West European Bureau of the Comintern. Arrested by the Nazi authorities on 9 March 1933, he was groundlessly accused of setting fire to the Reichstag. At the trial in Leipzig (September–December 1933) he delivered several famous speeches against Nazism, and as a result he became a hero among leftists and liberal internationalists. In February 1934 Dimitrov returned to the USSR and obtained Soviet citizenship. In 1937 he was elected to the USSR Supreme Soviet. At the Seventh Congress of the Comintern in 1935 he read the main report, which supported an offensive against fascism in Europe and pointed to the tasks of the Comintern. He was then elected a member of the Presidium of the Executive Committee and secretary general of the Communist International.

In this role, Dimitrov directed the creation of "uniform people's fronts" in France and Spain. He oversaw Stalinist purges in various Communist Parties that were sections of the Comintern—for example, in the Latvian, Hungarian, Polish, Romanian, and Yugoslav parties. These purges claimed the lives of thousands of people. In September 1939 he published an article in the *Komunisticheski Internatsional*. In it, he interpreted the war in Europe as a result of the aggression of Anglo-French imperialism against the "forces of peace and socialism"—that is, the USSR and Nazi Germany. Under his leadership, from 1939 to 1941 the Communist parties followed a pro-German or neutral policy, which changed radically in June 1941, after the invasion of the USSR by the Third Reich. In May 1943 Dimitrov signed an act that formally dissolved the Comintern, but actually the entire Comintern apparatus under his leadership went over to a special department of the CC of the All-Union Communist Party (Bolsheviks). The aim of this operation was to give the appearance of greater independence for Communists parties from the Kremlin; however, it actually increased their subordination to the leadership of the Soviet party. In 1942 Dimitrov co-formed the Bulgarian Fatherland Front, and then he was the architect of the Communist takeover in Bulgaria.

After the coup of 9 September 1944 Dimitrov remotely directed the Sovietization of Bulgaria; for example, in January 1945 he ordered death sentences against a few dozen representatives of the Bulgarian political elite. In September 1945 he returned to Sofia, assuming the post of secretary general of the Bulgarian Communist Party, and from November 1946 he simultaneously served as prime minister. He represented Bulgaria at a conference in Paris where the "sovereignty" of the new Bulgaria was recognized. This conference also led to the signing of a peace treaty between the Allies and Bulgaria in February 1947. Dimitrov was in charge of the bloody suppression of his political opponents as well as of his one-time allies from the Fatherland Front; for example, in 1947 he was responsible for the sentencing and then for the execution of **Nikola Petkov**. Dimitrov was one of the founders of the Information Bureau of the Communist and Workers' Parties (Cominform), which was created during a conference in Szklarska Poręba in September 1947. At that time, he planned to create a federation of Communist Balkan countries—Albania, Bulgaria, and Yugoslavia. However, since this project was ahead of Stalin's plans, in January 1948 in Moscow Dimitrov was officially subjected to criticism. In February 1948 in Moscow he signed a treaty of friendship between Bulgaria and the USSR. At the Fifth Congress of the BCP in December 1948 he was reelected secretary general. He was also in charge of the first stage of the collectivization of agriculture. Seriously ill, in 1949 Dimitrov went for treatment to the USSR, where he soon died at a sanatorium near Moscow. It was suspected that he was killed because of his influence in the Communist movement and because of his plans for a Balkan federation.

In 1981–89 fifteen volumes of Dimitrov's writings, *Sychinenia* (Works), were published in Bulgaria. They repeatedly appeared in various languages, but the period between 1939 and 1941, when the USSR and the Comintern were cooperating with the Third Reich, was carefully avoided in those publications. After Dimitrov's death his body was embalmed, in the same way as was done with Lenin's body, and it was placed in a specially built mausoleum in the center of Sofia. On 18 July 1990 the body was cremated and buried at the Orlandovtsi Cemetery in Sofia, and the mausoleum was demolished. (WR)

Sources: *Entsiklopediya Bulgariya*, vol. 1 (Sofia, 1981); Lazitch; *Communist International: 7th Congress, Moscow, 1935, Resolutions; including also the closing speech of Georgi Dimitroff* (New York, 1935); Joseph Rothschild, *The Communist Party of Bulgaria: Origins and Development, 1883–1936* (New York, 1959); Kamen Kalchev and Georgi Dimitrov, *Kratyk biograficheski ocherk* (Plovdiv, 1971); Nisan Oren, *Bulgarian Communism: The Road to Power, 1933–1944* (New York, 1971); *Devetdeset godini ot rozhdenieto na Georgi Dimitrov* (Sofia, 1972); Georgi Dimitrov, *And Yet It Moves: Concluding Speech before the Leipzig Trial* (Sofia, 1978); *Dimitroff contra Göring* (Berlin, 1981); John D. Bell, *The Bulgarian Communist Party from Blagoev to Zhivkov* (Stanford, 1986).

DIMITROVA Blaga (2 January 1922, Byala Slatyna–4 May 2003, Sofia), Bulgarian writer and dissident. Dimitrova spent her childhood in Velyko Tyrnovo. In 1945 she graduated in Slavic studies from the University of Sofia, and then she continued studies at the Gorki Institute in Moscow and in Leningrad, where she received a Ph.D. After her studies she edited periodicals for children and youngsters and popular scientific publications. Her knowledge of several Slavic languages, as well as of Swedish, German, and Vietnamese, made her a leading translator. For instance, she translated *Pan Tadeusz*, by Adam Mickiewicz, and several classical ancient poets. She also wrote poems herself. After the Socialist realist period, in 1956 Dimitrova changed her style, frequently experimenting in poetry. She published her first volume, *Lirika* (Lyrics), in 1959. For a long time she combined her "disobedient" literature with political engagement. In 1966–72 she lived in Vietnam and was active in trying to draw the war to a close. She also took part in Communist peace congresses in Berlin in 1969 and in Moscow in 1971. But her "deviations" from the official literary line were already clear from the mid-1960s—for instance, in the collection *Pytuvanye kym sebe si* (1965; *Journey to Oneself*, 1969), the novel *Otklonyenye* (Detour; 1967), and the volume of poems *Lavinata* (Avalanche; 1971). This is why from the early 1970s Dimitrova faced increasing problems with publishing her works. She was strongly criticized for a biography (written together with her husband, Yordan Vasilyev) of Elisaveta Bagriana. Its third volume was banned from publication. In 1981 the censors banned her novel *Liceto* (Face), and finally most of her works were banned.

Dimitrova belonged to those Bulgarian intellectuals who from the mid-1980s began to demand systemic reforms. She bravely defended the forcibly Bulgarized Turks, writing a short story about them, *Ime* (Name; 1985). In 1988 she joined the Club for the Support of Glasnost and Perestroika, founded at Sofia University and headed by **Zhelyu Zhelev**. During a congress of the Association of Bulgarian Writers in 1989 she sharply criticized her colleagues' silence in the face of the drastic abuses of human rights by the **Todor Zhivkov** regime. Her engagement in political opposition added to her popularity, which resulted in her assuming the position of vice-president alongside Zhelev in January 1992. On 30 June 1993 she resigned, arguing that she had had no influence on state affairs. Her decision was connected with her links to the right wing of the Union of Democratic Forces, which Zhelev criticized. Later Dimitrova presided over the Raina Kabaivanska Memorial Foundation, supporting talented children. She wrote for *Liberation* and other Western papers and was among the leading and most influential Bulgarian intellectuals. In 1993 she published a volume of poetic philosophical essays, *Uraniya* (Urania). Many of her poems were translated into English—for instance, in the collections *Because the Sea Is Black* (1989), *Last Rock Eagle* (1992), *Forbidden Sea* (2000), and *Scars* (2002). (AG)

Sources: *Syvremienna Bulgarska Entsiklopediya*, vol. 2 (Sofia, 1994); Heike Rader, *Auf Umwegen zu sich selbts* (Marburg, 1997); www.centrenationaldulivre.fr/actualites/biographies-bulgares.htm; Jerzy Jackowicz, *Bułgaria od rządów komunistycznych do demokracji parlamentarnej 1988–1991* (Warsaw, 1999); Raymond Detrez, *Historical Dictionary of Bulgaria* (Lanham, Md., 1997).

DINESCU Mircea (11 October 1950, Slobozia), Romanian poet and dissident. Born into a laborer's family, in 1969 Dinescu graduated from high school in Slobozia. In the early 1970s he moved to Bucharest, where he made his literary debut in the periodical *Luceafărul*, and in 1971 he published his first volume, *Invocaţia nimănui* (Calling nobody), for which he received an award of the Association of Romanian Writers (ARW). At first his works were marked by a sense of the tragic nature of the world. With time Dinescu evolved toward contesting reality and then toward sarcasm. He considered the world as alien to human spirituality. In 1976 he published *Proprietarul de poduri* (Owner of bridges), for which he was again awarded by the ARW. In 1979–84 he studied journalism at the Stefan Gheorghiu Party Academy. He gradually evolved toward a critical assessment of the Communist reality of Romania. He expressed his objections most clearly in the volume *Moartea citeşte ziarul* (Death reading a newspaper), which was banned by the censors from publication in 1988 but was printed in Amsterdam in 1989. In 1976–82 Dinescu edited the periodical *Luceafărul*, and in 1982–89, the periodical *România literară*. In 1981 he was awarded by the ARW for the third time. In the second half of the 1980s he was increasingly open in criticizing the Communist system and gained the reputation of a dissident. In 1989 he was fired from *România literară* and placed under house arrest; he then gave an interview to the French daily *Liberation*. Released on 22 December 1989, a few hours after the coup that toppled the **Nicolae Ceauşescu** regime, Dinescu was brought to the central TV headquarters in Bucharest, where, along with other dissidents and coup leaders, he announced the end of the dictatorship. They founded the National Salvation Front (Frontul Sălvari Naţionale [NSF]), which took over power. On the next day Dinescu and several other dissidents joined the NSF National Council, making it credible to the society. Soon, however, he left the NSF, and in 1991 he established the weekly *Academia Caţavencu* and became chairman of the ARW. In 2000 he ceased to publish his weekly and started another periodical, *Plai cu boi*. He also became a member of the National Council for the Study of Archives of the Former Security Police. (LW)

Sources: Józef Darski, *Rumunia: Historia, współczesność, konflikty narodowe* (Warsaw, 1995); *Dictionar Enciclopedic*, vol. 2 (Bucharest, 1996); romania-on-line.net/whoswho/DinescuMircea.htm.

DINNYÉS Lajos (16 April 1901, Alsódabas–14 May 1961, Budapest), Hungarian Peasant Party politician. Born into a landowner's family, Dinnyés was educated at a Calvinist gymnasium in Budapest, and then he graduated from the Agricultural Academy in Keszthely. From 1930 he ran a hundred-hectare farm. He began his political activities in rightist youth organizations. A member of the Independent Smallholders' Party (ISP) from 1930 and MP between 1931 and 1939, in 1934 he was elected a member of the local government commission of Pest County. In the press as well as in parliament, Dinnyés expressed definitely anti-German and anti–Arrow Cross Party views. He did not vote in favor of the anti-Jewish laws of 1938–39. During World War II he served in the army.

After the Germans entered Hungary in March 1944, Dinnyés went into hiding and was in the resistance movement. When the Soviet troops entered the country, he became involved in political life as a member of the National Committee in Alsódabas. From April 1945 until the end of his life, Dinnyés sat in parliament. In August 1945 he joined the National Executive Committee of the ISP and was president of the organization in Pest County. Between September 1946 and September 1947 and then from April 1948 he was again a member of the top party leadership. He had good personal relations with many leading Communist activists, including **Mihály Farkas**. Between March and September 1947 Dinnyés served as minister of national defense. On 31 May 1947, on the motion of the Hungarian Communist Party (HCP), Dinnyés agreed to assume the post of prime minister, replacing **Ferenc Nagy**, who, while on leave in Switzerland, was forced to resign. Dinnyés cooperated with the Communists, who aimed at the total takeover of power. He also carried out the nationalization of schools, big banks, and plants that employed more than one hundred people. On 10 December 1948, after Finance Minister István Nyárády escaped abroad, Dinnyés resigned. From December 1948 he was president of the United Research Institute of Agriculture; from 1952, head of the National Agricultural Library and head of the Documentation Center; from 1954, a member of the National Council of the Patriotic People's Front (PPF); and from 1960, a member of the Presidium of the National Council of the PPF. In October 1956 Dinnyés was a member of the Provisional National Council of the Fifth Budapest district. After the failure of the revolution he joined the victorious camp of **János Kádár**. After the elections of 1958 Dinnyés served as vice-president of the parliament. (JT)

Sources: Ferenc Nagy, *The Struggle behind the Iron Curtain* (New York, 1948); Imre Kovacs, ed., *Facts about Hungary: The Fight for Freedom* (New York, 1966); *Magyar Nagylexikon*, vol. 6 (Budapest, 1998); *A magyar forradalom és szabadságharc enciklopédiája* (Budapest, 1999).

DIONISIUS [originally Konstantin Valedinsky] (4 May 1876, Murom–15 March 1961, Warsaw), Orthodox Metropolitan of Warsaw and of all of Poland. The son of a clergyman, in his youth Dionisius was involved in missionary work in Siberia. In 1900 he graduated from the Kazan Theological Seminary, and from 1902 he was in charge of the Chełm (Kholm) Theological Seminary. In 1911 he became chaplain of the Russian legation in Rome, and in 1913 he was consecrated bishop and head of the Krzemieniec diocese in Volhynia. After the fall of tsarism, he supported the Ukrainian government of **Pavlo Skoropadsky**. In 1921 the Polish authorities recognized him as an ally in their efforts to gain autocephaly for the Orthodox Church in Poland. In the face of the resistance of some Russian bishops who recognized the supremacy of the Moscow Patriarchate, in February 1923 the Polish authorities supported the selection of Dionisius as head of the Warsaw diocese and his elevation to metropolitan. Between 1923 and 1924, under government pressure, Dionisius unsuccessfully sought the consent of Patriarch Tikhon of Moscow for the creation of an autocephalous church in Poland. Patriarch Tikhon would not agree to more than its autonomy. Finally, autocephaly was established in an uncanonical way. As a result of the efforts of the Polish authorities, on 13 November 1924 the patriarch of Constantinople confirmed the autocephaly of the Polish Orthodox Church. Dionisius accepted it because it also strengthened the position of the Church in relation to the Polish state.

Despite the breakup with Moscow, by continuing his moderate approach and patient diplomacy, Dionisius managed to prevent a split in the Polish Orthodox Church, and he succeeded in gaining the acceptance of its new status by Orthodox metropolitans from other countries. In November 1938, in agreement with state authorities, Dionisius managed to normalize the internal legal status of the Polish Orthodox Church. He defended the status of the Russian language. Nevertheless, under pressure he allowed, to a limited extent, the native languages of the faithful—that is, Ukrainian, Belorussian, and Polish—to be used for religious services, sermons, and publications. However, he did not agree to demands for the nationalization of the Orthodox Church in Volhynia. When these demands were supported by Polish authorities, promoting the development of the Ukrainian movement in Volhynia, in 1933 Dionisius resigned as head of the diocese of Krzemieniec. He was also in conflict with the authorities in 1938–39, when they started a Polonization of the Orthodox faithful in the regions of Lublin and Chełm and in the western part of Volhynia.

After the fall of Poland in 1939, Dionisius was temporarily placed under house arrest. German authorities brought about a compromise between Dionisius and Ukrainian activists. From September 1940 until the end of the occupation Dionisius served as metropolitan only in German-occupied Poland, and the two other (Ukrainian) bishops, with the consent of the Germans, were given a free hand in the Ukrainization program. Dionisius was also a "protector" of the Ukrainian Autocephalous Orthodox Church, which functioned in the territory of the Ukraine. In January 1945 the Orthodox episcopate of German-occupied Poland was evacuated to Austria. Dionisius was the only hierarch who decided to return to the territories ruled by the Communists. In June 1945 he again assumed charge of the Orthodox Church in Poland. The authorities did not accept his explanations about the occupation period and insisted on his resignation. He was not recognized as head of the autocephalous church by the Moscow Patriarchate; he held out until February 1948. Excommunicated by the Moscow Patriarchate and kept under house arrest in Sosnowiec, Dionisius declared loyalty to the state. He was supported only by the Constantinople Patriarchate and by the Polish government-in-exile. At the end of his life he was allowed to return to Warsaw, where he died in extreme poverty. (TS)

Sources: *Encyclopedia of Ukraine*, vol. 5 (Toronto, 1993); Mirosława Papierzyńska-Turek, *Państwo wobec prawosławia 1918–1939* (Warsaw, 1989), K. Urban, *Kościół prawosławny w Polsce 1945–1970 (rys historyczny)* (Kraków, 1996).

DIZDAREVIĆ Raif (9 December 1926, Fojnica, Bosnia and Herzegovina), Bosnian politician. From 1943 Dizdarević took part in the Communist guerrilla movement of **Josip Broz Tito**. In March 1944 he joined the

Communist Federation of Yugoslav Youth, and in March 1945, the Communist Party of Yugoslavia. He worked in the security service (1945–51), then in the Ministry of Foreign Affairs (1951–74), and on various diplomatic missions: as secretary and chargé d'affaires in Bulgaria (1951–54), first secretary in the Soviet Union and Mongolia (1956–59), and consul in Czechoslovakia (1963–67). He also held other posts, such as secretary of the Presidium of the Confederation of Yugoslav Trade Unions (1967–72), chairman of the Confederation of Trade Unions of Bosnia and Herzegovina (1974–78), and adviser to the federal secretary (minister) of foreign affairs (1972–74). From 1974 Dizdarević was a member of the Presidium of the Central Committee of the League of Communists of Bosnia and Herzegovina, and from 1978 to 1983 he was a member of the Presidium of the Socialist Republic of Bosnia and Herzegovina. He was an MP to the Federal Assembly and its speaker in 1982–83. From May 1984 to the end of 1987 he was federal secretary of foreign affairs. From 15 May 1984 to 15 May 1988 he was a member of the Presidium of the Socialist Federative Republic of Yugoslavia, and then, until 15 May 1989, he was its chairman. Then he retired. During the war in the former Yugoslavia Dizdarević lived in his home village of Fojnica. (AO)

Sources: Juliusz Stroynowski, ed., *Who's Who in the Socialist Countries of Europe* (Munich, London, and Paris, 1989); www.mfa. gov.yu/history/ministri/RDizdarevic_e.html.

DJAKOVIĆ Djuro (30 November 1886, Brodski Varoš, Bosnia–25 April 1929, Sveti Duh, Slovenia), Croatian Communist activist from Bosnia. As a teenager Djaković worked as a metalworker's apprentice. After joining a trade union organization, he started his political career in the Social Democratic Party of Bosnia and Herzegovina in 1909. During World War I he was sentenced by the Austrian authorities to hard labor. In late 1918 he returned to his home region, and in April 1919 he took part in a meeting at which the Socialist Workers' Party of Yugoslavia was founded. At its subsequent congress in June 1920 the party was dominated by followers of Bolshevism, including Djaković, who was elected to its Central Committee (CC), and the party's name was changed to the Communist Party of Yugoslavia (CPY). In 1920 Djaković won a parliamentary seat, and in June and July 1921 he was the CPY delegate to the Third Congress of the Communist International (Comintern) in Moscow. After returning home, he was temporarily put under house arrest. When the party was outlawed, he took part in its congress in Vienna in July 1922 and was again elected to the CC. Officially he was a trade union activist, and in 1926 he became the leader of the Croatian Metalworkers'

Trade Union. In 1927 he left for the USSR, where under the pseudonym "Georg Friedman" he studied at the Lenin School of the Comintern. In August 1928, as "Bosnić," he took part in the Sixth Congress of the Comintern and became a deputy member of its Executive Committee. In October 1928, at the Fourth CPY Congress, he was elected CC secretary. While crossing the border, Djaković was shot by the police. Recognized as a martyr of the Communist movement, he was included in the hall of fame of postwar Communist Yugoslavia. (WR)

Sources: Lazitch; *Enciklopedija Jugoslavije*, vol. 3 (Zagreb, 1958); *Djuro Djaković: Život i djelo* (Slovenski Brod, 1984).

DJILAS Milovan (12 June 1911, Podbišće, Montenegro–20 June 1995, Belgrade), Yugoslav Communist activist, politician, and writer. Djilas was born into a Montenegrin peasant family, the fourth of nine children. His father took part in both Balkan Wars (1912–13) and in World War I and was police commander in Kolašin from 1918. Djilas went to high school in Kolašin and Beran. In 1929–33 he studied literature at the University of Belgrade. Already then he was a keen Communist. The Bolshevik victory in Russia made him consider the possibility that a similar revolution was possible in Yugoslavia. During his studies, which he did not complete, he became a radical student leader, engaged in a struggle against the royal dictatorship of King **Alexander I**. He was first arrested in March 1932 for taking part in an anti-government demonstration. In April 1933 he was detained again and tortured, and he spent three years in the Sremska Mitrovica prison. It was there that he met influential Communist leaders, such as **Moša Pijade** and **Aleksander Ranković**, and he joined the zealous followers of Stalinism. After his release in 1936 he recruited volunteers for the Spanish Civil War. As **Josip Broz Tito** needed Djilas at home, he did not agree to his departure for Spain. In 1938 Djilas became a member of the Central Committee (CC) of the Communist Party of Yugoslavia (CPY), and in 1939 he joined its Politburo. During World War II he belonged to the top organizers of the Communist guerrilla movement. He commanded guerrilla troops in Montenegro and Bosnia, and he edited the party papers *Borba* and *Nova Jugoslavija*. During the war his father, two brothers, and one sister were killed by the Nazis or the Chetniks.

After the war Djilas became one of the top leaders of Communist Yugoslavia. In 1945 he was minister for Montenegro, and in 1946 he assumed the post of minister without portfolio. In 1944 he headed a mission to Moscow and met Stalin for the first time. In 1945 he belonged to a Yugoslav delegation, headed by Tito, negotiating conditions for a Yugoslav-Soviet treaty of mutual aid. In 1948 he went to Moscow for the third time to coordinate the policies of the Yugoslav and Soviet governments toward Albania. Discrepancies between the two governments were growing, and, under Soviet pressure, in June 1948 the Information Bureau of Communist and Workers' Parties (Cominform) condemned Tito's leadership of Yugoslavia. Along with **Edvard Kardelj** and **Boris Kidrić**, Djilas was considered an architect of the so-called self-government model of Yugoslav communism, which aimed at a limitation of the role of the central authorities in the economy. In January 1953 Djilas became one of the country's vice-presidents, and in December 1953 he also assumed the position of speaker of the Federal People's Assembly.

In 1953–54 Djilas published a series of articles in the daily *Borba* and the weekly *Nova Misao* in which he criticized the Communist monopoly of power. He suggested a democratic reconstruction of the system through the introduction of political pluralism. At the Third Extraordinary Plenum of the CC of the League of Communists of Yugoslavia (LCY), on 17 January 1954 he was removed from all positions. In March 1954 he gave up his party membership. When in 1955 Nikita Khrushchev came to Belgrade on a visit that was intended to repair Yugoslav-Soviet relations, Djilas was arrested for "spreading hostile propaganda" in an interview he gave to the *New York Times*, and he was sentenced to a year and a half in prison with suspended execution. When in the fall of 1956 Soviet troops bloodily suppressed the Hungarian Revolution, which jeopardized Yugoslav-Soviet relations, in December 1956 Djilas was detained again in the Sremska Mitrovica prison in connection with his article "The Storm over Eastern Europe," published in *The New Leader* in the United States, in which he supported the Hungarian uprising. He was sentenced to three years of hard labor.

An additional four years of prison were added to Djilas' sentence after he published *The New Class* (1957), smuggled from prison to the West. The book shook intellectual opinion in the West and brought him world fame. In the book he argued that the Communist revolution, started for the sake of a classless society, had resulted in the stabilization of a new ruling class that enjoyed a monopolistic access to power and special privileges. He also argued that under communism a political career was ideal for those who want to live a parasitic life at the expense of others. He considered "Socialist property" a disguise that hid the real ownership of the new class. He was particularly critical of the USSR. For instance, he called the collectivization of agriculture a "horrendous and devastating war, bearing symptoms of madness." He argued that Soviet troops had imposed communism in Poland, Czechoslovakia, and Hungary. He found that in

practice in the Soviet bloc "all that was left of the Marxist dialectics and materialism was formalism and dogmatism, serving cementing power, justifying tyranny, and violating human conscience."

Djilas was released in 1961, but returned to prison in 1962 after he published his *Conversations with Stalin* in the West; in it he called Stalin one of the worst criminals in history. Sentenced to nine years in prison, he was released after four years. All together he spent nine years in the same Sremska Mitrovica prison in which he had spent three years before the war. The 1968 Warsaw Pact intervention in Czechoslovakia had a strong impact on Yugoslav-Soviet relations. While in 1956 Tito had reacted very angrily to Djilas's criticism of the Soviets, in 1968 Tito used the same criticism to warn international opinion against the possibility of Soviet intervention in the Balkans. Djilas was even allowed to tour Western Europe and the United States. Until his death he lived in isolation in Belgrade. He was banned from political activity, but he could write and publish his works abroad, although not at home. The domestic ban on his publications was not lifted until 1988. In May 1989 the Yugoslav authorities officially rehabilitated him. With surprise and horror he watched the war in a decaying Yugoslavia in the 1990s. He put the blame for it on the nationalism of **Slobodan Milošević**, who, in his opinion, was using it as a means to stay in power. (AO)

Sources: Milovan Djilas, *Land without Justice* (New York, 1958); Milovan Djilas, *Memoir of a Revolutionary* (New York, 1973); Milovan Djilas, *Wartime* (New York, 1977); Milovan Djilas, *Rise and Fall* (San Diego, 1985); Milovan Djilas, *Tito: The Story from Inside* (New York, 1980), Stephen Clissold, *Djilas: The Progress of a Revolutionary* (Hounslow, Middlesex, 1983); Dennis Reinhartz, *Milovan Djilas: A Revolutionary as a Writer* (New York, 1981).

DJINDJIĆ Zoran (1 August 1952, Bosanski Šamac–12 March 2003, Belgrade), Serbian politician. The son of a Yugoslav general, Djindjić spent his childhood in several garrison towns. In 1970–74 he studied philosophy at the University of Belgrade and was active in the independent student movement. Arrested and sentenced to one year in prison but released after the intervention of the German chancellor, Willy Brandt, he started doctoral studies in Konstanz, Germany. In 1979 he defended a Ph.D. thesis written with Jürgen Habermas. Upon returning to Yugoslavia, Djindjić worked in the Institute of Philosophy and Social Theory, lectured in philosophy at the university in Novi Sad, and edited the periodical of the Serbian Philosophical Society, *Teorija*. In 1989 he was co-founder of the opposition Democratic Party (Demokratska Stranka [DS]); in 1990 he became head of its Supreme Board and in 1994 its chairman. Elected to the Serbian parliament in 1990, he was head of the DS faction until the elections of 1993, when he was elected to the Upper House of the federal parliament of the new Yugoslavia. In 1996 he co-organized and became one of the leaders of the opposition coalition Together (Zajedno), which included the Serbian Renewal Movement (Srpski Pokret Obnove) of **Vuk Drašković** and the Democratic Party of Serbia (Srpska Demokratska Stranka) of **Vojislav Koštunica**. Djindjić was the coalition's candidate for mayor of Belgrade in November 1996. The election was announced invalid in several dozen towns where opposition candidates won (including Belgrade), which resulted in eighty-eight days of mass anti-government demonstrations coordinated by Djindjić (among others). Under such pressure and after the intervention of the European Union, President **Slobodan Milošević** recognized the election results, and in February 1997 Djindjić became the first non-Communist mayor of Belgrade since World War II. In the summer of 1997 the coalition split, and Djindjić was recalled from office.

In 1998 Djindjić co-organized a liberal opposition coalition, the Alliance for Change, and in 2000 he became its coordinator. The alliance and the DS were in firm opposition to Milošević, accusing him of responsibility for the NATO air raids on Yugoslavia in 1999, and they maintained good relations with NATO diplomats. The government media accused Djindjić of treason, so he left for Montenegro. After the termination of the NATO air raids, he led the Alliance for Change into the Democratic Opposition of Serbia (Demokratska Opozicija Srbije [DOS]), a broad coalition against the Milošević government. Djindjić directed the campaign before the elections of December 2000. After the DOS won, he was elected prime minister of Serbia. He played an important role in internal reforms and in rapprochement with the West. During 2002 the DOS split, but its components supported his government, which entered into conflict with President Koštunica, who was more moderate in dealing with the post-Communists. Among other works, Djindjić published *Subjektivnost i nasilje* (Subjectivity and violence; 1984); *Jesen dijalektike* (The autumn of dialectics; 1986); *Jugoslavija kao nedovršena država* (Yugoslavia as an unfinished state; 1987); and *Srbija ni na istoku ni na zapadu* (Serbia—Neither East nor West; 1996). Djindjić was assassinated by the mafia structures in an incident that shook Yugoslavia. (AW)

Sources: Leonard Cohen, *Broken Bonds: The Disintegration of Yugoslavia* (Boulder, Colo., 1993); Susan L. Woodward, *The Balkan Tragedy: Chaos and Dissolution after the Cold War* (Washington, D.C., 1995); Christopher Bennett, *Yugoslavia's Bloody Collapse: Causes, Course and Consequences* (London, 1995); Karen Dawisha and Bruce Parrot, eds., *Politics, Power and the Struggle for Democracy in South-East Europe* (Cambridge, 1997); www.serbia.sr.gov.yu.

DJUKANOVIĆ Milo (15 February 1962, Nikšić), Montenegrin Communist and post-Communist activist. Djukanović graduated in economics from the University of Titograd (now Podgorica) in 1986. From 1979 he belonged to the League of Communists of Yugoslavia (LCY), and in 1986–89 he was a member of its Central Committee. He was active in transforming the Montenegrin section of the party into the Democratic Party of Socialists (Demokratska Partija Socijalista [DPS]), which won the first democratic elections in 1990 and has ruled Montenegro ever since. In January 1991 Djukanović was elected prime minister of the Montenegrin republic as a close aide of the DPS leader and president of the republic, **Momir Bulatović**. At the turn of 1997 Djukanović he entered into conflict with Bulatović because of the latter's support for the Serbian post-Communists of **Slobodan Milošević**, particularly in the context of Milošević's attempt to invalidate local elections won by the opposition.

Djukanović gained the support of a firm majority in the DPS, and in October 1997 he defeated Bulatović in the presidential elections. He took office in January 1998. His main goals were to change the Yugoslav federation into a confederation and to achieve rapprochement with the West, irrespective of the Serbian standpoint on these matters. In May 1998 the DPS, running in the coalition For a Better Life, defeated the Socialist People's Party of Bulatović and won an absolute majority in the Montenegrin parliament. During the Kosovo conflict and the NATO air raids on Yugoslavia in 1999, Djukanović distanced himself from Milošević, trying to follow an independent foreign and economic policy. He introduced the German mark as the sole currency, and he accelerated privatization. He also maintained good relations with the Serbian opposition. At the same time he tolerated the growth of a local oligarchy and its links with the local and Italian mafia. In 2000, when Milošević changed the Yugoslav constitution without regard to Montenegrin opinion, Djukanović started preparations to declare Montenegrin independence, and he gained support for his policies. The coalition Victory for Montenegro under his leadership defeated the pro-Serbian bloc of Bulatović, Together for Yugoslavia, in the parliamentary elections of April 2001, winning 47 percent of the mandates. In the elections of October 2002 the coalition For a European Montenegro won 52 percent of the mandates. After his term as president was over in November 2002, Djukanović became prime minister of the republic in January 2003. His program for a Yugoslav confederation was finally implemented when the name of the country was changed to Serbia and Montenegro in February 2003. (AW)

Sources: *Europa Środkowo-Wschodnia*, 1991–1998 (Warsaw, 1992–2000); Stojan Cerovic, "Divorce by Mutual Consent," *East European Constitutional Review*, 2002, nos. 1–2; Gregory O. Hall, "The Politics of Autocracy: Serbia under Slobodan Milosevic," *East European Quarterly*, 1999, no. 2; www.cpa.org.yu/news/elections/republic_mtn_president.htm; www.dps.cg.yu; www.izbori.org.yu/e-dps.html.

DJURANOVIĆ Veselin (17 May 1925, Martinići, near Danilovgrad, Montenegro–30 August 1997), Communist activist from Montenegro, Yugoslav head of state. During World War II Djuranović belonged to the Union of Communist Youth of Yugoslavia and fought in the guerrilla movement of **Josip Broz Tito**. From April to August 1943 he was imprisoned in an Italian concentration camp near Podgorica. From 1944 he belonged to the Communist Party of Yugoslavia and then to the League of Communists of Yugoslavia (LCY). After the war he advanced in the party structures, and he was active in the Communist youth organization. In 1953–58 he headed Radio Titograd and was editor-in-chief of the periodical *Pobjeda*. From 1958 to 1962 he headed the ideological commission of the LCY Central Committee (CC). In 1963–66 he was chairman (prime minister) of the Executive Council (government) of the Socialist Republic of Montenegro; from 1966 to 1968 he was secretary of the Executive Committee of the CC of the League of Communists of Montenegro (LCM), and from 1968 to 1977 he was its first secretary. He also belonged to the Presidium of the Montenegrin republic and was its president from May 1982 to May 1983. He was a long-term member of the LCY CC and belonged to its Presidium (March 1969–May 1974). In 1974 and 1984 he was elected to the Presidium of the LCY CC. After the sudden death of **Džemal Bijedić**, on 15 March 1977 Djuranović assumed the position of chairman of the Federal Executive Council (government) of Yugoslavia, and he held it until 16 May 1982. In May 1984 he became a member of the Presidium (collective head of state) of Yugoslavia, and from May 1984 to May 1985 he was its rotating chairman. (AO)

Sources: *Who's Who in the Socialist Countries of Europe* (Munich, London, and Paris, 1989); Slobodan Stanković, *The End of the Tito Era: Yugoslavia's Dilemmas* (Stanford, 1981).

DLOUHÝ Vladimír (31 July 1953, Prague), Czech economist and politician. In 1977 Dlouhý graduated from the Higher Economic School in Prague, and then he became a lecturer there. In 1984–89 he worked as a researcher at the Forecasting Institute of the Czechoslovak Academy of Sciences, working on mathematic and econometric models and studying the command economy and economic growth. In 1989 he was briefly deputy director of this institute. From 1974 he belonged to the Communist Party of Czechoslovakia (CPC), which he left in December 1989. From December 1989 to June 1990 he was deputy prime minister in the government of **Marian Čalfa** and chairman of the State Planning Commission. Later he temporarily directed the ministries of metallurgy, engineering, power and fuel, and agriculture, and after their liquidation he was minister of the national economy from July 1990 to June 1992. From December 1989 until its dissolution in June 1991 he was the Czechoslovak representative in the Comecon. From June 1990 to June 1992 he was an MP to the Chamber of the People of the Federal Assembly, at first on behalf of the Civic Forum (Občanské Fórum [OF]) and, after its split, on behalf of the Civic Democratic Alliance (Občanská Demokratická Aliance [ODA]). From 1990 he was one of the ODA leaders, and in 1992 and 1993–97 he was its deputy chairman. After the elections of June 1992, when the dissolution of Czechoslovakia became inevitable, Dlouhý assumed the post of minister of trade and industry in the government of the Czech Republic. He was one of the most popular Czech politicians of that time, and he had a significant impact on economic transformation and on privatization in particular. Because of accumulating economic problems, Dlouhý lost in the rankings and had to resign in May 1977. Soon he also gave up his parliamentary mandate but won it again in June 1996. From September 1997 he was an adviser and member of the board of the Prague branch of the ABB concern. In November 1997 he resigned from his position in the ODA, and in February 1998 he left the party. (PU)

Sources: *ČBS; Československí politici: 1918–1991* (Prague, 1991); *Kdo byl kdo v našich dějinach ve 20. stoleti*, vol. 1 (Prague, 1998).

DŁUGOSZOWSKI-WIENIAWA Bolesław (22 July 1881, Maksymówka, Dolina County [now in the Ukraine]–28 June 1942, New York), Polish general, doctor by profession. In 1906 Długoszowski-Wieniawa graduated in medicine from the University of Lwów (Lviv), and in 1909 he graduated from the Academy of Fine Arts in Paris. In 1910 he joined the Rifle Association. An officer in the First Brigade of the Polish Legions from 1914 to 1917, he served there in the cavalry unit led by Stanisław Belina-Prażmowski (later this unit became the First Uhlan Regiment). He took part in all the battles of this brigade in the Pripet Marshes (Polesie). From September 1915 to October 1916 Długoszowski-Wieniawa was an aide-de-camp of **Józef Piłsudski**. He was immensely devoted to Piłsudski, on behalf of whom he carried out many secret missions. In 1917 in Warsaw he completed a training course for adjutants and staff officers. During the so-called oath crisis (i.e., when Piłsudski's units refused to swear allegiance to the Germans and Austrians) in July 1917, Długoszowski-Wieniawa sided with Piłsudski. He was arrested, demoted to private, and sent to Kraków. After his escape from hospital, where he feigned illness, he joined the Polish Military Organization (Polska Organizacja Wojskowa [POW]). Working as a doctor in Nowy Sącz, he became a member of the High Command of the POW. In March 1918 he went on behalf of the POW to the Ukraine, from where he was to go to France, where, on the orders of **Edward Rydz-Śmigły**, the commander-in-chief of the POW, he was to monitor the activities of General **Józef Haller**. However, in June 1918 he was arrested by the Bolsheviks. After his release from prison, Długoszowski-Wieniawa unsuccessfully tried to get to France via Finland.

In November 1918 Długoszowski-Wieniawa returned to Warsaw and joined the then forming Polish Army (Wojsko Polskie). From 1918 to 1921 he served as an aide-de-camp to Commander-in-Chief Piłsudski. During the Kiev expedition in 1920 he was chief of staff of the First Cavalry Division. From 1920 he was a member of the National Grand Lodge, Łukasiński. In November 1921 he became a military attaché in Bucharest, and in 1922, a liaison officer of the General Staff of the Ministry of Foreign Affairs. Between August 1923 and August 1924 he was in the reserves. In 1924 he was promoted to colonel. From October 1925, as head of the Army Inspectorate in Warsaw, Długoszowski-Wieniawa took part in the preparations for the May coup d'état. After the coup, from 1926 to 1928 he was in command of a cavalry regiment in Warsaw. In March 1929 he became acting commander of the Warsaw garrison; in October 1930, commander of the First Cavalry Brigade; and between January 1932 and April 1938, commander of the Second Cavalry Division. In 1932 he was promoted to brigadier general, and in 1938 he rose to the rank of major general.

In 1938 Długoszowski-Wieniawa was appointed Polish ambassador to Italy. On 21 September 1939 President **Ignacy Mościcki** designated him as his successor. However, owing to the objections of France, he did not assume the post. As the Polish ambassador to Rome, he greatly contributed to the neutral attitude of the Fascist authorities toward Polish refugees who, via Italy, made their way to the Polish Army in France. In 1940, after Italy entered the war against France, Długoszowski-Wieniawa left for New York. In 1942 General **Władysław Sikorski** appointed him ambassador to Cuba. Długoszowski-Wieniawa committed suicide. He was decorated with (among other things) the Order of Virtuti Militari. He was a very interesting figure, not only as a military man and

politician, but also as a poet and a satirist from the circle of *Wiadomości Literackie* and *Skamander.* He was a music lover, hero of many anecdotes, and a popular frequenter of Warsaw cafés. His ashes were brought to Kraków and buried in the quarters of the Polish Legions at Rakowice Cemetery. (JS)

Sources: Piotr Stawecki, *Słownik biograficzny generałów Wojska Polskiego, 1918–1939* (Warsaw, 1994); *Słownik polityków polskich XX wieku* (Poznań, 1998); Jacek M. Majchrowski, *Ulubieniec Cezara–Bolesław Wieniawa Długoszowski: Zarys biografii* (Wrocław, 1990); Marian Romeyko, *Wspomnienia o Wieniawie i o rzymskich czasach* (Warsaw, 1990); Mariusz Urbanek, *Wieniawa—szwoleżer na pegazie* (Wrocław, 1991); Witold Dworzyński, *Wieniawa: Poeta—żołnierz—dyplomata* (Warsaw, 1993); Jacek M. Majchrowski, *Pierwszy ułan Drugiej Rzeczypospolitej* (Warsaw, 1993); Tadeusz Wittlin, *Szabla i koń* (London, 1996).

DMOWSKI Roman, pen name "Kazimierz Wybranowski" (9 August 1864, Kamionek, near Warsaw–2 January 1939, Drozdów, near Łomża), Polish politician and ideologist of Polish nationalism. Dmowski was born into an impoverished family with roots in the gentry, but his father was a blue-collar laborer. Dmowski graduated from the Third High School in Warsaw, and in 1886 he started studies in the Department of Physics and Mathematics of Warsaw University. In 1891 he received a candidate's degree, the equivalent of a doctorate. From 1887 he belonged to the Polish Youth Union–Zet, organized in Warsaw by **Zygmunt Balicki**. Dmowski brought about the removal of Socialist students from the union. In 1890 he effectively opposed an anti-tsarist demonstration prepared jointly by Polish and Russian students. From 1889 he belonged to the Polish League (Liga Polska), and on 3 May 1891 he organized a demonstration in Warsaw to commemorate the centenary of the 3 May Constitution. In 1891 he went to Paris, where he met leaders of the Polish League in exile. Arrested upon his return in August 1892, Dmowski was put in the Warsaw Citadel Prison and released in early 1893. In April 1893 he was instrumental in the dissolution of the Polish League and in the creation of the National League (Liga Narodowa). He became head of its Central Committee.

Dmowski published his first articles in *Głos* in 1890. He also authored the National League program, *Nasz patriotyzm* (Our patriotism), in which he outlined the foundations of Polish nationalism. Banned from Russian Poland by the tsarist authorities in 1893, Dmowski settled in Mitau (Jelgava) in Latvia, and in 1895 he left for Lemberg (Lwów, Lviv), where he started publishing *Przegląd Wszechpolski.* Subsequent versions of the program of the National Democratic Party, which he co-authored, were published there. In 1902 he published *Myśli nowoczesnego*

Polaka (Thoughts of a modern Pole), the basic work of contemporary Polish nationalism, in which he explained the premises of Polish nationalism. Dmowski traveled extensively in Great Britain, France, and Brazil. In March 1904 he went across the United States and Canada to Japan. He was not only fascinated by the Japanese society, but also managed to discourage the Japanese from supporting the anti-Russian revolutionary activities in Russian Poland that were advocated by **Józef Piłsudski**, whom he by chance met in Tokyo.

In March 1905 Dmowski returned to Warsaw. When the Russian authorities introduced martial law in the former Kingdom of Poland in November 1905, he went to Petersburg and talked to the Russian prime minister, Sergei Witte, encouraging him to cede power in the Kingdom of Poland to the Poles in order to calm the revolutionary atmosphere. During the 1905–6 revolution Dmowski advocated autonomy for the kingdom. He organized squads to resist the Fighting Organization of the Polish Socialist Party. Elected to the Second State Duma in February 1907, he became head of the Polish Club. In the Duma he opposed land reform projects. Despite anti-Polish steps by the Pyotr Stolypin government, Dmowski thought that Poland could regain independence only by allying itself with Russia against Germany. In 1908 he explained his views on the European situation after the annexation of Bosnia and Herzegovina by Austria-Hungary in his work *Niemcy, Rosja i kwestia polska* (Germany, Russia, and the Polish question). He opposed an armed struggle, considered Russia less dangerous to the Poles, and advocated unification of all Polish territories under Russian protection. In July 1908 he took part in the Neo-Slavic Congress in Prague, where he voted for a resolution on the reconciliation and equality of all Slavonic nations. His strategy became the cause of several splits in the National League. The groups Rzeczpospolita, Fronda, Secesja, and Zet left the league. Members of the league's Central Committee, including Dmowski, gave up their mandates. At the same time Dmowski opposed a school strike as harmful to Polish-Russian relations. In 1912 he lost an election to the Russian Duma in Warsaw and put the blame for it on the Jewish community. In consequence the league organized a boycott of Jewish shops.

After the outbreak of World War I, Dmowski went to Petersburg and in 1915 to Great Britain. He also traveled to France and Switzerland, lobbying for the recognition of Polish independence by the Entente and by Russia. Until the fall of the tsar he was ineffective, but in August 1917 he managed to co-found the National Committee of Poland (Komitet Narodowy Polski [KNP]) in Paris and became its chairman. In February 1918 he submitted to the French government a map of Polish territorial postulates and was active in the creation of the Polish Army in France under the command of General **Józef Haller**. Dmowski favored the fragmentation of Austria-Hungary as a region of potential German expansion. In the late summer and fall of 1918 he went to the United States again, where he met President Woodrow Wilson (on 8 October he tried to persuade Wilson to accept Lithuanian autonomy within Poland); with the Jewish community (he rejected a suggestion to accept Jewish representatives into the KNP); and with Polish Americans. He returned to Paris on 19 November 1918, when the Socialist government of **Jędrzej Moraczewski** was already installed by Piłudski in Warsaw. Although Dmowski recognized Piłsudski as provisional head of state, he opposed recognition of the Moraczewski cabinet. After the takeover by the **Ignacy Paderewski** government in January 1919, Dmowski became Polish delegate to the Paris Peace Conference. On 29 January 1919 he made a five-hour speech on the future borders of Poland. Despite the negative impression he made by his anti-Semitism, Dmowski was instrumental in the Entente's understanding of the Polish point of view at the conference.

From 1919 Dmowski was an MP to the Constituent Assembly (Sejm). After signing the Treaty of Versailles of 28 June 1919 and the Treaty of Saint-Germain of 10 September 1919, he returned to Warsaw. He was a fierce critic of the eastern policy of Piłsudski, and he opposed the Polish-Ukrainian offensive of April 1920, but he agreed to sit on the Council of State Defense. He also opposed the federalist program of Piłsudski and favored a unitary character for the Polish state and the assimilation of Slavonic minorities. From 1923 he was less and less active and spent much time in his Chludów estate, avoiding official positions. He was briefly foreign minister in the government of **Wincenty Witos** (28 October–15 December 1923). He criticized the excessive powers of the Polish parliament (*sejmokracja*) and was increasingly inspired by Italian fascism. He opposed the May 1926 coup of Piłsudski. In response he founded the Camp of Great Poland (Obóz Wielkiej Polski [OWP]) and became its leader. The organization's structure was similar to that of the Italian Fascist Party, and its program was aimed at the formation of younger generations of Polish nationalists. Current policy was entrusted to the Popular National Union (Związek Ludowo-Narodowy [ZLN]). At this time Dmowski authored *Polityka polska i odbudowanie państwa* (Polish politics and the reconstruction of statehood; 1925); *Zagadnienie rządu* (The question of government; 1927); and *Kościół, naród i państwo* (The church, nation, and state; 1927). In these works he abandoned the program of nationalism in favor of a Catholic state in a Polish nation. In March 1928 he established the National Party (Stronnictwo Narodowe [SN]), but his success lay rather in the expanding OWP Youth Council, which became the strongest political opposition force in the early 1930s. In March 1933 the *sanacja* government outlawed the OWP, which stimulated its members to join the official SN Youth Section, as well as to create the separate National Radical Camp (Obóz Narodowo-Radykalny [ONR]). In the early 1930s Dmowski published *Świat powojenny i Polska* (The postwar world and Poland; 1931) and *Przewrót* (Upheaval; 1934). He also published, under his pen name, novels in which he blamed Polish problems on the activities of Freemasons and Jews. Because of ailing health, Dmowski was less and less active in the late 1930s. A year before his death he returned to the Catholic Church. (PK)

Sources: *PSB*, vol. 5; *Słownik Polityków Polskich XX w.* (Poznań, 1998); Władysław Pobóg-Malinowski, *Narodowa Demokracja 1887–1918* (Warsaw, 1933); Marian Kiniorski, *Z czterdziestu pięciu lat wspomnień o Romanie Dmowskim* (Warsaw, 1939); *Roman Dmowski* (Poznań, 1939); Andrzej Micewski, *Roman Dmowski* (Warsaw, 1971); Roman Wapiński, *Roman Dmowski* (Lublin, 1988); Krzysztof Kawalec, *Roman Dmowski* (Warsaw, 1999).

DOBI István (31 December 1898, Szőny–24 November 1968, Budapest), Hungarian politician. Dobi came from a poor peasant family. He completed a six-grade primary school and a higher peasant school in 1949. He fought in World War I. In 1919 he served in the Hungarian Red Army and was taken captive by the Romanians at Szolnok. After his return home he again worked as an agrarian laborer. At the beginning of the 1920s Dobi joined the National Association of Agrarian Workers and the Social Democratic Party of Hungary. In 1930 he became president of the party in Szőny, but in 1936 he switched to the Independent Smallholders' Party (ISP). With the support of the party, Dobi was given a post in the Chamber of Agriculture in Kisalföld. He became the organizational secretary of the party and joined its national presidium. From 1937 he was the president of the ISP department for agrarian workers' affairs. Elected the national secretary of the Peasant Association in 1941, between 1943 and 1947 Dobi was president of the Section of Agrarian Workers and executive president of the ISP. After the seizure of the country by the Germans he joined the Hungarian Front.

In June 1945, in his absence, Dobi was elected to the Provisional National Assembly. From 20 August 1945 he was the vice-president of the ISP, a member of the Politburo and of the national executive committee of the party, and a member of the parliament from 4 November 1945. On 15 November 1945 he became minister without portfolio in the government of **Zoltán Tildy**. From February 1946 to November 1946 he was minister of agriculture, and from November the same year, minister without portfolio. He was again minister of agriculture in the government of **Ferenc Nagy**. A member of the committee investigating trumped-up Communist charges against MPs of his party, in May 1947 Dobi was elected president of the increasingly divided ISP. He also headed the Hungarian Peasant Association and was the editor-in-chief of its organ, *Kis Újság*. Dobi collaborated with the Communist Party in all his activities. Between 10 December 1948 and 14 August 1952 he was prime minister; in 1949–60, vice-president of the Patriotic People's Front; from 1951, president of the Council of Collective Farms; and in 1952–67, president of the Presidential Council.

During the 1956 revolution Dobi did not leave the parliament building. He appointed and swore in the government of **Imre Nagy**. After 4 November 1956 Dobi alone exercised and performed the functions of the Presidential Council. On 7 November 1956 he unlawfully dissolved the Nagy government and appointed members of the Hungarian "Revolutionary Peasant-Worker Government" of **János Kádár**. In 1959 Dobi formally joined the Hungarian Socialist Workers' Party and was soon elected a member of its Central Committee. In 1961 he was awarded the Lenin Peace Prize, and in 1967, when he was retiring, he was given the title of Hero of Socialist Labor. In 1968 he was appointed president of the National Cooperative Council. In 1962 his memoirs, *Vallomás és történelem* (Confessions and history), were published. (JT)

Sources: Bennet Kovrig, *Communism in Hungary from Kun to Kádár* (Stanford, 1979); Miklós Molnár, *From Béla Kun to János Kádár: Seventy Years of Hungarian Communism* (New York, 1990); *Magyar Nagylexikon*, vol. 6 (Budapest, 1998); *A magyar forradalom és szabadságharc enciklopédiája*, CD-ROM (Budapest, 1999).

DOBOSZYŃSKI Adam (11 January 1904, Kraków–29 August 1949, Warsaw), Polish nationalist politician. In 1920 Doboszyński fought in the Polish-Soviet war as a volunteer. After the end of the war he graduated from high school and took up studies at the Gdańsk Polytechnic College, from which he graduated in 1925. In the 1920s he was active in the National Popular Union (Związek Ludowo-Narodowy [ZLN]), and in 1934–40, in the National Party (Stronnictwo Narodowe [SN]) as a member of its radical and anti-Semitic wing of the "young." From 1931 to 1933 he belonged to the Camp of Great Poland (Obóz Wielkiej Polski [OWP]). In his book *Gospodarka narodowa* (National economy; 1936), he presented a plan for a corporatist system for Poland designed after the model of Italian fascism. On 23 June 1936, along with around a hundred of his supporters, Doboszyński made a "march on Myślenice." He decided to publicly flog the local mayor (*starosta*), who persistently persecuted the group National Democracy (Narodowa Demokracja, or Endecja [ND]); however, he could not get to him. After Doboszyński and his supporters entered the town, the local police station was disarmed, and the Jewish shops were robbed. In November 1938 he was arrested and sentenced to three and a half years in prison. Released ahead of time, in February 1939 he became a member of the Chief Committee of the SN. He fought in the September campaign of 1939 and was taken POW by the Germans but escaped and managed to get to France, where he fought in the Polish Army (May–June 1940). After the collapse of France, having avoided internment, Doboszyński left for Britain, where he was a critic of the conciliatory policy toward the USSR followed by General **Władysław Sikorski**. In December 1946 he secretly returned to Poland to conduct conspiratorial activities in nationalist groups. Arrested in 1947, he was sentenced to death in July 1949. Despite being severely tortured during investigation, he did not admit to collaboration with the Germans, of which he was falsely accused. Nevertheless, he was executed. In 1989 he was rehabilitated. (WR)

Sources: *Słownik polityków polskich XX wieku* (Poznań, 1998); *Proces Adama Doboszyńskiego* (Warsaw, 1949); Roman Wapiński, *Narodowa Demokracja 1893–1939* (Wrocław, 1980); Szymon Rudnicki, *Obóz Narodowo-Radykalny: Geneza i działalność* (Warsaw, 1985); B. Nitschke, *Adam Doboszyński: Publicysta i polityk* (Kraków, 1993).

DOBRACZYŃSKI Jan (20 April 1910, Warsaw–5 March 1994, Warsaw), Polish writer and political activist. Born into a clerk's family, Dobraczyński graduated in economics from the Warsaw College of Commerce (Wyższa Szkoła Handlowa) and in law from Warsaw University. He made his literary debut in the Catholic press in 1933 and then published articles in *Prostu z Mostu*. During the Nazi occupation he wrote for the underground press—for example, for the monthly *Sprawy Narodu*. A member of the National Military Organization (Narodowa Organizacja Wojskowa) and of the Home Army (Armia Krajowa), he fought in the Warsaw Uprising, and then he spent the rest of the war in a POW camp in Germany. After his return to Poland, Dobraczyński joined the Dziś i Jutro group of **Bolesław Piasecki**, and then he became active in the PAX Association. In 1946 he published a novel, *W rozwalonym domu* (In the demolished house), about the fate of the Warsaw Uprising generation. From May 1952 to November 1956 he was deputy to the Assembly of the Polish People's Republic. In March 1953, after *Tygodnik Powszechny* was closed down, he took over the editorship of the weekly, subordinating himself to the Stalinist authorities. From June 1971 to July 1983 he belonged to the Presidium of the All-Polish Committee of the National Unity Front (Front Jedności Narodu). He actively supported the introduction of martial law in Poland. From September 1982 he was in charge of the establishment of the facade organization Patriotic Movement for National Revival (Patriotyczny Ruch Odrodzenia Narodowego [PRON]); from December of that year he served as president of the Provisional National Council of the PRON; and between May 1983 and November 1989 he was president of the PRON National Council. In October 1988 he was appointed retired general. Issues of war and occupation, literary visions of biblical events, and the history of Christianity and Poland dominated his literary output. Dobraczyński won special recognition for his work *Listy Nikodema* (Letters of Nicodemus; 1958), as well as for his novels and collections of sketches. He also published his memoirs, *Gra w wybijanego* (Game of elimination; 1962), and *Tylko w jednym życiu* (In one life only; 1972). (WR)

Sources: *Literatura polska: Przewodnik encyklopedyczny*, vol. 1 (Warsaw, 1984); Mołdawa; *Słownik polityków polskich XX wieku* (Poznań, 1998); Andrzej Micewski, *Współrządzić czy nie kłamać* (Paris, 1978); Antoni Dudek and Grzegorz Pytel, *Bolesław Piasecki* (London, 1990).

DOBROGEANU-GHEREA Alexandru (30 November 1879, Iaşi–4 December 1937, Moscow), Romanian Communist activist. Dobrogeanu-Gherea was the eldest son of **Constantin Dobrogeanu-Gherea**, a veteran Romanian Social Democrat. In 1910 he became active in the Socialist group in Ploieşti. He completed philosophical and engineering studies in Germany. In 1919 he was elected to the parliament on behalf of the Romanian Social Democratic Party. Later, he went to Moscow, where he established contacts with the Communist International. This confirmed his critical attitude toward the moderate wing of Social Democracy, which he attacked for abandoning revolutionary ideals. He pinned special hopes on the revolution in Germany. Therefore he allied himself with the "maximalist" wing of the Social Democrats, and at the founding congress of the Socialist Communist Party of Romania in May 1921 he became a member of the top leadership of the party. He was temporarily arrested by the Romanian authorities but was released in June 1922. In September 1923 he again went to Moscow. There he allied himself with the faction of Leon Trotsky; he was criticized for that at the Third Congress of the Communist Party of Romania (CPR) in Vienna in September 1924. In Romania he was sentenced in absentia to ten years' imprisonment in the spring of 1925. Although in 1926 he spoke at the Plenum of the Executive Committee of the Comintern, in June 1928 he was allowed to attend the Sixth Congress of the CPR in only a consultative capacity. At the end of 1928 Dobrogeanu-Gherea returned to Romania and was arrested there. However, as a result of workers' protests he was released. At the beginning of 1932 he finally went to the USSR and worked there in the International Organization for Aid to Revolutionaries. Arrested along with a group of other Romanian Communists in 1937, he was murdered in Lubyanka Prison. (WR)

Sources: Ghita Ionescu, *Communism in Romania, 1944–1962* (Oxford, 1964); Lazitch; Marius Mircu, *Dosar Ana Pauker* (Bucharest, 1991); Şerban N. Ionescu, *Who Was Who in Twentieth Century Romania* (Boulder, Colo., 1994); Dennis Deletant, *Communist Terror in Romania: Gheorghiu-Dej and the Police State, 1948–1965* (New York, 1999).

DOBROGEANU-GHEREA Constantin [originally Mihai Solomon Katz] (21 May 1855, Slovianka, Kharkiv region–7 May 1920, Bucharest), Romanian literary critic and Socialist theoretician of Jewish descent. In 1872 Dobrogeanu-Gherea graduated from high school in Yekaterinoslav (Dniepropetrovsk), and then he studied natural sciences at Kharkiv University, where he joined the Narodnik organization. In 1875 he escaped from the Russian police to Iaşi, Romania. After a year he moved to Bucharest, where he became a co-founder of the first Romanian Socialist circles, maintaining contacts with Russian political émigrés in Western Europe. He worked as a blue-collar laborer and artisan and married the translator of Anton Chekhov into Romanian, Sofia Gherea. During the Romanian war of independence (1877–78) Dobrogeanu-Gherea was captured by the Russian police and imprisoned in the Petropavlovsk fortress and then in Mezen on the White Sea. He managed to escape, and via Norway, England, France, and Austria he returned to Bucharest in 1879. He edited the first Romanian Socialist dailies, *Besarabia* and *Înainte* (1879), and the monthly *România viitoare* (1880). In 1881 he was co-founder of the periodical *Contemporanul*, edited by a Socialist circle in Iaşi. In this periodical he argued with the then popular catchphrase, "art for art's sake," and claimed that artists had a social role to play. In 1882 he settled in Ploieşti, where he ran a restaurant so that he would be able to sponsor Socialist organizations. In 1883 he started writing political columns under the pen names "Caius Grachus," "Spartacus," and "I. Vasiliu."

In April 1893 Dobrogeanu-Gherea co-founded the Social Democratic Workers' Party of Romania (Partidul Social Democrat al Muncitolilor din România), and he represented it at the congresses of the Second International in 1893 and 1912. He published several books on socialism in which he initially advocated Russian Narodnik ideas, such as *Karl Marx şi economiştii noştri* (Karl Marx and our economists; 1884); *Ce vor socialiştii români* (What do Romanian Socialists want; 1886); and *Neoiobăgia. Studiu economico-social al problemelor noastre agrare* (New serfdom. A study of the economic and social problems of our agriculture; 1910). He thought advanced industrialization in Romania was impossible and advocated the development of agriculture and an improvement in the peasant standard of living—for example, by the takeover of large estates by the state and cheap land leases for peasants. At the end of his life Dobrogeanu-Gherea abandoned radical revolutionary ideas and criticized the Bolshevik revolution in Russia in 1917, parting ways with his son, **Alexandru Dobrogeanu-Gherea**. He was also involved in literary criticism. In 1893–94 he published the periodical *Literatura şi ştiinţa* and contributed to many other periodicals. He also published several books, such as *Studii critice* (Critical studies, 3 vols.; 1889–97); *Asupra criticei* (On criticism; 1890); *Arta pentru artă şi arta cu tendinţi* (Art for art's sake and purposeful art; 1894); and biographies of artists such as Mihai Eminescu. (LW)

Sources: *Biographisches Lexikon*, vol. 1; *Dictionar Enciclopedic*, vol. 2 (Bucharest, 1996); Damian Hurezeanu, *Constanin Dobrogeanu-Gherea* (Bucharest, 1974); Şerban N. Ionescu, *Who Was Who in Twentieth Century Romania* (Boulder, Colo., 1994); Keith Hitchins, *Rumania 1866–1947* (Oxford, 1994); Dorina N. Rusu, *Membrii Academiei Române 1866–1999* (Bucharest, 1999); Ion Alexandrescu, Ion Bulei, Ion Mamina, and Ioan Scurtu, *Enciclopedia de istorie României* (Bucharest, 2000).

DOBROVSKÝ Luboš (3 February 1932, Kolín), Czech journalist and politician. After high school Dobrovský worked as a teacher. In 1960 he graduated in Czech and Russian studies from the Department of Philosophy of Charles University in Prague. From 1959 to 1968 he was editor and commentator for the foreign policy section of Czechoslovak Radio, and in 1967–68 he was its Moscow correspondent. He was also involved in literary criticism and translations from Russian and Polish. In 1969 he worked at the periodical *Listy*, and in 1969–70, at *Plamene*. During the Prague Spring he was engaged in the democratization movement, and in 1968–69 he argued against the Soviet occupation. He was fired; in 1970 his publications were banned; and all through the period of "normalization" he worked as a store-keeper, window cleaner, and stoker. He translated a lot and edited the uncensored periodical *Kritický sborník*; in 1988–89 he worked with the uncensored *Lidové noviny*. In 1977 Dobrovský was one of the founding signatories of Charter 77, and after the Velvet Revolution of 1989 he was briefly a spokesman for the Civic Forum (Občanské Fórum [OF]). From January to June 1990 he was spokesman for the Ministry of Foreign Affairs, and from June to October 1990, deputy minister of foreign affairs. From October 1990 to June 1992 he was the minister of defense of Czechoslovakia. After a split in the OF in the spring of 1991 Dobrovský became a member of the Civic Movement (Občanské Hnutí). After he lost in the 1992 elections, until 1996 he was head of the chancellery of President **Václav Havel**; from 1996 to 2000 he was ambassador to Russia and then again an adviser to Havel. (PU)

Sources: *ČBS*; *Československí politici: 1918–1991* (Prague, 1991).

DOBRZAŃSKI Henryk, pseudonym "Hubal" (22 June 1897, Jasło–30 April 1940, Anielin, Kielce region), Polish officer, legend of the anti-German guerrilla movement. Born into a landowner's family, in 1914 Dobrzański graduated from a high school in Kraków. From 1912 he served in the Riflemen Teams, a Polish paramilitary organization in Galicia. During World War I he served in the *ulhans* (cavalry) of the Polish Legions and took part in several battles against the Russian Army. He was awarded the Virtuti Militari Order, as well as the Cross of the Brave four times. In 1918–39 Dobrzański was a cavalry officer and achieved the rank of major. Among the best Polish equestrians, he received many awards in international competition. During the German invasion, from 10 September 1939 he was deputy commander of the 110th Reserve Ulhan Regiment, reconstructed in Wołkowysk (Vaukavysk). A week after his appointment his regiment broke through to the Augustów Forest in fighting against the Red Army and Communist diversion bands. After the dissolution of his detachment, Dobrzański took command of the remaining volunteers and led them on to Warsaw and then to the St. Cross Mountains in the Kielce region. Meanwhile, the group swelled to three hundred men (infantry and cavalry) and became a guerrilla unit called the Fighting Kielce Region. In December 1939 Dobrzański subordinated it to the commander of the Service of Polish Victory, General **Michał Tokarzewski-Karaszewicz**. After two battles against the Germans, on 1 April 1940 the unit was dispersed, and Dobrzański was killed in a subsequent battle. He was posthumously awarded the wartime Virtuti Militari Order. In revenge for Dobrzański's operations the Germans burned down several villages in which he had been stationed and murdered their male population. According to popular belief, Dobrzański was the first Polish guerrilla commander of World War II, but actu-

ally the first such group was organized in the Pszczyna Forest on 6 September 1939. (TSt)

Sources: *Wielka encyklopedia PWN*, vol. 7 (Warsaw, 2002); Marek Szymański, *Oddział majora "Hubala"* (Warsaw, 1977); Tomasz Strzembosz, *Saga o "Łupaszce," podpułkowniku Jerzym Dąmbrowskim (1889–1941)* (Warsaw, 1996).

DOGAN Ahmed (29 March 1954, Pchelarovo, Dobrich region), Bulgarian politician and philosopher of Turkish descent. In 1981 Dogan graduated in philosophy from the University of Sofia, and then he received a Ph.D. in philosophy at the Bulgarian Academy of Sciences. In 1985 he joined protests against the so-called renaissance operation, consisting in the forced Communist assimilation of Bulgarians of Turkish descent—for instance, by the imposition of Bulgarian names. In 1986 Dogan was arrested and sentenced to ten years for founding an "anti-state" organization. He was detained in a Sofia prison. He was released thanks to an amnesty in November 1989, and on 4 January 1990 he founded the legal Movement for Rights and Freedoms (Dvizheniye za Prava i Svobody [MRF]), which was the continuation of a similar organization that had acted without formal authorization since 1985. From January 1990 he was chairman of the MRF Central Council and of its Central Executive Bureau. He was also editor-in-chief of its press organ, *Prava i Svobody*. In 1990–91 Dogan was an MP to the Great National Assembly and head of the MRF parliamentary faction. In May 1991 he left the assembly, protesting the draft constitution designed by the post-Communists. From the elections of October 1991 he sat in subsequent parliaments. In October 1992 he and the MRF parliamentary club contributed to the fall of the **Filip Dimitrov** government, expressing a vote of no-confidence because of the unfavorable effects of state farmland redistribution for the Bulgarian Turks. Dogan's support for the government of **Luben Berov**, which emerged afterwards as the result of a post-Communist faction, and accusations directed against Dogan for cooperation with the former Communist security police weakened his position and the MRF ratings. In the elections of April 1997 the MRF ran in a coalition called the Alliance for National Salvation, along with monarchists and the Bulgarian Agrarian National Union–Nikola Petkov; in the elections of June 2001 it ran with other ethnic minority parties and with the liberals, each time winning about 7.5 percent of the vote. (JJ)

Sources: *Europa Środkowo-Wschodnia 1991–1992* (Warsaw, 1992–94); Raymond Detrez, *Historical Dictionary of Bulgaria* (Lanham, Md., 1997); *Koy koy e v Bulgariya* (Sofia, 1998); Bugajski.

DOLANSKÝ Jaromír (25 February 1895, Prague–16 July 1973, Prague), Czech Communist activist. In 1921 Dolanský graduated in law from Charles University in Prague. In 1922 he joined the Communist Party of Czechoslovakia (CPC), and in 1924–28 he was editor-in-chief of the periodical *Komunistická revue*. In 1928–29 he was CPC regional secretary in Brno, and from 1929 he belonged to the CPC Central Committee. From 1930 to 1935 he was a leading activist of the Red Trade Unions, and in 1935 he became an MP and secretary of the Communist parliamentary club. When at the beginning of 1939 the CPC went underground, Dolanský, along with **Antonín Zapotocky**, was in the illegal leadership of the party. He was arrested while trying to cross the Polish border in April 1939 and sent to the Sachsenhausen concentration camp, where he stayed until the end of the war. From 1945 to 1968 he belonged to the Presidium of the CPC Central Committee, and from 1945 to 1969 he was an MP. From July 1946 to April 1949 he was minister of finance and later minister-chairman of the State Planning Office. From December 1951 to September 1963 he was deputy prime minister. He belonged to a relatively moderate wing of the Stalinist leadership and mainly dealt with the economy. At the end of the 1950s Dolanský was the author of a plan to reform the inefficient economic system. With the fall of **Antonín Novotný**, Dolanský disappeared from political life. (PU)

Sources: *ČBS; Kdo byl kdo v našich dějinach ve 20. stoleti, vol. 1* (Prague, 1998); Edward Taborsky, *Communism in Czechoslovakia 1948–1960* (Princeton, 1961).

DOMOKOS Géza (18 May 1928, Braşov), Hungarian politician, writer, and journalist from Transylvania. In 1948 Domokos started studies at the Maksim Gorki Institute in Bucharest, and in 1949–54 he studied at the Institute of World Literature in Moscow. Later he worked as a journalist. In 1957–61 he worked for the daily *Ifumunkas*, and in 1969–90 he was director of the Kriterion Press, which published books in the languages of national minorities. Domokos started his political career in the Office of the Central Committee of the Working Youth Union, whose member he was from 1956 to 1965. In 1965 he joined the Romanian Communist Party (RCP). From 1969 to November 1984 he was a deputy member of the RCP CC; from 1972 he was secretary of the Association of Romanian Writers; in 1971–78 he was a member of the National Council of Radio and Television; and from 1971 he belonged to the Council of the Working People of Hungarian Nationality. On 22 December 1989 he was invited, as a representative of the Hungarian minority, along with Reverend **Lászlo Tökés**, to join the National Salvation Front, and soon he entered its government. On 25 December Domokos was among the founders of the Democratic Alliance of Hungarians in Romania (DAHR), and he became its provisional chairman. During the First DAHR Congress in April 1990 it was decided that a united Hungarian organization would represent this minority on the Romanian political scene. Domokos was a rival for leadership with the poet and dissident **Géza Szöcs**. Ultimately Domokos won, and Szöcs became general secretary of the organization. In 1991 it had more than five hundred thousand members. Domokos represented a moderate line, arguing that a more radical program would antagonize even the liberal elements of Romanian public opinion against the Hungarians. Nevertheless, in response to the nationalist slogans of Romanian extremists, in October 1992 in Cluj (Kolozsvár) the DAHR adopted a declaration stating that Hungarians were a nation "co-constituting" the Romanian state and not a national minority; this led to even sharper Romanian reactions. During the Third DAHR Congress in January 1993, Domokos and Szöcs were dismissed, and the organization took a more conciliatory line, especially toward democratic Romanian parties. (PC)

Sources: *Dictionar Enciclopedic*, vol. 2 (Bucharest, 1996); *Who's Who in the Socialist Countries of Europe* (Munich, London, and Paris, 1989); Bugajski.

DONÁTH Ferenc (5 September 1913, Jászárokszállás–15 July 1986, Budapest), Hungarian Communist activist. Donáth's father was a barrister. From 1930 Donáth studied at the Department of Law at Péter Pázmány University in Budapest. In 1932 he joined an illegal Communist youth organization, and in 1934 he was admitted to the Hungarian Communist Party (HCP). In 1937 he co-organized the leftist March Front and established contacts with the Foreign Committee of the HCP. In 1939 he took part in a meeting in Makó where the decision was made to create the National Peasant Party. In the spring of 1940 Donáth was arrested. After his release in the fall of 1940, he was sent to the labor service, from which he was exempted in the spring of 1942 because he was suffering from lung hemorrhages. Donáth played a major role in the reorganization of the illegal HCP, carried out at the beginning of the 1940s, and he joined the leadership of the party. From February 1945 he worked in a committee preparing an agrarian reform under **Imre Nagy**, and then he supervised the implementation of the reform. From 1945 to 1948 he was political secretary of state in the Ministry of Agriculture. From June 1948 he was head of the Secretariat of the CC of the Hungarian Workers' Party (HWP). On 15 February 1951 he was arrested and sentenced to fifteen years of prison under trumped-up charges. He was released in July 1954. In the late spring of 1956, as vice-director of the Institute of Economics of the Hungarian Academy of Sciences, Donáth returned to public life.

On the night of 23 October 1956, in his absence, Donáth was elected secretary of the CC of the HCP, but the next day he resigned, as he did not agree with the assessment of the Hungarian uprising as a counterrevolution. Along with **Géza Losonczy**, he influenced Nagy's decision to return to political life. After 28 October Donáth joined negotiations in support of the consolidation process. On 1 November he became a member of the Executive Committee of the Hungarian Socialist Workers' Party, which was formed to replace the Hungarian Workers' Party. Along with Nagy, on 4 November Donáth formulated a manifesto condemning the Soviet military intervention, and after that he was granted asylum at the embassy of Yugoslavia. At the end of November, Donáth and others were interned in the town of Snagov in Romania. Donáth was delivered to the Hungarians, and in June 1958 he was sentenced to twelve years of prison as a secondary accused in the trial of Nagy. In April 1960 he was released under an individual pardon. In the 1960s Donáth withdrew from public life and concentrated on agrarian history and agricultural policy.

At the end of the 1970s Donáth became one of the leading figures of the political opposition that was forming at that time. He was one of the first to sign a manifesto, in 1979, expressing solidarity with the imprisoned members of the Czechoslovak Charter 77 group. He was the president of the editorial committee of *Bibó István—emlékkönyv* (The visitors' book of István Bibó), which was published in Switzerland. He supported efforts aiming at the creation of independent publications. He played a major role in building a dialogue among different groups of the opposition and also in the organization of meetings of these groups in Monor in 1985. (JT)

Sources: Bennet Kovrig, *Communism in Hungary from Kun to Kádár* (Stanford, 1979); Miklós Molnár, *From Béla Kun to János Kádár: Seventy Years of Hungarian Communism* (New York, 1990); *Magyar Nagylexikon*, vol. 6 (Budapest, 1998); *A magyar forradalom és szabadságharc enciklopédiája*, CD-ROM (Budapest, 1999); *Nagy Képes Milleniumi Arcképcsarnok* (Budapest, 1999).

DONTSOV Dmytro (29 August 1883, Melitopol, Tauris Province–30 March 1973, Montreal), Ukrainian journalist and politician, theoretician of Ukrainian nationalism. Dontsov came from a family of agrarian entrepreneurs but was orphaned at an early age. In 1900 he graduated from high school in Tsarskoe Selo, near Petersburg. During his law studies in Petersburg between 1900 and 1907 he was active in the Ukrainian revolutionary movement. In 1900 he was one of the founders of the Revolutionary Ukrainian Party (RUP) and in 1905 of the Ukrainian Social Democratic Workers' Party (USDWP). He remained a member of the Socialist Party at least until 1914, but his views evolved toward state ideology and later to integral nationalism, with a clearly declared sympathy for fascism and romantic conservatism. Dontsov began his journalistic career in 1906 with the Moscow *Ukrainskaia Zhizn*. He first began to publish books after his escape from Russia to Lvov in 1908. He presented his consistent anti-Russian and pro-independence standpoint for the first time in two books of 1913, *Moderne moskvofilstvo* (Modern Moscowphilism) and *Suchasne politychne polozheniie natsii i nashi zavdania* (Present political position of the nation and our tasks).

In 1914 Dontsov co-founded the pro-Austrian Union for the Liberation of Ukraine (ULU) in Lvov; he later moved to Berlin, where from 1914 to 1916 he organized the official news agency of the Ukrainian Parliamentary Club of the State Council in Vienna and published its bulletin, *Korrespondenz*. During that period he wrote works addressed to German government circles in which he attempted to explain that the reconstruction of an independent Ukrainian state was fundamental to the European balance of power, especially in view of the necessity of confining the spread of Russian influence in the central part of the continent after the war. From 1916 to 1917 Dontsov resided in Bern, where he headed the Office of the Peoples of Russia, an emigration center for refugees from the tsarist state. As the revolution in Russia broke out, he decided to return, first to Lvov, where he earned a Ph.D. in law, and then to Kiev. Among successive governments of the Ukrainian revolution he actively supported only the government of Hetman **Pavlo Skoropadsky**. As director, Dontsov co-founded its press bureau. He also established the Ukrainian Telegraphic Agency. In 1918 in Kiev he published (among other works) *Mizhnarodnoe polozhennia Ukrainy i Rossiia* (The international position of the Ukraine and Russia) and *Ukrainska derzhavna dumka i Ievropa* (Ukrainian state thought and Europe), in which he argued that the Ukraine was the eastern bastion of European culture. During the rule of the Directory Dontsov again lived in Bern (1919–21), where he directed the press and information section of the Ukrainian diplomatic mission. In 1921 in Vienna he published *Pidstavy nashoi polityky* (Foundations of our policy), in which, after the defeat of the Central Powers, he based the concept of Ukrainian statehood upon the Entente and Central European states that stood in the way of communism—Poland and Hungary.

Dontsov spent 1921–39 under the Polish government in Lvov, above all concentrating on programmatic and publishing activities. It was there in the mid-1920s that he formulated his final standpoint, which made him a proponent of Ukrainian nationalism. From 1923–24 he edited the biweekly *Zahrova*, where he displayed his anti-democratic and anti-egalitarian beliefs, as well as his sympathy for Italian fascism. Between 1922 and 1932 he was the editor-in-chief of *Literaturno-Naukovy Vistnyk* and from 1933, of *Vistnyk*, his own ideologically consistent periodical. He then rallied a group of writers of nationalist orientation and had a great influence upon the Galician younger generation. However, he was not a member of the Organization of Ukrainian Nationalists, which did not officially accept his ideology. In 1926 in Lvov his work *Natsionalizm* (Nationalism), a lecture on the doctrine of so-called active nationalism, was published. In it, Dontsov utterly criticized the national ideology hitherto accepted by the Ukrainian intelligentsia and depicted reality as a biologically understood space of conflicts among species-nations.

In the 1930s Dontsov developed an affinity to the Axis powers in Europe; he proposed to base Ukrainian policy on that of Hitler's Germany, and he outlined the prospects for a forthcoming downfall of the USSR. Arrested by the Polish authorities on 2 September 1939 and imprisoned in Bereza Kartuska, he soon escaped and fled to Bucharest, where, from 1940 to 1941 he edited the magazine *Batava*. After the outbreak of the German-Soviet war Dontsov moved to Prague, where he wrote articles about the Ukraine for the popular German press. He became increasingly absorbed in a mystical cult of the nation as set forth in the historic ideal of social harmony (*Dukh nashoi davnyny*—The spirit of our past; 1944). In 1945 he emigrated first to Paris, then to London, and finally to the United States. From 1947 Dontsov resided permanently in Montreal. Between 1949 and 1952 he lectured in Ukrainian literature at a local university, but above all he continued writing. Despite certain editorial changes in his works, especially concerning his attitude toward the Axis powers, he maintained the views he had formed between the wars. The assessment of his ideology, as well as his influence upon the political events of the 1930s and 1940s, remains a subject of heated dispute in Poland and the Ukraine. (TS)

Sources: *Encyclopedia of Ukraine*, vol. 1 (Toronto, 1984); Myroslav Sosnowskyi, *Dmytro Dontsov: Politycznyi portret* (New York and Toronto, 1974); Hryhoriy Vaskovych, *Dvi kontseptsji ukraiinskoyi politychnoyi dumky: Vyacheslavw Lypynskyi—Dmytro Dontsov* (New York, 1990); Rostyslav Yendyk, *Dontsov: Ideoloh ukraiinskoho natsionalizmu* (Munich, 1955); Volodymyr Martynets, *Idelohija orhanizovanoho i t. zv. volevoho natsionalizmu* (Winnipeg, 1954); Stanisław Jedynak, *Destruam et aedificabo: Studia z filozofii i myśli społecznej Zachodu* (Lublin, 1998); Tomasz Stryjek, *Ukraińska idea narodowa okresu międzywojennego* (Wrocław, 2000).

DOROSHENKO Dmytro (8 April 1882, Wilno [Vilnius]–19 March 1951, Munich), Ukrainian historian and politician. Doroshenko came from a Cossack family that farmed in the Chernihiv region and was descended from the seventeenth–century hetman Petro Doroshenko. After completing his secondary education at the Vilnius Gymnasium, Doroshenko began historical studies in 1901 in Warsaw, continuing in Petersburg and graduating in 1909 in Kiev. From the beginning of his studies he was active in the Revolutionary Ukrainian Party and the Ukrainian Radical Party. In 1906 in Kiev he became involved in editorial work (*Rada*, *Ukraiina*) and scientific work (the Ukrainian Scientific Society). From 1908 he was a member of the Society of Ukrainian Progressives. From 1909 to 1913 he worked as a teacher in Ekaterinoslav and carried out extensive educational activities in Ukrainian villages (the Prosvita Society). During World War I he undertook charity work in the All-Russian Union of Towns. In April 1917 he joined the Ukrainian Socialist Federalist Party, and in August 1917 the Central Council (Rada) of the Ukraine nominated him provincial commissar of the Chernihiv region.

After the German Army entered the Ukraine and the government of Hetman **Pavlo Skoropadsky** was established in May 1918, Doroshenko became minister for foreign affairs in the hetman's government. He attempted to bring a national Ukrainian character to the regime. When the regime fell in the winter of 1919, he organized a university in Kamenets Podolski and later conducted the Ukrainian Red Cross mission in Belgrade and Bucharest. He spent 1920–21 in Vienna, and in 1922 he edited the periodical *Ukrains'ke Slovo* in Berlin. From 1922 to 1926 he lectured in Ukrainian history at the Ukrainian Free University in Czechoslovakia and at Charles University in Prague. In 1926 he assumed the management of the newly founded Ukrainian Institute of Sciences in Berlin. He held this post until 1930 and at the same time continued his academic work in Prague. Because of increasing personal conflicts among the hetman's people (Doroshenko was, for example, a mediator in a conflict between Skoropadsky and **Vyacheslav Lypynsky**), Doroshenko resigned from the institute in 1930. Between 1931 and 1939 he lived in Warsaw, where he lectured in the Department of Orthodox Theology at Warsaw University and worked at the Ukrainian Institute of Sciences. After the Polish defeat in 1939 Doroshenko went to Prague and resumed lecturing at the Ukrainian Free University, continuing his scholarly work until the spring of 1945. Fearing arrest by the Soviets, he fled with the staffs of the Ukrainian scientific institutions to the American safety zone in Augsburg and Munich. From 1946 until his death Doroshenko remained president of the Ukrainian Free Academy of Sciences. In 1948–50 he was in Canada, where he lectured at, for example, St. Andrew College in Winnipeg.

Doroshenko left nearly one thousand publications on the history of Ukrainian statehood, biographies, Slavic history, the history of Ukrainian churches, regional history, records of Ukrainian relations with Western Europe, political thought, and Ukrainian historiography. Among his works the most noteworthy are the syntheses *Narys istorii Ukrainy* (An outline of Ukrainian history, 2 vols.; 1939) and *Istoriia Ukrainy 1917–1923* (The history of the Ukraine, 1917–1923; 1930–32); the definitive work to date on the history of Ukrainian historiography, *Ohliad ukrains'koi istoriohrafii* (A survey of Ukrainian historiography; 1923; English edition, with O. Ohloblyn, under the title *A Survey of Ukrainian Historiography*, 1957); biographies of Mykola Kostomarov (1920), Vyacheslav Lypynsky (1925), Taras Shevchenko (1929), and Volodymir Antonovych (1942); *Die Ukraine und das Reich: Neuen Jahrhunderte deutsch-ukrainischer Beziehungen* (Ukraine and the Reich: Recent centuries of German-Ukrainian relations; 1941); *Z istorii ukrains'koi politychnoi dumky za chasiv svitovoi viiny* (The history of Ukrainian political thought during World War I; 1936); *Pravoslavna tserkva v mynulomu i suchasnomu zhyttii ukrainskoho narodu* (The Orthodox Church in the past and present life of the Ukrainian nation; 1940); and *Slovianskyi svit v joho mynulomu i suchasnomu* (The Slavic world in the past and at present, 3 vols.; 1922). His biography of Petro Doroshenko remains in manuscript form. (TS)

Sources: *Encyclopedia of Ukraine*, vol. 1 (Toronto, 1984); *Bibliografia prac profesora D. Doroszenka za 1899–1942 roky* (Prague, 1942); Leonid Biłećkyj, *Dmytro Doroszenko* (Winnipeg, 1949); Iwan Korowytsky, ed., *Vyacheslav Lypynsky. Arkhiv. Tom 6. Lysty Dmytra Doroshenka do Vyacheslava Lypynskoho* (Philadelphia, 1973).

DOROSHENKO Volodymyr (30 October 1879, St. Petersburg–25 August 1963, Philadelphia, Pa.), Ukrainian historian of literature, bibliographer, and social activist. Doroshenko studied in Moscow, where he was active among Ukrainian students; later he was active in the Ukrainian Revolutionary Party and the Ukrainian Social Democratic Party. Monitored by the police, he escaped to Lemberg (Lviv, Lwów), where from 1908 to 1944 he worked in the library of the Taras Shevchenko Research Society (an informal Ukrainian academy of sciences). From 1925 he was an ordinary member of the society; in 1937–44 he was its director. From 1913 he was also a member of the Ukrainian Research Society in Kiev. During World War I Doroshenko sat on the Presidium of the Union of Liberation of Ukraine (Soyuz Vyzvolennia

Ukraiiny), which advocated the secession of the Dnieper Ukraine from Russia and the formation of a Ukrainian state in connection with the Austro-Hungarian monarchy. In 1944–49 Doroshenko lived in Germany and then in the United States. He authored several bibliographical works, including a two-volume bibliography of **Ivan Franko**, sixteen volumes on Taras Shevchenko, and bibliographies of **Olha Kobylyanska** and Panteleymon Kulish. He translated into Ukrainian works by Nikolay Gogol, Leo Tolstoy, and Johann Wolfgang von Goethe. He published a volume of polemics with **Serhiy Yefremov**, *Żhyttia i slovo* (Life and word; 1918) and monographs on **Vasyl Stefanyk** (1921) and Franko (1926), as well as a history of Ukrainian literature. He summed up the activities of the Taras Shevchenko Research Society in *Ohnyshche ukraiinskoyi nauky* (Center of Ukrainian science; 1951). In 1929–39 Doroshenko published the yearbook *Dnipro* in Lviv. He also published a great number of articles in the major Ukrainian periodicals: *Ukrainskaya Zhizn, Kiyevskaya Starina, Literaturno-Naukovyi Vistnyk, Rada, Dilo, Svoboda*, and *Ameryka*. (TS)

Sources: *Encyclopedia of Ukraine*, vol. 1 (Toronto, 1985); N. F. Korolevych, *Bibliohrafichna diyalnist V. V. Doroshenki 1879–1963* (Kiev, 1995); Orest Subtelny, *Ukraine: A History* (Toronto, 2000).

DOUNAR-ZAPOLSKI Mitrafan (14 June 1867, Rechitsa [Rechytsa]–30 November 1934 or 1935), Belorussian historian, ethnographer, and economist. In 1894 Dounar-Zapolski graduated from Kiev University. Between 1895 and 1897 he worked in the archives of the Russian Ministry of Justice in Moscow and taught at a private gymnasium. In 1899–1901 he was a *docent* (associate professor) in the Department of History and Philology of Moscow University, and in 1901–5, at Kiev University. From 1902 he was a full professor at this university. In 1907 he founded the Economic Institute in Kiev, and for ten years he was its director. In 1918 he directed the Belorussian Chamber of Commerce in Kiev. He took part in the formation of the Belorussian People's Republic (BPR). He was a member of the BPR commission on the creation of the Belorussian University in Minsk. In 1922–25 he worked as vice-rector of Baku University. He was also the founder of the Industrial and Commercial Museum of Azerbaijan. From 1925 to 1926 he was head of the History Department of the Belorussian State University, and then he worked in various research institutions in Moscow. In 1929 party reviewers questioned the contents of his book *Historyia Belarusi* (The history of Belorussia); it was completed in 1926, but the censors did not allow it to be printed. Subsequently, he was forced into an early retirement. The circumstances of Dounar-Zapolski's death are not clear. Arrested at the beginning of the 1930s, he was sent to a labor camp, and most probably died in the region of Narym.

Dounar-Zapolski's works are of great significance to Belorussian literature. In his first publications, he analyzed the natural environment of Belorussia and the culture of its people. He hypothesized that cultural and social processes would lead to the creation of a Belorussian political nation. He edited *Kalandiary Paunochno-Zakhodniaha Kraiu* (Calendars of the northwestern country), in which he published articles on the specificity of the Belorussian language, history, ethnography, and literature. From 1890 to 1895 he focused mainly on research on the family. In 1891 he published a work on the history of the lands of the Krivichi and Dregovichi (ancient slavonic tribes) until the end of the twelfth century. He also wrote about the history of the Union of Lublin and about the Polish-Lithuanian fight for Volhynia. In 1901 he published *Dzarzhaunaia haspadarka Vialikaha Kniastva Litouskaha pry Jahielonakh* (The economy of the Grand Duchy of Lithuania in the Jagiellonian period). The revolution of 1905 inspired him to do further research on the history of social revolts in Russia. He wrote several scholarly articles on the subject. In 1919 he edited *Asnovy dzerzhavnoustsi Bielarusi* (The basis of Belorussian statehood), which was translated into English and French. During the purge of "Belorussian nationalists," initiated in 1930, Dounar-Zapolski's writings were officially designated for destruction. (EM)

Sources: *MERSH*, vol. 9; *Bielaruskaia savietskaia entsiklopedia*, vol. 6, 1971; *Bielaruskaie Slova* (Ludwigsburg), 1955, no. 10; *Batskaushchyna*, 1964, nos. 617–618; N. Palonskaia-Vasilenka, "Dounar-Zapolski," *Zapisy* (New York), 1953, no. 1(3); Nicholas P. Vakar, *Belorussia: The Making of a Nation* (Cambridge, Mass., 1956); Vitaut Kipel and Zora Kipel, eds., *Byelorussian Statehood* (New York, 1988); P. Kruczok, *Mitrafan Dounar-Zapolski* (Minsk, 1995); Jan Zaprudnik, *Historical Dictionary of Belarus* (Lanham, Md., 1998).

DOVZHENKO Oleksandr (10 September 1894, Vyunyshche, near Chernikhov–25 November 1956, Moscow), Soviet Ukrainian film director. In 1914 Dovzhenko graduated from the Training Institute for Teachers in Glukhov, and later he worked as a teacher in Zhytomyr. From 1917 to 1919 he studied at the Trade Institute in Kiev. In 1917–20 he took part in the revolution as a member of the radical Socialist Borotbist Party. After the Bolshevik Revolution he worked in the Department of Folk Education and Art in Kiev, and in 1921–22, in the Soviet legations in Poland and Germany. In 1922–23 he studied painting in Berlin, and from 1923 to 1926 he worked as an illustrator for the newspaper *Visti VUTsVK*. He was a member of the Union of Proletarian Writers–Hart and of the All-

Ukrainian Academy of Proletarian Literature (Vseukrainska Akademiya Proletarskoyi Literatury [VAPLITE]). In 1926–28 Dovzhenko worked in a film studio in Odessa, where he shot his first movies, *Vasya—Reformator* (Vasya the Reformer; 1926) and *Yahidka kokhannia* (The fruit of love; 1926). His film *Zwenyhora* (1928) was recognized for its innovativeness. In 1929–41 Dovzhenko worked in a film studio in Kiev (later named after him), where he created a clear-cut satire of the Ukrainian national movement in 1918–20, *Arsenal* (1929), and an apotheosis of collectivization, *Zemla* (Land; 1930). The latter was rated among the twelve best films ever at the International Film Festival in Brussels in 1958. Dovzhenko's first sound film was *Ivan* (1932), about the construction of a power plant on the Dnieper River.

During World War II Dovzhenko used his talents on behalf of Soviet propaganda. After the Soviet invasion of the Eastern Borderland of Poland in September 1939, he shot a propaganda movie, *Vyzvolennia* (Liberation; 1940), praising the aggression as a "unification of Western Ukrainian territories with the Soviet Ukraine." In 1943 he created a documentary, *Bytva za nashu Radyansku Ukraiinu* (Struggle for our Soviet Ukraine), and he wrote a novel, *Ukraiina v ohni* (Ukraine on fire), that was, nevertheless, condemned by Stalin for "nationalist deviation" and was banned from publication. As a result Dovzhenko was not allowed to go to Kiev. In 1944 he shot a documentary, *Peremoha na Pravoberezhniy Ukraiini* (Victory in the Ukraine west of the Dnieper). From 1944 he lived and worked in Moscow. In 1949–56 he lectured in the All-Union State Institute of Cinematography; from 1955 he was a professor there. In 1957 his autobiographical novel, *Zacharovana Desna* (Enchanted Desna; 1979), was published posthumously. From 1941 until his death he wrote a diary; it was not published until 1994. His selected writings were published as *The Poet as Filmmaker* by MIT Press in 1973. The most complete edition of his works is *Tvory* (Works, 5 vols.; 1964–66). (BB)

Sources: *Encyclopedia of Ukraine*, vol. 1 (Toronto, 1984); *Ukraiinska Literaturna Entsyklopediya*, vol. 2 (Kiev, 1990); *Pisarze świata: Słownik encyklopedyczny* (Warsaw, 1995); *Malyi Slovnyk Istoriyi Ukraiiny* (Kiev, 1997); *Dovidnyk z Istoriyi Ukraiiny* (Kiev, 2001); Roman Korohodskyi, *Dovzhenko v poloni* (Kiev, 2000).

DOWBOR-MUŚNICKI Józef (25 October 1867, Garbów, near Sandomierz–26 October 1937, Batorów), Polish general. After graduating from high school in 1884 Dowbor-Muśnicki joined the cadet corps in Petersburg, and in 1886–88 he studied at the Constantine Military Academy. Later he served in the 140th infantry regiment and in the 11th regiment of grenadiers. In 1899 he entered the Petersburg Military Academy, from which he graduated with distinction in 1902. During the Russo-Japanese War of 1904–5 Dowbor-Muśnicki was an officer on the staff of the First Siberian Corps. From 1910 he was chief of staff in subsequent infantry divisions. During World War I he fought on many fronts and advanced in the ranks. In November 1914 he became commander of the Fourteenth Regiment of Siberian Riflemen. In August 1915 he was promoted to major general. He fought in Asia Minor and on the German front. In January 1917 he became chief of staff of the First Army, and in May 1917 he was promoted to general of division. On 6 August 1917 he became commander of the First Polish Corps and started to form it in Belorussia, where Polish troops were trying to prevent the assaults, murder, and pillaging of Polish manor houses by Bolshevized squads. In March 1918 he recognized the Regency Council, but under German pressure he had to demobilize his corps, and he settled on the Staszów estate.

After the restoration of independent Poland, on 6 January 1919 Dowbor-Muśnicki became commander-in-chief of the Polish armed forces in the former German partition. In a short time he managed to form an army that was successful in the Greater Polish Uprising. On 19 March 1919 he was promoted to general of arms, but he was on a collision course with **Józef Piłsudski**. He opposed a war with Soviet Russia and the sending of the Poznań army to the eastern front, and in particular he disagreed with the way Piłsudski unified the Polish troops from the three partitions. Piłsudski was also ill-disposed toward a talented, experienced, and popular general, so he tried to marginalize him. After the failed Kiev operation in the spring of 1920, Dowbor-Muśnicki sharply criticized Piłsudski, but when in late August the Bolshevik offensive was repelled eastward, he offered his services. Piłsudski wanted to entrust him with the command of the southern front, but Dowbor-Muśnicki refused and stayed passive until the end of the war. With this refusal Dowbor-Muśnicki lost a lot of his earlier popularity. On 14 September 1921 he retired and settled in Batorów, where he ran an estate and wrote his memoirs. He returned to public life during the May 1926 coup, when the Poznań authorities wanted to send troops under his command to defend the legal authorities against Piłsudski. When President **Stanisław Wojciechowski** and Prime Minister **Wincenty Witos** resigned, this plan was abandoned, and although Dowbor-Muśnicki favored an armed defense of democracy, he decided not to lead the Poznań troops on Warsaw. He authored *Krótki szkic do historii I Polskiego Korpusu* (Outline history of the First Polish Corps; 1919); *Na marginesie książki o pułkowniku Lisie-Kuli* (Marginal notes on the book on Colonel Lis-Kula; 1933); and *Moje wspomnienia* (My memoirs; 1935). (PU)

Sources: *PSB*, vol. 5; *Kto był kim w Drugiej Rzeczypospolitej* (Warsaw, 1994); *Encyklopedia historii Drugiej Rzeczypospolitej* (Warsaw, 1999); Piotr Bauer, *Generał Józef Dowbor-Muśnicki* (Poznań, 1988); Tadeusz Kryska-Karski, Stanisław Żurakowski, *Generałowie Polski Niepodległej* (Warsaw, 1991); Piotr Stawecki, *Słownik biograficzny generałów Wojska Polskiego* (Warsaw, 1994); Grzegorz Łukomski and Bogusław Polak, *Powstanie Wielkopolskie 1918–1919* (Koszalin and Warsaw, 1995).

DRACH Ivan (17 October 1936, Telizhentsy, Kiev region), Ukrainian poet and political activist. In 1961 Drach graduated in Ukrainian philology from Kiev University. In 1962–64 he worked on the editorial board of *Literaturna Ukraiina*, the weekly of the Association of Ukrainian Writers. From 1962 to 1964 he also studied at the Higher Course in Screenplay Writing of the State Cinema in Moscow, and then he worked as a screenplay writer for the **Oleksandr Dovzhenko** Memorial Film Studios in Kiev. After 1974 he was mainly involved with literary work. He was one of the pioneers of the revival of Ukrainian literature in the 1960s (the generation of *shestidesiatniki*). His poetry was distinguished by the freshness of its metaphors and neologisms and a variable rhythm, in contrast to the standards of Socialist realism. Drach was sharply criticized for the collections *Nizh u sontsi* (A knife in the sun; 1961) and *Oda chesnomu boyahuzevi* (Ode to an honest coward; 1963), but he nonetheless managed to publish a number of other collections, such as *Sonyashnyk* (Sunflower; 1962); *Protuberantsi sertsa* (Prominence of the heart; 1965); *Balady budniv* (Ballads of commonplaceness; 1967); and *Khram sontsia* (The sun temple; 1988). He authored screenplays for popular Ukrainian films: *Krynytsia dla sprahlykh* (The well for the thirsty; 1967); *Kaminnyi khrest* (Stone cross[based on short stories by **Vasyl Stefanyk**]; 1968); *Idu do tebe* (I am coming to you; 1971); and *Propala hramota* (The missing message [based on short stories by Nikolay Gogol]; 1972). A collection of Drach's poems was published in English as *Orchard Lamps* in 1989.

In 1989–92 Drach was first secretary of the Kiev branch of the Association of Ukrainian Writers. In 1989 he was among the organizers and leaders of the National Movement of Ukraine for Perestroika (Narodnyi Rukh Ukraiiny za Perebudovu). From 1990 he was a deputy to the Supreme Council of the Ukrainian SRR and then of independent Ukraine (with a break in 1994–98). From 1991 he was chairman of the Council of the Society for Relationships with Ukrainians Abroad, and from 1995, chairman of the Congress of the Ukrainian Intelligentsia. In 1992–2000 he was chairman of the Ukrainian World Coordination Council (Ukraiinska Vsesvitnia Koordynatsyina Rada), and in 2000–1 he presided over the State Committee for Information Policies, Television, and Radio. (BB)

Sources: *Encyclopedia of Ukraine*, vol. 1 (Toronto, 1984); *Ukraiinska Literaturna Entsyklopediya*, vol. 2 (Kiev 1990); *Pisarze świata: Słownik encyklopedyczny* (Warsaw, 1995); *Khto ye khto v Ukraiini 2000* (Kiev, 2000); Mykola Inytskyi, *Ivan Drach: Narys tvorchosti* (Kiev, 1986); A. O. Tkachenko, *Ivan Drach: Narys tvorchosti* (Kiev, 1988).

DRAGANOV Pyrvan (5 February 1890, Lom–2 February 1945, Sofia), Bulgarian diplomat. According to some sources, Draganov was the illegitimate son of Tsar **Ferdinand I** and the stepbrother of Tsar **Boris III**. In 1909 he graduated from the Higher Military School in Sofia, and then he continued his studies in Germany. In 1914–18 he was a personal aide to Prince Boris, and in 1920–32 he was his aide-de-camp. From 1932 to 1936 he served as military attaché in Berlin and in 1936–38 as envoy to Vienna and then to Berlin. After the fall of Poland in September 1939, Draganov held talks with the Germans to secure Bulgaria's position in the case of Soviet ambitions to expand into the Balkans, but Berlin avoided giving any guarantees. When Bessarabia was annexed by the USSR in 1940, he tried to make Germany press Romania to cede Southern Dobrudja to Bulgaria, and he succeeded. In accord with Tsar Boris' tactics, he played for time in order to keep Bulgaria out of the Tripartite Pact as long as possible without jeopardizing relations with Germany. As early as September 1941 Draganov expected trouble for Germany on the eastern front and even the defeat of the Third Reich by the Soviet Union, but given the delicate situation, Tsar Boris had to support the Third Reich.

From 1942 Draganov was an envoy to Spain. In the name of the tsarist government he started negotiations with the Americans and the British. In February 1944 he became minister of foreign affairs in the government of **Ivan Bagrianov**. He tried to loosen the relationship with Germany, but a reduction in the number of trains going through Bulgaria to the eastern front and the evacuation of German troops from Bulgarian ports was not enough for the Allies, who demanded that Bulgaria renounce its territorial gains of 1940 and 1941. Bulgaria was not ready to comply. When **Stoycho Moshanov** became the main negotiator of the peace treaty in Cairo in August 1944, Draganov made an impolitic step by putting the blame for Bulgaria's alliance with the Third Reich on the Allies. Later he held talks with the Soviets, promising Bulgarian neutrality and disarmament of the Germans in return for the Soviets' not entering Bulgaria. The Kremlin rejected this condition, which resulted in the resignation of the Bagrianov cabinet on 1 September 1944. After the Red Army entered Bulgaria in September 1944, Draganov was arrested by the Soviet authorities and handed over to the Bulgarian authorities. Although the prosecution preparing the trial of the tsarist elite suggested that Draganov should remain alive, the Politburo of the Bulgarian Communist Party decided in December 1944 to include him in the group to be sentenced to death. The verdict was announced on 1 February 1945, and it was executed the following night. (AG)

Sources: *Entsiklopediya Bulgariya*, vol. 2 (Sofia, 1981); Marshall Lee Miller, *Bulgaria during the Second World War* (Stanford, 1975); Jerzy Jackowicz, *Partie opozycyjne w Bułgarii 1944–1948* (Warsaw, 1997).

DRĂGHICI Alexandru (27 September 1913, Tisău, near Buzău–13 December 1993, Budapest), Romanian Communist activist. Drăghici completed five grades of primary school, and then he worked as a railroader. In 1933 he took part in a strike in Grivița. The following year he joined the Communist Party of Romania (CPR). In July 1935 he was sentenced to nine years' imprisonment in the trial of **Ana Pauker. Lucrețiu Pătrășcanu** was his lawyer. Drăghici served his sentence in Doftana Prison, where he met **Gheorghe Gheorghiu-Dej** and became a member of his group. From 1941 to 1944 he was incarcerated in Caransebeş and Tîrgu-Jiu. After the coup of August 1944 he was released, and with the support of the Communist Party, he assumed the post of prosecutor, although he did not have even a secondary education. In 1945 he was already a prosecutor in political trials, and in 1946, in the trial of Marshal **Ion Antonescu**. From October 1946 he was a deputy member, and from February 1948 a member, of the Central Committee (CC) of the CPR. As deputy head of the Political-Administrative Department of the party's CC, already in April 1948 he interrogated Pătrășcanu. A trusted partner of Gheorghiu-Dej, in December 1950 Drăghici was appointed head of the General Political Board of the Ministry of Interior and deputy minister of interior. He oversaw the preparations for the trial of Pătrășcanu. After the fall of **Teohari Georgescu**, in May 1952 Drăghici assumed the post of minister of interior. In September 1952 he became head of the new Ministry of Public Security. In October 1952 he was promoted to general. In September 1953 the Ministry of Interior and the Ministry of Public Security were merged, and Drăghici, as a member of the Secretariat of the CC of the CPR, was in charge of them. A deputy member of the Politburo from April 1954, on 20 August 1954 he was appointed deputy prime minister. In March 1957 he again became head of the integrated Ministry of Interior.

Drăghici was personally responsible for cruel Stalinist

terror in Romania. He was in control of around 180,000 prisoners in concentration camps. He oversaw the construction of the Danube–Black Sea Canal, where forced labor was used. The security forces, of which he was in charge, bloodily suppressed the peasant resistance to collectivization; the suppression claimed the lives of tens of thousands. Drăghici approved of the use of torture to coerce testimony. When, at the CC plenum of the Romanian Workers' Party (RWP) at the beginning of April 1956, **Iosif Chişinevschi** and **Miron Constantinescu** attacked Gheorghiu-Dej for slowing down the de-Stalinization process, Drăghici stood up in his defense and became the backbone of Gheorghiu-Dej's regime. In October 1962 he also subordinated military intelligence to himself. After the death of Gheorghiu-Dej in March 1965 Drăghici was even mentioned as his successor, but he was too dangerous for other members of the leadership. Drăghici was the only member of the party leadership to vote against the succession of **Nicolae Ceauşescu** to the party leadership. In July 1965 Drăghici resigned as head of the Ministry of Interior, but as secretary of the CC of the RWP, he still had a powerful influence upon this ministry. On 25 April 1968, soon after the rehabilitation of Patraşcanu, Drăghici was dismissed from all his posts for "crimes and abuses" (the trial of Patraşcanu was also mentioned), and he was demoted to private. The authorities even considered putting him on trial, but they were afraid that he might divulge that the majority of party leaders were responsible for similar crimes. It was only after the dismissal of Drăghici that Ceauşescu could consolidate his power.

During the Ceauşescu regime Drăghici was completely sidelined. After the overthrow of Ceauşescu in December 1989 he left for Hungary, where he lived with his daughter in Budapest. The new Romanian authorities filed a request for his extradition, but the democratic Hungarian government refused. In May 1993 Drăghici was tried in absentia, but the trial was canceled owing to his death. (WR)

Sources: Silviu Brucan, *The Wasted Generation* (Boulder, Colo., 1993); Dennis Deletant, *Ceauşescu and the Securitate: Coercion and Dissent in Romania, 1965–1989* (Armonk, N.Y., 1995); Dennis Deletant, *Communist Terror in Romania: Gheorghiu-Dej and the Police State, 1948–1965* (New York, 1999); Robert Levy, *Ana Pauker: The Rise and Fall of a Jewish Communist* (Berkeley, 2000).

DRAGOYCHEVA Tsola (18 August 1898, Byala Slatina–26 May 1993, Sofia), Bulgarian Communist activist. In 1918 Dragoycheva graduated from a high school for girls in Varna and in 1920 from the Higher Pedagogical Institute in Sofia. In 1919 she joined the Bulgarian Communist Party (BCP). In 1919–23 she worked as a teacher, but she frequently lost her jobs because of her illegal activities. She participated in the preparations for the September 1923 uprising. After its failure she was arrested and sentenced to fifteen years in prison. She was amnestied in May 1924, and she returned to clandestine work in the BCP military section in Ruse and Plovdiv. After the failed attempt on the life of Tsar **Boris III** in Sveta Nedela Church in Sofia—carried out by the BCP military section—Dragoycheva was arrested and sentenced to death. The execution was stopped as she was expecting a baby, and in January 1926 the sentence was commuted to life imprisonment. After Dragoycheva was released owing to another amnesty in 1932, she left for the USSR, where she worked with the Foreign Bureau of the BCP Central Committee. She also worked in the Women's Secretariat of the Communist International (Comintern) and studied in the Lenin School of the Comintern in Moscow (1933–35). In 1935 she took part in the Seventh Congress of the Comintern. In June 1936 she secretly returned to Bulgaria, where she was entrusted with editing the BCP organ, *Zasztita*. At the Second BCP Conference in the Vitosha Mountains in 1937 Dragoycheva was elected to the CC and remained a member until February 1990.

After the outbreak of World War II, in September 1940 Dragoycheva promoted the idea of a pact with the USSR that would guarantee Bulgaria its sovereignty and frontiers. In January 1941 she was elected a member of the Politburo and Secretariat of the BCP CC. After the German invasion of the Soviet Union in June 1941, the underground BCP authorities adopted the policy of "anti-Fascist armed struggle." In August 1941 Dragoycheva was arrested and detained in the Sv. Nikola Camp near Asenovgrad, from which she escaped at the end of 1941. During the trial of the BCP leadership in July 1942 she was again sentenced to death, this time in absentia. In the party leadership she was responsible for maintaining contacts with the Yugoslav Communist guerrillas of **Josip Broz Tito.**

Dragoycheva took part in the preparations for the uprising of 9 September 1944 and in the takeover of power by the Fatherland Front (FF). In 1944–48 she was general secretary of the FF National Committee, and from 1945 to 1950 she presided over the Bulgarian National Women's Union. With the decline of "home Communists" and with the purge of **Traycho Kostov**, in the late 1940s Dragoycheva lost her previous influence. From December 1947 to January 1957 she was minister of post, telephone, and telegraph. In 1948 she was dismissed from the top BCP leadership. From 1949 to 1952 she presided over the National Committee for the Defense of Peace, and in 1957–77 she presided over the All-National Committee of Bulgarian-Soviet Friendship. In 1966 she was reelected to the BCP CC Politburo.

She retired from this position in January 1984, but until 1986 she remained a member of the Council of State. She was a deputy to the parliament for forty-five years (1945–90). She authored the memoirs *Powela na dylga: Spomeni i razmisli* (Fulfillment of obligations: Memoirs and reflections, 3 vols.; 1972–79) and propaganda pieces on Bulgarian-Soviet friendship. (JJ)

Sources: Lazitch; *Entsiklopediya Bulgariya*, vol. 2 (Sofia, 1981); Elena Savova, *Tsola Dragoycheva: Biobibliografiya* (Sofia, 1974); J. F. Brown, *Bulgaria under Communism* (New York, 1975); Tasho Tashev, *Ministrite na Bulgariya 1879–1999: Entsiklopedichen spravochnik* (Sofia, 1999); Evgeniya Kalinova and Iskra Baeva, *Bulgarskite prekhodi 1944–1999* (Sofia, 2000); Angel Tsurakov, *Entsiklopediya: Pravitelstvata na Bulgariya. Khronologiya na politicheskiya zhivot 1879–2001* (Sofia, 2001).

DRAŠKOVIĆ Vuk (29 November 1946, Medja, Voivodina), Serbian politician. Drašković, who lost his mother in early childhood, graduated from a high school in Gacko and from the Law Department of the University of Belgrade in 1968. As a member of the Communist youth organization, he took part in the 1968 student demonstrations. Later he joined the League of Communists of Yugoslavia (LCY). From 1969 he worked as a journalist in the state press agency TANJUG, at first in Yugoslavia and then in Lusaka, Zambia. Recalled in 1978, after his disinformation about the outbreak of war between Zambia and Rhodesia caused a diplomatic incident, in 1978–80 he was press adviser to the Yugoslav Union of Trade Unions (Savez Sindikata Jugoslavije) and then editor-in-chief of the trade union paper *Rad*. In 1981 he made his debut as writer, publishing a novel, *Sudije* (Judges), in which he described a judge who resisted political pressure. In the novels *Nož* (Knife; 1982), *Molitva 1–2* (Prayer 1–2; 1985), and *Ruski konsul* (Russian consul; 1988) he described the sufferings of the Serbs during World War II, and in *Noć generala* (The general's nights; 1994), he described the last days of **Dragoljub (Draža) Mihailović**.

At the beginning of the 1980s Drašković was expelled from the LCY and joined the opposition. At first, as a declared nationalist, he cooperated with **Vojislav Šešelj** in the Saint Sava Association. In January 1990 it turned into an extreme nationalist party called the Renewal of the Serbian Nation, which soon broke up. Drašković took the lead of a huge anti-government demonstration in Belgrade on 9 March 1990 in which two people were killed and dozens were wounded in scuffles with the police. Drašković was briefly arrested. On 14 March 1990 the Serbian National Renewal movement (Srpski Pokret Obnove [SPO]) was founded with Drašković at its head. When the war broke out in the former Yugoslavia, in the summer of 1991 the SPO created a paramilitary group that took part in the fighting against the Croats. Soon Drašković moved to a more moderate opposition, exhorting the Serbs during anti-war demonstrations not to take part in a war that would lead to the breakup of Yugoslavia. On 1 June 1993 he was imprisoned along with his wife. In prison he was beaten and went on a hunger strike. Both he and his wife were released in July 1993 as a result of external pressure.

Under Drašković's lead the SPO joined an opposition coalition called the Democratic Movement of Serbia (DEPOS), which in the parliamentary elections of December 1993 won forty-five mandates. In the November 1996 local elections the SPO ran in the coalition Together (Zajedno), along with the Democratic Party of Serbia and the Serbian Civic Alliance, winning in many places. When the authorities intended to invalidate the elections, Drašković was one of the organizers of demonstrations that lasted eighty-eight days and ended with success. Drašković demonstrated his charismatic leadership, capable of appealing to the crowds. He had more problems in dealing with his opposition partners and with **Zoran Djindjić** in particular. As a result, the coalition Together broke up. Drašković ran in the presidential elections of 1997, although other opposition parties boycotted them. In the first round he gained 20.6 percent of the vote, and in the second round, in December 1997, a mere 15.4 percent. In the elections to the Serbian parliament in September 1997 the SPO again won 45 out of 250 mandates. Drašković lost many followers when, in January 1999, he sided with **Slobodan Milošević** and joined his government as deputy prime minister responsible for foreign policy. During the NATO intervention Drašković condemned the Western operation, but when he began to criticize President Milošević and spoke in favor of inviting UN troops to Kosovo, on 28 April 1999 he was dismissed. In October 1999 he barely escaped death in a car crash, which was an attempt on his life. He was again wounded by two sniper bullets in his apartment in Budva (Montenegro) in June 2000. He accused Milošević's special services of both attempts. In 2000 he stayed out of the Democratic Opposition of Serbia (Demokratska Opozicija Srbije [DOS]), in which his rival Djindjić played a major role. While in the September 2000 elections the DOS defeated the Socialists of Milošević, the SPO failed to exceed the threshold and stayed out of the Serbian parliament. (AO)

Sources: Bogoljub Pejcić, *Pisma Vuku* (Belgrade, 1991); Milena Popović, *Junska dogadanja* (Belgrade, 1994); Laura Silber and Allan Little, *The Death of Yugoslavia* (London, 1995); Warren Zimmermann, *Origins of a Catastrophe* (New York and Toronto, 1996); Dejan Anastasijević, *Out of Time* (N.p., 2000); Bugajski; www.mirhouse.com/ce-review/anastasijevic1.pdf; www.rferl.org.

DRENCHEV Milan (12 March 1917, Vinnitsa), Bulgarian Peasant Party politician. Drenchev studied law and economics. In 1941 he joined the youth organization of the Bulgarian Agrarian National Union (Bylgarski Zemedelski Naroden Syjuz [BANU]). He was imprisoned during World War II for organizing a protest against Bulgaria's alliance with the Axis. Released after the coup of September 1944, he resumed his BANU activities. After the party's leader, **Nikola Petkov**, was sentenced to death and the party broke up, Drenchev was arrested, and in 1948 he was sentenced to fourteen years in prison. Amnestied after several years, in 1955 he was detained again for trying to restore the BANU organization. He was sentenced to ten years. Released in 1962, until 1989 he remained under police surveillance; he was persecuted and forced to work as a blue-collar laborer at the most difficult "Socialist construction" sites.

In November 1989 Drenchev restored the BANU, taking Petkov as a symbol of the renewed organization and assuming the position of its general secretary. The party's program included the constitutional rule of law, the reprivatization of land, and respect for private property. After the collapse of the Communist dictatorship, the BANU quickly won wide support, and in 1990 it had fifteen thousand members. Drenchev tried to merge into it the BANU structure that had existed under Communist control, but in view of the mistrust of its leaders, especially with regard to Petkov's death, the attempt failed. The BANU–Nikola Petkov joined the Union of Democratic Forces (UDF), in which Drenchev became deputy chairman of the National Coordination Council. In the parliamentary elections of June 1990 the BANU candidates were not too successful.

In the spring of 1991 Drenchev favored a gradual dismissal of the post-Communists, and, contrary to the leaders of the UDF right wing, he opposed speeding up new elections. As a leader of the largest UDF faction (apart from that of the Social Democrats), Drenchev joined the UDF Center, founded in April 1991. In August 1991, however, the BANU–Nikola Petkov left the union as a result of the downgrading of its candidates on UDF lists. This step proved to be very costly, since in the elections of October 1991 the BANU–Nikola Petkov failed to exceed the 4 percent threshold and stayed out of the parliament. In February 1992 Drenchev was close to reaching an agreement with the post-Communist BANU, but the congress of the BANU–Nikola Petkov did not accept the agreement and removed Drenchev from the leadership, electing **Anastasya Moser** in his place. This choice split the party, since some of its members stayed loyal to Drenchev, who founded the Unifying Center of the Agrarian Movement and took the lead of the BANU–Nikola Petkov (Independent). In the elections of 1997 Drenchev tried to win a seat on behalf of the Alliance for National Salvation, but he lost. In 1998 his party left the alliance. (AG)

Sources: *Koy koy e v Bulgariya* (Sofia, 1998); Jerzy Jackowicz, *Bułgaria od rządów komunistycznych do demokracji parlamentarnej 1988–1991* (Warsaw, 1997); Raymond Detrez, *Historical Dictionary of Bulgaria* (Lanham, Md., 1997).

DRLJEVIĆ Sekula (25 August 1884, Morača–1945, Austria), Montenegrin politician. Drljević graduated from a high school in Sremski Karlovac and in law from the University of Zagreb. In 1906 he became secretary of the Ministry of Finance of Montenegro; from April 1907 to January 1910 he was minister of justice, and from June 1912 to April 1913, minister of finance. In the elections of 1913 he won a seat in the National Assembly (Skupština), staying in opposition to the government of Janko Vukotić. In May 1917 he was temporarily interned by the Austrian authorities. In 1918 he was elected to the National Assembly, which abolished the monarchy and decided to merge Montenegro with the Kingdom of Serbs, Croats, and Slovenes (SHS). From the early 1920s Drljević was active in the Montenegrin Federalist Party (Crnogorska Federalistička Stranka) and sat in the SHS parliament on its behalf in 1925–29. In 1938 he was elected MP from the lists of the United Opposition. After the breakup of Yugoslavia, in April 1941 Drljević went to Cetinje, where in July 1941 he took the lead of the national committee set to cooperate with the Italian occupation authorities. From 1942 he was active in Zagreb, where he cooperated with the Ustashe regime. After the war he escaped to Austria, where he died. He authored a popular song, *Oj, svijetla majska zoro!*, considered by Montenegrin nationalists as a national anthem, as well as the book *Balkanski sukobi* (Balkan encounters; 1944). (WR)

Sources: *Enciklopedija Jugoslavije*, vol. 3 (Zagreb, 1958); www.montenegro.org.au/crnogorske_vlade.html.

DRNOVŠEK Janez (17 May 1950, Celje), Slovene Communist activist and post-Communist politician. Drnovšek graduated in economics from the University of Ljubljana. In 1986 he received a Ph.D. in economics from the University of Maribor. At first he worked in the economic apparatus. From 1975 he was manager of the economics department of the construction enterprise Zasavje in Zagorje; from 1979 he was its deputy director, and from 1982 he was director of a branch of the Yugoslav Bank in Trbovlje. He was also economic counselor to the Yugoslav Embassy in Cairo, Egypt. From 1986 he was a deputy to the Lower House of the Federal Assembly and head of the Slovene trade union committee for foreign relations. From April 1989 he was Slovene representative to the Presidium of the Socialist Federative Republic of Yugoslavia; the Presidium served as a collective head of state. From May 1989 to May 1990 Drnovšek was chairman of the Presidium. He supported the Slovene proclamation of independence of 25 June 1991 and took part in negotiations that led to the conclusion of the Brioni Agreement of 7 July 1991 and to the withdrawal of the Yugoslav People's Army from Slovenia. In March 1992 he took the lead of the Liberal Democratic Party, which, after merging with other groups, as of 1994 was called the Liberal Democracy of Slovenia (Liberalna Demokracija Slovenije [LDS]). In April 1992 the National Assembly elected Drnovšek prime minister. He assumed this post on 14 May 1992. After the elections of December 1992 he remained as head of the government. He also remained prime minister after the elections of November 1996.

During his term Drnovšek focused on the economic and political transformation of Slovenia. He was very successful, maintaining the highest per capita GNP among the transforming East Central European countries and a steady economic growth rate. In foreign policy he made progress toward the integration of Slovenia into the European Union. On 10 June 1996 he signed a treaty of association, and in March 1998 he started accession negotiations. Since Slovenia failed to join NATO at the first stage of NATO's expansion in 1999, Drnovšek was criticized by the opposition. In April 2000 the Slovenian People's Party (Slovenska Ljudska Stranka [SLS]) withdrew from the ruling coalition, which included the LDS and the Democratic Party of Pensioners of Slovenia (DPPS). On 8 April 2000 Drnovšek's government failed to win a vote of confidence, and on 3 May 2000 Drnovšek resigned. As a result of the October 2000 elections the LDS reconstructed the coalition government with the SLS and DPPS, and Drnovšek again became prime minister. On 1 December 2002 he was elected president, and on 22 December he assumed the post of head of state. Under his presidency in a referendum on 23 March 2003, 54 percent of the Slovenes voted for entry into the European Union, and it took place on 1 May 2004. Drnovšek is an honorary doctor of Boston University and of Illinois Wesleyan University. (AO)

Sources: Leopoldina Plut-Pregelj and Carole Rogel, *Historical Dictionary of Slovenia* (Lanham, Md., 1996); Public Relations and Media Office, *Government of the Republic of Slovenia 1999* (Ljubljana, 1999); Polish Press Agency, *Noty biograficzne*; Bugajski; www.gov.si.

DROBNER Bolesław (28 June 1883, Kraków–21 March 1968, Kraków), Polish Socialist politician. From 1898 Drobner was a member of the Polish Social Democratic Party of Galicia and Teschen Silesia, and in 1901 he started studies in Berlin. In December 1901 he was arrested for defending Germanized Polish children of Września. In 1902 he enrolled at the Polytechnic of Lemberg (Lwów, Lviv). Expelled for taking part in a student strike, he continued his studies in Switzerland. From 1902 he belonged to the leadership of the Polish Socialist Party–Proletariat. In 1905 he took part in revolutionary actions in Warsaw, Łódź, Częstochowa, and Sosnowiec. In December 1905 he returned to Zurich, where he received a Ph.D. in chemistry in 1907. After the outbreak of World War I he joined the Polish Legions, and from May 1915 he served in the Austrian Army. Drobner represented the Kraków Socialists at the Sixteenth Unification Congress of the Polish Socialist Party (Polska Partia Socjalistyczna [PPS]) in Kraków in April 1919. With a group of radical followers, in December 1921 he began to edit the periodical *Głos Niezależnych Socjalistów*. In March 1922 he left the PPS, and in 1924 he founded the Independent Socialist Party of Labor (ISPL), advocating Socialist revolution in cooperation with Communists and the creation of a dictatorship of the proletariat.

In view of marginal support for the ISPL and the PPS move into opposition against the *sanacja* government, in June 1928 Drobner returned to the PPS. Elected to the PPS Supreme Council in 1928, with Adam Próchnik (among others) he worked out the so-called yellow program (from the color of the cover) of the PPS left in 1935. He also took part in the activities of the Society of the Workers' University, and from December 1933 he was a member of the Kraków City Council. In January 1936 he visited the USSR, and after his return he delivered a number of lectures and published an apologetic booklet, *Co widziałem w Rosji Sowieckiej?* (What did I see in Soviet Russia?). In May 1936 Drobner called for a united front with the Communists, which led to his expulsion from the PPS. In 1937 he edited the Kraków version of the daily *Dziennik Popularny*. Arrested several times for brief periods of time, he had more than twenty trials for his speeches during strikes and rallies.

After the outbreak of World War II Drobner went to Lwów. Arrested by the NKVD on 28 June 1940, in October 1941 he was released and went to Cheboksary (Chuvash ASSR), where his family was deported. In 1942 he resumed contact with **Wanda Wasilewska**, and from May 1943 he was active in the Soviet-sponsored Union of Polish Patriots [ZPP]. At the First ZPP Congress in Moscow on 9–10 June 1943 Drobner was elected to its Main Board. He also became acting head of the ZPP Social Welfare Department and inspector of supplies for the Poles at the Soviet Commissariat of Trade. In July 1944 he joined the Home National Council (Krajowa Rada Narodowa [HNC]) delegation to the territories liberated from the Germans, and in September 1944 he became an HNC deputy and then head of the Department of Labor, Social Welfare, and Health of the Polish Committee of National Liberation. On its behalf Drobner co-organized the Communist authorities on the territories liberated from the Germans and became the first mayor of Wrocław (Breslau) from March to June 1945. At a PPS conference in Lublin (10–11 September 1944), later called the Twenty-fifth Congress, in the absence of most party leaders independent from Communists, Drobner was elected chairman of the PPS Provisional Supreme Council. From July 1945 to December 1947 he was deputy chairman of the new PPS. He supported a merger of the PPS with the (Communist) Polish Workers' Party and was a delegate to the Unification Congress in Warsaw in December 1948, at which the Polish United Workers' Party (Polska Zjednoczona Partia Robotnicza [PUWP]) was founded. For twenty years Drobner belonged to the PUWP, accepting both its Stalinist line and the reforms of the **Władysław Gomułka** period. From late October 1956 to mid-February 1957 he was the first secretary of the PUWP Provincial Committee in Kraków. Among other works, Drobner authored the memoirs *Bezustanna walka* (Never-ending struggle, 2 vols.; 1962–67). (WD)

Sources: Mołdawa; *Słownik Biograficzny Działaczy Polskiego Ruchu Robotniczego* (Warsaw, 1978); Henryk Jabłoński, *Polityka PPS 1917–1919* (Warsaw, 1958); Józef Kowalski, *Trudne lata* (Warsaw, 1966); Krystyna Kersten, *Narodziny systemu władzy: Polska 1943–1948* (Poznań, 1990); Andrzej Albert [Wojciech Roszkowski], *Najnowsza historia Polski 1914–1993*, vol. 2 (Warsaw, 1995).

DRTINA Prokop (13 April 1900, Prague–16 October 1980, Prague), Czech lawyer and politician, son of the philosopher František Drtina. After receiving a law degree from Charles University in Prague, Drtina worked as a clerk in a Czech financial prosecutor's office. In the 1920s he was active in the student movement; between 1925 and 1928 he presided over the student faction of the National Labor Party (Narodná Strana Práce). In 1928 he entered the Socialist-Nationalist Party, and a year later he began to work in the office of the president of the republic. He linked his political career with **Edvard Beneš**, and soon after Beneš had assumed the presidency, Drtina became his personal secretary. In the spring of 1939, Drtina, along with other Beneš co-workers, founded a conspiratorial organization, the Political Center (Politické Ústředi). When it had been exposed, he emigrated in the fall of 1939 and worked with Beneš, who was living in London. Among other things, under the alias of "Pavel Svaty," he spoke as political commentator in the Czech broadcasts of London Radio.

Between 1944 and 1945 Drtina was a member of the government delegation to the regained territories, and after the end of the war he was an MP, elected as one of the Socialist nationalist leaders; from November 1945 he was minister of justice. He remained at this post until the coup of February 1948, fighting for law abidance and the independence of the courts. Drtina was one of the most fervent defendants of democracy and the rule of law, opposing the Communists and their totalitarian methods. In the postwar period he was also an ardent supporter of the massive deportations of Germans from Czech territories. On 20 February 1948, along with eleven ministers from the democratic parties, Drtina resigned his post, and President Beneš accepted his resignation under pressure from the Communists. After the establishment of the Communist government Drtina had a nervous breakdown and attempted to commit suicide. From March 1948 he was under arrest, but not until December 1953 was he tried and sentenced to fifteen years' imprisonment. In 1960 he was released under an amnesty, and in 1969 he was fully vindicated, but at the time of "normalization," at the beginning of the 1970s, the vindication was suspended. At the end of his life Drtina used his authority to support Charter 77. He wrote *Československo—Můj osud: Kniha života českého demokrata 20. stoleti* (Czechoslovakia—My assessment: A book of the life of a Czech democrat of the twentieth century, 4 vols.; Toronto, 1982; Prague, 1991–92). (PU)

Sources: *ČBS*; Josef Korbel, *The Communist Subversion of Czechoslovakia, 1948–1960* (Princeton, 1959); Karel Kaplan, *The Short March: The Communist Takeover in Czechoslovakia, 1945–1948* (London, 1981); *Kdo byl kdo v našich dějinách ve 20. stoleti*, vol. 1 (Prague, 1998).

DUBČEK Alexander (27 November 1921, Uhrovec, Topolčany district–7 November 1992, Bratislava), Czechoslovak Communist leader. Dubček's parents got married as emigrants in Chicago. Both belonged to Slovak Socialist groups. In 1921 they returned to Czechoslovakia, and in 1925 they decided to go to the USSR, where they were members of the Czechoslovak cooperative Interhelpo in Pishpek (Bishkek), Kyrgyzstan, and (from 1935) in Gorki (Nizhny Novgorod). In 1938 they returned to Slovakia, where Dubček joined the Slovak Communist Party in 1939. He worked as a metalworker in the Škoda factory in Dubnica nad Váhom. Along with his brother, he took part in the Slovak National Uprising of 1944, in which his brother was killed and Dubček was wounded. After the war he worked in a yeast factory in Trenčín, and in 1949 he became a party functionary. From 1949 to 1951 he was first secretary of the District Committee of the Communist Party of Slovakia (CPS) in Trenčín, and then he worked in the CPS Central Committee (CC) in Bratislava. From 1952 he was first secretary of the CPS Provincial Committee in Banská Bystrica, and in 1953–55 he was a deputy member of the CPS CC. In 1955–58 he studied at the Higher Party School of the CC of the Soviet party in Moscow. In May 1958 he became a member of the CPS CC and soon also secretary of the CPS District Committee in Bratislava. From 1960 he worked in Prague as secretary of the CPS CC and was a member of the Presidium of the CC of the Czechoslovak Communist Party (CPC), responsible for metallurgy, the engineering and chemical industry, and construction, lobbying for funds to develop these lines in Slovakia.

At the Twelfth CPC Congress in December 1962 Dubček became a member of the so-called Kolder Commission, which investigated Stalinist repression against CPC members. This work changed his views on the role of the party in the society and convinced him of the necessity for reforms and for compensation for the harm done in the Stalinist period. Dubček appealed for the rehabilitation of many Slovak Communists, including **Gustav Husak**. He gained popularity by his public criticism of the Stalinist *apparatchik* **Karel Bacilek**. In April 1962 Dubček was elected first secretary of the CPS CC and member of the CPC CC Presidium. He supported the program of economic reforms designed by **Ota Šik**, and he demanded that Stalinist functionaries be made responsible for the repressions. It was against this background that Dubček entered into conflict with the first secretary of the CPC CC and president, **Antonín Novotný**. The conflict was aggravated by their differing views on the place of Slovakia in the Czechoslovak state system, as Dubček thought that the Slovaks were economically and culturally discriminated against in the unitary state.

The conflict reached a climax in the fall of 1967. At the CPC CC Plenum on 30 October 1967 Dubček demanded a decisive change in the way the Communist Party ruled the country and self-criticism by those responsible for Stalinist crimes. On 4 January 1968 he was elected first secretary of the CPC CC. He began to reform the party apparatus, aiming at a limitation of its role. He supported economic reforms aiming at a combination of planning and market mechanisms. He also developed a new party, the Program of Action. He strove to transform Czechoslovakia into a federal state. Despite protests by other Communist leaders from the Soviet bloc, he was determined to continue with these changes. During the Prague Spring of 1968 Dubček won enormous popularity and used it to promote reforms. His efforts to create "socialism with a human face" also won him great prestige abroad. He thought that as long as Czechoslovakia fulfilled its international obligations, it had the right to decide about its internal affairs. He rehabilitated all victims of Stalinism, agreed to eliminate censorship, and gave up control of cultural institutions. In June 1968 he supported the idea of an extraordinary congress of the CPC, which was to bring a substantial change in the mechanisms of power. During his meetings with Soviet leaders he defended his program and argued that each Communist Party had the right to determine its own lines of development and socioeconomic model. At the same time he declared his readiness to defend the Socialist system within the Warsaw Pact.

After the Warsaw Pact invasion, on 21 August 1968 Dubček condemned the military action, but he appealed to the society and to the army not to resist by force. On 22 August 1968, along with other members of the top leadership, he was interned by a Soviet special unit and transported to Moscow. On 26 August he signed the so-called Moscow Protocol, which sanctioned the Warsaw Pact intervention. From the text Dubček managed to remove only a clause reading that the Czechoslovak reforms were a counterrevolution. He also gained consent to make Czechoslovakia a federal state in September 1968. He still hoped that some of the reforms could be introduced in an evolutionary way. Soon, however, his hopes proved to be illusionary. He did not support the secret Fourteenth CPC Congress in Prague's Vysočany quarter. He appealed to the society to cooperate with the occupation authorities, thinking that diffusing the social mood would accelerate the withdrawal of foreign troops. Increasingly isolated in the party leadership, in April 1969 Dubček resigned from the position of first secretary, and three months later he was recalled from the CPC CC Presidium. From April to September 1969 he was speaker of the Federal Assembly. In this capacity he signed Decree No. 99, which allowed the authorities to legitimately use force against those recognized as "anti-Socialist elements." In December 1969 he became ambassador to Turkey. Realizing that the new party leadership wanted to force him to emigrate, after a few months Dubček returned to Czechoslovakia. Dismissed from the CPC CC, in December 1970 he took a job as a mechanic in the West Slovak State Forest Administration in Krasňany, near Bratislava. In 1981 he retired. At all times he was kept under strict police surveillance.

From November 1989 Dubček was active in the Slovak movement Public against Violence. His appearance at the side of **Václav Havel** during a demonstration on 26 November 1989 symbolized an alliance of the

Czech and Slovak opposition. He became speaker of the Federal Assembly, which on 29 December 1989 elected Havel as president. Dubček supported the continuation of the Czechoslovak federation, and from March 1992 he presided over the Social Democratic Party in Slovakia. On 1 September 1992 he was severely wounded in a car crash and soon died as a result. His funeral in Bratislava was a mass demonstration of support for the joint state, which nonetheless soon split. Dubček authored the memoirs *Nádej zomiera posledná* (Hope dies last; 1993). (AGr)

Sources: *ČBS*; *Kdo byl kdo v našich dějinách ve 20. stoleti* (Prague, 1994); Gordon H. Skilling, *Czechoslovakia's Interrupted Revolution* (Princeton, 1976); Vladimir V. Kusin, *From Dubcek to Charter 77: A Study of "Normalization" in Czechoslovakia 1968–1978* (New York, 1978); *Zatajony dokument: Raport Komisji KC KPcz o procesach politycznych i rehabilitacji w Czechosłowacji w latach 1949–1968* (Warsaw, 1985); Zdeněk Mlynař, *Nightfrost in Prague* (New York, 1983); Dušan Kováč, *Dejiny Slovenska* (Prague, 1998); Petr Pithart, *Osmašedesáty* (Prague, 1990); *Slovenska otázka v dejinách Česko-Slovenska (1945–1992)* (Bratislava, 1994).

DUBOIS Stanisław (9 January 1901, Warsaw–21 August 1942, Oświęcim), Polish Socialist activist. Dubois graduated from a high school in Warsaw. From 1914 he was active in scouting, and in 1916 he established a Socialist self-education circle. From September 1918 he belonged to the Polish Socialist Party (Polska Partia Socjalistyczna [PPS]), and in November 1918 he took part in the disarmament of German soldiers in Warsaw. In 1919 he participated in the First Silesian Uprising; in 1920, in the Polish-Soviet war (for which he received the Cross of the Brave); and in 1921, in the Third Silesian Uprising. In 1921–39 he was secretary of the editorial board of the periodical *Robotnik*. When in December 1922 the Society of the Workers' University (Towarzystwo Uniwersytetu Robotniczego [TUR]) was established, he joined its Central Youth Department. At the congress of the TUR cells in Warsaw in early February 1926, when these cells took the name TUR Youth Organization (Organizacja Młodzieży TUR [OMTUR]), Dubois was elected to its Central Committee. From 1926 he was chairman of the Supreme Council of Red Scouting. In the elections of 1928 he won a seat on behalf of the PPS, becoming one of the youngest MPs in the assembly. He advocated an intensification of opposition activities against the *sanacja* government. He took part in the formation of the centrist and leftist opposition bloc, the Centrolew, and in its Kraków congress on 29 April 1930. In September 1930 Dubois was arrested, along with other Centrolew leaders, and detained in the Brest Fortress Prison. Released on bail, he returned to political activity. At the Twenty-second PPS Congress in Kraków in May 1931, Dubois was elected to the PPS Supreme Council. In the Brest trial of January 1932, he was sentenced to three years in prison. Released in September 1934, at a meeting of the PPS Supreme Council in July 1935 he spoke in favor of a united front of the left, and in August 1935 he co-organized the first joint action of the OMTUR, the Communist Union of Polish Youth, and the Tzukunft.

After the German invasion of Poland in September 1939, Dubois volunteered for the Polish Army and served in an engineering battalion. After the lost campaign, in October 1939 he returned to Warsaw and joined the leftist conspiracy. He organized a group of left-wing Socialists, and from April 1940 he edited an underground periodical, *Barykada Wolności*. The left-wing group became the nucleus of the Polish Socialists' organization, which later adopted the name of the Workers' Party of Polish Socialists (Robotnicza Partia Polskich Socjalistów). In October 1940 Dubois was arrested by the Gestapo and detained in the Pawiak Prison in Warsaw, from where he was moved to the concentration camp in Auschwitz. In the camp he was one of the organizers of resistance. He died in the camp. In 1968 his *Artykuły i przemówienia* (Articles and speeches) was published. (WD)

Sources: *PSB*, vol. 5; *Słownik biograficzny działaczy polskiego ruchu robotniczego* (Warsaw, 1978); I. Rydłowski, *Żołnierze lat wojny i okupacji* (Warsaw, 1971).

DUCA Ion Gheorghe (26 December 1879, Bucharest–29 December 1933, Sinaia), Romanian lawyer and politician. Duca studied law in Paris (1897–1900). In 1902 he obtained a Ph.D. in trade law at the Sorbonne. He was an active member of the Romanian Union in Paris (1898–1902); a journalist of the leading Romanian newspaper, *Universul*, from 1902; and a contributor to the magazine *Viaţa românească* between 1906 and 1916. From 1903 he practiced in his profession. He was a member of the National Liberal Party (NLP). In 1907 he was elected to parliament, in which he sat until his death. In 1914–16 he was minister of education. During World War I he worked closely with **Ion I. C. Brătianu**, whom he represented in the negotiations with the Allies in August 1916. As a result of these talks Romania came out against the Central Powers. Duca accompanied King **Ferdinand** and Brătianu into exile in Iaşi (December 1916–December 1918). During the war he was particularly devoted to the idea of unity of the Romanian nation and represented the concept in London, Paris, and Washington.

Duca was a member of the Romanian delegation to the Paris Peace Conference in 1919. He favored the Little Entente, advocated reaching an alliance with Poland in 1921, and supported the establishment of close relations with France. Between March 1922 and March 1926 he was minister of foreign affairs. He was also one of the authors of the constitution of March 1923 and of the Dynastic Act of 4 January 1926, by which Prince Charles was excluded from the succession. Later, this led to tensions between **Charles II** and the NLP and finally brought about a split in the party. From January 1930 Duca was the president of the NLP, and from 14 November 1933, prime minister. He outlawed the Iron Guard under an act of 10 December 1933. On 29 December 1933, after a meeting with the king in Sinaia, Duca was shot dead by a fighting squad of the Iron Guard at the railway station. He was the author of several works, including *Politica noastră externă* (Our foreign policy; 1913); *Raporturile unui ministru tânăr cu regele Carol I* (Relations of certain young statesman with King Carol I; 1933); and *Portrete şi amintiri* (Portraits and memoirs; 1935). In 1991–92 his *Memorii* (Memoirs) were published. (FA/TD)

Sources: *Biographisches Lexikon*, vol. 1; Larry L. Watts, *Romanian Cassandra: Ion Antonescu and the Struggle for Reform, 1916–1941* (Boulder, Colo., 1993); Tadeusz Dubicki and Krzysztof Dach, *Żelazny Legion Michała Archanioła* (Warsaw, 1996); Stephen Fischer-Galati, *Twentieth Century Romania* (New York, 1991); Nicolae Iorga, *Oameni care au fost*, Bucureşti 1936, vol. III; Paul Ştefanescu, *Asasinatele politice în istoria României* (Bucharest, 2000).

DUDÁS József (22 September 1912, Marosvásárhely–19 January 1957, Budapest), one of the leaders of the 1956 revolution in Hungary. An engineer by education, at the end of the 1920s Dudás joined a Communist cell in his hometown in Transylvania. In 1933 he was arrested by the Romanian authorities and spent five and a half years in prison. In August 1940, when Northern Transylvania was returned to Hungary, Dudás moved to Budapest, where he joined the local illegal Communist organization. He was a liaison among various groups of the opposition, and in September 1944 he belonged to an unofficial delegation to Moscow that discussed the conditions for armistice. Dudás co-founded the Hungarian National Insurgent and Liberation Committee, which aimed at the liberation of Hungary in cooperation with the Red Army. In 1945 he joined the Independent Smallholders' Party (ISP), and in 1946 he was elected to the Budapest City Council on its behalf. During a repression of ISP members he was arrested. In 1948 he was released but soon detained again and handed over to the Romanian security authorities, which, however, failed to prove that he had been a police informer before World War II. In 1954 Dudás was handed back to the Hungarian Communist authorities, which freed him. In August 1956 the Hungarian Foreign Ministry found his imprisonment in 1948–54 groundless.

After the outbreak of the revolution, on 29 October 1956, in the headquarters of the central press organ of the Communist party, *Szabad Nép*, Dudás founded the Hungarian National Committee, which demanded a coalition government, a multiparty political system, and the country's neutrality. He also founded the daily *Magyar Függetlenség*, which refused to recognize the **Imre Nagy** government. Dudás attracted about four hundred insurgents and tried to make the Soviets recognize him and not Nagy as the leader of the Hungarian authorities. He failed to make **Attila Szigethy** form a government alternative to that of Nagy. On 3 November Dudás and his subordinates entered into a conflict, which resulted in his dismissal from command and his brief arrest, based on false information. The next day, he was wounded and taken to hospital. Despite warnings, he did not leave the country, considering himself the leader of the insurrection. He trusted János Kádár and the party leadership, which lured him, on the pretext of negotiations, into the parliament building, where he was arrested by Soviet officers on 21 November. On 14 January 1957 the Supreme Military Court sentenced him to death without the right to a pardon for leading a plot against "the power of the people." A few days later he was executed. (JT)

Sources: *Magyar Nagylexikon*, vol. 6 (Budapest, 1998); *A magyar forradalom és szabadságharc enciklopédiája*, CD-ROM (Budapest, 1999); *Új Magyar Életrajzi Lexikon*, vol. 2 (Budapest, 2001); Ferenc A. Vali, *Rift and Revolt in Hungary* (Cambridge, Mass., 1961); Paul E. Zinner, *Revolution in Hungary* (New York, 1962).

DULA Matúš (28 June 1846, Blatnica–13 June 1926, Ružomberok), Slovak lawyer and politician. Born into a Protestant peasant family, Dula studied law in Vienna and Pest. In 1871 he opened his own barrister's office in Turčiansky Svätý Martin. In 1877–1901 and 1907–14 he served as vice-president, and, in 1914–18 as president, of the Slovak National Party (Slovenská Národná Strana [SNP]). He was the defense attorney in the trials of many national activists in Hungary. In 1900 he was sentenced to six months' imprisonment for organizing an ostentatious welcome for Ambro Pietor, a well-known national activist who was returning from prison. In 1906 he defended Reverend **Andrej Hlinka** and **Vavro Šrobár** in the courts in Ružomberk. In May 1914 he initiated the organization of the nonparty Slovak National Council (Slovenská Národná Rada [SNC]). The SNC followed the tradition of the main Slovak political organ from the period between 1848 and 1849. The formation of the SNC was interrupted by the outbreak of war.

In August 1914 Dula signed a declaration in which the SNP suspended its political activities. In September 1918 the leadership of the party entrusted him with the task of recreating the SNC. The SNC was formed mainly of SNP activists, and Dula became its president. The other main political currents—the Ludaks of Reverend Hlinka and the Social Democrats—recognized the authority of Dula and the SNP. In a forum of the Hungarian parliament on 19 October 1918, on behalf of the SNC, MP **Ferdinand Juriga** demanded the right of self-determination for the Slovak nation. After meeting with **Mihaly Károlyi**, the leader of the Hungarian opposition, at the beginning of October 1918, Dula talked in Prague about uniting the Czechs and Slovaks. Next, he summoned Slovak activists to Turčiansky Svätý Martin, where they finally established the SNC and formulated a program after the defeat of Austria-Hungary. On 30 October 1918 Dula co-created and signed, on behalf of the SNC, the so-called Martin Declaration, which proclaimed that the Slovak nation was a part of a "single Czechoslovak nation" and had the right to self-determination. In July 1919 Dula became vice-president of the Revolutionary National Assembly in Prague. In 1920 he was elected to the senate from the lists of the Slovak National Agrarian Party (Slovenská a rol'nícka národná strana), and after the party's breakup he switched over to the Czechoslovak National Democracy (Československá Národní Demokracie). Dula was one of the presidents of the Slovak Matrix (Matica Slovenská), reactivated in 1919. He published (among other works) *Stařešina národních pracovniků slovenských* (The elders of the Slovak national activists; 1926). (MG)

Sources: *Biographisches Lexikon*, vol. 1; *SBS*; *Reprezentačný biografický lexikón Slovenska* (Martin, 1999); *Politická elita meziválečného Československa 1918–1938: Kdo byl Kdo* (Prague, 1998); M. Slávik, ed., *Slovenský národovci do 30. októbra 1918* (Trenčín, 1945); *Muži deklarácie* (Martin, 1991); M. Peknik, ed., *Slovenske národné rady* (Bratislava, 1998).

DULGHERU Mişu [originally Dulbergher] (16 January 1909, Tecuci–?), Romanian functionary of the Communist political police. From the late 1920s Dulgheru worked as a bank officer and owner of an underwear shop in Galaţi. In 1940 he and his wife were employed in the Soviet legation in Bucharest; thus after the German invasion of the USSR, Dulgheru was suspected of contacts with Soviet intelligence and was detained in the Tîrgu-Jiu camp, where he met the top Romanian Communist leaders. Released after the coup of August 1944, he joined the Patriotic Guard of **Emil Bodnaraş** and then the Communist-controlled political police. From March 1945 he was an inspector, and after the establishment of the General Directorate of National Security (Direcţia Generală Securităţi Poporului [DGSS]) in August 1948, he was head of the DGSS Investigation Directorate. Dulgheru was responsible for bestialities during the interrogation of prisoners. He personally interrogated many key political prisoners, including **Lucreţiu Patraşcanu**. Since he failed to prove or did not want to prove Patraşcanu's guilt, in November 1952 Dulgheru himself was arrested. He underwent the "conveyer" and torture for about two years. He was accused of espionage and involvement in a Zionist plot, and then he was released without formal accusation. In the fall of 1967 Dulgheru testified before the party commission investigating the Patraşcanu case, pointing to the key role of **Alexandru Draghici** in this affair; the testimony was part of **Nicolae Ceauşescu**'s efforts aiming at the dismissal of Draghici. (WR)

Sources: Dennis Deletant, *Communist Terror in Romania: Gheorghiu-Dej and the Police State, 1948–1965* (New York, 1999); Robert Levy, *Ana Pauker: The Rise and Fall of a Jewish Communist* (Berkeley, 2000).

DURAY Miklós (18 July 1945, Lučenec [Losonc]), Hungarian politician from Slovakia. Duray graduated in geology and in 1977 he received a Ph.D. in geochemistry from the University of Bratislava. Initially he worked in the Institute of Pedology and the Institute of Geology of the Slovak Academy of Sciences; in 1977–90 he worked in a construction company. From 1964 he organized Hungarian youth clubs, and in 1968–69 he presided over the Hungarian Youth Association and was a member of the Presidium of the Democratic Community of Hungarians in Slovakia. In 1978 Duray founded the illegal Committee for the Defense of Hungarian Minority Rights in Czechoslovakia, which strove to eliminate the national and political discrimination of Hungarians. He signed Charter 77, and in numerous publications, both at home in the uncensored press and abroad, he criticized the nationality policy of Communist Czechoslovakia. Among other works, he published *Szlovákiai jelentés* (A report from Slovakia; 1982); *Kutyaszorító I* (Dead end I; 1983); *Kutyaszorító II* (Dead end II; 1989); *Tegnap alighanem bolondgombát etettek velünk* (Yesterday they probably fed us poisonous nushrooms; 1983); and *Kettős elnyomásban* (Under double pressure; 1989). From 1979 Duray was under constant surveillance by the security service. Arrested in 1982 and tried in 1983, he was released under international pressure. In 1984 he was arrested again, but after a year he was released owing to an amnesty.

In 1988 Duray was allowed to go on a year-long scholarship to the University of Indiana. After the Velvet Revolution, in December 1989 he was a candidate for minister of national minorities in the new Czechoslovak government, but the idea was opposed by the deputy prime minister and soon-to-be prime minister, **Marian Čalfa**. In February 1990 Duray co-founded the Coexistence movement (Együttélés-Spolužitie-Wspólnota-Soužití [ESWS]), aimed at a democratic state of law, a market economy, and equal rights for national minorities. From 1990 to 1998 he was its chairman. From January 1990 until the breakup of Czechoslovakia at the end of 1992, he was an MP to the Federal Assembly. In 1993 he worked out the idea that the Hungarians were not a national minority but "co-creators" of the Slovak state. The ESWS adopted this idea as the foundation of its program. Before the elections of 1994, the Hungarian parties from Slovakia founded the Party of the Hungarian Coalition (Magyar Koalíció Pártja/Strana Maďarskej Koalicie [MKP]). Duray was its chairman and (from 1999) deputy chairman. In 1994 he was elected MP on behalf of the MKP, and in 1994–96 he was the head of its parliamentary club. Elected to the parliament in 1998 and 2002, he was the co-author of an agreement with the Slovak Democratic Coalition that provided for the participation of representatives of the Hungarian minority in both governments of **Mikulaš Dzurinda**. (JT)

Sources: *Magyar Nagylexikon*, vol. 6 (Budapest, 1998); *Ki kicsoda 2000* (Budapest, 2001); *Slovensko 1996: Súhrnná správa o stave spoločnosti* (Bratislava, 1997); *Slovensko 1997: Súhrnná správa o stave spoločnosti* (Bratislava, 1998); *Slovensko 1998–1999: Súhrnná správa o stave spoločnosti* (Bratislava, 1999); *Slovensko 2000: Súhrnná správa o stave spoločnosti* (Bratislava, 2000); www.nevyberajusmev.sk/lidri-smk-duray.php.

ĎURČANSKÝ Ferdinand (18 December 1906, Rajec–15 March 1974, Munich), Slovak lawyer, politician, and journalist. Ďurčanský came from a landowner's family. After studying law in Bratislava, Paris, and The Hague, in 1933 he started working as an international law specialist at the Law Department of Komensky University in Bratislava. From 1936 he also worked as a publicist, writing for *Nástup*, a journal run and edited by his brother, Ján. Politically aligned with the Populists (Ludaks) of Reverend **Andrej Hlinka**, he was a member of the radical anti-Czechoslovak wing of Hlinka's Slovak People's Party (HSL'S). In June 1938 he was one of the main authors of a proposal for Slovak autonomy, which soon was adopted by parliament. On 6 October 1938 in Zlín Ďurčanský took part in a proclamation of autonomy. In the government of autonomous Slovakia, he initially served as minister of justice and minister of health and welfare. Then he was minister of transport and social work. From 1938 he maintained contacts with the Germans. He was an avowed supporter of close cooperation between Slovakia and Nazi Germany, which, he believed, would bring independence to the Slovaks. From December 1938 he sat in the Slovak parliament.

On 13 March 1939, along with Reverend **Jozef Tiso**, Ďurčanský took part in negotiations with Hitler in which the Nazi leader presented an ultimatum: either Slovakia announced its independence or Hungarian troops would invade the country. The next day the Slovak parliament proclaimed independence, and Ďurčanský became minister of foreign affairs. From 2 September 1939 he was also minister of interior and deputy prime minister. As a member of the government, he belonged to the radicals and substantially contributed to the suppression of civil rights in Slovakia. He was also much involved in the persecution of Jews. On 20 July 1940 he was dismissed from the government on the personal request of Hitler, who disapproved of his attempts to pursue a policy that was getting more independent from Germany. In the following years Ďurčanský, as a representative of the conservative wing of the HSL'S, was in opposition to **Vojtech Tuka** and **Alexander Mach**. He resumed his academic activities. Between 1940 and 1945 he was professor of international law at Bratislava University. In 1944 he organized propaganda against the Slovak National Uprising, and in January 1945 he initiated a congress of the youth wing of the HSL'S. Before the invasion of Slovakia by the Red Army in the spring of 1945 Ďurčanský fled to Austria and then to Italy. From 1947 to 1952 he hid in Argentina. In 1952 he arrived in the Federal Republic of Germany, where he was a spokesman for Ludak émigrés. He continued to criticize the Czechoslovak state and propagated the idea of an independent Slovakia. In 1947, as a war criminal, he was sentenced to death in absentia by the Czechoslovak National Court. (PU)

Sources: *ČBS*; *Kdo byl kdo v našich dějinach ve 20. stoleti*, vol. 1 (Prague, 1998); *Politická elita meziválečného Československa 1918–1938: Kdo byl kdo za prvni republiky* (Prague, 1998); Joseph A. Mikus, *Slovakia: A Political History, 1918–1950* (Milwaukee, 1963); Jerzy Tomaszewski, *Czechosłowacja* (Warsaw, 1997); *Ferdinand Ďurčanský (1906–1974)* (Martin, 1998); Dušan Kováč, *Dejiny Slovenska* (Bratislava, 1998).

DURCOVICI Anton (17 May 1888, Bad Deutsch Altenburg–10 December 1951, Sighet), Roman Catholic bishop of Iaşi. Durcovici was born into an Austrian family. After his father's death in 1895, the extremely impoverished family moved to Iaşi and in 1898 to Bucharest, where Durcovici attended high school. In 1906 he graduated from the Sfîntîi Iosif Theological Seminary, and then he studied in Rome, receiving a Ph.D. in philosophy and theology. In 1911 he was ordained in Rome, and after his return to Romania he worked as a catechist in a high school in Bucharest and administrator of the Tulcea parish. After the outbreak of World War I, Durcovici was interned owing to his Austrian origins (his brother served in the Austro-Hungarian Army) but was released in 1915. In 1917 he was entrusted with the administration of the Tîrgovişte and Giurgiu parishes. In 1924 he became rector of the theological seminary and then of the newly founded Catholic Theological Academy, where he taught philosophy, theology, and canon law. From 1935 he was chief vicar of the Bucharest archdiocese and minister to its intellectual community. He also founded a theological research periodical, *Farul Nou*.

On 30 October 1947 Durcovici was appointed bishop of Iaşi. He also presided over the Church Tribunal. On 3 August 1948 the Communist authorities passed a law on the nationalization of all schools and other education institutions, hospitals, monasteries, and other institutions of the Roman Catholic Church. Priests were threatened with losing their wages and state subsidies if they failed to recognize the new law. After the imprisonment of most bishops, the authorities started arresting priests. Durcovici encouraged the clergy to keep the faith and to decline state subsidies. Along with Bishop **Aron Marton**, he drafted a church constitution maintaining the church's loyalty to the Holy See. On 26 June 1949 functionaries of the political police, Securitate, surrounded Durcovici's residence. He tried to escape the siege but was captured by the security officers. Placed in a Bucharest prison, he was then moved to the Jilava and Sighet prisons. He was accused of spying for the Vatican and the United States, insulted, and tortured. He died of hunger and from horrible torture. Securitate officers later showed a photo of him after he had been tortured to terrorize other prisoners. It showed a starving figure covered with wounds and dirt. Durcovici was buried in the local village cemetery, but in order to make identification of the grave impossible, it was soon leveled and ploughed as a regular field. (ASK)

Sources: Florian Műlker, *Viaţa episcopului de Iaşi Anton Durcovici martir* (Iaşi, 1993); Denis Deletant, *Communist Terror in Romania: Gheorghiu-Dej and the Police State, 1948–1965* (New York, 1999); Robert Royal, *Catholic Martyrs of the Twentieth Century* (New York, 2000).

DVARCHANIN Ihnat (8 June 1895, Pohiry, near Slonim–8 December 1937, the White Sea–Baltic Canal), Belorussian national activist, poet, educator, and theoretician of literature. Between 1912 and 1915 Dvarchanin worked as a teacher in the village of Khmialnitsa, near Slonim. In May 1915 he was mobilized into the tsarist army. From the autumn of 1916 he fought on the western front. In June 1917 he joined the Belorussian Socialist Hromada in Minsk. Then he was a co-organizer of the All-Belorussian Congress. He also worked in the Belorussian Central Military Council. In April 1918 he became the secretary of the department of education of the Belorussian National Commissioners in Moscow. In July 1918 he spoke at a conference of the Belorussian schools and urged that the teaching of the Belorussian language be expanded. He also advocated the development of the national literature and historical research. After completing a gymnasium in Wilno (Vilnius) (as an extern), Dvarchanin studied in the history and philology department of Prague University, where in 1925 he received a Ph.D. in philosophy. He also worked in various organizations of Belorussian students and landowners in Prague.

After his return to Wilno, Dvarchanin lectured at a Belorussian gymnasium, directed Belorussian publishing houses, and (from 1926) belonged to the Belorussian Peasant and Worker Hromada, led by **Bronislau Taraszkiewicz**. He published *Chrestomathy of the New Belorussian Literature (from 1905)*. After the delegalization of the Hromada by the Polish authorities in 1927, Dvarchanin continued to direct its cadres. In 1928 he was elected an MP to the Polish Assembly (Sejm) and took part in the creation of the Belorussian peasant and worker parliamentary club called Zmahannie, which continued the ideals of the Hromada and was considered by the Polish authorities as anti-state. In 1926 Dvarchanin published his doctoral thesis in Polish: *Franciszek Skaryna jako kulturalny działacz i humanista na niwie białoruskiej* (Franciszek Skaryna as a cultural activist and humanist in the Belorussian field). Dvarchanin was one of the directors of the Society of the Belorussian School. In 1930 he was arrested and sentenced to eight years of prison. On 15 September 1932 he left for the USSR as the result of an exchange of political prisoners between Poland and the Soviet Union. From November 1932 he worked in the Committee of Research on Western Belorussia at the Academy of Sciences of the Belorussian Soviet Socialist Republic (BSSR) and served as director of its Linguistics Institute. On 16 August 1933 he was arrested by the security organs of the BSSR in connection with the case of the so-called Belorussian Nationalist Center. On 9 January 1934 the council of the OGPU of the BSSR sentenced him to death, but the sentence was commuted to ten years of labor camp. Dvarchanin served the sentence on the Solovets Islands, and later he labored in the construction of the White Sea–Baltic Canal. On 25 November 1937 an NKVD *troika* sentenced him to death by firing squad. He was posthumously rehabilitated on 18 April 1956. (AS/SA)

Sources: *Belarus: Entsyklapedychny daviednik* (Minsk, 1995); Aleksander Barszczewski, Aleksandra Bergman, and Jerzy Tomaszewski, *Ignacy Dworczanin, białoruski polityk i uczon/Ihnat Dvarchanin, bielaruski palityk i vuchony* (Warsaw, 1990); V. Holubiev, "Ofiary rosyjskiego caratu i bolszewizmu na Białorusi," *Narodnaia Vola*, 25 February 2000.

DYNOV Petur, pseudonym "Beinsa Duno" (12 July 1864, Hadyrcha [now Nikolaevka, near Varna]–27 December 1944, Sofia), Bulgarian theologian, philosopher, and religious reformer. Dynov's father, Konstantin Dynovski, was a well-known activist in the Bulgarian national revival, and his mother was a mystic. Dynov graduated from the American High School in Svishtov in 1887, and then he lived in the United States for seven years, where he worked as a blue-collar laborer and studied. In 1891 he graduated from Drew University in Madison, NJ, and then he studied medicine at Boston University. He acquired a sound knowledge of philosophy, astronomy, mathematics, and biology. In 1895 he returned to Bulgaria, and in 1896 he published his first work on the natural and social foundations of human life. In 1900 in Varna he founded a religious community called the White Brotherhood, guided by Divine Love, Wisdom, and Truth. From 1904 he lived in Sofia, expanding the circle of the community's followers in Bulgaria and abroad, in, among other places, Yugoslavia, France, Italy, and the United States. One of his followers was Albert Einstein. Dynov's social doctrine was based on the Gospel, but he opposed the formal hierarchical structures of Christian churches and preferred small groups of believers (*dynovists*) who met in open spaces, seeking contact with nature, in which they sought the source of existence. In his doctrine humanity was climbing from lower to higher civilizations; it had recently reached the stage of the "sixth race" and had an improved organization and clairvoyance. Dynov was respected by Tsar **Boris III**. Dynov supported the ruler's attempts to loosen Bulgaria's ties to the Third Reich and to save Bulgarian Jews from deportation and extermination. After the takeover of power, Bulgarian Communists persecuted Dynov's followers and disbanded the White Brotherhood communities. (WDj)

Sources: *Entsiklopediya Bulgariya*, vol. 1 (Sofia, 1978); Atanas Slavov, *Pytiat i vremeto: Svetska biografia na Petyr Dynov*, vol. 1 (Sofia, 1998); Milka Kraleva, *The Master Peter Dynov: His Life and Teaching* (Sofia, 2001).

DŽABIĆ Ali Fehmi (1853, Mostar–5 August 1918, Istanbul), Muslim clergyman and politician from Bosnia. Džabić learned the Koran in his hometown of Mostar. When Bosnia was occupied by Austria-Hungary, he represented Muslims in the Bosnian delegation that went to Vienna and Budapest in November 1878. From then on he continued to be one of the leaders of the Muslim minority in the Habsburg monarchy. In 1884 he became the mufti of Mostar. From 1886 he openly advocated autonomy for Bosnia and Herzegovina. Under his influence the Muslim Congress in Sarajevo in 1893 adopted his stance.

In 1899 a proposal for an autonomous Muslim Bosnia-Herzegovina was launched, and Džabić was suggested as its leader. The tendencies toward autonomy resulted not only from historical and demographic circumstances, but also from a conflict between Muslims and Christians, mostly Roman Catholics supported by the bishop of Sarajevo, Josip Stadler, and the majority of Habsburg officials. Negotiations that Džabić held with the imperial officials failed. He was more successful in his talks with representatives of the Eastern Orthodox Church; these helped to widen religious and educational freedoms for both communities. Nevertheless, for his opposition activities, the Habsburg authorities deprived Džabić of the office of mufti of Mostar. Džabić also maintained contacts with religious and lay authorities of the Ottoman Empire. When in 1902 he went on an official visit to the Porte, the Austro-Hungarian authorities refused him the right to return. He became a professor at the University of Istanbul and lectured in Arabic studies. Meanwhile, lay landowners began to represent the interests of Bosnian Muslims, and the religious conflict faded away. A year after Austria-Hungary annexed Bosnia-Herzegovina, in 1909 Emperor Francis Joseph granted Bosnian Muslims cultural autonomy. (MC)

Sources: *Biographisches Lexikon*, vol. 1; Nusret Šehić, *Autonomi pokret muslimana za vremije Austrougarske Uprave u Bosni Hercegovini* (Sarajevo, 1980); Mushin Rizvić, *Bosansko-muslimanska knjizevnost u doba preporoda (1887–1918)* (Sarajevo, 1990); H. T. Norris, *Islam in the Balkans: Religion and Society between Europe and the Arab World* (Columbia, S.C., 1993); "Ali Fehmi Dzabic (1853–1918)," www.bosanskialim.com/arhiva/alimi/ali_fehmi_dyabic.htm.

DZEMYANTSIEY Mikalay (25 May 1930, Khotlino), Belorussian Communist activist. During the Nazi occupation Dzemyantsiey fought in a guerrilla unit. After graduating from high school he worked as a teacher in the Vitebsk region. In 1958 he started working in the Communist Party apparatus in Vitebsk. In 1959 he graduated from the Belorussian Agricultural Academy, and in 1964 from the Higher Party School of the Central Committee (CC) of the Soviet party. In 1964–74 he headed the Department of Agriculture of the Vitebsk Regional Committee of the Communist Party of Belorussia (CPB), and in 1974–77 he was secretary of the CPB Regional Committee in Vitebsk. In 1977 he became head of the Department of Agriculture of the CPB CC, and in 1979, secretary and member of the Politburo of the CPB CC. In 1989–90 he was chairman of the Supreme Council of the Belorussian SSR and deputy chairman of the Supreme Council of the Soviet Union. After the Supreme Council of the Belorussian SSR announced its sovereignty on 27 July 1990,

Dzemyantsiey acted as the head of state. He was recalled for supporting the Moscow putsch of Gennady Yanayev in August 1991. From 1997 he was an MP to the National Assembly of Belarus, founded by President **Alyaksandr Lukashenka**. (EM)

Sources: *Kto jest kto w Białorusi* (Białystok, 2000); *Kto iest kto v Respublike Belarus* (Minsk, 1999); *Entsyklapiedyia historyi Belarusi*, vol. 2 (Minsk, 1994); Jan Zaprudnik, *Historical Dictionary of Belarus* (Lanham, Md., 1998); *Belarus: Entsyklapedyczny davednik* (Minsk, 1995).

DZERZHINSKY Feliks, pseudonyms "Astronom," "Domański," "Krzeczkowski," "Żebrowski" (11 September 1877, Dzierżynowo, near Oszmiana–20 June 1926, Moscow), top Bolshevik leader of Polish origin, head of the Cheka. Dzerzhinsky was born into a noble family of Edmund Dzerzhinsky and Helena née Januszewska. His father died when he was five years old. The widow with her children moved to Vilnius, where Dzerzhinsky began his education. After nine years of trouble he left school, intending to become a revolutionary. From 1894 he belonged to a Socialist circle, and in 1895 he joined the Social Democracy movement of Lithuania. In 1897 he was arrested and sent to Nolinsk, near Vyatka, from where he escaped two years later. He went to Warsaw, where he played a major role in the reorganization of the party and its transformation into the Social Democracy of the Kingdom of Poland and Lithuania (Socjal-Demokracja Królestwa Polskiego i Litwy [SDKPiL]). The aim of this internationalist party was social revolution. Dzerzhinsky already maintained that the struggle for the independence of Poland conflicted with the aims of the revolution. Arrested again in 1902 and sent to Siberia, he instigated a prisoner revolt in Irkutsk and fled, this time to Berlin. In 1904 he returned to Warsaw.

During the 1905 revolution Dzerzhinsky belonged to the chief agitators in Warsaw and Łódź. In 1906 his party became a part of the Bolshevik faction of Russian Social Democracy. He joined the CC of the Bolshevik party and personally met Vladimir Lenin. At the SDKPiL congress in Zakopane in 1906 Dzerzhinsky made the main speech and declared his support for a close union with the Bolsheviks. He even criticized the slogan of "the self-determination of nations." In 1908 he was arrested again and placed in Warsaw Citadel, where he wrote *Pamiętnik więźnia* (Prisoner's diary; 1951). He again escaped while being transported to Siberia and via Berlin arrived in Italy, where he visited Maksim Gorky in Capri. In 1912 he resumed underground activities in Warsaw, Częstochowa, and Dąbrowa Górnicza. Arrested again in 1914, he was sentenced to three years of prison and in 1916 to a further six years.

Released after the February 1917 revolution, Dzerzhinsky again became very active in the Bolshevik party. On 29 October 1917 he became a member of the Military-Revolutionary Committee, which prepared the Bolshevik coup. During the coup he was responsible for the post and telegraph, as well as for communications between the Smolny Institute and Bolshevik troops. After seizing power, he agreed with Lenin that they should establish a dictatorship rather than share the victory with other parties. On 20 December 1917 Dzerzhinsky was appointed head of the All-Russian Extraordinary Commission for Combating Counterrevolution and Sabotage (Cheka). He fanatically directed the Red Terror in the spirit of "revolutionary morality." From April 1918 Cheka *troikas* executed "enemies of the revolution" without trial. Lenin approved of the atrocities perpetrated by Dzerzhinsky and the Cheka. During negotiations with the Central Powers in Brest Litovsk Dzerzhinsky opposed Lenin's peace plans. In March 1919 he became commissar for internal affairs, and in spring 1920, a member of the Organization Bureau of the Bolshevik party's CC.

When in July 1920 the Red Army began an offensive against Poland, Dzerzhinsky headed the Polish Bureau of the party, which formed the Provisional Polish Revolutionary Committee (Tymczasowy Komitet Rewolucyjny Polski [TKRP], or Polrevkom). He also became head of the committee after it was established in Białystok as the highest organ of the Bolshevik government in Poland. After the Polish counteroffensive the Polrevkom was dissolved in August 1920.

In March 1921, still as head of the Cheka, Dzerzhinsky became commissar for transport. When in February 1922 the Cheka was renamed the State Political Administration (Gosudarstvennoe Politicheskoe Upravlenie [GPU]) he remained its head, keeping at the same time the post of commissar for internal affairs. At the Tenth Congress of the Bolshevik party Dzerzhinsky sharply criticized "worker opposition" and consorted with Stalin. In 1922 he found himself in opposition to Lenin as he supported Stalin's standpoint on terminating the autonomy of Georgian Bolsheviks. Gradually but steadily he increased his power. In September 1923 the GPU was renamed the OGPU (Obedinennoe Gosudarstvennoe Politicheskoe Upravlenie), and in February 1924 Dzerzhinsky was appointed head of the Supreme Council of the National Economy. He supported the New Economic Policy but monitored it so that it did not become a threat to party rule. In June 1924 he became a deputy member of the Politburo. Dzerzhinsky died suddenly during a debate of the CC.

For the interwar generation of Poles Dzerzhinsky was

a symbol of revolutionary terror and crime. When the Communists seized power after World War II in Poland, Dzerzhinsky became one of their heroes. His memory was honored especially in the security organs of the Polish People's Republic. A monument was built to him in Warsaw, and streets and factories were named after him, but for many Poles he remained a symbol of Bolshevik lawlessness. On 17 November 1989 his monument in Warsaw was toppled, much to the joy of the public; it presaged the recovery of sovereignty and democracy in Poland. (WR)

Sources: *MERSH*, vol. 10; Feliks Dzierżyński, *Listy do siostry Aldony* (Warsaw, 1951); Aleksander Solzhenitsyn, *Archipelag Gulag*, vols. 1–3 (Warsaw, 1990); Leonard Shapiro, *The Origin of the Communist Autocracy* (Cambridge, Mass., 1977); Edward Barszcz, *Feliks Dzierżyński: Wielki Polak i internacjonalista* (Warsaw, 1972); Michał Heller and Aleksander Niekricz, *Utopia u władzy*, vol. 1 (Warsaw, 1986); Richard Pipes, *Rewolucja rosyjska* (Warsaw, 1994).

DZHEMILEV Mustafa [also known as Adbul Dzhemil] (13 November 1943, Ayserez, Crimea), leader of the Crimean Tatars. In 1944 Dzhemilev, his family, and the whole Crimean Tatar community were deported to Uzbekistan. After graduating from high school in 1959, Dzhemilev tried to enroll in the Eastern Department of Tashkent University but was unsuccessful because Tatars were not accepted. He worked as a blue-collar laborer in Mirzachul and in an aircraft factory in Tashkent. At the end of 1961 he co-founded the illegal Union of Crimean Tatar Youth. When the organization was exposed and its leaders were arrested, he was fired from work and put under KGB surveillance. During the "second thaw," in 1962 he started to study at the Institute of Land Drainage Engineering in Tashkent, from which he was expelled in 1965 for "nationalist and anti-Soviet views" and for questioning the deportation of the Crimean Tatars. In May 1966 he was sentenced to one and a half years in prison for refusing to serve in the Soviet Army.

In November 1967 Dzhemilev entered into contact with a Moscow group of human rights defenders and with foreign correspondents; through them he informed the world about the situation of the Crimean Tatars. He took part in the human rights movement—for instance, by signing protests against the repression of dissidents and against the Warsaw Pact intervention in Czechoslovakia. In May 1969 he was one of the fourteen organizers of the Initiative Group for the Defense of Human Rights in the USSR (Initsiativnaia Gruppa Zashchity Prav Cheloveka v SSSR). Arrested again in September 1969, Dzhemilev was sentenced to three years in prison. He was arrested for the third time in June 1974, tried, and sentenced to one

year in prison for declining to serve in the Soviet Army. Three days before his term was up, he was accused of preparing documents "slandering Soviet state order" and expressing "anti-state propaganda." In protest Dzhemilev started a hunger strike, which he continued for 303 days and which brought him world renown. In April 1976 he was sentenced to two and a half years in a hard labor camp. In February 1979 he was sentenced again to one and a half years. In November 1983 he was arrested again and sentenced to three years for "organizing unrest" when he tried to bury his father in the Crimea. In April 1987, at the First All-Union Congress of the Crimean Tatar Activists, Dzhemilev was elected to the Central Initiative Group of the Crimean Tatar National Movement (Organizatsia Krymskotatarskogo Natsionalnogo Dvizheniia). In May 1989 he became chairman of its Central Council, and he was allowed to settle in the Crimea. In June 1991 he became speaker of the Crimean Tatar parliament (Medzhlis). He was reelected to this position in 1996 and 2001. In March 1998 he became a deputy to the Supreme Council of the Ukraine on behalf of the National Movement of Ukraine, and in 2003 he was reelected on behalf of the Our Ukraine (Nasha Ukraina) coalition. (BB)

Sources: *Khto ye khto v Ukraini 2000* (Kiev, 2000); Andrey Grigorenko, *A kagda my vernyomsa* (New York, 1977); *Shest dney: "Belaya kniga"* (New York, 1980); Svetlana Chervonnaya, *Krym '97: Kurultay protiv raskola* (Moscow, 1998); *Rossiiskaia Federatsiia protiv Mustafy Dzhemileva: Omskii protsess, Aprel 1976* (Kiev, 1998).

DZHUROV Dobri (5 January 1916, Vrabevo, near Troyan–17 June 2002, Sofia), Bulgarian general and Communist activist. In 1932 Dzhurov joined the Workers' Youth Union, and in 1938, the Bulgarian Communist Party (BCP). He graduated from high school in Sofia in 1937. In the same year he was sentenced to one year in prison for his revolutionary activities. During military service Dzhurov directed an illegal BCP cell in the infantry regiment in Dragoman (March 1939–December 1940). After he was released from service, he worked in the military party organization in Sofia. Arrested in 1942 and interned in the Krysto Pole concentration camp, he escaped. Sentenced to death in absentia, from June 1942 he operated in the Communist guerrilla movement; he was political commissar of the Chavdar unit from September 1942 and commander of the Chavdar Brigade from April 1944. After the uprising of 9 September 1944, he was promoted to the rank of colonel. In 1950–64 he advanced through successive ranks of general, and in 1978 he received a "marshal's star," which distinguished him among the generals, although he was not formally nominated a marshal.

After the September 1944 coup Dzhurov served in the Ministry of Interior, and from June 1945, in the army. He graduated from the Frunze Military Academy in Moscow in 1947 and from the Military Academy of the Soviet General Staff in 1959. He commanded a division and then an army. In 1956 he became deputy minister of national defense, and from March 1972 to September 1990 he was minister of national defense. In 1958–62 he was a deputy member, and from 1962 to 1990 a member, of the BCP Central Committee (CC); in 1974–77 he was a deputy member, and from 1977 to 1990 a member, of the BPC CC Politburo. In 1962–90 he was a deputy to the National Assembly. In early November 1989 Dzhurov joined the reformers in the BCP leadership who ousted **Todor Zhivkov** on 10 November 1989. After the BCP was transformed into the Bulgarian Socialist Party (BSP), Dzhurov was a member of the Presidium of the BSP Supreme Council (2 February–25 September 1990). In June 1990 he was elected deputy to the Grand National Assembly. He left it in January 1991, attacked for his Communist past, having, for instance, placed the military as guards in concentration camps. Dzhurov authored *Murgash: Spomeni* (Murgash: Memoirs; 1966); *Za voennata politika na partiyata* (On the wartime policy of the party; 1977); and *S vyarata i mech prez godinite: Izbrani proizvedeniya* (With faith and sword: Selected works; 1984). (JJ)

Sources: *Entsiklopediya Bulgariya*, vol. 2 (Sofia, 1981); Raymond Detrez, *Historical Dictionary of Bulgaria* (Lanham, Md., 1997); *Koy koy e v Bulgariya* (Sofia, 1998); Tasho Tashev, *Ministrite na Bulgariya 1879–1999: Entsiklopedichen spravochnik* (Sofia, 1999); Evgeniya Kalinova and Iskra Baeva, *Bulgarskite prekhodi 1944–1999* (Sofia, 2000); Angel Cyrakov, *Entsiklopediya na pravitelstvata na Bulgariya: Khronologiya na politicheskiya zhivot 1879–2001* (Sofia, 2001).

DZIAMIDAU Mikalay [also known as Mikolay Demidov] (10 December 1888 Gródek, near Białystok–23 May 1967, Chicago, Ill.), Belorussian colonel and social activist. Dziamidau's parents—Stanisław Kontarowski and Aleksandra née Kalinowska—were Poles, but Dziamidau chose to use the Belorussian version of the name of his stepfather, Jan Demidov. He was brought up by his grandfather, Aleksander Kalinowski, who was the brother of Konstanty Kalinowski, one of the leaders of the January insurrection of 1863 in Belorussia. Dziamidau attended high school in Łomża, and in 1905 he graduated from a teachers' seminary in Świsłocz. In 1911–12 he worked for the railways in Białystok and simultaneously studied at the Vilnius Pedagogical Institute. Mobilized by the Russian Army in 1914, he did office work and also studied at two military academies. After the October 1917 revolution he was a Bolshevik commissar in Novgorod. During the in-

spection of Russian troops at Dvinsk (German Dünaburg, now Daugavpils) Dziamidau was taken captive by the Germans. Released at the end of 1918, he left for Wilno (Vilnius), where he took part in the formation of Belorussian military formations in Lithuania.

In December 1918 Dziamidau arrived with a group of Belorussian officers in Grodno, and on behalf of the government of the Belorussian People's Republic he became the commandant of the town. There he created a few-hundred-strong garrison, as well as centers of recruitment for the Belorussian army in Grodno, Białystok, and many other towns. After the Poles entered Grodno in June 1919, Dziamidau was arrested and imprisoned in Białystok. In September 1919 he was released and incorporated into the Belorussian Military Commission, which was established with the consent of **Józef Piłsudski**. In the summer of 1920 Dziamidau joined the corps of General **Stanisław Bułak-Bałachowicz**, and, with the rank of colonel, he was in command of the seven-hundred-strong Independent Belorussian Battalion, which was formed of soldiers who came from the region of Białystok. In November 1920 he took part in the offensive on Mozyrz led by Bułak-Bałachowicz. Then he covered the retreat of these troops. Dziamidau stayed on Soviet territory until the middle of January 1921 and conducted guerilla warfare.

Forced to withdraw to Polish territory, Dziamidau was interned and imprisoned, along with his soldiers, in a camp in Radom. Released in June 1921, he got a job as a schoolmaster in Gródek, near Białystok. He organized a cooperative movement there and joined the electoral campaign of the Bloc of National Minorities. Under his influence the people of Gródek drove out the Polish teachers and demanded a school with Belorussian as the language of instruction. In November 1922 Dziamidau was accused of anti-state activities and was arrested. Released pending trial, he did not wait for his trial but managed to illegally get to Latvia. There he organized two Belorussian educational societies and worked as a teacher. After the Soviets occupied Latvia in 1940, he was put in a Moscow prison. Released in June 1941, he returned to Latvia. During the German occupation he organized and supervised Belorussian education in Latgalia. In 1943 he moved to Lida, where he organized schools and units of Belorussian self-defense.

In August 1944 Dziamidau went to Berlin and became deputy headmaster of a non-commissioned officers' school of the Belorussian National Defense. In December 1944 he tried to form Belorussian military formations in the army of General Alexander Vlasov. After the capitulation of Germany, he remained in the French occupation zone and organized aid for refugees from Belorussia. He also initiated the convention of the Council of the Belorussian Autocephalous Orthodox Church. In 1950 he went to the United States. He lived in Lansing and in Chicago, where he organized the religious and national life of the Belorussians in America. Dziamidau was a member of the board of the Belorussian-American National Council and of the board of the Belorussians of the State of Illinois. (EM)

Sources: O. Łatyszonek, "Mikołaj Demidow (1888–1967)," in *Białoruskie Zeszyty Historyczne*, vol. 1(3) (Białystok, 1995); *Biełarus* (New York), 1967, nos. 123–124; Vitaut Kipel and Zora Kipel, eds., *Byelorussian Statehood* (New York, 1988).

DZURINDA Mikulaš (4 February 1955, Spišský Štvrtok, Spišská Nová Ves district), Slovak politician. In 1979 Dzurinda graduated in the economics of transportation at the university in Žilina, where he also received a Ph.D. in 1989. From 1980 he worked in the Bratislava railway administration, and from 1988 he was the head of its management automation department. In 1991–92 he was deputy minister of transportation and telecommunications of the Slovak Republic. After the split of Czechoslovakia, from March 1994 to December 1994 Dzurinda was minister of transportation, telecommunications, and public works in the Slovak government of **Jozef Moravčik**. In 1990 he was co-founder of the Christian Democratic Movement (Krest'anskodemokratické Hnutie [KDH]), and from 1993 he was its deputy chairman for economic affairs. In November 1996 he ran for chairman of the party but lost to **Ján Čarnogurský**. In 1992 he became a deputy to the Slovak National Council, and from November 1994 to September 1998 he was a deputy to the Slovak parliament.

In 1997 Dzurinda co-founded the Slovak Democratic Coalition (Slovenská Demokratická Koalicie [SDK]), and from 4 July 1998 he was its chairman. The SDK included five parties: the KDH, the Democratic Party, the Democratic Union of Slovakia, the Social Democratic Party of Slovakia, and the Green Party of Slovakia. After the SDK victory over **Vladimír Mečiar**'s party, Dzurinda, as the leader of the largest faction of the coalition, assumed the position of prime minister on 30 October 1998. His cabinet, based on a coalition of the SDK, the post-Communists, the Party of the Hungarian Coalition, and the Party of Civic Understanding, radically changed the course of Slovak politics. Slovakia restored its credibility in the eyes of the West and made intensive efforts to accelerate its entry into NATO and the European Union. Dzurinda's government undertook economic reforms that aimed at a restructuring of the economy and an accelerated rate of growth. It also improved human rights standards and introduced direct presidential elections. All these policies resulted in the admission of Slovakia into the OECD in September 2000.

Dzurinda favored transforming the SDK into one party, which resulted in a conflict with the leaders of the parties that formed the coalition, especially the KDH chairman, Čarnogurský. In February 2000 Dzurinda left the KDH, created the Slovak Democratic and Christian Union (Slovenská Demokratická Krest'anská Únie [SDKÚ]), and took over its leadership. Despite numerous tensions in the ruling coalition, mainly with the post-Communists and the Hungarian minority, Dzurinda's government survived until the parliamentary elections of September 2002. Before these elections the four-group coalition was given little chance of success, but Dzurinda undertook effective steps to improve its ratings—for instance, by concluding alliances with a few small center and rightist parties—and he succeeded in winning 15 percent of the vote for the SDKÚ. Since his former coalition partners also did well, a new ruling coalition was created that included the KDH, the Hungarian minority, and the Alliance of the New Citizen, and Dzurinda became prime minister again on 16 October 2002. In a May 2003 referendum the entry of Slovakia into the European Union was supported by 92 percent of the Slovaks, and on 1 May 2004 Dzurinda led Slovakia into the union. (PU)

Sources: *Slovensko 1996: Súhrnná správa o stave spoločnosti* (Bratislava, 1997); *Slovensko 1997: Súhrnná správa o stave spoločnosti* (Bratislava, 1998); *Slovensko 1998–1999: Súhrnná správa o stave spoločnosti* (Bratislava, 1999); *Slovensko 2000: Súhrnná správa o stave spoločnosti* (Bratislava, 2000); www.sdkuonline.sk/predseda.php3; www.vlada.gov.sk/dzurinda/ktoje/zivotopis.php3; Bugajski.

DZYUBA Ivan (26 July 1931, Mykolayivka, Donetsk region), Ukrainian theoretician of literature, leader of the "generation of the 1960s" (*shestidesiatniki*). In 1953 Dzyuba graduated in Russian studies from the Pedagogical Institute in Donetsk, and in 1953–57 he completed doctoral studies at the Institute of Literature of the Academy of Sciences of the Ukrainian SSR. In 1957–62 he headed the review section of the monthly *Vitchyzna*, from which he was fired for "ideological errors." In 1964–65 he was a literary consultant of the Molod Publishing House. Fired for taking part in a protest against the arrests of dissidents in 1965, in 1966–69 Dzyuba was a proofreader for a biochemical periodical. In 1966 he published in the uncensored press (*samvydav*); in his major work, *Internatsyonalizm chy rusyfikatsia?* (Internationalism or Russificaton? 1968), he unmasked the Soviet Russification policy in the Ukraine. From 1969 to 1972 he was an editor of foreign literature books in the Dnipro Publishing House. Arrested and interrogated by the KGB many times, in April 1972 Dzyuba was excluded from the Association of Ukrainian Writers (AUW) and imprisoned. In May 1973 he was sentenced to five years for "anti-Soviet activities"; he submitted a self-criticism and was released in November 1973.

In 1974–82 Dzyuba was a proofreader and then a literary correspondent for the newspaper of a Kiev aircraft factory. In 1980 he was accepted back into the AUW, and from 1982 he did research. From 1988 to 1991 he presided over the Republican Association of Ukraine Specialists, and from 1991 he was editor-in-chief of the monthly *Suchasnist*, which he had earlier published in exile. Between April and October 1992 he was a member of the College for Humanitarian Policies of the Ukrainian State Duma. In November 1992 he became a member of the National Academy of Sciences of Ukraine (Nastyonalna Akademiya Nauk Ukrainy [NANU]). From October 1992 to June 1994 he was minister of culture. In 1996 he became secretary of the NANU Department of Literature, Language, and History of Art. From 1999 he was chairman of the Taras Shevchenko Committee of Ukrainian State Awards. Head of the editorial board of *Entsyklopediya suchasnoyi Ukraiiny* (Encyclopedia of contemporary Ukraine), Dzyuba authored many books on history of literature, including the following: *Zvychayna lyudyna chy mishchanyn?* (A common man or a burgher? 1959); *Hrani krystała* (Edges of crystal; 1978); *Avtohrafy vidrodzhenniya* (Autographs of revival; 1986); and *U vsyakoho svoya dola* (Everyone has his own fate; 1989). (BB)

Sources: *Encyclopedia of Ukraine*, vol. 1 (Toronto, 1984); *Ukrainska Literaturna Entsyklopediya*, vol. 2 (Kiev, 1990); *Khto ye khto v Ukraiini 2000* (Kiev, 2000); Roman Rakhmannyi, *Vohon i popil: Poryv i zlam Ivana Dzyuby* (Montreal, 1974); Bogumiła Berdychowska and Ola Hnatiuk, eds., *Bunt pokolenia: Rozmowy z intelektualistami ukraińskimi* (Lublin, 2000).

E

ECKHARDT Tibor (26 October 1888, Makó–10 September 1972, New York), Hungarian politician. Eckhardt studied in Berlin and Paris, and in 1908 he graduated in law from the University of Budapest. From 1908 he was head of the Makó district; in 1911–13 he was secretary of a province; from 1913 to 1914 he worked in the Ministry of Interior; from 1914 to 1916, as secretary of the government commissioner for Transylvania; and from 1916 to 1918, as head of a Transylvanian district. After the fall of the Habsburg monarchy, in the fall of 1918 Eckhardt formed a military unit that fought against Romanian insurgency in Transylvania but had to give up when the bulk of the Romanian Army entered this area. From June to August 1919 Eckhardt was head of the press department of the Foreign Ministry and Office of the Prime Minister (OPM) of the Szeged government; from November 1919 he headed the Foreign Policy Department of the High Command of the National Army of **Miklós Horthy**. In 1920–22 he headed the OPM Press Bureau, and from 1922 to 1926 he was an MP. In 1923 he left the ruling Unity Party. Along with **Gyula Gömbös** and **Endre Bajcsy-Zsilinszky** he founded a Fascist-like Hungarian National Independence Party (HNIP) and was one of its leaders. In the elections of 1926 he failed to win a mandate, and at the end of 1927 he left the HNIP and broke with the Fascist movement.

In 1928–30 Eckhardt was deputy chairman of the Hungarian Revisionist League, founded by **Pál Teleki**. During a trip to Western Europe and the United States he promoted the idea of a peaceful revision of the Hungarian borders fixed at Trianon in 1920. From December 1930 he belonged to the Independent Smallholders' Party (ISP), and in 1931–41 he was its MP. After the death of the ISP leader, **Gaszton Gaál**, in 1932 Eckhardt took the lead of the party. From 1933 to 1935 he was a delegate to the General Assembly of the League of Nations, where in 1934 he refuted accusations against Hungary connected with the assassination of the Yugoslav monarch, King **Alexander I**, and the French foreign minister, Louis Barthou. In the spring of 1934, in the name of the ISP, he concluded a secret cooperation agreement with Prime Minister Gömbös, but in view of electoral abuses he broke with Gömbös altogether. In the late 1930s Eckhardt was one of the leaders of the so-called defenders of the constitution, acting against dictatorial and Fascist tendencies. In foreign policy he favored a pro-British line. In 1940 he gave up the ISP leadership, and in the spring of 1941 he went to the United States to develop political contacts there. He founded the Movement for Independent Hungary there, but he failed to establish a government in exile. He also failed to improve the image of Hungary, since it finally declared war on the United States.

After World War II Eckhardt stayed in America. He lectured at Georgetown University in Washington, D.C. In 1948–54 he was a member of the Executive Committee of the Hungarian National Committee and headed its national defense commission. After numerous conflicts with key émigré politicians, in 1954 Eckhardt finally resigned from the committee. After the 1956 revolution he established First Aid for Hungary. Later he headed a Hungarian group in the American Republican Party. (JT)

Sources: *Magyar Életrajzi Lexikon*, vol. 3 (Budapest, 1981); *Magyar Nagylexikon*, vol. 6 (Budapest, 1998); *Új Magyar Életrajzi Lexikon*, vol. 2 (Budapest, 2001); Paul Nadanyi, *The "Free Hungary" Movement* (New York, 1942); John F. Montgomery, *Hungary: The Unwilling Satellite* (New York, 1947); Nicholas Horthy, *Memoirs* (Paris, 1954); Paul Ignotus, *Hungary* (London, 1972).

EDELMAN Marek (1 January 1919, Warsaw), Polish doctor and social activist of Jewish descent. From his youth Edelman was connected with the Socialist Bund. After 1939 he organized social life in the Warsaw Ghetto, strengthening the spirit of anti-German resistance; it resulted in the outbreak of an uprising on 19 April 1943. Edelman belonged to the command of the Jewish Fighting Organization (Żydowska Organizacja Bojowa [ŻOB]), and after the death of its leader, **Mordekhai Anielewicz**, he took the lead in the last stages of the fighting. After the uprising was suppressed by the Germans, Edelman was one of few survivors who managed to get out from the ruins. Along with a small ŻOB unit, he fought in the Warsaw Uprising of 1944. After the war he decided to stay in Poland, despite the Kielce pogrom of July 1946. In spite of pressure, he never joined the Communist Party. In the late 1950s he graduated in medicine from Łódź University and worked as a cardiologist in a hospital. Fired during the anti-Semitic Communist purge of 1967–68, he was also prevented from receiving his postdoctoral degree (*habilitacja*). Nevertheless, he continued to do research, the results of which were highly appreciated in Poland and abroad (for example, his study *Zawał serca: Z doświadczeń oddziału intensywnej terapii* [The infarct: From experience in an intensive care ward; 1979]).

In 1975 Edelman was a signatory of the "Letter of 101," protesting an amendment to the constitution that sanctioned the Communist Party's monopoly of power and a forced alliance with the USSR. From 1976 he was connected with the Committee for the Defense of Workers, and in September 1980 he joined the board of Solidarity for the Łódź region. Interned during the martial law period and released after protests from Western intellectuals, Edelman supported the underground Solidarity. In May 1984 he co-founded and was a member of a secret Łódź Solidarity Regional Executive Commission, rivaling the informal continuation of the union's Regional Board. In December 1988 he joined the Civic Committee of the Solidarity chairman, **Lech Wałęsa**, and became head of its commission for national minorities. In the spring of 1989 he took part in the Round Table Talks. During the dissolution of the Solidarity camp Edelman took the side of the Civic Movement–Democratic Action (Ruch Obywatelski-Akcja Demokratyczna [ROAD]) and then of the Democratic Union and Union of Freedom. As the last survivor of the Warsaw Ghetto Uprising command, Edelman belonged to the intellectual leaders whose opinions have always been noticed by the media. In 1999, his opinion, expressed in Germany, contributed to the decision to send Bundeswehr troops to the Balkans within the NATO land forces. He often criticized Israeli policies toward the Palestinians. He also sharply criticized the idea of the construction of a museum about Germans displaced from Eastern Europe after World War II. He authored the memoirs *Ghetto Fights* (1946; *Getto walczy*, 1983) and *Strażnik: Marek Edelman opowiada* (Guardsman Marek Edelman tells his story; 1999), and he co-authored a book interview by Hanna Krall, *Zdążyć przed Panem Bogiem* (1977; *To Steal a March on God*, 1996). In 1998 Edelman was awarded the Order of the Polish White Eagle, and in 1999 he became an honorary citizen of Łódź. He was awarded honorary doctorates from Yale University and the University of Brussels. (AG)

Sources: *Wielka encyklopedia PWN*, vol. 8 (Warsaw, 2002) *Opozycja w PRL: Słownik biograficzny 1956–89*, vol. 1 (Warsaw, 2000); www.uml.lodz.pl/indeksik.php; zsm.interpab.com.pl/~comenius/jewish/edelman.htm, www.uw.org.pl/main/o_unii_wladze.php?id=18; www.midrasz.home.pl/1999/lis/lis99_1.html.

EENPALU Kaarel (originally Karl Einbund) (28 May 1888, Vesneri–28 January 1942, Kirov), Estonian politician. Eenpalu graduated in law from universities in Dorpat (Tartu) and Moscow. Later he worked as a journalist and belonged to a radical cultural-political organization, Noor Eesti (Young Estonia). From 1914 he was in the Russian Army. After graduating from an officer training school in St. Petersburg, he commanded an artillery division on the Austrian front. From 1918 he took part in the Estonian war of independence, organizing the police and territorial defense of Tartu, and he also commanded artillery units in battles against the Bolsheviks at Narva. From 1920

Eenpalu was president of the constitutional commission of the parliament and then minister of interior. He organized an efficient police force, so when on 1 December 1924 the Communists attempted a coup in Tallinn, the government quickly brought the situation under control. Eenpalu escaped an assassination attempt on his life. In 1926 he became president of the parliament, and he contributed to the consolidation of small peasant parties. From 19 July to 1 November 1932 he was *riigivanen* (president and prime minister), and then he again served as president of the parliament.

When in a referendum on 14–16 October 1933 the Fascist Estonian Union of Veterans of the War of Independence (Eesti Vabadussojalaste Liit [EVL]) gained ratification for its proposals for the constitution by a majority of Estonians (57 percent), Eenpalu supported the creation of a new government with **Konstantin Päts** at the head. This government was based on the Farmers' Party, Socialists, small groups from the center, and the minorities. When in January 1934 the constitution was implemented, Päts, as head of the government, was given great powers as interim head of state, and he would not renounce his prerogatives. Eenpalu joined the Farmers' Party, resigned from presiding over the parliament, and assumed the post of deputy prime minister and minister of interior. With arrests, he suppressed the discontent of the EVL, whose leadership planned an armed coup. As part of the Estonization of the country, in 1935 he changed his name to Eenpalu. After he stabilized his power, he pursued a more moderate policy and attempted to gain the support of wider circles of society for the government. From 9 May 1938 to 12 October 1939 Eenpalu was prime minister. He resigned after a treaty of mutual assistance between Estonia and the USSR was signed. The treaty provided for the partial occupation of the country by the Red Army. After Estonia was brought under complete control and was finally incorporated into the USSR, in July 1940 Eenpalu was arrested by the NKVD. Deported far inside the USSR, he died in a Soviet prison. (WR)

Sources: *Eesti Noukogude Entsuklopeedia*, vol. 2 (Tallinn, 1974); *Estonia: Population, Cultural and Economic Life* (Tallinn, 1937); Jüri Poska, *Probaltica* (Stockholm, 1965); Piotr Łossowski, *Kraje bałtyckie na drodze od demokracji parlamentarnej do dyktatury (1918–1934)* (Wrocław, 1972).

EGLĪTIS Andrejs (21 October 1912, Ļaudona, Livonia), Latvian poet. Eglītis graduated from high school in Riga in 1935. In 1937–40 he worked as a correspondent for the periodicals *Brīvā Zeme* and *Rīts*, and from 1939 to 1943 he edited Riga radio broadcasts. In 1943–45 he worked as a war correspondent at the Latvian Legion in Courland, created under the auspices of the Third Reich. In May 1945 he managed to escape to Sweden, where he settled down. His first collections, including *Kristus un mīla* (Christ and love; 1934), were characterized by a Romantic perception of the world and by trust in the vitality of a person and a nation. During the German occupation Eglītis published *Nīcība* (Meanness; 1942), and during his first years in exile, *Uz vairoga* (On the shield; 1946) and *Nesaule* (Nonsun; 1953), in which he contrasted good and evil, creating apocalyptic visions of the Latvian struggles for freedom and survival. The cantata-prayer *Dievs, Tava zeme deg* (O, God, Your land is burning! 1943) won recognition for its religious expression of the nation's suffering. In his five subsequent collections as well Eglītis combined a biblical style with Latvian folk song motifs, expressing the feelings of a nation in chains. He won numerous awards from Latvian organizations in exile. In 1998 he returned to Latvia, where he was awarded the Order of the Three Stars of Latvia. (EJ)

Sources: *Latviešu rakstniecība biogrāfijās* (Riga, 1992); *Wileka encyklopedia PWN*, vol. 8 (Warsaw, 2002); Vitauts Kalve, *Mūžs un dziesma: Eglītis A. Uguns un vārdi* (Eslingen, 1949); J. Zanders, *Eglītis A. Vai vēl dievkociņš zied mātes kapu laukā* (Stockholm, 1955); Edmunds Zirnītis, *Andrejs Eglītis* (Linkolna, 1980).

EHRLICH Lambert (18 September 1878, Žabnice–26 May 1942, Ljubljana), Slovene Catholic priest and politician. Ehrlich studied in Innsbruck, Rome, Paris, and Oxford, and he earned his doctorate from the university in Innsbruck. He worked as a priest in Beljak and Klagenfurt, where between 1910 and 1919 he was professor at a theological seminary. As an expert on the issues of his native Carinthia, Ehrlich became a member of the Yugoslav delegation to the Paris Peace Conference in 1919. Then he lectured on the study of religion and on ethnography at the University of Ljubljana. An avowed opponent of communism, he was the spiritual leader of the Slovene Catholic youth. He had charge of the moderate academic club Straža (Guard), which was situated between the radical nationalism of the group Mladci (The Young) and the Christian socialism of the group Zarja (The Dawn). According to Ehrlich, Slovenia should have remained an independent country, confederated with a broader, supranational European union. As an opponent of the guerrilla movement of **Josip Broz Tito**, Ehrlich was shot dead on the street in Ljubljana by a special Communist unit of the security service (Varnostno-Obščevalna Služba). (WR)

Sources: *Slovenski bijografski leksikon*, vol. 1 (Ljubljana, 1925); *Enciklopedija Slovenije*, vol. 1 (Ljubljana, 1987); Leopoldina Plut-Pregelj and Carole Rogel, *Historical Dictionary of Slovenia* (Lanham, Md., 1996).

ĒĶIS Ludvigs (11 September 1892, Dobeles, Courland–7 July 1943, Washington, D.C.), Latvian diplomat. Ēķis was born into a peasant family. After graduating from a school in Riga, he studied at the Riga Polytechnic Institute. In 1914 he volunteered for the Russian Army. From September 1914 he was in German captivity, from which he was released in 1918. From December 1918 he was in the Latvian Army. In 1919, in recognition of his military merits, he was promoted to officer. Demobilized in 1920, he started working in the Ministry of Foreign Affairs. From 1922 he was secretary of the legation in Germany and later in Finland. In 1925 he was appointed head of department in the Ministry of Foreign Affairs. In 1928 he became councillor of the Latvian legation in London, and from 1931 he headed the Western States Department of the Ministry of Foreign Affairs. From May 1934 to June 1938 he served as minister of finance, and then he was envoy to Poland and Hungary, with his headquarters in Warsaw. From September 1939 he was in Romania. He arrived there from Warsaw with the diplomatic corps and with the Polish government. From April to August 1939 he was also a Latvian envoy to Turkey. In July 1940 he left Romania for the United States. From January 1941 he served as economic councillor of the Latvian legation in Washington. In the United States, he published several works that promoted the Latvian cause—for example, *Latvia: Struggle for Independence* (1942) and *The Truth about Bolshevik and Nazi Atrocities in Latvia*. (EJ)

Sources: *Latvijas darbinieku galerija* (Riga, 1928); *Latvijas vadošie darbinieki* (Riga, 1935); *Es viņu pazīstu* (Riga, 1939).

EKREM Vlorë bey (1 December 1885, Valona [Vlorë]–29 March 1964, Vienna), Albanian politician. Ekrem was the son of Sürey bey Vlorë and Mihr Toptani, members of the most powerful Albanian families. Ferid Pasha Vlorë, the great vizier of Turkey from the beginning of the twentieth century, was his uncle. Ekrem was educated at home, and then in 1903 he graduated from the Gymnasium Theresianum in Vienna. In 1904, on the recommendation of his uncle, he became secretary for legal affairs in the Ministry of Foreign Affairs of Turkey. In 1905 in Cannes he wrote his dissertation, *Ziele und Zukunft der Albanesen* (Goals and future of the Albanians), which was published in *Österreichischen Rundschau* in 1908. He increasingly identified with the issue of the independence of Albania, and after the Young Turk revolution of 1908 he founded the club Bashkimi (Unity) in Istanbul. At the beginning of the First Balkan War in 1912, Ekrem unsuccessfully attempted to gain support in Vienna for the cause of Albanian independence. After the proclamation of Albanian independence on 28 November 1912, **Ismail Kemali** appointed him senator and soon after vice-president of the Senate. In the summer of 1913, along with Ismail Kemali, Ekrem unsuccessfully tried to convince the Western powers to recognize Albania. When in March 1914, by will of the Western powers, **Wilhelm von Wied** became the ruler of Albania, Ekrem assumed the post of secretary general of the department of foreign affairs. After Wied left at the beginning of September 1914, Ekrem went to Italy, where he was interned throughout World War I. Released, he traveled in Western Europe.

In the elections at the end of 1922, Vlorë won a seat as a representative of Valona, and he aligned himself with **Ahmed Zogu**. After **Fan Noli** assumed power, Vlorë was temporarily arrested but was soon released. After the overthrow of Noli's government and the establishment of Zogu's dictatorship and his coronation, Ekrem again became an MP and a senator. In 1928 he became an envoy to London. After the Italian occupation of Albania in 1939 he took part in the Albanian government-in-exile, which was connected with King Zog. In 1944 he emigrated to Italy, where he was engaged in historical research and in writing his memoirs. He was the author of, for example, *Kalaja e Kanines* (Fortress in Kanines; 1961) and of two volumes of memoirs, published in 1968–73. A 1,500-page manuscript on the history of Turkish rule in Albania, written by Ekrem with Marie Amelie von Godin, is in the archives of the Südost-Institut in Munich. (WR)

Sources: *Biographisches Lexikon*, vol. 6; Adalbert Gottfried, *Das Problem der Albanischen Unabhängigkeit in den Jahren 1908–1914* (Vienna, 1970); John Swire, *Albania: The Rise of a Kingdom* (New York, 1971); Stefanaq Pollo and Arben Puto, *The History of Albania from Its Origins to the Present Day* (London, 1981); Jerzy Hauziński and Jan Leśny, *Historia Albanii* (Wrocław, 1992).

ELIADE Mircea (9 March 1907, Bucharest–22 April 1986, Chicago), Romanian historian of religions, writer, philosopher, and ethnologist. Eliade studied philosophy at the University of Bucharest and then at the University of Calcutta in India in 1928–31. In his youth, he was ideologically close to the extreme nationalist right. From 1933 to 1939 he lectured at the University of Bucharest. In 1940 he became cultural attaché in London and in 1941–44 in Lisbon. As he did not agree about the Sovietization of Romania, after the end of World War II he remained in exile. From 1945 to 1956 he lived in Paris, where he lectured at the École des Hautes Études for some time. Already then he was one of the leading researchers on myth and religion. From 1956 he lived in Chicago, where he was appointed to the chair of the history of religions at the University of Chicago. He was a critic of the Communist system, and he repeatedly spoke in defense of human rights, in Romania as well; therefore his works were not mentioned in Romania.

Eliade had a broad knowledge and tried to create an integral, autonomous scientific discipline. In his opinion, the modern world had lost the sense of the sacred. His philosophy aimed at trying to reconstruct human spirituality and a connection between humanity and the cosmos through giving a cosmic dimension to this connection and through uncovering the primordial myths and restoring the internal harmony of the world. Eliade won fame for his studies on the history of religion: *Traité d'histoire des réligions* (1949; *Patterns of Comparative Religion*, 1958); *Le mythe de l'éternel retour* (1949; *The Myth of the Eternal Return*, 1954); *The Sacred and the Profane* (1959); *De Zalmoxis à Gengis Han* (1970; *Zalmoxis, the Vanishing God: Comparative Studies in the Religions and Folklore of Dacia and Eastern Europe*, 1972); and *Histoire des croyances et des idées religieuses* (1976; *History of Religious Ideas*, 1978). He also dealt with Indology—for example, he published *Patanjali et le yoga* (1962; *Patanjali and Yoga*, 1969); with Orientalism: *Alchimia asiatică* (Asiatic alchemy; 1934); *Le chamanisme* (1951; *Shamanism: Archaic Techniques of Ecstasy*, 1964); and with mythology: *Images et symboles* (1952; *Images and Symbols: Studies in Religious Symbolism*, 1961). Eliade thought that the revival of literature was possible only through discovering the function of myth. According to him, the role of literature was to capture the sacred in everyday life. In his prose we distinguish a realistic level—for example, in his works *Isabel și apele diavolului* (Isabel and the devil's waters; 1930); *Maitreyi* (1933; *Bengal Nights*, 1994); and *Huliganii* (The hooligans; 1935)—and a fantastic-mystical level—for example, *La forêt interdite* (1955; *The Forbidden Forest*, 1978; Romanian edition: *Noaptea de Sânziene*, 1971) and *În curte la Dionis* (1977; *In Dionysus' Court*, 1981). Sometimes a Hindu level is distinguished, as in *Secretul Doctorului Honigberger* (The secret of Dr. Honigberger; 1940). Diaries and memoirs play a special place in his writings: *Șantier* (1935); *Mémoires (1907–1937)* (*Journey East, Journey West: 1907–1937*, 1981); *Fragments d'un journal* (Fragments from a diary; 1973). Eliade also wrote essays: *Soliloquii* (1932); *Oceanografie* (Oceanography; 1934); *Fragmentarium* ("trans" 1939); *Insula lui Euthanasius* (The island of Euthanasius; 1943); *Comentarii la legenda Mașterului Manole* (Comments on the legend of Master Manole; 1943). Eliade went a long way from modernist obsessions to a peaceful and impersonal art of storytelling. He was also editor-in-chief of the sixteen-volume *Encyclopedia of Religion* (1987). (LW)

Sources: *Dictionar Enciclopedic*, vol. 2 (Bucharest, 1996); *New York Times*, 23 April 1986; Leonard S. Klein, *Encyclopedia of World Literature in the Twentieth Century*, vol. 2 (New York, 1982).

ELIAŠ Alois (29 September 1890, Prague–19 June 1942, Prague), Czech general, prime minister of the Protectorate of Bohemia and Moravia. During World War I Eliaš was an officer of the Czechoslovak Legions in Russia, and in 1917 he managed to get to France via the United States. In 1919 he took part in the Polish-Czechoslovak and the Czechoslovak-Hungarian fights in Slovakia. In 1921–23 he studied at a military academy in Paris. From 1924 he worked in the organization section of the general staff, and in 1929–31 he was head of the Czechoslovak delegation in the disarmament commission to the League of Nations in Geneva. In 1931–33 he was in command of an infantry brigade in Litoměřice; from 1933 to 1935 he commanded a division, and in 1935–38 he was commander of the Fifth Corps in Trenčin. From 1936 he was a major general. On 1 December 1938 he assumed the portfolio of communications. He served as minister of communications until the German invasion, and then on 27 April 1939 he became prime minister of the Protectorate of Bohemia and Moravia. Assuming this post, Eliaš pledged to President **Edvard Beneš** that he would do all he could for the occupied country, and he stated that if he did not accept the post, it would be taken over by villains. He repeatedly opposed Fascist pressure; for example, he refused to sign anti-Jewish laws and declined to swear loyalty to Hitler. Eliaš cooperated with the national resistance movement and was also in touch with the Czechoslovak government in London. After Berlin dismissed the diplomat Konstantin von Neurath as protector (*Reichsprotektor*) and Reinhard Heydrich assumed the post, on 27 September 1941 Eliaš was arrested, sentenced to death, and executed for cooperation with the resistance movement. He was promoted posthumously to the rank of general of the army. (PU)

Sources: *ČSB; Kdo byl kdo v našich dějinách ve 20. Století*, vol. 1 (Prague, 1998); Vojtech Masny, *The Czechs under Nazi Rule* (New York and London, 1971); T. Pasák, *Generál Alois Eliaš a odboj, Slovo k historii* (Prague, 1991); Robert Kvaček and Dušan Tomášek, *General Alois Eliaš* (Třebič, 2001).

ENESCU Gheorghe (19 August 1881, Liveni, Romania–4 May 1955, Paris), Romanian composer, violinist, pianist, conductor, and teacher. Gifted with prodigious musical talent, at the age of five Enescu had already composed his first violin and piano work, *România*. At age seven he began his education at the Vienna Conservatory. As an eight-year-old, he played the violin part in the *First Symphony* by Johannes Brahms, under the baton of the composer. A year later he started to study at the Paris Conservatory, under the direction of Gabriel Fauré and Jules Massenet (among others). In January 1898 his *Poema Română* was performed publicly for the first time. After his studies, in 1899 Enescu began to tour the most important music stages of the world. He lived mostly in Paris, Bucharest, and Iaşi, where he conducted the local orchestras. Between 1901 and 1902 he composed the *Romanian Rhapsodies*, which won him great success. In 1902 in Paris he founded a trio, and in 1904 a quartet, named after him. In 1912 he funded an award for Romanian composers; it was granted until 1946. In 1920 he founded the Union of Romanian Composers and was its leader until 1948. As a violinist and conductor, he gave many concerts in (among other places) the United States and Great Britain. Each year he performed in France and Romania. He was a member of many artistic and scientific societies—for example, the Romanian Academy of Sciences and the Insitut de France in Paris. Enescu's violin repertoire included works by Johann Sebastian Bach, Wolfgang Amadeus Mozart, and French composers. He educated many outstanding violinists—for example, Yehudi Menuhin.

Enescu's output in his early period is categorized under Neoromanticism. He used string instruments perfectly, and he often used counterpoint structures whose particular threads constantly dissipate. In this respect, he can be compared with such composers as Jean Sibelius, **Béla Bartók**, Manuel de Falla, and **Karol Szymanowski**. From Neoromantic technique and expression (e.g., *The First Symphony* of 1905), he moved toward a search in the field of Romanian folk music; therefore he is considered as the creator of the national style in Romanian music. He created many works of a national character—for example, *Vox Maris*. In 1936 the monumental opera *Oedipus*, the only one Enescu composed, was premiered. All together, he wrote five symphonies, the *Violin Concerto* (1921), two piano concertos, three orchestral suites, and many chamber works. After the overthrow of King **Michael I** in 1947 Enescu settled for good in Paris. Since he criticized the totalitarian system, he was almost ignored in Communist Romania. (LW)

Sources: *Dictionar Enciclopedic*, vol. 2 (Bucharest, 1996); *Wielka encyklopedia PWN*, vol. 8 (Warsaw, 2002); Bernard Gavoty, *Les souvenires de George Enescu* (Paris, 1955); B. Kotlarov, *George Enescu* (Moscow, 1967); Gheorghe Sbârcea, *Povestea vieţii lui George Enescu* (Bucharest, 1982).

ENGLIŠ Karel (17 August 1880, Hrabyně, Opava district–13 June 1961, Hrabyně), Czech economist, philosopher, lawyer, and politician. In 1904 Engliš graduated in law at the Czech University in Prague. After a short stay on scholarship in Munich, he worked as a clerk in a district statistical office in Prague. In 1908–11 he worked in the Ministry of Trade in Vienna. In 1910 he submitted his postdoctoral degree thesis; from 1911 he was associate professor, and from 1917 full professor, of economics at the Czech Polytechnic in Brno. On 15 November 1918, along with Alois Jirásek, he submitted a draft bill in parliament on the establishment of a second Czech university, with its seat in Brno, and soon he became a professor and the first rector of this university. From 1927 he was a member of the Czechoslovak Academy of Sciences and Arts. In 1939 he became professor at the Law Department of Charles University in Prague. From December 1947 to February 1948 he was its rector. In 1947 he was awarded the title of doctor *honoris causa* from Masaryk University in Brno.

In 1913–18, as a representative of the People's Progressive Party (Lidovo-Pokrokova Strana), Engliš had a seat in the Moravian district parliament. In 1918 he was a member of the National Committee, and then until 1925 he was an MP of Czechoslovak National Democracy (Československá Národní Demokracie). He also sat on the parliamentary finance commission. In 1921, along with **Jaroslav Stránský**, Engliš formed the Moravian opposition wing of the party, which frequently criticized the party authorities. In the culmination of parliamentary conflict in 1925, he left the parliamentary club of the National Democrats, and he resigned his parliamentary seat. On three occasions—in 1920–21, 1925–28, and 1929–31—he served as minister of finance. Between 1934 and 1939, he was president of the Czechoslovak National Bank. In 1927 he carried out a budget and tax reform, cutting taxes and budget expenditures. In 1934 he devalued the Czech crown (*koruna*).

Engliš was the author of a teleological theory of the national economy. This theory put emphasis on the cognition of purposefulness in economic behavior. He was the author (among other works) of the following: *Teleologie jako forma vědeckého poznání* (Teleology as a form of scientific understanding; 1930); *Peníze* (Money; 1918); *Národní hospodářství* (1924; *Economics: A Purpose Oriented Approach*, 1992); *Finanční věda* (The science of finance; 1929); *Teorie státního hospodářství* (Theory of the state economy; 1932); *Hospodářské soustavy* (Economic systems; 1946); and the two-volume *Soustava národního hospodářství* (The system of the national economy; 1938), a synthesis of his economic views. Engliš developed his theory in *Malá logika* (Small logic; 1947) and in the manuscript "Velká logika" (Great logic). After the Communist coup in February 1948 Engliš was dismissed as rector of Charles University, and his works were removed from libraries. In 1952 he was forced to leave Prague. He went to his native

Hrabyně, where he wrote philosophical and economic works, the majority of which were never published. His scientific legacy is held in the archives of the National Museum in Prague. In 1990 in Prague the Karel Engliš Society was founded, and since 1994 Masaryk University in Brno has awarded the Karel Engliš Prize each year. (PU)

Sources: *ČBS*; *Českoslovenští politici: 1918–1991* (Prague, 1991); *Kdo byl kdo v našich dějinach ve 20. stoleti*, vol. *1* (Prague, 1998); *Politická elita meziválečného Československa 1918–1938: Kdo byl kdo za prvni republiky* (Prague, 1998); *Slovník českých filozofů* (Brno, 1998); Jaroslav Kolařík, *Peníze a politika: Karel Engliš, bojovník o stabilizaci* (Prague, 1937); František Vencovský, *Karel Engliš* (Brno, 1993); František Vencovský, *Dějiny českého ekonomického myšlení* (Brno, 1997).

ERBAN Evžen (18 June 1912, Vsetín–26 July 1994, Prague), Czech trade union activist and politician. From 1931 to 1935 Erban studied law at Charles University in Prague. In 1936–40 he was the secretary of several trade unions; between 1944 and 1945 he was a member of the Presidium of the illegal Central Council of Trade Unions, and until 1950 he was the council's secretary general. From 1945 to 1952 he had a seat in the National Assembly. Until 1948 he was a member of the leadership of Czechoslovak Social Democracy, and along with **Zdeněk Fierlinger** he sought cooperation with the Communist Party of Czechoslovakia (CPC). After the coup of February 1948 Erban was instrumental in liquidating the Social Democratic Party and incorporating it into the CPC. In June 1948 he became member of the Presidium of the Central Committee (CC) of the CPC, on which he sat until 1951. At that time he also served as minister of labor and social welfare. In 1952–63 he was head of the State Office for Social Welfare, and between 1963 and 1968 he was head of the State Administration of Material Reserves. In 1956 he became vice-president of the World Labor Confederation. In 1968 he was again made a member of the CC of the CPC; this was to show former Social Democrats that they were welcome in the CPC and that they should therefore not attempt to revive the Czech Social Democratic Party (ČSSD). However, the Social Democrats remembered Erban's role in the liquidation of the party and ignored the Communists' gesture. In 1969 Erban belonged to a commission that expelled reformers from the CC, and in 1971 he became a member of the Presidium of the CC of the CPC. In 1968 he initially served as secretary general of the CC of the National Front of the Czechoslovak Socialist Republic, and after **František Kriegel** was dismissed as chairman of the National Front, Erban took over Kriegel's post. In 1968–86 Erban was a member of the Czech National Council (CNC), and between 1969 and 1981 he served as CNC chairman. Between 1969 and

1990 he was also a member of the National Chamber of the National Assembly. In 1975–85 he was in charge of the Czechoslovak Society for International Relations. After an unsuccessful attempt to attend a congress of the revived Social Democracy, to which he was denied entrance, Erban left political life in 1990. (PU)

Sources: *ČBS*; *Kdo byl kdo v našich dějinach ve 20. stoleti*, vol. 1 (Prague, 1998); *Politická elita meziválečného Československa 1918–1938: Kdo byl kdo za prvni republiky* (Prague, 1998); *Who's Who in the Socialist Countries of Europe*, vol. 1 (Munich, London, and Paris, 1989).

ERDEI Ferenc (24 December 1910, Makó–11 May 1971, Budapest), Hungarian writer and politician. The son of a landless peasant who acquired land through work, in 1933 Erdei graduated in law from the University of Szeged. Drafted into the army, he was sentenced to seven months in prison for an anti-government demonstration. As a student he was already interested in economics and sociology. His sociographic work, *Futóhomok* (Drift sand; 1937), won him recognition. Erdei joined a group of writers who explored the Hungarian countryside; in 1937 he was a co-founder of the leftist March Front, demanding land reform and political liberalization. In 1939 he co-founded the National Peasant Party (NPP), the creation of the so-called populist writers. In the 1930s and 1940s he published, among other things, *Parasztok* (Peasants; 1938); *Magyar falu* (Hungarian countryside; 1940); *Magyar paraszt-társadalom* (Hungarian peasant community; 1941); and *Magyartanyák* (Hungarian farms; 1942), in which he presented the situation of the Hungarian countryside. In 1939–44 he was active in the leftist political movement, and in 1943 he was briefly arrested.

In October 1944 Erdei joined the Hungarian National Independence Front, and in December 1944 he became deputy to the Provisional National Assembly in Debrecen. Later he was an MP until his death. From December 1944 to November 1945 he was minister of interior. In 1945 he was elected the NPP deputy chairman and in 1947, secretary general. Erdei favored unconditional cooperation with the Communists. From 1948 he was a corresponding member, and from 1956 a member, of the Hungarian Academy of Sciences (HAS), and from 1949 he was deputy chairman of the Hungarian Patriotic Front. From September 1948 to June 1949 he was minister of state, and until July 1953, minister of agriculture. He favored collectivization of the countryside. During the first government of **Imre Nagy** Erdei was minister of justice (July 1953–October 1954). From October 1954 to November 1955 he was minister of agriculture again, and then, until late October 1956, deputy prime minister. On 30 October 1956 he joined

the second government of Nagy. He spoke in favor of a multiparty system and took part in the reorganization of the NPP. On 2 November he was appointed head of a delegation to negotiate the evacuation of Soviet troops from Hungary. The next day, during talks in the Soviet headquarters in Tököl, near Budapest, Erdei was arrested, along with other members of the delegation, by General Ivan Serov. After a month, he decided to support **János Kádár**, and he was released. From 1957 to 1964 he was the HAS general secretary; in 1964–70 he was secretary general of the Hungarian Patriotic Front and the HAS deputy chairman, and from 1970 until his death, he was HAS general secretary. From 1965 Erdei was a member of the Presidential Council and played an important role in the preparation of economic reforms that were never implemented. (JT)

Sources: *Magyar Nagylexikon*, vol. 7 (Budapest, 1998); *A magyar forradalom és szabadságharc enciklopédiája*, CD-ROM (Budapest, 1999); *Új Magyar Életrajzi Lexikon*, vol. 2 (Budapest, 2001); Paul Ignotus, *Hungary* (London, 1972); Ferenc Fekete, *Erdei Ferenc agrárközgazdasági munkáirol, különös tekintettel a szövetkezeti elmétre* (Budapest, 1984); Hans-Detlev Grothusen, ed., *Ungarn* (Göttingen, 1987); Steven Béla Várdy, *Historical Dictionary of Hungary* (Lanham, Md., 1997).

ERLICH Henryk [originally Hersz Wolf] (25 August 1882, Lublin–4 December 1941, Kuibyshev [now Samara]), Jewish Socialist activist and lawyer in Poland. The son of a miller, from his youth Erlich was active in Jewish leftist movements, and in 1903 he joined the Bund. Arrested in May 1904 and expelled from his studies at the University of Warsaw, after his release he went to study in Berlin, but after the outbreak of the 1905 revolution he returned to Warsaw, where he led a youth strike and edited the Bund paper *Nasze hasło*. Fearing arrest, Erlich left for Petersburg, where he graduated in law in 1908. Upon his return to the Congress Kingdom of Poland, he joined in Bund activities but was soon arrested and banned from the kingdom. In 1909–12 he traveled a lot on behalf of the party and was a consultant on Jewish affairs to Russian Social Democratic deputies in the Russian State Duma. He also represented the Bund in the Organization Committee of the Social Democratic Workers' Party of Russia (Mensheviks). In 1913 he was coopted to the Central Committee of the Bund, arrested, and released owing to tuberculosis.

From 1914 Erlich spoke in favor of the toppling of the tsar. After the February 1917 revolution he represented the Bund in the Executive Committee of the Petrograd soviet. He accepted the Bolshevik coup unwillingly and protested the idea of a dictatorship of the proletariat at the Second All-Union Congress of the Soviets (7–8 November

1917). From August 1918 he was back in Warsaw, where he co-organized the Executive Council of the Soviets. In 1919 Erlich was elected to the Warsaw City Council. He opposed the war against the Bolsheviks, which led to his brief arrest by the Polish authorities in 1920. From 1920 to 1939 he was active in the trade unions and in the Warsaw City Council, defending the interests of the Jewish poor. He was editor-in-chief of the Bund organ, *Folks Tsaytung*. He was against the entry of the Bund into the Communist International and opted for the party's cooperation with the Second International. He took part in its subsequent congresses as the Bund representative. Despite this, he defended Communists sued by the Polish authorities, and in 1934 he came out in favor of a united front of the left with the Communists.

After the German invasion of September 1939, Erlich left for eastern Poland, where, after the Soviet invasion, he was arrested by the NKVD on 4 October 1939. In July 1941 he was sentenced to death. The sentence was then commuted to ten years in a labor camp. After the outbreak of the German-Soviet war, Erlich was released as a Polish citizen in September 1941. Lavrenty Beria suggested that he preside over the International Jewish Anti-Fascist Committee. He agreed, but at the same time he resumed cooperation with the Polish government and favored the reconstruction of a united Polish army without separate Jewish units; the idea was supported by Polish National Democrats, on the one hand, and some Zionists, on the other. On 4 December 1941 Erlich was arrested again, along with **Wiktor Alter**, by the NKVD in Kuibyshev, this time on account of his alleged cooperation with Germany. On 23 December 1941 a Soviet court broke international law again by treating him as a Soviet citizen and sentencing him to death. Erlich was reported to have committed suicide. (AG)

Sources: *Wielka encyclopedia PWN*, vol. 8 (Warsaw, 2002); *Słownik biograficzny działaczy polskiego ruchu robotniczego*, vol. 2 (Warsaw, 1987); *The Case of Henryk Erlich and Wiktor Alter* (London, 1943); *Henryk Erlich i Wiktor Alter* (New York, 1951); Łukasz Hirszowicz, "NKVD Documents Shed New Light on the Fate of Ehrlich and Alter," *East European Jewish Affairs*, 1992, no. 2.

ESSAD Pasha Toptani (1863, Tirana–13 June 1920, Paris), Albanian politician. Essad was a member of a powerful feudal family from the area near Tirana. His family played an important role in the Turkish policy in Turkey and Albania. Essad was the son of Ali bey Toptani. From his father, he inherited one of the largest estates in Albania, between Tirana and Durrës. He started his career thanks to the support of his brother, Gani bey, a confidant of Sultan Abdulhamid. On behalf of the sultan, his brother committed many political murders, and then in 1902 he himself was murdered. After acquiring the family fortune, Essad served for some time as commander of the Turkish gendarmerie in Janina (now Ioánnina, Greece). In 1908 he joined the Young Turk movement and became deputy for Durrës in the Turkish parliament. During the Balkan Wars he played a rather dubious role, seeking to establish control over Albania. With his knowledge, and perhaps even on his orders, in January 1913 the Turkish commander of Shkodër, besieged by the Montenegrins, was murdered. This strengthened Essad's position as the rival of the Albanian government, which was created in December 1912 in Vlorë, under the leadership of **Ismail Kemali**. As a reward, Serbia and Montenegro supported his claims to the Albanian throne. At that time, the troops that were faithful to Essad controlled the middle of Albania, with Tirana and Durrës. In July 1913 Essad became minister of interior in the government of Ismail Kemali, but a month later he rebelled against him, and in October he established the Senate of Albania. When in February 1914 the great powers imposed Prince **Wilhelm von Wied** as the ruler of Albania, Essad was appointed minister of interior and of war in Wied's government. In May 1914 he attempted to lead another Albanian rebellion but was dismissed by the prince, and it was only owing to Italian intervention that he was allowed to leave for Brindisi.

The outbreak of World War I revived Essad's hopes. In August 1914 he arrived in Niš, where the Serb government evacuated from Belgrade was stationed. Essad obtained financial aid from **Nikola Pašić**, the Serb prime minister, in exchange for military actions against the Central Powers. After the departure of Prince Wied, in October 1914 Essad arrived in Durrës with a group of warriors, proclaiming himself head of the Albanian government and commander-in-chief of the army. Meanwhile, an anti-feudal uprising led by Haxhi Qamil undermined his power. The People's Assembly in Tirana, which was an emanation of the insurgent troops, issued a manifesto to the countries that were fighting. In this manifesto, they declared their neutrality and announced their intention of overthrowing Essad's government. The Serbian Army intervened, saving Essad from being surrounded in Durrës and bloodily suppressing the insurgents. When the Bulgarian Army seized Macedonia, the Serbs had to withdraw. Following the Serbian Army, Essad again escaped to Italy. The Italian government was willing to place him on the Albanian throne on condition that he severe ties with other countries. Essad did not agree to that, and he sought support in France. The French authorities were counting on the Albanian troops in the war in the Balkans; therefore they supported Essad and helped him to establish an Albanian "government-in-exile" in Salonika; however, they did not intend to give him power. Essad's ambitions became unrealistic in the face of a secret London treaty in April 1915; in it the Entente agreed to the partition of Albania between Greece and Italy. In exchange, Greece and Italy would enter the war on the side of the Entente.

When the Austro-Hungarian Army seized a great part of Albanian territory in the spring of 1916, Essad again went to France. At the Paris Peace Conference in 1919 he still attempted to gain the Entente's mandate for his "government-in-exile" but without success. Later, with the help of Osman Bali and Halida Lleshi, his co-workers, he tried to instigate a rebellion in Albania. In June 1920 he made an agreement with the Yugoslav authorities that in exchange for incorporating Albania into the Kingdom of Serbs, Croats, and Slovenes, he would be given a life governorship in the Albanian part of the kingdom. Essad was so hated in the country that many Albanians sought an opportunity to kill him. On 13 June 1920 he was shot and killed at the Hotel Continental in Paris by **Avni Rustemi**, an Albanian student. In 1919 in Paris Essad published his *Mémoire sur l'Albanie* (Memoirs from Albania). (WR)

Sources: *Biographisches Lexikon*, vol. 4; *Neue Zürcher Zeitung*, 11–15 June and 29–30 November 1920; Vlora Eqrem Bey, *Lebenserinnerungen*, vols. 1–2 (Munich, 1969–73); John Swire, *Albania: The Rise of a Kingdom* (New York, 1971); Stefanaq Pollo and Arben Puto, *The History of Albania from Its Origins to the Present Day* (London, 1981); Jerzy Hauziński and Jan Leśny, *Historia Albanii* (Wrocław, 1992); Miranda Vickers, *The Albanians: A Modern History* (London, 1995); Tadeusz Czekalski, *Albania w latach 1920–1924–aparat państwowy i jego funkcjonowanie* (Katowice, 1998).

ESTERHÁZY János (14 March 1901, Nyitraújlak [now in Slovakia]–8 March 1957, Mírov, Bohemia), count, Hungarian politician from Czechoslovakia. Esterházy graduated from the Trade Academy in Budapest. After the Treaty of Trianon (1920) he stayed in Czechoslovakia and managed an estate of some six hundred acres, left after the confiscation of the family latifundium of about six thousand acres during the Czechoslovak land reform. In 1932–36 he presided over the Home Christian Socialist Party, and from July 1936 to November 1938, over the United Hungarian Party (UHP). From 1935 to 1938 he was a member of the Czechoslovak parliament. He spoke in favor of the full autonomy of Slovakia and Transcarpathian Ruthenia within the Czechoslovak state and of minority rights for the Hungarians compatible with international standards. An opponent of Nazism and communism, in the late 1930s Esterházy distanced his party from the radical methods of the Sudeten Germans, and he did not take part in the partition of Czechoslovakia.

After the First Vienna Award in November 1938, when Hungary was given South Slovakia, 85 percent of whose inhabitants were Hungarians, Esterházy remained within Czechoslovakia. After its dismemberment in March 1939, as the leader of the Hungarian Party (successor to the UHP), he became the leader of about seventy thousand Hungarians within the Slovak state. In 1939 he founded the so-called Hungarian Household Movement, aiming at the preservation of Hungarian national identity. Despite German and Slovak pressures, Esterházy refused to reorganize this movement along Fascist lines, and he distanced himself from the extreme right. In 1941 he founded and presided over the only Hungarian institution in Slovakia, the Savings Bank in Bratislava, and he was the only Hungarian deputy to the Slovak parliament. In May 1942 he was the only deputy to vote against the deportation of Slovak Jews. In December 1944 the (Fascist) Arrow Cross activists arrested him briefly in Budapest, and at the end of the war he went into hiding since he was wanted by the German police. In April 1945 he was arrested by the Czechoslovak authorities, which in June 1945 handed him over to the Soviet military organs. Deported to Russia, in June 1946 Esterházy was sentenced in Moscow to ten years of forced labor. In September 1947 in Bratislava he was tried in absentia for contributing to the "Fascistization" of Slovakia, and he was sentenced to death for "national treason." In April 1949 the Soviet authorities transferred him to Communist Czechoslovakia, where his sentence was commuted to life imprisonment and, in May 1955, to twenty-five years in prison. Esterházy was already seriously ill with tuberculosis, which accelerated his death. In January 1993 he was rehabilitated in Russia and later also in Slovakia. (JT)

Sources: *Magyar Nagylexikon*, vol. 7 (Budapest, 1998); *Nagy Képes Milleniumi Arcképcsarnok* (Budapest, 1999); *Új Magyar Életrajzi Lexikon*, vol. 2 (Budapest, 2001); Gabor Szent-Irany, *Count Janos Esterhazy: Life and Work of the Great Son of the Hungarian Highland* (Astor, Fla., 1987); Imre Molnár, *Esterházy János, 1901–1957* (Dunaszerdahely, 1997).

ESTREICHER Stanisław (26 November 1869, Kraków–28 December 1939, Oranienburg), Polish historian of law and bibliographer. Estreicher belonged to a well-known family of Kraków scholars. He was the son of the bibliographer and historian of literature Karol Józef Estreicher (1827–1908), brother of the chemist Tadeusz Estreicher (1871–1952), and father of the bibliographer Karol Estreicher (1906–1984). He graduated from the Jagiellonian University in Kraków; from 1902 he was a professor there, and in 1919–21, rector. From 1912 he was a member of the Academy of Arts and Sciences, and from 1919, a member of the Polish Academy of Arts and Sciences. During World War I he supported the Supreme National Committee and the pro-Austrian orientation. In independent Poland he was active in the (conservative) National Right Party (Stronnictwo Prawicy Narodowej). Although he opposed the May 1926 coup d'état by **Józef Piłsudski**, he favored the cooperation of the conservatives with the ruling *sanacja*. After the Brest Trial of the opposition leaders (1931–33), Estreicher went into opposition against the *sanacja*'s authoritarianism, and in 1933 he protested the limitations on the autonomy of universities. His major scholarly accomplishment was the continuation of the monumental *Bibliografia polska* (Polish bibliography), which recorded Polish publications and foreign Polonica from the fifteenth to the twentieth centuries; he started co-editing it with his father in 1887. After the latter's death, Estreicher edited the work by himself and published volumes 23 to 33 between 1910 and 1939; he also supplemented the bibliographical entries and subject bibliographies and made corrections. He also authored *Początki prawa umownego* (The beginnings of contract law; 1901); *Kodeks Hammurabiego* (The Code of Hammurabi; 1905); *Najstarsze kodeksy prawne świata* (The oldest legal Codes in the world; 1931); and *Kultura prawnicza w Polsce XVI wieku* (The legal culture in Poland in the sixteenth century; 1931). After Kraków was seized by the Germans, in early November 1939 Estreicher, along with a group of university professors, was arrested by the Gestapo, and he died in a concentration camp. (WR)

Sources: *PSB*, vol. 6; *Encyklopedia historii Drugiej Rzeczypospolitej* (Warsaw, 1999); *Wielka encyklopedia PWN*, vol. 8 (Warsaw, 2002); *Lista strat kultury polskiej*, vol. 2 (Glasgow, 1945); Henryk Barycz, "Stanisław Estreicher i rozwój jego tworczości naukowej," *Pamiętnik Literacki*, 1946, nos. 1–2.

EVANGJELI Pandeli (1859, Korçë–September 1949, Korçë), Albanian independence activist and diplomat.

From his youth Evangjeli lived in Bucharest, where he was engaged in trade. His café there was a meeting place for the local Albanians. He also distributed printed materials that were published in Istanbul and Egypt and were devoted to the Albanian cause. In 1896 Evangjeli was elected president of the Dituria (Knowledge) association, and a year later he became head of the Albanian colony in Bucharest. After the creation of the government of **Ismail Kemali** in 1912 Evangjeli offered the government financial aid from the colony in Bucharest. After his return to Albania, in 1914 he served for a short time as prefect of Berat. He spent the war period in Bucharest, and in 1919 he was elected as a representative of the Albanian colony in Romania to the Paris Peace Conference. In 1921 he moved to Tirana, and the same year he became an MP for the Korçë district in the Constituent Assembly. He became minister of foreign affairs in the Ilias Bey Vrioni government, which was created in February 1921. On 16 October 1921 Evangjeli was elected prime minister for the first time, but on 6 December of that year he was forced to resign. He returned to politics after King **Ahmed Zogu** took over power in 1925. In 1927–30 he served as president of the parliament, and between 5 March 1930 and 22 October 1935 he was again head of the government. In 1935, confronted with famine, he called for aid from the International Red Cross. In 1937 he was reelected president of the parliament. He resigned after the Italian aggression, and he did not accept any political proposals put forward by the Italians. In 1947, owing to his difficult financial situation, Evangjeli left Tirana and moved to his native Korçë, where he spent the last years of his life. (TC)

Sources: *Biographisches Lexikon*, vol. 1; Michael Schmidt-Neke, *Enstehung und Ausbau der Konigsdiktatur in Albanien (1912–1939), Regierungsbildungen, Herrschaftsweisen und Machteliten in Einen Jungen Balkanstaat* (Munich, 1987); Sejfi Vllamasi, *Ballafaqime politike në Shqipëri (1897–1942)* (Tirana, 1995); Tadeusz Czekalski, *Albania w latach 1920–1924* (Katowice, 1998); Blendi Fevziu, "Pandeli Evangjeli, politikani pa fame," *Klan*, 14 January 2001.

F

FADENCHECHT Yosif (24 November 1873, Trapezunt–27 October 1953, Sofia?), Bulgarian lawyer and politician. Fadenchecht came from a Jewish family from the Habsburg empire. His mother came from Vienna and his father from Kraków. They were one of the few Ashkenazi families in the Bulgarian Jewish society, which was dominated by the Sephardim. Fadenchecht attended a gymnasium in Plovdiv and Sofia. He studied law and philosophy at the University of Leipzig and received a Ph.D. in 1897. He continued his studies in Sofia, Bologna, and Turin. After returning to Bulgaria, he became a professor of law at the university in Sofia, and in 1906 he became a member of the Academy of Sciences. He published many works, including the famous *Sistema na bylgarskoto veshtno pravo* (The system of Bulgarian press law; 1902). In 1908 he started to practice law and he gave up teaching. At that time he aligned himself with the opposition Radical Party, which was of a democratic and liberal nature. He was against Bulgaria's entry into World War I on the side of Germany. However, at the end of the war he accepted the post of minister of justice in the cabinet of **Aleksandur Malinov** (June–November 1918). In 1922–23, together with other members of the cabinet, he was imprisoned by the regime of **Aleksandur Stamboliyski**. After the war Fadenchecht was initially active as a member the Bar Council, and in 1930 he became its president. He also joined the Democratic Party. He published the monumental work *Bylgarsko grazhdansko pravo* (Bulgarian civic law; 1929). He was a champion of cooperation between Yugoslavia and Bulgaria. He survived World War II, and, like the majority of Bulgarian Jews, he avoided anti-Semitic persecutions. In July 1944 he was reelected president of the Bar Council. (MC)

Sources: *Biographisches Lexikon,* vol. 1; *Entsiklopediya Bulgariya,* vol. 7 (Sofia, 1996); *Wer ist's? Zeitgenossenlexikon* (Leipzig, 1909); Angel Dzhambazov, *Pravosudatna sistema na Bylgariia, 1878–1944* (Sofia,1990); Boris Spasov et al., *Almanakh na uridicheskii fakultet pri Sofiiskii universitet "Sv. Kliment Okhridski," 1892–1992* (Sofia, 1992); Tzvetan Todorov, ed., *The Fragility of Goodness: Why Bulgaria's Jews Survived the Holocaust* (London, 1999).

FALTER Alfred (25 July 1880, Ropa–1954, New York), Polish businessman of Jewish descent, one of the richest industrialists in interwar Poland. Initially Falter was a spokesman of the Upper Silesian tycoons, mainly those connected with German coal mining. He was a delegate to the International Commission of War Indemnities, founded according to the Treaty of Versailles of June 1919. In 1922 he was an economic expert of the Polish delegation to the Geneva conference on Upper Silesia. In 1922–32 he was among the authorities of the Upper Silesian Union of Coal and Steel Entrepreneurs, and from 1932 he was one of the chairmen of the Central Union of Polish Industry. From 1924 to 1939 he was a member of the board of the Bank of Poland (Bank Polski), and from 1932 to 1939, a member of the board (and from 1935, deputy chairman) of the Polish Steel Convention and the International Trade Chamber. He chaired and owned the majority of shares in the Upper Silesian Union of Coal Mines–Robur, which controlled 35 percent of coal sales in Poland. In 1928 he founded the Polish-Scandinavian transportation society Polskarob S.A. From October 1939 he was deputy minister in the government-in-exile of General **Władysław Sikorski**. In 1942 he left for the United States, where, making use of capital deposited there before the war, he managed a shipping company. (WR)

Sources: *Encyklopedia historii gospodarczej Polski,* vol. 1 (Warsaw, 1981); *Wielka encyklopedia PWN,* vol. 8 (Warsaw, 2002); Jan Kofman, *Lewiatan a podstawowe zagadnienia ekonomiczno-polityczne Drugiej Rzeczypospolitej* (Warsaw, 1986).

FALUDY György (22 September 1910, Budapest), Hungarian poet, writer, and translator. After graduating from a Calvinist high school in his hometown in 1928, Faludy studied at the universities in Budapest, Berlin, and Graz. He made his literary debut in periodicals of the Hungarian Social Democratic Party, which he joined in 1931. He won recognition for his translations of François Villon. From 1938 he lived in Paris; after the German invasion he lived in Algiers, and from 1941, in the United States. He was active in the Hungarian anti-Fascist émigré community, and for three years he also served in the U.S. Army. After returning to Hungary in 1946, Faludy contributed literary articles to the trade union daily *Népszava*. In 1950 he was arrested by the Communist police and put in a special camp for the intelligentsia in Recsk (in northern Hungary). For almost three years he created moving poems, memorized and later recorded by his prison mates after his release. After Stalin's death, in 1953 Faludy was released, but he refused to apply for rehabilitation. In 1954–56 he made his living by translating. After the suppression of the 1956 revolution he emigrated to Great Britain and later to Italy, Malta, and the United States. From 1967 he lived either in the United States or in Canada. From 1957 to 1962 he was editor of the leading periodical of the Hungarian émigré community, *Irodalmi Újság*. At the same time he was secretary of the International PEN club. From the mid-1960s he taught literature at

American and Canadian universities. He returned to Hungary in 1989 and continued his literary activity. He founded his own cultural foundation (Faludy Alapítvány) and twice ran in parliamentary elections, though without success. Faludy's fascination with French lyrics and his great erudition placed him in the last generation of writers connected with the leading interwar literary periodical, *Nyugat*. Wartime travels, Communist repression, and long-term emigration added to Faludy's works a sad reflection on human nature. His major works include *Villon balladái* (Villon's ballads; 1937); *My Happy Days in Hell* (1962); *East and West* (1978); *Notes from the Rainforest* (1988); and *Börtönversek 1950–1953* (Prison poems, 1950–1953; 1989). (MS)

Sources: *Mały słownik pisarzy węgierskich* (Warsaw, 1977); Béla Pomogáts, "Ezeregyszáz vers," *Élet és Irodalom*, 1989, no. 15; *Faludy György költő*, film, 1987; Béla Pomogáts, *Faludy György* (Budapest, 2000).

FARKAS Mihály (18 July 1904, Abaújszántó–6 December 1965, Budapest), Hungarian Communist activist. From his youth, Farkas was involved in the Communist movement in Hungary and Czechoslovakia. In the 1920s he went to the USSR, where he was active in Youth International. In July 1929, under the name "Wolf," he spoke on behalf of the Hungarian Communist Party (HCP) at a meeting of the Executive Committee of the Comintern. In 1935 he became a deputy member of the Presidium of the Comintern's Executive Committee. At that time he used the alias "Mikhail." In this role he went on special missions—for example, to Spain. During World War II he was the secretary of the Executive Committee of the Comintern, the highest-ranking Hungarian in this organization.

In 1944 Farkas came to Hungary and assumed the post of deputy minister of interior in the coalition government of General **Béla Miklós-Dálnoki**. In this role he co-organized many arrests and much torture and blackmail, which enabled the Communists, who were supported by the occupying Red Army, to come to power in Hungary. Farkas was responsible for (among other things) the arrest and investigation of **Béla Kovács**, the secretary general of the Smallholders' Party, and the arrests of other activists of the party. In September 1947 Farkas was a member of the Hungarian delegation to the founding congress of the Communist Information Bureau (Cominform) in Szlarska Poręba. In 1948 he became minister of defense, and in this role he carried out a brutal purge of the Hungarian Army. After the Communists absorbed the rest of the Social Democratic Party in June 1948 Farkas remained in the Secretariat and in the Politburo of the Central Committee (CC) of the Hungarian Workers' Party. In June 1948 he represented the party at the Cominform meeting in which

Tito was denounced. Despite his Jewish origins, Farkas had no scruples about the anti-Semitic purge that was conducted at the end of the 1940s. In 1949, under the eye of **Mátyás Rákosi**, he supervised the case of **László Rajk** and prepared his trial. In 1952 Farkas was promoted to general. After Stalin's death and following the establishment, under pressure from Moscow, of the "collective leadership" in the summer of 1953 Farkas supported **Imre Nagy**, who became prime minister. After Nagy's fall in 1955 Farkas lost his post, and after the Twentieth CPSU Congress he was ousted from the party's CC.

Even before the revolution, on 13 October 1956, Farkas was arrested, soon after the arrest of his son, a colonel in the security police AVH (Államvédelmi Hatóság). However, he was released after the revolution was suppressed. Soon after he was imprisoned again; in April 1957 he received a fourteen-year prison sentence for the "infringement of socialist law and order," and he became the main scapegoat of Stalinism in Hungary. Released ahead of time in 1960, Farkas died of a heart attack. (WR)

Sources: *Magyar Eletrajzi Lexikon,* vol. 1; Tamas Aczel and Tibor Meray, *The Revolt of the Mind* (London, 1961); Bennet Kovrig, *Communism in Hungary from Kun to Kadar* (Stanford, 1970); Branko Lazitch, *Biographical Dictionary of the Comintern* (Stanford, 1986).

FAZEKAS György (6 June 1914, Miskolc–22 May 1984. Budapest), Hungarian writer and journalist. After graduating from high school in Miskolc, Fazekas worked as a journalist, publishing mostly in the local paper, *Felső-Magyarország*. During World War II he served in the army and was taken prisoner of war by the Soviets. After the war he joined the Hungarian Communist Party (from 1948 the Hungarian Workers' Party) and worked for the central party organ, *Szabad Nép*. During the "thaw" after Stalin's death, Fazekas joined the group of reform-oriented followers of **Imre Nagy**. At the same time he published the novels *Emberrabló* (Thief of people; 1953) and *Csodálatos utazás* (Miraculous journey; 1954). During the 1956 revolution Fazekas was a member of Nagy's secretariat. When the Soviet troops entered Budapest, in November 1956 he sought shelter in the Yugoslav Embassy. On leaving it, he was deported to Romania. In the trial of Nagy and his aides in the summer of 1958, Fazekas was sentenced to ten years in prison. Amnestied in 1963, he was banned from working as a journalist and took casual jobs. In 1968 he was accepted back as editor of the Budapest daily *Magyar Hirlap*. In the 1970s and 1980s he wrote his memoirs, publishing *Miskolci toronyóra* (The Miskolc clock tower; 1976) and *Menedékjog—1956* (The right of asylum—1956; 1989). (MS)

Sources: *The Truth about the Nagy Affair: Facts, Documents, Comments* (London, 1959); András Pályi, "Az újságíró önéletrajza," *Élet és Irodalom*, 1977, no. 6; Judit Ember, *Menedék jog—1956: A Nagy Imre csoport elrablása* (Budapest, 1989); *Új magyar irodalmi lexikon* (Budapest, 1994).

FEDAK Stepan (9 January 1861, Przemyśl–6 January 1937, Lwów [Lviv]), Ukrainian lawyer, banker, and social activist. Fedak graduated from the Academic Gymnasium in Lwów, and he completed his law studies at the local university. From 1890 he practiced law. He co-founded and participated in the government of many of the institutions of economic life in Lwów: the cooperative bank, Centrobank; the Audit Union of Ukrainian Cooperative Societies; the Land Mortgage Bank; and the life insurance society Karpatiia. He was a member of the board of Narodna Torhivlia, a founding member of the mutual insurance society Dnister, and its director between 1909 and 1920; in 1913–18 he was vice-president of the National Bank in Lwów. In 1915 he was deported by the Russians to Kiev, where he conducted activities to aid war victims in Galicia. He returned to Lwów in 1916. From November 1918 he was secretary for provisions in the Western Ukrainian National Republic. In December 1918, after the capture of Lwów by Polish troops, Fedak founded the Civic Committee, which represented the Ukrainian people to the authorities and which helped captives, internees, and political prisoners. Until the end of his life Fedak chaired an unofficial committee for aid to political prisoners. He also remained a member of the Stauropigial Institute and an honorary member of the Prosvita Society. His daughters married the leaders of the Organization of Ukrainian Nationalists (OUN): **Yevhen Konovalets** and **Andriy Melnyk**. His son, Stepan Fedak (pseudonym "Dragon," 1901–45), a member of the Ukrainian Military Organization, made an unsuccessful attempt on the life of **Józef Piłsudski**, head of the Polish state, on 25 November 1921 in Lwów. (TS)

Sources: *Encyclopedia of Ukraine*, vol. 1 (Toronto, 1985); Matthew Stachiv and Jaroslav Sztendera, eds., *Western Ukraine at the Turning Point of Europe's History, 1918–1923*, vols. 1–2 (New York, 1971); Ryszard Torzecki, *Kwestia ukraińska w Polsce 1923–1929* (Kraków, 1989).

FEDORCHUK Vitalyi (December 1918, Zhytomyr), Communist security officer in the Ukraine. After graduating from a military school and from a higher NKVD school, in 1939 Fedorchuk started his career in the security apparatus, quickly gaining the reputation of a ruthless Chekist. In 1940 he joined the Communist Party. In 1943–47 he was an officer of the "Smersh" and then, until 1970, of the military intelligence, GRU (glavnoe razvedyvatelnoe upravlenie). In 1944–47 he commanded MVD (Ministerstvo vnutryennikh del) troops fighting against the Ukrainian Insurgent Army, and in 1946 he took an active part in the liquidation of the formal structures of the Greek Catholic Church and in the persecution of its bishops and clergy. Then he was sent on a mission to Vienna. In December 1953 he took part in the kidnapping of the Czech émigré politician **Bohumil Laušman**, who was later imprisoned in Czechoslovakia. In 1955 he returned to Moscow, where he graduated from the Higher School of the KGB. From 1957 he headed the counter-intelligence of the Soviet Army stationed in East Germany. In 1967, when Yuri Andropov took over the KGB, Fedorchuk became head of its Military Intelligence Department.

In July 1970 Fedorchuk took over the KGB of the Ukrainian SSR. He used all means of repression against independent activists: arrests and deportations to labor camps, treacherous assassinations, and imprisonment in psychiatric wards. After the fall of **Petro Shelest** in 1973, in September 1974 Fedorchuk became a deputy member, and in 1976 a member, of the Politburo of the Central Committee of the Communist Party of Ukraine. In January 1972 he intensified the repression against the democratic opposition—for instance, against the Ukrainian Helsinki Group; therefore democratic opposition circles called him the "butcher of Ukraine." In the summer of 1981 Fedorchuk publicly warned about the dangers of alleged counterrevolution in Poland. Connected with the "Dniepropetrovsk Mafia" of Leonid Brezhnev and with the head of the KGB, Andropov, he gained a powerful position in the Soviet hierarchy. When Andropov was getting ready to succeed Brezhnev and resigned from the KGB, on 26 May 1982 Fedorchuk was appointed his successor. When Brezhnev died in November 1982 and when Andropov became secretary general of the Soviet party, Fedorchuk ceded the position of head of the KGB to Victor Chebrikov and assumed the position of the Soviet minister of interior. These steps strengthened Andropov's control of the ministry, which had rivaled the KGB. As minister of interior, Fedorchuk implemented Andropov's policies, which were aimed at sharpening discipline in the party and in the society. During perestroika, in January 1986 Fedorchuk was sidelined to the position of inspector in the Ministry of National Defense, and then he retired. He was never held responsible for his policies. (WR)

Sources: *Encyclopedia of Ukraine*, vol. 1 (Toronto, 1984); Archie Brown, ed., *The Soviet Union: A Biographical Dictionary* (London, 1990); Peter Deriabin and T. H. Bagley, "Fedorchuk, the KGB, and the Soviet Succession," *Orbis*, 1982, vol. 26, no. 3; Zhores Medvedev, *Andropov* (New York, 1983); Michael Parrish, *Soviet Security and Intelligence Organizations, 1917–1990* (New York, 1992); Bohdan Nahaylo, *The Ukrainian Resurgence* (Toronto, 1999).

FEDORYK Yosafat Yosif (20 December 1897, Yaroslavl–28 December 1979, Stryi), bishop of the Ukrainian underground Greek Catholic Church in the USSR. In 1924–28 Fedoryk studied theology in Rome, and he earned a Ph.D. there. Until 1939 he worked in a Greek Catholic parish in Ostrów, near Przemyśl. During the Soviet and German occupations he served as prior (hegumen) of the Basilian monasteries in the diocese of Przemyśl. In September 1945 he was arrested by the Soviet authorities but was released. After the decision of the "Lviv ecumenical council" of March 1946 to dissolve the Greek Catholic Church and after its absorption into the Orthodox Church, Fedoryk continued his unofficial pastoral work. Arrested again in 1952, he spent many years in prisons in Lviv and the Donbas and in many labor camps (for example, in Karaganda), where at the end of his life he was ordained bishop by Bishop **Oleksandr Khira**. Fedoryk died soon after his release. (WR)

Sources: *Martirolohia ukrain's'kikh tserkov u chetyriokh tomakh*, vol. 2 (Toronto, 1985); Bohdan R. Bociurkiw, *The Ukrainian Greek-Catholic Church and the Soviet State (1939–1950)* (Edmonton, 1996).

FEDUN Petro (also known under the pseudonym of **Petro Poltava**) (1919, Shniryv, county of Brody–23 December 1951, near Ivano-Frankivsk), Ukrainian nationalist politician. In 1940 Fedun was inducted into the Red Army. After the outbreak of the German-Soviet war he was taken prisoner but was released thanks to the efforts of his parents. In 1941 he enrolled in the department of medicine in the university in Lviv (Lwów). Between 1940 and 1943 he organized the OUN Youth (Yunatstvo OUN, the youth unit of the Organization of Ukrainian Nationalists), and he was the editor of its press organ, *Yunak*. In 1944 Fedun became a member of the OUN-B, Provid; a major in the Ukrainian Insurgent Army (UPA); and deputy president of the General Secretariat of the Ukrainian Supreme Liberation Council (USLC) and head of its Information Bureau. He was one of the most famous and one of the most imaginative publicists of the Ukrainian underground. He thought that the organized struggle of the underground and the insurgent units of the UPA helped to mobilize the masses and prevented them from capitulation. He emphasized the similarities between Nazism and communism. He also advocated the democratization of the OUN. In August 1950 he sent the *Appeal of the Ukrainian Underground* to the U.S. Department of State and to the Voice of America. Fedun was killed in the Ukraine in a clash with the functionaries of the Soviet security organs. He authored such works as *Kontseptsia samostiinoi Ukrainy i osnovna tendentsiia politychnoho rozvytku suchasnoho svitu* (The concept of an independent Ukraine and the basic tendencies of political development of the modern world; 1947) and *Bezposeredn'o za shcho my vedemo nash bii* (What we are actually fighting for; 1949). His works were secretly conveyed by couriers to the West, and in 1959 they were published under the title *Zbirnyk pidpilnykh pysan'* (Collection of underground writings) in Munich. (GM)

Sources: *Entsyklopediia Ukrainoznavstva*, vol. 4; *Encyclopedia of Ukraine*, vol. 4 (Toronto, 1993); *The Ukrainian Insurgent Army in a Fight for Freedom* (New York, 1954); Ryszard Torzecki, *Polacy i Ukraińcy: Sprawa ukraińska w czasie II wojny światowej na terenie Ii Rzeczpospolitej* (Warsaw, 1993); Anatol Kaminskyi, *Vasyl Okhrymovich* (Toronto, New York, and London, 1999).

FEIERABEND Ladislav (14 June 1891, Kostelec, on the Orlice River–15 August 1969, Villach, Austria), Czech politician and economist. Feierabend completed high school in Hradec Králové, and in 1915 he graduated in law from the Czech University in Prague. During his studies he was also on scholarship in Oxford and Neuchatel, Switzerland. In 1915–17 he worked in the judiciary system, and then he co-organized the agricultural cooperative movement. In 1917–25 he was secretary of the Central Association of Cooperative Societies; then he was director, and from 1930 managing director, of Kooperativa, an association for purchasing agricultural farms. From 1930 he was president of Prague's agricultural exchange, and from 1934, president of the Czechoslovak Grain Association and vice-president of Czechoslovak Export Enterprises. One of the leading economists of the Agrarian Party, Feierabend published extensively. During the Second Republic (1938–39) he served as minister of agriculture, and initially he was also minister of justice. Until January 1940 he served as minister of agriculture in the government of the Protectorate of Bohemia and Moravia, and at the same time he was one of the co-founders of the national resistance movement. He represented the Agrarians in the Political Center (Politické Ústředí), and he maintained foreign contacts. In January 1940 he fled to France via Hungary and Yugoslavia. In France he started to work with the resistance movement. From 1941 he was finance minister in the Czechoslovak government-in-exile. He was often critical of President **Edvard Beneš**, especially about the latter's attitude toward the Communists and the USSR. In February 1945 Feierabend resigned in protest against the Beneš government policies and against the ban on the Agrarian Party after the war.

After his return to the country, Feierabend farmed on his estate in Mirošov, near Rokycany. Between 1946 and 1948 he was active in the Czechoslovak National Socialist

Party (Československá Strana Národně Socialistická); in 1946 he was the party's candidate in the elections to the National Assembly, but he lost. After the Communist coup in February 1948 Feierabend went into hiding, and in April of the same year he left the country along with his family. Until 1950 he was in Great Britain and then in the United States, where he worked in the Center for Central European Studies, was editor of the Voice of America, worked with Radio Free Europe, and was active in the Council of Free Czechoslovakia (Rada Svobodného Československa). In the 1960s in the United States Feierabend published eight volumes of his memoirs from the period 1938–48. A selection of these memoirs was published in London under the title *Soumrak Československé demokracie* (The decline of Czechoslovak democracy; 1986–88), and in Czechoslovakia the whole work was published under the title *Politické vzpomínky I–III* (Political memoirs I–III; 1994–96). (PU)

Sources: *ČBS*; *Českoslovenští politici: 1918–1991* (Prague, 1991); *Politická elita meziválečného Československa 1918–1938: Kdo byl kdo za první republiky* (Prague, 1998); *Kdo byl kdo v našich dějinach ve 20. stoleti*, vol. 1 (Prague, 1998); Eduard Beneš, *From Munich to a New War and New Victory* (London, 1954).

FEJÉRVÁRY Géza (15 March 1833, Josefstadt [now Josefov]–25 April 1914, Vienna), Hungarian politician and general. Fejérváry was born into a family with a strong patriotic and military tradition. He graduated from the military academy in Bécsújhely in 1851 and from the Vienna Military Academy in 1857. As a staff officer in the rank of captain, he distinguished himself in the battle of Solferino (1859). He took part in wars against Denmark (1864) and Prussia (1866). In 1865, in the rank of major, he became personal aide-de-camp to Emperor Francis Joseph. After the Austro-Hungarian Agreement of 1867 he was entrusted with the task of organizing the Hungarian Army, assuming the position of deputy minister (1872–84) and then minister of defense (1884–1903). In 1904 he assumed command of the Imperial Guard. During the so-called crisis of dualism, when the conflict over the range of Hungarian autonomy caused street demonstrations and a deadlock in parliamentary proceedings, on 18 June 1905 Fejérváry took over a non-parliamentary Hungarian government formed by the emperor. The opposition scornfully called it the "government of dragoons." A supporter of cooperation with Vienna on the condition of Hungarian autonomy, he mediated between the leaders of the Hungarian opposition and Emperor Francis Joseph. After resigning (8 April 1906), Fejérváry returned to the position of commander of the Imperial Guard and held it until his death. Among the Hungarian politicians, he was one of the most trustworthy supporters of the 1867 agreement. In domestic policy he favored a Bismarck type of rule. His strong personality and his commanding skills made him one of the leading Hungarian politicians at the turn of the twentieth century. (MS)

Sources: Gusztáv Gratz, *A dualizmus kora* (Budapest, 1934); Paul Ignotus, *Hungary* (London, 1972); *19. századi magyar történelem, 1790–1918* (Budapest, 1998).

FELCZAK Zygmunt (2 May 1903, Chorki, near Łęczyca–3 July 1946, Bydgoszcz), Polish political activist. From 1915, after finishing a village primary school, Felczak attended secondary school in Łęczyca, where in 1920 he volunteered to fight in the Polish-Soviet war. He graduated from high school in 1923 and began studying at Warsaw University and later at Poznań University, but he never graduated. At the same time he was active in the National Workers' Party (Narodowa Partia Robotnicza [NPR]) and in the Union of Working Youth–Unity (from 1934 he was president of the latter). He also edited the newspapers *Obrona Ludu* and *Demokrata*. He was a member of the left wing of the NPR, which opposed cooperation with the Christian Democrats. However, when in 1937 the NPR and the Christian Democratic Party merged into the Labor Party (Stronnictwo Pracy [SP]), Felczak became a member of the SP Main Board and deputy editor-in-chief of *Dziennik Bydgoski*. As he was well known in Bydgoszcz, in September 1939 Felczak escaped from the Germans to Warsaw, where he was active in the underground. From March 1942 he was an SP representative in the Coordinating Political Committee (Polityczny Komitet Porozumiewawczy [PKP]). He favored cooperation with the Socialist and Peasant Parties, as well as radical social changes in Poland. This resulted in a clash between Felczak and SP leaders on 18 October 1942. Removed from the PKP, he became a leader of a group publishing the paper *Zryw*, and from May 1943 he was vice-president of the Party of National Upsurge (Stronnictwo Zrywu Narodowego [SZN]).

During the Warsaw Uprising Felczak fought in a Home Army unit in downtown Warsaw, and after the failure of the uprising he escaped from a transport to a POW camp. He went into hiding in Włochy, near Warsaw, where he began to work with the Communists. In February 1945, on behalf of the Provisional Government, he was appointed governor (*voivode*) of Pomerania Province. On behalf of the SZN and with the approval of the Polish Workers' Party (Polska Partia Robotnicza [PPR]) he brought about the reactivation of the SP and in July 1945 became its president. He also founded the publishing cooperative Zryw, which published the *Ilustrowany Kurier Polski* (Illustrated

Polish daily). After **Karol Popiel** returned to Poland Felczak became vice-president of the reactivated SP, and from December 1945 he was an MP of the National Home Council (Krajowa Rada Narodowa [KRN]) and leader of the SP Club. In 1946 during the campaign before a June referendum, Felczak supported the PPR's slogan, "Three times yes," against the majority of party members. He then led a campaign to take over the party by those members who favored collaboration with the Communists and opted for the removal of Popiel's followers from the leadership of the SP. Felczak died after he was severely beaten by unknown assailants in Bydgoszcz. (WR)

Sources: *PSB*, vol. 6; Kunert, vol. 1; Konstanty Turowski, "Dzieje Stronnictwa Pracy w latach 1945–1946," *Chrześcijanin w Świecie*, 1982, no. 1; Mirosław Piotrowski, *Służba idei czy serwilizm? Zygmunt Felczak i Feliks Widy-Wirski w najnowszych dziejach Polski* (Lublin, 1994).

FELDMANIS Jūlijs (21 July 1889, Nīgrandas, Courland–16 August 1953, Washington, D.C.), Latvian diplomat. After graduating from a teachers' college in 1909, Feldmanis worked for two years as a teacher of German in Tukums. In 1915 he graduated in law from Moscow University. In 1915–18 he served in the Russian Army as a clerk, and he was also a social activist in the Caucasus. From January to July 1919 he was a lawyer in the government of Aleksandr Kolchak in Omsk, and then he returned to Latvia. From November 1919 he worked as head of the Eastern Department of the Ministry of Foreign Affairs, and then he was a legal adviser of the ministry. Between 1921 and 1923 he worked as secretary of the legation in Paris, in 1923–25 he was head of a department in the League of Nations, and between 1925 and 1928 he served as chargé d'affaires in France. After his return to Latvia in 1928, Feldmanis became head of the Eastern Department, and in 1929 head of the Western Department, of the Ministry of Foreign Affairs. From 1930 he served as a permanent delegate to the League of Nations; from 1932 he was also an envoy to Switzerland, and from September 1939 he was also an envoy to Denmark. In 1936 he was president of the League of Nations' commission for the affairs of Syrian refugees, and in 1939 he served as president of the commission for labor in the colonies. After Latvia's occupation by the Red Army and its incorporation into the USSR in 1940, Feldmanis was dismissed from his position. However, he was in charge of the legation to the League of Nations until 1946, and in Switzerland he was in charge of the legation until 1948. In 1948 he left for the United States. Appointed chargé d'affaires to the U.S. government in March 1949, he took an active part in the work of the Assembly of Captive European Nations (ACEN), and

he sought the maintenance of the recognition of Latvian independence by the American government. (EJ)

Sources: *Latvijas vadošie darbinieki* (Riga, 1929); *Es viņu pazīstu* (Riga, 1939); "Miris Latvijas sūtnis Vašingtonā Jūlijs Feldmans," *Laiks*, 19 August 1953; "Miris Jūlijs Feldmans," *Latvija*, 22 August 1953; O. Rozītis, "Manas atmiņas par sūtni J. Feldmani," *Austrālijas Latvietis*, 29 August 1953; Adolfs Blodnieks, *The Undefeated Nation* (New York, 1960); "Latvijas pastāvīgais delegāts," *Diena*, 3 October 1992.

FERDINAND I Sachsen-Coburg-Gotha (26 February 1861, Vienna–10 September 1948, Berlin), tsar of Bulgaria. Ferdinand was the son of Prince August and the daughter of the king of France, Louis-Philippe Bourbon. In his youth he served in the Austrian Army. After Prince Alexander Battenberg was toppled in 1887, the Bulgarian National Assembly offered the crown to Ferdinand, who despite the opposition of some European powers, decided to take it. After ascending the throne, he initially remained in the shadows of Prime Minister Aleksandur Stambolov, who actually ruled, but in 1895 Ferdinand dismissed him, and later he probably organized the plot that resulted in his assassination. This paved the way for Ferdinand to assume full power. In domestic policy he played on the conflicts among party leaders; having little social support, the parties were largely dependent on the royal court. Ferdinand opened Bulgaria to foreign investments, which contributed to economic development. In 1893 he married Maria-Louise Bourbon-Parma, and after her death in 1908, he married a German princess, Eleonor von Reuss-Köstritz.

In foreign policy Ferdinand aimed at strengthening Bulgaria's political and territorial position. Taking advantage of the Young Turk revolution, on 5 October 1908, he assumed the title of tsar and proclaimed full independence from Turkey. Striving for domination in the Balkans, in October 1912 Ferdinand entered into an alliance with Serbia and Greece and ordered an attack on Turkey. Despite initial successes, the Bulgarian Army failed to seize Istanbul, while conflicts with the allies—with Serbia over Macedonia and with Greece over Western Thrace—made the victory problematic. Under the influence of nationalist officers and radical Macedonian organizations, which wanted the unification of Macedonia with Bulgaria, in June 1913 Ferdinand ordered an attack on Serbia. In the Second Balkan War Serbia and Greece allied with Turkey, and Bulgaria was defeated, losing a part of already occupied territory. There were rumors of Ferdinand's possible abdication.

After the Balkan Wars Ferdinand changed his tactics and entrusted the government to a follower of the Central Powers, **Vasil Radoslavov**, with a rapprochement with Austria-Hungary in mind. While Vienna and Berlin initially treated Ferdinand as an adventurer and did not trust him, after the outbreak of World War I they changed their minds. After a series of German victories on the eastern front, in September 1915 Ferdinand decided to send the Bulgarian Army to occupy a part of Serbia and Macedonia. This decision raised objections among the traditionally Russophile part of the Bulgarian society and elite. Several opponents of his policy, including the Peasant Party leader **Aleksandur Stamboliyski**, were imprisoned. Ferdinand did not change course even after it became clear that the defeat of the Central Powers was assured. Trying to save face, he dismissed Radoslavov, but his successor as prime minister, **Aleksandur Malinov**, continued the previous policy.

A drastic decline in the standard of living and the hopeless situation of troops on the front lines were symptoms of the coming revolution. When at the end of August 1918 the Allied Salonika offensive broke through the Macedonian front and the one-hundred-thousand-man Bulgarian Army was surrounded and forced to surrender, a part of the troops rebelled. On 24 September 1918 the general staff was imprisoned by the soldiers, and a military revolutionary committee was founded in Radomir. Ferdinand released Stamboliyski from prison and sent him to calm the troops. On 27 September, however, Stamboliyski proclaimed a republic. Troops loyal to the tsar temporarily mastered the situation, but on 29 September Ferdinand had to accept harsh conditions of armistice with the Entente, including his own abdication in favor of his son, **Boris III**; this followed on 3 October 1918. Ferdinand left for Berlin and then for his residence in Coburg, where he later took up ornithology and entomology. (AG)

Sources: *Biographisches Lexikon*, vol. 2; *Ferdinand of Bulgaria: The Amazing Career of a Shoddy Czar* (London, 1916); Josef Knodt, *Ferdinand der Bulgare: Die Balkanmission eines Prinzen aus dem Hause Sachsen-Coburg und Gotha-Konary, 1887–1918* (Bielefeld, 1947); John M. A. Macdonald, *Czar Ferdinand and His People* (New York, 1971); Stephen Constant, *Foxy Ferdinand, 1861–1948, Tsar of Bulgaria* (London, 1979); Holger H. Herwig and Neil M. Heyman, *Biographical Dictionary of World War I* (Westport, Conn., 1982); Stefan Vlakhov-Mitsov, *Vladiteli v primka: Kniga za knyaz Batenberg, tsar Ferdinand I i tsar Boris III* (Sofia, 1992).

FERDINAND I Hohenzollern-Sigmaringen (24 August 1865, Sigmaringen, Prussia [now in Germany]–20 July 1927 Sinaia, Romania), king of Romania. The son of Prince Leopold of Hohenzollern-Sigmaringen and Infanta Antónia of Portugal and the nephew of the childless King Charles I of Romania, Ferdinand was a descendant of the Swabian line of the Hohenzollern family. He was educated at the university in Tübingen and in Leipzig.

He did his military service in Kassel. On 29 December 1892 he married Lady Marie, daughter of the Duke of Edinburgh and granddaughter of Queen Victoria. On 18 March 1899 he was formally adopted as crown prince of Romania by Charles I. At the beginning of the twentieth century Ferdinand kept out of the limelight—an attitude that was consistent with his nature, described by his wife and his contemporaries as a combination of moderation and personal modesty. During the Second Balkan War in 1913 Ferdinand served as commander-in-chief of the Romanian Army.

When Charles died, Ferdinand succeeded him to the Romanian throne on 11 October 1914. His personal sympathies were on the side of the Central Powers because his two brothers served in the German Army, Emperor Wilhelm II was his cousin, and Emperor Francis Joseph was a close acquaintance. Moreover, Ferdinand expected that the Central Powers would win the war. However, from the beginning of the conflict Ferdinand supported the cautious and neutral policies of Prime Minister **Ion I.C. Brațianu**. In the summer of 1916, influenced by the Romanian political elite and by his wife, who firmly supported England and France, he accepted Brațianu's decision to enter the war on the side of the Entente. Although Ferdinand was pressed by German and Austrian diplomats and was described in Berlin as a "renegade from the Hohenzollern family," he realized that he could not risk losing the throne. Formally, he was still commander-in-chief of the army, which in 1916 suffered a series of defeats and had to evacuate its soldiers to the eastern end of the kingdom at the beginning of 1917. The collapse of tsarism and the crisis in Russia additionally weakened the position of Romania. The morale of the Romanian Army was at its lowest ebb. Because of this, Ferdinand courageously decided to take an extraordinary step. At the beginning of April 1917 he gave a speech to the soldiers, who were mostly peasants. In this speech he promised them a radical land reform and greater participation in the public life of the country. The Constitutional Assembly gathered in Iași in July 1917 and amended the constitution to that effect. These steps definitely raised the morale of the army, although after the Bolshevik revolution in Russia and after the Brest-Litovsk Treaty of March 1918 Romania's situation became critical. However, Ferdinand was able to avoid personally signing the Bucharest peace treaty of May 1918 in which Romania agreed to cease activities against the Central Powers. In the summer of 1918 the position of Austria-Hungary deteriorated and Germany began seeking a truce, and on 10 November 1918 the Romanian Army resumed its activities against the Central Powers. At the end of November the royal family triumphantly returned to Bucharest.

At the Paris Peace Conference Ferdinand wrote a letter to the heads of the governments of England, France, and Italy presenting Romania's merits to the Entente. Thanks to the diplomatic talents of Brațianu and because of the activity of the Romanian Army against the Hungarian Soviet Republic, Romania finally achieved considerable territorial gains: Transylvania, Bukovina, Bessarabia, and a part of Dobruja were incorporated into a Greater Romanian state. On 15 October 1922 Ferdinand was crowned king of Greater Romania at Alba Iulia. Until the end of his life, he promoted a pro-Western foreign policy based on alliances with France, Czechoslovakia, Poland, and Yugoslavia and on the fulfillment of his 1917 promise of land reform. In 1926, at the request of Brațianu, Ferdinand appointed his grandson, Prince Michael, as crown prince instead of his son Charles, who had left his wife and was living with **Magda Lupescu**, which had aroused public indignation. Ferdinand also supported a system of rotating parties in power, as he wanted the royal court to remain the arbiter of political disputes. (WR)

Sources: *Biographisches Lexikon*, vol. 1; Holger H. Herwig and Neil M. Heyman, *Biographical Dictionary of World War I* (Westport, Conn., 1982); Marie Queen of Romania, *The Story of My Life*, vols. 1–2 (New York, 1934); Gheorghe Tuțui and Mircea Popa, *Hohenzollerni în România* (Bucharest, 1962); Sherman Spector, *Rumania at the Paris Peace Conference: A Study of the Diplomacy of I. C. Brațianu* (New York, 1962); Robert William Seton-Watson, *History of the Roumanians* (Hamden, Conn. 1963); Vasile Alexandrescu, *Romania in World War I* (Bucharest, 1985); Glenn Torrey, *General Henri Bertholet and Romania 1916–1919* (Boulder, Colo., 1987); Emile Turdeanu, *Modern Romania: The Achievement of National Unity 1914–1920* (Los Angeles, 1988); Keith Hitchins, *Rumania 1866–1947* (Oxford, 1994).

FESHCHENKO-CHOPIVSKYI Ivan (19 January 1884, Chudnov, Volhynia–2 Sept. 1952, Karelo-Finnish ASSR), Ukrainian politician. In 1908 Feshchenko-Chopivskyi graduated from the Polytechnical College in Kiev, and he started working there as an assistant in the Department of Metallurgy. He was active in the Ukrainian Party of Socialists-Federalists. In 1917 he became a member of the Ukrainian Central Council (Rada). At the end of February 1918 he was appointed minister of industry and trade. During the rule of Hetman **Pavlo Skoropadsky** he was in the opposition. At the beginning of 1919 he again joined the government of the Directorate of the Ukrainian National Republic (UNR). After the fall of the UNR he went to Poland. In 1922 he became professor of metallurgy at the Academy of Mining and Metallurgy in Kraków. In 1928 he became consultant in Baildon Steelworks in Katowice and director of the laboratory in Pokój Steelworks. During the Nazi occupation he was not active in politics. Arrested by the NKVD in March 1945 in Katowice, he was deported to a labor camp in the Karelo-Finnish ASSR, where he died. Feshchenko-Chopivskyi authored many works in the field of metallurgy, and he was a member of prestigious scientific societies. (WR)

Source: *Encyclopedia of Ukraine,* vol. 1 (Toronto, 1984).

FIELDORF Emil August, pseudonym "Nil" (20 March 1895, Kraków–24 February 1953, Warsaw), Polish general of the Home Army (Armia Krajowa [AK]). The son of a railroad worker, after completing high school in Kraków, Fieldorf attended a teacher training college. In 1912 he joined the Rifle Association. During World War I he fought in the Polish Legions and received the Order of Virtuti Militari for his courage in the battle of Hulewicze. After the oath crisis in July 1917 he was incorporated into the Austrian Army and fought on the Italian front. In September 1918 he joined the Polish Military Organization (Polska Organizacja Wojskowa [POW]) and in November 1918, the Polish Army. He participated in the disarmament of the Austrians in Kraków and in the fight for Lwów (Lviv) and Wilno (Vilnius). At the beginning of 1920 he fought in the battle of Dvinsk (Dünaburg, now Daugavpils). In April 1920 he took part in the Kiev campaign. Decorated with four Crosses of Valor, after the end of war he stayed in the army. As a company commander of the First Infantry Division, in May 1926 he supported **Józef Piłsudski**. In 1927 he completed a specialist training course for officers in Rembertów. From November 1935 he was a battalion commander of the Frontier Guards Corps in Troki, near Wilno, and from January 1938 he commanded an infantry regiment of the Frontier Guards Corps in Brzeżany.

In September 1939 Fieldorf's regiment fought in the Twelfth Tarnopol Infantry Division of General Gustaw Paszkiewicz. In October 1939 Fieldorf attempted to go to the West but was interned in Hungary. However, in January 1940 he reached France, where he served as an officer on General **Kazimierz Sosnkowski**'s staff. After the fall of France, on 17 July 1940 he was sent from London to Poland as the first emissary of the Polish Armed Forces (Polskie Siły Zbrojne [PSZ]). At the beginning of September 1940 he reached Warsaw, where he became inspector of the High Command of the Union of Armed Struggle (Związek Walki Zbrojnej [ZWZ]). From the spring of 1942 he commanded the AK Białystok region, and from the fall of 1942 he had the Command of Diversion (Kedyw). He supervised all units involved in current actions, training, and production of weapons for sabotage and diversion. Involved in the work of the Command of Underground Struggle, in February 1944 he was recalled from the Kedyw command and formed the rudiments of the Nie organization in case of Soviet occupation. On 29 September 1944 the commander-in-chief promoted him to brigadier general. From October 1944 he was a deputy to **Leopold Okulicki**, the AK commander-in-chief. After the AK was dissolved and Okulicki assumed the command of Nie in January 1945, Fieldorf remained his deputy and commander of the South Region of the organization.

Arrested accidentally on 7 March 1945 under the name Walenty Gdanicki, unrecognized, Fieldorf was deported by the Soviets to a labor camp in the Ural Mountains. He then worked in a forced labor camp near Kazan, from which he was released in October 1947 and returned to Poland. In February 1948 he disclosed his identity. Applying for reinstatement to military service, in October 1950 Fieldorf contacted his former commander, General Paszkiewicz, not knowing that he was responsible for many arrests. On 10 November 1950 Fieldorf was imprisoned. The arrest warrant was signed in the General Military Prosecutor's Office only eleven days later. Fieldorf was charged with an alleged attempt to overthrow the system by force, actions against the USSR, and the liquidation of Communist activists. On 16 April 1952 he was sentenced to death under a decree that was issued by the Polish Committee of National Liberation for the prosecution of "Fascist-Nazi" criminals. Appeals had no effect, and Fieldorf was executed. In 1958 investigation into his case was "discontinued," but he was fully rehabilitated on 7 March 1989. (WR)

Sources: Kunert, vol. 1; Maria Fieldorf and Leszek Zachuta, *Generał "Nil" August Emil Fieldorf: Fakty, dokumenty, relacje* (Warsaw, 1993); Andrzej Przewoźnik and Adam Strzembosz, *Generał "Nil"* (Warsaw, 1999).

FIERLINGER Zdenek (11 July 1891, Olomouc–2 May 1976, Prague), Czech Socialist, collaborator with Communists in their takeover of power in Czechoslovakia. After graduating from a trade school in Olomouc, from 1910 to 1914 Fierlinger worked as a representative of the MacCormick Company in Russia. During World War I he volunteered for the Russian Army, and in 1917 he took command of the Jan Hus Regiment of the Czechoslovak Legion in Siberia. In 1918–19 he was head of a military mission in France, where he became a colonel. After his return to Czechoslovakia in 1920 he joined the Social Democratic Party. In 1921 he started a diplomatic career and became ambassador to the Netherlands. In 1924–25 he was ambassador to Romania; in 1925–28, to the United States; and in 1928–32, to Switzerland. He subsequently represented Czechoslovakia in the League of Nations. At the beginning of 1937 he returned to Czechoslovakia, becoming head of the political department of the Ministry

of Foreign Affairs. From the summer of 1937 to December 1939 he was ambassador to Moscow, where he became aligned with communism.

Between January 1940 and July 1941 Fierlinger was in London, working in the government-in-exile. At the beginning of 1942 he again became ambassador to Moscow. On 12 December 1943 in Moscow, Fierlinger, along with President **Edvard Beneš**, signed a treaty of friendship and mutual assistance with the USSR. Afterwards, Fierlinger mediated in talks between the Communists and the government-in-exile. These talks led to the formation of a coalition cabinet, and on 7 April 1945 Fierlinger became the head of this government. On 26 April 1945 he signed a treaty with Vyacheslav Molotov through which the Transcarpathian Ukraine, the prewar territory of Czechoslovakia, was ceded to Moscow. After elections, on 3 July 1946 Fierlinger resigned as head of government, retaining the post of deputy prime minister. As leader of the Social Democratic Party, he endeavored to merge his party with the Communist Party. However, at the Congress of Social Democrats in November 1946 he did not have the support of the majority for his efforts; therefore he had to resign as head of the party in favor of **Bohumil Laušman**. In September 1947 Fierlinger brought about an agreement with the Communists on the taxation of large incomes.

During the Communist coup of February 1948 Fierlinger supported **Klement Gottwald**. Soon afterwards, the supporters of a union with the Communists prevailed in the Social Democratic Party, and Fierlinger again assumed the leadership of the party. In June 1948 his efforts led to the incorporation of his party into the Communist Party of Czechoslovakia (Komunisticka Strana Československa [CPC]). He also organized a purge of the opponents of this decision. At the same time he himself became a member of the Presidium of the Central Committee (CC) of the CPC. Between June 1948 and September 1953 he served as deputy prime minister. From April 1950 to January 1953 he was president of the state council for church affairs, and in this role he supervised the suppression of the church hierarchy, including the arrests and trials of Archbishop **Josef Beran** and Bishop **Jan Vojtaššak**. From September 1951 to June 1954 Fierlinger was a member of the political secretariat of the CC of the CPC, taking part in all decisions of the Stalinist leadership of the party. From September 1953 to June 1964 he was president of the National Assembly, and from June 1954 he belonged to the Politburo of the CC of the CPC. In the spring of 1968 he left the top leadership of the party but remained in the CC until 1971, when he retired as a "meritorious" party and national activist. His opportunism allowed him to stay at the top in politics throughout his life. He published *Národní fronta: Vychovatelka revoluce* (1945; The National Front: Teacher of the revolution; 1945); *Poslání sociální demokracie v novém státě* (The mission of social democracy in the new state; 1947); *Ve službách ČSR* (In the service of the Czechoslovak Republic, 2 vols.; 1948–49); and other works. (WR)

Sources: *ČBS*; H. Kuhn and O. Böss, *Biographisches Handbuch der Tschechoslovakei* (Prague, 1961); William E. Griffith, ed., *Communism in Europe*, vol. 2 (Cambridge, Mass., 1966); Josef Korbel, *The Communist Subversion of Czechoslovakia, 1948–1960* (Princeton, 1959); Karel Kaplan, *The Short March: The Communist Takeover in Czechoslovakia, 1945–1948* (London, 1981).

FILARET [originally Mykhailo Denisenko] (23 January 1929, Blahodatne near Donetsk), metropolitan of the Ukrainian Orthodox Church (UOC). In 1946–48 Filaret studied at the theological seminary in Odessa and later in the Moscow Theological Academy (MTA). In January 1950 he chose the monastic vocation and adopted the name Filaret. In 1952 he received a Ph.D. in theology. In 1953 he became associate professor and senior lecturer at the MTA. Appointed head of a seminary (*hegumen*), he worked as an inspector of the Saratov and Kiev seminaries. In July 1958 he became archimandrite and rector of the Kiev theological seminary. In 1960 he was appointed parish priest of St. Vladimir Cathedral in Kiev. In 1961–62 he was in Alexandria (Egypt), where he directed the Alexander Nevski Church. In February 1962 he was consecrated bishop and became vicar of the Leningrad archdiocese. He was also to run the Riga bishopric, but in June 1962 he was appointed vicar of the Central European Exarchate, and in October 1962 he became bishop of Vienna and Austria. He worked there until December 1964, when he was appointed bishop of Dmitrov, vicar of the Moscow archdiocese, and rector of the MTA.

Following the resignation of Metropolitan Ioan, on 14 May 1966 Filaret became the exarch of Ukraine, archbishop of Kiev and Halich, and a member of the Holy Synod of the Russian Orthodox Church (ROC). On 25 February 1968 he was elevated to the rank of metropolitan. In connection with the role that the Communist authorities attached to the Orthodox Church in their international peace propaganda campaign, Filaret, as a member of the commission of the Holy Synod on Christian unity and inter-church relations, visited almost one hundred countries. In 1977 he became a member of the World Peace Council. In the 1980s he took part in the Communist-controlled preparations for the millennium of the baptism of Kievan Ruthenia in 1988. In this role he actively combated autocephalic tendencies in the Ukrainian Orthodox Church. After the death of the ROC

patriarch, Pimen, in May 1990 Filaret was elected *locum tenens* of the patriarchic throne. Nevertheless, on 8 June 1990 he lost the position of patriarch to the metropolitan of Leningrad, Aleksiy II.

Supported by the new Ukrainian authorities and by **Leonid Kravchuk** in particular, in 1991 Filaret contributed to the proclamation of Ukrainian independence. In October 1990 the ROC Council (Sobor) granted the UOC, as the Ukrainian Exarchate was called, administrative autonomy, while Filaret was nominated metropolitan of Kiev and all of the Ukraine. On 1–3 November 1991 the UOC Council appealed to Patriarch Aleksiy for full autocephaly. In April 1992 the ROC Council refused the appeal, and on 27 May 1992 at the Council of Kharkiv some of the Ukrainian bishops opposing Filaret elected Volodymir (Sobodan), recommended by Moscow, as the metropolitan of Ukraine. This part of the Orthodox Church stayed with the name UOC. Filaret rejected these decisions and, appealing to extreme nationalist forces, on 26 June 1992 united his followers with the Ukrainian Autocephalous Orthodox Church in the UOC-Kiev Patriarchate (UOC-KP). **Mstyslav** (Skrypnik) was elected its patriarch, and Filaret was to be his deputy. The unification failed since Filaret was not credible and was widely suspected of earlier cooperation with the KGB. In order to render the UOC-KP credible, Filaret brought about the election of a new patriarch, former dissident **Volodymyr** (Romanyuk), while he remained his deputy. They soon entered into a conflict that overshadowed later attempts to explain the sudden death of Volodymir in July 1995. Violent demonstrations in Kiev on 18 July 1995, when Filaret, opposing an official ban, tried to bury the deceased patriarch in St. Sophia Cathedral, led to the strengthening of Filaret's image as a representative of the UOC national wing. At the subsequent council, on 21 October 1995, Filaret finally became the UOC-KP patriarch. He drew closer to President **Leonid Kuchma**, so in subsequent years he could sponsor the reconstruction of St. Michael Cathedral in Kiev, blown up owing to a decision by Stalin in 1935. In contrast to other Orthodox bishops, in June 2001 Filaret met with Pope John Paul II during his pilgrimage to the Ukraine. (TS)

Sources: *Encyclopedia of Ukraine*, vol. 1 (Toronto, 1984); Stephen K. Batalden, *Seeking God: The Recovery of Religious Identity in Orthodox Russia, Ukraine, and Georgia* (De Kalb, 1993); Bohdan Nahaylo, *The Ukrainian Resurgence* (Toronto, 1999); www.uaoc.org.ua; www.saveouruoc.com.

FILIPESCU Nicolae (17 December 1862, Bucharest–26 October 1916, Bucharest), Romanian politician. Filipescu graduated in law from the Sorbonne in Paris. In 1885 he took the lead of the Epoce Press and of a daily of the same name. He started his political career by winning a parliamentary seat in January 1888. In March 1888 he was arrested for anti-government pronouncements. In 1891–95 he was the mayor of Bucharest. In this capacity he contributed to the development of the capital—for instance, by building many boulevards. Then he was the mayor of Draite, and from July 1900 to February 1901 he was minister of agriculture in the conservative government of **Petre Carp**. Afterwards he stayed in the opposition, to both liberal and conservative governments. He favored the unification of all territories inhabited by Romanians under Habsburg rule. From January 1911 to April 1912 Filipescu was minister of war, contributing to the modernization and reorganization of the army. In the government of **Titu Liviu Maiorescu** (March 1912–January 1914), he was minister of agriculture again. In 1914 he founded National Action (Acţiunea Naţională), which favored Romania's entry into war on the side of the Entente. In October 1915 he co-founded the Unionist Federation (Federaţia Unionista), and later, along with the Conservative Democratic Party, he co-founded the National Conservative Party (Parditul Naţionalist Conservator). (PC)

Sources: Biographisches Lexikon, vol. 1; Constantine Gane, *P. P. Carp şi locul său în istoria politică a ţarii*, vols. 1–2 (Bucharest, 1936); George Taşcă, *Politica economico—sociala a lui P. P. Carp* (Bucharest, 1938); Titu Maiorescu, *Inseminări zilnice* (Bucharest, 1939–40).

FILIPOV Georgi (Grisha) (13 July 1919, Kadiyewka, Ukraine–2 November 1994, Sofia), Bulgarian Communist activist. Born into a family of Bulgarian refugees in the USSR, until the end of his life Filipov spoke with a Russian accent. In 1936 he came to Bulgaria with his family. He graduated from high school in Lovech (1938), and then he started his studies at the Physics and Math Department of the University of Sofia (1938–40); he failed to complete them owing to his Communist activities. In 1936 he became a member of the Workers' Youth Union, and in 1940, the Bulgarian Communist Party (BCP). Arrested for this activity, in 1942 he was sentenced to twelve years in prison. In 1943 this sentence was increased to fifteen years. Released as a result of the uprising of 9 September 1944, Filipov worked in the Fatherland Front and in the BCP structures in Lovech and Pleven and later in the Ministry of Industry in Sofia. In 1951 he graduated in the economics of industry and trade in Moscow, and in 1954 he became a candidate (doctor) in economics. Upon his return to Bulgaria he became head of the Higher Education Department in the Committee for Research, Art, and Culture, and he held the chair of Marxism-Leninism at the Higher Institute

of Machines and Engineering in Sofia. He also lectured in political economy there. From 1957 Filipov was deputy head of the State Planning Commission and later head of the Department of Planning, Finance, and Trade of the BCP Central Committee (CC) (1958–64). From 1962 he was a deputy member, and from 1966 a member, of the BCP CC; from 1971 he was CC secretary and from 1974 also a CC Politburo member. In 1964 he became chairman of the government commission for economic reform and management (1964–68); he was then first deputy chairman of the State Planning Commission (December 1968–July 1971), and in 1971 he became a member of the Council of State. From 1966 to 1989 he was an MP.

From 16 June 1981 to 24 March 1986 Filipov was prime minister. Because of this he temporarily left the CC Secretariat and the Council of State. Although he was presented as an economist, he only simulated reforms, attempting to avoid real changes and strictly following the dogmatic line of **Todor Zhivkov**. After leaving the government, Filipov returned to the CC Secretariat and the Council of State, and he became chairman of the commission for economic and social affairs of the BCP CC Politburo (1986–89). After the fall of Zhivkov in November 1989, Filipov left the BCP leadership, and when the party was transformed into the Bulgarian Socialist Party (BSP), he was accused of contributing to the economic crisis of the 1980s, removed from the BSP in April 1990, and temporarily imprisoned for embezzlement in July 1990. Filipov authored Marxist economic works such as *Izmeneniya v sistemata na pokazatelite w planiraneto* (Changes in the system of planning indicators; 1966). (JJ)

Sources: Entsiklopediya Bulgariya, vol. 7 (Sofia, 1996); Raymond Detrez, *Historical Dictionary of Bulgaria* (Lanham, Md., 1997); Tasho Tashev, *Ministrite na Bulgariya 1879–1999: Entsiklopedichen spravochnik* (Sofia, 1999); Evgeniya Kalinova and Iskra Baeva, *Bulgarskite prekhodi 1944–1999* (Sofia, 2000); Angel Tsyrakov, *Pravitelstvata na Bulgariya: Khronologiya na politicheskiya zhivot 1879–2001* (Sofia, 2001).

FILIPOVIĆ Filip (9 June 1879, Čačak–April 1938, Moscow), Yugoslav Communist activist. After graduating from high school in Belgrade, in 1899 Filipović left for St. Petersburg, where he studied mathematics. In 1904 he completed his studies and started working as a teacher in a trade school in the Russian capital. As a student, he had joined the Russian Social Democratic Party, and he favored the Bolshevik faction of the party. In 1912 he returned to Serbia, and he became secretary of the Chamber of Labor and one of the leaders of the Serbian Social Democratic Party. During World War I Filipović edited the party's press. During the Austrian occupation of Serbia he was interned in Vienna. After the fall of the Habsburg monarchy he went to Budapest, where he worked with the Hungarian Communists, and in February 1919 he arrived in Belgrade and co-organized the founding congress of the Communist Party of Yugoslavia (CPY) in April 1919. As a secretary, he headed the CPY with **Sima Marković**. In August 1920 Filipović was elected mayor of Belgrade and an MP to the parliament of the Kingdom of Serbs, Croats, and Slovenes. After the CPY was declared illegal in 1921, he was stripped of his immunity, and in February 1922 he was sentenced to two years' imprisonment. Released in September 1923, he resumed his CPY activities, organizing the CPY's legal facade, the Independent Workers' Party of Yugoslavia. In March 1923 he became secretary general of the party, and in June 1924 he went to the Fifth Congress of the Communist International in Moscow, where he spoke as "Bošković" and became a member of the Executive Committee of the Comintern. Later he also used the pseudonym "Baum." In March 1926 he became a deputy member of the Presidium of the Executive Committee of the International and the Yugoslav delegate to the Balkan Bureau of the Comintern. During Stalin's struggle for power in the Bolshevik party, Filipović managed to maintain his position in the leadership of the Comintern, and in August 1930 he became interim president of the CPY. In June 1932 he was transferred to the International Agricultural Institute, which was the traditional place of employment for downgraded functionaries. However, in 1935 he was still a CPY delegate to the Seventh Congress of the Comintern. Arrested by the NKVD in February 1938, he was sentenced to death on 8 April, and he was soon executed by firing squad. He was rehabilitated posthumously by the Supreme Military Court of the USSR in October 1957. (WR)

Sources: Lazitch; *Enciklopedija Jugoslavije*, vol. 3 (Zagreb, 1958); Milutin Jakovljević, *Filip Filipović: Životni put i revolucionarno delo* (Gorni Milanovac, 1979); J. Bojović, ed., *Filip Filipović: Revolucionarna misao i delo* (Belgrade, 1983).

FILOV Bogdan (28 March 1883, Stara Zagora–2 February 1945, Sofia), professor of archaeology and regent of Bulgaria. In 1901 Filov received a scholarship from the Ministry of Education. He studied classical philology, ancient history, and archaeology in Würzburg, Leipzig, and Freiburg in Germany. In 1906 he defended his Ph.D. dissertation, and from 1907 to 1909 he worked in Bonn, Paris, and Rome. In 1910 he became head of the National Museum in Sofia, and in 1921–29 he directed the Bulgarian Archaeological Institute. In 1914 he also began working at St. Kliment Ohridsky University in Sofia. In 1926 he became full professor and in 1931–32

rector of Sofia University. In 1923 he joined a Berlin Freemasons' lodge. He published many scholarly works, such as *Pomoshnite voiski na rimskata provintsia Miziia* (The auxiliary forces in the Roman province of Moesia; 1906); *Antichni pametnitsi v Narodniia Muzei* (Ancient monuments in the National Museum; 1912); and *Starobylgarskoto iskustvo* (Old Bulgarian art; 1924); these works were also published in English, French, and German. Filov also published *Starobylgarska tsyrkovna arkhitektura* (Old Bulgarian church architecture; 1930) and *Rimsko vladichestvo v Bylgariia* (Roman rule in Bulgaria; 1931). Among other things, he was a full member of the German Archaeological Institute in Berlin and the Austrian Archaeological Institute in Vienna.

In 1937–44 Filov served as president of the Bulgarian Academy of Sciences and was also president of the Bulgarian PEN club. Between November 1938 and February 1940 he was minister of education. He favored the pro-German line of Bulgarian diplomacy. He enjoyed scholarly authority, but he did not have any significant political experience; for these reasons, on 15 February 1940, Tsar **Boris III** appointed him prime minister of the government, so that Filov would be a willing tool in the tsar's hands. In 1942 Filov published *Ideitie i delata no dneshniia bezpartiien rezhim* (The objectives and achievements of the modern nonparty system).

Filov's government became entangled in a subtle struggle for influence in the Balkans between the Third Reich and the USSR; at first the latter two were allies, but from the end of 1940, they were more and more clearly rivals in this area. Moscow's pressure to conclude a Bulgarian-Soviet treaty of mutual assistance intensified in November and December of 1940, following the visit of a Soviet delegation to Sofia and the Communist-led collection of signatures on a petition demanding such a treaty. Nonetheless, Filov's government increased cooperation with the Third Reich; on 1 March 1941 Bulgaria acceded to the Tripartite Pact and on 25 November of the same year joined the anti-Comintern Pact. Despite a sudden deterioration of Bulgarian-Soviet relations after the Nazi invasion of the USSR in June 1941, Bulgaria did not join the war on the side of the Third Reich and retained its diplomatic agency in Moscow. In a way, Filov's government tried to pursue the Bulgarian raison d'état, but it more and more clearly yielded to pressure from Berlin. For example, on 13 December 1941 Filov declared a state of war with Great Britain and the United States.

After the German defeat at Stalingrad, Filov anxiously observed the collapse of German power. His situation changed suddenly with the death of Tsar Boris III. Filov became one of the key political figures. On 8 September

1943 the National Assembly elected him, General **Nikolai Michov**, and **Kiril**, Prince of Preslav as regents to rule on behalf of Tsar **Simeon**, who was not yet of age. Michov and Kiril had much less experience and less authority than Filipov. Filipov was more aware of the inevitability of the collapse of the Third Reich, and he realized that it was necessary for Bulgaria to join the Allied side. Because the stance of the USSR made such a step impossible, **Konstantin Muraviev**'s government was not established until 2 September 1944, based on a broader coalition and attempting to reach an agreement with the Allies. It was too late: the opposition of the Fatherland Front, led by the Communists, was so strong that the concession only speeded up the coup of 9 September 1944 and the over-throw of the regency. Along with the other regents and with dozens of leading tsarist politicians, Filipov was arrested, sentenced to death, and executed. His *Dnevnik* (Diary) was published in 1986 in Sofia, and *Putuvaniia iz Trakiia, Rodopite i Makedoniia, 1912–1916* (A voyage through Thrace, the Rhodopes, and Macedonia, 1912–1916) appeared in 1993. (WR)

Sources: *Entsiklopediia Bylgariia*, vol. 7 (Sofia, 1996); Hans-Joachim Hoppe, *Bulgarien: Hitlers eigenwilliger Verbündeter* (Stuttgart, 1979); Stephane Groueff, *Crown of Thorns* (Lanham, Md., 1987); Jerzy Jackowicz, *Partie opozycyjne w Bułgarii 1944–1948* (Warsaw, 1997); Tasho Tashev, *Ministrite na Bylgariia 1897–1999* (Sofia, 1999).

FINDER Paweł [originally Pinkus Finder] (17 September 1904, Leszczyny, near Bielsko-Biała–20 July 1944, Warsaw), Polish Communist activist of Jewish origin. Educated in a German gymnasium in Bielsko, in 1920 Finder left for Palestine, where he was a laborer. In 1922 he returned to Bielsko, finished school, and then went to Austria, where he joined the local Communist Party. He also headed the Free Socialist Students' Union (Freie Sozialistische Studentenvereinigung). In 1926 he graduated from the Chemical Institute at Mulhouse in France, where he obtained a degree as an engineer. Later, he worked on his Ph.D. thesis under the supervision of Frédéric Joliot-Curie and was active in the Communist Party of France. In 1927 he joined the Paris committee of the party and worked in the Organization Department of the CC. He published in a German version of *L'Humanité* under the name Paul Reynot. In 1928 he was arrested for possession of a false passport and expelled from France. He returned to Poland and started working in a factory in Bielsko. After a short military service between 1928 and 1929 he was promoted in the Communist Party of Poland (Komunistyczna Partia Polski [KPP]). At that time he was active in the KPP Military Department. Temporarily arrested in

1931 and 1932, he continued to work as party secretary in Łódź and Zagłębie Dąbrowskie, and at the end of 1933 he became secretary of the KPP Warsaw organization. Imprisoned in April 1934 and sentenced to twelve years for anti-state activities on 25 April 1936, he served his sentence in the Mokotów and Rawicz prisons.

After the outbreak of war in September 1939 Finder escaped from prison and managed to get to Białystok, which was seized by the USSR. He worked there as president of a district planning committee. In 1941 he joined the All-Union Communist Party (Bolsheviks) in Mogilev. In July 1941 he went to special Comintern schools in Pushkino and Kushnarenkovo. On the night of 27–28 December 1941 he was parachuted into Poland near Warsaw in the first Initiative Group sent to reconstruct the Communist Party in Poland. He lived in Warsaw under the name "Stanisław Pilecki" and worked in the Warsaw power plant. At the same time he was an active member of the ruling *troika* of the CC of the Polish Workers' Party (Polska Partia Robotnicza [PPR]) and wrote articles for *Trybuna Wolności*. After the death of **Marceli Nowotko**, the party leader, on 28 November 1942, Finder became the first secretary of the party and was also responsible for communications with headquarters in Moscow. As first secretary, he tried to establish contact with the Polish independence underground. However, the conditions Finder proposed were unacceptable. Finder was the co-author of the PPR's program declaration of 1943, titled *O co walczymy?* (What are we fighting for?). Arrested by the Gestapo on 14 November 1943, Finder was identified during a brutal investigation on Szucha Avenue and executed by firing squad in the ruins of the Warsaw Ghetto. (WR)

Sources: Kunert, vol. 2; *Paweł Finder we wspomnieniach towarzyszy walki* (Warsaw, 1956); S. Topol, *Paweł Finder 1904–1944: Życie i działalność* (Warsaw, 1978).

FISHTA Gjergj (23 October 1871, Zadrimë–30 December 1940, Shkodër), Albanian writer, folklorist, independence activist, and Catholic priest. After finishing school in his home town, Fishta left for Sutjeska (Bosnia), where he studied philosophy. After completing his studies, he returned to Albania, where he lectured at a seminary in Troshani. He then was a parish priest in Gomsiqe. From 1902, when he became director of a Franciscan school in Shkodër, he made efforts to replace the Italian language, which was obligatory in the schools, with Albanian. In 1908 he presided over a congress in Monastir (Bitoli), where he presented a proposal for the standardization of the Albanian alphabet. Fishta started his literary activities in the periodical *Albania*, which was edited by **Faik**

Konitza. He initiated the creation of a religious-cultural journal, *Hylli i Drites*, which is still published today by the Albanian Franciscans. From 1917 to 1918 he oversaw the journal *Posta e Shqypnies* in Shkodër. He was a member of the Albanian delegation to the Paris Peace Conference in 1919. As a representative of the Shkodër district, he was elected to the parliament (1921–24) and became head of a committee on educational affairs. In 1930–31 he represented Albania at conferences of the Balkan states. The art gallery in Shkodër was created on his initiative, as well as the museum, of which he was the director.

Fishta has been ranked among the most outstanding Albanian writers. His most famous work, *Lahuta e Malcis* (The lute of the highlands; 1937), often called the "Albanian Iliad," is a vast epic poem that reveals the richness of the Albanian folk culture. Fishta took a favorable attitude toward the Italian occupation of Albania. After the Communists came to power, he was regarded as a collaborator, and his body was removed from its grave. His corpse was found during the reconstruction of a Franciscan church in Shkodër, and a second funeral took place in December 1996. Fishta's publications include *Shqyptari i gjytetnuem* (The Albanian townsman; 1911); *Mrizi i zanawe* (The muses' siesta; 1913); *Juda Makabe* (Judas Maccabeus; 1920); *Vallja e Parrizit* (Paradise dance; 1925); collections of poetry: *Anzat e Parnasit* (Parnassus' wasps; 1907); *Pika voeset* (Drops of dew; 1909); *Gomari i Babatasit* (1923); and a work of criticism, *Tarraloqja e Ballkanit* (Balkan thoughtlessness; 1944). (TC)

Sources: *Biographisches Lexikon*, vol. 1; Eqrem Çabej, "Der albanische Dichter Gjergj Fishta 1871–1940," *Südostforschung*, 1941, no. 6; Dukagjini Pal, *Gjergj Fishta–jeta dhe veprat* (Shkodër, 1992); Ressuli Namik, "Tribut Gjergj Fishtes, poetit shqiptar," *Hylli i Drites*, 1993, no. 1; Tadeusz Czekalski, *Zarys dziejów chrześcijaństwa albańskiego w latach 1912–1993* (Kraków, 1996).

FISZBACH Tadeusz (4 November 1935, Dobraczyn, near Lwów [Lviv]), Polish Communist and post-Communist activist. Born into a working-class family, Fiszbach received a Ph.D. in the technical sciences. From 1959 he was a member of the Polish United Workers' Party (Polska Zjednoczona Partia Robotnicza [PUWP]), and from 1963 he worked in the party apparatus as secretary of the PUWP district committees in Elbląg and Tczew. In 1971–75 he was secretary of the PUWP Provincial Committee in Gdańsk, and from 1975 to January 1982 he was its first secretary. From 1975 to July 1981 he belonged to the PUWP Central Committee (CC). From December 1980 to July 1981 he was a deputy member of the PUWP CC Politburo. He lost the election to the CC during the Ninth Extraordinary PUWP Congress in July

1981. He was an MP from 1976 to 1985. Thought to be one of the supporters of party democratization, during the summer strikes of 1980 Fiszbach favored a compromise with the striking workers and took part in negotiations with the Interfactory Strike Committee in the Gdańsk shipyard. Respected by Solidarity and attacked by the party hardliners, after the declaration of martial law he was deprived of his party position in Gdańsk and sent to the embassy in Finland (1982–86). Later he was an adviser to the minister of foreign affairs. He returned to active political life at the beginning of 1989. Elected to the "contract" Assembly (Sejm) in June 1989, he became its deputy speaker. When the PUWP was dissolved at the Eleventh Congress in January 1990, Fiszbach opposed the group headed by **Aleksander Kwaśniewski** and **Leszek Miller**; he distanced himself from the PUWP tradition and co-founded the minority Social Democratic Union, which soon changed its name to the Polish Social Democratic Union. In 1990–91 Fiszbach was its chairman, but the party failed to played any significant role. From 2001 he was ambassador to Latvia. (PK)

Sources: Mołdawa; Jerzy Holzer, *"Solidarność"* (Warsaw, 1983); Antoni Dudek, *Pierwsze lata III Rzeczpospolitej 1989–1995* (Kraków, 1997).

FLONDOR Iancu (16 August 1865, Flondoreni, Bukovina–19 October 1924, Flondoreni), Romanian politician and lawyer. Flonder was descended from a boyar family that was well known in Bukovina. He studied law and philosophy at Francis Joseph I University in Cernăuţi (Chernivtsi) and in Vienna (1885–93), where in 1894 he earned his doctorate in law. He was one of the leaders of the Romanian National Movement in Bukovina; nevertheless, he initially accepted cooperation with the Austrian authorities. The Austrians trusted him and appointed him to important administrative posts. He was even given the title of baron by Emperor Francis Joseph. In March 1892 Flondor was one of the founders of the National Party of Romanian Bukovina (NPRB), which propagated the slogan of unification with Romania. In 1898–1918 he sat in the parliament of Bukovina. Between 1908 and 1910 he was president of the NPRB.

After the outbreak of World War I Flondor was interned by the Austrians until the winter of 1915, and between the spring and summer of 1918 he served as mayor of Storojineţ in Bukovina. On 27 October 1918 he was elected president of the Romanian National Council in Bukovina. This council proclaimed solidarity with the Romanians in Transylvania and Hungary. Flondor was against handing over power in Bukovina to the Ukrainian legionnaires. The president of Bukovina, Joseph Count Etzdorf, handed over power to the representatives of both National Councils, the Romanian council and the Ukrainian council. Meanwhile, in November 1918 Romanian troops entered Cernăuţi and then seized all of Bukovina. Between 12 and 28 November Flondor was head of the provisional government of Bukovina, and he simultaneously served as its minister of justice. At the General Congress of Bukovina, which was convened on 28 November 1918 in Cernăuţi and was chaired by Flondor, the decision was made to incorporate Bukovina into Romania. This decision was backed by a delegation of Poles from Bukovina. From December 1918 to April 1919 Flondor served as minister of state for Bukovina in the Romanian central government, but he was in conflict with another Bukovinian, Minister Ion Nistor. Between September 1919 and April 1920 Flondor was president of the newly created Democratic and United Party of Bukovina. On 2 May 1920 he resigned all his public and political positions. (FA/TD)

Sources: Aurel Morariu, *Bucovina, 1774–1914* (Bucharest, 1915); Simion Reli, *Din Bucovina vremurilor grele: Schiţe istorice* (Cernăuţi, 1926); Ilie Toronţiu, *Românii şi clasa intellectuală din Bucovina* (Cernăuţi, 1911); Ion Nistor, ed., *Amintirii răzleţe din timpul Unirii* (Cernăuţi, 1938); Ion Nistor, *Unirea Bucovinei 28 Noemvrie 1918* (Bucharest, 1928); Erich Prokopowitsch, *Das Ende der österreichischen Herrschaft in der Bukowina* (Munich, 1959); Emil Biedrzycki, *Historia Polaków na Bukowinie* (Kraków, 1973).

FOCK Jenő (17 May 1916, Kispest), Hungarian Communist activist. Born into a working-class family, Fock worked as a mechanic. In 1932 he joined the Trade Union of Metalworkers and then the illegal Hungarian Communist Party (HCP). He was also active in the illegal Communist Union of Young Workers and in the Red Fund, which supported families of arrested and/or fired Communist activists. In 1939 Fock was called up, and in 1940 he was accused of spying and sentenced to three years in prison. In 1943 he was sent to the front, from which he escaped and went into hiding in 1944. From 1945 he worked in the Budapest HCP committee and from 1947 in the economic administration; from January 1951 he was deputy minister of metallurgy and the machine-building industry. At the same time he graduated from the Economic Technical Academy. From October 1954 he was commercial councillor in East Germany, and from April 1955 to February 1957, secretary of the National Council of Trade Unions. From July to October 1956 he was a deputy member of the Central Committee (CC) of the Hungarian Workers' Party; from October 1956 to October 1989, a member of the CC of the Hungarian Socialist Workers' Party (HSWP); and in 1957–80 a member of the HSWP Politburo. From February 1957 to 1961 he was CC secretary for economic policy. Considered a supporter of reforms, in September 1961 Fock became deputy prime minister.

From 14 April 1967 Fock was prime minister. He took part in the elaboration and implementation of the so-called New Economic Mechanism (1968), which consisted of the abandonment of stiff planning procedures and the decentralization of economic decisions. Enterprises were to directly react to changes in domestic demand and to world prices. At the same time, the subsidization of factories bearing a deficit was maintained, along with central investment plans. When the reforms were curtailed in October 1973, Flondor wanted to resign, but it was not until 15 May 1975 that he was dismissed, along with other supporters of these reforms, such as **György Aczél** and **Rezső Nyers**. Nevertheless, Flondor stayed in the Politburo for five more years and in the HSWP CC for fourteen more years. In 1980 he was elected chairman of the Union of Technical and Natural Science Societies. At the end of December 1981 he was a member of a delegation that advised General **Wojciech Jaruzelski** on how to implement economic reforms during the period of martial law in Poland. In 1945–47, 1958–67, and 1971–85 Flondor was an MP. At a CC meeting in May 1988 he suggested that **János Kádár** resign from the position of HSWP general secretary and assume a purely representative function as its chairman. After the fall of the Communist regime Flondor retired. (JT)

Sources: *Magyar Nagylexikon*, vol. 8 (Budapest, 1999); *A magyar forradalom és szabadságharc enciklopédiája*, CD-ROM (Budapest, 1999); *Ki kicsoda 2000* (Budapest, 2001); I. Friss, ed., *Reform of the Economic Mechanism in Hungary* (Budapest, 1971); Paul Ignotus, *Hungary* (London, 1972); Bennet Kovrig, *Communism in Hungary from Kun to Kádár* (Stanford, 1979); Miklós Molnár, *From Béla Kun to János Kádár: Seventy Years of Hungarian Communism* (New York, 1990).

FOKIN Vitold (25 October 1932, Novomykolayivka, Zaporozhye), Soviet Communist and post-Communist activist in the Ukraine. The son of a teacher, in 1954 Fokin graduated in mining studies in Dniepropetrovsk, and in 1970 he received a Ph.D. in this field in Moscow. From 1954 to 1963 he worked in a coal mine in Bokovoantratsyt in the Lugansk region, attaining the position of head engineer. In 1963–71 he was deputy head of Donbasantratsyt Works, head of the coal mining holdings in Pervomaysk, chief engineer of Kadiyivka Works, and head of Sverdlovantratsyt Works in Sverdlovsk. From 1971 he worked in the Planning Office of the Ukrainian SSR. In 1972 he became deputy chairman, and in 1987 chairman, of this office. He was also a member of the Central Committee (CC) of the Communist Party of Ukraine, a member of the CC of the Communist Party of the Soviet Union (1990–91), and a deputy to the Supreme Council of the Soviet Union (1989–91). In July 1989 Fokin took part in a government commission that negotiated conditions for the termination of a strike by Donbas miners, the first such mass protest of Ukrainian workers during perestroika. On 23 October 1990 he assumed the position of prime minister of the Ukrainian SSR. This appointment was a rather unexpected move by President **Leonid Kravchuk**, who decided to meet the demands of striking students and fired the former prime minister, **Vitaliy Masol**. During Fokin's term, Ukraine proclaimed sovereignty, held a referendum on independence, and had its first presidential elections. Fokin played no major role in these events, concentrating on economic policy, which was designed in accordance with the populist ideas of President Kravchuk and the parliament. As a result, the budget of 1992 closed with a deficit of 33 percent. When on 1 October 1992 Kravchuk decided to implement reforms and dismissed Fokin, the new government faced a dramatic financial crisis. Later Fokin lectured at the Institute of World Economy and International Relations, chaired the International Endowment for Charity and Economic Links with the Russian Federation, and sat on the Economic Council of the President of Ukraine. (TS)

Sources: *Europa Środkowo-Wschodnia 1992* (Warsaw, 1994); Bohdan Nahaylo, *The Ukrainian Resurgence* (Toronto, 1999); Stanisław Kulczycki, ed., *Uryady Ukraiiny u XX st.* (Kiev, 2001).

FORIŞ Ştefan (9 May 1892, Tărlungeni, near Braşov–summer 1946, Romania), Romanian Communist activist. Born into a family of Transylvanian Hungarians, after graduating in physics and mathematics from the University of Budapest in September 1919, Foriş returned to Braşov, where he founded *Munkas*, a Hungarian Socialist newspaper. In 1921 he joined the Romanian Communist Party (RCP), and in 1922 he moved to Bucharest, where he was active in the Communist underground. In 1926 he became secretary of Red Aid (Ajurotul Roşu), the Romanian section of the International Organization for Aid to Revolutionaries. In 1927 he became a member of the Central Committee (CC) of the RCP. In July 1928 he was arrested but was released owing to ill health, and he went to Moscow. At the end of 1930 he returned to Romania, where in August 1931 he was imprisoned again. Released in 1935, in 1938 he joined the secretariat of the CC of the Romanian party. In accord with the tactics of the Communist International, the RCP favored the separation of Transylvania, Bessarabia, and Dobrudja from Romania. It was also a result of the fact that the party was dominated by national minorities. While Romanians made up around 72 percent of the population of Romania, in the party they constituted only some 23 percent. In the case of Hungarians, Jews, Russians, Ukrainians, and Bulgar-

ians, the proportions were reversed. In addition, the party was fractured because of arrests, and it did not have any financial support.

After Romania lost some territories to the USSR, Hungary, and Bulgaria, in October 1940 Foriş went to Moscow, where the Comintern appointed him secretary general of the RCP in place of the late Béla Brainer. After the outbreak of the German-Soviet war in June 1941 Foriş' contact with the Kremlin became more difficult and was often interrupted. When in 1942 Petre Gheorghe, the head of the party in Bucharest who acted as a liaison with the Kremlin, demanded on behalf of the Comintern that Foriş increase sabotage actions in the rear of the German Army, Foriş refused, justifying his decision by noting a lack of means and excessive risk. Soon Gheorghe was arrested and executed by the authorities of Marshal **Ion Antonescu**. This induced other members of the RCP leadership, who were in prison, to accuse Foriş of treason. In June 1943, in a prison hospital in the camp in Tîrgu-Jiu, **Gheorghe Gheorgiu-Dej**, **Emil Bodnăraş**, **Chivu Stoica**, **Iosif Ranghet**, and **Constantin Parvulescu** decided to remove Foriş from his position. It is not clear whether Foriş actually cooperated with the police of Antonescu, as it was later alleged by the propaganda of Gheorghiu-Dej, nor to what extent his removal was arranged with the cooperation of the Comintern. Bodnăraş played a key role. After being released, Bodnăraş hid Foriş, and on 4 April 1944 he demanded that Foriş hand over all party materials. After the coup of August 1944 Foriş was held under house arrest on the orders of Gheorghiu-Dej. On 7 June 1945 he was seen for the last time. Most probably, he was arrested two days later. As late as 1947 his mother was still inquiring in the Securitate about the fate of her son, and because of this she was cruelly murdered. According to a version established in 1967, Foriş was killed in the summer of 1946 by Panteleimon Bondarenko, an agent of the GRU who, as **Gheorghe Pintilie**, became head of the Securitate in August 1948. Foriş was buried in an unmarked grave, and his body was never found. (WR)

Sources: A. G. Savu, "Ştefan Foriş: Schiţă pentru o viitoare biografie," *Magazin Istoric*, 1968, no. 7; N. I. Florea, "Ştefan Foriş," *Analele de Istorie*, 1972, no. 3; Robert R. King, *History of the Romanian Communist Party* (Stanford, 1980); T. A. Pokivailova, "1939–1940: Cominternul şi Partidul Comunist din România," *Magazin Istoric*, 1997, no. 3; Denis Deletant, *Communist Terror in Romania: Gheorghiu-Dej and the Police State, 1948–1965* (New York, 1999).

FORMAN Miloš (18 December 1932, Čáslav, Kutná Hora district), Czech and American film director and screenplay writer. In 1956 Forman graduated from the Film and TV Department of the Academy of Musical Arts in Prague.

Later he worked in Czechoslovak TV and in the Laterna Magica Theater in Prague. He made his debut with satirical movies showing the hypocrisy of small-town dwellers: *Konkurs* (Contest; 1963); *Černý Petr* (Black Peter; 1963); and *Lásky jedné plavovlásky* (Loves of a blonde; 1965). These films brought him world recognition as one of the leaders of the Czechoslovak New Wave. Soon he received an offer from Carlo Ponti, with whom he directed *Hoří má panenko* (The firemen's ball; 1967). During the Warsaw Pact invasion of Czechoslovakia in 1968 Forman was in the West, where he learned that his recent movie had been banned; thus he decided to stay abroad, and in 1977 he received American citizenship. From 1975 he was a professor in the Film Department at Columbia University in New York. In his first American film, *Taking Off* (1971), he used the techniques of his earlier works, but the commercial failure of this film made him adapt an American prose style. This brought him success with the adaptation of Ken Kesey's *One Flew Over the Cuckoo's Nest* (1975), for which he received an Oscar in 1975. Later he filmed the famous musical *Hair* (1979) and directed a masterpiece movie on Wolfgang Amadeus Mozart, *Amadeus* (1984), which was awarded eight Oscars, including Forman's second Oscar as director. His *People vs. Larry Flynt* (1997), about the porn tycoon, raised some doubts about why Forman had portrayed Flynt as a champion of the freedom of speech but brought him commercial success and a Golden Bear award at the Berlin Film Festival. Forman has received many other awards, including an honorary doctorate from the Prague Academy of Musical Arts (1997). He authored the memoirs *Turnaround: A Memoir* (1993). (PU)

Sources: *ČBS*; *Kdo byl kdo v našich dějinach ve 20. stoleti*, vol. 1 (Prague, 1998); *International Dictionary of Films and Filmmakers*, vol. 2 (Chicago and London, 1991); Geoffrey Nowell-Smith, *The Oxford History of World Cinema* (Oxford, 1996); Josef Škvorecký, *All the Bright Young Men and Women* (Toronto, 1971); Antonin Liehm, *Closely Watched Films* (New York, 1974); Antonín Liehm, *The Miloš Forman Stories* (New York, 1975); Jan Foll, *Miloš Forman* (Prague, 1989); Jasmin Dizdarević, *Konkurs na režiséra Miloše Formana* (Prague, 1990).

FRANK Josip (10 April 1844, Osijek–17 December 1911, Zagreb), Croatian lawyer and politician. After graduating from a high school in Osijek, Frank studied law in Vienna; after graduation, from 1872 he worked as a lawyer in Zagreb. A close aide to the head of the Zagreb part of the province (*banat*), from the 1870s Frank was active in the Party of Law (Stranka Prava), and from 1877 he edited *Agramer Presse* and *Kroatische Post*. He won fame in 1880, publishing a study of the economic failure of the Hungarian-Croatian agreement, and for it he received a

Ph.D. After the electoral defeat of 1893 the Party of Law split, and Frank, along with Ante Starčević and his son, founded the True Party of Law (Čista Stranka Prava [TPL]) in 1895. The party's program was nationalist, anti-Serbian, anti-Hungarian, and anti-clerical. For tactical reasons the TPL leaders sought support in Vienna. After the senior Starčević died, in 1896 Frank took the lead of the party and made its program and style even more radical. In 1905 he refused to join the Rijeka Resolution and the Croatian-Serbian Coalition, which won the May 1906 elections. Going against the coalition and seeking a compromise with Budapest, Frank worked with the court in Vienna and used fanatical anti-Serb rhetoric, appealing to nationalist xenophobia and nationalist myths. He failed to create paramilitary Croatian "legions." In 1895 he published *Govori dra Josipa Franka* (Speeches by Doctor Josip Frank). After his death he became an ideological model for the Ustasha movement of **Ante Pavelić**. (WR)

Sources: *Enciklopedija Jugoslavije*, vol. 3 (Zagreb, 1958); Franjo Supilo, *Politika u Hrvatksoj* (Rijeka, 1911); Iso Kršnjavi, *Zapisci iza kulisa hrvatske politike*, vols. 1–2 (Zagreb, 1986); Robert Stallaerst and Jeannine Laurens, *Historical Dictionary of Croatia* (Lanham, Md., 1995); Aleksa Djilas, *The Contested Country: Yugoslav Unity and Communist Revolution, 1919–1953* (Cambridge, Mass., 1996).

FRANKO Ivan (27 or 25 August 1856, Nahuyewychi, near Drohobich–18 May 1916, Lviv [Lwów]), Ukrainian poet, writer, translator, and political activist. From 1864 to 1867 Franko studied in a Basilian school in Drohobich; in 1875 he graduated from a Drohobich high school and enrolled in philological studies at the University of Lemberg (Lviv). Later he also studied in Tchernowitz (Chernivtsi) (1890) and Vienna (1890–93). In 1893 he received a Ph.D. from the University of Vienna. At the same time he was active in the Academic Circle. In 1878–81 he co-edited the first Socialist newspaper in Galicia, *Praca*, and was a member of a Polish-Ukrainian-Jewish Socialist committee connected with it. In 1881 he was one of the key authors of the *Prohrama sotsialistiv polskykh i ruskykh Skhidnoyi Halychyny* (Program of the Polish and Ukrainian Socialists of East Galicia). He agitated among the workers of Lviv, Boryslav, and Drohobich and among Galician peasants. He was imprisoned for this activity four times in 1877–93. He was also fired from working on Ukrainian papers and prevented from taking over the chair of Ukrainian literature at the University of Lviv.

At the turn of the twentieth century Franko's views evolved from Socialist to nationalist. In 1886–96 he worked on Polish and Ukrainian papers, trying to establish a political party capable of modernizing the Ukrainian society and economy in Galicia. In 1890 he co-founded the Ruthenian-Ukrainian Radical Party (Rusko-Ukraiinska Radykalna Partiya) and was its chairman until 1898. On its behalf he ran for the Vienna parliament, but he lost in 1897 and 1898. In 1899 he left the party, and until 1904 he belonged to the Ukrainian National Democratic Party (Ukraiinsko Natsionalno-Demokratychna Partiya [USND]). His entry into the USND was connected with the arrival of **Mykhailo Hrushevskyi** to Lviv. Thanks to Hrushevskyi's support, in 1899 Franko became a full member of the Taras Shevchenko Research Society (TSRS). In 1989–1901 and 1903–12 he presided over the Philological Section of the society, and in 1898–1900 and 1908–13, over its Ethnographical Section. He edited a number of TSRS publications. In 1898–1907, along with Hrushevskyi and Volodymir Hnatyuk, Franko co-edited the periodical *Literaturno-Naukovyi Visnyk*. In 1906 he received an honorary doctorate from the University of Kharkiv.

Franko authored many literary, scholarly, and journalistic pieces in Ukrainian, Polish, and German. He translated from fourteen languages. He made his literary debut in 1874. His best known works include the following: *Kamenyari* (Stonecutters; 1878); *Vichnyi revolutsioner* (The eternal revolutionary; 1880); *Ne pora, ne pora* (Not the time, not the time; 1880); the poem *Moysey* (1905; *Moses*, 1987); *Zachar Berkut* (1883; English edition, 1944); the drama *Ukradene shchastya* (Stolen happiness; 1893); and the fable-poem *Łys Mykyta* (1890). Franko edited several Ukrainian and Polish periodicals, including *Druh* (1878), *Svit* (1881), *Zorya* (1883–86), *Pravda* (1888), *Tovarysh* (1888), *Narod* (1890–95), *Hromadskyi holos* (1895), *Zhytye i slovo* (1894–97), *Dilo* (1883–86), *Przyjaciel Ludu* (1886), *Kurjer Lwowski* (1887–97), *Przegląd społeczny* (1886), and *Khliborob* (1891). In 1897 he gave up journalism because of an article of his in the Vienna paper *Die Zeit* in which he called Adam Mickiewicz a "poet of treason." The most complete editions of Franko's works are *Tvory u 30 tomakh* (Works in thirty volumes; 1924–31) and *Zibrannya tvoriv u 50 tomakh* (Collected works in fifty volumes; 1976–86). English translations include *Poems and Stories* (1956), *Stories* (1972), and *Short Stories* (1977). (BB)

Sources: *Wielka encyklopedia PWN*, vol. 9 (Warsaw, 2002); *Dovidnyk z istoriyi Ukraiiny* (Kiev, 2001); *Entsyklopediya ukraiinoznastva*, vol. 9 (Lviv, 2000); Clarence A. Manning, ed., *Ivan Franko: The Poet of Western Ukraine* (New York, 1968); Karl Treimer, *Ivan Franko* (Vienna, 1971); Nicholas Wacyk, *Ivan Franko: His Thoughts and Struggles* (New York, 1975); Myroslav Moroz, *Ivan Franko: Bibliohrafichnyi pokazchyk* (Kiev, 1987); Yaroslav Hrytsak, *"Dukh shcho tilo rve do boyu . . .": Sproba politychnoho portreta Ivana Franka* (Lviv, 1990); *Ivan Franko i nacyonalne ta dukhovne vidrodzeniia Ukraiiny* (Ivano-Frankovsk, 1997).

FRASHËRI Mehdi (15 or 28 February 1872, Frashëri–25 May 1963, Rome), Albanian writer, politician, and diplomat. The son of Ragib Frashëri, Frashëri was a member of a powerful family of great influence in the Turkish empire. After completing schools in Ioánnina and Monastir (Bitola), he studied at the Istanbul Polytechnic, from which he graduated in 1897. From 1901 he worked as the subprefect of Peqin (1901–3) and Ohrid (1903–6). Later he was the prefect of Seridze (1908) and Serres (1908–9). In 1909 he became the Turkish governor-general in Samsun and subsequently in Palestine. He worked with the Balkan Committee in London. At the news of the proclamation of the independence of Albania in 1912, Frashëri resigned his post and returned home. Initially, he became prefect of Berat, and then, until September 1914, he was Albania's representative to the International Control Commission. During World War I, he was in Switzerland and Italy. He became minister of interior and later minister of foreign affairs in the government that was created by the all-Albanian congress in Durrës (1918). He was a member of the Albanian delegation to the Paris Peace Conference. In 1921 he again became minister of foreign affairs. From 1921 to 1924 he sat in parliament as a deputy from Elbasan.

In 1922 Frashëri became Albania's representative to the League of Nations. He headed the Albanian delegation at the conference in Lausanne (1923) and also participated in the work of the Delimitation Commission, responsible for the demarcation of the Albanian-Greek and Albanian-Yugoslav borders. In June 1926 he headed an Albanian delegation that held talks on a trade treaty and a consular convention with Greece in Athens. In 1928–30 he again represented Albania in the League of Nations. From 1929 on he served as speaker of the upper chamber of the Albanian parliament, except for a brief interval in 1930, when he assumed the portfolio of the ministry of the national economy. On 21 October 1935 Frashëri became head of the "government of liberals," which had an ambitious reform program involving the development of the infrastructure, the extension of democratic liberties, and the ending of corruption. He also favored cooperation with Italy. After a month the conservative opposition caused the collapse of the government, and Frashëri abandoned his intensive political activities. On 16 October 1943, during the German occupation, he became head of the Regency Council. His policy of loyalty toward Germany in return for independence in foreign policy proved a failure. In 1944 he left his country and went to Italy, where he lived for many years. He authored a book on the philosophy of the Turkish revolution that was published in Turkish in 1911. He also wrote political pamphlets, novels, the drama *Tradhti* (Treason; 1925), and *Lidhja e Prizrenit* (The League of Prizren; 1927). (TC)

Sources: *Biographisches Lexikon*, vol. 1; Hugh Seton-Watson, *The East European Revolution* (London, 1950); Ernesto Koliqi, "Mehdi Frashëri si shkrimtar," *Shêjzat*, 1973, no. 17; Bernd J. Fischer, "German Political Policy in Albania 1943–1944," in R.B. Spence & L.L. Nelson, ed., *Scholar, Patriot, Mentor: Historical Essays in Honor of Dmitrije Djordjević* (New York, 1992); Michael Schmidt-Neke, *Entstehung und Ausbau der Königsdiktatur in Albanien (1912–1939): Regierungsbildungen, Herrschaftsweise ind Machteliten in einem jungen Balkanstaat* (Munich, 1987).

FRASHËRI Midhat (25 March 1880, Istanbul–3 October 1949, New York), Albanian journalist, writer, and politician. Born into one of the richest aristocratic families of central Albania, Frashëri was the son of Abdyl bey Frashëri, a co-founder of the League of Prizren. He started his journalistic career by editing the periodical *Kalendari kombinar* in Sofia. He also edited the periodicals *Liria* (1908–10) and *Dituria* (1909), published by the Albanian community in Salonika. From 1905 he worked in the Turkish administration in Salonika and presided over the local political club. After returning to Albania in 1911, he took part in the anti-Turkish rebellion. At the Congress of Vlorë in 1912 he represented Gjirokaster. In the government of **Ismail Kemali** he became minister of public works. In 1915 he published *Hi edhe shpuzë* (Ashes and glowing embers). During World War I he was interned in Romania and then in Switzerland. Upon his return home in December 1918 he joined the government of Turchan Pasha Përmeti in Durrës, which failed to gain international recognition for Albanian independence in terms of ethnic borders at the Paris Peace Conference. In 1923–26 he was ambassador to Greece. Between the two world wars he wrote a lot and published under the pseudonym "Lumo Skendo."

After the Italian invasion of April 1939, Frashëri organized opposition activities and was interned by the Italians. Released in early 1942, he returned to his secret activities. In April 1942 he refused to participate in a conference of representatives of republican resistance, organized by the Communists in Pezë, because he did not trust them. In October 1942 he took the lead of the National Front (Belli Kombatër), whose aim was the liberation of Albania in its ethnic borders, including Kosovo, and the establishment of democratic rule. The organization planned a land reform and industrialization. On 2 August 1943, at a conference in Mukje (Mukaj), near Tirana, Frashëri agreed to work with the Communist guerrillas of **Enver Hoxha** against the Italians in the Committee of the Defense of the Homeland and on an effort to incorporate Kosovo into Albania.

This agreement was vetoed by the Yugoslav Communists, who were sponsoring Hoxha, so the Communist partisans started attacking activists of the National Front and slandering them in the eyes of the Albanians. Under these circumstances, after the Germans replaced the Italians as occupiers, Frashëri and his organization made use of the opportunity to organize substitute autonomous authorities in the shape of the Constitutional Assembly, called into being on 18 October 1943. Frashëri joined the Regency Council, representing monarchists and nationalists; this gave the Communists a reason to accuse him of treason. Conflicts among the nationalists and Allied support for the Communist guerrillas undermined the position of the National Front.

When the Communists brought Albania under their control, in mid-1944 Frashëri left for France, where he took the lead of the Committee of Free Albania, founded on 26 July 1949, the strongest political organization of Albanian émigré politicians. Then he went to the United States, where he suddenly died of a heart attack. It was suspected that the heart attack was caused by the Soviets. Frashëri's library, the largest in Albania (twenty thousand volumes), was taken over by the Communist authorities and became the core of the National Library created in Tirana. After the fall of the Communist regime, some of his works were published in Albania. (WR)

Sources: *Communist Takeover and Occupation of Albania: Special Report No. 13 of the House of Representatives Select Committee on Communist Aggression* (Washington, D.C., 1954); Stavro Skendi, *Albania* (New York, 1956); Stefanaq Pollo, Arben Puto, Kristo Frashëri, and Skënder Anamali, *The History of Albania* (London, 1981); Raymond Hutchings, *Historical Dictionary of Albania* (Lanham, Md., 1996); Jerzy Hauziński and Jan Leśny, *Historia Albanii* (Wrocław, 1992); Ressuli Namik, *Albanian Literature* (Boston, 1987).

FRASYNIUK Władysław (25 November 1954, Wrocław), Polish trade union activist and politician. Frasyniuk graduated from a technical high school and worked as a driver and mechanic in the Town Transportation Enterprise. In August 1980 he co-organized a strike in the Wrocław bus depot, and from September 1980 he was a member of the Inter-Factory Founding Committee (IFC) of Solidarity. From 5 March 1981 he presided over the IFC and then over the Lower Silesian Regional Board (LSRB) of Solidarity. He was also a member of the National Coordination Commission and then of the Presidium of the National Commission of Solidarity. When martial law was introduced on 13 December 1981, Frasyniuk avoided arrest and worked as head of the underground LSRB and a member of the all-Polish Provisional National Coordination Commission of

Solidarity. Arrested on 5 October 1982 and sentenced to six years, he was released through the amnesty of 1984. Arrested again in February 1985 and sentenced to four and a half years in prison, he was amnestied in the fall of 1986. From September 1986 he belonged to the open Solidarity authorities: the Provisional Council and (from November 1987) the National Executive Commission. At the same time he presided over the LSRB. A member of the Civic Committee from 1988, in early 1989 he took part in the Round Table Talks. In 1990 he was one of the Civic Committee leaders. In 1990–91 he belonged to the Presidium of Solidarity's National Commission and was in opposition to its chairman, **Lech Wałęsa**. In October 1990 he resigned from chairing the LSRB. In July 1990 he co-founded the Civic Movement–Democratic Action (Ruch Obywatelski-Akcja Demokratyczna [ROAD]). He was one of its two plenipotentiaries, and from January 1991 he was chairman of the ROAD Main Board. He favored the unification of the ROAD with other groups supporting **Tadeusz Mazowiecki** as candidate for president. From 1991 to 1994 Frasyniuk was deputy chairman of the Democratic Union, which had resulted from this unification, and later he was a member of the National Council of the Union of Freedom (Unia Wolności [UW]). Frasyniuk belonged to its liberal wing. He was an MP from 1991 to 2001, and in 1991–93 he was deputy chairman of an extraordinary parliamentary commission to investigate the effects of martial law. After the electoral defeat of the UW in September 2001, Frasyniuk became head of the party. In October he lost in local elections for the mayor of Wrocław. (AF)

Sources: *Kto jest kim w Polsce* (Warsaw, 2001); Jerzy Holzer, *"Solidarność,"* (Warsaw, 1983); Jerzy Holzer and Krzysztof Leski, *"Solidarność" w podziemiu* (Łódź, 1990); *Opozycja w PRL: Słownik biograficzny 1956–89* (Warsaw, 2000); Antoni Dudek, *Pierwsze lata III Rzeczpospolitej 1989–2001* (Kraków, 2002).

FRENŢIU Valeriu Traian (25 April 1875, Reşiţa–11 July 1952, Sighet Marmaţiei), Romanian Greek Catholic bishop, victim of communism. Fremţiu graduated from high school in Blaj. In 1894–98 he studied theology at the University of Budapest. In September 1898 he was ordained. Later he continued his studies in Vienna, where he received a Ph.D. in theology in 1902. After returning to Transylvania, he was chancellor of a parish, parish priest in Oraştie and Heţeg, and vicar of the Lugoj bishopric. In 1912 he was consecrated bishop of Lugoj. In early December 1918 he was, along with Bishop **Iuliu Hossu**, a delegate to the National Assembly in Alba Iulia that proclaimed the unification of Transylvania with Romania. In 1922 he was appointed bishop of

Oradea (Arad). He strove to introduce the Marian and Pauline orders into Romania and to establish religious schools. When a part of Transylvania was incorporated into Hungary according to the terms of the 1940 Vienna Award, Frenţiu protested against the discrimination of the local Romanian population; for this he was expelled to Romania. In 1941 he became apostolic administrator of the Alba Iulia and Fargaş archdioceses, and in 1947 he returned to his duties as bishop of Oradea. When the Communist authorities started to repress the Greek Catholic Church, on 28 October 1948 Frenţiu was arrested; along with five other Greek Catholic bishops, he was placed in the Dragoslavele Monastery (a summer residence of the Orthodox patriarchs of Romania, turned into a prison). In early 1949 they were all moved to the Căldăruşani Monastery, also turned into a prison, and from there Frenţiu was the last of the group to be moved to the Sighet Marmaţiei Prison. After two years spent under inhuman conditions, he fell seriously ill and died. He was secretly buried at night in a collective grave in the prison yard. In order to avoid pilgrimages by believers, the cemetery was soon leveled. Frenţiu's beatification proceedings are under way. (LW)

Sources: Józef Darski, *Rumunia: Historia, współczesność, konflikty narodowe* (Warsaw, 1995); Paul Caravia, Virgiliu Constantinescu, and Flori Stănescu, *The Imprisoned Church of Romania, 1944–1989* (Bucharest, 1999); Denis Deletant, *Communist Terror in Romania: Gheorghiu-Dej and the Police State, 1948–1965* (New York, 1999); www.bru.ro.

FRIEDRICH István (1 July 1883, Malacka [now in Slovakia]–25 November 1951, Vác), Hungarian politician. In 1905 Friedrich graduated in engineering from the Budapest Polytechnic. Then he studied at the polytechnic in Berlin, where he later worked as chief engineer in Allgemeine Elektrizitäts-Gesellschaft. In 1908 he founded a machine-building factory in Budapest, which he sold in 1920. He started political activities in 1912, joining the opposition Independence and 48 Party. In the fall of 1914 he volunteered for the army as a lieutenant in the artillery. Later, unable to fight on the front lines, he was directed to work in Plzeň and Vienna, and in 1917 he retired. He became famous for organizing a mass demonstration of support for the Hungarian National Council on 28 October 1918. Three days later he became secretary of state for political affairs in the Ministry of Defense in the government of **Mihaly Károlyi**. He entered into closer contacts with the radical opposition to Karolyi's rule, so in February 1919 he resigned.

During the Hungarian Soviet Republic (HSR) Friedrich was active in the opposition. He was arrested and sentenced to death. He managed to escape and became one of the leaders of a counterrevolutionary organization called the White House. On 6 August 1919, with the support of the Italian mission of the Entente and the Romanian command, he forced the "trade union" government of Gyula Peidl to resign. The next day Archduke Joseph Habsburg entrusted him with the formation of a new government and on 15 August nominated him prime minister. Friedrich annulled the HSR legislation and introduced summary procedures that allowed for the mass persecution of the revolutionaries. Friedrich failed to stabilize his power, as the Hungarian territory east of the Danube was occupied by the Romanians, and the western part of the country, by the National Army under **Miklós Horthy**. The Entente and the successor states of the Habsburg monarchy did not recognize his government, fearing a restoration of the Habsburgs. On 24 November 1919 Friedrich resigned. In the new government of **Károly Huszár** he received the portfolio of national defense. After Horthy was elected regent in March 1920, Friedrich resigned with the whole cabinet. In 1920–39 he was an MP on behalf of small Christian Democratic parties. In the summer of 1921 he was accused of taking part in the murder of Prime Minister **István Tisza**, but he was acquitted. In November 1921 he was temporarily arrested for participation in the second return of Charles IV Habsburg. For this reason he worked with the opponents of **István Bethlen**. Soon, however, he was marginalized in political life and fell into oblivion. In July 1951 he was arrested by the Communists in connection with the show trial of Archbishop **József Grősz**. He was sentenced to fifteen years in prison under the false accusation of initiating and leading a plot aimed at overthrowing the government. Friedrich died in prison. In 1990 his sentence was invalidated, and Friedrich was rehabilitated. (JT)

Sources: *Magyar Életrajzi Lexikon*, vol. 1 (Budapest, 1967); *Magyar Nagylexikon*, vol. 8 (Budapest, 1999); *Új Magyar Életrajzi Lexikon*, vol. 2 (Budapes, 2001); Oszkar Jaszi, *Revolution and Counterrevolution in Hungary* (London, 1924); Rudolf L. Tőkés, *Bela Kun and the Hungarian Soviet Republic* (New York, 1967); Paul Ignotus, *Hungary* (London, 1972).

FRLEC Boris (10 February 1936, Ljubljana), Slovene diplomat. After high school in Ljubljana, in 1959 Frlec graduated in the natural sciences and technology from the University of Ljubljana, and in 1965 he received a Ph.D. in chemistry. From 1959 he worked in the Jožef Stefan Institute, and from 1975 he was its director. An associate professor from 1968 and a full professor at the University of Ljubljana from 1976, he also stud-ied in the United States and the United Kingdom. He published numerous articles in inorganic chemistry. From 1982 to 1989 he was deputy chairman of the Executive Council (government) of the Slovene republic, and in 1989 he assumed the position of ambassador to Germany. After the breakup of Yugoslavia, in 1992 he became ambassador of Slovenia to Germany. After the dismissal of **Zoran Thaler**, in September 1997 Frlec became foreign minister. He pursued intense efforts to lead his country into the European Union. On 31 March 1998 Slovenia formally started accession negotiations. In the Slovene relationship with Croatia Frlec made some progress, but he failed to solve many problems, such as the final delimitation of the land and sea borders. In January 2000 he resigned for personal reasons, and in the summer of 2000 he became ambassador to the Netherlands. (AO)

Sources: *Government of the Republic of Slovenia, 1999* (Ljubljana, 1999); *Europa Środkowo-Wschodnia 1997–2000* (Warsaw, 1999–2002); www.rferl.org.

FUNDO Llazar (1894?, Korcë–October 1944, Bicaj, near Kukës), Albanian Communist activist. Fundo came from a family of Wallachian origin. He was a member of the Bashkimi (Unity) organization. After the murder of **Avni Rustemi**, the founder of the organization, by **Ahmed Zogu**'s people in 1924, Fundo assumed the leadership of the organization. At the same time he became editor-in-chief of the organization's newspaper, also called *Bashkimi*. He took part in the revolution of June 1924 in Albania, and after the fall of the **Fan Noli** government he went to Vienna. There he probably met groups of Balkan Communists. From Vienna he went to Moscow, and he was the first Albanian to attend the school of the Communist International there. In 1929 he attended the Eighth Conference of the Balkan Communist Federation. During the Stalinist purges Fundo left the USSR and went to Switzerland and then to Paris, where he studied law and became aligned with Trotskyism. During his stay in Moscow he had already been sending letters to Fan Noli, emphasizing his negative attitude toward Stalinism and the Soviet system. In 1938 **Sejfulla Malëshova** denounced him as a participant in Nikolay Bukharin's plot. Fundo was called to Moscow, but he did not go. In France he acted against the recruitment of Albanians to the International Brigades that fought in Spain. After he again refused to return to Moscow, the Comintern ordered his assassination. In Paris, Malëshova tried to kill him with an axe. After returning to Albania, Fundo made an unsuccessful attempt to found a Socialist party. In November 1939 he took part in a demonstration that was organized in Korcë on the anniversary of the proclamation of Albania's independence. Captured by the Italian police and interned in a camp on the island of Ventotene, from 1939 to 1943 Fundo was held there with the Kryeziu brothers. After his release from the camp, he joined the troops led by the Kryeziu brothers, which were active in the borderland between Kosovo and Albania. Captured by Communist guerrillas in September 1944, Fundo was tortured on the personal orders of **Enver Hoxha**, who wanted to extort information from him about the troops' aims and activities, as well as information about the British mission. After a short trial, Fundo was killed as an "agent of British intelligence." (TC)

Sources: Lazitch; Julian Amery, *Sons of the Eagle: A Study in Guerilla War* (London, 1948); Uran Butka, *Ringjallje* (Tetovë, 1996); Reginald Hibbert, *Albania's National Liberation Struggle: The Bitter Victory* (London and New York, 1991); Arshi Pipa, *Albanian Stalinism: Ideo-Political Aspects* (New York, 1990).

G

GAÁL Gaszton (30 November 1868, Székesfehérvár–26 October 1932, Balatonboglár), Hungarian politician. In 1889 Gaál graduated from the higher agricultural school in Magyaróvár. From 1890 he worked on various landed estates, and in 1894–1900 he worked in the Hungarian Ornithological Center as an assistant to Ottó Herman. From 1900 he ran his own farm, and from 1902, an estate in Balatonboglár. In 1905–6 he took part in the so-called national resistance action against the government of **Géza Fejérváry**, whom Emperor Franz Joseph had nominated prime minister without regard to the results of the parliamentary elections, which had been won by the so-called national coalition, which was critical of the 1867 agreement. In 1906–10 Gaál was an MP on behalf of the Independence and 48 Party, which belonged to this coalition. During the Hungarian Soviet Republic in 1919 his estate was taken over by the state administration and he had to go into hiding. From September 1919 to January 1920 he was a government commissioner for Baranya, Somogy, and Tolna Counties, as well as governor of Somogy County. In 1920–26 and from 1927 until his death he was an MP; from July 1920 it was as a member of the Christian Smallholders', Agrarian Laborers', and Burghers' Party. Two month later he left this party, but in February 1921 he returned and became its head. From January to August 1922 he was deputy chairman of the ruling Party of Unity of Count **István Bethlen**, and from August 1921 he was speaker of the parliament for a year. In protest against the government tax policy, unfavorable to the countryside, in August 1922 Gaál left the Party of Unity. He stayed in the opposition, appealing for a reduction of the tax burden imposed on agriculture and for the abolition of industrial protective tariffs. Having attracted well-to-do and medium-income farmers and peasants, in 1926 he founded the Hungarian Agrarian Party (HAP), which he headed and which won three seats in the elections of 1927. in December 1930 the HAP joined the Independent Smallholders' Party of **Zoltán Tildy** and **Ferenc Nagy**. From January 1931 until his death Gaál was its chairman and headed its parliamentary club. (JT)

Sources: *Magyar Életrajzi Lexikon*, vol. I (Budapest, 1967); *Magyar Nagylexikon*, vol. 8 (Budapest, 1999); *Új Magyar Életrajzi Lexikon*, vol. 2 (Budapest, 2001).

GABROVSKI Petar (9 July 1898, Razgrad–1 February 1945, Sofia), Bulgarian lawyer and politician. Gabrovski graduated from high school in Turnovo (now Veliko Turnovo) in 1916. After training at the Reserve Officers' School, he took part, as a platoon commander, in the final stages of World War I (1917–18). After the war he started to study law at Sofia University, graduating in 1923. Then he went to Vienna to pursue his field of specialization. After his return to Bulgaria, from 1924 he worked as a defense attorney in Sofia, and he was at the same time a member of the Supreme Bar Council and a member of the Presidium of the Union of Bulgarian Attorneys. In 1936 he was co-founder and one of the leaders of the pro-Fascist organization Soldiers for the Consolidation of Bulgarian National Identity (Ratnichestvo za Napredyka na Bylgarshtinata). During World War II he served as minister of railways, post, and telegraphs in the governments of **Georgi Kioseivanov** and **Bogdan Filov** (October 1939–September 1943), and between 9 and 14 September 1943 he simultaneously served as prime minister. After the coup of 9 September 1944 Gabrovski was arrested, sentenced by the People's Court to death, and executed. In August 1996 the Supreme Court of Bulgaria quashed that sentence in extraordinary appeal proceedings. Gabrovski was the author of *Politicheskite zadachi na momenta* (Political tasks for today; 1943). (JJ)

Sources: *Entsiklopediya Bulgariya*, vol. 2 (Sofia, 1981); Jerzy Jackowicz, *Partie opozycyjne w Bułgarii 1944–1948* (Warsaw, 1997); Tasho Tashev, *Ministrite na Bylgaria 1879–1999: Entsiklopedichen spravochnik* (Sofia, 1999).

GAFENCU Grigore (30 January 1892, Bucharest–30 January 1957, Geneva), Romanian lawyer and diplomat. Gafencu studied law at the University of Geneva. He earned a Ph.D. in law at the Sorbonne (1914). During World War I he fought as an aviator, receiving the Order of Michael the Brave in 1918 for his courage. He founded the magazine *Revista Vremei*, the economic periodical *Argus*, and one of the most popular Romanian daily journals, *Timpul*. He also directed the Orient-Radio (Rador) news agency in Bucharest. His press published works by Gheorghe M. Cantacuzino, **Nicolae Iorga**, **Gheorghe Brătianu** and others. In 1926 Gafencu was one of the founders of the National Peasant Party. He was an MP in 1928–30 and a senator between 1934 and 1937. He was secretary general of the Romanian Ministry of Foreign Affairs in 1928, deputy minister of public works and transportation (1929–30), deputy minister of foreign affairs (1932), deputy minister of industry and trade (1932–33), and foreign minister from December 1938.

As head of the Romanian diplomatic corps, Gafencu made efforts to preserve the neutrality of his country and peace in Europe. In September 1939, under his ministry, the Polish government and military units were interned in Romania, while other refugees found shelter there as well. After his departure from the Ministry of Foreign Affairs, in July 1940 Gafencu was appointed envoy and minister plenipotentiary to the USSR. Although he was a political opponent of the regime that came into power after the abdication of **Charles II** in September 1940, he served as minister to Moscow until Romanian troops entered the war against the USSR on the side of Germany in June 1941. Gafencu was interned by the Soviet authorities, and in July 1941 he was sent to Turkey along with members of the legations of Italy, Finland, and Slovakia. He went into political exile in Switzerland, where he maintained contacts with other opposition politicians in exile. He did not accept various posts that the Romanian authorities offered him, and he maintained contacts with the Polish government-in-exile.

After the war, Gafencu was an avowed opponent of the Communist regime, and he was the founder of the Romanian National Committee (1948). He was in constant touch with King **Michael I**, former prime minister General **Nicolae Rădescu**, and other politicians in exile. In November 1947, the Communist court in Bucharest sentenced Gafencu in absentia to twenty years' imprisonment for the "betrayal of his homeland." Gafencu was a member of the Academy of International Law. He attended the congresses of the European Movement in The Hague (1948) and Brussels (1949). He lectured in the United States, and in 1951 he was a signatory of the "Declaration of Aims and Principles of Liberation of the Central and Eastern European Peoples." He was also active in the Assembly of Captive European Nations in New York. In 1968 his body was buried in Budapest. Gafencu is known in historiography for his memoirs of his official visits in April and May 1939 and his talks with **Józef Beck**, Adolf Hitler, Neville Chamberlain, Benito Mussolini, and politicians in Paris, Brussels, Belgrade, and the Vatican: *Prèliminares de la guerre a l'Est* (1944; *Prelude to the Russian Campaign*, 1945). In 1991 his *Inseminari politice 1929–1939* (Political memoirs 1929–1939) were published, and in 1992, *Jurnal* (*iunie 1940–iulie 1942*) (Journal [June 1940–July 1942]). (FA/TD)

Sources: *Biographisches Lexikon*, vol. 2; *The Times*, 31 January 1957; Tadeusz Dubicki, *Wojsko polskie w Rumunii 1939–1941* (Warsaw, 1994); Archive of New Records in Warsaw, Legation Bern, catalogue numbers: 320, 322, 327, 328, 331.

GAJDA Radola [originally Rudolf Geidl] (14 February 1892, Kotor–15 April 1948, Prague), Czech general and politician of German origin. Between 1912 and 1913 Gajda volunteered to serve as an artilleryman in the First

Balkan War. During World War I he enlisted in the Montenegrin Army (1915), and after its defeat he managed to get to Russia, where he first joined the Serbian division in Odessa and then the Czechoslovak Legion (1917). As a battalion commander, he took part in a battle at Zborov (2 August 1917), after which he became a regiment commander. Following the "incident of Chelyabinsk," where the legionnaires at first lynched one of the prisoners on their way to Siberia and then forcefully released the participants of that event who were arrested by the Red Army, Gajda called for action against the Bolsheviks. In May 1918 he assumed the leadership of a military unit on the Omsk-Irkutsk trunk line in Siberia. Promoted to major general and divisional commander in September, in October 1918 he became commander of the northern Ural front, where he led the offensive that ended in the capture of Perm in December 1918. In 1919, in agreement with **Milan R. Štefanik**, Gajda fought in the Siberian army of Admiral Aleksandr Kolchak, and for a short period he was his chief of staff. However, because of a conflict with the Russian generals, Gajda left the army, and in November 1919 he tried to organize a rebellion against Kolchak. After the rebellion was put down owing to the intercession of the legionnaires, he was released on condition that he immediately leave Russia. His days in Siberia are described in *Moje pamĕti* (My memoirs; 1921).

Soon after returning to Czechoslovakia, Gajda left for Paris for one year, and he studied at the military academy. He later commanded an infantry division in Košice until 1924. In 1924–26 he was deputy chief of the General Staff, and from March to July 1926, chief of the General Staff. In 1925 he was co-founder of the National Fascist Community (Národni Obec Fašistická [NFC]). In 1926 rumors spread that Gajda, along with members of Andrej Hlinka's People's Party, was preparing a coup d'état. Gajda was put on leave and suspended from military duties but was not brought to trial until 1929, when he was sentenced to two months' imprisonment and expulsion from the army on the charge of betraying military secrets. His guilt was never proved beyond a reasonable doubt, the mild sentence attesting to the court's doubts. After his release from prison, Gajda became leader of the NFC and sat as its representative in the National Assembly from 1929 to 1931 and from 1935 to 1939. In 1933 a group of Fascists attempted to attack the barracks in Brno, a move that was intended to be the beginning of a coup. The coup perpetrators named Gajda as their leader, but he denied having been involved in the plot and was acquitted by the court. In August 1938, in the face of the collapse of Czechoslovakia, Gajda offered his services to President **Edvard Beneš**, who until then had been his enemy. However, his offer was rejected. In 1938–39 he was vice-president of the Party of National Unity, led by **Rudolf Beran**. On 11 March 1939 he was rehabilitated by a decree of **Emil Hácha**, and he was restored to the rank of general. After the proclamation of independence of Slovakia, at the negotiations for the creation of a new government Gajda offered to restore order in Slovakia within twenty-four hours. After 15 March 1939 he offered to collaborate with the occupier, and along with the Czech Fascists he tried to take over power in the Protectorate of Bohemia and Moravia. However, the Germans were not interested in his offer. Arrested in May 1945, two years later Gajda was sentenced to two years in prison, not for collaboration but only for promoting fascism. Since he had been held in detention pending trial, he was soon released. (PU)

Sources: *ČBS*; *Kdo byl kdo v našich dějinách ve 20. století*, vol. 1 (Prague, 1998); *Politická elita meziválečného Československa 1918–1938: Kdo byl kdo za první republiky* (Prague, 1998); F. G. Campbell, *Confrontation in Central Europe* (Chicago, 1975); Jerzy Tomaszewski, "Brno 1933: Porucznik Kobsinek maszeruje przeciw Masarykowi i Republice," in *Przewroty i zamachy stanu: Europa 1918–1939* (Warsaw, 1981); Antonín Klimek and Petr Hofman, *Vítěz, který prohrál: General Radola Gajda* (Prague, 1995).

GÁL Fedor (20 March 1945, Terezín), Slovak sociologist and politician. Gál graduated from the Bratislava Polytechnic. In 1972–82 he worked in the Institute of Labor and Social Affairs and in the Institute of the Standard of Living, and from 1982 to 1989, in the Institute of Forecasting of the Slovak Academy of Sciences in Bratislava. In November 1989 he took part in student protests that initiated the Velvet Revolution, and then he co-founded the movement Public against Violence (Verejnost' proti Násiliu [VPN]). In 1990 he headed the VPN coordination center; in 1990–91 he chaired its Slovak council and was director of the Institute of Social Analysis of Comenius University in Bratislava. As a member of the liberal-democratic wing of the VPN, Gál supported the economic reforms of **Václav Klaus**, which led to internal tensions within the VPN. In the spring of 1991, when a group of followers of **Vladimir Mečiar** founded the faction For a Democratic Slovakia and then transformed it into the Movement for a Democratic Slovakia (Hnutie za Demokratické Slovensko [HZDS]), breaking up the VPN, Gál resigned from his position. In 1991–92 he was an adviser to Prime Minister **Marian Čalfa**, and he took an active part in the negotiations on the Czechoslovak federation. He supported maintaining the federation, so when Czechoslovakia split up, he retired from political life. From 1992 he was an associate professor in the Sociology Department of Charles University in Prague, where he established the Center for Political Analysis. From 1990 he co-owned the G-Plus Press, and in 1993–94 he co-founded a private television station, NOVA. Gál co-authored *Svet vedy a poznávania* (The world of science and cognition; 1988) and *Dnešní krize česko-slovenských vztehů* (Today's crisis of Czecho-Slovak relations; 1992); and he authored *Možnost' a skutočnost'* (Ability and reality; 1990), *Z prvej ruky* (At first hand; 1991), and *O jinakosti* (On dissimilarity; 1998). (PU)

Sources: *ČBS*; Jan Rychlík, *Rozpad Československa: Česko-slovenské vztahy 1989–1992* (Bratislava, 2002); Eric Stein, *Czecho/Slovakia: Ethnic Conflict, Constitutional Fissure, Negotiated Breakup* (Ann Arbor, 1997); *Verejnost' proti nasiliu 1989–1991: Svedectva a dokumenty* (Bratislava, 1998).

GAŁCZYŃSKI Konstanty Ildefons (23 January 1905, Warsaw–6 December 1953, Warsaw), Polish poet. Following graduation from high school, Gałczyński started philological studies at the University of Warsaw, but he never completed them. During the 1920s he belonged to the Kwadryga (Quadriga) poetry group, and in 1926–33 he wrote for the satirical periodical *Cyrulik Warszawski*. Between 1930 and 1933 he worked as a censor at the Government Commissariat in Warsaw and then as an official at the Polish consulate in Berlin. From 1935 until 1939 he was affiliated with the right-wing *Prosto z mostu*. He fought the invading Nazis in September 1939 but was taken prisoner and spent the war in a German POW camp in Altengrabow, near Magdeburg. In 1946, he returned to Poland. Initially, he lived in Kraków, writing for the weekly *Przekrój*. Then he moved to Szczecin and Warsaw. Because of the official introduction of Socialist realism, from 1950 he was criticized for "formalism" and "petty bourgeois tastes," which were alien to Communism.

Porfirion osiełek czyli Klub Świętokradców (Porfirion the Donkey or the Club of the Sacrilegious; 1929) was Gałczyński's prose debut, a novel full of humor and imagination. His novels combined the satirical and the grotesque with a touch of Romantic lyricism. In his rhymed novel, *Koniec świata* (The end of the world; 1929), and *Utworach poetyckich* (Poetic works; 1937), he expressed his catastrophic premonitions, masked by an absurdist ambience and surrealistic humor. At the end of the 1930s, Gałczyński's hero was a member of the Polish intelligentsia, full of dreams but powerless and backward. Gałczyński's lyrical output is dominated by love poems and depictions of a happy family life. In the POW camp, he wrote patriotic poems (for example, *Pieśń o żołnierzach z Westerplatte* [Song about the soldiers of Westerplatte]), often adhering to the Romantic tradition. After his return to Poland, he continued lampooning the Polish intelligentsia—for instance, in his cycle of grotesque miniatures,

Teatrzyk Zielona Gęś (The green goose theater), which was published in *Przekrój*. In it he created an original surrealistic cabaret starring literary figures, animals, and even abstract ideas. His comprehensive collection, *Zaczarowana dorożka* (The magic cab; 1948), contained, among other pieces, his lyrical poems about Kraków. During Socialist realism Gałczyński succumbed to official pressure and wrote the propaganda song *Ukochany kraj* and a satirical poem, "Chryzostoma Bulwiecia podróż do Ciemnogrodu" (Chrysostom Bulwieć goes to Ignoranceville; 1954). His concept of "Ignoranceville" entered colloquial Polish as a symbol of backwardness and petty bourgeois conservatism. Between 1957 and 1960 his *Dzieła w pięciu tomach* (Works in five volumes) were published. (WR)

Sources: *Literatura polska XX wieku: Przewodnik encyklopedyczny*, vol. 1 (Warsaw, 2000); *Wielka encyklopedia PWN*, vol. 4 (Warsaw, 2001); Andrzej Stawar, *O Gałczyńskim* (Warsaw, 1959); *Wspomnienia o Gałczyńskim* (Warsaw, 1961); Andrzej Drawicz, *Konstanty Ildefons Gałczyński* (Warsaw, 1973).

GALICA Shote [originally Qerime Halili] (1895 Radishevë, near Drenica–July 1927, Derven, near Fushe Krujë), Albanian fighter for the independence of Kosovo. In 1909 her native village was burned down by Turkish troops led by Dzhevit Pasha. Her family went into hiding in the mountains. After returning to the village, her family lived in extreme poverty. In 1911 Galica joined one of the units fighting in Kosovo against the Turks, and from 1912, against the Serbs. In 1915 she married Azem Galica, one of the most famous warriors in Kosovo at that time, and joined his unit. In 1916–17 this unit was active on the borderland between two occupation zones: the Austro-Hungarian and the Bulgarian. During World War I Galica took part in dozens of battles against Serbian, Austro-Hungarian, and Bulgarian units. During an encounter in March 1917, when Azem's unit was encircled by the Bulgarians in Obrij, Galica was one of the few who managed to escape from the siege, though she was wounded. When in 1919 the Serbian units were disarming the Albanian population in Kosovo, Azem and Shote decided to continue their struggle in the region of Drenica. Galica was a liaison to the Kosovo Committee, which was active in Albania. In 1922, when a neutral zone was established between Albania and Kosovo, the town of Junik, situated within that zone, became the unit's base. Hoping for more active support from Tirana for the Kosovar cause, Azem and Shote backed **Hasan bey Prishtina** and **Bajram Curri**.

While the victory of the revolution in June 1924 in Albania created hopes for the internationalization of the Kosovar cause, it also brought an end to the neutral zone. When on 17 July 1924 Azem died of severe wounds, Galica took

his place. She delivered reports on the situation in Kosovo to the Kosovo Committee, which was active in Shkodër, and she organized bases for the wounded members of the unit in northern Albania. When in December 1924 **Ahmed Zogu** came to power in Tirana, her unit fought in the region of Has against Serbian troops that supported Zogu. Galica led the guerrilla warfare in Kosovo until 1926, when she was seriously wounded again and decided to return to Albania. At first she lived in Shullaz, then in Derven. Although her friends appealed to the authorities for help for Galica, she lived in extreme poverty, without social or medical assistance. Thanks to her friends from Kosovo, in 1927 she was admitted to a hospital in Tirana, but after a few days of treatment she returned to Derven, where she died. (TC)

Sources: *Fjalor Enciklopedik Shqiptar* (Tirana, 1985); Ajet Haxhiu, *Shota dhe Azem Galica* (Tirana, 1982); *Historia e popullit shqiptar* (Tirana, 1994).

GALVANAUSKAS Ernestas (20 November 1882, Zizonys, near Panevežys [Poniewież]–24 July 1967, Aix-les-Bains, France), Lithuanian politician. In 1908 Galvanauskas completed engineering studies at the Institute of Mining in St. Petersburg. While a student, he became involved in independence activities. In 1905 he took part in the Grand Lithuanian Assembly in Vilnius (Wilno), and then he was a co-founder of the populist Lithuanian Peasant Union (Lietuvos Valstiečiu Sąjunga). From 1908 to 1912 he studied at the university in Liege in Belgium, and then he worked in a French firm in Serbia. At the beginning of 1919 he returned to Lithuania and became secretary of the Lithuanian delegation to the Paris Peace Conference. From 7 October 1919 he served as prime minister. Among other matters, he dealt with the codification of laws and the organization of the administration and the army. He also had to deal with economic difficulties. In February 1920 he put down a rebellion in a garrison in Kaunas. He unsuccessfully attempted to force Poland to renounce its claims to the Vilnius (Wilno) region, and he did not gain international support for the Lithuanian stance. Galvanauskas held elections in April 1920, but as a result of these elections he had to resign on 19 June 1920. However, he remained minister of finance and trade. On 2 February 1922 he again became head of the government. He was unsuccessful in his efforts to prevent the international recognition of the incorporation of the Vilnius region into Poland. On 10 June 1924 he resigned his post.

In 1924–27 Galvanauskas was an envoy to London, from where he returned after the nationalist regime consolidated its power. He was in charge of the administration of the port in Klaipeda and worked as editor of the newspaper *Vakarai*; in 1934 he founded the Trade Institute and was its rector. In November 1939 he became minister of finance in the government of **Antanas Merkys**, and remained in office until the arrival of the Red Army in mid-June 1940. After the creation of the government of **Justas Paleckis**, Galvanauskas was appointed to a ministerial post, but realizing that this meant cooperation in the enslavement of the country, on 5 July he resigned and secretly left the country. In September 1940 he became head of the Lithuanian National Committee, which sought German support for the rebuilding of an independent Lithuania. After the Germans invaded Lithuania in June 1941 and arrested members of the Lithuanian provisional government, including **Kazys Škirpa**, the leader of this government, Galvanauskas withdrew from political life. After the war he lived in France, and between 1947 and 1962, in Madagascar, where he founded a technical high school for trade and handicrafts in Majunga (now Mahajanga). Owing to his state of health, at the end of his life Galvanauskas returned to France, where he died. (WR)

Sources: *EL*, vol. 2; Saulius Sužiedelis, *Historical Dictionary of Lithuania* (Lanham, Md., 1997); Alfred E. Senn, *The Great Powers, Lithuania, and the Vilna Question, 1920–1928* (Leiden, 1966); Bronis J. Kaslas, ed., *The USSR-German Aggression against Lithuania* (New York, 1973); David M. Crowe, *The Baltic States and the Great Powers: Foreign Relations, 1938–1940* (Boulder, Colo., 1993).

GANEV Dimitur [originally Vurbanov] (28 October 1898, Gradets, Sliven County–20 April 1964, Sofia), Bulgarian Communist activist. After graduating from a high school in Varna in 1915, Ganev fought in World War I. From 1918 he was a member of the Bulgarian Communist Youth Union, and in 1921 he joined the Bulgarian Communist Party (BCP). From 1921 to 1923 he worked as a teacher in Sliven County. He took part in the preparation of the Communist uprising of September 1923. After the failure of the uprising he was temporarily arrested. From 1924 he served as secretary of the Supply Workers' Union. In 1925–29 he belonged to the Central Committee (CC) of the Independent Workers' Trade Union and was a member of the Regional Committee of the BCP in Sofia. In 1929, as a member of the CC of the BCP, Ganev went to Romania, where he was a secretary of the Revolutionary Organization of Dobruja. From 1934 he was a member of the CC and of the Secretariat of the CC of the Romanian Communist Party (RCP). From 1926 to 1934 he edited the newspaper *Free Dobruja*. Arrested and sentenced to ten years' imprisonment, he was released in 1940 after Bulgaria took over southern Dobruja. He then served as secretary of the county committee of the Bulgarian Workers' Party (BWP) in Dobrich (also spelled Dobrič). In 1942

he became a member of the Politburo of the CC of the BWP, secretary of the District Committee of the BWP in Sofia, and editor of the illegal newspaper *Rabotnichesko Delo*. From February 1944 he was a plenipotentiary of the CC of the BWP in the insurgents' operational zone in Varna.

On 9 September 1944 Ganev became a member of the Bulgarian delegation set up to establish contact with the staff of the Soviet Third Ukrainian Front in order to conclude a truce. He later served as head of the public relations department of the CC of the BWP; was again editor-in-chief of the daily, *Rabotnichesko Delo* and secretary of the BWP town committee and district committee in Sofia; and was a member of the National Council of the Fatherland Front. In 1947–48 he was an envoy to Romania, and from 1949, a deputy member of the Politburo of the CC of the BCP, which was formed from the merger of the BWP with a part of the Social Democratic Party. Between December 1948 and September 1952 Ganev was minister of foreign trade. In 1952 he fell into disfavor and spent two years as minister plenipotentiary in Czechoslovakia, but at the Sixth Congress of the BCP in March 1954 he returned to the Secretariat of the CC, and from September 1957 he was a member of the Politburo. He also represented the BCP at the Twentieth Congress of the CPSU in Moscow in February 1956. After the April plenum of the CC of the BCP in 1956 Ganev became head of a commission set up to investigate the case of **Traicho Kostov**. The commission found irregularities, but its verdict was not made public; it was used only in the internal strife among the top leaders. From 1945 until his death Ganev was a deputy to successive National Assemblies. In 1954–57 and 1962–64 he also served as president of the Presidium of the Second and Fourth National Assemblies. In 1987 his *Izbrani proizvedeniia 1944–1964* (Selected works 1944–1964) were published. (JJ)

Sources: *Entsiklopediya Bulgariya*, vol. 2 (Sofia, 1981); J. F. Brown, *Bulgaria under Communist Rule* (New York, 1970); Tasho Tashev, *Ministrite na Bulgariya 1879–1999: Entsiklopedichen spravochnik* (Sofia, 1999).

GANEV Stoyan (23 July 1955, Pazardzhyk), Bulgarian lawyer and politician. Ganev graduated in law from the University of Sofia in 1973, and in 1985 he received his candidate's degree (doctorate) at the University of Moscow. In 1985–89 he lectured in constitutional law at the Law Department of the University of Sofia. From 1989 he began to play an important role in the opposition against the Communist regime, co-founding the Union of Democratic Forces (Sayuz na Demokratichnite Sili [UDF]). After the fall of **Todor Zhivkov** in November 1989, Ganev was deputy to the Grand National Assembly and then to the National Assembly (1991–94). He was also deputy chairman of the UDF parliamentary club (1991–92) and chairman of the United Democratic Center, which was a part of the UDF. From 8 November 1991 to 20 May 1992 he was deputy prime minister, and from November 1991 to the end of December 1992, also minister of foreign affairs in the government of **Filip Dimitrov**. In 1992 he presided over the Forty-seventh Session of the UN General Assembly. After leaving the government, he was dismissed from the UDF for his favorable attitude toward President **Zhelyu Zhelev** and for his close contacts with Dimitrov. He joined the Bulgarian Business Bloc. Ganev co-authored *Dyrzhavnoto pravo na sotsialisticheskite strani* (State law in the Socialist countries; 1986). (JJ)

Sources: *Demokratsiya*, 9 September 1991; Raymond Detrez, *Historical Dictionary of Bulgaria* (Lanham, Md., 1997); Tasho Tashev, *Ministrite na Bulgariya 1879–1999: Entsiklopedichen spravochnik* (Sofia, 1999).

GANEV Venelin (4 February 1880, Ruse–25 March 1966, Sofia), Bulgarian politician and lawyer. Ganev completed his studies in philosophy and law in Leipzig (1897–98) and Geneva (1898–1901), and he received a higher musical education in Geneva (1901). From 1908 he worked as an associate professor (*docent*) at the Department of Encyclopedia and the Philosophy of Law of Sofia University. From 1913 he worked there as a professor of philosophy and the general theory of law, and between 1918 and 1947 he was full professor at the Department of Commercial Law. In 1914–15 and 1916–18 he served as dean of the Law Department. In 1919 he was elected a member of the Bulgarian Academy of Sciences. From 1908 Ganev belonged to the Radical Democratic Party, which he left after the military coup of 9 June 1923, and he joined the newly created Democratic Alliance. He was a member of the Bulgarian delegation to the Paris Peace Conference in 1919. Between May and October 1919 he served as minister of justice in the government of **Teodor Teodorov**. From 1920 to 1922 he was envoy extraordinary and minister plenipotentiary to France, and in 1923–27 he was deputy to the Twenty-first National Assembly. In 1925 he left the Democratic Alliance and joined the opposition. In 1926–40 he worked as a lawyer in Sofia. Along with **Petko Stoyanov**, he led a group of so-called independent intellectuals, creating the League for the Defense of Human Rights.

During World War II Ganev took part in the formation of the Fatherland Front (1942–43), and from 1944 he was a member of the National Committee of the Fatherland Front. From 9 September 1944 to 18 September 1946 he was one of the three regents of Bulgaria on behalf of the minor monarch, Tsar **Simeon II**, and he worked with the Communists. In March 1945 he put forward an initiative to revive the Radical Party, and the party was legalized in September of that year. Ganev was the author of a letter to the Allied Control Commission on the postponement of elections in Bulgaria, which had been called for 26 August 1945. Along with a group of independent intellectuals gathered around him, Ganev showed a growing disappointment with the Communists; therefore in 1947 he was removed from Sofia to Drianovo and deprived of his pension, to which he was entitled as a former regent. In 1948 he was stripped of his membership in the Bulgarian Academy of Sciences, to which he was posthumously reinstated (March 1991) after his full rehabilitation (March 1990). Ganev was the author of (among other works) *Chopin* (1919); *Istoricheskoto razvitie na tyrgovskoto pravo* (Historical development of commercial law; 1921); *Sistematicheski kurs po nesystoiatelnostta* (Systematic course in bankruptcy law; 1926); *Kurs po tyrgovsko pravo* (Course in commercial law; 1923); *Kurs po obshta teoriia na pravoto: Uvod, Metodologiia na pravoto* (Course in the general theory of law: Introduction, methodology of law; 1921–32, 1946); *Uchebnik po obshta teoriia na pravoto* (Textbook on the general theory of law, 2 vols.; 1932–38); *Stopanska deistvitelnost: Opit za edna sotsiologicheska sistema* (Economic reality: Attempt at sociological synthesis; 1945); and *Demokratsiia* (Democracy; 1946). (JJ)

Sources: *Entsiklopediya Bulgariya*, vol. 2 (Sofia, 1981); Georgi Dimitrov, *Sychineniia*, vol. 13 (Sofia, 1987); Jerzy Jackowicz, *Partie opozycyjne w Bułgarii 1944–1948* (Warsaw, 1997); Tasho Tashev, *Ministrite na Bulgariya 1879–1999: Entsiklopedichen spravochnik* (Sofia, 1999).

GANIĆ Ejup (3 March 1946, Sebečevo, near Novi Pazar), Bosnian scholar and politician. In 1972 Ganić graduated from the Department of Technology of the University of Belgrade, and then he worked in the Institute of Chemistry, Technology, and Metallurgy in Belgrade. In 1976 he defended his Ph.D. thesis at the Massachusetts Institute of Technology in Cambridge and he worked as an assistant professor there. Later he worked in the Union Cambridge Corporation–Linde Division in New York, lectured at universities in New York and Chicago, and was a professor at the University of Illinois in Chicago. He authored many works in the thermo mechanics of liquids and co-authored six scholarly books in the United States. He founded and edited the periodical *Experimental Thermal and Fluids Science*, and he received a number of international awards. In 1982 Ganić returned to Bosnia and Herzegovina (B&H). He was a member of the board for research and development at UNIS in Sarajevo, professor at the Department of Engineering of the University of Sarajevo, and visiting professor at Lomonosov University in Moscow. On 18 November 1990 he was elected a member of the B&H presidency, and then he joined the Party of Democratic Action (Strana Demokratske Akcije [PDA]). He was its deputy chairman, and in 1992 he became de facto deputy president of B&H. During the kidnapping of President **Alija Izetbegović** (2–3 May 1992) Ganić was appointed acting president by Izetbegović, and he disapproved of the withdrawal of the whole Yugoslav People's Army (YPA) garrison from Sarajevo in exchange for Izetbegović's release. On 31 May 1994 Ganić was elected first vice-president of the Federation of Bosnia and Herzegovina, in which the president and vice-president rotated every year. From 1 January 2000 to 28 February 2001 he was president of the federation again. He headed the federation's commission in the Brčko arbitrage. Considered a Muslim extremist, Ganić entered into conflict with Prime Minister **Haris Silajdzić** and was expelled from the PDA in May 2000. According to President **Vojislav Koštunica**, Ganić bears the responsibility for the murder of YPA recruits on Dobrovoljacka Street in Sarajevo in 1992. Ganić is a member of the American Nuclear Society, and he authored *Bosanska otrovna jabuka* (Bosnian poisoned apple; 1995). (JD)

Sources: *Ko je ko u bošnjaka: Vijeće Kongresa Bošjačkih intelektualaca* (Sarajevo, 2000); Warren Zimmermann, *Origins of a Catastrophe* (New York and Toronto, 1996); Bugajski.

GANOVSKI Sava (1 March 1897, Kunino–24 April 1993, Sofia), Bulgarian Communist activist. After graduating from the Reserve Officers' School, Ganovski fought in World War I. He was sentenced to fifteen years' imprisonment for his anti-war activities, but after the end of the warfare he was released under an amnesty. From 1918 he was a member of the Bulgarian Social Democratic Workers' Party (the so-called narrow Socialists). In 1922 he graduated in pedagogy and philosophy from Sofia University, and in 1923–28 he pursued specialization studies in Halle and Berlin. In Berlin, he became a member of the Communist Party of Germany. He was one of the initiators of Narstud, a Bulgarian radical leftist union of students abroad. In 1928–31 he graduated in philosophy from the Institute of Red Professorship in Moscow, and he simultaneously lectured at the University for Western Minorities in Moscow, at Moscow University (1929–30), and at the Institute of Literature in Moscow, where he held the chair of dialectical and historical materialism (1930–31). After his return to Bulgaria in 1931 Ganovski organized teachers' trade unions, co-founded the Union

of Working and Struggling Writers (1932), and edited the newspapers *Syvremennik, Zvezda, Syvremenna misyl,* and *Nauchen pregled.* In 1941–43 he was repeatedly arrested and interned. At the beginning of 1944 he joined a guerrilla unit, becoming deputy political commissar in the military operational zone in Pleven. After the coup of 9 September 1944 Ganovski was a delegate of the government to Thrace, director of the press (1944–45), and envoy to Romania (1945–47) and Yugoslavia (1947–48). Then he was deputy minister for foreign affairs (1948–49); president (in the rank of minister) of the Committee of Science, Art, and Culture (December 1949–February 1952); and head of the Department of Science, Education, and Art of the CC of the Bulgarian Communist Party (1953–57).

In 1945 Ganovski was appointed professor at Sofia University; working in the Stalinist spirit, he held the chair of philosophy (1949–51) and then the chair of dialectical materialism and history of philosophy. In 1952 he became a member of the Bulgarian Academy of Sciences (BAS); a member of its Presidium; and secretary of the Department of History, Archaeology, and Philosophy of the BAS. In 1957–59 he was vice-president of the BAS; from 1959 to 1967 he was director of the BAS Institute of Pedagogy, and in 1977–87 he was director of the BAS Institute of Philosophy. Between 1954 and 1990 he was a member of the CC of the BCP and a deputy to the National Assembly. In 1965 and in 1966–71 he was president of the Bureau of the National Assembly. He was elected to membership in the Academies of Sciences of Czechoslovakia, the German Democratic Republic, Romania, and the USSR. Ganovski was the author of (among other works) *Osnovni napravleniia v filosofiiata* (Basic trends in philosophy; 1934); *Shto e zhivot* (What is life; 1935); *Osnovni zakoni na nauchnata filosofiia* (Basic principles of scientific philosophy; 1940); and *Kratka istoriia na filosofiiata ot drevnostta do nainovoto vreme* (Short history of philosophy from ancient times to modern times; 1941, reissued many times). (JJ)

Sources: *Entsiklopediya Bulgariya,* vol. 2 (Sofia, 1981); *100 godini na BAN,* vol. 1 (Sofia, 1969); *Akademik Sava Ganovski: Iubileen sbornik* (Sofia, 1971); Tasho Tashev, *Ministrite na Bulgariya 1979–1999: Entsiklopedichen spravochnik* (Sofia, 1999).

GARAMI Ernő (13 December 1876, Budapest–28 May 1935, Budapest), Hungarian writer and politician. From 1898 Garami was one of the leaders of the Hungarian Social Democratic Party (HSDP). An adherent of Marxist revisionism, in 1905–6 and 1907–18 he was editor of the party daily, *Népszava,* where he intensively campaigned for the introduction of universal suffrage in Hungary. In 1906 he founded *Szocializmus,* a theoretical organ of the

Hungarian Social Democrats, and he co-edited it until 1918. Garami translated the works of Karl Marx, Friedrich Engels, and Karl Kautsky. He also wrote short stories and plays—for example, the play *Megváltás felé* (Toward the breakthrough; 1908). During the republican revolution in Hungary (November 1918–March 1919) Garami was minister of trade in the government of **Mihaly Károlyi.** After the proclamation of the Hungarian Soviet Republic (HSR) in March 1919 he emigrated to Austria and then to Switzerland, as he disagreed with the policy of the HSDP, particularly with the party's decision to merge with the Hungarian Communist Party. Garami edited the newspaper *Jövő*, which was published in Vienna from 1921. In it, he sharply criticized the government of Regent **Miklós Horthy**, as well as Communist policies. Because of his articles, legal proceedings were instituted against him in Hungary. After his trial was discontinued in 1929, Garami returned to Hungary. From 1930 he was again a member of the leadership of the HSDP, and from 1934 he was editor of the daily *Népszava*. Rejecting the principle of the dictatorship of the proletariat, Garami promoted the need for a social agreement between workers and the bourgeoisie. In his public speeches as well as in his journalism, Garami warned against communism, pointing out to its anti-humanistic and anti-worker nature. (MS)

Sources: *Biographisches Lexikon*, vol. 1; *Garami Ernő: Emlékkönyv* (Budapest, 1939); Ferenc Mucsi, *A Kristóffy-Garami-paktum* (Budapest, 1970); Paul Ignotus, *Hungary* (London, 1972); Lajos Varga, *Garami Ernő: Politikai életrajz* (Budapest, 1996).

GARBAI Sándor (27 March 1879, Kiskunhalas–7 November 1947, Paris), Hungarian politician. After completing primary school, Garbai worked as a farm laborer (1892–94) and then as a bricklayer in Budapest (1894–97). He later became a journeyman and joined the Hungarian Social Democratic Party (HSDP). In 1901–19 he was one of the HSDP leaders. In 1903 he co-founded the All-National Union of Hungarian Construction Workers and until 1919 served as its president. In 1903–19 he was president of the Workers' Insurance Institute. In 1907 he became vice-president, and in the following year head, of the All-National Workers' Insurance Fund. He became well known in Hungary after 1905, when his party started a struggle for universal suffrage and the secret ballot. From June 1917, as an HSDP delegate, Garbai was vice-president of the Suffrage Bloc, established under the leadership of Count **Mihály Károlyi.** After the victory of the republican revolution in Hungary, between November 1918 and March 1919 Garbai was president plenipotentiary of the All-National Housing Council.

Garbai declared himself in favor of merging the HSDP

and the Communist Party. The two parties merged on 21 March 1919. Under the Hungarian Soviet Republic (HSR) he presided over the Revolutionary Governing Council, which served as the government. However, actual power was concentrated in the hands of **Béla Kun**, who formally was only the people's commissar for foreign affairs. Garbai served as minister of education in the so-called trade union government of Gyula Peidl, which was founded after the fall of the HSR and lasted only six days (1–6 August 1919). After the capture of Budapest, the Romanian troops arrested Garbai. They then released him and escorted him to Transylvania in November 1919. In February 1920 he traveled via Czechoslovakia to Vienna, where he lived until 1934 as one of the leaders of the Hungarians in exile. Between 1920 and 1927 he belonged to a Social Democratic group called Világosság (The Light). Later he founded the group Előre (Forward), which aimed at bringing about the unification of various factions in exile. Between 1927 and 1932 Garbai also edited his own newspaper, *Előre*. In the 1930s Garbai once again became an advocate of Social Democracy, and he condemned Bolshevism. Arrested in February 1934 during the Schutzbund uprising in Vienna, he was released on condition that he leave the country. He went to Bratislava and joined the Slovak Social Democratic movement. In November 1938 he moved to Paris. After the end of World War II he wanted to return to Hungary, but his former comrades in the country opposed that. In 1965 a special commission of the Politburo of the Hungarian Socialist Workers' Party, set up to investigate his activities in exile, decided that he represented an "inappropriate attitude" at that time. The authorities also refused permission for Garbai's ashes to be brought back to Hungary. (JT)

Sources: *Magyar Nagylexikon*, vol. 8 (Budapest, 1999); *Új Magyar Életrajzi Lexikon*, vol. 2 (Budapest, 2001); Rudolf L. Tőkes, *Bela Kun and the Hungarian Soviet Republic* (New York, 1967); Lajos Varga, *Garbai Sándor, 1879–1947: A Forradalmi Kormányzótanács elnóke* (Budapest, 1987).

GARMUS Antanas (19 February 1881, Tursonas, near Kaunas–23 July 1953, Chicago, Illinois), Lithuanian doctor and politician. During the revolution of 1905 Garmus was arrested by the Russian authorities for his activities in the Social Democratic Party. In 1907–14 he studied medicine in Bern, Switzerland, where he earned his doctorate. After his return to Lithuania he was inducted into the Russian Army. During World War I he worked as a military doctor. Between the wars he lectured at the university, and he also worked in the Red Cross and in the Lithuanian anti-tuberculosis society. He was one of the leaders of the international movement against tuberculosis. In June 1940

Garmus agreed to stand as a candidate for the People's Assembly in the elections controlled by the occupying Red Army. He cherished the illusion that the assembly would be able to preserve at least the partial sovereignty of Lithuania. After Germany invaded Lithuania in 1942, Garmus publicly revealed Communist methods of fraud and abuse during the elections. Before the arrival of the Red Army in 1944, he was imprisoned in a German concentration camp. Liberated by the U.S. Army in the spring of 1945, he settled in Germany. In 1949 he moved to the United States, where he gave extensive testimony before the House of Representatives Select Committee to Investigate Incorporation of the Baltic States. (WR)

Sources: *EL*, vol. 2; Bronis J. Kaslas, ed., *The USSR-German Aggression against Lithuania* (New York, 1973); Joseph Pajauvis-Javis, *Soviet Genocide in Lithuania* (New York, 1980).

GAROFLID Constantin (14 September, Buzău–14 June 1943?), Romanian politician. Born into a landowner's family, after high school Garoflid studied medicine in Paris and graduated in 1894. His main interest, however, was in the disproportional land ownership structure in Romania, which he analyzed in *Problema agrară şi deslegarea ei* (The agrarian question and its solution; 1908). He suggested the parceling out of selected large estates. He was elected to the parliament for the first time in 1914. Initially he belonged to the Conservative Party, and in 1919 he joined the People's Party of General **Alexandru Avarescu**. From February to October 1918 he was minister of agriculture, trying to implement King **Ferdinand**'s promise of December 1917 concerning an extensive parceling out of land. Garoflid realized the necessity of parceling out for social reasons, but he feared that a radical liquidation of the large estates would undermine agricultural output. From April 1920 to July 1921 he was minister without portfolio, and from July to December 1921, minister of agriculture in the second government of Avarescu. In this capacity he worked out a draft land reform law that was passed by the parliament on 14 July 1920 and was implemented with July 1921 amendments referring to newly acquired territories (Transylvania, Bessarabia, and Banat). The land reform started a radical transformation of the Romanian system of land ownership. The proportion of large estates in the total area was seriously reduced, while about 1,400,000 settlers received land. Since the average allotment was small, the reform reduced the purchasing power of the countryside and hampered economic development. From March 1926 to June 1927 Garoflid was minister of agriculture again in the third government of Avarescu. In 1930–38 he was one of the founders of the Agrarian League. All through the interwar years he also presided over the Romanian Union of Vineyard Owners. (FAWR)

Sources: David Mitrany, *The Land and the Peasant in Rumania* (Oxford, 1930); *Politics and Political Parties in Roumania* (London, 1936); Şerban N. Ionescu, *Who Was Who in Twentieth Century Romania* (Boulder, Colo., 1994); Keith Hitchins, *Rumania 1866–1947* (Oxford, 1994); Wojciech Roszkowski, *Land Reforms in East Central Europe after World War I* (Warsaw, 1995).

GÁSPÁR Sándor (15 April 1917, Pánd–16 April 2002, Budapest), Hungarian Communist activist. Born into a peasant family, after completing a vocational school, Gáspár worked as a mechanic. From 1935 he was a member of the Metalworkers' Trade Union; from 1936 he was in the Hungarian Social Democratic Party (HSDP), and in 1940 he joined the Hungarian Communist Party (HCP). In 1945–46 he was a member of the leadership of the Metalworkers' Trade Union and an organizer of the District Committee of the HCP in the Sixth District of Budapest. From 1946 he was a member of the CC of the HCP, and between 1948 and 1956 he belonged to the CC of the Hungarian Workers' Party (HWP). In 1947–88 he was an MP in the parliament. Between 1946 and 1947 he was a full timer in the CC of the HWP; in 1947–50 he served as deputy secretary general of the Metalworkers' Trade Union, and in 1950–52, as its secretary general. Between 1951 and 1952 he studied at the Higher Party School of the CPSU in Moscow. In 1952–54 he was deputy secretary general, and between 1954 and 1956 president, of the National Council of Trade Unions (NCTU).

From July 1956 Gáspár was a deputy member, and between 23 and 28 October a member, of the Politburo of the CC of the HWP. In September 1956 he co-organized the funeral of **László Rajk** and his associates. During the revolution of 1956 he tried above all to maintain his position. After 4 November he declared himself in favor of **János Kádár**, and he was one of the organizers of the Hungarian Socialist Workers' Party (HSWP). In a radio address of 13 November on behalf of Kádár's National Council of the Hungarian Free Trade Unions, formed in opposition to the workers' councils, Gáspár called on workers to resume work, and at the same time he stressed the necessity of a multiparty system. Between November 1956 and 1988 he was a member of the CC of the HSWP. A typical representative of the party apparatus, from the beginning of 1957 to 1959 Gáspár was secretary general of the reactivated NCTU; until 1961 he served as the first secretary of the Budapest Committee of the HSWP; until 1962 he was secretary of the CC; and until 1965 he again served as the first secretary of the Budapest Committee of the HSWP. In 1965–83 he again held the post of secretary general of the NCTU, and until 1988 he was its president. In 1959–62 he was a deputy member, and between 1962 and 1988 a member, of the Politburo of the CC of the HSWP. In 1954–88 he was a member, and between 1963 and 1988 vice-president, of the Presidential Council. From 1960 to 1964 he was also vice-president of the National Patriotic Front. One of the party dogmatists, at the beginning of the 1970s he contributed to the collapse of economic reforms. In 1972 along with (among others) **Béla Biszku** and Zoltán Komócsin, Gáspár took part in an attempt to remove Kádár from power, but he finally withdrew and took Kádár's side. Between 1978 and 1989 he was president of the Communist World Federation of Trade Unions (WFTU). In May 1988, as one of the conservatives, Gáspár left the leadership of the HSWP; a month later he resigned as president of the NCTU, and in March 1989 he left the WFTU. (JT)

Sources: *Magyar Nagylexikon*, vol. 8 (Budapest, 1999); *A magyar forradalom és szabadságharc enciklopédiája*, CD-ROM (Budapest, 1999); *Ki kicsoda 2000* (Budapest, 2001); Bennet Kovrig, *Communism in Hungary from Kun to Kádár* (Stanford, 1979); Miklós Molnár, *From Béla Kun to János Kádár: Seventy Years of Hungarian Communism* (New York, 1990).

GAŠPAROVIČ Ivan (27 March 1941, Poltár, Lučenec district), Slovak lawyer and politician. In 1964 Gašparovič graduated in law from the University of Bratislava, and then he practiced in the Martin and Trenčín town prosecutor's offices for two years. In 1966–68 he was town prosecutor in Bratislava. From 1968 to 1990 he was assistant professor and then associate professor of criminal law at Bratislava University, and in 1990 he was briefly its deputy rector. From July 1990 to the beginning of March 1992 he was general prosecutor of Czechoslovakia. He was recalled from this office under pressure from MPs and the media, as he was accused of slowing down the prosecution of Communist crimes. In April 1992 he joined the Movement for a Democratic Slovakia (Hnutie za Demokratické Slovensko [HZDS]) of **Vladimir Mečiar**. He quickly gained Mečiar's trust and became one of Mečiar's closest aides as deputy chairman of his party. As a result of the June 1992 elections Gašparovič won a seat in the Slovak National Council, renamed the National Council of the Slovak Republic after the split of Czechslovakia in January 1993. He was later reelected, and in 1992–98 he was deputy speaker of the parliament. Before the elections of 2002 he entered into conflict with Mečiar, who did not agree to place Gašparovič on the list of candidates for the parliament. In July 2002 Gašparovič left the HZDS, and, along with a group of activists displeased with Mečiar's leadership, he established the Movement for Democracy

(Hnutie za Demokraciu [HZD]). This secession harmed Mečiar's standing, as the HZDS won only 19.5 percent of the vote in the elections of September 2002. It did not help Gašparovič, though, as the HZD won only 3.3 percent and failed to reach the electoral threshold. Surprisingly Gašparovič got to the second round of the presidential elections; on 17 April 2004 he defeated Mečiar and became president, taking over office in mid–June 2004. (PU)

Sources: *ČBS*; Eric Stein, *Czecho/Slovakia: Ethnic Conflict, Constitutional Fissure, Negotiated Breakup* (Ann Arbor, 1997); Miroslav Pekník, ed., *Slovenské Národné Rady* (Bratislava, 1998); Jan Rychlík, *Rozpad Československa: Česko-slovenské vztahy 1989–1992* (Bratislava, 2002); www.hnutie-za-demokraciu.sk.

GAVRILO [originally Djordje Dožić] (17 May 1881, Vrujci u Morači, Montenegro–7 May 1950, Belgrade), Serbian patriarch. Gavrilo attended a people's school run by the monastery in Morača. His uncle, Mihailo Dožić-Medenica, was archimandrite at that monastery. Gavrilo was later educated at a high school in Belgrade, at a theological seminary in Prizren, and at a seminary on the island of Chalke, near Istanbul. In February 1900 he was ordained a monk at the monastery in Sićevo, and he adopted the monastic name Gavrilo. Later, he resided in the monasteries of Jošanica and Visoki Dečani. In 1905–9 he studied in the Department of Orthodox Theology in Athens. After graduation he was secretary of the Hilandar Monastery on Mount Athos, and he was the Serbian representative to the Ecumenical Patriarchate in Constantinople. On 1 December 1911 he was elected metropolitan of the Prizren diocese. After the end of the Balkan War in 1913, he was elected metropolitan of Peć (Ipek) in Montenegro. After the occupation of Serbia by the troops of the Central Powers and the capitulation of Montenegro at the end of 1915, he was interned in Cegléd in Hungary. However, owing to illness, he was released and transferred to Ulcinj.

After the collapse of Austria-Hungary Gavrilo attended the Grand National Assembly in Podgorica and headed the Serbian delegation that concluded an agreement with the Montenegrins. Following the death of Mitrofan Ban, the metropolitan of Montenegro, Gavrilo became his successor, and after the death of Patriarch Varnava, on 8 February 1938 Gavrilo was elected patriarch of the entire Serbian Orthodox Church. One of his first decisions was to annul the excommunication that Varnava had imposed on Prime Minister **Milan Stojadinović** for submitting a concordat with the Vatican to be ratified by the Skupština (Assembly). (That concordat did not come into effect, however.) Later, Gavrilo lent his support to a group of officers who, led by General **Dušan Simović**, executed a coup d'état and took over power in Yugoslavia from the pro-Axis government (27 March 1941); consequently, the Germans, after conquering Yugoslavia in April of that same year, recognized Gavrilo as one of their opponents. He was imprisoned for a short time in the Gestapo prison in Belgrade. Released, the patriarch was interned at the monasteries of Rakovica, near Belgrade, and Vojilovica, near Pančevo, for the next three years. In mid–September 1944 he was deported to the concentration camp at Dachau, and later he was sent to Vienna and Kutzbuehel, where in the spring of 1945 he was liberated by the U.S. Army. After a short stay in Rome and London, where he took part in the baptism of Alexander, the successor to the throne, Gavrilo accepted an invitation from **Edvard Beneš**, the president of Czechoslovakia, and he went to Karlovy Vary. In November 1946 Gavrilo decided to return to Yugoslavia, where he again ascended the throne of the patriarchate and remained in office until the end of his life. In 1974 his *Memoari* (Memoirs) were published in Paris. (AG)

Sources: *Biographisches Lexikon*, vol. 2; *Enciklopedija Jugoslavije*, vol. 3 (Zagreb, 1958); Robert J. Kerner, ed., *Yugoslavia* (Berkeley, 1949); Djoko Slijepčević, *Istorija srpske pravoslavne crkve*, vol. 2 (Munich, 1966); Wacław Felczak and Tadeusz Wasilewski, *Historia Jugosławii* (Wrocław, 1985).

GAVRILOVIĆ Mihailo (8 May 1868, Aleksinac–1 November 1924, London), Serb historian and diplomat. Gavrilović completed high school in Niš and then graduated from the Department of Philosophy of Belgrade University (1891), where he started to work, and he was gradually promoted to the post of professor. He published extensively and dealt mainly with the history of the Middle Ages and nineteenth-century Serbia. In 1900 he became director of the State Archives in Belgrade. He investigated not only the Serbian archives, but also the Austrian, French, and Russian archives. On the basis of his research he wrote his main work, *Knez Miloš Obrenović* (Prince Miloš Obrenović, 3 vols., 1908–12). In 1910 he became an envoy of Serbia to Montenegro, and in 1914, envoy to the Holy See in Rome. In 1917 he assumed the post of adviser to the minister of foreign affairs of the Serbian government, which was on the island of Corfu. In 1918 he was deputy minister of foreign affairs, and in 1919–24 he was an envoy to London. A fourth volume of his work on Miloš Obrenović, which was in manuscript, was destroyed during World War I. (WR)

Sources: *Enciklopedija Jugoslavije*, vol. 3 (Zagreb, 1958); *R. W. Seton-Watson and the Yugoslavs: Correspondence*, vol. 1, *1906–1918*; vol. 2, *1918–1941* (London and Zagreb, 1976); *Istorija srpskog naroda*, vol. 6 (Belgrade, 1983).

GAWLINA Józef (18 November 1892, Strzybnik, Opole region–21 September 1964, Rome), Polish Roman Catholic bishop. After graduating from a high school in Rybnik, Gawlina studied theology in Breslau (now Wrocław, Poland). Mobilized into the German Army in 1914, he took part in the war as a stretcher bearer on the French front and later in Palestine, where he was taken captive by the English. After returning to Poland, he completed his studies and earned a doctorate. In June 1921 he received holy orders. He worked in various parishes of the Katowice diocese. In 1927 in Warsaw he organized the Catholic Press Office, which he directed for two years. In 1933 he was consecrated field bishop of the Polish Army. Wounded during the September campaign in 1939, he performed his duties in France and Great Britain, but he also visited Polish soldiers on many fronts of World War II. In May 1942 he made a pastoral visitation of the Polish Army in the USSR and later also in the Middle East, North Africa, and Italy. After the war he served as the ordinary for the Poles in Germany. He resided in Rome, where he was rector of St. Stanislaus Church. In 1949 the Holy See appointed him the spiritual patron of Poles in exile. He made numerous pastoral visits to the Polish communities in many countries. In 1952 Pope Pius XII named him archbishop and member of the Supreme Council of Exiles, and in 1954, director of the World Federation of Marian Sodality. Gawlina was secretary of the Preparatory Commission of the Second Vatican Council. A gifted preacher and a prolific publicist, he published extensively in the Catholic press in the interwar period. During World War II he edited the newspaper *W imię Boże* and supported the Veritas Publishing House in London. He was also the publisher of *Hosianum* and of the series *Sacrum Poloniae Millennium*. His writings were collected in the volume *Z wojny i wygnania* (From war and from exile; 1952). He also published his memoirs, *Z teki biskupa polowego* (From the portfolio of a field bishop; 1943) and *Biskup polowy na biblijnym Wschodzie* (Field bishop in the biblical East; 1943). Gawlina also organized and presided over the World Committee for the Celebration of Poland's Millenium of Christianity. However, he did not live to see the celebrations. (WR)

Sources: Stanisław Łoza, *Czy wiesz kto to jest* (Warsaw, 1938); J. Bańka, *Arcybiskup Józef Gawlina* (Rome, 1970); K. Biegun, *Arcypasterz Polski wygnańczej: Bp polowy Józef Gawlina* (Warsaw, 1993); Krzysztof Dybciak and Zdzisław Kudelski, eds., *Leksykon kultury polskiej poza krajem od roku 1939* (Lublin, 2000).

GEDVILAS Mečislovas (19 September 1901, Bubiai, near Šiauliai–1981, Vilnius), Lithuanian Communist activist. After high school Gedvilas studied at the Institute of Technology in Petrograd between 1919 and 1922. After returning to Lithuania, he worked as a teacher at a gymnasium (high school) in Palanga (1923–27). He was engaged in conspiratorial Communist activities. He also took part in an unsuccessful revolt of Socialists and members of people's parties in Tauragė in 1927, for which he was imprisoned for four years in an internment camp in Varniai. From 1931 to 1940 he was district director of the Health Insurance Fund in Telšiai, and from 1934 he was involved in the underground activities of the Communist Party of Lithuania (CPL). When the troops of the Red Army entered the country on 15 June 1940, Gedvilas became minister of interior in the government of **Justas Paleckis**. One of his first steps was to legalize the CPL on 25 June 1940. He falsely assured Lithuanians that the Red Army did not intend to incorporate Lithuania into the USSR but wanted only to restore "order." However, following the manipulated elections to the National Assembly in mid–July 1940, Lithuania was incorporated into the USSR, and Paleckis became president of the Supreme Soviet of the Lithuanian SSR. In August of that year Gedvilas was appointed president of the republic's Council of People's Commissars (government). In that role, he supervised the arrests of thousands of Lithuanians and their deportations deep into the USSR. He was responsible for the deaths of thousands of innocent people. After the reoccupation of Lithuania by the Red Army in 1944, Gedvilas resumed the duties of head of the republic's government, and he held his post until 1956. He was in charge of the administrative apparatus of the Lithuanian SSR during the worst years of the Stalinist persecutions. From 1956 to 1968 he served as minister of education and then he retired. (WR)

Sources: *EL*, vol. 2; Joseph Paujaujis-Javis, *Soviet Genocide in Lithuania* (New York, 1980); Romuald J. Misiunas and Rein Taagepera, *The Baltic States: Years of Dependence, 1940–1990* (Berkeley, 1993).

GEGA Liri (1917, Gjirokastra–December 1956), Albanian Communist activist. Gega came from an intellectual family and graduated from a pedagogical school for girls in Tirana, and then she studied in Florence. Arrested during her stay in Italy in 1940, she spent twenty-one months in a prison in Florence. After returning to Albania, she became aligned with a Communist group from Shkodër. She was the only woman in the group of founders of the Communist Party of Albania (CPA). From March 1943 to November 1944 she was a member of the Politburo of the CC of the CPA. In 1944, on the orders of Yugoslav Communists, she murdered Mustafa Gjinishi, a member of the Politburo of the CPA who had entered into an agreement with the National Front (Belli Kombëtar) in August 1943

in Mukaj. From August 1944 she was secretary general of the Albanian Anti-Fascist Youth Union, and between 1944 and 1946, secretary general of the Anti-Fascist Women's Union. In 1945 she was elected deputy for Vlorë district. In the spring of 1948, at the Eighth Plenum of the CC of the CPA, Gega was accused of sectarianism, "political terror," and, above all, favoring separatist tendencies in the north of Albania. The accusations were connected with the fact that she had opposed the elimination of the units led by Gani bey Kryeziu and **Muharrem Bajraktari**, which had operated there soon after the war. As a result of attacks by **Koçi Xoxe**, Gega was expelled from the leadership of the Democratic Front. At a party conference in Tirana in April 1956, she was among a group of activists who dared to publicly attack **Enver Hoxha**. Arrested while attempting to escape abroad with her husband, Dali Ndreu, a member of the CC of the CPA, Gega was executed by firing squad at the end of 1956. She was charged with, among other things, collaboration with foreign intelligence. Nikita Khrushchev publicly claimed that at the time of execution Gega was pregnant, but his accusation was met with official denial by the Albanian authorities. (TC)

Sources: *Bashkimi*, 20 November 1945; William E. Griffith, *Albania and the Sino-Soviet Rift* (Cambridge, Mass., 1963); Hans-Detlev Grothusen, ed., *Albanien* (Göttingen, 1993); Uran Butka, *Ringjallje* (Tetovë, 1996); *Marrëdhëniet shqiptaro-jugosllave 1945–1948: Dokumente* (Tirana, 1996).

GEMINDER Bedřich (19 November 1901, Moravská Ostrava–3 December 1952, Prague), Czechoslovak Communist activist. Geminder came from a lower-middle-class Jewish family. As a high school student he belonged to a Zionist group. In 1919–21 he studied in Berlin. After returning to Czechoslovakia, he joined the Communist Party of Czechoslovakia (CPC). In 1924–26 he was in the USSR, where he worked in the Communist International apparatus. Later, using the pseudonyms "Otto Kramer" and "Vitavski," he was active in Czechoslovakia and in Western Europe. Between 1934 and 1935 he was again in Moscow, where, under the pseudonym "G. Friedrich," he worked in the Department of Agitation and Propaganda of the Comintern. After a short stay in Czechoslovakia he settled in the USSR, where he continued his work in the Comintern apparatus. Sent to Czechoslovakia in 1945, he became a member of the Secretariat of the Central Committee (CC) of the CPC, and he was in charge of the party's foreign relations department. In September 1947 he was a member of the Czechoslovak delegation to the founding congress of the Information Bureau of the Communist and Workers' Parties at Szklarska Poręba. During anti-Semitic purges connected with the disclosure of alleged "Titoists," in November 1951 Geminder was arrested in connection with the case of Noel Field, and he was accused of spying for the United States and Israel. In the trial of **Rudolph Slánský** and his comrades (20–27 November 1952), Geminder was tortured during interrogation and confessed to even the most absurd charges. As a "Jewish, bourgeois nationalist," he was sentenced to death and then executed by firing squad. (WR)

Sources: Lazitch; Edward Taborsky, *Communism in Czechoslovakia, 1948–1960* (Princeton, 1961); Eugen Loebl, *Stalinism in Prague: The Loebl Story* (New York, 1969); Jiři Pelikán, *The Czechoslovak Political Trials, 1950–1954* (Stanford, 1971).

GEORGESCU Teohari (31 January 1908, Bucharest–2 September 1976, Bucharest), Romanian Communist activist. After completing four grades of primary school, Georgescu started working as a printer's apprentice. In 1928 he joined the printers' trade union and co-organized a strike, for which he drew the attention of the security police. From 1929 he belonged to the Romanian Communist Party (RCP). In November 1933 he was arrested but was released after a few months. Arrested again in 1935, he was released pending trial, and in 1940 he was sentenced to two months in prison. In August 1940, on the orders of **Georgi Dimitrov**, the RCP sent Georgescu to Moscow, where he underwent NKVD training in cryptographic methods. In October 1940, after obtaining Soviet instructions, he became a deputy to **Ştefan Foriş**, the new head of the party. Rearrested in April 1941, Georgescu spent the following years in prisons in Bucharest, Caransebeş, and Tîrgu-Jiu, where he was held along with the leaders of the RCP—for example, **Gheorghe Gheorghiu-Dej**, **Gheorghe Apostol**, and **Alexandru Drăghici**.

Released in August 1944, Georgescu became deputy minister of interior, representing the RCP in the government of General **Nicolae Rădescu**. In mid–January 1945 he defied orders from Rădescu, who was not only prime minister, but also his immediate superior in the ministry, to dissolve the Communist Patriotic Guard, and he subordinated the entire security apparatus to the Soviet services. Georgescu also refused to obey the prime minister's demand that he resign. With **Ana Pauker** and **Alexandru Nicolschi**, Georgescu was in charge of expanding the RCP by recruiting around two hundred thousand former members of the Iron Guard and criminals. In August 1945 he even signed an agreement to that effect with Nicolae Pătraşcu, the head of the Iron Guard. At the party's national conference in October 1945 Georgescu joined the Central Committee (CC) of the RCP and the Politburo of the CC. He also became one of the four secretaries of the CC. In 1947 he became minister of interior and supervised the

organization of forced labor camps providing labor for the construction of the Danube–Black Sea Canal. He was also responsible for the suppression of the Greek Catholic Church and for cruel persecutions of its hierarchy. In 1948 he was in charge of manipulating parliamentary elections. At the party congress on 22 February 1948, he attacked **Lucreţiu Pătrăşcanu**; later, along with Aleksander Sakharovski, chief Soviet adviser in the Ministry of Interior, Georgescu supervised the investigation against Pătrăşcanu. Georgescu belonged to the group of Pauker and **Vasile Luca**. Attacked at the Plenum of the CC on 6 March 1952 for "rightist deviation" and for "loss of alertness and a class instinct," two months later Georgescu was dismissed from all his posts. (WR)

Sources: Ghita Ionescu, *Communism in Romania, 1944–1962* (Oxford, 1964); Robert R. King, *History of the Romanian Communist Party* (Stanford, 1980); Şerban N. Ionescu, *Who Was Who in Twentieth Century Romania* (Boulder, Colo., 1994); Dennis Deletant, *Communist Terror in Romania: Gheorghiu-Dej and the Police State, 1948–1965* (New York, 1999).

GEORGESCU Vlad (29 October 1937, Bucharest–13 November 1988, Munich), Romanian dissident and émigré activist. A trained historian, between 1959 and 1963 Georgescu worked at the Romanian-Russian Museum in Bucharest. At the time he became an informer for the secret police, the Securitate. From 1963 through 1979 he was a scholar at the Institute for Southeast European Studies, earning his doctorate in history and publishing a number of valuable historical works. In 1972, he lectured at Columbia University in New York. Following his return, he cooperated with the U.S. ambassador in Bucharest, Harry Barnes, who clandestinely sent Georgescu's dispatches, critical of the regime of **Nicolae Ceauşescu**, to the West. Consequently, in March 1977 Georgescu was fired, but the Communist Party suppressed the investigation and reinstated him in his job in May 1977. He was awarded a Wilson Foundation fellowship, but the Romanian government refused to give him an exit visa. Only the intervention of **Zbigniew Brzezinski** allowed him to leave in April 1979. Between 1982 and 1988 Georgescu was the director of the Romanian section of Radio Free Europe. He rejuvenated the staff, released many of the old émigrés, and supported the people who had experienced life under communism. He penned several important historical works, including *Politica şi istorie: Cazul comuniştilor români 1944–1977* (Politics and history: The case of the Romanian Communists, 1944–1977; 1981). (AB)

Sources: Mihai Pellin, *Opisul emigraţiei politice: Destine în 1222 de fişe alcătuite pe bază dosarelor din arhivele Securităţii* (Bucharest, 2002).

GEORGIEV Kimon [originally Stoyanov] (11 August 1882, Pazardzhik–28 September 1969, Sofia), Bulgarian politician. After high school, Georgiev graduated from the Military Academy in Sofia. He took part in both Balkan Wars and in World War I. After the end of the war he belonged to the leadership of the radical national Military League (Voenen Syiuz [ML]). The ML gained support because people were deeply disillusioned with the results of the war: the Treaty of Neuilly of 27 November 1919 and the reduction in the Bulgarian Army to twenty thousand soldiers. The ML reached an agreement with National Concord (Naroden Sgovor), a secret organization led by **Aleksandur Tsankov**; with the Constitutional Bloc, created in July 1922; and with the Internal Macedonian Revolutionary Organization (IMRO). Then the ML played an important role in the overthrow of the dictatorship of **Aleksandur Stamboliyski** in June 1923. Georgiev represented the left wing of the ML. In the cabinet of **Andrei Liapchev** he held the portfolio of minister of railways, post, and telegraphs (1926–28). In 1927 he was one of the founders of the Zveno Group, a political organization of officers who from January 1933 planned to take over power. As the result of a bloodless coup d'état that overthrew the democratic cabinet of **Nikola Mushanov**, on 19 May 1934 Georgiev became prime minister of the government which was backed by and partially personally based on the army. The parliament was dissolved, and political parties were abolished. Georgiev represented a pro-Russian orientation, and he established diplomatic relations with the USSR. On 22 January 1935 he resigned his post under pressure from Tsar **Boris III**, who feared anti-monarchic attitudes in the army and wanted to improve relations with the Third Reich. The ML was dissolved, and some of its members were arrested. Removed from power, Georgiev did not enter parliament in the elections of 1938.

During World War II Georgiev was one of the leaders of the anti-tsarist opposition and was against aligning Bulgaria with the Third Reich. On 1 September 1940 he signed a protest letter to the government of **Bogdan Filov** against the adoption of a law for the "protection of the nation." In the first half of 1942 he established contact with Communists and the agrarian left, and they formed the Fatherland Front. The program of the Fatherland Front, announced from Moscow on Khristo Botev Radio on 17 July 1942, provided for close cooperation with the USSR. After the death of Tsar Boris III, at the beginning of September 1943 Georgiev, along with other opposition activists, signed an appeal for the dissolution of the National Assembly, new elections, a broad government coalition, and the neutralization of foreign policy. Since none of these claims were granted, Georgiev questioned the legality of the election of the regents. On 7 August 1944, along with twelve other members of the opposition, he signed a declaration to the regents and to the government insisting on a fundamental change in foreign policy, rapprochement with the USSR, and the creation of a people's government. He was temporarily held under house arrest in Burgas, and after his release he became involved in the preparation of the September 1944 coup.

Although he was influential in the army, Georgiev was unable to control the Fatherland Front, which was dominated by the Communists. After the coup of 9 September 1944 in Sofia, the victory of which he announced on the radio, Georgiev was formally appointed prime minister. However, his government was controlled by the Communists. Although he never formally joined the Bulgarian Communist Party (BCP), he rendered great services to it. He accepted the bloody suppression of the entire political elite of the tsarist period, but he gradually lost influence. Removed as head of the government on 23 November 1946, he became a puppet in the hands of the Communists. Until December 1947 he still served as minister of foreign affairs, and until January 1950 he was also deputy prime minister, but he was gradually removed from power. From December 1947 to March 1959 he served as minister of electrification, and later he was president of a committee for construction and architecture. Georgiev accepted all the Communist policies and authorized terror directed against his former opponents, as well as against his former associates from the Zveno Group and the Fatherland Front. From December 1959 to March 1962 he again served as deputy prime minister, and then he retired. In 1982 his *Izbrani proizvedeniia* (Selected works) were published. (WR)

Sources: *Entsiklopediya Bulgariya*, vol. 2 (Sofia, 1981); Dimo Kazasow, *Burni godiny* (Sofia, 1949); J. F. Brown, *Bulgaria under Communist Rule* (New York, 1970); Marshall Lee Miller, *Bulgaria during the Second World War* (Stanford, 1975); Jerzy Jackowicz, *Partie opozycyjne w Bułgarii 1944–1948* (Warsaw, 1997); Tasho Tashev, *Ministrite na Bulgariya 1879–1999: Entsiklopedichen spravochnik* (Sofia, 1999).

GEORGIEVSKI Ljubcho (17 January 1966, Shtip), Macedonian politician. Georgievski graduated from the Philological Faculty of Ss. Cyril and Methodius University in Skopje. A member of the League of Communists of Macedonia, in 1990 he became leader of the Internal Macedonian Revolutionary Organization–Democratic Party for Macedonian National Unity (Vnatrešno-Makedonska Revolucionerna Organizacija–Demokratska Partija za Makedonsko Edinstvo [IMRO–DPMNU]), a nationalist party that adopted the name of the legendary liberation movement that sought to free Macedonian lands in the late nineteenth and early twentieth centuries.

In 1991 Georgievski served briefly as vice-president of the Republic of Macedonia. From 1992 to 1995 he was an MP on behalf of the IMRO-DPMNU. When the party won the 1998 elections, he became prime minister and held the post from 30 November 1998 to 7 October 2002. Accused of being pro-Bulgarian (a Macedonian taboo) in his early days as party leader, Georgievski is a nationalist and is opposed to according equal rights to ethnic minorities. This position was modulated somewhat when he took office as prime minister. Confronted with a mass influx of Albanians from Kosovo to Macedonia and the subsequent Albanian insurgency of 2001, his views hardened. He employed various tactics to delay the implementation of the Ohrid Agreement (signed in August 2001), which were aimed at bringing peace to the land. His policies were chaotic and erratic. His relations with Western states were strained by his government's failure to cooperate fully in addressing the Albanian insurgency. By 2002, Georgievski had become avowedly right wing, to the extent that he even attacked moderates in his own party; this brought the IMRO-DPMNU a serious defeat in the September 2002 elections. (DP)

Sources: Valentina Georgieva and Sasha Konechni, *Historical Dictionary of the Republic of Macedonia* (Lanham, Md., 1998); Duncan Perry, "Macedonia's Quest for Security and Stability," *Current History*, March 2000; Duncan Perry, "Macedonia: Melting Pot or Meltdown?" *Current History*, November 2001; Bugajski; *RFE/RL Newsline*; *OMRI Daily Digest*; www.rulers.org.

GEREMEK Bronisław (6 March 1932, Warsaw), Polish historian and politician. Geremek graduated in history from Warsaw University in 1955, received a Ph.D. in 1960, and received a postdoctoral degree (*habilitacja*) in 1970. From 1989 he was a full professor. In 1955–85 and from 1989 he worked in the Institute of History of the Polish Academy of Sciences (PAS). In 1956–58 he was a fellow, and from 1962 to 1965 a lecturer, at the Sorbonne in Paris. From 1962 to 1965 he also worked as director of the Center of Polish Culture at the University of Paris, and from 1970 to 1985 he was head of the PAS Medieval History Workshop. From 1950 he belonged to the (Communist) Polish United Workers' Party, which he left in 1968, after the Warsaw Pact invasion of Czechoslovakia. In 1975 he joined the protests against the amendment of the constitution, signing the so-called Letter of Seven. From 1978 he was a member of the Society of Scientific Courses and its Program Board. In August 1980 he belonged to the Commission of Experts of the Inter-Factory Strike Committee in Gdańsk. Later he was one of the key advisers of the Inter-Factory Founding Committee of Solidarity and its National Coordination Commission. Head of the group of advisers to **Lech Wałęsa**, he also presided over the Program Board of the Center for Social and Professional Studies of the Solidarity National Commission. He headed the commission to work out the Solidarity program adopted by the union's First Congress in September 1981. Like **Tadeusz Mazowiecki**, he favored a moderate and cautious strategy for Solidarity.

After the introduction of martial law, on 13 December 1981 Geremek was interned. Released in December 1982, he was viciously attacked by the Communist propaganda. Fired from the PAS, he collaborated with the underground structures of Solidarity and was Wałęsa's adviser. He participated in several meetings with foreign politicians visiting Poland. In February 1988, in the official monthly *Konfrontacje*, he offered a compromise with Communist authorities in the form of an "anti-crisis pact." In 1988 he co-organized and became a member of the Civic Committee of the Solidarity Chairman. He was one of the architects and key negotiators during the Round Table Talks (February–April 1989), co-presiding over the political reform negotiating group. From 1989 to 2001 he was an MP. Initially he presided over the Civic Parliamentary Club and the parliamentary foreign relations commission, but during the "war at the top" in 1990 he was attacked by Wałęsa and his followers for slowing down systemic transformation, and he left the club. He co-founded Civic Movement–Democratic Action (Ruch Obywatelski–Akcja Demokratyczna [ROAD]), and later he was head of the parliamentary club of the Democratic Union (1991–94) and the Freedom Union (Unia Wolności) (1994–97). In 1992–93 he was professor with a chair in international affairs at the College de France. From October 1997 to June 2000 he was foreign minister. Thanks to his personal contacts, Geremek contributed to Poland's entry into NATO and played a key role in negotiations with the European Union. From December 2000 he presided over the Freedom Union. He resigned as a result of the electoral defeat of this party in September 2001. From early 2002 he headed the Chair of European Civilization at the College of Europe in Natolin, Warsaw. He authored a number of works in the medieval history of Europe, including the following: *Najemna siła robocza w rzemiośle Paryża XIII–XV wieku* (Hired labor in Paris handicrafts from the thirteenth to the fifteenth centuries; 1962); *Ludzie marginesu w średniowiecznym Paryżu* (1967; *Margins of Society in Late Medieval Paris*, 1987); *Litość i szubienica: Dzieje nędzy i miłosierdzia* (1989; *Poverty: A History*, 1994); and *Common Roots of Europe* (1996). In 2002 he received the Grand Prix de la Francophonie from the French Academy. He also received the Polish Order of the White Eagle. (AF)

Sources: *Wielka encyklopedia PWN*, vol. 10 (Warsaw, 2002); *Nasi w Sejmie i Senacie* (Warsaw, 1990); *Geremek opowiada, Żakowski pyta* (Warsaw, 1990); Jan Skórzyński, *Ugoda i rewolucja: Władza i opozycja 1985–1989* (Warsaw, 1995); Antoni Dudek, *Pierwsze lata III Rzeczpospolitej 1989–2001* (Kraków, 2002); Janusz A. Majcherek, *Pierwsza dekada III Rzeczpospolitej 1989–1999* (Warsaw, 1999).

GERMENJI Themistokli (1871, Korçë–9 November 1917, Salonika), Albanian independence activist and journalist. Germenji came from a merchant family. After completing his education at a Greek school in his home town, he left for Romania, where he was engaged in trade. He also worked with the Albanian national organizations Drita and Dituria. From 1901 he continued his patriotic activities, first in Albania and then in Monastir in Macedonia. In 1903 he worked with Macedonian organizations, supplying weapons for an anti-Turkish uprising that was being prepared. Germenji originally advocated the creation of an autonomous Albanian-Macedonian state, but he abandoned the idea a few years later. In 1911 he was imprisoned by the Turkish authorities on charges of preparing an uprising. For seven months he served his sentence in Ioánnina (Janina) and later in Korçë. Demonstrations by the Albanian population accelerated his release. In 1911–12 Germenji traveled to Italy and Corfu, where he sought support for the Albanian cause and coordinated the activities of the Albanian diaspora. Between 1913 and 1914 he was allied with **Ismail Kemali**, and he organized the state administration. When the Albanians got control of Korçë in March 1914, Germenji became head of a unit of local volunteers who were responsible for security in the town.

After the outbreak of World War I, in September 1914 Germenji left for Romania, where he co-founded the National League (Lidhja Kombëtare), which represented the interests of local Albanians. In January 1915 he moved to Bulgaria, where he edited the newspaper *The Library of Zeri and Shqipërise*. He returned to Albania when a chance arose to organize the Albanian administration under the French occupation. From December 1916 to June 1917 he was in charge of the autonomous republic in Korçë. He also organized the Albanian units that in the future would fight against the city's takeover by the Greeks. Germenji fell into disfavor with the French when he did not agree to the formation of Albanian units paid by the French. Probably his position was also undermined by the political intrigues of the Greeks and by the animosity of the adherents of **Essad Pasha Toptani**. Germenji was officially charged with maintaining contacts with representatives of Austria-Hungary and Bulgaria. The military court in Salonika sentenced him, as a foreign intelligence agent, to death by firing squad. His last words before the execution were, "Long live Albania; long live France." In 1933 his body was brought from Salonika to Korçë. (TC)

Sources: *Fjalor Enciklopedik Shqiptar* (Tirana, 1985); Stefanaq Pollo and Arben Puto, *The History of Albania from Its Origins to the Present Day* (London, 1981); Tako Piro, *Themistokli Germenji* (Tirana, 1988); Sejfi Vllamasi, *Ballafaqime politike ne Shqiperi (1897–1942)* (Tirana, 1995).

GERŐ Ernő [original name Singer] (8 July 1898, Terbegec (now Slovakia)–12 March 1980, Budapest), Hungarian Communist leader. Gerő's father was an agricultural tenant and later a merchant. After finishing high school, Gerő was admitted to the Medical Academy in Budapest (1916), but he did not complete his studies. During World War I he worked in the Socialist Union of Young Workers, and in 1918 he became a member of the Hungarian Communist Party. During the Hungarian Soviet Republic he was active in the Communist Union of Young Workers (CUYW). He volunteered for the Hungarian Red Army but was not sent to the front. After the fall of the Soviet Republic Gerő fled to Vienna and joined the faction of **Jenő Landler** in the Hungarian Communist movement in exile. He worked in the office of the CUYW and later participated in the creation of unions of young workers in Slovakia and Romania. Sent to Hungary to direct the Communist organizations in the country (1922), Gerő was soon arrested and in May 1923 was sentenced to fifteen years' imprisonment.

As the result of an exchange of prisoners, in 1924 Gerő was sent to the USSR. At first he worked in a factory, and from 1925 he was active among Hungarian Communist exiles in France. In 1928 he returned to Moscow, where he studied at the International Lenin School. From 1931 Gerő worked in the Executive Committee of the Communist International, and on its behalf, he was active in France, Belgium, Spain, and Portugal. As an instructor of the Comintern, he took part in the Spanish Civil War. He became notorious for his purges of Trotskyites and anarchists. Between 1939 and 1941 he represented the Hungarian party in the Communist International. After its formal dissolution in 1943, he joined the ranks of the Red Army, where he led agitation and propaganda work in the enemy's rear and among captives. In November 1944 he took part in cease-fire talks with the Hungarian delegation in Moscow.

After his return to Hungary Gerő was elected to the parliament in December 1944. Until the return of **Mátyás Rákosi** to Hungary in February 1945, Gerő headed the Communist Party and was a member of its Central Committee (CC) and Politburo. In May 1945 he was put in charge of the Ministry of Trade and Transport, and in November 1945 he was appointed minister of transport.

In June 1948, at the founding congress of the Hungarian Workers' Party (HWP), Gerő became a member of the CC Secretariat and soon deputy secretary general of the party. From December 1948 he was minister of finance, and until February 1949 he was again minister of transport. In June 1949 he became president of the Council of the National Economy. From 1949 he was an honorary member of the Hungarian Academy of Sciences. On 14 November 1952 he became deputy prime minister.

After Stalin's death in March 1953 Gerő became aligned with the faction of Vyacheslav Molotov. After a conference in Moscow in June 1953 he was dismissed as deputy secretary general of the CC of the HWP, although he remained a member of the Politburo. In the first government of **Imre Nagy** in 1953 Gerő held the posts of deputy prime minister and minister of the interior until July 1954. Under his leadership the Committee of Economic Policy of the CC was created, and it was used to attack Nagy's economic policies. Gerő contributed to Nagy's fall in 1955. At a plenum of the CC of the HWP in July 1956 he was elected first secretary in place of Rákosi. This choice was an attempt to continue the "hard line" of his predecessor but without him.

On the evening of 23 October, 1956 Gerő gave a radio speech that was perceived as provocative. In a vague way, he spoke about chauvinists, anti-Semites, and reactionaries, as well as the manifestations of "nationalistic character." The speech contributed to the spread of the uprising; therefore Gerő soon phoned Nikita Khrushchev, asking for the assistance of Soviet troops. On the motion of Anastas Mikoyan and Mikhail Suslov, who arrived in Budapest for a meeting of the CC of the HWP, on 25 October 1956 Gerő was dismissed as first secretary of the party. He was also removed from all his posts, and on 28 October he was taken to Moscow, along with his family. In February 1957 the leadership of the Hungarian Socialist Workers' Party (HSWP) decided to ban him from returning to Hungary for five years. Finally, at the beginning of 1961, he was allowed to return. The CC of the HSWP found him guilty of violating laws in the period of the "cult of personality," and in 1962 he was expelled from the party. As a pensioner, Gerő made a living doing translations. In 1977 he asked for admission to the HSWP, but the party leadership rejected his request. Apart from Rákosi, Gerő best incarnated the Stalinist dictatorship in Hungary. (JT)

Sources: *The Annual Obituary*, 1980; Bennet Kovrig, *Communism in Hungary from Kun to Kádár* (Stanford, 1979); Miklós Molnár, *From Béla Kun to János Kádár: Seventy Years of Hungarian Communism* (New York, 1990); *Magyar Nagylexikon*, vol. 8 (Budapest, 1999); *A magyar forradalom és szabadságharc enciklopédiája*, CD-ROM (Budapest, 1999); *Nagy Képes Milleniumi Arcképcsarnok* (Budapest, 1999).

GESHOV Ivan (20 February 1849, Plovdiv–24 March 1924, Sofia), Bulgarian economist and politician. Geshov graduated from high school in Plovdiv, and in 1865–69 he studied finance and political science in Manchester. In 1872 he returned to Plovdiv, where he worked in trade. Because of information he published in *The Times* on Turkish atrocities against the Bulgarians during the April 1876 uprising, he was arrested and sentenced to death by the Turkish authorities in 1877. In prison he wrote *Zapiski na edin osyden* (Records of a condemned man). Thanks to the intervention of the British ambassador in Turkey, Geshov was pardoned. After Bulgaria gained independence in 1878, he was active in the political life of East Rumelia as one of the leaders of the pro-unification National Party (NP). He was a deputy and first speaker of the Regional Assembly (1879–80) and minister of finance of East Rumelia (1882–83). Later he moved to Sofia, where he was director of the Bulgarian National Bank (1883–86) and head of the Bulgarian delegation to the peace talks in Bucharest in 1886. He also presided over the first Bulgarian agricultural and industrial congress in Plovdiv in 1892. In 1887–94 he was in opposition to the government of Stefan Stambolov. From 1901 he headed the NP and then the United National Progressive Party, created when the NP and the Liberal Progressive Party merged in 1920.

Geshov held several government positions. He was minister of finance (August–November 1886 and May 1894–August 1897), head of the Ministry of Trade and Agriculture (October 1894–February 1986 and July 1896–January 1897), and prime minister and minister of foreign affairs (16 March 1911–1 June 1913). As the head of the diplomatic corps, he prepared Bulgarian-Serbian and Bulgarian-Greek agreements that were the foundations of the Balkan Alliance. After World War I he was considered one of the most responsible people for the Bulgarian defeat in the Second Balkan War of 1913. He was a deputy to the National Assembly (1894–99 and 1901–20) and to the Grand National Assembly (1886–87 and 1911). He was speaker of the National Assembly in 1901 and 1913. In 1915 he opposed Bulgaria's entry into the war on the side of the Central Powers. After the war he was in opposition to the Bulgarian Agrarian National Union government. In 1922 he emigrated to France, where he was active against the **Aleksandur Stamboliyski** regime. He took parting in the creation of the Constitutional Bloc, and after the coup of 9 June 1923 he joined the Democratic Alliance.

Geshov was a full member of the Bulgarian Society of the Friends of Books from 1884, its treasurer (1884–98), and its chairman (1898–1911). When the society became the Bulgarian Academy of Sciences, he became its chairman (1911–24). Moreover, he was chairman of the Bulgarian Red Cross (1884–1924). One of the few Bulgarians awarded the Order of Ss. Cyril and Methodius, Geshov published (among other works) the following: *Dumi i dela: Ikonomicheski i finansovi studii* (Words and deeds: Economic and financial studies; 1899); *Narodna partija* (The national party; 1908); *Balkanskiyat suyuz: Spomeni i dokumenti* (The Balkan alliance: Memoirs and documents; 1915); and *Spomeni i studii* (Memoirs and studies; 1928). Geshov was also founder and editor-in-chief of the newspaper *Maritsa* (1878–85). (JJ)

Sources: *Biographisches Lexikon*, vol. 2; *Entsiklopediya Bulgariya*, vol. 2 (Sofia, 1981); Stefan Bobchev, *Koy e Ivan Geshov? Rech* (Sofia, 1908); Richard J. Crompton, *Bulgaria 1878–1983: A History* (Boulder, Colo., 1983); E. Statelova, *Ivan E. Geshov* (Sofia, 1994); *Bulgarski dyrzhavnitsi* (Sofia, 1995); Raymond Detrez, *Historical Dictionary of Bulgaria* (Lanham, Md., 1997); Tasho Tashev, *Ministrite na Bulgariya 1879–1999: Entsiklopedichen Spravochnik* (Sofia, 1999).

GHEORGHIU-DEJ Gheorghe (8 November 1901, Bîrlad, Moldavia–19 March 1965, Bucharest), Romanian Communist leader. Gheorghiu-Dej came from a working-class family. After primary school, he started working as a porter at the port of Galati at the age of eleven. Then after completing the third grade of a vocational high school, he was a factory worker and a railroad electrician. From 1923 to 1925 he served in the army, attaining the rank of sergeant. In the mid-1920s he joined the Communist Party. He was arrested several times for revolutionary agitation. In 1931 he was sent by the party to work in Dej; hence he later added "Dej" to his surname. In February 1933 he was arrested for organizing the Grivița railway strike and was sentenced to twelve years' imprisonment. At that time he was already a member of the Central Committee (CC) of the Romanian Communist Party. He served his sentence in the Doftana prison, near Câmpina; it was infamous for hard material conditions and the cruelty of the warders. In prison, he met the leading Romanian Communists and became their informal leader. Released, he came into conflict with the general secretary of the party, **Ştefan Foriş**, who refused to start sabotage actions in the rear of the German Army on the orders of the Comintern. In 1942 Gheorghiu-Dej was imprisoned again and accused of spying for the USSR. Along with the majority of Romanian Communists, he was held in a camp in Tîrgu-Jiu, where in April 1944 he caused the removal of Foriş as general secretary. On the orders of Gheorghiu-Dej, Foriş was killed in the summer of 1946.

Shortly before the coup of August 1944, which overthrew the dictatorship of Marshal **Ion Antonescu**, Gheorghiu-Dej escaped from prison, and after the establishment of the coalition government of General **Constantin Sănătescu** he assumed the minister of communications. In December 1944 and January 1945 Gheorghiu-Dej stayed with **Ana Pauker** in Moscow. Although Stalin had initially considered making Pauker head of the party, during this visit he appointed Gheorghiu-Dej secretary general of the party. After his return to Bucharest Gheorghiu-Dej started implementing a plan to accelerate the Communist takeover of power. For example, he personally directed the attacks of Communist raiding parties on the Malax plants in Bucharest at the beginning of 1945. He also played a key role in the removal of the government of General **Nicolae Radescu**. In 1945–48 a balance of power was maintained in the party leadership, in which Gheorghiu-Dej represented the "national wing"; therefore his leadership was at first rather nominal, and the decisive voice was that of the activists of non-Romanian origin who came from the USSR and Soviet MVD agents, who organized the General Department of State Security (Direcţia Generală a Securităţii Poporului; for short, Securitate).

Gheorghiu-Dej gradually consolidated his position and was one of the most ardent Stalinists. In December 1947 he forced King **Michael I** to abdicate. In February 1948, after the incorporation of the remains of a split Social Democracy, he became the head of the Romanian Workers' Party (Partidul Muncitoresc Român [RWP]). In the government that followed the overthrow of democracy in 1945, he was primarily responsible for economic affairs. In 1945–48 he headed the Supreme Economic Council; in 1946–48 he was minister of the national economy; between 1948 and 1949 he was head of the Planning Committee, and from 1948 he was also deputy prime minister in the cabinet of **Petru Groza**. He supervised extremely unrealistic economic plans, which were implemented with the use of the forced labor of prisoners. During the collectivizations of 1949–62 he played a key role in breaking up the opposition of peasants who tried to organize active resistance—for example, in the regions of Arad, Argeş, Bihor, and Timişoara. At that time, over eighty thousand people were arrested and sent to camps. He was co-responsible for the Stalinization of social life and purges connected with an anti-Titoist campaign. In 1946 he launched attacks against **Lucreţiu Patraşcanu**, who was a leading Communist of a more pro-national orientation. Later, Gheorghiu-Dej caused the expulsion of Patraşcanu from the party, his imprisonment in August 1948, his sentencing to death, and his execution in April 1954. In agreement with Andrey Vyshinsky and with the assistance of Soviet advisers in the Ministry of Interior, in 1952 Gheorghiu-Dej conducted a purge that affected leading functionaries of non-Romanian origin—for example, Pauker and **Vasile**

Luca. Next, he dismissed Groza, and in June of the same year he assumed the post of prime minister, concentrating all power in his hands.

After Stalin's death in March 1953 Gheorghiu-Dej followed the Kremlin's directives concerning "collective leadership," and on 20 April 1954 he resigned as head of the party, retaining the post of head of government. Having realized that this step meant the risk of losing total power, on 30 September 1955 he changed posts, assuming the leadership of the party again. After the Twentieth Congress of the CPSU Gheorghiu-Dej decided that in Romania de-Stalinization had already taken place in the form of the purge of 1952; therefore the hard-line policy should be maintained. He closely cooperated with the Kremlin during the suppression of the Hungarian Revolution in the fall of 1956. At that time he consolidated the forces of the Securitate and in 1957 arranged the removal of potential rivals, such as **Miron Constantinescu** and **Iosif Chişinevski**, from party leadership. In 1958 he unleashed a campaign of "revolutionary vigilance," which resulted in widespread purges of the cultural circles. A new penal code in July 1958 increased the punishment for "anti-state" activities. The arrests intensified, and there was an increase in the number of labor camp prisoners, especially in the Danube delta (e.g., in Balta Brăilei, Feteşti, and Periprava), where the Danube–Black Sea Canal was being built.

Steadily consolidating his power, in 1961 Gheorghiu-Dej also became president of Romania. It is estimated that between 1949 and 1960, under his rule, 134,000 political trials were held, and around 550,000 people were convicted. Ruling by terror, at the same time he clearly sought a more independent foreign policy course. Romania stressed its national interests within the framework of the Council for Mutual Economic Assistance (Comecon). The personal dislike between Gheorghiu-Dej and Nikita Khrushchev grew. At the Third Congress of the RWP in June 1960, Gheorghiu-Dej backed the Chinese formula of equality among Socialist countries. At a CMEA meeting on 15 February 1963, the Romanian delegation openly opposed a coordination of the plans of member states, emphasizing the principle of national sovereignty. Despite pressure from the Kremlin, which put forward a plan for an ethnic referendum in Transylvania that would be dangerous for Bucharest, Gheorghiu-Dej did not yield. At the time of the mounting Chinese-Soviet conflict, the Romanian delegation went to Beijing in February 1963, and in March of the same year Bucharest restored diplomatic relations with Albania, which had been broken off by Moscow's satellites. Gheorghiu-Dej's efforts also led to an improvement of relations with Yugoslavia. Khrushchev's fall consolidated Gheorghiu-Dej's position in relation to

the Kremlin. On 21 October 1964 he asked the USSR ambassador to withdraw KGB advisers from Romania. His determined stance toward Moscow won him much popularity among the Romanians, especially because he also released some political prisoners. In January 1965 it turned out that he was seriously ill, and soon he was diagnosed with lung cancer. However, information about his disease was announced to the public only a day before his death. (WR)

Sources: Robert R. King, *History of the Romanian Communist Party* (Stanford, 1980); Vladimir Tismaneanu, *Fantoma lui Gheorghiu-Dej* (Bucharest, 1995); Stelian Tanase, *Elite si societate: Guvernarea Gheorghiu-Dej, 1948–1965* (Bucharest, 1998); Dennis Deletant, *Communist Terror in Romania: Gheorghiu-Dej and the Police State, 1948–1965* (New York, 1999).

GHIBU Onisifor (31 May 1883, Sălişte–31 October 1972, Sibiu), Romanian pedagogue and politician. In 1902, Ghibu graduated from a high school in Braşov. Between 1902 and 1905 he studied at the Theological Institute in Sibiu (Transylvania), and from 1905 through 1909, at universities in Bucharest, Budapest, Strasbourg, and Jena. In 1909, he successfully defended his Ph.D. dissertation in philosophy and pedagogy at Jena. Between 1910 and 1914, he worked at the Orthodox Archbishopric in Sibiu. His field of responsibility was the Romanian educational system. Concurrently, between 1911 and 1912, he was a substitute professor at the Theological-Pedagogical Institute in Sibiu. From 1912 through 1914 he served as secretary of the department of education of the Transylvanian Society of Literature and Culture of the Romanian Nation (Asociaţiunii Transilvane pentru Literatura Româna şi Cultura Poporului Român [ASTRA]) in Braşov. During World War I, he resided in Bucharest, Iaşi, and Kishinev, advocating the creation of a unified Romanian state embracing all Romanians. To expedite this goal, he founded and edited the periodical *Scoala moldoveneasca* and the dailies *Ardealul in Basarabia* and *România noua*. He also contributed to *Cuvânt moldovenesc* and *Luminatorul*. In 1919, he became a member of the Romanian Academy of Sciences. From 1919 he was a professor of pedagogy and the history of pedagogy at Cluj University.

Ghibu stressed the necessity to organize education in accord with the national spirit and based upon modern standards. His numerous works include the following: *Ziaristica bisericească la români: Studiu istoric* (Church periodicals of the Romanians: A historical study; 1910); *Despre educaţie* (On education; 1911); *Şcoala românească în Transilvania şi Ungaria: Dezvoltarea ei istorică şi situaţia ei actuală* (The Romanian school in Transylvania and Hungary: Its historical development and the current situation; 1915); *Din istoria literaturi didactice româneşti* (From the history of Romanian didactic literature, 3 vols.; 1916); and *Dictatura şi anarhie: Priviri critice asupra evoluţiei şi directivelor învăţământului şi educaţiei româneşti sub regimul Antonescu 1940–1944* (Dictatorship and anarchy: Critical studies on the evolution and development of Romanian teaching and education under the Antonescu regime, 1940–1944; 1944). Ghibu criticized the Communist regime in Romania in a two-volume work, *Chemare la judecata istoriei* (A call before the court of history), which was not published until 1992 and 1993. After World War II Ghibu was imprisoned for many years in forced labor camps. Released at the beginning of the 1960s, he was removed from public life and died in obscurity in 1972. He left behind his unpublished memoirs. (LW)

Sources: *Dictionar Enciclopedic*, vol. 2 (Bucharest, 1996); Şerban N. Ionescu, *Who Was Who in Twentieth Century Romania* (Boulder, Colo., 1994); Dorina N. Rusu, *Membrii Academiei Române 1866–1999* (Bucharest, 1999).

GICHEV Dimitur (28 November 1893, Perushchytsa–26 April 1964, Sofia), Bulgarian Peasant Party politician. Born into a teacher's family, Gichev studied in a theological seminary, but he chose a political career. From 1911 he belonged to the Bulgarian Agrarian National Union (BANU) of **Aleksandur Stamboliyski**. In 1923 he was elected to the National Assembly. After the fall of the Stamboliyski regime Gichev worked in the underground, and in 1925 he was arrested. After his release he returned to active political life in 1931, becoming minister of agriculture (June 1931–December 1932) and minister of trade (until May 1934) in the governments of **Aleksandur Malinov** and **Nikola Mushanov**. In the 1930s he became one of the leaders of the BANU Vrabcha-1 faction, more moderate and pro-Western than the leftist BANU Pladne. BANU Vrabcha-1 refused to support the military group Zveno, which staged a coup in May 1934. After the coup, Gichev was temporarily detained in the Klisura Monastery. The Vrabcha-1 faction stayed in opposition under the autocratic regime of Tsar **Boris III** after 1935. In 1939–40 Gichev favored cooperation with Great Britain, for which he was criticized by government circles.

Gichev opposed Bulgaria's accession to the Tripartite Pact. After the death of Boris III, he was one of the signatories of an appeal on 8 September 1943 by democratic leaders for new elections to the Grand National Assembly and the elaboration of a neutral foreign policy based on the broad consent of all political parties. Gichev maintained contacts with the Soviet embassy in Sofia, but he refused to join the Fatherland Front, which he considered too

dependent on Moscow. At the same time he thought that the Communists and Zveno were threats to democracy. In the summer of 1944 he reconciled with the idea of close cooperation with the Soviet Union and stayed in touch with the Soviet chargé d'affaires in Sofia. In August 1944, along with twelve other politicians, he signed a declaration demanding a substantial change in Bulgarian foreign policy, rapprochement with the USSR, and the formation of a populist government. After a declaration of neutrality by the **Ivan Bagrianov** government was rejected by Moscow, on 2 September 1944 Gichev agreed to join the "government of last chance" headed by **Konstantin Muraviev**, a moderate BANU politician. This government was toppled by the coup of 9 September 1944. As a result Gichev was arrested, and in early 1945 he was sentenced to one year in prison. Released in September 1945, he resumed activity in the BANU faction of **Nikola Petkov**. Arrested again in October 1947, on 16 April 1948 he was sentenced by a Communist court to life imprisonment. Released in 1959, he did not return to politics. (WR)

Sources: *Entsiklopediya Bulgariya*, vol. 2 (Sofia, 1978); Marshall Lee Miller, *Bulgaria during the Second World War* (Stanford, 1975); Stephane Groueff, *Crown of Thorns* (Lanham, Md., 1987); *Entsiklopediya na Bulgariya 1879–1999: Entsiklopedichen spravochnik* (Sofia, 1999).

GIEDROYĆ Jerzy (27 July 1906, Mińsk Litewski–14 September 2000, Maisons Laffite, near Paris), Polish pundit, politician, and lawyer. Giedroyć came from an aristocratic family of Lithuanian origin. As a youth, he fought in the Polish-Soviet war. Later, he studied at the University of Warsaw. Following the May 1926 coup d'état, he supported **Józef Piłsudski**. Between 1929 and 1935 he was employed with the press office of the Council of Ministers, then at the Ministry of Agriculture, and between 1935 and 1939, he was the supervisor of a department at the Ministry of Industry and Trade. In 1930, at the behest of the Ministry of Foreign Affairs, he initiated the publication of *Wschód-Orient*, editing its first issue. Between 1930 and 1939, he edited the bi-monthly *Bunt Młodych* and also the weekly *Polityka*. He was an ideologist of statism and of the anti-Soviet minorities' Promethean Movement; he was also the chairman of the Myśl Mocarstwowa organization. At the same time, he advocated concord with Poland's ethnic minorities and opposed nationalism and communism.

After the outbreak of World War II in September 1939, together with his government, Giedroyć left Poland for Romania. Between 1939 and 1940, he was secretary to the Polish ambassador, Roger Raczyński, in Bucharest, serving also as a liaison between the Polish and British embassies. After leaving the embassy, he served in the Independent Carpathian Rifle Brigade in Palestine between 1941 and 1943 and afterwards in the Second Free Polish Corps, participating in the battle of Tobruk. Between 1942 and 1944 he was the supervisor of publishing at the Department of Propaganda and Culture of the Second Corps. He founded its publishing house and published a daily and weekly *Orzeł Biały*. In 1945, he briefly sojourned in London, where he served as a department supervisor at the Ministry of Information. In 1946 he founded the Literary Institute (Instytut Literacki) in Rome. In 1947 the institute moved to Maisons Laffite, near Paris. A year later, Giedroyć began publishing the monthly *Kultura* and then books of the Literary Institute. In 1962, he started editing and publishing *Zeszyty Historyczne*, which continued to appear after his death. Between 1974 and 1982, he co-edited *Kontinent*. Along with Zofia and Zygmunt Hertz, as well as **Józef Czapski**, Giedroyć created an unreplicable center of Polish cultural life. Miniature editions of *Kultura* were smuggled into Poland illegally. They immensely influenced the nation's intellectual and political life. To a large extent, they shaped the Polish dissident milieu, in particular in its tolerant attitude toward Ukrainians, Belorussians, and Lithuanians.

After Poland regained its independence in 1989, numerous honors were piled upon Giedroyć. He received honorary doctorates from the Jagiellonian University in Kraków, the University of Wrocław, the University of Białostok, the University of Warsaw, the University of **Maria Curie-Skłodowska** in Lublin, and the University of Friburg. He was critical toward the Third Polish Republic and its new elite. He refused to accept the Order of the White Eagle from President **Lech Wałęsa**. However, he displayed an accommodationist attitude toward former Communists, and this made him many enemies. He advocated an active Eastern policy, based in particular upon good relations between Poland and Ukraine. In 1997, he accepted honorary citizenship from the Republic of Lithuania. In 1996, he published his memoirs in Warsaw: *Autobiografia na cztery ręce* (An autobiography for four hands). Yet Giedroyć never visited Poland after 1989. Following his death, according to his will, the publication of *Kultura* was discontinued. (PK)

Sources: *Kto jest kim w polityce: Świat po roku 1860* (Warsaw, 1996); *Słownik polityków polskich XX w.* (Warsaw, 1998); *Leksykon kultury polskiej poza krajem od roku 1939*, vol. 1 (Lublin, 2000); Andrzej Friszke, *Życie polityczne emigracji* (Warsaw, 1999); Rafał Habielski, *Życie społeczne i kulturalne emigracji* (Warsaw, 1999); *Jerzego Giedroycia doktoraty honoris causa* (Lublin, 1999); *Więź*, 2000, no. 12; Krzysztof Pomian, *W kręgu Giedroycia* (Warsaw, 2000).

GIEREK Edward (6 January 1913, Porąbka–29 July 2001, Cieszyn), Polish Communist leader. Gierek came from a coal miner's family. In 1923 he left Poland with his mother for France, where in 1926 he began working in coal mining. In 1931 he joined the French Communist Party. In 1937, he moved to Belgium and joined the Belgian Communist Party. During World War II he was active in the Communist underground. From 1946 to 1948, as a member of the (Communist) Polish Workers' Party, he chaired the Council of Poles in Belgium. In 1948 he returned to Poland and quickly advanced through the ranks of the (Communist) Polish United Workers' Party (Polska Zjednoczona Partia Robotnicza [PUWP]) in Upper Silesia. First he worked in the Central Committee (CC) apparatus in Warsaw, but then he was transferred to Upper Silesia. He enjoyed the support of the top Communist leader, **Aleksander Zawadzki**, for having broken up a strike in the Dąbrowa Basin. Between 1951 and 1954 Gierek served as a secretary of the PUWP Provincial Committee in Katowice. In March 1953 he was appointed a member of the PUWP CC. From April 1954 through March 1956 he was head of the CC Department of Heavy Industry. In March 1956, during the Sixth Plenum of the CC, he was elevated to the membership of the CC Secretariat. On 28 June he was included in a party task force in charge of crushing demonstrations in Poznań. During the Seventh Plenum he was coopted to the PUWP CC Politburo. The reasons for the meteoric rise of such an activist, who enjoyed the trust of the Stalinists despite his sojourn of twenty years in the West, remain unclear.

On 19 October 1956, Gierek joined a top PUWP leadership delegation in negotiations with a Soviet delegation headed by **Nikita Khrushchev** concerning the takeover of power by **Władysław Gomułka**. At the Eighth Plenum Gierek was dropped from the Politburo but retained his post with the CC Secretariat. He remained neutral between the "liberal" Puławska group and the "conservative" Natolin faction. In March 1957 he was nominated as the first secretary of the PUWP Provincial Committee in Katowice. He played a moderating role in a conflict between Silesians and Dąbrowa Basin denizens and was adjudged a "good master" who was able to coerce the central authorities into channeling additional funds for the development of Katowice Province. He became the main representative of the heavy industry lobby, which thus enjoyed preferential treatment in budgetary matters. An increase in investments after 1959 allowed him to hone his lobbying skills further to benefit his province. In March 1959, during the Third PUWP Congress, Gierek was once again coopted to the Politburo. During the Fourth Congress, however, he lost his post with the Secretariat but remained in the Politburo.

Constantly solidifying his power in the Katowice region, he became the leader of the top economic bureaucrats, and his realm was dubbed "the Polish Katanga."

During the political crisis of March 1968, Gierek prevented the spread of anti-government demonstrations in his realm by threatening the use of force. On 19 March 1968, during a rally of party activists with Gomułka, some of those present chanted their support for Gierek, who, like the first secretary, delivered a strongly anti-Semitic speech. During an inter-party struggle between Gomułka and the secret police boss, **Mieczysław Moczar**, Gierek emerged as the third force in the PUWP. In July 1968, during the Twelfth Plenum of the CC, he remarked that "the ways of governing must change because times are changing"; the comment reflected his growing self-assurance. According to an official communiqué following the parliamentary "elections" of June 1969, Gierek received the best results, topping even those of Gomułka.

In mid-December 1970, when Gomułka ordered that firearms be used to crush a workers' rebellion on the Baltic Coast, Gierek adopted a wait-and-see attitude in Upper Silesia. On 18 December 1970 most top PUWP leaders backed a political solution to the crisis, thus spelling the end of Gomułka and his closest collaborators. Late on the night of 18 December 1970 Gierek arrived in Warsaw, where the members of the Politburo and the CC agreed to install him as first secretary. The CC approved this decision the following day. Gierek spoke on national television, admitting that some of the blame for the bloody events on the Baltic Coast also lay with the authorities.

Upon the assumption of power, Gierek attempted to consolidate his leadership and calm the nation. In February 1971, another batch of Gomułka's followers was purged from the CC and Politburo. In May and June Gierek managed to sideline Moczar. Meanwhile, he personally traveled to Szczecin and Gdańsk, where he managed to convince the striking workers to end their protest. The government rescinded the price increases that had caused the rebellion and promised to rebuild the Royal Castle in Warsaw. The new first secretary endeavored to buy social peace by embarking upon a program of spectacular investments in consumption, including the production of the Fiat 125, the construction of highways, and a purchase of the Coca Cola license for Poland. As a result, levels of optimism rose among the population. At the same time, Gierek supported the Kremlin's plans to use détente to build up the weapons potential of the Soviet bloc. To this end, he ordered the building of the gigantic Katowice Steelworks and embarked on other projects. The "great leap" in investments was facilitated by the

willingness of Western nations to grant enormous credits to the Communists. However, the inefficient and wasteful economic system of Communist Poland prevented anyone from taking advantage of the opportunities, and the Gierek team never contemplated any serious changes, undertaking only cosmetic and counterproductive "reforms." In February 1976, Gierek and his regime amended the constitution with a law about "the leading role of the party" and Poland's alliance with the Soviet Union. The amendments triggered objections from the dissident intelligentsia. The regime's relations with the Catholic Church were also poor. As early as 1975 there were signs of a looming economic crisis. Instead of improvements, loudly touted as imminent by Gierek's propaganda machine, there were shortages. An attempt to raise the prices of basic necessities in June 1976 caused violent protests by workers in Radom and Ursus. The Communists brutally crushed the demonstrations, but they retracted the price increases. The incident led to the formation of an institutionalized democratic opposition, most notably the Committee for the Defense of Workers.

From the mid–1970s, the Gierek regime, which suffered from internal divisions, appeared increasingly rudderless. The deterioration of the economic situation fostered oppositionist attitudes and activities. The authorities were unable to crush them because they had pledged to respect human rights: the government of Poland was a signatory to the Helsinki Accord of August 1975, and it needed more bank credit in the West, the granting of which was increasingly tied to a nation's human rights record. As a result, between 1976 and 1980, Poland's economy deteriorated further, dissident activities intensified, and the bankrupt nature of Communist ideology was laid bare. In October 1978, the Polish nation was presented with an ideological alternative with the election of Cardinal Karol Wojtyła as Pope **John Paul II**, who made a pilgrimage home in June 1979. In 1979 and 1980, the Polish GNP continued to decline, and the Gierek team failed to elucidate any program of reform. Strikes in the summer of 1980 threatened the stability of the regime, but Gierek failed to react to the situation even then. At the end of August 1980, he admitted openly during a Politburo meeting that he had no idea what to do. The Gdańsk Agreement of 31 August 1980 and the permission of the regime for the founding of independent trade unions spelled the end of his rule. On 6 September, during the Sixth CC Plenum, Gierek was replaced by **Stanisław Kania**. On 2 December 1980, he was purged from the CC and the Council of State (he had occupied the latter post since 1976). On 19 December 1980 he resigned his parliamentary seat (which he had held since 1952). On 15 July 1981, during the Ninth Extraordinary

PUWP Congress, he was expelled from the party. After martial law was imposed, he was even briefly interned.

The balance of Gierek's rule is negative. His "propaganda of success" spread optimistic slogans about building "a second Poland," but the nation sank into a swamp of economic and social crises. Although Gierek was impressed by the West, which he knew from his youth, he paid effusive homage to Leonid Brezhnev and the rulers of the USSR. He opened up Poland's economy to the West, but he also paved the way to corruption at the top. From being debt free, during the Gierek regime Poland became a debtor nation, saddled with gigantic financial obligations. Most of the U.S.$25 billion borrowed by his team was wasted or stolen. Despite all this, after Poland regained its independence in 1989, some of the temporarily destitute Poles recalled the "good old times," and Gierek was rehabilitated in the public opinion. In 1990, he published two massive interviews, *Przerwana dekada* (The interrupted decade) and *Replika* (A response). In 1993, he published his memoirs, *Smak życia* (The taste of life), in which he justified his policies. (WR)

Sources: Mołdawa; Andrzej Micewski, *Współrządzić czy nie kłamać* (Paris, 1978); Jean Woodall, ed., *Policy and Politics in Contemporary Poland* (London, 1982); Jakub Karpiński, *Countdown: The Polish Upheavals of 1956, 1968, 1970, 1976, 1980* (New York, 1982); George Sanford, *Polish Communism in Crisis* (London and Canberra, 1983); Zbigniew Błażyński, *Towarzysze zeznają: Dekada Gierka 1970–1980 w tzw. Komisji Grabskiego* (London, 1987); Andrzej Albert [Wojciech Roszkowski], *Najnowsza historia Polski 1914–1993*, vols. 1–2 (Warsaw, 1993); Andrzej Paczkowski, *Pół wieku dziejów Polski* (Warsaw, 1995); Jacek Wegner, *Sternicy: Od Nowotki do Rakowskiego* (Kraków, 1997); Jerzy Eisler, *Grudzień 1970* (Warsaw, 2000); Janusz Rolicki, *Gierek* (Warsaw, 2002).

GIERTYCH Jędrzej (7 January 1903, Sosnowiec–8 October 1992, London), Polish nationalist politician and pundit. Giertych came from an intelligentsia family. From 1913 he was active in the scouting movement. In 1920, he was wounded outside of Warsaw while fighting as a volunteer in the Polish-Soviet war. He graduated from high school in Wilno (1921). Afterwards, he completed a law degree at the University of Warsaw (1925) and a degree in international affairs at the School of Political Science in Warsaw (1926). Between 1925 and 1929 he supervised the Foreign Department of the Union of Polish Scouting (Związek Harcerstwa Polskiego). During the coup d'état of May 1926, he fought on the side of the government. From 1927 through 1929, he served in the Polish Navy. Later he worked at the Ministry of Foreign Affairs as an official in charge of the Polish diaspora (Polonia). In 1931, he was posted as an attaché to the Polish Consulate in Allenstein, Germany. From his youth, he was active in the nationalist movement. He advocated a corporatist nation-state,

along with anti-liberalism, anti-Semitism, and extreme anti-Germanism. In 1932, he openly plunged into politics, joining the radical wing of the National Party (Stronnictwo Narodowe [SN]). First, he became the secretary of the Youth Department of the Executive Committee of the Camp of Great Poland (1932–33) and then a member of the SN Main Committee (1936–39) and Main Board (1937–39). He was coopted to the leadership of a secret part of the SN, where he opposed the majority group of his main rival, **Tadeusz Bielecki**. In 1933 he was elected to the Warsaw City Council on behalf of the SN.

During the September 1939 campaign, Giertych fought on the Hel Peninsula. Taken prisoner by the Nazis, he attempted to escape six times, and therefore he was the first Allied officer to be imprisoned in a special POW camp at Colditz. Liberated at the beginning of April 1945, he returned to active military service. In the fall of 1945, he clandestinely traveled to Poland as an emissary of the Polish government-in-exile and the SN. On the way back, he smuggled his family out to the West. Released from the military in 1947, for the next two years he was entrusted by the Polish government-in-exile with the mission of beaming radio programs to Soviet-occupied Poland from the *SS Maria*, a ship he commanded. However, he was critical of the Polish émigré authorities for their involvement with Western intelligence agencies. In 1961 he was expelled from the SN for having written an open letter to **Nikita Khrushchev**. He was active in the Latin Mass Society in Great Britain, which advocated the Tridentine Rite in the Catholic Church. Nonetheless, he was opposed to any break with Rome. He concentrated mainly on journalism, literature, history, and publishing. After 1956, he leaned toward cooperation with the regime in Warsaw.

Giertych's first article appeared in 1917 in the scouting movement's periodical *Młodzież*. Between 1932 and 1939, he was an editor of *Warszawski Dziennik Narodowy*. He also published in *Myśl Narodowa, Kurier Warszawski, Kurier Poznański*, and *Słowo Narodowe*. After the war, he worked with the following émigré periodicals: *Horyzonty* (Brussels), *Życie* (London), and *Przemiany* (Rome). He also wrote for the Catholic press, including *The Tablet, The Catholic Herald*, and *The Catholic Times*. Between 1969 and 1988, he published *Opoka*. He also ran a few of his own publishing ventures, putting out (among other things) the historiosophical works of Feliks Koneczny. He published a few dozen books in several languages. His most important works include *My nowe pokolenie!* (We, the new generation! 1929); *Tragizm losów Polski* (The tragedy of Poland's fate; 1936); *Hiszpania bohaterska* (Heroic Spain; 1837); *O wyjście z kryzysu* (To emerge from the crisis; 1938); *Nacjonalizm chrześcijański* (Christian nationalism;

1948); *Poland and Germany* (1958); *Deutschland und die Polen von 1795 bis heute* (Germany and Poland from 1795 until today; 1962); *Józef Piłsudski 1914–1919* (1979); *In Defense of My Country* (1981); and *Tysiąc lat histori polskiego narodu* (A thousand years of history of the Polish nation; 1986). He also wrote memoirs: *Wrześniowcy* (The September war soldiers; 1957); *Wspomnienia ochotnika 1920 r.* (The memories of a volunteer of 1920; 1958); and *Europa w niewoli* (Europe enslaved; 1959). As an émigré, he supported himself as a blue-collar laborer and a language teacher. He raised nine children. (MC)

Sources: Jerzy Janusz Terej, *Rzeczywistość i polityka: Ze studiów nad dziejami najnowszymi Narodowej Demokracji* (Warsaw, 1979); Krzysztof Kawalec, *Narodowa Demokracja wobec faszyzmu 1922–1939* (Warsaw, 1989); Zdzisław Zakrzewski, "Wspomnienia," tape, June 1989; Barbara O'Driscoll, *Just Say Hail Mary: The Story of Maria and Jedrzej Giertych* (London, 1999); Leszek Żebrowski, "Jędrzej Giertych (1903–1992)," 25 October 2001; "Giertych, Jędrzej (1903–1992)," wiem.onet.pl/wiem/0041d6.html.

GIEYSZTOR Aleksander (17 July 1916, Moscow–9 February 1999, Warsaw), Polish historian and social activist. Gieysztor graduated from the Historical-Philosophical Department at the University of Warsaw in 1937. From 1935 to 1937 he worked at the Main Archive of Old Documents. In 1938 he enrolled at the École Pratique des Hautes Études in Paris, concentrating on medieval history. During World War II, in Poland under the Nazi occupation, he clandestinely defended his doctorate in 1942. He lectured at the Free Polish University (1943–44). In 1940 he joined the Union for Armed Struggle, and in 1942, the Home Army (Armia Krajowa [AK]). He worked at the Bureau of Information and Propaganda of the AK Main Command, eventually becoming its supervisor in June 1944. He participated in the Warsaw Uprising. Imprisoned in a German POW camp, he and Stanisław Płoski penned their account of the insurrection: *Powstanie Warszawskie* (The Warsaw Uprising), which was published in the underground only in 1981.

In June 1945 Gieysztor began to work at the Institute of Art History and Inventory of Historical Objects of the Ministry of Culture and Art, and in September 1945, at the Institute of History at the University of Warsaw. In 1946 he was awarded a postdoctoral degree. In 1949 he became an assistant professor and in 1960 a full professor. Between 1953 and 1955, he served as deputy director of the Institute of the History of Material Culture and from 1969 as the editor-in-chief of *Kwartalnik Historii Kultury Materialnej*. Between 1951 and 1953 he was deputy dean and between 1956 and 1959 deputy rector of the University of Warsaw. From 1955 to 1975 he was director of the

Institute of History at the University of Warsaw. He was on the editorial board of *Kwartalnik Historyczny* and of the serial *Polski Słownik Biograficzny* (Polish biographical dictionary). In 1971 he became a corresponding member, and in 1980 a full member, of the Polish Academy of Sciences (PAS). In 1981–83 and 1990–92 he was the PAS president. After its reactivation in 1989, he became a member of the Polish Academy of Arts and Sciences. From 1947 Gieysztor was involved in an effort to reconstruct the Royal Castle in Warsaw. In 1971 he was coopted to the Civic Presidium for the Reconstruction of the Castle, and between 1980 and 1991 he served as director of the reconstructed castle. The deputy chairman of the Council for the Preservation of the Memory of Struggle and Martyrdom from 1990, he also served for many years as the president of the National Committee of the International Council of Museums (ICOM) and an honorary member of the International Council on Monuments and Sites (ICOMOS). In 1965 he was included on the board of the very prestigious International Committee for Historical Sciences, serving as its deputy chairman between 1975 and 1980 and as its chairman from 1980 through 1985. He was a member of many foreign scholarly academies and a honorary doctor of ten foreign and three Polish universities.

Although Gieysztor shied away from politics, his civic and patriotic involvement was significant. In 1964, he signed the "Letter of 34," a protest by Polish intellectuals against the cultural policies of the Communist regime. During the period of martial law, he was an advocate for the prisoners and internees. In February 1989, he was endorsed by both the Communists and the opposition as an independent participant in the Round Table Talks. Gieysztor's scholarly output comprises over one thousand items. His most important works include *Władza Karola Wielkiego w opinii współczesnych* (The power of Charlemagne according to contemporaries; 1938); *Zarys pisma łacińskiego* (An outline of Latin; 1973); and *Mitologia Słowian* (Mythology of the Slavs; 1982). He also co-edited many other works. (WD-JK)

Sources: *Wielka Encyklopedia PWN*, vol. 10 (Warsaw, 2002); *Muzealnictwo*, 1999, no. 41; Danuta Gawin, Ewa Gieysztor, Marian Sołtysiak, and Andrzej Tomaszewski, *Aleksander Gieysztor o dziedzictwie kultury* (Warsaw, 2000); *Wielka Internetowa Encyklopedia Multimedialna*.

GIGURTU Ion [originally Gigârtu] (24 June 1886, Turnu Severin–1959, Sighet), Romanian engineer, businessman, and politician. After completing a lycée in Craiova, Gigurtu studied at the Polytechnic College in Paris between 1906 and 1910. After 1918 he was active as an industrialist in several areas of the economy, including the mining industry, metallurgy, railways, and banking. Before 1937 he did not take an active part in political life, although from 1930 he financially supported King **Charles II** and his favorite, **Elena Lupescu**. Gigurtu belonged to the court camarilla of the king. Between December 1937 and February 1938 he served as minister of industry and trade, and when Charles II assumed full dictatorial power, Gigurtu became involved in the financial support of the regime. From 1937 he kept in close touch with German political and industrial circles—for example, with Hermann Göring. From November 1939 to July 1940 he was minister of public works. As prime minister of the last government during the reign of Charles II (between 4 July and 5 September 1940), Gigurtu allowed members of the Iron Guard to join the government for the first time. **Horia Sima** became minister of religious affairs, and Vasile Noveanu was appointed minister of finance in his government. This maneuver did not save Charles II from having to abdicate; the abdication came as a result of general discontent in the country caused by Romania's loss of nearly one-third of its former territory under the Second Vienna Award of 30 August 1940. Gigurtu was dismissed on 5 September 1940, when General **Ion Antonescu** came to power. After World War II Gigurtu was a long-term political prisoner. He died in the Sighet prison, but the exact date of death and place of burial are not known. (FA/TD)

Sources: *Politics and Political Parties in Roumania* (London, 1936); *The International Who's Who* (London, 1941); Şerban N. Ionescu, *Who Was Who in Twentieth Century Romania* (Boulder, Colo., 1994); M. Muşat and I. Ardeleanu, *România după Marea Unire*, vol. 2 (Bucharest, 1986); Al. Gh. Savu, *Dictatura regală 1938–1940* (Bucharest, 1970); A. Simon, *Regimul politic din România septembrie 1940–ianuarie 1941* (Cluj, 1976).

GIMES Miklós (22 December 1917, Budapest–16 June 1958, Budapest), Hungarian Communist activist, victim of the 1956 revolution. Gimes wanted to become a doctor, like his parents, but he did not complete his studies. In 1942 he established contact with the illicit Communist movement. Being of Jewish origin, he was called to labor service, but in summer 1944 he managed to escape and subsequently joined the Yugoslav guerrilla army of **Josip Broz Tito**. From January 1945 he was in Budapest, where he joined the Hungarian Communist Party and worked as a journalist for the party's central organ, *Szabad Nép* (1946–54). From February 1947 he was a member of the editorial board; he also authored a number of ideological articles. Initially Gimes was a protégé of **József Rév**, but after 1953 he became a supporter of reforms introduced by Prime Minister **Imre Nagy**. In 1954, he worked as

a correspondent for *Szabad Nép* in Geneva, Berlin, and Paris. When Nagy was dismissed, Gimes was moved to another daily. In May 1955, at a party meeting, he demanded a review of the sentences pronounced in the **László Rajk** trial, as well as the show trials related to it; as a result, he was removed from the party and dismissed from his job. Gimes worked as a librarian and lecturer. He was one of the central figures of the so-called party opposition gathered around Nagy, but Gimes's views were more radical than those of the majority of his comrades as he supported a multiparty system. In July 1956, after **Mátyás Rákosi** had lost the position of first secretary of the party, Gimes was accepted back into the party. During the revolution he co-founded the *Magyar Szabadság* daily; after 4 November he became one of the most important figures of the intellectual resistance: he edited an illegal magazine, *Október Huszonharmadika*, and he established the Hungarian Democratic Independence Movement. On 5 December 1956 he was arrested by Soviet officers. On 15 June 1958, in the trial of Imre Nagy and his comrades, Gimes was sentenced to death without the right of appeal on a charge of initiating and leading a conspiracy against "the rule of the people." He was executed the following day. In June 1989, he had a solemn burial along with Nagy and other victims executed after the trial. (JT)

Sources: *Magyar Nagylexikon*, vol. 8 (Budapest, 1999); *A magyar forradalom és szabadságharc enciklopédiája*, CD-ROM (Budapest, 1999); *Új Magyar Életrajzi Lexikon*, vol. 2 (Budapest, 2001); Ferenc A. Vali, *Rift and Revolt in Hungary* (Cambridge, Mass., 1961); Paul E. Zinner, *Revolution in Hungary* (New York, 1962); György Litván, ed., *Rewolucja węgierska 1956 roku* (Warsaw, 1996); Sándor Révész, *Egyetlen élet: Gimes Miklós története* (Budapest, 1999).

GIRA Liudas (27 August 1884, Vilnius [Wilno]–1 July 1946, Vilnius), Lithuanian poet and literary critic. Gira graduated from the theological seminary in Vilnius in 1905. In December 1905, on behalf of the Catholic Church, he was secretary of the Grand Lithuanian Assembly in Vilnius, where he demanded autonomy for Lithuania. He did not take holy orders but undertook social, political, and literary activities instead. In 1913–14 he edited the first Lithuanian journal of literary criticism, *Vaivorykšté*. In 1912 he published his first volume of poetry, *Lauku Dainos* (Songs of the fields). He was among the founders of the Lithuanian Union of Farmers, and during World War I he joined the Christian Democratic Party. In 1915 he belonged to the Vilnius Civic Committee. From the end of 1918, despite a lack of military training, he was briefly head of the Lithuanian garrison in Vilnius. When the Bolsheviks seized the city at the end of December 1918, Gira was briefly arrested. After his release he went to the

Lithuanian side of the front. In August 1919 he took part in putting down a plot by the Polish Military Organization in Kaunas aiming at the establishment of a pro-Polish Lithuanian government there. In 1921–26 Gira was director of the Lithuanian State Theater, and later he worked in the Ministry of Education. In 1921 he published *Žiežyrbos* (Sparks), and in 1929, *Silko gijos* (Silk threads). He also wrote dramas. Disappointed by subsequent Lithuanian governments, he went through an ideological evolution toward communism, and during the first Soviet occupation (1940–41) he was deputy commissar of education. After the German Wehrmacht entered Lithuania in June 1941, he escaped to the USSR and joined the Red Army. He served in it until 1944, when he was demobilized in the rank of captain and returned to Lithuania.

Under postwar Soviet rule Gira was one of the most touted Lithuanian writers, contributing to the intellectual Sovietization of his homeland. In 1945 he received the title of "people's poet" and membership in the Academy of Sciences of the Lithuanian SSR. In 1949 he published the collection *Thrys berželiai* (Three birch trees). Gira's literary output is subject to controversial evaluations. Appreciated by some as a folk poet, between the wars he mostly wrote in the spirit of patriotic pathos, and after 1940 he evolved toward Socialist realism in the Stalinist style. In 1952 his collected works were published in Russian as *Izbrannoye* (Selections), and in 1960–63 five volumes of his *Raštai* (Writings) were published in Lithuanian. (AG)

Sources: *EL*, vol. 2; *Lietuvių literatūros istorija*, vol. 4 (Vilnius, 1968).

GIRGINOV Aleksandur (29 April 1879, Turnovo–1 November 1953, Belene), Bulgarian politician and lawyer. Girginov graduated and received a Ph.D. in law in Leipzig. After returning home, he worked as a lawyer. He was one of the leaders of the Democratic Party and represented it in the National Assembly (1908–11 and 1913–34). After the June 1923 coup he joined the Democratic Alliance, but he left it in early 1924. Later he stayed in the opposition. He was minister of finance in the government of **Aleksandur Malinov** (June–October 1931) and minister of interior and minister of health in the government of **Nikola Mushanov** (October 1931–May 1934). He was the author of a restrictive press law. During World War II he declared himself in favor of Bulgaria's neutrality, opposing the pro-German policies of subsequent governments. On 27 August 1944, along with twelve opposition politicians, he signed a declaration demanding the termination of the alliance with the Third Reich, a rapprochement with the Soviet Union, and the formation of a constitutional national government. In the short-lived government of **Konstantin Muraviev**

(2–9 September 1944) Girginov assumed the position of minister of finance and acting minister of trade, industry, and labor. After the coup of 9 September 1944 he was arrested and sentenced to one year in prison. After his release in early September 1945, Girginov, along with Mushanov, reactivated the Democratic Party, which, along with the Bulgarian Agrarian National Union and the Social Democratic Party, was active in opposition to the Communist-dominated Fatherland Front. For this activity he was detained in the Belene concentration camp on the Danube island of Persin, where he died. Girginov authored (among other works) the following: *Parlamentarizum i poemaneto na wlastta* (Parliamentarism and the acquisition of power; 1907); *Durzhavnoto ustroystvo na Bulgariya* (The state system of Bulgaria; 1921); *Bulgariya pred velikata voyna* (Bulgaria before the Great War; 1932); *Narodnata katastrofa: Voynata 1912–1913* (The national disaster. The war of 1912–1913; 1926); and *Izpitaniyata vuv voynata 1915–1918* (The experience of the 1915–1918 war; 1936). In 1946 he edited the daily *Zname*. (JJ)

Sources: *Entsiklopediya Bulgariya*, vol. 2 (Sofia, 1981); Charles A. Moser, *Dimitrov of Bulgaria* (Ottawa, Ill., 1979); Jerzy Jackowicz, *Partie opozycyjne w Bułgarii 1944–1948* (Warsaw, 1997); Tasho Tashev, *Ministrite na Bulgariya 1879–1999: Entsiklopedichen spravochnik* (Sofia, 1999).

GJINI Frano (20 February 1886, Shkodër–11 March 1948, Shkoder), Albanian Catholic bishop. Gjini studied at St. Francis Xavier College and then in Rome, where he was ordained. After returning home, he worked as a parish priest in Laç, Vlorë, and Durrës. In 1930 he was consecrated bishop. He worked as auxiliary bishop in Durrës and (from 1932) in Oroshi, where he also became the abbot of the Mirdytes. After the expulsion from Albania of the apostolic delegate, Archbishop Giovanni Nigris, in 1945, Gjini was the first Albanian in history to assume these duties. In 1946, after the death of Archbishop **Gasper Thaçi**, Gjini became head of the Catholic Church in Albania; the Church worked under enormous pressure from the Communist authorities, which demanded the Church's breach with Rome and its assistance in the construction of the totalitarian system. These demands were accompanied by threats that Gjini would meet the fate of Catholic priests who had been shot earlier. Gjini rejected the demands to break with Rome but offered assistance in the reconstruction of Albania. In an open letter to **Enver Hoxha** he stated that it was necessary to meet not only the material, but also the spiritual needs of the nation. As a result Gjini was arrested for "anti-Communist propaganda." His imprisonment was also connected with repressions following an anti-Communist Mirdyte rebellion in Postrriba (9 September 1946). Gjini was accused of collaboration with the Vatican and the British mission and with taking part in the preparation of the rebellion. Weapons allegedly found in a church in Oroshi served as proof. Gjini was tortured in prison and tried in a show trial. He was sentenced to death and shot along with eighteen other priests and lay Catholics. According to the official report, his last words were, "Long live Christ the King, the Catholic religion, and all the Catholics in the world! Long live the Pope! Though my blood and flesh will stay here, my heart is with the Pope. Long live Albania!" His burial place has not been found. (TC)

Sources: Tadeusz Czekalski, *Zarys dziejów chrześcijaństwa albańskiego w latach 1912–1993* (Kraków, 1996); *Martirizimi i kishës katolike shqiptare (1944–1990)* (Shkodër, 1993); Pjeter Pepa, *Dosja e diktaturës* (Tirana, 1995); Ndoc Dom Nogaj, *Kisha Katolike Shqiptare 1944 nëntor 1990: Humbje dhe fitore* (Shkodër, 1999); Robert Royal, *Catholic Martyrs of the Twentieth Century* (New York, 2000).

GŁĄBIŃSKI Stanisław (25 February 1862, Skole–1943, Moscow), Polish economist and politician. Upon graduating from high school in Sambor, Głąbiński enrolled in the Law School at the University of Lemberg (Lwów, Lviv) in 1880. He received his Ph.D. there in 1887 and a postdoctoral degree in 1888, becoming assistant professor in 1892 and full professor in 1895. For many years he served as dean of the Law School and, between 1908 and 1909, as rector of the University of Lwów. In 1902 he started his political career by winning a seat in the Council of State in Vienna. In 1904 he was also elected to the Galician Home Parliament. He served on both bodies until 1918. He was involved with the nationalist camp and in 1905 co-founded the Democratic National Party. Following the elections of 1907, as the leader of the strongest party in the Polish Club, Głąbiński became its deputy chairman and then chairman, serving until 1911. From January to June 1911, he was minister of railroads. He attempted to carry out the decentralization and commercialization of the railroads, as well as to Polonize the Galician administration. During World War I, until 1917 he advocated loyalty toward Austria. In 1918 he came out for the independence of Poland, attacking the pro-Austrian orientation of the conservatives in the Council of State. From 23 October to 4 November 1918, he was foreign minister in the Regency Council government of **Józef Świeżyński**. Later, as an extraordinary government commissioner, he organized the Polish Liquidation Commission in Kraków and the Ruling Commission in Lwów. In January 1919 he was dispatched to Romania to secure permission to concentrate Polish military units in Constantinople, Odessa, and Bessarabia and to transfer them through Romanian territory to Poland.

From 1919 to 1928, Głąbiński was an MP for the Popular National Union (Zjednoczenie Ludowo-Narodowe [ZLN]). He chaired the ZLN Supreme Council, and after the resignation of **Roman Dmowski** from this post, he became chairman of the ZLN parliamentary club. On 1 July 1920, he joined the Council for the Defense of the State. In 1923 he participated in negotiations with the Polish Peasant Party–Piast (PSL–Piast), which resulted in the so-called Lanckorona Pact, creating a coalition government of the Christian Union of National Unity and the PSL–Piast. On 28 May 1923 Głąbiński became deputy prime minister and minister for religious confessions and public enlightenment. On 14 November 1923 he resigned and returned to chair the ZLN parliamentary club. From 1928 to 1935 he was senator and chair of the national-democratic club in the Senate. As a representative of the old, moderate, so-called professorial wing of the party, he lost influence in the 1930s. In September 1939 he was arrested by the Soviet NKVD and kidnapped to Moscow, where he died in jail. Głąbiński's main scholarly focus was macroeconomics. He co-authored (with Ludwik Finkel) *Historia i statystyka monarchii austro-węgierskiej* (History and statistics of the Austro-Hungarian monarchy; 1897) and authored *Wykład ekonomii społecznej* (A lecture on social economy; 1912); *Nauka skarbowości* (A study of the treasury; 1925); *Ustrój skarbowy Rzeczpospolitej Polskiej* (The treasury system of the Polish Republic; 1926); *Ekonomika narodowa* (The national economy, 2 vols.; 1927–28); *Polskie prawo skarbowe* (The Polish treasury law; 1928); and *Historia ekonomiki* (History of economy, 2 vols.; 1939). He also penned *Wspomnienia polityczne* (Historical memoirs; 1939). (PU)

Sources: *PSB*, vol. 8; *Kto był kim w Drugiej Rzeczypospolitej* (Warsaw, 1994); *Encyklopedia Historii Drugiej Rzeczypospolitej* (Warsaw, 1999); Roman Wapiński, *Narodowa Demokracja 1893–1939* (Wrocław, 1980); Adam Próchnik, *Pierwsze piętnastolecie Polski niepodległej* (Warsaw, 1983); Władysław Pobóg-Malinowski, *Najnowsza historia polityczna Polski*, vol. 2 (London, 1983).

GLEMP Józef (18 December 1929, Inowrocław), cardinal, Primate of Poland. In 1950–56 Glemp studied at the Higher Theological Seminary in Gniezno and Poznań, and in 1956 he was ordained. From 1956 to 1957 he worked as a notary in the metropolitan curia in Gniezno; from 1957 to 1964 he was vicar in various parishes; and in 1958–64 he studied at the Pontifical University at the Lateran. From 1964 to 1967 he was secretary at the Higher Theological Seminary in Gniezno; from 1965 to 1967, notary in the metropolitan tribunal in Gniezno; and from 1970 to 1978, consultor of the Gniezno tribunal. From 1967 he worked at the Secretariat of the Primate of Poland in Warsaw and was personal secretary to Primate **Stefan Wyszyński**. From 1976 he was canon of the primate's chapter in Gniezno. On 4 March 1979 he was appointed bishop of Warmia and made his ingress in Frombork Cathedral on 6 May 1979. Later he presided over the Iustitia et Pax commission of the Polish Episcopate and was a member of its commission for ministry among workers.

After the death of Cardinal Wyszyński, on 7 July 1981 Glemp was appointed the archbishop metropolitan of Gniezno and Warsaw. He made his ingress in Gniezno on 13 September and in Warsaw on 24 September 1981. On 2 February 1983 he was appointed cardinal. In the fall of 1981 he tried to mediate between the Polish Communist authorities and Solidarity, meeting with General **Wojciech Jaruzelski** and **Lech Wałęsa** on 4 November, but it was in vain. He established the Primate's Social Council, which was inaugurated on 12 December. After the introduction of martial law, on 13 December 1981 Glemp appealed for peace and calm, at the same time undertaking efforts to release those interned and to moderate living conditions in internment camps and prisons. On 17 December he established the Primate's Committee of Relief for the Detained and Their Families. He followed a policy of cautious support for Solidarity but distanced himself from the ongoing political struggle and from underground Solidarity activities. He initiated the pilgrimages of Pope **John Paul II** to Poland in 1983 and 1987, which were aimed at keeping up spirits and integrating the society along the lines of religious and national values. In his contacts with the authorities Glemp appealed for an easing of the martial law regime. In 1984 he supported the official pressure aiming at the forced emigration of imprisoned Solidarity leaders; the effort failed because the leaders refused to leave. Glemp attempted to register the Church Agricultural Endowment. This initiative was blocked by the Communists, but it brought some foreign aid for individual farmers. In 1986 he encouraged lay Catholic activists to join the Consultative Council of the Chairman of the Council of State, hoping against all odds to establish a dialogue between the authorities and the moderate opposition.

In 1989 Glemp delegated representatives of the Episcopate as observers to the Round Table Talks. He succeeded in making the Communist authorities pass legislation concerning the legal status of the Roman Catholic Church, the freedom of conscience and religion (17 May 1989), and the resumption of diplomatic relations between Poland and the Holy See (17 July 1989). During the systemic transformations after 1989 Glemp strove to strengthen the Church's position in public life. He supported endeavors to regain Church property confiscated under communism,

he managed to restore religious instruction in the schools (1990), and he strongly supported the ban on abortion and the anti-abortion campaign. Many times he criticized the liberal circles of Solidarity. After the dissolution of the union of the Gniezno and Warsaw archdiocese, on 25 March 1992 Glemp was released from his duties as archbishop of Gniezno, but he retained the title of Primate of Poland. He succeeded in bringing about a concordat with the Holy See (28 July 1993). In 1997 he criticized the version of the constitution that was finally passed by the parliament. Under his leadership the Episcopate supported Polish accession to the European Union. During the celebration of the Jubilee Year in May 2000, Glemp publicly confessed to the neglect and sins of the Church in Poland. He was a member of the Congregation of Eastern Churches, the Papal Council of Culture, and the Council of the Conference of European Episcopates. In March 2004 his last term as chairman of the Conference of the Polish Episcopate ended. Glemp authored several collections of homilies: *Kościół na drogach ojczyzny* (The Church on the roads of the homeland; 1985); *Służyć Ewangelii słowem* (To serve the Gospel with the word; 1991); *Gniezno—ciągła odnowa* (Gniezno–constant renewal; 1992); and *Od Kalwarii na drogi Europy* (From Calvary onto European ways; 1997). (AF)

Sources: Grzegorz Polak, *Kto jest kim w Kościele?* (Warsaw, 1999); *Kto jest kim w Polsce* (Warsaw, 2001); Andrrzej Micewski, *Kościół wobec "Solidarności" i stanu wojennego* (Paris, 1987); Jarosław Gowin, *Kościół w czasach wolności 1989–1999* (Kraków, 1999); Antoni Dudek, *Pierwsze lata III Rzeczpospolitej: 1989–2001* (Kraków, 2002); *Caritati in iustitia: Dwadzieścia lat posługi prymasowskiej kardynała Józefa Glempa* (Warsaw, 2001).

GLIGOROV Kiro (3 May 1917, Shtip), Macedonian politician. Born into a middle-class family, Gligorov graduated from high school in Skopje and in law from the University of Belgrade (1938). After his return to Skopje, he worked as a lawyer in a private bank. In 1941 he joined he Communist Party and the guerrilla movement of **Josip Broz Tito**. He was a member of the Anti-Fascist Council of the National Liberation of Macedonia and the Anti-Fascist Council of the National Liberation of Yugoslavia. After World War II he was secretary of the constitutional commission of the Macedonian republic. Delegated to Belgrade, from 1945 he worked in federal government institutions. In 1953–55 he was deputy director of the Federal Institute of Economic Planning and then secretary (minister) in the Federal Executive Economic Council. From 1962 to 1967 he was federal secretary (minister) of finance, and in 1967–69, deputy chairman of the Federal Executive Council. At this time he was a supporter of the centralization of power in Yugoslavia.

In the 1960s Gligorov co-authored the Yugoslav economic reform. In the spring of 1969 he resigned from the government, and in 1971–78 he was a member of the Presidium of the Socialist Federative Republic of Yugoslavia (SFRY). From 1974 to 1978 he was speaker of its parliament. As a result of his conflict with Tito over economic policy, in 1978 he was dismissed from all state positions. After the death of Tito, Gligorov was eliminated from the Central Committee of the League of Communists of Yugoslavia as he advocated full respect for market mechanisms. At the end of the 1980s he cooperated with Prime Minister **Ante Marković**, introducing market reforms. During the breakup of Yugoslavia, on 27 January 1991 the republican parliament elected Gligorov president of the Socialist Republic of Macedonia (as of November 1991, the Republic of Macedonia). In the spring of 1991 Gligorov, along with **Alija Izetbegović**, presented a plan to transform the SFRY into a loose federation; the plan was rejected by the Serbs.

On 8 September 1991, as a result of a referendum, Macedonia proclaimed independence, and Gligorov continued as its president. In October 1994 he won the presidential elections and remained the head of the new state, trying to overcome the country's international isolation. On 12 September 1995 he concluded an agreement with Greece, which for historical and national reasons initially did not accept "Macedonia" as the name of the country. The name that was settled on was the Former Yugoslav Republic of Macedonia. Gligorov also established a formal relationship with Bulgaria, and despite economic problems, he kept his multi-ethnic country in equilibrium. On 3 October 1995 he was wounded in a bomb attack in Skopje, the perpetrators of which were never found. Owing to ailing health, Gligorov did not run in the presidential elections of November 1999. (AO)

Sources: Valentina Georgieva and Sasha Konechni, *Historical Dictionary of Macedonia* (Lanham, Md., 1998); *Biographical Notes*, Polish Press Agency PAP; Laura Silber and Allan Little, *The Death of Yugoslavia* (London, 1995); Warren Zimmermann, *Origins of a Catastrophe* (New York and Toronto, 1996); Irena Stawowy-Kawka, *Historia Macedonii* (Wrocław, 2001); Bugajski.

GLIWIC Hipolit (24 March 1878, Warsaw–9 April 1943, Warsaw), Polish economist and businessman of Jewish origin. Gliwic graduated from the University of Odessa in 1901 and in 1906 from the Mining Institute in St. Petersburg, where he became an assistant professor in 1909. Between 1903 and 1907, he was active in the Polish Socialist Party. In 1911 he became the manager of the Warsaw branch of the Prodamet Company and joined the White Eagle Masonic lodge, which was a subsidiary of the Grand Orient lodge.

From 1914 to 1918 in St. Petersburg, Gliwic was active in Polish independence organizations, and in 1918 he became the trade adviser to the plenipotentiary office of the Regency Council in Russia. At the end of 1918 he returned to Warsaw, where he co-organized the Union of Polish Democracy and the grand national lodge Copernicus. Between 1919 and 1922 he was the trade adviser for the Ministry of the Treasury, and from 1922 through 1925, the adviser and chargé d'affaires of Poland in the United States. Upon his return home, he became director of the Department of Trade at the Ministry of Industry and Trade. Following the coup d'état of May 1926, he served briefly as the minister of industry and trade in the government of **Kazimierz Bartel**. From 1927 to 1930, Gliwic represented Poland at the League of Nations, including its Economic Advisory Committee. Closely tied to the industrial circles, he sat on many boards of banks and industrial enterprises. Among others, he co-organized the Unity of Mining and Steel Mill Interests in 1927 and 1928. From 1926 to 1934 he was on the board of overseers of the Trade Bank in Warsaw, chairing it from 1928 through 1932. Between 1928 and 1939, he was a professor at the Free Polish University (Wolna Wszechnica Polska) and a lecturer at the University of Lwów (1931–39) and the Jagiellonian University in Kraków (1934–39). From 1926 to 1928, he was active in the Labor Party and later in the Nonparty Bloc of Cooperation with the Government (BBWR). From 1928 through 1930 he served in the Senate and was its deputy speaker. He authored many books and articles on economic matters, including *Ewolucja syndykatów* (The evolution of syndicates, 2 vols.; 1916) and *Podstawy ekonomiki światowej* (Foundations of the world economy, 3 vols.; 1926–38). During the Nazi occupation Gliwic was active in the underground. From 1942 to 1943 under the code name "Tomasz," he supervised the Economic Council with the Second Department (Intelligence) of the Supreme Command of the Home Army. Gliwic was arrested by the Gestapo on 8 April 1943 and committed suicide in jail. (WR)

Sources: *PSB*, vol. 8; *Encyklopedia historii gospodarczej Polski do 1945 roku*, vol. 1 (Warsaw, 1981); Ludwik Hass, *Masoneria polska XX wieku* (Warsaw, 1996).

GOCŁOWSKI Tadeusz (16 September 1931, Piski, near Ostrołęka), archbishop metropolitan of Gdańsk. Gocłowski studied philosophy and theology in the Theological Institute of the Priests of the Mission in Kraków (1951–56). In June 1956 he was ordained in Kraków. Later he studied canon law at the Catholic University of Lublin (1956–59) and in 1969–70 at the Canon Law Department of the Angelicum Pontifical University in Rome, where he received a Ph.D. in 1970. He then lectured at the Theological Institute of the Priests of the Mission in Kraków and at the Episcopal Theological Seminary in Gdańsk, whose rector he was in 1970–73 and 1982–83. From 1973 to 1982 he was provincial of the Polish province of the Congregation of Priests of the Mission in Kraków. On 17 April 1983 he was consecrated bishop and appointed auxiliary bishop of Gdańsk. From 31 December 1984 he was ordinary bishop of Gdańsk. One of the chaplains of Solidarity, during martial law Gocłowski protected the underground activists of the union. In 1988–89, he represented the Episcopate in talks between the Communist authorities and the opposition in Magdalenka, near Warsaw, where the Round Table Talks were prepared. Gocłowski proved to be a sophisticated negotiator. He was also engaged in secret mediations in the political conflicts of the early 1990s. As the crisis in the Civic Committee of the Chairman of Solidarity grew, on 7 and 8 April 1990 Gocłowski organized a meeting in Gdańsk between **Lech Wałęsa** and Prime Minister **Tadeusz Mazowiecki**; **Adam Michnik**, **Jacek Kuroń**, and **Bronisław Geremek** also took part, along with a few other opposition leaders. The meeting failed to resolve the growing personal strife between Wałęsa and Mazowiecki. Trying to unite the dispersed anti-Communist groups before the parliamentary elections, in July 1993 Gocłowski helped establish the Homeland (Ojczyzna) Election Committee, headed by **Wiesław Chrzanowski**. In connection with changes in the Catholic Church organization in Poland, on 25 March 1992 Gocłowski became archbishop metropolitan of Gdańsk. One of the leading Polish Roman Catholic hierarchs, co-chairman of the Joint Commission of the State and Episcopate, and a member of the Permanent Council of the Polish Episcopate, he was responsible for the pilgrimage to Poland of Pope John Paul II in 1999. (PK)

Sources: Grzegorz Polak, *Kto jest kim w Kościele?* (Warsaw, 1999); Peter Raina, *Droga do "Okrągłego Stołu": Zakulisowe rozmowy przygotowawcze* (Warsaw, 1999); Antoni Dudek, *Pierwsze lata III Rzeczpospolitej: 1989–2001* (Kraków, 2002).

GODMANIS Ivars (27 November 1951, Riga), Latvian politician. Godmanis graduated from the Department of Physics and Mathematics of the Latvian State University in 1974. Later he worked there as a lecturer, and in 1984–88 he was assistant professor at the Institute of Solid Body Physics. From 1986 to 1989 he lectured in informatics and received a Ph.D. in mathematics and physics. From the foundation of the Latvian Popular Front (LPF) he was an active member, working in its political committee. At the Second Congress of the LPF in May 1989 Godmanis was elected deputy chairman of its council. On 4 May 1990 the Supreme Council of the Latvian SSR proclaimed de jure sovereignty of the republic, removing the terms "Socialist" and "Soviet" from the country's official name and electing Godmanis as prime minister of a new government. When Soviet special forces attacked the Ministry of Interior in Riga in January 1991, Godmanis continued efforts to secure the country's freedom; during a referendum concerning the future shape of the Soviet Union in March 1991 he supported independence, so the referendum was not held in Latvia. During the Moscow putsch, on 19 August 1991, Godmanis, along with the chairman of the Latvian Supreme Council, **Anatolijs Gorbunovs**, signed an announcement refusing to recognize the new power in Moscow.

On the second day of the Moscow coup, on 20 August 1991 the Supreme Council of Latvia announced the country's full independence. Godmanis remained prime minister and was the most popular Latvian politician at the time. The new state faced enormous problems, connected with having been the most highly Russified among the Baltic republics, the necessity to create an army and police force from scratch, and economic collapse and hyperinflation. One of the most difficult tasks was the introduction of a national currency. In July 1992 the Latvian ruble was initiated, and in March 1993 the Latvian lat was introduced. Privatization of the economy started. In foreign policy the Godmanis government established a special relationship with Sweden. Economic cooperation with Estonia and Lithuania was initially very weak owing to the substitutive nature of their economies. Struggling with these problems, Godmanis frequently reconstructed his cabinet, sacrificing ministers for the sake of the government. Despite Godmanis's many successes in the systemic transformation of a Soviet republic into an independent state, the breakup of the LPF into various parties and a decline in the standard of living quickly eroded his popularity. In the spring and summer of 1992 nationalist radicals and post–Communists attempted to overthrow his government, but Godmanis managed to stay in power. In the elections of June 1993 his party won only 4 percent of the vote, and Godmanis lost his parliamentary seat. On 22 July 1993 he resigned as prime minister. In 1994–95 he was deputy chairman of a private company in Riga, and in 1995–97 he was chairman of the state bank, Latvijas Krājbanka. In 1998 he was elected to the parliament (Saeima) on behalf of the liberal Latvia's Way (Latvijas Ceļš) party. As minister of finance in the government of Vilis Kristopans from November 1998 to July 1999, Godmanis counteracted the influence of the Russian financial crisis on the Latvian economy. (EJ-WR)

Sources: *Who Is Who in Latvia 1996: Biographical Dictionary* (Riga, 1996); *Kas ir kas Latvijâ* (Riga, 1999); Romuald J. Misiunas and Rein Taagepera, *The Baltic States: Years of Dependence*

1940–1990 (Berkeley, 1993); Anatol Lieven, *The Baltic Revolution* (New Haven, 1993); *Europa Środkowo-Wschodnia 1993* (Warsaw, 1995); Juris Dreifelds, *Latvia in Transition* (Cambridge, 1996); *Policy of the Occupation Powers in Latvia, 1939–1991* (Riga, 1999); Andrejs Plakans, *Historical Dictionary of Latvia* (Lanham, Md., 1997).

GOGA Octavian (1 April 1881, Răsiniani–7 May 1938, Ciucea), Romanian poet, publicist, and politician. From 1900 to 1904 Goga studied philology and philosophy at Budapest University. He was one of the greatest Romanian poets of the twentieth century and also one of the leaders of the Romanian movement in Transylvania before 1918. The creator of "Romanism" and an ardent supporter of Greater Romania, he made his literary debut with a collection of patriotic poems, *Luceafărul* (Morning star), in 1904. The next year he published *Poezii* (Poems), which was a Bible of sorts for Romanian nationalists before 1918. Goga spent 1912–13 in a Hungarian prison in Szeged, where he was put for his anti-Hungarian activities. After his release he was engaged in intensive propaganda for the unification of Romania, which was also conducted outside the country—in France, Italy, and Russia. During World War I Goga represented a pro-Entente orientation.

In 1919 Goga joined the People's Party of General **Alexandru Averescu**. In 1921 he became a member of the Romanian Academy. From 5 to 16 December 1919 he served as minister of education, and then he held this post on an interim basis until 18 March 1920, when he was appointed minister of education and religious affairs. Between 30 March 1926 and 14 July 1926 he was minister of interior. In 1932, having left the People's Party, he formed the National Agrarian Party. In July 1935 his party merged with the League of National Christian Defense, the extremely rightist and anti-Semitic party of **Alexandru C. Cuza**. As a result, the National Christian Party was created, led by Goga and Cuza. This party had a strong Fascist tinge in the spirit of Italian corporativism, but it remained marginal on the Romanian political scene. At the same time Goga supported King **Charles II** in his political struggle against the National Peasant Party and the Iron Guard. After the elections of December 1937 Goga was appointed prime minister by the king, a move that was supposed to facilitate the assumption of full power by Charles II. Goga served as prime minister between 28 December 1937 and 10 February 1938, introducing anti-Semitic laws and shifting Romanian foreign policy toward Germany and Italy. After the royal coup d'état of 10 February 1938 he withdrew from political life. He died a few months later in unexplained circumstances.

His wife, Veturia Goga, was an adviser to Marshal **Ion Antonescu** in the field of social policy.

Goga authored a number of collections of poems and prose and political commentaries, including the following: *O seamă de cuvinte* (A handful of words; 1908); *Inseminările unui trecător: Crâmpeie din zbuciumarile de la noi* (Notes of a passerby: Our disturbances and tensions; 1911); *Strigăte în pustiu: Cuvinte din Ardeal într—o țară neutră* (Scream in the dessert: Words on Transylvania and the neutral country; 1915); *Mustul cara fierbe* (Boiling juice; 1927); *Precursori* (Precursors; 1930); and . . . *Aceași luptă* (. . .The same struggle; 1930). (FA/TD)

Sources: *Biographisches Lexikon*, vol. 2; Stephen Fischer-Galati, *Twentieth Century Rumania* (New York, 1991); M. Musat and I. Ardeleanu, *România după Marea Unire*, vol. 2 (Bucharest, 1986); I. D. Bălan, *Octavian Goga* (Bucharest, 1966); Al. Gh. Savu, *Dictatura regală 1938–1940* (Bucharest, 1970).

GOJDIČ Pavel (17 July 1888, Ruski Peklani, near Prešov–17 July 1960, Leopoldovo), Greek Catholic bishop of Prešov. Gojdič was the son of a Greek Catholic priest. After completing a gymnasium in Prešov in 1907, between 1909 and 1911 he studied theology in Budapest. In July 1922 he joined the Order of St. Basil the Great in Mukačevo, and on 25 March 1927 in Rome he was ordained bishop of the Prešov diocese. In the fall of 1938 he supported the autonomy movement of the Transcarpathian Ukraine, and in October 1938 he mediated on the issue of changing the borders of Slovakia in favor of Hungary. After the liquidation of the Greek Catholic Church by the Communists in 1946, Gojdič continued his pastoral activities until his arrest on 28 April 1950. In January 1951 in Bratislava he was sentenced to life imprisonment. He served the sentence in Leopoldovo, where he died. In 1968 his body was buried in the Cathedral of St. John the Baptist in Prešov. On 5 November 2001 he was beatified by Pope **John Paul II**. (WR)

Sources: *Martirologia ukrain'skikh tserkov u chetyriokh tomakh*, vol. 2; *SBS*, vol. 2; J. E. Pavel Gojdič-jepiskop prjaševskij (Prešov, 1947); *Proces proti vlastizradným biskupom Jánovi Vojtašš akovi, Michalovi Buzalkovi, Pavlovi Gojdičovi* (Bratislava, 1961).

GOLDELMAN Solomon (5 December 1885, Soroka, Bessarabia–3 January 1974, Jerusalem), Jewish scholar and cultural activist in the Ukraine. From his youth Goldelman was connected with the Zionist left. In 1913 he graduated in economics from the Trade Institute in Kiev and worked there until 1915, when he started working in the Association of Landed Administrations (zemstvos). From July 1917 he represented the Zionist Socialist party Poale Zion in the Central Ukrainian Council (Rada). During the rule of Hetman **Pavlo Skoropadskyi**, Goldelman edited the Poale Zion daily *Unser Leben* in Odessa. In December 1918 he was appointed minister of labor and secretary for national minorities in the government of the Directorate of the Ukrainian National Republic in Kiev. Later he was deputy minister of trade and industry, and from August 1919 to April 1920, deputy minister of labor in the government of **Izaak Mazepa**. In mid-1920 Goldelman left for Vienna, and in 1922 he co-organized the Ukrainian Agricultural Academy in Poděbrady in Bohemia. He lectured there until 1939, when he emigrated to Palestine. Until his death Goldelman maintained contacts with Ukrainian political exiles and promoted Ukrainian-Jewish cooperation. He authored numerous works, including a textbook on economics and industrial policy (1923), a work on international economic policy (1924), and a study on the theory of joint stock companies (1925). In 1921 he published *Lysty zhydivskoho sotsialdemokrata pro Ukraiinu* (Letters of a Jewish Social Democrat on the Ukrainian question), in 1937 *Löst der Kommunismus die Judenfrage?* (Does communism solve the Jewish question?), and in 1973 *Juden-Bauern in der Ukraine* (Jewish peasants in the Ukraine). (WR)

Sources: *Encyclopedia of Ukraine*, vol. 2 (Toronto, 1988); L. Bykovsky, *Solomon I. Goldelman: A Portrait of a Politician and Educator (1885–1974)* (New York and Toronto, 1980).

GOLIAN Ján (26 January 1906, Dombóvár, Hungary–April 1945, Flossenbürg, Germany), Slovak general, leader of the Slovak National Uprising. Golian graduated from the Higher Military School in Prague. In 1938 he was attached to the Tenth Division in Banska Bystrica, and after the dismemberment of Czechoslovakia he was appointed a major and officer of the Slovak general staff. Despite his service in the Slovak army, he could not reconcile himself to the fall of the Czechoslovak Republic and did not identify himself with the new Slovak state. In 1942 and 1943 he fought on the eastern front, where he entered into contact with Soviet guerrillas. On his return to Slovakia he was relocated to Banska Bystrica, where he started an underground military organization. From the beginning of 1944 he held talks with the illegal Slovak National Council (SNC), and after a secret meeting in Bratislava, on 27 April 1944 he assumed military command of a planned armed uprising. The SNC entrusted him with the task of preparing the strategy and contacting guerrilla units acting in Slovakia. The uprising was to be coordinated with Red Army operations.

On 29 August 1944 Golian ordered insurgent troops to attack the German military units entering Slovakia. Thanks to this decision, after the war Slovakia was not marked as Hitler's ally. On 1 September 1944 President **Edvard Beneš** appointed Golian commander of the First Czechoslovak Army in Slovakia, and four days later he was appointed brigadier general by the London government in exile. For over a month he served as commander-in-chief of the Czechoslovak armed forces in Slovakia. After the assumption of this post by General **Rudolf Viest**, who was sent from London, Golian became Viest's deputy. The Soviet command, considering the Slovak resistance movement "politically suspicious," did not inform the Slovaks about its change of strategy in the fight against the Germans. As a result, the insurrection collapsed in October 1944 and the partisans went into hiding in the mountains, where they continued the struggle. On 3 November 1944 the Germans captured both leaders in Pohronsky Bukovec. Golian perished in unknown circumstances in Flossenbürg. (PU)

Sources: *ČBS*; *Kdo byl kdo v našich dějinách ve 20. století*, vol. 1 (Prague, 1998); Joseph A. Mikus, *Slovakia: A Political History 1918–1950* (Milwaukee, 1963); *Reprezentačný biografický lexikón Slovenska* (Martin, 1999); Dušan Kováč, *Dejiny Slovenska* (Prague, 2000); http://www.muzeumsnp.sk/golian_s.htm.

GOMA Paul (2 October 1935, Mâna, Bessarabia), Romanian writer and dissident. After Bessarabia and Northern Bukovina were annexed by the USSR in June 1940, Goma's family escaped to Romania. At the age of seventeen he was temporarily arrested by the political police, the Securitate, for "anti-state" views recorded in his personal diary. In 1956 he was expelled as a student of Bucharest University for stating that Romania was under Soviet occupation. He was sentenced to two and a half years in prison and five years of house arrest. After his release, he worked as a blue-collar laborer, a photographer, and a trumpet player. When **Nicolae Ceauşescu** refused to send Romanian troops into Czechoslovakia in August 1968, Goma was carried away with enthusiasm and joined the (Communist) Romanian Workers' Party, becoming a loyal follower of the regime. In early 1977 he failed to organize a Romanian equivalent of the Czechoslovak Charter 77. He sent out letters of support for Charter 77, including a letter encouraging Ceauşescu to endorse it, but his movement failed to gain wide support. He managed to collect two hundred signatures for a letter demanding a liberalization of the Romanian regime, but to no major avail.

On 1 April 1977 Goma was arrested, and in the fall of 1977 he was forced to leave Romania. He settled in Paris. He wrote most of his books while in France. The most important of them include the following: *Ostinato* (1971); *Ura noastră cea de toate zilele* (Our daily bread; 1972); *Gherla* (1976); *În cerc* (In a circle; 1977); *Garda inversă*

(Opposite guard; 1979); *Culoarea curcubeului* (The color of the rainbow; 1979); *Patimile după Pitești* (Redemption after Pitești; 1981); *Bonifacia* (1986); *Sabina* (1991); *Astra* (1992); and an autobiographical novel, *Altina—gradina scufandata* (Altina—submerged garden; 1998). In 1988 a Securitate agent was assigned to kill him, but the agent himself revealed this plan. Called the "Romanian Solzhenitsyn," Goma criticized Romanian writers for their submission to the Ceaușescu regime. He continued this criticism after 1989, contesting the post–Ceaușescu reality. He thinks of himself as an author not understood by contemporary Romanians. He created the so-called public novel, a sort of personal diary. Analyzing the human condition, Goma identified the most important issues of the twentieth century. Frequently his abstract meditations and reflections turned into polemics with specific Romanian authors. In 1991 he received an award from the Association of Romanian Writers for *Ostinato*. (LW)

Sources: Gheorge Glodeanu, *Incursiuni in literatura diasporei și a disidenți* (Bucharest, 1999); Costin Scorpan, *Istoria României: Enciclopedie* (Bucharest, 1997); Virgil Ierunca, *Subiect și predicat* (Bucharest, 1993).

GÖMBÖS Gyula (26 December 1886, Murga–6 October 1936, Munich), Hungarian right-wing politician. In 1905 Gömbös graduated from a cadet school in Pécs, in 1912 he took a course for senior officers in Budapest, and in 1914 he graduated from the Military Academy in Vienna. In May 1915 he was appointed captain of the General Staff. After the outbreak of World War I, he was sent to the Serbian front. From 1915 he fought against the Russians in the Carpathian Mountains. In June 1916 he was wounded; after his recovery, he was transferred to the National Defense Ministry (NDM). In 1917–18 he served in the army's logistical department in Vienna. After the fall of the Austro-Hungarian monarchy in October 1918, Gömbös was recalled to Budapest. From December 1918 he was in charge of the Balkan office in the NMD Operations Department. He acted in right-wing officer organizations aimed at overthrowing the republican rule of Count **Mihály Károlyi**. In January 1919 he co-founded and soon afterwards assumed the leadership of the Hungarian Defense Association (Magyar Országos Véderö Egyesülete [HDA]). Dismissed from the ministry and threatened with detention after the Hungarian Soviet Republic (HSR) had been proclaimed in March 1919, he escaped to Vienna, where he joined the anti-Bolshevik committee of Count **István Bethlen**. As a committee representative, he went to Belgrade, where he held talks with French commanders about joint operations against the HSR. He made contact with the government-in-exile in Szeged, and he was ap-

pointed secretary of state in charge of national defense. He took an active part in organizing the National Army, whose commander was Admiral **Miklós Horthy**, and in creating the latter's legend.

After the counterrevolutionary forces had entered Budapest, Gömbös moved to the reserves at the end of 1919. In January 1920 he was elected MP, and he soon became a leader of the extreme nationalist right wing and an advocate of the so-called free elections of the king. He demanded the introduction of a dictatorship, anti-Jewish laws, and a crackdown on HSR adherents and the "destructive" press. Mobilizing the HDA, in October 1921 he helped avert a second attempt by Charles IV Habsburg to return to the Hungarian throne. Owing to his anti-revolutionary attitude and considerable popular support, Gömbös became a politician with a future in the eyes of Regent Horthy. In February 1922, Gömbös became deputy chairman of the ruling Unity Party (Egységes Párt), newly established by Prime Minister Bethlen, but the conservative-liberal party majority, disapproving of Gömbös' radicalism, pushed him into the background. Because of an ever-growing conflict with Bethlen, in August 1923 Gömbös left the party and founded the racist Hungarian National Independence Party. The success of Bethlen's consolidation policy weakened Gömbös' influence. Therefore, he dissolved his party in September 1928 and returned with the majority of its members to the government party.

From September 1928 to October 1929, Gömbös was secretary of state in the NDM. In 1929 Horthy awarded him the title of "hero" (*vitéz*) and promoted him to the rank of retired general. From October 1929 he was national defense minister, gaining considerable success in modernizing the army. On 1 October 1932, when the Great Depression was at its worst, Gömbös became prime minister, at the same time remaining minister of national defense. His so-called National Labor Plan, consisting of ninety-five points, was the first government program in Hungary. The plan included agrarian and fiscal reforms, debt conversion, support for exporters, and enhanced social benefits. However, its implementation encountered difficulties. Giving up some of his radical ideas, Gömbös had to search for compromise with more moderate political and economic groups. Initially, he was distinctly successful in matters to do with the economy and foreign policy. His government helped the country recover from the Great Depression. German-Hungarian trade agreements of 1933 and 1934 and the development of Hungarian-Italian-Austrian economic and political cooperation as of 1934 made it possible for Hungary to export large quantities of agrarian products at figures above world prices. As a result, the situation in the country improved. The economy also got a boost in 1932, when the Entente states wrote off the remainder of war damages, and in 1933, when the League of Nations lowered the installments on loans that Hungary had incurred in the 1920s. In foreign policy, Gömbös took advantage of the temporary vacuum in Central Europe, declaring, with Italian and Austrian support, a peaceful revision of the Treaty of Trianon. He also hoped for German support and was the first foreign politician to pay Hitler a visit in June 1933.

In spring 1934 Gömbös announced an accelerated implementation of reforms. He intended to abolish public elections, commence a wide-scale program of peasant colonization, and introduce a corporationist system similar to the one in Italy. He also sought to turn the government National Unity Party (Nemzeti Egység Pártja [NUP]), reorganized in 1932, into a mass, Fascist-type organization. Both conservative-liberal politicians and the legal left-wing opposition attacked the plans vigorously. Trying to break the resistance, in March 1935 Gömbös persuaded Horthy to dissolve the parliament and call for a new election. Gömbös won the election, and the regent again entrusted him with creating a cabinet. When Bethlen left the government party in March 1935, Gömbös assumed its de facto leadership, but his attempts to turn the NUP into a mass totalitarian organization ended in failure. In addition to Horthy's growing distrust of Gömbös and the resistance from conservative circles and left-wing forces, a major factor that thwarted Gömbös's plans was kidney disease. Terminally ill, he was treated in a clinic in Munich, but the treatment was unsuccessful. (JT)

Sources: *Biographisches Lexikon*, vol. 1; *Magyar Nagylexikon*, vol. 8 (Budapest, 1999); *Nagy Képes Milleniumi Arcképcsarnok* (Budapest. 1999); *Új Magyar Életrajzi Lexikon*, vol. 2 (Budapest, 2001); C. A. Macartney, *October Fifteenth: A History of Modern Hungary*, vols. 1–2 (Edinburgh, 1957–61); *The Confidential Papers of Admiral Horthy* (Budapest, 1965); *1932–1935: Drei Jahre Regierung Gömbös* (Budapest, 1935); Steven Bela Vardy, *Historical Dictionary of Hungary* (Lanham, Md., 1997); Jenó Gergely, *Gömbös Gyula politikai pályakép* (Budapest, 2001); József Vongó, *Gömbös Gyula és a jobboldali radikalizmus: Tanulmányok* (Pecs, 2001).

GOMBROWICZ Witold (4 August 1904, Małoszyce, near Opatów–25 July 1969, Vence, France), Polish writer. Gombrowicz graduated from St. Stanislas Kostka High School in Warsaw in 1922 and from the Law Department at the University of Warsaw in 1927. Then he moved to Paris, where he studied philosophy and economics. After his return home, he briefly practiced law in Warsaw but soon devoted himself exclusively to literature. From 1934 he worked with the daily press and literary magazines, concentrating on literary criticism in (among others) *Kurier Poranny*. In August 1939 he traveled to Argentina, where he spent World War II. He remained without a steady job for some time until he was employed by the Polish Bank in Buenos Aires (1947–53). Because of his mocking attitude toward patriotism, he was ignored by most of the émigré community. In 1963 he received a Ford Foundation fellowship to travel to West Berlin. Later, he moved to France. In 1967, he was awarded the International Literary Prize of Publishers (Prix Formentor).

Gombrowicz's literary debut was a collection of semi-fantastic stories published as *Pamiętnik z okresu dojrzewania* (A memoir from the period of becoming mature; 1933), later enlarged and put out as *Bakakaj* (1957). The novel that brought him international acclaim was *Ferdydurke* (1937; *Ferdudurke*, 1961), a jeering attack on traditional morality and culture. In his drama *Iwona, księżniczka Burgunda* (1938, staged in 1959; *Ivona, Princess of Burgundy*, 1970), he focused on ugliness that, once allowed in, wreaks havoc in the ducal court. In Argentina he penned the drama *Ślub* (1953; *Marriage*, 1970) and the novel *Trans-Atlantyk* (1953; *Trans-Atlantyk*, 1994). The former was a transcript from a dream that served simultaneously as a parody of a Shakespearian tragedy. The latter best reflects Gombrowicz's critical attitude toward his native cultural tradition. In his *Pornografia* (1960; *Pornografia*, 1967), which is set in Poland under Nazi occupation, the author focused on the vital strength of youth but also its capacity for crime. In *Kosmos* (1965; *Cosmos*, 1967) he delved into the psychology of the erotic. The last play he wrote was *Operetka* (Operetta), published in the third volume of his *Dziennik* (Diary; 1988). Written in the convention of a historiosophical grotesque, the play reviews the events of the twentieth century cast as a fashion show. From 1953, Gombrowicz kept a diary, which was published in Paris in three volumes (1957–66). He mixed in it personal, often banal, observations with polemics and philosophical considerations, thus constructing a peculiar portrait of himself. He was a subversive and often sacrilegious writer, annoying with his egotism, skepticism, and anarchy but at the same time dazzling and intellectually prolific. The generation that survived World War II had a negative attitude toward his move to Argentina, which was treated as an escape, and his open dissociation from the war. He was sharply criticized both in the émigré community and in Poland for undermining the sense of Polishness. However, he was also appreciated for his originality and the acuteness of his criticism of the Polish national psyche. Almost all of his works have been translated into over a dozen languages. His eleven-volume *Dzieła zebrane* (Collected works; 1969–77) were published in the West and his fifteen-volume *Dzieła* (Works; 1986–97) in Poland. (PU)

Sources: *Literatura polska XX wieku. Przewodnik encyklopedyczny*, vol. 1 (Warsaw, 2000); Tadeusz Kępiński, *Witold Gombrowicz i świat jego młodości* (Kraków, 1974); Tadeusz Kępiński, *Witold Gombrowicz: Studium portretowe*, vols. 1–2 (Kraków, 1988), Jean-Claude Dedieu, *Witold Gombrowicz* (Paris, 1993); Jan Błoński, *Forma, śmiech i rzeczy ostateczne: Studia o Gombrowiczu* (Kraków, 1994); Joanna Siedlecka, *Jaśnie panicz* (Warsaw, 1997); Janusz Margański, *Gombrowicz—wieczny debiutant* (Kraków, 2001); Jerzy Jarzębski, *Podglądanie Gombrowicza* (Kraków, 2001); Agnieszka Stawiarska, *Gombrowicz w przedwojennej Polsce* (Kraków, 2002).

GOMUŁKA Władysław, pseudonym "Wiesław" (6 February 1905, Białobrzegi Franciszkańskie, near Krosno–1 September 1982, Warsaw), Polish Communist leader. Gomułka came from a working-class family. At fourteen, he finished his education, completing seven grades of school. Then he worked as a locksmith in Krosno, Drohobycz, and Warsaw. He joined the Polish Socialist Party–Left, and from 1925 to 1926 he belonged to the National Peasant Party. In 1926 he joined the Communist Party of Poland (Komunistyczna Partia Polski [KPP]). He also was a full-time organizer of the Trade Union of Chemical Industry Workers, a member of the KPP Central Trade Department (1931–32), and an activist in the Cultural-Educational Association of Workers–Siła (Strength). In 1930 and 1931 he traveled to Moscow to attend congresses of the Trade Unions of the Red International. In 1932 he was arrested and imprisoned in Poland. In 1934, with the assistance of the KPP, he fled to the USSR. He traveled to the Crimea and then to Moscow, where he attended the Lenin School of the Communist International. He returned to Poland under an alias, but he was rearrested and jailed between 1936 and 1939.

During the September campaign of 1939, Gomułka was freed and took part in the defense of Warsaw. Between 1939 and 1942 he lived in Białystok and Lwów (Lviv), joining the Soviet party in 1941. In 1942 he returned to Krosno and became involved with the (Communist) Polish Workers' Party (Polska Partia Robotnicza [PPR]). He also founded the People's Guard in Subcarpathia and later left for Warsaw. Gomułka became the secretary of the PPR Warsaw Committee, a member of the PPR Provisional Central Committee, and the party's propaganda chief. From 18 to 25 February 1943 he negotiated with Poland's official underground Office of the Delegate of the Government in Exile for the Homeland and with clandestine Jewish organizations. However, the PPR demands were unacceptable to those seeking independence for Poland, and the negotiations were broken off. Meanwhile Gomułka co-founded the People's Army and from November 1943 served as the secretary of the PPR Central Committee (CC). His rise in the party hierarchy was facilitated by the deaths of the former leaders, **Marceli Nowotko** and Bolesław Mołojec, as well as by the Gestapo's arrest of **Paweł Finder**. The turnover at the top involved a temporary lack of radio contact with Moscow and mutual suspicions regarding the infiltration of the Communist movement by the Nazi police. That notwithstanding, in August 1944 Gomułka became one of the founding members of the newly established Politburo, and in December 1945 he was proclaimed general secretary of the PPR.

Gomułka was one of the main co-founders of the Home National Council (Krajowa Rada Narodowa [KRN]); the KRN usurped power in Poland to the detriment of the Polish government-in-exile, which it did not recognize. After the KRN assembled a provisional government, Gomułka became the first deputy prime minister. In June 1945 he participated in negotiations in Moscow to create the Provisional Government of National Unity. In July 1945 he was a member of the Polish delegation to the Big Three Conference in Potsdam. In November 1945 he was appointed minister for the Recovered Territories, which greatly enhanced his political standing. Although the Soviet intelligence and security services most influenced the power balance in Poland, Gomułka, as the head of the PPR, condoned their actions, accepting brutal repressions against the independence forces. He was involved in the struggle against the post–Home Army organizations and the Polish Peasant Party, fanatically believing in the righteousness of communism and proclaiming that "we shall never give up the power that we have once captured." His ideas are reflected in his book *W walce o demokrację ludową: Artykuły i przemówienia* (In the struggle for a people's democracy: Articles and speeches; 1947). From 1947, Gomułka served as a deputy in the Constitutional Parliament.

Between 22 and 27 September 1947 Gomułka represented the PPR at the conference of representatives of Communist and proletarian parties in Szklarska Poręba, when the Information Bureau (Cominform) was founded. He delivered two speeches there, even though his position in the power structure was already weakened. Despite embracing communism, he opposed copying certain Soviet models on the "Polish road to socialism," including an acceleration in the collectivization of agriculture. During the PPR CC Plenum of 3 June 1948 Gomułka was accused of "right-nationalist deviation." In September 1948 he was purged as the general secretary of the PPR. However, during the Unification Congress of the Polish Socialist Party and the PPR in December 1948, at Stalin's suggestion, Gomułka was included in the CC of the newly formed Polish United Workers' Party (Polska Zjednoczona Partia Robotnicza [PUWP]). Following the liquidation of the Ministry for the Recovered Territories in January 1949, Gomułka was stripped of his post as deputy prime minister and demoted to deputy chairman of the Supreme Chamber of Control and then to director of the Warsaw branch of the Enterprise for Social Insurance. He was attacked in the media and investigated by the secret police, purged from the PUWP CC (November 1949), arrested (August 1951), stripped of his parliamentary seat, and, finally, thrown out of the party (October 1951). A show trial for him was prepared that involved the arrest and torture of many of his followers.

Gomułka was freed in December 1954 in the wake of the "thaw" following Stalin's death. During an inter-party struggle within the top leadership, he became a candidate for chief of the PUWP. Both the dogmatic Natolin group and the more liberal Puławska faction wooed him. In October 1956 he returned to power triumphantly. Despite the pressure from Soviet armed forces stationed in Poland and the initial objections of the Soviet delegation under **Nikita Khrushchev**, who suddenly visited Warsaw, ultimately the Kremlin accepted the decision of the Eighth Plenum of the PUWP CC of 19–21 October 1956, when Gomułka was coopted to the CC and elected to the Politburo and to the post of PUWP CC first secretary. On 24 October 1956, Gomułka criticized Stalinism, speaking to several hundred thousand Warsaw citizens gathered at Parade Place. On 18 November 1956 he concluded an agreement in Moscow regulating bilateral relations, in particular the status of the Soviet Army in Poland. He accepted the decollectivization of agriculture and concluded a new agreement with the Catholic Church, permitting the release of Primate Cardinal **Stefan Wyszyński** from jail. From 1957 he served as a parliamentary deputy and a member of the Council of State.

Soon, however, Gomułka went back to his old ways. Widespread hopes engendered in the society by his return were quickly extinguished as he halted systemic and cadre changes, even restored some compromised party functionaries to their former positions, and turned to exercising power in an autocratic manner. The Gomułka team's economic policies—renewed investments in heavy and industry and armaments at the expense of consumption, a halt in organizational changes, the promotion of a policy of autarky for Poland, and closing the nation off to modern technologies—brought about economic stagnation. In his intra-party policies, Gomułka struggled against so-called revisionism. The termination of the "liberal" party youth weekly *Po prostu*, the increase in censorship, and anti-revisionist undertakings caused the defection of many intellectuals from the party. Gomułka initiated the great move to build schools: "One thousand schools for the Millennium of Poland"; but during the Millennium of Poland's Christianity (966–1966), he stressed its secular character. His anti-clericalism ushered in a serious crisis in church-state relations during the celebration of the Baptism of Poland in 1966. He constantly invoked the danger from Germany. After the Polish Catholic episcopate published its famous letter to its German counterpart, vowing to "forgive and beg forgiveness," Gomułka led a hostile propaganda campaign spreading hatred against the Church and Germany in 1965 and 1966.

Purges undertaken in Poland's leadership following the Israeli victory over the Arab states in 1967 were of an openly anti-Semitic character. Following the banning of the play *Dziady* (Forefathers' Eve) by Adam Mickiewicz, student demonstrations broke out in March 1968 calling for the freedom of speech. The demonstrations brought about an anti-Semitic and anti-intelligentsia propaganda campaign of the chauvinistic PUWP faction under **Mieczysław Moczar**. To defend his political standing, Gomułka temporarily supported the campaign. As a result, several thousand members of the intelligentsia of Jewish origin left Poland, damaging the nation's reputation all over the world. The events of March 1968 weakened Gomułka. He strengthened his hand by unequivocally supporting the Soviet invasion of Czechoslovakia in August 1968. The March 1968 events negatively affected education and university life and further demoralized society.

In foreign policy, Gomułka believed that loyalty to the Kremlin would preempt any threat stemming from a possible accord between the USSR and West Germany. Along with other Warsaw Pact nations, on 7 December 1970 Poland concluded a pact with West Germany that normalized mutual relations. Since the pact confirmed Poland's western borders, it is considered to be the most important achievement of Gomułka's foreign policy. Increases in meat prices announced on 13 December 1970 triggered worker riots on the Baltic Sea Coast; the riots broke out the following day and were bloodily put down on Gomułka's orders. Consequently, on 20 December 1970, he was purged as the first secretary of the PUWP CC. In February 1971 he was suspended as a member of the CC; in May 1972 he lost his membership in the Council of State and soon after was stripped of his parliamentary seat. When he retired, Gomułka wrote his memoirs, which were published in 1994 as *Pamiętniki* (Memoirs) in two volumes. (PK)

Sources: *Słownik polityków polskich XX w.* (Poznań, 1998); *Słownik biograficzny działaczy polskiego ruchu robotniczego*, vol. 2 (Warsaw, 1987); *The Cambridge Biographical Encyclopedia* (Cambridge, 1998); Nicholas Bethell, *Gomulka, His Poland and His Communism* (London, 1969); *Nowotko-Mołojec: Z początków PPR. Nieznane relacje Władysława Gomułki i Franciszka Jóźwiaka* (London, 1986); Andrzej Werblan, *Władysław Gomułka, sekretarz generalny PPR* (Warsaw, 1988); Paweł Machcewicz, *Władysław Gomułka* (Warsaw, 1995);

Antoni Dudek, *Państwo i Kościół w Polsce 1945–1970* (Kraków, 1995); Jerzy Eisler, *Grudzień 1970* (Warsaw, 2000); Dariusz Stola, *Kampania antysyjonistyczna w Polsce 1967–1968* (Warsaw, 2000).

GÖNCZ Árpád (10 February 1922, Budapest), Hungarian politician. Born into an educated family, in 1944 Göncz graduated in law from the University of Budapest. In February 1944 he was recruited into the army. He was taken prisoner of war by the Soviets several times but always managed to escape. In early 1945 he ran away from his unit in Germany and took part in the armed anti-German resistance as a member of the Freedom Front of Hungarian Students. In the summer of 1945 he joined the Independent Smallholders' Party (ISP). From 1946 to 1948 he worked in the ISP headquarters, and for some time he was a personal secretary to the party's general secretary, **Béla Kovács**. In 1947–48, Göncz presided over the Budapest committee of Independent Youth, which was the ISP youth organization. He also edited its weekly, *Nemzedék*, and was secretary of the ISP parliamentary club. When in February 1947 the Soviet security organs arrested Kovács, Göncz was arrested by the Hungarian security police, but he was released after a few weeks. After the ISP was crushed by the Communists, from 1948 Göncz worked as a blue-collar laborer. In 1951 he was employed as senior construction worker in a drainage company, and in 1952 he enrolled at the Crop Production Department of the Agricultural Academy in Gödöllő, near Budapest, where he completed four years of studies but did not graduate.

During the 1956 revolution Göncz worked in the re-organized Hungarian Peasant Union. He passed a memorandum to the ambassador of India, Krishna Menon, from the Hungarian Democratic Independence Movement; the memorandum was based on the work by **István Bibó**, *Tervezet a magyar kérdés megoldására* (Draft compromise solution to the Hungarian question). In February 1957 Göncz passed abroad a manuscript by **Imre Nagy** written in 1955–56. In May 1957 Göncz was arrested and tried, along with Bibó and his aides. On 2 August 1958 he was sentenced to life imprisonment. In March 1960 he took part in a hunger strike of political prisoners in Vác Prison. He learned English there and practiced translation. In 1963 he was amnestied, and from 1964 he worked in the drainage company again. He attempted to complete his agricultural degree but was expelled from the Agricultural Academy. From 1965 he worked as a writer and translator of literature. In 1978–81 he lectured at the University of Szeged. In 1979–80 he co-edited *Bibó István-emlékkönyv* (The István Bibó memorial book), finally published in the samizdat press and in Switzerland. He also signed democratic opposition addresses to the authorities.

In the fall of 1988 Göncz was one of the founders of the (liberal) Alliance of Free Democrats (Szabad Demokraták Szövetsége [AFD]); then he was its spokesman and a member of the AFD National Council. He also was among the founders and deputy chairman of the Committee for Historical Rectification, which succeeded in organizing a solemn memorial service for Imre Nagy, his aides, and all the victims of the 1956 revolution; it was aimed at maintaining the memory of the revolution and recognizing and honoring the insurgents. From 1989 Göncz presided over the Budapest committee of the League of Human Rights, and from December 1989 to September 1990, over the Association of Hungarian Writers. Later he was its honorary chairman. In May 1990 he was elected an MP on behalf of the AFD. On the basis of an agreement between the Hungarian Democratic Forum, which won the election, and the largest opposition faction, the AFD, Göncz became speaker of the parliament and, in accord with the constitution, provisional president. On 3 August 1990 he was elected president for the first term, and on 19 June 1995, for the second term. He held this position until 4 August 2000. During his terms in office, Göncz was the most popular politician in Hungary. He contributed substantially to the stabilization of the young Hungarian democracy and gained much prestige abroad. He strongly supported the economic transformation toward a market economy and a pro-Western course in foreign policy. He translated into Hungarian a number of contemporary and classical works by English, American, and Japanese authors, including J. R. R. Tolkien. In 1990 his *Plays and Other Writings* were published in the United States, and in 1994 he published his memoirs, *Beszélgetések az elnökkel* (Conversations with the president). (JT)

Sources: *Magyar Nagylexikon*, vol. 8 (Budapest, 1999); *Ki kicsoda 2000* (Budapest, 2001); *Europa Środkowa i Wschodnia, 1991–1999* (Warsaw, 1993–2001); Steven Bela Vardy, *Historical Dictionary of Hungary* (Lanham, Md., 1997); Jerzy Kochanowski, *Węgry* (Warsaw, 1997); Attila Szakolczay, *Az 1956-os forradalom és szabadságharc* (Budapest, 2001); www.rulers.org.

GOPPERS Karlis (2 April 1876, Planu, near Valka–June 1941, Dreilini, near Riga), Latvian general. In 1896 Goppers graduated from an officer training school in Vilnius. Afterwards he served in the Russian Army. In 1912 he became captain. During World War I he commanded a battalion, and from 1915, already a colonel, he was in command of a regiment. In 1917 he became commander of the First Brigade of the Latvian Rifles. Sent far inside Russia in December 1917, he took part in the domestic war; he commanded military units of the Whites at Samara and later assumed the command of the Twenty-first Infantry

Division in Siberia. In June 1920 he returned to Latvia. On 13 August 1920 he was promoted to general. At this time he directed the founding group of Latvian scouting. He remained the chief of this scouting organization until his death. From 1924 he commanded an infantry division. Goppers published many works on the history and theory of military science. After the Soviet invasion of Latvia, in September 1940 he was arrested by the NKVD. He was kept in prison in Riga and was executed there before the German invasion. In 1944 his body was recognized among the victims murdered by the NKVD. (WR/EJ)

Sources: *Latvijas darbinieku galerija 1918–1928* (Riga, 1929); *Latviešu konversacijas vardnica*, vol. 6 (Riga, 1931); Testimony by Ants Grantskalns before the House of Representatives Select Committee to Investigate Incorporation of the Baltic States, *First Interim Report*, 1st Session (Washington, D.C., 1954).

GORBUNOVS Anatolijs (10 February 1942, Pildas), Latvian post–Communist politician. Born into a Russified Latvian peasant family, Gorbunovs graduated from a technical high school in Riga in 1959, from the Construction Department of the Riga Polytechnic Institute in 1970, and from the Academy of Social Sciences in Moscow in 1978. From 1959 he worked as a technician in a kolkhoz. From 1966 he was a member of the Communist Party of the Soviet Union, and in 1967 he became head of the Komsomol in Riga. From 1974 he was active in various levels of the party structure in Riga, and from 1980 to 1985 he was secretary and first secretary of the Riga regional and city committee. As a result of his association with intellectuals, mainly the poet Jānis Peters, Gorbunovs' views evolved toward national communism. In 1984–85 he headed the Administration Department of the Central Committee (CC) of the Communist Party of Latvia (CPL), and in 1985–88 he was CC secretary for ideological affairs and a member of the CPL CC Politburo. On 30 September 1988 he became chairman of the Supreme Council of the Latvian SSR.

When on 4 May 1990 the Supreme Council of the Latvian SSR declared de jure the sovereignty of Latvia, removing the terms "Socialist" and "Soviet" from the country's name, Gorbunovs was recognized as the head of the new state. On 12 May, along with the chairmen of the Supreme Councils of the Estonian and Lithuanian republics, **Arnold Rüütel** and **Vytautas Landsbergis** respectively, Gorbunovs renewed the treaty of Baltic cooperation of 1934. Under threats from Moscow, in mid-May Gorbunovs suggested a suspension of the declaration of sovereignty, but he was outvoted in the Supreme Council. When Soviet special forces attacked the Ministry of Interior in Riga in January 1991, Gorbunovs continued efforts in

favor of Latvia's independence. During a referendum on the future shape of the Soviet Union in March 1991, he stood up for Latvia's independence. During the Moscow putsch, on 19 August 1991 he, along with Prime Minister **Ivars Godmanis**, issued a declaration that the coup leaders had acted illegally. The next day, the Latvian Supreme Council proclaimed full independence, and Gorbunovs stayed in office as Latvia's head of state. After the breakup of the CPL, from April 1990 Gorbunovs belonged to the Independent Communist Party of Latvia. When the new constitution was passed, from 15 September 1992 he was the provisional president of Latvia. His very high ratings were hurt by his stand on the citizenship rights of Russians (he opposed excessively restrictive policies in this respect) and the economic problems of the new state, but he managed to avoid the most unpopular decisions. On 8 July 1993 he handed over power to the newly elected president, **Guntis Ulmanis**. From 1993 Gorbunovs was an MP on behalf of the liberal Latvia's Way (Latvijas Ceļš) party, and in 1993–95 he was speaker of the parliament. Later he headed several parliamentary commissions. From December 1995 to July 1999 he was deputy prime minister and then, until December 2002, minister of transportation. (EJ)

Sources: *Latvijas Padomju Enciklopēdija*, vol. 3 (Riga, 1983); *Who Is Who in Latvia 1996: Biographical Dictionary* (Riga, 1996); *Kas ir kas Latvijâ* (Riga, 1999); Romuald J. Misiunas and Rein Taagepera, *The Baltic States: Years of Dependence, 1940–1990* (Berkeley, 1993); Anatol Lieven, *The Baltic Revolution* (New Haven, 1993); *Europa Środkowo-Wschodnia 1993* (Warsaw, 1995); Juris Dreifelds, *Latvia in Transition* (Cambridge, 1996); Andrejs Plakans, *Historical Dictionary of Latvia* (Lanham, Md., 1997).

GÓRECKI Henryk Mikołaj (6 December 1933, Czernica, near Rybnik), Polish composer. Górecki graduated from high school in Rydułtowy, and in 1955–60 he studied composition at the State Higher Musical School in Katowice. Later this school changed its name to the Musical Academy, and Górecki was its rector from 1975 to 1979 and professor from 1977. From 1994 he was a member of the Polish Academy of Arts and Sciences. Initially his compositions, such as *Epitafium* (1958), were influenced by dodecaphony and pointillism. The first performances of his works were spectacular events at International Festivals of Contemporary Music known as Warsaw Autumn. Górecki was one of the pioneers of aleatoric music but maintained his own style, characterized by vitality and an intensity of emotion. In his *First Symphony* (1959), *Zderzenia* (Clashes; 1960), and *Genesis I–III* (1961–63) he employed masses of sound and obsessional repetitions. Through archaizing his music in the late 1960s— recognizable in *Trzy utwory w dawnym stylu* (Three pieces in the old style; 1963) and *Muzyka staropolska*

(Old Polish music; 1969)—he arrived at the neo-tonalism of his *Second* and *Third Symphonies* (1972 and 1976), the psalm *Beatus Vir* (1979), and *Concerto for Harpsichord and String Orchestra* (1980). In 1993 his *Third Symphony* became an unprecedented best seller, entering the charts and competing with pop music. More than seven hundred thousand copies of the record of this composition were sold, the most ever in the history of contemporary symphonic music. Górecki received the Recording of the Year award in 1993 and the Classical Music Award in 1994. (WR)

Sources: Thomas Adrian, *Górecki* (Oxford, 1997); *Britannica: Edycja polska*, vol. 14 (Poznań, 2000).

GÓRECKI Roman (27 August 1889, Stara Sól, Eastern Galicia–9 August 1946, Whitchurch, Shropshire, England), Polish general and politician. Upon graduating from a high school in Tarnów, Górecki enrolled in the law school at the University of Lvov, where he received his doctorate in 1914. He belonged to the Zarzewie (Spark) group, which was a splinter organization of the secret Union of Polish Youth–Zet. In 1909 he joined the Polish Riflemen Teams, training independent cadres for the struggle against Russia. Between 1914 and 1916, he fought in the Second Brigade of the Polish Legions. During the Oath Crisis, he remained in the service, but in 1918 he co-authored a plan for the Polish Auxiliary Corps to abandon the Austro-Hungarian forces and break through the Russian front near Rarańcza. Consequently, he was imprisoned at Huszt and court-martialed, but the charges against him were dropped because of an amnesty. Górecki described his adventures in *Z moich wspomnień* (From my recollections; 1924) and *W obliczu śmierci* (Facing death; 1933). He joined the Polish Army at the end of 1918. In 1919 he was dispatched to France to study military administration. In July 1923 he was promoted to general and appointed chief of the Military Controller Corps. Following the coup d'état of May 1926, he became deputy minister of military affairs. In 1927 he was nominated chairman of the Bank of the Home Economy (Bank Gospodarstwa Krajowego [BGK]) as a close confidant of **Józef Piłsudski**. He also sat on numerous boards of state-owned companies, exerting enormous influence on the functioning of the so-called state complex. From October 1935 to May 1936, he served as minister of industry and trade but later returned to his old post at the BGK. At the beginning of the 1920s he became a member of the Grand National Lodge. In 1928 he was appointed chairman of the largest veterans' organization subordinated to the ruling regime. Following the collapse of Poland in September 1939, he was an émigré in Paris, London, and Glasgow, where he lectured on banking. Górecki authored several works, including *Rola BGK w życiu gospodarczym Polski* (The role of the BGK in Poland's economic life; 1928); *Le développement économique de la Pologne* (1935; *Poland and Her Economic Development*, 1935); and *Gospodarczy dorobek Polski w latach 1918–1938* (The economic achievements of Poland between 1918 and 1938; 1946). (WR)

Sources: *PSB*, vol. 8; Stanisław Łoza, *Czy wiesz kto to jest* (Warsaw, 1937); Janusz Jędrzejewicz, ed., *Wspomnienia legionowe*, vol. 1 (Warsaw, 1924); Stanisław Głąbiński, *Wspomnienia polityczne* (Pelplin, 1939); Zbigniew Landau, *Bank Gospodarstwa Krajowego* (Warsaw, 1993); Ludwik Hass, *Masoneria polska XX wieku* (Warsaw, 1996).

GORKIĆ Milan [originally Josip Čižinski] (1904, Sarajevo–1937? USSR), Yugoslav Communist activist. The son of an Austro-Hungarian official from Transcarpathian Ruthenia, in 1919 Gorkić joined the radical leftist groups that founded the Communist Party of Yugoslavia (CPY). In 1922 he took part in a conference of Communist youth in Vienna, and then he went to Moscow. He studied in the Comintern school and advanced in the apparatus of the Communist Youth International (CYI) under his adopted name. From 1924 he was a member of the CYI Executive Committee, and in 1928 he became its secretary. He also joined the CPY Central Committee and its Politburo. Supported by Nikolay Bukharin, in 1932 Gorkić became CPY general secretary. He directed the party from Moscow and Vienna. He also undertook secret trips to Yugoslavia. For instance, in 1934 he presided over a clandestine national party conference in Ljubljana. In 1935 he headed the Yugoslav delegation to the Seventh Congress of the Comintern and became deputy member of its Executive Committee and the only representative of the Yugoslav party. In 1936 the party headquarters were moved to Paris, so Gorkić commuted between the Soviet and French capitals. In June 1937 he was called to Moscow by the Comintern leadership. Upon arrival, he was arrested, sentenced to death, and soon executed. His first wife, Betty Glane, met the same fate. (WR)

Sources: Lazitch; Adam B. Ulam, *Tito and the Cominform* (Westport, Conn., 1952); Milovan Džilas, *Memoir of a Revolutionary* (New York, 1973); Ivan Ocak, *Gorkić: Život, rad i pogibja* (Zagreb, 1988).

GOTOVAC Vlado (18 September 1930, Imotski, Dalmatia–7 December 2000, Rome), Croatian writer and politician. During the "Croatian Spring" of 1971 Gotovac edited the weekly *Hrvatski Tjednik*, demanding democracy and national freedoms. He was arrested for an interview he gave on Swedish television and spent three years in prison. In 1977 he was temporarily arrested again. In June 1981 he was sentenced to two years in prison for his contacts with émigré circles. In May 1989 he co-founded the Croatian Social Liberal Party (Hrvatska Socijalno-Liberalna Stranka [HSLS]), the first non-Communist party in Croatia. During the rule of **Franjo Tudjman** it was the second largest political party in Croatia. Gotovac openly criticized the nationalist and authoritarian regime of Tudjman. In 1993, along with five other intellectuals, he demanded Tudjman's resignation because of Croatia's intervention in the Bosnian war. From 1995 Gotovac was an MP, and in 1996–97 he was the HSLS chairman. In 1997 he ran in the presidential elections against Tudjman, but he lost. After the elections of January 2000 the HSLS entered the ruling coalition. Gotovac authored intellectual lyricsthat alluded to the poetry of T. S. Eliot, including *Pjesme od uvijek* (Eternal poems; 1956), *Tri slučaja* (Three cases; 1981), as well as essays collected in *Princip dela* (The principle of the work; 1966) and *Moj slučaj* (My case; 1989). (WR)

Sources: *Wielka encyklopedia PWN*, vol. 10 (Warsaw, 2002); Ante Čuvalo, *The Croatian National Movement 1966–1972* (Boulder, Colo., 1990); Milovan Baletić, ed., *Ljudi iz 1971: Prekinuta šutnja* (Zagreb, 1990); Robert Stallaerst and Jeannine Laurens, *Historical Dictionary of Croatia* (Lanham, Md., 1995); www.rulers.org.

GOTTWALD Klement (23 November 1896, Dedice–14 March 1953, Moscow), Communist leader of Czechoslovakia. Gottwald came from a peasant family but was born out of an illegitimate relationship. At the age of twelve he was sent to Vienna, where he was to learn the trade of carpentry. It was there that he joined the youth unit of the Social Democratic Party. After his return to his native Moravia, in 1915 he was inducted into the Austrian Army. On the wave of radical Socialist agitation in October 1918 he deserted from the Italian front, and he joined the then forming Czech army in Brno. There he was one of the most ardent revolutionary agitators, and Lenin's work *State and Revolution* was a beacon for him. When the Czechoslovak Social Democratic Party split in September, Gottwald supported the Bolshevik faction, which founded the Communist Party of Czechoslovakia (Komunisticka Strana Československa [CPC]). From 1922 to 1925 Gottwald edited the Communist paper *Pravda* in Ostrava and also co-organized the Communist Party of Slovakia. At the Third Congress of the CPC in October 1925 he joined the Central Committee (CC) of the party, and in 1926 he entered its Politburo, where he was responsible for propaganda and agitation. In 1928 he was a member of the CPC delegation to the Sixth Congress of the Communist International, and he joined the Executive Committee of the Comintern.

At the Fifth Congress of the CPC in February 1929 Gottwald assumed the post of secretary general of the party, and soon he was elected an MP in Prague. As a member of official party delegations, he repeatedly went to congresses and plenums of the Executive Committee (EC) of the Comintern to Moscow. From 1929 he belonged to the Presidium of the EC, where he was a member of its strict leadership. From August 1934 he lived almost uninterruptedly in Moscow, taking part in Stalin's game as one of his close associates. From 1935 he was also a member of the EC Secretariat. As a representative of the Stalinist leadership of the Comintern, in 1937 Gottwald communicated the Kremlin's directives on the civil war in Spain to seventeen representatives of West European parties. In November 1938, after the Munich Agreement, he returned to Moscow, where he worked in the Comintern's executive until its formal dissolution in 1943. In fact, he continued to exercise his functions within the framework of a special department of the CC of the All-Russian Communist Party (Bolsheviks). At that time he translated Stalin's *Problems of Leninism* into the Czech.

During talks with President **Edvard Beneš** in Moscow (December 1943) Gottwald came to the fore as the leading representative of Communists within the framework of the Czechoslovak National Front. In the coalition cabinet that was installed in Košice in April 1945, Gottwald served as deputy prime minister, supporting, for example, the ceding of the Transcarpathian Ukraine to the USSR. In return, he counted on the Kremlin's support on the incorporation of the western part of Teschen Silesia (Zaolzie) and the Kłodzko Basin into Czechoslovakia, but Stalin agreed to only the former. After the elections of 26 May 1946 Gottwald, as leader of the party that obtained a relative majority of votes (31 percent), became head of the government, formed of nine Communists and twelve members of other parties. He still presented himself and the Communist Party as the guardians of democracy, but in practice he supervised the CPC's takeover of full power, appointing party functionaries to the key posts of ministers of interior and information. After a meeting with Stalin in September 1946 Gottwald announced that Czechoslovakia would follow its own version of socialism, planned by the CPC and based upon a parliamentary majority. At the same time, though, he supported the arrests of the Slovak Ludaks (the followers of Reverend **Andrej Hlinka**) and the Czech agrarians, who were accused of "plotting" against the state. Although at first Gottwald did not want to recognize the Polish minority in Zaolzie, under Soviet pressure in March

1947 he finally signed a treaty of friendship and cooperation with the Polish government of **Józef Cyrankiewicz**. In July 1947 Gottwald's government rejected the American offer to include Czechoslovakia in the Marshall Plan. In September 1947 he signed an agreement on a special property tax bill with the Socialists; this added to the popularity of the Communists, who dominated the trade unions and the security apparatus and had collaborators in all other parties, especially among the Socialists.

On 17 February 1948 Gottwald suspended a government meeting, at which non-Communist ministers demanded the withdrawal of the appointments of Communists to key posts in the Ministry of Interior. When on 20 February these ministers resigned, Gottwald did not announce the resignation of the government, but taking advantage of Communist-prompted street demonstrations and blackmail on the part of the USSR Embassy, a few days later he reconstructed the cabinet with a Communist majority. Despite his declarations that the government's activities would be "constitutional" and "democratic," in practice he forced ailing President Beneš to step down, and on 14 June 1948 Gottwald assumed the presidency. In a short time the CPC leadership, with Gottwald as head, carried out the Sovietization of Czechoslovakia by outlawing opposition parties, persecuting their activists, and unleashing police terror. Gottwald supervised changes in the economic system, the collectivization of agriculture, mass arrests, and purges in the party, all in the name of a struggle against Titoism and cosmopolitanism. During the party purges he removed (among others) his close party associate **Rudolph Slánský**, against whom he gave extensive testimony. Slánský and thirteen others were sentenced to death and executed in 1952. Gottwald was known for his excessive use of alcohol. At Stalin's funeral in March 1953 he was taken ill, and soon after he died. His publications include *Deset let* (Ten years; 1946). After his death a collection of his writings was issued as *Spisy* (10 vols.; 1955–58). (WR)

Sources: *ČBS*; Lazitch; *The Times*, 16 March 1953; *Klement Gottwald: Bibliografická pomůcka* (Brno, 1976); Jitka Bilková, *Klement Gottwald: Život a dílo. Výberove bibliografie* (Prague, 1983); *Klement Gottwald: Revolucionař a politik. Sborník statí* (Prague, 1986); Karel Kaplan, *The Short March: The Communist Takeover in Czechoslovakia 1945–1948* (London, 1987).

GOŹDZIK Lechosław (21 January 1931, Tomaszów Mazowiecki), Polish social activist. From 1945 Goździk belonged to the (Communist) Union of Struggling Youth and then to the Polish Youth Union (Związek Młodzieży Polskiej [ZMP]). In 1946 he joined the Polish Workers' Party, and from December 1948 he was a member of the (Communist) Polish United Workers' Party (Polska Zjednoczona Partia Robotnicza [PUWP]). From 1953 he worked in the Passenger Car Factory in the Warsaw quarter of Żerań. In 1955 he became secretary of its PUWP Factory Committee. He criticized social and political relations in Poland at a meeting of Warsaw PUWP activists in April 1956. He entered into contact with critical journalists—for example, from the weekly *Po prostu*—and with ZMP activists from Warsaw University, making the Żerań factory a center of spontaneous political activity. He co-initiated the first workers' council, the statute for which was announced in September 1956. During the breakthrough days of 19–21 October 1956 Goździk organized rallies in support of party reformers, which made it difficult for the neo-Stalinists to act. In agreement with the PUWP Warsaw Committee, he spoke at a rally in the Warsaw Polytechnic, bringing emotions under control and stopping a demonstration heading for the Soviet Embassy. Goździk enjoyed huge popularity as the leader of Warsaw workers. After the October 1956 breakthrough he favored extending the power of the workers' councils by granting them the right to elect directors and to share in management responsibilities. This was meant as a step toward a truly socialized Socialist economy. He also advocated the necessity to reform the party itself—for instance, through vertical contacts among party organizations and direct elections of delegates to the party congresses in large factories and offices.

Gradually sidelined by the party apparatus, before the parliamentary elections of January 1957 Goździk was placed low on the candidate lists, which practically prevented him from being elected. In 1958 he was recalled from his party functions, and in 1959 he was moved to an electronics factory, Warel. In 1964 he graduated from an evening technical high school, and in 1965 he left for Świnoujście, where he became a fisherman and owner of a fish cutter. In 1970 he left the PUWP. In September 1981 he was an honorary guest at the Solidarity congress. In 1984–90 he was deputy chairman of the Main Administration of the Fishermen's Association; in 1991 he co-organized the Association of Fish Shipowners and was its chairman from 1991 to 1994. In 1993 he ran in the parliamentary elections on behalf of the Democratic Union, but he lost. In 1994–95 he presided over the Świnoujście City Council. (AF)

Sources: *Wielka encyklopedia PWN*, vol. 10 (Warsaw, 2002); Kazimierz Kloc, *Historia samorządu robotniczego w PRL 1944–1989* (Warsaw, 1992); Jerzy Eisler and Robert Kupiecki, *Na zakręcie historii—rok 1956* (Warsaw, 1992); Paweł Machcewicz, *Polski rok 1956* (Warsaw, 1993); Wiesław Władyka, *Październik '56* (Warsaw, 1994); Paweł Machcewicz, ed., *Kampania wyborcza i wybory do Sejmu 20 stycznia 1957* (Warsaw, 2000).

GRABSKI Stanisław (5 April 1871, Borów, near Łowicz–6 May 1949, Sulejówek), Polish politician, economist, and pundit. Grabski was born into a family of landed nobility and was the brother of **Władysław Grabski**. He encountered socialism at his Warsaw high school. Subsequently, he began to work with the editorial board of *Głos* and participated in educational activities for the working class. In 1890 he joined the Union of Polish Workers (UPW). While at the mathematical-biological department of the University of Warsaw, he met **Roman Dmowski**. After beginning studies in the social sciences and philosophy in Berlin in 1991, he established contacts with the local worker activists and edited *Gazeta Robotnicza*. To escape arrest, he fled to Paris, where he enrolled at the École des Sciences Politiques. He represented the UPW at a Paris congress in 1892 that founded the Polish Socialist Party (Polska Partia Socjalistyczna [PPS]). As a PPS representative, Grabski participated in the International Socialist Congress in Zurich. Gradually, however, he came to embrace the ideology of the National League. In 1893 he enrolled at the University of Bern, where he received a Ph.D. in 1894. In 1899 he became the librarian of the National Polish Museum in Rapersville. He contributed articles to *Przedświt*. He came to abandon the principles of class struggle in favor of social and national solidarity. However, he continued to maintain good personal relations with various Socialists, including **Józef Piłsudski**.

In 1903, Grabski arrived in Kraków, where he taught at the Philosophy Department of the Jagiellonian University. He also lectured in economics and became involved in charity and social work, supporting the Farming Society and participating in the founding of milk firms. In 1905 he moved to Lwów (Lviv), where he became an agricultural official in the Homeland Department and a professor at the Agricultural Academy in Dublany. As an assistant professor, he taught philosophy and methodology in the social sciences at the University of Lwów. In 1906 he joined the National League and was coopted to its Central Committee. In 1906 he became a secretary and an expert on agriculture and homeland autonomy in the Polish Club in the Russian State Duma. Following the dissolution of the First Duma, Grabski returned to Lwów, where he was active in the National Democratic Party as its deputy chairman. He supervised the publication of *Słowo Polskie*. On his initiative, the National Democrats began organizing paramilitary units to compete with the Riflemen Teams and Unions.

In 1914 Grabski co-founded the Galician Central National Committee, which opposed insurrection against Russia. He published *Zjednoczenie*. In 1915, as Austro-Hungarian troops approached Lwów, he left for Kiev. Following the fall of the tsar in March 1917, he advocated the formation of a Polish army in Russia. He participated in the Council of the Polish Inter-Party Union in Moscow, working for its Department of Foreign Affairs. After the Bolshevik revolution, Grabski was coopted in Kiev to the Supreme Polish Military Committee (Naczpol), leading the organization of Polish military units in Russia. Then he traveled via England to France, where he was invited to join the National Polish Committee (Komitet Narodowy Polski [KNP]), a legally recognized representative of Poland in the West. He authored an ethnographic map of Poland and a proposal for its eastern borders; Grabski's version was more moderate than that espoused by Dmowski. Grabski assisted in the work of the Polish delegation at the Paris Peace Conference. Following the establishment of the government of **Jędrzej Moraczewski** in Warsaw, Grabski returned home as a delegate of the KNP and of the supreme commander of the Allied armies, Marshal Ferdinand Foch. In 1919, Grabski was elected to the Constituent Assembly (Sejm). He also continued to represent the National Democrats in the parliament between 1922 and 1928. He initiated the foundation of the rightist Popular-National Union. As chairman of the parliamentary commission for foreign affairs, he participated in negotiations with the Czechs to resolve the conflict over Tsechen. He opposed the agreement between Piłsudski and **Symon Petlura**. Following the armistice of October 1920, Grabski participated in the Polish delegation negotiating with the Bolsheviks. He opposed the annexation of Minsk to Poland. In the Treaty of Riga of March 1921, his concept of the Polish-Soviet border was the one accepted; it included the annexation of a swath of land known as "the Grabski Corridor." In 1921 he participated in a Polish diplomatic mission to Paris concerning Upper Silesia; there he convinced the French to delegate the matter to the League of Nations.

In 1920 Grabski advocated the dissolution of the National League, and when his proposal was rejected, he left the organization. His political influence visibly waned. He opposed secret and Fascist nationalist organizations. The slogan "Poland for the Poles" he answered with "Poles for Poland." He returned to lecturing at the university and took over as editor-in-chief of *Słowo Polskie*. In October 1923 he was nominated minister for religious confessions and public enlightenment, but in December 1923 he quit, along with the entire government of **Wincenty Witos**. In 1924 Grabski joined a commission to establish the official language in the eastern territories. He submitted a proposal about the language for the schools, but it was vetoed by the left and the national minorities. Grabski then led a mission to the Holy See to conclude a concordat, and he became its co-author in February 1925. In March

1925 he was once again nominated minister of religious confessions and public enlightenment, conducting a school plebiscite in eastern Poland. Following the collapse of the government led by his brother Władysław, he remained at his post in the succeeding governments of **Aleksander Skrzyński** and Witos.

After the coup d'état of May 1926, Grabski withdrew from public life. Following the Soviet invasion of 17 September 1939, he was arrested in Lwów and later sent to Moscow. Released in 1941 because of a Soviet-Polish treaty, he left Moscow for London, where he supported the policy of General **Władysław Sikorski**. He launched the bi-monthly *Jutro Polski*. In 1942 he joined the National Council of the Polish Republic, an advisory organ of the president and government-in-exile, and was elected its chairman. He drew close to the populists. In August 1944, with **Stanisław Mikołajczyk**, Grabski participated in talks with Stalin in Moscow. Accepting the Yalta agreement and the pact founding the Provisional Government of National Unity for Poland, he returned home on 30 June 1945 and became deputy chairman of the Communist-controlled National Home Council. He participated in the Potsdam conference. In 1947 he took over the chair of social systems at the Law School of the University of Warsaw. Grabski authored numerous works in political science and economics, including the following: *Rewolucja* (Revolution; 1921); *Uwagi o bieżącej chwili historycznej Polski* (Remarks on the contemporary historical moment of Poland; 1922); *Kryzys myśli państwowej* (A crisis in state thought; 1927); *Ekonomia społeczna* (Social economics; 1927–32); *Państwo narodowe* (A nation-state; 1929); *Ku lepszej Polsce* (Toward a better Poland; 1937); and *Na nowej drodze* (On a new road; 1946). In 1989 his *Pamiętniki* (Memoirs, 2 vols.) were published. (JS)

Sources: *PSB*, vol. 8; *Słownik polityków polskich XX wieku* (Poznań, 1998); Roman Wapiński, *Narodowa Demokracja 1893–1939* (Wrocław, 1980); Adam Próchnik, *Pierwsze piętnastolecie Polski niepodległej* (Warsaw, 1983); Władysław Pobóg-Malinowski, *Najnowsza historia polityczna Polski*, vol. 2 (London, 1983), vol. 3 (London, 1986); Krystyna Kersten, *Narodziny systemu władzy: Polska 1943–1948* (Poznań, 1990); Jan Zamoyski, *Powrót na mapę* (Warsaw, 1991); Andrzej Nowak, *Polska i trzy Rosje: Studium polityki wschodniej Józefa Piłsudskiego (do kwietnia 1920)* (Kraków, 2001).

GRABSKI Tadeusz (14 March 1929, Warsaw–2 February 1998, Warsaw), Polish Communist activist. In 1951 Grabski graduated from the Higher School of Economics in Poznań, where he received a doctorate in economics. He then served in the military. In 1956 he joined the (Communist) Polish United Workers' Party (Polska Zjednoczona Partia Robotnicza [PUWP]) and assumed managerial posts in industry, including one as the director of the Provincial Conglomerate of Regional Industry Enterprises in Poznań and one as chairman of the board of the Provincial Union of Labor Cooperatives in Poznań. Between 1972 and 1973 he served as chairman of the presidium of the Provincial National Council in Poznań, and from 1973 through 1975, as the provincial governor (*voivode*) of Poznań. Between 1975 and 1979 he was first secretary of the PUWP Provincial Committee in Konin. He was a parliamentary deputy (1976–80) and a member of the PUWP Central Committee (CC) (from December 1975 to February 1980 and from August 1980 to July 1981). In 1979 and 1980, he worked as chief executive of Metra Automatic Systems Enterprises in Poznań. Between 1980 and 1981, Grabski was considered to be the most conservative and pro-Soviet and pro-East German activist in the Communist leadership of Poland. In August 1980 he joined the Politburo, and in September he became secretary of the PUWP CC, while holding the post of deputy prime minister (August–September 1980). In the party leadership he oversaw industry, construction, transportation, and finance. He advocated the need to crush Solidarity with force; this accounted for his popularity with the Kremlin. Relying on the protection of the Communist Party of the Soviet Union, he openly criticized the top PUWP leadership for its lack of resolve in dealing with Solidarity. During a meeting of the PUWP CC on 9 June 1981 Grabski attempted to procure the dismissal of First Secretary **Stanisław Kania**, openly accusing him of lacking the trust of Poland's Soviet ally. During the PUWP Ninth Congress in July 1981, Grabski failed to be included in the top leadership of the party. Afterwards, he was sidelined and shifted to diplomatic work. (PK)

Sources: Mołdawa; Włodzimierz Janowski and Aleksander Kochański, *Informator o strukturze i obsadzie personalnej centralnego aparatu PZPR 1948–1990* (Warsaw, 2000); Andrzej Paczkowski, *Droga do "mniejszego zła": Strategia i taktyka obozu władzy lipiec 1980–styczeń 1982* (Kraków, 2002).

GRABSKI Władysław (7 July 1874, Borów, near Łowicz–1 March 1938, Warsaw), Polish politician, economist, and historian. Grabski came from a family of landed nobility; he was the brother of **Stanisław Grabski**. While at a Warsaw high school (1883–92), he became a Socialist. He studied in Paris at the École des Sciences Politiques (1892–94) and at the Sorbonne (1892–95). His views evolved toward liberalism and national solidarity. Between 1896 and 1897 Grabski studied agriculture in Halle, Germany. After returning home, he took over the management of the family estate. In 1899 he established an experimental agricultural post in Kutno. He also organized village cooperatives. His *Historia Towarzystwa Rolniczego, 1858–61*

(History of the Agricultural Society, 1858–61; 1904) won a prize from the Academy of Arts and Sciences in Kraków. In 1904 Grabski co-founded the illegal Union of National-Political Work (Związek Pracy Narodowo-Politycznej), and in 1905 he joined the National League. He was then briefly imprisoned by the Russian authorities. In 1906 he became involved with National Democracy. Between 1905 and 1912 he was a deputy to the State Duma. He refused to run for the Fourth Duma and instead concentrated on social and charity work at the Central Agricultural Society and the Office for Social Work, which published his *Rocznik Statystyczny Królestwa Polskiego* (The statistical yearbook of the Polish kingdom).

Following the outbreak of World War I, Grabski joined the National Committee of Poland (Komitet Narodowy Polski [KNP]), and in 1915 he founded and chaired the Central Civic Committee. Before the Germans took Warsaw, he left for Russia. He was active in the Council of the Societies to Assist War Victims in Poland. After the fall of the Romanovs, Grabski became involved in the Polish Liquidation Commission. Following the Bolshevik revolution of 1917, he returned home, where he was arrested by the Germans and imprisoned at Modlin. While in jail, he wrote a textbook on the agricultural history of Poland. After the collapse of the German administration in Poland, on 26 October 1918 Grabski became minister of agriculture in the government of **Józef Świeżyński**. In the resurrected Poland he focused on economic matters, including organizing and chairing the Main Liquidation Bureau. In 1919 he participated in the Polish delegation to the Paris Peace Conference. Between 1919 and 1922 he was an MP on the ticket of the Popular-National Union. From December 1919 through November 1920 he served in the government of **Leopold Skulski**. On 23 June 1920 he became prime minister and organized the Council for the Defense of the State. He quit on 24 July 1920, objecting to the decisions of the conference at Spa in which the Western powers offered to compromise with the Soviets at the expense of Poland. However, he remained minister of the treasury until November 1920. From 1921 to 1922 he served as extraordinary commissar for the repatriation of Poles from Russia, and in 1922 he was director of the Polish-American Committee to Aid Children.

In January 1923 Grabski once again became minister of the treasury in the government of General **Władysław Sikorski**. In May 1923, after the majority government of **Wincenty Witos** took over, he kept his post. He intended to introduce a new currency (replacing the Polish mark with the złoty) but first planned to balance the budget and decrease inflation. Since Witos failed to support him, Grabski quit on 1 July 1923. However, after the Witos cabinet collapsed, Grabski assembled his own "extraparliamentary" government and became prime minister and minister of the treasury on 19 December 1923. Facing hyperinflation and economic crisis, he managed to balance the budget by introducing an extraordinary property tax and reducing spending. He also succeeded in reforming the currency. On 28 April 1924 the newly created Polish Bank introduced the złoty. Grabski carried out his plans relying solely on domestic resources. His intention was to maintain Poland's independence of action; this was reflected in, among other things, a rejection of the expert services of the British mission under Hilton Young. However, Grabski's reforms collapsed because of economic recession, the inauspicious international situation, and the return of inflation (the so-called second inflation). The reforms also suffered because of the opposition of **Józef Piłsudski** and his followers to the government. In the fall of 1925, Grabski lost the confidence of leaders in banking, industry, and commerce. He tendered his resignation on 14 November 1925.

In May 1926 Grabski was a candidate for prime minister in an "extraparliamentary" government. However, he failed to gain sufficient support from the political parties. This put an end to his political career, and he began to focus on academic work. From 1923 he was a professor at the Main School of Agricultural Economics in Warsaw. Between 1928 and 1934 he headed the Society of Polish Economists and Statisticians in Warsaw. Later, he was elected an honorary member of the society. In 1936 he organized the Institute for the Sociology of the Countryside and launched the *Rocznik Socjologii Wsi* (The yearbook for the sociology of the village). He believed that a land reform would facilitate economic development in the Polish countryside and, as a consequence, in the entire national economy. He founded and became an ordinary member of the Warsaw Scientific Society. Along with **Eugeniusz Kwiatkowski**, Grabski was considered to be the most outstanding political economist of the Second Polish Republic. He was decorated with the Order of the White Eagle. He authored numerous scholarly works, including the following: *Materiały w sprawie włościańskiej* (The evidence on the peasant question, 3 vols.; 1907–19); *Społeczne gospodarstwo agrarne* (A social agrarian economy; 1923); *Reforma agronomii społecznej* (The reform of the social agrarian economy; 1928); *Historia wsi w Polsce* (History of the Polish countryside; 1929); *Wieś i folwark* (The village and the demesne; 1930); *Idea Polski* (The idea of Poland; 1935); and "Parcelacja agrarna wobec struktury, koniunktury i chwili dziejowej Polski" (Agricultural partitioning in the light of the structure, timing, and history of Poland, *Ekonomista*, 1938, vol. 4). He also published his memoirs: *Dwa lata pracy u podstaw państwowości naszej 1924–1925* (Two years of work at the foundations of our state; 1927). (JS)

Sources: *PSB*, vol. 8; *Słownik polityków polskich XX wieku* (Poznań, 1998); Jan Hupka, *Z czasów wielkiej wojny* (Lwów, 1927); Stefan Dziewulski, "Profesor Władysław Grabski i jego prace," *Przegląd Statystyczny*, 1938, no. 2; Antoni Żabko-Potopowicz, "Śp. Władysław Grabski," *Ekonomista*, 1938, no. 1; Jerzy Tomaszewski, *Stabilizacja waluty w Polsce* (Warsaw, 1961); Zbigniew Landau and Jerzy Tomaszewski, *W dobie inflacji* (Warsaw, 1967); Władysław Pobóg-Malinowski, *Najnowsza historia polityczna Polski*, vol. 2 (London, 1983); Stanisław Grabski, *Pamiętniki*, vols. 1–2 (Warsaw, 1989).

GRANIĆ Mate (19 September 1947, Baska Voda), Croatian politician. Granić studied medicine in Zagreb (1966–71) and specialized in diabetes in 1976–77. In 1977 he became assistant professor at the Vuk Vrhovac Institute of Diabetes and Endocrinology. In 1980 he received a Ph.D. in medical science, and in 1985 he became professor and deputy director of the institute. In 1990 he became dean of the Department of Medicine of the University of Zagreb. He was also a visiting professor at Harvard University and at the University of Munich. In 1989 he joined the Croatian Democratic Union (Hrvatska Demokratska Zajednica [HDZ]) and soon became its deputy chairman. In June 1993 he assumed the position of deputy prime minister and minister of foreign affairs. He played an active role in shaping Croatian foreign policy, taking part in the peace talks in Dayton, Ohio, where on 21 November 1995 a peace treaty was signed terminating the war in Bosnia and Herzegovina. Granić made efforts to facilitate the rapprochement of Croatia with the European Union and NATO, but he faced the reluctance of the Western powers, who accused the Zagreb authorities of insufficient support for the Dayton agreement and violations of democratic principles. Croatia's relations with the Western powers improved after 24 March 1999, when NATO started an intervention in Yugoslavia. The next day Granić issued a statement fully supporting the NATO operation. After the death of **Franjo Tudjman** in December 1999, the ruling HDZ was defeated in the parliamentary elections of 3 January 2000. In consequence Granić left the HDZ Presidium and gave up all his party and government positions. He ran in the presidential elections of January 2000 but came in third and failed to qualify for the second round. In March 2000 he left the HDZ, which, in his opinion, had become too rightist. He co-founded the Croatian Democratic Center, later renamed the Democratic Center, and became its chairman. (AO)

Sources: *Europa Środkowo-Wschodnia 1993–1999* (Warsaw, 1995–2001); Richard Holbrooke, *To End a War* (New York, 1998); Saša Cvijetić, "News Report for Croatia," *Central Europe Review*, 10 January 2000; *Biographical Notes*, Polish Press Agency PAP, November 2001; Bugajski; www.rferl.org.

GRAŻYŃSKI Michał, pseudonym "Borelowski" (12 May 1890, Gdów, near Wieliczka–10 December 1965, Putney, Great Britain), Polish politician. The son of a teacher, after graduating from Nowodworski High School in Kraków, Grażyński studied at the Philosophy Department of the Jagiellonian University (1909–14), where he received his doctorate. While a student, he joined the Polish Riflemen Squads. In October 1914 he volunteered for the Thirteenth (Austro-Hungarian) Infantry Regiment and left for the eastern front. In 1915 he was seriously wounded at the battle of Gołaczów. In 1918, he joined the newly created Polish Army. He participated in preparing the plebiscite in Spiš and Orava. In August 1920, he arrived in Upper Silesia on an assignment from the Second Department (Intelligence) of the General Staff of the Polish Army. His orders were to prepare the clandestine structure of the Upper Silesian Polish Military Organization, which he commanded from December 1920. Upon the outbreak of the Third Silesian Uprising in May 1921, Grażyński became chief of staff of the East Operation Group, the largest of the insurgent units. He endeavored to intensify insurgent operations as much as possible, which led to a serious conflict with the political leadership of the uprising, **Wojciech Korfanty** in particular. An attempt by the officers of the East Operation Group to take over political leadership ended with Grażyński's arrest in June 1921. However, the charges against him were soon dropped.

Following his dismissal from the armed forces, Grażyńsk returned to Kraków. Between 1921 and 1923 he worked in various official capacities, including a position at the Ministry of Land Reform. At the behest of military intelligence, he conducted operations among the Polish minority in Opole Silesia. After the May 1926 coup d'état, he was nominated provincial governor of Silesia, holding that post for over a decade (August 1926–September 1939). He contributed to the manifold development of the province. He also established his own political camp. To this end, he took advantage of the specific autonomous cultural and economic institutions of Silesia, positioning himself in the Union of Silesian Insurgents (Związek Powstańców Śląskich) and the Union for the Reform of the Republic (Związek Naprawy Rzeczypospolitej). However, he opposed local separatism. Contrary to Korfanty, who was ready to obey international agreements, Grażyński used all methods at his disposal to try to weaken German influence in Upper Silesia. In education policy in particular, he often curtailed German minority schooling, which led to numerous complaints against Poland in the League of Nations and the International Justice Tribunal in The Hague. He opposed both the Volksbund, which represented the German minority, and the Christian National camp of Korfanty. Grażyński initiated numerous economic and cultural undertakings in Upper Silesia. From 1931 he headed the Union of Polish Scouting, attempting to carry out a program of "civic formation." In September and October 1938, he prepared and completed a plan for the annexation of Zaolzie to Poland. In September 1939 he became minister for information and propaganda. When the war began, he escaped to Romania and then to France. He spent the war in Great Britain, sidelined by the government of General **Władysław Sikorski**. Grażyński died in an accident. He published numerous scholarly articles on numismatics and social and educational topics. (AGr)

Sources: *PSB*, vol. 8; *Kto był kim w Drugiej Rzeczypospolitej* (Warsaw, 1994); *Encyklopedia Historii Drugiej Rzeczypospolitej* (Warsaw, 1999); Henryk Rechowicz, *Wojewoda śląski dr Michał Grażyński* (Warsaw and Kraków, 1988); Wanda Musialik, *Michał Tadeusz Grażyński 1890–1965: Biografia polityczna* (Opole, 1989); Tomasz Falęcki, *Powstańcy śląscy 1921–1939* (Wrocław and Warsaw, 1990); Jan Łączewski, *Michał Grażyński (1890–1965): Sylwetka polityka* (Częstochowa, 2000).

GRĪNBERGS Teodors (2 April 1870, Dundaga, Courland–14 June 1962, Eslingen, Germany), Lutheran archbishop of Latvia. Grīnbergs graduated from a high school in Jelgava and from the Department of Theology at the University of Dorpat (Tartu) in 1896. He also studied history and philosophy there. He was auxiliary pastor and tutor in Pope, Courland. From 1899 he was vicar in Lutriņi, Courland, and from 1907 to 1934, pastor in Ventspils. In 1918–19 he presided over the commission of education in this town. In 1922–23 he was an MP on behalf of the Union of Christian Democrats, and from 1919 to 1932, high school headmaster in Ventspils. In 1931 he was appointed deputy archbishop of the Lutheran Church in Latvia, and in March 1932 he was elected archbishop. From 1931 he was also associate professor and chair of the Institute of Theology and later full professor at the University of Riga. He edited a number of religious periodicals, including one for children, *Bitīte*. He authored several articles on the history of the Lutheran Church and theology. During the first Soviet occupation (1940–41) he avoided deportation. In 1943 he signed a letter of protest against German occupation policies, demanding Latvia's independence. In October 1944 he left for Germany, where in 1944–62 he continued as archbishop of the Latvian Lutheran Church in exile. (EJ)

Sources: *Latviešu konversācijas vārdnīca*, vol. 6 (Riga, 1931); *Es viņu pazīstu* (Riga, 1939); *Arhibīskaps Dr. Teodors Grīnbergs: Rakstu krājums 100. dzimumdienas atcerei* (n.p., 1970).

GRINIUS Kazys (17 December 1866, Selema Buda, near Marijampole–4 June 1950, Chicago), Peasant Party politician, president of Lithuania. The son of wealthy peasants, Grinius became familiar with the Lithuanian literature and national traditions in his childhood. After graduating from a gymnasium in Marijampole, in 1887 he began medical studies in Moscow, where he became involved in the secret Lithuanian Student Association, headed by **Petras Leonas**. In 1888 Grinius, along with Vincas Kudirka and others, co-organized a conference of Lithuanian Democrats in Marijampole. He was arrested for the first time in 1889. After completing medical studies in Moscow in 1893, he worked as a doctor in the Russian fleet, and then he started a private practice in Marijampole. He took part in the underground Liberal Peasant Movement and co-founded the newspaper *Varpas*; in 1902 he was a co-author of the program of the Democratic Party of Lithuania. In 1905 the tsarist authorities forced him to go to Vilnius (Wilno), where he wrote for the local Lithuanian periodicals. He subsequently returned to Marijampole, where he organized the theater, took part in the work of the educational association Sviesa, and initiated many patriotic demonstrations. Arrested in 1906 and 1908, he was forced to go to Vilnius again. After his return to Marijampole in 1911, he organized the first agrarian exhibition in Lithuania.

During World War I Grinius was in Russia. In 1917 he was a member of the Lithuanian Council. During the Bolshevik revolution, in 1918 his wife, Joana, and his daughter, Gražina, were murdered in Kislovodsk. At the end of 1919 Grinius returned to Lithuania via Turkey and France, where he temporarily directed the repatriation of Lithuanians to their country. Elected an MP to the Lithuanian Constituent Assembly, he served as prime minister from 19 June 1920 to 1 February 1922. On 12 July 1920 he signed a peace treaty with Soviet Russia and proclaimed Lithuania's neutrality in the Polish-Soviet conflict. He also signed the Suwałki agreement of 7 October 1920, concerning a demarcation line. After the Vilnius region had been seized by Polish units under the command of General Lucjan Żeligowski, Grinius asked the League of Nations to intervene. As a result, a special commission put an end to the Polish-Lithuanian struggle. In 1922 Grinius took charge of the health service in Kaunas. On 7 June 1926 he was elected president as a representative of the Populists (Laudininkai) and signed a treaty of non-aggression with the USSR on 28 September 1926. As an anti-clericalist, Grinius pursued a conciliatory policy toward the extreme leftist opposition, which consolidated the rightist camp.

Nationalist conspirators began a coup d'état on 17 December 1926, Grinius's birthday, when many officers arrived in the capital to celebrate. As a result of the coup (led by Major Povilas Plechavičius), the leader of the Nationalists, **Antanas Smetona**, became head of state. Grinius accepted the resignation of the government of **Mykolas Sleževičius** and entrusted **Augustinas Voldemaras** with the mission of forming a new cabinet. Then he resigned on 19 December 1926. He returned to the municipality of Kaunas, where he served as head of the local health service. After the Soviet invasion of 1940, he avoided arrest. When in June 1941 the Germans invaded Lithuania, he supported national opposition, and therefore he was temporarily put under house arrest in Azoulu Buda. Before the return of the Red Army, in the summer of 1944 he went to Germany, where after the end of the war he found shelter in a refugee camp in Hanau. In 1947 he emigrated to the United States, where he lived in Philadelphia and Chicago. He represented the Lithuanian peasant activists in the International Peasant Union. He published *Lithuania in a Post-War Europe as a Free and Independent State* (1943) and the memoirs *Atsiminimai ir mintys (Memoirs and Reflections)* (vol. 1, 1947; vol. 2, 1962). His work on the coup d'état of 1926, *Apie 1926 m. gruodžio 17-os dienos perversmą (The Coup of 17 December 1926)*, was published posthumously in 1954. (WR)

Sources: *EL*, vol. 2; Piotr Łossowski, *Kraje bałtyckie na drodze od demokracji parlamentarnej do dyktatury 1918–1934* (Wrocław, 1972); Algirdas Banevicius, *111 Lietuvos valstybes 1918–1940 politikos veikeju* (Vilnius, 1991); Liudas Truska, Algimantas Lileikis, Gediminas Ilgunas, and Rimgaudas Gelezevicius, *Lietuvos prezidentai* (Vilnius, 1995); Alfonsas Eidintas and Vytautas Žalys, *Lithuania in European Politics: The Years of the First Republic, 1918–1940* (New York, 1997); www.ktl.mii.lt/prezidentai.

GRĪNS Aleksandrs Jēkabs (15 August 1895, Biržu, Courland–25 December 1941, Astrakhan), Latvian writer. After graduating from a gymnasium in Cesis (1914), Grīns volunteered for the Russian Army in 1915. The same year he graduated from the Aleksei Cadet School in Moscow. From August 1916 he fought in the Fourth Latvian Regiment of Riflemen and was severely wounded in August 1917. Later, he described his experiences of that period in his novel *Dvēseļu putenis* (Blizzard of souls; 1932–34). Mobilized into the army of Soviet Latvia in April 1919, he deserted the next month and joined the Latvian army. From 1920 he was a captain. Between 1920 and 1924 he was the deputy editor of *Latvijas Kareivis*, a journal of the War Ministry. Transferred to the reserves in 1924, he worked on the editorial staffs of several magazines. In 1936–40 he returned to military service in the corps for the territorial defense of the country, and from 1939 he was an officer in the army staff. Grīns wrote plays, poetry, and historical novels. He was the author of (among other works) the trilogy *Saderinātie*

(Plights: 1938–40). After the seizure of Latvia by the USSR in September 1940 he was enlisted into the Red Army, and on 14 June 1941 he was arrested along with other Latvian officers. Deported to a prison in Astrakhan, he was executed by firing squad. (EJ/WR)

Sources: P. Ērmanis, *Aleksandra Grīna dzīve: Grīns A. Kopotie raksti* (Riga, 1939); Rolfs Ekmanis, *Latvian Literature under the Soviets, 1940–1975* (Belmont, Mass., 1978); H. Hiršs, *Vēl viena atgriešanās: Grīns A. Dvēseļu putenis* (Riga, 1989); Romuald J. Misiunas and Rein Taagepera, *The Baltic States: Years of Dependence, 1940–1980* (Berkeley, 1993); A. Bambals, "Orderis man paziņots . . .," *Latvijas Arhīvi*, 1997, no. 2.

GRIŠKEVIČIUS Petras (19 July 1924, Kriaunai–14 November 1987, Vilnius), Lithuanian Communist activist. After the Soviet invasion of Lithuania in June 1940 Griškevičius joined the Communist youth organization Komjaunimas, and during World War II he fought in the Soviet guerrilla movement in Lithuania. In 1945 he became a member of the Communist Party of Lithuania (CPL). From 1948 he worked in the Department of Propaganda of the CPL Central Committee (CC), and in 1956–64 he advanced in the Vilnius party organization, reaching the position of secretary. In 1964 he became head of the Organization Department of the CPL CC, and in 1971, head of the CPL Vilnius City Committee. After the death of the head of the Lithuanian party, **Antanas Sniečkus**, in 1974 Griškevičius became his successor as first secretary of the CPL CC. He was known as a colorless apparatchik, zealous in implementing the Kremlin's policies and supporting all the decisions of Leonid Brezhnev and his aides, including those having to do with the Russification of Lithuania. He was hostile to the Catholic Church and religion, and he suppressed all hints of social discontent and the nuclei of the democratic opposition. Perestroika and glasnost catalyzed the national and democratic movements and undermined the determination of the party apparatus. In 1986 many writers from the Association of Writers of the Lithuanian SSR signed a petition defending the natural environment, threatened by the search for oil under the Baltic Sea bottom, and in November 1987 they elected new authorities supporting perestroika. Soon after that Griškevičius died of a heart attack. (WR)

Sources: Saulius Sužiedelis, *Historical Dictionary of Lithuania* (Lanham, Md., 1997); *The International Who's Who 1984/85* (Europa 1985); Alfred Erich Senn, *Lithuania Awakening* (Berkeley, 1990).

GROL Milan (31 August 1876, Belgrade–3 December 1952, Yugoslavia), Yugoslav writer and politician of Serb nationality. After graduating from the Department of Philosophy of Belgrade University in 1899, Grol studied literature in Paris. Later he returned to Serbia and worked in the National Theater in Belgrade, and between 1918 and 1924 he was its director. At the same time he wrote and published extensively. He was the author of, for example, *Pozorišne kritike* (Theater criticism; 1931) and *Iz predratne Serbije* (From prewar Serbia; 1939). From 1901 he belonged to leftist groups of the Serb intelligentsia, which stood in opposition to the regime of King **Alexander Obrenović**. After World War I he joined the Serbian Democratic Party (SDP), which advocated equal rights for the nations of Yugoslavia and a federal system of government. In 1929 he criticized the royal coup d'état. Between 1925 and 1927 he was an MP. He favored the Serbo-Croatian compromise of August 1939. In February 1940 he was elected president of the SDP. He supported the coup of 27 March 1941, and he joined the coalition government of General **Dušan Simović**. After the German invasion he along with the government went into exile.

As the result of an agreement in November 1944 between **Josip Broz Tito** and **Ivan Šubašic**, Grol joined the government dominated by the Communists as deputy prime minister. At first King **Peter II** wanted to name him one of his temporary regents, but Tito did not agree to that. After his arrival in Belgrade (February 1945), Grol was helpless in the face of the Communists' totalitarian methods of political struggle. Initially, he was allowed to publish the magazine *Demokratija*, but after six issues the Titoist authorities closed it down, despite the fact that Grol remained deputy prime minister. On 8 March 1945 he resigned his post, explaining to Tito that he could not perform his functions: the government met very seldom, and the most important decisions were made in the executive of the Communist Party, outside the government. Temporarily arrested, after his release Grol withdrew from political life. In 1990 his *Londonski dnevnik, 1941–1945* (London diary, 1941–1945) was published in Belgrade. (WR)

Sources: *Enciklopedija Jugoslavije*, vol. 3 (Zagreb, 1958); Constanin Fotitch, *The War We Lost* (New York, 1948); J. Jukic, *The Fall of Yugoslavia* (New York and London, 1974); Michał Jerzy Zacharias, *Jugosławia w polityce Wielkiej Brytanii 1940–1945* (Wrocław, 1985).

GRONKIEWICZ-WALTZ Hanna (4 November 1952, Warsaw), Polish lawyer and political activist. Gronkiewicz-Waltz graduated in law with distinction from the University of Warsaw in 1975, and later she worked there, specializing in banking law, in particular the legal position of central banks. From 1980 she belonged to Solidarity. In 1982 she got involved with the Catholic Movement of Renewal in the Holy Spirit. In 1981 she received a Ph.D. and in 1993 a post-doctoral degree (*habilitacja*). She au-

thored several dozen scholarly works. In 1989 she became a parliamentary expert in public law. In 1990–92 she was an associate professor at the Canon Law Department of the Academy of Catholic Theology (now the Cardinal Stefan Wyszyński University) in Warsaw. In 1991 she ran in the parliamentary elections on behalf of Victoria, the **Lech Wałęsa** committee. In 1992 she became adviser to the Supreme Council of Control. In March 1992 she was elected chairwoman of the National Bank of Poland (Narodowy Bank Polski [NBP]). During her term a banking reform was implemented in Poland. The Polish złoty was denominated, and its rate of exchange was made liquid in relation to hard currencies. In November 1995 Gronkiewicz-Waltz ran in the presidential elections on behalf of a group of small rightist parties, but she failed to get to the second round of the voting. In February 1998 she was reelected as NBP chairwoman. In 1998–2000 she also presided over the Council of Monetary Policy. She was rated among the best central bank chairpersons by the U.S. periodical *Global Finance*, and she was named the European Banker of 1998. In January 2001 she assumed the position of deputy chairperson of the European Bank of Reconstruction and Development in London. (IS)

Sources: *Kto jest kim w Polsce* (Warsaw, 2001); *Wielka encyklopedia PWN*, vol. 10 (Warsaw, 2002); Janusz A. Majcherek, *Pierwsza dekada III Rzeczypospolitej* (Warsaw, 1999); Antoni Dudek, *Pierwsze lata III Rzeczyspospolitej 1989–2001* (Kraków, 2002); Wojciech Roszkowski, *Historia Polski 1914–2001* (Warsaw, 2002).

GRŐSZ József (9 December 1887, Féltorony [now in Austria]–3 October 1961, Kalocsa), archbishop and leader of the Hungarian Catholic Church. Grősz graduated from a Benedictine high school in Győr. After completing theological studies in the Vienna Pazmaneum in 1911, he took holy orders. He was sent to Farád and after a year to Oroszvár, where he worked as a vicar. From 1913 he worked in the bishop's chancellery in Győr. In 1914, he was appointed liturgist to the bishop, and in 1921, secretary to bishop Antal Fetser. From 1924, he managed the bishop's chancellery. In December 1928, he was appointed auxiliary bishop of Győr, and in 1931 he was appointed canon. From 1933 he was the vicar of the chapter and subsequently chief vicar. From January 1936 he was the apostolic administrator of the Szombathely diocese. In July 1939 he was appointed diocesan bishop. As such, he became a member of the Upper Chamber of the parliament. In May 1943, he was appointed archbishop of Kalocsa; until March 1944 he was also in charge of the administration of the see in Szombathely. For most of the 1943–46 period, he was a member of the leadership of the Hungarian Academy of Sciences. After the death of Cardinal **Jusztinián Serédi**, from 25 March 1945 until the nomination of his successor, **József Mindszenty**, and then after his arrest, from February 1949 Grősz was the head of the Catholic Church in Hungary on the basis of an authorization issued by the Holy See. After Primate Mindszenty was arrested, the government urged Grősz to resign. Brutally pressed by the Communists, on 30 August 1950 he signed an agreement with the state on behalf of the Episcopate. The agreement, which was null and void in terms of canon law, guaranteed state control over the church, at the same permitting certain church activities. The majority of bishops still sought to retain independence. They refused to support the "peace priests" movement, organized by the Communist authorities, and declined to take an oath of loyalty to the Communist constitution. Moreover, they voiced their objections to the brutal abuses occurring in the denominational policies of the state.

In May 1951, Grősz was arrested and sentenced to fifteen years in prison on the fabricated charges of organizing activities aimed at the overthrow of the system. His trial, combined with another twenty-four cases, resulted in a total of fifteen death sentences. These verdicts were designed to intimidate the clergy and the faithful, as well as to facilitate the promotion of priests who obeyed the authorities. During Grősz's trial, a number of bishops were kept under house arrest and forced to appoint the "peace priests" as vicars. Eventually, in July 1951 the Episcopate took an oath of loyalty to the Stalinist constitution. In October 1955, Grősz's sentence was annulled, but he was still kept under house arrest. He was pardoned in May 1956 on the request of the Episcopate, and he was able to return to the position of archbishop. As chairman of the Episcopate for a second time, he collaborated with Communist authorities in order to secure conditions under which the Church could function. In 1957, a conference of bishops under his leadership joined a state-controlled peace movement of priests (which they had opposed before) and established its own peace committee, Opus Pacis. From 1957, Grősz was a board member of the National Front of the Patriotic People's Front. On the occasion of his seventieth birthday, he was awarded the Order of the Flag of the Hungarian People's Republic. In May 1990, the 1951 conviction was rendered invalid. (JT)

Sources: *The Trial of József Grősz and His Accomplices* (Budapest, 1951); *Da Mindszenty a Grősz* (Rome, 1952); *Magyar Nagylexikon*, vol. 8 (Budapest, 1999); *A magyar forradalom és szabadságharc enciklopédiája* (Budapest, 1999).

GRÓSZ Károly (1 August 1930, Miskolc–7 January 1996, Gödöllő), Hungarian Communist activist. Grósz's father worked in a machine factory in Diósgyőr and in the 1930s was a member of the illegal Communist Party.

At first, Grósz did his apprenticeship in the same factory, and from the spring of 1945, in a printing house in Borsod. The same year he joined the Hungarian Communist Party. In 1948 he became the secretary of Borsod County's National Union of Hungarian Youth, and he moved to Budapest. In 1950 he became a political worker of the Central Committee (CC) of the Hungarian Workers' Party (HWP). Drafted into the army in 1950, he graduated from the Petőfi Military and Political Academy. He served as a political officer in Kaposvár and Marcali. In 1954 he completed his military service and became the head of the Agitation and Propaganda Department of the HWP's party committee in Borsod County.

During the revolution of 1956 Grósz retained his posts. On 26 October 1956 he forbade journalists to write on current events, and on 28 October he removed the historical Hungarian emblem from the masthead of the newspaper *Északmagyarország*, which had been put there in place of the "Socialist" emblem of Rakosi. On 4 November Grósz became a member of the Revolutionary Council of Workers and Peasants and the head of the party organization of Borsod County. After the suppression of the revolution the authorities of the Hungarian Socialist Workers' Party (HSWP) investigated Grósz's activities during the October events and in December 1956 dismissed him from his posts. In 1958 he was in charge of publishing the newspaper *Északmagyarország*. Between 1959 and 1961 he attended the Higher Party School. After completing his studies at the school, Grósz started work in the CC Propaganda and Political Departments. In 1962 he was secretary of the party committee of Hungarian Radio and Television. From 1968 he was deputy head of the Agitation and Propaganda Department of the CC. From 1970 he was a member of the editorial team of the party paper, *Pártélet*. In 1973 he became the first secretary of the party committee of Fejér County, and in 1974, head of the Agitation and Propaganda Department of the CC of the HSWP. From 1979 he was the first secretary of the party committee of Borsod County.

In 1980–89 Grósz was a member of the CC of the HSWP, and from 1985 to 1989, a member of the Politburo. From 1984 he was the first secretary of the party committee in Budapest. On 25 June 1987 he became prime minister and held the post until 23 November 1988. In May 1988 he was elected first secretary of the HSWP, in place of **János Kádár**. However, between June and October 1989 the party was actually ruled by a quadrumvirate, in which Grósz did not have full power. He did not approve of the transformation of the HSWP into the Hungarian Socialist Party (HSP) and did not join the HSP. From December 1989 Grósz was a member of the CC of the splinter group that continued to function under the name of the HSWP. (JT)

Sources: Bennet Kovrig, *Communism in Hungary from Kun to Kádár* (Stanford, 1979); Miklós Molnár, *From Béla Kun to János Kádár: Seventy Years of Hungarian Communism* (New York, 1990); *Magyar Nagylexikon*, vol. 8 (Budapest, 1999); *A magyar forradalom és szabadságharc enciklopédiája*, CD-ROM (Budapest, 1999).

GROSZKOWSKI Janusz (21 March 1898, Warsaw–3 August 1984, Warsaw), Polish electronics and radio engineer. Between 1915 and 1919 Groszkowski studied at the Warsaw Polytechnic (WP). From 1918 to 1921 he served in the Polish Army, attaining the rank of captain in the corps of sappers. In 1922 he graduated from the Officers' School of Communications in Paris, and then he was hired as a lecturer at the WP, becoming an assistant professor in 1929. From 1929 to 1939 he served as the director of the Radio Technical Institute, and from 1933, the State Institute for Telecommunications. In 1934 he became a corresponding member, and the following year a regular member, of the Academy of Technical Sciences. Between 1926 and 1938 he belonged to the Freemasonic Grand National Lodge. During the Nazi occupation, Groszkowski was assigned by the Office of the Government Delegate for the Homeland and the intelligence services of the Union of Armed Struggle–Home Army to crack the Nazi V1 and V2 rocket systems. The fruit of his investigations and the parts of the rockets captured by the Polish underground were passed on to London. Between 1945 and 1946 Groszkowski worked at the Łódź Polytechnic but later returned to the WP. Between 1953 and 1963 he was also employed at the Institute of Basic Technical Problems. In 1949 he became a member of the Warsaw Scientific Society, and in 1953, the Polish Academy of Sciences (PAS). Between January 1963 and December 1971 he was the PAS chairman. He also served as deputy chairman (June 1968–June 1971) and chairman (June 1971–February 1976) of the All-Polish Committee of the Front of National Unity. Between 1972 and 1976 he was a deputy in the parliament, and from March 1972 through March 1976 he was deputy chairman of the Council of State. (WR)

Sources: Mołdawa; Ludwik Hass, *Masoneria polska XX wieku* (Warsaw, 1996).

GROTOWSKI Jerzy (11 August 1933, Rzeszów–14 January 1999, Pontedera, near Pisa, Italy), Polish director, theater reformer, and theoretician. Grotowski studied acting (1951–55) and directing (1956–60) at the Higher State Theatrical School in Kraków. In 1955 and 1956, he also studied directing at the State Institute for Theatrical Art in Moscow. In 1959 in Opole he founded the Theater of 13 Rows (later called Laboratorium). He moved his theater to Wrocław and continued as its supervisor until 1984. His was a "participatory theater," where the emotional interaction between an actor and the audience was more important than the script. At the end of his life, Grotowski concentrated on theoretical and pedagogical work. He was internationally recognized as an innovator who changed the face of contemporary theater. He was greatly influenced by the Romantic output of Adam Mickiewicz. He authored a popular manifesto, *Ku teatrowi ubogiemu* (Toward a poor theater; 1968). Contending with frail health all his life and concentrating on his work, Grotowski was dubbed "the Magician of the Theater." He preferred the reductionist mode of expression (empty sets and no seats for the audience). He was fascinated by Hindu mysticism (in 1970 he spent a few months in India) and Christian anthropology, even though his *Apocalypsis cum figuris* (1968) was criticized by the Catholic Church. From 1978 to 1982 Grotowski traveled extensively, studying the rituals of human behavior. After the imposition of martial law in Poland, he left for the United States in August 1982, and in 1986 he settled in Pontedera, Italy. In cooperation with the University of California and the Peter Brook Center, he created a theatrical group there, realizing his own artistic and research program. He received numerous honorary doctorates. The Chair of Theater Anthropology was established especially for him at the College de France. Considered the greatest reformer of European theater at the end of the twentieth century, he visited Poland several times in the 1990s; his last trip was in 1997.

Grotowski's creative career can be divided into four periods. First, it was performance theater (1957–69), when he staged plays based upon his own scripts of George Byron's *Cain* (1960); Adam Mickiewicz's *Dziady* (Forefathers' Eve; 1961); Stanisław Wyspiański's *Akropolis* (1962); Juliusz Słowacki's *Książę niezłomny* (Prince Valiant; 1965), based upon Don Pedro Calderóna de la Barca; and *Apocalipsis cum figuris* (1968), and when he started implementing the idea of "a poor theater." Second was the period of "participatory theater" (1969–78), when Grotowski conducted paratheatrical experiments combined with research on various forms of human expression; this period includes *Uniwersytet Poszukiwań Teatru Narodów* (The University in search of a theater of nations; 1975); *Przedsięwzięcie Góra* (The mountain undertaking; 1977); and *Drzewo ludzi* (The tree of humans; 1979). Third, Grotowski introduced the theater of sources (1976–82), which was a period of transcultural research and experimentation carried out in an international group. Fourth, Grotowski supervised the Ritual Arts (from 1983); this period included his time in California (1983–85) and Italy (1985–99). (JS)

Sources: *Wielka encyklopedia PWN*, vol. 10 (Warsaw, 2002); Tadeusz Burzyński and Zbigniew Osiński, *Grotowski's Laboratory* (Warsaw, 1979); Timothy J. Wiles, *The Theater Event: Modern Theories of Performance* (Chicago, 1980); Jennifer Kumiega, *The Theatre of Grotowski* (London, 1985); *The Grotowski Sourcebook* (London, 1997); Zbigniew Osiński, *Grotowski: Źródła, inspiracje, konteksty* (Gdańsk, 1998); Józef Kelera, *Grotowski wielokrotnie* (Wrocław, 1999); Stephan Wangh, *An Acrobat of the Heart* (New York, 2000); www.teatry.art.pl/!inne/grotowski/.

GROZA Petru (7 December 1884, Bačia, near Hunedoary–7 January 1958, Bucharest), Romanian Peasant Party activist, cooperator with the Communists in their takeover. Groza came from the petty bourgeoisie. After completing studies in a Protestant school in Szászváros, he studied law at the universities in Budapest, Berlin, and Leipzig and received a Ph.D. In 1921–22 and 1926–27 he was in the Peasant Party governments. In 1927 he left the Peasant Party of **Ion Mihalache** after serious financial corruption had been revealed. In 1933 he founded the leftist Peasant Ploughmen's Front, linked with the Communist underground. During World War II Groza grew rich after taking over confiscated Jewish properties. In the fall of 1943 his organization entered into an agreement with the Communists and Socialists in the Patriotic Anti-Fascist Front. Temporarily arrested by the regime of **Ion Antonescu**, after Antonescu's overthrow Groza became deputy prime minister in the second government of General **Constantin Sănătescu** in November 1944. He remained in this post in the next cabinet of General **Nicolae Rădescu**.

The crisis caused by the Communists in February 1945 and the resignation of Rădescu's government caused great tension. As a result of a Soviet ultimatum presented unceremoniously to King **Michael I** by the Soviet deputy minister for foreign affairs, Andrei Vyshinsky, Groza was assigned the mission of forming a government. Although the leaders of the Peasant Party (**Iuliu Maniu**) and Liberal Party (**Dinu Brătianu**) demanded the majority in the government, Groza manipulated its membership in such a way that it gave the Communists full control over the country. On 6 March 1945 Groza became prime minister. He endorsed all the moves of the Communists: a bloody suppression of high-ranking officials of the Antonescu regime and the liquidation of the democratic opposition, mainly the National Peasant Party; these meant the death of thousands of people. On 30 December 1947, along with the head of the Communist Party, **Gheorghe Gheorghiu-Dej**, Groza submitted a demand to King Michael to abdicate. On 4 February 1948 he signed a treaty of "friendship" in Moscow that subjected Romania to the USSR. He also accepted the constitution of 13 April 1948 and a policy of rapid industrialization and brutal collectivization, as a result of which thousands of peasants were murdered. On 2 June 1952, when Gheorghiu-Dej became prime minister, Groza was appointed president of the Grand National Assembly. In 1955 he had a heart attack that removed him from active political life, but until his death he formally remained the head of the parliament of Communist Romania. Groza was a cynic and sybarite who frenziedly amassed material goods. (WR)

Sources: Arthur Gould Lee, *Crown against Sickle: The Story of King Michael of Romania* (London, 1950); Ghita Ionescu, *Communism in Rumania, 1944–1962* (Oxford, 1964); Andrzej Koryn, *Rumunia w polityce wielkich mocarstw 1944–1947* (Wrocław, 1983); Josif Toma Popescu, *Świadectwo* (Warsaw, 1996); Dennis Deletant, *Communist Terror in Romania: Gheorghiu-Dej and the Police State, 1948–1965* (New York, 1999).

GRUDZIEŃ Zdzisław (6 October 1924, Escaudain, France–30 January 1982, Warsaw), Polish Communist activist. The son of a coal miner who emigrated to France, Grudzień himself worked as a coal miner in France and Belgium. In 1941 he joined the French Communist Party and became active in the Communist resistance against the Nazis. In 1946, he returned to Poland and joined the (Communist) Polish Workers' Party. From December 1948 he was active in the (Communist) Polish United Workers' Party (PUWP) and became a functionary of the Union of Youth Struggle and then the Union of Polish Youth (UPY). At the Second UPY Congress in 1955 Grudzień was coopted to its presiding body, along with **Jan Szydlak** and **Stanisław Kania**. In 1957 he graduated from the Academy of Mining and Metallurgy. He was one of the closest collaborators of **Edward Gierek**, who facilitated his ascent in the party hierarchy. In 1957 Grudzień became secretary of the PUWP Provincial Committee in Katowice. Between 1965 and 1981 he was a parliamentary deputy, where he served as, among other things, chairman of the national defense commission. After Gierek became first secretary of the PUWP Central Committee (CC) in December 1970, Grudzień was promoted to his sponsor's post of first secretary of the PUWP Provincial Committee in Katowice. At the Sixth PUWP Congress in December 1971 he became a deputy member, and later a member, of the Politburo (December 1975–October 1980). Between 1973 and 1980 he also served as the chairman of the Provincial National Council in Katowice. He used the construction of the Katowice Steel Works as the symbol of the Communist "propaganda of success." Grudzień was stripped of all of his party and government posts following the purge of Gierek at the Sixth Plenum of the PUWP CC on 6 September 1980. In June 1981 he was expelled from the PUWP, and in July 1981 he gave up his parliamentary seat. (PK)

Sources: Mołdawa; *Słownik polityków polskich XX wieku* (Poznań, 1998); Antoni Czubiński, *Dzieje najnowsze Polski 1944–1989* (Poznań, 1992).

GRUEV Damian (Dame) (January 1871, Smilevo, near Bitola–10 December 1906, Rusinovo, near Maleševo), Macedonian revolutionary activist. In 1889–91 Gruev studied history in Belgrade and Sofia, where he got in touch with Macedonian freedom fighters. Expelled from the university and arrested on account of his alleged participation in the assassination of Minister Khristo Belchev in 1891, after his release he left for Macedonia under Turkish rule. From 1899 he worked as a teacher in Salonika, Smilevo, Shtip, and Prilep. In 1893 he tried to establish a Macedonian revolutionary committee in Bitola, similar to the one existing in Bulgaria, but he failed. In November 1893, at a meeting in Salonika, he was among the founders of the Internal Macedonian Revolutionary Organization (Vnatrešna Makedonska Revolucionerna Organizacija [IMRO]), and he became its secretary. Along with **Goce Delchev**, Gruev created a network of Macedonian revolutionary conspiracy. In 1900 he was arrested and sent deep into Asia Minor. He returned home in early 1903, on the eve of an anti-Turkish uprising. During a Bitola insurrection committee meeting in Smilevo on 2–7 May 1903, Gruev expressed skepticism as to the chances of the uprising, but he joined the closed circle of its leadership and took part in the final stages of its preparation. After its outbreak on 2 August 1903, St. Elijah Day (thence the name Illinden Uprising), he fought in several battles against the Turkish troops. After the uprising was suppressed, Gruev remained in the country and restructured the IMRO organization. During the Macedonian Congress in the Rila Monastery in 1906 Gruev joined the IMRO Central Committee and was one of its top leaders. After the organization split, he supported the IMRO left against its pro-Bulgarian wing. Gruev was killed in a skirmish with Turkish troops. (WR)

Sources: *Entsiklopediya Bulgariya*, vol. 2 (Sofia, 1981); Gane Todorovski, *Dame Gruev* (Skopje, 1968); Duncan M. Perry, *The Politics of Terror: The Macedonian Liberation Movements, 1893–1903* (Durham, N.C., 1988); Dušan Konstantinov, *Damjan Gruev: Diplomat, Strateg i državnik* (Skopje, 1993); Raymond Detrez, *Historical Dictionary of Bulgaria* (Lanham, Md., 1997); Irena Stawowy-Kawka, *Historia Macedonii* (Wrocław, 2000); www.vmro-istorija.com.mk/Foto/Dame.g.htm.

GRUJIĆ Sava (25 November 1840, Kolari, near Smerdevo–21 October 1913, Belgrade), Serb politician. In 1861 Grujić graduated from the School of Artillery in Serbia, and then he studied in military academies in Prussia (1861–63) and Russia (1864–70). From June 1876 he commanded the Serbian artillery in the war against Turkey. He advanced to the rank of colonel, and in October 1876 he became minister of war. He carried out a reform of the military and stayed in office until the end of the war with

Turkey in 1878. Later he worked in diplomacy. In 1879 he was the Serbian envoy to Bulgaria, in 1882 to Greece, and from 1885 to Russia. In 1887 he was promoted to the rank of general. From June to December 1887 he was minister of the armed forces, and then, until April 1888, prime minister. He was one of the leaders of the Radical Party. From February 1889 to February 1891 he was prime minister again, combining this position with that of foreign minister, and from March 1890 he was minister of the armed forces. From 1891 to 1893 he was the Serbian envoy to Istanbul. From June to November 1893 he was minister of the armed forces again, and then, until January 1894, prime minister, minister of war, and foreign minister. From 1897 to 1899 he was envoy to Russia, and from 1900 to 1903, envoy to Turkey. After the coup of May 1903, when a group of officers assassinated King **Alexander Obrenović** and helped **Peter Karadjordjević** ascend the throne, Grujić became head of the Council of State (June 1903). On 21 November 1903 he became prime minister again and stayed in power until 27 November 1904. Later he was prime minister and minister of war again from 1 March 1906 to 17 April 1906. From 1906 to 1910 he presided over the Council of State. He authored many works, including *Vojna organizacija Srbije* (The military organization of Serbia; 1874) and *Osnovi vojnog uredzienja kneževine Bugarske* (Foundations of the military structure of the principality of Bulgaria; 1880). (AO)

Sources: *Enciklopedija Jugoslavije*, vol. 3 (Zagreb, 1958); Michael Petrovic, *A History of Modern Serbia, 1804–1918*, vol. 2 (New York, 1976); www.mfa.gov.yu/History/ministri/SGrujic_s.html.

GRÜNBAUM Icchak (24 November 1879, Warsaw–1970, Gan Shemuel, Israel), Zionist politician in Poland. Grünbaum spent his childhood in Płońsk, where he joined the Zionist movement in 1898. He participated in the Zionist Congress in Basel in 1905. During the congress in Helsinki in 1906, he advocated *Gegenwartsarbeit*, or working for Jewish rights in individual states . In 1908 he became secretary general of the Central Committee of the Zionists of Russia in Vilnius (Wilno). He was arrested on numerous occasions by the Russian authorities. He graduated from the law school at the University of Warsaw and worked as a litigator. In 1914, he launched the journal *Dos Yidishe Folk* in Warsaw. Following the outbreak of World War I, Grünbaum was evacuated to Russia. From 1915 to 1917 he published the *Petrograder Togblat* in St. Petersburg. In 1918 he returned to Poland, where he unveiled a plan of cultural and national autonomy for the Polish Jews. He was elected MP to the Constitutional Assembly in January 1919, and he was a member of its Constitutional Commission. He was consistently reelected in 1922, 1928, and 1930. In 1922 he initiated and co-organized the National Minorities Bloc in the parliament, which led to altercations within the Zionist movement. He opposed the Polish-Jewish agreement of 1924. He spoke critically about the Polish state on numerous occasions. He competed for power within the Zionist movement with **Leon Reich**. After the coup d'état of May 1926, Grünbaum opposed the *sanacja* regime. He co-founded the Tarbut movement to promote the use of Hebrew by Polish Jews. In the early 1920s he became the editor-in-chief of *Hajnt*.

In 1932 Grünbaum left for France, and then he settled in Palestine, where he was elected a member of the executive board of the Jewish Agency. He also supervised the Committee to Rescue Polish Jews. In 1946 he was arrested by the British. Upon his release, he became a signatory to the act of Israeli independence. Between May 1948 and February 1949 he served as the minister for internal affairs in the first government of Israel. He organized the first parliamentary elections, but upon the defeat of his Zionist party he withdrew from public life and concentrated on academic pursuits. Two of his children were active in the Communist movement. Among other works, Grünbaum published the *Encyclopedia of the Jewish Diaspora*. (WR)

Sources: *Who's Who in Israel, 1968* (Tel Aviv, 1968); *Encyclopedia Judaica*, vol. 7 (Jerusalem, 1971); *New Encyclopedia of Zionism and Israel*, vol. 1 (New York, 1994); *Posłowie i senatorowie Rzeczpospolitej Polskiej 1919–1939: Słownik biograficzny*, vol. 1 (Warsaw, 1998); J. Marcus, *Social and Political History of Jews in Poland, 1919–1939* (New York, 1983); R. Prister, *Without Compromise: Yitzhak Gruenbaum, Zionist Leader and Polish Patriot* (N.p., 1987).

GRYDZEWSKI Mieczysław [originally Grützhändler] (27 December 1894, Warsaw–9 January 1970, London), Polish journalist and editor. During law studies in Moscow and Warsaw Grydzewski worked with the periodical *Pro Arte et Studio*, and in 1918–19 he was its editor-in-chief. After graduation he worked on the editorial staff of the Warsaw daily *Kurier Polski*. During the Polish-Soviet war of 1919–21 he volunteered to work in the Press Office of the High Command. In 1922 he received a Ph.D. in history. From 1920 to 1928 and from 1935 to 1939 he was editor-in-chief of the poetry periodical *Skamander*. He also co-founded and was editor-in-chief of *Wiadomości Literackie* (1922–39) and *La Pologne Littéraire* (1926–36). In 1931–32 he wrote the "Foreign Chronicle" column in the periodical *Kultura*. In September 1939 he left for France and then moved to London in 1940. In 1939–44 he edited *Wiadomości Polskie, Polityczne i Literackie*, closed down by the British authorities in 1944. In 1944–46 he wrote

reviews of English books on Poland for Polish émigré periodicals. From 1946 to 1966 he was publisher and editor-in-chief of *Wiadomości*, the leading periodical of the Polish political émigrés in London. He signed his columns "Silva Rerum." On the basis of the results of a questionnaire in *Wiadomości* in 1957, which aimed at ranking Polish writers abroad, Grydzewski established the Academy of Literature and an annual award for the best book published in exile and the best work published in his periodical. These awards were granted until 1990. Grydzewski authored (among other works) the following: *Kalejdoskop warszawski* (The Warsaw kaleidoscope; 1945); *Niezłomni* (The unshaken; 1946); and *Listy do Tuwima i Lechonia, 1940–43* (Letters to Tuwim and Lechoń, 1940–1943; 1986). He edited and published the anthologies *Kraj lat dziecinnych* (The homeland of the childhood years; 1942 and 1987) and *Wiersze polskie wybrane* (Selected Polish poems; 1946). He also edited the book series *Biblioteka wczoraj i dziś* (The library of yesterday and today) and *Biblioteka Ziemi Naszej* (The library of our land). (JS)

Sources: *Współcześni polscy pisarze i badacze literatury: Słownik biobibliograficzny*, vol. 3 (Warsaw, 1994); Rafał Habielski, *Niezłomni, nieprzejednani: Emigracyjne "Wiadomości" i ich krąg 1940–1981* (Warsaw, 1991); Adam Supruniuk, ed., *"Wiadomości" i okolice: Szkice i wspomnienia*, vols. 1–2 (Toruń, 1995–96); *Leksykon kultury polskiej poza krajem od roku 1939*, vol. 1 (Lublin, 2000).

GRZEŚKOWIAK Alicja (10 June 1941, Świrz), Polish lawyer and political activist. In 1963 Grześkowiak graduated in law from the Department of Law and Administration of Nicholas Copernicus University in Toruń. In 1971 she received a Ph.D. and in 1978 a postdoctoral degree (*habilitacja*); in 1990 she became a professor of criminal law. In 1969 she qualified to be a judge. From 1966 to 1996 she worked at Toruń University and from 1990 at the Catholic University of Lublin. In 1968–85 she belonged to the Communist-controlled Democratic Party, and from 1980, to Solidarity. In the 1980s she participated in several citizen initiatives, including the Association against the Death Penalty and the Polish Helsinki Committee. From 1988 she also practiced as a lawyer. In June 1989 she was elected to the Senate. She chaired its constitutional commission and headed the Polish delegation to the European Parliamentary Assembly. She was elected to the Senate in 1991, 1993, and 1997. In 1991–93 she was deputy speaker, and in 1997–2001 she was speaker of the Senate. From 1992 she was a member of the Administrative Council of the John Paul II Foundation in Rome, and from 1993, a consultant to the Pontifical Council for the Family. She was awarded the pontifical order Pro Ecclesia et Pontifice. She is Dame of the Order of the fratres Cruciferi Dominici

Sepulchri Hierosolymitani. Among other works she has authored *Kara śmierci w polskim prawie karnym* (The death penalty in Polish criminal law; 1978); *Zagadnienie prawnokarnej ochrony dziecka poczętego w pracach Sejmu i Senatu Rzeczpospolitej Polskiej w latach 1990–91* (The question of legal protection of the fetus in the proceedings of the Assembly and Senate, 1990–91; 1994); and *W trosce o rodzinę* (Taking care of the family; 1996). (IS)

Sources: *Kto jest kim w Polsce* (Warsaw, 2001); *Wielka encyklopedia PWN*, vol. 10 (Warsaw, 2002); Antoni Dudek, *Pierwsze lata III Rzeczyspospolitej 1989–2001* (Kraków, 2002).

GUCWA Stanisław (18 April 1919, Przybysławice, near Brzesko–14 August 1994, Warsaw), Polish Communist peasant activist. Before World War II Gucwa was active in the Beacon's Fire Union of Rural Youth of the Polish Republic (Związku Młodzieży Wiejskiej Rzeczypospolitej Polskiej "Wici"). During the war he belonged to the Peasant Battalions; from 1945 he was a member of the Communist-controlled Peasant Party (Stronnictwo Ludowe), and from 1949, the United Peasant Party (Zjednoczone Stronnictwo Ludowe [ZSL]). Later he advanced in the economic administration. In 1956–57 he worked in the Ministry of State Purchasing; in 1957–69 he was deputy minister of agriculture, and from 1969 to 1971, minister of the food-processing industry and state purchasing. From 1961 to 1989 he was an MP. Gucwa climbed the ZSL apparatus all the way up, always strictly following the directives of the ruling (Communist) Polish United Workers' Party. In 1959–84 he was a member of the ZSL Chief Committee (CC), and in February 1971 he took over the position of chairman of the ZSL CC, succeeding **Czesław Wycech** and proclaiming a renewal of the party, a task in which he failed altogether. In 1971–72 he was deputy chairman of the Council of State, and from 1971 to 1985, speaker of the Assembly. Gucwa symbolized the submission of the parliament to the Communist Party. In the Solidarity era, after **Stefan Ignar** was elected head of the ZSL in May 1981, Gucwa lost his top position in the party, and he was slowly dropped from the top state positions. (PK)

Sources: Mołdawa; *Słownik polityków polskich XX w.* (Poznań, 1998); Michał Czajka and Marcin Kamler, *Leksykon Historii Polski* (Warsaw, 1995); *VII Kongres Zjednoczonego Stronnictwa Ludowego* (Warsaw, 1976).

GURAKUQI Luigji (20 February 1879, Shkodër–2 March 1925, Bari), Albanian politician, diplomat, and journalist. Gurakuqi was educated in a school run by the Italians in Shkodër. Because of his exceptional abilities, he was sent to San Demetrio School in Calabria, where he continued his education under the direction of outstanding representatives of the Albanian diaspora in Italy. He attended the Albania national activist congress in Monastir in 1908 at which the latin alphabet was adopted for the Albanian language. In 1909 he was appointed director of the pedagogical school in Elbasan, the first institution on Albanian soil that educated teachers. In 1910–11 he took part in an anti-Turkish insurrection, at first in Kosovo and then in the region of Malesia e Madhe. He represented Shkodër at a congress in Vlorë (November–December 1912), and he was one of the closest associates of **Ismail Kemali**. In the provisional government that was formed in December 1912, Gurakuqi assumed the post of minister of education. After the seizure of Shkodër by Montenegro (1914), he was interned in Cetinje. During the Austro-Hungarian occupation, he founded new schools in the region of Shkodër. When Albania regained independence, in January 1920 Gurakuqi assumed the Ministry of Education. In 1921–24 he was a deputy to the parliament, representing the district of Shkodër. He directed the political weekly *Ora e Maleve*, which was edited in Shkodër. During the revolution of 1924 he was a close associate of **Fan Noli**, served as finance minister in his government, and sought international recognition for the new cabinet. After the fall of Noli's government Gurakuqi went into exile in Italy. An active opponent of **Ahmed Zogu**, he was shot by one of Zogu's agents in Bari. In 2000, at the seventy-fifth anniversary of Gurakuqi's death, a monument to him was unveiled in Bari. His publications include *Vargimi ne gjuhen shqipe* (Foundations of the Albanian language; 1906). (TC)

Sources: *Biographisches Lexikon*, vol. 2; Selenica Teki, *Shqipria me 1927* (Tirana, 1928); Piro Tako, *Luigj Gurakuqi, jeta dhe vepra* (Tirana, 1980); Vllamasi Sejfi, *Ballafaqime politike ne Shqiperi (1897–1942)* (Tirana, 1995).

GUZEVIČIUS-GUDAITIS Aleksandras (12 May 1908, Moscow–18 April 1969, Vilnius), Lithuanian Communist activist and writer. From his youth Guzevičius-Gudaitis acted in the underground Communist Party of Lithuania (CPL). In 1928 he was sent to Germany, where he edited a Lithuanian paper. After two years of work for the Communist International (1929–31) he returned to Lithuania. Almost immediately arrested, he spent the years 1931–38 in prison. After the Red Army occupied Lithuania in mid–June 1940, he became co-organizer of the apparatus of Communist terror and deputy minister of interior in the government of the Lithuanian SSR. He played a key role in the organization and execution of mass arrests and the deportation of thousands of Lithuanians during the first Soviet occupation (1940–41). Among others, on 28

November 1940 he signed a deportation instruction in which he broadly defined various categories of "enemies of the people." Therefore he was directly responsible for the genocidal actions that followed. Until June 1941 about twenty-eight thousand people were deported from Lithuania. After three years spent in the USSR, in the summer of 1944 Guzevičius-Gudaitis returned as minister of state security to continue the same activities, ruthlessly persecuting Lithuanian and Polish freedom fighters. He was a member of the Central Committee (CC) of the CPL from 1940. In 1949 he temporarily fell out of favor, but in 1952 he returned to the CPL CC. In 1953–56 he was minister of culture of the Lithuanian SSR and deputy to the republican Supreme Council. His widely publicized literary works were just typical Socialist realist propaganda. For example, in the two volumes of *Kalvio Ignoto teisybė* (The truth about Ignoto the locksmith; 1948–49) he tried to create a legend about the Communist movement in Lithuania. (WR)

Sources: *EL*, vol. 2; Joseph Paujaujis-Javis, *Soviet Genocide in Lithuania* (New York, 1980).

GWIAZDA Andrzej (14 April 1935, Pińczów), Polish social activist. Gwiazda graduated from the Gdańsk Polytechnic in 1966. Until 1973 he worked there as an assistant professor, and then he was employed in the Elmor Company. In 1976 he sent a letter to the Assembly supporting the demands of the Committee for the Defense of Workers (Komitet Obrony Robotników [KOR]) that the Communist authorities release participants of the June 1976 protests and allow those who had been fired to return to work. On 29 April 1978 he was one of the three members of the Founding Committee of the Free Trade Unions (Wolne Związki Zawodowe [WZZ]) in Gdańsk. Later he was also editor of its periodical, *Robotnik Wybrzeża*. Gwiazda was arrested many times for forty-eight-hour periods. In August 1980 he belonged to the Inter-Factory Strike Committee in Gdańsk. From September 1980 to July 1981 he was deputy chairman of the Inter-Factory Founding Committee of Solidarity's Gdańsk Region and then a member of the union's Gdańsk Regional Board. From February to September 1981 he was deputy chairman of the National Coordination Commission of Solidarity. Gwiazda gradually came to oppose **Lech Wałęsa**, attracting more radical activists of the Gdańsk WZZ from before 1980. In September 1981 he was a delegate to the First Congress of Solidarity. He was elected to its National Commission, but he lost the election for chairman to Wałęsa. Upon the introduction of martial law, on 13 December 1981 Gwiazda was interned, and in 1982 he was arrested. Amnestied in 1984, he was active in the underground Solidarity in opposition to Wałęsa. In 1987 he co-founded the so-called Working Group, demanding that the National Commission elected in 1981 be convened. He opposed the Round Table Talks. After the breakup of the Working Group, in 1990 Gwiazda tried to organize free trade unions in opposition to Solidarity, but he failed. (AF)

Sources: Jerzy Holzer, *"Solidarność*, (Warsaw, 1983); Jerzy Holzer and Krzysztof Leski, *"Solidarność" w podziemiu* (Łódź, 1990); Jan Skórzyński, *Ugoda i rewolucja: Władza i opozycja 1985–1989* (Warsaw, 1995); *Opozycja w PRL: Słownik biograficzny 1956–89* (Warsaw, 2000).

H

HABRMAN Gustáv (24 January 1864,Česká Třebová–22 March 1932, Prague), Czech journalist and Social Democratic politician. Habrman came from a poor working-class family. At seventeen he left for Vienna, where he learned the trade of a wood-carver and a turner. It was there that he was introduced to Socialist thought, and he became active in the Czech workers' movement. In 1884 he was arrested and sentenced to three years of prison for his activities. After his release he emigrated to France and then to the United States, where he spent eight years, acting in the workers' movement. After his return to Bohemia, he edited the Brno magazine *Rovnost* from 1897. In 1901 he moved to Plzen, where he became editor-in-chief of *Nova doba* and the leader of local Social Democracy. In 1907, as a representative of Social Democracy, he was elected to the Viennese parliament, in which he sat until the collapse of Austria-Hungary.

After the outbreak of World War I Habrman took a stand against Austria-Hungary, opposing the Social Democratic faction of **Bohumír Šmeral**. In 1915 he left for Switzerland, where he started working with **Tomáš Garrigue Masaryk**, becoming a member of the "Mafia," a committee established to coordinate activities with the emigrant community. In 1917 he attended the international conference of Socialists in Stockholm, where he advocated the formation of an independent Czechoslovakia. In July 1918 he became a member of the National Committee, and in October in Geneva he took part in the negotiations on the creation of the state. After his return to Bohemia, he became a member of the Revolutionary National Assembly (provisional parliament) and minister of schools and education in the first government of **Karel Kramář**. He held this post until 1920, and in 1921–25 he was minister for social affairs. After the electoral defeat of the Social Democrats in 1925 Habrman left the government, became a senator, and held the post until his death. In 1924 he published *Z mého života vzpominký* (The memoirs of my life). (PU)

Sources: *ČBS*; *Kto bol kto za I. ČSR* (Bratislava, 1993); *Kdo byl kdo v našich dějinach ve 20. stoleti*, vol. 1 (Prague, 1998); *Politická elita meziválečného Československa 1918–1938: Kdo byl kdo za prvni republiky* (Prague, 1998).

HÁCHA Emil (12 July 1872, Trhové Sviny, district of České Budějovice–27 June 1945, Prague), lawyer and politician, president of Czechoslovakia and of the Protectorate of Bohemia and Moravia. Born into the family of a fiscal clerk, after graduating from high school in České Budějovice, in 1895 Hácha graduated in law from the Czech University in Prague. After doing a legal internship as a trainee from 1895 to 1898, he started working as a clerk in a Bohemian district council. He also worked as a legal counselor of the Supreme Administrative Tribunal in Vienna. During World War I he cooperated with Ferdinand Pantůček, who was active in a secret committee that was later called the "Mafia" (Maffie). After the war Pantůček was appointed president of the Supreme Administrative Court (SAC), and Hácha became a member of the SAC. In 1925 Hácha assumed the post of president of the SAC. In 1920 he became a *docent* (associate professor) at Charles University. In his academic work he mainly dealt with English public law. He was the author of *O správním soudnictvi v Anglii* (On the administrative judiciary system in England; 1913) and other works and a contributor to *Slovník československého práva veřejného* (The dictionary of Czechoslovak public law, 4 vols.; 1929–38). He was also a literary scholar and a translator of English fiction. A recognized professional, Hácha was a judge of The Hague Tribunal and a member of the legislative council of the Czechoslovak government.

On 30 November 1938, following the Pact of Munich; the resignation of President **Edvard Beneš**; the passage of a law on the autonomy of Slovakia and Subcarpathian Ruthenia and the change of the name of the state to Czechoslovakia; and given the reluctance of other politicians to assume the leadership of the state, Hácha became president of the Second Republic. In December 1938, on a visit to Slovakia, he was assured by Father **Jozef Tiso** that autonomy was the highest aspiration of the Slovaks. On 14 March 1939 he went with **František Chvalkovsky** to Berlin, where he conducted negotiations with Adolf Hitler. After Slovak independence was hurriedly declared that very day under German pressure, the unified Czech and Slovak state ceased to exist. A day later, before dawn, blackmailed by Hitler and Hermann Göring, who threatened to bomb Prague, Hácha agreed to the incorporation of Czech territories into the Third Reich, accepted the creation of the Protectorate of Bohemia and Moravia, and assumed the post of president of the Protectorate.

During the first two years of the Protectorate, while showing loyalty to the Germans, Hácha also tried to maintain a minimum of autonomy. He was supported in his efforts by a group of his associates led by **Jiři Havelka**. In October 1939 Hácha refused to swear allegiance to Hitler. He also intervened on behalf of prisoners and protested against the Germanization of the Protectorate of Bohemia and Moravia. He also objected to the enactment of anti-Jewish laws, and after they were introduced by Konstantin von Neurath, Hácha tried to minimize the number of people affected by such laws. With Prime Minister **Alois Eliáš**, Hácha maintained contact both with the national and foreign resistance movement and with President Beneš in London. A breakthrough came after Reinhard Heydrich's appointment as Reich protector of Bohemia and Moravia, the arrest and execution of Eliáš, and the imprisonment of Havelka. Hácha succeeded in the difficult task of saving Havelka's life, but he did so at the price of significant concessions to Germany, such as the introduction of Walter Bertsch, a German, and **Emanuel Moravec**, an open collaborator, into the government. Hácha finally broke down after the assassination of Heydrich (27 May 1942). At Heydrich's funeral Hitler announced the end of the Protectorate, and Hácha expressed his condemnation of the assassins. Soon afterwards, Hácha withdrew from public life and lived at Lány castle. In 1943, owing to progressing arteriosclerosis, he ceased to perform his duties. From May 1944, those duties were routinely performed by the prime minister of the Protectorate (first **Jaroslav Krejči**, then **Richard Bienert**). On 13 May 1945 Hácha was arrested and taken to a prison hospital in Pankrac, where he died. (PU)

Sources: *ČBS*; *Československí politici: 1918–1991* (Prague, 1991); *Kdo byl kdo v našich dějinach ve 20. stoleti*, vol. 1 (Prague, 1998); *Politická elita meziválečného Československa 1918–1938: Kdo byl kdo za první republiky* (Prague, 1998); Vojtech Masny, *The Czechs under Nazi Rule* (New York and London, 1971); Vladimír Kadlec, *Podivné konce našich presidentů* (Hradec Králové, 1991); Robert Kvaček and Dušan Tomášek, *Causa Emil Hácha* (Prague, 1995); Tomáš Pasák, *JUDr. Emil Hácha* (Prague, 1997); Vít Machálek, *Prezident v zajetí: Život činy a kríž Emila Háchy* (Prague, 1998); http://www.hrad.cz/president/hacha.html.

HADLEUSKI Vintsuk (16 December 1898, Porazovo, near Volkovysk–December 1942, Trostsianets), Catholic priest, Belorussian national activist. The son of a peasant, Hadleuski graduated from a seminary in Wilno (Vilnius) in 1912 and from the Catholic Theological Academy in Petrograd in 1917. Ordained while a student in 1914, he joined the Belorussian movement. After completing his studies, he was a curate in one of the parishes of Minsk. In March 1917 he attended the First Congress of Belorussian Parties and Organizations, which called for autonomy for Belorussia within the framework of a federal Russia; Hadleuski became a member of the Belorussian National Committee. He initiated the congress of Belorussian Catholic priests in May 1917 and advocated the Beloruthenization of religious life in the Catholic Church on Belorussian territory. After the Belorussian People's Republic (BPR) proclaimed its independence on 25 March 1918,

Hadleuski became a member of its council (parliament). He co-organized the Belorussian Catholic seminary in Minsk and the Belorussian Christian Democratic Party. He was also an editor of the party's organ, *Krynitsa* (later *Byelaruskaya Krynitsa*).

From January 1920 Hadleuski was in Wilno (Vilnius), where he participated in the creation of the Belorussian National Committee and of the Frantsysk Skaryna Belorussian Publishing House. Appointed parish priest of Żodziszki in 1924, he celebrated one of the Sunday masses in Belorussian; this gave rise to protests by the local Poles and caused the intervention of the authorities. Arrested on 25 June 1925, Hadleuski was accused of anti-state activities but was released on bail after a few months. Arrested again in March 1926, in March 1927 he was sentenced to two years in prison for instigating a rebellion against the government. Released in 1929, he became a chaplain in a hospital in Wilno. He took an active part in the national life of the Belorussians in the Wilno region. In 1930 he completed a translation of the New Testament into Belorussian. In 1936 he started publishing the periodical *Belaruski Front*, in which he analyzed the international situation in Europe, predicted an imminent war, and called on the Belorussian elite to take advantage of the anticipated change in the European order to unite the country and establish an independent state.

Escaping from the Red Army, in September 1939 Hadleuski went to Kaunas and in June 1940 to German-occupied Warsaw. On 19 June 1941 he became a member of the Belorussian National Committee in Berlin. He was in favor of cooperation with the Germans, the end goal of which was an independent Belorussian state. From September 1941 he worked as a school inspector for the General District of Belorussia created by the occupiers. He was also one of the senior leaders of the Belorussian People's Mutual Aid Association; in his plans, the leadership of this organization was to serve as the Belorussian government. While forming the structures of the Belorussian government, Hadleuski went beyond the limits allowed by the occupiers. Arrested by the Gestapo on 24 December 1942, he probably perished in a concentration camp at Trostsianets, near Minsk. (EM)

Sources: V. Panutsevich, "Ks. Vintses Hadleuski—dziarzhauny muzh i pravadyr narodu," *Belaruskaia tsarkva* (Chicago), 1965, no. 28; *Batskaushchina* (Munich), 1965, no. 632; *Belaruskaia Trybuna* (New York), 1952, nos. 1–2; Vitaut Kipel and Zora Kipel, eds., *Byelorussian Statehood* (New York, 1988).

HADZHIYSKI Ivan (13 October 1907, Troyan–3 October 1944, Visoka Čuka, Yugoslavia), Bulgarian writer, psychologist, and sociologist. Hadzhiyski graduated in philosophy (1932) and law (1936) from the University of Sofia. During his studies he became engaged in the activities of a leftist student union, and in 1929 he joined the Bulgarian Workers' Party, a legal superstructure of the illegal Bulgarian Communist Party. He was a white-collar worker in Velyko Turnovo and Troyan and then a lawyer in Sofia. He was arrested several times, and in 1936 he was sentenced to three months on the basis of the state protection law. After the coup of 9 September 1944 and Bulgaria's entry into the war on the Soviet side, Hadzhiyski volunteered for the army and was killed as a war correspondent in unknown circumstances. He authored several works, including the following: *Avtoritet, dostoyinstvo i maska* (Authority, dignity, and mask; 1933); *Psykhologia na Aprilskoto vystaniye* (Psychology of the April uprising; 1943); and *Byt i dushevnost na nashiya narod* (The existence and spirituality of our nation, 3 vols.; 1940–45). In the last work he presented an extensive image of various groups of Bulgarian society over the centuries. (JW)

Sources: *Entsyklopediya Bulgariya*, vol. 7 (Sofia, 1996); *Wielka encyklopedia PWN*, vol. 11 (Warsaw, 2002); Yordan Vasiliev, *Ivan Hadzhiyski v bulgarskata kultura* (Sofia, 1988).

HAJDARI Azem (11 March 1963, Tropojë–12 September 1998, Tirana), Albanian politician, youth movement and trade union activist. Hajdari came from a Muslim family. He studied at the Philosophy Department at the University of Tirana. In recognition of his role in the creation of an independent student movement he was called a hero of the events of December 1990. After the failure of Prime Minister Adil Çarçani's negotiations with striking students, on 9 December 1990 a group of fourteen students under Hajdari's leadership was received by **Ramiz Alia**, leader of the party. Soon after Hajdari co-formed the first non-Communist Democratic Party. He contended with **Sali Berisha** for the post of party chairman and after losing the elections assumed the post of deputy chairman of the party. During the election campaign of March 1991 Hajdari was often attacked by the post-Communist press, which suggested that he had avoided military service on account of mental disturbances. He spent 1992 at an American university, where he continued his education. From 1996 to 1997 he was deputy from Tropojë, and until 1996 he served as president of a parliamentary commission for special services. At the end of 1996 he was elected president of the Federation of Independent Trade Unions. He was unsuccessful in his attempts to take political control of a student strike in 1997. When the financial pyramids collapsed in the same year, Hajdari began to openly criticize Berisha, but a few months later

the two politicians became reconciled again. In July 1997 Berisha even proposed Hajdari as minister of interior, but his candidacy was not accepted by the parliament. On 18 September 1997 Hajdari fell victim to an assassination attempt by Gafurr Mazreku, a Socialist deputy, who shot at him several times in the parliament building. The shooting was a consequence of a conflict in parliament over a value added tax rate increase by the government. Hajdari survived the attempt, but one year later he was shot dead along with his bodyguard near the head office of the Democratic Party in Tirana. Speculating about the motive for the murder, the press suggested a family vendetta or Hajdari's links with weapons trafficking. (TC)

Sources: Nicolas J. Costa, *Albania: A European Enigma* (Boulder, Colo., 1995); Panajot Barka, *Kryengritja e tradhtuar* (Tirana, 1998); Elez Biberaj, *Shqipëria në tranzicion: Rruga e vështrisë drejt Demokracisë* (Tirana, 2001).

HÁJEK Jiří (6 June 1913, Krhanice–22 October 1993, Prague), Czech Communist activist, lawyer, historian, diplomat, and democratic opposition activist. In 1936 Hájek graduated in law from Charles University in Prague and later he worked as a financial clerk. After the partition of Czechoslovakia he was active in the then forming resistance movement, but in November 1939 he was arrested by the Gestapo, and throughout World War II he was held at a Nazi camp. An active member of the Social Democratic movement since his student days, he resumed this work after the war. In 1945–48 Hájek belonged to the left wing of the Social Democratic movement, actively promoting its incorporation into the Communist Party of Czechoslovakia (CPC). From 1945 to 1946 he was an MP of the Provisional National Assembly, and from 1946 to 1948, secretary general of a workers' academy. After Social Democracy joined the Communist Party, Hájek was a member of the CC of the CPC (1948–69). From 1948 to 1954 he was an MP; in 1949–53 he was a professor in the School of Political and Economic Sciences in Prague, and from 1954 he was a professor at Charles University. In 1955 he became ambassador to Great Britain, and in 1958, deputy foreign minister. From 1962 to 1965 he was permanent representative of Czechoslovakia to the United Nations. In 1965 he became minister of education and culture, and from 1967 to 1968 he served as minister of education.

In the 1960s Hájek was one of the initiators and supporters of the reform process in Czechoslovakia. Between April and September 1968 he was minister of foreign affairs. In August 1968 he protested at the United Nations against the invasion of Czechoslovakia by the Warsaw Pact troops. Soon he was dismissed from his post, and in 1970 he was expelled from the CPC. Until 1972 he was a researcher at the Historical Institute of the Czechoslovak Academy of Sciences, but in 1973 he was retired and in 1976 he was deprived of membership in the Academy by government decision. In late 1976 and early 1977 Hájek was a co-founder of Charter 77, a manifest of the then forming democratic opposition, and he was one of its first three spokesmen (along with **Jan Patočka** and **Václav Havel**). He served as Charter 77 spokesman until April 1978 and subsequently from June 1979 until the beginning of 1980. He was constantly kept under surveillance by the Czechoslovak special services. Detained on many occasions, in May 1981 he spent a short time in jail, pending trial. From November 1988 he presided over the Czechoslovak Helsinki Committee, and in November 1989 he was one of the founders of the Civic Forum. From 1990 to 1992 he was the adviser to the president of the National Assembly, **Alexander Dubček**, and he served as a consultant to the Institute of State and Law of the Czechoslovak Academy of Sciences. Hájek was the author of many historical works, including the following: *Wilsonovská legenda v dějinách ČSR* (The Wilson legend in the history of Czechoslovakia; 1953); *Německá otázka a československá politika* (The German cause and Czechoslovak policy; 1954); *Mnichov* (Munich; 1958); *Deset let poté* (Ten years later; 1978); and *Paměti* (Memoirs; 1997), which were published posthumously. (PU)

Sources: *ČBS*; *Českoslovenští politici: 1918–1991* (Prague, 1991); *Who's Who in the Socialist Countries of Europe*, vol. 1 (Munich, London, and Paris, 1989); Gordon H. Skilling, *Czechoslovakia's Interrupted Revolution* (Princeton, 1976); Vladimir V. Kusin, *From Dubcek to Charter 77: A Study of "Normalization" in Czechoslovakia, 1968–1978* (New York, 1978); Vilém Precan, ed., *Charta 77 (1977–1989). Od morální k demokratické revoluci: Dokumentace* (Bratislava, 1990); Alexander Dubcek, *Hope Dies Last* (New York, 1993).

HALECKI Oskar (26 May 1891, Vienna–17 September 1973, White Plains, New York), Polish historian. The son of an Austrian general and a Croatian woman, Halecki graduated from high school in Vienna and later completed historical studies at the Jagiellonian University in Kraków, where he earned a Ph.D. in 1913 and was awarded a postdoctoral degree in 1916. Between 1916 and 1918 he lectured as a *docent* (associate professor) at the Jagiellonian University, and in 1918 he took the chair of East European history at Warsaw University, where he lectured until 1939. In the academic year 1920–21 he was dean of the Philosophy Department and in 1930–31, dean of the Humanities Department. He was a member, and between 1930 and 1939 president, of the Polish Academy of Arts and Sciences (Polska Akademia Umiejętności). He also belonged to the Polish Heraldic Society, the Warsaw Sci-

entific Society, and the Lwów (Lviv) Scientific Society. In 1919 Halecki was an expert in the Polish delegation to the Paris Peace Conference; between 1921 and 1924 he was secretary of the Commission for Intellectual Cooperation (Commission de Coopération Intellectuelle) of the League of Nations; and from 1924 to 1926 he was director of the University Section of the Institut de Coopération Intellectuelle in Paris. The outbreak of war in 1939 found him in Switzerland. From there he went to France, where he organized the Polish University in Exile. After the fall of France Halecki went to the United States, where he co-organized the Polish Institute of Arts and Sciences under the auspices of the Kościuszko Foundation. From 1942 he was its director and from 1952 its president. In 1944 he took the chair of East European history at Fordham University, where he worked until his retirement in 1961. He also lectured at Columbia University in New York, the University of Montreal, the University of California at Los Angeles, and Saint Ignatius Loyola University in Rome.

Halecki left a vast scholarly legacy; it includes a two-volume history of the Polish-Lithuanian Commonwealth, *Dzieje Unii Jagiellońskiej* (The history of the Jagiellonian Union; 1919–20); works on the history of Western and Eastern Christianity: *Rome et Byzance au temps du Grand Schisme* (Rome and Byzantium at the time of the Great Schism; 1937) and *From Florence to Brest* (1958; also published in Polish in 1997); a synthesis of Polish history, *The History of Poland* (1942; also published in French, Spanish, and Polish); and syntheses of European history: *The Limits and Divisions of European History* (1950; also published in German) and *Borderlands of Western Civilization* (1952; also published in German and Polish). Halecki was also the author of dozens of monographs and articles in many languages. He stressed the unique character and historical significance of the Polish-Lithuanian Union, the Brest-Litovsk Union of 1596, and the role of Christianity in the history of Europe. The theme underlying many of his later works was the distinctive character and sense of European culture, in which he saw a synthesis of Greek philosophy, Roman law, and Christianity. He strongly emphasized the place and role of Poland in the history of Europe, a role that had been belittled either deliberately for political reasons or out of ignorance. Enjoying great respect among American historians, Halecki was awarded honorary doctorates by the universities in Lyon, Montreal, and New York. (WR)

Sources: *Polacy w historii i kulturze krajów Europy Zachodniej* (Poznań, 1981); Hans A. Schmitt, ed., *Historians of Modern Europe* (Baton Rouge, 1971); Walerian Meysztowicz, *To, co trwałe* (London, 1974); Janusz Pajewski, "In memoriam Oskar Halecki," *Kwartalnik Historyczny*, 1975, no. 4; Rafał Habielski, *Życie społeczne i kulturalne emigracji* (Warsaw, 1999).

HALIPPA Pantelimon (Pan) (1 August 1883, Cubolta, Moldavia–30 April 1979, Bucharest), Romanian journalist and politician. After finishing a seminary in Edineţ and an Orthodox theological seminary in Kishinev (Chişinău), in 1903 Halippa took up studies at the Department of Physics and Mathematics of the University of Dorpat (Tartu), but in 1905 he discontinued his studies because of the outbreak of the revolution in Russia. He returned to Kishinev and joined the young Romanian intellectuals who were calling for the independence of Bessarabia, which was then part of the Russian empire. From 1905 to 1908 Halippa contributed to the periodical *Revistă Basarabiei*, in which he published the Romanian national anthem, *Deşteaptă-te române!* (Awaken thee, Romanian), for which he was arrested and tried by the Russian authorities. At that time he also founded the national daily *Basarabia*. In 1908 Halippa published a book, *Pilde şi poveţe* (Examples and pieces of advice), and left for Romania. Until 1913 he lived in Iaşi, where from 1908 to 1913 he studied at the Department of Literature and Philosophy of the University of Iaşi. In 1912 he published *Basarabia, schiţă geografică* (Bessarabia, a geographical outline). He contributed to the periodical *Viaţa românească*, in which he published *Scrisori din Basarabia* (Letters from Bessarabia). In 1913 he returned to Kishinev, where he edited the daily *Cuvânt Moldovenesc*.

After the outbreak of World War I Halippa actively worked for the unification of Moldavia and Romania. In 1917 he founded the Moldavian National Party (Partidul Naţional Moldovenesc) and the People's University in Kishinev. Between 1917 and 1918 he was vice-president, and then president, of the Council of the Country (Sfatul Ţării), which in January 1918 voted for the creation of the Independent Republic of Moldavia and in April of that year, for its unification with Romania. Halippa was a member of similar Romanian national assemblies in Bukovina and Transylvania that voted to unite with Romania. In 1918–21 Halippa was leader of the National Peasant Party of Bessarabia (Partidul Naţional Ţărănesc din Basarabia). In 1921, after a conflict within the National Peasant Party of Bessarabia, he joined the Peasant Party (Partidul Ţărănesc). In 1918 he became a member of the Romanian Academy of Sciences. After 1918 he held numerous government positions in Romania. Between 1919 and 1920 he was minister/secretary of state for the affairs of Bessarabia, in 1927 minister of public works, and in 1930 minister of public works and transport and minister of health and social welfare. In addition, from 1928 to 1930, in 1932, and from 1932 to 1933, he was minister/secretary of state, and between 1918 and 1934 he served as senator or MP. In 1932 he published and edited the periodical *Viaţa Basarabiei*. In 1940 he founded the Bessarabian Writers' and Publishers' Association. After World War II Halippa was critical of the Communist government. Consequently, he was removed from public life, and in 1950 he was arrested and imprisoned without trial in a prison in Şighet Marmaţiei. After two years he was handed over to the NKVD in Kishinev, where he was tried and sentenced to twenty-five years of hard labor in Siberia. In 1955 the deportation sentence was commuted to a prison term, and he was handed over to the Romanian authorities. Until 1957 Halippa was held in prisons in Aiud and Gherla. After his release from prison he settled in Bucharest. (LW)

Sources: *Dictionar Enciclopedic*, vol. 3 (Bucharest, 1999); Juliusz Demel, *Historia Rumunii* (Wrocław, 1986); Şerban N. Ionescu, *Who Was Who in Twentieth Century Romania* (Boulder, Colo., 1994); Dorina N. Rusu, *Membrii Academiei Române 1866–1999* (Bucharest, 1999); Ion Alexandrescu, Ion Bulei, Ion Mamina, and Ioan Scurtu, *Enciclopedia de istorie României* (Bucharest, 2000).

HALL Aleksander (20 May 1953, Gdańsk), Polish politician. Hall graduated in history from the University of Gdańsk in 1977. From his school years he was connected with the democratic opposition and was active in academic ministry groups. In 1977–79 he was active in the Movement for the Defense of Human and Civic Rights, and in 1977–81 he co-founded and edited an uncensored periodical, *Bratniak*. In 1979 he co-organized and became leader of the Movement of Young Poland, whose program was based on democratic, national, and Catholic values and which played an important role in the Gdańsk region, particularly during the summer strikes of 1980 and after the formation of Solidarity. From September 1980 Hall was a member of Solidarity. After the introduction of martial law on 13 December 1981, he went into hiding. In 1981–84 he belonged to the Solidarity Regional Coordination Commission in Gdańsk. After coming out of hiding, in 1984–89 Hall wrote for the periodical *Przegląd Katolicki* and from 1982 for the underground *Polityka Polska*. In 1986–89 he was a member of the Social Council of the Primate of Poland, and in 1988–89 he was deputy chairman of the Dziekania Political Thought Club. In December 1988 he joined the Civic Committee of Solidarity Chairman **Lech Wałęsa**. He took part in the Round Table Talks (February–April 1989), and from September 1989 to December 1990 he was minister for contacts with political organizations. During the so-called war at the top in 1990 Hall supported Prime Minister **Tadeusz Mazowiecki**. From November 1990 he presided over the Forum of Democratic Right (FDR), and from May 1991 he was deputy chairman of the Democratic Union (DU). In 1992, along with the FDR Hall left the DU and co-founded the Conservative Party. In 1991–93 he was an MP. From 1997 he was chairman of the Political Council of the Conservative Popular Party (Stronnictwo Konserwatywno-Ludowe), which joined Solidarity Electoral Action (Akcja Wyborcza Solidarność [AWS]). An MP from 1997 to 2001, Hall was deputy head of the AWS parliamentary club. He authored several works, including *Polemiki i refleksje* (Polemics and Reflections; 1989); a book-interview, *Spór o Polskę* (Debate over Poland; 1993); *Polskie patriotyzmy* (Polish patriotisms; 1997); and *Widziane z prawej strony* (Seen from the right side; 2000). (AF)

Sources: Mołdawa; *Kto jest kim w Polsce* (Warsaw, 2001); Jan Skórzyński, *Ugoda i rewolucja: Władza i opozycja 1985–1989* (Warsaw, 1995); Antoni Dudek, *Pierwsze lata III Rzeczypospolitej 1989–2001* (Kraków, 2002).

HALLER Józef (Haller de Hallenburg) (13 August 1873, Jurczyce–4 June 1960, London), Polish general. Haller attended a high school in Košice and Hranice and then studied at the Jagiellonian University in Kraków and the Technical Military Academy in Vienna. He joined the Austrian Army, where he rose to the rank of captain. In 1912 he retired from active service and devoted himself to the Falcon Movement (Ruch Sokoli) and to scouting among the Galician Poles. After the outbreak of World War I Haller organized the Eastern Legion (Legion Wschodni), which was dissolved by the Austrians; therefore he joined the Polish Legions, assuming command of the Second Brigade. During the crisis of July 1917 he remained in the army and pledged an oath of loyalty to the emperors of Austria-Hungary and Germany, becoming the head of the Polish Auxiliary Corps. At the news of the Brest-Litovsk peace treaty between the Central Powers and the Bolsheviks, the conditions of which were unfavorable to Poland, Haller and his units fought their way through the front, fighting a severe battle against the Austrians at Rarańcza. Haller attached his units to the Second Polish Corps in Russia and assumed its command. On 11 May 1918 the corps lost a battle at Kaniów, was surrounded by the Germans, disarmed, and interned. However, many officers and soldiers, including Haller, escaped captivity and in the spring of 1918 forced their way to Murmansk via territories controlled by the Bolsheviks. On 12 July 1918 Haller arrived in France. In Paris he became a member of the Polish National Committee, and on 4 October 1918 he was appointed commander-in-chief of the Polish Army in France.

In June 1919 Haller, at the head of his army (called the "Blue Army"), crossed the borders of the Republic of Poland and then was the commander in battles against the Ukrainians in Eastern Galicia. Later he organized the defense of Pomerania. On 10 February 1920 in Puck he conducted a symbolical "marriage" of Poland with the Baltic Sea. In the Polish-Soviet war he commanded the northern section of the front. He was politically tied with Christian Democracy and was its representative in the Assembly (1922–27). During the crisis connected with the election and assassination of President **Gabriel Narutowicz** in 1922, the national right considered Haller a charismatic leader. After the coup of May 1926 he was dismissed from service. In February 1936 he joined the agreement of the Center Right, which was formed in the Swiss residence of **Ignacy Paderewski** in Morges (Morges Front) and was in opposition to the *sanacja* (i.e., moral and political cleansing) regime. In 1937 Haller was one of the founders of the Labor Party.

In October 1939 Haller joined the government of General **Władysław Sikorski** as a minister without portfolio and held the post until July 1943. After the end of the war Haller remained in England, where he was active in the political life of the Polish emigrant community. In December 1949 he became a member of the Political Council, which was in opposition to President **August Zaleski**. In February 1952, as a representative of the Labor Party, Haller became a member of the Presidium of the Political Council. He signed the Act of Unification of the Polish emigration in March 1953. He gradually withdrew from politics owing to declining health. (WR)

Sources: *Dziesięciolecie Rzeczpospolitej Polskiej 1918–1928* (Warsaw, 1928); *Polacy w historii . . .* ; Andrzej Friszke, *Życie polityczne emigracji* (Warsaw, 1999); Janusz Zabłocki, *Chrześcijańska Demokracja w kraju i na emigracji 1947–1970* (Lublin, 1999).

HALLER Stanisław (26 April 1872, Polanka-Haller, near Bielsko–April 1940, Kharkiv), Polish general. Haller came from a landowning family of bourgeois origin and was the cousin of **Józef Haller**. After graduating from high school in Bielsko in 1892, he volunteered for the Austrian Army, and in 1894 he became a regular soldier. In 1901 he graduated from the Military College in Vienna. He commanded a battalion and was a general staff officer and chief of staff of the Kraków fortress. He served as chief of staff until 1915 and then became deputy chief of the corps staff and commander of an artillery regiment. From May 1918, as colonel, he commanded an artillery brigade on the Italian front. In November 1918 he volunteered for the Polish Army and became deputy commander of Kraków and later chief of staff of the Kraków district of the Polish Army. On 1 January 1920 Haller was nominated general, and he assumed the duties of chief of the General Staff of the Polish Army. With **Józef Piłsudski**, he worked out the plan for the Kiev expedition of April 1920. During the retreat from the Ukraine he resigned and took command of the Thirteenth Infantry Division and then the Sixth Army. He was also a member of the War Council. After the end of the Polish-Soviet war Haller served as an army inspector in Lwów (Lviv), and in 1923 he became chief of the General Staff. His hitherto good relations with Piłsudski deteriorated when Haller became aware of preparations for a coup d'état. In December 1925 he resigned and withdrew to his family estate. During the coup of May 1926, he was appointed chief of staff of the government forces in Warsaw, and he cooperated in the defense of the constitutional government. After the coup he was interned. Following his release, he obtained a dismissal from the army and settled permanently at Polanka. In 1926 he published a book about the May coup, *Wypadki warszawskie* (Warsaw events), and *Naród i armia* (The nation and the army), in which he was critical of Piłsudski. Haller was a member of Catholic Action, and in his political sympathies he became increasingly closer to National Democracy. In September 1939 he declared his readiness to serve in the army. Seeking an assignment, he went eastward, where he was captured by the Red Army. Haller was sent to the camp in Starobielsk, and in the spring of 1940, by decision of the Kremlin leadership, he was murdered by the NKVD in Kharkiv. (WR)

Sources: *PSB*, vol. 9; *Kto był kim w Drugiej Rzeczypospolitej* (Warsaw, 1994); *Encyklopedia historii Drugiej Rzeczypospolitej* (Warsaw, 1999); Norman Davies, *White Eagle Red Star: The Polish-Soviet War, 1919–20* (London, 1972); Andrzej Nowak, *Polska i trzy Rosje: Studium o polityce wschodniej Józefa Piłsudskiego (do kwietnia 1920 roku)* (Kraków, 2001).

HALUBOK Uladzimir (15 May 1882, Lasnaia, near Nowogródek [now Novogrudok, Belarus]–28 September 1937), Belorussian writer, actor, and director. After completing primary school in Minsk, Halubok worked as a porter, locksmith, and warehouseman. In 1906 he started publishing his poems and stories in the newspaper *Nasha Niva* in Vilnius and later in the newspapers *Luchinka* and *Maladaya Belarus*. From 1915 he was one of the organizers of the Belorussian Relief Committee for War Victims. In 1920 he was involved in the organization of theater life in Slutsk. Between 1920 and 1922 he worked at the Art Department in the People's Commissariat of Education of the Belorussian SSR and was also in charge of the theater section of the Belorussian Workers' Club in Minsk. Halubok was the director of a workers' theater and belonged to the writers' societies Maladnyak and Polymia. He wrote forty plays, gathering motifs from the everyday life of Minsk and from local folklore. He staged some of

his plays in the theater he directed. He also wrote many theater reviews and published newspaper articles on the Belorussian theater. In the late 1920s, like most Belorussian culture activists, Halubok was accused of nationalism. In 1931 the Soviet authorities banned the publication of his works. Until 1937 he worked as an actor. Arrested in September 1937, according to the official report, Halubok died of coronary disease in prison. (EM)

Sources: *Entsyklapiediya historyi Bielarusi*, vol. 2 (Minsk, 1994); A. Atroshchanka, *Uladzimir Halubok* (Minsk, 1969).

HAMPL Antonín (12 April 1875, Jaroměř–17 May 1942, Berlin), Czech Social Democratic politician. A graduate of the State Industrial School in Prague, Hampl was already taking part in the workers' movement as a student. From 1910 he was secretary of the Metalworkers' Union, an organization that grew rapidly to become the strongest trade union in Bohemia. From 1918 he was a member of the leadership of the Czechoslovak Social Democratic Party, and from 1924 to 1938, president of the party. In 1918 he was a member of the Czechoslovak National Committee, and later he was an MP throughout the interwar period. From 1919 and 1920 he served as minister of public works in the cabinet of **Vlastimil Tusar**. At that time he worked for social welfare legislation, the protection of workers' rights, social insurance, and workers' self-government. From the beginning of the 1920s Hampl was the de facto leader of the Social Democratic movement, which was then going through hard times because its left wing had broken off to form the Communist Party. Hampl tried to consolidate Czech Social Democracy. Thanks to his leadership abilities, by the mid-1930s the party doubled its membership. Many former secessionists returned to the party. As a result of the Munich Agreement and the stance of the international community, Czechoslovak Social Democracy left the Socialist International. In the autumn of 1938 a new political party was created, the National Labor Party (NLP), which grouped anti-Nazi political activists. Hampl became president of the NLP. However, when Hitler created the Protectorate of Bohemia and Moravia on 15 March 1939, the National Labor Party was dissolved. Arrested by the Gestapo in May 1941, Hampl died in prison in Berlin. (PU)

Sources: *ČBS*; *Kto bol kto za I. ČSR* (Bratislava, 1993); *Kdo byl kdo v našich dějinách ve 20. stoleti*, vol. 1 (Prague, 1998); *Politická elita meziválečného Československa 1918–1938: Kdo byl kdo za první republiky* (Prague, 1998).

HAMVAS Béla, pseudonym "Pál Antal" (24 March 1897, Eperjes [Prešov]–7 November 1968, Budapest), Hungarian philosopher and writer. After graduating from a high school in Bratislava, Hamvas volunteered for the army and fought on the eastern front. Displaced along with his family from Bratislava in 1919, he settled in Budapest, where he studied Hungarian and German language and literature. After graduating in 1923, he contributed to the daily *Budapesti Hirlap*, in which he published short stories, as well as articles on art and literature. From 1927 Hamvas worked as a librarian and devoted himself mostly to philosophy. Among other projects, he interpreted and creatively developed observations made by Bertrand Russell in *The Prospects of Industrial Civilization* and by Sigmund Freud in *Das Unbehagen in der Kultur*. In 1935 he established a debating salon and a periodical, both named *Sziget*, where, along with friends like **László Németh**, he published on the topics of culture, beauty, and the capacities of human cognition. In 1937 Hamvas married Katalin Kemény, with whom he wrote *Forradalom a művészetben: Absztrakció és szürrealizmus Magyarországon* (Revolution in art: Abstraction and Surrealism in Hungary; 1947). The work was later sharply criticized by the Marxists.

In World War II, Hamvas again fought on the eastern front, from where he deserted in 1944. During the war he lost some of his notes and parts of the study *Scientia Sacra*, which consisted of nearly twenty essays. The study, devoted to interrelations among metaphysics, anthropology, and culture, was finally published in 1988. One of the conclusions he reached was that religion is the foundation of all human civilizations. He continued his scholarly work after the war. From 1945 to 1948 he edited a series of papers presenting the most prominent figures among twentieth-century European historians of the idea. In 1946 he published his collected essays, *Anthologia humana: Ötezer év bölcsessége* (Anthologia humana: Five thousand years of wisdom). Hamvas was criticized and attacked by adherents of Marxism, and in 1948 a ban was placed on the publication of his works that was maintained nearly until the end of Communist rule in Hungary. Hamvas lost his job as a librarian and made his living working as an unskilled laborer. In 1951 he started work on another monumental work, *Karnevál* (Carnival; 1997), a novel that is a catalogue of ethical positions available to individuals, depicted in the context of different epochs, traditions, and continents. *Patmosz* (1992), a three-volume collection of essays written in 1959–66, is the quintessence of his work; in it Hamvas arrived at the conclusion that contemporary civilization was in deep crisis. His works are being edited and published by the Hamvas Institute, established in Budapest in 2001. (MS)

Sources: *Gyémántnál keményebb: 100 éve született Hamvas Béla* (Budapest, 1997); Zoltán Bódis, *Hamvas-írás: A hamvasi nyelvszelétet megközzelítése* (Debrecen, 1997); *Új magyar irodalmi lexikon* (Budapest, 2000); Pál Darabos, *Hamvas Béla: Egy életmű fiziognómiája* (Budapest, 2002).

HANCHAR Viktar (29 April 1957, Augustovo, near Lahoisk–1999?, Minsk), Belorussian politician. Hanchar graduated from the Law Department of the Belorussian State University in Minsk. From 1986 he worked at the Belorussian Institute of the National Economy. He was deputy to the Supreme Council of Belarus from 1990 to 1995 and from 1995 to 1999. In 1994 President **Alyaksandr Lukashenka** appointed him deputy prime minister of the Belorussian government. From September 1996 Hanchar served as president of the Central Electoral Committee (CEC). He opposed Lukashenka's policy of restricting the role of parliament and objected to a referendum on constitutional amendments planned by Lukashenka. In November 1996 Hanchar stated that the referendum ordered by Lukashenka was being held in violation of the law. In retaliation he was dismissed as head of the CEC. After the referendum, he was one of the leaders of the Supreme Council, which was not recognized by the president, and a member of the liberal United Citizens' Party of Belarus, created in the autumn of 1995. Hanchar often spoke out against Lukashenka's dictatorship and his aim to unite Belarus with Russia. Kidnapped on a street in Minsk on 16 September 1999, Hanchar disappeared without a trace. According to opposition sources, he was a victim of the so-called death squads headed by Lukashenka's security officers. (EM)

Sources: *Kto iest kto v Respublike Belarus* (Minsk, 1999); Jan Zaprudnik, *Historical Dictionary of Belarus* (Lanham, Md., 1998); David R. Marples, *Belarus: A Denationalized Nation* (Amsterdam, 1999); Jan Czuryłowicz, "Trójkąt białoruski," *Wprost*, 1 July 2001.

HARASZTI Sándor (18 November 1897, Czinderybogád–19 January 1982, Budapest), Hungarian Communist activist and publicist. After passing his high school graduation exams in Pécs, Haraszti worked as a railway clerk. In 1919 he joined the Hungarian Social Democratic Party (HSDP), and under the Hungarian Soviet Republic he fought in the Red Army. In 1920 he went into exile in Austria and in the Kingdom of Serbs, Croats, and Slovenes, where he worked as a journalist. In 1929 he returned to Hungary. He was active in the Hungarian Communist Party (HCP) and was arrested on several occasions. In 1930 he began working as the Budapest editor of the Transylvanian newspaper *Korunk*. During World War II Haraszti was active in various anti-Fascist organizations, and when the Germans occupied Hungary in March 1944, he went underground. Between 1945 and 1948 he worked as editor of the daily *Szabadság* and as deputy head of the Propaganda and Agitation Department of the CC of the HCP. From 1949 he was director of the Athenaeum Publishing House. Arrested in November 1950, a year later Haraszti was sentenced to death in the trial of **János Kádár** and comrades. After spending a few years in a death cell, Haraszti had his sentence commuted to life imprisonment. Released and rehabilitated in mid-1954, he assumed the post of editor-in-chief of the newspaper *Béke és Szabadság*. A close associate of **Imre Nagy** in 1956, Haraszti presided over the Hungarian Union of Journalists. During the 1956 revolution he was editor-in-chief of the central party daily, *Népszabadság*. After the Soviet Army occupied Budapest, Haraszti took refuge in the Yugoslav Embassy, and after he left the embassy, he was interned in Romania. In the trial of Nagy and associates in the summer of 1958 Haraszti was sentenced to six years in prison. Released under an amnesty in 1960, he worked in the Akadémia Publishing House between 1963 and 1979. His political memoirs, *Befejezetlen számvetés* (Unfinished accounts; 1986), were published posthumously. (MS)

Sources: Judit Ember, *Menedék-jog 1956* (Budapest, 1989); Ferenc Donáth, "Haraszti Sándor és amiért nem kellett," *Liget*, 1989, no. 2.

HARETSKI Maksim, pseudonyms "Maksim Bielarus," "A. Mstsislauski," "Dzed Kuzma," "Maciej Myszka," "Mizerus Monus" (18 February 1893, Malaya Bahatskauka, near Mstsislav–10 February 1938, Smolensk), Belorussian writer and literary critic. After graduating from the School of Bailiffs and Agronomists in Gorki in 1913, Haretski worked as a bailiff in Lithuania. Mobilized into the Russian Army in 1914, he was seriously wounded in Prussia. In 1916 he graduated from the Military College in Petrograd. In 1918 he worked in the editorial offices of the newspapers *Izvestia Smolenskovo Sovieta* and *Zviazda* in Smolensk, and from 1920 he was a teacher at a Belorussian high school in Wilno (Vilnius), where he edited the newspapers *Nasha Dumka* and *Belaruskiia Vedamastsi*. In 1922 he was arrested by the Polish authorities for cooperation with the Communists. In 1923 he went to the Belorussian SSR. He lectured in literature at the Belorussian State University and at the Belorussian Communist University, and he worked as a professor at the Belorussian Academy of Sciences. In July 1930 he was arrested along with other intellectuals for being a member of an actually nonexistent organization, the Belarus Liberation Union, and he was sentenced to five years in a labor camp in Viatka. Arrested again in November 1937 and sentenced to death by an NKVD court, Haretski was executed by firing squad.

In 1913 Haretski made his literary debut with a short story published in the newspaper *Nasha Niva* in Vilnius.

His writing reflected the life of the Belorussian nation during the epoch of war, revolution, and political and territorial rift. His novels—*Dzvie Dushy* (Two souls; 1919); *Melankholia* (Melancholy; 1920); *U chim zakluchalasia iaho kriuda?* (What is his harm? 1926); *Tsihaia plyn* (Silent current; 1930)—were literary analyses of the spiritual life of the Belorussians, their constant choices and inner conflicts caused by the existing political and social reality. In the novel *Na imperialistycznej wojnie* (At the imperialistic war; 1926) Haretski presented the drama of soldiers fighting on the German-Soviet front. The novel *Usiebielaruski Ziezd 1917 hoda* (The All-Belorussian Congress of 1917), written to "uplift hearts," depicted a nation that was bursting the fetters of alien domination. Haretski was the author of the first history of Belorussian literature, *Historiia belaruskai literatury* (History of Belorussian literature; 1920) and of works about past and contemporary Belorussian literature. (EM)

Sources: Nicholas P. Vakar, *Belorussia: The Making of a Nation* (Cambridge, Mass., 1956); D. Buhaiou, *Maksim Haretski* (Minsk, 1968); T. Dasayeva, *Letapis zhytsia i tvorchastsi Maksima Haretskaha* (Minsk, 1993); Jan Zaprudnik, *Historical Dictionary of Belarus* (Lanham, Md., 1998).

HARETSKI Radzim (7 December 1928, Minsk), Belorussian geologist and social activist. In 1952 Haretski graduated from the Oil Institute in Moscow. In 1952–71 he worked in the Institute of Geology of the Academy of Sciences of the USSR; in 1972–93 he was director of the Institute of Geochemistry and Geophysics of the Belorussian Academy of Sciences (BAS); and in 1992–97 he was deputy chairman of the BAS. From 1993 he was chairman of the Belorussian Geological Society and a member of the American Geophysical Society. From 1995 he held a chair at the Belorussian State University in Minsk. In 1993–2001 he was chairman of Batskaushchyna, the World Association of Belorussians. Haretski organized a number of conferences and congresses of Belorussians living abroad. He is the author of several scholarly works, including *Tektonika Belarusi* (Tectonics of Belorussia; 1976). (EM)

Sources: *Kto iest kto w Respublike Belarus* (Minsk, 1999); Jan Zaprudnik, *Belarus: At a Crossroads in History* (Boulder, Colo., 1993); Jan Zaprudnik, *Historical Dictionary of Belarus* (Lanham, Md., 1998); *Kto jest kim w Białorusi* (Białystok, 2000).

HARUN Ales [originally Aleksandar Prushynski] (11 March. 1887, Novy Dvor–28 July 1920, Kraków), Belorussian politician, writer, and poet. Born into the large and poor family of a craftsman, in 1897 Harun finished a parish school in Minsk and in 1902 a school of crafts.

He worked as a carpenter in Minsk. A member of the Russian Socialist Revolutionary Party from 1904, he was involved in printing and distributing revolutionary literature. Arrested in 1907, he was sentenced to two years in prison by a court in Wilno (Vilnius) but was later acquitted. Arrested again in 1908, he was sentenced to exile in the Irkutsk *guberniya* (province). While in exile, Harun wrote poems that were published in the periodicals *Nasha Niva* and *Belarus*. Harun worked floating wood on the Lena River and in gold mines. After the February 1917 revolution he first lived in Moscow, becoming a member of the Belorussian People's Hromada; then in September of that year he went to Minsk, and in October 1917 he joined the Central Committee (CC) of the Belorussian Socialist Hromada. Harun participated in the preparations for the First All-Belorussian Congress in December 1917, and as its vice-president, he took part in the formation of the Belorussian People's Republic (BPR). As editor of the newspaper *Belaruski Shlakh*, he promoted the idea of an independent Belorussian state. During the German and Bolshevik occupations of Minsk Harun was in charge of shelters for orphans and homeless children. After the arrival of the Polish troops in the spring of 1919, he became president of the Belorussian Provisional National Committee, and in that role he greeted **Józef Piłsudski**, thanking him for the liberation of Belorussia from Russian imperialism. In October 1919 Harun became a member of the Belorussian Military Committee (BMC). He founded publishing houses, promoted BMC activities, and edited the periodical *Run'*. In July 1920, following the Polish troops, Harun withdrew to Poland, where he died and was buried at the Rakowice Cemetery in Kraków.

Harun made his literary debut as a poet in 1905. In 1918 he published *Matchin dar* (A gift from mother), his collected poems from 1907–14, in which the fate of Belorussia and the Belorussian nation was the main theme. The "mother" in the title refers to his enslaved homeland. The liberation of Belorussia from alien domination is even more strongly emphasized in Harun's second collection, *Novaia pesnia* (New song), from the years 1917–20. In his journalism, Harun treated the Bolshevik slogans of freedom, equality, and social justice as demagogy and the 1919 Polish declarations and assurances of freedom for the Belorussians as hypocrisy. The idea of independence for Belorussia was of crucial importance in his writing. Unlike most Belorussian intellectuals of his time, Harun considered social and economic issues as less important. Between 1912 and 1915 Harun also wrote several stories, the best known of which are *Maladoie* (The young), *Chalavek bez kryvi* (A man without blood), and *Pan Szabuniewicz* (Mr. Szabuniewicz). (EM)

Sources: *Entsyklapiedyia historyi Bielarusi*, vol. 2 (Minsk, 1994); *Bielaruskiia pismenniki 1917–1990: Davednik* (Minsk, 1994); *Bielaruskaia entsyklapiedyia*, vol. 5 (Minsk, 1997); Maksim Haretski, *Historyia bielaruskai litaratury* (Vilnia, 1920); M. Larchanka, "Tvorchasts Alesia Haruna," *Belarus*, 1945, no. 5; Nicholas P. Vakar, *Bielorussia: The Making of a Nation* (Cambridge, Mass., 1956); Vitaut Kipel and Zora Kipel, eds., *Byelorussian Statehood* (New York, 1988); A. Loika, *Historyia belaruskai litaratury: Dakastrychnitski peryiad*, vol. 2 (Minsk, 1989); U. Kazbiaruk, *Svetlai voli zychny zvon: Ales Harun* (Minsk, 1991).

HASANI Sinan (14 May 1922, Požaranje, near Kosovska Vitina), Yugoslav Communist activist of Albanian nationality, writer, and journalist. Hasani graduated from the **Djuro Djaković** Higher Party School in Belgrade. In 1942 he joined the Yugoslav Communist Party. He was a political commissar in one of the Communist guerrilla units in Serbia. After the war he was secretary of the regional committee of the League of Communists of Yugoslavia (LCY) in Gniljane and secretary of the regional committee of the Popular Front. Advancing in the party ranks, he joined the ideological commission in the regional party structure in Kosovo, where he was responsible for cultural policy. In 1965–67 he headed Rilindja, the Albanian language press. In 1959–85 he was a member of the Central Committee of the League of Communists of Serbia; in 1967–71 he was deputy speaker of the Serbian parliament, and from 1971 to 1974 he was ambassador to Denmark. In 1975 Hasani became deputy speaker of the federal parliament. At the end of the 1980s, he was, apart from **Fadil Hoxha**, the only Albanian among the top federal authorities. In March 1981 he belonged to those Kosovo leaders who condemned the demonstrations of Albanian students. From May 1982 he belonged to the party leadership in the autonomous region of Kosovo-Metohija. From 15 May 1986 to 15 May 1987 he was chairman of the Presidium of the Socialist Federative Republic of Yugoslavia. In 1987 he was dismissed from the leadership. Hasani published a couple of novels, including *Gde se reka deli* (Where the river forks; 1967), and a collection of essays, *Kosovo istine i zablude* (Kosovo truths and errors; 1986). (TC)

Sources: *Jugoslavenski savremenici: Ko je ko u Jugoslavii* (Belgrade, 1970); Ana Lalaj, *Kosova: Rruga egjate drejt vetevendosjes 1948–1981* (Tirana, 2000); *Who's Who in the Socialist Countries of Europe* (Munich, London, and Paris, 1989).

HAŠEK Jaroslav (30 April 1883, Prague–3 January 1923, Lipnica, Havlíčkův Brod district), Czech writer. In 1899–1903 Hašek studied at a trade academy, and then he worked as a shop assistant and bank officer. Soon he gave up steady employment, and for four years he wandered around Central Europe, writing columns, humorous sketches, and short stories that were published in various periodicals. From 1907 he lived in Prague, where he contributed to satirical magazines and was a habitual guest of the Prague pubs. Mobilized during World War I, he went over to the Russian side and joined the Czechoslovak Legion in 1916. Hašek edited the *Čechoslovan*, the press organ of the Legion, in which he led anti-Habsburg and pro-Russian agitation. At this time he favored the restitution of Czech statehood under the Russian Romanovs. Demoted, in 1918 he joined the Red Army and the Bolshevik party. He returned home in 1920 with revolution in mind, but in view of the unreceptive atmosphere among Czech workers, he took a job as a comedian. He performed in the Red Seven Cabaret and returned to the lifestyle of a bohemian. From 1921 he lived in Lipnica.

From the beginning of his literary career Hašek was fascinated with folktales and the simple country folk life. He made his literary debut in 1900 with columns written from his trip to Slovakia. In the collection of tales from his trips around Central Europe, *Průvodči cizinců a jiné satiry z cest i domova* (A guide for foreigners and other satires from my trips and from home; 1913), he described the everyday life of simple people, based on stories heard in pubs, full of humor and satire. A double-dealing trickster, in 1909 Hašek published articles about fictitious animals in a professional zoological periodical, *Svět Zvířat*. In 1911 he founded the Party of Moderate Progress within the Limits of the Law, ridiculing Austro-Hungarian political life, ideological programs, and election campaigns. In the parliamentary campaign of the party in 1911 he was joined by (among others) **Franz Kafka** and Egon Erwin Kisch, and the party's program included (for instance) the rehabilitation of dogs and the nationalization of doorkeepers. He described the party's activities in 1912 in *Politické a sociální dějiny Strany mírného pokroku v mezích zákona* (The political and social history of the Party of Moderate Progress within the Limits of the Law).

Hašek was skeptical of any authority and norm of behavior. He thought that all political systems limited personal freedom and the pursuit of happiness. He stressed the absurdity of human life and of the world order. His anarchic or even nihilistic attitude is revealed in the collections *Trampoty pana Tenkráta* (Mr. Tenkrat in trouble; 1912); *Můj obchod se psy* (My dog trade; 1915); *Dva tucty povídek* (Two dozen stories; 1920); *Pepíček Nový a jiné povídky* (New Joe and other stories; 1921); *Tři muži se žralokem a jiné poučné historky* (Three men with a shark and other instructive stories; 1921); and *Mírová konference a jiné humoresky* (The peace conference and other humorous sketches; 1922). Hašek contrasted folk wisdom with the absurdity of politics, ideology, and the state administration. His most famous novel, which brought him

world renown, *Osudy dobrého vojáka Švejka za světové války* (1921–23; *Good Soldier Schweik*, 1930; *The Good Soldier Svejk and His Fortunes in the World War*, 1973), was constructed with such a contrast. The hero of the title is a simpleton who thoughtlessly but exactly follows orders, unmasking the stupidity of the Austro-Hungarian Army. Hašek worked on the novel for a great part of his life. The adventures of Švejk were to be the story of a man entangled in history. Hašek never completed his novel. The unfinished work was rather unsuccessfully continued by Karel Vaněk. Hašek's work was twice translated into English and also into many other languages. It was also filmed and adapted as a play in Czechoslovakia and abroad. (PU)

Sources: *Kdo byl kdo v našich dějinach ve 20. stoleti*, vol. 1 (Prague, 1998); Gustav Janouch, *Jaroslav Hašek, der Vater des braven Soldaten Schwejk* (Bern and Munich, 1967); Cecil Parrott, *The Bad Bohemian: The Life of Jaroslav Hašek* (London, 1978); Radko Pytlík, *Lidský profil Jaroslava Haška* (Prague, 1979); Cecil Parrott, *Jaroslav Hašek: A Study of Švejk and the Short Stories* (Cambridge, 1982); Ladislav Soldan, *Jaroslav Hašek* (Prague, 1982); Jiří Hájek, *Jaroslav Hašek* (Prague, 1983); Zdeněk Hoření, *Jaroslav Hašek novinář* (Prague, 1983); Boris Mědílek, *Bibliografie Jaroslava Haška* (Prague, 1983); Přemysl Blažíček, *Haškův Švejk* (Prague, 1991).

HAURYLIK Yazep (6 April 1893, Kalodchin, near Vileika–8 December 1937, Leningrad), Belorussian activist. In 1914 Haurylik graduated from a teachers' college in Boruny. He worked in schools run by the Orthodox Church in the region of Kaunas and was a conductor of an Orthodox choir. In 1919 he was dismissed from work for criticizing the clergy. In 1920 he became aligned with the Belorussian national movement and promoted the idea of struggle for Belorussian statehood. Between 1921 and 1922 he worked in a school in Oszmiana, and in 1922 he organized a Belorussian high school in Radoszkowicze. From 1924 he was active in the Belorussian School Society, and from 1925 he was a member of the Belorussian Peasant and Worker Hromada. In 1927, after he refused to cooperate with the Polish police, Haurylik was deprived of the right to practice as a teacher. In 1928 he was elected an MP from the lists of the Union of Workers and Peasants. In May 1930 he joined the Communist Party of Western Belorussia. Arrested in August 1930 for anti-state activities, in January 1931 he was sentenced to eight years. In September 1932, as a result of the exchange of political prisoners, he was sent to the USSR. He worked in the Commissariat of People's Education of the Belorussian SSR in Minsk. Arrested by the NKVD in 1933 for being a member of a nonexistent organization called the Belorussian National Center, Haurylik was sentenced to ten years in a labor camp. He was held prisoner on the Solovets Islands, and he labored on the construction of the White Sea Canal. On 25 November 1937 the NKVD Leningrad District Court sentenced Haurylik to execution by firing squad. (EM)

Sources: *Entsyklapiedyia historyi Bielarusi*, vol. 2 (Minsk, 1994); *Posłowie i senatorowie Rzeczpospolitej Polskiej 1919–1939: Słownik biograficzny*, vol. 1 (Warsaw, 1998); Nicholas P. Vakar, *Belorussia: The Making of a Nation* (Cambridge, Mass., 1956).

HAVEL Václav (5 October 1936, Prague), Czech playwright and dissident, president of Czechoslovakia and the Czech Republic. Born into an upper-middle-class family from Prague, owing to his "bourgeois" origins, Havel was not allowed to study in a regular high school under Stalinist rule. In 1951–55 he worked as a laboratory assistant and took classes in an evening high school. In 1955–57 he studied in the Department of Economics of the Prague Polytechnic. In 1957–59 he did his military service. In 1951 he became interested in literature. His first texts were reviewed by **Jaroslav Seifert**. From the mid-1950s Havel published in the periodicals *Květen, Divadlo, Literárni noviny, Tvář*, and *Sešity pro mladou literaturu*. In 1959–60 he worked as a stage assistant in the ABC Theater and then as directorial assistant and playwright in the Na Zábradlí Theater in Prague (1961–68). In 1967 he graduated from the Academy of Theater and Musical Arts in Prague. In the mid-1960s he attracted attention as the author of dramas of the absurd, publishing *Zahradní slavnost* (1963; *Garden Party*, 1969) and *Vyrozuměni* (1965; *Memorandum*, 1967). From 1965 Havel was a member, and from 1968 chairman, of the editorial board of the literary monthly *Tvář*, which was suspended during "normalization" in 1969. After a conflict with the Communist-controlled Association of Czechoslovak Writers, in 1968 he became chairman of the Club of Independent Writers.

During the "Prague Spring" of 1968 Havel supported reforms and joined the Club of Engaged Nonparty Members (Klub Angažovaných Nestraníků), acting in favor of the reconstruction of the Czechoslovak Social Democracy. After the Warsaw Pact invasion he helped edit radio broadcasts condemning the "brotherly help" of the Soviet bloc. In August 1969 he was the key author of the "Ten Points" address to the federal government, the Federal Assembly, the Czech government, the Czech National Council, and the Central Committee of the Czechoslovak Communist Party; the address protested the "normalization." In the early 1970s Havel was banned from publishing for political reasons, so in 1974 he took a blue-collar job in the Trutnov Brewery. In 1975 he authored an extensive letter to **Gustáv Husák** analyzing the social and political situation in Czechoslovakia. The letter was not answered by the authorities but was widely noticed at home and strengthened Havel's reputation as one of the leaders of the intellectual opposition. In the 1970s he wrote several plays: *Audience* (Audience; 1975); *Vernisáž* (Varnishing day; 1975); *Horský hotel* (Mountain hotel; 1976); and *Protest* (1978), published and staged only abroad or in the uncensored press at home. He also authored the famous essay *Moc bezmocných* (1978; *Power of the Powerless*, 1985).

In 1976 Havel was one of the initiators and authors of Charter 77, announced on 1 January 1977. A year later he became its spokesman. Soon he was arrested for the first time, but he was released in the same year. On 24 April 1978 he co-founded the Committee for the Defense of the Unjustly Prosecuted (Výbor na Obranu Nespravedlivě Stíhaných). In 1978 he was arrested again, and in 1979 he was sentenced to four and a half years in prison for an "attempt to overthrow the republic." Released in March 1983 for health reasons, he was already an unquestionable leader of the democratic opposition in Czechoslovakia. He still wrote a lot—for instance, the dramas *Largo desolato* (1984; English version, 1987); *Pokoušeni* (1985; *Temptation*, 1987); and *Asanace* (Garbage removal; 1987). In 1987–89 he belonged to the editorial board and wrote for the uncensored *Lidové Noviny*. He was true to liberal and democratic values, resisting the illusion of "socialism with a human face." He also pointed to the egoism of Western societies, interested in consumption and unwilling to help the nations enslaved by communism.

On 16 January 1989 Havel took part in a demonstration in Venceslas Square in Prague on the twentieth anniversary of the death of **Jan Palach**. After the demonstration he was arrested, but in May 1989 he was conditionally released. After a demonstration on 17 November 1989 commemorating the fiftieth anniversary of the death of **Jan Opletal**, brutally crushed by the police, Havel took the lead of the Velvet Revolution. On 19 November he co-founded the Civic Forum (Občanské Forum [OF]). After negotiations with the Communist authorities and the creation of the "government of national reconciliation," Havel agreed to run for president. His election on 29 December 1989 sealed the fall of the Communist regime in Czechoslovakia. Havel tried to remove the adjective "Socialist" from the name of the country; this led to his first conflict between the Czechs and Slovaks concerning their relationship within the federation.

Havel's legitimacy was confirmed by the first free parliamentary elections in June 1990: the newly elected parliament reelected him president in July 1990. He was very active on the international scene and tried to save the

Czechoslovak federation. Nevertheless he made mistakes in relation to the Slovak question, antagonizing the ambitious Slovak leaders. After the parliamentary elections of June 1992 the breakup of Czechoslovakia seemed inevitable, and on 3 July 1992 the Federal Assembly refused, owing to the Slovak votes, to approve Havel's presidency for the next term. On 20 July 1992 he resigned from the remaining three months of his presidency. On 1 January 1993 the federation ceased to exist, and on 26 January 1993 the Czech National Council elected him the first president of the Czech Republic. On 20 January 1998 he was re-elected for another five-year term. As president Havel did not have broad powers, but thanks to his unquestionable authority and the support of most Czechs, he had a strong influence on Czech politics, especially in crisis situations. As a nonparty person, he frequently criticized various actions of politicians, especially those of Prime Minister **Václav Klaus**; this resulted in frequent conflicts between the two men. Havel remained a key figure in Czech foreign policy. As someone who was very popular in the West, he was undoubtedly responsible for the Czech entry into NATO (12 March 1999) and the European Union (1 May 2004). (PU)

Sources: *ČBS*; *Kdo byl kdo v našich dějinách ve 20. století*, vol. 1 (Prague, 1998); *Slovník českých spisovatelů od roku 1945*, vol. 1 (Prague, 1998); Eda Kriseová, *Václav Havel: Životopis* (Brno, 1991); Ortwin Ramadan, *Václav Havel: Ein Portrait* (Munich, 1991); Michael Simmons, *The Reluctant President: A Political Life of Václav Havel* (London, 1991); Halina Janaszek-Ivančikova, ed., *Literatury zachodniosłowiańskie czasu przełomów 1890–1990*, vol. 2: *Literatura czeska* (Katowice, 1999); John Keane, *Václav Havel: A Political Tragedy in Six Acts* (London, 1999).

HAVELKA Jiří (25 July 1892, Oryol, Russia–5 June 1964, Hostomice pod Brdy, near Beroun), Czech lawyer and politician. Havelka completed law studies at the Czech University in Prague. Between 1919 and 1921 he worked in the State Roads Administration, and from 1921 to 1933, in the Ministry of Railways. From 1931 he was a *docent* (associate professor) in the Law Department of Charles University in Prague. In 1933 he became legal counselor to the Supreme Administrative Court in Prague, where he met **Emil Hácha** and became his closest co-worker. Havelka was the author of many works in the field of railway and administrative law. He also edited *Slovník československého veřejného prava* (Dictionary of Czechoslovak public law). After the Pact of Munich, from December 1938 to April 1939 Havelka was minister without portfolio and minister of transport, and he simultaneously acted as head of the chancellery of the president, later receiving a formal appointment to this position. In 1939–40 he also served as deputy prime minister of the government of

Alois Eliáš. Havelka had a great influence on the policy of Hácha. Havelka himself often represented the government in talks with Konstantin von Neurath, the Reich protector of Bohemia and Moravia, and other Nazi officials, and he did not hesitate to oppose them on many occasions. In September 1939 he protested the arrests of Jews; a month later, he persuaded Hácha not to adopt anti-Jewish laws. With Eliáš, he worked with the national and foreign resistance movement. The information that Havelka provided was valuable for the Czech underground. Dismissed from all his government positions in April 1941, he resumed work in the Supreme Administrative Court. After Reinhard Heydrich was appointed as Reich protector in September 1941, Havelka was arrested and imprisoned. Released from Pankrac Prison owing to the intervention of President Hácha, who threatened to resign, he was held under house arrest until the end of World War II. After the war he was accused of collaboration and imprisoned, but in March 1947 the People's Court acquitted him of charges. Persecuted by the Communists in the 1950s, Havelka had to leave Prague, and until the end of his life he lived in seclusion in the countryside. (PU)

Sources: *ČBS*; *Českoslovenští politici: 1918–1991* (Prague, 1991); *Politická elita meziválečného Československa 1918–1938: Kdo byl kdo za prvni republiky* (Prague, 1998); *Kdo byl kdo v našich dějinach ve 20. stoleti*, vol. 1 (Prague, 1998).

HÁY Gyula (5 May 1900, Abony–7 May 1975, Ascona, Switzerland), Hungarian writer. After graduating from high school, Háy studied at the Budapest Polytechnic but did not complete his studies. In 1919 he worked in the People's Commissariat of Education of the Hungarian Soviet Republic (HSR). From 1920 he was in exile in Germany, where he worked as an interior decorator. After returning to Hungary in 1923, he worked with the press and with leftist organizations. In 1929 he again went to Germany, where he joined the Communist Party. Later, he was in exile in Austria, Switzerland, and the USSR (1935–45). Háy made his debut as a writer in the 1920s. In 1929 he published the novel *Színhely: Budapest; idó: tíz év előtt* (Place of action: Budapest; Time: Ten years ago), which included numerous autobiographical elements, yet the historical drama *Isten, császár, paraszt* (God, Caesar, and peasants), staged in Berlin in 1932, brought him greater acclaim. From then on Háy turned to writing drama. After returning to Hungary, he also wrote film scripts, and as head of the chair of drama in the School of Drama in Budapest, he promoted Socialist realism. After Stalin's death in 1953, Háy became a prominent figure of the Hungarian thaw in literary circles. He also wrote articles in which he ironically commented on the Communist reality. During the invasion of Budapest by the Soviet Army in November 1956, Háy was the author of the Hungarian Writers' Union's dramatic call for resistance broadcasts on the radio. Arrested and sentenced to six years' imprisonment in a show trial in 1957, Háy was released under amnesty in 1960. In 1964 he emigrated to Switzerland, from where he contributed to the leading periodicals issued by Hungarians in exile, *Irodalmi Újság* and *Új Látóhatár*, which also published his later dramas. Háy was also occupied with translations, particularly of works by German and Russian authors. In 1974 he published his memoirs, *Born in 1900: Memoirs*. (MS)

Sources: Paul Ignotus, *Hungary* (London, 1972); Péter Gál Molnár, "Nekrológ helyett," *Kritika*, 1975, no. 6; Lóránt Czigány, *Nézz vissza haraggal! Államosított irodalom Magyarországon, 1946–1988* (Budapest, 1990); János Szabó, *Der "vollkommender Macher" Julius Hay: Ein Dramatiker im Bann der Zeitgeschichte* (Munich, 1992); Éva Háy, *Auf beiden Seiten der Barrikade* (Leipzig, 1994).

HEBRANG Andrija (21 October 1899, Bačevac, near Virovitica–11 June 1949, Belgrade), Croatian Communist activist. Born into a peasant family, Hebrang studied in a trade school (1912–14), and in 1917 he joined the army, serving in an artillery regiment in Osijek and Zagreb. From 1919 he belonged to the Socialist Workers' Party of Yugoslavia, renamed the Communist Party of Yugoslavia in June 1920. From 1923 he lived in Zagreb, and in 1925 he became secretary of the local party committee. In 1928 he was sentenced to twelve years in prison for his Communist activities. He served in prisons in Leopoglava and Sremska Mitrovica. After his release, in 1941 he returned to Zagreb and became a member of the Central Committee of the Croatian Communist Party and head of its military committee. Wounded in action, in February 1942 Hebrang was caught by the Ustasha authorities, but in September 1942 he was exchanged. He was active in the Zagreb Anti-Fascist Council of National Liberation of Croatia, created in 1943. From October 1944 he was commissar of trade and industry, and from March 1945, minister of industry. In January 1948 he became head of the Federal Planning Commission. Probably owing to Soviet provocation, **Josip Broz Tito** lost confidence in Hebrang. Monitored from March 1948, the following month Hebrang was put under practical house arrest, and in May 1948 he was dismissed from his position and arrested. He was accused of sending secret reports to Moscow. Tito considered him a rival who enjoyed the support of the Kremlin; this was particularly dangerous for Hebrang after the Cominform's condemnation of Tito in June 1948. Hebrang was put in the Belgrade prison of Glavnjač, where he was brutally interrogated and died or committed suicide. His burial place is not known. After decades of effort by his family, Hebrang was rehabilitated in 1989. (AO)

Sources: Stephen Clissold, ed., *Yugoslavia and the Soviet Union 1939–1973: A Documentary Survey* (London, 1975); Zvonko Ivanković-Vonta, *Hebrang* (Zagreb, 1988); Živorad Mihajlović, *Hebrang: Izdajnik ili žrtva političke igre* (Belgrade, 1989); Nada Kisić-Kolanović, *Andrija Hebrang: Iluzije i otrežnjenja* (Zagreb, 1996); www.posta.hr/markeasp/index_e.asp; www.andrija-hebrang.com.

HEGEDÜS András (31 October 1922, Szilsárkány–23 October 1999, Budapest), Hungarian Communist activist. Born into the family of a medium-size estate owner, Hegedüs lost his father in early childhood. During the German occupation he was the secretary of the Union of Communist Youth, and in January 1945 he became regional secretary of the Hungarian Union of Democratic Youth, which was created at the initiative of the Communists. Later, he was appointed national organizational secretary of the union. In 1946 he underwent a three-month training course at a higher party school. From the end of 1947 Hegedüs was agricultural adviser to **Ernő Gerő** and deputy head, later becoming head, of the Department of Agriculture and Collective Farms of the Central Committee (CC) of the Hungarian Communist Party. From 1950 he was a member of the CC of the Hungarian Workers' Party (HWP) and its Secretariat. At the Second Congress of the HWP, held in February 1951, Hegedüs was elected to the organizational committee of the Politburo and to the CC. From November 1951 he was deputy minister of agriculture, and from January 1952 he was minister of the state-owned agricultural and forest farms. In the first government of **Imre Nagy** in 1953 Hegedüs served as first deputy prime minister and minister of agriculture. On 18 April 1955 he was appointed president of the Council of Ministers, and in this capacity he signed, on behalf of Hungary, the treaty establishing the Warsaw Pact.

During the revolution, on 24 October 1956 Hegedüs was dismissed as premier and was appointed deputy prime minister. On 28 October he signed the government's formal request for the assistance of Soviet troops, which were stationed in Hungary. He antedated the document five days. The Politburo had already made this decision on the night of 23–24 October. On 29 October, along with other discredited executive activists Hagedüs was taken to the USSR. In Moscow, he worked at the Institute of Philosophy of the Soviet Academy of Sciences. After his return to Hungary in September 1958, he worked at the Institute of Economic Sciences of the Hungarian Academy of Sciences (HAS), and from 1962 he was vice-president of the Central Statistical Office. From 1963 he headed the Sociology Research Group, which was created at the HAS, and from 1966 he lectured at the Karl Marx University of Economics.

In the mid-1960s Hegedüs's views underwent a gradual metamorphosis. In 1968 he condemned the intervention of Warsaw Pact troops in Czechoslovakia. As a result, he was dismissed from his post and went to work at the Industrial Research Group of the HAS. In 1973 the Politburo of the Hungarian Socialist Workers' Party passed a resolution on the "anti-Marxist views of certain sociologists," among them Hegedüs; in May the same year he was accused of revisionism in the so-called trial of philosophers, expelled from the party, and dismissed from work. In 1975–90, because of the great interest he attracted (owing, for example, to his complicated career path), Hegedüs toured the world, giving lectures; in these lectures he subjected socialism to scholarly and political criticism, trying to draw the world's attention to Eastern Europe. In 1979 he signed a declaration of solidarity with the imprisoned members of the Czechoslovak Charter 77 movement. In December 1986 he took part in an illegal conference devoted to the events of 1956. In December 1988 he delivered a lecture at the first legal and public conference on the revolution of 1956. In 1988 he was elected titular professor of the Karl Marx University of Economics. Among other works, Hegedüs published his memoirs, *A történelem és a hatalom igézetében* (Life under the spell of history and power), and *Élet egy eszme árnyékában* (Life in the shadow of one idea). (JT)

Sources: Bennet Kovrig, *Communism in Hungary from Kun to Kádár* (Stanford, 1979); Miklós Molnár, *From Béla Kun to János Kádár: Seventy Years of Hungarian Communism* (New York, 1990); *Magyar Nagylexikon*, vol. 9 (Budapest, 1999); *A magyar forradalom és szabadságharc enciklopédiája*, CD-ROM (Budapest, 1999).

HEL Ivan (17 July 1937, Klitsko, near Horodka), Ukrainian dissident and politician. The son of a soldier of the Organization of Ukrainian Nationalists who was sentenced to twenty years in 1950, Hel was expelled from tenth grade in 1952 for refusing to join the Komsomol. In 1954 he graduated from high school in Sambor. In view of his background, he was not allowed to study at Lviv University, so he became a metalworker. He was accepted into an extramural program of the study of history only after he did military service (1956–59). Thanks to his acquaintance with **Mykhailo Horyn**, Hel joined the opposition and mainly dealt with the distribution of uncensored samizdat publications. Arrested in August 1965, in March 1966 he was sentenced to three years of labor camp. He served his term in Mordovian camps. In 1967 he twice addressed the Presidium of the Supreme Council of the Ukrainian SSR to legalize the Ukrainian Greek Catholic Church. After his return to Lviv, he was not allowed to complete his studies, and he worked as a metalworker and teacher in Sambor. From 1968 to 1971 he published eleven uncensored books, including those by **Valentyn Moroz** and **Ivan Dziuba**. In November 1970 he turned to the Supreme Court of the Ukrainian SSR in defense of Moroz. In January 1972 Hel was arrested again, and in August 1972 he was sentenced to ten years in labor camp and five years of forced settlement. All together he spent three hundred days on hunger strikes in the camps of the Mordovian and Komi ASSRs, demanding the status of a political prisoner. Under the pseudonym "Stepan Howerlja," he wrote and published in London *Hrani kultury* (Edges of culture; 1984), which was a polemic with Dziuba's *Hrani krystala* (Edges of crystal). From the spring of 1987, along with **Vyacheslav Chornovil** and Horyn, Hel co-edited the reconstructed *Ukraiinskyi Visnyk*. When **Yosif Terelya** emigrated, Hel took the lead of the Committee for the Defense of the Ukrainian Catholic Church. He edited the informal organ of the committee, *Khrystyanskyi Holos*, and then *Vira batkiv*. In 1989 he co-founded the Ukrainian Popular Movement (Rukh). In 1990–94 he was deputy chairman of the Lviv regional Council of Deputies, and then he presided over the regional commission for rehabilitation of those repressed under communism. (TS)

Sources: *Encyclopedia of Ukraine*, vol. 2 (Toronto, 1988); *Visnyk represiy v Ukraiini, Zakordonne predstavnyctvo Ukraiinskoyi Helsinskoyi Hrupy* (New York, 1980–81); Ludmila Alekseyeva, *Istoriya inakomysla v SSSR* (Vilnius and Moscow, 1992); Heorhiy Kasyanov, *Nezhodni: Ukraiinska intelihentsiya v rusi oporu 1960–80 rokiv* (Kiev, 1995); Anatoli Rusnachenko, *Natsionalno-vyzvolnyi rukh v Ukraiini* (Kiev, 1998); T. Batenko, "*Ya povstayu, otzhe, i isnuyu...*": *Politychnyi portret Ivana Hela (Narysy z istoriyi ukraiinskoho rukhu oporu kintsia 1950-kh–pochatku 1990-kh rokiv)* (Lviv, 1999).

HENDRYCH Jiří (28 December 1913, Lom, near Most–16 May 1979, Prague), Czech Communist activist. Between 1932 and 1933 Hendrych studied law at Charles University in Prague, but because of his political activities, he was expelled from the university. In 1931–34 he was a member of a Communist youth organization, and in 1934 he joined the Communist Party of Czechoslovakia (CPC). In the late 1930s he was active as a party functionary in the districts of Teplice and Kladno. Between 1937 and 1938 he was editor of the party newspaper, *Svoboda*, in Kladno, and from 1939 to 1941 he was a member of an illegal district committee of the CP in Kladno. Arrested in 1941, Hendrych was held at the concentration camp of Mauthausen until the end of the war. In 1945–71 he was a member of the CC of the CPC; from 1951 to 1952 and from 1954 to 1968 he was secretary and member of the Secretariat of the CC of the CPC, and between 1958 and 1968 he was a member of the Politburo (later Presidium) of the CC of the CPC. In 1963–65 Hendrych was president of an agricultural commission, and between 1965 and 1968 he was president of an ideological commission of the CC of the CPC. Between 1950 and 1969 he sat in the National Assembly, and then, until 1971, in the Federal Assembly. In the 1950s and 1960s he was the main party ideologist, and he actively fought against revisionism and against "ideological diversion." He was a close associate of **Antonín Novotný**, whom he knew from the concentration camp. Before the Prague Spring Hendrych was considered the second most important figure in the party, and during the struggle within the party in 1967 he declared himself against the reformation movement. Denounced in the spring of 1968, he was dismissed from all important party and state posts. Hendrych's downfall was considered the greatest success of the cabinet policy of the reformers. (PU)

Sources: *ČBS*; *Kdo byl kdo v našich dějinach ve 20. stoleti*, vol. 1 (Prague, 1998); Galia Golan, *Reform Rule in Czechoslovakia: The Dubček Era, 1968–1969* (Cambridge, 1973); Kieran Williams, *The Prague Spring and Its Aftermath* (Cambridge, 1997); Jaromir Navrátil, ed., *The Prague Spring 1968* (Prague, 1998); Kenneth N. Skoug, Jr., *Czechoslovakia's Lost Fight for Freedom, 1967–1969* (Westport, Conn., 1999).

HENIUSH Larysa (9 August 1910, Voupa, near Volkovysk–7 April 1983, Zelva), Belorussian poet. In 1928 Heniush graduated from a Polish gymnasium in Volkovysk, and in 1937 she went to Prague, where her husband, Ivan, was studying. She was secretary to **Vasil Zakharka**, the president of the Belorussian People's Republic (BPR) in exile. She also cared for the Belorussian émigrés from Poland and the USSR and was in charge of the documentation of the BPR. She made her literary debut in 1939, and in the 1940s she published poems in *Ranitsa* and *Belaruski Rabotnik*, Belorussian newspapers that came out in Berlin. She attended the Second All-Belorussian Congress convened in German-occupied Minsk in June 1944. In 1948 she was arrested by the NKVD in Prague, although she had Czechoslovak citizenship. She was held in Soviet prisons in Vienna and Lviv. In 1949, in a trial held in a Minsk court, she was sentenced to twenty-five years in a concentration camp in the Komi ASSR for collaboration with the Germans. In 1956 a commission of the Supreme Soviet of the USSR commuted the sentence to eight years but did not rehabilitate her. After returning from the camp, Heniush settled in Zelva, where she spent the rest of her life. In 1942 the first collection of her poems, *Ad rodnykh niu* (From native fields), appeared in Prague. From 1963 her poems were published in the Soviet press. The most important collections of her works include *Nevadam z Niomana* (With a fishing net from the Neman River; 1967); *Bely son* (White dream; 1992); and a work for children written in verse, *Kazki dla Michaśki* (Fairy tales for Michaśka; 1972). Heniush's autobiography, *Spoved* (Confession; 1993), was published after her death. In it, the tragic fate of the Belorussian intelligentsia of the twentieth century was depicted. (EM)

Sources: Nicholas P. Vakar, *Belorussia: The Making of a Nation* (Cambridge, Mass., 1956); B. Sachanka, "Larysa Heniush," *Maladosts*, 1988, no. 10; *Bielaruskiya pismienniki (1917–1990): Davednik* (Minsk, 1994); *Bielaruskaia entsiklopiediya*, vol. 5 (Minsk, 1995).

HENLEIN Konrad (6 May 1898, Maffersdorf bei Reichenberg [now Vratislavice, near Liberec, Czech Republic]–10 May 1945, Plzeň), German politician in Czechoslovakia. During World War I Henlein volunteered for the Austro-Hungarian Army and in 1917 was taken captive in Italy. It was there that his nationalistic and Greater Germany views crystallized. In 1919 he returned to his newly created fatherland, Czechoslovakia, where he initially worked as a bank clerk. From 1925 he worked as a gymnastics teacher. He perceived gymnastics as a vital element in bringing up the youth in a nationalistic spirit. From 1931 he was leader of the German Gymnastic Union in Czechoslovakia. After the activities of the NSDAP (Nationalsozialistische Deutsche arbeiterpartei) were outlawed in Czechoslovakia, in October 1933 Henlein founded the Sudeten German Home Front (Sudetendeutsche Heimatfront), which later changed its name to the Sudeten German Party (Sudetendeutsche Partei [SdP]). The SdP initially tried to distance itself from Fascist Germany, declaring formal support for the republic. During the Great Depression the SdP became a leading force in Czechoslovak politics, gaining 1.2 million votes in 1935, becoming the second strongest party in the parliament. Henlein increasingly firmly demanded autonomy for the Germans in Czechoslovakia, and from 1937 he began openly to call for the incorporation of the Czech Sudetenland into the Third Reich; a secret memorandum to this effect was presented to Hitler in the autumn. Over the course of the following year German demands, transmitted by Henlein (which were, in fact, Hitler's demands), gradually increased, and the Czechoslovak side submitted to virtually all of them in an attempt to save the country. Following the Munich Diktat and the German annexation of the lands inhabited by the German population, Henlein became *Gauleiter* (regional governor) of the Sudetenland (Reichsgau Sudetenland). At the beginning of May 1945 Henlein was taken captive by the Americans, and he committed suicide in a Plzeň camp. (PU)

Sources: *Deutsche Biographische Enzyklopädie*, vol. 4 (Munich, 1996); *Kto bol kto za I. ČSR* (Bratislava, 1993); *Kdo byl kdo v našich dějinách ve 20. stoleti*, vol. 1 (Prague, 1998); Stanislav Biman, *Kariéra ucitele tělocviku* (Usti n. Labou, 1983); Ralf Gebel, *Heim ins Reich! Konrad Henlein und der Reichsgau Sudetenland (1938–1945)* (Munich, 2000).

HERBERT Zbigniew (29 October 1924, Lwów [now Lviv, Ukraine]–28 July 1998, Warsaw), Polish poet, essayist, and playwright. The son of a bank director, Herbert was a student at the Kazimierz Wielki Gymnasium when the Red Army entered Lwów in 1939. He attended an underground high school during the wartime German occupation of Poland and also completed a cadet officers' school of the Polish Home Army in 1942. In 1943 he passed his high school final exams and began studying at the underground Jan Kazimierz University in Lwów. In 1944 he went with his family to Kraków. After the war he simultaneously gained admission to drama, economics, and art studies in Kraków. He chose the Academy of Commerce, from which he graduated in 1947. He also studied law and philosophy, first at the Jagiellonian University in Kraków and then at the Mikołaj Kopernik University in Toruń, under the direction of Henryk Elzenberg, his professor and mentor. In 1946 he moved to the Gdańsk-Sopot-Gdynia area (the Triple City) and in 1949 to Toruń.

In 1948 Herbert started writing columns for *Tygodnik Wybrzeża* and *Arkona*, and he became a candidate member of the Gdańsk branch of the Polish Writers' Union, but he left it that very year, before the political verification of its members. In 1949 he earned a degree in law from Toruń University. In order to avoid training as a prosecutor for the military, he moved to Warsaw, where for a number of years he worked at a variety of odd jobs, such as shop assistant, calculator and time-study man at a cooperative society, designer in the peat industry, and administrative manager of the Union of Polish Composers. In 1950 Herbert made his literary debut with the poems *Napis* (Register), *Pożegnanie września* (Goodbye to September), and *Złoty środek* (Golden mean). Before 1956 he wrote columns, reviews, and short essays in *Słowo Powszechne* (1949–51), *Dziś i jutro* (1950–53, under the pseudonyms of Patryk and Stefan Martha), *Przegląd Powszechny* (1952, under the pseudonym of Bolesław Hertyński), and *Tygodnik Powszechny* (1950–53). From 1955 he contributed to the literary review *Twórczość*.

During the "thaw" Herbert published his first collection of poems, *Struna światła* (The Chord of light; 1956), which, along with the drama *Jaskinia filozofów* (Philosophers' den; 1956) and his second collection of poems, *Hermes, pies i gwiazda* (Hermes, a dog and a star; 1957), put him among the most prominent Polish postwar poets. Herbert resumed writing for the revived *Tygodnik Powszechny*. In 1958 he went abroad for the first time, traveling to France, England, Italy, and Greece. He came into contact with émigré circles, including the Paris-based *Kultura* group. The year 1961 saw the publication of a volume of his poems, *Studium przedmiotu* (A study of the object). In 1962 he published *Barbarzyńca w ogrodzie* (A Barbarian in the Garden; 1985), a collection of essays inspired by his visits to France and Italy, and in 1969 another collection of poems, *Napis* (Register), came out. He also wrote dramatic works and plays for the radio. In recognition for his work, both in Poland and abroad, Herbert received the Kościelski Foundation Prize (1963), the Jurzykowski Foundation Award (1965), the Internationaler Nikolaus Lenau Preis (1965), and the Herder Prize; he was also granted membership in the Akademie der Kunste in Berlin and the Akademie der Schönen Kunste in Munich. His poetry was translated into English, German, Danish, Czech, Hungarian, Serbo-Croatian, Norwegian, Swedish, and Romanian. The German editions (1964 and 1967, translated by Karl Dedecius) and the English editions (1968, translated by Czesław Miłosz and Peter Dale Scott) have influenced contemporary German- and English-language poetry. After 1965 Herbert traveled a lot, and he lived in France, the Federal Republic of Germany, the United States, and other countries.

In 1971 Herbert returned to Warsaw. The 1974 publication of *Pan Cogito* (Mr. Cogito; 1993), a volume of his verse, was an important literary and social event. This work was read as a program for reconstructing the foundations of individual existence within a totalitarian or consumerist order that erodes the human conscience. For the leading poets of the younger generation, the so-called New Wave (including Stanisław Barańczak, Adam Zagajewski, and Ryszard Krynicki), Herbert was the main reference. In 1975 Herbert signed the "Letter of 59," a protest against amendments to the constitution of the Polish People's Republic. This act consolidated his position as the leading poet of moral resistance against the Communist dictatorship. Polish Communist censors imposed a ban on the publication of his works. Between 1975 and 1981 Herbert lived in Germany, Austria, and Italy. In 1977 he became a member of the clandestine literary periodical *Zapis*. Upon returning to Poland in 1981, he became involved in the Solidarity movement. After the imposition of martial law in Poland he worked with underground publishing houses. In 1983 Polish independent publishers and the Literary Institute in Paris published Herbert's *Raport z oblężonego miasta* (Report from the Besieged City; 1985), a volume of verse that was a continuation of the poetic and moral program of *Pan Cogito*. From 1986 to 1992 Herbert lived in France. The year 1990 saw the publication of another collection of his poetry, *Elegia na odejście* (Elegy for the Departure and Other Poems). After returning to Poland, Herbert published a collection of essays, *Martwa natura z wędzidłem* (Still life with a bridle; 1993), and his last two volumes of poetry, *Rovigo* (1993) and *Epilog burzy* (Epilogue of the storm; 1998). Herbert received awards in Poland and abroad, including the German Petrarch Prize (1978), the Andrzej Strug Award (1981), the Solidarity Honorary Cultural Award (1983), the Sęp-Szarzyński Award (1984), the Hungarian Bethlen Prize (1987), the Polish-Jewish-American Bruno Schulz Prize (1988), and the Jerusalem Prize (1990). He died after a prolonged illness in Warsaw. A volume of his essays, *Labirynt nad morzem* (Labyrinth by the sea), was published in 2000. Herbert exerted a powerful influence upon Polish poetry in the second half of the twentieth century, and since the 1970s, his work has shaped the attitudes of both the intellectual elite and a wider audience. (DT)

Sources: Jan Błoński, "Tradycja, ironia i głębsze znaczenie," *Poezja*, 1970, no. 3; Julian Kornhauser and Adam Zagajewski, *Świat nie przedstawiony* (Kraków, 1974); Karl Dedecius, *Polnische Profile* (Frankfurt am Main, 1975); R. Przybylski, *To jest klasycyzm* (Warsaw, 1978); B. Carpenter and J. Carpenter, "The Poet as Conscience," *Slavic and East European Journal*, 1980, no. 1; Stanisław Barańczak, *Uciekinier z Utopii: O poezji Zbigniewa Herberta* (London, 1984); E. Balcerzan, *Poezja polska w latach 1939–1965* (Warsaw, 1988); A. Franaszek, *Ciemne źródło (o twórczości Zbigniewa Herberta)* (London, 1998); Joanna Siedlecka, *Pan od poezji: Rzecz o Zbigniewie Herbercie* (Warsaw, 2002).

HERCZEG Ferenc (22 September 1863, Versec [Vršac], Banat–24 February 1954, Budapest), Hungarian writer and politician. Born into a middle-class German family, Herczeg wrote his first works in German since he only learned the Hungarian language at the Piarist Gymnasium in Szeged later on. Between 1878 and 1881 he studied law at the university in Budapest, where he also started his law practice, which he continued in his native Versec and in Timişoara. Leading a stormy life and gambling, Herczeg began writing and publishing novels. After a duel that ended in the death of his adversary, Herczeg landed in prison for a few months. His first novel, *Fenn és lenn* (Up and down; 1890), was a history of nightclub and casino life. In 1891 Herczeg became editor-in-chief of the capital's daily, *Budapesti Hírlap*, and one year later he published a

short story collection, *Mutamur* (We are changing), about the love adventures of women. This collection earned him nationwide fame and culminated with a trilogy on the life of the Gyurkovics family (1893–99), the first part of which, *A Gyurkovics leányok* (The Gyurkovics girls), was adapted for the theater and was staged throughout Europe. From 1894 to 1944 Herczeg was editor-in-chief of *Új idők*, the most popular magazine of the conservative upper and middle classes of Hungary.

Herczeg began his political career in 1896, becoming a member of the lower chamber of the parliament and, in 1927, an MP in the upper chamber. An adviser and close friend of Prime Minister **István Tisza**, in 1899 Herczeg became a member of the Hungarian Academy of Sciences, where he served as vice-president on several occasions. Under the Hungarian Soviet Republic (HSR) Herczeg was dismissed from his job and was even imprisoned for a short time. Herczeg belonged to many literary societies. He wrote and published a lot, including fairy tales—*Napnyugati mesék* (Fairy tales at sunset; 1894); serious novels—*Simon Zsuzsa* (1894), *Az aranyhegedű* (Golden violin; 1916); historical novels—*Pogányok* (Pagans; 1902), *Hét sváb* (Seven Swabians; 1916), *Az élet kapuja* (The gates of life; 1919); and dramas, the most popular of which were *Ocskay brigadéros* (Brigadier Ocskay; 1901), *Bizánc* (Byzantium; 1904), and *Kék róka* (The blue fox; 1917). Herczeg's works were characterized by simple composition and dialogues that contained imaginative ideas and references to old Hungarian mythology. During the interwar period Herczeg was called the "prince of literature" and was the Hungarian government's most promoted writer, exerting a significant influence upon the literary life of his country during the first decades of the twentieth century. Beginning in 1929, he held the influential position of president of the Revisionist League, an association of intellectuals who aimed at changing the Hungarian borders established by the Treaty of Trianon. Herczeg was fascinated by Italian fascism. However, he rejected German Nazism from the beginning and tried to influence Regent **Miklós Horthy** against it. After the end of World War II Herczeg was dismissed from all his positions, and his works were banned from publication in Hungary until the mid-1980s. (MS)

Sources: Erzsébet Hamvai, *Herczeg Ferenc stílusa és nyelve* (Budapest, 1911); Herczeg Ferenc, *Emlékkönyv* (Budapest, 1943); József Fitz, *Herczeg Ferenc irodalmi munkássága* (Budapest, 1944); *Mały słownik pisarzy węgierskich* (Warsaw, 1977).

HERLING-GRUDZIŃSKI Gustaw (20 May 1919, Kielce–4 July 2000, Naples, Italy), Polish writer and publicist. Born into an impoverished landowning family, between 1929 and 1937 Herling-Grudziński attended high school in Kielce. In 1935 he made his literary debut in the Warsaw youth periodical *Kuźnia Młodych*. In 1937 he began studying Polish philology at Warsaw University, but his studies were interrupted by the war. As a student, he contributed to the periodicals of the Union of Polish Democratic Youth. He wrote for the bi-weekly *Przemiany*, where he worked as editor of the literary section, and in 1938 he started publishing in *Orka na Ugorze*. Before 1939 he published a number of reviews and critical essays in major literary magazines—*Ateneum, Nasz Wyraz, Pion*, and *Pióro*.

In October 1939 Herling-Grudziński co-founded and was chief-of-staff of the underground Polish People's Independence Action (Polska Ludowa Akcja Niepodległościowa [PLAN]). He went to the territories occupied by the USSR. In December 1939 he was in Białystok, then in Lwów (Lviv), where he became acquainted with Polish literary circles. Lacking prospects for further activities, he went to Grodno and worked there as a carpenter's apprentice in a puppet theater. Warned of possible arrest, in March 1940 he went into hiding near Sokółka. Arrested by the NKVD while trying to cross the Lithuanian border, he was sentenced to five years in prison on the charge of spying for Germany. His German-sounding name was used as evidence in his case. He was taken from the prison in Vitebsk to Leningrad and Vologda, and finally he was sent to a labor camp in Yertsevo in the region of Archangel. He worked unloading railway cars, and after the outbreak of the German-Soviet war, he was employed in the so-called general works section. In November 1941, following the proclamation of "amnesty" for the Poles imprisoned in the USSR, Herling-Grudziński went on a hunger strike in protest against being held in the labor camp. Thanks to his protest, in January 1942 he was released, and in March, along with the Tenth Division of the army of General **Władysław Anders**, he left the USSR. Via Iran, Iraq, Palestine, and Egypt, he reached Italy, where in May 1944 he served as a radio operator for the Third Carpathian Rifle Division in the battle of Monte Cassino. Decorated with the Virtuti Militari Cross for his valor in the battle, he also fought in the battles of Ancona and the Gothic Line. As a soldier, he wrote articles for *Kurier Polski* (published in Baghdad), the monthly *W drodze* (published in Jerusalem), the weekly *Orzeł Biały*, and other periodicals.

In 1945 in Rome, Herling-Grudziński published his first book, *Żywi i umarli* (The living and the dead), a collection of essays from 1943–45, and he took over the literary section of *Orzeł Biały*. In June 1947, also in Rome, along with **Jerzy Giedroyć, Jerzy Czapski**, and Zofia and Zygmunt Hertz, he founded the monthly *Kultura* and the Literary Institute. However, he did not move with the *Kultura* group to Paris but went to London, where he began contributing to *Wiadomości*. In 1951 *Inny Świat* (The other world), a literary account of his prison and labor camp experiences, was published in English as *A World Apart*, with a preface by Bertrand Russell. The book, whose original Polish edition appeared in 1953 in London, was translated into Swedish, Spanish, German, Italian, French, Russian, Czech, Arabic, Chinese, and Japanese and became a classic of labor camp literature. After the death of his first wife in 1952 Herling-Grudziński moved to Munich, where he worked in the Polish section of Radio Free Europe. He was in charge of the cultural desk, reviewed Polish publications, and gave a regular talk, "A Letter to a Communist."

In 1955 Herling-Grudziński settled in Naples. He married Lidia Croce, daughter of Benedetto Croce. At the invitation of the writers Ignazio Silone and Nicola Chiaromonte, he began contributing to *Il Tempo Presente*, and he continued doing so until 1968. He also contributed to *Il Corriere della Sera, Il Mondo, Il Giornale*, and other periodicals. In 1956 he resumed his work with *Kultura*, where he published stories, essays, sketches, articles, reviews, and translations. In the Literary Institute in Paris his subsequent collections of stories and sketches were published: *Skrzydła ołtarza* (1960; *The Island: Three Tales*, 1994); *Drugie przyjście* (Second coming; 1963); and *Upiory rewolucji* (Specters of revolution; 1969). In 1971 in *Kultura*, he began to publish his *Dziennik pisany nocą* (The journal written at night; 1996), an intellectual record of everyday impressions and opinions interwoven with pieces of literary fiction. In 1974, along with Czapski and Giedroyć, Herling-Grudziński joined the editorial committee of a Russian émigré quarterly, *Kontinent*. In the second half of the 1970s, the independent Polish periodicals (among them *Zapis, Puls*, and *Krytyka*) and publishing houses (such as NOWa, KOS, CDN, BAZA, and Enklawa) began to publish his works. Herling-Grudziński supported the opposition in Poland. He was, among other things, a trustee of the underground Polish Alliance for Independence (Polskie Porozumienie Niepodległościow [PPN]) and a member of the Fund to Aid Independent Polish Literature and Science. Until 1988 his works were officially banned in Poland. From 1989 onward, he was a frequent visitor to Poland and commented on current Polish political and cultural events. He received many foreign and Polish awards, as well as awards from the émigré community, including the Jurzykowski Foundation Award (1965), the French PEN Club Prize and the Prix Gutenberg Award (1986), the Polish PEN Club Prize (1990), and the Premio

Viareggio Prize (1994). In 1996, as a result of differences in political opinions with Giedroyć, Herling-Grudziński left *Kultura* and transferred his *Journal Written at Night* to *Rzeczpospolita*, published in Poland. (DT)

Sources: Włodzimierz Bolecki, *Ciemny staw: Trzy szkice do portretu Gustawa Herlinga-Grudzińskiego* (Warsaw, 1991); R. K. Przybylski, ed., *Być i pisać: O prozie Gustawa Herlinga-Grudzińskiego* (Poznań, 1991); J. Paszek, *Gustaw Herling-Grudziński* (Katowice, 1992); Włodzimierz Bolecki and Gustaw Herling-Grudziński, *Rozmowy w Dragonei* (Warsaw, 1997); Zdzisław Kudelski, ed., *Herling-Grudziński i krytycy: Antologia tekstów* (Lublin, 1997); Włodzimierz Bolecki and Gustaw Herling-Grudziński, *Rozmowy w Neapolu* (Warsaw, 1999).

HERMAIZE Josyf (1892, Kiev–?), Ukrainian historian of Karaite origin. During the revolution in the Ukraine Hermaize was a member of the Ukrainian Social Democratic Workers' Party (USDWP). He took part in the Ukrainian Military Congress and in the Small Council (Rada), an organ of the Ukrainian Central Council. He completed his studies in history and then lectured at Kiev University. In the 1920s he also served as secretary of the historical section and director of the archaeographic commission of the All-Ukrainian Academy of Sciences. He was a student and a close co-worker of **Mykhaylo Hrushevsky**. Arrested and accused of being a member of the Union for the Liberation of Ukraine in 1929, in 1930 Hermaize was sentenced to six years in prison. He served his sentence in Yaroslavl and on the Solovets Islands. After his release he settled in Saratov but was arrested again and sentenced to ten years. His further fate is unknown. Hermaize published *Narysy z istorii revolutsiinoho rukhu na Ukraiini* (Essays in the history of the revolutionary movement in the Ukraine; 1926); *Koliyivshchyna v svitli novoznaidenykh materiialiv* (Koliyivshchyna in the light of newly discovered materials; 1924); and a number of articles devoted to important figures of Ukrainian social and political life in the nineteenth century (for example Decembrists, Mykhaylo Drahomanov and Volodymyr Antonovych). He also edited and published *Kodenska khyha sudovykh aktiv* (The Koden judicial book; 1931), a collection of documents about the Polish trials of participants of the Koliyivshchyna (peasant uprising). (TS)

Sources: *Encyclopedia of Ukraine*, vol. 2 (Toronto, 1988); W. Prystayko and Yu. Shapoval, *Sprava "Spilki vyzvolennia Ukraiiny"* (Kiev, 1995); *Mykhaylo Hrushevskyi i GPU-NKVD: Trahichne desiatylittia: 1924–1934* (Kiev, 1996).

HEYROVSKÝ Jaroslav (20 December 1890, Prague–27 March 1967, Prague), Czech chemist and physicist, Nobel Prize winner. The son of a lawyer, from childhood Heyrovský showed an interest in the natural sciences. After a year of studies in Prague, he moved to University College in London, where he began to work with the Nobel Prize winner William Ramsay. World War I found Heyrovský in Prague. He was mobilized and worked in a military hospital as a druggist and X-ray operator. In 1920 he received a postdoctoral degree at Charles University in Prague, and in 1926 he became a professor of physical chemistry there. Heyrovský's major accomplishment was the creation of a new line of electrochemistry—polarography. In 1922 he discovered electrolysis by means of a mercury drop electrode, and in 1925 he co-created the first polarograph. From 1925 Heyrovský belonged to the National Scholarly Council (Národná Rada Badatelská); from 1932 he was a full member of the Czech Royal Scholarly Society; in 1933 he lectured at the University of California at Berkeley; and from 1938 he was a full member of the Czech Academy of Science and Art. In 1929, along with Emil Votoček, he founded the scholarly periodical *Collection of Czechoslovak Chemical Communications*. In 1950 he organized the Institute of Polarography of the Czechoslovak Academy of Sciences, and until 1963 he was its first director. In 1959 he received the Nobel Prize in chemistry for discovering polarography and its applications in analytic chemistry. In 1965 he became a member of the Royal Society in London and an honorary doctor at Charles University in Prague. He authored and co-authored several works, including *Použití polarografické metody v praktické chemii* (The uses of the polarographic method in practical chemistry; 1933); *Polarographie* (Polarography; 1941); and *Základy polarografie* (Foundations of polarography; 1962 [with Jaroslav Kůta]). His works were translated into many languages. (PU)

Sources: *ČBS*; *Wielka encyklopedia PWN*, vol. 11 (Warsaw, 2002); Jiří Koryta, *Jaroslav Heyrovský* (Prague, 1990); *Kdo byl kdo v našich dějinach ve 20. stoleti*, vol. 1 (Prague, 1998); *Le prix Nobel en 1959* (Stockholm, 1960).

HLINKA Andrej (27 September 1864, Černová–16 August 1938, Ružomberok), Roman Catholic priest, founder of the Slovak national movement. Born into a peasant family, Hlinka was ordained in 1889. He worked for the revival of national consciousness among the Slovaks and was also active in the temperance movement. Along with Anton Bielek, he edited the periodical *L'udóve Novíny*, which soon became immensely popular among peasants. Proceeding from the principles of the papal encyclical *Rerum novarum* of Pope Leo XIII, Hlinka appealed for the creation of a Slovak social program based upon the principles of Catholic social teaching. Following his example, many Slovak priests began establishing cooperative societies, people's banks, and temperance organizations.

Hlinka also defended the Catholic and national identity of the Slovaks and protested the introduction of Hungarian as a compulsory language in rural elementary schools because it led to an increase in illiteracy in Slovakia and made teaching religion among Slovak children more difficult. From 1905 Hlinka worked as a parish priest in Ružomberok. In 1913 he co-founded the Slovak People's Party (Slovenská L'udová Strana) and sat as its representative in the parliament in Budapest. Initially he supported Slovak autonomy within the Hungarian state and was against a union of Slovakia with the Czechs within the framework of a projected federalist Habsburg monarchy. At that time he formed an electoral alliance with the Hungarian Catholic People's Party. In 1906 his involvement in the political campaign led to a conflict between him and his diocesan bishop, Sándor Párvy, an ardent advocate of the policy of denationalization of the Slovaks, who suspended Hlinka in his pastoral duties. Slovak as well as Moravian Catholics stood in defense of Hlinka. Pope Pius X also took his side and ordered the lifting of all church penalties that had been imposed on him.

In October 1907 dramatic events took place at Černova, Hlinka's native village. On his initiative, the local Catholics built a church there and wanted Hlinka to consecrate it. The Hungarian state and church authorities refused permission and sent another priest. As a result of protests by the local people, the Hungarian gendarmerie intervened, discharging a volley at the defenseless crowd and killing fifteen people. The killings in Černova led to protests in Europe and America, especially after a series of articles by Robert W. Seton-Watson, a British scholar, and after speeches by the Nobel Prize winner M. Bjørnstjerne Bjørnson. The Hungarian authorities arrested Hlinka, accusing him of anti-Hungarian agitation, but this only consolidated his position as one of the most important leaders of the Slovak nation. While in prison in Szeged (1907–10), Hlinka translated the Old Testament into the Slovak language. After his release he still maintained that autonomy within the Hungarian kingdom was the goal of the Slovaks. He rejected proposals for a common state with the Czechs as he feared that it would result in domination by liberal and Masonic elites. In 1917 he was appointed apostolic prothonotary.

With the collapse of the Habsburg state and the revolution in Hungary in 1918, Hlinka supported a program of federation with the Czechs. On 24 May 1918, as one of the leaders of the Slovak National Party, Hlinka stated at a meeting in Turčiansky Svätý Martin that it was time for the Slovaks to choose whether they wanted to be with the Hungarians or with the Czechs. Declaring for union with the Czechs, he joined the supporters of the Czechoslovak

orientation. He was one of the signatories of a declaration issued on 30 October 1918 in Turčiansky Svätý Martin. The declaration was a political manifesto of Slovakia's sovereignty within a federal Czechoslovakia. In December 1918 Hlinka founded the Slovak People's Party, a Christian party later renamed the Slovak People's Party of Hlinka (Hlinkova Slovenská L'udová Strana [HSL'S], also known as the Ludaks). The HSL'S supported the integration of the Slovaks and the Czechs but according to principles specified in the so-called Pittsburgh agreement of May 30, 1918, which foresaw the creation of a federation of two equal nations. The Ludak movement dominated the political life of Slovakia in the interwar period. From 1919 Hlinka edited the newspaper *Slovak*, the largest Slovak daily, in which he promoted Slovak autonomy and opposed the imposition by Prague of so-called Czechoslovakism, which in practice denied the Slovaks the right to their own national identity and viewed the Slovak language as a variant of Czech. In 1919, using a false passport, Hlinka traveled via Poland to Paris. At the Paris Peace Conference he made efforts to secure favorable provisions for Slovakia. After his return he was imprisoned by the Czechoslovak authorities.

In the 1920s Hlinka grew more and more disappointed with the development of national relations in Czechoslovakia. He considered the possibility of a federation of Slovakia with Poland, which he regarded as closer to Slovakia in terms of religion. However, when in 1927 a chance appeared for a change in the centralist policy of the Prague government, he decided that two HSL'S politicians would take part in a Czechoslovak government. After the arrest of **Vojtech Tuka**, who spied for Hungary but in whose guilt Hlinka did not believe, the members of the HSL'S left the government and until the end of the interwar period remained in opposition. The respect that Hlinka enjoyed allowed the HSL'S to maintain unity within its ranks in the 1930s, despite the clashing views of four factions: pro-Czech, pro-Hungarian, pro-Polish, and (the biggest one) the Slovak autonomists. Hlinka himself wanted to save the federation with the Czechs, although he criticized the current policies of the Prague government. During the celebration of the 1100th anniversary of the consecration of the first church in Nitra and the creation of the petty state of Prince Pribina, Hlinka did not support the radical Slovak nationalists, who openly called for the dismantling of Czechoslovakia. In 1935 he supported the election of **Edvard Beneš** to the post of president of Czechoslovakia. In the late 1930s he again considered the possibility of a federation with Poland. In the summer of 1937, on the initiative of the Polish Ministry of Foreign Affairs, Hlinka made a visit to Krynica and Zakopane, where he was greeted enthusiastically and was assured that Poland supported the autonomy aspirations of Slovakia. Hlinka was then decorated with the Grand Ribbon of the Order of Polonia Restituta.

Disappointed by the lack of major changes in the policies of the Prague government, in 1938, along with the leaders of German and Hungarian national minority organizations, Hlinka demanded that the Prague government declare Slovak autonomy. At that time he favored the nationalist, extremely anti-Czech wing in his party. At the end of his life Hlinka still considered that a federation with the Czechs was the best solution for the Slovaks, and he opposed attempts at control of the HSL'S by politicians like Tuka and **Ferdinand Ďurčanský**, who sought inspiration in the Third Reich. Hlinka's *Zápisky z Mírova* (Notes from Mírov) were published posthumously in 1941. (AGr)

*Sources: Kdo byl kdo v našich déjinách ve 20 stole*ti (Prague, 1994); *The Political Trial against the Rev. Father Andrew Hlinka, the Rev. Father Joseph Tomik, Dr. Srobar, and Others* (New York, 1906); Alois Kolísek, *Andrej Hlinka* (Bratislava, 1924); Karol Sidor, *Andrej Hlinka* (Bratislava, 1934); *Słowacja i Słowacy,* vol. 2 (Kraków, 1938); Janusz Bazydło, "Hlinka Andrej," *Encyklopedia katolicka,* vol. 6 (Lublin, 1993); Joseph Mikus, *Slovakia, A Political History: 1918–1950* (Milwaukee, 1963); Henryk Batowski, *Z polityki międzynarodowej XX wieku: Wybór studiów z lat 1930–1975* (Kraków, 1979); Ewa Orlof, *Dyplomacja polska wobec sprawy słowackiej w latach 1938–1939* (Kraków, 1980); Bohdan Cywiński, *Ogniem próbowane: Z dziejów najnowszych Kościoła katolickiego w Europie Środkowo-Wschodniej,* vols. 1–2 (Rome, 1982; Lublin, 1990); Dušan Kováč, *Dejiny Slovenska* (Prague, 2000).

HLOND August (5 July 1881, Brzęczkowice, Upper Silesia–22 October 1948, Warsaw), cardinal, Primate of Poland. Born into the large family of a railwayman, in October 1893 Hlond started his secondary education in a Salesian school in Valsalice, near Turin, Italy. Later he studied at Lombriasco and Rome. In October 1897 he took vows in the Salesian Order. In 1904 he graduated from high school in Lemberg (Lwów, Lviv), and in July 1905 he was ordained a priest. Later he studied in Kraków and Lwów, but he did not graduate, as he started his ministry in Przemyśl. From 1909 Hlond was the superior of a Salesian monastery in Vienna, and in 1912 he obtained confirmation in the order in the Habsburg monarchy. In 1919, he became provincial of the Austro-Hungarian-German province of the Salesian Order. During the Polish uprisings in Silesia (1919–21) Hlond was active in favor of Poland. On 7 November 1922 he was appointed apostolic administrator of the part of the Breslau (Wrocław) archdiocese that had been granted to Poland after World War I. From June 1923 he was a permanent participant of the Conference of the Polish Episcopate. He organized the Episcopal curia and

diocese institutions, and he established the weekly *Gość Niedzielny* (1923), the Diocese Charity Secretariat, and the Silesia Relief Committee to aid the jobless. He co-organized a Holy Year pilgrimage to Rome and the coronation of the picture of the Holy Virgin Mary in Piekary Śląskie. After Pope Pius XI reorganized the Polish Church by means of the papal bull *Vixdum Poloniae unitas* (28 October 1925), on 14 December 1925 Hlond became the first ordinary bishop of the Katowice diocese.

After the death of Cardinal **Edmund Dalbor**, on 24 June 1926 Hlond was appointed archbishop of Gniezno and Poznań, the Primate of Poland, and chairman of the Conference of the Polish Episcopate. He made his ingress in both towns in October 1926. In January 1927 he established the Chancellery of the Primate of Poland, and on 23 June 1927 he was appointed cardinal. He contributed to the reactivation of religious life by organizing Catholic Action and establishing its Chief Institute in 1930. He cared for the ministry among the Polish diaspora and received special authority in this respect from Pope Pius XI in 1931. For this purpose he established the Christ Society for the Emigration. In November 1933 he established the Social Council of the Primate of Poland. In August 1936 in the Jasna Góra Monastery in Częstochowa he convened the first synod of the Polish Church after the regaining of independence. In numerous homilies and pastoral letters Hlond stressed the necessity of the Church's engagement in contemporary social problems, including those of unemployment. In view of the totalitarian threats stemming from the Third Reich and the Soviet Union he stressed the importance of strengthening Polish statehood. He supported Christian trade unions, as well as youth and cooperative organizations. After the death of Cardinal **Aleksander Kakowski**, Hlond took over the duties of the head of the Warsaw archbishopric in December 1938.

After the German invasion of Poland, on 14 September 1939 Hlond left via Romania to Rome, where he informed Pope Pius XII about the dramatic situation in Poland and made his case in favor of Poland. In 1940 Hlond published in Italian, French, English, and Spanish a report on the persecution of the Polish Church under the German occupation. From 1940 he lived in Lourdes, France, and from June 1943, in Hautecombe in French Savoy. Arrested by the Germans in February 1944, Hlond was interned in Bar-le-Duch in the Department of Meuse and in the Wiedenbrück Monastery in Westphalia. Released on 1 April 1945 by the U.S. Army, he went to Rome, where on 8 July 1945 he received special authority from the Pope to organize the church administration of the northern and western territories newly gained by Poland after the war. At the end of July he went to Poznań, and on 15 August

1945 he erected five apostolic administrations for the dioceses whose German bishops were still alive: in Wrocław, Gorzów, Opole, Gdańsk, and Olsztyn. For political reasons, the new Communist authorities did not recognize this decision and demanded that Hlond make the Pope appoint Polish ordinary bishops, which was impossible in the light of Church tradition. In view of the Church's refusal, the Communists started arguing that the Church question the Polish nature of these territories. Contrary to this propaganda, Hlond did a lot to help the new Polish settlers take root in the new Catholic parishes established in the acquired territories. In June and July 1947 he made a long visitation to these territories. On 4 March 1946 Hlond resigned from the Poznań archbishopric and took over the Warsaw archbishopric, remaining the Primate of Poland. In this way he wanted to avoid the traditional rivalry of the Gniezno and Warsaw provinces over primacy. He made his ingress into the Warsaw cathedral on 10 May 1946. The bibliography of Hlond's works includes about four hundred articles, pastoral letters, and homilies. A collection of his writings and speeches was published in the United States as *Na straży sumień* (On guard of the conscience; 1951). (WR)

Sources: *Encyklopedia historii Drugiej Rzeczpospolitej* (Warsaw, 1999); *Nasza przeszłość*, vol. 42 (Kraków, 1974); Feliks Lenort, ed., *Na stolicy prymasowskiej w Gnieźnie i Poznaniu: Szkice o prymasach Polski w oresie niewoli narodowej i w II Rzeczpospolitej* (Poznań, 1982); Jerzy Lis, *August Hlond 1881–1948: Prymas Polski, kardynał, działacz społeczny, pisarz* (Katowice, 1987); Franz Scholz, *Zwischen Staatsräson und Evangelium: Kardinal Hlond und die Tragödie der ostdeutschen Diözesen* (Frankfurt am Main, 1988).

HODŽA Milan (1 February 1878, Sučany, Slovakia–27 June 1944, Clearwater, Florida), Slovak politician. Hodža came from a Protestant landowning family. He studied in Budapest and Cluj and completed law and philosophical studies in Vienna. He worked with **Vavro Šrobár** and **Pavol Blaho**, members of a group of editors for the periodical *Hlas*. They saw hope for Slovak autonomy in the democratization of Austria-Hungary. From 1900 to 1902 Hodža edited *Slovenský dennik*, and from 1903 to 1914, *Slovenský týždennik*. From 1905 to 1910 he was a deputy to the parliament in Budapest and secretary of the parliamentary club of national minorities. From 1906 he served as vice-president of the Slovak National Party (Slovenská Narodná Straná [SNS]) and was leader of its agrarian wing. In the program of the SNS, he declared that the peasants were the social base of the modern political movement that was struggling for equal rights for Slovaks. Hodža and **Alexandru Vaida-Voevod**, a Romanian Peasant Party politician, worked with Archduke Franz Ferdinand, aiming at the transformation of the Habsburg monarchy into a federation of national states. After the assassination of Franz Ferdinand in Sarajevo this plan had to be abandoned.

After the outbreak of World War I, Hodža served as an officer in the Austro-Hungarian Army. From 1915 to 1916 he was a military censor and later an editor in an Austrian press agency. At that time his views shifted to a pro-Czechoslovak orientation, and in 1918 he participated in the preparation of a proposal to organize a joint state of Czechs and Slovaks. During Czech and Slovak negotiations in Geneva in October 1918 Hodža represented the Slovak side. Soon after the adoption of the Declaration of Turčiansky Svätý Martin on the Slovak accession to a common state with the Czechs, he arrived there on 30 October 1918 with the information that the state had been proclaimed two days earlier in Prague. As a result of Hodža's efforts, an article on sending a separate Slovak delegation to the Paris Peace Conference was removed from the declaration.

From 1918 to 1919 Hodža was a plenipotentiary representative of Czechoslovakia in Budapest. On 6 December 1918 he signed a treaty with the war minister of the Hungarian Republic on the withdrawal of Hungarian troops from the greater part of Slovakia. He described his mission in his work *Slovenský rozchod z Maďarami roku 1918* (The Slovak parting with the Hungarians in 1918; 1928). The book was a response to attacks by Šrobár and **Edvard Beneš**, who accused Hodža of a pro-Hungarian attitude. In 1920 Hodža published *Československy rozkol* (Czechoslovak split) about the political aspects of the creation of the Slovak literary language. In 1921 he became professor of the modern history of Slavic nations at Komenský University in Bratislava. In 1919 he formed the Peasant Party (Národná Republikanska Strana Rol'nická), which represented the Czechoslovak program and competed with the autonomists of Reverend **Andrej Hlinka**, who sharply criticized Hodža for favoring the Czech policy toward Slovakia. Hodža's party worked in alliance with the Czech Agrarians of **Antonin Švehla** and in 1922 united with them. Hodža became vice-president of the National Executive Committee of the Republican Agrarian Party (Republikánská Strana Zemědělského a Malorolnického Lidu) and co-founder and member of the leadership of the International Agrarian Bureau in Prague, an organization that consisted of fifteen European agrarian parties. From 1919 to 1920 and from 1926 to 1927 Hodža served as minister for unification of legislation; from 1922 to 1926 and from 1932 to 1935, as minister of agriculture; and between 1926 and 1929, as minister for education. In 1929, after the fall of Švehla's government, Hodža withdrew from political life in the midst of a corruption scandal. Between 1930 and 1934 six volumes of his collected works, *Články,* *reči, štúdie* (Articles, speeches, studies), were published.

In 1932 Hodža was again appointed minister of agriculture, and on 5 November 1935, prime minister of the Czechoslovak government. He declared a need for rapprochement among the states of Central Europe, particularly in the economic sphere. He was against a treaty between Czechoslovakia and the USSR, which was signed by Beneš in 1935. In 1937 he unsuccessfully attempted to reduce tension in the Danube Basin through an agreement of the Little Entente, Hungary, and Austria. In the face of German provocations and the increasingly aggressive claims of the Third Reich, in February 1937 Hodža's cabinet worked out a plan for the decentralization of the administration in the Sudetenland to satisfy German demands. However, the agreement with moderate German groups was not enough to prevent a crisis. Hitler constantly used the demonstrations of the Sudeten Nazis to fuel war hysteria. As the policy of concessions pursued by France and Great Britain was ineffective, Hodža accepted the ultimatum of Berchtesgaden, and on 22 September 1938 he resigned as prime minister. Hodža saw an increase in the popularity of the Slovak People's Party of Hlinka (Hlinkova Slovenská L'udová Strana [HSL'S]) and Hlinka's program for the emancipation of Slovaks; therefore, after the Munich conference of 1938, he also expressed himself in favor of the decentralization of the state and Slovak autonomy, signing an agreement with the HSL'S at the beginning of October 1938.

Hodža later emigrated to France, where he organized the Slovak National Council (Slovenská Narodná Radá), which was in opposition to the Czechoslovak National Council (Československý Národni Výbor). Unlike the camp of President Beneš, Hodža and his council opted for the future autonomy of Slovakia. In 1940 he refused to accept the post of deputy prime minister in the London government-in-exile. In 1941 he left for the United States, where he was one of the initiators of the Green International. In 1942 in London he published *Federation in Central Europe*, in which he warned against the expansionism of the USSR and called for the creation of a union of Central European nations as a protectorate of the United States. However, his concepts did not gain much support, and after 1945 they were no longer valid. Hodža died before the end of World War II. His son Fedor was a secretary of the Democratic Party between 1945 and 1948, and after the upheavals of 1948 he emigrated to the United States. (MG/WR)

Sources: *ČBS*; *Encyklopedia Slovenska*, vol. 2 (Bratislava, 1978); *Mala československa encyklopedie*, vol. 2 (Prague, 1987); *Who's Who in Central and Eastern Europe 1933–34* (Zurich, 1935); Risto Kovijanić, *Milan Hodža a Juhoslavania* (Bratislava, 1938); *Słowacja i Słowacy*, vol. 2 (Kraków, 1938); Anton Štefanek, *Milan Hodža* (Bratislava, 1938); Joseph A. Mikus, *Slovakia: A Political History, 1918–1950* (Milwaukee, 1963); *Milan Hodža—štatnik a politik* (Bratislava, 1994); Karol Kollár, *Milan Hodža: Moderný teoretik—pragmatický politik* (Bratislava, 1994); Jan Juríček, *Milan Hodža: Kapitola z dejin slovenskej, československej a europskej politiky* (Bratislava, 1994); Jan Kukli and Jan Němeček, *Hodža versus Beneš: Milan Hodža a slovenska otázka v zahraničnim odboji za druge světove války* (Prague, 1999); Samuel Cambel, *Štátnik a národohospodar Milan Hodža* (Bratislava, 2001).

HOŁÓWKO Tadeusz, pseudonyms "Kirgiz," "Otwinowski," and "Hołodyński" (17 September 1889, Semipalatinsk, Kazakhstan–29 August 1931, Truskawiec), Polish politician. Hołówko's father was head of a customs house and a participant of the January 1863 Insurrection. As a high school student in Verny (now Almaty) in 1905–7, Hołówko had contacts with a military organization of Socialists-revolutionists. From 1909 he studied in the Department of Natural History at St. Petersburg University, and later he was a student at the Jagiellonian University in Kraków (1912) and at the law school of St. Petersburg University. Linked with the Polish Socialist Party (PPS)–Revolutionary Faction, he took part in the Coalition Committee, which headed strikes at universities in 1911. In 1912 he was arrested in Moscow but was acquitted after a trial. Along with **Mieczysław Niedziałkowski**, he published *Głos Młodych*. In 1914 he co-organized the Polish Military Organization (Polska Organizacja Wojskowa [POW]) in Warsaw. Arrested after the German seizure of Warsaw, Hołówko spent 1915–16 in Salzwedel and Stendal. After his release, between 1917 and 1918 he edited the press organ of the POW, *Rząd i Wojsko*. At the beginning of 1918 he traveled via the Ukraine to Moscow, where, as a representative of the PPS–Revolutionary Faction and the POW, he tried to consolidate pro-independence trends among Polish military units in Russia. He also talked with Bolshevik leaders, among them Leon Trotsky and Vladimir Lenin. However, he failed to persuade them to support the Polish Socialists in their quest for the independence of Poland.

Hołówko was one of the co-founders of the Lublin government of **Ignacy Daszyński** (7–11 November 1918), co-author of its manifesto, and deputy minister of propaganda in the Daszyński cabinet. He was later head of a department in the Ministry of Labor and Social Welfare and a Warsaw councillor (1919–27). He fought in the Polish-Soviet war and was wounded. From 1921 to 1925 he was a member of the PPS leadership and editor-in-chief of *Trybuna*. He was a leading representative of the Promethean current in Polish eastern thought among **Józef Piłsudski**'s followers. From 1925 Hołówko stayed in Paris, where in 1926 he participated in the creation of the society called La Prométhée, as well as a periodical of the same name; they propagated the idea of the separation of non-Russian nations from Russia. Hołówko had wide contacts among the emigrants from Russia. As a representative of the PPS, he took an active part in the congress of the Labor and Socialist International in Marseilles (1925). After returning to Poland, he dealt with "prometheism," national minorities, and Poland's eastern policy. He also directed the Ethnic Research Institute.

In 1926 Hołówko supported the May coup d'état staged by Piłsudski. In 1927 he left the PPS and was appointed head of the Eastern Department of the Ministry of Foreign Affairs. He strove for the consolidation of Ukrainian anti-Soviet forces in Poland, called for a liberal treatment of national minorities, and opposed anti-Semitism but allowed for the re-Polonization of the Germanized Polish population. In 1930 he was elected MP of the Nonparty Bloc for Cooperation with the Government (BBWR), representing Vilnius, and he became head of the Assembly club of the BBWR. He resigned from his post at the Ministry of Foreign Affairs. Along with **Janusz Jędrzejewicz**, Hołówko held talks with Ukrainian organizations on the implementation of federative concepts. Hołówko was murdered by Ukrainian nationalists who held him responsible, against the facts, for the pacification actions in Eastern Galicia. (PK)

Sources: *PSB*; *Słownik Polityków Polskich XX w.* (Poznań, 1998); Jerzy Lewandowski, *Litwa i Białoruś w polityce obozu belwederskiego* (Warsaw, 1962); Piotr Wandycz, "Czy Hołówko rozmawiał z Leninem i Trockim w 1918 roku?" *Zeszyty Historyczne* (Paris), 1974, no. 41; Iwo Werschler, *Z dziejów obozu belwederskiego: Tadeusz Hołówko-życie i działalność* (Warsaw, 1984); B. Stoczewska, *Litwa, Białoruś, Ukraina w myśli politycznej Leona Wasilewskiego* (Kraków, 1998), W. Bączkowski, *O wschodnich problemach Polski* (Kraków, 2000).

HOLUBOVYCH Vsevolod (February 1885, Moldavka, Podolia–16 May 1939, Yaroslav), Ukrainian politician. The son of a priest, Holubovych graduated from a theological seminary and from the Kiev Polytechnic Institute (1915). In 1916–17 he worked as head of the road department on the Romanian front. From 1903 he belonged to the Ukrainian Revolutionary Party, and in February 1913 he joined the Kiev organization of the Ukrainian Party of Socialist Revolutionaries (UPSR). In the spring of 1917 he took the lead of the UPSR committee in Odessa. Elected to the Odessa City Council and to the Ukrainian and Russian Constituent Assemblies, at the Second UPSR Congress he became a member of the Ukrainian Central Council

(UCC). In July 1917 he became minister of transportation, and in October 1917, minister of industry and trade in the UCC General Secretariat (government). He did his best to secure war supplies and means of transportation for the army of the Ukrainian National Republic (UNR). From December 1917 to January 1918 he was a member and later head of the Ukrainian delegation to the peace talks in Brest-Litovsk.

In view of the Ukrainian declaration of independence (Fourth UCC Universal) and the resignation of the **Volodymir Vynnychenko** government, on 18 January 1918 Holubovych became prime minister of the UNR, holding on to the Ministry of Industry and Trade. From the end of January 1918 to the conclusion of the Brest-Litovsk Peace Treaty in early March 1918, the Bolshevik offensive forced Holubovych to leave Kiev, and his government stayed in Volhynia. He returned to Kiev with the German troops, but from then on his activity was largely depending on their consent. Since he planned a land reform, his cabinet was toppled on 29 April 1918 by the followers of Hetman **Pavlo Skoropadksyi**, who had German support. In June 1918 Holubovych was arrested and sentenced to two years in prison. Released as a result of the takeover by the Directorate on 16 December 1918, in the winter of 1918–19 Holubovych stayed in opposition to the new authorities, but he soon agreed to edit the government newspaper, *Trudova Hromada* (1919–20). While in Kamenets Podolskyi, in the second half of 1919 Holubovych took part in leading a UNR anti-Bolshevik insurgency, also directed against General Anton Denikin. An opponent of the Directorate's alliance with Poland, he stayed in Kamenets Podolskyi until June 1920, when the town was taken by the Red Army. He joined in organizing the local university, but in August 1920 he was arrested. Accused of preparing an anti-Bolshevik uprising, in May 1921 he was sentenced to five years of forced labor. Amnestied at the end of 1921, he worked as head of the construction department in the Ukrainian Council of the National Economy. In March 1931 he was arrested again for alleged participation in the so-called Ukrainian National Center. Tortured, he confessed to being guilty and died in prison. (TS)

Sources: *Encyclopedia of Ukraine*, vol. 2 (Toronto, 1988); Hryhory Kostiuk, *Stalinist Rule in the Ukraine* (New York, 1960); Matthew Stachiv and Jaroslav Sztendera, eds., *Western Ukraine at the Turning Point of Europe's History, 1918–1923*, vols. 1–2 (New York, 1971); Stanisław Kulczycki, ed., *Uryady Ukraiiny u XX st.* (Kiev, 2001).

HÓMAN Bálint (29 December 1885, Budapest–2 June 1951, Vác), Hungarian historian and politician. Born to a

German burgher family, in 1908 Hóman graduated from the History Department of Budapest University, where he later worked as a librarian, lecturer (from 1918), and professor and head of the chair of Hungarian medieval history (1925–31). Between 1922 and 1923 he was director of the National Széchenyi Library and later managing director of the National Museum until 1932. From October 1932 to May 1938 and from February 1939 to March 1942 he served as minister of religious affairs and education in the governments of **Gyula Gömbös**, **Kálmán Darányi**, **Pál Teleki**, and **László Bárdossy**. Hóman designed and implemented a program to develop elementary education and to establish new institutions of higher education, particularly technical and economic universities, so as to enhance the competitive abilities of the Hungarians and the Hungarian economy in the world. In foreign policy he advocated rapprochement with Germany. From 1932 he was an MP. At the end of 1944 he fled to Austria. Wanted as a war criminal by the postwar Hungarian government and handed over to Hungary by the Western Allies in 1945, Hóman was charged with treason and in 1946 sentenced to life imprisonment. He served his sentence in Vác, the most severe penal institution for political prisoners, where he died.

An outstanding medievalist, Hóman was an expert on and a popularizer of the era of the Árpáds, whose politics and activity he considered paragons to be followed. Initially he was a representative of the positivist school but was gradually drawn to the concept of the creative role of the spirit (*Geistesgeschichte*). His most important works include *Magyar pénztörténet 1000–1325* (History of finance in Hungary; 1916); *A magyar királyság pénzügyei és gazdaságpolitikája Károly Róbert korában* (Finances and economic policy of Hungary under Charles Robert; 1921); *Szent István* (St. Stephen; 1939); and *Geschichte des ungarischen Mittelalters* (History of the Hungarian Middle Ages, 2 vols.; 1940–43). Along with **Gyula Szekfű**, Hóman authored the monumental seven-volume *Magyar Történet* (History of Hungary; 1929–33) and co-authored the four-volume *Egyetemes történet* (General history; 1935–37). Hóman described his experiences from his first term as minister in *Művelődéspolitka* (Cultural and educational policy; 1938). (MS)

Sources: *Biographisches Lexikon*, vol. 2; László Tóth, *Hóman Bálint, a történetíró* (Budapest, 1939); Ferenc Glátz, *Nemzeti kultúra—kulturált nemzet* (Budapest, 1988); Béla László, *Hóman Bálint utolsó évei* (Budapest, 1993); Steven Bela Vardy, *Historical Dictionary of Hungary* (Lanham, Md., 1997).

HONCHAR Oles (Oleksandr) (3 April 1918, Sukha, Poltava province–14 July 1995, Kiev), Ukrainian writer, journalist, and political activist. In 1933–37 Honchar studied at the Technical School for Journalists in Kharkiv. He made his literary debut in 1937. From 1937 to 1941 he studied philology at the universities in Kharkiv and Dniepropetrovsk. After the outbreak of the German-Soviet war in June 1941, he volunteered for the front. Twice wounded and captured by the Germans, Honchar spent a few months in a German camp. After escaping from captivity, he returned to the front. He ended his military activity in Prague at the end of war. In 1946–48 Honchar wrote the novels *Alpy* (The Alps; 1946); *Holubyi Dunay* (Blue Danube; 1948; awarded the Stalin Prize); and *Zlata Praha* (Golden Prague; 1949; awarded the Stalin Prize); these constituted a trilogy, *Praporonostsi* (The standard-bearers). In 1959–71 Honchar presided over the Association of Ukrainian Writers (Spilka Pysmennykiv Ukraiiny), and in 1959–86 he was secretary of the Association of Writers of the USSR. He was a deputy to the Supreme Councils of the Ukrainian SSR and the USSR and editor-in-chief of the monthly *Vitchyzna*. In the 1950s and 1960s he wrote several novels, of which the most important was *Sobor* (Assembly; 1968), referring to the protection of Ukrainian cultural relics. Although Honchar always behaved the way the authorities expected, in April 1968 he was attacked by official propaganda because the regional party secretary in Dniepropetrovsk recognized himself in one of the negative characters in Honchar's work.

Honchar authored screenplays for several films produced in the Oleksandr Dovzhenko Film Studios, including *Partyzanska iskra* (Partisan spark; 1958); *Abituryentka* (Woman graduate; 1973); and *Vse peremahaye lyubov* (Love will overcome all; 1987). From 1973 Honchar was chairman of the Ukrainian republican Committee for the Defense of Peace and a member of the World Peace Council. In 1978 he became a member of the Academy of Sciences of the USSR. At the turn of the 1990s he worked with the Taras Shevchenko Society of the Ukrainian language and with the Ukrainian National Movement for Perestroika (Narodnyi Rukh Ukraiiny za Prebudovu). During a student strike in 1990, whose aim was to accelerate political change in the Ukraine, Honchar gave up his party membership. The most complete collection of his works, *Tvory* (Works), was published in Kiev in 1987–88. His works were translated into almost forty languages. (BB)

Sources: *Encyclopedia of Ukraine*, vol. 2 (Toronto, 1988); *Pisarze świata: Słownik encyklopedyczny* (Warsaw, 1995); *Dovidnyk z istoriyi Ukraiiny* (Kiev, 2001); *Shevchenkivski laureaty 1962–2001: Entsyklopedychnyi dovidnyk* (Kiev, 2001); Mykhailo Strelbytskyi, *Proza monumentalnoho istoryzmu: Dorobok Olesia Honchara* (Kiev, 1988); *Vinok pamyati Olesia Honchara* (Kiev, 1997).

HOPKO Wasyl (21 April 1904, Hrabské, near Prešov–23 July 1976, Prešov), Greek Catholic auxiliary bishop of Prešov. Hopko graduated from a theological seminary in Prešov and from theological studies in Prague, and then he worked in various parishes in Czechoslovakia, among them Prague, where he earned a Ph.D. in theology at Charles University. In 1934 he founded the first Greek Catholic parish in Prague. In 1936 he was appointed papal chamberlain. From 1945 he edited the newspaper *Blagovisnik*. On 11 May 1947 he was ordained auxiliary bishop of Prešov. During the suppression of the Greek Catholic Church by the Communist authorities, on 28 April 1950 Hopko was arrested by the Czechoslovak security police and was sentenced to fifteen years in prison. Meanwhile, the Uniate Church was formally incorporated into the Orthodox Church under the jurisdiction of the Russian metropolitan. Hopko served his sentence in Leopoldov, Waldince, Mirovo, Ružin Prison in Prague, and other prisons. Released in 1964, he was kept under surveillance. In 1968 he returned to Prešov and sought the legalization of the Greek Catholic Church. However, as part of the policy of "normalization," on 2 April 1969 he was again removed from the administration of the eparchy of Prešov. In September 2003 Pope **John Paul II** beatified Hopko during a pilgrimage to Slovakia. (WR)

Sources: *Martirologia ukrainskikh tserkov u chetyriokh tomakh*, vol. 2 (Toronto, 1985); *Encyclopedia of Ukraine*, vol. 2 (Toronto, 1988).

HORAKOVA Milada (25 December 1901, Prague–27 June 1950, Prague), Czech lawyer and politician. From 1929 Horakova belonged to the Czechoslovak National Socialist Party and was active in the women's movement. After the German invasion of Czechoslovakia in March 1939, she started activities in the resistance, cooperating with the Political Center (Politické Ustředi) of **Prokop Drtina** and the largest non-Communist clandestine group, We Shall Remain Faithful (Věrni Zůstaneme). On 2 August 1940 she was arrested along with her husband by the Gestapo and imprisoned in Pankrác Prison and in Terezín. In October 1944 she was sentenced to eight years but was released in April 1945. After returning to Prague and to political activity, Horakova joined the National Socialist leadership and won a parliamentary seat. In 1945–48 she presided over the Council of Czechoslovak Women and was deputy chairperson of the Union of Liberated Political Prisoners. After the Communist coup of February 1948, she gave up her parliamentary mandate and worked in the Prague City Council. On 27 September 1949 she was arrested. Between 31 May and 8 June 1950 she was the main defendant of the first show trial in Czechoslovakia, staged by the Soviet advisers. As a result Horakova, along with three other defendants, was sentenced to death. Despite numerous protests (by, among others, Albert Einstein), she was executed. Her rehabilitation, started during the Prague Spring of 1968, was suspended during the "normalization" of the 1970s. Horakova was not fully rehabilitated until 1990, after the Velvet Revolution. (PU)

Sources: *ČBS*; *Kdo byl kdo v našich dějinách ve 20. století*, vol. 1 (Prague, 1998); Jiří Pelikán, *The Czechoslovak Political Trials, 1950–1954* (Stanford, 1971); Miroslav Ivanov, *Justiční vražda aneb smrt Milady Horakové* (Prague, 1991); Karel Kaplan, *Největší politický proces "M. Horáková a spol"* (Prague and Brno, 1995); Zora Dvořaková and Jiří Doležal, *O Miladě Horákové a Milada Horáková o sebě* (Prague, 2001).

HORBOVYI Volodymir (30 January 1889, Dolina–21 May 1984, Obolonia, near Dolina), Ukrainian lawyer and nationalist activist. Horbovyi completed law studies in Prague, where he started his political activities. After World War I, he practiced law in Poland and Czechoslovakia. At the beginning of the 1930s he joined the Ukrainian Military Organization and for some time commanded one of its units, carrying on activities against the Polish authorities in Eastern Galicia. On 28 October 1933 he was arrested and sent to a camp in Bereza Kartuska. Released in December 1934, he joined a group of lawyers representing the defendants charged with the murder of Minister **Bronisław Pieracki**, and he also defended **Stepan Bandera** and **Yaroslav Stetsko** in Lwów (May and June 1936).

After the occupation of Eastern Galicia by the USSR in September 1939, Horbovyi arrived in Kraków, where he headed the Relief Committee for Ukrainian POWs and for refugees from Soviet labor camps. He became aligned with the Bandera faction of the Organization of Ukrainian Nationalists (OUN), and in April 1941 he became head of its commission for statehood planning. At the end of June 1941 he was named president of the Ukrainian National Committee, which demanded independence for the Ukraine from the Germans. Horbovyi was arrested by the Gestapo, but in July 1942 he was released owing to ill health. For some time he lived in German-occupied Prague and later became a judge of the Court of Appeals in German-occupied Poland. Having Czechoslovak citizenship, at the end the war Horbovyi went to Prague, where he worked as a legal counselor in the Ministry of Agriculture. On 1 August 1947 he was arrested for collaboration with the Germans and expelled to Poland. In July 1948 he was handed over to the Soviet Ministry for Internal Affairs and deported to the USSR. On 1 August 1949 he was sentenced to twenty-five years in labor camp. He wrote numerous protests against his imprisonment and his trial, citing, among other things, his Czechoslovak citizenship, but to no avail. Released in August 1972, Horbovyi had to settle in his native village and was not even allowed to visit his son, who lived in Czechoslovakia. (WR)

Sources: S. P. de Boer, E. J. Driessen, and H. L. Verhaa, eds., *Biographical Dictionary of Dissidents in the Soviet Union* (The Hague: Martinus Nijhoff, 1982); *ABN Correspondence*, 1984, nos. 3–4.

HORN Gyula (5 July 1932, Budapest), Hungarian Communist and post-Communist activist. The son of a laborer murdered by the Gestapo in 1944, after high school Horn studied at the Higher Economic and Financial School in Rostov (USSR), from which he graduated in 1954. In the same year he joined the (Communist) Hungarian Workers' Party (HWP). In 1954–59 he was a white-collar worker in the Ministry of Finance. During the revolution, from late October to early November 1956, he belonged to the Revolutionary Home Guard. After 4 November he joined the Hungarian Socialist Workers' Party (Magyar Szocialista Munkáspárt [HSWP]). From December 1956 to June 1957—on the orders of the party Central Committee (CC)—Horn belonged to a special group of political police whose aim was to search for and arrest insurgents. From 1959 he worked in the Department of the USSR of the Ministry of Foreign Affairs, dealing with economic matters. From 1961 he was attaché in Bulgaria, and in 1963–69, in Yugoslavia. Later he advanced in the HSWP CC apparatus, first as deputy head (1969–83) and then head of the Foreign Affairs Department. In 1970 he graduated from the Higher Political School in Budapest, and in 1977 he received a Ph.D. in economics on the basis of a study of the Yugoslav economic model. In March 1985, at the Thirteenth HSWP Congress, he was elected to the CC, and in the same month he became undersecretary of state in the Foreign Ministry.

From May 1989 to May 1990 Horn was minister of foreign affairs in the government of **Miklós Németh**. In September 1989 he decided to open the Hungarian-Austrian border to thousands of East German refugees; this accelerated the fall of the Berlin Wall in November 1989. For this decision, in January 1990 Horn was awarded a gold medal from the Gustav Stresemann Society, and later he received the Charlemagne Prize in Aachen, Germany; the Great Cross of the Order of Merit of the German Federal Republic; and other German awards for his contribution to the unification of Europe. In 1991 he became a member of the Honorary European Senate. During Horn's term as minister, Hungary entered into diplomatic relations with South Korea, the Holy See, Israel, and South Africa. In the presence of the representatives of the Hungarian opposi-

tion, in early March 1990, Horn signed an agreement in Moscow on the withdrawal of Soviet troops from Hungary by the end of June 1993. From June to October 1989 he was a member of the Politburo of the HSWP CC, and then he was elected to the top leadership of the newly created Hungarian Socialist Party (Magyar Szocialiszta Párt [HSP]). In May 1990 he was elected the HSP chairman. In September 1992 the HSP was accepted into the Socialist International. In the first free elections in March 1990 Horn won a parliamentary seat on behalf of the HSP and became head of the parliamentary commission of foreign affairs. In January 1993 he resigned from this position in view of the strong criticism of the ruling parties.

In the elections of May 1994 Horn led his party to victory. The HSP won 54 percent of the mandates. In order to strengthen the legitimacy of his government abroad, Horn invited the (liberal) Alliance of Free Democrats into the ruling coalition. From 15 July 1994 to 6 July 1998 Horn was prime minister. His government negotiated Hungary's entry into NATO (finally materialized in March 1999), stabilized the economy, and stimulated its growth. Because of a number of corruption scandals, in the elections of May 1998, both coalition parties lost. As a result, in September 1998 Horn resigned from the chair of the HSP and from its top leadership, but he stayed in the party and retained his parliamentary seat. He was reelected in May 2002, when the HSP returned to power. From 1996 Horn was deputy chairman of the Socialist International. In 1991 he published one part of his memoirs, *Cölöpök* (Border stones), and in 1999, a second part, *Azok a kilencvenes évek!* (Oh, these 1990s!). (JT)

Sources: *Magyar Nagylexikon*, vol. 9 (Budapest, 1999); *Ki kicsoda 2000* (Budapest, 2001); Steven Bela Vardy, *Historical Dictionary of Hungary* (Lanham, Md., 1997); *Europa Środkowo-Wschodnia 1994–1999* (Warsaw, 1996–2000); *Eastern Europe and the Commonwealth of Independent States 1999* (London, 1999).

HORTHY Miklós (18 June 1868, Kenderes–9 February 1957, Estoril, Portugal), regent of Hungary. Horthy came from a noble family. After graduating from the Naval Academy at Fiume (now Rijeka, Croatia), in 1886 he began his military service in the Austro-Hungarian Navy. Between 1892 and 1894 Horthy sailed around the world as an officer on the corvette *Saida*. Later, he went on numerous foreign missions, gaining diplomatic experience. From December 1909 to July 1914 Horthy served as aide-de-camp to Francis Joseph, the emperor of Austria and king of Hungary. From December 1914 he was captain of the *Novara*, one of the monarchy's most modern cruisers. At the beginning of May 1916 he twice broke through the English and French naval blockades on the Strait of

Otranto. He repeated a similar feat the following year, using three cruisers. Horthy was wounded during the struggle but continued to command the battle lying on a stretcher. In February 1918 King **Charles IV** appointed Horthy rear admiral and commander-in-chief of the monarchy's navy. After the collapse of the Habsburg monarchy, in the autumn of 1918 Horthy presided over the Austro-Hungarian fleet's transfer to the Yugoslav National Council, and then he returned to his family estate in Kenderes.

Under the Hungarian Soviet Republic (HSR), on 6 June 1919 Horthy became national defense minister in **Gyula Károlyi**'s counterrevolutionary government, formed in Szeged. Three days later he issued a manifesto on organizing a new army, and in August he established the High Command of the National Army, independent from the revolutionary Ministry of Defense. Soon afterwards, Horthy was officially appointed commander-in-chief of all Hungarian military forces. In reaction to the "Red Terror" of the HSR, Horthy tolerated the "White Terror" against leaders and activists of the HSR. Around one thousand people fell victim to the "White Terror." On 16 November 1919, mounted on a white horse, Horthy led the National Army into Budapest. On 1 March 1920 the Hungarian parliament elected him regent. He served as regent for twenty-five years, though this was initially intended to be only an interim position. Horthy's powers were similar to those of the king, except for the right to grant nobility. In order to avoid military actions by the Entente but also because of personal ambition, on two occasions (March–April and October 1921) Horthy thwarted the efforts of Charles IV to recover his throne. He also contributed to the dethronement of the Habsburgs in November of that year. Horthy supported the social and political consolidation of the government of **István Bethlen** (1921–31). He was instrumental in the establishment of the Order of Heroes (Vitézi Rend), a society of well over ten thousand Hungarians considered to be the most effective in the "struggle for the homeland." From then on, the status of hero bestowed by Horthy was a substitute for a noble title.

With his modesty and exemplary family life, Horthy won great respect and popularity. Initially he had little to do with public affairs, but from the mid–1930s he was more and more involved in politics. His conservative views led him to take a stand not only against the Communist left, but also against the extreme right. For example, in 1938 **Ferenc Szálasi**, the leader of the fascist Arrow Cross Party, was sentenced to three years in prison. In domestic affairs, Horthy tried to maintain the political balance and constitutionality of the government. He opposed tendencies to solidify the dictatorship, and he supported Bethlen's efforts to leave some room for

maneuver to the liberal-democratic and Social Democratic opposition. At the same time, he considered Fascist Italy and later the Third Reich as allies in his efforts to revise the 1920 Treaty of Trianon. At a time when Hungary was regaining some of the territories it had lost through the Treaty of Trianon—southern Slovakia in November 1938, Transcarpathian Ruthenia in March 1939, a part of Transylvania in August 1940, and Voivodina in April 1941—Horthy enjoyed great popularity among the Hungarians, although Hungary had to pay a price for these territorial gains by joining the anti-Comintern Pact in February 1939 and the Tripartite Pact in November 1940. In September 1939 Horthy called for neutrality but played a major role in ensuring that tens of thousands of Poles, and later French and English prisoners of war, as well as Jews, could find refuge in Hungary.

Gradually, however, Horthy increasingly yielded to German pressure. In April 1941 he abandoned the policy of military neutrality pursued by Prime Minister Count **Pál Teleki**; under Horthy's leadership, Hungary became part of the German-led alliance. After the German aggression against the USSR on 21 June 1941, Horthy called for severing diplomatic relations with Moscow, and five days later he decided to declare war on the USSR. In 1942 Horthy's eldest son was elected deputy regent by the parliament, but in the same year he died in an air crash on the eastern front. For a long time Horthy believed that Germany would not be able to defeat the Anglo-Saxon powers but that it would be able to control the European continent. He agreed to the enactment of laws that restricted the rights of Jews (1938, 1939, and 1941), but he refused permission for their deportation or liquidation. After Germany occupied Hungary on 19 March 1944, Horthy remained the country's head of state and appointed a government that met German expectations. However, he entrusted the mission of forming the government to General **Döme Sztójay** instead of **Béla Imrédy**, the man proposed by the Germans. Horthy left the majority of Hungarian Jews to their own fate and tolerated their confinement in ghettos, although in July he still managed to prevent the deportation of Budapest Jews to death camps. He passively observed the German arrests of both leftist and conservative underground activists.

After Romania joined the Allies in August 1944, Horthy dismissed the government of Sztójay and made efforts to extricate Hungary from the war. On October 11 of that year the Hungarian delegation, authorized by Horthy, signed a preliminary cease-fire with the USSR in Moscow. According to the provisions of the cease-fire, four days later the regent was to announce the breakup of the alliance with Germany, but because of the quick reaction of the Germans, the plan ended in failure. Since the Germans had abducted Horthy's youngest son, Miklós, and threatened to kill him, Horthy withdrew his cease-fire proclamation, and on 16 October resigned as regent and appointed Szálasi as prime minister. The following day the Germans interned Horthy along with his wife in Hirschberg Palace, near Weilheim in Bavaria, where he was under house arrest until May 1945. After the end of World War II he was taken captive by the Americans. The Allies unanimously agreed not to denounce Horthy as a war criminal and refused to hand him over to Yugoslavia, which considered him as such. At the same time the Allies recommended that he remain out of Hungary. During the Nuremberg trial Horthy was twice interrogated as a witness. In December 1948 he left Weilheim and along with his family settled in Estoril in Portugal. Horthy attentively followed the events of the Hungarian Revolution in 1956; the suppression of the revolution shook him so deeply that he died soon afterwards. His ashes and the remains of his wife were brought back to Hungary in September 1992, and they were buried with ceremony in Kenderes. In 1954 Horthy's *Memoirs* were published. (JT)

Sources: *Biographisches Lexikon*, vol. 2; Steven Bela Vardy, *Historical Dictionary of Hungary* (Lanham, Md., 1997); *Magyar Nagylexikon*, vol. 9 (Budapest, 1999); *Nagy Képes Milleniumi Arck-épcsarnok* (Budapest, 1999); *Magyarország 1944–1956*, CD-ROM (Budapest, 2001); C. A. Macartney, *October Fifteenth: A History of Modern Hungary*, vols. 1–2 (Edinburgh, 1957–61); *The Confidential Papers of Admiral Horthy* (Budapest, 1965); Zoltan Vas, *Horthy* (Budapest, 1977); Peter Gosztony, *Miklós von Horthy: Admiral und Reichsverweser* (Göttingen, 1973); Tibor Zsiga, *Horthy ellen, a királyért* (Budapest, 1989); Thomas L. Sakmyster, *Hungary's Admiral on Horseback: Miklós Horthy, 1918–1944* (Boulder, Colo., 1994); Gábor Bencsik, *Horthy Miklós: A kormányzó és kora* (Budapest, 2001).

HORVÁTH Márton [originally Schiller] (8 October 1906, Budapest–7 June 1987, Budapest), Hungarian Communist activist. The son of an antiquarian, in 1931 Horváth joined the illegal Hungarian Communist Party (HCP) and discontinued his studies at a polytechnic in Budapest. In 1932 he was arrested and interned for organizing strikes. Imprisoned in 1935 for distributing *Vasas*, an opposition trade union newspaper, he was released in 1939; despite being banned from Budapest, he remained in the capital and continued underground activities. As one of the party leaders, in 1941 Horváth conducted talks with **Árpád Szakasits** on cooperation between the Communists and Socialists. From the end of 1941 Horváth was editor of *Szabad Nép*, an illegal central organ of the HCP. Horváth was arrested again in 1942 and sentenced to twelve years in prison, but in March 1944 his term was suspended owing to a simulated illness. After taking part in blowing up the monument of **Gyula Gömbös** in October 1944, Horváth

was arrested again but managed to escape.

From 1944 Horváth was a member of the HCP CC, and from June 1948, a member of the CC of the Hungarian Workers' Party (HWP). Between January 1945 and October 1946 he was a member of the Politburo of the HCP. From June 1948 to September 1949 he was a deputy member, and until June 1953 a member, of the Politburo of the CC of the HWP. From 1945 he was an MP, and between 1949 and 1953, a member of the Presidium Council. From 1945 to 1950 he was editor of *Szabad Nép*. Between 1950 and 1954, as head of the Propaganda and Agitation Department of the CC of the HWP, Horváth was also a member, and from 1954 to 1956 president, of the editorial board of *Szabad Nép*. From 1948 to 1953, as a co-worker of **József Révai**, Horváth played a major role in the implementation of Stalinist educational and cultural policies, which included a transformation of the fine arts in the spirit of Socialist realism. His collected articles, *Lobogónk: Petófi* (Our banner: Petófi; 1950), came to symbolize the ideology of the time of **Mátyás Rákosi**. In June 1956 Horváth took part in the famous debates of the Petófi Circle on the state of the Hungarian press, after which the CC of the HWP banned the Petófi Circle's activities. On October 23, in an editorial in *Szabad Nép*, Horváth agreed with the demands of a the young demonstrators and gave his support to **Imre Nagy**. After 4 November Horváth did not hold any political positions. In May 1957 he was deprived of his parliamentary seat. From 1957 he was director of the Petófi Literary Museum; from 1960 he was head of Hunnia Film Studios, and from 1963 until his retirement in 1966, he was again head of the Petófi Literary Museum. (JT)

Sources: *A magyar forradalom és szabadságharc enciklopédiája*, CD-ROM (Budapest, 1999); *Magyar Nagylexikon*, vol. 9 (Budapest, 1999); Bennet Kovrig, *Communism in Hungary from Kun to Kádár* (Stanford, 1979); Miklós Molnár, *From Béla Kun to János Kádár: Seventy Years of Hungarian Communism* (New York, 1990).

HORWITZ-WALECKI Maksymilian [originally Horwitz] (6 September 1877, Warsaw–after June 1937, USSR), Polish Communist activist. Born into an assimilated Jewish middle-class family, Horwitz-Walecki graduated from Wojciech Górski High School in Warsaw, and then he left to study in Ghent, Belgium. From 1895 he belonged to the Belgian Socialist Party and the Foreign Union of Polish Socialists. After his returned to Russian Poland in 1898, he was active in the Polish Socialist Party (Polska Partia Socjalistyczna [PPS]). Arrested in December 1899, in August 1901 he was sentenced to exile in Siberia, but he escaped during transport and went to the European west, where he criticized both the pro-independence followers of **Józef Piłsudski** and the internationalist extreme left of the party. During the 1905 revolution Horwitz-Walecki was active in Kraków and then in Warsaw, where he was imprisoned again but released on bail. In December 1905 he was arrested again, but in April 1906 he organized a daring escape of prisoners facing the death penalty. Caught and sentenced to exile, he escaped during transport and returned to underground Socialist activities. At the Third PPS Council he opposed both wings of the party, but he was closer to the internationalist wing, and he co-founded the PPS–Left.

During World War I Horwitz-Walecki was engaged in the anti-war faction of the Second International and took part in both Zimmerwald conferences in 1915 and 1916. He gradually drew closer to the Social Democracy of the Kingdom of Poland and Lithuania (Socjaldemokracja Królestwa Polskiego i Litwy [SDKPiL]). After returning to Poland, in December 1918 he took part in the conference at which the PPS–Left and the SDKPiL merged into the Communist Workers' Party of Poland (Komunistyczna Partia Robotnicza Polski [KPRP]). Arrested by the Polish police in October 1919, in the summer of 1920 Horwitz-Walecki escaped from the Dąbie camp near Kraków, and from then on he was mainly active abroad. On behalf of the Communist International he took part in the activities of the Italian and French Communist Parties, and in 1922 he was active in the United States. From 1923 he lived in Berlin, where he edited *Die Rote Fahne* and headed the local KPRP post.

An opponent of the extreme left of the party, along with **Maria Kostrzewa-Koszutska** and **Adolf Warszawski-Warski**, Horwitz-Walecki advocated the necessity of creating a broad front of workers and peasants and elaborating a party program attractive to Poles. Such a program prevailed at the Second KPRP Congress in Bolshevo, near Moscow, in September and October 1922. Horwitz-Walecki joined the KPRP Central Committee and the Politburo. He was also a member of the Presidium of the Executive Committee (EC) of the Communist International (CI). The Polish Commission of the Fifth CI Congress in July 1924, headed by Stalin, condemned this program, and Horwitz-Walecki was removed from the KPRP leadership. He continued his Comintern activities, especially with regard to CI relations with the Second International. He was also active in the Spanish, Greek, and Belgian Communist Parties. In 1928–35 he was deputy head of the EC of the CI Secretariat; from 1935 he edited the periodical *Kommunisticheski Internatsional*. Arrested during the Great Purge on 22 June 1937, Horwitz-Walecki was killed in prison. He was rehabilitated after the Twentieth Congress of the CPSU. In 1967 his *Zbiór pism* (Collection of writings) was published. (WR)

Sources: *PSB*, vol. 10; Lazitch; *Słownik biograficzny działaczy polskiego ruchu robotniczego*, vol. 2 (Warsaw, 1987); Jan Kancewicz, "Maksymilian Horwitz-Walecki," *Z pola walki*, 1958, no 4; Feliks Tych, *PPS-Lewica w latach 1914–1918* (Warsaw, 1960); Anna Żarnowska, *Geneza rozłamu w PPSP 1904–1906* (Warsaw, 1965); Aleksander Kochański, *SDKPiL 1907–1910* (Warsaw, 1971); James P. Cannon, *The First Ten Years of American Communism* (New York, 1973).

HORYN Bohdan (10 February 1936, Kniselo, Bóbrka [Bibrka] County), Ukrainian politician and art historian, brother of **Mykhailo Horyn**. In 1959 Horyn graduated from the University of Lviv, and then he worked in a folk culture house in Lviv. Later he taught painting and drawing in a Lviv high school. In 1960 he started publishing in literary and art journals. From 1962 he worked in the Museum of Ukrainian Art in Lviv (Lvivskyi Muzey Ukraiinskoho Mystetstva). He organized the publication and distribution of materials in the uncensored press (samizdat). Arrested in August 1965 and accused of anti-Soviet agitation and propaganda, Horyn was sentenced to four years of labor camp. After his release, in 1968–76 he worked as a blue-collar laborer. In 1976–89 he worked as a junior scholar in the Lviv Gallery of Painting, and in 1988 he was co-founder of the Ukrainian Helsinki Union (Ukraiinska Helsinska Spilka [UHS]), the first official opposition organization in the Ukraine. In 1988–90 Horyn chaired the UHS Lviv organization. In 1989 he co-founded the Ukrainian Popular Movement for Perestroika (Narodnyi Rukh Ukraiiny za Perebudovu), and in 1990, the Ukrainian Republican Party (Ukraiinska Respublikanska Partiya [URP]). In 1990–92 he headed its Lviv organization. From 1990 to 1997 Horyn was a member of the URP Board and Council. He was a deputy to the Supreme Council of the Ukrainian SSR and then Ukraine in 1990–94 and 1994–98. In 1994–96 he was director of the Research Institute of the Diaspora (Instytut Doslidzhen Diaspory). Horyn was a member of the editorial boards of several *samvydav* periodicals, such as *Ukraiinskyi visnyk* (1988–89), *Kafedra* (1988–89), and *Lvivski novyny* (1989, editor-in-chief). He authored books on foreign policy and the arts, including the following: *Na puti v Yevropu* (On the road to Europe; 1994), *Krym ne tilky zona vidpochynku* (Crimea is not only a holiday resort; 1994; co-author); *Opanas Zalyvakha: Vybir shlakhu* (Opanas Zalyvakha: Choice of the way; 1995). (BB)

Sources: *Encyclopedia of Ukraine*, vol. 2 (Toronto, 1988); *Khto ie khto v Ukraiini 2000* (Kiev, 2000); *Lykho z rozumu: Portrety dvanadtsiaty "zlochyntsiv." Zbirnyk materialiv uklal Vyacheslav Chornovil* (Paris, 1967); Taras Batenko, *Opozytsiyna osobystis': Druha polovyna XX stolittia. Politychnyi portret Bohdana Horynia* (Lviv, 1997); Bohdan Nahaylo, *The Ukrainian Resurgence* (Toronto, 1999).

HORYN Mykhailo (20 June 1930, Kniselo, Bóbrka [Bibrka] County), Ukrainian dissident and politician, brother of **Bohdan Horyn**. From 1949 Horyn studied logic and psychology at Ivan Franko University in Lviv. In 1953 he was expelled from the university for refusing to join the Komsomol, but he graduated thanks to the help of the rector. In 1954–61 he taught logic, psychology, and Ukrainian language and literature in a high school. From 1961 he was a researcher in an experimental laboratory of psychology and the physiology of labor in a truck factory in Lviv. From the early 1960s he organized the publication and distribution of materials in the uncensored press (samizdat). In August 1965 he was arrested and accused of anti-Soviet agitation and propaganda. In April 1966 he was sentenced to six years of hard labor camp and in July 1967 to an additional three years in prison for distributing samizdat materials among his prison mates. Released in August 1971, Horyn worked as an engine driver and stoker and from 1977 as a psychologist once again. At this time he published the underground *Byuletyn* of the Ukrainian Helsinki Group (Ukraiinska Helsinska Hrupa) and helped the families of political prisoners. In November 1981 he was arrested again, and in June 1982 he was sentenced to ten years of hard labor camp and five years of forced settlement as a "dangerous recidivist." Horyn served his sentence in the Kuchino camp, along with **Vasyl Stus**, **Valery Marchenko**, **Levko Lukyanenko**, and **Oleksa Tykhyi**.

Released in July 1987, one month later Horyn joined **Vyacheslav Chornovil** in publishing the periodical *Ukrainskyi Visnyk*. In 1988, along with his brother Bohdan and Chornovil, he co-founded the Ukrainian Helsinki Union (Ukraiinska Helsinska Spilka). At the founding congress of the Ukrainian Popular Movement for Perestroika (Narodnyi Rukh Ukraiiny za Perebudovu) in September 1989, Horyn was elected chairman of its secretariat. He organized spectacular actions, such as the "chain of unification" between Lviv and Kiev and celebrations of the Cossack tradition. In 1990 Horyn co-founded the Ukrainian Republican Party (Ukraiinska Respublikanska Partiya [URP]). In 1990–94 he was a deputy to the Supreme Council of the Ukrainian SSR (from 1991, Ukraine), where he headed the Popular Council (Narodna Rada) faction. In 1992–95 he was the URP chairman, and then he became its honorary chairman. After a split in the URP in 1997, Horyn co-founded the Ukrainian Christian Republican Party (Ukraiinska Khrystyansko-Respublikanska Partiya), and in May 2000 he became head of the Ukrainian World Coordination Council (Ukraiinska Svitova Koordynatsyina Rada), dealing with Ukrainians abroad. (BB)

Sources: *Encyclopedia of Ukraine*, vol. 2 (Toronto, 1988); *Khto ie khto v Ukraini v 2001* (Kiev, 2001); Bohdan Nahaylo, *The Ukrainian Resurgence* (Toronto, 1999); *Ukraiinska Hromadska Hrupa spryiannia vykonanniu Helsinskych uhod* (Kharkiv, 2001); Tadeusz Andrzej Olszański, *Historia Ukrainy XX w.* (Warsaw, n.d.).

HOSSU Iuliu (30 June 1885, Milasul Mare [Transylvania]–5 March 1970, Caldarusami), Romanian cardinal, Eastern-rite bishop of Cluj-Gherla diocese, political prisoner of communism. The son of a Uniate priest, Hossu was ordained in March 1910 and then went to Rome to continue his studies at the college of the Congregation for the Propagation of the Faith. On 21 April 1917 he was consecrated bishop and was appointed diocesan bishop of the Eastern-rite diocese of Cluj. Because of his involvement in efforts toward the unification of Transylvania and Romania, Hossu was persecuted by Hungarian authorities, who accused him of promoting Romanian nationalism. Hossu attended the Grand National Assembly, which was held in Alba Iulia on 1 December 1918, to vote on behalf of the Romanian people for the incorporation of Transylvania and Banat into the Old Kingdom of Romania. He and the Orthodox bishop, **Miron Cristea**, were delegated to submit the resolution to King **Ferdinand I**, who signed the union of Romania and Transylvania on 14 December 1918. Between the wars Hossu was engaged in social work, supported the development of the Christian Democratic movement, and he organized many educational and charitable events in his diocese. Although under the Romanian constitution of March 1923 the Uniate Church was recognized as a national religion on an equal footing with the Orthodox Church, the authorities, on the initiative of the Bucharest Patriarchate, encouraged the Uniates to unite with the Orthodox Church. Hossu protested and exhorted the people of Transylvania to remain faithful to the Holy See. Persecutions of the Uniates during the interwar period ceased in 1929, when a coalition led by **Iuliu Maniu**, a Uniate from Transylvania and the head of the National Peasant Party, came to power. In the 1930s Hossu was one of the initiators of the establishment of the Pontifical Romanian College in Rome.

Between 1940 and 1944, when the Transylvanian territories became part of Hungary under the so-called Second Vienna Award of August 1940, Hossu protested the persecutions of Jews. He sheltered many Jews, saving them from deportation to concentration camps. He also defended members of the Orthodox Church, particularly the bishop of Cluj, Nicolae Colan, who subsequently turned against the Uniates and personally seized the cathedral of Bishop Hossu in 1948. The Hungarian authorities tried to suppress Hossu, considering him a Romanian nationalist. They also attempted to force the Catholicization of the Transylvanian people.

After the Communists took power in Romania, they began to introduce a plan to destroy Christianity there. Particularly repressive measures were taken against the Uniate Church. Hossu defended the rights of the faithful, especially the right to teach religion in schools. The situation became more difficult in August 1948, when the government broke a concordat with the Holy See and issued decrees on education and against cults. The Catholic episcopate and the Uniate episcopate refused to obey these decrees. On 3 October 1948 the authorities assembled the Uniate clergy in Cluj-Napoca, where they urged them to break off the union with Rome and join the Romanian Orthodox Church. Hossu protested and exhorted the priests and the people to remain faithful to Rome. The state authorities formally abolished the union in Romania on 1 December 1948. The faithful and the clergy were forced into the Romanian Orthodox Church, and those who resisted were arrested. On 29 December 1948 Hossu, along with six other Romanian Uniate bishops, was arrested on charges of working in support of global imperialism, allegedly represented by the Vatican. He was visited in prison by Jeremiah, the Romanian patriarch of the Orthodox Church, who promised Hossu freedom at the price of his joining the Orthodox Church, but Hossu, like the other Uniate bishops, rejected this offer. Hossu was transferred to a penitentiary in Sighet and was held there for years. Five Uniate bishops died in prison, and Hossu was released in 1956. He was interned in Orthodox monasteries and was banned from performing any pastoral duties until the end of his life. Despite persecution, he managed to get in touch with the underground Uniate clergy. Hossu was a symbol of the persevering resistance of the Romanian Uniates. He died at the Orthodox monastery of Caldarusami. In 1969 the Pope appointed him cardinal *in pectore*—that is, without public announcement of the nomination. The appointment was revealed in March 1973. The beatification process of Hossu is under way. (AGr)

Sources: Franz Hummer, *Bischöfe für den Untergrund: Zur Praxis der Geheimbischöfe in der katholischen Kirche* (Vienna and Munich, 1971); Robert Royal, *The Calvary of Romania*; Bohdan Cywiński, *Ogniem próbowane: Z dziejów najnowszych Kościoła katolickiego w Europie Środkowo-Wschodniej*, vols. 1–2 (Rome, 1982; Lublin, 1990); S. A. Prunduş, O.S.B.M., and C. Plăianu, *Cardinalul Iuliu Hossu* (Cluj, 1995); Dennis Deletant, *Communist Terror in Romania: Gheorghiu-Dej and the Police State, 1948–1965* (New York, 1999).

HOXHA Enver (16 October 1908, Gjirokastër–11 April 1985, Tirana), Albanian Communist leader. The son of a Muslim cloth merchant from the southern Albanian Tosks, Hoxha was educated at the French lycée in Tirana, and from 1930 to 1934 he studied at the University of Montpellier. Because of his poor academic performance, his state scholarship was withdrawn. However, he remained in France, where he met **Ali Kelmendi** and other Albanian Communist activists. He worked at the Albanian consulate

general in Brussels and wrote, under a pseudonym, articles for *L'Humanité* in which he vehemently attacked the government of King **Zog I**. In 1936 he returned to Albania and taught French at a lycée. In 1939 he was imprisoned for a short time for his criticism of the royal dictatorship. After Italy invaded Albania, in November 1941 Hoxha organized a small party, called the Communist Party of Albania, and guerrilla units that developed broader activities with the support of the Yugoslav Communists after the attack of Germany against the USSR (June 1941). At a state conference of the party in Labinot (March 1943) Hoxha was elected secretary general, and he headed the party for the next forty-two years. In July 1943 he became commander of the Communist National Liberation Front. On 2 August 1943 Hoxha reached an agreement with other parties of the national resistance—royalists and the democratic organization of Belli Kombëtar; however, he almost immediately started to suppress them. When on 28 May 1944 the Communists formed the Anti-Fascist Council for National Liberation, based on the Yugoslav model, they concealed the true nature of the council in the guise of "national" and "people's" rhetoric. In October 1944 Hoxha became head of the provisional government and commander-in-chief of the army, with the rank of general.

After the invasion of Tirana, on 4 December 1944 Hoxha announced the total liberation of Albania from Nazi occupation. Industry, banking, and transportation were nationalized, and the political system began to be changed along the Soviet pattern. The Allies recognized the provisional government of Hoxha on condition that free elections would be held. Meanwhile, from the beginning of 1945 Hoxha and the Communists conducted a bloody crackdown on the opposition, mainly against royalists and Belli Kombëtar. In the elections of 2 December 1944, which despite obvious falsifications were recognized as valid by the Great Powers, the Communists gained complete domination of the country. Because the party had support mainly among the Tosks in the south, their dialect was recognized as the official language of Albania. On 11 January 1946 Hoxha assumed the post of prime minister of Albania, and he also became Albanian foreign minister, defense minister, commander-in-chief of the armed forces, and head of the party. After the liquidation of the opposition he started to remove members of the party executive who were not obedient enough.

In 1946 Hoxha signed a political and economic agreement with Yugoslavia. In Belgrade, the unification of Albania and Yugoslavia into one state was considered. However, Hoxha aimed at maintaining a separate state. In connection with Albania's role as a base for the Communists during the continuing civil war in Greece, as well as Albania's blowing up English ships in the Corfu Channel, the Western powers withdrew recognition of Hoxha's regime. Because of Belgrade's economic help and Stalin's vague attitude toward the independence of Albania, Hoxha cooperated closely with **Josip Broz Tito**. In May 1947 mass arrests were made among Hoxha's opponents, who favored a pro-Yugoslav course at that time. Albania signed a treaty of friendship and cooperation with Bulgaria, which was a sign of its independence, but it was not invited to the founding conference of the Cominform at Szklarska Poręba in September 1947. At the Eighth Plenum of the Central Committee (CC) of the party in February 1948 the pro-Yugoslav course won, and Hoxha's position was weakened. Thus, he welcomed the denunciation of Tito by the Cominform in June 1948, and he vehemently attacked the Yugoslav leader. All relations with Belgrade were broken off, and the adherents of cooperation with Tito fell victims to another bloody purge. At the First Congress of the Albanian Party of Labor in November, Hoxha's main rival, **Koci Xoxe**, was expelled from the party. In May 1949 Xoxe was secretly sentenced to death and executed. Thanks to Kim Philby's cooperation with the Soviet services in 1949, Hoxha foiled an attempt at the overthrow of his regime by a group of Albanians who were trained in Greece and the Federal Republic of Germany. Nearly all participants of the action were caught and executed. Having concentrated all power in his hands, Hoxha also increased the persecution of religious organizations, above all the Catholic Church.

After Stalin's death in March 1953 and the Twentieth Congress of the CPSU in February 1956, Hoxha became a spokesman of doctrinal Stalinism; he not only failed to change course, but he organized new purges as well. For example, all the delegates to the party conference of April 1956 who expected democratization were arrested, and most of them were murdered. Such a fate befell **Liri Gega**, for example. As an open supporter of the Stalinist terror, Hoxha found himself in conflict with **Nikita Khrushchev**'s pragmatic course and his policy of "thaw." Thus, during his visit to Beijing in May 1956 Hoxa reached rapprochement with China. During Khrushchev's visit to Albania in May 1959, Hoxha did not agree to improve relations with Yugoslavia and refused to begin de-Stalinization. At the congress of the Romanian party in June 1960 Khrushchev openly criticized the attitude of the Albanians, and at a conference of the Communist parties in Moscow (November 1960), Hoxha sharply attacked the Soviet leader, gaining the support of the Chinese delegation. This sealed the split in the Communist movement.

In 1961 Hoxha finally broke off relations with the USSR and its European satellites, choosing the People's Republic of China as his strategic partner. This resulted in another purge, the victims of which were (among others) the secretary of the CC, **Liri Belishova**, and Admiral Teme Sejko. In the second half of the 1960s in Albania the "Cultural Revolution" was carried out. It was based on the Chinese model and had similar results. For example, parents were induced to give "Illyrian" rather than Christian or Muslim names to their children. In 1967 Albania was declared the first atheist country in the world because religious practices were regarded as a crime. All temples were closed; the Church of the Virgin Mary of Shkodër, Patroness of Albania, was destroyed; all Muslim, Orthodox, and Catholic clerics were put in prisons or in camps, and many of them perished. For example, Father Shtjefen Kurti was executed by a firing squad for baptizing a child.

In the 1960s and 1970s Hoxha's Albania was a completely isolated country, dependent on economic assistance from Beijing. Hoxha's xenophobic policy was evident, for example, in the fact that the country was surrounded by a net of thousands of concrete bunkers; this led to stagnation in the housing industry. The first tensions between Tirana and Beijing appeared with the normalization of relations between China and the United States. After the death of Mao Zedong in 1976 and the adoption of a more pragmatic course by the Chinese leadership, Hoxha also broke off relations with Beijing, considering himself the only true follower of Marxism in the Leninist and Stalinist tradition. He began another purge, whose victim were (among others) Minister of Defense **Beqir Balluku** and (in 1980) Prime Minister **Mehmet Shehu**. There are suppositions that Hoxha took a direct part in Shehu's killing, which was staged as a suicide. The conflict between Serbs and Albanians in the Yugoslav province of Kosovo was an additional source of trouble for Hoxha's regime, and from 1981 this conflict intensified. Tirana wanted to believe that the conflict was the effect not only of Serb chauvinism, but USSR influence as well.

Hoxha's totalitarian regime, one of the bloodiest in history, engineered great social transformations. However, although illiteracy was eliminated and the emancipation of women was achieved, the regime, ruling by terror, kept the Albanian people in blind obedience, fear, and isolation. Armaments took up most of the public funds, and this led to a domestic poverty that was unprecedented in Europe. An intelligent and gifted tactician, Hoxha raised the principles of the Balkan vendetta to the rank of a factor organizing social life. At the end of his life Hoxha ruled with the assistance of a narrow camarilla, in which the leading role was played by his wife, **Nexhmije Hoxha**, and his potential successor, **Ramiz Alia**. There was no chance for creating the rudiments of a democratic opposition; therefore several years had to pass after his death before the system he had built collapsed. In Albania, countless works by Hoxha were issued in various languages, mainly his speeches and memoirs (e.g., *With Stalin*, 1981; *Titoites: Historical Notes*, 1982; and *Laying the Foundations for a New Albania*, 1984); these have to be approached with a critical eye because they are written in "newspeak" and often contain false information. (WR)

Sources: *Current Biography*, 1950; Peter R. Prifti, *Socialist Albania since 1945* (Cambridge, Mass., 1978); *New York Times*, 12 April 1985; Rodger Swearingen, ed., *Leaders of the Communist World* (New York, 1971); Pero Zlatar, *Enver Hodza: Politička biografia* (Belgrade, 1986); Arshi Pipa, *Albanian Stalinism* (Boulder, Colo., 1990); Gabriel Jandot, *L'Albanie d'Enver Hoxha: 1944–1985* (Paris, 1994); Miranda Vickers, *The Albanians: A Modern History* (London, 1995); James S. O'Donnell (James Salibur), *A Coming of Age: Albania under Enver Hoxha* (Boulder, Colo., 1999).

HOXHA Nexhmije [née Xhuglini] (7 February 1921, Monastir), Albanian Communist activist, from January 1945 wife of **Enver Hoxha**. Hoxha graduated from a pedagogical school for girls in Tirana in 1941, and then she worked as a teacher in a Tirana school. From 1937 she was connected with a group of Communists from Shkodër. From 1941 she belonged to the Communist Party, and from 1943 she edited the periodical for women *Gruaja Shqiptare*. Sentenced in absentia to twelve years in prison for her Communist activities, in 1944 Hoxha fought in the First Striking Division of the Communist guerrilla army. She took part in all the most important sessions of the Front of National Liberation; from 1943 she belonged to its Supreme Council, and from 1944, to the Secretariat of the First Albanian Anti-Fascist Union of Women. From 1946 she presided over this organization, which soon took the name of the Albanian Union of Women. From 1945 to 1991 Hoxha was a deputy to the parliament, initially as a member of its foreign affairs commission and then the commission of culture. From 1948 she was a member of the Central Committee (CC) of the Albanian Party of Labor (APL), holding various positions connected with culture, education, and propaganda. From 1966 she directed the Institute of Marxist-Leninist Studies of the CC. Between 1950 and 1962 she was chairperson of the Society of Albanian-Soviet Friendship. In 1976 she belonged to a commission for the elaboration of a new constitution. After her husband's death in April 1985, Hoxha was considered to be at the core of the group of hard-liners, and from March 1986 she was presented as the chairperson of the Democratic Front. In June 1991 she was expelled from the APL and criticized by the party organ, *Zeri i Popullit*, for her pompous way of life. On 4 December 1991 she was arrested. At the end of January 1993 she was sentenced to nine years in prison for the embezzlement of 750,000 leks. After appeal, this sentence was increased to eleven years, but Hoxha was released from prison in January 1997. She authored *Jeta imë më Enverin: Kujtime* (My life with Enver: Memoirs; 1998). (TC)

Sources: Raymond Hutchings, *Historical Dictionary of Albania* (Lanham, Md., 1996); Stavro Skendi, *Albania* (New York, 1956); *Fjalori Enciklopedik Shqiptar* (Tirana, 1985); Arshi Pipa, *Albanian Stalinism: Ideo-Political Aspects* (New York, 1990); Elez Biberaj, *Shqipëria në tranzicion: Rruga e veshtrise drejt Demokracise* (Tirana, 2001).

HRABAL Bohumil (28 March 1914, Brno–3 February 1997, Prague), Czech writer. In 1934 Hrabal graduated from high school in Nymburk, and then he started law studies at Charles University in Prague. In 1939 he interrupted them owing to the closing of the university by the Germans, but in 1945 he began to study again, and in 1946 he received a Ph.D. in law. During the German occupation he worked as a notary assistant, teacher, storekeeper, and railway worker; after graduation he was a travel agent, ironmaster, and theater worker. From 1962 he devoted himself only to writing. His literary debut was difficult. An early volume of lyrics, *Ztracená ulička* (Lost street), was not published because the press was closed down in 1949; in the 1950s the Communist censors banned his collection of short stories, *Skřivánek na niti* (Fettered lark); and his first book, *Hovory lidí* (People's talks; 1956), went unnoticed. The breakthrough came with *Perlička na dně* (Pearl at the bottom; 1963). Both this collection of stories and the subsequent volumes—*Pábitelé* (Petty chatterbox; 1964); *Taneční hodiny pro starší a pokročilé* (Dance classes for the elderly and advanced; 1964); and *Ostře sledované vlaky* (1965; *Closely Watched Trains*, 1968)—were based on the counterpoints of ugliness and beauty, brutality and sensitivity, and life and death. Hrabal combined the literary with the colloquial language and showed a deep knowledge of various groups of people. He also combined satire or even the grotesque with naturalism. He wrote in contrast to the obligatory, artificial, and bombastic prose of Socialist realism. In his subsequent books, such as *Inzerát na dům, ve kterém už nechci bydlet* (House for sale in which I do not want to live anymore; 1965) and *Obsluhoval jsem anglického krále* (1971; *I Served the King of England*, 1989), he was increasingly critical of the social reality, particularly in the latter book, which presents the agony of the Czech middle class.

Hrabal turned to memoirs in the trilogy *Městečko u vody* (A town on the water), comprised of *Postřižny* (Hair clipping; 1976), *Krasosmutnění* (Beautiful mourning; 1979), and *Harlekýnovy milióny* (Harlequin's millions; 1981). His tales in the volumes *Slavnosti sněženek* (The snowdrop festival; 1978) and *Příliš hlučná samota* (1976; *Too Loud a Solitude*, 1990) were in the Czech tradition of "beer stories" and brought back the charm of the Prague suburbs. Hrabal continued to present the panorama of Czech social life in the novel *Kouzelná flétna* (The magic flute; 1990). In the 1980s he published an autobiographical trilogy abroad: *Proluky* (Empty spaces in urban development; 1986); *Vita nuova* (1987); and *Svatby v domě* (Wedding at home; 1987). His *Sebrané spisy Bohumila Hrabala* (Collected works of Bohumil Hrabal) were published in 1992–97. His works were translated into many languages and in various collections. They were also staged and filmed by **Jiří Menzel**. (PU)

Sources: *ČBS*; *Kdo byl kdo v našich dějinách ve 20. stoleti*, vol. 1 (Prague, 1998); *Slovník českých spisovatelů od roku 1945*, vol. 2 (Prague, 1998); Susanna Roth, *Laute Einsamkeit und bitteres Glück: Zur poetischen Welt von Bohumil Hrabals Prosa* (Bern, 1986); Radko Pytlík, *Bohumil Hrabal* (Prague, 1990); Jaroslav Kladiva, *Literatura Bohumila Hrabala: Struktura a metoda Hrabalových del* (Prague, 1994); Monika Zgustová, *V rajské zahradě trpkých plodů: O životě a díle Bohumila Hrabala* (Prague, 1997); Alexander Götz, *Bilder aus der Tiefe der Zeit: Erinnerung und Selbststilisierung als ästhetische Funktionen im Werk Bohumil Hrabals* (Frankfurt am Main, 1998); Radko Pytlík, *The Sad King of Czech Literature, Bohumil Hrabal: His Life and Work* (Prague, 2000).

HRECHUKHA Mykhailo [also known as Grechukha] (19 September 1902, Moshny, near Cherkasy–15 May 1976, Kiev), Ukrainian Communist activist. The son of a peasant, from 1916 Hrechukha worked in a sugar refinery. In 1922 he began his career in the Komsomol in his home region. Quickly promoted during the Great Purge, in 1938 he graduated from the Institute of Motorization and Highways in Kharkiv and became party secretary of the town and district committee in Zhytomyr and a member of the Politburo of the CC of the Communist Party (Bolshevik) of Ukraine. In 1939 he moved to Kiev and assumed the post of president of the Supreme Soviet of the Ukrainian SSR. After the Red Army occupied the then Polish territories of Eastern Galicia and Volhynia in September 1939, in October of that year Hrechukha arrived in Lwów (Lviv), where he monitored the preparations for and the course of the manipulated elections to the People's Assembly of Western Ukraine, as well as the motion to incorporate those territories into the Ukrainian SSR. He also authorized religious persecution and the deportation of Polish citizens to the Soviet interior. A close associate of **Nikita Khrushchev**, in 1954 Hrechukha moved from the post of formal head of the republic to the post of deputy prime minister of the Ukrainian SSR, and in 1956 he became a deputy member of the CC of the CPSU. In 1961 he resigned from all his party and government posts.

For some time he served as transportation adviser to the administration, and then he retired. (WR)

Sources: *Encyclopedia of Ukraine*, vol. 2 (Toronto, 1988); *Prominent Personalities in the USSR* (Metuchen, N.J., 1968); Boris Levytsky, *The Soviet Political Elite* (Stanford, 1969); *Istoria Ukrainskoi SSR*, vols. 7–8 (Kiev, 1984); David R. Marples, *Stalinism in Ukraine in the 1940s* (London, 1992).

HRIBAR Ivan (19 September 1851, Trzin (Trnovče)–18 April 1941, Ljubljana), Slovene politician. After graduating from high school in 1867, Hribar started working in the banking sector, serving as manager of the Ljubljana branch of the Czech Banka Slavija from 1876 to 1919. His interests in culture and literature led to his involvement in the Slovene national movement. He was influenced by the Young Czech movement and later the neo-Pan-Slavic movement promoted by **Karel Kramář**. In 1884 Hribar founded the periodical *Slovan*, and soon afterwards, along with **Ivan Tavčar**, he assumed the leadership of a radical national group that opposed the conciliatory policy of the Slovene liberals. He called for national unity of the Slovenes and endeavored to create a political group that would counterbalance both the liberals and the Slovene clerical conservatives. In the elections to the local parliament of Krajina in 1883 and 1886 the radical nationalist faction failed to win the support of the voters. At the beginning of the 1890s Hribar was drawn to social Catholicism, working with the theologian Anton Mahnič. In 1894, along with Tavčar, Hribar formed the National Liberal Party, renamed the National Progressive Party in 1905. This brought him success. He was repeatedly elected to the local parliament of Krajina (1886–1906), and then he sat in the Vienna parliament (1907–11). He was a long-time mayor of Ljubljana (1886–1910), where he founded a Slovene bank and a university and implemented an ambitious modernization program. During World War I Hribar was interned by the Austrian authorities because he promoted Pan-Slavism and Russophilia. After the war he played an active role in the establishment of the Kingdom of Serbs, Croats, and Slovenes, serving as its ambassador to Prague and Sofia (1919–23) and then as viceroy in Slovenia. In 1925 he withdrew from active politics in protest against the Serb domination of the state. Between 1928 and 1932 he published four volumes of memoirs, *Moji spomini* (My memoirs). After the German invasion and defeat of Yugoslavia Hribar committed suicide. (MC)

Sources: *Biographisches Lexikon*, vol. 2; *Enciklopedija Slovenija*, vol. 4 (Ljubljan, 1990); Taja Cepic and Janja Rebolj, eds., *Homo sum: Ivan Hribar in njegova Ljubljana: Zbornik ob razstavi Mestnego muzeja Ljubljana* (Ljubljana, 1997); Irena Gantar Godina, "Novoslovanska ideja in Slovenci," *Zgodovinski Casopis*, 1989, no. 4; "Ivan Hribar (1851–1941)," www2.arnes.si/~fyakel/hribar.htm.

HRINCHENKO Borys, pseudonyms "Vartovyi," "Vilkh-ivskyi," "Yavorenko," and others (9 December 1863, Vilkhovyi Yar, Kharkiv Province–6 May 1910, Ospedaletti, Włochy), Ukrainian writer and social and political activist. Born into an impoverished noble family, after graduating from high school, Hrinchenko worked as a teacher in eastern Ukraine. In 1891 (or 1892), along with Ivan Lypa, **Mykola Mikhnovskyi**, and others, he founded the secret nationalist Taras Brotherhood (Bratstvo Tarasivtsiv). In 1894 he settled in Chernikhov, where he worked in the local land office. Thanks to the support of Ukrainian patrons, he organized the largest press in the Russian part of Ukraine, publishing popular Ukrainian literature. From 1902 he lived and worked in Kiev. From 1904 he was one of the leaders of the Ukrainian Democratic Party (Ukraiinska Demokratychna Partiya [UDP]), belonging to its left wing. The left wing soon turned into the Ukrainian Radical Party (Ukraiinska Radykalna Partiya), which, in turn, reunited with the UDP to form the Ukrainian Democratic Radical Party (Ukraiinska Demokratychno-Radykalna Partiya [UDRP]) at the end of 1905. From 1906 Hrinchenko contributed to the newspaper *Hromadska dumka* and edited the periodical *Nowa hromada*, and in 1906–9 he presided over the Kievan organization Prosvita (Education). On behalf of Hromada (Community), a Kievan organization of the Ukrainian intelligentsia, in 1902–9 he edited *Slovar ukraiinskoyi movy* (Dictionary of the Ukrainian language).

Hrinchenko made his literary debut in the 1880s. He authored almost fifty short stories, including "Chudova divchyna" (Magic girl; 1884), "Sama, zovsim sama" (Alone, all alone; 1885), and "Olesya" (1890); the novels *Sonyashnyi promin* (Sunray; 1890) and *Sered temnoyi nochi* (In the middle of a dark night; 1900); the collections of poetry *Pid silskoyu strikhoyu* (Under a village roof; 1886) and *Pid khmarnym nebom* (Under clouded skies; 1893); and historic dramas, such as *Sered buri* (In the storm; 1897). He translated works by Friedrich Schiller, Johann Wolfgang Goethe, Heinrich Heine, Victor Hugo, and Henrik Ibsen. His ethnographic output includes the three-volume *Ethnohrafichni materialy, zibranni v Chernihivskiy i susidnykh z neyu huberniakh* (Etnographic materials gathered in Chernikhov and neighboring provinces; 1895–96) and a couple of collections of folktales. Hrinchenko was an outstanding pedagogue, fighting for instruction in the Ukrainian language in the schools. He presented his views on this subject in *Yaka teper narodna shkola v Ukraiini* (What should be a popular school in the Ukraine today; 1896). He authored a number of school textbooks—for instance, on Ukrainian grammar. He was among the leaders of the Ukrainian Narodnik movement.

Hrinchenko presented his political views in detail in the UDRP program, which he authored, and in *Lysty z Naddni-pryanskoyi Ukraiiny* (Letter from the Dnieper Ukraine), published in the newspaper *Bukovyna* in 1892–93. (BB)

Sources: *Encyclopedia of Ukraine*, vol. 2 (Toronto, 1988); *Dovidnyk z istoriyi Ukraiiny* (Kiev, 2001); Borys Hrinchenko and Mykhailo Drahomanow, *Dialohy pro ukraiinsku natsionalnu spravu* (Kiev, 1994); Valentyna Statieyeva, *Ukrainski pysmennyky pro problemy literaturnoy movy ta movoznavstva XIX-pochatku XX st.* (Uzhhorod, 1997); Adventyna Zhyvotenko-Pyankiv, *Pedagohichno-prosvitnytska pratsia Borysa Hrinchenka* (Kiev, 1999).

HRONSKÝ Jozef [originally Cíger] (23 February 1896, Zvolen–13 July 1960, Luján, Argentina), Slovak writer. Hronský graduated from a pedagogical college in Léva (now Levice, Slovakia). From 1914 he worked as a teacher in Krupina, Kremnica, and Martin, and between 1917 and 1918 he fought in the Austro-Hungarian Army on the Italian front. From 1928 to 1937 he was editor-in-chief of *Slniečko*, a well-known magazine for children. In 1933 he became secretary of the Slovak Matrix (Matica slovenská [MS]), and in May 1940 he was appointed head of the MS. After the creation of the Slovak state on 14 March 1939, Hronský backed the idea of independence. Under his leadership, the MS became the main institution representing Slovak science and culture. During the Slovak National Uprising in August 1944 Hronský was held prisoner by the insurgents. In 1945 he went into exile. He lived in Austria, Bavaria, and Italy, and in 1948 he settled in Argentina. Because he was in conflict with **Ferdinand Ďurčanský**'s radical camp, which formed the nucleus of the Slovak political émigré community in Buenos Aires, until the mid–1950s Hronský kept away from émigré organizations. In 1956 he became honorary president of the Society of Slovak Writers and Artists in exile, and that very year he assumed the leadership of the Slovak National Council Abroad (Slovenská Národná Rada v Zahraniči [SNRvZ]), replacing **Karol Sidor** (who had died in 1953). In 1959 he founded the MS in exile.

Hronský is considered one of the leading Slovak prose writers. He began his literary career by publishing three collections of short stories: *U nás* (Here; 1923); *Domov* (Homeland; 1925); and *Medové srdce* (Heart of honey; 1929); these reveal the influences of the native realistic tradition combined with European modernism and impressionism. In *Podpolianske rozprávky* (Podpoliany stories; 1932) Hronský reassessed Slovak myths about highland robbers. He emphasized the relationship between mankind and the earth and a faith in the positive values of rural life. His novels *Chlieb* (Bread; 1931) and *Jozef Mak* (1933; English publication in 1985) constitute a transition between turn-of-the-century realism and contemporary Slovak literature. His novel *Pisár Gráč* (The writer Gráč; 1940) involved a clash between nature and civilization. In the novel *Na Bukvovom dvore* (At the Bukva court; 1944) Hronský analyzed the irrational sources of human behavior. In exile, he published *Andreas Búr Majster* (Mayor Andreas; 1948), a novel inspired by folk legends, and the famous novel *Svet na trasovisku* (The world in the swamp; 1960), a diatribe against the Slovak National Uprising, which he condemned as an act directed against Slovak statehood and instigated by external Communist forces. Hronský is also regarded as a precursor of the modern Slovak literature for children and youth. (MG)

Sources: *Slovník slovenských spisovateľov* (Prague, 1999); *Literatury zachodniosłowiańskie czasu przełomów 1890–1990*, vol. 1 (Katowice, 1994); *Pamiatke Jozefa Cígera Hronského* (Middletown, Pa., 1960); Jozef M. Rydlo, *"Svet na Trasovisku" nell' opera letteraria di J . C. Hronský* (Padua, 1971); Jozef M. Rydlo, *Jozef Cíger Hronský, 1896–1960: Abbozzo bibliografico* (Vatican City, 1973); Alexander Matuška, *J. C. Hronský* (Bratislava, 1979); *Biografické štúdie*, vol. 19, 1992; Augustín Maťovčík, *Jozef Cíger-Hronský: Životná drama* (Martin, 1995); *Biografické štúdie*, vol. 24, 1997.

HROZNÝ Bedřich (6 May 1879, Lysá on the Elbe, near Nymburk–12 December 1952, Prague), Czech orientalist, pioneer of Hittite studies. The son of a Protestant minister, in 1897–1901 Hrozný studied in Vienna, first Protestant theology and then old oriental languages and the ancient history of Asia Minor. In 1901–2 he also studied Assyrian civilization in Berlin and London, and later he worked in the Vienna university library. In 1904–5 he went to explore in the Middle East for the first time. From 1905 he was associate professor, and from 1915 full professor, at the University of Vienna. In 1919 he became full professor at Charles University in Prague, and in 1922 he co-founded the Institute of Oriental Studies in Prague. From 1929 he was editor-in-chief of the periodical *Archiv orientální*. A member of the Czech Academy of Sciences and Arts and the Czech Royal Research Society, in 1939 and 1945 he was rector of Charles University.

Hrozný made his literary debut with works on ancient Babylon—for instance, *Das Getreide im alten Babylonien* (Grain in ancient Babylon; 1914). In 1914 he started studying cuneiform texts written in an unknown language. He discovered that it was the Hittite language of the seventeenth–thirteenth centuries B.C. and that it belonged to the Indo-European group. In the course of further research Hrozný managed to decipher the Hittite records and elaborated Hittite grammar and history. His major works of this time included *Die Sprache der Hethiter, ihr Bau und Zugehörigkeit zum indogermanischen Sprachstamm*

(The Hittite language, its structure and Indo-European nature; 1917); *Hethitische Keilschrifttexte aus Boghazköy in Umschrift mit Übersetzung und Kommentar* (Hittite cuneiform texts from Boghazköy phonetically recorded with translation and interpretation; 1919); and *Základy chetitského jazyka* (Foundations of the Hittite language; 1922). During archaeological excavations in 1924–25 Hrozný discovered the old Assyrian city of Kanesh and its archive of Assyrian merchants from the nineteenth century B.C., including about one thousand Cappadocian tablets with the oldest form of Assyrian cuneiform records. He also conducted excavations in Syria and Palestine, where he discovered the first traces of the Amurru culture. In the 1930s Hrozný partially deciphered Hittite hieroglyphs. He gathered his discoveries into two syntheses: *Die älteste Geschichte Vorderasiens* (The oldest history of Asia Minor; 1940) and *Nejstarší dějiny Přední Asie, Indie, a Kréty* (The oldest history of Asia Minor, India, and Crete; 1943). (PU)

Sources: *ČBS*; Lubor Matouš, *Bedřich Hrozný: The Life and Work of a Czech Oriental Scholar* (Prague, 1949); Lubor Matouš, *Stopami zašlých kultur: O práci prof. Bedřicha Hrozného* (Prague, 1949); Vojtěch Zamarovský, *Za tajemstvím říše Chetitů* (Prague, 1961); Jiří Prosecký, *Akademik Bedřich Hrozný: Bibliografie 1902–1979* (Prague, 1979).

HRUSHEVSKYI Mykhailo (29 September 1866, Chełm [now in Poland]–25 November 1934, Kislovodsk), prominent Ukrainian historian, academic organizer, and politician. Hrushevskyi was born into the family of a Slavist and pedagogue from the Kiev region. In 1869 the family moved to Transcaucasia, where in 1886 Hrushevskyi graduated from a gymnasium (high school) in Tiflis (Tbilisi, Georgia). From 1886 to 1890 he studied in the Department of Philology and History of Kiev University under the supervision of Volodymyr Antonovych. Hrushevskyi remained at Kiev University, where he wrote and defended his Ph.D. thesis, *Ocherk istorii Kievskoi zemli ot smerti Iaroslava do kontsa 14 veka* (An outline of the history of the Kievan lands from the death of Yaroslav to the end of the fourteenth century; 1891), and his post-doctoral thesis, *Barskoe starostvo: Istoricheskie ocherki* (Bar County: A historical survey; 1894). From 1894 to 1913 he held the chair of world history, with special emphasis on the history of Eastern Europe, at the University of Lemberg (Lwów, Lviv). In view of the Polish character of this university, apart from his university work, Hrushevskyi concentrated on developing the Shevchenko Scientific Society (NTSh), and through concerted organizational, fund-raising, and research efforts he successfully promoted its transformation into a genuine Ukrainian academy of sciences. In 1894

Hrushevskyi became director of the Historical-Philosophical Section of the NTSh, and from 1897 to 1913 he was its president. Between 1895 and 1913 he published the bi-monthly *Zapysky NTSh*. He also initiated, and served as chief editor of two series of NTSh source publications, *Zherela do istorii Ukrainy-Rusy* (Sources for the study of the history of Ukraine-Rus) and *Pam'iatky ukrains'ko-rus'koi movy i literatury* (Souvenirs of the Ukrainian-Ruthenian language and literature). In these series he published his collected articles and theses, *Rozvidky i materiialy do istorii Ukrainy-Rusy* (Studies and materials on the history of Ukraine-Rus, 5 vols.; 1896–1902). He also taught many Ukrainian historians who would later become prominent.

In 1898, along with **Ivan Franko**, Hrushevskyi began publishing the periodical *Literaturno-Naukovyi Visnyk*. Until 1914 this periodical was the most important forum for the exchange of views among the Ukrainian cultural and political elite (from 1907 it was published in Kiev). In 1898 in Lviv, Hrushevskyi published the first volume of his *opus magnum*, *Istoriia Ukrainy-Rusy* (The history of Ukraine-Rus; 1997). By 1937, ten volumes of this work had been published, covering Ukrainian history from the earliest times to 1658. The series contributed not only to the consolidation of Ukrainian national consciousness, but also to the widespread adoption of the name "Ukraine." Hrushevskyi offered a new interpretation of the nation's history and established a paradigm for a separate Ukrainian historical process. This was a challenge to Russian historiography, which depicted the history of the so-called Little Russia from the perspective of the imperialist tsarist state, as a result of which the existence of a Ukrainian nation had not been recognized. In *Zvychaina skhema "ruskoi" istorii i sprava ratsional'noho ukladu istorii skhidnoho Slov'ianstva* (A schematic of "Russian" history and the question of a rational system of East Slavonic history, published in Stati po slavianovedeniiu, part 1, 1904) Hrushevskyi rejected the Russian concept of the continuity of the history of Eastern Europe from the ninth to the nineteenth centuries, from Kiev through Vladimir on the Klyazma River to Moscow, in favor of a concept that excluded Russia (Kiev—Halicz-Volhynian Duchy—southern part of the Grand Duchy of Lithuania —the Cossack state—Ukrainian revival of the nineteenth century). Although his interpretation of Ukrainian history, the so-called Narodnik interpretation, had been the subject of criticism and conflicting interpretations for twenty years already, the above-mentioned scheme was accepted by independent twentieth-century Ukrainian historiography as the basic scheme for the periodization of Ukrainian history.

In his later publications, Hrushevskyi put more emphasis upon the history of statehood in Ukraine, yet his "Narodnik" point of view manifested itself in, among other things, the rejection of the so-called Norman theory of the origin of Rus. A concise version of his synthesis was published in 1904 as *Ocherk istorii ukrains'koho naroda* (An outline of Ukrainian history). A more popular version of the work, titled *Iliustrovana istoriia Ukrainy* (Illustrated history of Ukraine), was published in 1911. After the 1905 revolution, Hrushevskyi was more and more strongly associated with Ukrainian scholarly and political life in Russia. In 1906 he worked in St. Petersburg and from 1907 in Kiev. His views on the Ukrainian question crystallized as Socialist, democratic, and federalist and found their expression in, among other works, *Osvobozhdenie Rossii i ukrainskii vopros* (The liberation of Russia and the Ukrainian question; 1907). An active publicist, Hrushevskyi was the founder of the Ukrainian Scientific Society in Kiev (1907) and the Society of Ukrainian Progressives (1908). He emerged as an established leader of the Ukrainian movement already before World War I.

Arrested after the outbreak of World War I, Hrushevskyi was exiled to Simbirsk, then to Kazan, and finally to Moscow, and he remained under police supervision. Released soon after the outbreak of the February 1917 revolution, on 17 March 1917 he was elected president of the Kiev-based Ukrainian Central Rada (UCR), which served as a provisional Ukrainian parliament. Hrushevskyi became one of the leaders of the Ukrainian Party of Socialist Revolutionaries (UPSR), which dominated within the UCR. Immediately after the Bolshevik coup in Petrograd, he supported the proclamation of independence of the Ukrainian People's Republic (UPR), and on 29 April 1918 the UCR elected him its first president. However, because of the coup staged in Kiev by Hetman **Pavlo Skoropadsky** and because of the collapse of the UPR, Hrushevskyi's nomination was only symbolic. During the revolution Hrushevskyi published *Vilna Ukraina* (Free Ukraine; 1917), *Na porozi novoi Ukrainy: Hadki i mrii* (On the threshold of a new Ukraine: Thoughts and dreams; 1918), and other works. In 1919 he emigrated to Vienna, where he sought the support of European countries for the UPR. He was a member of the UPSR Foreign Committee and published the party's organ, *Boritesia—Poborete!* (1920–22). Above all, however, he continued his scholarly work. In 1919 he founded the Ukrainian Sociological Institute in Vienna (which was later moved to Prague). Hrushevskyi's publications include *Pochatky hromadians'tva (henetychna sotsiolohiia)* (Origins of society [genetic sociology]; 1921) and *Z istorii relihiinoi dumky na Ukraini* (On the history of religious thought in Ukraine; 1925). He also began writing another work, *Istoriia ukrains'koi literatury* (History of Ukrainian literature, 5 vols.; 1922–27). His autobiography, *Autobiohrafiia*, was published posthumously in 1965.

Encouraged by the announcement of the Ukrainization policy of the Ukrainian SSR, in 1924 Hrushevskyi decided to accept an invitation from Kharkiv and returned to the Ukraine, where he continued his scholarly work. Elected a member of the All-Ukrainian Academy of Sciences, he assumed the leadership of an archaeographic commission and held the chair of modern Ukrainian history. He initiated a series of historical and ethnological research projects, published the periodical *Ukraina* (1924–30), and edited publications by young historians. He established relations with the NTSh in Lwów, paving the way for the transborder unity of Ukrainian scholarly activity. After the Ukrainization policy was abandoned and the Stalinization of science began, Hrushevskyi was accused of nationalism and of defying the Marxist vision of the historical process. In March 1931 he was transferred to Moscow, while the institutions as well as the school of history he had established were abolished. He continued his scholarly work until the end of his life. He died in 1934 in the Caucasus, where he went for medical treatment. He was buried in Kiev. Until the end of the USSR, the Soviet regime continued to combat his scheme of Ukrainian history. Hrushevskyi left over 1,800 publications in the field of history, archaeology, sociology, and ethnology, as well as fairytales, dramas, and stories. (TS)

Sources: *Encyclopedia of Ukraine*, vol. 2 (Toronto, 1988); *MERSH*, vol. XIC; Dmytro Doroshenko, *Ohliad ukrains'koi istoriohrafii* (Prague, 1923); *Iuvilei akademika M. S. Hrushevs'koho 1866–1926* (Kiev, 1927); *Ukrains'kyi istoryk*, (1966 and 1984, special editions); Lubomyr Vynar, *Mykhailo Hrushevs'kyi i Naukove Tovarystvo im. Tarasa Shevchenka 1892–1930* (Munich, 1970); Lubomyr Vynarm ed., *Mykhailo Hrushevs'kyi 1866–1934: Bibliographic Sources* (New York, Munich, and Toronto, 1985); T. Prymak, *Mykhailo Hrushevsky and the Politics of National Culture* (Toronto, 1987); O. Kopilenko, *"Ukrains'ka ideia" Mykhaily Hrushevs'koho: Istoriia i suchasnist'* (Kiev, 1991); Ruslan I. Pyrik, *Zhyttia Mykhailo Hrushevskoho ostannnie diesiatylettia, 1924–1934* (Kiev, 1993); Gennadii Strels'kyi, *Mykhailo Hrushevs'kyi, ioho spodvyzhnyky i oponenty* (Kiev, 1996); I. Hrytsak and I. Dashkevych, eds., *Mykhailo Hrushevs'kyi i ukrains'ka istorychna nauka* (Lviv, 1999).

HRYB Miechyslau (28 September 1938, Saviche, Grodno region), Soviet security officer, Belorussian post-Communist activist. In 1967 Hryb graduated extramurally from the Belorussian State University in Minsk. In 1959–81 he worked in the Vitebsk regional structures of the Ministry of Interior of the Belorussian SSR (BSSR). From 1981 he was head of the Public Order Protection Aministration of the Belorussian Ministry of Interior, and from 1985, head of the Administration of Internal Affairs of the Regional Committee in Vitebsk. In 1985 the Vitebsk militia managed to arrest a serial killer of women (forty-three victims), but the success proved to compromise the Soviet judiciary because thirteen innocent people had already been sentenced for these crimes. In 1993 Hryb was promoted to the rank of militia general. From 1990 he was deputy of the BSSR Supreme Council and head of its Commission of National Security, Defense, and Combating Crime. On 28 January 1994, on the initiative of hard-liner deputies of the former Communist nomenklatura, Hryb replaced **Stanislau Shushkevich** as chairman of the Belorussian Supreme Council, serving as the formal head of state. He was reelected to the Supreme Council in 1995, and he was its chairman until 10 January 1996. From November 1996 Hryb went into opposition to the system created by **Alyaksandr Lukashenka**. Later he was chairman of the Belorussian Euroatlantic Association, a member of the Belorussian Helsinki Committee, and (from 1999) deputy chairman of the Belorussian Social Democratic party Narodnaya Hramada (National Community). Hryb authored *Belarus na shlakhakh nezalezhnastsi* (Belarus on the roads to independence; 1994). (EM)

Sources: *Bielaruskaia entsiklopiedyia*, vol. 5 (Minsk, 1995); *Belarus: Entsyklapedychny davednik* (Minsk, 1995); Jan Zaprudnik, *Historical Dictionary of Belarus* (Lanham, Md., 1998); *Kto iest kto v Respublike Belarus* (Minsk, 1999); David R. Marples, *Belarus: A Denationalization of a Nation* (Amsterdam, 1999).

HRYHORENKO Petro [also known as Grigorenko] (16 October 1907, Borysivka, Zaporozhye–21 February 1987, New York), Soviet general and dissident of Ukrainian descent. From his youth Hryhorenko was active in the Komsomol, and in 1929–31 he was a member of its Central Committee in the Ukraine. A member of the Communist Party from 1927, in 1929–31 he studied at the Technological Institute in Kharkiv. From 1931 he was in the army, and he graduated from the Kuibyshev Military Engineering Academy. In 1934–37 he served in the Belorussian military district and studied at the Academy of the General Staff; in 1939–43 he served in the Far East. In 1944–45 he fought on the front line and was twice wounded. He ended the war as the chief of staff of a division with the rank of colonel. Awarded the Order of Lenin and other orders, from 1945 to 1961 he lectured at the Frunze Military Academy and from 1959 was chair of one of its departments, with the rank of major general.

At a party conference in 1961, Hryhorenko spoke in favor of free elections, so he was banned from teaching and sent to serve in the Far East. In 1963 he organized the illegal Union of Struggle for the Rebirth of Leninism. He published seven leaflets condemning the Soviet bureaucracy and its policies toward workers. He distributed them in Moscow, Kaluga, and the Leningrad and Middle Asiatic Military Districts. Arrested in 1964, Hryhorenko was sent to the psychiatric ward of the Serbski Institute, where, according to the Soviet practice of that time, he was found mentally ill. In July 1964 the Supreme Court of the USSR sent him to Leningrad for forced psychiatric treatment. A month later he was expelled from the army and demoted. After his release in 1965 Hryhorenko worked as a watchman, guide, and construction worker. He drew closer to the Moscow dissidents and became engaged in the struggle for the rights of deported nationals, mainly the Crimean Tatars.

In the fall of 1967 Hryhorenko wrote a secretly distributed pamphlet, *Sokrytye istoricheskoy pravdy: Prestupleniye pered narodom!* (Hiding historical truth: Crime against the nation!), in which he accused Stalin for the Red Army defeats in 1941. In 1967–68 he was one of the organizers of a petition campaign in defense of Aleksandr Ginzburg and Yuriy Galanskov; in 1968 he spoke in favor of the Prague Spring and co-authored a letter to members of the Communist Party of Czechoslovakia and the Czechoslovak nation in which he enthusiastically welcomed "socialism with a human face." At the end of 1968 he wrote an essay on Soviet psychiatric wards that was included in Natalya Gorbanevskaya's *Red Square at Noon* (1972). In May 1969, just before another trial of Crimean Tatars in Tashkent, in which he wanted to appear as their defense counsel, Hryhorenko was arrested again. In 1970 he was again sent for forced psychiatric treatment. The academician Andrei Sakharov and the international community spoke in his defense. In 1973 a collection of Hryhorenko's texts was published as *Mysli sumasshedshego* (Thoughts of a madman). Released on 24 June 1974, on the eve of Richard Nixon's visit to the USSR, Hryhorenko spoke in defense of **Mustafa Dzhemilev**, leader of the Crimean Tatars, and of Sakharov, who was attacked by Soviet propaganda after receiving the Nobel Prize. The *Grigorenko Papers*, illustrating his case, were published in the United States in 1976. In 1976–77 Hryhorenko was one of the key organizers and activists of the Moscow Helsinki Group. On his initiative a commission was established to examine the use of psychiatry as a tool for political repression. In 1976 Hryhorenko co-founded the Ukrainian Helsinki Group (UHG), and in 1977 he published a booklet, *Nashi budni* (Our everyday), on the KGB operations against the Helsinki movement. In November 1977 he was allowed to go to the United States for half a year; while there, he was deprived of his Soviet citizenship. He stayed in America, where he was the UHG representative. He finally abandoned communism. In 1981

he published the memoirs *W podpole mozhno vstretit tolko krys* (You can only meet rats in the underground; translated as *Memoirs*, 1982). By virtue of a decree by Russian president Boris Yeltsin, in 1993 Hryhorenko's military rank was posthumously restored to him. A street in Kiev and several streets in the Crimea bear his name. In 1997 Hryhorenko was posthumously awarded the Ukrainian Order for Bravery. (BB)

Sources: *Encyclopedia of Ukraine*, vol. 2 (Toronto, 1988); Bohdan Nahaylo, *The Ukrainian Resurgence* (Toronto, 1999); *Ukrainska Hromadska Hrupa spryiannia vykonanniu Helinskykh uhod* (Kharkiv, 2001); *Dovidnyk z istoriyi Ukraiiny* (Kiev, 2001).

HRYHORIIV Matvii Nykyfor (1885, Zastavie, Podolia–27 July 1919, Ukraine), Ukrainian military leader. Hryhoriiv served in the Russian Army and attained the rank of captain. Under the rule of Hetman **Pavlo Skoropadsky** and later under the rule of the Directorate of the Ukrainian National Republic, he assembled around 6,000–8,000 soldiers under his command in the region of Alexandria and Mykolayiv (also spelled Nikolayev). He recruited his soldiers mainly among anarchists and splinter groups of Socialist revolutionaries, called "Borotbists" after the title of a newspaper. In January 1919 Hryhoriiv rebelled against the Directorate when it forbade his soldiers to fight against the Allied troops that had intervened against the Bolsheviks. He became allied with the Bolshevik government in Kharkiv, and between February and April 1919 his fifteen-thousand-strong troops played a key role in offensives against the Whites and Allied forces in the regions of Mykolayiv, Kherson, and Odessa. In early May 1919 the Bolsheviks ordered Hryhoriiv to lead his troops against the Romanians to support the Hungarian Soviet Republic, but he refused. He proclaimed himself ataman of the Ukraine and organized an anti-Bolshevik uprising in the region of Kherson and Yekaterinoslav. During the revolt his troops committed pogroms against the Jewish population. Since the Red Army managed to crush the revolt, his troops joined forces with the anarchist units of **Nestor Makhno**. Soon a sharp conflict broke out between Hryhoriiv and Makhno. Hryhoriiv demanded that that they support the army of General Anton Denikin against the Bolsheviks. Makhno opposed Hryhoriiv's plans and ordered that he be shot. (WR)

Sources: *Encyclopedia of Ukraine*, vol. 2 (Toronto, 1988); Matthew Stachiv and Jaroslav Sztendera, eds., *Western Ukraine at the Turning Point of Europe's History, 1918–1923*, vols. 1–2 (New York, 1971); Paul R. Magocsi, *A History of Ukraine* (Seattle, 1996); Orest Subtelny, *Ukraine: A History* (Toronto, 2000).

HURBAN VAJANSKÝ Svetozár [originally Svetozár Miloslav Hurban] (16 January 1847, Hlboké–17 August

1916, Turčiansky Svätý Martin [Martin]), Slovak politician, writer, and conservative national ideologist. Hurban Vajanský came from a small-town Protestant family. His father, Pastor Jozef Miloslav Hurban, was one of the most prominent representatives of the Slovak national movement. Hurban Vajanský completed law studies in Bratislava, and in 1878 settled in Turčiansky Svätý Martin. From 1878 he was editor of the newspaper *Národnie noviny*; from 1898 to 1899 and from 1906 to 1916 he was its editor-in-chief. From 1878 to 1880 he also edited the periodical *Orol*, and from 1881, *Slovenské pohl'ady*, of which he became the owner in 1890. He continued to publish it until 1916. Hurban Vajanský was imprisoned several times for his journalism. From the end of the 1870s he was the leading ideologist of the Slovak National Party (Slovenská Národná Strana [SNP]), and he co-formed the so-called Martin center of the national movement. He held high posts in the leadership of the party, but it was his extensive journalistic work that assured his position. His editorials in *Národnie noviny* were regarded as the official line of the SNP.

Hurban Vajanský is regarded as a leading representative of the conservative trend in the Slovak national movement at the turn of the twentieth century. An ardent Russophile, he transferred Russian Pan-Slavic ideas to the Slovak soil. As he believed that ethnic issues in Central Europe would be resolved by Russian intervention, he advocated passive resistance. He feared the political engagement of the masses and assigned the task of preserving the national culture to the intelligentsia, which he regarded as the "nation *pars pro toto*." The work *Nálady a vyhl'ady* (Attitudes and perspectives; 1897) is considered a synthesis of his views. From the launch of the periodical *Hlas*, edited by **Pavol Blaho** and **Vavro Šrobár** in 1897, Hurban Vajanský carried on intense disputes with young Slovak intellectuals who rejected his elitist concept of the nation and his Pan-Slavism. He accused them of destroying the unity of the national movement, as well as cosmopolitanism and yielding to the Czechs. Hurban Vajanský was seen as the most important critic of the idea of the "Czechoslovak nation" and as the main ideological opponent of **Tomáš Garrigue Masaryk** in Slovakia. He is regarded as a co-founder of modern literary criticism and a precursor of artistic criticism. In 1880 Hurban Vajanský made his debut as a poet with the collection *Tatry a more* (The Tatras and the sea). In his prose works—for example, the novella *Letiace tiene* (Passing shadows; 1883) and the novel *Suchá ratolesť* (Dry shoot; 1884)—he dealt with the concerns of the upper classes, unfolding Utopian visions of the Magyarized nobility of Slovak origins uniting with the nationally conscious intelligentsia. The novel *Kotlín*

(1901), a polemic with the Hlasists (Hlasisty), gave rise to Slovak modernism. Hurban Vajanský's selected works of literary criticism were published in the volumes *State o slovenskej literatúre* (Articles on Slovak literature; 1956) and *State o svetovej literatúre* (Articles on world literature; 1957). (MG)

Sources: *Biographisches Lexikon*, vol. 2; *Reprezentačný biografický lexikón Slovenska* (Martin, 1999); *Literatury zachodniosłowiańskie czasu przełomów 1890–1990*, vol. 1 (Katowice, 1994); Ol'ga Nagyová, *Mladý Vajanský ako novinár* (Bratislava, 1973); Ján Juríček, *Vajanský: Portrét odvážneho* (Bratislava, 1988); Ivan Kusý, *Zrelý Vajanský* (Bratislava, 1992); Zdzisław Niedziela, *Słowacja znana i nieznana: Szkice z dziejów literatury słowackiej* (Kraków, 1995); Zdenek Janči, *Svetozár Hurban Vajanský: Kritik výtvarného umenia* (Nitra, 1998).

HUSÁK Gustav (10 January 1913, Dúbravka, near Bratislava–18 November 1991, Bratislava), Czechoslovak Communist leader. Born into a peasant family, at sixteen Husák joined the Communist Youth Union in Bratislava. He joined the Slovak branch of the Communist Party of Czechoslovakia (CPC) in 1933 while studying at the Law Department of the university in Bratislava. He co-founded a circle of leftist intellectuals that centered around **Vladimir Clementis** and the periodical *DAV*. These intellectuals actively participated in ideological discussions about the future of Slovakia. At that time Husák became known as an opponent of a centralized state model. After the outbreak of World War II, he was in opposition to the government of Reverend **Jozef Tiso**. In August 1943 Husák joined the Central Committee (CC) of the Communist Party of Slovakia (CPS). Following the guidelines laid down by the leadership of the CPC in Moscow, at that time he insisted on the necessity of creating a broader platform in the struggle against the local regime and Nazi Germany. He took part in signing the so-called Christmas Treaty (concluded on 24 December 1943) and in the establishment of the underground Slovak National Council (SNC). As a representative of the SNC, he established contact with representatives of the military underground who supported Lieutenant Colonel **Jan Golian**. After the outbreak of the Slovak National Uprising in August 1944, Husák moved to Banská Bystrica, the center of the insurgency, where he became vice-president of the SNC and was in charge of its interior department. After the collapse of the uprising, he became a member of the Presidium of the Board of Commissioners of the SNC in February 1945, and he tried to recruit members of all opposition groups into the SNC. In January 1945, along with a group of Slovak Communists, Husák was in Moscow, where they were presented with a project to establish a new government center in Czechoslovakia. This government center was to include representatives of the government-in-exile and the local Communists. In February 1945 Husák joined the Presidium of the CC of the CPS and, as its interim president, prepared the program for Slovak autonomy within the Czechoslovak state.

After the elections to the National Assembly (May 1946), on 13 August 1946 Husák became president of the Board of Commissioners of the SNC. Among other things, he was in charge of the interior department and of the state security organs. He called for moving the German and Hungarian minorities out of Slovakia and for the radical suppression of Reverend Tiso's lieutenants. His security services prepared a number of actions against the opponents of the Communist regime—for example, against the Slovak Democratic Party—and they launched persecutions against the Catholic Church. After the coup of February 1948, despite Husák's protests, a tight rein was put on the autonomy of the Slovaks and the CPS. Husák's career collapsed in May 1950, when the Ninth Congress of the CPS denounced "Slovak bourgeois nationalism" among party members. In February 1951 Husák and other leading activists were expelled from the party and arrested for so-called nationalist deviation. Despite being tortured during interrogations, Husák refused to testify against the other accused, and he did not confess guilt in the crimes for which he was accused. Sentenced to life imprisonment in April 1954, he was released in 1960 and was fully rehabilitated in 1963. Husák rejected the post of deputy prime minister, which was offered to him, and took up research at the Institute of State and Law of the Slovak Academy of Sciences. In August 1964 he published his memoirs from the period of his underground activity; in them he defended the model and strategy of the CPS. The publication of these memoirs was an important event.

Husák was one of **Alexander Dubček**'s associates when the latter launched his reform program. In April 1968 he became deputy prime minister. After the invasion of Czechoslovakia by Warsaw Pact troops, between 23 and 26 August 1968, along with other party and state leaders, Husák took part in talks in Moscow in which the Czechoslovak delegation accepted the reversal of the Prague Spring reforms. During the talks in Moscow he gained the trust of Leonid Brezhnev. It is believed that during confidential talks Brezhnev promised Husák that Moscow would accept a federal model for the Czechoslovak state. Soon after returning to Czechoslovakia, Husák sharply criticized the Fourteenth Extraordinary Congress of the CPC, the so-called Vysočany Congress, which protested the intervention of Warsaw Pact troops and called for the continuation of reforms. Husák stressed that the Vysočany Congress was not representative because less

than 10 percent of the Slovak delegates attended it. At the end of August 1968 Husák became first secretary of the CC of the CPS and a member of the Presidium of the CC of the CPC. In the autumn of 1968 he was appointed head of a government commission that drafted a bill on the Czechoslovak federation, passed on 27 October 1968. However, as a ruler, Husák aimed at maintaining a centralist model of the state.

On 17 April 1969 Dubček had to resign, and Husák succeeded him as first secretary of the CC of the CPC. Using the slogan of "normalization," he brought about the pacification of the reformist forces within the party and in the society at large. On 6 May 1970 he signed an agreement of friendship, cooperation, and mutual assistance with the USSR that sanctioned the "temporary" stationing of Soviet troops on Czechoslovak territory. In May 1971, at a session of the Fourteenth Congress of the CPC, Husák was elected secretary general of the party. The ruling team formed at that time remained virtually unchanged until November 1989. On 29 May 1975 Husák added the post of president to his other titles.

After 1969 Husák carried out a great purge of the CPC that resulted in expelling all party activists who did not accept the policy of total subordination to Moscow. Within a few years the number of party members dropped by over half a million, and around 140,000 people emigrated. People considered enemies of the system were not allowed to practice in their professions. As part of the "normalization" process, a tough struggle was introduced against independent intellectuals and against the structures of the Catholic Church. This struggle involved attempts to recruit the clergy into pro-government organizations and block the appointment of new bishops. Although in the spring of 1969 Husák announced that he would not persecute his political opponents, after the launch of Charter 77, its leading signatories were sentenced in political trials.

The advent of Mikhail Gorbachev in Moscow and the changes he initiated gradually undermined the power of Husák, who was an avowed opponent of glasnost and perestroika. On 17 December 1987 he resigned as secretary general of the CC of the CPC. Until the end he refused to enter into talks with the opposition. After mass demonstrations and strikes, in December 1989 he had to accept the so-called government of national agreement of **Marian Čalfa**, which consisted of representatives of both the CPC and the opposition. On 10 December 1989 Husák resigned as president of Czechoslovakia and was soon thereafter expelled from the CPC. (AGr)

Sources: *Kdo był kdo v našich dějinách ve 20 století* (Prague, 1994); Gordon H. Skilling, *Czechoslovakia's Interrupted Revolution* (Princeton, 1976); Vladimir V. Kusin, *From Dubcek to Charter 77:*

A Study of "Normalization" in Czechoslovakia 1968–1978 (New York, 1978); Jerzy Tomaszewski, *Europa Środkowo-Wschodnia 1944–1968: Powstanie, ewolucja i kryzys realnego socjalizmu* (Warsaw, 1992); Jan Pešek, *Štátna bezpečnost na Slovensku 1948–1953* (Bratislava, 1999); Dušan Kováč, *Dejiny Slovenska* (Prague, 2000); Jan Pešek, *Nástroj represie a politickej kontroly: Štátna bezpečnost na Slovensku 1953–1970* (Bratislava, 2000).

HUSZÁR Károly [originally Schorn] (10 September 1882, Vienna–29 October 1941, Budapest), Hungarian politician. A teacher by training, from 1903 Huszár became actively engaged with Christian Democratic peasant movements and parties. From 1910 to 1918 he represented the Catholic National Party in the parliament. At the same time he was editor-in-chief of its newspaper, *Néppárt*. During World War I he fought on a number of fronts as a volunteer. Just before the republican coup in November 1918, he was appointed minister of education and denominations. He was arrested in 1919, when the Hungarian Soviet Republic was established. After his release he emigrated to Vienna. In 1919–22 he was a leader of the Christian National Union (Keresztény Nemzeti Egyesülés Partja), a base for all Hungarian governments since the beginning of the 1920s. Huszár belonged to its Christian Social wing. In the cabinet of **István Friedrich** (August–November 1919) he was again in charge of the Ministry of Education and Denominations. As prime minister (24 November 1919–1 March 1920), Huszár forced the calling of a basically democratic parliamentary election and insisted upon sending a Hungarian delegation to Paris for the peace talks. In the conflict between legalists, who demanded the reinstatement of the former emperor, Charles IV, and the advocates of handing power over to **Miklós Horthy**, Huszár eventually took sides with the latter. In 1920–28 Huszár was an MP and deputy chairman of the National Assembly; subsequently, he was a senator. From 1928 to 1934 he was president of the National Institute of Social Security. In the last years of his life, he gradually retreated from political life. (MS)

Sources: *Ki kicsoda* (Budapest, 2001); *20 századi magyar történelem 1900–1994* (Budapest, 1997).

HUZAR Lubomyr (26 February 1933, Lwów [Lviv]), cardinal, head of the Greek Catholic Church. After graduating from the first grade of high school in Lviv, in 1944 Huzar left with his family for Austria and in 1949 for the United States. He graduated from the theological seminary in Stamford, Connecticut, and then he studied philosophy at St. Basil College and theology at the Catholic University in Washington, D.C. In March 1958 he was ordained, and in 1958–59 he taught at the Stamford Theological

Seminary and was minister to the Ukrainian Popular Union (Ukraiinskyi Narodnyi Soyuz) and the house of education of the Society of Ukrainian Youth of America (Spilka Ukraiinskoyi Molodi Ameryky) in Hellenville, New York. From 1965 he was parish priest, and in 1967 he graduated with an M.A. in philosophy. To continue theological studies, in 1969 Huzar went to Rome, where in 1972 he received a Ph.D. and entered the Studite Order in Grottaferrata, near Rome. In 1978 Cardinal **Yosyp Slipyi** appointed him archimandrite (prior) of St. Theodore Monastery, responsible for Studite monasteries outside Ukraine. In 1973–84 Huzar lectured at the Pontifical Urbaniana University in Rome. On 2 April 1977 he was consecrated bishop by Cardinal Slipyi, and in 1984–91 he was vicar general of the Lviv Archdiocese in Rome. In 1993 he returned to the Ukraine. In 1993–94 he lectured at the Holy Spirit Seminary in Lviv, and from April 1996 he was exarch of Kiev and Vyshhorod. In October 1996 Huzar was appointed auxiliary bishop of Lviv. After the death of Cardinal **Myroslav Lubachivskyi**, on 25 January 2001, the synod of Ukrainian bishops elected Huzar archbishop of Lviv, and on 21 February 2001 Pope **John Paul II** appointed him cardinal. In June 2001, along with the Roman Catholic archbishop of Lviv, Cardinal **Marian Jaworski**, Huzar co-organized the Pope's pilgrimage to the Ukraine. Huzar was engaged in the Polish-Ukrainian reconciliation; for instance, he published a special pastoral letter concerning the Polish Youth War Veterans' (Orlęta) Cemetery in Lviv in July 2002. (BB)

Sources: "Zhyttiepys novoho Halytskoho Mytropolyta," *Postup*, 27–28 January 2001; "Kardynał Lwowiak," *Gazeta Wyborcza*, 14–15 July 2002; *Annuario Pontificio 2001*; "Krótki życiorys Kardynała Lubomyra Huzara," www.opoka.org.pl; www.catholic-hierarchy.org.

HVIEZDOSLAV Pavol [originally Országh] (2 February 1849, Vyšný Kubín–8 November 1921, Dolný Kubín), Slovak poet, writer, and playwright. Born into a landowner's family, Hviezdoslav wrote his first poems in Hungarian and German. During his high school years in Kiežmark (1864–70) he began to write in Slovak. In 1872 he graduated in law in Prešov. From 1875 he worked as a lawyer in Námestovo and then in Dolný Kubín. He made his literary debut with a collection of poems, *Básnické prviesenky Jozefa Zbranského* (Poetic primroses of Jozef Zbranský; 1868), in which he expressed his attachment to Orava, the spiritual values of the Slovak people, and Slavophilism. In 1871 he published the poem *Otčim* (Stepfather), in which he departed from patriotic feelings toward more universal issues. Later he mainly published in the periodical *Slovenské pohľady*. Hviezdoslav wrote reflective lyrics, contemplating the world, the individual, and the nation. He glorified nature and human beings in the poem *Hájnikova žena* (The gamekeeper's wife; 1884–86). He expressed his fears concerning his oppressed nation in the cycle *Žalmy a hymny* (Psalms and hymns; 1896). He also praised the Oravian landscape, expressing his pantheist beliefs. Hviezdoslav reflected on the forces of nature in the cycle *Stesky* (Longings; 1903–8). In the eposes *Ežo Vlkolinský* (1890) and *Gabor Vlkolinský* (1901) he critically assessed the relationship between landowners and peasants in Slovakia. In 1909 he created his most outstanding drama, *Herodes a Herodias* (Herod and Herodiad). In the collection *Krvavé sonety* (1914; *Bloody Sonnets*, 1950) he considered war atrocities as divine punishment for human sins. His writings reflected Polish-Slovak border disputes over Orava (1919–20), which shook his earlier Polonophilism.

Hviezdoslav is considered the most outstanding Slovak writer of the turn of the twentieth century. His works were both national and universal and show his unique, individual style. He introduced Slovak poetry into European literature. In his program for the creation of Slovak "high culture" an important place was taken by his translations of William Shakespeare, Johann Wolfgang Goethe, Friedrich Schiller, Adam Mickiewicz, Aleksandr Pushkin, Sandor Petófi, and many others. Also Hviezdoslav's own works were translated into many languages. (MG)

Sources: *SBS; Slovník slovenských spisovateľov* (Prague, 1999); Augustín Matovčik et al., *Reprezentačný biografický lexikón Slovenska* (Martin, 1999); Pavol Bujnák, *Pavol Országh Hviezdoslav* (Liptovský Mikuláš, 1919); Władysław Bobek, "Hviezdoslav: Największy poeta Słowacji," *Kurier Literacko-Naukowy*, 1936, no. 42; Stanislav Šmatlák, *Hviezdoslav: Básnik národný a svetový* (Bratislava, 1969); Augustín Matovčik, *Herold svitajúcich časov: Hviezdoslav* (Martin, 1988); Augustín Matovčik, *Hviezdoslav a rodná Orava* (Martin, 1999).

I

IERUNCA Virgil [originally Untaru] (16 August 1920, Lădeşti), Romanian journalist and émigré activist. In 1939–47 Ierunca edited the Communist periodical *România Liberă*. In February 1947 he emigrated to France, where he worked with **Mircea Eliade** on the editorial board of the cultural magazine *Luceafărul*. Soon after his departure from Romania, Ierunca married **Monica Lovinescu**. From 1951 to 1974 he edited Romanian broadcasts on French Radio. In 1974–90 he also worked in the Romanian Section of Radio Free Europe, where he, along with his wife, edited the very popular series "Actualitatea Culturală Românească" (Contemporary Romanian culture) and "Povestea vorbei: Pagini uitate, pagini cenzurate, pagini exilate" (Tales of the word: Forgotten, censored, and exiled pages). Ierunca became the leading personality among the Romanian exiles. He worked with all the major émigré periodicals, including *Caiete de Dor* and *Fiinţa Românească*. In April 1989 he signed an appeal demanding the liberalization of cultural life in Romania. After the fall of the **Nicolae Ceauşescu** regime, Ierunca retired. (AB)

Sources: Mihai Pellin, *Opisul emigraţiei politice: Destine în 1222 de fişe alcătuite pe bază dosarelor din arhivele Securităţii* (Bucharest, 2002).

IGNAR Stefan (17 February 1908, Bałdrzychów, near Łęczyca–23 January 1992, Warsaw), Polish peasant activist. While a student of philosophy at Poznań University (1927–31), Ignar was active in the Polish Academic Peasant Youth and the Union of Rural Youth (Związek Młodzieży Wiejskiej [ZMW]). From 1937 to 1939 he was a member of the ZMW Main Board. In 1932 he joined the Peasant Party (Stronnictwo Ludowe [SL]), and from 1935 to 1939 he was a member of the SL Chief Council. From 1933 to 1935 he lectured at Orkan Rural University in Gać, near Przeworsk, and later he was a co-founder and editor-in-chief of the bi-weekly *Chłopskie Życie Gospodarcze* (1935–37). From 1938 to 1939 Ignar was editor-in-chief of the weekly *Wici*. In 1937 he organized a peasant strike in Łódź Province. During the Nazi occupation he co-formed the underground SL–Roch and the Peasant Battalions (Bataliony Chłopskie [BCh]). In 1940–44 he was president of the Provincial Leadership of the Roch Peasant Movement in Łódź and a member of the Fifth District Command of the BCh.

In 1944 Ignar drew closer to the Polish Workers' Party (Polska Partia Robotnicza [PPR]) and the Polish Committee of National Liberation (Polski Komitet Wyzwolenia Narodowego [PKWN]), and as result he broke off with the Central Leadership of the Peasant Movement (Centralne Kierownictwo Ruchu Ludowego [CKRL]). In March 1945 he left the SL–Roch. In 1945 he again joined the Union of Rural Youth of the Republic of Poland–Wici (ZMW RP–Wici); between 1946 and 1947 he was its vice-president, and from 1947 to 1948, president of its Main Board. Ignar substantially contributed to the consolidation of the youth movement under Communist tutelage and to the establishment of the Union of Polish Youth (Związek Młodzieży Polskiej [ZMP]). In 1948–49 he presided over the ZMP Chief Council. In 1947 he joined the SL, which cooperated with the Communists, and from 1948 to 1949 he was a member of the Presidium of the SL Chief Executive Committee. From 1948 to 1950 he presided over the Main Board of the Peasant Mutual Aid Association. He supported forced collectivization. From 1949 to 1989 Ignar was a member of the United Peasant Party (Zjednoczone Stronnictwo Ludowe [ZSL]), serving as vice-president (1949–56) and president (1956–62, 1981) of the ZSL Chief Committee. In 1949–76 Ignar lectured at Warsaw Agricultural University (Szkoła Główna Gospodarstwa Wiejskiego). From 1952 to 1976 he was an MP in the Assembly, and from 1952 to 1956, deputy president of the State Council. He also served as deputy prime minister (October 1956–June 1969). From 1955 to 1957 he was president of the Main Board of the Polish-Soviet Friendship Society. From 1958 to 1983 he was a member of the Presidium of the All-Polish Committee of the National Unity Front. In 1964 he became a professor of economics. He authored numerous propagandist and scholarly publications, such as *Sojusz robotniczo-chłopski w świetle niektórych doświadczeń ruchu ludowego* (Alliance between peasants and workers in light of some experiences in the peasant movement; 1950); *Agraryzm: Społeczno-gospodarczy program burżuazji wiejskiej* (Agrarianism: Social and economic program of the rural bourgeoisie; 1956); and *Polityka agrarna* (Agrarian policy; 1968). (JS)

Sources: Mołdawa; *Słownik biograficzny działaczy ruchu ludowego* (Warsaw, 1989); *Encyklopedia historii Polski: Dzieje polityczne*, vol. 1 (Warsaw, 1994); Krystyna Kersten, *Narodziny systemu władzy: Polska 1943–1948.* (Poznań, 1990); Stanisław Giza, *Kalendarz wydarzeń historii ruchu ludowego, 1895–1965.* (Warsaw, 1967).

IGNOTUS Pál (1 July 1901, Budapest–1 April 1978, London), Hungarian writer and radical politician. The son of Hugó Veigelsberg Ignotus, the founder and editor-in-chief of Nyugat, a periodical of the Hungarian classical avant garde, in 1923 Ignotus began contributing to the daily Esti Kurír, and later he was editor of this newspaper's foreign column. He wrote literary reviews and political analyses for the daily Magyar Hírlap and published in the periodicals Nyugat, A Toll, Századunk, and Szocializmus. In the discussions between the representatives of the "peasant" and "urban" movements, Ignotus was one of the most radical "urbanists." At the end of 1938, after the passage of the first anti-Jewish law, Ignotus went to England, where he led anti-Nazi propaganda for the BBC. In 1944 he joined the circle of the Hungarian Council in England, led by **Mihály Károlyi**. After returning to Hungary, Ignotus accepted the post of press attaché in London at the request of the Hungarian Social Democratic Party. He started work in November 1947. Recalled in 1949, despite warnings, Ignotus returned to Hungary because his father was dying. He was arrested and sentenced to long-term imprisonment on trumped-up charges of spying.

At the end of March 1956 Ignotus was released. On 16 September 1956, at a general meeting of the Union of Hungarian Writers, he was elected a member of its presidium. On 1 November 1956, along with eight other writers, Ignotus signed a manifesto denouncing sporadic street lynchings and defending the moral purity of the revolution. After the suppression of the revolution on 4 November, he again left Hungary. Ignotus greatly contributed to the creation of a forum for the literature of Hungarian émigrés. Until 1962 he was editor-in-chief of *Irodalmi Újság*, a literary periodical published in London, and was in charge of the work of the Union of Hungarian Writers Abroad until its dissolution. In 1964 Ignotus published his prison memoirs, *Fogságban* (In confinement) and in 1972, *Hungary*, a short account of its recent history. (JT)

Sources: *Magyar Nagylexikon*, vol. 9 (Budapest, 1999); *A magyar forradalom és szabadságharc enciklopédiája* (Budapest, 1999).

IHNATOUSKI Usevalad (19 April 1881, Takary, Kamenets County–4 February 1931, Minsk), Belorussian historian and social and political activist. The son of a teacher, in 1911 Ihnatouski graduated from the University of Dorpat (Tartu). In June 1914 he became a member of the Council of the Belorussian Social Democratic Hramada, and in 1918, a member of the Central Committee (CC) of the Belorussian Party of Socialist Revolutionaries. After the occupation of Belorussia by the Polish Army Ihnatouski founded a Belorussian Communist organization. Admitted to the Russian Communist Party (Bolsheviks) in 1920, he became commissar of education of the Belorussian Soviet Socialist Republic (BSSR). Between 1926

and 1928 he was president of the Institute of Belorussian Culture (Inbelkult). From December 1928 he served as president of the Belorussian Academy of Sciences (BAS) and director of the Institute of History of the BAS. From 1922 to 1930 he was a member of the Central Executive Committee of the BSSR, and in 1924–26, head of the Department of Agitation and Propaganda of the CC of the Communist Party (CP) of Belorussia. He carried out the mission assigned to him by Soviet propaganda, which involved information activities needed to secure the return of Belorussian exiles to the BSSR.

Ihnatouski greatly contributed to the creation of Belorussian higher education and to the revival of Belorussian culture. In 1915 he founded a cultural and political society called Nash Kray (Our Country). In 1919 he published *Krotki narys historii Bialorusi* (An outline of Belorussian history). The year 1925 saw the publication of a history of Belorussia in the nineteenth and early twentieth centuries; it described the territory, population, economy, and history of the country as seen from the contemporary Soviet perspective and was co-authored by I. Smolich and **Arkad Smolich**. In 1928 Ihnatouski published *1863 rok na Białarusi* (The year 1863 in Belorussia). When in 1929 the Soviet authorities launched a campaign against Belorussian "nationalism" within the party, Ihnatouski attempted to defend the cultural autonomy of the republic; consequently he became a target of attacks. During a brutal propaganda campaign in 1930 he was accused of "national opportunism." On 30 November 1930 he wrote a letter to the CC of the CP of Belorussia in which he attempted to explain that he was not a "nationalist" but a "true Communist," and he asked for a chance to continue his work in the BAS. However, on 22 January 1931, labeled a "leader of the national democratic counterrevolution" and a "kulak agent," he was expelled from the party and dismissed from the post of director of the BAS. Fearing arrest, Ihnatouski committed suicide. His works were burned -and recycled. (AS/SA)

Sources: *Belarus: Entsyklapedychny davednik* (Minsk, 1995); *Skarynich: Rochnik literaturna-navukovy* (Moscow, Minsk, and Smolensk, 1997); Nicholas P. Vakar, *Belorussia: The Making of a Nation* (Cambridge, Mass., 1956); Vitaut Kipel and Zora Kipel, eds., *Byelorussian Statehood* (New York, 1988); Rainer Lindner, *Historiker und Herrschaft: Nationsbildung und Geschichtspolitik in Weissrussland im 19. und 20. Jahrhundert* (Munich, 1999).

ILIESCU Ion (3 March 1930, Oltenița), Romanian Communist activist and post-Communist politician, president of Romania. In the 1940s Iliescu studied in Bucharest. He joined the Communist Party of Romania in 1944. In 1948 he co-founded the Union of High School Student Unions of Romania. In 1955 he graduated in electrical engineering from the Polytechnic Institute in Bucharest and the Power Engineering Institute in Moscow, where he met Mikhail Gorbachev. Upon his return to Romania, Iliescu started working at the Research and Design Institute of Power Engineering in Bucharest, dealing with water power plants and the economy. In 1956 he co-founded the Union of Student Unions of Romania. In the 1960s he represented Romanian students in international student organizations. In 1967 he became first secretary of the Communist Youth Union and minister for youth questions in the government of **Ion Maurer**, promoting the nationalist line of **Nicolae Ceauşescu**. In 1968 he became an MP, and in 1971, a member of the Central Committee (CC) of the Romanian Communist Party (RCP). Half a year later he entered into conflict with Ceauşescu because he opposed the so-called cultural revolution. Accused of "intellectual deviation" and deprived of all functions except for his CC membership, Iliescu was sent to Timişoara, where he was party secretary until 1974. In 1974–79 he was party secretary in Iaşi. Gradually sidelined, in 1979–84 he presided over the National Council of Water Resources, and from 1984 he was director of a technical press. In 1989 he belonged to the group of Communist activists dismissed by Ceauşescu and opposing his policies; they were probably supported by Gorbachev as an alternative leadership for Romania.

After the Timişoara riots, on 22 December 1989 Iliescu took the lead of the Council of the National Salvation Front (Frontul Salvării Naţionale [NSF]), which arrested, sentenced to death, and executed Ceauşescu and his wife on 25 December 1989. In February 1990 Iliescu became head of the Provisional Council of National Unity (Consiliul Provizoriu de Uniune Naţionala), and in May 1990 he was elected president for a two-year term. He relied on the former Communist apparatus and the political police, Securitate, and he slowed down market reforms. In December 1992 he was reelected president, formally resigning from the leadership and membership of the NSF, which, after a split and the departure of its liberal and anti-Communist activists, changed its name to the Democratic National Salvation Front (Frontul Democrat Salvări Naţionale) in 1992 and to the Party of Social Democracy in Romania (Partidul Democraţiei Sociale din România [PSDR]) in 1993. In 1992–96 market reforms were slowly introduced, but Iliescu and the PSDR-based government were reluctant to integrate the country within the European Union and NATO. Until 1995 Iliescu and the PSDR cooperated with the extreme nationalists.

After the lost parliamentary and presidential elections of November and December 1996, Iliescu became chairman of the PSDR and a senator. Owing to popular discontent with the center-right governments, in December 2000 Iliescu again won the presidency. Although in 1999 he and his party had criticized the NATO air raids on Yugoslavia, after the elections Iliescu spoke in favor of Romania's entry into the European Union and NATO. Both Iliescu and his party gradually evolved toward a West European-style social democracy. Iliescu published *Probleme globale: Creativitate* (Global problems: Creativity; 1990); *Revoluţie şi reformă* (Revolution and reform; 1993); *România în Europa şi in lumne* (Romania in Europe and in the world; 1994); and *Momente de istorie* (Historical moments; vol. 1, 1995; vols. 2 and 3, 1996). (LW)

Sources: *Dictionar Enciclopedic* (Bucharest, 1999); Andrei Codrescu, *The Hole in the Flag* (New York, 1991); Daniel N. Nelson, ed., *Romania after Tyranny* (Boulder, Colo., 1992); *Personalităţi politice, publice* (Bucharest, 1994); Józef Darski, *Rumunia: Historia, współczesność, konflikty narodowe* (Warsaw, 1994); Tom Gallagher, *Romania after Ceausescu* (Edinburgh, 1995); Costin Scorpan, *Istoria României: Enciclopedie* (Bucharest, 1997); Ion Alexandrescu, Ion Bulei, Ion Mamina, and Ioan Scurtu, *Enciclopedia de istorie României* (Bucharest, 2000); http://members.tripod.com; www.cidob.org/bios; www.rferl.org/nca.

ILLYÉS Gyula (2 November 1902, Felsőrácegrespuszta–15 April 1983, Budapest), Hungarian poet and writer. The son of a peasant who worked as a mechanic on a manor, between 1918 and 1919 Illyés took part in the leftist movement of students and young workers. In the autumn of 1920 he enrolled in the university in Budapest. Fearing arrest, at the end of that year he emigrated to France, where, among other things, he worked in a book bindery, was involved in a trade union movement of Hungarian émigrés, and was active in workers' educational circles. For some time he studied at the Sorbonne. After an amnesty, in 1926 he returned to Hungary and got a clerical job in Budapest. From 1927 he worked in an insurance company, and in 1938 he became an officer in the National Bank of Hungary. Initially, Illyés wrote for *Dokumentum* and *Munka*, periodicals founded and edited by *Lajos Kassák*. He later also published in *Nyugat*, a periodical of the Hungarian avant garde. Illyés made his literary debut with a volume of poems in 1928. At the beginning of the 1930s he was already a recognized writer and received the Baumgarten Prize for best poet of the year four times. In 1934 Illyés attended a congress of Soviet writers in Moscow, and as a result, he wrote a book about Russia (1934). His best prose works from that period include *Puszták népe* (People of the Puszta 1967; 1936) and a collection of essays, *Magyarok* (The Hungarians; 1938).

In 1937 Illyés was the leading figure of the "peasant writers' movement" and one of the founders of the leftist March Front. Beginning in 1941 he edited the literary weekly *Magyar Csillag.* After Germany occupied Hungary in March 1944, Illyés went into hiding in the countryside. In 1945 he was elected to the parliament on behalf of the National Peasant Party (NPP), and until 1946 he was one of the NPP leaders. From 1946 to 1949 he edited a literary periodical, *Válasz.* In 1946 the Hungarian People's Educational Institute was established on his initiative, and Illyés became its first president. In 1945 he became a member of the Hungarian Academy of Sciences but was expelled for political reasons in 1949. He was removed from public life, and his works were not published. It was not until 1954, under the premiership of **Imre Nagy**, that Illyés became a member of the National Council of the reorganized Hungarian Patriotic Front. In September 1956 he again joined the leadership of the Hungarian Writers' Union (HWU). During the 1956 revolution he took part in the revival of the NPP. On 2 September 1956 the weekly *Irodalmi Újság* published *Egy mondat a zsarnokságról* (A sentence about tyranny), a poem Illyés wrote in 1950, which depicted the essence of Stalinism under **Mátyás Rákosi**. The poem could not be republished officially until 1986. On 10 November 1956, along with **Tibor Déry**, **István Örkény**, and others, Illyés asked for political asylum in the Polish Embassy in Budapest. They were given temporary refuge, but a few hours later they all left the embassy building. After the suppression of the revolution Illyés did not write for years.

A 1958 resolution of the CC of the Hungarian Socialist Workers' Party on "peasant writers" also denounced the stance of Illyés. Despite this, however, in 1959 Illyés joined the HWU, which was reorganized after the revolution. In the 1950s and 1960s Illyés enriched Hungarian literature with numerous historical dramas. He was one of the most respected writers of the **János Kádár** period. The novels *Kháron ladikján* (1969; Charon's Ferry, 2000) and *Ebéd a kastélyban* (Dinner at the palace; 1962) are his best works of that period. In the late 1970s and early 1980s Illyés supported the newly formed opposition and regularly stood up in the defense of Hungarians living in neighboring countries. *Szellem és erószak* (Spirit and violence), his collected essays on the subject, was banned from publication, allegedly to protect "Hungarian international interests." In 1987 Illyés published *Teremteni: Összegyűjtött versek, 1946–1968* (Memoirs and notes, 1946–68). English publications of his works include *Selected Poems* (1971) and *What You Have Almost Forgotten: Selected Poems of Gyula Illyés* (1999). (JT)

Sources: *Magyar Életrajzi Lexikon*, vol. 3 (Budapest, 1994); *Magyar Nagylexikon*, vol. 9 (Budapest, 1999); *Magyarország 1944–1956*, CD-ROM (Budapest, 2001); Thomas Kabedebo and Paul Tabori, eds., *A Tribute to Gyula Illyes* (Washington, D.C., 1968); Paul Ignotus, *Hungary* (London, 1972); Miklós Béládi, *Illyés Gyula* (Budapest, 1987); György Litván, ed., *Rewolucja węgierska 1956 roku* (Warsaw, 1996); Steven Bela Vardy, *Historical Dictionary of Hungary* (Lanham, Md., 1997).

ILVES Toomas Hendrik (23 December 1953, Stockholm), Estonian politician. Ilves graduated in psychology from Columbia University in New York in 1976, and then he worked in the United States as a teacher of Estonian and English. In 1984–88 he was an analyst in Radio Free Europe (RFE), and from 1988 to 1993 he was head of the RFE Estonian Section. From 1993 he worked in the diplomatic service of Estonia. In 1993–96 Ilves was ambassador to the United States, also accredited in Canada and Mexico. From March 1997 to October 1998 he was minister of foreign affairs, and then he became director of the North Atlantic Institute. He headed Estonian diplomacy again in the government of **Mart Laar** (March 1999–March 2002). In 1998 he founded the (liberal conservative) Estonian People's Party and won a parliamentary seat on its behalf in the elections of March 1999. After the party's merger with the Party of Moderates, in November 1999 Ilves became deputy chairman of the People's Party Moderates (Rahvaerakond Mõõdukad [PPM]). In view of the shift of the constituency toward the right in 1999–2001, Ilves gained influence in the party, which had been center-left before. He enjoyed high social ratings, and in 2001 he became PPM chairman. As head of diplomacy, he consistently led Estonia toward the European Union and NATO. At the end of his term he managed to draw Estonia closer to these goals, both through the signing of the Baltic Charter by the American, Estonian, Latvian, and Lithuanian presidents, and through American support for the modernization of the Estonian Army. He also attempted to approach some of the former Soviet republics, but he was rather skeptical about a closer relationship with Latvia and Lithuania. His policy toward Russia, which opposed Estonia's entry into NATO, was additionally complicated by his support for the independence of Chechnya. In view of the breakup of the ruling center-right coalition, in January 2002 Ilves resigned from his position and went into the opposition. In June 2004 he was elected a member of the European Parliament. (AG)

Sources: *Eesti Entsuklopeedia*, vol. 14 (Tallinn, 2000); *Eastern Europe and the Commonwealth of Independent States 1999* (London, 1999); Mel Huang, "And the Winner Is . . . ," *Central European Review*, 1999, no. 24; Mel Huang, "Right-Wing Socialists," *Central European Review*, 1999, no. 37; Mel Huang, "Does Estonia Have a Left?" *Central European Review*, 2000, no. 13.

IMRÉDY Béla (29 December 1891, Budapest–28 February 1946, Budapest), Hungarian economist and right-wing politician. Imrédy came from a family of German origin that had gained Hungarian nobility. His father was vice-president and deputy director of the National Small Landowners' Credit Office. After earning a doctorate in law in 1913, Imrédy began a career as a government official. From August 1914 he served as a second lieutenant in the reserves and later as first lieutenant. Demobilized in 1918, he passed his exams in finance, and in 1919 he began working in the Ministry of Finance. In 1922 he left the government administration and became secretary of the Union of Savings Associations and Banks. In 1924 he was made secretary general of this union. From 1926 he served as deputy director of the National Bank of Hungary, becoming its director in 1928. As an internationally recognized expert in finance, Imrédy served his country as finance minister in the government of **Gyula Gömbös** (October 1932–January 1935), which aimed at developing close ties with Hitler. Imrédy was in charge of restructuring the agricultural debt and protecting peasant farms. Between January 1935 and May 1938 he was president of the National Bank of Hungary.

In 1936 Imrédy was elected president of the ruling Party of National Unity (Magyar Egység Pártja). In March 1938 he became minister of the economy without portfolio, a position created especially for him, and he was in charge of the Győr investment program, aimed at an intensive development of the Hungarian Army. The program, initiated under prime minister **Kálmán Darányi**, had been prepared under Imrédy's leadership. On 13 May 1938 Regent **Miklós Horthy** appointed Imrédy prime minister. At the beginning of his rule, Imrédy followed the policy laid down by conservative circles. In May 1938 he oversaw the parliament's passage of the first so-called Jewish Law, which restricted the rights of the Hungarian Jews. At the same time, however, he took measures aimed at limiting the activities of the Arrow Cross Party, as well as those of the Social Democratic movement. In the spirit of a peaceful revision of the 1920 Treaty of Trianon, Imrédy sought an agreement with the Little Entente, and at the end of August he rejected a proposal by Hitler that promised the reincorporation of Slovakia into Hungary in exchange for Hungarian involvement in military actions against Czechoslovakia. Following the First Vienna Award (2 November 1938), under which Hungary regained some of the territories it had lost after the Treaty of Trianon, Imrédy developed an uncritical pro-German attitude and dictatorial leanings. In October 1938 he tried to rule by decree, but the Council of Ministers resisted his pressure. At the end of November 1938 over sixty people left his party, and the parliament voted against the prime minister. However, Horthy, who feared the discontent of Germany

and the extreme right, again entrusted Imrédy with the mission of forming a government. Imrédy allowed for the creation of the Volksbund, a so-called people's union of Germans in Hungary that sympathized with Hitler, and he began preparing a second anti-Jewish law based upon racial principles. This law was adopted by Imrédy's cabinet in May. In January 1939 Imrédy's government joined the anti-Comintern Pact.

The parliamentary opposition, in the shape of a so-called front for the defense of the constitution, united in an effort to depose Imrédy, and when it was disclosed that one of Imrédy's great-grandmothers was a Jew, he was forced to resign (16 February 1939). Seeking to regain power, he moved closer to the extreme right. In October 1940 Imrédy effected a split in the ruling party, which he represented as a member of parliament, and formed his own Party of Hungarian Renewal (Magyar Megújulás Pártja). This party was more moderate than the Arrow Cross Party but still had a Fascist character. After the occupation of Hungary by the German Army in March 1944, the Germans wanted to make Imrédy prime minister, but Horthy resisted the pressure. From the end of May until August 1944 Imrédy served as minister without portfolio for economic affairs in the pro-German government of General **Döme Sztójay**. Owing to a conflict with the Hungary-based command of the SS (*Schutzstaffeln*) over the destination of Jewish property, Imrédy resigned from the government. He finally joined the extreme right-wing National Union of Legislators. In the spring of 1945, following **Ferenc Szálasi**, Imrédy went to Germany. He was arrested by American authorities and handed over to the Hungarians in October. On 23 November 1945 Imrédy was sentenced to death for war crimes by the People's Tribunal in Budapest, and he was executed. (JT)

Sources: Miklos Horthy, *Memoirs* (New York, 1954); *Az Imrédy-per; a vád, a vallomások és az ítélet* (Budapest, 1945); *Magyar Nagylexikon*, vol. 9 (Budapest, 1999); *A magyar forradalom és szabadságharc enciklopédiája* (Budapest, 1999).

INCULEȚ Ion (5 April 1884, Rezeni, Bessarabia–15 August 1940, Bucharest), Romanian politician from Bessarabia. In 1902–8 Inculeț studied theology in Kishinev (Chişinău) and mathematics at the university in Yuryev in Russia. He began lecturing in mathematics at the university in St. Petersburg in 1909, becoming *privatdozent* in 1910. He was active during the February 1917 revolution, joining the Petrograd Soviet of Workers', Peasants', and Soldiers' Deputies, where he worked with Aleksandr Kerensky. Politically he was increasingly drawn to the Socialist revolutionaries. In August 1917, Kerensky sent Inculeț to Bessarabia as a representative of the Provisional Government. After the Bolshevik Revolution, on 4 December 1917, Inculeț became head of the Bessarabian National Council (Sfatul Țării), which was dominated by Romanians and which sought to separate Bessarabia from Russia and incorporate it into the Old Kingdom of Romania. On 15 December 1917 in Kishinev, the National Council proclaimed the autonomy of the Moldavian province between the Prut and Dniester Rivers within a federal Russia. When the Bolsheviks invaded Kiev in January 1918, Inculeț called for support from the Romanian Army. The Romanian offensive pushed the Bolsheviks eastward; thus, on 8 February 1918 the council proclaimed an independent Moldavian Republic, and in April of that year, with a majority of Romanian votes, the council voted for union with Romania. This union became possible after Austro-Hungarian troops were pushed out of the greater part of the Old Kingdom. On 9 December 1918 the council finally decided to incorporate Bessarabia into Romania, without granting Bessarabia autonomous rights. From 1918 to 1940 Inculeț served as a member of parliament in Bucharest. Between April 1918 and February 1919; from September to December 1919; between March and May 1920; and from January 1922 to March 1926 he was minister for Bessarabia in successive Romanian governments. Between June 1926 and November 1928 he was minister of health; from November 1933 to August 1936, minister of interior; and then until November 1937, deputy prime minister. As a member of the Royal Council, Inculeț had good relations with King **Charles II**. (FA/WR)

Sources: R. W. Seton-Watson, *A History of the Romanians* (Hamden, CT, 1963); Șerban N. Ionescu, *Who Was Who in Twentieth Century Romania* (Boulder, Colo., 1994); Keith Hitchins, *Rumania 1866–1947* (Oxford, 1994).

INDRA Alois (17 March 1921, Medzev, near Košice–2 August 1990, Prague), Czechoslovak Communist activist. Before the war Indra worked as a railway clerk. In 1937 he joined the Communist Party of Czechoslovakia (CPC), and in the 1950s he was active in the executive of the party in Źlin, which at that time was renamed Gottwaldov. Indra rose to the position of first secretary of the provincial committee. In 1962–63 he headed the State Planning Committee, and from April 1968 he occupied the post of minister of transport. From 1962 to 1989 he was a member of the Central Committee (CC) of the CPC, attaining the highest party posts. From 1964 he was a deputy to the National Assembly. Indra owed his rise mainly to his extremely doctrinal and conservative views, as well as to his support of the Soviet intervention in August 1968. He and several other "hard-core" members of the party executive (e.g., **Vasil Bil'ak**) submitted a letter

to Leonid Brezhnev in which they called for the Soviet intervention in Czechoslovakia. Indra was to be one of the key figures in the "revolutionary government of workers and peasants," which was to be formed after the invasion of Czechoslovakia by the Warsaw Pact forces. However, President **Ludvik Svoboda** did not appoint this government. From 23 to 26 August 1968 Indra participated in talks in Moscow, representing an extremely pro-Moscow stance. From 1968 he was secretary of the CC, and from 1971, a member of the Presidium of the CC of the CPC. In 1971–89 he served as president of the Federal Assembly. As a member of the highest party and state authorities, Indra was an avowed supporter of the "normalization" after the Soviet intervention; therefore he also enjoyed the great trust of the Kremlin. He withdrew from political life after being deprived of all his posts at a special plenum of the CC of the CPC that was assembled under the pressure of anti-Communist demonstrations at the end of November 1989. On 17 February 1990 Indra was expelled from the party. (PU)

Sources: *ČBS*; *Kdo byl kdo v našich dějinách ve 20. století*, vol. 1 (Prague, 1998); *Who's Who in the Socialist Countries of Europe*, vol. 2 (Munich, London, and Paris, 1989); *Českoslovenští politici: 1918–1991* (Prague, 1991); Gordon H. Skilling, *Czechoslovakia's Interrupted Revolution* (Princeton, 1976); Vladimir V. Kusin, *From Dubcek to Charter 77: A Study of "Normalization" in Czechoslovakia, 1968–1978* (New York, 1978).

INGR Jan Sergej (2 September 1894, Vlkoš–17 June 1956, Paris), Czech general. Ingr graduated form a high school in Kiev. In 1914 he volunteered for the Austro-Hungarian Army, and in October 1915 he was taken captive by the Russians. In May 1916 he joined a Serbian volunteer division, and in January 1917, the Czechoslovak Legion in Russia. He later traveled via Murmansk to Great Britain and France to join a military unit that was being formed there. As a member of this unit, he took part in the fighting on the western front, and he returned with this unit to Czechoslovakia. In 1919 Ingr participated in the Polish-Czechoslovak conflict in Teschen Silesia and in the struggle against the Hungarian Red Army in Slovakia. After the end of the war he joined the Czechoslovak Army. He took a general staff course in Prague and later completed studies at the Military College in Paris. In 1923 Ingr became chief of the operations unit of the military district command in Prague, and in 1929 he was promoted to a similar position in the General Staff. In 1931 he became commander of a regiment, in 1934 of a brigade, and in 1935 of a division. In 1934 he was promoted to brigadier general and in 1938 to major general. In 1936 he became deputy commander of the Third Corps in Brno, and at the time of mobilization in 1938 he was its commander.

Ingr was against the Munich capitulation, and after the partition of Czechoslovakia he was in charge of the Defense of the Nation, a resistance organization in Moravia. In the summer of 1939 he traveled via Poland to France, where he became a member of the Czechoslovak National Committee and chief of the Military Command, which organized the formation of a Czechoslovak army in France. After the capitulation of France, Ingr managed to get to Great Britain, where between July 1940 and September 1944 he served as defense minister in the Czechoslovak government-in-exile. In September 1944 he became chief of the General Staff, which was also formally in charge of the Czechoslovak units in the USSR. As chief of staff, Ingr got in touch with General **Heliodor Píka**, head of the military mission in the USSR, in order to establish cooperation between the Red Army and the insurgents in Slovakia. However, the Soviet command allowed the uprising to bleed out. In April 1945, under Soviet pressure, Ingr was dismissed as chief of staff, and a month later, after returning to Prague, he was not allowed to continue serving in the army for political reasons. In October 1947, on the motion of President **Edvard Beneš**, Ingr was appointed ambassador to Holland. After the coup of February 1948 he resigned his post and remained in exile. He initially lived in Great Britain and later in the United States, where he worked with General **František Moravec**. (PU)

Sources: *ČBS*; *Svaz československých důstojnikův v exilu* (Washington, D.C., 1957); *Českoslovenští politici: 1918–1991* (Prague, 1991); *Kdo byl kdo v našich dějinach ve 20. stoleti*, vol. 2 (Prague, 1998); *Politická elita meziválečného Československa 1918–1938: Kdo byl kdo za prvni republiky* (Prague, 1998).

IONESCO Eugene [originally Ionescu] (13 November 1909, Slatina–28 March 1994, Paris), French playwright of Romanian descent. Ionesco's mother was a French Jew, and his father was Romanian. He spent his childhood in Paris. In 1922 he went to Romania, where until 1926 he lived with his father, who in the meantime had divorced his mother. From 1926 Ionesco lived with his mother, who moved to Bucharest. In 1928 he graduated from high school in Craiova and made his literary debut as a poet in the daily *Bilete de papagal*. In 1929–33 he studied Romance languages and literature at the University of Bucharest. From 1930 to 1938 he published vanguard articles and essays with anti-totalitarian overtones in such periodicals as *Critică*, *Universul Literar*, *Facla*, *Rampa*, *Parerile Libere*, and *Vremea*. In 1934 he published a series of provocative articles titled *Nu* (No), in which he criticized the most outstanding Romanian writers of that time. He worked as a teacher of French in Cernavodă, and then, until 1938, he was a white-collar worker in the

Ministry of Education, responsible for foreign relations. In 1938 he received a government scholarship and left for doctoral studies in Paris. In 1939 he returned to Romania and taught French.

In 1942 Ionesco left for France again. He lived in Marseilles and then in Vichy, where in 1943–44 he was the Romanian cultural attaché to the Vichy government. In 1945 he moved to Paris. Initially he earned his living by translating. He was interested in Surrealism, the literature of the absurd, and "anti-prose." At the end of the 1940s he began to write plays in French, becoming a pioneer of the theater of the absurd. In 1949 he wrote *La cantatrice chauve* (The Bald Prima-Donna; 1966), and in 1951, *La leçon* (The lesson), which brought him world fame. The most famous of his play include the following: *Les chaises* (1952; Chairs, 1973); *Le rhinocéros* (1959; Rhinoceros, 1960); *La soif et la faim* (1966; Hunger and Thirst, 1971); *Macbett* (1972); *L'homme aux valises* (1975; Man with Bags, 1977); and *Thème et variations; ou, Voyages chez les morts* (Theme and variations, or journeys among the dead; 1980). Ionesco rejected the conventions of classical theater and created the theater of the situation, crossing the limits of reality into nightmare. In his plays he opposed totalitarian regimes. At the same time he was convinced of the paradox and absurdity of human existence. He showed how language was used unthinkingly and revealed its secrets. Thence apparently simple things turned out to be complicated and have many meanings. In his works contemporary man was fated to suffer depersonalization and dehumanization. From 1970 Ionesco was a member of the Académie Française. He was awarded the Legion of Honor and many other literary and theater honors. He received a number of honorary doctorates in the United States and Europe. In France he maintained sporadic contacts with Romanian émigrés. His friendship with **Mircea Eliade** did not survive because of the latter's sympathy for the Fascist Iron Guard. Until 1989 Ionesco's plays were banned by the Communist regime in Romania. Ionesco authored the memoirs *Present Past, Past Present* (1972). (LW)

Sources: Leonard S. Klein, *Encyclopedia of World Literature in the Twentieth Century* (New York, 1982); *Dictionar Enciclopedic*, vol. 3 (Bucharest, 1999); Philippe Sénart, *Ionesco* (Paris, 1966); Ronald Hayman, *Eugene Ionesco* (London, 1972); Richard Coe, *Eugene Ionesco* (Ann Arbor, 1979); Deborah Gaensbauer, *Eugene Ionesco* (New York, 1996); Harold Bloom, ed., *Eugene Ionesco* (Philadelphia, 2003); www.imagi-nation.com; www.cpcug.org.

IONESCU Dumitru (Take) (25 October 1858, Ploieşti–4 July 1922, Rome), Romanian politician. Ionescu attended Sfântul-Sava High School in Bucharest, later received a bachelor's degree from Bucharest University, and in 1881 earned a Ph.D. in law from the Sorbonne in Paris. Later he worked as a journalist and was a member of the Liberal Party. Elected an MP in 1884, in 1889 he switched over to the Conservative Party and contributed to the periodicals *La liberté roumaine* and *Timpul*. Ionescu won recognition as an outstanding lawyer and a gifted speaker; he was called "Guriţa de Aur" (the Golden Tongue). From December 1891 to October 1895 Ionescu served as minister of culture, implementing reforms in education. In the government of **Gheorghe Grigore Cantacuzino**, he played the role of gray eminence, serving as minister of justice from April 1899 to January 1900 and as minister of finance until July 1900. Ionescu struggled with the effects of bad harvests, as well as with the repercussions of the world economic crisis. He again held the post of minister of finance between 1904 and 1907 in the subsequent government of Cantacuzino, which resigned as the result of a peasant uprising in Moldavia. After the government of **Dimitrie Sturdza** brutally suppressed that uprising, Ionescu left the Conservative Party and on 16 February 1908 founded his own Conservative Democratic Party. In October 1912 he became minister of interior and played an important role in negotiations that led to the Bucharest Peace Treaty, which granted southern Dobrudja to Romania.

After the outbreak of World War I Ionescu advocated military neutrality. However, he co-formed National Action (Acţiunea Naţională) and vigorously worked for the incorporation of Transylvania and Bessarabia into Romania. When Romania entered the war on the side of the Entente, Ionescu became aligned with the liberals. In December 1916 he became minister without portfolio, and in July 1917 deputy prime minister, in the government of **Ion I.C. Brațianu**, which was evacuated to Iaşi. When peace negotiations with the Central Powers began in the spring of 1918, Ionescu resigned and went to Paris, where he edited the periodical *La Roumanie* and from 3 October 1918 presided over the National Council for Romanian Union (Consiliul Naţional al Unităţii Române) and led a vigorous campaign for the Romanian cause. Thanks to his contacts, during the Paris Peace Conference Ionescu contributed to the promotion of Romanian territorial claims. From June 1920 to December 1921 he served as minister of foreign affairs in the government of General **Alexandru Averescu**, concluding treaties on mutual assistance with Poland in March 1921, Czechoslovakia in April, and Yugoslavia in June 1921. The treaties with Czechoslovakia and Yugoslavia laid the foundations for the Little Entente. From 17 December 1921 to 19 January 1921 Ionescu served as prime minister and minister of finance, but he resigned after the parliament passed a vote of no confidence. Soon afterwards he died. Ionescu

authored, among other works, *The Origins of the War; the Testimony of a Witness* (1917), *Souvenirs* (1919), and *Some Personal Impressions* (1922). (WR)

Sources: *Biographisches Lexikon*, vol. 2; Constantin Xeni, *Take Ionescu (1858–1922)* (Bucharest, 1933); Marie, Queen of Romania, *The Story of My Life*, vols. 1–2; (New York, 1934); Henri Prost, *Destin de la Roumanie 1918–1954* (Paris, 1954); Vasile Alexandrescu, *Romania in World War I* (Bucharest, 1985); Mircea Muşat and Ion Ardeleanu, *România dupa Marea Unire*, vols. 1–2 (Bucharest, 1986); Emile Turdeanu, *Modern Romania: The Achievement of National Unity, 1914–1920* (Los Angeles, 1988); Şerban N. Ionescu, *Who Was Who in Twentieth Century Romania* (Boulder, Colo., 1994).

IONESCU NICOLAE (Nae) (16 July 1890, Brăila–15 March 1940, Bucharest), Romanian philosopher and pundit. Ionescu attended Nicolae Bălcescu High School in Brăila. Subsequently, he studied philosophy in Bucharest, Vienna, and Munich, where he received a Ph.D. in 1919. After his return to Romania in 1920 he became a professor, and he lectured in the history of philosophy, logic, and metaphysics at Bucharest University. His right-wing philosophical views quickly extended to politics and religion. In his opinion, the factors that guaranteed the maintenance of the identity, independence, and well-being of Romania were nationalism, monarchy, and Orthodoxy, which he considered the most essential qualities of the "Romanian national spirit." Ionescu created an intellectual system in which philosophy was not only an act of reason, but also an act of volition and should be lived through and realized in everyday existence, art, and politics. He rejected modernism, popular in the West, advocating instead a return to traditional and specifically Romanian values. In 1924–29 Ionescu co-founded and was editor-in-chief of a radical, right-wing Orthodox magazine, *Cuvântul*, and from 1929 to 1934 and in 1938 he was its director.

Backing nationalism and authoritarian rule and at the same time opposing parliamentarian democracy, Ionescu supported the return to the throne of King **Charles II** in 1930, hoping that the latter would implement his illiberal ideas. In 1933, however, when the king became close to the liberals, Ionescu turned against him, taking sides with the Fascist Iron Guard (Gărdia de Fier [IG]) and becoming one of its ideologues. In 1933, Ionescu was arrested for a short time and charged with moral co-responsibility for the murder of the liberal prime minister, **Ion G. Duca**, who was killed by Iron Guard members. In 1938, when the king dissolved all political parties and when bloody persecutions of Iron Guard members and sympathizers began, Ionescu was sent to a labor camp in Miercurea Ciuc. After his release in 1939, he was kept under house arrest. In 1940 he was probably poisoned by a royal agent who was his jailer. As a lecturer and pundit, Ionescu exerted a great influence on the views of Romanian elites in the 1930s. He authored books such as *Doctrinele partidelor politice: Sindicalism* (Doctrines of political parties: Syndicalism; 1924); *Fenomenul Legionar* (The phenomenon of the Legion; 1940); and *Istoria logicei* (History of logic; 1941). Ionescu's students include **Mircea Eliade, Emil Cioran, Constantin Noica**, and Mircea Vulcănescu. (LW)

Sources: *Dictionar Enciclopedic*, vol. 3 (Bucharest, 1999); Vlad Georgescu, *Istoria Românilor de la origini pînă în zilele noastre* (Oakland, 1984); Dan Ciachir, *Gînduri despre Nae Ionescu* (Iaşi, 1994); Józef Darski, *Rumunia: Historia, współczesność, konflikty narodowe* (Warsaw, 1995); Krzysztof Dach and Tadeusz Dubicki, *Żelazny Legion Michała Archanioła* (Warsaw, 1996); Isabela Vasiliu-Scrabu, *Metafisica lui Nea Ionescu* (Slobozia, 2000); www.miscarea-legionara.org; www.bautz.de.

IONESCU-QUINTUS Mircea (18 March 1917, Kherson, Ukraine), Romanian politician. In 1938 Ionescu-Quintus graduated in law from the University of Bucharest. In 1940–87 he worked as a lawyer in Prahova. During World War II he served in the Romanian Army, advancing to the rank of major. In 1945 he joined the National Liberal Party (Partidul Naţional Liberal [PNL]). After the suppression of all opposition parties, liquidation of the PNL, and arrest or killing of its leaders, Ionescu-Quintus suspended all political activities and worked as a lawyer. After the fall of the **Nicolae Ceauşescu** regime, in early 1990 Ionescu-Quintus joined the restored PNL. In 1990–92 he was its deputy chairman. He was elected MP on its behalf, and in 1990–91 he was deputy speaker of the Lower Chamber. After the resignation of the government of **Petru Roman** in October 1991, the PNL entered the new ruling coalition, and Ionescu-Quintus became minister of justice in the government of **Theodor Stolojan**, holding this position until the parliamentary elections of September 1992. At this time the PNL broke ties with the anti-Communist Democratic Convention of Romania (Convenţia Democratica din România [DCR]). In the 1992 elections the PNL failed to win any parliamentary seats. In 1991–93 Ionescu-Quintus lectured in constitutional law at the University of Ploieşti. In 1993 he assumed the leadership of the PNL, which drew closer to the DCR and joined it in 1994. In 1996 Ionescu-Quintus ran from the DCR lists and won a senator's mandate. As a part of the DCR, the PNL belonged to the ruling coalition. In 1996–99 Ionescu-Quintus was deputy speaker of the Senate, and in 1999–2000, its speaker. In 1997 he was reelected PNL chairman. In 2000 he was reelected senator on behalf of the PNL, which, correct in predicting the defeat of the DCR, ran alone. In 2001 Ionescu-Quintus retired from leading the PNL and was replaced by Valeriu Stoica. (LW)

Sources: Józef Darski, *Rumunia: Historia, współczesność, konflikty narodowe* (Warsaw, 1995); Ion Alexandrescu, Ion Bulei, Ion Mamina, and Ioan Scurtu, *Enciclopedia de istorie României* (Bucharest, 2000); Duncan Light and Daniel Phinnemore, *Post–Communist Romania* (Palgrave, 2001); www.electionworld.org; www.tripod.com; www.romania-on-line.net; www.cdep.ro.

IONIŢA Ion (14 June 1924, Matasaru–1987? Bucharest), Romanian general. Ioniţa was a nephew of the Romanian Communist Party (RCP) leader **Nicolae Ceauşescu**. In 1944, he joined a Communist youth organization, and from 1945 he was a member of the RCP, where he made a quick career owing to his family connections. Consequently, he attended a military high school, and then he graduated from the Romanian Military Academy in Bucharest. After his studies, at the beginning of the 1950s, he became deputy head of the Political Board of the army. Until 1966, he was commander of air force and anti-aircraft units. In 1955–65 he was a deputy member of the Central Committee (CC) of the Romanian Workers' Party. From 1961 to 1984, he was an MP. From 1962 he was deputy minister of defense, and from September 1966 to June 1976, minister of defense. In 1965–69 he was a deputy member of the Executive Committee of the RCP CC, and from 1969 to 1984, a member of the RCP CC. From 19 June 1976 to 21 May 1982 Ioniţa was deputy prime minister. It was probably then that he began a clandestine collaboration with Moscow-supported, Ceauşescu-opposing groups within the army, security service, and Communist Party. As a consequence, he lost his positions in 1982. In 1983 he established a conspiracy in the Romanian Army, aimed at overthrowing Ceauşescu; several other generals joined the conspiracy. In 1984, he planned to carry out a coup d'état with the help of a motorized military unit and to take control of the television station during Ceauşescu's visit to West Germany. In the same year, two conspiracy members revealed the plans to Securitate, and Ioniţa was deprived of all his functions except for the military ones. In 1985, Ioniţa and several other Romanian generals made fresh attempts to reestablish contacts with one another and with envoys of the Soviet military intelligence, GRU. This conspiracy was uncovered too. Most of its members were arrested, and Ioniţa was murdered in 1987 under unclear circumstances. (LW)

Sources: *Who's Who in the Socialist Countries of Europe* (Munich, London, and Paris, 1989); Józef Darski, *Rumunia: Historia, współczesność, konflikty narodowe* (Warsaw, 1995); Ion Alexandrescu, Ion Bulei, Ion Mamina, and Ioan Scurtu, *Enciclopedia de istorie României* (Bucharest, 2000).

IORGA Nicolae (17 June 1871, Botoşani–28 November 1940, Bucharest), Romanian historian, writer, poet, and politician. Expelled from a gymnasium in Botoşani, Iorga moved to Iaşi, where he studied history at the university, earning an M.A. degree after only one year of studies. From 1890 to 1892 he studied in Paris, then in Leipzig, where he received a Ph.D. in history (1893). In 1894 he was appointed professor of universal history at the University of Bucharest. In 1890–1900 he belonged to the Social Democratic Party but left it as a result of an ideological evolution. In 1891 he founded the League for the Cultural Unity of All Romanians, which for all Romanians abroad. Iorga was also one of the promoters of the so-called sowers' movement. From 1903 to 1910 he edited *Sămănătorul* (Sower), a periodical devoted to rural issues. In 1908 he founded a people's university at Văleni de Munte. In 1910 he became a member of the Romanian Academy of Sciences. In the same year, along with **Alexandru Cuza**, he founded a nationalist party, the National Democratic Party. In 1914 he co-founded the Southeast European Institute (Institutului de Studii Sud-Est Europene), which still exists today. During World War I Iorga led a campaign for the Entente. In 1918 he played a major role in the Grand National Assembly, which voted for the realization of a Greater Romania.

In 1920 Iorga established and directed the Romanian School at Fontenay-aux-Roses in Paris. He also held lectures at the Sorbonne. In 1920 Cuza broke with Iorga to form a Fascist party, the League of National Christian Defense (1923). In 1924 Iorga held the first Byzantine congress. In 1937 he founded the Institute for Byzantine Studies and the Institute of Universal History. In 1925 he joined the National Peasant Party led by **Iuliu Maniu**, but after one year he left this party to become an independent politician. Iorga supported **Charles II**, who returned from exile to claim the Romanian throne in 1930. From 18 April 1931 to 6 June 1932 Iorga held the post of prime minister in the government based on his National Democratic Party and the National Agrarian Union of **Constantin Argetoianu**. In February 1938 he served briefly in the government of **Miron Cristea**, and between 1938 and 1940 he was the king's adviser. Iorga followed a nationalist doctrine but was against radical methods. His opposition to both the radical left and the radical right led to his assassination by members of the Iron Guard, an ultra-nationalist and Fascist organization.

A prolific writer and publicist, Iorga published over one thousand books and brochures and around twenty-five thousand articles. He published and edited many national periodicals, such as *Neamul românesc*, *Revista istorică*, *Revue Historique Sud-Est-Européen*, and *Floarea darurilor*. He also edited many volumes of historical sources. He was against the subordination of history to one philosophical system. His historiography was dominated by a spiritual element. The five-volume *Geschichte des Osmanischen Reiches* (History of the Ottoman Empire; 1908–13) was his most important work before World War I. Iorga was the author of works of great significance to Romanian history, such as *Studii şi cercetări cu privire la istoria românilor* (Studies and research on the history of Romanians, 41 vols.; 1901–16); *Istoria Bisericii româneşti* (History of the Romanian Orthodox Church, 2 vols.; 1930); *Istoria armatei româneşti* (History of the Romanian Army, 2 vols.; 1929); and *Istoria comerţiului românesc* (History of Romanian trade, 2 vols.; 1925); Iorga integrated Romanian history with world history. From 1935 to 1939 he published a monumental ten-volume work, *Istoria Românilor* (Romanian history). An outstanding specialist in universal history, Iorga published, among other works, studies on the Crusades and works about the history of Byzantium and Venice. He also wrote poems, dramas, and memoirs, and he translated American poetry. The author of numerous syntheses on the history of Romanian and Romance literatures—including *Istoria literaturii româneşti contemporane* (History of contemporary Romanian literature, 2 vols.; 1934) and *Istoria literaturii româneşti* (History of Romanian literature, 3 vols.; 1925–33)—Iorga was also a member of many foreign scholarly societies. (LW)

Sources: *Biographisches Lexikon*, vol. 2; *Dictionar Enciclopedic*, vol. 3 (Bucharest, 1999); Barbu Theodorescu, *Nicolae Iorga* (Bucharest, 1968); Walter Markow, *Nicolae Iorga, 1871–1940: Historiker, Literaturhistoriker, Byzantinist* (Berlin, 1972); William O. Oldson, *The Historical and Nationalist Thought of Nicolae Iorga* (New York, 1973); Halina Mirska-Lasota, *Maly słownik pisarzy rumuńskich* (Warsaw, 1975); Petre Turlea, *Nicolae Iorga în viaţa politica României* (Bucharest, 1991); Costin Scorpan, *Istoria României: Enciclopedie* (Bucharest, 1997); Nicholas Nagy-Talavera, *Nicolae Iorga: A Biography* (Iaşi and Portland, Ore., 1998).

ISĂRESCU Mugur (1 August 1949, Drăgăşani), Romanian politician and financial expert. In 1971 Isărescu graduated from the Department of International Economics of the Academy of Economic Studies (AES) in Bucharest. In 1971–90 he worked in the Institute of World Economy in Bucharest, and from 1975 to 1990 he lectured in finance, monetary policies, and international economics there. Moreover, in 1980–89 he lectured in these fields at the Foreign Ministry, the Popular University in Bucharest, and the University of Iaşi. In 1989 Isărescu received a Ph.D. in economics. After the fall of the **Nicolae Ceauşescu** regime and the takeover by the National Salvation Front (Frontul Sălvarii Naţionale) in December 1989, Isărescu started working in the Foreign Ministry and was sent to the United States. In 1990 he returned to Romania and, thanks to the support of the **Petre Roman** government, he was elected president of the Romanian National Bank. He held this position until the end of 1999, introducing a banking reform compatible with international standards. In 1991 Isărescu was also vice-president of the World Bank. In 1994–96 he lectured at the Western University in Timişoara and at the AES in Bucharest. From 22 December 1999 to 28 December 2000 he was a non-partisan prime minister on behalf of the center-right Democratic Convention of Romania (Convenţia Democratica din România [DCR]), suspending his presidency of the Romanian National Bank. In November 2000 Isărescu ran in the presidential elections as an independent candidate but ended up fourth, with 9.5 percent of the vote, and he returned to the presidency of the central bank. Isărescu authored several books and articles on contemporary Romanian and world economic problems. (LW)

Sources: *Dictionar Enciclopedic*, vol. 3 (Bucharest, 1999); Ion Alexandrescu, Ion Bulei, Ion Mamina, and Ioan Scurtu, *Enciclopedia de istorie României* (Bucharest, 2000); Józef Darski, *Rumunia: Historia, współczesność, konflikty narodowe* (Warsaw, 1995); Tom Gallagher, *Romania after Ceauşescu* (Edinburgh, 1995); Duncan Light and Daniel Phinnemore, *Post–Communist Romania* (New York, 2001); www.mugur.isarescu.ro; www.romania-on-line.net.

IVÁN-KOVÁCS László (18 August 1930, Debrecen–30 December 1957, Budapest), one of the leaders of the Hungarian revolution of 1956. Born into a family of clerks, in 1951 Iván-Kovács graduated from an economic high school but failed to gain admission to a law school. He successfully completed two semesters of extramural studies at the Higher School of Economics. In 1951–53 he worked as a civil servant in the army. On 23 October 1956 he took part in a demonstration in front of the Hungarian Radio building. He gained access to weapons and fought against the Soviet troops invading the capital. On 25 October he joined the Corvin Lane insurgents, becoming commander of that largest group of fighters. Iván-Kovács negotiated the conditions of disarmament with the party leadership. On 29 October a delegation of insurgents was received by **Imre Nagy**, to whom Iván-Kovács presented the demands of the Corvin Lane fighters: the securing of independence for the country, the withdrawal of Soviet troops, abolition of the one-party system, and the creation of a Revolutionary National Guard formed from the insurgents. Although on 1 November he was dismissed as commander, Iván-Kovács remained with the fighters. On 4 November he started a struggle against the Soviet forces, but on that very day he was denounced as a traitor by the Corvin Lane fighters. He was arrested by the insurgents but managed to escape. Holding on to his weapons, he took refuge at his family home in the countryside. In February

1957 he founded an illegal party to defend the ideals of the revolution. Along with his friends, he wrote leaflets and planned to free **Pál Maléter**, assuming that Maléter was on Hungarian territory. Arrested on 12 March 1957, on 22 August of that year Iván-Kovács was sentenced to death for leading a conspiracy against the "people's government." On 27 December 1957 the Supreme Court confirmed the sentence, and three days later he was executed. (JT)

Sources: *Magyar Nagylexikon*, vol. 10 (Budapest, 2000); Attila Szakolczay, *Az 1956-os forradalom és szabadságharc* (Budapest, 2001); György Litván, ed., *Rewolucja węgierska 1956 roku* (Warsaw, 1996).

IVANKA Milan (25 October 1876, Turčiansky Sv. Martin–26 August 1950, Bratislava), Slovak politician and journalist. Born into a landowner's family, Ivanka graduated in law in Budapest. He started his law career in **Matuš Dula**'s office in his hometown. From 1904 he worked in Trnava. At first, he remained under the influence of the conservative center of the Slovak national movement in Turčiansky Sv. Martin, and then he drew closer to the pro-Czech group of the periodical *Hlas*, and in 1906–14 he edited the periodical *Národný hlásnik*. In 1907 Ivanka was elected to the Hungarian parliament in Budapest, but in 1909 he was deprived of the mandate and sentenced to one year in prison for "anti-state" proclamations during the electoral campaign. In numerous publications Ivanka criticized the Magyarization policies of the Hungarian government. His best known work was *Slováci a Maďari* (Slovaks and Hungarians; 1914). During World War I Ivanka cooperated with **Milan Hodža**. In 1918 he joined the Slovak National Council and headed the department of home affairs in the Ministry for Slovak Administration. In 1918–20 and 1929–34 he sat in the Czechoslovak parliament, where he belonged to the Slovak leaders of the Czechoslovak National Democracy (Československa Národná Demokracia). Ivanka opposed the demands for Slovak autonomy and criticized the People's Party of Reverend **Andrej Hlinka**. Ivanka's booklet, *Proti tajnej irredente* (Against secret irredentism; 1928), initiated the proceedings that led to the imprisonment of **Vojtech Tuka**. In 1934 Ivanka gave up his mandate and joined the Agrarian Party. In 1939 he moved to Prague and took part in the Czechoslovak resistance, for which he was imprisoned by the Gestapo in Terezín. After the war he returned to Slovakia, but he retired from politics. (MG)

Sources: *SBS*; *ČBS*; *Kdo byl kdo v našich dějinách ve 20. století*, vol. 1 (Prague, 1998), *Politické strany na Slovensku 1860–1989* (Bratislava, 1992); Marián Hronský, *Boj o Slovensko a Trianon 1918–1920* (Bratislava, 1998).

IVANOUSKI Vatslau (7 June 1880, Lebiodka, near Shchuchyn–7 December 1943, Minsk), Belorussian social and political activist. Ivanouski was one of the five children of Leonard Iwanowski, the owner of Lebiodka estates. His father was a typical *gente Polonus, natione Lituanus* (Pole of Lithuanian nationality). In 1891 the family moved to Warsaw to educate the children. Ivanouski attended the Fifth Classical Gymnasium for boys, graduating in 1899. In Warsaw, the Iwanowski brothers chose different national identities. Jerzy, the eldest, chose Polish nationality and in November 1918 became the first Polish minister of trade and industry; Vatslau identified as a Belorussian, while the youngest, Tadeusz, assumed Lithuanian nationality. In 1904 Ivanouski graduated from St. Petersburg Technological Institute and started working there, first as a research and teaching assistant and, after receiving his doctoral degree, as an assistant professor. Along with **Aleksander Ulasau** and the brothers **Anton** and **Ivan Lutskevich**, in 1902 Ivanouski established the Belorussian Revolutionary Party, later the Belorussian Socialist Hromada. In 1903 he began legal and illegal publishing activities in St. Petersburg. Under the title of the "Belorussian People's Education Group," he published literature that invoked memories of Belorussian history, traditions, and culture. At that time Ivanouski supported organic work among the peasants and privileged education over politics. In 1906 in St. Petersburg he founded an official publishing house, Zahlanie Sontsa i u Nasha Akontsa (The sun will also shine in our window), which promoted the Belorussian national idea. Ivanouski contributed to the periodical *Nasha Niva*. In 1912 he made Wilno (Vilnius) the center of Belorussian publishing, establishing there the largest publishing house, which also dealt with the professional distribution of books.

During World War I Ivanouski founded and was the first head of the Belorussian Relief Committee for War Victims. Arrested by the Bolsheviks, he managed to escape and resumed his journalistic activities. After the proclamation of independence by the Council of the Belorussian People's Republic, Ivanouski became minister of education in the cabinet of Anton Lutskevich. At that time he was in favor of Polish-Belorussian cooperation. He planned the establishment of the Belorussian University in Minsk. He succeeded in establishing the Pedagogical Institute, and from March to October 1920 he was its rector. After the signing of the Treaty of Riga in March 1921, which ended the Polish-Soviet war, Ivanouski withdrew from political life and settled in Warsaw. In the fall of 1922 he became the Chair of Food Fermentation Technology at Warsaw Polytechnic. In 1924 he became associate professor, and in 1935, full professor. In the 1930s he was dean of the

Chemistry Department, head of the Military College, and a member of the senate of the Polytechnic.

In September 1939 Ivanouski left for Wilno (Vilnius), which the Soviets soon handed over to the Lithuanian administration. Thanks to his brother Tadeusz, a zoology professor at Kaunas University, Ivanouski was given the Chair of Chemical Technology at Vilnius University. Both brothers hoped that the German-Soviet conflict would debilitate both countries and allow for the establishment of an independent Belorussia in a loose union with Poland. In that spirit, Ivanouski tried to reach an agreement with the intelligence section of the Polish Union of Armed Struggle (Związek Walki Zbrojnej [ZWZ]) but failed to reach a compromise on the issue of the Polish-Belorussian borders. After the Nazi invasion of the USSR in June 1941, Ivanouski waited for a declaration concerning Belorussia. At the beginning of July 1941 the Germans granted permission only for the reactivation of the Belorussian National Committee, and Ivanouski chaired this committee. In December 1941 the Germans named him mayor of Minsk. He followed the program of Wilhelm Kube, general commissioner for the District of Belorussia, who supported Belorussian nationalism. Ivanouski served as president of the Belorussian Trust Council, established in June 1943, which represented the interests of the Belorussian people to the German authorities, and he was also president of the Belorussian Scientific Society. After the assassination of Kube in October 1943, by pointing out the Soviet assassins, Ivanouski managed to convince the Germans not to persecute the Belorussian people. He also went to Berlin to Kube's funeral. According to the official version, Ivanouski was killed in an assassination arranged by the Soviet underground; this version is more probable than the one stating that the assassination was carried out by supporters of Ivanouski's political rival, **Radaslau Astrouski**. (EM)

Sources: Nicholas P. Vakar, *Belorussia: The Making of a Nation* (Cambridge, Mass., 1956); August Iwański, Sr., *Pamiętniki 1832–1876*; August Iwański, Jr., *Wspomnienia 1881–1939* (Warsaw, 1968); Vitaut Kipel and Zora Kipel, eds., *Byelorussian Statehood* (New York, 1988); Jerzy Turonek, *Białoruś pod okupacją niemiecką* (Wrocław, 1989); Jerzy Turonek, *Wacław Iwanowski i odrodzenie Białorusi* (Warsaw, 1992).

IVANOV Tsveti (24 August 1914, Oriakhovo–23 July 1950, Svishtov), Bulgarian journalist and leftist activist. A member of the Union of Socialist Youth from 1932, Ivanov received a law degree from Sofia University in 1937. He published extensively in the leftist press—for example, in the periodicals *Sotsialisticheska Mladezh* and *Trezva Borba*. Between 1940 and 1944 he was editor and publisher of the Khemus Publishing House. After the Communist coup of September 1944 he declared his support for the Bulgarian Social Democratic Workers' Party. As editor-in-chief of the newspapers Literaturen Front and Svoboden Narod, Ivanov criticized Communist methods of governing based on violations of the freedom of speech and the use of force to break up opposition meetings. In June 1946 he questioned the sentencing of **Krystio Pastukhov**, one of the leaders of the Social Democratic movement, citing examples of blatant violations of the law during Pastukhov's trial; consequently, Ivanov was arrested and accused of "disseminating false information." On 13 August 1946, in a rigged trial in which he defended the freedom of the press, Ivanov was sentenced to one year and seven months in prison, a fine, and the deprivation of his public rights for two years. After serving his sentence, Ivanov was taken to a concentration camp in Belene, where he contracted tetanus. He died in a prison hospital. (AG)

Sources: *Entsiklopediya Bulgariya*, vol. 3 (Sofia, 1982); Jerzy Jackowicz, *Partie opozycyjne w Bułgarii 1944–1948* (Warsaw, 1997).

IVASHKO Volodymyr (28 October 1932, Poltava), Ukrainian Communist activist. After graduating in engineering, from 1956 Ivashko lectured in a mining institute in Kharkiv. A member of the CPSU from 1960, from 1973 he was a professional party worker. In 1978 he became secretary of the Regional Committee in Kharkiv, and in 1980 he worked as a political instructor in Afghanistan. In 1986 he became secretary of the Central Committee (CC) of the Communist Party of Ukraine (CPU). In 1987 he became first secretary of the Dniepropetrovsk Regional Committee, heading the most powerful group of the nomeklatura, connected with the military-industrial complex. In 1986 Ivashko became a deputy member of the CPSU CC and in 1987 a deputy to the Supreme Council of the USSR. From December 1988 he was second secretary of the CPU CC for ideology, becoming, thanks to the support of Mikhail Gorbachev, a potential successor to **Volodymyr Shcherbytskyi**, a dogmatic member of the old Brezhnevite guard. In view of the establishment of a strong opposition organization—the Ukrainian Popular Movement for Perestroika—on 28 September 1989 the CPU CC Plenum entrusted Ivashko with the post of first secretary.

Initially Ivashko tried to adjust his policies to the growing social aspirations, but he failed to gain the support of the opposition and began to lose the support of the party apparatus, so in November 1989 he returned to a more orthodox rhetoric. After decades of the repression of Ukrainian national culture and as a result of the criminal neglect of the authorities after the Chernobyl disaster, staying in power was too difficult a task for him. In the free elections to the Supreme Council of the Ukrainian SSR in March 1990 Ivashko won in one of the Kiev districts, took the lead of the Communist majority faction For a Sovereign Soviet Ukraine (Za Suverennu Radyansku Ukraiinu), and on 4 June 1990 was elected chairman of the Supreme Council. Nevertheless, he failed to adjust party policies to the changing situation and failed to make consistent personnel changes. Soon, at the Twenty-Eighth CPU Congress in June 1990, Ivashko resigned from the CPU leadership, and at the Twenty-Eighth CPSU Congress on 2 July 1990 he agreed to become Gorbachev's deputy general secretary of the all-Soviet party. On 5 July in Kiev, the pro-independence deputies made the Supreme Council of the Ukrainian SSR prepare a "Declaration of the State Sovereignty of the Ukraine" and demanded a recall of the Ukrainian deputies from the Moscow conference of deputies or, in case they refused, their dismissal. Since the motion was supported by the majority of Communist deputies, Ivashko accepted the ultimatum and resigned from chairing the Ukrainian Supreme Council on 9 July 1990. During the Moscow putsch of August 1991 Ivashko was passive, and his career ended with the dissolution of the CPSU. (TS)

Sources: Alexander Rahr, ed., *A Biographical Directory of 100 Leading Soviet Officials* (Boulder, Colo., 1990); Kathleen Mihalisko, "Volodymir Ivashko and Ukraine," *Radio Liberty Report on the USSR*, 20 July 1990; Taras Kuzio and Andrew Wilson, *Ukraine: From Perestroika to Independence* (New York, 1994); Bohdan Nahaylo, *The Ukrainian Resurgence* (Toronto, 1999); V. M. Lytvyn, *Ukraiina na mezhi tysiacholit (1991–2000 rr.)* (Kiev, 2000).

IWASZKIEWICZ Jarosław, pseudonym "Eleuter" (20 February 1894, Kalnik, Ukraine–2 March 1980, Warsaw), Polish writer and social activist. Iwaszkiewicz was born into an impoverished landowner's family, and his father died while Iwaszkiewicz was still young. In 1902–4 he lived in Warsaw, and then he returned to the Ukraine, where he graduated from high school. In 1912 he enrolled in law and music studies in Kiev. He witnessed the revolution in Kiev, and in 1918 he went to Warsaw, where he made a living by private tutoring. Initially he was connected with the periodical Pro Arte et Studio and took part in the cabaret Pod Picadorem (At Picador's). In 1918 Iwaszkiewicz published his first collection of poems, *Oktostychy* (Octastichs). Later he drew close to the Expressionist group of the periodical *Zdrój*, and in 1920 he co-founded the literary group Skamander. In 1923–25 Iwaszkiewicz was secretary to the speaker of the Assembly, **Maciej Rataj**, and he published a lot in the daily and literary press. In 1925 he went to Paris on a scholarship, where he studied Arabic and Turkish. He was friends with **Karol Szymanowski** and wrote the libretto for his opera,

Król Roger (King Roger; 1926). Thanks to his marriage to Anna Lilpop, the daughter of a rich family, in 1928 Iwaszkiewicz settled in Podkowa Leśna, near Warsaw, in a house called Stawisko. In 1932–35 he was secretary to the Polish legation in Denmark and Belgium, and in the 1930s he traveled a lot in France and southern Italy. He was also active in the International PEN Club. His best known works of that time included *Panny z Wilka* (Lasses from Wilk; 1933); *Brzezina* (1933; Birch Grove, 2002); and *Młyn nad Utratą* (Mill on the Utrata River; 1936).

During the German occupation Iwaszkiewicz lived in Stawisko, which became a shelter for many Polish artists and writers. He also wrote new works, such as *Matka Joanna od Aniołów* (Mother Joanna of the Angels; 1946). In 1945 he briefly edited the weekly *Życie Literackie*, and then he was the literary director of the Teatr Polski in Warsaw. In 1945–49 he was chairman of the Trade Union of Polish Writers and a member of the board of the Polish PEN Club. In 1947–48 he edited the weekly *Nowiny Literackie*. Engaged in the new political system, in 1948 he took an active part in the Congress of Intellectuals in Defense of Peace in Wrocław, and he wrote in the Socialist realist style. From 1952 he was an MP. In 1953 he took part in the public mourning of Stalin. From 1955 until his death he was editor-in-chief of the monthly *Twórczość*. His best known novel, *Sława i chwała* (Fame and glory, 3 vols.; 1956–62), covered a wide social panorama of the first half of the twentieth century. From 1959 to his death Iwaszkiewicz was chairman of the Association of Polish Writers. He enjoyed the support of the Communist authorities and, in return, he was always cooperative with them—for instance, he opposed the "Letter of 34," written by intellectuals against the official cultural policy in 1964. Nevertheless, Iwaszkiewicz's prose belongs among the best achievements of Polish literature of the twentieth century. Iwaszkiewicz received many national and foreign awards, including the Righteous among the Nations medal of the Yad Vashem Institute in Jerusalem. His ten-volume *Dzieła* (Works) were published in 1958–59 and his two-volume *Dramaty* (Dramas) in 1980–84. Iwaszkiewicz also translated from French, Spanish, German, and Russian and translated the works of Søren Kierkegaard. (PK)

Sources: *Literatura polska XX w. Przewodnik encyklopedyczny*, vol. 1 (Warsaw, 2000); Ryszard Przybylski, *Eros i Tanatos: Proza Jarosława Iwaszkiewicza 1916–1938* (Warsaw, 1970); Eugenia Łoch, *Pisarstwo Jarosława Iwaszkiewicza wobec tradycji i współczesności* (Lublin, 1987); Andrzej Zawada, *Jarosław Iwaszkiewicz* (Warsaw, 1994); Tadeusz Drewnowski, *Próba scalenia: Obiegi-wzorce-style* (Warsaw, 1997); Jerzy Eisler, *List 34* (Warsaw, 1993).

IZETBEGOVIĆ Alija (8 August 1925, Bozanski Samac–19 October 2003, Sarajevo), Bosnian Muslim politician.

Under the German occupation during World War II Izetbegović became active in the movement of Bosnian Muslims, for which he was imprisoned for three years after the war. He graduated in law from Sarajevo University and qualified as a lawyer. In 1970 he published "The Islamic Declaration" in the underground press; in it he called Muslims to a moral revival. In 1982 he published *Islam between East and West*. In 1983 he was sentenced to fourteen years of prison for anti-state activities, but he was released in November 1988. In May 1990 he was one of the founders of the Party of Democratic Action (Strana Demokratske Akcije), and in October 1990 he was elected the leader of the party. Until 2001 Izetbegović ruled the party in an autocratic way, using radical religious and ethnic rhetoric. From December 1990 he was the president of the Presidency of the Republic of Bosnia and Herzegovina (serving as the head of state). In June 1991, along with **Kiro Gligorov**, he proposed a plan for the transformation of the Socialist Federative Republic of Yugoslavia into a looser federation (the so-called plan of asymmetrical federation), but the plan was rejected.

After the proclamation of independence by Slovenia and Croatia on 25 June 1991, Izetbegović decided that Bosnia and Herzegovina could not remain in a Yugoslavia dominated by Serbs. Bosnian Serbs strongly opposed a separation from Yugoslavia, but on 3 March 1992, on behalf of the presidency, Izetbegović nonetheless proclaimed the independence of Bosnia and Herzegovina. He repeatedly expressed his disappointment with the reluctance of the international community to intervene in the face of the escalation of war in Bosnia and Herzegovina, in which the Bosnian Muslims became the main victims of ethnic cleansing. In March 1993 Izetbegović accepted the plan of Cyrus Vance and David Owen, but it was not implemented because the Bosnian Serbs rejected it. Izetbegović was one of the signatories of the peace agreement negotiated in Dayton, Ohio, on 21 November 1995 and signed in Paris on 14 December 1995. By virtue of this agreement Bosnia and Herzegovina formally remained one state composed of two territorial units: the Croat-Muslim Federation and the Bosnian Serb Republic. After the elections of September 1996 Izetbegović again held the post of president of the Presidency of the Republic of Bosnia and Herzegovina until September 1998, and he remained a member of the presidency until 2000, when he again resumed the position of president for eight months. (AO)

Sources: *Noty biograficzne*, Redakcja Dokumentacji Prasowej PAP; Laura Silber and Allan Little, *The Death of Yugoslavia* (London, 1995); Warren Zimmermann, *Origins of a Catastrophe* (New York and Toronto, 1996); Ante Čuvalo, *Historical Dictionary of Bosnia and Herzegovina* (Lanham, Md., 1997); Bugajski; www.rulers.org.

J

JAAKSON Ernst (11 August 1905, Riga–4 September 1998, New York), Estonian diplomat and politician. Jaakson studied economics in Riga and law in Tartu. Between 1926 and 1928 he served in the army. From 1928 on he uninterruptedly worked in diplomacy, first in the Information Department of the Estonian Ministry of Foreign Affairs (1928–29) and from 1932 in the General Consulate of Estonia in New York. Jaakson deserves credit for ensuring the continuity of Estonian statehood following the aggression by the USSR in June 1940, the reoccupation of Estonia in 1944, and through more than forty years of Soviet occupation. It was, among other things, thanks to his perseverance that the United States never recognized the annexation of Estonia de jure and that the prewar diplomatic and consular services performed their duties as representatives of a formally recognized state until 1991—that is, until the end of the Soviet occupation of Estonia. In 1965 Jaakson became Estonia's top-ranking diplomatic representative in the United States, and in that capacity he saw the recovery of Estonian independence. Upon the recognition of Estonian sovereignty by the Western nations in 1991, Jaakson was appointed Estonian ambassador to the United States. He held this position until 1993, when he was formally transferred to the post of consul general in New York. He remained in office until his death. He bequeathed around 500,000 euros to Tartu University. Jaakson left his memoirs, *Eestile* (For Estonia), and received the highest national medals and awards. (AG)

Sources: *Eesti Enstuklopeedia*, vol. 14 (Tallinn, 2000); Anne Velliste, *Ernst Jaaksonile* (Tallinn, 2000); Ernst Jaakson, "Noteworthy Estonians," http://www.vm.ee/eng/famous/Jaakson.htm.

JAAKSON Jüri (16 January 1870, Karuli [later Uue-Võidu], near Viljandi–20 April 1942, Sosva, near Sverdlovsk), Estonian politician and social activist. Jaakson studied law in Dorpat (Tartu) in 1892–96 and worked as a lawyer in Viljandi (1897–1901). Later he moved to Riga, where he ran a law firm until 1914. After the outbreak of World War I, he became a member of the board of the Tallinn City Bank. He was active in various social organizations; for example, he was president of the Viljandi Farmers' Society and the Koit (Dawn) society. During his stay in Riga Jaakson was president of the Estonian Sobriety Society and also presided over the Imanta Society (1902–5), as well as the Estonian Education and Assistance Society in Riga (1906–14). He also initiated the private

Tsar Alexander Estonian School and was president of its Board of Superintendents. In addition, during the war he presided over the Union of Northern Estonian Farmers and the Tallinn Economic Union. After the outbreak of the February 1917 revolution, Jaakson became assistant to the commissar of Estonia Province, and from 1917 to 1918 he was vice-president of the Estonia Province Assembly (Eesti Maanõukogu). In February 1918 he joined the commission that drew up the Estonian declaration of independence. In the Provisional Government he served as general commissioner responsible for taking over property from the German occupation authorities. From 1918 to 1920 Jaakson was minister of justice. A member of the parliament (Riigikogu) for its first four terms and one of the more influential politicians of the national-liberal Estonian People's Party of **Jaan Tõnisson**, between 16 December 1924 and 25 November 1925 Jaakson served as head of state (riigivanem, equivalent to president and prime minister). He became head of state after an unsuccessful Communist coup d'état; therefore his was a nonparty government, supported by parties of both the right and the left. Jaakson also had the support of 72 percent of the deputies. Attempts to amend the constitution to strengthen the executive power were thwarted by the Socialist opposition. This conflict was one of the reasons for his government's resignation.

Until 1940 Jaakson served as president of the Bank of Estonia and was temporarily a member of the National Economic Council (1935–38) and the parliament (1938–40). Unlike Tõnisson, Jaakson was not involved in activities against the dictatorship of **Konstantin Päts**. As president of the Central Bank, in 1928 Jaakson promoted the introduction of the Estonian national currency, the kroon, and tried to maintain its exchange rate at a stable level of 4 kroon to US\$1, guaranteed by reserves of gold and foreign currencies. Under his management, the Central Bank ceased granting loans and concentrated on monetary policy. From 1927 the bank was also formally independent from the government. Jaakson's efforts greatly contributed to the establishment of a more orderly foreign exchange market and strengthened investors' trust in Estonia. These policies became one of the main springs of economic growth in the second half of the 1920s. During the Great Depression the bank changed its tactics. With a monopoly on foreign currency exchange for an interim period, it resumed its lending activities, offering cheaper loans than commercial banks and thus boosting economic growth in the second half of the 1930s. After the occupation of Estonia by the Red Army in June 1940, Jaakson was arrested by the NKVD on 14 June 1941, and he was deported to a camp in Sosva, where he was executed by firing squad. (AG)

Sources: Tönu Parming, *The Collapse of Liberal Democracy and the Rise of Authoritarianism in Estonia* (London, 1975); Tõnu Tannberg, Matti Laur, Tõnis Lukas, Ain Mäesalu, and Ago Pajur, *History of Estonia* (Tallinn, 2000); Rein Taagepera, *Estonia: Return to Independence* (Boulder, Colo., 1993); www.president. ee/eng/riigipead/JuriJaakson.html; www.htg.tartu.ee/eng/index. html; "Strona obchodów 80-lecia niepodległości Estonii," ew80. www.ee/eng/chronicle/1918.html; "Eesti Pank 1919–1999," in: Strona Banku Estonii, www.ee/epbe/en/history.html.

JABŁOŃSKI Henryk (27 December 1909, Waliszewo. near Łowicz–27 January 2003, Warsaw), Polish Socialist and Communist activist and historian. Born into a working-class family, after graduating in history from Warsaw University in 1931, Jabłoński started working at this university, and he joined the Polish Socialist Party (Polska Partia Socjalistyczna [PPS]). In 1939 he fought in the September campaign and later served in the Polish Armed Forces (PSZ) in the West. He fought in the battle of Narvik and in France (among other places), after which he returned to Poland in 1945. Initially moderately and later more firmly, Jabłoński was in favor of cooperation with the Communist Polish Workers' Party (Polska Partia Robotnicza [PPR]) within the framework of the Alliance Commission of the Democratic Parties, as well as the struggle against the Polish Peasant Party (PSL). As a representative of the Communist-backed PPS, he became a member of the National Home Council (KRN). In 1946 he was in charge of the PPS Political and Propaganda Department. From 1945 to 1947 he served as president of the Executive board of the Workers' University. From November 1945 to December 1948 he was a member of the PPS Chief Council, and from April 1946 to December 1948, a member of the PPS Central Executive Committee. Jabłoński advocated the merger of the PPS with the PPR. In December 1948 he became a member of the CC of the Polish United Workers' Party (Polska Zjednoczona Partia Robotnicza [PUWP]), and until March 1954 he was a member of the Organizational Bureau of the PUWP CC. In 1947–53 he was deputy minister of education, and as such he implemented a Stalinist program. In 1947 he became professor at the Academy of Political Sciences in Warsaw and in 1950 at Warsaw University. In 1952 he became a member of the Polish Academy of Sciences. From March 1953 to the fall of 1955 he was scientific secretary of the First Department of Social Sciences of the Polish Academy of Sciences and subsequently scientific secretary of the Polish Academy of Sciences until December 1965. Jabłoński authored numerous publications on the Socialist theory of science, the history of the Polish left, and its relations with Vladimir Lenin.

In the mid-1950s Jabłoński was considered a supporter of the Puławska group, and later he supported the ruling team of **Władysław Gomułka**. In 1965–66 he was minister of higher education, and from 1966 to 1972, minister of education and higher learning. On 4 March 1968, after the first wave of student protests, Jabłoński yielded to the pressure of party authorities and the Ministry of Internal Affairs, and, as minister of education, he made the decision to expel two students, **Adam Michnik** and Henryk Szlajfer, from Warsaw University. This decision was illegal in light of the regulations then in force, and it greatly increased tensions. When **Edward Gierek** came to power, Jabłoński became one of the main leaders of the new ruling team. In December 1970 he became a deputy member, and in December 1971 a member, of the PUWP CC Politburo. In March 1972 he assumed the post of president of the Council of State and authorized the disastrous economic policy of the Gierek administration. Between 1976 and 1983 he was president of the All-Polish Committee of the National Unity Front.

A member of parliament in 1947–89, from December 1975 to February 1976 Jabłoński presided over the select committee for drafting amendments to the constitution of the Polish People's Republic. The proposed changes included a provision about the alliance between the Polish People's Republic and the USSR and about the leading role of the PUWP. These proposals caused social protests. In late 1980 Jabłoński spoke aggressively against Solidarity, which was being established at that time. Although at the Ninth Congress of the PUWP in July 1981 Jabłoński resigned from the CC and from its Politburo, in December 1981, as president of the Council of the State, he was instrumental in confirming the decision of General **Wojciech Jaruzelski** to impose martial law in Poland. In November 1985 Jabłoński resigned as president of the State Council, and he was succeeded by Jaruzelski. At the Tenth Congress of the PUWP in July 1986 Jabłoński returned to the CC of the party and remained a member until the dissolution of the party in January 1990. Between 1983 and 1990 he served as president of the Chief Council of the Association of Fighters for Freedom and Democracy (ZBOWiD). He was loyal to the subsequent rulers of Communist Poland and accepted all subsequent political shifts in the Polish People's Republic. Jabłoński's works include *Polityka Polskiej Partii Socjalistycznej w czasie wojny 1914–1918* (Policy of the Polish Socialist Party during the war of 1914–1918; 1958) and *Pisma wybrane* (Selected writings, 3 vols.; 1985–86). (PK)

Sources: Mołdawa; *Słownik polskich polityków XX w.* (Warsaw, 1998); Michał Czajka and Marcin Kamler, *Leksykon Historii Polski* (Warsaw, 1995); Jerzy Eisler, *Marzec 1968* (Warsaw, 1991); Włodzimierz Janowski and Aleksander Kochański, *Informator* o strukturze i obsadzie personalnej centralnego aparatu PZPR 1948–1990 (Warsaw, 2000); Jerzy Eisler, Grudzień 1970 (Warsaw, 2000).

JABLONSKIS Jonas, pseudonym "Jonas Rygiškių" (30 December 1860, Kubiliai–23 February 1930, Kaunas), Lithuanian linguist and codifier of the Lithuanian language. After graduating from high school, Jablonskis studied classical languages at Moscow University (1881–85). Because he was a Catholic, after graduating he could not to find a job in the schools. He supported himself by giving private lessons and by working as a judicial officer in Marijampole. In 1889 he found a job as a Greek and Latin teacher in Jelgava, Latvia. Because he frequently spent his summer vacations in Lithuania, where he collected linguistic information, the Russian authorities dismissed him from his job in 1896. Jablonskis took up a teaching position in Tallinn while continuing to collect linguistic data and compile a Lithuanian dictionary commissioned by the Russian Academy of Sciences and initiated by Antanas Juška. Expelled from Tallinn in 1901, he continued his work in Pskov. In the same year, he published Lietuviškos kalbos gramatika (Lithuanian grammar). This work, in which he systematized the foundations of the Lithuanian language, was published under the pseudonym "P. Kriaušaitis" in Tilsit (now Sovetsk), Eastern Prussia, because on Russian territory the tsar had imposed a ban on publications in Lithuanian using the Latin alphabet. In 1902 the Russian authorities banned Jablonskis from coming to Lithuania. When both bans were lifted in 1904, he returned to Vilnius and worked in the editorial offices of the periodicals Vilniaus Žinios and Lietuvos Ūkininkas. He also founded the Aušra publishing house. In 1906–8 Jablonskis taught in a pedagogical seminary in Panevėžys; from 1908 to 1912 he taught in Brest-Litovsk and later in Grodno.

After the outbreak of World War I, the Grodno school in which Jablonskis was teaching was evacuated to the interior of Russia. Between 1915 and 1918 he lectured at a gymnasium for Lithuanian refugees in Voronezh. As a result of bad living conditions there, in 1918 he returned to Lithuania almost paralyzed. In 1919 he arrived in Kaunas, and when a university was established there in 1922, he became an honorary professor. Because his health was declining, Jablonskis had to retire in 1926, but he continued his intensive scholarly work until his death. His most important works include Lietuvių kalbos sintaksė (Syntax of the Lithuanian language; 1911); Rašomosios kalbos dalykai (Issues of literary language; 1912); Lietuvių kalbos vadovėlis (Lithuanian language textbook; 1925); and Linksniai ir prielinksniai (Grammatical cases and preposi-

tions; 1929). Thanks to Jablonskis's excellent linguistic education, his works were rigorous and innovative, as was his theoretical approach. Jablonskis formulated standard modern Lithuanian, enriching literary patterns with the colloquial speech of Lithuanian peasants; standardizing the orthography; removing loan words; and systematizing the grammar, particularly the syntax. A complete edition of his works was published under the title Jablonskio raštai (The works of Jablonskis, 5 vols.; 1932–36). (WR)

Sources: EL, vol. 2; P. Skardžius, "J. Jablonskis ir dabartinė lietuvių bendrinė kalba," Archivum Philologicum (Kaunas), vol. 6, 1937; J. Palionis, Įžymusis lietuvių kalbininkas Jonas Jablonskis (Vilnius, 1955); Jerzy Ochmański, Litewski ruch narodowo-kulturalny w XIX wieku (Białystok, 1965); Arvydas Vidziūnas, Jono Jablonskis akcentologija (Vilnius, 1997).

JAGIELSKI Mieczysław (12 January 1924, Kolomyia–28 February 1997, Warsaw), Polish Communist activist. Born into a peasant family, Jagielski completed his studies at the Central School of Planning and Statistics and at the Academic Staff Training Institute of the CC of the Polish United Workers' Party (Polska Zjednoczona Partia Robotnicza [PUWP]) in Warsaw. In 1944 he joined the Fighting Youth Union (Związek Walki Młodych [ZWM]), and in 1946, the Polish Workers' Party (Polska Partia Robotnicza [PPR]). From December 1948 he belonged to the PUWP. From 1946 to 1950 he worked in the Peasant Mutual Aid Association (Związek Samopomocy Chłopskiej [ZSCh]) and later in the Central Administration of State-Owned Farms. In 1952 he started working in the Agricultural Department of the CC of the PUWP and was soon promoted to head of this department. He held this position until 1957. Jagielski initially implemented the party's policy of the accelerated collectivization of agriculture, but during the "thaw" he did not oppose the dissolution of most agricultural cooperatives in the summer of 1956. In 1957–59 Jagielski was deputy minister of agriculture. In 1959 he became minister of agriculture, implementing quasi-collectivization policies for the development of "agricultural circles." From March 1954 to March 1959 he was a deputy member of the CC of the PUWP; from March 1959 to July 1981 he was a member of the CC; in 1964–81 he was a deputy member of the Politburo; and in July 1981 he became a member of the Politburo of the CC of the PUWP. In June 1970 Jagielski became deputy prime minister. From 1971 to 1975, as president of the government Planning Commission, he was co-responsible for an increase in investment spending, which led to the waste of enormous resources and the collapse of the economy in the late 1970s. From 1971 to 1981 Jagielski was the permanent representative of Poland to the Council for Mutual Economic Assistance (Comecon) in Moscow. In 1975 he became a professor at the Central School of Planning and Statistics in Warsaw. He authored *Niektóre problemy rozwoju rolnictwa w latach 1966–1970* (Some issues in the development of agriculture in the years 1966–70; 1965), *O nowej polityce partii na wsi* (About the new agricultural policy of the party; 1957), and other works. In 1957–85 he was a member of parliament.

On 21 August 1980 Jagielski was head of a special government commission to negotiate with the Inter-Factory Strike Committee at the Gdańsk shipyard. During the negotiations he held a rather uncompromising stance until the strike at the shipyard turned into a general strike in the Gdańsk area (Triple City). When on 24 August the Fourth Plenum of the CC of the PUWP decided to adopt a political solution to the conflict, Jagielski negotiated in that spirit and brought about an agreement with the Inter-Factory Strike Committee on 31 August. The scene of his signing the agreement with **Lech Wałęsa**, the president of the Inter-Factory Strike Committee, was immortalized in the world media. Soon afterwards Jagielski was sharply criticized by party hard-liners for his concessions. In July 1981 he resigned as deputy prime minister, and at the end of 1981 he withdrew from political activity. In 1988 he retired. Jagielski was given the Order of the Builder of the People's Poland, the highest state award. (WD)

Sources: Mołdawa; Jean Woodall, ed., *Policy and Politics in Contemporary Poland* (London, 1982); George Sanford, *Polish Communism in Crisis* (London, 1983); Timothy Garton Ash, *The Polish Revolution: Solidarity* (New York, 1985); *Słownik biograficzny działaczy polskiego ruchu robotniczego* (Warsaw, 1987); *Tajne dokumenty Biura Politycznego: PZPR a "Solidarność" 1980–1981* (London, 1992); Lech Wałęsa, *Droga nadziei* (Kraków, 2000).

JAKEŠ Miloš (12 August 1922, České Chalupy), Czech Communist activist. In 1937–50 Jakeš worked in the Bata shoe factory in Żlin. In 1944 he graduated from an industrial electro-technical school. In 1945 he joined the Communist Party of Czechoslovakia (CPC). Initially he was active in the Czechoslovak Youth Union, advancing to the level of its national secretary. In 1955 he left for Moscow, where he studied at the Higher Party School of the CPSU CC for three years. After returning home, he began to advance in the party hierarchy. In 1966 he became deputy minister of interior and a member (and in April 1968 chairman) of the Central Control Commission of the CPC CC. During the Prague Spring of 1968, Jakeš sided with the conservatives, and in this capacity he participated in the Moscow talks of 23–26 August 1968. He fully supported the so-called normalization, as well as purges in the party. In 1977 he became a member and

secretary of the CPC CC, and in 1981 he joined the CPC CC Presidium. In 1977–81 Jakeš presided over the CPC CC Commission for Agriculture and Supplies, and from 1981 to 1989, the Commission of the National Economy. After the resignation of **Gustav Husák** from the post of general secretary of the CPC CC, on 17 December 1987 Jakeš was elected to this position as a compromise candidate, but he was rather a hard-liner. He assumed the leadership under worsening economic conditions and growing social discontent, and he could not cope with the accumulating problems. He tried to maintain the monopoly of CPC power through superficial economic reforms and a tough political line. He had no intellectual skills nor any personal charisma to preserve the Communist power. As a result of the Velvet Revolution, in November 1989 Jakeš was forced to resign from the position of general secretary, and on 5 December 1989 he was expelled from the party. In 1996 he was accused of having betrayed his homeland in 1968, but in September 2002 he was acquitted. Jakeš published the memoirs *Dva roky generálním tajemníkem* (Two years as general secretary; 1996). (PU)

Sources: *ČBS*; *Kdo byl kdo v našich dějinách ve 20. století*, vol. 1 (Prague, 1998); *Who's Who in the Socialist Countries of Europe*, vol. 2 (Munich, London, and Paris, 1989); *Československí politici: 1918–1991* (Prague, 1991).

JAKOBSON August (2 September 1904, Pärnu–23 May 1963, Tallinn), Estonian writer and Communist activist. In 1922 Jakobson was a co-founder of the Estonian Writers' Union (EWU). In 1926–29 he studied economics, and between 1931 and 1935 he was a medical student. He gained publicity after publishing the grotesque *Vaeste-Patuste alev* (Village of poor sinners) in 1927. Along with other Socialist writers, Jakobson attempted to found a literary group affiliated with the weekly *Kirjanduslik orbiit*, of which only a few issues were published. Before the war he gained fame after publishing the series *Tuhkur Hobune* (1928–33) and a few other novels such as *Andruksonide suguvósa* (The Andruksonide Clan; 1934–38). In 1939 he was elected president of the EWU. After the invasion of the Red Army in June 1940 and the incorporation of the Estonian SSR into the USSR, Jakobson became a member of a commission established by the Ministry of Education of the Estonian SSR that prepared an index of books banned from publication. Over 1,500 books, mainly Estonian literature, fell victim to this commission, and twenty authors had all their works banned from publication. At that time Jakobson was a member of the editorial staff of *Kommunist*, an organ of the Communist Party of Estonia (CPE), and he was also the editor-in-chief of *Ilukirjandus ja Kunst*, a leading organ of Socialist realism. Jakobson actively helped to suppress the EWU and to transform it into the Estonian Soviet Writers' Union. In his activities, Jakobson was driven by the faith that leftist ideals could be embodied in the Estonian SSR. He was also encouraged by a good financial standing, granted by the Communists to obedient intellectuals.

After June 1941 Jakobson went to the USSR. In 1942 he joined the CPE, and in 1943 along with (among others) Johannes Vares, he co-founded the Writers' Union of the Estonian SSR. After the Red Army again occupied Estonia in 1944, Jakobson was elected president of the Writers' Union of the Estonian SSR and held the position from 1944 to 1946 and from 1950 to 1954. His second nomination to that position especially was proof of the trust the Stalinist leaders placed in him because it came after the Eighth CPE CC Plenum, which was followed by a purge of artists under the slogan of "eliminating bourgeois nationalism." Between 1950 and 1958 Jakobson was president of the Presidium of the Supreme Soviet of the Estonian SSR; in 1951–58 he was a member of the CC of the CPE; and from 1947 to 1963 he was a member of the Supreme Soviet of the USSR. Jakobson subordinated his writing to the requirements of the propaganda for a "struggle for peace" and the "doctrine of Socialist realism." He was the author of *Elu tsitadellis* (Life in a citadel; 1946), a model Socialist realist novel for which he received the Stalin Prize. After Stalin's death, Jakobson's influence began to diminish. In 1954 he resigned as president of the Writers' Union of the Estonian SSR, and in 1958 he was replaced as president of the Supreme Soviet of the Estonian SSR by Johan Eichweld, a man brought up in the USSR. (AG)

Sources: *Bolshaia Sovetskaia Entsiklopediia*, vol. 30 (Moscow, 1978); *Eesti Entsuklopeedia*, vol. 14 (Tallinn, 2000); P. Järv, *August Jakobson* (Tallinn, 1972); Toivo V. Raun, *Estonia and the Estonians* (Stanford, 1987); Romualdas J. Misiunas and Rein Taagepera, *The Baltic States: Years of Dependence, 1940–1990* (Berkeley, 1993); "Estonian Cultural History Short Overview," *Estonian Literary Magazine*, 1996, no. 2; http://www.okupatsioon.ee/english/overviews/index.html.

JAKOPIĆ Rihard (12 April 1869, Ljubljana–21 April 1943, Ljubljana), Slovene painter. Jakopić graduated from a high school in Ljubljana. Then he studied painting in Vienna (1887–89), Munich (1889–90), and Prague (1903–4). In Munich he met Anton Ažbé, with whom he founded a painting school. In 1904–6 he exhibited in Vienna, Belgrade, Berlin, London, and Sofia, along with other Slovene Impressionists, such as Ivan Grohar, Matija Jama, and Matej Sternen. In 1900 he co-founded the Slovene Society of Arts (Slovensko Umetniško Društvo), and he became its secretary. In 1900 he also organized the first art exhibition in Ljubljana, and in 1907 he founded the Slovene School of Impressionist Drawing and Painting. In 1909 he financed the first art gallery in Ljubljana, known as the Jakopićiev Paviljon. This building lasted until 1962, when it was torn down. In 1938 Jakopić became a member of the Slovene Academy of Science and Arts. A special award in his name (Jakopićieva Nagrada) for outstanding artistic achievements was initiated in 1969. Jakopić left about 1,200 paintings and 650 drawings, as well as several articles on art. He is considered an Impressionist, although he evolved toward Post-Impressionism and Symbolism and (after World War I) toward Expressionism. His best know works include the following: *Alkoholik* (The alcoholic; 1901); *Breze* (Birch trees; 1902); *Med gabri* (Between hornbeams; 1904); *Sestrici* (Sisters; 1912); *Spomini* (Memoirs; 1912); *Sava* (The Sava River; 1912); and *Slepec* (The blind man; 1926). *Rihard Jakopić v besedi* (Conversations with Rihard Jakopić; 1947) was published posthumously. (AO)

Sources: *Enciklopedija Slovenije*, vol. 4 (Ljubljana, 1990); *Encikolpedija Jugoslavije*, vol. 4 (Zagreb, 1961); Anton Podbevšek, *Rihard Jakopić* (Ljubljana, 1983); *L'impressionisme et la peinture de plein air* (Paris, 1992).

JAKOVA Tuk (26 April 1914, Shkodër–26 August 1959, Tirana), Albanian Communist activist. Jakova was born into a Catholic family from the northern Albanian ethnic group of Gegs. After attending primary school in Shkodër, he completed two grades of a gymnasium but discontinued his education because of financial problems. It was probably during his military service that Jakova came into contact with the Communist movement. After doing his military service, he worked as a carpenter in a firm that made furniture. At the end of the 1930s he was one of the founders of a Communist group in Shkodër. In January 1939 he was arrested and sentenced to six years. Released in April 1939, he fled to Yugoslavia but returned to his country after a few months. He was a member of the Communist Party of Albania (CPA) from the time the party was founded. In June 1942 he formed one of the first partisan units. Tried in absentia on two occasions, in 1942 Jakova was sentenced to death. He served as a member of the General Staff of the National Liberation Army, a member of the General Council of the National Liberation Front, and political commissar of the First Partisan Brigade.

When in February 1945 a central organization of trade unions was established at a congress of workers' delegates, Jakova assumed its leadership and continued at its helm until 1947. Among the CPA leaders, he was one of the few representatives of the northern part of Albania. He was frequently assigned crucial missions, such as negotiations with the Catholic Church or with representatives of

Western countries. In August 1946 he conducted talks with U.S. State Department representatives on the recognition of the new Albanian government by Washington. In 1946 Jakova submitted Albania's request for admission to the United Nations to the UN Security Council. From February to October 1947 he was ambassador to Yugoslavia, accredited also to Hungary. In 1945–55 he was a deputy to the People's Assembly, and between January and March 1946, president of the parliament. In September 1948 Jakova supported **Enver Hoxha** against **Koçi Xoxe**, and he joined the Politburo of the CC. Soon afterwards he was promoted to second secretary of the CC of the Albanian Labor Party (ALP), and on 28 November 1948 he became deputy prime minister. In 1950–54 he headed the ministry of industry and the ministry of finance.

In February 1951 Jakova was expelled from the Politburo for his protests against the terror that Hoxha wanted to unleash after a bomb exploded in the building of the Soviet legation in Tirana. At the Second Congress of the ALP in late March and early April 1952 Hoxha attacked Jakova for "opportunism" and for "defying party orders concerning religious issues." Jakova did a self-criticism, and therefore he was not expelled from the CC. After Stalin's death in 1953, Jakova began to advocate the rehabilitation of Xoxe, whose liquidation he had helped to bring about. In July 1953 he resigned as deputy prime minister but returned to that post one year later. He was finally dismissed on 24 June 1955 on charges of revisionism and pro-Yugoslav activities. After the Twentieth Congress of the CPSU, demands for Jakova's rehabilitation were voiced at ALP conferences in April 1956, including a national conference, but in vain. Through repression, Hoxha broke down the opposition within the CC of the ALP that had allegedly been instigated by Jakova. During a wave of persecutions in 1957 Jakova was arrested and sentenced to twenty years' imprisonment. He served his sentence in Vlorë and Zvernec, and in 1958 he was transferred to Tirana, where he died in a prison hospital. In 1999 his letters to his wife from prison were published. (TC)

Sources: *Bashkimi*, 22 November 1945; Stavro Skendi, *Albania* (New York, 1956); William E. Griffith, *Albania and the Sino-Soviet Rift* (Cambridge, Mass., 1963); Henry Hamm, *Albania: China's Beachhead in Europe* (London, 1963); Arshi Pipa, *Albanian Stalinism: Ideo-Political Aspects* (New York, 1990); Mita Jakova and Tuk Jakova, *Leterkëmbim dhimbshem 1957–1959* (Tirana, 1999).

JAKUBISKO Juraj (30 April 1938, Kojšov, near Spišská Nová Ves), Slovak film director. In 1966 Jakubisko graduated from the Film and Television Department of the Theater and Music Academy in Prague. During his studies he had already attracted attention, winning awards at the short-feature film festivals in Mannheim, Oberhausen, and Bergamo. He made his feature film debut with *Kristove roky* (Christ's years; 1967), in which he dealt with the complicated relationship between Czechs and Slovaks. Then he directed the experimental movies *Zbehovia a pútnici* (Refugees and pilgrims; 1968), *Vtáčkovia, siroty a blázni* (Birds, orphans, and clowns; 1969), and *Dovidenia v pekle priatelia* (See you in hell, friends; 1970); these were banned in Czechoslovakia during the "normalization" after the suppression of the Prague Spring. Forced into silence for years, in 1983 Jakubisko directed his best film, *Tisícročná včela* (The thousand-year-old bee), based on the novel by Petr Jaroš; in it folk naturalism was combined with mystic poetry, and it was interpreted as a symbol of the Slovak experience and an homage to the common people. The influence of his experimental style can also be seen in Jakubisko's later films, such as *Perinbaba* (1985); *Sedím na konári a je mi dobre* (I sit on a branch and I feel fine; 1989); *Lepšie byt' bohatý a zdravý ako chudobný a chorý* (It is better to be rich and healthy than poor and sick; 1992); and *Nejasná zpráva o konci světa* (Unclear report of the end of the world; 1997). Jakubisko's films were presented at many international festivals and won him several awards. Since the breakup of Czechoslovakia, Jakubisko has lived in Prague, where, with his wife, he runs a Film Studio, J&J Jakubisko Film. (PU)

Sources: *ČBS*; *Kdo byl kdo v našich dějinach ve 20. století*, vol. 1 (Prague, 1998); Jan Jaroš, *Juraj Jakubisko* (Prague, 1989); Jerzy Płażewski, *Historia filmu 1895–2000* (Warsaw, 2001); Jean Loup Passek, ed., *Dictionnaire du cinéma* (Paris, 1991); www.jakubisko.cz.

JAŁBRZYKOWSKI Romuald (7 February 1876 Łętowo-Dąb, near Łomża–19 April 1955, Białystok), Polish Roman Catholic archbishop of Wilno (Vilnius). Jałbrzykowski graduated from high school in Łomża, from the theological seminary in Sejny (1898), and from the Theological Academy in St. Petersburg in 1902. Ordained in March 1901, he taught at the Sejny seminary, and from 1910 he was canon of the cathedral chapter in Sejny. Evacuated to Mohylev in 1915, from 1916 he lived in Minsk, where he worked in the Polish Relief Society for the Victims of War. In 1917 he returned to Sejny, where he became vicar general of this part of the Sejny diocese, which was incorporated into Poland. On 28 July 1918 Jałbrzykowski was consecrated auxiliary bishop of the Sejny diocese, and on 14 December 1915 he became ordinary bishop of the newly created Łomża diocese. On 24 June 1926 he was appointed the first archbishop metropolitan of the Wilno (Vilnius) archdiocese. Close to the National Democracy and supported by the Polish majority of this diocese,

Jałbrzykowski was not popular among the Lithuanian minority. After the Vilnius region was incorporated into Lithuania in October 1939, despite Lithuanian pressure, he did not resign, but after the Soviet invasion of June 1940 he was expelled from office and put under house arrest. In 1942–44 Jałbrzykowski was imprisoned by the Germans. In 1945 he left for Białystok in Poland; from there he administered the Polish part of the Wilno archbishopric until his death. (WR)

Sources: *PSB*, vol. 10; *Encyklopedia historii Drugiej Rzeczypospolitej* (Warsaw, 1999); Piotr Łossowski, *Litwa a sprawy polskie 1939–1940* (Warsaw, 1982); Jan Żaryn, *Stolica Apostolska wobec Polski i Polaków w latach 1944–1958* (Warsaw, 1998).

JANÁČEK Leoš (3 July 1854, Hukvaldy, Moravia–12 August 1928, Ostrava, Czechoslovakia), Czech composer. At eleven Janáček entered a music school at the Augustinian monastery in Brno. From 1869 to 1874 he attended a teacher training institute, and in 1880 he earned the title of music teacher at the Prague Organ School. In 1879 he entered the Leipzig Conservatory and in 1880 moved to study in Vienna, but he never completed his studies. In 1881 in Brno, Janáček founded the Society for the Promotion of Church Music in Moravia, under whose auspices an organ school was established. He directed this school until 1919. From 1886 to 1902 he also worked as a voice teacher at a high school. He was active as a conductor, choirmaster, organizer of musical life (for example, in the Beseda choral society in Brno), and a critic and theoretician of music. In 1886 Janáček entered into a collaboration with František Bartoš, who encouraged his interest in Moravian folk songs. This interest resulted in the works *Národní písně moravské* (Moravian folk songs, 1901; co-authored with Bartoš) and *Moravské písně milostné* (Moravian love songs, 1930; co-authored with Pavel Vaša). An outstanding authority on Moravian folk music, in 1919 Janáček became president of the Brno branch of the State Institute of Folk Songs. After 1904 he devoted himself to composing and gave up most other occupations. In 1909–11 he was president of the Club of the Friends of Art in Brno. After the Organ School was transformed into a conservatory in 1919, Janáček became a professor and lectured there until 1925. In 1925 he was named an honorary doctor of Masaryk University in Brno. In 1912 he became a member of the Czech Academy of Sciences and Arts, and in 1927, a member of the Prussian Academy of Arts.

Janáček's first works show the distinct influence of other composers, mainly Antonín Dvořák, Bedřich Smetana, Richard Strauss, and Richard Wagner. In 1888 he turned to Moravian folk music and later to Czech and Slovak folk music. *Lašské tance* (Lachian dances; 1889–90) is the first notable work of that period. He enriched the harmonic structure of this work while preserving the folk rhythms and melodic schemes. *Její pastorkyňa* (Jenůfa; 1904), the first Moravian national opera, is the most important work of his folk music period. In this opera, Janáček employed vocal exclamations and his own "speech melody" concept, bringing out the poetic charm of folk language and folk music. The topics of his operas were often inspired by Russian literature, on the wave of Slavophilism popular in Bohemia. Works arising from that inspiration include the operas *Kát'a Kabanová* (1921) and *Z mrtvého domu* (From the house of the dead; 1930), as well as instrumental works such as *Piano Trio* (1908), *First String Quartet*, and *Taras Bulba* (1921). Janáček increasingly used autobiographical motifs in his works—for instance, in the opera *Osud* (Fate, 1903–6; premiere in 1958). In his later instrumental music he also employed Impressionistic techniques. The works written toward the end of his life, *Concertino* (1925) and *Sinfonietta* (1926), represent a modern approach to form and tone color. Janáček left nine operas, four cantatas, four choral works, five symphonic works, the ballet *Rákós Rákoczy* (1891), and many chamber and piano works. (PU)

Sources: *ČBS*; Max Brod, *Leoš Janáček: Život a dílo* (Prague, 1924); Hans Hollander, *Leoš Janáček* (London, 1963); Erik Chrisholm, *The Operas of Leoš Janáček* (Oxford, 1971); Bohumír Štědroň, *Leoš Janáček: K jeho lidskému a uměleckému profilu* (Brno, 1976); Michael Ewans, *Janáček's Tragic Operas* (London, 1977); William D. Curtis, *Leoš Janáček* (Utica, N.Y., 1978); Milan Šolc and Jarmil Burghauser, *Leoš Janáček: Souborné kritické vydání* (Prague, 1979); Kurt Honolka, *Leos Janácek: Sein Leben, sein Werk, seine Zeit* (Stuttgart, 1982); Bohumír Štědroň, ed., *Leoš Janáček: Vzpomínky, dokumenty, korespondence a studie* (Prague, 1986); Paul Wingfield, ed., *Janácek Studies* (Cambridge, 1999); Meinhard Saremba, *Leos Janácek: Zeit-Leben-Werk-Wirkung* (Kassel, 2001); Mirka Zemanová, *Janáček* (Boston, 2002).

JANCSÓ Miklós (27 September 1921, Vác), Hungarian film director. After graduating from the Law Department of the university in Kolozsvár (Cluj) in 1944, Jancsó served in the army and was taken POW by the Soviets. After his release and return home, he graduated from the Higher Theater and Film School in Budapest (1950). At the same time he was active in Communist youth organizations. In the 1950s he mostly directed documentaries and propaganda newsreels. After 1956 he dealt with cartoon films and in the 1960s with feature films. All together he directed more than twenty films. His films were full of subtle dramaturgy and generalized national and universal experience. He created a unique film narrative. Applying long shots, he showed his characters in a crowd or against the background of a wide outdoor panorama. Jancsó also directed stage plays, adapting several classical works of

Hungarian and foreign literature. His most outstanding movies included moral and philosophical analyses of human behavior in breakthrough moments of Hungarian history from the Spring of Nations to the Hungarian Soviet Republic: *Szegénylegények* (The desperate; 1965); *Csillagosok, katonák* (Stars on caps; 1967); *Csend és kiáltás* (Silence and scream; 1968); *Még kér a nép* (The red psalm; 1972), an award winner at the Cannes Festival; *Szerelmem, Elektra* (Electra, my love; 1974); *Magyar rapszódia* (Hungarian rhapsody; 1978); and *Jézus Krisztus horoszkópja* (The horoscope of Jesus Christ; 1988). Jancsó received special awards for his overall work at Cannes (1979) and Venice (1987). (MS)

Sources: *International Dictionary of Films and Filmmakers*, vol. 2 (Chicago and London, 1991); *Miklós Jancsó: Seminarium filmowe* (Wrocław, 1979); Jozsef Marx, *Jancsó Miklós két és több élete* (Budapest, 2000); *Ki Kicsoda 2002* (Budapest, 2001).

JANKOWSKI Jan Stanisław, pseudonyms "Doktór" and "Soból" (6 May 1882, Krassowo Wielkie, Wysokie Mazowieckie County–13 March 1953, USSR), Polish Christian Democratic politician, delegate of the Polish Government-in-Exile for the Homeland. Jankowski came from a landowning family and graduated from high school in Piotrków Trybunalski in 1900. He studied physics, mathematics, and chemistry in Warsaw. After a school strike in 1905 he went to study in Prague, where he received a diploma as a chemical engineer in 1906. In 1912 he also completed an agricultural college at the Jagiellonian University in Kraków. In 1901 he joined the Union of Polish Youth called Zet. In 1906 he co-organized the National Workers' Union (Narodowy Związek Robotniczy [NZR]), and in 1908 he became a member of the NZR Main Board. In 1912–13 he represented the NZR in the Provisional Commission of Confederated Independence Parties, and, from 1915, in the Chief Committee of the United Independence Parties. Between September and December 1915 Jankowski served in the First Regiment of the Polish Legions, and later he became a member of the Central National Committee in German-occupied Warsaw. Beginning in 1917 he administered estates in the former Kingdom of Poland. In April 1920 he became head of the Main Land Office. In May 1920 he co-founded the National Workers' Party (Narodowa Partia Robotnicza [NPR]), formed from the NZR. Between March and May 1921, as a representative of his party, Jankowski was minister of labor and social welfare. In February 1925 he was deputy minister of labor and social welfare, and between April and May 1926 he was again minister. From September 1920 to May 1923 he was NPR president and then vice-president until 1933. In 1928–35 he was an MP,

and from 1926 to 1936 he was vice-president of the Polish Trade Union (Zjednoczenie Zawodowe Polskie [ZPP]). In 1937 he joined the Labor Party (Stronnictwo Pracy [SP]), which was formed by the merging of the NPR and the Christian Democratic Party.

During the Nazi occupation Jankowski formally worked for the City Board and in various social welfare institutions. At the same time, from the beginning of the German occupation, he was active in the SP underground structures. In 1941 he became director of the Department of Labor and Social Welfare of the Delegation of the Polish Government-in-Exile for the Homeland, and in 1943 he was appointed to a three-member advisory committee to Julian Kulski, the administrator of Warsaw. Jankowski was also active in the Information and Propaganda Bureau of the Home Army Headquarters. In December 1942 he became a deputy to **Jan Piekałkiewicz**, the delegate of the Polish Government-in-Exile for the Homeland. Following Piekałkiewicz's arrest on 19 February 1943, Jankowski replaced him as delegate, and his nomination was confirmed by President **Władysław Raczkiewicz** in April 1943. On 22 May 1943 Jankowski was also nominated deputy premier of the Polish government in London. As such, from May 1944 he was in charge of the National Council of Ministers (Krajowa Rada Ministrów [KRM]). On 25–26 July 1944 the Polish government-in-exile authorized Jankowski to "make all decisions necessitated by the pace of the Soviet offensive" and to "announce the uprising at a time of your choosing." Jankowski made that dramatic decision on 31 July, following consultations with the Home Army command. During the uprising he was in the capital, and after its failure he was secretly taken to Pruszków, where he continued his underground work. Jankowski was arrested by the NKVD on the night of 27–28 March 1945, when he was supposed to have talks with General Ivan Serov. In the Trial of the Sixteen, on 21 June 1945 Jankowski was sentenced to eight years for alleged "hostile activities" in the rear of the Red Army. According to the Soviet Red Cross, he died in prison. (WR)

Sources: Kunert, vol. 1; T. Monasterska, *Narodowy Związek Robotniczy 1905–1920* (Warsaw, 1973); Bohdan Kroll, *Opieka i samopomoc społeczna w Warszawie 1939–1944* (Warsaw, 1977); Henryk Przybylski, *Chrześcijańska Demokracja i Narodowa Partia Robotnicza w latach 1926–1937* (Warsaw, 1980); W. Ciechomski, "Jan Stanisław Jankowski," *Ład*, 1984, no. 10; Waldemar Grabowski, *Delegatura Rządu Rzeczypospolitej Polskiej na Kraj* (Warsaw, 1995); Andrzej K. Kunert and Eugeniusz Piontek, *Proces moskiewski przywódców polskiego państwa podziemnego* (Warsaw, 2000).

JÁNOSI Ferenc (13 January 1916, Sárospatak–2 September 1968, Budapest), Hungarian priest and politician. After theological studies in Sárospatak, where he was ordained a Calvinist pastor, Jánosi studied theology at the university in Wittenberg (1937–38) and graduated in Hungarian, Latin, and Greek pedagogy from the university in Debrecen in 1941. He also received a Ph.D. there. During World War II he worked as a chaplain in the army and was taken POW by the Soviets. He undertook propaganda activities among Hungarians POWs, editing the Red Army periodical *Új Szó* (1944). In 1944 he married Erzsébet Nagy, daughter of **Imre Nagy**. In December 1944 he co-organized the Provisional National Government, obedient to the Kremlin. In 1944–51 Jánosi worked in the Ministry of Defense, advancing to the rank of general and later becoming secretary of state in the Ministry of Culture. From 1954 he was general secretary of the National Council of the Patriotic People's Front, and in 1955–57, director of the Sándor Petőfi Literary Museum. During the 1956 revolution Jánosi stood by Nagy. Interned and tried along with him in 1958, he was sentenced to eight years in prison. Released in 1960 through an amnesty for political prisoners, he worked as a planning officer in a food processing plant in Budapest and later as archivist of Pest County. In 1963 Jánosi co-founded the so-called movement of local chronicle writers. (MS)

Sources: *Magyar Nagylexikon*, vol. 10 (Budapest, 2000); Judit Ember, *Menedékjog—1956* (Budapest, 1989); *In memoriam Nagy Imre* (Budapest, 1989); György Litván and Janós M. Bak, eds., *Die ungarische Revolution 1956* (Vienna, 1994).

JANOUŠEK Karel (30 October 1893, Přerov–27 October 1971, Prague), Czech air force general. After graduating from high school, Janoušek worked as a clerk. Sent to the Russian front in 1914, he was taken prisoner and subsequently joined the Czechoslovak Legion. As a soldier of the Czechoslovak Legion, he took part in many battles, including the battle of Zborov, and he fought in Siberia. After returning to Czechoslovakia in 1920, he entered the Military College in Prague as an auditor, and in 1923 he finished his studies. Later he served as a general staff officer in the land command operations unit in Prague. Janoušek greatly contributed to the development of the Czechoslovak air force, and in 1934–39 he was commander of the air force in Bohemia. In 1937 he was promoted to major general (in British English: air vice-marshal). In June 1939 he began underground activities, but in November of that year he emigrated to France and became chief of the Third (air force) Department of the Czechoslovak military command. After the fall of France Janoušek was active in Great Britain, where he served as commander of the Czechoslovak air force. In 1940 he became air marshal of the Czechoslovak Air Force in Britain and air vice-marshal in the Royal Air Force. After

the war Janoušek served for three years as deputy chief of the general staff for special tasks, and later he served for a short time as inspector-general of anti-aircraft defense. After the Communist coup of February 1948 he was dismissed from the army. During an attempt to emigrate in April 1948, provoked by an agent of the special services, Janoušek was arrested and sentenced to nineteen years' imprisonment. Two years later his sentence was increased to life imprisonment. Amnestied in 1960, he was rehabilitated in 1968. In 1990 he was reinstated to the rank of lieutenant general, and one year later he was posthumously promoted to general. (PU)

Sources: *ČBS*; *Kdo byl kdo v našich dějinách ve 20. stoleti*, vol. 1 (Prague, 1998); Z. Vališ, *Generál Karel Janoušek* (Prague, 1997); John O. Crane and Sylvia Crane, *Czechoslovakia: Anvil of the Cold War* (New York, 1982).

JANOWICZ Sokrat (4 September 1936, Krynki), Belorussian writer and social activist in Poland. In 1955 Janowicz graduated from an electro-technical school in Białystok. From 1956 he worked on the editorial board of the weekly *Niva*, edited in Belorussian. In 1973 he graduated in Polish studies from Warsaw University. He was active in the Belorussian Social and Cultural Society. In 1970 he was expelled from the (Communist) Polish United Workers' Party for "anti-Sovietism and Belorussian nationalism." During martial law Janowicz edited the uncensored Belorussian press. In 1988 he co-founded an unregistered Belorussian club, and in 1989 he ran in the elections to the Senate, but he lost. In 1990–92 he presided over the Belorussian Democratic Union (Białoruskie Zjednoczenie Demokratyczne), the only party representing national minorities in Poland. In 1994 he withdrew from political activity. In 1997 Janowicz founded a society called Willa Sokrates, and later he organized literary meetings of writers, translators, and literary critics from Poland, Belarus, and other countries. He made his literary debut in *Niva* in 1956. In 1969 he published his first collection of short stories, *Zahony* (Field patches). His short literary pieces were sort of philosophical treatises by the heroes he found in his social environment. In 1979 Janowicz published the novel *Ściana* (The wall), and in 1981, *Samasiey* (Self-seeding), but he gained the widest renown for his social and political journalism, which is represented by the historical essay *Białoruś, Białoruś* (Belarus, Belarus; 1987) and the volume *Dolina pełna losu* (The fateful valley; 1993). (EM)

Sources: *Bielaruskiya pismienniki (1917–1990): Davednik* (Minsk, 1994); *Bielaruskiya pismienniki: Biblijahraficzny slounik*, vol. 6 (Minsk, 1995).

JANŠA Janez (17 September 1958, Ljubljana), Slovene politician. Janša graduated in military studies in Ljubljana, and then he joined the League of Communists of Slovenia. He taught at a high school and was a consultant to the republican defense secretariat in Ljubljana. He was also active in the League of Communist Youth of Slovenia. In 1986 he organized a conference on the security of the Slovene republic. His criticism of the condition of the Yugoslav People's Army (YPA) led to his expulsion from the Communist Party. Janša worked in a private computer company, and he continued to write critical articles on the YPA—for instance, in the periodical *Mladina*. In July 1988 he was temporarily arrested for possessing a classified document. His case catalyzed the movement for Slovene independence. In the summer of 1989 Janša co-founded the Slovenian Democratic Union (Slovenske Demokratične Zveze). After the elections of April 1990 Janša became minister of defense in the government of **Lojze Peterle**. During the ten-day war with the YPA (27 June–6 July 1991) Janša worked out a plan for national defense through guerrilla operations, and he played an important role in stabilizing the independence of Slovenia.

Janša continued as minister of defense in the government of **Janez Drnovšek**. He created serious controversy by publishing his memoirs, *Premiki: Nastajanje in obramba slovenske države 1988–1992* (Memoirs: Emergence and defense of Slovene statehood, 1988–1992; 1992). From 1993 he chaired the Social Democratic Party of Slovenia (Socialdemokratska Stranka Slovenije [SPS]). In 1993 he entered into conflict with President **Milan Kučan**, who feared his strong position. Janša, on the other hand, suspected Kučan of having been at least partly responsible for Janša's imprisonment in 1988. In July 1993 arms and munitions destined for Bosnia were found in the Maribor airport; they violated the international embargo. Janša was accused of engineering the operation. Information about his involvement came from the Ministry of Interior, which was a counterpart to military intelligence. It was thought that this was the ministry's revenge for Janša's having revealed information on the military's secret handling of gambling profits. For his part Janša accused Kučan of organizing illegal arms dealings, but the president denied these accusations. In March 1994 Janša was forced to resign, and the SPS joined the opposition. In the elections of November 1996 the SPS won 18 percent of the mandates, and Janša won a seat for himself. He was one of the leaders of the opposition. In May 2000 he regained the portfolio of defense minister in the government of Andrej Bajuk. In the elections of October 2000 the SPS won almost 16 percent of the mandates but was in opposition to the subsequent government of Drnovšek, and in November 2000 Janša resigned from chairing the SPS. (WR)

Sources: *Slovenski kdo je kdo* (Ljubljana, 1999); Leopoldina Plut-Progelj and Carole Rogel, *Historical Dictionary of Slovenia* (Lanham, Md., 1996); Jill Benderly and Evan Kraft, eds., *Independent Slovenia: Origins, Movements, Prospects* (London, 1994); James Gow and Cathie Carmichael, *Slovenia and the Slovenes* (London, 2000); Bugajski; www.sds.si.

JAROSS Andor (23 May 1896, Komáromcsehi–11 April 1946, Budapest), Hungarian politician from Slovakia. Jaross was an activist of Hungary's ruling Party of Unity in the region of Feldivék, which was incorporated into Hungary under the First Vienna Award in November 1938. At that time, he became minister for the regained territories in the government of **Béla Imrédy**. In 1939, along with Imrédy, Jaross switched over to the Party of Hungarian Life, founded by **Pál Teleki**. In October 1940 Jaross was one of the founders of the extreme right-wing Party of Hungarian Renewal (Magyar Megújulás Pártja). An aggressive and brutal anti-Semite, when Germany occupied Hungary in March 1944, Jaross became minister of interior in the government of General **Döme Sztójay**. In that role, he concentrated the Jewish population into ghettos and subsequently began deporting Jews to extermination camps. In August 1944 Regent **Miklós Horthy** dismissed Jaross when he realized what he was doing, but under **Ferenc Szálasi**, Jaross again became a member of the government and continued the extermination of Hungarian Jews. Captured after the war and tried in Budapest, Jaross was sentenced to death and executed. (WR)

Sources: Philip Rees, *Biographical Dictionary of the Extreme Right since 1890* (New York, 1990); C. A. Macartney, *October Fifteenth: A History of Modern Hungary*, vols. 1–2 (Edinburgh, 1957–61); M. Lacko, *Arrow Cross Men, 1935–1944* (Budapest, 1969).

JAROSZEWICZ Piotr (8 October 1909, Nieśwież–1 September 1992, Anin, near Warsaw), Polish Communist activist. Brought up in a teachers' family, Jaroszewicz graduated from the Free Polish University. Before the war he directed a primary school near Garwolin. During the war he was in the USSR; in 1943 he joined the Polish units that were being formed by General Zygmunt Berling. In 1944 Jaroszewicz joined the Polish Workers' Party (Polska Partia Robotnicza [PPR]), and in 1948 he became a member of the Polish United Workers' Party (Polska Zjednoczona Partia Robotnicza [PUWP]). In 1944–45 Jaroszewicz served as deputy commander of the First Polish Army for political and educational affairs, and from 1945 to 1946 he was deputy chief of the Main Political and Educational Board of the Soviet-controlled

Polish Army. From 1946 to 1950 he served as deputy minister of national defense and as chief quartermaster of the Polish Army. In 1947 he became a deputy member of the CC of the PPR. From December 1948 to February 1980 he was a member of the CC of the PUWP, and in 1964 he became a deputy member of its Politburo. In 1950 he was appointed deputy president of the State Committee for Economic Planning. From 1954 to 1955 he was minister of mining, and from 1955 to 1956, minister of coal mining. He subsequently assumed the post of permanent Polish representative to the Council for Mutual Economic Assistance (Comecon), and he held this post until 1970. From 1958 to 1970 Jaroszewicz was president of the Committee for Economic Cooperation of the Council of Ministers. Between November 1952 and December 1970 he also held the post of deputy prime minister. Owing to his special loyalty to the Kremlin, he managed to keep senior posts despite leadership reshuffles. From 1972 to 1980 Jaroszewicz was one of the leaders of the Association of Fighters for Freedom and Democracy (ZBOWiD). From 1947 to 1980 he was an MP.

After the fall of **Władysław Gomułka**, Jaroszewicz joined the Politburo and became head of the government on 23 December 1970. One of the architects of the economic policy of **Edward Gierek**, Jaroszewicz believed that a modernization of the economy, the introduction of new technologies, and an inflow of investments would afford an additional chance to discreetly expand military potential. On that issue, he followed the Moscow party line, and he promoted only those sectors of the economy that were important to the Kremlin. At the Seventh Congress of the PUWP (8–12 December 1975) Jaroszewicz read the program paper, "The Main Principles of the Social and Economic Development of Poland between 1976 and 1980." His loyalty to the USSR was often cited as a source of contention during intra-party strife.

In 1976–77, the practice of settling accounts with Comecon countries via the so-called transfer ruble, which was disadvantageous to Poland, led to a deep economic crisis that was compounded by irresponsible investment policies. A proposal to raise prices, presented by Jaroszewicz in the Assembly on 24 June 1976 and approved by top party leaders, was the direct cause of strikes, which were brutally suppressed in Radom and Ursus. As a result of the crisis, Jaroszewicz was subjected to severe criticism for economic failures in the decade 1970–80. At the Eighth Congress of the PUWP (11–15 February 1980) Jaroszewicz was made a scapegoat, failed to get to the CC, and was removed from the post of prime minister. In December 1980 he was forced to resign his parliamentary seat and was subsequently expelled from the PUWP. After martial law was imposed, he was briefly interned, for show, by the regime of General **Wojciech Jaruzelski**. In 1984, by decision of the Assembly, Jaroszewicz was brought before the Tribunal of State, but after a few months the proceedings against him were discontinued. In 1991 Jaroszewicz published an extended interview, *Przerywam milczenie* (I break the silence). Jaroszewicz and his wife, Alicja Solska, who was a journalist for *Trybuna Ludu*, were murdered in unexplained circumstances. (PK)

Sources: Mołdawa; *Słownik polityków polskich XX w.* (Poznań, 1998); Zbigniew Błażyński, *Towarzysze zeznają. Z tajnych archiwów Komitetu Centralnego* (London, 1987); Andrzej Albert [Wojciech Roszkowski], *Najnowsza historia Polski 1914–1993*, vol. 2 (Warsaw, 1995); *Kto jest kim w Polsce* (Warsaw, 1985).

JARUZELSKI Wojciech (6 July 1923, Kurów, near Puławy), Polish general, Communist activist, and politician. Born into an impoverished family of landed gentry with patriotic traditions, from 1933 Jaruzelski studied in a high school run by the Marian Order in Warsaw. After the outbreak of the war in September 1939 his parents sought shelter in Lithuania; from there they were deported by the Soviets to Siberia in June 1941. Jaruzelski's father perished in the Gulag, while Jaruzelski and his mother were forced to settle in Turachak, in the Altai region, where he worked at felling trees and did other hard labor. In 1943 Jaruzelski joined the Polish Army formed under Soviet control; he graduated from officer training school in Ryazan, and he fought with the First Army all up until its final operations on the Oder and Elbe. After the war Jaruzelski remained in the army, supporting the new Communist power. He took part in operations against the Polish pro-independence fighters and against the Ukrainian Insurgent Army near Hrubieszów. In 1947 he joined the (Communist) Polish Workers' Party, and from December 1948 he was a member of the Polish United Workers' Party (Polska Zjednoczona Partia Robotnicza [PUWP]), which, along with his work for the military intelligence, helped him toward a brilliant career in the (Communist) Polish Army (Wojsko Polskie [WP]). In 1953 he was promoted to the rank of colonel.

In 1955 Jaruzelski graduated with distinction from the Higher School of Infantry (HSI) and from the Academy of the General Staff. In July 1956 he became the youngest WP brigadier general. In 1947–57 Jaruzelski lectured at the HSI and was head of the Administration of Military Academies and deputy head of the Chief Administration of Combat Training, enjoying a solid reputation and the trust of the Soviet command in Poland. In October 1956 he appealed to the Soviet generals to stay in WP and two of them with Polish roots—Jerzy Bordziłowski and Józef

Urbanowicz—stayed and helped Jaruzelski in his career. From 1957 Jaruzelski commanded the Twelfth Mechanized Division in Szczecin, and from June 1960 he was chief of the WP Main Political Administration. In October 1960 he was promoted to general of division, and in 1961 he became an MP. From 1962 he was deputy minister of defense, and from 1964, a member of the PUWP Central Committee (CC). Clever, effective, and totally loyal to the party leadership, Jaruzelski advanced steadily. In February 1965 he became chief of the General Staff. He took part in the purge of officers of Jewish descent that was carried out in the 1960s by military counterintelligence. On 11 April 1968 he became minister of defense and supervised the Polish participation in the Warsaw Pact invasion of Czechoslovakia in August 1968. In October 1968 he was promoted to the rank of general of arms. In December 1970 he implemented the decision of the PUWP head, **Władysław Gomułka**, to use guns against striking workers on the Polish Baltic Coast. As a result, several dozen people were killed. After the toppling of Gomułka, on 19 December 1970 Jaruzelski suspended his orders. The next day, when **Edward Gierek** became the new party first secretary, Jaruzelski was promoted to deputy member of the PUWP CC Politburo.

In the new ruling team Jaruzelski played a rather independent role, supporting Gierek against **Mieczysław Moczar** in the summer of 1971. At the Sixth PUWP Congress in December 1971 Jaruzelski became a member of the Politburo. From 1972 he was deputy chairman of the war veterans' Union of Fighters for Freedom and Democracy, and in October 1973 he became the first general of the army. In the late 1970s he worked with **Stanisław Kania**, responsible in the PUWP leadership for the apparatus of coercion, including the army. Both Jaruzelski and Kania remained passive during the summer 1980 strikes. When at the Sixth PUWP CC Plenum on 6 September 1980 Kania became the new first secretary, Jaruzelski's position was enhanced because the army played an important role in the political game between Solidarity, expressing the aspirations of Polish society, and the Kremlin. On 22 October 1980 Jaruzelski ordered a special task force of the General Staff under General **Florian Siwicki** to elaborate a plan for the introduction of martial law. In early December 1980 Jaruzelski received signals from Moscow that a massive Soviet invasion of Poland was likely. During a summit meeting of the Warsaw Pact countries in Moscow on 5 December 1980, Jaruzelski presented an outline plan for the suppression of Solidarity by Polish forces. When the pressure on Poland intensified again, on 11 February 1981 Jaruzelski became prime minister. He appealed for ninety days of peace and quiet.

Jaruzelski's appeal hung in the air in mid–March 1981, when, during the Soyuz 81 maneuver of the Warsaw Pact in Poland, a militia unit seriously beat three Solidarity activists in Bydgoszcz. During the crisis that followed, Jaruzelski accused Solidarity of provocation and delayed an investigation into the affair. After the so-called Warsaw agreement of 30 March saved Poland from a general strike and unforeseeable consequences, on 3 April Jaruzelski was summoned to Brest-Litovsk, along with Kania, where they both managed to convince the KGB chief, Yuri Andropov, and defense minister, Dmitri Ustinov, that a suppression of Solidarity through martial law was possible. In the summer of 1981 the economic and social situation turned even worse, and Jaruzelski's government could do nothing to improve it. At an extraordinary PUWP congress in July, Jaruzelski was one of the key players, stabilizing the party apparatus, and on 14 August he reported to the Kremlin on the state of preparations for the anti-Solidarity action. While Kania tended to delay the action, Jaruzelski succumbed to the Kremlin's blackmail and was more eager to start it. At the Fourth PUWP CC Plenum on 17 October 1981 Jaruzelski became the party's new first secretary.

Having concentrated all the reins of power in his hands, on 13 December 1981, ignoring binding legislation, Jaruzelski introduced martial law and took the lead of the unconstitutional Military Council of National Salvation (Wojskowa Rada Ocalenia Narodowego). This decision has become the subject of heated debates. According to current evidence, a Soviet invasion could not have been dismissed, but it was rather unlikely in the fall of 1981. Jaruzelski suppressed Solidarity and saved the power of the party nomenklatura, putting the blame for the crisis on Solidarity. He bears responsibility for the use of force and for the victims of the martial law. Although from February 1981 to January 1986 Jaruzelski was head of the Commission for Economic Reform and he temporarily stopped the economic decline, he failed to introduce the necessary systemic reforms and relied on conservative activists, the military, and the security police. Leading the party, he maneuvered between its extreme pro-Muscovite faction and the moderates. From November 1983, when he ceased to be minister of defense, to December 1990, he chaired the Committee of National Defense and was commander-in-chief of the army. On 13 November 1985 he resigned from chairing the Council of Ministers and assumed the post of chairman of the Council of State.

From the mid-1980s the economic and social situation began to worsen again, but the Communist authorities, led by Jaruzelski, reacted slowly and inconsistently. An illusory economic reform and an alleged political opening could not prevent the decline of the economy and of social morale. The country was facing collapse. After the failure of a referendum on reform in November 1987 and in view of the Soviet perestroika, Jaruzelski started preparations for sharing responsibility, but not power, with the democratic opposition. The summer strikes of 1988 attested to the inadequacy of this policy, so at the Tenth PUWP CC Plenum in December 1988 and January 1989, Jaruzelski decided to start the Round Table Talks with Solidarity and convinced the rest of the leadership to accept this decision. He did not take part in these talks, and he did not run in the partly free elections of 4 June 1989. He also hesitated to run for president, but finally, on 19 July 1989, he was elected to this post by the National Assembly by a margin of one vote. As a result he gave up the position of PUWP first secretary. Despite some hesitation, Jaruzelski approved of the formation of the **Tadeusz Mazowiecki** government in early September 1989. In view of the fall of Communist regimes in East Central Europe in late 1989, the dissolution of the PUWP in January 1990, and the decline of the Soviet empire, Jaruzelski cared only about the safe retreat of the party nomenklatura. Under pressure from the new political elites he agreed to early presidential elections in the fall of 1990, declined to run, and retired. Jaruzelski made great and rather successful efforts to present himself as the savior of the nation from a Soviet invasion. In 1992 he published his memoirs, *Stan wojenny: Dlaczego . . .* (Martial Law: Why . . .). Owing to the complicated social and political situation after the collapse of Communist power, Jaruzelski avoided responsibility before the Tribunal of State for the imposition of martial law. The trial concerning his responsibility for the 1970 Baltic Coast massacre, delayed for years, did not start until 2001, and there is not a great chance that it will be concluded in the near future. (PK/WR)

Sources: Mołdawa; *Wielka encyklopedia PWN*, vol. 12 (Warsaw, 2002); Michael Checinski, *Poland, Communism, Nationalism, Anti-Semitism* (New York, 1982); Andrzej Albert [Wojciech Roszkowski], *Najnowsza historia Polski 1914–1993*, vol. 2 (Warsaw, 1995); Vladimir Bukovski, *Judgement in Moscow* (Paris, 1995); Jan Skórzyński, *Ugoda i rewolucja: Władza i opozycja 1985–1989* (Warsaw, 1995); Anton Palinka, *Jaruzelski oder die Politik des kleineren Übels* (Frankfurt am Main, 1996); *O stanie wojennym w sejmowej Komisji Odpowiedzialności Konstytucyjnej* (Warsaw, 1997); Christopher Andrew and Vasili Mitrokhin, *The Sword and the Shield: The Mitrokhin Archive and the Secret History of the KBG* (New York, 1999); Jerzy Eisler, *Grudzień 1970* (Warsaw, 2000); Lech Kowalski, *Generał ze skazą* (Warsaw, 2001); Antoni Dudek, *Pierwsze lata III Rzeczpospolitej 1989–2001* (Kraków, 2002); Andrzej Paczkowski, *Droga do "mniejszego zła"* (Kraków, 2002).

JASIENICA Paweł [originally Lech Beynar] (10 November 1909, Symbirsk, Russia–19 August 1970, Warsaw), Polish writer. Jasienica was born into an intelligentsia family that returned to Poland from Russia in 1920; after high school in Grodno (Hrodna) he graduated in history from Stefan Bathory University in Wilno (Vilnius) in 1932. In 1934–37 he taught in a Grodno high school, and then he worked for the Polish Radio station in Wilno. He fought in the September 1939 campaign and was taken POW by the Germans. After escaping, from 1941 Jasienica was active in the Union of Armed Struggle (Związek Walki Zbrojnej [ZWZ]), and from 1942, in the Home Army (Armia Krajowa [AK]) in (among other places) the village called Jasienica (thence his pen name). From 1944 Jasienica edited an underground periodical, *Pobudka*, of the Bureau of Information and Propaganda of the Wilno AK district. In July 1944 he took part in the Wilno operations of the AK; then, along with AK troops that had avoided being shattered by the NKVD, he continued fighting in the unit of Major Zygmunt Szyndzielarz (pseudonym "Łupaszka") and was his aide-de-camp and later his deputy commander. After the dissolution of the "Łupaszka" unit, in September 1944 Jasienica settled in Kraków. After the war he wrote for various periodicals, and from 1946 he belonged to the editorial board of the weekly *Tygodnik Powszechny*. Arrested in July 1948 in connection with an investigation concerning the Wilno AK, he was released after the intervention of **Bolesław Piasecki**.

From 1950 Jasienica lived in Warsaw, publishing in *Życie Warszawy, Nowa Kultura, Po prostu, Twórczość*, and *Przegląd Kulturalny*. In 1951 he joined the Association of Polish Writers (Związek Literatów Polskich [ZLP]), and in 1959–62 he was deputy chairman of its Main Board. After 1956 he belonged to the Club of the Crooked Circle (Klub Krzywego Koła), a discussion group, and just before its dissolution in 1962 he was its chairman. From 1961 he belonged to the Polish PEN Club, and in 1966–70 he was its deputy chairman. Jasienica authored extremely popular syntheses of the early history of Poland: *Polska Piastów* (Poland under the Piasts; 1960); *Polska Jagiellonów* (Poland under the Jagiellons; 1963); and *Rzeczpospolita Obojga Narodów* (The Commonwealth of Two Nations, 3 vols.; 1967–72). In 1964 Jasienica signed the "Letter of 34," written by intellectuals against the abuses of censorship. In March 1968 he supported protesting students, which resulted in a furious propaganda attack against him. Jasienica was condemned at mass rallies in Białystok and Katowice, where his role during World War II was totally distorted. On 19 March 1968 **Władysław Gomułka** publicly insinuated that Jasienica had cooperated with the Communist security apparatus. The authorities demanded his expulsion from the ZLP and banned the publication of his works. Nevertheless, later Jasienica's works became classics of Polish historical literature. Some of his works—such as *Rozważania o wojnie domowej* (Reflections on the civil war; 1978)—were later published in the underground press. In 1986 his *Pamiętnik* (Diary) was published secretly. In 1980 the ZLP Congress resolved to clear Jasienica of the 1968 slander. (PK)

Sources: *Wielka Encyklopedia PWN*, vol. 12 (Warsaw, 2002); *Literatura polska XX w. Przewodnik encyklopedyczny* (Warsaw, 2000); Bernard Wiaderny, *Paweł Jasienica. Fragment biografii* (Warsaw, 1991); Jerzy Eisler, *List 34* (Warsaw, 1993); *Współcześni polscy pisarze i badacze literatury: Słownik bibliograficzny* (Warsaw, 1994); Tadeusz Drewnowski, *Próba scalenia: Obiegi-wzorce-style* (Warsaw, 1997).

JASIUKOWICZ Stanisław (8 December 1882, St. Petersburg–after September 1946, USSR), Polish politician. The son of a Polish entrepreneur in Russia, after graduating from a gymnasium in Yekaterinoslav (now Dniepropetrovsk), Jasiukowicz studied at the Technological Institute in St. Petersburg and at the university in Munich, where in 1911 he received a Ph.D. in economics. After returning to Poland, he settled in Chodów, his father's estate near Kutno. He later went to the Canary Islands for treatment of a lung disease. While a student in St. Petersburg, he joined the Union of Polish Youth, Zet, and in 1911, the National Democratic Party (Stronnictwo Narodowo-Demokratyczne [SND]). In 1917 he joined the National League and financed some of its political initiatives. In 1920 he became an MP on behalf of the National Democrats and was reelected in 1923, each time filling a vacant seat. At the same time he ran his family estate in Chodów. Jasiukowicz was elected from the lists of the National Party (Stronnictwo Narodowe [SN]) in the elections of 1928, 1930, and 1935. In 1928 he became a member of the SN Main Board and Political Committee, and in February 1935, a member of the SN Chief Committee, as well as one of the party's three vice-presidents and head of its Financial Department.

After the defeat of Poland in September 1939, Jasiukowicz took part in a meeting of the SN Chief Committee on 13 October 1939, when a decision was made to continue the party's activities in the underground. In March 1940, after the confiscation of his estate, which was now within the territory of the Third Reich, Jasiukowicz left for Warsaw and joined the advisory group to the commander-in-chief of the Union of Armed Struggle (Związek Walki Zbrojnej [ZWZ]), later the Home Army (Armia Krajowa [AK]). Between January and April 1942 he was jailed by the Gestapo. Released, he became vice-president of the SN. From June to December 1943 he served as party president, and after the leadership of the SN was taken over by Aleksander Zwierzyński, Jasiukowicz again became party vice-president. In May 1943 he was appointed Deputy Delegate of the Polish Government-in-Exile for the Homeland (Delegat Rządu RP na Kraj). At that time, he used the pseudonyms "Kucieński" and "Opolski." When the Home Council of Ministers (Krajowa Rada Ministrów), headed by the Delegate of the Government-in-Exile, was established (3 May 1944), Jasiukowicz was made one of its three member-ministers, along with **Adam Bień** from the Peasant Party and **Antoni Pajdak** from the Polish Socialist party Freedom-Equality-Independence. During the Warsaw Uprising Jasiukowicz performed his duties in the Śródmieście district in the city center, and after the failure of the uprising he left the capital along with the civilian population. He continued his activities in Kraków, Piotrków Trybunalski, and Pruszków. Arrested by the NKVD on 28 March 1945 in Pruszków, he was taken to Moscow and imprisoned in the Lubyanka Prison. Tried in the Trial of Sixteen, he was sentenced to five years' imprisonment on 21 June. He served his sentence in the Lubyanka Prison. Jasiukowicz was last heard from in a letter to his son in September 1946. The circumstances of his death are unknown. (WR)

Sources: Kunert, vol. 3; *PSB*, vol. 11; *Proces szesnastu: Dokumenty NKWD* (Warsaw, 1995); Waldemar Grabowski, *Delegatura Rządu Rzeczypospolitej Polskiej na Kraj* (Warsaw, 1995); Andrzej Chmielarz, Andrzej K. Kunert, and Eugeniusz Piontek, *Proces moskiewski przywódców polskiego państwa podziemnego* (Warsaw, 2000).

JASZCZUK Bolesław (25 October 1913, Warsaw–1 January 1990, Warsaw), Polish Communist activist. Jaszczuk came from a family of the urban intelligentsia. In 1939 he graduated in electrical engineering from the Warsaw Polytechnic College. While a student, he became affiliated with the Communist youth movement. From 1939 to 1941 he worked as a teacher and electrician in Białystok and Warsaw. In 1942 he joined the Polish Workers' Party (Polska Partia Robotnicza [PPR]). Between 1943 and 1945 he was a prisoner in the Mauthausen-Gusen concentration camp. After the war he held numerous positions in the PPR and later in the Polish United Workers' Party (Polska Zjednoczona Partia Robotnicza [PUWP]). From 1945 to 1947 he was in charge of the Economic Department and subsequently served as secretary for economic affairs of the Warsaw Committee of the PPR. From the founding of the PUWP in December 1948 until March 1959 Jaszczuk was a deputy member and subsequently a member of its Central Committee. On 21 November 1964 he became a deputy member of the Politburo, and from 16 November 1968 to 20 December 1970 he was a member of the Politburo.

Between 1948 and 1949 Jaszczuk was deputy mayor

of Warsaw; in 1948–50 he was provincial governor (*woje-woda*) in Dąbrowa Górnicza Silesia; from 1950 to 1952 he was president of the Presidium of the Provincial National Council in Katowice; from February 1952 to July 1956 he was minister of power engineering; from July 1956 to February 1957 he was minister of the machine industry and was subsequently vice-president of the Planning Commission of the Council of Ministers between March 1957 and November 1959. From 1959 to 1963 he served as ambassador to Moscow. After his return Jaszczuk became economic secretary of the PUWP CC. Regarded as one of the closest associates of **Władysław Gomułka**, he was responsible for the economic policy of the 1960s, which was bringing increasingly worse results. In 1970 Jaszczuk co-authored an economic reform based on the so-called material interest incentive system and was in charge of its implementation. This reform involved a reduction of the bureaucracy and the introduction of a more rational cost accounting system, and it tied pay raises to increased labor productivity. In practice, though, it meant an increase in the prices of food and manufactured goods. Food price increases in December 1970 led to worker riots on the Baltic Coast and massive bloodshed. As a result, Gomułka, along with other top party officials, had to step down. At the Seventh CC Plenum on 20 December 1970, Jaszczuk was expelled from the Politburo and the CC Secretariat and, on 7 February 1971, from the CC and the party. Between January 1957 and February 1961 and from April 1965 to February 1972 Jaszczuk served as an MP. (PK)

Sources: Mołdawa; Włodzimierz Janowski and Aleksander Kochański, *Informator o strukturze i obsadzie personalnej central-nego aparatu PZPR 1948–1990* (Warsaw, 2000); Andrzej Albert [Wojciech Roszkowski], *Najnowsza historia Polski 1914–1993*, vol. 2 (Warsaw, 1995); Jerzy Eisler, *Grudzień 1970* (Warsaw, 2000).

JÁSZI Oszkár (2 March 1875, Nagykároly–13 February 1957, Oberlin, Ohio), Hungarian politician. Born into an intellectual family of Jewish origins from Transylvania, Jászi studied law at the university in Budapest (1892–96) and subsequently in France and England. After graduating, he worked as a clerk in the Ministry of Agriculture (1898–1906). In 1899 he was one of the founders of the periodical *Huszadik Század*, and between 1906 and 1919 he was editor-in-chief of this periodical. He published extensively, speaking out against the dominant position of the landed aristocracy, clericalism, and ethnic oppression. He also called for universal suffrage and civil liberties. He was secretary general of the Social Sciences Association (1907–18) and director of the Free School of Social Sciences, which conducted free courses for workers. In 1911 he became a private professor of constitutional studies at

the university in Kolozsvár (now Cluj). In 1914 he was the founder and president of the All-National Bourgeois Radical Party.

One of the leading figures of the republican revolution of October 1918 in Hungary, Jászi was a member of the Hungarian National Council (Magyar Nemzeti Tanács), and from October 1918 to January 1919 he was minister without portfolio responsible for ethnic issues in the government of **Mihály Károlyi**. He also directed the Council for Foreign Affairs. In November 1918 Jászi took part in cease-fire negotiations in Belgrade, and later he became chairman of the Hungarian delegation sent for similar talks with Romania in Arad (now Oradea). When Károlyi resigned as prime minister to assume the post of provisional president in January 1919, Jászi also gave up his position and became a sociology professor at the university in Budapest. After the Hungarian Soviet Republic (HSR) was proclaimed in March 1919, he left his country in May of that year. Between 1919 and 1925 he lived in Vienna as one of the leaders of the Hungarians in exile. As editor-in-chief of the periodical *Bécsi Magyar Újság*, Jászi firmly condemned the "White Terror" in Hungary, which was conducted with the consent of **Miklós Horthy** against HSR activists, yet he equally strongly criticized the Communists.

Between 1923 and 1924 Jászi was invited to the United States for a series of lectures. In 1925 he settled in the United States for good and became a sociology professor at Oberlin College near Cleveland, Ohio. During World War II he was president of the Democratic Union of Hungarians in the United States. In 1947 he made a short visit to Hungary. In 1991 his ashes were brought to Budapest.

Jászi was instrumental in legitimizing the modern social sciences, particularly sociology, in Hungary. He was the leading theoretician of the radical faction of bourgeois liberalism. A scholar and a politician, he considered the democratization of Hungary his main task. He was deeply involved in ethnic issues. His concept of cooperation among the Danube nations became very influential. Jászi was the author of a proposal to resolve Hungary's ethnic problems along the lines of the Swiss model, on the basis of liberal and democratic principles. His publications include *Revolution and Counterrevolution in Hungary* (1924) and a well-known book, *The Dissolution of the Habsburg Monarchy* (1929). Much of his legacy is kept in the Library of Congress in Washington, D.C. (JT)

Sources: *Nagy Képes Milleniumi Arcképcsarnok* (Budapest, 1999); *Magyar Nagylexikon*, vol. 10 (Budapest, 2000); *Magyarország 1944–1956*, CD-ROM (Budapest, 2001); Paul Ignotus, *Hungary* (London, 1972); Nicholas Horthy, *Memoirs* (Paris, 1954); C. A. Macartney, *October Fifteenth: A History of Modern Hungary*, vols. 1–2 (Edinburgh, 1957–61); Steven Bela Vardy, *Historical Dictionary of Hungary* (Lanham, Md., 1997); *Jászi Oszkar hazatérése* (Budapest, 1996); János Pelle, *Jászi Oszkar: Életrajze, észme—és kortörténeti esszé* (Budapest, 2001).

JAWOROWSKI Rajmund, pseudonyms "Włodzimierz," "Antoni," and others (31 August 1885, Birzhula, Ukraine–24 April 1941, Warsaw), Polish Socialist activist. Jaworowski joined the Polish Socialist Party (Polska Partia Socjalistyczna [PPS]) in 1904. He was active in its Military Organization (Organizacja Bojowa), producing bombs and running military training in the Congress Kingdom of Poland. In 1906 he became aligned with the PPS–Revolutionary Faction, and in 1918–19 he was a member of its Central Workers' Committee. Between 1907 and 1909 he was in exile in Siberia but escaped and managed to get to Galicia. In 1909 he joined the Union of Active Struggle (Związek Walki Czynnej [ZWC]). In 1914 he worked for the Commission of Confederated Independence Parties. In 1914–18 he was a member of the Polish Legions and co-organized the Polish Military Organization in the Congress Kingdom of Poland. From 1918 to 1928 Jaworowski served as president of the Warsaw District Workers' Committee of the PPS. In 1920 he volunteered for the Polish Army, and from 1920 to 1921 he was a member of the Polish delegation for negotiations with Soviet Russia in Riga. Between 1922 and 1930 he was an MP on behalf of the PPS. After the murder of President **Gabriel Narutowicz** in December 1922, Jaworowski began organizing a leftist coup to remove the nationalist right from power. During the coup of May 1926, he supported **Józef Piłsudski** and co-organized the general strike of railwaymen. In 1921–28 he was a member of the PPS Chief Council, and from 1926 to 1928, deputy chairman of the PPS Central Executive Committee. In October 1928 he effected a split in the PPS by organizing the pro-Piłsudski PPS–Former Revolutionary Faction and becoming leader of its Central Executive Committee. In 1919–27 Jaworowski was vice-president, and from 1927 to 1931 president, of the Warsaw City Council. Between 1931 and 1939 he served as president of the Central Association of Class Trade Unions (later the Central Organization of Class Trade Unions), which was linked with this party. However, as a result of the split within the party that he himself had caused, Jaworowski lost his former political influence. During the Nazi occupation in 1939 Jaworowski joined the underground Service for the Victory of Poland and later the Union of Armed Struggle. (JS)

Sources: *PSB*, vol. 11; *Encyklopedia historii Drugiej Rzeczypospolitej* (Warsaw, 1999); *Encyklopedia historii Polski: Dzieje polityczne*, vol. 1 (Warsaw, 1994).

JAWORSKI Marian (21 August 1926, Lwów [Lviv]), Roman Catholic archbishop of Lviv, philosopher, and theologian. As did most Poles, Jaworski left Lwów when the Red Army took over the city in 1944. He graduated from a theological seminary in Kalwaria Zebrzydowska, near Kraków, and in June 1950 he was ordained. Then he worked as a vicar in Basznia Dolna and Poronin, and in 1956–58 he was chaplain of the archbishop of Kraków, Eugeniusz Baziak. At the time he became friends with Reverend Karol Wojtyła, later Pope **John Paul II**. From 1967 he taught at the Pontifical Theological Academy in Kraków; from 1973 to 1982 he was its dean, and in 1982–83, its rector. From 1970 Jaworski was secretary of the Commission for Catholic Doctrine of the Polish Episcopate, and from 1973, secretary of its Research Council. On 21 May 1984 he was consecrated auxiliary bishop of the Lviv archdiocese, acting in Lubaczów, on a piece of its territory situated within Poland. From 16 January 1991 Jaworski was archbishop of Lviv, and from 1998, cardinal, initially *in pectore* and from 21 February 2001, overt. He established close contacts with the Lviv hierarchy of the Greek Catholic Church, and with its archbishop of Lviv, **Lubomyr Husar**, Jaworski co-organized the pilgrimage of John Paul II to the Ukraine in June 2001. Jaworski authored *Religijne poznanie Boga według Romano Guardiniego* (The religious cognition of God according to Romano Guardini; 1967); *Zwycięzcy dam spożyć owoc z drzewa życia* (I will give the winner the fruit of the tree of life to eat; 1987); and *Metafizyka* (Metaphysics; 1998). (WR)

Sources: *Wielka encyklopedia PWN*, vol. 12 (Warsaw, 2002); George Weigel, *Witness to Hope* (New York, 1999); www.catholic-hierarchy.org.

JĘDRYCHOWSKI Stefan (19 May 1910, Warsaw–26 May 1996, Warsaw), Polish Communist activist. After graduating from a high school in Wilno (Vilnius) in 1928, Jędrychowski took up law studies at Stefan Batory University in Wilno, graduating in 1932. While a student, he belonged to the Union of Polish Democratic Youth and the Youth Legion, which supported the Józef Piłsudski government. In 1932 he joined the editorial committee of the periodical *Żagary*, a supplement to the conservative daily *Słowo*. In the same year, however, he was drawn to the radical left. In 1935 he was imprisoned for several months for his participation in an illegal group led by Henryk Dembiński that attracted young pro-Communists. Arrested again in 1937 for his journalism in *Po prostu* and *Karta*, after his release in August 1939 Jędrychowski received a Ph.D. in law for the treatise *Bankructwo państwowe i pożyczka przymusowa. Patologia kredytu w okresie* *powszechnego kryzysu kapitalizmu* (State bankruptcy and compulsory loans: The pathology of credit during the general crisis of capitalism).

After the German invasion of Poland in September 1939, Jędrychowski organized a workers' militia in Wilno. Since he was a well-known leftist activist, after the Red Army entered Vilnius, he was elected to the People's Assembly and later to the Supreme Soviet of the Lithuanian SSR. Until December 1940, he worked in the editorial offices of *Prawda Wileńska*. After Germany attacked the USSR in June 1941, Jędrychowski traveled to the Soviet interior and began contributing to the Communist periodical *Nowe Widnokręgi*. He was one of the founders and leaders of the Union of Polish Patriots (Związek Patriotów Polskich [ZPP]), which was inspired by Stalin. Co-founder of the Tadeusz Kościuszko First Division, in 1944 Jędrychowski joined the Polish Workers' Party (Polska Partia Robotnicza [PPR]). Beginning with the First Congress of the PPR in December 1945 until 1975, he was a member of its Central Committee (CC), and after December 1948 he was a member of the CC of the Polish United Workers' Party (Polska Zjednoczona Partia Robotnicza [PUWP]). Jędrychowski actively participated in the Stalinization of Poland by, among other things, helping to eliminate party members who were accused of so-called rightist-nationalist deviation. From July to October 1956 he was a deputy member, and from October 1956 a member, of the PUWP CC Politburo. From July 1944 to February 1972 he was a deputy to the National Home Council (KRN) and subsequently an MP in the Legislative Assembly and in the Assembly of the Polish People's Republic. He also held many government and party posts. At the beginning of 1945 Jędrychowski was a representative of the Provisional Government to France; from June 1945 to February 1947 he was minister of shipping and foreign trade; from December 1947 to April 1948 he was head of the Economic Department of the PPR CC; from April 1948 to April 1949 he was vice-president of the Central Planning Office; and subsequently he was deputy chairman of the State Committee for Economic Planning until December 1951.

Jędrychowski was co-responsible for the preparation and implementation of the Six-Year Plan (1950–55) and the successive Five-Year Plans. From December 1951 to October 1956 he was deputy prime minister, from July to December 1956 he was chairman of the State Committee for Economic Planning, and from December 1956 to December 1968 he was chairman of the Planning Commission of the Council of Ministers. In March 1968 he dismissed people of Jewish origin from this commission. From December 1968 to December 1971 he served as minister of foreign affairs. After the events of December

1970 Jędrychowski, who was seen as a close associate of **Władysław Gomułka**, gradually withdrew from the political scene. In December 1971 he left the Politburo but continued to serve as finance minister until November 1974. As a result of a conflict with Prime Minister **Piotr Jaroszewicz**, Jędrychowski was dismissed from the government. Between January 1975 and February 1978 he was ambassador to Hungary, and subsequently he retired. After 1989 he spoke publicly against the transformation of the system. His psychological portrait was depicted in *Zniewolony Umysł* (The captive mind), by **Czesław Miłosz**, who had been his friend in Wilno. (WD)

Sources: Mołdawa; Nicholas Bethell, *Gomułka: His Poland, His Communism* (London, 1969); Andrzej Albert [Wojciech Roszkowski], *Najnowsza historia Polski 1914–1993*, vols. 1–2 (Warsaw, 1993); Jerzy Eisler, *Marzec 1968* (Warsaw, 1991); Włodzimierz Janowski and Aleksander Kochański, *Informator o strukturze i obsadzie personalnej centralnego aparatu PZPR 1948–1990* (Warsaw, 2000); Jerzy Eisler, *Grudzień 1970* (Warsaw, 2000).

JĘDRZEJEWICZ Janusz (21 June 1885, Spichintsy, near Kiev–16 March 1951, London), Polish politician. The son of a chemist employed as a deputy director of a sugar refinery in the Ukraine, Jędrzejewicz was the brother of **Wacław Jędrzejewicz**. While still at school, he was involved in pro-independence youth organizations, and in 1904 he joined the Polish Socialist Party (PPS). He studied mathematics and chemistry in Kraków and Paris. In 1914 he became active in the Polish Military Organization (Polska Organizacja Wojskowa [POW]), and between 1915 and 1916 he served in the Polish Legions. A close associate of **Józef Piłsudski**, in 1917 Jędrzejewicz started working in the Military Commission of the Provisional Council of State, and in the summer of that year he began publishing the periodical *Rząd i wojsko*. He was also a member of the Convention of Organization A (Konwent Organizacji A), a conspiratorial group of trusted activists of parties that supported Piłsudski. This group led the pro-independence camp at the time when Piłsudski was interned. Jędrzejewicz published numerous articles and brochures, such as *Józef Piłsudski* (1918), that supported the tactics of the pro-independence left.

In the fall of 1918 Jędrzejewicz joined the Polish Army and fought in the Polish-Bolshevik war. He retired from the army in 1923 and started working as a teacher. In 1926 he founded the monthly *Wiedza i Życie*. A member of the National Grand Lodge, after the coup of May 1926 he worked in the chancellery of the prime minister, where he was in charge of education and the school system. In the 1928 elections Jędrzejewicz ran successfully as a candidate of the Nonparty Bloc of Cooperation with the Government (BBWR), and between 1930 and 1935 he was vice-president of the BBWR. In 1929 he founded the educational organization Zrąb. He was also interested in eastern policy. In 1930 he co-founded the Eastern Institute in Wilno (Vilnius) and lectured in its School of Political Sciences. He was a supporter of the Promethean idea that stipulated the liberation of the nations in the USSR's sphere of influence from the Kremlin's domination. Between August 1931 and February 1934 Jędrzejewicz was minister of religious affairs and public education. At that time he authorized a 1932 law on the school system and a 1933 law on state academic schools. These laws were called the "Jędrzejewicz Reform" of the Polish school system. A uniform system of elementary schools, gymnasiums (high schools), comprehensive high schools, and vocational schools was introduced. Relations between the administration and state institutions of higher education were regulated. The Jędrzejewicz Reform caused much controversy, but it also won many supporters and is looked upon favorably today. Promoting a model of upbringing in the national spirit typical of the *sanacja* (moral and political cleansing) regime, Jędrzejewicz focused on the development of youth organizations supporting the government system after the May coup. Accordingly, he co-founded the Advance Guard (Straż Przednia), which targeted high school students, and the Youth Legion, which targeted older students.

On 11 May 1933 Jędrzejewicz assumed the post of prime minister. It was during his term in office that a new constitutional bill was pushed through the Assembly in violation of parliamentary procedures and that the Polish-German non-aggression declaration of January 1934 was signed. Jędrzejewicz resigned on 14 May 1934. After Piłsudski's death, he supported **Walery Sławek**, but both men gradually lost power in the *sanacja* circles. In 1935–38 Jędrzejewicz served as a senator. In 1937 he did not support the establishment of the pro-totalitarian Camp of National Unity (Obóz Zjednoczenia Narodowego [OZN]). In September 1939 he went to Romania and then to Palestine, trying to consolidate *sanacja* circles, which were blamed for the September 1939 defeat. In the fall of 1947 he settled in London. Jędrzejewicz wrote his memoirs, *W służbie idei: Fragmenty pamiętnika i pism* (In service to the idea: Fragments of memoirs and of writings; 1972). (WR)

Sources: *PSB*, vol. 11; *Encyklopedia historii Drugiej Rzeczypospolitej* (Warsaw, 1999); Władysław Pobóg-Malinowski, *Najnowsza historia polityczna Polski*, vol. 2 (London, 1983); Władysław T. Kulesza, *Koncepcje ideowo-polityczne obozu rządzącego w Polsce w latach 1926–1935* (Wrocław, 1985); Tomasz Nałęcz, "Janusz Jędrzejewicz, premier Rzeczypospolitej 10 V 1933–13 V 1934," in Andrzej Chojnowski and Piotr Wróbel, eds., *Prezydenci i premierzy Drugiej Rzeczypospolitej* (Wrocław, 1992).

JĘDRZEJEWICZ Wacław (21 January 1893, Spichintsy, near Kiev–30 November 1993, Cheshire, Connecticut), Polish politician. The son of a chemist employed as a deputy director of a sugar refinery in the Ukraine, Jędrzejewicz was the brother of **Janusz Jędrzejewicz**. He studied in Kraków, where he joined the Union of Polish Youth, Zet, and the Rifle Association. In August 1914 he was one of the co-founders of the Polish Military Organization (Polska Organizacja Wojskowa [POW]), and he became a member of the POW High Command. In 1915 he served in the Polish Legions, but in March 1916 he again devoted himself to work in the POW. In July 1917 he refused to swear allegiance to the emperors of Germany and Austria-Hungary, and he was arrested. Released from prison in September 1918, Jędrzejewicz became head of the personnel department of the POW High Command. After the Polish Army was formed in November of that year, he started working in the Second Department of the General Staff. He was a negotiator and co-signatory of the Polish-Ukrainian agreement of 24 April 1920 and a military adviser at the peace negotiations with Soviet Russia in Riga. Between 1925 and 1928 Jędrzejewicz served as military attaché to Tokyo; therefore he did not personally take part in the May coup of 1926. However, he was a close associate of **Józef Piłsudski**. In 1928 Jędrzejewicz became director of the Administrative Department, and in 1931 director of the Consular Department, of the Ministry of Foreign Affairs. In September 1933 he was made deputy minister of the treasury in the government of his brother, Janusz. In February 1934 he succeeded his brother as minister of religious affairs and public education and held this position in the cabinets of **Leon Kozłowski** and **Walery Sławek** until October 1935. After Piłsudski's death, Jędrzejewicz gradually withdrew from public life.

In September 1939 Jędrzejewicz took part in shipping the treasury of the National Defense Fund out of Poland. In March 1941 he settled in the United States. In June 1942 he took an active part in the establishment of the National Committee of Americans of Polish Origin and subsequently in the establishment of the Józef Piłsudski Institute in New York. From 1943 to 1948 he served as president of this institute. He devoted himself to research, compiling and editing documentation on the *sanacja* government and Piłsudski's life. He wrote *Poland in the British Parliament* (3 vols.; 1946–62); the detailed *Kronika życia Józefa Piłsudskiego 1867–1935* (Chronicle of Józef Piłsudski's life 1867–1935; 1977); the biography *Józef Piłsudski 1867–1935: Życiorys* (Józef Piłsudski, 1867–1935: A biography; 1982); and other works. (WR)

Sources: *Encyklopedia historii Drugiej Rzeczypospolitej* (Warsaw, 1999); Władysław Pobóg-Malinowski, *Najnowsza historia polityczna Polski*, vol. 2 (London, 1983); Władysław T. Kulesza, *Koncepcje ideowo-polityczne obozu rządzącego w Polsce w latach 1926–1935* (Wrocław, 1985).

JEFTIĆ Bogoljub (24 December 1886, Kragujevac–7 June 1960, Paris), Serb politician. In his youth Jeftić was allied with the Radical Party. In 1926 he became an envoy to Tirana. When King **Alexander I** took power in 1929, he was made a court minister. In 1931 he was one of the founders of the ruling Yugoslav National Party (YNP), which became the only legal political party after other political parties and associations were declared illegal. The YNP worked for the centralization of the state. In July 1932 Jeftić became minister of foreign affairs and held this position for two and a half years in four successive cabinets. At that time, the main aims of Yugoslavia's foreign policy were to strengthen relations with France and Britain and develop cooperation within the Little Entente and the so-called Little Balkan Entente. In February 1934 the Balkan Pact was signed with Turkey, Greece, and Romania, and relations with Bulgaria improved. This effectively thwarted Italian plans to establish a regional coalition against Yugoslavia. Jeftić played a major role in securing those agreements.

Jeftić was a witness to the Ustaša attempt on the life of King Alexander on 9 October 1934 in Marseilles. He recalled that the last words of the dying king were an order addressed to his entourage to "take care of my Yugoslavia." On 19 December 1934 Jeftić was assigned the mission of forming a new government. Talks on forming a government of national unity, conducted with political parties that lacked representation in the parliament dominated by the supporters of the assassinated king, reached a deadlock because Jeftić did not want to abandon a unitary and centrist line in the domestic policy dominated by the Serbs. His resistance became one of the factors that led to the unification of a divided non-parliamentary opposition under the leadership of the Radical Party and the Slovene People's Party. The elections of May 1935, held in an atmosphere of terror and marked by "miracles at the ballot box," directly impinged on the political and moral standing of the prime minister; finally, as a result of an increase in social support for the opposition, Jeftić was forced to resign on 24 June 1935. He resigned under pressure from a coalition formed by **Milan Stojadinović**. When Stojadinović dissolved the ruling party, Jeftić, along with **Petar Živković**, revived the YNP in June 1936. After the parliamentary elections of December 1938 this party joined the opposition led by the Croat leader **Vladko Maček**.

After the coup staged by General **Dušan Simović** on 27 March 1941, provoked by the concessions made to the Third Reich and Italy, Jeftić again joined the government and assumed the portfolio of minister of transportation. After the German aggression in April 1941, he went to Great Britain, where he served as a member of successive Yugoslav governments-in-exile. From September 1943 to July 1944 he was ambassador of the royal government to London. He was dismissed from this position as a result of an agreement between **Josip Broz Tito** and the Yugoslav government-in-exile. Jeftić did not return to Yugoslavia. In 1946 he became a member of the émigré Yugoslav National Council in London. (AG)

Sources: Biographisches Lexikon, vol. 2; *Osteuropa-Handbuch: Jugoslawien* (Cologne and Graz, 1954); Jacob B. Hoptner, *Yugoslavia in Crisis, 1934–1941* (New York, 1962); Ljubo Boban, *Sporazum Cvetković-Maček* (Belgrade, 1965); Johann Wuescht, *Jugoslawien und das Dritte Reich* (Stuttgart, 1969); Wacław Felczak and Tadeusz Wasilewski, *Historia Jugosławii* (Wrocław, 1985); Michał J. Zacharias, *Jugosławia w polityce Wielkiej Brytanii 1940–1945* (Wrocław, 1987).

JEGLIČ Anton Bonaventura (29 May 1850, Begunje na Gorenjskem–2 July 1937, Stična), Slovene Catholic bishop. After attending a theological seminary in Ljubljana, Jeglič completed theological studies in Vienna in 1876, and he was ordained in 1879. He subsequently lectured in history, cannon law, and church doctrine at a theological seminary and at the Theological Department of the University of Ljubljana. In 1882 he became a canon in Sarajevo, and in February 1898 he was consecrated bishop of Ljubljana. From the end of the nineteenth century, Jeglič had a major influence in shaping Slovene social Catholicism. An opponent of modernism, he ordered most copies of *Erotika*, by **Ivan Cankar**, to be bought up and burned. He was one of the spiritual animators of the Catholic National Party (Katoliška Narodna Stranka) and (from 1905) the Slovene People's Party (Slovenska Ljudska Stranka [SLS]). He worked closely with **Ivan Šušteršič**, the leader of the SLS. A promoter of Catholic education, Jeglič brought about the establishment of a Catholic gymnasium in Ljubljana in 1905. In opposition to Sokol (Falcon), a liberal gymnastic society, he supported Orel (Eagle), a similar conservative organization. In 1916 he backed the left wing of the Slovene national Catholic movement led by **Janez Krek**, and he supported Krek's work in the agricultural cooperative movement. Jeglič supported the May Declaration of 1917 and activities aimed at the establishment of a Slovene state, but at the end of 1918 he accepted the incorporation of Slovenia into the Kingdom of Serbs, Croats, and Slovenes. He repeatedly defended the rights of the Slovenes in Austria and Italy. Jeglič's views were influenced by the philosophy of Aleš Ušeničnik, but he supported various factions within the Catholic people's movement. In May 1930 Jeglič retired and in 1932 settled in a monastery in Stična. (WR)

Sources: Slovenski bijografski leksikon, vol. 3 (Ljubljana, 1928); *Enciklopedija Slovenije*, vol. 2 (Ljubljana, 1990); Joza Jagodić,

Nadškof Jeglič (Celovec, 1952); J. Prunk, "Škof Jeglič—politik," *Kronika*, 1971, no. 19; Edo Sukulj, ed. *Jegličev simpozij v Rimu* (Celje, 1991); Leopoldina Plut-Pregelj and Carole Rogel, *Historical Dictionary of Slovenia* (Lanham, Md., 1996).

JEHLIČKA František, pseudonyms "Margin" and "Pater Salezius" (24 January 1879, Kúty, Slovakia–3 January 1939, Vienna), Slovak priest, politician, and philosopher. Jehlička completed theological studies in Vienna, where in 1902 he was ordained and in 1905 he successfully defended his doctoral thesis. At that time he worked with Father **Ferdinand Juriga** in organizing the political movement of the Slovak Catholics. One of the leading representatives of Slovak conservative thought, in the treatise *Novoveká filozofia a Slováci* (Modern philosophy and the Slovaks; 1903) Jehlička condemned empiricism and rationalism, arguing against, among other things, the liberal movement of the Hlasists. In 1906 he was elected to the Hungarian parliament from the lists of the independent Slovak faction of the Hungarian Catholic People's Party and in 1913 from the lists of the Slovak People's Party (Slovenská ľudová strana [SLS]). However, soon afterwards he distanced himself from Slovak national claims, resigned his parliamentary seat, and pursued an academic career. In 1907 he began lecturing in theology at the university in Budapest, where he was promoted to associate professor in 1910.

After Czechoslovakia was created, Jehlička returned to Slovakia and declared his loyalty to the new state. He took a seat in parliament in Prague and was appointed administrator of the university in Bratislava. An associate of Reverend **Andrej Hlinka**, he helped to revive the SLS. On Jehlička's initiative, Hlinka went to the Paris Peace Conference. Jehlička also prepared a memorandum that the Slovak delegation submitted to the representatives of the victorious powers in September 1919. In this memorandum, the Slovaks demanded autonomy and a plebiscite on Slovak national status. Seeing that all these actions were unsuccessful, Jehlička began to call for the reincorporation of Slovakia into Hungary. In Budapest, he founded the Party of Hungarian-Slovak Friendship (Magyarbarát Tót Párt) and prepared a plan for Slovak autonomy within the Hungarian state. This plan was approved by the Hungarian government in January 1921. In 1920 Jehlička became professor of theology at Warsaw University. In agreement with the Hungarian authorities, in May 1920 he established the Slovak National Council in Warsaw, and he began forming the Hungarian-Slovak Legion. He also worked with Polish intelligence. In Kraków, he published the periodical *Slovák*, in which he called for a union of the Polish and Slovak states in September 1920 and continued to uphold this view thereafter. Jehlička helped to prepare a military action in Slovakia and established a center for anti-Czech propaganda in Cieszyn. His actions failed to win support in Slovakia and were condemned by the SLS leadership. Nonetheless, by using his contacts in Catholic circles, he continued to agitate against the Czechoslovak state. In 1933 he was one of the founders of the Slovak Council in Geneva, which frequently submitted manifestos on the Slovak cause to the League of Nations. From 1933 on, Jehlička stayed in close touch with the Italian authorities, the Sudeten Germans, and German intelligence. He was the author of numerous political brochures, including *Quo vadis, the Slovak Nation?* (1935). (MG)

Sources: *SBS*; Konštantín Čulen, "Dr. Rudolf František Jehlička," in *Literárny almanach Slováka v Amerike* (Middletown, Pa., 1957); Juraj Kramer, *Iredenta a separatizmus v slovenskej politike* (Bratislava, 1957); Vladimír Bakoš, *Kapitoly s dejín slovenského myslenia* (Bratislava, 1995); Marián Hronský, *Boj o Slovensko a Trianon 1918–1920* (Bratislava, 1998); Béla Angyal, "Magyar szervezetek és mozgalmak Csehszlovákiában 1918–1921," *Fórum Társdalomtudományi Szemle*, 2000, no. 1.

JELAVIĆ Ante (21 August 1963, Podprolog, Croatia), Croatian politician from Bosnia-Herzegovina (BH). An officer of the Yugoslav People's Army, in the early 1990s Jelavić joined the Bosnian Croatian militia. During the war in Bosnia he advanced to the position of chief of logistics of Croatian units. In 1996 he became minister of defense of the Muslim-Croat Federation, one of the two parts constituting Bosnia-Herzegovina, and from 1998 he was a member of the Presidium of the Republic of Bosnia and Herzegovina—that is, the collective head of state—on behalf of the Croatian Democratic Union (Hrvatska Demokratska Zajednica [HDZ]). Although Croatian president **Franjo Tudjman** declared his support for another candidate, Jelavić managed to win nonetheless. From 15 June 1999 to 14 February 2000 Jelavić presided over the BH Presidium. He strove to maintain strong links with Croatia and opposed the liquidation of Herceg-Bosnia, thought to be a Croatian state within Bosnia-Herzegovina, on the basis of the Washington Agreement of March 1994 and the Dayton Agreement of November 1995. As long as Tudjman was in power, Zagreb supported the separatism of Bosnian Croats, but the new Croat president, **Stipe Mesić**, announced in 2000 that he would withhold financial support for Herceg-Bosnia and would give up plans of dividing BH between Serbia and Croatia. Jelavić's position was weakened by changes in the electoral law before the elections of November 2000; these led to the loss of power by the HDZ in BH. In March 2001 Jelavić declared that the Croats would leave the Muslim-Croat Federation and demanded an amendment of the electoral law. A separate Bosnian Croat government was created in

Mostar. As a result, the international mediator for Bosnian civil reconstruction, Wolfgang Petritsch, responsible for the implementation of the Dayton Agreement, removed Jelavić from the BH Presidium on 7 March 2001. In May 2002 Jelavić resigned from leading the HDZ in BH. (WR/AO)

Sources: Bugajski; www.rulers.org; www.ohr.int; www.rferl.org.

JIČÍNSKÝ Zdeněk (26 February 1929, Ostřešany, Pardubice district), Czech lawyer and politician. After graduating in law from Charles University in Prague in 1952, Jičínský worked as an assistant professor at this university. In 1951 he joined the Communist Party of Czechoslovakia (CPC), and from 1954 to 1964 he worked as a lecturer at the party school of the party's Central Committee. Between 1959 and 1960 he sat on a committee responsible for drafting a new constitution that contributed greatly to the federalization of the state. In 1964 he became a *docent* (associate professor) and in 1969 a professor at the Law Department of Charles University. Jičínský was an advocate of the democratization of the country. From 1968 to 1969 he was a deputy to the Czech National Council and deputy chairman and then chairman of its national law committee. In 1969 he also became a deputy to the Chamber of Nations of the Federal Assembly. In November 1969, during the so-called normalization period, he was deprived of both parliamentary seats. Expelled from the CPC and dismissed from the university in 1970, he worked as a lawyer in an insurance society. After signing Charter 77 in 1977, Jičínský was dismissed from work, and for two years he could not find a job. In 1979–89 he worked as a lawyer in the Mototechna Prague firm, and he published abroad as well as in the underground press in Czechoslovakia.

In November and December 1989, as one of the leaders of the Civic Forum (Občanské Fórum [OF]), Jičínský represented the opposition during negotiations with the Communist authorities. From the end of 1989 to the end of 1992 he was a deputy to the Chamber of Nations of the Federal Assembly, and until June 1992 he was deputy chairman of the Federal Assembly. Until 1991 he represented the Civic Forum, and after its breakup, the Civic Movement (Občanské Hnutí [OH]). From the spring of 1992 on he was a representative of the Czechoslovak Social Democracy (Československá Sociální Demokracie), renamed the Czech Social Democratic Party (Česká Strana Sociálně Demokratická) in 1993. Jičínský called for the recognition of the legal continuity of Czechoslovakia and advocated the maintenance of the common state of Czechs and Slovaks. In June 1996 he became a member

of the Chamber of Deputies in the Czech parliament, in which he sat until June 2002, and deputy chairman of its Constitutional Law Committee. He was the author and co-author of such works as *Ústava ČSSR* (The constitution of the CSSR; 1961; co-authored with Pavel Levit); *Vznik České národní rady v době Pražského jara 1968 a její působení do podzimu 1969* (The establishment of the Czech National Council during the Prague Spring of 1968 and its activity until the autumn of 1969; Cologne, 1984; Prague, 1990); *Československý parlament v polistopadovém vývoji* (The Czechoslovak parliament during the post–November period; 1993); and *Problémy české politiky* (Issues of Czech policy; 1993). (PU)

Sources: *ČBS*; *Kdo je kdo v České Republice na přelomu 20. století* (Prague, 1998); *Českoslovenští politici: 1918–1991* (Prague, 1991); *Kdo byl kdo v našich dějinách ve 20. století*, vol. 1 (Prague, 1998); Eric Stein, *Czecho/Slovakia: Ethnic Conflict, Constitutional Fissure, Negotiated Breakup* (Ann Arbor, 1997); Jan Rychlík, *Rozpad Československa: Česko-slovenské vztahy 1989–1992* (Bratislava, 2002).

JODKO-NARKIEWICZ Witold, pseudonyms "Aleksander Wroński," "Jowisz," "Judym," and others (29 April 1864, Warsaw–22 October 1924, Warsaw), Polish politician and Socialist journalist. In 1884 Jodko-Narkiewicz joined the International Social Revolutionary Party Proletariat (First Proletariat), and later he was active in the Social Revolutionary Party Proletariat (Second Proletariat). From 1885 to 1898 he was in exile. He studied medicine in Dorpat (Tartu), Würzburg, and Paris. In 1892, as a representative of the Second Proletariat, he co-organized the Paris congress of Polish Socialists, and he was the secretary of this congress. Thus he became co-founder of the Union of Polish Socialists Abroad (Związek Zagraniczny Socjalistów Polskich [ZZSP]). From 1894 to 1897 he was a member of the Board of the ZZSP and the Polish Socialist Party (Polska Partia Socjalistyczna [PPS]), and in 1902 he became a member of the PPS Central Workers' Committee. A close associate of **Józef Piłsudski**, Jodko-Narkiewicz was considered a theoretician of socialism. From 1893 to 1897 and in 1905 he edited the periodical *Przedświt*. After the split in the Socialist movement in 1906, he was a member of the PPS–Revolutionary Faction. He helped organize pro-independence organizations in Galicia. In 1912 he was a co-founder of the Commission of Confederated Independence Parties, and he served as its secretary until 1914. In 1914 he co-founded and was the leader of the Polish National Organization (Polska Organizacja Narodowa [PON]). From 1915 to 1916 he was a member of the Central National Committee (Centralny Komitet Narodowy [CKN]). He called for an alliance with the Central Powers. In 1918–19 Jodko-Narkiewicz served as deputy minister for foreign affairs. From 1919 to 1921 he served as ambassador to Turkey, and from 1921 to 1923, as ambassador to Latvia. In the spring of 1922 he represented Poland in negotiations among the representatives of the Baltic states in Riga. He was the author of program brochures and articles on the political system and the international position of Poland. (JS)

Sources: *PSB*, vol. 11; *Słownik polityków polskich XX wieku* (Poznań, 1998); *Encyklopedia Historii Polski: Dzieje polityczne*, vol. 1 (Warsaw, 1994); Jerzy Holzer, *Polska Paria Socjalistyczna w latach 1917–1919* (Warsaw, 1962); Wacław Jędrzejewicz, *Kronika życia Józefa Piłsudskiego 1867–1935* (London, 1986).

JOHN PAUL II [originally Karol Wojtyła] (18 May 1920, Wadowice–2 April 2005, Rome), Polish Pope. John Paul's mother died while he was young, and he soon lost his older brother. He was brought up by a pious father, a retired lieutenant of the Polish Army, in humble material conditions. In 1938 he graduated from high school in Wadowice. He started Polish studies at the Jagiellonian University (Uniwersytet Jagielloński [UJ]) in Kraków. After the German invasion of Poland in 1939 he had to interrupt his studies, and he worked as a blue-collar laborer in the Solvay chemical factory and in a quarry near Kraków. In October 1942, after his father's death, John Paul started theological studies at the clandestine UJ Theological Department and at a secret theological seminary. At the same time he performed in the clandestine Rhapsodical Theater (Teatr Rapsodyczny). In March 1946 he published a collection of poems, *Pieśń o Bogu ukrytym* (Hymn of the hidden God). In August 1946 he graduated, and on 1 November 1946 he was ordained. Inspired by Cardinal **Adam Sapieha,** in 1946–48 John Paul continued his studies at the Pontifical Angelicum University in Rome, where he received a Ph.D. Upon his return to Poland, he started to work as a vicar in a rural parish in Niegowici (1948–51), studying and lecturing at the UJ and the Catholic University of Lublin (Katolicki Uniwersytet Lubelski [KUL]), where in 1951 he received a Ph.D. and in 1953 a postdoctoral degree (*habilitacja*) in moral theology. He taught social ethics at the Theological Seminary in Kraków and (from 1954) philosophy at the KUL. Until 1953 and after 1956 he also published in the Kraków Catholic weekly, *Tygodnik Powszechny*.

On 4 July 1958 John Paul was consecrated as bishop of Kraków. He faced a serious challenge when the Communist authorities removed religious instruction from the schools, which was in contradiction to the church-state agreement of 1956, and he also had to cope with obstacles that arose during the construction of a church in Nowa Huta. Believers in this new industrial town de-

manded a Catholic church and, facing official obstructions, demonstrated in defense of the cross in 1960. Thanks to John Paul's skillful diplomacy, the Nowa Huta church was finally erected. In 1960 John Paul published *Miłość i odpowiedzialność* (*Love and Responsibility*, 1981) on Catholic sexual morality, of which Pope Paul VI availed himself while preparing his encyclical *Humanum vitae*. Also in 1960 he published the drama *Przed sklepem jubilera* (In front of the jeweller's store). On 16 June 1962 John Paul was elected vicar of the Kraków chapter. The Polish Communist authorities agreed that he would succeed Archbishop Eugeniusz Baziak as metropolitan of Kraków, counting on the possibility of winning him over against Primate **Stefan Wyszyński**. On 30 December 1963 he was appointed archbishop metropolitan of Kraków. Soon he totally frustrated the hopes of the Communists.

A member of the preparatory commission of the Second Vatican Council in 1962–65, John Paul took an active part in the council, and he greatly contributed to its debates on religious freedom. After his work on the council he co-authored letters inviting bishops from many countries to the celebrations of the Millennium of Polish Christianity; among these was a letter to the German bishops that had the famous phrase "we forgive and ask forgiveness." On 29 May 1967 Pope Paul VI appointed him cardinal. In 1969 John Paul published *Osoba i czyn* (The acting person), in which he stressed the particular dignity of the human being. From 1971 he was a member of the Council of the Secretariat of the Synod of Bishops, and he became known for his work in other Roman Curia congregations. On the invitation of Pope Paul VI, in 1976 he led the Vatican Lenten retreat. He visited the United States twice, and in September 1978, along with a delegation of the Polish Episcopate, he toured West Germany, receiving an enthusiastic welcome.

On 16 October 1978 John Paul was elected pope. He adopted the name John Paul II in reference to the tradition of his two great predecessors, John XXIII and Paul VI. His election was a world sensation since he was the first non-Italian to become the head of the Catholic Church in 455 years and since he came for a Communist country, where, despite thirty-five years of official struggle against religion, the Catholic Church and faith had remained alive among the majority of the population. This election changed Poland, where John Paul became not only a religious leader, but also a national hero. The election of a Polish Pope drew the world's attention to the political nature of the divisions in Europe and to its actual unity.

From the very beginning John Paul II attracted attention by his new style, enormous energy, and spiritual personality. Everywhere he went he drew the enthusiasm of the crowd. In a short time he published the encyclicals *Redemptor hominis* (1979) and *Laborem Exercens* (1981), which provided for the theological foundations of his pontificate. His new style included numerous pilgrimages. By the twenty-fifth anniversary of his pontificate he had paid more than one hundred visits to most countries of the world. In 1979 he went to Mexico, Poland, Ireland, the United States, and Turkey; in 1980, to several African countries, Germany, France, and Brazil; and in 1981, to Pakistan, the Philippines, and Japan. Everywhere he was welcomed by huge crowds. His visit to Poland in June 1979 played an enormous role in the awakening of the civil society in his homeland. His activities raised a lot of anxiety in the Kremlin. During a meeting of Soviet bloc party secretaries in Berlin on 3–5 June 1979 plans were prepared to oppose his mission. The local pro-Soviet press brutally attacked him. His theology of labor and the peaceful method of achieving social goals that he advocated substantially contributed to the formation of Solidarity after the summer 1980 strikes on the Polish Baltic Coast. When in December 1980 the Kremlin made preparations to invade Poland, John Paul planned to come to his homeland. It may be assumed that the attempt on his life made in Rome by the Turkish terrorist Mehmet Ali Agca on 13 May 1981 was no accident. There are hints indicating that the attempt was prepared by the Bulgarian special services in cooperation with the KGB, but the case remains unsolved.

After convalescence, John Paul II resumed his pilgrimages. In 1982 he went to Africa, Fatima (Portugal), Great Britain, Argentina, Brazil, and Spain, and he paid a visit to the International Labour Organization headquarters in Geneva, Switzerland. In 1983 he visited Central America, the Caribbean islands, and Poland. His homilies to the Poles kept up their determination during the period of martial law. In January 1984 the Holy See restored diplomatic relations with the United States, severed in 1867. In May 1984 John Paul went on another trip to Asia and the Pacific, meeting President Ronald Reagan in Alaska. He paid special attention to Third World countries and the threats of spreading violence resulting from the so-called theology of liberation, particularly popular in Latin America. In September 1984 a special instruction of the Congregation for the Doctrine of Faith was published on the matter. Supporting efforts at liberation from economic, political, cultural, social, and racial discrimination, the instruction criticized the theology of liberation for accepting the principle of the class struggle and the use of violence.

The Pope met all kinds of political leaders, even those who openly violated principles advocated by the Church

and even suppressed religion. For instance, in February 1985 he met the Soviet foreign minister, Andrei Gromyko. In August 1985 he went to Africa, where he appealed for a dialogue with Islam. In 1986 he visited India (where he met Mother Teresa), East Asia, Australia, and New Zealand. In December 1987 he received the Patriarch of Constantinople, Dimitrios II, in the Vatican and signed with him a declaration of hope for the development of a dialogue and rapprochement between the Catholic and Orthodox Churches.

Apart from enthusiasm, his mission raised objections. In Latin America and the Philippines, a part of the clergy did not abandon the theology of liberation. Many believers, including many priests in the United States and Western Europe, criticized his negative attitude toward abortion and the acceptance of women into the priesthood. Radical theologians even questioned the right of the Pope to state what was within the limits of Catholic doctrine and what was not. An extraordinary Synod of Bishops in Rome in November and December 1985 defined the limits of political engagement by the clergy; stressed the importance of women in Church life and the substantial meaning of the protection of the fetus; and condemned the consumerist way of life, race discrimination, and violations of human rights. Defined as a social "liberal" and a doctrinal "conservative," the Pope was convinced that the protection of human dignity and the necessary modernization of Church activity did not imply a democratic debate over Catholic doctrine. In 1987 he published another social encyclical, *Sollicitudo rei socialis*. He supported the development of religious movements, but he opposed integrism, which rejected the accomplishments of the Second Vatican Council. When in late June 1988 the integrist leader, Archbishop Marcel Levebvre, consecrated four bishops without consent of the Holy See, he was excommunicated; this started the first twentieth-century schism in Catholicism.

John Paul II greatly contributed to the relatively peaceful fall of the Communist system in the Soviet bloc. This was also stressed by Mikhail Gorbachev, whom the Pope met on 1 December 1989. After 1989 the Pope normalized the legal and organizational standing of the Catholic Church in the Soviet Union and the East European countries. He also visited most of the former Communist countries. Apart from Poland, he visited Czechoslovakia in 1990; Hungary in 1991 and 1996; Albania, Estonia, Latvia, and Lithuania in 1993; Croatia in 1994 and 2003; the Czech Republic and Slovakia in 1995; Slovenia in 1996; Bosnia and Herzegovina in 1997; Romania in 1999; Ukraine, Armenia, and Kazakhstan in 2001; and Bulgaria in 2002. He also went to Cuba in 1998. Thanks to the mediation of the Vatican and local churches, peaceful transitions from dictatorship to democracy were made possible in the Philippines, Nicaragua, and some African countries. The Pope also took an active part in negotiating a border agreement between Chile and Argentina.

Inspired by the Second Vatican Council's stance toward non-Christian religions, John Paul II was particularly active in the process of reconciliation between the Catholic Church and Jews, and he made several breakthrough steps in this direction. In April 1986 he was the first pope to pay a visit to the Rome synagogue. He established relations between the Holy See and the state of Israel. On 30 December 1993 the first agreement between them was signed in Jerusalem. On 17 March 1994 the Israeli prime minister paid an official visit to the Vatican, and on 15 June 1994 diplomatic relations were established between the two states. On 25 October 1994 the Vatican also established official relations with the Palestinian Liberation Organization. In view of the spread of militant Islam, the Pope decided to go to Sudan in February 1993, where he defended Christian rights, which had been violated by the bloody repression of the local fundamentalist regime.

The pontificate of John Paul II gave the Catholic Church a new dynamism, but the challenges to Catholicism remained. Scandals involving priests and even bishops and the erosion of religious belief required not only words, but also deeds. For instance, the Pope suspended French bishop Jacques Gaillot for supporting ideas contrary to Catholic doctrine. Despite the tensions and problems within the U.S. Catholic community, he consistently opposed abortion, homosexuality, and women's entry into the priesthood. During a visit to the United States in August 1993 he strongly criticized the "civilization of death" that accepted abortion and euthanasia. At the same time, opposing the ordination of women, he stressed the unique dignity of women. During his visit to South Africa in September 1995 he said that women were more sensitive to peace and justice since they were closer to the mystique of life. On the occasion of a UN conference in Beijing in the summer of 1995, he published a letter apologizing for centuries of the unequal treatment of women and for the sins of "those sons of the Church" who bore responsibility for this. He always stressed the role of family and motherhood in diminishing the crisis of human civilization. In 1986 in Rome he initiated Catholic youth meetings, held every year or every other year in various countries all over the world.

In 1991 John Paul II published the encyclical *Centisimus Annus* to commemorate the centenary of the *Rerum Novarum* encyclical of Pope Leo XIII. In November and December 1991 he organized the Synod of European Bishops, which launched a new evangelization of the Old Continent. In November 1992 in Rome a new catechism was announced, and in October 1993 the encyclical *Veritatis Splendor* was published. Although many Catholics failed to follow his teachings, his popularity was enormous. In 1994 *Time* magazine announced that John Paul was Man of the Year. In June 1994 he called on all Catholics to do self-examinations and demanded repentance for intolerance and violence. In 1994 his book, *Przekroczyć próg nadziei* (Crossing the Threshold of Hope; 1994), became a worldwide best seller. In March 1995 he announced the encyclical *Evangelium vitae* in defense of life against the "culture of death," and in May 1995 another encyclical, *Ut unum sint*, on a possible unity among Christians. On the occasion of fifty years of his priesthood in 1996, he announced his memoirs, *Dar i tajemnica* (Gift and Mystery; 1996). The theological culmination of his pontificate was the encyclical *Fides et ratio* (1998), in which he stated that in its departure from faith, European culture was also departing from reason and that it was essential to combine faith and reason.

John Paul II told the world what he thought necessary, disregarding hasty, everyday opinions. He opposed both the Iraqi invasion of Kuwait in 1990 and the military operations against Iraq in 1991 and 2003. He also criticized the UN action in Somalia. He tried to create a basis for the solution of political problems by formulating a moral diagnosis. For instance, during the religious celebrations on the five hundredth anniversary of Columbus's landing in America in October 1992, he stressed the importance of the Christianization of the new continent, but he criticized the crimes committed by the colonizers, including priests. He did not conceal truth, even if it was troublesome for the Church. In October 1992 he rehabilitated Galileo, calling the Inquisition verdict of 1632 a "painful misunderstanding." As a scholar, he cared for the development of contacts between the Church and academia.

John Paul II canonized and beatified more than one thousand people, more than any other pope in history. Thus he showed his contemporaries the examples of faith, heroism, and even martyrdom in the defense of faith. He introduced the one-billion-man Catholic community into the new millennium through the celebration of the Jubilee Year 2000. In the spring of 2000 he visited the Holy Land, praying at Mount Sinai and at the Tomb of Christ in Jerusalem. During the Jubilee Year he led the Church in self-examination, apologizing to other communities—for instance, the Jewish community—for sins committed in the name of the Church, and he encouraged personal self-examinations of this kind. Fighting Parkinson's disease, he relentlessly continued his mission. He often appealed to his audience to "be not afraid!" and he posed fundamental questions vital for any human being: "What should we do?" and "How do we recognize good and evil?" John Paul's death and funeral witnessed an unprecedented mass grievance all over the world, especially in Poland and Italy. (WR)

Sources: *Habemus papam* (Kraków, 1978); Claire Sterling, *The Time of the Assasins* (New York, 1983); Paul Henze, *Plot to Kill the Pope* (New York, 1983); André Frossard, *"Be Not Afraid!"* (New York, 1984); Rocco Buttiglione, *Karol Wojtyła: The Thought of the Man Who Became Pope John Paul II* (Grand Rapids, Mich., 1997); J. N. D. Kelly, *The Oxford Dictionary of Popes* (Oxford, 1986); John Moody, *Pope John Paul II* (New York, 1997); Mieczysław Maliński, *Przewodnik po życiu Karola Wojtyły* (Kraków, 1997); Avery Dulles, SJ, *The Splendor of Faith: The Theological Vision of Pope John Paul II* (New York, 1999); George Weigel, *Witness to Hope* (New York, 1999); Luigi Accatolli, *Man of the Millennium: John Paul II* (Boston, 2000).

JOVANOVIĆ Dragoljub (6 April 1895, Pirot–1977), Yugoslav Peasant Party politician and sociologist of Serb descent. During World War I Jovanović served in the Serbian Army. At the end of the war he started studies in Paris and received a Ph.D. there. Later he worked as a professor of sociology at the University of Belgrade. In the 1920s he belonged to the opposition against the royal dictatorship and Serbian nationalist parties. In an article published in 1928 he accused the Belgrade press of sowing a nationalist psychosis that led to the assassination of **Stjepan Radić** and other MPs. Accused of anti-state activities, Jovanović spent a year under house arrest. He supported the idea of a federal Yugoslavia. In the 1930s he worked with the leader of the Croatian Peasant Party, **Vlatko Maček**, and he co-organized the Peasant Democratic Coalition. He published a lot on various issues of the Yugoslav countryside. During World War II, he favored the cooperation of federalist organizations with the Communists. Although he spent the war years in Belgrade, he was included in the Anti-Fascist Council of the National Liberation of Yugoslavia—that is, the Communist quasi-parliament. After the war he remained an MP. When in July 1946 he criticized the plans for collectivization and an excessive dependence on the USSR, he was deprived of his mandate, arrested, and sentenced to nine years in prison in September 1947. While in prison, Jovanović recorded his reflections on scraps of toilet paper, and after many years he edited them into two volumes of short essays about persons whom he had met and who had since died: *Ljudi, ljudi: Medaljony 56 umrilih savremenika* (People, people: Lockets of 56 deceased contemporaries; 1973) and *Ljudi, ljudi: Medaljony 46 umrilih savremenika* (1975; People, people: Lockets of 46 deceased contemporaries). Disappointed with communism, Jovanović remained true to the idea of a federal Yugoslavia, although in the census

of 1971 he declared himself to be a Serb. He authored *Le rendement optimum du travail ouvrier* (Optimum productivity of the labor force; 1923); *Les effets économiques et sociaux de la guerre en Serbie* (The economic and social consequences of the war in Serbia; 1930); and *Agrarna politika* (Agrarian policy; 1930). (WR)

Sources: *Enciklopedija Jugoslavije*, vol. 4 (Zagreb, 1960); Richard Frucht, ed., *Encyclopedia of Eastern Europe* (New York and London, 2000); Hugh Seton-Watson, *The East European Revolution* (London, 1956); *Dragoljub Jovanović—sloboda od straha: Izabrane političke rasprave* (Belgrade, 1991).

JOVANOVIĆ Slobodan (21 November 1869, Novi Sad–12 December 1958, London), Yugoslav historian and politician of Serb nationality. In 1890 Jovanović graduated in law from Geneva University. In 1897 he started working in the Serbian Ministry of Foreign Affairs, but he soon devoted himself to a scholarly career. In 1905 he became a professor of history at the University of Belgrade. He was one of the leading experts on Serbian history of the nineteenth century. He also dealt with the history of the state and law and European political thought. For some time he was the president of the University of Belgrade. In the 1930s he anxiously observed the pro-German course of the autocratic government headed by Regent **Paul Karadjordjević**. Jovanović supported the coup d'état of 27 March 1941 and became deputy prime minister in the government of **Dušan Simović**. At the end of March he visited Berlin and Rome but failed to reduce the hostility of Germany and Italy toward the new authorities of the state. When the Third Reich subjugated Yugoslavia in April 1941, Jovanović, along with the government, left for England.

On 12 January 1942 King **Peter II** appointed Jovanović prime minister of the government-in-exile. As a scholar of international reputation, Jovanović was supposed to raise the prestige of the government-in-exile and to mitigate the Serb-Croat conflict. This mission failed in the face of the increasingly strong position of the Communist guerrillas and **Josip Broz Tito** in occupied Yugoslavia. Jovanović's talks with the ambassador of the USSR in London, Alexander Bogomolov, in May 1942, did not bring any results except for the Kremlin's false assurances of non-interference in the domestic affairs of Yugoslavia. On 28 June 1943 Jovanović resigned his post in favor of **Božidar Purić**, who also failed to change the course of events. After the war Jovanović remained in England. The hostility of the Communists reached him even there. In June 1946 in Belgrade, he was tried in absentia in the trial of **Draža Mihailović** and was sentenced to sixteen years of hard labor. Jovanović was politically active in exile—for example, he directed the Yugoslav National Committee in England. In 1993 *Slobodan Jovanovic u emigraciji: Razgovori i zapisi* (Slobodan Jovanovic in exile: Talks and writings) was published in Belgrade. (WR)

Sources: *Enciklopedja Jugoslavije*, vol. 4 (Zagreb, 1960); *Biographishes Lexikon*, vol. 2; K. Fotitch, *The War We Lost* (New York, 1948); Kosta Pavlović, *Razgovori sa Slobodanom Jovanovićem 1941–1945* (Windsor, 1969); Michał Jerzy Zacharias, *Jugosławia w polityce Wielkiej Brytanii 1940–1945* (Wrocław, 1985); Aleksandar Pavkovic, *Slobodan Jovanovic: An Unsentimental Approach to Politics* (Boulder, Colo., 1993); Vladan Mihajlović, *Slobodan Jovanović i gradanaska država* (Belgrade, 1996).

JOVANOVIĆ Vladislav (9 June 1933, Zitni Potok), Serb Communist activist and diplomat. Jovanović's parents were teachers. In 1951 he graduated from high school and then from law studies in Belgrade. In 1957 he started a diplomatic career. From 1960 to 1964 he worked in the Yugoslav Embassy in Brussels, and from 1964, in the Ministry of Foreign Affairs in Belgrade. In 1967–71 he served in the embassy in Turkey, then again in the Ministry of Foreign Affairs in Belgrade. From 1975 to 1979 he was councillor of the embassy in London, from 1980 he headed the Department of Western Europe, and in 1985–89 he was ambassador to Turkey. From 1991 to 1993, with a short break in 1992, Jovanović was foreign minister of the Serb republic. In July 1992 he became foreign minister of the Federal Republic of Yugoslavia (FRY), but he resigned in September 1992 in protest against the policies of the **Milan Panić** government, which he found contrary to Serbian interest. From March 1993 he was FRY foreign minister again. In accordance with the policy of **Slobodan Milošević**, Jovanović tried to make the Bosnian Serbs agree to the Cyrus Vance and David Owen plan, but in vain. In August 1995 he resigned, and in September 1995 he took the lead of the FRY mission to the United Nations. In December 1995 before the UN Security Council he protested the accusations leveled against the Bosnian Serbs for the Srebrenica massacre of July 1995. His argument that the Muslim victims had been killed in fraternal fighting among themselves was perceived as cynical and absurd. Jovanović defended Milošević's policy during the Kosovo crisis in 1999, appealing for termination of the NATO air raids on the FRY. (AO)

Sources: David Owen, *Balkan Odyssey* (New York, 1995); Željan E. Šuster, *Historical Dictionary of the Federal Republic of Yugoslavia* (Lanham, Md., 1999); www.rferl.org; www.mfa.gov.yu/history/Ministri/VJovanovic_s.html.

JOVANOVIĆ Živadin (14 November 1938, Oparić), Yugoslav Communist activist of Serb nationality. Jovanović

graduated from high school in Jagodina and in law from the University of Belgrade in 1961. For many years he worked in the diplomatic service—as adviser to the Presidium of the Serb republic (1970–74) and councillor at the Yugoslav Embassy in Kenya (1974–78). He was also undersecretary of the Presidium of the Socialist Federative Republic of Yugoslavia (1984–88), and he headed the diplomatic mission to Angola (1988–93). In 1994–97 he was deputy minister of foreign affairs of the Federal Republic of Yugoslavia (FRY). Then he was deputy chairman of the Socialist Party of Serbia (SPS), headed by **Slobodan Milošević**. In September 1997 he was elected deputy to the National Assembly of Serbia. In January 1998 the FRY prime minister, **Radoje Kontić**, appointed Jovanović foreign minister. He served in this capacity during the aggravation of the Albanian-Serb relationship in Kosovo. After the failure of the Kosovo peace talks, on 24 March 1999 NATO began air raids on targets in the FRY. Jovanović remained foreign minister until 17 October 2000, when the Democratic Opposition of Serbia took over power. After Milošević was handed over to The Hague International Criminal Tribunal for Former Yugoslavia in June 2001, Jovanović acted as the SPS chairman, and in December 2001 he passed his duties on to Mirko Marjanović. (AO)

Sources: www.mfa.gov.yu/history/Ministri/ZJovanovic_s.html.

JÓZEWSKI Henryk, pseudonyms "Przemysław," "Niemirowicz," and "Olgierd" (6 August 1892, Kiev–23 April 1981, Warsaw), Polish politician. Józewski studied mathematics at the university in Kiev, where he became associated with Polish pro-independence organizations. Drawn to the PPS–Revolutionary Faction, during World War I he co-organized the Polish Military Organization (Polska Organizacja Wojskowa [POW]) in the east. Following a reorganization of the POW, he became a senior staff member of the Second Department of the General Staff of the Polish Army in 1919. He directed Area Three of the Intelligence Office, where he was in charge of active intelligence work. He played a role in the establishment of the Polish Partisan Unit, one of whose functions was to serve as a platform for Polish-Ukrainian military cooperation against the Red Army. Wanted by the Soviet Cheka from the end of 1919, Józewski was summoned to Warsaw. **Józef Piłsudski** delegated him as a representative of Poland to the government of the Ukrainian People's Republic, where he served as deputy minister of interior. From 1922 on he lived in Volhynia, where he painted as an amateur.

After the coup of May 1926, which Józewski had

helped to prepare, from August 1926 to June 1928 he was a member of the staff of the Office of the Prime Minister, and he was head of this office for some time. He combined the work of minister of military affairs and minister of interior. On 30 June 1928 he became the provincial governor (*wojewoda*) of Volhynia. A promoter of cooperation between the Poles and the Ukrainians in Volhynia, from December 1929 to June 1930 he served as minister of interior, trying to regulate relations between the state and the Orthodox Church. Subsequently, he again became the provincial governor of Volhynia. He believed that the Ukrainian nationalists from Galicia posed a threat to the integrity of Poland and to Polish-Ukrainian cooperation in Volhynia. He was in favor of maintaining the so-called Sokal border, a special administrative frontier that was intended to isolate Volhynia from the influence of Ukrainians from Galicia. At the same time he supported, and even initiated, the development of Ukrainian economic, political, and social organizations that favored cooperation with Poland. He supported parceling farmland out to Ukrainians but at the same time protected Polish military settlements and worked to effectively abolish Ukrainian schools. Nevertheless, he was able to win the support of many Ukrainian intellectuals.

After Piłsudski's death, under pressure from Polish and Ukrainian nationalist circles, Józewski was dismissed from his position in April 1938, and he became the provincial governor of Łódź. After the outbreak of World War II, he moved the office of the provincial governor of Łódź to Volhynia. In the autumn of 1939 Józewski became active in the Service for the Victory of Poland (SZP) and in the Union of Armed Struggle (ZWZ) in Warsaw. Because of objections to his *sanacja* past, he was dismissed as commander of the ZWZ Warsaw City District. He established the elitist Grupa Olgierda (Olgierd's Group), which published the periodicals *Polska Walczy* and *Ziemie Wschodnie Rzeczypospolitej*. Wounded in an assassination attempt, Józewski was less active in underground activities after 1943. He continued underground work until 1945, leading the Polish Democratic Party, an organization of little importance. He worked with the Delegation of Armed Forces for the Homeland (Delegatura Sił Zbrojnych na Kraj) from May to August 1945 and with the Freedom and Independence association (Zrzeszenie Wolność i Niezawisłość [WiN]). He remained in hiding until 1953, when he was arrested. Sentenced to life imprisonment in September 1954, he was released on the wave of the "thaw" in 1956. Until the end of his life he kept busy mainly with painting. Józewski was the author of the memoirs *Zamiast pamiętnika* (Instead of a memoir), published in *Zeszyty Historyczne* (1982–83). (PK)

Sources: Kunert, vol. 1; *Słownik Polityków Polskich XX w.* (Poznań, 1998); Stefan Korboński, *Polskie państwo podziemne* (Paris, 1975); Iwo Werschler, *Z dziejów obozu belwederskiego: Tadeusz Hołówko-życie i działalność* (Warsaw, 1984); J. Kęsik, *Zaufany komendanta: Biografia polityczna Jana Henryka Józewskiego 1892–1981* (Wrocław, 1995).

JÓZSEF Attila (11 April 1905, Budapest–3 December 1937, Balatonszárszó), Hungarian poet. The son of a washerwoman and a soap maker who deserted the family in 1908, József was placed with a foster family for two years in 1910. He later lived alternately in harsh poverty with his family and in various institutions. While in primary school, he made a living as a laborer. After his mother's death in 1919, his brother-in-law took care of him. In 1920 József attended a lower theological seminary of the Salezian order for a short time. From 1920 to 1922 he studied at a gymnasium in Makó, but he had to leave this school following an attempt at suicide. He went to Budapest, where he continued his education, earning a living by giving private lessons. At the same time he wrote poems. One year after the publication of the first volume of his poetry, *Szépség koldusa* (Beggar of beauty; 1922), his poems began to be published in *Nyugat*, the most prestigious literary periodical at that time. In 1924 József began to study Hungarian language and literature, as well as Romance language and literature, at the university in Szeged, but he had to discontinue his studies because of a scandal that erupted when the local press published his poems, which were seen as blasphemous and nihilistic. He spent the following academic year at the university in Vienna, where he became friends with almost all of the pro-Communist Hungarian émigrés. In 1926–27 József studied at the Sorbonne and became fascinated with the French avant garde and with Marxism-Leninism. After returning to Hungary, he studied at the university in Budapest, but because of financial problems and a conflict with the authorities of this university, he was unable to complete his studies. In 1928, following a nervous breakdown, he went to a sanatorium.

In 1930 József became active in the then illegal Hungarian Communist Party (HCP), writing and editing leaflets, manifestos, and articles. In 1931 he published *Döntsd a tőkét, ne siránkozz!* (Do not lament, overthrow the capital!), a volume of poetry that was confiscated by the police because in it József called for the establishment of a dictatorship of the proletariat in Hungary. One year later he was brought to trial, accused of public incitement to class hatred. As a result of sectarian conflicts within the party and because of his own temporary mental disturbance, József broke off organizational ties with the HCP in 1934. One year later he left Judit Szántó, his life companion, whom he had met in the party in 1930. From 1935 on, his periods of intense work were interrupted by increasingly frequent periods in institutions for the mentally ill. In December 1937 József committed suicide by throwing himself under a train. József was one of the greatest Hungarian lyric poets of the first half of the twentieth century. He introduced European avant-garde ideas into Hungarian poetry. A committed poet, he often directly or indirectly referred to a Stalinist version of Marxism-Leninism. He used very rich language and a variety of verse forms, which gave his poems an immense esthetic and emotional charge. He was also the author of poems devoted to his mother, which were full of tenderness and subtle lyricism; these are some of the most beautiful poems in Hungarian literature. After World War II, József's poetry was widely exploited to serve the needs of Communist propaganda in Hungary. (MS)

Sources: *Biographisches Lexikon*, vol. 2; Laszló Balogh, *József Attila* (Budapest, 1970); *"Miért fáj ma is": Az ismeretlen József Attila* (Budapest, 1992); *A Dunánál: Tanulmányok József Attiláról* (Budapest, 1995); Steven Bela Vardy, *Historical Dictionary of Hungary* (Lanham, Md., 1997); Jolán József, *József Attila élete* (Budapest, 1999).

JÓŹWIAK Franciszek, pseudonym "Witold" (20 October 1895, Huta Baranowska, near Puławy–23 October 1966, Warsaw), Polish Communist activist. Jóźwiak came from a peasant family and completed primary school. During World War I he fought in the Polish Legions, and from 1921 he was in the Polish Communist Workers' Party. He spent 1929–30 in Moscow, where he started working for the Comintern. He was imprisoned for his Communist activities in Poland between 1931–36 and 1937–39. After the outbreak of war in September 1939 Jóźwiak went to the Soviet-occupied territories, where in 1941 he joined the All-Union Communist Party (Bolshevik). From June 1941 he was in the Soviet guerrilla movement in the rear of the German front. In March 1942 he came to Warsaw and became a member of the CC of the Polish Workers' Party (Polska Partia Robotnicza [PPR]). After **Marceli Nowotko** was killed, in January 1943 Jóźwiak joined the Secretariat of the CC, the three-member leadership of the party. From August 1942 he served as chief of staff of the People's Guard, and from January to July 1944, of the People's Army (Armia Ludowa). He was closely connected with **Bolesław Bierut**.

In October 1944 Jóźwiak became commander-in-chief of the Civil Militia (Milicja Obywatelska), and from March 1945 to March 1949 he was undersecretary of state in the Ministry of Public Security (Ministerstwo Bezpieczeństwa Publicznego [MBP]). From 1944 he was brigadier general; in April 1946 he was nominated general of division. Jóźwiak was among the main organizers of the Communist terror. At a plenum in August 1948 he sharply attacked **Władysław Gomułka** for "rightist-nationalist deviation," and he joined the Politburo of the CC of the PPR. From December 1948 Jóźwiak was a member of the Politburo of the CC of the Polish United Workers' Party (Polska Zjednoczona Partia Robotnicza [PUWP]). In March 1949 he left the MO (Milicja obywatelska) and the MBP to chair the Supreme Chamber of Control, and he became a member of the Council of State. His departure from the MBP came as a result of his conflict with the head of the MBP, **Stanisław Radkiewicz**, who proved to be stronger. From April 1949 to January 1955 Jóźwiak also presided over the Party Central Control Commission. From September 1949 to December 1956 he was president of the Association of Fighters for Freedom and Democracy. For some period of time he was married to Helena Wolińska, head of a department in the Supreme Military Prosecutor's Office. During the "thaw" Jóźwiak belonged to the Natolin faction of hard-liners. In April 1955 he was named deputy prime minister. At the Eighth Plenum of the CC of the PUWP in October 1956 Jóźwiak defended Marshal **Konstantin Rokossovski** and was dropped from the central party leadership. On 24 October 1956 he was dismissed as deputy premier. At the Third Congress of the PUWP in March 1959 he was also ousted from the CC. To the end of his life Jóźwiak remained a Stalinist, which manifested itself in (among other things) his support of the Chinese orthodoxy. (WR)

Sources: Mołdawa; Z. Jakubowski, *Franciszek Jóźwiak "Witold"* (Warsaw, 1974); Marek Łatyński, *Nie paść na kolana* (London, n.d.); Krystyna Kersten, *Narodziny systemu władzy: Polska 1943–1948* (Poznań, 1990); Władysław Gomułka, *Pamiętniki*, vol. 2 (Warsaw, 1994); *Tajne oblicze GL-AL. I PPR. Dokumenty*, vol. 1 (Warsaw, 1997).

JURCZYK Marian (16 October 1935, Karczewice, near Częstochowa), Polish trade union activist. Jurczyk graduated from an economic high school. From 1954 he worked in the Szczecin shipyard as a blue-collar laborer. He took part in the strike of December 1970. In August 1980 he was elected chairman of the Strike Committee of the shipyard and of the Inter-Factory Strike Committee in Szczecin. On 30 August 1980 he signed the Szczecin agreement with representatives of the Communist authorities. In 1980–81 Jurczyk chaired the Inter-Factory Workers' Commission of Solidarity in Szczecin and the West Pomeranian Regional Board of the union. Thought to be a radical, at the First Solidarity Congress in September 1981 Jurczyk was elected to its National Commission, but he lost the election for union chairman to **Lech Wałęsa**. On 13 December 1981 Jurczyk was interned, and in 1982 he was arrested. Amnestied in 1984, until 1986 he worked as head of the Szczecin shipyard warehouse. From 1986 on an invalid pension, Jurczyk took part in underground Solidarity activities in Szczecin, opposing Wałęsa and his tactics. From 1987 he was one of the leaders of the Working Group, demanding a convention of the Solidarity National Commission elected in 1981. He opposed the Round Table Agreement and attacked the government of **Tadeusz Mazowiecki** and later President Wałęsa. In 1990 he co-organized and until 1994 he presided over the National Coordination Commission, and from 1996 he presided over the National Commission of the Solidarity 80 trade union. From 1997 Jurczyk was an independent senator, and in 1998–2001 he was mayor of Szczecin on behalf of the Independent Social Movement in coalition with the post-Communists. Jurczyk was accused of having cooperated with the Communist security services. He explained that his cooperation was the result of blackmail and that it ended with the death of two members of his family. In March 2000 he gave up his senator's mandate. In December 2002 the Supreme Court relieved him of the "lustration lie," arguing that he had done no damage. From November 2002 Jurczyk was mayor of Szczecin, again in cooperation with the post-Communists. (WR)

Sources: *Kto jest kim w Polsce* (Warsaw, 2001); Jerzy Holzer, "Solidarność" (Warsaw, 1983); Małgorzata Szejnert and Tomasz Zalewski, *Szczecin, grudzień, sierpień, grudzień* (London, 1986); Jerzy Holzer and Krzysztof Leski, *"Solidarność" w podziemiu* (Łódź, 1990).

JURIGA Ferdinand (12 October 1874, Gbely–23 November 1950, Bratislava), Slovak Catholic priest and politician. Juriga studied theology in Esztergom and Vienna. In 1898 he took holy orders. In 1905 he became a parish priest in Vajnory. When in 1905 the Catholic People's Party (Katolikus Néppárt [CPP]) of Ferenc Zichy joined the ruling coalition and abandoned its demands for the mitigation of ethnic policy, Juriga, along with Reverend **Andrej Hlinka**, **František Jehlička**, František Skýčak, and other Slovak activists, announced the establishment of the Slovak People's Party (Slovenská Ľudová Strana [SPP]), a local faction of the CCP. Juriga became very popular as a people's judge and an uncompromising critic of Magyarization and corruption in state offices. In 1906 in Stúpava, near Bratislava, he was elected an MP from the SPP lists. In 1907 he was sentenced to a two-year imprisonment for "anti-state" publications. In 1910, as a representative of the Catholic wing of the Slovak National Party (SNP), he won a seat in parliament. After

conflicts with the Protestant leadership of the SNP in 1913, along with Hlinka, Juriga brought about the foundation of an independent SPP. During World War I Juriga was the only Slovak member of the Hungarian parliament. On 19 October 1918, in the Hungarian parliament, he demanded on behalf of the newly established Slovak National Council (Slovenská Národná Rada [SNR]) the right of self-determination for the Slovak nation. One of the organizers of the SNR assembly in Turčiansky Svätý Martin (today Martin), Juriga was co-author and signatory of the declaration of 30 October 1918, which called for the creation of a common state of Czechs and Slovaks. In 1918–29 Juriga sat in the parliament in Prague. As a result of a conflict with Hlinka, he left the SPP before the elections of 1929. Juriga formed his own party but failed to win a seat in parliament, and he withdrew from politics. (MG)

Sources: *SBS*; Augustín Mat'ovčik et al., *Reprezentačný biografický lexikón Slovenska* (Martin, 1999); *Muži deklarácie* (Martin, 1991); *Politické strany na Slovensku* (Bratislava, 1992); Marián Hronský, *Boj o Slovensko a Trianon 1918–1920* (Bratislava, 1998).

JUSTINIAN [originally Ioan Marina] (22 February 1901, Sueşti, near Rîmnicu Vîlcea–26 March 1977, Bucharest), Patriarch of the Romanian Orthodox Church. After completing a theological seminary in Rîmnicu, Justinian took holy orders in 1924. He studied theology at the university in Budapest and in 1929 earned a bachelor's degree. He later taught at a theological seminary in Rîmnicu. As a widower, he entered a monastery in Cetatuia, near Iaşi, taking the name Justinian. In August 1944 for a short time he gave shelter in the parsonage to **Gheorghe Gheorgiu-Dej**, the future leader of the Communists. In 1945 Justinian was consecrated bishop and was appointed curate to the Moldavian metropolitan in Iaşi. In 1947 he became the metropolitan of Moldavia, and on 24 May 1948, Patriarch of the Romanian Orthodox Church. Justinian's career was supported by such people as **Ana Pauker**, who was responsible for the religious policy of the Communist Party. Justinian recognized the subordination of Church structures to the state and tolerated the policy of clergy recruitment by the Securitate, the secret political police. A new Church statute, prepared under Justinian's supervision, was approved by the Synod of the Orthodox Church in 1948 and by the Ministry for Religious Affairs in 1949. Justinian supported the pro-government Union of Democratic Priests, led by Father Ion Burducea, a former member of the Iron Guard who represented Communists as the minister for religious affairs. In the 1930s and 1940s Justinian combated the Orthodox Church's support for the authoritarian government of Marshal **Ion Antonescu**, but he tolerated the fact that clergymen formerly linked with the Iron Guard were members of the Church's ruling body. Justinian was an uncompromising opponent of the Uniate Church and supported activities aimed at its abolishment. He took part in an attack against the Greek Catholic clergy, accepting the unlawful and cruel persecutions of Greek Catholic clergymen. Justinian often visited Greek Catholic bishops in prison and unsuccessfully tried to persuade them to joined the Orthodox Church. He ordered a takeover of the Uniate churches. The Orthodox monasteries were used by the authorities to intern Uniate hierarchs.

At the same time, Justinian implemented a reform of the system and a reorganization of the Orthodox Church and its pastoral work. He attempted to modernize the organization of the Orthodox Church. He was committed to revitalizing the priests' pastoral work, promoted education, and founded charities. His work brought him recognition, especially in the provinces. He reformed theological studies, founded a publishing house, set up museums, and collected Church archives. He also man-aged to maintain ties with the Romanian mission in Jerusalem and with the Romanian mission in Detroit. The latter mission was elevated to the rank of archbishopric of America, with the status of an autonomous church. Justinian established a Romanian diocese of Central and Western Europe for émigrés. In the 1960s, when Romania began to emphasize greater independence from the USSR, he supported Romanian theologians' studies in the West and took an active part in the ecumenical movement. In 1961, on his initiative, the Romanian Orthodox Church joined the Ecumenical Council of Churches and the Conference of European Churches. In 1962 Justinian sent an observer to the Second Ecumenical Council, and in 1967 he established an official relationship with the Catholic Church. (AGr)

Sources: *Encyklopedia katolicka*, vol. 8 (Lublin, 2000); *Die Rumänische Orthodoxe Kirche* (Bucharest, 1962); E. Ch. Suttner, *Beiträge zur Kirchengeschichte der Rumänen* (Vienna, 1978); Bohdan Cywiński, *Ogniem próbowane: Z dziejów najnowszych Kościoła katolickiego w Europie Środkowo-Wschodniej* (Lublin, 1990); Dennis Deletant, *Communist Terror in Romania: Gheorghiu-Dej and the Police State, 1948–1965* (New York, 1999).

K

KABAKCHIEV Khristo (2 January 1878, Galati–6 October 1940, Moscow), Bulgarian Communist activist. After graduating from high school, Kabakchiev studied in Bulgaria and Switzerland. From 1897 he belonged to the Bulgarian Social Democratic Party, and in 1903 he supported its Bolshevik faction, Tesnyaki. From 1905 he was a member of its Central Committee. In 1908 he was elected MP to the National Assembly. When in April 1919 the Bulgarian Communist Party was created, Kabakchiev joined its Central Committee (CC). In 1920 he was the party's delegate to the Second Congress of the Communist International. In January 1923 he became the organizational secretary of the CC of the party, directing the preparations for a coup that began in September of that year. After the failure of the coup, Kabakchiev was sentenced to twelve and a half years of prison. Released under the amnesty of 1926, he left for the USSR, where he assumed the post of member of the Executive Committee of the Comintern, a position that until then he had held in absentia. In 1928 he was removed from the party executive and from the International; he then worked at the Comintern school and at the Marx-Engels-Lenin Institute. At that time Kabakchiev was a member of the All-Union Communist Party (Bolsheviks). He was arrested during the great purge in 1937. Released the next year in a bad state of health, he died soon afterwards. (WR)

Sources: Lazitch; *Who Was Who in the USSR* (Metuchen, N.J., 1972).

KÄBIN Johannes (24 September 1905, Kalvi–26 October 1999, Tallinn), Soviet Communist activist of Estonian origin. Käbin was born into a peasant family that in 1910 had left for Russia and had been Russified, becoming, as it was called in Estonia, "Yestonians." Until the 1950s he used the Russian version of his name, Ivan Kebin. From 1923 to 1925 he was a seasonal laborer. After graduating from the Leningrad party school in 1926, Käbin became a member of the All-Union Communist Party (Bolsheviks) in 1927. In 1927–31 he was head of the soviet in Susanino in the region of Gatchina. From 1931 he worked as a party instructor in Leningrad, and from 1935 to 1936, after completing a course in Marxism-Leninism, he became head of propaganda and agitation in the Omsk district in Siberia. In 1936–38 Käbin studied in Moscow at the Institute of Red Professorship, from which he did not graduate. Later, he was a party instructor at the Gubkin Institute, and in 1938–41, thus during the first Soviet occupation of Estonia, he served as head of the Propaganda and Agitation Department of the Central Committee (CC) of the Communist Party of Estonia (Bolsheviks) (CPE[B]).

From 1941 Käbin was a member of the CC of the CPE(B), responsible for training party cadres in the territory of the USSR, and he was also the head of the Party History Institute of the CPE(B). Between 1944 and 1947 he was deputy secretary of the CC for propaganda and agitation affairs, and from 1948, secretary and member of the Politburo of the CC of the CPE(B). On the wave of purges connected with accusations against those who had underestimated "bourgeois nationalism," directed against the previous leadership of the party with **Nikolai Karotamm** at its head, in 1950 Käbin became first secretary of the CC of the CPE(B) and a member of the CC of the CPSU. He came to the post of head of the Estonian party as an ardent Stalinist functionary and a Russifier. However, he was a skillful tactician, which allowed him to survive de-Stalinization, change political course, and, thanks to good relations with **Nikita Khrushchev**, improve the supply of goods in the Estonian SSR. After 1956 Käbin returned to the Estonian version of his surname and even tried to improve his Estonian, although his language gaffes were proverbial in the Estonian SSR. In the 1960s and 1970s he tolerated the cultural identity of the republic and gave up his efforts to impose Socialist realism. By 1978 his policy was no longer approved of by the Kremlin. Käbin resigned from his post of first secretary of the CC and became president of the Presidium of the Supreme Council of the Estonian SSR and deputy president of the Presidium of the Supreme Council of the USSR. This was a typical "blow to the leadership" because at the same time **Karl Vaino**, an ardent Russifier, was made head of the Estonian party. In 1983 Käbin finally retired and was succeeded as president of the Presidium of the Supreme Council by **Arnold Rüütel**. He also resigned from the Politburo of the CC of the CPE. Käbin continued to hold a seat in the CC of the CPE until 1986, and later he left even this position. (AG/WR)

Sources: *Who's Who in the Socialist Countries of Europe* (Munich, London, and Paris, 1989); Romualdas Misunas and Rein Taagepera, *The Baltic States: The Years of Dependence, 1940–1970* (Berkeley, 1993); Rein Taagepera, *Estonia: Return to Independence* (Boulder, Colo., 1993); Valdemar Pinn, *Kes oli Nikolai Karotamm?* (N.p., 1996); http://www.sada.ee/inimesed.php; P. Ernits, "Kebba Jürri võrsed," *Luup*, 1998, no. 4.

KACZMAREK Czesław (16 April 1895, Lisewo Małe, near Sierpc–26 August 1963, Lublin), Polish bishop. The son of a peasant, after graduating from a training college in 1914, Kaczmarek taught in Tłuchów. In 1916 he enrolled in a theological seminary in Płock. He volunteered to fight in the Polish-Soviet war in 1920. In August 1922 he was ordained. Later he continued his studies at the University of Lille, France, where he received a Ph.D. in 1927. Until 1928 he worked as a minister of Polish parishes in France. After returning to Poland, he was secretary general of the Union of Catholic Youth in Płock, organizing retreats and courses for the local youth. From 1932 he was director of the Institute of Catholic Action in Płock, and he founded a few periodicals promoting Catholic social teachings. He also founded the so-called evening universities aiming at the religious instruction of adults. On 24 May 1938 Kaczmarek was appointed bishop of Kielce. He founded the Institute of Higher Religious Culture in Kielce, and he reactivated Catholic Action activities and the Jedność Press. He was thought to be close to the National Democracy. From September 1939 to May 1940 Kaczmarek published three Episcopal letters encouraging believers to respect the regulations of the German occupants; this resulted in some criticism from the pro-independence activists in the underground. At the same time he ran an underground theological seminary and aided more than two hundred priests from outside his diocese. Moreover, he delegated chaplains to guerrilla units and supported secret education.

After the war Kaczmarek organized the reconstruction of devastated churches and the distribution of material aid for the victims of the war through Caritas. In 1946 Communist propaganda accused him of co-responsibility in the Kielce pogrom of Jews, although in practice he had had no chance to act and had been isolated by the Communist security officers. Kaczmarek was critical of the agreement that Primate **Stefan Wyszyński** reached with authorities on 14 April 1950. He protested the involvement of the clergy in the Communist-sponsored movement of "patriotic priests." Arrested on 20 January 1951, during a long investigation, Kaczmarek was interrogated personally by **Józef Różański** and was repeatedly tortured, so he confessed to having headed an "anti-state and anti-people's center." He was the only member of the Polish Episcopate to undergo a show trial; on 22 September 1953 he was sentenced to twelve years in prison. In May 1956, owing to ailing health, he was moved to the Rywałd Królewski Monastery, which he left without permission and went to Warsaw. On 28 December 1956 the Supreme Military Court lifted his sentence, and in 1957 the Supreme Military Prosecutor discontinued the case "for lack of proof." In April 1957 Kaczmarek returned to the Kielce diocese and implemented the Great Novena before the Millennium of Polish Christianity. He dismissed "patriotic priests," so he was attacked again by propaganda. In a homily delivered in February 1959 he defended Christians persecuted in

Red China, so the Communist authorities tried to ban his activities as ordinary bishop. Supported by a personal letter from Pope John XXIII, Kaczmarek stayed in Kielce and continued his mission despite obstacles and harassment. In November 1990 the Prosecutor General fully rehabilitated him and other priests sentenced with him in 1953. (AGr)

Sources: *Encyklopedia Katolicka*, vol. 8 (Lublin, 2000); *Leksykon duchowieństwa represjonowanego w PRL w latach 1945–1989*, vol. 1 (Warsaw, 2002); Andrzej Micewski, *Kardynał Wyszyński: Prymas i mąż stanu* (Paris, 1982); Jan Śledzianowski, *Ksiądz Czesław Kaczmarek biskup kielecki 1895–1963* (Kielce, 1991); Jan Żaryn, *Kościół a władza w Polsce (1945–1950)* (Warsaw, 1997).

KACZOROWSKI Ryszard (26 November 1919, Białystok), Polish politician. Kaczorowski graduated from a trade school in Białystok. From his youth he was active in scouting. In August 1939 he was deputy commander of the Scouting Emergence in Białystok, and under the Soviet occupation he became deputy commander of the Białystok troop, included in the Gray Ranks (underground scouting) in November 1939. In June 1940 he became commander of the Gray Ranks troop and liaison officer between this organization and the commander of the Union of Armed Struggle in Białystok. Arrested by the NKVD in July 1940 and held in the Białystok and Minsk prisons, in February 1941 Kaczorowski was sentenced to death by the Supreme Court of the Belorussian SSR. In May 1941 this sentence was commuted to ten years of labor camp in Kolyma. Released from camp after the conclusion of the Polish-Soviet agreement of July 1941, in March 1942 Kaczorowski joined the Polish Army formed by General **Władysław Anders**. Evacuated from the USSR, he fought with the Second Polish Corps in Italy, which was at the battle of Monte Cassino in May 1944.

After the war Kaczorowski lived in Great Britain. In 1947 he graduated from high school and in 1949 from the School of Foreign Trade in London. Until 1986 he worked as a bookkeeper in industry. From 1949 he belonged to the Headquarters of Scouting in exile; in 1955–67 he was Head of the Scouts, and from 1967, president of the Polish Scouting Association in exile. He commanded Polish World Scouting congresses in Monte Cassino in 1969 and Belgium in 1982. Kaczorowski belonged to the leadership of the Association of Polish War Veterans (Stowarzyszenie Polskich Kombatantów), the Federation of Poles in Great Britain, Polish Social and Cultural Center, Polish School Matrix, Institute of Polish Catholic Action, and Coordination Council of the Polonia of the Free World. In March 1986 he was included in the National Council of the Polish

Republic and the Polish Government-in-Exile. In 1986–89 he was minister of homeland affairs in the government of Edward Szczepanik, maintaining wide contacts in Poland. In accord with the constitution of April 1935, in January 1988 President Kazimierz Sabbat designated Kaczorowski as his successor. After Sabbat's death, on 19 July 1989 Kaczorowski assumed the duties of Polish president in exile. On 22 December 1990 at Warsaw Castle, he symbolically passed his insignia to the first freely elected president of Poland, **Lech Wałęsa**. Kaczorowski continued to live in London, taking an active part in the social life of Poland and British Polonia and enjoying the authority of a politician who combined the traditions of the Second and Third Polish Republics. (JS)

Sources: *Władze Rzeczypospolitej Polskiej na Uchodźstwie* (London, 1990); *Polonia: Słownik biograficzny* (Warsaw, 2000); Adam Dobroński, *Ostatni Prezydent II Rzeczypospolitej Ryszard Kaczorowski: Osiem wieczorów z prezydentem* (Białystok, 1999); Rafał Habielski, *Życie społeczne i kulturalne emigracji* (Warsaw, 1999); *Ryszard Kaczorowski doctor honoris causa Uniwersytetu w Białymstok* (Białystok, 1999).

KACZYŃSKI Jarosław (18 June 1949, Warsaw), Polish lawyer and politician, twin brother of **Lech Kaczyński**. In 1971 Kaczyński graduated in law from the University of Warsaw, in 1976 he received a Ph.D. in law, and from 1977 he worked at the University of Warsaw campus in Białystok. In 1976 he sent out a personal letter protesting the amendment of the constitution, and then he worked with the Committee for the Defense of Workers and its Intervention Bureau in particular. He contributed to the uncensored monthly *Głos*, and in 1980–81 he headed the law section of the Center for Social Research of Solidarity's Mazowsze Regional Board. After the introduction of martial law in December 1981, from 1982 Kaczyński was active in the underground structures of Solidarity and the Polish Helsinki Committee. He became a close aide of **Lech Wałęsa**, heading the social and political administration of the Provisional Coordination Commission of Solidarity from 1986. In 1987–89 he was one of the secretaries of Solidarity's National Executive Commission, and from 1988 to 1991 he was a member of the Civic Committee of the Solidarity Chairman. He took part in the Round Table Talks (February–April 1989).

In June 1989 Kaczyński was elected to the Senate, and in August 1989 he played an important role in the creation of a coalition of the Civic Parliamentary Club (Obywatelski Klub Parlamentarny [OKP]), the United Peasant Party, and the Democratic Party; it led to the formation of the **Tadeusz Mazowiecki** government. From October 1989 to December 1990 he was editor-in-chief of the weekly *Tygodnik Solidarność*. In 1990 he headed an OKP faction opposing the club's leadership and supporting Wałęsa in a conflict with Mazowiecki (the so-called war at the top). In May 1990 he co-founded the Center Alliance (Porozumienie Centrum [PC]) and became its chairman. From December 1990 to November 1991 he was chief of the Chancellery of President Wałęsa. He entered into conflict with the president over the role of former Communist activists in Wałęsa's camp, and from early 1992 he became his keen opponent. From May 1993 Kaczyński headed the PC parliamentary club. After the party was defeated in the elections of September 1993, he remained its chairman. He advocated de-communization and scrutiny of former security collaborators. He referred to national and Catholic values and supported Polish integration with NATO and the European Union. From 1996 he was active in Solidarity Electoral Action (Akcja Wyborcza Solidarność), but in the elections of September 1997 he won a seat on behalf of the Movement for the Reconstruction of Poland, and then he was an independent MP. Kaczyński authored a few books and co-authored *Lewy czerwcowy* (The left-handed blow in June; 1993), an anti-Wałęsa pamphlet. From early 2001 he was chief aide to his brother Lech, with whom he created the Law and Justice party (Prawo i Sprawiedliwość [PiS]). In the elections of September 2001 the party gained 9.5 percent of the vote, and Kaczyński won a seat. From October 2002 he was the PiS chairman. After the party won the election of September 2005 he did not assume the position of prime minister but rather focused on chairing the party.

Sources: *Nasi w Sejmie i Senacie* (Warsaw, 1990); Teresa Torańska, *My* (Warsaw, 1994); Jan Skórzyński, *Ugoda i rewolucja: Władza i opozycja 1985–1989* (Warsaw, 1995); Janusz A. Majcherek, *Pierwsza dekada III Rzeczpospolitej 1989–1999* (Warsaw, 1999); Wojciech Roszkowski, *Historia Polski 1914–2000* (Warsaw, 2001); Antoni Dudek, *Pierwsze lata III Rzeczpospolitej 1989–2001* (Kraków, 2002).

KACZYŃSKI Lech (18 June 1949, Warsaw), Polish lawyer and politician, twin brother of **Jarosław Kaczyński**. Kaczyński graduated in law from the University of Warsaw in 1971. He received a Ph.D. in 1980 and a postdoctoral degree (*habilitacja*) in 1990. He worked at the Academy of Catholic Theology in Warsaw (as of 1999, the Cardinal Stefan Wyszyński University) and the University of Gdańsk. From 1977 he worked with the Committee for the Defense of Workers, and from 1978, with the Free Trade Unions in Gdańsk. In August 1980 he was one of the advisers of the Inter-Factory Strike Committee and later of the Inter-Factory Founding Committee and the Solidarity Regional Board in Gdańsk. In 1981 he headed the Center for Social and Professional Studies of Solidarity's National Commission and was a delegate to the First Solidarity Congress in Gdańsk. Interned on 13 December 1981 and released in October 1982, Kaczyński was active in the Solidarity underground structures, working closely with **Lech Wałęsa**. From January 1986 he represented the Gdańsk region in the Solidarity Provisional Coordination Commission; he was its secretary and later the secretary of the National Executive Commission. From 1988 to 1991 he belonged to the Civic Committee of the Chairman of Solidarity. He took part in the Round Table Talks (February–April 1989).

In 1989–90 Kaczyński was a member of the Presidium of Solidarity's National Executive Commission, and from May 1990 to March 1991 he was first deputy chairman of the union. In June 1989 he was elected to the Senate, where he belonged to a group that questioned the policy of the leadership of the Civic Parliamentary Club during the so-called war at the top between Wałęsa and Prime Minister **Tadeusz Mazowiecki**. In 1991 Kaczyński was elected to the Lower House (Sejm) on behalf of the Center Alliance (Porozumienie Centrum). From March to October 1991 he was minister of state for national security in the Office of President Wałęsa. He left this position disagreeing with Wałęsa's personnel policy. In 1991–92 Kaczyński chaired the parliamentary commission of administration and home affairs. From February 1992 to May 1995 he was chairman of the Supreme Chamber of Control. In September 1995 he was registered as a presidential candidate, but he withdrew in October. In June 2000 he became minister of justice in the government of **Jerzy Buzek**, gaining huge popularity thanks to his determination to combat corruption and inefficiency in the judiciary. He was recalled from this position in July 2001. From March 2001 he was the leader of the Law and Justice party (Prawo i Sprawiedliwość). In the elections of September 2001 his party gained 9.5 percent of the votes, and Kaczyński won a seat, becoming one of the leaders of the parliamentary opposition. In the direct elections of October 2002 he was elected president of Warsaw. In the first round of presidential election, on 9 October 2005, he came in second after Donald Tusk, but two weeks later he won the presidency with 54 percent of the vote.

Sources: *Nasi w Sejmie i Senacie* (Warsaw, 1990); Jan Skórzyński, *Ugoda i rewolucja: Władza i opozycja 1985–1989* (Warsaw, 1995); Janusz A. Majcherek, *Pierwsza dekada III Rzeczpospolitej 1989–1999* (Warsaw, 1999); Wojciech Roszkowski, *Historia Polski 1914–2000* (Warsaw, 2001); Antoni Dudek, *Pierwsze lata III Rzeczpospolitej 1989–2001* (Kraków, 2002).

KACZYŃSKI Zygmunt (15 October 1894, Kaczyń, near Łomża–13 May 1953, Warsaw), Polish priest and politician. After graduating from a seminary in Warsaw, in 1914 Kaczyński began to study at the Theological Academy in St. Petersburg, where he received the degree of candidate in canon law. Ordained in 1917, he returned to Poland and assumed the post of secretary general of the Association of Christian Workers. In January 1919 he was elected to the Constituent Assembly as a representative of the National Popular Union (Związek Ludowo-Narodowy [ZLN]), but he soon founded the Christian National Workers' Club. In 1920, during the Polish-Soviet war, he served as a chaplain in the Polish Army. In the elections of 1922, he ran successfully as a Christian Democratic Party candidate. He was the editor of *Pracownik Polski* and *Rzeczpospolita*. In 1922 Kaczyński was appointed papal chamberlain and was honored with the Pro Ecclesia et Pontifice award. In 1923 he visited Polish parishes in the United States. In 1928 he withdrew from active political life and assumed the post of director of the Catholic Press Agency. He often criticized the Socialist left and Communist infiltration into the Polish Teachers' Union (ZNP). In Christian Democratic circles, he represented a faction that was critical of the *sanacja* regime. In 1937 he was one of the organizers of the Front Morges, and he supported the union of Christian Democratic parties within the Labor Party (Stronnictwo Pracy [SP]).

After the German invasion of Poland in September 1939, Kaczyński made his way to France via Hungary. In France he worked in the administration of the Polish government-in-exile. He also represented the SP in the National Council of the Republic of Poland, an advisory organ to the president and the government. In 1942 he accompanied Prime Minister **Władysław Sikorski** during his visit to the United States. After Sikorski's death, Kaczyński assumed the post of minister of religious affairs and public education in the government of **Stanisław Mikołajczyk**. In November 1944 he resigned, but he continued to support Mikołajczyk in his efforts to reach a compromise with the USSR. When the Provisional Government of National Unity was established in June 1945, Kaczyński decided to return to Poland, and, along with **Karol Popiel**, he started to revive the SP in Poland. However, the Communists quickly got control of this party. In October 1945 Kaczyński became the priest of All Saints Parish in Warsaw and was one of the co-founders of *Tygodnik Warszawski*, a weekly that drew on the social teachings of the Church and opposed communism. However, this weekly was abolished, and in April 1949 Kaczyński was arrested and sentenced to ten years' imprisonment for "anti-state activities." He died in Mokotów Prison in Warsaw. (WR)

Sources: *PSB*, vol. 11; Józef Haller, *Pamiętniki* (London, 1964); *Nauka Polska na Obczyźnie*, 1955, no. 1; Karol Popiel, *Na mogiłach przyjaciół* (London, 1966).

KÁDÁR János [originally Csermanek] (26 October 1912, Fiume [Rijeka]–6 July 1989, Budapest), Hungarian Communist leader. Kádár was the son of a maidservant who, forced by circumstances of poverty, gave him up temporarily to foster parents in Kapoly, Somogy County. In 1918 he went to live in Budapest. After graduating from a vocational school, Kádár became an apprentice to a mechanic and repaired typewriters. At the age of seventeen he joined a group of trade union youth activists in the district of Vasas. In 1931, under the pseudonym of János Barna, Kádár joined the illegal Communist Union of Young Workers (CUYW) and the Communist Party. The same year he was arrested but was released for lack of evidence. From the spring of 1932 he was a member of the North District Committee of the CUYW, and a year later he was secretary of its Central Committee (CC). In 1933 he was again arrested and sentenced to two years of prison; there he met many Communists, among others **Mátyás Rákosi**. At the end of 1933, because of his "cowardly" behavior at the police station when he was arrested, Kádár was expelled from the CUYW. After being released from prison, he worked as a part-time laborer; then at the party's command, he joined the Social Democrats, becoming head of their youth structure in 1940.

In the spring of 1941 Kádár joined the Budapest Committee of the Hungarian Communist Party (HCP). From May 1942 he was a member of the CC; from December of the same year he was secretary of the CC, and from February 1943, its executive secretary. At that time he was given a new organizational pseudonym, János Kádár. After the reform of the Communist International in 1943, the illegal secretariat headed by Kádár decided to dissolve the party. In June 1943 he co-organized the Peace Party, a cover for the Communist Party. In April 1944 he was sent to Yugoslavia to establish contacts with the Hungarian Communist activists there. Arrested at the border by the Hungarian authorities but unrecognized, he was accused of desertion from the Hungarian Army and received a two-year prison sentence.

In November 1944 Kádár escaped from prison and returned to Budapest. In January 1945 his post of secretary general was taken over by **Ernő Gerő**, who gave Kádár a party reprimand for the dissolution of the Communist Party. In April 1945 Kádár was elected secretary of the CC of the HCP, secretary of the Budapest Committee of the party, and head of the cadres department of the CC. In May of the same year he joined the then created Politburo. From 1946 Kádár was deputy secretary general of the HCP and later of the Hungarian Workers' Party (HWP). In 1948–50 he was minister of the interior. Despite his close relations with **László Rajk**, in 1949 Kádár played

an important role in preparing and conducting Rajk's trial. He was also responsible for the sentences that were pronounced in other show trials—for example, against Cardinal **Jozsef Mindszenty**, the Social Democrats, and high-ranking military and economic activists. From May 1950 he was head of the Department of Party and Mass Organizations of the CC, and in June of the same year he was resigned from the post of minister.

In the spring of 1951 Kádár was arrested by the Office of State Protection (Államvédelmi Hatóság [ÁVH]), and at the May meeting of the CC of the HWP, he was fired from all his party posts. In December 1952 the Supreme Court sentenced him to life imprisonment. Released and rehabilitated in July 1954, he became secretary of the party's committee in the Thirteenth District of Budapest, and from September 1955 he was first secretary of the HWP organization in Pest County. At the plenum of the CC of the HWP in July 1956, at which Gerő was appointed first secretary of the party in place of Rákosi, Kádár was again elected a member of the CC and the Politburo and also deputy secretary of the CC.

On 25 October 1956, during the revolution, Kádár was elected, in place of Gerő, to the post of first secretary of the CC of the HWP. At a meeting of the CC on 26 October he became a member of the Directorate formed in place of the Politburo, and two days later he became president of the Presidium of the HWP, which was in deep crisis. On 30 October he was appointed minister without portfolio in the government of **Imre Nagy**, and the next day he joined the executive committee preparing the founding congress of the party, under the new name of the Hungarian Socialist Workers' Party (Magyar Szocialista Munkáspárt [HSWP]). On 1 November, in a radio speech, Kádár talked about the "praiseworthy people's uprising, which overthrew the rule of Rákosi" and announced that the newly created HSWP, of which he became chairman, would, above all, defend the sovereignty and national honor of Hungary. At the time his speech was broadcast, Kádár was already outside the country. Along with **Ferenc Münnich** he secretly went to Moscow. Between 2 and 4 November Kádár took part in meetings of the Presidium of the CC of the CPSU, at which the Soviet leadership appointed him head of the new puppet government created in Moscow. On 3 November Kádár was appointed minister without portfolio in the transformed Hungarian coalition government of Nagy since no one in Budapest knew where he was or what he was doing. On 4 November Kádár informed Hungarians in a radio announcement that the "Hungarian Revolutionary Government of Workers and Peasants" had been formed. He justified the creation of this government by saying that it was necessary to put an end to the "rowdy excesses of counterrevolutionaries." On 7 November Soviet troops escorted Kádár to Budapest, and the president of the Presidential Council, **István Dobi**, officially appointed him president of the Council of Ministers.

From February 1957 Kádár was a member of the Politburo and first secretary of the CC of the HSWP, and between 1985 and 1989 he was general secretary of the party. He concentrated all the power in his hands. Thus he was primarily responsible for conducting the persecutions that followed the suppression of the revolution—for example, the execution of Imre Nagy and his associates. On 28 January 1958 he resigned as prime minister, but from 13 September 1961 to 30 June 1965 he again held the premiership. His name is associated with a period referred to as "goulash communism" (1965–85), during which Kádár bought the peace and passivity of society at the price of a pro-consumer economic policy. As a result of the country's huge debt, Kádár's Hungary appeared to be the second "happiest barrack" in the Communist camp, trailing only the Polish People's Republic. Despite this, at turning points, Kádár did not hesitate to support the orthodox line of the Kremlin. For example, in 1968 he sent Hungarian troops to Czechoslovakia.

In the autumn of 1986, during Kádár's visit to Moscow, Mikhail Gorbachev gave him to understand that he expected reforms or a resignation from him, but Kádár objected. At a state party conference that was convened in May 1988 because of a deepening political-economic crisis in the country and Kádár's resistance to reforms, a new post was created for him: president of the HSWP. However, he was removed from the Politburo. The actual leadership was taken over by the new general secretary of the party, **Károly Grósz**. At a meeting of the CC of the HSWP in April 1989 Kádár was removed from the party presidency and from the CC on account of his ill health. In his last public speech, showing a sense of guilt and seeking to justify himself at the same time, Kádár, in a vague way, awkwardly attempted to account for his past. The end of his life coincided with the collapse of the system that he had headed. Kádár died on the day that the Supreme Court posthumously rehabilitated Imre Nagy and his associates, clearing them of false charges. In 1989 Kádár's memoirs were published titled *Végakarat* (The testament). (JT)

Sources: *A magyar forradalom és szabadságharc enciklopédiája,* CD-ROM (Budapest, 1999); *Nagy Képes Milleniumi Arcképcsarnok* (Budapest, 1999); *Magyar Nagylexikon,* vol. 10 (Budapest, 2000); William Showcross, *Crime and Compromise: Janos Kadar and the Politics of Hungary since the Revolution* (New York, 1974); Bennet Kovrig, *Communism in Hungary from Kun to Kádár* (Stanford, 1979); Miklós Molnár, *From Béla Kun to János Kádár: Seventy Years of Hungarian Communism* (New York, 1990).

KADARE Ismail (28 January 1936, Gjirokaster), Albanian writer. In the late 1950s Kadare studied at the University of Tirana and then at the Maksim Gorky Literary Institute in Moscow. He returned to Albania in 1960, when Albanian-Soviet relations had dramatically worsened. After publishing a few volumes of poetry, in 1961 he was accepted into the Albanian Union of Writers. His earliest collections include *Ëndërrimet* (Dreams; 1957); *Shekulli im* (My century; 1961); and the most valued, *Përse mendohen këto male* (What do these mountains think about? 1964). Kadare won international recognition with his novels, several of which were translated into English, such as *Gjenerali i ushtrisë së vdekur* (1964; *General of the Dead Army,* 1971); *Dasma* (1968; *Wedding,* 1968), in which he showed the emancipation of women in postwar Albania; and *Kështjella* (1970; *The Castle,* 1980), about the Albanian national movement in the times of Skander bey. In his *Autobiografi e popullit në vargje* (1971; *Autobiography of People in Verse,* 1987) Kadare turned to folk poetry and legends. Political purges among intellectuals made him write the "politically correct" novels *Nëntori i një kryeqyteti* (November in the capital; 1973) and *Dimri i madh* (Great winter; 1977) about Albania's breakaway from the Soviet bloc and **Enver Hoxha**'s role in this process.

From the 1970s Kadare dominated Albanian literature. Many of his novels and short stories, such as *Gjakftohtësia* (Blood for blood; 1980); *Koha e shkrimeve* (The age of writing; 1986); and especially *Nëpunësi I pallati të ëndrrave* (1981; *Palace of Dreams,* 1993), referred to Albanian history under Turkish rule. His historical novel, *Ura mi tri harque* (1978; *Three-Arched Bridge,* 1993), reaching back to the mythical beginnings of Albanian history, was enthusiastically welcomed by critics. In 1988 he published the monumental volume *Koncert në fund të dimrit* (Concert, 1994), situated at the time when Albania broke off relations with China (1978). Kadare hardly fit into the Communist cultural patterns, but he was officially tolerated because of his international renown. He even had some access to the inner circles of power. In 1990, he received permission to leave for medical treatment in France, where he gave a number of interviews, appealing for Western aid to the Albanian nation striving toward democratization. In 1997 Kadare published his collective works in Albanian and French. In 1995 he published *Albanian Spring: The Anatomy of Tyranny.* Kadare's works stimulate reflection on the political involvement of the individual and show the threats to which a man is exposed when facing tyranny, officially sanctioned crime, and political taboos. (WD)

Sources: *Wielka encyklopedia PWN*, vol. 13 (Warsaw, 2003); Raymond Hutchings, *Historical Dictionary of Albania* (Lanham, Md., 1996); Tefik Çaushi, *Universi letrar i Kadarese* (N.p., 1993); Fabien Terpan, *Ismail Kadare* (Paris, 1992); Robert Elsie, "Modern Albanian Literature," in Franz-Lothar Altmann, ed., *Albanien in Umbruch* (Munich, 1990); www.britannica.com/bcom/eb/article/0/0/.

KAFKA Franz (3 July 1883, Prague–3 June 1923, Kierling, near Vienna), German-language writer of Jewish origin who was linked with Prague. Brought up in the Jewish community in Prague, Kafka studied law at Prague's German university. Initially loosely associated with Jewish traditions, he later became interested in Zionism and Hasidism. Kafka's tyrannical father, as well as his proneness to migraines and sleeplessness, had an overwhelming influence on his psyche. Moreover, at the end of World War I, Kafka was a witness to the growing wave of anti-Semitism. In 1917 he contracted tuberculosis and spent the rest of his life in sanatoriums in Austria. Kafka never married, but two women played an important roles in his life: Milena Jesenska, a journalist, and Dora Dymant, a Polish Jewess who took care of him at the end of his life. During his lifetime Kafka published only a few works, including *Das Urteil* (The judgment; 1916); *Die Verwandlung* (Metamorphosis; 1916); and *In der Strafkolonie* (In the penal colony; 1919). Kafka left most of his works with Max Brod, his friend and future biographer. When he was dying, Kafka asked Brod to destroy his works. Brod disregarded his instructions and published them in order: *Der Prozess* (The trial; 1925), *Das Schloss* (The castle; 1926), and *Amerika* (America; 1927). Brod also published Kafka's collected works as *The Diaries 1910–1923, Letters to Milena*, and *Letters to Felice*.

Soon after his death, Kafka became famous throughout the world, and literary critics recognized him as one of the most outstanding and original writers of the twentieth century. His writing is not easy to interpret. His characters are embroiled in tragic quests for identity and in hopeless attempts to understand their dependence on the omnipresent hierarchical structure of power. For example, the protagonist of *The Trial*, Joseph K., fails to understand what he has been accused of; nor does he perceive the true nature of the court that tries him. Some interpreters see in Kafka's works a psychological reflection of his life situation, while others consider the alienation of his characters a symbolic representation of modern anti-Semitism or the fate of man in a world without religion. Kafka's visions anticipated twentieth-century totalitarianism, which placed millions of people in "Kafkaesque" situations, in an absurd and at the same time tragic enslavement by anonymous institutions and irrational ideologies. The nations of the Soviet bloc, which were not only ruled by totalitarian Communist parties, but were also deprived of sovereignty and still forced to describe their positions in terms of freedom and independence, constitute a particular example of such entanglements. Therefore, in countries like Communist Czechoslovakia, the publication of Kafka's works was prohibited for many years. The most complete edition of his works was published in Frankfurt am Main as *Gesammeltwerke* (9 vols., 1951–58). (WR)

Sources: *Encyclopedia Judaica*, vol. 10 (Jerusalem, 1971); Max Brod, *Franz Kafka als Weg weisende Gestalt* (St. Gallen, 1951); Max Brod, *Franz Kafka: A Biography* (New York, 1960); Roman Karst, *Drogi samotności: Rzecz o Franzu Kafce* (Warsaw, 1960); Charles Osborne, *Kafka* (Edinburgh, 1967); Erich Heller, *Kafka* (London, 1974); Ronald Hayman, *Kafka: A Biography of Kafka* (London, 1981); Peter U. Beicken, *Franz Kafka: Leben und Werk* (Stuttgart, 1986); Thomas Anz, *Franz Kafka* (Munich, 1989); František Kautman, *Franz Kafka* (Prague, 1992); Jeremy Adler, *Franz Kafka* (Woodstock, N.Y., 2002).

KAGANOVICH Lazar (22 November 1893, Kabany, near Kiev–25 July 1991, Moscow), Soviet Communist activist, executor of Stalin's policies in the Ukraine. Born into a poor Jewish family, Kaganovich left school early to begin an apprenticeship as a shoemaker. In 1911 he joined the Bolshevik party. After the outbreak of the revolution, he was elected a delegate to the Third All-Russian Congress of Soviets (December 1917). He owed his rise to the top of the government to Stalin, who, after becoming secretary general of the Central Committee (CC) of the Russian Communist Party (Bolsheviks) (RCP[B]) in 1921, entrusted Kaganovich with personnel policy in the CC. Kaganovich's loyalty to Stalin, shaped at that time, never wavered. Stalin used him in his policy toward the Ukraine mainly because Kaganovich was one of the few party leaders who spoke fluent Ukrainian. The aim of Kaganovich's first mission to the Ukraine was to accelerate the Ukrainization process. Such a line was considered urgent in Moscow because of the rapid revival of Ukrainian culture that had been instigated by the non-Bolshevik intelligentsia, whose outstanding representatives (among them **Mykhailo Hrushevsky**) had returned from exile. In April 1925 Kaganovich became the first secretary of the CC of the Communist Party (Bolshevik) of the Ukraine (CP[B]U) and accelerated the Ukrainization process, though under the party's control, in the administration, the army, and the trade union movement.

In the spring of 1926 the Ukrainization process began to slow down. Stalin decided to decelerate it in order to gain support among the Russians in the Ukraine who did not want to be forced to learn a "peasant" language and might have turned to the Trotskyist opposition. This was in keeping with Stalin's previous decisions since the removal the year before of Emmanuel Kviring, Kaganovich's predecessor as head of the CP(B)U, had also been motivated by the need to fight Trotsky's influence. Kviring, an ethnic German, was known as a supporter of Russian dominance over Ukrainian culture and a representative of the eastern, Russian-speaking part of the Ukraine. Kaganovich accused **Olexander Shumsky**, commissar of education and a supporter of intensive Ukrainization, of nationalist deviation in the CP(B)U and then removed him from office. This case was also affected by a personal conflict, as Shumsky had previously put pressure on Stalin to oust Kaganovich from the party leadership. Subsequently Kaganovich conducted a purge of the leadership of the Communist Party of Western Ukraine, the majority of which supported Shumsky. Under Kaganovich's rule in the Ukraine, a campaign of accusations was launched against the writer **Mykola Khvylovy**. Kaganovich was ordered back from the Ukraine in 1928, after fulfilling all his tasks. The local Bolsheviks again assumed leadership positions. Stalin once more needed the support of Ukrainian activists, this time against the Bukharinist opposition among leaders of the All-Union Communist Party (Bolsheviks). Kaganovich returned to Moscow and was reinstated as a member of the Secretariat of the CC.

In the first half of the 1930s Kaganovich performed many important tasks, including that of supervising the collectivization of agriculture in the Ukraine. The Ukraine failed to produce enough grain to fulfill an overestimated plan of grain supplies, and mass famine began in the autumn of 1932. At that point Kaganovich, along with Vyacheslav Molotov, headed a special committee that, by a ruthless confiscation of grain, virtually deprived the country of food and increased the extent of the catastrophe. Thus, both Kaganovich and Molotov were responsible for the starvation of millions of Ukrainians. Later, Kaganovich was in charge of the great reconstruction of Moscow (including the construction of the first subway), as well as the administration of the industrial and raw material departments. He was also one of the chief executors of the "Great Purge" in the Ukraine at the end of the 1930s.

In the late 1940s, when the Ukraine was exhausted by war and failed to fulfill the grain quota in 1946, Kaganovich was again appointed first secretary of the CC of the CP(B)U (March–December 1947), and his actions brought results comparable to those of the 1930s. Later, as an anti-Semitic campaign grew during the last years of Stalin's rule, Kaganovich's position within the Politburo clearly weakened. After Stalin's death, especially after the Twentieth CPSU Congress, his position was endangered by de-Stalinization. In June 1957, together with other Stalinists, such as Molotov and Georgy Malenkov, Kaganovich attempted to depose **Nikita Khrushchev**, secretary general of the CPSU CC. The attempt failed, and the group members (labeled as "anti-party") were ousted from the Politburo and from the CC. In 1961 Kaganovich retired, and his name disappeared from encyclopedias of Soviet history for a long time. The year 1996 saw the publication of his *Pamiatnye zapiski rabochego kommunista-bolshevika, profsoiuznogo, partiinogo i sovetsko-gosudarstvennego rabotnika* (Notes by a Communist-Bolshevik activist and trade union, party, and Soviet government worker). (TS)

Sources: *MERSH*, vol. 16; Roy Medvedev, *Ludzie Stalina* (Warsaw, 1989); *Encyclopedia of Ukraine*, vol. 2 (Toronto, 1988); Jeanne Vronskaya and Vladimir Chuguev, *The Biographical Dictionary of the Former Soviet Union: Prominent People in All Fields from 1917 to the Present* (London, 1992); Archie Brown, Michael Koser, and Gerald Smith, eds., *The Cambridge Encyclopedia of Russia and the Former Soviet Union* (Cambridge and New York, 1994).

KAIRYS Steponas (20 December 1878, Užnevėžiai, near Ukmergė–16 December 1964, New York), Lithuanian Socialist politician. While a student at a gymnasium in Šiauliai, Kairys protested that Catholic students were being forced to take part in Orthodox services, and because of this, he was expelled from school in 1897. After passing his high school final exams, he studied at the Technological Institute in St. Petersburg, where he was twice suspended for taking part in political demonstrations. In 1900 he joined the Lithuanian Social Democratic Party (LSDP) and favored the independence of this party from the Russian Social Democratic Party. The following year he became a member of the Central Committee (CC) of the LSDP. During the sessions of the Grand Lithuanian Assembly in 1905, he was elected a member of its five-member presidium. Elected to the Russian State Duma from the lists of the Lithuanian Social Democrats in 1907, Kairys served as secretary of the seven-member parliamentary representation of the LSDP. At that time he was in favor of the federation of an independent Lithuania with Poland, Belarus, and Latvia. In 1908–11 he worked on the construction of railway bridges in the region of Samara and Kursk. He subsequently worked in the Vilnius (Wilno) sewage department. As a representative of the LSDP, he attended congresses of the Russian Social Democrats in London and congresses of the Polish Social Democrats in Kraków.

After the Germans occupied Vilnius in 1915, Kairys became more involved in the cause of Lithuanian independence. When on 18 September 1917 the Germans agreed to the establishment of the Lithuanian Council (Lietuvos Tarybe), he became its vice-president. In protest against the conciliatory attitude of the majority of this council, he resigned at the end of January 1918, but he joined it again after its members agreed to abandon all constraints regarding the sovereignty of a future Lithuanian state. On 16 February 1918 Kairys was one of the signatories of the Lithuanian independence declaration. He again withdrew from the Lithuanian Council (which in July of that year changed its name to State Council) when, under German pressure, its members accepted Wilhelm von Urach, Duke of Württemberg, as the future king of Lithuania. After Lithuania regained its independence, Kairys worked in the Ministry of Industry and Trade. Between April and October 1919 he was minister of supplies. From 1923 to 1938 he headed the Kaunas sewage department and served as consultant for sewage projects in other Lithuanian cities. In 1920 he became an MP as a representative of the LSDP. Elected again in 1923 and in 1926, he served as president of the party and of its parliamentary representation. After the elections of May 1926, Kairys became deputy speaker of the parliament. Following the nationalist coup d'état of December 1926, he joined the opposition, but in 1936–37 he repeatedly rejected Communist offers to establish a common people's front. In 1923 he began lecturing at Kaunas University, where he received a professorship in 1939. In 1939 he published *Miestu kanalizacija* (The city sewage system).

During the first Soviet occupation (1940–41), Kairys avoided deportation. Between 1941 and 1943 he was the dean of the Engineering Department of Kaunas University. From the end of 1943, he served as president of the Supreme Committee for the Liberation of Lithuania (Vyriausias Lietuvos Islaisvinimo Komitetas [VLIK]), which called for a struggle against the USSR and against communism. In April 1944 most VLIK leaders were arrested by the Gestapo. Kairys tried to leave for Sweden under the name Juozas Kaminskas, but he was arrested by the Germans and imprisoned in Libau (Liepāja). Unrecognized and released during the evacuation of the town, he left for Germany before the Red Army entered Lithuania. In Germany, he revived the activities of the VLIK and took the leadership of the Social Democratic Party in exile. In 1952 he went to the United States, where he was less active owing to ill health. In 1957 he published his famous memoirs, *Lietuva budo* (Lithuania was awakening), and in 1964, its second volume, *Tau, Lietuva* (For you, Lithuania). (WR)

Sources: *EL*, vol. 3; L. Sabaliūnas, "Social Democracy in Tsarist Lithuania," *Slavic Review*, 1972, no. 2; Jerzy Ochmański, *Historia Litwy* (Wrocław, 1967); Constantine R. Jurgėla, *Lithuania: The Outpost of Freedom* (St. Petersburg, Fla., 1976); Vladas Krivickas, "The Programs of the Lithuanian Social Democratic Party 1896–1931," *Journal of Baltic Studies*, 1980, no. 2; Alfonsas Eidintas and Vytautas Žalys, *Lithuania in European Politics: The Years of the First Republic, 1918–1940* (New York, 1997).

KAJKA Michał (27 September 1858, Skomack Wielki, near Ełk–5 September 1940, Orzysz), Polish poet and Masurian activist. Born into a peasant family, Kajka completed a few grades of a rural elementary school in the village of Rostki and continued his learning through self-education. He started to work at fourteen, often as a farmhand. In 1875 he also took up carpentry and bricklaying. At seventeen he began writing poems. From 1883 on he lived permanently in the village of Ogródek, near Ełk. In 1884 he began publishing in the Masurian press (for example, in *Mazur, Nowiny Śląskie, Gazeta Ludowa, Gazeta Olsztyńska, Mazurski Przyjaciel Ludu, Życie Młodzieży*, and *Kalendarz dla Mazurów*). He was very active in Masurian social-political and cultural life. In 1890 in Ogródek, he founded a secret library of the Society of Peasant Libraries, and in 1896 he was a co-founder of the Masurian Peasant Party in Ełk. For defending Polish national identity in Masuria, Kajka incurred persecution by the German authorities. In 1920, during a plebiscite in Warmia and Masuria, he was a champion of Polish interests. He co-organized the Masurian Union, and in 1923 he became its president. He took part in the work of the Union of Poles in Eastern Prussia, the Union of Polish School Societies, and the Masurian Mutual Aid Association. He attended congresses of Polish organizations and associations. He wrote a great deal about injustices to peasants and discrimination against the Poles in Masuria. Kajka withdrew from active social work in 1933 because of his advanced age and because of an increasingly difficult political situation in Masuria after the Nazi takeover of power, but he continued to write. His writing, influenced by religious books, classics of Polish literature, and the tradition of peasant writing, praised the beauty of nature and referred to current issues. He was also the author of many religious songs. Kajka is regarded as the most outstanding Masurian peasant poet. Various efforts were made to perpetuate his memory—for instance, in 1946 the village of Buchwald in Ostróda County was renamed Kajkowo. The following collections of Kajka's poems were published: *Pieśni mazurskie* (Masurian songs; 1927); *Wybór wierszy* (Selection of poems; 1954); *Zebrałem snop plonu* (I have gathered a sheaf of crops; 1958); *Wiersze wybrane* (Selected poems; 1958); and *Z duchowej mej niwy* (From my spiritual soil; 1982). (JS)

Sources: *PSB*, vol. 11; *Słownik biograficzny działaczy ruchu ludowego* (Warsaw, 1989); Witold Piechocki, *Michał Kajka* (Warsaw, 1958); Melchior Wańkowicz, *Na tropach smętka*. (Warsaw,

1958); Władysław Chojnacki, *Sylwetki mazurskie: Szkice z dziejów Pomorza* (Warsaw, 1961); Jerzy Oleksiński, *Bard ziemi mazurskiej* (Warsaw, 1972); Janusz Jasiński, *Michał Kajka, 1858–1940: Droga do Polski* (Suwałki, 1990); Zbigniew Chojnowski, *Michał Kajka: Poeta mazurski* (Olsztyn, 1992).

KĄKOL Kazimierz (22 November 1920, Warsaw), Polish Communist activist. The son of a railway worker, during the German occupation (1939–45) Kąkol belonged to the pro-independence Home Army and worked in secret education organizations. He graduated from the University of Łódź, and in 1949 he received a Ph.D. in economics. From 1957 he was a member of the (Communist) Polish United Workers' Party (PUWP), gradually advancing in its hierarchy. From December 1971 to February 1980 he was a deputy member of the PUWP Central Committee, and from February 1980 to July 1981 he belonged to the PUWP Central Control Commission. From 1957 he was editor-in-chief of the bi-weekly *Prawo i Życie*, and from 1968 he directed the School of Journalism at Warsaw University. From 1974 he was a professor, and in 1973–74, director of the Institute of Journalism of Warsaw University. Politically Kąkol was connected with **Mieczysław Moczar**. In 1968 he orchestrated an anti-Zionist campaign in which his *Prawo i Życie* played an important role. Kąkol was active in the propaganda campaign against the Prague Spring and for the Warsaw Pact intervention in Czechoslovakia, including the participation of Polish troops in this operation. From May 1974 to April 1980 he was minister/head of the Office for Religious Affairs (Urząd do Spraw Wyznań). The Communist authorities hoped Kąkol would improve their relationship with the Holy See behind the back of the Polish Episcopate and Primate **Stefan Wyszyński** after foreign minister **Stefan Olszowski** was received by Pope Paul VI on 12 November 1973. These hopes soon proved to be in vain. In 1985–89 Kąkol headed the Main Commission of Investigation of Hitlerite Crimes in Poland, and in 1983–89 he belonged to the Socioeconomic Council of the parliament. (PK)

Sources: *Popularna Encyklopedia Powszechna*, vol. 9 (Kraków, 1996); Mołdawa; Andrzej Micewski, *Współrządzić czy nie kłamać* (Paris, 1978); Jerzy Eisler, *Marzec 1968* (Warsaw, 1991).

KAKOWSKI Aleksander (5 February 1862, Dębiny, near Przasnysz–30 December 1938, Warsaw), Polish archbishop and cardinal. Kakowski successfully passed his high school final exams in Pułtusk and later graduated from a theological seminary in Warsaw. He studied at the Roman Catholic Theological Academy in St. Petersburg and then at the Gregorian University in Rome, where in 1885 he received a Ph.D. in canon law. On 30 May 1885 he took holy orders. In 1887 he began lecturing at a seminary in Warsaw, and later he was a secretary of the bishop's court. In 1901 he became a canon of the Warsaw chapter. Because of Kakowski's moderate political stance, the Holy See was able to get the Russian authorities to accept his nomination to the post of archbishop of Warsaw. On 22 June 1913 he was consecrated in St. Petersburg, and on 14 September he made a ceremonious entry into Warsaw Cathedral. Thereafter, he used the title of Primate of the Kingdom of Poland until the end of his life. After the Germans entered Warsaw in 1915, Kakowski forbade his subordinate priests to become involved in political activities, but when new Polish institutions began to be organized, he allowed the clergymen to participate in charity and mutual aid organizations. Kakowski was indirectly linked with the pro-Russian Inter-Party Political Circle, and he had reservations about the Act of 5 November 1916, which was issued by the emperors of Germany and Austria-Hungary. After the February 1917 revolution, on 16 April 1917 Kakowski issued a pastoral letter written in a spirit of cooperation with the German authorities. He was instrumental in the establishment of the People's Union (Zjednoczenie Ludowe [ZL]), which was a conservative Catholic party.

On 12 October 1917 Kakowski became a member of the Regency Council, a provisional Polish government in the former Kingdom of Poland. The Regency Council was subordinate to the Central Powers. In November 1918 Kakowski opposed the transfer of power to **Józef Piłsudski**, as he thought that the Regency Council should delegate the power to a parliament chosen through general elections. On 15 December 1919 Kakowski was appointed cardinal. He was a member of the Vatican Congregation of Sacraments, Propaganda of Faith, and Seminaries and Universities. In July 1920 he was the co-author of a pastoral letter calling for the defense of Poland against the Bolshevik invasion. He was instrumental in the signing of the concordat of 10 February 1925. An efficient organizer, Kakowski summoned an archdiocesan synod in 1922 and a synod of Polish bishops in 1936. He was a co-founder of Catholic Action and initiated the establishment of the diocese of Łódź. He was also a co-founder of the Theological Department at Warsaw University, and in 1937 he was a co-founder of the Institute of Higher Religious Culture in Warsaw. Kakowski left extensive memoirs, *Z niewoli do niepodległości* (From slavery to independence; 2000). (WR)

Sources: *PSB*, vol. 11; *Encyklopedia historii Drugiej Rzeczypospolitej* (Warsaw, 1999); Ks. Stefan Wyszyński, "Kardynał Kakowski," *Ateneum Kapłańskie*, 1939, nos. 163–165; Władysław Pobóg-Malinowski, *Najnowsza historia polityczna Polski*, vol. 2 (London, 1983).

KALANTA Romas (1953–14 May 1972, Kaunas), Lithuanian student who set himself on fire. While attending an evening high school, Kalanta under pressure enrolled in the Komsomol. In protest against the violation of Lithuanian national and religious freedoms by the Kremlin, on Sunday, 14 May 1972, in the square in front of the theater in Kaunas, where in 1940 the People's Assembly had voted for the incorporation of Lithuania into the USSR, Kalanta doused himself with gasoline, set himself ablaze, and soon thereafter died of burns. This case became very famous throughout the capital. Fearing an outbreak of demonstrations, on 18 May the authorities ordered that his funeral be two hours earlier than planned. However, thousands of Lithuanians displayed their patriotic feelings, chanting "Freedom for Lithuania!" Two people were killed, and many were injured and arrested by consolidated KGB forces during the suppression of two-day demonstrations. The authorities attempted to prove that Kalanta had been unstable and had acted under the influence of drugs. Few people were convinced by such claims, especially since on 29 May another student set himself on fire in Varėna and on 3 June a similar act was committed by a worker from Kaunas. In October 1972 eight people were given sentences ranging from one to three years in prison for participating in the May demonstrations. The memory of Kalanta's tragic gesture to a considerable extent shaped the consciousness of the Lithuanian opposition. (WR)

Sources: *EL*, vol. 3; Saulius Sužiedelis, *Historical Dictionary of Lithuania* (Lanham, Md., 1997); "Romas Kalanta," *Kultura*, 1972, nos. 7/8; Romuald J. Misiunas and Rein Taagepera, *The Baltic States: Years of Dependence, 1940–1990* (Berkeley, 1993).

KALCHENKO Nikifor (9 February 1906, Koshmanivka, near Poltava–14 May 1989, Kiev), Soviet Communist activist in the Ukraine. The son of a peasant, from 1921 to 1924 Kalchenko studied at a horticultural school and in 1925–28 at the Agricultural Institute in Poltava. In 1932 he joined the Communist Party. An active implementer of the policy of collectivization in agriculture, in 1928–38 he worked as an agronomist, kolkhoz director, and head of department in the administration of the Kharkiv district. Between 1938 and 1941 he headed an executive committee of the district soviet of Workers' Deputies in Odessa. In 1938–40 he was a deputy member, and from 1940 to 1976 a member, of the Central Committee (CC) of the party in the Ukraine. From 1954 to 1976 he was a member of the Politburo of the CC of the Communist Party of Ukraine. From 1952 to 1956 and from 1966 to 1976 he was also a deputy member, and from 1956 to 1966 a member, of the CC of the Communist Party of the Soviet Union (CPSU). In 1941–46 Kalchenko belonged to the Military Council

of the Red Army and to the Military Council of the First Ukrainian Front. He was rose to the rank of lieutenant general. In 1946 he became minister of technology, in 1947 minister of state farms (sovkhozy), and in 1950–52 minister of agriculture of the Ukrainian SSR. In 1952–54 he was first vice-president of the Council of Ministers of the Ukrainian SSR; from 1954 to 1961 he was head of the government of the Soviet Ukraine, and in 1961–76 he was deputy prime minister of the Ukrainian SSR. For many years Kalchenko also served as deputy to the Supreme Soviet of the Ukrainian SSR and deputy to the Supreme Soviet of the USSR. The peak of his career coincided with the rule of **Nikita Khrushchev**. Along with **Oleksy Kyrychenko**, Kalchenko took part in the Ukrainization of the cadres of the Ukrainian SSR following the Twentieth Congress of the CPSU. Like Kyrychenko, however, in 1961 Kalchenko fell victim to Khrushchev's reshuffling of the party and government leadership. (TS)

Sources: *Ukrains'ka Radians'ka Entsyklopediia*, vol. 6 (Kiev, 1961); Borys Levytsky, *Politics and Society in Soviet Ukraine, 1953–1980* (Edmonton, 1984).

KALECKI Michał (22 June 1899, Łódź–27 April 1970, Warsaw), Polish economist. The son of a small merchant of Jewish origin, after graduating from a gymnasium in Łódź, Kalecki studied at Warsaw Technical University. He interrupted his studies when he was drafted into the army in June 1919. After returning from the front in the Polish-Bolshevik war, Kalecki continued his studies at the Technical University in Gdańsk, where he received a half-diploma (i.e., he completed two years of studies) in 1923. Between 1923 and 1929 he did odd jobs and subsequently worked at the Institute for Economic Research. In the periodicals he edited, including *Prace* and *Koniunktura Gospodarcza*, he published a number of important studies on price, income, and consumption indexes, as well as indexes of "investment movements." Along with Ludwik Landau, Kalecki also published pioneering works on social income in Poland between 1929 and 1933. In October 1933, at a conference in Holland, he read the paper "Macro-Dynamic Theory of Business Cycles," which included elements of the theory of saving, investment, and employment. At that time he also published *Essays in the Theory of Economic Fluctuations* in London. Kalecki contributed to *Przegląd Gospodarczy* and *Polska Gospodarcza*, where in 1935 he published the article "Istota poprawy koniunkturalnej" (The essence of cyclical economic upswings), which later came to be cited as the introduction to the modern theory of employment. In the same year Kalecki published *Próba teorii koniunktury* (An attempt at a theory of business cycles), which was considered a pioneering contribution to the theory of the cycle. This study was later compared to contemporary works by John Maynard Keynes. In 1936 Kalecki received a stipend from the Rockefeller Foundation that enabled him to continue his research in Sweden and England, where he studied Keynes's theory. Keynes was unenthusiastic about Kalecki's works, yet he helped him find employment in Cambridge. In 1937 Kalecki published *A Theory of Business Cycles*.

During World War II, Kalecki conducted research at Oxford on the war economy. After a short stay in Poland in 1946, in the following eight years he worked in the economic department of the Secretariat of the United Nations. In 1954 he returned to Poland and worked as a state planner. In 1955 and 1956 he served as an adviser to Deputy Prime Minister **Hilary Minc**. After October 1956 Kalecki was appointed a professor and vice-president of the government Economic Council. From 1957 to 1964 he worked in the Planning Commission. At that time he drafted a prospective plan for 1961–75, but this plan was not implemented. From 1957 to 1961 Kalecki was an economic adviser to the governments of Israel, India, and Cuba. In 1961 he began lecturing at the Central School of Planning and Statistics (Szkoła Główna Planowania i Statystyki [SGPiS]), and in 1966 he became a full member of the Polish Academy of Sciences. Kalecki believed that economic development was determined by technological progress. He created a theory of the planned economy that was presented in *Zarys teorii wzrostu gospodarki socjalistycznej* (An outline of the theory of growth in a Socialist economy; 1963). During the "March events" of 1968, on the wave of an anti-Semitic campaign, Kalecki was attacked by party zealots in the SGPiS and was relegated to a minor post; therefore, he gave up work at this school. In 1969 he worked as a lecturer in Cambridge. He died soon after returning to Poland. Six volumes of his *Dzieła* (Works) were published in 1979–87, and an eight-volume edition, *Collected Works of Michael Kalecki*, edited by Jerzy Osiatyński, was published between 1990 and 1997. (WR)

Sources: *The International Who Is Who 1963–1964* (London, 1963); George R. Feiwel *The Intellectual Capital of Michal Kalecki* (Knoxville, Tenn., 1975); Malcolm C. Sawyer, *The Economics of Michal Kalecki* (Armonk, N.Y., 1985); Krzysztof Leowski, "Michał Kalecki," *Poczet wybitnych profesorów SGH-SGPiS* (Warsaw, 1986); Jerzy Osiatyński, *Michal Kalecki on a Socialist Economy* (New York, 1988); Mario Sebastiani, *Kalecki's Relevance Today* (New York, 1989); Mark Blang, ed., *Michal Kalecki (1899–1970)* (Aldershot, 1992).

KALFOV Khristo (16 October 1883, Kalofer–1 February 1945, Sofia), Bulgarian politician. After graduating from the Military Academy in Sofia (1903) and the Military Academy in Turin (1907–11), Kalfov returned to Bulgaria and served in an artillery regiment (1911–12). He participated in the Balkan Wars (1921–13) as an officer for special tasks to the commander-in-chief. He later served in the bodyguard of Tsar **Ferdinand I**. From 1914 to 1917 he was the martial arts instructor of Prince **Boris**, and when Boris became king, Kalfov became his aide-de-camp (1918–22). After resigning from service at the tsar's court and retiring from the army with the rank of colonel in September 1922, Kalfov was one of the organizers of the coup of 9 June 1923. During the premiership of **Aleksandur Tsankov**, between June 1923 and January 1926 Kalfov served as minister of foreign and religious affairs and was responsible for various tasks, including the drafting of a treaty of friendship with Turkey (1925) and a protocol with Greece on respecting the rights of minorities. He was a Bulgarian representative at two sessions of the Council of the League of Nations in Geneva. In 1923–26 Kalfov served as secretary of the Democratic Alliance, and after the split within this party in 1932, he joined the National Social Movement (NSM) of Tsankov, becoming a member of the central leadership of the NSM. In 1934 he left the NSM and supported the regime of Tsar Boris III. In 1936 Kalfov made an unsuccessful attempt at establishing a Fascist state social party. He was a deputy to the National Assembly from 1927 to 1934 and from 1940 to 1944 and served as its speaker during the second term. After 9 September 1944 Kalfov was arrested and sentenced by the so-called people's court to death and confiscation of property for his activities in parliament between 1940 and 1944. The sentence was carried out immediately. Kalfov was rehabilitated by a decision of the Supreme Court in April 1996. (JJ)

Sources: *Entsiklopediya: Bylgariya*, vol. 3 (Sofia, 1982); *Sbornik na obiknoveno narodno sybranie* (Sofia, 1940); Tasho Tashev, *Ministrite na Bylgariya 1879–1999: Entsiklopedichen spravochnik* (Sofia, 1999); Angel Tsurakov, *Entsiklopediya Pravitelstvata na Bylgariya: Khronologiia na politicheskiia zhivot 1879–2001* (Sofia, 2001).

KÁLLAI Gyula (1 June 1910, Berettyóújfalu–12 March 1996, Budapest), Hungarian Communist activist. The son of a shoemaker, Kállai graduated from high school in 1930, and then he studied at the universities in Budapest and Debrecen. He joined the Hungarian Communist Party (HCP) in 1931 and was one of the organizers of the March Front, for which he was expelled from the university in 1937. He then started working as a journalist in Debrecen. Between 1939 and 1944 he worked for the Social Democratic daily newspaper *Népszava*. He co-organized a demonstration on 15 March 1942 at which people protested Hungary's participation in the war. Arrested in July 1942, Kállai was released in November for lack of evidence. In September 1944 he took part in the founding meeting of the Central Committee (CC) of the illegal Communist Party. As a representative of the party, he participated in the work of the Executive Committee of the Hungarian National Independence Front.

In 1945 Kállai became a member of the CC of the HCP and then of the Hungarian Workers' Party, as well as head of the Propaganda Department of the CC. From July 1945 he was political secretary of state to the Presidium of the Council of Ministers, and between November 1945 and May 1946 he was political secretary of state for information. In 1946–49 Kállai headed the party's Press Department, then the Department for Intellectuals, and finally the Department for Cultural Policy. Between 1948 and 1949 he was head of the Office of the President of the Republic of Hungary. In June 1949 he was appointed minister of foreign affairs. In April 1951 he was arrested on false charges, dismissed from all his posts, and sentenced to life imprisonment in a secret trial. Released in July 1954, he became head of the publishing section at the Ministry of People's Education. Between February 1955 and the end of October 1956 he was deputy minister of people's education. In July 1956 he was again elected a member of the CC, becoming head of the Science and Culture Department of the CC.

At the CC Plenum on 24 October 1956 Kállai was elected a member of the Politburo and secretary of the CC. During the revolution he remained in hiding in the flat of one of his friends. Between 1956 and 1989 he was a member of the CC and of the Politburo of the Hungarian Socialist Workers' Party (HSWP). From February 1957 he held the post of secretary of the CC, and until 1975 he was head of the Science and Culture Department of the CC of the HSWP. At a meeting of the HSWP in January 1957 Kállai gave an account of talks that had been conducted by the **Imre Nagy** group in Romania, and he suggested taking the group to court. From May 1957 Kállai was minister of culture. In 1957, in his book *A magyarországi ellenforradalom a marxizmus-leninizmus fényében* (Counterrevolution in Hungary in the light of Marxism-Leninism), Kállai presented a "scientific" evaluation of the revolution. In 1958–89 he was president of the State Council of the Patriotic People's Front. Between 1960 and 1965 he was first deputy premier and deputy premier. From 30 June 1965 to 14 April 1967 he held the post of premier, and between 1967 and 1971 he was president of the parliament. From 1967 he was a member of the Presidential Council of the Hungarian People's Republic. In 1945–51 and 1958–90 he was an MP. Kállai's memoirs, *Megkésett börtönnapló* (Late journal from prison), appeared in 1987. (JT)

Sources: Bennet Kovrig, *Communism in Hungary from Kun to Kádár* (Stanford, 1979); Miklós Molnár, *From Béla Kun to János Kádár: Seventy Years of Hungarian Communism* (New York, 1990); *Magyar Nagylexikon*, vol. 10 (Budapest, 2000); *A magyar forradalom és szabadságharc enciklopédiája*, CD-ROM (Budapest, 1999).

KALLAS Siim (2 October 1948, Tallinn), Estonian politician. After graduating in banking and finance from the University of Tartu, Kallas worked in the Ministry of Finance of the Estonian SSR, and in 1979–86 he was director of the Central Administration of Savings Banks. In 1987–89 he was deputy editor-in-chief of the party newspaper, *Rahva Hääl*. Kallas became popular when he published, with **Edgar Savisaar**, a program of economic reforms that included the autonomy of the Estonian economy, the introduction of a national currency and budget, and the development of trade based on a market economy. Despite the negative reaction of the Communist authorities, the wide social support for the program became an inspiration for the "Principles of an Independent Estonian Economy," adopted in 1989. In 1989–91 Kallas was chairman of the Central Council of Trade Unions and deputy to the Supreme Council of the Estonian SSR. After Estonia regained independence in 1991, Kallas took a decisive turn to the right. From 1991 to 1994 he chaired the Bank of Estonia, becoming known for his consistent support for the privatization of the whole economy. He resigned in a cloud of scandal because he was accused of the embezzlement of US$10 million. Although he was cleared of this accusation in 2000, the Supreme Court sent the case back for further examination. The whole affair became the core of attacks on the center-right government and on Kallas himself. On the eve of the parliamentary elections of September 1995, Kallas founded the Estonian Reform Party (Eesti Reformierakond [ERP]), and he became its chairman. From 1995 he sat in the parliament.

From October 1995 to November 1996 Kallas was foreign minister in the government of **Tiit Vähi**. The fall of that government caused the reformers to move into the opposition. Kallas returned to power as a result of the March 1999 elections, when his party entered a coalition with other center and right-wing parties and joined the government of **Mart Laar**; Kallas became minister of finance and continued market reforms. Perceived as an advocate of monetarism, Kallas consistently supported wide privatization, including that of the railways and the health service. Although prospects for entering the European Union (whose program is much more socially oriented than the ERP would like), eased Kallas's pronouncements on privatization, Kallas tried to complete the changes in ownership. In 2002 the ruling coalition broke up. On 28 January 2002 Kallas entered into a coalition with the Estonian Center Party and created a new government under his leadership. As result of the March 2003 elections, on 10 April 2003 Kallas resigned from the position of prime minister. In December 2004 he was nominated European commissioner for administrative affairs, audits, and anti-fraud and vice-president of the European Commission. (AG)

Sources: *Eesti Enstuklopeedia*, vol. 14 (Tallinn, 2000); Matti Laur, Tõnis Lukas, Ain Mäesalu, Ago Pajur, and Tõnu Tannberg, *History of Estonia* (Tallinn, 2000); Mel Huang, "Does Estonia Have a Left?" *Central European Review*, 2000, no. 13; Mel Huang, "The News from Estonia: All Important News since 1 April 2000," *Central European Review*, 2000, no. 14; eng.reform.ee/cv_siimkallas. html.

KÁLLAY Miklós (23 January 1887, Nyíregyháza–14 January 1967, New York), Hungarian politician. Born into an aristocratic family, after attending school in Geneva and Munich, Kállay received a Ph. D. in law in Budapest in 1910. In 1920–22 he was head of a county and then of Szabolcs Province in eastern Hungary. From 1929 he was secretary of state in the Ministry of Trade, from 1931 an MP, and from 1937 a senator. From October 1932 to January 1935 Kállay was minister of agriculture in the government of **Gyula Gömbös**, from which he resigned in protest against the authoritarian inclinations of the prime minister. For some time Kállay was head of the National Land Drainage Administration. On 9 March 1942 Regent **Miklós Horthy** invited him to become prime minister, and until mid–1943 Kállay combined this position with the office of foreign minister. In domestic affairs Kállay tried—with some success—to reduce the influence of extreme parties (the Arrow Cross Fascists and the Communists) and to minimize the impact of war on the Hungarian economy. His basic foreign policy goal was to extricate the country from war without jeopardizing it with a German or Soviet occupation. As a result of the Big Three's policies, and of Stalin in particular, this strategy ultimately failed. When Germany occupied Hungary, on 22 March 1944 Kállay was dismissed. He initially hid from the Arrow Cross people in the Turkish Embassy. After leaving it, he was arrested and imprisoned in the German concentration camps of Mauthausen and Dachau. After World War II Kállay lived in Italy, and from 1951, in the United States. He was active in the pro-independence organizations of Hungarian émigrés and wrote articles. In 1954 Kállay published his memoirs in New York, *Hungarian Premier: A Personal Account of a Nation's Struggle in the Second World War*. (MS)

Sources: *Biographisches Lexikon*, vol. 2; György Ránki, *Emlékiratok és valóság* (Budapest, 1964); *20 századi magyar történelem, 1900–1994* (Budapest, 1977); John F. Montgomery, *Hungary: The Unwilling Satellite* (New York, 1947); Nicholas Horthy, *Memoirs* (New York, 1954); Paul Ignotus, *Hungary* (London, 1972); Steven Bela Vardy, *Historical Dictionary of Hungary* (Lanham, Md., 1997); *Magyar életrajzi lexikon*, CD-ROM 2000.

KALNBĒRZINŠ Jānis (17 September 1893, Katlakana–4 February 1986, Riga), Latvian Communist activist. In 1908 Kalnbērzinš began to work as a laborer in the Riga port. In 1914 he joined the Bolshevik party and was sent to work in Lithuania. From 1918 to 1922 he served as a volunteer in the Red Army. Later, he attended the Communist University of Western Nations, and in 1925–28 he worked in the Communist underground in Latvia. He subsequently went to study at the Institute of Red Professorship in Moscow. After completing his studies in 1933, Kalnbērzinš worked in the party apparatus. In 1931 he joined the Central Committee (CC) of the Communist Party of Latvia (CPL). In 1936 he returned to Latvia, where he led the Communist underground in Riga. In 1939 he was imprisoned by the Latvian authorities, but when the Red Army marched into Latvia in June 1940 he was released and officially appointed first secretary of the CC of the CPL. At that time, along with the special emissary of the Kremlin, Andrey Vyshinsky, and NKVD functionaries, Kalnbērzinš organized the Communist takeover of power in Latvia, the incorporation of the republic into the Soviet Union, and the arrests and deportation of Latvian people. Thousands of Latvians lost their lives as a result of these actions. After the German invasion in June 1941, Kalnbērzinš went to the Soviet interior, where he became a member of the Military Council of the Northwestern Front. In 1941–52 he was a deputy member of the CC of the All-Union Communist Party (Bolsheviks). He subsequently became a member of the CC, and in 1957–61 he served as a deputy member of the Presidium of the CC. In 1945 Kalnbērzinš returned to Latvia as first secretary of the CC of the Latvian Communist Party (Bolsheviks) and directed a mostly Russian party apparatus. He supervised the second stage of the Sovietization of Latvia, which involved the arrests and deportation of all non-Communist activists, the collectivization of agriculture, and the deportation of peasants. These actions led to thousands more victims. A vicious Russifier of Latvia, in 1951 Kalnbērzinš published a work about a decade of Soviet rule. In this work, he maintained that from its beginning the Latvian nation had developed nothing but gratitude for its contacts with Russia.

The "thaw" and the de-Stalinization movement between 1953 and 1956 changed political conditions in Latvia. Since the Russians constituted the majority of party members in Latvia, changes in the Kremlin resulted in a greater openness of the Kremlin authorities toward the Latvians, whose cooperation they wanted to secure. The Latviazation of the party increased during the first years of **Nikita Khrushchev**'s rule, but since the Kremlin decided that this process had gone too far, in 1959 a purge of the Latvian party leadership was launched. Kalnbērziņš was dismissed as first secretary. Although he personally was not accused of anything, **Arvids Pelše**, who succeeded him, pointed out his "deficiencies in working with the youth in the spirit of a proper internationalism." Kalnbērziņš was transferred to the post of president of the Supreme Soviet of the Latvian SSR and in 1960 to the post of vice-president of the Supreme Soviet of the USSR. In 1970 he retired but continued to serve as deputy to the Supreme Soviet of the USSR until 1974. (EJ/WR)

Sources: *Prominent Personalities in the USSR* (Metuchen, N.J., 1968); *Great Soviet Encyclopedia*, vol. 11; Archie Brown, ed., *The Soviet Union: A Biographical Dictionary* (New York, 1990); Romuald J. Misunas and Rein Taagepera, *The Baltic States: The Years of Dependence, 1940–1970* (Berkeley, 1993); Andrejs Plakans, *Historical Dictionary of Latvia* (Lanham, Md., 1997).

KALNIŅŠ Bruno (7 May 1899, Tukums, Courland–26 March 1990, Stockholm), Latvian Socialist politician. The son of **Pauls Kalniņš**, he went to high school in Dubulti, and in 1913 he joined the Social Democratic Workers' Party of Latvia (SDWPL). In 1916 he graduated from high school in Helsingfors (Helsinki). In 1916–17 he studied law at the University of Petrograd. In 1917 he was elected to the Executive Committee of the Riga Council (Soviet) of Workers' and Peasants' Delegates. In 1918–34 he was a member of the SDWPL Central Committee (CC), and from 1918 to 1926 he was its secretary. A member of the Latvian National Council that proclaimed Latvia's independence on 18 November 1918, in 1919 Kalniņš volunteered to fight in defense of the country, and until 1921 he presided over the Central Bureau of Trade Unions. In 1921–34 he chaired the Socialist youth paramilitary organization, the Workers' Sporting Union (Strādnieku Sporta Savienība), later called the Sports and Workers' Guard (Strādnieku Sports un Sargs). A deputy to the Constituent Assembly (1920–22) and subsequent terms of the parliament and the editor of several Socialist periodicals, during the coup of 15 May 1934 Kalniņš was arrested and in 1935 sentenced to four years in prison. Thanks to the intervention of the Scandinavian Social Democrats, he was released in November 1936. In 1937 he left for Finland, where he was press attaché of the Spanish Republican representation. A member of the Foreign Committee of the Socialist Workers' and Peasants' Party of Latvia, which was banned at home, in November 1939 he was deprived of Latvian citizenship.

After the Soviet invasion of Latvia in June 1940, Kalniņš returned home and applied to the Communist Party of Latvia, but in vain. From July to October 1940 he was a political adviser in the reorganized Latvian Army, trying to protect officers from repression. After Latvia was incorporated into the USSR, he worked as an associate professor at Riga University. Arrested by the Germans in July 1941 but released thanks to the guarantees of some Latvian officers, he resumed his SDWPL activities. In 1943 Kalniņš co-founded and became deputy chairman of the Central Council of Latvia, aiming at independence from Germany and the USSR. He was arrested in July 1944 and sent to the Stuthoff concentration camp.

After his release from camp in 1945, Kalniņš went to Sweden, where he lectured and worked as a librarian at the Slavic Institute of the University of Stockholm in 1945–70. In 1956 he received a Ph.D. From 1960 to 1970 he also lectured at the Higher Military Academy. In 1945 he co-founded the Social Democratic Club of Latvians in Sweden, and later he became chairman of the SDWPL Foreign Committee. In 1947–86 he represented Latvia in the Union of East European Socialists in London; from 1961 to 1986 he was the union's president and representative in the Socialist International (SI). From 1983 he was the SI's honorary president. Kalniņš authored several works, including: *Sociāldemokrātijas militārpolitika* (The military policy of Social Democracy; 1928); *Der sowjetische Propagandastaat* (The Soviet propaganda state; 1950); *Latvijas Sociāldemokrātijas piecdesmit gadi* (Fifty years of Latvian Social Democracy; 1956); *Revolūcija vai evolūcija Padomju Savienībā* (Revolution or evolution in the Soviet Union; 1957); *Die Staatsgründung Lettlands* (The foundation of the Latvian state; 1971); *Sociāldemokrātu kustība Latvijā* (1972; *The Social Democratic Movement in Latvia*, 1977); and the memoirs *Vēl cīņa nav galā . . . 1899–1920* (The struggle is not yet over . . . 1899–1920; 1983). (EJ)

Sources: Edgars Andersons, *Latvijas Bruņotie spēki un to priekšvēsture* (Toronto, 1983); *Latviešu nacionālā pretestības kustība 1943–1945* (Upsala, 1994); Leonards Lapiņš, *Latvijas Universitātes Tautsaimniecības un tiesību zinātņu fakultātes Tiesību zinātņu nodaļas absolventu dzīves un darba gaitas (1919–1944)* (Riga, 1999); Aivars Stranga, *LSDSP un 1934. gada 15. maija valsts apvērsums: Demokrātijas likteņi Latvijā* (Riga, 1998); Ādolfs Šilde, *Latvijas vēsture 1914–1940: Valsts tapšana un suverēnā valsts* (Stockholm, 1976); Baiba Vītoliņa, "Dažas liecības par Bruno Kalniņa darbību 1940–1944. gadā," *Latvijas Vēsture: Jaunie un Jaunākie Laiki*, 2001, nos. 1–3; Andrejs Plakans, *Historical Dictionary of Latvia* (Lanham, Md., 1997).

KALNIŅŠ Pauls (3 March 1872, Vilces district, Courland–26 August 1945, Lustenau, Austria), Latvian Socialist politician. Born into a peasant family, Kalniņš completed a gymnasium in Libau (Liepāja) in 1892, and in 1898 he graduated from the Medical School of the university in Dorpat (Tartu). In 1897 he spent a few months in jail for taking part in a movement known as the "New Current." In 1898 he began working as a doctor in Tukums. In 1899 he was expelled from Courland for his political activities, and he went to work as a doctor in Žagare, Lithuania. In 1901 he returned to Latvia and began working in Mitau (Jelgava), where, along with his wife Klara, he organized and led a group of Latvian Social Democrats in Courland. In 1903, threatened with arrest, Kalniņš was forced to emigrate to Switzerland, where he worked as an assistant at a clinic in Zurich and was active among Latvian and Russian Socialists. From November 1905 to January 1906 he took part in the revolution in Latvia and organized Socialist activities in Libau. After the failure of the revolution Kalniņš emigrated again but returned to Latvia in December 1906. From 1907 to 1909 he was a member of the editorial staff of the newspaper *Cīņa*, an organ of the illegal Latvian Social Democratic Party (LSDP), and he also worked as a doctor in Riga. In 1914 he was mobilized into the Russian Army as a military doctor. After the February 1917 revolution, in August 1917 Kalniņš was elected as a deputy to the municipal Duma (legislative assembly) in Riga. In 1918 he again took up LSDP activities. On 17 November 1918 he was elected a member of the Latvian National Council. Between March and July 1919 he was a special envoy of Latvia to Germany. From 1920 to 1921 he was deputy mayor of Riga. In 1920 he was elected deputy to the Constitutional Assembly, in 1922 he became a member of the parliament (Saeima), and in 1925 he was elected its president. After a coup d'état staged by **Kārlis Ulmanis** in May 1934, Kalniņš was interned for a few months. After his release, he resumed his medical practice in Riga. He avoided deportation by the Soviets in 1940–41. In 1943 he was one of the founders of the Central Council of Latvia under the auspices of the Third Reich. At the end of the war Kalniņš managed to get to Austria via Germany. He died while waiting for permission to enter Switzerland. (EJ)

Sources: *Latvijas darbinieku galerija* (Riga, 1928); *Latvijas vadošie darbinieki* (Riga, 1935); Ēriks Jēkabsons, "Paulam Kalniņam," *Latvijas Ārsts*, 1997, no. 3; Andrejs Plakans, *Historical Dictionary of Latvia* (Lanham, Md., 1997).

KALVODA Jan (30 October 1953, Prague), Czech lawyer and politician. In 1978 Kalvoda graduated in law from Charles University in Prague. Then he began to practice law; in 1983–90 he practiced in Rokycany. In November 1989 he was a co-founder of the local Civic Forum (Občanské Fórum [OF]) organization. In February 1990,

as a result of the reconstruction of the parliament, Kalvoda became a member of the Czech National Council. In the first free parliamentary elections of June 1990 he won a seat on behalf of the OF, and in January 1991 he became deputy speaker of the Czech parliament. After the breakup of the OF in the spring of 1991, he joined the Civic Democratic Alliance (Občanská Demokratická Aliance [ODA]); in it he soon advanced, pushing its founders, from the circle of former dissidents, into the shadows. In March 1992 Kalvoda became the ODA chairman, and in June 1992 he was reelected to the Czech parliament, in which he sat until 1996. From July 1992 to July 1996 he was deputy prime minister of the Czech Republic and head of the office for legislation and public administration in the government of **Václav Klaus**. In Klaus's next cabinet, Kalvoda was deputy prime minister and minister of justice. In December 1996 he resigned from the government and in early 1997 from his party position, in connection with a groundless use of scholarly titles. In June 1997 he opened his own law office in Prague and retired from political life. In 1998 Kalvoda left the ODA. (PU)

Sources: *ČBS*; *Kdo byl kdo v našich dějinach ve 20. stoleti*, vol. 1 (Prague, 1998); Jan Rychlík, *Rozpad Československa: Česko-slovenské vztahy 1989–1992* (Bratislava, 2002); Eric Stein, *Czecho/Slovakia; Ethnic Conflict, Constitutional Fissure, Negotiated Breakup* (Ann Arbor, 1997)

KALYNETS Ihor (9 July 1939, Chodorów [Khodoriv], near Lwów [Lviv]), Ukrainian poet and dissident. Brought up in a pro-independence tradition, in 1961 Kalynets graduated in philology from the University of Lviv. In 1961–72 he worked in the Lviv archive. His first volume of poems, *Ekskursiya* (Excursion), was banned by Soviet censorship, and the second, *Vohon Kupala* (Kupala's fire; 1966), was the only one published officially in the USSR. Kalynets distributed his works through the uncensored press, so from 1965 he was under constant KGB surveillance. The ban of his next volume meant the permanent loss of publishing opportunities. Kalynets published the volume in Belgium, and the subsequent one—*Pidsumovuyuchi movchannia* (Summing up silence; 1971)—in Munich, Germany. His wife, also a poet, was arrested in January 1972 for her contacts with the Western media and with the human rights movement, and Kalynets was arrested in August 1972. Both were sentenced to six years of labor camp and three years of forced settlement. Kalynets served in the Kuchino camp near Perm. In the camp he went on a hunger strike to protest the ban on seeing his mother and his newly born daughter. His subsequent volumes—*Koronuvannia opudala* (Coronation of the scarecrow; 1972) and *Spohady pro svit* (Memoirs of the world; 1973)—were published in the West. In 1975 Kalynets became a member of the International PEN club, and in 1977 he received the Ivan Franko Award in Chicago. He spent the forced settlement years along with his family near Chyta in Siberia.

In 1981 Kalynets returned to Lviv, where he worked in the library of the Academy of Sciences of the Ukrainian SSR from 1983 to 1990. From 1987 he, along with his wife, was active in the renaissance of the social and cultural life in Lviv. He edited the periodical *Yevshan-Zilla* (1990–92), co-founded the Taras Shevchenko Society of Ukrainian Language, and organized actions to commemorate the victims of Stalinist terror. In 1990 he was elected deputy to the Lviv regional council. Poems that Kalynets had written before his arrest were collected in the volume *Probudzhena muza* (The awakened muse; 1991), and those created while he was in captivity, in *Nevolnycha muza* (The enslaved Muse; 1991). In 1997 Kalynets published a full collection of his poetry as *Slovo tryvayuche* (Lasting word). In 1991 Kalynets was given the Vasyl Stus Award and in 1992 the Taras Shevchenko State Award. All together he published seventeen volumes of poetry and a lyrical novel, *Molimos zoryam dalnym* (Let us pray to distant stars; 1994). His poetry was translated into many languages. (TS)

Sources: *Visnyk represiy v Ukrajini* (New York, 1980, 1982); Heorhiy Kasyanov, *Nezhodni: Ukraiinska intelihentsiya v rusi oporu 1960–80 rokiv* (Kiev, 1995); Anatoliy Rusnachenko, *Natsionalno-vyzvolnyi rukh v Ukraiini* (Kiev, 1998).

KAMIŃSKI Aleksander, pseudonyms "Dąbrowski," "Juliusz Górecki," and others (28 January 1903, Warsaw–15 March 1978, Warsaw), Polish scouting activist. In 1917–19 Kamiński organized Polish scouting in Uman, Russia. After returning to Poland in February 1921, he was an instructor of the Polish Scouting Association (Związek Harcerstwa Polskiego [ZHP]), and he directed schools for instructors in Nierodzim and Górki Wielkie. He was the founder of the Polish wolf cub movement for children aged 9–11 and the organizer of this movement on a national scale. In September 1939 Kamiński fought in the defense of Warsaw, and in October of that year he joined the Service for the Victory of Poland (Służba Zwycięstwu Polsce [SZP]), which was the central underground military organization. He subsequently became a member of the Union of Armed Struggle (Związek Walki Zbrojnej [ZWZ]) and in 1942, a member of the Home Army (Armia Krajowa). From November 1939 to October 1944 Kamiński edited *Biuletyn Informacyjny*, the most important underground military periodical, whose circulation reached 50,000. He was a member of the Polish Home Army Main Headquar-

ters Information and Propaganda Bureau, and in 1941–44, he was head of the Information and Propaganda Bureau of the Warsaw District of the Home Army. In October 1939 he joined the headquarters of the Szare Szeregi (Gray Ranks), an underground scouting organization. In 1941 he became a consultant to the Chief of the Scouts. In 1940 Kamiński began working with the Jewish resistance in the Warsaw Ghetto. After the Warsaw Ghetto Uprising (April–May 1943) he delivered false documents to fighters in the Jewish Defense Organization (Żydowska Organizacja Bojowa [ŻOB]) who survived the uprising.

In 1945–50 Kamiński worked in the Department of Social Pedagogy of Łódź University. In 1947 he earned a Ph.D. After he was expelled from Łódź University for political reasons in 1950, he did research on the history of the Saduvian tribe. In 1958 he resumed his work at Łódź University. In 1962 he earned his postdoctoral degree and became professor and head of the Department of Social Pedagogy. From 1946 to 1947 Kamiński was vice-president of the Polish Scouting Association, which was disbanded in 1949. After the revival of this organization, he served as its president from December 1956 to April 1958. Kamiński authored around six hundred articles and a dozen or so books, including *Antek Cwaniak* (1932); *Andrzej Małkowski* (1934); *Książka wodza zuchów* (The book of the Wolf Cub scout leader; 1935); and *Wielka gra* (The great game; 1942). His novels—*Kamienie na szaniec* (Stones for the rampart; 1943) and *Zośka i Parasol* (1957), which documented the military actions of the Gray Ranks—won him the greatest acclaim. Kamiński's most important research works are *Prehistoria polskich związków młodzieży* (Prehistory of Polish youth unions; 1959); *Polskie związki młodzieży 1804–1831* (Polish youth associations 1804–1831; 1963); *Polskie związki młodzieży 1831–1848* (Polish youth associations 1831–1848; 1968); *Jaćwierz* (Saduvians; 1963); and *Funkcje pedagogiki społecznej* (Tasks of social pedagogy; 1972). (TS)

Sources: *Nowa encyklopedia powszechna PWN*, vol. 3 (Warsaw, 1995); Kunert, vol. 2; Władysław Bartoszewski, "Z kart wojennej służby Aleksandra Kamińskiego," *Tygodnik Powszechny*, 1978, nos. 18–19; Andrzej Janowski, *Być dzielnym i umieć się różnić: Szkice o Aleksandrze Kamińskim* (Warsaw, 1992).

KANDYBA Ivan (7 June 1930, Stulno, near Włodawa), Ukrainian lawyer, dissident, and nationalist politician. Kandyba's family was resettled to the Ukrainian SSR on the basis of an agreement on a population exchange between Poland and the USSR in 1945. In 1953 he graduated in law from the University of Lviv, and then he worked as a notary, judge, and lawyer in Glinyany, near Lviv. In 1959–60, along with **Levko Lukyanenko**, he founded the illegal (Marxist) Ukrainian Workers' and Peasants' Union (Ukraiinska Robotnicho-Selanska Spilka), which aimed at the secession of the Ukraine from the USSR on the basis of a constitutional referendum and the right of self-determination of nations. Arrested along with seven other people in January 1961, Kandyba was sentenced to fifteen years of labor camp for "betraying the homeland." While serving in Mordovia and near Perm, owing to his protests about living conditions in the camp, he received an additional sentence of one year in 1962 and three years in 1967. In July 1969, along with Lukyanenko and **Mykhailo Horyn**, Kandyba passed a letter to the UN Committee of Human Rights concerning the genocide of political prisoners in the Soviet Union. Released in January 1976, he was not allowed to return to Lviv, so he settled in nearby Pustomyty, where he worked as an electrician and doorkeeper. In 1976 he co-founded the Ukrainian Helsinki Group (UHG); therefore he was under constant KGB surveillance. In 1978–80 he was refused permission several times to reunite with his family in the United States. He was arrested again in March 1981 as the last remaining UHG member in the Ukraine. In July 1981 Kandyba was sentenced to ten years of labor camp and five years of forced settlement. He served in the Kuchino camp, and in 1988 he was moved to Perm. Released in September 1988, in April 1990 he co-founded and became head of the organization State Independence for Ukraine, and he edited its organ, *Neskorena natsiya*. In November 1992 Kandyba became a member of the Organization of Ukrainian Nationalists (OUN) in exile, and then he legalized this organization in the Ukraine. In May 1993 he became deputy chairman, and in January 1996 chairman, of the OUN. His headquarters are in Lviv. (TS)

Sources: *Encyclopedia of Ukraine*, vol. 2 (Toronto, 1988); *Ukraiinska Helsinkska Hrupa 1978–1982: Dokumenty i materiyaly* (Toronto and Baltimore, 1983); Ludmila Aleksieyeva, *Istoriia ina-komysliia v SSSR* (Vilnius and Moscow, 1992); Heorhiy Kasyanov, *Nezhodni: Ukraiinska intelihentsiya v rusi oporu 1960–80 rokiv* (Kiev, 1995); Anatoliy Rusnachenko, *Natsionalno-vyzvolnyi rukh v Ukraiini* (Kiev, 1998).

KANDYBA Oleh, pseudonym "Olzhych" (8 July 1907, Zhytomyr–9 June 1944, Sachsenhausen), Ukrainian politician, archaeologist, and poet. In 1923 Kandyba went into exile in Prague, where in 1929 he completed archaeological studies at Charles University and then received a doctorate. He worked in the Czech National Museum, and in the 1930s he made several research journeys to Western Europe and the Balkans. He published extensively, including *Schipenitz: Kunst und Geräte neolitischen Dorfes* (Shipenyts: Art and tools of a Neolithic village; 1937). In 1938 he lectured at Harvard University and

helped organize the Ukrainian Scientific Institute in St. Paul, Minnesota. In 1929 Kandyba became aligned with the Organization of Ukrainian Nationalists (OUN) and headed its cultural and educational departments. After a split within the OUN in 1940, he supported **Andriy Melnyk**. On Melnyk's orders, in post-Munich Czechoslovakia Kandyba represented the OUN leadership to Subcarpathian Ruthenia, and from 1938 to 1939 he participated in the establishment of the Carpathian Sich, which was the embryo of the Ukrainian military force. Kandyba was a member of Melnyk's "derivative group," the members of which established the Ukrainian National Council in the summer of 1941, shortly after the German troops entered Kiev. Kandyba worked for the revival of social and cultural life in the capital and was particularly successful in activating the nationalists. He helped to edit the newspaper *Ukrains'ke Slovo* and the periodicals *Rozbudova natsii* and *Ukrains'kyi visnyk*. When the German authorities tightened their control, Kandyba went underground and led the conspiratorial activities of the Melnyk faction in Lwów (Lviv). Arrested in May 1944, Kandyba was later killed in a concentration camp. Ukrainian history and the Ukraine's right to independence was the main subject of Kandyba's poetry. He avoided lyricism, glorified action, and praised the sense of duty. Two volumes, *Rin'* (Gravel; 1935) and *Vezhi* (Towers; 1940), were published in his lifetime, while four other volumes were published posthumously: *Pidzamche* (Castle grounds; 1946); *Poezii* (Poems; 1956); *Velychnist'* (Majesty; 1969); and *Neznanemu boiakovi: Zapovidane zhivim* (To the unknown soldier: Handed down to the living; 1994). Under the pseudonym "K. Kostiantyn," Kandyba also wrote satirical poems. A complete edition of his works was published in 1991 in Prešov, Slovakia. In 1996, a documentary was filmed about him in the Ukraine. (TS)

Sources: *Encyclopedia of Ukraine*, vol. 3 (Toronto, 1993); Ryszard Torzecki, *Polacy i Ukraińcy: Sprawa ukraińska w czasie II wojny światowej na terenie II Rzeczypospolitej* (Warsaw, 1993).

KANIA Stanisław (8 March 1927, Wrocanka, near Jasło), Polish Communist activist. Born into a peasant family, in 1945 Kania joined the (Communist) Polish Workers' Party, and from December 1948 he was a member of the Polish United Workers' Party (Polska Zjednoczona Partia Robotnicza [PUWP]). He graduated from the Higher School of Social Sciences of the PUWP Central Committee (CC). From 1952 to 1956 he worked in the apparatus of the Polish Youth Union, and then he advanced in the PUWP apparatus. In 1958 he became head of the Department of Agriculture of the PUWP Warsaw Provincial Committee, and from 1962 to 1968 he was secretary of this committee. From June 1964 he was a deputy member, and from November 1968 a member, of the PUWP CC. In December 1968 Kania assumed the position of head of the PUWP CC Administration Department, gaining a wide range of powers and supervising the party's personnel policy, the army, and special services. He was also responsible for the party policy toward the Catholic Church. As head of the CC Administrative Department, Kania communicated directly with the administration of the CC of the Soviet party and the KGB in Moscow.

During the crisis of party leadership in December 1970, resulting from the Baltic Coast workers' riots, Kania supported the election of **Edward Gierek** to the position of first secretary, so at the Ninth CC Plenum in April 1971 he was promoted to CC secretary. In late May 1971, when **Mieczysław Moczar** tried to organize his followers in Olsztyn, Kania helped Gierek organize a counteraction and dismiss Moczar from the top party leadership at the Tenth CC Plenum in June 1971. In December 1971 Kania became a deputy member, and in December 1975 a member, of the Politburo, joining the inner circle of Communist power. From 1972 he was an MP. In June 1974 he helped Gierek dismiss another rival, **Franciszek Szlachcic**. In the 1970s Kania supervised the Ministry of Interior operations against the Catholic Church and the emerging democratic opposition. Among other things, he unsuccessfully tried to divide and rule the Episcopate of Poland by instigating a rivalry between Cardinal Karol Wojtyła (later Pope **John Paul II**) and Primate **Stefan Wyszyński**. In view of détente and Gierek's policy of seeking Western credits, political repression, for which Kania was responsible, was not so drastic as in earlier decades, but it was sometimes very painful.

When in July 1980 workers' strikes began to spread throughout Poland as a result of price increases, Kania, along with **General Wojciech Jaruzelski**, was responsible for the so-called repressive ministries. It is not clear why all through the summer of 1980 they failed to try to prevent the spread of strikes while Gierek was on holiday in Russia. In August 1980 Kania took the lead of the party crisis task force. The moment the Gdańsk strike turned into a general strike, directed by the Inter-Factory Strike Committee (Międzyzakładowy Komitet Strajkowy [MKS]) and led by **Lech Wałęsa**, Kania decided to support a political solution to the conflict and an agreement with the MKS. At the Sixth CC Plenum on the night of 5–6 September 1980, Kania became the new PUWP first secretary. After the formation of Solidarity, he initially represented a moderate line, going back and forth between the reformers ready to compromise with Solidarity and the hard-liners who favored confrontation, as well as between most of the Polish society, which supported Solidarity,

and the Kremlin, which constantly threatened military intervention. On 5 December 1980 in Moscow, Kania had to explain why "counterrevolution" was being tolerated in Poland, but the Kremlin leaders gave him more time to figure out how to cope with Solidarity.

Kania faced a similar crisis in March 1981, when during the Soyuz 81 Warsaw Pact maneuver three Solidarity activists were beaten by the militia in Bydgoszcz. The union threatened a general strike, and the maneuver could have changed into an intervention. At the last minute an agreement was reached with Solidarity. On 3 April 1981 Kania and General Jaruzelski, who in the meantime had become prime minister, met with Leonid Brezhnev and other top Kremlin leaders in Brest-Litovsk and probably agreed to introduce martial law in Poland. During the campaign before the Ninth PUWP Extraordinary Congress, Kania was strongly attacked by the hard-liners. The congress, which took place in July 1981, strengthened his position, but the worsening economic situation, the increasing social conflicts, and the impossibility of reaching an agreement with Solidarity and the Kremlin at the same time led Kania's dilatory tactics into a dead end. In mid-August 1981 Kania and Jaruzelski spoke with Brezhnev again. The latter probably came to the conclusion that only Jaruzelski had guaranteed the suppression of Solidarity by using the Polish forces. At the Fourth CC Plenum on 16–18 October 1981 Kania resigned as leader of the PUWP. Jaruzelski became the new first secretary, and on 13 December 1981 he introduced martial law.

Kania found himself in the shadows. From May 1982 to November 1985 he was a member of the Council of State; from January 1981 to July 1983 he belonged to the Presidium of the All-Polish Committee of the National Unity Front; and from November 1985 to June 1989 he presided over the parliamentary commission of self-government. After 1989 he retired from politics. Kania authored the memoirs *Zatrzymać konfrontację* (Stop the confrontation; 1991), in which he presented the events of 1980–81 in a different way than General Jaruzelski. (WR)

Sources: Mołdawa; Andrzej Micewski, *Współrządzić czy nie kłamać* (Paris, 1978); Timothy Garton Ash, *The Polish Revolution: "Solidarity"* (New York, 1983); Zbigniew Błażyński, *Towarzysze zeznają: Dekada Gierka 1970–1980 w tzw. Komisji Grabskiego* (London, 1987); Andrzej Albert [Wojciech Roszkowski], *Najnowsza historia Polski 1914–1993*, vols. 1–2 (Warsaw, 1993); Jacek Wegner, *Sternicy: Od Nowotki do Rakowskiego* (Kraków, 1997); Włodzimierz Janowski and Aleksander Kochański, *Informator o strukturze i obsadzie personalnej centralnego aparatu PZPR 1948–1990* (Warsaw, 2000); Jerzy Eisler, *Grudzień 1970* (Warsaw, 2000).

KANTOR Tadeusz (6 April 1915, Wielopole, near Kraków–8 December 1990, Kraków), Polish artist of Jewish origin. In 1939 Kantor graduated from the Academy of Fine Arts in Kraków. During the German occupation he organized underground exhibitions and an underground Independent Theater. After the war, he founded the Group of Young Artists (1945). Kantor's work was influenced by surrealism, constructivism, expressionism, and futurism. In 1947 he was in Paris. After returning to Poland in 1948, he initiated an exhibition of Polish modern art. In 1956 along with Maria Jarema, he founded the avantgarde theater, known as the Cricot 2 Theater. In all genres of art, Kantor strove to express reality by reducing it to simple things. In Poland his work was a precursor of the Informel Theater, the assemblage, the happening (*Cricotage*, 1965; *Panoramic Sea Happening*, 1967). Kantor gained international recognition at the Cricot 2 Theater as the creator of performances based not only on the works of **Witkacy (Stanisław Ignacy Witkiewicz)**—*W małym dworku* (Country house; 1961), *Wariat i zakonnica* (The madman and the Nun; 1963)—but also on his own scripts: *Umarła klasa* (The dead class; 1975); *Wielopole, Wielopole* (1980); *Niech szczezną artyści* (Let the artists perish; 1985); and *Nigdy tu już nie powrócę* (I shall never come back here; 1988). In these plays, in an original and impressive way, Kantor expressed his anxiety about the modern degradation of human life. His publications include a manifesto, *Teatr Śmierci* (The theater of death; 1975); *Metamorphosis* (1982); and the collection *Wielopole, Wielopole* (1984). (WR)

Sources: *Nowa encyklopedia powszechna PWN*, vol. 3 (Warsaw, 1995); *The Dictionary of Art*, vol. 17 (London, 1996); Wiesław Borowski, *Tadeusz Kantor* (Warsaw, 1982); Klaus Dermutz, *Totes Leben: Zur Anthropologie und Theologie von Tadeusz Kantors Teater des Todes und der Liebe* (Graz, 1994); Krzysztof Miklaszewski, *Encounters with Tadeusz Kantor* (London, 2002).

KAPETANOVIĆ Izudin (1 September 1953, Tuzla), Bosnian politician and engineer. Kapetanović graduated from the Department of Electrical Technology of the University of Sarajevo in 1976 and received a second degree in power-plant engineering there in 1985. He also completed doctoral studies in numerical calculus in the electromagnetic field at the Technische Hochschule Ilmenau in Germany (1985–86), and he specialized in this field. Kapetanović received a Ph.D. in electrical engineering at the University of Tuzla (1988), where he worked, advancing from assistant professor to full professor. There he was deputy dean (1986–88) and dean (1988–98) of the Department of Electrical and Machine Technology and then rector from November 2000. From 1997 he also lectured in the Department of Traffic and Communications at the University of Sarajevo. Kapetanović authored about eighty scholarly works, including three books. In 1996–99 he was director of the Elektrodistribucija Power Plant in Tuzla. From 31 January to 18 December 1996 he was prime minister of Bosnia-Herzegovina. During his term, normal living conditions were restored in a country ravaged by war—among them, water, electricity, and heating supplies. Kapetanović was minister of power engineering, mining, and industry from December 1996 to March 1998; one of the leaders of the Party of Democratic Action (Strana Demokratske Akcije) of **Alija Izetbegović**; a member of the leadership of the Association of Bosnian Intellectuals; and founder and director of the Institute of Electrical Current–Energoinvenst in Sarajevo (1998–2000). (JD)

Sources: *Ko je ko u Bosnjaka: Vijeće Kongresa Bosnjackih Intelektualaca* (Sarajevo, 2000).

KAPLIŃSKI Jaan (22 January 1941, Tartu), Estonian poet. Kapliński's father, Jerzy Kapliński, was a lecturer of Polish at the University of Tartu who stimulated Estonian-Polish cultural links, and his mother, Nora Raudsepp-Kapliński, was a ballet dancer. His father was arrested by the NKVD in 1941, and he perished in the Gulag. Kapliński studied Romance languages and mathematical linguistics at the University of Tartu, as well as sociology and ecology. From 1968 he belonged to the Union of Estonian Writers. In 1965–72 he worked at Tartu University, and in 1974–80, in the Tallinn Botanical Garden. At the turn of the 1970s, in connection with the intensified Russification policies of the Communist authorities, Kapliński became a leader of the intellectual opposition. On his initiative, in October 1980 a group of forty intellectuals sent an open letter to the party authorities of the Soviet Union and the Estonian SSR demanding the discontinuation of the Russification policies. The authorities answered with repression. In the late 1980s Kapliński worked as a journalist; taking advantage of perestroika, he traveled to the West, promoting the restitution of Estonian statehood. After Estonia regained independence in 1991, Kaplinski was elected to the parliament (Riigikogu) and was a deputy on behalf of the Estonian Center Party (1992–95). He was connected with the leftist faction of the party, led by **Edgar Savisaar**. Before the end of his term he gave up his mandate and returned to literary work.

Kapliński authored several volumes of poems, mostly in Estonian, such as *Tolmust ja värvidest* (Dust and colors; 1967) and *Valge joon Võrumaa kohale* (White line over Voru; 1972), but also in English: *The Same Sea in Us All* (1985), *Wandering Border* (1987), *I Am the Spring in Tartu and Other Poems Written in English* (1991), and *Through the Forest* (1996). He also wrote in Swedish and Finnish. The trauma of World War II and his problems with self-identity—Kapliński said if it were not for his father's arrest, he could have returned to Poland—as well as existential problems with the Soviet reality, led Kapliński to Buddhism. He experimented in his writing, adapting typically East Asian forms of literature to the Estonian language. His radical message, including Taoist motifs and an ecological sensitivity—combined, for instance, in the volume *See ja teine* (This and the other; 1996)—brought him renown in the West, while Western consumerism became a frequent topic of his poems and essays. (AG)

Sources: *Eesti Entsuklopeedia*, vol. 14 (Tallinn, 2000); Piotr Łossowski, *Stosunki polsko-estońskie 1918–1939* (Gdańsk, 1992); Tõnu Tannberg, Matti Laur, Tõnis Lukas, Ain Mäesalu, and Ago Pajur, *History of Estonia* (Tallinn, 2000); www.mv.helsinki.fi/helsinkiforum/english/people/kaplinski.html; jaan.kaplinski.com/life/memories.html; www.einst.ee/literary/spring98/06transc.htm.

KAPO Hysni (4 March 1915, Terbaç, near Vlorë–23 September 1979, Paris), Albanian Communist activist. Kapo came from a Muslim family. After completing a school of commerce in Vlorë, he worked as a bookseller and a male nurse at a hospital in Vlorë between 1936 and 1940. In the Communist movement, he became aligned with a splinter group of the "young" that broke away from a group from Korçë. A member of the Communist Party of Albania (CPA) from the party's foundation in 1941, Kapo was the leader of a party organization in Vlorë. He is credited with having founded, in 1941, one of the first partisan units linked with the Communists. He was a staff member of the National Liberation Army (NLA) and a member of the General Council of the National Liberation Front. In 1943 he became a political commissar in the Fifth Brigade of the NLA. Official historiography credits him with having played an important role in the battle of Drashovicë against the Germans (15 September 1943). In practice, Kapo distinguished himself in combating the units of non-Communist resistance, particularly the units of the National Front (Balli Kombëtar). Along with Shefqet Peçi, he commanded a unit that was responsible for bloody pacification campaigns carried out as a part of "purge actions" in the northern part of the country.

In 1944 Kapo became the NLA inspector general, with the rank of colonel. As a member of a special Communist court that punished "war criminals and enemies of the people" after the war, he was responsible for many judicial crimes. From July 1945 to February 1947 he served as ambassador to Belgrade. In 1945 he became a deputy to the parliament. From 1945 to 1947 he served as minister of foreign affairs and was a member of the Albanian delegation to the Paris Peace Conference in 1946. In 1946 he became a member of the Politburo of the CPA CC, and in 1948, a member of the Albanian Labor Party (ALP). Until the time

Albania broke off relations with the USSR, Kapo served as president of the Albanian-Soviet Friendship Society. In 1949 he was promoted to general. From July 1950 to June 1958 he was deputy prime minister, and from September 1951 to July 1954, minister of agriculture. A close associate of **Enver Hoxha**, Kapo showed the greatest skill in adjusting to changes in Hoxha's policy. Hoxha, referring to the pseudonym that Kapo used during the occupation, called him "Besniku i Partisë" (Faithful to the Party). In 1948 Kapo was in favor of breaking off relations with Yugoslavia, and in June 1960 he was an ALP delegate to a congress of the Romanian party in Bucharest, where it came to an open conflict with the Soviet leadership. Kapo was also sent to Moscow in November of that year for negotiations with **Nikita Khrushchev**, as a result of which the ALP broke off relations with the Kremlin. In 1980 Kapo's house in Terbaç was turned into a museum. A monument to Kapo was built in Vlorë. In 1991 this monument was destroyed. Kapo received many honors, including the Order of Hero of Socialist Work (1965). Between 1980 and 1983 his *Vepra të zgjehura* (Selected works, 5 vols.) were published. Kapo's wife, Vito Kondi, was a deputy member (1952–61) and a member (1962–91) of the ALP CC. (TC)

Sources: *Bashkimi*, 22 November 1945; *Fjalor Enciklopedik Shqiptar* (Tirana, 1985); Raymond Hutchings, *Historical Dictionary of Albania* (Lanham, Md., 1996); William E. Griffith, *Albania and the Sino-Soviet Rift* (Cambridge, 1963); Arshi Pipa, *Albanian Stalinism* (Boulder, Colo., 1990); Klaus-Detlev Grothusen, ed., *Albanien* (Göttingen, 1993).

KAPSUKAS-MICKEVIČIUS Vincas [originally Mickevičius] (7 April 1880, Būdviečiai, near Vilkaviškis–17 February 1935, Moscow), Lithuanian Communist activist. Born into a family of rich peasants, Kapsukas-Mickevičius completed high school in Marijampolė in 1897, and then his parents enrolled him in a theological seminary in Sejny. Expelled in 1898 for protesting against the tsarist government in Lithuania, from 1902 to 1904 he studied sociology and economics in Bern, Switzerland, where he wrote under the pseudonym "Kapsukas" for underground Lithuanian periodicals published in East Prussia. He initially favored the liberal-democratic line of the periodicals *Ūkininkas* and *Varpas*. For some time, he worked on the editorial staff of the latter periodical in Tilsit (Sovetsk). Under the influence of Russian Marxists, he lost interest in the cause of Lithuanian independence and gave priority to world revolution. In 1904 he founded a Socialist youth organization, Dragas (Comrade), which merged with the Lithuanian Social Democratic Party the following year. He became a member of its Central Committee (CC). He failed to persuade Social Democratic leaders to cooperate with the Bolsheviks. In 1907–13 he served a prison sentence, and subsequently he was exiled to Siberia. At the end of 1913 he escaped, and after long travel he reached the United States in 1916. There he published Socialist newspapers in Philadelphia, and he even gained the support of the Lithuanian Socialists in the United States for the Bolshevik cause.

After the February 1917 revolution, Kapsukas-Mickevičius returned to Russia, where he co-established the Central Office of the Lithuanian Section in the Bolshevik party. After the October Revolution, he became commissar for the treasury, and on 8 December 1917 he was appointed commissar for Lithuanian affairs in Stalin's Commissariat of Nationalities. He disbanded Lithuanian mutual aid committees because they favored the cause of Lithuanian independence. After Bolshevik troops captured Dvinsk (Daugavpils), on 8 December 1918 Kapsukas-Mickevičius announced the establishment of the Provisional Government of Workers and Peasants, and he became its head. A few days later he proclaimed the foundation of the Lithuanian Soviet Republic. On 5 January 1919 the government moved to Vilnius (Wilno), which was occupied by the Red Army. When on 16 January a decision was made to establish the Lithuanian-Belorussian SSR, Kapsukas-Mickevičius became head of its Council of People's Commissars. He was in charge of establishing the Bolshevik administration, and he led the revolutionary terror. When the Polish troops marched into Vilnius in April 1919, he withdrew to Smolensk, where he published the Bolshevik newspaper Zvezda. In July 1920 he returned to Vilnius with the new offensive of the Red Army. He remained in Vilnius after the Red Army withdrew, and he edited Pochodnia, a legal trade union newspaper. In the summer of 1921 he left for Moscow, where he joined the CC of the Communist Party of Lithuania (CPL). He wrote numerous articles and brochures that promoted communism, but the CPL managed to attract only around one thousand members, and the majority of them were non-Lithuanians. In 1926 he joined the Executive Committee of the Communist International. Kapsukas-Mickevičius died of natural causes. In 1955 the Communist authorities renamed the city of Marijampolė and Vilnius University after him. The former names were restored when Lithuania regained independence in 1991. Between 1960 and 1966 eight volumes of his propaganda writings were published. (WR)

Sources: EL, vol. 3; MERSH, vol. 15; Saulius Sužiedelis, Historical Dictionary of Lithuania (Lanham, Md., 1997); Mykolas Biržiška, Lietuvių tautos keliu, vols. 1–2 (Los Angeles, 1952–53); Alfred E. Senn, The Emergence of Modern Lithuania (New York, 1959); Jerzy Ochmański, Historia Litwy (Wrocław, 1967); Henryk Wisner, Litwa dzieje państwa i narodu (Warsaw, 1999).

KAPUŚCIŃSKI Ryszard (4 March 1932, Pińsk), Polish journalist and writer. In 1955 Kapuściński graduated in history from Warsaw University. He worked for the daily Sztandar Młodych (1950–56), the weeklies Polityka (1957–61) and Kultura (1974–81), and the monthly Kontynenty (1973), publishing correspondence from various countries affected by military conflicts and undergoing political change. He published Chrystus z karabinem na ramieniu (Christ with a carbine on his shoulders; 1975); Jeszcze jeden dzień życia (1976; Another Day of Life, 1986); Cesarz (1978; Emperor, 1984), in which he presented the ambience and lifestyle of the Ethiopian court (allusions to the Communist reality were traced in this book); and Wojna futbolowa (1978; Soccer War, 1990), on the war between Honduras and El Salvador. Apart from serving as Polish Press Agency correspondent (1962–72), Kapuściński lectured in many countries—for instance, as visiting professor in universities in Bangalore (India), Caracas (Venezuela), and Philadelphia (United States), as well as a Fellow at St. Anthony's College in Oxford (1986). In 1981–85 he was deputy chairman of Poland 2000, a forecasting committee of the Polish Academy of Sciences. He was also a member of many Polish and international organizations, such as the Polish Sociological Society, the European Academy of Science and Arts, the International Parliament of Writers, and the International PEN Club. He received many Polish, German, Italian, and American awards. His books—such as Szachinszach (1982; Shah of Shahs, 1985); Lapidarium (1990); Imperium (1993; English translation, 1994), on the collapse of the Soviet Union; and Heban (Ebony; 1998), on the disaster of civilization in Africa—were translated into more than a dozen languages, making him one of the most popular Polish writers. (WR)

Sources: Nowa encyklopedia powszechna PWN, vol. 3 (Warsaw, 1995); Kto jest kim w Polsce (Warsaw, 2001); Kazimierz Wolny, O twórczości Ryszarda Kapuścińskiego (Rzeszów, 1998); Zbigniew Bauer, Antymedialny reportaż Ryszarda Kapuścińskiego (Warsaw, 2001).

KARADŽIĆ Radovan (19 June 1945, Petnjica), Serb nationalist politician, war criminal. Born in a Montenegrin village, in 1960 Karadžić moved to Sarajevo, where he graduated from a medical high school and the Medical Academy. He specialized in psychiatry. His hobby was poetry, and he published several volumes. In 1967 he met **Dobrica Ćosić**, a nationalist writer who encouraged him to become active in politics. In 1968 Karadžić made a passionate speech to students from the roof of a university building in Sarajevo. For many years he worked in psychiatric wards and hospitals, developing his skills, and he also worked in the United States. He worked for a soccer club in Sarajevo, and in 1983–84, for the Belgrade soccer team Crvena Zvezda. In 1985 Karadžić spent eleven months in prison, accused of fraud. In 1990 he co-founded the Serbian Democratic Party in Bosnia-Herzegovina (SDP BH), and he became its leader. When in 1992 the Bosnian Serbs proclaimed the independence of the Bosnian Serb Republic, Karadžić became its first president. In cooperation with **Slobodan Milošević** and **Ratko Mladić**, he started the construction of an "ethnically clean" Serbian state in Bosnia that could be united with Serbia and other former Yugoslav territories inhabited by Serbs. Milošević supported Karadžić all the way until under Western pressure, he closed the border between Serbia and Bosnia-Herzegovina.

In 1995 Karadžić was twice accused of genocide and crimes against humanity by the International Criminal Tribunal for Former Yugoslavia (ICTY) in The Hague. Along with General Mladić, he was blamed for the siege of Sarajevo (April 1992–May 1995); the murder of about six thousand Muslims from Srebrenica (July 1995); rapes; the detention of thousands of Bosnian Muslims and Croats in concentration camps; and the use of UN peace-keeping forces as human shields against NATO air raids (May–June 1995). Initially Karadžić took part in peace talks, but after he was accused of war crimes, it was Milošević and not Karadžić who represented Bosnian Serbs during the talks in Dayton, Ohio. One of the stipulations of the Dayton agreement was that Karadžić had to retire from politics. Under pressure from Milošević and Bosnian Serb leaders, on 16 June 1996 it was announced that Karadžić would no longer hold the offices of president of the Bosnian Serb Republic and leader of the SDP BH and that he would withdraw from politics. This decision was a prerequisite for the international community to supervise elections in Bosnia-Herzegovina in September 1996. Despite his resignation, Karadžić maintained authority and influence among Bosnian Serbs. From time to time he went into hiding, and despite the ICTY indictment, he has not been arrested. In 2001 his popular autobiography was published under the title *Radovan i Serbia* (Radovan and Serbia). (AO)

Sources: Lenard J. Cohen, *The Disintegration of Yugoslavia* (Boulder, Colo., 1993); Edgar O'Ballance, *Civil War in Bosnia, 1992–94* (New York, 1995); David Owen, *Balkan Odyssey* (New York, 1995); Laura Silber and Allan Little, *The Death of Yugoslavia* (London, 1995); Warren Zimmermann, *Origins of a Catastrophe* (New York and Toronto, 1996); Richard Holbrooke, *To End a War* (New York, 1998); International Criminal Tribunal for the Former Yugoslavia, www.un.org/icty/indictment.

KARASZEWICZ-TOKARZEWSKI Michał, pseudonyms "Stolarski," "Torwid," "Stawski," and "Doktor" (5 January 1893, Lemberg [Lwów, Lviv]–22 May 1964, Casablanca), Polish general. After graduating from a high school in Drohobych, Karaszewicz-Tokarzewski studied law and medicine at the Jagiellonian University in Kraków. He was a member of the Polish Socialist Party (Polska Partia Socjalistyczna [PPS]). Inducted into the Austrian Army, he graduated from a reserve officers' school in Vienna. In 1912 he joined the Rifle Association, under whose auspices he completed a secondary and an academic officers' school. He was also a member of the Union of Active Struggle (Związek Walki Czynnej [ZWC]). In August 1914 he joined the Polish Legions, where he rose to the rank of commander of an infantry regiment. He fought in many battles, including those of Anielino and Laski. After the oath crisis, Karaszewicz-Tokarzewski served in the Austrian Army from December 1917 to May 1918 and subsequently in the Polish Military Organization (Polska Organizacja Wojskowa [POW]), where he held various posts, such as POW commandant in Lublin. Until October 1918 he was a POW representative to European Russia, the Ukraine, the French Military Mission in Moscow, and the Polish Military Committee in Moscow.

From November 1918 Karaszewicz-Tokarzewski served in the Polish Army. He founded the Fifth Infantry Regiment in Kraków and was its commander in the battle of Lwów and other battles. In March 1919 he became commander of the First Infantry Brigade. Later, he held various positions, including deputy general inspector of the infantry and deputy head of the Infantry Department of the Ministry of Military Affairs. In May 1921 Karaszewicz-Tokarzewski took command of the First Lithuanian-Belorussian Division (the future Nineteenth Infantry Division in Vilnius). In August 1924 he was promoted to brigadier general. In March 1927 he became head of the Personnel Office of the Ministry of Military Affairs, and in March 1929, commander of the Twenty-Fifth Infantry Division in Kalisz. Between 1932 and 1936 he was commander of Corps Area Three in Grodno, then commander of Corps Area Six in Lwów, and in 1938 he became commander of Corps Area Eight in Toruń. In 1924 he joined the Polish Theosophical Society and the National Grand Lodge–Tomasz Zan; in 1925 he joined the Liberal Catholic Church.

During the September campaign of 1939, Karaszewicz-Tokarzewski commanded the Operation Group of the Pomorze Army in the battle of the Bzura River. Until 19 September, as deputy commander of the Warszawa (Warsaw Army), he fought in the defense of Warsaw. He initiated the establishment of an underground resistance command center authorized by Marshal **Edward Rydz-Śmigły**. From 27 September to 13 November 1939

Karaszewicz-Tokarzewski served as commander of the Service for the Victory of Poland (Służba Zwycięstwu Polsce [SZP]). He co-founded the Chief Council, which was to take political command of the SZP, but because he was too closely linked with the *sanacja* circles, Prime Minister **Władysław Sikorski** dismissed him as the SZP commander. In November 1939 Karaszewicz-Tokarzewski became commander of the Lwów area of the Union of Armed Struggle (Związek Walki Zbrojnej [ZWZ]). Arrested by the NKVD on 6–7 March 1940 while crossing the Soviet-German border, he was held in a Soviet prison until August 1941, and then he was released under the Sikorski-Mayski Agreement. In August 1941 he became commander of the Sixth Infantry Division of the Polish Army in the USSR, and in January 1943 he was appointed major general. In March 1943 he became deputy commander of the Polish Army in the East, led by General **Władysław Anders**, and in December 1944, commander of the Third Corps in the Middle East. From August 1946 to December 1946 he served as commander of the Second Corps, and later he was in the Polish Resettlement Corps (Polski Korpus Przysposobienia i Rozmieszczenia). After the war, Karaszewicz-Tokarzewski settled in London, where he worked in a factory. In August 1954 he became general inspector of the armed forces in exile. In March 1964, shortly before his death, he was promoted to lieutenant general. He was active in the leadership of several Masonic lodges in London, including Le Droit Humain, the International Concord Lodge, and the Egyptian Rite of Ancient Mysteries. In September 1992 the urn with Karaszewicz-Tokarzewski's ashes was brought to the Powązki Cemetery in Warsaw. (JS)

Sources: *Kto był kim w Drugiej Rzeczypospolitej* (Warsaw, 1994); *Encyklopedia Historii Polski: Dzieje polityczne*, vol. 2 (Warsaw, 1995); Zbigniew Mierzwiński, *Generałowie II Rzeczypospolitej*, vol. 1 (Warsaw, 1990); Stefan Korboński, *Polskie Państwo Podziemne* (Paris, 1975); T. Kryska-Karski and S. Żurakowski, *Generałowie Polski Niepodległej.* (London, 1976); Władysław Pobóg-Malinowski, *Najnowsza historia polityczna Polski 1864–1945*, vol. 3 (London, 1986); Ludwik Hass, *Masoneria polska XX wieku* (Warsaw, 1996).

KARATKEVICH Uladzimir (26 November 1930, Orsha–25 July 1984, Minsk), Belorussian writer and poet. From 1951 to 1954 Karatkevich studied in the Philological Department of Kiev University, and in 1954–58 he worked as a teacher in the Ukraine and Belorussia. He made his literary debut in 1955. His collections of poetry are *Matchina dusha* (Mother's soul; 1958); *Vyacherniia vetrazi* (Evening sails; 1960); *Maia Iliada* (My Iliad; 1969) and *Byu. Ios'ts.' Budu* (I am. I was. I shall be; 1986), a work published after his death. As a prose writer, Karatkevich

was inspired mainly by historical motifs. He placed the characters of his novels in the midst of major historical events, binding their fate with that of Belorussia. He created a Belorussian historical mythology modeled on that of **Henryk Sienkiewicz**, whose historical mythology pervaded the historical consciousness of the Poles. Karatkevich planned to write a trilogy about the January 1863 *Insurrection* but completed only the first part, *Kalasy pad serpom tvaim* (Grain under your sickle; 1962). His novel *Zbroya* (Armor), written in 1964 and published in 1981, was also devoted to the January insurrection. *Kastus Kalinouski*, a novel written in 1963, was not published until 1978. The novel *Khrystos pryzamliusia u Harodni* (Christ stopped in Grodno; 1972) was devoted to the epoch of King Sigismund I Jagiellon. The novel *Dzikaie palavanie karala Stakha* (King Stakh's wild hunt), which was reissued many times, was devoted to the clash of cultures and ethical systems in Belorussia at the turn of the nineteenth century. Karatkevich's publications also include the novel *Chorny zamak Alshanski* (Black Olszany Castle; 1979) and a drama about Josaphat Kuncewicz, *Zvany Vitsiebska* (The bells of Vitebsk; 1974). (EM)

Sources: V. Tichina, *Mahchymastsi realizmu* (Minsk, 1982); Adam Maldzis, *Zhytstsio i uzniasiennie Uladzimira Karatkievicha* (Minsk, 1990); A. Rusetski, *Uladzimir Karatkievich: praz historyiu u suchasnasts* (Minsk, 1991); Jan Zaprudnik, *Historical Dictionary of Belarus* (Lanham, Md., 1998).

KARAVANSKYI Svyatoslav (24 December 1920, Odessa), Ukrainian poet and dissident. At the end of World War II, in 1945 Karavanskyi was sentenced to twenty-five years in a forced labor camp for taking part in the struggle for Ukrainian independence. After seventeen years in the camps of Kolyma, Magadan, and Mordovia, he was amnestied in 1962 and returned to Odessa, where he reunited with his wife, **Nina Strokatą-Karavanska**. He published poems and articles, referring to the Stalinist repression. In 1965 Karavanskyi was arrested again and sentenced to five years in prison. He served in Volodymir Prison and other places. Still in prison, he joined the Ukrainian Helsinki Group; in November 1979 he was released on condition that he emigrate. Along with his wife, he settled in the United States, where he published a number of volumes of poetry and translations, including *Sutychka z tayfunom* (Encounter with a typhoon; 1980); *Moje remeslo* (My handicraft; 1981); *Yaryna z horodu Khomy Chereshni* (Vegetables from the Khoma Chereshna Garden; 1981); and *Humorystychnyi samvydav* (A satirical uncensored publication; 1982). (WR)

Sources: *Encyclopedia of Ukraine*, vol. 2 (Toronto, 1988); S. P. de Boer, E. J. Driessen, and H. L. Verhaar, eds., *Biographical Dictionary of Dissidents in the Soviet Union* (The Hague, 1982).

KARAVELOV Petko (24 March 1843, Koprivshtitsa–24 January 1903, Sofia), Bulgarian politician. Karavelov was the brother of the writer Luben Karavelov. From 1860 he lived in Moscow, where he graduated from high school and where he studied at the Historical-Philological and Law Departments of the Moscow State University. After returning home in 1878, he entered the public scene, and for twenty-five years he was active in Bulgarian political life. In 1879 he became an MP on behalf of the Liberal Party, which he chaired from 1879 to 1883. Later he was the leader of the faction of extreme liberals. In 1894 he founded the Democratic Party and was its leader. From December 1880 to May 1881 and from July 1884 to August 1886 he was prime minister, and in the first government he was also minister of finance. During Karavelov's second term as head of government, in 1885 the Bulgarian Principality merged with East Rumelia and won the war against Serbia. Karavelov opposed the deposition of Prince Battenberg, and in August 1886 he assumed the duties of the regent for a few days. After Prince **Ferdinand** ascended the throne and after Stefan Stambolov introduced his dictatorship (1887–94), Karavelov found himself in opposition to the new regime. Arrested and sentenced to long-term imprisonment, he was released after the fall of Stambolov. After the failure of the government of General Racho Petrov, which bloodily suppressed a peasant rebellion, from 5 March 1901 to 4 January 1902 Karavelov he was prime minister again, but internal friction in the ruling elite caused him to resign. One of his daughters, Lora, married the poet **Peyo Yavorov**. (JW)

Sources: *Entsiklopediya Bulgariya*, vol. 3 (Sofia, 1982); Angel Tsurakov, *Pravitelstvata na Bulgariya, chast II, 1879–1913* (Sofia, 1996); Milen Kumanov and Tanya Nikolova, *Politicheski partii, organizatsii i dvizheniya v Bulgariya i tekhnite lideri* (Sofia, 1999).

KARDELJ Edvard (27 January 1910, Ljubljana–10 February 1979, Ljubljana), Communist activist of Slovene nationality. Born into a working-class family, Kardelj graduated from a teachers' college in Ljubljana. In 1926 he joined the outlawed League of Communist Youth, and in 1929, the Communist Party of Yugoslavia (CPY). Arrested in 1930, he spent two years in prison. From 1932 to 1934 he organized a CPY section in Slovenia. He published a great deal in the spirit of orthodox Stalinist communism. For example, in 1934, under the pseudonym "Tone Brodar," he published *Fašizem* (Fascism). In 1934 Kardelj traveled via Czechoslovakia to the Soviet Union, where, under the pseudonym "Birk," he received intelligence training at the Leninist School of the Comintern. In January 1937 he returned to Yugoslavia, and in April of that year he attended the founding congress of the Communist Party of Slovenia

in Čebinje. In 1939, under the pseudonym "Sperans," he published *Razvoj slovenskego narodnego vprašanja* (The development of the Slovene national question), in which he emphasized the separate national identity of the Slovenes. He also published under the pseudonym "Jože Beve," and he was arrested several times. He rose through the party ranks, becoming a member of the CPY Central Committee (CC) and Politburo in 1940.

After the fall and partition of Yugoslavia in April 1941, Kardelj, along with other Communists, adopted a wait-and-see attitude. When the Nazis invaded the USSR in June of that year, he helped to organize Communist underground activities in Slovenia and Croatia, and he joined the Partisans led by **Josip Broz Tito**. At that time Kardelj was leader of the Slovene party, and he participated in the work of Tito's staff. On 29 November 1943 Kardelj became deputy prime minister in Tito's provisional government and retained this post after March 1945, when he also became the minister responsible for drafting a new constitution. Kardelj was also head of the Party Central Control Commission. Like Tito, Kardelj for a while favored a Balkan federation based on Yugoslav-Bulgarian integration. In 1946 he became head of the Yugoslav delegation to the Paris Peace Conference. Along with **Milovan Djilas**, he represented the CPY at the founding congress of the Information Bureau of the Communist and Workers' Parties (Cominform) at Szklarska Poręba in September 1947. He was also a Yugoslav delegate at the sessions of the UN General Assembly in 1945 and 1948–51. After the Cominform denounced Tito at the Fifth Congress of the CPY in July 1948, Kardelj firmly supported the party leader and his political line, and he also joined the Politburo and Secretariat of the CPY CC. From 1948 to 1953 Kardelj served as minister of foreign affairs. From 1963 to 1967 he was president of the federal National Assembly. He supported not only Tito's political line, but also such systemic changes as the decollectivization of agriculture and the economic system of workers' self-management. One of the major theoreticians of Socialist self-management, Kardelj was a co-author of the constitutions of 1953, 1963, and 1974. He published many works in this field. He was also the author of *The Communist Party of Yugoslavia in the Struggle for the New Yugoslavia's People's Authority and for Socialism* (1948), *The Way of New Yugoslavia* (1949), *Socialism and War* (1960), and other works. In 1979 his *Izbor iz dela* (Selected works, 7 vols.) was published. (WR)

Sources: *Enciklopedija Slovenije*, vol. 5 (Ljubljana, 1991); Lazitch; Leopoldina Plut-Progelj and Carole Rogel, *Historical Dictionary of Slovenia* (Lanham, Md., 1996); Adam Ulam, *Titoism and the Cominform* (Westport, Conn., 1952); Milovan Džilas, *Memoirs of a*

Revolutionary (New York, 1973); Dennison Rusinow, *The Yugoslav Experiment, 1948–1974* (Berkeley, 1977); Duncan Wilson, *Tito's Yugoslavia* (Cambridge, 1979); Š. Bulovec, *Bibliografija Edvarda Kardelja* (Ljubljana, 1980); Sabrina P. Ramet, *Nationalism and Federalism in Yugoslavia, 1962–1991* (Bloomington, 1992); John Lampe, *Yugoslavia as History* (Cambridge, 1996).

KAREVIČIUS Pranciskus (30 September 1861, Graš- iunai, near Kretinga–30 May 1945, Marijampolė), Lithu- anian bishop. In 1886 Karevičius completed his studies at the Theological Academy in St. Petersburg, and in May 1886 he was ordained a priest. He lectured at the same academy for two years and then worked in a Catholic parish in Samara. In 1892 he began working in St. Cath- erine Parish in St. Petersburg. He served as the parish priest of that parish from 1908 on, defending the rights of Lithuanians and Latvians to use their native languages in church services. On 27 February 1914 Karevičius was appointed bishop of Samogitia. With his ingress into Kaunas Cathedral, the Lithuanization of the Samogitia diocese began. This led to protests by the local Poles. After the outbreak of World War I, the Russian authorities made it impossible for Karevičius to continue his work; therefore, he moved to Panevėžys, but when the Germans occupied Lithuania, he returned to Kaunas in August 1915. In 1917–18 Karevičius supported the Lithuanian Council in its efforts to gain independence for Lithuania. He ad- ministered the oath of allegiance to the first units of the Lithuanian Army, and he attended the opening ceremonies of the Constituent Assembly in May 1920. In April 1926, following the reorganization of the church in Lithuania, the diocese of Samogitia ceased to exist, and the majority of its territory was incorporated into the archdiocese of Kaunas. Karevičius retired and resided in the monastery in Marijampolė. He also entered the Marian order, which was revived by Archbishop **Jurgis Matulaitis-Matulevičius**. Karevičius died soon after the Red Army again occupied Lithuania. (WR)

Sources: *EL*, vol. 3; Alfred E. Senn, *The Emergence of Modern Lithuania* (New York, 1959).

KARMASIN Franz (2 September 1901, Olomouc–25 June 1970, Steinbach, Federal Republic of Germany), Ger- man politician active in Slovakia. After graduating from high school in Olomouc, Karmasin completed agricultural studies at a German polytechnic in Česky Tešin. He then began working with German political organizations, becoming a member of a student organization called Fre- inschar Arndt. After receiving a diploma in engineering, Karmasin worked for a short time as a clerk in Moravia, but soon the German organization Kameradschaftsbund sent him to Slovakia, where he became active in the Spiš

German Party (Zipser Deutsche Partei [ZdP]). However, he soon left this organization. In 1927 he became secretary of the German Cultural Union (Deutsche Kulturverband), an organization operating throughout Slovakia, and he founded the Carpathian German Party (Karpatendeutsche Partei [KdP]). After Hitler's rise to power in Germany in 1933, the KdP became the Slovak branch of the Su- deten German Party (Sudetendeutsche Partei [SdP]) of **Konrad Henlein**. The two parties submitted a joint list of candidates for the parliamentary elections of 1935, in which Karmasin obtained a seat in the Czechoslovak parliament. Two years later he became Henlein's deputy in Slovakia.

After the Czechoslovak authorities banned KdP activi- ties in September 1938, Karmasin founded the German Party (Deutsche Partei [DP]), which became possible when Slovak autonomy was declared. He established his party along the lines of the Nazi party. In the Slovak autonomous government (1938–39) Karmasin served as secretary for the German minority. In February 1939, along with **Voj- tech Tuka**, Karmasin was received by Hitler, to whom both declared their readiness to proclaim Slovak independence under the auspices of the Third Reich. On 14 March 1939 Karmasin organized anti-Czech actions and helped to provide arms for Hlinka's Guards (Hlinkova Garda [HG]). Also, on behalf of the German minority, he demanded the separation of Slovakia, in line with the strategic interests of the Third Reich. An established leader of the German minority, Karmasin sat in the Slovak parliament during World War II. He supported the pro-German orientation of the Slovak government and organized the recruitment of Slovak Germans into the SS units. During the Slovak National Uprising, Karmasin established Homeland De- fense (Heimatschutz), a military organization that fought against the insurgents and took part in the persecution of the civil population. In April 1945, along with members of the Slovak government, Karmasin fled to Austria, where he remained in hiding under the name Franz Dibak. In June 1948 the National Court in Bratislava sentenced him to death in absentia, but in 1949 he managed to escape to the Federal Republic of Germany, whose authorities refused to extradite him. (PU)

Sources: *Kdo byl kdo v našich dějinach ve 20. stoleti*, vol. 1 (Prague, 1998); *Politická elita meziválečného Československa 1918– 1938: Kdo byl kdo za prvni republiky* (Prague, 1998); *Kto bol kto za I. ČSR* (Bratislava, 1993); Jerzy Tomaszewski, *Czechosłowacja* (Warsaw, 1997); *SBS*, vol. 3; Dušan Kovač, *Dejiny Slovenska* (Bratislava, 1998).

KÁROLYI Gyula (7 May 1871, Nyírbakta–23 April 1947, Budapest), Hungarian politician, count, cousin of **Mihály**

Károlyi. After graduating in law from the universities in Budapest, Berlin, and Bonn, Károlyi managed his landed estate in Arad (Oradea) Province in Transylvania. In 1905–18 he was a member of the Upper House. He took part in the so-called national opposition to the **Géza Fejérváry** government (1905–6). From 1906 to 1910, during the rule of the "national coalition," Károlyi was governor of Arad city and province and a member of the opposition Constitutional Party (1913–18). During World War I he volunteered to fight on the Russian front. After the breakup of the Habsburg monarchy he withdrew to his estate. During the Hungarian Soviet Republic (HSR), from 5 May 1919, Károlyi headed a counter-government in Arad, then in Romania. The Romanian authorities inactivated this government and interned several of its members, including Károlyi, for two weeks. On 30 May 1919 Károlyi reconstructed his government in Szeged, occupied by the French troops. Into his government he invited **Miklós Horthy**, who became minister of national defense and head of the new Hungarian Army. Since the French found this cabinet "too reactionary," they insisted on its transformation and opposed its activities against the HSR government in Budapest, so on 12 July 1919 Károlyi resigned.

In the 1920s Károlyi lived on his estates within Trianon Hungary. In 1927 he became a member of the reconstructed Upper House, and in 1928–30 he held a prestigious position in the crown guard. In December 1930 he became foreign minister, and on 24 August 1931, during the worst of the Great Depression, as a trusted aide to Horthy, Károlyi assumed the position of prime minister. Despite foreign exchange controls, reductions in budgetary spending, and tax increases, Károlyi's government failed to overcome the depression, and it aggravated social discontent. After the Biatorbágy railway bridge was blown up in September 1931 and twenty-two people were killed, Károlyi introduced a state of emergency, believing that this was an act of Communist terrorism. In fact the perpetrator turned out to be a rightist extremist. After the execution of two Communist activists, Károlyi's government found itself under strong pressure, not only from the opposition, but also from the leadership of the ruling Unity Party of **István Bethlen**. On 1 October 1932 Károlyi resigned, gave up his parliamentary mandate, and retired from political life. During World War II Károlyi belonged to the inner circle of Horthy advisers, supporting a separate peace treaty with the Western Allies and the cautious attempts of the **Miklós Kállay** government to leave the alliance with Germany. (JT)

Sources: *Magyar Életrajzi Lexikon*, vol. 1 (Budapest, 1967); *Magyar Nagylexikon*, vol. 10 (Budapest, 2000); Oszkar Jaszi, *Revolution and Counterrevolution in Hungary* (London, 1924); C. A. Macartney, *October Fifteenth: A History of Modern Hungary*, vols. 1–2 (Edinburgh, 1957–61); Rudolf L. Tőkés, *Bela Kun and the Hungarian Soviet Republic* (New York, 1967); Paul Ignotus, *Hungary* (London, 1972); Steven Bela Vardy, *Historical Dictionary of Hungary* (Lanham, Md., 1997).

KÁROLYI Mihály (4 March 1875, Budapest–19 March 1955, Vence, France), count, Hungarian statesman. A member of an aristocratic family with a proud history, Károlyi was the son of Gyula and Georgina Károlyi, Gyula's cousin. After graduating from a private high school, Károlyi studied law at the university in Budapest from 1893 to 1899. Initially, he was a member of the ruling Liberal Party (Szabadelvű Párt), but he soon clashed with **István Tisza**, who was prime minister and leader of the party; shortly before the elections of 1905 Károlyi joined the Party of Independence and 1848 (Függetlenségi és 48-as Párt), an opposition party that drew on the tradition of the Hungarian revolution of 1848–49. In 1909–12 Károlyi served as president of the All-National Hungarian Economic Union, which attracted the great landowners. From 1905 to 1906 and from 1910 to 1918 he was a member of parliament. When Tisza, the speaker of the parliament, overcame the opposition's filibustering (June 1912), Károlyi became his implacable enemy. Károlyi represented opposition views particularly in international affairs, as he proposed a pro-Entente orientation instead of an alliance with Germany. Since he called for universal suffrage and cared about social issues, he stood out among his contemporary politicians of aristocratic origin.

Following a merger between the two factions of the independence movement, in 1913, Károlyi became leader of the Party of Independence and 1848, whose program called for the transformation of the Habsburg monarchy into a personal union. Although Károlyi was against World War I, in 1915 he served at the front for a short time. However, in December of that year in parliament, he insisted on the conclusion of peace. Since his party supported the war, in 1916, along with his followers, Károlyi founded the Independence Party of '48. In respect to the war and social issues, Károlyi's views became close to those of the Social Democrats and the bourgeois radicals. In 1917 Károlyi became president of the Suffrage Bloc, which called for universal suffrage and the secret ballot, and he urged the conclusion of peace without territorial annexations. At the beginning of 1918 Károlyi was accused of treason and collaboration with the enemy, but after the monarchy's defeat, he became a leading figure of the republican revolution. On 24 October 1918 Károlyi was elected president of the Hungarian National Council (Magyar Nemzeti Tanács), which consisted mainly of Social Democrats and liberal radicals. On 31 October he was appointed prime minister and minister of foreign affairs, and on 25 November, minister of finance; from 12 to 29 December he served as minister of national defense. Assuming the office, Károlyi took an oath to "Hungary and the Hungarian nation" instead of to the king. Károlyi initiated peace negotiations with the Entente, as a result of which on 13 November he signed a cease-fire in Belgrade.

On 16 November 1918 Hungary was proclaimed an independent republic. Both as its prime minister and as president (from 11 January 1919) Károlyi failed to consolidate the country, whose economy was in ruins and whose society was in a state of turmoil. The country was surrounded by succession states that wanted to gain as much of the territory of the former monarchy as possible, including territories that were historically Hungarian. Because of this, Károlyi was sharply attacked both by the left and by the right. In February 1919, to mark the symbolic launch of an agrarian reform, Károlyi parceled out his own estate in Kápolna. His foreign policy suffered a defeat. On 20 March 1919 Károlyi received a note from French general Fernand Vix in which the administration and the remnants of the Hungarian Army were ordered to leave much of the territory of the Great Hungarian Plain under threat of a resumption of warfare. Károlyi dismissed the government and entrusted the mission of forming a new cabinet to the Social Democrats, who reached an agreement with the Communists and established the Ruling Revolutionary Council. On 21 March the council proclaimed the Hungarian Soviet Republic (HSR) and dismissed Károlyi from office.

In July 1919 Károlyi went to Czechoslovakia. He later lived in Italy, Yugoslavia, and London, and in 1925 he settled in Paris. He was an avowed opponent of the regime of Regent **Miklós Horthy**. In 1922 in Munich Károlyi published his memoirs, which appeared also in English as *Fighting the World: The Struggle for Peace* (1925). Tried in absentia in 1923 in Budapest, Károlyi was sentenced for "treason" and deprived of his property. In exile, he became a supporter of communism and the USSR. In 1931 he visited the Soviet Union. In 1938 he moved to London, where he was active in the Movement for New Democratic Hungary. This movement was established to work against Nazism. Károlyi also served as president of the Hungarian Council in England. At the end of the war, he cherished the hope that he would play an important role in Hungarian politics, but he had to be satisfied with an act of parliament proclaiming his historical merits, passed after the proclamation of the Hungarian Republic in February 1946, and a parliamentary seat given to him as a nonparty candidate. In that same year Károlyi returned to Hungary, where he was greeted with ceremony and received the Grand Cross of the Order of Merit of the Hungarian Republic, the most prestigious Hungarian award. The sentences he had been given in the trial of 1923 were quashed. In July 1947 Károlyi was appointed Hungary's ambassador to Paris, but the day after the arrest of **László Rajk** in June 1949, he resigned and went into exile for the second time. He attempted to mobilize international public opinion against the organizers of Rajk's show trial. At the end of his life Károlyi wrote an autobiography that was published in 1956 as *Faith without Illusion*. In 1962 his ashes were returned to Hungary and buried with ceremony in Budapest. (JT)

Sources: *Biographisches Lexikon*, vol. 3; Steven Bela Vardy, *Historical Dictionary of Hungary* (Lanham, Md., 1997); *Nagy Képes Milleniumi Arcképcsarnok* (Budapest, 1999); *Magyar Nagylexikon*, vol. 10 (Budapest, 2000); *Magyarország 1944–1956*, CD-ROM (Budapest, 2001); Oszkar Jaszi, *Revolution and Counterrevolution in Hungary* (London, 1924); C. A. Macartney, *October Fifteenth: A History of Modern Hungary*, vols. 1–2 (Edinburgh, 1957–61); Catherine Andrassy Karolyi, *A Life Together* (London, 1966); Rudolf L. Tőkés, *Bela Kun and the Hungarian Soviet Republic* (New York, 1967); Tibor Hajdu, *Károlyi Mihály: Politikai életrajz* (Budapest, 1978); Holger Fischer, *Oszkar Jaszi und Mihály Károlyi* (Munich, 1978).

KAROTAMM Nikolai (23 October 1901, Pärnu–26 September 1969, Moscow), Estonian Communist activist. The son of a carpenter, after the Bolshevik revolution Karotamm went to Russia. He studied in the Communist School for Western National Minorities in Leningrad. In 1928 he joined the Communist Party. He later worked in the Communist underground in Estonia and organized a party unit in Tallinn. In 1930 he again went to the USSR, where in 1933 he began lecturing and publishing in Moscow. Between 1935 and 1936 he worked in the Comintern, and from 1938 to 1940 he ran a technical school in Leningrad. After the incorporation of Estonia into the USSR in 1940, he became party secretary in Tartu and second secretary of the CC of the CP of Estonia. In June 1941 he took part in organizing the deportation of around ten thousand Estonians far into the interior of the USSR.

During the German-Soviet war Karotamm was chief of the Estonian staff of the Partisan Movement. When the Red Army again occupied Estonia, he was made first secretary of the CC of the Estonian Communist Party (Bolsheviks) in September 1944. He supervised the deportations of 1945. In 1948 Karotamm announced the collectivization of Estonian agriculture. Although it seems that he attempted to limit the extent and speed of collectivization, in January 1949 he informed Stalin that he was ready to "get rid of the kulaks as a class" through deportation. This action began on 23 March 1949. Deportation orders for about twenty-one thousand families were signed by Karotamm himself. In a short period about eighty thousand people were deported to Kazakhstan and to the Novosibirsk oblast (province). Because of the conditions under which the deportations were carried out, there was a high mortality rate among the deportees; thus the action can be described as planned genocide. As a result of a purge of the Estonian party leadership, in March 1950 Karotamm was dismissed from his post for "errors of rightist opportunism." He worked in the Academy of Sciences of the CPSU CC and at the Institute for Economic Sciences of the USSR Academy of Sciences. In 1966 he received the title of professor. His publications include a Russian–Estonian dictionary (1944); *Ekonomicheskaia effektivnost kapitalnykh vlozhenii* (The economic effectiveness of capital investments; 1957); and *K istorii ucheniia o sotsialisticheskom selskom khoziaistve* (From the history of studies of the Socialist agricultural farm; 1959). In 1964 Karotamm received a Ph.D. in economics. (WR)

Sources: *MERSH*, vol. 16; *Eesti NSV Kolhoosnikute Kongress 1st* (Tallinn, 1948); Rein Taagepera, "Soviet Collectivization of Estonian Agriculture: The Deportation Phase," *Soviet Studies*, 1980, no. 3; Romuald J. Misiunas and Rein Taagepera, *The Baltic States: Years of Dependence, 1940–1980* (Berkeley, 1983); Voldemar Pinn, *Kes oli Nikolai Karotamm?* vols. 1–2 (Uppsala, 1996–97); www.sada.ee/php/query.

KARPENKA Henadz (17 September 1949, Minsk–6 April 1999, Minsk), Belarusian scientist and political activist. After graduating from the Belorussian Pedagogical Institute in 1972, Karpenka worked at the Institute of Nuclear Energy of the Academy of Sciences of the Belorussian SSR. In 1983–90 he was the director of the Powder Metallurgy Enterprise in Molodechno. From 1991 to 1994 he served as president of the Municipal Executive Committee in Molodechno; thus he was head of the local administration. In 1990 he earned a Ph.D. in metallurgical sciences and became a corresponding member of the National Academy of Sciences of Belorussia. He authored over one hundred publications in the field of metallurgy. In 1990–96 Karpenka was deputy to the Supreme Soviet of the Belorussian SSR, and in 1996 he became its vice-president. In November 1993 he disclosed a letter from Eduard Shirkovsky, head of the Belorussian KGB, and Vladimir Yegorov, minister of interior, to **Stanislau Shushkevich**, president of the Supreme Soviet, in which they criticized the reforms of the Belorussian state. After the election of **Alyaksandr Lukashenka** as president in July 1994, Karpenka joined the firm opposition to Lukashenka's government. When Lukashenka established his own parliament, Karpenka remained a member of the Supreme Soviet, which was not recognized by Lukashenka, and he became a determined opponent of the regime.

In January 1997 he was elected president of the National Economic Council, which, along with other organizations independent from Lukashenka, became the foundation of a shadow cabinet. A co-founder of the United Civic Party, in December 1997 Karpenka became head of the National Executive Committee of the opposition. He died suddenly of a heart attack. (EM)

Sources: Jan Zaprudnik, *Historical Dictionary of Belarus* (Lanham, Md., 1998); David R. Marples, *Belarus: A Denationalized Nation* (Amsterdam, 1999); *Kto est kto v Respublike Bielarus* (Minsk, 1999).

KARPIŃSKI Stanisław (23 October 1870, Raducz–24 December 1943, Warsaw), Polish banker and politician. The son of a landowner, Karpiński graduated from the Leopold Kronenberg School of Commerce in Warsaw and from the Department of Economics of Leipzig University. In 1893 he started working in the Commercial Bank (Bank Handlowy) in Warsaw. In 1909 he was a co-founder of the Bank of Cooperative Societies (Bank Towarzystw Spółdzielczych), and then he served as the managing director of this bank from 1910 to 1918 and from 1919 to 1924. After the outbreak of World War I, Karpiński became more active in politics, and he assumed the post of treasurer of the Central Civic Committee. He gave many public lectures and published extensively on economic topics. In 1918 he became involved in preparing the principles of the financial system of the future Poland. In *Projekt ustawy Banku Polskiego w związku ze sprawą waluty* (The Bank of Poland bill and the currency issue; 1918) Karpiński advocated that the future Polish currency be based on the currencies of the partitioning powers. In November 1918, on behalf of the Polish state, he became head of the board of the Polish National Loan Association (Polska Krajowa Kasa Pożyczkowa), which had until then served as the bank of issue for the Kingdom of Poland under German occupation. In April 1919 Karpiński became minister of the treasury. Faced with the difficulty of increasing revenues and unable to stop inflation because of increased budgetary spending, he resigned in July 1919. A senator from the lists of the National Popular Union (Związek Ludowo-Narodowy [ZLN]) in 1922–27, he took part in the work of the Senate's Treasury and Budget Commission.

Karpiński participated in consultations with former treasury ministers and President **Stanisław Wojciechowski** to work out a program for strengthening the treasury. Only Karpiński supported the proposals of **Władysław Grabski**; therefore, when Grabski became prime minister, he appointed Karpiński president of the Organization Committee of the new Bank of Poland in January 1924 and chairman of the bank on 29 April of that year. For half a year Karpiński worked closely with Grabski, but in November 1925 he refused any further stock market interventions to maintain the Polish złoty, which was threatened by a growing "second inflation." This led to the resignation of Grabski, who later sharply criticized Karpiński for his decision. In May 1927 Karpiński explained the reasons for his decision in a special open letter. He was against allowing foreign capital into the central bank, and he defended the independence of the Bank of Poland from the government. This, in turn, led to a conflict with the *sanacja* government because **Józef Piłsudski** wanted to subordinate the central bank to the executive power. Thus, when in 1929 Karpiński's five-year term ended, its extension was not even contemplated. Karpiński retired from public life. In 1931 he published *Pamiętnik dziesięciolecia 1915–1924* (Memoirs of the decade 1915–1924). (WR)

Sources: *PSB*, vol. 12; *Encyklopedia historii Drugiej Rzeczypospolitej* (Warsaw, 1999); Jerzy Tomaszewski, *Stabilizacja waluty w Polsce* (Warsaw, 1961); Zygmunt Karpiński, *O Wielkopolsce, złocie i dalekich podróżach* (Warsaw, 1971); Feliks Młynarski, *Wspomnienia* (Warsaw, 1971).

KARSKI Jan [originally Kozielewski] (24 April 1914, Łódź–13 July 2000, Washington, D.C.), courier of the Polish underground during World War II, political scientist. After completing law and diplomatic studies at Jan Kazimierz University in Lwów (Lviv), Karski began working at the Ministry of Foreign Affairs. He fought in the September campaign in 1939. Captured and placed in a Soviet prison, he managed to escape from a transport to the East. He got to Warsaw, where he joined the Polish anti-Nazi underground. He was also active in the Front for the Rebirth of Poland (Front Odrodzenia Polski), which was a Catholic underground organization, and the Information Bureau of the Home Army High Command. Arrested by the Gestapo and tortured, Karski tried to commit suicide because he feared that he might reveal secret information to the Germans, but he was saved. He was soon sprung by Home Army soldiers. After recuperating, he resumed his underground work. In August 1942 in the Warsaw Ghetto, he met Leon Feiner, an activist and representative of the Bund to the Home Delegation of the Polish Government-in-Exile (Delegatura Rządu na Kraj). Feiner asked Karski to relay the Jewish demands to the leaders of the Big Three. These demands included a a declaration that preventing the Holocaust would be one of the aims of the war against the Third Reich. As a representative of the Home Delegation, Karski went to Great Britain and the United States to report on the extermination of Jews and to present Jewish demands to the Allied leaders. At the beginning of 1943 he was received by British foreign secretary Anthony Eden, President Franklin D. Roosevelt, U.S. secretary of state Cordell Hull, and leaders of American Jews, but Karski failed to make them believe the shocking reports about the Holocaust or to convince them to take action in defense of European Jews. After the war, Karski remained in the United States, where in 1952 he began lecturing in international relations and in the theory of communism at Georgetown University in Washington, D.C. His publications include *The Story of the Secret State* (1944), and *The Great Powers and Poland 1919–1945: From Versailles to Yalta* (1985). (WR)

Sources: Jan Nowak Jeziorański, *Kurier z Warszawy* (Kraków, 1993); *New York Times*, 15 July 2000; *Gwiazda Polarna*, 19 July 2000; Tadeusz Zachurski, "Świadek Jan Karski (1914–2000)," *Wprost*, 23 July 2000.

KARVAŠ Imrich (25 February 1903, Levice-Kalinčiakovo–22 February 1981, Bratislava), Slovak lawyer and economist. In 1925 Karvaš graduated in law from Komenský University in Bratislava, where he became a *docent* (associate professor) in 1930 and a university professor in 1940. He mainly dealt with economic law, both in teaching and in his practice. From 1926 to 1930 Karvaš was secretary of the Chamber of Commerce and Industry in Bratislava; from 1930 to 1933 he was secretary of the Union of Slovak Banks; from 1932 to 1938 he was general secretary of the National Economic Institute of Slovakia and Carpathian Ruthenia; and from 1936 to 1938 he was vice-president of the Export Institute in Prague. In 1938 he served for a short time as minister without portfolio and later as minister of industry, trade, and craft in the government of General **Jan Syrový**. After the establishment of the Slovak state in March 1939, Karvaš became chairman of the Slovak National Bank. In 1942 he was also appointed chairman of the Supreme Office for Supplies. In 1940 he established the School of Economics in Bratislava. He worked with the Slovak resistance and maintained contacts with the group led by **Vavro Šrobar** and the Slovak National Council. Karvaš ordered that a part of the treasury of the Slovak National Bank be transferred from Bratislava to Banská Bystrica so that the insurgents could use it. Following the disclosure of his contacts with the resistance in September 1944, Karvaš spent the rest of the war in Nazi concentration camps.

After returning home, Karvaš served as dean of the School of Law at the university in Bratislava from 1947 to 1948 and as government adviser for the reconstruction of Slovakia from 1945 to 1948. After the Communist coup of February 1948, he refused to cooperate with the regime. Accused of high treason in 1949, he was sentenced to two years' imprisonment and the forfeiture of property. After one year he was released but was forced to leave Bratislava in 1953. In 1958 Karvaš was arrested again and sentenced to seventeen years in prison for espionage and high treason. Released under amnesty in 1960, he was rehabilitated by court order in 1969. In his scholarly views, Karvaš was a follower of the teleological school of **Karel Engliš** and was the main ideologist of Slovak regionalism. He advocated the economic development of Slovakia as a separate territorial entity and called for the improvement of Slovakia's position in the Czechoslovak state. In 1926 he was a co-founder of *Hospodárske rozhľady*, the first Slovak economic periodical, and in 1939 he became its editor-in-chief. Karvaš was the author of such works as *Hospodárska štatistika Slovenska* (Economic statistics of Slovakia; 1928); *Štátne príjmy a konjunktúra* (State revenues and economic growth; 1931); *Kartely a konjunktúra* (The influence of cartels on economic prosperity; 1932); *Čas v hospodárskej teórii* (Time in the theory of economics; 1938); and *Základy hospodárskej vedy* (The basics of economic science, 2 vols.; 1947). (PU)

Sources: *ČBS*; *Politická elita meziválečného Československa 1918–1938: Kdo byl kdo za první republiky* (Prague, 1998); *SBS*, vol. 3 (Martin, 1989); *Reprezentačný biografický lexikón Slovenska* (Martin, 1999); Stanislav J. Kirschbaum, *A History of Slovakia* (London, 1995); Peter A. Toma and Dušan Kováč, *Slovakia from Samo to Dzurinda* (Stanford, 2001); Rudolf Chmel, ed., *Kwestia slowacka w XX wieku* (Gliwice, 2002); http://www.muzeumsnp.sk/karvas_s.htm.

KAŠPAR Karel (16 May 1870, Mirošov, near Rokycany–21 April 1941, Prague), Czech cardinal, Primate of Bohemia. After studying theology and philosophy in Rome in 1888–93, Kašpar was ordained a priest. In 1896–98 he continued his education, studying law at the Pontifical Institute of St. Apollinaris (now known as the Pontifical Lateran University). At that time he wrote the famous work *Církevní zákonodárství v náboženských kongregacích* (Church legislation in religious congregations, 2 vols.; 1903–4). After returning to Bohemia, Kašpar lectured at a theological seminary in Prague, and from 1907 to 1920 he was a canon of the Prague metropolitan chapter. In 1920 he was consecrated bishop, and the following year he was appointed diocesan bishop of Hradec Kralové. In 1926 he attended the Eucharistic Congress in the United States, and in 1930 he traveled to Palestine and Egypt, as a result of which he wrote *Po stopach božského Spasitela v Egyptě a Svaté zemi* (Tracing the Holy Savior in Egypt and the Holy Land; 1931). Kašpar's moderation and diplomatic talents helped to improve relations between the Czechoslovak state and the Catholic Church. In 1931 he was appointed archbishop of Prague and Primate of Bo-

hemia, and in 1935 he was made a cardinal; domestically this was seen as the Holy See's recognition of Czechoslovakia. During the Sudeten crisis of 1938 Kašpar called for a peaceful settlement of the conflict. His efforts included meeting with the British mediator, Lord Walter Runciman. Following the partition of Czechoslovakia in 1938 and 1939, Kašpar tried to raise the spirits of the Czech people, and he supported efforts aimed at the sovereignty of Czechoslovakia. (WR)

Sources: *ČBS*; Josef Tomeš et al., *Česky Biografický Slovník XX. stoleti* (Prague, 1999); Charles Roux, *Huit ans au Vatican* (Paris, 1947).

KASPRZYCKI Tadeusz (16 January 1891, Warsaw–4 December 1978, Montreal), Polish general. In 1910 Kasprzycki began studies in the social sciences, natural sciences, and law at the Sorbonne and at the School of Social Sciences in Paris. In 1911 he joined the Union of Active Struggle (Związek Walki Czynnej [ZWC]). He was commander of a ZWC unit in Paris and commander of ZWC units in the district of Switzerland and southern France. In 1912 he switched to studying in Geneva, where he founded a Riflemen's Association. He also organized a riflemen's movement in the Russian sector of partitioned Poland. In 1913 Kasprzycki completed an officers' summer school run by the Riflemen's Association. In July 1914 he served as commander of an officers' summer school in Oleandry, near Kraków. Closely connected with **Józef Piłsudski**, in August 1914 Kasprzycki became commander of the First Cadre Company of the First Brigade of the Polish Legions. His company was involved in an unsuccessful attempt to instigate an anti-Russian uprising in the Kingdom of Poland. In September 1915 Kasprzycki was transferred to work in the Polish Military Organization (Polska Organizacja Wojskowa [POW]). He served as POW commander in Warsaw and Lublin. In 1917 he founded the Union of Polish Military Organizations. From January to July 1917 he acted as head of the general and organizational section of the Military Commission of the Provisional Council of State. He co-founded the Convention of Organization A (Konwent Organizacji A), a group that led the independence movement. From 1918 he served in the Polish Army.

After Piłsudski returned from Magdeburg to Warsaw in November 1918, Kasprzycki became his aide-de-camp. From the beginning of December 1918 to November 1919, as a lieutenant colonel, he served as chief of the general aide-de-camp section of the Head of State and Commander-in-Chief. In 1921 he graduated from the Military College and from the Diplomatic Department of the École des Sciences Politiques in Paris. Upon his return he was promoted to colonel. From March 1922 Kasprzycki held various posts in the General Staff; in 1926 he became head of the Office of the Supreme Council of War; and in July 1927 he became head of the Second Department of the General Staff (intelligence). From 1927 to 1931 Kasprzycki served as commander of the Nineteenth Infantry Division. He was a Polish delegate to the disarmament conference and to the Preparatory Consultative Commission of the League of Nations. In 1929 he was promoted to brigadier general. In July 1934 he was appointed deputy minister for military affairs, and after Piłsudski's death, he became minister for military affairs in October 1935. In 1936 he was promoted to major general. In September 1939 Kasprzycki left Poland with the government and traveled via Romania, Turkey, and France to Great Britain. He co-founded the Polish University in Exile. He was a member of the Józef Piłsudski Institute and other organizations. In 1954 he settled in Canada. In exile, he did not take part in active politics. Kasprzycki was the author of *Kartki z dziennika oficera I Brygady* (Pages from the diary of an officer of the First Brigade; 1934). (JS)

Sources: *Kto był kim w Drugiej Rzeczypospolitej* (Warsaw, 1994); Tomasz Nałęcz, *Polska Organizacja Wojkowa 1914–1918* (Warsaw, 1984); Piotr Stawecki, *Słownik biograficzny generałów Wojska Polskiego, 1918–1939* (Warsaw, 1994); *Encyklopedia historii Drugiej Rzeczypospolitej* (Warsaw, 1999); Zbigniew Mierzwiński, *Generałowie II Rzeczypospolitej* (Warsaw, 1995); Tadeusz Kryska-Karski and Stanisław Żurakowski, *Generałowie Polski Niepodległej* (London, 1976); "Śp. generał Tadeusz Kasprzycki," *Niepodległość*, 1980, vol. 13.

KASSÁK Lajos (21 March 1887, Érsekújvár [now in Slovakia]–22 July 1967, Budapest), Hungarian poet and writer. Kassák's father, who was of Slovak origin, worked as a drugstore assistant, and his mother was a washerwoman. Having dropped out of secondary school, Kassák became an apprentice locksmith and worked as a blue-collar laborer. He was active in the trade union movement and in the Social Democratic Party. He organized strikes, and because of this he was often dismissed from work. An autodidact, Kassák became interested in poetry. He published his first piece of work in 1905. In 1909, without money, he set off on foot to Paris. On the way he did many odd jobs. In 1910 he was deported from Paris by the Hungarian legation. These experiences shaped his avant-garde understanding of esthetics, as well as his program for an artistic revolution. In 1915 Kassák published the first volume of his poems and founded a periodical, *Tett*. In 1916 he began editing the periodical *Ma*. Under the Hungarian Soviet Republic (HSR) in 1919 Kassák was a member of the leadership of the writers' directorate. However, because he criticized the regime

and its cultural policy, the government suspended *Ma*. After the collapse of the HSR in August 1919 Kassák was arrested. Released in 1920, he left for Vienna, where he again edited *Ma*. This journal soon gained international fame. Kassák's poems reveal the influences of futurism, and his paintings reflect the influences of constructivism and cubism. In 1926 Kassák returned to Hungary; edited the periodicals *Dokumentum* and *Munka*; and published his autobiography, *Egy ember élete* (A man's life). He also wrote for the Social Democratic daily, *Népszava*, and for the periodical *Szocializmus*. In 1940 he was sentenced to two months' imprisonment.

In 1946 Kassák became vice-president of the Hungarian Arts Council. As a prominent artist, on his sixtieth birthday he was given a pension and a house in Budapest. In 1947 he became president of the Arts Commission of the Hungarian Social Democratic Party (HSDP). In January 1948, as a party representative, he became an MP, replacing a person who had been forced to resign. In 1948 Kassák joined the Hungarian Workers' Party (HWP), which was a Communist party. In 1949 Kassák fell into disfavor, and his works ceased to be published. At a party meeting of the Hungarian Writers' Union in September 1953, Kassák criticized the HWP cultural policy, and as a result he was expelled from the party. In 1956 he resumed his artistic work. At a general meeting of the Writers' Union in September of that year he was elected to its Presidium. In 1965 Kassák received the Kossuth Award. The Kassák Lajos Museum in Budapest is in charge of his literary and artistic legacy. (JT)

Sources: *Lajos Kassak Retrospective Exhibition, April–May 1984* (New York, 1984); *A magyar forradalom és szabadságharc enciklopédiája* (Budapest, 1999); *Magyar Nagylexikon*, vol. 10 (Budapest, 2000).

KAVAN Jan (17 October 1946, London), Czech journalist and politician. Kavan is the son of an Englishwoman and a Czech diplomat who was imprisoned in 1952–55 in connection with the case of **Rudolf Slansky**. In 1964–68 he studied in the Department of Education and Journalism of Charles University in Prague, contributing to the periodicals *Mladá fronta*, *Student*, and *My*. In 1966–68 he edited the periodical *Universita Karlova*. Kavan was active in the student opposition, and in 1968–69 he was a member of the Presidium of the Union of Higher School Students. In January 1969 he co-organized the funeral of **Jan Palach**. Expelled from the university, Kavan emigrated to Great Britain, where he studied at St. Anthony College in Oxford, the London School of Economics and Political Science (1970–74), and Reading University. He wrote for British and American newspapers (*The Times*, *The Observer*, the

New York Times, and *New Statesman*), and he was active in the leftist student movement. In 1974–90 Kavan directed the Palach Press Agency; from 1982 to 1989 he was deputy director of the Jan Palach Information and Research Trust; and from 1985 to 1990 he was deputy editor-in-chief of the *East European Reporter* and vice-president of the East European Cultural Foundation. From 1982 to 1990 he was a member of the British Labour Party. Kavan maintained contacts with the Czechoslovak opposition, operating a channel through which émigré publications and duplication equipment could enter his homeland. In 1979 he was deprived of Czechoslovak citizenship.

On 25 November 1989 Kavan returned to Prague and joined the Coordination Center of the Civic Forum (Občanské Fórum [OF]). From June 1990 to June 1992 he was an MP to the Chamber of the People of the Federal Assembly and a member of its foreign affairs commission. In the spring of 1991, to explain the events of 17 November 1989, the commission accused Kavan of cooperation with the Communist security service, but in 1996 he was cleared of these charges. In 1992–93 Kavan lectured at American universities, and upon his return to the Czech Republic in 1993 he joined the Czech Social Democratic Party (Česká Strana Sociálně Demokratická [ČSSD]) and chaired its foreign affairs department. In November 1996 he was elected to the Senate, and after the electoral victory of the Social Democrats in July 1998 he became minister of foreign affairs in the government of **Miloš Zeman**. From 10 December 1999 Kavan was also deputy prime minister. His major achievement was the accession of the Czech Republic to NATO on 12 March 1999. Kavan also initiated a renewal of cooperation within the Višegrad Group (Czech Republic, Hungary, Poland, and Slovakia), neglected by the previous government of **Václav Klaus**. After a repeat victory of the Social Democrats in the elections of June 2002, Kavan won a parliamentary seat and belonged to the foreign affairs commission, but he did not stay in the government. In the summer of 2002 Kavan was accused of shielding the corruption of his subordinate, Karel Srba, who was also suspected of ordering a political murder. (PU)

Sources: *ČBS*; *Kdo je kdo v České Republice na přelomu 20. století* (Prague, 1998); "Co wiedział Jan Kavan," *Rzeczpospolita*, 24 July 2002; www.vlada.cz/1250/vlada/vlada_clenove.htm.

KAVČIĆ Stane (30 October 1919, Ljubljana–27 March 1987, Ljubljana), Slovene Communist activist. Kavčić joined the Communist Party in July 1941. During the war he served as, among other things, secretary of a party district committee in Vrhnika. He underwent training in the USSR. After the war, he became secretary of

the Central Committee (CC) of the Communist Party of Slovenia (1945–49). Subsequently, he held the position of vice-president of the Presidium of the People's Assembly of the People's Republic of Slovenia (1949–50) and vice-president of the Executive Committee, which served as the government of the Socialist Republic of Slovenia (1951–56). Secretary of the chief committee of the Socialist Union of the Working People of Slovenia (1956–58) and president of the Council of Slovenian Trade Unions (1958–63), Kavčić headed the commission for ideological affairs of the CC of the League of Communists of Slovenia (1963–66) and the government of the federal Republic of Slovenia (1967–72). He was a member of the Executive Committee of the League of Communists of Yugoslavia (LCY) in 1966 and a member of the Presidium of the LCY in 1969–72. He also belonged to the CC of the League of Communists of Slovenia (1967–69).

In the 1960s and 1970s Kavčić favored an export-oriented, liberal, and decentralized economy. He strove to develop cooperation between Slovenia and its Western neighbors. His views, which were considered insufficiently class-conscious and Yugoslav, led to a conflict with some of the Slovene and Yugoslav leaders. After the so-called Croat spring of 1971, the Presidium of the LCY decided that the "Croat spring" had been initiated by people with pro-Western views, as well as nationalists and extreme liberals. In the face of a change of policy and the consolidation of the leading role of the party, Kavčić was dismissed as president of the government of the Slovene Republic. He also resigned from the Presidium of the LCY and then retired. He had to withdraw from politics and public life. Kavčić wrote *Samoupravljanje* (Self-management, 4 vols.; 1964–67). His *Dnevnik in spomini* (Diary and memoirs; 1988) was published posthumously. (AO)

Sources: *Enciklopedija Slovenije*, vol. 5 (Ljubljana, 1991); Wiesław Walkiewicz, *Jugosławia* (Warsaw, 2000); *Who's Who in the Socialist Countries of Europe*, vol. 2 (Munich, London, and Paris, 1989); Sabrina P. Ramet, *Nationalism and Federalism in Yugoslavia, 1962–1991* (Bloomington, 1992); Leopoldina Plut-Pregelj and Carole Rogel, *Historical Dictionary of Slovenia* (Lanham, Md., 1996).

KAZASOV Dimo (5 October 1886, Trjavna–28 July 1980, Sofia), Bulgarian writer and politician. The son of a teacher, after graduating from a gymnasium in Ruse in 1907, Kazasov also worked as a teacher. In 1918 he completed law studies at Sofia University. In his youth he was aligned with the Narodnik movement and later with the Social Democratic movement. In 1895 he joined the trade union movement, and from 1910 to 1919 he served as president of the Bulgarian Teachers' Union. Shortly after the war, Kazasov became an MP on behalf of the Social Democratic Party. In 1919–20, along with the Communists, he organized strikes of transportation workers that were crushed by the government. Later, he conspired against the government of **Aleksandur Stambolyski**. After the overthrow of Stamboliski in June 1923, Kazasov assumed the portfolio of minister of post and communication in the cabinet of **Aleksandur Tsankov**. In this role, he helped to suppress a revolutionary Communist uprising in September 1923. However, in February 1924 he left the government and joined the opposition. In 1924–28 Kazasov served as president of the Bulgarian Journalists' Union, and he published a great deal. In 1927 he was a co-founder of the Zveno group, which advocated the establishment of an authoritarian state. The Zveno group maintained close contacts with other influential organizations such as the Military League. In May 1934 the groups linked to Zveno and the Military League staged a coup d'état. At this point, Kazasov left Zveno and joined the National Social Movement (NSM) led by Tsankov. After Tsar Boris III dismissed the government of **Kimon Georgiev** in January 1935, Kazasov became Bulgaria's ambassador to Yugoslavia. After returning to Bulgaria in 1936, he again drifted to the left. At that time he published *Dneshna Yugoslaviia* (Today's Yugoslavia; 1938) and other works. In 1940 he opposed the anti-Jewish legislation that was being passed. He served as chairman of the Committee for Victims of Political Persecution. In 1943 he joined the Communist-led underground Fatherland Front. After the coup of 9 September 1944, Kazasov worked with the Communists. In the government of Kimon Georgiev, he served as minister of propaganda (September 1944–September 1945), and from September 1945 to December 1947 he held the post of minister for information and arts. From 1950 to 1958 he was head of the publishing operations of the government. Until the end of his life Kazasov wrote and published memoirs and comments on the recent history of Bulgaria. In 1987 his memoirs, *Iskri ot burni godini* (Sparks of the turbulent years), were published. (JJ/MC)

Sources: *Biographisches Lexikon*, vol. 2; *Entsiklopediya Bulgariya*, vol. 3 (Sofia, 1982); Vicki Tamir, *Bulgaria and Her Jews: The History of a Dubious Symbiosis* (New York, 1979); Robert J. McIntyre, *Bulgaria: Politics, Economics and Society* (London and New York, 1988); Boika Vasileva, *Evreite v Bylgaria, 1944–1952* (Sofia, 1992); Tzvetan Todorov, ed., *The Fragility of Goodness: Why Bulgaria's Jews Survived the Holocaust* (London, 1999).

KAZLOUSKI Pavel (9 March 1942, Vaukaunia, near Pruzhany–2000?), Belorussian Soviet general. Kazlouski graduated from the School of Commanders in Tashkent in 1965, from the Frunze Military Academy in 1974, and from the General Staff Academy in 1987. He did military service in Central Asia, Transcaucasia, and the North Caucasian District. In 1989 he became commander of the Twenty-eighth Army, which was headquartered in Grodno. In 1991 he became chief of staff and deputy commander of the Belorussian Military District. Despite the fact that in August 1991 he supported the Moscow coup staged by Gennady Yanayev, which nearly cost him expulsion from the army, Kazlouski retained his position and served as minister of national defense of the Republic of Belarus from 1991 to 1994. He opposed the Beloruthenization and de-Sovietization of the military. At that time he planned to negotiate concessions from the West in exchange for Belarus' giving up nuclear weapons. In 1996 he joined the opposition against **Alyaksandr Lukashenka**. Kazlouski disappeared without a trace, kidnapped by "unknown assailants" in a street in Minsk. (EM)

Sources: *Entsyklapedyia historii Belarusi*, vol. 4 (Minsk, 1997); Jan Zaprudnik, *Belarus: At a Crossroads in History* (Boulder, Colo., 1993); Jan Zaprudnik, *Historical Dictionary of Belarus* (Lanham, Md., 1998).

KEBICH Vyacheslau (10 June 1936, Koniuszewszczyzna), Belorussian Communist and post-Communist activist. Kebich graduated from the Belorussian Polytechnic Institute in 1958 and the Higher Party School in Minsk in 1984. He worked as an engineer in the Minsk Factory of Automatization of Factories, and from 1973 he was director of the Minsk Factory of Machine Tools. In 1980–85 Kebich started working in the party apparatus. He was secretary of the Minsk Regional Committee of the Communist Party of Belorussia (CPB) and head of the Department of Industry of its Central Committee (CC). In 1985 he became deputy prime minister of the Belorussian SSR (BSSR) and head of its Planning Commission. In 1986–91 he was a member of the CPB CC, and in 1990–91 he belonged to the CC of the CPSU. In April 1990 Kebich became prime minister of the BSSR. After the proclamation of independence of the republic on 25 July 1991, in November 1991 Kebich signed a statement from the government of the "Republic of Belarus" that the Soviet "super empire" had collapsed. On 8 December 1991, Kebich and the chairman of the BSSR Supreme Council, **Stanislau Shushkevich**, were the Belorussian signatories of the agreement with the Ukraine and Russia dissolving the Soviet Union. Initially Kebich supported a market orientation in the country's internal transformation and favored seeking economic and political links with the West, but in view of a worsening financial situation and a dramatic decline in economic activity, in 1993 he decided to reorient Belorussian policy toward Russia. Kebich ruled by means of his "power party." He was the actual head of state and a favorite in the presidential elections of July 1994. Nevertheless, he lost to **Alyaksandr Lukashenka**, who outdid him with demagogic and populist slogans, especially on the theme of combating corruption. After his resignation from the government on 21 July 1994, Kebich was chairman of the Belorussian Trade and Finance Association, and from 1996 he was an MP. (EM)

Sources: *Kto iest kto v Respublike Belarus* (Minsk, 1999); *Bielaruskaiya entsyklapiedyia*, vol. 8 (Minsk, 1999); Jan Zaprudnik, *Belarus: At a Crossroads in History* (Boulder, Colo., 1993); Siergiej Owsiannik and Jelena Striełkowa, *Władza a społeczeństwo: Białoruś 1991–1998* (Warsaw, 1998); David R. Marples, *Belarus: A Denationalized Nation* (Amsterdam, 1999).

KELAM Tunne (10 July 1936, Taheva), Estonian politician. Kelam graduated in history from the University of Tartu in 1959, following which he worked in the Main Historical Archives of the Estonian SSR. In 1965–75 he worked for the Estonian Encyclopedia Press (Eesti Nõukogude Entsüklopeedia) and the Valgus Press. From the end of the 1960s he was active in the human rights movement, and in the early 1970s he organized an independent philosophical seminar. Kelam planned to send a memorandum to the United Nations and its general secretary, Kurt Waldheim, demanding the restitution of Estonian independence based on the 1920 borders. The authors of the memorandum were discovered by the KGB in 1975, and it led to several arrests. Kelam avoided imprisonment but was fired from his job, and in 1980–88 he worked on a state farm (sovkhoz) in Ranna.

In January 1988 Kelam co-founded the Estonian National Independence Party (Eesti Rahvusliku Sõltumatuse Partei [ERSP]), whose program included demands for wider autonomy and, later, the restitution of Estonian independence. The party recognized the Estonian SSR as a product of Soviet occupation and acknowledged Estonian citizenship only for those who had had it in 1940, as well as their descendants. The ERSP did not admit Communist Party members. The ERSP demanded a stop to the immigration that was aimed at the Russification of Estonia, an explanation of the "blank spots" in recent history, and an improvement in the quality of the natural environment. Because of his criticism of the Popular Front of Estonia, which supported perestroika, Kelam was perceived at home and abroad as a "rightist extremist." Nevertheless, his efforts to create civic committees as alternative administrative structures and the registration of people entitled to Estonian citizenship according to the above-mentioned criterion, which started in February 1989, ended in success. In February 1990 the pro-independence parties held elections to the Estonian Congress, which was meant as an alternative to the Supreme Council of the Estonian SSR. Kelam became the chairman of the congress but entered into a complicated game, recognizing the Supreme Council as a provisional authority acting under the congress' supervision until the complete restitution of independence. Kelam deemed the steps taken by the Supreme Council chairman, **Arnold Rüütel**, and Prime Minister **Edgar Savisaar** as too conciliatory to the Kremlin, so he tried to remove them from power but failed. He then returned to the idea of cooperation with the Supreme Council; after the failure of the Moscow putsch in August 1991, both bodies delegated their representatives to the Constituent Assembly (Põhiseaduse Assamblee).

Kelam and his party were defeated in the first parliamentary elections after Estonia regained independence, in September 1992, gaining only 7 percent of the vote. Fragmentation in the parliament allowed Kelam to win the position of deputy speaker. In the government of **Mart Laar** the ERSP won four ministerial portfolios. Later the anti-Communist rhetoric of the ERSP softened, and after the resignation of its defense minister the party faced a crisis. Some of its activists vetoed the election of Kelam as chairman, accusing him of a departure from the original program—for instance, by his giving up de-Communization and tolerating non-citizens in high administrative positions and in the police in particular. Before the elections of 1995 Kelam entered into a coalition with the Pro Patria Union (Isamaaliit) of Laar, but the coalition won only 8 percent of the vote. As a result, Kelam resigned as the ERSP leader. He retained only the position of deputy speaker of parliament. In 1996 he ran in the presidential elections but lost. (AG)

Sources: *Eesti entsüklopeedia*, vol. 14 (Tallinn, 2000); Rein Taagepera, *Estonia: Return to Independence* (Boulder, Colo., 1993); *Eastern Europe and the Commonwealth of Independent States, 1999* (London, 1999); republika.pl/darski1/kraje/estonia/chronb.htm; www.riigikogu.ee/parliament.html.

KËLCYRA Ali bey [originally Klisura Ali] (28 May 1891, Këlcyrë–24 September 1963, Rome), Albanian politician and lawyer. Këlcyra studied in Istanbul and earned a Ph.D. in law in Rome in 1919. In May 1920 he was one of the organizers of an action that aimed at pushing the Italians out of the Tepelene area. He served as an MP from 1921 to 1924. A gifted speaker who often resorted to demagogy, he was considered an opponent of aristocratic rule and a supporter of democratization. Këlcyra belonged to a group that initiated the revolution of 1924. After the failure of the revolution, he left Albania and co-founded the National Union (Bashkimi Kombëtar). At that time, he mainly lived in Paris. Këlcyra returned to Albania in the 1930s. He belonged to a group of politicians with whom the Italians conducted exploratory talks before their 1939 aggression. In November 1942 Këlcyra was one of the founders of the National Front (Balli Kombëtar), an underground organization that was in competition with the Communist National Liberation Front. Këlcyra's reputation suffered as a result of his involvement with the Albanian administration, which collaborated with the Italians, and also because he had signed an agreement with General Lorenzo Dalmazzo, commander of the Italian Ninth Army (the so-called Dalmazzo-Këlcyra agreement) that was a kind of non-aggression pact that gave the Italians a free hand in operations against the Communists in the southern part of the country. (Some historians deny the existence of this agreement.) On 23 October 1944 Këlcyra was evacuated on a fishing boat from Shkodër to Brindisi. In exile, he was active in the revived National Front. In 1950 he brought about a crisis in this organization, and he was accused by some of its leaders of crypto-communism. The splinter groups established the Albanian Democratic Union. In 1953 Këlcyra became a member of the Radio Free Europe Committee, and he worked in the Albanian section. (TC)

Sources: *Biographisches Lexikon*, vol. 2; Ekrem Bey Vlora, *Lebenserinnerungen*, vols. 1–2 (Munich, 1968–73); Wiliam Bland and Ian Price, *A Tangled Web: A History of Anglo-American Relations with Albania (1912–1955)* (London, 1986); Michael Schmidt-Neke, *Enstehung und Ausbau der Konigsdiktatur in Albanien (1912–1939), Regierungsbildungen, Herrschaftsweisen und Machteliten in Einen Jungen Balkanstaat* (Munich, 1987); Sejfi Vllamasi, *Ballafaqime politike në Shqipëri (1897–1942)* (Tirana, 1995).

KELMENDI Ali (3 November 1900, Pejë [Peć]–11 February 1939, Paris), Albanian Communist activist. Born into the family of an agricultural worker, Kelmendi attended an Albanian school in Pejë. In 1920 he joined a Socialist group that was active in Pejë. After the elections to the parliament of the Kingdom of Serbs, Croats, and Slovenes, in which he failed to obtain a seat, in July 1921 Kelmendi illegally crossed the border and arrived in Shkodër. In 1922 he was one of the co-organizers of the radical youth union called Bashkimi (Union), and he served as commander of the gendarmerie headquarters in Krumë. Kelmendi became politically involved in the support of **Fan Noli** and **Bajram Curri**. During the revolution of 1924 he fought against the local gendarmerie commander, who did not subordinate himself to the revolutionary government. After the collapse of the revolution Kelmendi went to Bari and from there a few months later to Vienna, where he joined a leftist organization, the National Revolutionary Committee (Komiteti Nacional Revolucionar [KONARE]). In June 1925 he arrived in Pejë to acquaint himself with the situation of the

Albanians in Kosovo, but because he was kept under police surveillance, after a few months he returned to Vienna. In October 1925 the KONARE leadership selected Kelmendi as one of the fourteen activists who went for training to the USSR, where, in the "villa of Prince Yusupov" and in other places in Leningrad, they underwent special training. Trained in border control, under the name of "Rezinov" Kelmendi served as a trainee in Odessa and then worked as a blue-collar laborer in Leningrad, where he simultaneously continued his education at a Comintern school.

As a Comintern envoy, Kelmendi returned to Albania in 1930. He set off to establish the first Albanian Communist group. Despite persistent agitation in Tirana, Elbasa, Kruji, and Vlorë, he failed to unite several fractious groups into one uniform party. In 1932–35 Kelmendi was arrested and imprisoned several times. Released, he went to Turkey to establish cooperation with the local Communist activists. In June 1936 he illegally arrived in Albania for the last time, but after three days he was arrested and expelled without the right to return. After a short stay in Paris, Kelmendi returned to Moscow and worked for a few months in the Balkan section of the Comintern. Because of the ongoing war in Spain, he was sent to France, where he established recruitment centers and tried to convince the Albanians who lived in France to fight on the side of the Spanish republican government. Under the pseudonym "Çuni," he also wrote articles for the leftist press. Suffering from tuberculosis, Kelmendi died as a result of complications after a lung operation. The view promoted by Communist propaganda—that is, that Kelmendi met **Enver Hoxha** in Albania and recognized Hoxha as his successor—remains unconfirmed. (TC)

Sources: *Biographisches Lexikon*, vol. 2; *Fjalor Enciklopedik Shqiptar* (Tirana, 1985); *Ali Kelmendi: Militant i shquar i levizjes komuniste shqiptarë* (Tirana, 1960); Kersta Aleksić, *Ali Kelmendi* (Prishtina, 1970); Reginald Hibbert, *Albania's National Liberation Struggle: The Bitter Victory* (London and New York, 1991).

KEMALI Ismail Vlorë bey (16 January 1844, Valona [Vlorë]–24 January 1919, Perugia), head of the first government of Albania. A descendant of a powerful Albanian family and the grandson of one of the leaders of the 1829 insurrection, Kemali was the son of Mahmud bey Vlorë. He graduated from Zosima Gymnasium in Ioánnina, where he mastered French, Greek, Turkish, and Italian. He later studied law and worked in the Turkish administration in northern Greece and Bulgaria thanks to the support of his uncle, Midhat Pasha, governor of the Danube *vilayet* (province). In 1869 Kemali became *sanjak-bey* (bey of the district) of Southern Dobruja and head of the international Danubian commission. At that time he traveled to France,

England, and Italy, becoming acquainted with the European political elite. After Murad V ascended the throne in 1876, Midhat Pasha planned to establish a united Albanian *vilayet* with Kemali as governor. However, Midhat Pasha fell into disfavor, and the plan was abandoned. In 1884 Kemali became *sanjak-bey* of Bolu, and in 1890 he was appointed the governor of Beirut. In his activities and writings at that time, he showed pro-British sympathies and a dislike of the Central Powers. At that time he founded the periodical *Mecrayi Efkâr*, which was devoted to the reform of the Ottoman Empire.

Seeing that hopes for autonomy of the united Albanian territories within the Ottoman Empire were unrealistic, in 1900 Kemali gave up work in the administration but continued as leader of the Albanian faction in the Turkish parliament. Over the following years he maintained intensive contacts with Greek and British authorities. In 1902 he attended the Young Turk Congress in Paris. Under the threat of an Albanian armed rebellion, in July 1908 Sultan Abdülhamid granted a constitution to Albania. When the Young Turks overthrew the sultan, this decision was annulled, as a result of which the public mood in the country worsened. Kemali entered the new parliament, where he was a member of the opposition. In April 1909 he took part in an unsuccessful coup attempt against the Young Turks; consequently he had to flee to Athens. After reaching a compromise with the government, he returned to Istanbul, where he founded Ahrar, a liberal party that called for the decentralization of the empire and its component parts, including Albania.

The dissolution of the parliament in Istanbul in January 1912 and the brutality of the police in the territories inhabited by the Albanians led to an Albanian insurrection in the mountains of Gjakova under the leadership of **Hasan Prishtina** (April 1912). However, the other Balkan states did not want a united Albania and felt threatened after the insurgents captured Skopje and marched on Salonika. In the First Balkan War, Turkey surrendered to Serbia and Greece, whose troops invaded Albanian territories from the south and north. The only option left for the Albanians was full independence. Kemali traveled to Budapest and Vienna, promoting this idea. He realized that because the Entente favored Greece and Serbia, only Austria-Hungary might support this idea and that it was necessary to create *faits accomplis*. On 28 November 1912 the Albanian National Assembly met in Vlorë. During the assembly, eighty-three delegates proclaimed the creation of an independent Albanian state and declared its neutrality in the ongoing conflict. Kemali gave the main speech and became head of the provisional Albanian government.

The situation of this government was very difficult because it controlled only a small part of the Albanian-inhabited territory, which the Greeks and Serbs wanted to divide between themselves, while Durrës and Tirana were governed by **Essad Pasha Toptani**, who wanted to become the governor of Albania. The Great Powers supported a united Albania under Turkish supremacy. In April 1913 Kemali unsuccessfully attempted to gain support in Rome, Vienna, Paris, and London, but the decisions made at a London conference of the Great Powers in July 1913 were unfavorable for him. The Great Powers did not recognize his government. Albania gained the status of an autonomous state under international control with a territory reduced so much that half of the Albanian-speaking population was left outside its borders. The lost territories included northern Macedonia and Kosovo, which were given to Serbia, and southern Macedonia, which was given to Greece. Essad Pasha recognized Kemali's government, becoming its minister of interior. However, he soon started a rebellion against Kemali. When in January 1914 Essad's supporters threatened Vlorë, Kemali dissolved his powerless government, left the city, and went to Nicaea (Iznik). Meanwhile, the Great Powers agreed on the candidacy of **Wilhelm von Wied** as Prince of Albania. Thereafter, Kemali did not play any major political role. In 1918–19 he dictated his memoirs, which were published in 1921 as *The Memoirs of Ismail Kemali Bey*. (WR)

Sources: *Biographisches Lexikon*, vol. 4; Adalbert Gottfried, *Das Problem der Albanischen Unabhängigkeit in den Jahren 1908–1914* (Vienna, 1970); John Swire, *Albania: The Rise of a Kingdom* (New York, 1971); Stefanaq Pollo and Arben Puto, *The History of Albania from Its Origins to the Present Day* (London, 1981); Jerzy Hauziński and Jan Leśny, *Historia Albanii* (Wrocław, 1992); Miranda Vickers, *The Albanians: A Modern History* (London, 1995).

ĶENIŅŠ Atis (28 July 1874, Grenču, Courland–9 March 1961, Riga), Latvian poet and politician. Born into the family of a servant, Ķeniņš finished a teacher training college in Irlava in 1894 and subsequently worked as a teacher in Courland (Jelgava and Līvbērze). At that time he began writing poems. He also translated stage plays. Between 1897 and 1900 he worked as the director of a rural school. In 1900 he settled in Riga, where he founded a private school of commerce in 1904, transformed into a *Realgymnasium* (science-oriented high school) for boys in 1907. Ķeniņš took part in the 1905 revolution, and later emigrated to Finland. During World War I he was active in Latvian charity and social organizations in Moscow. In 1918 he graduated in law from Moscow University. He was one of the founders of the Latvian National Democratic Party. At the end of 1918 Ķeniņš returned to Latvia, and as a member of the Latvian Provisional National Council, he took part in the proclamation of Latvia's independence. In

November 1919 he was appointed head of the diplomatic mission in Poland. Because of his firm position on some of the contentious issues, he was in disfavor with the Polish authorities. Recalled de facto in December 1920 and formally in April 1921, he worked as a lawyer in Riga. From 1931 to 1933 he served as minister of education and justice. After the Soviet invasion, in July 1940 he attempted to prepare and put forward an alternative list for the parliamentary "elections" held under the control of USSR representatives. Arrested in 1941, Ķeniņš was deported to Kazakhstan, where he worked as a teacher. After the war he returned to Latvia and started working at a college, but in 1951 he was again deported to Kazakhstan. Allowed to return in 1955, he lived in Riga until the end of his life. (EJ)

Sources: *Latvijas darbinieku galerija* (Riga, 1928); Jēkabs Līgotņu, "Gara cīnītāja un dzejnieka Ata Ķeniņa 60 gadu šūpļa svētkos," *Piesaule*, 1934, no. 7; *Latvijas vadošie darbinieki* (Riga, 1935); *Es viņu pazīstu* (Riga, 1939); *Ķeniņš A. Mājup: Dzeja un piemiņa* (Riga, 1999).

KĘPA Józef (18 May 1928, Rzeczyca, near Rawa Mazowiecka), Polish Communist activist. From August 1945 Kępa was active in the (Communist) Union of Youth Struggle in Łódź. In 1950–54 he worked in the administration of the (Communist) Polish Youth Union. From 1954 to 1958 he was an assistant in the Institute of Social Sciences of the Central Committee (CC) of the Polish United Workers' Party (PUWP). In 1958 he graduated in history from this school, and then he worked at various posts in the PUWP apparatus. In 1959–60 Kępa was secretary of the PUWP Warsaw-Mokotów Quarter Committee; from 1960 to 1961 he headed the Department of Education and Science of the PUWP Warsaw Committee, and from 1961 he was its secretary. From December 1967 to December 1976 he was first secretary of the PUWP Warsaw Committee. From 1966 he was identified as a member of the **Mieczysław Moczar** faction. At a session of the Warsaw PUWP activists on 11 March 1968 Kępa called for a struggle against "revisionism," "cosmopolitanism," and "Zionism." He was one of the main engineers of the party's anti-Semitic campaign, which led to the firing of hundreds of people from their jobs. They were then deprived of Polish citizenship and forced to emigrate. At the Fifth PUWP Congress in November 1968 Kępa became a member of its CC. Despite a political counteroffensive by **Władysław Gomułka**, in 1968–70 Kępa strengthened his position in the party. In December 1970 he became a deputy member, and in December 1975 a member, of the party Politburo. He continued in this capacity until the Eighth PUWP Congress in February 1980. After the

June 1976 workers' riots Kępa opposed **Edward Gierek**. At closed meetings of the party leadership he criticized Gierek's economic and social policy from a dogmatic point of view, Gierek's domestic policy (in Kępa's view it was too liberal), and the opening to the West. In particular Kępa advocated a repressive policy toward the democratic opposition. From December 1976 to February 1979 Kępa was deputy prime minister, and from February 1979 to July 1981 he was minister of administration, local economy, and environmental protection. In 1969–80 he was an MP. Paradoxically he was dismissed along with the Gierek team in 1980. After the introduction of martial law in December 1981 Kępa tried to return to the party leadership, but in vain. (WD)

Sources: Mołdawa; Andrzej Albert [Wojciech Roszkowski], *Najnowsza historia Polski 1918–1980*, vol. 2 (Warsaw 1995); Jerzy Eisler, *Marzec 1968* (Warsaw, 1991); Krzysztof Lesiakowski, *Mieczysław Moczar "Mietek": Biografia polityczna* (Warsaw, 1998); Włodzimierz Janowski and Aleksander Kochański, *Informator o strukturze i obsadzie personalnej centralnego aparatu PZPR 1948–1990* (Warsaw, 2000); Jerzy Eisler, *Grudzień 1970* (Warsaw, 2000).

KERESZTES-FISCHER Ferenc [until 1929 Fischer] (18 February 1881, Pécs–3 March 1948, Vöcklabruck, Austria), Hungarian politician. After graduating and receiving a Ph.D. in administration from the Department of Law of the University of Budapest, Keresztes-Fischer worked as a lawyer in Pécs and was a legal counselor of the local savings bank. During World War I he served as an officer in the reserves. After the breakup of the Habsburg monarchy, in October 1918 Keresztes-Fischer returned to Pécs, where he was temporarily arrested by the Serb authorities. After their withdrawal and after the stabilization of the regency system, from October 1921 he was governor of Baranya Province and of the city of Pécs and from December 1925 also of Somogy Province. From August 1931 he was minister of interior in the governments of **Gyula Károlyi** and **Gyula Gömbös**. He reorganized the ministry, modernizing its operations. In January 1935 he left he government in protest against the radical rightist policies of Gömbös. In consequence, following **István Bethlen**, he also left the ruling Unity Party, on behalf of which he had been MP from 1932. From January 1936 to May 1938 Keresztes-Fischer chaired the Center of Financial Institutions, and in 1936–39 he was a senator. From May 1938 to March 1944 he was minister of interior again. In 1939–44 he was an MP on behalf of the ruling party. He strongly criticized both extreme movements—the (Fascist) Arrow Cross and the Communist Party—and suppressed their activities by means of the political police. (After September 1939 the Ministry of Interior included a special Tenth Department for the problems of war refugees, including the Poles, whose head was **József Antall**.) After the resignation of **László Bárdossy**, from 7 to 9 March 1942 Keresztes-Fischer was acting prime minister. He belonged to the pro-English group of Bethlen and Prime Minister **Miklós Kállay**. In August 1943 he joined the inner circle of advisers of Regent **Miklós Horthy**. After the German occupation of Hungary in March 1944, Keresztes-Fischer was arrested by the Gestapo and sent to a concentration camp in Germany. One of the streets in Warsaw, Poland, was named after him to commemorate his assistance to the Polish wartime refugees. (JT)

Sources: *Magyar Életrajzi Lexikon*, vol. 1 (Budapest, 1967); *Magyar Nagylexikon*, vol. 10 (Budapest, 2000); Artúr Benisch, *Vármegyei határkigazítások: Keresztes-Fischer Ferenc* (Budapest, 1938); John F. Montgomery, *Hungary: The Unwilling Satellite* (New York, 1947); Paul Ignotus, *Hungary* (London, 1972).

KERTÉSZ Imre (9 November 1929, Budapest), Hungarian writer. Because of his Jewish descent, in 1944 Kertész was sent to the German nazi concentration camp in Auschwitz and then to Buchenwald. After World War II he returned to Hungary, where, after graduating from high school (1948), he worked as a journalist until 1951 and then in the Press Department of the Ministry of Metallurgy and Industrial Machinery and as a blue-collar laborer. From 1953 Kertész made his living by writing and translating. The main topic of his works is the Holocaust. From the notes that he took in the 1950s, in 1960–73 Kertész wrote the novel *Sorstalanság* (1975; *Fateless*, 1992), an autobiographical story of a boy in a concentration camp who describes the horrible reality in simple words. Kertész's subsequent novels—*A kudarc* (Failure; 1988) and *Kaddis a meg nem született gyermekkért* (1990; *Kaddish for a Child Not Born*, 1997)—completed a trilogy of the "fateless people," full of original reflections on an individual's fate, totalitarianism, and references to the twentieth-century history of Central Europe. In 1992 Kertész's *Gályanapló* (Galley diary), a diary in fictional form, was published, covering the years 1961–1991. Kertész also wrote several short stories and essays, such as *A holokauszt mint kultúra* (Holocaust as culture; 1993), and he translated the works of many German philosophers and writers. Kertész received many Hungarian awards, including the Kossuth State Award (1997), and in 2002 he was the first Hungarian to receive the Nobel Prize for Literature. (MS)

Sources: *Wielka encyklopedia PWN*, vol. 13 (Warsaw, 2003); *Új magyar irodalmi lexikon* (Budapest, 2000); György Spiró, "Non habent sua fata: A Sorstalanság-újraolvasva," *Élet és Irodalom*, 1983, no. 30; http://culturelover.com/imrekertesz.html.

KÉTHLY Anna (16 November 1889, Budapest–7 September, 1976 Blankenberge, Belgium), Hungarian politician. Born into a large working-class family, Kéthly began working as a young girl to earn money for her education. After becoming a qualified typist and bookkeeper, from 1907 she worked as a clerk. In 1913 she joined the trade union of private clerks, serving as its vice-president from 1920 on, secretary general from 1939 to March 1944, and honorary president from 1945 on. In 1917 Kéthly joined the Hungarian Social Democratic Party (Magyarországi Szociáldemokrata Párt [HSDP]). In December 1919 she was elected a member of the HSDP Central Women's Organizational Committee and soon afterwards was appointed its secretary. In 1920 Kéthly became a contributor to the periodical *Nómunkás*, and in 1926–38 she worked as its editor and publisher. Kéthly was the second woman in Hungarian history to serve as a member of parliament (1922–39), and for a long time she was the only female MP. Elected as a member of the leadership of the HSDP in 1922, between 1943 and 1944 she conducted talks with politicians of other orientations on the possibility of Hungary's withdrawal from the war. When Germany occupied Hungary, she joined the underground resistance movement in March 1944.

After the end of World War II, Kéthly became a member of the HSDP Political Bureau. A member of parliament between April 1945 and April 1948, she served as head of the HSDP parliamentary representation and as deputy speaker of the parliament from November 1945 to February 1948. In the party, she was responsible for foreign relations and for women's issues. Although she was a proponent of a moderate line, she firmly called for the independence of the HSDP and was against the "unification" of the Hungarian Communist Party and the HSDP under Communist leadership. In February 1948, on the initiative of a group that supported the Communists, Kéthly was expelled from the party leadership, and at a party congress in March she was expelled from the party. Deprived of her parliamentary seat, she was held under house arrest for two years. Arrested in June 1950, she was sentenced to life imprisonment for "espionage" and "anti-state activities" in January 1954. Pardoned under international pressure in November 1954, she was kept under constant police surveillance.

In April 1956 Kéthly refused to ask for a new trial and to take up a position in the Patriotic People's Front. After the outbreak of the 1956 revolution, she was one of the initiators of the reorganization of the HSDP, and on 31 October she was elected as party president. On 1 November she went to a congress of the Socialist International in Vienna. The following day, in her absence, the government of **Imre Nagy** delegated her to the UN General Assembly, and on 3 November she was appointed minister of state in

Nagy's coalition government. Because of the second Soviet intervention, Kéthly could not return to Budapest; therefore she flew to New York to attend the UN General Assembly session on the situation in Hungary. In January 1957 she was elected president of the Hungarian Revolutionary Council, which was established at that time in Strasbourg and which consisted of representatives of the democratic parties that had taken part in the revolution and other prominent people who had been forced to emigrate. Kéthly settled in Brussels. From 1957 to December 1963 she was the editor-in-chief of the newspaper *Népszava*, which was published in London, and from 1970 to 1973 she worked as an editor of the periodical *Szociáldemokrata Szemle*. Kéthly was the Hungarian representative in the International Confederation of Free Trade Unions, a member of the HSDP leadership in exile (in 1958 becoming president of the HSDP), and a member of the Socialist International. In 1962, in her absence, the Supreme Court in Budapest quashed the sentence Kéthly had been given in the trial of 1954 but simultaneously sentenced her to four years' imprisonment for "anti-state" activities during the 1956 events. In October 1990 Kéthly's ashes were brought to Hungary and buried in a Budapest cemetery, in the same section as the remains of the participants of the 1956 revolution who had been convicted or executed. In 1994 the Supreme Court fully rehabilitated Kéthly and quashed the sentence she had received in the trial of 1962. (JT)

Sources: *Nagy Képes Milleniumi Arcképcsarnok* (Budapest, 1999); *Magyar Nagylexikon*, vol. 10 (Budapest, 2000); *Magyarország 1944–1956*, CD-ROM (Budapest, 2001); Méray Tibor, *Thirteen Days That Shook the Kremlin* (New York, 1959); Bennet Kovrig, *Communism in Hungary from Kun to Kadar* (Stanford, 1979); Hans-Detlev Grothusen, ed., *Ungarn* (Göttingen, 1987); György Litván, ed., *Rewolucja węgierska 1956 roku* (Warsaw, 1996).

KHADYKA Yuriy (23 June 1938, Minsk), Belorussian scholar and politician. Khadyka graduated in physics from the Belorussian State University in 1960, and then he worked in the Institute of Physics of the Belorussian Academy of Sciences (BAS). He went through all the levels of the professorial career, from assistant to full professor. He was head of a laboratory dealing with space early-warning systems aimed at the prevention of rocket attacks. He also headed a section of the Soviet Academy of Sciences, developing optical and electronic intelligence devices. At the end of the 1960s Khadyka created a Belorussian art seminar attached to the BAS. Ten years later, along with his aides, he established the Museum of Old Belorussian Art. He authored about 150 publications in physics and about 30 in the history of old Belorussian art. In 1988 Khadyka joined the democratic movement. In 1989 he was elected deputy chairman of the Belorussian National

Front (BNF), and after **Zyanon Paznyak** emigrated, he became the BNF's chief spokesman. After the takeover of power by **Alyaksandr Lukashenka**, Khadyka was arrested several times (for instance, in 1996) for taking part in opposition demonstrations. (EM)

Sources: A. Ulitsyonak, *Inshadumtsy* (Minsk, 1991); Jan Zaprudnik, *Historical Dictionary of Belarus* (Lanham, Md., 1998); *Kto jest kim na Białorusi* (Białystok, 2000).

KHIRA Oleksandr (17 January 1897, Vilkhivtsi, Subcarpathian Ruthenia–26 May 1983, Karaganda, Kazakhstan), bishop of the underground Ukrainian Greek Catholic Church in the USSR. Khira studied theology at the seminary in Uzhhorod (Užhorod) but completed his studies in Budapest in 1920. From 1924 he worked as a lecturer in canon law, in the history of the church, and in moral and pastoral theology at Uzhhorod Seminary. He also founded the Subcarpathian movement of the Apostolate of Suffering. Appointed papal chamberlain in 1934, Khira made missionary visits to the Ukrainian communities in France and Belgium. In 1934 he became rector of Uzhhorod Seminary, but in March 1939 he was dismissed from his post after Subcarpathia was incorporated into Hungary. In 1943 he was appointed prelate and in 1944 vicar general of the Mukachevo eparchy. Secretly consecrated by Bishop **Theodore Romzha** in 1945, Khira avoided the first wave of arrests of the Uniate hierarchy after Subcarpathia was incorporated into the Ukrainian SSR, but on 10 February 1949 he was imprisoned by Soviet security functionaries and was sentenced in Kiev to twenty-five years of labor camp. He was held in camps near Irkutsk, Kemerovo, and Omsk and had to work in coal mines (among other places). Released and rehabilitated on 6 September 1956, Khira returned to his native village, where he resumed his duties as priest and bishop of Mukachevo. On 17 January 1957 Khira was deported to forced labor in Kazakhstan. After many years of carrying on his pastoral work secretly, in 1978 he managed to obtain permission to officially conduct Catholic activities. He was deeply committed to his work; as a result of his efforts, for example, a church was built in Karaganda. (WR)

Sources: "Smert vladyky movchaznoy Tserkvy," *Ukraiinski Vistii* (Edmonton), 10 August 1983; *Martirologia ukraiinskikh tserkov u chetyriokh tomakh*, vol. 2 (Toronto, 1985); *Encyclopedia of Ukraine*, vol. 2 (Toronto, 1988); Bohdan R. Bociurkiw, *The Ukrainian Greek-Catholic Church and the Soviet State (1939–1950)* (Edmonton, 1996).

KHMARA Stepan (12 October 1937, Bobyatyn, near Sokal), Ukrainian dissident and politician. The son of a peasant, Khmara initially worked as a driver, first in the

Ukraine, and then in Kazakhstan (1955–59). In 1964 he graduated in dentistry in Lviv, and he worked as a dentist in Girnik, near Sokal. Engaged in the distribution of uncensored samizdat publications, after the arrest of **Vyacheslav Chornovil**, the editor-in-chief of *Ukraiinskyi visnyk*, in 1972 Khmara managed to publish another issue of the periodical, which included, among other things, his own article (signed "Maksym Sahaydak"), "Etnotsyd Ukraiintsiv v SSSR" (The ethnocide of Ukrainians in the USSR). Despite police surveillance and terror, in 1975 Khmara prepared another issue, in which he published the article "Holos iz pekla" (A voice from hell), criticizing Western policies toward the Soviet Union. Arrested on 31 March 1980, in December of that year Khmara was sentenced to seven years of labor camp, five years of forced settlement, and the confiscation of property. He spent his prison years in the Perm camps. Since he continued to demand respect for human rights, he spent almost a year in a dark cell. Against his will, in February 1987 he was pardoned.

In 1988–89 Khmara was still frequently arrested for short periods of time. In July 1988 he joined the Executive Committee of the Ukrainian Helsinki Group (UHG), and he took part in a meeting in Lviv of national and democratic representatives of the Soviet nations. From May to October 1989, as a member of the Committee for the Defense of the Ukrainian Greek Catholic Church, Khmara organized a hunger strike in Moscow, demanding the legalization of this church. Elected to the Ukrainian Supreme Council in 1990, he demanded a declaration of state sovereignty for the Ukraine. He took part in a student strike in Kiev in October 1990, supporting the students with a thirteen-day hunger strike. Provoked by a militia colonel, Khmara was accused of assault and deprived of immunity by a Communist majority of the Supreme Council. After his arrest in December 1990, he went on hunger strikes twice. Signatures appealing for his release were gathered in neighboring countries. Released under the pressure of democratic forces, Khmara became deputy chairman of the Ukrainian Republican Party (UPR, successor of the UHG). In May and June 1992 he led a group of his followers out of the UPR and founded the Ukrainian Conservative Republican Party (Ukraiinska Konservatyvna Respublikanska Partiya). Reelected to the Supreme Council in 1994, Khmara demanded the confiscation of Communist Party property, as well as the de-Communization of the administration and judiciary. Khmara's program includes element of populism, anti-Semitism, zealous anti-communism, and Russophobia. (TS)

Sources: *Encyclopedia of Ukraine*, vol. 2 (Toronto, 1988); Zakordonne Predstavnytstwo Ukraiinskoii Helsinskoii Hrupy, *Visnyk represiy v Ukraini* (New York, 1980–84); Heorhij Kasyanov, *Nezhodni: Ukraiinska intelihentsiya v rusi oporu 1960–80 rokiv*

(Kiev, 1995); Anatoliy Rusnachenko, *Natsionalno-vyzvolnyi rukh v Ukraiini* (Kiev, 1998); Bohdan Nahaylo, *The Ukrainian Resurgence* (Toronto, 1999).

KHOMYSHYN Hryhoriy (25 March 1867, Hadynkivtsi, near Tarnopol [Ternopil]–28 December 1945, Kiev), Greek Catholic bishop, martyr for the faith. After graduating from a seminary, in November 1893 Khomyshyn was ordained a priest. He continued his studies in Vienna, graduating in 1899. In 1902 he was appointed rector of the Lwów (Lviv) seminary, and in 1904, bishop of Stanisławów (now Ivano-Frankivsk). During the Russian occupation of Eastern Galicia, between September 1914 and June 1915 Khomyshyn remained in Vienna. As an advocate of bringing the Greek rite closer to the Latin rite, in 1916 he unsuccessfully attempted to introduce the Gregorian calendar, which caused protests from the clergy of the diocese. Despite his sympathy for the Ukrainian pro-independence movement, along with Archbishop **Andrey Sheptytsky** Khomyshyn opposed the priority of politics in pastoral work. Khomyshyn was known as an energetic organizer of social and charity work. He also cared for callings to the priesthood. In 1921 he introduced the requirement of celibacy of priests and founded the Saint Josaphat Society of Unmarried Priests. In the 1930s he opposed the politicization of priests and was against radical nationalism, as well as communism. He sympathized with the moderate Catholic national movement. In the autumn of 1939 Khomyshyn was temporarily arrested by the NKVD but was soon released. In June 1941, before its withdrawal from Stanisławów, the NKVD attempted to poison him. During the German occupation Khomyshyn maintained political neutrality. After the invasion of the Red Army, in October 1944 he signed a pastoral letter condemning fratricidal fighting and urging an end to violence and bloodshed. Arrested again on 11 April 1945 by the NKVD, Khomyshyn was transported to a prison in Lviv and then to Lukianivka Prison in Kiev. Despite his advanced age, he was subjected to a brutal interrogation, as a result of which he died. On 27 June 2001 Pope John Paul II beatified Khomyshyn at a solemn Holy Mass in Lviv. (WR)

Sources: *Encyclopedia of Ukraine*, vol. 1 (Toronto, 1984); Bohdan R. Bociurkiw, *The Ukrainian Greek-Catholic Church and the Soviet State (1939–1950)* (Edmonton, 1996); Bohdan Vivchar, "Povernenia," *Tserkovni visnyk* (Chicago), 17 March 1996; *Osservatore Romano* (weekly edition in English), 2001, nos. 25 and 27.

KHRUSHCHEV Nikita (17 April 1894, Kalinovka, Kursk Province–11 September, 1971 Moscow), Soviet leader and head of the Communist Party in the Ukraine (1938–49). Khrushchev was born into a poor peasant family and finished a few grades of primary school. In 1909–17 he worked as a miner in the Donetsk region. In 1918 he joined the Bolshevik party, and from 1919 he served in the Red Army. After the termination of the civil war he advanced in the party ranks in the Ukraine thanks to his close links with Stalin. From 1929 he formally studied at the Industrial Academy but was rather involved in the local party committee work. In 1930 he was sent by Stalin to supervise the collectivization of agriculture in the Ukraine, which resulted in the starvation and death of millions of Ukrainians. In 1931 Khrushchev became party secretary in one of the Moscow quarters and in January 1932 second party secretary of the Moscow city party organization. In 1934 he became a member of the Central Committee (CC) of the All-Union Communist Party (Bolsheviks) and then secretary of the Moscow organization of the party. In this capacity he played a key role in the purge that followed the assassination of Sergey Kirov in December 1934.

After a series of bloody purges in the Ukrainian party leadership, in January 1938 Khrushchev was appointed first secretary of the CC of the Communist Party (Bolsheviks) of Ukraine. From 1939 he was also a member of the Politburo of the All-Union party. He was responsible for the introduction of Russian as the language of instruction in Ukrainian schools at all levels, as well as for the last stage of the Great Purge of Nikolay Yezhov. As a result, he was responsible for the deaths of thousands of Ukrainians. After 17 September 1939 Khrushchev supervised the incorporation of the Southeast Borderland of Poland (Eastern Galicia and Volhynia) into the Ukrainian SSR, as well as the arrest and deportation of the inhabitants of this territory, mostly Poles. In the summer of 1940 he supervised a similar takeover in North Bukovina, detached from Romania and incorporated into the Ukrainian SSR. During World War II Khrushchev represented Stalin in various political missions and organized Soviet guerrillas in the Ukraine. After the war he mostly dealt with the reconstruction of the Ukrainian economy and with combating Ukrainian independent guerrillas. He ruthlessly destroyed the kulaks and the national elites of the newly acquired territories. Those who fell victim to his activities were mainly Poles from the Home Army, falsely accused of cooperation with the Third Reich; fighters of the Ukrainian Insurgent Army; and independent artists, such as **Maksym Rylskyi** and **Volodymyr Sosyura**. Khrushchev failed to rapidly reconstruct Ukrainian agriculture. In March 1947 he was recalled from the party position, but he was appointed prime minister of the Ukrainian SSR. In December 1947 he resumed the Ukrainian party leadership and held it until December 1949, when he again became secretary of the All-Union party CC and first secretary of the Moscow committee.

Despite his failures Khrushchev was recognized as an "expert" in agriculture. He advocated the concentration of kolkhozes and the creation of agricultural towns (*agrogorod*). During the Nineteenth Congress in October 1952 Stalin entrusted Khrushchev with the recording of amendments in the party statute; these changed the name of the party to the Communist Party of the Soviet Union (CPSU). After Stalin's death, on 14 March 1953 Khrushchev became CC secretary, and after Lavrenty Beria was removed from the ruling *troika* in June and executed in December 1953, Khrushchev joined the collective leadership of the party in his place. In September 1953 he became first secretary of the CPSU CC. In January 1955 he removed Georgy Malenkov from the position of prime minister, and it was taken over by Khrushchev's protégé, Nikolay Bulganin. In an attempt to win over the party apparatus, at the end of the Twentieth Congress of the CPSU in February 1956, Khrushchev made the famous "secret speech," in which he condemned the "personality cult" of Stalin and physical liquidation as a method of personnel changes. When his opponents joined hands and tried to remove him, in June 1957 Khrushchev counterattacked, defeating Malenkov, Vyacheslav Molotov, and **Lazar Kaganovich**. In March 1958 he removed Bulganin and took over the position of prime minister of the USSR.

In foreign policy Khrushchev continued imperial policies, stressing either "international détente" (1954–55) or contradictions between "socialism" and "capitalism." He eased Soviet–Yugoslav relations, and in May 1955 he came in a mission of reconciliation to Belgrade. In October 1956 he accepted **Władysław Gomułka** as the new Polish party leader, but he almost immediately ordered a brutal intervention in Hungary, where the situation had slipped out of the hands of the Communist leadership. From early 1957 he carried out a successful global offensive, consolidating the Soviet bloc and gaining new footholds in the Third World. This was made possible by huge armaments spending and by the successes of Soviet technology, such as the launch of the first intercontinental ballistic missile and the first satellite in 1957. In the late 1950s Khrushchev introduced a school reform consisting in the removal of local languages from the basic curricula. He openly argued that instruction in these languages was not necessary from the point of view of science and technology. After a temporary "thaw" in 1962 Khrushchev strengthened the reins of censorship, especially in Ukraine. Those who fell victim to his hostility to "formalism" and "modernism" were, among others, representatives of the generation of the 1960s (*shestidesiatniky*), such as **Ivan Dziuba**, **Yevhen Sverstiuk**, and **Ivan Svitlychnyi**.

At the turn of the 1960s Khrushchev's policies led to

a new split in the world Communist movement, this time between the CPSU and the Chinese party. In 1958 and 1961 he demanded the withdrawal of Western powers from West Berlin, while he included East Berlin in the Communist-controlled German Democratic Republic. This led the world to the edge of nuclear war, just as did Khrushchev's irresponsible policy in Cuba, where he placed Soviet rockets in October 1962. During the Twenty-second CPSU Congress in October 1961 Khrushchev announced that communism would be realized in the USSR by 1980. He strengthened the reform process within the party and criticized Stalin again, but the new "thaw" was short-lived. Without de-collectivization Khrushchev failed to modernize agriculture. He was consistent only in his anti-religious policies. Inefficiency in the economy and extravagant imperialist steps led to his fall. On 13 October 1964 the Presidium of the CPSU CC deprived him of the position of first secretary and excluded him from all party bodies. Khrushchev retired unharmed. In the 1970s his memoirs, *Khrushchev Remembers* (1970) and *The Last Testament* (1974), were published in the West. At the end of the 1990s his granddaughter was granted American citizenship. (WR)

Sources: *MERSH*, vol. 16; *Encyclopedia of Ukraine*, vol. 2 (Toronto, 1988); Viktor Alexandrov, *Khrushchev of the Ukraine: A Biography* (London, 1957); Horvath G. Paloczi, *Khrushchev: The Making of a Dictator* (Boston, 1960); Hryhory Kostiuk, *Stalinist Rule in the Ukraine* (New York, 1960); *Khrushchev's Crimes in Ukraine* (London, 1962); Wolfgang Leonard, *Nikita Sergejewitsch Chruschtschow: Aufstieg und Fall eines Sowjetführers* (Lucerne, 1965); Edward Crankshaw, *Khrushchev: A Career* (New York, 1966); William Hyland, *The Fall of Khrushchev* (New York, 1968); Roy A. Medvedev, *Khrushchev: The Years in Power* (New York, 1976); David R. Marples, *Stalinism in Ukraine in the 1940s* (London, 1992).

KHUEN-HÉDERVÁRY Károlyi [originally Khuen] (23 May 1849, Gräfenberg–16 February 1918, Budapest), Hungarian politician. Khuen-Héderváry graduated in law from universities in Pressburg (Pozsonyi, Bratislava) and Zagreb, and then he worked in the judiciary of Syrmien Province. In 1874 he adopted the second part of his name in accord with the last will of Count Héder Viczay von Vicza und Hédervár, and he inherited the latter's huge landed estate in Slavonia. In 1875 he was elected to the Hungarian parliament for the first time. In 1883 he was appointed *ban* (governor) of Croatia, where the Magyarization policies of his predecessor, Koloman Tisza, had led to great social tension. Khuen-Héderváry made use of the poor rootedness of Croatian political parties and conflicts between Slavonian Croats and Serbs, he managed to gain the majority for his line in the Croatian Assembly (Sabor), and he legalized his absolutist rule.

As a result he managed to continue a hardly softened Magyarization policy for about twenty years. In the course of the crisis connected with demands for a wider autonomy for the Hungarian Army, from 27 June to 3 November 1903 Khuen-Héderváry was prime minister, and in 1904–5, a "personal royal minister" in the government of **István Tisza**. He again held the position of prime minister from 17 January 1910 to 22 April 1912. In February 1910 Khuen-Héderváry co-founded and then until his death he chaired the (Conservative) National Labor Party (Nemzeti Munkapárt), which won the elections of June 1910, allowing for the continuation of Tisza's policy until World War I. (WR)

Sources: *Biographisches Lexikon*, vol. 2; *Magyar Életrajzi Lexikon*, vol. 1 (Budapest, 1967); Martin Polić, *Ban Dragutin grof Khuen-Héderváry i njegovo doba* (Zagreb, 1901); Robert W. Seton-Watson, *Corruption and Reform in Hungary* (London, 1911); Josip Horvath, *Politička povijest Hrvatska* (Zagreb, 1936); Jerzy Kochanowski, *Węgry* (Warsaw, 1997).

KHVYLOVY Mykola [originally Fitilov] (14 December 1893, Trostianets, Kharkiv Province–13 May 1933, Kharkiv), Ukrainian poet and writer, Communist, symbol of the so-called Executed Renaissance (those representatives of the Ukrainian cultural renaissance that were mostly executed by Stalin). Born into a family of village teachers, Khvylovy completed only five grades of a gymnasium, but thanks to the help of his relatives, he gained a good knowledge of both Ukrainian and world literature. From 1916 to 1917 he fought on the eastern front. Later, he was active in an insurgent movement that was of an anti-hetman, anti-Denikin, and later anti-Petlura character. In 1919 he joined the Communist Party (Bolshevik) of Ukraine (CP[B]U). In 1921 he settled permanently in Kharkiv. Khvylovy began his literary activities around 1913, writing poetry that with his full creative maturity gave way to novels and stories. His poems—which were included in the collections *Molodist* (Youth; 1921), *Dosvitni symfonii* (Symphonies of the dawn; 1922), and *Stari poezii* (Old poetry; 1931)—had features characteristic of symbolism and futurism. Khvylovy was a eulogist of industrialization and urbanization and their historic instrument, the proletariat. It was his prose that won him popularity and critical recognition. His subsequent works—including the collections *Syni etiudy* (Blue études; 1922); *Osin'* (The autumn; 1924); the novel *Ya* (Me; 1924); and the stories "Sanatoriina zona" (The sanatorium zone; 1924) and "Valdshnepy" (Wild ducks; 1925)—show an evolution of topics and means of description. That evolution, consistent with the official Soviet critique, had its political consequences, and the edition of the second part of "Wild Ducks" was confiscated.

From the pathos of the revolution and the expressionistic style of his novels, Khvylovy gradually moved toward a deeper psychological analysis and a more realistic description of the life of the Ukrainian intelligentsia in the post–revolutionary period. His literary career gained a political character, as he became involved in creative societies in the Ukraine and in the so-called literary discussion between 1925 and 1928. In 1923 he co-founded Hart, a group of proletarian writers; along with its equivalent addressed to peasants, Hart was meant to give a mass character to Ukrainian literature. However, in October 1925 Khvylovy founded his own Free Academy of Proletarian Literature (Vaplite). In his struggle for the quality of art, he gained the support of a group of Ukrainian non-Communist writers, the so-called neo-classicals. As a Communist, though, Khvylovy tried to change their literary activities to make them truly proletarian. At the peak period of the struggle within the CPU(B) leadership for the direction of Ukrainization (1925–26), Khvylovy published three series of polemic articles in which he presented his own concepts, formed under the influence of Oswald Spengler, among others. In *Kamo hriadeshy?* (Quo vadis? 1925); *Dumky proty techii* (Thoughts against the stream; 1926); and *Apolohety pysaryzmu* (Apologists of hack writing; 1926), he outlined the contrast between European culture and the provincialism of Ukrainian culture, which was expressed in the symbolic formula of a society called Prosvita (Education).

The idea of increasing the cultural distance between Ukraine and Russia (expressed in the famous slogan *Het' vid Moskvy* [Out of Moscow]) and seeking rapprochement with Europe led Khvylovy to emphasize the political independence of Ukraine. That concept also included the idea of an "Asian Renaissance" in which Ukraine would play a special role. Struggling against the manifestations of Russian imperialism, Khvylovy saw the exhaustion of the "cultural-historical cycle" in Western Europe. Therefore, he thought that the revolutionary nations of Eastern Europe and the nations of Asia might give Western Europe a renewed spirit. Ukrainian literature, as a promoter of the new literary style, the "romanticism of vitalism," was to be in the avant garde of that process. The last of Khvylovy's polemic works, *Ukraina chy Malorosiia?* (Ukraine or Little Russia?), was banned from publication by the authorities. With Stalin's personal involvement, the Vaplite was liquidated, and its members, including Khvylovy, were forced to do self-criticism. Khvylovy spent the winter of 1928 in Berlin and Vienna. He could have stayed abroad but returned to the USSR and attempted to accept the limitations placed on his creative work. He continued editing *Literaturnyi iarmarok* (1930) and *Politfront* (1930–31) but under the party's dictation. His

attempts at adjustment proved to be a failure. Khvylovy's suicide in 1933 was a form of protest against the enormity of persecution and the extent of the famine in the Ukraine under the government of **Pavlo Postyshev**. Khvylovy's works were published as *Tvory v piatokh tomakh* (Works in five volumes; 1978–86). (TS)

Sources: *Encyclopedia of Ukraine*, vol. 1 (Toronto, 1984); George Luckyj, *Literary Politics in the Soviet Ukraine 1917–1934* (New York, 1956); Yuri Lavrynenko, ed., *Rozstrilane vidrodzhennia: Antolohiya 1917–1933* (Paris, 1959); Yuri Lutskiy, ed., *Vaplitansky zbirnyk* (Edmonton and Toronto, 1977); James Mace, *Communism and the Dilemmas of National Liberation: National Communism in Soviet Ukraine 1918–1933* (Cambridge, 1983).

KIDRIĆ Boris (10 April 1912, Vienna–11 April 1953, Belgrade), Yugoslav Communist activist of Serb nationality. In 1927 Kidrić became active in the Communist movement, for which he was imprisoned in Maribor between 1927 and 1928. Released, he began to study in the Chemistry Department of the University of Ljubljana. Arrested again in 1933, he spent several months in prison. In May 1935 he became the secretary of the Central Committee (CC) of the League of Yugoslav Communist Youth (Savez Komunističke Omladine Jugoslavije [SKOJ]), and in September he attended a congress of the Communist Youth International in Moscow. After returning to Vienna, in May 1936 Kidrić was arrested and spent one year in prison. In 1938, on the orders of **Josip Broz Tito**, he went to Paris, where he conducted activities among students from Yugoslavia. He returned to Yugoslavia in the autumn of 1939.

A member of the CC of the Communist Party of Yugoslavia from September 1940 on, Kidrić put forward a proposal for cooperation among Slovene anti-Fascist parties within the framework of the Anti-Imperialistic Front (renamed the Liberation Front later), and he joined its Executive Committee. Elected to the Presidium of the Anti-Fascist Council for the National Liberation of Yugoslavia (Antifašističko Veće Narodnog Oslobodenja [AVNOJ]), in May 1945 Kidrić became head of the Slovene government, and in December of that year, the political secretary of the CC of the Communist Party of Slovenia. In July 1946 he became minister of industry in the government of the Federal People's Republic of Yugoslavia. Appointed president of the Economic Council later on, Kidrić called for a decentralized model of the economy, as he considered the system of central planning less effective. Kidrić contributed to the introduction of the self-management system for companies and associations in 1950, which limited the role of the state in the economy. Elected to the Communist Party of Yugoslavia (CPY) Politburo at the Fifth CPY Congress in 1948, he was reelected at the Sixth CPY Congress in 1952, when the CPY changed its name to the League of Communists of Yugoslavia. Kidrić authored numerous works on the political economy of socialism; these were published as *Sabrana dela* (Collected works, 7 vols.; 1985). (AO)

Sources: *Enciklopedija Jugoslavije*, vol. 5 (Zagreb, 1962); *Enciklopedija Slovenije*, vol. 5 (Ljubljana, 1991); Janko Prunk, *Boris Kidrić* (Ljubljana, 1984); Lev Modić, *Boris Kidrić* (Ljubljana, 1986); Ivo Banac, *With Stalin against Tito* (Ithaca, N.Y., 1988); Wiesław Walkiewicz, *Jugosławia* (Warsaw, 2000); James Gow and Cathie Carmichael, *Slovenia and the Slovenians* (London, 2000).

KIERNIK Władysław (27 July 1879, Bochnia–23 August 1971, Warsaw), Polish Peasant Party politician and lawyer. In 1902 Kiernik graduated in law from the Jagiellonian University in Kraków and earned a Ph.D. there in 1903. He subsequently ran a law practice in Bochnia. While in high school, he was active in secret pro-independence organizations. In 1903 he joined the Polish Peasant Party (Polskie Stronnictwo Ludowe [PSL]). He participated in the activities of the People's School Society, serving as a member of its Main Board in 1906–21. He also sat on the Chief Council of the Union of Agricultural Associations. After the outbreak of World War I in 1914 Kiernik organized the county National Committee in Bochnia. He served as military commissioner of the Polish Legions in Bochnia County. As the commissioner of the Polish Liquidation Commission (Polska Komisja Likwidacyjna) for Bochnia, in October 1918 he helped to abolish Austrian authority and subsequently became head (*starosta*) of Bochnia County.

From 1913 Kiernik was a leading activist of the Polish Peasant Party–Piast (PSL–Piast). From 1921 to 1931 he was a member of its Chief Council, from 1925 to 1931 a member of the party's Main Board, and from 1930 to 1931 its vice-president. In 1919–33 he was a PSL–Piast MP, from 1919 to 1927 a member of the presidium of the party's parliamentary representation, and in 1922–23 vice-president of the party. Kiernik was responsible for agricultural reforms, the development of cooperatives and rural self-government, the organization of administration, and the promotion of education. Kiernik was a close associate of **Wincenty Witos**. In 1920, during the Polish-Soviet war, he was a member of the State Defense Council. He belonged to the Polish delegation to the peace negotiations in Minsk and Riga. In 1921–22 he was president of the Main Land Office. As minister of interior in the government of Witos from May to December 1923, Kiernik was responsible for the use of the army against demonstrators in several towns in Lesser Poland, as a result of which many people were wounded or killed. From November 1925 to May 1926 he served as minister of agriculture

and state property. In 1924–25 he was editor-in-chief of the weekly *Piast*. After the coup of May 1926, he was in the opposition to the *sanacja* regime. In 1929 he was one of the leaders of the so-called Centrolew, a center-left coalition that was established to restore democracy. He also co-organized the Congress for the Defense of the Law and Freedom of the People in Kraków in 1930. Arrested for two months in September 1930, in 1932 Kiernik was sentenced in the Brześć trial to two and a half years in prison. In 1931 he co-founded the Peasant Party (Stronnictwo Ludowe [SL]) and co-authored its program. Until 1939 he served as a member of the SL Chief Council and vice-president of the SL Chief Executive Committee. To avoid serving his sentence, he emigrated to Czechoslovakia, where he lived from 1933 to 1939. After the German invasion of Czechoslovakia, he returned to Poland, where he was imprisoned for several weeks.

During World War II Kiernik belonged to the leadership of the Peasant Party–Roch (SL–Roch) in Kraków. Arrested by the Gestapo in July 1940, he was held in prison for half a year. After the war, he became vice-president of the Chief Executive Committee of the Polish Peasant Party (PSL), led by **Stanisław Mikołajczyk**, and in January 1946 he became president of its Chief Council. In June 1945 he attended a Moscow conference that led to the establishment of the Provisional Government of National Unity (Tymczasowy Rząd Jedności Narodowej). From July 1945 to February 1947 he served as minister of public administration. Kiernik was more submissive to the Communists than Mikołajczyk, supporting their plan to establish the Bloc of Democratic Parties, which the PSL did not join. From 1945 to 1947 Kiernik was a deputy to the National Home Council (Krajowa Rada Narodowa). In January 1947 he became MP. After Mikołajczyk fled the country, Kiernik continued cooperation with the Polish United Workers' Party (Polska Zjednoczona Partia Robotnicza [PUWP]). In November 1949 he joined the Chief Council of the United Peasant Party (Zjednoczone Stronnictwo Ludowe [ZSL]) and served as deputy chairman of its Chief Audit Committee. He belonged to the Polish delegation to UN sessions in London (1946) and New York (1956). From 1956 to 1966 Kiernik served as vice-president of the Polonia Society. He also sat on the governing bodies of many window-dressing community organizations sponsored by the Communists. (JS)

Sources: *Słownik Biograficzny Działaczy Ruchu Ludowego* (Warsaw, 1989); *Encyklopedia historii Drugiej Rzeczypospolitej* (Warsaw, 1999); *Encyklopedia Historii Polski: Dzieje polityczne*, vol. 1 (Warsaw, 1994); Roman Buczek, *Stronnictwo Ludowe w latach 1939–1945* (London, 1975); Krystyna Kersten, *Narodziny systemu władzy: Polska 1943–1948* (Poznań, 1990); Stanisław Łach, *Polskie Stronnictwo Ludowe w latach 1945–1947* (Gdańsk, 1995).

KIEŚLOWSKI Krzysztof (27 June 1941, Warsaw–13 March 1996, Warsaw), Polish film director. Kieślowski lost his father early. In 1968 he graduated from the Direction Department of the Higher State Film, Television, and Theater School in Łódź. He made his television film debut with *Zdjęcie* (Photograph; 1968). Initially Kieślowski directed documentaries, of which *Byłem żołnierzem* (I was a soldier; 1970) and *Siedem kobiet w różnym wieku* (Seven women in various ages; 1978) became classic works of Polish documentary film. Kieślowski worked in the Documentary Film Studio in Warsaw, taking up topics hardly acceptable to the Communist authorities—for instance, *Z miasta Łodzi* (From the city of Łódź, 1969) and *Robotnicy 71* (Workers 71; 1972, co-director). His early films were severely censored. In 1973 he directed his first feature film, *Przejście podziemne* (Underpass). From 1974 he belonged to the film group Tor, later a film studio. Kieślowski is considered one of the leaders of the "cinema of moral concern." His subsequent films—*Personel* (Personnel; 1975), *Spokój* (Quiet; 1976), and *Amator* (Amateur; 1979)—belonged to this trend. He presented the complicated and mendacious lives of people under totalitarian rule, which forced them to make dramatic moral choices.

In the 1980s Kieślowski more often reflected on human fate and existential problems. Discouraged by politics, he less often referred to social problems. He won fame with his television series *Dekalog* (The Decalogue; 1989), which referred to universal problems but was set against the dull background of the Polish reality of the late 1980s. Kieślowski found himself among the elite of European cinema with his *Podwójne życie Weroniki* (The double life of Veronique; 1991), and his position was sealed with the trilogy *Trzy kolory: Niebieski* (Three colors: Blue; 1993), *Trzy kolory: Biały* (Three colors: White; 1994), and *Trzy kolory: Czerwony* (Three colors: Red; 1994), alluding to the French flag. The last received three Oscar nominations. Kieślowski worked with the director of photography Piotr Sobociński and the screenplay writer, lawyer, and politician Krzysztof Piesiewicz. Kieślowski lectured at the film and theater school in Katowice, as well as in Germany, Switzerland, and Finland. He won the Gold Lion in Venice and the Silver Bear in Berlin. He also authored the book *Decalogue* (1989). (PK)

Sources: *Kto jest kim w Polsce 1984: Informator biograficzny* (Warsaw, 1984); *International Dictionary of Films and Filmmakers*, vol. 2 (Chicago and London, 1991); Phil Cavendish, "Kieślowski's Decalogue," *Sight and Sound*, Summer 1990; *Rzeczpospolita*, 14 March 1996.

KIIVIT Jaan (27 February 1906, Pahuvere–3 August 1971. Tallinn), Estonian Lutheran clergyman. After graduating in theology from Tartu University in 1932, Kiivit worked as a pastor in the region of Viru-Jaagupi. In 1940 he additionally became head of the Lutheran Church in the district of Virumaa. On the wave of nominations of clergy people who were loyal to the Communist regime, in 1946 Kiivit resigned his position to become an assessor in the consistory. In 1948 he was promoted to head of the Estonian Evangelical Lutheran Church (EELC) in Tallinn, and on 2 February 1949 he was appointed acting bishop of the EELC. This nomination, made a day before the mass deportation of Estonians far into the interior of the USSR, was a turning point in the relations between the state and the Lutheran Church. Kiivit took the place of **August Pähn**, who, although registered as an NKVD agent, maintained some semblance of the Church's independence from the state. The elevation of Kiivit to head of the EELC was directly linked to his being recognized as more loyal than his predecessor, who was arrested and deported to Siberia. Documents found after 1991 indicate that at least several years prior to becoming head of the EELC, Kiivit was registered as an NKVD agent under the pseudonym "Yuri I." Upon the appointment of a new head of the Church, the membership of the consistory was also changed through the recruitment of people who were more submissive to the Communists than the previous members. On 23 October 1949 Kiivit was appointed archbishop of the EELC; it was a new position in the Church's practice, because until then bishop was the highest Church dignitary. This peculiar promotion was instigated by the authorities, the objective being to raise the prestige of the Church dominated by Communist agents.

With the nomination of Kiivit, the struggle against religion reached a new stage. As a result of the deportations of 1949, Church attendance dropped, and Church documents and sermons adopted some of the terms of Communist propaganda. EELC dignitaries attended state ceremonies, and lower-ranking clergy were forced to promote loyalty to the atheist state. The clergymen also supported the USSR "peace" propaganda abroad. Stalin's death in 1953 brought a temporary liberalization of religious policy in the USSR, but these changes had little influence on Kiivit's attitude. He traveled abroad, advertising the alleged religious freedom in the Soviet Union; took part in the "struggle for peace"; and probably collected information for the KGB about the work of other Protestant churches. The atheist campaign led by the authorities after 1959 resulted in a decrease in public interest in the affairs of the EELC, and the number of the faithful dropped within a few years to 10 percent. When Kiivit was retiring as archbishop in 1967, the churches stood empty, and religion had been relegated from the consciousness of most Estonians. Kiivit's son,

Jaan Kiivit, Jr., who became the archbishop of the EELC in 1994, attempted to regain the public trust, yet it is estimated that merely 15 percent of Estonians belong to the Lutheran Church. (AG)

Sources: *Eesti Noukogude Entsuklopeedia*, vol. 4 (Tallinn, 1989); Tõnu Parming and Elmar Järvesöö, *A Case Study of a Soviet Republic: The Estonian SRR* (Boulder, Colo., 1978); Indrek Jürjo, Pagulus ja *Nõukogude Eesti: Vaateid KGB, EKP ja VEKSA arhiividokumentide põhjal* (Tallinn, 1996); Riho Altnurme, "Religion in Estonia," in "Okupatsioon Museum," http://www.okupatsioon.ee/english/overviews; http://www.eelk.ee/~eelk109/kogudus; http://www.ekspress.ee/Arhiiv/Vanad/1997/02/areen/raamat1.

KILAR Wojciech (17 July 1932, Lwów [Lviv]), Polish composer. In 1955 Kilar graduated from the Higher State Musical School in Katowice, and in 1959–60 he continued his studies with Bolesław Wóytowicz and Nadia Boulanger in Paris. Initially he composed under the influence of the classical composers of twentieth-century music, such as Igor Stravinsky and Béla Bartók. He was also inspired by jazz. Many of Kilar's works were presented for the first time during the International Festivals of Contemporary Music known as "Warsaw Autumn." Kilar made his debut in 1955 with *Mała uwertura* (Small overture); then he composed his first and second symphonies (1955–56), *Riff 62* (1962), *Generique* (1963), and *Diphtongos* (1964). Later he developed his own style, combining experimental harmony and sound with elements of folklore. This style was best represented in his *Krzesany* (1974), *Kościelec 1909* (1976), and *Orawa* (Orava; 1986). In the 1980s and 1990s Kilar's increasingly sophisticated compositions included more and more mystical elements. He did not conceal the Christian inspiration of such works as *Angelus* (1984) and *Missa pro pace* (2000). He also wrote music for about 150 films, including *Dracula*, by Francis F. Coppola; *Pan Tadeusz*, by **Andrzej Wajda**; and *Pianist*, by **Roman Polański**. Since 1979 Kilar has been vice-president of the Union of Polish Composers. He received many awards, including that of the American Association of Composers (1993) and the (Polish) Grand Award of the Cultural Foundation (2001). (WR)

Sources: *Kto jest kim w Polsce* (Warsaw, 2001); *Cieszę się życiem: Rozmowy z Wojciechem Kilarem* (Kraków, 1997).

KINGISEPP Viktor (12 March 1888, Kaarma-Suure, Saaremaa–4 May 1922. Tallinn), Estonian Bolshevik activist. At the age of seventeen, Kingisepp took part in the 1905 revolution. In 1906–11 he studied law at the university in St. Petersburg, where in 1917 he passed his final exams. From 1906, as a member of the Bolshevik faction of the Russian Social Democratic Party, he was active in Tallinn and St. Petersburg. A co-founder of the Bolshevik newspaper *Kiir*, he also published in *Pravda*. From 1914 to 1916 Kingisepp was active in the region of Tver and Kazan. After the overthrow of tsarism, he returned to Petrograd, but in June 1917 he was again sent to Tallinn, where he was to establish a Bolshevik organization. In October 1917 he became vice-president of the Estonian Military and Revolutionary Committee and helped to organize the Red Guard. A coup that began a few days after the Bolshevik revolution in Petrograd led to a brief takeover of power by the Bolsheviks in Estonia. Kingisepp was responsible for expropriations; depriving the higher social classes of the protection of the law; terror against opponents; desecration of the churches; persecution of the clergy; and forcible suppression of the authorities that enjoyed public support, including in particular the Estonian National Council (Maapäev) (27 November 1917). The German offensive of February 1918 removed the Bolsheviks.

In the spring of 1918 Kingisepp returned to Moscow, where he joined the Cheka and worked in the Supreme Military Tribunal. As an investigator, he took part in the trials of leftist Socialist revolutionaries and in the also in case of Bruce Lockhart (a British diplomat tried by the Soviets for espionage). In November 1918 Kingisepp managed to illegally get to Estonian territory, where he supported the Bolshevik troops in the war against the emerging state. He was responsible for an attempt to stir up a rebellion in Tallinn in December 1918 that was suppressed by the government, and for the bloody pacification of a revolt in Saaremaa in February 1919. Kingisepp represented Moscow's interests at the First and Second Congresses of the Communist Party of Estonia (CPE), where he was elected a member of the Central Committee and the Politburo of the Party. Despite this, in the Tartu Peace Treaty of 2 February 1920, Soviet Russia recognized Estonia's sovereignty. However, Kingisepp's work had some influence on Estonian workers, nearly 10 percent of whom supported the Communists, owing to postwar difficulties. Arrested by the police on 3 May 1922, Kingisepp was tried under martial law regulations by a court martial and was executed by firing squad the following day. His body was burned at an unknown place to prevent the spread of a cult centered around him, but a cult developed nonetheless. Owing to the circumstances of his death, Kingisepp's story was widely exploited by Soviet propaganda at the time of the Soviet occupation of Estonia. The town of Kuressaare was renamed Kingispepp after him. Moreover, he was the hero of stories for the youth, and a great number of squares, streets, and institutions were named after him. After 1991 his cult ended. (AG)

Sources: *Eesti Entsuklopeedia*, vol. 14 (Tallinn, 2000); *Bolshaia Sovetskaia Entsiklopediia*, vol. 12 (Moscow, 1973); Rolf Parve, *Põranda all: Lugusid ja laaste Viktor Kingisepp* (Tallinn, 1967); Matti Laur, Tõnis Lukas, Ain Mäesalu, Ago Pajur, and Tõnu Tannberg, *History of Estonia* (Tallinn, 2000); Rein Taagepera, *Estonia: Return to Independence* (Boulder, Colo., 1993).

KINIORSKI Marian (1 December 1868, Pokrzywnica, near Sandomierz–23 May 1943, Warsaw), Polish national politician. Kiniorski came from a landowning family. Expelled from a gymnasium for his patriotic attitude about Poland, he passed his high school final exams in 1888 in Vyazma, Smolensk Province. He subsequently studied in the National Agricultural School in Dublany, near Kraków. At that time he was a member of the first group of the Union of Polish Youth called Zet and headed an organization called Bratnia Pomoc (Fraternal Help). Along with dozens of other students, he left Fraternal Help after a conflict with the authorities of the university. Kiniorski farmed on his family estate, and in 1892 he joined the Polish League (Liga Polska). In 1899, after a two-year course of studies, he graduated from the École des Sciences Politiques in Paris. At that time he became friends with **Władysław Reymont** and Zenon Przesmycki (Miriam). After graduation, he bought an estate in Suchodębie, near Kutno. Apart from his farming activities, he worked in the National Education Society (Towarzystwo Oświaty Narodowej [TON]), a secret organization that he supported financially. From 1901 to 1903 he was editor-in-chief of *Ekonomista*. Kiniorski was one of the co-founders of National Democracy (Narodowa Demokracja [ND]) in the Congress Kingdom of Poland. In 1906, as a representative of the ND, he was a deputy to the first Russian State Duma, and from 1912 to 1914, a deputy to the fourth Duma. In 1912 he became a member of the Chief Council of the ND, and in 1907, the vice-president of the Central Agricultural Society (Centralne Towarzystwo Rolnicze [CTR]). Kiniorski published extensively in the agricultural press. For example, in 1911, under the pseudonym "Rusticus," he published *Listy z dworu wiejskiego* (Letters from a country manor). During World War I, he was the secretary of the Inter-Party Political Circle (Międzypartyjne Koło Polityczne), an organization with a pro-Russian and pro-coalition orientation. In March 1918 he became president of the CTR. When Poland regained independence, Kiniorski was active in the Union of Landowners (Związek Ziemian), and in 1920 he was one of the founders of the Union of Polish Agricultural Organizations. From 1922 to 1928 he held a senatorial seat; therefore, in 1923 he resigned as leader of the CTR. A firm opponent of the *sanacja* regime, in 1930 he withdrew from politics and devoted himself to the administration of his estate. After the Germans captured central Poland in 1939, they removed him from his farm. Kiniorski moved to Warsaw, where he died. His publications include *W służbie ziemi* (In the service of the land; 1929). (WR)

Sources: *PSB*, vol. 12; Kazimierz Konarski, *Dalekie i bliskie: Wspomnienia szczęśliwego człowieka* (Wrocław, 1965); Roman Wapiński, *Narodowa Demokracja 1893–1939* (Wrocław, 1980); Czesław Brzoza and Kamil Stepan, *Posłowie polscy w parlamencie rosyjskim 1906–1917* (Warsaw, 2001).

KIOSEIVANOV Georgi (19 January 1884, Peštera–27 July 1960, La Tour de Peilz, Switzerland), Bulgarian politician. After completing law studies and earning a doctorate at the Sorbonne, Kioseivanov returned to Bulgaria, where he started working in the Ministry for Foreign Affairs. Until 1923 he mostly served in diplomatic missions in such cities as Rome, Istanbul, and Berlin, where he held the post of chargé d'affaires. He was later appointed Bulgarian minister to Bucharest, Athens, and Belgrade. Kioseivanov belonged to a group of nonparty professional diplomats and ardent supporters of Tsar **Boris III**, who, after assuming authoritarian power in January 1935, installed Kioseivanov as head of his chancellery. In April 1935 he became minister of foreign affairs, and on 23 September 1935 he was appointed prime minister, while keeping the foreign affairs portfolio.

Kioseivanov's main task was to stabilize the new system of government. He suppressed opposition in the army by instituting legal proceedings against officers who held opposition views and disbanding all organizations of career officers. In 1936 he reshuffled the cabinet by recruiting some ministers from the extreme right; this caused protests and led to another reconstruction of the cabinet. Political parties were abolished, and an authoritarian constitution, which greatly increased the tsar's powers, was introduced. However, Kioseivanov failed to completely crush the opposition, which all together received about 40 percent of the mandates in the elections of March 1938. In foreign policy, he attempted to strengthen relations with Yugoslavia (treaty of friendship of 24 January 1937) and Greece (Salonika convention of 31 March 1938). His government unsuccessfully attempted to bring about Romania's peaceful withdrawal from the disputed area of Southern Dobrudja. Kioseivanov led a complicated game with Germany, which was putting pressure on Bulgaria. He saw the Third Reich as a possible source of weapons for the Bulgarian Army; this led to a secret agreement in March 1938 on the supply of German arms; Kioseivanov also hoped Germany could be used to exert pressure on Romania. However, he rejected German demands that Bulgaria join the Axis. After the outbreak of World War II, Bulgaria declared neutrality on 24 October 1939. Kioseivanov tried to prevent Bulgaria from entering the war. This policy led to a divergence of opinions with the tsar, who dismissed Kioseivanov on 16 February 1940 and sent him to the embassy in Switzerland. In 1943 Kioseivanov realized that in the face of the possible defeat of Germany, Bulgaria should seek guarantees for its borders with the Allies; therefore, he entered into negotiations with the Office of Strategic Services (OSS) resident, Allen Dulles, but he abandoned these contacts owing to German pressure. After the coup of 9 September 1944 in Sofia, Kioseivanov was dismissed from his post. Fearing for his life, he remained in the West. Until 1951 he lived in Geneva and then in Madrid, where he contacted Tsarina Joanna and Tsar **Simeon II**. In 1956 Kioseivanov returned to Switzerland, where he died. (AG)

Sources: *Biographisches Lexikon*, vol. 2; Marshall Lee Miller, *Bulgaria during the Second World War* (Stanford, 1975); Stefane Groueff, *Crown of Thorns: The Reign of King Boris III of Bulgaria, 1918–1943* (Lanham, Md., 1987); Tadeusz Wasilewski, *Historia Bułgarii* (Wrocław, 1988); Raymond Detrez, *Historical Dictionary of Bulgaria* (Lanham, Md., 1997); Tasho Tashev, *Ministrite na Bulgariya 1879–1999: Entsiklopedichen spravochnik* (Sofia, 1999).

KIRÁLY Béla (14 April 1912, Kaposvár), Hungarian officer, politician, and historian. The son of a head of a railway station, after high school Király enrolled in the Ludovika Military Academy in Budapest. From 1935 to 1940 he served in the army, and in 1942 he graduated with distinction from the Military Academy of the General Staff. From December 1942 he worked in the Ministry of National Defense. In the summer of 1943 he was sent to the eastern front. After the Arrow Cross takeover in October 1944, Király stayed in the army, and in March 1945 he volunteered to defend the town of Kőszeg in western Hungary against the Red Army. Nevertheless, he soon passed over to the Russian side. Treated as a prisoner of war, he escaped from a transport into Russia. After returning home in the summer of 1945, he joined the Hungarian Communist Party (HCP), and in early 1946 he became lieutenant colonel and chief of staff of a division in the town of Pápa. From 1947 Király headed the Training Department of the Ministry of Defense. From 1948 he was a deputy commander and in 1949–50 a commander of infantry. From September 1950 he commanded the Military Academy in Budapest. He was promoted to brigadier general and organized military parades in Budapest. In the summer of 1951 Király was arrested and in January 1952 sentenced to death for "anti-state activities" and "plotting against the power of the people." The sentence was then commuted to life in prison.

In September 1956 Király was released, and he joined the followers of **Imre Nagy**. On 31 October he was rehabilitated by the Supreme Court. During the revolution he became chairman of the Revolutionary Committee of National Defense, coordinating the command of the Hungarian Army, the Revolutionary Defense Committee, and the operations of the Revolutionary National Guard (RNG). On 31 October Király was appointed RNG commander in chief and military commander of Budapest. In compliance with the instructions of Imre Nagy, on 4 November Király ordered his troops not to resist the Soviet Army. He himself, however, took up the struggle against the Soviets, commanding a few units until he finally crossed the Austrian border in late November 1956. In January 1957 Király was elected deputy chairman of the Hungarian Revolutionary Council in Strasbourg, France; it included leaders of the revolution who had been forced to leave the country. Later Király settled in the United States, where he organized the Hungarian Committee and belonged to several Hungarian émigré organizations.

In 1966 Király retired from political life and started a scholarly career. In 1957 he graduated in history from Columbia University; in 1962 he received a Ph.D.; and in 1963–83 he lectured at Brooklyn College and the City University of New York, where he became professor of military science. In 1994 Király received honorary doctorates from both universities. The state of Kentucky appointed him colonel, while the state of Maryland and the city of Baton Rouge, Louisiana, granted him honorary citizenship. On 16 June 1989 Király spoke in Budapest during the solemn funeral of Imre Nagy and his aides. After the fall of communism, Király recovered his Hungarian citizenship, and in 1990 he was promoted to retired general of arms. In 1990–94 he was an MP on behalf of the Alliance of Free Democrats. Király edited a number of books on the 1956 revolution and the history of communism in East Central Europe. His memoirs, *Honvédségből Néphadsereg* (From the Honved Army to the People's Army), were published in the West in 1986 and in Hungary in 1989. In 2001 Király published *The Basic History of Modern Hungary, 1867–1999*. (JT)

Sources: *A magyar forradalom és szabadságharc enciklopédiája*, CD-ROM (Budapest, 1999); *Magyar Nagylexikon*, vol. 11 (Budapest, 2000); Paul Ignotus, *Hungary* (London, 1972); *Society in Change: Studies in Honor of Béla Király* (Boulder, Colo., 1983); *Ki kicsoda 2000* (Budapest, 2001); György Litván, ed., *Rewolucja węgierska 1956 roku* (Warsaw, 1996).

KIRÁLY Karoly (26 September, 1930 Târnăveni), Hungarian Communist activist and dissident in Romania. Király graduated from the Academy of Economic

Sciences in Bucharest and the Ştefan Gheorghiu Higher Party School. He started his career in the early 1950s in the apparatus of the Romanian Workers' Party (as of 1965, the Romanian Communist Party [RCP]) in Transylvania. Among other things, he was first secretary of the RCP organization in the Covaşna region, where the share of Hungarians reached 86 percent. From 1970 Király was a deputy member of the Politburo of the RCP Executive Committee. He was also deputy chairman of the Council of the Hungarian Working People. Known as an organizer of hunting and partying for RCP officials in the Transylvanian forests, in 1972 Király radically changed his stance, protesting before the top RCP leadership against the discrimination of the Hungarian minority. He criticized the reduction of Hungarian instruction in schools; the *numerus clausus* principle in university, government, and party admittance; and the elimination of the use of bilingual geographical names. He also criticized the **Nicolae Ceauşescu** regime. Called to Bucharest in 1974, he talked with Prime Minister **Ilie Verdeţ**, reiterating his protests. He also passed open letters to the West. In February 1978 Király was arrested and exposed to radioactivity, following which he was interned in the Caransebeş prison. Released in October 1978, he continued dissident activities and was kept under surveillance by the political police, the Securitate. In 1985, along with other opposition activists, Király signed a declaration in defense of Hungarian minority rights in Romania. After the revolution of December 1989 Király was co-founder of the Democratic Alliance of Hungarians in Romania (DAHR) and deputy chairman of the Council of the National Salvation Front. In the elections of May 1990 he was elected to the Senate on behalf of the DAHR and sat in the Upper House until the end of the term in May 1992. (ASK)

Sources: *Relatara Karoly Király* (N.p., 1998); Dennis Deletant, *Ceauşescu and the Securitate: Coercion and Dissent in Romania, 1965–1989* (New York, 1995); Ion M. Pacepa, *Red Horizons* (New York, 1987); George Schöpflin and Henry Poulton, *Romania's Ethnic Hungarians* (London, 1990).

KIRCHENŠTEINS Auguss (18 September 1872, Waldenberg [Mazcalaca]–3 September 1963, Riga), Latvian microbiologist and political activist. Kirchenšteins came from a peasant family and completed veterinary studies in Dorpat (Tartu). He took part in the revolution of 1905 and then emigrated. From 1907 to 1908 he studied in Zurich, then worked in Switzerland and in Serbia. In 1914–17 he served in the Serbian Army as a doctor. In 1917 he returned to Latvia, and in 1919 he created the veterinary department at the University of Riga. Between June and October 1919 he was the head of the Veterinary

Inspectors' Office of the Latvian Army. From 1923 he was a professor, and he worked on vaccines against tuberculosis. As president of the Society of Latvian-Soviet Friendship, Kirchenšteins was a frequent guest at the embassy of the USSR in Riga, and he established close contacts with the representatives of the Kremlin.

After the Soviet invasion on 18 June 1940, a special Soviet envoy, Andrei Vyshinsky, submitted to President **Kārlis Ulmanis** a list of new government members, with Kirchenšteins as prime minister. After the list had been signed, Kirchenšteins assumed power, and Ulmanis was soon arrested. On 6 July 1940 Kirchenšteins announced elections to the new National Assembly, stressing that previous governments had not guaranteed friendly relations with the USSR and that his cabinet would implement the resolutions of the agreements between the two states. He also stated that "the presence of the Red Army serves the defense of freedom and the preservation of statehood." Vyshinsky also publicly supported the idea of a "free Latvia." The electoral law, however, was illegally changed so that only candidates approved by the Communists could run for seats. "The elections" of 14–15 July 1940 obviously brought success to the Communist list. On 18 July the New Assembly passed the incorporation of Latvia into the USSR as a Soviet republic, and Kirchenšteins became president of Latvia's Supreme Council. On 25 July 1940 he recalled Latvia's diplomatic representatives from abroad, but the great majority of them ignored this demand and refused to return home. In the new constitution the principle of the "dictatorship of the proletariat" was introduced. Kirchenšteins signed arrest and deportation orders for the Latvian national elite, actions that followed in 1940–41. After the German aggression in June 1941 Kirchenšteins took refuge in Moscow, where he assumed the post of vice-president of the Supreme Council of the USSR. He returned to Riga with the Red Army. Between 1944 and 1952 he again presided over the Supreme Council of the Latvian SSR and signed a great many deportation orders of Latvians in 1944 and 1949. After that he returned to his scientific work as the director of the Institute of Microbiology of the Latvian Academy of Sciences. Kirchenšteins published around eight hundred scientific works. He received many awards, including that of Hero of Socialist Work. (WR)

Sources: Alfred Bilmanis, *A History of Latvia* (Princeton, 1951); Albert N. Tarulis, *Soviet Policy toward the Baltic States* (Notre Dame, Ind., 1959); *Who Was Who in the USSR* (Metuchen, N.J., 1972).

KIRIL, Prince of Preslav (5 November 1895, Sofia–2 February 1946, Sofia), younger brother of Tsar **Boris III**, regent of Bulgaria. Kiril was the son of **Ferdinand**. As his older brother, Boris, was to succeed to the throne, he was not involved in politics. He liked to surround himself with expensive women. During his stay in Vienna at the end of World War I, he accumulated debts that caused great trouble for the royal family. Although it was common knowledge that Kiril was not interested in public life, this did not hinder the court camarilla from appointing him general. After Boris died, in August 1943 Prime Minister **Bogdan Filov** used his influence to get Kiril elected as one of the regents, against the terms of the constitution, which stipulated that only a person known for his public activity might become regent. On 8 September 1943 the National Assembly elected Kiril, along with Filov and General **Nikola Mihov**, to the Regency Council, which was to exercise power on behalf of Simeon, who was under age. As Kiril continued to show little interest in state affairs, the other two regents coordinated those affairs themselves, presenting them to Kiril in ready form; therefore his rather moderate attitude toward cooperation with the Germans was of no great importance. When on 9 September 1944 the Communist uprising in Sofia led to the overthrow of the rule of the regents, Kiril was arrested, and along with about a hundred associates he was sentenced to death and executed. In fact, the verdict was dictated by **Georgi Dimitrov** from Moscow. (WR)

Sources: *Entsiklopediya Bulgariya*, vol. 3; M. L. Miller, *Bulgaria during the Second World War* (Stanford, 1975); Hans-Joachim Hoppe, *Bulgarien–Hitlers eigenwilliger Verbündeter* (Stuttgart, 1979); Stephane Groueff, *Crown of Thorns* (Lanham, Md., 1987); Jerzy Jackowicz, *Partie opozycyjne w Bułgarii 1944–1948* (Warsaw, 1997).

KIRYL [originally Konstantin Konstantinov] (3 January 1901, Sofia–7 February 1971, Sofia), patriarch of the Bulgarian Orthodox Church, historian, and theologian. After graduating from the theological seminary in Sofia in 1920, Kiryl studied theology in Belgorod and Cernauţi (Chernivtsi) (1920–25) and philosophy in Berlin (1928–30). In 1923 he was ordained, and in 1927 he received a Ph.D. in theology. He taught in the Sofia seminary. He was also secretary of Rila Monastery and chief secretary of the synod. In 1938 Kiryl was elected metropolitan of Plovdiv, and he was one of the key organizers of the Bulgarian Orthodox Church's pronouncements against anti-Jewish legislation. Starting with a memorandum on 15 November 1940 through protests in 1943, the Bulgarian Synod (thanks to Kiril, among others) appealed to Tsar **Boris III** and state authorities in defense of the Bulgarian Jews, remembering Christ's command to love one's brother. On 10 March 1943 Kiryl stated in Plovdiv that he would leave with the 1,500 Jews who had been arrested, and his declaration prevented their deportation. After the coup of 9 November 1944 Kiryl was arrested

and brutally interrogated. Later Communist tactics minimized the moral influence of the church and reduced it to a pure decoration, so Kiryl was released. In the summer of 1948 he took part in an Orthodox conference in Moscow chaired by the patriarch of Moscow. On 10 May 1953 the Bulgarian church recovered its own patriarchy, lost under the Turkish occupation in 1393, and the national council elected Kiryl patriarch. Swathed in the appearance of splendor, the Bulgarian Orthodox Church lost real independence and moral authority. Kiryl authored a number of works on the history of the Bulgarian church and received honorary doctorates from theological academies in Sofia, Moscow, and Leningrad. In 2001 the Yad Vashem Institute in Jerusalem posthumously awarded him the title of Righteous among the Nations. (WDj)

Sources: *Entsiklopediya Bulgariya*, vol. 2 (Sofia, 1978); *Bulgariya 20. vek. Almanakh* (Sofia, 1999); *Kiryl Patriarkh Bulgarski: Jubileyna nauchna sesiya* (Plovdiv, 2001).

KIŠ Danilo (2 February 1935, Subotica–15 October 1989, Paris), Yugoslav writer. Kiš was born into a Hungarian Jewish family from Bačka. During the war, he witnessed pogroms against Jews, and his father perished in the Auschwitz death camp in Oświęcim. He was sixteen when his mother died, causing another shock. Kiš passed his high school graduation exams in Cetinje, and in 1958 he completed philosophical studies in Belgrade, specializing in world literature. After doing his military service (1961–62), he published his first two novels: *Mansarda* and *Psalam 44* (Psalm 44; 1962). He worked as a teacher of the Serbo-Croatian language in Strasbourg (1962–64) and Bordeaux (1974–76). Kiš spent the last years of his life in Paris. He wrote in Serbian. In his writings, which reveal postmodernist features, he included conspicuously autobiographical motifs, depicting the fate of a Jewish child and his father, who becomes an almost mythical figure. Kiš's literary works include the novels *Bašta, pepeo* (1965; *Garden, Ashes*, 1975) and *Peščanik* (1972; *Hourglass*, 1990); the collections of essays *Poetika I* and *Poetika II* (1972); stories devoted to the victims of Stalinism: *Grobnica za Borisa Davidoviča* (1976; *Tomb for Boris Davidovich*, 1978) and *Enciklopedija mrtvih* (1987; *Encyclopedia of the Dead*, 1989); a collection of sketches, *Čas anatomije* (The anatomy lesson; 1978); and numerous translations of French, Russian, and Hungarian poetry. Kiš received many Yugoslav and foreign awards, including awards from France. (WR)

Sources: *Nowa encyklopedia powszechna PWN*, vol. 3 (Warsaw, 1995); Jovan Delić, *Književni pogledi Danila Kiša* (Belgrade, 1995); Susan Sontag, ed., *Homo poeticus: Essays and Interviews with Danilo Kiš* (New York, 1995); Mihailo Pantić, *Kiš* (Novi Sad, 1998); Krzysztof Varga, "Szalona jasność umysłu," *Gazeta Wyborcza*, 16–17 October 1999; www.kis.org.yu.

KIS János (17 September, 1943 Budapest), Hungarian dissident and politician. A graduate in philosophy from Eötvös Lóránd University in Budapest in 1967, in 1967–73 Kis worked in the Institute of Philosophy of the Hungarian Academy of Sciences, from which he was expelled for his political views. His publications were banned. From the early 1970s, he was active in the democratic opposition. He signed its most important pronouncements and documents; in 1981–89 he edited the leading Hungarian periodical of the uncensored press, *Beszéló*; and from 1989 to 1991 he presided over its program council. Kis was a founding member of the Alliance of Free Democrats (Szabad Demokraták Szövetsége [AFD]), and until 1999 he belonged to its National Council. As the leading leftist and later liberal intellectual, Kis exercised a strong influence on AFD circles, whose stance evolved from anti-communism to cooperation with the Communists after 1989; in 1994–98 and from 2002 the AFD entered into the ruling coalition with the Communists. Gradually withdrawing from a direct engagement in politics, Kis remained active in public life, frequently appearing in the media and speaking on contemporary domestic and foreign policy issues. In the fall of 2002 he left the AFD in protest against its unconditional support for Prime Minister **Péter Medgyessy**, accused of cooperation with the former Communist secret services. Kis authored *Hogyan lehetséges kritikai gazdaságtan?* (Is critical economics possible? 1973); *Vannak-e emberi jogaink?* (Are we entitled to human rights? 1986); *Politics in Hungary: For a Democratic Alternative* (1989); and *Az állam semlegessége* (Neutrality of the state; 1997). (AH)

Sources: *Ki Kicsoda 2002* (Budapast, 2001); *Magyar Nagylexikon* (Budapest, 2000).

KISIELEWSKI Stefan (7 March 1911, Warsaw–27 September 1991, Warsaw), Polish writer, composer, and music critic. The son of Zygmunt Kisielewski, a writer and Socialist activist, in 1937 Kisielewski graduated from the Warsaw Conservatory. He also studied in the Department of Humanities at Warsaw University. While a student, he made his literary debut in the magazine *Bunt Młodych*, edited by **Jerzy Giedroyc**, and he became a regular contributor to the magazine and to its successor, *Polityka* (from 1935). Kisielewski took part in the September campaign of 1939, and during the Nazi occupation he was active in the cultural underground—for example, in a unit of the Delegation of the Polish Government-in-Exile for the Homeland, which was preparing the reactivation of Polish Radio. He fought in the Warsaw Uprising in the ranks of the Home Army.

In 1945 Kisielewski began to work with the Kraków weekly *Tygodnik Powszechny*, in which he criticized romantic attitudes and the armed struggle against the new government. Under the pseudonym of "Kisiel" he also published popular columns. After the Pax Association took over the weekly in 1953, Kisielewski stopped contributing to *Tygodnik Powszechny*. Between 1945 and 1949 Kisielewski was a professor at the Higher School of Music in Kraków; in 1945–46 and 1956–59 he was the editor of the magazine *Ruch Muzyczny*; and between 1956 and 1961 he served as president of the Polish Composers' Union. He composed several symphonies and many other musical works. In 1956–57 Kisielewski was the co-author of the concept of "neopositivism," which recognized the necessity of respecting the political and geopolitical realities of the Polish People's Republic but did not accept the ideological principles of socialism. Such a concept of realism was a starting point for postulating a gradual liberalization of the system, as well as the extension of human rights. After October 1956 Kisielewski returned to the revived *Tygodnik Powszechny*, where he wrote a popular series of feature articles—for example, *Łopatą do głowy* (Explaining in the simplest terms), *Gwoździe w mózgu* (Nails in the brain), and, in 1976–81, *Wołanie na puszczy* (A cry in the desert).

As a journalist and an MP on behalf of the parliamentary group Znak (1957–65), Kisielewski urged the rationalization of the economy; a lifting of restrictions on the development of the small private sector; an extension of the freedom of speech; limitations on the powers of censorship; and a facilitation of contacts with the West. He made similar proposals as a member of the executive of the Polish Writers' Union. In 1964 he signed the "Letter of 34" against the excessive interference of censorship. These deeds made Kisielewski a target of attacks by Communist authorities. On 29 February 1968, at the General Assembly of the Warsaw branch of the Polish Writers' Union, Kisielewski made a famous speech on the "dictatorship of blockheads" in Polish culture. In the weeks that followed he became one of the main objects of an aggressive propaganda campaign. He was also beaten by "unknown perpetrators" and was temporarily banned from publishing.

Between 1967 and 1976 at the Paris-based Literary Institute (Instytut Literacki) Kisielewski, under the pseudonym of "Tomasz Staliński," published five popular novels devoted to the realities of the Polish People's Republic, among them *Cienie w pieczarze* (Shadows in the cavern;

1971), *Romans zimowy* (Winter romance; 1972), and *Śledztwo* (Investigation; 1974). His commentaries and feature articles, banned by censorship in *Tygodnik Powszechny*, ran periodically in the magazine *Kultura*. In 1975–76 Kisielewski participated in a protest campaign against amendments to the constitution. From 1976 he worked with the Committee for the Defense of Workers (Komitet Obrony Robotników [KOR]) and later with the Committee for Social Self-Defense KOR and with the uncensored press, where he published political brochures, such as *Na czym polega socjalizm?* (What does socialism consist of?) and *Czy istnieje walka o świat?* (Is there a struggle for the world?). Kisielewski advocated that the opposition seek an agreement with Moscow, leaving out the authorities of the Polish People's Republic. He regarded the bankruptcy of the Socialist economic system as irreparable, and, especially after 1981, he advocated a shift toward a market economy and economic liberalism. In the late 1980s he established ties with a group that created the Movement of Real Politics (Ruch Polityki Realnej) in 1987 and later the Union of Real Politics (Unia Polityki Realnej), of which he was an honorary president. In 1990 he supported the candidacy of **Lech Wałęsa** for president, which led to his parting with *Tygodnik Powszechny*. He moved his feature articles to the weekly *Wprost*. Kisielewski also authored numerous essays and feature articles; a novel, *Sprzysiężenie* (Conspiracy; 1949); works published under his real name or under pseudonyms; a volume of sketches about composers, *Gwiazdozbiór muzyczny* (Musical constellation; 1958); and *Dzienniki* (Diaries), published in 1996. (AF)

Sources: *Opozycja w PRL: Słownik biograficzny 1956–89* (Warsaw, 2000); *Literatura polska: Przewodnik encyklopedyczny* (Warsaw, 1984), vol. 1; Marta Fik, *Kultura polska po Jałcie: Kronika lat 1944–1981* (London, 1989); Jerzy Eisler, *Marzec 1968* (Warsaw, 1991); Andrzej Friszke, *Opozycja polityczna w PRL 1945–1980* (London, 1994).

KISS János (24 March 1883, Erdőszentgyörgy [Sângeorgiu de Pădure, Romania]–8 December 1944, Budapest), Hungarian general. Born into a Szekler soldier's family in Transylvania, Kiss graduated from a cadet school in Nagyszeben (Sibiu) in 1902. He fought in World War I, and then he served in the Hungarian Army. In 1929 he was promoted to the rank of colonel. He commanded the Fifth Honved Regiment (1928–32) and the First Bicycle Brigade, and he was instructor of sports in Baranya Province (1933–36). In 1936 he was promoted to general and assigned to the High Command of the Hungarian Army. In 1938, as general of division, he became inspector of infantry of the High Command. In 1939, in protest against the High Command's pro-German line, he retired. Kiss was a close friend of **Endre Bajcsy-Zsilinszky**. In the spring of 1944 he worked out a strategic plan according to which the Hungarian Army would withdraw to the Balkans and join the Yugoslav guerrillas. When the Arrow Cross Party seized power in October 1944, Kiss became commander of the Hungarian National Insurgent and Liberation Committee. He elaborated a plan for an uprising in Budapest, but before it could be implemented, Arrow Cross learned about the committee and arrested Kiss and his aides on 22 November 1944. After two weeks of cruel interrogations, a military tribunal of the Arrow Cross government sentenced Kiss to death, and he was soon executed. In March 1945 he was posthumously promoted to the rank of general of arms. (JT)

Sources: *Magyar Életrajzi Lexikon*, vol. 1 (Budapest, 1967); *Magyar Nagylexikon*, vol. 11 (Budapest, 2000); Sándor Kiss, *Emlékeim Kiss János altábornagyról* (Budapest, 1979).

KISTIAKOVSKYI Bohdan (4 November 1868, Kiev–16 April 1920, Yekaterinodar [now Krasnodar] on the Kuban River), Ukrainian sociologist and philosopher of law. Kistiakovskyi was a nephew of the historian Volodymyr Antonovych and the son of Oleksander Kistiakovskyi, a professor of law and president of the Law Society in Kiev. Kistiakovskyi declared himself a Ukrainian already in his youth, although he did not learn to speak Ukrainian until he was an adult. He advocated that the Ukraine remain in a union with Russia. During his law studies in Kiev (1888–90), Kharkiv (1890), and Dorpat (Tartu, 1890–92), he was active in Marxist and national groups. Imprisoned from 1892 to 1893, he was kept under police surveillance until 1895 for spreading revolutionary ideas. He continued his studies in Berlin, Paris, and Strasbourg, where he earned a doctorate in theoretical sociology for his work *Gesellschaft und Einzelwesen: Eine methodologische Untersuchung* (1899). At that time Kistiakovskyi was already being influenced by Ferdinand Tonnies, Georg Simmel, formal sociology, and the neo-Kantians. He himself exerted influence on such scientists as Georg Jellinek, Max Weber, and Hans Kelsen. Persecuted in Russia (his wife was exiled for taking part in the national movement), Kistiakovskyi returned to Germany. He cooperated with Russian liberal circles in exile, co-edited *Osvobozhdenie* (1902–5), and became a member of the Russian Constitutional Democratic Party (the so-called Kadets). He also stayed in touch with Galician radicals, including **Ivan Franko**.

Kistiakovskyi returned to Russia after the tsar's manifesto of October 1905. He lectured at the Institute of Trade and, from 1909 on, also at Moscow University. In 1909 he published *Stranitsy proshlogo: K istorii konstitutsion-*

nogo dvizheniia v Rossii (Pages from the past: From the history of the constitutional movement in Russia). In 1911 he resigned in protest against the conservative policy of tsarism and became a teacher of the philosophy of law and political science at Demidov High School. From 1907 to 1910 he edited *Kriticheskoe obozrenie*, a periodical that published translations of works by Western authors, and from 1912 to 1917 he was editor-in-chief of *Pravovoi Vestnik*. In 1916 he published *Sotsialnye nauki i pravo (Social sciences and law),* which was considered his life's work. He also wrote for the Moscow periodical *Ukrainskaia zhizn* (1912–17). Disappointed with the Kadets's approach to the Ukrainian cause, in 1917 Kistiakovskyi returned to Kiev, where he took up the chair of law at the university. Under the government of Hetman **Pavlo Skoropadskyi**, he became a member of the Senate and the Administrative Court and helped to draft a law on citizenship and a statute on the Ukrainian Academy of Sciences. In 1919 he became a member of the Ukrainian Academy of Sciences, where he held the chairs of law and sociology. His article about Russian "legal nihilism," which was published in the famous collection *Vekhi* (Landmarks; 1909), became the subject of a national debate. (TS)

Sources: *Encyclopaedia of Social Sciences*, vol. 8 (New York, 1932); A. Vucinich, *Social Thought in Tsarist Russia: The Quest for a General Science of Society, 1861–1917* (Chicago and London, 1976); Andrzej Walicki, *Filozofia prawa rosyjskiego liberalizmu* (Warsaw, 1995); S. Heuman, *Kistiakovsky: The Struggle for National and Constitutional Rights in the Last Years of Tsarism* (Cambridge, Mass., 1998).

KISZCZAK Czesław (19 October 1925, Roczyny, near Bielsko), Polish Communist activist and general. Born into a peasant family, during World War II Kiszczak was active in the Communist underground. From 1945 he served in the Communist Polish Army, working in intelligence and counterintelligence. Among other things, he supervised the return of Polish officers from Great Britain to Poland after the war. In 1945 he joined the (Communist) Polish Workers' Party, and he attended the central party school. From December 1948 he was a member of the Polish United Workers' Party (Polska Zjednoczona Partia Robotnicza [PUWP]). In 1957 Kiszczak graduated from the Academy of the General Staff. In 1972–79 he was deputy chief of the General Staff and the head of military intelligence. In 1970 he was active in a special task force connected with the workers' riots on the Baltic Coast. From 1973 he was a brigadier general, and from 1979, general of division. In 1979–81 he was chief of the Military Internal Service (Wojskowa Służba Wewnętrzna), or counterintelligence; in 1983 he was promoted to the rank of general of arms. At the same time he advanced in the party structures. In

February 1980 Kiszczak became a deputy member, and in July 1981 a member, of the PUWP Central Committee (CC); in February 1982 he became a deputy member, and in July 1986 a member, of the Politburo. Thanks to the support of General **Wojciech Jaruzelski**, in July 1981 Kiszczak became minister of interior, replacing **Mirosław Milewski**, with whom he was in conflict. This nomination strengthened Jaruzelski's control of the security apparatus. In 1985–89 Kiszczak was also an MP.

Kiszczak was one of the key architects of martial law, introduced on 13 December 1981, and a member of the non-constitutional Military Council of National Salvation. As minister of interior, at the beginning of the period of martial law, he instructed the lower levels of command to use firearms; this led to the shooting to death of several striking miners of the Wujek coal mine on 16 December 1981. Kiszczak also directed the repression of the Solidarity leadership and other participants of the protests. In 1983–89 Kiszczak chaired the government Committee for the Respect of Law, Public Order, and Social Discipline, and after the abolishment of martial law he retained special authority to use coercion. As a result of new strikes, in August and September 1988 Kiszczak was empowered by Jaruzelski to start negotiations with the Solidarity leadership. On 31 August 1988 he met with **Lech Wałęsa**. One of the initiators of the Round Table Talks and co-chairman of the party and government delegation to the talks (February–April 1989), despite the PUWP defeat in the parliamentary elections of June 1989, on 2 August 1989 Kiszczak became prime minister. His attempts to create a government failed. In September 1989 he assumed the position of deputy prime minister and minister of interior in the government of **Tadeusz Mazowiecki**. In this capacity he slowed down the personnel shifts in his ministry. During his term a significant amount of crucial PUWP and security apparatus evidence was destroyed or taken over by private hands. Kiszczak left the government in July 1990. In 1997 he was tried before the Tribunal of State for allowing the duty-free import of alcohol, but he was acquitted. Kiszczak's trial concerning his responsibility for the shooting of the Wujek miners ended in March 2004 with a suspended sentence of two years in prison, but he appealed. (PK)

Sources: Mołdawa; *Słownik polityków polskich XX wieku* (Poznań, 1998); Witold Bereś and Jerzy Skoczylas, *Generał Kiszczak mówi . . . Prawie wszystko* (Warsaw, 1991); Generał Pawłow, *Byłem rezydentem KGB w Polsce* (Warsaw, 1994); Jan Skórzyński, *Ugoda i rewolucja: Władza i opozycja 1985–89* (Warsaw, 1995).

KITZBERG August (8 January 1856, Põlde, near Laatre–10 October 1927, Tartu), Estonian writer and dramatist. Born into a poor peasant family, Kitzberg could not attend school because of a lack of finances, and he became an autodidact. Initially he worked as a municipal clerk, and in 1894 he took up a job with a bank in Dvinsk (now Daugavpils). From 1901 to 1904 he headed the sales department of the newspaper *Postimees*, and from 1904 to 1920 he worked in a mortgage bank in Dorpat. In 1920 he retired. Although he began writing in the 1870s, his literary career developed slowly. He gained some popularity after writing the novel *Maimu* (1889). He also wrote novels for the daily or weekly press, and a collection of these novels was published in 1915. Initially Kitzberg's writing was imbued with optimism, while social criticism was reduced to a humorous element—for instance, in *Punga Maart a Uba Kaarel* (Wise Martin and Dumb Charles; 1894); *Pila-Peteri Testament* (The testament of Pila-Peteri; 1897); and *Rädsep Óhk* (Tailor Óhk; 1903). Under the influence of realist writers, particularly **Eduard Vilde**, Kitzberg's social criticism became sharper. His collaboration with Vanemuine, the first professional theater in Estonia, was a turning point in his career; there he finally found a place where his plays were staged, and he developed a friendship with Karl Menning, the theater director, who became his patron. Kitzberg became the most prominent Estonian dramatist of the turn of the century, and his plays were also staged abroad—for example, in Hungary and Italy. In the drama *Kauka jumal* (1906; *In the gale of winds*; 1906), Kitzberg condemned social inequities and exonerated the poor, even if they fought for their rights by means of revolution. In the drama *Libahunt* (Werewolf; 1912) he depicted the reactions of a rural community to new social phenomena. The emancipation-seeking heroine comes into conflict with people around her; consequently she becomes the victim of a plot, and she is ousted from the village. She lives the life of a savage in the woods, and one day she is shot by her former fiancé, who, mistaking her for a wild animal, kills her out of fear. (AG)

Sources: *Kto est kto v kulture Estonii: Izobrazitelnie isskustva, literatura, teatr, muzika, kino* (Avenaris, 1996); *Eesti Entsuklopeedia*, vol. 14 (Tallinn, 2000); mapage.noos.fr/estonie/Kitzberg.html; www.miksike.ee/lisakogud/kirjandus/kitzberg.htm.

KLAUS Václav (19 June 1941, Prague), Czech economist and politician, president of the Czech Republic. In 1963 Klaus graduated in foreign trade from the Higher School of Economics in Prague, and then he worked in the Institute of Economics of the Czechoslovak Academy of Sciences (CAS). He went to Italy (1966) and the United States (1969) for additional training. In the 1960s he published articles criticizing the economic system, and in 1968 he became head of the economic section of *Lidové noviny*. After the suppression of the Prague Spring, Klaus was forced to leave the Institute of Economics in 1969. For fifteen years he worked in the central bank, and in 1987–89, in the Forecasting Institute of the CAS. In the 1970s and 1980s he mostly dealt with macroeconomics, monetary policy, and comparative economic systems. He published both in official periodicals and in the uncensored press, as well as abroad. He attracted a group of economists who developed monetarist views.

In November 1989 Klaus was one of the founders of the Civic Forum (Občanské Fórum [OF]), and he took part in talks between the opposition and the Communist authorities. In the government of **Marian Čalfa**, Klaus was minister of finance from December 1989. He retained this position after the first free elections of June 1990, and from 3 October 1991 he was simultaneously deputy prime minister. In October 1990 he became head of the OF, and after its split in April 1991 he became chairman of the (conservative-liberal) Civic Democratic Party (Občanská Demokratická Strana [ODS]). From June 1990 he was a deputy to the Chamber of the People of the Federal Assembly. After the elections of June 1992, when the breakup of Czechoslovakia became inevitable, Klaus resigned from the federal government and assumed the position of prime minister of the Czech Republic, which he held until 2 January 1998. Klaus was the chief architect of transformation to a market economy. He opposed the "third way" of **Valtr Komárek**, as well as the "non-political politics" of **Václav Havel**, which resulted in his conflicts with many politicians. He authored and implemented a controversial plan of coupon privatization. He helped both republics rejoin the International Monetary Fund and the World Bank, but his reforms were a source of frustration and protests, especially in Slovakia, which was an additional reason for the breakup of the federation. After the 1992 elections, as the ODS chairman, Klaus took part in talks on the dissolution of the federation with **Vladimir Mečiar**'s Movement for a Democratic Slovakia, which won in Slovakia. As the Czech prime minister, Klaus was not in favor of the Slovak "brake" on market reforms but supported an efficient separation and regulation of Czech-Slovak relations.

After the Czech Republic became independent, Klaus continued the market and democratic reforms. He supported privatization, although he opposed the restitution of nationalized property, especially that of the Catholic Church. He was skeptical about prospects for Central European cooperation and slowed down cooperation within the Višegrad Group (the Czech Republic, Hungary, Poland, and Slovakia). Initially he was also not enthusiastic about European integration. After the 1996 elections the ODS retained its position as the strongest Czech party, but a coalition with the Christian and Democratic Union–Czechoslovak People's Party (Křest'anská a Demokratická Unie–Československa Strana Lidová [KDU–ČSL]) and the Civic Democratic Alliance (Občanská Demokratická Aliance [ODA]) did not constitute a majority in the parliament. Klaus's new government faced a deteriorating economic and social situation and tensions within the coalition. The latter was also a result of Klaus's political style because he seemed convinced of his infallibility. In November 1997 a scandal broke out connected with irregularities in ODS financing; it led to the collapse of Klaus's government on 30 November 1997 and the departure of many disappointed activists from his party. Notwithstanding, Klaus managed to keep his position as ODS chairman and led the party to unexpected success in the early elections of June 1998. The ODS came in second after the Social Democrats. In view of the Social Democrats' inability to create a majority coalition, Klaus made an "opposition agreement" with them, providing for the formation of a minority Social Democratic government, the election of speakers of both houses from the ODS, and consultation on major government policies with the ODS.

On 17 July 1998 Klaus assumed the position of speaker in the parliament. Despite various challenges, the "opposition agreement" survived a full term of parliament, and Klaus was its speaker until the June 2002 elections. Since he was not a coalition member, he could criticize government policies while maintaining some influence over them. Contrary to widespread expectations, the ODS was defeated in 2002, and the Social Democrats entered into a new coalition with the KDU-ČSL and the Freedom Union, thereby discontinuing the "opposition agreement." Klaus and the ODS were forced into the opposition. Klaus declared that he would not run for the ODS chairmanship in the next election, and during the party congress in December 2002 he became its honorary chairman. Despite an unfavorable parliamentary configuration, Klaus attracted a number of leftist votes, and, after several rounds, he was finally elected president on 28 February 2003. (PU)

Sources: *ČBS*; *Českoslovenští politici: 1918–1991* (Prague, 1991); *Kdo byl kdo v našich dějinach ve 20. stoleti*, vol. 1 (Prague, 1998); Jan Rychlík, *Rozpad Československa: Česko-slovenské vztahy 1989–1992* (Bratislava, 2002); Eric Stein, *Czecho/Slovakia: Ethnic Conflict, Constitutional Fissure, Negotiated Breakup* (Ann Arbor, 1997); Oldřich Dědek et al., *Ekonomické aspekty zániku Československa* (Prague, 1997); www.ods.cz; wtd.vlada.cz/scripts/detail.php?id=457; www.klaus.cz.

KLAUSON Valter (20 December 1913, Tolmachov, near St. Petersburg–5 December 1988, Tallinn), Estonian Communist activist. The son of a laborer, Klauson was brought up in the USSR. In 1933 he finished a technical high school and subsequently worked as head of a technical department, taking part in the construction of roads, bridges, and railway lines. After the outbreak of the German-Soviet war in June 1941, he was inducted into the Red Army. He initially commanded a company and later a battalion. In 1943 he joined the Communist Party. After Soviet troops captured Estonia, Klauson went there as one of the "Yestonians" (Estonians who had been Russified in the USSR), and from 1944 to 1953 he held executive positions in the Administration of Roads of the Estonian SSR. In 1953–54 he served as minister of transport and roads of the Estonian SSR. In 1954 he became first deputy prime minister, and from October 1961 to January 1984 he served as prime minister of the Estonian SSR. In 1965 he graduated from a party university of the Central Committee (CC) of the Communist Party of the Soviet Union (CPSU). He was also a member of the USSR Supreme Soviet (1958–74), the CPSU CC (1961–86), and the Politburo of the Communist Party of Estonia (CPE) CC (1956–84). Klauson's career was closely linked with that of **Johannes Käbin**, first secretary of the CPE CC, as Klauson was one of his most trusted associates. Consequently, Klauson was to a great extent responsible for the persecutions in the 1960s and 1970s, but at the same time he helped to make living conditions in Estonia slightly better than in other Soviet republics. The dismissal of Käbin and the takeover of power by **Karl Vaino**, who was even more dogmatic, initially did not result in the dismissal of Klauson, who undoubtedly bears partial responsibility for the Russification policy during the early 1980s. Klauson was finally dismissed as prime minister in 1984, simultaneously losing his position in the ECP CC Politburo, which meant the end of his career. (AG)

Sources: *Bolshaia Sovetskaia Entsiklopediia*, vol. 12 (Moscow, 1973); *Eesti Enstuklopeedia*, vol. 14 (Tallinn, 2000); Toivo V. Raun, *Estonia and the Estonians* (Stanford, 1987); Tõnu Tannberg, Matti Laur, Tõnis Lukas, Ain Mäesalu, and Ago Pajur, *History of Estonia* (Tallinn, 2000).

KLEBELSBERG Kunó (13 November 1875, Magyarpécska [now in Romania]–11 October 1932, Budapest), Hungarian politician, count. After completing law studies at the university in Budapest in 1898, Klebelsberg worked in the Office of the Council of Ministers. He subsequently served as head of a department (1898–1910) and judge in the Administrative Court. During the second government of **István Tisza** (1913–17), he was secretary of state for administrative affairs in the Ministry for Religious Affairs and National Education (January 1914–March 1917) and secretary of state for political affairs in the Office of the Council of Ministers (March–June 1917). From 1917 to 1918 he was an MP on behalf of the majority National Labor Party of Tisza. In February 1919, along with Count **István Bethlen**, Klebelsberg founded the rightist anti-revolutionary Party of National Unity. Under the Hungarian Soviet Republic he went into hiding in the countryside. In 1920–31 he was again an MP, representing the ruling United Party (Egységes Párt) from 1922 on. In the government of Bethlen, Klebelsberg assumed the portfolio of minister of interior (December 1921–June 1922) and subsequently served as minister of education and religious affairs until August 1931.

Klebelsberg thought that the development of culture was the basis for the development of Hungary. His conservative reforms, based on so-called neo-nationalism, aimed at creating a strong and well-educated middle class. Under a law enacted in 1926, he implemented a policy that led within three years to the construction of nearly 6,000 modern classrooms in rural elementary schools and over 2,000 dwellings for teachers. A network of agricultural schools was established, 1,500 rural libraries and an equal number of school libraries were founded, and 500 kindergartens were organized. Illiteracy was greatly reduced. A network of *real* schools (emphasizing practical education) was established, secondary schools for girls were founded, more modern teaching aids were introduced, and an institutional system of higher education and research was set up. Klebelsberg attached great importance to the reorganization of the universities transferred from territories lost by Hungary. The university in Bratislava was moved to Pécs, and the university in Cluj was relocated to Szeged. The university in Debrecen was also developed. Klebelsberg also brought about the establishment of a network of Hungarian foreign institutes, the so-called Collegium Hungaricum (in 1924 in Vienna and Berlin; in 1927 in Rome, Paris, and Zurich), and with the help of the National Scholarship Council, established in 1927, he organized and expanded a system of academic scholarships. In 1922 Klebelsberg became a member of the Hungarian Academy of Sciences, and as president of the Hungarian Historical Society (1917–32), he initiated the publication of a series of source documents for the study of recent Hungarian history: *Fontes Historiae Hungaricae Aevi Recentoris*. Klebelsberg's publications include *Neónacionalizmus* (Neo-nationalism; 1928); *Beszédei, cikkei, törvényjavaslatai, 1916–1926* (Speeches, studies, and parliamentary bills, 1916–1926; 1927); and *Világváltságban* (In a Global Crisis; 1931). His *Tudomány, kultúra, politika* (Science, culture, politics) was published in 1990. (JT)

Sources: *Biographisches Lexikon*, vol. 2; *Nagy Képes Milleniumi Arcképcsarnok* (Budapest, 1999); *Magyar Nagylexikon*, vol. 11 (Budapest, 2000); József Huszti, *Gróf Klebelsberg Kunó életmúve* (Budapest, 1942); C. A. Macartney, *October Fifteenth: A History of Modern Hungary*, vols. 1–2 (Edinburgh, 1957–61); William M. Batkay, *Authoritarian Politics in a Transitional State: Istvan Bethlen and the United Party in Hungary, 1919–1926* (Boulder, Colo., 1982); *Gróf Klebelsberg Kunó emlékezete* (Szeged, 1995); Steven Bela Vardy, *Historical Dictionary of Hungary* (Lanham, Md., 1997).

KLEEBERG Franciszek (1 February 1888, Tarnopol [Ternopil]–5 April 1941, Weisser Hirsch, Germany), Polish general. Kleeberg finished a military *Realschule* in Hranice, passed his high school final exams in Vienna, and graduated from the Military Technical Academy in Mödling. In 1908 he became a professional officer in the Austrian artillery. In 1913 he began studying at the Military College in Vienna, but his studies were interrupted by the outbreak of World War I. From August 1914 to May 1915 he held various staff positions on the Russian front, and later he was assigned to the Polish Legions. Initially he served as staff officer of the Second Brigade of the Polish Legions; until May 1916 he was deputy chief of staff of the Legions' headquarters, and later he joined the staff of the Third Brigade. From February to July 1917 Kleeberg was deputy commander of the First Artillery Regiment of the Legions and subsequently served in the Polish Military Force (Polska Siła Zbrojna), which was subordinated to the German occupation authorities but remained under the auspices of the Provisional Council of State. In December 1917 Kleeberg became commander of an artillery training course in Garwolin, and in April 1918 he was again called up to staff service in the Austrian Army.

In November 1918 Kleeberg began serving in the Polish Army with the rank of lieutenant colonel. Until March 1919 he was chief of staff of the Wschód (East) Command during fighting against the Ukrainians in East Galicia. He subsequently worked in the Ministry for Military Affairs and served as head of the First Department of the General Staff. From July to October 1920, during the Polish-Soviet war, he was chief of staff of the First Army and the Operational Group. Later, he served as chief of staff of the General District Headquarters and chief of staff of the Corps Area Headquarters in Poznań. From October 1922 to May 1924 he was in command of the Fourteenth Infantry Division in Poznań. In 1925 he completed a course at the Military College in Paris. From November 1925 to March 1927 he was the academic director at the Military College in Warsaw, and afterwards he assumed command of the Twenty-ninth Infantry Division in Grodno. In 1928 he was promoted to the rank of general, and in 1934 he became commander of Corps Area Three in Grodno. In 1936 he was transferred to the post of commander of Corps Area Nine in Brześć on the Bug River. In September 1939 Kleeberg organized and then took command of the Polesie Operational Group, which fought against Soviet and German troops and then, marching to relieve Warsaw, took part in the last battles of the September campaign near Kock and Wola Gułowska (2–5 October 1939). The Polesie Group capitulated on 6 October. Kleeberg was taken prisoner by the Germans and held as a POW in harsh conditions in the fortress of Königstein. He died in a military hospital near Dresden. In 1943 he was posthumously promoted to major general. After the war, his body was brought to Poland and buried at the military cemetery in Kock. Kleeberg's works include *O organizacji artylerii* (On the organization of artillery, 3 vols.; 1920) and *Organizacja obrony państwa* (The organization of national defense, 7 vols.; 1922). (JS)

Sources: *PSB*, vol. 12; T. Kryska-Karski and S. Żurakowski, *Generałowie Polski Niepodległej* (London, 1976); Feliks Przyłubski, *Opowieść o generale Kleebergu: Wrzesień-październik 1939* (Warsaw, 1989); Zbigniew Mierzwiński, *Generałowie II Rzeczypospolitej* (Warsaw, 1990); Piotr Stawecki, *Słownik biograficzny generałów Wojska Polskiego 1918–1939* (Warsaw, 1994); *Encyklopedia Historii Polski: Dzieje polityczne*, vol. 1 (Warsaw, 1994).

KLEPACZ Michał (23 July 1893, Wola, near Warsaw–27 January 1967, Łódź), Polish Roman Catholic bishop. After graduating from a high school in Warsaw, in 1910 Klepacz entered the theological seminary in Kielce. In 1915–18 he studied at the Petrograd Theological Academy, where he was ordained in June 1916. After returning home, he became general secretary of the Catholic Youth Union of the Kielce diocese. After the establishment of the Catholic University of Lublin (Katolicki Uniwersytet Lubelski [KUL]) in 1918, Klepacz graduated from this university. From 1919 he taught dogmatics and the history of philosophy at the theological seminary in Kielce. He was co-founder of the Society of the Catholic School. In 1932 he received a Ph.D. in theology at the KUL. From 1937 he was professor of philosophy at the Department of Theology of the University of Wilno (Vilnius), and after it was closed at the end of 1939, he worked at the theological seminary and the secret Department of Theology in Wilno. On 3 March 1942, along with other professors and alumni of the seminary, Klepacz was arrested by the Germans and later sent to labor camps in Kaunas and Prowieniszki (Prowenischken).

After his release at the end of 1944, Klepacz returned to Wilno and taught in the local seminary. In 1945 Archbishop **Romuald Jałbrzykowski** sent him to Białystok in Poland, with the mission of organizing the seminary that was to be moved from Wilno. On 20 December 1946 Klepacz was appointed bishop of Łódź, and he was consecrated on 13 April 1947. In 1949–56 he belonged to the Joint Commission of the Government and Episcopate. After Primate **Stefan Wyszyński** was arrested on

28 September 1953, Klepacz became the only candidate to preside over the Conference of the Polish Episcopate who was acceptable to the Communist Party, so he was elected by the bishops. In an extremely difficult situation, he endorsed the official communiqués distancing the Episcopate from Primate Wyszyński. Klepacz tried to protect the Church from further attacks but had to accept increased interference from the Communist Party and the security apparatus in church life. He maintained good relations with **Bolesław Piasecki** and accepted the activities of his PAX Association against the unity of the Church. Notwithstanding, he maintained contact with the imprisoned Primate Wyszyński, and he strove to liberate him. On 26 August 1956 in Częstochowa, Klepacz read the Jasna Góra Vows of the Nation. After Wyszyński was freed, in the fall of 1956 Klepacz took part in talks with the government; these led to the signing of the so-called little agreement of 8 December 1956 on church-state relations. In 1958 Klepacz organized the synod of the Łódź diocese. He was active in the proceedings of the Second Vatican Council. Klepacz authored many works in theology, philosophy, and pedagogy, as well as numerous sermons and pastoral letters. (AGr)

Sources: *Słownik Polskich Teologów Katolickich 1918–1981* (Warsaw, 1983); *Encyklopedia Katolicka*, vol. 9 (Lublin, 2002); Andrzej Micewski, *Kardynał Wyszyński: Prymas i mąż stanu* (Paris, 1982); Antoni Dudek, *Państwo i Kościół w Polsce w latach 1945–1970* (Kraków, 1995); Jan Żaryn, *Stolica Apostolska wobec Polski i Polaków w latach 1944–1958* (Warsaw, 1998); Andrzej Grajewski, *Wygnanie: Diecezja katowicka w latach stalinowskich* (Katowice, 2002).

KLISZKO Zenon (8 December 1908, Łódź–4 September 1989, Warsaw), Polish Communist activist. Born into a working-class family, Kliszko graduated in law from Warsaw University and began working for the leftist press, joining the illegal Communist Party of Poland (Komunistyczna Partia Polski [KPP]) in 1931. After September 1939 he worked in the Soviet-occupied territories in Białystok and Lwów. In 1941 he arrived in Warsaw and joined the Polish Workers' Party (Polska Partia Robotnicza [PPR]) at the beginning of 1942. He fought in the Warsaw Uprising. A close associate of **Władysław Gomułka**, in August 1944 Kliszko became a member of the Central Committee (CC); in October of that year he became head of the CC Cadres Department, and in April 1945, secretary of the PPR CC. He was instrumental in organizing the PPR apparatus. Linked with the "home" faction of the PPR leadership, he closely followed the PPR policy aimed at gaining total power. In 1944–47 Kliszko was a deputy to the National Home Council (KRN) and then an MP in the Legislative Assembly. In 1945–48 he served as president of the PPR parliamentary representation. In October 1947 he was head of a special commission to investigate the "escape of **Stanisław Mikołajczyk** and his associates." When in August 1948 the "internationalists" attacked Gomułka's position and engineered his dismissal from the party leadership, Kliszko dissociated himself from his patron but did not avoid falling into disfavor. In September 1948 he was dismissed from his position in the PPR apparatus and was demoted to deputy member of the CC. At the December 1948 congress at which the Polish United Workers' Party (Polska Zjednoczona Partia Robotnicza [PUWP]) was founded, Kliszko was elected deputy member of the PUWP CC and undersecretary of state in the Ministry of Justice. On 13 November 1949, at the Third Plenum of the PUWP CC, he was dismissed from all his posts, arrested, and submitted to a harsh investigation.

Kliszko was released during the "thaw," and, together with Gomułka, he returned to politics. In August 1956 he was reelected deputy minister of justice. After the elections of January 1957, he assumed the post of deputy speaker of the Assembly, joining the Secretariat in May 1957 and the Politburo of the PUWP CC in March 1959. Kliszko's responsibilities included controlling the United Peasant Party (Zjednoczone Stronnictwo Ludowe [ZSL]) and the Democratic Party (Stronnictwo Demokratyczne [SD]). He was also responsible for relations with the Episcopate. He was in charge of the CC Agricultural Department and the PUWP parliamentary representation. In February 1960, Kliszko left the Agricultural Department and assumed control of the CC Foreign Department and Cadres Department and also took charge of parliamentary issues. In this last capacity, he was a particularly bothersome supervisor of the Catholic parliamentary group Znak. In 1963 Kliszko also became chairman of the PUWP CC Ideological Commission. He was known as a narrow-minded dogmatist in such areas as the struggle against the Catholic Church and independent culture.

When strikes erupted in northern Poland, Kliszko was sent there by Gomułka as his special representative. Along with **Ignacy Loga-Sowiński** and General Grzegorz Korczyński, he arrived in Gdańsk on the evening of 14 December 1970 to monitor events. As he saw that the authorities were losing control of the situation, the following day, with Gomułka's consent, Kliszko ordered the army and the Citizens' Militia (Milicja Obywatelska) to "pacify" Gdańsk. Without coordinating his actions with **Stanisław Kociołek**, who had called on the workers in Gdynia to resume work on 17 December, Kliszko made the decision to crush the protests by force, in Gdynia as well. This decision led to dozens of deaths. As one of the closest aides to Gomułka, Kliszko bore some of the responsibility for the bloodshed in northern Poland; thus on 20 December 1970 at the Seventh CC Plenum he was expelled from the CC Secretariat and Politburo, and in February 1971 at the Eighth Plenum he was also expelled from the CC. A party commission headed by **Władysław Kruczek** was to investigate the responsibility of the Gomułka administration for the tragedy in northern Poland, but it failed to reach any conclusions. Kliszko retired and was never held responsible for his decisions. (WR)

Sources: Mołdawa; *Słownik polityków polskich XX wieku* (Poznań, 1998); Nicholas Bethell, *Gomułka: His Poland, His Communism* (London, 1969); Andrzej Micewski, *Współrządzić czy nie kłamać* (Paris, 1978); Jan Nowak, *Polska z oddali* (London, 1988); *Tajne dokumenty państwo-Kościół 1960–1980* (London, 1996); Krzysztof Lesiakowski, *Mieczysław Moczar "Mietek": Biografia polityczna* (Warsaw, 1998); Włodzimierz Janowski and Aleksander Kochański, *Informator o strukturze i obsadzie personalnej centralnego aparatu PZPR 1948–1990* (Warsaw, 2000); Jerzy Eisler, *Grudzień 1970* (Warsaw, 2000).

KLJUSEV Nikola (2 October 1927, Shtip), Macedonian politician. In 1953 Kljusev graduated in economics from the University of Belgrade, and in 1964 he received a Ph.D. He worked as an assistant professor at the Institute of Macedonian Industrial Research (1953–59) and the Institute of Economics (1960–67). From 1968 he was a lecturer, and from 1972 a professor, in the Department of Economics of Ss. Cyril and Methodius University in Skopje. In 1988 he was elected a member of the Macedonian Academy of Sciences and Arts, in which he presided over the Council of Demographic Research and directed studies in economic theory and policy. After the elections of November and December 1990, as a follower of the Internal Macedonian Revolutionary Organization–Democratic Party for Macedonian National Unity (Vnatrešno-Makedonska Revolucionerna Organizacija–Demokratska Partija za Makedonsko Edinstvo [IMRO–DPMNU]), on 17 January 1991 Kljusev became a nonparty prime minister of a government of experts that led Macedonia to independence. He organized a referendum on secession from the Yugoslav federation and the formation of a sovereign state (8 September 1991). He also carried out a monetary reform and brought about the withdrawal of the Yugoslav People's Army from Macedonia. In view of Greek protests, Kljusev failed to gain recognition for the name of the new state by the European Union. In this connection, after a non-confidence vote on 7 July 1992, he resigned. He joined the IMRO-DPMNU and was elected chairman of its Supreme Council in September 1997. In the government of **Ljubcho Georgievski** Kljusev assumed the position of minister of defense (November 1998–October 2000), advocating Macedonia's entry into NATO, the deployment of NATO troops in Macedonia, and military cooperation with Albania, as well as a treaty on Kosovo between Macedonia and Albania. Kljusev authored *Koristenje na proizvodnite kapaciteti vo industrijata na SV Makedonija* (The utilization of Macedonian industrial capacity; 1967) and *Efektivnost na investicite vo industrijata na SR Makedonija* (The productivity of industrial investments in Macedonia; 1969), and he co-authored *Ekonomske funkcije federacije* (Economic functions of the federation; 1970), *Antiteza* (Anti-thesis; 1994), and *Pogledi i promeni* (Views and changes; 1995). (JD)

Sources: *Europa Środkowo-Wschodnia 1992* (Warsaw, 1994); Valentina Georgieva and Sasha Konechni, *Historical Dictionary of the Republic of Macedonia* (Lanham, Md., 1998); Irena Stawowy-Kawka, *Historia Macedonii* (Wrocław, 2000); Bugajski.

KLOFAČ Václav (21 September 1868, Havlíčkův Brod–10 July 1942, Prague), Czech journalist and politician, leader of the National Socialist Party. Klofač became active in politics in the 1890s as a student of philosophy. Between 1890 and 1899 he worked in the editorial offices of *Národný Listy*. At first he worked with the radical wing of the Young Czech Party, and in 1897 he co-founded the National Social Party (Strana Národné Sociálni). In 1907 he was one of the founders and the first editor-in-chief of *České slovo*, a press organ of the National Socialist Party. From 1901 Klofač sat in the Viennese parliament. He was an opponent of the Austro-Hungarian Empire and a proponent of Slavic cooperation. From this position, in 1908 he protested the annexation of Bosnia and Herzegovina, and he also developed contacts with Russian, Serbian, Croatian, and Slovenian politicians. Because of his convictions Klofač was imprisoned after the outbreak of World War I. He was the last Czech politician released in July 1917. Soon after he became deputy president of the association of Czech members in parliament, and from July 1918 he was deputy president of the Czechoslovak National Council (Národni Výbor Československý). At the end of October 1918 Klofač was a member of the Czech delegation at the Geneva negotiations on creating the first Czechoslovak government. In 1918–20 he served as defense minister in the first two cabinets. The post involved serious challenges, such as the introduction of state authority in the territory of Czechoslovakia and the defense of the borders of the newly created state. Klofač also joined the Revolutionary National Assembly (Revoluční Národní Shromáždění). Then, until the outbreak of World War II he was senator and deputy president of the Senate, and between February and November 1926, president of the Senate. Despite the attempts by **Jiři Stříbrny** to take over

power in the 1920s, for almost the entire interwar period Klofač headed the Czechoslovak National Socialist Party (Československá Strana Národně Socialistická). (PU)

Sources: *ČBS*; *Kto bol kto za I. ČSR* (Bratislava, 1993); B. Šantrůček, *Václav Klofač: Pohledy do života a díla* (Prague, 1928); *Kdo był kdo v našich dějinach ve 20. stoleti*, vol. 1 (Prague, 1998); *Politická elita meziválečného Československa 1918–1938: Kdo byl kdo za první republiky* (Prague, 1998).

KMET'KO Karol (12 December 1875, Veľ'ké Držkovce–22 Decembe, 1948 Nitra), Slovak Catholic bishop and social activist. Kmet'ko graduated in theology in Budapest and earned a Ph.D. in 1906. In addition to his pastoral service, he was devoted to educational and cultural work among peasants, founding cooperatives and mutual aid associations. He was a member of the St. Adalbert Society and the Slovak Museum Association. During World War I he was kept under police surveillance. In October 1918 he became a member of the Slovak National Council (Slovenská Národná Rada [SNR]). Kmet'ko was one of the signatories of the Martin Declaration of 30 October 1918, in which the SNR called for the creation of a common state of Czechs and Slovaks. From 1918 to 1922 he sat in the parliament in Prague, where he opposed the parceling out of the Church's estate and the nationalization of Catholic schools. In 1920 he became one of the first Slovak bishops in Czechoslovakia. As diocesan bishop of the diocese of Nitra, he resigned his parliamentary seat in 1922. He was friends with Reverend **Andrej Hlinka**, but he criticized Hlinka's choice of associates, and unlike Hlinka, he called for cooperation with members of the People's Party, led by Reverend **Jan Šramek**. In 1921 Kmet'ko became president of the Catholic School Council, helping to develop Church-run education. He supported missionary work and the development of monasteries. After the establishment of the Slovak Republic in March 1939, Kmet'ko supported the political ambitions of Reverend **Jozef Tiso**, but in 1941 he condemned the racist legislation. He opposed the persecution of Jews, particularly at the time of the deportation of Jews to German concentration camps in 1942. In 1944 Kmet'ko was appointed titular archbishop. After the restitution of Czechoslovakia, he served as chairman of the Conference of Slovak Bishops, enjoying great social respect. He protested the dissolution of Catholic organizations and the restriction of religious freedom. (MG)

Sources: Augustín Mat'ovčík et al., *Reprezentačný biografický lexikón Slovenska* (Martin, 1999); *Lexikón katolíckych kňazských osobností Slovenska* (Bratislava, 2000); *J. E. Dr. Karol Kmet'ko 25 rokov biskupom v Nitre* (Trnava, 1946); Martha Kristina Kona and Viliam Kona, eds., *Arcibiskup Dr. Karol Kmet'ko* (Cambridge, Ont., 1989); Bohdan Cywiński, *Ogniem próbowane*, vol. 2 (Rome, 1990).

KŇAŽKO Milan (28 August 1945, Horné Plachtince, Veľký Krtíš district), Slovak actor and politician. In 1968 Kňažko graduated from the Higher School of Musical Arts in Bratislava, following which he studied in a theater school in Nancy, France. He worked as an actor in the Theater on the Promenade in 1970–71, in the New Stage Theater in 1971–85, and in the Slovak National Stage in Bratislava in 1985–90. From 1967 to 1989 he belonged to the Party of Slovak Renaissance (Strana Slovenskej Obrody), a Communist satellite. In November 1989 he co-founded the Civic Forum (Občanské Fórum) in Prague, and then he returned to Bratislava, where he joined the Public against Violence (Verejnosť Proti Nasiliu [VPN]) and its Coordination Committee. Kňažko took part in talks with the authorities that resulted in the formation of the government of **Marian Čalfa**. From January to June 1990 he was an adviser to President **Václav Hável**, and from June 1990 to June 1992 he was a deputy to the Chamber of the People of the Federal Assembly. In the spring of 1991 Kňažko left the VPN and co-founded the Movement for a Democratic Slovakia (Hnutie za Demokratické Slovensko [HZDS]). From September 1990 to May 1991 he was the first minister of international relations of the Slovak Republic. Owing to an unclear division of authority, he often entered into conflict with the foreign minister of Czechoslovakia, **Jiří Dienstbier**. Deputy chairman of the HZDS from June 1991 to March 1993, in June 1992 Kňažko was elected to the Slovak National Council (renamed the National Council of the Slovak Republic after the breakup of the federation), and he remained Slovak minister of international relations.

After the breakup of the federation, from January 1993 Kňažko was the first foreign minister of Slovakia, but in March 1993 he entered into conflict with the HZDS leader, **Vladimír Mečiar**. He left the party and co-founded the Democratic Alliance (DA), following a more liberal political line and opposing Mečiar. After another group of activists left the HZDS and formed the Union for a Democratic Slovakia, the DA joined it. In April 1994 Kňažko became the union's deputy chairman and an MP. When a group of secessionists from the Slovak National Party joined, his party adopted the name of Democratic Union (Demokratická Únia [DU]). To prevent another HZDS victory, in 1997 the DU joined the Slovak Democratic Coalition (Slovenská Demokratická Koalicia [SDK]). In the elections of September 1998 the HZDS won one mandate more than the SDK, but Mečiar, lacking allies, could not form a new government. Under these circumstances, the SDK and other anti-Mečiar factions formed a coalition. In the government of **Mikuláš Dzurinda**, based on this coalition, Kňažko became minister of culture in October

1998. He favored changing the SDK into one party, so when in 2000 Prime Minister Dzurinda established the Slovak Democratic and Christian Union (Slovenská Demokratická Kresťanská Únie [SDKÚ]), Kňažko joined it and became its deputy chairman for media and cultural affairs. (PU)

Sources: *ČBS*; *Kdo byl kdo v našich dějinach ve 20. stoleti*, vol. 1 (Prague, 1998); Jan Rychlík, *Rozpad Československa:Česko-slovenské vztahy 1989–1992* (Bratislava, 2002); Eric Stein, *Czecho/Slovakia: Ethnic Conflict, Constitutional Fissure, Negotiated Breakup* (Ann Arbor, 1997); www.sdkuonline.sk/podpreds4.php3.

KÖBLÖS Elek, pseudonym "Bǎdulescu" (17 April 1887, Dumbravioara, Mureş–November or December 1937, Moscow), Romanian Communist activist. Köblös was born into a Jewish family in Transylvania, where he worked as a woodcutter and was active in the trade unions. At the end of World War I he joined a Hungarian Socialist revolutionary organization that pursued both social and national aims. After the incorporation of Transylvania into Romania, Köblös supported the Hungarian Soviet Republic (HSR), and in October 1920 he took part in a general strike attempt that was suppressed by the government. In May 1921 he represented Transylvanian Communists at the founding congress of the Communist Party of Romania (CPR). At the Second Congress of the CPR he became a member of the Central Committee (CC) and subsequently a member of the Politburo of the party, where he was in charge of the trade union section. Köblös supported the Comintern's policy aimed at partitioning Romania and establishing a separate Transylvanian statehood. Consequently, in the spring of 1924 the Communist International entrusted him with the leadership of the Romanian party. In May and June 1924 he attended the Fifth Congress of the Comintern, where he consolidated his position; following that, at the Third Congress of the CPR in August 1924 in Vienna he gave the main speech and was elected secretary general of the party. After the CPR was declared illegal in April 1924, Köblös unsuccessfully attempted to use the legal Peasants' and Workers' Bloc as a front. Fearing arrest, in the autumn of 1925 he left for the Soviet Union. He directed party activities from Moscow and Vienna. He was arrested by Czechoslovak authorities while attempting to return to Romania but was allowed to return to the Soviet Union. Attacked at the Fourth Congress of the CPR in Kharkiv in June 1928 for following a "Trotskyist political line," Köblös was dismissed from his position, although he had performed a self-criticism, and the leadership of the party was assumed by Vitali Holostenko, a Ukrainian. In December 1929 Köblös was also denounced by the CC of the All-Union Communist Party (Bolsheviks) and by the Comintern, and then he was completely removed from political life. Arrested by the NKVD in 1937, he was sentenced to death and executed. (WR)

Sources: Lazitch; Florin Constantiniu, ed., *O ancheta stalinista 1937–1938: Lichidarea lui Marcel Pauker* (Bucharest, 1995); Dennis Deletant, *Communist Terror in Romania: Gheorghiu-Dej and the Police State, 1948–1965* (New York, 1999).

KOBYLYANSKA Olha (27 November 1863, Gura Humorului–21 March 1942, Chernivtsi [Cernăuţi, Czernowitz]), Ukrainian writer linked with Bukovina. Born into the large family of an Austrian clerk, Kobylyanska finished only four grades of a German elementary school, but she later gained knowledge of the Ukrainian and European literary culture by studying on her own. In 1891 she settled permanently in Czernowitz. She wrote her first works in German, but after 1891 she wrote only in Ukrainian. Her writing was much influenced by Ukrainian writers of the turn of the century, such as **Lesya Ukrainka**, **Ivan Franko**, and **Mykhailo Kotsiubynsky**. Contacts with Galician circles, as well as her own experience, led to Kobylyanska's involvement in the Ukrainian women's movement, evidence of which appeared in her early works. In the novels *Liudyna* (A person; 1891) and *Tsarivna* (The princess; 1894) and in the stories *Vin i vona* (He and she; 1892), *Impromptu phantasie* (1895), and *Valse melancholique* (1898), Kobylyanska presented poor young women who opposed the provincial middle-class communities that condemned them to social isolation. Many of these characters had the features of a spiritual aristocratism, inspired by the work of Friedrich Nietzsche. Kobylyanska's stories written in 1914–18 had anti-war overtones. The workings of the forces of nature and passions, which direct human fate, are presented in such novels as *Zemlia* (Land; 1902) and *V nediliu rano zillia kopala* (She was gathering herbs on Sunday morning; 1909). The main characters in these novels are Bukovinian peasants and workers. Kobylyanska addressed issues of social service in the novels *Nioba* (1905); *Cherez kladku* (Across the bridge; 1912); and her last great work, *Apostol cherni* (Apostle of the Black, 2 vols.; 1936).

Because Kobylyanska was an avowed social activist and a democrat, during the so-called Ukrainization period her work aroused interest in the Soviet Union, where nine volumes of her works were published between 1927 and 1929; the year 1928 saw official celebrations of forty years of her creative work. The authorities of the Ukrainian SSR gave her material assistance but failed to encourage her to come to the Ukraine. When in August 1940 the Soviet authorities arrived in Bukovina, Kobylyanska became a member of the Union of Ukrainian Writers, and her image was exploited to serve the needs of unification propaganda.

Kobylyanska died after the return of the Romanian authorities to Bukovina. (TS)

Sources: O. Makovei, "Olha Kobylyanska," *Literaturno-Naukovyi Vistnyk*, 1902, no. 12; L. Kohut, ed., *Olha Kobylyanska: Almanakh u pamyatku ii soroklitnoy pysmennytskoy diialnosty (1887–1927)* (Chernivtsi, 1928); L. Luka, *O. Kobylyanska i F. Nichshe* (Lviv, 1928); O. Kushch, *Olha Kobylyanska: Bibliohrafichnyi pokazhchyk* (Kiev, 1960); N. Tomashuk, *Olha Kobylyanska* (Kiev, 1969); V. Vozniuk, *Pro Olhu Kobylyansku* (Kiev, 1983).

KOC Adam, pseudonyms "Witold" and "Szlachetny" (31 August 1891, Suwałki–3 February 1969, New York), Polish officer and politician. In 1909 Koc joined the Union of Active Struggle, organized by **Józef Piłsudski**, and then he belonged to the Riflemen's Union and commanded its Warsaw district. After the outbreak of World War I, he organized the Polish Military Organization and was its Warsaw commander. In 1915 he got through to the Polish Legions, where he became an officer of the First Brigade. In 1917–18 he led diversionary maneuvers during the German occupation, and in November 1918 he commanded the disarmament of German troops. After the war Koc stayed in the Polish Army, and in 1919 he graduated from the School of the General Staff; then he worked in its Second Department (intelligence and counterintelligence). Later he was chief of propaganda in the High Command, and he organized and commanded the 201st Regiment of the Polish Army. From July to December 1920 he commanded a volunteer division in the Polish-Soviet war. From 1921 he worked in Inspectorate No. 2 of the army; in 1924–26 he was chief of the Department of Non-Catholic Denominations in the Ministry of Military Affairs; and from 1926 to 1928 he was chief of staff of the District Corps Command in Lwów (Lviv).

In 1928 Koc retired with the rank of colonel and became an MP on behalf of the *sanacja* Nonparty Bloc of Cooperation with the Government. He also headed its parliamentary club. In 1929–30 he was editor-in-chief of the pro-government weekly *Głos Prawdy* and the daily *Gazeta Polska*. In 1930 he became undersecretary of state in the Ministry of the Treasury; in 1932 he became a member and from 1936 he was chairman of the board of the Bank of Poland (Bank Polski). In 1936 Koc began to organize a new government party, the Camp of National Unity (Obóz Zjednoczenia Narodowego [OZN]). In February 1937 he became its head, and he announced the "OZN Declaration," which included authoritarian and nationalist elements and with which he wanted to attract the younger generation of radical nationalists. In June 1937 Koc organized the Union of Young Poland and took its lead. This union failed, and Koc got himself into trouble with the Piłsudski old guard, so in December 1937 he was dismissed from the OZN leadership.

In 1938 he became a senator of behalf of the OZN. After the outbreak of World War II he left for France, where from October to December 1939 he was minister of treasury in the government-in-exile of General **Władysław Sikorski**. In 1940 Koc settled in New York, where he was active in the *sanacja* émigré community. (PU)

Sources: *Kto był kim w Drugiej Rzeczypospolitej* (Warsaw, 1994); *Encyklopedia historii Drugiej Rzeczypospolitej* (Warsaw, 1999); Tadeusz Katelbach, "'Szlachetny' (Wspomnienie o Adamie Kocu)," *Zeszyty Historyczne*, 1969, no. 16; Edward D. Wynot, *Polish Politics in Transition: The Camp of National Unity and the Struggle for Power, 1925–1939* (Athens, Ga., 1974); Jacek Majchrowski, *Silni-zwarci-gotowi: Myśl polityczna Obozu Zjednoczenia Narodowego* (Warsaw, 1985).

KOCBEK Edvard (27 September 1904, Videm, Gornja Radgona–3 November 1981, Ljubljana), Slovene writer, poet, and politician. During the interwar period, Kocbek belonged to the supporters of Slovene Christian socialism and worked as the editor of the periodical *Križ*. He also wrote for the periodicals *Ogenj* and *Dom in svet*. Because he criticized clericalism and the Slovene church's support for General Francisco Franco in Spain, he came into conflict with the conservative faction of the Slovene Catholic peasant party. During World War II Kocbek supported the partisans of **Josip Broz Tito**. After the war he held various positions in the apparatus of power in Belgrade and Ljubljana. However, he did not accept the ideological mentality of Communists and consequently came into conflict with them as well. Forced to take compulsory retirement in 1952, he withdrew from political life and took up writing and translating. Kocbek published his first poems as early as the 1920s. At that time he wrote under the influence of expressionism and symbolism, reflecting on the condition of man and his place in society. In 1964 his collection *Groza* received the France Prešeren Literary Award. At that time he also wrote diaries and literary sketches. In 1975 in the periodical *Zaliv*, published in Triest, Kocbek criticized the massacre of members of the Home Guard (*domobranci*) committed by the Communists after the war; consequently he fell into disfavor. In 1977 he published his famous novels, *Žerjavica* (Embers) and *Nevesta v črnem* (The bride in black). Highly acclaimed as well were the collection of novels *Strah in pogum* (Fear and courage; 1951); the diaries *Tovarišja* (Comrades; 1949) and *Listina* (Document; 1967); and the collection of essays *Svoboda in nujnost* (Freedom and necessity; 1974). Kocbek also translated works by Honoré de Balzac, Guy de Maupassant, and Antoine de Saint-Exupéry. (WR)

Sources: *Enciklopedia Slovenije*, vol. 5 (Ljubljana, 1991); *Mały słownik pisarzy zachodnio-słowiańskich i południowo-słowiańskich* (Warsaw, 1973); S. Hribar, *Edvard Kocbek in križansko gibanje* (Maribor, 1990); Jill Benderly and Evan Kraft, eds., *Independent Slovenia: Origins, Movements, Prospects* (London, 1994); Leopoldina Plut-Progelj and Carole Rogel, *Historical Dictionary of Slovenia* (Lanham, Md., 1996); James Gow and Cathie Carmichael, *Slovenia and the Slovenes* (London, 2000).

KOCIOŁEK Stanisław (3 May 1933, Warsaw), Polish Communist activist. Born into an intelligentsia family, in 1951–52 Kociołek was a schoolmaster in Piotrków, Iława County. In 1957 he graduated from Warsaw University. From 1953 he belonged to the (Communist) Polish United Workers' Party (Polska Zjednoczona Partia Robotnicza PUWP]). In 1956–58 he was first secretary of the PUWP committee at Warsaw University, from 1958 to 1960 he was first secretary of the Warsaw Committee of the Union of Socialist Youth, and in 1963–64 he was first secretary of the Downtown Warsaw PUWP Committee. Promoted by **Władysław Gomułka**, in 1964 Kociołek became first secretary of the Warsaw City PUWP Committee. He was considered a hard-liner. For instance, he was active in the attacks on intellectuals demanding a freedom of speech. From 1967 to 1970 he was first secretary of the Gdańsk Provincial PUWP Committee; from June to November 1964 he was a deputy member, and from November 1964 to December 1971 a member, of the PUWP Central Committee (CC). From November 1968 to March 1971 he was a member of the Politburo, and in 1970–71 he was secretary of the PUWP CC. In 1965–72 he was an MP. In April 1968 he made a speech in the parliament brutally attacking deputies from the Catholic club Znak (Sign) who had spoken in defense of the writers and students slandered after the March 1968 events.

From 30 June to 23 December 1970 Kociołek was deputy prime minister. In this capacity he went to the Baltic Triple City (Gdańsk-Sopot-Gdynia) to control the operations against the striking workers. On 15 December, in a television speech, he justified the police crackdown in Gdańsk, and the next day, without coordinating his move with another top party leader, **Zenon Kliszko**, he called on the Gdynia workers to go back to work on 17 December. While on the way, the workers were shot at, and several dozen people were killed. Kociołek was one of the leaders of a movement aimed at dismissing Gomułka. In this respect he was thought to have cooperated with **Mieczysław Moczar**. On 19 March 1971 Kociołek left the Politburo, and from June 1971 to August 1978 he was ambassador to Belgium and Luxembourg. From September 1978 to March 1980 he chaired the board of the Central Administration of Labor Cooperatives, and from June to November 1980 he was ambassador to Tunisia. During a counteroffensive of hard-liners, in November 1980

Kociołek again became first secretary of the Warsaw City PUWP Committee, advocating a crackdown on Solidarity, especially in the fall of 1981. After the introduction of martial law in December 1981 he strove to intensify the repression against Solidarity and democratic opposition leaders. Dismissed by General **Wojciech Jaruzelski**, from mid-1982 to the end of 1985 Kociołek was ambassador to the USSR and later editor-in-chief of the periodical *Polish Perspectives*. After 1989 an investigation was started concerning his responsibility for the 1970 Gdynia massacre. Kociołek became one of the main defendants in a trial that began in September 2001. (PK)

Sources: Mołdawa; Andrzej Albert [Wojciech Roszkowski], *Najnowsza historia Polski 1914–1993*, vols. 1–2 (Warsaw, 1993); *Popularna Encyklopedia Powszechna*, vol. 9 (Kraków, 1996); Krzysztof Lesiakowski, *Mieczysław Moczar "Mietek": Biografia polityczna* (Warsaw, 1998); Włodzimierz Janowski and Aleksander Kochański, *Informator o strukturze i obsadzie personalnej centralnego aparatu PZPR 1948–1990* (Warsaw, 2000); Jerzy Eisler, *Grudzień 1970* (Warsaw, 2000).

KODÁLY Zoltán (16 December 1882, Kecskemét–6 March 1967, Budapest), one of the two most outstanding Hungarian composers and ethnographers of the twentieth century (the other one being **Béla Bartók**). In 1900 Kodály began to study both at the Budapest Academy of Music and at the Humanities Faculty of Budapest University. In 1904 he received a diploma in composition, and in 1906, a Ph.D. in Hungarian and German philology. In 1905 he toured Hungary in his first quest for folk song sources and later continued his research with Bartók. From 1907 to 1940 Kodály lectured at the Budapest Academy of Music, becoming a full professor in 1912. In December 1918 he became deputy director of this academy. Along with Bartók and Ernő Dohnányi, he was elected to the music directorate of the People's Commissariat of Education in the government of the Hungarian Soviet Republic. In the autumn of 1919, because of his role in the revolution, disciplinary proceedings were instituted against him, and in September 1921 he was forced to take a compulsory leave.

The works that Kodály composed in the 1920s brought him acclaim throughout the world. At that time he also began to work in the field of musical pedagogy. He developed a method—named the Kodály method—of teaching music to children and adolescents. From the 1930s, Kodály sympathized with the movement of peasant writers and supported the leftist March Front, which strove to develop the Hungarian countryside and which was proscribed by the authorities in 1938, after two years of existence. In 1938, along with many other public figures and representatives of the intelligentsia, Kodály protested the first anti-Jewish law. In March 1942 he signed an anti-war and anti-German manifesto issued by the Committee for Historical Memory. In 1944 he went into hiding from the Germans. A prominent representative of intellectual life, in November 1945 Kodály became an MP. In 1945 he became director of the Budapest Academy of Music, and from 1946 to 1949 he served as president of the Hungarian Academy of Sciences. In 1951 he became head of the Musicology Committee of the Academy of Sciences and was in charge of a folk music research group.

As a person with close links to the National Peasant Party (which was revived under the name of Petőfi Party), during the 1956 revolution Kodály was put forward as a candidate for the position of chairman of a provisional organ that served as the head of state. On 21 November 1956 he became president of the Revolutionary Committee of Hungarian Intellectuals, whose activities were suspended a month later. Kodály was awarded the Kossuth Prize (1948, 1952, 1957) and granted honorary doctorates at Oxford University (1960) and Humboldt University in Berlin (1964). His work contributed greatly to the revival of musical culture in Hungary and to the consolidation of national cultural values. Kodály's most famous works include editions of folk songs, the opera *Háry János*, and the *Psalmus Hungaricus* (1923), written to celebrate the fiftieth anniversary of the union of Buda and Pest, as well as *Te Deum* (1936), *Missa Brevis* (1943–44), and some chamber works. (JT)

Sources: *A magyar forradalom és szabadságharc enciklopédiája* (Budapest, 1999); *Magyar Nagylexikon*, vol. 11 (Budapest, 2000); *Kodály Centenary 1982*, Sound Recording, Fuga (Finland), 1960; Katinka S. Daniel, *Kodály Approach: Method Book* (Champaign, Ill., 1979); Lois Choksy, *The Kodály Context: Creating Environment for Musical Learning* (Englewood Cliffs, N.J., 1981).

KOFLER Remus (1902–17 April 1954, Bucharest), Romanian Communist activist. In the early 1940s Kofler was deputy leader of the Romanian Communist Party (RCP). During the **Ion Antonescu** dictatorship he was at large, maintaining contacts with a group of younger activists, headed by **Gheorghe Gheorghiu-Dej**, who were detained or interned by the regime. Kofler took part in the preparations for the coup of 23 August 1944, which removed Antonescu from power. After the Communist takeover in early 1945, Kofler was dismissed from the party leadership, and on 13 December 1949 he was arrested. The prosecution wanted to prove that he took part in a plot against "the power of the people," allegedly led by **Iuliu Maniu**. As a result of torture, Kofler confessed that he had cooperated with the Antonescu police. There were attempts to prove that he was also responsible for "anti-party" and "anti-state" activities in connection with the trial of **Laszló Rajk** in Hungary and **Traycho Kostov** in Bulgaria. Ultimately Kofler was accused of high treason and cooperation with "Fascist" police and British intelligence. In mid–April 1954 the Communist Party Politburo decided to close the case in which he was tried along with **Lucreţiu Pătrăşcanu** and his aides. Kofler was sentenced to death and almost immediately executed. (ASK)

Sources: Lavinia Betea, "'Recunoştiinţa' partidului pentru cei care 1-au subvenţionat," *Magazin Istoric*, 1997, no. 7; Dennis Deletant, *Communist Terror in Romania: Gheorghiu-Dej and the Police State, 1948–1965* (New York, 1999).

KOKALARI Musine (25 October 1917, Adana, Turkey–13 August 1983, Rreshen), Albanian writer, democratic activist, and political prisoner. The daughter of a lawyer, Kokalari first went to school in Gjirokastër and then attended Naim Frashëri High School in Tirana. Between 1937 and 1941 she studied literature in Rome, where she earned a doctorate. After returning to Albania, she was affiliated with pro-Western intellectual circles, and she also wrote for the illegal political press. After Italy capitulated in September 1943 and the politicians who had been previously interned returned to Albania, Kokalari helped to establish the Social Democratic Party, which was joined by leftist activists from the National Front (Balli Kombëtar) and by some of the former activists of the Communist Party of Albania. Kokalari was also in charge of *Zeri i Lirisë*, an organ of the party. An attempt to form a military unit in the region of Vlorë ended in the arrest and execution of most party leaders by the Gestapo. Kokalari avoided arrest but was forced to abandon her political activities. In November 1944 her two brothers were executed by firing squad without trial. She was arrested on 16 November 1944 but was released after seventeen days.

In 1945 Kokalari refused to join the Communist-dominated Union of Albanian Writers. She got in touch with democratic and anti-Communist circles and with representatives of the British mission. In March 1945, along with Gjergji Kokoshi and Suad Asllani, she founded an anti-Communist group that entered into cooperation with similar groups led by Sami Çeribashi and Qenan Dibra. Their work resulted in a memorandum on the situation in Albania that was presented to diplomatic missions based in Tirana. On Kokalari's initiative, on 6 November 1945 the Democratic Union (Bashkimi Demokratik) was established in Tirana. This organization issued a memorandum that demanded that Western countries intervene and help to create an appropriate political atmosphere before the elections that were to be held on 2 December 1945. Kokalari's contacts with the English prompted her arrest (23 January 1946). On 2 July of that year she was sentenced to twenty years in prison. She initially served her sentence in a prison attached to an iron ore mine in Burrell, and in 1952 she was transferred to one of the penal institutions in Tirana. Released in 1961, she was interned in Rreshen, where she had limited freedom of movement and worked on the land and on construction sites. Kokalari's publications include a collection of stories, *Siç më thotë nëna plakë* (Like my old mother told me; 1941), in which she depicted folk customs and traditions. (TC)

Sources: Eglantina Mandia, *Sonata e hënës: Rrefim për nje jete* (Tirana, 1995); Agim Musta, *Mandelët e Shqiperise* (Tirana, n.d.); Pepa Pjeter, *Dosja e diktaturës* (Tirana, 1995); Musine Kokalari, *Si lindi Partia Socjal Demokrate: Artikuj, shkrime, esse, kujtime* (Tirana, 2000).

KOŁAKOWSKI Leszek (23 October 1927, Radom), Polish philosopher. Kołakowski graduated in philosophy from Warsaw University (1950); in 1953 he received a Ph.D. and in 1956 a postdoctoral degree (*habilitacja*); in 1964 he became a professor. He worked as an assistant professor at Łódź University (1947–49) and Warsaw University (1949–51). In 1952–54 he worked at the Institute of Social Sciences of the Central Committee (CC) of the Polish United Workers' Party (Polska Zjednoczona Partia Robotnicza [PUWP]), and from 1952 to 1968 he was at Warsaw University, where he was chair of History of Modern Philosophy (1959–68). In 1946–48 Kołakowski belonged to the (Communist) Polish Workers' Party, and from December 1948 he belonged to the PUWP. Initially he was a spokesman of vulgar Marxism, active on the "ideological front." He contributed to party periodicals, such as *Kuźnica* and *Nowe Drogi*, and he fiercely criticized Christian philosophy, the Catholic Church, and religion—for instance, in the collection *Szkice o filozofii katolickiej* (Essays on Catholic philosophy; 1955). From 1956 Kołakowski sympathized with the so-called revisionism, opposing Marxism as an institutional doctrine but still supporting Marxism as an intellectual offer capable of change. He treated the concept of socialism as a utopia that should be approached with the awareness that there was no guarantee of its implementation. He stressed the necessity of analyzing all dogmas and allegedly absolute truths—for instance, in *Kapłan i Błazen* (Chaplain and clown; 1959). Kołakowski strove toward a humanist Marxism, based on the autonomy of the human being and his/her responsibility. In philosophical treatises, popular essays, and plays, he gradually evolved from criticism to a dialogue with Catholic philosophy. In 1957 Kołakowski was attacked by **Władysław Gomułka**, and in 1966 he was expelled from the PUWP for criticizing its political line; this led to the resignation from the party of several outstanding writers. In March 1968 Kołakowski was recognized as one of the main ideologues and protectors of the student movement, for which he was deprived of his position as chair and expelled from Warsaw University.

From November 1968 Kołakowski lectured in Montreal and Berkeley and, from 1970, at Oxford. He published in outstanding Western and émigré periodicals, such as *Kultura* and *Aneks*. Some of his articles—such as "Tezy o nadziei i beznadziejności" (Theses of hope and hopelessness; 1971)—were significant for the formation of the democratic opposition in Poland. In 1976–79 Kołakowski published his opus magnum, *Główne nurty marksizmu* (Main Currents of Marxism, 1978), in which he critically assessed Marxist philosophy; it was translated into many languages. In the 1970s and 1980s he mainly searched for the permanent foundation of culture and civilization; ultimately he found it in religion (*Jeśli Boga nie ma*, 1988; *Religion: If There Is No God*, 1982). A member of the scholarly academies of many countries and a winner of many prestigious awards, in 1976–77 Kołakowski worked with the Committee for the Defense of Workers in Poland, and he contributed to its popularity in the West. Until 1980 and again in 1982–87 his publications, or even quotations from them, were banned in Poland. Kołakowski also authored, among other things, the following: *Trzynaście bajek z królestwa Lailonii dla dużych i małych* (1963; *Tales from the Kingdom of Lailonia*, 1989); *Klucz niebieski* (1964; *Key to Heaven*, 1972); *Rozmowy z diabłem* (Conversations with the devil; 1965); *Obecność mitu* (1972; *Presence of Myth*, 1989); *Czy diabeł może być zbawiony* (Can the devil be saved? 1982); *Metaphysical Horror* (1988); *Pochwała niekonsekwencji* (Eulogy of inconsistence, 3 vols.; 1989); and *Mini wykłady o maxi sprawach* (Mini-lectures on maxi-problems; 1997). Kołakowski's works are translated into most Western languages. In November 2003 he was selected by the Library of Congress for its first John W. Kluge Prize for Lifetime Achievement in Humanities and Social Sciences.

Sources: *Nowa encyklopedia powszechna PWN*, vol. 3 (Warsaw, 1995); *Opozycja w PRL: Słownik biograficzny 1956–89*, vol. 1 (Warsaw, 2000); Gesine Schwan, *Leszek Kolakowski: Eine marxistische Philosophie der Freiheit* (Stuttgart, 1971); Mariola Flis, *Leszek Kołakowski: Teoretyk kultury europejskiej* (Kraków, 1992); Maria Kaczmarska, *Leszek Kołakowski: Bibliografia podmiotowo-przedmiotowa* (Radom, 1994); Jan Andrzej Kłoczowski, *Więcej niż mit: Leszka Kołakowskiego spory o religię* (Kraków, 1994); Christian Heidrich, *Leszek Kolakowski: Zwischen Skepsis und Mystik* (Frankfurt, 1995); Stanley Pierson, *Leaving Marxism* (Stanford, 2001).

KOLAROV Vasil (16 July 1877, Shumen–23 January 1950, Sofia), Bulgarian Communist leader. The son of a shoemaker, after high school Kolarov studied law at Ge-

neva University. In 1897 he joined the Bulgarian Social Democratic Party, and in 1903 he supported its Bolshevik faction, the Tesnyaki. Between 1904 and 1912 he headed the party organization in Plovdiv. From 1905 he sat on the Central Committee of the party, and from 1913 he sat in parliament. Kolarov attended conferences of the Socialist International in Stuttgart (1907) and Copenhagen (1910). At a conference in Zimmerwald he did not support the Leninist faction. In April 1919, when the Communist Party of Bulgaria was created, Kolarov became secretary of its CC. From then on, he frequently went to Russia. In 1920 he was the Bulgarian delegate to the Second Congress of the Communist International, and in 1921 he presided over its Third Congress. At the Fourth Congress in 1923 Kolarov joined the Executive Committee, Presidium, and Secretariat of the Comintern. At the beginning of 1923, as the Comintern's representative, he made a journey to France, Czechoslovakia, Germany, and Norway. At the end of June 1923 he returned to Bulgaria. Temporarily arrested, after his release he became head of a revolutionary committee that attempted to assume power during a coup in September 1923. After the failure of the action, Kolarov fled to Yugoslavia and then, via Austria, reached the USSR, where he stayed for the next twenty-two years, assuming Soviet citizenship. As a member of the Comintern leadership, Kolarov closely cooperated with its leader, his compatriot **Georgi Dimitrov**, and he loyally supported the Stalinist line. In 1928–29 he headed the Balkan Secretariat of the Comintern. Along with Dimitrov, he headed a group of Bulgarian Communists in the USSR. He went on special missions to various countries of Western Europe and to Mongolia. From 1928 to 1939 he was president of Peasant International. In May 1943 he signed an act dissolving the Comintern but continued to work in its apparatus, which was transferred to a special department of the CC of the All-Union Communist Party (Bolsheviks).

Kolarov returned to Bulgaria in September 1945, assuming the post of deputy president of the Fatherland Front. After the abolition of the monarchy, between 15 September 1946 and 9 December 1947 he was provisional president of the Bulgarian People's Republic, and between 21 November 1946 and 9 December 1947 he served as president of the Communist-dominated National Assembly. Kolarov authorized a brutal crackdown on the Peasant Party, ignoring the letters sent to him by **Nikola Petkov**, who was sentenced to death. On 11 December 1947 he became deputy prime minister and foreign minister. After the death of Georgi Dimitrov, on 20 July 1949 Kolarov assumed the post of head of government. In this role, he supervised the case of **Traicho Kostov**, who was sentenced to death and executed in

December 1949. Kolarov died while serving as prime minister. (WR)

Sources: Lazitch; *V pamet na Vasil Kolarov* (Sofia, 1951); Joseph Rothschild, *The Communist Party of Bulgaria* (New York, 1959); Nevena Krumova, *Prez buri: Iz zivota na Vasil Kolarov* (Sofia, 1964); Paulina Edreva, *Vasil Kolarov* (Sofia, 1972); Jerzy Jackowicz, *Partie opozycyjne w Bułgarii 1944–1948* (Warsaw, 1997).

KOLAS Yakub [originally Kanstantsin Mitskevich] (3 November 1882, Akinchitse, near Stoubtsy–13 August 1956, Minsk), Belorussian poet, writer, and journalist. The son of a forester, Kolas completed a teacher training college in Niasvizh in 1902. Between 1902 and 1906 he worked as a teacher. Banned from practicing his profession for taking part in an illegal congress of Belorussian teachers, in 1906–7 he worked in private schools and on the editorial staff of *Nasha Niva*, a weekly that initiated the development of Belorussian intellectual life. In September 1908 the court in Vilnius (Wilno) sentenced Kolas to three years in prison for breaking the ban that forbade him to work as a teacher and for spreading revolutionary propaganda. In 1915 he was mobilized into the army. After finishing a school for non-commissioned officers in a reserve regiment in Perm, in the summer of 1917 he was sent to the Romanian front with the rank of second lieutenant. Demobilized in the autumn of 1917, he went to live with his family in Kursk Province. From 1918 to 1920 Kolas worked as a teacher. In 1921 he returned to Minsk, where he found a job with the scientific and terminological commission of the Commissariat of Education. He taught classes at teacher training institutions in Slutsk, at a pedagogical technical high school in Minsk, and at the Belorussian State University. In 1928 he became a professor of the Academy of Sciences of the Belorussian SSR, and a year later, vice-chairman of the academy. Kolas held leadership positions in the Union of Soviet Writers. During the war he went to Klyazma and then to Tashkent. He was involved with journalism as well as radio and press propaganda. In the autumn of 1944 he returned to Minsk. A member of the Central Committee of the Communist Party of Belorussia, he served as deputy to the Supreme Soviet of the Soviet Union and the Supreme Soviet of the Belorussian SSR.

Kolas was one of the fathers of the modern literary Belorussian language. He published his first poems in the newspaper *Nasha Dolia* in 1906. The subsequent collections of his poetry—*Pesni Zhal'by* (Songs Complaints; 1910), *Niomanaŭ dar* (Gift from the Neman; 1913), and *Toŭ stae palena* (Stout logs; 1913)—depicted the spiritual life of peasants and carried the message that a beautiful, just, and affluent Belorussia would be reborn thanks to Belorussian peasants. In the poems Kolas wrote at the beginning of the 1920s, particularly in the volume *Vodhulle* (In general; 1922), he attempted to define the life philosophy of the Belorussian people as compared with that of their neighbors. In the poem *Novaia ziamlia* (New land; 1923) he painted a fairytale picture of the Belorussian nature. In the trilogy *Na rastanniakh* (At the Crossroads; 1921–54) he wrote about the dilemmas of the Belorussian intelligentsia. Kolas returned to the recent history of Belorussia in the novels *Na prastorakh zhytstsia* (On life's expanses; 1926), *Adshchapenets* (Renegade; 1932), and *Dryhva* (The swamp; 1934) and in the poems *Sud u lese* (Trial in the forest; 1943) and *Adplata* (The payment; 1944). (EM)

Sources: *Wielka Encyklopedia Powszechna*, vol. 5 (Warsaw, 1965); Anton Adamowicz, *Iakub Kolas u supratsive savetyzatsii* (Munich, 1955); Nicholas P. Vakar, *Belorussia: The Making of a Nation* (Cambridge, Mass., 1956); M. Muszynski, *Jakub Kołas: Letapis zhytstsia i tvorchastsi* (Minsk, 1982); V. Zhuraulou, *Iakub Kolas i paetyka belaruskaha ramana* (Minsk, 1991); Jan Zaprudnik, *Historical Dictionary of Belarus* (Lanham, Md., 1998); Rainer Lindner, *Historiker und Herrschaft: Nationsbildung und Geschichtspolitik in Weissrussland im 19 und 20. Jahrhundert* (Munich, 1999).

KOLBE Maksymilian Maria [originally Rajmund] (7 January 1894, Zduńska Wola–14 August 1941, Oświęcim), martyr, saint of the Roman Catholic Church. The son of a weaver of German descent, Kolbe entered the novitiate in 1910 and made his first vows in Lemberg (Lviv, Lwów) in 1911. After passing his high school graduation exams in 1912, he studied philosophy at the Pontifical Gregorian University in Rome, and in November 1914 he took his final vows in the Franciscan order. In 1915 he earned a Ph.D. in philosophy. In the winter of 1917–18 he developed tuberculosis, from which he suffered until the end of his life. In April 1918 he was ordained a priest. After earning a Ph.D. in theology in July 1919, he returned to Poland. He taught Church history at a seminary in Kraków, and in January 1922 he began editing the periodical *Rycerz Niepokalanej*, initially in Grodno and from 1927 in Niepokalanów (Mary Immaculate's Place), a friary near Teresin, not far from Warsaw. In January 1930 Kolbe went to China, but since his mission was unsuccessful, in May 1930 he settled in Nagasaki, Japan, where he taught philosophy at a theological seminary and edited *Rycerz Niepokalanej* in Japanese. In 1936 he returned to Poland in very poor health. He worked in Niepokalanów, where he edited *Mały Dziennik* (circulation of 150,000), a daily that attacked leftist and liberal parties and represented anti-Semitic views. At the end of September 1939 Kolbe was detained by the Germans but was then released. He refused to sign the *Deutshce Volksliste* (German Folk List—a Nazi register of people in

Nazi occupied territories of Poland, divided into four categories according to their loyalty to the German nation) and continued to provide shelter to people who were displaced from northern Poland, including many Jews. Arrested in February 1941, he was sent to the concentration camp of Auschwitz, near Oświęcim (prisoner number 16670) in May 1941. During the selection of prisoners condemned to death, Kolbe volunteered his life in the place of Franciszek Gajowniczek, a forester who had a wife and children. Condemned to death in a starvation bunker, after two weeks of suffering Kolbe was killed by an SS man by an injection of carbolic acid. Beatified in 1963, Kolbe was canonized in 1982 by Pope John Paul II. Kolbe's selected writings were published in 1982 under the title *Myśli i rozważania* (Thoughts and considerations). (WR)

Sources: *PSB*, vol. 13; Maria Winowska, *Death Camp Proved Him Right* (Kenosha, Wisc., 1971); Mary Craig, *Blessed Maximilian Kolbe OFM Conv. Priest Hero of a Death Camp* (London, 1973); Diana Dewar, *Saint of Auschwitz* (San Francisco, 1982); Leon Dyczewski, *Święty Maksymilian Kolbe* (Warsaw, 1984); Kinga Strzelecka, *Maksymilian Maria Kolbe* (Kraków, 1982); Ozaki Tomei, *Nagasaki no Korube Shinpu* (Tokyo, 1983); Francis M. Kalvelage, ed., *Kolbe: Saint of the Immaculata* (New Bedford, Mass., 2001).

KOLIQI Ernest (20 May 1903, Shkodër–15 February 1974, Rome), Albanian writer, linguist, and politician. The brother of **Mikel Koliqi**, Koliqi completed literary studies in Padua. He was one of the founders of *Ora e Maleve*, a political and cultural periodical, well known in Shkoder, that attracted radical politicians led by **Luigji Gurakuqi**. In 1924 Koliqi supported the revolution led by **Fan Noli** and began working in the central administration. After the revolution, he went into political exile in Italy, where he completed his studies and then took the chair of Albanian language and literature at the University of Rome. After the Italian invasion of Albania in April 1939, he was one of the few widely respected people who joined the collaborationist government, in which he headed the ministry of education until December 1941. This decision harmed his reputation and led to accusations that he had been paid by the Italian authorities. In 1940 Koliqi began editing the periodical *Shkëndija*. In July 1939, on the orders of the Italian foreign minister, Galeazzo Ciano, he drafted a propaganda proposal of the "Albanian irredenta" that was to promote the liberation of Albanian territories that were part of Yugoslavia. During the Italian occupation, Kolbe directed the Institute of Albanian Studies, attracting the top specialists. After the war he emigrated to Italy, where he brought together a group of pro-Italian politicians with whom he founded the Independent National Bloc (Blloku Kombëtar Indipendent) in 1946. In 1957 he began editing the periodical *Shejzat* in Rome. He published numerous literary and critical works, including *Kushtrimi i Skenderbegut* (Skanderbeg's appeal; 1924); *Hija e Malevë* (Shadows of the mountains; 1928); *Gjurmat e Stinve* (Traces of the summer; 1933); *Tregtar flamujsh* (Trader of flags; 1935); and *Symfonija e Shqypevet* (1941; Symphony of eagles, 1972). As a translator, Koliqi introduced Albanians to the outstanding works of Italian poetry. (TC)

Sources: Stavro Skendi, *Albania* (New York, 1956); Galeazzo Ciano, *Pamiętniki 1939–1943* (Warsaw, 1991); Anton Nikë Berisha, *Ernest Koliqi: Poet i prozator* (Tirana, 1997); Bernd Fischer, *Albania at War, 1939–1945* (London, 1999); Malish Shestani, *Ernest Koliqi ne mendimin e bashkekohësve dhe studjuesve* (Tirana, 2000).

KOLIQI Mikel (29 September 1902, Shkodër–28 January 1997, Shkodër), Albanian Catholic cardinal, prisoner of conscience. The brother of **Ernest Koliqi**, Koliqi attended a Jesuit college in Shkodër and subsequently completed technical studies in Italy. While in Italy, he undertook philosophical and theological studies in Milan. In May 1931 he took holy orders. After returning to Albania, he worked in the parish of Shkodër as a curate, parish priest, and finally vicar general of the archdiocese of Shkodër. He published journalistic commentaries and edited the periodical *Kumbona e së diellës*. He simultaneously directed a religious music group. Arrested in February 1945, on the first wave of Communist persecutions of the Church in Shkodër, Koliqi was sentenced to four years in prison. Released, he was soon arrested again and sentenced to a forty-four-year imprisonment. All together, he spent thirty-eight years in prisons and camps in Lushnjë, Kuç, Kurveleshë, and Gjazë. In 1986 he was released under an amnesty. Koliqi was the oldest of the priests who had survived the period of religious persecution. He resumed his liturgical work, assuming the duties of parish priest in Shkodër. He also revived the weekly *Kumbona e së diellës*. On 31 January 1992 he became a prelate. After Pope John Paul II visited Albania in 1993, in recognition of Koliqi's unbroken faith, on 26 September 1994, the Pope elevated him to cardinal. He was the first Albanian cardinal. However, because of his age, Koliqi did not join the College of Cardinals. Koliqi composed scores for three musical melodramas: *Rozafa*; *Rrethimi i Shkodres* (Around Shkodër); and *Ruba e Kuqe* (Red scarf). He received prestigious national awards and was honored with the title of Pishtar i Demokracise (Martyr for the Faith), conferred by parliament. (TC)

Sources: *Martirizimi i Kishes Katolike Shqiptare* (Shkodër, 1993); Didier Rance, *Albanie: Ils ont voulu tuer Dieu. La persécution contre l'Église catholique (1944–1991)* (Paris, 1996); *Acta Apostolicae Sedis*, 1997, no. 3; *Annuario Pontificio*, 1997; Robert Royal, *The Catholic Martyrs of the Twentieth Century* (New York, 2000).

KOLISHEVSKI Lazar (12 February 1914, Sveti Nikola, Serbia [now in Macedonia]–6 July 2000, Skopje), Macedonian Communist activist. Brought up in an orphanage, in 1932 Kolishevski graduated from a trade school in Kragujevac and worked as a metalworker. He joined the illegal Communist Party in 1935. He attended the University of Belgrade and worked as party secretary in Kragujevac and Smederevo Palanka before World War II. The leader of the Communist Party in Macedonia, in October 1941 Kolishevski was posted to Skopje by the Yugoslav Communist Party (YCP) Central Committee (CC) to combat the influence of the competing Bulgarian Communist Party, which had approved the incorporation of Macedonia into Bulgaria. Kolishevski overshadowed his Bulgarian rivals when the Regional Committee of which he was head issued an order to promulgate an armed uprising against the Bulgarian Army. He was arrested by the Bulgarian police and was sentenced to death for treason. He remained in prison in Pleven, Bulgaria, until 1944; his sentence was commuted to life. In 1943, he was elected (in absentia) to the Anti-Fascist Council for the National Liberation of Yugoslavia (Antifašističko Vijeće Narodnog Oslobodenja Jugoslavije [AVNOJ]) and in 1944 to the Anti-Fascist Assembly for the National Liberation of Macedonia. In 1943 he was also elected (in absentia) chair of the CC of the LCY in Macedonia. Kolishevski held that post until 1963. After the capitulation of Bulgaria, upon his release from prison, Kolishevski was involved in negotiations in 1944 in Bulgaria intended to lead to the amalgamation of Pirin Macedonia with the Yugoslav Macedonian Republic. Later, in 1947, at a Lake Bled conference, he doggedly demanded the union, but in vain.

In early 1945 Kolishevski became the Yugoslav Socialist Republic of Macedonia's first prime minister. He was elected a candidate member of the Politburo of the LCY in 1948 at the Fifth Party Congress. He was elected a member of the LCY CC's Executive Committee and a member of the presidency at the Sixth and Seventh Congresses. In 1953, Kolishevski became the president of the Assembly of the Peoples' Republic of Macedonia. He served as a deputy to both the national and Macedonian assemblies from 1945 to 1972. In 1946, he was one of only two Macedonians on the Presidium of the National Constituent Assembly. In 1958, he was the only Macedonian on the Party Executive Committee. Kolishevski was pro-Belgrade. He set the tone and made the rules for Macedonia's revisionist history. In *Aspekti na makedonskoto prašanje* (1962; *Aspects of the Macedonian Question*, 1980) he sought to ensure that Macedonia's history reflected little Bulgarian influence, while he sought to maximize that of Serbia. He advocated the preservation of the separation of nationali-

ties. Kolishevski received the Great Star of Yugoslavia, the Partisan 1941 Medal, and other decorations. In May 1980, he was the first president of the new rotating presidency of Yugoslavia. (DP)

Sources: *Enciklopedija Jugoslavije*, vol. 5 (Zagreb, 1962); Valentina Georgieva and Sasha Konechni, *Historical Dictionary of the Republic of Macedonia* (Lanham, Md., 1998); Stephen E. Palmer, Jr. and Robert R. King, *Yugoslav Communism and the Macedonian Question* (Hamden, Conn., 1971); Stoyan Pribichevich, *Macedonia: Its People and History* (University Park, Pa. and London, 1982); www.rulers.org.

KOŁODZIEJSKI Henryk (12 May 1884, Warsaw–18 April 1953, Warsaw), Polish economist and social activist. During the 1905 revolution Kołodziejski was a member of the Military Revolutionary Committee of the Social Democracy of the Kingdom of Poland and Lithuania. Arrested and sent to the Russo-Japanese front, he escaped and returned to the Kingdom of Poland. Arrested for the second time, after six months he again escaped from the Warsaw Citadel and went to Galicia. In 1907 Kołodziejski graduated from the Jagiellonian University in Kraków, and in 1912 he earned a doctorate there. In 1914 he was interned in Vienna. In 1915 he began working in the Public Library in Warsaw. In 1918 he became a member of the Grand East of France Masonic Lodge, and in 1920, a member of the Poles United Grand National Lodge in Warsaw. In 1920 he served in the Polish Army. He subsequently founded and became the director of the Assembly Library. In this role he was able to take part in many backstage negotiations and political activities, becoming one of the best-informed people in Poland. In 1926 Kołodziejski was a co-founder and member of the Main Board of the Union of Polish Socialist Intellectuals and a co-initiator and member of the Survey Committee for the Investigation of the Conditions and Costs of Production and Exchange. In 1931–39 he was a member of the Scientific Council of the Institute for Social Affairs. During the Nazi occupation Kołodziejski lived in Warsaw, and, as a member of the Cooperative Committee, he worked with the Delegation of the Polish Government-in-Exile for the Homeland. At the beginning of 1945 he took part in consultations on the establishment of the Provisional Government of National Unity. By gaining, in a rather enigmatic way, the trust of **Bolesław Bierut**, Kołodziejski became a member of the National Home Council (KRN), and in January 1947 he successfully ran for a seat in the Legislative Assembly as a nonparty candidate. From February 1947 to March 1949 he served as president of the Supreme Chamber of Control, and from February 1947 until his death he was a member of the State Council. In 1949 he became head of the Supreme Cooperative Council, which authorized the collectivization of agriculture. His publications include *Wnioski z kryzysu* (Conclusions from the crisis; 1932), *Automatyzm czy gospodarka planowa* (Automatism or planned economy; 1933), and *Z zagadnień bezrobocia* (Some unemployment issues; 1938). (WR)

Sources: *PSB*, vol. 13; Mołdawa; Stanisław Łoza, *Czy wiesz kto to jest* (Warsaw, 1938); Ludwik Hass, *Masoneria polska XX wieku* (Warsaw, 1996).

KOMÁREK Valtr (10 August 1930, Hodonín), Czech economist and political activist. In 1954 Komárek graduated from the Moscow State Economic Institute and from the Higher Economic School in Prague, where in 1962 he became an associate professor and (in 1990) full professor. In 1946–90 he was a member of the Communist Party of Czechoslovakia (CPC). In 1954–58, 1960–64, and 1967–68 he worked in the State Planning Commission, and between 1964 and 1967 he was an adviser to the Cuban minister of industry. In 1968–70 Komárek was general secretary of the Economic Council of the Czechoslovak government and a member of the commission for economic policy of the CPC Central Committee's Presidium. Expelled from the council because of its activity during the Prague Spring of 1968, Komárek became an adviser to the government and to the chairman of the Federal Price Administration. From 1978 to 1984 he worked in the Institute of Economics of the Czechoslovak Academy of Sciences. Later he co-founded and until 1992 chaired the Forecasting Institute of the academy.

In the late 1980s Komárek was a representative of the reform faction in the CPC, especially favoring economic reform. After the Velvet Revolution he entered into cooperation with the Civic Forum (Občanské Fórum [OF]), and in December 1989 he became deputy prime minister and chairman of the Economic Council in the government of **Marian Čalfa**. In January 1990 Komárek left the CPC and joined the OF. After the OF split, from 1991 to 1993 he belonged to Czechoslovak Social Democracy (Československá Sociální Demokracie [ČSD]). From 1990 to 1992 he was a deputy to the Chamber of the People of the Federal Assembly; from June 1992 he chaired its foreign affairs commission, and before the elections of June 1992 he was the head of the ČSD electoral committee. During the first stage of systemic transformation Komárek gained a reputation as a key critic of the policies of **Václav Klaus**. He opted for a more gradual economic transformation and a more developed social welfare policy. For these reasons after the 1990 elections he stayed out of the second Čalfa government, dominated by liberals. In 1993, after the breakup of Czechoslovakia, which he thought a major mistake, Komárek retired from political

life. He authored *Inovace a intenzifikace v hospodářství* (Innovation and intensification in the economy; 1986); *Souhrnné prognózy vývoje československé společnosti a ekonomiky do roku 2010* (General forecast of the development of the Czechoslovak society and economy until 2010; 1988 [co-author]); *Ohrožená revoluce* (Revolution in danger; 1991); and *Mé pády a vzestupy* (My falls and rises; 1992). (PU)

Sources: *ČBS*; *Kdo byl kdo v našich dějinách ve 20. století*, vol. 1 (Prague, 1998); *Kdo je kdo v České Republice na přelomu 20. století* (Prague, 1998).

KOMINEK Bolesław (23 December 1903, Radlin–10 March 1974, Wrocław), Polish cardinal, archbishop of Wrocław. The son of an Upper Silesian miner, Kominek completed secondary school in Rybnik and then began theological studies at the Jagiellonian University in Kraków. After his ordination in 1927, he left for Paris, where he graduated from the Institut Catholique. In 1931 he gained a doctorate in philosophy and in Catholic social science. From 1930 to 1931 he was curate in Dębie, near Katowice, and from 1931 to 1939, he was a diocesan secretary for Catholic Action in Upper Silesia. During the German occupation Kominek worked in the Katowice curia and secretly helped prisoners in Nazi concentration camps. In September 1945 Primate August Hlond appointed him the apostolic administrator of Opole. Kominwk greatly contributed to the stabilization of the Polish community in the Opole region and to the rebuilding of dozens of churches. He set up the Holy Cross Publishing House in Opole. On 28 January 1951 Kominek was forced by the Communist authorities to leave his office. From 1951 to 1953 he worked in the Kraków curia and lectured in sociology at the theological department of the Jagiellonian University. Kominek was consecrated bishop on 10 October 1954, but only in December 1956, in the wake of **Władysław Gomułka**'s temporary liberalization, he was able to become the first Polish bishop of Wrocław.

In March 1962 Pope John XXIII named Kominek archbishop, and in June of the same year he became the metropolitan of Wrocław. Although the Polish authorities at first refused to give him a passport, he later took an active part in the Second Vatican Council. At the end of the council he was an initiator and main author of the famous letter addressed to the German bishops, in which the words "we forgive and ask for forgiveness" appear. In November 1965 censorship blocked his article "Dialog z Niemcami" (Dialogue with the Germans) in *Tygodnik Powszechny*, in which he explained to Polish Catholics the meaning of this letter. Kominek was one of the main targets of the Communist propaganda campaign unleashed against the

Polish bishops. In 1968 the authorities initiated the construction of a monument to John XXIII in Wrocław. This was a propaganda ploy created to give political credibility to the pro-Communist Catholics of the PAX Association and to cause a split among the clergy. Kominek called the action a ruse and proposed that the collected funds be spent on the construction of a church commemorating the work of the deceased pope. In February 1973 Kominek was named cardinal. For many years he presided over the Pastoral Commission of the Polish Episcopate and over a special commission for the western dioceses. He was vice-president of the Council of European Episcopal Conferences. Kominek was buried in Wrocław Cathedral. His memoirs, *W służbie Ziem Zachodnich* (In the service of the Western Territories), were published posthumously in 1977. (WR)

Sources: *Tygodnik Powszechny*, 1974, no. 11; *Verbum Crucis—Dei Virtus: Księga pamiątkowa w hołdzie kardynałowi Bolesławowi Kominkowi* (Wrocław, 1974); Rudolf Buchała, "W służbie narodowi. Kard. Bolesłw Kominek (1903–1974)," *Chrześcijanin w świecie*, 1980, no. 89; Antoni Dudek, *Państwo i Kościół w Polsce 1945–1970* (Kraków, 1995).

KOMOROWSKI Tadeusz, pseudonyms "Bór," "Korczak," "Lawina," and "Znicz" (1 June 1895, Chorobrów, Eastern Galicia–24 August 1966, London), Polish general and politician. Komorowski came from a family of landowners. After graduating from a military academy in Vienna, in 1913–18 he was a professional soldier in the Austrian cavalry. In November 1918, along with his squadron, he arrived in Dębica, where the Second Polish Regiment of Legionary Uhlans was being organized. After the war he served in the Prince Józef Poniatowski Eighth Uhlan Regiment in Kraków. From August 1920 he commanded the Twelfth Uhlan Regiment. Komorowski practiced the art of equitation professionally. In 1925 he was appointed commanding officer of the School for Regular Non-Commissioned Cavalry Officers in Jaworowo. In 1928 he became commander of the Ninth Regiment of Little Poland Uhlans in Trembowla. During the Olympic Games in Berlin (1936), Komorowski led the team competing in the three-day equestrian event, and his team won the silver medal. In 1938 he was transferred to Grudziądz, to the post of commanding officer of the Cavalry Training Center (CTC).

At the end of August 1939, after the CTC was dissolved, Komorowski was transferred to a reserve center in Garwolin. He fought in the September campaign until 23 September 1939. He managed to escape captivity, getting to Kraków, where he participated in the creation of underground structures. Komorowski co-organized and commanded the Military Organization of Kraków, which in January 1940 joined the Union of Armed Struggle (Związek Walki Zbrojnej [ZWZ]). From 1940 to 1941 he was commander of the Kraków-Silesian region of the ZWZ. Between July 1941 and July 1943 he was deputy commander-in-chief of the ZWZ and deputy commander of the Home Army (Armia Krajowa [AK]). After the arrest of General **Stefan Grot-Rowecki** by the Germans, Komorowski became commander-in-chief of the Home Army, with the rank of brigadier general. He held the post between 17 July 1943 and 2 October 1944, being the commander of the Armed Forces in the Homeland. At the end of July 1944, along with the government's delegate for the homeland, **Jan Stanisław Jankowski,** and with the AK Warsaw command, Komorowski made a decision to start the Warsaw Uprising on 1 August, and he led it. After signing the capitulation on 2 October 1944, Komorowski was taken captive by the Germans. During the fighting in Warsaw, on 30 September 1944, Komorowski had been appointed commander-in-chief of the Polish Armed Forces. He rejected the German proposal to take part in anti-Soviet sabotage in return for his release.

At the end of the war Komorowski was delivered to Switzerland; from there he went to London. He assumed the duties of the commander-in-chief on 28 May 1945 and held the post until 8 November 1946. After the war he remained in exile in London. He held various posts among the Polish émigrés. From July 1947 to April 1949 he served as prime minister of the Polish government-in-exile; in 1949–54 he was a member of the Political Council, and from 1956, a member of the Council of the Three; he was a co-founder (1947) and president of the Chief Council of the Home Army Circle and president of the Council of the Polish Underground Movement Study Trust (Studium Polski Podziemnej). Among other works Komorowski wrote *The Secret Army* (1950; *Armia Podziemna*, 1951), which was translated into Polish, French, and Spanish. Komorowski repeatedly wrote about his decision to start the fighting in Warsaw—for example, in *Biuletyn Informacyjny Koła AK* (Informational bulletin of the Home Army Circle; 1947) and *Dziennik Polski* (Polish daily; 1954 and 1964). (JS)

Sources: Kunert, vol. 2; Tadeusz Pełczyński, "Generał Bór-Komorowski żołnierz i obywatel," *Dziennik Polski i Dziennik Żołnierza*, 1966, no. 210; Marek Ney-Krwawicz, *Komendanci Armii Krajowej* (Warsaw, 1992); Henryk Piotr Kosk, *Generalicja polska: Popularny słownik biograficzny*, vol. 1 (Pruszków, 1998); Juliusz L. Englert, *Generał Bór-Komorowski* (London, 1994); Andrzej K. Kunert, ed., *Generał Tadeusz Bór-Komorowski w relacjach i dokumentach* (Warsaw, 2001).

KONDRATIUK Yuriy (21 June 1897, Poltava–1941 or 1942, near Kozielsk), Ukrainian engineer, pioneer in rocketry. After studying at the St. Petersburg Polytechnic Institute, Kondratiuk worked in various plants in the Ukraine, Russia, the Caucasus, and Siberia. In 1919 he published *Tem, kto budet chitat,chtoby stroit* (To those who will read in order to build), and in 1929, *Zavoevanie mezhplanetnykh prostranstv* (The conquest of interplanetary space). In the latter work he presented equations for rocket motion, calculated optimal flight trajectories, explained the theory of multi-stage rockets, and proposed the use of new rocket fuels. In a visionary way, Kondratiuk described the functioning of space stations, supply crafts, and planetary landing modules, as well as the use of gravitational fields of celestial bodies for spacecraft acceleration and deceleration. In 1933 he became head of a task force at the Energy Engineering Research Institute in Kharkiv, which designed one of the largest wind power plants in the world. Kondratiuk died during World War II in unclear circumstances. The results of his work are still used in space flights. One of the craters on the Moon has been named after Kondratiuk. (WR)

Sources: *Encyclopedia of Ukraine*, vol. 2 (Toronto, 1988).

KONESKI Blazhe (19 December 1921, Nebregovo, near Prilep–7 December 1993, Skopje), Macedonian poet and linguist. After graduating from high school in Kragujevac, Koneski studied philology at Ss. Cyril and Methodius University in Skopje and at the universities in Belgrade and Sofia. He became a professor at Skopje University and was its rector from 1958 to 1960. He was editor of the periodicals *Nov den* and *Makedonski jazik*. The first president of the Macedonian Academy of Arts and Sciences, Koneski was a corresponding member of the Yugoslav Academy of Sciences, as well as the Serbian and Slovene academies. He was head of the Cultural Department of the Ministry for Education of the Macedonian republic, and he presided over a committee that codified Macedonian vocabulary and grammar in *Gramatika na makedonskijot literaturen jazik* (Grammar of the literary Macedonian language, 2 vols.; 1952–52). Koneski edited Macedonia's first dictionary of Macedonian, *Rečnik na makedonski jazik* (1965). He received honorary doctorates from the University of Chicago and the Jagiellonian University of Kraków. He was also a poet, writer, and translator, translating the works of Heinrich Heine and William Shakespeare into Macedonian. Koneski's works were also translated into many languages, including English, Polish, and Russian. Among other works, he wrote the following: *Zemljata i ljubovta* (Land and love; 1948); *Lingvistika* (Linguistics; 1948); *Pesni* (Songs; 1953); collection of short stories *Lozje* (Vineyard; 1955); *Istorija na Makedonskijat jazik* (History of the Macedonian language; 1965); and *Towards the Macedonian Renaissance* (1961). (DP)

Sources: *Enciklopedija Jugoslavije*, vol. 5 (Zagreb, 1962); *Mały słownik pisarzy zachodnio-słowiańskich i południowo-słowiańskich* (Warsaw, 1973); "Blaze Koneski," in Mine Holton and Graham W. Reid, eds., *Reading the Ashes: An Anthology of the Poetry of Modern Macedonia* (Pittsburgh, 1977).

KONIK Konstantin (31 December 1873, Dorpat–3 August 1936, Tartu), Estonian doctor and politician. In 1899 Konik graduated from Dorpat (Tartu) University and began his medical practice. In 1908 he received a doctorate degree. In 1913–15 he published some articles in *Trevis*, the first professional medical periodical in the Estonian language. After the February 1917 revolution, Konik became a member of the Provincial Government. On 19 February 1918, along with **Konstantin Päts** and **Jüri Vilms**, he made up the three-member Estonian Salvation Committee (Eestimaa Päästmises Komitee), the highest state authority appointed by the Estonian National Council (Maapäev). Konik represented the Estonian Labor Party. In 1918–20 he served as head of the Health Care Department of the Estonian Provisional Government. From 1920 to 1931 he was a professor of surgery and dean of the Tartu University Medical School. Apart from teaching classes, which were popular with students, Konik managed to provide the university hospital with heliotherapy, X-rays, and other equipment. His work earned him great respect, and in the late 1920s, he returned to politics. He won a seat in the parliamentary elections, and from May to October 1928, he served as minister of education and social welfare in the government of **Jaan Tõnisson**. Konik later returned to the university, where he worked until his death. (AG)

Sources: *Eesti Entsuklopeedia*, vol. 14 (Tallinn, 2000); Georg von Rauch, *The Baltic States: The Years of Independence, 1917–1940* (Berkeley, 1970); "Strona szpitala klinicznego Uniwersytetu w Tartu," http://www.cut.ee/index.php?1,2,2; "Strona Ministerstwa Spraw Socjalnych Republiki Estonii," www.sm.ee/gopr030/Web/gpweb.nsf/pages/sotsiaalministeerium0003.

KONITZA Faik, pseudonym "Trank Spiro bey" (15 March 1876, Konicë–14 December 1942, Boston), Albanian diplomat, writer, and translator. Born into an aristocratic family, Konitza initially attended St. Francis Xavier Jesuit College in Shkodër. In 1886 he went to Istanbul, where he attended the Galatasaray Gymnasium. He studied in France (Grenoble, Dijon, Paris); Sweden (Uppsala); and the United States. In 1895 he received a diploma in Romance philology in Dijon. Konitza was a co-founder and editor of *Albania* (1896–1909), one of the most important opinion-making publications of the Albanian émigrés and regarded as the first modern Albanian-language periodical. Initially, this periodical was published in Brussels and then in London. In *Albania* Konitza promoted autonomy for the Albanian territories under the rule of Austria-Hungary. His great knowledge and erudition impressed Guillaume Apollinaire, whom he befriended in 1903 and who called Konitza "the Voltaire of the Balkans." In 1909 Konitza assumed the editorship of *Dielli*, a periodical published in Boston, and in 1911, the editorship of *Trumbeta e Krujës*, a periodical published in St. Louis. He was also chief editor of seven other periodicals that were published by the Albanian diaspora. Konitza published his articles in 130 periodicals, which appeared in nine different languages. The aim of a great majority of the articles was to publicize the Albanian cause in Europe. In 1912 in the United States Konitza became secretary of a literary society called Vatra. In 1913 he was a delegate of this society to conferences in London and Trieste. At that time he abandoned pro-Habsburg ideas in favor of Albanian independence. In 1914 he served for a short time as consul general of the government of **Essad Pasha Toptani** to Washington.

During World War I Konitza was initially in Austria and then in Switzerland, from where he criticized the Balkan policy of the Central Powers. After the war he returned to the United States. In 1924 he was elected a member of the Albanian parliament. When **Ahmed Zogu** took over power, Konitza became Albanian ambassador to the United States in May 1926. In 1929 he visited Albania for the last time and then left the diplomatic service, criticizing the policy of King **Zog I**. Until his death Konitza was the most influential figure in the Albanian diaspora in the United States, remaining independent despite pressure from King Zog, who sought political support in the United States. The Communist authorities refused permission for Konitza's body to be brought back to Albania; therefore, he was buried in Boston. His works, denounced during the Communist era, were finally published in Albania in 1992. Konitza wrote, among other things, *Jeta e Skënderbeut* (The life of Skanderbeg; 1912); *Doktor Gjëlpëra zbulon rrenjet e drames së Mamurrasit* (Dr. Gjëlpëra reveals the lies behind the events in Mamurrasit; 1924); *Ne hijen e hurmavë* (In the shadow of date palms; 1926); and *Si m'u duk Shqipëria* (My perception of Albania; 1929). (TC)

Sources: *Biographisches Lexikon*, vol. 2; Stavro Skendi, *Albania* (New York, 1956); *Fjalori Enciklopedik Shqiptar* (Tirana, 1985); Stuart E. Mann, *Albanian Literature* (London, 1955); Giuseppe Schiro, *Storia della litteratura albanese* (Milan, 1959); Federata Panshqiptare e Amerikes VATRA, *Faik Konitza 1876–1976* (New York, 1976); Namik Ressuli, *Albanian Literature* (Boston, 1987); Fevziu Blendi, *Histori e shtypit shqiptar 1848–1996* (Tirana, 1996).

KONOVALETS Yevhen (14 June 1891, Zashkov, near Lemberg [Lwów, Lviv]–23 May 1938, Rotterdam), Ukrainian officer and nationalist politician. The son of a teacher, Konovalets completed a gymnasium in Lemberg. During his law studies at the University of Lemberg he

was a secretary of the Prosvita Society. He co-organized an educational association of students whose members traveled around to villages and presented scholarly papers to village people. In 1910, in the "case of the 101 students," Konovalets was tried for activities aimed at the establishment of a Ukrainian university in Lemberg. He was a political representative for youth in the Central Committee of the Ukrainian National Democratic Party. During World War I he served as a warrant officer in the Austro-Hungarian Army. Taken captive in the battle of Makivka in 1915, he was held in a prisoner of war camp in Tsaritsyn (now Volgograd), where, along with **Andrii Melnyk**, **Roman Sushko**, and others, he formed a group of Ukrainian prisoners of war. After his release from the camp in 1917, Konovalets went to Kiev, where he organized a brigade of Sich Riflemen, the best unit of the Ukrainian Army between 1918 and 1919. He suppressed the Bolshevik uprising in Kiev and was commander in the battle against the forces of Mikhail Muravyov. After the signing of the Brest-Litovsk peace treaty (March 1918), Konovalets took part in the counterattack on Kiev. He expanded his unit to regiment level, but after Hetman **Pavlo Skoropadskyi** came to power, the Germans disarmed his regiment. Avoiding political conflicts, he later revived his unit in Belaya Tserkov, where he formed troops faithful to the hetman.

On 16 November 1918, after Skoropadsky signed a federal treaty with Russia, Konovalets joined an uprising against the hetman, declaring his support for the Ukrainian National Republic (UNR). He expanded his Sich Riflemen first to division and then to corps level. He fought on the side of the UNR until the end of 1919. In December 1919 he was interned briefly by the Poles in Łuck (Lutsk). In the spring of 1920 he went abroad. On **Symon Petlyura**'s recommendation Konovalets attempted to organize a reserve army composed of Ukrainian soldiers interned in Czechoslovakia and Ukrainians who had been captured by the Italians. However, Prime Minister **Yevhen Petrushevych** did not support him, so his mission ended in failure. He returned to Lwów in the summer of 1921 and was a co-organizer of **Yurko Tyutyunnyk**'s expedition to the USSR. In 1920 he joined a group of officers who founded the Ukrainian Military Organization (UVO) in Prague. He reorganized the UVO by creating its modern general headquarters.

At the end of November 1922 Konovalets left Poland. He lived in Berlin until 1929, then in Geneva (1929–36) and Rome (1936–38). He consolidated the UVO structures and established relations with political circles in Germany, Great Britain, Lithuania, Spain, Italy, and other countries. For a time he enjoyed the friendly neutrality of the Czechoslovak authorities and received subventions from Germany and Lithuania. He organized a political information service and established Ukrainian offices in various countries. The UVO used terror on a large scale; its victims were not only Poles, but compromise-minded Ukrainians as well. Konovalets laid the foundations for the consolidation of Ukrainian nationalists, which took place in 1929 in Vienna, where the Organization of Ukrainian Nationalists (OUN) was formed. By means of an armed struggle against Poland and the USSR, the OUN attempted to create Ukrainian statehood in the territories populated by Ukrainians. During his frequent visits abroad, Konovalets contributed to the formation of OUN branches in the United States, Canada, France, Belgium, and other countries. At the League of Nations he submitted many protests, such as those against Polish pacifications in Volhynia in 1930, in an attempt to internationalize the Ukrainian cause. He headed the activities of the Ukrainian underground in Poland and organized the sabotage and assassinations of the representatives of Polish authorities. In the 1930s the OUN won the support of young Ukrainians in Poland. Konovalets also tried to establish an underground network in the USSR. He met with Hitler twice to negotiate the training of Ukrainian soldiers in the Third Reich. In 1938 Konovalets was killed by an NKVD agent Pavel Sudoplatov, who won his trust and then planted a bomb in a box of chocolates that he handed Konovalets. (GM)

Sources: *Encyclopedia of Ukraine*, vol. 2 (Toronto, 1988); Matthew Stachiv and Jaroslav Sztendera, eds., *Western Ukraine at the Turning Point of Europe's History, 1918–1923*, vols. 1–2 (New York, 1971); *Ievhen Konovalets ta joho doba* (Munich, 1974); Ryszard Torzecki, *Kwestia ukraińska w Polsce w latach 1923–1929* (Kraków, 1989); Ryszard Torzecki, *Polacy i Ukraińcy. Sprawa ukraińska w czasie II wojny światowej na terenie II Rzeczypospolitej* (Warsaw, 1993); Stepan Ripetskyi, *Ukrains'ke Sichove Striletstvo* (Lviv, 1995); Pavel Sudoplatov, *Spietsoperatsii. Lubianka i Kreml 1930–1950 gody* (Moscow, 1997).

KONRÁD György (2 April 1933, Debrecen), Hungarian writer. Born into a rich family of Jewish descent from northeastern Hungary, in 1944 Konrád hid with his family in Budapest. In 1951–56 he studied Hungarian language and literature at the University of Budapest, and during the 1956 revolution he belonged to a university unit of the National Guard. For this reason he later faced problems with finding a job. From 1959 to 1965 he worked in an educational institution, and in 1965–1973 he worked as a sociologist at the Institute of Planning and Architectural Studies. From 1960 he worked in the Helikon Press. Konrád made his literary debut in the 1960s, publishing popular articles about the leaders of French existentialism and the *nouveau roman*. Struggling with censorship, he also wrote sociological works, of which the best known

were studies of hooliganism and lifestyles in the large housing quarters. He presented a literary version of these studies in the novel *A látogató* (The guest; 1969), which raised heated debates in the media.

In the 1970s Konrád developed an interest in the links between communism and intellectuals, and he presented his assessment in the novel *A városalapító* (1977; *The City Builder*, 1977) and in the study (with Iván Szelényi) *Az étrelmiség útja az osztályhatalomhoz* (The road of the intelligentsia to class rule; 1978). As a result of constant police repression and censorship, from the late 1970s Konrád mostly published abroad and in the uncensored press, becoming one of the best-known Hungarian author in the West. He wrote *The Case Worker* (1974); *Der Komplize* (The accomplice; 1980); *Antipolityk* (Anti-politics; 1985); and *Die Melankolie des Wiedersgeburts* (The melancholy of rebirth; 1992). After the fall of Communist rule, Konrád became involved in political life, serving as an adviser to the Alliance of Free Democrats and initiating the leftist Democratic Charter (Demokratikus Charta). In 1990–93 he was chairman of the International PEN Club, and from 1997 he was chairman of the Academy of Arts in Berlin. (MS)

Sources: *Magyar alakok* (Budapest, 1994); *Új magyar irodalmi lexikon* (Budapest, 1994); *György Konrad: Eine Stimme aus Mitteleuropa* (Rehburg and Loccum, 1996); *Ki Kicsoda 2002* (Budapest, 2001).

KONSTANTINOVA Elka (25 May 1932, Sofia), Bulgarian historian of literature and politician. The daughter of an activist of the Radical Democratic Party (RDP), Konstantinova studied at the University of Sofia, and then she worked at the Institute of Literature of the Bulgarian Academy of Sciences (BAS), publishing biographical essays and theoretical works on science fiction. In 1978–83 she taught the Bulgarian language at the Jagiellonian University in Kraków, Poland, where she became fascinated with Solidarity. In 1988 she joined the Club for the Support of Glasnost and Perestroika, led by **Zhelyu Zhelev**. In December 1989 Konstantinova restored the RDP and took its lead. On behalf of this party she became a member of the National Coordination Council of the Union of Democratic Forces (UDF). After the split of the UDF in the spring of 1991, she joined the Right Bloc, which demanded the full elimination of Communist influence, the nationalization of Bulgarian Communist Party property, and an immediate dissolution of the Grand National Assembly (GNA). In view of the resistance of the UDF leadership, Konstantinova, along with thirty-nine other deputies, left the GNA. Demanding early elections, Konstantinova opposed the passage of a new constitution by a parliament dominated by the post-Communists. When the GNA passed a law stipulating that deputies who did not sign the constitution would lose their mandates, Konstantinova and several other people started a hunger strike. She demanded the dismissal of UDF activists who insisted that the constitution be passed by a GNA elected in 1990. She succeeded, and the UDF ran in the elections of October 1991 as a rightist organization. Konstantinova won a mandate and became minister of culture in the new government of **Filip Dimitrov**. After a few months she resigned, protesting the reduction of budgetary spending on culture. As a result of conflicts within the RDP, in 1993 Konstantinova was dismissed from its leadership. Two months before the 1994 elections she left the RDP and joined the Popular Union (Naroden Sayuz), but she was sidelined. From 1999 Konstantinova headed the BAS modern Bulgarian literature section. (AG)

Sources: Jerzy Jackowicz, *Bułgaria od rządów komunistycznych do demokracji parlamentarnej 1988–1991* (Warsaw, 1992); Raymond Detrez, *Historical Dictionary of Bulgaria* (Lanham, Md., 1997); www.cit.bg/rrech/e.konstantinova.htm; www.omda.bg/engl/news/party/sds_engl.htm; www.ilit.bas.bg/en/sections/novalit.htm.

KONTIĆ Radoje (31 May 1937, Nikšić, Montenegro), Montenegrin Communist and post-Communist activist. In 1956 Kontić joined the League of Communists of Yugoslavia (LCY). After graduating from Belgrade University in 1961, he became director of the Boris Kidrić Steelworks in the town of Nikšić. In 1974 he became a member of the LCY Central Committee, and in 1978–82 and 1986–89 he was minister without portfolio in the federal government. From 1982 through 1986 Kontić was deputy prime minister and (in 1989–91) prime minister of the Montenegrin republic. In June 1991 he was among the LCY activists in Montenegro who changed the name of the party into the Democratic Party of Socialists (Demokratska Partija Socijalista). In July 1992 Kontić became deputy prime minister in the federal government of **Milan Panić**. On 29 December 1992 the federal parliament dismissed Panić and appointed Kontić as acting prime minister. From December 1992 to February 1993 he was also minister of defense. On 3 March 1993 the federal parliament elected Kontić prime minister. Kontić repeatedly appealed to the United Nations for the abolishment of sanctions against the new Yugoslav federation, arguing that the perception of Yugoslavia as aggressor in Bosnia-Herzegovina was groundless. After the parliamentary elections of November 1996, Kontić continued as head of the federal government created in March 1997. He attempted to stay neutral in the conflict between the presidents of Serbia and Montenegro—**Slobodan Milošević** and **Milo Djukanović.**

This conflict intensified after the presidential elections in Montenegro in October 1997, in which **Momir Bulatović**, supported by Milošević, lost to Djukanović. On 18 May 1998 the federal parliament recalled Kontić from the position of prime minister. The official reason was his delay of economic reforms. Kontić was replaced by Bulatović, but the decision of the federal parliament was opposed by the Montenegrin parliament. (AO)

Sources: Polish Press Agency, *Biographical Notes, Press Documentation*, 1998; *Who's Who in the Socialist Countries of Europe* (Munich, London, and Paris, 1989); Bugajski.

KOPÁCSI Sándor (5 March 1922, Miskolc–2 March 2001, Toronto), one of the leaders of the 1956 revolution in Hungary. The son of a laborer and activist in the Hungarian Social Democratic Party (HSDP), at the age of fifteen Kopácsi took part in a leaflet action against the Arrow Cross Party, and he was shot in the leg. He finished a basic vocational school and worked as a turner during the war. After the Germans occupied Hungary in March 1944, he joined the anti-Nazi resistance movement, and his family provided shelter for Jewish people who were in hiding. After the war, Kopácsi joined the Hungarian Communist Party (HCP) and the new police force. After graduating from a police officers' school in 1949, he was transferred to the department of public security at the headquarters of the HCP in Budapest. Sent to a two-year course at the Higher Party School in the autumn of 1949, he was subsequently appointed head of the party apparatus of the police. In 1952 he became chief of the Budapest police, and in 1953, a member of parliament.

After the Twentieth CPSU Congress, at an open party meeting of the police Kopácsi spoke out against **Mátyás Rákosi**, head of the party. Influenced by the events of June 1956 in Poznań, Poland, Kopácsi, like some of his colleagues, said at a meeting of army and police officers that he would not "shoot at people." On 23 October 1956 he ordered the police to return to the barracks, and he entered into talks with the insurgents. On 31 October he joined the provisional leadership of the Hungarian Socialist Workers' Party (HSWP) and became a member of the Revolutionary Defense Committee. He gained the trust of the insurgents, and on 3 November he was elected deputy commander of the Revolutionary National Guard. On 5 November, after the second Soviet intervention, Kopácsi was arrested by General Ivan Serov, head of the KGB. On 15 June 1958, in the trial of **Imre Nagy** and his associates, Kopácsi was sentenced to life imprisonment. Released under an amnesty in 1963, he worked as a turner in a telephone factory until 1965, later becoming a technical clerk. In 1969 he was allowed to finish his studies, but after receiving a degree in law, he did not get a job that was appropriate for his level of education. In 1975 he emigrated to Canada. In 1987 he retired. In 1989 Kopácsi, along with his deceased parents, was honored with the title of Righteous among Nations by the Yad Vashem Institute in Jerusalem. In the same year he returned to Hungary, where he was rehabilitated. In 1990 his officer's rank was restored to him, and he was promoted to brigadier general. Kopácsi published an autobiographical novel, *Életfogytiglan* (Life sentence), which came out in English as *In the Name of the Working Class: The Inside Story of the Hungarian Revolution* (1987). (JT)

Sources: *A magyar forradalom és szabadságharc enciklopédiája*, CD-ROM (Budapest, 1999); *Magyar Nagylexikon*, vol. 11 (Budapest, 2000); *Ki kicsoda 2000* (Budapest, 2001); Paul Ignotus, *Hungary* (London, 1972); György Litván, ed., *Rewolucja węgierska 1956 roku* (Warsaw, 1996).

KOPAŃSKI Stanisław (19 May 1895, St. Petersburg–23 March 1976, London), Polish general and engineer. Conscripted into the Russian Army in 1915, Kopański gave up his technical studies in St. Petersburg and graduated from the Mikhailov Artillery School. He served in the mounted artillery, and during World War I he fought on the German front. After the February 1917 revolution, he served in the First Polish Corps in Russia between 1917 and 1918. In November 1918 he joined the Polish Army. With the First Mounted Artillery Division, he fought in the battles of Lwów (Lviv) and Wilno (Vilnius), where in 1919 he lost an eye. During the Polish-Soviet war in 1920 he fought with General Juliusz Rómmel's Mounted Division. In 1923–24 Kopański completed engineering studies in Warsaw, and in 1924–27 he was the academic director of an officer cadet school and held the rank of major. In 1929 he graduated from the Military College in Paris. After returning to Poland, he began serving in the Third Department of the General Staff in 1934. From 1935 to 1936 he was deputy armor commander in the Ministry of Military Affairs, and from 1937 to 1938 he was commander of the first motorized artillery regiment. In 1938–39 Kopański completed a course at the Military Studies Center, rising to the rank of colonel. From March to September 1939 he was head of the Third (Operational) Department of the Staff of the Commander-in-Chief.

After the September 1939 defeat, Kopański made his way, via Romania, to France, where he became the armor commander in the High Command. At the beginning of 1940 he was sent to Syria to form the Polish Independent Carpathian Rifle Brigade, and he was promoted to general. He was in command of this brigade until 1942. From 1942 to 1943 he commanded the Third Carpathian Rifle Division.

He led the African campaign of this division, which fought at Tobruk, Gazala, and in the Libyan desert. In July 1943 Kopański became chief of staff of the commander-in-chief. In 1944 he was promoted to major general. After the death of General **Władysław Sikorski**, he became a leading figure of the Polish Armed Forces in the West. In September 1946 he was appointed inspector general of the Polish Adjustment and Resettlement Corps (Polski Korpus Przysposobienia i Rozmieszczenia), and he continued to hold this position until 1949. After the demobilization, Kopański remained in Great Britain. He organized assistance for the Polish servicemen who had fought in the West. In 1946 the authorities of the Polish People's Republic stripped him of Polish citizenship. From 1970 to 1972 Kopański was a member of the Council of Three (Rada Trzech), which served as a collective head of state in exile. He was also active in war veterans' organizations. He published *Wspomnienia wojenne, 1939–1945* (War memoirs, 1939–45; 1961) and *Moja służba w Wojsku Polskim, 1917–1939* (My service in the Polish Army, 1917–39; 1965). (JS)

Sources: Tadusz Kryska-Karski and Stanisław Żurakowski, *Generałowie Polski Niepodległej.* (London, 1976); Józef Garliński, *Polska w drugiej wojnie światowej* (London, 1982); Henryk Piotr Kosk, *Generalicja polska: Popularny słownik biograficzny*, vol. 1 (Pruszków, 1998); Zbigniew Mierzwiński, *Generałowie II Rzeczypospolitej*, vol. 1 (Warsaw, 1990); Jan Nowak Jeziorański, *Kurier z Warszawy* (Kraków, 1993); *Encyklopedia Historii Polski: Dzieje polityczne*, vol. 1 (Warsaw, 1994); Krzysztof Dybciak and Zdzisław Kudelski, eds., *Leksykon kultury polskiej poza krajem od roku 1939* (Lublin, 2000).

KOPECKÝ Václav (27 August 1897, Kosmonosy, district of Mladá Boleslav–5 August 1961, Prague), Czech Communist activist and journalist. Kopecký studied at Charles University in Prague but never graduated. Until 1924 he worked as a government official. In 1919 he was one of the founders of the Marxist Association (Marxistické Sdružení), an organization of leftist intellectuals, and in 1921 he was a co-founder of the Communist Party of Czechoslovakia (CPC). Kopecký was a member of a faction led by **Klement Gottwald** that subordinated all its activities to the Stalinist version of internationalist communism. In the mid-1920s he became an editor of Communist newspapers, initially *Dělnický deník* in Ostrava and, from 1928 on, *Rude Právo*. From 1929 to 1938 he was a member of the Central Committee (CC) and a deputy to the National Assembly, and from 1931 to 1938 he was a member of the Politburo of the CC of the CPC. From the time he joined the leadership of the party, Kopecký eagerly complied with Kremlin directives and informed the Soviet authorities about the situation within the CPC and in the country at large. He spent the World War II period in Moscow, where, as a member of the leadership

of the party abroad, he helped to shape Gottwald's policies. In December 1943 Kopecký took part in negotiations
with **Edvard Beneš** and was a co-author of the so-called
Christmas agreement, which initiated cooperation between
the government-in-exile and the center of the Communist
émigré community in Moscow.

In 1945 Kopecký was one of the authors of the Košice
program, which was announced by the government of the
National Front of Czechs and Slovaks. In 1945 he also became a member of the CC and the Presidium of the CC of
the CPC and a deputy to the National Assembly. A member
of the Politburo of the CPC CC from 1954 on, Kopecký
served as deputy prime minister from October 1949 to
April 1950 and from January 1953 to August 1961, holding the post of first deputy prime minister from January to
September 1953. In addition, he was minister of information and, from 1953 to 1954, minister of culture. One of
the main party ideologists during the Stalinist period, he
shaped the Communist cultural policy in the 1940s and
1950s. As one of the senior leaders of the CPC, Kopecký
actively participated in unlawful party activities and took
part in staging political trials in the 1950s, showing inge-
nuity in fabricating and presenting trumped-up charges
against members of non-Communist parties, Catholic
clergy, and "internal enemies" within the party. Kopecký's
publications include *Třicet let KSČ* (Thirty years of the
CPC; 1951) and *ČSR a KSČ* (ČSR and the CPC; 1960),
which justified the unlawful political trials and expounded
the Stalinist interpretation of history. (PU)

Sources: *ČBS*; *Českoslovenští politici: 1918–1991* (Prague, 1991);
Kdo byl kdo v našich dějinach ve 20. stoleti, vol. 1 (Prague, 1998);
Vratislav Busek and Nicolas Spulber, eds., *Czechoslovakia* (New
York, 1957); Josef Korbel, *The Communist Subversion of Czecho-
slovakia, 1938–1948* (Princeton, 1959); Vladimir Reisky de Dubnic,
Communist Propaganda Methods: The Case of Czechoslovakia (New
York, 1960); Edward Taborsky, *Communism in Czechoslovakia,
1948–1960* (Princeton, 1961); Paul E. Zinner, *Communist Strategy
and Tactics in Czechoslovakia, 1918–48* (New York, 1963).

KÕPP Johan (9 November 1874, Holdre–21 October
1970, Stockholm), Estonian Lutheran bishop. Kõpp graduated from high school in 1896 and completed theological
studies in Tartu in 1906. He then worked for two years as
a high school teacher in Pärnu, and from 1909 to 1922 he
was a pastor in Laiuse. Kõpp was one of the first Estonians
to take up a chair at the University of Tartu in 1916. In
1917 he was one of the leading organizers of a church congress at which the Estonian Evangelical Lutheran Church
(EELC) was founded as an institution independent from
German church structures. Between world wars Kõpp was
one of the leaders of the Christian People's Party (Kristlik
Rahvaerakond), a Christian-democratic party that called

for increasing the role of the Lutheran Church in society
and opposed reforms that might diminish the ownership
rights of Protestant congregations. Still, secularization
among the Estonian people began to increase in the late
1920s. From 1920 to 1927 Kõpp was deputy rector, and
from 1928 to 1937 rector, of Tartu University. He had
broad international contacts, and his writings were known
abroad. In 1939 he was elevated to bishop, after Hugo Rahamägi, the former head of the EELC, had been dismissed
in an atmosphere of public scandal that led to a deep rift
among the hierarchs and the faithful. As a result of the
Molotov-Ribbentrop Pact of August 1939, most Baltic
Germans emigrated. After the German pastors, many of
whom had worked in Estonian parishes, left Estonia, the
numbers of the Lutheran clergy on the eve of the Soviet
invasion diminished by one-fifth.

When the Red Army entered Estonia in June 1940, the
role of the head of the EELC became even more difficult.
Kõpp was not deported to the Soviet Union, but his work
was severely limited and the Lutheran Church suffered
harassment, including a ban on the printing of religious
books, the removal of religion from the schools, the takeover of church farmlands and some other real property by
the state, and persecutions of the clergy. When the Germans occupied Estonia in 1941, Kõpp managed to restore
most of the rights and freedoms that the Lutherans had enjoyed before the war, but the theological schools were not
reopened until 1943, and their reopening did not prevent a
further drop in the number of pastors. Relations with the
Germans, although correct, were not free from tensions
over such issues as the confiscation of church bells for war
production and the status of the Theological Institute. The
reoccupation of Estonia by the Soviet Union and a mass
exodus of Estonians in 1944 influenced Kõpp's decision to
leave the country. As a result, the Lutheran Church found
itself in a very difficult situation, because seventy-two
pastors—half the total number—left Estonia along with
Kõpp. Before leaving, Kõpp wrote a letter authorizing
Anton Eilart to act as bishop assessor of the consistory.
However, Eilart was soon arrested by the NKVD and was
later forced to go underground. As a result, the EELC was
deprived of its legal authorities, which made it easier for
the Communists to control it.

Kõpp managed to prepare the EELC to work in exile.
In 1943 the consistory and the Church Council enacted
a law authorizing the bishop to act in situations when
neither of these organs could assemble. This law made
possible the transfer of the Church's activities abroad.
Although the small Estonian community settled in several
countries, Kõpp, who resided in Sweden, succeeded in
establishing an efficient network of parishes and deaner-

ies. The establishment of foundations for pastoral work successfully prevented the incorporation of Estonians into the local congregations of the countries where they had settled and preserved their native language in the liturgy. The EELC abroad easily gained acceptance by other Protestant churches and was put on the list of founders of the Lutheran World Federation (Lund 1947). The Theological Institute, which educated future pastors, was established during Kõpp's time, as was the periodical *Estonian Church*, which is still published today. In 1965 Kõpp retired. (AG)

Sources: *Eesti Entsuklopeedia*, vol. 5 (Tallinn, 1990); Tõnu Parming and Elmar Järvesöö, *A Case Study of a Soviet Republic: The Estonian SRR* (Boulder, Colo., 1978); Mati Laur, Tõnis Lukas, Ain Mäesalu, Ago Pajur, and Tõnu Tannberg, *History of Estonia* (Tallin, 2000); http://www.eelk.ee/EELCabroad.html; http://www.okupatsioon.ee/english/overviews/index.html; http://www.eelk.ee/~eelk109/kogudus.htm; http://www.htg.tartu.ee/eng/index.html.

KORBOŃSKI Stefan (2 March 1901, Praszka, near Częstochowa–23 April 1989, Washington, D.C.), Polish politician. While still a high school student, Korboński volunteered for the Polish Army, which was being formed at the end of 1918. He fought in the defense of Lwów (Lviv), and in 1920 he served in the Twenty-ninth Regiment of the Kaniów Riflemen. In 1921 he took part in the Third Silesian Uprising. Korboński completed legal studies in Poznań and then practiced in local courts and worked in the State Attorney General's Office of the Republic of Poland. In the 1930s, with his cousin Zygmunt Graliński, Korboński ran a law firm in Warsaw. In 1925 he joined the Polish Peasant Party–Liberation (Polskie Stronnictwo Ludowe–Wyzwolenie). After the unification of the peasant movement in 1931 Korboński joined the leadership of the Peasant Party (Stronnictwo Ludowe [SL]). In 1936–39 he was president of the Białystok executive board of the SL and a member of the Supreme Party Court. In September 1939 Korboński fought as a reserve officer and was captured by the Soviets in Włodzimierz Wołyński (now Volodymyr-Volynskyi). He escaped from a transport heading far into the USSR and returned to Warsaw, where he co-organized the underground SL. In October 1939 he joined its Chief Political Council. After the arrest of **Maciej Rataj** in March 1940, Korboński replaced him as party representative in the inter-party Political Agreement Committee (Polityczny Komitet Porozumiewawczy).

In 1941, after Korboński's resignation from the committee, the commander-in-chief of the Home Army and the government delegate appointed chief of the Directorate of Civil Resistance (Kierownictwo Walki Cywilnej [KWC]).

In this role he organized sabotage actions, passive resistance, and an underground judiciary that passed sentences on the traitors to the nation. He also ran a radio station called Świt, which kept the London government of the Republic of Poland, as well as Poles at home and abroad, informed about events in occupied Poland. Korboński's wife, Zofia, managed the Cipher Bureau. After the KWC merged with the Directorate of the Conspiratorial Struggle (which had been formed by the High Command of the Home Army to organize sabotage) and when the Directorate of Underground Struggle (Kierownictwo Walki Podziemnej) was established in July 1943, Korboński was appointed chief of civil resistance. During the Warsaw Uprising he also became head of the Interior Department of the Government Delegation. After the collapse of the uprising Korboński, along with the civilian population, left Warsaw. In March 1945 the Soviet services treacherously arrested sixteen leaders of Underground Poland, among them delegate **Jan Stanisław Jankowski**, and Korboński took over Jankowski's duties.

After the Yalta Conference, the London authorities of the SL found themselves in opposition to the government-in-exile. On 27 June 1945 Korboński resigned from his duties, and the following day Soviet functionaries arrested him in Kraków. The Communists agreed to the creation of the Polish Peasant Party (Polskie Stronnictwo Ludowe[PSL]) and since Korboński was one of the leaders he was released. In August 1945 Korboński became president of the PSL in Warsaw, and in 1946 he was elected to the Chief Executive Committee of the party. In the elections of January 1947 he won a seat in the capital. Korboński delivered two courageous speeches in the Assembly, stigmatizing the violations and abuses of power by the Communists. Both speeches were censored, not only in the press, but also in the parliamentary stenographic records. Threatened with the loss of his immunity and with arrest, on 5 November 1947 Korboński and his wife secretly went to Sweden and then, via England, arrived in the United States at the end of the month.

Initially, Korboński was linked with the Polish National Democratic Committee (Polski Narodowy Komitet Demokratyczny) of **Stanisław Mikołajczyk**, and after the organization disintegrated, he was one of the leaders of the PSL in exile in the United States, cooperating, for example, with **Stanisław Bańczyk**. In the conflict between the London government-in-exile and the Political Council, Korboński supported the latter, and he led the representation of the council in the United States. In 1954 he testified before the U.S. House of Representatives Committee to Investigate Communist Aggression. From 1954 on, as a representative of the Polish Political Council, Korboński sat in the Assembly of Captive European Nations (ACEN). In 1958–59, 1966–67, and 1971–85 he was president of the ACEN. For many years he also presided over the Polish Unity Council in the United States and was a member of the Polish Institute of Arts and Sciences.

Korboński was the author of many books: the trilogy *W imieniu Rzeczypospolitej* (1954; *Fighting Warsaw*, 1968), *W imieniu Kremla* (1956; *Warsaw in Chains*, 1959), and *W imieniu Polski Walczącej* (1963; *Warsaw in Exile*, 1966; published also in Spanish), as well as *Polskie Państwo Podziemne* (1975; *The Polish Underground State: A Guide to the Underground, 1939–1945*, 1981) and *The Jews and the Poles in World War II* (1989). Korboński was awarded the Virtuti Militari Cross for the war of 1920, the Home Army Cross, the 1939–45 war medal, and other decorations. In 1980 the Yad Vashem Institute in Jerusalem bestowed the Medal of the Righteous on him for his participation in saving Jews during the war. (WR)

Sources: Kunert, vol. 1; Andrzej Pomian, "Stefan Korboński 2 III 1901–23 IX 1989," *Nowy Dziennik*, 26 April 1989; Krystyna Kersten, *Narodziny systemu władzy: Polska 1943–1948* (Poznań, 1990); Stanisław Łach, *Polskie Stronnictwo Ludowe w latach 1945–1947* (Gdańsk, 1995).

KORCZAK Janusz [originally Henryk Goldszmit] (22 July 1878 or 1879, Warsaw–6 [?] August 1942, Treblinka), Polish doctor, writer, and teacher. Korczak was born into an assimilated Jewish family connected with the secular enlightenment Haskala movement. In 1905 he graduated in medicine from Warsaw University, and then he practiced in Berlin, Paris, and London clinics. After returning home in 1905, he worked as a pediatrician in Warsaw; this led to his lifetime passion and mission: aid to children. In 1907 he became connected with the Aid to Orphans society, and in 1912 he co-founded and until his death headed the Jewish Orphanage in Warsaw. In 1919, with Maryna Falska, Korczak established and until 1936 directed the Polish orphanage Our Home (Nasz Dom) in Warsaw. He was also active in many charity institutions, wrote for the periodicals *Głos* and *Przegląd Społeczny*, and gave lectures on the radio. Korczak explored child psychology and upbringing. In his orphanages he introduced his own educational programs, stimulating the activities of children (for instance, he engaged them in the editing of *Mały Przegląd*). Korczak described his pedagogical methodology in *Momenty wychowawcze* (Educational moments; 1919), *Jak kochać dzieci* (How to love children; 1920), and *Prawo dzieci do szacunku* (Children's right to dignity; 1929), and he presented his findings at the Institute of Special Pedagogy and the

Free University in Warsaw. After the German invasion in September 1939, Korczak made radio presentations for children, and after the capitulation of Poland he focused on securing safe living conditions for his Jewish pupils. In the fall of 1940 his Jewish orphanage was forced to move within the Warsaw Ghetto, and Korczak was arrested. After a few months he was released on bail, but on 5 August 1942 the orphanage was closed and his pupils were sent to the death camp of Treblinka. Although Korczak was offered a pardon, he accompanied his children to the very end and perished with them.

Korczak wrote a lot for children, but his works include important messages for adults as well. Some of these works are valuable documents of the time—for example, *Jośki, Mośki i Srule* (Joseks, Moseks, and Sruls; 1910) and *Józki, Jaśki i Franki* (Joes, Jacks, and Frankies; 1911). His most famous novel, *Król Maciuś Pierwszy* (1922; *King Matt the First*, 1986), along with its follow-up, *Król Maciuś Pierwszy na bezludnej wyspie* (King Matt on a deserted island; 1923), include serious philosophical reflections on human nature and power. Korczak also authored *Sława* (Fame; 1913), *Bankructwo małego Dżeka* (The bankruptcy of Little Jack; 1924), and *Kajtuś czarodziej* (Kajtuś the magician; 1934). His works were translated into many languages, gaining international recognition. In 1990 **Andrzej Wajda** directed the movie *Korczak*. In 1992–96 the first six volumes of Korczak's *Dzieła wszystkie* (Complete works) were published in Poland. His *Selected Works* were published in the United States in 1967, *Ghetto Diary* in the United States in 1978, and the *Ghetto Years* in Israel in 1980. (PU)

Sources: *PSB*, vol. 8; *Literatura polska XX wieku: Przewodnik encyklopedyczny*, vol. 1 (Warsaw, 2000); Alicja Szlązakowa, *Janusz Korczak* (Warsaw, 1978); Maria Falkowska, ed., *Kalendarium życia, działalności i twórczości Janusza Korczaka* (Warsaw, 1978); Ludwika Barszczewska and Bolesław Milewicz, eds., *Wspomnienia o Januszu Korczaku* (Warsaw, 1981); Aleksander Lewin, ed., *Janusz Korczak w getcie: Nowe źródła* (Warsaw, 1992); Adir Cohen, *The Gate of Light: Janusz Korczak, the Educator and Writer Who Overcame the Holocaust* (Rutherford, N.J., 1994); Betty Jean Lifton, *The King of Children: A Biography of Janusz Korczak* (New York, 1997); www.korczak.pl/biography.htm.

KORDAČ František (11 January 1852, Seletice, near Libán, district of Nymburk–26 April 1934, Prague), Czech archbishop. In 1878 Kordač completed philosophical and theological studies in Rome. In 1879, after taking holy orders, he began his ministry in Liberec. In 1885 he became a professor and in 1889 the rector of a theological seminary in Litoměřice. In 1905 he became a professor of philosophy and Christian apologetics at the Theological Department of Charles University in Prague. From 1918 to 1919 he was a deputy to the revolutionary National Assembly as a representative of the Czechoslovak People's Party (Československá strana lidová [ČSL]). After he was consecrated bishop and appointed archbishop of Prague and Primate of Bohemia in September 1919, Kordač resigned his parliamentary seat. During the internal conflicts within the Czech Church, he firmly defended the authority of Rome and rejected calls for reforms from a part of the clergy, such as a demand to abolish celibacy. The only reform he supported was one that called for the use of the Czech language in pastoral services. Despite Kordač's efforts to maintain the unity of the Church, in 1920 a group of radical priests proclaimed the establishment of the Czechoslovak Church, which led to their excommunication. This, along with an agricultural reform that deprived the Church of much of its property, weakened the position of the Church in Czechoslovakia. In the second half of the 1920s Kordač successfully completed the construction of the archbishop's gymnasium and a theological seminary in Prague. After the papal nuncio ostentatiously left in 1925 in protest against the participation of the government in a commemoration of the death of Jan Hus, Kordač tried to explain in the Vatican that for the Czech people Hus had a national rather than a religious dimension. Kordač was actively involved in forging an agreement between Czechoslovakia and the Holy See; it was reached at the beginning of 1928, when the Vatican sent a new nuncio, Pietro Ciriaci. Kordač came into conflict with Ciriaci over the latter's financial claims. As a result, Kordač resigned as archbishop in 1931, although old age and ill health were given as the official reasons for his resignation. (PU)

Sources: *ČBS*; J. Dejmek, "Československo-vatikánská jednání o modus vivendi 1927–28," *Český časopis historický*, 1994; Milan Buben, *Encyklopedie českých a moravských sídelních biskupů* (Prague, 2000); *Kdo byl kdo v našich dějinách ve 20. stoleti*, vol. 1 (Prague, 1998).

KOREC Jan Chryzostom SJ (22 January 1924, Bošany), Slovak cardinal. Korec started theological studies in Trnava. In 1939 he entered the Jesuit monastic seminary in Ružomberok, where he studied philosophy and theology. After the dissolution of the male orders in Slovakia by the Communists on 14–15 April 1950, Korec was interned in the Jasov, Podolínec, and Pezinok monasteries. Ordained secretly in Rožňava in October 1950, he started working as a minister in a Jesuit seminary. On 24 August 1951 he was secretly consecrated by Bishop Pavol Hnilica SJ. Unable to work as an official minister, for ten years he worked as a blue-collar laborer. In March 1960 Korec was arrested, and in May 1960 he was sentenced to twelve years for

"betraying the Socialist homeland" by, for instance, carrying on a religious ministry among the youth and secretly ordaining of priests.

For seven years Korec was detained in the worst Czechoslovak prisons, often under inhuman conditions. Conditionally released in February 1968, despite health problems, he joined in the official ministry—for instance, in the creation of the Work of the Council of Renewal, the most important church initiative during the Prague Spring. On 8 July 1969 Korec was received in a private audience by Pope Paul VI, who presented him with his own episcopal insignia. After returning home, Korec was prevented from taking over his diocese. Perceived by the Communists as the main organizer of Church structures independent from the state, during the so-called normalization he was banned from all official religious duties. From 1970 he lived in Bratislava under constant police surveillance. Nevertheless, until the fall of Communist rule in 1989 Korec was active in the underground Catholic Church in Slovakia, and he ordained 120 priests. He also stayed in contact with the leaders of the democratic opposition. He publicly protested the obligation of the clergy to belong to the state-controlled Pacem in terris Association. He belonged to the top moral authorities in Slovakia.

When on 25 March 1988 a demonstration in defense of believers was brutally dispersed by the riot police in Bratislava, Korec signed an open letter defending those repressed. He returned to his normal ministry in November 1989. In January 1990 he assumed the position of rector of Ss. Cyril and Methodius Catholic Seminary in Bratislava, and on 6 February 1990 he became bishop of Nitra, the oldest Slovak diocese. On 28 June 1991 Pope **John Paul II** appointed him cardinal. In 1991 Korec supported the dissolution of Czechoslovakia and the proclamation of an independent Slovakia. On 30 June 1995 he welcomed John Paul II in Nitra, where the Pope met the Slovak youth. During ten years of his episcopal service Korec consecrated about sixty new churches. He played an important role in negotiating the concordat between the Holy See and the Slovak state in 2000. He received many prestigious awards. In 1986 he became an honorary doctor of the University of Notre Dame in South Bend, Indiana. In 1993 he received the Legion of Honor for his human rights work. Korec authored sixty-five works, among them works on dialectic materialism and atheist humanism, as well as textbooks on spiritual training. He translated works by Karl Ranner SJ into Slovak. His memoirs, *Od barbarskiej noci* (1994; *Night of the Barbarians*, 2002), were translated into many languages and won him fame. In 1997 he also published *Človek na cestách Zeme* (Man on earthly roads). In 1998 Korec was invited to deliver the Lenten retreat for the Pope and the Roman Curia workers. (AGr)

Sources: Norbert Kmet, *Postavenie Cirkvi na Slovensku 1948–1951* (Bratislava, 2000); Jan Pešek and Michal Barnovský, *Pod kuratelou moci: Cirkvi na Slovensku v rokoch 1953–1970* (Bratislava, 1999); František Mikloško, *Nebudete ich moct rozvrātit: Z osudov katolickej cirkvi na Slovensku v rokoch 1943–1989* (Bratislava, 1991); *Gość Niedzielny*, 7 February 1999; *Annuario Pontificio 2000*.

KORFANTY Wojciech (20 April 1873, Sadzawka, near Katowice–17 August 1939, Katowice), Polish national and Christian Democratic politician. The son of a miner, shortly before his final exams Korfanty was expelled from a German gymnasium for his contacts with the Polish independence movement; therefore he passed his high school final exams in 1895 extramurally (i.e., without attending school). He began to study at the polytechnic school in Charlottenburg and later studied law at Breslau (now Wrocław) University. In 1898 he was admitted to the Union of Polish Youth called Zet, the junior arm of the National Democratic Party. He worked as a journalist for Polish magazines in Silesia, *Górnoślązak* and *Praca*. In 1904 he began writing for *Polak*, a periodical that he founded. In 1902 Korfanty was sentenced to four months in prison for the articles he published. He served the sentence in a "strict regime" prison in Wronki. Owing to his staunch resistance to the German authorities and to the policies of Germanization, Korfanty soon became a hero of the Polish people in Silesia, and on 25 June 1903 he was elected MP to the Reichstag. He sat in the German parliament between 1911 and 1918, repeatedly opposing the German policies toward the Poles. In 1904–18 he also sat in the Prussian Diet. In 1910 he reached an agreement with another independence activist in Silesia, Adam Napieralski, and this consolidated Polish political movements in the region.

During World War I Korfanty initially supported the German side, but in October 1914 he abandoned his loyalty to Germany since it had not abolished its anti-Polish laws. As the situation on the front was worsening for Germany, Korfanty became radicalized, and his last speech in the Reichstag on 25 October 1918 was a culmination of this change of attitude. In his address, Korfanty demanded the incorporation of all ethnically Polish lands, including Upper Silesia, into Poland. On 14 November 1918 he arrived in Warsaw, where along with **Wincenty Witos**, he tried to prevent the Socialists from forming a government. In December 1918 he left for Poznań, where he was one of the main negotiators with the Germans during the Great Poland Uprising (Powstanie Wielkopolskie). In 1919 he

was elected MP to the Constituent Assembly and president of the National Democratic Club. In 1920 he became the Polish plebiscite commissioner in Silesia. After the failure of the plebiscite of 20 March 1921, having received confidential information that Poland would get only two administrative districts, at the beginning of May Korfanty made a decision to start the Third Silesian Uprising, announcing himself as dictator of the insurrection. As a result of the success of the uprising, Poland obtained more area in Silesia than previously intended. This success was the main reason for Korfanty's later attacks against **Józef Piłsudski**, whom he blamed for the lack of military support for the uprising.

On 27 October 1923, during the rule of the center-right Chjeno-Piast coalition, Korfanty became minister without portfolio and deputy prime minister in the government of Witos, but this government collapsed on 19 December 1923. After the coup of May 1926 Korfanty stood in firm opposition to Piłsudski and the *sanacja* regime. In 1927 he was accused of connections with big German business in Upper Silesia. On 9 September 1930 he was arrested and put in the Brześć fortress. While in prison, he was elected senator and chairman of the Christian Democratic Party. On 20 December 1930 Korfanty left prison. In 1931 he became president of the Main Board of the Christian Democratic Party. In 1935, after the disintegration of the Christian Democratic Party, new political attacks were launched against Korfanty; therefore he decided to emigrate to Czechoslovakia. While abroad, he was elected president of the Labor Party (Stronnictwo Pracy [SP]) in 1937. He was a co-founder of the Morges Front, which rallied all centrist activists and parties in opposition to the *sanacja* regime. Having witnessed the Munich decision on Czechoslovakia and as a person who knew Germans well, Korfanty was aware of the danger that loomed over Europe; therefore, in April 1939 he returned to Poland. Arrested and placed in the Mokotów prison, he was released owing to ill health on 20 July 1939. (PU)

Sources: *PSB*, vol. 14; *Kto był kim w Drugiej Rzeczypospolitej* (Warszaw, 1994); Grzegorz Łukomski and Bogusław Polak, *Powstanie Wielkopolskie 1918–1919* (Koszalin and Warsaw, 1995); *Encyklopedia Powstań Śląskich* (Opole, 1982); *Encyklopedia historii Drugiej Rzeczypospolitej* (Warsaw, 1999); Marian Orzechowski, *Wojciech Korfanty: Biografia polityczna* (Wrocław, Warsaw, Kraków, and Gdańsk, 1975); Jan Przewłocki, *Wojciech Korfanty: Polityka, wzloty i niepowodzenia* (Kielce, 1993); Ks. Jan Kudera, *Wojciech Korfanty* (Katowice, 1999); Edward Balawajder, *Wojciech Korfanty: Myśl katolicko-społeczna i działalność* (Katowice, 2001).

KORNAI János (21 January 1928, Budapest), Hungarian economist. Kornai studied history and philosophy at the University of Budapest. In 1947–55 he edited the central Communist Party daily, *Szabad Nép*. From 1955 he worked in the Hungarian Academy of Sciences, first at the Institute of Economics (until 1958); then as director of the Institute of Textile Industry (until 1963); as head of the Center for Computer Technology (until 1967); and then as director and professor of the Institute of Economics from 1967. From 1986 he was a professor at Harvard University in Cambridge, Massachusetts, and from 1989, at the Collegium Budapest. In 1972–77 Kornai was deputy chairman of the UN Planning Commission. In the 1960s and 1970s he was a visiting professor at leading American and West European universities. One of the top experts on command economies, Kornai initially saw shortcomings in excessive centralization. Later he tried to develop mathematical models to improve the mechanisms of command economies, but finally he concluded that there were unsolvable contradictions in the Socialist economies. Kornai's best-known books include *Anti-equilibrium* (1971; English edition, 1972) and *Hiány* (1980, *Economics of Shortage*, 1980), translated into many languages. In these books he showed that the command economy is limited by resources and that its problems result from inherent inefficiencies and constant shortages. Kornai created a dynamic model of the command economy, taking into account such phenomena as shortages, expansion drives, and soft budget constraints. After 1989 he focused on the transition from a command to a market economy, and in 1990 he formulated a general model of economic transformation based on the Hungarian case. Kornai also authored *Highways and Byways: Studies on Socialist Reform and Postsocialist Transition* (1995) and *Struggle and Hope* (1997). (MS)

Sources: *Ki Kicsoda 2002* (Budapest, 2001); *Magyar Nagylexikon* (Budapest, 2000); http://post.economics.harvard.edu/faculty/kornai/kornai.html.

KORNIŁOWICZ Władysław (5 August 1884, Warsaw–26 November 1946, Laski), Polish Catholic priest, charity worker, and journalist. Korniłowicz was born into a Warsaw intelligentsia family with gentry roots. Aligned with the independence movement in his youth, he was expelled from high school in 1898 for protesting a ban on the use of the Polish language that was imposed by the Russian authorities. Korniłowicz graduated from another high school, where he was the leader of Filarecja, a youth group that pursued both patriotic and Catholic aims. He studied the natural sciences at the university in Zurich (1903–5) and then at a theological seminary in Warsaw (1905–6). He subsequently graduated from the department of philosophy and theology at the University of Fribourg. In Switzerland Korniłowicz was an active member in

an association of Polish students, along with such other students as the Socialist **Bolesław Drobner** and the anthropologist Jan Czekanowski. Ordained on 11 April 1912, Korniłowicz started working as chaplain in the Jadwiga Zamoyska School in Zakopane. During World War I, along with Andrzej Małkowski, he started the Polish scouting movement among the students and alumni of this school. He also worked in the Diocesan Curia in Warsaw. In 1920, during the Polish-Soviet war, Korniłowicz served as chaplain on the front lines and in the Włocławek garrison. On the initiative of Mother Elżbieta Róża Czacka, the superior of the Franciscan Sisters and founder of the Society for the Care of the Blind, he became chaplain of the Franciscan Sisters. He simultaneously lectured in liturgy and ethics at the Catholic University of Lublin (1923–30).

From 1930 on Korniłowicz devoted himself primarily to work at the Institute for the Blind in Laski, where he settled permanently. He was also active in landed gentry circles and among scouts and university students, some of whom were members of the leftist Catholic organization Odrodzenie (Rebirth). Korniłowicz pleaded with the authorities on behalf of imprisoned political opponents of the *sanacja* regime, particularly members of left-wing parties. Thanks to his efforts, a number of people, including the Communist Henryk Dembiński, were released from prison. Korniłowicz held community retreats for converts, Catholic progressives, and liberal members of the so-called Circle. A proponent of neo-Thomism, he also put emphasis on active participation in the Holy Mass. He promoted his views in the periodical *Verbum*, of which he was editor-in-chief (1934–39). In Poland Korniłowicz popularized the ideas of Jacques Maritain, who was a friend of his. During the German occupation Korniłowicz went into hiding in a Franciscan convent in the Lublin region. Seriously ill, in 1945 he returned to Laski, where he died soon afterwards. Korniłowicz was considered a precursor of ecumenism and one of the spiritual fathers of the Second Vatican Council. (MC)

Sources: *PSB*, vol. 14; Stefan Wyszyński, "Ksiądz Władysław Korniłowicz," *Tygodnik Powszechny*, 1946, no. 50; Antoni Marylski, "Ksiądz Władysław Korniłowicz," *Znak*, 1966, no. 144; *Tadeusz Mazowiecki, ed., Ludzie Lasek* (Warsaw, 1987).

KORNIYCHUK Oleksander (25 May 1905, Khrystynivka, Kiev Province–14 May 1972, Kiev), Ukrainian writer and dramatist, Soviet party and state activist. Born into the family of a railroad worker, in 1929 Korniychuk graduated in philology from the Institute of Folk Culture in Kiev. Already a member of the Communist Party, from 1929 to 1934 he worked as a screenwriter in Kiev, Kharkiv, and Odessa. His first plays on "the building of socialism" are little known. It was his drama about the civil war, *Zahybel eskadry* (Loss of the squadron; 1933), that brought him fame. Korniychuk's subsequent plays, such as *Platon Krechet* (1934) and *Pravda* (Truth; 1937), aroused the interest of Stalin himself. In the latter, he touched on the subject of "brotherly help," which the Russian nation was supposed to give to the Ukrainians during the revolution of 1917. In 1934 Korniychuk became an executive member of the newly founded Union of Ukrainian Writers; in 1937 he became a deputy to the Supreme Council of the USSR, and a year later, also a deputy to the Supreme Council of the Ukrainian SSR. From January 1938 he presided over the Union of Ukrainian Writers. In 1939 he became a full member of the Academy of Sciences of the Ukrainian SSR and in 1943 also of the Academy of Sciences of the USSR.

For purposes of propaganda in favor of the unification of the Western Ukraine with the USSR, after 17 September 1939 Korniychuk wrote *Bohdan Khmelnytsky*, a play in the style of Soviet monumentalism praising the Pereyaslav agreement. The play became the basis for a film (1939) and then an opera (1951) under the same title. In 1939 Korniychuk married the Polish Communist activist **Wanda Wasilewska**. During the war, Korniychuk's literary creativity was still connected with the political needs of the authorities. In the works *Partyzany v stepakh Ukraiiny* (Partisans in the steppes of the Ukraine; 1942) and *Front* (1942), he depicted the drama of the war in a propagandist way. Despite the alliance between the USSR and the United States, in 1944 he wrote an anti-American play, *Misija mistera Perkinsa v krajinu bilshovikiv* (Mr. Perkins's mission in the Bolshevik state). In February 1944 Korniychuk was appointed minister for foreign affairs of the USSR. In accordance with Stalin's policy of extending the formal powers of the republic, Korniychuk even prepared the establishment of diplomatic relations between the Ukraine and the United States and Great Britain, but in July 1944 he lost his post because Stalin, having seized the entire territory of the Ukraine, abandoned his plan. Korniychuk's next plays—for example, *Kalynovyi hai* (Cranberry grove; 1950)—closely followed the criteria of Socialist realism. In 1947–55 and 1959–72 he served as president of the Supreme Council of the USSR. He also became a member of the CC of the Communist Party of Ukraine (1949) and of the CC of the CPSU (1952). After Stalin's death Korniychuk supported de-Stalinization. In 1954, in connection with another round of "Ukrainization" of the cadres in the USSR, he became deputy prime minister of the Ukrainian SSR. The same year he wrote a play, *Kryla* (The wings), a kind of satire on the Stalinist bureaucracy. (TS)

Sources: Yurii Kobyletskyi, *Dramaturh i chas: Tvorchist' Oleksandra Korniychuka* (Kiev, 1965); D. Vakulenko, *Oleksandr Korniychuk: Narys zhyttia i tvorchosti* (Kiev, 1980).

KOROŠEC Antun (12 May 1872, Biserjane–14 December 1940, Belgrade), Slovene priest and politician. After graduating from high school in 1892, Korošec studied theology in Maribor and later earned a Ph.D. from the University of Graz. In 1895 he was ordained a priest and worked for three years in the parishes of Sladki Gori and Radljah. In 1898 he assumed the editorship of the newspaper *Slovenski Gospodar*. He later contributed to *Südsteirischen Presse* and edited *Naš dom* and the newspaper *Straža*. In 1906 he obtained a seat in the parliament in Vienna. In the autumn of that year he founded the Slovene Union of Peasants from Styria (Slovensko Kmečko Zvezo za Štajersko), which soon became the Slovene People's Party (Slovenska Ljudska Stranka [SLS]). At that time Korpšec began working more closely with **Janez Krek**, who exerted an ideological influence on him. Together, they propagated a peasant form of the Slovene version of Social Catholicism.

In 1914 Korošec became head of the Croat and Slovene parliamentary representation in Vienna. In May 1917 he was elected president of the Yugoslav Club. On 30 May 1917 in the parliament in Vienna he read the so-called May Declaration, which he had helped to draft and which called for the unification of all Slovene, Croat, and Serb-populated territories of the monarchy into a democratic state under Habsburg rule. Korošec became head of the National Committee, which was established by all the major political parties of Slovenia—that is, the SLS under his leadership, the Liberal Party, and the Yugoslav Social Democratic Party. He served as president of the National Council of Slovenes, Croats, and Serbs, which was established on 5 October 1918 in Zagreb and which served as the chief political organ of the South Slavs in the Habsburg empire. On 29 October Korošec announced the secession of the South Slavs from Austria-Hungary. In October 1918, during negotiations on the establishment of a state with **Nikola Pašić**, prime minister of Serbia, and **Ante Trumbić**, a representative of the Yugoslav Committee, Korošec proposed a confederate model. These negotiations led to the signing of the Geneva Declaration on 9 November 1918 concerning a joint state.

When the South Slav nations united into the Kingdom of Serbs, Croats, and Slovenes, Korošec became deputy prime minister of its first government, established on 20 December 1918. He was disappointed by the adoption of the constitution (28 June 1921), which dashed federalist hopes. Following an unprecedented attack in 1928 inside the parliament building (Skupština), in which **Stjepan**

Radić and other Croatian deputies were assassinated, plunging the country into a deep crisis, Korošec performed the duties of prime minister from 28 July 1928 to 7 January 1929, the first ever non-Serbian politician to do so. Initially loyal to King **Alexander**, he gradually moved to the opposition as he saw that the Serbs were beginning to concentrate all power. Korošec supported the so-called Zagreb Manifesto of November 1932, announced by the Peasant Democratic Coalition, in which absolutism, centralism, and unitarism were condemned. He drafted the so-called Ljubljana Manifesto, passed by the Slovenes in December 1932, which not only criticized the royal regime, but also called for the establishment of a federation of the Yugoslav nations. As a result, Korošec was interned on the island of Hvar, along with other members of the SLS leadership. After the death of King Alexander in 1934, Korošec resumed political activities, hoping for an evolutionary change in the Serbian policy. In 1936 he joined the Yugoslav Radical Union, a political group established by Prime Minister **Milan Stojadinović**, which gained a significant majority in the parliament. From 1935 to 1938 Korošec served as minister of the interior. Elected Senate speaker in 1939, he supported the negotiations between the Serbs and Croats that resulted in the Sporazum (Agreement) of 26 August 1939. However, the Sporazum did little to improve the situation of the Slovenes. In foreign policy Korošec favored cooperation with the Germans. Shortly before his death he served as minister of education. (AO)

Sources: *Enciklopedija Slovenije*, vol. 5 (Ljubljana, 1991); *Biographisches Lexikon*, vol. 2; Carole Rogel, *The Slovenes and Yugoslavism, 1890–1914* (Boulder, Colo., 1977); Alex N. Dragnich, *The First Yugoslavia* (Stanford, 1983); Wacław Felczak and Tadeusz Wasilewski, *Historia Jugosławii* (Wrocław, 1985); "Življenje in delo dr. Antona Korošca," *Prispevky za zgodovino delavskega gibanja*, 1991, no. 1; Feliks Bister, *Anton Korošec, državnozborski poslanec na Dunaju: Življenje in delo, 1872–1918* (Ljubljana, 1992).

KORVIN Otto (24 March 1894, Nagybocskó–28 December 1919, Budapest), head of the political police of the Hungarian Soviet Republic. Korvin was born into the family of a sawmill worker, and after school he worked as a clerk in the Budapest Timber Bank. In 1917 he joined the leftist anti-war movement of Ervin Szabó. After the arrest of the leading activists of the left in the summer of 1918, Korvin became radicalized and joined the Hungarian Bolsheviks in Budapest. When **Béla Kun** came from Russia to Budapest, on 17 November 1918 the Hungarian Communist Party was created (Kommunisták Magyarországi Pártja), and Korvin became a member of its Central Committee, serving at the same time as the secretary of

propaganda. Between March and August 1919 he was head of the political department in the Commissariat of Internal Affairs in the Hungarian Soviet Republic (HSR), and he directed the secret police, which he organized along the pattern of the Bolshevik Cheka. He worked with the groups of "Lenin's Boys" (Lenin Fiúk), mostly criminals released from prisons at the beginning of the revolution who plundered the civil population and took hostages to extort information and ransom. Korvin was responsible for the unlawful arrests of "enemies of the people," torture during investigations, and executions carried out by his security apparatus. After the fall of the HSR Korvin did not manage to escape. Arrested in August 1919, he was sentenced to death and executed. (WR)

Sources: Rudolf L. Tőkes, *Bela Kun and the Hungarian Soviet Republic* (New York, 1967); *Életrajzi Lexikon*, vol. 1 (Budapest, 1967).

KÓS Károly [originally Kosch] (16 December 1883, Temesvár [Timisoara]–25 August 1977, Kolozsvár [Cluj]), Hungarian architect, graphic artist, and writer. Kós graduated from the Architecture Department of Budapest Technical University in 1907. Before World War I, he used traditional, Transylvanian architectural motifs to design a number of buildings, including Calvinist churches in the Óbuda district of Budapest and in Kolozsvár, the Székely National Museum of Sfintu Gheorghe, and the buildings of the Budapest Zoo. Kós designed the decorations prepared for the coronation ceremony of Emperor Karl I as King of Hungary (1916). In 1917–18 Kós traveled in Turkey, where he compiled materials for a monograph about the architecture of Istanbul, published in 1918, and then he returned to his native Transylvania. In 1919, after the 1918 presidential address of Woodrow Wilson, Kós proclaimed a republic in the region of Călătea, whose national symbols, currency, and postal stamps he designed personally. Over the following years he mainly earned his living working as a graphic artist. He helped to organize the political and cultural life of the Hungarians in Transylvania, which was given to Romania by the 1920 Treaty of Trianon. Kós founded many periodicals, book publishing houses, and artistic associations. In 1925 he published the novel *Varjú nemzetség* (Nation of crows), a kind of chronicle of seventeenth-century Transylvania. He won the greatest acclaim as the author of *Az Országépítő* (The country builder; 1934), a romantic historical novel about King Stephen I that was later successfully adapted into a play.

Kós enthusiastically welcomed the incorporation of southern Transylvania into Hungary under the Second Vienna Award in August 1940, but he remained skeptical about a rapprochement between Hungary and Germany.

In 1940 he began lecturing at the School of Agriculture in Kolozsvár. In 1944 he moved there and got involved in public life, becoming head of the provincial branch of the Hungarian People's Union (1945–46), head of the Hungarian Union of Plastic Artists in Romania, a member of the board of the Economic Association of Transylvanian Hungarians, an editor of the periodical *Világosság*, and a member of the Romanian parliament (1946–48). In 1952 Kós retired. He was a codifier, but at the same time a creative transformer, of Transylvanian architecture. His literary and graphic output contributed to the maintenance of a separate regional identity for Transylvania. (MS)

Sources: Pál Balázs, *Kós Károly* (Budapest, 1971); János Varró, *Kós Károly, a szépiró* (Kolozsvár, 1973); Samu Benkő, "Búcsú Kós Károlytól," *Tiszatáj*, 1977, no. 10; György Száraz, "Búcsú Kós Károlytól," *Élet és Irodalom*, 1977, no. 36; *Kós Károlyi emlékezete: Születésének 100 érfurdulójára* (Szentendre, 1984); Samu Benkő, *Kós Károly* (Budapest, 1991); Béla Köpeczi, ed., *History of Transylvania* (Boulder, Colo., 2001).

KOŚCIAŁKOWSKI-ZYNDRAM Marian, pseudonym "Jerzy Orwid" (16 March 1892, Ponedel, Lithuania–12 April 1946, Brookwood, United Kingdom), Polish officer and politician. In 1910 Kościałkowski-Zyndram began to study at the Psychoneurological Institute in St. Petersburg but after two years he switched to studying agriculture at the Riga Polytechnic. In 1911 he co-founded the Union of Active Struggle (Związek Walki Czynnej [ZWC]) in St. Petersburg and Riga. In 1912 he was commander of the ZWC Baltic district. In August 1914 he went to Warsaw, where he joined the Polish Legions. He played an important role in the so-called flying squadrons of the Polish Military Organization (Polska Organizacja Wojskowa [POW]), which carried out sabotage actions behind the lines of the Russian Army. In February 1915 he became second lieutenant and commander of the Warsaw flying squadron. From June 1915 he commanded all such units in the Russian-occupied territories. In August 1915 he became platoon commander in the First Brigade of the Legions. On the orders of **Józef Piłsudski**, Kościałkowski-Zyndram returned from the front to Warsaw, where he became commander of the POW district and later adjutant and inspector of the POW High Command. In 1917 he was active in the Military Commission of the Provisional Council of State of the Kingdom of Poland, which was established under the control of the German authorities-in-occupation.

In November 1918, as head of the department of active struggle of the POW High Command and commander of the flying squadrons, Kościałkowski-Zyndram was in charge of disarming the Germans in Warsaw. In April 1919 he served as head of an intelligence section of the Head-quarters of the Commander-in-Chief, and he participated in the seizure of Vilnius. He fought in the Polish-Soviet war, holding various positions in the army, including that of head of the Second (Intelligence) Department of the Command of the Lithuanian-Belorussian Front. He organized POW and self-defense units in Lithuania and Belorussia. In August 1920 he took over command of the Union for the Defense of the Homeland, which carried out sabotage actions in the territories occupied by the Red Army. During the Vilnius expedition of General **Lucjan Żeligowski** in October 1920, he led a group called Bieniakonie, which was the first to enter the city. From 1920 to 1922 he served on the staff of the Armed Forces of Central Lithuania. On the orders of Piłsudski, in 1922 Kościałkowski-Zyndram retired from military service and became involved in politics as an activist of the Polish Peasant Party–Liberation (Polskie Stronnictwo Ludowe–Wyzwolenie [PSL–Liberation]). In March 1925 he joined the Main Board of the PSL–Liberation and became its vice-president. Kościałkowski-Zyndram belonged to the Masonic Lodge of Vilnius. In 1925 he co-founded the Labor Club, and in October 1926 he became president of the Labor Party, into which the Labor Club was transformed and which supported the *sanacja* government. From 1927 to 1930 he was vice-president of the Nonparty Bloc of Cooperation with the Government (Bezpartyjny Blok Współpracy z Rządem [BBWR]), and from October 1928 to December 1929 he was president of the Urban and Rural Labor Union. From 1922 to 1930 and from 1935 to 1939 he was an MP, and from July 1930 to March 1934 he was the provincial governor of Białystok. In 1932 he was appointed a reserve lieutenant colonel. In March 1934 Kościałkowski-Zyndram became president-commissioner of Warsaw. From June 1934 to October 1935 he served as minister of interior, and in the summer of 1935 he contributed to the conclusion of an agreement with the parliamentary representation of the Ukrainian National Democratic Alliance (UNDO). In the *sanacja* camp, he represented the liberal wing.

After Piłsudski's death, Kościałkowski-Zyndram joined the group led by President **Ignacy Mościcki**. On 13 October 1935 he became prime minister of the government and passed through parliament policy that gave special powers to the president, thereafter he ruled on the basis of presidential decrees. Although this government achieved a balanced budget by introducing a deflation policy, increasing taxes, cutting administrative expenses, and rationing foreign currency, these steps became factors that gave rise to workers' protests in Kraków and Lwów (Lviv) in the spring of 1936. After the government's resignation on 15 May 1936, Kościałkowski-Zyndram became minister of social welfare in the government of **Feliks Sławoj-Składkowski**. In September 1939, along with the government, he went to Romania; from there he made his way to France. In 1940 he settled in Great Britain. (JS)

Sources: *PSB*, vol. 14; *Encyklopedia Historii Polski: Dzieje polityczne*, vol. 1 (Warsaw, 1994); *Encyklopedia historii Drugiej Rzeczypospolitej* (Warsaw, 1999); Tadeusz Jędruszczak, *Piłsudczycy bez Piłsudskiego* (Warsaw, 1963); Władysław Pobóg-Malinowski, *Najnowsza historia polityczna Polski*, vol. 2 (London, 1983).

KOSHELIVETS Ivan [originally Yareshko] (10 November 1907, Koshelivka, Chernihiv region–5 February 1999, Munich, Germany), Ukrainian historian of literature and translator. In 1930 Koshelivets graduated from the Institute of Folk Literature in Nizhyn. In 1940–41 he was a doctoral student at the Taras Shevchenko Institute of Literature. From 1944 he lived in exile. In 1947 he settled in Munich, where in 1955–60 he co-edited the monthly *Ukraiinska literaturna hazeta*. From 1961 to 1984 he was editor-in-chief of the monthly *Suchasnist* (with a break in 1968–75 and 1979–82). Koshelivets belonged to the Taras Shevchenko Scholarly Society and the Ukrainian Free Academy of Sciences. He was a professor at the Free Ukrainian University and a member of the editorial board of *Entsyklopediya Ukraiinoznastva*. Among other works, Koshelivets authored *Narysy z literatury* (Literary essays; 1954); *Suchasna literatura v USRR* (Contemporary literature in the USSR; 1964); *Mykola Skrypnyk* (1972); *Z-pid yakykh bryl?* (From under what solid figures? 1975); *Oleksandr Dovzhenko* (1980); and the memoirs *Rozmowy po dorozi do sebe* (Conversations on the way home; 1985). He edited the anthology *Panorama naynovishoyi literatury v USRR* (Panorama of recent literature in the USSR; 1963). He translated into Ukrainian works by Denis Diderot and Franz Kafka. On the orders of **Jerzy Giedroyć**, in 1969 Koshelivets edited the anthology *Ukraina 1956–1968* (The Ukraine 1956–1968), which included documents concerning the generation of the 1960s among Ukrainian writers. This work was published by the (Polish) Literary Institute in Paris. (BB)

Sources: *Encyclopedia of Ukraine*, vol. 2 (Toronto, 1988); *Ukraiinska Literaturna Entsyklopediya*, vol. 3 (Kiev, 1995); *Khto ye khto v Ukraiini 1997* (Kiev, 1997).

KOSIOR Stanislav (18 November 1889, Węgrów–26 February 1939, Moscow), Soviet Communist activist in the Ukraine. Kosior was born into a Polish working-class family that settled in the Donbas in 1896. At thirteen he began working at a factory, and in 1907 he joined the Russian Social Democratic Party. From 1907 to 1918 he was a Bolshevik activist in the Donbas region. During World War I he organized Bolshevik units in Kiev. He was imprisoned several times, and in 1915–17 he was in exile in Siberia. From March 1917 to March 1918 Kosior was involved in party activities in Petrograd. From March to April 1918 he served as people's commissar of finance in the Ukrainian Bolshevik government. One of the founders of the Communist Party (Bolshevik) of Ukraine (Komunistychna Partiya [Bilshovykiv] Ukrayiny [CP(B)U]), Kosior was a member and the secretary of the Central Committee (CC) from 1919 to 1920 and the head of the Organizational Department of the CC from 1922 to 1925. As a close associate of Stalin, Kosior was quickly promoted in the central party apparatus. From 1925 to 1928 he was secretary and from 1928 a member of the Politburo of the CC of the All-Union Communist Party (Bolsheviks) and a member of the Presidium of the Central Executive Committee of the Soviet Union.

In 1928 Kosior returned to Kiev and became secretary general (and from 1934 first secretary) of the CP(B)U CC. As the person in charge of collectivization, at the Third All-Ukrainian Conference of the CP(B)U in July 1932 he supported **Lazar Kaganovich** and Vyacheslav Molotov, who insisted that the Ukraine fulfill an excessive grain supply plan, although Kosior knew that there was not enough grain even for the Ukrainian people. On his initiative, grain reserves were established at the kolkhozes in the fall of 1932. The confiscation of these reserves and of seed grain, carried out on the orders of Stalin and Molotov with Kosior's support, was one of the main reasons for the great famine in the Ukraine in 1932–33, which caused the death of many millions of people. Kosior also opposed the policy of Ukrainization. Dismissed from his posts in the Ukraine in January 1938, he was appointed deputy prime minister of the Soviet Union. However, he was soon removed from all his party and government posts. Arrested in April or May 1938, he was falsely accused of being a member of the Polish Military Organization (Polska Organizacja Wojskowa [POW]). He was subjected to prolonged torture. He was allegedly interrogated by Stalin himself. Sentenced to death on 26 February 1939, Kosior was probably executed by firing squad on the spot. He was rehabilitated after the Twentieth CPSU Congress. (BB)

Sources: *MERSH*, vol. 17; *Entsyklopediia Ukraiinoznavstva*, vol. 3 (Lviv, 1994); *Malyi slovnyk istoriï Ukraiiny* (Kiev, 1997); *Dovidnyk z istorii Ukraiiny* (Kiev, 2001); Hryhory Kostiuk, *Stalinist Rule in the Ukraine* (New York, 1960); M. B. Pohrebinskyi, *Stanislav Vikentiovych Kosior* (Kiev, 1963); *O Stanislave Kosiore: Wospominaniia, ocherki, stati* (Moscow, 1989).

KOSTELNYK Havryil (1886, Ruski Krstur, near Bačka, Serbia–20 September 1948, Lviv [Lemberg, Lwów]), priest of the Greek Catholic (Uniate) Church, representative of its anti-Vatican wing. Kostelnyk studied philosophy and theology in Zagreb, Lemberg, and Friburg, where in 1913 he earned a Ph.D. From 1920 to 1928 he lectured at a seminary in Lwów. Dismissed for his anti-Vatican leanings by the rector of this seminary, Father **Yosyf Slipyi**, Kostelnyk became the parish priest of the Transfiguration Church, the biggest church in Lwów. He was a firm critic of communism, but because he had distanced himself from the Latin tendencies in the Uniate Church and from the Vatican's eastern policy, after the Red Army seized Lwów in September 1939, he became the Kremlin's candidate to lead the separation of the Uniate Church from Rome. Kostelnyk remained loyal to the Greek Catholic church as long as his patron and mentor, Archbishop **Andrey Sheptytskyi**, was alive. At the end of June 1941 he supported the Ukraine's declaration of independence, proclaimed by the Bandera faction of the Organization of Ukrainian Nationalists (OUN-B). Since his two sons were serving in the SS Galizien division, Kostelnyk became an easy target for blackmail by the Soviets when the Red Army again entered East Galicia. He called for an end to the fighting. With the support of Serhiy Danylenko ("Karin"), in April 1945, following the arrest of Archbishop Slipyi, Kostelnyk became administrator of Lviv Province and agreed to assume the chairmanship of the so-called Initiating Committee for the Reunification of the Greek Catholic Church with the Russian Orthodox Church.

Under close surveillance by the political police, the Initiating Committee staged a "unification" agitation campaign among the Uniate clergy, who were intimidated by arrests. On 8–10 March 1946 over two hundred delegates held a "council" (*sobor*) in St. George's Cathedral in Lviv, during which a decision was made to subordinate the Uniate Church to the Orthodox Church and appoint leaders of the Initiating Committee as bishops of the Orthodox Church. A Requiem Mass for the late Archbishop Sheptytskyi, as the precursor of Orthodox Christianity in East Galicia, was the extreme of hypocrisy. On 3 April 1946 Kostelnyk and his co-workers were admitted to see **Nikita Khrushchev**, head of the party in the Ukraine, and **Mykhailo Khrechukha**, president of the Supreme Soviet of the Ukrainian SSR. On 7 April the Patriarch of Moscow, Alexey I, accepted the Galician Church into the "mother Orthodox Church" and appointed Kostelnyk protopresbyter, which was the highest honor for a married Orthodox priest. As a result of the "council," 986 Greek Catholic priests joined the Orthodox Church and only 280 remained faithful to the Vatican. The majority of the latter were soon arrested and deported to labor camps. Uniate churches were taken over by the Orthodox Church.

Kostelnyk pleaded on behalf of the persecuted, but to no effect. After a Holy Mass in the Transfiguration Church, Kostelnyk was fatally shot on the street by an unknown assassin. The assassin was in turn shot dead from a car waiting for him. The Soviet authorities blamed the murder on the Ukrainian nationalist underground, but it is probable that the assassination was masterminded by the Soviet secret police. (WR)

Sources: *Encyclopedia of Ukraine*, vol. 2 (Toronto, 1988); *Diiannia soboru hreko-katolyts'koi tserkvy u Lvovi, 8–10 bereznia 1946* (Lviv, 1946); Bohdan R. Bociurkiw, *The Ukrainian Greek-Catholic Church and the Soviet State (1939–1950)* (Edmonton, 1996).

KOSTENKO Lina (19 March 1930, Rzhyshchiv, near Kiev), Ukrainian poet, one of the leaders of the 1960s generation (*shestidesiatniki*). After graduating from high school, Kostenko studied at the Kiev Pedagogical Institute and in 1952–56 at the Maksim Gorky Literary Institute in Moscow. She made her literary debut in the early 1950s. In 1957 she published her first volume, *Prominnia zemli* (Earth rays), and in 1958 another collection, *Vitryla* (Sails), but it was the volume *Mandrivky sertsia* (1961; *Wanderings of the Heart*, 1990) that won her wider recognition. Kostenko's subsequent collections of poems, *Zorianyi horal* (Star chorale; 1963) and *Knyazha hora* (Princely mountain; 1972), were banned from publication as a result of her involvement in protests against the Russification policies of Soviet Ukrainian authorities and her open support for arrested Ukrainian intellectuals (for instance, **Mykhailo Horyn** and **Vyacheslav Chornovil**). Kostenko's personal lyrics and poems analyzing the social role of a poet under totalitarianism were banned by censorship for many years. She was able to publish *Nad berehami vichnoyi riky* (On the banks of the eternal river) in 1977. She won great popularity with her poetic novel *Marysia Churay* (1979), initially ignored by official critics but awarded the Taras Shevchenko State Award in 1987. In the 1980s Kostenko's subsequent collections were published: *Nepovtornist* (Non-recurrence; 1980) and *Sad netanuchykh skulptur* (The garden of non-melting sculptures; 1987). She also co-authored and authored screenplays. A collection of English translations of Kostenko's poems was published as *Lilac King: Poems* (1990). (BB)

Sources: *Encyclopedia of Ukraine*, vol. 2 (Toronto, 1988); *Khto ye khto v Ukraiini 2000* (Kiev, 2000); Vyacheslav Briukhovetskyi, *Lina Kostenko: Narys tworczosti* (Kiev, 1990); *Ukraiinska Literaturna Encyklopedija*, vol. 3 (Kiev, 1995); Bogumiła Berdychowska and Ola Hnatiuk, eds., *Bunt pokolenia: Rozmowy z intelektualistami ukraińskimi* (Lublin, 2000); *Shevchenkivski laureaty 1962–2001: Entsyklopedychnyi dovidnyk* (Kiev, 2001).

KOSTOV Ivan (23 December 1949, Sofia), Bulgarian politician and economist. After graduating in economics from the Karl Marx Institute of Economics in Sofia, Kostov worked there as an assistant professor. From 1979 he was a senior lecturer at the Department of Scientific Communism of the Lenin Memorial Higher Institute of Mechanical and Electric Engineering in Sofia. In 1982 he received a Ph.D. in mathematical modeling. During the Bulgarian Round Table Talks in early 1990 Kostov was an economic expert, and he authored a reform based on the Polish "shock therapy" of **Leszek Balcerowicz**. In the parliamentary elections of June 1990 Kostov won a seat on behalf of the Union of Democratic Forces (Sayuz na Demokratichnite Sili [UDF]). From December 1990 to November 1991 he was minister of finance in the government of **Dimitur Popov**. He negotiated an agreement with the trade unions, suspending strikes for half a year; this allowed for the liberalization of prices, given a partial freeze on wages. In view of the social costs of these steps, Kostov became a target of fierce attacks by the post-Communists and radical trade unions, including Podkrepa. On the other hand, his firmness and consistency in carrying out the reform won him supporters. As a result he retained his position in the government of **Filip Dimitrov** (November 1991–October 1992).

Kostov lost in the parliamentary elections of December 1994, but he won the election for UDF leader, and on 29 December 1994 he assumed this position. Under his influence economic liberalism became a key element of the UDF program. The economic disaster and the ineptitude of the government of **Zhan Videnov** led to an outburst of social discontent. Given the support of President **Zhelyu Zhelev**, Kostov succeeded in the early parliamentary elections of April 1997, in which the UDF won 52.2 percent of the vote. On 21 May 1997 he became prime minister. Within two years he had curbed inflation; he connected the leva with the Deutsche mark; restored agricultural and forest land property; succeeded in privatizing some large companies (e.g., the Balkan airline company); and reoriented foreign policy toward the West. In 1999 Bulgaria refused to grant air space for Russian air supplies to Yugoslavia during the NATO Kosovo operation. The army was reorganized so as to conform more closely with NATO standards. Appreciating these efforts, the European Union invited Bulgaria to accession talks. Kostov also strengthened his position as the UDF leader. Under his influence the UDF evolved from a loose federation of conflicting groups toward a steerable federative party, similar to German Christian Democracy. Thus after losing in the local elections in the fall of 1999, within one month Kostov managed to change two-thirds of his cabinet without much resistance within the UDF. Despite these successes Kostov and his government confronted serious problems: material conditions for most people were still bad; there was excessive bureaucracy, and there were corruption scandals involving his ministers. All this led to electoral defeat for the UDF in June 2001. On 24 July 2001 Kostov resigned as prime minister. He also gave up his UDF leadership in favor of Ekaterina Mikhailova, one of his closest aides who thus far had headed the UDF parliamentary club. Notwithstanding, Kostov remained one of the key figures in the UDF. (AG)

Sources: *Koy koy e v Bulgariya* (Sofia, 1998); Tasho Tashev, *Ministrite na Bulgariya 1879–1999: Entsiklopedichen spravochnik* (Sofia, 1999); Jerzy Jackowicz, *Bułgaria od rządów komunistycznych do demokracji parlamentarnej 1988–1991* (Warsaw, 1992); Raymond Detrez, *Historical Dictionary of Bulgaria* (Lanham, Md., 1997); www.omda.bg/engl/news/party/sds_engl.htm; www.omda.bg/engl/personalia/kostov_engl.htm; www.electionworld.org/election/bulgaria.htm; www.ecn.org/est/balcani/bulga/bulgaria50.htm.

KOSTOV Traycho [originally Dzhunev] (17 June 1897, Sofia–17 December 1949, Sofia), Bulgarian Communist activist. Born into the family of a railroad worker, Kostov finished high school in Sofia and went on to study law at Sofia University, but he never graduated. In April 1919 he joined the then forming Bulgarian Communist Party (BCP). He served as secretary of a Communist youth organization in Sofia and was a member of the Central Committee (CC) of the Communist Youth Union. Arrested for taking part in preparations for the unsuccessful Communist uprising of September 1923, Kostov was sentenced to eight years the following year. Released in 1929, he left for Moscow, where he worked in the Executive Committee of the Communist International, studied at a Leninist school, and joined the Foreign Bureau of the BCP CC. After returning to Bulgaria in 1931, he became a member of the BCP CC. In 1934–35 he was in Moscow, where he served as a BCP delegate in the Comintern and worked in the Balkan Secretariat of the Communist International. In February 1936 Kostov returned to Bulgaria and became a member of the BCP CC Politburo. In 1938 he also joined the CC Secretariat and assumed the editorship of *Rabotnicheski Vestnik*, a party organ. In 1938–39 he was repeatedly arrested for anti-state activities but was released for lack of evidence. In 1940 he went underground, serving as secretary of the CC for political affairs. During the German-Soviet war he organized military resistance to the regime of Tsar **Boris**. Arrested in 1942 and sentenced to life imprisonment, Kostov was released by the government of **Konstantin Muraviev** on 2 September 1944. Only a week later he led a coup that overthrew Muraviev's government.

When the Communist-controlled Fatherland Front ruled in Bulgaria, Kostov served as secretary general of the party's CC until the return from Moscow of Georgi Dimitrov, to whom he yielded his position in November 1945. In March 1946 Kostov became deputy prime minister in the government of **Kimon Georgiev**; he continued to hold this post from 1946 to 1948 in Dimitrov's government, in which he was also responsible for economic issues as minister for electrification, water, and natural resources, minister without portfolio, and president of the State Committee for Economic and Financial Affairs. On two occasions he traveled to Moscow to speak with Stalin (June 1946 and February 1948). In June 1948 he represented Bulgaria at the congress of the Information Bureau of the Communist and Workers' Parties, at which **Josip Broz Tito** and the Yugoslav leadership were denounced. Arrested in connection with the case of Noel Field in April 1949, Kostov was accused of "nationalism," hostility to the Soviet Union, spying for England and the United States, "Titoism," and collaboration with the Bulgarian tsarist police. The case was part of a wave of purges within the parties of the Communist bloc, but it was also part of a struggle for power between Bulgarian Communists who, like Kostov, had experience working in Bulgaria and those who from the 1930s had uninterruptedly resided in Moscow. As a result of the trial, in which he did not plead guilty despite being tortured, on 17 December 1949 Kostov was sentenced to death and executed. The press wrote widely about his allegedly having pleaded guilty. Partially rehabilitated in 1956, Kostov was fully vindicated in December 1989. His *Izbrani proizvedenia* (Collected works) were published in 1978. (WR)

Sources: Lazitch; Blagoi Popovski, *Sudskata provokatsiia vo Sofiia* (Skopje, 1950); *Ob osnovnykh urokakh ot raskrytiia bandy Traicho Kostova* (Sofia, 1950); Adam Ulam, *Titoism and the Cominform* (Cambridge, Mass., 1952); J. F. Brown, *Bulgaria under Communist Rule* (New York, 1970); S. Steven, *Operation Splinter Factor* (Philadelphia and New York, 1974); Marshall Lee Miller, *Bulgaria during the Second World War* (Stanford, 1975); Jerzy Tomaszewski, *Bułgaria 1944–1971* (Warsaw, 1989); Mito Isusov, *Poslednata godina na Traicho Kostov* (Sofia, 1990).

KOŠTUNICA Vojislav (24 March 1944, Belgrade), Serbian lawyer and politician, president of Yugoslavia. The son of a judge, in 1970 Koštunica graduated in law from the University of Belgrade, and in 1974 he received a Ph.D. there. From 1970 he worked there as an assistant professor, but in 1974 he was forced to leave the university for co-organizing a petition in defense of an arrested professor. He worked at the Institute of Social Sciences and from 1981 at the Institute of Philosophy and Social Theory. For some time he was the director of the latter institute. Koštunica published

several articles in constitutional law and political philosophy; he translated from English (for example, *The Federalist Papers*); and he edited the scholarly periodicals *Arhiv za pravne i društvene nauke*, *Filozofske studije*, and *Filozofija i društvo*. In the 1980s he was active in the human rights movement and joined the Committee for the Defense of the Freedom of Thought and Speech. In 1989 he co-founded the anti-Communist (Serbian) Democratic Party (Demokratska Stranka [DS]). He became its deputy chairman, and in 1990 he won a Serbian parliamentary seat on its behalf.

In 1992 the DS split because of differing opinions about participation in an opposition coalition called the Democratic Movement of Serbia (Demokratski Pokret Srbije [DEPOS]), created around the Serbian Renewal Movement (SRM) of **Vuk Drašković**. Along with a group of DEPOS adherents, Koštunica left the DS, founded the Democratic Party of Serbia (Demokratska Stranka Srbije [DSS]), and became its leader. In the 1992 elections the DSS won nineteen out of fifty mandates gained by the DEPOS. In 1993 the DSS left the DEPOS in protest against SRM support for the Bosnian Serb leader **Radovan Karadzić**. Running alone, in the elections of 1993 the DSS won a mere 2.7 percent of the vote, but Koštunica stayed an MP. In the federal elections of 1996 the DSS joined the coalition Together (Zajedno), which included the SRM and the DS of **Zoran Djindjić**. During the student protests of 1996–97 Koštunica was the only leader of the opposition invited to speak at the rallies. He also took part in a long sit-down strike in downtown Belgrade in January 1997. His party joined a boycott of republican and presidential elections. During the Kosovo conflict and the NATO air raids in 1999, contrary to the SRM, the DSS did not support **Slobodan Milošević**, but it was critical of NATO and maintained a distance from the liberal opposition cooperating with NATO diplomats.

Because of the DSS stance, Koštunica became the compromise candidate of a wide coalition of Milošević opponents, called the Democratic Opposition of Serbia (Demokratska Opozicija Srbije [DOS]), in the elections for president of Yugoslavia. According to the calculations of the opposition, Koštunica won more than 50 percent of the vote in the first round of voting on 24 September 2000, but the state electoral commission, controlled by Milošević, announced that it would be necessary to hold a second round. After mass demonstrations and after a part of the army and security forces had passed over to the opposition, Milošević admitted defeat, and Koštunica was officially announced as the new president. After he officially took over power on 7 October 2000, he adopted a cautious attitude toward settling accounts with Milošević and his clique. After the Serbian parliamentary elections in December 2000, Koštunica's ratings reached their highest point, but the DOS began to crumble, and Koštunica entered into a conflict with Prime Minister Djindjić regarding the new government's stance toward the defeated post-Communists and the Yugoslav Crimes Tribunal in The Hague. On both issues Koštunica was much more moderate than Djindjić. In April 2001 he agreed to hand over Milošević to The Hague tribunal. In the presidential election of 8 December 2002 Koštunica won 57.5 percent of the vote, but owing to the lack of a 50 percent participation rate, the election was determined to be invalid. From 3 March 2004 Koštunica was prime minister of Serbia. He authored several books, including *Politički sistem kapitalizma i opozicija* (The political system of capitalism and the opposition; 1978); *Stranački pluralizam ili monizam* (Party pluralism or monism; 1983 [with Kosta Cavoški]); and *Izmedju sile i pravde* (Between force and truth; 2000). (AW)

Sources: Lenard J. Cohen, *Broken Bonds: The Disintegration of Yugoslavia* (Boulder, Colo., 1993); Christopher Bennett, *Yugoslavia's Bloody Collapse: Causes, Course and Consequences* (London, 1995); Susan L. Woodward, *The Balkan Tragedy: Chaos and Dissolution after the Cold War* (Washington, D.C., 1995); Gregory O. Hall, "The Politics of Autocracy: Serbia under Slobodan Milošević," *East European Quarterly*, 1999, no. 2; www.predsednik.gov.yu.

KOSTURKOV Stoyan (25 November 1866, Panagyurishte–17 December 1949, Sofia), Bulgarian politician. After graduating from a theological school in a monastery in Liaskovets in 1890, Kosturkov worked as a teacher in Pazardzhik, Vratsa, Pomorie, Varna, and Sofia until 1906, except for the academic year 1891–92, when he studied law in Geneva. In 1905 Kosturkov was one of the founders of the Radical Democratic Party, which was renamed the Radical Party (RP) in 1922, and he served as secretary of the central leadership of this party from 1906 to 1934, except for an interval from 1922 to 1923. He was the editor of the party press organs, *Demokrat* (1905–10) and *Radikal* (1910–34), and a contributor to the party's theoretical organ, *Demokraticheski pregled*. Kosturkov supported the proclamation of Bulgaria's independence in 1908 but opposed the consolidation of the monarchy. In 1915 he protested against Bulgaria's entering World War I on the side of Germany and Austria-Hungary. From 1913 to 1927 and 1931 to 1934 Kosturkov was a deputy to the National Assembly. Despite his opposition to Bulgaria's involvement in the war, in June 1918 he assumed the post of minister of education in the government of **Aleksandur Malinov** and continued to hold this post in the cabinet of **Teodor Teodorov** until October 1919.

Kosturkov was one of the leaders of the Constitutional Bloc, which was in opposition to the government of the Bulgarian Agrarian National Union (BANU), led by **Aleksandur Stamboliyski**. Arrested after an unsuccessful anti-government action organized by the Constitutional Bloc in Tyrnovo (17 September 1922), Kosturkov was to stand trial as one of those who had brought about the second "national catastrophe" in Bulgaria in 1918, but his trial was prevented by the coup of 9 June 1923. Kosturkov was against the accession of the RP to the Democratic Alliance and was in opposition to the government of **Aleksandur Tsankov**. In 1931 the RP, under his leadership, joined the National Bloc, and he became minister of railways, post, and telegraphs in the government of Malinov and in the subsequent government of **Nikola Mushanov** (June 1931–May 1934). Kosturkov took part in congresses of the International Radical Entente in Paris, London, Copenhagen, and Sofia. In 1935–44 he defended the Tyrnovo Constitution, and in 1943 he stood up in defense of Bulgarian Jews. During World War II he tried to avoid contacts with the Communists and refused to cooperate with the Fatherland Front but did not stand up against it. After the coup of 9 September 1944, as a result of Kosturkov's efforts, the RP was revived, joining the Fatherland Front in 1945. Kosturkov became minister of education in the government of **Kimon Georgiev** (November 1945–November 1946). He also served as deputy to the National Assembly (1945–46). In 1946 he withdrew from politics. (JJ)

Sources: *Entsiklopediya Bulgariya*, vol. 3 (Sofia, 1982); Tadeusz Wasilewski, *Historia Bułgarii* (Wrocław, 1988); Georgi Dimitrov, *Sychineniia*, vol. 16 (Sofia, 1990); Milen Kumanov and Tania Nikolova, *Politicheski partii, organizatsii i dvizheniia v Bulgariia i technite lideri 1879–1999: Kratyk spravochnik* (Sofia, 1999); Tasho Tashev, *Ministrite na Bulgariia 1879–1999: Entsiklopedichen spravochnik* (Sofia, 1999); Angel Tzurakov, *Entsiklopediia: Pravitelstvata na Bulgariia. Khronologiia na politicheskiia zhivot 1879–2001* (Sofia, 2001).

KOSZTOLÁNYI Dezső (29 March 1885, Szabadka [Subotica]–3 November 1936, Budapest), Hungarian writer and journalist. From 1903 to 1906 Kosztolányi studied Hungarian and German language and literature at Budapest University, and for a few months in 1904 he also attended the university in Vienna. After dropping out of university, he began working as a journalist. From 1908 on he contributed to *Nyugat*, the most important literary magazine in Hungary during the interwar period. In 1907 he published his first poetry volume, *Négy fal között* (Within four walls), in which he advocated "art for art's sake." In subsequent collections of poems—such as *A szegény kisgyermek panaszai* (The complaints of a poor little child; 1910); *Mágia* (Magic; 1912); *Mák* (Poppy; 1916); *Kenyér és bor* (Bread and wine; 1920); and *A bús* *férfi panaszai* (The sad man's laments; 1924)—Kosztolányi increasingly combined the concept of "art for art's sake" with reflections on the human condition. He also wrote stories that were published in 1908 in the collection *Boszorkányos esték* (Magic evenings) and press articles that were published in great numbers in all kinds of papers and periodicals. At the beginning of the 1920s Kosztolányi concentrated on prose writing. His novel *Nero, a véres költő* (1922; *Bloody Poet Nero*, 1927), about the clash between tyranny and humanism, is considered one of the best Hungarian historical novels. The novels *Pacsirta* (1924; *Skylark*, 1993); *Aranysárkány* (Golden kite; 1924); *Édes Anna* (1926); and the collection of novellas *Esti Kornél* (1933) are innovatively composed studies on man, human relations, and middle-class society. At the end of the 1920s Kosztolányi became actively involved in the literary life of Hungary and Europe. In 1930 he became the first president of the Hungarian PEN Club. He corresponded with and personally met most of the greatest writers of his time, including Thomas Mann, Maksim Gorky, and John Galsworthy. He was also an outstanding translator of William Shakespeare and Oscar Wilde. The publication of Kosztolányi's works was prohibited in Hungary in 1947–54 due to his critical attitude toward the Hungarian Soviet Republic. (MS)

Sources: Ferenc Baráth, *Kosztolányi* (Zalaegerszeg, 1938); László Rónay, *Kosztolányi* (Budapest, 1977); Ernő Kulcsár Szabó and Mihály Szegedy-Maszák, *Tanulmányok Kosztolányiról* (Budapest, 1998).

KOSZUTSKA Maria, pseudonyms "Kostrzewa," "Vera," and "Anna" (2 February 1876, Główczyn, near Kalisz–9 July 1939, Yaroslavl?), Polish Socialist and Communist activist. Born into a noble family and brought up in the tradition of independence, Koszutska finished a girls' boarding school in Warsaw (1893) and obtained qualifications for teaching in private schools (1901). At the end of 1902 she joined the Polish Socialist Party (Polska Partia Socjalistyczna [PPS]), and with her husband, Józef Ciszewski, she conducted revolutionary agitation among workers. Arrested in 1903, she was sentenced to a three-year exile in Arkhangelsk Province. Released because of her mother's illness, she took part in the 1905 revolution. Arrested in January 1906 and released again, she went underground. An advocate of increasing the revolutionary struggle, in November of the same year Koszutska helped to establish the PPS-Left. From 1907 to 1914 she lived in Galicia, from where she directed party activities in the Kingdom of Poland and where she drafted the party program, according to which Poland would be a part of a Socialist Russia. At the beginning of 1916 she returned to German-occupied Warsaw, where she conducted intensive agitation and published extensively in various periodicals, including *Głos Robotniczy*. After the Bolshevik revolution in Russia, Koszutska advocated similar tactics in the struggle for power. In the autumn of 1918 she actively supported the extreme left, and in December of that year she brought about the establishment of the Communist Workers' Party of Poland (Komunistyczna Partia Robotnicza Polski [KPRP]). From the foundation of the party, Koszutska was a member of its Central Committee (CC), and in 1919–20 she served as the secretary of the CC.

During the Polish-Soviet war Koszutska was twice arrested for supporting the Red Army. Released on bail in January 1921, she went abroad. She was active in the KPRP and from 1925 in the Communist Party of Poland (Komunistyczna Partia Polski [KPP]) in Berlin, Gdańsk, Sopot, and Moscow. She was the co-author of *Tezy Agrarne* (Agrarian theses; 1922), in which she called for parceling out the great estates among smallholders and landless peasants in order to attract them to the Socialist revolution. This was a departure from the concept of land nationalization, predominant among the Bolsheviks. Koszutska expressed a similar view in a paper that she read at the Fourth Congress of the Communist International in Moscow in December 1922. In late September and early October 1922, at the Second KPRP Congress in Bolshevo, near Moscow, Koszutska's agrarian theses and the view that it was necessary to create "an alliance of peasants and workers" became incorporated into the resolutions of the congress, and she was elected to the Politburo of the party's CC abroad. At the Fifth Comintern Congress in July 1924, Stalin fiercely attacked her views, and Koszutska was expelled from the Politburo. At the Third KPRP Congress in February 1925 she did not join the CC. She was sent to work in the Peasant International. After the coup of May 1926 in Poland, which had been supported by the KPP, Koszutska criticized the so-called May mistake of the leadership of the party and again joined the CC. At the Fourth KPP Congress in May–August 1927 she returned to the party Politburo. However, the faction led by **Julian Leński-Leszczyński** received enough support from Stalin to expel her from the CC for her "rightist deviation." After the Seventh Comintern Congress in 1935, when the KPP adopted the "united front" tactic, Koszutska wrote a letter in which she conducted self-criticism and stated that she wanted to join the leadership of the party again, but the CC found her self-criticism insufficient. In August 1937 she was arrested by the NKVD. In the August 1938 Comintern resolution dissolving the KPP, Koszutska was declared guilty of "instigating factional struggle." She died in prison. In 1956 she was rehabilitated by the authorities of the Polish United Workers' Party. Her three-volume *Pisma i przemówienia* (Writings and speeches) were published between 1961 and 1962. (WR)

Sources: *PSB*, vol. 14; *Słownik biograficzny działaczy polskiego ruchu robotniczego*, vol. 3 (Warsaw, 1992); M. K. Dziewanowski, *The Communist Party of Poland* (Cambridge, Mass., 1959); Feliks Tych, *PPS-Lewica 1914–1918* (Warsaw, 1960); *Tragedia KPP* (Warsaw, 1989).

KOT Stanisław (22 October 1885, Ruda, near Ropczyce– 26 December 1975, London), Polish Peasant Party politician and historian of culture and education. Born into a peasant family, Kot participated in the pro-independence movement while a high school student. He completed university studies at Lemberg (Lviv, Lwów) and earned a Ph.D. there in 1909. During World War I he was a close associate of **Władysław Sikorski**, head of the Military Department of the pro-Austrian Supreme National Committee. From 1914 to 1918 Kot directed the press bureau of this department and edited *Wiadomości Polskie*. In 1919 he settled in Kraków. In 1920 he became professor at the Jagiellonian University, where he held the chair of History of Culture until 1933. In 1921 he became a member of the Polish Academy of Arts and Sciences. An opponent of the ruling camp, he organized a protest against the arrest of the leaders of the center-left opposition (Centrolew) in 1930 and a protest against the reform of the school system. As a result, Kot was forced to retire, and his chair at the university was abolished. In 1933 he joined the Peasant Party (Stronnictwo Ludowe [SL]) and was a member of its Chief Council from 1935 to 1939 and a member of its Chief Executive Committee from 1936 to 1939. He represented the right wing of the party, but in 1937, working closely with **Wincenty Witos**, he co-organized peasant strikes.

In September 1939 Kot helped to reconstruct the Polish government-in-exile, in which he served as deputy prime minister and minister of interior from December 1939 to August 1941. In 1941–42 he was assigned to the Polish Embassy in the Soviet Union, the most difficult diplomatic post at that time. Trying to provide assistance to Polish citizens in the Soviet territories, Kot was unable to avoid conflicts with the Soviet authorities and with many Polish politicians. From 1942 to 1943 he served as minister of state for Polish affairs in the Middle East, and from March 1943 to November 1944, as minister of information. In April 1943 Kot issued a communiqué about the Katyń massacre. In July 1945 he returned to Poland and was one of the founders of the Polish Peasant Party (Polskie Stronnictwo Ludowe [PSL]). From 1945 to 1947 Kot served as ambassador to Rome, representing the Government of

National Unity. In 1947, when Communist pressure was growing, he resigned and remained in exile. Kot's roles included that of president of the PSL Chief Council and president of the PSL European Council. He was active in the International Peasant Union. He left a vast scholarly legacy in the history of education and the history of culture, including particularly the history of the Reformation. His literary works on anti-Trinitarianism are especially highly regarded. Kot dealt with the history of sixteenth- and seventeenth-century political thought. He was a co-founder and editor of *Biblioteka Polska* (Polish library; 1919–39), a series that published masterpieces of literature. From 1921 to 1939 he edited the quarterly *Reformacja w Polsce* (Reformation in Poland). His publications include the following: *Andrzej Frycz Modrzewski* (1919); *Rzeczpospolita Polska w literaturze politycznej Zachodu* (The Republic of Poland in Western political literature; 1919); *Ideologia polityczna i społeczna Braci Polskich zwanych arianami* (Political and social ideology of the Polish Brethren, also called the Arians; 1932); *Historia wychowania* (History of education, 2nd rev. ed., 2 vols.; 1934); *Listy z Rosji do generała Sikorskiego* (Letters from Russia to General Sikorski; 1955); and *Rozmowy z Kremlem* (Talks with the Kremlin; 1959). (JS)

Sources: *Słownik biograficzny działaczy ruchu ludowego* (Warsaw, 1989); *Encyklopedia historii Drugiej Rzeczypospolitej* (Warsaw, 1999); *Sprawa polska w czasie drugiej wojny światowej na arenie międzynarodowej: Zbiór dokumentów* (Warsaw, 1965); Roman Buczek, *Stronnictwo Ludowe w latach 1939–1945* (London, 1975); Jan Karski, *The Great Powers and Poland (1919–1945)* (Lanham, Md., 1985); Tadeusz Rutkowski, *Stanisław Kot 1885–1975: Biografia polityczna* (Warsaw, 2000).

KOTAŃSKI Marek (11 March 1942, Warsaw–18 August 2002, Nowy Dwór Mazowiecki), Polish social worker. After graduating in psychology from Warsaw University (1965), Kotański worked at the Sanatorium for People with Nervous Disorders in Warsaw. In 1968 he began working with the Social Anti-Alcoholic Committee. In 1978 he founded the Drug Addicts Resocialization Center in Głosków, and in 1981, he founded MONAR, the Youth Movement for Drug Abuse Prevention. He was also the founder of the association Solidarity against AIDS-PLUS. In 1986–89 Kotański was a member of a consultative council to the president of the Council of State. In January 1994 he founded Markot, an organization whose objective was to combat homelessness. He created shelters where young drug addicts could find support. While working with these young people, he tried to involve them in helping others. He also founded dozens of drug treatment centers, as well as shelters for the homeless. Initially Kotański believed in a liberal value system; for example, he stated that condoms were the most effective means of preventing HIV transmission. Before the visit of John Paul II to Poland in June 1999, Kotański called on young people to practice abstinence, and from then on he openly spoke about the religious motivation behind his work, promoting the Clean Hearts Movement. A charismatic leader and a strong personality immensely popular among the people with whom he worked, Kotański died in a car crash. He was the author of *Ty zaraziłeś ich narkomanią* (You turned them into drug addicts; 1982) and *Sprzedałem się ludziom* (I sold myself to the people; 1992). (WR)

Sources: *Kto jest kim w Polsce* (Warsaw, 1993); "Był miłosierny," *Gość Niedzielny*, 1 September 2002.

KOTSIUBYNSKYI Mykhailo (originally Zakhar Kozub) (17 September 1864, Vinnytsya, Ukraine–25 April 1913, Kiev), Ukrainian writer and social activist. Kotsiubynskyi spent his childhood in Podolia. After graduating from Shargorod Seminary in 1880, he studied in a theological seminary in Kamyanets-Podilsky. In 1882 he was expelled from school for his involvement in the Narodnik movement, and until the end of his life he was kept under surveillance. After his father's death, Kotsiubynskyi had to support his family, working as a private teacher in and around Vinnytsya. A member of the Vinnytsya town council (1888–90), in 1891 he became qualified as an elementary school teacher and started working in the village of Lopatyntsy, near the town of Jampol, Podolia. In 1892–97 he worked on a commission appointed to exterminate a grapevine parasite. At the same time he was a member of the secret Taras Fraternity. He was the editor of the newspaper *Volyn'* in Zhytomyr. In 1898 Kotsiubynskyi began working as a clerk in the Chernigov zemstvo (local self-government), where he also served as president of the local section of an education society called Prosvita from 1906 to 1908. In 1905 he traveled to Germany, Italy, Switzerland, and Austria, where in Lemberg (Lwów, Lviv) he became acquainted with such prominent people as **Ivan Franko**. He spent the years 1909–11 in Capri, where he went for reasons of health and where he got in touch with Maksim Gorky.

Kotsiubynskyi's writing was influenced by the works of Taras Shevchenko, Fyodor Dostoevsky, and contemporary Western writers. Under the influence of Ludwig Feuerbach, he became an atheist. His first novels were realistic in character but included innovative elements, particularly in the way that landscape was presented. At the turn of the twentieth century Kotsiubynskyi deepened the psychological complexity of his characters. In the novels and collections of stories *V putakh shaitana i inshi opovidannia* (In the fetters of satan; 1899), *Opovidannia z besarabskoho zhyttia* (Stories from Bessarabian life; 1900), and *Pid mineratamy*

(Under the minarets; 1904), the protagonists are exotic characters: Moldovians, gypsies, and Turks. The works of that period, which show the influence of impressionism, made Kotsiubynskyi the leading Ukrainian writer of the modernist period. In the 1905 manifesto *Z potoku zhyttia* (From the stream of life), Kotsiubynskyi called for abandoning ethnographic topics in favor of social issues and for developing a style that would be understood by the contemporary reader. He realized the ideal of a committed artist in *Smikh* (Laughter; 1906) and *Vin ide* (He is coming; 1906), his stories from the period of the revolution of 1905–7; these depicted, among other things, processions and pogroms organized by members of the Russian nationalist organization Black Hundreds (Chernaia Sotnia), as well as other tsarist persecutions. In the novel *Fata Morgana* (2 vols.; 1904–10) Kotsiubynskyi presented a wide panorama of the fate of contemporary Ukrainian peasants. *Intermezzo* (1909) is an analysis of the dilemmas of an artist. Kotsiubynskyi's last outstanding novel, *Tini zabutykh predkiv* (Shadows of forgotten ancestors; 1912), contains a lyrical picture of the life of the Hutsuls, Ukrainian highlanders. Complete editions of Kotsiubynskyi's works were published in the Soviet Union in 1929–30 (5 vols.), 1961–62 (6 vols.), and 1973–75 (8 vols.). Many of his literary works were translated into foreign languages, and a number of his writings were adapted as films—for example, *Tini zabutykh predkiv* (1967). Kotsiubynskyi is considered the first Ukrainian prose writer of European stature. (TS)

Sources: *Encyclopedia of Ukraine*, vol. 2 (Toronto, 1988); Zoia Kotsiubynska-Iefimienko, *Mykhailo Kotsiubynskyi: Zhyttia i tvorchist* (Kiev, 1955); Myroslav Moroz, *Mykhailo Kotsiubynskyi: Bibliohrafichnyi pokazhchyk* (Kiev, 1964); Mykhailo Kostenko, *Khudozhnia maisternist Mykhaila Kotsiubynskoho* (Kiev, 1969); Elżbieta Wiśniewska, *O sztuce pisarskiej Michajła Kociubyńskiego* (Wrocław, 1973); Oleksandra Chernenko, *Mykhailo Kotsiubynski—impresiionist: Obraz ludyny v tvorchosti pysmennyka* (Munich, 1977).

KOTSIUBYNSKYI Yuri (7 December 1896, Vinnytsya–8 March 1937, Kiev), Ukrainian Communist activist. The son of the outstanding writer **Mykhailo Kotsiubynskyi**, Kotsiubynskyi attended a gymnasium in Chernihov. In 1913 he joined the Russian Social Democratic Workers' Party. Mobilized by the Russian Army in 1916, he studied at an officer training school in Odessa and did his military service in Petrograd. In October 1917 in Petrograd he took part in the Bolshevik coup. In December 1917 he was appointed deputy to the people's secretary for military affairs, later becoming the acting people's secretary for military affairs. In January 1918 he became commander-in-chief of the Ukrainian Bolshevik army. In March 1918 he became a member of the Central Executive Committee (Tsentralnyi Vykonavchyi Komitet) and the people's secretary of interior of the Ukrainian Soviet People's Republic. At the end of November 1918 he joined the Provisional Workers' and Peasants' Government of the Ukraine. Between 1919 and 1920 he headed the Bolshevik state and party organs in Chernihov and Poltava.

In 1920 Kotsiubynskyi began working in the Soviet diplomatic service, first in Austria (1920–22 and 1925–27), then in Poland (1927–30). In February 1930 he became deputy president, and in February 1934 president, of the Planning Office and deputy prime minister of the Council of People's Commissars of the Ukrainian SSR. He was a member of the Central Committee (CC) of the Communist Party (Bolshevik) of Ukraine (Komunistychna Partiia [Bilshovykiv] Ukraiiny [CP(B)U]) and a member of the Ukrainian Central Executive Committee (Vseukrainskyi Tsentralnyi Vykonavchyi Komitet). In November 1934 Kotsiubynskyi was dismissed from work, expelled from the CP(B)U CC, and later expelled from the party. Arrested along with twenty-two prominent Communists in February 1935, he was accused of anti-Soviet activities and sentenced to six years in exile. In October 1936, while still in exile, he was arrested again and deported to Kiev, where he was accused of organizing and directing, on the orders of **Georgii Piatakov**, a counterrevolutionary Trotskyite organization in the Ukraine (Ukraiinskyi Trotskistskyi Tsentr). On 8 March 1937 he was sentenced by the USSR Supreme Court to execution by firing squad, and he was executed the same day. Kotsiubynskyi was rehabilitated in December 1955. (BB)

Sources: *Encyclopedia of Ukraine*, vol. 2 (Toronto, 1988); *Entsyklopediya ukraiinoznavstva*, vol. 3 (Lviv, 1994); *Dovidnyk z istorii Ukraiiny* (Kiev, 2001); Hryhory Kostiuk, *Stalinist Rule in the Ukraine* (New York, 1960); Iurii Shapoval, Volodymyr Prystaiko, and Vadym Zolotariov, *ChK—GPU—NKVD v Ukraiini: Osoby, fakty, dokumenty* (Kiev, 1997).

KOTSYLOVSKYI Iosyf (3 March 1876, Pakoshivka, Lemkiv district–17 November 1947, Chapayevka, near Kiev), Greek Catholic bishop of Przemyśl. The son of an MP in the Galician Assembly, in 1895 Kotsylovskyi joined the Austro-Hungarian Army and then finished an officer training school. In 1901–7 he studied in Rome, earning two doctorates, one in philosophy (1903) and one in theology (1907). Ordained in 1907, he lectured at a theological seminary in Stanisławów (Ivano-Frankivsk), serving as its deputy rector. In 1911 he entered the Basilian order, taking the name of Yosafat. Appointed bishop of Przemyśl and Samborsk on 23 September 1917, Kotsylovskyi supported the Ukrainian (Galician) National Republic, which was proclaimed on 1 November 1918. After the fall of this republic, he worked in the territory of Poland, where he founded many social and religious organizations, as well as the periodical *Ukrains'kyĭ Beskid*. In 1921 he established a theological seminary in Przemyśl. He was initially opposed to the Polish state but gradually started making attempts to ease tensions and conflicts between the Ukrainians and the Poles. He also cooperated with the Roman Catholic Episcopate.

At the end of World War II the new Polish-Soviet border separated two-thirds of the faithful of the diocese from the diocesan capital; therefore, in the autumn of 1944 Kotsylovskyi appointed two vicars general: Father Mykhailo Melnyk in Drohobych and Father Mykola Panas in Sokal. Arrested by the State Security Office on 20 September 1945, Kotsylovskyi was held in a prison in Rzeszów, and on 18 January 1946 he was handed over to the Soviet NKGB (Narodnyi kommissariat gosudarstvennoi bezopasnosti). As the Soviet authorities wanted to avoid a confrontation with the Uniate Church before the elections to the USSR Supreme Soviet, Kotsylovskyi was temporarily released and returned to Przemyśl. He did not accept the decision of the "Ecumenical Council" of Lviv in March 1946 by which the Greek Catholic Church was incorporated into the Orthodox Church. On 22–24 June 1946, as the only Greek Catholic bishop not to have been imprisoned, Kotsylovskyi attended a conference of the Polish Episcopate in Częstochowa; there the Polish bishops sent a memorandum informing the Provisional Government of National Unity that they accepted the Greek Catholic bishop as a member of the Episcopate. Under pressure from the NKGB, the Polish Communist authorities decided to forcibly deport Kotsylovskyi to the Soviet Union. Although informed about these plans, he refused to escape to the West, and on 26 June 1946 he was arrested by the Polish security organs, handed over to the Soviet authorities, and imprisoned in Lviv. He was later deported to Kiev. As a Polish citizen, he refused to participate in the rigged trial. He was deported to a labor camp near Kiev, where he died. On 27 June 2001 Pope John Paul II beatified Kotsylovskyi at a solemn Holy Mass in Lviv. (WR)

Sources: *Pamiati peremyskoho vladyki kyr Iosafata Kotsylovskoho* (N.p., 1956); "Iak pomer Kyr Iosafat," *Ukraiinski Vistii* (Edmonton), 18 March 1957; *Na Khrystovyi nivi, Spomyny* (New York, 1978); *Encyclopedia of Ukraine*, vol. 2 (Toronto, 1988); Bohdan R. Bociurkiw, *The Ukrainian Greek-Catholic Church and the Soviet State (1939–1950)* (Edmonton, 1996); *Osservatore Romano* (weekly edition in English), 2001, nos. 25 and 27; Dariusz Iwaneczko, "Historia dwóch aresztowań przemyskiego biskupa greckokatolickiego Jozafata Kocyłowskiego," *Biuletyn Instytutu Pamięci Narodowej*, 2001, no. 7.

KOTTA Kostaq Koço (1889, Korçë [Korça]–1949, Burrell), Albanian politician. Born into an Orthodox family, Kotta studied medicine in Athens and then at one of the Italian universities. In 1913 he began working as a clerk in Korçë and later as secretary in the Ministry of Education.

In 1919 he was a school inspector in the district of Berat. In 1921–23 he served as prefect of Berat. As a member of parliament, he was politically aligned with the group of "localists," who aimed at reducing the powers of the central government. Before 1924 Kotta served as minister of public works on two occasions. In 1924 he became a member of parliament. During the revolution of June 1924 he fled to Greece, from where he returned in December of the same year. Kotta was one of the organizers of a military operation to overthrow the revolutionary government of **Fan Noli**. In the first cabinet after the victory of **Ahmed Zogu**, Kotta assumed the ministry of the national economy and public works. On 3 October 1925, as a deputy from Korçë, he was elected speaker of the Chamber of Deputies. From 10 September 1928 to 5 February 1930 he headed the first cabinet appointed after the establishment of the monarchy. At that time he introduced modern civil and penal codes based on European legal principles. On 9 September 1936 Kotta became prime minister for the second time. After the Italian invasion, he resigned on 8 April 1939. During the war he was linked with the Legaliteti (Legality) Movement. In 1944 Kotta fled to Greece. Captured with the help of Greek Communists in Salonika and handed over to Albania, he was sentenced to life imprisonment in a public trial on 1 March 1945. He was incarcerated in a new prison in Burrell, which had been built in the 1930s when he was serving as prime minister. Kotta died as a result of torture. (TC)

Sources: Michael Schmidt-Neke, *Enstehung und Ausbau der Konigsdiktatur in Albanien (1912–1939): Regierungsbildungen, Herrschaftsweisen und Machteliten in Einen Jungen Balkanstaat* (Munich, 1987); Sejfi Vllamasi, *Ballafaqime politike në Shqipëri (1897–1942)* (Tirana, 1995).

KOVÁČ Michal (5 September 1930, Ľubiša, Humenné district), Slovak economist and politician. After high school in Humenné, in 1954 Kováč graduated from the Higher School of Economics in Bratislava. In 1955–71 he worked in the local apparatus of the Czechoslovak central bank in Bratislava, belonging to the Communist Party of Czechoslovakia (CPC). In 1964–65 he lectured at the school of the central bank of Cuba, and in 1967–69 he was deputy director of the London office of Źivnobanka. During the so-called normalization after the Warsaw Pact invasion of Czechoslovakia, in 1970 Kováč was expelled from the CPC and demoted. From 1971 to 1978 he worked in the Bratislava city office of the central bank, and then until 1989 he was a researcher at the Central Economic Planning Institute in Bratislava. During the Velvet Revolution he joined Public against Violence (Verejnost' proti Nasiliu [VPN]). From December 1989 to May 1991 he was minister of finance in the Slovak government, and in June 1990 he won a seat in the Chamber of the People of the Federal Assembly on behalf of the VPN. In March 1991, along with **Vladimir Mečiar** and other advocates of a "social market economy," Kováč established the faction For a Democratic Slovakia, which soon left the VPN, and Kováč and his friends from the SAID faction founded a party called the Movement for a Democratic Slovakia (Hnutie za Demokratické Slovensko [HZDS]). In 1991–93 Kováč was its deputy chairman. In June 1992 he took part in negotiations between the victorious parties—the Slovak HZDS and the Czech Civic Democratic Party—on the future of Czechoslovakia. From June to December 1992 Kováč was the last speaker of the Federal Assembly.

After the breakup of Czechoslovakia, on 15 February 1993 Kováč was elected the first democratic president of Slovakia, and on 2 March 1993 he was sworn in. He left the HZDS and entered into an ever-growing conflict with his former ally, Mečiar. On Kováč's initiative, on 11 March 1994 the parliament passed a vote of no confidence on the Mečiar government. The conflict intensified after the early parliamentary elections of the fall of 1994, when the HZDS created a coalition with the Slovak National Party (Slovenská Národná Strana), the Association of Slovak Workers (Združenie Robotníkov Slovenska) and another government headed by Mečiar. In view of the latter's authoritarian style and his tendency to marginalize the opposition, Kováč remained the last mainstay of democracy. In his policies he could count on the support of the opposition and of the Catholic Church, but the ruling coalition attempted to make him resign. In 1995 Mečiar's special services kidnapped Kováč's son and drove him to Austria. All attempts to bring those responsible to court were fruitless. The Mečiar government tried to limit the authority of the president and to compromise him in the eyes of the Slovaks. Kováč managed to survive until the end of his term on 2 March 1998. Then Mečiar took over the presidential duties and amnestied all those involved in the kidnapping of Kováč's son. After the electoral victory of the anti-Mečiar coalition in September 1998 and the introduction of direct presidential elections, Kováč planned to run, but four days before the voting in May 1999, he withdrew, asking his supporters to vote for the candidate of the ruling coalition, **Rudolf Schuster**. (PU)

Sources: *ČBS*; *Kdo byl kdo v našich dějinách ve 20. stoleti*, vol. 1 (Prague, 1998); Jan Rychlík, *Rozpad Československa: Česko-slovenské vztahy 1989–1992* (Bratislava, 2002); Eric Stein, *Czecho/Slovakia: Ethnic Conflict, Constitutional Fissure, Negotiated Breakup* (Ann Arbor, 1997); www.referaty.sk/index.php?referat=4434; www.president.sk/.

KOVÁCS Béla (20 April 1908, Mecsekalja–21 June 1959, Pécs), Hungarian Peasant Party politician. For many years Kovács farmed in his home village. After meeting **Ferenc Nagy** in 1932, he became active in the revived Independent Smallholders' Party (Fügetlen Kisgazdapárt [ISP]). In 1941 he became the secretary of a bipartisan peasant alliance that was in opposition to the Horthy regime and demanded radical agrarian reform. At the end of 1944 Kovács became undersecretary of state in the Ministry of Interior of the Provisional Government, first in Debrecen, then in Budapest. In 1945 he became deputy secretary general of the ISP, and on 19 August 1945, secretary general of the ISP. After the ISP victory in the elections of 4 November 1945, Kovács was the party's candidate for the post of minister of interior, but he was thwarted by Marshal Kliment Voroshilov, the head of the Allied Control Commission for Hungary. Kovács assumed the portfolio of minister of agriculture. In the autumn of 1946 he proposed the establishment of the Peasant Federation, composed of the ISP and the National Peasant Party (NPP). Until then, the NPP had been in a leftist bloc together with the Communists. Kovács's proposal, as well as his great popularity among the peasants, was a thorn in the Communists' side. The Communists attempted to tie him to an alleged conspiracy against the state. In January 1947 Kovács was accused of being involved in the espionage activities of alleged conspirators against the Red Army. He resigned as secretary general of the ISP, and on 26 February 1947 he was imprisoned by the Soviet authorities. Kovács's testimony, extracted by the use of torture, was used as the basis for the fabrication of charges against the current prime minister, Ferenc Nagy, who was accused of involvement in a "plot" and forced to resign in May 1947. Kovács was deported to the USSR, where he spent many years in prisons and camps.

Released under an amnesty in April 1956, Kovács was allowed to return to Hungary. On 27 October 1956 **Imre Nagy** invited him to take part in a coalition government as the representative of the ISP, which was revived after Stalinism. Kovács began to work on the reconstruction of the party and supported the neutralization of Hungary. After the suppression of the insurrection in Budapest, he fell seriously ill and avoided arrest. He withdrew from political life and was not persecuted. In January 1957 **János Kádár** tried to persuade Kovács to join the new state authorities, but he refused. Only in the autumn of 1958, after the execution of Nagy, did he agree to stand for parliamentary "elections," lending support for the policy of Kadarism. Kovács won a seat in parliament, but as a result of his prison ordeals his health declined rapidly, and he died prematurely. (WR)

Sources: Steven Bela Vardy, *Historical Dictionary of Hungary* (Lanham, Md., 1997); *Nagy Képés Milleniumi Arcképcsarnok* (Budapest, 1999); *Magyar Nagylexikon*, vol. 10 (Budapest, 2000); *Magyarország 1944–1956*, CD-ROM, Budapest 2001; Ferenc Nagy, *The Struggle Behind the Iron Curtain* (New York, 1948); *Newsweek*, 6 July 1959; *New York Times*, 23 June 1959.

KOVÁCS Imre (19 March 1913, Felsögöböjárás–28 October 1980, New York), Hungarian Peasant Party politician. Born into a peasant family on the estates of Archduke Joseph Habsburg, after completing high school Kovács enrolled at the economics university in Budapest. During his studies he joined a radical literary group called Country Discoverers. In his book, *A néma forradalom* (Mute revolution; 1937), he depicted the misery of the Hungarian countryside and its social stratification. The Horthy government banned the publication of the book. Kovács was expelled from his studies and sentenced to three months of prison. After his release, he joined the liberal Peasant March Front, which was in opposition to the government and insisted on the implementation of an agrarian reform and the liberalization of the political system. In June 1939 Kovács was one of the co-founders of the small National Peasant Party (Nemzeti Parasztpárt) and became its secretary general. At first he held the post officially, and from 1944 in secret. Imprisoned by the Germans in the autumn of 1944 and released at the beginning of 1945, Kovács could not control his party, which was penetrated by the Communists.

In November 1945 Kovács was elected to the parliament, but the following year he resigned the leadership of the party, which was now dominated by the Communists. After the arrest at the beginning of 1947 of **Béla Kovács**, secretary general of the Independent Smallholders' Party, and the defeat of the main forces of the peasant opposition, Kovács left for Switzerland. He later went to France and England and finally settled in the United States, where he was active in Hungarian organizations in exile. He belonged to the Hungarian National Council and, from 1958, to the Hungarian Committee and the Free Europe Committee. As the president of the Hungarian Calvinist Reformed Church in New York, in 1956 Kovács led protests against the Soviet invasion of Hungary. In 1958 he founded *Új Látóhatár*, an exile literary monthly. He was also the editor of the volume *Facts about Hungary* (1959) and of the memoirs *From One Occupation to Another* (1949), published in German, Hungarian, French, and English. Kovács also authored novels and essays on political and agricultural topics. (WR)

Sources: *The Annual Obituary*, 1980; István Hartyányi, *Kovács Imre bibliográfia* (Budapest, 1993).

KŐVÁGÓ József [originally Küronya] (8 April 1913, Csömödér–10 December 1996, Linwood, New York), Hungarian Peasant Party politician. After graduating from the Military Technical Academy in Budapest, Kővágó received a diploma in engineering from the Budapest Polytechnic. In 1939 he began working at the Military Technical Institute and served in the army for a short time. When the Arrow Cross Party took over power on 15 October 1944, Kővágó joined the military resistance movement. He was a member of the group led by Jenő Nagy, a colonel in the General Staff. As aide-de-camp to General **János Kiss**, he took part in the work of the Hungarian National Insurrection and Liberation Committee. On 22 November 1944 Kővágó was arrested. Although the case was referred to a military court, he was released and sent to the front lines, from which he escaped in March 1945. In November 1944 Kővágó had joined the Independent Smallholders' Party (ISP). In May 1945, on the party's request, he became deputy mayor of Budapest, and in the fall of that year, after local and parliamentary elections, he became mayor of Budapest and an MP. He played a major role in the reconstruction of Budapest and the normalization of life in the capital. In 1947 he was forced to resign his post under Communist pressure, and he consequently withdrew from public life.

Arrested on false charges in 1950, Kővágó was sentenced to life imprisonment. He was released in September 1956. During the revolution he helped to revive the ISP. On 3 November 1956 he was elected secretary general of the party. On 1 November 1956 he again became mayor of Budapest. After the suppression of the revolution, on 30 November he fled abroad and settled in the United States. In January 1957, at an open session of the United Nations, he defended the cause of the Hungarian Revolution. At the founding general meeting of the Hungarian Revolutionary Council in Strasbourg, Kővágó was elected vice-president and held the post until 1960. While in exile, he helped preserve the memory of the revolution and played an active role in protests initiated by Western countries against the Soviet occupation of Hungary. From 1961 to 1978, he conducted research as an engineer. From 1973 to 1983 he worked as a university professor. In 1991 he received the Middle Cross of the Order of the Hungarian Republic, and in 1992 he became an honorary citizen of Budapest. In January 1997 Kővágó was buried in Budapest. His writings include *You Are All Alone* (1959). (JT)

Sources: *A magyar forradalom és szabadságharc enciklopédiája* (Budapest, 1999); *Magyar Nagylexikon*, vol. 11 (Budapest, 2000); Ferenc Nagy, *The Struggle behind the Iron Curtain* (New York, 1948).

KOVALYK Zinoviy (18 August 1903, Ivachev, near Ternopil–22 June 1941, Lviv), Ukrainian Greek Catholic priest, martyr for the faith. After finishing secondary school, Kovalyk entered the Redemptorist order, and on 28 July 1926 he took his vows. He later completed philosophical and theological studies in Belgium. Ordained a priest in September 1932, he worked in a parish in Volhynia. After the Red Army seized the Polish eastern territories in September 1939, Kovalyk continued his pastoral work despite persecution by the new authorities. Arrested by the NKVD while preaching a sermon in church on 20 December 1940, he was held and interrogated in the Brygidki Prison in Lviv. When the Soviet troops and authorities were withdrawing from Lviv after the Third Reich attacked the Soviet Union, Kovalyk was cruelly murdered: he was crucified on a prison wall. On 27 June 2001 at a Solemn Mass in Lviv, Pope John Paul II beatified him as a martyr for the faith. (WR)

Sources: *Osservatore Romano* (weekly edition in English), 2001, nos. 25 and 27.

KOVPAK Sydor (25 May 1887, Kotelva, near Poltava–11 December 1967, Kiev), Soviet general of Ukrainian descent. Kovpak took part in World War I. In 1919 he joined the Bolshevik party. In his native village he was in command of a guerrilla unit fighting against the Germans, and he also commanded the troops of General Anton Denikin. In 1920 he fought against the army of General Pyotr Wrangel in the twenty-fifth "Chapayev" division. After the Bolshevik victory Kovpak worked on military committees in various towns of the USSR, among others Kryvyi Rih. From 1937 to 1941 he was president of the town military commission in Putivl, Sumy district. Between 1941 and 1944 he was in command of a partisan group, first of a brigade, and later of a division. From 1941 he led partisan attacks in the districts of Sumy, Kursk, Orlov, and Bryansk. From 1942 to 1943 he led a raid from the Bryansk forests through the districts of Homel, Pinsk, Volhynia, Rovno, Zhytomyr, and Kiev, as well as the famous raid from the Dnieper River to the Carpathians. In 1944 the partisan group that he commanded was renamed the First S. Kovpak Ukrainian Partisan Division. In 1947 Kovpak became deputy chairman of the Presidium of the Supreme Council of the USSR. In April 1967 he joined the Presidium of the Supreme Council of the USSR. At the Sixteenth—Nineteenth and Twenty-first–Twenty-third Congresses of the Communist Party (Bolshevik) of Ukraine, Kovpak was elected to the Central Committee. He was a deputy to the Second—Seventh Supreme Soviets of the USSR. Kovpak wrote the memoirs *Od Putivla v*

Karpaty (From Putivl to the Carpathians). He was twice decorated with the star of the Hero of the USSR (1942 and 1944). Four times decorated with the Order of Lenin, Kovpak also held the Order of the Red Banner. (GM)

Sources: Andrii Chaikovsky, *Nevidoma viina* (Kiev, 1994); *Ukraiinska radianska entsyklopediya*, vol. 5 (Kiev, 1980); Werszyhora Petro, *Karpacki rajd* (Warsaw, 1951).

KOWALCZYK Stanisław (12 December 1924, Pabianice–30 January 1998, Warsaw), Polish Communist activist. Born into a working-class family, Kowalczyk graduated from the Academy of Mining and Metallurgy in Kraków. In 1947 he joined the Polish Socialist Party (Polska Partia Socjalistyczna [PPS]) and in December 1948 the Polish United Workers' Party (Polska Zjednoczona Partia Robotnicza [PUWP]). After the war he served in the army and subsequently worked in the chemical industry, gradually rising through the party ranks. From 1960 to 1968 Kowalczyk served as secretary of the PUWP Executive Committee in Katowice. In 1964 he became a deputy member and in 1968 a member of the PUWP Central Committee (CC). In 1968 he began working in the CC apparatus, serving as head of the Department of Industry and Transport.

A close associate of **Edward Gierek**, Kowalczyk became CC secretary in December 1971 and minister of interior in March 1973. In June 1973 he became a deputy member and in December 1975 a member of the PUWP CC Politburo. As a minister, he came into conflict with **Franciszek Szlachcic**, the CC member responsible for the Ministry of Interior. When Szlachcic left the party leadership in June 1974, Kowalczyk consolidated his position as a functionary who was in charge of the ministry of interior on Gierek's behalf. In 1974 Kowalczyk became brigadier general and in 1977 major general of the police. During his term in office the Ministry of Interior apparatus was in touch with the criminal world abroad and smuggled valuables into Poland that had been gained illegally (Operation Iron). It remains unclear to what extent Kowalczyk was aware of these activities. He was responsible for the persecution of workers who protested price increases in June 1976 and for attempts to suppress the emerging democratic opposition, also by illegal means. The Fourth Department of the Ministry of Interior intensified actions against the Catholic Church and against priests. In the summer of 1980 Kowalczyk became a member of a government task force to prepare the suppression of strikes by force. The plan prepared in the Ministry of Interior, code named "Summer 80," included the pacification of strikes in the Gdańsk Shipyard and the abduction of **Lech Wałęsa**. In October 1980 Kowalczyk left the Ministry of Interior.

On 1–2 December 1980 at the Seventh CC Plenum he was expelled from the Politburo as part of a broader action aimed at eliminating Gierek's associates. Kowalczyk become deputy prime minister but resigned in February 1981, and at the Ninth PUWP Congress he did not even became a member of the CC. An MP in the Assembly of the Polish People's Republic from 1969 on, Kowalczyk resigned his seat in January 1982. After 1989 he was never held responsible for his activities. (PK)

Sources: Mołdawa; Włodzimierz Janowski and Witalij Pawłow, *General Pawłow: Byłem rezydentem KGB w Polsce* (Warsaw, 1994); Andrzej Albert [Wojciech Roszkowski], *Najnowsza historia Polski 1914–1993*, vol. 2 (Warsaw, 1995); Henryk Dominiczak, *Organy bezpieczeństwa PRL 1944–1990* (Warsaw, 1997); Aleksander Kochański, *Informator o strukturze i obsadzie personalnej centralnego aparatu PZPR 1948–1990* (Warsaw, 2000).

KOWALSKA Faustyna [originally Helena] (25 August 1905, Głogowiec–5 October, 1938), saint of the Catholic Church. One of ten children in a peasant family, Kowalska completed only three grades of primary school. At eighteen she decided to enter a convent, but her parents could not afford to provide her with a dowry. Following her calling to a religious life, she went to Warsaw, where, after much effort, she was finally accepted into the Congregation of the Sisters of Our Lady of Mercy in 1925. Members of this congregation took care of wayward or neglected girls. Kowalska was a sister of the "second choir"—that is, one of the uneducated sisters assigned to humble manual chores. Despite her poor health, Kowalska worked beyond her strength and often suffered humiliation from other nuns. Kowalska began to have visions, and as time went on, her visions became more frequent; in them, Christ ordered her to spread devotion to the Divine Mercy, but no one believed her. In 1933 her confessor, Father Michał Sopoćko, became interested in her visions and encouraged her to write down her experiences. She wrote the five-hundred-page *Dzienniczek* (published in English as *Divine Mercy in My Soul: The Diary of St. Faustina*). Psychiatric examinations did not show any deviations from normality, and the contents of Kowalska's diary went beyond the theological knowledge of an uneducated nun. Based on one of her visions, a picture was painted showing Christ with two rays shining forth from his breast and the words "Jesus, I Trust In You," which Christ supposedly told her to use in prayers. After a stay in convents in Płock and Wilno (Vilnius), Kowalska died of tuberculosis in a convent near Kraków. Thanks to the efforts of Father Sopoćko, the message of Divine Mercy continued to spread in Polish parishes, despite the doubts of the Church hierarchy. In November 1958, on the basis of an inaccurate translation of Kowalska's *Dzienniczek*, the Congregation of the Holy Office stated that the cult of Divine Mercy had no supernatural sources. In 1965 a new investigation into her life and diary was launched by Karol Wojtyła, Archbishop of Kraków. After his election as pope, **John Paul II** beatified Kowalska on 18 April 1993 and canonized her on 30 April 2000. In August 2002, during his visit to Poland, John Paul II consecrated the huge Sanctuary of the Divine Mercy in Łagiewniki, near Kraków. In 1994 the film *Faustyna*, directed by Jerzy Łukasiewicz, enjoyed great popularity. (WR)

Sources: Ks. Stanisław Urbański, *Mistyczny świat ducha: Kanonizacja s. Faustyny Kowalskiej* (Warsaw, 2000); Jan Grzegorczyk, *Każda dusza to inny świat* (Poznań, 2000); Jan Turnau, "Faustyna, święta drugiego choru," *Wysokie Obcasy*, 17 August 2002; http://www.vatican.va/news_services/liturgy/saints.

KOWALSKI Władysław (26 August 1894, Paprotnia, near Rawa Mazowiecka–14 December 1958, Warsaw), Polish Peasant Party and Communist activist. Born into the family of a horse groom, early on Kowalski became allied with the radical peasant movement. After the outbreak of World War I he was in the Puławy Legion, and from 1914 to 1917 he served in the Russian Army. In 1919 he joined the Polish Peasant Party–Liberation (Polskie Stronnictwo Ludowe–Wyzwolenie [PSL–Liberation]). At the same time he was also a member of the Communist Party of Poland (Komunistyczna Partia Polski [KPP]). In 1925 he went over to the crypto-Communist Independent Peasant Party (Niezależna Partia Chłopska [NPCh]), and in 1926 he became a member of its Central Committee (CC). When the NPCh was declared illegal in 1927, Kowalski helped to found the Union of the Peasant Left–Mutual Aid, which was a legally operating agency of the KPP in the countryside, and in 1928 he became the editor-in-chief of *Samopomoc Chłopska*, a press organ of the party. He joined the Central Agricultural Department of the KPP CC. Arrested in 1932, Kowalski was sentenced to three months in jail. From 1937 he was active in the Democratic Club in Warsaw, becoming a member of its Main Board.

During World War II Kowalski lived in Warsaw and was active in the underground. He was arrested and caught in street roundups several times. In 1941 he was a member of a Communist group called Proletariusz, and he edited a periodical under the same title. In 1942 he joined the Polish Workers' Party (Polska Partia Robotnicza [PPR]). In 1942–43 he edited *Trybuna Chłopska*. In late 1943 and early 1944 he helped to establish the National Home Council (Krajowa Rada Narodowa [KRN]) and became its vice-president. On the orders of the PPR, Kowalski helped

to found the Peasant Party–People's Will (Stronnictwo Ludowe–Wola Ludu) and became its vice-president in February 1944. One of the founders of the pro-Communist Peasant Party (Stronnictwo Ludowe [SL]) in the autumn of 1944, Kowalski served as vice-president of the SL from March to September 1945 and as a member of the SL Chief Council and the Chief Executive Committee from January 1946 on. He edited *Zielony Sztandar*. From June 1945 to February 1947 Kowalski was minister of culture in the Provisional Government of National Unity. In February 1947 he became leader of the SL parliamentary representation and speaker of the Legislative Assembly. He tolerated abuses of power against MPs by granting permission for the temporary arrest of many them, often after the fact. He canvassed for support of peasant movement activists for the PPR. After the remains of the debilitated Polish Peasant Party (Polskie Stronnictwo Ludowe [PSL]) were incorporated into the SL in November 1949, Kowalski was elected president of the Chief Executive Committee of the United Peasant Party (Zjednoczone Stronnictwo Ludowe [ZSL]). From 1952 to 1956 he was a member of the State Council. He strictly subordinated the ZSL to the Polish United Workers' Party (Polska Zjednoczona Partia Robotnicza) and supported the collectivization of agriculture. Kowalski committed suicide at the time of political transformations in Poland after October 1956. He was the author of stories and novels, including *W Grzmiącej* (In Grzmiąca; 1936). (JS)

Sources: *PSB*, vol. 14; Roman Buczek, *Stronnictwo Ludowe w latach 1939–1945* (London, 1975); Tadeusz Błażejewski, *Polityka i pióro: O Władysławie Kowalskim* (Łódź, 1978); Zygmunt Hemmerling, *Władysław Kowalski* (Warsaw, 1977); *Słownik biograficzny działaczy ruchu ludowego* (Warsaw, 1989); Krystyna Kersten, *Narodziny systemu władzy: Polska 1943–1948* (Poznań, 1990); Stanisław Łach, *Polskie Stronnictwo Ludowe w latach 1945–1947* (Gdańsk, 1995).

KOZAL Michał (25 September 1893, Nowy Folwark, near Krotoszyn–26 January 1943, Dachau), Polish Roman Catholic bishop, martyr. The son of a manorial clerk, after graduating from high school in Krotoszyn, Kozal studied in a theological seminary in Poznań and Gniezno (1914–18). Ordained in February 1918, he worked as a curate in rural parishes, a religion teacher in a girls' high school in Bydgoszcz, and a lecturer in theology and liturgics at a seminary in Gniezno. In 1933 he was named papal chamberlain. On 12 June 1939 Kozal was appointed bishop auxiliary of Włocławek. When the Germans occupied Włocławek in September 1939 and Bishop Karol Radoński left the town, Kozal was left in charge of the diocese, but on 7 November he was arrested by the Gestapo. Cesare Orsenigo, the papal nuncio in Berlin, was able to negotiate his release on condition that he be placed in charge of the Lublin diocese, to which Pope Pius XII agreed. Kozal rejected that proposal, as he believed that such a decision, made under duress, would amount to cooperation with the occupier. In April 1941 Kozal was transferred to the Dachau concentration camp. Subsequent requests for his release, made by Orsenigo on behalf of Bishop Radoński and the Holy See, were rejected by the Nazi authorities, who claimed that he had engaged in "anti-German activities." Kozal died in the Dachau concentration camp. Pope John Paul II beatified him during his visit to Poland in June 1987. (WR)

Sources: *PSB*, vol. 14; Jacek Wilczur, "Biskup Michał Kozal—więzień nr 24544," *Narodowiec*, 1966, no. 105; "Ofiary zbrodni niemieckich spośród duchowieństwa diecezji włocławskiej," *Kronika Diecezji Włocławskiej*, 1947; *Ateneum Kapłańskie*, 1946 and 1957.

KOZICKI Stanisław (4 April 1876, Łempice, near Pułtusk–28 September, 1958 Polanica Zdrój), Polish journalist, historian, and politician. Kozicki studied in the Higher Agricultural School in Berlin and in Halle, where he received a Ph.D. in philosophy in 1899. In 1899–1902 he worked as an assistant professor at the Jagiellonian University in Kraków. During his student years he belonged to the Union of Polish Youth–Zet. Upon his return home in 1900 Kozicki joined the National League (NL) and, in 1902, the National Democratic Party (Stronnictwo Narodow-Demokratyczne [NDP]). In 1902 he went to Warsaw, where he headed the NDP's organizational work. He was also active in the Society of National Education and published a lot. In 1905 Kozicki co-organized the National Workers' Union. He organized the NDP campaign before the elections to the Russian Duma. In 1910 he became a member of the NL Central Committee and the NDP Chief Board. He worked closely with **Roman Dmowski**, fully supporting his anti-German line based on cooperation with Russia. In 1910 he was an observer at the Slavic Congress in Sofia.

When in 1915 the German Army was approaching Warsaw, Kozicki, along with some of the most anti-German politicians, left for Russia; there he published in National Democratic periodicals *Sprawa Polska* and *Gazeta Polska*, and he was active in the National Committee of Poland (Komitet Narodowy Polski [KNP]). In 1917, on Dmowski's request, Kozicki moved to London, where he worked in the KNP office, heading its Civil and Press Department and promoting the Polish cause in Great Britain. In 1919–20 he was general secretary of the Polish delegation to the Paris Peace Conference. After returning to Poland, he was active in the National

Democratic Party, renamed the Popular National Union (Związek Ludowo-Narodowy [ZLN]). In 1922 Kozicki was editor-in-chief of *Przegląd Wszechpolski*, and until May 1923 he was editor-in-chief of *Kurier Poznański*. In 1922–26 he was an MP, and from June to December 1923 he headed the ZLN parliamentary club. In February 1926 he became minister plenipotentiary in Italy, but as a result of the May 1926 coup he was recalled from this post. In 1926 Kozicki co-organized the Camp of Great Poland, designed according to the Italian Fascist pattern and meant as a reaction to the system introduced by **Józef Piłsudski**. In 1928 Kozicki was elected to the Senate on behalf of the ZLN. He was a senator until 1935, also belonging the Chief Committee of the National Party (Stronnictwo Narodowe) in 1934–39. During World War II Kozicki retired from politics, and after the war he published in *Tygodnik Warszawski*, *Tygodnik Powszechny*, and *Kierunki*. He authored several works, including *Niemcy i Polska na tle polityki powojennej* (Germany and Poland in postwar politics; 1927); *Na Sycylii* (In Sicily; 1928); and *Historia Ligi Narodowej (1889–1907)* (History of the National League, 1889–1907; 1964). (PU)

Sources: *PSB*, vol. 14; *Kto był kim w Drugiej Rzeczypospolitej* (Warsaw, 1994); *Encyklopedia historii Drugiej Rzeczypospolitej* (Warsaw, 1999); Marian Seyda, *Polska na przełomie dziejów*, vols. 1–2 (Warsaw and Wilno, 1927–31); Władysław Pobóg-Malinowski, *Narodowa Demokracja 1887–1918* (Warsaw, 1933); Marian Leczyk, *Komitet Narodowy Polski a Ententa i Stany Zjednoczone 1917–1919* (Warsaw, 1966); Krzysztof Kawalec, *Roman Dmowski* (Warsaw, 1996).

KOZŁOWSKI Leon (6 June 1892, Rembieszyce, Kielce region–11 May 1944, Berlin), Polish archaeologist and politician. After graduating from high school in 1910, Kozłowski started studies in the natural sciences and archaeology at the Jagiellonian University in Kraków and then continued them in Tübingen, Germany, in 1912–13. He belonged to the Union of Progressive Youth and then to the Union of Active Struggle and the Riflemen's Association, both connected with **Józef Piłsudski**. After the outbreak of World War I Kozłowski interrupted his studies, and in 1914–17 he served in the Polish Legions. In 1917–18 he completed his studies in Tübingen and received a Ph.D. In 1920 he volunteered to fight in the Polish-Soviet war. Later in 1920 he became an associate professor of prehistory at the Jagiellonian University, and in 1921–31 and 1935–39 he was a professor at John Casimir University in Lwów (Lviv). Kozłowski authored many scholarly works, including *Groby megalityczne na wschód od Odry* (Megalith tombs east of the Oder River; 1921); *Starsza epoka kamienna w Polsce* (The Old Stone Age in Poland; 1922); *Młodsza epoka kamienna w Polsce* (The New Stone Age in Poland;

1924); and *Zarys pradziejów Polski południowo-wschodniej* (Outline of prehistory of Southeast Poland; 1939). From 1935 Kozłowski was a corresponding member of the Polish Academy of Arts and Sciences.

Kozłowski started his political career after the May 1926 coup, organizing the Union for the Reform of the Republic (Związek Naprawy Rzeczypospolitej) in Lwów. In 1928–35 he was an MP on behalf of the ruling Nonparty Bloc of Cooperation with the Government. He was a member of its leadership and senator on its behalf in 1935–39. From August 1930 to March 1932 he was minister of agrarian reforms in the governments of **Józef Piłsudski**, **Walery Sławek**, and **Aleksander Prystor**. In 1932–33 he was undersecretary of state in the Ministry of Treasury, and from 15 May 1934 to 28 March 1935 he was prime minister. After the assassination of **Bronisław Pieracki**, in June 1934 Kozłowski was also acting minister of interior. Thought to be an ally of the group of legionnaires and its elite—the "colonels"—after the death of Piłsudski, Kozłowski supported Sławek. In 1937–38 he was a member of the Camp of National Unity (Obóz Zjednoczenia Narodowego [OZN]). After the outbreak of World War II and the Soviet invasion of East Poland, on 26 September 1939 Kozłowski was arrested by the NKVD in Lwów. In July 1941 he was sentenced to death. The sentence was then commuted to ten years. Following the Polish-Soviet agreement, in September 1941 he was released, and in October 1941 he joined the army of General **Władysław Anders**. Soon he disappeared, got through the front lines, and was interned by the Germans. Sentenced to death by a Polish martial court for desertion, Kozłowski died in prison in Berlin. (PU)

Sources: *PSB*, vol. 15; *Encyklopedia historii Drugiej Rzeczypospolitej* (Warsaw, 1999); *Kto był kim w Drugiej Rzeczypospolitej* (Warsaw, 1994); Władysław T. Kulesza, *Koncepcje ideowo-polityczne obozu rządzacego w Polsce w latach 1926–1935* (Wrocław, 1985); Władysław Pobóg-Malinowski, *Najnowsza historia polityczna Polski*, vol. 3 (London, 1986).

KOZOVSKI Ferdinand (27 January 1892, Knezha–12 September 1965, Sofia), Bulgarian Communist activist and general. While a high school student, Kozovski joined the Socialist movement, and in 1911 he became a member of the "narrow" faction of the Bulgarian Workers' Social Democratic Party (Tesnyaki), close to the Bolsheviks. He established a party organization in Knezha. He fought in the Balkan Wars (1912–13) and subsequently finished a school for reserve officers. During World War I Kozovski agitated for peace. After the war he graduated in law from the university in Sofia and practiced as an attorney in Knezha. After the failure of the Communist uprising in 1923, Kozovski emigrated to Yugoslavia. In 1926 he left for the Soviet Union, where he graduated from the Frunze Military Academy. He subsequently served as an officer in the Red Army and taught military subjects at a Moscow university to émigrés from Western countries. During the Civil War in Spain, under the pseudonym "Petrov," Kozovski commanded the Twelfth International Brigade and served in the command of the Fourth Corps of the Republican Army; he was wounded. After the outbreak of World War II, Kozovski worked as an editor in the Bulgarian section of Moscow Radio and in Khristo Botev Radio. He returned to Bulgaria after the coup of 9 September 1944 and was assigned to the Defense Ministry, where he conducted a purge of officers. Between 1944 and 1945 he was assistant to the commander-in-chief of the Bulgarian Army, subsequently becoming deputy minister of national defense and head of the Political Board of the army. From 1948 to 1950 Kozovski was in the diplomatic service in Hungary and Poland. After returning to Bulgaria, he became one of the senior leaders of the Fatherland Front. (AG)

Sources: *Entsiklopediya Bulgariya*, vol. 3 (Sofia, 1982); Jerzy Tomaszewski, *Bułgaria 1944–1971* (Warsaw, 1989).

KRAIGHER Sergej (30 May 1914, Postojna, Slovenia–17 January 2001, Ljubljana), Slovene Communist activist. Kraigher studied in Ljubljana and then in Zagreb, where he graduated from the medical school. In February 1934 he joined the Communist Party of Yugoslavia (CPY). Arrested in 1934, he spent two years in prison in Sremska Mitrovica. From 1941 to 1945 he fought with the Communist partisans. He served as secretary of party committees in Trbovlje, Grosuplje, Celje, and Maribor. In 1945 he became secretary of the CPY city committee in Ljubljana and vice-president of the local city council. In 1946–50 he served as vice-president of the government of the Slovene Republic, and in 1948 he became a member of the CC of the Communist Party of Slovenia. From 1951 to 1953 Kraigher was chairman of the National Bank of Yugoslavia, and from 1963 to 1967, vice-president of the Federal Executive Council—that is, the federal government of Yugoslavia. From 1963 to 1967 he headed a commission for socioeconomic relations appointed by the Federal Council of the Assembly of the Socialist Federal Republic of Yugoslavia (SFRY). From 1967 to 1974 he was president of the National Assembly of the Socialist Republic of Slovenia, and from May 1974 to May 1979, chairman of the Presidium of the Socialist Republic of Slovenia. In 1969–74 Kraigher was a member of the Presidium of the CC of the League of Communists of Yugoslavia (LCY), and from 1974 to 1982, a member of the Presidium of the CC of the League of Communists of Slovenia (LCS). He was a member of the presidency of the SFRY (1971–74 and 1979–84), its vice-president (1980–81), and its president (1981–82), holding the highest position in the state at that time. Kraigher was the author of numerous articles on socioeconomic relations. In 1982 he headed a commission that drafted an anti-inflation program to stabilize the economy, but the implementation of that program did not prevent the economic collapse of the country in the late 1980s. (AO)

Sources: *Enciklopedija Jugoslavije*, vol. 5 (Zagreb, 1962); *Who's Who in the Socialist Countries of Europe* (Munich, London, and Paris, 1989); *Enciklopedija Slovenije*, vol. 5 (Ljubljana, 1991).

KRAJIŠNIK Momčilo (20 January 1945, Zabrlje, near Sarajevo), Bosnian Serb activist. The speaker of the parliament of Bosnia-Herzegovina in 1991, in 1992 Krajišnik resigned from this position and took over the position of speaker of the Bosnian Serb assembly. Controlling the local authorities, the police, military units, and the arms trade, he gained enormous power. Along with **Biljana Plavšić**, Krajišnik represented the nationalist "hawks" in the leadership of the Serbian Democratic Party (SDP) in Bosnia-Herzegovina. As a result of the elections of September 1996, he became a member of the three-man presidency of the Republic of Bosnia-Herzegovina on behalf of the Serbian Republic of Bosnia. In 1997 he was defeated by its president, Plavšić, who, with the support of NATO units, took over control of the police and chose a more conciliatory line. After the SDP lost the majority in the parliament of Bosnia-Herzegovina in November 1997, Krajišnik's position was further weakened when the government of Bosnia-Herzegovina was taken over by a moderate prime minister, Milorad Dodik. In August 1998 Krajišnik was accused of killing an officer connected with Plavšić, and in February 2000 he was accused by the International Yugoslav War Crimes Tribunal in The Hague of co-responsibility for the genocide of Bosnian Muslims. Arrested by French soldiers in Pale in April 2000, he was brought before the tribunal in February 2004, but he pleaded not guilty. (WR)

Sources: Laura Silber and Allan Little, *The Death of Yugoslavia* (London, 1995); Ante Čuvalo, *Historical Dictionary of Bosnia and Herzegovina* (Lanham, Md., 1997); www.diplomatiejudiciaire.com/UK/Tpyuk/KrajisnikUK.htm; www.rulers.org.

KRAMÁŘ Karel (27 December 1860, Vysoké nad Jizerou–26 May 1937, Prague), Czech politician, lawyer, and economist. Kramář's father secured the social advancement of his family, starting as a bricklayer and gradually acquiring a considerable fortune as an entrepreneur. Kramář took up law studies in Prague, which he completed in 1884. Then he studied public economics and political science in Berlin, London, and Paris. In Vienna, he entered political life, founding, along with **Tomáš Garrigue Masaryk**, the so-called realist movement. Kramář was the author of the political part of the movement's program, stressing the need for cooperation among the Slavic nations within the framework of the Austro-Hungarian Empire. Such cooperation was supposed to lead to the transformation of the empire into a federal state. In 1891 Kramář was elected an MP, representing the Young Czech party. Quite soon, he became one of its leaders, and at the turn of the century he was considered the leading Czech politician in Vienna. Although in the first general elections to the Viennese parliament in 1907 Kramář's party lost its position as the strongest Czech political force, he himself retained his position among the Czech politicians. (He was an ardent advocate of the elections in any case.)

In the ideological sphere, Kramář was the creator of "New Slavism," a concept according to which cooperation among the Slavic nations (including Russia) would be a counterbalance for the increasing influence of Germany in Austria-Hungary. In accordance with this idea, he organized two all-Slavic rallies, in Prague (1908) and Sofia (1910). In 1914 Kramář submitted, to the foreign minister of Russia, Sergey Sazonov, a project for the creation of a Slavic "Reich" under the scepter of the Romanovs. From the beginning of World War I Kramář was oriented against Austria. Along with Masaryk, **Alois Rašin**, **Edward Beneš**, and Josef Scheiner, he founded an organization called Mafia, which led the movement for independence in the Czech and Slovak territories. Along with Rašin, Kramář was arrested in 1915, and on 3 June 1916, sentenced to death. A year later the sentence was changed to twenty years of prison, but then Kramář was amnestied, and he returned to political life. On 9 February 1918 his efforts led to the unification of the "young Czechs" with the "old Czechs" and to the creation of the conservative Czech State Democratic Party (Česka Státopraprávní Demokracie).

In July 1918 Kramář became the head of the Czechoslovak National Committee (Československý Národni Výbor), which was joined by members of all political parties. Next, he headed a delegation to Geneva, where he met with representatives of the Czechoslovak National Council (Národni Výbor Československý) under the leadership of Beneš. On 14 November 1918 Kramář gave a speech in the National Assembly in which he announced the removal of the Habsburgs from the Czech throne and the appointment of Masaryk to the post of president of the new state. Between 14 November 1918 and 8 July 1919 Kramář was the first Czechoslovak prime minister.

In 1919 he was the head of the Czechoslovak delegation during the Paris Peace Conference, at which there were differences on foreign policy between Masaryk and Beneš. Kramář proposed to organize an anti-Bolshevik intervention in Russia that was supposed to ensure the security of the smaller Slavic countries in case of a German aggression. In 1919 the conservatives, led by Kramář, lost the parliamentary elections, and he himself ceased to be prime minister. His party changed its program and its name to Czechoslovak National Democracy (Československá Narodní Demokracie).

As a result of his conflict with Masaryk and Beneš, Kramář soon lost his position as one of the most influential politicians in Czechoslovakia. From 1919 to 1934 he was an MP and leader of National Democracy. In 1934, along with **Jiři Stříbrny** and František Mareš, he created the National Union (Národni Sjednocení), a group with a nationalistic program that did not gain great social support. Kramář was the author of many theoretical and historical works, among them the following: *České státní právo* (Czech state law; 1896); *Les parties politiques et la situation parlementaire en Autriche* (Political parties and the parliamentary situation in Austria; 1899); *Dějiny české politiky od roku 1879* (A history of Czech politics from 1879; 1909); *Austrian Terrorism in Bohemia* (1916); *Ruská krise* (The Russian crisis; 1921); and *Československi stát a Slovanstvo* (The Czechoslovak state and Slavism; 1927). In 1938 the first part of Kramář's memoirs, *Paméti*, appeared. (PU)

Sources: *ČBS*; *Kto bol kto za I. ČSR* (Bratislava, 1993); *Kdo był kdo v našich dějinach ve 20. stoleti*, vol. 1 (Prague, 1998); *Politická elita meziválečnéhoČeskoslovenska 1918–1938: Kdo byl kdo za prvni republiky* (Prague, 1998); Vladimir Sis, *Karel Kramář* (Prague, 1930); Kamil Krofta, *Politická postava Karla Kramáře* (Prague, 1930); Vincenc Červinka, *Karel Kramář, jého život a význam* (Prague, 1930); *První ministerský predseda ČSR dr: Karel Kramář* (Prague, 1938); Karel Herman, *Slovanska politika Karla Kramáře* (Prague, 1971).

KRASSÓ György (19 October 1932, Budapest–13 February 1991, Budapest), Hungarian journalist and political activist. At the age of fourteen Krassó joined the Hungarian Communist Party (HCP). From 1949 to 1951 he served his apprenticeship as a turner and studied for his high school final examinations at an evening school. In 1951 he began studying at the Academy of Economics in Budapest. Accused of spreading "revisionist" views, he was thrown out of the party in 1952 and expelled from the university in 1955. Involved in the armed struggle from the beginning of the 1956 revolution, Krassó took part in the assault on the radio station and other operations. Arrested for distributing leaflets after the fall of the revolution, he was sentenced to ten years' imprisonment. He was released under an amnesty in 1963. Arrested again in the same year, he was held under investigation for several months and accused of "anti-state agitation." From 1964 to 1970 Krassó worked as a turner. In 1970 he was dismissed from work for his opposition activities, such as illegal publications. In 1973 he retired on a pension. He organized protests against the arrests of members of Charter 77 in Czechoslovakia. In the 1980s he set up the underground publishing house Magyar Október (Hungarian October) and organized activities commemorating the 1956 revolution, as a result of which he was placed under house arrest in 1984. In 1985 Krassó emigrated to Great Britain, where he worked with the BBC and Radio Free Europe. In 1989 he returned to Hungary, calling for a thorough de-Communization modeled on the de-Nazification process in Germany. In 1990, the Hungarian October Party (Október Párt), which Krassó had founded, did not gain the required 5 percent of the vote in the first democratic parliamentary elections in Hungary. (MS)

Sources: Péter Sneé, *Meghalt Krassó György,* "Magyar Nemzet," 1991, no. 37; *Új magyar irodalmi lexikon* (Budapest, 1994); György Litván, ed., *Rewolucja węgierska 1956 roku* (Warsaw, 1996).

KRAVCHUK Leonid (10 January 1934, Velykyi Zhytyn, Volhynia), Ukrainian Communist activist and post-Communist politician. After graduating from a technical high school in Rivne, Kravchuk studied economics at Kiev University. In 1958–60 he lectured in political economy in Chernihiv. In 1960–67 he worked in the Department of Propaganda and Agitation of the Chernihiv regional committee of the Communist Party of Ukraine (Komunistychna Partiya Ukraiiny [CPU]). From 1967 he was a doctoral student at the Academy of Social Sciences of the Central Committee (CC) of the CPSU, where he received a Ph.D. in 1970. Then he started working in the CPU apparatus. From 1980 Kravchuk was head of the Department of Propaganda and Agitation of the CPU CC. From October 1988 to October 1989 he was head of the Ideological Department of the CPU CC. An adherent of perestroika, from October 1989 to June 1990 he was CPU CC secretary for ideology and a deputy member of the CPU Politburo. In June 1990 he became a member of the Politburo and second secretary of the CPU CC. In March 1990 he was elected a deputy to the Supreme Council of the Ukrainian SSR. Kravchuk supported the autonomy of the Ukrainian party and republic. When on 16 July 1990 the Supreme Council announced Ukrainian sovereignty—meaning the priority of local laws before all-Soviet legislation—Kravchuk became the council's chairman.

As a result of the August 1991 putsch in Moscow, Kravchuk gave up his party membership. After the failure of the putsch, on 24 August the Supreme Council passed the declaration of Ukrainian independence. On 1 December 1991 Kravchuk was elected president, winning 61.6 percent of the vote. On the same day, about 90 percent of Ukrainians supported the independence declaration in a referendum. Realizing that the breakup of the Soviet Union was inevitable, in the fall of 1991 Kravchuk supported a loose federation of Soviet republics, but when this attempt to save the Soviet state failed, on 7–8 December 1991 Kravchuk met with the presidents of Russia, Boris Yeltsin, and Belorussia, **Stanislau Shushkevich**, in Belovyezha Forest and signed an agreement on the formation of the Commonwealth of Independent States, which led to the dissolution of the Soviet Union.

Under Kravchuk's rule Ukraine had no exact borders, its economy was in ruins, and the new political system was only in the making. Kravchuk was one of the leaders of the Social Democratic Party of Ukraine (United) (Sotsialdemokratychna Partiya Ukraiiny [Obyednana]). There were serious tensions with Russia over borders, the division of the armed forced, and the nuclear arsenal. In August 1992 Kravchuk agreed with Yeltsin on the division of the Black Sea Fleet; the agreement finally came into force after another meeting with Yeltsin in June 1993. Kravchuk did not accept the secession of the Crimean Republic and did not recognize Sevastopol as a part of Russia. On 14 January 1994 he signed with U.S. president Bill Clinton and with Russian president Yeltsin an agreement on the delivery of the Ukrainian nuclear arsenal to Russia in exchange for American and Russian guarantees of Ukrainian independence and American economic aid. Kravchuk established diplomatic relations with most countries of the world and established good neighbor agreements with Poland and Romania. From the spring of 1993 a conflict grew between Kravchuk and Prime Minister **Leonid Kuchma** over economic reform. Because of delays in the reform, the economic situation of the country worsened. In the presidential elections of July 1994 Kravchuk came first in the first round but lost to Kuchma in the second round. From September 1994 Kravchuk was a deputy to the Supreme Council of Ukraine, but his party was sidelined. Kravchuk authored the memoirs *Mayemo te, shcho mayemo: Spohady i rozdumy* (We have what we have: Memoirs and reflections; 2002). (BB)

Sources: *Khto ye khto v Ukraiini 2000* (Kiev, 2000); *Ukraina: Znaki zapytania* (Warsaw, 1990); Tadeusz Andrzej Olszański, *Historia Ukrainy XX w.* (Warsaw, n.d.); Mykola Mikhalchenko and Viiktor Andrushchenko, *Belovyezhe. L. Kravchuk. Ukraiina 1991–1995* (Kiev, 1996); Andrzej Chojnowski, *Ukraina* (Warsaw, 1997); Bohdan Nahaylo, *The Ukrainian Resurgence* (Toronto, 1999); Bugajski.

KRECHEUSKI Pyotr (7 August 1879, Kobryn–8 March 1928, Prague), Belorussian writer, historian, and politician. The son of a village deacon, Krecheuski graduated from the Wilno (Vilnius) Theological Seminary (1909) but decided to pursue a teaching career. From 1902 to 1909 he worked as a teacher in the counties of Białystok and Wołkowysk (Volkovysk). From 1909 to 1914 he was employed in the Wilno State Bank. From 1914 he served in the Russian Army. In December 1917 he took part in the preparations for and the work of the First All-Belorussian Congress and became one of the senior leaders of the Belorussian People's Republic (BPR). In 1918, after the Belorussian Socialist Hromada split into three groups, Krecheuski became one of the leaders of the Belorussian Party of Socialists-Federalists. He was an avowed supporter of the struggle to maintain the independence of the BPR. He believed that an alliance with neither the Poles nor the Bolsheviks offered a compromise solution to the Belorussian question. In May 1918 Krecheuski became secretary of trade of the BPR and, in October 1918, secretary of the Council of the BPR, which served as a provisional legislative government of the republic. On 13 December 1919 he became president of the Council of the BPR. After the council withdrew from Belorussian territory, Krecheuski held his position in exile: in Kaunas, in Berlin, and finally in Prague. At that time he established a network of BPR representatives in various countries. He kept Western governments—as well as public opinion—informed about the situation of the Belorussian people under the Soviet and Polish governments. In September 1921 he convened a Belorussian conference in Prague, at which representatives of various organizations in exile recognized his government. Despite intrigues by the Soviet services, Krecheuski managed to maintain unity within the Belorussian government-in-exile. In Prague, he also founded the Belorussian Archive, which was intercepted by the Red Army in 1945.

Krecheuski was the author of works on the Polish-Soviet Treaty of Riga of 1921 and on the Belorussian National-Political Conference in Prague in September 1921. These works were published in Berlin in 1925. Krecheuski defined both Poland and Soviet Russia as occupiers of Belorussian territories. The drama *Rahneda*, written in 1921, depicted the political situation in the Polotsk Duchy in the tenth century; it was a metaphorical picture of the situation of Belorussia at the beginning of the twentieth century. Krecheuski was the editor of *Zamezhnaia Belarus* (Foreign Belorussia; 1926), a compendium about the history, culture, and economy of Belorussia. (EM)

Sources: *Khrystsianskaia Dumka* (Vilnius), 20 March 1938; *Batskaushchyna* (Munich), 15 March 1953; *Byelorussian Times* (Flushing, N.Y.), January 1978; Vitaut Kipel and Zora Kipel, eds.,

Byelorussian Statehood (New York, 1988); *Entsyklapiedyia historyi Bielarusi*, vol. 4 (Minsk, 1997).

KREJČI Jaroslav (27 June 1892, Křemenec–18 May 1956, Leopoldovo), Czech lawyer and politician. In 1915 Krejči graduated from law studies at the university in Prague. During World War I he served in the rear of the Austro-Hungarian Army. From 1918 to 1920 he worked in a land office in Brno. In 1919 he joined the Czech National Socialist Party. In 1920 he became a government official, later an adviser to the prime minister, and from 1936 to 1938 he was president of the secretariat of the Law Council, an advisory body at the office of the prime minister. From 1921 to 1938 Krejči served as secretary, and from 1938 to 1939 as president, of the Constitutional Tribunal. He also pursued academic work at the university in Brno, where in 1938 he became a professor of constitutional law. In his views at that time, Krejči was close to the ideas of **Tomáš Garrigue Masaryk**, and between 1928 and 1938 he was one of the leaders of the National Socialist Party. From 1928 to 1945 he published the periodical *Moderní stát* and was the author of numerous studies in the field of constitutional law and the legal system.

In the governments of the Second Republic (1938–39) Krejči served as minister of justice and head of the government commission for the German minority in the Czech territories. In the second government of the Protectorate of Bohemia and Moravia in 1940 he served briefly as minister of agriculture. After the arrest of **Alois Eliaš**, in September 1941 Krejči took over his duties, and from 19 January 1942 to 19 January 1945 he served as prime minister of the puppet Czech government of the Protectorate of Bohemia and Moravia. As head of the government, he performed the duties of head of state in place of the ailing president, **Emil Hácha**, de facto from 1943 and officially from May 1944. In the final stages of the war Krejči again served as deputy prime minister. After the appointment of Reinhard Heydrich as Reich Protector of Bohemia and Moravia and the appointment of Krejči as prime minister, the situation of the people in the Protectorate of Bohemia and Moravia worsened. Arrests and death sentences became more frequent, the extermination of Jewish people was stepped up, and the powers of the Czech administration were restricted. As head of the government, Krejči not only endorsed German policies and gave assurances of the Czech people's support for Hitler, but he also carried out the Nazis' orders. Arrested in May 1945, Krejči was accused of collaboration with the occupation authorities. One year later the People's Court sentenced him to twenty-five years' imprisonment. He died in prison. (PU)

Sources: *ČBS*; *Kdo byl kdo v našich dějinach ve 20. stoleti*, vol. 1 (Prague, 1998); *Politická elita meziválečného Československa 1918–1938: Kdo byl kdo za první republiky* (Prague, 1998); *Českoslovenští politici: 1918–1991* (Prague, 1991); Jerzy Tomaszewski, *Czechosłowacja* (Warsaw, 1997).

KREK Janez Evangelist (27 November 1865, St. Gregor pri Ribnici–8 October 1917, Johannisthal [Šentjanž]), priest, writer, politician, and leader of the Slovene national movement. The son of a teacher, Krek was ordained a priest in Laibach (Ljubljana) in 1888 and subsequently studied theology in Vienna, where in 1892 he received a Ph.D. After returning to Ljubljana, he became a lecturer in fundamental theology and Thomism at a local seminary. Already in Vienna, he had become aware of the increasingly crucial working-class question and unresolved social problems. In his writings, Krek tried to outline a plan for the future organization of Slovene society based on Pope Leo XIII's Social Encyclical *Rerum Novarum* and on the thought of Karl von Vogelsang. Krek's theoretical principles became the basis for the program of the Catholic National Party (Katoliška Narodna Stranka [CNP]), announced in 1895. Over the following years Krek actively participated in Slovene national life and was one of the main founders of a network of savings and loan associations modeled on the system of Friedrich W. Raiffeisen. He also helped to found agricultural associations and cooperatives. In 1910 the Central Cooperative Union consisted of as many as 560 organizations. On Krek's initiative, a school training staff for cooperative societies was established in 1908 and a school of agriculture and housekeeping for women in 1913, both in Ljubljana. These successes were accompanied by the increase of importance of the CNP, renamed the Slovene People's Party (Slovenska Ljudska Stranka [SLS]) in 1905. The SLS was supported by small and medium Slovene farmers, whose financial situation improved as a result of the developing cooperative movement.

Krek also managed to attract the majority of workers to the SLS. In 1894 he founded the Slovene Catholic Workers' Union (Slovensko Katoliško Delavsko Društvo), whose influence quickly spread across industrial centers where Slovene workers were employed. He also founded the Consumers' Union, the School Union, and the dynamic Union for the Construction of Workers' Housing Estates. In October 1895, at the first meeting with workers' delegates, Krek presented "A Social Plan to Improve the Situation of Slovene Workers," which for many years provided the main program guidelines for the Slovene Christian Democratic Party. In 1897 Krek initiated the establishment of the Slovene Christian Social Workers' Union, which was later transformed into the apolitical Union of School Circles.

As a result of Krek's efforts, the socially engaged ideology of the Christian Democratic movement became the main influence on the institutions of the Slovene national revival, and after 1918 the Catholic parties gained a dominant position in Slovene political life, relegating Social Democrats to defensive positions. At the same time Krek opposed the nationalist extremists. A member of the Reichsrat of Austria-Hungary (1897–1900, 1907–17) and the provincial parliament of Krajina (1902–17), Krek called for intensive cooperation among the South Slavic nations, which, according to his plan, were to be united in a separate administrative district within the framework of the Habsburg empire. He designated a special role for the Slovenes in the economy and cultural life of the future province of the Southern Slavs. Krek played a key role in drafting the May Declaration of 1917, submitted by Slovene, Croat, and Serb politicians, who called for unity within a single state but still under Habsburg rule. Thanks to Krek, the cooperative movement also successfully developed in Croatia and on the Dalmatian coast. Krek's literary and journalistic legacy consists of four volumes, but a complete edition did not come out until 1922–23 in Ljubljana, where his *Izbrani Spisi* (Selected writings) were published posthumously. Krek was instrumental in shaping the intellectual attitudes of several generations of Slovene intelligentsia and politicians. (AG)

Sources: *Biographisches Lexikon*, vol. 2; *Enciklopedija Jugoslavije*, vol. 5 (Zagreb, 1962); *Enciklopedija Slovenije*, vol. 6 (Ljubljana, 1992); Fran Erjavec, *Zgodovina katoliškega gibanja na Slovenskem* (Ljubljana, 1928); R. Jurčec, *Krek* (Ljubljana, 1935); Ferdo Gestrin and Vasilij Melik, *Slovenska zgodovina od konca osemnajstega stoletja do 1918* (Ljubljana, 1966); Vinko Brumen, *Srce v sredini: Življenje, delo in osebnost Janeza Evangelista Kreka* (Buenos Aires, 1968); Carole Rogel, *The Slovenes and Yugoslavism, 1890–1914* (Boulder, Colo., 1977); Wacław Felczak and Tadeusz Wasilewski, *Historia Jugosławii* (Wrocław, 1985).

KREK Miha (29 September 1897, Leskovica–18 November 1969, Cleveland, Ohio), Slovene politician. Krek studied law in Zagreb and Ljubljana, where he earned a doctorate in 1930. An active member of the Slovene People's Party, he joined Slovene Catholic Action and edited the periodical *Slovenec*. In 1935 **Anton Korošec** supported his candidacy for the post of minister without portfolio in the government of **Milan Stojadinović** (June 1935–February 1939). In 1940 Krek became head of the Slovene branch of the Bank Committee. After the German invasion in April 1941, he left for London, where he served as minister and deputy prime minister of the government-in-exile until Prime Minister **Ivan Šubašić** concluded an agreement with the Communists led by **Josip Broz Tito**. Krek did not accept this agreement and warned the Allies against

recognizing the Communist regime in Yugoslavia. In 1944 in Rome he founded an anti-Communist national committee that favored the liberation of Slovenia by the Allies. In the spring of 1945 Krek protested the Allies' handing over Home Guard (Domobranci) members to the Communists. He helped Slovene refugees in Italy. In 1947 he settled in the United States, where he was active in émigré circles. Krek served as a member of the leadership of the Union of Christian Democratic Parties of Eastern Europe. (WR)

Sources: *Enciklopedia Slovenije*, vol. 6 (Ljubljana, 1992); Leopoldina Plut-Progelj and Carole Rogel, *Historical Dictionary of Slovenia* (Lanham, Md., 1996).

KREVE-MICKEVIČIUS Vincas [originally Mickevičius] (19 October 1882, Subartonys, near Merkyne–7 July 1954, Philadelphia, Pennsylvania), Lithuanian writer, philologist, and politician. "Kreve" was his pen name. Between the wars he used both names, and after the war he signed himself as Kreve only. From 1898 to 1900 Kreve attended a theological seminary in Vilnius (Wilno). In 1902 he moved to a gymnasium in Kazan, and he graduated in 1904. Between 1904 and 1905 he studied at the historical and philological department of the university in Kiev, but because of the outbreak of the revolution, the tsarist authorities closed the university, and Kreve moved to study in Lviv (Lwów). There he defended his thesis in comparative philology, and in 1908 he obtained a Ph.D. in philosophy. He started working as a high school teacher in Baku and continued part-time linguistic studies in Kiev, where he earned an M.A. in comparative philology based on his thesis on the origin of the names of Buddha and Pratekhabuddha. After the fall of tsarism and the proclamation of independence by Azerbaijan, Kreve was appointed Lithuanian consul in Baku. After the seizure of Azerbaijan by the Bolsheviks, he returned to Lithuania, where from 1920 to 1921 he worked in the Ministry of Education. In 1922 he was appointed professor at the university in Kaunas, where he lectured in Slavic literature until 1940. He published extensively and was the editor and publisher of many periodicals—for example, *Tauta ir Žordis* in 1924–31 and *Musu Tautosaka* in 1930–35. His literary and scholarly activities, as well as intensive journalism, brought him many awards and distinctions, including an honorary doctorate at the University of Riga.

After the Soviet invasion in June 1940 Kreve assumed the post of deputy prime minister in the so-called people's government of **Justas Paleckis**, and he endeavored to prevent the final incorporation of Lithuania by the USSR. To achieve his aim on 1 July he met with Vyacheslav Molotov, but the latter stated that the decision to deprive Lithuania of sovereignty would not be withdrawn. Later,

Kreve publicly revealed the substance of the talk with Molotov; it became one of the key pieces of evidence in a 1954 report by the U.S. Congress that determined that the actions of the USSR toward the Baltic States could be regarded as aggression. After his return from Moscow, Kreve withdrew from political life and devoted himself to scholarly work. He assumed the post of director of the Institute of Lithuanian Studies, which was later transformed into the Lithuanian Academy of Sciences. After 22 June 1941 he temporarily lectured at the University of Vilnius, but fearing arrest by the Gestapo, he went into hiding. With the arrival of the Red Army in 1944, he decided to emigrate. He managed to get to the United States via Austria. In the United States he assumed the post of lecturer in Slavic literature at the University of Pennsylvania in Philadelphia. (AG)

Sources: *EL*, vol. 3; "Vinca Kreve's Place in Lithuanian Literature," *Studi Baltici* (Florence), 1952, no. 9; B. Vaškelis, "Vincas Kreve: The Lithuanian Classic," *Lithuanus*, Fall 1965; Joseph Pajauvis-Javis, *Soviet Genocide in Lithuania* (New York, 1980).

KRIEGEL František (10 April 1908, Stanisławów [now Ivano-Frankivsk]–3 December 1979, Prague), Czech doctor and political activist. Born into a Jewish family in Galicia, at the end of the 1920s Kriegel went to Czechoslovakia, where in 1934 he graduated in medicine from Charles University in Prague. By then he was already a member of the Communist Party of Czechoslovakia (CPC). From 1934 to 1936 he worked in an internal medicine clinic in Prague and subsequently was a doctor in the republican army in Spain until 1939. In 1939 he was interned in France for a short time. From 1940 until the end of the war Kriegel worked as a doctor in the Chinese Communist Army, and then he returned to Czechoslovakia and until 1949 served as the organizational secretary of the Provincial Committee of the CP of Czechoslovakia in Prague. During the Communist coup d'état in February 1948 Kriegel was deputy chief of the general staff of the People's Militia (Lidové Milice), fighting squadrons that played a major role in controlling the public during the coup. From 1949 to 1952 he held the post of deputy minister of health but was dismissed as part of the anti-Semitic purges conducted under the slogan of the "struggle against Zionism." After his dismissal, Kriegel worked as a doctor, and from 1960 to 1963 he was a health adviser to the government of Cuba. In 1964–65 he headed the hospital ward of the Institute for Research on Rheumatic Diseases in Prague, and later he became head of the internal medicine ward of Thomayer Hospital in Prague. From 1964 to 1969 he sat in the National Assembly and later, for a short time, in the People's Chamber of the Federal Assembly. During the Prague Spring of 1968 Kriegel became one

of the senior leaders of the party, where he represented a reformist faction. From 1966 to 1969 he sat on the Central Committee (CC) of the CPC, and from 4 June to 31 August 1968 he was a member of the CC Presidium. In 1968 he also served as president of the CC of the National Front. After the invasion of Czechoslovakia by Warsaw Pact troops on 21 August 1968, along with other government representatives Kriegel was taken to Moscow. However, he did not take part in negotiations with the Soviet leadership. He was asked to sign the final protocol ending the Moscow negotiations, but as the only member of the Czechoslovak delegation, he refused. On 18 October 1968, together with three other deputies, Kriegel voted in the Federal Assembly against the adoption of an agreement allowing Soviet troops to be stationed on Czechoslovak territory. In 1969 he was expelled from the CC of the CPC and then from the party itself. He was subsequently stripped of his parliamentary seat. In the 1970s Kriegel was active in the opposition, and in 1977 he was one of the first signatories of Charter 77. (PU)

Sources: *ČBS*; *Českoslovenští politici: 1918–1991* (Prague, 1991); *Kdo byl kdo v našich dějinách ve 20. stoleti*, vol. 1 (Prague, 1998); Gordon H. Skilling, *Czechoslovakia's Interrupted Revolution* (Princeton, 1976); Vilém Precan, ed., *Charta 77 (1977–1989)*. *Od morální k demokratické revoluci: Dokumentace* (Bratislava, 1990); Andrzej Garlicki and Andrzej Paczkowski, eds., *Zaciskanie pętli: Tajne dokumenty dotyczące Czechosłowacji 1968 r.* (Warsaw, 1995).

KRILYK Osyp, pseudonym "Vasylkiv" (22 July 1898, Krakowiec, near Jaworów, Galicia–11 September 1941, Orlov), Ukrainian Communist activist. In 1918, while a law student at the University of Lemberg (Lwów, Lviv), Krilyk was a co-founder of International Revolutionary Social Democracy, a group drawing on the ideas of Mykhailo Drahomanov; it represented the national faction in the Ukrainian Communist movement. In 1919 the members of this group joined the Communist Party of Eastern Galicia (CPEG). In 1920 Krilyk began organizing Communist circles among soldiers of the Ukrainian Galician Army who had been interned in Czechoslovakia. He also founded the Committee to Aid the Revolutionary Movement of Eastern Galicia in Prague and the CPEG Foreign Committee in Vienna. After returning to Galicia at the end of 1920, Krilyk assumed the post of secretary of the CPEG Central Committee. Arrested by the Polish police on 30 October 1921 along with several members of the Communist Workers' Party of Poland (Komunistyczna Partia Robotnicza Polski [KPRP]), Krilyk was tried in a trial of thirty-nine Communists in Lwów (the so-called St. George trial, November 1922–January 1923). Acquitted of charges of high treason, he became head of the nationalist faction within the CPEG (Vasylkiv's faction, known as the Vasylkivtsi).

In November 1922, like most Ukrainian parties in Galicia, the CPEG boycotted the elections to the Polish Assembly. Trying to increase the autonomy of the CPEG vis-à-vis the KPRP, in 1923 Krilyk brought about the transformation of the CPEG into the Communist Party of Western Ukraine (Komunistychna Partiia Zakhidnoi Ukrainy [KPZU]). He contributed to an increase in the popularity of the nationalist-Communist orientation among the Ukrainians in Eastern Galicia through the activities of the Ukrainian Peasants' and Workers' Socialist Union (known as the Sel-Rob), a party independent from the KPZU, in 1926–32. Krilyk implemented the resolution of the Fifth Comintern Congress of 1924 and the policies of the authorities of the Ukrainian Soviet Socialist Republic. The secretary of the KPZU CC, Krilyk also joined the KPRP CC, and in 1927 he entered the Politburo of the Communist Party of Poland (Komunistyczna Partia Polski [KPP]), becoming a KPZU representative in the Polish section of the Comintern in Moscow. In April 1927 the Vasylkivtsi faction, who had a majority within the KPZU, refused the request of the leaders of the Communist Party (Bolshevik) of Ukraine (CP[B]U) and the Communist International that they too denounce the so-called nationalist deviation of **Oleksandr Shumsky**, minister of education of the Ukrainian SSR. As a result, in 1928 Krilyk was expelled from the Comintern, and Stalinists assumed control of the KPZU leadership. Expelled from the KPZU in March 1929, in 1932 Krilyk left for the Ukrainian SSR, where he became a member of the management of a publishing house in Kharkiv. Arrested in May 1933, he was deported to Karelia. After the German Army invaded Ukraine, on 11 September 1941, Krilyk was executed, along with **Khristian Rakovsky** and others, by an NKVD firing squad in a prison in Orlov. (TS)

Sources: *Encyclopedia of Ukraine*, vol. 2 (Toronto, 1988); *Proces komunistów we Lwowie* (Warsaw, 1958); Janusz Radziejowski, *Komunistyczna Partia Zachodniej Ukrainy 1919–1929: Węzłowe problemy ideologiczne* (Kraków, 1976); Roman Solchanyk, "The Communist Party of Western Ukraine 1919–1938," Ph.D. diss., University of Michigan, 1973.

KRLEŽA Miroslav (7 July 1893, Zagreb–29 December 1981, Zagreb), Croatian writer. Krleža came from a lower-middle-class family. His father was a clerk in Zagreb. In 1908 Krleža entered the Cadet School in Pécs and was later educated at the Ludoviceum, a military academy in Budapest. During the Balkan Wars he twice tried to join the Serbian Army but was unsuccessful. However, in 1913 he went to the front lines anyway, to fight on the Serbian side, but was arrested by the Serbs, who suspected him of spying. Upon his return to Austria-Hungary, Krleža was in turn arrested as a deserter and expelled from the Austro-Hungarian Army. After the outbreak of World War I, he was again inducted into the Austro-Hungarian Army in December 1915. As he had symptoms of tuberculosis, he was sent to a hospital. Later he fought in Galicia. After the war he devoted himself to writing. The year 1917 saw the publication of *Tri simfonije* (Three symphonies), a collection of poems that was highly acclaimed by the critics. Krleža was also the author of many dramas, of which *Golgota* was staged in 1922 and *Michelangelo Buonarroti* and *Adam i Eva* (Adam and Eve) in 1925.

Krleža was against the establishment of the monarchy in the Kingdom of Serbs, Croats, and Slovenes. From 1918 to 1939 he was a member of the Communist Party. His fascination with Marxism and with the Bolshevik revolution in Russia was reflected in his publications in the bi-weekly *Plamen*, first issued in 1919. In 1922 he published the collection of novellas *Hrvatski bog Mars* (The Croatian God Mars). From 1923 to 1927 he published the monthly *Književna republika*. After the introduction of the authoritarian regime of King **Alexander I** in 1929, for a short time the Croatian opposition formed a united front: Communists, including Krleža, sat on the board of Matica Hrvatska, the leading Croatian cultural society, side by side with clericals.

Krleža's drama *U agoniji* (In agony) was published in 1928. With *Gospoda Glembajevi* (The Glembajs; 1928) and *Leda* (1932) it formed a trilogy about the Glembaj family. Krleža used the disintegration of a family as a vehicle to criticize the downfall of bourgeois society. He regarded this trilogy as his greatest achievement, although some critics received it unfavorably. After moving to Czechoslovakia, Krleža finished the novel *Povratak Filipa Latinovića* (1932; *The Return of Philip Latinovich*, 1959). In the spring of 1932 he went to Warsaw, where he met the Polish writer Zofia Nałkowska, with whom he formed a friendship. After Krleža's return to Zagreb in 1933 a sort of "poster war" occurred: in response to posters announcing a public speech by Krleža, there appeared posters calling for its boycott. In additional posters, prominent people of culture defended Krleža. The speech was cancelled, and Krleža severed his ties with Matica Hrvatska. In 1934, attacked by both the right wing and some left-wing parties, Krleža founded *Danas*, a literary monthly that attracted Communist writers. After the intervention of the authorities, this monthly was suspended. In 1939 Krleža published the periodical *Pečat*.

Arrested by the Ustashe during World War II, Krleža was de facto held under house arrest in Zagreb. After the war he founded the monthly *Republika*. He was in the executive of the League of Communists of Yugoslavia (LCY) and the executive of the League of Communists of Croatia (LCC). Elected a member of the Yugoslav Academy of Science and Art, he became its vice-president in 1947. From 1958 to 1961 he served as president of the Yugoslav Writers' Union. The director of the Yugoslav Lexicographic Institute (Leksikografski Zavod Jugoslavije) from 1951 on, Krleža was editor-in-chief of *Enciklopedija Jugoslavije* (Encyclopedia of Yugoslavia, 8 vols.; 1955–71). Krleža's most important works also include *Balade Petrice Kerempuha* (Ballads of Petrica Kerempuh; 1936); *Na rubu pameti* (1938; *On the Edge of Reason*, 1976); *Bankiet u Blitvi* (1939; *Banquet in Blitva*, 2002); *Davni dani* (Bygone days; 1956), *Zastave* (Flags; 1967); and *Dnevnik* (Diary; 1977). (AO)

Sources: *Enciklopedija Jugoslavije*, vol. 5 (Zagreb, 1962); *Mały słownik pisarzy zachodnio-słowiańskich i południowo-słowiańskich* (Warsaw, 1973); Jan Wierzbicki, *Miroslav Krleža* (Warsaw, 1975); Marijan Matković, *La vie et l'oeuvre de Miroslav Krleža* (Paris, 1977); Stanko Lasić, *Krleža: Kronologija života i rada* (Zagreb, 1982); Vojislav Djurić, ed., *Miroslav Krleža* (Belgrade, 1967).

KROFTA Kamil (17 July 1876, Plzen–16 August 1945, Prague), Czech historian and diplomat. After graduating from high school in Plzen, Krofta studied history at the university in Prague and Austrian history at the Institute of Vienna. In 1899 he commenced two years of studies in Rome, where he did research in the Vatican archives. After returning from Italy, he accepted a job in the Czech Land Archives in Prague, where he worked until 1912. In 1911 Krofta was appointed associate professor of Austrian history, and after the establishment of independent Czechoslovakia he became a full professor of Czech history at Charles University in Prague. Krofta mainly dealt with the history of the Czech reformation, the development of national consciousness in Central Europe, and the history of Slovakia. He wrote many studies, including *Bila hora* (White mountain; 1913); *Mistř Jan Hus v živote a památkách českého lidu* (Master Jan Hus in the life and memory of the Czech people; 1915); *Přehled dějin selského stavu v Čechach a na Moravě* (Overview of the history of agriculture in Bohemia and Moravia; 1920); *Cechy do válek husitských* (Bohemia before the Hussite wars; 1930); *Nesmrtelny narod* (The immortal nation; 1940); and *Dějiny československé* (Czechoslovak history; 1946).

After the establishment of the Czechoslovak state, Krofta worked in the Ministry of Education. From 1920 on he was active in the diplomatic service, initially serving in the Vatican. He later worked in the Czechoslovak embassies in Vienna (1921–25) and Berlin (1925–27); then he returned to Prague and became head of the Presidium of the Ministry of Foreign Affairs. In that capacity Krofta was the deputy to and the closest co-worker of minister **Edvard Beneš**. Krofta had much genuine influence on Czechoslovak foreign policy; for example, he worked out the modus vivendi adopted by Czechoslovakia and the Vatican in 1927, after the Holy See had recalled the papal nuncio from Prague in 1925.

After Beneš became president, Krofta was appointed foreign minister in March 1936. In accordance with Beneš's line, he based Czechoslovak foreign policy on the inviolability of borders guaranteed by the Treaty of Versailles, an alliance with France, and an agreement with the Soviet Union. The efforts of Czechoslovak diplomacy were unsuccessful, though; therefore, following the Pact of Munich of September 1938, Krofta resigned and withdrew from politics. After the outbreak of World War II, he was active in the anti-Fascist resistance movement. From 1942 to 1944 he was one of the representatives of the National Preparatory Revolutionary Committee and a co-author of its program. Arrested by the Gestapo in June 1944, Krofta was held in prison in Terezín (Theresienstadt) until the end of the war. The stay in prison seriously undermined his health, and he died shortly after the liberation. Krofta was the author of the memoirs *Z dob naši prvni republiký* (From the times of the First Republic; 1939). (PU)

Sources: *ČBS*; *Kto bol kto za I.ČSR* (Bratislava, 1993); *Kdo byl kdo v našich dějinach ve 20. stoleti*, vol.1 (Prague, 1998); *Politická elita meziválečného Československa 1918–1938: Kdo byl kdo za prvni republiky* (Prague, 1998); Henri Nogueres, *Munich: "Peace for Our Time"* (New York, 1963); Jindrich Dejmek, *Historik v cele diplomacie, Kamil Krofta: Studie z dejin československé zahranicní politiky v letech 1936–1938* (Prague, 1998).

KROSS Jaan (19 February 1920, Tallinn), Estonian writer and translator. During the German occupation Kross was mobilized. For supporting Estonian independence he was arrested for a few months. After his release in 1944, he graduated in law at the University of Tartu. After the war he lectured in constitutional and international law there, but in 1948 he was arrested. Detained in Tallinn, he was later sent to a labor camp in the Komi ASSR. After his release in 1954 he started writing, although he was hardly tolerated by the authorities. In 1959 Kross became the target of propaganda attacks. In 1976–80 he was secretary of the Association of Writers of the Estonian SSR. Kross thought the Estonians had survived as a nation thanks to their innate skepticism, and he promoted national revival through the "recovery of history." In the 1980s he was increasingly active in the national movement. On 24 February 1988, a prewar national holiday, Kross signed an appeal by Estonian intellectuals to celebrate the anniversary of independence. In 1992–93 Kross was an MP, and he chaired a parliamentary commission to investigate cooperation with the KGB. He received honorary doctorates from the universities in Tartu (1989) and Helsinki (1990).

Kross made his literary debut before the war, but he started his literary career in 1958 when he published *Söerikastaja* (Coal concentrator). Later he published *Kivist viiulid* (Violin of stone; 1964), *Lauljad laevavööridel* (Singing aboard; 1966), and *Vihm teeb toredaid asju* (The rain creates funny things; 1969). For the collection *Voog ja Koolmpii* (The wave and the trident; 1971) Kross received the J. Smull Award (1972). He received this award several times—for the novels *Kolme katku vahel* (Between three plagues, 2 vols.; 1970–72), *Keisri hull* (Imperial madman; 1978), and *Profesor Martensi äraső̈it* (1984; *Professor Martens' Departure*, 1994). Kross also wrote *Neli monoologi Püha Jüri asjus* (Four appeals to St. George; 1970); *Michelsoni immatrikuleerimine* (Matriculation of Michelson; 1971); and *Taevakivi* (1975; *The Rock from the Sky*, 1983). His novels, including *Mesmeri ring* (The Mesmer ring; 1995), were translated into many languages. Kross also translated from Bertold Brecht, Heinrich Heine, Paul Eluard, and William Shakespeare.

Kross's writing evolved from a poetic reflection on the fate of his country and the hopes for a better future, connected with a rising standard of living, to a more critical approach in the 1970s. His typical hero was a man involved in unresolvable moral dilemmas, forcing him to make heroic choices between compromises with a hostile social environment and moral resistance that would mean destruction. In view of the heavy censorship Kross frequently described figures from Estonian history. He placed them in positions typical of Greek tragedies, making clear allusions to the realities of the Soviet occupation. He also reached back into his memory—for instance, in *Silmade avamise päev* (The open door day; 1988) and *Väljakaevamised* (Exhumations; 1990)—describing the Stalinist era through the eyes of its victims. One of the most outstanding Estonian intellectuals, Kross has been mentioned as a serious candidate for the Nobel Prize in Literature. (AG)

Sources: *Kto yest kto v kulture Estonii: Izobrazitielnyie isskustva, litieratura, teatr, muzika, kino* (Avyenaris, 1996); *Eesti Entsuklopeedia*, vol. 14 (Tallinn, 2000); Tönu Parming and Elmar Järvesoo, *A Case Study of a Soviet Republic: The Estonian SSR* (Boulder, Colo., 1978); Toivo U. Raun, *Estonia and the Estonians* (Stanford, 1991); Anatol Lieven, *The Baltic Revolution* (New Haven, 1993); Rein Taagepera, *Estonia: Return to Independence* (Boulder, Colo., 1993).

KRUCZEK Władysław (27 April 1910, Zwięczyca, near Rzeszów–5 November 2003, Warsaw), Polish Communist activist. Kruczek was a member of the Communist Party of Poland (Komunistyczna Partia Polski [KPP]) before World War II, and during the war he joined the People's Guard (Gwardia Ludowa). He organized Communist power in the Rzeszów region. In 1945 he joined the Polish Workers' Party (Polska Partia Robotnicza [PPR]), becoming a member of the Polish United Workers' Party (Polska Zjednoczona Partia Robotnicza [PUWP]) in 1948. As a PUWP member, Kruczek supported ideological orthodoxy and Stalinist iron-fisted rule. From 1955 to 1956, at the time of the struggle for power within the PUWP, Kruczek was close to the Natolin faction, working with people like **Franciszek Mazur**, Wiktor Kłosiewicz, and Kazimierz Mijal. This group enjoyed the support of Marshal **Konstantin Rokossovsky** and propagated anti-intellectual and anti-Semitic slogans. After October 1956 Kruczek remained a dogmatist. For example, at the beginning of the 1960s he attacked the editorial staff of the periodical *Polityka*, specifically **Mieczysław F. Rakowski** personally for "revisionist" leanings. From 1956 to 1971 Kruczek was first secretary of the PUWP Provincial Committee in Rzeszów, and from 1968 to 1980, a member of the PUWP CC Politburo. As a result of his efforts, the position of the city of Rzeszów in the region improved through investments, the establishment of local offices of government agencies, and the opening of a higher pedagogical school. This came about at the expense of other cities, particularly Przemyśl.

Kruczek supported the removal of **Władysław Gomułka** from power in December 1970. After Gomułka's overthrow, Kruczek became head of a commission appointed at the Ninth Plenum of the PUWP CC to investigate the December 1970 Baltic Coast events. This commission failed to arrive at any conclusion. Its final report, presented at the Sixth PUWP Congress on 6–11 December 1971, put the blame for the December 1970 events on the leaders who had been removed from power. From 1971 to 1980 Kruczek served as president of the Central Council of Trade Unions; therefore, the strikes in the summer of 1980 strongly undermined his position in the apparatus of power. At a session of the Politburo on 28 August 1980 Kruczek went so far as to demand that a state of emergency be declared. At the Seventh CC Plenum on 1–2 December 1980 he was dismissed from his position. From 1961 to 1985 Kruczek was an MP; from 1972 to 1982 he was a member of the Council of State, and from March 1972 to 1980 he was vice-president of the Council of State. (PK)

Sources: Mołdawa; Michał Czajka and Marcin Kamler, *Leksykon Historii Polski* (Warsaw, 1995); P. Pasławska and Z. Przywara, *Władysław Kruczek: 60 lecie urodzin 27 kwietnia 1910–27 kwi-*

etnia 1970. Bibliografia prac wydanych drukiem oraz artykułów zawartych w czasopismach (przemówienia, wywiady, artykuły) w latach 1956–1969 (Rzeszów, 1970).

KRUJA Mustafa Merlika (15 March 1887, Kruja–27 December 1958, Niagara Falls), Albanian politician, linguist, and writer. After finishing school in his native Kruja, Kruja continued his education in Ioánnina. He later studied at the university in Istanbul, where, under the pseudonym "Asim Dzhenan," he wrote articles for liberal Turkish newspapers. Expelled from the university for taking part in student protests in Istanbul in 1909, Kruja continued his education thanks to the intercession of the Albanian deputies to the Turkish parliament. After completing his studies in administration and political science (1910), Kruja worked as a mathematics teacher at a high school in Durrës. In the spring of 1912 he joined an uprising in the north of the country. He attended the Albanian assembly in Vlorë that ended with a declaration of independence (28 November 1912). In 1915, on the orders of **Essad Pasha Toptani**, Kruja was arrested and placed in a prison in Bari. He was later interned in Sicily. Released in 1917, he went to Rome, where he became editor-in-chief of *Kuvendi*, a political and literary periodical. In December 1918 he returned to Albania. He became minister of post and telegraphs in the government established under Italian auspices in Durrës. He was the secretary of the Albanian delegation to the Paris Peace Conference in 1919. Elected to parliament from the Kosovo district in 1921, Kruja became aligned with the Progressive Party (Partia Perparimtare). He also belonged to the Kosovo Defense Committee and cooperated with the units led by **Bajram Curri**. During the revolution of 1924 he served as secretary general in the Ministry of Interior. In practice, he was in control of Central Albania.

After the collapse of the revolution, along with a group of the closest associates of **Fan Noli**, Kruja fled, via Vlorë, to Brindisi. He later lived for a few years in Zadar, where he worked with the National Union (Bashkimi Kombëtar). Before the Italian invasion of Albania, Kruja was one of the best-known activists of the anti-Zog émigré community in Italy. After the invasion, he returned to his country in April 1939 and served as cultural adviser to the Italian authorities. In April 1940 he became director of the Institute of Albanian Studies in Tirana. He succeeded Shefqet Vërlaci as prime minister in the collaborationist government and held his post from 4 December 1941 to 9 January 1943. He also assumed the ministry of interior in this government. During his term in office, the Italians made some concessions, increasing Albanian autonomy. After resigning from his post, Kruja became politically close to the pro-Western **Abas Kupi** and to the monarchist movement known as Legaliteti (Legal-

ity). Kruja was particularly hated by the Communists, who regarded him as a symbol of collaboration with the Italian occupiers. On 12 October 1943, in the center of Tirana, an attempt was made on his life, as a result of which he was lightly wounded. Captured by the Communist partisans, he was released under British pressure and went to Rome. From there he made his way to Egypt, where he met King **Zog I**. Subsequently, via France, he went to the United States, where he lived until the end of his life. His signature on the Declaration of Independence of 1912 was covered up in publications from the Communist period. Kruja was the author of numerous historical publications and an Albanian dictionary. (TC)

Sources: *Fjalori Enciklopedik Shqiptar* (Tirana, 1985); *Biographisches Lexikon*, vol. 2; John Swire, *Albania: The Rise of a Kingdom* (London, 1929); Ernest Koliqi, "Shtatëdhetëvjetori i lindjes së Mustafa Kruja," in *Shêjzat—Le Pleiadi*, 1957; Francesco Jacomini di San Savino, *La politica dell'Italia in Albania* (Bologna, 1965); Sejfi Vllamasi, *Ballafaqime politike në Shqipëri (1897–1942)* (Tirana, 1995); Mustafa Kruja, *Anthologji historike: Shkrime e përkthime* (Elbasan, 2001).

KRUMINŠ Janis, pseudonym "Pilate" (25 September 1894, Skriveri Volost, near Riga–15 March 1938, Moscow), Latvian Communist activist. Born into a peasant family, Kruminš joined the Latvian Social Democratic Party in 1912, gradually drifting toward the Bolsheviks. In March 1917 he began spreading Leninist slogans in Livonia. In June 1917 he became deputy chairman of the Executive Committee of the Latvian Soviet of Delegates. At the beginning of 1918, during the German occupation of Latvia, Kruminš worked in the Communist underground in Livonia. In 1919, he worked in Courland, by then under Latvian rule. At the beginning of 1919 he helped to found the Communist Party of Latvia (CPL), which chose to function within the Comintern. He also joined the Central Committee (CC) of the CPL, and in March 1919 he represented this party at the congress of the Russian Communist Party (Bolsheviks). After the CPL was declared illegal in 1929, Kruminš went to the Soviet Union, where he settled permanently. In 1931 he became head of the foreign bureau of the party, which he represented on the Executive Committee of the Communist International. In 1935 he spoke at the Seventh Congress of the Comintern. Accused of "Latvian nationalism," Kruminš was arrested by the NKVD in 1938 and was murdered. He was rehabilitated by the authorities of the Soviet Union in 1956. (WR)

Sources: Lazitch; *MERSH*, vol. 18; *Who Was Who in the USSR* (Metuchen, N.J., 1972); Andrew Ezergailis, *The 1917 Revolution in Latvia* (New York, 1974); *Latvijas Kominististkas Partijas kongresu, konferencu un CK plenumu resolucijas un lemumi, 1904–1940* (Riga, 1958).

KRUPAVIČIUS Mykolas (1 October 1885, Balbieriškis, near Mariampole–4 December 1970, Chicago, Illinois), Roman Catholic priest, politician, leader of the Lithuanian Christian Democratic Party. In 1913 Krupavičius completed a seminary in Sejny. Ordained a priest in June 1914, during World War I he graduated from the Theological Academy in Petrograd. In 1917 he worked as a chaplain in a Lithuanian gymnasium in Voronezh, where he was sentenced to death in absentia by the Bolsheviks. Krupavičius left for Lithuania, where he co-organized the Christian Democratic Party. From 1918 he worked in the Ministry of Interior and later in the Ministry of Agriculture of Lithuania, where he prepared a draft agrarian reform aiming at the expropriation of the large Polish landowners. From 1920 to 1926 Krupavičius was a Christian Democratic MP to parliament. At that time he was a member of the chief leadership of the Christian Democratic movement, which headed not only the party itself, but also its appendages—the Peasant Union in the countryside and a workers' labor federation. In 1923–26, as minister of agriculture, Krupavičius supervised the implementation of an agrarian reform that had been passed by the parliament in 1922. After the nationalist coup of December 1926 he left for France, where he studied sociology, economics, and law. In the 1930s he lectured at a seminary in Vilkaviškis.

In 1940 Krupavičius escaped being arrested by the NKVD, and in June 1941, along with **Kazys Grinius** and other Lithuanian politicians, he submitted a memorandum to the Germans warning against actions that the Lithuanians would not accept—for example, the extermination of Jews. It is all the more noteworthy that Krupavičius was known for anti-Semitism and a dislike of Poles. As the Soviet offensive arrived in 1944, Krupavičius emigrated to Germany, and the end of the war found him there. In 1945 he was elected president of the Supreme Committee for the Liberation of Lithuania (Vyriausias Lietuvos Islaisvinimo Komitetas [VLIK]) in exile. From 1948 he was a domestic prelate of Pope Pius XII. After his resignation as head of the VLIK in 1957, Krupavičius left for the United States, where he died. He was one of the main theoreticians of Lithuanian social Catholicism, especially sensitive about the peasantry. He published (among other works) *Zemes klausimas Lietuvoje* (The agrarian question in Lithuania; 1919), *Krikščioniskoji demokratija* (Christian Democracy; 1948), and his memoirs, which end in 1926 (1972). (WR)

Sources: *EL*, vol.3; Saulius Sužiedelis, *Historical Dictionary of Lithuania* (Lanham, Md., 1997); Petras Maldeikis, *Mykolas Krupavicius* (Chicago, 1975); *Valstybininkas politikos sukuriuose: Prelatas Mykolas Krupavicius 1885–1970. Biografine apybraiza:* *Amzininku atsiminimai, dokumentai, laiskai* (Chicago, 1980); Alfonsas Eidintas and Vytautas Žalys, *Lithuania in European Politics: The Years of the First Republic, 1918–1940* (New York, 1997).

KRUSHELNYTSKYI Anton (4 August 1878, Łańcut–13 November 1941, Soviet Union), Ukrainian writer, journalist, and politician. While a student, Krushelnytskyi was associated with the monthly *Moloda Ukraïna*, and with **Ivan Franko** he edited *Literaturo-naukovyĭ vistnyk*. He subsequently worked as a high school teacher and was active in the Ukrainian Radical Party. From April to August 1919 he served as minister of education in the Borys Martos government of the Ukrainian National Republic. After the war he worked in the Viennese publishing house Chaika, which specialized in textbooks and translations of classical literature. After returning to Galicia in 1925, Krushelnytskyi could not find a job as a teacher. From 1929 to 1933 in Poland, he edited pro-Soviet periodicals, *Novi Shliakhy* and *Krytyka*. Arrested by the authorities on many occasions, in 1934, along with his family, he went to the Ukrainian SSR. However, the family was arrested on charges of taking part in a "White Guard" organization. Along with his wife, Krushelnytskyi was sent to a labor camp, while their two sons, Ivan and Taras, were executed by firing squad. In his writing Krushelnytskyi was influenced by the traditions of West European modernism. His literary output includes the collections of stories *Proletari* (Proletarians; 1899) and *Svitla i tini* (Lights and shadows; 1900); the dramas *Artistka* (An artist; 1901) and *Cholovik chesti* (A man of honor; 1904); the comedy *Orly* (Eagles; 1906); and the novels *Rubaiut' lis* (The forest is being felled; 1919), *Iak promovyt zemlia* (When the earth speaks; 1920), *Iak pryhorne zemlia* (When the earth takes one in; 1920), and *Budenny Khlib* (Daily bread; 1920). Krushelnytskyi was also the author of literary essays, critical pieces, and translations. (WR)

Sources: *Ukraine: A Concise Encyclopedia*, vols. 1–2 (Toronto, 1963–71); *Encyclopedia of Ukraine*, vol. 2 (Toronto, 1988); Hryhory Kostiuk, *Stalinist Rule in the Ukraine* (New York, 1960).

KRUUS Hans (10 October 1891, Tartu–30 June 1976, Tallinn), Estonian historian and Communist activist. Born into a working-class family, early on Kruus became allied with the radical movement. In 1917 he helped to found the Estonian Party of Socialist Revolutionaries, and for some time he served as chairman of the party. After Estonia gained independence, he became a member of the Constitutional Assembly (1919) and then a member of the first parliament (Riigikogu). From 1920 to 1921 he was one of the senior leaders of the crypto-Communist Estonian Independent Socialist Workers' Party. In 1922 he graduated from Tartu University and began a brilliant academic career. The work *Eesti: Maa, Rahva, Kultur* (Estonia: Territory, people, culture), published in 1926, was one of the major achievements of Estonian interwar historiography. In 1927 Kruus received a Ph.D. Until the end of the 1930s he lectured in history at Tartu University and served as its deputy rector from 1934 to 1937. He was also the editor-in-chief of *Ajaloolise Ajakirja*, the main Estonian historical periodical. Under his editorship the first three volumes of a collective history of Estonia were published in 1935–40, and the publication of an Estonian biographical dictionary was launched. Kruus was also a member of the editorial staff of the first Estonian encyclopedia and a member of many scholarly organizations.

After the Soviet invasion in June 1940, Kruus became deputy prime minister of the so-called people's government of **Johannes Vares**, in which he was the only prominent representative of the prewar Estonian elite. In the same year he joined the Communist Party and was elected to the Supreme Soviet of the Estonian SSR. Along with **Nigol Andresen**, he supervised the transformation of the Ministry of Foreign Affairs (MFA) of Estonia into the People's Commissariat of Foreign Affairs of the Estonian SSR, and he accepted the purge of the ministry of which he was in charge. In June 1941 Kruus also became the rector of Tartu University. He was responsible for personnel purges, the closing of one of the most prestigious schools of Protestant theology in Europe, and the introduction of Marxist-Leninist indoctrination. He dissolved student organizations and decided that admittance to the university would be conditional on a "proper" social background and that tuition fees would be obligatory only for those students whose parents' income "was not a result of their own work." He even agreed to the loss of degree-granting rights by the university.

In June 1941 Kruus fled to the Soviet Union. He returned to Estonia in 1944 and was charged with reestablishing the People's Commissariat of Foreign Affairs of the Estonian SSR. In 1946 the People's Commissariat of Foreign Affairs was transformed into the MFA of the Estonian SSR. At the same time Kruus headed the Academy of Sciences of the Estonian SSR until 1950 and sat in the Supreme Soviet of the Estonian SSR from 1940 to 1950. To some extent he believed that the existence of the MFA of the Estonian SSR could play a constructive role in preserving the symbols of Estonian sovereignty. He put a great emphasis on educating a diplomatic staff, and he preferred to employ Estonians who often spoke little Russian or none at all. The price was that the MFA of the Estonian SSR played the role of a propaganda mouthpiece among the Estonian émigré community. The very existence of the MFA gave credibility to the 1940 annexation and to Soviet propaganda claims about the alleged freedom of the Estonian SSR as a sovereign member of the Soviet Union, when the truth was that the top positions in the MFA were occupied by Moscow's agents or even by NKVD functionaries and that the activities of the MFA were closely subordinated to the Kremlin's directives. Dismissed from his position at the party CC plenum in March 1950, Kruus was accused of "bourgeois nationalism." The publication of all his works was banned until 1955, when he was reinstated as senior lecturer at Tartu University. In 1958 Kruus became president of the Commission for Research on the Homeland of the Academy of Sciences of the Estonian SSR. (AG)

Sources: *Eesti Nokogrida Entsuklopeedia*, vol. 5 (Tallinn, 1990); *Eesti Entsuklopeedia*, vol. 14 (Tallinn, 2000); Evald Uustalu, *The History of the Estonian People* (London, 1952); Eero Medijainen, "Foreign Ministry of the Estonian SSR"; Väino Sirk, "The Soviet Educational System in Estonia 1940–1991"; Piret Lotman, "Censorship during the Occupation of Estonia," all in Strona Muzeum Okupacji, www.okupatsioon.ee/english/overviews/index.html.

KRYMSKYI Ahatanhel (15 January 1871, Volodymyr Volynsky–25 January 1942, Kustanay, Kazakhstan), Ukrainian writer, translator, and literary scholar. Krymskyi attended high school in Ostroh and Kiev. In 1885 he entered the Pavlo Galagan College in Kiev and later studied at the Lazarev Institute of Oriental Languages and at the university in Moscow. In 1898 he became an associate professor (*docent*). From 1900 to 1918 Krymskyi worked as a professor of Arabic literature and Oriental history at the Lazarev Institute. In 1896–98 he was in Syria and Lebanon. In 1918 he became a professor at Kiev University. In the autumn of 1918 he helped to found the All-Ukrainian Academy of Sciences (Ukraiinska Akademiya Nauk [UAN]) and served as the first UAN permanent secretary. Krymskyi greatly contributed to the development of the UAN, particularly its historical and philological department, which he directed until 1929, when he was forced to resign his post. In 1921–29 he was in charge of the Institute of Oriental Studies (Instytut Skhodoznavstva) in Kiev. In May 1928 the authorities did not approve his reelection to the post of permanent secretary of the UAN and soon abolished all the institutions that he directed. In 1930 Krymskyi was removed from scholarly and pedagogical work. Arrested in July 1941 by the NKVD, he was accused of nationalist anti-Soviet activities and imprisoned. The circumstances of his death are unclear.

Krymskyi wrote many scholarly works on the history

and culture of Arab countries, Iran, and Turkey, including *Istoriia musulmanstva* (The history of Islam, 3 vols.; 1904–12); *Istoriia Arabiv i arabskoy literatury svitskoyi i dukhovnoy* (The history of the Arabs and Arabic secular and religious literature; 1911–12); *Istoriia Persi ta yi pismenstva* (The history of Persia and its literature; 1923); and *Istoriia Turechchyny ta yi pismenstva* (The history of Turkey and its literature; 1924–27). Krymskyi's interests also included the history of the Ukrainian language and literature, and his most important works in this field include *Ukrainskaia gramatika* (Ukrainian grammar; 1907) and *Narysy z istorii ukraiiskoy movy* (An outline of the history of the Ukrainian language; 1922 [co-authored by Oleksiy Shakhmatov]). Krymskyi's most important literary works include three volumes of lyrical poetry, *Palmove hillia* (Palm branches; 1901, 1908, and 1922); the collection *Povistky i eskizy z ukraiinskoho zhyttia* (Narratives and sketches from Ukrainian life; 1895); *Beyrutski opovidannia* (Beirut stories; 1906); and the novel *Andriy Lahovskyi* (1905; full edition, 1972). Krymskyi translated many Turkish and Persian literary works as well as literary classics into Ukrainian. (BB)

Sources: *Encyclopedia of Ukraine*, vol. 2 (Toronto, 1988); *Dovidnyk z istorii Ukraïny* (Kiev, 2001); Oleh Babyshkin, *Ahatanhel Krymskyi* (Kiev, 1967); Kazimir I. Gurnitskyi, *Agatangel Efimovich Krymskyi* (Moscow, 1980); Solomiia D. Pavlychko, *Natsionalizm, seksualnist, oriientalizm. Skladnyi svit Ahatanhela Krymskoho* (Kiev, 2000).

KRYPYAKEVYCH Ivan (25 June 1886, Lemberg [Lwów, Lviv]–21 April 1967, Lviv, Ukraine), Ukrainian historian. In 1904 Krypyakevych graduated from high school in Lemberg, and in 1909 he completed studies at Lemberg University. In 1907 he was detained for taking part in the struggle for the Ukrainization of this university. Until 1914 Krypyakevych was influenced by **Mykhailo Hrushevskyi**. Under Hrushevskyi's guidance, in 1911 he earned a Ph.D. for a thesis about the Cossacks during Stefan Batory's times; Hrushevskyi also shaped Krypyakevych's research interests, which included the history of the Cossacks and the history of Lviv and the Halych District from the thirteenth to the seventeenth centuries. Later their paths parted, as Hrushevskyi remained involved in Narodnyk (national) historiography while Krypyakevych became closer to the so-called statehood approach to Ukrainian history. Because of his negative assessment of the historical role of Poland in the Ukraine, Krypyakevych could not hope to get a position at the University of Lwów, dominated by the Poles. From 1911 to 1939 he worked in Ukrainian and Polish high schools in Rohatyn, Lwów, and Żółkiew (now Zhovkva). He was involved in the work of the underground Ukrainian university in Lwów (1921–24) and lectured at the Greek Catholic Theological Academy (1934–39). His research work was mostly carried out within the framework of the Shevchenko Scientific Society (NTSh). In 1911 he became a full member of the NTSh and later also the president of its historical and philosophical commission. In 1934 he began editing *Zapysky Naukovoho Tovarystva im. Shevchenka* (ZNTSh).

Between 1925 and 1931 Krypyakevych wrote his pioneering work, *Studiï nad derzhavoiu Bohdana Khmelnytskoho* (Studies on the rule of Bohdan Khmelnytskyi,). *Ukraiinska istoriohrafiia* (Ukrainian historiography), written in 1923, was another of his important works. Krypyakevych maintained relations with scholars from the Ukrainian SSR, and in 1929 he visited Kiev and Kharkiv. In 1931 these contacts were severed by the Soviets, and he was attacked as a "Fascist." In the 1930s, in collaboration with other historians, Krypyakevych wrote the syntheses *Velyka istoriia Ukraiiny* (Great history of Ukraine; 1935); *Istoriia ukraiinskoho viyska* (The history of the Ukrainian Army; 1936); *Istoriia ukraiinskoy kultury* (The history of Ukrainian culture; 1937); and *Vsesvitnia istoriia* (General history; 1938–39). He also worked on his own synthesis, *Istoriia Ukraiiny* (History of Ukraine), but it was not published until 1949 in Munich, with Krypyakevych using the pseudonym of Ivan Kholmskyi.

As part of the Kremlin's pro-Ukrainian tactics after the annexation of Eastern Galicia in October 1939, Krypyakevych was appointed professor and took up the chair of Ukrainian history at Lviv University. In 1940 he became the director of the Lviv branch of the Historical Institute of the Academy of Sciences of the Ukrainian SSR. At that time the Soviet authorities abolished the NTSh. Krypyakevych continued his scholarly work during the German occupation of Lviv. When the Soviet authorities returned in 1944, he again assumed his former posts, but from 1946 to 1948 he worked at the central branch of the institute in Kiev since its Lviv branch had been closed. In 1948 he returned to Lviv and worked in an ethnographic museum. In 1953 he became the director of the Institute of Social Sciences of the Academy of Sciences of the Ukrainian SSR. In the postwar years he wrote the monograph *Bohdan Khmelnytskyi* (1954); the collection of source documents *Dokumenty Bohdana Khmelnytskoho (1648–1657)* (Documents of Bohdan Khmelnytskyi [1648–1657]; 1961); and *Halytsko-Volynske kniazivstvo* (The Halych-Volhynia Duchy; 1984). In 1958 Krypyakevych was elected a full member of the Academy of Sciences of the Ukrainian SSR. All together, he published over five hundred historical works. (TS)

Sources: *Encyclopedia of Ukraine*, vol. 2 (Toronto, 1988); D. Doroshenko and O. Ohlobyn, "A Survey of Ukrainian Historiography," *Annals of the Ukrainian Academy of Arts and Sciences in the US*, vols. 5–6 (New York, 1957); I. Dashkevych, "Ivan Krypyakevych: Istoryk Ukraiiny," in I. Krypyakevych, *Istoriia Ukraiiny* (Lviv, 1990).

KRZAKLEWSKI Marian (23 August 1950, Kolbuszowa), Polish trade union activist and politician. Krzaklewski graduated from the Department of Automatics of the Silesian Polytechnic in Gliwice. In 1976–84 he worked at the Department of Complex Automatic Systems of the Polish Academy of Sciences (PAS) in Gliwice. From 1985 he worked at the Katowice branch of the Silesian Polytechnic. In 1986 he received a Ph.D. in computerizing industrial processes. From August 1980 he belonged to Solidarity, and from September 1980 he was deputy chairman of the PAS Upper Silesian Coordination Commission of Solidarity. From the beginning of martial law in December 1981, Krzaklewski worked in the secret PAS commission and with the regional underground structures of the union. He also edited its publications. In 1985 he was arrested and sentenced for trade union activity. Amnestied in 1986, he was forced to leave the PAS. From 1986 he belonged to the Silesian underground structure of Solidarity and was responsible for the printing and distribution of publications. From 1989 he belonged to the National Executive Commission of Solidarity and to the Civic Committee of the Chairman of Solidarity. He was secretary of the Silesian Regional Civic Committee; when **Lech Wałęsa** was elected president, in February 1991 Krzaklewski was elected chairman of Solidarity. From 1991 he was a member of the board of the International Confederation of Free Trade Unions. In 1996 he co-organized Solidarity Electoral Action (Akcja Wyborcza Solidarność [AWS]), which united small and fragmented centrist and right-wing parties and won the parliamentary elections in September 1997. An MP on behalf of the AWS and chairman of its parliamentary club, Krzaklewski substantially influenced the policies of the government of **Jerzy Buzek**. In 1997–2001 he belonged to the Polish delegation to the Parliamentary Assembly of the Council of Europe and was deputy chairman of the Group of the European People's Party. An AWS candidate in the presidential elections of October 2000, Krzaklewski won 15.6 percent of the vote, coming in third. In 2001 he co-initiated the AWS–Solidarity of the Right, which lost the parliamentary elections of September 2001, failing to reach the required 5 percent threshold. In September 2002 Krzaklewski lost in the elections for Solidarity chairman, but he remained in the union's leadership. (IS)

Sources: Janusz A. Majcherek, *Pierwsza dekada III Rzeczypospolitej* (Warsaw, 1999); Antoni Dudek, *Pierwsze lata III Rzeczyspospolitej 1989–2001* (Kraków, 2002); Wojciech Roszkowski, *Historia Polski 1914–2001* (Warsaw, 2002).

KRZYŻANOWSKI Adam (19 January 1873, Kraków–29 January 1963, Kraków), Polish economist and politician. Krzyżanowski was the son of a bookseller from a landed gentry family. After graduating from high school in Kraków, he studied law and administration at the Jagiellonian University (Uniwersytet Jagielloński [UJ]), earning a doctorate in 1894. The following year he studied in Berlin and Leipzig, attending lectures by such scholars as Gustav Schmoller. In 1895 he published his first treatise on the social and economic aspects of the parceling out of land. From 1896 to 1904 Krzyżanowski worked in the Kraków Agricultural Society, publishing a number of works on economic and agricultural issues, including *Projekt reformy agrarnej* (Agrarian reform proposal; 1897), *Studia agrarne* (Agrarian studies; 1900), and *Rolnictwo wobec polityki handlowej* (Agriculture and trade policy; 1901). Krzyżanowski was influenced by the German Historical School and "Academic Socialism" (*Kathedersozialismus*), although he was also a member of the Conservative Club. In 1908 he received his postdoctoral degree, and in 1911 he published the theoretical work *Pieniądz* (Money). In 1916 he became a professor of state finance at the UJ. During World War I, Krzyżanowski changed his interests and views, drifting toward the neo-liberal school in *Socjalizm a prawo natury* (Socialism and natural law; 1911), *Gospodarka wojenna* (War economy; 1919), and *Założenia ekonomiki* (Principles of economics; 1919).

During the first years of independence, Krzyżanowski published a great deal on inflation, taking a stance as its opponent and as an advocate of reductions in budget expenditures. His works *Bolszewizm* (Bolshevism; 1920); *Socjalizm po wojnie* (Socialism after the war; 1920); *Waluta i kredyt* (Currency and credit; 1921); and *Walka z drożyzną* (Struggle against high prices; 1922) consolidated his position as a prominent Polish economist and leader of the so-called liberal Kraków school. He criticized the treasury and currency reform implemented by **Władysław Grabski**, as he believed that it would fail without foreign assistance. Krzyżanowski did not change his stance after the initial success of this reform and considered the so-called second inflation in 1925 a confirmation of his opinion. He believed that the weakness of the Polish economy was a result of the lack of capital. Hoping the coup of May 1926 would bring about political stabilization, Krzyżanowski assumed the post of head of the Polish bureau of the Edwin Kemmerer mission. He negotiated the terms of the American loan, which was finalized in the autumn of 1927. In 1928 he was elected an MP representing the Nonparty Bloc of Cooperation with the Government (Bezpartyjny Blok Współpracy z Rządem [BBWR]), a political organization that supported the *sanacja* regime, and he was in charge of the Treasury Committee of the Assembly. Krzyżanowski was one of the few economists who foresaw the great economic crisis. In 1930, despite his critical attitude toward the BBWR, he again represented the BBWR in the 1930 parliamentary elections, in which he won a seat. However, he refused to support the position of the BBWR parliamentary representation in a vote on the detention of opposition leaders, and in February 1931 he resigned his seat. In 1932 he sent a memorandum to the authorities in which he urged that the deflation policy be abandoned, and in 1937 he even called for the introduction of controlled inflation to stimulate economic development. However, he was an avowed opponent of economic statism. In politics, Krzyżanowski drifted toward the Union of Conservative Political Organizations. He again became involved in social issues, publishing *Demograficzne oblicze kryzysu* (Demographic aspects of the crisis; 1932); *Moralność współczesna* (Contemporary morality; 1935); and *Dolar i złoty* (The dollar and the złoty; 1936). From 1933–34 to 1937–38 Krzyżanowski was deputy rector of the UJ. As a scholarly authority, he opposed the anti-Semitic excesses of some universities.

Arrested along with other UJ professors by the Nazis on 6 November 1939, after the German invasion of Poland, Krzyżanowski was sent to the Sachsenhausen concentration camp. Released in February 1940, he was involved in underground academic teaching in Kraków. Invited by the Yalta Good Offices Commission, he took part in Moscow negotiations that led to the establishment of the Communist-dominated Provisional Government of National Unity in June 1945. He was also co-opted to the National Home Council (Krajowa Rada Narodowa [KRN]). In the rigged elections of January 1947 Krzyżanowski obtained a seat from the slate of the Democratic Party (Stronnictwo Demokratyczne [SD]). He also served as chairman of the SD Provincial Committee in Kraków. After the Stalinization of the universities, Krzyżanowski was retired, despite objections of the UJ Senate in December 1948. On 12 July 1949 he resigned his parliamentary seat and his party position. At that time he published *Wiek XX: Zarys dziejów najnowszych* (The Twentieth Century: An outline of recent history; 1947) and *Chrześcijańska moralność polityczna* (Christian political morality; 1948). Banned from publishing his works after 1949, Krzyżanowski worked on his memoirs, a history of nineteenth- and twentieth-century Poland, a history of Russia, and "Nauka o ludności" (Population studies), which remained in manuscript form. After October 1956 he resumed lecturing at the UJ. He was also elected president of the Polish Academy of Arts and Sciences (Polska Akademia Umiejętności), which was revived for a short time. Active in the Club of Catholic Intellectuals in Kraków, in 1958 Krzyżanowski was awarded an honorary doctorate by the UJ. (WR)

Sources: *PSB*, vol. 15; *Encyklopedia historii gospodarczej Polski do 1945 roku*, vol. 1 (Warsaw, 1981); *Encyklopedia historii Drugiej Rzeczypospolitej* (Warsaw, 1999); Ferdynand Zweig, *Adam Krzyżanowski* (Kraków, 1937).

KRZYŻANOWSKI Aleksander, pseudonym "Wilk" (18 February 1885, Bryansk–29 September 1951, Warsaw), colonel of the Polish Home Army. During World War I Krzyżanowski served in the Russian Army and in the First Polish Corps of General **Józef Dowbór-Muśnicki**. In 1919–20 he took part in the Polish-Soviet war. Decorated with the Cross of the Brave for his action at Lida, after the war he remained in the army. During the coup of May 1926 he sided with the government; therefore after the victory of **Józef Piłsudski**, he considered retirement from the service. Krzyżanowski remained and commanded different units of artillery in Bydgoszcz, Prużany, and Tarnopol. In 1934 he was promoted to major. In the September campaign of 1939 he commanded Poznań, an artillery unit in the twenty-sixth army regiment. In October 1939 he was sent from Warsaw to Wilno (Vilnius) with a mission to organize and subordinate the local conspiracy against the command of the Polish Victory Service (Służba Zwycięstwu Polski [SZP]). Krzyżanowski assumed the post of chief of staff and deputy district commander of the SZP in Wilno. When in June 1940 the Red Army entered the city, he escaped arrest.

After the imprisonment of his superior, Colonel Nikodem Sulik, in May 1941, Krzyżanowski assumed the command of the Wilno District of the Union of Armed Struggle (Związek Walki Zbrojnej [ZWZ]). After the German invasion of the USSR he considerably developed the military conspiracy in the Wilno region. He also tried, in vain, to come to terms with representatives of the local Lithuanians and Belorussians. From mid-1943 the Home Army (Armia Krajowa [AK]) in the Wilno region steadily moved from organizational and diversionary activities toward armed struggle. This was also dictated by the increasing activity of the Soviet guerrillas, who acted against the AK. In January 1944 Krzyżanowski negotiated an agreement with the commander of the Soviet guerrilla group in the Wilno area, but already in February 1944 the agreement was broken by a guerrilla attack on the fifth brigade of the AK. In the face of the approaching Soviet offensive, Krzyżanowski held talks with representatives of German intelligence, aiming at an exchange of captives and at gaining reconnaissance about German positions. However, no agreements were reached. During Operation Burza (Tempest) Krzyżanowski commanded the units of the Home Army of the Wilno District. In July 1944 he agreed with the commander of the Third Belorussian Front on cooperation in the Wilno operation. The operation was successful. After capturing Wilno, the commander of the front invited Krzyżanowski and his chief of staff to negotiate. They both were arrested, like most officers of the district who were gathered in Bogusze. On 28 September 1944, while in prison, Krzyżanowski was promoted to the rank of colonel by the Polish commander-in-chief and was decorated with the Order of Virtuti Militari by the chief commander of the AK. Krzyżanowski was transported from Wilno to Butyrki Prison and in October 1946 to the camp in Diagilevo. On 17 August 1947 he escaped from there but was arrested in Wilno. After a short inquiry in Moscow, in November 1947 he was evacuated to Poland, and he arrived in Gdańsk.

Krzyżanowski then assumed the post of director of a scutching plant in Pakość, near Mogilno. On 3 July 1948 he was arrested there by the Communist security police and transported to the prison on Rakowiecka Street in Warsaw. He was falsely charged with collaboration with the Germans, the liquidation of Communist activists, and the continuation of postwar underground activities. After three years of investigation, in which he did not plead guilty, Krzyżanowski died in prison as a result of tuberculosis and exhaustion. (WR)

Sources: *PSB*, vol. 15; Krzysztof Tarka, "Pułkownik Aleksander Krzyżanowski 'Wilk'—Komendant Okręgu Wileńskiego Związku Walki Zbrojnej—Armii Krajowej," *Zeszyty Naukowe Uniwersytetu Opolskiego*, 1996.

KUBILIŪNAS Petras (16 May 1894, Rokiškis–22 August 1946, Moscow), Lithuanian officer and politician. After graduating from the Military Academy in Vilnius (1914), Kubiliūnas served in the Russian Army during World War I. In 1919 he returned to Lithuania, where he joined the army and took part in military operations on the front lines. From 1925 to 1927 he studied in the Military Academy in Prague, and in 1929 he was appointed chief of the general staff with the rank of colonel in the Lithuanian Army. In 1934 Kubiliūnas joined the supporters of **Augustinas Voldemaras**. After the failure of an attempted coup d'état by Voldemaras in May of that year, Kubiliūnas was arrested and sentenced to death. President **Antanas Smetona** exercised his power of pardon, and the sentence was commuted to life imprisonment, and then it was quashed in 1936. Arrested after the Soviet invasion of Lithuania in June 1940, Kubiliūnas avoided deportation and was released when the Germans seized Lithuania in June 1941. In August 1941 he was appointed first general counselor to the Nazi commissioner-general of Lithuania, Theodor von Renteln. The highest-ranking Lithuanian collaborator with the German authorities-in-occupation, Kubiliūnas was widely criticized by pro-independence Lithuanians for his unconditional submissiveness to the occupiers, especially after he applied for German citizenship in 1943.

He called on the Lithuanians to join the Reichsarbeitsdienst and auxiliary Lithuanian units that fought on the side of the German Army against the Soviets. Because the Lithuanians generally remembered the Soviet occupation as worse than the Nazi occupation, toward the end of the war Kubiliūnas's urgings achieved considerable results. In the summer of 1944 Kubiliūnas withdrew along with the German Army, and after the end of the war he settled in the British zone of occupation in Germany. Abducted by the Soviet services in December 1945, Kubiliūnas was taken to Moscow, where, after long interrogations and tortures, he was sentenced to death and executed. (WR)

Sources: *EL*, vol. 3; Saulius Sužiedelis, *Historical Dictionary of Lithuania* (Lanham, Md., 1997).

KUBILIUS Andrius (8 December 1956, Vilnius), Lithuanian politician. In 1979 Kubilius graduated in physics from Vilnius University, and in 1979–90 he worked there as an assistant professor. In 1988 he joined the Lithuanian Movement for Perestroika (Sąjūdis). He became known as an efficient organizer, good in human relations, so he was elected executive secretary of the Sąjūdis. After Lithuania regained independence in 1991, in 1992 Kubilius was elected to the parliament. After Sąjūdis, a party emerged called the Homeland Union–Lithuanian Conservatives (Tėvynės Sąjunga–Lietuvos Konservatoriai); for a short time Kubilius headed its parliamentary club. After the electoral victory of this party in October and November 1996, he became speaker of the parliament and head of its European commission. From 3 November 1999 to 26 October 2000 Kubilius was prime minister. He resigned after his party lost the elections of October 2000, but he won a seat and stayed an MP. (WR)

Sources: Richard J. Krickus, *Showdown: The Lithuanian Rebellion and the Breakup of the Soviet Empire* (Washington, D.C., 1997); www.rulers.org; www.lrs.lt; www.tlst.lt.

KUBINA Teodor Filip (16 April 1890, Świętochłowice–13 February 1951, Częstochowa), Polish bishop. The son of a miner, Kubina graduated from high school in Königshütte (Królewska Huta). From 1901 he studied at the Theological Department of Breslau (Wrocław) University and at the Collegium Germano-Hungaricum in Rome, where he received a Ph.D. in philosophy in 1904. Later he defended another Ph.D. dissertation in theology at the Gregorianum University in Rome. Contacts with Polish Jesuits strengthened his Polish consciousness and encouraged him to improve his Polish. Ordained in Rome in October 1906, after returning home Kubina worked as a vicar in Königshütte and was active in Polish social organizations. As a result, in 1911 his was transferred to Berlin, where he was a minister to Polish workers. In September 1917, he was the first Poleto become parish priest of the Holy Virgin Mary parish in Kattowitz (Katowice). After World War I Kubina actively supported the incorporation of Upper Silesia into Poland (for instance, as head of the Silesian Academic Union). At the end of 1920 he took part in a delegation of the Polish Plebiscite Commissariat to Rome, aimed at convincing the Holy See that Polish priests should participate in the plebiscite campaign. For his nationalist activities Kubina became the target of German fighting squadrons. After the plebiscite and division of Upper Silesia, Kubina joined the Supreme National Council in the Polish part of the region, and in 1923 he became the first editor-in-chief of the weekly *Gość Niedzielny*. After the creation of the Częstochowa diocese, on 14 December 1925 he was appointed its first ordinary bishop. In this capacity he organized diocese institutions and founded the weekly *Niedziela*. In 1926 he visited the Polish American communities. In 1931 he established the Society of Polish Emigrants under the Protection of the Queen of the Polish Crown. Kubina developed charity work among the poorest, especially in the Dąbrowa industrial region. His work *Akcja katolicka a akcja społeczna* (Catholic action and social action; 1930), as well as his pastoral letters from the time of the Great Depression, belong among the sharpest Church criticisms of social and political relations in Poland. As a result Kubina even had to explain his position in the Roman Curia, where he was suspected of stimulating social radicalism.

During the German occupation Kubina stayed in Częstochowa, organizing the religious life of the diocese, which was divided by the border between the Reich and the General Gouvernement (the official name of the Nazi occupation authority in Poland). He supported various charity efforts and maintained contact with the delegate of the Polish Government-in-Exile for the Homeland. He co-authored a memorandum of bishops on 25 May 1940 that demanded freedom for the Church from the German authorities. He organized a ministry among Polish forced laborers in Germany—for instance, by financing the Polish Protective Committee. He also organized aid for the Polish refugees from Warsaw, especially after the suppression of the Warsaw Uprising in the fall of 1944. In 1945 Kubina elaborated a new administrative division of his diocese, reorganized the Episcopal curia, and founded the diocese charity committee, Caritas. In 1946 he joined in signing a letter condemning the Kielce pogrom. After 1945 he repeatedly spoke in defense of religious freedom. Kubina authored more than two hundred books and articles. (AGr)

Sources: *PSB*, vol. 16; *Słownik biograficzny katolicyzmu społecznego w Polsce*, vol. 2 (Warsaw, 1994), *Słownik biograficzny katolickiego duchowieństwa śląskiego XIX i XX wieku* (Katowice, 1996); Jan Żaryn, *Kościół a władza w Polsce (1945–1950)* (Warsaw, 1992).

KUBIYOVYCH Volodymyr (23 September 1900, Nowy Sącz–2 November 1985, Sarcelles, near Paris), Ukrainian geographer, demographer, encyclopedist, and political activist. Kubiyovych began studying at the Jagiellonian University in Kraków in 1918 and completed his studies in 1923, after a break caused by his participation in the Polish-Ukrainian war. From 1918 to 1919 he served in the artillery in the Ukrainian Galician Army. In 1928 he became an associate professor (*docent*) at the Jagiellonian University. In 1931 he was elected a full member of the Shevchenko Scientific Society (NTSh) and headed its geographic commission. In 1939 he was dismissed as docent at the Jagiellonian University. During the war, in 1940 Kubiyovych was appointed professor at the Ukrainian Free University in Prague, and in April of the same year he became head of the Ukrainian Central Committee (Ukrayiinskyi Tsentralyi Komitet [UCC]) in Kraków, which coordinated the work of Ukrainian social and cultural organizations in German-occupied Poland. In April 1943 Kubiyovych was one of the initiators and then head of the Military Board (Viyskova Uprava) in Lviv, which was in charge of organizing the Ukrainian Division of the Ukrainian National Army (SS Galizien division). In 1944 he appealed for an end to the hostilities between the Poles and the Ukrainians. From 1945 Kubiyovych lived in exile, where he devoted himself mostly to scholarly work. He was the initiator and chief editor of *Entsyklopediia Ukraiinoznavstva*, whose three general volumes were published in 1949–52 and eleven alphabetical volumes in 1952–95. He also edited and contributed numerous entries to the six-volume *Encyclopedia of Ukraine* (Toronto, 1984–93). From 1947 to 1963 Kubiyovych served as secretary general of the NTSh abroad, and from 1952 until his death he was president of the NTSh in Europe.

In his scholarly work, Kubiyovych's interest turned to the anthropogeography of the Carpathian region and to the demographic processes in Galicia, the Carpathian region, Volhynia, and the Pripet Marshes. He was the author of nearly eighty scholarly works, including *Życie pasterskie w Beskidach Wschodnich* (Pastoral life in the Eastern Beskyds; 1926); *Terytoriia i liudnist ukraiinskykh zemel* (The territory and population of the Ukrainian lands; 1935); *Atlas Ukraiiny i sumezhnykh krayiv* (An atlas of Ukraine and adjacent countries; 1937); *Heohrafiia ukraiinskykh i sumezhnykh zemel* (A geography of Ukraine and adjacent lands; 1938); and *Etnichni hrupy Pivdenno-zakhidnoyi Ukraiiny (Halychyny)* (Ethnic groups of Southwestern Ukraine [Galicia]; 1953).

Kubiyovych was also the author of wall maps of the Ukraine and Galicia. His memoirs include *Meni 70* (I am 70; 1970) and *Ukraiintsi v Heneralniy Hubernyi 1939–41* (Ukrainians in the General Gouvernrment 1939–41; 1975). (BB)

Sources: *Encyclopedia of Ukraine*, vol. 2 (Toronto, 1988); *Entsyklopediia Ukraiinoznavstva*, vol. 4 (Lviv, 1994); *Dovidnyk z istorii Ukraiiny* (Kiev, 2001); *Vydatni diiachi Ukraiiny mynulykh stolit* (Kiev, 2001); *Malyi slovnyk istorii Ukraiiny* (Kiev, 1997); Oleh Shablyi, *Volodymyr Kubiyovych: Entsyklopediia zhyttia i tvorennia* (Paris and Lviv, 1996).

KUČAN Milan (14 January 1941, Krizevci), Slovene Communist activist and post-Communist politician, president of Slovenia. The son of a teacher, at the age of three Kučan lost his father, who was killed by the Nazis. He graduated in law from the University of Ljubljana. From 1958 he belonged to the Communist Party of Slovenia, and from 1964 he was active in the Slovene Youth Union. In 1968–69 he was its chairman. From 1969 to 1973 Kučan was a member of the Secretariat of the Central Committee (CC) of the League of Communists of Slovenia (LCS); in 1973–78 he was secretary of the Socialist Union of Working People (Socialisticna Zveza Delovnega Ljudstva), and then he was chairman of the Assembly of the Slovene Socialist Republic. From 1982 to 1986 he represented Slovenia in the Presidium of the CC of the League of Communists of Yugoslavia, and from 1986 to 1989 he was chairman of the LCS CC. At this time Kučan supported political reforms and the liberalization of social life. He tolerated the development of new political movements that led to the so-called Slovene Spring of 1988. In April 1990 Kučan became chairman of the Presidium of the Slovene Republic. He supported the declaration of Slovene independence on 25 June 1991, taking the lead of the new state. After the beginning of the Yugoslav People's Army (YPA) intervention, Kučan declared he would resist it by all available means. He took part in the negotiations that led to the agreement of Brioni of 7 July 1991. Yugoslav leader **Slobodan Milošević** agreed that the YPA would leave Slovenia, where, unlike Croatia or Bosnia-Herzegovina, there was no Serb population.

In December 1992 Kučan was elected president of Slovenia by a 64 percent majority of the vote. In November 1997 he was reelected in the first round, gaining 56 percent of the vote. His second term was over in December 2002. In foreign policy Kučan represented a definitely pro-Western line. He not only managed to avoid Slovenia's involvement in the war in the former Yugoslavia, but he also established good relations with all of Slovenia's neighbors. Kučan fully supported efforts by the government of **Janez Drnovšek** that aimed at the integration of Slovenia into NATO and the European Union. On 10 June 1996 Slovenia signed an association treaty with the union, and in March 1998 accession talks began. Although Slovenia was not included in the first round of NATO enlargements in 1999, Kučan continued with efforts that ultimately led to the country's entry into NATO and the European Union in 2004. Kučan also supported the systemic transformation of Slovenia from a command to a market economy and from totalitarianism to democracy. In surveys by Slovene Public Opinion in 1995 and 1998, Kučan was recognized as the third most important figure in all of Slovene history. (AO)

Sources: *Enciklopedija Slovenije*, vol. 6 (Ljubljana, 1992); Jill Benderly and Evan Kraft, eds., *Independent Slovenia: Origins, Movements, Prospects* (London, 1994); Leopoldina Plut-Pregelj and Carole Rogel, *Historical Dictionary of Slovenia* (Lanham, Md., 1996); Warren Zimmermann, *Origins of a Catastrophe* (New York and Toronto, 1996); Bugajski; www.sigov.si/up-rs/enpredmk.htm.

KUCHARZEWSKI Jan (27 May 1876, Wysokie Mazowieckie–4 July 1952, New York), Polish politician, lawyer, and historian. Born into an intellectual family, Kucharzewski received a law degree from Warsaw University (1898) and then completed further studies in law, sociology, and economics in Berlin. He subsequently worked as an attorney. He lectured in law and political economics at the Society for Scientific Courses. He was a member of the Union of Polish Youth called Zet. From 1905 to 1908 he was active in the National Democratic Party (Stronnictwo Narodowo-Demokratyczne [SND]) and from 1905 to 1911 in the National League. Kucharzewski severed his ties with the national parties after they decided that Germany, rather than Russia, was the biggest threat to Poland. During World War I, in Switzerland from 1914 to 1917, Kucharzewski promoted the cause of Polish independence. After the issue (on 5 November 1916) of the Two Emperors' Manifesto, which proclaimed the creation of a Polish kingdom under German control, he began favoring the Central Powers. After returning to Poland, he started working in the organs of the Provisional Council of State in June 1917 and later in the Regency Council in Warsaw. From 26 November 1917 to 11 February 1918 Kucharzewski served as prime minister of the government of the Kingdom of Poland. He resigned in protest against the Treaty of Brest-Litovsk. In February 1918 he became a member of the board of the Union for the Establishment of the Polish State. On 2 October 1918 he was again designated prime minister but gave up the task of forming a government.

After 1920 Kucharzewski withdrew from politics and devoted himself to scholarly and journalistic pursuits.

In general, though, he supported the policies of **Józef Piłsudski**. He considered Soviet Russia to be the greatest threat to Poland. He supported a plan for a wide federation of East Central European countries. In April 1940 he left occupied Poland. After a stay in Italy, France, and Portugal, in July 1940 he settled in the United States, where he was active as a journalist and scholar. Kucharzewski helped to establish the Polish Institute of Arts and Sciences of America (Polski Instytut Naukowy w Ameryce [PIASA]), and in 1942 he became president of its board. From 1911 he belonged to the Warsaw Scientific Society and from 1926 to the Polish Academy of Arts and Sciences (Polska Akademia Umiejętności). He was an independent researcher and was not connected to any university. Kucharzewski was initially interested in law and sociology, but from World War I on he focused his attention on the history of nineteenth-century Poland and Russia. In his works he analyzed the ideology and methods of the Russian revolutionary movement. He argued that Bolshevism was the continuation of tsarist despotism. Kucharzewski was the author of many highly acclaimed works on Polish and Russian history, including *Socjalizm prawniczy* (Legal socialism; 1906); *Narodowość a państwo* (Nationality and the state; 1907); *Sprawa polska w parlamencie frankfurckim, 1848 r.* (The Polish cause in the Frankfurt parliament; 1908); and particularly the unfinished monumental work *Od białego caratu do czerwonego* (From white to the red tsarism, 7 vols.; 1923–35) and *The Origins of Modern Russia* (1948). (JS)

Sources: *PSB*, vol. 16; Oskar Halecki, "Śp. Jan Kucharzewski," *Teki Historyczne*, vol. 5, 1952; W. Kamieniecki, *Historycy i politycy warszawscy, 1900–1950* (Warsaw, 1992); *Encyklopedia Historii Polski: Dzieje polityczne*, vol. 1 (Warsaw, 1994); Krzysztof Dybciak and Zdzisław Kudelski, eds., *Leksykon kultury polskiej poza krajem od roku 1939* (Lublin, 2000).

KUCHMA Leonid (9 August 1938, Chaykyne, Chernihiv region), Ukrainian Communist activist and post-Communist politician. In 1955–60 Kuchma studied at the Department of Physics and Technology of the Dniepropetrovsk university, where he specialized in rocket technology. From 1960 to 1972 he was an engineer, and then until 1975, he was deputy chief engineer at the Pivdenne (South) Design Office, which produced SS-18 and SS-24 rockets, as well as Kosmos, Interkosmos, Tsyklon, and Zenith rockets and various types of satellites. Kuchma was also technical director of Soviet rocket testing at the Baykonur cosmodrome. In 1975–81 he was secretary of the party committee in the Pivdenne office, and in 1981–82, secretary of the party committee of the Southern Production Association of Machine Construction (Vyrobnyche Obyednannia Pivdennyi Mashynobudivnyi Zavod [SPAMC]). In 1982–86 Kuchma was first deputy engineer designer of the Pivdenne office, and from 1986 to 1992, general director of the SPAMC, which was then one of the largest armaments factories in the world. In 1990–92 Kuchma was a deputy to the Supreme Council of the Ukrainian SSR and from 1991 of Ukraine. He also belonged to the council's Commission of Defense and Security.

From 13 October 1992 to 22 September 1993 Kuchma was prime minister and a member of the Council of National Security. A supporter of economic reforms, he found himself in conflict with a more conservative president, **Leonid Kravchuk**. After leaving the government, Kuchma headed the Ukrainian Union of Industrialists and Entrepreneurs (Ukraiinskyi Soyuz Promyslovtsiv ta Pidpryiemtsiv), gaining the full support of the economic administration, especially in the armaments sector. In March 1994 he was reelected to the Supreme Council, where he belonged to the Inter-Regional Group of deputies and co-chaired the Constitutional Commission.

In July 1994 Kuchma was elected president, gaining 52.2 percent of the vote in the second round and defeating Kravchuk. He assumed the office on 19 July 1994. One of his main successes was the passing of a new constitution by the Supreme Council on 28 June 1996. Kuchma followed a cautious foreign policy, maintaining correct relations with the West and Poland, which he treated as a bridge to the West, and with Russia, with which Ukraine was closely connected in economic terms. During his term the foundations of Ukrainian statehood were strengthened, as were the state capitalist structures, which he skillfully steered. In November 1999 Kuchma was reelected, gaining 56.3 percent of the vote in the second round. In the fall of 2000 the Socialist leader **Oleksandr Moroz** accused Kuchma of having masterminded the kidnapping and murder of a journalist, Georgi Gongadze. In 2002 protests against his rule reached mass dimensions. Participants at huge rallies demanded Kuchma's resignation. Suspected of selling Kolchuga radar systems to Iraq, Kuchma was also isolated internationally, but he survived the crisis. During the elections in the fall of 2004 he supported Victor Yanukovych, but after an election fraud was disclosed, Kuchma agreed to repeating the second round. In January 2005 Kuchma finally turned presidential power over to the newly elected **Viktor Yushchenko**. (BB)

Sources: *Khto ye khto v Ukraiini 2000* (Kiev, 2000); Leonid Lukanov, *Tretiy prezydent: Politychnyi portret Leonida Kuchmy* (Kiev, 1996); Andrzej Chojnowski, *Ukraina* (Warsaw, 1997); Ihor Sharov, *100 vydatnych imen Ukraiiny* (Kiev, 1999); Bohdan Nahaylo, *The Ukrainian Resurgence* (Toronto, 1999); Bugajski; Dmytro Czobit, *Chas pidlod vlady abo Chy ye "Sprava Honhadze" spravoyu Kuchmy?* (Kiev, 2001); www.president.gov.ua.

KUHARIĆ Franjo (15 April 1919, Gornij Pribić, near Krasić–11 March 2002, Zagreb), Croatian cardinal. The son of a peasant, after elementary school Kuharić graduated from a theological seminary in Šalati, near Zagreb, in 1939. Later he studied philosophy and theology in the higher theological seminary in Zagreb. In July 1945 he was ordained by Archbishop **Alojzije Stepinac**. In 1946 he administered the Rakov Potok parish, whose parish priest was killed by the Communists. In 1947 Kuharić barely avoided an attempt on his own life. For some time he went into hiding, and in 1948 he was wounded during a pilgrimage to the Marija Bistrica sanctuary. From 1950 Kuharić was parish priest in Okiča. In December 1956 he was repeatedly interrogated by the security office in Zagreb because of alleged counterrevolutionary activities. From 1957 he was parish priest in Sambor, and on 30 May 1964 Archbishop **Franjo Šeper** consecrated him bishop. Kuharić participated in the Second Vatican Council. He was editor-in-chief of the bi-weekly *Glas Koncila*, transforming it into an opinion-shaping weekly with a circulation of more than one hundred thousand. After Cardinal Šeper became prefect of the Congregation of the Doctrine of Faith, in 1969 Pope Paul VI appointed Kuharić apostolic administrator of the Zagreb metropolis, and on 16 June 1970, archbishop of Zagreb. For more than fifteen years Kuharić also presided over the Conference of Yugoslav Bishops. During his term he created sixty new parishes and erected twenty-three new churches. He initiated the renovation of many sacral buildings, including the Gothic cathedral of Zagreb. Kuharić prepared and led the celebration of the 1,300th anniversary of Christianity in Croatia, which ended with a national eucharistic congress in Marija Bistrica in 1984. Kuharić opposed the propagation of atheism in the schools and demanded freedom of religion. He developed a ministry for the Croatian diaspora worldwide. The Communist authorities labeled him a "provocateur" and an "enemy of the system" for his public denunciations of Communist policies. On 2 February 1983 Pope **John Paul II** appointed him cardinal, which the Communist authorities considered a "hostile act" toward Yugoslavia.

In the summer of 1991 Kuharić supported Croatian efforts at independence. He contributed to the recognition of the Croatian state by the Holy See. From the beginning of the war in the former Yugoslavia, Kuharić was engaged in the defense of human rights and demanded international sanctions against the aggressors. He maintained contacts with Orthodox and Muslim clergy. For instance, he met with Patriarch Pavle, head of the Serbian Orthodox Church, and together they appealed for a termination of military operations. Kuharić organized assistance for the refugees from territories occupied by the Yugoslav Army and Serbian squadrons. He also condemned war crimes committed by Croatian soldiers against Bosnian Muslims during the war in Bosnia-Herzegovina. In 1994 Kuharić visited a besieged Sarajevo, where he met with the Patriarch of Moscow, Alexey II. In July 1995 he supported the Croatian military action in Krajina, inhabited mostly by Serbs; this raised some controversy. When the Conference of the Croatian Episcopate was created in May 1993, Kuharić became its chairman. In October 1994 he organized the pilgrimage of John Paul II on the occasion of the 900th anniversary of the Zagreb metropolis. Kuharić repeatedly defended the memory of Cardinal Stepinac, slandered by the Communists as a Croatian nationalist and alleged war criminal. Kuharić started Stepinac's beatification trial, which ended on 3 November 1998 with the proclamation that Stepinac was blessed. In 1997 John Paul II accepted Kuharić's retirement. (AGr)

Sources: Darko Pavicić, *Razgovori s kardinalom* (Zagreb, 1995); *Annuario Pontificio, 2002*; Polish Catholic Information Agency, 11 and 12 March 2002; *Glas Koncila*, 17 March 2002; www.catholic-hierarchy.org.

KUKABAKA Mikhas (1936, Babruysk), Belorussian dissident. Kukabaka's father perished in the Finnish-Soviet war in 1939, and his mother, engaged in pro-independence guerrilla activities, died of wounds in 1947. Kukabaka was brought up in an orphanage. He graduated from a trade school, and in 1953 he was sent to work on the construction of an oil refinery on the Angara River in Siberia. Then he served in the army and worked as an electrician in Babruysk. Kukabaka started political activities in March 1968, when he protested the Warsaw Pact invasion of Czechoslovakia. He repeatedly protested the Russification of Belorussia. Arrested in 1970, he was detained and released many times. All together he spent more than seventeen years in prison, including seven years in psychiatric wards in Sychovka and Mogilev, owing to a so-called schizophrenia without symptoms. In 1977 Kukabaka gave up his Soviet citizenship and applied for emigration from the USSR, but in vain. He was not allowed to leave until December 1988. Kukabaka settled in Moscow, where he wrote and published announcements and political essays. (EM)

Sources: S. P. de Boer, E. J. Driessen, and H. L. Verhaar, eds., *Biographical Dictionary of Dissidents in the Soviet Union, 1956–1975* (The Hague and Boston, 1982); Jan Zaprudnik, *Historical Dictionary of Belarus* (Lanham, Md., 1998); *Karta*, 2002, no. 34.

KUKAN Eduard (26 December 1939, Horný Jatov), Slovak politician. Kukan graduated from the Moscow Institute of International Relations in 1964, and later he received a Ph.D. in law from Charles University in Prague. From 1964 he worked in the Foreign Ministry, and in 1968–73 he was attaché, second secretary, and chargé d'affaires in Lusaka, Zambia. Later he served as councillor and deputy ambassador in the United States; from 1981 to 1985 he was director of the Department of Sub-Saharan Africa; in 1985–88 he was ambassador to Ethiopia; then until 1990 he was director of the Department of Latin America in the Foreign Ministry. From the early 1960s to 1989 Kukan belonged to the Czechoslovak Communist Party. In 1990 he was appointed ambassador to the United Nations. From the breakup of Czechoslovakia in January 1993 to 1994 he was Slovak ambassador to the United Nations. In March 1994 Kukan became minister of foreign affairs in the government of **Jozef Moravčik**. In the early parliamentary elections of September 1994 he won a seat on behalf of the Democratic Union of Slovakia (Demokratická Únie Slovenska [DUS]), which he joined in March 1995. He sat on the parliamentary foreign affairs and European integration commissions. In December 1994, when the government of Moravčik collapsed, Kukan resigned from his position.

In March 1997 Kukan was elected chairman of the DUS. One of the architects of an agreement among opposition parties and of the formation of the Slovak Democratic Coalition (Slovenská Demokratická Koalicia [SDK]), he became its deputy chairman in July 1998. After the elections of September 1998 and an SDK victory, in late October 1998 Kukan became foreign minister again. He had considerable influence on the pro-Western reorientation of Slovak foreign policy, aimed at making up for time lost during the **Vladimir Mečiar** regime. Slovakia began to be perceived as a serious candidate for the European Union and NATO. In 1999–2001 Kukan was an envoy of UN Secretary General Kofi Annan to the Balkans. After another electoral victory of the center and right parties in the elections of September 2002, Kukan retained the position of foreign minister, ultimately leading Slovakia into NATO and the European Union in March and June 2004 respectively. A supporter of the transformation of the SDC into one party, he co-founded and became deputy chairman of the Slovak Democratic and Christian Union (Slovenská Demokratická Krest'anská Únie [SDKÚ]). Kukan received an honorary doctorate from Uppsala College, New Jersey, and received the Pontifical Order of St. Gregory for his contribution to a concordat with the Holy See. In April 2004 Kukan ran in the presidential elections but came in third in the first round. (PU)

Sources: *Slovensko 1996: Súhrnná správa o stave spoločnosti* (Bratislava, 1997); *Slovensko 1997: Súhrnná správa o stave spoločnosti* (Bratislava, 1998); *Slovensko 1998–1999: Súhrnná správa o stave spoločnosti* (Bratislava, 1999); *Slovensko 2000: Súhrnná správa o stave spoločnosti* (Bratislava, 2000); www.home.sk/www/slovpolitika/kukan.htm; www.referaty.sk/?referat=1610; www.government.gov.sk; www.sdkuonline.sk/podpreds2.php3.

KUKIEL Marian (15 May 1885, Dąbrowa Tarnowska–15 August 1973, London), Polish general, historian, and politician. Kukiel was allied with the independence movement in his youth. In 1905 he was active in the military structures of the Polish Socialist Party (Polska Partia Socjalistyczna [PPS]). In 1908 he was a co-founder of the Union of Active Struggle (Związek Walki Czynnej [ZWC]) in the Austrian partition of Poland; later, as a close associate of **Józef Piłsudski**, he played a leading role in organizing the rifle corps. At the same time Kukiel studied history in Lwów under the guidance of **Szymon Askenazy**. He specialized in the history of the Polish military from the eighteenth century to modern times. In 1909 he received a Ph.D. During World War I Kukiel served in the Polish Legions. In 1915 he was promoted to officer in the First Brigade of the Polish Legions. He fought in the Polish-Soviet war as commander of a regiment and an infantry brigade. On 1 July 1923 he became a general. At that time he published *Dzieje Wojska Polskiego w dobie napoleońskiej, 1795–1815* (The history of the Polish Army in the Napoleonic period, 1795–1815, 2 vols.; 1918–20) and *Zarys historii wojskowości w Polsce* (An outline of Polish military history, 2 vols.; 1921). From 1925 to 1926 Kukiel was the head of the Historical Bureau of the General Staff. During the coup of May 1926 he supported the legitimate authorities, and as a result, he was expelled from the army. From 1927 to 1935 he was an associate professor (*docent*) and subsequently a full professor at the Jagiellonian University in Kraków. From 1930 to 1939 he worked as a curator at the Czartoryski Museum in Kraków. In 1927 he published *Wojny napoleońskie* (The Napoleonic Wars). In 1932 Kukiel became a member of the Polish Academy of Arts and Sciences (Polska Akademia Umiejętności). In 1937 he published the two-volume *Wojna 1812 roku* (The War of 1812). Kukiel gradually moved into the opposition to Piłsudski, and at the end of the 1930s he was one of the founders of the Christian-Democratic Labor Party (Stronnictwo Pracy [SP]).

During the September campaign of 1939, Kukiel was the military commander of Tarnów and an officer of the staff in the defense of Lwów. He subsequently made his way to France and Great Britain, where General **Władysław Sikorski** appointed him deputy minister for military affairs and later commander of the First Corps of the Polish Armed Forces (Polskie Siły Zbrojne [PSZ]) in Scotland. In September 1942 Kukiel became minister for military affairs in Sikorski's government. After

Sikorski's death, Kukiel continued to hold this post in the governments of **Stanisław Mikołajczyk** (until 1944) and **Tomasz Arciszewski** (until February 1949). On 16 April 1943, on behalf of the Government of the Republic of Poland, Kukeil requested that the International Red Cross investigate the killing of Polish officers in Katyń. After World War II Kukiel worked as the director of the London-based Władysław Sikorski Historical Institute from 1947 to 1973 and lectured as a professor at the Polish University Abroad (Polski Uniwersytet na Obczyźnie) from 1945 to 1973. He co-edited sixteen volumes of *Teki historyczne* (Historical papers; 1947–71). Kukiel's publications include a work about Prince Adam Czartoryski, *Książę Adam* (Prince Adam; 1950), and its English version, *Czartoryski and European Unity 1770–1861* (1955); the synthesis *Dzieje Polski porozbiorowej 1795–1921* (The history of Poland after the partition 1795–1921; 1961); and the biography *Generał Sikorski: Żołnierz i mąż stanu Polski walczącej* (General Sikorski: Soldier and statesman of fighting Poland; 1970). Kukiel published extensively in the London-based *Wiadomości* and in other émigré periodicals. (MC)

Sources: *Teki Historyczne*, vol. 17 (London, 1978–80); Zbigniew Mierzwiński, *Generałowie II Rzeczpospolitej*, vol. 1 (Warsaw, 1990); Janusz Zuziak, *Generał Marian Kukiel 1885–1973: Żołnierz, historyk, poliyk* (Pruszków, 1997); Rafał Habielski, *Życie społeczne i kulturalne emigracji* (Warsaw, 1999); *Leksykon kultury polskiej poza krajem od roku 1939*, vol. 1 (Lublin, 2000).

KUKK Juhan (13 April 1885, Käru, near Viru–December 1945, Soviet Union), Estonian politician. Kukk studied in Dorpat (Tartu), at the Department of Commerce of Riga Polytechnic College (1904–10), and in Germany. After returning to Estonia in 1910, he worked in the Dorpat Loan and Insurance Company. In 1911 he became editor-in-chief of the cooperative newspaper *Ühistegevusleht* and was active in the cooperative movement. During World War I Kukk was a member of the Estonian Nutrition Committee. In 1917 he obtained a seat in the Estonian Provincial Assembly (Eestimaa Maanõukogu) and became head of the Financial Department of the Estonian Provincial Government. Kukk was one of the authors and the editor of the final version of the declaration of Estonian Independence of 23 February 1918. In the Estonian Provisional Government, he became minister of finance and state property, then minister of finance (1919–20), and then minister of industry and trade (1921–22). Kukk managed to establish the foundations of the state's financial apparatus: the Ministry of Finance and the Central Bank, of which he became the director in 1919. Although the bank's exposure to political influences proved unfavorable for

the economy, to some extent Kukk succeeded in bringing the chaos in public finances under control through such measures as the introduction of the Estonian mark, which replaced the Finnish and German marks and the Russian ruble, which had previously been in circulation.

One of the senior leaders of the Estonian Labor Party (ELP), Kukk served as member of the Constitutional Assembly and as speaker of the first parliament (*Riigikogu*). From 21 November 1922 to 2 August 1923 he was head of state (*riigivanem*). The rejection of one of the bills in a referendum forced the authorities to call an early election, as a result of which the ELP lost nearly half of its twenty-two seats. Kukk served as an MP for the following three years, and later he devoted himself to social and economic work. From 1919 to 1930 he was president of the Central Council of Cooperative Unions. After retiring from active politics, he served as president of the Estonian Consumer Union in 1926–30. In 1920 he became a member of the board of the People's Bank (Rahvapank) and of several of the largest commercial companies in the country, such as Balti Manufakuur and Kreenbalt. From 1937 to 1940, as a representative of large-scale industry, Kukk was a member of the board of the Chamber of Commerce and Industry. From 1936 to 1940 he served as president of the All-Estonian Union of Textile Manufacturers. He believed in parliamentary democracy; therefore he anxiously observed the development of authoritarianism. After the coup of 1934, led by **Konstantin Päts**, Kukk joined the opposition. In 1938, along with **Jaan Tõnisson**, **Jaan Teemant**, and **Ants Piip**, he sharply protested the restrictions imposed by the new electoral law. After the Red Army seized Estonia in June 1940, Kukk was arrested and died in unexplained circumstances. (AG)

Sources: Evald Uustalu, *The History of the Estonian People* (London, 1953); Matti Laur, Tõnis Lukas, Ain Mäesalu, Ago Pajur, and Tõnu Tannberg, *History of Estonia* (Tallinn, 2000); Strona Urzędu Prezydenta Republiki Estonii, http://www.president.ee/eng/riigipead/JuhanKukk.html; Strona Ministerstwa Finansów Estonii http://www.fin.ee/pages.php/011805; Strona obchodów 80-lecia niepodległości Estonii, ew80.www.ee/eng/chronicle/1918.html; http://www.kirmus.ee/Valjaanded/ekmar/milleks.html.

KUKK Jüri (1 May 1940, Pärnu–27 March 1981, Vologda), Estonian Democratic activist, victim of Communist repression. From 1958 to 1963 Kukk studied chemistry at Tartu University, where he worked at the chemistry department from 1965. At that time he joined the CPSU. In 1972 he received the Candidate of Science degree. In 1975–76, along with his wife, Kukk completed a scientific internship program in Paris. The stay in the West induced him to leave the party in May 1978 as he had had enough of dishonesty. In July 1979 the authorities expelled him from university. Along with a group of forty-five Lithuanians, Latvians, and Estonians, Kukk signed the Baltic Appeal in August 1979; in it they demanded the admittance of the fact that the Molotov-Ribbentrop Pact had been unlawful from the beginning. Kukk applied for permission to emigrate, but to no effect. He signed an open letter to Leonid Brezhnev in protest against the aggression of the USSR in Afghanistan. He also protested the deportation of Andrei Sakharov to Gorki. After turbulent events in Tallinn that occurred on the day of the prewar Independence Day, in February 1980 Kukk was arrested and subjected to psychiatric "treatment." In January 1981 he was sentenced to two years in the Gulag. He died on his way to Siberia. The authorities fixed a marker with the number 23781 upon his grave and forbade a tombstone there. Only after a long time was his family allowed to place a gravestone and a cross on his grave. (WR)

Sources: Rein Taagepera, *Softening without Liberalization in the Soviet Union: The Case of Juri Kukk* (Lanham, Md., 1984).

KUKLIŃSKI Ryszard (13 June 1930, Warsaw–11 March 2004, Washington, D.C.), Polish colonel. In 1947 Kukliński joined the (Communist) Polish Army. In 1950 he graduated from the Officers' School of Infantry in Wrocław, and later he served in various units in Piła and Kołobrzeg. In 1961 he enrolled in the Academy of the General Staff, and from 1963 he worked in the General Staff, where he soon became a trusted aide to General **Wojciech Jaruzelski**. At the beginning of 1968, for half a year Kukliński served in Vietnam as a member of the International Arbitrage Commission. Upon his return to Poland he became a liaison officer between the commander-in-chief of the Warsaw Pact, Marshal Viktor Kulikov, and the Polish minister of defense, General Jaruzelski, during the preparations for the invasion of Czechoslovakia. In 1975 Kukliński trained at the Kliment Voroshilov Academy of the Soviet Armed Forces, where he met General **Czesław Kiszczak**. After returning to Poland, he became head of the Strategic Planning Section and later of the Operations Administration of the General Staff. He also served as a liaison officer in the General Staff of the Soviet Army, gaining access to top classified information. In 1980–81 he took part in the preparations for the introduction of martial law in Poland.

From 1971 Kukliński worked with U.S. intelligence, delivering to the Americans about thirty-five thousand pages of top secret Warsaw Pact documents. He started this cooperation on his own initiative, supplying, for instance, an extensive memorandum on the weakness of NATO forces in Europe. Thanks to Kukliński, the Americans learned about Soviet plans, including those for a Warsaw Pact invasion of Western Europe and the details of martial law in Poland. In view of the growing risk of Kukliński being unmasked, on 7 November 1981 the CIA evacuated him, along with his family, to the United States. On 23 May 1984 the Martial Court of the Warsaw Military District sentenced him to death in absentia for high treason. On the basis of the amnesty of 1989 this sentence was commuted to twenty-five years in prison. Kukliński's case became known in Poland in April 1987, when the Paris-based monthly *Kultura* published an extensive interview with him titled "Wojna z narodem widziana od środka" (The war against the nation as seen from within). After the fall of communism in Poland, Kukliński's rehabilitation raised a heated debate. In 1994 his two sons, Bogdan and Waldemar, perished in mysterious circumstances. There are hints that they may have been murdered by Communist special services. In May 1995 the Polish Supreme Court repealed Kukliński's sentence, in September 1997 he was acquitted, and in May 1998 he went to Poland for the first time since 1981. (PU)

Sources: *Bohater czy zdrajca: Fakty i dokumenty* (Warsaw, 1992); Zbigniew Kumoś, ed., *Nikt czyli Kukliński (Rzecz o zdradzie)* (Warsaw, 2002); Józef Szaniawski, *Samotna misja: Pułkownik Kukliński i zimna wojna* (Warsaw and Chicago, 2003); Benjamin Weiser, *A Secret Life: The Polish Officer, His Covert Mission, and the Price He Paid to Save His Country* (New York, 2004).

KULISH Mykola (5 December 1892, Chaplyntsi, Tavriya Province–3 November 1937, Solovets Islands), Ukrainian playwright. After graduating from high school, Kulish entered a school for warrant officers in Odessa (1913). During World War I he fought on the front lines. At the beginning of 1918 he became president of the Soviet of Workers' and Peasants' Delegates in Oleshkiv. From 1919 to 1921 he served in the army, fighting against the army of General Anton Denikin. Demobilized, he was in charge of education in Oleshkiv County, and he edited the journal *Chervonyi shliakh* in Zinovyevsk (now Kirovohrad). In 1922 Kulish began working in the provincial department of people's education in Odessa. In 1924 he wrote the drama *97* about the great famine of 1921–22. The following year he wrote the drama *Komuna v stepakh* (Commune in the steppes). Both plays were staged in Kharkiv and won him great acclaim. In 1925 Kulish moved to Kharkiv, where he became friends with **Mykola Khvylovi** and **Les Kurbas**. In the 1920s Kulish was a member of Hart, a writers' group, and later a member of the Free Academy of Proletarian Literature (Vilna Akademiya Proletarskoyi Literatury [VAPLITE]). From November 1926 to January 1928 he served as president of the VAPLITE. At the end of 1929 he joined the presidium of a new writers' organization, Politfront.

Kulish was one of the co-founders of the new Ukrainian theater. His first dramas were realistic and social in character. The comedy *Khuliy Khuryna* (1926) reveals expressionist influences, and *Zona* (1926) was a criticism of party careerism. In *Otak zahynuv Huska* (That's how Huska died; 1927) he was influenced by symbolism. Kulish's best dramas include *Narodnyi Malakhiy* (The people's Malachi; 1928); *Myna Mazaylo* (1929); and *Patetychna sonata* (Sonata pathétique; 1929). The first two dramas present a clash between revolutionary ideas and Soviet reality and between Ukrainian national aspirations and Communist ideology, while the third depicts the Ukraine of the years 1917–18 and the struggle for the Ukraine among the Whites, the Communists, and the national-patriotic camp. In the 1930s Kulish wrote, among other things, *Maklena Grasa* (1933), *Proshchay, selo* (Farewell, countryside; 1933), and *Povorot Marka* (Marko's return; 1934). Most of his dramas were staged by the Berezil Theater in Kharkiv under the direction of **Les Kurbas**, the most famous Ukrainian theater director at that time. Kulish's popularity was accompanied by increasing criticism from conservative party circles, particularly after the publication of *Narodyi Malakhiy*. Arrested in December 1934, Kulish was accused of being a member of a terrorist organization linked with the Organization of Ukrainian Nationalists (Orhanizatsiya Ukrayinskykh Natsionalistiv [OUN]). In 1935 he was sentenced to ten years in an isolation cell in a concentration camp on the Solovets Islands. In November 1937, by judgment of an NKVD troika, he was executed by firing squad, along with a group of other Ukrainian writers. Kulish was rehabilitated posthumously in 1956. (BB)

Sources: *Encyclopedia of Ukraine*, vol. 2 (Toronto, 1988); Roman Bzheskyi, *Polityczni ideii tvoriv Mykoly Kulisha* (Munich, 1955); Ivan Semenchuk, *Slukhaiu muzyku liudskoï dushi: Stanovlennia Mykoly Kulisha* (Kiev, 1997); Volodymyr Pratsovytyi, *Ukrainskyi natsionalnyi kharakter u dramaturhii Mykoly Kulisha* (Lviv, 1998); Iuriy Lutskyi, *Literaturna polityka v radianskiy Ukraiini* (Kiev, 2000); *Dovidnyk z istorii Ukraiiny* (Kiev, 2001).

KUN Béla (20 February 1886, Szilágycseh, Transylvania–29 August 1938?, Moscow), Hungarian Communist leader. The son of an impoverished clerk of Jewish origin, in 1902 Kun joined the Social Democratic Party and worked in the editorial offices of leftist journals in Kolozsvár, Nagyvárad, and Budapest. During World War I he served in the Austro-Hungarian Army. He attained the rank of lieutenant on the eastern front. In 1916 the Russians captured him. Kun was put into a prison camp near Tomsk, where he led Marxist agitation, mainly among the Hungarian captives. Released after the February 1917 revolution, he wrote for the revolutionary press, through which he attracted the attention of the Bolsheviks. After the October Revolution of 1917 Kun went to Petrograd, where Karol Radek named him his assistant in the Commissariat for Foreign Affairs. Kun also edited *Nemzetközi Szocialista*, a Bolshevik newspaper for Hungarian soldiers who were still fighting on the side of Austria-Hungary.

On 24 March 1918 Kun founded a Hungarian section in the Bolshevik party, and soon after that he became the president of the Federation of Foreign Groups in the Russian Communist Party (Bolsheviks). After the fall of the Austro-Hungarian monarchy, on 17 November 1918 Kun arrived in Budapest on Lenin's orders and founded the Hungarian Communist Party there, propagating Bolshevik tactics used in the struggle for power. The economic crisis, inflation, an external trade embargo, and the Entente's harsh conditions of armistice—all these created a breeding ground for revolutionary agitation in Hungary. Kun demanded the resignation of the republican government of **Mihály Károlyi** and aimed at acquiring full power. On 20 February 1919 the Union of the Unemployed, which was controlled by the Hungarian Bolsheviks, organized street demonstrations in Budapest in which several people were killed. Kun and sixty-seven other organizers of the demonstration were arrested. Battered by the guards, Kun became the hero of the crowd. Already in a prison hospital he prepared an open letter calling for the establishment of a "dictatorship of the proletariat" and the unification of the entire left under the slogan of "full power for the Soviets." The Károlyi government lost control over the army and had to yield to the Entente's ultimatum that the Hungarian Army withdraw to its "ethnic boundaries." Giving power to the left seemed the only way to calm the masses.

The Social Democrats and the Hungarian Communist Party formed a new government under the leadership of **Sándor Garbai**. On 21 March 1919 this government proclaimed the Hungarian Soviet Republic (HSR). Released from prison, Kun was appointed head of the Commissariat for Foreign Affairs and became the gray eminence of the ruling alliance. The Social Democrats also accepted his program. However, the HSR authorities failed to solve any of the pressing problems of the country. Kun rejected the ultimatum of the Entente but could not oppose the Entente's allies, the Czechs and the Romanians. Efforts to export revolution to Slovakia, a prewar territory of the Kingdom of Hungary, were unsuccessful. Endeavors to reach an agreement with the Socialists, who were holding power in Austria, failed. Attempts at collectivization and the uncontrollable terror in towns caused many people to be disappointed with the HSR; therefore on 1 August 1919 the revolutionary government fell, and Romanian forces invaded Budapest. Kun fled to Austria; after a short time he managed to get to Germany and in August 1920 to Russia.

In October 1920 Kun became a member of the Military Council of the Southern Front in the struggle against General Peter Wrangler, and he took part in a bloody crackdown on White officers in the Crimea. As early as February 1921 he began to organize groups of Hungarian Bolsheviks for an action in Hungary. In the spring of 1921 he went to Germany to support the local Communists. At a Comintern Congress in July 1921, he became a member of the Executive Committee (EC). In the Hungarian Communist Party Kun represented a radical course aiming at the revival of the Communist movement in the country and at another revolution, but a strong party opposition, under the leadership of **Jenő Landler**, preferred longer preparations. When one of his close associates embezzled Comintern funds to set up a private shop in Transylvania, Kun was sent to Sverdlovsk, where he headed the propaganda department (Agitprop) of the Urals office of the Bolshevik party. In 1923 he returned to Moscow, where he became a member of the Central Committee (CC) of the Comsomol, and in 1924 he was promoted to head of the Propaganda Department of the CC of the party. In 1925 Kun distanced himself from Leon Trotsky, and in 1926, from his former patron, Grigoryi Zinovyev. In the summer of 1926 in Berlin Kun held talks with Károlyi on commuting the sentence of Mátyás Rákosi, who was under threat of capital punishment in Hungary. On a trip with a Comintern mission to Austria in 1928, Kun was arrested, but he was sent back to the USSR. At the Sixth Comintern Congress in July and August 1928 Kun joined the Presidium of the EC of the Communist International, and in August 1929 he became head of its Balkan Secretariat, which coordinated the activities of the Bulgarian, Cypriot, Greek, Yugoslav, and Romanian parties.

In the summer of 1929 Kun lost in the elections in the Hungarian club in Moscow and in retaliation ordered a GPU (security police) associate to arrest the opponents of Landler's faction on charges of Trotskyism. However, the Comintern did not support Kun's accusation. At the beginning of the 1930s Kun was among the leading ideologists of the Comintern. He also lectured at the International Leninist School and at the Institute of the Red Professorship. At a meeting of the EC of the Comintern in December 1933 Kun sharply criticized West European Social Democracy and the "uniform front." At the Seventh Congress of the Comintern in the summer of 1935 Kun did not join the Presidium of the EC because

of an open conflict in the Hungarian party. In May 1936 the Presidium submitted the case for examination by the Control Committee, and after its negative assessment on 5 September 1936 Kun was expelled from the party and from the Comintern. In 1937 false news of his death was announced in Budapest. The Presidium of the EC of the Comintern attacked him for "Hungarian nationalism." Kun was arrested in connection with the trial of Nikolai Bukharin and comrades, but for a long time his fate was unknown. Even the date of his death is the subject of controversy. According to information provided by the USSR Embassy in Hungary in 1989, Kun was executed immediately after the announcement of his death sentence in prison. His wife and two children survived exile. In 1986 Kun's works were published in Moscow. (WR)

Sources: *MERSH*, vol. 18; Géza Herczeg, *Kun Béla* (Budapest, 1929); Bélané Kun, *Kun Béla* (Budapest, 1966); Rudolf L. Tőkes, *Béla Kun: The Man and the Revolutionary* (New York, 1966); Rudolf L. Tőkes, *Bela Kun and the Hungarian Soviet Republic* (New York, 1967); György Borsányi, *The Life of a Communist Revolutionary: Béla Kun* (Boulder, Colo., 1993).

KUNDERA Milan (1 April 1929, Brno), Czech writer. After graduating from a high school in Brno in 1948, Kundera started studies in literature at Charles University in Prague, but soon he moved to the Department of Film and Television at the Academy of Theater and Musical Arts, where he graduated in screenplay writing. In 1952–70 he lectured there in world literature, advancing to associate professor in 1964. In 1964 he also received the State Award and in 1968 the award of the Association of Czechoslovak Writers. In 1948–50 and 1956–70 Kundera belonged to the Communist Party of Czechoslovakia. From the late 1960s he was one of the leaders of the Czech cultural opposition. After the suppression of the Prague Spring, during the so-called normalization, Kundera was banned from publishing, and in 1975 he emigrated to France, where he delivered guest lectures. In 1980 he became a professor at the École des Hautes Études in Paris. In 1979 he was deprived of his Czechoslovak citizenship, and in 1981 he became a citizen of France.

Kundera made his literary debut in 1946, and his first volume of poetry was titled *Člověk: zahrada šírá* (A man: A wide open garden; 1953). Initially he wrote Socialist realist works, but he departed from this style in a collection of erotic poetry, *Monology* (Monologues; 1957). Kundera's poems were very personal and belonged to the vanguard style, officially rejected in Czechoslovakia. In 1963 he published his first drama, *Majitelé klíčů* (Key wwners), in which he considered the choice between an active but risky life and passivity and safety. In the late 1950s Kundera joined in the debate on cultural policy and contemporary art, which resulted in the book *Umění románu* (1960; *The Art of the Novel*, 1988). In 1963–69 he published three volumes: *Směšné lásky* (1963; *Laughable Loves*, 1974), in which he expressed skepticism about life; the novel *Žert* (1967; *Joke*, 1982), a political resume of the past; and the play *Ptákovina* (Bird; 1969), a black comedy showing a reality full of hypocrisy, dullness, and cruelty. In 1967–69 Kundera was very active, publishing a lot on Czech history, culture, and politics.

In exile Kundera continued writing prose, publishing *Život je jinde* (1979; *Life Is Elsewhere*, 1986) and *Valčík na rozloučenou* (1979; *Farewell Waltz*, 1998). In France he wrote his best known works, *Kniha smíchu a zapomnění* (1981; *Book of Laughter and Forgetting*, 1980), *Nesnesitelná lehkost bytí* (1981; *Unbearable Lightness of Being*, 1984), and *Nesmrtelnost* (1990; *Immortality*, 1991). In these works he dealt with the situation of a man in a totalitarian system and his internal freedom in the face of a dangerous and unfriendly world. His hero is a person seeking security and finding it only within himself, in the ability to judge. Kundera drew close to the French rationalism of Denis Diderot, his master. Among other works, he wrote a play, *Jakub a jeho pán* (1970, *Jacques and His Master*, 1985). In one of his essays Kundera presented his own controversial vision of Central European cultural identity. He became one of the best known contemporary Czech writers, and he received many literary awards. His books served as the foundations for many screenplays and were translated into many languages. (PU)

Sources: *ČBS*; *Slovník českých spisovatelů od roku 1945*, vol. 2 (Prague, 1998); Marketa Goetz-Stankiewicz, *The Silenced Theatre* (Toronto, 1979); Maria Nemcová Banerjee, *Terminal Paradox: The Novels of Milan Kundera* (New York, 1990); Miloslav Hoznauer, *Milan Kundera* (Prague, 1991); *Proměny*, 1991, no. 31; Fred Misurella, *Understanding Milan Kundera: Public Events, Private Affairs* (Columbia, S.C., 1993); Květoslav Chvatík, *Svět románů Milana Kundery* (Brno, 1994); Helena Kosková, *Milan Kundera* (Jinočany, 1998); Peter Petro, ed., *Critical Essays on Milan Kundera* (New York, 1999); Harold Bloom, ed., *Milan Kundera* (Philadelphia, 2002).

KUPALA Yanka [originally Ivan Lutsevich] (7 July 1882, Vyazhynka, near Minsk–28 June 1942, Moscow), Belorussian poet, dramatist, and journalist. Born into a family of lesser gentry, from 1902 to 1909 Kupala worked as a traveling teacher, a court secretary in Radoszkowicze (Radashkovichy), and a clerk in a brewery near Minsk. Between 1909 and 1913 he studied in St. Petersburg and worked at a local public library. In 1908 he began contributing to *Nasha Niva*. In October 1913 he settled in Vilnius,

where he worked as secretary of the Belorussian Publishing Society, and in March 1914 he became the secretary of *Nasha Niva*. In August 1915 Kupala fled to Moscow. Mobilized in January 1916, he served in a construction battalion in Minsk, Polotsk, and Smolensk. At the beginning of 1919 he settled in Minsk. He edited the literary periodicals *Run'* and *Vol'ny Shtandar*. He supported every government that promised freedom for Belorussia, irrespective of whether it was Soviet or Polish. The signing of the Treaty of Riga (March 1921) caused Kupala to have a nervous breakdown and a long illness.

From 1921 to 1922 Kupala worked in the Commissariat of Education of the Belorussian SSR, serving as head of its Publishing Department. He was one of the initiators of the Belorussian National Theater, the Belorussian State University, the Institute of Belorussian Culture, and an association of writers called Polymia. In 1928 he became a member of the Academy of Sciences of the Belorussian SSR, and in 1929, a member of the Academy of Sciences of the Ukrainian SSR. In the summer of 1930 Kupala was accused of promoting "bourgeois nationalism." His family was deported to Siberia as part of the drive to "get rid of the kulaks." Soon after that he was accused of leading a counterrevolutionary organization called the Belarus Liberation Union. As a result of repeated public humiliation, Kupala attempted suicide on 27 November 1930. Saved by doctors, he had no more strength to resist; he publicly admitted his "erroneous views" and promised to fight against the "kulak nationalist rebirth movement." In October 1939 he took part in the proceedings of the People's Assembly, which made a decision to incorporate Belorussian territories that until then had belonged to Poland into the Belorussian SSR. During the German-Soviet war Kupala engaged in propaganda to mobilize people to fight the German invaders. He died in unexplained circumstances in the Hotel Moscow. He was probably murdered.

Kupala wrote his first literary works in Polish. In 1903 he began to publish them in the periodical *Ziarno*. In 1905 he wrote his first poem in Belorussian, *Muzhyk* (Peasant), and published it in the Minsk newspaper *Severno-Zapadnyĭ Kraĭ*. From then on, he was one of the chief contributors to the canon of the modern Belorussian literary language. From 1908 on Kupala regularly published in *Nasha Niva*. In 1909 he published *Zhaleika*, the first collection of his poems, but a part of its edition was confiscated. The enslaved Belorussian peasant, presented against the background of the beautiful world of nature, is a recurring motif in his writing. In the collection *Huslar* (Wizard; 1910) a romantic view of the world was predominant. In the collection *Shliakh zhytstsia* (Along the path of life; 1913) Kupala focused on patriotic and moral values. Dignity, honor, and freedom for the Belorussian people became the motifs of his subsequent literary works. These were predominant in the poems *Son na kurhanie* (Dream on a Kurgan; 1910) and *Mahila lva* (Tomb of a lion; 1913), in the drama *Razburanaie hniazdo* (Ravaged nest; 1913), and in the collection *Pesni vainy* (Songs of war; 1915). In the collection *Spadchyna* (The heritage; 1922) Kupala was very critical of the revolution, which he saw as a source of destruction and devastation. Kupala gained his greatest renown as the author of *Tuteyshyia* (The natives; 1922), a comedy that depicted the shaping of the national consciousness of Belorussian peasants. Kupala's works written during the period of Socialist realism—*Pesnia budaunitstvu* (Song about construction; 1936) and *Ad sertsa* (Coming from my heart; 1940)—are of less literary value. Six volumes of collected works, titled *Zbor tvorau*, were published in 1961–63 in Minsk. (EM)

Sources: *Wielka Encyklopedia Powszechna*, vol. 6 (Warsaw, 1965); *Bielaruskaia SSR: Kratkaia entsiklopediia*, vol. 5 (Minsk, 1982); Nicholas P. Vakar, *Belorussia: The Making of a Nation* (Cambridge, Mass., 1956); Irina Bahdanovich, *Ianka Kupala i ramantyzm* (Minsk, 1989); A. Bialatski, *Litaratura i natsiia* (Minsk, 1991); Uladzimir Hnilamiodau, *Ianka Kupala: Novy pohliad* (Minsk, 1995); Jan Zaprudnik, *Historical Dictionary of Belarus* (Lanham, Md., 1998); Rainer Lindner, *Historiker und Herrschaft: Nationsbildung und Geschichtspolitik in Weissrussland im 19. und 20. Jahrhundert* (Munich, 1999); Dzmitri Saniuk, *Estetyka tvarchosti Ianki Kupaly* (Minsk, 2000).

KUPERJANOV Julius (11 October 1894, Likhowo, near Novorzhevsk–2 February 1919, Tartu), Estonian military commander. Kuperjanov was the son of Estonian peasants who escaped to Russia following a conflict with the local landowner. In 1904 he returned to Estonia, went to school in Sipe, and then, against the will of his parents, he continued his education in a teacher training college at the University of Dorpat (Tartu). During his studies he took part in the activities of young radicals. In early 1914 Kuperjanov worked as a teacher in a parish school in Kambja. Upon the outbreak of war in the summer of 1914, he was drafted into the Russian Army, and in 1915 he graduated from the Reserve Officers' School in Petrograd. During World War I he commanded a reconnaissance unit, and from 1917 he was an officer in the Estonian supply battalion, which he co-organized. In 1918 he organized and commanded a guerrilla group of youngsters and peasants threatened by Bolshevik terror; he managed to transform it into a disciplined and well-armed unit. This unit was moved to the rear of the advancing Bolshevik army and efficiently disorganized its operations. The unit made history as the Kuperjanov Battalion, thanks to the recapture of

Tartu in mid-January 1919. The reopening of the railway line leading to this town made possible the entry of an armored train into the Tartu railway station and the seizure of the town by surprise. Despite fierce attacks by the more numerous Bolshevik troops, Tartu was held until the Estonian rescue came. This operation probably saved the town from Bolshevik slaughter. The Bolsheviks managed to shoot only about a dozen people, including Orthodox bishop Platon. At the end of January 1919, the Kuperjanov unit fought in the bloodiest battle of the Estonian War of Independence, at Valka, which was captured mainly thanks to Kuperjanov's personal engagement. Severely wounded near the Paju estate, he soon died. In independent Estonia exclusive Estonian troops bore his name. (AG)

Sources: *Eesti Entsuklopeedia*, vol. 14 (Tallinn, 2000); Jaan Soots, "Wojna Estonji o wyzwolenie 1918–1920," *Przegląd Wojskowy*, 1929, vol. 6, no. 20; Jan Lewandowski, *Estonia* (Warsaw, 2001).

KUPI Abas, pseudonym "Bazi Canës" (August 1891, Bilajt, near Fush Kruje–9 January 1976, Freeport, Long Island, New York), Albanian officer, politician, pro-independence activist, and member of the pantheistic sect Bektashi. Initially Kupi was involved in criminal activities in the region of his native Kruje, but by 1914 he was already known as one of the leaders of the self-defense units that maintained order there. In 1920 Kupi fought against units from the Kingdom of Serbs, Croats, and Slovenes in the region of Koplik. During the democratic revolution of June 1924, he supported the current government authorities, organizing a defense of Lezhe that lasted a few days. When King **Zog** returned to power, Kupi was promoted to the rank of officer and became commander of the gendarmerie in Kruje. On 7 April 1939, during the Italian invasion of Albania, Kupi, who held the rank of major, was one of the few officers who tried to organize a defense. His unit, fighting in the region of Dürres, was defeated after several hours of struggle, and he himself emigrated to Turkey.

In 1940 Kupi made his way to Yugoslavia, where he helped to establish the Unity Front, regarded as the first organized group of the Albanian resistance movement and linked with British intelligence. Plans to instigate an anti-Italian uprising in Albania failed. Kupi returned to Albania and became leader of a guerrilla unit that was active in the region of Kruje. In April 1942 he became a member of the General Council of the National Liberation Front, which was to represent a broad political coalition in the Albanian resistance movement. In July 1943 Kupi became a member of the General Staff of the National Liberation Army. The monopolist tendencies of the Communists prompted him to establish his own group. At that time his unit was active in the region of Diber-Mati. In October 1943 he became a member of the Regency Council. In consultation with the British, on 20 November 1943, at a congress of royalists faithful to King **Zog** in Herri, Kupi established an organization called Legality (Legaliteti) and became its leader. The organization, influential mainly in the north of the country, had two thousand armed men. During negotiations with the British, who tried to persuade Kupi to take more a decisive stance against the Germans, he made his own demands. He insisted that the Allies recognize King **Zog I** and Greater Albania, including Kosovo. As his demands were not met, Legality became involved in actions against the Communist partisans rather than against the Germans. In September 1944 Kupi began to form the general staff of a military organization, but his plans were thwarted after the Communists seized the region of Mati, where Legality had the greatest influence.

In November 1944 Kupi left Albania for Italy. On 26 August 1949 in Paris, he announced the establishment of the Albanian National Committee, based on an agreement between royalists like him and republicans led by **Midhat Frashëri**. In 1949 Kupi helped to prepare English sabotage actions against the Communist government in Tirana. Despite heavy Communist losses, none of the guerrilla groups sent from Italy fulfilled their mission because the Communists had been informed about their plans by the Soviet agent Kim Philby. In 1967 Kupi went to the United States, where he lived until his death. He left eight children. (TC)

Sources: *New York Times*, 11 January 1976; Hugh Seton-Watson, *The East European Revolution* (London, 1950); Robert Lee Wolff, *The Balkans in Our Time* (Cambridge, Mass., 1956); Kim Philby, *My Silent War* (London, 1968); Nicholas Bethell, *Betrayed* (London, 1984); Reginald Hibbert, *Albania's National Liberation Struggle: The Bitter Victory* (London and New York, 1991); Gjergj Titani, *Hasani Proletar: Personalitete ushtarake shqiptare ne vite 1912 Dhjetor–1997, vellimi i pare* (Tirana, 1997); Sejfi Vllamasi, *Ballafaqime politike ne Shqiperi (1897–1942)* (Tirana, 1995).

KURBAS Les (25 February 1887, Sambor–3 November 1937, Solovets Islands?), Ukrainian director, actor, and theater theorist. Born into a family of actors, after passing his high school final examinations in Tarnopol (Ternopil), Kurbas studied philosophy at the University of Vienna. In 1908 he transferred to the University of Lemberg (Lviv, Lwów), where in 1909 he organized a drama society. In 1910, when relations between Poles and Ukrainians deteriorated, he was expelled from the University of Lemberg. For some time he studied drama in Vienna, and in the summer of 1911 he was invited by the Hutsul Theater in Verkhovyna to work as a stage manager. From 1912 to 1914 he performed in a theater run under the auspices of the Ruska Besida (Ruthenian Conversation) Society. In September 1915 he founded and directed the Ternopilski Teatralni Vechory (Ternopil Theater Evenings), a theater company in Ternopil. In March 1916 Kurbas moved to Kiev, where from August 1917 to April 1919 he helped to establish the Molodyy Teatr (Young Theater), becoming its artistic director and stage manager. In June 1920, along with a group of actors, he formed the Kiev Drama School (Kyivdramte [KDS]), in which he played various roles, including that of Macbeth, his last theater role. In the same year Kurbas staged Shevchenko's *Haidamaky* (The Haidamaks) in the Taras Shevchenko Theater in Kiev. This production played a major role in the development of Ukrainian theater. In May 1921 the KDS group moved to Kharkiv, where it changed its name to the State Exemplary Touring Theater.

In 1922 Kurbas founded the Berezil Artistic Association, an avant-garde theater. It initially functioned in Kiev and from 1926 on in Kharkiv. It was during the Kharkiv period of the Berezil Theater that Kurbas was most successful as a director. In his creative work he combined literature, theater, music, painting, and philosophy, particularly Expressionism and Constructivism. At that time he befriended the playwright **Mykola Kulish**, who became his closest associate. They both believed that theater was an instrument capable of shaping the public opinion and national consciousness of the Ukrainian people. Kurbas presented his views on theater in *Molodyi Teatr: Heneza–zavdannia–shliakhy* (The Young Theater: Origins–tasks–paths; 1917), *Shliakhy ukraiinskoho teatru i Berezil* (The paths of the Ukrainian theater and the Berezil; 1927), and other works. He lectured at the Kiev and Kharkiv music and drama institutes (1922–26 and 1926–33 respectively). He was also one of the initiators of the theater journals *Teatralni visti, Barykady teatru*, and *Radians'kyi teatr*.

At the end of 1930 Kurbas became the director of the reorganized Veselyi Proletar (Happy Proletarian) Small Forms Theater. Earlier, a Ukrainian opera house and a theater for children had been founded in Kharkiv on his initiative. From 1927 on, Kurbas's work was the subject of increasing official criticism. He was accused of (among other things) nationalism, formalism, and detachment from Soviet reality. He was banned from staging Kulish's *Sonata Pathétique* and other plays. At the beginning of 1931 a campaign was launched against Kurbas, and in September 1933 **Pavel Postyshev**, first secretary of the Central Committee of the Communist Party (Bolshevik) of Ukraine, demanded that he perform a self-criticism and denounce **Mykola Khvylovyi** and

Mykola Skrypnyk. Kurbas refused, and in October of that year he was dismissed as artistic director of the Berezil Theater. Later he was stripped of the title of People's Artist, which he had received in 1925. Arrested in December 1933, he was sent to a prison camp and was later executed. In some sources, 15 November 1942 is given as the date of his death. *Filosofiia teatru* (Philosophy of the theater; 2001) is the most complete edition of his writings. (BB)

Sources: *Encyclopedia of Ukraine*, vol. 2 (Toronto, 1988); *Ukrainska Literaturna Entsyklopediia*, vol. 3 (Kiev, 1995); *Dovidnyk z istorii Ukraiiny* (Kiev, 2001); *Les Kurbas u teatralniy diialnosti, v otsinkakh suchasnykiv—dokumenty* (Baltimore and Toronto, 1989); Nelli Korniienko, *Les Kurbas: Repetytsiia maibutnioho* (Kiev, 1998).

KUROŃ Jacek (3 March 1934, Lwów [Lviv]–17 June 2004, Warsaw), Polish social and political activist. Kuroń graduated in history from Warsaw University in 1957. In 1949–53 and 1955–56 he was active in the (Communist) Union of Polish Youth, and from 1955 to 1961, in the Walter Circle of Red Scouting. In 1956 he took part in the youth "renewal" movement at Warsaw University, and he worked with the workers' council of the Żerań Motor Car Factory. In 1953 and from 1956 to 1964 Kuroń belonged to the Polish United Workers' Party (Polska Zjednoczona Partia Robotnicza [PUWP]). In 1962 he co-founded a political discussion club at Warsaw University. The club was dissolved by the Communist authorities in 1963. In 1964–65, along with **Karol Modzelewski**, Kuroń prepared and signed an "Open Letter to PUWP Members," in which he and Modzelewski pointed to the divergence between Communist ideas and practice. In March 1965 he was arrested and sentenced to three years in prison, and in 1967 he was released. The "Open Letter" was smuggled to the West and published there. It was translated into many languages and made both signatories famous, especially among the Western left. Kuroń took part in many activities of the "rangers" (extreme leftist critics of the Communist system in Poland)—for instance, he took part in demonstrations to protest the banning of Adam Mickiewicz's play *Dziady* (Forefathers). Arrested on 8 March 1968 and sentenced to three and a half years in prison for organizing student protests, Kuroń was released in 1971. In 1975 he co-organized protests against the amendment of the constitution, and he signed the "Letter of 59" on this issue. In July 1976 he wrote a letter to the Italian Communist leader, Enrique Berlinguer, asking his assistance in the defense of Polish workers arrested after protests in June 1976.

On 23 September 1976 Kuroń was among the founding members of the Committee for the Defense of Workers (Komitet Obrony Robotników [KOR]). He co-authored the concept of overcoming totalitarianism by social self-organization outside of official Communist structures (*Myśli o programie działania* [Thoughts on the program of action]; 1976). Detained from May to July 1977, Kuroń was one of the leaders of Committee of Social Self-Defense KOR. He published a lot in the uncensored press. He was editor of the periodical *Kwartalnik Polityczny Krytyka* and a member of and lecturer in the Society of Scientific Courses. Repeatedly detained for forty-eight-hour periods, in 1979 Kuroń was the target of an assault by a squad from the Socialist Union of Polish Students, inspired by the Security Service. He took part in the KOR's meetings with Czech Charter 77 representatives. From September 1980 he was an adviser to the Inter-Factory Founding Committee of Solidarity in Gdańsk and then to its National Coordination Commission and the National Commission. One of the key experts of Solidarity and co-author of the concept of the self-limiting revolution, Kuroń was treated by the Communist authorities as an extremist. The Kremlin demanded his arrest. After the introduction of martial law on 13 December 1981, Kuroń was interned and then arrested because of an attempt to overthrow the system by force. Amnestied in 1984, he worked with the Solidarity underground structures and the uncensored press.

In 1988 Kuroń joined the Civic Committee of the Chairman of Solidarity, and from February to April 1989 he took part in the Round Table Talks. From June 1989 to 1997 he was an MP. From September 1989 to December 1990 and from July 1992 to September 1993 he was minister of labor and social welfare. A member of the Presidium of the Civic Parliamentary Club and deputy chairman of the Democratic Union and later of the Union of Freedom, Kuroń was active in numerous charity efforts whose aim it was to ease the social costs of the economic transformation—for instance, the SOS Foundation. In 1993 he initiated the Pact on State Enterprise. In 1993–97 he chaired the parliamentary commission of national and ethnic minorities. For many years he was the most popular politician in Poland. In 1995 he was a candidate in the presidential elections, but he won only 9 percent of the vote. Kuroń authored many works, including the following: *Zasady ideowe* (Ideological principles; 1978); *Polityka i odpowiedzialność* (Politics and responsibility; 1984); *Wiara i wina* (Faith and guilt; 1990); *Gwiezdny czas* (Star times; 1991); *Moja zupa* (My soup; 1991); *Spoko! czyli kwadratura koła* (Play it cool or squaring the circle; 1992); *Na krawędzi* (On the edge; 1997); and *Działanie* (Acting; 2002). (AF)

Sources: *Nasi w Sejmie i Senacie* (Warsaw, 1990); *Opozycja w PRL: Słownik biograficzny 1956–1988,* vol. 1 (Warsaw, 2000); Andrzej Friszke, *Opozycja polityczna w PRL 1945–1980* (London,

1994); Jan Skórzyński, *Ugoda i rewolucja: Władza i opozycja 1985–1989* (Warsaw, 1995); Janusz A. Majcherek, *Pierwsza dekada III Rzeczpospolitej 1989–1999* (Warsaw, 1999); Wojciech Roszkowski, *Historia Polski 1914–2000* (Warsaw, 2001); Antoni Dudek, *Pierwsze lata III Rzeczpospolitej 1989–2001* (Kraków, 2002).

KUSHAL Frantsishak (16 February 1895, Pershay, near Volozhin [Valozhyn]–25 May 1968, Rochester, New York), Belorussian general and national activist. Born into a peasant family, Kushal graduated from a high school in Ivanets. In 1915 he was mobilized into the Russian Army, and in February 1916 he finished an officer training school. As a company commander on the German front lines, he received many awards and was promoted to staff captain. After the February 1917 revolution, Kushal became involved in the Belorussian pro-independence movement. In the autumn of 1917 he retired from military service and settled in Minsk and Vilnius, where he took part in Belorussian political life. In April 1919 he was briefly detained by the Polish authorities for working in support of the cause of Belorussian independence. When the Belorussian Military Commission was established, Kushal served as a member until the end of the Polish-Soviet war. In 1921 he became a career officer in the Polish Army. He served in Chełm, Pułtusk, and Małkinia. In September 1939 he fought in the battle of Lwów (Lviv) and was taken prisoner by the Soviets. He was held in prison camps in Starobelsk and Paulishchy Bor, near Smolensk, and the Lubyanka Prison in Moscow. In mid–June 1941 he was taken to Minsk and placed under surveillance by the local NKVD.

After the Nazi invasion of the Soviet Union in June 1941, Kushal collaborated with the Germans. In December 1941 he became commander of a school for non-commissioned officers that trained cadres for the Belorussian Self-Defense organization. In July 1942 he was put in charge of a training course for officers of Belorussian Self-Defense and appointed head of the department of military affairs of the Belorussian People's Mutual Aid Association, whose founders intended it to become a form of Belorussian government allied with the Third Reich. In December 1943 Kushal joined the Belorussian Central Council (BCC), which operated with the consent of the Germans and which described itself as the political representation of the nation. In March 1944 the BCC appointed Kushal commander of Belorussian National Defense, military units formed of recruits. In the summer of 1944 Kushal went to Germany, and one year later he emigrated to the United States. While there, he founded the Association of Belorussian War Veterans in 1947, and from 1952 to 1954 he served as president of the Belorussian and American Union. Kushal was one of the founders of and contributors to the émigré periodicals *Belarus* and *Bats'kaŭshchyna*. He also wrote numerous works on Belorussian military history. In 1999 Kushal's *Sproby stvarennia belaruskaha voiska* (Efforts to establish the Belorussian Army) was published in Minsk. (EM)

Sources: *Entsyklapiedyia historyi Bielarusi*, vol. 4 (Minsk, 1997); *New York Times*, 27 May 1968; *Belarus* (New York), 1968, no. 134; Vitaut Kipel and Zora Kipel, eds., *Byelorussian Statehood* (New York, 1988).

KUSTURICA Emir (24 November 1954, Sarajevo), Yugoslav film director. Born into a Muslim family in Bosnia, Kusturica graduated from the FAMU Film Institute in Prague, Czechoslovakia. In 1978 he received the first prize at a student film festival in Prague. Upon returning home, he worked in Sarajevo television. Kusturica made his directorial debut in 1979, and he gained a wider reputation for a television adaptation of **Ivo Andrić**'s *Buffet Titanic* (1980). All his later movies were successes. For *Sječas li se Dolly Bell?* (Do you remember Dolly Bell? 1981) he won the Golden Lion in Venice in 1981; for *Otac na službenom putu* (When father was away on business; 1985) he received the Golden Palm in Cannes in 1985. He won the Golden Palm again in 1989 for *Dom za vešanje* (*Time of the Gypsies*), in which he combined improvisation by amateur actors with surreal visions of Balkan gypsies. Kusturica was always fascinated by the gypsy culture, and he thought the secret of his success was his own version of a Federico Fellini-like creativity. In the 1980s Kusturica was one of the leaders of the Sarajevo movement of New Primitivism, which filled the Communist authorities with consternation. He also performed in the musical group Zabranjeno Pušenje (No Smoking), which won great popularity. The music for the *Time of the Gypsies* was composed by Goran Bregović, with whom Kusturica worked out a specific style, called *umza-umza*, combining Balkan and gypsy folk music with funky and punk rock. After the breakup of Yugoslavia and the outbreak of war in its former territory, Kusturica stressed that he was a Yugoslav. He opposed Serbian nationalism, and he challenged one of its leaders, **Vojislav Šešelj**, to a duel.

From 1990 Kusturica frequently worked in the United States—for instance, at Columbia University in New York. It was in America that his movie *Arizona Dreams* (1992) was directed, with an international cast, winning him the Golden Bear in Berlin in 1993. Nevertheless, Kusturica became disappointed with the American movie industry and returned home, where he directed his best-known film, *Bila jednom jedna zemlja* (*Underground*; 1995), for which he won his third Golden Palm in Cannes in 1995. In the movie, in a symbolic and surrealist way, he presented half a century of Communist Yugoslav history and its final destruction. In 1998 Kusturica directed *Crna mačka, beli mačor* (*Black Cat, White Cat*). (WR)

Sources: Jean-Marc Bouineau, *Mala knjiga o Emiru Kusturici* (Belgrade, 1995); Georgio Bertellini, *Emir Kusturica* (Milan, 1996); Paolo Vecchi, *Emir Kusturica* (Rome, 1999); Stach Szabłowski, "Emir Kusturica," www.e-zone.pl/lk/lk_kusturica.php; www.actustar.com/biographies/kusturicaemir.html.

KUSÝ Miroslav (1 December 1931, Bratislava), Slovak dissident philosopher and political scientist. In 1954 Kusý graduated in philosophy from Charles University in Prague. Later he worked as assistant professor, associate professor, and (from 1967) full professor at the Department of Philosophy of Comenius University in Bratislava. During the Prague Spring of 1968 he was one of the reform leaders of the Communist Party of Slovakia (CPS). From October 1968 to April 1969 he headed the Ideological Department of the CPS Central Committee. As a result of the Warsaw Pact invasion, during the so-called normalization Kusý was expelled from the CPS and from the university (1970), and he started dissident activities for which he was further repressed. He became one of the leaders of the democratic opposition in Slovakia, closely cooperating with Czech dissidents. In 1977 he signed Charter 77. He published a lot in the uncensored press and abroad, mainly on the political and social situation in Czechoslovakia. In the 1970s and 1980s Kusý worked as a blue-collar laborer. In August 1989 he was arrested, but in late November 1989 he was released during the "Velvet Revolution." In 1989 he was a co-founder of the Czechoslovak Helsinki Committee, and in 1990, of the Slovak Helsinki Committee. In 1990–91 he was an MP and member of the Presidium of the Slovak National Council, and then he worked as head of the Bratislava office of President **Václav Havel**. He was also rector of Bratislava University and founded the chair of political science there in 1990. In 1992 he founded and became UNESCO chair of human rights at this university. From the elections of 1998 Kusý worked as an adviser for human rights and national minorities to **Prime Minister Mikuláš Dzurinda**. Kusý authored many works, including *Zakázané písomnosti* (Forbidden writings; 1990); *Na vlnách Slobodnej Európy* (On the waves of Free Europe; 1990); *Eseje* (Essays; 1991); and *Čo s našimi Maďarmi?* (What about our Hungarians? 1998). (PU)

Sources: *ČBS*; Rudolf Chmel, ed., *Kwestia słowacka w XX wieku* (Gliwice, 2002); www.ceu.hu/sun/SUN%202002/Descriptions/CVs/Kusy.htm.

KUTLVAŠR Karel (27 January 1895, Michalovice–2 September 1961, Prague), Czech general. Before World War I Kutlvašr worked as a clerk in Kiev. After the outbreak of the war he joined a Czech unit and took part in intelligence operations. In 1917 he became an officer of the Czechoslovak Legions, and on 2 July 1917 he fought at Zborov, the Legions' first battle in Russia. In 1918 he distinguished himself in fighting against the Bolsheviks, and in October of that year he became commander of the first regiment, with which he fought in Siberia in 1919. In February 1920, as commander of this regiment, Kutlvašr returned to Prague, where he was put in command of an infantry regiment until 1923. From 1923 to 1931 he served as commander of an infantry brigade in Chomutov, and then he directed an infantry school in Milovice until 1934. In 1932 he became brigadier general. From 1934 to 1939 he commanded a division in Hradec Králové. During the German occupation Kutlvašr was active in the national resistance movement as a member of an organization called Defense of the Nation (Obrana Národa). In May 1945 he was military commander of the Prague Uprising. In this role he accepted the capitulation of the German forces. The Communists claimed that Kutlvašr had thus prevented the Red Army from liberating Prague and never forgave him. Initially after the war Kutlvašr was promoted to major general and served as commander of the Greater Prague military district, and in 1946 he assumed command of a corps in Plzen. From 1946 to 1948 he was deputy district commander in Brno. After the coup of February 1948 Kutlvašr was forced to retire. In the autumn of 1948 he assumed the leadership of an anti-Communist organization founded by Josef Hruška, a provocateur working for **Bedřich Reicin**, head of military intelligence. Arrested in December of that year, Kutlvašr was sentenced to life imprisonment in May 1949. Amnestied in 1960, he was rehabilitated in 1968, during the Prague Spring. In 1991 he was posthumously promoted to army general. (PU)

Sources: *ČBS*; *Kdo byl kdo v našich dějinach ve 20. století*, vol. 1 (Prague, 1998); Libor Vukoupil, *Slovník českých dějin* (Brno, 2000).

KUTRZEBA Stanisław (15 November 1876, Kraków–7 January 1946, Kraków), Polish legal historian. From 1894 to 1898 Kutrzeba studied at the School of Law of the Jagiellonian University (Uniwersytet Jagielloński [UJ]) in Kraków, earning a doctorate. From 1899 to 1900 he attended lectures at the Collège de France and the École des Hautes Études. From 1901 to 1908 he was an assistant professor at the City and Land Archives in Kraków. In 1902 he received his postdoctoral degree from the UJ for his work on the history of Polish law, and in 1908 he was offered a UJ professorship. In the academic years 1913–14 and 1920–21 Kutrzeba was dean of the UJ School of

Law. In 1914 he became a corresponding member of the Department of History and Philosophy of the Academy of Arts and Sciences in Kraków. In 1918 he became an active member of the Polish Academy of Arts and Sciences (Polska Akademia Umiejętności [PAU]) and chairman of the PAU Legal Committee. From 1919 to 1926 he was secretary of the PAU Department of History and Philosophy, and in 1926 he became secretary general of the PAU. In the academic year 1932–33 Kutrzeba was the rector of the UJ, and from 1939 to 1946 he was president of the PAU. He was also a foreign member of the Czech Academy of Arts and Sciences, a foreign member of the Hungarian Academy of Sciences, and a corresponding member of the Académie des Sciences Morales et Politiques in Paris. He was an expert on the Polish delegation to the Paris Peace Conference in 1919 and headed a delegation that negotiated an arbitration treaty with Czechoslovakia in 1925. He increasingly embraced federalist views.

After the outbreak of World War II, Kutrzeba became deputy chairman of the Civic Assistance Committee in Kraków. Arrested along with other UJ professors by the Nazis during the Sonderaktion Krakau, on 6 November 1939, he was sent to the Sachsenhausen concentration camp. Returning to Poland in February 1940, Kutrzeba refused an offer to work with the Institut für Deutsche Ostarbeit. He was involved in clandestine teaching, serving as dean of the underground UJ school of law. In 1945 in Moscow he attended negotiations on the establishment of the Provisional Government of National Unity. At that time he was coopted to the National Home Council (Krajowa Rada Narodowa [KRN]). Kutrzeba wrote articles for *Tygodnik Powszechny* and helped found *Tygodnik Warszawski*. He left a vast and wide-ranging legacy. Recognized as an expert on the history of Polish law and the political system, he also published legal and political source documents. Kutrzeba is the author of several hundred publications, including the following: *Sądy ziemskie i grodzkie w wiekach średnich* (Land and town courts in the Middle Ages; 1901–2); *Mężobójstwo w prawie polskim XIV i XV wieku* (The crime of husband killing in Polish fourteenth- and fifteenth-century law; 1907); *Historia ustroju Polski w zarysie* (An outline history of the Polish political system, 4 vols.; 1905–17); *Dawne polskie prawo sądowe* (Old Polish law of courts, 2 vols.; 1921); *Polska Odrodzona 1914–21* (Poland reborn 1914–21; 1921); *Sejm walny dawnej Rzeczypospolitej Polskiej* (The National Diet of the Old Republic of Poland; 1922); *Polskie prawo polityczne według traktatów* (Polish political law according to treaties; 1923); and *Historia źródeł dawnego prawa polskiego* (History of sources of old Polish law, 2 vols.; 1925–26). (JS)

Sources: *PSB*, vol. 16; Adam Vetulani, *Stanisław Kutrzeba: Historyk prawa* (Kraków, 1947); *Słownik historyków polskich* (Warsaw, 1994); *Stanisław Kutrzeba, 1876–1946: Materiały z Uroczystego Posiedzenia PAU w dniu 24 czerwca 1996* (Kraków, 1998).

KUTRZEBA Tadeusz (15 April 1885, Kraków–8 January 1947, London), Polish general and historian. The son of an officer of the Austrian Army, Kutrzeba studied at a military high school, and in 1906 he graduated from the Technical Academy in Vienna as a second lieutenant of sappers. He studied at the Austrian General Staff Academy, and he took a higher course in military engineering. During World War I he fought in the Austro-Hungarian Army, but in late 1918 he joined the Polish Army as a captain. He quickly advanced. During the Polish-Soviet war Kutrzeba was chief of staff and commander of the first Legionary division of infantry, and from April 1920 he commanded the southeastern and middle fronts. During the May 1926 coup Kutrzeba supported President **Stanisław Wojciechowski** and fought on the government's side, but after the victory of **Józef Piłsudski** he stayed in the army. Promoted to the rank of brigadier general in 1928, he took over the command of the Higher Military School and held it until the outbreak of war in 1939. From 1935 Kutrzeba also worked in the General Inspectorate of the Armed Forces.

On the eve of war, Kutrzeba was appointed general of division and assumed command of the Poznań Army. During the September 1939 campaign, after the Polish troops had retreated from the German border, Kutrzeba commanded the Poznań and Pomorze Armies at the Battle of the Bzura River. On 9 September he started a counteroffensive that took the Germans by surprise. This move started a battle that lasted a few days, the largest in the Polish defense war of 1939; it forced the Germans to change their plans and move several divisions, aircraft, and armored units to the Bzura area. The Polish counteroffensive delayed the capture of Warsaw. Since the units commanded by Kutrzeba could not receive Polish support, he ordered the retreat to Warsaw. With the remnants of the Poznań Army he made his way to the capital and was appointed deputy commander of the Warsaw Army. After the capitulation of Warsaw, Kutrzeba was taken prisoner of war, and he spent the war years in a POW camp in Germany. After the war he did not come back to Poland; he settled in London, where he worked at the Historical Commission of the September Campaign. Kutrzeba authored several works, including *Bitwa nad Niemnem (wrzesień-październik 1920)* (The Battle of the Niemen River, [September–October 1920;] 1926); *Wyprawa Kijowska 1920 roku* (The Kiev Operation of 1920; 1937); and *Bitwa nad Bzurą* (The Battle of the Bzura River; 1958). In 1957 Kutrzeba's ashes were transported to and buried in Warsaw. (WD)

Sources: *PSB*, vol. 16; J. Godlewski, "Bitwa nad Bzurą," *Wojskowy Przegląd Historyczny*, 1962, nos. 1–4, and 1963, no. 1; *Wielka Internetowa Encyklopedia Multimedialna, Encyklopedia II wojny światowej* (Warsaw, 1975).

KVATERNIK Eugen Dido (29 March 1910, Zagreb–10 March 1962, Rio Cuarto, Argentina), Croatian nationalist politician. Kvaternik was the son of **Slavko Kvaternik**, the grandson of **Josip Frank**, and the great-grandson of Eugen Kvaternik (1825–71). In 1930, along with his father and **Ante Pavelić**, he co-founded the Ustasha (Insurgent) movement. He was its leading activist in Italy (1930–34). As chief of staff of its revolutionary operations, acting under the pseudonym "Longin," Kvaternik planned and carried out the assassination of Yugoslav King **Alexander I** on 9 October 1934. In late September 1934 he went from Italy to Switzerland to instruct the assassins, who arrived from the Jankapuszta camp, near Nagykanizsa, in Hungary. After the assassination Kvaternik fled from France to Italy. Arrested in Turin, he was place under house arrest until April 1941. In France he was sentenced to death in absentia. After the proclamation on 10 April 1941 of the Independent Croatian State (Nezavisna Država Hrvatska [NDH]), under Nazi auspices, Kvaternik became its chief ideologue. He was also an MP, the minister of interior, and head of the security (Ravsigur). He approved of the arrests of Jews and of paying the German authorities the equivalent of 30 German marks for each person transported to the death camps. Jewish property was confiscated by the NDH. Kvaternik also directed the extermination of Croatian Serbs, announcing that irrespective of the final outcome of the war, after its termination there would no Serbs at all in Croatia. In October 1942 Kvaternik was dismissed by the Germans owing to the chaos caused by his genocidal policies. It is estimated that about 125,000 Serbs and many thousands of Jews were killed in Croatia during World War II. A 1964 estimate by the Center for Scholarly Documentation of the Institute of the History of the Workers' Movement in Zagreb fixed the number of victims at 249,000. According to the Jewish commune of Zagreb, the number of victims of the Jasenovac concentration camp was 85,000. In independent Croatia Kvaternik's memoirs were published as *Sjećanja i zapažanja 1925–1945* (Memoirs and reflections, 1925–1945; 1995). (JD)

Sources: Branimir Yelitch, *Fight for the Croatian State* (Buenos Aires, 1960); Ivo Omrčanin, *Dramatis Personae and Finis of the Independent State of Croatia in British and American Documents* (Bryn Mawr, Pa., 1983); Bogdan Krizman, *Ante Pavelić i Ustaše* (Zagreb, 1983).

KVATERNIK Slavko (25 August 1878, Vučinić Selo–8 June 1947, Zagreb), Croatian marshal and nationalist politician. Kvaternik was the son of Eugen Kvaternik, the leader of an unsuccessful uprising against the Hungarians in 1871. After graduating from the Infantry Cadet School in Karlstadt (Karlovac), he began to serve in the Austro-Hungarian Army. From 1904 to 1906 he studied at the Military Academy and was promoted to captain. During World War I he served as a staff officer of the forty-second Honved division, chief of staff of the fifty-fifth infantry division, and then colonel in the Austro-Hungarian military government in Belgrade. In December 1918 Kvaternik supported the Yugoslav cause, but after a short period of service in the army of the newly founded Kingdom of Serbs, Croats, and Slovenes, he became disenchanted and left the army. Through his marriage with the daughter of **Josip Frank**, leader of the Croatian Party of Rights (Hrvatska Stranka Prava), he became involved with the Croatian nationalists who negated the constitution of 1921. His son, **Eugen Dido**, was one of the major Ustasha leaders. As the director of the Croatian Worker cooperative (Hrvatski Radiša), Kvaternik was one of the leading figures in the country supporting **Ante Pavelić**.

On 10 April 1941 in Zagreb, before the city was captured by the Germans, Kvaternik proclaimed the establishment of the Independent State of Croatia. When the head of state, Pavelić, arrived in Croatia, Kvaternik became his deputy. He was also appointed defense minister in the government established on 15 April and commander-in-chief with the rank of marshal of the Croatian military forces. Almost immediately he began to form the Croatian Home Army (Domobranstvo). However, lacking the required skills, he was neither successful in his work nor respected. In addition, because of his pro-Habsburg sympathies, Kvaternik was not the kind of politician with whom the leaders of the Third Reich wanted to work. He resigned his position owing to ill health at the beginning of October 1942, at the time of the purge of former supporters of the Habsburgs. In November of that year Pavelić finally dismissed him, as well as his son, from all their official duties, though the fact was not announced until January 1943. From then on Kvaternik lived in Bratislava, Vienna, and Semmering. While abroad, he criticized the Ustasha regime in Zagreb. Handed over to the Titoist authorities, Kvaternik was sentenced to death (7 June 1947) and executed. (WR)

Sources: *Biographisches Lexikon*, vol. 2; Rudolf Kiszling, "Die Wehrmacht des unabhängingen Staates Kroatien 1941–1945," *Österreichische Militärische Zeitschrift*, 1965, nos. 261–266; Jerzy Kozeński, *Agresja na Jugosławię* (Poznań, 1979); Ivo Omrčanin, *Dramatis Presonae and Finis of the Independent State of Croatia in British and American Documents* (Bryn Mawr, Pa., 1983); Bogdan Krizman, *Ustaše i Treći Reich*, vols. 1–2 (Zagreb, 1983); Bogdan Krizman, *Ante Pavelić i Ustaše* (Zagreb, 1983); Marcus Tanner, *Croatia: A Nation Forged in War* (New Haven, 1997).

KVIESIS Alberts (22 December 1881, Tērvetes, Courland–9 August 1944, Riga), Peasant Party politician, president of Latvia. Born into the family of a municipal clerk, in 1902 Kviesis graduated from a high school in Mitava (Jelgava). In 1907 he graduated from the Law School of the university in Dorpat (Tartu). He later worked as an attorney in Mitava, taking an active part in the city's public life. In 1915, as a war refugee in Dorpat, he headed the Committee for Aid to Latvian Refugees. In 1917 he was elected to the Provisional Council of Courland, based in Dorpat. In 1917 he became a member of the Latvian Peasant Union. In 1918 he returned to Mitava and later moved to Riga, where in November of that year he joined the Latvian Provisional National Council. In 1919 he became a member of the Judiciary Council and subsequently its chairman from May 1920 to 1930 (except for the period from 1921 to 1923, when he served as minister of interior). As a deputy to the Constitutional Assembly and member of parliament (Saeima) for three terms, Kviesis represented the Peasant Union and worked closely with **Kārlis Ulmanis**. In 1926 he became deputy speaker of the parliament.

In 1930 Kviesis was elected president of the state for the first time and was reelected in 1933. He continued to perform his duties after the coup staged by Ulmanis in May 1934. After his second term as president ended, Kviesis resumed his work as an attorney in Riga. During the Soviet occupation of 1939–41 he avoided deportation and lived in the countryside. After the German invasion in July 1941, he returned to his job in Riga, and in 1942 he became a legal adviser to the justice department of the Latvian self-government under German supervision. In 1943 Kviesis became director general of the department. In November 1944 he protested in vain against the conscription of men born in ten successive years into the Latvian Waffen SS Legion. Kviesis died of a heart attack after he had boarded a ship bound for Germany during the evacuation of the city. He was buried in Riga. (EJ)

Sources: *Latvijas darbinieku galerija* (Riga, 1928); *Latvijas vadošie darbinieki* (Riga, 1935); *Es viņu pazīstu* (Riga, 1939); Andrejs Plakans, *Historical Dictionary of Latvia* (Lanham, Md., 1997).

KWAPIŃSKI Jan [originally Piotr Chałupka] (12 November 1885, Warsaw–4 November 1964, Penley, United Kingdom), Polish Socialist activist. Kwapiński graduated from a factory school, and from 1900 he worked at the rolling mill in Ostrowiec Świętokrzyski. In 1901 he joined the Polish Socialist Party (Polska Partia Socjalistyczna [PPS]). A participant in the 1905 revolution, because of his role in the so-called Ostrowiec Republic, he had to go into hiding. Kwapiński left for Kraków, where he gradu-ated from a course for PPS fighting squadron instructors. From 1906 he was active in the PPS–Revolutionary Faction and directed many armed operations. Arrested in April 1907, he was brought to the ill-famed Tenth Pavilion of the Warsaw Citadel. In December 1907 he was sentenced to death, but the sentence was then commuted to fifteen years of forced labor. In 1908 Kwapiński was sent to Orel Province. Released after the February 1917 revolution, he represented political prisoners in the Executive Committee of the Orel soviet. He founded a PPS cell there and helped Polish refugees.

In November 1918 Kwapiński returned to Poland, taking over the Ministry of Interior administration in Piotrków Trybunalski. In March 1919 he was suspended as a PPS member for his attempts to turn the Polish workers' councils into organs of power. In April 1919, after resuming his PPS membership, Kwapiński was elected to the party's Supreme Council and evolved toward reformism. In 1920 he became a member of the PPS Central Executive Committee. In 1919 he co-organized the Trade Union of Farm Hands of the Polish Republic, and he was chairman of its Main Board until 1939. In 1922–39 he was also chairman of the Central Commission of Trade Unions. Kwapiński combated Communist influence in the trade unions. As an MP (1922–30), he favored legal methods of struggle against the *sanacja* regime. Co-organizer of the Centrolew opposition bloc, in 1930 Kwapiński was sentenced to a year in prison for a speech in which he attacked **Józef Piłsudski**. In the mid–1930s he strove to create a democratic opposition bloc and wrote for the Socialist press. In March 1939 he became mayor of Łódź.

In September 1939 Kwapiński went eastward. In June 1940 he was arrested by the NKVD and detained in Altai Yakutsya. Released after the Polish-Soviet Treaty of July 1941, in October 1941 he became a delegate of the Polish Embassy in Tashkent. He left for London, where in January 1942 he became head of the PPS Foreign Committee and a member of its Commission for Homeland Affairs. From June 1942 he was minister of industry and trade; from July 1943, deputy prime minister and minister of industry, trade, and navigation; and from November 1944, also minister of the treasury in subsequent governments-in-exile. Kwapiński firmly opposed concessions concerning Poland's eastern border. After the war he stayed in London and worked in the Central Foreign Committee of the PPS. In 1952–54 he was its deputy chairman and from 1954 to 1961, chairman. Kwapiński authored many works, including the following: *O jaką reformę rolną walczy Polska Partia Socjalistyczna?* (What kind of land reform is the Polish Socialist Party fighting for? 1925); *Organizacja Bojowa. Katorga. Rewolucja rosyjska. Z moich wspomnień*

1905–1919 (Fighting Squads. Exile. Russian Revolution. My memoirs 1905–1919; 1928); *Pod Rogowem: Ze wspomnień bojowca* (At Rogów: Memoirs of a fighter; 1928); *1939–1945: Kartki z pamiętnika* (1939–1945: Notes from a diary; 1947); and *Moje wspomnienia, 1904–1939* (My memoirs, 1904–1939; 1965). (JS)

Sources: *PSB*, vol. 16; *Słownik biograficzny działaczy polskiego ruchu robotniczego*, vol. 3 (Warsaw, 1992); *Kto był kim w Drugiej Rzeczypospolitej* (Warsaw, 1994); *Encyklopedia historii Polski: Dzieje polityczne*, vol. 1 (Warsaw, 1994); Jerzy Holzer, *Polska Partia Socjalistyczna w latach 1917–1919* (Warsaw, 1962); Tadeusz Wolsza, *Rząd RP na obczyźnie wobec wydarzeń w kraju, 1945–1950* (Warsaw, 1998).

KWASIBORSKI Józef, pseudonyms "Dębicki" and "Rafał" (14 October 1898, Minsk–17 October 1980, Pruszków), Polish politician. The son of an artisan metalworker, while a student at Mikołaj Rej Gymnasium in Warsaw, Kwasiborski joined the Polish Military Organization (Polska Organizacja Wojskowa [POW]), and in 1918 he became deputy commander of the POW district of Grodzisk Mazowiecki-Błonie. In 1919 he passed his high school final examinations and began to study medicine at Warsaw University. He discontinued his studies in 1920, when he volunteered to serve in the Polish Army during the Polish-Soviet war. In 1921 he resumed his studies but discontinued them because of financial problems in 1923. Kwasiborski worked at an institution for the mentally ill in Pruszków while simultaneously studying at the School of Journalism; at the Warsaw University Medical School; and, from 1930 to 1931, at the Law School of Warsaw University, but he never completed his studies. In 1924 he became chairman of the provincial board of the Polish Christian Democratic Party, and in 1928 he became a member of the Main Board of this party. From 1937 to 1939 he served as deputy secretary of the Main Board of the Labor Party (Stronnictwo Pracy [SP]).

Kwasiborski fought in the September 1939 campaign, and when it ended, he returned home to Pruszków. In March 1940 he was one of the two vice-chairmen of the underground SP, which he represented in the Coordinating Political Committee from October 1942 to May 1943. From 1941 until the end of the war Kwasiborski served as district delegate of Warsaw Province of the Polish government-in-exile. He fought in the Warsaw Uprising; a few days after its capitulation, he left the city and continued his underground activities in Milanówek and Pruszków. In April 1945 he became a member of the National Unity Council (Rada Jedności Narodowej [RJN]). When **Karol Popiel** returned from exile in July 1945, Kwasiborski helped to revive the SP, but the original SP leaders had to reconcile themselves to sharing party leadership equally with the Zryw group, known as the Party of National Upsurge (Stronnictwo Zrywu Narodowego [SZN]), led by **Zygmunt Felczak** and **Feliks Widy-Wirski**. In December 1945 Kwasiborski became a deputy to the National Home Council (Krajowa Rada Narodowa [KRN]), but when the members of the SZN took control of the SP, he resigned his seat in September 1946. On 31 August 1948 Kwasiborski was arrested by the State Security Office. On 6 April 1951, after a long interrogation in a rigged trial, he was sentenced to life imprisonment on charges including "Fascist and Nazi crimes." In October 1956 he was released under an amnesty, and in July 1958 his sentence was declared null and void *ab initio*. Kwasiborski was active in the Literary Archconfraternity in Warsaw and served as chairman of the Community Temperance Committee in Pruszków. In 1972 he received the papal award Pro Ecclesia et Pontifice. (WR)

Sources: Kunert, vol. 2; *Sojusznicy Gestapo: Proces Kwasiborskiego i innych* (trial transcript) (Warsaw, 1951); Stefan Korboński, *Polskie państwo podziemne* (Paris, 1975); F. Galewicz, "Józef Kwasiborski," *Chrześcijanin w Świecie*, 1979, no. 11; Henryk Przybylski, *Chrześcijańska Demokracja i Narodowa Partia Pracy w latach 1926–1937* (Warsaw, 1980); Konstanty Turowski, "Dzieje Stronnictwa Pracy w latach 1945–1946," *Chrześcijanin w Świecie*, 1982, no. 1; Janusz Zabłocki, *Chrześcijańska Demokracja w kraju i na emigracji 1947–1970* (Lublin, 1999).

KWAŚNIEWSKI Aleksander (15 November 1954, Białogard), Polish Communist activist and post-Communist politician. In 1973–77 Kwaśniewski studied in the Department of Transportation Economics at Gdańsk University, but he did not graduate. During his studies he was active in the Socialist Union of Polish Students (SUPS). In 1977 he joined the (Communist) Polish United Workers' Party (Polska Zjednoczona Partia Robotnicza [PUWP]) and continued his career in the SUPS apparatus as deputy chairman of its provincial administration in Gdańsk (1977–79) and head of the Department of Culture of its Main Board (1979–80). In November 1981 Kwaśniewski became editor-in-chief of the student periodical *Itd*. Scrutinized during martial law, he continued in this capacity until February 1984, when he became editor-in-chief of the daily *Sztandar Młodych*. From November 1985 Kwaśniewski was minister for youth affairs, and in October 1987 he assumed the chair of the government Committee for Youth and Physical Culture. In 1988–91 he was also chair of the Polish Olympics Committee. It was then that he made numerous contacts with other youth and sports activists, often connected with special services. From October 1988 to August 1989 Kwaśniewski was minister without portfolio, a member of the Government

Presidium, and chairman of the Socio-Political Committee of the Council of Ministers. In this capacity he played a key role in the preparation of the Round Table Talks, and he took part in them as co-chairman of the trade union pluralism group. In the parliamentary elections of 4 June 1989 he ran for the Senate, but he lost.

In late 1989, during the growing crisis in the Communist Party, Kwaśniewski mobilized younger cadres, and with the support of the party leadership he took the lead of the "renewal" wing of the party. At the Eleventh PUWP Congress in January 1990, when the party was dissolved, Kwaśniewski assumed leadership of the post-Communist Social Democracy of the Polish Republic (Socjaldemokracja Rzeczypospolitej Polskiej [SdRP]). He gained the support of the former PUWP apparatus and rank-and-file membership since he successfully nourished their hopes for political survival. In the parliamentary elections of October 1991 Kwaśniewski won a seat and took the lead of the parliamentary Club of the Democratic Left. Former Communists not only managed to appropriate a significant part of state property, becoming the new business class, but they also benefited from the social costs of transformation and a growing discontent with the post-Solidarity elites. Thence the SdRP ratings grew, along with those of a wider coalition, the Democratic Left Alliance (Sojusz Lewicy Demokratycznej [SLD]). In the elections of September 1993 the SLD gained more than 20 percent of the vote and became the largest parliamentary faction. Kwaśniewski made use of the resistance of President **Lech Wałęsa** and avoided heading the government; this made it possible for him to maintain a distance from the coalition government of the SLD and the Polish Peasant Party under **Waldemar Pawlak** (1993–95), and even from the governments headed by his SLD colleagues, **Józef Oleksy** and **Włodzimierz Cimoszewicz** (1995–97). Kwaśniewski chaired the parliamentary constitutional commission and contributed substantially to the preparation of the constitution that came into force in October 1997.

In the presidential campaign of 1995 Kwaśniewski enjoyed the highest ratings, and the competition among post-Solidarity candidates made him the key challenger to Wałęsa. During the campaign Kwaśniewski skillfully utilized Wałęsa's mistakes and the social costs of transformation, promoting the slogan "let us choose the future." He was unharmed by lies he told about his education (he claimed he had a master's degree) and by inaccuracies in his property statement. Finally, Kwaśniewski defeated Wałęsa by a slight margin in the second round of voting on 19 November 1995, winning 51.7 percent of the vote. Contrary to the expectations of the Kremlin and some of the post-Communists, as president, Kwaśniewski continued his pro-Western foreign policies, supporting the Polish application to NATO and the European Union. He established good personal relations with the leaders of Germany, France, and Great Britain. He also frequently visited Brussels and other European capitals. He succeeded in maintaining close relations with Ukraine and Lithuania without antagonizing Russia. Despite a controversial visit to Minsk in March 1996, Kwaśniewski harbored no illusions as to the **Alyaksandr Lukashenka** regime in Belorussia.

After the victory of Solidarity Electoral Action in the parliamentary elections of September 1997 and the formation of the government of **Jerzy Buzek**, Kwaśniewski effectively become its counterweight, vetoing several bills and strengthening his personal position as the ultimate arbitrator. In foreign policy he continued the previous line, endorsing the entry of Poland into NATO in March 1999. In domestic policy he generally supported the SLD opposition. Even obvious lapses did not reduce his popularity. Before the presidential elections of 8 October 2000 Kwaśniewski was a firm favorite and was reelected in the first round, winning 53.9 percent of the vote. When in addition the SLD won the parliamentary elections of September 2001, Kwaśniewski co-ruled with his own political base, and he maintained high ratings in the society. He was actively in favor of a reconciliation of the Poles with the Germans, Ukrainians, and Jews. In early 2003 he entered into a conflict with Prime Minister **Leszek Miller** on several issues, ranging from financial policies to issues of corruption. In May 2004 Kwaśniewski led Poland into the European Union. (WR)

Sources: Mołdawa; *Wielka encyklopedia PWN*, vol. 15 (Warsaw, 2003); Andrzej Albert [Wojciech Roszkowski], *Najnowsza historia Polski 1914–1993*, vol. 2 (Warsaw, 1995); Jan Skórzyński, *Ugoda i rewolucja: Władza i opozycja 1985–1989* (Warsaw, 1995); Antoni Dudek, *Pierwsze lata III Rzeczpospolitej 1989–1995* (Kraków, 1997); Janusz A. Majcherek, *Pierwsza dekada III Rzeczpospolitej 1989–1999* (Warsaw, 1999).

KWIATKOWSKI Eugeniusz (30 December 1888, Kraków–22 August 1974, Kraków), Polish politician. Born into an intelligentsia family possessing a landed estate, in 1907 Kwiatkowski graduated from a prestigious high school in Chyrów. He studied in Lemberg (Lwów, Lviv) and from 1910 at the Königliche Bayerische Technische Hochschule in Munich, Germany, where he graduated in chemical engineering in 1912. Until 1909 Kwiatkowski belonged to the Union of Polish Youth–Zet and then to the Organization of Pro-Independence Youth–Zarzewie (Embers). In 1909–10 he was a member of the Polish Military Union. From 1913 he worked as a deputy director of a private gas works in Lublin. In the spring of 1916 he joined the Polish Legions. He also worked with the Polish Military Organization (Polska Organizacja Wojskowa). In November 1918 he took part in the disarming of the Austrian garrison in Łuków, following which he joined the Polish Army. Kwiatkowski served as deputy head of the Chemical Department of the Main Supply Administration of the army. Then he lectured in chemistry at the Warsaw Polytechnic, where he became friends with **Ignacy Mościcki**. Thanks to him, Kwiatkowski later played an important role in economic policy. He worked at the State Factory of Wood Distillation in Hajnówka, and in 1923–26 he was technical director of the Factory of Nitric Compounds in Chorzów.

Kwiatkowski became an active politician after the May 1926 coup d'état, assuming the portfolio of industry and trade (June 1926–August 1930). In 1928–30 and 1938–39 he was an MP on behalf of the Nonparty Bloc of Cooperation with the Government and the National Unity Camp. He advocated a widely planned industrialization. He was associated with the construction of the port and town of Gdynia, a showcase of the modern Polish economy. Suspected by the ruling group of contacts with the opposition, owing to intrigues of the group of Legionnaires, Kwiatkowski was dismissed by **Józef Piłsudski**. Despite efforts by President Mościcki, Kwiatkowski stayed out of the government until the end of the Great Depression. In 1930 he returned to industry and worked as director of the State Factory of Nitric Compounds in Mościce, near Tarnów, and later of the United State Factories of Nitric Compounds in Chorzów, Mościce, and Jaworzno (1931–35). Kwiatkowski published a lot on current economic issues. In 1932 he published *Dysproporcje: Rzecz o Polsce dawnej i obecnej* (Disproportions: On past and present Poland), analyzing Poland's position in the world and its economic chances for the future. He drew attention to the German threat and to the necessity for the state stimulation of social and economic activity. This book, handed to the president and prime minister, played an important role in the elaboration of the *sanacja* economic program. From 1934 Kwiatkowski was a member of the Academy of Technical Sciences in Warsaw, and in 1935 he published *Kryzys współczesny i zagadnienia odbudowy życia gospodarczego* (The contemporary crisis and the question of economic reconstruction). From 1936 he was an honorary member of the Polish Chemical Association and an ordinary member of the Warsaw Scientific Society.

After the death of Piłsudski, Kwiatkowski returned to political life. On 13 October 1935 he joined the government of **Marian Zyndram-Kościałkowski** and then that of **Felicjan Sławoj-Składkowski**. Until September 1939 he was deputy prime minister and minister of the treasury.

He belonged to the liberal wing of the ruling group, connected with President Mościcki. Kwiatkowski favored the development of Polish industry on the basis of local raw materials and domestic demand and by means of state intervention. He supervised the implementation of economic plans aimed at reducing the gap between Poland and other European nations. His chief investment at this time was the development of the Central Industrial Region (Centralny Okręg Przemysłowy [COP]) within the Four-Year Investment Plan (1936–39), aimed at strengthening Poland's security and reducing unemployment. Located at the confluence of the Vistula and San Rivers, the COP included several modern heavy-industry projects. After the Four-Year Plan was fulfilled ahead of time, in mid-1939 Kwiatkowski announced a comprehensive Fifteen-Year Plan of social and economic development for 1939–54, aimed at the modernization of the army; at the development of a transportation network, agriculture, and education; and at closing the gap between the more and less developed regions of Poland.

After the German invasion of Poland in September 1939, along with the whole government, Kwiatkowski left for Romania. He declared his readiness to cooperate with General **Władysław Sikorski**, but as a *sanacja* politician, he was not trusted. Interned in Romania, he stayed there for the whole of the war. He studied economic history and wrote *Zarys dziejów gospodarczych świata* (Outline of world economic history; vol. 1, 1947; vol. 2 was banned by Communist censorship in Poland).

After World War II, in June 1945 Kwiatkowski was encouraged to return to Poland. In 1945–48 he headed the Office of the Government Delegate for the Reconstruction of the Baltic Coast. In January 1947 he was elected to the parliament on behalf of the Communist-dominated Democratic Bloc. Initially the Communist propaganda was successful in convincing Kwiatkowski to return to Poland, but his planning methodology was contrary to the logic of the centralized and armament-oriented strategy of the Communists, who expelled him from public positions. In 1950 he became chairman of the Committee of Technical Sciences of the Polish Academy of Arts and Sciences, but the academy was soon dissolved by the authorities. From 1948 Kwiatkowski was attacked in public and placed under police surveillance. He was banned from living in Warsaw and the Baltic Coast, so he settled in Kraków. For some time he was allowed to teach at the School of Political Science of the Jagiellonian University, but in the early 1950s he became totally isolated. Until his death Kwiatkowski did chemical research. In the early 1970s the Communist authorities remembered him during the implementation of the economic policy of **Edward**

Gierek. Kwiatkowski was given a few awards, and he was invited to consult in the construction of the Northern Port in Gdańsk. In 1974 Gdańsk University awarded him an honorary doctorate. (PK)

Sources: *Słownik Polityków Polskich XX w.* (Poznań, 1998); *Encyklopedia historii Drugiej Rzeczypospolitej* (Warsaw, 1999); Janusz Rakowski, *Eugeniusz Kwiatkowski: Szkic biograficzny młodych lat na tle ruchu niepodległościowego 1886–1920* (London, 1977); Marian M. Drozdowski, *Eugeniusz Kwiatkowski: Człowiek i dzieło* (Kraków, 1989); Janusz Zaręba, *Eugeniusz Kwiatkowski: Romantyczny polityk* (Warsaw, 1998); Andrzej Zwoliński, *Eugeniusz Kwiatkowski* (Wrocław, 2001).

KYRYCHENKO Oleksiy (25 February 1908, Chornobaivka, near Kherson–29 December 1975, Moscow), Ukrainian Communist activist. Kyrychenko began to work in the apparatus of the Central Committee (CC) of the Communist Party (Bolshevik) of Ukraine (CP[B]U) in 1938. During World War II he served as a political officer. From 1949 to 1953, as second secretary of the CP(B)U CC, Kyrychenko was the highest-ranking Ukrainian in the party at that time. At the CP(B)U CC Plenum in June 1953, shortly after the death of Stalin, Kyrychenko was elected first secretary of the Ukrainian party. He was the first Ukrainian to fill this post, except for the short-lived leadership of **Dmytro Manuilsky** in the 1920s. Aligned with **Nikita Khrushchev**, who was first secretary of the CP(B)U CC from 1947 to 1949, Kyrychenko helped to strengthen the Ukrainian representation in the party leadership and to increase Ukraine's economic autonomy. These changes were introduced at the Eighteenth Congress of the Communist Party of Ukraine (CPU) in 1954 and at the Nineteenth Congress in 1956. The authorities of the Ukrainian SSR supported Khrushchev's denunciation of Stalin at the Twentieth Congress of the Communist Party of the Soviet Union (CPSU) (February 1956). The year 1954 saw the beginning of new relations between Kiev and Moscow, marked by the transfer of the Crimean Peninsula from the Russian Soviet Federated Socialist Republic to the Ukrainian SSR on the occasion of the 300th anniversary of the Pereyaslav Agreement. After suppressing the so-called anti-party group led by Georgy Malenkov, Lazar Kaganovich, and Vyacheslav Molotov in June 1957, Khrushchev decided to promote Kyrychenko. Already a member of the CPSU CC Politburo since 1955, in December 1957 Kyrychenko was transferred to Moscow; the position he vacated in Kiev was filled by Nikolay Podgorny. The late 1950s and early 1960s saw the gradual development of political opposition in the Ukraine, and a part of the intelligentsia pinned its hopes on Kyrychenko as a possible successor to Khrushchev as first secretary of the CPSU. However, Khrushchev chose a policy line aimed at increasing central control and extended it to the Ukraine. In January 1960 Khrushchev unexpectedly removed Kyrychenko from party leadership, relegating him to the role of secretary of a district committee in Rostov. Kyrychenko held this post only for half a year. Khrushchev's decision was probably motivated by his fear that Kyrychenko, who described himself as the "second person in the state," might seize power. Later Kyrychenko disappeared from public life. (TS)

Sources: *Prominent Personalities in the USSR* (Metuchen, N.J., 1968); *Encyclopedia of Ukraine*, vol. 2 (Toronto, 1988); Robert S. Sullivant, *Soviet Politics and the Ukraine 1917–1957* (New York and London, 1962); Borys Lewytzkyj, *Politics and Society in Soviet Ukraine 1953–1980* (Edmonton, 1984).

L

LAAR Mart (22 April 1960, Viljandi), Estonian politician. Laar graduated in history from the University of Tartu. In 1983–85 he taught history at a high school in Tallinn, and in 1987–90 he was head of the Department of National Heritage Protection at the Ministry of Culture of the Estonian SSR. In 1987 he co-founded the Estonian Society for the Protection of Monuments, a social organization aimed at cultivating Estonian national traditions, and he became head of the historical section of the society. A member of the Estonian Congress and the Estonian Committee, alternative organs striving for the restitution of independence in 1989–91, Laar was also a deputy to the Supreme Council of the Estonian SSR and of Estonia from April 1990 to August 1992. After the restitution of Estonian independence in August 1991, in the elections to the parliament (Riigikogu) of August 1992 Laar won a seat on behalf of the Estonian Christian Democratic Party, running within the Pro Patria (Isamaa) coalition.

On 21 October 1992 Laar became prime minister. In the same month he was also elected chairman of the Pro Patria Union (Isamaaliit [PPU]). In June 1993 the parliament passed a law on foreigners, imposing an obligation on the Russians living in Estonia to either gain citizenship within two years or obtain a residence permit; in consequence tension grew between Russia and Estonia, all the more so because significant numbers of Russian troops were still stationed in the country. When the parliament eased the law in September 1993, Laar negotiated the withdrawal of Russian troops by the end of August 1994. His government managed to overcome the economic decline connected with the collapse of the Soviet and Russian markets. Accused of embezzlement in the course of an exchange of rubles for Estonian crowns, on 27 October 1994 Laar resigned after his coalition lost the parliamentary majority. In the parliamentary elections of March 1995 the PPU and the Estonian National Independence Party lost, gaining only a few mandates. Laar himself won a seat but remained in the opposition. After new elections, when the PPU won 18 percent of the mandates, on 25 March 1999 Laar became prime minister of the government based on a coalition of the PPU, the Estonian Reform Party (Eesti Reformierakond), and the People's Party Moderates (Rahvaerakond Mõõdukad). He became known as a radical reformer who liberalized the Estonian economy. In foreign policy he strove for Estonian membership in NATO and the European Union. Laar resigned on 28 January 2002 following the dissolution of the ruling coalition. (MK)

Sources: *Kes on Kes? Eesti 2000* (Tallinn, 2000); Józef Darski, *Estonia: Historia, współczesność, konflikty narodowe* (Warsaw, 1995); *The Baltic States: A Reference Book* (Tallinn-Riga-Vilnius, 1991); *Europa Środkowo-Wschodnia 1994–1995* (Warsaw, 1997); Matti Laur, Tõnis Lukas, Ain Mäesalu, Ago Pajur, and Tõnu Tannberg, *History of Estonia* (Tallinn, 2000); www.ee/eng/govmin/curricula.html; www.rulers.org.

LĀCIS Mārtins, pseudonyms "Jan Sudrabs," "Dyadya," and "Garais" (16 December 1888, Večpiebalga Volost, near Cesis–20 March 1938?, USSR), Latvian Communist activist, leading functionary of the Bolshevik political police. Born into a family of farm workers, after graduating from high school, Lācis studied at Shanyavski University in Moscow (1912–1915). He was one of the main founders of the Bolshevik faction of the Social Democratic movement in Latvia. Arrested in 1915 and deported to Irkutsk, he managed to escape. Lācis took part in the February 1917 revolution, during which he headed a Bolshevik organization in the Vyborg district of Petrograd. In July 1917 he became a member of the Petrograd Military Revolutionary Committee and took part in the preparations for a coup. After the October Revolution of 1917, Lācis became one of the top figures in the People's Commissariat of Internal Affairs. In May 1918 he became a member of the Presidium of the Cheka, and in August of that year he was made head of the Cheka in the Fifth Army on the eastern front. On 6 July 1918, during an unsuccessful revolt attempt organized by members of the Socialist Revolutionary Party (SR Party), Lācis was briefly detained by the SR functionaries of the Cheka. After the attempted assassination of Lenin, Lācis advocated bloody reprisals against the opponents of the regime. From 1919 to 1921 he headed the Cheka in the Ukraine and was responsible for mass killings and atrocities. He attended the first congresses of the Bolshevik party after the revolution, but when Stalin consolidated his position and the "Bolshevik old guard" was removed from power, Lācis's position was gradually undermined. At the end of the 1920s he served as deputy chairman of the Central Mining Council. In 1928 he became a party lecturer, and in 1932, the director of the Plekhanov Economics Institute. In 1937, during a purge of Latvian Communists, Lācis was arrested and then executed. His publications include *Dva goda borby na vnutrennem fronte* (Two years of struggle on the internal front; 1920) and *Cherezvychainye komisii po kontrrevolutsii* (The Cheka in the struggle against counterrevolution; 1921). These works are important sources for the history of the Bolshevik terror. (WR)

Sources: *MERSH*, vol. 19; *Geroi Oktiabria*, vol. 2 (Leningrad, 1967); *Who Was Who in the USSR* (Metuchen, N.J., 1972); Alexander Rabinovitz, *The Bolsheviks Come to Power: The 1917 Revolution in Petrograd* (New York, 1976); Adam B. Ulam, *The Bolsheviks* (New York, 1978); Ilga Gore, *Mārtins Lācis: Cekists un literāts* (Riga, 1989).

LACIS Vilis (29 April 1904, Rinuži, near Riga–6 February 1966, Riga), Latvian Communist activist. The son of a docker, Lacis spent the years from 1917 to 1921 in Russia. He later worked in the dockers' trade union and at the same time was active in the Communist underground in Latvia. He also wrote novels about the lives of fishermen and dockers, including *Putni bez sparniem* (The wingless birds, 3 vols.; 1931–33). From 1928 Lacis secretly belonged to the All-Union Communist Party (Bolsheviks). During the Russian invasion in June 1940 he assumed the post of minister of interior, and after the "elections" of July 1940 and the incorporation of Latvia into the USSR, he became head of the Latvian SSR government. After the German invasion Lacis headed partisan activities in the rear of the front. Following the Soviet reconquest, he became head of the Latvian SSR government and held this post until 1959. From 1952 he was also the president of the Supreme Council of the republic. In 1944 and 1949 Lacis approved major deportations of Latvians far into the USSR; he was responsible for the deaths of thousands. Between 1952 and 1961 Lacis was a deputy member of the Central Committee of the CPSU. He was a member of the Soviet delegation to the founding conference of the Warsaw Pact in May 1955 and also represented the Supreme Council of the USSR during official visits to Belgium and Finland. In 1954 he presided over a session of the Council of Nationalities of the USSR. Lacis continued to write and publish extensively; he was the author of novels, stories, and dramas, such as *Vedekla* (Daughter-in-law; 1943) and *Uzvara* (The victory; 1945)— model products of Socialist realism for which Lacis was granted the Stalin Award in 1948 and 1952. In July 1959 Lacis was deprived of his post but remained a member of the Central Committee of the Republican Party. In 1987 his letters were published in the volume *Vestules*. (WR)

Sources: *MERSH*, vol. 19; Romuald J. Misiunas and Rein Taagepera, *The Baltic States: Years of Dependence, 1940–1980* (Berkeley, 1983); Ingrida Sokolova, *Vilis Lacis: Ocherk tvorchestva* (Moscow, 1959); Vilhelmina Kairisa, *Tautas rastnieks Vilic Lacis* (Riga, 1964); *Miesta zhizni i dieiatielnosti Vilisa Licisa* (N.p., 1974); Biruta Gudrike, ed., *Atminas par Vili Laci* (Riga, 1975).

LAIDONER Johan (12 February 1884, Viiratsi, near Viljandi–13 March 1953, Vladimir), Estonian general and politician. The son of a farm laborer, after graduating from high school in Vilnius, Laidoner studied at the Nikolayev Academy of the General Staff, graduating in 1912. During World War I he fought as a Russian staff officer on the western front. In 1916 he became a divisional chief of staff. In December 1917 he assumed command of an Estonian division, and until 1920 he commanded units

that fought against the Bolsheviks for the independence of Estonia. On 23 December 1918 Laidoner formally became commander-in-chief of the Estonian Army. In 1919 he was promoted to major general, and in 1920 he became lieutenant general. In January 1919 the Red Army was thirty kilometers from Tallinn but was driven back eastward owing to the mobilization of all military forces, English and Finnish material assistance, and Laidoner's military talents. In the spring of 1919 the Estonian troops and the Russian units led by Nikolay Yudenich combined their forces to fight against the Bolsheviks. After the end of the war and the signing of the treaty of 2 February 1920, in which Soviet Russia recognized the independence of Estonia, Laidoner transferred to the reserves in March 1920. As a member of parliament for its first three terms, he represented the Union of Farmers (Põllumeeste Kogu), led by **Konstantin Päts**, and sat on the budget, finance, and national defense committees.

On 1 December 1924 Laidoner returned to the army as commander-in-chief to put down an attempted Communist coup d'état in Tallinn. He subsequently left the army again and became involved in political and economic activities. He became a member of the supervisory boards of several companies but was not successful in that role. The Estonian political system was undermined by the supremacy of parliament and the excessive fragmentation of the political parties. Therefore, many politicians, including Laidoner, sought ways to change the constitution so as to improve the functioning of the state. At the end of 1933 Päts and Laidoner made unsuccessful attempts at reaching an agreement with the Union of Veterans of the War of Independence (Eesti Vabadussõjalaste Liit [EVL]), an extreme rightist organization. When in January 1934 a new constitution came into force and the EVL put forward its own candidate in the presidential elections, Laidoner was proposed by the parties of new settlers and the political center. The course of the campaign indicated that the EVL, which had many supporters, might use force to gain power if it lost the elections. In that situation, Päts decided to take preventive measures. On 12 March 1934 he again appointed Laidoner as commander-in-chief of the army, granting him special powers to restore "law and order." Over four hundred EVL leaders were arrested, and the organization itself was abolished. By restoring Laidoner to active duty, Päts secured the loyalty of the army because Laidoner was very popular among the military. After the new government consolidated its position, Laidoner continued as commander-in-chief, responsible for the army and for domestic security. Laidoner was a co-founder of the ruling party, the Fatherland League (Isamaaliit), and, as the second-ranking person in the state, he supported the authoritarian regime of Päts. From 1934 to

1940 he also served as chairman of the Estonian Olympics Committee.

In foreign policy, Laidoner was skeptical about the prospects of the Baltic Entente and sought to strengthen Estonia's security by establishing relations with Germany and the Soviet Union. He also advocated the strengthening of political and military relations with Poland; one of the reasons was that his wife, Maria Kruszewska, was Polish. From 1930 to 1940 he was an honorary chairman of the Estonian-Polish Society. He visited Poland for the first time in 1928, during the celebrations of the tenth anniversary of Poland's independence, and for the second time in April 1939, when he and the Polish government analyzed threats to security in Eastern Europe from Germany and the Soviet Union. After the Molotov-Ribbentrop Pact was signed on 23 August 1939, the situation in Estonia became hopeless; therefore Laidoner did not protest the Soviet ultimatum, and, under threat of invasion by the Red Army, he endorsed a new Estonian-Soviet treaty of 28 September 1939 that forced Estonia to agree to the establishment of Soviet bases on the islands of Saarema and Hiiumaa and in the Paldiski port. Given the Soviet ultimatum of 15 June 1940, Laidoner supported the decision of President Päts that Estonia offer no resistance, and two days later he signed a formal consent allowing Red Army units, eighty thousand strong, to enter Estonia. On 19 July 1940 Laidoner was deported to Penza. In the spring of 1941 he was arrested and taken to a prison in Kirov and then sent from there to Ivanovo. Shortly afterwards he was transferred to Butyrki Prison in Moscow and finally to Vladimir, where he died. (WR)

Sources: *Johan Laidoner: Mälestusi kaasaeglasilt* (Tallinn, 1934); *Johan Laidoner* (Stockholm, 1953); Piotr Łossowski, *Kraje bałtyckie na drodze od demokracji parlamentarnej do dyktatury (1918–1934)* (Wrocław, 1972); Georg von Rauch, *The Baltic States, the Years of Independence: Estonia, Latvia, Lithuania, 1917–1940* (Berkeley, 1974); V. Raudvassar, ed., *Johan Laidoner, 1884–1953* (Tartu, 1991); K. Deemant, "Johan Laidoneri riigikaitselisest pärandist," *Looming*, 1994, no. 2; H. Tõnismägi, *Ülekohtu toimikud* (Tallinn, 1998; Andres Kasekamp, *The Radical Right in Interwar Estonia* (London, 2000).

LAKOTA Hryhoriy (31 January 1883, Holodivka, Lemkiv region–12 November 1950, Abez, near Vorkuta), Uniate bishop, martyred by the Communists. Lakota was born into a peasant family. He graduated from high school and then completed theological studies in Lemberg (Lviv). Ordained in 1908, he continued his studies in Vienna (1909–13), earning a Ph.D. in theology in 1913. He subsequently taught homiletics, canon law, and church history at a seminary in Przemyśl. From 1918 to 1926 he was its rector. In 1924 he became vicar general, and on 16 May 1926, auxiliary bishop of the diocese of Przemyśl and Sambor (Sambir). After the Red Army invaded Poland in September 1939, Lakota moved to Jarosław, which was occupied by the Germans, and in June 1941 he returned to Przemyśl. At the end of World War II, the administration of the diocese became difficult because the new Polish-Soviet border separated two-thirds of the faithful of the diocese from the diocesan capital. Lakota did not accept the decision of the "Ecumenical Council" of Lviv in March 1946 incorporating the Uniate Church into the Orthodox Church. Consequently, as part of the Soviet effort to abolish the Uniate Church, on 9 June 1946 Lakota was arrested by the Polish Security Service and handed over to the Soviet NKGB. Sentenced to ten years, he was held in Vorkuta labor camps, where he became seriously ill and died. Lakota was the author of (among other works) a commentary on matrimonial law and *Try synody Peremys'ky v XVI–XIX st.* (Three synods of Przemyśl in the sixteenth–nineteenth centuries; 1939). On 27 June 2001 Pope John Paul II beatified Lakota at a solemn Holy Mass in Lviv. (WR)

Sources: Atanasiï Pekar, *Ispovidniky viry nashoï suczastnisti: Prychynok do martirolohii Ukraïn's'koï Katolitskoï Tserkvi pid sovitami* (Toronto, 1982); *Martirolohia ukraïn's'kikh tserkov u chetyriokh tomakh*, vol. 2 (Toronto, 1985); *Encyclopedia of Ukraine*, vol. 3 (Toronto, 1993); *Kto był kim w Drugiej Rzeczypospolitej* (Warsaw, 1994); Bohdan R. Bociurkiw, *The Ukrainian Greek-Catholic Church and the Soviet State (1939–1950)* (Edmonton, 1996); *Osservatore Romano* (weekly edition in English), 2001, nos. 25 and 27.

LAMPE Alfred (14 May 1900, Warsaw–10 December 1943, Moscow), Polish Communist activist. Born into a working-class family, Lampe studied in Warsaw and Paris. In 1917 he became a member of Jugend, a youth organization linked with the Jewish Social Democratic Workers' Party–Poale Zion (Workers of Zion), and in 1921 he joined the Communist Workers' Party of Poland (Komunistyczna Partia Robotnicza Polski [KPRP]; renamed the Communist Party of Poland [Komunistyczna Partia Polski, KPP] in 1925). In 1922 Lampe helped to found the Union of Communist Youth in Poland. Arrested and sentenced to imprisonment after a long interrogation, he was released in 1926. In the same year he became a member of the Central Committee (CC) and in 1929 a member of the Politburo and the Secretariat of the CC of the KPP. Arrested again in 1933, he was sentenced to fifteen years in prison for Communist activities. Lampe was released after the outbreak of World War II in September 1939. He went to the territories occupied by the Red Army, and later, after the German attack on the Soviet Union in June 1941, he went further eastward. In 1942, along with **Wanda Wasilewska**, **Jerzy Borejsza**, and Jerzy Putrament, Lampe began working on the editorial staff of the periodical *Nowe Widnokręgi*, and in 1943, on the editorial board of *Wolna Polska*. On 4 January 1943, together with Wasilewska, he sent a letter to Vyacheslav Molotov proposing the establishment of a new center in charge of Polish affairs, to which Stalin consented. Lampe played a key role among the leaders of the Union of Polish Patriots (Związek Patriotów Polskich [ZPP]) and was one of the leading Polish Communist ideologists in the Soviet Union. He was the author of the ZPP ideological declaration of May 1943 and co-founder of the Tadeusz Kościuszko First Infantry Division, which fought with the Red Army. In the autumn of 1943 he drafted the program of the Polish National Committee, but he did not hold any formal position in it. Lampe died suddenly. (PK)

Sources: Maria Turlejska, "Rozwój myśli politycznej Alfreda Lampego," in *Twórcy polskiej myśli politycznej*, vol. 2 (Warsaw, 1978); Krystyna Kersten, *Narodziny systemu władzy: Polska 1943–1948* (Poznań, 1990); Andrzej Albert [Wojciech Roszkowski], *Najnowsza historia Polski 1914–1993*, vol. 1 (Warsaw, 1995); *Słownik polityków polskich XX w.* (Poznań, 1998).

LANDLER Jenő (23 November 1875, Gelse–25 February 1928, Cannes, France), Hungarian Communist activist. The son of a rich land leaser, Landler graduated from a Piarist high school in Nagykanizsa and in law from Budapest University. Later he worked as a lawyer. He was a legal adviser to the Hungarian Railwaymen's Trade Union. After the national railwaymen's strike of 1904 Landler defended the organizers of the strike (the Trial of the Thirteen). In 1906 he was one of the leaders of the Budapest tramway workers' strike, and in 1908 he joined the Hungarian Social Democratic Party (Magyarországi Szociáldemokrata Párt [MSP]), belonging to its left wing. During World War I Landler was one of the leaders of anti-war movements. He was arrested for three months for organizing a strike. From October 1918 Landler headed the office of the Hungarian National Council. On 21 March 1919, as one of the leaders of the MSP left wing, he took part in negotiations with imprisoned Communist leaders on the unification of their parties and on a common takeover of power.

After the Hungarian Soviet Republic (HSR) was formed, Landler became commissar of interior (March–April and May–August 1919), railways and navigation (April–May), and trade (March–April 1919). He organized the Red Guard (militia) and a united armed force of internal security. When Romanian and Czechoslovak troops intervened against the HSR, on 7 May, Landler was appointed commander of the Third Corps of the Hungarian Red Army, leading a victorious campaign in Upper Hungary (Slovakia) in May and June 1919. On 14 July the Governing Revolutionary Council appointed him commander-in-chief of the Hungarian Red Army. After the fall of the HSR, Landler fled to Austria, where he took part in the reconstruction of the Hungarian Communist Party (Kommunisták Magyarországi Pártja [KMP]) and joined its provisional Central Committee. His main task was to reorganize the illegal Communist movement in Hungary by combining legal and clandestine measures. As head of the Hungarian Communist émigré community in Vienna, Landler soon entered into a conflict with the Moscow group of **Béla Kun**. In 1925 the conflict eased up, and Landler joined in the preparations for the First KMP Congress near Moscow. In 1920–22 in Vienna Landler edited the Hungarian-language Communist periodical *Proletár*, and he wrote for the Vienna periodicals *Bécsi Vörös Újság* and *Új Március*, the Košice *Kassai Munkás*, the Paris *Párisi Munkás*, and the Moscow *Moszkvai Vörös Újság*. On the orders of the Communist International Landler joined the Communist Party of Austria and took part in the third and fourth congresses of the Comintern. Landler died of a heart attack. After cremation in Paris, his ashes were placed at the Kremlin Wall in Moscow in August 1928. (JT)

Sources: *Magyar Életrajzi Lexikon*, vol. 2 (Budapest, 1969); *Magyar Nagylexikon*, vol. 11 (Budapest, 2000); *Biographisches Lexikon*, vol. 3; Rudolf L. Tőkés, *Bela Kun and the Hungarian Soviet Republic* (New York, 1967); Péter Földes, *Az utca hadvezére: Dr Landler Jenő élete* (Budapest, 1970); Bennet Kovrig, *Communism in Hungary from Kun to Kadar* (Stanford, 1979).

LANDSBERGIS Vytautas (18 October 1932, Kaunas), Lithuanian politician. Landsbergis was born into a family with patriotic traditions. One of his grandfathers was **Jonas Jablonskis**, and the other, Gabrielius Landsbergis, was an associate of Vincas Kudirka. In 1955 Landsbergis graduated from a music conservatory, with piano as his subject, and in 1969 he received a Ph.D. in musicology. In the 1960s and 1970s he taught at the conservatory and at the Vilnius Pedagogical Institute. He became an expert in and interpreter of works by **Mikolajus Čiurlonis**. In 1986 he published *Čiurlioniu muzika* (The music of Čiurlonis), and in 1992, *M. K. Čiurlonis: Time and Content*. In June 1988 Landsbergis joined the pro-independence movement, taking the lead of the Lithuanian Movement for Perestroika (Lietuvos Persitvarkymo Sąjūdis). In the period of perestroika, when the Soviet empire was declining and international changes were increasingly favorable, Landsbergis strove for the reconstruction of a sovereign Lithuanian state. He played the key role in demonstrations during the August 1988 anniversary of the Molotov-

Ribbentrop Pact and in a brutally crushed demonstration at Gediminas Square in Vilnius on 28 September 1988. At the First Sąjūdis Congress on 22–24 October 1988 Landsbergis consolidated his position in the movement. In March 1989 he was elected a delegate to the Congress of People's Deputies of the USSR, and in May 1989 he led the Lithuanian delegates out of the congress in protest against Mikhail Gorbachev's opposition to Lithuanian demands for autonomy. Owing to Landsbergis's growing personal popularity, he was perceived as the leader of the pro-independence movement. After the elections to the Lithuanian Supreme Council in February 1990, won by the Sąjūdis, Landsbergis was elected chairman of the council, which, by a large majority, announced the independence of Lithuania and the restitution of national symbols on 11 March 1990. This step caused serious international repercussions. The Kremlin protested, but at the same time it annulled the Molotov-Ribbentrop Pact, giving the Lithuanians a substantial boost in their quest. In the West it was feared that the secession of Lithuania might strengthen conservative opposition to Gorbachev and jeopardize perestroika.

From March 1990 to August 1991 Landsbergis zigzagged between defending the independence declaration and responding to Soviet and Western pressure. On 12 May 1990 he met with the leaders of Estonia (**Arnold Rüütel**) and Latvia (**Anatolijs Gorbunovs**) to renew the Baltic Council of the three nations that had been established in 1934. On 13 January 1991 a limited Soviet intervention started in Vilnius, leading to about a dozen victims. Landsbergis bravely defended the Lithuanian desire for independence but decided to suspend the independence declaration. Immediately after the collapse of the Moscow putsch of August 1991, he reactivated the declaration. From this moment Lithuania began to gain international recognition as a sovereign state. Landsbergis faced growing opposition from both the extreme nationalists and the post-Communists. The former attacked him for having risked the Soviet intervention, while the latter fueled the social discontent connected with economic shortages. Therefore in the parliamentary elections of 25 October 1992 the moderate post-Communist Lithuanian Democratic Labor Party of **Algirdas Brazauskas** won. When Brazauskas also defeated a pro-independence candidate, Stasys Lozoraitis, in the presidential elections of February 1993, Lansbergis seemed completely ousted. In May 1993 Sąjūdis changed its name to the Homeland Union–Lithuanian Conservatives (Tėvynės Sąjunga–Lietuvos Konservatoriai [TSLK]). After four years of economic problems, the parliamentary elections of October and November 1996 brought victory to center and right-wing groups, and

Landsbergis was elected speaker of the parliament (Seimas). He held this position until the elections of October 2000. Landsbergis won a seat on behalf of the TSLK, but the party lost and moved into the opposition. In December 1997 Landsbergis was defeated in the first round of the presidential elections. Apart from collections of speeches and documents from 1988–94, in 2000 Landsbergis published his memoirs, *Lithuania Independent Again*, in Great Britain. From July 2004 Landsbergis was a member of the European Parliament on behalf of the European People's Party. (WR)

Sources: *Wielka encyklopedia PWN*, vol. 15 (Warsaw, 2003); Saulius Sužiedelis, *Historical Dictionary of Lithuania* (Lanham, Md., 1997); Alfred E. Senn, *Lithuania Awakening* (Berkeley, 1990); Anatol Lieven, *The Baltic Revolution* (New Haven, 1993); Romuald J. Misiunas and Rein Taagepera, *The Baltic States: Years of Dependence, 1940–1990* (Berkeley, 1993); V. Stanley Vardys and Judith B. Sedaitis, *Lithuania: The Rebel Nation* (Boulder, Colo., 1997); Bugajski; www.lrs.lt; www.tslt.lt.

LANGE Oskar (27 July 1904, Tomaszów Mazowiecki–2 October 1965, London), Polish economist and political activist. After graduating from high school in Tomaszów Mazowiecki, Lange studied economics at the university in Poznań and at the Jagiellonian University (Uniwersytet Jagielloński [UJ]) in Kraków, where he also worked as an assistant to **Adam Krzyżanowski**. In 1928 Lange earned a doctorate from the UJ. He contributed to *Economic Review* and *Przegląd Współczesny*. In 1929 he studied in England. In 1931 he became an associate professor (*docent*) at the UJ. From 1934 to 1936 he held a Rockefeller Foundation scholarship in Great Britain and the United States, where he lectured at the London School of Economics, the University of Michigan, and other schools. After a short stay in Poland, Lange again went to the United States. From 1938 to 1945 he was a professor of economics and statistics at the University of Chicago. His publications include "On the Economic Theory of Socialism" in the *Review of Economic Studies* (1936–37) and *Price Flexibility and Employment* (1944). Lange was one of the founders of econometrics and a co-founder of the Econometric Society. He also edited *Econometrica*, a journal of this society. In 1927 Lange joined the Polish Socialist Party (Polska Partia Socjalistyczna [PPS]). In the United States he was a member of the Union for Democratic Action and was active in trade unions.

In 1944 Lange was in the Soviet Union, invited by the Union of Polish Patriots (Związek Patriotów Polskich [ZPP]), a political organization controlled by Stalin. He believed that it would be possible to introduce an innovative model of a Socialist economy in Poland. In November 1945 Lange became an ambassador of the Provisional

Government of National Unity (Tymczasowy Rząd Jedności Narodowej) to Washington, and later he was the Polish delegate to the UN Security Council. In December 1947 he returned to Poland and took up the chair of statistics at the Warsaw School of Economics (Szkoła Główna Handlowa [SGH]). After the SGH was transformed into the Central School of Planning and Statistics (Szkoła Główna Planowania i Statystyki [SGPiS]) and program changes in the Stalinist spirit were introduced, Lange served as rector of the SGPiS from 1952 to 1955. In 1947 he became a member of the Central Executive Committee of the PPS; in December 1948, a member of the Central Committee (CC) of the Polish United Workers' Party (Polska Zjednoczona Partia Robotnicza [PUWP]); and until August 1952 he served as chairman of the PUWP parliamentary representation in the Assembly. Lange accepted the principles of the Six-Year Plan, which was modeled on similar Soviet plans. A supporter of the new system, he also held a chair at the Institute of Social Sciences of the PUWP CC (1950–54). From 1955 to 1956 he was a planning adviser to the government of India and later to the governments of Ceylon, Egypt, and Iraq. Lange's advisory experiences resulted in, among other things, publications on the economies of developing countries. In 1956 Lange took the chair of economics at Warsaw University. In April 1955 he became a member of the Council of State, and in February 1957, its vice-chairman. From 1957 to 1962 Lange was president of the Economic Council, advising the Council of Ministers of the Polish People's Republic, but the Economic Council was marginalized by the PUWP leadership. Despite this, Lange belonged to the Communist establishment until the end of his life. From 1957 to 1959 he was chairman of the UN Economic Commission for Europe. Lange's *Wstęp do ekonometrii* (Introduction to econometrics; 1958) was translated into many languages and was highly regarded as an academic textbook, as was another one of his works, *Ekonomia polityczna* (1959; *Political Economy*, 1963), which, although a Marxist synthesis, was far from schematic in its approach. From 1973 to 1986 eight volumes of Lange's *Dzieła* (Works) were published. (WR)

Sources: *PSB*; Mołdawa; Jerzy Topolski, "Oskar Lange," *Kwartalnik Historyczny*, 1966; Stanisław Jankowski, "Oskar Lange," *Poczet wybitnych profesorów SGH-SGPiS* (Warsaw, 1986); Tadeusz Sierocki, *Oskar Lange* (Warsaw, 1989).

LARKA Andres (5 March 1879, Pilistvere, near Vilijandi–8 January 1943, Malmoz, near Kirov), Estonian general and politician. Born into the family of a miller, Larka served as a volunteer in the tsarist army. In 1902 he graduated from the Vilnius Military Academy and then fought in the 1904–5 Russo-Japanese War. In 1912 Larka graduated from the General Staff Academy in St. Petersburg. He served as an officer in World War I. After the 1917 Bolshevik revolution, Larka was one of the organizers of the first Estonian division and commanded an artillery brigade that was stationed in Haapsalu. Larka became defense minister in the Estonian Provisional Government, and in March 1918 he was promoted to major general. From November to December of 1918 he also served as chief of staff. As minister, Larka helped to form self-defense units (*omakaitse*) that served as the army, the police, and the civil defense during the critical times of late 1918 and early 1919. Larka supervised the development of Estonian military terminology and the design of uniforms; this work had to be done partly in secret because the German occupation authorities did not recognize the Estonian state. Larka himself had to go into hiding in September 1918. After the capitulation of Germany, he failed to control the situation during the war against the Bolsheviks. The fate of the war of independence changed after **Konstantin Päts** assumed the portfolio of minister of war and General **Johan Laidoner** was appointed to the newly established post of commander-in-chief of the army. At the beginning of 1919 Larka became deputy minister of defense. He was seen as a professional without political ambitions, but because of the frequent changes of war ministers, his role was more important than his position would suggest.

In 1925 Larka retired because of ill health (tuberculosis). He bought a farm and a mill in Saue, near Tallinn. In 1926 he joined the Union of Veterans of the War of Independence (Eesti Vabadussõjalaste Liit [EVL]) and was one of its leaders until the end of its existence. Larka was not a charismatic figure, but the pro-Fascist founders of the EVL hoped that he would attract new members and win public support for the EVL. Although he had little influence on EVL members, Larka unreservedly endorsed all EVL activities, which aimed at changing the constitution to support authoritarianism. Larka was the EVL candidate in the presidential elections of 1934. A well-organized campaign, led by **Hjalmar Mäe**, promoted Larka as the major candidate for president, but a coup d'état staged by Päts thwarted the EVL's success. Unlike other EVL leaders, Larka was not arrested, and he attempted to challenge Päts's activities in the Supreme Court. He also became entangled in the activities of the EVL leaders, who planned a coup to remove the Päts regime from power (December 1935). Arrested along with other EVL leaders after a failed coup attempt, Larka was sentenced to twenty years in prison but was released after two years. He resigned as head of the EVL and withdrew from political life. After the Red Army occupied Estonia, Larka was arrested on 23 July 1940 in Tallinn. He died in a labor camp. (AG)

Sources: *Eesti Entsuklopeedia*, vol. 14 (Tallinn, 2000); Jaan Soots, "Wojna Estonji o Wyzwolenie 1918–1920," *Przegląd Wojskowy*, 1929, no. 20; Piotr Łossowski, *Kraje bałtyckie na drodze od demokracji parlamentarnej do dyktatury 1918–1934* (Wrocław, 1972); Tõnu Parming, *The Collapse of Liberal Democracy and the Rise of Authoritarianism in Estonia* (Beverly Hills, Calif., 1975); Andres Kasekamp, *The Radical Right in Interwar Estonia* (London, 2000); www.mod.gov.ee/english/history/defhistory.html; www.mod.gov.ee/english/history/history.html.

LASTOUSKI Vaclau, pen names "Artsiom Muzyka," "Juri Vereshchanka," "Vlast," and others (8 November 1883, Kalesniki estate, near Dzisna–23 January 1938, Saratov), Belorussian political activist, historian, ethnographer, and writer. In 1902 Lastouski joined the Polish Socialist Party in Lithuania. In 1906–17 he was member of the Belorussian Social Democratic Hramada. From 1909 to 1915 he was secretary of the editorial staff of the *Nasha Niva* newspaper; in 1916–17 he was editor of the *Homan* newspaper, and from 1918 he was editor of the journal *Kryvichanin*. Lastouski initiated an extensive discussion about the development of Belorussian literature; in it **Yanka Kupala**, **Maksim Haretski**, and others took part. Lastouski was the owner of the Belorussian Kniharnia (Bookshop) and of the Lastouski Belorussian Publishing Society in Wilno (Vilnius), and he printed and wrote textbooks for schools. He was one of the authors of the "Memorandum of the Representatives of Belorussia," written for an international conference in Lausanne in 1916 and including the Belorussian demand for a national state. At the end of 1918 Lastouski was the head of the Belorussian representation in Lithuania and the Belorussian attaché at the Lithuanian Embassy in Berlin. In 1919 he became the leader of the Belorussian Socialist Revolutionaries.

In December 1919 Lastouski became the head of the first independent government of Belorussia. The Polish authorities did not acknowledge the independence of Belorussia, and on 17 December 1919 Lastouski was put in prison in Minsk. Released in February 1920, he went to Riga. In 1920 he addressed the Entente states with a request for help for the government of the Belorussian People's Republic (BPR). On his initiative the Bloc of Belorussian Parties for the Struggle for an Independent and Unified Belorussia against Soviet Rule and against Polish Occupation was created on 20 October 1920 at a Belorussian conference in Riga. From 1920 to 1923 Lastouski went on diplomatic missions to Belgium, Germany, the Vatican, Italy, Czechoslovakia, France, Switzerland,

and other countries. In 1923 he resigned from the post of prime minister of the BPR. Between 1923 and 1927 he edited the journal *Kryvich* in Kaunas. In 1927 he agreed to come to Soviet Belorussia to create the Belorussian Academy of Sciences (BAS). He also became a member of the BAS. He held the post of director of the Belorussian State Museum, worked at the Institute of Belorussian Culture (Inbelkult), and was head of the BAS ethnographic department. During an ethnographic expedition organized by Lastouski, one of the Belorussian symbols was found, the Cross of Efrasinia Polatskaia. In October 1929 Lastouski was dismissed as secretary of the BAS, and on 21 July 1930 he was arrested and accused of creating the Belorussian Liberation Union. Deprived of his academic title (which was restored to him posthumously in 1990), after ten months of prison he was exiled for five years to Saratov, where he directed the department of old prints and manuscripts of the university library. Arrested again on 20 August 1937, he was convicted by the Supreme Military Court of the USSR and executed in Saratov. Lastouski was vindicated, and his first sentence was overturned in 1958 and the second in 1988.

Lastouski was the author of many works significant for Belorussian culture. In 1910 he published his first scholarly work, *Karotkaia historiia Belarusi* (Short history of Belorussia). In 1924 he published a concise Russian-Kryuski (Belorussian) dictionary in Kaunas, and in 1926 his *Historyia bielaruskai (kryuskai) knihi* (History of Belorussian [Kryuski] books) appeared in print, a survey of over one thousand of the most significant manuscripts, old documents, and old prints, dating from the beginning of Belorussian literature in the tenth century to the nineteenth century. Lastouski was the author of the historical fantasy novel *The Labyrinth* (1923). He translated into Belorussian (for example) the works of Alexander Tolstoy from Russian, Rudyard Kipling from English, Eliza Orzeszkowa and Kazimierz Tetmajer from Polish, and Christian Andersen from Danish. (AS/SA)

Sources: Nicholas P. Vakar, *Belorussia: The Making of a Nation* (Cambridge, Mass., 1956); Vitaut Kipel and Zora Kipel, eds., *Byelorussian Statehood* (New York, 1988); Jazep Januszkiewicz, "Nieadmienny sakratar adradzeńnia Wacłau Łastouski," *Nawuka i technika* (Minsk, 1995); Jan Zaprudnik, *Historical Dictionary of Belarus* (Lanham, Md., 1998).

LATKOVSKIS Vikentijs (20 June 1899, Dagdas, Livonia–3 November 1983, Riga), Latvian Communist activist. After graduating from high school, Latkovskis began to work as a teacher in rural elementary schools in Livonia in 1918. From 1919 to 1921 he served in the Red Army and later returned to Latvia. From 1921 to 1928 he again worked as a teacher. In 1928–30 Latkovskis was a member of the board of Dünaburg (Daugavpils) County. In 1930 he began to work as a teacher in Riga. He simultaneously studied agriculture at the University of Latvia in Riga. After a coup staged by **Kārlis Ulmanis** in May 1934, Latkovskis was dismissed as a teacher. He moved to his native municipality of Dagdas and took part in the Communist underground. In 1938 he resumed his studies. After the Red Army entered Latvia in June 1940, Latkovskis became deputy minister of interior in the "people's government" of **Augusts Kirchenšteins** and chief of the political police of the State Security Board. As a deputy to the People's Assembly of Latvia, Latkovskis was instrumental in the formal annexation of Latvia by the Soviet Union. From 1940 to 1941 he was one of the main organizers of the terror and deportations of Latvians. He also took an active part in the reconstruction of the Communist Party of Latvia (CPL). In September 1940 he was appointed people's commissar for the food industry of the Latvian SSR, and later he also became a member of the Supreme Soviet of the Latvian SSR. During the Soviet-German war, Latkovskis served as deputy to the plenipotentiary of the Central Committee (CC) of the CPL and of the Council of People's Commissars (government) of the Latvian SSR in Omsk and Novosibirsk Provinces (1941–44). In 1944 he returned to Latvia, together with the Red Army, but he played a less important role than previously. From 1954 to 1957 and from 1966 to 1971 he served as deputy minister of the food industry of the republic. (EJ)

Sources: Latvijas PSR Mazā enciklopēdija, vol. 2 (Riga, 1969); *Latvijas padomju enciklopēdija*, vol. 5 (Riga, 1984).

LATYSHEVSKYI Ivan (17 October 1879, Bohorodczany–27 November 1957, Ivano-Frankivsk [Stanisławów]), Uniate bishop of Stanisławów. Latyshevskyi studied theology in Lemberg (Lviv, Lwów) and then in Vienna, where he earned a doctorate in 1905. He later completed biblical studies in Innsbruck and Vienna. Ordained in October 1907, he worked as a religion teacher at a high school in Stanisławów and taught church history at a local seminary. In November 1918 he began working in the Department for Religious Affairs of the Western Ukrainian National Republic. After the collapse of this republic, he resumed his pastoral work in Polish territories. On 26 January 1930 Latyshevskyi was appointed auxiliary bishop of Stanisławów. He had many duties; for example, he was in charge of the activities of Catholic Action. During the Soviet occupation between 1939 and 1941, Latyshevskyi was frequently interrogated. He continued his pastoral work also during the German occupation. After the return

of the Red Army, Latyshevskyi was arrested on 11 April 1945 as part of the campaign to abolish the Uniate Church. Placed in prison in Kiev and held under investigation for one and a half years, he was subsequently sentenced to ten years in a labor camp. He served the sentence in labor camps in Merke, Chulak-Tau, and other places. On 3 June 1955 he was allowed to return to Stanisławów (renamed Ivano-Frankivsk after the war), where he assumed the duties of bishop; these included consecrating his successor, Bishop **Ivan Slezyuk**. Latyshevskyi died shortly afterwards as a result of the ordeal he had suffered in labor camps. (WR)

Sources: Atanasiy Pekar, *Ispovidniky viry nashoy suczastnisti: Prychynok do martirolohii Ukraiinskoy Katolitskoy Tserkvi pid sovitami* (Toronto, 1982); *Encyclopedia of Ukraine*, vol. 2 (Toronto, 1985); *Martirolohia ukraiinskikh tserkov u chetyriokh tomakh*, vol. 2 (Toronto, 1988); Bohdan R. Bociurkiw, *The Ukrainian Greek-Catholic Church and the Soviet State (1939–1950)* (Edmonton, 1996).

LAURISTIN Johannes (29 October 1899, Tallinn–28 August 1941, Tallinn), Estonian Communist activist and writer. Born into a working-class family, Lauristin finished only a primary school (1914). He took an active part in the October Revolution and became a member of the Bolshevik party (1917). However, during the war for Estonian independence Lauristin fought on the side of the emerging Estonian republic. He served in the Estonian Army until 1922. A laborer, he was quickly promoted in the structures of the Estonian trade unions. He was one of the organizers of the illegal Union of Communist Youth of Estonia and a co-founder of the Estonian Union of Young Proletarians. He also became a member of the Central Committee (CC) of the Communist Party of Estonia (CPE). From 1923 to 1933 Lauristin was editor-in-chief of *Noor Tooline*. In 1922 he was elected to the Central Council of Trade Unions of Estonia. At the Third Congress of the CPE he was coopted to the top leadership of the party. In March 1923 Lauristin won a seat in the parliamentary elections as a candidate of the United Front of Working People, but he did not take his seat because on the day before the elections, he was arrested and then sentenced to seven years in prison. While in prison, Lauristin wrote *Riigiikukutajad* (Destroyers of the state). In 1932 he was released from prison, but after a trial in 1932–34 he was sentenced to an additional six years of hard labor. At that time he began writing the novel *Vabariik* (Republic), which he did not complete. Released from prison under an amnesty in 1938, Lauristin was coopted to the underground Politburo of the CC of the CPE. Officially, he worked as an inspector of the Health Care Fund in Tallinn. After Estonia was occupied by the Red Army in June 1940 and then incorporated into the USSR as the Estonian SSR in July 1940, Lauristin became first chairman of the Council of People's Commissars of the Estonian SSR, secretary of the CC of the CP (Bolshevik) of Estonia (the name of the party was expanded in October 1940), and a member of the USSR Supreme Soviet. Because of his positions, Lauristin held the primary responsibility, together with **Nikolai Karotamm** and **Karl Säre**, for the crimes against the Estonian people committed by the Soviet regime between 1940 and 1941. According to the official version of his death, Lauristin attempted to escape to the Soviet Union on the ship *Yakov Sverdlov* shortly before the German Army entered Tallinn, but he died at sea. However, there is suspicion that he was murdered by the NKVD. (AG)

Sources: *Bolshaia Sovetskaia Entsiklopediia*, vol. 14 (Moscow, 1973); *Eesti Entsuklopeedia*, vol. 14 (Tallinn, 2000); Romuald J. Misunas and Rein Taagepera, *The Baltic States: The Years of Dependence, 1940–1970* (Berkeley, 1993); Pekka Erelt, "Kas Lauristin tapeti," *Eesti Ekspress*, 21 October 1999.

LAURISTIN Marju (7 April 1940, Tallinn), Estonian political activist. The daughter of **Johannes Lauristin**, in 1966 Lauristin graduated in Estonian philology from the University of Tartu, and then she worked as a radio journalist. From 1970 she was connected with the University of Tartu, where in 1976 she received a Ph.D. in philology. She was interested in the sociology of culture, and in the 1980s she worked at the chair of journalism. In 1968–90 she belonged to the CPSU. In 1980, along with **Jaan Kaplinski** and other intellectuals, Lauristin sent the "Letter of 40," whose signatories demanded the discontinuance of discrimination against the Estonian language; the discrimination increased when **Karl Vaino** took over as first secretary of the Communist Party of Estonia (CPE). Lauristin's involvement in opposition activities, although still as a party member, brought her authority as a leading representative of party reformers, supporting perestroika and opposing the policies of the Vaino party apparatus.

As dean of the Department of Journalism of Tartu University, on 13 April 1988 Lauristin, along with the head of the Planning Commission, **Edgar Savisaar**, appeared on television and called for the creation of the People's Front (Rahvariine [PF]), aimed at supporting Mikhail Gorbachev's reforms but with a strong emphasis on the need for a new union agreement for the Soviet republics. At this time the PF opposed overly radical demands, "separatist" tendencies, and full independence, which was demanded by the anti-Communist opposition. During the October 1988 congress of the PF, Lauristin joined its leadership. Under the pressure of anti-Communist civic committees, in September 1989 she supported the

civic committee movement and full independence from the USSR. In January 1990 Lauristin left the CPE and took the lead of the Estonian Social Democratic Party of Independence (Eesti Sotsialdemokrate Iseseisvuspartei). After this party merged with two small similar groups, in September 1990 Lauristin co-founded the Estonian Social Democratic Party, renamed the Party Moderates (Mõõdukad [PM]), which joined the Socialist International. In the elections to the Estonian Congress in February 1990 Lauristin won a seat and joined the Estonian Committee, but because of rivalry between the PF leaders and the anti-Communists, as well as Lauristin's opposition to Prime Minister Savisaar's policies, in October 1990 she was expelled from the committee. In 1989–91 Lauristin was a member of the Supreme Council of the USSR, and in 1990–92, of the Supreme Council of the Estonian SSR. In the government that emerged after the first free elections of October 1992 under **Mart Laar**, Lauristin became minister of social affairs, but owing to her conflict with the prime minister, she left the government.

In the 1995 elections Lauristin lost and stayed out of the parliament. In 1999 she managed to win a seat again. Later her ratings declined, and in 1999 she lost in the local elections in Tartu. The fusion of her party with a conservative faction led by **Toomas Hendrik Ilves** into the People's Party Moderates further eroded her influence, and in 2000 Ilves took over the party's leadership. Lauristin authored many scholarly works, including the following: *Towards a Civic Society* (1993); *Return to the Western World: Cultural and Political Perspectives on the Estonian Postcommunist Transition* (co-author; 1997); *Political Control and Ideological Canonisation: The Estonian Press during the Soviet Period* (1997); *Transformations of the Public Sphere and the Changing Role of the Media in Postcommunist Society* (1998). (AG)

Sources: *Eesti Enstuklopeedia*, vol. 14 (Tallinn, 2000); Anatol Lieven, *The Baltic Revolution* (New Haven, 1993); Rein Taagepera, *Estonia: Return to Independence* (Boulder, Colo., 1993); Mel Huang, "Does Estonia Have a Left?" *Central European Review*, 2000, no. 13; Józef Darski Web site: http://republika.pl/darski1/kraje/estonia/chronb.htm.

LAUŠMAN Bohumil (30 August 1903, Žumberk–9 May 1963, Prague), Czech Social Democratic politician. In his youth Laušman worked at a bank. Between 1935 and 1939 he was an MP, and in 1938–39 he was secretary of the National Labor Party (Národni Strana Práce). In 1939 he emigrated to France and then to Great Britain, where he was active in the Czechoslovak National Council. After his return to Czechoslovakia in the fall of 1944 Laušman, as a representative of the party, worked in Banská Bystrica in the government-in-exile for the affairs of the liberated territories. In 1946 he was elected to the parliament. Although he was closely connected with **Zdenek Fierlinger**, Laušman was a member of the wing of the Social Democratic Party (Československa Sociální Demokracie) that was independent from the Communists. After the elections of May 1946 Laušman assumed the post of minister of industry in the government of **Klement Gottwald**. At a congress in Brno on 16 November 1947 the Social Democrats made a shift toward greater independence from the Communists, and Laušman became secretary general of the party. In February 1948 at Laušman's house ministers gathered who had resigned from the government in protest against the Communization of the police. Laušman unsuccessfully attempted to mediate, criticizing both the decision of the non-Communist ministers and the Communist undertakings. He let the most vigorous opponents of communism resign from the leadership of Social Democracy, but in March 1948, after a coup, Laušman was dismissed as head of the party. He then managed a power plant in Bratislava. In 1949 he emigrated, at first to Yugoslavia and then to Austria. He worked in the Czechoslovak section of Radio Free Europe. In December 1953 Laušman was abducted from Austria by agents of Soviet and Czechoslovak "security." Imprisoned during an investigation and sentenced to seventeen years' imprisonment in 1957, he died in Ruzyne Prison in Prague under vague circumstances. Laušman published (among other works) *Hospodářská výstavba republiky* (Economic development of the republic; 1946), *Řeknu pravdu* (I will tell the truth; 1947), and *Kdo bol vinen?* (Who was to blame? 1953). (WR)

Sources: *ČBS*; *Encyklopedia Slovenska*, vol. 3 (Bratislava, 1979); Kurt Glaser, *Czecho-Slovakia: A Critical History* (Caldwell, Idaho, 1961); Stefan Pagác, *Svedek z cely císlo 13: Dokument* (New York, 1979); Stefan Pagac, *State Secret No. 1: Warning for the Free World* (New York, 1981).

LÁZÁR György (15 September 1924, Isaszeg), Hungarian Communist activist. A draftsman by trade, in 1945 Lázár joined the Hungarian Communist Party, quickly advancing in its ranks. From 1948 he held directorial positions in the State Planning Commission. In 1958 he became the commission's deputy chairman, and in 1973, chairman. In this capacity he counteracted a more rational economic policy. From February 1970 to June 1973 Lázár was minister of labor, and from June 1973 to May 1975, deputy prime minister. Until 1968 he was a member of the Central People's Revisory Commission and then a member of the Central Committee (CC) of the Hungarian Socialist Workers' Party (HSWP). In 1975 he became a member of the HSWP CC Politburo and an MP. Lázár was among the closest friends of **János Kádár**. From 15 May 1975 to 25 June 1987 he was prime minister. In this position, he impeded the economic reforms of his predecessor, **Jenő Fock**. Lázár tried to avoid ideologically risky reforms and to shield the inefficiency of the economic system by accepting huge foreign loans, especially in the 1980s. He became a symbol of the so-called goulash socialism, based on spreading social opportunism and apathy. Lázár signed an agreement with Czechoslovakia on the construction of the ecologically disastrous Nagymaros-Gabčikovo Dam on the Danube River. He stepped down in the face of aggravated economic crisis. He became the HSWP deputy general secretary, but as a result of pro-democratic and pro-market movements, in May 1988 Lázár was expelled from his party positions, and then he lost his parliamentary mandate. (AH)

Sources: Bennet Kovrig, *Communism in Hungary from Kun to Kádár* (Stanford, 1979); *A nép támogatásával a szocializmus útján: Válogatott beszédek, cikkek* (Budapest, 1983); Miklós Molnár, *From Béla Kun to János Kádár: Seventy Years of Hungarian Communism* (New York, 1990); *20 századi magyar történelem* (Budapest, 1997).

LAZARENKO Pavlo (23 January 1953, Karpivka, near Dniepropetrovsk), Ukrainian Communist and post-Communist activist. The son of a kolkhoz director, after primary school Lazarenko worked as a driver in his father's enterprise, and from 1971 to 1973 he served in the Soviet Army in Central Asia. In 1978 he graduated from the Institute of Agrarian Economics in Dniepropetrovsk. In 1978–79 he worked as an agronomist, and from late 1979, as director of the Mikhail Kalinin kolkhoz in the New Moscow region. From December 1985 Lazarenko headed the Agricultural Department of the regional Communist Party committee in Dniepropetrovsk, and from August 1990 he was deputy chairman of the regional executive committee. In early 1992 **Leonid Kravchuk** appointed Lazarenko presidential representative in Dniepropetrovsk. The promotion of an agronomist to a key position in the Ukrainian industrial center was intended to reduce the influence of the local lobby, but Lazarenko took the lead of the Dniepropetrovsk oligarchy and helped it build a leading position in the Ukraine. Lazarenko became co-owner of a number of local presses and television channels. From 1994 he was a member of the Ukrainian Supreme Council, and in May 1995 he became deputy prime minister responsible for the power sector in the government of **Yevhen Marchuk**. When President **Leonid Kuchma** dismissed Marchuk, on 27 May 1996 Lazarenko became prime minister.

Lazarenko's key success as prime minister was the

introduction of a Ukrainian currency—the hryvna. He also consolidated the position of his oligarchs on the fuel market. In July 1996 Lazarenko barely avoided a bomb attack in Kiev, believed to be an attempt by the rival Donetsk group to eliminate him. On 1 July 1997, pressured by Kuchma, Lazarenko stepped down. He became head of the Dniepropetrovsk regional council and a member of the Supreme Council. In September 1997 he took the lead of the All-Ukrainian Association Community (AUAC; Hromada [AUAC]), which proclaimed itself to be a Social Democratic party opposing President Kuchma. In December 1998 Lazarenko was arrested in Switzerland on charges of the embezzlement of the equivalent of U.S.$20 million in connection with financial settlements for the supply of gas from Russia. He was let out on a bail of U.S.$3 million, and in early 1999 he returned to the Ukraine. Lazarenko explained the accusation against him as a part of Kuchma's presidential campaign. When in February 1999 the prosecutor's office moved to deprive him of parliamentary immunity, he left the Ukraine. He applied for political asylum in the United States, but he was arrested there. His extradition was requested by both the Ukraine and Switzerland (money laundering in local banks). In early 2000 Lazarenko accused Kuchma's aides of illegal financial deals. He declared his readiness to return to the Ukraine on condition of immunity, but the Supreme Council did not grant it. In March 1999 the AUAC dissolved, and most of its MPs joined a new party, Fatherland (Batkivshchyna), led by Lazarenko's hitherto ally, Yulia Tymoshenko. (TS)

Sources: *Europa Środkowo-Wschodnia 1996* (Warsaw, 1998); Radzisława Gortat, *Ukraińskie wybory* (Warsaw, 1998); Bohdan Nahaylo, *The Ukrainian Resurgence* (Toronto, 1999); Bugajski; www.rulers.org.

LEBED Dmytro (11 January 1893, Nikolayevka, Yekaterinoslav Province–30 October 1937?), Ukrainian Communist activist. Born into a poor peasant family, Lebed began working as a locksmith in 1908. In 1909 he became a member of the Bolshevik party and was active in its structures in Yekaterinoslav (now Dniepropetrovsk, Ukraine) until 1920. From 1918 to 1920 he was in the Commissariat of Internal Affairs of the Soviet Ukraine, and in 1920 he became a member of the Central Committee (CC) of the Communist Party (Bolshevik) of Ukraine (CP[B]U). Lebed was one of the representatives of the "Yekaterinoslav orientation," which aimed to establish a so-called Donetsk–Kryvy Rih Soviet Republic. They wanted to introduce Soviet rule only in the eastern, industrialized part of the Ukraine and did not hope for a revolution in the central and western Ukraine, which was dominated by the peasants. Lebed considered the revolution in the Ukraine to be part of the Russian Revolution, which was to grow into a world revolution. He believed that any compromise between the Communist ideas of internationalism and the national ideas amounted to ushering in counterrevolution. Lebed's view, according to which the "building of socialism" required that the proletarian urban culture assume leadership over the peasant rural culture, meant a subordination of the Ukrainian people—as the more "backward"—to the Russian culture and language. Lebed developed these views in *Sovetskaia Ukraina i natsionalnyi vopros za piat' let* (Soviet Ukraine and the national question during the last five years; 1924). From 1921 to 1923 Lebed held the post of second secretary of the CP(B)U CC. When in 1925 in Moscow it was decided to increase the pace of Ukrainization, Emanuel Kviryng, head of the CP(B)U, was replaced by **Lazar Kaganovich**; this meant the end of Lebed's career as well. **Mykola Skrypnyk**, the main strategist of Ukrainization until its end in the early 1930s, described Lebed's theory as an expression of Great Russian nationalism in the Ukraine and compared it to Ukrainian nationalism, regarding both as equally dangerous for efforts to resolve the national question in the Soviet Union. Arrested during the Great Purge, Lebed died in prison. (TS)

Sources: *MERSH*, vol. 19; *Encyclopedia of Ukraine*, vol. 3 (Toronto, 1993); E. Hirchak, *Na dva fronta v borbe s natsionalizmom* (Moscow and Leningrad, 1930); Mykola Skrypnyk, *Do teorii borotby dvokh kultur* (Kharkiv, 1926).

LEBED Mykola, pseudonyms "Skyba" and "Maksym Ruban" (23 November 1909, Strilychi Novi, near Bóbrka–19 July 1998, Pittsburgh, Pennsylvania), Ukrainian nationalist politician. From 1932 to 1934 Lebed was a liaison officer between the National Executive of the Organization of Ukrainian Nationalists (OUN), based in Poland, and its Directorate (Provid) abroad. In June 1934, on **Stepan Bandera**'s recommendation, he organized the assassination of the Polish interior minister, Bronisław Pieracki. In the preparations for the assassination he was assisted by (among others) his future wife, Daria Hnatkivs'ka. After Pieracki's assassination, Lebed fled, at first to Gdańsk and then to Germany. At the demand of the Polish authorities he was arrested, on the orders of Heinrich Himmler, and delivered to Poland. In 1936 in Warsaw, Lebed was sentenced to death in a trial of OUN activists (among them Bandera); the sentence was then changed to life imprisonment. Lebed served the sentence first in Święty Krzyż, then in Rawicz and Siedlce. On 5 September 1939 he escaped and returned to his native land.

In 1940 in Rome, Lebed took part in a mediation effort between members of the Bandera faction and **Andriy Melnyk**. After the split of the OUN into a revolutionary faction (i.e., the followers of Bandera [OUN-B]) and a Melnyk faction, Lebed became a member of the OUN-B Directorate (Provid). In June 1941 he joined the government of **Yaroslav Stetsko**, which was established on the initiative of Bandera followers after the outbreak of the German-Soviet war. After the Germans arrested members of this government, as well as numerous activists of the OUN-B, on 15 September 1941 Lebed assumed the duties of head of the OUN-B. He organized three OUN conferences. He was hunted by the Gestapo, which arrested his mother, his sister, and (in January 1944) his wife and child. On 13 May 1943 his duties as *providnik* (head) of the OUN-B were taken over by a three-member Bureau of the Provid, headed by **Roman Shukhevych**. Lebed's opposition to the democratization of the OUN program was the reason for his leaving. According to another, less likely version, Lebed was forced to step down from his post because he opposed the extensive development of the Ukrainian guerrilla movement.

Lebed rejected Shukhevych's proposal to join the Bureau of the Provid. Finally, he became responsible for directing the foreign policy of the OUN-B. Between 1941 and 1944 he headed talks with the Polish Home Army (Armia Krajowa [AK]) and with the Delegation of the Polish Government-in-Exile. In the Ukrainian Supreme Liberation Council (UHVR), which was established in July 1944 and was the political superstructure of the Ukrainian Insurgent Army (Ukraiinska Povstancha Armiia [UPA]), Lebed served as secretary general for foreign affairs. In that capacity he directed talks with the Hungarians that led to the establishment of local agreements between the Ukrainian guerrillas and Hungarian units. He mediated in talks between the UPA and the Germans that resulted in (among other things) the release of many members of the Bandera faction (including Bandera and Stetsko) from Nazi concentration camps. Lebed left the Ukraine in July 1944, when the war front was passing, and he was given the task of gaining the support of Western allies for the Ukrainian cause.

From 1945 Lebed was in exile in Italy, Germany, and (from 1949) the United States, where he held the post of secretary general of the foreign representation of the UHVR. He was one of the initiators of another split in the OUN, as a result of which the so-called OUN abroad was created. In 1952–73 Lebed was head of Prolog, a research and publishing institute in New York that informed Western public opinion about the policies of the USSR in the Ukraine. He left commentaries and the monograph *UPA*, which was published in 1946. Lebed's attitude toward the mass murders of Poles in Volhynia (Wołyń) remained vague. According to some interpretations, he opposed them, while according to others, it was Lebed who had ordered the liquidation of thousands of Polish civilians. In 1988 and 1992, the American press presented information about Lebed's cooperation with the Gestapo and his participation in the murders of Jews in Eastern Galicia. His responsibility for the death of Minister Pieracki was noted, as well as his cooperation with the CIA after the war. Lebed consistently denied these accusations, maintaining that they were based upon fabrications by the KGB. (GM)

Sources: *Entsyklopediia Ukraiinoznavstva*, vol. 6; *Encyclopedia of Ukraine*, vol. 3 (Toronto, 1993); *The Ukrainian Weekly*, 26 July 1998; Ryszard Torzecki, *Polacy i Ukraińcy: Sprawa ukraińska w czasie II wojny światowej na terenie II Rzeczpospolitej* (Warsaw, 1993); Anatol Kaminskyi, *Vasyl Okhrymovich* (Toronto, New York, and London, 1999); Petro Mirchuk, *Ukraiinska Povstanska Armiia 1942–1950* (Lviv, 1993); *Chicago Sun*, 17 April 1988; *New York Times*, 17 September 1992.

LECHOWICZ Włodzimierz (16 January 1911, Szczucin, near Dąbrowa Tarnowska–25 November 1986, Warsaw), Polish political activist. Lechowicz graduated in philosophical studies from Warsaw University and then worked in the government administration. From 1936 to 1939 he was secretary general of the Association of Government Officials. Before World War II he belonged to the illegal Communist Party of Poland (Komunistyczna Partia Polski [KPP]). During the German occupation he was active in the underground resistance movement; for example, he participated in the work of the State Security Corps, which was the embryo of a police force, and in the work of the sabotage department of the Command of the Underground Struggle. He also cooperated with the General Staff Information Department of the Communist People's Guard (later the People's Army) and with Soviet intelligence. In 1942 Lechowicz became a member of the Democratic Party (Stronnictwo Demokratyczne [SD]). From 1945 to 1947 he worked in the Ministry of Regained Territories. In November 1945 he became a member of the SD Central Committee (CC); in July 1946, a member of the Political Committee of the SD CC; and in November of that year, deputy chairman of the party. Lechowicz won a parliamentary seat in the rigged elections of January 1947. From February to March 1947 he served as minister for supplies and trade and subsequently as minister for supplies. In September 1948 he was dismissed from his ministerial post. Arrested in October of that year, Lechowicz was held in prison for seven years although he had not been convicted. Because of his double role during the occupation, he was subjected to torture by the Communists, who wanted to extort testimony against **Władysław Gomułka** and other activists of the national Communist underground to incriminate them as collaborators with the pro-independence ("reactionary") underground movement. Lechowicz was stripped of his parliamentary immunity in April 1949—that is, after his imprisonment. In July 1955 he was sentenced to fifteen years in prison. Released in May 1956, he was rehabilitated in December 1956. From 1956 to 1969 Lechowicz again served as deputy chairman of the SD CC. In 1957–61 he was editor-in-chief of the newspaper *Kurier Polski*. He was also president of the board of the Epoka Publishing House. From July 1961 to December 1970 he was chairman of the Small-Scale Producers' Committee, which was in charge of crafts. From 1970 to 1974 Lechowicz served as ambassador to Holland. From 1957 to 1972 he was an MP in the Assembly of the Polish People's Republic. (WR)

Sources: Mołdawa; Maria Turlejska, *Te pokolenia żałobami czarne . . . Skazani na śmierć i ich sędziowie 1944–1954* (London, 1989); Stanisław Marat and Jacek Snopkiewicz, *Ludzie bezpieki* (Warsaw, 1990).

LEDERER Jiří (15 July 1922, Kvasiny, district of Rychnov nad Kněžnou–12 October 1983, Birnbach, Germany), Czech journalist, translator, and commentator. From 1945 to 1948 Lederer studied in the Department of Philosophy at Charles University and at the Higher Political and Social School in Prague. From 1948 to 1949 he studied at the Jagiellonian University in Kraków. In 1951–54 he worked as a turner. In 1946 he began to contribute articles to Social Democratic newspapers. In 1954 he started working as a journalist for the periodical *Svět sovětů*, then for the newspaper *Večerní Praha*, and then for *Technické noviny*. Between 1962 and 1967 he was head of a research group of Czechoslovak radio. One of the leading journalists during the Prague Spring, Lederer wrote for *Literární listy* and *Reportér*. During the so-called normalization period, he took part in opposition activities, for which he was imprisoned several times (1970, 1972–73, 1977–80). In 1977 Lederer signed Charter 77. In 1980 he emigrated to the Federal Republic of Germany, where he worked as a journalist. In underground periodicals and abroad, he published a number of commentaries and essays, including *České rozhovory* (Czech conversations; 1979; published in Cologne). He wrote a book devoted to **Jan Palach**, *Palach: Zpráva o životě, činu a smrti českého studenta* (Jan Palach: An account of the life, activities, and death of a Czech student; 1990); it was published posthumously. (PU)

Sources: *ČBS*; J. Brabec et al., *Slovník zakázaných autorů 1948–80* (Prague, 1991); František Knopp, *Česká literatura v exilu 1948–89: Bibliografie* (Prague, 1996).

LEDNICKI Aleksander (15 July 1866, Minsk–11 August 1934, Warsaw), Polish lawyer and politician. The son of small landowners who took part in the January Insurrection of 1863, after losing his father, Lednicki was brought up by his grandfather in a patriotic spirit. In 1885 he passed his high school final examinations in a gymnasium in Minsk, and in 1889 he completed law studies in Yaroslavl. He subsequently worked as an attorney in Moscow, gaining fame and fortune, and in 1903 he became a member of the local bar association. Lednicki's high earnings allowed him to buy several landed estates in Lithuania and Belorussia. He also owned a lot of real estate in Moscow, Minsk, Smolensk, and Vilnius. After becoming the chairman of the United Bank in Moscow in 1910, he was active among the Poles in Russia and in Russian liberal circles. One of the founders of the Progressive Democratic Union in 1904, Lednicki served as the party's vice-president. In 1906 he was elected to the first State Duma. After the dissolution of the Duma, he wrote a protest manifesto, as a result of which he was imprisoned for three months in 1908. From 1907 to 1910 Lednicki was a member of the Grand East of the Peoples of Russia lodge, and he maintained Masonic contacts later on. In 1905 he helped to found the Constitutional Democratic Party (also known as the Kadets), and he was a member of its Central Committee until 1916. In April 1916 a conference of this party was held in Lednicki's apartment in Moscow, at which his proposal that the Kingdom of Poland be granted autonomy was adopted as part of the party's program.

During World War I Lednicki was active in the Central Civic Committee. He was also the founder of the Polish Committee for Aid to War Victims and served as its chairman from 1914 to 1917. He initially supported Polish-Russian rapprochement as a means to secure the autonomy of the Polish territories, and he worked with the National Democrats and the Party of Real Politics (Stronnictwo Polityki Realnej [SPR]). As the Russian position on the issue of Polish autonomy was unclear and the tsarist army suffered defeats, in 1916 Lednicki called for the independence of Poland and joined the underground Polish Independence Association, whose members included activists of the pro-Piłsudski Polish Military Organization (Polska Organizacja Wojskowa [POW]). After the February 1917 revolution, the Provisional Government appointed him chairman of the Liquidation Commission for the Affairs of the Kingdom of Poland (Komisja Likwidacyjna do spraw Królestwa Polskiego) on 15 March 1917. Thanks to Lednicki's efforts as chairman of this commission, the Provisional Government issued a declaration on 30 March that accepted the principle of Polish independence. Lednicki also founded Polish democratic committees in

Russia that recognized the Provisional Council of State and the Regency Council; consequently, he came into conflict with members of the National Democratic movement. After the Bolshevik revolution, when the Regency Council appointed Lednicki as its representative to liaise with the new government, the National Democrats increased their attacks against him, accusing him not only of wrong political choices, but also of dishonesty.

The attacks by the National Democrats, particularly by Zygmunt Wasilewski, a journalist, did not stop after Lednicki's arrival in Warsaw in October 1918. From 1919 to 1923 Lednicki edited the periodical *Tydzień Polski*. His numerous publications of that period include *Z lat wojny: Artykuły, listy, przemówienia 1915–1918* (The war years: Articles, letters, speeches 1915–1918; 1921), *Nasza polityka wschodnia* (Our eastern policy; 1922), and *Zadania chwili* (Tasks of the moment; 1922). In 1926 Lednicki successfully sued Wasilewski for slander but retired from active politics. He nonetheless continued to serve as president of the Polish Pan-European Union. He also worked as a legal counselor to (among others) Western entrepreneurs who invested in Poland, and he was a member of the supervisory boards of many banks and companies. In May 1934 Lednicki mediated an agreement, very disadvantageous for Poland, between the Polish government and the French shareholders of a factory in Żyrardów. Under fire from part of the government press, for whom he was a scapegoat, Lednicki committed suicide. (WR)

Sources: *PSB*, vol. 16; Antoni Pieretiatkowicz, *Współczesna encyklopedia życia politycznego* (Warsaw, 1931); *Who's Who in Central Europe, 1935/36* (Zurich, 1937); Wacław Lednicki, *Pamiętniki*, vols. 1–2 (London, 1963–67); Janusz Pajewski, *Wokół sprawy polskiej Paryż-Lozanna-Londyn, 1914–1918* (Poznań, 1970); Andrew Kier Wise, "Aleksander Lednicki: Polish Patriot and Russian Liberationist," Ph.D. diss., University of Virginia, 1996; Ludwik Hass, *Masoneria polska XX wieku* (Warsaw, 1996).

LEDNICKI Wacław (28 April 1891, Moscow–20 October 1967, Berkeley), Polish literary historian. The son of **Aleksander Lednicki**, Lednicki graduated from a gymnasium (high school) in Moscow in 1910. He subsequently studied Polish philology at the Jagiellonian University in Kraków and Romance and German philology at Moscow University. After completing his studies in 1915, he worked as a teacher. In 1918 he served as secretary of the Regency Council representation, liaising with the Bolshevik government. This representation was directed by his father. After returning to Poland, Lednicki served in the Polish Army (1919–20), and then he devoted himself to scholarly work. In 1922 he earned a Ph.D. in Romance philology, but he later became primarily involved in Russian literature. In 1926 he received the postdoctoral degree for a study on Aleksandr Pushkin.

However, for political reasons, Lednicki did not obtain a professorship at the Jagiellonian University until 1928. He also held the chair of Russian literature at the Université Libre in Brussels. After the Nazi invasion of Poland, Lednicki managed to escape to Belgium; from there he made his way, via Portugal, to the United States. From 1940 to 1944 he lectured at Harvard University, subsequently becoming a professor of Slavic studies at the University of California in Berkeley. In 1947 he was awarded an honorary doctorate by the Université Libre in Brussels. Lednicki was one of the founders of the Polish Institute of Arts and Sciences in New York. In 1962 he retired. Lednicki was one of the pioneers in the study of Russian literature in the United States. He studied Aleksandr Pushkin, Leo Tolstoy, and Fyodor Dostoevsky. He also investigated the relations between Russian writers and Poland. Lednicki's publications include the following: *Przyjaciele Moskale* (Muscovite friends; 1935); *Panslavism* (Pan-Slavism; 1948); *Russia, Poland, and the West* (1954); *Pushkin's Bronze Horseman* (1955); and his extensive *Pamiętniki* (Diary; 1963–1967). *The Adventures of a Modern Gil Blas during the Last War* (1971) was published posthumously. (WR)

Sources: *PSB*, vol. 16; W. Jakubowski, "Droga naukowa Wacława Lednickiego," *Zeszyty Naukowe UJ*, 1970, vol. 17; *Polacy w historii i kulturze krajów Europy Zachodniej* (Poznań, 1981).

LEKA I (6 April 1939, Tirana), successor to the Albanian throne. The son of **Ahmed Zogu (King Zog)** and Geraldine Apponyi, Leka was born on the eve of the Italian invasion of Albania and left it as a baby only a few days old. He graduated from Sandhurst Military Academy in Great Britain. After his father died in 1961, Leka was proclaimed king of Albania by a group of Albanian monarchists in Paris. Arrested several times for the illegal possession of arms—for instance, in Thailand and Spain—in 1972 Leka held a conference in Madrid and announced the formation of the Military Council of Liberation of Ethnic Albania, which he would head. According to press accounts, he dealt with the military training of Albanian volunteers. Expelled from Spain, in February 1979 Leka went to Rhodesia, where he dealt in the arms trade. From 1980 he lived in Johannesburg, South Africa. From 1989 he repeatedly announced plans to return to Albania, where he claimed to have a major influence. Leka's vision of monarchy was similar to that of King Juan Carlos of Spain. In order to gain support in Albania, Leka established the National Democratic Party, which later assumed the historical name of the Movement for Legality; it gained 2–3 percent of the vote in subsequent elections. Leka returned to Albania on 19 November 1993, but he was expelled because he held an invalid passport (he indicated "King of Albania" as his profession). After the crisis connected with financial pyramids, in 1997 Leka managed to return to Albania, where the parliamentary elections were connected with a referendum on the political system. On 29 June 1997 the majority of Albanians rejected monarchy. On 3 July 1997 Leka organized a rally in downtown Tirana and accused the ruling Socialists of having falsified the referendum. He appeared armed, and the Socialists interpreted this as an attempt at a coup. Leka left the country, and he was sued in absentia. Late he lived on a farm near Randberg in South Africa with his wife, Susan Cullen-Ward, and his children. (TC)

Sources: William Bland and Ian Price, *A Tangled Web: A History of Anglo-American Relations with Albania (1912–1955)* (London, 1986); Gwen Robyns, *Geraldine of the Albanians* (London, 1987); Miranda Vickers and James Pettifier, *Albania: From Anarchy to a Balkan Identity* (New York, 1997); www.rulers.com.

LÉKAI László [originally Lung] (12 March 1910, Zalalövö–30 June 1986, Esztergom), Primate of Hungary. In 1934 Lékai graduated in theology and philosophy in Rome and was ordained. In 1936 he received a Ph.D. in theology. Later he worked as a diocese priest, catechist in a pedagogical institute for boys, and lecturer in the theological seminary in Veszprém. From 1944 he was an adviser to the Hungarian Episcopate, and in 1944–48 he was secretary to Primate **József Mindszenty**. During the German occupation of Hungary Lékai was imprisoned along with Mindszenty. In 1946 he was appointed papal camerlengo. From 1948 to 1972 he was parish priest in Balatonlelle, Zalaszentiván, and Badacsony on Lake Balaton. On 8 February 1972 he was appointed apostolic administrator of the Veszprém diocese, and on 16 March 1972 he was consecrated as bishop. In 1973 Lékai failed to make Primate Mindszenty to give up his position. In 1974 he became apostolic administrator of Esztergom, and after the death of Mindszenty, on 12 February 1976, he was appointed archbishop of Esztergom and Primate of Hungary. On 24 May 1976 Lékai became cardinal. He joined the Vatican Congregation of Catholic Education. Initially perceived as a follower of the uncompromising line of Mindszenty, Lékai later became known as a supporter of the eastern policies of Cardinal Agostino Casaroli. In the atmosphere of the so-called goulash communism, Lékai's policies provided the hierarchy and believers with apparent security at the cost of some priests sitting on the Communist parliament and helping out Communist authorities by discriminating against anti-Communist priests (for example, the Bokor youth movement of Father György Bulányi). As a result the official Catholic Church was made an ally of the atheist authorities. Many priests were released from prisons and the hierarchy was reconstructed, but the Church lost authority among the believers, many of whom thought Lékai's "small steps" policies were leading nowhere. Lékai was awarded several state honors. (MS)

Sources: *"A megnyesett fa kizöldül": Portré dr. Lekai Lászlóról* (Budapest, 1984); Alceste Santini, *Ungheria quarantanni dopo* (Rome, 1985); Jenő Gergely, "Lékai László," *Világosság*, 1986, nos. 8–9; Hansjakob Stehle, *Tajna dyplomacja Watykanu* (Warsaw, 1993); Andrzej Grajewski, *Kompleks Judasza* (Poznań, 1999); www.catholic-hierarchy.org.

LEM Stanisław (12 October 1921, Lwów [Lviv]—27 March 2006, Kraków), Polish writer. In 1940 Lem enrolled in medical studies, which he pursued in 1944–45 in the Lviv Institute of Medicine and which he completed at the Jagiellonian University in Kraków, where he settled after World War II. He made his literary debut in 1946; his first novel to attract attention was *Astronauci* (Astronauts; 1951), a work of science fiction atypical of the Socialist realist pattern of the early 1950s. Later Lem published a number of short stories and novels in this genre, including *Obłok Magellana* (Magellanic cloud; 1955); *Dzienniki gwiazdowe* (1957; *Star Diaries*, 1976); and *Solaris* (1961; English edition 1970); these won him fame in Poland and soon also abroad. Constantly improving his style and deepening the psychology of his characters, Lem asked fundamental questions about the future of human beings during a period of scientific and technological revolution, as well as about the nature of the world and the limits of knowledge. His views evolved toward a skeptical or even pessimistic vision of the development of human civilization. Lem's subsequent works—such as *Summa technologiae* (1964), *Bajki robotów* (1964), *Cyberiada* (1965), *Filozofia przypadku* (1968; *Chain of Chance*, 1978), and *Kongres futurologiczny* (1973; *Futurological Congress*, 1974)—were like philosophical treatises, full of paradoxes and subtle grotesqueness. Lem was increasingly interested in literary creativity and the cognitive value of literature, as well as in the debate on the links between technological progress and the evolution of humans as a species. The reviver of science fiction, a futurologist, and a theoretician of literature, Lem became one of the most frequently published Polish authors, both at home and abroad. His works were translated into thirty languages. Selections from his works were published many times. The most extensive of these was *Dzieła* (Works, 19 vols.; 1994–97). (WR)

Sources: *Literatura polska: Przewodnik encyklopedyczny*, vol. 1 (Warsaw, 2000); *Stanislaw Lem an der Grenzen Science Fiction* (Meitingen, 1985); Jerzy Jarzębski, ed., *Lem w oczach krytyki światowej* (Kraków, 1989); J. Madison Davis, *Stanislaw Lem* (Mercer Island, Wash., 1990); Antoni Smuszkiewicz, *Stanisław Lem* (Poznań, 1995); Małgorzata Szpakowska, *Dyskusje ze Stanisławem Lemem* (Warsaw, 1996).

LENÁRT Jozef (3 April 1923, Liptovská Porúbka), Slovak Communist activist. A chemist by trade, in 1939–44 Lenárt worked in the Bat'a shoe factory. In the summer of 1944 he took part in the Slovak National Uprising. From 1946 he was active in the Communist Party of Slovakia (CPS). In 1950–53, 1957–66, and 1970–88 Lenárt was a member of the CPS Central Committee (CC). From 1950 to 1951 he was director of the 29 August Factory, and then, until 1953, he was deputy minister of light industry. In 1953 he was sent to study at the Higher Party School of the CPSU CC in Moscow. After returning to Czechoslovakia, he became first secretary of the Bratislava party committee (October 1956–January 1958). In 1958 he joined the CC of the Communist Party of Czechoslovakia (CPC) and became secretary of the CPS CC. From 1962 to 1989, with a short break (1968–70), Lenárt belonged to the Presidium of the CPC CC. In 1962–63 he presided over the Slovak National Council, and from 20 September 1963 to 8 April 1968 he was prime minister of Czechoslovakia. He was dismissed as an aide of **Antonín Novotný**. From 1960 to 1969 Lenárt was a member of the National Assembly, and then, until 1990, a member of the Chamber of the People of the Federal Assembly. During the Prague Spring he avoided taking a clear position, but after the Warsaw Pact intervention of August 1968 he supported the "brotherly help" of the Warsaw Pact nations. From 23 to 26 August 1968 Lenárt took part in talks in Moscow, and upon returning home, he became one of the leading spokesmen of "normalization." At the end of November 1989 Lenárt retired from politics, and in February 1990 he was expelled from the CPC. In 1996 he was accused of treason after the events of 1968, but in October 1997 the case was dismissed. In January 1998 the Supreme Court resumed the case, and in September 2002 Lenárt was tried, along with **Miloš Jakeš**, but both were acquitted. (PU)

Sources: *ČBS*; *Who's Who in the Socialist Countries of Europe*, vol. 2 (Munich, London, and Paris, 1989); *Českoslovenští politici 1918/1991* (Prague, 1991); *Kdo byl kdo v našich dějinach ve 20. stoleti*, vol. 1 (Prague, 1998).

LEONAS Petras (16 November 1864, Leškava, near Marijampole–12 May 1938, Kaunas), Lithuanian lawyer and politician. In 1889 Leonas received a law degree from Moscow University. While a student, he led a secret organization of Lithuanian students and was a co-founder of *Varpas*, one of the first underground national periodicals. After completing his studies, Leonas worked as a deputy public prosecutor and later as a judge. In 1905 he was one of the leading Lithuanian journalists of the revolutionary period. Dismissed as a judge because of his contacts with the radical movement, Leonas settled in Kaunas in 1906 and ran a law practice there. Elected to the second Russian Duma in 1907, he focused his attention on Lithuanian autonomy, drafting a bill on that issue, but it was never implemented. He also dealt with agrarian reform. After the outbreak of World War I Leonas became a member of the Lithuanian Central Committee for Assistance and was sent to St. Petersburg, where he directed institutions providing aid to Lithuanian refugees in the capital and in Moscow. After the February 1917 revolution, he co-founded the populist National Democratic Freedom League–Santara, the origin of the future Lithuanian Peasant Union. Over the years his ties with this party weakened.

Leonas's professional qualifications and the respect he enjoyed among the Lithuanian people led to his appointment as minister of justice in the first government of independent Lithuania, established on 11 November 1918. In 1919 he was appointed minister of interior. He significantly contributed to the development of legislation—for example, acts on the judicial system and laws regulating the functioning of local self-government were prepared under his direction. After leaving the government, Leonas became chairman of the Central Electoral Committee, which supervised parliamentary elections for three successive terms. When the university in Kaunas was founded, Leonas was made dean of the School of Law. He held this post for eleven years and simultaneously lectured in law and sociology. His views, emphasizing individual rights and the advantages of liberal democracy, were not approved of by the regime of **Antanas Smetona**; therefore, in 1933 Leonas was dismissed as dean and was banned from lecturing. In response, the School of Law defiantly granted him the title of honorary professor. This position did not have to be confirmed by the authorities, so Leonas could continue lecturing to students.

Leonas was one of the most prominent Lithuanian lawyers of the interwar period. A supporter of legal positivism, he tried to use the achievements of sociology in his work. In 1933 he was granted an honorary doctorate from Kaunas University. He was one of the founders of the Lithuanian Law Society, and from 1929 to 1933 he served as chairman of the Lithuanian Bar Association. Leonas published numerous works and articles in scholarly periodicals. His publications include *Teise enciklopedijos paskaitos* (An introduction to lectures in law; 1924), *Teises filosofijos istorija* (History of the philosophy of law; 1928), and *Sociologijos paskaitos* (A lecture in sociology; 1938). (AG)

Sources: *EL*, vol. 3; A. Rimka, *Lietuvių tautos atgimimo socialiniai pagrindai* (Kaunas, 1931); *Kultura*, 1938, no. 5; Z. Toliusis, "Petro Leono gyvenimas ira darbai," *Naujoji Romuva*, 1938; Wojciech Roszkowski, "Litewskie partie chłopskie (1905–1970)," in Krzysztof Jasiewicz, ed., *Europa nieprowincjonalna* (Warsaw, 1999).

LESZCZYŃSKI-LEŃSKI Julian (8 January 1889, Płock–June 1937?, Moscow), Polish Communist activist. The son of a laborer, Leszczyński-Leński joined the Social Democracy of the Kingdom of Poland and Lithuania (Socjaldemokracja Królestwa Polskiego i Litwy [SDKPiL]) in 1905. After graduating from high school in Płock (1909), he studied history and literature at the Jagiellonian University in Kraków. Expelled from the university in 1911 for directing a student strike, he moved to Warsaw. In October 1913 he attended a Bolshevik conference in Poronin, where he met Vladimir Lenin. Arrested shortly afterwards in Warsaw, he was deported to Russia. Released on bail in 1915, he made a living by working as a tutor in Moscow. In March 1917 Leszczyński-Leński became an SDKPiL delegate to the April conference of the Bolshevik party, and he joined the SDKPiL Central Executive Committee in Russia. In June 1917 he was elected to the Petrograd Executive Committee of the Soviet of Workers', Peasants', and Soldiers' Deputies and later to the Constituent Assembly. During the October Revolution, along with a group of soldiers, Leszczyński-Leński occupied the Main Telegraph building. At the Second All-Russian Congress of Soviets (7–8 November 1917) he became a deputy member of the All-Russian Central Executive Committee of Soviets (Vserossiiskii Tsentralnii Ispolnitelnii Komitet [VTsIK]). On 7 December 1917 he was named a full member of the VTsIK. Four days later he was appointed commissar for Polish affairs at the People's Commissariat for Ethnic Affairs in Russia.

When the Red Army launched its westward offensive in November 1918, Leszczyński-Leński helped to establish the Bolshevik administration in the territories seized from the Germans. In January 1919 he became commissar of education in the government of the Belorussian and Lithuanian Soviet Republic and one of the leaders of the Communist Workers' Party of Poland (Komunistyczna Partia Robotnicza Polski [KPRP]) in Russia. After the Polish troops captured Wilno (Vilnius), Leszczyński-Leński returned to Minsk and conducted Bolshevik agitation among the Poles. In August 1920 he was a delegate of the Polish Provisional Revolutionary Committee at the command of the southwestern front of the Red Army. At the end of 1920 he was an expert for the Bolshevik delegation to negotiations with Poland in Riga, and from March 1921 to December 1923 he served as a member of the Polish Bureau at the Central Committee (CC) of the All-Russian Communist Party (Bolsheviks). In late September and early October 1923 Leszczyński-Leński attended the Second Congress of the KPRP, at which he criticized the "opportunism" of the party's leadership. The conflict between him and the KPRP leaders continued after they forbade him to take any executive positions in the party. As a delegate to the Fifth Congress of the Communist International, Leszczyński-Leński was influential in the headquarters of the Communist movement and gradually recovered control of the situation. The Polish Commission, elected at this congress, annulled the decision of the KPRP and sent Leszczyński-Leński to Poland. His intensive work to win allies was interrupted by his arrest in October 1924. In October 1925 he escaped from prison in Warsaw and made his way to the Soviet Union. In December 1925, during a conference of the KPRP at which it changed its name to the Communist Party of Poland (Komunistyczna Partia Polski [KPP]), Leszczyński-Leński became a member of the party's CC. At a CC plenum in June 1929 he was elected secretary general of the KPP. His triumph was linked with the fact that he supported Stalin, who at that time gained full power within the All-Union Communist Party (Bolsheviks). At the Sixth Comintern Congress Leszczyński-Leński became a deputy member of the Presidium of the Comintern Executive Committee. In mid-1934, in agreement with the Comintern leaders, he introduced changes of policy toward the Socialists, supporting the idea of a "united front." In August 1935 he became a member of the Presidium of the Comintern Executive Committee. In 1936 he settled in Paris, where the headquarters of the KPP CC Politburo was based. In June 1937 he was summoned to Moscow. Arrested shortly after his arrival, he was accused of enabling Polish intelligence to infiltrate the KPP leadership. He was executed soon afterwards. (WR)

Sources: *PSB*, vol. 17; M. K. Dziewanowski, *The Communist Party of Poland* (Cambridge, Mass., 1959); K. Gruda, "Sprawa polska na V Kongresie Międzynarodówki Komunistycznej," *Z Pola Walki*, 1962, no. 4; *Księga Polaków uczestników rewolucji październikowej* (Warsaw, 1967).

LETTRICH Jozef (17 June 1905, Turčianské Teplice-Divaky–29 September 1968, New York), Slovak lawyer and politician. Lettrich studied law at Comenius University in Bratislava. In 1929 he earned a master's degree. From 1931 to 1935 he was an attorney's assistant in Zvolen. He subsequently worked as a clerk (1935–41) and attorney (1941–44) in Bratislava. In the 1930s he was among the young intelligentsia of the Slovak agrarian movement. These intellectuals supported Slovak nationalism and questioned the policies of the Agrarian Party, which promoted "Czechoslovakism." After the collapse of Czechoslovakia Lettrich did not accept the establishment of the Slovak Fascist state, and from 1939, he worked with the civic wing of the resistance movement led by Ján Lichner. In 1940 Lettrich became a member of an organization called Demec. The Nazis detained him twice:

in 1939 and 1941. Lettrich took part in negotiations with the Communists on cooperation in the struggle against the Germans. In December 1943, after long talks, he was one of the signatories of the "Christmas Agreement," which concerned cooperation between the civic and Communist resistance movements. From 1943 to 1944 Lettrich was a member of the illegal Slovak National Council (Slovenská Národná Rada [SNR]), established as a result of the Christmas Agreement; he served as an unofficial secretary of the SNR and participated in the preparations for an uprising. During the Slovak National Uprising he was one of the SNR leaders and served as a commissioner for education and the school system.

From 1945 to 1948 Lettrich was head of the Democratic Party, president of the SNR, and a deputy to the National Assembly. In 1946 he was a co-author of the "April agreement" with the Slovak Catholic movement. He subsequently represented the Slovak democratic center. After the elections of May 1946, which were won by the Democratic Party, Lettrich opposed the growing centralism of the government in Prague and the increasing Communist influence. He also protested the death sentence against Reverend **Jozef Tiso**. During the Communist coup in February 1948 Lettrich agreed that ministers of the Democratic Party should resign from the government, and he called on other members of the party not to join Communist-initiated action committees. Forced to resign as president of the SNR on 26 February 1948, Lettrich emigrated to the United States, where he was active in various émigré organizations, including the Council of Free Czechoslovakia and the Permanent Conference of Slovak Democratic Exiles. He also wrote and published extensively. *The History of Modern Slovakia* (1955) is one of his best-known works. (PU)

Sources: *ČBS*; *SBS*, vol. 3; *Reprezentačný biografický lexikón Slovenska* (Martin, 1999); Libor Vykoupil, *Slovník českých dějin* (Brno, 2000).

LEVYTSKYI Borys [also known as Lewytzkyj] (19 May 1915, Vienna–28 October 1984, Munich), Ukrainian journalist, politician, and political scientist. While a student of philosophy and psychology at Jan Kazimierz University in Lwów (Lviv), Levytskyi became the editor of the periodical *Nove Selo* (1936–39) and an activist in the Organization of Ukrainian Nationalists (OUN). He completed his studies in 1938. After the German invasion of the Soviet Union in June 1941, Levytskyi, together with **Ivan Mitrynga**, went to Central Ukraine and attempted to found the Ukrainian Democratic Peasant Party there. After the war, he went to the Western world, where he left the OUN and became one of the founders of the Ukrainian Revolutionary Democratic

Party. He also edited the periodical *Vpered* (1949–56). In 1948 Levytskyi established his own center for research on the Soviet Union that published a monthly bulletin about the Soviet authorities. In the 1950s he published a great deal—for example, as a regular contributor to the *Süddeutsche Zeitung* in Munich (under the pseudonym "Paul Sikora"). In the 1970s Levytskyi was an adviser on Soviet affairs to the West German Social Democratic Party (SPD). He also published through the Paris-based Polish Instytut Literacki (Literary Institute) and in the periodical *Kultura*. He was the author of important works on the history and practices of communism, including the following: *Vom Roten Terror zur sozialistischen Gesselschaft* (1961); *Die Sowjetukraine, 1944–1963* (1964); *Die Rote Inquisition* (1967; *The Uses of Terror*, 1971); *The Soviet Political Elite* (1969); *Die sowjetische Nationalitätspolitik nach Stalins Tod, 1953–1970* (1970); *Die Marschälle und die Politik* (1971); *Sowjetische Entspannungspolitik heute* (1975); and *Politics and Society in Soviet Ukraine, 1953–1980* (1984). Levytskyi also edited biographical publications, including *Who's Who in the Socialist Countries* (1978), *Who's Who in the Soviet Union* (1984), and *The Stalinist Terror in the Thirties* (1974). (WR)

Sources: *Encyclopedia of Ukraine*, vol. 3 (Toronto, 1993).

LEVYTSKYI Dmytro (1877 Dobrachyn, near Sokal–31 October 1942, Bukhara, Uzbekistan), Ukrainian lawyer and politician. After graduating in law from the university in Vienna, Levytskyi worked as an attorney in Rawa Ruska (Rava Rus'ka) and Brzeżany (Berezhany) from 1912 to 1914. During World War I he served as an officer in the Austro-Hungarian Army. Taken prisoner, he was held in Tashkent. In 1917 he organized the Galicia and Bukovina Committee in Kiev. During the rule of Hetman **Pavlo Skoropadsky**, Levytskyi was the secretary of the opposition Ukrainian National Union. He subsequently served as head of the diplomatic mission of the Ukrainian People's Republic (UPR) to Denmark (1919–21). After the war he returned to Galicia, which was under Polish rule, and he published the daily *Dilo* (1923–25). He was also one of the founders and leading activists of the Ukrainian National Democratic Alliance (Ukraiinske Natsionalno-Demokratychne Obiednaniie [UNDO]), which called for a compromise with Poland. From 1925 to 1935 Levytskyi was chairman and then (until 1939) vice-chairman of the UNDO. From 1928 to 1930 and from 1930 to 1935 he was an MP in the Assembly of the Republic of Poland and chairman of the Ukrainian parliamentary representation. From the end of 1930 to 1931 Levytskyi was imprisoned for criticizing Polish policies. The *sanacja* government prevented him from running in the elections to the Assembly. From 1936 to 1939 Levytskyi was the founder and then the leader of the Ukrainian Coordinating Committee, which represented all Ukrainian groups that were allowed to function in Poland. In September 1939 Levytskyi was arrested by the NKVD. Released after the German invasion of the Soviet Union in June 1941, he was ordered to settle in Uzbekistan, where he died in a Polish nursing home. (WR)

Sources: *Encyclopedia of Ukraine*, vol. 3 (Toronto, 1993); *Kto był kim w Drugiej Rzeczypospolitej* (Warsaw, 1994); *Encyklopedia historii Drugiej Rzeczypospolitej* (Warsaw, 1999); Ryszard Torzecki, *Kwestia ukraińska w Polsce 1923–1929* (Kraków, 1989).

LEVYTSKYI Kost (18 November 1859, Tysmenytsya, near Tlumach–12 November 1941, Lviv [Lemberg, Lwów]), Ukrainian lawyer and politician. Levytskyi graduated in law from the university in Lemberg, where he subsequently opened a law practice (1890). He was an editor and the publisher of the periodical *Chasopys pravnycha* (1899–1900). One of the leaders of the Prosvita Society, he succeeded in changing it from a purely educational group into an educational and economic organization. Levytskyi was the founder and benefactor of many Ukrainian economic organizations, including Narodna Torhovla; the insurance company Dnister; Tsentrobank (from 1898 to 1939 he was its director); the Audit Commission of Ukrainian Cooperative Societies (from 1904 to 1914 he was its chairman); the Mortgage and Land Bank; and the Karpatia Reinsurance Company. In 1899 he became a member of the Shevchenko Society. Levytskyi was a nationalist and populist in his views. He organized the People's Council and served as its president from 1885 to 1899. After joining the Ukrainian National Democratic Party, he served as its secretary and president of its board from 1902 on. In 1907 he became an MP in the Austrian parliament (Reichsrat) and in 1908 also in the Galician Assembly. As the leader of the strongest Ukrainian party in both parliaments, Levytskyi played a major role in Galician political life at that time.

During World War I Levytskyi was one of the leaders of the movement for Ukrainian independence. In 1914 he was elected president of the Supreme Ukrainian Council (Holovna Ukraiinska Rada) in Lviv, and in 1915 he was also elected president of the General Ukrainian Council (Zahalna Ukraiinska Rada) in Vienna. Although most of the population of Lviv spoke Polish and the Ukrainians were a minority there, Levytskyi believed that because of the Ukrainian-speaking majority in the surrounding area, the city should become the center of the Ukrainian government. As head of the Lviv branch of the Ukrainian National Rada (Council), established on 18 October 1918 and led by **Yevhen Petrushevych**, on 1 November Levytskyi ordered Ukrainian units to forcibly occupy Lviv, and they seized power from the retreating Austrian authorities. This caused resistance from the Polish insurgents in the city, who were supported by units of the newly formed Polish Army sent from central Poland. Although the Ukrainian authorities had to escape from Lviv, on 7 November Levytskyi assumed the post of head of the Secretariat (provisional government) of the Western Ukrainian National Republic (Zakhidno-Ukraiinska Narodna Republika [ZUNR]). However, in mid-December he resigned from this position. After the Polish troops gained full control of Eastern Galicia, Levytskyi, together with the ZUNR authorities, left for Vienna, where he served as press secretary and then secretary for foreign affairs of Petrushevych's government-in-exile.

In 1923 Levytskyi returned to Galicia, which was under Polish rule. He worked energetically to consolidate Ukrainian trade, economic, and cultural organizations. He served as chairman of the Ukrainian Lawyers' Union, editor of the periodical *Zhyttia i pravo*, and director of Tsentrobank. He was one of the leaders of the Ukrainian National Democratic Alliance (Ukraiinske Natsionalno-Demokratychne Obiednannya [UNDO]) but was not directly involved in politics. After the Red Army occupied Eastern Galicia in September 1939, Levytskyi became head of the delegation of the Ukrainian National Committee to conduct talks with the new authorities. Arrested and taken to Moscow, he was released in the spring of 1941, and he returned to Lviv. On 30 June 1941, after the Nazis occupied Lviv, Levytskyi established the Ukrainian National Council, which proclaimed Ukrainian independence and a "Promethean" program that called for the liberation of all nations enslaved by Russia. However, the council did not gain German support, and shortly afterwards Levytskyi died. Levytskyi was the author of several monographs, including the following: *Istoriia polytychnoy dumky halytskykh Ukraiintsiv 1848–1914* (The history of political thought of the Galician Ukrainians 1848–1914, 2 vols.; 1926); *Istoriia vyzvolnykh zvahan halytskikh Ukraiintsiv z chasu svitovoy viyny* (The history of the liberation struggle of the Galician Ukrainians during the world war, 3 vols.; 1929–30); *Velykyi Zryv* (The great effort; 1931); and *Ukraiinski polytyki* (Ukrainian politicians; 1936). (WR)

Sources: *Encyclopedia of Ukraine*, vol. 3 (Toronto, 1993); Matthew Stachiv and Jaroslav Sztendera, eds., *Western Ukraine at the Turning Point of Europe's History, 1918–1923*, vols. 1–2 (New York, 1971); Maciej Kozłowski, *Między Sanem i Zbruczem: Walki o Lwów i Galicje Wschodnią 1918–1919* (Kraków, 1990); Tadeusz Andrzej Olszański, *Historia Ukrainy XX w.* (Warsaw, n.d.); Paul R. Magocsi, *A History of Ukraine* (Seattle, 1996); Orest Subtelny, *Ukraine: A History* (Toronto, 2000).

LEXA Ivan (18 August 1961, Bratislava), Slovak political activist. Lexa graduated in chemical technology from the Higher Technical University in Bratislava in 1983, in chemical doctoral studies in 1987, and from a managerial school at the Industrial Institute in Bratislava in 1991. In 1983–90 he worked for the Slovnaft Company. In the early 1990s he became one of the most trusted aides of **Vladimír Mečiar**. From January to April 1991 Lexa headed Mečiar's Office of the Slovak Prime Minister. After the resignation of Mečiar's government, until June 1992 Lexa headed the chancellery of the Movement for a Democratic Slovakia (Hnutie za Demokratické Slovensko [HZDS]). In 1992–93 he was the HZDS plenipotentiary for the creation of the office of president of the Slovak Republic, and later he was secretary of the Ministry of Administration and the Privatization of National Property, where he helped Mečiar's people with the appropriation of state assets. In November 1994 Mečiar wanted to make Lexa head of this ministry, but President **Michal Kováč** refused to endorse this decision.

In the elections of 1994 Lexa won a seat in the parliament on behalf of the HZDS. Despite President Kováč's opposition, Mečiar succeeded in forcing an amendment of the law on the Slovak Information Service (Slovenská Informačná Služba [SIS]), achieving the right to nominate the SIS head. Thus on 18 April 1995 Lexa was appointed head of the SIS. He continued in this capacity until 28 October 1998, becoming a symbol of the lawless operations of the Mečiar elite. Among other things, Lexa was instrumental in the kidnapping of President Kováč's son and in his deportation to Austria, in attempts to compromise Bishop Rudolf Balaž, and in the eavesdropping and intimidation of opposition politicians and journalists. In all these operations Lexa was supported by Mečiar. Immediately after Mečiar took over the duties of president, all functionaries involved in the capture of Kováč's son were amnestied. After the elections of September 1998, in order that Lexa could retain immunity, Mečiar gave up his mandate in his favor. This step did not shield Lexa from investigation, since the new prime minister, **Mikulaš Dzurinda**, annulled the amnesty and on 15 April 1999 the parliament repealed Lexa's immunity. In July 1999 the court decided that Lexa might stay at liberty during the investigation. In May 2000 Lexa fled abroad, so in July 2000 the Slovak authorities issued a warrant for his arrest. On 14 July 2002 Lexa was arrested in South Africa and deported to Slovakia. (PU)

Sources: Marian Leško, *Mečiar a mečiarizmus* (Bratislava, 1998); *Slovensko 1996: Súhrnná správa o stave spoločnosti* (Bratislava, 1997); *Slovensko 1997: Súhrnná správa o stave spoločnosti* (Bratislava, 1998); *Slovensko 1998–1999: Súhrnná správa o stave spoločnosti* (Bratislava, 1999); Ľuba Lesna, *Únos demokracie: Zo zákulisia slovenskéj tajnej služby* (Prague and Bratislava, 2001); *Slovensko 2000: Súhrnná správa o stave spoločnosti* (Bratislava, 2000); *Sme,* 18 July 2002.

LIBOHOVA Myfit bey (July 1876, Libohovë–10 February 1927, Tirana), Albanian writer and diplomat. Born into a Muslim landowning family, Libohova was the eldest son of Neki Pasha, governor of Gjirokastër and deputy to the first Turkish parliament. After graduating from high school in Ioánnina, Libohova studied law in Istanbul and France. After graduating, he worked in diplomacy, beginning as first secretary in the Turkish Embassy in Belgium and later assuming the post of Turkish consul in Lárisa. In 1908 he was an MP for the Gjirokastër district in the Young Turk parliament. From November 1912 to January 1914 he headed the ministry of interior in the government of **Ismail Kemali**, and then he became minister of justice in the cabinet of Turhan Pasha Përmeti. Libohova represented Albania in the International Control Commission, which supervised the Albanian state from 1913 to 1914. In 1918, on his initiative, a congress was held under Italian auspices in Dürres. This congress established a government in which Libohova assumed the ministry of foreign affairs. A supporter of the monarchy, from 1920 to 1924 he was politically aligned with the Beys' Party, which was active in Gjirokastër and represented the large landowners. From March to June 1924 Libohova headed the ministry of justice in the government of Shefqet Vërlaci. After the outbreak of the revolution in the south, he was appointed a special government representative to conduct talks with the rebels in Vlorë, but they imprisoned him for some time. After **Fan Noli** became prime minister, Libohova fled to Greece. In December 1924, when **Ahmed Zogu** returned to regain power, Libohova, who was Zogu's trusted associate, was supposed to capture the south of the country but managed to gain control only of the frontier post at Kakavi. From January 1925 to March 1928 Libohova headed the ministries of finance, justice, and foreign affairs in Zogu's first government. In 1925 he was elected a member of parliament for the Gjirokastër district. A supporter of cooperation with the Italians, Libohova, together with his brother Eqrem, became involved in negotiations leading to the conclusion of treaties in 1926–27 that made Albania politically dependent on Italy in exchange for economic aid. Libohova's publications include his memoirs, *Politika ime ndë Shqipëri 1916–1920* (My policy in Albania; 1922). Libohova's brother Eqrem (1882–1948) served as prime minister (19 January–13 February and 12 May–9 September 1944) in the government that collaborated with the Italians. (TC)

Sources: *Biographisches Lexikon*, vol. 2; Michael Schmidt-Neke, *Enstehung und Ausbau der Konigsdiktatur in Albanien (1912–*

1939); Regierungsbildungen, Herrschaftsweisen und Machteliten in Einen Jungen Balkanstaat (Munich, 1987); Bardhosh Gaçe, *Ata që shpallën Pavarësinë Kombëtare* (Tirana, 1997).

LIEBERMAN Herman (3 January 1870, Drohobych–21 October 1941, London), Polish lawyer and socialist activist of Jewish origin. While a high school student in Boryslav and Stryy, Lieberman organized pro-independence and socialist circles. In 1889 he began studying law in Paris. Expelled from France in 1890, he returned to Galicia and completed law studies at the Jagiellonian University in Kraków, earning a Ph.D. in 1894. In 1899 he opened a law practice in Przemyśl. From 1893 to 1919 he was a member of the Polish Socialist Democratic Party of Galicia and Teschen Silesia (Polska Partia Socjalno-Demokratyczna Galicji i Śląska Cieszyńskiego [PPSD]), and from 1901 to 1919 he was a member of the board of this party. From 1907 to 1918 Lieberman sat in the Austrian parliament (Reichsrat) in Vienna as a PPSD representative. In 1914 he joined the Polish Legions, from which he was expelled in 1917 for anti-German agitation. After the oath of allegiance crisis of July 1917 Lieberman became counsel for the defense of legionnaires accused of high treason. In 1918 he co-organized the Soviet of Soldiers and Workers and the Polish National Council in Przemyśl. From 1919 to 1933 he was an MP in the Assembly. An expert on constitutional law, Lieberman contributed significantly to the drafting of the constitution of March 1921. As an MP in the Assembly, he also dealt with military affairs. In 1919 he joined the Polish Socialist Party (Polska Partia Socjalistyczna [PPS]). From 1920 to 1939 he was a member of the PPS Chief Council, and from 1931 to 1934, vice-president of the PPS Central Executive Committee. He represented the PPS in the Bureau of the Socialist International (from 1932 to 1939) and in its Executive Committee (from 1937 on).

After the coup of May 1926 Lieberman opposed the *sanacja* government. In 1929 he was the chief Assembly prosecutor in the Tribunal of State trial of Treasury Minister Gabriel Czechowicz. He was also active in the so-called Centrolew, a center-left coalition of opposition parties that defended democracy. In September 1930, along with other opposition leaders, Lieberman was arrested and imprisoned in the Brest fortress. In January 1932 he was sentenced to two and a half years in prison. Upon learning that the sentence had become final and binding, Lieberman emigrated to Czechoslovakia (October 1933) and later to France. He worked in Paris and earned a living by contributing to leftist periodicals. He also edited the periodical *Świat i Polska*. He worked with left-wing and peasant parties in Poland. During the Spanish Civil

War Lieberman was the chairman of a committee for aid to wounded Polish volunteers. After the outbreak of World War II, he worked closely with General **Władysław Sikorski**, supporting Sikorski's policy toward the Soviet Union. In December 1939 Lieberman became vice-president of the National Council in exile. In March 1940 he was elected president of the PPS Central Executive Committee in exile. In September 1941 he became minister of justice in Sikorski's government. Lieberman successfully completed many projects; for example, as a result of his efforts, the government passed a symbolic resolution to abolish the isolation camp at Bereza Kartuska. Lieberman was the author of many articles and agitation brochures, as well as *Pamiętniki* (Memoirs; 1996). (JS)

Sources: *PSB*, vol. 17; *Kto był kim w Drugiej Rzeczypospolitej* (Warsaw, 1994); *Encyklopedia historii Polski: Dzieje polityczne* (Warsaw, 1994); Artur Leinwand, *Poseł Herman Lieberman* (Kraków, 1983); Marian Leczyk, ed., *Sprawa brzeska* (Warsaw, 1987); Janusz Gmitruk, *Herman Lieberman, Stanisław Mikołajczyk: Zmagania z totalitaryzmem* (Warsaw, 2001).

LIICEANU Gabriel (23 May 1942, Râmnicu Vâlcea), Romanian writer and cultural activist. In 1965 Liiceanu graduated from the Department of Philosophy and in 1973 from the Department of Classical Philology of Bucharest University. In 1976 he received a Ph.D. there. In 1965–75 he worked at the Institute of Philosophy and from 1975 to 1989 at the Institute of Arts of the Romanian Academy of Science. In 1982–84 he worked as a Humboldt Foundation Fellow in Heidelberg. One of the close associates of **Constantin Noica**, in 1983 Liiceanu published *Jurnalul de la Păltiniş: Un model paideic în cultura umanistă* (Păltinişu dairy: Paeideia as a model in humanist culture), and in 1987, *Epistolar* (Letters), in which he promoted Noica's theories. Both books brought Liiceanu wide recognition. In 1983 he received an award from the Association of Romanian Writers for *Jurnalul de la Păltiniş* and became one of the leading Romanian intellectuals. In 1990 Liiceanu became head of the political press Editura Politică (later renamed Humanitas), which soon gained a dominant position on the Romanian book market. From 1992 Liiceanu was a professor in the Department of Philosophy at Bucharest University. (AB)

Sources: Romania-on-line.net/whoswho/LiiceanuGabriel.htm.

LILIĆ Zoran (27 August 1953, Brza Palanka, near Kladovo), Serb politician. Lilić was born into a poor family with many children. He studied metallurgical technology, at the same time working sporadically as a model and a conductor. After his studies, for twelve years Lilić worked in the Rekord Factory in the Rakovica outskirts of Belgrade. In 1990 he became a member of the Serbian parliament on behalf of the Socialist Party of Serbia (SPS). Rapidly advancing, he became the deputy chairman of the SPS and the chairman of the Serbian parliament. After the resignation of **Dobrica Ćosić** from the presidency of the Federal Republic of Yugoslavia (FRY), on 25 June 1993 Lilić took over this position and remained head of state for four years as an obedient executor of the policies of **Slobodan Milošević**. When in July 1997 Milošević was elected FRY president, in the September 1997 elections Lilić was supported by the SPS in the elections for the Serbian presidency, but he lost to **Vojislav Šešelj**. Owing to a low turnout, the election results were annulled, but Lilić did not run again. He refused to testify in the Milošević trial before The Hague Tribunal for War Crimes in the Former Yugoslavia, but in July 2002 Lilić was arrested by the Serbian police and brought to The Hague as a witness. (AO)

Sources: Željan E. Šuster, *Historical Dictionary of the Federal Republic of Yugoslavia* (Lanham, Md., 1999); Bugajski; *Europa Środkowo-Wschodnia* 1993–1999 (Warsaw, 1995–2001); www.rferl.org.

LILOV Aleksandur (31 August 1933, Granichak), Bulgarian Communist activist. Lilov entered into contact with the Communist movement in 1947, when he joined the Dimitrov People's Youth Union (DPYU). In 1954 he became a member of the Bulgarian Communist Party (BCP). In 1962 he graduated in Bulgarian philology from Sofia University. Gradually advancing through the party ranks, in 1962 Lilov became a member of the DPYU Central Committee (CC) Bureau, and in 1963–66 he was secretary of the DPYU CC. Later he studied in Moscow, where he received a Ph.D. in literature and arts at the Soviet CC party school. After returning to Bulgaria, Lilov worked as editor of the party press. In 1971 he became a member of the BCP CC; in 1972 he became CC secretary; and in 1974 he became a member of the BCP Politburo. A member of the National Assembly and of the Fatherland Front, in 1981 Lilov received a Ph.D. in Marxist philosophy, and from 1975 he worked at the Institute of Art and Science of the Bulgarian Academy of Science (BAS) as a close aide of **Ludmila Zhivkova**.

After Zhivkova died in 1981, Lilov's political career was interrupted. Lilov's conflict with Ludmila's father, **Todor Zhivkov**, led to his dismissal from the CC Politburo and Secretariat. For six years he was director of the BAS Institute of Contemporary Social Theories. At the end of 1989, realizing the inevitability of change in Bulgaria in view of perestroika and the collapse of the Communist system in the Soviet bloc, Lilov joined the BCP opposition

against Zhivkov and contributed substantially to his toppling. As a result, Lilov became the party's top ideologist, who was to adjust the BCP to its new role in a pluralist society. This new task required renaming the party the Bulgarian Socialist Party (BSP); the dismissal of its most dogmatic leaders; support for the free market system; and opposition to de-Communization, which was advocated by some of the opposition leaders. These changes were carried out at the party congress in January and February 1990, at which Lilov was elected its leader. When the BSP lost the elections and was removed from power, in December 1991 another party congress dismissed Lilov from the leadership and chose **Zhan Videnov** in his place. Two years later Lilov was accused of the illegal financing of pro-Soviet Third World countries. The parliament deprived him of immunity, but he was soon acquitted. Lilov remained one of the BSP leaders, heading its strategic center. After the crisis in early 1997, when the BSP's ratings fell dramatically and its structures disintegrated, Lilov played a leading role in the dismissal of Videnov and in the stabilization of the party. (AG)

Sources: *Koy koy e v Bulgariya* (Sofia, 1998); *Entsiklopediya Bulgariya*, vol. 3 (Sofia, 1982); Jerzy Jackowicz, *Bułgaria od rządów komunistycznych do demokracji parlamentarnej 1988–1991* (Warsaw, 1992); Ivan Stoyanov, *Nova saga za Lilov* (Plovdiv, 1993); Raymond Detrez, *Historical Dictionary of Bulgaria* (Lanham, Md., 1997); www.ceri-sciencespo.com/publica/etude/etude31.pdf; www.nato.int/acad/fellow/94–96/dimitrov/04–03.htm; www.house.gov/csce/bulgarep93.html.

LIMANOWSKI Bolesław (18 October 1835, Podgórze, near Dvinsk [now Daugavpils, Latvia]–1 February 1935, Warsaw), Polish Socialist activist, historian, and sociologist. After graduating from a high school in Moscow in 1854, Limanowski studied medicine in Moscow and Dorpat (Tartu) in 1854–69. While a student, he was sentenced to six years in exile in Arkhangelsk Province for organizing and taking part in a patriotic demonstration in 1861. In 1870 he settled in Galicia. From 1873 to 1875 Limanowski studied philosophy in Lemberg (Lwów, Lviv), earning a Ph.D. In 1878 he went to live in Switzerland. Limanowski was one of the main founders of the Polish Socialist movement, in which he combined Socialist ideas with the struggle for Polish independence. In 1881, at a Socialist congress in Chur, he defended the position that Polish independence was consistent with the Socialist program, clashing on this point with Ludwik Waryński and Kazimierz Dłuski. From 1881 to 1882 Limanowski co-founded the Polish People Socialist Association, which supported the struggle for a free Poland based on the working class. In 1882 he published *Historia ruchu narodowego od 1861 do 1864* (The history of the national movement from 1861 to 1864), the first history of the January Insurrection of 1863 written from the perspective of the "Reds." In 1887 Limanowski became a member of the Polish League (Liga Polska), but because of his social views, he later distanced himself from the national movement. In 1889 he became secretary of the board of the Association of Polish Émigrés. In November 1892 he served as chairman of a conference in Paris at which the Polish Socialist Party (Polska Partia Socjalistyczna [PPS]) was founded. He was also a co-author of the party's program. In 1893 Limanowski returned to Paris, where he found a job in an insurance company. He continued to write extensively. His publications include *Stuletnia walka narodu polskiego o niepodległość* (The century-long struggle of the Polish nation for independence; 1894) and *Historia demokracji polskiej w epoce porozbiorowej* (The history of Polish democracy after the partition; 1901). In 1900 Limanowski represented the PPS at the International Socialist Congress in Paris. By then he was very popular, both among the émigrés and in partitioned Poland. During the split within the Polish Socialist movement he supported the PPS–Revolutionary Faction.

In 1907, after returning from exile, Limanowski settled in Kraków, where he devoted himself to intensive scholarly work. At that time he wrote *Historia powstania narodu polskiego 1863–1864* (A history of the 1863–1864 uprising of the Polish people; 1909), *Szermierze wolności* (Champions of freedom; 1911), *Historia ruchu rewolucyjnego w Polsce 1846 roku* (A history of the 1846 revolutionary movement in Poland; 1913), and other works. Limanowski often represented Polish Socialists at international congresses and conferences. Despite his partial deafness, from which he suffered from the end of the nineteenth century and which hampered his political activities, he was engaged in supporting the pro-independence efforts of **Józef Piłsudski**, and in 1912 he became head of the Polish Military Treasury. He also conducted lectures for the youth of the Riflemen's Association and other Polish organizations in Galicia. During World War I Limanowski supported Piłsudski, although he criticized the Piłsudski associates who began to abandon Socialist ideas.

After Poland regained independence, in 1919 Limanowski moved to Warsaw, where he completed his *Socjologia* (Sociology, 2 vols.; 1915–19) and wrote *Walerian Łukasiński* (1920) and *Mazowsze pruskie* (Prussian Mazovia; 1925). The last, a brochure, was a result of his travels around the northeastern part of the Second Republic of Poland. In November 1922 Limanowski was elected to the Senate on behalf of the PPS. After the coup of May 1926, which he criticized, Limanowski joined the opposition to the government. He repeatedly criticized the

new form of government, as well as Piłsudski's struggle against parliamentarism. In 1928 the government did not allow Limanowski to act in the capacity of senior senator. He continued to serve as senator, though, until the end of his life. Among Limanowski's numerous writings, his historical treatises, which educated two generations of pro-independence activists, are particularly valuable. Although an autodidact in the field of history, he strictly followed the principles of scholarly work. He did not consider himself a Marxist. A researcher and an activist strongly concerned with social injustice, Limanowski aimed at combining the national struggle with the struggle for better living conditions for wide circles of society. In 1957 his *Pamiętniki* (Memoirs) were published. (WR)

Sources: *PSB*, vol. 17; Wiktor Feldman, *Dzieje polskiej myśli politycznej w okresie porozbiorowym*, vol. 3 (Warsaw, 1920); *Księga jubileuszowa Polskiej Partii Socjalistycznej 1892–1932* (Warsaw, 1933); Marceli Handelsman, *Historycy: Portrety i profile* (Warsaw, 1937); Zbigniew Żechowski, *Socjologia Bolesława Limanowskiego* (Poznań, 1964); Jerzy Targalski, *Szermierz wolności: Stuletni żywot Bolesława Limanowskiego, 1835–1935* (Warsaw, 1973); Kazimiera Janina Cottam, *Bolesław Limanowski (1835–1935): A Study in Socialism and Nationalism* (Boulder, Colo., 1978).

LIPIŃSKI Edward (24 November 1888, Nowe Miasto on Pilica–13 July 1986, Warsaw), Polish economist. Lipiński studied at the College of Commerce in Leipzig (1909–12) and at the university in Zurich (1912–13). Back in Warsaw, from 1907 to 1918 he was a member of the Polish Socialist Party–Left (Polska Partia Socjalistyczna–Lewica [PPS–Lewica]), and between 1914 and 1918 he was active in the Society for the Propagation of Knowledge on Commerce and Industry, a sort of workers' university. Lipiński was one of the pioneers of labor protection in Poland. In 1918–20 he headed the labor inspection of the Governing Board of the City of Warsaw, served as an adviser to the Ministry of Labor, and was head of the Labor and Industry Statistics Department of the Central Statistical Office of Poland. From 1923 Lipiński was a lecturer, and from 1929 a professor, at the Warsaw School of Economics (Szkoła Główna Handlowa [SGH]). In 1937 he became vice-president of the SGH. Between 1928 and 1939 he was an initiator and director of the Institute for Market and Price Research (Instytut Badania Koniunktur Gospodarczych i Cen); from 1929 he served as editor-in-chief of the quarterly *Ekonomista*; and from 1934 he held the post of president of the Society of Polish Economists and Statisticians in Warsaw. Lipiński was the first in Poland to lecture on the theory of economic fluctuations and the theory of economic growth. He also initiated research on labor, salary, and price statistics. In the 1920s he was a member of the Polish Socialist Party (Polska Partia Socialistyczna [PPS]) and a co-founder of and activist in the League for the Defense of Human and Civil Rights.

During the German occupation Lipiński was an organizer and director of the Municipal Trade School, which formally was a technical school but in fact ran academic classes. From 1945 to 1949 he was professor and vice-president of the SGH; in 1945–47 he was director of the Institute of the National Economy in the Presidium of the Council of Ministers; from 1946 to 1948 he was director of the National Economy Bank; and in 1946–65 he was president, and then honorary president of the Polish Economic Society. Between 1946 and 1948 Lipiński was a member of the PPS and then, until 1976, a member of the Polish United Workers' Party (Polska Zjednoczona Partia Robotnicza [PUWP]). From 1951 he was a member of the Polish Academy of Sciences, and from 1954, dean of the Department of Economics of Warsaw University. Lipiński also lectured at the Central School of Planning and Statistics (formerly the SGH). He belonged to many international scientific societies. During the Stalinist years Lipiński mainly conducted research on the history of Polish economic thought and the theory of political economics; he was a follower of Marxism, which he attempted to develop in an original way, posing questions about the future of mankind and civilization during transformations in the economic system. In 1956–62 Lipiński was vice-president of the Economic Council to the Council of Ministers, which was supposed to prepare a plan for economic reform but did not as a result of the reluctant attitude of the PUWP executive. In 1958 Lipiński retired, but he continued to take an active part in public life. In 1964 he signed the "Letter of 34" against the tightening of censorship.

Between 1971 and 1976 Lipiński was consulted by the Communist administration, and he used the opportunity to plead for the release of political prisoners. From 1972 he belonged to the Kopernik Masonic lodge. In 1975 he was one of the initiators of a protest against amendments to the constitution and a signatory of the "Letter of 59." In May 1976 Lipiński submitted an open letter to **Edward Gierek** in which he criticized Gierek's economic policies and the political system of the Polish People's Republic. Lipiński was a co-founder and one of the major leaders of the Committee for the Defense of Workers (Komitet Obrony Robotników [KOR]), founded on 23 September 1976, and then of the KOR Committee for Social Self-Defense (Komitet Samoobrony Społecznej KOR [KSS KOR]). Lipiński used his position to protect younger KOR activists (from 1978 the meetings of the committee were held in his flat), and he won the sympathy of the West for the committee (through his visits to the United States in the autumn of 1976 and his appeals for the release of the imprisoned between 1976 and 1977.) From 1978 Lipiński was a member of the informal Society for Scientific Courses (Towarzystwo Kursów Naukowych). At a Solidarity congress on 28 September 1981 Lipiński read an announcement about the dissolution of the KSS KOR.

Lipiński was the author of a few hundred scientific and popular works in economics. He had already published the first of his works during World War I. Among other works, he authored *Teorie ekonomiczne Erazma Majewskiego* (The economic theories of Erasmus Majewski; 1920) and edited *Koniunktura gospodarcza w Polsce 1924–1927* (Polish business conditions, 1924–1927, 4 vols.; May 1928–December 1931). Lipiński contributed to the theory of economic fluctuations in *Ekonomista* (1934–36), the theory of investment (*Polityka Gospodarcza*, 1936), and the theory of growth in *Z problemów gospodarczych wzrostu* (On the economic issues of growth; 1930). He was also the author of lectures on the theory of economics (1945–46), *Historia myśli ekonomicznej* (The history of economic thought; 1950), and of works about Mikołaj Kopernik as an economist (1953). After October 1956 Lipiński dealt with the model of the "socialist economy" (*Nowe drogi*, 1956, no. 11), but in the 1970s he also wrote *Historia polskiej myśli ekonomicznej do końca XVIII wieku* (The history of Polish economic thought until the end of eighteenth century; 1975). At the end of his life Lipiński was increasingly skeptical about the prospects of the command economy—for example, in *Problemy, pytania, wątpliwości: Z warsztatu ekonomisty* (Problems, questions, doubts: From the economist's workshop; 1981). (AF)

Sources: *Opozycja w PRL: Słownik biograficzny 1956–89* (Warsaw, 2000); Józef Nowicki, "Edward Lipiński (1888–1986)," in *Poczet wybitnych profesorów SGH-SGPiS* (Warsaw, 1986); *Wyższa Szkoła Handlowa, Szkoła Główna Handlowa, Miejska Szkoła Handlowa* (Warsaw, 1984); Andrzej Friszke, *Opozycja polityczna w PRL 1945–1980* (London, 1994); *Encyklopedia historii Drugiej Rzeczypospolitej* (Warsaw, 1999).

LIPIŃSKI Wacław, pseudonyms "Aleksander" and "Gwido" (28 September 1896, Łódź–4 April 1949, Wronki), Polish officer, historian, and politician. Born into a craftsman's family, from childhood Lipiński was active in scouting. In 1914 he joined the Polish Legions. In July 1917 he refused to swear allegiance to the emperors of Germany and Austria-Hungary, but he avoided internment. He became secretary of the League for the Independence of Poland, which called for a sovereign Poland federated with an independent Lithuania. He also became a member of the High Command of the Polish Military Organization (Polska Organizacja Wojskowa [POW]).

In November 1918 Lipiński took part in the fighting for Lwów (Lviv), and in the spring of 1919 he took part in the Polish Army's campaign leading to the takeover of Wilno (Vilnius). He later served as a press officer in the command of the Lithuanian-Belorussian front, becoming deputy head of the Second Department of the Poznań Area Military Command in February 1920. In 1921 Lipiński received a law degree from the Jagiellonian University in Kraków and earned a doctorate there in 1922. He also studied history at the Jagiellonian University and at the School of Political Sciences in Kraków. In 1917 he began working at the Military Historical Office, where he wrote *Walka zbrojna o niepodległość Polski 1905–1918* (The armed struggle for the independence of Poland 1905–1918; 1935). In 1932 Lipiński became secretary of the Niepodległość publishing house. From 1934 to 1936 he was secretary general of the Institute for Research in the Modern History of Poland, and in 1936 he became the director of this institute, which changed its name to the Józef Piłsudski Institute. In 1936 Lipiński received the postdoctoral degree in history. His book *Wielki Marszałek* (The great marshal) was a popular hagiography of Piłsudski. Lipiński was also the editor-in-chief of *Pisma zbiorowe Józefa Piłsudskiego* (Collected writings of Józef Piłsudski, 10 vols.; 1937–38).

During the September campaign in 1939, Lipiński served as head of the propaganda department in the Command of the Defense of Warsaw. His radio talks lifted public morale. After the capitulation of Warsaw, Lipiński made his way, via Zakopane, to Hungary, where, at the end of 1940, he got in touch with Marshal **Edward Rydz-Śmigły**, who had fled from internment in Romania. In March 1942 Lipiński returned to Warsaw and began working with a pro-Piłsudski group called Myśl Państwowa (State Thought) and with the Convention of Pro-Independence Organizations. Lipiński's underground publications include *Pakt polsko-rosyjski* (The Polish-Russian pact; 1942), *Bilans czterolecia* (Four years: An assessment; 1944), and *Wojna polsko-niemiecka: Kampania wrześniowa w Polsce r. 1939* (The Polish-German war: The September 1939 campaign in Poland; published under the pseudonym "W. Gel" and co-authored by "A. Szański," probably the pseudonym of Rydz-Śmigły). Arrested by the Gestapo in February 1944, Lipiński was ransomed by his family in May of the same year. He settled near Grodzisk Mazowiecki and did not take part in the Warsaw Uprising. At the beginning of 1945 Lipiński returned to a devastated Warsaw and unsuccessfully sought employment at Warsaw University. In the spring of 1946 he founded the pro-Piłsudski National Independence Party (Stronnictwo Niezawisłości Narodowej [SNN]) and published the underground *Głos Opozycji*. On 25 September 1946 he initiated the establishment of the Coordinating Committee of Polish Underground Organizations (Komitet Porozumiewawczy Organizacji Polski Podziemnej [KPOPP]), an association of organizations that had not been legalized by the Communists, including the Freedom and Independence Association (Zrzeszenie Wolność i Niezawisłość [WiN]), the National Party (Stronnictwo Narodowe [SN]), the SNN, and the Polish Socialist Party/Freedom-Equality-Independence (PPS/Wolność-Równość-Niezawisłość). Arrested on 7 January 1947 at a KPOPP meeting, Lipiński was sentenced to death on 17 December of that year. The sentence was commuted to life in prison, where he was murdered. (WR)

Sources: *PSB*, vol. 17; Kunert, vol. 2; *Słownik polityków polskich XX wieku* (Poznań, 1998); *Gazeta Ludowa*, 4–28 December 1947; Władysław Pobóg-Malinowski, "Wacław Socha-Lipiński," *Kultura* (Paris), 1949, no. 3; Tomasz Nałęcz, *Polska Organizacja Wojskowa 1914–1918* (Warsaw, 1984); Marek Gałęzowski, *Wzór Piłsudczyka: Wacław Lipiński 1896–1949* (Warsaw, 2001).

LIPSKI Jan Józef (25 May 1926, Warsaw–10 September 1991, Kraków), Polish historian of literature and social activist. During the Nazi occupation Lipski fought in the underground scouting units of the Gray Ranks (Szare Szeregi) and in the Home Army (Armia Krajowa). He took part in the Warsaw Uprising, was wounded, and was decorated with the Cross of Valor. In 1953 he graduated in Polish philology from Warsaw University and became an editor at the State Publishing Institute; he was expelled from there in 1959 for political reasons. From 1956 to 1957 he was head of the literary department in the editorial offices of *Po prostu*. In 1961–82 Lipski was a researcher at the Institute for Literary Research of the Polish Academy of Sciences. In 1965 he earned a Ph.D. From 1956 he belonged to a discussion society called the Club of the Crooked Circle (Klub Krzywego Koła); in 1957–58 he was its president, then vice-president and secretary until 1962, when the club was dissolved by the authorities. In 1961 Lipski co-initiated the revival of an underground Freemasons' lodge called Kopernik; in 1962–81 and 1986–88 he was its president, and between 1988 and 1990, its secretary. Lipski was active in many protest actions—for example, he was co-initiator of the "Letter of 34" in 1964. From 1965 he administered a secret fund that was set up to provide aid to people arrested for political reasons, as well as to their families. Lipski attracted a multigenerational group of intellectuals critical of the regime. In 1975 he was one of the initiators of a protest against amendments to the constitution, and he was a signatory of the "Letter of 59."

Lipski co-organized help for workers who were subjected to repressive measures for taking part in demonstrations on 25 June 1976, and he co-founded the Committee for the Defense of Workers (Komitet Obrony Robotników [KOR]) on 23 September 1976. Later he was one of the most committed activists of the KOR Committee for Social Self-Defense (Komitet Samoobrony Społecznej KOR [KSS KOR]); he was responsible for its finances and was imprisoned in May and June 1977. Lipski belonged to the Society of Scientific Courses (1978–81) and its Stipend Committee. He worked with the uncensored press. From 1980 Lipski was an activist in Solidarity and was the union's expert during negotiations over the censorship law. A member of the Executive Committee of the Solidarity Mazowsze Region, he was a delegate to the union's congress in September 1981. After the imposition of martial law in Poland Lipski took part in a strike in the Ursus factory, was arrested, and was tried. His trial was interrupted owing to his ill health, and he was allowed to go to Great Britain for treatment. He returned in September 1982, after an announcement that a trial of KSS KOR members had been prepared. Arrested and then released on January 1983 owing to ill health, Lipski was amnestied in 1984. He collaborated with the underground structures of Solidarity and its secret press and publications.

In November 1987 Lipski co-initiated the formation of the Polish Socialist Party and became president of its Chief Council. From 1988 he was a member of the Civic Committee of the Chairman of Solidarity, and from 1989 he was a senator of the Civic Parliamentary Club (Obywatelski Klub Parlamentarny [OKP]). Lipski referred to the traditions and thought of the non-Communist left. He combined ideological and ethical ideas and sharply stigmatized nationalism and national xenophobia in *Dwie ojczyzny—dwa patriotyzmy* (Two motherlands—two patriotisms; 1981). Because of this he was attacked by the national wing of Solidarity. Opposition to Lipski became obvious in 1989, for example, when his candidacy for senator from Radom was challenged by a candidate supported by the local bishop's curia and by some union activists. From 1989 Lipski was critical of the so-called Balcerowicz Plan, and the radical turn of the OKP and the government toward economic liberalism. He stood for a protective state and opposed the rapid increase of social stratification. Lipski authored several works in the history of literature, including *Twórczość Jana Kasprowicza 1878–1906* (The literary works of Jan Kasprowicz 1878–1906; 1975); *Szkice poezji* (Poetry drafts 1992); a collection of essays, *Tunika Nessosa* (Nessos's tunic 1987); and the historical monographs *KOR* (KOR: A history of the Workers' Defense Committee in Poland, 1976–1981; 1985) and *Katolickie Państwo*

Narodu Polskiego (The Catholic state of the Polish nation, 1994). (AF)

Sources: *Nasi w Sejmie i Senacie* (Warsaw, 1990); Andrzej Friszke, *Opozycja polityczna w PRL 1945–1980* (London, 1994); *Jan Józef: Spotkania i spojrzenia* (Warsaw, 1996).

LIPSKI Józef (5 June 1894 Breslau [Wrocław]–1 November 1958, Washington, D.C.), Polish diplomat. Lipski came from a landed gentry family. After graduating in law from Lausanne University in Switzerland, he worked in the legal section of the Polish National Committee in Paris. In June 1919 he began working in the Polish diplomatic corps. Until January 1922 he was secretary in the legation of the Republic of Poland in London and subsequently served at diplomatic missions in Paris and Berlin. In 1925 he became deputy head, and in 1928 head, of the Western Section of the Political and Economic Department at the Ministry of Foreign Affairs. In July 1933 he was appointed envoy extraordinary and minister plenipotentiary to Berlin. After the legation was elevated to the status of embassy in October 1934, Lipski became ambassador to Germany. He was a co-author of the Polish-German declaration of non-aggression of January 1934. In October 1938 the German authorities presented him with demands that an extraterritorial corridor be created across northern Poland and that Gdańsk be incorporated into the Third Reich, as well as a demand for Polish cooperation against the Soviet Union. The Polish government rejected these demands. On 31 August 1939, after the deadline, Lipski was given Hitler's ultimatum, the rejection of which was to be a pretext for Hitler to attack Poland. In September 1939 Lipski made his way to France, where he volunteered to serve in the Polish Army. Until June 1940 he served as a private in the Polish Armed Forces in the West and from 1940 to 1946 on the staff of the commander-in-chief. At that time Lipski traveled a lot with Generals **Władysław Sikorski**, **Kazimierz Sosnkowski**, and **Władysław Anders**. After the war Lipski remained in exile. In 1951 he became an official representative of the Polish government-in-exile in the United States. In 1968 his memoirs, *Diplomat in Berlin, 1933–1939: Papers and Memoirs of Józef Lipski, Ambassador of Poland*, were published in the United States. (JS)

Sources: *Kto był kim w Drugiej Rzeczypospolitej* (Warsaw, 1994); Simon Newman, *March 1939: The British Guarantee to Poland* (Oxford, 1976); Olgierd Terlecki, *Pułkownik Beck* (Kraków, 1985); Tadeusz Wolsza, *Rząd RP na obczyźnie wobec wydarzeń w kraju, 1945–1950* (Warsaw, 1998).

LIVYTSKYI Andriy (9 April 1879, Poltava region–17 January 1954, Karlsruhe), lawyer, president of the Ukrainian National Republic (UNR). Born into an old Cossack family, Livytskyi was educated at Halahan College in Kiev. He graduated from the law school of Kiev University. He worked as an attorney and a justice of the peace in Łubnie, Kaniów, and other places. From his youth he was active in the sociopolitical life. He was president of the Students' Hromada (Community) in Kiev. In 1901 he joined the Revolutionary Ukrainian Party (RUP), which opted for the autonomy of the Ukraine. He was arrested and tried for taking part in the revolution in 1905. The Court of Appeals quashed the verdict of the Court of First Instance, and Livytskyi regained his freedom. After the transformation of the RUP into the Ukrainian Social Democratic Workers' Party (USDWP) in 1905, Livytskyi became one of its leading activists, along with (among others) **Volodymyr Vynnychenko** and **Symon Petlyura**.

In 1917 Livytskyi became a member of the Central Rada (Council) and commissar of the Poltava guberniya (province). In 1918 he joined the Ukrainian National Union; during the rule of the Directory he was one of the organizers and members of the Labor Congress. In April 1919 he became minister of justice and deputy prime minister of the UNR. In August 1919 he became head of the Ministry for Foreign Affairs of the UNR; in October 1919 he was appointed head of a diplomatic mission that was sent to Poland. On 22 April 1920 Livytskyi signed the Treaty of Peace and Alliance between Poland and the Ukraine, known in Poland as the Piłsudski-Petlyura Alliance and in the Ukraine as the Treaty of Warsaw. After the failure of the Polish-Ukrainian military campaign, on October 1920 Livytskyi became prime minister of the UNR. In the following years, at Petlyura's side, he directed, the diplomatic activities of the UNR government-in-exile. After Petlyura's assassination in May 1926, Livytskyi became his successor. From that moment until his death he directed UNR activities. At the outbreak of World War II Livytskyi lived in Warsaw, where he was interned by the Germans. It is believed that in 1940 he delegated **Taras Borovets** to Polesie with a mission to organize an anti-Communist underground there. In 1944 he nominated **Pavlo Shandruk** to the Ukrainian committee formed in support of the Third Reich. He transformed the Ukrainian SS Galizien Division into the First Division of the Ukrainian National Army, which saved its soldiers from deportation to the USSR. In 1945 he resumed the work of the UNR government-in-exile and invited recent émigrés to join this government. In 1946 he entrusted **Izaak Mazepa** with the mission of conducting negotiations with all Ukrainian groups in exile; this led to the establishment of the Ukrainian National Council in 1948. The council was a substitute for the Ukrainian parliament. Livytskyi died in Germany and was buried in Munich. (GM)

Sources: *Derzhavnyi tsentr Ukraiinskoyi Narodnoyi Respubliky v ekzyli: Statti i materiialy* (Philadelphia, Kiev, and Washington, D.C., 1993); *Entsyklopediia Ukrainoznavstva*, vol. 4 (Lviv, 1994); Robert Potocki, *Idea restytucji Ukraińskiej Republiki Ludowej (1920–1939)* (Lublin, 1999); Ryszard Torzecki, *Kwestia ukraińska w Polsce w latach 1923–1929* (Kraków, 1989); Jan Jacek Bruski, *Petlurowcy: Centrum państwowe Ukraińskiej Republiki Ludowej na wychodźstwie 1919–1924* (Kraków, 2000).

LIVYTSKYI Mykola, pseudonym "V. Tkach" (9 January 1907, Kiev–8 December 1989, Philadelphia, Pennsylvania), Ukrainian politician, son of **Andriy Livytskyi**. After the Treaty of Riga was signed in 1921, Livytskyi lived with his parents in Warsaw, where he went to school and then to university. He was active in the community of Ukrainian students, and from 1925 to 1927 he headed the Ukrainian Students' Hromada. In the 1930s he went to Geneva, where he completed economic and journalism studies. He served as secretary of the delegation of the government of the Ukrainian National Republic (UNR) to the League of Nations and directed a branch of the Ukrainian Press Bureau. In 1937, on the orders of the UNR government, Livytskyi made diplomatic visits to Italy, Germany, Czechoslovakia, Austria, Poland, and France. From 1938 to 1939 he served as the representative of the UNR in Khust, in Subcarpathian Ruthenia. In 1942 he arrived in Kiev. Briefly detained by the Gestapo, he was sent to the part of Poland known as the General Government. From 1945 to 1946 Livytskyi helped establish the Ukrainian National State Union, of which he became head in 1951. In 1949 he became a member of the Ukrainian National Council, which served as the UNR parliament in exile. In 1957 he was appointed head (prime minister) of the executive of the Ukrainian National Council, as well as director of foreign affairs; in that capacity, he made numerous foreign visits, during one of which he met the prime minister of Canada. In 1967 Livytskyi was elected president of the UNR government-in-exile, and he held this position until his death. He made official visits to Australia (1973) and Canada and the United States (1976). He initiated the establishment of the Symon Petlyura Foundation (1976). In 1979 he reformed the UNR government-in-exile. Livytskyi was the author of numerous publications; these came out in two volumes: *Vidnosyny Zakhid–Skhid i problemy ponevolenykh Moskvoiu natsii* (West–East relations and the affairs of the nations enslaved by Moscow; 1975) and *DTS UNR v ekzyli mizh 1920 in 1940 rokamy* (The State Center [*Derzhavnyĭ Tsentr*] of the UNR in exile in the years 1920–1940; 1984). (GM)

Sources: *Encyclopedia of Ukraine*, vol. 3 (Toronto, 1993); *Entsyklopediia Ukraiinoznavstva*, vol. 4 (Lviv, 1994); *Derzhavnyi Tsentr Ukraiinskoyi Narodnoyi Respubliky v ekzyli: Statti i materialy* (Philadelphia, Kiev, and Washington, D.C., 1993).

LJOTIĆ Dimitrije (12 August 1891, Belgrade–23 April 1945, Ajdovcina, Slovenia), Serbian nationalist politician. Ljotić came from an affluent family that supported the Karadjordjević dynasty. His grandfather, Dimitrije, was a close associate of Prince Alexander. After graduating from high school, Ljotić commenced law studies. Initially he was fascinated by Leo Tolstoy and pacifism, but his views changed as a result of his experiences during the Balkan Wars (1912–13). In the autumn of 1913 a scholarship funded by **Peter I Karadjordjević** allowed Ljotić to go to Paris, where he continued his education. Ljotić was greatly influenced by Charles Maurras and his nationalist ideas. After the Sarajevo assassinations in 1914, Ljotić returned to Serbia and was inducted into the army. For a short time he considered entering a monastery. From 1920 to 1929 he was a member of the Radical Party and served as head of its youth section. He supported the authoritarian rule of King Alexander that began in January 1929. In February 1931 he assumed the post of minister of justice in the government of **Petar Živković** but resigned after King Alexander rejected his plans for a constitution.

After the assassination of Alexander I in 1934, Ljotić founded the Yugoslav national movement Zbor and became its leader. He always emphasized that Zbor was not a political party—he had a negative attitude toward parties—but a way of organizing the nation. Estimates of the number of his supporters range from several hundred to several thousand. On 6 January 1935—the anniversary of the establishment of an authoritarian government by the king—Zbor's program was announced. In it, Ljotić presented an apocalyptic vision of the world. According to his mystical doctrine, in order to save the nation it was necessary to preserve its "holy" values: the monarchy, the nation, and morality. He considered individualism, liberalism, communism, democracy, feminism, and modernity as the main threats. He was against freemasonry and the Jews. His ideas were akin to fascism, although he denied it. His views were promoted in the Belgrade weekly *Otadžbina*. Ljotić gained a reputation as an excellent speaker, and some even considered him a prophet. He was arrested on several occasions, and the distribution of *Otadžbina* was prohibited by the authorities. However, in the elections of 1935 and 1938 neither Ljotić nor any of his supporters became members of parliament.

Zbor did not join in the demonstrations against Yugoslavia's accession to the Tripartite Pact. Ljotić served in the Yugoslav Army during the Nazi invasion of April 1941, but after the capitulation he collaborated with the German occupation authorities. In April 1941 he helped to prepare an agreement with the Germans and to establish an administrative council to which two members of Zbor were appointed. In September 1941 he helped to establish the collaborationist government of General **Milan Nedić**. Ljotić put his most loyal soldiers in the Serbian Voluntary Corps, which was established on 15 September 1941. Informally, it was the Zbor army, whose aim was to struggle against the Communist partisans. In the anticipation of German defeat, Ljotić joined the Chetniks and tried to unite the national forces. After the victory of the partisans of **Josip Broz Tito**, Ljotić attempted to escape, via Slovenia, to the West, but he died in a car crash. His memoirs, *Iz moga života* (From my life), were published in 1952, and *Light of Truth* was published in 1984. (AO)

Sources: Philip Rees, *Biographical Dictionary of the Extreme Right since 1890* (New York, 1990); Alex N. Dragnich, *The First Yugoslavia* (Stanford, 1983); M. Stefanović, *Zbor Dimitrija Ljotića, 1934–1945* (Belgrade, 1984); Nebojša Popov, *Serbski dramat: Od faszystowskiego populizmu do Miloševicia* (Łódź ,1994); John Lampe, *Yugoslavia as History* (Cambridge, 1996).

LOGA-SOWIŃSKI Ignacy (20 January 1914, Vankewitz, Germany–10 December 1992, Warsaw), Polish Communist activist. The son of a farmhand, in his youth Loga-Sowiński worked in the building trade. From 1935 he was a member of the Communist Party of Poland. From 1939 to 1941 he worked in the Soviet-occupied part of Poland, where he entered into cooperation with Soviet intelligence. Transferred to the German-occupied part of Poland, in 1942 he joined the (Communist) Polish Workers' Party (Polska Partia Robotnicza [PPR]), and from 1943 he was a member of its Central Committee. In 1944 Loga-Sowiński was the party's plenipotentiary in the Lublin region, and in early 1945 he was the plenipotentiary of the (Communist) Provisional Government in the Łódź region. From 1946 to 1948 he was the PPR first secretary of the Łódź region. From 1944 to 1947 Loga-Sowiński belonged to the National Home Council, and from 1947 to 1952 he was a member of the (Communist) Constitutent Assembly. From December 1948 in the Polish United Workers' Party (Polska Zjednoczona Partia Robotnicza [PUWP]), he was closely connected with **Władysław Gomułka**. In 1951 Loga-Sowiński was arrested and imprisoned. He returned to political life along with Gomułka. At the Eighth Plenum of the PUWP Central Committee (CC) in October 1956, he joined the CC and the Politburo of the PUWP. In 1956–71 Loga-Sowiński chaired the Central Council of Trade Unions, and from 1957 to 1971 he was a member of parliament. In 1957 he became a member of the Council of State, and from 1965 to 1971 he was the council's deputy chairman. In December 1970, along with **Zenon Kliszko** and General Grzegorz Korczyński, Loga-Sowiński came to the Baltic Coast, where he joined a special task force responsible for the pacification of workers' protests in the Triple City (Gdańsk, Gdyna, and Sopot). During a Politburo meeting on 19 December 1970 Loga-Sowiński opposed the removal of Gomułka. In February 1971 he was dismissed from the Politburo and in December 1971 from the CC. In 1971–78 Loga-Sowiński was ambassador to Turkey. Later he retired from political life. (PK)

Sources: Mołdawa; *Słownik polityków polskich XX wieku* (Poznań, 1998); Krzysztof Lesiakowski, *Mieczysław Moczar "Mietek": Biografia polityczna* (Warsaw, 1998); Jerzy Eisler, *Grudzień 1970* (Warsaw, 2000).

LONČAR Budimir (1 April 1924, Preko, Croatia), Yugoslav Communist activist and diplomat of Croatian nationality. After graduating from high school, Lončar studied at a military school, and in 1941 he joined the guerrilla movement of **Josip Broz Tito**. During World War II he held various positions in the Union of Communist Youth of Yugoslavia and in the Communist Party of Dalmatia. In 1947–49 he worked in the security service. In 1950 he became consul in New York and councillor at the Yugoslav standing mission to the United Nations. From 1956 Lončar worked in the Foreign Ministry in Belgrade. In 1965 he became ambassador to Indonesia and simultaneously held the position of auxiliary ambassador to Malaysia and Singapore. From 1969 he was an adviser to the foreign minister. In 1973 he became ambassador to West Germany, and in 1977, undersecretary of state in the Foreign Ministry. From 1979 to 1983 Lončar was ambassador to the United States. In 1983–87 he was deputy federal secretary (deputy minister), and from December 1987, federal secretary (minister) of foreign affairs. Lončar tried to prevent the dissolution of the Yugoslav federal republic, seeking assistance from the European community, but in vain. After Slovenia and Croatia proclaimed independence on 25 June 1991, the federal government of **Ante Marković** gradually lost power. In December 1991 Lončar resigned from his position and retired. (AO)

Sources: Warren Zimmermann, *Origins of a Catastrophe* (New York, 1996); www.mfa.gov.yu/history/Ministri/B Lončar _s.html.

LORKOVIĆ Ivan (17 June 1876, Zagreb–24 February 1926, Zagreb), Croatian politician. As a student of law at Zagreb University, Lorković belonged to the founders of the Union of Croatian and Serbian Academic Youth, which edited the periodical *Narodna misao* from 1897. Co-founder and leader of the Croatian Progressive Party (Hrvatska Napredna Stranka), in December 1905 Lorković belonged to the founders of the Croatian-Serbian Coalition, uniting political efforts of the two nations under Habsburg rule. From 1906 he was a member of the Croatian Assembly (Sabor). After **Frano Supilo** withdrew from the coalition, Lorković became the key spokesman for cooperation between Serbs and Croats. At the end of March 1918 he joined the Croatian Committee, which declared itself in favor of a joint state with the Serbs and Slovenes. After the Kingdom of Serbs, Croats, and Slovenes (SHS) came into being in December 1918, Lorković was increasingly disappointed by the centralist policies of the Serbs, and in 1919 he founded the Croatian Union (Hrvatska Zajednica), which adopted a federalist program. After the passing of the June 1921 constitution, along with the Croatian Republican Peasant Party of **Stjepan Radić** and the Croatian Party of Law, Lorković established the Croatian Bloc, acting in sharp opposition to the political system of the SHS. (WR)

Sources: *Enciklopedija Jugoslavije*, vol. 5 (Zagreb, 1962); Mark Biondich, *Stjepan Radić, the Croat Peasant Party, and the Politics of Mass Mobilization, 1904–1928* (Toronto, 2000).

LORKOVIĆ Mladen (1 March 1909, Zagreb–25 April 1945, Lepoglava), Croatian nationalist politician. Lorković was the son of **Ivan Lorković**, leader of the Croatian Progressive Party. The political failure of his father, who had called for a national union of the Southern Slav nations and who died prematurely, increased his patriotic feelings. While a student, Lorković took part in military actions against the regime of King **Alexander I** (**Karadjordjević**). Fearing arrest, he fled to Berlin, where he worked closely with **Ante Pavelić**. Lorković was imprisoned after returning to Yugoslavia but was released after a hunger strike. In 1939 he published *Narod i zemlja Hrvata* (The nation and the land of the Croats). After becoming minister of foreign affairs of the Independent State of Croatia in June 1941, Lorković followed the pro-German line of Pavelić. He resigned in April 1943, after a protest by the Italians, who did not like his comments about their policy toward Croatia. Lorković remained a member of the Ustasha government until **Nikola Mandić** became prime minister in September 1943, when he resigned for a short time in protest against expected changes in the political line. However, in October 1943 he returned to the government, assuming the portfolio of minister of interior. In July 1944 he was arrested by the Ustasha authorities for taking part in an alleged pro-Allied plot. Along with a dozen or so other Croatian politicians and officers, Lorković was murdered by the Ustasha in a prison near Zagreb shortly before the end of the war. (WR)

Sources: Jere Jareb, *Pola stoleća hrvatske politike: Povodom Mačekove autobiografije* (Buenos Aires, 1960); Ivo Omrčanin,

Dramatis Presonae and Finis of the Independent State of Croatia in British and American Documents (Bryn Mawr, Pa., 1983); Bogdan Krizman, *Ustaše i Treći Reich*, vols. 1–2 (Zagreb, 1983); Bogdan Krizman, *Ante Pavelić i Ustaše* (Zagreb, 1983); Marcus Tanner, *Croatia: A Nation Forged in War* (New Haven, 1997).

LOSIK Yazep (6 November 1883, Mikalaieushchina, Minsk County–1 April 1940), Belorussian political and social activist, philologist, writer, and teacher. Losik was the uncle of **Yakub Kolas**. He was educated in a teacher-training college in Molodechno (1898–99) and graduated from a municipal school in Novgorod (1902). In 1905 he was active in the revolutionary movement and was exiled to Siberia. In 1907 he escaped from prison and went into hiding. Captured in 1911, he was again exiled for life to Siberia. In Irkutsk he began to write for the Wilno (Vilnius) paper *Nasha Niva*. After the February 1917 revolution, Losik returned to Belorussia. He was one of the founders of the Belorussian Social Democratic Hramada (BSDH). In 1917–18 he edited the *Wolna Belarus* paper. In 1917 he campaigned for the autonomy of Belorussia within the Russian federation. After the dissolution of the All-Belorussian Congress and signing of the Brest-Litovsk Treaty, Losik declared his support for the independence of Belorussia. At a congress of Belorussian organizations and national parties he was elected to the Executive Committee of the Central Council of the Belorussian Organizations and became a member of the Great Belorussian Council. During the German occupation Losik worked in Minsk. He was one of the initiators of the proclamation of the Belorussian People's Republic (BPR). On 25 April 1918 Losik was among the signatories of a telegram from the BPR to Emperor Wilhelm II of Germany in which the signatories stated that "they saw the future of Belorussia only under the patronage of the German state." After a split in the BSDH Losik was one of the leaders of the Belorussian Social Democratic Party, and from June 1918 he was president of the Council of the BPR. After a split in the BPR on 13 December 1919 Losik took the leadership of its Higher Council.

After the end of World War I Losik remained in the Belorussian SSR and was one of the first to recognize the Soviet authorities. From 1921 he lectured at Minsk University, at courses for instructors, and at the School of Pedagogy. He translated *The Communist Manifesto*, by Marx and Engels, into Belorussian. In 1922 Losik was elected a member of the Institute of Belorussian Culture (Inbelkult). The same year he published a practical grammar of the Belorussian language (*Hramatyka belaruskai movy: Fonetyka*). The Bolshevik paper *Zviazda* labeled the book as counterrevolutionary. Losik was arrested but was released after the intervention of the people's commissar

of the BSSR, **Usievalad Ihnatouski**. In November 1926 Losik organized a conference devoted to the reform of the Belorussian grammar and alphabet. In July 1930 he was arrested again in allegedly because of hisconnection with the Belorussian Liberation Union which did not acutally exist. On 6 December 1930 Losik was deprived of his academic title. By a decision of the OGPU of the BSSR on 10 April 1931, Losik was exiled to Kamyshyn in the Saratov district for five years. In November 1934 he was amnestied but was not allowed to return to Belorussia. He lived with his family in the district of Bryansk. In June 1938 Losik was arrested again and in 1940 sentenced to five years for "anti-Soviet agitation." According to the official version, Losik died in prison. In 1958 he was vindicated, and his 1938 sentence was quashed; in 1988 his 1931 sentence was quashed. Losik published extensively on the history and national revival of Belorussia—for example, the essays *1517–1917* (1917), a history of the Great Lithuanian-Belorussian Duchy (1918), and a depiction of the battle of Grunwald in medieval chronicles. Between 1921 and 1927 he published dozens of linguistic works. In 1994 *Tvory: Apaviadanni, kazki, artykuly* (Works: Short stories, tales and articles) was published, and in 1995 Losik's Belorussian grammar was reissued. (AS/SA)

Sources: Miasnikou Anatol, *Natsdemy: Los i trahiediia Fabiiana Shantyra, Usievalada Ihnatouskaha i Jazepa Losika* (Minsk, 1993).

LOSONCZY Géza (5 May 1917, Érsekcsanád–21 December 1957, Budapest), Hungarian Communist activist, victim of the 1956 revolution. Born into the family of a clergyman of the Evangelical Reformed Church, after passing his high school exams, Losonczy studied Hungarian and Romance languages and literatures at Debrecen University. In 1937 he joined the leftist March Front, one of the aims of which was to revitalize the Hungarian countryside. In 1939, while on a scholarship in France, Losonczy joined the Hungarian Communist Party (HCP), which was illegal in Hungary. After returning home, he worked as a journalist with *Népszava*, the central organ of the Social Democratic movement. In 1940 he was arrested for his political activities. He was subsequently kept under police surveillance. In 1941 Losonczy completed his studies in Budapest. He helped to publish an anti-war issue of *Népszava* with articles by major representatives of the anti-Nazi movement. In 1942 he went underground. After Germany occupied Hungary in March 1944, Losonczy was active in the resistance movement and helped to organize the Hungarian National Independence Front. In March 1945 he became the editor of *Szabad Nép*, the central organ of the HCP. He was also a member of its

Central Committee (CC) from 1946 to 1951, a member of parliament from 1945 to 1951, and secretary of state for political affairs in the Ministry of People's Education from 1949 to 1951. Arrested in 1951 on false charges, Losonczy was sentenced to fifteen years' imprisonment. Seriously ill, he was released in the summer of 1954. He spent one year in a hospital and sanatorium. In April 1955 he was rehabilitated.

After recovering, Losonczy became one of the leading figures of the so-called party opposition centered around **Imre Nagy**. In 1955 he signed a memorandum presented to the CC of the Hungarian Workers' Party (HWP) by writers protesting the retightening of censorship. On the night of 23–24 October 1956 Losonczy was coopted to the leadership of the HWP and elected a deputy member of the Politburo, but, along with **Ferenc Donáth**, he resigned from these positions in protest against the policy of First Secretary **Ernő Gerő** and the entire CC, and he supported the demands of the insurgents. On 26 October at a CC meeting Losonczy insisted that the HWP start negotiations with the insurgents. On 30 October he joined the government of Imre Nagy, becoming the minister of state in charge of press and propaganda. He was also a member of the provisional leadership of the Hungarian Socialist Workers' Party (HSWP). On 3 November, along with **Zoltán Tildy**, Losonczy conducted the last press conference of Nagy's government. The day after the second Soviet intervention started, Losonczy took refuge in the Yugoslav Embassy in Budapest. On 22 November, along with other members of Nagy's group, he was abducted and interned in Romania. In mid-April 1957 Losonczy was brought to Budapest. During investigations, his lung disease recurred. However, he began and continued a hunger strike. Before his trial began, Losonczy died in jail in unexplained circumstances. Information about his death was not announced to the public until June 1958, when a communiqué was issued about the trial and execution of Imre Nagy and his associates, together with whom Losonczy was ceremoniously reburied in June 1989 in Budapest. (JT)

Sources: *A magyar forradalom és szabadságharc enciklopédiája*, CD-ROM (Budapest, 1999); *Magyar Nagylexikon*, vol. 12 (Budapest, 2001); Ferenc A. Vali, *Rift and Revolt in Hungary* (Cambridge, Mass., 1961); Paul E. Zinner, *Revolution in Hungary* (New York, 1962); György Litván, ed., *Rewolucja węgierska 1956 roku* (Warsaw, 1996).

LOTOTSKYI Oleksandr (22 March 1870, Bronitsa, Podolia–22 October 1939, Warsaw), Ukrainian politician, scholar, and Orthodox Church activist. Born into a clergyman's family, Lototskyi studied at the Podolian Theological Seminary, and from 1892 to 1896 he studied canon law at the Kiev Theological Academy. After his studies he started working as a state controller in Kiev and then in St. Petersburg (1900–17). In both centers Lototskyi was active in Ukrainian social and Orthodox Church life; for example, he translated the Bible into the Ukrainian language and participated in the founding of the Vik publishing house in Kiev (1896). In 1917 he co-founded the Ukrainian Party of Socialists-Federalists (UPS-F), a centrist pro-independence party that continued the tradition of the Society of Ukrainian Progressives. At the beginning of 1917 Lototskyi became president of the Ukrainian National Rada (Council) in Petrograd. In May 1917, on the motion of the Ukrainian Central Rada (UCR), the Provisional Government of Russia appointed him commissar of Bukovina and Pokutia (Pokucie). From September to November 1917 Lototskyi was general secretary in the General Secretariat of the UCR, from which he resigned because of its radicalization. He returned to the government during the presidency of the Socialist Revolutionary **Vsevolod Holubovych** at the beginning of 1918, but he again stepped down because he opposed Holubovych's overly leftist policy. At the end of the regime of Hetman **Pavlo Skoropadskyi**, Lototskyi, as minister for religious affairs, joined (in October 1918) the second cabinet of Fedor Lyzohub, which was established to negotiate with the Ukrainian left—that is, the Directory of **Volodymir Vynnychenko**.

At an ecumenical council in Kiev on 12 November 1918 Lototskyi firmly supported the autocephaly of the Orthodox Church in the Ukraine. He prepared a law about autocephaly that was promulgated by a decree of 1 January 1919 issued by the Directory of the Ukrainian People's Republic (UPR). From January 1919 to March 1920 Lototskyi served as the UNR ambassador to Istanbul, with a mission of gaining the recognition for the autocephaly by the Patriarch of Constantinople. After the fall of the UNR Lototskyi emigrated to Vienna and then to Prague, where between 1922 and 1929 he was an assistant professor and professor of Orthodox law at the Ukrainian Free University. There, he continued his political activities within the framework of the Ukrainian Radical Democratic Party, and he remained deputy prime minister and minister for religious affairs in subsequent UPR governments-in-exile.

In 1928 Lototskyi moved to Warsaw, where he assumed the position of professor at the School of Orthodox Theology of Warsaw University and the post of head of the Department of Slavic Orthodox Churches and Romanian Orthodox Church History. On his initiative, in 1930 the Ukrainian Scientific Institute was founded in Warsaw, the only Ukrainian research institution financed by government funds in Poland before 1939. Lototskyi headed the institute until 1938. His efforts led to the publication of around fifty-four volumes of scholarly works in the fields of literature and literary studies, history and Orthodox Church history, statistics, economics, and jurisprudence. Lototskyi was buried in the Orthodox cemetery in Warsaw. In 1971 his son Boris obtained the consent of the authorities of the Polish People's Republic to take his father's ashes to the United States, where they were buried in Bound Brook, New Jersey.

Lototskyi was the author of many articles in Ukrainian and Russian periodicals. He helped to obtain the permission of St. Petersburg for the publication of a series of Ukrainian books (for example, a full edition of *Kobzar*, by Taras Shevchenko, 1907). Lototskyi himself also wrote several fundamental works in Orthodox Church history: *Prawo cerkiewne* (Orthodox Church law; 1924); *Ukrains'ki dzherela tserkovnoho prava* (Foundations of the Ukrainian Orthodox Church law; 1931); and "Autokefalia" (Autocephaly, 2 vols.; 1935–38); he also wrote a biography of Symon Petlyura (1936). Lototskyi also left his memoirs: *Storinky mynuloho* (Stories of the past, 3 vols.; 1932–1934) and *U Tsarhorodi* (In Tsarigrad; 1939), which contain invaluable materials on the history of Ukrainian sociopolitical life, especially in the period between 1900 and 1917. (GM)

Sources: *Encyclopedia of Ukraine*, vol. 3 (Toronto, 1993); *Lytsar pratsi i oboviazku: Zbirnyk prysviachenyi pamiati prof. O. Lototskoho-Bilousenka* (Toronto and New York, 1983); Stefan Kozak, "Ołeksandr Łotoćkyj: Uczony, dyplomat, i polityk," *Warszawskie Zeszyty Ukrainoznawcze*, vol. 3.

LOVINESCU Monica (20 November 1923, Bucharest), Romanian journalist and émigré activist. Lovinescu graduated in linguistic and philosophical studies at Bucharest University. She made her literary debut in the periodical *Vremea*. Later she contributed to *Revista Fundaţilor Regale* and, after World War II, also to the weekly *Democraţia*. In September 1947 Lovinescu went to Paris on a scholarship from the French government, and in January 1948 she asked for political asylum there. Soon after coming to Paris, Lovinescu married **Virgil Ierunca**. In 1958 the Romanian Communists arrested her mother, Ecaterina Bălăcioiu, and sentenced her to a long-term imprisonment, during which she died. In 1961–75 Lovinescu edited Romanian musical and literary broadcasts on French radio. From 1962 she worked with Radio Free Europe, editing (along with her husband) the very popular broadcasts *Actualitatea culturală românească* (Contemporary Romanian culture and *Teze şi Antiteze la Paris* (Theses and antitheses in Paris). In 1977

Lovinescu strongly supported **Paul Goma**. In April 1989 she signed a demand for the liberalization of cultural life in Romania. After the fall of the **Nicolae Ceauşescu** regime in 1989, Lovinescu continued her cultural activities, both in Romania and abroad. In 2002 she published her *Jurnal 1981–1984* (Diary 1981–1984) and *Jurnal 1985–1988* (Diary 1985–1988). (AB)

Sources: Mihai Pellin, *Opisul emigraţiei politice: Destine în 1222 de fişe alcătuite pe bază dosarelor din arhivele Securităţii* (Bucharest, 2002).

LOZORAITIS Stasys (5 September 1898, Kovno [Kaunas]–24 December 1983, Rome), Lithuanian politician. After Lithuania regained its independence, Lozoraitis worked in the Ministry of Interior and in the chancellery of the government. In 1923 he entered the diplomatic service, becoming first secretary and later councillor at the legation in Berlin. He simultaneously studied international law at Berlin University. In 1929 he was sent to the diplomatic mission at the Holy See, where in 1931 he became chargé d'affaires. After returning to Lithuania in 1932, Lozoraitis became director of the political department in the Ministry of Foreign Affairs, and in June 1934 he became head of this ministry. He strengthened the ties between Lithuania and the other states of the Baltic Entente (Latvia and Estonia) and called for the normalization of relations with Poland; he expressed his views in memoranda presented to President **Antanas Smetona**. However, Lozoraitis resigned as minister in protest against the Polish ultimatum of March 1938. In February 1939 he was appointed minister plenipotentiary to Italy. In the face of mounting pressure from the Soviet Union, in May 1940 the minister of foreign affairs, **Juozas Urbšys**, authorized Lozoraitis to act on behalf of the Lithuanian government in the case that the Soviet Union occupied the country. After Lithuania was seized by the Soviet Union in June 1940, Lozoraitis made numerous attempts to draw the attention of Western governments and public opinion to the unlawful annexation of Lithuania and to the mass terror introduced into the country by the Kremlin. After World War II, he continued his efforts; for example, he sent letters to the United Nations and other international organizations. His son, also Stasys Lozoraitis (1924–94), was a representative of the Lithuanian government-in-exile at the Holy See and later in the United States; in the autumn of 1992 he returned to Lithuania, where he ran in the February 1993 presidential elections, in which he obtained around 40 percent of the votes but lost to **Algirdas Brazauskas**. (WR)

Sources: *EL*, vol. 3; Saulius Sužiedelis, *Historical Dictionary of Lithuania* (Lanham, Md., 1997).

LOZYNSKYI Mykhailo (30 July 1880, Babyn, Galicia–3 November 1937, Solovets Islands), Ukrainian lawyer and politician. Lozynskyi graduated in law. Before World War I he was the editor of *Dilo* (later *Hromads'ka Dumka*) and a contributor to *Haslo*, an organ of the Ukrainian Radical Party in Tschernowitz (now Chernivtsi); he also worked with the Rada (Council) in Kiev. During the war he belonged to the Union for the Liberation of Ukraine and supported the Central Powers. In March 1919 he became deputy secretary for foreign affairs of the Western Ukrainian National Republic (Zakhidno-Ukrayins'ka Narodna Republika [ZUNR]), a member of the ZUNR delegation to talks with Poland, and a Ukrainian delegate to the Paris Peace Conference. From 1921 to 1927 Lozynskyi was a professor of international law at the Ukrainian Free University in Prague. Disappointed by the Entente's March 1923 decision to give Eastern Galicia to Poland and by the lack of an autonomous government there and encouraged by the initial successes of the Ukrainization policy in the Ukrainian SSR, Lozynskyi decided to move to Kharkiv. In 1927 he took up the chair of law at the Institute of the National Economy. He also worked at the Ukrainian Institute of Marxism-Leninism. Arrested in 1930 in connection with the case of the so-called Union for the Liberation of Ukraine, Lozynskyi was deported to the Urals and then to the Solovets Islands, where he was sentenced to death and executed.

Lozynskyi published extensively on Ukrainian-Polish relations. His first work was devoted to the liberation struggle in the Ukraine in the seventeenth and eighteenth centuries. Emphasizing the traditions of freedom of the Cossacks, in the treatise *Marks-Engels-Liebknecht pro vidbudovanie Polshchi* (Marx, Engels, and Liebknecht on the reconstruction of Poland; 1906), he criticized thinkers who had a preconceived idea of Poland and its "historical" borders. Lozynskyi was drawn to Mikhail Bakunin's proposals to dismember Russia and separate the Ukraine as a member of a future federation of East European nations. His book *Polsky i ruskyi revoliutsiinyi rukh i Ukraina* (The Polish and Russian revolutionary movement and the Ukraine; 1908) was a polemic against the views of Polish and Russian political parties. In *Avtonomiia kraiv v avstriyskii konstytutsii* (Autonomy of the countries in the Austrian constitution; 1912) and *Podil Halychyny* (The division of Eastern Galicia; 1913) he addressed current issues. In the collection *Akt 12 kvitnia 1908 r.* (The Act of 12 April 1908; 1909) Lozynskyi tried to justify the killing of Alfred Potocki, governor of Galicia, by stressing the miserable living conditions of Ukrainians under Polish rule. During World War I Lozynskyi worked in Vienna to change the status of Eastern Galicia and have it made into a separate province (*Die Schaffung einer ukrainischen Provinz in Oesterreich*; 1915); he challenged

the Polish influence with the Central Powers (*Dokumente des polnischen Russophilismus*; 1915), as well as with the Entente countries (*Les "droits" de la Pologne sur la Galicie*; 1917). In 1919 he published a political and propaganda treatise, *L'Ukraine Occidentale (Galicie): L'invasion polonaise en Ukraine Occidentale est crime contre le Droit*. During a stay in Prague, Lozynskyi wrote many works on international law and the history of Ukrainian constitutional law, including his principal work, *Halychyna v rr. 1918–1920* (Eastern Galicia 1918–1920; 1922). (TS)

Sources: *Encyclopedia of Ukraine*, vol. 3 (Toronto, 1993); Kost Levytskyi, *Istoriia politychnoyi dumky halytskykh ukraiintsiv 1848–1914* (Lviv, 1926); Kost Levytskyi, *Istoriia vyzvolnykh zmahan halytskych ukraiintsiv z chasiv svitovoyi viyny 1914–1918 rr.* (Lviv, 1928); M. Lytvyn and K. Naumenko, *Istoriia ZUNR* (Lviv, 1995); G. Cvengros, *La République Démocratique Ukrainienne—la République Française (1917–1922)* (Lviv, 1995).

LUBACHIVSKYI Myroslav Ivan (24 June 1914, Dolina–14 December 2000, Lviv), cardinal and head of the Ukrainian Greek Catholic Church. In 1938 Lubachivskyi graduated in theology from the University of Lwów (Lviv), and later he studied theology in Innsbruck. He was ordained by Metropolitan **Andriy Sheptytskyi** in September 1938. Later he worked in the Greek Catholic archdiocese of Lviv. In 1942–47 he lived and worked at the Biblical Institute and the Gregorianum in Rome and at the Rome Medical Academy. In May 1947 Lubachivskyi left for the United States and received American citizenship. Until 1980 he worked there among Ukrainian Greek Catholics as (among other things) secretary to the archbishop of Philadelphia for Ukrainians of the Byzantine rite. Lubachivskyi translated the catechism into Ukrainian, and he edited homilies, reflections, and catecheses. He also worked in Austria, Switzerland, and Italy. In 1967–68 he edited Radio Vatican broadcasts. On 13 September 1979 the Synod of the Ukrainian Greek Catholic Church elected him archbishop of Philadelphia for the Ukrainians. He was personally consecrated by Pope **John Paul II** on 12 November 1979. On 27 March 1980 the Synod appointed Lubachivskyi coadjutor with the right of succession to the archbishop of Lviv, Cardinal **Josyf Slipyi**. After Slipyi's death, on 7 September 1984, Lubachivskyi became archbishop of Lviv, and on 25 May 1985 John Paul II appointed him cardinal. In October 1987 Lubachivskyi met with the Primate of Poland, Cardinal **Józef Glemp**, and started reconciliation talks between the Greek and Roman Catholic Churches and between the Poles and Ukrainians. In November 1987 he made a similar effort toward the patriarchate of Moscow, but to no avail.

Lubachivskyi returned to the Ukraine in March 1991, during the breakup of the Soviet Union. He dealt with the reconstruction of Greek Catholic structures after forty-five years of Communist oppression. He tried to ease the tensions with the Orthodox Church. On 25 March 1994 Lubachivskyi wrote a pastoral letter on the unity of the Christian churches in which he appealed for the termination of inter-Christian hostilities and the reconstruction of church unity in the Ukraine. In view of his ailing health, in 1996 Lubachivskyi asked the Pope for an assistant bishop to deal with the current administration of the Uniate Church and the Lviv archdiocese. On 14 October 1996 the Synod elected Bishop **Lubomyr Huzar** for this role, and the next day the Holy See confirmed this choice. Lubachivskyi took an active part in the synods of the Catholic Church in 1980, 1983, 1985, 1987, and 1990 (as co-chairman), as well as in the First Special Synod of European Bishops in 1991. After the death of Cardinal Slipyi, Lubachivskyi chaired all the synods of the Greek Catholic Church. In 1986 he published a booklet, *Was It Really Russia That Was Christianized in 988?* In 1988 he also chaired the celebrations for the Millennium of the Baptism of Kievan Ruthenia in various countries. Lubachivskyi was buried in St. Yur (George) Cathedral in Lviv, which he had reconstructed after the years of Communist destruction. (AGr)

Sources: *Encyclopedia of Ukraine*, vol. 3 (Toronto, 1993); Bohdan Nahaylo, *The Ukrainian Resurgence* (Toronto, 1999); *Annuario Pontificio, 2000*; Andrzej Kaczyński, "Arcybiskup większy Lwowa," *Rzeczpospolita*, 22 December 2000; Rev. Bogdan Pańczak, "Wielki sercem i Duchem," *Tygodnik Powszechny*, 7 January 2001.

ŁUBIEŃSKI Konstanty (21 March 1910, Zassów, near Dębica–25 September 1977, Warsaw), Polish politician. Born into a landowner's family, Łubieński completed studies in law and economics at the Jagiellonian University in Kraków in 1934, and from 1936 to 1939 he worked in the Ministry of the Treasury. Active in a conservative group called Big Power Ideology (Myśl Mocarstwowa), he contributed to the periodicals *Bunt Młodych* and *Polityka*, edited by **Jerzy Giedroyć**. During the Nazi occupation Łubieński was a soldier in the Home Army (Armia Krajowa), and in 1944 he commanded its Mielec district. In 1945 he joined a group founded by **Bolesław Piasecki** and centered around the weekly *Dziś i jutro*. Łubieński was the author of *List otwarty do Pana Tadeusza Łady* (An open letter to Mr. Tadeusz Łada; 1948), encouraging Catholics to support the Socialist system. After the creation of the pro-government Catholic organization Pax in 1952, Łubieński became one of its leaders. From 1952 until his death, he was an MP. In the fall of 1956 he was one of the main opponents of Piasecki's policies within Pax. In November 1956 Łubieński left the organization and co-founded a group centered around the weekly *Za i przeciw*.

After this group split in the fall of 1957, he joined the Club of Catholic Intellectuals (Klub Inteligencji Katolickiej [KIK]) in Warsaw. From 1958 to 1962 he was a member of the KIK board, then its vice-president (1962–69) and president (1969–72). In 1957 he joined a parliamentary group called Znak, in which he mainly dealt with economic issues but also defended the ownership rights of the Roman Catholic Church and the rights of the faithful. In June 1971 he became vice-president of the All-Polish Committee of the National Unity Front (Ogólnopolski Komitet Frontu Jedności Narodu) and advocated a greater involvement of the Znak movement in political life. This was opposed by a majority of KIK members and led to Łubieński's resignation from the KIK leadership. In 1976 he belonged to a special committee for drafting amendments to the Constitution of the Polish People's Republic, and he supported the amendments. This led to a sharp conflict with most members of the Znak movement. After the elections of 1976 Łubieński became a member of the State Council and president of the parliamentary group called Znak, which was not recognized by most members of the movement as representative. In June 1976 he left the KIK. The following month Łubieński co-founded the Polish Club of Catholic Intellectuals (Polski Klub Inteligencji Katolickiej) and became its president. (AF)

Sources: Andrzej Micewski, *Współrządzić czy nie kłamać? PAX i "Znak" w Polsce 1945–1976* (Paris, 1978).

LUBOMIRSKI Zdzisław, prince (4 April 1865, Nizhny Novgorod–31 July 1943, Maławieś, near Grójec, Poland), Polish conservative politician from an aristocratic family. The son of a participant in the January Insurrection of 1863, Lubomirski was born in exile. He was brought up and educated in Galicia. He received a law degree from the Jagiellonian University in Kraków and from the university in Graz. In 1893 he settled in the so-called Kingdom of Poland. Lubomirski was involved in charity and educational work, joining the Warsaw Philanthropic Society and the Society for School Tuition Fees. He was also an initiator of the Society of National Education (Towarzystwo Oświaty Narodowej [TON]). Lubomirski was the leader of conciliatory circles; in 1904, along with other activists, he issued a servile memorandum to the tsarist government. From 1908 to 1909 he took part in negotiations with the Russophile Pan-Slavic movement in Bohemia and the Kingdom of Poland, as a result of which he drifted toward the National Democratic Party.

After the outbreak of World War I, Lubomirski became chairman of the Civic Committee of the City of Warsaw (3 August 1914). He cooperated with the Party of Real

Politics (Stronnictwo Polityki Realnej [SPR]) and the Polish National Committee. He remained in Warsaw after the withdrawal of the Russians, who had appointed him mayor of the city on 4 August 1915. After the Germans occupied Warsaw, they recognized Lubomirski's appointment. Under his leadership, the Central and Warsaw National Committees dealt de jure with educational and charity work, while de facto they handled many of the administrative and political responsibilities of the nonexistent Polish government. Lubomirski tried to prevent the establishment of a Polish army under the auspices of Germany and to ease tensions in the capital. He opposed extreme Germanophile tendencies, cooperated with the Provisional Council of State, and maintained contacts with **Józef Piłsudski**. Shocked by the revolution in Russia, Lubomirski began to work closely with the pro-Polish activists. On 15 October 1917 the emperors of Austria-Hungary and Germany appointed Lubomirski, together with Archbishop **Aleksander Kakowski** and Count Józef Ostrowski, as members of the Regency Council of the Kingdom of Poland. In the fall of 1918 an attempt to appoint Lubomirski head of state ended in failure. However, he managed to take control of the Polish military units that had been established by the Germans. On 10 November at the railway station in Warsaw, Lubomirski welcomed Piłsudski back to Poland, and on 14 November the Regency Council passed its duties on to Piłsudski.

Lubomirski returned to politics during the coup of May 1926, undertaking mediation negotiations among the parties. He later became deputy chairman of the pro-Piłsudski Polish Conservative Organization of Pro-State Work. From 1931 to 1935 he also served as chairman of the Chief Council of Landed Gentry Organizations. From 1928 to 1938 he sat in the Senate, first as a representative of the Nonparty Bloc of Cooperation with the Government (Bezpartyjny Blok Współpracy z Rządem) and later as a presidential nominee. Lubomirski protested the authoritarian leanings of the *sanacja* regime, particularly during the co-called Brześć Trial. Because of his contacts with the opposition, Lubomirski lost his senatorial seat. During the defense of Warsaw in September 1939, he acted in the Civic Committee. Under the German occupation he was involved in charity work and maintained contacts with the underground circles of the landed gentry. Arrested by the Gestapo on 10 November 1942, Lubomirski was released in January 1943, with his health broken. He died shortly afterwards on his family estate. (MC)

Sources: *PSB*, vol. 18; Władysław Pobóg-Malinowski, *Najnowsza historia polityczna Polski*, vols. 1–3 (London, 1983–86); Krzysztof Jasiewicz, *Lista strat ziemiaństwa polskiego 1939–1945* (Warsaw, 1995).

LUCA Vasile (8 June 1898, Cătălina, Transylvania–23 July 1963, Aiud), Romanian Communist activist. Born into a family of Transylvanian Hungarians, Luca lost his parents when he was seven and was brought up in an orphanage in Sibiu. In 1913 he became an apprentice to a locksmith and later worked on the railways. Inducted into the army in 1915, he fought on various fronts in World War I. From April to August 1919 he was a soldier of the Red Guard of the Hungarian Soviet Republic (HSR). As a member of the Hungarian Communist Party (HCP), in the autumn of 1919 Luca returned to Transylvania, which had been incorporated into Romania. When the Communist Party of Romania (CPR) was founded in 1922, Luca became a member. From 1924 to 1927 he was imprisoned for his Communist activities. Released in 1927, he joined the CPR Central Committee (CC). In accordance with the Comintern line, he called for the establishment of a separate state of the "Transylvanian proletariat." Luca was active in the trade union movement in Transylvania, organizing strikes at the Lupeni mines in 1929 and at the Grivița plants in Bucharest in 1933. From 1933 to 1938 and from 1939 to 1940 he was imprisoned again. In April 1940 he attempted to cross the Soviet border. Captured by the Romanian authorities, he spent three months in prison. He was released after the Soviet Union seized Bessarabia in June 1940. In 1940 Luca was elected to the Supreme Soviet of the Ukrainian SSR. From 1941 to 1944 he was in Moscow, where he was in charge of the Romanian section of Moscow Radio (Radio România Liberă). He also helped to establish the Tudor Vladimirescu Division, which was recruited from Romanian prisoners of war.

In June 1944 Luca arrived in Moldavia, together with the Red Army. In September 1944, after the overthrow of the regime of Marshal **Ion Antonescu**, he returned to Bucharest and became leader of the National Democratic Bloc (NDB), a pro-Communist coalition against the so-called historical parties and against the king. Luca served as the NDB leader until November 1946. From 1944 to 1952, along with **Ana Pauker**, **Teohari Georgescu**, and **Gheorghe Gheorghiu-Dej**, Luca was one of the senior leaders of the Romanian Communist Party (RCP), serving as secretary of the CC and a member of the RCP Politburo. He co-organized the parliamentary pseudo-elections of 19 November 1946 and was co-responsible for the political persecutions and brutal Sovietization of Romania in 1944–52. Luca's name was associated with the "internationalist" faction in the party, which competed with the "national" faction of Gheorghiu-Dej.

Between November 1947 and May 1952 Luca served as minister of finance. Aligned with Pauker and Georgescu, he became a target of attacks by Gheorghiu-Dej and his supporters. The party purge in these years was caused by many factors, including attempts to "Romanize" the party, but the monetary reform that had deprived people of their savings was the main pretext. Although a decision to launch the reform had been taken by the entire leadership of the party, Luca was responsible for its implementation. At a CC meeting on 29 February–1 March 1952 Luca was attacked for errors and abuses during the implementation of this reform. A special commission was appointed whose findings contributed to Luca's expulsion from the CC at its next meeting on 26 May. Soon afterwards Pauker and Georgescu were also purged. Arrested in August of that year, Luca was sentenced to hard labor for life on 10 October 1954. He served his sentence in various places, including Râmnicul Sărat, where he met the Peasant Party activists **Ion Mihalache** and **Corneliu Coposu**. In 1963 Luca's sentence was commuted to twenty-five years, but he died in prison soon after. In 1956 Gheorghiu-Dej stated that the expulsion of Georgescu, Luca, and Pauker had been part of the de-Stalinization process in Romania, but in 1968 Luca was rehabilitated by **Nicolae Ceauşescu** as a "victim of Stalinism." (FA/TD/WR)

Sources: Vladimir Tismăneanu, *Arheologia terori* (Bucharest, 1992); Gheorghe Apostol, *Eu şi Gheorghiu Dej* (Bucharest, 1998); Stelian Tanase, *Elite şi societate în timpul lui Gheorghiu Dej* (Bucharest, 1999); Dennis Deletant, *Communist Terror in Romania: Gheorghiu-Dej and the Police State, 1948–1965* (New York, 1999); Robert Levy, *Ana Pauker: The Rise and Fall of a Jewish* Communist (Berkeley, 2000).

LUCACIU Vasile (21 January 1852, Apa, near Satu Mare, Transylvania–29 November 1922, Sisesti, near Satu Mare), Romanian Greek Catholic priest, writer, and politician. In 1868 Lucaciu began to study theology and philosophy in Rome. In 1874 he earned a Ph.D. from the University of Rome. In 1878, after returning to Romania, he began to teach in Transylvanian high schools. In the 1880s he became active in the Romanian National Party (RNP), serving as its secretary general from 1892 to 1918. Lucaciu was a co-author and signatory of a memorandum from Transylvanian Romanian activists to Emperor Francis Joseph in 1892; in it they called for autonomy for Transylvania within the empire rather than the Kingdom of Hungary. They also sharply criticized the Hungarian electoral, legal, and educational systems. Lucaciu was arrested; during his trial in 1894 he courageously defended the Romanian cause. A supporter of the radical line of the party, he called for the union of Transylvania with the Old Kingdom. Imprisoned on several occasions, Lucaciu became a legend in the Romanian national movement in Transylvania. In 1905 he became a member of the Hungarian parliament, where he firmly criticized the policies of Budapest toward the national minorities. After the outbreak of World War I, in December 1914 Lucaciu became leader of the League for the Cultural Unity of All Romanians. Consequently, he was expelled from Transylvania by the Hungarian authorities. He went to the Old Kingdom and then abroad. In April 1917 he visited the United States, presenting the demands of Transylvanian Romanians to the American government. In September 1918 he became vice-president of the Romanian Provisional National Committee in Paris. Lucaciu was one of the main organizers of the National Assembly in Alba Iulia on 1 December 1918, at which the union of Transylvania and the Old Kingdom of Romania was proclaimed. From 1919 to 1920 Lucaciu served as minister of the Governing Council of Transylvania. From 1919 to 1922 he was a member of the Romanian parliament, initially representing the RNP and from 1920 onwards the People's Party, led by General **Alexandru Averescu**. (FA/WR)

Sources: R. W. Seton-Watson, *A History of the Romanians* (Hamden, CT, 1963); Ştefan Pascu and Miron Constantinescu, eds., *Unification of the Romanian State: The Union of Transylvania with Old Romania* (Bucharest, 1971); Ştefan Pascu, *A History of Transylvania* (Detroit, 1982); Béla Köpeczi, ed., *History of Transylvania* (Budapest, 1994); Şerban N. Ionescu, *Who Was Who in Twentieth Century Romania* (Boulder, Colo., 1994).

LUCHIAN Ştefan (1 February 1868, Stefaneşti–28 June 1916, Bucharest), Romanian painter. Luchian came from Northern Moldavia. In 1873 his family moved to Bucharest, where in 1889 he graduated from the School of Fine Arts. Later he also studied in the Akademie der Bildenden Künste in Munich, Germany, and in the Académie Julian in Paris, where his tutor was William-Adolphe Bouguereau. Soon Luchian gave up academism and became influenced by impressionism. After the death of his mother in 1883, Luchian inherited a considerable fortune, but he soon spent it and found himself in poverty. After returning to Romania in 1892, he worked out his own style, combining expressionism, symbolism, and impressionism. He belonged to the movement of Independent Artists. In 1900 Luchian was partially paralyzed, and it influenced the emotional intensity of his works—for instance, his *Self-Portrait* (1907). Luchian also painted landscapes and scenic pieces. In several works he presented the living conditions of the poor in the countryside; therefore he was later treated as the forerunner of Socialist realism. At the end of his life Luchian was fully immobilized and mainly painted flowers and still lifes. Luchian committed suicide. (WR)

Sources: Richard Frucht, ed., *Encyclopedia of Eastern Europe* (New York and London, 2000); Vasile Drăguţ, *Luchian* (Bucharest, 1963); Zoe Dumitrescu Busulenga, *Ştefan Luchian* (Bucharest, 1993); Jacques Lassaigne, *Ştefan Luchian* (Bucharest, 1994); www.artnet.com/library/05/0523/T052321.asp.

LUCINSCHI Petru (27 January 1940, Radulenii Vechi), Moldavian Communist and post-Communist politician. In 1962 Lucinschi graduated in philology and history from Kishinev University. Later he joined the League of Young Communists, and in 1963, the Komsomol and the Higher School for Personnel at the Central Committee (CC) of the CPSU. In 1964 he became a member of the Communist Party of Moldavia (Partidul Comunist din Moldova [CPM]) and then of the CPSU. In 1971 Lucinschi moved from the Komsomol to the CC Secretariat of the CPM. In 1976 he became first secretary of the Kishinev Town Planning Committee, and in 1977 he received a Ph.D. in Marxist philosophy at Kishinev University. In 1978 he went to Moscow, where until 1986 he was deputy head of the Department of Propaganda of the CPSU CC. Promoted to deputy member of the CPSU CC, Lucinschi was sent to Tajikistan, where he became second secretary of the local republican party and deputy to the Supreme Council of the USSR. In 1989, on Mikhail Gorbachev's request, he returned to the Moldavian SSR to introduce perestroika there. A delegate to the Congress of People's Deputies and a member of the last Politburo of the CPSU CC, in 1990 Lucinschi became first secretary of the CPM. In early 1991 he returned to Moscow, where he joined the CPSU CC Secretariat.

After the CPSU dissolved itself in late August 1991 and after the USSR broke up in December 1991, Lucinschi stayed in Moscow, where he headed the Institute of Sociopolitical Studies and later the Foundation for the Development of the Social Sciences. In 1992 he returned to the then independent Moldova, and after a few months he became its ambassador to Moscow. In 1993 Lucinschi went back to Kishinev, where, supported by Communists and other groups opposing unification with Romania, he became speaker of the parliament. He spoke in favor of Moldova's integration with the Commonwealth of Independent States (CIS) and for a special autonomous status for the mostly Russian-speaking Transnistria and the Gagauz areas. Also in 1993 Lucinschi took the lead of the pro-Russian Agrarian Democratic Party of Moldova (Partidul Democrat Agrar din Moldova), which won the 1994 parliamentary elections. As a result, he regained the position of speaker of parliament. In 1995 Lucinschi left this party and formed the Bloc for a Democratic and Prosperous Moldova (Pentru Moldova Democrată şi Prosperă), although he was formally not a member. He sharply criticized President **Mircea Snegur**, who spoke in favor of rapprochement with Romania, while Lucinschi favored a close relationship with the CIS and a "socially oriented" market economy.

Supported by leftist and pro-Russian parties, at the end of 1996 Lucinschi won the presidential elections, and on 15 January 1997 he took over Moldova's presidency. In order to widen his political base he turned toward centrist and rightist groups, thus antagonizing the leftist and pro-Russian forces. In 1997 a coalition of centrist and leftist groups that supported Lucinschi came into being under the name of Prosperous and Democratic Moldova (Moldova Prosperă şi Democrată). Also in 1997 Lucinschi made an agreement with Boris Yeltsin on the withdrawal of the Russian Fourteenth Army from Transnistria, but the Russian Duma did not ratify this agreement. In 1998 Lucinschi introduced Moldova into an alliance with Georgia, Ukraine, Azerbaijan, and (from 1999) Uzbekistan (GUUAM). In 1998 he gave up his pro-Russian rhetoric and commenced rapprochement with Western Europe and Romania, stressing the independence of Moldova. In 1998 he lost the support of the parliamentary majority. In 1999 he won support for the extension of presidential powers in a referendum that the Constitutional Court found contradicted the constitution. In 2000 the parliament, united against Lucinschi, transformed Moldova into a parliamentary republic. In early 2001 conflicts in the parliament made it possible for Lucinschi to dissolve it and to announce new parliamentary elections in which the Party of Moldovan Communists (Partidul Comunist al Republicii Moldova [PMC]) won an absolute parliamentary majority. The bloc Republic, supporting Lucinschi, was completely defeated. On 7 April 2001 Lucinschi resigned from the presidency. (LW)

Sources: Aleksander Rahr, ed., *A Biographical Directory of 100 Leading Soviet Officials* (Boulder, Colo., 1990); Józef Darski, *Rumunia: Historia, współczesność, konflikty narodowe* (Warsaw, 1995); *Dictionar Enciclopedic*, vol. 4 (Bucharest, 2001); www.cidob.org; Bugajski; www.rulers.com.

LUDZHEV Dimitur (27 March 1950, Burgas), Bulgarian politician, economist, and sociologist. After graduating from the Karl Marx Economic Institute in Sofia, Ludzhev worked in the regional apparatus of the Communist Youth Union and later in its central headquarters. He lectured at Sofia University and was a researcher at the Institute of History of the Bulgarian Academy of Sciences (1976–83). In 1983 he went on scholarship to Poland, and in 1989 and 1995, to the United States. In 1988 Ludzhev joined the Club for the Support of Glasnost and Perestroika, led by **Zhelyu Zhelev**, and in the June 1990 elections he won a mandate on behalf of the Union of Democratic Forces (Sayuz na Demokratichnite Sili [UDF]). In December 1990 he became deputy prime minister for economic affairs in the government of **Dimitur Popov**, whose policy of "shock therapy" led to dramatic price increases and a decline in the standard of living. After the parliamentary elections of October 1991, won by the UDF, Ludzhev became minister of national defense. In May 1992 he stepped down as a result of an illegal arms sale in which he was involved.

In the spring of 1993 Ludzhev left the UDF and founded the New Policy Center (NPC). In the parliament his group was called the New Choice (Now Izbor). The NPC program favored negotiations with striking trade unions and was quite popular for some time as an alternative to the government of **Filip Dimitrov**, which introduced socially painful reforms. Moreover, Ludzhev remained on friendly terms with President Zhelev. After the government of **Luben Berov** resigned, in June 1993 Zhelev asked Ludzhev to form a new cabinet, but he failed to accomplish this mission. In the parliamentary elections of December 1994 the NPC was defeated, winning only 1.5 percent of the vote. On the eve of the 1997 elections Ludzhev began working with the (Turkish) Movement for Rights and Freedoms of **Ahmed Dogan**, and, along with a few small groups, he established the Alliance for National Salvation. Ludzhev became its deputy chairman and won a parliamentary seat. He opposed the UDF government of **Ivan Kostov**, and he played no major role. In July 1998 Ludzhev joined the Liberal Democratic Coalition, aiming at winning local elections, but a lack of cooperation with his main allies—Zhelev and Dogan—caused the coalition to fail. (AG)

Sources: Raymond Detrez, *Historical Dictionary of Bulgaria* (Lanham, Md., 1997); Jerzy Jackowicz, *Bułgaria od rządów komunistycznych do demokracji parlamentarnej 1988–1991* (Warsaw, 1992); www.omda.bg/engl/personalia/ludjev_engl.htm; www.icn.bg/bgnews/pointarticles/liberalunion/en.htm; www.online.bg/politics/who/govern/assemblies/pgdps.htm,

LUKÁCS György (13 April 1885, Budapest–5 June 1971, Budapest), Hungarian philosopher, theoretician of Marxism, and politician. Lukács was the son of a credit bank director of Jewish origin. After graduating from high school, in 1902 Lukács became an auditor in law at the University of Budapest. In 1906 he earned his doctoral degree in Kolozsvár (now Cluj in Romania), and subsequently, until 1907, he studied in Berlin. Lukács was a student of Max Weber. In 1908 his work on the history of modern drama won the Kisfaludy Society Prize. In 1910 his first book, a volume of essays, was published: *Lélek és formák* (Soul and form; 1974). Until 1911 Lukács lived mainly in Berlin, and from 1912 he lived in Heidelberg for five years (except for brief intervals). Between the fall of 1915 and the summer of 1916 Lukács did his military service in the office that censored letters in Budapest. In November 1917 he moved to Budapest, and in December 1918 he joined the Communist Party of Hungary. In February 1919 he became a member of the party's illegal Central Committee (CC), and on 1 March he became one of the editors of *Vörös Újság*.

From the moment the Hungarian Soviet Republic (HSR) was proclaimed on 21 March 1919, Lukács was a deputy people's commissar, and on 3 April he became the people's commissar for education. In May and June he was a political commissar in one of the divisions of the Hungarian Red Army. After the fall of the HSR, in August 1919 Lukács went into exile in Vienna. In 1920 he became a member of the provisional CC of the Hungarian Communist Party that was active in Vienna. In October 1921, as a result of factional strife, he left the CC. In 1921 he attended the Third Congress of the Communist International in Moscow. In 1923 he published *History and Class Consciousness* (English edition in 1971), a work on the history of class consciousness that was condemned by the Comintern. It was only in June 1926 in Berlin that Lukács was again coopted into the CC. In 1929 his program project, *Blum-tézisek* (Blum's theses), was rejected by the Central Committee. These theses set as an aim the "democratic dictatorship of peasants and workers," instead of the "dictatorship of the proletariat." At the Second Congress of the Communist Party of Hungary in 1930 Lukács was again expelled from the CC. He began to work in the Marx-Engels-Lenin Institute in Moscow. From the summer of 1931 he again lived in Berlin. In March 1933 he returned to Moscow, where he was a researcher in various scientific institutes. After the German attack against the USSR, Lukács was arrested by the NKVD but was soon released, having conducted an ideological self-criticism. At the end of 1941 he was transferred from Moscow to Tashkent, and in 1943 he was allowed to return to Moscow with his family.

In August 1945 Lukács again returned to Budapest, where in his absence he had been appointed a deputy to the Provisional National Assembly. In 1949 he became a member of parliament. He resigned his seat in December 1951, but in 1953 he again became an MP. From 1945 Lukács lectured at Budapest University and dealt with cultural policy. From 1948 he was a full and honorary member of the Hungarian Academy of Sciences and was also elected to the presidium of the academy. During the so-called Lukács Debate in 1949–50, the crux of which was Lukács's understanding of democracy, Lukács was forced to carry out an open self-criticism. At an extraordinary conference of the CC of the Hungarian Workers' Party between 23 and 24 October 1956 Lukács was elected a member of the CC. Between 27 October and 3 November he was minister of people's education in the government of **Imre Nagy**. On 31

October 1956 he became a member of the committee that prepared the founding congress of the Hungarian Socialist Workers' Party (HSWP). Lukács opposed Hungary's withdrawal from the Warsaw Pact. Along with Nagy, on 4 November Lukács asked for asylum in the Yugoslav Embassy. On 18 November he left the embassy, was arrested by the Russians, and was interned in Romania.

In April 1957 Lukács and his wife were allowed to return to Hungary, and no legal proceedings were instituted against him. In 1958 he retired. His works were published in the West. In 1967 Lukács again became a member of the Communist Party. Under the influence of the events of 1968 in Czechoslovakia, he submitted a study to the CC of the HSWP. In this study, he called "Socialist democracy" a real alternative to Stalinism. In the late 1960s Lukács began writing *A társadalmi lét ontológiájáról* (1976; *Ontology of Social Being*, 1980). In 1989 his memoirs were published: *Megélt gondolkodás: Életrajz magnószalagon* (Life memoirs: A biographical record). (JT)

Sources: *Magyar Életrajzi Lexikon*, vol. 3 (Budapest, 1985); *Biographisches Lexikon*, vol. 3; *The Times*, 5 June 1971; George Lichtheim, *György Lukács* (Munich, 1971); Fritz Raddatz, *György Lukács* (Reinbeck bei Hamburg, 1972); Tibor Hanák, *Lukács was anders* (Meisenheim/Glan, 1973); Andrew Arato and Paul Breines, *The Young Lukács and the Origins of Western Marxism* (New York, 1979); *A magyar forradalom és szabadságharc enciklopédiája*, CD-ROM (Budapest, 1999).

LUKANOV Andrey (26 September 1938, Moscow–2 October 1996, Sofia), Bulgarian Communist activist. The son of **Karlo Lukanov**, Lukanov graduated from the Institute of International Relations in Moscow (1963). In 1957 he joined the Dimitrov Communist Youth League, and in 1966, the Bulgarian Communist Party (BCP). In 1976 he became a deputy member, and in December 1977 a member, of the BCP Central Committee (CC). After returning to Bulgaria, Lukanov worked in the Ministry of Foreign Affairs (1963–65), served as head of the International Organizations Department in the Ministry of Foreign Trade (1966–68), and was first secretary of Bulgaria's representation to the United Nations in Geneva (1969–72). From 1972 to 1976 he served as deputy minister of foreign trade. In July 1979 he became a deputy member of the Politburo and chairman of the Currency Commission of the BCP CC. From 17 June 1976 to 19 June 1986 Lukanov was deputy prime minister, and on 19 August 1987 he became first deputy prime minister in the government of **Georgi Atanasov**. From 1981 to 1986 he was Bulgaria's permanent representative to the Comecon in Moscow. From August 1987 to November 1989 he served as minister of foreign economic relations. From 1976 to 1996 he was a deputy to the National Assembly.

In the face of a crisis of the system, Lukanov was one of those who initiated the removal of **Todor Zhivkov** from power at the BCP CC Plenum on 10 November 1989. On 16 November Lukanov joined the CC Politburo and Secretariat, and the following day he became a member of the Council of State. From 2 February to 25 September 1990 he was a member of the Presidium of the Supreme Council of the Bulgarian Socialist Party (BSP), as the BCP was renamed. He later became BSP deputy chairman. He presided over a parliamentary committee established to investigate mismanagement and corruption; the committee prepared a report on the economic crisis in Bulgaria. On 5 February 1990 Lukanov became prime minister. Although he strove to establish a coalition government, he headed a one-party post-Communist government that failed to implement any reforms. On 22 December 1990 he was forced to resign under pressure from the trade unions and as a result of public discontent.

On 27 August 1991, after the unsuccessful coup in Moscow, Lukanov resigned as BSP deputy chairman in protest against the wavering policies of **Aleksandur Lilov**, chairman of the BSP. He subsequently helped to establish new capital investment groups in Bulgaria and, as a representative of a company called Multigroup, he coordinated natural gas trades with Russia. On 7 July 1992, upon the demand of the public prosecutor general, Lukanov was deprived of his parliamentary immunity and subsequently arrested on a charge of issuing grants to aid pro-Soviet Third World countries. He was released from prison on 3 December 1992. In 1996 Lukanov was shot and killed by a gunman in front of his house. In March 1997 the European Court of Human Rights in Strasbourg punished Bulgaria for the improper handling of this case by the Bulgarian prosecutorial services. The compensation was awarded to Lukanov's family. In 2000 the case was discontinued owing to a lack of suspects. Lukanov's publications include *Chetirideset godini sotsialisticheska vunshna turgoviia na NR Bulgariia* (Forty years of Socialist foreign trade of the Bulgarian People's Republic; 1985); *Za krizata* (About the crisis; 1992); *Sotsialnata demokratsiia: Alternativa za Bulgariia* (Social Democracy: An alternative for Bulgaria; 1992); and *Bulgarskata korida: Pismo ot "Razvigor"* (The Bulgarian corrida: Letters from "Razvigor"; 1993). (JJ)

Sources: *Entsiklopediya Bulgariya*, vol. 3 (Sofia, 1982); *Deputatite na VII Velikoto narodno subranie*, 1991; *Deloto "Lukanov"* (Sofia, 1993); Raymond Detrez, *Historical Dictionary of Bulgaria* (Lanham, Md., 1997); Nora Ananieva, *Andrei Lukanov v Parlamenta* (Sofia, 1998); Tasho Tashev, *Ministrite na Bulgariya 1879–1999: Entsiklopedichen spravochnik* (Sofia, 1999); Evgeniia Kalinova and Iskra Baeva, *Bulgarskite prekhodi 1944–1999* (Sofia, 2000); Angel Tsurakov, *Entsiklopediia. Pravitelstvata na Bulgariya: Khronologiia na politicheskiia zhivot 1879–2001* (Sofia, 2001).

LUKANOV Karlo (20 October 1897, Pleven–15 July 1982. Sofia), Bulgarian politician. The son of a Socialist activist, Lukanov joined the Union of Social Democratic Working Youth in 1913 and the Bulgarian Workers' Social Democratic Party (the so-called narrow Socialists) in 1917. In the same year he graduated from a school for reserve officers and then fought in World War I as an officer of the Twenty-sixth Artillery Regiment. After graduating in law from Sofia University in 1921, he worked as an attorney in Pleven. In 1921 he became a member of the Bulgarian Communist Party (BCP), and in 1923 he began working with the BCP Foreign Bureau. Lukanov was arrested for those activities and sentenced to four and a half years' imprisonment in 1925. Released under an amnesty in 1926, he emigrated to the Soviet Union at the beginning of 1927. From 1927 to 1936 Lukanov worked as a judge in Moscow. He belonged to the Soviet All-Union Communist Party (Bolsheviks) until 1944. He fought in the Spanish Civil War (1936–39) as chief of staff of the Twelfth International Brigade and head of the international brigades' training base in Albacete. After returning to Moscow, he worked for the Communist International. From 1941 to 1944 Lukanov was a journalist and anchorman with the Moscow-based Bulgarian-language radio station Khristo Botev. After returning to Bulgaria in October 1944, he became the director of Bulgarian Radio. In 1947 he became deputy chairman of the State Planning Commission, and in 1949, chairman of the Commission for Science, Arts, and Culture. Lukanov subsequently served as chairman of the State Planning Commission (until February 1952), deputy prime minister in the government of **Vulko Chervenkov** (until January 1954), ambassador to the Soviet Union and Mongolia and minister plenipotentiary to Finland (1954–56), deputy prime minister in the government of **Anton Yugov** (April 1956–February 1957), minister of foreign affairs (August 1956–November 1962), and ambassador to Switzerland (1962–64). From 1964 to 1982 he served as deputy chairman of the All-National Committee of Bulgarian-Soviet Friendship, and from 1976 to 1982, as a member of the National Council of the Fatherland Front. From 1950 to 1982 Lukanov was a deputy to the National Assembly. (JJ)

Sources: *Entsiklopediya Bulgariya*, vol. 3 (Sofia, 1982); Lazitch; *Narodni predstaviteli v Sedmo narodno subranie* (Sofia, 1982); Georgi Dimitrov, *Sychineniia*, vol. 15 (Sofia, 1989); Tasho Tashev, *Ministrite na Bulgariya 1879–1999: Entsiklopedichen spravochnik* (Sofia, 1999); Angel Tsurakov, *Entsiklopediya. Pravitelstvata na Bulgariya: Khronologiya na politicheskiia zhivot 1879–2001* (Sofia, 2001).

LUKASHENKA Alyaksandr (30 August 1954, Kopys, near Orsha), Belorussian Communist activist, dictator of Belarus. In 1971–75 Lukashenka studied at the Pedagogical Institute in Mogilev. From 1975 he was Komsomol secretary in a school in Shklov, and in 1975–77 he was an instructor in the political section of the Western Frontier Region of the Frontier Protection Force of the all-Soviet KGB in Brest. From 1977 he was Komsomol secretary of the Mogilev town administration and an instructor in its executive committee. In 1978–80 he worked as secretary of Znaniye, a political propaganda society in Shklov. In 1979 he joined the CPSU. In 1982–83 he was deputy chairman of the Udarnik Kolkhoz in the Shklov region, and from 1983 to 1985 he was deputy director of the building materials combine in Shklov. In 1985 he graduated extramurally from the Belorussian Agricultural Academy and became party secretary of a kolkhoz in the Shklov region. From 1987 to 1990 he headed the Gorodyets Sovkhoz in this region.

During the election of Soviet deputies in 1989 Lukashenka lost to the then chairman of the Council of Ministers of the Belorussian SSR, **Vyacheslav Kebich**. Lukashenka took part in a few rallies of the Belorussian National Front. Elected to the Belorussian Supreme Council in 1990, in 1991 he co-founded Communists of Belorussia for Democracy, whose aim it was to create alternative structures in the Communist Party. Lukashenka criticized the Central Committee of the Communist Party of Belorussia for "detaching itself from the masses." His rhetoric was emotionally charged, appealing to the common folk. He condemned the nomenklatura for its appropriation of party and state assets, and he gained support among democratic journalists. On 25 August 1991 he signed a motion for the dismissal of the chairman of the Supreme Council of the Belorussian SSR, **Mikalay Dziamantsiey. Stanislau Shushkevich** was elected in his place. During the voting Lukashenka entered the hall carrying the red-and-white banner of Belarus. During the ratification of the agreement on the Commonwealth of Independent States Lukashenka abstained from voting, but he later claimed to have voted against it. In July 1993 he took the lead of a provisional parliamentary commission to investigate the economic activities of republican and local party structures. In November 1993 he announced the findings of this commission: the chairman of the Supreme Council, the prime minister, and a number of other leaders were accused of embezzlement. On 25 January 1994 Lukashenka gained a Communist majority on a motion to dismiss Shushkevich.

In the presidential elections of July 1994 Lukashenka won in the second round, having promoted the themes of social justice and the combating of corruption. In 1994–99 he intensified dictatorial policies. In December 1994, when the MP **Siarhiey Antonchik** announced a report on corruption in the administration, Lukashenka banned its publication. In January 1995 he announced a decree on the Office of Presidential Protection, providing it with the right to invigilate the opposition. In April 1995 he ordered special services to remove nineteen opposition MPs who were on a hunger strike against the tariff union with Russia, a referendum on national symbols, and the introduction of Russian as a second official language in Belarus. The referendum was held on 14 May 1995, confirming changes proposed by Lukashenka. As a result, Belarus returned to the symbols of the Belorussian SSR but without the hammer and sickle. On 24 November 1996 Lukashenka organized another referendum that was an outright violation of the constitution; therefore no serious international organization recognized its results. (Among other things, a citizen allegedly gave up his interest in the sources of financing of the ruling group.) A new version of the constitution was prepared, and a pseudo-parliament was convened to rubber-stamp the presidential decrees. In 1997–98 Lukashenka carried out an authoritarian and anti-market economic reform. Local authorities were banned from economic activity, and 70 percent of private firms were also banned. The authorities gained the right to confiscate private property without court procedures. Repression of the opposition became a permanent mode of governance, and the independent press was constantly threatened and fined for spreading "false information." Private radio and television stations were not allowed to operate.

Lukashenka isolated Belarus from abroad and limited its sovereignty. When in September 1995 a military helicopter shot down an American balloon and its two pilots were killed, instead of apologizing, Lukashenka fell back on the old Cold War rhetoric. On 17 June 1998 representatives of twenty-two embassies were asked to move to new locations. Ambassadors from the European Union and the United States left Belarus for a couple of months. On 2 April 1996 and again in 1997 Lukashenka and Russian president Boris Yeltsin signed agreements on the formation of the Union of Belarus and Russia (UBR), and on 25 December 1999 they signed an agreement on the "unification" of the two countries. From 2000 Lukashenka was chairman of the UBR State Supreme Council. He financed Russian strategic military bases, including an anti-rocket command, from the Belorussian budget. In May 1999 Lukashenka suppressed attempts to organize free presidential elections. During the campaign, hundreds of opposition activists were arrested, including one of the candidates, **Mikhail Chyhir**. After the elections, in August 1999 the chairman of the Supreme Council of Belarus,

Syamyon Sharetsky, left the country, fearing for his life. In September 1999 the chairman of the Central Electoral Commission, **Viktar Hanchar**, disappeared. From 20 July 1999 Lukashenka exercised presidential power without a constitutional foundation, quoting the results of the 1996 referendum, which, however, did not include the issue of an extension of the presidential term in office. (AS/SA)

Sources: *Belarus: Encyklapedychny davednik* (Minsk, 1995); Siergiej Owsiannik and Jełena Striełkowa, *Władza a społeczeństwo: Białoruś 1991–1998* (Warsaw, 1998); Yanka Zaprudnik, *Belarus na histarychnykh skryzavanyakh* (Minsk, 1996); *Tsentrum Karta, Archiu naynoushaye historii, Demakratychnaja apazytsia Belarusi 1956–1991. Dawiednik* (Minsk, 1999); Volha Paulava, *Syklouskiya strastsi* (Moscow, 1999); David R. Marples, *Belarus: A Denationalized Nation* (Amsterdam, 1999); Bugajski.

ŁUKASZEWICZ Jerzy (24 September 1931, Warsaw–18 July 1983, Warsaw), Polish Communist activist. In his youth Łukaszewicz worked as a blue-collar laborer. From 1949 he was active in the (Communist) Union of Polish Youth, and from 1951 he belonged to the (Communist) Polish United Workers' Party (Polska Zjednoczona Partia Robotnicza [PUWP]). In 1956 he started to work at the Nowotko Factory in Warsaw. In 1957–60 he was deputy head of the Department of Organization of the Central Committee (CC) of the Union of Socialist Youth (Związek Młodzieży Socjalistycznej [ZMS]), and in 1960–62 he was first secretary of the ZMS Warsaw Committee. Later he worked in the PUWP apparatus. Until 1964 Łukaszewicz headed a department in the Warsaw PUWP Committee. Later he was first secretary of the Wola Quarter PUWP Committee, and from 1969, the Warsaw Provincial PUWP Committee. From June 1964 a deputy member and from November 1968 a member of the PUWP CC, Łukaszewicz was close to the so-called partisan faction of **Mieczysław Moczar**. He graduated from the Higher School of Social Sciences at the PUWP CC. During the events of December 1970 Łukaszewicz declared himself in favor of **Edward Gierek**, so in December 1971 he joined the CC Secretariat, and in January 1972 he became head of the Department of Propaganda, Press, and Publications of the PUWP CC. From March 1972 he was also an MP. From December 1975 he was a deputy member and from February 1980 a member of the Politburo of the PUWP CC. Responsible for ideology, in the 1970s Łukaszewicz was a key engineer of cultural policies. In this role he became known as narrow-minded and dogmatic, personally supervising the loyalty of artists and scholars and penalizing their disobedience. According to Łukaszewicz's own assessment in 1981, he held the press, radio, and television in a stranglehold. In this connection he had a very bad reputation in cultural circles. As a result of the Baltic Coast strikes, as early as August 1980 Łukaszewicz was dismissed from the CC Secretariat and Politburo; in October 1980, from the CC; and in December 1980, he gave up his parliamentary mandate. (WR)

Sources: Mołdawa; Zbigniew Błażyński, *Towarzysze zeznają: Z tajnych archiwów Komitetu Centralnego* (London, 1987); Andrzej Albert [Wojciech Roszkowski], *Najnowsza historia Polski 1914–1993*, vol. 2 (Warsaw, 1993).

LUKOV Khristo (1887, Varna–13 February 1943, Sofia), Bulgarian general and politician. Lukov graduated in military studies in Sofia in 1907. He quickly advanced, and during World War I, already a general, he commanded the Second Army on the Macedonian front. In 1924 he was appointed commander of the School of Artillery, and in 1928–34 he headed the Department of Education at the Ministry of War. In 1932 Lukov founded the Union of Bulgarian National Legions, an extreme rightist organization with an anti-Turkish and anti-Semitic program. From November 1934 to January 1935 Lukov was minister of war in the cabinet of **Kimon Georgiev**. Although he initially favored the Zveno group, he later changed his mind and supported Tsar **Boris III**, helping him gain control of the army. Lukov declared his loyalty to the monarch, but the legionnaire movement was suspended in January 1936 and went underground. Fearing that Lukov had excessively close contacts with the Nazis, the tsar dismissed him from command in January 1938. Later Lukov tried to draw closer to **Aleksandur Tsankov**, aiming at a unification of the extreme right, but to no avail. During World War II, the Third Reich used Lukov as a means of pressure on Boris III. Lukov himself planned to gain power with German help, but he was assassinated. According to one version, the assassins were the Communists; according to another, they were the followers of Zveno, while a third version points to the agents of the tsar. (WR)

Sources: Philip Rees, *Biographical Dictionary of the Extreme Right since 1890* (New York, 1990); Z. Kolev, *Suyuz na Bulgarskite Natsionalni Legioni* (Sofia, 1976); Marshall Lee Miller, *Bulgaria during the Second World War* (Stanford, 1975); John D. Ball, *The Bulgarian Communist Party* (Stanford, 1985).

LUKŠA Juozas (1921, Juodbudžiai–September 1951, near Prienai), anti-Soviet Lithuanian partisan leader. Lukša graduated from a high school in Kaunas. He was arrested when the Red Army seized Lithuania in 1940. Released after the outbreak of the German-Soviet war in June 1941, he commenced architectural studies in Kaunas and was also active in the anti-German underground. After the Red Army again occupied Lithuania in the summer of 1944, Lukša continued his studies, as well as his underground activities which were now directed against the Soviet authorities. In 1945, Lukša went into hiding, and at the beginning of 1946, along with his brother Stasys, he joined a forest-based partisan unit. In November 1946 he was appointed captain. In 1947 he secretly made his way, via Poland, to Scandinavia and then to Rome, where, as a special representative of the Lithuanian underground, he presented a letter to Pope Pius XII about the dire situation of Catholics in Lithuania under Soviet rule. Under the pseudonym "J. Daumantas," Lukša wrote *Partizanai už Geležinės Uždangos* (English translation: *Fighters for Freedom*, 1975) and published it in the United States. In it he described the Lithuanian resistance movement against communism. He also established contacts with the Lithuanian Liberation Committee in exile. At the end of 1950 Lukša returned to Lithuania and continued the military struggle against the Soviet authorities. He was killed during a battle against NKVD units. His father, five brothers, and eleven relatives were murdered in retaliation for his activities. Lukša became a legendary hero in the struggle for Lithuanian independence. (WR)

Sources: *EL*, vol. 3; N. E. Sūduis, *Vienų vieni* (Brooklyn, 1954); Zeznanie Grigorija Burlickiego, *Fourth Interim Report of the House of Representatives Select Committee on Communist Aggression* (Washington, D.C., 1954); Constantine R. Jurgėla, *Lithuania: The Outpost of Freedom* (St. Petersburg, Fla., 1976).

LUKYANENKO Lev (Levko) (24 August 1928, Khrypivka, Chernihiv region) Ukrainian dissident and politician. The son of a peasant, in 1944 Lukyanenko was drafted into the Red Army. Until 1950 he served, among other places, in the Soviet occupation zone in Austria and in the Caucasus. In 1951–53 Lukyanenko belonged to the Komsomol and then to the Communist Party. After completing law studies in Moscow in 1958, he worked in the propaganda apparatus in the Lviv region and then he worked in law. Disapproving of official policies toward collectivization, Lukyanenko decided to undertake underground activities. In 1959 he co-founded the Ukrainian Workers' and Peasants' Union (Ukraiinska Robotnicho-Selanska Spilka). At its first meeting on 7 November 1960, the founding members thought Lukyanenko's program was too radical, and on the eve of the second meeting, in January 1961, all the founders were arrested. In May 1961 in Lviv Lukyanenko was sentenced to death by firing squad, but the Supreme Court changed the verdict to fifteen years in prison. He served in Mordovian camps, where, along with representatives of the "generation of the 1960s" (*shestidesiatniki*)—that is, victims of the post-1965 arrests in the Ukraine—Lukyanenko became engaged in the defense of prisoners' rights. For organizing a strike in one of the Perm camps, in 1974 Lukyanenko was sent to Vladimir Prison and underwent a forced psychiatric examination. Released in 1976, he worked as an electrician. In September 1976 he joined the Ukrainian Helsinki Group. He reported to the Belgrade Conference on Security and Cooperation in Europe, sending information on the violation of human rights in the USSR. Arrested again in December 1977, Lukyanenko refused to testify and started a hunger strike. In June 1978 he was sentenced to ten years in camp and five years of forced settlement. He served in Sosnovka, Mordovia, and (from February 1980) Kuchino, near Perm. In December 1987 he was forced to settle in Berezivka in the Tomsk region in Siberia. In March 1988 he was elected chairman of the Ukrainian Helsinki Union (UHU) in absentia. Offered release on the condition that he emigrate, Lukyanenko refused and was released in November 1988.

In April 1990 Lukyanenko was elected chairman of the Ukrainian Republican Party (Ukraiinska Respublikanska Partiya [URP]), which was based on the UHU. He was also elected to the Supreme Council of the Ukrainian SSR and became deputy chairman of the People's Council, an opposition parliamentary group. He co-wrote the act of Ukrainian independence of 24 August 1991. In the presidential elections of December 1991 Lukyanenko won 4.5 percent of the vote. From May 1992 to November 1993 he was the first Ukrainian ambassador to Canada. He gave up this position in protest against government policies. From May 1992 he was an honorary URP chairman. In 1994 he led the electoral bloc Ukraiina, and in 1998–99 he represented the National Front, which coordinated right-wing parties. Lukyanenko received the St. Vladimir Order and a Ph.D. in law at the University of Alberta, Canada. He authored *Shcho dali?* (What next? 1989); *Spovid u kameri smertnykiv* (Confession on death row; 1991); *Za Ukraiinu, za yiyi volu . . .* (For the Ukraine, for its freedom . . . ; 1991); *Viruyu v Boha i v Ukraiinu* (I believe in God and in the Ukraine; 1991) *Ne dam zahynut Ukraiini!* (I will not let the Ukraine perish! 1994); *Narodzhennia nowoyi ery* (Birth of a new era; 1997); and *U kraiini klenowovo lystka* (In the land of the maple leaf; 1998). (TS)

Sources: *Encyclopedia of Ukraine*, vol. 3 (Toronto, 1993); *Visnyk represiy v Ukraiini* (New York, 1982); *Veesti iz SSSR*, vol. 1, 1978–81; Taras Kuzio and Andrew Wilson, *Ukraine: Perestroika to Independence* (Edmonton, 1994); Heorhiy Kasyanov, *Nezhodni: Ukraiinska intelihentsiya v rusi oporu 1960–80 rokiv* (Kiev, 1995); Anatoliy Rusnachenko, *Natsionalno-vyzvolnyi rukh v Ukraiini* (Kiev, 1998); Bohdan Nahaylo, *The Ukrainian Resurgence* (Toronto, 1999); Bugajski.

LULCHEV Kosta (9 March 1882, Oryakhovo–31 January 1965, Oryakhovo), Bulgarian Socialist politician. Lulchev joined the Bulgarian Workers' Social Democratic Party (BWSDP) in 1895. After its split in 1903 he followed the faction that supported an evolutionary change of the political system toward socialism—the so called broad Socialists. In 1913–31 Lulchev was an MP on behalf of the BWSDP, and in 1924–33 he was secretary of its Central Committee. In October 1944 he was elected secretary general of the party. Lulchev's election was a compromise in the course of the intensifying Sovietization of Bulgaria and a factional struggle among the Social Democrats, whose right wing, headed by **Krystyo Pastukhov**, opposed the Communists, while the left wing, led by Dimitur Neykov, demanded close cooperation with the Communists and on their terms. Lulchev supported cooperation with the Communists but with a separate identity for the Social Democrats. On 29 May 1945, the crypto-Communists of Neykov attempted to take over the leadership of the BWSDP and to merge the party with the Communist Party. Since the Communists managed to attract a part of the BWSDP leadership, Lulchev was forced to organize new party structures. On 10 June 1945 the Bulgarian Workers' Social Democratic (United) Party was created with Lulchev as its secretary general and **Gregor Cheshmedzhiev** as its chairman. Under pressure from Western countries, the new party was finally registered in September 1945.

In the campaign before the parliamentary elections Lulchev repeatedly protested the violations of the law by the Communists, and on 14 November 1945 he, along with Pastukhov, **Nikola Petkov**, and **Petur Stoyanov**, signed a memorandum to the regents and the prime minister demanding the resignation of the cabinet and a postponement of the elections. Lulchev also warned Western diplomats about what was happening, but he could not prevent repression nor the abuses of power. In the elections of November 1945 Lulchev won a seat in the parliament, where he protested the violation of democratic freedoms and defended his colleagues who had been arrested and sentenced on false grounds (among others, Pastukhov and **Cveti Ivanov**). After the arrest of the Peasant Party leader, Nikola Petkov, in 1947, Lulchev made dramatic appeals, pointing to the groundlessness of the accusations and the political nature of Petkov's trial. In July 1948 the Communists arrested Lulchev, by then the last opposition leader. After a show trial, in which, under the threat of a death sentence, Lulchev was forced to plead guilty, on 15 November 1948 he was sentenced to fifteen years in prison. He served eleven years of this sentence, in, among other places, the forced labor camps of Belene and Lovech. (AG)

Sources: *Entsiklopediya Bulgariya*, vol. 3 (Sofia, 1982); Hugh Seton-Watson, *The East European Revolution* (London,

1956); Jerzy Jackowicz, *Partie opozycyjne w Bułgarii 1944–1948* (Warsaw, 1997); Petur Kuzmanov, *Kosta Lulchev: Edin zhivot v sluzhbe na sotsialdemokratsiyata* (Sofia, 1998); www.fes.de/fes-publ/mitarbeiter/dauderstaedt/probe.html.

LUPESCU Magda Elena [née Wolff] (15 September 1895, Iaşi–28 June 1977, Estoril, Portugal), influential concubine and second wife of **Charles II**, the king of Romania. The daughter of a Jewish shopkeeper and a Romanian woman, in 1919 Lupescu married an officer in the Romanian Army who was promoted to the General Staff and moved with his wife to Bucharest in 1921. In 1923 they divorced, and she Romanized her maiden name to Lupescu (*lupu* in English means *wolf*). In 1924 Charles II started a romance with her, causing a court scandal. The next year he left with Lupescu for Italy and gave up his claims to the throne. Soon they settled in Paris, and in 1928 Charles formally divorced his Greek wife, Queen Helen. In 1930, in agreement with the head of the National Peasant Party, **Iuliu Maniu**, Charles returned to the throne on the condition that he break off his relationship with Lupescu. Nevertheless, he brought Lupescu with him to Bucharest and continued the relationship. Aiming at an authoritarian model of monarchy, Charles stirred up conflicts among and within the political parties, establishing a system based on his court camarilla, in which Lupescu played an important role. She had significant influence on Charles's political decisions and on his personnel policies. Acting behind the scenes, the camarilla became a new center of power in Romania, but the public did not welcome the royal concubine—because of her Jewish origins, among other reasons. Her name was frequently paraphrased into Lupeasca (She-Wolf). The political elite and upper echelons of officers, headed by General **Ion Antonescu**, held Charles and Lupescu responsible for the territorial concessions to the Soviet Union, Hungary, and Bulgaria in 1940, forcing Charles to abdicate and leave the country. He left along with Lupescu by a special train that included twelve cars of art objects from the royal palace; these were the national patrimony. In 1947 Charles and Lupescu married and settled in Portugal, where she lived until her death. (ASK)

Sources: Paul Quinlan, "Lupescu: Romania's Grey Eminence," *East European Quarterly*, 1994, no. 1; Ioan Scurtu, *Istoria României în Anii 1918–1940* (Bucharest, 1995); Ion Bulei, *Scurtă Istorie a Românilor* (Bucharest, 1996); www.uk-genealogy. uk/Database/D0021/I7090.html; lesmadeleines.free.fr/celebrites/ lupescu.htm.

LUTOSŁAWSKI Kazimierz (4 March 1880, Drozdów–5 January 1924, Drozdów), Polish Catholic priest, journalist, and politician. Lutosławski came from a landed gentry family and was the half-brother of **Wincenty Lutosławski**. He studied medicine in Germany and Switzerland, earning a Ph.D. at the University of Zurich in 1903. From 1909 to 1911 he studied at a seminary in Fribourg. Ordained in 1912, he earned a Ph.D. in theology two years later. While in Switzerland, Lutosławski became a member of the secret Union of Polish Youth–Zet and later a member of the National League (Liga Narodowa), which was the beginning of a long-term collaboration with Roman Dmowski. After returning to the Kingdom of Poland, Lutosławski organized village education, published articles in nationalist newspapers, and wrote books. He also helped to found the Polish scouting movement in the Russian and later in the Prussian partition of Poland. In 1914 he protested the militarization of the scouting movement; consequently, he came into conflict with the leadership of the movement.

In 1915, during World War I, Lutosławski was evacuated to Russia, where he was involved in scouting and organized the Polish school system. In 1916 he became a military chaplain to the Polish Rifle Brigade. He edited nationalist newspapers and published articles. He was politically active among the Polish émigrés. From August 1917 Lutosławski represented the National League in the Council of Polish Parties' Union (Rada Polska Zjednoczenia Międzypartyjnego) in Moscow, which hoped for the victory of the Allies. Along with his brothers, Marian and Józef, he supported the formation of Polish military forces. After the Bolsheviks arrested and then executed his brothers in the spring of 1918, Lutosławski went into hiding, shifting his activities to the Ukraine. After returning to Poland, he participated in the activities of the National Popular Union (Związek Ludowo-Narodowy [ZLN]). As an MP for the Podlasie region from 1919 to 1924, he gained a reputation as a fiery, aggressive, and controversial speaker and an active legislator. He also continued his journalistic and scouting activities. In 1920 he served as a military chaplain and was decorated with the Cross of Valor for his bravery in the battles against the Bolsheviks. Lutosławski died suddenly on his family estate in Drozdowo. His publications include *Hasła rewolucji w świetle nauki katolickiej* (Revolutionary demands in the light of Catholic teaching; 1919); *Teologia* (Theology, 3 vols.; 1919); and *Wychowanie młodzieży wobec współczesnych potrzeb i zadań* (The upbringing of youth and contemporary tasks; 1923). (MC)

Sources: *PSB*, vol. 18; Wojciech Wasiutyński, *Czwarte pokolenie: Szkice z dziejów Nacjonalizmu Polskiego* (London, 1982); Olaf Bergman, *Narodowa Demokracja wobec problematyki żydowskiej w latach 1918–1929* (Poznań, 1998); Władysław Pobóg-Malinowski, *Najnowsza historia polityczna Polski*, vols. 1–2 (London, 1983–86).

LUTOSŁAWSKI Wincenty (6 June 1863, Warsaw–28 December 1954, Kraków), Polish philosopher and educator. Lutosławski came from a landed gentry family and was the half-brother of Reverend **Kazimierz Lutosławski**. He studied chemistry at the polytechnic in Riga and then in Dorpat (Tartu), where he also took up philosophy. He subsequently studied Romance languages at the Ecole Pratique des Hautes Etudes in Paris. He published his M.A. thesis from Dorpat as *Erhaltung und Untergang der Staatsverfassungen nach Plato, Aristoteles und Machiavelli* (1888). He received a Ph.D. at the University of Helsinki for a dissertation about the individualistic worldview, published as *Über die Grundvoraussetzungen und Konsequenzen der individualistischen Weltanschauung* (1898). From 1890 to 1893 Lutosławski worked as an associate professor (*docent*) at the university in Kazan in Russia, studying Plato's logic. He also investigated Plato's ideas during a stay in London and while traveling through North America. Lutosławski succeeded in determining the chronology of Plato's dialogues, which facilitated the study and interpretation of the development of Plato's thought. In his work Lutosławski used a methodology developed by the Scottish philologist Lewis Campbell; Lutosławski improved upon it and named it stylometry. He published his findings in *O pierwszych trzech tetralogiach dzieł Platona* (On the first three tetralogies of Plato's works; 1896) and *The Origin and Growth of Plato's Logic with an Account of Plato's Style and the Chronology of His Writings* (London, 1897). The latter work consolidated his position as a philosopher.

From 1895 to 1905 Lutosławski lived mainly in Spain, where he developed an intellectual system based upon Platonic idealism and Polish Romantic messianism. This was a spiritualist idea of progressive reincarnation inspired by the poetry of Juliusz Słowacki. According to Lutosławski, the world was based on a multi-level hierarchy of souls, from individual souls through collective (national and all-human) to the universal (cosmic) soul. The Polish national soul played quite an important role in this hierarchy. Lutosławski presented this theory in *Seelenmacht: Abriss einer zeitgemäßen Weltanschauung* (1899). From 1899 to 1900 Lutosławski lectured at the Jagiellonian University in Kraków and later at the universities in Lausanne and Geneva in Switzerland. From 1904 to 1906 he worked at the University College of London. In 1907 and 1908 he traveled throughout the United States, giving lectures at all major intellectual centers. Later, he lectured in Warsaw for one year. He also traveled throughout the territories of the former Polish-Lithuanian Commonwealth and visited émigré communities, giving lectures in which he promoted his philosophy among wider circles. In 1913 he settled in Savoy and lectured at the University of Geneva. At that time he published *Rozwój potęgi woli przez psychofizyczne ćwiczenia* (The development of willpower through psychophysical exercise; 1910) and *Volonté et Liberté* (Will and freedom; 1913).

At the beginning of the twentieth century Lutosławski became attracted to the National League (Liga Narodowa). He developed close contacts with **Roman Dmowski**, Jan Ludwik Popławski, and **Zygmunt Balicki**. Their collaborative efforts were not very harmonious, though, and Lutosławski founded his own esoteric group of people interested in temperance and the spiritual aspect of nationalist thought. This group published the periodical *Eleusis*. However, in 1912 Lutosławski severed ties with them. During World War I he resumed his contacts with members of the National Democratic Party. At that time he was a very active current affairs commentator, writing in several languages. He supported Polish diplomats during the 1919 peace negotiations. In 1920 he became a professor at Stefan Batory University in Wilno (Vilnius). He strove to reconcile his university work with his educational passion, which involved frequent travels throughout Poland. He tirelessly published works in which he developed increasingly eccentric theories of the soul in a futurological context. These works had clearly nationalist overtones. According to Lutosławski, the Polish national spirit, imbued with freedom, would vanquish the German and Jewish spirits, which had poisoned the world with the doctrines of materialism and determinism. He covered these issues in *The World of Souls* (1924), *Nieśmiertelność duszy* (The immortality of the soul; 1925), and *Knowledge of Reality* (1934), as well as in other works. In 1931 Lutosławski retired and settled in Dzięgielów, near Cieszyn. In 1933 he published his memoirs, *Jeden łatwy żywot* (One easy life). During World War II and the German occupation he initially lived in Dzięgielów, and then he moved to Kraków. From 1946 to 1947 Lutosławski taught philosophy at the Jagiellonian University. (MC)

Sources: *PSB*, vol. 18; Wojciech Wasiutyński, *Czwarte pokolenie: Szkice z dziejów Nacjonalizmu Polskiego* (London, 1982); Stanisław Kozicki, *Historia Ligi Narodowej* (London, 1964); Wit Jaworski, *Eleuteryzm i mesjanizm: U źródeł filozofii społecznej Wincentego Lutosławskiego* (Kraków, 1994).

LUTOSŁAWSKI Witold (25 January 1913, Warsaw–7 February 1994, Warsaw), Polish composer, pianist, and conductor. Lutosławski came from a landed gentry family aligned with the national movement. His father Józef, executed by the Bolsheviks in 1918, had dedicated to Lutosławski his posthumously published book, *Chleb i Ojczyzna* (Bread and the Fatherland). At home, Lutosławski was imbued with a love of classical music, particularly that of Frédéric Chopin and Ludwig van Beethoven. He began taking piano lessons when he was a child. He composed his first work at the age of nine. In 1932 he began studying at the Frédéric Chopin Music Academy in Warsaw. He studied composition with Witold Maliszewski and piano with Jerzy Lefeld. In the 1930s he was greatly influenced by Igor Stravinsky and Albert Roussel. In 1937 he graduated from the Warsaw Conservatory. He subsequently served in a communications officers' cadet school in Zgierz for one year. It was then he completed the *Symphonic Variations*. Lutosławski's further studies in Paris were interrupted by the war. In September 1939 he fought on the front lines. He was taken prisoner by the Germans but managed to escape. During the German occupation Lutosławski was active in various cultural initiatives of the underground resistance movement. To earn a living, he played piano in cafés. At that time he wrote *Variations on a Theme by Paganini* for two pianos (1941) and *Symphony No. 1* (1941–47). His *Melodie Ludowe* (Folk melodies; 1945) for string orchestra did not cause protests by the Communist authorities, but his other works were banned. During the Stalinist period Lutosławski was accused of "formalism." His other works of that period include *Little Suite for Orchestra* (1951), *Concerto for Orchestra* (1954), and *Dance Preludes for Clarinet and Piano* (1954), but they were not performed during his life. He earned a living by writing popular songs under pseudonyms.

Lutosławski's creative work developed greatly after October 1956, especially after the authorities of the Polish People's Republic stopped combating contemporary music and the annual Warszawska Jesień (Warsaw Autumn) festivals were launched in Warsaw. The *Funeral Music* for string orchestra (1958), an innovative composition dedicated to the memory of Béla Bartók, brought Lutosławski international recognition and the prize of UNESCO's Tribune Internationale des Compositeurs. Lutosławski experimented with asynchronous compositions and was one of the first composers to employ aleatory methods—as, for example, in *Venetian Games* for orchestra (1961). Most of his subsequent works, though, were harmonically organized and monumental; these include *Symphony No. 2* (1967), *Symphony No. 3* (1983), and *Symphony No. 4* (1993), and concertos for cello (1970) and for oboe and harp (1980). Lutosławski followed this trend in writing compositions for male voices and choral music for poems by Henri Michaux (1963). Lutosławski educated many students in Poland and abroad. He was also active as a conductor of his own music. He worked with many celebrities, including Mstislav Rostropovich, Sir Peter Pears, Anne-Sophie Mutter, and Dietrich Fischer-Dieskau. He received many awards, including the UNESCO Prize (1959, 1968), the French order of Commandeur des Arts et des Lettres (1982), the Grawemeyer Award (1985), the Royal Philharmonic Society Gold Medal (1986), the Polar Music Prize (Sweden, 1993), and the Inamori Foundation Prize (Japan, 1993). Posthumously he received the International Music Award (1994). From the 1970s on, Lutosławski was spiritually aligned with the democratic opposition. (MC)

Sources: *New Encyclopedia Britannica*, vol. 7 (Chicago, 1990); *The Times*, 10 February 1994; Bohdan Pociej, *Lutosławski a wartość muzyki* (Kraków, 1976); *The Norton/Grove Concise Encyclopedia of Music* (New York, 1994); Stanley Alexandrowicz, "A Transcription and Analysis of Witold Lutoslawski's Melodie Ludowe," Ph.D. diss., Manhattan School of Music, New York, 1993; Irina Nikolaskaya, *Conversations with Witold Lutosławski, 1987–92* (Stockholm, 1994); Charles Rodman Rae, *The Music of Lutoslawski* (London, 1994); Jadwiga Paja-Stach, *Witold Lutosławski* (Kraków, 1996); Zbigniew Skowron, *Lutoslawski Studies* (New York, 2001); Stanisław Będkowski, *Witold Lutoslawski* (Westport, Conn., 2001).

LUTSKEVICH Anton (29 January 1884, Šiauliai–1946, Kazakhstan?), Belorussian political activist, ideologue of the national revival movement, and journalist. Lutskevich came from a noble family and was the younger brother of **Ivan Lutskevich**. After graduating from high school in Minsk (1902), he began studying at the Department of Mathematics and Physics of the University of Dorpat (Tartu). In 1902 he co-founded the Belorussian Revolutionary Party. After a split within this party, Lutskevich, along with his brother, founded the Belorussian Revolutionary Hromada in 1903. In 1904 he was arrested for distributing anti-tsarist literature. He took part in the 1905–7 revolution and was one of the founders of the Belorussian newspapers *Nasha Dola* and *Nasha Niva* in 1906. In 1907 he moved to Vilna (Wilno, Vilnius), where he helped to establish a Belorussian library and reading room. In 1915 Lutskevich became president of the Belorussian Committee for Aid to War Victims and chairman of the Belorussian National Committee. In 1916 he began publishing the periodical *Homan* in Vilna. During the February 1917 revolution and the Bolshevik revolution in 1917, his articles helped to consolidate the independence movement. Lutskevich advocated the establishment of a confederation of the grand duchy of Lithuania, which would include Lithuania, Latvia, and Belorussia. He discussed the issue with representatives of the Polish, Jewish, Lithuanian, and Latvian communities. At the beginning of 1918 he became president of the Vilna Belorussian Council and called for the establishment of a Belorussian state within its ethnic borders.

After the Germans occupied most of Belorussia, the Belorussian People's Republic (BPR) was proclaimed on 25 March 1918 as a result of an agreement with a similar council in Minsk. The weakening of the German position in the summer of 1918 and controversies over the extent of Belorussian dependence on the Germans undermined the union of the BPR government. In September 1918 the

BPR Council appointed Lutskevich prime minister and minister of interior. He strove for international recognition of the BPR and established diplomatic relations with nineteen countries. In December 1918, the BPR government managed to escape the Bolsheviks, moving to Hrodna (Grodno). In January 1919 Lutskevich issued a protest against the entry of Polish troops into the Białystok and Bielsk districts, which, according to the BPR authorities, were part of the Belorussian state. After the Hrodna and Vilna regions were under the control of the Polish Army, Lutskevich went to Berlin, where he insisted that the Belorussian issue be put on the agenda of the Paris Peace Conference. In Paris, he met the Polish prime minister, **Ignacy Paderewski**, with whom he agreed on a plan of cooperation between the Polish and Belorussian governments. Arrested by the Polish authorities on his way back to Belorussia via Warsaw in September 1919, Lutskevich was released at the end of November; by then he had lost most of his supporters in the BPR Council.

At the end of February 1920 Lutskevich moved to Vilna, where he resumed publishing *Nasha Niva*. He also established the Belorussian National Committee and the Ivan Lutskevich Belorussian Museum. He worked as a teacher at the Belorussian Gymnasium in Vilna. He organized the parliamentary elections of 1922, in which eleven representatives of the Belorussian communities won seats in the Polish Assembly and Senate. In 1925 he became a member of the Belorussian Peasants' and Workers' Hromada. Accused of cooperation with the Communists and arrested in October 1927, Lutskevich was acquitted after a few months in prison. In 1930 he established a new group, the Central Union of Belorussian Cultural and Economic Organizations (Tsentrsayuz), which received financial help from the Polish authorities. This union published newspapers for peasant communities. Tsentrsayuz and Lutskevich were generally ostracized for their contacts with the Polish authorities. In 1933 Lutskevich lost his job as a teacher at the Belorussian Gymnasium and withdrew from public life. Arrested on 30 September 1939 by the Soviet authorities, he was sentenced by a NKVD court to six years in prison. According to the official version, he died in Kazakhstan in 1946. Lutskevich wrote a great number of articles and several analytical works on Belorussian history, including *Ekonomiczna ewolucja i ruch białoruski* (Economic evolution and the Belorussian movement; 1917); *Polskaya akupatsyia u Belarusi* (The Polish occupation of Belorussia; 1920); *Èvaliutsyia belaruskay adradzhènskay idèaliohii i iae adliustravanne u litaratury* (The evolution of Belorussian revival ideology and its reflection in literature; 1926); and *Za 25 hadou: 1903–1928* (Twenty-five years: 1903–1928; 1928). (EM)

Sources: *Entsyklapiedyia historyi Bielarusi*, vol. 4 (Minsk, 1994); Nicholas P. Vakar, *Belorussia: The Making of a Nation* (Cambridge, Mass., 1956); Aleksandra Bergman, *Sprawy białoruskie w II Rzeczypospolitej* (Warsaw, 1984); Vitaut Kipel and Zora Kipel, eds., *Byelorussian Statehood* (New York, 1988); Jerzy Turonek, *Białoruś pod okupacją niemiecką* (Warsaw, 1993); J. Januszkiewicz, "Lutskevichy," in *Shliakham hadou: Histarychna-litaraturny zbornik* (Minsk, 1994); Jan Zaprudnik, *Historical Dictionary of Belarus* (Lanham, Md., 1998).

LUTSKEVICH Ivan (9 June 1881, Šiauliai–20 August 1919, Zakopane, Poland), Belorussian social activist, ethnographer, and archaeologist. The brother of **Anton Lutskevich**, Lutskevich graduated from the Moscow Archaeological Institute. At the beginning of the twentieth century, along with **Vatslau Ivanouski**, he organized the Belorussian People's Education and Culture Group in St. Petersburg. In 1902 he helped to establish the Belorussian Revolutionary Party, and in 1903, the Belorussian Revolutionary Hromada. In 1906 he was one of the founders of the newspapers *Nasha Dola* and *Nasha Niva*. During World War I he organized Belorussian schools in the Hrodna and Vilna regions. From his student days at a high school in Minsk, Lutskevich had collected exhibits and materials about the earliest history of Belorussia. Gradually, his collection became the basis for the establishment of the Belorussian Museum in Vilna (Wilno, Vilnius) in 1919. Along with his brother and **Vatslau Lastouski**, Lutskevich originated the concept of reconstructing the grand duchy of Lithuania, and from 1918 on he supported the declaration of independence by the Belorussian People's Republic. According to Lutskevich, the restoration of the Uniate (Greek Catholic) Church as the national church of the Belorussian people would be a chance to build a Belorussian state. As Belorussians associated Catholicism with Poland and the Orthodox Church with Russia, the Uniate Church would promote the development of Belorussian national consciousness. Later, this idea was often revived by Belorussian national activists. As a result of Lutskevich's efforts, the Belorussian issue was raised at international forums during conferences of nations in Stockholm and Lausanne in 1916, at which Lutskevich demanded an equality in relations among Belorussians, Ukrainians, Russians, and Poles through the establishment of national states within ethnic borders. At the end of his life Lutskevich suffered from tuberculosis. He died in Zakopane, where he went for treatment. A symbolic funeral was held for him in Vilnius in 1991. (EM)

Sources: *Pamiatsi Ivana Lutskevicha: U pershyia uhodki s'mertsi jaho* (Vilnius, 1920); Nicholas P. Vakar, *Belorussia: The Making of a Nation* (Cambridge, Mass., 1956); A. Kaval, "Ivan Lutskevich 1881–1919," *Niva*, 1981, no. 23; Vitaut Kipel and Zora Kipel, eds., *Byelorussian Statehood* (New York, 1988); Jerzy Turonek, *Białoruś pod okupacją niemiecką* (Warsaw, 1993); J. Januszkiewicz, "Lutskevichy," in *Shliakham hadou: Histarychna-litaraturny zbornik* (Minsk, 1994); Jan Zaprudnik, *Historical Dictionary of Belarus* (Lanham, Md., 1998).

LUX Josef (1 February 1956, Ústi at Orlici–22 November 1999 Seattle, Washington), Czech politician. Lux graduated in agriculture from Brno University in 1980, and then he managed a collective farm. He began his political activity in 1982, when he joined the Czechoslovak People's Party (Československá Strana Lidová [ČSL]); it was a way to avoid joining the Communist Party. Lux became seriously involved in politics only after the Velvet Revolution, when in January 1990 he was elected a deputy to the Federal Assembly of Czechoslovakia and in November 1990 became the leader of his party. After the elections of 1992 his party joined the parliament and the ruling coalition, and Lux assumed the post of deputy prime minister and minister of agriculture in the government of **Václav Klaus**. Lux gave his party a new profile. Under his leadership the party thrived, extending its name to the Christian Democratic Union–Czechoslovak People's Party (Krest'anska a Demokratická Unie–Československá Strana Lidová [KDU–ČSL]) and forming a rather stable (8–10 percent) electorate of Christian Democratic views. It paid off in the elections of 1996, when the KDU–ČSL was the only party in the coalition whose social support increased. At the same time Lux gained the reputation of an independent politician, often critical of his party's coalition partner, the Civic Democratic Party (Občanská Demokratická Strana [ODS]). The lack of acceptance of his political style and the obscure sources of finance for this party made Lux and the KDU–ČSL leave the coalition government on 29 November 1997, which caused its fall. At the beginning of December 1997 President **Václav Havel** entrusted Lux with forming a government, but he failed. In the provisional government of **Josef Tošovski**, which was formed in January 1998, Lux assumed the portfolio of minister of agriculture. After the early elections of 19–20 June 1998 the KDU–ČSL went into the opposition, and Lux disapproved of the political system of the Czech Social Democratic Party (Ceská Strana Sociálne Democratická [ČSSD]) and the ODS, accusing them of an attempt to eliminate other parties from the political scene. On 24 September 1998 Lux left all his party posts, announcing that he was suffering from leukemia. He died after postoperative complications. (PU)

Sources: *ČBS*; *Kdo byl kdo v našich dějinách ve 20. století*, vol. 1 (Prague, 1998); Eva Rolečková, *Josef Lux: Muž se světlem v srdci* (Prague, 2000).

LUXEMBURG Rosa, pseudonym "Róża Kruszyńska" (5 March 1870, Zamość–15 January 1919, Berlin, Germany), activist of the Polish and German workers' movements, theorist of socialism and the political economy. Born into the family of an assimilated Jewish merchant, Luxemburg spent her childhood in Warsaw, where she graduated from the Second Warsaw High School for Girls (1887). In 1888 she joined activists who were attempting to reestablish the Proletariat Party. Fearing arrest, she left for Zurich, where she studied the natural sciences and mathematics. After two years she transferred to the School of Law and Economics of Zurich University, where she received a Ph.D. for her dissertation, "Die industrielle Entwicklung Polens" (The industrial development of Poland), in 1897. In her dissertation, Luxemburg argued that it would be impossible to rebuild the Polish state owing to increasingly tight economic ties between the Kingdom of Poland and Russia. While a student, Luxemburg was active in Polish and Russian Socialist groups in Switzerland. In the conflict between supporters of Polish independence, who later formed the Polish Socialist Party (Polska Partia Socjalistyczna [PPS]), and supporters of the Russian Revolution, who called for abandoning the idea of an independent Poland, Luxemburg, as leader of the Social Democracy of the Kingdom of Poland (Socjaldemokracja Królestwa Polskiego [SDKP]) and the author of its ideological program, supported the latter group. She considered a national state to be a tool of exploitation and believed that the aim of world revolution was to improve the situation of the proletariat; consequently, she called for the abolition of borders altogether.

After completing her studies, Luxemburg settled in Berlin and worked with the Social Democratic Party of Germany (Sozialdemokratische Partei Deutschlands [SPD]). Her sharp speeches and non-German origins did not win her supporters. However, she soon became a leading spokesperson of the party's left wing, publishing *Sozialreform oder Revolution* (1899; *Reform or Revolution*, 1973), as well as articles in *Leipziger Volkszeitung*, an organ of the left wing. At the turn of the century, along with Marcin Kasprzak, Luxemburg attempted to break up the PPS in the Prussian partition by winning the support of members who represented a more internationalist attitude. When the Social Democracy of the Kingdom of Poland and Lithuania (Socjaldemokracja Królestwa Polskiego i Litwy [SDKPiL]) was founded in 1900, Luxemburg treated it with reserve at first, but, after program changes were introduced, she served as an SDKPiL delegate in the Bureau of the Second International from 1904 to 1918. In 1904 Luxemburg was briefly detained for insulting the German emperor. In her article "Organisationsfragen der russischen Sozialdemokratie" (Organizational questions of Russian Social Democracy) Luxemburg argued with Lenin, whom she accused of dictatorial leanings in the Russian Social Democratic Workers' Party (RSDWP).

After the outbreak of the 1905 revolution in Russia, Luxemburg went to Warsaw to participate in the struggle and was arrested. She managed to escape to Finland, where a conflict with Lenin was averted. She expressed herself in favor of Lenin's tactics, and at a 1907 congress of the RSDWP in London she sharply attacked the Mensheviks. Luxemburg advocated mass strikes as powerful tools with which to exert pressure upon state authorities (*Massenstreik, Partei und Gewerkschaften*, 1906; [*The Mass Strike, the Political Party, and the Trade Unions*; 1971]). Luxemburg's demands for mass action led to a sharp conflict with the SPD leadership, as well as with Karl Kautsky, who until then had been favorably disposed to her. As a result of this conflict, she was expelled from the editorial staff of *Leipziger Volkszeitung*. From 1907 to 1914 Luxemburg taught at the SPD school in Berlin, where she wrote *Einfuehrung in die Nationaloekonomie* (Introduction to political economy; 1925) and *Akkumulation des Kapitals* (1913; *The Accumulation of Capital*, 1951), in which she criticized the theses of Marx and Engels, emphasized the relationship between the activities of the state and the accumulation of capital, and described imperialism as a sort of passageway to Socialist society. She also published in the SDKPiL newspapers (*Czerwony Sztandar, Trybuna*, and *Nasza Sprawa*). After the SDKPiL split into two factions, one supporting the left wing of the SPD and the other supporting the Bolsheviks, Luxemburg supported the former faction. This led to a conflict with Lenin, who favored the latter faction and condemned her because she did not support his decision to expel the Mensheviks from the RSDWP and even attempted to impose arbitration by the International and the SPD on this issue.

In 1914 Luxemburg opposed the majority of the SPD, who had voted in the Reichstag in favor of war credits for the government. She founded a separate group within the party, Die Internationale, and sharply protested the war, which led to her imprisonment. While in prison, Luxemburg wrote *Die Kriese der deutschen Sotzialdemokratie* (1919; *The Crisis in the German Social Democracy*, 1969), which was distributed illegally. Freed from prison by the German Revolution at the end of November 1918, Luxemburg, supported by the Spartacus League, began to organize a Bolshevik-type revolution in Germany. She co-founded the Communist Party of Germany (CPG) and co-authored its program. According to the prevailing view, the Communist uprising of January 1919 in Berlin began against Luxemburg's recommendations because she realized that the chances for victory were slim. On 15 January 1919, during the persecutions after the uprising, Luxemburg was arrested, and while being transported to prison, she was murdered by German Freikorps troops. Her views were combated in the Communist movement as so-called Luxemburgism. Nonetheless, Luxemburg holds a place in the pantheon of the international revolutionary left. (AG)

Sources: *PSB*, vol. 18; Charles E. Rothwell, *Rosa Luxemburg and the German Social Democratic Party* (Stanford, 1942); Aleksander Kochański, *Róża Luksemburg* (Warsaw, 1976); Adam Ciołkosz, *Róża Luksemburg a rewolucja rosyjska* (Paris, 1961); Elzbieta Ettinger, *Rosa Luxemburg: A Life* (Boston, 1986); Richard Abraham, *Rosa Luxemburg: A Life for the International* (Oxford, 1989); Sebastian Haffner, *Niemiecka rewolucja 1918/1919* (Lublin, 1996).

LYAPCHEV Andrei (30 November 1866, Resen, Macedonia–8 November 1933, Sofia), Bulgarian politician. Lyapchev graduated from a high school in Plovdiv. In 1885 he volunteered to fight in the Serbo-Bulgarian war. He subsequently studied finance in Zurich and political economy in Paris and Berlin (until 1893). After returning to Bulgaria, he worked in the Ministry of Finance (1894–1905) and was engaged in journalism. At the end of the nineteenth century Lyapchev was active in the Bulgarian liberation movement in Macedonia. From 1885 to 1896 he edited the newspaper *Mlada Bulgariia*. He later founded, and from 1899 to 1905 edited, the newspaper *Reformi*, an organ of the Supreme Macedonian Committee. After joining the Democratic Party, Lyapchev became one of its leaders and held many ministerial posts. He served as minister of agriculture and commerce (January 1908–September 1910) and minister of finance (September 1910–March 1911 and June–November 1918) in the government of **Aleksandur Malinov** and as minister of war in the government of **Teodor Teodorov** (November 1918–May 1919). Lyapchev was the first Bulgarian civil minister of war since the country's liberation from the Turkish yoke. On 28 September 1918 Lyapchev headed the Bulgarian delegation that signed an armistice with the Entente at Salonika. He was elected a deputy to the fourteenth and sixteenth through twenty-third National Assemblies (1908–11 and 1913–33). An opponent of the Bulgarian Agrarian National Union (BANU), Lyapchev took part in an unsuccessful action organized by the Constitutional Bloc against the government of **Aleksandur Stamboliyski** (17 September 1922). Arrested along with other ministers of Malinov's cabinet after the failure of this action, in March 1923 Lyapchev was brought before the State Court, which was established to try those who had brought about the "second national catastrophe" in Bulgaria.

After the coup of 9 June 1923, which overthrew the government of Stamboliyski, Lyapchev was released and became one of the leaders of the newly established Democratic Alliance (DA). The collapse of the government of **Aleksandur Tsankov** offered Lyapchev a chance to take up the post of head of government and minister of the interior and health (4 January 1926–29 June 1931). In domestic policy, Lyapchev followed Tsankov's political line and tried to initiate a policy of reconciliation. He legalized the Bulgarian Workers' Party, which continued the activities of the outlawed Bulgarian Communist Party. In foreign policy, he sought rapprochement with Great Britain and tried to encourage foreign investments in Bulgaria. As a result of his efforts, Bulgaria was included in the stabilization plan of the Financial Committee of the League of Nations and secured a loan to facilitate the settlement of refugees in the region (1926) and a stabilization loan (1928). Owing to an economic crisis, the DA lost its position in the elections of June 1931, and Lyapchev resigned as prime minister. After the DA split in 1932, Lyapchev became the leader of a moderate faction of a movement that opposed Tsankov's Fascist program. (JJ)

Sources: *Entsiklopediya Bulgariya*, vol. 3 (Sofia, 1982); Tadeusz Wasilewski, *Historia Bułgarii* (Wrocław, 1988); Milen Kumanov and Tania Nikolova, *Politicheski partii, organizatsii i dvizheniia v Bulgariia i tekhnite lideri 1879–1999: Kratyk spravochnik* (Sofia, 1999); Tasho Tashev, *Ministrite na Bulgariia 1879–1999: Entsiklopedichen spravochnik* (Sofia, 1999); Veselin Tepavicharov, *Bulgarski dyrzhavnitsi i polititsi 1918–1947* (Sofia, 2000); Angel Tsurakov, *Entsiklopediia. Pravitelstvata na Bulgariia: Khronologiia na politicheski zhivot 1879–2001* (Sofia, 2001).

LYPA Yuriy (5 May 1900, Odessa–20 August 1944, Shutiv), Ukrainian writer. Because his father Ivan, a poet and minister of the Ukrainian National Republic, settled in Poland after World War I, Lypa graduated in medicine from the University of Poznań in 1929. Later he practiced medicine in Warsaw, becoming one of the key figures among Ukranian émigrés in Poland. In 1929 he founded a literary group, Tank. Lypa made his literary debut in 1919, and later he published three volumes of poetry—*Svitlist* (The light; 1925), *Surovist* (Severity; 1931), and *Viruyu* (I believe; 1938); a novel, *Kozaky v Moskovii* (Cossacks in Moscow; 1931); the collections of short stories *Notatnyk* (Notebook, 3 vols.; 1936–37) and *Kinnotchyk ta inshi opovidannia* (The horseman and other stories; 1946); and a collection of essays on Ukrainian literature, *Biyi za ukraiinsku literaturu* (Struggles for Ukrainian literature; 1935). In the 1930s Lypa contributed to the Lviv (Lwów) monthly, *Vistnyk*, edited by **Dmytro Dontsov**. Lypa's literary output was strongly connected with politics, and in the late 1930s he worked out a nationalist "Black Sea" doctrine. In 1938–41 he published a trilogy: *Pryznachennia Ukraiiny* (The fate of the Ukraine), *Chornomorska doktryna* (The Black Sea Doctrine), and *Rozpodil Rosiyi* (The disintegration of Russia). Lypa's theories were based on the assumption that race was a group of uniform psychological features. The survival of races was, in his opinion, determined by three factors: religion, morality, and a stable geopolitical orientation. In the case of the Ukraine it was to be based on the North–South, and not on the East–West, axis. According to Lypa, the "fate" of the Ukraine depended on control of the Crimea, a key to the Black Sea, and on northward expansion, following the pattern of the early Kievan rulers of the ninth to eleventh centuries. Lypa's medical works include *Fitoterapia* (Phytotherapy; 1933), *Tsilyushchi roslyny v davniy i suchasniy medytsyni* (Healing plants in old and contemporary medicine; 1937), and *Liky pid nohamy* (Medicines under our feet; 1943). Lypa was killed by Soviet security forces while serving as a doctor in the Ukrainian Insurgent Army. (TS)

Sources: *Encyclopedia of Ukraine*, vol. 3 (Toronto, 1993); *Dovidnyk z istorii Ukraiiny*, vol. 2 (Kiev, 1995); L. Bykovskyi, *Apostol novitnoho ukraiinstwa Yuriy Lypa* (Geneva, 1946); Borys Kukhta, *Z istorii ukraiinskoy politycznoyi dumky* (Kiev, 1994).

LYPKIVSKYI Vasyl Ivan (19 March 1864, Popudnia, near Lipovets, Kiev Province–27 November 1937, USSR), co-founder and head of the Ukrainian Autocephalous Orthodox Church (UAOC), metropolitan of Kiev. In 1873 Lypkivskyi entered a theological school in Uman. He later studied at the Kiev Theological Seminary (1879–84) and at the Theological Academy in Kiev, graduating in 1889. Ordained in 1891, he served as dean of a cathedral in Lipovets from 1892 to 1903. From 1903 to 1905 Lypkivskyi lectured on canon law at an Orthodox church school for teachers in Kiev, but he lost his job because he supported a separate Ukrainian Orthodox Church. After the fall of tsarism, Lypkivskyi strove to establish an autocephalous church in the Ukraine. He was elected president of the Kiev Eparchial Council and the Resurrection Brotherhood, which was soon changed into the All-Ukrainian Orthodox Church Council. In May 1919 in St. Nicholas Cathedral in Kiev, Lypkivskyi celebrated the first liturgy in Ukrainian. Although the Russian Orthodox hierarchs strongly opposed his activities, he gained wide support among Ukrainians. In the summer of 1919 he became a parish priest of St. Sofia Cathedral in Kiev.

In May 1920, after **Symon Petlyura**'s troops (supported by the Polish Army) seized Kiev, the All-Ukrainian Orthodox Church Council proclaimed the establishment of the UAOC. After the Bolsheviks seized power in the Ukraine, Lypkivskyi was appointed the first UAOC metropolitan in October 1921. Since the Russian Orthodox bishops recognized neither the UAOC nor the appointment of Lypkivskyi as its metropolitan and since they refused to consecrate him, the council decided to consecrate him without the consent of other bishops, through the ancient ritual of the laying on of hands. However, Lypkivskyi's appointment was questioned by some of the Orthodox bishops and clergy in the Ukraine. Nonetheless, he began vigorously to organize the new Church. He traveled throughout the Ukraine, establishing over 500 parishes. In 1927 the UAOC consisted of 36 bishops and 2,500 priests. Lypkivskyi placed great emphasis on involving laypeople in church life. He also consecrated married priests as bishops. One of his main aims was to maintain the independence of the UAOC from the Moscow Patriarchate, which had become increasingly controlled by the Soviet authorities. In October 1927 the authorities managed to win the support of some members of the All-Ukrainian Orthodox Church Council, who dismissed Lypkivskyi from his office. He settled in the suburbs of Kiev, where he remained under de facto house arrest and lived in extreme poverty. Arrested by the NKVD in November 1937 and accused of anti-Soviet activities, he was executed by a firing squad shortly afterwards.

Lypkivskyi was the author of numerous works on canon law and the history of the Church and theology, but most of them remained in manuscript form and were destroyed during World War II. Only the last of his seven volumes on the history of the Ukrainian Orthodox Church was published posthumously in Canada: *Vidrodzhennia Tserkvy v Ukraiini 1917–1930* (The revival of the Orthodox Church in the Ukraine in 1917–1930; 1961). In 1936 Lypkivskyi's autobiography was published in *Nasza Kultura* in Warsaw. Some of Lypkivskyi's articles were published in Ukrainian periodicals in exile after the war, including "Ukraiinska Avtokefalna Tserkva i radianska komunistychna vlada" (The Ukrainian Autocephalous Orthodox Church and the Soviet government, in *Vil'na Ukraiina*, 1955–58) and "Iak Ukraiinska Tserkva povernula sobi voliu" (The road of the Ukrainian Church to freedom, in *Ukraiinske pravoslavne slovo*, 1956). (WR)

Sources: *Encyclopedia of Ukraine*, vol. 3 (Toronto, 1993); F. Heyer, *Die Orthodoxe Kirche in der Ukraine von 1917–1945* (Cologne and Braunsfeld, 1953); W. Kolarz, *Religion in the Soviet Union* (London, 1961); *Russian Oppression in the Ukraine* (London, 1962); M. Sadylenko, *Sumni naslidky lypkivshchyny v Ukraiinskyi Pravoslavniy Tserkvy* (Toronto, 1978); R. Armstark, *Die Ukrainische Autokephale Orthodoxe Kirche: Erinnerungen des Metropoliten Vasyl K. Lypkivskyj* (Würzberg, 1982).

LYPYNSKYI Vyacheslav [real name Wacław Lipiński] (17 April 1882, Zaturce in Wołyń [Volhynia]–14 June 1931, Wienerwald, near Vienna), politician, publicist, and ideologist of Ukrainian conservatism and national thought (*derzhavnytstvo*). Born into a Polish landowning family, Lypynskyi was educated in a gymnasium in Zhytomyr

between 1893 and 1898 and later (1898–1902) in the First Kiev Gymnasium. Most probably, he had already by then been introduced to the Ukrainian national movement and despite his noble Polish birth he began to feel and declare himself a Ukrainian, without, however, renouncing Roman Catholicism. In 1903–8 Lypynskyi studied history at the Jagiellonian University in Kraków (among other places). Having settled in Galicia, from 1908 he devoted himself entirely to journalism and independent research. In 1909 in Kraków he published *Szlachta na Ukrainie* (Nobility in the Ukraine), and in 1912 in Kiev, along with other authors, he issued *Z dziejów Ukrainy* (From the history of the Ukraine). Lypynskyi tried to prove the Russian and Ukrainian origins of the local gentry, as well as the participation of their ancestors in Ukrainian state building during the time of Bohdan Khmelnitsky's uprising.

Even before 1914 Lypynskyi had put forward a territorial concept of the Ukrainian nation. He proposed that the problem of a lack of a "leading stratum" in the Ukrainian nation be solved by the transfer of all the Ukrainian nobility, regardless of its Polish or Russian origins, to the Ukrainian camp and that the existing traditions and culture of this class be preserved. This proposal led to a proposal for an independent Ukrainian state. In *Memorandum* (1912) Lypynskyi tried to go beyond the vision of policies based on the two occupying countries, Russia and Austria-Hungary, and to move toward propaganda in support of the Ukrainian cause in Germany and the Entente states.

Lypynskyi spent the first year of World War I as a Russian officer in a campaign in Eastern Prussia. However, in 1915, owing to ill health (lung disease), he was sent to convalesce. Between 1917 and 1919 he founded a conservative peasant and pro-independence party, the Ukrainian Democratic Farmers' [Khliborobs'ka] Party. Lypynskyi was an ambassador of Hetman **Pavlo Skoropadskyi** in Vienna. In November 1918 he supported a federal treaty between the Ukraine and "White" Russia. As the Directory of **Symon Petlyura** assumed power in the Ukraine, in July 1919 Lypynskyi left the diplomatic service and remained in exile in Austria. There he became involved in forming a conservative camp that was centered around the hetman. In 1926 in Vienna he published *Lysty do brativ-khliborobiv* (Letters to brothers-farmers [*khliboroby*]), which presented his social and political thought—from the foundations of the philosophy of politics to concrete proposals for the political system. At that time Lypynskyi also wrote *Ukraiina na perelomi: 1657–59* (The Ukraine at the turning point: 1657–59) and *Relihiia i tserkva v istorii Ukraiiny* (Religion and the Church in the history of the Ukraine), in which he advocated that the cultural influences of East and West should be synthesized in the

Ukraine. In 1920 Lypynskyi had already founded the Ukrainian Union of Farmers [Khliboroby] and State-Supporters, and from 1919 to 1926 he published the periodical *Khliborobs'ka Ukraina*. In 1926–27, on the request of Hetman Skoropadskyi, Lypynskyi took part in the establishment of the Ukrainian Scientific Institute in Berlin. Having disagreed with the hetman about the political system of the future Ukraine, he returned to Reichenau, where in 1930 he founded his own party, the Ukrainian Fraternity of "Classocrats"-Monarchist. Lypynskyi was buried in his native Zaturce, in the then Polish part of Volhynia. (TS)

Sources: *Encyclopedia of Ukraine*, vol. 3 (Toronto, 1993); Ivan Mirchuk, *Dvi kontseptsii ukrainskoyi politychnoyi dumky: Viacheslav Lypynskyi—Dmytro Dontsov* (Munich, 1980); Hryhoriy Vaskovych, *Dvi konceptsii ukraiinskoyi politychnoyi dumky: Viacheslav Lypynskyi—Dmytro Dontsov* (New York, 1990); *Ukrainian Harvard Studies*, 1985, nos. 3–4 (issue devoted entirely to Lypynskyi).

LYSIAK-RUDNYTSKYI Ivan (27 October 1919, Vienna–25 April 1984, Edmonton, Canada), Ukrainian historian and pedagogue. Lysiak-Rudnytskyi was the son of Pavlo Lysiak and **Milena Rudnytska**. His uncle was **Ivan Rudnytskyi-Kedryn**. In 1937 Lysiak-Rudnytskyi graduated from the Academic Gymnasium in Lviv (Lwów); in 1937–39 he studied law at Lviv University, and in 1940–43, international relations at the University of Berlin. In 1945 he received a Ph.D. from Charles University in Prague. In the 1940s Lysiak-Rudnytskyi belonged to Mazepynets, a Ukrainian student organization; he chaired the Ukrainian Academic Hromada; and he was a member of the Organization of Ukrainian Nationalist Students, which, contrary to its name, attempted to detach Ukrainian youth from integral nationalism. Initially Lysiak-Rudnytskyi sympathized with the conservative movement of Hetman **Pavlo Skoropadskyi**, but in the 1940s, under the influence of Mihailo Drahomanov and **Vyacheslav Lypynskyi**, his views evolved toward liberal conservatism.

After World War II, Lysiak-Rudnytskyi went to Austria and in 1947 for Switzerland; in June 1951 he came to the United States. In 1951–52 he studied at Columbia University, and from 1954 to 1956 he worked as an urban transportation controller in Philadelphia. In 1956–67 he lectured in Russian and West European studies at La Salle College in Philadelphia, and in 1967–71, at the American University in Washington, D.C. In 1971 Lysiak-Rudnytskyi became a professor of Ukrainian and East European history at the University of Alberta in Edmonton, Canada. In the 1950s and 1960s he worked with the Free Ukrainian Academy of Arts and Sciences (Ukraiinska Vilna Akademiya Nauk i Mystetstv) in the United States. He was a full member of the Taras Shevchenko Research Society (Naukove Tovarystvo im. T. Shevchenka), and in 1976 he co-founded the Canadian Institute of Ukrainian Studies at the University of Alberta. In 1961–67 Lysiak-Rudnytskyi worked with the key Ukrainian émigré monthly *Suchasnist*. In 1967 he co-authored a letter in which thirty-five American intellectuals of Ukrainian origin demanded from the Soviet Union the establishment of Ukrainian citizenship, relations between the Ukrainian SSR and other countries, recognition of the Ukrainian language as the official state language of the Ukrainian SSR, and legalization of the Ukrainian Autocephalous Orthodox Church and the Ukrainian Greek Catholic Church. Lysiak-Rudnytskyi authored and edited about two hundred works in Ukrainian history, including *Drahomanov* (1952), *Mizh istorieyu i politykoyu* (Between history and politics; 1973), and *Rethinking Ukrainian History* (1981). The most complete collection of his works was published as *Istorychni ese* (Historical essays, 2 vols.; 1994). (BB)

Sources: *Encyclopedia of Ukraine*, vol. 4 (Toronto, 1993); *Dovidnyk z Istorii Ukraiiny* (Kiev, 2001); Yaroslav Hrytsak, "Ivan Lysiak-Rudnytskyi: Narys intelektualnoyi biohrafii," *Suchasnist*, 1994, no. 11.

LYUBCHENKO Panas (14 January 1897, Kaharlyk, Kiev region–29 August 1937, Kiev), Ukrainian Socialist and Communist activist. From 1917 to 1918 Lyubchenko was a member of the Ukrainian Central Rada (Council). A member of the Central Committee (CC) of the Ukrainian Party of Socialist Revolutionaries, in 1918 he became the leader of the party's leftist faction, which became a separate party, the so-called Borotbists. When in 1920 the internationalist part of the Borotbist faction merged with the Bolsheviks into the Communist Party (Bolshevik) of Ukraine (CP[B]U), Lyubchenko became the secretary of a provincial party organization in Kiev. From 1921 to 1922 he was head of the provincial Executive Committee in Chernihiv, and from 1922 to 1925 he was head of the All-Ukrainian Union of Agricultural Cooperatives. Promoted to first secretary of the CC in 1927, Lyubchenko became a member of the CP(B)U CC Politburo in 1934. In March 1933 he became deputy head, and in January 1934 head, of the Council of People's Commissars of the Ukrainian SSR. Lyubchenko was considered one of the most talented but at the same time one of the most ruthless Communist activists in the Ukraine. As a representative of the All-Ukrainian Council of Trade Unions, in March and April 1930 he served as the "people's prosecutor" during the show trial of a fictitious organization, the Union for the Liberation of Ukraine. At a CC plenum at the beginning of July 1933, Lyubchenko brutally attacked **Mykola**

Skrypnyk; the attack was one of the factors that led to Skrypnyk's suicide. Lyubchenko was instrumental in the implementation of the policy of forced collectivization in Ukrainian agriculture and in the confiscation of grain; these steps led to an unnecessary and tragic famine that caused the death of several million Ukrainians. Attacked from the beginning of 1937 as a member of the "Borotbist conspiracy" within the party and then as a "Fascist spy," Lyubchenko was dismissed from his position. Fearing arrest and the fate of many of his victims, Lyubchenko, together with his wife, committed suicide. (WR)

Sources: *MERSH*, vol. 20; *Encyclopedia of Ukraine*, vol. 3 (Toronto, 1993); Hryhory Kostiuk, *Stalinist Rule in the Ukraine* (New York, 1960); Andrzej Chojnowski, *Ukraina* (Warsaw, 1997).

M

MAČEK Vladimir (Vladko) (20 July 1879, Jastrebarsko–15 May 1964, Washington, D.C.), Croatian lawyer and politician. After graduating in law in Zagreb in 1903, Maček practiced as an attorney in Zagreb, Petrinja, and Samobor and as a judge in Ivanec. In 1905 he joined the Croatian Peasant Party (CPP). During World War I he served as an officer in the Austro-Hungarian Army on the Serbian and Russian fronts. In the parliament of the Kingdom of Serbs, Croats, and Slovenes Maček represented a moderate wing of the CPP. The party assumed the name Croatian Republican Peasant Party (Hrvatska Republikanska Seljačka Stranka [HRSS]) in 1920. As a result of an agreement between its head, **Stjepan Radić**, and **Nikola Pašić** in June 1925, the party dropped the adjective "republican," which was provocative for the monarchy, and Maček became deputy speaker of the parliament. In 1927 he became head of the Peasant Democratic Coalition, formed by the CPP and the Democratic Party—groups demanding the establishment of a federation instead of a centralized state dominated by the Serbs. After the death of Radić, Maček was elected leader of the CPP (18 August 1928). After King **Alexander I** strengthened the centralized Serb dictatorship, Maček stepped up his protests against it. In November 1932 he was one of the signatories of the Zagreb Manifesto, which called for equal rights for the Yugoslav nations. As a result, in January 1933 Maček was arrested and in April 1933 sentenced to three years in prison.

After the assassination of Alexander in October 1934, Maček was soon released as part of the attempts by Regent **Paul Karadjordjević** to liberalize domestic relations. Paul invited Maček to talks in Belgrade, during which the latter agreed to the continuation of the monarchy on condition of the democratization and federalization of the state. The reorganization of Bosnia and Herzegovina, Dalmatia, Montenegro, and Macedonia remained a contentious issue. Maček maintained that if Montenegro and Macedonia were to come within the orbit of Serb influences, then Croatia should take up all of the territory that had belonged to Austria-Hungary before World War I. Before the elections of May 1935, Maček's efforts resulted in a joint list of candidates submitted by the opposition bloc formed by the Peasant Democratic Coalition, in which the CPP was the most important party. Despite manipulations by the regime, this list obtained over 37 percent of the vote. In the elections of December 1938 the extent of vote rigging was even greater; still, the coalition gained almost 45 percent of the vote. Because of worsening geopolitical conditions, both sides became more willing to reach a compromise, and on 26 August 1939, on behalf of the majority of the Croatian parties, Maček signed an agreement (*sporazum*) with the government of **Dragiša Cvetković**. This agreement gave Croatia and the provincial parliament in Zagreb considerable autonomy within Yugoslavia. Maček became deputy prime minister of the central government. To some extent the agreement helped to ease tensions between the Croats and the Serbs, although it did not satisfy the Ustashe, who considered it a betrayal and continued their struggle for independence, even resorting to terrorism. At the beginning of 1941 Maček maintained that Yugoslavia should continue its passive resistance to pressure from the Axis countries; consequently, he supported its accession to the Tripartite Pact (25 March 1941).

After the coup d'état of 27 March 1941, to which the Croats generally had a negative reaction, Maček hesitated a few days before finally supporting the government of **Dušan Simović** on 3 April. Although Maček considered the coup an irresponsible step by Serb officers, he decided that the unity of the country was more important. However, his appeal to Croats for support of the Simović government in the face of the German invasion failed, and a great number of soldiers surrendered without fighting. When on 10 April 1941 the Germans occupied Zagreb, Maček decided to stay in Croatia. However, he refused to support a puppet Croat state established by the Ustashe under the leadership of **Ante Pavelić**. As a result Maček was arrested and placed in a concentration camp near Graz. During negotiations between the government-in-exile of King **Peter II** and the Communists led by **Josip Broz Tito**, Maček was proposed as prime minister of a coalition government, but the Communists did not agree to that. Released from the concentration camp at the end of the war, Maček returned to Yugoslavia, which was controlled by the Communists. As he could not reconcile himself to the fact that Croatia was now under Communist rule, Maček left his country on 6 May 1945. Via Germany and France he traveled to the United States, where he maintained intensive contacts with political émigrés from other Central and East European countries. He died in the United States. Maček authored *In the Struggle for Freedom* (1957), in which he described his political quandaries and choices. In 1992 his *Memoari* (Memoirs) were published in Zagreb. (WR)

Sources: *Biographisches Lexikon*, vol. 3; *Enciklopedija Jugoslavije* vol. 5 (Zagreb, 1962); Constantine Fotich, *The War We Lost* (New York, 1948); Todor Stojkov, "O stvaranju bloka narodnog sporazuma," in *Istorija XX wieka*, 1964, vol. 6; Ljubo Boban, *Sporazum Cvetković-Maček* (Belgrade, 1965); Ljubo Boban, *Maček i politika Hrvatse sejlačke stranke 1928–1941*, vols. 1–2 (Zagreb, 1974); Mark Biondich, *Stjepan Radić, the Croat Peasant Party, and the Politics of Mass Mobilization, 1904–1928* (Toronto, 2000).

MACH Alexander (11 October 1902, Palárikovo–15 October 1980, Bratislava), Slovak journalist and politician. Mach intended to become a Catholic clergyman. In 1916 he began studies at a theological seminary in Esztergom, and he continued them in Trnava. In 1922 he stopped his studies and devoted himself to political and journalistic work. From 1922 Mach was a functionary of the party of Reverend **Andrej Hlinka**, the Slovak People' Party (Slovenská L'udová Strana), which in 1925 extended its name to Hlinka's Slovak People's Party (Hlinkova Sloveská L'udová Strana [HSL'S]). He soon became known as an opponent of the Czechoslovak state. For a long time the leadership of the party was dominated by those who supported autonomy for Slovakia within the framework of a common state of Czechs and Slovaks, but Mach was among those who advocated a sovereign Slovak state.

In the 1930s Mach was a co-founder of a paramilitary organization within the HSL'S, the Hlinka Guard (Hlinkova Garda [HG]). After the proclamation of Slovakia's independence (14 March 1939), Mach became head of the Office of Propaganda. He also directed the HG. He supported the further Fascization of Slovakia and close relations with the Third Reich. He propagated the slogans of "completing the Slovak national revolution" and "the march on Bratislava" to assume power by the radicals. Mach initiated a meeting of cultural activists in Tatranska Lomnica (August 1940), where the so-called Lomnica Manifesto was passed. In it, the principles of Slovak totalitarianism were expounded; these were a mixture of concepts gathered from papal encyclicals and from the ideology of the Third Reich. At the same time Mach maintained contacts with liberal and leftist intellectuals, to whom he liked to present himself as a patron of Slovak culture and a promoter of artists. Some of the intellectuals who were linked with the Communist movement—for example, **Laco Novomeský**—used their connections with Mach to intervene on behalf of political prisoners.

Along with Prime Minister **Béla Tuka**, Mach promoted anti-Semitic policies. As early as 1938 HG functionaries actively supported the deportation of Jews from the territories of southern Slovakia. In August 1940 Mach resigned as the head of the Office of Propaganda, criticizing the policy of President **Josef Tiso**, whom he accused of excessive submission to liberal-democratic politicians and of failure to cooperate with the Germans. In May 1940 President Tiso received Mach's resignation, dismissing him at the same time as head of the HG. Mach went to Berlin, where he was the guest of Joseph Goebbels and Joachim von Ribbentrop (among others). In June 1940 a Slovak-German conference took place in Salzburg, where Hitler expressed his discontent that Mach and Tuka had been removed from power. As a result both politicians returned to the government. Mach was appointed minister of interior and held the office until March 1945. He also resumed the leadership of the HG. At the beginning of 1941 at an HG conference in Trenčianske Teplice Mach took part in passing a resolution for "the final solution of the Jewish question is Slovakia"; a similar plan was prepared for the gypsies, who were labeled "anti-social elements." As minister of interior and head of the HG, Mach was responsible for the deportation of over fifty thousand Slovak Jews, the majority of whom were transported to death camps and perished. In 1944 on Mach's orders, HG units, along with German forces, took part in quelling the Slovak National Uprising. In March 1945 Mach fled to Austria. Interned there by the Americans, he was handed over by them to the Czechoslovak government. In 1947 he was sentenced to thirty years of prison by the Supreme Court in Bratislava. He was released under amnesty in 1968. Mach settled in Bratislava, where he lived until his death. Mach was the author of many articles, published mainly in *Gardista*, an organ of the HG. (AGr)

Sources: *Kdo byl kdo v našich dějinách ve 20 stoleti* (Prague, 1994); Ivan Kamenec, *Slovenský Stát 1939–1945* (Prague, 1992); Ewa Orlof, *Dyplomacja Polska wobec sprawy słowackiej w latach 1938–1939* (Kraków, 1980); *Słowacja na przełomie: Powstanie słowackie 1944* (Warsaw, 1969).

MACIEREWICZ Antoni, pseudonyms "Marcin Ankwicz," "Scriptor," and others (3 August 1948, Warsaw), Polish politician and historian. The son of a Christian Democratic politician murdered by the Communists after World War II, Macierewicz graduated in history from Warsaw University. In 1975–76 he worked there in the Department of Iberian Studies. A participant in the student protests of March 1968 and held in prison from March to July 1968, Macierewicz was commander of the Romuald Traugutt Memorial Warsaw Scouting Squad, called the Black One. In 1969 he co-founded the Senior Scouting Group and the Gang of Tramps connected with it. In 1972–73 he taught in a Warsaw high school, and in 1975–76 he took part in protests against the amendment of the constitution. From July 1976 Macierewicz co-organized relief efforts for workers repressed after the June 1976 protests. On 23 September 1976 he co-founded the Committee for the Defense of Workers (Komitet Obrony Robotników [KOR]), which supplied financial and legal aid to those imprisoned and fired, as well as to their families. Dismissed from work, from May to July 1977 Macierewicz was imprisoned. After his release, in September 1977 he joined the Committee of Social Self-Defense of the KOR, stimulating social organization outside of official structures. From 1977 to 1981 Macierewicz was editor-in-chief of the secretly published monthly *Głos*, attracting KOR followers opposing **Jacek Kuroń** and **Adam Michnik**. In August 1980 he organized a strike in the Town Cleaning Enterprise. From the fall of 1980 to December 1981 Macierewicz was the organizer and de facto head of the Center of Public Opinion Studies in the Mazowsze region of Solidarity.

After the introduction of martial law in December 1981, Macierewicz worked in the underground—for example, as editor of *Głos*. In early 1989 he opposed the Round Table Talks. In October 1989 he co-founded the Christian National Union (Zjednoczenie Chrześcijańsko-Narodowe [ZChN]) and became deputy chairman of its Supreme Board. In 1990 he joined the Civic Committee of **Lech Wałęsa**. In 1991 Macierewicz became a member of the Advisory Committee of President Wałęsa, and in 1991–93 he was an MP on behalf of the ZChN. In December 1991 he became minister of interior in the **Jan Olszewski** government. A radical advocate of lustration, on 4 June 1992, realizing that a parliamentary resolution was imminent, Macierewicz publicized a list of alleged secret collaborators in the Communist special services who still worked in the parliament and government. This became an immediate reason for the collapse of the Olszewski cabinet. Removed from the ZChN for a badly prepared move, from November 1992 Macierewicz presided over the Christian National Movement Polish Action, which in 1995 became allied with Olszewski's Movement for the Reconstruction of Poland (Ruch Odbudowy Polski [ROP]). From 1997 to 2001 Macierewicz was an MP on behalf of the ROP, and from 2001, on behalf of the League of Polish Families, which he left in 2002 and founded the Catholic National Caucus. The spokesman for radical de-Communization and lustration, Macierewicz is rated among the keen opponents of Poland's entry into the European Union. (AF)

Sources: Janusz A. Majcherek, *Pierwsza dekada III Rzeczpospolitej 1989–1999* (Warsaw, 1999); *Opozycja w PRL: Słownik biograficzny 1956–89*, vol. 1 (Warsaw, 2000); Wojciech Roszkowski, *Historia Polski 1914–2001* (Warsaw, 2002); Antoni Dudek, *Pierwsze lata III Rzeczpospolitej 1989–2001* (Kraków, 2002).

MACKIEWICZ Józef (1 June 1902, St. Petersburg–31 January 1985, Munich), Polish journalist and writer. The brother of **Stanisław Mackiewicz**, Mackiewicz came from a family tracing its origins to the landed gentry. While a high school student in Wilno (Vilnius), he served as a volunteer in the Polish-Soviet war (1919–20). In 1921 he began studying at the School of Natural Sciences and Mathematics of Warsaw University and at the School of Law of Wilno University. In 1923 he discontinued his studies and became involved in journalism. A supporter of the "homeland idea," as opposed to Polish and Lithuanian nationalisms, Mackiewicz emphasized the multicultural character of the lands of the former Grand Duchy of Lithuania and called for equal rights for its inhabitants. In 1938 he published *Bunt rojstów* (The rebel of the moors), in which he criticized Poland's policy toward national minorities. He advocated cooperation between the Baltic States and Poland in the face of the Soviet threat. An enemy of totalitarian systems, particularly communism, Mackiewicz also criticized nationalism; as a result, he came into conflict with leftist groups, nationalists, and pro-Piłsudski groups.

After the capture of Wilno by the Red Army in September 1939, Mackiewicz fled to Kaunas. He established cooperation with the Lithuanians, which he continued after Lithuanian troops entered Wilno on 14 October 1939. After publishing "My Wilnianie" (We, the people of Vilnius) in *Lietuvos Zinios*, where he included a criticism of Poland before September 1939, Mackiewicz was appointed by the Lithuanian authorities as the editor of *Gazeta Codzienna*, which promoted anti-communism and the "homeland idea" (November 1939–May 1940). After Lithuania was invaded by the Soviet Army and then incorporated into the Soviet Union, Mackiewicz went into hiding in the Rudniki Forest, where he worked as a woodcutter (June 1940–June 1941). When the Germans occupied Wilno, he returned to the city. Optimistic about the new occupier, he published several articles in *Goniec Codzienny*, a "reptile" newspaper (i.e., Polish language but German-controlled and collaborationist), from July to October 1941. In 1942 a special court of the Home Army sentenced Mackiewicz to death for collaboration. The reality of the German occupation, particularly the killings of Jews, made Mackiewicz change his views; therefore, the sentence was overturned at the beginning of 1943. In May 1943, most probably with the consent of the Home Army, Mackiewicz went to Katyń to observe the exhumation, by the Germans, of Polish officers murdered by the NKVD. After returning to Wilno, he gave an interview on the subject to *Goniec Codzienny* (3 June 1943).

From May to July 1944 in Warsaw Mackiewicz published the anti-Communist periodical *Alarm*, warning about the Soviet threat. In January 1945 he made his way, via Vienna, to Rome, where he became aligned with the Second Corps, led by General **Władysław Anders**. Mackiewicz edited a book about Katyń, *Zbrodnia katyńska w świetle dokumentów* (The Katyń massacre in the light of documents; 1946). He published articles in *Orzeł Biały*, where, among other things, he reminded the world about the extermination of the Jews from the Wilno region. From 1947 to 1955 Mackiewicz lived in London and then, until his death, in Munich. He published articles in Polish émigré periodicals, including *Kultura*, as well as in the periodicals of Russian, Lithuanian, and Ukrainian émigrés. In 1955 he published the novel *Droga do nikąd* (*The Road to Nowhere*, 1964), about life in Lithuania under Soviet occupation, and in 1957 the book *Kontra*, in which he described the handing over by the Allies of the Cossacks from the Don region to the NKVD. The novels *Sprawa pułkownika Miasojedowa* (The case of Colonel Myasoyedov; 1962), *Lewa wolna* (Free Left; 1965), and *Nie trzeba głośno mówić* (No need to speak out loud; 1969) are also important. Both Mackiewicz's political journalism and his literary prose were characterized by extreme anticommunism. In 1962 he published *Zwycięstwo prowokacji* (The victory of provocation), a collection of essays attacking the Kraków *Tygodnik Powszechny*, a weekly that attempted to maintain an independent position within the limits of the political system of the Polish People's Republic. In the collections of commentaries *W cieniu krzyża* (1972; *In the Shadow of the Cross*, 1973) and *Watykan w cieniu czerwonej gwiazdy* (The Vatican in the shadow of the red star; 1975) Mackiewicz criticized the Vatican and the Western Allies for their policy of appeasement toward the Soviet Union. (MC)

Sources: *Literatura polska XX wiek: Przewodnik encyklopedyczny*, vol. 1 (Warsaw, 2000); Marek Adamiec, *"Cień wielkiej tajemnicy . . .": Norwid, Grabiński, Leśmian, Tyrmand, Mackiewicz, Herbert, Vincenz* (Gdańsk, 1995); J. Malewski [Włodzimierz Bolecki], *Ptasznik z Wilna* (Kraków, 1991); *Leksykon kultury polskiej poza krajem od roku 1939*, vol. 1 (Lublin, 2000); Włodzimierz Bolecki and Krzysztof Masłoń, "Zrozumieć Mackiewicza," *Rzeczpospolita*, 2 March 2002; "Moje credo pisarskie? . . . Prawda," *Tygodnik Powszechny*, 31 March 2002.

MACKIEWICZ Stanisław, penname, "Cat" (18 December 1896, St. Petersburg–18 February 1966, Warsaw), Polish politician and journalist. The brother of **Józef Mackiewicz**, Mackiewicz came from a family tracing its roots to the landed gentry. From 1906 to 1916 he attended high schools in St. Petersburg and Wilno (Vilnius). In 1914 he entered the Jagiellonian University in Kraków. Later, he studied law at Warsaw University and at the Jagiellonian University, finally graduating from Stefan Batory University in Wilno (1924). In 1911 Mackiewicz became aligned with a secret national youth group called Pet, and he edited its periodical, *Pobudka*. During World War I he was active in the secret pro-independence Union of Polish Youth –Zet and in the Polish Military Organization (Polska Organizacja Wojskowa [POW]) in St. Petersburg

and Wilno. At that time he published a work about **Henryk Sienkiewicz**. Arrested by the Germans in 1917 in Warsaw, Mackiewicz fled to Kraków, where he began working for the conservative *Czas*. He soon volunteered to serve in the Thirteenth Regiment of the Vilnius Uhlans and fought with the Bolsheviks. He also contributed to the conservative and monarchist press, including *Dziennik Poznański* and the Warsaw *Straż Kresowa*. In 1922 Mackiewicz became editor-in-chief and later publisher of the daily *Słowo* in Vilnius and headed this paper until 1939. Despite his extremely conservative views, his periodical published articles by intellectuals representing various orientations, including those with Communist leanings, such as Henryk Dembiński and Czesław Miłosz (who wrote for Slowo's literary supplement *Żagary*). Mackiewicz published treatises about the necessity to form an alliance with the Germans (for example, *Kropka nad i* [Spelling it out]; 1927), as well as treatises about communism (*Myśl w obcęgach* [Russian minds in fetters]; 1931) and conservative politics (*Książka moich rozczarowań* [The book of my disappointments]; 1939). Michał Bobrzyński, Wacław Studnicki, and Charles Maurras were his ideological masters. In his journalism, Mackiewicz combined imperialistic ideas in foreign policy with monarchism and economic liberalism in domestic policy. He was active in the Monarchist Organization (1925), the Union of Polish Monarchists (1926), the Polish Conservative Organization of Pro-State Work (1926), and the Conservative Party (1937). Mackiewicz initially supported **Józef Piłsudski**, organizing his so-called Nieśwież agreement with the conservative camp (1926). In the Assembly, to which he was elected on the ticket of the Nonparty Bloc of Cooperation with the Government (Bezpartyjny Blok Współpracy z Rządem [BBWR]), Mackiewicz represented the Polish Conservative Organization of Pro-State Work. After Piłsudski's death, Mackiewicz criticized his successors for etatism and mono-party leanings, as well as the foreign policy of **Józef Beck** and Poland's lack of military preparation for the imminent war. In March 1939 he was briefly detained in the camp at Bereza Kartuska.

After the Third Reich and the Soviet Union attacked Poland in September 1939, Mackiewicz left for France, where he continued to publish *Słowo*. He was active as a member of the Polish government-in-exile and sat on the National Council. Immediately after the defeat of France, Mackiewicz suggested that it was necessary to begin capitulation negotiations with Germany, but at the beginning of September 1940 he left for Great Britain. Initially ostracized for Germanophilia, he soon again became active in the National Council. He opposed General **Władysław Sikorski**. He particularly criticized negotiations between the Soviet Union and the Polish Communists. He accused the Western Allies, particularly the British, of treachery. Mackiewicz published extensively, including *Historia Polski od 11 listopada 1918 do 17 września 1939* (The history of Poland from 11 November 1918 to 17 September 1939; 1941) and *Klucz do Piłsudskiego* (The key to Piłsudski; 1943). After the war Mackiewicz wrote for *Dziennik Polski, Wiadomości*, and *Lwów i Wilno*, a periodical that he edited. His publications include *Lata nadziei* (Years of hope; 1946) and *Stanisław August* (1953), a book about the last Polish king. One of the most implacable anti-Communists, on 7 June 1954 Mackiewicz became prime minister of the government-in-exile in London and held this position until 8 August 1955. On 14 June 1956 he unexpectedly returned to Poland. This decision was influenced both by his conviction that the work of the government-in-exile was pointless and by economic factors. Mackiewicz settled in Warsaw. At odds with the Poles in emigration, he sharply criticized postwar émigré circles in *Londyniszcze* (1957) and *Zielone oczy* (1958; Green eyes; 1958). Later he became involved in historical journalism. When his health deteriorated, Mackiewicz also wrote dramas, with aid from the PAX Association of **Bolesław Piasecki**. (MC)

Sources: *PSB*, vol. 19; Władysław Pobóg-Malinowski, *Najnowsza historia polityczna Polski*, vols. 2–3 (London, 1983–86); Jerzy Jaruzelski, *Stanisław Cat-Mackiewicz, 1896–1966: Wilno-Londyn-Warszawa* (Warsaw, 1994); Artur Górski, *Władza polityczna w myśli Stanisława Cata-Mackiewicza* (Kraków, 1999); *Leksykon kultury polskiej poza krajem od roku 1939*, vol. 1 (Lublin, 2000).

MACZEK Stanisław (31 March 1892, Szczerzec, East Galicia–11 December 1994, Edinburgh), Polish general. Maczek graduated from the Department of Philosophy and Polish Philology of the University of Lemberg (Lwów, Lviv), where, while a student, he underwent military training in the Riflemen's Association. During World War I he was an officer in the Austrian Army. He served in the Second Regiment of Tyrolean Riflemen, at first on the Russian front and later on the Italian front. From the fall of 1918 he was in the Polish Army. In the Polish-Soviet war (1919–20) he commanded a company in the Fourth Infantry Division. After the end of the war he commanded an infantry battalion of the Twenty-sixth Infantry Regiment in Lwów and then studied for one year at the War College. Afterwards, he was deputy commander of the Seventy-sixth Infantry Regiment and for five years commander of the Eighty-first Regiment of Grodno Riflemen.

In 1937 Maczek began to organize the Tenth Armored Cavalry Brigade, of which he became commander in 1938. With his brigade, a part of the "Kraków Army," he fought in the September campaign of 1939. After the Soviet invasion of Poland, on 19 September 1939 Maczek, along with a group of his soldiers, crossed the Hungarian border and was interned there. In October 1939 he managed to get to France, where in 1940 he reconstructed the Tenth Armored Cavalry Brigade. In recognition of his merits in the September campaign, he was promoted to general. After the collapse of France in July 1940, Maczek went to Britain, where he again organized and commanded the Tenth Armored Cavalry Brigade. In 1942 he began to form the First Armored Division of soldiers and officers who fought under his command in Poland and France. His division started fighting on 1 August 1944 and took part in the Allied invasion of Normandy—for example, in the battle of Falaise, where it played a crucial role. Maczek's division then fought in Belgium and in the Netherlands, playing a special role in the battle of Breda. The division gained the gratitude of the local people because Maczek tried to avoid the destruction of towns during battles. The battle trail of this division ended in Wilhelmshaven in Germany.

From 1945 to 1947 Maczek commanded the First Corps of the Polish Armed Forces in the West, which were stationed in Scotland. After the war he remained in exile in Edinburgh. The Communist government in Warsaw stripped him of his Polish citizenship. Maczek published his memoirs, *Od podwody do czołga: Wspomnienia wojenne, 1918–1945* (From the wagon to the tank: War memoirs, 1918–1945; 1961). In 1990 Maczek was appointed lieutenant general. In 1994 he was decorated with the Order of the White Eagle. In accordance with his wishes, he was buried in Breda. (JS)

Sources: Franciszek Skibiński, *Pierwsza pancerna* (Warsaw, 1979); T. Wysocki, *1. Polska Dywizja Pancerna 1939–1945* (Warsaw, 1994); Juliusz L. Englert and Krzysztof Barbarski, *Generał Maczek i żołnierze 1 Dywizji Pancernej* (London, 1992); Zbigniew Tomkowski, *Generał Maczek: Najstarszy żołnierz Rzeczypospolitej* (Warsaw, 1994); Piotr Stawecki, *Słownik biograficzny generałów Wojska Polskiego, 1918–1939* (Warsaw, 1994).

MADGEARU Virgil (14 December 1887, Galați–27 November 1940, near Snagov), Romanian economist and politician. After graduating from high school in Galați, Madgearu studied economics at the university in Leipzig, where in 1911 he earned a Ph.D. in economic sciences for a dissertation on the industrial development of Romania. He subsequently continued his studies in London. In 1912 he returned to Romania, where he was appointed head of the Workers' and Craftsmen's Central Insurance Fund, later becoming editor-in-chief of the insurance periodical *Monitorul asigurărilor muncitorești*. Madgearu published articles on the Romanian economy, especially agriculture.

In 1916 he became a professor at the Academy of Commerce and Industry in Bucharest. On his initiative, the chair of social policy and cooperative studies was established at this academy. From 1918 he edited the periodical *Independenţa economică* in Iaşi.

After World War I Madgearu was a co-founder of the Union for Social Reform Studies, which later became the Romanian Social Institute (Institutul Social-Român), and he served as its secretary general and then as chairman of the Social Policy Department. A member of the agrarian Peasant Party (*Partidul ţărănesc*) from 1919 to 1926, its ideologue, and then its secretary general, Madgearu called for radical agrarian reform and advocated the development of the Romanian economy based on farming and small-scale manufacturing. He believed that peasants who acquired land in land reforms—the largest social group—should play a decisive role in a democratically governed Romania. When in 1926 the Peasant Party merged with the Transylvanian National Romanian Party (Partidul Naţional Român), forming the National Peasant Party (Partidul Naţional Ţărănesc [NPP]), Madgearu became its secretary general. He served as a NPP member of parliament (1926–38); minister of trade and industry (November 1928–November 1929, July–October 1930, August–October 1932); minister of finance (November 1929–January 1930, October 1932–November 1933); and minister of agriculture (October 1930–April 1931). He called for the establishment of a bloc of agrarian countries to become more competitive with the industrialized Western countries, through the establishment of peasant cooperatives (among other things). He advocated a so-called third way of development, neither socialist nor capitalist. In 1935 Madgearu founded the Romanian Institute for the Study of Economic Cycles. After the royal dictatorship was established, Madgearu joined the opposition. After the abdication of King **Charles II** and the coming to power of General **Ion Antonescu**, as a critic of the Fascist Iron Guard Madgearu was abducted by Guardists in November 1940, subjected to torture, and shot dead in the forest near Snagov.

Madgearu's publications include the following: *Structura şi tendinţele băncilor populare în România* (The structure and tendencies of the people's banks in Romania; 1914); *Revoluţia agrară şi evoluţia clasei ţărăneşti* (The agrarian revolution and the evolution of the peasant class; 1923); *Înţelegerea economică a statelor dunărene* (Economic cooperation of the Danubian countries; 1932); *Reorganizarea sistemului de credit* (Reorganization of the credit system; 1934); and *La politique économique extérieure de la Roumanie 1927–1938*. In 1990 Madgearu was posthumously recognized as a member of the Romanian Academy of Sciences. (LW)

Sources: *Dictionar Enciclopedic*, vol. 4 (Bucharest, 2001); Vlad Georgescu, *Istoria Românilor de la origini pînă în zilele noastre* (Oakland, 1984); Józef Darski, *Rumunia: Historia, współczesność, konflikty narodowe* (Warsaw, 1995); Krzysztof Dach and Tadeusz Dubicki, *Żelazny Legion Michała Archanioła* (Warsaw, 1996); Dorina N. Rusu, *Membrii Academiei Române 1866–1999* (Bucharest, 1999); Ion Alexandrescu, Ion Bulei, Ion Mamina, and Ioan Scurtu, *Enciclopedia de istorie României* (Bucharest, 2000).

MÁDL Ferenc (29 January 1931, Bánd, near Veszprém), president of Hungary. In 1955 Mádl graduated in law from Eötvös Lóránd University in Budapest, and in 1956 he started working in the Institute of Legal Studies of the Hungarian Academy of Sciences (HAS). In 1961–63 he studied in the Department of Law of the University of Strasbourg, France. In 1964 he received a Ph.D. in political science, and in 1973 he became a professor at Eötvös Lóránd University in Budapest. In 1978 he received his postdoctoral degree at the HAS. From this time Mádl was head of the Institute of Civil Law, and in 1985–87 he was dean of the Department of Law of his university. He also lectured at Harvard University in Cambridge, Massachusetts. From 1987 Mádl was a member of the HAS and later also a member of many foreign institutions dealing with international law. He was not a Communist Party member. From May 1990 to February 1993 he was minister without portfolio in the **József Antall** government, dealing with education, research policy, and privatization; then, until June 1994 he was minister of education and culture. In the presidential elections of June 1995 Mádl was supported by the Hungarian Democratic Forum, the Christian Democrats, and the Alliance of Young Democrats–Fidesz, but he lost to **Árpád Göncz**. From 1996 Mádl was chairman of the Hungarian Association of Civic Cooperation, politically close to Fidesz. On 6 June 2000 Mádl was elected president, and he continued the pro-Atlantic and pro-European policies of his predecessor. (WR)

Sources: www.cidob.org/bios/castellano/lideres/m-049.htm.

MADZHAROV Mikhail (31 January 1854, Koprivshtitsa–23 January 1944, Sofia), Bulgarian politician. In 1877 Madzharov graduated from Robert College in Istanbul. From 1877 to 1879 he worked as a teacher in Pazardzhik. After Bulgaria's liberation from the Turkish yoke in 1878, he became leader of the National Party (1879) and editor of the newspaper *Marica* (1882–85). Madzharov served as deputy to the District Assembly, a member of the Standing Committee for Eastern Rumelia (1880–85), and director (minister) of finance in the directorate (government) of this province (1882–85). From 1880 to 1912 and from 1919 to 1920 he was a deputy to the National Assembly, and in

1911, a deputy to the Grand National Assembly, of which he was vice-president. In 1884 Madzharov became a corresponding member and subsequently a full member of the Bulgarian Literary Society (later the Bulgarian Academy of Sciences). Because of his Russophile views, Madzharov had to emigrate to Odessa and then to Istanbul. After three years he returned to Bulgaria. He worked as an attorney in Sofia and edited the periodical *Bulgarska sbirka* (1893) and the newspaper *Mir* (1894–1912). He served as minister of public housing, roads, and transportation (1894–99); minister of interior and health in the cabinet of **Stoyan Danev** (June 1913); and minister plenipotentiary to Great Britain (1913–14). In 1913 he signed a peace treaty in London ending the Second Balkan War. From 1914 to 1915 he was minister plenipotentiary to Russia.

Madzharov opposed Bulgaria's entering World War I on the side of Germany. After the war, he served as minister of war in the government of **Teodor Teodorov** (May–October 1919) and minister of foreign and religious affairs in the cabinet of **Aleksandur Stamboliyski** (October 1919–June 1920). From then on, Madzharov was an opponent of Stamboliyski's autocratic rule. After the 1922 congress of the Constitutional Bloc in Tŭrnovo, Madzharov was arrested and then sentenced on the grounds of being partly responsible for the national catastrophe in Bulgaria. Released after the coup of 9 June 1923, he became one of the leaders of the United National Progressive Party. A member of the opposition in 1935–44, Madzharov was against rapprochement with the Germans. Madzharov was killed during the Allied bombing of Sofia. His publications include *Zashto me sŭdiat* (Why they are trying me; 1923); *Iztochna Rumelia* (Eastern Rumelia; 1925); *Poslednite godini na K. Stoilov* (The last years of K. Stoilov; 1927); *Od samovlastie kŭm svoboda i zakonnost* (From autocratic rule to the rule of law; 1936); and *Spomeni 1854–1889* (Memoirs 1854–1889; 1968). Madzharov translated *War and Peace* by Leo Tolstoy into Bulgarian (1889–92). (JJ)

Sources: *Entsiklopediya Bulgariya*, vol. 4 (Sofia, 1984); *100 godini na BAN*, vol. 1 (Sofia, 1969); Tasho Tashev, *Ministrite na Bulgariya 1879–1999: Entsiklopedichen spravochnik* (Sofia, 1999); Georgi Milen Kumanov and Tania Nikolova, *Politicheski partii, organizatsii i dvizheniia v Bulgariya i tekhnite lideri 1879–1999: Kratuk spravochnik* (Sofia, 1999); Angel Tzurakov, *Entsiklopediia. Pravitelstvata na Bulgariya: Khronologiia na politicheskiia zhivot 1879–2001* (Sofia, 2001).

MÄE Hjalmar (24 October 1901, Kuivajõe–10 April 1978, Graz, Austria), Estonian politician, Nazi collaborator. Mäe studied in Berlin and Innsbruck. He earned a Ph.D. in philosophy in 1927 and in political science in 1930. After returning to Estonia, he joined the National Centrist Party (NCP) of **Jaan Tõnisson** and became a member of the municipal board in the region of Harju. Mäe was chairman of the Estonian Radio Union and served as editor-in-chief of a periodical devoted to radio. Until the end of his life he considered propaganda as the most important element in politics, even more important than military force. In 1931 Mäe left the NCP and joined the extremely rightist Estonian War of Independence Veterans' League (Eesti Vabadussõjalaste Liit [EVL]). He rose rapidly through the ranks of the EVL movement, becoming the de facto chief of its propaganda operations. He won many new members to the EVL, contributing to the support of constitutional amendments in an October 1933 referendum and to the victory of the EVL in the local elections to town councils in January 1934.

As the person in charge of the presidential campaign of General **Andres Larka** in 1934, Mäe made the mistake of expecting that General **Johan Laidoner** would be the main contender. This allowed **Konstantin Päts** to stay in the shadows and then, in agreement with Laidoner, to stage a coup d'état in March 1934. Briefly detained, Mäe was soon released and helped in the preparations for a coup that was to install the EVL in power. However, the plot was revealed, and Mäe was sentenced to twenty years' imprisonment in a trial of EVL leaders. Released under an amnesty of 1938, he was elected the new head of the EVL after the death of **Artur Sirk**. However, after the EVL was disbanded by the regime of Päts, who gradually gained wide public acceptance, Mäe retired from politics. He founded his own firm, dealing with imports from Germany. He frequently traveled to Berlin, where he established contacts with high officials of the Third Reich, including Werner Best, Heinrich Himmler's deputy. At the end of 1939, Mäe claimed German origins and repatriated to Germany; the move saved him from a massacre of EVL members that the Soviet authorities conducted from 1940 to 1941. In the spring of 1941 in Helsinki Mäe established the Estonian Liberation Committee, which aimed at the restitution of Estonian independence under German tutelage.

After the Germans occupied Estonia in June 1941, Mäe returned home as a German citizen and became general land director (*General Landesdirektor*), the top-ranking functionary of the Estonian self-government. Against the hopes of his former colleagues, Mäe did not revive the EVL. Without the restitution of Estonian independence and with the increasing economic exploitation of the Estonian people, the killings of Jews by the local police, and the formation of Estonian SS units, Mäe, who imitated Hitler's behavior, failed to gain wide support, and appeals to the Estonian people urging them to join the war against the Soviet Union had little effect. When the Red Army approached the borders of Estonia in 1944, Mäe declared a second war of independence, but it was only after a special radio appeal by **Jüri Uluots** that Estonian men began to join the army. After the war, from 1945 to 1947, Mäe was imprisoned in Austria, where he worked in local émigré organizations. He was an adviser on Soviet affairs to the governments of the Federal Republic of Germany and Austria, and he died undisturbed by anyone. (AG)

Sources: *Eesti Entsuklopeedia*, vol. 14 (Tallinn, 2000); Andres Kasekamp, *Radical Right in Interwar Estonia* (London, 1995); "Report of the Estonian International Commission for the Investigation of Crimes Against Humanity, Phase II—The German Occupation of Estonia, 1941–1944," Strona Estońskiej Międzynarodowej Komisji dla Badania Zbrodni Przeciwko Ludzkości www.historycommission .ee/temp/conclusions.htm

MĂGUREANU Virgil [originally Virgil Astaliş] (5 March 1941, Satu Mare, Transylvania), head of Romanian intelligence. During World War II Măgureanu's Romanian family name was Magyarized into Asztalos. After primary school Măgureanu went to a textile trade school, where he became secretary of the local Communist youth organization. In 1964 he started studies in the Department of Philosophy at Bucharest University. During that time he got a scholarship to study in Moscow, where he was probably recruited by the KGB. During his studies he also started collaborating with the Romanian political police, Securitate, serving in its counterintelligence. After graduating, in 1969 Măgureanu started working in the Ştefan Gheorghiu Party Academy in Bucharest, adopting his mother's maiden name, Măgureanu, to avoid any suspicion of Hungarian descent. After Colonel Muammar Qaddafi took power in Libya in 1969, Măgureanu was sent there to help create a new Libyan security police. During this mission he developed close contacts with KGB officers, for which he was recalled to Romania. In the fall of 1971 he was moved to the Department of Scientific Socialism at the University of Bucharest, and in September 1972 he started working in foreign intelligence under the alias of "Captain Mihăil Mihai." In March 1973 Măgureanu retired and returned to the Ştefan Gheorghiu Party Academy, maintaining his contacts with the Securitate. In 1983 he was appointed professor. After the fall of **Nicolae Ceauşescu** the new post-Communist president, **Ion Iliescu**, appointed Măgureanu head of the Romanian Information Service, established in place of the dissolved Securitate. After the Iliescu group lost the elections in 1996, Măgureanu resigned. Soon afterwards he established the National Romanian Party (Partidul Naţional Român), which failed to win wide support. (ASK)

Sources: Bugajski; Kieron Williams and Dennis Deletant, *Security Intelligence Service in New Democracies* (London, 2001).

MAIORESCU Titu Liviu (15 February 1840, Craiova–2 July 1917, Bucharest) Romanian philosopher, journalist, and politician. The son of Ioan Maiorescu-Trifu, a well-known journalist and politician, Maiorescu studied at the Theresianum in Vienna (1856–58); at the universities in Berlin and Giessen; and at the Sorbonne in Paris (1858–61), earning a Ph.D. in 1861. From 1862 to 1870 he was a professor and subsequently the rector of the University of Iaşi. Maiorescu was the founder of modern Romanian philology, philosophy, and literary criticism. In 1863 in Iaşi he founded the Junimea (Youth) Society, a literary and political group that was opposed to democracy, considering it a phenomenon introducedinto Romania in an artificial way. Maiorescu was also co-founder and publisher of *Convorbiri Literare*, the most important literary review in Romania, which first came out in 1867 in Iaşi and which is still published today. He was the founder of the Romanian Academy, established in 1867. He was also the first publisher of Mihai Eminescu, the greatest Romanian poet. One of the most prominent Romanian logicians, Maiorescu authored *Logica* (1876). From 1884 to 1901 he was a professor of logic at Bucharest University, and from 1885 to 1897 he was rector of this university. He translated German, English, and Scandinavian literature into Romanian.

Maiorescu belonged to the Conservative Party, which he represented in the Romanian parliament from 1871 onwards. From April 1874 to January 1876 he served as minister of national education; from May to July 1876, as Romanian minister to Berlin; and from 1888 to 1891, as minister of national education. From July 1900 to February 1901 he was minister of justice, and from December 1911 to March 1912, minister of foreign affairs. From 28 March 1912 to 4 January 1914 he simultaneously served as prime minister and minister of foreign affairs. In the summer of 1913, despite the reluctance of **Charles I**, Maiorescu decided that Romania would enter the Second Balkan War against Bulgaria, during which the Romanian troops reached the outskirts of Sofia. Maiorescu served as chairman of the Bucharest Peace Conference in August 1913, during which Romania obtained southern Dobrudja from Bulgaria. During World War I he represented a pro-German orientation, opposing Romania's entering the war on the side of the Entente. Maiorescu remained in German-occupied Bucharest, where he died. Maiorescu was the author or editor of a great number of publications, including the following: *Critice* (Critical pieces, 3 vols.; 1892); *Discursuri parlamentare* (Parliamentary speeches, 5 vols.; 1897–1915); *Istoria contemporană a României 1860–1900* (Contemporary Romanian history 1860–1900; 1925); *Inseminări zilnice (1855–1891)*

(Diaries 1855–1891, 3 vols.; 1937–43); and *Inseminări zilnice 1892–1917* (Diaries 1892–1917, 6 vols.; 1985–88). (FA/TD)

Sources: *Biographisches Lexikon*, vol. 3; Eugen Lovinescu, *Titu Maiorescu*, vols. 1–2 (Bucharest, 1936); Zigu Ornea, *Junimea şi junimirsul* (Bucharest, 1969); Gheorghe Ivaşcu, *Titu Liviu Maiorescu* (Bucharest, 1973); Zigu Ornea, *Viata lui Titu Maiorescu*, vols. 1–2 (Bucharest, 1986–87); Ion Bulei, *Sistemul politic al. României moderne: Partidul Conservator* (Bucharest, 1987); Keith Hitchins, *Rumania 1866–1947* (Oxford, 1994); Simion Ghita, *Titu Maiorescu şi filosofia europeana* (Galaţi, 1995).

MAIRONIS-MAČIULIS Jonas [originally Mačiulevičius-Mačiulis] (21 October 1862, Pasandravys, Raseiniai County–28 June 1932, Kaunas), Lithuanian poet and Catholic priest. After finishing school in Kaunas, Maironis-Mačiulis began to study literature at the university in Kiev in 1883. Discouraged by the low standard of lectures and by the atmosphere among students there, he dropped his studies and entered the Kaunas Theological Seminary in 1884. After graduating, he continued his studies at the Theological Academy in St. Petersburg (1888–92), earning M.A. and Ph.D. degrees in theology. He taught moral theology at this academy from 1894 to 1909. From 1909 until his death Maironis-Mačiulis served as rector of the Kaunas Theological Seminary, where he introduced lectures in Lithuanian instead of the previously used Latin or Polish. He also supported pro-independence and cultural organizations. In 1905 he attended the Grand Lithuanian Assembly in Vilnius and was co-founder of the Christian Democratic movement. In 1922, after Lithuania gained independence, he became a professor at Kaunas University, where he taught moral theology, world literature, and Lithuanian philology. In 1932 Kaunas University granted him an honorary doctorate. Earlier he had been promoted to prelate of the Samogitian diocese and to the rank of protonotary apostolic.

Maironis-Mačiulis began his literary career while a student, when, under the tutelage of Bishop Antanas Baranauskas, he studied the classics of world literature. In 1885 in the illegally published periodical *Aušra*, he published his first poem, *Lietuvos vargas* (Lithuanian sorrow), later changed to *Miškas ūžia* (The sighs of the forest). Because in the tsarist empire all publications in Lithuanian were prohibited, Maironis-Mačiulis had to publish his works in Tilsit (then in Germany; now Sovetsk, Russia). In 1891, under the pseudonym Stanislovas Zanavykas, he published *Lietuvos istorija* (The history of Lithuania). He first used the pseudonym Maironis in 1895, publishing the first collection of his poems, *Pavasario balsai* (Voices of spring). In his description of the Lithuanian past, he idealized the period from the thirteenth to the sixteenth centuries, emphasizing in particular the achievements of Vytautas the Great

(1350–1430), grand duke of Lithuania. Maironis-Mačiulis had nothing against the lighter genres; for example, he wrote the libretto of the operetta *Kame išganymas?* (Where is deliverance?). In the poem *Trab skausmų i garbę* (Through suffering to glory; 1895), published as part of the collection *Jaunoi Lietuva* (Young Lithuania), he depicted the ideals of young people who devoted their lives to the national cause, overcame class antagonisms, and strove for the development of Lithuanian culture. By publishing the poem *Znad Biruty* (From Biruta; 1904) in Polish, Maironis-Mačiulis wanted to win the support of the Polonized nobility for the cause of Lithuanian revival. During the independence period he wrote a three-part historical drama with anti-Polish overtones: *Kęstučio mirtis* (The death of Kęstutis; 1921); *Vytautas pas kryžioučius* (Vytautas the Great and the Teutonic knights; 1924); and *Vytautas karalius* (King Vytautas; 1930). During the independence period this trilogy was regularly staged on Independence Day, 16 February, in the State Theater in Kaunas.

Maironis-Mačiulis's writing greatly influenced twentieth-century Lithuanian literature. *Pavasario balsai* was published six times in the author's lifetime, and each successive edition included new poems; the first edition consisting of only 45 poems, while the last edition had 131 poems. Though greatly influenced by Romanticism, Maironis-Mačiulis did not yield to the conflict between emotion and reason, the two constituting a harmonious whole in his writings, leading to the victory of moral principles and heroism characteristic of patriotic poetry. He often used expressions of everyday speech. He replaced the traditional Lithuanian syllabic verse with tonic verse; as a result, his poetry became an inspiration for many composers, who wrote music to his poems. For example, his *Marija, Marija* became one of the most popular Lithuanian religious hymns, and *Lietuva brangi* (Dear Lithuania) was an unofficial national anthem during Soviet rule. After 1944 the Soviet authorities attempted to place a ban on the publication of Maironis-Mačiulis's works, but under public pressure, after 1956 his poems began to be published again. (AG)

Sources: *EL*, vol. 3; J. Tumas, *Lietuvių literatūros pasjaitos: Jonas Mačiulis-Maironis* (Kaunas, 1924); Vanda Zaborskaite, *Maironis* (Vilnius, 1987); Constantine R. Jurgela, *Lithuania: The Outpost of Freedom* (St. Petersburg, Fla., 1976); *Lithuania: An Encyclopedic Survey* (Vilnius, 1986); Irena Slavinskaite, *Mairoinis* (Kaunas, 1987); Romas Adomavičius, *Maironio rastu bibliografija 1883–1989* (Vilnius, 1990); Saulius Sužiedelis, *Historical Dictionary of Lithuania* (Lanham, Md., 1997); Henryk Wisner, *Litwa dzieje państwa i narodu* (Warsaw, 1999).

MAISTER Rudolf (29 March 1874, Kamnik–26 July 1934, Unec, near Rakek), Slovene general and poet. Maister completed six grades of high school in Ljubljana and then went to a cadet school in Vienna. He began his military career in the Austro-Hungarian Army, becoming a lieutenant in 1885. He was stationed at Przemyśl in Galicia and in other places. During World War I, with the rank of major, Maister fought in Maribor. He worked with many Slovene politicians and also with the National Council of Styria. After the collapse of the Austro-Hungarian Empire, Maister took control of Maribor and all of Lower Styria (1 November 1918). Promoted to general, in November 1918 he established Slovene units consisting of four thousand soldiers and two hundred officers, and he brought about the disarmament of the units of the former Austro-Hungarian Army. He also occupied the Slovene outposts in Styria. On 27 November 1918 Maister signed an agreement with the local Austrian commander on the border between Styria and Carinthia. In May 1919 he commanded one of the five units that launched an offensive in Carinthia. After victory was achieved and a truce was signed, Maister assumed control of the Slovene outposts in Carinthia around St. Lenart and Ettendorf.

Under the Saint-Germain-en-Laye 1920 Treaty of southern Styria, with Maribor and a small part of Carinthia, was incorporated into the Kingdom of Serbs, Croats, and Slovenes (SHS), and the fate of southern Carinthia was to be decided by a plebiscite on 10 October 1920. Maister was elected honorary president of the National Council of Carinthia but failed to win the support of the Carinthian people for the SHS: 59 percent of the votes were in favor of the area becoming part of Austria. As a result, according to the decision of the plebiscite committee, Maister and his subordinates left Carinthia on 19 September 1919. He became the governor of Maribor and from 1921 to 1923 served as chairman of a commission in charge of demarcating the border with Italy. After retiring in 1923, Maister wrote several articles that were published in *Boj za Maribor 1918–1919: Spominski zbornik ob sedemdesetletnici bojev za Maribor* (Battle for Maribor 1918–1919: A collection of memoirs on the seventieth anniversary of the struggle for Maribor; 1988). Maister made his debut as a poet in the periodical *Vrtec* in 1890. He later published several collections of poems, including *Poezije* (Poetry; 1904). Monuments honoring Maister were built in his native Kamnik, as well as in Maribor (1987) and Ljubljana (1999). His portrait can be seen on Slovene banknotes. (AO)

Sources: *Enciklopedija Slovenije*, vol. 6 (Ljubljana, 1992); *Enciklopedija Jugoslavije*, vol. 5 (Zagreb, 1962); B. Hartman, *Rudolf Maister* (Ljubljana, 1989); Arnold Suppan, ed., *Deutsche Geschichte in Osten Europas: Zwischen Adria und Karawanken* (Berlin, 1998).

MAJER Václav (22 January 1904, Pochválov, near Rakovník–26 January 1972, College Park, Maryland), Czech Social Democratic politician. A miner by trade, in 1935–38 Majer was head of the Union of Lease and Smallholders connected with the Social Democratic Party. After the Pact of Munich, in the fall of 1938 he tried in vain to establish the National Labor Party (Národná Strana Práce) in opposition to the Party of National Unity (Strana Národní Jednoty). At the beginning of the Nazi occupation Majer worked in the underground, but threatened with arrest, he fled through Hungary and Yugoslavia to France in 1940. He joined a Czechoslovak military unit there, but after the collapse of France, he moved to Great Britain. From 1942 to 1945 Majer belonged to the Czechoslovak State Council (Státní Rada Československa) and in 1944–45 was minister of industry, trade, and handicrafts in the government-in-exile. In March 1945 he took part in Moscow talks that led to the creation of a coalition government, which included the Communists. After World War II Majer was a member of the National Assembly and minister of supplies. He belonged to the top leadership of the Social Democratic Party, where he represented the right wing, opposing the Communists. During a coup in February 1948 he protested the Communist activities and stepped down on 25 February, the sole minister from his party to do so. He demanded that other Social Democratic ministers do the same, but he was outvoted by the party's left wing, headed by **Zdenek Fierlinger**, and center, headed by **Bohumil Laušman**. Majer left for Great Britain, where he presided over the Czech Social Democracy in exile. Later he emigrated to the United States, where he was active in the Council of Free Czechoslovakia, the Assembly of Captive European Nations, and the Socialist International. Majer published a lot and worked with Radio Free Europe and the Voice of America. (PU)

Sources: *ČBS*; *Československí politici: 1918–1991* (Prague, 1991); *Kdo byl kdo v našich dějinách ve 20. stoleti*, vol. 1 (Prague, 1998); Karel Kaplan, *The Short March: The Communist Takeover in Czechoslovakia, 1945–948* (London, 1981); John O. Crane and Sylvia Crane, *Czechoslovakia: Anvil of the Cold War* (New York, 1982).

MAKHNO Nestor (27 October 1889, Gulay Pole, near Yekaterinoslav–25 July 1934, Paris), anarchist, leader of the Ukrainian peasant guerrillas. Makhno was born into a poor peasant family. Deprived of his father at an early age, from his youth he worked as a farm laborer. In 1906 he joined an anarchist circle. Makhno was sentenced to life imprisonment for his participation in the assassination of a local police officer. He served the sentence in Butyrki Prison in Moscow, where he met the anarchist Piotr Arshynov, who gave him a thorough introduction to philosophy and the tactics of anarchism.

Released under an amnesty after the February 1917 revolution, Makhno returned to his home village and organized a council of delegates there. In August 1917 he formed an armed band that plundered the neighboring gentry and gave away land to the poor peasants. Makhno's cruelties soon earned him the reputation of a new Stepan (Stenka) Razin. During the occupation of the Ukraine by the Central Powers Makhno remained in hiding and then went to Moscow, where he met his idol, Piotr Kropotkin, as well as Vladimir Lenin. After his return to Gulay Pole in the fall of 1918, Makhno became active again, this time against the Austrians and the supporters of Hetman **Pavlo Skoropadskyi**. Makhno's detachments, having strong support in the countryside and becoming increasingly better organized, could carry out activities on a large scale. During an encirclement they hid among apparently quietly working peasants, only to start an attack at the least expected moment. Makhno was a commander with unusual instincts, an iron will, and a sense of humor that won him authority and commanded obedience among his subordinates. After the fall of the hetman's government, Makhno's troops took a stand against the Directory of the Ukrainian People's Republic. In the first half of 1919 the territory around Gulay Pole was virtually independent. Realizing here the anarchist experiment, Makhno based his rule upon provisional rallies, as well as congresses of peasant and partisan delegates. Public education was introduced that was Ukrainian in character. This petty statehood was based upon agrarian communes and perfectly organized military troops, which Makhno kept in an iron grip. The local Jews played quite an important role in this anarchic structure since Makhno strove against anti-Semitism.

In January 1919 Makhno signed an alliance with the Bolsheviks against the army of General Anton Denikin. The Ukrainian insurgency under Makhno's command was incorporated into the Red Army, preserving only the customary black banner. Along with the Bolsheviks Makhno occupied Kharkiv. After the first Bolshevik attempt to gain control over his movement, in May 1919 Makhno broke off the alliance and ordered the execution of two Cheka agents who had come to kill him. In June 1919 the Red Army captured the Rosa Luxemburg Memorial Commune in Gulay Pole, and soon after Denikin's armed forces completed its destruction. Makhno's detachments withdrew and in the summer of 1919 resumed cooperation with the Bolsheviks against Denikin. In October and November 1919 Makhno occupied Yekaterinoslav and Alexandrovsk and introduced the principles of anarchism into the municipal organizations. This ended with a wave of atrocities. At the end of 1919 Makhno was ordered by the command of the Red Army to move westward to the Polish front, but he refused to comply with the orders as he did not want to leave his home area. In October 1920 the Bolsheviks again made an agreement with Makhno, offering amnesty for all anarchists and freedom for anarchist propaganda in exchange for help against General Peter Wrangel's army. Makhno rebuilt the communes of Gulay Pole and took part, along with the Bolsheviks, in the Crimean offensive. The Red Army, after defeating Wrangel's army, attacked Makhno's troops. On 25 November 1920 the Bolsheviks destroyed his forces in the Crimea. The next day Leon Trotsky ordered the final attack at Gulay Pole. The Bolsheviks captured the staff and a great number of Makhno's soldiers and then murdered most of them.

Makhno escaped the roundup and in August 1921 fled to Romania. After nearly one year of wayfaring through Romania and Poland and after a stay in Gdańsk and Berlin, he reached Paris, where he spent the last years of his life in misery. He worked in a car factory, but most of the time he drank. In 1929–37 three volumes of his memoirs, *Russkaia revoliutsiia na Ukraine* (The Russian revolution in the Ukraine), appeared in Paris. Makhno died of tuberculosis. In the 1970s his activities gained considerable popularity among the New Left, and in 1992 his memoirs were published in Moscow. (WR)

Sources: *MERSH*, vol. 21; Joseph Kassel, *Makhno et sa juive* (Paris, 1925); David Footman, *Makhnovshchina* (Oxford, 1956); Victor Peters, *Nestor Makhno* (Winnipeg, 1970); Michael Palij, *The Anarchism of Nestor Makhno, 1918–1921* (Seattle, 1977); *Die Machno-Bewegung: Texte und Dokumente* (Berlin, 1980); Yves Ternon, *Makhno: La révolte anarchiste* (Brussels, 1981); Valerii Volkovinskii, *Makhni i ievo krakh* (Kiev, 1991); W. F. Verstiuk, *Makhnovshchina: Seliańsky povstańkyi rukh na Ukraini* (Kiev, 1991); Rostyslav Sambuk, *Makhno: Ostannia pravda* (Kiev, 1997).

MAKOVECZ Imre (20 November 1935, Budapest), Hungarian architect. Makovecz graduated from the Budapest Polytechnic College in 1959. In the 1960s and 1970s he worked as an architect in small towns. From 1981 he headed a design cooperative, Makona, simultaneously lecturing at the Budapest Polytechnic College and at the Central School of Industrial Design. From 1992 Makovecz was president of the Hungarian Academy of Fine Arts, and from 2000, deputy chairman of the Hungarian Chamber of Architecture. Makovecz is a chief representative of "organic architecture." He designed more than a hundred buildings of various types, combining the typical features of Hungarian national style with functionalism in an original way. He frequently used religious and plant motifs, as well as treatments that violated the traditional concept of symmetry. From the end of the 1980s Makovecz actively participated in public life, using his authority as an intellectual to support Christian Democratic and conservative initiatives. He exhibited numerous times in Europe and the United States. His major achievements include the following: the House of Culture in Sárospatak (1983); a church in Paks (1988); the Catholic University in Piliscsaba (1992–95); and the Hungarian pavilion at the World Exhibition in Seville (1992). Makovecz is the co-author (with János Gerle) of *A századforduló magyar épitészete* (Hungarian Architecture at the turn of the century; 1990). (MS)

Sources: Attila Komjáthy, *Makovecz Imre* (Budapest, 1977); János Frank, *Makovecz Imre* (Budapest, 1980); Jeffrey Cook, *Seeking Structure from Nature: The Organic Architecture of Hungary* (Basel and Boston, 1996); *Magyar Nagylexikon* (Budapest, 2000).

MAKOWSKI Wacław (15 November 1880, Wilno [Vilnius]–28 December 1942, Bucharest), Polish politician and lawyer. Makowski was born into an intelligentsia family tracing its origins to the landed gentry. He attended high school in Vilnius. In 1902 he completed law studies at Warsaw University and graduated in philosophy from the Jagiellonian University in Kraków and from the university in Lemberg (Lwów, Lviv). While a law student, Makowski was active in a secret Socialist pro-independence organization called Spójnia, and he published in underground leftist periodicals, including *Głos, Ogniwo,* and *Społeczeństwo.* He also published two progressive and moralistic novels. From 1901 to 1906 the tsarist police arrested him twice for political reasons. Makowski was active in the Association of Public Defenders (1905–7) and pursued scholarly work, studying summary law and the sociology of law. He published articles in *Ateneum* and *Gazeta Sądowa Warszawska.* In 1911 he published *Zbrodnie, kary i sądy wyjątkowe* (Crime, punishment, and special courts). After the outbreak of World War I and the German occupation of Warsaw in 1915, Makowski supported the so called, activists who favored the Central Powers and established local government institutions in Warsaw, including the judicial system and the home guard. He supported **Józef Piłsudski.** In July 1916 he became a member of the Warsaw City Council and then was appointed deputy director of the Justice Department in the Provisional Council of State and justice minister in the government of the Regency Council (February–April 1918).

During the Polish-Soviet war Makowski served in the Polish Army. After being transferred to the reserves in 1922, he was promoted to colonel. The minister of justice in successive governments from June 1922 until May 1923, Makowski played an active role in standardizing Polish legislation. For example, he was a co-author of the penal code. A lecturer, professor, and dean of the Department of Law of Warsaw University, after the coup of May 1926 he again became minister of justice (May–September 1926) and was instrumental in the introduction of constitutional amendments (August 1926). In 1928 Makowski became an MP on behalf of the pro-government Labor Party and later as a representative of the Nonparty Bloc of Cooperation with the Government (Bezpartyjny Blok Współpracy z Rządem). He increasingly embraced corporatist and authoritarian ideas. He published a number of treatises on constitutional law, including *Na drodze do reformy konstytucyjnej* (On the way to constitutional reform; 1928). In a similar spirit he edited the quarterly *Nowe Państwo.* Makowski was active in the international arena, speaking in favor of Poland's right to access to the sea. In 1933 he co-authored (with Georges Cruzen and Andre Tibal) *La question de Dantzig.* Makowski was one of the authors of the Polish constitution of April 1935. From 1935 on he sat in the Senate. In 1938, elected on the government ticket of the Camp of National Unity (Obóz Zjednoczenia Narodowego), Makowski became Senate speaker. After the last session of parliament on 2 September 1939, he escaped to the south of Poland and later to Romania, where he was interned along with the authorities of the Republic of Poland. The new Polish authorities in France considered Makowski an important person of the former *sanacja* regime, and they prevented him from going to the West. (MC)

Sources: *PSB,* vol. 19; Władysław Pobóg-Malinowski, *Najnowsza historia polityczna Polski,* vols. 1–3 (London, 1983–86); Władysław T. Kulesza, *Koncepcje ideowo-polityczne obozu rządzącego w Polsce w latach 1926–1935* (Wrocław, 1985); *Kto był kim w Drugiej Rzeczypospolitej* (Warsaw, 1994).

MALANCHUK Valentyn (13 November 1928, Ploskirov–25 April 1984, Kiev), Soviet party activist and historian of Ukrainian origin. After graduating from Lviv University in 1950, Malanchuk worked in the Lviv district committee of the Komsomol from 1950 to 1952 and in the Lviv district committee of the Communist Party of Ukraine (Komunistychna Partiya Ukrayiny [CPU]) from 1952 to 1967. While working in Lviv, Malanchuk showed a particular zeal in suppressing "Ukrainian bourgeois nationalists," which led to numerous conflicts with the cultural intelligentsia. In order to end these conflicts, **Petro Shelest** decided to transfer Malanchuk to Kiev. In 1967 Malanchuk became deputy minister of higher education, and in 1968 he became a professor at Kiev University. In 1972 he was appointed secretary for ideology of the Central Committee (CC) of the CPU and held the post until April 1979. From 1972 to 1981 he served as a deputy member of the CPU CC Politburo. Malanchuk's time in office in the CPU CC coincided with the greatest wave of anti-Ukrainian persecutions after World War II. An advocate of accelerated Russification and Sovietization of the Ukraine, he supported these persecutions. When more liberal policies toward the intelligentsia were introduced, Malanchuk left his post, becoming head of the department of CPSU history at Kiev Polytechnic. Malanchuk wrote numerous ideological articles on the history of the Communist movement in the Western Ukraine, as well as the books *Istoriia Komsomolu Zakhidn'oï Ukraïny* (The history of the Komsomol in the Western Ukraine; 1959) and *Radians'ka natsionalna polityka* (Soviet ethnic policies; 1963). (BB)

Sources: *Who's Who in the Socialist Countries of Europe* (Munich, London, and Paris, 1978); Oleh Bazhan, "Mene nazyvaiut' suchasnym Kochubeiem...," *Literaturna Ukraiina*, 2 December 1993; Jarosław Hrycak, *Historia Ukrainy 1772–1999* (Lublin, 2000).

MALANIUK Yevhen (20 January 1897, Kherson–16 January 1968, New York), Ukrainian poet and politician. In 1917 Malaniuk became an officer in the army of the Ukrainian National Republic (UNR). After this army was defeated, he was interned by the Polish authorities in Kalisz. He subsequently went to Czechoslovakia and completed studies at the Academy of Agriculture in Poděbrady (1923). Malaniuk lived in Czechoslovakia until the end of World War II, and then he made his way via Germany to the United States. His publications include *Hebariy* (Herbarium; 1926); *Zemlia i zalizo* (Earth and iron; 1930); *Zemna madonna* (Earthly madonna; 1934); *Persten Polikrata* (The ring of Polycrates; 1939); *Vlada* (Power; 1951); and *Ostannia vesna* (The last spring; 1954). In 1953 Malaniuk published a longer poem, *Piata symfoniia* (Fifth symphony), and the collections of essays *Narysy z istoriï nashoï kultury* (An outline of the history of our culture; 1954), *Do problemy bo'shevyzmu* (1956; On Bolshevism; 1956), and *Knyha sposterezhen* (Book of observations; 1962). Malaniuk was one of the contributors to *Vistnyk*, a periodical under the editorship of **Dmytro Dontsov**. He exerted great influence on the culture of the Ukrainian diaspora, but in the Ukrainian SSR he was attacked as a "Fascist" writer. Malaniuk's passionate style and the themes of his poems reflect his frustration over the failure of the Ukrainian struggle for independence and with the Ukrainian tragedy under Communist rule. (WR)

Sources: *Encyclopedia of Ukraine*, vol. 3 (Toronto, 1993); Ann Lencyk Pawliczko, *Ukraine and Ukrainians throughout the World* (Toronto, 1994).

MALËSHOVA Sejfulla (1900, Malëshovë–9 June 1971, Fier), Albanian Communist activist, poet, and journalist. Malëshova finished primary school in Vlorë and graduated from San Demetrio Corone High School in Cosenza, Italy. For a few years he studied medicine in Italy. In 1923 he returned to Albania and became a member of a youth organization called Bashkimi (Union). During the 1924 revolution Malëshova was the personal secretary of **Fan Noli**. After the failure of the revolution, he went to Vienna and joined the leftist National Revolutionary Committee (Komiteti Nacional Revolucionar [KONARE]), founded in 1925. The KONARE appointed Malëshova to a fourteen-member youth group sent him for training to Moscow and Leningrad. In Leningrad he graduated from a military school and translated *The Communist Manifesto* into Albanian. After leaving Moscow, Malëshova settled in France, where in 1938, on the orders of the Comintern, he attempted to murder **Llazar Fundo**, a Communist activist who was aligned with Trotsky. In 1942 Malëshova returned to Albania. In July 1943 he was appointed to the General Staff of the National Liberation Army. He rose quickly through the ranks of the Communist Party of Albania (CPA), becoming a member of its Central Committee (CC) in 1944 and then a member of the CC Politburo. He was also made secretary of the National Liberation Front.

Among the party leaders, Malëshova had the best knowledge of Marxist-Leninist theory. As a result, he was appointed to many responsible positions. Working in the spirit of Stalinist orthodoxy, he directed the department of press and propaganda, served as head of the central bank, and also helped to establish the Albanian Writers' Union and the first post-1944 sports clubs. In 1946 he served briefly as minister of education. On his initiative, translations of Soviet texts glorifying Lenin and the Stakhanovite movement were introduced into the schools. Nevertheless, Malëshova was one of the few party leaders who called for maintaining relations with the West and opposed overly close cooperation with Yugoslavia. In December 1945 the party leaders began to accuse Malëshova of "rightist deviation" and opportunism, and in February 1946 he was expelled from the Politburo and from the CC of the party. **Enver Hoxha** publicly labeled him a "lackey of the bourgeoisie" and a proponent of the abolition of the Communist Party. On the orders of **Koçi Xoxe**, Malëshova was arrested for opposing cooperation with Yugoslavia. Released after the fall of Xoxe in 1948, he spent the rest of his life in isolation, first working as a clerk in Berat and then in Fier, where he was banned from talking to local people. Malëshova died of appendicitis as a result of the lack of proper medical care. Malëshova first published his works in the 1930s under the pseudonym "Lame Kodra"

(Red Poet). In 1945 a collection of his poetry, *Vjersha* (Poems), was published in Tirana. (TC)

Sources: Lazitch; *Bashkimi*, 14 November 1945; Edmund Davies, *Ilyrian Venture: The Story of the British Military Mission in Enemy-Occupied Albania* (London, 1952); William E. Griffith, *Albania and the Sino-Soviet Rift* (Cambridge, Mass., 1963); Sejfi Vllamasi, *Ballafaqime politike në Shqipëri (1897–1942)* (Tirana, 1995).

MALÉTER Pál (4 September 1917, Eperjes [now Slovakia]–16 June 1958, Budapest), Hungarian general. Born into an intellectual family, after graduating from high school, Maléter was a student at the Medical Academy in Prague. He continued his medical studies in Budapest, but because of financial problems he could not finish his studies. He volunteered for the military in order to obtain Hungarian citizenship. In the fall of 1940 he was admitted to the Ludovika Military Academy in Budapest. After graduating from the academy, Maléter served in Kassa (now Košice, Slovakia), and then in 1944 he was sent to the eastern front, where he was taken captive. In captivity he volunteered to fight against the Germans. After completing a guerrilla training school, in the fall of 1944 Maléter, along with his unit, found himself in Transylvania. In January 1945 he became commander of a battalion that was created to defend the Provisional National Government, and from the spring of that year he commanded the battalion protecting the Ministry of National Defense. Until the outbreak of the revolution of 1956 Maléter served in lower-level positions in the people's army before attaining the rank of colonel.

On 25 October 1956, on the orders of the head of the general headquarters, Maléter, accompanied by the students of the Military Academy and equipped with five tanks, set off to help one of his units, which was located in the Kilián Barracks. As only one tank managed to get to the barracks, Maléter, with the consent of his superiors, concluded a cease-fire agreement with the insurgent units fighting in that district. On 27 and 28 October, after the end of the cease-fire agreement, Maléter, along with his soldiers, took control of the buildings surrounding the barracks. Having received the information that the government of **Imre Nagy** had ordered a cease-fire, Maléter complied with the government order. Maléter took part in cease-fire talks in Corvin Alley (Corvin Köz), where the biggest insurgent group was located. At Nagy's invitation Maléter participated in talks that were held in the parliament with the delegates of the workers' councils, and on 31 October he took part in a conference on the creation of the National Guard. The same day Nagy appointed him first deputy minister of national defense, and on 3 November, minister with the rank of major general. The same day

Maléter took part in negotiations conducted with the Soviet command in the parliament. In the evening Maléter, heading the Hungarian delegation, went for further talks to the headquarters of the Soviet troops in Tököl, near Budapest, where he was arrested along with all the other members of the delegation on the orders of the KGB head, General Ivan Sierov, who was present. On 15 June 1958, in a secret trial of Nagy and his associates, the People's Judicial Council of the Supreme Court charged Maléter with treason against the homeland, rebellion, and also with the fact that as a military leader of the insurrection, he had initiated and led the uprising. He was sentenced to death, without the right of appeal. Maléter did not plead for clemency, and until the end he believed in the ideas of the uprising. The day after the sentence was pronounced he was executed. (JT)

Sources: Horváth Miklós, *Maléter Pál: 1956-os Intézet-Osiris-Századvég* (Budapest, 1995); *1956 kézikönyve*, vol. 3: (*Megtorlás és Emlékezés*) (Budapest, 1996); *A magyar forradalom és szabadságharc enciklopédiája*, CD-ROM (Budapest, 1999).

MALINOV Aleksandur (21 April 1867, Pandykli, Bessarabia–20 March 1938, Sofia), Bulgarian politician. The son of a merchant, Malinov graduated from a high school in Belgrade and in law studies in Kiev. After returning to Bulgaria, he worked as a judge, public prosecutor, and defense attorney (1891–1902). One of the leaders of the Democratic Party, Malinov took the helm of this party in 1903 and held the top position until the end of his life. In 1903 Malinov was appointed president of the Tribunal of State, which sentenced former ministers Todor Ivanchov, Dimitur Tonchev, and **Vasil Radoslavov** to eight month's imprisonment for violating the constitution, embezzlement, and damage caused by their rule. Malinov served as deputy to the National Assembly (1901, 1908–34) and chairman of the Grand National Assembly in 1911. After the collapse of the government of **Stoyan Danev** (6 May 1903), he did not accept the proposal of Prince **Ferdinand I** to establish a new government. Under Malinov's leadership, the Democratic Party joined the Patriotic Bloc (1907–8), and on 16 January 1908 he became the head of a one-party government, serving also as minister of public housing, roads, and transportation (January 1908–November 1910) and minister of foreign and religious affairs (November 1910–March 1911). As prime minister, Malinov contributed to the establishment of the university in Sofia; took part in the preparations for and the proclamation of Bulgaria's independence as a kingdom (22 September 1908); and helped to draft amendments to the Turnovo Constitution and to consolidate the position of Tsar Ferdinand in Bulgaria. Malinov resigned on 16 March 1911.

Known for his pro-Western and pro-Russian sympathies, in September 1915 Malinov did not support Ferdinand's decision that Bulgaria enter World War I on the side of the Central Powers, and he called for neutrality. In the face of a deteriorating situation on the front and shortages of supplies in the cities, on 21 June 1918 Ferdinand appointed Malinov head of a coalition cabinet formed by the Democratic Party and the Radical Democratic Party. Until October he also served as minister of foreign and religious affairs and subsequently as minister of justice. In August Malinov warned the tsar and the German command about the military situation, but to no effect. After the collapse of the Macedonian front in mid-September, Malinov put down a military uprising in Radomir (27 September) and signed the armistice with the Entente in Salonika (29 September). Tsar Ferdinand had to abdicate, and Bulgaria was occupied by French, English, and Italian troops. In order to contain social unrest, in October Malinov introduced the moderate Socialists and the Bulgarian Agrarian National Union (BANU), led by **Aleksandur Stamboliyski**, into the governing coalition. However, on 28 November he resigned in protest against the Entente's decision to hand over southern Dobruja to Romania.

Under the rule of Stamboliyski (1919–23), Malinov played a leadership role in the establishment of the Constitutional Bloc (1922) and took part in an anti-government action organized by this bloc in Turnovo, for which he was arrested and imprisoned in Shumen. In March 1923 he was put on trial as one of those who had brought about the "national catastrophe" in Bulgaria, but he was released after the coup of 9 June 1923. In August 1923 he helped to establish the Democratic Alliance but left it at the beginning of 1924 and joined the opposition. At the end of May 1931 Malinov co-founded the National Bloc, which won the parliamentary elections in June. From 29 June to 12 October 1931 he served as prime minister and minister of foreign and religious affairs for the third time. As president of the National Assembly, he became the godfather of Princess Maria Luisa. After the coup of 9 May 1934 he again joined the opposition. Malinov died during an election campaign meeting in Sofia; he was a candidate of the democratic opposition. His publications include *Pod znaka na ostrasteni i opasni politicheski borbi* (Amid ardent and dangerous political struggle; 1934) and *Stranichki ot nashata nova politicheska istoriia. Spomeni* (Pages from our recent political history; 1938). (JJ)

Sources: *Entsiklopedyia Bulgariya*, vol. 4 (Sofia, 1984); *Biographsches Lexikon*, vol. 3; John D. Bell, *Peasants in Power: Alexander Stamboliski and the Bulgarian Agrarian National Union 1899–1923* (Princeton, 1977); Milen Kumanov, *Aleksandur Malinov: Poznatiyat i nepoznatiyat* (Sofia, 1993); A. Pantev and B. Gavrilov, *100-te nai-vliiatelni bulgari v nashata istoriia* (Sofia, 1997); Raymond Detrez, *Historical Dictionary of Bulgaria* (Lanham, Md., 1997); Tasho Tashev, *Ministrite na Bulgariya 1879–1999: Entsiklopedichen spravochnik* (Sofia, 1999); *Bulgarski durzhavnitsi i polititsi 1918–1947* (Sofia, 2000).

MALINOWSKI Bronisław (7 April 1884, Kraków–16 May 1942, New Haven, Connecticut), Polish anthropologist and sociologist. After graduating from a high school in Kraków, Malinowski studied mathematics, physics, and the history of philosophy at the Jagiellonian University (1902–6), earning a Ph.D. in philosophy (1908) there. In 1909 he continued his studies in Berlin, and in 1910 he went to the London School of Economics, where, influenced by James Frazer, A. C. Haddon, and W. H. R. Rivers, he developed his own anthropological studies. From 1913 Malinowski lectured at the London School of Economics and also traveled extensively, conducting field studies. From 1914 to 1918 he was based in Melbourne and studied the peoples of New Guinea and the Trobriand Islands. The results of these studies, published in *Argonauts of the Western Pacific* (1922), *Crime and Custom in Savage Society* (1926), *The Sexual Life of Savages in North-Western Melanesia* (1929), and *Coral Gardens and Their Magic* (1935), brought him international fame. In 1927 Malinowski was appointed to the chair of anthropology at the University of London. In 1934 he conducted studies in southern and eastern Africa, and in 1940–41, among the Zapotecs in Mexico. In 1936 he received an honorary doctorate from Harvard University. In 1938 he went to the United States, where he obtained a professorship at Yale University the following year. As a member of the Polish Academy of Arts and Sciences (Polska Akademia Umiejętności), Malinowski maintained close ties with Poland. Apart from **Oskar Halecki** and **Jan Kucharzewski**, he was one of the main founders of the Polish Institute of Arts and Sciences (Polski Instytut Naukowy) in America, serving as its first chairman from 1940 to 1942.

Malinowski's major theoretical works were published posthumously. These are *A Scientific Theory of Culture and Other Essays* (1944), *The Dynamics of Culture Change* (1945), *Freedom and Civilization* (1947), and *Magic, Science and Religion* (1948). Malinowski advocated that anthropological studies be based on a solid empirical foundation and that hypotheses be verified by the investigation of human activities. He believed that culture distinguished man from other creatures. He considered economy, family and upbringing, the political system, law, magic, religion, art, knowledge, and recreation as the main structural elements of culture. In his functionalist theory of cultural change Malinowski distinguished between endogenous elements (spontaneous evolution) and exogenous ones (external influences). He stressed the role of the clashes of cultures and changes as the disturbance of an existing culture balance. Malinowski's academic output is being published in Poland in his *Dzieła* (Works); seven volumes have already come out (1980–90). In 2002 his *Dzienniki* (Diaries) were published. (WR)

Sources: International Encyclopedia of the Social Sciences, vol. 9 (London, 1968); *Polacy w historii i kulturze krajów Europy Zachodniej: Słownik biograficzny* (Poznań, 1981); *Uczeni polscy XIX iXX stulecia*, vol. 3 (Warsaw, 1997); Raymond Firth, ed., *Man and Culture: An Evaluation of the Work of Bronislaw Malinowski* (London, 1957); Andrzej K. Paluch, *Malinowski* (Warsaw, 1981); Mariola Flis and Andrzej K. Paluch, eds., *Antropologia społeczna Bronisława Malinowskiego* (Warsaw, 1985); Ernst Gellner, *Language and Solitude* (Cambridge, 1989); Krzysztof Dybciak and Zdzisław Kudelski, eds., *Leksykon kultury polskiej poza krajem od roku 1939* (Lublin, 2000).

MALINOWSKI Roman (26 February 1935, Białystok), Polish Peasant Party activist. Born into a family of peasants and workers, in 1956 Malinowski graduated from the Central School of Planning and Statistics in Warsaw. From 1956 he belonged to the United Peasant Party (Zjednoczone Stronnictwo Ludowe [ZSL]), and he advanced in both the party, which was fully controlled by the Communists, and the state administration. In 1956–57 Malinowski was a member of the Chief Administration of the Association of Peasant Mutual Aid, from 1958 to 1963 he worked in the Central Association of Savings and Loan Cooperatives, and in 1969–71 he was deputy chairman of the Central Board of Dairy Cooperatives. From 1971 to 1973 he was deputy chairman of the Provincial National Council in Łódź, and from December 1973 to May 1975 he was the governor (*wojewoda*) of Łódź. From 1976 to 1989 he was a deputy to the parliament (Sejm), and from April 1980 to November 1985 he was deputy prime minister. The minister of the food industry and the state purchasing system from April to October 1980, from 1987 to 1991 he presided over the National Council of Polish-Soviet Friendship.

From November 1981 to September 1989 Malinowski was the ZSL chairman. He supported the introduction of martial law in December 1981. From 1983 to 1989 he belonged to the National Council of the facade organization, the Patriotic Movement of National Renaissance, and from 1985 to 1989 he was the speaker of the Sejm. Active abroad, Malinowski tried to overcome the international isolation of the Polish Communist authorities, paying visits to Italy and the Holy See (October 1984), Finland, Austria, Germany, and the United States (May–June 1987). A participant of the Round Table Talks, after the Communist defeat in the June 1989 elections and the failure of an

attempt by General **Czesław Kiszczak** to create a new government, Malinowski entered into a new coalition. **Lech Wałęsa**'s initiative of 7 August 1989, aimed at the creation of a coalition of former Communist satellites—the ZSL and the Democratic Party (Stronnictwo Demokratyczne [SD])—and the opposition Civic Parliamentary Caucus, gained the support of Malinowski and the SD leadership. The new coalition came into being on 17 August 1989, and **Tadeusz Mazowiecki** soon emerged as the first non-Communist head of the Polish government since World War II. Malinowski authored the memoirs *Wielka koalicja. Kulisy* (The great coalition: Behind the scenes; 1992). From 1989 Malinowski belonged to the Polish Peasant Party–Renaissance and then to the Polish Peasant Party (Polskie Stronnictwo Ludowe). (PK)

Sources: Mołdawa; *Słownik polityków polskich XX w.*; Michał Czajka, Marcin Kamler and Witold Sienkiewicz, *Leksykon historii Polski* (Warsaw, 1995); Jan Skórzyński, *Ugoda i rewolucja: Władza i opozycja 1985–1989* (Warsaw, 1995).

MALY Václav (21 September 1950, Prague), Czech bishop. The son of a teacher, Maly's decision to enter a theological seminar in Litoměřice cost his father his job. In June 1976 he was ordained, and for two years he worked as a vicar. After signing Charter 77, Maly lost the permission of the Communist authorities to minister. Despite the administrative ban he performed his duties secretly; for this he was imprisoned from May to December 1979. In 1980–89 Maly worked in the underground Catholic Church, employed as a geodesist, stoker, and toilet cleaner. In 1981 he became a Charter 77 spokesman. From 1978 he was a member of the Committee for the Defense of the Unjustly Prosecuted (Výbor na Obranu Nespravedlivě Stihaných [VONS]); later he was also a member of Polish-Czechoslovak Solidarity, and from 1988 he was a member of the Czech Helsinki Committee. Maly lectured at the secret Czech "Flying University." Frequently harassed by the political police, he became a popular personality in November 1989, when he led a demonstration of the Civic Forum on Letenské Sady in Prague. He encouraged its participants to say the Lord's Prayer, which was prohibited by the Communists outside of sacral buildings. The first spokesman of the Civic Forum, in January 1990 Maly returned to the ministry in St. Gabriel Parish in Prague Smichov, and in 1991–96 he worked in St. Anthony Parish in Prague Holešovice. He was also the first chairman of the Czech Catholic Charity (Česka Katolicka Charita). He accompanied many dissidents in their peregrinations of the soul. A close friend of **Václav Havel**, Maly was the chairman of the Organization Committee for the pilgrimage of Pope John Paul II to the Czech Republic in 1997.

Appointed auxiliary bishop of Prague on 8 December 1997, Maly was consecrated by Cardinal **Miloslav Vlk** on 11 January 1998. (AGr)

Sources: *Kdo byl kdo w našich dějinách ve 20. stoleti* (Prague, 1994); Information service of the (Polish) Catholic Information Agency, 8 December 1997 and 11 January 1998; www.totalita.cz; www.catholic-hierarchy.org.

MALYPETR Jan (21 December 1873, Klobouky–27 September 1947, Slaný), Czech Agrarian Party politician. After graduating from the Agricultural College in Kadani, Malypetr ran his family farm in Klobouki. From 1899 he was active in the Agrarian Party, and a year later he was elected to the local government. In 1906 he became a member of the Executive Committee of the party, in 1911 he was made *starost* (local representative of the authorities) in Klobouki, and in 1914 he was made district *starost* in Slaný. Malypetr became known as an efficient organizer; he was (among other things) a co-founder of the Union of Central Czech Power Plants. After World War I Malypetr became one of the leaders of the Agrarian Party (as of 1922, the Republican Party of Peasants and Smallholders), and during the First Republic he sat in the parliament. In 1922–25 he was minister of interior in the government of **Antonin Švehla**, contributing to political stabilization in Slovakia and Subcarpathian Ruthenia. After the elections of 1925 and the fall of Švehla's cabinet, Malypetr became speaker of the parliament, and he held the post until 1932. After the resignation of the government of **Fratišek Udržal** in October 1932, President **Tomáš Garrigue Masaryk** assigned Malypetr the task of forming a cabinet. Malypetr assumed the post of prime minister on 29 October 1932, at the time of the Great Depression and mounting problems in domestic policy connected with the resignation of the National Democrats from the government. Malypetr tried to save the situation by establishing tighter state controls over the economy. The parliament passed the necessary laws on 9 June 1933. Malypetr held the post of prime minister in the three subsequent cabinets, until 5 November 1935. In 1935–39 he was again speaker of the parliament. At the time of the Munich crisis in 1938, Malypetr advocated concessions toward Hitler. During the occupation he maintained a conciliatory attitude toward the Germans. In 1946 Malypetr was brought before the National Court and was charged with collaboration, but the court cleared him of the accusations. (PU)

Sources: *ČBS*; *Kto bol kto za I. ČSR* (Bratislava, 1993); *Kdo byl kdo v našich dějinach ve 20. stoleti*, vol. 1 (Prague, 1998); *Politická elita meziválečného Československa 1918–1938: Kdo byl kdo za prvni republiky* (Prague, 1998).

MANDIĆ Ante (2 June 1881, Trieste–15 November 1959, Lovran), Croatian lawyer and politician. After studying law in Vienna and Graz, Mandić worked as an attorney in Trieste and Abbazia (now Opatija, Croatia). During World War I he was in Russia, where in 1915 he helped to establish the Yugoslav Committee (Jugoslavenski Odbor), which was involved in various activities, such as recruiting Croatian prisoners of war to a volunteer legion in Odessa. In September 1917 Mandić became head of the London-based Bureau of the Yugoslav Committee. After returning to his country in 1919, he worked with the Adriatic Committee and the Yugoslav-Czechoslovak League. From 1921 to 1937 he worked in Opatija and then in Belgrade. After the collapse and partition of Yugoslavia in April 1941, Mandić again went to Opatija. In 1943 he moved to the territories controlled by **Josip Broz Tito**'s partisans. In November 1943 he attended the Second Congress of the Anti-Fascist Council for the National Liberation of Yugoslavia (Antifašističko Veće Narodnog Oslobodenja Jugoslavije [AVNOJ]) in Jajce. In 1944 Mandić was chairman of a commission for investigating war crimes, and from March to the end of November 1945 he was a member of the three-man Regency Council (Namjesništvo), which was in control of the government from the abdication of King **Peter** until the formal abolition of the monarchy. Mandić subsequently pursued scholarly work. His publications include *Fragmenti za historiju ujedinjenja* (Contributions to the history of the unification; 1956), a collection of documents for the study of the history of the Yugoslav Committee. (WR)

Sources: *Enciklopedija Jugoslavije*, vol. 6 (Zagreb, 1965); Michał Jerzy Zacharias, *Jugosławia w polityce Wielkiej Brytanii 1940–1945* (Wrocław, 1985).

MANDIĆ Nikola (15 January 1869, Dolac, near Travnik–7 June 1945, Zagreb), Croatian national politician. Mandić studied law in Sarajevo and Vienna. After graduation, he practiced as an attorney in Sarajevo. He was a member of the Croatian Party of Rights (led by Ante Starčević), which sought to unify all Croat-populated territories, first within the Habsburg monarchy and subsequently within a national state. In 1908 Mandić was a co-founder of the Croatian Peasant Party. In 1910 he was elected an MP and speaker of the Bosnian parliament. During World War I he was a civil commissioner, assisting the military governor of Bosnia. After the establishment of the Kingdom of Serbs, Croats, and Slovenes, Mandić served as a deputy to the Constitutional Assembly. He vigorously protested the 1921 constitution, and when it came into force, he retired from politics, resuming his professional career. At the end of the 1930s Mandić was known for his nationalist views, but he never joined the Ustasha movement. He also did not take an active part in the establishment of the Independent State of Croatia in April 1941. In September 1942 **Ante Pavelić** appointed Mandić secretary of state, and on 2 September 1943, prime minister—to the surprise of the Ustasha elite. Some politicians from Pavelić's entourage even resigned in protest. On 11 October 1944 Mandić reorganized his cabinet, bringing in politicians from the Croatian Peasant Party, which was to enhance the credibility of the Ustasha regime in the eyes of the Allies. Mandić fled from Zagreb on 6 May 1945. Caught by the British and handed over to the Communists on 18 May, he was sentenced to death and executed. (WR)

Sources: Ladislaus Hory and Martin Broszat, *Der kroatische Ustascha-Staat 1941–1945* (Stuttgart, 1964); Ivo Omrčanin, *Dramatis Presonae and Finis of the Independent State of Croatia in British and American Documents* (Bryn Mawr, Pa., 1983); Bogdan Krizman, *Ustaše il Treći Reich*, vols. 1–2 (Zagreb, 1983); Bogdan Krizman, *Ante Pavelić i Ustaše* (Zagreb, 1983); Marcus Tanner, *Croatia: A Nation Forged in War* (New Haven, 1997).

MĂNESCU Corneliu (8 February 1916, Ploeşti–26 June 2000, Bucharest), Romanian Communist diplomat. Mănescu came from an intelligentsia family with liberal views. He completed law studies at the university in Bucharest. In the second half of the 1930s he became involved in a student movement and secretly joined the Romanian Communist Party (RCP). He officially wrote for the leftist newspapers. Following the Communist takeover after World War II, Mănescu served as deputy minister of national defense (1948–55), vice-president of the State Planning Committee (1955–60), ambassador to Hungary, and minister of foreign affairs (March 1961–October 1972). As head of the foreign service and one of the closest associates of Prime Minister **Ion Maurer** from 1961 to 1974, Mănescu significantly contributed to overcoming Romania's dependency on the Soviet Union and helped to broaden and diversify Romania's foreign relations. Mănescu's establishment of diplomatic relations with the Federal Republic of Germany in 1964, when the countries subordinated to the Soviet regime recognized the German Democratic Republic as the only representative of the German nation, was one of Romania's major moves independent of the Soviet Union. In September 1967 Mănescu became the first politician from the Soviet bloc to serve as chairman of the UN General Assembly; he chaired the twenty-second session, which investigated (among other things) the crucial issues of the 1967 Six Day Arab-Israeli War and the 1968 invasion of Czechoslovakia by Warsaw Pact troops (with the exception of Romania).

Gradually moved into the background as an opponent of the domestic policies of **Nicolae Ceauşescu**, Mănescu

was forced to resign his last position, that of ambassador to France, and to retire in 1982. In March 1989 he was one of the co-authors of the "Letter of the Six," written by former top-ranking Communist officials and criticizing the disastrous policies of the leaders of the Romanian Communist Party, as well as denouncing Ceauşescu's personality cult. As punishment, Mănescu was placed under house arrest. After the revolution in December 1989, Mănescu served as a member of the Provisional Council of the National Salvation Front and chairman of a parliamentary committee for foreign policy from 1990 to 1992. (ASK)

Sources: *Chronological History of Romania* (Bucharest, 1974); Silviu Brucan, *The Wasted Generation* (Boulder, Colo., 1993); Şerban N. Ionescu, *Who Was Who in Twentieth Century Romania* (Boulder, Colo., 1994); *Adevărul*, 27 June 2000.

MĂNESCU Manea (9 August 1916, Braila), Romanian Communist activist, son-in-law of **Nicolae Ceauşescu**. The son of a Communist activist, after graduating from the Academy of Trade and Industry in Bucharest, in 1944 Mănescu, along with Ceauşescu began restoring the Association of Communist Youth. In 1951 he was appointed dean of the Department of Economics of Bucharest University, and in 1951–55 he was chairman of the Central Statistical Office. He also became a member of the Romanian Academy of Sciences. From October 1955 to March 1957 Mănescu was minister of finance, and then he became deputy chairman of the State Planning Commission and chairman of the State Commission of Labor and Wages. From 1959 he was secretary general of the National Sociological Committee and then deputy chairman of the Economic Research Society. In 1960 he became a member of the Central Committee (CC) of the Romanian Communist Party (RCP), for four years working as head of its Department of Culture and Science. In 1961 he became an MP, and in 1961–69 he headed the parliamentary commission for finance and economy. From 1965 Mănescu was a member of the State Council for Research; from 1966 to 1968 he was a deputy member of the CC Executive Committee and then a full member. From February 1971 he was a member of the CC Standing Presidium, the highest executive organ of the Communist Party. From 1969 to 1972 he was deputy chairman of the Council of State, and in October 1972 he became chairman of the State Planning Commission.

On 29 March 1974 Mănescu became prime minister, and in 1974–79 he also headed the Council for Economic and Social Relations. He implemented the diplomatic line of Ceauşescu, visiting France, the United States, and other Western countries. In contrast to other Communist countries, Romania maintained contacts with Israel and also entered into relations with the Palestinian Liberation Organization. On 29 March 1979 Mănescu resigned, formally for health reasons. Soon he was also removed from other party and state positions. In November 1982 he suddenly returned as deputy chairman of the Council of State and became chairman of the National Council for Consolidated Land Administration. In March 1983 he returned to the CC Executive Committee, and in December 1984 he became a CC Politburo member. Mănescu authored numerous works on economic development and mathematical modeling. After the fall of the Ceauşescu regime, Mănescu retired. (PC)

Sources: *International Year Book and Statesmen's Who's Who* (London,1990); *Who's Who in the Socialist Countries of Europe* (Munich, London, and Paris, 1978).

MANIU Iuliu (8 January 1873, Simleu Silvanei–July 1953?, Sighet), Romanian Peasant Party politician. Maniu was born into a peasant family in Transylvania. In February 1905 he was elected as a representative of the Romanian National Party (Partidul Naţional Romanesc [RNP]) to the Hungarian parliament, where he demanded equal rights for the Romanian people in Transylvania. During World War I Maniu served in the Austro-Hungarian Army. In May 1918 he organized a revolt of the Romanian troops, which joined the side of the Entente. Maniu was a member of a delegation of Transylvanian Romanians who on 14 November 1918 rejected the conditions set by the National Council of Hungary on the matter of self-determination and voted for full secession. On 1 December 1918 Maniu presided over the Great Assembly of Transylvanian Romanians in Alba Iulia that proclaimed union with the Old Kingdom of Romania. He also became head of the RNP and of the Transylvanian Directing Council. The council's demands were supported by the Entente and ratified by the peace treaty signed with Hungary in Trianon in June 1920.

From 1926 Maniu headed the National Peasant Party (Partidul Naţional Ţărănesc [NPP]), known as the Tsaranists and formed by the merger of the Transylvanian RNP with the Peasant Party of **Ion Mihalache** from the Old Kingdom. Between 10 November 1928 and 10 October 1930 (with a short break), Maniu served as prime minister. He agreed to the return of King **Charles II** from exile in July 1930, but he resigned after the king broke his promise to leave his mistress, **Magda Lupescu**, and reconcile with Queen Helen. Two years later Maniu reconciled with the king, and from 20 October 1932 to 14 January 1933 he again served as the head of government. However, as Charles showed increasingly explicit dictatorial tendencies and accepted the Fascists from the Iron Guard in his regime, Maniu broke off his relations with the king and joined the opposition. After the king's conflict with the Iron Guard in 1937 Maniu formed a tactical electoral alliance with the Iron Guard. However, he failed to win the elections, which were manipulated by the royal administration, and he went against his own interests by entering into an alliance with forces representing aims contradictory to his own.

After Romania was divested of Transylvania and Bessarabia in the summer of 1940 and General **Ion Antonescu** came to power, the NPP was declared illegal, and a part of its base, northern Transylvania, was again included within the boundaries of Hungary. Despite this, Maniu enjoyed great respect in the countryside. He thought at that point that the regime of Antonescu might be a shield protecting Romania against extreme Fascists and against the conquest of the country by Germany. He accepted Romania's involvement in the war against the USSR in 1941 in order to regain Bessarabia, which had been incorporated by the Soviets, but when the involvement of the Romanian Army went beyond this aim, in January 1942 Maniu, along with the leader of the liberal opposition, **Constantin Bratianu**, sent a note to Antonescu demanding the withdrawal of Romanian forces to the west of the Dniester River. In August 1943, in agreement with groups close to Antonescu, Maniu authorized a letter to the United States and Great Britain proposing that Romania join the Allied side on condition that the Allies guarantee Romanian rule in Bessarabia. The letter went unanswered because of the role that the Allies attributed to the USSR on the eastern front. The Kremlin, on the other hand, considered Maniu's offer contrary to its interests and demanded the unconditional capitulation of Romania. With the approach of the Soviets, in June 1944 Maniu agreed to the preliminary conditions for negotiations with the Allies that were presented by Stalin: Romania would join the Allies against Germany; it would give up claims to Bessarabia; Transylvania would be returned to Romania; and the Red Army would be allowed to march through Romania. Maniu also began to form a national front that prepared a coup and brought Romania to the Allied side.

On 23 August 1944, the day of Antonescu's arrest by King Michael's guards and the establishment of a coalition government of the National Democratic Front, Maniu became a member of the cabinet. In November 1944 the USSR introduced its own military administration in Transylvania; removed the voluntary National Guard, a paramilitary organization that had remained under the influence of the NPP; and diminished the influence of the non-Communists. On 6 March 1945 under pressure from the Kremlin, a government dominated by the Communists and the left was established, and **Petru Groza** was installed as its head. Maniu and his party went into the opposition. On 18 July 1945 Maniu gave a speech in which he demanded the restoration of a broad coalition cabinet. Because the Allies had given the USSR leeway, this claim could not be realized, especially since in February 1946 the United States, Great Britain, and France recognized Groza's government. During negotiations on a peace treaty with Romania in 1946, the Peasant Party opposition protested the interference of the USSR in Romania's domestic affairs. However, in the falsified elections of November 1946, according to official statistics, Maniu's party gained only 12 percent of the vote.

In April 1947 Maniu, along with some leaders of the opposition, bravely sent a letter to a conference of foreign ministers of the great powers, accusing Groza's government of human rights abuses. In the beginning of July 1947 Maniu supported the acceptance of the Marshall Plan for Romania, but in the middle of the same month he was arrested by the Communists. In November 1947 he was sentenced to life imprisonment under the false accusations of spying against and the sabotage of "the people's democracy," as well as the fascization of Romania before World War II. Maniu died in prison. Different dates are given for his death, including 1951, 1953, and 1955. After the fall of communism in Romania some of Maniu's works were published, including *Testament moral politic* (A moral-political testament; 1991) and *Trei discursuri* (Three conversations; 1991). (WR)

Sources: *Trial of the Former National Peasant Party Leaders: Maniu, Michalache, Penesco, Nicolesco-Buzesti, and Others from Shorthand Notes* (Bucharest, 1947; also published in French); Andrzej Koryn, *Rumunia w polityce wielkich mocarstw 1944–1947* (Wrocław, 1983); Ion Calafeteanu, ed., *Iuliu Maniu, Ion Antonescu: Opinii si confruntari politice 1940–1944* (Cluj and Napoca, 1994); Josif Toma Popescu, *Świadectwo* (Warsaw, 1996); Ioan Scurtu, *Iuliu Maniu: Activitatea politica* (Bucharest, 1996); Dennis Deletant, *Communist Terror in Romania: Gheorghiu-Dej and the Police State, 1948–1965* (New York, 1999).

MANOILESCU Mihail (10 December 1891, Tecuci–1950, Sighet), Romanian economist and politician. In 1915 Manoilescu graduated in engineering studies from the Budapest Polytechnic Institute. In 1920 he became director of a department at the Ministry of Industry and Trade, and from 1926 to 1927 he was a member of the People's Party (Partidul Poporului) and undersecretary of state in the Ministry of Finance. A member of the National Peasant Party (Partidul Naţional Ţărănesc [NPP]) from 1927, Manoilescu was in opposition to the NPP's "peasant" wing, as he believed that peasants could not be the dominant force in a state undergoing modernization. He advocated industrialization and protectionism and supported the efforts of **Charles II** to regain the Romanian throne. In October 1927 Manoilescu was arrested while returning to Romania with secret letters from Charles to the Romanian opposition. Accused of a conspiracy that aimed to stage a coup d'état, he was tried and placed in Jilava Prison but was soon acquitted. After Charles assumed the Romanian throne in 1930, Manoilescu was cleared of charges and appointed minister of public works and transport.

From October 1930 to April 1931 Manoilescu was minister of industry and trade. Later he served as chairman of the central bank (June–November 1931) and worked as a professor of political economy at the university in Bucharest (1932–44). His views evolved from neo-liberalism to authoritarian corporatism and a fascination with Italian fascism. In 1932 Manoilescu founded the corporatist periodical *Lumnea Nouă*, and in 1933, the National Corporate League (Liga Naţional-Corporatistă), a group that combated the dominance of party politics in public life. In 1936 Manoilescu was a guest at a Nazi congress in Nuremberg. In 1937 he became a senator on the ticket of All for the Fatherland (Totul pentru Ţară), an organization established by the Iron Guard (Gărdia de Fier). Manoilescu's views corresponded to a great extent with the ideology of the Iron Guard, although he was a supporter of the concentration of property and promoted protectionism and the introduction of protective anti-import customs duties. According to Manoilescu, free international trade strengthened only the developed Western countries at the expense of agricultural countries like Romania. King Charles II approved of his views. Consequently, after the 1938 coup d'état and the abolition of all political parties, when Charles assumed full control of the government, he made Manoilescu one of his closest associates. From June to September 1938 Manoilescu served as minister of foreign affairs and headed a delegation that accepted the Vienna Award on 30 August 1938. Under the Vienna Award around one-third of Romania's territory was ceded to Hungary and Bulgaria. After General **Ion Antonescu** came to power in September of that year, Manoilescu retired from politics.

In 1948 Manoilescu was arrested by the Communists and imprisoned without trial in Sighet Prison, where he died. Manoilescu's publications include the following: *Politica Statului în chestiunea refacerii industriale* (State policy on industrial reconstruction; 1920); *Organizarea financiară a economiei naţionale* (The financial organization of the national economy; 1924); *La théorie du protectionisme industriel* (The theory of industrial protectionism; 1929); *Echilibrul economic european* (European economic equilibrium; 1931); *România, stat cooperatist* (Romania, a corporate state; 1933); *Secolul corporatismului* (The age of corporatism; 1934); *Le parti unique* (One party; 1937); and *La situation économique de la Roumanie en 1929* (Romania's economic situation in 1929; 1940). Manoilescu also authored *Memorii* (Memoirs; 1993). (LW)

Sources: Philip Rees, *Biographical Dictionary of the Extreme Right since 1890* (New York, 1990); *Dictionar Enciclopedic*, vol. 4 (Bucharest, 2001); Vlad Georgescu, *Istoria Românilor de la origini pînă în zilele noastre* (Oakland, 1984); Vasile C. Nechita, ed., *Mihail Manoilescu, creator de teorie economica* (Iaşi, 1993); Józef Darski, *Rumunia: Historia, współczesność, konflikty narodowe* (Warsaw, 1995); Krzysztof Dach and Tadeusz Dubicki, *Żelazny Legion Michała Archanioła* (Warsaw, 1996); Dorina N. Rusu, *Membrii Academiei Române 1866–1999* (Bucharest, 1999); Ion Alexandrescu, Ion Bulei, Ion Mamina, and Ioan Scurtu, *Enciclopedia de istorie României* (Bucharest, 2000); pages.prodigy.net; www.miscarea-legionara.org.

MANOLESCU Nicolae (27 November 1939, Râmnicu Vâlcea), Romanian literary critic and politician. In 1956 Manolescu graduated from a high school in Sibiu, and in 1962 he graduated in philological studies at the University of Bucharest. In 1962–72 he published in the literary periodical *Contemporanul* and in 1972–93 in *România literară*. From 1971 to 1974 he was deputy editor-in-chief and from 1990 director of the latter periodical. In 1974 Manolescu received a Ph.D. in literature from the University of Bucharest, and in 1990 he became a professor of philology at this university. In 1990 he co-founded the democratic Civic Alliance (Alianţa Civica [SO]), which aimed at the development of civic society in Romania. The organization split in 1991, when its Bucharest branch, headed by Manolescu, decided to turn into a political party, the Civic Alliance Party (Partidul Alianţei Civice [PSO]). In 1991–95 the PSO, led by Manolescu, was a part of the Democratic Convention of Romania (Convenţia Democrată Română [CDR]), which included parties opposing the post-Communist rule. In 1992–96 Manolescu was a senator on behalf of the CDR. In 1994–95 the PSO belonged to the Civic Citizens' Alliance, a failed attempt to unify the liberal parties. In 1995, owing to Manolescu's personal conflicts in the CDR, the PSO left the convention. Before the parliamentary and presidential elections of November 1996 the PSO merged with the Liberal Party into the National Liberal Alliance (Alianţa Naţional-Liberală), but the alliance was defeated, while Manolescu, running for president, won only 0.7 percent of the vote. In 1998 Manolescu merged his party with the National Liberal Party (Partidul Naţional Liberal), and for some time he was a member of its National Council. Manolescu authored *Literatura română de azi* (Contemporary Romanian kiterature; 1965); *Metamorfozele poeziei*

(Metamorphoses of poetry; 1968); *Eseuri critice* (Critical essays, 7 vols.; 1971–89); *Despre poezie* (On poetry; 1987); *Istoria critică a literaturii române* (Critical history of Romanian literature; 1990); and *Teme* (Themes; 2001). In 1997 Manolescu became a member of the Romanian Academy of Sciences. (LW)

Sources: *Dictionar Enciclopedic*, vol. 4 (Bucharest, 2001); Józef Darski, *Rumunia: Historia, współczesność, konflikty narodowe* (Warsaw, 1995); Dorina N. Rusu, *Membrii Academiei Române 1866–1999* (Bucharest, 1999); Ion Alexandrescu, Ion Bulei, Ion Mamina, and Ioan Scurtu, *Enciclopedia de istorie României* (Bucharest, 2000); romania-on-line.net/whoswho/ManolescuNicolae.htm.

MANOLIĆ Josip (22 March 1920, Kalinovac, near Djurdjevac), Croatian Communist activist and post-Communist politician. Manolić graduated in law in Zagreb. In 1939 he joined the Communist Party of Yugoslavia, and during World War II he fought with the Communist guerrillas. After the war he worked in the Public Security Office, in the Croatian republican Ministry of Interior (1948–60), and in the Secretariat of Internal Affairs in Zagreb (1960–65). In 1965 and 1969 Manolić won a seat in the Croatian republican assembly and chaired its legislative commission. After the "Croatian Spring" and the purge in the League of Communists of Croatia in December 1971, Manolić was accused of "nationalism." He lost his mandate and withdrew from political life. In 1989 he co-founded the Croatian Democratic Union (Hrvatska Demokratska Zajednica [HDZ]) and was the first chairman of its Executive Council. In 1990 and 1992 Manolić was elected to the Croatian parliament. In 1990 he became deputy chairman of the Croatian Presidium, still within the Socialist Federative Republic of Yugoslavia.

On 24 August 1990 Manolić became prime minister of Croatia, which proclaimed its independence in June 1991. He remained in office until 3 August 1991. In 1991–93 he chaired the Office of Protection of the Constitutional Order (Ured za Zaštitu Ustavnog Poretka). In 1993 he became chairman of the House of Districts, the upper house of the Croatian parliament. In April 1994 a number of HDZ activists criticized President **Franjo Tudjman**. Manolić himself objected to Tudjman's anti-Muslim policies in Bosnia-Herzegovina and to his dictatorial style. As a result Manolić was dismissed from the HDZ, along with **Stipe Mesić**. In April 1994 Manolić co-founded the Croatian Independent Democrats (Hrvatski Nezavisni Demokrati [HND]) and became the party's deputy chairman. In May 1994 Manolić was also dismissed from the position of chairman of the House of Districts, which led to a parliamentary crisis that was resolved in the fall of 1994. After Mesić left the HND in 1997, Manolić became head of the party, but in the subsequent elections the party failed to gain more than one mandate. (AO)

Sources: *Hrvatski Leksikon*, vol. 2 (Zagreb, 1997); Robert Stallaerts and Jeannine Laurens, *Historical Dictionary of the Republic of Croatia* (Lanham, Md., 1995); *The International Who's Who 1996–97* (London, 1996); *Europa Środkowo-Wschodnia 1994–95* (Warsaw, 1996–97); Bugajski.

MANSFELD Péter (10 March 1941, Budapest–21 March 1959, Budapest), victim of the Communist oppression. Mansfeld was the son of a barber. His parents divorced, and he was brought up by a single mother. After primary school, Mansfeld studied in a vocational school. In October 1956 he joined the insurgents in Szén Square in Budapest. He did not take part in the fighting but supplied arms and food and was a liaison between various groups of insurgents. On 5 November 1956 Mansfeld broke into the villa of former interior minister **László Piros** and took weapons that the latter hid at home. After the suppression of the revolution, Mansfeld continued his education. In February 1958, along with a friend, he decided to establish an armed group. They captured a militiaman from the post in front of the Austrian Embassy, disarmed him, and set him free. They also planned to free imprisoned friends and to take revenge against those who had informed on the insurgents, but they failed. Two days after the capture of the militiaman, Mansfeld was arrested. On 21 November 1958 he was sentenced to life imprisonment for taking part in a "plot against the power of the people." On 19 March 1959 the Supreme Court changed this sentence to a death penalty. Two days later he was executed as an adult. (JT)

Sources: *A magyar forradalom és szabadságharc enciklopédiája*, CD-ROM (Budapest, 1999); *Magyar Nagylexikon*, vol. 12 (Budapest, 2001); György Litván, ed., *Rewolucja węgierska 1956 roku* (Warsaw, 1996).

MANUILSKYI Dmytro (3 October 1883, Sviatets, Volhynia–22 February 1959, Kiev), Soviet and Communist activist of Ukrainian origin. In 1903 Manuilskyi began to study at St. Petersburg University and joined the Bolshevik faction of the Russian Social Democratic Workers' Party (RSDWP). From 1900 to 1906 he was involved in agitation work in St. Petersburg. In 1906 he was sentenced to five years' exile for his part in the mutiny of the sailors in Kronstadt, but he escaped to Kiev and joined the local RSDWP (Bolshevik) committee in 1907. In the autumn of that year Manuilskyi went to Paris, where in 1911 he graduated in law from the Sorbonne. From 1912 to 1913 he illegally stayed in Moscow and St. Petersburg and then again went abroad. In May 1917 he returned to Russia and later that year took part in the October Revolution. On 12 June 1918, along with **Khristian Rakovsky**, Manuilskyi signed the Preliminaries of Peace with the Ukrainian National Republic. Then he was sent by the Central Committee (CC) of the party to the Ukraine to organize the Bolshevik movement there. For some time he was drawn to the so-called federalist faction of the Communist Party (Bolshevik) of Ukraine (Komunistychna Partiya [Bilshovykiv] Ukrayiny [CP(B)U]), which called for a federal union in which the Ukrainian SSR and the RSFSR would have equal rights. From 1919 to 1920 Manuilskyi belonged to the All-Ukrainian Revolutionary Committee (Vseukrayins'kyy Revkom), and from 1920 to 1921 he was a delegate to the Polish-Soviet peace negotiations in Riga.

From 1920 to 1922 Manuilskyi was the people's commissar for agriculture of the Ukrainian SSR, and in 1921 he served for a short time as first secretary of the CP(B)U CC and editor of the newspaper *Kommunist*. From 1920 to 1923 and from 1949 to 1952 he was a member of the Politburo of the CP(B)U CC, and from 1924 to 1949, a member of the CC Presidium. In the struggle for power in the Kremlin, Manuilskyi gave his unreserved support to Stalin. From 1928 to 1943 he held the post of secretary of the Executive Committee of the Communist International. Head of the party delegation to the Third International, Manuilskyi was one of the main executors of Stalinist policies in this organization, including the bloody Stalinist purges in the Comintern apparatus and in foreign Communist parties. In 1944 Manuilskyi became deputy prime minister and the people's commissar for foreign affairs of the Ukrainian SSR. In April 1945 he was head of the Ukrainian delegation to the international conference in San Francisco where the United Nations was established. He was also head of the Ukrainian delegation to the Paris Peace Conference in 1946 and attended the first sessions of the UN General Assembly. From the UN rostrum he attacked, among other things, the work of Ukrainian émigré communities. From 1945 to 1946 Manuilskyi was one of the initiators and ideologues of yet another campaign against "Ukrainian bourgeois nationalism," and he organized attacks against such prominent representatives of Ukrainian culture as the historians Mykola Petrovsky and **Ivan Krypyakevych** and the writers **Oleksandr Dovzhenko**, **Volodymyr Sosyura**, **Yury Yanovsky**, and **Maksym Rylsky**. From 1946 to 1953 Manuilskyi was deputy prime minister of the Ukrainian SSR, and from 1946 to 1952 he was also minister of foreign affairs. He subsequently retired. (BB)

Sources: *MERSH*, vol. 21; *Encyclopedia of Ukraine*, vol. 3 (Toronto, 1993); *Malyi Slovnyk Istorii Ukraiiny* (Kiev, 1997); Lazitch; *Dovidnyk z istorii Ukraiiny* (Kiev, 2001); Hryhory Kostiuk, *Stalinist Rule in the Ukraine* (New York, 1960); Leonid Suyarko, *D. Z. Manuilskyi: Revoliutsioner, diplomat, uchenyi* (Kiev, 1983).

MÁRAI Sándor [originally Grosschmid] (11 April 1900, Kassa [Košice]–21 February 1989, San Diego, California), Hungarian writer, poet, and journalist. Márai's father was a successful attorney and a senator in Kassa, and his elder brother, Géza Radványi, was a film director. After graduating from a high school in Eperjes (Prešov), Márai went to Budapest, where he briefly attended the School of Arts at the university and subsequently worked as a journalist. Under the Hungarian Soviet Republic (HSR) he published in the Communist press. After the fall of the HSR he went to Vienna and then to Germany. In Leipzig, Berlin, and Frankfurt Márai published his articles in *Frankfurter Zeitung, Prager Tageblattnak,* and the Budapest-based *Újság.* He wrote many reports from his foreign journeys. In 1928 he returned to Hungary, and for twenty years he was one of the most popular and prolific writers. In that time Márai published thirty-nine novels, poetry volumes, collections of novellas, and essays. He also wrote articles for newspapers. In 1934 he published *Egy polgár vallomásai* (Confessions of a burgher), a novel about the life of Kassa burghers that had numerous autobiographical elements. This book made Márai one of the most famous twentieth-century Hungarian prose writers. He was also an acclaimed playwright. His plays *Kaland* (Adventure; 1940) and *Kassai polgárok* (Kassa burghers; 1942) were successfully staged. In 1942 Márai became a member of the Hungarian Academy of Sciences. In 1943 he began to write a diary; the first volume, devoted to the period from 1943 to 1944, contains a moving description of war events (*Napló* [A diary]; 1946). The subsequent volumes of this diary, which Márai wrote and published until the end of his life, were a record of reflections of an émigré from Communist-ruled Central Europe and an analysis of relations between culture and authority, art and kitsch, and past and present.

In 1945 and 1946 Márai took a long journey around Western Europe and finally left Hungary in 1948 as a result of his troubles with the censors when writing the novel *Sértődöttek* (The offended; 1947–48), the third volume of which was eventually sent to a paper mill. After living in Switzerland for around two years, Márai went to Italy and in 1952 to the United States. From 1951 to 1967, under the pseudonym "Candidus," Márai worked with the Hungarian section of Radio Free Europe. He published extensively in the Munich-based *Látóhatár,* the most important political and literary periodical of Hungarians in exile. He also rewrote his old novels and wrote new ones. Márai spent the last years of his life in solitude and poverty, finally committing suicide. After the fall of communism in Hungary, he was posthumously awarded the most important national distinctions and lit-

erary prizes, becoming one of the most widely published writers. Márai's characters were merchants, entrepreneurs, and artists who strove for freedom of belief and behavior. Márai believed that an individual was socially and culturally predetermined and that only a depiction of an individual's fate allowed for philosophical reflections upon history. Other strong points of Márai's writing are its concise, emotionally aphoristic nature and its well-chosen composition. Márai was a great eulogist of Central European middle-class culture. (MS)

Sources: Gábor Thurzó, *Magyar írók: Márai Sándor,* "Erdélyi Helikon," 1934; Aladár Komlós, *Írók és elvek. Márai Sándor* (Budapest, 1937); Béla Horváth, "Márai estéje," *Látóhatár,* 1962, no. 1; Albert Tezla, *Márai Sándor. Hungarian Authors* (Cambridge, Massachusetts, 1970); Emil Csonka, "A legnagyobb élő magyar író. A 80 éves Márai Sándor," in *Új Látóhatár,* 1980, no. 1; Mihály Szegedy-Maszák, *Márai Sándor* (Budapest, 1991); *Mały słownik pisarzy węgierskich* (Warsaw, 1977).

MARCHENKO Valery [originally Umrilov] (1947, Kiev–7 October 1984, Leningrad), Ukrainian democratic activist, victim of the Soviet terror. The grandson of the historian Mykhailo Marchenko, after graduating in philology from Kiev University in 1970, Marchenko worked for the literary periodical *Literaturna Ukraina* from 1970 to 1973 and at the same time published in underground journals and studied the Azer language. Arrested on 25 June 1973, Marchenko was sentenced to six years in a labor camp and two years in exile on 29 December of that year. In 1974 he participated in a hunger strike in labor camp No. 35 in Perm. On 9 August 1974, along with thirteen other prisoners, he sent a letter to the International Red Cross, protesting the conditions in the labor camp, and in December of that year he sent a letter to the Supreme Soviet of the Soviet Union demanding recognition of the status of political prisoner. In 1975 Marchenko wrote *Pismo dedu* (A letter to grandfather), in which he criticized the servile attitude of his grandfather to the Communist regime, and *Moia prekrasnaia ledi* (My beautiful lady), describing the role of a beautiful KGB agent who had drawn him into making political confessions that led to his arrest. Both works appeared as samizdat publications. Because the authorities refused to grant him the status of political prisoner, on 10 December 1975 Marchenko renounced his Soviet citizenship. Temporarily released, he was again sentenced to twenty-three years in a labor camp in 1976. Marchenko died in prison because of delayed medical care. (WR)

Sources: S. P. de Boer, E. J. Driessen, and H. L. Verhaar, eds., *Biographical Dictionary of Dissidents in the Soviet Union, 1956–1975* (The Hague and Boston, 1982); *Encyclopedia of Ukraine,* vol. 3 (Toronto, 1993).

MARCHLEWSKI Julian, pseudonyms "Karski" and "Kujawiak" (17 May 1866, Włocławek–22 March 1925, Nervi, Italy), activist in the Polish and international Communist movement, economist, and journalist. While a high school student, Marchlewski became involved in revolutionary activities as a member of a circle of the International Social Revolutionary Party Proletariat. In 1889 he was one of the founders of the Polish Workers' Union (Związek Robotników Polskich [ZRP]). Persecuted by the tsarist authorities, Marchlewski was imprisoned between 1891 and 1892. In 1893 he emigrated to Switzerland and in 1895 moved to Germany. At that time he became active as a journalist, writing for *Sprawa Robotnicza* (1893–95). In 1893 he was one of the founders of the Social Democracy of the Kingdom of Poland, which in 1900 changed its name to the Social Democracy of the Kingdom of Poland and Lithuania (Socjaldemokracja Królestwa Polskiego i Litwy [SDKPiL]). Marchlewski was one of the leaders and ideologues of this party. In 1897 he published his doctoral dissertation, *Fizjokratyzm w dawnej Polsce* (Physiocracy in old Poland), and in 1903 he published *Stosunki społeczno-ekonomiczne na ziemiach polskich Zaboru Pruskiego* (Socioeconomic relations in the Polish territories of the Prussian partition). Marchlewski published articles in various periodicals of the Social Democratic movement, including *Przegląd Robotniczy* and *Czerwony Sztandar*.

In 1902 Marchlewski became a member of the Main Board of the SDKPiL. He represented the SDKPiL at many congresses of the Second International. Also in 1902 in Berlin he founded a company that published translations of Slavic and Scandinavian literature into German. In just over two years he published nearly fifty volumes, including works by Adolf Dygasiński, Wacław Sieroszewski, **Stefan Żeromski**, and Kazimierz Przerwa-Tetmajer. During the 1905–7 revolution Marchlewski was initially in Kraków and then in Warsaw. From 1906 to 1907 he was imprisoned by the tsarist authorities. Released, he went to Germany. In exile, Marchlewski was one of the leaders and main journalists of the left wing of the German Social Democratic movement. During World War I Marchlewski took a pro-internationalist stance, condemning the leaders of Social Democratic parties who supported their governments. In 1916, along with other activists of the radical German left wing, he co-founded the Spartacus League. Arrested by the Prussian authorities, he was imprisoned in a camp at Havelberg.

In 1918, as part of an exchange of prisoners of war, Marchlewski went to Soviet Russia and joined the All-Russian Central Executive Committee of the Soviets of Workers' and Soldiers' Deputies. In 1919 he was again in Germany for a few months and was active in the Ruhr area. At that time he was a member of the Central Committee (CC) of the Communist Party of Germany. After returning to Russia in the same year, he took part in the establishment of the Communist International and represented the Communist Workers' Party of Poland (Komunistyczna Partia Robotnicza Polski [KPRP]) in the Executive Committee of the Comintern. He also worked in the Soviet diplomatic service. For example, in July and October 1919 in Białowieża and Mikaszewice, as a representative of the Soviet authorities, Marchlewski negotiated with representatives of the Polish government. During the Polish-Soviet war he was head of the Polish Provisional Revolutionary Committee (Tymczasowy Komitet Rewolucyjny Polski [TKRP]), established by the Polish Bureau of the CC of the All-Russian Communist Party (Bolsheviks) in July 1920 in Moscow. The TKRP sought to establish a Polish Soviet Socialist Republic within the borders of Western Galicia and the former Kingdom of Poland. Marchlewski was depicted by Żeromski in his famous literary report, *Na probostwie w Wyszkowie* (At the rectory in Wyszków), which condemned the national treason of Polish Communists. In 1922, after the failure of revolutionary plans in Poland, Marchlewski helped to establish the Communist University of Western National Minorities, subsequently serving as its rector and a lecturer. An initiator of the International Organization for Aid to Revolutionaries, in 1922 Marchlewski also helped to establish this organization, becoming first president of its CC. Marchlewski died while being treated for an illness in Italy.

In the Communist movement Marchlewski was considered an expert on agrarian issues. His publications include *Polskie programy burżuazyjne w kwestii rolnej* (Polish bourgeois programs on the agrarian issue; 1908) and *Komuniści a wiejski lud roboczy* (The Communists and the rural working class; 1919). In 1920 Marchlewski worked on an agrarian program that was adopted at the Second Congress of the Communist International (*Sprawa rolna a rewolucja socjalistyczna* [The agrarian issue and the Socialist revolution]; 1926) and that was an official exposition of the Comintern's strategy and tactics on the issue. In this program Marchlewski called for revolutionary expropriation and a collective agricultural economy. Marchlewski was also the author of Marxist works devoted mainly to Polish history and economy, including the following: *Walka robotnicza pod caratem* (Worker struggle under tsarist rule; 1905); *O dochodzie* (On income; 1907); *Antysemityzm a robotnicy* (Anti-Semitism and the workers; 1913); *Kriegssozialismus in Theorie und Praxis* (1915); and *Wobec kwestii rolnej w Polsce* (About the agrarian issue in Poland; 1918). *Sochineniia* was published in the Soviet Union in 1931, and *Pisma Wybrane* (Selected writings, 2 vols.) was published in Poland in 1952–56. In post-1945 Communist Poland Marchlewski was considered one of the main leaders of the Polish Communist left. Streets, squares, schools, kindergartens, and military structures were named after him. After 1989 they were renamed, and Marchlewski's monuments and busts disappeared from public sight in Poland. (WD)

Sources: *PSB*, vol. 19; *MERSH*, vol. 21; *Słownik biograficzny działaczy polskiego ruchu robotniczego*, vol. 3 (Warsaw, 1993); J. Kaczanowska, *Bibliografia prac Juliana Marchlewskiego* (Łódź, 1954); M. K. Dziewanowski, *The Communist Party of Poland* (Cambridge, Mass., 1959); Feliks Tych, *Julian Marchlewski; Szkic biograficzny* (Warsaw, 1966); Walentyna Najdus, *Lewica polska w Kraju Rad 1918–1920* (Warsaw, 1971).

MARCHUK Yevhen (28 January 1941, Dolynivka, Kirovohrad region), Ukrainian Communist activist and post-Communist politician. In 1963 Marchuk graduated from the Pedagogical Institute in Kirovohrad. From 1963 he was a KGB functionary, first in the Kirovohrad region and from 1965 on the republican level. From 1988 he was head of the KGB administration in the Poltava region, and in 1990 he was promoted to first deputy chairman of the KGB of the Ukrainian SSR. Between June and November 1991 Marchuk was minister of defense, national security, and emergency situations of the Ukrainian SSR and then of the Ukraine. From November 1991 to July 1994 he was head of the Security Service of the Ukraine (Służba Bezpeky Ukrajiny). Appointed general of the army, from July 1994 he was deputy prime minister. In September 1994 Marchuk was appointed a special presidential representative in the Crimean Autonomous Republic, and in October 1994, first deputy prime minister and head of the Coordination Committee to Combat Corruption and Organized Crime. In 1994–95 he headed the Coordination Council for the Development of the Ukrainian Frontier. From 1 March 1995 to 28 May 1996 he was Ukraine's prime minister. In 1995–2000 he served as MP of the Supreme Council. In 1999 he ran for the presidency, but he came in fifth in the first round, with 8.1 percent of the vote. In November 1999 President **Leonid Kuchma** appointed Marchuk secretary of the Council of National Security and Defense, and in December 1999, chairman of the State Inter-Ministry Commission for Ukraine's Cooperation with NATO. (BB)

Sources: *Khto ye khto v Ukraiini 2000* (Kiev, 2000); Bohdan Nahaylo, *The Ukrainian Resurgence* (Toronto, 1999); Bugajski.

MARGHILOMAN Alexandru (10 February 1854, Buzau–11 May 1925. Bucharest), Romanian politician, lawyer, and journalist. Marghiloman completed law studies at the Sorbonne and continued his studies at the School of Political Studies in Paris (1874–79), earning a doctorate. In 1884 he joined the Conservative Party and became a member of parliament on its behalf. Marghiloman was an influential politician, with a substantial fortune and with family connections, thanks to his marriage to Princess Eliza Ştirbey. In 1888–89 and 1891–95 he was minister of justice. In that capacity he carried out a radical reform of the administration of the judiciary and the commercial code. Between 1889 and 1891 he was minister of public works. At that time Romania bought out the Romanian section of the Lemberg-Chernovitsy-Iaşi railway line. He also approved the construction of a strategic connection via the Danube between Feteşti and Cernavoda. Marghiloman subsequently served as foreign minister (1900–1), interior minister (1910–12), and finance minister (1912–14). He was the author of the financial clauses included in the Bucharest Treaty of August 1913.

On 4 June 1914 Marghiloman became leader of the Conservative Party. Between 1914 and 1916 he advocated that Romania should remain neutral, with an option for possible cooperation with the Central Powers against Russia. When the Romanian authorities left Bucharest in November 1916, Marghiloman remained in the capital as president of the Romanian Red Cross. He probably reached an agreement with the head of the Liberal Party, **Ion I. C. Brătianu**, and when on 15 August 1916 Romania entered the war, he represented a pro-German option and Brătianu a pro-Allied option. For this reason, during the German occupation Marghiloman collaborated with the occupying authorities. Between 1 March and 12 November 1918 he was prime minister and took part in the National Assembly in Chişinău (Kishinev) that announced the incorporation of Bessarabia into Romania (27 March 1918). After the end of World War I Marghiloman was accused of collaboration with the Germans, but he was never brought to court. In 1919–20 he was an MP on behalf of the Conservative Party for the last time. Marghiloman was known for his elegance in private as well as in political life and also for his original memoirs, *Note politice* (Political notes; 1927). (FA/TD)

Sources: Holger H. Herwig and Neil M. Heyman, *Biographical Dictionary of World War I* (Westport, Conn., 1982); Mircea Muşat and Ion Ardeleanu, *România dupa Marea Unire*, vols. 1–2 (Bucharest, 1986); Glenn Torrey, *General Henri Berthelot and Romania 1916–1919* (Boulder, Colo., 1987).

MARINKOVIĆ Vojislav (13 May 1876, Belgrade–18 September 1935, Belgrade), Serbian politician. The son of the politicians Dimitrije and Velika Marinković,

Marinković graduated from a gymnasium in Belgrade. He later completed law studies in Paris, where he also studied economics and political science. After returning to Belgrade, he began to work in the Ministry of Finance in 1901. He soon left the civil service to become the director of the United Commercial Bank. Marinković began his political career in 1906, entering the parliament (Skupština), where he was one of the founders of the Serbian Progressive Party (Srbska Napredna Stranka [SPP]), led by **Stojan Novaković**. Marinković sat in the parliament from 1906 until the end of his life, holding various positions in the coalition cabinets of **Nikola Pašić** (November 1914–June 1917 and November 1918–December 1918), including that of minister of economy. After the death of Novaković, Marinković became leader of the SPP. As a representative of the opposition, he took part in negotiations with the Pašić government in Corfu (15 June 1917–20 July 1917). These negotiations ended in the drafting of the Corfu Declaration, which announced the intention of founding a unified Southern Slav state. Marinković was also one of the co-authors of the Geneva Agreement, which was a compromise between the Slavs who had lived in the Habsburg monarchy before 1917 and the government of the Kingdom of Serbs.

In the Kingdom of Serbs, Croats, and Slovenes, established after World War I, Marinković was one of the founders of the Democratic Union (Demokratska Zajednica [DU]), which united various political forces. The DU was a supranational platform of political cooperation that promoted a state ideology of a moderately rightist profile. In 1920 the DU was transformed from a confederation of parties into the Serbian Democratic Party (Demokratska Stranka [DP]). From December 1921 to June 1922 Marinković was minister of interior in the coalition cabinet of Pašić. After the wing led by **Svetozar Pribićević** was expelled from the DP in April 1924, Marinković, along with other Serbian parties, helped to establish an opposition bloc that was joined by the Slovene People's Party and the Yugoslav Muslim Organization. This agreement among the parties led to the collapse of the government based on a coalition formed by the Pašić party and the Pribićević group, and it also offered Marinković a chance to assume the post of head of diplomacy in the coalition cabinet of **Ljubomir Davidović** (July–November 1924). In 1927 Marinković was again appointed minister of foreign affairs, becoming a member of seven subsequent cabinets, and from 4 April to 1 July 1932 he served as prime minister. As minister of foreign affairs, Marinković signed a treaty of friendship with France (11 November 1927). He also succeeded in improving relations with neighboring countries and in thwarting Italian attempts to surround Yugoslavia and to force it to make territorial concessions. Marinković called for the softening of the royal dictatorship. However, as a result of an increase in party conflicts, Marinković was dismissed as head of government. From October 1934 to December 1934 he was a member of the government for the last time, serving in the cabinet of **Nikola Uzunović**. Unlike the majority of DP members, who opposed the dictatorship of King **Alexander I**, Marinković supported the royal regime, helping to draft the constitution of 3 November 1931, granted by a royal decree, and an electoral law that considerably restricted electoral rights. (AG)

Sources: *Biographisches Lexikon*, vol. 3; *Enciklopedija Jugoslavije*, vol. 6 (Zagreb, 1965); *Osteuropa-Handbuch; Jugoslawien* (Cologne and Graz, 1954); Kosta Pavlović, *Vojislav Marinković i njegovo doba 1876–1935*, vols. 1–5 (London, 1955–60); Branislav Gligorijević, *Demokratska stranka i politički odnosi u Kraljevini Srba, Hrvata i Slovenaca* (Belgrade, 1970); Dimitrije Djordjevic, ed., *The Creation of Yugoslavia 1914–1918* (Santa Barbara, Calif., 1980); Wacław Felczak and Tadeusz Wasilewski, *Historia Jugosławii* (Wrocław, 1985).

MARKOV Georgi (1 March 1929, Sofia–11 September 1978, London), Bulgarian writer, journalist, and dissident, victim of communism. A chemical engineer by profession, Markov published his first works at the beginning of the 1960s. His novel *Muzhe* (Men; 1962) received Bulgaria's top literary award. His publications also include the poetry collections *Patent* (1966) and *Komunisty* (Communists; 1969). As a member of the privileged elite, Markov personally met many top leaders, including **Todor Zhivkov**. Markov's problems with the censors began after the 1968 invasion of Czechoslovakia by Warsaw Pact troops. In 1969 he obtained permission to visit his brother in Italy and decided to stay in the West. He settled in London. He became a broadcast journalist for the BBC, the Deutsche Welle, and Radio Free Europe, where he broadcast *Zadochni reportazhi za Bŭlgariia* (Correspondence reports from Bulgaria), in which he described everyday life under Communist rule, particularly the party and government elite's life behind the scenes. Markov's biting tongue and criticism of party leaders, including Zhivkov, made him one of the regime's most hated people. In 1972 the court in Sofia sentenced Markov in absentia to four years and eight months in prison. His wife, Zdravka Lekova, was subjected to persecution and pressured to divorce Markov, to which she finally agreed. As a result of the rise of the opposition movement in Bulgaria after 1978, which expressed itself in (among others things) "Declaration 78," the authorities decided that Markov was very harmful to the regime, and the security services made several attempts to kill him. Finally, on 7 November 1978 at a London bus stop, a Bulgarian agent, using a device hidden in an umbrella, secretly injected Markov with poison. Four days later Markov died in a hospital. The people responsible for his murder have never been brought to justice, and documents relating to the case were destroyed by the Bulgarian services. (AG)

Sources: *Suvremenna Bulgarska Entsiklopediya*, vol. 3 (Sofia, 1994); *Georgi Markov: The Truth That Killed* (New York, 1983); Kalin Todorov, *Koi ubi Georgi Markov* (Sofia, 1991); *Interviu na Iliana Benovska z Georgi Markov* (Sofia, 1993); Raymond Detrez, *Historical Dictionary of Bulgaria* (Lanham, Md., 1997); www.rferl.org/nca/features/1996/09/F.RU.960918155306.html; www.videofact.com/english/defectors_33_en.html.

MARKOVIĆ Ante (25 November 1924, Konjic, Bosnia-Herzegovina), Yugoslav Communist activist of Croatian descent. Marković fought in the Communist guerrilla movement during World War II. In 1954 he graduated in electrical engineering studies in Zagreb. In 1961–86 he was director of the Rade Končar Company, from 1982 to 1986 he was speaker of the Croatian republican assembly, and until 1988 he headed the Croatian republican Presidium. On 17 March 1989 the all-Yugoslav parliament appointed Marković head of the Federal Executive Council (government). He initially tried to modify the Socialist economic model but finally decided to introduce a market economy. In cooperation with Jeffrey Sachs, Marković worked out a program of economic reform close to the Polish "shock therapy" of **Leszek Balcerowicz**. The basic elements of the reform, which started on 18 December 1989, were the following: 10,000 old dinars were exchanged for one new dinar; the rate of exchange of the new currency was established at seven dinars for one German mark; the internal convertibility of the dinar was introduced; there was a partial liberalization of imports and prices, privatization, and privileges for foreign investors. Within the first six months, Marković managed to curb inflation from more than 2,500 percent per annum to almost zero. On 29 July 1990 Marković formed his own party, the Alliance of Reform Forces of Yugoslavia (Savez Reformskih Snaga Jugoslavije [SRSJ]), striving to maintain the unity of Yugoslavia. Nevertheless, in the elections of April and May 1990, most of the voters supported parties advocating national goals. Even in multiethnic Bosnia-Herzegovina the SRSJ gained only 5.4 percent of the vote and in Macedonia, 9.2 percent.

Marković failed to prevent the declarations of Slovene and Croatian independence on 25 June 1991. While the election of **Stipe Mesić** as Yugoslav president was blocked by the Serbs for months and the position of head of the Yugoslav armed forces was vacant, Marković authorized the Yugoslav People's Army (YPA) to defend the Yugoslav borders. On 27 June 1991 the YPA started operations against Slovenia, which cost several dozen lives. Marković denied having ordered the use of force. In response the minister of defense, Veljko Kadijević, accused Marković of lying. The conflict was aggravated when Marković criticized the YPA operations against Croatia. In October 1991 the presidential palace in Zagreb, where Marković was talking with **Franjo Tudjman**, was bombed. Marković found that it was a YPA attempt on his life. Marković did not accept the budget for 1992, calling it a "war budget," and he resigned on 20 December 1991. (AO)

Sources: Susan Woodward, *Balkan Tragedy* (Washington, D.C., 1995); Misha Glenny, *The Fall of Yugoslavia* (London, 1992); Warren Zimmermann, *Origins of a Catastrophe* (New York and Toronto, 1996); Laura Silber and Allan Little, *The Death of Yugoslavia* (London, 1995); Željan E. Šuster, *Historical Dictionary of the Federal Republic of Yugoslavia* (Lanham, Md., 1999); Bugajski.

MARKOVIĆ Sima (8 November 1888, Kragujevac–after July 1939, USSR), Serb Communist leader, victim of Stalinist purges. The son of a teacher, Marković graduated in mathematics from Belgrade University, and in 1913 he obtained a Ph.D. there. From 1907 he was in the Serbian Social Democratic Party, belonging to the *direktaši* faction, formed by the supporters of the syndicalistic "direct action." After World War I and the creation of the Kingdom of Serbs, Croats, and Slovenes (SHS) in 1918, Marković lectured at Belgrade University but was expelled for his revolutionary views. From the creation of the Communists Party of Yugoslavia (CPY) in April 1919, Marković was a member of its leadership. In June 1920 he was elected secretary general of the party and an MP to the parliament. In June 1921 he attended the Third Congress of the Communist International and was elected to its Executive Committee. After his return to the SHS, he was arrested and sentenced to a two-year imprisonment. After his release Marković went to Moscow, where, under the pseudonym "Semić," he took an active part in Comintern activities. In April 1925 he clashed with Stalin, criticizing his approach to nationalist issues; therefore the Comintern suspended him from the party executive. Despite this, in 1926 at the party congress in Vienna Marković was again elected the CPY secretary general. Under pressure from the Comintern, the next congress of the CPY in Dresden ousted Marković from the party leadership, and in 1929 he was expelled from the party itself for his "rightist views." Following his return to Yugoslavia, Marković, under the pseudonym "V. Bunić," wrote several works in mathematics and philosophy. From 1931 he was kept a prisoner by the Yugoslav authorities. In 1934 he was allowed to leave for the USSR, where he lived as "Milan Milić." In 1935 Marković was again admitted to the CPY, in which he did not hold any positions, working only at the Institute of Philosophy of the USSR Academy of Sciences. In July 1939 he was arrested as an "agent of imperialism" and sentenced to ten years of hard labor. After that Marković disappeared without a trace. (WR)

Sources: *Enciklopedija Jugoslavije*, vol. 6 (Zagreb, 1965); Branko Lazitch, *Biographical Dictionary of the Comintern* (Stanford, 1986).

MAROSÁN György (15 May 1908, Hosszúpályi–20 December 1992, Budapest), Hungarian Communist activist. The son of a teacher and organist in a Greek Catholic church, from 1917 Marosán was brought up in an orphanage in Debrecen. In 1926 he moved to Budapest. In 1927 he joined the Hungarian Social Democratic Party (HSDP). In 1939 he was secretary general of the National Union of Food Industry Workers and from 1943 its president. From 1941 Marosán was a member of the Budapest executive of the HSDP. Temporarily arrested in 1942, in 1943 he was regional organizational secretary of the party. In 1944, during the German occupation, Marosán was arrested and interned in Nagykanizsa. Until August 1945 he was national secretary and from 1945 to 1947 secretary general of the HSDP. From February 1947 Marosán was deputy secretary general of the party; from April 1945 he was a member of the Provisional National Assembly; and until 1963 he was a member of parliament. One of the main initiators of the "unification" of the HSDP and the Hungarian Communist Party, Marosán took an active part in the removal of the right wing and the center of the Social Democratic Party. In 1948 he received a decoration from Tito; it was later used as one of the bases for accusations against him. At the "unification" congress of the two workers' parties in June 1948 Marosán was elected third deputy secretary general and also a member of the CC, the Politburo, and the Secretariat of the Hungarian Workers' Party (HWP). From August 1948 to July 1949 he was first secretary of the Budapest Committee of the HWP while keeping his other positions. Between June 1949 and August 1950 he served as minister of light industry. At the beginning of July 1950 Marosán was arrested and sentenced to death. The sentence was changed to life imprisonment. At the end of March 1956 Marosán was released, and three months later he was rehabilitated. At a meeting of the CC of the HWP in July 1956 he was elected a member of the Politburo. Between 30 July and 27 October that year he served as vice-premier.

At a congress of the Politburo of the HWP on 23 October 1956, Marosán, citing the threat of a counter-revolution, demanded that orders be given to shoot at demonstrators. On 31 October he was arrested for a short time by the insurgents at Szén Square. On 2 November he went to the Soviet headquarters in Tököl. He joined the so-called Hungarian Revolutionary Government of Workers and Peasants and also the CC and the Politburo of the Hungarian Socialist Workers' Party (HSWP). In February 1957 Marosán became administrative secretary of the CC and deputy to **János Kádár**. Between February 1957 and January 1960 he was minister without portfolio, and from April 1957, secretary of the Budapest party committee. Marosán was an advocate of severe repressive measures against the insurgents. In 1962, during the preparation of an HSWP resolution that would put an end to the law-infringing Stalinist trials against activists of the workers' movement, Marosán formulated a separate statement that led to a conflict with Kádár. In October 1962 the CC of the HSWP removed Marosán from the Politburo and Secretariat and expelled him from the CC. In 1965 Marosán left the HSWP, but in 1972 he again became a party member. In the autumn of 1989 Marosán opposed the dissolution of the HSWP, and he took part in the formation of a new HSWP, which at that time was already a splinter group. In 1989 Marosán's memoirs, *A tanúk még élnek* (The witnesses are still alive), were published. (JT)

Sources: *A magyar forradalom és szabadságharc enciklopédiája*, CD-ROM (Budapest, 1999); William Shawcross, *Crime and Compromise: Janos Kadar and the Politics of Hungary since the Revolution* (New York, 1974); Bennet Kovrig, *Communism in Hungary from Kun to Kádár* (Stanford, 1979).

MARTANESHI Baba Faja [originally Xhani Mustafa] (1910, Luzin e Madhe, near Kavajë–19 March 1947, Tirana), Albanian clergyman of the Muslim Bektashis (a sect of Sufis) and participant in the resistance movement. In 1934 Martaneshi took charge of the parish of Martanesh. After the Italian invasion in 1939, he was among the first to form a unit that fought against the occupiers and was based in the region of Elbasan. Martaneshi rallied the Bektashis and other Muslims, who were convinced that the Italians had a negative attitude toward Islam. In 1944 his unit expanded into a battalion, and Martaneshi rose to the rank of colonel. He was one of the people most wanted by the Italians. He became a member of the General Council of the National Liberation Front, established in September 1942. In July 1943 he joined the General Staff of the (Communist) National Liberation Army. After the mysterious death of the Bektashi leader, Saliha Niyazi Dede, in November 1941, the Bektashi movement was split. Martaneshi enjoyed the support of the Communists. He became famous for his proposal to execute those who did not want to fight with the Communists and chose to fight independently. From May

1944 to January 1946 Martaneshi served as vice-president of the Council of the Anti-Fascist Front for National Liberation. An enthusiast of social reforms introduced by the Communists, he was one of those who called for changes aimed at decentralizing the Bektashi community. Martaneshi served as chairman of the Fourth Congress of the Bektashi Clergy (3–5 May 1945), at which he was elected secretary general of this community. In 1945 he became a deputy for the Elbasan district to the People's Assembly. Martaneshi died in unexplained circumstances, murdered in Tirana in a Bektashi shrine by Ded Baba Abazi, who committed suicide shortly afterwards. Some believe that Martaneshi's cooperation with the Communists was the reason for this murder. (TC)

Sources: *Bashkimi*, 18 November 1945 and 20 March 1947; Bernd Fischer, *Albania at War 1939–1945* (London, 1999); Baba Selim R. Kaliçani, *Histori e baballarëve te teqese se Martaneshit* (Tirana, 1997); David Smiley, *Albanian Assignment* (London, 1984); Klaus-Detlev Grothusen, ed., *Albanien* (Göttingen, 1993).

MARTINOVIĆ Mitar (8 November 1870, Bajice, near Cetinje–11 February 1954, Belgrade), Montenegrin general and politician. In 1890 Martinović completed military studies in Turin. He subsequently served in the Montenegrin Army and was promoted to general in 1902. From 1907 to 1910 he served as minister of war. During the Balkan Wars King **Nicholas** appointed him prime minister, a position he held from 19 June 1912 to 8 May 1913. He also served as minister of war and foreign affairs in the government he headed. Martinović's government failed to retain control over the region of Shkoder, gained during the First Balkan War; it was awarded to Albania. Hoping for Serbian and Russian support, Montenegrin forces captured Shkodër in April 1913, and it was only the threat of war with Austria-Hungary and pressure from the Western powers that made King Nicholas and Martinović abandon their plans. As a result, Martinović resigned as prime minister. During World War I Martinović was in command of the Montenegrin forces on the Herzegovina and Drina front, and he also commanded the Sarajevo offensive. From April to December 1915 he was a delegate of the Montenegrin Army to the Russian Supreme Command and then served as a commander in the region of Kotor. After Montenegro became part of the Kingdom of Serbs, Croats, and Slovenes in 1918, Martinović joined the army of this kingdom and served as deputy commander of an army district. He was the author of *Vojni duh i disciplina u vojsci* (Military spirit and discipline in the army). (WR)

Sources: *Enciklopedija Jugoslavije*, vol. 6 (Zagreb, 1965); John D. Treadway, *The Falcon and the Eagle: Montenegro and Austria-Hungary, 1908–1914* (West Lafayette, Ind., 1983); www.rulers.org.

MARTNA Mihkel (17 September 1860, Paimpere–24 May 1934, Tallinn), Estonian Social Democratic politician. Aligned with the Marxist movement from the 1880s, at the turn of the century, along with **Konstantin Päts**, Martna was co-founder of the radical newspaper *Teataja*, which promoted the cause of Estonian independence and called for radical social reforms. He was an active member of the group led by Päts for only a short time, though, because when the Social Democratic periodical *Uused* was founded Martna transferred most of his articles there. Aligned with a group of Estonian Social Democrats who acted independently from the Russian Social Democratic Workers' Party, Martna called for the transformation of Russia into a democratic republic in which the rights of ethnic minorities would be respected. This program became the basis of the Estonian Social Democratic Workers' Union (Eesti Sotsiaaldemokraatlik Tööliste Ühisus [ESTÜ]), established in 1905. The ESTÜ called for autonomy for Estonia within the framework of a Russian federal republic proposed by the Russian left.

Martna took an active part in the 1905 revolution. After its defeat, he emigrated and lived in England and Switzerland from 1906 to 1917. A member of the first foreign delegation of the Estonian National Council (Maapäev), he was assigned the task of getting to Germany and Switzerland to promote the Estonian struggle for independence there. This plan failed, though; on the way Martna got stuck in Copenhagen and stayed there. In 1919 he became an unofficial Estonian representative to Germany, but after a short mission he returned to Estonia owing to illness. In independent Estonia Martna was one of the leaders of the Estonian Social Democratic Workers' Party (Eesti Sotsiaaldemokraatlik Tööliste Partei [ESTP]), which sought to establish a Socialist system in Estonia in an evolutionary way; Martna represented the radical wing of this party. It seems that because of this, although generally respected (in 1930 he was awarded an honorary doctorate by the University of Tartu), Martna never held any ministerial positions. From 1931 to 1932 he was chairman of the ESTP. He was a member of parliament (Riigikogu) for five terms, serving as its speaker during the third and fourth terms. Martna published numerous works on contemporary political issues, including *Estland, die Esten und die estnische Frage* (Estonia, the Estonians, and the Estonian question; 1919). (AG)

Sources: *Eesti Entsuklopeedia* vol. 14 (Tallinn, 2000); Evald Uustalu, *The History of the Estonian People* (London, 1952); Tõnu Tannberg, Matti Laur, Tõnis Lukas, Ain Mäesalu, and Ago Pajur, *History of Estonia* (Tallinn, 2000).

MÁRTON Áron (28 August 1896, Csíkszentdomokos [now Sândominic, Romania]–29 September 1980, Alba

Iulia [Gyulafehérvár], Romania), Hungarian Roman Catholic bishop from Transylvania. Márton came from a Szekler family of farmers from Transylvania. During World War I he was wounded three times. After Transylvania was ceded to Romania under the 1920 Treaty of Trianon, Márton decided to stay in the Romanian territories. After completing theological studies, he was ordained a priest in 1924 and worked as a curate. From 1928 to 1929 he served as deputy headmaster of a Catholic high school in Tîrgu Mureş (Marosvásárhely). From 1930 to 1932 he served as a curate and archivist in Alba Iulia (Gyulafehérvár), and in October 1932 he became a minister of Hungarian students in Cluj-Napoca (Kolozsvár). From 1933 to 1938 Márton edited the pedagogical periodical *Erdélyi Iskola*, which he had helped to found and to which he regularly contributed articles on rural education. He established a non–school-based education network in the territories of the diocese of Alba Iulia. From 1934 to 1938 he was director of the reorganized Transylvanian Roman Catholic National Union.

In December 1938 Pope Pius XI appointed Márton bishop of Alba Iulia, the biggest of the then existing four Roman Catholic dioceses in Transylvania. At that time Márton became the spiritual leader of Hungarians from southern Transylvania who had remained in Romania after the Second Vienna Award of 1940. Márton was against the war, condemned anti-Semitism, and protested the racial persecutions and deportations of Jews. After the end of the war he opposed the Romanian Communist authorities on such issues as the independence of Church-run schools and religious practices. He consistently called for improving the situation of the Hungarian minority, which was deprived of its rights after the war. Márton was arrested in June 1949. Initially his trial was planned as part of the trial of **László Rajk**, who also came from Transylvania. Finally, in 1951, in a rigged trial Márton was sentenced to ten years in a high-security prison and to forced labor for life on false charges of treason and taking part in a conspiracy. In February 1955 Márton was released on the initiative of former prime minister **Petru Groza**. However, from 1956 to 1967 Márton was kept under house arrest, which was lifted only after the intervention of Franz König, archbishop of Vienna. (JT)

Sources: *Nagy Képes Milleniumi Arcképcsarnok* (Budapest, 1999); *Magyar Nagylexikon*, vol. 12 (Budapest, 2001); Jeromos Szalay, *The Truth about Central Europe* (Paris, 1955); Pál Péter Domokos, *Rendületlenül: Márton Áron Erdélyi püspöke* (Budapest, 1990); Dennis Deletant, *Communist Terror in Romania: Gheorghiu-Dej and the Police State, 1948–1965* (New York, 1999); László Virt, *Nyilott szívvel: Márton Áron erdélyi püspök élete és eszmei* (Budapest, 2002).

MASARYK Jan (14 September 1886, Prague–10 March 1948, Prague), Czech diplomat and politician. The younger son of **Tomáš Garrigue Masaryk**, from 1897 to 1906 Masaryk attended a *Realschule* and a gymnasium in Prague but failed to pass his high school final examinations. From 1906 to 1913 he worked in the United States, mainly at the Crane railway plant in Bridgeport, Connecticut. During World War I he served in the Austro-Hungarian Army. In 1919 Masaryk entered the Czechoslovak diplomatic service, initially serving as chargé d'affaires in the United States, then as counselor in the Ministry of Foreign Affairs until 1924, and then as ambassador to Great Britain from 1925 to 1938. He pursued the foreign policy laid down by President **Edvard Beneš**, which was based on alliances with England and France and on the League of Nations. Masaryk enjoyed great popularity in British diplomatic circles and was a frequent guest at the royal court. His broad contacts and charming manners contributed to a positive image of the new state. Masaryk also tried to influence British foreign policy. In the 1930s he was a firm opponent of the Western policy of appeasement and repeatedly warned against Nazism. In 1938 he attempted to thwart German plans to annex Czechoslovakia. As early as February 1938 he intervened with Lord Halifax, urging that the British government abandon its policy of concessions to Germany, and he undertook similar efforts after the incorporation of Austria. Masaryk described the policy of appeasement as dangerous to the entire world. On 25 September 1938 he sent a letter to Prime Minister Neville Chamberlain in which, on behalf of Czechoslovakia, he rejected Hitler's demands. After the Pact of Munich (30 September 1938), Masaryk resigned as ambassador and asked for political asylum. Early in 1939 he went to the United States, where he gave a series of lectures.

After the German invasion and then the partition of Czechoslovakia in March 1939, Masaryk returned to London and resumed his political activities. One of the closest associates of Beneš, he served as minister of foreign affairs (1940–45) and as deputy prime minister (1942–45) in the London-based Czechoslovak government-in-exile headed by Beneš. From 1944 to 1945 Masaryk was also minister of national defense. He made regular wartime broadcasts from London to the Czechoslovak people. Thanks to his efforts as minister of foreign affairs, the Allies recognized the Czechoslovak government-in-exile, Great Britain annulled its signature on the Munich agreement, and Czechoslovakia was accepted as a member of the anti-Nazi coalition.

In April 1945 Masaryk became minister of foreign affairs of the government established on the basis of the Košice program. He attended the founding conference of the United Nations, and as a representative of Czechoslovakia, he signed the UN Charter on 26 June 1945. Masaryk tried to pursue a policy of balance between the Soviet Union and the Western powers, but he increasingly lost independence. In July 1947 he was forced by Stalin to reject postwar U.S. reconstruction aid under the Marshall Plan. During the Communist coup in February 1948 Masaryk criticized the resignation of other non-Communist ministers, considering their step to be erroneous and shortsighted. He represented Beneš as foreign minister in the newly established Communist cabinet of **Klement Gottwald**, but he never reconciled himself to the fact that the Communists had taken over power in Czechoslovakia. The circumstances of Masaryk's death are not clear to this day. He may have committed a protest suicide, or it may have been a political murder. On 10 March 1948 his body was found in the garden of Czernin Palace, where he had lived in an apartment on the top floor. Masaryk was buried beside his father at Lány Cemetery.

Before his death Masaryk enjoyed great public popularity and support, both because he was the son of President Masaryk, the "father of the nation," and because of his stance before and during the war. The most popular politician between 1945 and 1948, after his death Masaryk became a symbol of democratic ideals. In 1946 his broadcasts from London were published in the book *Volá Londýn* (London calling). His wartime broadcasts to occupied Czechoslovakia were published in English as *Speaking to My Country* (1944). Masaryk's parliamentary speech in which he described his concept of Czechoslovakia's postwar foreign policy was reproduced in *Ani opona ani most* (Neither a curtain nor a bridge; 1947). (PU)

Sources: *ČBS*; *Politická elita meziválečného Československa 1918–1938: Kdo byl kdo za první republiky* (Prague, 1998); *Kdo byl kdo v našich dějinách ve 20. století*, vol. 1 (Prague, 1998); R. H. Bruce Lockhart, *Jan Masaryk: A Personal Memoir* (London, 1951); Claire Sterling, *The Masaryk Case* (New York, 1968); Telford Taylor, *Munich: The Price of Peace* (New York, 1979); Vladimír Vaněk, *Jan Masaryk* (Prague, 1994); Pavel Kosatík and Michal Kolář, *Jan Masaryk: Pravdivý příběh* (Prague, 1998); Zdeněk Šedivý, *Jan Masaryk . . . při jméně, které nosil . . . musel zemřít* (Vimperk, 1998); Antonin Sum, *Otec a syn: Tomaš Garrigue a Jan Masarykové ve vzpomínkách prátel a pametinků* (Prague, 2000).

MASARYK Tomáš Garrigue (7 March 1850, Hodonín–14 September 1937, Lány), Czech philosopher, sociologist, politician, and co-founder and first president of Czechoslovakia. Born into a family of limited means, in 1872 Masaryk passed his high school final examinations and began to study classical philology at the School of Philosophy in Vienna. Two years earlier, Masaryk, formerly a Roman Catholic, had joined the Uniate Church. That decision influenced his future views on the place of the church in the state. While a student, Masaryk devoted himself to philosophy, which he believed should help to establish a new, better order in the world. He identified with the concepts of Plato and Auguste Comte. Masaryk was also engaged in social work; he was a member of the Bohemian Academic Society, serving as its chairman from 1874 to 1875. In 1876 Masaryk graduated; his thesis was "The Nature of the Soul According to Plato." He subsequently studied for a year in Leipzig, where he met an American, Charlotte Garrigue, whom he married in 1878. The following year he earned a postdoctoral degree from the University of Vienna for a study in which he analyzed suicide as a mass phenomenon of modern civilization. Over the following four years Masaryk worked as a *Privatdozent* at the university in Vienna. After the university in Prague was divided into a German university and a Czech university, Masaryk was appointed associate professor by the Czech university. He taught the history of philosophy, logic, ethics, the foundations of psychology, and sociology.

By then Masaryk already exerted great influence on Czech scholarly and intellectual life. He founded the monthly *Athenaeum* (1883), becoming its editor-in-chief, and initiated the publication of a new Czech encyclopedia. He was also one of the leading challengers of the authenticity of two thirteenth-century manuscripts: *Rukopis královédvorský* and *Rukopis Zelenohorský*; the controversy led to a sharp conflict with the senior academic staff, undermined his position at the university, and fueled numerous political attacks against him. In 1887 Masaryk entered politics, joining, along with **Karel Kramař**, a group of "realists" that became part of the Young Czech Party in 1890. One year later Masaryk became an MP in the parliament in Vienna and an MP in the Czech provincial parliament. In 1893 he resigned from both seats as a result of conflicts with the leadership of the Young Czech Party. At that time he called for autonomy for the Czech lands within the Habsburg empire and rejected any kind of radicalism. He believed that more could be gained through a steady democratization of Austria-Hungary and through the strengthening of the cultural and economic position of Bohemia within the monarchy and that sovereignty would be gained gradually. Masaryk based his political program upon his own concept of Czech history, which he presented in many works written in the 1890s, including the tetralogy *Česká otázka* (The Czech question), *Naše nynější krise* (Our present crisis), *Jan Hus*, and *Karel Havlíček Borovský* (1895–96). Masaryk maintained that humanism and freedom, particularly religious freedom, were the most important values in Czech history. He contrasted historical facts with myths and democracy with theocracy, absolutism, and dictatorship. He paid much attention to social issues and to the workers' movement. He called for, among other things, an eight-hour work day and universal suffrage, but he criticized Marxism and rejected revolution as an anachronistic phenomenon. He expounded his views in *Otázka sociální* (The social question; 1898), as well as in the periodical *Naše doba*, which he founded in 1893 and edited until 1914.

From 1900 to 1914 Masaryk was leader of the so-called Realist Party, initially known as the Czech People's Party and later—after merging with the Radical Progressive Party—as the Czech Progressive Party. This new party demanded autonomy for the Bohemian lands within the monarchy through changes to the electoral law and the introduction of universal suffrage—for women as well as for men. After 1907, when general elections were introduced, Masaryk again sat in the parliament in Vienna. At that time he dealt with the Slavic issue and worked for integration between the Slovaks and the Czechs, supporting so-called Czechoslovakism—that is, a concept according to which the Czechs and the Slovaks were one nation, speaking different dialects of the same language. Masaryk criticized Vienna's policy in the Balkans (the annexation of Bosnia and Herzegovina, political trials of Serbian and Croatian activists) and the dependency of the Habsburg empire on Germany. He was curious about Russia, which resulted in the work *Rusko a Evropa* (Russia and Europe; 1913). He was skeptical of pro-Russian sympathies, although he tried not to criticize Russia.

After the outbreak of the war in 1914, Masaryk began to organize an anti-Habsburg movement at home, and in December of the same year he traveled to the West to seek allies for the establishment of an independent state of Czechs and Slovaks. Masaryk worked with **Edvard Beneš** and **Milan Štefánik**, striving for international recognition of the future state's right to independence. In 1915 in France he founded the Czech Foreign Committee, which was renamed the Czechoslovak National Council in Paris in 1916. It was an organ that united Czech and Slovak emigrants, and Masaryk served as its president until 1918. Masaryk gained the support of many influential politicians in the West; "Czechoslovakia's liberation from foreign rule" was one of the issues mentioned by U.S. president Woodrow Wilson in 1917. Masaryk also co-organized a secret committee of Czech politicians at home; later it was called the "Mafia." In May 1917, after the fall of tsarism, Masaryk went to Russia, where he became involved in organizing Czechoslovak legions. While in Russia, he witnessed the Bolshevik revolution, toward which he reacted negatively, announcing the neutrality of the Czechoslovak troops. In March 1918, after Bolshevik Russia signed the Treaty of Brest-Litovsk with the Central Powers, Masaryk traveled via Japan to the United States, believing that the Americans would have a decisive influence on the shape of Europe after the war. In America he established contacts with President Wilson and brought about the signing of the Pittsburgh Convention (30 May 1918), which provided for the establishment of an independent Czech and Slovak state with autonomous organs for Slovakia. On 14 October 1918 Beneš informed the Allies that a provisional Czechoslovak government-in-exile was established and Masaryk was its president and prime minister. This government was officially recognized by the Western powers. Four days later Masaryk published the Washington Declaration—a declaration of Czechoslovakia's independence, in which he described the principles for the establishment of the new state. Elected the first president of Czechoslovakia by acclamation of the Revolutionary National Assembly on 14 November, Masaryk returned to his country on 21 December of the same year and took the presidential oath.

A politician who enjoyed the greatest prestige, Masaryk was reelected president in 1920, 1927, and 1934. He strove to consolidate the young state and to strengthen its parliamentary democratic system. As a supporter of Czechoslovakism, Masaryk was against autonomy for the Slovaks, but realizing that there were many nationally conscious minority groups, he advocated that their rights be respected so that they would accept the new Czechoslovak state. Masaryk became leader of an informal political group called Hrad (Castle), which consisted of his faithful friends and associates, who had liberal and reformist views and who exerted strong influence on the Czech political scene. Masaryk advocated that the presidential powers be increased according to the American model. He frequently represented Czechoslovakia abroad but left the implementation of the country's foreign policy to Beneš, his closest associate and successor. Masaryk based the security of Czechoslovakia on the Western powers and had a negative attitude toward the Bolshevik government in Russia. On 14 December 1935 Masaryk resigned as president for health reasons. Until the end of his life he lived at Lány Castle. Already during his lifetime he was honored for what he had done for the country. For example, in 1930 the parliament pronounced that "T. G. Masaryk deserves credit for his services to the state," and after his resignation he was styled "President-Liberator." Masaryk became the symbol of Czech democracy and moral authority, and he was the subject of folk legends.

In his philosophical views, Masaryk was a proponent of critical realism, which was based on positivism and which combined empirical research and rational criticism with the recognition of the role of man's emotional attitude to the world. He understood divinity as a creative and ruling power that gave sense and aim to everything. Masaryk's views had much influence on future Czech and Slovak thinkers. Masaryk left his memoirs from the time when the Czechoslovak state was being created: *Světová revoluce za války a ve válce, 1914–1918* (1925; *The Making of a State: Memoirs and Observations, 1914–1918*, 1927). (PU)

Sources: *ČBS; Kto bol kto za I. ČSR* (Bratislava, 1993); *Politická elita meziválečného Československa 1918–1938: Kdo byl kdo za první republiky* (Prague, 1998); *Kdo byl kdo v našich dějinach ve 20. stoleti, vol. 1* (Prague, 1998); Karel Čapek, *Hovory z T. G. Masarykiem,* vols. 1–3 (Prague, 1928–35); Zdeněk Nejedlý, *T. G. Masaryk,* vols. 1–4 (Prague, 1930–35); R. W. Seton-Watson, *A History of the Czechs and Slovaks* (Hamden, Conn., 1965); Milan Machovec, *T. G. Masaryk* (Prague, 1968); Emil Ludwig, *Defender of Democracy* (New York, 1971); Jan Galandauer, *T. G. Masaryk a vznik ČSR* (Prague, 1988); *T. G. Masaryk (1850–1937),* vols. 1–3 (London, 1989–90); Jan Patočka, *Tři studie o Masarykovi* (Prague, 1991); Janusz Gruchała, *Tomasz G. Masaryk* (Wrocław, 1996).

MĀSĒNS Vilis (17 November 1902, Dikļi, Livonia–15 July 1964, New York), Latvian diplomat. After graduating from a *Realschule* in Valmiera, Māsēns studied chemistry (1920–22) and law (1922–24) at the University of Riga. From 1923 to 1927 he worked as a clerk at the consulate general in London. In 1928 he graduated from the London School of Economics and Politics. From 1930 to 1931 he was a secretary at a legation in Kaunas, and in 1931 he became an attaché. From 1933 to 1937 he served as secretary at a legation in Paris. After returning to his country, Māsēns became head of the Western Department and (in 1938) head of the Baltic Department of the Ministry of Foreign Affairs. After the Red Army seized Latvia, he was dismissed from his position in September 1940, but he avoided deportation. In 1944 Māsēns went to Germany. In 1947 he earned a doctorate in law from the University of Heidelberg and subsequently worked as a counselor at the International Refugees Organization. In 1950 he left for the United States and became an activist in the Assembly of Captive European Nations (ACEN), where he served as Latvia's representative and chairman of its general committee (1958–62). (EJ)

Sources: *Es viņu pazīstu* (Riga, 1939); *Daugavas Vanagu Mēnešraksts,* 1964, no. 5; *Daugavas Vanagi,* 1964, no. 5; A. Rumpēters, "Dr. iur. Vili Māsēnu pieminot," *Latviešu Juristu Raksti,* 1968, no. 9.

MASHERAU Pyotr [known as Masherov in the USSR] (26 February 1918, Shyrki, Vitebsk region–4 October 1980), Belorussian Communist activist. Born into a peasant family, Masherau graduated from the Vitebsk Pedagogical Institute (1939) and subsequently worked as a physics teacher in Rasonsk (1939–41). In August 1941 he helped organize a partisan movement in the Vitebsk region, becoming the commander of a unit in October 1942 and of a brigade in March 1943. In October 1943 Masherau was transferred to party work. After the Vilnius region was seized by the Red Army, he became secretary of the Komsomol for the Vileyka region and subsequently head of a Komsomol organization in the Molodechno district. In October 1947 he was made first secretary of its Central Committee (CC). In July 1954 he became second secretary of the Brest City Committee of the Communist Party of Belorussia (CP of Belorussia); in August 1955 he became first secretary of the District Committee in Brest, and in October 1959, secretary of the CC of the CP of Belorussia. In March 1965 Masherau succeeded **Kiryl Mazurau** as first secretary of the CC of the CP of Belorussia and held this post until his death. From 1961 to 1964 he was also a member of the CC of the Communist Party of the Soviet Union (CPSU). Under his leadership the Belorussian SSR enjoyed economic prosperity, boosted by large investments in heavy industry. Monuments to **Yakub Kolas** and **Yanka Kupala** were built in Minsk, but at the same time the intensity of Russification and Sovietization increased—all young people belonged to the Komsomol, and every eleventh citizen was a member of the Communist Party. Masherau died in a car crash on the way from Baranovichi to Minsk in rather mysterious circumstances. (EM)

Sources: Archie Brown, ed., *The Soviet Union: A Biographical Dictionary* (London, 1990); *Entsyklapiedyia historyi Bielarusi,* vol. 5 (Minsk, 1999); V. Yakutov, *Petr Masherov* (Minsk, 1992); Jan Zaprudnik, *Historical Dictionary of Belarus* (Lanham, Md., 1998); S. Antanovich, *Petr Masherov: Zhizn', sud'ba, pamiat'. Dokumentalnaia povest'* (Minsk, 1998).

MASOL Vitaliy (14 November 1928, Olyshivka, near Chernihiv), Soviet party and state official, prime minister of the Ukraine. In 1951 Masol graduated in mechanical engineering from the Kiev Polytechnic Institute. In 1953–71 he worked in a machine-building factory in Novokramatorsk, first as an engineer and later as the director. In 1972 he became deputy chairman of the Planning Commission of the Ukrainian SSR, and in 1979 he became its chairman and the first deputy prime minister of the Ukrainian SSR. From 1976 Masol was a member of the Central Committee (CC) of the Communist Party of the Ukraine, and in 1981–86 he was a member of the Central Inspection Commission of the CPSU. On the wave of personnel changes after the Chernobyl disaster, on 10 July 1987 Masol became prime minister of the Ukrainian SSR, continuing with conservative policies. In

March 1990 he became deputy to the Supreme Council of the Ukrainian SSR. In view of the Communist domination in the council (the so-called Group of 239) over the independence-minded opposition, it proved impossible to oust the Masol government in a parliamentary way. Therefore, on 1 October 1990 the opposition undertook a failed attempt at a general strike. Hunger strikes by Kiev and Lviv students (2–16 October 1990), who were demanding Ukrainian sovereignty, had one goal: the dismissal of Masol. In order to prevent social upheaval, the chairman of the Supreme Council, **Leonid Kravchuk**, sacrificed Masol, who resigned on 14 November 1990. For the second time Masol became prime minister of the independent Ukraine on 16 June 1994, when President Kravchuk wanted to gain the support of the Russian-speaking and pro-Communist constituency of Eastern Ukraine in forthcoming presidential elections. After his victory, the new president, **Leonid Kuchma**, confirmed Masol as prime minister, but Masol proved unprepared for the job and unwilling to introduce reforms. His government lasted until 1 March 1995, when Masol stepped down under pressure from Kuchma. (TS)

Sources: *Encyclopedia of Ukraine*, vol. 3 (Toronto, 1993); W. Baran and V. Danylenko, *Ukraiina v umovakh systemnoyi kryzy (1946–1980-i rr.)* (Kiev, 1999); Bohdan Nahaylo, *The Ukrainian Resurgence* (Toronto, 1999); Volodymyr Lytvyn, *Ukraiina na mezhi tysyacholit (1991–2000 rr.)* (Kiev, 2000).

MATEŠA Zlatko (17 July 1949, Zagreb), Croatian politician. Mateša graduated in law from the University of Zagreb. He also studied at the Henley Management College in the United Kingdom. In 1978 he became assessor in a Zagreb court. He worked as a legal adviser for the INA petrochemical combine (1978–80); he was then head of its legal department (1980–82), director of the legal and personnel departments (1982–85), and general manager (1985–89). Later he became deputy chairman of the INA board of trustees and then general director of the board (1990–92). In 1992–93 Mateša was director of the Agency for Restructuring and Development. A close aide of President **Franjo Tudjman** and one of the leaders of the Croatian Democratic Union (Hrvatska Demokratska Zajednica [HDZ]), from April 1993 to September 1995 he was minister without portfolio and from September to November 1995, minister of the economy. From 7 November 1995 to 27 January 2000 Mateša was prime minister. During his term Croatian relations with the Western countries were rather cold. Croatian authorities were accused of violations of democracy and a lack of support for the Dayton Agreement of November 1995. Mateša made clear his critical assessment of The Hague Tribunal for War Crimes in Former Yugoslavia. Relations improved in 1999, when Mateša supported the NATO intervention in the Federal Republic of Yugoslavia. Croatia emerged from international isolation when Tudjman died and the opposition took over power after the parliamentary elections of January 2000. The ruling HDZ was defeated, and Mateša stepped down, drawing closer to the Croatian Democratic Center (Hrvatski Demokratski Centar). (AO)

Sources: *Europa Środkowo-Wschodnia 1996–1999* (Warsaw, 1999–2001); *Biographical Notes*, Polish Press Agency PAP, February 2000.

MATSKEVICH Uladzimir (1 March 1947, Marina Gorka, near Mahilyow [Mogilev]), Soviet general, head of the Belorussian KGB. In 1970 Matskevich graduated from the Belorussian Technological Institute and in 1978 from the KBG Institute of the Belorussian Soviet Socialist Republic. From 1970 he worked as an engineer at the oil refinery in Mozyr, and from 1973 he was active in the Komsomol structures in the region of Homel. From 1976 he was a KGB official in Homel and in the Vitebsk region. From 1990 to 1993 Matskevich was head of the KGB administration of Minsk and the Minsk region, and in 1993–94, of the Brest district. In 1995 President **Alyaksandr Lukashenka** appointed Matskevich head of the KGB of Belorussia with the rank of lieutenant general. Matskevich has played a major role in strengthening and maintaining the dictatorial regime of Lukashenka, supervising the apparatus that has terrorized opponents of the regime. Some of the opposition leaders, such as, for instance, **Viktar Hanchar**, have disappeared under mysterious circumstances. (WR)

Sources: *Bielaruskaia entsyklapiedyia*, vol. 10 (Minsk, 1999); *Kto yest kto w Respublike Belarus* (Minsk, 1999); Jan Zaprudnik, *Historical Dictionary of Belarus* (Lanham, Md., 1998).

MATULAITIS-MATULEVIČIUS Jurgis (13 April 1871, Marijampolė–27 January 1927, Kaunas), Lithuanian bishop beatified by the Catholic Church. One of eight children born into a poor peasant family, Matulaitis-Matulevičius was orphaned at an early age and remained under the care of an uncle. He studied at a seminary in Kielce, enrolled under the Polish surname of Matulewicz. Later on he also used the Lithuanized version of this surname, Matulevičius. He completed seminary studies in Warsaw and St. Petersburg. Ordained a priest in 1899, he worked in a parish in the diocese of Kielce and then continued his studies in Fribourg, Switzerland, earning a Ph.D. in 1902. After returning home, Matulaitis-Matulevičius was appointed professor and vice-rector of the seminary in Kielce. He was an ardent supporter of the social teachings of Pope Leo XIII. An expert in the field of Catholic social thought, he was active among workers, helping to establish (among other things) the Christian Democratic movement. He also edited *Pracownik Polski*. In 1907 he began teaching at the newly established Department of Sociology at the Theological Academy in St. Petersburg. In 1909 he entered the Marian order, reestablished its structures in Lithuania, and subsequently became the superior of this order. From 1911 to 1914 he was head of the Marian order in Fribourg, and then he worked in Warsaw, where in 1915 he restored the Marian monastery at Bielany.

In October 1918 Pope Benedict XV appointed Matulaitis-Matulevičius bishop of Vilnius. Vilnius changed hands several times in 1918–20because it was the subject of a sharp dispute between the Poles, who were the majority of the Vilnius population, and the Lithuanians, who wanted Vilnius—the former Lithuanian capital—to be part of the Lithuanian state. Thus Matulaitis-Matulevičius found himself in the center of a conflict between two Catholic communities. He constantly strove to understand and reconcile the Poles and the Lithuanians. At the same time, though, he supported the right of Belorussians and Lithuanians to use their own language; because of this stance, he was sharply attacked by Polish nationalists. These attacks increased after the Vilnius region was finally incorporated into Poland in 1922. After Poland signed the concordat in 1925, Matulaitis-Matulevičius resigned as bishop and went to Rome to dedicate himself to the development of the Marian order. Appointed titular archbishop of Adulis and apostolic visitator to Lithuania by Pope Pius XI, he sought to establish a Lithuanian metropolis in Kaunas, and he laid the groundwork for a concordat with the Lithuanian Republic. Lithuanian nationalists never forgave him that he had resigned as bishop of Vilnius. In the summer of 1926 Matulaitis-Matulevičius went to the United States, where he visited Marian monasteries he had founded. Shortly after returning to Rome, he fell ill and died. Taking into account his moral virtues as well as his work for Polish-Lithuanian reconciliation, Pope John Paul II completed his beatification process, declaring him a Blessed of the Catholic Church on 28 June 1987. (WR)

Sources: *EL*, vol. 3; Saulius Sužiedelis, *Historical Dictionary of Lithuania* (Lanham, Md., 1997); K. Čibiras, ed., *Arkivyskupas Jurgis Matulevičius* (Marijampolė, 1933); C. Reklaitis, *Il Servo di Dio Giorgio Matulaitis* (Rome, 1955); Stanley C. Gaucias, *Archbishop George Matulaitis* (Chicago, 1981); Tadeusz Górski, MIC, *Rozmiłowany w Kościele: Błogosławiony arcybiskup Jerzy Matulewicz* (Warsaw, 1987).

MATULIONIS Teofilis (4 July 1873, Kadariškiai–20 August 1962, Šeduva), Lithuanian bishop. After completing theological studies at a seminary in St. Petersburg (1900), Matulionis worked in a parish in Latvian Latgalia. In 1910 he became a priest in the parish of the Most Sacred Heart of Jesus in St. Petersburg and worked among the working class. In 1923 he was arrested and sentenced in the Moscow trial of Archbishop **Jan Cieplak** to a three-year imprisonment for protesting the expropriation of churches. Released after two years, Matulionis was secretly consecrated bishop in 1929. He became auxiliary bishop in the apostolic administration of the archdiocese of Mogilev (now Mahilyow, Belarus), covering all of Russia. Arrested and interrogated for one year, in 1930 Matulionis was sentenced to ten years of forced labor on the Solovets Islands. Ill and emaciated, after two years he was transferred to a prison, then to a labor camp near Leningrad, and later to a prison hospital in Moscow. Exchanged for imprisoned Lithuanian Communists in 1933, he went to Lithuania. In 1934–36 Matulionis visited the United States and several West European countries. He was also received by Pope Pius XI, to whom he gave an account of conditions in the Soviet Union. After returning to Lithuania, Matulionis served as a judge in an ecclesiastic court in the archdiocese of Kaunas and as chaplain to the Benedictine order and chaplain to the Lithuanian armed forces (1940). In 1943 he was appointed ordinary bishop of Kaišiadorys. After the Red Army seized Lithuania in 1944, Matulionis continued his pastoral duties for some time, but in 1946 he was arrested and imprisoned, first in the Vladimir Prison and then in a labor camp in Potma in the Mordoviian ASSR. Released in 1956, he was banned from exercising his pastoral ministry and was held under house arrest in Birštonas and then in Šeduva, where he died. In February 1962, shortly before his death, Matulionis was elevated to archbishop by Pope John XXIII. (WR)

Sources: *EL*, vol. 3; *Annuario Pontificio*, 1958; T. Narbutas, *Four Martyred Bishops* (N.p., 1953); Pranas Gaida, *Nemarus mirtingasis arkivyskupas Teofilus Matulionis* (Rome, 1981); Irena Mikłaszewicz, *Polityka sowiecka wobec Kościoła katolickiego na Litwie 1944–1965* (Warsaw, 2001).

MATUSZEWSKI Ignacy (10 September 1891, Warsaw–3 August 1946, New York), Polish politician. Born into an intelligentsia family, after graduating from high school in Warsaw, Matuszewski studied philosophy in Kraków, law in Dorpat (Tartu), and architecture in Milan. In 1913 he began studying agriculture in Warsaw. Mobilized into the Russian Army, he fought on the Galician front. In April 1917 he was promoted to captain, and in June of that year, he was one of the organizers of the First General Congress of Polish Military Men in Petrograd. Matuszewski helped to establish Polish military units in Russia and then served in the First Polish Corps and joined the Polish Military Organization (Polska Organizacja Wojskowa [POW]). In February 1918 he led the military capture of Minsk by Polish troops and then assumed command of this city. In May of that year he unsuccessfully attempted to remove General **Józef Dowbór-Muśnicki** from the command of the First Corps and to send his units to fight against the Germans. In the summer of 1918 Matuszewski was head of POW intelligence for Russia, Ukraine, and Belorussia. In late October he became a member of the POW High Command, and in early November he helped organize the Polish Army. Assigned to the General Adjutancy of Commander-in-Chief **Józef Piłsudski**, at the end of 1918 Matuszewski began serving in the Sixth Department and then in the Second Department (Intelligence) of the General Staff. In August 1920 he became head of this department and was a military expert to the Polish delegation at the peace negotiations with the Bolsheviks in Riga. In July 1923 he resigned as head of intelligence and took a one-year course at the Military College.

Promoted to colonel in August 1924, after the coup of May 1926 Matuszewski became head of a department in the Ministry of Foreign Affairs, and in April 1927 he became director of the Administrative Department of the Ministry of Foreign Affairs. Regarded as a member of the so-called group of colonels, he was an envoy to Hungary until September 1929; from April 1929 to May 1931, during the initial stage of the Great Depression, he served as head of the Ministry of the Treasury. At that time he signed a "match loan" agreement in Sweden, the terms of which were rather disadvantageous for Poland. Matuszewski also unsuccessfully attempted to balance the budget. He considered his main task to be the protection of a fixed exchange rate for the Polish zloty. A supporter of deflation policy, Matuszewski resigned as a result of a conflict with Piłsudski over the budget for the army. Later, he became a leading journalist of the pro-government *Gazeta Polska*. An adherent of **Edward Rydz-Śmigły**, in May 1936 Matuszewski resigned from the editorial staff after a conflict with the government of **Felicjan Sławoj Składkowski**, and he became chairman of Towarzystwo Kredytowe Miejskie (City Credit Company) in Warsaw. In September 1939 he was in charge of evacuating the gold reserves of the Bank of Poland to France. After the capitulation of France, Matuszewski made his way to the United States in July 1940 and became one of the founders of the National Committee of Americans of Polish Descent (Komitet Narodowy Amerykanów Polskiego Pochodzenia). He published extensively in the Polish émigré press, criticizing the policies of the governments led by General **Władysław Sikorski** and **Stanisław Mikołajczyk**. Matuszewski's publications include *Próby syntez* (Attempts at syntheses; 1937).

Sources: *PSB*, vol. 20; *Kto był kim w Drugiej Rzeczpospolitej* (Warsaw, 1994); Zygmunt Karpiński, *O Wielkopolsce, złocie i dalekich podróżach* (Warsaw, 1971); Feliks Młynarski, *Wspomnienia* (Warsaw, 1971); Władysław T. Kulesza, *Koncepcje ideowo-polityczne obozu rządzącego w Polsce w latach 1926–1935* (Wrocław, 1985).

MATUSZEWSKI Stefan (2 December 1905, Giżyn, near Mława–21 March 1985, Warsaw), Polish Communist activist. Born into a peasant family, Matuszewski graduated in theology from Warsaw University in 1930. He was ordained a priest but then left the priesthood. In 1937 he joined the Polish Socialist Party (Polska Partia Socjalistyczna [PPS]) and was active in the Society of Workers University. During World War II he was in the Soviet Union, serving, from 1943 to 1944, in the Polish Army, which was being formed there under the auspices of the Kremlin. After returning to Poland, in cooperation with the Communists, Matuszewski organized Communist-dependent PPS structures. In September 1944 he became deputy head of the Information and Propaganda Department of the Polish Committee of National Liberation (Polski Komitet Wyzwolenia Narodowego [PKWN]). In 1945 he served as secretary general and deputy chairman of the Central Executive Committee of the so-called licensed (i.e., permitted by the authorities) Polish Socialist Party (Polska Partia Socjalistyczna [PPS]) and advocated that the PPS be incorporated into the Polish Workers' Party (Polska Partia Robotnicza [PPR]). In August 1946 Matuszewski was suspended as a PPS member for his vehement speeches in support of this merger. From December 1944 to September 1946 he was minister of information and propaganda, and from 1944 to 1947, he was a deputy to the National Home Council (Krajowa Rada Narodowa [KRN]). When in 1948 the pro-Communist orientation prevailed within the PPS, Matuszewski again became one of the PPS leaders and worked for the incorporation of the PPS into the PPR. He served as chairman of the PPS Provincial Committee in Warsaw Province, a member of the Chief Council and Central Executive Committee of the PPS, and secretary of the Central Commission of Trade Unions (Komisja Centralna Związków Zawodowych [KCZZ]). After the Polish United Workers' Party (Polska Zjednoczona Partia [PUWP]) was established, Matuszewski served as first secretary of the PUWP Executive Committee in Warsaw from 1948 to 1949 and as a member of the Central Committee (CC) and deputy member of the

PUWP CC Politburo from 1948 to 1954. In 1949–52 he was president of the Mass Organizations Commission of the PUWP CC and government plenipotentiary responsible for a program to eliminate illiteracy. From 1952 to 1954 he was head of the PUWP CC Administrative Department. Matuszewski's influence diminished after the March 1954 congress of the PUWP, when he left the Politburo. From 1952 to 1956 he was an MP, and from 1952 to 1957, a member of the Council of State. In October 1956 he supported the dogmatic Natolin faction. Later Matuszewski taught at Warsaw University. (PK)

Sources: Mołdawa; Włodzimierz Janowski and Aleksander Kochański, *Informator o strukturze i obsadzie personalnej centralnego aparatu PZPR 1948–1990* (Warsaw, 2000); Krystyna Kersten, *Narodziny systemu władzya: Polska 1943–1948* (Poznań, 1990); Marek Łatyński, *Nie paść na kolana: Szkice o opozyji lat czterdziestych* (Warsaw, 1987).

MATWIN Władysław (17 July 1916, Grodziec), Polish Communist activist. The son of a miner, Matwin graduated from high school. In the 1930s he was active in the Communist Party of Poland, and he spent 1938–39 in exile in Czechoslovakia. During World War II he was in the Soviet Union, where he joined the Soviet-sponsored Union of Polish Patriots and was its representative in Tehran, Iran. In 1945–46 Matwin was secretary of the Polish Embassy in Moscow. In 1946–48 he was secretary of the Provincial Committee of the Polish Workers' Party (Polska Partia Robotnicza [PPR]) in Wrocław, and from March to October 1947 and July to December 1948 he was its first secretary. During a party congress in December 1948, when the Polish United Workers' Party (Polska Zjednoczona Partia Robotnicza [PUWP]) came into being, Matwin sharply criticized **Władysław Gomułka**. From December 1948 to June 1949 Matwin was first secretary of the PUWP Provincial Committee in Wrocław, and then until November 1952 he was chairman of the Main Board of the Union of Polish Youth (Związek Młodzieży Polskiej [ZMP]). During his term, the Polish Scouting Association was incorporated into the ZMP, and the union's daily, *Sztandar Młodych*, was started. From December 1952 to February 1954 Matwin was first secretary of the PUWP Warsaw Provincial Committee, and from January 1954 to March 1956 and from November 1956 to March 1957 he was editor-in-chief of the party daily, *Trybuna Ludu*.

From 24 January 1955 to 30 November 1963 Matwin was secretary of the PUWP Central Committee (CC), and from March 1957 to October 1963 he was also first secretary of the PUWP Provincial Committee in Wrocław. After **Nikita Khrushchev** made his secret speech at the Twentieth CPSU Congress in February 1956, Matwin declared

himself in favor of a new line for the Polish Communist Party. He criticized the overgrowth of the CC apparatus and its low standards. He suggested structural changes in the party organization. His duties included supervision of the Democratic Party, the Main Political Administration of the army, and youth organizations. He controlled CC departments of education, planning and finance, and administration. Initially Matwin opposed the rehabilitation of Gomułka. At the same time party dogmatics accused him of loosening censorship. Matwin was one of the "young secretaries" of the PUWP, considered to be in the Puławska faction. From October 1952 to April 1965 Matwin was an MP, and from August 1952 to November 1956, a member of the Presidium of the All-Polish Conference of the National Front. Gradually sidelined, he studied mathematics and later worked in this field. In the course of time Matwin drew closer to the revisionist opposition. (PK)

Sources: Mołdawa; Antoni Czubiński, *Dzieje Najnowsze Polski 1944–1989* (Poznań, 1992); Włodzimierz Janowski and Aleksander Kochański, *Informator o strukturze i obsadzie personalnej centralnego aparatu PZPR 1948–1990* (Warsaw, 2000); Andrzej Albert [Wojciech Roszkowski], *Najnowsza historia Polski 1914–1993*, vol. 2 (Warsaw, 1995).

MAURER Ion (23 September 1902, Bucharest–8 February 2000, Bucharest), Romanian Communist activist and lawyer. Maurer's mother was Romanian and his father was a German from Alsace who had taught French to Crown Prince Charles of Romania. After finishing high school in Craiova, Maurer studied law at the University of Bucharest, graduating in 1923 and then earning a Ph.D. from this university. He subsequently practiced as a counsel for the defense in political trials. In the 1930s he defended some leaders of the Communist Party and favored revolutionary Marxism. In 1936 Maurer joined the Communist Party of Romania. From 1941 to 1943 he was imprisoned in a concentration camp for his Communist activities. In August 1944 he helped the leaders of the party, including **Gheorghe Gheorghiu-Dej**, to escape from the camp. After the coup d'état and the arrest of Marshal **Ion Antonescu**, Maurer served as deputy minister of transportation and public works (1944–46). From 1945 to 1955 he was a member of the Central Committee (CC) of the Romanian Communist Party, which from 1948 to 1965 was known as the Romanian Workers' Party (RWP). From 1946 to 1947 Maurer was minister of national education; from 1947 to 1948, minister of industry and trade. From 1946–47 he was a member of the Romanian delegation to the Paris Peace Conference. From 1948 to 1952 he was first deputy president of the Council of Ministers, and from 1952 to 1957, director of the Institute of Legal

Studies of the Romanian Academy of Sciences. In 1955 Maurer became a member of the Romanian Academy of Sciences. From 1957 to 1958 he was minister of foreign affairs. In 1960 he again became a member of the RWP CC, and in 1965, a member of the Standing Presidium of the Executive Committee of the RCP CC. He served as chairman of the Grand National Assembly until 1961.

On 21 March 1961 Maurer became prime minister and held this post until 29 March 1974. From 1965 to 1974 he also served as vice-president of the Council of State. As prime minister and a close associate of Gheorghiu-Dej, Maurer implemented Gheorghiu-Dej's neo-Stalinist concepts of economic policy, the nationalist line in domestic policy, and a foreign policy that was relatively independent of the Soviet Union. In March 1964 Maurer went to Beijing and unsuccessfully attempted to bring about a resumption of the Soviet-Chinese dialogue. After the death of Gheorghiu-Dej in March 1965, Maurer was instrumental in **Nicolae Ceauşescu**'s succession. Although Gheorghiu-Dej had wanted **Gheorghe Apostol** as his successor, Maurer proposed the candidacy of Ceauşescu, who promised Maurer that he would keep him on as prime minister. Maurer also hoped that Ceauşescu would be more efficient in maintaining a relative independence from Moscow. Ceauşescu initially continued the policy of abandoning intensive industrialization and laying greater emphasis on consumer goods, which characterized the last years of Gheorghiu-Dej's rule, but in 1971 he returned to neo-Stalinist methods in economic policy and to intensive industrialization, and he also began to build an extensive personality cult around himself. Maurer, who advocated a greater decentralization of the state and the economy, became an opponent of Ceauşescu and his personality cult. In 1974, like many other former associates of Gheorghiu-Dej, Maurer was forced to resign and to retire from politics. In the 1980s he maintained secret contacts with the anti-Ceauşescu opposition within the party, and in 1987 he was the co-author of a letter with proposals for reforms in Romania; the letter was addressed to Mikhail Gorbachev and delivered to the embassy of the Soviet Union. (LW)

Sources: Ion Alexandrescu, Ion Bulei, Ion Mamina, and Ioan Scurtu, *Enciclopedia de istorie României* (Bucharest, 2000); *Dictionar Enciclopedic*, vol. 4 (Bucharest, 2001); Ion Raţiu, *Contemporary Romania* (Richmond, 1975); Vlad Georgescu, *Istoria Românilor de la origini pînă în zilele noastre* (Oakland, 1984); Juliusz Demel, *Historia Rumunii* (Wrocław, 1986); Lavinia Betea, *Maurer şi lumea de ieri* (Arad, 1995); Józef Darski, *Rumunia: Historia, współczesność, konflikty narodowe* (Warsaw, 1995); Dorina N. Rusu, *Membrii Academiei Române 1866–1999* (Bucharest, 1999); Dennis Deletant, *Communist Terror in Romania: Gheorghiu-Dej and the Police State, 1948–1965* (New York, 1999).

MAZEPA Izaak (16 August 1884, Kostobobriv, Chernihiv Province–18 March 1952, Augsburg, Germany), Ukrainian politician. Mazepa studied in St. Petersburg, where he was an active member of the Ukrainian Student Hromada (community). In 1905 he joined the underground Ukrainian Social Democratic Workers' Party (Ukrayins'ka Sotsial-Demokraticheskaya Rabochaya Partiya [USDRP]) and soon became one of its leaders. From 1911 to 1917 Mazepa worked as an agronomist. After the February 1917 revolution he was a member of the Yekaterinoslav City Duma and the Yekaterinoslav Soviet of Workers' and Peasants' Deputies. In April 1918 he became head of the Yekaterinoslav Provincial Revolutionary Soviet. Under the rule of Hetman **Pavlo Skoropadskyi**, Mazepa co-edited the USDRP paper, *Nasha Sprava*. In January 1919 Mazepa was a delegate to the Labor Congress in Kiev and was elected secretary of the USDRP Central Committee (CC). In April 1919 he became minister of interior in the government of the Ukrainian National Republic (Ukrayins'ka Narodna Republika [UNR]). On 29 August 1919 Mazepa was appointed prime minister of the UNR government. He opposed territorial concessions and announced his resignation in protest against the Piłsudski-Petlyura treaty of April 1920, but when the Polish-Ukrainian forces entered Kiev, Mazepa formally continued to serve as head of government until late May 1920. Later, he held the post of UNR minister of agriculture. In late 1920 Mazepa settled in Lwów (Lviv), and in 1923 he emigrated to Czechoslovakia. From 1927 he was an associate professor (*docent*) at the Ukrainian Husbandry Academy and its successor, the Ukrainian Technical and Husbandry Institute (UTHI), in Poděbrady. He represented the USDRP at international Socialist conferences and was a member of the Executive Committee of the Labor and Socialist International.

In 1945 Mazepa settled in Germany. In 1946 he became a professor at the UTHI in Munich. He co-founded the Ukrainian National Rada—a parliament of Ukrainians in exile—and was the first chairman (prime minister) of its executive organ from 1948 to 1952. He was also a founding member of the Ukrainian Socialist Party in exile (established in 1950). Mazepa's publications include the following: *Bolshevyzm i okupatsiia Ukrainy* (Bolshevism and the occupation of the Ukraine; 1922); a two-volume outline of Ukrainian policies, *Pidstavy nashoho vidrodzhennia* (Foundations of our rebirth, 1946); and memoirs of the years 1917–21, *Ukraïna v ohni i buri revoliutsiï* (Ukraine in the fire and storm of revolution, 2 vols.; 1941). Mazepa also wrote scholarly works on such topics as Carpathian mountain pastures. (GM)

Sources: *Encyclopedia of Ukraine*, vol. 3 (Toronto, 1993); *Entsyklopediia Ukraïnoznavstva*, vol. 4 (Lviv, 1994); Panas Fedenko, *Issak Mazepa: Botets za voliu* (London, 1954); "Issakovi Mazepi na vichnu pamiat," *Nashe Slovo*, 1973, no. 3; Ryszard Torzecki, *Kwestia ukraińska w Polsce w latach 1923–1929* (Kraków, 1989).

MAZOWIECKI Tadeusz (18 April 1927, Płock), Polish politician. Mazowiecki studied law at Warsaw University. In 1949–55 he was connected with the periodical *Dziś i Jutro* and with the (Catholic) association PAX of **Bolesław Piasecki** that cooperated with the Communist Party. In 1950–52 he was deputy editor-in-chief of the PAX daily, *Słowo Powszechne*, and from 1953 to 1955 he was editor-in-chief of the PAX weekly, *Wrocławski Tygodnik Katolików*. In 1955 Mazowiecki led the so-called Fronda and was suspended as a PAX member. In October 1956 he co-founded the All-Polish Club of the Progressive Catholic Intelligentsia. From 1957 he belonged to the board of the Catholic Intelligentsia Club (Klub Inteligencji Katolickiej [KIK]), and in 1975–81 and 1988–90 he was its deputy chairman. In 1958 Mazowiecki co-founded the monthly *Więź* and was its editor-in-chief until 1981. Inspired by the personalist thought of Emanuel Mounier, Mazowiecki advocated an opening of the Catholic Church to contemporary social change; he initiated dialogue with non-believers, supported ecumenism, and pointed to the necessity to democratize the Communist system. From 1961 to 1971 he was an MP on behalf of the club Znak (Sign). In 1968 he co-authored a parliamentary interpellation concerning repression of students taking part in the March 1968 events.

In the 1970s Mazowiecki belonged to the non-conformist wing of the Znak movement, favoring a dialogue with the secular revisionist opposition. In 1976 he co-initiated protests against amendments to the constitution. He was a spokesman for the hunger strike in St. Martin Church in Warsaw (May 1977). He organized a session on human rights in the Warsaw KIK (October 1977), was an active member of the Society of Scientific Courses (1978–81), and published in the uncensored press. In August 1980 Mazowiecki chaired the Commission of Experts of the Inter-Factory Strike Committee in Gdańsk, and he was one of the architects of the August Accord. Later he was one of the key advisers to **Lech Wałęsa** and the National Coordination Commission of Solidarity. He was also editor-in-chief of the weekly *Tygodnik Solidarność*. Supporter of a moderate line, Mazowiecki tried to avoid confrontation with the Communist powers and to allow Solidarity to survive and democratize the Communist system. Interned from 13 December 1981 to 23 December 1982, in 1983–84 Mazowiecki chaired the KIK Program Council and was an adviser to Wałęsa. In the summer of 1988 he advised the strike committee in the Gdańsk Shipyard and co-organized the Civic Committee of the Chairman of Solidarity. A key negotiator during preparations for the Round Table Talks (February–April 1989), as well as one of the participants, Mazowiecki chaired the negotiating group on trade union pluralism. From June 1989 he was again editor-in-chief of *Tygodnik Solidarność*. He did not run in the parliamentary elections of 4 June 1989, disagreeing with the way "social" candidates were selected.

On 24 August 1989 Mazowiecki was appointed prime minister, forming a cabinet with only a few Communist ministers—the first postwar government in Poland not fully controlled by the Communists. As prime minister, he started systemic transformations: a limitation of links with the Soviet Union and rapprochement with the West; the liquidation of the system of nomenklatura; local self-government reforms; the abolition of censorship; and scrutiny of the Civic Militia and security service functionaries. Mazowiecki's government started an economic transformation toward a market economy (**Leszek Balcerowicz**'s "shock therapy") and concluded a Polish-German treaty confirming the existing border between the two countries (14 November 1990). From early 1990 Mazowiecki's policies were increasingly criticized by a more radical part of the Civic Parliamentary Club and by Wałęsa as too cautious in dismantling the old system; this started the so-called "war at the top." The conflict among the Solidarity elite made Mazowiecki run against Wałęsa in the presidential elections. On 25 November 1990 Mazowiecki won 18 percent of the vote, coming in third. He lost not only to Wałęsa, but also to an obscure candidate, Stanisław Tymiński. As a result, he resigned from the premiership, and his resignation was accepted by the parliament on 14 December 1990. From 2 December 1990 Mazowiecki chaired the Democratic Union (Unia Demokratyczna), formed by his followers from the presidential campaign. After it merged with the Gdańsk Liberals into the Union of Freedom (Unia Wolności [UW]) in 1994, Mazowiecki was UW chairman until April 1995. From 1991 to 2001 he was an MP, and in 1992–93 he chaired the Constitutional Commission of the National Assembly. From 1992 to 1995 Mazowiecki was a special reporter of the UN Committee on Human Rights in Former Yugoslavia. Co-author of the constitutional compromise of 1997, Mazowiecki authored numerous books and articles, including *Rozdroża i wartości* (Crossroads and values; 1970) and *Internowanie* (Internment; 1983). Mazowiecki retired from politics in 2002. (AF)

Sources: Mołdawa; *Kto jest kim w Polsce* (Warsaw, 2001); Andrzej Micewski, *Współrządzić czy nie kłamać?* (Paris, 1978); Jerzy Holzer, *"Solidarność"* (Warsaw, 1983); Timothy Garton Ash, *The Polish Revolution: Solidarity* (New York, 1985); Zbigniew Domarańczyk, *100 dni Mazowieckiego* (Warsaw, 1990); *Tadeusz Mazowiecki: Polityk trudnych czasów* (Warsaw, 1997); Jan Skórzyński, *Ugoda i rewolucja: Władza i opozycja 1985–1989* (Warsaw, 1995); Antoni Dudek, *Pierwsze lata III Rzeczpospolitej 1989–2001* (Kraków, 2002).

MAZUR Franciszek [originally Horodenko] (1 August 1895, Volkovtse, Podolia–7 March 1975, Warsaw), Polish Communist activist of Ukrainian descent. Mazur's biography is obscure at some points and contains gaps. Born into the family of a farm worker, he took part in the Bolshevik revolution of 1917 and in the civil war in Russia. In 1919 he joined the All-Russian Communist Party (Bolsheviks). He later probably worked for the NKVD and the judicial persecution apparatus in the Ukraine. In 1930 Mazur came to Poland and became a member of the Central Committee (CC) of the Communist Party of Poland (Komunistyczna Partia Polski [KPP]). He also directed the work of the Communist Party of Western Ukraine (KPZU) and was imprisoned by the Polish authorities. In September 1939 he was in the Soviet Union. In 1945 he came to Poland, and in August of that year he became secretary of the CC of the Polish Workers' Party (Polska Partia Robotnicza [PPR]). From 1946 to 1948 Mazur headed the Organizational Department of the PPR CC. In November 1948 he became a deputy member of the Politburo and a member of the Organizational Bureau of the PPR CC. In 1946 he joined the National Home Council (Krajowa Rada Narodowa [KRN]). In 1947 he became an MP in the Constituent Assembly, and in 1948 he served as president of the PPR parliamentary representation.

Elected to the CC of the Polish United Workers' Party (Polska Zjednoczona Partia Robotnicza [PUWP]) in December 1948, Mazur was in charge of the CC Organizational Department and served as a member of the Organizational Bureau and a deputy member of the Politburo of the PUWP CC. In May 1950 he became a member of the Politburo, secretary of the PUWP CC Organizational Bureau, and secretary of the PUWP CC. One of the Kremlin's most trusted co-workers in the party executive, Mazur was a very influential figure, supervising (among other things) the cooperative movement, youth organizations, and the clergy. He was also one of the people in charge of the ministry of national defense and security. He was responsible for the economic, foreign, financial and administrative departments, as well as others. In 1953 Mazur was in charge of establishing a "special sector" within the CC for controlling the security police. He was deputy speaker of the first Assembly (1952–56). From 1952 to 1957 he served as vice-president of the Council of State. He was one of the chief implementers of the policy to persecute the Catholic Church in 1950–56.

He signed an agreement with the Episcopate on 14 April 1950, but he was also co-responsible for the decision to arrest Cardinal **Stefan Wyszyński** in September 1953. On his initiative, in March 1953 the PAX association of **Bolesław Piasecki** took over *Tygodnik Powszechny*, removing the legitimate editorial staff. Mazur was a close associate of **Bolesław Bierut** and was aligned with the dogmatic Natolin faction in the PUWP. In May 1956 he took part in negotiations with **Władysław Gomułka** on Gomułka's return to power. From late September to mid-November 1956 Mazur was in the Soviet Union. At the Eighth CC Plenum in October 1956 he left the Politburo and Secretariat of the PUWP CC, and in March 1959 he was dropped from the CC. Mazur was a member of the PUWP Central Audit Committee from 1959 to 1964 and an ambassador to Czechoslovakia from 1957 to 1965. He subsequently retired. (PK)

Sources: Mołdawa; Józef Światło, *Kulisy partii i bezpieki* (N.p., n.d.); Jan Nowak, *Wojna w eterze* (London, 1985); Antoni Czubiński, *Dzieje Najnowsze Polski 1944–1989* (Poznań, 1992); Włodzimierz Janowski and Aleksander Kochański, *Informator o strukturze i obsadzie personalnej centralnego aparatu PZPR 1948–1990* (Warsaw, 2000).

MAZURAU Kiril [known as Mazurov in the Soviet Union] (7 April 1914, Rudnia Prybytkouskaya, near Homel–19 December 1989, Moscow), Soviet activist in Belorussia. In 1933 Mazurau finished a course in road construction in a technical high school in Homel, and in 1947 he graduated from the Higher Pedagogical School of the Central Committee (CC) of the Communist Party (Bolshevik) of Belorussia [CP(B)B]). From 1936 to 1939 he served in the Red Army and was a political worker of the Belorussian railways. From 1939 to 1941 he worked in the Komsomol apparatus. In June 1941 Mazurau began serving on the front line, initially as a political officer of a company, and in 1942, of the Twenty-first Army, with the rank of lieutenant colonel. In September 1942 he became a representative of the Red Army General Staff in the partisan movement in the territories of German-occupied Belorussia. In 1943 he was again transferred to work in the Komsomol. After the war Mazurau became first secretary of the Komsomol. From 1947 onwards he worked in the apparatus of the CP(B)B CC, holding a variety of posts, including that of secretary of the Municipal Committee and the District Committee in Minsk. From 1953 to 1956 he served as chairman of the Council of Ministers of the Belorussian SSR. He was the first Belorussian to assume the post of first secretary of the CP(B)B CC (July 1956). Mazurau served as head of the party and head of the political authorities of the Belorussian SSR until 1965 and was instrumental in increasing the degree of Sovietization of Belorussia in all areas of social and cultural life. At the same time Belorussia went into a new stage of industrialization, modeled on that of the Soviet Union. Mazurau had ambitions to make Belorussia a leader among other Soviet-dominated republics in building a "developed Communist" society. From 1965 to 1978 Mazurau was a member of the Politburo of the CC of the Communist Party of the Soviet Union and first deputy prime minister of the Soviet Union. From 1950 to 1979 he was a deputy to the Supreme Soviet of the USSR. Dismissed at the end of Leonid Brezhnev's rule, Mazurau served as president of the All-Union Council of War and Labor Veterans from 1986 until the end of his life. (EM)

Sources: Archie Brown, ed., *The Soviet Union: A Biographical Dictionary* (London, 1990); Jan Zaprudnik, *Historical Dictionary of Belarus* (Lanham, Md., 1998); *Entsyklapedyia historyi Bielarusi,* vol. 5 (Minsk, 1999); *Bielaruskaia entsyklapiedyia,* vol. 9 (Minsk, 1999).

MEČIAR Vladimír (26 July 1942, Zvolen), Slovak politician. After graduating from high school in 1959, Mečiar was a white-collar worker in the county National Committee (NC) in Źiar nad Hronem. In 1962 he joined the Communist Party of Czechoslovakia (CPC), and he became active in its youth organizations. In 1967–68 he chaired the regional committee of the Socialist Union of Czechoslovak Youth. From 1967 to 1969 he was deputy chairman of the Committee of People's Control in the county NC. In 1970 Mečiar was expelled from the CPC for supporting the Prague Spring of 1968. Until 1973 he worked as a blue-collar laborer in Western Slovakia. He also graduated in law from the University of Bratislava. In 1973–90 Mečiar was a legal adviser to the Skloobal Nemšova Company.

Mečiar started his political career during the Velvet Revolution of 1989. He was one of the founders and leaders of the Public against Violence (Verejnost' proti Nasiliu [VPN]). From January to June 1990 he was minister of interior and the natural environment of the Slovak republic. As a result of the first free elections in June 1990, Mečiar won a seat in the Chamber of the People of the Federal Assembly on behalf of the VPN. From 27 June 1990 to 23 April 1991 he was head of the Slovak government. In March 1991 he entered into conflict with the VPN leadership and created a platform called For a Democratic Slovakia. This led to his dismissal from the premiership. Mečiar left the VPN, and at the end of April 1991 he created the Movement for a Democratic Slovakia (Hnutie za demokratické Slovensko [HZDS]). At the founding congress of the party, on 22 June 1991, Mečiar was elected its chairman. The party adopted a populist program with the slogan of a "social market economy" and with particular reference to the "Slovak question." Mečiar was increasingly critical of the economic reforms of **Václav Klaus**, combining his criticism with nationalist rhetoric. He demanded a Czechoslovak confederation and a separate "Slovak economic road." He gained massive support, so the HZDS won the June 1992 elections in Slovakia. Mečiar became an MP to the Slovak National Council, and on 24 June 1992 he resumed the position of Slovak prime minister. In view of the simultaneous victory of his main opponent, Klaus, in the Czech lands, the Czechoslovak federation was doomed. After negotiations with Klaus, on 1 January 1993 Czechoslovakia was dissolved.

Mečiar was the first prime minister of the newly independent Slovak state, but soon he had to face inter-party struggles. Due to his autocratic style, the HZDS split twice. In March 1993 a group led by **Milan Kňažko** left, and a year later a group led by **Jozef Moravčik** seceded. Also, President **Michal Kovač**, elected by the ruling majority, increasingly distanced himself from Mečiar. Mečiar's government could not handle these pressures, and on 14 March 1994 the parliament voted Mečiar out of government. Nevertheless, he managed to force early elections. On 30 September and 1 October 1994 the HZDS won almost 35 percent of the vote and created a new cabinet with the extreme right-wing Slovak National Party and the populist Association of Slovak Workers. Mečiar became prime minister again and held this position from 13 December 1994 to 29 October 1998. His term was marked by an authoritarian style, a violation of democratic rules, and an incoherent foreign policy. Mečiar carried out a purge in an effort to marginalize the opposition. His main target was President Kováč, the only political figure he could not dismiss. Mečiar limited presidential powers and used various forms of pressure to make Kováč resign. These efforts culminated with the kidnapping of Kováč's son and his deportation to Austria by the special services headed by a trusted aide of Mečiar, **Ivan Lexa**. Despite these pressures, Kováč did not resign. With the termination of his term, on 2 March 1998 Mečiar took over most of his powers and amnestied those involved in the kidnapping of Kováč's son. Mečiar performed presidential duties until 29 October 1998.

"Mečiarism" also had negative effects in Slovakia's foreign relations. Because of the twists and turns in Mečiar's foreign policy and his undemocratic rule, the country was dropped from the first group of possible candidates to NATO and the European Union. Despite pro-Western declarations, in practice Mečiar forced rapprochement with Russia and sent discouraging signals to the West. In

1997 he manipulated a referendum on Slovakia's entry into NATO. In fact he isolated Slovakia in the international arena. Despite his autocratic style, Mečiar hesitated to falsify the elections of September 1998. Although the HZDS won the largest number of votes, the anti-Mečiar coalition won a majority, and the HZDS was forced into the opposition. Mečiar announced his withdrawal from politics, but when direct presidential elections were announced, he decided to run. In May 1999 he came in second in the first round but lost in the second round to the candidate of the ruling coalition, **Rudolf Schuster**. Before the parliamentary elections of September 2002, Mečiar raised new fears, since his return to power could have slowed down Slovakia's integration with the Euro-Atlantic structures. In July 2002 **Ivan Gašparovič** left the HZDS because he was disappointed that his name was not on the list of candidates; he then formed the Movement for Democracy (Hnutie za Demokraciu [HZD]). Gašparovič's departure seriously weakened the HZDS, which won only 19.5 percent of the vote and remained in the opposition. In a referendum in 2003 Mečiar called on his followers to support entry into the European Union, but this did not help him in the presidential elections of April 2004, in which he lost to Gašparovič. (PU)

Sources: *ČBS*; *Kdo byl kdo v našich dějinach ve 20. stoleti*, vol. 1 (Prague, 1998); Eric Stein, *Czecho/Slovakia: Ethnic Conflict, Constitutional Fissure, Negotiated Breakup* (Ann Arbor, 1997); Ján Liďák, Viera Koganová, and Dušan Leška, *Politické strany a hnutia na Slovensku po roku 1989* (Bratislava, 1999); Marian Leško, *Mečiar a mečiarizmus* (Bratislava, 1998); Dana Podracká and L'uba Šajdová, *Slovenské tabu: Vladimír Mečiar* (Bratislava, 2000); Svätoslav Mathé, *Slovenská politika v rokoch 1848–1993* (Martin, 2001); Jan Rychlík, *Rozpad Československa: Česko-slovenské vztahy 1989–1992* (Bratislava, 2002).

MEDENIS Janis (31 May 1903, Praulienas–10 May 1961, Murjanos), Latvian writer and poet. In 1922–33 Medenis studied philology in Riga, and from 1927 to 1937 he was secretary of the editorial staff of a multi-volume dictionary of the Latvian language, *Latviešu Konversacijas Vārdnica*. Medenis's collections of poems—*Torņi pamale* (The towers on the horizon; 1926), *Tecila* (Whetstone; 1933), *Verenība* (Power; 1936), and *Teiksmu raksti* (Symbols from legends; 1942)—belong among the greatest achievements of twentieth-century Latvian lyrical poetry. During the Soviet and German occupation of 1940–44 Medenis lived in Latvia. In 1945 he attempted to go to Sweden but was captured by Soviet security forces. He was held for several years in a prison in Latvia, and at the end of the 1940s he was sent to the mines on the Kolyma River. His poem *Milky Way* is an evocation of the traumatic experiences of that period. In 1955 Medenis was allowed to return to his native land, but he was relegated to total oblivion, and his creative work was passed over in silence. His collection *Dienu krāšņums* (Beauty of the days) was not published until 1958. Medenis never regained his health and died prematurely as a result of the labor camp ordeals. (WR)

Sources: Rolfs Ekmanis, *Latvian Literature under the Soviets, 1940–1975* (Belmont, Mass., 1978); Romuald J. Misiunas and Rein Taagepera, *The Baltic States: Years of Dependence, 1940–1980* (Berkeley, 1993).

MEDGYESSY Péter (19 October 1942, Budapest), Hungarian post-Communist politician. The son of a white-collar worker from Transylvania, in 1962–66 Medgyessy studied economics at the Karl Marx Economics University in Budapest, and later he received a Ph.D. there. From 1966 he worked in the Ministry of Finance, heading its price, international finance, and budget departments in the 1980s. From 1982 deputy minister and from 1987 the minister of finance, Medgyessy authored a tax reform. From 23 November 1988 to 3 May 1990 Medgyessy was deputy prime minister in the government of **Miklós Németh**, responsible for economic liberalization and privatization. In 1990–94 he chaired the Magyar Paribas Bank, connected with a French capital group, and from 1994 to 1996 he was chairman of the Hungarian Bank of Investments and Development (MBFB). From July 1994 to July 1998 Medgyessy was minister of finance again, this time in the government of **Gyula Horn**. He managed to slightly curb inflation and to accelerate economic growth, as well as to introduce a new pension system. From 1998 to 2001 he chaired the Inter-Europa Bank and the insurance company Atlasz. After the parliamentary elections of April 2002, in which a coalition of the (post-Communist) Hungarian Socialist Party and the Alliance of Free Democrats won a slight majority, on 27 May 2002 Medgyessy became prime minister of the government based on this coalition. In August 2002 the daily *Magyar Hirlap* disclosed that in 1977–82 Medgyessy had cooperated with Communist counterintelligence. He initially denied this accusation, but when solid proof was presented, he admitted this had been the case; however, the affair hardly damaged his reputation as prime minister. Medgyessy's government played an important role in encouraging Hungarians to vote for accession to the European Union in a referendum in May 2003. Because of a conflict with the Free Democrats, Medgyessy had to resign from the government on 29 September 2004. (WR)

Sources: Rudolf L. Tőkes, *Hungary's Negotiated Revolution: Economic Reforms, Social Change, and Political Succession, 1957–1990* (Cambridge, 1996); *Rzeczpospolita*, 26 August 2002; www.kancellaria.gov.hu/miniszterelnok/index_e.html; www.cidob.org/bios/castellano/lideres/m-010.htm.

MEIDANI Rexhep (17 August 1944, Tirana), Albanian physicist and politician. In 1966 Meidani graduated in physics from Tirana University and started working at its Department of Physics. In 1973–76 he specialized in spectrometry and magnetic resonance at the Universities of Caen and Paris XI (Orsay). From 1977 Meidani lectured at the university in Prishtina, and in May 1981 he returned to Paris, where in 1984 he received a Ph.D. in the physics of solid substances. In 1987 he became a professor. Accepted by the **Enver Hoxha** regime, Meidani was fully loyal, so in 1988 he became dean of the Natural Sciences Department, and in 1992, chair of Theoretical Physics. Until 1997 he mostly dealt with research at Tirana University. Well known in the international community of solid substance physicists, he took part in many international conferences and worked as a visiting professor at universities in Cluj (Romania), Siegen (Germany), Portsmouth (UK), and Boston, Massachusetts. In 1990 Meidani was appointed head of the State Electoral Commission. From November 1994 he was active in the Albanian Center for Human Rights, editing its press organ. From July 1996 he belonged to the (post-Communist) Albanian Socialist Party (Partia Socialiste ë Shqipërisë [APS]), and a month later he became its secretary general. In the elections of June 1997 Meidani won a seat in the parliament, which elected him president. He assumed the office on 24 July 1997, resigning from the ASP. Meidani strove to strengthen relations with the European Union, supporting the Albanian government's attempts to avoid a spillover from the Kosovo conflict of 1999 and to prevent the penetration of Muslim fundamentalist fighters into Albania. Meidani authored twenty-three books and textbooks, as well as several dozen articles in theoretical physics that were published abroad. He received honorary doctorates from universities in Sofia (Bulgaria) and Salonika (Greece). Meidani's term ended on 24 July 2002. (TC)

Sources: Elez Biberaj, *Shqipëria ne tranzicion: Rruga e vështrisë drejt Demokracisë* (Tirana, 2001); Józefa Wiśniewska, "Redżep Mejdani," *Przegląd Albański*, 1997; *Europa Środkowo-Wschodnia 1999* (Warsaw, 2000); president.gov.al/biograph.htm.

MEIEROVICS Sigfrids (5 February 1887, Durbe, Courland–22 August 1925, Tukums), Latvian politician, economist, and diplomat. The son of a doctor, Meierovics completed a trade school in Riga in 1908, and in 1911 he graduated from the Department of Trade of the Riga Polytechnic Institute. In 1915 he started working at a bank in Moscow, and in 1916 he moved to Rēzekne, where he worked as a clerk in a food supply department of the Union of Russian Towns on the north front. From February 1917 Meierovics was active in Riga, where he was among the founders of the Peasant Union. In October 1917, along with **Janis Cakšte** and Latvian deputies to the Duma, he became a member of the Latvian Refugee Committee. In St. Petersburg, this committee worked on (among other things) plans for the autonomy of and social reforms in Latvia. Meierovics was elected to the Presidium of the first Latvian National Assembly, which became the Latvian Provisional National Council (LPNC) on 18 November 1917. He was head of the foreign affairs department of the council.

In January 1918 Meierovics became a member of the first foreign diplomatic mission of the LPNC, sent to establish relations with the Entente states and to gain recognition for Latvia as a sovereign state, independent of both Russia and Germany. The talks, between Meierovics and the ambassadors of Great Britain, France, and the United States, coincided with the signing of the Treaty of Brest-Litovsk, in which Soviet Russia ceded the Latvian territories to Germany. This hindered Latvia's aspirations for independence. To prevent the cession of these territories to Germany, in the summer of 1918 Meierovics left for England, where on 11 November 1918 he succeeded in obtaining the recognition of the LPNC as the government of Latvia and confirming his own status as an informal representative of Latvia. On 19 November Meierovics was formally appointed the first Latvian foreign minister. In 1919 he represented Latvia at the Paris Peace Conference. In July 1919 he returned to Latvia, and in October 1919 he took part in the struggle against the intervention of White Russian troops. From 1920 Meierovics was a member of the Latvian Constituent Assembly, and from 1922, of the parliament. He held the post of foreign minister until January 1924, serving simultaneously as prime minister between 19 June 1921 and 26 January 1923 and between 28 June 1923 and 26 January 1924. He headed talks with the governments of Estonia and Lithuania that led to the creation of the so-called Baltic Entente, and in 1921 he gained de jure international recognition for Latvia. In December 1924 he resumed the post of foreign minister. Meierovics died tragically in a car accident and was buried in Riga. (AG/EJ)

Sources: Emile Doumergue, *La Lettonie et la Baltique* (Paris, 1919); [A. Tupiņš], *Sigfrids A. Meierovics* (Riga, 1925); *Latvijas ārlietu ministra Z. A. Meierovica piemiņai (biogrāfija un ģīmetnes)* (Riga, 1925); *Divu cilvēku traģēdija* (Riga, 1925); *Zigfrīda un Kristīnes Meierovics Piemiņas albums* (Riga, 1926); Alfreds Bilmanis, *A History of Latvia* (London, 1952); Gore, "Zigfrīds Anna Meierovics (1887–1925) un Latvijas ceļš uz neatkarību," *Latvijas Vēsture*, 1993, no. 2; A. Lerhis, "Zigfrīds Anna Meierovics (1887–1925)," *Latvijas Vēstures Institūta Žurnāls*, 2000, no. 3.

MEKSI Aleksander Gabriel (8 March 1939, Tirana), Albanian archaeologist and politician. Born into an Eastern

Orthodox family, in 1960 Meksi graduated in engineering from the Polytechnic University of Tirana. After two years of work at the water power plant in Shkopeti, he started doing research at the Institute of Cultural Monuments and the Institute of Archaeological Studies, specializing in medieval and Byzantine architecture. In 1988 Meksi received a Ph.D. He co-authored a couple of textbooks for students. He belonged to a group of intellectuals who co-founded the Albanian Democratic Party (Partia Demokratike e Shqipërisë [PDS]) and was **Sali Berisha**'s main rival for its leadership. From April 1991 to March 1992 Meksi was a member of parliament and deputy chairman of its presidium. On 13 April 1992 he became prime minister of the government dominated by the PDS. In September 1992, speaking before the UN General Assembly, Meksi pointed to Serb nationalism as the main obstacle to a resolution of the conflicts in the former Yugoslavia. Meksi's term coincided with an aggravation of conflicts with Albania's neighbors: with Yugoslavia the problem was Kosovo, and with Greece it was the Greek minority in Albania and the trial of members of the Omonia organization. In February 1997 Meksi's government became a target of attacks as a result of the collapse of the financial pyramid schemes. Interviewed by *The Economist*, Meksi stated that his government did not fear a civil war if the post-Communists caused it. As a result of this interview, he gained the nickname "Aleksander i Vogel" (Alexander the Small). On 1 March 1997 Meksi resigned along with his government. He left the PDS and became engaged in economic activities. After the elections of 2001 Meksi returned to the PDS. (TC)

Sources: Miranda Vickers and James Pettifier, *Albania: From Anarchy to a Balkan Identity* (New York, 1997); Biberaj Elez, *Shqipëria ne tranzicion: Rruga e vështrisë drejt Demokracisë* (Tirana, 2001); Bugajski.

MELNYK Andriy (12 December 1890, Volia Yakubova, Drohobych County–1 November 1964, Cologne, Germany), Ukrainian political and military activist. Melnyk studied at the Higher School of Agriculture in Vienna (1912–14), but his studies were interrupted by the outbreak of World War I. In 1914–16 he commanded companies (*sotnyas*) of the Ukrainian Sich Riflemen. After the battle of Lysonia, he was taken prisoner by the Russians and interned in Tsaritsyn, where he became a close aide to **Yevhen Konovalets**. Melnyk was one of the organizers of a Ukrainian POW group that was later formed into a military unit. Released toward the end of 1917, Melnyk helped to organize the Sich Riflemen and became commander of one of their battalions. He served on the staff of a regiment, a division, a corps, and a group of the Sich Riflemen. In January 1919 he became chief of staff of the army of the Ukrainian National Republic (UNR). After a short period as a Polish prisoner of war, Melnyk served as inspector of a UNR military mission in Prague from 1920 to 1921. At that time he completed his studies, receiving a diploma in forestry engineering. In 1922 he settled in Galicia. After Konovalets had left the country, Melnyk assumed home command of the Ukrainian Military Organization (Ukrajinska Viiskova Orhanizatsiia [UVO]). In the spring of 1924 he was arrested and sentenced to five years' imprisonment. He was released toward the end of 1928, partly as a result of the efforts of the UNR president, **Andriy Livytskyi**. Melnyk began working in metropolitan property administration in Lwów (Lviv). He served as president of the Chief Council of the Orly (Eagles) Catholic Association of Ukrainian Youth and was involved with the Moloda Hromada (Young Company) society. In 1934 he became a member of the UVO senior staff. After the assassination of Konovalets in 1938, Melnyk went abroad and became head of the leadership (*provid*) of the Organization of Ukrainian Nationalists (Orhanizatsiia Ukraiinskykh Natsionalistiv [OUN]). His leadership was confirmed at the OUN Second Grand Assembly in Rome in August 1939.

After a split in the OUN in 1940, Melnyk became head of an OUN faction that came to be known as the OUN-Melnyk Faction (OUN-M). During World War II Melnyk advocated cooperation with the Germans and organized OUN-M mobile units (*pokhidni grupy*), which were to take over power in the Ukrainian territories after the outbreak of the German-Soviet war. After the German attack on the Soviet Union in June 1941, Melnyk offered military cooperation to the Third Reich, but the offer was turned down. During the war he was kept under house arrest in Berlin. In January 1942, along with Archbishop **Andriy Sheptytskyi**, Livytskyi, and other Ukrainian activists, Melnyk submitted a memorandum to Hitler demanding an end to German persecutions in the Ukraine. Arrested in 1944 for his attempts to establish contacts with the Allies, Melnyk was imprisoned for a few months in the Sachsenhausen concentration camp. After the war, Melnyk settled in Luxembourg. He was a co-founder of the Ukrainian National Council. In 1947, at the OUN Third Grand Assembly, he was appointed head of the OUN for life. In 1959 he proposed the idea of a world congress of Ukrainians and a Ukrainian union. Melnyk was also an initiator and then the head of a foundation in memory of Konovalets. (GM)

Sources: *Encyclopedia of Ukraine*, vol. 3 (Toronto, 1993); *Entsyklopediia Ukraiinoznavstva*, vol. 4 (Lviv, 1994); *Andriy Melnyk 1890–1964* (N.p., 1966); *Nepohasnyi ohon' viry* (N.p., 1974); Ryszard Torzecki, *Kwestia ukraińska w Polsce w latach 1923–1929* (Kraków, 1989); Paul R. Magocsi, *A History of Ukraine* (Seattle, 1996); Orest Subtelny, *Ukraine: A History* (Toronto, 2000).

MENZEL Jiří (23 February 1938, Prague), Czech screenplay writer, film director, and actor. In 1962 Menzel graduated from the Department of Film and Television of the Academy of Musical Arts in Prague. He made his debut in 1965 with the movies *Zločin v dívčí škole* (Crime in a girls' school), based on a story by **Josef Škvorecký**, and *Smrt pana Baltisbergra* (The death of Mr. Balisberger). Menzel became famous for his film version of **Bohumil Hrabal**'s *Ostře sledované vlaky* (Closely watched trains; 1966), for which he received an Oscar in 1967. In a masterly way Menzel connected the drama of wartime with the comic happenings of everyday life, perfectly reflecting Hrabal's prose. The movie placed Menzel among the leaders of the Czechoslovak "New Wave." He confirmed his mastery of subtle style and comic expression in the movies *Rozmarné leto* (Wanton summer; 1967), *Zločin v šantánu* (Crime in a nightclub; 1968), and *Skřivánci na niti* (Larks on a string; 1969). During the so-called normalization after 1968 Menzel's films were banned, and he had to distance himself from his works in public. Nevertheless, he rejected an official demand to return the Oscar because it was an award of the "Zionists." Menzel had problems realizing his subsequent films, such as *Postřižiny* (Hair clipping; 1980), also based on a work by Hrabal; *Slavnosti sněženek* (Snowflake festival; 1983); *Vesničko má středisková* (My sweet little village; 1985); and *Konec starých časů* (The end of old times; 1989). In the 1990s he put **Václav Havel**'s play, *Žebrácká opera* (Beggar's opera; 1991), on the screen. In 1969–74 Menzel directed plays in Prague theaters—Semafor, Disk, Divadlo na Zábradlí, and Činoherní Klub—and abroad. He played in numerous films and television series, including *Hospoda* (The inn; 1996). He also published two collections of columns, *Tak nevím* (Yes, I don't know; 1996) and *Tak nevím podruhé* (Yes, I don't know for the second time; 1998). In 1988 he co-founded the European Cinema Society. In 1996 Menzel was awarded the Czech Lion for his contributions to Czech cinema. (PU)

Sources: *ČBS*; *Kdo byl kdo v našich dějinach ve 20. století*, vol. 1 (Prague, 1998); *International Dictionary of Films and Filmmakers*, vol. 2 (Chicago and London, 1991); Geoffrey Nowell-Smith, *The Oxford History of World Cinema* (Oxford, 1996); Josef Škvorecký, *All the Bright Young Men and Women* (Toronto, 1971); Antonin Liehm, *Closely Watched Films* (New York, 1974); Michael Stoil, *Cinema beyond the Danube* (Metuchen, NJ, 1974); Josef Škvorecký, *Jiří Menzel and the History of the Closely Watched Trains* (Colorado 1982); Peter Hames, *The Czechoslovak New Wave* (Berkeley, 1985).

MERI Lennart (29 March 1929, Tallinn—14 March 2006, Tallinn), Estonian politician, journalist, and director of documentary movies. Meri's father, Georg Meri, was a diplomat and translator of William Shakespeare's works.

Because of his father's foreign travels, young Meri attended schools in various countries and learned four languages. When the Red Army occupied Estonia in June 1940, the Meris were in Tallinn, and in 1941 they were deported to Siberia. As a teenager Meri worked felling trees and harvesting potatoes. After World War II, the family was allowed to return to Estonia. In 1953 Meri graduated with distinction from the Department of History and Philology of the University of Tartu, but owing to his past, he was not allowed to work as a historian. As a result he worked as a playwright and director of radio plays. He published a number of reports from remote areas of the Soviet Union in which he presented a fascinating and picturesque world, drawing attention to the growing conflict between local communities and the central bureaucracy. These reports, also published abroad, brought him renown and served as screenplays. Meri's major success was the movie *Linnutee Tuuled* (Winds of the Milky Road; 1977). Some of Meri's works were shown only outside the USSR. In 1986 Meri received an honorary doctorate from the University of Helsinki. He also translated the works of Western writers (among others, Graham Greene and Erich Maria Remarque) into Estonian, as well as the works of Alexander Solzhenitsyn. Meri made use of his foreign travels to inform the outside world about the situation in Estonia, and he made numerous contacts with Western politicians.

In the 1980s Meri was more and more explicit in criticizing the Soviet reality. He joined protests against plans to mine phosphates in Estonia because such mining would spell ecological disaster. In 1988 he established the Estonian Institute (EI), aiming at cultural cooperation with foreign countries and helping Estonian youth to study abroad. Foreign branches of the EI became informal outposts of independent Estonia, and after 1991 they turned into Estonian embassies. In the breakthrough years 1988–91 Meri sympathized with the Popular Front, demanding perestroika in Estonia. After the elections of 12 April 1990 Meri became minister of foreign affairs in the government of **Edgar Savisaar**, with a mission to reconstruct the foundations of Estonian diplomacy. After leaving the foreign affairs post in January 1991, from April 1991 to October 1992 Meri was ambassador to Finland.

In the presidential elections of October 1992 Meri ran as a candidate of the non-Communist camp. His opponents published materials from his student years that implied he had cooperated with the KGB, but this attack produced the opposite effect of what was intended—that is, it consolidated the opponents of the post-Communist candidate, **Arnold Rüütel**. In the second round, on 6 October 1992, Meri won the presidency. As president, he was more cautious concerning relations with Russia than he had been in the past. Nevertheless, he favored Estonia's accession to NATO and the European Union. In domestic policy Meri opposed granting Estonian citizenship to Russians. He supported (though with some objections) the economic reforms introduced by the centrist and rightist governments. On 20 September 1996 Meri was reelected, despite the fact that the parliament was then dominated by the left. During his second term Meri continued the earlier policies, but under pressure from the European Union, he agreed to a liberalization of the policy toward the Russian minority. In view of the instability of government coalitions, Meri tried to extend presidential powers with regard to the highest-level appointments in the military and central bank. As a result, the opposition accused him of an excessively liberal interpretation of the constitution. After his second term was over on 8 October 2001, Meri retired from politics. (AG)

Sources: *Rocznik Europa Środkowo—Wschodnia 1992* (Warsaw, 1994); Mel Huang, "Estonia's Military Musical Chairs Continue," *Central European Review*, 2000, no. 20; Bugajski; www.president. ee/eng/president.html; www.rulers.com; www.britannica.com/ bcom/eb/article.

MERKYS Antanas (1 February 1887, Bajorai, near Rokiskis–March 1955, USSR), Lithuanian politician. Merkys studied law in Dorpat (Tartu) and Kiev. During World War I he served as an officer in the transport section of the Russian Army. In 1918 he joined the then forming Lithuanian Army. Between March and July 1919 Merkys was defense minister, and in 1922 he went into the civil service. He worked as an attorney, was active in the Nationalist League (Tautininku Sąjunga) of **Antanas Smetona**, and was Smetona's secretary for some time. After the nationalist coup, between December 1926 and August 1927 Merkys again served as defense minister; between 1927 and 1932 he was governor of the autonomous region of Klaipeda, and in 1933–39 he held the post of mayor of Kaunas.

On 21 September 1939 Merkys was appointed prime minister and signed a treaty of mutual assistance with the USSR. The treaty ceded bases in Lithuania to Moscow in exchange for the district of Wilno (Vilnius). Despite the conciliatory attitude of Merkys's government, the Soviet blackmail continued, and the Kremlin multiplied threatening incidents and accusations. On 7 June 1940 Merkys was summoned to Moscow. Molotov accused two Lithuanian ministers of hostile activities and Merkys himself of transforming the Baltic Entente into an alliance directed against the USSR. Merkys tried to mitigate the incidents provoked by the USSR, but to no effect. On 14 June the Kremlin submitted an ultimatum urging the punishment of the two

government ministers, the creation of a cabinet that could support the objectives of the treaties with the USSR, and Lithuania's consent to the entry of additional Red Army units. Merkys resigned his post, but as President Smetona fled to East Prussia, Merkys performed Smetona's duties for some time. However, he was not recognized in that capacity by the special Soviet supervisor, Vladimir Dekanozov, who announced that Smetona's leaving meant his resignation, and on 17 June Dekanozov appointed **Justas Paleckis** as prime minister. The new government soon organized new "elections" to the People's Parliament (Seimas), as well as the incorporation of Lithuania into the USSR. On 16 July 1940 Merkys was arrested by the NKVD and deported far inside the USSR, where he died in unknown circumstances. (WR)

Sources: *EL*, vol. 3; Statys Raštikis, *Kovose del Lietuvos* (Los Angeles, 1957); Bronis J. Kaslas, ed., *The USSR-German Aggression against Lithuania* (New York, 1973); Georg von Rauch, *The Baltic States: The Years of Independence, 1917–1940* (London, Berkeley, and Los Angeles, 1974); Romuald J. Misiunas and Rein Taagepera, *The Baltic States: Years of Dependence, 1940–1980* (Berkeley, 1993).

MESIĆ Stjepan (Stipe) (24 December 1934, Orahovica), Croatian politician. In 1961 Mesić graduated in law from the University of Zagreb, and then he returned to his hometown to become its mayor. In the late 1960s he became an MP of the republican assembly. In 1971 he supported liberalization efforts, known as the Croatian Spring, including initiatives aimed at the strengthening of Croatian autonomy. During the repressions that followed, Mesić was sentenced to one year in prison. After his release he ran a building firm. At the end of the 1980s he became involved in the movement that led to the formation of the Croatian Democratic Union (Hrvatska Demokratska Zajednica [HDZ]). From 1990 Mesić was its secretary and was later chairman of its Main Board. After the first free elections, in May 1990 Mesić became prime minister of the Croatian republic, and he represented it in the Presidium of the Socialist Federal Republic of Yugoslavia (SFRY). Despite Serb protests but in accordance with the constitution, in July 1991 Mesić was elected chairman of the SFRY Presidium and held this position until December 1991, when the SFRY ceased to exist.

After Croatia gained independence, in September 1992 Mesić was elected speaker of the House of Representatives. In 1994, criticizing the authoritarian rule of President **Franjo Tudjman** and his policies toward Bosnia-Herzegovina, Mesić left the HDZ. As a result, he was recalled from his office. Along with about 20 percent of the HZD members, Mesić formed a new party, the Croatian

Independent Democrats (Hrvatski Nezavisni Demokrati [HND]). Since the HND was not successful, in 1997 Mesić and most of its members joined the Croatian People's Party (Hrvatska Narodna Stranka [HNS]), and he became its deputy chairman. Before the January 2000 elections, the HNS created a coalition with three other centrist parties. The coalition won 14 percent of the vote and supported the center-left government of **Ivica Račan**. Despite the fact that Mesić enjoyed considerable personal authority, Mesić rather surprisingly won the presidential elections of January and February 2000, gaining 41 percent of the vote in the first round (twice the pre-election predictions) and 56 percent in the second round. In October 2002 he testified before The Hague Tribunal for War Crimes in Former Yugoslavia, accusing **Slobodan Milošević** of such crimes. Mesić authored several works, including *Kako smo srušili Jugoslaviju: Politicki memoari posljednjeg predsjednika Predsjednistva SFRJ* (How we broke apart Yugoslavia: Political memoirs of the last chairman of the SFRY; 1992). In January 2005 Mesić was reelected president. (AW)

Sources: *Tko je tko u Hrvatskoj* (Zagreb, 1993); *Europa Środkowo-Wschodnia 1991–1998* (Warsaw, 1992–2000); Karen Dawisha and Bruce Parrot, eds., *Politics, Power and the Struggle for Democracy in South-East Europe* (Cambridge, 1997); Alex J. Bellamy, "Croatia after Tudjman: The 2000 Parliamentary and Presidential Elections," *Problems of Post-Communism*, 2001, no. 5; Zoran Kusovac, "The Prospects for Change in Post-Tudjman Croatia," *East European Constitutional Review*, 2000, no. 2; www.predsjednik.hr/zivotopis.html.

MESSNER Zbigniew (13 March 1929, Stryj [Stryi, now in Ukraine]), Polish Communist activist. In 1951 Messner graduated from the Higher Economic School in Katowice, and from 1950 he worked there as a researcher. From 1953 he belonged to the Polish United Workers' Party (Polska Zjednoczona Partia Robotnicza [PUWP]). In 1961 he received a Ph.D. and in 1969 his postdoctoral degree; in 1977 he became a professor. From 1968 to 1975 Messner was deputy rector, and from 1975 to 1982 rector, of the Economic Academy in Katowice. He authored several Marxist works on the political economy. From November 1980 to December 1983 he was chairman of the Provincial National Council in Katowice. At the Ninth Extraordinary PUWP Congress in July 1981 Messner joined the party's Central Committee (CC) and its Politburo. From early 1982 to late 1983 he was first secretary of the Provincial PUWP Committee in Katowice. In November 1983 he became deputy prime minister and, on 6 November 1985, prime minister. In 1986–88 Messner chaired the Commission for Economic Reform, endorsing the so-called second stage of reform; it was a cosmetic change in the system, which began to show symptoms of structural crisis. In 1988–89 Messner was also a member of the Council of State, and from 1985 to 1989 he was an MP. After the summer strikes of 1988, realizing the depth of the crisis, the leadership of the (Communist) All-Polish Accord of Trade Unions (a rival to Solidarity) made the Messner government resign on 19 September 1988. After he retired from politics in 1989, Messner was head of the Research Board of the Association of Polish Accountants, which enjoyed the monopoly of chartered accountants. (IS/WR)

Sources: Mołdawa; *Kto jest kim w Polsce* (Warsaw, 2001); Jan Skórzyński, *Ugoda i rewolucja: Władza i opozycja 1985–1989* (Warsaw, 1995); Wojciech Roszkowski, *Historia Polski 1914–2001* (Warsaw, 2002).

MEŠTROVIĆ Ivan (15 August 1883, Vrpolje–16 January 1962, South Bend, Indiana), Croatian sculptor. Meštrović was born into a peasant family. His father—the only literate person in his village—helped his son to gain an education. In 1899 Meštrović went to Split, where he was apprenticed to a stonecutter who noticed his talent. A year later he went to Vienna. Thanks to the help of a rich entrepreneur, he was accepted into the Academy of Fine Arts, from which he graduated in 1905. After joining the Vienna Secession Group (1903), Meštrović could exhibit his works more often. He lived for some time in France and Italy. His works soon gained the appreciation of August Rodin and other artists. Meštrović's sculpture of the 1389 Battle of Kosovo Field won first prize at an international exhibition in 1911, and critics acclaimed him the greatest sculptor of modern times. In 1914 Meštrović was one of the founders of the Yugoslav Committee (Jugoslavenski Odbor), which sought to realize the Yugoslav idea and unsuccessfully tried to dissuade the Entente states from making territorial concessions to Italy at the expense of the South Slavic nations. After World War I, Meštrović settled in the Kingdom of Serbs, Croats, and Slovenes. He stayed away from politics and rejected a senatorial seat offered him by King **Alexander I**. He worked as a sculptor and architect. He was also a professor and rector of the Academy of Art in Zagreb. In 1924–25 he was in the United States.

During World War II Meštrović refused to cooperate with the Independent State of Croatia, ruled by the Ustashas. Imprisoned in 1941 but released in 1942, he went to Italy and then to Switzerland, where he came down with an illness and was seriously ill for nearly a year. **Josip Broz Tito** personally invited Meštrović to come back to Yugoslavia, and, by way of an exception, the new Communist authorities would not confiscate his property. However, he refused to return. In 1949 Meštrović donated his houses in Zagreb and Split to be made into museums; these contain his numerous works. In January 1947 he left for the United States, and in 1952 he took American citizenship. He became a professor at Syracuse University, and in 1955 he transferred to Notre Dame University in South Bend, Indiana. Before his death Meštrović visited Yugoslavia to meet with the ailing cardinal **Alojzije Stepinac**, who had been released from prison. Meštrović is buried in the village of Otavice, where he built his family mausoleum. During the 1991–95 war in the former Yugoslavia this mausoleum was desecrated and damaged. Meštrović created many works on historical, religious, and biblical themes. His most important works include the Kosovo series, *My Mother, Self-Portrait, Madonna and Child, Job's Complaint, Desperation, Crucifix*, the monument of Bishop Grgur Ninski (Gregory of Nin), two statues of Indians in Chicago, the Tomb of the Unknown Soldier in Avala (near Belgrade), *The Victor* at Kalemegdan in Belgrade, and the mausoleum of the Račić family. (AO)

Sources: Milan Curcin, *Ivan Meštrović: A Monograph* (London, 1919); Laurence Schmeckebier, *Ivan Meštrović: Sculptor and Patriot* (Syracuse, 1959); Dusko Keckemet, *Ivan Meštrović* (Belgrade, 1983); Ana Adamec, *Ivan Meštrović 1883–1962* (Belgrade, 1983); Tadeusz Wasilewski and Wacław Felczak, *Historia Jugosławii* (Wrocław, 1985); www.croatia.net/html/mestrovic.

MEZŐ Imre [originally Izsák Ignác Mehrel] (13 December 1905, Ramocsaháza–1 November 1956, Budapest), Hungarian Communist activist, victim of the 1956 revolution. Born into a poor peasant family, Mező worked as a tailor's apprentice. In 1927 he emigrated to Belgium, where he joined the Communist Party of Belgium in 1929. In 1936, along with his wife, he joined the International Brigades and fought in the Spanish Civil War. He was twice wounded. Interned by the French authorities in 1939, Mező served in the French Army from 1940 to 1941 and then helped to organize the resistance movement. In 1943 he took command of an underground unit of foreign Communists organized by the French Communist Party. In August 1944 he fought in the Paris uprising as one of the leaders of the Patriotic Militia. In June 1945 Mező returned to Hungary and began working in the municipal committee of the Hungarian Communist Party (HCP) in Budapest. In 1948 he became head of the Organizational Department of the Budapest Committee of the Hungarian Workers' Party (HWP). From 1950, except for an interval in 1953–54, he served as secretary of the Budapest Committee. In July 1953 Mező became a supporter of **Imre Nagy**. In July 1956 he joined the Central Committee (CC) of the HWP. A supporter of

reforms, in June 1956 he took part in the famous debates of the Petőfi Circle on the state of the Hungarian press, after which the HWP CC banned the activities of the Petőfi Circle. On 23 October 1956, as head of the HWP Budapest Committee delegation, Mező asked the party leadership for permission to organize a demonstration in front of the statue of General Józef Bem. Subsequently, he was appointed a member of the CC Military Commission. On 30 October, when a delegation of insurgents came to negotiate in the headquarters of the Budapest Committee of the party in Köztársaság Square, a gunfight ensued that turned into a siege of the building. The party and security forces who were defending the building shot even at doctors and nurses who were trying to save the wounded. When the defenders gave up the fight and a group of delegates, among them Mező, started to walk out of the building, they were shot at. A few days later Mező died of his wounds. (JT)

Sources: *A magyar forradalom és szabadságharc enciklopédiája*, CD-ROM (Budapest, 1999); *Magyar Nagylexikon*, vol. 13 (Budapest, 2001); György Litván, ed., *Rewolucja węgierska 1956 roku* (Warsaw, 1996).

MICEWSKI Andrzej (3 November 1926, Warsaw), Polish journalist and political activist. In 1949 Micewski graduated in law from Warsaw University. In 1946–56 he worked for the periodical *Dziś i Jutro* and for the daily *Słowo Powszechne*, published by the PAX association, a Catholic organization cooperating with the Communist authorities. After October 1956 Micewski distanced himself from the dogmatic Natolin faction, supported by PAX leader **Bolesław Piasecki**, and from 1957 he was deputy editor-in-chief of the weekly *Za i przeciw*. In 1960–70 Micewski was active in the Znak movement and was a member of the editorial board of the monthly *Więź*. From 1967 he worked with **Janusz Zabłocki** and his Center of Documentation and Social Studies, which chose closer cooperation with the Communist authorities. In 1971–73 Micewski was editor-in-chief of Verum Press; in 1974–87 he was a member of the editorial board of *Tygodnik Powszechny*; and in 1985–88 he was editor-in-chief of the Vienna monthly *Znaki Czasu*, which was close to the Polish Episcopate. From 1984 to 1987 Micewski was a member of the Social Council of the Primate of Poland. In 1997–2001 he was an MP, from 1997 to 1999 on behalf of the Polish Peasant Party and later as an independent. Micewski authored a number of books and articles, including such valuable monographs as *Współrządzić czy nie kłamać: PAX i Znak w Polsce 1945–1976* (To co-rule or not to lie: PAX and Znak in Poland, 1945–1976; 1978) and *Kardynał Wyszyński:*

Prymas i mąż stanu (Cardinal Wyszyński: Primate and statesman; 1982). (IS)

Sources: *Kto jest kim w Polsce* (Warsaw, 1993); *Nowa encyklopedia powszechna PWN*, vol. 4 (Warsaw, 1996); Antoni Dudek, *Państwo i Kościół w Polsce 1945–1970* (Kraków, 1995).

MICHAEL I Hohenzollern-Sigmaringen (25 October 1921, Sinaia), king of Romania. Michael's father was **Charles II**, king of Romania (1930–40), and his mother was Queen Helen from the Greek ruling family. Soon after Michael's birth, Charles started a romance with **Magda Elena Lupescu**, and in 1925 he gave up the throne in favor of his son, who was then a minor. After the death of his grandfather, King **Ferdinand**, on 20 July 1927, Michael was declared king of Romania. Because he was a minor, a regency council was created that included Michael's uncle, Prince Nicolae; the patriarch of the Romanian Orthodox Church, **Miron Cristea**; and the chairman of the Supreme Court, Gheorghe Buzdugan. When in 1930 Michael's father returned to Romania and took over the throne as Charles II, Michael was deprived of the crown and given the purely symbolic title of grand duke (*voievode*) of Alba Iulia. After getting his primary education at the Sinaia Palace, Michael continued his education in a special class taught by outstanding Romanian scholars. In 1932 his parents formally divorced, and his mother was forced to leave Romania. In 1939 Michael was appointed a senator and a lieutenant in the Romanian army.

After Romania's humiliating loss of about one-third of its territories to its neighbors, on 5 September 1940 Charles II abdicated and ceded power to General **Ion Antonescu**. The next day Michael was enthroned for the second time as Michael I. However, the real power remained in the hands of Antonescu and his aides, who allied Romania with the Third Reich. Michael's influence on current affairs was very limited, and it was only in his New Year's speeches that he appeared before the nation. In view of the anticipated defeat of the Third Reich, in 1943 Michael, along with some representatives of the opposition, began secret negotiations with the Allies. Helped by the leaders of the Liberal, Peasant, Social Democratic, and Communist Parties, he tried to make Antonescu change the political line; in case this did not work, he planned to topple him.

On 23 August 1944 Michael invited Antonescu to the royal palace, and since Antonescu refused to change his pro-German policies, Michael ordered his arrest. Then Michael appointed General **Constantin Sănătescu** as prime minister of a government based on a coalition of the opposition parties, including the Communists. After the Red Army entered Romania, special Soviet envoy Andrey Vyshinsky issued an ultimatum; as a result, on 6 March

1945 Michael was forced to appoint a government headed by **Petru Groza** and dominated by the Communists, who consistently strove to eliminate the democratic opposition and subordinate Romania to the Soviet Union. Michael opposed these policies, and in 1945–46 he went on a "royal strike," refusing to endorse government decrees. On 8 November 1945, during a demonstration in his honor in Bucharest, the Communists provoked a scuffle that led to bloodshed. In 1947 Michael went to London, where he was unsuccessful in trying to gain Western support. At the end of December 1947 the royal palace was surrounded by Soviet tanks and Communist troops. On 30 December 1947 Michael was forced to abdicate, and in early 1948 he left Romania. He was deprived of Romanian citizenship, and his property was confiscated. Michael left for London, where he made known the circumstances of his abdication, and after a few months he settled in Switzerland. In 1948–89 Michael worked with Romanian émigré circles organized within the Romanian National Committee, but he had no contact with his father. Every year he made radio speeches to the nation.

After the **Nicolae Ceauşescu** regime was toppled in December 1989, in 1990 members of the Communist-dominated National Salvation Front (Frontul Sălvari Naţionale) refused Michael an entry visa to Romania. At the end of 1990 he was granted a visa, but upon his arrival in Romania Michael was arrested and forced to leave the country. In 1992 President **Ion Iliescu** agreed to Michael's visit for Easter. Michael was welcomed by about one million people when he came to Bucharest. Fearing increased support for the restoration of the monarchy and for the center-right opposition parties, in 1992–96 the post-Communists repeatedly refused Michael the right to return to Romania. In 1997, when the post-Communists lost the elections, Michael finally regained his Romanian citizenship and returned to Romania. He took no part in current politics but was active in advocating Romania's entry into NATO. (LW)

Sources: *Dictionar Enciclopedic*, vol. 4 (Bucharest, 2001); *Biographisches Lexikon*, vol. 3; Arthur Gould Lee, *Crown against Sickle: The Story of King Michael of Rumania* (London, 1953); Andrzej Koryn, *Rumunia w polityce wielkich mocarstw 1944–1947* (Wrocław, 1983); Vlad Georgescu, *Istoria Românilor de la origini pînă în zilele noastre* (Oakland, 1984); Dennis Deletant, *Communist Terror in Romania: Gheorghiu-Dej and the Police State, 1948–1965* (New York, 1999); Robert Levy, *Ana Pauker: The Rise and Fall of a Jewish Communist* (Berkeley, 2000); www.msci.memphis.edu.

MICHNIK Adam (27 October 1946, Warsaw), Polish journalist and politician. Born into a family of Communist activists of Jewish origin, in his school years Michnik took part in "Red scouting," and in 1961 he organized the Club of Seekers of Contradictions, which was dissolved by the

Communist authorities. During his studies in history at Warsaw University, Michnik organized numerous acts of contestation and was one of the leaders of the so-called "rangers," a group of young revisionist activists. In 1965 he was imprisoned for two months, and in 1965 and 1967 his student rights were suspended. In early 1968 Michnik co-organized student protests against the suspension of Adam Mickiewicz's play *Dziady* (Forefathers) at the National Theater in Warsaw. He was ousted from the university, and this became a reason for a student demonstration at Warsaw University on 8 March 1968, marking the beginning of the so-called March 1968 events. In 1969 Michnik was sentenced to three years in prison, but he was soon released. He worked as a blue-collar laborer, and then he was secretary to **Antoni Słonimski**. In 1975 he graduated in extramural historical studies from Poznań University. In 1975–76 Michnik co-organized protests against amendments to the constitution, and he signed the "Letter of 59." He spent 1976–77 in Western Europe, where he organized support for workers oppressed after the June 1976 protests and for the Committee for the Defense of Workers (Komitet Obrony Robotników [KOR]). Upon returning to Poland, Michnik was imprisoned from May to July 1977. A member of the KOR and later of the Committee of Social Self-Defense–KOR, Michnik was co-author of a program for social organization outside the structures licensed by the Communists; he described the program in *Nowy ewolucjonizm* (New evolutionism; 1976). In *Kościół, lewica, dialog* (1977; *The Church and the Left*, 1993) he advocated cooperation between the secular opposition and the Catholics in their struggle for a pluralist civic society. Michnik wrote a lot for the uncensored press in Poland and for the Western media. From 1978 he co-edited the uncensored *Kwartalnik Polityczny Krytyka* and co-organized the underground press NOWa. In 1978–81 Michnik was a member of the Society of Scholarly Courses and a lecturer there. He took part in meetings of representatives of the KOR and the Czechoslovak Charter 77. Michnik was frequently arrested for brief periods and beaten several times by the security police.

In 1980–81 Michnik was an adviser in the Mazowsze region of Solidarity. On 13 December 1981 he was interned, and in September 1992 he was accused of an attempt to overthrow the Communist system. In April 1984 he rejected an offer to emigrate, and in July 1984 he was amnestied. He worked with underground Solidarity structures and presses. In February 1985 he was arrested and sentenced to three years in prison, and in July 1986 he was released on the basis of another amnesty. In 1985 in prison Michnik wrote "Takie czasy: Rzecz o kompromisie" (Such times: On compromise), in which he stated that it would

be possible to come to terms with the Communists who were ready to recognize Solidarity as a partner. In 1988 he supported the idea of talks between Solidarity leaders and the Communist authorities. At that time Michnik was one of the closest aides of **Lech Wałęsa**. In 1988–90 Michnik belonged to the Civic Committee of the Chairman of Solidarity, and from February to April 1989 he was one of the key participants of the Round Table Talks. Elected to the parliament on 4 June 1989, he belonged to the Civic Parliamentary Club, and he substantially influenced its line—for example, by working out the idea of "Your president, our prime minister" (July 1989), which became the foundation for the formation of the government of **Tadeusz Mazowiecki** in August 1989. In 1990 Michnik co-founded the Civic Movement–Democratic Action, which supported Mazowiecki in the presidential elections in fierce opposition to Wałęsa.

Since May 1989 Michnik has been editor-in-chief and ideological godfather of *Gazeta Wyborcza*, which has gradually become the largest-circulation newspaper in Poland. A pundit with a powerful impact on the thinking and political tactics of the democratic opposition, Michnik has gained a great deal of authority, especially abroad. As a result of a series of polemics and controversial pronouncements (for example, a sympathy toward General **Wojciech Jaruzelski**, an overestimation of the dangers of rightist populism, easy forgiveness of Communist crimes in the name of society, and criticisms of lustration), Michnik has lost some of his followers. In December 2002, half a year after it happened, he revealed an offer from film producer Lew Rywin that involved corruption; this started a wide-ranging political scandal. Michnik has also authored the following: *Szanse polskiej demokracji* (Chances for Polish democracy; 1984); *Z dziejów honoru w Polsce* (From the history of honor in Poland; 1985); *Polskie pytania* (Polish questions; 1985); *Letters from Prison* (1985); *Diabeł naszego czasu* (The devil of our times; 1995); a conversation with Reverend **Józef Tischner** and Jacek Żakowski: *Między panem a plebanem* (Between the master and the priest; 1995); and *Letters from Freedom* (1998). (AF)

Sources: *Nasi w Sejmie i Senacie* (Warsaw, 1990); *Nowa encyklopedia powszechna PWN*, vol. 4 (Warsaw, 1996); Jan Skórzyński, *Ugoda i rewolucja: Władza i opozycja 1985–1989* (Warsaw, 1995); Janusz A. Majcherek, *Pierwsza dekada III Rzeczpospolitej 1989–1999* (Warsaw, 1999); *Opozycja w PRL: Słownik biograficzny 1956–89*, vol. 1 (Warsaw, 2000); Antoni Dudek, *Pierwsze lata III Rzeczpospolitej 1989–2001* (Kraków, 2002).

MIEDZIŃSKI Bogusław, pseudonym "Andrzej Świtek" (22 March 1891, Miastków, near Garwolin–8 May 1972,

London), Polish politician and journalist. Miedziński was the son of a manor clerk. After passing his high school final examinations in Siedlce, he studied chemistry at the Technical University of Lemberg (Lwów, Lviv) in 1910–12 and then completed agricultural studies at the Jagiellonian University (1912–14). While in high school, Miedziński began his political activities, participating in a school strike (1905), and in 1906 he became active in the Military Organization of the Polish Socialist Party (Polska Partia Socjalistyczna [PPS]) in Siedlce. In 1907 he joined the PPS–Revolutionary Faction, and in 1910, the Union of Active Struggle (Związek Walki Czynnej [ZWC]) and the Riflemen's Association. After the outbreak of World War I, Miedziński was one of the co-founders and commanders of the Polish Military Organization (Polska Organizacja Wojskowa [POW]). Until September 1915 he served as commander of the Warsaw district and a member of the POW High Command, subsequently transferring to the First Brigade of the Polish Legions. He fought in many battles, including those of Kukle, Kamieniucha (now Kamenukha, Ukraine), and Kostiuchnówka (now Kostyukhnivka, Ukraine). In June 1916 **Józef Piłsudski** again assigned him to the POW. In the spring of 1917 Miedziński became second deputy to the commander-in-chief of the POW, and in the summer of that year he became a member of the Convention of Organization A (Konwent Organizacji A), the top elite of the pro-Piłsudski camp. From February to July 1918 Miedziński was in charge of the POW activities in Russia, Ukraine, and Belorussia, where he tried to take over control of the Polish corps in Russia. In October of that year he joined the staff of the POW High Command under the direct command of Commander **Edward Rydz-Śmigły**, and in early November 1918 he helped to establish the people's government in Lublin headed by **Ignacy Daszyński**.

In July 1919 Miedziński became head of the Second Department in the Ministry of Military Affairs and later head of the Second Information Department of the Staff of the Ministry of Military Affairs—that is, intelligence. In October 1920 he became a special task officer in the office of the minister of military affairs, and in January 1922, deputy aide-de-camp general to the commander-in-chief. Miedziński was one of Piłsudski's most trusted associates. When Piłsudski retired from public life, Miedziński's role in politics also diminished. In 1922 he was elected to the Assembly on behalf of the Polish Peasant Party–Piast (Polskie Stronnictwo Ludowe–Piast [PSL–Piast]), and after a split in its parliamentary representation, he went over to the PSL–Liberation (Polskie Stronnictwo Ludowe–Wyzwolenie). From 1923 to 1926 Miedziński published extensively in *Kurier Poranny* and *Głos Prawdy*, presenting the political line of Piłsudski. Miedziński's articles, as well as his parliamentary speeches, prepared the ground for the coup d'état of May 1926, as he called for putting an end to party favoritism and praised iron-grip rule. He was also one of the main organizers of the coup, and after its success, he justified it as a necessary step. Miedziński was one of the "colonels"—a group that played a leading role in Poland at that time. From January 1927 to April 1929 he served as minister of post and telegraphs. After embezzlement was uncovered in the ministry he headed, he had to make a public apology. In the elections of 1928, 1930, and 1935 Miedziński was elected to the Assembly on the ticket of the Nonparty Bloc of Cooperation with the Government (Bezpartyjny Blok Współpracy z Rządem [BBWR]). From 1929 to 1938 he edited *Gazeta Polska*. In 1930 Piłsudski gave a series of interviews to this newspaper, explaining his vision of a new Polish constitution. Gradually, however, Miedziński, who was suspected of favoritism and excessive ambition in the army, lost some of Piłsudski's trust.

After the death of Piłsudski in 1935, Miedziński regained his influence by forming a friendship with General (later Marshal) Rydz-Śmigły. From 1935 to 1938 Miedziński was the deputy speaker of the Assembly, becoming a senator and deputy speaker of the Senate in 1938. He was one of the authors of the political declaration of the Camp of National Unity (Obóz Zjednoczenia Narodowego [OZN]). He actively contributed to the drafting of the April Constitution of 1935. He had considerable influence with publishers and distributors. In 1934 he became head of the press group Prasa Polska S.A., which he transformed into Dom Prasy S.A. in 1935. Through his associates, Miedziński also controlled several newspapers and the Polish Railway Bookshop Company. One of the most powerful politicians in the ruling camp, he generally preferred to keep out of the limelight. His great ambition and his tactlessness made him unpopular even in *sanacja* circles. In September 1939 he left Poland. He went to France, where he was completely removed from power. After the capitulation of France, he made his way, via Spain and Portugal, to England (1941); from there he was sent by the commander-in-chief, of the Polish army abroad, General **Władysław Sikorski**, to South Africa. In 1947 Miedziński settled in England, where he worked at a bakery and was active as a journalist. His extensive *Wspomnienia* (Memoirs) were published posthumously in *Zeszyty Historyczne* (nos. 33–37). (WR)

Sources: *PSB*, vol. 20; *Album sterników nawy państwa polskiego* (Warsaw, 1929); S. Benedykt, "Wspomnienia o Bogusławie Miedzińskim," *Orzeł Biały*, 1972, nos. 96–97; "Życiorys Bogusława Miedzińskiego," *Kultura* (Paris) 1972, no. 6; Janusz Jędrzejewicz, *W służbie idei* (London, 1972); Władysław T. Kulesza, *Koncepcje ideowo-polityczne obozu rządzącego w Polsce w latach 1926–1935* (Wrocław, 1985); *Kto był kim w Drugiej Rzeczypospolitej* (Warsaw, 1994).

MIEROSZEWSKI Juliusz (3 February 1906, Kraków–21 June 1976, London), Polish political journalist and writer. After graduating from high school, Mieroszewski studied law at the Jagiellonian University in Kraków, and he graduated from the Higher School of Commerce in Kraków. He published articles in periodicals that belonged to the "Pałac Prasy" (Press Palace) group: *Na szerokim świecie*, *Tempo dnia*, and *Ilustrowany Kurier Codzienny*. He specialized in international affairs. Because he criticized Nazism, he was regarded as a persona non grata in the Third Reich and was refused an entry visa to Germany. After the German invasion of Poland in September 1939, Mieroszewski made his way, via Romania and Turkey, to the Middle East. He served in the Independent Carpathian Rifle Brigade and later in the Second Corps of General **Władysław Anders**. After World War II, he settled in London and contributed to *Wiadomości Literackie*.

In 1949 Mieroszewski began a life-long association with the Paris-based *Kultura*. From 1950, under the pseudonym "Londyńczyk," he contributed to *Kronika londyńska* (London chronicle) and *Kronika emigracyjna* (Emigration chronicle); he was also the author of numerous political analyses in which he represented moderately Socialist and liberal views in response to the changes occurring in the Communist bloc and internationally. At the beginning of the 1950s Mieroszewski supported the American idea of "liberating" Eastern Europe, but realizing its inefficiency, in 1956 he supported the October transformations and **Władysław Gomułka** as the best choice for Poland. Mieroszewski sought international recognition of the Oder-Neisse border. In the 1960s he supported party revisionism and sketched a prospect of improved relations between Poland and the Soviet Union if Poland's mediation in the cultural and political rapprochement between the Soviet Union and Europe was successful. He also attached great importance to improving relations with Poland's closest neighbors: Lithuania, Belorussia, and Ukraine. He was able to foresee the development of a Polish workers' movement in defense of democratic freedoms and an increased intensity in their struggle for better living conditions. Mieroszewski's publications include *Ewolucjonizm* (Evolutionism; 1964); *Polityczne neurozy* (Political neuroses; 1967); *Modele i praktyka* (Models and practice; 1970); and *Materiały do refleksji i zadumy* (Materials for reflection and contemplation; 1976). From the mid-1970s Mieroszewski's works were often published by the underground press in Poland. Seen as one of the most dangerous ideological "subversives" by the Polish Communist authorities, Mieroszewski had a great impact on shaping the political thought of an entire generation of Polish independent intellectuals because his analyses also reached Poland through Radio Free Europe and other channels. (WR)

Sources: *Kultura*, 1976, nos. 7–8; Bohdan Osadczuk, "Refleksje o śmierci Juliusza Mieroszewskiego," *Kultura*, 1977, no. 7; Piotr Wandycz, "O Juliuszu Mieroszewskim," *Zeszyty Historyczne*, 1986, no. 78; Rafał Habielski, *Życie społeczne i kulturalne emigracji* (Warsaw, 1999).

MIERZWA Stanisław (27 January 1905, Biskupice Radłowskie–10 October 1985, Kraków), Polish lawyer and politician. Mierzwa was born into a peasant family. After finishing high school in Tarnów, he studied law at the Jagiellonian University in Kraków, graduating in 1934. Later he did a legal internship as a lawyer trainee. While still in school, Mierzwa became active in social and political life, joining the Lesser Polish Youth Union, an association of peasant youth. He became a local, and later a national, activist of the Polish Academic Peasant Youth and the Union of Rural Youth of the Republic of Poland, and he also contributed to their periodicals. Arrested in 1933 for helping to organize a student strike, Mierzwa was sentenced to two months in prison. In 1932 he joined the Peasant Party (Stronnictwo Ludowe [SL]), and he quickly rose through the party ranks. He was active at the local, regional, and national levels. In 1933 he became a member of the Chief Council, and in 1935, a member of the Chief Executive Committee. He also contributed to the party weekly, *Piast*. One of the main organizers of the great peasant strike on 15–25 August 1937 and a close political associate of **Wincent Witos**, Mierzwa belonged to the radical opponents of the camp supporting Piłsudski and the National Party (Stronnictwo Narodowe [SN]).

During World War II Mierzwa was one of the main organizers of the underground peasant movement. In 1940 he joined the district authorities of the underground Peasant Party called Roch (Stronnictwo Ludowe–Roch [SL–Roch]) and helped to edit secret pamphlets. In 1942 he joined the Central Leadership of the Peasant Movement–Roch (Centralne Kierownictwo Ruchu Ludowego–Roch [CKRL–Roch]), and in 1943 he became a representative of the CKRL in the coalition National Unity Council (Rada Jedności Narodowej [RJN]). Mierzwa supported **Stanisław Mikołajczyk**'s policy to seek compromise with the Soviet Union. Arrested through treachery by the NKVD on 28 March 1945, Mierzwa was taken to Moscow. In June of that year, in a trial of sixteen leaders of the Polish Underground State, he was sentenced to four months in prison. After returning to Poland, he worked as an attorney in Kraków and resumed his political activities, becoming secretary of the Provincial Board of the Polish Peasant Party (Polskie Stronnictwo Ludowe [PSL]) and a member of the PSL Provisional Chief Executive Committee. At a PSL congress in January 1946 Mierzwa joined the Chief Council and the Chief Executive Committee. He was known as a firm defender of the PSL's independence. He was also one of the most important associates of Mikołajczyk. In September 1946, during the election campaign, Mierzwa was arrested along with several other PSL activists from Kraków. On 10 September 1947, in a trial of activists from the PSL and the Freedom and Independence (Zrzeszenie Wolność i Niezawisłość [WiN]) association—the so-called Niepokólczycki trial—Mierzwa was sentenced to ten years' imprisonment and was also disbarred. In 1953 he was released owing to ill health, and in 1954 he was granted a pardon. After 1956 Mierzwa worked as an attorney but did not resume direct political activities. He refused to join the pro-Communist United Peasant Party (Zjednoczone Stronnictwo Ludowe [ZSL]), yet his initiatives, which were primarily aimed at commemorating the memory of Witos, attracted many former members of the SL, SL–Roch, and PSL. After the death of Mikołajczyk, émigré members of those parties regarded Mierzwa as the main authority. Mierzwa did not join the Independent Self-Governing Trade Union of Independent Farmers–Solidarity (Niezależny Samorządny Związek Zawodowy Rolników Indywidualnych–Solidarność [NSZZRI–Solidarity]) because he did not believe in the stability of the new political situation in 1980. (AP)

Sources: *Słownik biograficzny działaczy ruchu ludowego* (Warsaw, 1989); Alina Fitowa, *Stanisław Mierzwa "Słomka" na tle swoich czasów* (Wierzchosławice, 1994); Waldemar Strzałkowski, Andrzej Chmielarz and Andrzej K. Kunert, ed., *Proces szesnastu: Dokumenty NKWD*; (Warsaw, 1995); Andrzej K. Kunert and Eugeniusz Piontek, *Proces moskiewski przywódców polskiego państwa podziemnego* (Warsaw, 2000).

MIGJENI [originally Gjergji Millosh] (13 October 1911, Shkodër–26 August 1938, Torre Pelice, Italy), Albanian writer, poet, and journalist. Migjeni came from a family of Montenegrin origin. After graduating from a Serbian school in Shkodër, he continued his education at St. John Orthodox Theological Seminary in Monastir (Bitola). Despite this, he remained an atheist throughout his life. Migjeni started work as a teacher at a primary school in Vrake. It was then that he started writing his first literary works and began to publish them in the press in Shkodër. In 1937, as his health deteriorated (advanced tuberculosis), Migjeni left for Italy, where his sister was studying, and died there in a sanatorium. Because of his short, only five-year period of literary activity, he was called a "meteor of Albanian literary life." Migjeni wrote both poetic works and prose sketches. Filled with sorrow and pain, his works focus on the cruelty of human misery. Migjeni combined social criticism with a criticism of capitalism and religion, although his language was full of religious metaphors. The first volume of his poems, *Vargjet e lira* (Free verse; 1991), appeared posthumously in 1944. The Albanian Communists considered Migjeni a precursor of Socialist realism. They accepted his prophecy of the coming of a new man as a result of a people's revolution, but they rejected the humanitarian version of socialism that Migjeni propagated. (TC)

Sources: Pipa Arshi, *Contemporary Albanian Literature* (New York, 1991); Ismail Kadare, *Ardhja e Migjenit* (Tirana, 1991); Rinush Idrizi, *Migjeni* (Tirana, 1992); Saneja Mazllum, *Vetem Itaka mbetet. Tylko Itaka pozostanie: Antologia poezji albańskiej i polskiej XX w.* (Warsaw, 1993); Lazer Radi, *Nje verë me Migjeni* (Tirana, 1998).

MIHAIL [originally Metodij Gogov] (20 March 1912, Novo Selo, near Strumnica–6 July 1999, Skopje), Orthodox archbishop of Ohrid, head of the Macedonian Orthodox Church. Mihail entered a theological seminar in 1927. In 1936 he graduated with distinction from the Theological School of the University of Belgrade. During World War II he worked as a priest in the Macedonian territories and strove to reestablish the archbishopric in Ohrid. In 1945 he chaired a conference of around three hundred Orthodox priests in Macedonia who called for the independence of their Orthodox Church and the independence of their country. Shortly afterwards Mihail was arrested by the Communist authorities. Released after six months, he continued his work. Imprisoned again in 1948, he was released in 1953. From 1953 to 1966 he served as a priest in Skopje, and he subsequently went to Australia, where he established the first parish of the Macedonian Orthodox Church independent of the Serbian hierarchy. Mihail was instrumental in the 1967 proclamation of autocephaly of the Macedonian Orthodox Church; the proclamation was not recognized by other churches. In the following years Mihail made numerous missionary visits to various Macedonian communities scattered throughout the world. After the death of his wife, he was ordained bishop of Vardar in 1988. After Macedonia declared its independence, Mihail became archbishop and metropolitan of Ohrid in 1993. (WR)

Sources: Slavko Dimevski, *Istorija na Makedonskata pravoslavna crkva* (Skopje, 1989); www.rulers.org.

MIHAILOV Ivan, "Vancho" (26 December 1896, Novo Selo, near Shtip–5 September 1990, Rome), Macedonian revolutionary. Mihailov was born into a family of activists in the Internal Macedonian Revolutionary Organization

(IMRO), and he began his career as an aide to **Todor Aleksandrov**, the man most responsible for keeping IMRO alive during the post–Balkan War years. Mihailov was fanatical in his pursuit of an independent Macedonia, which he envisioned as a Switzerland of the Balkans in a book he wrote: *Macedonia: Switzerland of the Balkans* (1950). When what was to become the Republic of Macedonia became part of the Kingdom of Serbs, Croats, and Slovenes following World War I, Aleksandrov and Mihailov fought for independence from Yugoslavia and annexation to Bulgaria. Mihailov was a participant in the planning of a June 1923 coup against Bulgarian prime minister **Aleksandur Stamboliyski**, who was tortured and murdered by Mihailov's associates. In 1924, Aleksandrov was assassinated in a plot that some have linked to Mihailov and others to General **Aleksandur Protogerov**, IMRO's second in command. A deadly rivalry between Protogerov and Mihailov immediately sprang up, with the organization fracturing into Centralist (Mihailov) and Federalist (Protogerov) camps. The Federalists sought Macedonian autonomy within Yugoslavia. The 1923–34 period was violent in Bulgaria owing in part to IMRO's fraternal strife and in part to the fact that the people of southwestern Bulgaria's Petrich region, a stronghold of IMRO forces, were subjected to IMRO justice and taxation. Gangland-style wars erupted, sometimes even spilling over into the streets of Sofia, Bulgaria's capital, with incursions into Yugoslavia and Greece.

The Bulgarian government was unable to bring order to the chaos wrought by IMRO. Mihailov saw Serbia as the main obstacle to Macedonian independence and union with Bulgaria. While IMRO factions feuded, Mihailov did not attack Bulgaria's Tsar **Boris III**, even though Boris was seeking to improve relations with King **Alexander** of Serbia. A ruthless leader, Mihailov cooperated with the Croatian Ustashe of **Ante Pavelić**, supplying the assassin who was to murder King Alexander in Marseilles in 1934. A bloodless coup led by Bulgarian military leaders and civilian reformers unseated the government and expelled IMRO from Bulgaria in May 1934, destroying its infrastructure rapidly. Mihailov escaped to the West. After some time spent in the United States and Canada, he finally settled in Italy, living in seclusion. He died there peacefully, still promoting Macedonian independence. Mihailov published many articles and books about the Macedonian question and four volumes of *Spomeni* (Memoirs; 1958–73). (DP)

Sources: *Entsiklopediya Bulgariya*, vol. 4 (Sofia, 1984); Ivan Katardžiev, *Makedonsko nacionalno pitajne 1919–1930* (Zagreb, 1983); Raymond Detrez, *Historical Dictionary of Bulgaria* (Lanham, Md., 1997); Nadine Lange-Akhlund, *The Macedonian Question,* *1893–1908* (Boulder, Colo., 1998); Stoyan Pribichevich, *Macedonia, Its People and History* (University Park and London, 1982).

MIHAILOVIĆ Dragoljub (Draža) (27 April 1893, Ivanjica, Serbia–17 July 1946, Belgrade), Serbian officer, head of the Yugoslav underground army linked with the Yugoslav royal government-in-exile. The son of a teacher, Mihailović entered the Belgrade Military Academy in 1910, but in 1912 his studies were interrupted by the First Balkan War, in which he fought as a corporal. During the Second Balkan War Mihailović was promoted to second lieutenant. In World War I he became famous for his courage in the battle of Štip and was decorated with the Order of the White Eagle. After a truce was called, Mihailović resumed his studies and graduated from the Military Academy in Belgrade. In 1929 he also completed a six-month officer training course in France. In the 1930s Mihailović commanded a regiment in Slovenia and later worked in the General Staff in Belgrade. He also taught tactics at the Military Academy and served as Yugoslavia's military attaché in Prague and Sofia. After returning to his country, Mihailović analyzed the defense capacity and military plans of Yugoslavia. He pointed out that the defense of Yugoslavia's northern borders would be practically impossible and emphasized that it was necessary to set up defenses in the mountainous regions far inside the country. Mihailović wrote a book on guerrilla warfare. He recognized the dangers of the German "fifth column" in Croatia. He also did not deny his pro-British sympathies. In the delicate situation that Yugoslavia was in from 1939 to 1941, Mihailović was briefly kept under house arrest. During the German invasion in April 1941 he was chief of staff of a division that defended Sarajevo.

Mihailović refused to lay down arms, and in early May 1941 in Ravna Gora, he announced the beginning of a guerrilla war. Thousands of soldiers rallied around him, faithful to the royal government-in-exile in London led by **Dušan Simović**. Mihailović's troops were called Chetniks, to commemorate the Serbian partisans in the struggle for independence against Turkey. Mihailović's strategy, in line with the policies of the government-in-exile and initially consistent with British plans, was based on accumulating forces and weapons for a general uprising to be staged when the German occupation weakened. Meanwhile, Chetnik units carried out sabotage actions, breaking German communication lines and preventing the Germans from confiscating food. Mihailović's resistance to the Germans was recognized in the West, where his contribution to impeding the German offensive in the Soviet Union was emphasized. *Time* magazine named him "Man of the Year, 1941." From the beginning of the occupation the Chetniks had enemies not only among the Germans, but also among the Croatian Ustashe (led by **Ante Pavelić**) and the Communists. After the Third Reich invaded the USSR in June 1941, the Communists, led by **Josip Broz Tito**, also joined the struggle against the occupiers, but they did not change their hostile stance toward Mihailović.

In December 1941 Mihailović was promoted to general. In January 1942 he was appointed minister of war in the Yugoslav government-in-exile, and in June 1942 he became deputy commander-in-chief of the Yugoslav Army. Initially the Chetniks enjoyed the support of Great Britain, but from 1942 on, as the Allies began to make concessions to Stalin, British aid became increasingly nominal. In addition, the United States became more inclined to give credence to Communist reports of Mihailović's collaboration with the occupiers. The Allies were also disturbed by Mihailović's Serbian nationalism, as well as his clashes with the Communist Partisans. At the Tehran Conference in early December 1943, the Big Three accepted the principle that both the Chetniks and the Partisans should receive aid in proportion to their activities. As a result, in February 1944 Winston Churchill in effect took the side of Tito, accusing Mihailović of passivity and contacts with the occupiers. Allied liaison officers denied these accusations, but Churchill's point of view prevailed, and Mihailović's political role diminished. Although until the end of the war Mihailović was a supporter of the Allies, engaging substantial German forces in Serbia and liberating around five hundred Allied prisoners of war, his efforts to establish contacts with the Communists ended in failure. Toward the end of the war Tito's Partisans and secret police were involved not only in the struggle against the Germans, but also in hunting down Chetniks. Occasions of tactical cooperation with the Chetniks were used to disarm and then arrest them. Such was the fate of, among others, Colonel Dragutin Keserović and Colonel Velimir Pelitić, who was Mihailović's special emissary for talks with the Russians.

In April 1945 the Chetniks clashed with the Black Legion of the Croatian Ustashe at Levač Polje. Later, Mihailović mainly fought against Tito's army and police. For nearly one year after the end of the war, Mihailović was hunted by six Communist-led divisions. From the beginning, Tito and his associates admitted their intention to seize and then execute him. Captured by the Communists on 13 March 1946, Mihailović was accused of collaboration with the Croatian Ustashe and with the Germans. His trial began on 10 June 1946 in Topčider. The Communist court rejected the testimony of Allied officers who defended him. Despite protests by Serbian émigrés and by a special U.S. committee for his defense, Mihailović was sentenced to death in a rigged show trial on 15 July of that year. Two days later he was executed. This execution slightly undermined Tito's credibility in the West, but the denunciation of Tito by Moscow and its satellite states (June 1948) soon obscured this crime. (WR)

Sources: *Biographisches Lexikon*, vol. 3; Albert B. Seitz, *Mihailovic: Hoax or Hero?* (Columbus, Ohio, 1953); *The Trial of Dragoljub-Draža Mihailović* (Belgrade, 1946); *Tributes to General Mihailovich: Priznanja generalu Mihailovicu* (Windsor, Ontario, 1966); Yozo Tomasevich, *The Chetniks: War and Revolution in Yugoslavia, 1941–1945* (Stanford, 1975); Matteo Milazzo, *The Chetnik Movement and Yugoslav Resistance* (Baltimore, 1975); David Martin, ed., *Patriot or Traitor? The Case of General Mihailovic* (Stanford, 1978); *Spomenica dostojna divljenja ko je ubio generala Mihajlovića* (London, 1980); *Draza Mihailovic Memorial Book, 1946–1976: Dedicated to the Thirtieth Anniversary of the Death of the Leader of the Third Serbian Uprising* (Chicago, 1981); Lucien Karchmar, *Draža Mihailović and the Rise of the Četnik Movement 1941–1942*, vols. 1–2 (New York, 1987).

MIHALACHE Ion (3 March 1882, Topoloveni–5 March 1953, Râmnicu Sărat), Romanian Peasant Party politician. Mihalache was a village teacher in his native village of Topoloveni. In 1912 he founded the newspaper *Vremea Nova*. He also found a peasant union that was the origin of the Peasant Party in the Old Kingdom of Romania. The party was formed in 1918 in reaction to a speech by King **Ferdinand** in December 1917, in which he addressed the soldiers and announced a division of the great estates and the distribution of the land among peasant war veterans. As a result of the political revival of Romanian peasants during World War I, the Peasant Party gained much success in the elections of 1919. In the coalition government of **Alexandru Vaida-Voievoda** (December 1919–March 1920) Mihalache served as minister of agriculture, and he advocated radical agrarian reform. The right opposed his proposals; therefore, in March 1920, King Ferdinand dissolved the government and installed General **Alexandru Avarescu** as premier. In October 1926, Mihalache became vice-president of the united National Peasant Party (Partidul Naţional Ţărănesc; the so-called Tsaranists), formed by the merger of his Peasant Party with the National Peasant Party of Transylvania. Between 1928 and 1930 Mihalache served as minister of agriculture in the government of **Iuliu Maniu**, the leader of the party, and in 1930–33 he was minister of interior. He refused to take part in the dictatorial government of King **Charles II**, and during World War II he was one of the organizers of the underground opposition against the regime of **Ion Antonescu**.

In August 1944 on behalf of the opposition coalition Mihalache demanded that Antonescu conclude an armistice with the Allies. After the overthrow of the dictator on 23 August 1944, the Western powers proposed Mihalache as a member of the coalition government, but the Russians and their client, Prime Minister **Petru Groza**, ordered him to sever his association with Maniu and to split the Tsaranist party. Mihalache rejected these conditions. In the face of increasing Communist dictatorship, he planned to form a government-in-exile with Maniu, but he was captured while attempting to cross the border in December 1946. Deprived of his immunity, on 11 November 1947 Mihalache was sentenced by a military court in a show trial to life imprisonment. He probably died in prison. (WR)

Sources: *Encyclopedia Britannica*, vol. 6 (Chicago, 1948); Ghita Ionescu, *Communism in Rumania, 1944–1962* (London, 1964); *Chronological History of Romania* (Bucharest, 1972); Andrzej Koryn, *Rumunia w polityce wielkich mocarstw 1944–1947* (Wrocław, 1983); Dennis Deletant, *Communist Terror in Romania: Gheorghiu-Dej and the Police State, 1948–1965* (New York, 1999).

MIHALOVIĆ Antun (17 July 1868, Feričanci–21 September 1949, Zagreb), Croatian politician. Mihalović studied law in Vienna and Graz. In 1893 he began working in the administration in Osijek and later in Virovitica. In 1901 he became an MP in the Croatian parliament (Sabor). From 1904 to 1907 he served as governor (*veliki župan*) of the district of Virovitica and the town of Osijek. He resigned this post as a result of a conflict with Ban Teodor Pejačević over the Hungarian railway lines in Croatia. Mihalović was one of the most prominent politicians in the Croatian-Serbian Coalition, which was established after the adoption in October 1905 of the Rijeka (Fiume) Resolution by the Croatian politicians and the Zadar (Zara) Resolution by the Serbian politicians. In these resolutions the signatories declared themselves against Austrian domination and supported the Hungarians in their efforts to gain full independence. As a representative of the Croatian-Serbian Coalition, Mihalović was assigned to the upper house of the Hungarian-Croatian parliament. On 29 May 1917 he became *ban* (governor) of Croatia, Slavonia, and Dalmatia. His policy to protect the interests of these regions was often criticized by Vienna and Budapest. After the Kingdom of Serbs, Croats, and Slovenes was proclaimed, Mihalović resigned on 20 January 1919. From 1936 to 1941 he held a seat in the Yugoslav Senate. (AO)

Sources: *Biographishes Lexikon*, vol. 2; Ferdo Culinović, *Jugoslavija izmedju dva rata* (Zagreb, 1961).

MIJUŠKOVIĆ Lazar (24 December 1867, Pješivci, near Nikšić–1936, Belgrade), Montenegrin politician. Mijušković completed technical studies in Paris. In 1893 he entered Montenegro's diplomatic service. He was one of the close associates of Prince **Nicholas** (later King Nicholas). In late 1902 Mijušković became head of the Chief State Control, and in late 1903, minister of finance. On 19 December 1905 he became the first prime minister of a government based on the constitution and the parliament. On 24 November 1906 Mijušković resigned as a result of a tariff war with Serbia. He later served as minister of foreign affairs. After the annexation of Bosnia and Herzegovina by Austria-Hungary in 1908, Montenegro took the side of Russia and the countries that were against this annexation. Mijušković negotiated on the issue of annexation in St. Petersburg and Belgrade, strengthening Montenegro's political ties with Russia and Serbia. During the Albanian uprising in 1911 he tried to obtain Russian aid for the Albanian refugees, who were a serious burden on Montenegrin finances. However, after receiving this aid, Montenegro used it to supply the Montenegrin Army with weapons, and King Nicholas attempted to increase his influence in Albania by cooperating with Vienna; as a result, St. Petersburg expressed its discontent. Following the king's example, Mijušković changed his policies and cut his ties with Russia. Hoping for territorial gains in Albania at the expense of Turkey, Montenegro joined the Balkan League but failed to fulfill its ambitions in either of the two Balkan Wars. At the brink of World War I, Mijušković brought about an alliance with Serbia. On 2 January 1916 he again became head of the government, but after the defeat of the Montenegrin forces by the Austro-Hungarian Army, he was forced to resign on 12 May 1916, and, along with King Nicholas, he went into exile. After the monarchy was abolished in Montenegro and the country became part of the Kingdom of Serbs, Croats, and Slovenes, in late 1918 Mijušković settled in Serbia, where he lived until the end of his life. (WR)

Sources: *Enciklopedija Jugoslavije*, vol. 6 (Zagreb, 1965); John D. Treadway, *The Falcon and the Eagle: Montenegro and Austria-Hungary, 1908–1914* (West Lafayette, Ind., 1983); www.rulers.org.

MIKHALCHEV Dimitur (25 December 1880, Lozengrad, Edirne Thrace–18 January 1967, Sofia), Bulgarian philosopher and diplomat. Mikhalchev was born into an affluent middle-class family. While a philosophy student at Sofia University (1901–5), he made his literary debut in the prestigious periodical *Misa*. From 1906 to 1909 he worked at the universities in Berlin, Freiburg, and Munich. In 1909 he earned a Ph.D. from the University of Greifswald. In 1909 he published *Philosophische Studien: Beiträge zur Kritik des modernen Psychologismus* (Philosophical studies: Contributions to the critique of modern psychologism), based on his doctoral thesis. In 1910 Mikhalchev became a member of the Kantian Society (Kantgesellschaft), and in 1911 he lectured in St. Petersburg. In 1910 he became an associate professor and in 1915 a full professor of philosophy at Sofia University. He fought in the Balkan Wars. In the autumn of 1913 Mikhalchev was a member of a delegation that was intended to inform Europeans about the tragic results of the Balkan Wars for Bulgaria. From 1923 to 1927 he served as an envoy to Czechoslovakia and later worked at Sofia University. Mikhalchev favored historical materialism in its moderate form and argued with the supporters of dogmatic dialectical materialism. He was a co-founder and editor of *Filosofski Pregled* (1929–43). From 1934 to 1936 he served as an envoy to the Soviet Union. Again an envoy to Moscow after the coup of 9 September 1944, Mikhalchev took part in the signing of a peace treaty and was a witness to plans for a Balkan federation; however, these plans were not implemented. In 1946 Mikhalchev returned to Bulgaria. As president of the Bulgarian Academy of Sciences, he protested the persecution of scholars who were labeled by the authorities as "bourgeois" and tried to defend them. In 1947 he was forced to retire. In 1953 **Todor Pavlov** broke up Mikhalchev's philosophical school on the grounds that it was reactionary. Mikhalchev, whose works were not published, was persecuted and lived in poverty but continued his scholarly work. He studied (among other things) the philosophy of Henri Bergson, traditional logic, relations between dialectics and the philosophy of the Sophists, and pragmatism. In 1981 his *Izbrani suchineniia* (Selected works) appeared, and in the 1990s many more of his works were published, restoring Mikhalchev to his due place in contemporary Bulgarian philosophy. (WDj)

Sources: Kiril D. Darkovski, "Dimitur Mikhalchev: Opit za intelektualen portret," in Dimitur Mikhalchev, *Izbrani suchineniia* (Sofia, 1981); Dimitur Denkov and Dimitur Mikhalchev, *Istoriko-filosofski ocherk* (Sofia, 1988).

MIKHNOVSKYI Mykola (1873 Turivka, Chernihiv region–3 March 1924, Kiev), Ukrainian politician and ideologue. Mikhnovskyi graduated in law from Kiev University. He helped to found the Brotherhood of Taras in 1891 and the Young Ukraine (Moloda Ukraiina) society in 1896. In 1899 he settled in Kharkiv and opened a law practice. Among other things, he acted as defense counsel in political trials. In 1900 Mikhnovskyi wrote the program of the Revolutionary Ukrainian Party (RUP), printed in Lemberg (Lviv, Lwów) as *Samostiyna Ukraiina* (Independent Ukraine); in it independence for the Ukraine was demanded for the first time. In late 1901

and early 1902 Mikhnovskyi was one of the founders of the Ukrainian Popular Party (Ukraiinska Narodna Partiya [UNP]), which rallied supporters of a military struggle for independence. In articles and proclamations from 1902–4—including "Robitnycha sprava v prohrami UNP" (1902; The workers' question in the UNP program; 1902) and "Desiat zapovidii" (Ten commandments; 1903)—Mikhnovskyi formulated the theoretical principles of Ukrainian nationalism. In 1906 he issued a UNP program that foresaw the establishment of a united, independent, and democratic Ukraine encompassing the territory from the Carpathians to the Caucasus—a republic of the working class, with a presidential system, guarantees of social rights for the people, and land for the peasants. In 1903 Mikhnovskyi established a UNP paramilitary organization that carried out several terrorist attacks in Kharkiv (1904) and Kiev (1909). Mikhnovskyi edited the periodicals *Samostiyna Ukraiina* (Lemberg, 1905), *Khliborob* (Lubni, 1905), *Slobozhanshchyna* (Kharkiv, 1906), and *Snip* (Kharkiv, 1912–13).

During World War I Mikhnovskyi was mobilized into the tsarist army. In March 1917 he was the first to propose the idea of establishing Ukrainian military forces. On his initiative, the Ukrainian Military Club and the Military Organizational Committee were founded in Kiev. The aim of these organizations was to form Ukrainian military units. In May 1917 Mikhnovskyi helped to establish the Bohdan Khmelnytskyi First Ukrainian Cossack Regiment. In 1917, as a representative of the Ukrainian Military Club, Mikhnovskyi became a member of the Ukrainian Central Rada (Council) and a member of the Ukrainian General Military Committee. He was among the Council members who advocated that the Ukraine declare independence and that the Council assume full power in the Ukrainian territories; as a result of his views, he came into conflict with the majority of the Council. In the summer of 1917, after an unsuccessful insurrection attempt, Mikhnovskyi was arrested on the orders of **Volodymyr Vynnychenko**. He was subsequently sent to the Romanian front. In the autumn of 1917 he returned to the Poltava region and helped to establish the Ukrainian Democratic Agrarian Party (Ukraiinska Demokratychno-Khliborobska Partiya [UD-KhP]). During the rule of Hetman **Pavlo Skoropadskyi**, Mikhnovskyi was in the opposition. He also had a negative stance regarding the Directory, a competitive government center established by the Council. He believed that the Directory was seeking to establish a Socialist order. In early 1919, on the orders of the UDKhP, Mikhnovskyi tried to establish contacts with some commanders of the army of the Ukrainian National Republic (UNR), hoping for their help in controlling the increasing anarchy in the army. Arrested by the Bolsheviks, Mikhnovskyi was to be executed, but he was saved by an attack of troops led by Ataman (commander-in-chief) **Matviy Hryhoryiv**. In 1920 Mikhnovskyi went to Novorossiysk, from where he unsuccessfully attempted to go abroad. He subsequently worked in cooperatives and schools in Kuban. In the spring of 1924 he returned to Kiev and was arrested by the GPU. According to one version, Mikhnovskyi was executed by a firing squad; according to another version, he hanged himself after being released (this would most probably have been a suicide staged by the GPU). (BB)

Sources: *Encyclopedia of Ukraine*, vol. 3 (Toronto, 1993); *Entsyklopediia Ukrainoznavstva*, vol. 5 (Lviv, 1996); *Dovidnyk z istorii Ukraiiny* (Kiev, 2001); Viktor Andriievskyi, *Mykola Mikhnovskyi* (Munich, 1950); Petro Mirchuk, *Mykola Mikhnovskyi: Apostol Ukraiinskoy Derzhavnosty* (London, 1960); Mykola Horelov, *Peredvisnyki nezalezhnoy Ukraiiny* (Kiev, 1996); Vladislav Verstiuk and Tatiana Ostashko, *Diiachi Ukraiinskoy Tsentralnoy Rady: Biohrafichnyi dovidnyk* (Kiev, 1998).

MIKHOV Nikola (29 November 1891, Turnovo–1 or 2 February 1945, Sofia), general, regent of Bulgaria. In 1911 Mikhov graduated from the Sofia Military Academy, and later he studied in Germany. He began his career in the army fighting in the Balkan Wars and World War I. During the interwar period Mikhov held various positions, including those of commander of a division, commander of the army, and commander of the Sofia garrison in the 1930s. From 1938 to 1941 he was commander of the Sofia Military Academy. In 1941 he was commander of the Second Bulgarian Army in Macedonia and later commander of the First Bulgarian Army, which was stationed in Sofia. A supporter of rapprochement with Nazi Germany, Mikhov was appointed minister of war by **Bogdan Filov** (April 1942). In January 1943 he went to Germany to coordinate Bulgaria's military cooperation with the Third Reich, and in August of that year he accompanied Tsar **Boris III** on his last visit to Germany. After the death of Boris, on a motion by Filov, the National Assembly on 11 September 1943 elected Mikhov one of three regents who were to rule on behalf of the minor heir to the throne, **Simeon**. Mikhov showed little interest in politics, but his election would ensure the strong support of the army for the Regency Council. In early September 1944 Mikhov still believed that the Third Reich would win the war and was against entering negotiations with the Allies. After an uprising overthrew the regency on 9 September 1944, Mikhov was arrested. At the beginning of 1945, along with the other regents and dozens of other politicians, he was sentenced to death and executed. Mikhov published *Dnevnik* (Diary; *Svoboda*, 1944, nos. 91–100; *Naroden Soyuz*, 1945, nos. 3–7). On 29 August 1996 the Supreme Court quashed Mikhov's sentence. (WR)

Sources: *Entsiklopediya Bulgariya*, vol. 6 (Sofia, 1978); *Biographisches Lexikon*, vol. 3; Marshall Lee Miller, *Bulgaria during the Second World War* (Stanford, 1975); Stephane Groueff, *Crown of Thorns* (Lanham, Md., 1987); Bogdan Filov, *Dnevnik* (Sofia, 1990); Tasho Tashev, *Ministrite na Bulgariya 1879–1999: Entsiklopedichen spravochnik* (Sofia, 1999).

MIKLÓS Dálnoki Béla (11 June 1890, Budapest–21 November 1948, Budapest), Hungarian general and politician. Miklós came from a Szekler family of noble origins. His father was a teacher. At seventeen Miklós began to officially use the noble nickname indicating his father's place of birth (Dálnok). After graduating from high school in Sopron (1907), he attended the Ludovika Military Academy in Budapest. In 1910 he was promoted to second lieutenant of hussars. During World War I he served on many fronts. Under the Hungarian Soviet Republic (HSR) in 1919 Miklós served in the city headquarters until June, subsequently becoming a non-commissioned officer. After the collapse of the HSR in August 1919, he was again assigned to the city headquarters. From 1920 to 1921 he studied at the General Staff Academy and subsequently served in the Ministry of National Defense and in various units of the army. In 1929 he was awarded the title of "hero" (*vitéz*). From 1929 to 1933 he was deputy chief of the military office of Regent **Miklós Horthy** and subsequently served as military attaché to Berlin until 1936. In 1938 Miklós became commander of the Second Mounted Brigade, and in 1939 he was promoted to general. In 1940 he became commander of the First Armored Corps, at the head of which he took part in the campaign against Yugoslavia and the Soviet Union. In November 1941 he was promoted to major general. In February 1942 he became commander of the Ninth Corps, and in October of that year he was appointed chief aide-de-camp to Horthy and head of his military bureau. On 1 August 1943 he was promoted to lieutenant general.

In August 1944 Miklós took over command of the First Hungarian Army, which was stationed in the northeastern Carpathians. After Hungary's unsuccessful attempt to withdraw from the war (15 October 1944), along with the staff and twenty thousand of his men, Miklós defected to the Soviet side. In November he was involved in ceasefire negotiations in Moscow. The Soviet leaders asked him to become the leader of a provisional Hungarian government that they planned to establish. A member of the Provisional National Assembly that was established in Debrecen, Miklós served as prime minister of the Provisional National Government from 22 December 1944 to 15 November 1945. As head of the government, he complied with the demands of the local Communists and of Moscow, and many a time he endorsed decisions that were disadvantageous to Hungary. In November 1945, as a prominent public figure, Miklós was again invited to join the parliament. Before the 1947 elections, Miklós joined the Hungarian Independence Party, established by **Zoltán Pfeiffer**, and became a member of its Executive Committee. After the elections of 31 August 1947, the results of which were partly falsified by the Communists, Miklós became a member of parliament. On 20 November of that year, like all the MPs from the Hungarian Independence Party, Miklós was unlawfully deprived of his seat, and then he retired from public life. (JT)

Sources: John F. Montgomery, *Hungary: The Unwilling Satellite* (New York, 1947); Ferenc Nagy, *The Struggle Behind the Iron Curtain* (New York, 1948); *Magyar Életrajzi Lexikon*, vol. 2 (Budapest, 1969); *A magyar forradalom és szabadságharc enciklopédiája* (Budapest, 1999).

MIKLOŠKO František (2 June 1947, Nitra), Slovak dissident and politician. After completing courses at a technical high school in Nitra, in 1978 Mikloško graduated in mathematics from the University of Bratislava. He worked at the Institute of Cybernetics of the Slovak Academy of Sciences, but in 1983 he was fired for political reasons and then worked as a blue-collar laborer. In the 1970s and 1980s Mikloško was active in the underground Catholic Church. He also published in and helped organize the uncensored press. He was one of the organizers of the "candle demonstration" in Bratislava on 25 March 1988; the demonstration demanded that the authorities respect human rights, allow freedom of confession, and consent to to the Church's appointment of bishops for vacant dioceses. In November 1989 Mikloško co-organized the Public against Violence (Verejnost' proti Nasiliu [VPN]) and was a member of its coordinating center. As a result of the reconstruction of the Slovak parliament, on 1 March 1990 Mikloško became an MP of the Slovak National Council (SNC). In the first free elections of June 1990 he won a seat on behalf of the VPN and became speaker of the SNC for two years. After the VPN split, Mikloško became one of the leaders of the Civic Democratic Union–VPN. In March 1992 he left it and joined the Christian Democratic Movement (Krest'ansko-Demokratické Hnutie [KDH]). In 1990–92 he took part in talks concerning the new legal foundations of the Czechoslovak relationship; along with **Ján Čarnogurski**, Mikloško favored an inter-state agreement between the Czech and Slovak republics.

After the Czechoslovak federation collapsed Mikloško was an MP in all subsequent parliaments of independent Slovakia. He was one of the most adamant opponents of **Vladimír Mečiar** and his policies. In 1996 Mikloško became a member of the KDH Presidium, and in 2000, deputy chairman of the party for economic affairs. In 1997, along with all of the KDH, he joined the Slovak Democratic Coalition (Slovenská Demokratická Koalícia [SDK]), created before the elections of 1998 in order to remove Mečiar from power. As a result of a conflict in the coalition, connected with the plan of Prime Minister **Mikuláš Dzurinda** to turn the SDK into one party, in 2000 Mikloško, along with other KDH MPs, left the SDK parliamentary club. In the elections of 2002 the KDH ran alone, winning 8.25 percent of the vote. Mikloško authored *Nebudete ich môct't' rozvrátit't'* (You will not be able to crush them; 1991), on the Slovak Catholic Church in 1948–89, and *Čas stretnutí* (Time to meet; 1996), a collection of reflections on Slovakia's development after the Velvet Revolution. (PU)

Sources: *ČBS*; *Kdo byl kdo v našich dějinach ve 20. stoleti*, vol. 1 (Prague, 1998); Eric Stein, *Czecho/Slovakia: Ethnic Conflict, Constitutional Fissure, Negotiated Breakup* (Ann Arbor, 1997); Ján Čarnogurský, *Videné od Dunaja* (Bratislava, 1997); Svätoslav Mathé, *Slovenská politika v rokoch 1848–1993* (Martin, 2001); Jan Rychlík, *Rozpad Československa:Česko-slovenské vztahy 1989–1992* (Bratislava, 2002); www.kdh.sk/tvare/zivot_miklosko.htm#.

MIKOŁAJCZYK Stanisław (18 July 1901, Holsterhausen, Westphalia–13 December 1966, Washington, D.C.), Polish Peasant Party politician. Born into a family of miners, Mikołajczyk finished elementary school in Germany. After his family settled in Greater Poland (Wielkopolska, the Poznań region), where it purchased a small farm, he continued his education on his own. Mikołajczyk took part in the Great Poland Uprising against the Germans (1918–19), and in 1920 he fought in the Polish-Soviet war, during which he was wounded. After completing agricultural courses, he worked on his parents' farm and from time to time in a sugar factory. In 1930 he purchased his own farm. He worked for the development of agricultural associations and rural education; for example, he established an association of rural youth in Strzyżewo. In 1922 he joined the Polish Peasant Party–Piast (Polskie Stronnictwo Ludowe–Piast [PSL–Piast]). In 1927 he co-organized the Great Poland Union of Rural Youth and served as its vice-president (1927–28), subsequently becoming honorary president. From 1930 to 1931 Mikołajczyk was a member of the PSL–Piast Supreme Council. In 1930, on the ticket of the PSL–Piast, he became the youngest MP in the Polish Assembly. From 1931 to 1939 he was a member of the Supreme Council of the Peasant Party (Stronnictwo Ludowe [SL]), and from 1933 to 1939, a member of the SL Chief Executive Committee. When **Władysław Kiernik**, vice-president of the SL Chief Executive Committee, was in exile, Mikołajczyk substituted for him. He represented a moderate agrarian approach to social reforms, but in the late 1930s he called for parceling out the landed estates without compensation to their owners. Mikołajczyk sought allies against the ruling camp both in the centrist parties and on the right. He was one of the closest associates of **Wincenty Witos**, whose policies he supported. Mikołajczyk had a negative view of the Polish Socialist Party (Polska Partia Socjalistyczna [PPS]), as well as the National Party (Stronnictwo Narodowe [SN]). From 1936 to 1939 Mikołajczyk was president of the Great Poland Society of Agricultural Associations. In 1936 he called for a platform of centrist opposition forces in the form of the so-called Morges Front. In August 1937, as interim president of the SL, he led an all-Polish peasant strike, for which he was sentenced to four months' imprisonment.

Mikołajczyk fought in the September 1939 campaign and subsequently made his way, via Hungary, to France. He was the president of the SL Foreign Committee, and in December 1939 he became vice-president and acting president of the National Council, which was an advisory organ to the president and to the government-in-exile. On 3 September 1941 Mikołajczyk became deputy prime minister and minister of interior in the government of General **Władysław Sikorski**. He also served as president of the Committee for Home Affairs. In the structures of the Polish government-in-exile Mikołajczyk was known to have a negative opinion of General **Kazimierz Sosnkowski**, who represented the pro-*sanacja* forces. On 14 July 1943, after the death of Sikorski, Mikołajczyk became head of the government-in-exile in London. Faced with the Kremlin's tenacity and the Western Allies' passivity over the Polish issue, Mikołajczyk more and more clearly realized that it would be necessary to reach a compromise with the Soviet Union in order to save Poland's endangered sovereignty. Since the Big Three did not inform Mikołajczyk about the decisions they had reached on the Polish borders at the Tehran Conference (November–December 1943), Mikołajczyk devoted a great deal of fruitless effort trying to negotiate the reestablishment of Poland's prewar borders. Mikołajczyk was among those who decided to start the uprising in Warsaw. At the beginning of August 1944 he attempted to use the threat of an uprising in Warsaw as a trump card in the talks with Stalin in the Kremlin. However, Stalin had imperialistic inclinations and had no interest in assisting the Poles; he not only halted the Soviet offensive, but he also refused to allow Allied planes to supply the Warsaw insurgents, thus allowing the Germans to suppress the Warsaw Uprising. During his second visit to Moscow in mid-October 1944, Mikołajczyk was referred by Stalin to the National Home Council (Krajowa Rada Narodowa [KRN]) and the

Polish Committee of National Liberation (Polski Komitet Wyzwolenia Narodowego [PKWN]), but the Allies did not give him any support. Mikołajczyk also learned that the Curzon Line had already been accepted in Tehran. In the face of opposition in the Polish government-in-exile, and also because of the failure of his talks with President Franklin D. Roosevelt, on 24 November 1944 Mikołajczyk resigned as prime minister.

Mikołajczyk realized that it would be necessary to make ever greater concessions to the emerging Communist authorities in order to have a chance to take part in the legal political struggle in Poland; therefore, he recognized the Curzon Line as a basis for the Polish-Soviet border. He also accepted the agreements of the Yalta Conference (February 1945), and in June 1945 he attended a Moscow conference on the establishment of the Provisional Government of National Unity (Tymczasowy Rząd Jedności Narodowej [TRJN]). Mikołajczyk joined the TRJN as deputy prime minister and minister of agriculture and agricultural reforms (28 June 1945–8 February 1947). In July 1945 he attended the Potsdam Conference, and in August 1945 he took part in negotiations leading to the signing of an agreement on the Polish-Soviet border. At that time he succeeded in thwarting a project to build huge Polish-Soviet mixed enterprises but failed to enforce clear rules for the disbursement to Poland of German war reparations, which were to be paid through Soviet agency.

Mikołajczyk strove to consolidate the Polish non-Communist peasant movement. As he saw that the name "Stronnictwo Ludowe" had been arrogated by crypto-Communists, on 22 July 1945 he assumed the post of vice-president of the Provisional Chief Executive Committee of the Polish Peasant Party (Polskie Stronnictwo Ludowe [PSL]), becoming the de facto head of the party owing to Witos's illness. After Witos's death, Mikołajczyk was elected president of the PSL on 21 January 1946. From 1945 to 1946 he was a deputy to the KRN and chairman of the PSL parliamentary representation. He gathered around himself the majority of the political opposition in Poland. In February 1946, during talks with the Communists and the Communist-dominated PPS on the establishment of the electoral Bloc of Democratic Parties, Mikołajczyk rejected the proposal of a bloc in which the Communists offered the PSL 20 percent of the seats, and he demanded 75 percent of the seats for his party. He realized that he had great public support. At that time the PSL had more members than the Communist Polish Workers' Party (Polska Partia Robotnicza [PPR]) and the PPS together. In a referendum of 30 June 1946 the PSL, in opposition to the parties in the Communist bloc, called for a "no" vote on the abolition of the Senate. Three-fourths of the voters followed his recommendation, but the results of the referendum were falsified. During the election campaign the PPR, with the help of the security apparatus, made numerous attempts to destroy the unity within the PSL and organized opposition to Mikołajczyk within the party. The Communists terrorized the activists and the supporters of the PSL.

The rigged elections to the Constituent Assembly on 19 January 1947 gave the PSL only 28 out of the 444 seats. The anti-Mikołajczyk faction, the PSL–Left (PSL–Lewica) increased its activities. Facing the threat of arrest and a political trial, with the help of the American and British embassies, on 21 October 1947 Mikołajczyk secretly left Poland. Reluctantly received by his former associates from the London government, in early 1950 he established the Polish National Democratic Committee, intended as competition to the London government. However, the committee never played any major political role. Mikołajczyk finally settled in the United States. He became president of the PSL-in-exile and chairman of the International Peasant Union. He often spoke on Radio Free Europe. Although he was a champion of moderation and democracy, owing to the course of history in the second half of the twentieth century, Mikołajczyk became a controversial figure, viewed in diametrically opposite ways. The authorities of the Polish People's Republic always maligned him. The Communist-controlled United Peasant Party (Zjednoczone Stronnictwo Ludowe [ZSL], 1949–89) declared him its main enemy. Thus, when in 1990 the leaders of this party recognized Mikołajczyk as their ideological paradigm and renamed their party the PSL, it was historical usurpation. In 2000 Mikołajczyk's ashes were brought to Poland and reburied in the Cemetery of Distinguished Citizens of Great Poland in Poznań. Mikołajczyk's publications include *The Rape of Poland* (1948), published in Polish by the underground press as *Polska zniewolona* (1981). (JS)

Sources: *PSB*, vol. 21; *Słownik biograficzny działaczy ruchu ludowego* (Warsaw, 1989); Roman Buczek, *Stronnictwo Ludowe w latach 1939–1945* (London, 1975); Krystyna Kersten, *Narodziny systemu władzy: Polska 1943–1948* (Poznań, 1990); Andrzej Paczkowski, *Stanisław Mikołajczyk, czyli klęska realisty: Zarys biografii politycznej* (Warsaw, 1991); Michał Karalus, *Chłopak ze Strzyżewa: Młodość Stanisława Mikołajczyka, 1901–1930* (Dobrzyca, 1993); Stanisław Łach, *Polskie Stronnictwo Ludowe w latach 1945–1947* (Gdańsk, 1995); Andrzej Albert [Wojciech Roszkowski], *Najnowsza historia Polski 1914–1993*, vol. 2 (Warsaw, 1995); Roman Buczek, *Stanisław Mikołajczyk* (Toronto, 1996); Stanisław Stępka, *Stanisław Mikołajczyk* (Warsaw, 2001).

MIKULIĆ Branko (10 June 1928, Podgradje, near Gornji Vakuf, Bosnia and Herzegovina–12 April 1994, Sarajevo), Yugoslav Communist activist. In 1943 Mikulić joined the Partisans led by **Josip Broz Tito** and fought in the Seventeenth Brigade. In 1945 he became a member of the Communist Party of Yugoslavia (CPY). He later graduated from an economics school in Zagreb. He served as secretary of the League of Communist Youth of Yugoslavia (SKOJ) in the towns of Gornji Vakuf and Bugojno and subsequently held local-level party posts in Bugojno, Jajce, Livno, and Żenica. In 1965 Mikulić was elected a member of the Central Committee (CC) of the League of Communists of Bosnia and Herzegovina (LCBH). From 1967 to 1969 he was chairman of the Executive Council (prime minister) of Bosnia and Herzegovina, and from March 1969 to April 1978, he was chairman of the CC of the LCBH. From May 1974 to June 1982 Mikulić was a member of the Presidium of the CC of the League of Communists of Yugoslavia (LCY). He was a member of the presidency of Bosnia and Herzegovina (May 1974–April 1978 and April 1982–May 1984). From 19 October 1978 to 23 October 1979 he served as chairman of the LCY CC Presidium. From April 1982 to April 1983 he was chairman of the presidency of Bosnia and Herzegovina. From May 1984 to May 1986 he was a member of the presidency of the Socialist Federal Republic of Yugoslavia (SFRY). On 15 May 1986 Mikulić became president of the Federal Executive Council (prime minister) of the SFRY. In order to improve the economic situation he sought aid from the International Monetary Fund. This aid was conditional on Yugoslavia's fulfilling numerous requirements, including the curbing of inflation; therefore, the government made a decision to reduce salaries, the money supply, and budgetary expenses. However, inflation continued to rise: it was 190 percent in 1986, 419 percent in 1987, and 1,232 percent in 1988. At the end of 1988 Mikulić decided to resign, but he officially continued to serve as prime minister until 16 March 1989, when he was succeeded by **Ante Marković**. (AO)

Sources: *Who's Who in the Socialist Countries of Europe* (Munich, London, and Paris, 1989); Slobodan Stanković, *The End of the Tito Era: Yugoslavia's Dilemmas* (Stanford, 1981); Susan Woodward, *Balkan Tragedy* (Washington, D.C., 1995).

MILCZANOWSKI Andrzej (26 May 1939, Równe, Volhynia), Polish lawyer and politician. The son of a prosecutor executed by the NKVD during World War II, in 1962 Milczanowski graduated in law from the University of Poznań. Until 1968 he worked in the county prosecutor's office in Szczecin and until 1980 as a legal adviser in various enterprises. From 1978 he worked with the Intervention Bureau of the Committee of Social Self-Defense–KOR. Milczanowski took part in the August 1980 workers' strikes and became head of the Legal Office of the West Pomeranian Region of Solidarity and head of the Factory Commission of Solidarity in the Szczecin Shipyard. After martial law was introduced, from 13 to 15 December 1981 Milczanowski took part in the Regional Strike Committee, for which he was sentenced to five years in prison. Amnestied after two and a half years, he continued trade union activities in the underground Solidarity. In 1984–88 Milczanowski belonged to the secret Coordination Council of Solidarity's West Pomeranian Region and to the all-national Provisional Coordination Commission; from 1987 he belonged to the National Executive Commission of Solidarity. In the summer of 1988 he led the strike in the Szczecin Shipyard. From December 1988 he belonged to the Civic Committee of the Chairman of Solidarity, and from February to April 1989 he participated in the Round Table Talks.

From May 1990 Milczanowski was deputy head, and from August 1990 to January 1992 head, of the newly organized Office of State Protection. From July 1992 to December 1995 he was minister of interior in the governments of **Hanna Suchocka**, **Waldemar Pawlak**, and **Józef Oleksy**. He held this position on behalf of President **Lech Wałęsa**, carrying out his political line. Milczanowski opposed the exposure of former collaborators of the (Communist) Security Service (Służba Bezpieczeństwa [SB]) since he believed this would jeopardize current operations of special services. He also opposed the exchange of personnel in these services and the public release of SB documentation. His stance was often criticized by various politicians from the post-Solidarity camp. When Wałęsa lost the presidential elections in 1995, on the eve of the assumption of the presidency by the post-Communist **Aleksander Kwaśniewski** (21 December 1995), Milczanowski made a dramatic parliamentary speech in which he accused the acting prime minister, Oleksy, of contacts with Soviet and Russian intelligence. The investigation of this matter was suspended, while an investigation concerning Milczanowski's disclosure of state secrets was deadlocked for years. From 1996 Milczanowski worked as a notary in Szczecin. (AF)

Sources: *Biała Księga: Akta śledztwa prowadzonego przez Prokuraturę Warszawskiego Okręgu Wojskowego w Warszawie w sprawie wniosków Ministra Spraw Wewnętrznych z dnia 19.12.1995 r. i 16.01.1996 r.* (Warsaw, 1996); *Opozycja w PRL: Słownik biograficzny 1956–89* (Warsaw, 2000); Antoni Dudek, *Pierwsze lata III Rzeczpospolitej 1989–2001* (Kraków, 2002).

MILEWSKI Mirosław (1 May 1928, Lipsk), Polish Communist activist. In 1944 Milewski had already joined the security apparatus created by the Soviets in Poland and took part in its operations in the Suwałki region. In 1945–48 he was a member of the (Communist) Polish Workers' Party, and from 1948 to 1990, the Polish United Workers' Party (Polska Zjednoczona Partia Robotnicza [PUWP]). From 1944 to 1958 Milewski worked in military security and later in the Ministry of Interior in Warsaw, where he was deputy director and director of the Department of Intelligence; from 1971 to 1980 he was undersecretary of state, and from October 1980 to July 1981, minister of interior. In 1957 Milewski formally graduated from the Department of Agriculture of the Main School of Rural Economy in Warsaw. From 1971 he was a brigadier general, and from 1979, a general of division in the Civic Militia (Milicja Obywatelska). From 1974 a member of the Supreme Board and from 1979 deputy chairman of the Association of Combatants for Freedom and Democracy, Milewski advanced in the Ministry of Interior thanks to his close cooperation with the Soviet security apparatus.

From December 1971 to February 1980 Milewski was a deputy member and then a member of the PUWP Central Committee (CC), and from July 1981 he was CC secretary and a member of the CC Politburo. He advocated a crackdown on Solidarity. His departure from the Ministry of Interior and advancement in the party apparatus was connected with the consolidation of power by General **Wojciech Jaruzelski**. Although Milewski, believed to be a man of the Kremlin, gained overall control of the security forces on behalf of the party leadership, direct control was taken over by General **Czesław Kiszczak**, connected with Jaruzelski. It is assumed that Kiszczak's group, rooted in military intelligence and counterintelligence, had a hand in the Iron (Żelazo) affair, in which Milewski probably supervised the criminal operations of his functionaries in the West. The personal conflict between Milewski and Kiszczak, as well as a rivalry between two groups, the Legia (the sports club of the military) and the Gwardia (the sports club of the militiamen), continued into the martial law period. It probably culminated with the murder of Reverend **Jerzy Popiełuszko** in October 1984. In connection with this case, Milewski was dismissed from all party and state functions in May 1985 and expelled from the party in 1986. The mysterious affairs in which he was involved were not explained even after 1989. (IS/WR)

Sources: Mołdawa; Krystyna Daszkiewicz, *Uprowadzenie i morderstwo ks: Jerzego Popiełuszki* (Poznań, 1990); Jerzy Jachowicz, "Złoty wywiad PRL," *Gazeta Wyborcza*, 11 October 1990; Tadeusz Fredro-Bielecki, *Zwycięstwo księdza Jerzego* (Warsaw, 1991); Jan Widacki, *Czego nie powiedział generał Kiszczak* (Warsaw, 1992); *Generał Pawłow: Byłem rezydentem KGB w Polsce* (Warsaw, 1994); Henryk Dominiczak, *Organy bezpieczeństwa PRL 1944–1990* (Warsaw, 1997).

MIŁKOWSKI Stanisław (6 June 1905, Sikorzyce, near Dąbrowa Górnicza–April 1945, Bergen-Belsen), Polish economist and Peasant Party activist. Born into a peasant family, after graduating from high school in Tarnów, Miłkowski completed law studies and a higher cooperative course at the Jagiellonian University in Kraków (1934). In 1926 he joined the Union of Polish Academic Peasant Youth (Ogólnopolski Związek Akademickiej Młodzieży Ludowej) and served as its president from 1929 to 1930. In 1931 he joined the Peasant Party (Stronnictwo Ludowe [SL]). In 1934 Miłkowski became a member of the Main Board of the Union of Rural Youth called Wici and served as its deputy chairman from 1935 to 1938. From December 1935 to February 1938 he belonged to the SL Supreme Council, and in August 1935 he joined the SL Chief Executive Committee. In the 1930s he published extensively, becoming one of the main theoreticians of Polish agrarianism. Miłkowski believed that the Poles should follow the example of the Czech agrarians, and he supported unification tendencies in the peasant movement. In 1931 he initiated the development of the ideology of the peasant youth movement. He expounded his concepts in the brochure *Agraryzm jako forma przebudowy ustroju społecznego* (Agrarianism as a form of reconstruction of the social system; 1934). Miłkowski advocated that large landed estates be parceled out without compensation to their owners, and he supported the development of agricultural cooperatives. He was more critical of capitalism than of socialism or even communism, as he believed that the latter two were the future of the urban economy. He called for the industrialization of agriculture and the deglomeration of cities and advocated that local governments be granted broad powers. He presented his theses in the brochure *Walka o nową Polskę* (Struggle for a new Poland; 1936). Miłkowski's agrarian ideology gave rise to a programmatic discussion within the SL. Although he criticized the mass-rally–based methods of struggle used by the older generation of Peasant Party members, the SL adopted the majority of his objections as part of its program in 1935. During the Nazi occupation Miłkowski took part in activities of the underground peasant movement organized by the Peasant Party–Roch (Stronnictwo Ludowe–Roch [SL–Roch]). Along with **Zygmunt Zaremba**, he wrote the peasant-Socialist "Program of People's Poland" (Program Polski Ludowej; 1940–41). He also served as president of the Provisional Cooperative Council. In late August 1944 Miłkowski was arrested in Międzylesie, near Warsaw, where he lived. Deported to the camp in Bergen-Belsen, he died there in unknown circumstances. (WR)

Sources: *PSB*, vol. 21; Zygmunt Zaremba, *Wojna i konspiracja* (London, 1957); *Materiały źródłowe do historii polskiego ruchu ludowego*, vol. 4 (Warsaw, 1966); Józef Niećko, *Na drodze do Polski Ludowej* (Warsaw, 1967).

MILLER Leszek (3 July 1946, Żyrardów), Polish Communist activist and post-Communist politician. Born into a laborer's family, Miller started working as a blue-collar laborer in the Linen Industry Factory in Żyrardów. A member of the Polish United Workers' Party (Polska Zjednoczona Partia Robotnicza [PUWP]) from 1969, in 1977 he graduated from the Higher School of Social Sciences at the PUWP Central Committee (CC). From 1982 to 1985 Miller headed the Group for Youth Affairs, and in 1985–86 he was head of the CC Department for Youth, Physical Culture, and Tourism. In 1986–89 he was first secretary of the PUWP Provincial Committee in Skierniewice, and from December 1988 he was CC secretary and head of the CC Commission for Youth and Social Organizations. From July 1989 he belonged to the CC Politburo. Miller took part in the Round Table Talks in 1989, co-chairing the negotiating group for youth affairs. Miller was elected to the parliament in the breakthrough elections of 4 June 1989 and in subsequent elections in 1991, 1993, 1997, and 2001. In August 1989 he belonged to the PUWP working group negotiating the party's share in the government of **Tadeusz Mazowiecki**. He also played a major role in the privatization of the holdings of the Communist nomenklatura—for example, through a special economic agency of the PUWP CC.

After the PUWP was dissolved in January 1990, Miller became secretary general of the Social Democracy of the Polish Republic (Socjaldemokracja Rzeczypospolitej Polski [SdRP]). From March 1993 he was its deputy chairman, and from December 1997, its chairman. Miller was suspected of taking part in the transfer of a CPSU loan to the SdRP in violation of Polish currency laws, but an investigation into the matter was discontinued by a post-Communist minister of justice. After the SdRP was transformed into the Democratic Left Alliance (Sojusz Lewicy Demokratycznej [SLD]) in December 1999, Miller became chairman of the party. From October 1993 to February 1996 he was minister of labor and social policy; from February 1996 to October 1997 he was head of the Office of the Prime Minister, and then he was minister of interior and administration. As chairman of the SLD parliamentary club, in 1997–2001 Miller was in sharp opposition to the government of **Jerzy Buzek**. After the elections of September 2001 brought victory to the SLD, on 4 October 2001 Miller became prime minister of the government based on a coalition of the SLD and the Polish Peasant Party. His government checked the reform of education and the health service and slowed down privatization. In December 2002 Miller finalized the negotiations on Poland's accession to the European Union, confirmed by a referendum in June 2003. In the spring of 2003 he took part in the decision on Polish participation in the war in Iraq. Economic stagnation and high unemployment eroded social support for Miller's cabinet. Political struggles, failed legislation, and repeated scandals within the SLD ranks culminated in a corruption scandal involving SLD member Lew Rywin, who offered the media concern Agora (the publisher of *Gazeta Wyborcza*) help in changing the law in exchange for a bribe—allegedly in the name of Miller. All this, as well as Miller's escalating conflict with President **Aleksander Kwaśniewski** brought Miller's ratings to a record low, so on 2 May 2004 he resigned. (IS/WR)

Sources: Mołdawa; Katarzyna Kęsicka, "Ałganow i pożyczka KPZR," *Gazeta Wyborcza*, 12 January 1996; Rafał Kasprów, "Wszystkie pieniądze SLD," *Życie*, 26 February 1998; Andrzej Kulik and Jarosław Knap, "Bagno w Kotlinie," *Wprost*, 30 August 1998; Janusz A. Majcherek, *Pierwsza dekada III Rzeczypospolitej* (Warsaw, 1999); Antoni Dudek, *Pierwsze lata III Rzeczyspospolitej 1989–2001* (Kraków, 2002); Arnošt Bečka and Jacek Molesta, *Sprawozdanie z likwidcji majątku byłej Polskiej Zjednoczonej Partrii Robotncizej* (Warsaw, 2001).

MILOŠEVIĆ Slobodan (20 August 1941, Požarevac—12 March 2006, The Hague), Serb and Yugoslav Communist activist, president of Yugoslavia. Milošević's father was an Orthodox priest, and his mother a teacher. Both committed suicide, his father in 1962, and his mother in 1972. In 1959 Milošević joined the League of Communists of Yugoslavia (LCY), and in 1964 he graduated in law from the University of Belgrade. During his studies he was department secretary of the League of Communists of Serbia (LCS) and deputy chairman of the Student Union. In 1969–73 he was deputy director and from 1973 to 1978 director of the Tehnogas enterprise. In 1978–83 he was chairman of Beobank, the largest bank in Yugoslavia at the time. In 1984, thanks to the support of **Ivan Stambolić**, the LCS leader, Milošević became chairman of the LCS Committee in Belgrade. From May 1986 to July 1990 he chaired the Presidium of the LCS Central Committee. In May 1989 he became chairman of the Presidium of the Socialist Federal Republic of Yugoslavia (SFRY). After the dissolution of the LCY, in July 1990 the LCS joined the Socialist Union of Serbian Parties with the Socialist Party of Serbia (Socialistička Partija Srbije [SPS]), headed by Miloševič. In the elections of December 1990 and December 1992 Milošević won 65 and 56 percent of the vote respectively and strengthened his position as president of Serbia and de facto ruler of the new Yugoslavia, which was shrinking as a result of the secessions of its republics. Since according to the constitution Milošević could not run for a third time, on 15 July 1997 the Federal Assembly elected him president of the Federal Republic of Yugoslavia, consisting of Serbia and Montenegro.

Milošević strove to strengthen the position of Serbs in the SFRY, but his actions in fact led to the country's downfall, to the civil war, and to massive war crimes. The turning point in Milošević's career came on 24 April 1987, when he told the Kosovo Serbs that nobody would conquer them anymore. By appealing to Serb nationalism and by starting an anti-Albanian campaign, Milošević gained popularity among the Serbs. On 28 June 1989 he presided over the celebration of the six hundredth anniversary of the Serbian defeat by the Turks at Kosovo Field. Milošević inspired a demonstration that led to the takeover of power in the autonomous republics of Kosovo and Voivodina by nationalist politicians allied with him. In 1990 the Serbian constitution was changed to limit the autonomy of both regions. This aggravated relations between Serbia and other SFRY republics. Milošević referred to the idea of Greater Serbia and strove to centralize the state against the aspirations of the Slovenes and Croats, who wanted to turn the SFRY into a loose confederation. As a result, on 25 June 1991 Slovenia and Croatia proclaimed their independence. Soon they were followed by Macedonia and Bosnia-Herzegovina, inhabited by large numbers of Serbs. SFRY military intervention in Slovenia and Croatia and Serbian military operations in Bosnia led to a war during which ethnic cleansing and mass murders were recorded on a scale unseen in Europe after World War II. Milošević was largely responsible for this course of events, since he militarily supported Serbian operations in Croatia and Bosnia-Herzegovina. As a result of international pressures (economic sanctions and NATO air raids against Serbia), in 1995 Milošević had to give up his support for the Bosnian Serbs and their leader, **Radovan Karadžić**, who is accused of war crimes. Milošević took part in peace negotiations and was one of the signatories to the treaties of Dayton Agreement (21 November 1995) and Paris Agreement (14 December 1995), which ended the war in Bosnia-Herzegovina.

Milošević's policies were generally condemned abroad. He was accused of the violation of democratic rules and human rights, as well as war crimes. Nevertheless, in Serbia he continued to be very popular, especially in the countryside, where he was thought a national hero. His wife, professor of sociology Mirjana Marković, played an important political role in the system. The opposition was too weak and split to challenge Milošević's position. Milošević followed a skillful policy of divide and rule—for instance, he attracted one of the opposition leaders, **Vuk Drašković**, to the government in 1999. By that time

Milošević's ruthless policies toward the Kosovo Albanians had led to another crisis. In view of proofs of serious violations of human rights in Kosovo and the failure of diplomatic efforts to curb these violations, in March 1999 NATO started air raids over the new Yugoslavia. After the conclusion of a peace accord on 9 June 1999, the international community took over control in Kosovo. Although Milošević brought about the fall of the old and the new Yugoslavia, he made use of the NATO raids to consolidate his position at home and to attack the opposition. In May 1999 he was formally accused of war crimes by The Hague International Tribunal for War Crimes in Former Yugoslavia. In September 2000 Milošević lost the presidential election to **Vojislav Koštunica**. For some time Milošević did not accept the defeat, but finally, under domestic and foreign pressure, on 7 October 2000 he resigned. Although he counted on immunity, on 1 April 2001 he was arrested and handed over to The Hague tribunal. During the trial, which started on 12 February 2002, he was accused of war crimes and genocide, but he died before the end of the trial. (AO)

Sources: Lenard J. Cohen, *Serpent in the Bosom: The Rise and Fall of Slobodan Milosevic* (Boulder, Colo., 1995); Laura Silber and Allan Little, *The Death of Yugoslavia* (London, 1995); Warren Zimmermann, *Origins of a Catastrophe* (New York and Toronto, 1996); Dusko Doder and Louise Branson, *Milosevic: Portrait of a Tyrant* (New York, 1999); Slavoljub Djukić, *Milošević and Marković: A Lust for Power* (Montreal, 2001); Bugajski; www.gov.yu/institutions/president/president.html.

MIŁOSZ Czesław (30 June 1911, Szetejnie [Šateiniai], near Kėdainiai, Lithuania–14 August 2004, Kraków), Polish poet and writer. Miłosz graduated from high school in Wilno (Vilnius) in 1929, and he studied law at Wilno University from 1929 to 1934. In 1931 he co-founded the leftist literary group Żagary, and in 1933–34 he edited the periodical *Żagary*. Miłosz made his literary debut with the volume *Poemat o czasie zastygłym* (Poem on time standing still; 1933). After graduation, Miłosz received a scholarship from the National Culture Fund. He went to Paris, where he made friends with his relative Oskar Miłosz, who greatly influenced his work. Upon returning to Poland in 1935, Miłosz started working for the Polish radio station in Wilno. His sympathy for the national minorities caused him to lose his job, but from 1937 he worked at Polish Radio in Warsaw. He also published in the periodicals *Marchołt* and *Ateneum* and the daily *Słowo*. In September 1939 Miłosz went to Wilno, already incorporated by Lithuania. He wrote for the dailies *Gazeta Codzienna* and *Kurier Wileński*. After the Soviets occupied Lithuania, in the summer of 1940 Miłosz left for German-occupied Warsaw and worked as a caretaker at the university library.

Connected with the underground Socialist group Liberty (Wolność), he did not join the military underground but was active in the cultural underground. After the outbreak of the Warsaw Uprising in August 1944 Miłosz left for Lesser Poland, where he spent the winter of 1944–45 at the estate of friends. After the war he settled in Kraków, publishing in the periodicals *Odrodzenie*, *Przekrój*, and *Twórczość*. He also published *Ocalenie* (Salvation; 1945). In 1945 Miłosz won an award from the ministry of culture and started working in the Polish consulate in New York. In 1947 he became cultural attaché in the embassy in Washington, D.C., and in 1950 he became first secretary in the embassy in France. In 1948 he published *Traktat moralny* (Treatise on morality).

In February 1951 Miłosz asked for political asylum in France, becoming the target of a propaganda attack by the Polish Communist authorities; his works were banned in Poland. At the same time political émigrés were very critical of his cooperation with the Communist regime. Miłosz was helped by the Paris monthly *Kultura*. It was there that he explained his breakaway from the Communist government. In 1951 he published *Zniewolony umysł* (*Captive Mind*, 1953), which was also translated into other languages. In 1953 he published a novel, *Zdobycie władzy*, in French (Polish edition, 1955; *Seizure of Power*, 1955), for which he received the Prix Littéraire Européen. Thanks to these works, Miłosz won a reputation as a leading critic of communism and pro-Soviet leftist intellectuals. His subsequent works—such as the collections of poems *Światło dzienne* (Daylight; 1953) and *Traktat poetycki* (1958; *Treatise on Poetry*, 2001), the novel *Dolina Issy* (1955; *Issa Valley*, 1981), and his memoirs *Rodzinna Europa* (1959; *Native Realm*, 1968)—strengthened his literary position. In 1960 Miłosz was given the chair of Polish literature at the University of California in Berkeley. After a series of new volumes of poetry and prose—including a study on **Stanisław Brzozowski**, *Człowiek wśród skorpionów* (A man among Scorpios; 1962)—in 1969 Miłosz published the textbook *The History of Polish Literature*. In the United States he was initially known as the translator of **Zbigniew Herbert**'s works into English, but in the 1970s he gradually won a reputation among English-speaking readers, receiving the prestigious Neustadt International Prize for Literature (1978). Miłosz also published the volume of poetry *Gdzie słońce wschodzi i kędy zapada* (Where the sun rises and where it sets; 1974); the collections of prose *Prywatne obowiązki* (Private duties; 1972), *Ziemia Ulro* (1977; *Land of Ulro*, 1984), and *Ogród nauk* (Garden of arts and sciences; 1979); and dialogues with **Tomas Venclova** (1979).

In 1980 Miłosz received the Nobel Prize for Literature.

Since this award followed the formation of Solidarity, the Communist authorities in Poland removed the ban on his works. For the first time wider circles of Poles in Poland could not only read his poetry, but frequently could also simply learn his name. The publication of his works followed on a large scale. In June 1981 Miłosz made a triumphant tour of Poland, becoming a symbol of a new cultural freedom and political aspirations. When martial law was introduced in Poland, he chaired the Fund for Aid to Independent Polish Literature and Culture. In the 1980s Miłosz's publications included *Nieobjęta ziemia* (Unembraced land; 1984); *Kroniki* (Chronicles; 1987); and the essays and volumes of prose *Zaczynając od moich ulic* (Starting from my streets; 1985) and *Metafizyczna pauza* (Metaphysical pause; 1989). In 2002 Miłosz returned to Poland and settled in Kraków.

Miłosz translated a lot into Polish (for example, some books of the Bible) and into English. Starting in the 1990s he also published the collections of poetry *Dalsze okolice* (Distant neighborhood; 1991) and *To* (This; 2000); and the volumes of prose *Rok myśliwego* (1990; *Year of the Hunter*, 1994), *Abecadło Miłosza* (Miłosz's ABC's; 1997), *Życie na wyspach* (Life on the isles; 1997), and *Piesek przydrożny* (1997; *Road-Side Dog*, 1998). Miłosz was active in meeting readers and delivering lectures, and he won several awards, such as membership to the American Academy of Arts and Letters and the American Academy of Arts and Sciences (both in 1982); the U.S. president's special award for contributions to American culture; honorary citizenship in Lithuania (1992); the Italian Grinzane Cavour Award (1992); the Polish Nike Award (1998); and honorary doctorates from the University of Michigan (1977), the University of California (1978), the Catholic University of Lublin (1981), New York University (1981), Harvard University (1989), Kaunas University (1992), and the University of Rome (1992). He also received the U.S. National Medal of Arts, as well as the highest Polish and Lithuanian orders. In 1988 Miłosz's *Collected Poems* were published in the United States. (DT)

Sources: "Teksty," *Pamiętnik Literacki* (London), 1981, nos. 4–5; *Twórczość*, 1981 no. 6; *Miłosz '51* (London, 1983); Andrzej Walicki, *Spotkania z Miłoszem* (London, 1985); Jerzy K. Wiatkowski, ed., *Poznawanie Miłosza* (Kraków, 1985); D. Davie, *Czeslaw Milosz and the Insufficiency of Lyric* (Cambridge, 1986); Aleksander Fiut, *Moment wieczny: Poezja Czesława Miłosza* (Paris, 1987); Renata Górczyńska and Piotr Kłoczowski, eds., *Trzy zimy oraz głosy o wierszach* (London, 1987); Edward Możejko *Between Anxiety and Hope* (Edmonton, 1988); L. Nathan and A. Quinn, *The Poet's Work: An Introduction to Czeslaw Milosz* (Cambridge, Mass., 1991).

MILOVANOVIĆ Milovan (17 February 1863, Belgrade–18 June 1912, Belgrade), Serb politician and diplomat. Milovanović studied law in Belgrade and later in Paris,

where in 1888 he earned a doctorate. In the same year he was appointed professor at Belgrade University, where he worked from 1888 to 1891. Milovanović took an active part in the drafting of the Serbian constitution of 1888, which introduced modern parliamentarism. In 1891 he joined the Radical Party. From 1891 to 1892 and from 1893 to 1894 he was head of a department in the Ministry of Foreign Affairs. From 1896 to 1897 he served as minister of justice. After **Alexander Obrenović** came to the throne, Milovanović initially sought cooperation between the Radical Party and the king, but soon he began to protest Alexander's absolutist policy. In 1899 Milovanović was sentenced in absentia to two years' imprisonment. Pardoned and rehabilitated the following year, he became an envoy to Bucharest.

From February 1901 to May 1902 Milovanović served as minister of the national economy, and from March to May 1902 he also held the post of finance minister. From 1903 to 1907 he was head of a diplomatic mission to Rome. In 1907 he represented Serbia at the Second Hague Peace Conference, which was an important stage in the development of international law. In July 1908 he became foreign minister of Serbia and held this post until the end of his life. From 4 July 1911 to 1 June 1912 he also served as prime minister. Milovanović was highly esteemed as a diplomat. In October 1908, during the crisis that followed the annexation of Bosnia and Herzegovina by Austria-Hungary, Milovanović managed to avert the looming war with Austria-Hungary. He thought that Serbia could not wage a war against Vienna alone and that the Serbian question should be turned into a European cause and combined with the principle of the European balance of power. He sought rapprochement between Serbia and the Entente and strove for an agreement among the Balkan states. In 1909 Milovanović entered into negotiations with Bulgaria, which led to the signing of a Serbian-Bulgarian treaty of friendship and alliance on 13 March 1912. This was a step toward an alliance between the four Balkan states: Serbia, Bulgaria, Greece, and Montenegro, and it sparked off the First Balkan War. Milovanović's publications include *Srbi i hrvati* (The Serbs and the Croats; 1895) and *Krivično pravo* (Penal law; 1889). He published articles in *Odjek* and *Samouprava*, periodicals of the Radical Party. In 1894 he founded *Delo*, another periodical of the Radical Party. Milovanović's publications also appeared in the Paris *Journal des débats* and *Le Temps*, in the Vienna *Die Zeit*, and in other periodicals. (AO)

Sources: *Enciklopedija Jugoslavije*, vol. 6 (Zagreb, 1965); *Biographisches Lexikon*, vol. 3; Dimitrije Djordjević, "Pašić i Milovanović u pregovorima za Balkanski savez," *Istoricki Časopis*, 1959, nos. 9–10; Dimitrije Djordjević, *Milovanović Milovan* (Belgrade, 1962); Wacław Felczak and Tadeusz Wasilewski, *Historia Jugosławii* (Wrocław, 1985).

MILUTINOVIĆ Milan (19 December 1942, Belgrade), Serb post-Communist politician. In 1965 Milutinović graduated in law from the University of Belgrade. During his studies he was active in the Communist student organization and became friends with **Slobodan Milošević**. Milutinović belonged to the Presidium of the Union of Yugoslav Youth (Savez Omladine Jugoslavije) and joined the League of Communists of Yugoslavia. In 1969–74 he sat on the sociopolitical council of the federal parliament, and from 1977 to 1982 he was secretary (minister) of education and science of the republic of Serbia. From 1983 to 1987 he was director of the National Library of Serbia; then he was head of the Department of Press, Culture, and Information of the Yugoslav Foreign Ministry, and from 1989 he was ambassador to Greece. In August 1995 Milutinović became the new Yugoslavia's minister of foreign affairs and held this position for three years. He was the main Yugoslav negotiator of the Dayton agreement of November 1995 that ended the war in Bosnia-Herzegovina. On 29 December 1997 Milutinović became president of Serbia, replacing Milošević, who became president of Yugoslavia.

From the beginning of February 1999 Milutinović took part in the talks in Rambouillet, where an agreement between Kosovo Albanians and Serbs was being worked out. When the Serbs rejected the draft agreement and when NATO started air raids on the new Yugoslavia (March–June 1999), Milutinović appealed for a stop to the bombing, but to no avail. In May 1999 The Hague International Tribunal for War Crimes in former Yugoslavia accused Milutinović of crimes against humanity during the Kosovo conflict. He was found co-responsible for the military operations of Serb forces terrorizing and expelling Albanians from their homes. In October 2000 Milutinović became deputy chairman of the Socialist Party of Serbia (Socialistička Partija Srbije). He resigned from this position in April 2001, when an investigation was started concerning his participation in the illegal purchase of a villa. Prime minister **Zoran Djindić** opposed handing Milutinović over to The Hague Tribunal as long as he held the office of Serbian president, but when his term was over in December 2002, Milutinović surrendered to the tribunal. (AO)

Sources: Richard Holbrooke, *To End a War* (New York, 1998); Bugajski; www.mfa.gov.yu/history/Ministri/MMilutinovic_s.html; www.un.org/icty/glance/milutinovic.html; www.fact-index.com/m/mi/milan_milutinovic.html.

MINÁČ Vladimír (10 August 1922, Klenovec–25 October 1996, Bratislava), Slovak writer. After graduating from high school in 1940, Mináč studied Slovak and German philology at Comenius University in Bratislava. He participated in the Slovak National Uprising. Arrested by the Gestapo in December 1944, he was imprisoned in concentration camps at Mauthausen and Dachau. After the liberation, Mináč worked as a journalist. From 1956 to 1967 he was a member of the presidium of the Czechoslovak Writers' Union. From 1974 to 1990 he was president of the cultural organization Slovenska Matica in Martin. From 1953 to 1989 he belonged to the Communist Party of Czechoslovakia (CPC); from 1968 to 1971 he was a member of the CPC Central Committee (CC), and from 1971 to 1989 he was a member of the CC of the Communist Party of Slovakia. Mináč served as a deputy to the National Assembly (1964–68), a deputy to the People's Chamber of the Federal Assembly (1969–71), and a deputy to the Slovak National Council (1971–90). After the Velvet Revolution of 1989 he was elected to the Federal Assembly on the ticket of the post-Communist Slovak Party of the Democratic Left (Strana Demokratickej L'avice). Mináč made his literary debut with the novel *Smrt' t'chodí po horách* (Death walks the mountains; 1948), in which he described his experiences during the Slovak National Uprising. In the novel *Včera a zajtra* (Yesterday and tomorrow; 1949) he depicted the fate of a hero after the war. His subsequent novel, *Modré vlny* (Blue waves; 1951), was a typical Socialist realist work. The trilogy *Generácia* (Generation) is considered his best work; it consists of the novels *Dlhý čas čakania* (The long waiting time; 1958), *Živí a mŕtví* (The quick and the dead; 1959), and *Zvony zvonia na deň* (The bells ring for the day; 1961). It is a synthesis of the transformations in the lives of the Slovaks in 1944–48. In his later works Mináč gave a literary account of the Stalinist period of "errors and distortions" but always stayed within the limits ordained by the authorities. After the collapse of communism, Mináč published several volumes of essays that were critical of the social and national transformations taking place in Slovakia after 1989, including *Sub tegmine* (Under the plum tree; 1992) and *Návraty k prevratu* (Returns to the coup; 1993). (PU)

Sources: *Encyklopedia slovenských spisovateľov*, vol. 2 (Bratislava, 1984); *Who's Who in the Socialist Countries of Europe*, vol. 2 (Munich, London, and Paris, 1989); *Kdo byl kdo v našich dějinach ve 20. stoleti*, vol. 1 (Prague, 1998); *Reprezentačný biografický lexikón Slovenska* (Martin, 1999); Július Noge, *Prozaik Vladimír Mináč* (Bratislava, 1962); *V košeli zo žihľavy: Biografické rozhovory Petra Holku s Vladimírom Mináčom* (Bratislava, 1999).

MINC Hilary (24 August 1905, Kazimierz on the Vistula–26 November 1974, Warsaw), Polish Communist activist. Minc came from a Jewish lower-middle-class family. While in a gymnasium, he joined the Union of Polish Socialist Youth. During his studies at Warsaw University, in 1922 he joined the Communist Workers' Party of Poland (Komunistyczna Partia Robotniczej Polski [KPRP]). Fearing arrest, he left for France, where he completed law and economic studies in Paris and Toulouse, and he also obtained a Ph.D. in economics. Minc joined the French Communist Party and organized numerous strikes; therefore in 1928 he was ordered to leave France. After his return to Poland he worked as an editor in the Central Statistical Office of Poland.

In September 1939 Minc was in Lwów (now Lviv), and in December 1939 he began lecturing in economics at the university in Samarkand. From 1943 he belonged to the leading organizers of the Union of Polish Patriots and the Bureau of Polish Communists in the USSR, and he was one of the political officers of the First Tadeusz Kościuszko Infantry Division. In August 1944 Minc became a member of the CC and Politburo of the Polish Workers' Party (Polska Partia Robotnicza [PPR]). From July to December 1944 he headed the Economic Office of the Polish Committee of National Liberation (Polski Komitet Wyzwolenia Narodowego [PKWN]), and from December 1944 to March 1947 he was trade minister in the Provisional Government and in the Provisional Polish Government of National Unity. As an advocate of Stalinist central planning, in February 1948 Minc brought about the resignation of **Czesław Bobrowski** from the Central Planning Office (CPO) and the dissolution of this office. In April 1949 he became head of the State Commission for Economic Planning, which was established in place of the CPO. Throughout this time Minc also presided over the Economic Committee of the Council of Ministers. From March 1947 to April 1949 he was minister of industry and trade. These posts enabled him to play a key role in the introduction of the command economy in Poland. At a congress in December 1948 at which the Polish United Workers' Party (Polska Zjednoczona Partia Robotnicza [PUWP]) was founded, Minc became a member of the party's Central Committee (CC), the Politburo, and the Secretariat of the CC, joining the party's top leadership. In April 1949 he also became deputy prime minister responsible for the economy—and mainly for the implementation of the Six-Year Plan (1949–55). Minc firmly supported accelerated industrialization and the collectivization of agriculture. In 1952, during a mounting anti-Semitic campaign in the USSR, Minc's position in the party leadership was shaken, but after Stalin's death his troubles were over.

In 1955 and 1956 Minc was closer to the Puławianie faction of the PUWP, but because of his leading role under Stalinism, he could not make himself credible as the advocate of a more moderate political line, especially since the policy of intense industrialization, which was associated with him, had brought catastrophic results: the supply and distribution of goods to the public had collapsed. During talks on **Władysław Gomułka**'s return to power, held by the Natolin faction (Natolińczycy) and the Puławianie faction after the events of June 1956 in Poznań, Minc's position was already hopeless, and his resignation was a precondition issued by Gomułka. At the beginning of October 1956 Minc was removed from the Politburo and soon dismissed as deputy prime minister. In the spring of 1957, the public prosecutor general, Andrzej Burda, presented the Politburo with charges against top functionaries of the Ministry of Public Security. He also proposed an inquiry against the top representatives of the Stalinist administration, including Minc. However, it was decided that these functionaries should bear "political responsibility" only. In 1957 Minc retired, and in March 1959 he left the CC of the PUWP. (WR)

Sources: Mołdawa; Marek Łatyński, *Nie paść na kolana* (Warsaw, 1987); Krystyna Kersten, *Narodziny systemu władzy: Polska 1943–1948* (Poznań, 1990); Marek Nadolski, *Komuniści wobec chłopów w Polsce 1941–1956* (Warsaw, 1993); Andrzej Jezierski and Cecylia Leszczyńska, *Dzieje gospodarcze Polski w zarysie do 1989 r.* (Warsaw, 1994).

MINDSZENTY József [originally Péhm] (29 March 1892, Csehimindszent, near Szombathely–6 May 1975, Vienna, Austria), cardinal, Primate of Hungary. Born into a peasant family, Mindszenty graduated from St. Norbert Gymnasium in Szombathely in 1902 and from a diocesan seminary in Szombathely in 1912. In 1915 he was ordained, and in January 1917 he became a religion teacher at a high school in Zalaegerszeg. During the revolution of 1918–19 Mindszenty helped to organize right-wing Christian movements in Zalaegerszeg, and because of this he was briefly detained in February 1919. In October 1919 he was appointed parish priest in Zalaegerszeg, becoming a dean in 1921. In 1927 he was made a bishop's representative in the diocesan district of Zala. In 1940 Prime Minister **Pál Teleki** entrusted Mindszenty with organizing the movement of the National Policy Service in the Transdanubian district. Its aim was to prevent an increase of Nazi influence among the German minority in Hungary. In March 1944 Pope Pius XII appointed Mindszenty bishop of Veszprém. On 31 October 1944, along with the bishops of Székesfehérvár and Győr and the abbot of the monastery in Pannonhalma, Mindszenty sent a memorandum in which the signatories called for an end to the fighting; the memorandum was addressed to **Ferenc Szálasi**, a Fascist leader and prime minister appointed on Hitler's orders. On 27 November, along with his clerics, Mindszenty was arrested by members of the Arrow Cross Party and was imprisoned in Sopronkőhida, where he was held until April 1945, when the Soviet troops entered Hungary.

On 5 September 1945 Pope Pius XII appointed Mindszenty archbishop of Esztergom, and in February 1946 he elevated him to cardinal. A conservative faithful to tradition, Mindszenty was critical of social and political changes in Hungary. An uncompromising anti-Communist and royalist, he opposed the increasing Communist influence. Because of this, a press campaign was launched against him. Subsequently, on 26 December 1948, he was arrested on charges including his opposition to the secularization of Roman Catholic schools in Hungary. During an investigation of the charges Mindszenty was repeatedly tortured. In February 1949 the People's Court in Budapest sentenced him to life imprisonment on trumped-up charges that included treason and currency smuggling. The UN General Assembly condemned this sentence in a special resolution. In July 1955, under an agreement between the government and the Episcopate, owing to his deteriorating health Mindszenty was transferred to the town of Felsőpetény, where he was kept under house arrest. It was there that he learned about the outbreak of the revolution in October 1956.

On 30 October 1956 Mindszenty was set free, and the following day, under an escort of a special unit of officers from an armored regiment, he arrived at the archbishop's palace on Castle Hill in Buda. Over the following days he received guests from Hungary and abroad and made statements to the press. On 1 November he was visited by **Zoltán Tildy** and **Pál Maléter**, who represented the government of **Imre Nagy**. On the evening of 3 November, in a radio address, Mindszenty exhorted the nation to restore internal and external order and to establish a multiparty society in the "spirit of the national culture" and based on "justly restricted private property." He firmly advocated that national unity be maintained, but he also appealed to the "inheritors of the fallen system" to bring the guilty to a "nonparty" court. He called for the restoration of freedom of worship and insisted that the Catholic Church's institutions and associations be restored to it. Because of the Soviet intervention, Mindszenty did not describe the uprising as a revolution but as a struggle for freedom.

After the second Soviet intervention, on 4 November 1956 Mindszenty took refuge in the U.S. Embassy in Budapest and was granted asylum there. In September 1971, under a tentative agreement among the Hungarian state, the U.S. government, and the Vatican, he could safely leave the embassy to go abroad. Mindszenty settled in Pazmaneum in Vienna. He considered that his task was to give moral support to the Hungarians in exile. Therefore, he traveled extensively and visited places where they lived. In early November 1973 Pope Paul VI asked that Mindszenty resign his position for the sake of the Church's policy of opening a dialogue with Communist countries. Mindszenty refused, and on 8 December the Pope announced that the position of archbishop of Esztergom, the Primate of Hungary, was vacant. Mindszenty's autobiography, *Emlékirataim* (My memoirs), came out in 1974 and was translated into English (*Memoirs*, 1974), German, and French. Mindszenty died in a charity hospital in Vienna. In accord with his wishes, he was buried in the basilica at Mariazell. In 1989 he was rehabilitated by the Hungarian authorities. On 4 May 1991 Mindszenty's ashes were brought to Hungary and reburied in the crypt of the basilica in Esztergom. (JT)

Sources: *Documents on the Mindszenty Case* (Budapest, 1949); Béla Fabian, *Cardinal Mindszenty: The Story of a Modern Martyr* (New York, 1949); László Várga, *Revision of the Sentence against Cardinal Mindszenty* (New York, 1955); George Schuster, *In Silence I Speak* (New York, 1956); József Közi-Horváth, *Cardinal Mindszenty: Confessor and Martyr of Our Time* (Chichester, 1979); József Török, *Mindszenty József emlékezete/szerkesztette* (Budapest, 1995); István Mészáros, *Ki volt Mindszenty? Cikkgy űjtemény 1944–1998* (Budapest, 1999); *A magyar forradalom és szabadságharc enciklopédiája*, CD-ROM (Budapest, 1999); *Nagy Képes Milleniumi Arcképcsarnok* (Budapest, 1999).

MINEV Iliya (5 February 1917, Saranbey [now Septemvri]–11 January 2000, Septemvri), Bulgarian dissident and political prisoner. While a high school student in Pazardzhik, Minev joined the nationalist legionnaire movement led by **Khristo Lukov** and criticized Marxist views. He graduated from a lycée in Plovdiv and subsequently studied industrial chemistry at the university in Toulouse, France. After returning to Bulgaria, he worked as an engineer. Arrested shortly after the coup of 9 September 1944, he was released after one year. In 1946 Minev was imprisoned again for his opposition activities. The public prosecutor demanded a death sentence for him, but he was condemned to twenty-five years in prison. After a short period of freedom, in 1975 he was sentenced again, initially to six years in prison, subsequently to eight. Minev served his sentence in Pazardzhik, Plovdiv, Stara Zagora, and other places. He spent around three years in solitary confinement and 480 days on hunger strikes. Released in 1983, he was kept under house arrest in Septemvri. Minev never compromised with the authorities, and in 1987 he sent a letter to President Ronald Reagan describing the violation of human rights in Bulgaria; as a result, he was arrested again. After he was released, in

January 1988 Minev founded the Independent Association for the Defense of Human Rights, the first anti-Communist organization in Bulgaria. The authorities reacted with repression and confiscated the archives of this association. Thanks to the broadcasts of Radio Free Europe, Minev's two-month hunger strike gained publicity; the authorities capitulated and gave back the archives. However, the security police managed to infiltrate the executive board of this association; as a result, Minev was removed from politics. In 1990 he visited the United States, where he was enthusiastically greeted by political émigrés. One of the longest-held political prisoners of the twentieth century, Minev spent a total of thirty-two years in prison. (WDj)

Sources: "Iliya Minev: In Memoriam," *Anti*, 14–20 January 2000; Ivan Dochev, *Shest desetiletiia borbi sreshtu komunizma za svobodna Bulgariya* (Sofia, 1998).

MINIĆ Miloš (28 August 1914, Preljina, near Čačak), Yugoslav Communist activist of Serb nationality. Minić graduated from a high school in Čačak and in 1938 in law from the University of Belgrade. As a student, from 1935 he was active in the Union of Communist Youth of Yugoslavia. In 1936 he joined the Communist Party of Yugoslavia. From 1939 he was a party functionary in Čačak and later in Kruševac. During World War II Minić fought in the Communist guerrilla movement in Western Serbia. From October 1944 he worked in the security apparatus in Belgrade. From March 1945 to 1950 Minić was chief prosecutor of Serbia and a military prosecutor of the Yugoslav People's Army. In this role he acted as the chief prosecutor in the trial of **Dragoljub (Draža) Mihailović**, who was sentenced to death and executed in 1946. In 1953 Minić entered the Federal Executive Council (Yugoslav government) and became a member of the Executive Council of the Serbian republic. In 1957–62 he was chairman of the Executive Council (prime minister) of the Serbian republic. In 1962 he returned to the Federal Executive Council of Yugoslavia, and in 1963–1965 he was its deputy chairman. Then until 1966 he headed the commission for socioeconomic and political affairs of the Central Committee (CC) of the League of Communists of Yugoslavia. From 1966 to 1967 he was deputy speaker of the federal assembly and chairman of one of its chambers, the Federal Council. In 1967–69 he was speaker of the Serb parliament, and from December 1972 to May 1978 he was deputy chairman of the Federal Executive Council and the federal secretary (minister) of foreign affairs. (AO)

Sources: *Enciklopedija Jugoslavije*, vol. 6 (Zagreb, 1965); Slobodan Stanković, *The End of the Tito Era: Yugoslavia's Dilemmas* (Stanford, 1981); www.mfa.gov.yu/History/ministri/MMinic_s.html.

MIRONAS Vladas (22 June 1880, Panemunis–1954, Vladimir), Lithuanian priest and political activist. In 1904, after graduating from the Theological Academy in St. Petersburg, Mironas took holy orders. An old school friend of **Antanas Smetona**, he became one of the main promoters of nationalism among the Lithuanian clergy. In 1910 Mironas became a parish priest at Valkininkai, and in 1914, a parish priest in Daugai. In 1917 he was elected to the Lithuanian Council (Lietuvos Taryba) and served as its vice-president. Mironas was one of the signatories of the declaration of Lithuanian independence of 16 February 1918. In 1926 he was elected to parliament on the ticket of the Nationalist Union, led by Smetona. After the coup d'état led by Smetona in December of that year, Mironas became one of Smetona's closest associates. In 1929 he became the chief chaplain of the army. On 24 March 1938, during a crisis brought about by a Polish ultimatum, Mironas was appointed prime minister and, against his convictions, he was forced to establish diplomatic relations with Poland. His government lasted until 28 March 1939, when Nazi Germany's occupation of the region of Klaipėda (Memel) led to another crisis. Arrested by the NKVD after the invasion by Red Army in June 1940, Mironas was released in June 1941, when the Germans seized Lithuania. He resumed his work in the parish of Daugai. After Lithuania was again incorporated into the Soviet Union, Mironas was arrested in 1947. He died in prison. (WR)

Sources: *EL*, vol. 3; Saulius Sužiedelis, *Historical Dictionary of Lithuania* (Lanham, Md., 1997); Aleksandras Merkelis, *Antanas Smetona* (New York, 1964).

MIRONESCU Gheorghe G. (28 January 1874, Vaslui–1953, Sighet), Romanian lawyer and politician. Mironescu studied philology at the university in Bucharest (1891–94) and later earned a doctorate in law in Paris (1899). In 1918 he became a professor at the School of Law of the University of Bucharest. During World War I he lived in exile in France and conducted propaganda in support of the unification of the Romanian territories. Mironescu was the author of numerous articles devoted to the issue of Romania's unification, and from 1917 to 1918 he edited the newspaper *La Roumanie* in Paris. After returning to Romania, he worked with the People's Party of General **Alexandru Averescu**. In 1926 he began to work with the National Peasant Party (NPP). Mironescu was a member of many cabinets, starting with the short-lived government of **Take Ionescu** (December 1921–January 1922). From 7 to 13 June 1930 Mironescu was an interim head of the cabinet and subsequently a minister in the government established by the NPP (10 October 1930–18 April 1931).

From 1928 to 1931 he was minister of foreign affairs; in 1932, minister of finance; from 1932 to 1933, deputy prime minister; in 1933, minister of interior; and in 1938, minister without portfolio. Mironescu had a good relationship with King **Charles II**, whose return to Romania Mironescu, as prime minister, had approved in 1930. As minister of foreign affairs, he strove to improve relations with Poland; his efforts were successful, and during a visit of the Polish foreign minister **August Zaleski** to Bucharest in late October 1929, a conciliation and arbitration treaty was signed. The two countries also agreed that they had "common aims and policy concepts." From 30 March 1938 until the fall of the royal government, Mironescu served as an adviser to Charles II. In 1939 he was elected a member of the Romanian Academy. Arrested by the Communists after World War II, he died in prison. Mironescu's publications include *Din istoria dreptului privat roman* (On the history of Romanian private law; 1896); *România faţa de războiul european* (Romania and the war in Europe; 1915); *Aperçus sur la question roumaine* (Comments on the Romanian question; 1919); *The Problem of Banat* (1919); *France et Roumanie* (1930); and *Conversiunea agricolă* (Conversion of agriculture; 1932). (FA/TD)

Sources: Ioan Scurtu, *Istoria Partidului Naţional Tărănesc 1926–1947* (Bucharest, 1994); *Historia dyplomacji polskiej*, vol. 4 (Warsaw, 1995); H. Bułhak, "Polska a Rumunia 1918–1939," in *Przyjaźnie i Antagonizmy: Stosunki z państwami sąsiednimi w latach 1918–1939* (Wrocław and Warsaw, 1977).

MIŠIĆ Živojin (July 1855, Struganik, near Valjevo–20 January 1921, Belgrade), chief of staff and de facto commander of the Serbian Army during World War I. The son of a peasant, from 1876 to 1878, while a student at a cadet school, Mišić fought in the Serbo-Turkish war. In 1885 he commanded a battalion fighting against the Bulgarians. He subsequently studied in Austria. In 1891 he began working for the general staff of the Serbian Army and simultaneously taught at the Military Academy in Belgrade. The revolt of 1903, which put **Peter Karadjordjević** on the throne, impeded Mišić's brilliant career. Because the new Serbian authorities did not trust him, he was forced to retire. As a result of the Bosnian crisis, Mišić returned to active service in 1909, assuming the position of deputy chief of staff. He was instrumental in the modernization of the Serbian Army, which proved its military worth during the Balkan Wars. After a victory over the Turks at Kumanovo in October 1912, Mišić was promoted to the rank of general. In July 1913 he contributed to the defeat of the Bulgarians at Bregalnica. In September 1913 he again transferred to the reserves.

With the outbreak of World War I, Mišić resumed his military service, becoming deputy to the chief of staff and commander-in-chief of the Serbian Army, General **Radomir Putnik**. Mišić was commander of the First Army during the retreat in November 1914 and during a counteroffensive in December 1914, when the Serbs drove the Austrians back to the Sava River and recaptured Belgrade. For his part in the struggle Mišić was promoted to marshal. In the fall of 1915 he tried to persuade the other commanders to start a counteroffensive, but in the face of a Bulgarian invasion he had to withdraw his troops over the mountains toward the Adriatic. During the winter retreat of the Serbian Army, carried out under harsh conditions and known as the "Serbian Golgotha" because of heavy losses among the civilian population that followed the army, Mišić became ill. After a convalescence in France, he returned to the front line in September 1916. At that time the Serbian Army was in a very difficult situation, as it had been driven back to the region of Salonika (Thessaloniki). Mišić led a counteroffensive, recapturing Monastir (now Bitola, Macedonia) and the Kajmakcalan region from the Bulgarians. On 1 January 1918 Mišić became chief of staff, and although Prince **Alexander Karadjordjević** was the formal commander-in-chief, it was Mišić who de facto commanded the Serbian Army. At that time he planned a campaign that, in his opinion, would defeat the Central Powers in the Balkans. He managed to convince Alexander and the French commanders that this campaign was necessary. On 15 September 1918 Mišić ordered the Serbian forces and the Entente troops, which were under his command, to launch an attack from Salonika to the north. The immediate successes of the "Salonika offensive" led to the capitulation of Bulgaria on 29 September and to the capture of Belgrade on 1 November of that year. At the time of the establishment of the Kingdom of Serbs, Croats, and Slovenes, in late 1918 Mišić deployed the Serbian troops in Macedonia and Kosovo, strengthening the Serbian positions in the southern part of the newly established kingdom. Mišić's *Moje uspomnene* (My memoirs) were published in 1978. (WR)

Sources: John Clinton Adams, *Flight in Winter* (Princeton, 1942); Alan Palmer, *The Gardeners of Salonika* (New York, 1965); Holger H. Herwig and Neil M. Heyman, *Biographical Dictionary of World War I* (Westport, Conn., 1982); Djordje Popović, *Vojevoda Živojin Misić i njegovi ratnici* (Niš, 1988).

MISIRKOV Krste (18 November 1874, Postol, near Grčka–26 February 1926, Sofia), Macedonian linguist and political writer. Misirkov studied in Sofia, Belgrade, and St. Petersburg, where he established the Macedonian Society. The organization lobbied for the autonomy of Ottoman Macedonia. As president of the Macedonian

Society, Misirkov contributed to several periodicals. He is best known for a book published in 1903, *Za Makedonskite raboti* (On Macedonian matters). In this work he argued for a Macedonian identity separate from that of the neighboring Slavic peoples. He suggested the creation of a Macedonian language based on four regional dialects. Misirkov and his associates became known as the Macedonianists (Makedontskite). A journalist and teacher, Misirkov is regarded as a central figure in the Macedonian national movement's hagiography. (DP)

Sources: *Enciklopedija Jugoslavije*, vol. 6 (Zagreb, 1965); Blazhe Ristovski, *Krste P. Misirkov*, 2 vols. (Skopje, 1974); Duncan M. Perry, *The Politics of Terror: The Macedonian Liberation Movements, 1873–1903* (Durham, N.C., 1988); Valentina Georgieva and Sasha Konechni, *Historical Dictionary of the Republic of Macedonia* (Lanham, Md., 1998).

MITROVICA Rexhep bey (1888, Mitrovicë–28 May 1967, Ankara), Albanian politician and journalist. Born into a Muslim land-owning family from Kosovo, Mitrovica finished secondary school in Skopje, where he became active in the Albanian national movement. He was one of the signatories of the declaration of independence proclaimed by the Albanian National Assembly in Vlorë on 28 November 1912. In 1921 Mitrovica was elected MP and joined the Popular Party (Partia Popullorë). In 1921 he became minister of education and held this post in subsequent cabinets until 1924. He established a network of schools throughout the country. As minister, he supported secular schools and state control over private education; this led to a conflict with the Catholic clergy. From 1924 on, after **Ahmed Zogu** came to power, Mitrovica lived mainly in Vienna and Paris. He was one of the founders of the National Union (Bashkimi Kombëtar). He returned to Albania in 1939, becoming one of the founders of the National Front (Balli Kombëtar) in 1942 and a co-founder of the Second League of Prizren in 1943. From 4 November 1943 to 18 July 1944, after the Italian occupation ended and the German Army marched into Albania, Mitrovica headed a collaborationist government that pledged, among other things, to pay for the stationing of German troops in Albania and for the calling up of around thirty thousand volunteers. The ever-stronger position of the Communist partisans and a mounting economic crisis undermined public trust in Mitrovica's government. According to Mitrovica, his cabinet resigned because it could not work with other government structures, including the Regency Council. In 1944 Mitrovica left the country and, via Italy, went to France. He spent the last years of his life in Turkey. (TC)

Sources: Michael Schmidt-Neke, *Enstehung und Ausbau der Konigsdiktatur in Albanien (1912–1939): Regierungsbildungen, Herrschaftsweisen und Machteliten in Einen Jungen Balkanstaat* (Munich, 1987); Bardhosh Gaçe, *Ata që shpallën Pavarësinë Kombëtare* (Tirana, 1997); *Dokumente te institucioneve gjermane per historine shqiptare 1941–1944* (Prishtina, 1998); Bernd J. Fischer, *Albania at War, 1939–1945* (London, 1999).

MITRYNGA Ivan, pseudonym "Serhiy Oreliuk" (1909, Bóbrka, Galicia, [now Bibrka, Ukraine]–6 September 1943, Vilia, Volhynia), Ukrainian journalist and nationalist activist. In the 1930s Mitrynga studied history in Lwów (Lviv) and joined the Organization of Ukrainian Nationalists (OUN). He worked with nationalist publishing houses and edited the paper *Het z bolshevyzmom* (1938). He was critical of the OUN's Fascist tendencies. He severed his relations with the OUN after the outbreak of the Soviet-German war in 1941. In the Pripet Marshes (Polesie) Mitrynga set up the Ukrainian Revolutionary Party of Workers and Peasants, which merged with a number of other groups to form the Ukrainian People's Democratic Party in 1942. He became aligned with the Polesian Sich and with the so-called First Ukrainian Insurgent Army under the command of Ataman **Taras Borovets** (Bulba). Mitrynga served as chief of the political and propaganda staff in the Polesian Sich. He was killed in a skirmish either with the Germans or with Soviet guerrillas. Mitrynga wrote a number of political pamphlets, including *Hitler i Ukraïna* (Hitler and the Ukraine; 1939) and *Nash shliakh borotby* (Our path of struggle; 1940). (GM)

Sources: *Encyclopedia of Ukraine*, vol. 3 (Toronto, 1993); Ryszard Torzecki, *Polacy i Ukraińcy: Sprawa ukraińska w czasie II wojny światowej na terenie II Rzeczypospolitej* (Warsaw, 1993); *Entsyklopediya Ukraiinoznavstva*, vol. 5 (Lviv, 1993).

MLADENOV Petur (22 August 1936, Urbabintsi [now Toshevtsi], near Vidin–31 May 2000, Sofia), Bulgarian Communist activist. Mladenov's father, a Communist activist, was killed in 1944, fighting as a deputy commander for political affairs in the Georgi Benkovski partisan unit. In 1949 Mladenov became a member of the Dimitrov Communist Youth League (DCYL), and in 1964, a member of the Bulgarian Communist Party (BCP). He completed studies at the Suvorov School in Sofia (1954) and subsequently studied philosophy at Sofia University. In 1963 Mladenov graduated from the Moscow State Institute of International Relations. After returning to Bulgaria, he became first secretary of the DCYL district committee in Vidin in 1964 and head of the International Relations Department of the Central Committee (CC) of the DCYL in 1966. From 1966 to 1969 Mladenov served as secretary of the DCYL CC. He continued his political career in the BCP and in the government. He was first secretary of the BCP District Committee in Vidin (1969–71), a member of the BCP CC (1971–90), and a deputy member (1974–77) and member (1977–90) of the BCP CC Politburo. Mladenov succeeded Ivan Bashev as foreign minister after the latter died tragically on Mount Vitosha. He served in this position from December 1971 to November 1989, in the governments of **Stanko Todorov**, **Grisha Filipov**, and **Georgi Atanasov**. He also was a deputy to the National Assembly (1971–90).

Mladenov was the leader of the activists who, with the support of Mikhail Gorbachev, engineered a bloodless overthrow of **Todor Zhivkov**. In an open letter of 24 October 1989 addressed to BCP CC Politburo members, Mladenov accused Zhivkov of deepening the crisis in Bulgaria. When Zhivkov was removed from power (10 November 1989), Mladenov became secretary general of the BCP CC (until 2 February 1990) and chairman of the Council of State (17 December 1989–3 April 1990). He was also appointed chairman of the Constitutional Commission of the National Assembly. At the Fourteenth Extraordinary Congress of the BCP (January–February 1990) Mladenov was elected to the Supreme Party Council (1 February–25 September 1990) and designated chairman (president) of Bulgaria. Following an agreement reached in round table negotiations, on 3 April 1990 the parliament appointed Mladenov president and commander-in-chief of the armed forces. On 6 July 1990 Mladenov resigned these positions under the pressure of student demonstrations sparked off by Mladenov's words: "Tanks had better be used here" (*Pro-dobre e tankovete da doidat*), uttered on 14 December 1989 to protesters around the National Assembly building. For several months Mladenov unsuccessfully attempted to deny that he had said those words. His resignation ended his political career. Mladenov's publications include *Zhivotut: Plusove i minusi* (Life: Pluses and minuses; 1992). (JJ)

Sources: *Entsiklopediya Bulgariya*, vol. 4 (Sofia, 1984); *Narodni predstaviteli ot Deveto narodno subranie* (Sofia, 1987); Raymond Detrez, *Historical Dictionary of Bulgaria* (Lanham, Md., 1997); Tasho Tashev, *Ministrite na Bulgariya 1879–1999: Entsiklopedichen Spravochnik* (Sofia, 1999); Evgeniya Kalinova and Iskra Baeva, *Bulgarskite prekhodi 1944–1999* (Sofia, 2000); Angel Tsurakov, *Entsiklopediya. Pravitelstvata na Bulgariia: Khronologiya na politicheskiia zhivot 1879–2001* (Sofia, 2001).

MLADIĆ Ratko (12 March 1943, Kalinovnik, Bosnia-Herzegovina), Bosnian Serb general accused of war crimes. Mladić's father was a partisan in the Communist guerrilla army of **Josip Broz Tito** and was killed while fighting the Croatian Ustashe in 1945. Mladić graduated from the Higher Officers' School with distinction and made a quick career in the army. He commanded armored units in Mace-

donia and Kosovo, advancing to the rank of general. In 1991 he commanded the Ninth Corps of the Yugoslav People's Army in Knin in Croatia. Under his command, after half a year's siege, the Serb troops captured Vukovar. When the war broke out in Bosnia in 1992, **Slobodan Milošević** appointed him commander-in-chief of the Yugoslav Army in this republic. Soon Mladić transformed his units into an army of the self-appointed Serb Republic of Bosnia. Supported by Milošević and **Radovan Karadžić**, Mladić strove to create an "ethnically clean" Serbian state in Bosnia in order to merge it with Serbia and other Serb-dominated territories of the former Yugoslavia. In the summer of 1992 troops commanded by Mladić controlled about 70 percent of the territory of Bosnia-Herzegovina.

Mladić represented extreme nationalism. Compared to him, Bosnian Serbs considered Karadžić a moderate. Mladić enjoyed a high profile among his fanatic soldiers. He called himself a "Balkan Napoleon," while for the Croats, Muslims, and the Western media he was the "butcher of Bosnia." In May 1994 Mladić's daughter, Anna, committed suicide in protest against the massacre of Muslims at Goražde, which had been ordered by Mladić. After the NATO air raids started in 1995 and after Bosnian Serbs began to lose the struggle with the Muslim and Croatian forces, Karadžić accused Mladić of tactical errors and recalled him from command in August 1995; however, under pressure from the officer corps he had to change his mind, and he reinstalled Mladić. After the signing of the agreements of Dayton (21 November 1995) and Paris (14 December 1995), Mladić withdrew from public sight. In December 1996, under Western pressure, **Biljana Plavšić**, who succeeded Karadžić as president of the Serb Republic of Bosnia (which joined the Bosnia-Herzegovina federation), dismissed Mladić from command. In 1995 Mladić was twice accused by The Hague Tribunal for War Crimes in Former Yugoslavia of committing genocide and crimes against humanity. Along with Karadžić, Mladić is held responsible for the siege of Sarajevo (April 1992–May 1995); for the murder of about six thousand Muslims in Srebrenica (July 1995); for rape; for holding thousands of Bosnian Croats and Muslims in concentration camps; and for using UN peacekeeping troops as "live shields" against NATO air raids (May–June 1995). Mladić has continued to live in hiding. (AO)

Sources: Lenard J. Cohen, *The Disintegration of Yugoslavia* (Boulder, Colo., 1993); Edgar O'Ballance, *Civil War in Bosnia, 1992–94* (New York, 1995); Laura Silber and Allan Little, *The Death of Yugoslavia* (London, 1995); Warren Zimmermann, *Origins of a Catastrophe* (New York and Toronto, 1996), Richard Holbrooke, *To End a War* (New York, 1998); David Owen, *Balkan Odyssey* (New York, 1995); International Criminal Tribunal for the Former Yugoslavia, www.un.org/icty/indictment.

MLYNÁŘ Zdeněk (22 June 1930, Vysoké Mýto–15 April 1997, Vienna), Czech lawyer, political scientist, and Communist activist. In 1946 Mlynář became a member of the Communist Party of Czechoslovakia (CPC). In 1950–55 he studied in the law department of Lomonosov University in Moscow, where he met (among others) Mikhail Gorbachev. Between 1956 and 1964 Mlynář worked in the Institute of State and Law of the Czechoslovak Academy of Sciences in Prague; from 1963 he was an assistant professor in the Department of Law of Charles University. He wrote many works on the Marxist theory of politics. From 1964 to 1968 Mlynář was secretary of the law committee of the Central Committee (CC) of the CPC, and during the Prague Spring he joined the top leadership of the party. In 1968–69 he was a member of the CC, and between 4 April and 16 November 1968 he was secretary of the CC of the CPC. Mlynář was one of the main representatives of the reformist current; he developed the political part of the CPC's Program of Action, which was passed in April 1968. After the Warsaw Pact invasion, in August Mlynář took part in talks with Soviet leaders in Moscow. In November 1968 he was recalled from his prominent posts for "deviations from the political line of the party"; in September 1969 he was excluded from the CC of the CPC, and in 1970 he was expelled from the party.

In 1970–77 Mlynář worked in the entomological department of the National Museum in Prague. As one of the initiators and first signatories of Charter 77 in January 1977, he was dismissed from work and remained under house arrest until June 1977. He then emigrated to Austria. From 1982 to 1989 Mlynář was president of the Austrian Institute of International Politics in Luxembourg. In 1989 he became a professor of political science at the University of Innsbruck. Mlynář researched the events of the Prague Spring and became an international authority on the crisis of the Communist political systems and on perestroika. In 1989 he returned to Czechoslovakia but did not play a major role in the political transformations after the Velvet Revolution. In the parliamentary elections of 1996 Mlynář was honorary leader of the Leftist Bloc (Levy Blok), and after its electoral failure he resigned from this post owing to health problems. Mlynář became famous for his works *Československý pokus o reformu 1968* (The Czechoslovak reform attempt, 1968; 1975); *Krise sovětského systému a Západ* (The crisis of the Soviet system and the West; 1986); and the memoirs *Mráz přichází z Kremla* (1978; *Nightfrost in Prague: The End of Humane Socialism*, 1980). (PU)

Sources: *ČBS*; *Kdo byl kdo v našich dějinách ve 20. století*, vol. 1 (Prague, 1998); Gordon H. Skilling, *Czechoslovakia's Interrupted Revolution* (Princeton, 1976); Vladimir V. Kusin,

From Dubcek to Charter 77: A Study of "Normalization" in Czechoslovakia 1968–1978 (New York, 1978); Vilém Precan, ed., *Charta 77 (1977–1989): Od morální k demokratické revoluci; dokumentace* (Bratislava, 1990); Alexander Dubcek, *Hope Dies Last* (New York, 1993).

MŁYNARSKI Feliks (20 November 1884, Gniewczyn, near Przeworsk–13 April 1972, Kraków), Polish economist and politician. Młynarski was the son of an organist. Expelled from a gymnasium in Jarosław for taking part in a pro-independence organization, he passed his high school final examinations with distinction as an extramural student in Sanok in 1903 and began studying philosophy at the Jagiellonian University in Kraków. In the same year he became a member of the Union of Polish Youth called Zet, and in 1907, a member of the secret National League. An opponent of the pro-Russian orientation in the league, in 1908–9 Młynarski was one of the organizers of Fronda and one of the initiators of the withdrawal of Zet from the National League. In 1910 Młynarski became one of the leaders of the secret, academic Independence League. He subsequently helped to establish the Polish Riflemen Squads and then served as their chairman (1913–14). From 1911 to 1912 he took part in the establishment of the Provisional Commission of Confederated Independence Parties and became one of its leaders. In 1911, under the pseudonym "Jan Brzoza," Młynarski published the brochure *Zagadnienie polityki niepodległości* (On the pro-independence policy). After the outbreak of World War I, Młynarski joined the Polish Legions but was assigned to the Military Department of the Supreme National Committee and sent to the United States, where he failed to gain broad support from the Polish émigré community for the cause of independence. After returning to Poland, Młynarski dealt with economic issues and published several brochures, including *Siła nabywcza pieniądza* (The purchasing power of money; 1918).

In November 1918 Młynarski began working at the Ministry of Labor and Social Welfare. In the autumn of 1922 he joined the National Workers' Party. In April 1923 the minister of the treasury, **Władysław Grabski**, hired him as director of a department in his ministry. Młynarski became one of Grabski's closest aides and held similar views on the currency and treasury reform. After Grabski left the government, Młynarski also resigned, but when Grabski became prime minister, he appointed Młynarski vice-chairman of the Bank of Poland in August 1924. From 1925 to 1927 Młynarski negotiated a stabilization loan in the United States and Great Britain. Although an agreement about the loan was reached in October 1927, Młynarski was not treated favorably by the ruling camp after May 1926. After his term ended in 1929, he left the bank and began lecturing at the Warsaw School of Economics (Szkoła Główna Handlowa [SGH]) and became a professor there in 1933. He was also a member of several supervisory boards of banks and companies. As a result of his growing reputation as a financial expert and the author of *Gold and the Central Bank* (1929), Młynarski became a member of the Financial Commission of the League of Nations in 1929 and held this position from 1929 to 1937. At the end of the 1930s Młynarski drifted to the opposition Morges Front. At that time he published *Proporcjonalizm ekonomiczny* (Economic proportionalism; 1937) and *Totalitaryzm czy demokracja w Polsce?* (Totalitarianism or democracy in Poland? 1938).

At the end of October 1939 Młynarski prepared a plan for the establishment of a new banking institution for the part of Nazi-occupied Poland known as the General Gouvernement. As a result, the German authorities offered him the post of chairman of the Bank of Issue in Poland, based in Kraków. In order to enhance the credibility of the new currency, the Germans agreed to make an exception and include the word "Poland' in the name of the bank. After extensive consultations with the Polish independence underground, Młynarski accepted this offer and in January 1940 assumed the post of chairman of the bank. He had to constantly maneuver between pressure from the Nazi authorities and Polish interests, but his work was positively assessed by subsequent delegates of the Polish Government-in-Exile for the Homeland. The Polish złotys issued by the bank were colloquially called *młynarki*, after Młynarski.

After the war, Młynarski declared his willingness to work in the new political environment, but instead he was accused of collaboration. However, witnesses unanimously defended him against the accusations, and an investigation into the case was discontinued in November 1946. Młynarski lectured at the Academy of Commerce and the School of Law of the Jagiellonian University in Kraków but was dismissed in 1951. He became the director of the library of the School of Economics in Kraków, and in 1961 he retired. After the war, Młynarski wrote several works but published only *Pieniądz i gospodarstwo pieniężne* (Money and the monetary economy; 1947) and *Wspomnienia* (Memoirs; 1971), which were a short version of memoirs kept in the Jagiellonian Library in Kraków. (WR)

Sources: *PSB*, vol. 21; Zbigniew Landau, *Plan stabilizacyjny 1927–1930* (Warsaw, 1963); Czesław Madajczyk, *Polityka III Rzeszy w okupowanej Polsce* (Warsaw, 1970); Zygmunt Karpiński, *O Wielkopolsce, złocie i dalekich podróżach* (Warsaw, 1971); Zbigniew Landau, "Feliks Młynarski (1884–1972): Zarys życia i działalności na polu finansów," *Finanse*, 1973, no. 11.

MŇAČKO Ladislav (28 January 1919, Valašské Klobouky, Zlín district–24 February 1994, Bratislava), Slovak journalist and writer of Czech origin. From his childhood Mňačko lived in Slovakia, where his father worked in the government administration. He attended high school in Turčiansky Svätý Martin. During World War II Mňačko attempted to escape abroad and join the Czechoslovak Army but was arrested by the German police; for two years he was imprisoned in the concentration camp of Hunswinckel and sent to forced labor in a coal mine. Mňačko escaped from there to Moravia and fought in partisan units (1944–45). At the end of the war he was seriously injured. After the war he devoted himself to journalism. He was the editor of the Communist daily *Rudé Právo* (1945–48) and of the Bratislava *Pravda* (until 1954); subsequently he became a freelance journalist. In 1956 and 1964 Mňačko briefly served as editor-in-chief of the Slovak weekly *Kultúrny život*, which was instrumental in the liberalization process in the 1960s. Initially an ardent supporter of communism and a prominent journalist of the regime, from the 1950s Mňačko was increasingly critical of the Communist reality. In the autobiographical book *Smrt' sa volá Engelchen* (1959; *Death Is Called Engelchen*, 1961) he depicted the partisan struggle at the end of World War II. In *Kde končia prašné cesty* (Where dusty roads end; 1962) and *Oneskorené reportáže* (1963; Overdue reports; 1963), which sold several thousand copies, Mňačko dealt with the lawlessness of the Stalinist period. In the novel *Ako chutí moc* (1958; *The Taste of Power*, 1967) he exposed the regime's mechanisms.

In August 1967 Mňačko emigrated to Israel in protest against Czechoslovakia's position on the Arab-Israeli War; as a result, he was deprived of his Czechoslovak citizenship. He returned home in May 1968, but in August 1968, after the Warsaw Pact invasion of Czechoslovakia, he again left his country and settled in Austria. There he wrote two political essays, *Agresoři* (Aggressors; published in German in 1968) and *Siedma noc* (1990; *The Seventh Night*, 1969), and eight novels, of which *Súdruh Münchhausen* (Comrade Münchhausen; 1972) became the most famous. This book, a grotesque allegory of the Communist regime, was the first Slovak book published by Index, an émigré publishing house. Mňačko also authored a number of radio and television programs, mainly produced in Austria and West Germany. In 1990 he returned to Bratislava and protested the separatist aspirations of Slovakia. After the disintegration of the federation, Mňačko moved to Prague. (PU)

Sources: *ČBS*; *Kdo byl kdo v našich dějinách ve 20. století*, vol. 1 (Prague, 1998); *Reprezentačný biografický lexikón Slovenska* (Martin, 1999); H. Gordon Skilling, *Czechoslovakia's Interrupted Revolution* (Princeton, 1976).

MOCSONY-STÂRCEA Ion (16 May 1909, Cernâuţi), Romanian politician and political prisoner. Mocsony-Stârcea came from a landowner's family. In 1932 he graduated in modern languages from Cambridge University and started working in the Romanian Foreign Ministry. From April to August 1942 he was private secretary to King **Michael I** and head of his chancellery, and from 4 November 1944, his majordomo. Mocsony-Stârcea was an eye witness to the coup of 23 August 1944. He worked in the Foreign Ministry until the Communist purge of March 1945. On 6 August 1947 he was arrested on his estate of Bulci in the Banat region and forced to testify in the trial of **Iuliu Maniu** and his aides. In this trial Mocsony-Stârcea himself was sentenced to two years in prison. He served in Craiova Prison from December 1947 to October 1949. Soon he was accused again and imprisoned in Timişoara (November 1949–September 1950). In May 1950 he was taken by the political police, Securitate, and brutally interrogated (he lost all his teeth) in connection with the case of **Lucreţiu Pătrăşcanu**. From March 1952 Mocsony-Stârcea was held in the intelligence interrogation center until Pătrăşcanu's trial in April 1954, in which he was sentenced to fifteen years of hard labor. He served the sentence in Aiud, Jilava, Piteşti, and Dej. In October 1961 the minister of interior, **Alexandru Drăghici**, offered him a deal: in exchange for a written record of the coup of 23 August 1944, his imprisonment would be changed to house arrest. Mocsony-Stârcea agreed. In November 1962 he was brought to Câmpulung-Muscel, where he wrote a text that he had to correct several times to make it useful in the power game of the Communist leadership. After two years Mocsony-Stârcea was allowed to leave for Switzerland. (ASK)

Sources: Dennis Deletant, *Communist Terror in Romania: Gheorghiu-Dej and the Police State, 1948–1965* (New York, 1999).

MOCZAR Mieczysław [originally Nikolay Demko] (23 December 1913, Łódź–1 November 1986, Warsaw), Communist activist in Poland. Moczar was the son of a peasant of Belorussian origin who served in the tsarist army. His family belonged to the poor class in Łódź, and his father was an activist in the Communist Party of Poland (Komunistyczna Partia Polski [KPP]). Moczar finished primary school and a course in locksmithing. In 1937 he became a member of the KPP. Until the outbreak of World War II he was an active member of the International Organization for Aid to Revolutionaries, and because of this he was sentenced to two years' imprisonment. From 1939 to 1941 he was in the Soviet territories and entered into cooperation with Soviet security services. After the

outbreak of the German-Soviet war in June 1941, Moczar made his way to Łódź, where he helped to establish a conspiratorial organization called the Front of Struggle for Our Freedom and Yours (Front Walki za Naszą i Waszą Wolność). In March 1942 Moczar became a member of the (Communist) Polish Workers' Party (Polska Partia Robotnicza [PPR]), as a representative of which he established the seed of the Communist underground. He became commander of the Fifth District of the People's Guard (Gwardia Ludowa [GL]) and commander of the GL in Łódź. In April 1943 the GL High Command appointed him commander of the Lublin district, but after a conflict with Leon Kasman, who had been sent from Moscow, the PPR authorities transferred Moczar to the Kielce region. In April 1944 Moczar became commander of the Kielce district of the People's Army (Armia Ludowa). From January 1945 to May 1948 he was head of the Provincial Public Security Office in Łódź. In 1946 he was promoted to brigadier general. At that time he became known as a cruel persecutor of independence activists. From May to September 1948 Moczar was undersecretary of state in the Ministry of Public Security, and from August 1944 to December 1948 he was a member of the PPR Central Committee (CC). Until 1948 he was seen as **Władysław Gomułka**'s man. During the campaign against so-called rightist-nationalist deviation and after the establishment of the (Communist) Polish United Workers' Party (Polska Zjednoczona Partia Robotnicza; [PUWP]) in December 1948, Moczar dissociated himself from Gomułka and from his former allies. At that time, in a letter to the PUWP leadership, he declared that his—and every true party member's—homeland was the Soviet Union.

Moczar's declarations of loyalty to the PUWP leaders and to the Kremlin allowed him to keep his position in the power hierarchy. In December 1948 he became a deputy member of the PUWP CC. Transferred to the post of chairman of the Provincial National Council in Białystok and in 1952 to the Provincial National Council in Olsztyn, he became deputy chairman of the Warsaw Provincial National Council in 1954. In April 1956 Prime Minister **Józef Cyrankiewicz** appointed him minister for state farms. At the Seventh PUWP CC Plenum in July 1956 Moczar attacked Stalinist party leaders and became a member of the PUWP CC. At the Eighth Plenum he supported Gomułka's return to the position of first secretary of the CC and the election of Gomułka's closest associates to the Politburo. Appointed undersecretary of state in the Ministry of Interior in December 1956, Moczar became the minister of interior in December 1964. He held this post until July 1968, when he became secretary of the CC responsible for the police and internal armed forces. Promoted to major general in 1963, Moczar became chairman of the Main Board of the influential Association of Fighters for Freedom and Democracy (Związek Bojowników o Wolność i Demokrację [ZBoWiD]) in September 1964. He held this position until 1972. In 1963 he published *Barwy walki* (The colors of war), probably edited by someone else. Thanks to official propaganda, this book had a total of thirteen printings.

In the 1960s Moczar was the leader of the so-called partisan group in the PUWP ranks. This group promoted an anti-intellectual and anti-Semitic ideology. At the same time, by using patriotic phraseology and appealing to the common experiences of soldiers, Moczar wooed former Home Army soldiers. Moczar was the author of a peculiar chauvinist rhetoric and the main director of an anti-Zionist campaign after the Six-Day War of 1967. The demonstration of power in March 1968 by the Ministry of Interior, which Moczar headed, was seen as a kind of anti-Gomułka putsch, but it is not clear what Moczar's ultimate aims were. In any case, Moscow did not approve of his nationalist rhetoric. In July 1968 Moczar became a deputy member, and in December 1970 a member, of the PUWP CC Politburo. From 1957 to 1980 he was an MP in the Assembly of the Polish People's Republic.

During the events of December 1970 Moczar called for the use of force to suppress worker riots. The fall of Gomułka and the advent of **Edward Gierek** and his team repositioned Moczar as a contender for the party leadership. In mid-April 1971, preempting Moczar's intentions, Gierek dismissed him as head of the police and internal armed forces; therefore, at the end of May of that year Moczar attempted to organize his supporters in Olsztyn. On 25 June 1971 at the Tenth CC Plenum, Gierek successfully counteracted, ousting Moczar from the CC Secretariat. At the Sixth PUWP Congress in December 1971 Moczar left the Politburo and assumed the post of chairman of the Supreme Chamber of Control, a less important role at that time. In 1972 he also lost the post of chairman of the ZBoWiD. Until the events of August 1980 he clearly remained on the political sidelines, although as chairman of the Supreme Chamber of Control, he carefully compiled a dossier on the economic embezzlements committed by top officials of the Gierek administration. The fall of Gierek and a new first secretary of the CC in September 1980 allowed Moczar to again become a top party official. In December 1980 he returned to the PUWP CC Politburo, and in November 1980 he again assumed leadership of the ZBoWiD. He took part in the preparations for the Ninth Extraordinary Congress of the PUWP. Although he supported **Stanisław Kania** and tried to

exploit the Solidarity movement, at the Ninth Congress Moczar did not even join the CC; this meant the end of his career. During the period of martial law he was successively dismissed from all his positions. In March 1983 he ceased to serve as chairman of the Supreme Chamber of Control and was forced to resign as chairman of the ZBoWiD. In July 1983 he also resigned as vice-president of the All-Polish Committee of the National Unity Front. He was offered the post of ambassador to Yugoslavia, but he rejected this offer. Moczar allowed information from the archives he had compiled in the Supreme Chamber of Control to be published, but this did not help him to return to a top position. (WD/WR)

Sources: Mołdawa; Jakub Karpiński, *Countdown: The Polish Upheavals of 1956, 1968, 1970, 1976, 1980* (New York, 1982); Jerzy Eisler, *Marzec 1968* (Warsaw, 1991); Krzysztof Lesiakowski, *Mieczysław Moczar "Mietek": Biografia polityczna* (Warsaw, 1998); Włodzimierz Janowski and Aleksander Kochański, *Informator o strukturze i obsadzie personalnej centralnego aparatu PZPR 1948–1990* (Warsaw, 2000); Jerzy Eisler, *Grudzień 1970* (Warsaw, 2000); Dariusz Stola, *Kampania antysyjonistyczna w Polsce 1967–1968* (Warsaw, 2000); Marcin Zaremba, *Komunizm, legitymizacja, nacjonalizm: Nacjonalistyczna legitymizacja władzy komunistycznej w Polsce* (Warsaw, 2001).

MOCZARSKI Kazimierz, pseudonyms "Rafał" and "Grawer" (21 July 1907, Warsaw–27 September 1975, Warsaw), Polish politician. The son of a teacher, after graduating from a high school in Warsaw, Moczarski received a diploma from the Department of Law of Warsaw University in 1932 and subsequently studied at the School of Journalism in Warsaw and at the Institut des Hautes Etudes Internationales in Paris. While a student, he did his military service (1931–32) and completed consular training in the Polish Consulate in Paris. In 1935 Moczarski began working as a counselor at the Ministry of Labor and Social Welfare. In 1937 in Warsaw he helped to establish the Democratic Club, and subsequently he was an activist in the Democratic Party (Stronnictwo Demokratyczne [SD]). A participant in the September 1939 campaign, Moczarski fought in the defense of Warsaw and in other battles. During the German occupation he took part in SD underground activities and worked for the Information and Propaganda Bureau (Biuro Informacji i Propagandy [BIP]) of the High Command of the Union of Armed Struggle and then the Home Army (Armia Krajowa [AK]). In November 1943 Moczarski joined the Command of the Underground Struggle, and in May 1944 he became deputy head of the Command of the Underground Struggle for Warsaw. He considerably contributed to the combating of traitors and Gestapo informers. During the Warsaw Uprising Moczarski was in charge of telegraphic communication for the AK High Command and was the editor-in-chief of *Wiadomości Powstańcze*. In mid-October 1944 he became head of the revived BIP apparatus. He was a co-author of a proclamation in mid-July 1945 calling on AK soldiers to take up civilian work, as well as an order in a similar spirit issued on 24 July 1945 by Colonel Jan Rzepecki, head of the Delegation of Armed Forces for the Homeland (Delegatura Sił Zbrojnych na Kraj).

Arrested on 11 August 1945 by the (Communist) State Security Office, Moczarski was sentenced to ten years' imprisonment in January 1946. Under an amnesty in February 1947 his sentence was commuted to five years' imprisonment. At the end of his term, despite appeals by his colleagues from the SD, Moczar was not released. While still serving the sentence, he was subjected to a cruel investigation, the aim of which was to extort testimony against members of the Polish wartime pro-independence underground to incriminate them as collaborators with the Germans. Moczarski described the methods of torture in "List z Centralnego Więzienia w Sztumie" (A letter from the Central Prison in Sztum, *Kultura*, 1980, no. 53). Although he did not admit to the absurd charges, on 18 November 1952 Moczarski was sentenced to death. After he had waited for his execution for nearly a year, in October 1953 the Supreme Court commuted his death sentence to life in prison. Released during the "thaw" in April 1956 and rehabilitated in December 1956, Moczarski resumed work in the SD. From 1961 to 1965 he was a member of the SD Chief Council and worked on the editorial staff of *Kurier Polski*. For many years he was an activist in the Community Temperance Committee, and, along with Jan Górski, he published *Alkohol w kulturze i obyczaju* (Alcohol in culture and customs; 1972). Moczarski became famous as the author of the memoirs *Rozmowy z katem* (1978, *Conversations with an Executioner*, 1981), first published in the periodical *Odra* (1972–74) and in 1977, posthumously, as a book. It was an account of Moczarski's nine-month stay with Jürgen Stroop, annihilator of the Warsaw Ghetto, in one cell of Mokotów Prison. The book, repeatedly republished and translated into many languages, presented a psychological picture of a Nazi war criminal and at the same time—from a psychological perspective—depicted the tragic fate of soldiers of the Polish wartime pro-independence underground. This account also exposed the cruelties of the Stalinist period, which treated a Nazi criminal guilty of genocide and a Polish fighter for independence in the same way. (WR)

Sources: Kunert, vol. 1; *Kurier Polski*, 1975, no. 205; Władysław Bartoszewski and Aleksander Gieysztor, "Rafał," *Tygodnik Powszechny*, 1976, no. 41; Grzegorz Mazur, *Biuro Informacji i Propagandy SZP-ZWZ-AK* (Warsaw, 1987).

MOCZULSKI Leszek (7 June 1930, Warsaw), Polish journalist, dissident, and politician. Moczulski graduated from the Academy of Political Science in 1951 and in law from the University of Warsaw in 1952. A member of the (Communist) Polish Workers' Party and (in 1948–50) of the Polish United Workers' Party (Polska Zjednoczona Partia Robotnicza [PUWP]), Moczulski worked for the dailies *Trybuna Ludu* (1950) and *Życie Warszawy* (1950–53) and the weeklies *Wieś* (1953) and *Dookoła Świata* (1955–59). In 1958 he was accused of having contacts with the Western press, but he was acquitted. Later he worked for the weekly *Stolica* (1961–77), where he published a lot on the history of interwar Poland and World War II. Moczulski kept in touch with officers of the prewar Polish Army and the wartime Home Army. His first books were *Dylematy: Wstęp do historii Europy Zachodniej 1945–1970* (Dilemmas: Introduction to the history of Western Europe, 1945–1970; 1971) and *Wojna polska* (The Polish war; 1972) on the September 1939 campaign. The latter book was withdrawn from bookstores for political reasons. In 1976 Moczulski was the major author of the "Program of 44" and a "Memorial" to the Communist authorities suggesting systemic change. The co-initiator of a secret organization, the Independence Current (Nurt Niepodległościowy), on 26 March 1977 Moczulski co-organized the open Movement for the Defense of Human and Civic Rights (Ruch Obrony Praw Człowieka i Obywatela [ROPCiO]) and became one of its spokesmen. He edited the uncensored periodical *Opinia* (1977–78). In the summer of 1978, after a split in the ROPCiO, Moczulski took the lead of one of its splinter groups, and he edited the periodical *Droga*, where he published his political program, "Rewolucja bez rewolucji" (Revolution without revolution).

On 1 September 1979 Moczulski co-founded the Confederation for Independent Poland (Konfederacja Polski Niepodległej [KPN]), a political party with a pro-independence and anti-Communist program; it referred to the tradition of **Józef Piłsudski** and was critical of other opposition groups, the Committee for Social Self-Defense–KOR in particular. Moczulski was the KPN chairman. His arrest in September 1980 and his trial, which started in June 1981, played an important role in the extension of the KPN's influence. In October 1982 Moczulski was sentenced to seven years in prison. Amnestied in 1984, he resumed his KPN activities. Arrested again in March 1985, in April 1986 he was sentenced to four years in prison. Moczulski went abroad for medical treatment and established contacts with political émigrés. Upon his return to Poland in 1987, he continued his activities. In 1989 he opposed the Round Table Talks and a compromise with the Communists. In the elections of June 1989 the

KPN ran on its own but failed to win any parliamentary seats. In 1990 Moczulski ran for the presidency but gained only 2.5 percent of the vote. Before the elections of October 1991, the KPN advocated de-Communization and protested the decline of the standard of living, winning 8.9 percent of the vote. Moczulski became head of the KPN parliamentary club. In his speeches he sharply attacked post-Communist MPs, recalling the crimes of the Communist system; he demanded a scrutiny of top state personnel, and he criticized liberal economic reforms. He advocated rapprochement with NATO and the Ukraine. In June 1992 Moczulski's name was mentioned by minister of interior **Antoni Macierewicz** as being among former Communist informers. Moczulski tried to clear his reputation, but his trial went on for years without a resolution. In the elections of 1993 the KPN won 5.8 percent of the vote. Moczulski remained its chairman, but his leadership was questioned and the party lost support. In 1994 and 1996 the party split, and he was marginalized. Moczulski authored a number of works, including the following: *Trzecia Rzeczpospolita: Zarys ustroju politycznego* (The Polish Third Republic: Outline of the political system; 1984); an extensive interview, *Bez wahania* (Without hesitation; 1993); *Geopolityka* (Geopolitics; 1999); and *Lustracja: Rzecz o teraźniejszości i przeszłości* (Lustration: On the present and the past; 2001). (AF)

Sources: Mołdawa; *Opozycja w PRL: Słownik biograficzny 1956–89*, vol. 1 (Warsaw, 2000); Janusz A. Majcherek, *Pierwsza dekada III Rzeczypospolitej 1989–1999* (Warsaw, 1999); Antoni Dudek, *Pierwsze lata III Rzeczpospolitej 1989–2001* (Kraków, 2002).

MODZELEWSKI Karol (23 November 1937, Moscow), Polish historian and politician. The naturalized son of the Communist activist Zygmunt Modzelewski (1900–54), Modzelewski graduated in history from Warsaw University (Uniwersytet Warszawski [UW]) in 1959; he received a Ph.D. in 1974, a postdoctoral degree in 1978, and a professorship at the Polish Academy of Sciences in 1990 and at UW in 1994. A member of the (Communist) Union of Polish Youth from 1950, in 1956 Modzelewski was active in a reform youth movement at UW, worked with the Żerań Factory workers' council, and co-founded the Revolutionary Youth Union; in 1957–64 he belonged to the Union of Socialist Youth and the Polish United Workers' Party (Polska Zjednoczona Partia Robotnicza [PUWP]). An assistant professor at the UW History Department (1959–64), in 1962 he co-founded a discussion club that was dissolved by the authorities in 1963. In 1964–65, along with **Jacek Kuroń**, Modzelewski prepared an "Open Letter to PUWP Members," in which they pointed to the

divergence between Communist ideas and practice. In March 1965 Modzelewski was arrested and sentenced to three and a half years of imprisonment. The "Open Letter" was translated into many languages and gained wide publicity in the West. In 1967 Modzelewski was released. He took part in student protests against the ban of Adam Mickiewicz's play *Dziady* (Forefathers) at the Warsaw National Theater. Arrested on 8 March 1968, Modzelewski was again sentenced to three and a half years in prison.

Released in 1971, in 1972–83 Modzelewski worked at the Institute of Material Culture of the Polish Academy of Sciences in Wrocław. In the fall of 1976 he wrote a "Letter to Citizen E. Gierek," in which he appealed to the authorities to stop the repression that followed the June 1976 workers' protests, and he pointed to the necessity for political and economic reform. From September 1980 Modzelewski was one of the new trade union leaders in Wrocław. He took part in the founding conference of new trade union delegates on 17 September 1980 in Gdańsk, where he suggested an all-national organization and the name "Solidarity." A spokesman for the Solidarity National Coordination Commission (9 November 1980–1 April 1981) and a member of the National Commission elected during the Solidarity congress in September 1981, Modzelewski belonged to its radical wing, criticizing the style of **Lech Wałęsa** and favoring the creation of a mixed system, combining social self-organization with the leading role of the Communist Party on the national level, a proposal that was meant as a shield against Soviet intervention. After the introduction of martial law, on 13 December 1981 Modzelewski was interned, and in 1982 he was arrested on account of an alleged attempt to overthrow the political system. Amnestied in 1984, he returned to scholarly work. In 1989–91 he was a senator of the Civic Parliamentary Club (Obywatelski Klub Parlamentarny [OKP]). Critical of the **Leszek Balcerowicz** reforms, which he thought would destroy national industries and impoverish wide circles of society, Modzelewski favored state intervention and a more gradual systemic reform. In November 1989 he co-founded the Group for the Defense of Workers' Rights, and in 1990, the parliamentary club Solidarity of Labor, which left the OKP in 1991. In June 1992 Modzelewski co-founded the Union of Labor (Unia Pracy [UP]) and was its honorary chairman from 1992 to 1995. He left the UP when the party failed to support Kuroń for president. Modzelewski headed Kuroń's electoral committee, and after Kuroń lost the presidential election, Modzelewski withdrew from political life. Modzelewski authored a number of historical works on the Middle Ages, such as *Chłopi w monarchii wczesnopiastowskiej* (Peasants in the early Piast monarchy; 1987), and on current politics, such as *Dokąd od komunizmu* (From communism, where? 1993). (AF)

Sources: *Nasi w Sejmie i Senacie* (Warsaw, 1990); Andrzej Friszke, *Opozycja polityczna w PRL 1945–1980* (London, 1994); Jan Skórzyński, *Ugoda i rewolucja: Władza i opozycja 1985–1989* (Warsaw, 1995); Janusz A. Majcherek, *Pierwsza dekada III Rzeczpospolitej 1989–1999* (Warsaw, 1999); Antoni Dudek, *Pierwsze lata III Rzeczpospolitej 1989–2001* (Kraków, 2002).

MOISIU Spiro (3 May 1900, Kavajë–12 April 1981, Tirana), Albanian officer and Communist activist. Born into an Orthodox family, Moisiu was related to the famous actor Aleksandër Moisiu. He attended a Greek school in Kavajë, and in 1912 he went to an Albanian school in the same town. From 1914 to 1918 he continued his education at a military school in Austria. After returning to Albania, he joined the gendarmerie. In 1920 he was commissioned at the lowest rank of officer and assigned to a unit that guarded the sessions of the national congress in Lushnjë. As an adjutant to the chief of staff, Moisiu took part in battles against the Serbs in the region of Martanesh in 1921 and subsequently helped to suppress an uprising of the Catholic Mirdytes. In 1923 he served in the garrison in Tirana; from there he was sent to the newly formed Albanian Army. Although Moisiu had taken part in the 1924 revolution, after the victory of **Ahmed Zogu**, he remained in the army. He commanded a battalion, except in 1935, when he was briefly in charge of the Management of Prisons. In 1938 he was promoted to major. During the Italian invasion in April 1939 Moisiu commanded a battalion in the border region of Shkodër-Shengjin and did not resist the invaders. In the same year he joined the Albanian units established by the Italians and assumed command of the Tommorri battalion, which was part of the Italian Venice division and subsequently of the Ninth Army. Moisiu was arrested by the Italians for refusing to obey an order in November 1940 and sentenced to death for deserting the battlefield. However, the sentence was not carried out, and at the end of 1941 he was released from prison and ejected from the army.

At that point Moisiu moved to Lushnjë and ran a shop there. In October 1942 he assumed command of the local structures of the National Liberation Front and began to form his own partisan unit, which joined the Communist units of **Enver Hoxha**. Regarded as one of the best organizers of the partisan units, Moisiu became the chief of the General Staff of the National Liberation Army in July 1943. Promoted to general in May 1944, he served as chief of staff until 1946, when he retired.

Summoned by Hoxha, Moisiu resumed military service after Albania severed relations with Yugoslavia in 1948, becoming chief of the Tirana garrison. He served in the army until 1965. From 1945 to 1980 Moisiu was repeatedly elected to parliament and was a member of its presidium. From 1945 to 1964 he served as chairman of the Association for Aid to the Army and Defense of the Homeland (Shoqëria në Ndihme të Ushtrisë e Mbrojtjes [SHNUM]), an all-national paramilitary organization that was instrumental in the system of totalitarian control in Albania. In 1963 this organization consisted of 170,000 members. (TC)

Sources: *Fjalori Enciklopedik Shqiptar* (Tirana, 1985); Klaus-Detlev Grothusen, ed., *Albania* (Göttingen, 1993); Titani Gjergji and Hasani Proleter, *Personalitete ushtarake shqiptare në vite 1912–1997*, vol. 1 (Tirana, 1997); Vangjel Kasapi, *General Spiro Moisiu* (Tirana, 2000).

MOJSOV Lazar (19 December 1920, Negotino, Macedonia), Macedonian Communist activist. Mojsov earned a doctoral degree in law at the University of Belgrade. He served as a partisan during World War II and was a member of the Anti-Fascist Assembly of the People's Liberation of Macedonia (Antifašističko vijeće narodnog oslobodenja Makedonije [ASNOM]). From 1948 to 1951, Mojsov was Macedonia's public prosecutor, and in 1953 he was elected president of the Supreme Court. He served as a member of the Assembly of the Republic of Macedonia from 1948 to 1951. He was elected to the Yugoslav Federal Assembly four times between 1945 and 1958 and in 1964 and 1967. Mojsov was a practicing attorney in the Yugoslav Socialist Republic of Macedonia between 1953 and 1958 and served as the director and editor-in-chief of *Nova Makedonija*, Macedonia's chief daily newspaper at the time. In 1962–66, he was director and editor-in-chief of *Borba*, a leading Yugoslav newspaper published in Belgrade. Mojsov was appointed Yugoslav ambassador to the USSR and Mongolia from 1958 to 1961, and he again became an ambassador between 1967 and 1969, serving this time in Austria as Yugoslavia's representative on the International Atomic Energy Association. From 1969 to 1974, he was Yugoslavia's permanent representative at the United Nations. Between 1974 and 1978, Mojsov served as deputy federal secretary for foreign affairs, and he became the president of the thirty-second session of the UN General Assembly in 1977. From 1958 a member of the Central Committee and later a member of the presidency of the Central Committee of the League of Yugoslav Communists, Mojsov published on foreign affairs and history. Among other works, he authored *Bulgarska radnichka partija (komunista) i makedonsko nacionalno* *pitanje* (The Bulgarian Workers' Party [Communists] and the Macedonian national question; 1948) and *Macedonian Historical Themes* (1979). (DP)

Sources: *Enciklopedija Jugoslavije*, vol. 6 (Zagreb, 1965).

MOLNÁR Ferenc (12 January 1878, Budapest–2 April 1952, New York City), Hungarian playwright, writer, and journalist. After completing law studies in Geneva and Budapest, Molnár began working as a journalist and soon won readers with his style and ironic humor. At the same time he began writing novellas and soon afterward novels as well; these included themes and characters from the middle-class life of Budapest. In 1902 Molnár made his debut as a playwright with *A doktor úr* (The attorney-at-law). His later dramas and comedies were full of lyricism and irony; they include *Józsi* (1904); *Az ördög* (1907; *The Devil*, 1908); and particularly *Liliom* (1909; *Liliom: A Legend in Seven Scenes and a Prologue*, 1921), which depicts the Budapest demimonde; *A testőr* (1910; *Guardsman*, 1924) resembled the writings of Luigi Pirandello. These plays were frequently staged and were enormously popular both in Hungary and abroad. Molnár gained his greatest fame as the author of *A Pál utcai fiúk* (1907; *Paul Street Boys*, 1927), a novel for youth that was translated and adapted for film many times; it became part of the canon of world juvenile fiction as a work that exalted in a simple yet intense way the superiority of human reason and will over force and ruthlessness. During World War I Molnár was mostly engaged in short story writing, including fictionalized war reports. After the war he resumed writing plays in the style of the bourgeois burlesque or symbolic drama. From 1930 onward Molnár lived in France, Switzerland, and the United States. Although he visited Hungary only occasionally, many of his plays written at that time were still set in the realities of his homeland, particularly of Budapest. In 1950 Molnár published the autobiographical novel *Companion in Exile*. (MS)

Sources: *Új magyar irodalmi lexikon* (Budapest, 2000); Elisabeth M. Rajec, *Ferenc Molnár: Bibliography* (Vienna, Cologne, and Graz, 1986); István Várkonyi, *Ferenc Molnar and the Austro-Hungarian "Fin de Siecle"* (New York, 1991); Joel A. Smith, *The Romantic Comedy of Ferenc Molnar* (Louisville, Ky., 1995); Mátyás Sárközi, *Színház az egész világ: Molnár Ferenc regényes élete* (Budapest, 1995); Steven Bela Vardy, *Historical Dictionary of Hungary* (Lanham, Md., 1997).

MORACZEWSKI Jędrzej Edward (13 January 1870, Trzemeszno–5 August 1944, Sulejówek), Polish Socialist and pro-independence activist. While a high school student, Moraczewski was a member of a secret patriotic self-education group. From 1888 to 1894 he studied in the Department of Engineering at the Technical University of Lemberg (Lwów, Lviv). He was also a member of, and from 1892 the leader of, a secret pro-independence group in Lemberg. In 1894 Moraczewski joined the Galician Social Democratic Party, which in 1897 changed its name to the Polish Social Democratic Party of Galicia and Silesia (Polska Partia Socjalno-Demokratyczna Galicji i Śląska Cieszyńskiego [PPSD]). Moraczewski worked as an editor of the Lemberg biweekly *Życie* and as a clerk in the Road Office in Lemberg. From 1894 to 1895 he did voluntary military service and then took part in the construction of state railways in Galicia, Dalmatia, and other places. In 1899 he became an activist in the Adam Mickiewicz People's University Society. In 1907 he joined the PPSD board and became an MP on its behalf in the Austrian parliament. From 1907 to 1918 Moraczewski belonged to the Association of Socialist MPs. In 1912 he became affiliated with the riflemen movement of **Józef Piłsudski**. In August 1914, as a private, Moraczewski joined the First Brigade of the Polish Legions, and in September 1914, as a lieutenant, he served in the commissariat in Kielce, at the headquarters of the Legions. Later he was assigned to the Chief National Committee. In January 1916 he took part in the military operations of the First Brigade in Volhynia, and from July 1916 he served in a sapper company in Modlin. In May 1917 he was detained for his pro-independence activities. After the oath crisis of July 1917, Moraczewski became one of the leaders of the Polish Military Organization (Polska Organizacja Wojskowa [POW]). He also joined the Convention of Organization A (Konwent Organizacji A), where he was in charge of political activities. In October 1918 he became a member of the presidium of the Polish Liquidation Commission (Polska Komisja Likwidacyjna) in Kraków and subsequently a member of the presidium of its successor, the Governing Commission, in Lwów. He was also head of its supplies department. On 7 November 1918 Moraczewski assumed the portfolio of minister of post and communication in the Provisional Government of the Republic of Poland in Lublin.

On 18 November 1918, after Piłsudski's return to Warsaw, Moraczewski became prime minister and minister of communications. He was one of Piłsudski's close associates. Despite the difficult conditions, Moraczewski's government managed, among other things, to introduce an eight-hour workday; set minimum wages and establish social insurance; and introduce an electoral law providing for universal, equal, and direct suffrage, voting by secret ballot, and proportional representation. However, Moraczewski was attacked by various political groups, particularly the National Democrats. After the failure of an attempted coup d'état on 4–5 January 1919, staged by a group of rightist activists (who held Moraczewski captive for some time), Moraczewski resigned, along with the entire government, on 16 January. In the January 1919 elections he was elected to the Constituent Assembly, where he served as deputy speaker and chairman of the Union of Polish Socialist Deputies. At the unification congress of the Polish Socialist Party (Polska Partia Socjalistyczna [PPS]) in April 1919 Moraczewski became a member of the Supreme Council (1919–26) and the Central Executive Committee (1919–23) of the party. Moraczewski fought in the Polish-Soviet war. From 1922 to 1927 he was an MP and served as deputy speaker of the Assembly and deputy chairman of the PPS parliamentary club. From 1920 to 1922 he was deputy chairman of the Railway Workers' Trade Union, and from November 1925 to February 1926, minister of public works.

Moraczewski took an active part in the coup of May 1926, organizing a strike of railway workers and the occupation of the Warsaw East railway station, thus preventing the pro-government troops from moving into the capital. From October 1926 to December 1929 he again served as minister of public works. As the PPS joined the opposition to Piłsudski, Moraczewski resigned his membership in the PPS Supreme Council in November 1926 and was subsequently expelled from the PPS. In January 1927 he resigned his parliamentary seat. In 1928–30 he contributed to the periodical *Przedświt*, defending his views and the policies of Piłsudski. In October 1928 he joined the PPS–Former Revolutionary Faction, which supported Piłsudski. After the failure of this group in the elections of November 1930, Moraczewski was elected chairman of the Central Association of Class Trade Unions, and in May 1931, chairman of the Central Trade Department of the Association of Trade Unions (Centralny Wydział Zawodowy Związku Związków Zawodowych), which was established as a result of a merger of pro-government trade union organizations. He was also an editor of *Front Robotniczy*. Moraczewski's views gradually evolved from social solidarity to syndicalism and statism. In September 1939 in Sulejówek Moraczewski organized a citizens' committee for aid to war victims. He was critical of the activities of General **Władysław Sikorski**. Moraczewski was killed in warfare. His publications include the following: *Polityka polska a uwięzienie Piłsudskiego* (Polish politics and the imprisonment of Piłsudski; 1918); *Projekt rozwiązania trudności gospodarczych w Polsce* (A plan for solving the economic difficulties in Poland; 1932); *Strajk, bojkot, lokaut* (Strike, boycott, lockout; 1933); *Rozważania nad położeniem politycznym i gospodarczym Polski* (Deliberations on the political and economic situation of Poland; 1938); and (under the initials E. K.) the memoirs *Przewrót w Polsce; Część I: Rządy ludowe* (Coup in Poland; Part 1: People's rule; 1919). (JS)

Sources: *PSB*, vol. 21; *Prezydenci i premierzy Drugiej Rzeczypospolitej* (Wrocław, Warsaw, and Kraków, 1992); *Encyklopedia historii Drugiej Rzeczypospolitej* (Warsaw, 1999); *Encyklopedia Historii Polski: Dzieje polityczne*, vol. 1 (Warsaw, 1994); Jerzy Holzer, *Polska Partia Socjalistyczna w latach 1917–1919* (Warsaw, 1962); Seweryn Ajzner, *Związek Związków Zawodowych 1931–1939* (Warsaw, 1979); Władysław Pobóg-Malinowski, *Najnowsza historia polityczna Polski 1864–1945*, vol. 2 (London, 1983).

MORAVČÍK Jozef (13 March 1945, Očová, Zvolen region), Slovak lawyer and politician. In 1963–68 Moravčík studied law at the universities in Prague and Bratislava, and then he worked as an assistant professor at the Higher Economic School in Bratislava and in the Bratislava branch of the Chemapol enterprise. In 1972–85 he was assistant professor, then associate professor and chair of economic law in the School of Law at the University of Bratislava; in 1990–91 he became dean of the school. The author and co-author of numerous scholarly works and textbooks in economic law, in 1990–92 Moravčík was a member of the Slovak National Council on behalf of the Public against Violence (Verejnost' t'proti Nasiliu [VPN]). After its dissolution, he was active in the Movement for a Democratic Slovakia (Hnutie za Demokratické Slovensko [HZDS]). From June to December 1992 Moravčík was a member of the Chamber of the People of the Federal Assembly, and from July to December 1992, minister of foreign affairs of the last Czechoslovak government. After the emergence of independent Slovakia, he was adviser to the prime minister for legislative affairs, and from March 1993 to February 1994 he was minister of foreign affairs.

In early 1994 Moravčík entered into a sharp conflict with the HZDS chairman and prime minister, **Vladimír Mečiar**. In February 1994, along with Roman Kováč, Moravčík organized a faction called the Alternative for Political Realism, and then he was expelled from the HZDS. As a result, the ruling coalition lost its parliamentary majority, Mečiar's government collapsed, and Moravčík became the new prime minister. He held this position from 16 March to 13 December 1994, when the HZDS won early elections and Mečiar resumed power as prime minister. In April 1994 Moravčík co-founded the Democratic Union of Slovakia, soon renamed the Democratic Union (Demokratická Únia [DU]), which won almost 9 percent of the vote in the elections of September–October 1994 and remained in the opposition. From April 1994 to March 1997 Moravčík was the DU chairman, and in 1994–98 he was an MP. In 1996 he introduced the DU into a coalition aiming at the removal of Mečiar from power after the elections of 1998. In March

1997 Moravčík resigned from chairing the DU, remaining head of its Program Council. He grew skeptical about the Slovak Democratic Coalition (Slovenská Demokratická Koalicie [SDK]), and he did not join it before the elections of September 1998. From December 1998 Moravčík was mayor of Bratislava. (PU)

Sources: *ČBS*; *Slovensko 1996: Súhrnná správa o stave spoločnosti* (Bratislava, 1997); *Slovensko 1997: Súhrnná správa o stave spoločnosti* (Bratislava, 1998); *Slovensko 1998–1999: Súhrnná správa o stave spoločnosti* (Bratislava, 1999).

MORAVEC Emanuel (17 April 1893, Prague–5 May 1945, Prague), Czech officer, military theorist, and politician. In 1912 Moravec graduated from the School of Mechanical Engineering in Prague. During World War I, as a cadet in the Austro-Hungarian Army, he fought on the Galician front and was taken prisoner by the Russians in 1915. He joined the Czechoslovak Legions and fought in Siberia. In 1920 he returned to Czechoslovakia and served on the staff of the district army command in Užhorod (now Uzhhorod, Ukraine) and later, until 1927, in Prague. From 1927 to 1931 he commanded battalions in Znojmo and Humenné. In 1923 Moravec graduated from the Military College in Prague, and in 1931 he became a lecturer in the history of the armed forces and strategy at this college. In the same year he began working at the General Staff. In 1933 he was promoted to colonel, and in 1936 he took command of a regiment in Prague. One of the main Czech military theorists, Moravec dealt with the sociological aspects of war, the psychology of soldiers, and the influence of politics on Czechoslovakia's defense doctrine and strategy; he devoted two books to these issues: *Vojáci a doba* (Soldiers and time; 1934) and *Obrana státu* (Defense of the state; 1935). Moravec contributed military-political commentaries to *Lidové noviny* and *Přítomnost*, mainly under the pseudonym "Stanislav Yester." In the 1930s Moravec became more active in politics. He had close links with a political group called Hrad (Castle), led by President **Tomáš Garrigue Masaryk**, but he already started showing leanings toward authoritarianism.

In September 1938 Moravec commanded a regiment in south Moravia and firmly opposed Czechoslovakia's capitulation to the Munich agreement. On 28 September 1938 he went to Prague and demanded a meeting with President **Edvard Beneš**, which he was granted. He wanted to persuade the president to defend the country at all costs. After the Munich Pact, Moravec radically changed his views and in 1939 entered into cooperation with the Germans. He believed that collaboration was the only possible solution for the Czech nation under the circumstances and expressed his views in many articles, radio broadcasts, and books. Moravec became a fanatical supporter of Nazism and was in opposition to the government of **Alois Eliaš**. After Eliaš was imprisoned and then executed and when President **Emil Hácha** reluctantly agreed to Moravec's candidacy for a ministerial position, in 1942 Moravec became minister of education in the government of the Protectorate of Bohemia and Moravia; he held this post until May 1945, promoting a model of upbringing of youth in the Nazi spirit. In May 1942 Moravec established a Fascist organization called the Board of Trustees for the Education of Youth (Kuratorium pro Výchovu Mládeže). Moravec was one of the most hated dignitaries in the country and the personification and symbol of collaboration. He committed suicide after the outbreak of the Prague Uprising. (PU)

Sources: *ČBS*; *Českoslovenští politici: 1918–1991* (Prague, 1991); *Politická elita meziválečného Československa 1918–1938: Kdo byl kdo za první republiky* (Prague, 1998); *Kdo byl kdo v našich dějinách ve 20. století*, vol. 1 (Prague, 1998); Vojtech Masny, *The Czechs under Nazi Rule* (New York and London, 1971); Jiří Pernes, *Až na dno zrady: Emanuel Moravec* (Prague, 1997).

MORAVEC František (23 July 1895, Čáslav–26 July 1966, Washington, D.C.), general, chief of Czechoslovak intelligence. Moravec studied at Charles University in Prague. After the outbreak of World War I, he was inducted into the Austro-Hungarian Army and fought on the Russian front. In 1915 he went over to the Russian side and joined the Czechoslovak Legions, with which he fought against the Bolsheviks in Siberia. In 1919 he joined the Czechoslovak Army, which operated on the Slovak front against the Hungarian Red Army. In 1929 Moravec graduated from the Military College in Prague. He subsequently served in a division in Plzeň and in the information department of the military district in Prague. In 1934 he became chief of the Second Department (Intelligence) of the General Staff, and in 1936 he was promoted to colonel. Because Czechoslovakia was at the center of activities of various intelligence networks, the majority of Moravec's work was based on counterintelligence. In this work he showed great professionalism and had good results; for example, he accurately predicted the aggressive steps of the Third Reich. During a visit to Moscow in 1938 Moravec signed an agreement on the exchange of information with the Soviet services.

On 14 March 1939, shortly before the German invasion, along with eleven of his closest associates, Moravec went to London; from there he directed the intelligence of the Czechoslovak government-in-exile. His reports constituted an important contribution by Czechoslovakia to the Allied cause. For example, as early as March 1941

Moravec informed President **Edvard Beneš** about German plans to attack the Soviet Union. For this reason and also because of the information he provided to the Allies, Moravec figured on a list of people to be arrested after the German invasion of the British Isles. In May 1942, with the help of two of his agents, Jan Kubiš and Josef Gabčík, Moravec organized the successful assassination of Reinhard Heydrich, head of the Reich Central Security Office (*Reichssicherheitshauptamt*). Both assassins were soon hunted down and killed by the Germans. A few weeks later, as part of the reprisals for Heydrich's assassination, almost all the inhabitants of the Czech village of Lidice were executed, and the village itself was razed to the ground. In 1944 Moravec became general. In May 1945 he returned to Czechoslovakia, becoming chief of military intelligence of the republic. After the Communist coup of February 1948, fearing for his life, Moravec fled to the West and was granted political asylum in the United States. He also served as adviser to the U.S. Defense Department. In 1975 his interesting memoirs, *Master of Spies: The Memoirs of General František Moravec*, were published in the United States. In 1990 they were published in the Czech Republic under the title *Špion, jemuz neverili* (A spy who was not believed). (WR)

Sources: *ČBS*; Eduard Beneš, *From Munich to a New War and New Victory* (London, 1954); Charles Whitting, *The Spymasters* (New York, 1976); Jiři Solo, *Ve službách prezidenta: Generál František Moravec ve světle archívních dokumenů* (Prague, 1994); John Waller, *The Unseen War in Europe: Espionage and Conspiracy in the Second World War* (New York, 1996).

MORAWSKI Jerzy (11 August 1918, Warsaw), Polish Communist activist. Born into a laborer's family, Morawski studied at Warsaw University. During World War II he was active in the Communist underground. From 1942 he belonged to the Polish Workers' Party (Polska Partia Robotnicza [PPR]), and he edited its periodicals, *Trybuna Wolności* and *Walka Młodych*. In 1944–45 Morawski belonged to the Secretariat of the Central Committee (CC) of the PPR for the German-occupied territories, and then he became chairman of the Union of Youth Struggle. In 1945–48 he was its deputy chairman, and until 1949 he was deputy chairman of the (Communist) Union of Polish Youth (Związek Młodzieży Polskiej [ZMP]). In 1949–50 he was secretary of the ZMP Main Board. From 1945 to 1947 Morawski was a member of the National Home Council, and then, until 1965, an MP. From December 1948 he was a deputy member, and from March 1954 a member, of the CC of the Polish United Workers' Party (Polska Zjednoczona Partia Robotnicza [PUWP]). In 1950–52 he was secretary of the PUWP Provincial Com-

mittee in Poznań; until 1953 he was deputy head of the Department of Mass Propaganda of the PUWP CC; and then he was deputy head and (from 1954) head of the Department of Propaganda and Agitation of the PUWP CC. During the "thaw," in January 1955 he became CC secretary, and from May to July 1956 he was editor-in-chief of the CC daily, *Trybuna Ludu*. In 1956 Morawski radically changed his mind on the subject of **Władysław Gomułka**'s return to power. Initially he sharply criticized Gomułka, and then he supported the former PPR leader. In October 1956 Morawski played an important role as one of the "young secretaries" (along with **Władysław Matwin**) connected with the Puławska faction. From October 1956 Morawski was a Politburo member. From December 1956 (when he left the CC Secretariat) to March 1957 he chaired the CC Commission for Youth Problems, and from May 1957 he was CC secretary again. Morawski left the CC Politburo and Secretariat in January 1960, after Colonel Paweł Monat, connected with the Puławska faction, fled to the West. In 1957–61 Morawski chaired the parliamentary Foreign Affairs Commission. From 1959 to 1963 he was deputy chairman of the Supreme Chamber of Control. During the Fourth PUWP Congress in June 1964 Morawski was dropped from the CC; this meant not only the end of his party career, but also the elimination of the influence of the Puławska people. In 1964–69 Morawski was ambassador to London, and after returning to Poland he worked at the Institute of International Affairs and in journalism. (PK)

Sources: Mołdawa; Włodzimierz Janowski and Aleksander Kochański, *Informator o strukturze i obsadzie personalnej centralnego aparatu PZPR 1948–1990* (Warsaw, 2000); Antoni Czubiński, *Dzieje Najnowsze Polski 1944–1989* (Poznań, 1992); Andrzej Albert [Wojciech Roszkowski], *Najnowsza historia Polski 1914–1993*, vol. 2 (Warsaw, 1995).

MÓRICZ Zsigmond (29 June 1879, Tiszacsécse–5 September 1942, Budapest), Hungarian writer and journalist. Móricz's father was a peasant, and his mother was the daughter of a Calvinist pastor. He studied in elite Calvinist high schools in Debrecen, Sárospatak, and Kisújszállási. In 1899 he began to study theology, law, and philosophy at the university in Debrecen, and later in Budapest, but he did not pass his final exams. At the same time he also worked as a journalist. Móricz gained literary recognition as the author of *Hét krajcár* (1909; *Seven Pennies and Other Short Stories*, 1988) and *Tragédia* (Tragedy; 1910), two volumes naturalistically depicting rural life in Hungary, and *Sári bíró* (Judge Sári), a comedy staged in 1909. In the novels *Sárarany* (Gold in the mire; 1910), *Az Isten háta mögött* (A winter behind God's back; 1911), and

A fáklya (1917; *Torch*, 1931) he also depicted the everyday life of villages and small towns and the futile efforts of the Hungarian intelligentsia to spread education. Thanks to his friendship with **Endre Ady**, Móricz started writing for the biweekly *Nyugat* and became one of the leading contributors to this periodical, which played the most important role for Hungarian literature in the first half of the twentieth century.

During World War I Móricz worked as a war correspondent. In his reports and stories he emphasized the drama of a man forced into fighting and killing. He welcomed the republican revolution in Hungary (1918–19). Under the Hungarian Soviet Republic (HSR) in 1919 Móricz was a member of the Directorate of Writers and the author of articles and reports supporting the parceling out of large estates and the establishment of collective farms (kolkhozes). After the fall of the HSR, Móricz had problems getting his works published. Following the suicide of his first wife in 1925, he married the actress Mária Simonyi (1926–37), who played many parts in his dramas. After a period of fascination with the revolution, Móricz became a supporter of educational and economic development and gradual reforms. This attitude was reflected in *Erdély* (Transylvania; 1922–35), a historical trilogy depicting the harmony of social life, the development of culture, and the strength of a well-governed country, as illustrated by seventeenth-century Transylvania. The novels *Légy jó mindhalálig* (1920; *Be Faithful unto Death*, 1969) and *Pillangó* (Butterfly; 1925)—written in a different mood—praise the beauty of love and faithfulness. In 1929, along with **Mihály Babits** and Oszkár Gellért, Móricz assumed the editorship of *Nyugat*. In the 1930s he was drawn to the so-called peasant writers' movement, believing it was a panacea to the increasing popularity of fascism. After becoming the editor-in-chief of *Kelet Népe* (1939), Móricz drew peasant writers to this periodical. At that time he published *Életem regénye* (The story of my life; 1939), which included autobiographical elements, and *Rózsa Sándor* (1941–42), a two-volume historical novel based on the events of the Springtime of Nations in Hungary. Owing to his mastery in the use of elements of expressionism, naturalism, and realism, Móricz is considered one of the greatest Hungarian prose writers of the twentieth century. (MS)

Sources: Tamás Kiss, *Igy élt Móricz Zsigmond* (Budapest, 1979); Imre Bori, *Móricz Zsigmond prózája* (Újvidék, 1982); Károly Rádics, *Móricz Zsigmond a Nyugat szerkesztője* (Nyíregyháza, 1989); Mihaly Czine, *Móricz Zsigmond* (Debrecen, 1992); Steven Bela Vardy, *Historical Dictionary of Hungary* (Lanham, Md., 1997).

MOROZ Oleksandr (29 February 1944, Buda, near Kiev), Ukrainian Communist activist and post-Communist politician. The son of a poor peasant, Moroz graduated from the Ukrainian Agricultural Academy and from the Higher Party School of the Central Committee (CC) of the Communist Party of Ukraine (CPU). He worked as an engineer and manager. From 1976 he was deputy head, and from 1989 head, of the agricultural department of the Kiev regional party committee. In March 1990, as first secretary of the CPU regional committee in Tarashcha, Moroz was elected to the Supreme Council of the Ukrainian SSR. In cooperation with the opposition from the Ukrainian Popular Movement for Restructuring (Rukh), Moroz encouraged the Communists to vote for the declaration of the state sovereignty of Ukraine of 16 July 1990 and then for the declaration of Ukrainian independence of 24 August 1991. Since the Communist Party was banned in late August 1991, on 26 October 1991 Moroz co-organized the founding congress of a new party—the Socialist Party of Ukraine (Sotsyalistychna Partiya Ukraiiny [SPU])—and he became its leader. The SPU took over most of the Communist constituency and stayed in opposition to the governments appointed by presidents **Leonid Kravchuk** and **Leonid Kuchma** (October 1992–September 1993). Moroz remained chairman of the party from May 1994 to May 1998.

On 26 June 1994 Moroz ran in the presidential elections and came in third, winning 13.1 percent of the vote. Although his party advocated the elimination of the office of president, in the second round Moroz tactically supported Kuchma. Moroz's evolution toward a Social Democratic program was opposed by a part of the SPU leadership and led to a split in the party in 1996, when Natalya Vitrenko founded the Progressive Socialist Party. In 1994–96, along with Kuchma, Moroz co-chaired the parliamentary constitutional commission, checking Kuchma's ambition to introduce a presidential system of power. Despite his opposition to extended presidential powers, Moroz agreed to a compromise in June 1995 that served as the foundation for the constitution of 28 June 1996. In the March 1998 elections to the Supreme Council the SPU ran in alliance with the Peasant Party of Ukraine and won twenty-nine mandates, becoming the second largest group on the left after the reinvented Communists. Criticizing the economic policies of President Kuchma, on 31 October 1999 Moroz ran for the presidency and came in third for the second time. In the second round he supported Kuchma's rival, the Communist leader **Petro Symonenko**. In a conflict between Kuchma and the Supreme Council majority in January and February 2000, Moroz supported the antipresidential opposition and declared himself against a referendum on the extension of presidential powers (16 April 2000). In November and December 2000 Moroz participated in widespread debates in which Kuchma was accused of ordering the murder of an opposition journalist, Georgiy Gongadze. In the elections of March 2002 Moroz was reelected to the Supreme Council. Hs popularity, especially in Southern and Eastern Ukraine, was due to his combination of anti-market and anti-corruption rhetoric. During the Orange Revolution of the fall of 2004 Moroz supported **Viktor Yushchenko**. (TS)

Sources: Taras Kuzio and Andrew Wilson, eds., *Ukraine: From Perestroika to Independence* (New York, 1994); Andrew Wilson, *Ukrainian Nationalism in the 1990s* (Cambridge, 1997); Bohdan Nahaylo, *The Ukrainian Resurgence* (Toronto, 1999); Volodymyr M. Lytvyn, *Ukraiina na mezhi tysyacholit (1991–2000 rr.)* (Kiev, 2000); Sharon L. Wolchik and Volodymyr Zviglyanich, eds., *Ukraine: The Search for a National Identity* (Oxford, 2000).

MOROZ Valentyn (15 April 1936, Kholoniv, Volhynia), Ukrainian dissident and politician. The son of a peasant, Moroz graduated in history from the University of Lviv, and then he worked as a teacher in country schools. From 1964 he taught at pedagogical institutes in Lutsk and Ivano-Frankivsk. Arrested in 1965 for the distribution of uncensored materials, Moroz was sentenced to four years of labor camp in Mordovia. It was there that he wrote *Reportazh iz zapovidnyka imeni Beriya* (Report from the Beria Memorial Reservation), published abroad and in the uncensored press at home. Released in 1969, Moroz wrote the essays *Sered snigiv* (In deep snow), *Khronika oporu* (Chronicle of resistance), and *Moysey i Dantan* (Moses and Danton). Arrested again in June 1970 as a recidivist, in November 1970 Moroz was sentenced to six years of special prison, three years of labor camp, and five years of forced settlement. His trial resounded widely in the West and at home (forty protests were presented before the Supreme Court of the Ukrainian SSR). From July to November 1974 Moroz went on a hunger strike in Vladimir Prison, demanding a transfer to a camp. His extremely hostile attitude toward the Russians and the Jews and his lack of respect for other prisoners in the Sosnovka Camp in Mordovia led to a conflict among Ukrainian dissidents. A special committee of prisoners reprimanded him and announced a boycott of his works in the samizdat publications. As a result of the hunger strike and Moroz's popularity in the West, in April 1979 the Soviets exchanged Moroz and four other political prisoners for two Soviet spies imprisoned in the United States. At the same time Moroz lost his Soviet citizenship. He settled in America and lectured at Harvard University. Later he moved to Canada, where he worked as a radio commentator. In

1997 he returned to Ukraine and lived in Lviv, lecturing at the university. Moroz authored more than thirty books, including the following: *Eseyi, lysty, dokumenty* (Essays, letters, and documents; 1975); *Bumerang* (Boomerang; 1974); *Lektsii z istorii Ukraiiny* (Lectures in Ukrainian history; 1982); *Ukraiina v 20-u stolitti* (Ukraine in the twentieth century; 1992); and *Natsionalizm 20-ho stolittia* (Nationalism of the twentieth century; 1997). (TS)

Sources: *Encyclopedia of Ukraine*, vol. 3 (Toronto, 1993); Ludmila. Alekseyeva, *Istoriya inakomysliya w SSSR* (Vilnius and Moscow, 1992); Ivan Lysiak-Rudnytskyi, *Istorychni ese*, vol. 2 (Kiev, 1994); Heorhiy Kasyanov, *Nezhodni: Ukraiinska intelihentsiya v rusi oporu 1960–80 rokiv* (Kiev, 1995); Anatoliy Rusnachenko, *Natsionalno-vyzvolnyi rukh w Ukraiini* (Kiev, 1998).

MORUZOV Mihail (3 April 1890, Zebil–27 November 1940, Jilava), head of Romanian military intelligence. The son of an Orthodox priest of the Russian Old Believers, after completing three grades of high school, Moruzov joined the secret police in Dobrudja. He distinguished himself during World War I on the front in Dobrudja and during the incorporation of Bessarabia by Romania in 1918. For example, he abducted Friederich von Mayer, the chief of German military intelligence on the front in Dobrudja and the region of the Black Sea, and he arrested most of the German spies in Dobrudja. Moruzov resorted to deceit to take over command of the Bolshevik forces in Bessarabia in order to thwart their actions against the Romanian forces. During the war he was promoted to chief of intelligence in Dobrudja. Moruzov soon came into conflict with the director of intelligence, Romulus Vornescu, who accused him of being a double agent for the Soviet Union and of large-scale smuggling in Bessarabia and the Danube delta. As the result of an investigation Moruzov was arrested and expelled from the Special Information Services (SIS). He moved to Bucharest, where he lived in poverty.

Thanks to General Constantin Dragu, commander of the military district in Bessarabia to whom Moruzov had rendered important services during the war, Moruzov became head of the SIS in 1929. After King **Charles II** returned to Romania in 1930, Moruzov won the king's favor. He entered into a close relationship with Ernest Urdereanu, the leading figure of the court camarilla, and took part in its political games. As a result of initiatives to establish cooperation with German military intelligence (Abwehr)—made on the king's orders from 1937—after the defeat of Poland in 1939 Moruzov reached an agreement on cooperation with Admiral Wilhelm Canaris, head of the Abwehr. In this agreement Moruzov pledged to protect the Romanian oilfields but agreed to allow German troops to stay in that area. Moruzov supported the regime of Charles II in combating the Fascist Iron Guard. In 1938 Moruzov ordered that nearly all Iron Guard leaders be executed under the pretext of their having attempted to escape while in transit between prisons. In the summer of 1939, on the orders of the king, Moruzov interned General **Ion Antonescu** in the Bistriţa Orthodox monastery because of Antonescu's contacts with the Iron Guard; this gave rise to Antonescu's hostility toward Moruzov. Impressed by the German expansion, after Premier **Armand Calinescu** was murdered in September 1939, Moruzov began to seek good relations with the Iron Guard and to support the Iron Guard's rise to power. When in November 1939 **Horia Sima**, chief of the Iron Guard, and a close associate returned from Germany to Romania and were arrested on the border, Moruzov released them from prison and secretly transported them to the palace, where they held talks with Urdereanu, during which the Iron Guard's participation in the government was discussed. Moruzov employed a group of important Iron Guard leaders in the SIS, which saved them from mobilization for the war. However, when on 5 September 1940 Antonescu came to power (which he shared with the Iron Guard), Moruzov was regarded as an enemy. He was secretly tried and put in prison. Admiral Canaris personally pleaded with Antonescu and Sima on behalf of Moruzov. Both Antonescu and Sima assured him that they did not intend to take Moruzov's life; nevertheless, he was murdered by the Iron Guard in Jilava Prison. (ASK)

Sources: Michel Sturdza, *The Suicide of Europe* (Belmond, Mass., 1968); Paul Stefanescu, *Istoria servicilor secrete romanesti* (Bucharest, 1994); Ion Budunescu and Ion Rusu-Sireanu, *Descifrarea unei istorii necunoscute*, vol. 3 (Bucharest, 1977); Christian Troncota, *Eugen Cristescu asul servicilor secrete romanesti* (Bucharest, 1994).

MOŚCICKI Ignacy (1 December 1867, Mierzanów, near Ciechanów–2 October 1946, Versoix, near Geneva, Switzerland), chemist-technologist, president of Poland. Mościcki came from a landed gentry family. He began his secondary school education in Płock and finished it in Warsaw. From 1887 to 1891 he studied chemistry at the Technical University in Riga, where he organized pro-independence educational groups among students and Polish soldiers of the Riga garrison. He also pursued clandestine activities in the (Social Revolutionary) Second Proletariat. After returning home, Mościcki continued these activities in Skierbieszów and Warsaw. Because of his involvement in the production of explosives and in the preparations for the assassination of Josif Hurko, the governor general of Warsaw, Mościcki was threatened with arrest by the tsarist authorities, so in July 1892, along with his wife, he fled to London. Working mainly as a laborer, he was involved with the leadership of the Union of Polish Socialists Abroad and the editorial staff of the periodical *Przedświt*. It was in London that in 1896 Mościcki met **Józef Piłsudski**, and from then on he was aligned with his political camp.

In the autumn of 1897 Mościcki moved to Fribourg, Switzerland, where he worked as an assistant professor in the department of physics of the university for four years. In 1900 he developed a method to produce nitric acid on an industrial scale, obtaining nitric oxides by burning air in an electric arc. In 1901 in Fribourg Mościcki became head of a research group in a laboratory designed according to his specifications, and he gained recognition as an outstanding chemist. In 1901 he became a technical manager in the Société de l'Acide Nitrique, a firm that opened a small factory in Fribourg to produce nitric acid. Mościcki is also credited with many inventions in the field of electrochemistry and electrophysics. In 1912 he was given a professorship in physical chemistry and technical electrochemistry at the Technical University of Lemberg (Lwów, Lviv), where he became professor *ad personam*, and, from 1915 to 1917 he served as dean of the Department of Chemistry. In 1916 Mościcki established the Metan Institute for Scientific and Technical Research, later renamed the Chemical Research Institute. He was also active in the underground Polish Military Organization (1916–18) and the Polish Independence League. In 1917 Mościcki initiated the construction of an ammonium nitrate factory in Jaworzno and became its director. In 1922 he was appointed director of the Nitrogen Compound Factory at Królewska Huta (now Chorzów), recently taken over from the Germans. As a result of the innovations Mościcki introduced, Poland did not need to import nitric compounds. In October 1925 Mościcki was appointed chair of technical electrochemistry at the Warsaw Polytechnic. The holder of forty Polish and foreign patents, Mościcki was granted honorary doctorates by many Polish and foreign universities. A full member of the Polish Academy of Arts and Sciences (Polska Akademia Umiejętności) and the Warsaw Scientific Society and an honorary member of the Academy of Technical Sciences and the Polish Chemical Society, Mościcki authored over sixty works in Polish, French, and German.

On 1 June 1926, on a motion by Piłsudski, the National Assembly elected Mościcki president of Poland, one day after Piłsudski had refused to assume this position. On 2 August 1926, on Piłsudski's initiative, the 1921 constitution was amended (the so-called August amendment), extending the president's powers by granting him the right to dissolve the Lower House (Sejm) and the Senate and to issue decrees that had the force of acts of parliament; such powers gave the president a strong position in the state. Mościcki enjoyed the support of Piłsudski because he was unconditionally loyal to him and concentrated on developing industry. In 1930 Mościcki initiated the construction of a nitrogen compound factory near Tarnów, where the new industrial district was named Mościce. On 6 August 1926 he issued a decree that established the office of inspector general of the armed forces, to which he appointed Piłsudski on 27 August 1926. Piłsudski was also supported by Mościcki in skirmishes with the new parliament elected in 1928. After his seven-year term ended, on 8 May 1933 Mościcki was reelected, despite a boycott by the opposition. On 23 April 1935 he endorsed a new constitution that established an authoritarian system. It granted even greater powers to the president, making him responsible only to God and history.

After the death of Piłsudski in May 1935, under the provisions of the constitution, the role of Mościcki as president increased considerably. He became the leader of the so-called Castle group, the most liberal faction of the *sanacja* camp. This group wanted to increase the economic potential of Poland through state interventionism. After the so-called group of colonels, led by **Walery Sławek**, was eliminated from the political game, Mościcki shared power with a group led by Marshal **Edward Rydz-Śmigły**, and he actually left the political initiative to Rydz-Śmigły. The result of this power sharing was evident in the establishment of the government of **Felicjan Sławoj-Składkowski** on 15 May 1936. On 10 November 1936 Mościcki appointed Rydz-Śmigły marshal of Poland. Tensions between Rydz-Śmigły and Mościcki flared, though, after the former established the pro-totalitarian Camp of National Unity (Obóz Zjednoczenia Narodowego [OZN]), and especially after **Adam Koc**'s declaration on 21 February 1937 that Poland needed a strong government headed by Rydz-Śmigły as commander-in-chief.

After the outbreak of World War II, Mościcki moved to the village of Błota, near Warsaw, on 2 September 1939. When the German troops approached Warsaw, along with the government and the commander-in-chief, he went to Ołyka (Olyka) in Volhynia, and thence toward the Romanian border. While in Kuty, Mościcki received the news that on 17 September the Soviet troops had invaded Poland; therefore, in order to avoid arrest, along with the government, he decided to leave Poland and crossed into Romania. The Romanian authorities interned him in Craiova. On the night of 20–21 September Mościcki appointed General **Bolesław Wieniawa-Długoszowski** as president of Poland, but after French protests, Wien-

iawa-Długoszowski resigned. On 30 September Mościcki finally handed over his office to **Władysław Raczkiewicz**, who was in France at the time. On 25 December 1939 Mościcki left for Switzerland, as he had Swiss citizenship. Mościcki wrote memoirs that were published by the New York *Niepodległość*. Mościcki's ashes were brought to Poland and buried in the crypt of St. John's Cathedral in Warsaw. (JS)

Sources: *PSB*, vol. 22; *Kto był kim w Drugiej Rzeczypospolitej* (Warsaw, 1994); *Prezydenci i premierzy Drugiej Rzeczypospolitej* (Wrocław, 1992); Stanisław Łoza, *Profesor Ignacy Mościcki, prezydent Najjaśniejszej Rzeczypospolitej Polskiej* (Warsaw, 1928); Ignacy Mościcki, *Autobiografia* (Warsaw, 1993); Sławomir M. Nowinowski, *Prezydent Ignacy Mościcki* (Warsaw, 1994); Zofia Dobrowolska, ed., *Ignacy Mościcki, Ostatni prezydent Drugiej Rzeczypospolitej Polskiej: Bibliografia* (Ciechanów, 1991).

MOSDORF Jan (30 May 1904, Warsaw–11 October 1943, Oświęcim), Polish nationalist activist. Born into an intelligentsia family, Mosdorf attended several high schools, graduating from the Jan Zamoyski Gymnasium in Warsaw in 1922. He studied law and later philosophy and history at Warsaw University. He received a diploma in 1928 and subsequently studied at the Ecole des Sciences Politiques in Paris. In 1934 he received a Ph.D. from Warsaw University for a dissertation on August Comte's philosophy of history. Allied with the nationalist movement in his youth, Mosdorf was a member of the secret National High School Organization and later a member of the anti-Semitic Youth Movement of the Great Poland Camp. From 1928 to 1933 he headed the Chief Council of the All-Polish Youth. He was a member of the National Guard, the conspiratorial leadership of the nationalist movement. In 1934, along with a group of young radical activists, Mosdorf left the National Party (Stronnictwo Narodowe [SN]) and became one of the founders of the National Radical Camp (Obóz Narodowo-Radykalny [ONR]), which called for a national revolution. Mosdorf initially acted as the ONR leader. He lost that position after a split initiated by **Bolesław Piasecki**, who in 1935 established a competition group, the National Radical Movement, the so-called Falanga. Mosdorf also lost the trust of some of his colleagues because he hid from the authorities for a year to escape an arrest following the assassination of Minister **Bronisław Pieracki**. After 1935 Mosdorf gradually withdrew from the activities of the ONR and devoted himself to journalism.

After the German and Soviet invasions of Poland in September 1939, Mosdorf returned to the SN and was active in the underground propaganda department of the SN Main Board. In December 1939, along with Stanisław Piasecki, he established the underground periodical *Walka* and then served as its editor. Arrested in June 1940 by the Gestapo and imprisoned in Pawiak Prison in Warsaw, Mosdorf was transported to the Auschwitz concentration camp on 6 January 1941. In the autumn of 1941, along with Professor **Roman Rybarski**, he established an underground national organization there. He was involved in clandestine teaching and in aiding the Jews. Arrested for his underground work by the camp Gestapo, Mosdorf was executed in a mass execution. Before the war, Mosdorf's views were characterized by extreme nationalism, socioeconomic radicalism, and anti-Semitism. After 1939 he abandoned his extremist views, considering Poland's struggle against its two enemies, Germany and the Soviet Union, as his main goal. The evolution of his views can be traced in his articles in *Głos Akademicki, Akademik Polski, Gazeta Warszawska, Myśl Narodowa, Sztafety, Prosto z Mostu*, and *Walka*. Mosdorf also wrote several sociopolitical works, including *Akademik i polityka* (The academic and politics; 1926) and *Wczoraj i jutro* (Yesterday and tomorrow; 1938). (MC)

Sources: *PSB*, vol. 22; Mieczysław Sobczak, *Stosunek Narodowej Demokracji do kwestii żydowskiej w Polsce w latach 1918–1939* (Wrocław, 1938); Philip Friedman, *Their Brothers' Keepers* (New York, 1978); Szymon Rudnicki, *Obóz Narodowo-Radykalny: Geneza i działalność* (Warsaw, 1985); Jerzy Ptakowski, *Oświęcim bez cenzury i bez legend* (New York, 1985); Krzysztof Kawalec, *Narodowa Demokracja wobec faszyzmu 1922–1939* (Warsaw, 1989); Władysław Sznarbachowski, *300 lat wspomnień.* (London, 1997); Leszek Żebrowski, "Jan Mosdorf (1904–1943)," 23 October 2001.

MOSER Anastasya [née Dimitrova] (30 June 1937, Sofia), Bulgarian politician, daughter of **Georgi "Gemeto" Dimitrov**. Moser spent most of her life in the United States, where her father emigrated in 1945 and where she married Charles Moser, a lecturer in Bulgarian and dean of the Slavic Department at George Washington University in Washington, D.C. She returned to Bulgaria in 1991, joining in the activities of the reactivated Nikola Petkov Bulgarian Agrarian National Union (NP BANU). While the NP BANU leader, **Milan Drenchev**, demanded that the unification of the peasant movement be preceded by an investigation and dismissal of those compromised by having served the Communists in the satellite BANU, Moser preferred unification to clearing past accounts. In February 1992 she ousted Drenchev from the party leadership and helped in the unification of the two parties, taking over the leadership of the united BANU. In the elections of December 1994 Moser won a seat in parliament, taking the lead of a coalition called the Popular Union (Naroden Sajuz [NS]), which cooperated with the Union of Democratic Forces (UDF) but which remained a separate club. In the

parliamentary elections of April 1997 the two groups ran together, which brought them a landslide victory. Moser did not join the **Ivan Kostov** government, but her influence in the UDF grew. For some time she was even its deputy chairman. Moser did not welcome the return to Bulgaria of the former tsar, **Simeon II**. She even stated that he might jeopardize democracy, but after a landslide victory by Simeon's party in the elections of June 2001 she announced she was ready to talk about a possible coalition. Despite a significant decline in the UDF's rankings, the BANU managed to exceed the 5 percent threshold and win parliamentary seats, but it stayed in the opposition. In January 2001 Moser was elected chairman of the European People's Party. (AG)

Sources: Raymond Detrez, *Historical Dictionary of Bulgaria* (Lanham, Md., 1997); *Koy koy e v Bulgariya* (Sofia, 1998); Bugajski; www.hri.org/news/balkans/bta; www.economist.com/countries/Bulgaria; www.europeanforum.bot-consult.se/cup/bulgaria.

MOSHANOV Stoycho (25 May 1892, Drianovo–10 January 1975, Sofia), Bulgarian politician. The nephew of Prime Minister **Nikola Mushanov**, Moshanov completed law studies in Aix-en-Provence, France. He fought on the front during World War I, and subsequently he became one of the leaders of the Democratic Party, which he represented in parliament from 1923 to 1934. After the coup of 1934 Moshanov became aligned with the royal court and became minister of education in 1935, but he resigned this post in protest against the government's pro-German line in foreign policy. Although the National Assembly was dominated by supporters of Tsar **Boris III**, by mobilizing all the opposition parties and taking advantage of the differences of opinion within the government camp, Moshanov succeeded in becoming parliament speaker (1938–39). After the 1940 elections, which were held under police control and in violation of democratic principles, the opposition politicians (including Moshanov) who called for Bulgaria's cooperation with the Western countries were eliminated from the parliament. Moshanov went to Paris and London, where he lived until 1944, maintaining contacts with the Allies in case the fate of the war changed. In August 1944 Moshanov returned to Bulgaria and undertook to conduct negotiations with the Allies on Bulgaria's withdrawal from the war, insisting at the same time on guarantees of Western aid in the case of Soviet aggression. However, because of the Soviet veto, the negotiations ended in failure at the beginning of September 1944. From 1945 to 1947 Moshanov was in opposition to the Communist rule. He mediated in the contacts of **Nikola Petkov** and **Georgi "Gemeto" Dimitrov** with the U.S. Embassy. Thanks to Moshanov's help, "Gemeto" managed to escape to the West. Moshanov also attempted to transform the small Democratic Party into a locus uniting other small parties that had attracted the intelligentsia before the war, but his efforts were unsuccessful. Arrested by the Communist authorities and sentenced to a long prison term, Moshanov was sent to the Belene concentration camp. After his release, he died in obscurity in Sofia. (AG)

Sources: *Entsiklopedia Bulgariya*, vol. 4 (Sofia, 1984); *Suvremenna Bulgarska Entsiklopediya*, vol. 3 (Sofia, 1994); Marshall Lee Miller, *Bulgaria during the Second World War* (Stanford, 1975); Jerzy Jackowicz, *Partie opozycyjne w Bułgarii 1944–1948* (Warsaw, 1997); www.omda.bg/engl/inf-command/subversion.htm.

MOTHER TERESA OF CALCUTTA [originally Anjeze Gonxhe Bojaxhiu] (27 August 1910 Shkup, Albania, Ottoman Empire [now Skopje, Macedonia]–5 September 1997, Calcutta, India), Albanian nun, famous throughout the world for her services to the destitute. Born into a Catholic family of merchants, at eighteen Teresa went to Dublin and joined the Sisters of Loreto congregation. In December 1928 she took the name Maria Teresa and left for Darjeeling, India, where she spent seventeen years working as a teacher, both at a local school and at a convent school in Calcutta. She taught religion and geography. According to her own account, in 1946, while traveling on a train in Darjeeling, she received a call from God and pledged to devote her life to "the poorest of the poor." Teresa completed a course in nursing with the Medical Missionary Sisters in Patna, and in 1950 she founded the Congregation of the Missionaries of Charity. The nuns from this congregation pledged themselves to disinterested service to the destitute. Initially the order provided aid to the dying and then also started serving abandoned children and lepers. After 1965 the congregation began opening new centers and missions in various countries around the world. In recognition of her apostolate, Teresa was honored in 1971 by Pope Paul VI, who awarded her the first Pope John XXIII Peace Prize. In 1979 Teresa received the Nobel Prize for Peace, and in 1985 she received the American Medal of Freedom and honorary U.S. citizenship. The government of India also recognized her service and in 1980 awarded her the Jewel of India, the highest award granted to foreigners.

After World War II Albania was ruled by the Communists, who in 1967 declared Albania the first completely atheistic state in the world and decreed punishment for religious practices; thus Teresa was unable to maintain contact with her homeland for decades. Although her family lived in Albania, it was only on 15 August 1989 that she was allowed to go to Albania for a private visit, invited by **Nexhmije Hoxha**, chairperson of the Democratic Front and the widow of the former president of Albania. Observers consider that this visit had a major influence in changing the state's attitude toward religion. Although Teresa mainly worked in India, her congregation was known and popular in some East European countries, including Poland, where as early as the 1980s the Missionaries of Charity began to care for the poor and homeless. In March 1991 the Missionaries of Charity established their first center in Tirana, and the following year Teresa received an Albanian passport. Teresa's publications include *My Life for the Poor* (1995). Teresa was beatified by Pope **John Paul II** on 19 October 2003. (TC)

Sources: Edward Le Joly, *Mother Teresa of Calcutta* (San Francisco, 1983); Lush Gjergj, *Mother Teresa: Her Life, Her Works* (Brooklyn, 1991); Monique de Huertas, *Mère Teresa: Semez l'amour, il germera* (Paris, 1993); Roger Royle and Gary Woods, *Matka Teresa: Obrazy życia* (Warsaw, 1996); Mariola Woszkowska, "Bogini zaułków," *Przegląd Albański*, 1996, no. 1; Anne Sebba, *Mother Teresa* (New York, 1997); Navin Chawla, *Matka Teresa* (Warsaw, 1998); Renzo Allegri, *Teresa of the Poor: The Story of Her Life* (Ann Arbor, 1998); Christian Feldmann, *Miłość pozostaje: Życie Matki Teresy z Kalkutu* (Warsaw, 1998); Maryanne Raphael, *Mother Teresa: Called to Love* (Waverly, Ohio, 2000).

MROŻEK Sławomir (29 June 1930, Borzęcin, near Kraków), Polish writer, playwright, and humorist. Mrożek made his literary debut in 1950 in the Kraków weekly *Przekrój*. Initially strongly involved in communism, he published Socialist realist columns. From the mid-1950s Mrożek worked with the student satirical theater Bim-Bom in Gdańsk. In his first plays—such as *Policja* (Police; 1958), *Indyk* (Turkey; 1960), *Karol* (Charles; 1961), *Strip-tease* (1961; English edition, 1962), and *Zabawa* (A party; 1962)—he proved to be a master of absurdist humor, grotesque allegory, and anti-traditionalist provocation. Mrożek continued to contribute to *Przekrój*, where he published short literary pieces and cartoons. The collections of his satires *Słoń* (1957; *Elephant*, 1962) and *Wesele w Atomicach* (The wedding in Atomice; 1959) consolidated his reputation as a writer pointing to the absurdities of Communist reality in Poland. Saying that something looked as if it had been "taken out of Mrożek" became a proverbial expression. In the West Mrożek's works were considered close to those of **Eugene Ionesco** and the theater of the absurd. Mrożek won world renown for the play *Tango* (1965; English edition, 1968), in which he presented the roots of totalitarianism in the everyday behavior of contemporaries. In 1963 Mrożek went to Italy. In 1968 he spoke against the anti-Semitic campaign of the Polish Communist authorities and against the Warsaw Pact invasion of Czechoslovakia. Until 1989 he lived in

France and then, until 1996, in Mexico. From caricaturing reality Mrożek evolved toward a deeper reflection on the psychology of his contemporaries. His later works include *Emigranci* (Emigrants; 1974), *Vatzlav* (1979; English edition, 1972), and *Ambasador* (Ambassador; 1981). Mrożek showed the destruction of values and the ambivalence of human behavior, suspended between primitive carelessness and tragic helplessness, as well as between a desire for full freedom and the necessity for rules. At the end of the 1990s Mrożek returned to Poland. Mrożek's works have been translated into twenty languages and staged in many countries. (WR)

Sources: Alek Pohl, *Zurück zum From: Strukturanalysen zu Slawomir Mrozek* (Berlin, 1972); Jan Błoński, "Mrożek filozof: Próba interpretacji fantastyki współczesnej," *Pamiętnik Literacki*, 1977, no. 3; *Literatura polska: Przewodnik encyklopedyczny*, vol. 2 (Warsaw, 2000); Halina Stephan, *Mrożek* (Kraków, 1996); Małgorzata Sugiera, *Dramaturgia Sławomira Mrożka* (Kraków, 1997).

MSTYSLAV [originally Stepan Skrypnyk] (10 April 1898, Poltava–11 June 1993, Bound Brook, New Jersey), leader of the Ukrainian Autocephalous Orthodox Church (UAOC). Skrypnyk was a clergyman of the UAOC, established in the Ukraine by a decision of the Directory on 1 January 1919; he was also the nephew of **Symon Petlyura**. At the end of the 1920s in Poland, Skrypnyk joined a circle of Ukrainian émigrés centered around the Volhynian governor (*wojewoda*) **Henryk Józewski**, who, following the concept of Marshal **Józef Piłsudski**, between 1928 and 1938 implemented a policy of winning the support of Ukrainians for the Polish state. In 1930–39, as a representative of the Ukrainian Volhynian Unification (UVU), which ran in the elections on the ticket of the pro-government Nonparty Bloc of Cooperation with the Government (BBWR), Skrypnyk was a deputy to the Assembly of the Polish Republic. The UVU deputies represented a loyalist line, contrary to most deputies representing the Ukrainian parties from Galicia. In his parliamentary activities Skrypnyk became known as a supporter of the Ukrainization of the Orthodox Church in Poland. He opposed the decisions of Metropolitan **Dionisius Valedinsky** that preserved the Russian language character of the Orthodox Church. Skrypnyk defended the Orthodox Church's property, threatened by the so-called revindication action, which was conducted by the state between 1938 and 1939. Disappointed with the Polish policy, in 1938 Skrypnyk left the club of the Volhynian deputies and started to work with the opposition Ukrainian Parliamentary Representation of Galician deputies.

During the German occupation, within the framework of the revived Ukrainian autocephalous Orthodox Church (dissolved by the Bolsheviks in 1921), Skrypnyk was ordained bishop of Pereyaslav in 1942 in Kiev. From 1942 to 1943 he was temporarily imprisoned by the Gestapo, and in 1944 he evacuated to Germany, where he continued his activities as bishop until 1946. In 1947–49 he headed the autocephalous Orthodox Church in Canada. From 1950 he lived in the United States, where the synod of the local autocephalous Orthodox Church, established in 1919, appointed him president of the consistory and deputy to Metropolitan Ioan Teodorovych. In 1963 Skrypnyk was an observer at the sessions of the Second Vatican Ecumenical Council. In 1969 he replaced the deceased metropolitan, Nikanor Abramovych, as head of the UAOC in Europe (headquartered in Karlsruhe), and after the death of Teodorovych, he became metropolitan of the entire UAOC (1971).

In the face of the revival of the UAOC in the Ukraine, which came about as a result of a split in the Orthodox Church of the Moscow Patriarchate in June 1990, Skrypnyk became head of the UAOC. In September 1990 he arrived in the Ukraine for enthronement. However, owing to his autocratic style of governing the Orthodox Church and because of his questioning of the canonicality of the election of bishops, he got into a conflict with the bishops. He returned to the United States, while the bishops held an ecumenical council (June 1992) that was supported by the state authorities and that proclaimed the unification of the UAOC and the Ukrainian Orthodox Church. Until then, the Ukrainian Orthodox Church had been subordinated to the Moscow Patriarchate. Not all parishes of the two Orthodox churches recognized the new authorities. The ecumenical council actually acknowledged Skrypnyk as the head of the Orthodox Church and **Filaret Denisenko** as his deputy, but, as it turned out later, it did so without the latter's consent. Skrypnyk again arrived in the Ukraine; however, he did not find common ground with Filaret (a former exarch of the Moscow Patriarchate in the Ukraine who was suspected of collaboration with the KGB), and he rejected the resolutions of the ecumenical council. Despite Filaret's objections, Skrypnyk was considered head of the Ukrainian Orthodox Church–Kiev Patriarchate until his death. (GM)

Sources: *Encyclopedia of Ukraine*, vol. 4 (Toronto, 1993); Włodzimierz Mędrzecki, "Ukraińska Reprezentacja Parlamentarna w Drugiej Rzeczypospolitej," in *Warszawskie Zeszyty Ukrainoznawcze*, vol. 3; Włodzimierz Pawluczuk, *Ukraina: Polityka i mistyka* (Kraków, 1998).

MUCHA Alfons (24 July 1860, Ivančice, Moravia–14 July 1939, Prague), Czech painter, graphic artist, designer, leading representative of Art Nouveau. After he had failed to gain admission to the Prague Academy of Fine Arts in 1877, Mucha went to Vienna, where he found employment in the production of stage decorations. In 1881 he met Count Khuen-Belassi, who commissioned him to paint frescos in his castles in Hrušovany and Gandegg. The count subsequently sponsored Mucha's studies in Munich. From 1885 to 1887 Mucha studied at the Akademie der Bildenden Künste in Munich. In 1888 he went to Paris, where he studied at the Académie Julian and (from 1889 to 1894) at the Académie Colarossi. He earned a living by taking on various minor commissions, such as painting illustrations for *La Vie Populaire* and *Le Petit Français Illustré*. Mucha gained renown in 1894 as the designer of a poster for the play *Gismonde*, which featured a life-size picture of Sarah Bernhardt, the leading actress of the play. As a result of the poster's success, Mucha entered into a six-year exclusive contract with the actress for the design of posters showing Bernhardt. He also won many commissions to design advertising posters, stamps, calendars, illustrations, and the like. Apart from commissioned work, Mucha ran his own school of drawing (Cours Mucha), and from 1898 to 1900 he helped to organize the 1900 Paris Exhibition, preparing the Bosnia and Herzegovina Pavilion. He also designed jewelry for the Fouquet store in Paris. Around 1900 a "Mucha style" became recognized in Art Nouveau, although Mucha himself opposed the classification of his art as Art Nouveau. In 1904 Mucha moved to the United States, from where he frequently traveled to Paris. In 1910 he returned to Prague.

From 1910 to 1928 Mucha created his greatest works, a monumental series of paintings, *Slovanská epopej* (Slavic epic), in which his Slavophilism was expressed. The series consists of twenty paintings depicting the major events in the history of the Slavs. Mucha's style reveals the influences of Hans Makart and Eugène-Samuel Grasset. It is characterized by rich ornamentation and a balance between realistic and stylized elements. Elements of Byzantine art can also be seen, particularly in the mosaic backgrounds of the pictures and in richly adorned attire decorated with gold and jewels. (PU)

Sources: *ČBS*; Joseph S. Roucek, *Slavonic Encyclopaedia* (New York, 1949); Emanuel Poche et al., *Encyklopedie českého výtvarného umění* (Prague, 1975); *The Dictionary of Art*, vol. 22 (London and New York, 1996); *Kdo byl kdo v našich dějinách ve 20. století*, vol. 1 (Prague, 1998); Brian Reade, *Art Nouveau and Alphonse Mucha* (London, 1963); Jiří Mucha, *Alphonse Mucha: The Master of Art Nouveau* (Prague, 1966); Jiří Mucha, *Kankán se svatozáří: Život a dílo Alfonse Muchy* (Prague, 1969); Jiří Mucha, *Alphonse Maria Mucha: His Life and Art* (London, 1989); Renate Ulmer, *Alfons Mucha* (Cologne, 1993); Ann Bridges, *Alphonse Mucha* (London, 1991).

MUDRYI Vasyl (19 March 1893, Vikno, near Skalat–19 March 1966, Yonkers, New York), Ukrainian social activist and politician. While a university student in Lemberg (Lviv, Lwów), Mudryi served as chairman of the Ukrainian Student Union. From 1917 to 1920 he worked in the administration of the Ukrainian National Republic (Ukraiinska Narodna Republika [UNR]), serving as commissar of education and head of Proskuriv County. After returning to Lwów in 1921, Mudryi helped to organize the underground Ukrainian University, for which he served as finance officer and secretary (1921–25). He was also an active member of the Main Board of the Prosvita Society, becoming its vice-president in 1932. From 1921 to 1939 Mudryi was an executive member of the Taras Shevchenko Scientific Society. He was a member of the editorial staff of *Dilo*, a leading Ukrainian newspaper published in Lwów, and he served as its editor-in-chief from 1927 to 1935. Mudryi co-authored the program of the Ukrainian National Democratic Alliance (Ukraiinske Natsionalno-Demokratychne Obyednannya [UNDO]), which was the largest Ukrainian party in Poland; he served as its vice-president (1926–35) and subsequently its president. In 1935–39 Mudryi was an MP in the Polish Lower House (Sejm). A proponent of the normalization of Polish-Ukrainian relations, he became deputy speaker of the Sejm, a member of the Commission for Foreign Affairs, and leader of the Ukrainian Parliamentary Representation. He also maintained contacts with the Organization of Ukrainian Nationalists (OUN). The policies of the Polish authorities did not facilitate a Polish-Ukrainian agreement; among other things, they prompted the UNDO to submit, on 7 May 1938, a "Declaration on the Situation of the Ukrainian Nation in the Polish State," which included a demand for territorial autonomy in the areas populated by Ukrainians. In December 1938, along with thirteen UNDO MPs and MP Stepan Skrypnyk, Mudryi submitted a request to the Sejm for the establishment of such autonomy. On 2 September 1939, at the last session of the Sejm, he submitted a declaration that the Ukrainian minority would "fulfill its citizen duties of blood and property toward the State."

After the defeat of Poland, Mudryi limited his political activities. Until 1941 he lived in Kraków and then in Lviv, where he worked as a cinema manager from 1942 to 1943. He maintained contacts with the **Stepan Bandera** faction of the Organization of Ukrainian Nationalists (OUN-B). In June 1941 he joined the Ukrainian National Committee, established by the OUN-B. He also worked with *Ideya i Chyn*, an underground organ of the OUN-B. In July 1944 Mudryi became vice-president of the Ukrainian Supreme Liberation Council (Ukraiinska Holovna Vyzvolna Rada), a political superstructure of the Ukrainian Insurgent Army.

From 1944 to 1948 he was in western Germany, where he revived the UNDO and then served as its leader until his death. He was also president of the Central Representation of the Ukrainian Emigration in Europe. In 1949 Mudryi left for the United States, where he became executive director of the Ukrainian Congress Committee. Mudryi authored numerous articles and brochures on political topics. His publications also include *Borotba za ohnyshche ukraiinskoy kultury v zakhidnykh zemliakh Ukraiiny* (The struggle for the core of Ukrainian culture in Ukraine's western lands; 1923) and a monograph about Ivan Franko (1957). (GM)

Sources: *Encyclopedia of Ukraine*, vol. 3 (Toronto, 1993); *Kto był kim w Drugiej Rzeczpospolitej* (Warsaw, 1994); Ryszard Torzecki, *Kwestia ukraińska w Polsce w latach 1923–1929* (Warsaw, 1989); Ryszard Torzecki, *Polacy i Ukraińcy: Sprawa ukraińska w czasie II wojny światowej na terenie II Rzeczypospolitej* (Warsaw, 1993).

MÜNNICH Ferenc (16 November 1886, Seregélyes–29 November 1967, Budapest), Hungarian Communist activist. The son of a chemist, after high school Münnich studied law in Kolozsvar (now Cluj in Romania), and in 1910 he earned a doctoral degree. During World War I Münnich did his military service in Máramarossziget in Transylvania. In 1915 he was awarded the Silver Medal for Bravery and was promoted to lieutenant. In October 1915, along with his unit, Münnich was captured by the Russians. He was put in a prisoner of war camp in Tomsk, where he took part in the creation of a Socialist organization among the prisoners of war. In May 1917 Münnich joined the Russian Social Democratic Workers' Party, and later he became a member of the Tomsk organization of the All-Union Communist Party (Bolsheviks). He fought in the Russian Civil War as a commander of the international unit formed by the prisoners of war. In 1918 he became commander of a regiment. For some time he worked in the Cheka in Moscow. In November 1918 Münnich returned to Hungary, and a month later he joined the founders of the Hungarian Communist Party. Under the Hungarian Soviet Republic (HSR) in 1919 he became head of the Organizational Department of the People's Commissariat for Military Affairs, and in April he was appointed political commissar of the sixth division. He took part in the northern campaign and was appointed people's commissar for military affairs, with headquarters in Eperjes (now Prešov in Slovakia) at the territory of the newly created Slovak Soviet Republic. After the fall of the HSR, Münnich emigrated to Vienna, where he joined the faction of **Béla Kun**.

In March 1921, on the orders of the Communist International, Münnich took part in the so-called March action of Communists in Germany. After the failure of this action, he was arrested, sentenced to one month in prison, and subsequently expelled from Germany. Between 1922 and 1936 he was in the USSR. In 1922 he became president of the Auditing Commission of the Hungarian Oil Syndicate. In 1930 he joined the editorial staff of *Sarló és Kalapács*, a newspaper of Hungarian Communists in exile, and in 1931–33 he was its editor-in-chief. During the Spanish Civil War Münnich fought as a major in the Twelfth International Brigade, where he became deputy commander of the Forty-fifth Division and was later appointed chief of the general staff of the Fifteenth Spanish Division. In 1938 Münnich became commander of the Eleventh International Reserve Brigade. After the collapse of the Spanish republic in February 1939 Münnich fled to France, where he was placed in an internment camp. Released in 1941 following a Soviet intervention, Münnich returned to the USSR. After the German aggression against the USSR, Münnich trained partisans. Later he fought at Stalingrad. Between November 1942 and 1945 he was editor-in-chief of the Hungarian section of Radio Moscow. He wrote commentaries under the name of Nikolai Fiodorov. It was there that Münnich established closer contacts with **Mátyás Rákosi**, **Ernő Gerő**, and **József Révai**.

In September 1945 Münnich returned to Hungary and was appointed governor of the city of Pécs. Between May 1946 and 1949, as chief commanding officer of the Budapest police, he reorganized the chief command, created the department of economic police, and organized alarm units. Between 1949 and 1956 Münnich was in the diplomatic service: in 1949–50 as head of the legation in Finland, between 1950 and 1954 in Bulgaria, between September 1954 and August 1956 as ambassador to the USSR, and between August 1956 and 25 October 1956 as ambassador to Yugoslavia. In 1949–53 Münnich was also a member of parliament. In September 1956 he was chosen for the committee that prepared a second funeral for **László Rajk** and his associates. In his funeral speech, Münnich described Rajk's judges as "sadistic criminals who had crawled out of the swamps of personality cults into the daylight."

On 24 October 1956 Münnich was coopted to the CC of the Hungarian Workers' Party. Between 27 October and 3 November he was interior minister in the government of **Imre Nagy**. On 1 November, along with **János Kádár**, Münnich secretly went to Moscow, where on 2 and 3 November he took part in a meeting of the Presidium of the CC of the CPSU and in the creation of a puppet government in Hungary. On 4 November 1956 Münnich became minister of the armed forces and public security affairs in the "Revolutionary Government of Workers and Peasants." In November 1956 he joined the Politburo of the Hungarian Socialist Workers' Party (HSWP). Münnich helped to organize the armed battalions of the security services and workers' guard. In February 1957 Münnich was first deputy prime minister, and from 28 January 1958 to 13 September 1961 he was prime minister. Between 1961 and 1965 he was minister without portfolio. Between November 1956 and 1967 Münnich was a member of the CC of the HSWP, and until 1966 he served as a member of the Politburo. (JT)

Sources: *Current Biography*, 1959; *Obituaries from* The Times *1961–1970* (Reading, 1975); Lazitch; *Magyar Életrajzi Lexikon*, vol. 3 (Budapest, 1985); *A magyar forradalom és szabadságharc enciklopédiája*, CD-ROM (Budapest, 1999); *Tankok ellen, száz halálon át: Münnich Ferenc a spanyol polgárháborúban* (Budapest, 1976); *Három forradalom hőse: Münnich Ferenc válogatott beszédei és írásai* (Budapest, 1986).

MUNTERS Vilhelms (25 July 1898, Riga–11 January 1967, Riga), Latvian diplomat. The son of a merchant, Munters graduated from a school of commerce in Riga. Inducted into the Russian Army at the beginning of 1917 but demobilized in October of that year, he returned to Riga in July 1918. From July 1919 to October 1920 he served in the Estonian Army. In 1920 he returned to Latvia, and, encouraged by **Zigfrids Meierovics**, he began working in the Ministry of Foreign Affairs. From 1925 to 1931 Munters was head of the Department for the Baltic States, and from 1931 to 1933, director of the Administrative and Legal Department. In July 1933 he became secretary general of the Ministry of Foreign Affairs, and in July 1936, minister of foreign affairs. Munters spoke several foreign languages and was highly intelligent, but he was criticized for his irresolute character. In mid-June 1937 he visited Moscow, where he was received by Stalin. At this visit, which had a ceremonious character, an official announcement was issued stressing that Latvia and the Soviet Union enjoyed friendly relations. During his visits to Berlin in November 1937 and May 1938, Munters rebutted German criticism of legislation introduced by Latvian dictator **Kārlis Ulmanis** that had limited the freedoms of the national minorities. In September of that year Munters unsuccessfully attempted to obtain German guarantees for Latvia's neutrality. As head of the Latvian foreign service, Munters was elected chairman of the 101st session of the League of Nations in 1938.

After the collapse of Poland, under the Molotov-Ribbentrop Pact of 23 August 1939, the Kremlin demanded that Latvia, like Finland, Estonia, and Lithuania, allow for the establishment of Soviet garrisons and extra-territorial communication routes across their territories. Munters realized the hopelessness of the situation, and on 5 October 1939, after he made another visit to Moscow, the Latvian government signed a treaty with the Soviet Union under which Soviet bases were established in Liepāja and Ventspils. After the Soviet invasion Munters was dismissed as minister on 21 June 1940. On 16 July he was deported to Voronezh, where he taught foreign languages at the Voronezh Pedagogical Institute. The Soviet authorities wanted him to become a Latvian quisling, but Munters refused. Arrested on 26 June 1941, he was held in prisons in Voronezh, Saratov, Kirov (from 1942), and later Moscow. In 1952 he was sentenced to twenty-five years. Released in 1954 but banned from returning to Latvia, Munters worked as a translator in Vladimir. In 1959 he was allowed to return to Latvia, where he continued to work as a translator. He was the only former minister of Latvia to cooperate with the Soviet KGB, writing articles and books about the "criminal activities" of Latvian émigrés in the West, although it is not clear when this cooperation began. Munters held many awards and distinctions, including the Order of Polonia Restituta of the first and third degrees. He is buried in Riga. (EJ)

Sources: Georg von Rauch, *The Baltic States: The Years of Independence: Estonia, Latvia, Lithuania 1917–1940* (Berkeley, 1970); O. Niedra, "Ierēdnis," *Lauku Avīze*, 5 October 1990; V. Bērziņš, "Muntera padēls protestē," *Zvaigzne*, 1991, nos. 2–3; B. Daukšts, "Muntera oficiālā un neoficiālā vizīte: Padomju Savienībā," *Latvijas Vēsture*, 1992, no. 2; R. Ārmanis, "Rusofils, anglofils vai ģermanofils: V. Munters nacionālsociālistu vērtējumā," *Latvijas Vēstures Institūta Žurnāls*, 1993, no. 3; David M. Crowe, *The Baltic States and the Great Powers: Foreign Relations, 1938–1940* (Boulder, Colo., 1993); J. Labsvīrs, "Atmiņu skices par Vilhelmu Munteru," *Latvijas Vēstures Institūta Žurnāls*, 2000, no. 1; I. Feldmanis, "Latvijas ārlietu ministrs V. Munters par vācbaltiešu attieksmi pret Latviju 1939. gada pavasarī," *Latvijas Vēsture*, 2000, no. 4.

MURAVIEV Konstantin (21 February 1893, Pazardzhik–31 January 1965, Sofia), Bulgarian politician. Muraviev fought in both Balkan Wars. In 1918 he joined the Bulgarian Agrarian National Union (BANU). In 1919–20 he was a state security officer in the **Aleksandur Stamboliyski** regime. A nephew of Stamboliyski, Muraviev served as consul general in Rotterdam and chargé d'affaires in Holland and Turkey. From March to June 1923 he was minister of war. In this role, he proved incompetent, and his incompetence was blamed for Stamboliyski's fall. After the military coup of June 1923, Muraviev was arrested and sentenced to a long prison term. Released in April 1924, he lived in exile until 1926. In 1927 he became editor-in-chief of the periodical *Zemedelsko zname*, an organ of the BANU. At the beginning of the 1930s, as one of the leaders of the agrarian right wing of the Vrabcha 1 group, Muraviev worked closely with **Dimitur Gichev**. Muraviev served as minister of public education (June 1931–December 1932) and minister of agriculture and state property (December 1932–May 1934) in the coalition governments dominated by the Agrarians. After the coup of 1934, he went over to the opposition, both to the Zveno group and to the regime of Tsar **Boris III**. In August 1936 Muraviev signed a declaration in which the tsarist governments were denounced as anti-democratic and anti-people, and in June 1937 he was a co-founder of a political amnesty committee. After the death of Tsar Boris, Muraviev supported the September 1943 appeals by democratic groups for new elections, but when new elections were not held, he stated that the election of the new Regency Council was illegal. Muraviev continued to call for the establishment of a broad ruling coalition and was among the opponents of the regime of the three regents. On 7 August 1944 Muraviev signed a declaration addressed to the regents and to the government demanding a change in Bulgaria's foreign policy and calling for an agreement with the Soviet Union.

After Bulgaria's failure to reach an agreement with the Allies and because of the Soviet offensive, Muraviev was appointed prime minister by the regents on 2 September 1944. He invited politicians of the opposition and the pro-Soviet Fatherland Front to join his government, but they refused to cooperate and vehemently attacked his government, preparing to overthrow it. On 4 September Muraviev announced the program of his cabinet; in it he pledged to return to a constitutional form of government, ban Fascist organizations, dissolve the National Assembly and call new elections, grant amnesty to political prisoners, withdraw Bulgarian troops from Serbia, and enter into talks with the Allies. By releasing the opponents of the regents from prison, Muraviev unintentionally helped in the preparations for a pro-Soviet coup. Negotiations with the Allies did not make headway because of the opposition of the Kremlin. The Red Army had already reached the Danube, and Muraviev delayed granting permission for it to march through Bulgarian territory until an agreement was reached with the Soviet Union. Meanwhile, on 5 September the Soviets declared war on Bulgaria. On the same day, without delay, Muraviev's government broke off its ties with Germany, whose troops were retreating from Bulgaria. The minister of war, Ivan Marinov, who by then had started cooperating with the Communists, delayed the announcement of this decision for three days, giving more time to the plotters. On 8 September Soviet troops began to enter Bulgaria unopposed. At the last moment and against the will of

the regents, Muraviev declared war on Germany, but it was too late. On 9 September 1944 his government was overthrown by an uprising organized by the Communists and by officers supporting the Zveno group. Arrested by General Marinov, Muraviev was imprisoned for a short time in the Soviet Union, but at the beginning of 1945 he was sentenced in Sofia to life in prison. Released in 1955 but imprisoned again during the Hungarian Revolution in 1956, Muraviev was held in the Belene forced labor camp. Released toward the end of his life, he did not play any political role. His memoirs, *Subitiia i khora: Spomeni* (Events and people: Memoirs), were published in 1992 in Sofia. He was also the author of *Dogovorut za mir v Nuyi* (The Neuilly Peace Treaty; 1993). In 1996 the Supreme Court in Bulgaria quashed the sentence against Muraviev issued in 1945. (WR)

Sources: *Kratka bulgarska entsiklopediya*, vol. 3 (Sofia, 1963); *Biographisches Lexikon*, vol. 3; Marshall Lee Miller, *Bulgaria during the Second World War* (Stanford, 1975); Stephane Groueff, *Crown of Thorns* (Lanham, Md., 1987); Tasho Tashev, *Ministrite na Bulgariya 1879–1999: Entsiklopedichen Spravochnik* (Sofia, 1999).

MURAVSCHI Valeriu (1949, Orhei), Moldavian politician. Muravschi graduated in economics from the Polytechnic Institute in Kishinev. From June 1990 he was minister of finance of the Moldavian SSR, and on 28 May 1991, thanks to the support of President **Mircea Snegur**, he became head of the republican government. As a result of the failure of the Moscow putsch, both Moldavian leaders decided to support the independence of the republic, which the parliament declared on 27 August 1991. At the same time the new state of Moldova was introduced into the Commonwealth of Independent States. Muravschi's government was dominated by the Moldavian Romanians, and some of them thought Moldova should merge with Romania. Muravschi could not overcome the growing ethnic tensions: the Gagauz separatist movement and the secession of the Transnistrian Republic announced by the Russians under the auspices of the Soviet troops stationed on the Dniester River. In order to solve these problems President Snegur forced Muravschi's resignation on 30 June 1992 and was willing to create a multiethnic government. From 1992 Muravschi was an MP, and in 1993 he founded the short-lived Socialist Workers' Party. From 1995 he chaired the Union of Moldavian Banks, and from 1996, the Christian Democratic People's Party of Moldova (Partidul Ţăranesc Creştin Democrat din Moldova [PTCDM]), advocating privatization and Christian values. In the elections of February 2001 the PTCDM won 8.2 percent of the vote and 11 percent of the mandates, becoming the third largest faction. In November 2001 it merged with four other groups into the Liberal Party (Partidul Liberal). (WR)

Sources: *Europa Środkowo-Wschodnia 1992* (Warsaw, 1994); Bugajski; *RFE/RL Newsline*, 13 November 2002; www.terra.es/personal2/monolith/moldova.htm; www.1upinfo.com/country-guide-study/moldova/moldova51.html.

MUSHANOV Nikola (12 April 1872, Drianovo–10 May 1951, Turnovo), Bulgarian lawyer and politician. After graduating from high school, Mushanov completed law studies in Aix-en-Provence, France and subsequently worked as an attorney in Ruse. He entered politics in 1897, joining the Democratic Party. In 1902 he was elected an MP for the first time. From January 1908 to September 1910 he was minister of education and introduced a reform of the school system. Subsequently, until March 1911, he served as minister of interior in the government of **Aleksandur Malinov**. A supporter of West European-style democracy, after the victory of the Entente, Mushanov accepted the posts of minister of social welfare, railways, interior, and health in the first agrarian government after the war. He resigned in June 1919 because he opposed the autocratic governments of **Aleksandur Stamboliyski**. Arrested during the increasing dictatorship of Stamboliyski, Mushanov was not released until the coup of June 1923.

In the 1920s Mushanov worked as an attorney. On 12 October 1931, after the resignation of Malinov, Mushanov became head of a coalition cabinet formed with the Agrarians and the Liberals. On 14 May 1934 he announced his resignation and failed to fulfill the mission of forming a new cabinet. His government was de facto dismissed during the bloodless coup of 18 May 1934, but Mushanov kept his parliamentary seat. He was again elected to the parliament in the 1938 elections, which were manipulated by the tsarist camarilla. During World War II he was in opposition to the pro-German governments of **Georgi Kioseivanov** and **Bogdan Filov**, but he accepted the Bulgarian territorial gains of 1940–41: Macedonia, Southern Dobruja, and a part of Thrace. From the beginning of 1943 onwards Mushanov increasingly called for an agreement with the Allies. He maintained correct relations with Soviet diplomats in Sofia but refused to join the Fatherland Front, considering it openly pro-Soviet and hoping that Tsar **Boris III** would bring about an agreement with the Allies. At the beginning of September 1944 the regents considered entrusting Mushanov with the mission of forming a government, but he eventually joined the government of **Konstantin Muraviev** as minister without portfolio. After the coup of 9 September 1944 Mushanov was arrested and sentenced to life imprisonment. On the anniversary of the September coup he was released under an amnesty and again joined the Democratic Party, for which he was placed under house arrest in the countryside. Mushanov was murdered by the security services. In 1992 his *Spomeni: Dnevnik* (Memoirs) were published in Bulgaria. (WR)

Sources: *Entsiklopediya Bulgariya*, vol. 4 (Sofia, 1984); Marshall Lee Miller, *Bulgaria during the Second World War* (Stanford, 1975); Stephane Groueff, *Crown of Thorns* (Lanham, Md., 1987); Jerzy Jackowicz, *Partie opozycyjne w Bułgarii 1944–1948* (Warsaw, 1997); Tasho Tashev, *Ministrite na Bulgariya 1879–1999: Entsiklopedichen Spravochnik* (Sofia, 1999).

MÜÜRISEPP Aleksei (4 July 1902, Valta–7 October 1970, Tartu), Estonian Communist activist. Müürisepp's father was a sailor. In 1908, along with his parents, he was deported into the depths of Russia. He initially lived in Siberia. From 1924 to 1926 he served in the Red Army. Having completed his military service, he joined the Bolshevik party and was assigned to work in the trade unions. After graduating from the Tomsk Railway Electromechanical Engineering Institute in 1937, Müürisepp worked on the railways in Ordzonikidze and Krasnoyarsk (1942–44). He went to Estonia in 1944 and rose rapidly through the ranks of the Communist Party (Bolshevik) of Estonia (CP[B]E), becoming secretary of its Central Committee (CC) (1948–49). After **Johannes Käbin** came to power, Müürisepp became one of Käbin's closest associates. From 1949 to 1951 he was deputy prime minister; from 29 March 1951 to 12 October 1961 he was prime minister of the Estonian SSR; from 1952 to 1966 he was a member of the CPSU CC; and from 1950 to 1962 he also held the portfolio of minister of foreign affairs of the Estonian SSR. Müürisepp conducted a purge of the Ministry of Foreign Affairs of the Estonian SSR, expelling many officials who had been trained by **Hans Kruus**, his predecessor, who was accused of nationalism. After leaving the post of prime minister, Müürisepp became chairman of the Supreme Soviet of the Estonian SSR and deputy chairman of the Supreme Soviet of the Soviet Union. He held these positions until the end of his life. In the final stage of his career, Müürisepp also served as a member of the Audit Commission of the CPSU and the USSR Supreme Soviet. He sat on the CC and on the Politburo of the Communist Party of Estonia until the end of his life. (AG)

Sources: *Bolshaia Sovetskaia Entsiklopediia*, vol. 17 (Moscow, 1974); *Eesti Enstuklopeedia*, vol. 14 (Tallinn, 2000); Romuald J. Misunas and Rein Taagepera, *The Baltic States: The Years of Dependence, 1940–1970* (Berkeley, 1993); Eero Medijainen, "Foreign Ministry of the Estonian SSR," in Strona, "Okupatsioon Museum," www.okupatsioon.ee/english/overviews/index.html.

N

NAGY Ferenc (8 October 1903, Bisse–12 June 1979, Fairfax, Virginia), Peasant Party politician and prime minister of Hungary. Born into a peasant family, for many years Nagy worked as a farmer. In 1923 he joined the first Party of Smallholders, founded by **Istvan Szabó Nagyatádi**. In 1929 he published an article on political discrimination against peasants that made him popular in the Hungarian countryside. Since the Horthy authorities disregarded the demands of the peasants, Nagy left the party, which had become an appendage of the system, and with **Zoltan Tildy** he began to form a new Independent Smallholders' Party (ISP). The party was officially created on 12 October 1930 at a rally in Békés, and Nagy was elected its secretary general. Despite the pressure of the Horthysts, in the 1935 elections the party received 25 percent of the vote but only twenty-three seats in the parliament. Nagy was elected an MP. In September 1941 he also became the leader of the supraparty Peasant Union. After the defeat of the Hungarian Army at Voronezh in 1943, Nagy brought about an alliance between the peasant parties and the Social Democrats, in opposition to the Horthy policy.

On 17 April 1944 Nagy was arrested by the Gestapo in Pécs and was jailed in Budapest. The Horthy prison administration released him when the Arrow Cross Party took over power in mid-October 1944; the shift in administrations probably saved his life. Under the rule of **Ferenc Szálasi**, Nagy remained in hiding, but in January 1945 he started to revive his party in the Hungarian territory controlled by the Red Army. In the spring of 1945 Nagy became minister of reconstruction in the provisional coalition government and chairman of the National Cooperative Council. On 19 August 1945 he was again elected president of the ISP. After the ISP electoral victory of 4 November 1945, Nagy became president of parliament. When Prime Minister **Zoltan Tildy** assumed the presidency, on 3 February 1946 Nagy became the head of government. Despite the fact that the Smallholders had an absolute majority in parliament, Nagy's was a coalition government because of the demands of the Allied Control Commission, headed by Marshal Kliment Voroshilov. Deputy Prime Minister Mátyás Rákosi, the leader of the Communist Party, played a special role in this cabinet.

In the summer of 1946 Nagy held talks in Moscow and then in the United States, Great Britain, and France. The Communists, who controlled the departments of security and justice, made repeated attempts to undermine the position of the government and the Smallholders' Party through intrigues. They kept discovering a succession of "plots" against democracy, in which they finally entangled the secretary general of the Smallholders' Party, **Béla Kovács**. Nagy courageously defended his closest associate but could not prevent his arrest by Soviet services. In May 1947 Nagy went to Switzerland for a short holiday; there he learned that Kovács had been forced to testify against him. Rákosi demanded his resignation as prime minister, threatening that he could not otherwise guarantee the safety of his wife and five-year-old son, who had remained in Hungary. On 2 June 1947 Nagy resigned as head of government; having received an American visa, he left with his family for the United States.

In America Nagy bought a farm in Herndon, Virginia. He belonged to the Executive Committee of the Hungarian National Council, and in 1960 he joined the Hungarian Committee, in which he dealt with foreign affairs. As a representative of the committee, Nagy sat in the Assembly of Captive European Nations and in 1961–62 was its president. In 1948 Nagy published his memoirs, *The Struggle behind the Iron Curtain*, in the United States. The Hungarian edition came out in his homeland in 1990. (WR)

Sources: Peter Horvath, "Communist Tactics in Hungary between June 1944 and June 1947," Ph.D. diss., New York University, 1955; Paul A. Homori, "Soviet Influences on the Establishment and Character of the Hungarian People's Republic 1944–1954," Ph.D. diss., University of Michigan, 1964; Csicsery-Rónay István, ed. *Nagy Ferenc miniszterelnök: Visszamelékezések, tanulmányok, cikkek (összeállította és a bevezetot írta)*ed. (Budapest, 1995); Eric Roman, *Hungary and the Victor Powers, 1945–1959* (New York, 1996); Steven Bela Vardy, *Historical Dictionary of Hungary* (Lanham, Md., 1997).

NAGY Imre (6 June 1896, Kaposvár–16 June 1958, Budapest), Hungarian Communist politician, leader of the revolution of 1956. Nagy's father was a court servant, an orderly in a *comitat* (county), and an employee of the telegraph service. After completing four grades of a gymnasium, Nagy was apprenticed to a locksmith. In 1915 he was conscripted into the army, and in the summer of the next year he was taken captive by the Russians. From June 1918 he fought in the civil war with the Red Guards. In February 1920 he joined the Bolshevik party, and in March 1921 he returned to Hungary and worked as a clerk in an insurance company in his hometown. Nagy took part in the work of a local organization of the Hungarian Social Democratic Party, but in 1925 he was expelled from the party. In 1927, because of his Communist activities, Nagy was arrested for a short period. After his release he emigrated to Vienna, but he repeatedly illegally returned to Hungary. On behalf of the Communist Party he organized activity among the peasants, and he was head of the Department for the Countryside for the party. At the Second Congress of the Hungarian Communist Party (HCP) in Moscow in 1930 Nagy was criticized for his "rightist deviation." From 1930 he lived in the USSR. He worked at the Institute for Agrarian Sciences, at the Communist International, at the Central Statistical Office of the USSR, and in 1939–44 he also worked at Moscow radio, where he was the editor of broadcasts in Hungarian. In those years Nagy published many works on agrarian issues. In 1936 he was expelled from the party, but in 1938 he had his membership reinstated.

In November 1944 Nagy returned to Hungary as a member of the leadership of the HCP. From December 1944 he was an MP to the Provisional National Assembly and later to parliament. In the Provisional National Government he was the minister of agriculture and carried out the parceling of land; then he served as interior minister in the coalition government until 20 March 1946. Later, he was one of the secretaries of the HCP. Between 1947 and 1949 Nagy was president of parliament. Between 1944 and 1949 he was a member of the Central Committee (CC) of the HCP and (from 1948) the Hungarian Workers' Party (HWP). In 1945–49 and 1951–55 he was a member of the party's Politburo. Nagy did not support the rapid collectivization of agriculture nor the persecution of "kulaks." Nagy performed a self-criticism, but in 1949 he was openly denounced by Stalin, and he was excluded from the leadership of the party. Until the summer of 1950 Nagy lectured at the Hungarian Agricultural Academy in Budapest. It was then that he was appointed head of the Administrative Department of the CC of the HWP. From 1950 he was a corresponding member, and between 1953 and 1955 a full member, of the Hungarian Academy of Sciences. From December 1950 he was minister of food supply; from January 1952 he held the post of purchasing minister; and from November 1952 he served as deputy prime minister.

After Stalin's death, on 4 July 1953 at the initiative of the Soviet faction of Georgy Malenkov, Nagy became prime minister. He attempted then to implement moderate economic reforms that aimed at the improvement of public provision. For example, the negative attitude toward the individual agriculturalist was moderated, and collectivization was slowed down; moreover, forced labor camps began to be eliminated, and some political prisoners were released. On 18 April 1955 Nagy was dismissed as prime minister, and in December he was also expelled from the party and stripped of his academic degrees. These steps were connected with Malenkov's departure from the post of prime minister of the USSR. Nagy did not want to recant

and stuck to his program. He was considered a leading politician of the party opposition against the Stalinists. On 13 October 1956 he was readmitted to the party. His academic degrees were given back to him as well.

On 23 October 1956, at the demands of demonstrators in Budapest, Nagy became a member of the supreme party leadership, and he was reinstated as prime minister. Acting as premier, on the one hand, Nagy wanted the HWP authorities and the Soviet leadership to recognize the main aims of the revolution, but on the other hand, he attempted to curb the demonstrators' demands, which he felt were excessive. As Nagy increasingly identified with the demonstrators, on 28 October he announced a cease-fire, moved for the withdrawal of Soviet troops from Hungarian territory, and declared the introduction of a multiparty system. Despite the cease-fire, Soviet troops continued to arrive in Hungary, so on 1 November Nagy declared Hungary's neutrality and its withdrawal from the Warsaw Pact. On the morning of 4 November the Soviet troops attacked Budapest. Nagy took refuge in the Yugoslav Embassy. On 22 November he left the embassy, as he was granted a safe-conduct by the Soviet-installed provisional government of **János Kádár**; nonetheless, he was seized by the Soviet services and deported to the town of Snagov in Romania. Arrested there on 14 April 1957, Nagy was returned to Budapest. He did not want to resign as prime minister in favor of Kádár and would not renounce the idea of the revolution; had he done so, it might have saved his life.

By a resolution of the CC of the Hungarian Socialist Workers' Party on 21 December 1956, a political case was instituted against Nagy. After repeated postponements of a trial, on 15 June 1958 the People's Judicial Council of the Supreme Court accused Nagy, as the political leader at the time, of "counterrevolution," of initiating and directing the 1956 events, and of high treason; it then sentenced him to death. Nagy denied all the accusations, and he declined to defend himself. Nor did he ask for a pardon. The sentence was executed in the National Prison in Budapest. Nagy's body was put in an unmarked grave there, and in 1961 his remains were taken to the Ràkoskeresztúr Municipal Cemetery and buried in plot 301. In the spring of 1989, under pressure from democratic forces, his remains were exhumed, and on 16 June 1989 they were reburied in the same place, along with the remains of his associates in martyrdom. The funeral ceremonies became a symbolic breakthrough during the democratic transformations in Hungary. (JT)

Sources: *The Times*, 18 June 1958; *The Counterrevolutionary Conspiracy of Imre Nagy and His Accomplices* (Budapest, 1958); The *Truth about the Nagy Affair: Facts, Documents, Comments* (London, 1959); Méray Tibor, *Thirteen Days That Shook the*

Kremlin (New York, 1959); Tóbiás Áron, *In memoriam Nagy Imre: Emlékezés egy miniszterelnökre. Válogatta, szerkesztette és a bevezetűok szövegeit írta* (Budapest, 1989); Méray Tibor, *Nagy Imre élete és halála* (Budapest, 1989); Aleksander Nawrocki, *Jak zamordowano Imre Nagya?* (Warsaw, 1990); *1956 kézikönyve,* vol. 3 (*Megtorlás és Emlékezés*) (Budapest, 1996); *Nagy Képes Milleniumi Arcképcsarnok* (Budapest, 1999); *A magyar forradalom és szabadságharc enciklopédiája,* CD-ROM (Budapest, 1999).

NAJDER Zdzisław (31 October 1930, Warsaw), Polish historian of literature and politician. Najder graduated in philosophy and Polish studies from Warsaw University in 1954. In 1969 he received a Ph.D. and in 1977 his postdoctoral degree. He worked at the Institute of Literary Studies of the Polish Academy of Sciences (1952–57), published in *Twórczość* (1957–81), and lectured in the United States and Great Britain. An outstanding expert on Joseph Conrad, in 1976 Najder founded and until 1981 chaired the Polish Alliance for Independence (Polskie Porozumienie Niepodległościowe [PPN]), a secret organization that published analyses and essays shaping the political thought of the democratic opposition in the spirit of full independence and democracy. Najder worked closely with the Paris monthly *Kultura* (writing there under the pen name "Socjusz"). From 1977 he was harassed by the security services. When martial law was introduced in Poland on 13 December 1981, Najder was in Great Britain. Warned by the British Foreign Ministry that an investigation concerning the PPN was under way, he stayed in the West. From April 1982 to March 1987 Najder was head of the Polish Section of Radio Free Europe. In May 1983 he was sentenced to death in absentia and deprived of his Polish citizenship. After this sentence was annulled in 1989, Najder returned to Poland in February 1990. He joined the Civic Committee of the Chairman of Solidarity and managed its activities. In October 1990 he became the formal chairman of the committee. As a follower of **Lech Wałęsa**, Najder played an important role during the so-called war at the top between the followers of Wałęsa and those of **Tadeusz Mazowiecki**. In 1991 Najder belonged to the Advisory Committee of President Wałęsa. In 1992 he headed the group of advisers of Prime Minister **Jan Olszewski**, and then he chaired the Civic Institute in Warsaw. In 1992 Najder fell a political victim of the lustration for having signed an agreement to contact the security services in 1958. These contacts had been rare, and he broke them off in 1963. In the 1990s Najder was a professor at the University of Opole. Najder authored *Nad Conradem* (On Conrad; 1965); *Życie Conrada-Korzeniowskiego* (The life of Conrad-Korzeniowski; 1980); the collections of essays *Ile jest dróg?* (How many ways? 1982) and *Wymiary polskich spraw 1982–1990* (Di-

mensions of Polish affairs 1982–1990; 1990); and a diary of the years 1990–92, *Jaka Polska: Co i komu doradzałem?* (What kind of Poland: What and whom did I advise? 1993). Najder also published, in English, *Joseph Conrad: A Chronicle* (1983) and *Conrad in Perspective* (1997), and he edited a number of studies on Conrad. (AF)

Sources: *Nowa encyklopedia powszechna PWN,* vol. 4 (Warsaw, 1996); *Opozycja w PRL: Słownik biograficzny 1956–89,* vol. 1 (Warsaw, 2000); *Kto jest kim w Polsce* (Warsaw, 2001); Antoni Dudek, *Pierwsze lata III Rzeczypospolitej 1989–2001* (Kraków, 2002).

NANO Fatos (16 September 1952, Tirana), Albanian politician. The son of a journalist and director of Albanian Radio and Television, in 1975 Nano graduated in economics from the University of Tirana. He worked as an economist in the Elbasan Iron Mill and later at the Institute of Marxist-Leninist Studies of the Central Committee of the (Communist) Albanian Labor Party (ALP). From 1981 he worked as an economist at Priska, but he returned to the institute in 1984, at the same time lecturing in the Department of Economics of the University of Tirana. Nano started his political career in 1990 as general secretary of the Council of Ministers. In January 1991 he became deputy prime minister and minister of foreign trade, and on 22 February 1991, prime minister of the so-called government of reform. In an interview for *The Independent* he stated, "I am not a Stalinist, I am neither a Maoist nor a follower of Pol Pot. In fact, I am an Albanian and I want to integrate Albania with Europe." In the short run Nano could not uphold the credibility of the totalitarian party, so on 5 June 1991 he resigned and was elected head of the post-Communist Albanian Socialist Party (Partia Socialiste Shqipërisë [PSS]).

At the first national PSS conference, Nano rejected the idea of a continuation of the ALP line and refused to bear responsibility for Hoxha's regime and its crimes." In 1992 Nano was elected an MP from Kuçovë. On 28 February 1993 the parliament, dominated by the Albanian Democratic Party, deprived Nano of immunity, and on 3 April 1994 a Tirana court sentenced him to twelve years in prison for forging documents and the embezzlement of foreign aid funds. In November 1995 the Supreme Court reduced the sentence to four years. Nano served the sentence in Benca Prison, near Tepelene. In August 1996, while still in jail, he was elected the PSS leader again. During a deep political crisis, caused by the collapse of the financial pyramid schemes, on 4 March 1997 President **Sali Berisha** amnestied Nano. He was elected an MP from the Tepelene district, and after a victorious election, on 23 July 1997 Nano resumed duties as prime minister. On 2 October 1998 he resigned, after demonstrations connected with the death of **Azem Hajdari**, but he retained the PSS leadership. In February 1999 Nano gave up the PSS chairmanship, but he also caused the resignation of his successor, Pendeli Majko. In January 2002 Nano caused another crisis, forcing the dismissal of another PSS prime minister, Ilir Meta. (TC)

Sources: Elez Biberaj, *Shqipëria ne tranzicion: Rruga e vështrisë drejt Demokracisë* (Tirana, 2001); Miranda Vickers and James Pettifier, *Albania: From Anarchy to a Balkan Identity* (New York, 1997); Bugajski; www.rulers.org.

NARUTOWICZ Gabriel (17 March 1865, Telshe [Telšiai, Telsze], Samogitia region–16 December 1922, Warsaw), hydraulic engineer, first president of Poland. Narutiwucz came from a landed gentry family. He attended a German classical high school in Libau (Liepāja) from 1873 to 1883 and subsequently studied at the Department of Physics and Mathematics of St. Petersburg University but discontinued his studies for health reasons. In the spring of 1886 he went to Davos, Switzerland, for treatment. In the fall of 1886 he commenced studies at the Department of Civil Engineering of the Technical University in Zurich and graduated with distinction in March 1891. While a student, Narutowicz became loosely affiliated with an émigré group of the Second Proletariat Party; consequently, in 1889 he could not return to his country because the tsarist authorities issued a warrant for his arrest. In 1891 Narutowicz started his professional career. In 1895 he received Swiss citizenship. He soon won international recognition as a water power engineer. In 1907 he was appointed to the chair of Hydropower Engineering of the Technical University, Zurich. He established his own design office, which supervised the construction of water power plants in Austria, Spain, Switzerland, and Italy. He designed the Mühleberg hydroelectric power plant on the Aare River, one of the biggest and most modern hydroelectric plants at that time in Europe. He also designed an electricity plant powered by the water from melting glaciers; such a design was then an absolute novelty. Although Narutowicz's return to Poland prevented the implementation of this project, the idea was put into practice in Switzerland in 1955. In 1911 Narutowicz initiated river engineering works in Galicia. From 1913 to 1920 he held various positions, including that of dean of the School of Engineering at the Technical University, Zurich, and member of the Water Management Commission at the Department of Home Affairs of the Federal Council. He became a Swiss delegate to the International Commission for the Regulation of the Rhine in 1914 and chairman of the commission in 1915.

In 1914 Narutowicz established the Polish Mutual Aid Committee in Zurich, and in 1915 he became a member of the Committee for Aid to War Victims in Poland, which was founded by (among others) **Henryk Sienkiewicz**. Narutowicz initially supported the notion that Poland should regain independence without siding with any of the states that had partitioned it. He gave lectures and wrote press articles. He was a member of the La Pologne et la Guerre Society in Lausanne and a member of the editorial staff of the Polish Encyclopedia Publishers. He finally became an adherent of the ideas promoted by **Józef Piłsudski**. Narutowicz was responsible for money sent from the United States for the Polish Legions and was in charge of their press bureaus in Bern and Rapperswil. In January 1917 he expressed in print his disappointment with the policies of the Entente states and expressed his support for the Central Powers. However, he rejected political proposals from Germany. After the outbreak of the revolution in Russia, he again became a supporter of the Entente.

In July 1919 Narutowicz became a consultant to the Polish Ministry of Public Works and participated in various projects, including that of channeling the Vistula River. As minister of public works (June 1920–June 1922), he reorganized his ministry and successfully initiated the enactment of many laws, including pioneering water management and electricity laws. He also brought about the construction of numerous civil engineering projects. From 1920 to 1922 Narutowicz was the first president of the newly established Academy of Technical Sciences, and he was chairman of the National Reconstruction Council in 1921. Appointed by the government as a delegate for the incorporation of the Wilno (Vilnius) region, in 1922 Narutowicz went there to calm the anti-government sentiments. In April 1922 he became Poland's delegate to an international conference in Genoa at which postwar political and economic relations in Europe were discussed. In June 1922 Narutowicz became minister of foreign affairs. He drafted a proposal for the autonomy of Eastern Galicia. Considered a supporter of Piłsudski, to whom he was related by affinity, Narutowicz wanted to tighten relations with Romania and develop economic cooperation with Soviet Russia. He was a member of the Wolność Przywrócona (Restored Freedom) Masonic lodge, which belonged to the Grand National Lodge.

In November 1922 Narutowicz ran in the elections to the Assembly on the ticket of the National Union in the Polish Eastern Territories, a party supported by Piłsudski, but he lost. On 8 December 1922 **Stanisław Thugutt**, chairman of the Polish Peasant Party–Liberation (Polskie Stronnictwo Ludowe–Wyzwolenie [PSL–Liberation]), proposed Narutowicz as a presidential candidate. Narutowicz initially refused, declaring his support for **Stanisław Wojciechowski**, but finally he agreed to stand. Narutowicz's candidacy was one of five submitted on 9 December 1922. Elected in the fifth round of voting with support from the left-wing and centrist parties and the national minorities, Narutowicz defeated Count **Maurycy Zamoyski**, the representative of the right-wing parties. Narutowicz's election met with an attack by the right-wing parties, particularly the National Democrats. Accusations were made that he had been elected by the vote of the national minorities, mainly Jews. Attempts were made to prevent him from taking the presidential oath in the Assembly. Some politicians, including **Wincenty Witos**, suggested that Narutowicz renounce this election. On 11 December 1922 Narutowicz was sworn in, and on 14 December he took over power from Piłsudski. On 16 December 1922 at the opening of an art exhibit in the Zachęta Society of Fine Arts in Warsaw, Narutowicz was assassinated by Eligiusz Niewiadomski, a mentally disturbed painter and fanatic supporter of National Democracy. Narutowicz is buried in the crypt of St. John's Cathedral in Warsaw. (JS)

Sources: *PSB*, vol. 22; *Kto był kim w Drugiej Rzeczypospolitej* (Warsaw, 1994); Tadeusz Hołówko, *Prezydent Gabriel Narutowicz; Życie i działalność* (Warsaw, 1924); Marek Ruszczyc, *Pierwszy prezydent Gabriel Narutowicz* (Warsaw, 1967); Franciszek Bernaś, *Gabriel Narutowicz* (Warsaw, 1979); *Prezydenci i premierzy Drugiej Rzeczypospolitej* (Wrocław, 1992); Janusz Pajewski and Waldemar Łazuga, *Gabriel Narutowicz: Pierwszy prezydent Rzeczypospolitej* (Warsaw, 1993); Ludwik Hass, *Masoneria polska XX wieku* (Warsaw, 1996).

NĂSTASE Adrian (22 June 1950, Bucharest), Romanian lawyer and politician. In 1973 Năstase graduated in law from the University of Bucharest, and then he worked at the Institute of Legal Studies (ILS). In 1978 he also graduated in sociology. In 1987 he received a Ph.D. at the ILS. In 1977–79 and 1984–85 Năstase lectured in international public law at the Academy of Economic Studies in Bucharest. He spent the years 1980–82 on scholarships in Great Britain and Norway. He worked at the UNESCO Department of Human Rights and Peace in London and at the International Institute of Peace Studies in Oslo. A member of the Romanian Association of Scholars, in 1982 Năstase went to France, where he became director of the International Institute of Human Rights in Strasbourg and researcher at the French Society on International Law in Paris. Accepted by the **Nicolae Ceaușescu** regime, Năstase was loyal to it.

After the fall of Ceaușescu, in 1990 Năstase began a political career in the National Salvation Front (Frontul Sălvari Naționale [FSN]). He became an MP and was foreign minister until December 1992. From 1992 to 1996 he chaired the Chamber of Deputies of the Romanian parliament. After the FSN split in 1992, Năstase

remained in the group supporting **Ion Iliescu**; it created the Democratic National Salvation Front (Frontul Democrat Salvări Naționale), turned in 1993 into the Party of Social Democracy in Romania (Partidul Democrației Sociale din România [PDSR]). In 1993–97 Năstase was the PDSR chairman. In 1994 he lectured on international public law at the Sorbonne in Paris. In 1994 he initiated a parliamentary coalition of the PDSR with extreme nationalists and Communist members of the former nomenklatura. The coalition lasted until the end of 1995. Năstase was one of the closest aides of President Iliescu. When the PDSR lost the elections of November 1996, in 1997 Năstase was elected deputy chairman of his party and a member of the Romanian delegation to the Parliamentary Assembly of the Council of Europe. He criticized the NATO air raids on the new Yugoslavia in 1999, as well as concessions of the reform government to the Romanian Hungarians. When the PDSR won the parliamentary elections and Iliescu won the presidency again, on 28 December 2000 Năstase became prime minister. His government announced the creation of a "socially oriented" market economy, a struggle against corruption, and efforts toward Romania's integration into NATO and the European Union. In early 2001 Năstase was elected the PDSR chairman, replacing Iliescu, who resigned from the party.

Năstase authored more than 150 books and articles on international law and international relations, including the following: *The Right to Peace* (1991); *Drepturile omului: Religia secolului viitor* (Human rights: The religion of the future century; 1992); *Drepturile omului, socieatea civilă, diplomația parlamentară: Idei, acțiuni, evoluție* (Human rights, civil society, parliamentary diplomacy: Ideas, actions, evolution; 1994); and *Lupta pentru viitor* (The struggle for the future; 2000). Năstase held numerous positions in Romanian and international research societies, including the Euro-Atlantic Center in Bucharest, the Institute of East-West Security Studies in New York, and the American Association of International Law. (LW)

Sources: Józef Darski, *Rumunia: Historia, współczesność, konflikty narodowe* (Warsaw, 1995); Tom Gallagher, *Romania after Ceausescu* (Edinburgh, 1995); Ion Alexandrescu, Ion Bulei, Ion Mamina, and Ioan Scurtu, *Enciclopedia de istorie României* (Bucharest, 2000); David Phinnemore, *Post-Communist Romania* (New York, 2001); Bugajski; www.cidob.org; www.rulers.org; www.guv.ro.

NATLAČEN Marko (24 April 1886, Manče–13 October 1942, Ljubljana), Slovene politician. Natlačen completed law studies in Vienna. He subsequently became an activist of the Slovene People's Party and the president of Orel (Eagle), a conservative organization of Slovene Catholic youth. From September 1935 to April 1941 he served as governor (*ban*) of Drava Province (*banovina*), which comprised Slovenia. On 6 April 1941, after the German invasion of Yugoslavia, Natlačen established the National Council of Slovenia (Narodni Svet z Sloveniju), which sought autonomy for Slovenia under Italian tutelage. He wanted to extract some political concessions from the Italian occupiers, so he joined the Consultative Council of Ljubljana Province, established by the Italians, but he did not achieve much. Trying to prevent Italian persecutions, Natlačen destroyed the lists—in his possession—that included the names of members and supporters of the Communist Party. Despite his efforts, Natlačen was regarded as a traitor both by the Conservatives and by the Communists, and he was murdered by Communist security agents. (WR)

Sources: *Enciklopedia Slovenije*, vol. 7 (Ljubljana, 1993); Leopoldina Plut-Progelj and Carole Rogel, *Historical Dictionary of Slovenia* (Lanham, Md., 1996).

NAZARUK Osyp (31 August 1883, Nahiryanka, near Buchach–31 March 1940, Kraków), Ukrainian lawyer, politician, and journalist. Born into a family of peasants and craftsmen, Nazaruk was refused admission to all high schools in Galicia for taking part in democratic organizations and leftist student groups (1899–1904). In 1902 he finally graduated from high school in Lemberg (Lwów, Lviv), and he later studied in Vienna, earning a Ph.D. in law (1908). Nazaruk was a member of the executive of the Ukrainian Radical Party (URP) from 1905 to 1919 and co-edited *Hromadsky Holos* from 1916 to 1918. He became famous as a gifted rally speaker. From 1915 to 1918 Nazaruk served as director of the press bureau of the Ukrainian Sich Riflemen's Legion. A member of the Ukrainian National Rada (Council) of the Western Ukrainian National Republic (Zakhidno-Ukrayins'ka Narodna Republika [ZUNR]), he was delegated to negotiate with Hetman **Pavlo Skoropadskyi** for assistance against Poland. After arriving in the Dnieper region in November 1918, as a member of the Sich Riflemen's Council, Nazaruk participated in the revolt against the hetman's regime in Belaya Tserkov (Bila Tserkva). He held several positions in the first governments of the Ukrainian National Republic (UNR); for example, he directed the Ukrainian Telegraphic Agency and served as minister of press and propaganda. In early 1919 Nazaruk became aligned with **Volodymyr Vynnychenko** and began to doubt the effectiveness of democracy and evolving toward dictatorship. In mid-1919 Nazaruk became a close associate of **Yevhen Petrushevych**, dictator of the ZUNR, and he contributed to *Strilets*, an organ of the Ukrainian Galician Army.

From 1920 to 1922 Nazaruk edited the official periodicals of the ZUNR government-in-exile in Vienna and was subsequently sent to Canada, where he represented this government for the Ukrainians in exile (1922–23). Influenced by **Vyacheslav Lypynskyi**, Nazaruk definitely abandoned his democratic views. In 1923–26 he was in the United States, where he edited *Sich* in Chicago and co-edited *Ameryka* in Philadelphia, both of which were Conservative press organs. After returning to Lwów, Nazaruk became aligned with Bishop **Hryhoriy Khomyshyn**, and from 1928 to 1939 he served as editor-in-chief of *Nova Zoria*, a periodical of the Ukrainian Christian Organization. In 1930 Nazaruk was a founding member of the Ukrainian Catholic People's Party (Ukrayinska Katolytska Narodna Partiya), a party of Ukrainian Conservatives in Poland. He promoted the idea of Ukraine as a "synthesis" of the East and the West, expressed in Eastern-rite Catholicism. In the 1930s Nazaruk was the leading journalist of the Ukrainian Catholic press in Poland. He sought cooperation with Polish Conservatives and strove for a change in the Polish government's policies toward the Ukrainians. In October 1939 he moved from Lwów to Warsaw and later to Kraków, where he died. Nazaruk authored his memoirs, *Slidamy USS* (Tracing the Ukrainian Sich Riflemen; 1916) and *Rik na Velykiy Ukraiini* (One year in the Great Ukraine; 1920); the historical novels *Kniaz Iaroslav Osmomysl* (1920) and *Roksoliana* (1930); and sociopolitical brochures and reports. In the memoirs *Zi Lvova do Varshavy* (From Lviv to Warsaw; 1995), written on the eve of the fall of the Second Republic of Poland, Nazaruk sharply criticized the policies of the Polish state toward national minorities. (TS)

Sources: Ryszard Torzecki, *Kwestia ukraińska w Polsce w latach 1923–1929* (Warsaw, 1989); Ivan Lysiak-Rudnytskyi, "Nazaruk i Lypyns'kyi," in Ivan Lysiak-Rudnytskyi, *Istorychni ese*, vol. 2 (Lviv, 1996); M. Shwahulak, "Osyp Nazaruk i jego 'ucieczka' przed Sowietami," in Osyp Nazaruk, *Ucieczka ze Lwowa do Warszawy* (Przemyśl, 1999).

NAZOR Vladimir (30 May 1876, Postire, island of Brač–19 June 1949, Zagreb), Croatian poet and writer. In 1906 Nazor completed studies in the natural sciences at Graz. In his early volumes—*Slavenske legende* (Slavic Legends; 1910), *Živana* (1902), *Lirika* (Lyric poetry; 1910), *Hrvatski kraljevi* (Croatian kings; 1912), and *Nove pjesme* (New poems; 1913)—he drew on national history and sought inspiration from biblical, Greek, Roman, and Slavic mythology. Nazor was regarded as a spiritual leader for the supporters of a common state of Southern Slav peoples, but under the influence of World War I he abandoned the role of bard of the Yugoslav people. For many years Nazor worked in schools in Split, Pazin, Zadar, Koper, Kastav, Zagreb, Sušak, and Crikvenica. After retiring in 1931, he lived in Zagreb. At the end of 1942 he made his way from Ustasha-controlled Zagreb to the Partisans led by **Josip Broz Tito**. The daring feat of the aged poet became a legend in the Communist movement. In 1943 Nazor became the first chairman of the Zagreb Anti-Fascist Council for the National Liberation of Croatia (Zagrebačko Antifašističko Vijeće Narodnog Oslobodjenja Hrvatske [ZAVNOH]). Nazor's war experiences brought about a new period in his writing: he wrote poems about the Partisan movement, including *Legende o drugu Titu* (The legends of Comrade Tito; 1946). After the war, Nazor served as speaker of the Communist-dominated Croatian National Assembly until the end of his life. Nazor's other major works include the collections *Intima* (1915), *Pjesme ljuvene* (Love poems; 1915), *Niza od koralja* (String of beads; 1922), *Pjesme o četiri arhandjela* (poems about four archangels; 1927), *Pjesme o bratu gavanu i seki siromaštini* (Poems about a rich brother and a poor sister; 1931), and *Pjesme u šikari, iz močvare i na usjevima* (Poems about brushwood, from swamps, and over crops; 1931), as well as novels, including *Krvavi dani* (Bloody days; 1908), *Veli Jože* (Big Jože; 1908), and *Pastir Loda* (Loda the Shepherd; 1938–39). Some of his novellas and stories, including *Priče iz djetinstva* (Childhood stories; 1924), include autobiographical elements. Nazor also translated literary classics, including William Shakespeare and Dante Alighieri. (AO)

Sources: Tode Čolak, *Vladimir Nazor* (Belgrade, 1966); *Mały słownik pisarzy zachodnio-słowiańskich i południowo-słowiańskich* (Warsaw, 1973); Šime Vučetić, *Vladimir Nazor: Čovjek i pisac* (Zagreb, 1976).

NEDIĆ Milan (20 August 1877, Grocka–4 February 1946, Belgrade), Serbian general and politician. After graduating from a military academy, Nedić distinguished himself as the commander of Serbian units during the Balkan Wars and in World War I. In the Yugoslav kingdom he was the commander of a regiment, a brigade, and an army. Then he was chief of the General Staff and minister for military affairs. In this role he supported a right-wing Serbian organization called Zbor. In 1937 he published his memoirs, *Srpska vojska na albanskoj Golgote* (The Serbian Army on the Albanian Golgotha). In April 1941 Nedić was commander in the Yugoslav defensive war against Germany. After the capitulation, on 20 August 1941 he accepted the German offer and became head of the puppet Serbian government. He hoped that it would moderate the German policy of terror toward Serbs and stop the cruelties that the Serbs had suffered at the hands of the Croatian Ustashe. Nedić's collaboration did not help much, although he was able to refuse German demands to send Serbian units to war against the Allies. His administration lacked authority. Both the Chetniks of General **Dragoljub (Draža) Mihailović**, linked with the Yugoslav government-in-exile in London, and the Communists of **Josip Broz Tito** commanded greater respect in the region. Before the invasion of Belgrade by the Red Army Nedić fled to Austria but was imprisoned by the Allies and delivered to Tito's Communist government in September 1945. After many weeks of questioning, Nedić allegedly committed suicide by jumping out of a prison window. Most probably, however, the Communists wanted to prevent him from testifying in public hearings. If there were a trial, Nedić might have told about the cooperation of the Communists with the German invaders in the period between April and June 1941, when the German-Soviet friendship was still in force. (WR)

Sources: Milan Nedić, *Ratni govori Milana Nedicia srpskom narodu* (Belgrade, 1942); Constantin Fotitch, *The War We Lost* (New York, 1948); Andelka Cvijić and Milenko Vasović, eds., *Milan Nedić: Život, govori, saslušanja* (Belgrade, 1991).

NEGOVANI Kristo (1875, Negovani, near Florina–12 February 1905, Negovani), Albanian Orthodox priest and national martyr. The son of a merchant from the Albanian-Macedonian border, Negovani completed five grades of high school in Athens. His father was killed by the Haiduks (frontier guards); therefore, Negovani began to earn his own living at the age of sixteen. He first worked as a village teacher and later as a laborer at the Romanian port of Brăila. It was there that he met representatives of the Albanian revival movement. Encouraged to take up patriotic work, he returned to his native village and was ordained an Orthodox priest. Negovani was one of the first clergymen to celebrate the liturgy in Albanian in his country. He also pursued intensive educational work. He published, among other things, the Albanian-language periodicals *Drita* and *Kalendari Kombiar*. Negovani's activities brought him to the attention of Greek and Bulgarian nationalists and the Turkish authorities. In August 1902 the village of Negovani was attacked by Bulgarian partisans and in October 1903 by Greek partisans, who unsuccessfully attempted to discourage Negovani from continuing his work. In 1904 he was briefly detained in Monastir (now Bitola, Macedonia). On 10 February 1905 the village of Negovani was attacked by another unit of Greek *andartes*, and Negovani was murdered along with dozens of the villagers. Negovani's publications include the verse stories *Prishja e Hormovës* (The destruction of Hormovës; 1903) and the prose collections *I vogli Dho-*

nat Argjendi (Little Dhonat Argjendi; 1904) and *I drunjti kryq* (Wooden cross; 1906). Negovani's importance even increased after his death, as he became a symbol of martyrdom for the national cause. (WR)

Sources: *Biographisches Lexikon*, vol. 3; Dhimitër Fullani, "Papa Kristo Negovani," *Bulletin Univershtet Shkopje*, 1960, no. 2; Hysni Myzyri, *Shkollat e para kombëtare shqipe* (Tirana, 1973).

NEJEDLÝ Zdeněk (10 February 1878, Litomyšl, Svitavy district–9 March 1962, Prague), Czech historian, musicologist, and Communist activist. Nejedlý studied history and esthetics at the Department of Philosophy of the Czech university in Prague, and he also privately studied the theory of music. In 1905 he became an associate professor and in 1919 a full professor of music in the Department of Philosophy of Charles University. From 1903 Nejedlý was a member of the Royal Bohemian Society of Sciences and in 1907 a member of the Czech Academy of Sciences and Arts. He was primarily engaged in the music culture of the Hussite period, to which he devoted the monographs *Počátky husitského zpěvu* (The origins of Hussite songs; 1907) and *Dějiny husitského zpěvu za válek husitských* (The history of Hussite songs during the Hussite wars; 1913). The author of the four-volume work *Bedřich Smetana* (1924–33), Nejedlý also dealt with contemporary music and criticism, and he often passed subjective and unfair judgments—for example, concerning Antonin Dvořak and **Leoš Janaček**. He wrote the extensive but unfinished *Všeobecne dějiny hudby* (A general history of music; 1916–30), *Opera Národního divadla do roku 1900* (The National Theater opera until 1900; 1933), and *Opera Národního divadla od roku 1900 do převratu* (The National Theater opera from 1900 until the coup; 1936). He also dealt with the history of Czech culture and politics.

Initially Nejedlý was a member of the left wing of the Czech Progressive Party, known as the realist movement, and later he supported the Socialist Party. In 1921 he entered into cooperation with the Communist Party of Czechoslovakia (CPC). In 1924 he established the Society for Cultural and Economic Rapprochement with New Russia. From 1921 to 1930 he edited the cultural and political periodical *Var*, in which he promoted Communist ideas. In 1932 Nejedlý became chairman of the Leftist Front (Levá Fronta), an organization of the Czech leftist intelligentsia. After the outbreak of World War II, he went to the Soviet Union. He taught at the university in Moscow and at the Institute of History of the Soviet Academy of Sciences. He cooperated with the leadership of the CPC abroad, and in 1941 he became vice-chairman of the All-Slavonic Committee upon his return to Czechoslovakia. Nejedlý served as minister of education (1945–46), minister of labor and social welfare (1946–48), minister of education and art (1948–53), and minister without portfolio (1953). From January to September 1953 he also held the post of deputy prime minister. In 1946 he became a member of the CPC Central Committee (CC), and from 1946 to 1954 he was a member of the CC Presidium. One of the main Stalinist ideologues, Nejedlý became chairman of the Czechoslovak-Soviet Friendship Society in 1948. Nejedlý was the author of the theory of the "continuity of progressive traditions" from Hussitism to communism. He was instrumental in introducing Marxism-Leninism in education, research, and art. His name is associated with the 1948 reform of the school system, which introduced uniform, Soviet-style schools, and with political purges at the universities. From 1945 to 1952 Nejedlý served as chairman of the Czech Academy of Sciences and Arts. After the Czechoslovak Academy of Sciences was established in 1952, he became its chairman and held this post until the end of his life. (PU)

Sources: *ČBS*; *Kdo byl kdo v našich dějinách ve 20. století*, vol. 1 (Prague, 1998); A. Sychra, *Estetika Zdeňka Nejedlého* (Prague, 1956); Vratislav Busek and Nicholas Spulber, eds., *Czechoslovakia* (New York, 1957); Josef Korbel, *The Communist Subversion of Czechoslovakia, 1938–1948* (Princeton, 1959); Vladimir Reisky de Dubnic, *Communist Propaganda Methods: The Case of Czechoslovakia* (New York, 1960); Edward Taborsky, *Communism in Czechoslovakia, 1948–1960* (Princeton, 1961); *Zdeněk Nejedlý: Doba-život-dílo* (Prague, 1975); F. Červinka, *Zdeněk Nejedlý* (Prague, 1969); M. Ransdorf, *Zdeněk Nejedlý* (Prague, 1988).

NEKRASHEVICH Stsiapan (8 May 1883, Danilouka, near Mogilev [Mahilyow]–20 December 1937, Minsk), Belorussian linguist and social activist. Nekrashevich graduated from a teacher training college (1908) and from the Vilnius Teachers' Institute (1913). In 1914 he joined the Russian Army and fought on the Romanian front. After returning home in February 1917, he became involved in politics. He became a member of the Belorussian Socialist Hromada, and after its breakup in the spring of 1918, he joined the Belorussian Party of Socialist Revolutionaries. In the fall of 1917 he went to Odessa, where he organized cultural and educational activities for soldiers and refugees from Belorussia. After the Belorussian National Republic (BNR) proclaimed its independence on 25 March 1918, Nekrashevich became a representative of the BNR government in southern Ukraine. In agreement with the French military, which commanded the Entente forces, he attempted to form Belorussian military units to fight against the Bolsheviks. In 1920 Nekrashevich settled in Minsk and worked at the People's Commissariat of Education. He helped to establish the Institute of Belorussian

Culture and served as its director from 1922 to 1925. From 1926 to 1928 he was head of the Department of Arts of the Belorussian Academy of Sciences and head of the Commission for a Belorussian Dictionary. In 1928 Nekrashevich became vice-president of the Belorussian Academy of Sciences, and in 1929, director of the Institute of Linguistics. Arrested on charges of working for a nonexistent organization, the Belorussian Liberation Union, in 1930 Nekrashevich was sentenced to five years in exile in Siberia. In 1937 he was tried again and sentenced to death. Nekrashevich's publications include the following: *Belaruska-raseyski slounik* (Belorussian-Russian dictionary; 1925); *Raseyska-belaruski slounik* (Russian-Belorussian dictionary; 1928); *Prahrama dlia zbirannia asablivastsey belaruskikh havorak i havorak perakhodnykh da susednikh movau* (A program to study the peculiarities of local dialects of Belorussian and the transition dialects to neighboring languages; 1927); *Mova knihi Kasiiana Rymlianina Eramity* (The language of the Book of Cassian, the Roman hermit; 1928); and *Praekt belaruskaha pravapisu* (A project of Belorussian grammar; 1930). (EM)

Sources: *MERSH*, vol. 24; *Entsyklapiedyia historyi Bielarusi*, vol. 5 (Minsk, 1997); I. Hermanovich, "Ab navukovai dzeinastsi S. M. Nekrashevicha"; *Vesnik BDU*, 1972, series A, no. 3; Vitaut Kipel and Zora Kipel, eds., *Byelorussian Statehood* (New York, 1988); E. Yofe, "Pershy starshynia Inbelkultu," *Spadchyna*, 1995, no. 6; Rainer Lindner, *Historiker und Herrschaft: Nationsbildung und Geschichtspolitik in Weissrussland im 19. und 20. Jahrhundert* (Munich, 1999).

NÉMETH László (18 April 1901, Nagybánya [now Baia Mare, Romania]–3 March 1975, Budapest), Hungarian writer and journalist. Németh was born into a family of teachers and clerks. After graduating from high school in 1919, he studied Romance languages and literatures and medicine at the university in Budapest. After graduating in 1925, he opened a private dental practice. In 1925 Németh won a short story contest organized by the biweekly *Nyugat*, the most important Hungarian literary periodical of the first half of the twentieth century. From then on he devoted himself mainly to writing and literary criticism, becoming a leading contributor to *Nyugat*. In 1929 Németh developed tuberculosis. In 1932–37 he was the founder and then editor of and contributor to the periodical *Tanú*, becoming the leading ideologue of his generation. Németh believed that neither socialism nor capitalism could transform society; rather the moral rebirth of individuals was the only effective way toward an unrestrained association of free, educated, and financially independent people; Németh believed such a transformation was possible through the development of education, science, and art.

Németh described his proposal for this so-called third way in several books, including *Magyarság és Európa* (The Hungarians and Europe; 1935), *A minőség forradalma* (The revolution of quality; 1940), and *Kisebbségben* (In the minority, 2 vols.; 1942). From 1934 to 1935 Németh was in charge of Hungarian Radio's literary desk. In his novels—such as *Gyász* (Mourning; 1935), *Bűn* (1937; *Guilt*, 1966), and *Az utolsó kísérlet* (The Last Experiment; 1937–41)—Németh juxtaposed his vision of the "third way" with the reality of contemporary Hungary. He also addressed similar issues in his dramas.

Immediately after World War II, Németh concentrated his attention on the interdependences between the government and the nation, on the one hand, and among individuals, on the other. In the novels and dramas of that period he depicted a gallery of characters who, despite yielding to violence, were victorious in moral terms; examples include *Széchenyi* (1946), *Iszony* (1947; *Revulsion*, 1966), and *Husz János* (Jan Hus; 1948). At the peak of Socialist realism, Németh earned his living working as a teacher and translator. After 1953 he returned to historical writing. He wrote about (among others) Galileo Galilei, Emperor Joseph II, and Gandhi. In 1956 Németh became an executive member of the Association of Hungarian Writers, but he was not directly involved in the 1956 revolution. In 1957 he received the Kossuth Prize, the nation's highest award. In the 1960s he was engaged in writing essays and biographies, such as *Sajkódi esték* (Evenings at Sajkód; 1961) and *Kísérletező ember* (Experimenter; 1963). In 1970 Németh had a stroke that put an end to his writing career. Because of his frequent use of psychological analysis and the universality of his reflections, Németh is regarded as one of the greatest Hungarian writers of the twentieth century. (MS)

Sources: Steven Bela Vardy, *Historical Dictionary of Hungary* (Lanham, Md., 1997); Ferenc Grezsa, *Németh László Tanú-korszaka* (Budapest, 1990); István Lakatos, *Naplóm Németh Lászlóról, 1963–1975* (Tatabánya, 1995); *In memoriam Németh László, 1901–1975* (Nagybánya, 1995); István Lakatos, *Életrajzi kronológia*, vols. 1–2 (Budapest, 1997–98); *Németh László irodalomszemlélet*, ed. József Máriás (Debrecen, 1999); Tibor Tüskés, *Az édenalapító: Írasók Németh Lászlóról* (Pécs, 2001).

NÉMETH Miklós (24 January 1948, Monok), Hungarian Communist activist and post-Communist politician. In 1971 Németh graduated from the Higher Economic School in Budapest. In 1971–77 he was a lecturer there. He spent 1974–75 on a scholarship at Harvard University. From 1977 to 1981 Németh was deputy head of a department in the State Planning Commission, and in 1976 he joined the Hungarian Socialist Workers' Party (HSWP). From 1981 he worked in the Department of Economic Policy of the HSWP Central Committee (CC); from 1983 he was its deputy head and from 1986, its head. In 1987 Németh became a CC member and CC secretary for economic policy. In May 1988, along with two other reformers, **Rezső Nyers** and **Imre Pozsgay**, Németh was included in the CC Politburo, and from June 1989 until the dissolution of the party he belonged to the four-man HSWP Presidium, along with Pozsgay, Nyers, and **Károly Grósz**.

From 23 November 1988 Németh was prime minister. He was suggested for this position by Grósz, who, assuming the position of the party's general secretary, counted on retaining control of the government. Németh soon realized that Hungary was on the brink of an economic disaster and needed radical change. He made use of the growing freedom within the Soviet policy of perestroika, as well as the confusion in the HSWP ranks, and he initiated systemic changes. He allowed spontaneous privatization, selling state property for a song and giving preferential access to it to party functionaries. During the funeral of **Imre Nagy** and his aides in June 1989, Németh was one of the four HSWP leaders invited to take part in the ceremony. In September 1989 his government opened the border with Austria to thousands of East German tourists who were escaping to the West. Therefore, along with the foreign minister, **Gyula Horn**, Németh contributed to the fall of the Berlin Wall. In October 1989 Németh was elected to the leadership of the (post-Communist) Hungarian Socialist Party (Magyar Szocialista Párt [MSP]), but two months later he left the party. An HSWP member of parliament from 1988 to 1990, in the elections of March 1990 Németh won a seat as an independent candidate. He resigned as prime minister on 23 May 1990, when a new cabinet was formed by **József Antall**, Jr. In 1991 Németh gave up his mandate and became one of the deputy chairmen of the European Bank of Reconstruction and Development in London. In 1999 he received an honorary doctorate from the Higher Economic School in Budapest. Upon his return to Hungary in 2000 Németh tried to return to political life, but in vain. (JT)

Sources: *Magyar Nagylexikon*, vol. 13 (Budapest, 2001); *Ki kicsoda 2000* (Budapest, 2001); Timothy Garton Ash, *We the People* (Cambridge, 1990); Rudolf L. Tőkes, *Hungary's Negotiated Revolution: Economic Reforms, Social Change, and Political Succession, 1957–1990* (Cambridge, 1996); Bugajski.

NEYCHEV Mincho (23 March 1887, Stara Zagora–11 August 1956, Sofia), Bulgarian Communist activist. Neychev studied law and philosophy in Switzerland, earning a doctorate in 1908. After returning to Bulgaria in 1920, he joined the Bulgarian Communist Party (BCP). He ran a law practice and was a member of a BCP district committee in Stara Zagora. After an unsuccessful Communist coup in 1923, in which he participated, Neychev defended the Communists who were tried for taking part in the coup. During World War II he was arrested for his Communist activities. He was sent to the Kresto Pole camp, where he spent the years 1941–43. Released, he joined the Fatherland Front. After the coup of 9 September 1944, Neychev began his political career, organizing mass repressions against opponents of the Communist system. As minister of justice (September 1944–April 1946), he even increased show trial sentences passed on members of the prewar Bulgarian elite beyond those demanded by the Communist public prosecutors. As a reward, he was made a member of the Politburo of the BCP Central Committee (1949–54) and minister of foreign affairs (1950–56). From November 1946 to December 1947 Neychev served as minister of education; from 1947 to 1950 he was chairman of the Presidium of the Grand National Assembly and one of the main authors of a draft of the Communist constitution of 1947. Neychev was never brought to justice for his judicial crimes. (AG)

Sources: *Entsiklopediya Bulgariya*, vol. 4 (Sofia, 1984); *Suvremenna Bulgarska Entsiklopediya*, vol. 3 (Sofia, 1994); J. F. Brown, *Bulgaria under Communist Rule* (New York, 1970); Jerzy Tomaszewski, *Bułgaria 1944–1971* (Warsaw, 1989); Jerzy Jackowicz, *Partie opozycyjne w Bułgarii 1944–1948* (Warsaw, 1997).

NEYKOV Dimitur (21 May 1884, Tulcha, northern Dobrudja–16 February 1949, Sofia), Bulgarian politician. After graduating from high school in Ruse, Neykov studied philosophy at Sofia University but was expelled for taking part in student protests. At that time he was an activist in a student social democratic group. In 1905 he joined the Bulgarian Social Democratic Workers' Party (BSDWP). In 1908 he completed philosophical studies in Munich. After returning to Bulgaria, Neykov worked as a teacher in Dupnitsa and Burgas and as a school inspector in Sofia. He was also active in the cooperative movement, serving as chairman of the Napred (Forward) consumer cooperative in Sofia (1924–35), the Podslon (Protection) savings and building cooperative society, the People's Cooperative Banks Association, and the General Association of Popular Banks. After the end of World War I Neykov was a member of the Central Committee (CC) of the BSDWP (United) from 1919 to 1934 and the secretary of the BSDWP from 1923 to 1926. From 1920 to 1939 he was a deputy to the National Assembly.

Neykov condemned the coup d'état of 19 May 1934 and joined the legal opposition to the government of Tsar **Boris III**. In 1935 he entered into cooperation with leftist groups, including the Bulgarian Communist Party.

In 1938 he was tried for publicly offending the ruling dynasty of Sachsen-Coburg. In 1939, as a member of parliament, he visited the Soviet Union. Neykov was against Bulgaria's entry into World War II on the side of Germany. He helped to establish the Anti-Fascist People's Front and the Fatherland Front. He became chairman of the Sofia District Committee in 1943 and a member of the National Committee of the Fatherland Front in 1944. After the coup of 9 September 1944 Neykov became minister of trade, industry, and labor in the government of **Kimon Georgiev** (September–October 1944), minister of trade and industry (October 1944–March 1946), and minister of trade and supplies (March–November 1946). At the same time he strove to tighten relations between the BSDWP and other parties in the Fatherland Front. From 1945 to 1948—that is, until the BSDWP united with the Bulgarian (Communist) Workers' Party—Neykov served as secretary general of the BSDWP. From 1945 to 1946 he edited the periodical *Narod*. In 1946 he was a member of the Bulgarian delegation to the Paris Peace Conference, which set the terms and conditions of peace treaties with the Third Reich's satellites. From 1945 to 1946 Neykov was a deputy to the National Assembly, and from 1946 to 1949, vice-chairman of the Presidium of the Grand National Assembly. (JJ)

Sources: *Entsiklopediya Bulgariya*, vol. 4 (Sofia, 1984); Georgi Dimitrov, *Suchineniya*, vol. 13 (Sofia, 1987); Tasho Tashev, *Ministrite na Bulgariya 1879–1999: Entsiklopedichen Spravochnik* (Sofia, 1999); Milen Kumanov and Tania Nikolova, *Politicheski partii, organizatsii i dvizheniia v Bulgariya i tekhnite lideri 1879–1999: Kratuk spravochnik* (Sofia, 1999); Angel Tsurakov, *Entsiklopediya: Pravitelstvata na Bulgariya. Khronologiia na politicheskiia zhivot 1879–2001* (Sofia, 2001).

NICHOLAS I (7 October 1841, Njegos, Montenegro–2 March 1921, Antibes, France), descendant of the dynasty of Njegoš-Petrović, prince and king of Montenegro. Nicholas was educated in Paris and Trieste. In 1860 he came to the throne after the assassination of his uncle, Prince Danilo II, who was childless. As an outstanding leader and accomplished diplomat, Nicholas transformed his small principality into a sovereign nation. After the wars against the Ottoman Empire (1862, 1876–78), in which Montenegro took an active part, at the Congress of Berlin (1878) Montenegro was doubled in size and recognized as a sovereign state. Nicholas skillfully strengthened his dynastic connections. He won the friendship and support of Tsar Alexander II of Russia, which helped him save the sovereignty of his nation. Nicholas's daughter Elena married Victor Emmanuel III (1896), the future king of Italy. Another daughter, Zorka, married Peter Karadjordjević

(1883), but she died before he became king of Serbia. Two other daughters married Russian grand dukes. In 1905 Nicholas convened the Constituent Assembly and granted Montenegro a constitution, but in 1907 he dissolved the assembly and reassumed an autocratic system of government. In 1907 there was a plot against him. On the fiftieth anniversary of his assumption of power, on 28 August 1910, he declared himself king. After the Balkan War of 1912–13 the territory of Montenegro became considerably larger. During World War I Nicholas supported Serbia against Austria-Hungary. However, the Montenegrin Army of fifty thousand soldiers was unable to resist the Austro-Hungarian offensive and was defeated in January 1916. Nicholas went to Italy and then to France. On 26 November 1918 the National Assembly of Montenegro formally deposed him. Montenegro was incorporated into Serbia, which later became part of the Kingdom of Serbs, Croats, and Slovenes. Nicholas never acknowledged this decision and supported a Montenegrin government-in-exile until his death. (AO)

Sources: *Biographisches Lexikon*, vol. 3; Barbara Jelavich, *History of the Balkans; Twentieth Century*, vol. 2 (Cambridge, 1983); John D. Treadway, *The Falcon and the Eagle: Montenegro and Austria-Hungary, 1908–1914* (West Lafayette, Ind., 1983); Wacław Felczak and Tadeusz Wasilewski, *Historia Jugosławii* (Wrocław, 1985).

NICKELSBURG László (10 April 1924, Budapest–26 August 1961, Budapest), one of the leaders of the 1956 Hungarian Revolution. Nickelsburg's father, a soldier in the Hungarian Red Army in 1919, was imprisoned and died as a result of the prison ordeal, and his mother had to bring up four children on her own. In 1941 Nickelsburg finished a basic vocational school and started working. In 1944 he was inducted into the labor service units but managed to escape and remained in hiding until the end of World War II. His mother and three siblings were deported and died in a concentration camp. After 1945 Nickelsburg worked as a blue-collar laborer, and many times he was declared the most productive worker. In 1953 he became a member of the Hungarian Workers' Party (HWP). On 31 October 1956 he joined the fighters in Baross Square and almost immediately became their leader. He established contacts with other groups of fighters, including those from Corvin Lane, and with the main headquarters of the police in Budapest. After attempts to halt the advancing Soviet armored units failed and when Nickelsburg's group dispersed, he joined the voluntary ambulance service. While rescuing a wounded person, he became wounded himself. On 25 November he fled to Vienna but returned to Hungary on 5 December. Arrested on 14 December, he was soon released because the secret police wanted him to lead them to other members of the revolutionaries. However, Nickelsburg did not want to cooperate; therefore, in February 1957 he was arrested again and sentenced to life imprisonment. In 1959 the Ministry of Interior ordered an additional investigation of the group of fighters from Baross Square. On 15 July 1961 the Supreme Court sentenced Nickelsburg to death without the right of appeal on charges of leading a conspiracy against the "people's government." Soon afterwards Nickelsburg was executed as the last victim of the repression unleashed by the **János Kádár** regime. (JT)

Sources: *Magyar Nagylexikon*, vol. 13 (Budapest, 2001); György Litván, ed., *Rewolucja węgierska 1956 roku* (Warsaw, 1996); Attila Szakolczay, *Az 1956-os forradalom és szabadságharc* (Budapest, 2001).

NICOLSCHI Alexandru [originally Boris Grünberg] (2 June 1915. Kishinyov [Chişinău]–16 June 1992, Bucharest), Romanian secret police officer. Nicolschi came from a Jewish-Russian family from Bessarabia. In 1932 in the then Romanian Chişinău he joined a youth wing of the Communist Party. From 1937 to 1939 he served in the Romanian Army. In September 1940, after the Soviet annexation of Bessarabia, he entered the NKVD service and moved to Cernăuţi (Chernivtsi), where he underwent espionage training in the NKVD foreign intelligence. Subsequently, under the name of "Vasile Ştefănescu," Nicolschi crossed the Romanian border. Arrested after two weeks of activities, in July 1941 he was sentenced to hard labor for life. He served his sentence in Ploieşti and Aiud. Released from prison after the coup of August 1944, he joined the political police. In the spring of 1945 Nicolschi became deputy head of the Corps of Secret Agents. At that time he personally investigated political prisoners and became particularly notorious for his brutality. Nicolschi was directly responsible for the death of many prisoners. For example, in the summer of 1946 he took part in the killing of **Ştefan Foriş**, former head of the Communist Party. In April 1947 Nicolschi became inspector general of the secret police. After the establishment of the General Direction of National Security (Direcţia Generală a Securităţii Poporului [DGSP]) in August 1948, he became one of the two deputies to the DGSP head, **Gheorghe Pintilie** (Bondarenko). One of the main investigators in the case of **Lucreţiu Pătrăşcanu**, Nicolschi supervised the establishment of a network of concentration camps. From 1949 to 1952 he also implemented a program for the "reeducation" of prisoners through sophisticated methods of destroying their mental health, as well as through the use of drugs.

Notorious for his cruelty, Nicolschi also used the services of many other sadists, including Eugene Ţurcanu, a prisoner and former Iron Guard member who employed a wide range of physical and mental tortures. In 1953 Nicolschi became director general of the Ministry of Interior. Until 1954 he held a number of posts, including that of head of a technical department that supervised electronic surveillance. (WR)

Sources: Marius Oprea, "Alexandru Nikolski," *Cuvîntul*, 1992, nos. 112–115; Dennis Deletant, *Ceauşescu and the Securitate: Coercion and Dissent in Romania, 1965–1989* (Armonk, N.Y., 1995); Dennis Deletant, *Communist Terror in Romania: Gheorghiu-Dej and the Police State, 1948–1965* (New York, 1999).

NIEĆKO Józef (25 March 1891, Kozłówka, near Luartów–30 November 1953, Warsaw), Polish Peasant Party activist. Born into a poor peasant family, Niećko finished only three grades of primary school. In 1912 he joined the National Peasant Union. In 1913 he moved to Warsaw, where he worked on various publication staffs and attempted to write. In 1914 he joined the Polish Military Organization (Polska Organizacja Wojskowa [POW]) and conducted agitation among peasants. Arrested by the tsarist authorities in the spring of 1915, Niećko was placed in the Lublin Castle and then taken to a prison in Moscow. Released in January 1916, he was kept under police surveillance in Nizhny Novgorod. He returned to Poland in December 1918. In June 1919 he co-founded the Central Union of Rural Youth (Centralny Związek Młodzieży Wiejskiej [CZMW]) and then became its head. He developed a self-education movement among peasant youth, promoted modern methods of land cultivation and animal husbandry, and encouraged the establishment of agricultural cooperatives and associations. After the coup of May 1926, Niećko advocated that the CZMW remain independent of the ruling *sanacja* regime, and subsequently he left the organization. In June 1928 he co-founded the Union of Rural Youth of the Republic of Poland (Związek Młodzieży Wiejskiej Rzeczypospolitej Polskiej [ZMW RP]). From 1930 to 1939 Niećko was head of the ZMW RP Presidium, and from 1929 to 1938, editor-in-chief of the weekly *Wici*, in which he published many articles. A theorist of agrarianism, his stance gradually evolved from social solidarity to peasant radicalism. In 1931 he joined the Peasant Party (Stronnictwo Ludowe [SL]) and served as a member of its Supreme Council from 1938 to 1939.

After the outbreak of World War II, Niećko took part in the establishment of underground structures of the peasant movement. At the beginning of 1940 he became a member of the Central Leadership of the Roch

Peasant Movement (Centralne Kierownictwo Ruchu Ludowego [CKRL]), taking charge of military affairs. In the fall of 1940 he began to organize the Peasant Guard (Straż Chłopska [SCh])—the future Peasant Battalions (Bataliony Chłopskie [BCh])—and was their political chief. In 1942 he supported a plan for the BCh to take up the struggle against the Germans in defense of peasants who were being forced to leave the Zamość region. For a long time Niećko opposed subordinating the BCh to the High Command of the Union of Armed Struggle (Związek Walki Zbrojnej [ZWZ]—later the Home Army [Armia Krajowa]). However, in December 1942 he signed an agreement on uniting the BCh with the Home Army. During the Warsaw Uprising of 1944, Niećko became a representative of the Peasant Party–Roch (Stronnictwo Ludowe–Roch [SL–Roch]) in the National Unity Council (Rada Jedności Narodowej [RJN]), the underground representation of political parties and groups linked with the Polish government-in-exile in London.

In the fall of 1944 Niećko advocated that the CKRL leave the Home Council of Ministers and the RJN, which were linked with the London government. He called for negotiations with the (Communist) Polish Workers' Party (Polska Partia Robotnicza [PPR]), the National Home Council (Krajowa Rada Narodowa [KRN]), and the Polish Committee of National Liberation. He recognized the Yalta agreements as the basis for negotiations with the Communist-controlled Provisional Government. In mid-1945 Niećko encouraged the BCh and SL–Roch soldiers to come out of hiding. In August 1945 he became second vice-chairman of the Chief Executive Committee of the newly established Polish Peasant Party (Polskie Stronnictwo Ludowe [PSL]), and from 1946 to 1947 he was a member of the PSL Supreme Council. In December 1945 he became a PSL deputy to the KRN. Niećko was among the party members who were opposed to **Stanisław Mikołajczyk**. Niećko took part in negotiations with the PPR and the Socialists on the establishment of an electoral bloc, and he supported a vote of "three times yes" in the referendum of 30 June 1946. In March 1947, after he had been dismissed from the editorial staff of the monthly *Chłopski Świat*, Niećko began publishing *Chłopi i Państwo*, a weekly that was in opposition to the PSL leaders; consequently, he was expelled from the PSL. He then co-founded and in June 1947 became chairman of the Central Committee of the PSL–Left. After Mikołajczyk fled to the West in October 1947 and pro-Communist activists took over the leadership of the PSL, Niećko was appointed chairman of the PSL Provisional Chief Executive Committee. In mid-November 1948 he

became chairman of the Chief Executive Committee of the so-called revived PSL, which was subordinated to the Communists. When on 29 November 1949 the remnants of the PSL were merged with the SL, Niećko became deputy chairman of the Chief Executive Committee of the United Peasant Party (Zjednoczone Stronnictwo Ludowe [ZSL]) and chairman of the ZSL Supreme Council. From 1948 to 1953 he was a member of the Council of State, and from 1952 to 1953 he was an MP, supporting, among other things, the collectivization of agriculture. Niećko's publications include *O wewnętrzne życie wsi* (For the internal life of rural communities; 1930) and *Na wiciowych drogach* (The roads of the Union of Rural Youth; 1937). (JS)

Sources: *PSB*, vol. 22; Mołdawa; *Słownik Biograficzny Działaczy Ruchu Ludowego* (Warsaw, 1989); *Encyklopedia Historii Polski: Dzieje polityczne*, vol. 2 (Warsaw, 1995); *Encyklopedia historii Drugiej Rzeczypospolitej* (Warsaw, 1999); Roman Buczek, *Stronnictwo Ludowe w latach 1939–1945* (London, 1975); Krystyna Kersten, *Narodziny systemu władzy: Polska 1943–1948* (Poznań, 1990); Stanisław Łach, *Polskie Stronnictwo Ludowe w latach 1945–1947* (Gdańsk, 1995).

NIEDRA Andrievs (8 February 1871, Tirzas, Livonia–25 September 1942, Riga), Latvian Lutheran pastor and politician. In 1899 Niedra graduated from the Department of Theology of the University of Dorpat (Tartu). He began writing poems and stories of a national character in his early youth. After graduation, he worked as a journalist and literary editor at several Latvian periodicals. From 1903 to 1906 he was editor of the periodical *Austrums*. In 1905 he opposed the ideas of the revolution. In 1906 he began working as a Lutheran pastor in the diocese of Matisi and from 1908 to 1918 in the diocese of Kalsnava-Vietalva in Livonia. During the offensive of the Red Army in January 1919 Niedra went to Liepāja and became involved in politics, supporting cooperation with the Germans in the struggle against the Bolsheviks. From April to June 1919, after the German coup against the Provisional Government of **Kārlis Ulmanis**, Niedra served as head of the pro-German government of Latvia. In October and November 1919 he cooperated with the German and White Russian armies, led by Pavel Bermondt-Avalov. After Avalov's forces were forced to retreat from Latvia, Niedra went to Germany. From 1921 to 1924 he worked as a Lutheran pastor in Wilno (Vilnius). After returning to Latvia in 1924, he was arrested and sentenced to three years in prison on charges of treason. The sentence was commuted to a ban on his settling in Latvia. Niedra settled in East Prussia and worked as a pastor there. He returned to Latvia during the German occupation, in April 1942, and he died a few months later. Niedra's publications include

Dzīvais mironis (The living corpse; 1924) and the memoirs *Mana bērnība un puikasgadi* (My childhood and boyhood; 1924). In 1998 Niedra's *Tautas nodevēja atmiņas* (The memoirs of a traitor to the nation) were published. (EJ)

Sources: J. Asars, V. Dermanis, and Ko Andrievs, *Niedra mums sludina* (Riga, 1905); V. Eglītis, *Andrievs Niedra savā dzīvē un darbos* (Riga, 1924); *Andrievs Niedra* (Veiverlija, 1960); Andrejs Plakans, *Historical Dictionary of Latvia* (Lanham, Md., 1997).

NIEDZIAŁKOWSKI Mieczysław (19 September 1893, Wilno [Vilnius]–21 June 1940, Palmiry, near Warsaw), Polish Socialist politician. Niwsiałkowski came from a noble family. In 1909 he co-founded the Union of Progressive and Pro-Independence Youth (Związek Młodzieży Postępowo-Niepodległościowej). From 1910 he belonged to the Executive Bureau of this organization and to the editorial staff of *Głos Młodych* (Voice of youth). From 1912 he studied law at the university in St. Petersburg. In 1914 he joined the Polish Socialist Party (Polska Partia Socjalistyczna [PPS]), becoming head of its District Workers' Committee in Warsaw. From September 1916 to April 1919 Niedziałkowski was a member of the Central Workers' Committee of the PPS. While emphasizing the party's links to the workers, he consistently supported the Polish Military Organization, the Legions, and the position of **Józef Piłsudski**.

In November 1918 Niedziałkowski took part in negotiations leading to the establishment of the government of **Jędrzej Moraczewski**. From 18 November 1918, as head of the Assembly Department in the Ministry of Interior, Niedziałkowski was involved in work on the electoral law in the Constituent Assembly. Between January 1919 and 1935 he was an MP, and in 1929–35 he was president of the Parliamentary Union of Polish Socialists (Związek Parlamentarny Polskich Socjalistów). From 1 January 1919 Niedziałkowski headed the government's Constitutional Office. He belonged to the PPS Chief Council (Rada Naczelna PPS) and to the Central Executive Committee (Centralny Komitet Wykonawczy [CKW]) from the time of its unification congress in April 1919 until the dissolution of the party on 28 September 1939. From 1920 Niedziałkowski was secretary general of the PPS. From 1921, he acted as the party's secretary general for foreign affairs, and he was responsible for contacts with Socialist parties abroad and with the Socialist International. He attended the subsequent congresses of the Socialist International. In 1924–31 he was deputy president of the CKW PPS, and in 1927–39 he was editor-in-chief of *Robotnik*. He also published articles in *Przedświt*, *Trybuna*, and *Światło*. He published (for example) *Położenie międzynarodowe Polski i polityka socjalizmu polskiego* (1925; The international situation of Poland and the policy of Polish

socialism; 1925); *Teoria i praktyka socjalizmu wobec nowych zagadnień* (The theory and practice of socialism in the face of new issues; 1926); and *Do Polski Ludowej* (To people's Poland; 1941).

After the May 1926 coup Niedziałkowski initially supported Piłsudski's group (*Sanacja*). However, he became disaffected toward this regime, as its members became aligned with the landowning groups and inspired actions aiming at a split within the PPS. After 1928 he became one of the leaders of the parliamentary opposition to the *sanacja* regime. Niedziałkowski was also a co-organizer and ideologist of the center-left opposition (Centrolew). At the Twenty-third Congress of the PPS in 1934 he sought to gain the support of the peasants and the lower middle class for the party's program, and he accepted the idea of an interim dictatorship of the proletariat. He took part in negotiations with the Communist Party of Poland, which resulted in the signing of a non-aggression pact in 1935. However, as early as 1936 he opposed cooperation with the Communists and aimed at closer cooperation with democratic parties. Niedziałkowski was the author of the PPS program of 1937. In the face of the German threat, on behalf of the PPS, he proposed the establishment of a government of national defense, and on two occasions he visited President **Ignacy Mościcki** to discuss the issue.

In September 1939 Niedziałkowski was active in the civil defense of Warsaw. He was involved, for example, in recruitments to the Workers' Battalions for the Defense of Warsaw. From October 1939 he was a member of the Political Council of the Service for the Victory of Poland (Służba Zwycięstwu Polsce [SZP]) and civil commissioner to the commander of the SZP, General **Michał Koraszewicz-Tokarzewski**. Arrested by the Gestapo on 22 December 1939 and sentenced to death by a German court martial at Szucha Avenue on 18 February 1940, Niedziałkowski was executed in Palmiry. (PK)

Sources: *PSB*, vol. 22; M. Śliwa, *Myśl polityczna Mieczysława Niedziałkowskiego (1893–1940)* (Warsaw, 1980); Antoni Czubiński, *Centrolew* (Poznań, 1963); Janusz Żarnowski, *Polska Partia Socjalistyczna w latach 1935–1939* (Warsaw, 1965); Jerzy Holzer, *Mozaika polityczna II Rzeczypospolitej* (Warsaw, 1974); Ignacy Wilczek [Jerzy Holzer], "Mieczysław Niedzialkowski," *PPN*, 1978, no. 22; Andrzej Friszke, *O kształt niepodległej* (Warsaw, 1989); Lidia Ciołkoszowa, *Spojrzenie wstecz* (Paris, 1995).

NIEPOKÓLCZYCKI Franciszek, pseudonyms "Franek," "Szubert," and "Teodor" (27 October 1900, Zhytomyr–11 June 1974, Warsaw), Polish pro-independence activist and officer. The son of a carpenter, in 1919 Niepokólczycki graduated from high school in Zhytomyr. From 1918 to 1921 he was a member of the Polish Military Organization (Polska Organizacja Wojskowa [POW]). After graduating from a POW officer training school, he served as a commander of the POW Zhitomir District, a clerk in the Military Department of the POW High Command in the Ukraine, and head of the POW Liquidation Commission. In 1922 Niepokólczycki became an officer in the Polish Army and served in an infantry corps. From 1923 he served in a corps of sappers. He lectured at the Sapper Training Center and worked for the General Inspectorate of the Armed Forces. He took part in the September 1939 campaign as a commander of sappers in the Modlin Army, with the rank of major. On 15 September Niepokólczycki joined the defense of Warsaw. At the end of September he joined the Service for the Victory of Poland (Służba Zwycięstwu Polsce [SZP]), an underground organization that later became the Union of Armed Struggle (Związek Walki Zbrojnej [ZWZ]) and in 1942 became the Home Army (Armia Krajowa [AK]). In the fall of 1939 Niepokólczycki became head of a sabotage unit of the High Command of the SZP and ZWZ, and in April 1940 he became commander of a ZWZ organization for subversive struggle known as the Revenge Union (Związek Odwetu). In 1942 he also became chief of the Sapper Department of the AK High Command. In November 1941 he was promoted to lieutenant colonel. In the autumn of 1942 he helped to establish the Directorate of Sabotage (Kierownictwo Dywersji [Kedyw]), a large subversive-struggle division of the AK High Command. In January 1943 he became deputy commander of Kedyw. He co-designed a program to defend the Warsaw Ghetto, but it was not implemented in April 1943. Niepokólczycki fought in the Warsaw Uprising (August–October 1944); after its failure he was taken prisoner and sent to the officers' POW camp at Woldenberg. In February 1945 he returned to Poland and continued his underground work as deputy commander of the South District of the Delegation of Armed Forces for the Homeland. In September 1945 he joined an underground organization called Freedom and Independence (Zrzeszenie Wolność i Niezawisłość [WiN]), and in November of that year he became chairman of the WiN Main Board. WiN conducted intelligence and propaganda work, trying to limit the partisan struggle to self-defense against Communist security services. Arrested in October 1946, on 10 September 1947 Niepokólczycki was sentenced to death, but the sentence was commuted to life imprisonment. Released in December 1956, from 1958 on he worked in various firms. (TSt)

Sources: *PSB*, vol. 23; Kunert, vol. 2; Tomasz Strzembosz, *Oddziały szturmowe konspiracyjnej Warszawy 1939–1944* (Warsaw, 1983); Henryk Witkowski, *Kedyw Okręgu Warszawskiego Armii Krajowej w latach 1943–1944* (Warsaw, 1984); *Armia Krajowa: Dramatyczny epilog* (Warsaw, 1994).

NIESIOŁOWSKI Stefan (4 February 1944, Kałęczewo, near Łódź), Polish dissident and politician. During his studies in biology at the University of Łódź (1961–65) Niesiołowski was connected with the academic Catholic ministry of Father Hubert Czuma. From 1965 he worked in the Department of Zoology of Łódź University. In 1965, along with the brothers **Andrzej Czuma** and Benedykt Czuma, Niesiołowski co-founded the Movement (Ruch), a pioneer secret opposition organization. He co-authored its program declaration, *Mijają lata . . .* (As the years go by . . . ; 1969), advocating the regaining of independence and a respect for human rights. He published in the Movement's *Biuletyn* from 1969. Arrested and tried for the intention of setting fire to the Lenin Museum in Poronin, in the trial of the Movement in 1971 Niesiołowski was sentenced to seven years in prison. Released in 1974, from 1975 he was engaged in protests against amendments to the constitution (for example, amendments introducing the "leading role" of the Communist Party and an alliance with the USSR). He was also active in the defense of workers oppressed after the riots of June 1976. Connected with the Łódź group of the Movement for the Defense of Human and Civic Rights (Ruch Obrony Praw Człowieka i Obywatela [ROPCiO]), he published in its uncensored press (e.g., *Opinia*).

In 1980 Niesiołowski was active as an adviser to the workers striking in Łódź. He belonged to the initiators of the Łódź organization of Solidarity, and in 1981 he joined its Łódź Regional Management. He co-founded the weekly *Solidarność Ziemi Łódzkiej*. On 13 December 1981 Niesiołowski was interned in Jaworz and later in Darłówek. Released after almost a year, he headed a secret Solidarity commission at the University of Łódź. He encouraged publications in the uncensored press and published a lot himself. Under the pen name Ewa Ostrołęcka he published a book, *"Ruch" przeciw totalizmowi* (The Movement against totalitarianism; 1985). From 1989 Niesiołowski worked in the Łódź Regional Civic Committee. In June 1989 he was elected to the parliament on behalf of the Civic Committee of the Chairman of Solidarity, and in October 1991, on behalf of the Christian National Union (Zjednoczenie Chrześcijańsko-Narodowe [ZChN]), which he co-founded in 1989. Niesiołowski supported his party's coalition with the Democratic Union, which was the foundation of the government of **Hanna Suchocka**, and several times he intervened to quash conflicts in this coalition. In 1997–2001 Niesiołowski was an MP on behalf of the Solidarity Electoral Action (Akcja Wyborcza Solidarność) coalition, heading the ZChN parliamentary group. Elected to the parliament again in 2005 on behalf of the civic platform (Platforma obywatelska), he was a fierce critic of the law and justice (Prawo i sprawiedliwość) government. In 1979 he received a Ph.D. and in 1990 his postdoctoral degree, lecturing in entomology at the University of Łódź. Niesiołowski authored the memoirs *Wysoki brzeg* (High shore; 1989) and *Prosta drogaa: O Polskę z Bogiem* (Straight road: For a Poland with God; 1993). (PK)

Sources: *Nasi w Sejmie i Senacie* (Warsaw, 1990); Andrzej Friszke, *Opozycja polityczna w PRL 1945–1980* (London, 1994); Dobrosława Świerczyńska, ed., *Kto był kim w drugim obiegu? Słownik pseudonimów* (Warsaw, 1995); *Opozycja w PRL: Słownik Biograficzny 1956–1989,* vol. 1 (Warsaw, 2000); *Kto jest kim w Polsce* (Warsaw, 2001).

NIKLUS Mart-Olav (22 September 1934, Tartu), Estonian dissident and independence activist. In 1957 Niklus graduated from the Physics and Mathematics Department of the University of Tartu. In 1957–58 he worked as a translator and teacher of English. He also published a few articles in ornithology, for which he received awards. In August 1958 he was arrested for sending photos to the West illustrating life in Soviet Estonia. In January 1959 he was sentenced to ten years in prison. While in jail, he translated into Estonian three works by Charles Darwin and the UN Declaration of Human Rights. In 1965 Niklus organized a hunger strike in a Mordovian camp in protest against the living conditions there. Transferred to Vladimir Prison and released in July 1966, he could not find a job relevant to his education, so he worked as a blue-collar laborer and driver. From September 1968 Niklus taught English in the schools. In 1971 he was fired because of his membership in an unofficial anti-alcohol club, but in 1974 he was rehired as an English teacher. In August 1979 Niklus signed the Baltic Appeal, which pointed to the illegality of the Molotov-Ribbentrop Pact, and he lost his job again. In 1980 Niklus was refused the right to emigrate, and in January 1981 he was arrested again and sentenced, along with **Jüri Kukk**, to ten years of labor camp. He served in the Khristopol Camp in the Tatar ASSR, where he was exposed to chemical and psychiatric experiments. During perestroika, in early 1987 Niklus was transferred to Tallinn, but as he refused to sign an oath of loyalty, he was sent back to the camp in the Ural Mountains. In July 1988 he was released without any preconditions. Niklus's return to Tallinn on 13 July 1988 became an occasion for a patriotic demonstration. (WR)

Sources: *Baltic News*, 1985, no. 3; S. P. de Boer, E. J. Driessen, and H. L. Verhaar, eds., *Biographical Dictionary of Dissidents in the Soviet Union, 1956–1975* (The Hague and Boston, 1982); Rein Taagepera, *Estonia: Return to Independence* (Boulder, Colo., 1993).

NINČIĆ Momčilo (10 June 1876, Jagodina–23 December 1949, Lausanne, Switzerland), Yugoslav diplomat of Serbian origin. After graduating from high school in Belgrade, Ninčić studied law in Paris, graduating in 1899. He worked in the Serbian Ministry of Finance, and in 1902 he became a professor in the Department of Law of Belgrade University. In 1912 he was elected MP on the ticket of the Radical Party. He was a Freemason. From 1915 to August 1919 Ninčić was minister of finance in the government of **Nikola Pašić**, who was in exile on Corfu from November 1915. After the establishment of the Kingdom of Serbs, Croats, and Slovenes (SHS), Ninčić served in the cabinet of **Stojan Protić**. At that time he carried out a reform that standardized the monetary system of the state. In the second government of Protić (February–May 1920) Ninčić became minister of justice and later minister of trade and industry. He also held these posts in the cabinet of **Milenko Vesnic** (May–December 1920). In January 1921 he also assumed the post of minister of foreign affairs in the government of Pašić and held this post in the cabinet of **Nikola Uzunović** until December 1926, except for an interval between June and October 1924. Ninčić was one of the founders and a driving force behind the so-called Little Entente, which was based on the Yugoslav-Czechoslovak treaty of 14 August 1920, the Czechoslovak-Romanian treaty of 23 April 1921, and the Yugoslav-Romanian treaty of 7 June 1921. In these treaties Yugoslavia, Czechoslovakia, and Romania pledged mutual assistance in the case of a violation of the Treaty of Trianon with Hungary or the Treaty of Neuilly with Bulgaria. Ninčić also sought to strengthen Yugoslavia's position in the face of territorial pressures from Italy, and on 27 January 1924 he signed the so-called Adriatic Pact between Yugoslavia and Italy, in which the two states pledged to remain neutral in the case of an attack by another state. From 1920 to 1926 Ninčić was also an editor of the periodical *Novi život*.

After King **Alexander Karadjordjević** established a royal dictatorship in 1929, Ninčić retired from active politics, but he did not protest the king's policies. After the coup d'état of 27 March 1941 and the enthronement of King Peter, General **Dušan Simović** entrusted Ninčić with the portfolio of minister of foreign affairs. On 30 March Ninčić assured the governments of Italy and Germany that Yugoslav policies would not change, but Germany's attitude to the coup was hostile from the beginning. Seeking support, Ninčić entered into negotiations with Great Britain, and on the night of 5–6 April 1941 he also signed a treaty of friendship and non-aggression with the Soviet Union. However, his efforts did not prevent the invasion of Yugoslavia by the Third Reich on 6 April, and it forced Simović's government, along with Ninčić, to go into exile in Great Britain. In July 1942, along with the king, Ninčić visited the United States, where he signed a lend-lease agreement for Yugoslavia and was given assurances of U.S. support for the Yugoslav government-in-exile. Despite his efforts, Ninčić failed to obtain the Kremlin's ratification of the treaty of April 1941, and at the beginning of January 1943 he resigned. Ninčić died in exile. His publications include *Pitanje o svojini zemlje Srba pod Turcima* (The issue of Serbian land ownership under Turkish rule; 1913); *Spoljna politika Kralevjine SHS 1922–1924* (The foreign policy of the Kingdom of SHS from 1922 to 1924; 1924); *Spoljna politika Kralevjine SHS 1925–1926* (The foreign policy of the Kingdom of SHS from 1925 to 1926; 1926); and *La crise bosniaque 1908–1909 et les grandes puissances européennnes* (The Bosnian crisis of 1908–1909 and the great European powers, 2 vols.; 1937). (WR)

Sources: *Biographisches Lexikon*, vol. 3; Constantin Fotitch, *The War We Lost* (New York, 1948); Vlatko Macek, *In the Struggle for Freedom* (London, 1957); Ferdo Čulinović, *Jugoslavija izmedju dva rata*, vols. 1–2 (Zagreb, 1971); Ludwik Hass, *Ambicje, rachuby, rzeczywistość: Wolnomularstwo w Europie Środkowo-Wschodniej 1905–1928* (Warsaw, 1984); Michał Jerzy Zacharias, *Jugosławia w polityce Wielkiej Brytanii 1940–1945* (Wrocław, 1985).

NOICA Constantin (24 June 1909, Vităneşti–4 December 1987, Sibiu), Romanian philosopher and essayist. In 1928 Noica graduated from the Spiru Haret Lycée in Bucharest; one year earlier he had made his literary debut in the periodical *Vlăstarul*. From 1928 to 1931 he studied literature and philosophy at Bucharest University. From 1932 to 1934 he worked as a librarian at the Department of the History of Philosophy at Bucharest University. At that time he was also a member of the artistic, philosophical, and literary society Criterion. In 1934 Noica moved to Sinaia and began translating works by Descartes and Kant. A supporter of the pro-Fascist Iron Guard, in 1938 Noica left for France, after the regime of King **Charles II** began to persecute members of this organization. In France he continued his philosophical studies. After returning to Romania, Noica earned a Ph.D. in philosophy in 1940. In the same year he edited one issue of the periodical *Adsum*, in which he co-authored and published an article-manifesto on the Iron Guard movement. He also contributed to the nationalist dailies *Buna Vestire* and *Cuvântul*. From 1941 to 1944 Noica was in Berlin, working for the Romanian-German Institute, which dealt with international relations. In the periodical *Izvoare de filosofie* Noica published university lectures on metaphysics and logic authored by his mentor, **Nicolae (Nae) Ionescu**.

In 1944 Noica returned to Romania. After the Communist takeover he was persecuted. From 1949 to 1958 he was kept under house arrest in Câmpulung Muscel, and in 1958 he was sentenced in a political trial to twenty-five years' imprisonment, of which he served six. From 1965 to 1975 Noica founded and then worked for the Center for Logic of the Romanian Academy of Sciences. After retiring, he lived in Păltiniş, a small town in the mountains (1975–87). There he established a kind of private seminary of Romanian intellectuals that was tolerated by the authorities. Noica believed that under the dictatorship of **Nicolae Ceauşescu** the only possible form of resistance was intellectual opposition and independent philosophical and cultural research. His wide range of interests included the philosophy of culture, axiology, philosophical anthropology, ontology, logic, semantics, and the history of philosophy. Noica wrote a dozen or so books, including the following: *Mathesis sau bucurile simple* (Science or simple joys; 1934); *Viaţa şi filosofia lui René Descartes* (The life and philosophy of René Descartes; 1937); *Două introduceri şi o trecere spre idealism* (Two introductions and a transition to idealism; 1943); *Devenirea intru fiinţă: Încercare asupra filosofiei tradiţionale* (Becoming unto being: An essay on traditional philosophy; 1950); *Semnificaţia culturală a categoriilor lui Aristotel* (Cultural significance in Aristotle's categories; 1968); *Eminescu sau gânduri despre omul deplin în cultura română* (Eminescu or thoughts on the complete man of Romanian culture; 1975); and *Sentimentul românesc al fiinţei* (The Romanian feeling of being; 1978). (LW)

Sources: *Dictionar Enciclopedic*, vol. 4 (Bucharest, 2001); Józef Darski, *Rumunia: Historia, współczesność, konflikty narodowe* (Warsaw, 1995); Dorina N. Rusu, *Membrii Academiei Române 1866–1999* (Bucharest, 1999); www.ssmu.mcgill.ca; http//pages.prodigy.net; www.geocites.com.

NOLI Fan (Theofan) Stylian (1882, Ibrik Tepe, Thrace–13 March 1965, Fort Lauderdale, Florida), Albanian Orthodox bishop and politician. Noli was educated in Turkey, Greece, and Egypt, where he also taught in a Greek school and was introduced to the Albanian national movement. From 1908 to 1912 he studied at Harvard University. In March 1908 in Boston, Noli was ordained bishop of the U.S. Albanian Orthodox Church. In 1912 he founded a pan-Albanian federation, Vatra, which was the leading organization of the Albanian diaspora. Noli was greatly impressed by the American political system. In 1919 the Albanian community in the United States sent him to the National Assembly in Lushnja, where in January 1920 the principles of the Albanian political system were established. After returning to Albania, Noli was appointed bishop of Dürres, and he became active in Albanian public life—for example, he published the periodical *Dielli*. He used his contacts in America to help Albania gain the status of a member of the League of Nations after World War I. As an Albanian delegate to the League of Nations, Noli protested the occupation of northern Albania by the troops of the Kingdom of Serbs, Croats, and Slovenes (SHS). In November 1921 the Council of Ambassadors established the final shape of the Albanian territory, granting Albania the territories that had been occupied by the SHS, except for Kosovo.

After the first elections of 1921 Noli became head of the People's Party. As the result of a serious crisis brought about by a series of political murders, in the spring of 1924 a revolt arose against the conservative government of Ilias bey Vrioni, in which **Ahmed Zogu** played the role of *éminence grise*. On 16 June 1924 Noli became prime minister of a new government that promised basic democratic reforms. However, Noli's policies alienated part of the population. A long-promised land reform was a failure, and no financial assistance came from the League of Nations. At the same time Noli's government set up a tribunal that sentenced many supporters of the previous government to death in absentia and confiscated their property. Noli's social radicalism won him the label of the "red bishop." Noli's establishment of official relations with the USSR confirmed the validity of this title. Noli publicly humiliated his opponents and was reluctant to hold new elections. Under international pressure, he finally agreed to new elections in November 1924. Meanwhile, however, the officers' corps began to openly support Zogu, who, assisted by soldiers from the Russian Army forces of General Pyotr Wrangel and by Zogu's compatriots from the Mati clan, assembled a substantial armed force in Yugoslav territory. On 24 December 1924 Zogu's troops entered Tirana, and Noli fled to Italy.

In March 1925 Noli founded the National Revolutionary Committee (Komiteti Nacional Revolucionar [KONARE]) in Vienna, which established contacts with the Communist International, and some of its members turned to communism. In April 1927 the KONARE was renamed the Committee for National Liberation (Komiteti Nacional Clirimtar). In November 1927 Noli visited Moscow, attending the Congress of Friends of the Soviet Union, but that visit alienated him from communism. In 1930 he abandoned his political activities, and in 1932 he again left for the United States. He settled in Boston, where he conducted pastoral activities and pursued scholarly work, translating Anglo-Saxon literary works into Albanian, among them Shakespeare, Edgar Allan Poe, and George Bernard Shaw. Noli was also the author of the drama *Israelite e Filistine* (The Israelites and the Philistines; 1907), *Historise se Skanderbeut* (History of Skanderbeg; 1947), a book about Ludwig van Beethoven, and *Autobiography* (1960). Noli's works, as well as his translations, contributed greatly to the development of the Albanian literary language. Noli also composed Orthodox music. In 1945 Noli rejected **Enver Hoxha**'s offer to take the post of speaker of the parliament. (TC/WR)

Sources: *Biographisches Lexikon*, vol. 3; Lame Lefter, *Ligjëron Fan Noli* (Tirana, 1944); Vehbi Bala, *Jeta e Fan S. Nolit: Portret, monografi* (N.p.,1972); Idriz Ajeti, ed., *Fan S. Noli: Në 100-vjetorin e lindjes, 1882–1982* (Prishtina, 1984); Nasho Jordaqi, *Udhëtim me Fan Nolin: Nga Traka në ShBA* (Tirana, approx. 1994); Miranda Vickers, *The Albanians: A Modern History* (London, 1995); Eftim Dodona, *Noli i panjohur* (Tirana, 1996); Blendi Fevziu, *Histori e shtypit shqiptar* (Tirana, 1996).

NOSEK Václav (26 September 1892, Velká Dobra–22 July 1955, Prague), Czech Communist activist. A miner by trade, Nosek was active in the Socialist movement from his youth. Between 1919 and 1921 he was a member of the Marxist wing of the Social Democratic Party, and in 1921 he joined the Communist Party of Czechoslovakia (CPC). From 1924 to 1938 he served as secretary of the Red Trade Unions, and in 1929–36 he was a member of the Central Committee of the CPC. Under the Nazi occupation Nosek was temporarily imprisoned, and after his release in the summer of 1939 he left for London. There he was one of the leaders of the Communist émigrés, and in 1942–45 he served as deputy president of the Czechoslovak National Council (Státni Rada Československa) in London. From 1945 Nosek was a member of the Presidium of the CC of the CPC and an MP. From April 1945 he was minister of interior. In 1945–48 he used his power to suppress his political opponents. He conducted purges of the National Security Corps, replacing people who were not associated with the Communist Party by members of the CPC. Nosek's activities were the direct reason for the resignation of the non-Communist ministers and for the February crisis in 1948, after which the Communists assumed full power in Czechoslovakia. Later, Nosek's position was weakened considerably, especially after the establishment of the Ministry of National Security (1950), which took over most of the powers of the Ministry of Interior. Nosek held the post of minister of interior until 14 September 1953, and then until his death he served as minister of labor. (PU)

Sources: *ČBS*; *Českoslovenští politici: 1918–1991* (Prague, 1991); Vladimir Zdárský, *Václav Nosek: Hornik-ministr* (Prague; 1946); Jitka Klementová, *Václav Nosek* (Prague, 1987); Karel Kaplan, *The Short March: The Communist Takeover in Czechoslovakia 1945–1948* (London, 1987).

NOSI Lef (1876, Elbasan–March 1945, Tirana), Albanian pro-independence activist, linguist, historian, and writer. After graduating from high school in Elbasan, Nosi studied pharmacy in Athens, Greece. At that time he joined the national movement. He corresponded with, among others, **Fan Noli**. In 1909 in Elbasan he co-founded an Albanian club, Vllaznia, and became its deputy chairman. He also initiated the establishment of an educational group called Aferdita in Elbasan. In 1909 Nosi taught Albanian in the schools, and one year later he founded *Tomorri*, a periodical that was designed to promote pro-independence ideas. Nosi was one of the co-founders of a congress in Elbasan (September 1909) that debated the issue of standardizing the Albanian language. He also initiated the establishment of a school for teachers of Albanian. Imprisoned by the Turks during the quelling of an Albanian uprising in 1910, Nosi served his sentence in Monastir (Bitola) and Bursa, Turkey. Released in March 1911, he returned to Elbasan and devoted himself to writing a textbook on the Albanian language.

In 1912 Nosi was a delegate from Elbasan to a conference in Vlorë at which, in November of that year, Albanian independence was proclaimed. Nosi became minister of post and telegraphs in the government of **Ismail Kemali**. He was also a member of a delegation that was sent to Neuwied to ask Prince **Wilhelm von Wied** to accept the Albanian throne. In 1918 Nosi became a member of the government that was established under Italian auspices in Dürres. He attended the Paris Peace Conference. After returning to Albania, along with a group of renowned Albanian politicians, Nosi was an active member of a patriotic society called Atdheu (Homeland). In the 1923 parliamentary elections Nosi was one of the leading representatives of a group called As i Beut as i Pashës (Without the Beys and Pashas), which ran in Elbasan. After failure in these elections, Nosi retired from politics and became involved in linguistic research. In 1924 he began editing the major documents that illustrated Albania's road to freedom. He also collected folk songs. Nosi returned to politics in October 1943, joining the four-member leadership of the Regency Council, which was established by the Germans. In consequence, the Communists accused him of collaboration with the occupiers. Sentenced to death by the Special People's Tribunal, Nosi was executed by a firing squad. (TC)

Sources: Sejfi Vllamasi, *Ballafaqime politike në Shqipëri (1897–1942)* (Tirana, 1995); Bardhosh Gaçe, *Ata që shpallën Pavarësinë Kombëtare* (Tirana, 1997); Bernd Fischer, *Albania at War, 1939–1945* (London, 1999).

NOVAKOVIĆ Stojan (3 November 1842, Šabac–3 March 1915, Niš), Serbian historian, philologist, and politician.

Novaković attended a gymnasium in Šabac and a lycée in Belgrade. In 1863 he became a clerk in the Ministry of Finance. He later worked as a high school teacher in Belgrade. From 1872 to 1873 Novaković was a librarian and curator in a museum. In 1873 he became minister of education, and at the end of that year, head of the National Library. In 1874 he was again appointed minister of education and held this post until 1875. From 1875 to 1880 Novaković lectured at the university in Belgrade. From 1880 to 1883 he served as minister of education for the third time and was instrumental in promoting education in Serbia and the development of libraries and museums. In 1865 Novaković became a member of the Serbian Scientific Society (Srpsko Učeno Društvo), and in 1887, a member of the Serbian Royal Academy. In 1880 he helped to establish the conservative Progressive Party (Napredna Stranka) and was a member until its dissolution in 1896. In 1883 Novaković joined the State Council. He served as minister of interior in the cabinet of Milutin Garašanin (1884–85) but resigned in protest against the excessive influence of King Milan I Obrenović on the government's work. In 1885 Novaković opposed the declaration of war on Bulgaria. This war ended in defeat for the Serbian Army. From 1885 to 1892 Novaković was Serbia's envoy to Constantinople. In 1893 he became minister of foreign affairs, and from 25 June 1895 to 17 December 1896 he also held the post of prime minister. Novaković initially supported a pro-Austrian policy but then became a supporter of a pro-Russian orientation. From 1897 to 1900 he again was an envoy to Turkey, in 1899 to France, and from 1900 to 1904 to Russia.

In 1906 Novaković revived the Progressive Party and served as its leader until the end of his life. Although his was the smallest party in the coalition government, he again became prime minister (11 February 1909–21 October 1909) during the international crisis that followed the annexation of Bosnia-Herzegovina by Austria-Hungary, when Serbia was on the brink of war. Novaković was head of the Serbian delegation that negotiated peace terms with Turkey at the London Peace Conference in 1913. He described his political work in *Dvadeset godina ustavne politike u Srbiji 1883–1903* (Twenty years of legislative policy in Serbia 1883–1903; 1912). Among hundreds of works by Novaković, the most important are the following: *Vaskrs države srpske* (The revival of the Serbian state; 1904); *Zakonik Stefana Dušana* (The legal code of Stefan Dušan; 1898); *Istorija srpske književnosti* (The history of Serbian literature; 1867); *Srpska bibliografija* (Serbian bibliography; 1869); *Srbi i Turci u XIV i XV veku* (The Serbs and the Turks in the fourteenth and fifteenth centuries; 1863). (AO)

Sources: *Enciklopedija Jugoslavije*, vol. 6 (Zagreb, 1965); *Biographishes Lexikon*, vol. 4; Vasa Cubrilović, *Društveni elementi u delima Stojana Novakovića* (Belgrade, 1959); Vladimir Stojancević, ed., *Stojan Novaković, ličnost i delo: Naučni skup povodom 150-godisnjice rodjenja (1842–1992)* (Belgrade, 1995); Željan E. Šuster, *Historical Dictionary of the Federal Republic of Yugoslavia* (Lanham, Md., 1999).

NOVOMESKÝ Ladislav (Laco) (27 December 1904, Budapest–4 September 1976, Bratislava), Slovak poet, journalist, and Communist activist. After graduating from high school, Novomeský worked as a teacher and studied as an extramural student in the Department of Philosophy of Comenius University in Bratislava. In 1925 he joined the Communist Party of Czechoslovakia (CPC). He worked as a journalist for party papers and periodicals, initially for the Bratislava newspaper *Pravda chudoby* and later for the Prague *Rudý večerník*, *Rudé právo*, and *Rudá zářa*. A member of a leftist avant-garde literary group called DAV, Novomeský edited a periodical under the same title from 1935 to 1937. His first collections of poems, including *Nedeľa* (Sunday; 1927), belonged to proletarian literature, and his later volumes, including *Romboid* (1932) and *Otvorené okná* (Open windows; 1935), included elements of lyric poetry and symbolism. In his later collections, *Svätý za dedinou* (The saint beyond the village; 1939) and *Pašovanou ceruzkou* (With a smuggled pencil; 1948), Novomeský addressed current issues and protested against fascism. In 1933 he published the book *Marx a slovensky národ* (Marx and the Slovak nation).

During World War II Novomeský joined the Communist resistance movement in Slovakia. He was arrested in 1940 and 1942. In 1943, along with **Karol Šmidke** and **Gustav Husák**, he signed the so-called Christmas agreement on behalf of the CPC; it united the efforts of the Communist resistance movement and the democratic resistance movement in Slovakia. During the Slovak National Uprising in 1944 Novomeský was one of the leaders of the Slovak National Council (SNC), and at the end of 1944 he was a member of a delegation that conducted negotiations with President **Edvard Beneš** in London. In March 1945 Novomeský took part in negotiations in Moscow that led to the adoption of the Košice program of the first postwar government of Czechoslovakia. From 1945 to 1950 he held the post of commissioner for education (the equivalent of a ministerial position in Slovakia), and he served as deputy chairman of the SNC. In 1951, along with a group of leading Slovak Communists, including **Vlado Clementis**, Novomeský was arrested and accused of "Slovak bourgeois nationalism." He spent five years in prison. Released in 1956, he worked for the National Literature Monument in Prague. Rehabilitated in 1963, he worked at the Institute of Slovak Literature of the Slovak Academy of Science (1963–66). In 1969 he supported the "normalization" policy pursued by Husák. From 1968 to 1974 Novomeský was the chairman, and subsequently the honorary chairman of the national cultural institution Matica Slovenská. After he had been banned from writing in the 1950s, he returned to literature in the 1960s, writing *Vila Tereza* (1963), *Do mesta 30 minút* (Thirty minutes to the city; 1963), and *Stamodtiaľ a iné* (Out from there and other poems; 1964). Novomeský was a theorist of Czechoslovak context literature and an expert on modern culture, which was demonstrated in his political commentaries and essays, including *Čestná povinnosť* (An honorable duty; 1969), *Manifesty a protesty* (Manifestos and protests; 1970), and *Zväzky a záväzky* (Relations and commitments; 1972). He also translated Russian literature. (PU)

Sources: *ČBS; SBS*, vol. 4; *Kdo byl kdo v našich dějinach ve 20. stoleti*, vol. 2 (Prague, 1998); Halina Janaszek-Ivančikova, ed., *Literatury zachodniosłowiańskie czasu przełomów 1890–1990*, vol. 1, *Literatura łużycka i słowacka* (Katowice, 1994); Stanislav Šmatlák, *Básnik Laco Novomeský* (Bratislava, 1967); Zdenka Holotíková, *Ladislav Novomeský* (Bratislava, 1981); Stanislav Šmatlák, *Laco Novomeský* (Bratislava, 1984); Rudolf Chmel, ed., *Kwestia slowacka w XX wieku* (Gliwice, 2002).

NOVOTNÝ Antonín (10 December 1904, Letňany, near Prague–28 January 1975, Prague), Czechoslovak Communist leader. Born into a working-class family, in 1921 Novotný joined the Communist Party of Czechoslovakia (CPC), and in 1929 he received his first administrative post in the party. In 1935 he was a delegate to the Seventh Congress of the Communist International, and in 1937 he became secretary of a party committee in Prague. After the German invasion in March 1939, Novotný went underground. Arrested by the Gestapo in September 1941, he was placed in the Mauthausen concentration camp and was held there until the end of the war. After returning home in May 1945, Novotný again became head of the party in Prague, and in 1946 he was elected to the party's Central Committee (CC). He took a leading role in the Communist coup of February 1948. In September 1951 he was promoted to full membership in the CC Secretariat; this promotion was linked to his role in the dismissal of **Rudolf Slanský**. In December 1951 Novotný was elected to the Presidium of the CC of the CPC. In February 1953 he became deputy prime minister of Czechoslovakia. A dull apparatchik, Novotný owed all his promotions to his absolute faithfulness in following the Stalinist line of **Klement Gottwald**. After Gottwald died in March 1953, Novotný replaced him as first secretary of the CC of the CPC in September 1953. Initially he was a member of the "collective leadership," whose members included **Antonin Zápotocký** and Prime Minister **Viliam Široký**. Despite signs of "thaw" in the Soviet bloc that followed the Twentieth Congress of the CPSU and the 1956 events in Poland and Hungary, the Czechoslovak leaders did not introduce any changes in the Stalinist system of government in Czechoslovakia.

Novotný gradually subordinated the party apparatus to himself and extended his powers. On 19 November 1957, after the death of Zápotocký, Novotný became president of Czechoslovakia. From 1959 to 1968 he also served as chairman of the National Front. When in 1961 a bad economic situation and **Nikita Khrushchev**'s "second thaw" in the Soviet Union gave rise to ferment, Novotný impeded changes and tried to prevent the disclosure of his role in the crimes of the system. In June 1961 he was instrumental in the dismissal of his main rival, **Rudolf Barák**, from the Ministry of Interior, and in January 1962 he personally took part in Barák's arrest. Nevertheless, Novotný failed to deter the Slovak faction of the party in its efforts to square things with the past. Under a 1962 resolution of the Twelfth Congress of the CPC, the new CC reviewed some political trials from 1949–54 and in April 1963 decided that many "deserving comrades" had been unlawfully convicted. The removal of "scapegoats" did not help. Novotný was replaced as head of the Slovak party by **Alexander Dubček**. Khrushchev's thaw in the Soviet Union induced the party authorities to limit censorship for the time being, but it also gave rise to student demonstrations for greater freedoms. In May 1964, the police, using truncheons, dispersed a demonstration of around three thousand students.

Despite the problems caused by the Kremlin's thaw, the fall of Khrushchev in October 1964 actually weakened Novotný's position because he was linked with Khrushchev. In the middle of the decade, an attempt to return to Stalinist orthodoxy increased the ferment within the Slovak party and among party intellectuals. Criticism of the party leadership was also voiced at a congress of Czechoslovak writers in June 1967. A crisis emerged at a CC plenum in October 1967. After the brutal quelling of a student demonstration in Prague's Strahov district, Novotný and the hard-liners had to face increasing criticism. The pro-reform forces united with the Slovak autonomists in the party. Novotný tried to use the occasion of Leonid Brezhnev's visit to Prague in December 1967 to consolidate his power, but without success. The pro-reform groups became so strong that Novotný had to perform a self-criticism. The balance tipped in favor of the reformists after they discovered that the dogmatists were plotting a coup. On 5 January 1968 Novotný was replaced

as first secretary of the CC of the CPC by Dubček. On 22 March 1968, during the Prague Spring, he was also forced to resign as president of the state. He continued to serve, though, as a member of the party's CC. After the invasion of Czechoslovakia by Warsaw Pact troops in August 1968, Novotný did not return to power. In 1971 he was finally expelled from the CPC CC. According to **Milan Kundera**, Novotný was the personification of "the Czech genius of shallowness." (WR)

Sources: *ČBS*; Lazitch; *Enciklopedia Slovenska*, vol. 4 (Bratislava, 1980); Zdeněk Eliaš and Jaromír Netík, "Czechoslovakia," in William E. Griffith, ed., *Communism in Europe*, vol. 2 (Cambridge, 1966); Vladimir V. Kusin, *The Intellectual Origins of the Prague Spring: The Development of Reformist Ideas in Czechoslovakia, 1958–1967* (Cambridge, 1971); Otto Ulč and Jan F. Triska, *Politics in Czechoslovakia* (San Francisco, 1974); Vladimir Kadlec, *Podivné konce našich presidentů* (Hradec Králové, 1991); Rudolf Černy, *Ex-prezident: Vzpomínky Antonína Novotného*, vols. 1–3 (Prague, 1998–99); Ondrej Felcman, *Vláda a prezident: Obdobi prazského jara* (Prague, 2000).

NOWAK Zenon (27 January 1905, Pabianice, near Łódź–21 August 1980, Warsaw), Polish Communist activist. Born into a working-class family, from 1917 to 1920 Nowak was a miner in Westphalia and later in Silesia. He also worked as an agrarian laborer and weaver in Pabianice. In 1924 he joined the Communist Workers' Party of Poland (Komunistyczna Partia Robotnicza Polski [KPRP]), which in 1925 changed its name to the Communist Party of Poland (Komunistyczna Partia Polski [KPP]). From 1932 to 1938 Nowak was a member of the KPP Central Committee (CC). He cooperated with the Communist International and probably also with the NKVD. After KPP activists were murdered on Stalin's orders (1936–39), Nowak, together with **Bolesław Bierut**, dissolved the KPP units in the Polish territories. From 1942 to 1945, Nowak worked in a German labor camp in the Sudeten, and from 1945 to 1947 he served in the Soviet Army. After returning to Poland in 1947, he joined the (Communist) Polish Workers' Party (Polska Partia Robotnicza [PPR]) and served as secretary of the PPR Executive Committee in Poznań and Katowice, head of the PPR CC Cadres Department (September–December 1948), and member of the Organizational Bureau of the PPR CC (November–December 1948). In the summer of 1948 Nowak was one of the activists who attacked **Władysław Gomułka**.

From the foundation of the Polish United Workers' Party (Polska Zjednoczona Partia Robotnicza [PUWP]) in December 1948, Nowak served as a member of its CC, a member of its Organizational Bureau, and head of its CC Cadres Department. In May 1950 he became a deputy member and in March 1954 a member of the Politburo. From May 1950 to March 1954 he served as secretary of the PUWP CC. In the party leadership Nowak was responsible for organizational affairs and the cadres. He sought to increase the party's influence in society along the lines of the Soviet model. From 1952 to 1956 he was an MP. From November 1952 to March 1954 he served as deputy prime minister. After the death of Bierut, in February 1956 Nowak's role increased. At that time he was one of the leaders of the dogmatic Natolin faction (Natolińczycy) and the Kremlin's candidate to succeed Bierut as party head. Nowak was against the dissemination of the so-called secret report delivered by **Nikita Khrushchev** at the Twentieth Congress of the CPSU. In July 1956, on behalf of the Natolin faction, Nowak proposed a program to tighten cooperation with the Soviet Union and continue the collectivization policy; he also called for reducing the number of people of Jewish origin in the party leadership, releasing Primate Stefan Wyszyński from house arrest, and reinstating Gomułka as a member of the Politburo. At the Eighth Plenum of the CC in October 1956 Nowak was expelled from the Politburo but continued to serve as first deputy prime minister. Gradually, Gomułka began to cooperate with some members of the Natolin faction, including Nowak. From 1961 to 1972 Nowak again served as an MP. He left the post of deputy prime minister in December 1968. From 1968 to 1971 he was chairman of the Party Central Control Commission, and from 1969 to 1971 he was chairman of the Supreme Chamber of Control. From 1971 to 1978 Nowak was ambassador to Moscow, and from 1978 to 1980, a member of the Presidium of the All-Polish Committee of the National Unity Front. (PK)

Sources: Mołdawa; Józef Światło, *Kulisy partii i bezpieki* (N.p., n.d.); Jan Nowak, *Wojna w eterze* (London, 1985); Antoni Czubiński, *Dzieje Najnowsze Polski 1944–1989* (Poznań, 1992); Andrzej Albert [Wojciech Roszkowski], *Najnowsza historia Polski 1914–1993*, vol. 2 (Warsaw, 1995); Włodzimierz Janowski and Aleksander Kochański, *Informator o strukturze i obsadzie personalnej centralnego aparatu PZPR 1948–1990* (Warsaw, 2000).

NOWAK-JEZIORAŃSKI Jan [originally Zdzisław Antoni Jeziorański], pseudonyms "Janek" and "Jan Zych" (15 May 1913, Warsaw–20 January 2005, Warsaw), Polish journalist and political activist. Born into a family with patriotic traditions, Nowak-Jeziorański studied economics at the University of Poznań (1933–36), and then he worked there as an assistant professor (1937–39). In the September 1939 campaign he fought in Volhynia. Taken prisoner of war by the Germans, he escaped during transport, but he was arrested again and sent to the Vosswald Camp in Silesia. He escaped again and came to Warsaw in Octo-

ber 1939. Nowak-Jeziorański took part in underground activities, and from mid-1941 he worked for the Bureau of Information and Propaganda of the High Command of the Union of Armed Struggle (Związek Walki Zbrojnej [ZWZ]) and later of the Home Army (Armia Krajowa [AK]). With the consent of the Polish underground authorities, he worked in the Germany Commissary Management of Real Estate in Warsaw and managed several houses in which clandestine meetings took place. In the summer of 1941 he took part in an anti-German disinformation action, "N," organizing the dissemination of propaganda materials in the Polish territories incorporated into Nazi Germany and in the Third Reich itself. As a courier of the AK High Command, Nowak-Jeziorański made several trips between Warsaw and London, serving as a messenger between the Polish government-in-exile and the leaders of the Polish underground state and army. It was then that he adopted the pseudonym "Jan Nowak." In 1943 he was awarded the Cross of the Brave and in 1944 the Cross of Virtuti Militari. Before returning to Poland in the summer of 1944, Nowak-Jeziorański met with British prime minister Winston Churchill and foreign minister Anthony Eden. Upon arrival in Warsaw, he told the Polish underground leaders of his impression that the West was indifferent toward Poland and the planned uprising in Warsaw. During the Warsaw Uprising, in August and September 1944, he edited Lightning (Błyskawica), radio broadcasts in English.

At the end of the Warsaw Uprising Nowak-Jeziorański was ordered to get through to London with microfilms of the uprising. He left Poland in December 1944 and, via Switzerland, he got to London in January 1945. In February 1945 he was promoted to captain. After the war he stayed in London. In 1946–55 Nowak-Jeziorański belonged to the Main Board of the Polish freedom movement Independence and Democracy, and from 1947 he was active in the Association of Polish War Veterans (Stowarzyszenie Polskich Kombatantów). In 1948 he was decorated with the British King's Medal for Courage in the Cause of Freedom. In 1948–51 he edited Polish broadcasts on the BBC, and in 1951–76 he was director of the Polish section of Radio Free Europe (RFE) in Munich. The RFE's broadcasts were aimed against Communist propaganda and the Communist monopoly of information in Poland, but Nowak-Jeziorański frequently had to make political decisions that did not always correspond with the current policies of his American employers and German hosts. For instance, he always strove for the international recognition of the Oder-Neisse border. In October 1956 he worked to calm tensions in Poland, knowing that the West would not help Poland against the Soviets.

After retiring from the RFE, Nowak-Jeziorański moved to Washington, D.C., where in 1977–92 he was a National Security Council consultant. He also became a member of the Polish American Congress. Until 1996 he belonged to its Board of Directors, and in 1991–92 he was one of its deputy chairmen. He co-organized help for Solidarity. Nowak-Jeziorański visited Poland for the first time after the war in 1989. From 1990 to 1993 he edited a television series, *Poland from a Distance* (Polska z oddali), which was later continued on Polish Radio. Using his Washington contacts, Nowak-Jeziorański worked for Polish entry into NATO. Active in Polish affairs, he frequently spoke on sensitive issues—for instance, he explicitly defended Colonel **Ryszard Kukliński** and demanded an explanation of the **Józef Oleksy** case, which was before the court. In the presidential campaign of 2000 he supported **Andrzej Olechowski** against **Aleksander Kwaśniewski**. He was engaged in the Polish-Jewish reconciliation. In 1994 Nowak-Jeziorański received the Order of the White Eagle, in 1996 the U.S. Presidential Medal of Freedom, and in 1998 the Lithuanian Order of Gediminas. He authored numerous articles and several books, such as *63 Days: The Story of the Warsaw Uprising* (under the pen name J. Zych; 1945); *Rosja wobec Powstania Warszawskiego* (Russia and the Warsaw Uprising; 1947); *Polska droga ku wolności, 1952–1974* (The Polish road to freedom, 1952–74; 1974); *Kurier z Warszawy* (1978; edition in Poland, 1981; *Courier from Warsaw*, 1982); *Polska pozostała sobą* (Poland remained herself; 1980); *Wojna w eterze: Wspomnienia 1948–1956* (War on the air: Memoirs, 1956–78; 1986); *Polska z oddali: Wspomnienia 1956–1976* (Poland from a distance: Memoirs, 1956–74; 1988); *W poszukiwaniu nadziei* (In search of hope; 1993); *Rozmowy o Polsce* (Conversations about Poland; 1995); and *Polska wczoraj, dziś i jutro* (Poland yesterday, today, and tomorrow; 1999). Nowak-Jeziorański won numerous literary and journalism awards, honorary doctorates, and honorary citizenships in Polish towns. (JS)

Sources: *Who's Who in Polish America, 1996–1997* (New York, 1996); *Polonia: Słownik biograficzny* (Warsaw, 2000); "Promocja" Jana Nowaka-Jeziorańskiego na doktora honoris causa Uniwersytetu Wrocławskiego, Wrocław, 2000.

NOWOTKO Marceli, pseudonyms "Marian," "Stary," and others (8 August 1893, Warsaw–28 November 1942, Warsaw), Polish Communist activist. Born into a large family of an agrarian worker, after finishing four grades of a rural elementary school, Nowotko worked as an apprentice locksmith and in a sugar factory. In 1915 he lost his job. In 1916 he joined Social Democracy of the Kingdom of Poland and Lithuania (Socjaldemokracja

Królestwa Polskiego i Litwy [SDKPiL]). From 1916 to 1918 he was an economic émigré in Germany, where he met the local revolutionaries. After returning home in December 1918, Nowotko became secretary of the Council of Workers' Delegates in Ciechanów and a member of the Communist Workers' Party of Poland (Komunistyczna Partia Robotnicza Polski [KPRP]). In October 1919 he was arrested for organizing a strike of agricultural workers. After his release, he became an activist in the Trade Union of Agricultural Workers. Arrested again for revolutionary agitation and then released, he was in hiding from mid-1920 until the Red Army marched into Poland in August 1920. Nowotko then became the commissar of the Polish Provisional Revolutionary Committee (Tymczasowy Komitet Rewolucyjny Polski) in Wysokie Mazowieckie and directed the Bolshevik terror in the territories where he was in charge. Wanted by the police after the retreat of the Soviet troops, he went to the Dąbrowa Górnicza mining district, where, under the name of Marceli Nowakowski, he worked in a factory. He also served as a KPRP district secretary and the chairman of the Metalworkers' Trade Union. From 1921 to 1927 Nowotko directed the underground units of the KPRP in Poznania (Wielkopolska), the Dąbrowa Górnicza mining district, Lwów (Lviv), Warsaw, and Łódź. (The KPRP was renamed the Communist Party of Poland [Komunistyczna Partia Polski (KPP)] in 1925.) In 1927 Nowotko was a delegate to the Fourth Congress of the KPP in Moscow. Arrested in July 1929, one year later he was sentenced to four years in prison. After his release, he resumed his work for the KPP, becoming a member of the KPP National Secretariat. Arrested again in April 1935 and sentenced to twelve years in prison in October 1936, he was freed during the Nazi invasion in September 1939. In the meantime, the KPP had been dissolved and its leaders murdered on Stalin's orders.

After making his way to the territories occupied by the Soviet Union, Nowotko worked for a Białystok unit of the International Organization for Aid to Revolutionaries. In mid-1940 he became chairman of a district executive committee in Łapy. In the spring of 1941 he went to Moscow, where he underwent training in a school of the Communist International. On 28 December 1941 he was parachuted close to Wiązowna, near Warsaw, with the first Initiative Group, which was to establish a new Communist party. While landing, Nowotko broke his leg. At the founding congress of the Polish Workers' Party (Polska Partia Robotnicza [PPR]) on 5 January 1942 Nowotko was elected first secretary of the party. At that time he used the name of Jan Wysocki. Nowotko strictly adhered to the Soviet strategies, based on concealing ties to the Kremlin and on promoting a program of a national liberation struggle. He called for immediately taking up military struggle, which conflicted with the program of the pro-independence underground and with Polish interests because the German occupation forces had a disproportionate advantage in Poland, but it was advantageous to the Soviet Union, which was having difficulties on the front. As a result of internal rivalry in the PPR leadership, Nowotko was shot and killed by Zygmunt Mołojec, on the orders of the latter's brother, Bolesław, who aspired to become the leader of the party. (WR)

Sources: *PSB*, vol. 23; Nicholas Bethell, *Gomulka, His Poland and His Communism* (Harlow, 1969); *Nowotko-Mołojec: Z początków PPR. Nieznane relacje Wladyslawa Gomułki i Franciszka Jóźwiaka* (London, 1986); Krystyna Kersten, *Narodziny systemu władzy: Polska 1943–1948* (Poznań, 1990); Marek J. Chodakiewicz, Piotr Gontarczyk, Leszek Żebrowski, eds., *Tajne oblicze GL-AL. i PPR: Dokumenty*, vol. I (Warsaw, 1997).

NYERS Rezső (21 March 1923, Budapest), Hungarian Communist activist. The son of a laborer, after primary school Nyers worked in a printing house. From 1940 he belonged to the Hungarian Social Democratic Party (HSDP) and from 1942 to the Trade Union of Printers. In 1945–46 he was deputy secretary of the HSDP committee in the Budapest quarter of Kispest, and he worked for the central party organ, *Népszava*. In 1947–48 he was deputy secretary and secretary of the HSDP committee in Pest. From the merger of the HSDP and the Hungarian Communist Party into the Hungarian Workers' Party (HWP) in June 1948, Nyers was the HWP's secretary for organization in the Pest provincial committee. From 1948 to 1954 he was a deputy member, and from 1956 a member, of the HWP Central Committee (CC), and from 1948 to 1953 he was an MP. In 1949–51 Nyers worked in the CC apparatus, from 1951 to 1954 he headed a department in the Ministry of Domestic Trade, from 1954 to 1956 he was deputy chairman of the All-National Union of Consumer Co-Operatives (AUCC), and from July to October 1956 he was minister of consumer industry. In 1956 he graduated from the Higher Economic School in Budapest.

During the revolution, on 5 November 1956 Nyers joined the government of **János Kádár**, and a week later he became head of the Commissariat of Supplies. From February 1957 he belonged to the CC of the Hungarian Socialist Workers' Party (HSWP), and in 1958–98 he was an MP. From 1957 to 1960 Nyers chaired the AUCC again, and from January 1960 to November 1962 he was minister of finance. From 1962 he was a deputy member, and from 1966 a member, of the HSWP CC Politburo, and from 1962 he was CC secretary for economic policy and head of the State Planning Commission. Nyers co-authored the New Economic Mechanism of 1968, but in the early 1970s, when the reform was checked, he was dismissed. In March 1974 he left the CC Secretariat, and in 1975 he was dropped from the Politburo. From 1974 to 1988 he was director of the Institute of Economics of the Hungarian Academy of Sciences; from 1976, head of the editorial board of the periodical *Közgazdasági Szemle*; from 1983 to 1990, chairman of the Hungarian Economic Association; and from 1986, professor of the Higher Economic School in Budapest.

As the economic crisis became aggravated in the late 1980s, Nyers returned to the HSWP leadership. In December 1987 he co-founded and briefly led the New March Forum, referring to the March Front of 1937. In May 1988 he returned to the CC Politburo, and from November 1988 to June 1989 he was minister of state for coordinating economic reforms. From June 1989 to its dissolution in October 1989, Nyers was the HWSP chairman. From October 1989 to May 1990 he chaired the (post-Communist) Hungarian Socialist Party (HSP). In the first free elections in March 1990 the HSP won almost 11 percent of the vote, and Nyers became an MP again. In 1998 he retired from political life. (JT)

Sources: *A magyar forradalom és szabadságharc enciklopédiája*, CD-ROM (Budapest, 1999); *Magyar Nagylexikon*, vol. 13 (Budapest, 2001); *Ki kicsoda 2000* (Budapest, 2001); I. Friss, ed., *Reform of the Economic Mechanism in Hungary* (Budapest, 1971); Paul Ignotus, *Hungary* (London, 1972); Bennet Kovrig, *Communism in Hungary from Kun to Kádár* (Stanford, 1979); Klaus-Detlev Grothusen, ed., *Ungarn* (Göttingen, 1987); Tamás Vácsi, *Újra a reformatok élén* (Kecskemet, 1989).

O

OBBOV Aleksandur (2 February 1887, Pleven–18 October 1975, Sofia), Bulgarian politician. Obbov finished a wine-making school in Pleven (1905) and completed law studies in Sofia (1913). In 1904 he joined the Bulgarian Agrarian National Union (Bulgarski Zemedelski Naroden Sayuz [BANU]). He was a member of its Standing Committee from 1908 to 1919 and the secretary of the Standing Committee from 1914 to 1919. Obbov served as a member and deputy speaker (1919–20) and then again as a member (1920–23) of the National Assembly. He was minister of agriculture and state property (May 1920–June 1923) and minister of interior and health (February–March 1923) in the government of **Aleksandur Stamboliyski**. After the overthrow of Stamboliyski in June 1923, Obbov organized a peasant resistance to the government of **Aleksandur Tsankov** in the Pleven district. After the uprising was suppressed, Obbov emigrated to Romania and then to Czechoslovakia. Along with **Raiko Daskalov**, he was a founding member of the BANU Foreign Representation in Prague (1923–25). After a split in the peasant movement in exile (1925), Obbov became the leader of its right wing.

After returning to Bulgaria in 1933, Obbov entered politics. He condemned the coup d'état of May 1934 and joined the legal opposition to the government of Tsar **Boris III**. From 1935 to 1944 he was one of the leaders of the Aleksandur Stamboliyski BANU. During World War II Obbov was interned in the Gonda Voda concentration camp. After his release, he was one of the founders of the Fatherland Front (1944). After the coup of 9 September 1944, he helped to organize and consolidate the BANU; for example, he was the editor-in-chief of the newspaper, *Zemedelsko zname*, and a member (1945–47) and secretary (1946–47) of the BANU Standing Committee. Obbov was minister without portfolio (August 1945–March 1946), minister of agriculture and state property (August–September 1945), and deputy prime minister and minister of agriculture and state property (March–November 1946) in the government of **Kimon Georgiev**. As deputy prime minister and minister without portfolio (November 1946–December 1947) in the cabinet of **Georgi Dimitrov**, Obbov endorsed the suppression of the non-Communist opposition. He served as deputy to the National Assembly (1945–46) and to the Grand National Assembly (1946–49). He was a member of the delegation that signed a peace treaty for Bulgaria with the Allies in Paris (10 February 1947). In the summer of 1947 Obbov opposed the transformation of the BANU into an appendage of the Communist Party; consequently, he was stripped of his posts and persecuted. After the plenum of the Central Committee of the Bulgarian Communist Party in April 1956, at which the "personality cult" was denounced, Obbov again became a member of the Fatherland Front. (JJ)

Sources: *Entsiklopediya Bulgariya*, vol. 4 (Sofia, 1984); Georgi Dimitrov, *Suchineniia*, vol. 15 (Sofia, 1989); Ilcho Dimitrov, *Minaloto* (Sofia, 1992); Tasho Tashev, *Ministrite na Bŭlgariia 1879–1999; Entsiklopedichen Spravochnik* (Sofia, 1999); Milen Kumanov and Tania Nikolova, *Politicheski partii, organizatsii i dvizheniia v Bulgariia i tekhnite lideri 1879–1999: Kratuk spravochnik* (Sofia, 1999); Angel Tsurakov, *Entsiklopediia. Pravitelstvata na Bulgariia: Khronologiia na politicheskiia zhivot 1879–2001* (Sofia, 2001).

OBERSOVSZKY Gyula (1 January 1927, Pécs–15 March 2001, Budapest), Hungarian writer. Obersovszky was born into the family of an entrepreneur and cultural activist of Polish origin. For financial reasons, at the age of fifteen he began working as a trainee at a notary's office in Püspökladány. In 1944 he joined the Hungarian Communist Party, and in the spring of 1945 he worked on a commission for parceling out land. In 1949 he graduated from the Department of Drama of the School of Drama in Budapest and began working in the Department of Popular Education of the National Council in Debrecen. A co-founder of the provincial organization of the Association of Hungarian Writers and the periodical *Építők*, Obersovszky joined the Union of Hungarian Journalists in 1954. In the same year he was stripped of all his posts and expelled from the party. He moved to Budapest, and as an employee of the Institute of Popular Education, he organized drama courses. In the summer of 1956 he resumed his journalistic work.

On 23 October 1956 Obersovszky took part in the siege of the radio building in Budapest. The following day he founded and then edited *Igazság*, the first newspaper of the revolution. On 4 November he founded the underground periodical *Élünk* and joined a group of fighters from the hospital on Sándor Péterffy Street. He helped to organize the "silent" revolution of 23 November and a women's demonstration against the Soviet intervention and the suppression of the revolution on 4 December. Arrested in December 1956 and tried in the trial of **Ilona Tóth** and her comrades in April 1957, Obersovszky was sentenced to three years in prison. However, on 20 June 1957 the Supreme Court sentenced Obersovszky, along with another writer, József Gáli, to death on the charge of "plotting against the people's government." As a result of international protests, Obersovszky was reprieved and the case was reviewed. He was sentenced to life imprisonment and Gáli to fifteen years. Obersovszky was released under an amnesty in 1963. From 1967 to 1989 he was an editor of the newspaper *Sportfogadás*. He could publish his works only under a pseudonym, "Oby Gyula." It was only after the fall of communism that he could publish under his real name again. In 1988 Obersovszky was co-founder of the Historical Compensation Committee, whose aim it was to bring about a solemn reburial of **Imre Nagy**, his associates, and all the victims of the 1956 revolution and to preserve the memory of its fighters. In 1990 for a short period Obersovszky revived and edited the periodicals *Igazság* and *Élünk*. From 1991 to 2000 he was the only editor of the periodical *Vagyok*. (JT)

Sources: *A magyar forradalom és szabadságharc enciklopédiája*, CD-ROM (Budapest, 1999); *Ki kicsoda 2000* (Budapest, 2001); *Magyar Nagylexikon*, vol. 14 (Budapest, 2002); György Litván, ed., *Rewolucja węgierska 1956 roku* (Warsaw, 1996).

OCHAB Edward (16 August 1906, Kraków–1 May 1989, Warsaw), Polish Communist leader. The son of a clerk of peasant origin, Ochab graduated from the Cooperative College affiliated with the Jagiellonian University in Kraków in 1927, and two years later he joined the Communist Party of Poland (Komunistyczna Partia Polski [KPP]). Imprisoned five times for his Communist activities in the interwar period, he spent a total of six years in prison. In September 1939 he got out of a prison in Warsaw and fought in the defense of the capital. After the Red Army seized the eastern territories of the Second Republic of Poland in September 1939, Ochab found himself in the Soviet-occupied territories. After the German invasion of the Soviet Union in June 1941, he volunteered to serve in the Red Army. Assigned to a *stroybat* (construction battalion), in March 1943 he organized the Union of Polish Patriots (Związek Patriotów Polskich [ZPP]) under the aegis of the Kremlin. From 1943 to 1944 he served as political officer in the units of the Polish Army under Soviet command. He enjoyed the trust of the Kremlin; therefore, he was soon promoted to responsible positions.

From July to November 1944 Ochab served as deputy commander of the First Polish Army for political and educational affairs and subsequently as deputy head of the Department of Public Administration of the Polish Committee of National Liberation (Polski Komitet Wyzwolenia Narodowego [PKWN]). After the establishment of the Provisional Government, he served as undersecretary of state in the Ministry of Public Administration, and from April to June 1945 he was head of this ministry. From July 1945 to February 1946 he was secretary of the Central Committee (CC) of the (Communist) Polish Workers' Party (Polska Partia Robotnicza [PPR]), and subsequently he served as first secretary of the PPR Provincial Committee in Katowice until April 1948. From May to September 1948 Ochab was chairman of the Central Board of the Cooperative Union, and from 1948 to 1949 he was chairman of the Central Commission of Trade Unions (Komisja Centralna Związków Zawodowych [KCZZ]). After **Władysław Gomułka** was dismissed in September 1948, Ochab again joined the PPR CC Secretariat and became a deputy member of the party's Politburo. At that time he was one of the top-ranking members of the Stalinist leadership of the party. In December 1948 he became a member of the CC of the Polish United Workers' Party (Polska Zjednoczona Partia Robotnicza [PUWP]), a deputy member of the Politburo, and a member of the PUWP CC Organizational Bureau. In April 1949 Ochab was appointed deputy minister of national defense and was promoted to general. In the first half of 1950 he also served as chief of the Main Political and Educational Board of the Polish Army. In May 1950 he became CC secretary and a member of the secretariat of the CC Organizational Bureau. In March 1954 he joined the PUWP CC Politburo. He also held many posts in the regime of **Bolesław Bierut**; for example, he was chairman of the Main Board of the Polish-Soviet Friendship Society.

After Stalin's death and when factional strife within the PUWP leadership increased, Ochab represented a neutral position, although he initially spoke dogmatically. For example, in September 1953 he sharply attacked the Catholic Church and Primate Cardinal **Stefan Wyszyński**. After the death of Bierut, at the Sixth Plenum of the CC on 20 March 1956, under pressure from **Nikita Khrushchev**, Ochab was elected the new first secretary of the PUWP CC. He maneuvered between the Puławska faction (Puławianie) and the conservative Natolin faction (Natolińczycy) during the Poznań revolt in June 1956 and in the summer of that year, when both factions began to consider restoring Gomułka to power because they wanted to secure Gomułka's support for their position. Ochab still pointed to "kulaks," "imperialist agents," and "bourgeois scoundrels" as "class enemies," but he also promised "further democratization of the party and society."

At the beginning of October 1956, the Politburo, and particularly Ochab, along with **Józef Cyrankiewicz** and **Aleksander Zawadzki**, agreed to reelect Gomułka to the position of first secretary of the CC. Since the Puławska faction approved, the Natolin faction warned the Kremlin that a counterrevolution was breaking out in Poland. On 19 October 1956, shortly before the opening of the Eighth Plenum of the CC, a Soviet delegation headed by Khrushchev landed at the airport near Warsaw, and Soviet troops moved toward the capital. Ochab, Cyrankiewicz, and Zawadzki received this delegation and, after a dramatic discussion, succeeded in persuading Khrushchev that the reinstatement of Gomułka was the best solution. Ochab continued to be a member of the Politburo and the CC Secretariat.

As the man behind the compromise, Ochab joined the new ruling group. From January 1957 to October 1959 he served as minister of agriculture. In May 1961 he became deputy chairman of the Council of State, and in August 1964, after Zawadzki's death, he was appointed chairman of the Council of State. From April 1965 to April 1968 he also served as chairman of the All-Polish Committee of the National Unity Front. As a result of the anti-Semitic campaign launched by the PUWP leadership in March 1968, Ochab submitted a letter to the CC Politburo and Secretariat protesting this campaign, and he resigned all his party and government posts. On 11 April 1968 the Assembly removed him as chairman of the Council of State. At the Twelfth Plenum of the CC in July of that year Ochab was also dismissed from the party leadership, and he retired from politics. In October 1977, along with **Władysław Matwin**, **Jerzy Morawski**, and several other former activists of the PUWP, Ochab signed a letter to **Edward Gierek** warning the authorities of the mounting economic and social crisis and calling for changes in economic policies and a reform of the system in Poland. However, until the end of his life Ochab remained a dogmatic Communist, which was amply manifested in a long interview given to Teresa Torańska during the period of martial law. (WR)

Sources: Mołdawa; Jan Nowak, *Wojna w eterze* (London, 1985); Teresa Torańska, *Oni* (Warsaw, 1985); Jerzy Eisler, *Marzec 1968* (Warsaw, 1991); Andrzej Albert [Wojciech Roszkowski], *Najnowsza historia Polski 1914–1993*, vol. 2 (Warsaw, 1995); Krzysztof Lesiakowski, *Mieczysław Moczar "Mietek": Biografia polityczna* (Warsaw, 1998); Włodzimierz Janowski, *Informator o strukturze i obsadzie personalnej centralnego aparatu PZPR 1948–1990* (Warsaw, 2000).

OHIYENKO Ivan (monastic name Ilarion) (14 January 1882, Brusilov, Kiev region–29 March 1972, Winnipeg, Canada), Ukrainian historian, linguist, metropolitan of the Autocephalous Orthodox Church. In 1909 Ohiyenko completed his studies in Slavic philology and literature at the university in Kiev, and then he lectured at the Kiev Trade Institute, as well as at his alma mater. After the February 1917 revolution, he worked on the Ukrainization of higher education and received a professorship at the newly established Ukrainian State University in Kiev. After the seizure of Kiev by the Bolsheviks, Ohiyenko was rector of the Ukrainian State University in Kamyanets Podilskyy

(Kamieniec Podolski). In 1919, on behalf of the Ukrainian Party of Socialists-Federalists, he served as minister of education and religious affairs in the government of the Ukrainian National Republic (UNR). After the fall of the UNR Ohiyenko settled in Tarnów, Poland, where until 1924 he served as minister for religious affairs in the UNR government-in-exile. He taught at a gymnasium in Lwów, and in 1926 he took a professorship in the Old Church Slavonic language and paleography at the Department of Orthodox Theology of Warsaw University. In 1932, on the wave of anti-Ukrainian persecutions, Ohiyenko lost his post. He published in the magazines *Ridna mova* and *Nasha Kultura*. In 1937–39 he published the Ukrainian translation of the Old and New Testaments.

During the Nazi occupation Ohiyenko took holy orders and was consecrated bishop of the Chełm (Kholm) diocese in 1940. He carried out the Ukrainization of the Orthodox Church of Chełm, and in March 1944 he was elevated to the status of metropolitan. The day before the Chełm region was seized by the Red Army, Ohiyenko left for Austria, then for Switzerland, and in 1947 he was invited to Canada, where in 1951 he was appointed metropolitan of Winnipeg and became head of the Ukrainian Orthodox Church in Canada. He initiated the publication of the magazine *Vira i kultura*, revived *Nasha Kultura*, founded a theological society, and lectured at and served as dean at St. Andrew's College. Ohiyenko was the author of many important works in the field of the Ukrainian history and literature, among them the following: *Ukraiinska kultura* (Ukrainian culture; 1918); *Istoriia ukraiinskoho drukarstva* (History of Ukrainian printing; 1925); *Kostiantyn i Mefodii: Ikh zhyttia ta diialnist* (Constantine and Methodius: Their life and work, 2 vols.; 1927–28); and *Suchasna ukraiinska literaturna mova* (The Ukrainian modern literary language; 1935); Ohiyenko also wrote dictionaries of the Ukrainian language and works in the history of the Church in the Ukraine—for example, *Fortetsia pravoslaviia na Volyni: Sviata Pochaivska Lavra* (The fortress of the Orthodox Church in Volhynia: Holy Lavra Pochayivska; 1961) and *Kanonizatsiia sviatykh v ukraiinskii tserkvi* (The canonization of saints in the Ukrainian Orthodox Church; 1965). (WR)

Sources: *Encyclopedia of Ukraine*, vol. 3 (Toronto, 1993); V. Zaikin, *Profesor Ivan Ohiyenko iak tserkovnyi ta hromadskii diiakh i iak uchennyi* (Warsaw, 1925); *Zhalobna knyha v pamiat Metropolyta Ilarijona* (Winnipeg, 1973).

OKULICKI Leopold, pseudonyms "Kobra," "Kula," "Niedźwiadek," and "Termit" (12 November 1898, Bratucice, near Bochnia–24 December 1946 Moscow), Polish general, last commander-in-chief of the Polish Home Army (Armia Krajowa [AK]). Okulicki graduated from elementary school in Okulice and from high school in Bochnia, as an extramural student, in 1919. In May 1913 he joined the Riflemen's Association, and in May 1914 he became a non-commissioned officer. On 6 August 1914 he joined the Polish Legions, but in September he was dismissed for health reasons. Okulicki got his second assignment to the Third Infantry Regiment of the Second Brigade in September 1915. He fought in the battles of Rarańcza (Rarancha) and Kostiuchnówka (Kostyukhnivka), and in 1916 he was slightly wounded at the battle of Polska Góra. After the so-called oath of allegiance crisis of July 1917, Okulicki was inducted into the Austrian Army. In 1918 he finished a reserve officer training school in Košice. In August 1918 he deserted from the Austrian Army and joined the Polish Military Organization (Polska Organizacja Wojskowa [POW]) in Kraków. On 31 October 1918 he helped to disarm the Austrians and subsequently fought against the Ukrainians in the battle of Lwów (Lviv). He fought on the Polish-Soviet front near Volkovysk. In April 1920 he became a lieutenant. In June of that year he was slightly wounded at the battle on the Berezina River.

In 1925 Okulicki graduated from the Military College in Warsaw. He subsequently became head of the mobilization department of the Headquarters of Corps Area Three in Grodno. Promoted to major in March 1928, he later commanded a battalion of an infantry regiment in Rybnik and then taught tactics at the Infantry Training Center at Rembertów. From 1934 to 1935 he was chief of staff of the Thirteenth Infantry Division in Równe (Rivne) and then became head of the Wschód (East) Department of the Third Operational Department of the General Staff. In March 1936 he became lieutenant colonel, and on 1 April 1939 he was appointed deputy chief of the Third Department of the General Staff (from 1 September 1939 the Staff of the Commander-in-Chief). As officer for operational affairs of the local branch of the General Headquarters of the Commander-in-Chief, Okulicki remained in Warsaw after the Staff of the Commander-in-Chief left the capital on 6 September 1939. During the defense of Warsaw he served as chief of staff of the Warsaw West sector, and on 17 September he became commander of this sector.

After the capitulation of Warsaw, Okulicki helped to establish the underground Service for the Victory of Poland (Służba Zwycięstwu Polsce [SZP]). In October 1939 he became commander of the SZP for Łódź Province, and in January 1940, commander for the Łódź district of the Union of Armed Struggle (Związek Walki Zbrojnej [ZWZ]). In July 1940 Okulicki was promoted to colonel. Fearing arrest, in August 1940 he transferred to the ZWZ High Command in Warsaw. In October 1940 he was appointed commander of the ZWZ in Lviv. On 22 January 1941 Okulicki was arrested by the NKVD and placed in Lubyanka Prison, and in April 1941 he was transferred to Lefortovo Prison. After the outbreak of the Soviet-German war and the signing of the Sikorski-Maysky agreement, Okulicki was released under an amnesty. He took part in negotiations between General **Władysław Anders** and Stalin and was appointed chief of staff of the Polish Army in the Soviet Union. In March 1942 he became commander of the Seventh Infantry Division, formed in Kerman, Uzbekistan. He continued to hold this post after the army of General Anders left the Soviet Union.

After training in Great Britain for a special force of paratroopers to be dropped in occupied Poland, on 22 May 1944 he was parachuted to the Kos receiving unit near Wierzbno, not far from Kraków. Promoted to brigadier general on the same day, Okulicki became first deputy to the chief of staff and chief of operations in the AK High Command. On 27 July he became commander of the Independence organization (Niepodległość [NIE]), as a result of which he ceased working in the staff. However, he played a major role in the decision to start the Warsaw Uprising. After General **Tadeusz Pełczyński** was wounded, Okulicki served as interim chief-of-staff of the AK High Command. After the failure of the uprising, General **Tadeusz Bór-Komorowski** appointed Okulicki as his successor. On 2 October, along with the civilian population, Okulicki left Warsaw and went to Częstochowa, where on the following day he assumed the duties of the AK commander-in-chief. He was formally appointed in December 1944. On 19 January 1945 he ordered the dissolution of the AK and at the same time made the decision that the cadres should remain underground and weapons and equipment should be hidden.

On 27 March 1945, invited by the Soviet command of the First Belorussian Front, Okulicki went to negotiate with their representatives in Pruszków, where, along with fifteen other leaders of the Polish underground state, he was arrested by the NKVD for failure to obey the orders of the Soviet military command and was charged with organizing armed sabotage against the Red Army behind the front lines. They were all taken to Moscow and placed in Lubyanka Prison. In the so-called Trial of Sixteen (18–21 June 1945) before the Military Board of the Soviet Supreme Court in Moscow, a trial of the leaders of an Allied country, Okulicki received the stiffest sentence: ten years in prison. He died in Lubyanka Prison in Moscow. (JS)

Sources: *PSB*, vol. 22; Kunert, vol. 2; Jerzy R. Krzyżanowski, *Generał. Opowieść o Leopoldzie Okulickim* (London, 1980); Janusz Kurtyka, *Generał Leopold Okulicki "Niedźwiadek" (1898–1946)* (Warsaw, 1989); Andrzej Przemyski, *Ostatni komendant: Generał Leopold Okulicki* (Lublin, 1990); Zbigniew Mierzwiński, *Generałowie II Rzeczypospolitej* (Warsaw, 1990); Krzysztof A. Tochman, *Słownik Biograficzny Cichociemnych*, vol. 1 (Oleśnica, 1994).

OLECHOWSKI Andrzej (9 September 1947, Kraków), Polish economist and politician. In 1973 Olechowski graduated from the Socioeconomics Department of the Main School of Planning and Statistics (now the Warsaw School of Economics) in Warsaw. In 1979 he received a Ph.D. in economics. For many years he worked in the UN Conference on Trade and Development in Geneva and for the World Bank in Washington, D.C., cooperating with Polish Communist intelligence. In 1989 he became head of a department in the Ministry of Foreign Economic Relations. He took part in the Round Table Talks on behalf of the government. A member of the boards of directors of many banks and companies—including Bank Handlowy S.A. w Warszawie and Bank Inicjatyw Gospodarczych S.A., the latter being established by the Communist nomenklatura—from 1989 to 1991 Olechowski was deputy chairman of the Narodowy Bank Polski, and in 1991–92 he was secretary of state in the Ministry of Foreign Economic Relations. The main negotiator of a trade agreement between Poland and the European Communities, from December 1991 to June 1992 he was minister of finance in the government of **Jan Olszewski**. In 1992–93 he was an economic adviser to President **Lech Wałęsa**, and in 1993 he co-initiated and organized the Nonparty Bloc for the Support of Reforms. From October 1993 to January 1996 Olechowski was minister of foreign affairs in the governments of **Waldemar Pawlak** and **Józef Oleksy**. One of the most popular politicians of the 1990s, in 2000 Olechowski ran in the presidential elections, coming in second with 17.3 percent of the vote. In January 2001, along with **Maciej Płażyński** and Donald Tusk, he co-initiated the creation of the Civic Platform. In September 2002 he ran for mayor of Warsaw, but he came in third. (IS)

Sources: *Kto jest kim w Polsce* (Warsaw, 2001); Janusz A. Majcherek, *Pierwsza dekada III Rzeczypospolitej* (Warsaw, 1999); Antoni Dudek, *Pierwsze lata III Rzeczyspospolitej 1989–2001* (Kraków, 2002); Wojciech Roszkowski, *Historia Polski 1914–2001* (Warsaw, 2002).

OLEKSY Józef (22 June 1946, Nowy Sącz), Polish Communist activist and post-Communist politician. In 1969 Oleksy graduated from the Foreign Trade Department of the Main School of Planning and Statistics (now the Warsaw School of Economics) in Warsaw. In 1971–72 he studied at the European Department of Comparative Law in Strasbourg and Pescara. In 1977 he received a Ph.D. in economics. During his studies Oleksy was active in the Association of Polish Students, and from 1968 he belonged to the Polish United Workers' Party (Polska Zjednoczona Partia Robotnicza [PUWP]). In 1977–81 he worked in the Department of Ideological Education of the PUWP Central Committee (CC), from 1981 to 1986 he headed the Office of the PUWP Central Commission of Inspection, and in 1987–89 he was first secretary of the PUWP Provincial Committee in Biała Podlaska. After the PUWP was dissolved in January 1990, Oleksy became a member of the Presidium of the Main Board of the Social Democracy of the Polish Republic (Socjaldemokracja Rzeczypospolitej Polski [SdRP]). From 1993 he was its deputy chairman and in 1996–97, chairman. From March to August 1989 Oleksy was minister for contacts with trade unions in the government of **Mieczysław Rakowski**. Elected in the breakthrough elections of June 1989, Oleksy was also an MP in subsequent terms of the parliament, and from October 1993 to March 1995, speaker of the Lower House. From 1 March 1995 to 24 January 1996 he was prime minister of the government based on a coalition of post-Communists and the Polish Peasant Party. Oleksy resigned as a result of accusations raised by the minister of interior, **Andrzej Milczanowski**, who claimed that Oleksy had been a Soviet and later a Russian agent. The case has not been sufficiently explained. In October 2000 the Lustration Court found Oleksy guilty of lying about his cooperation with Communist special services, but he appealed. From December 1999 Oleksy was a member of the National Board of the Democratic Left Alliance (Sojusz Lewicy Demokratycznej [SLD]). From 2001 Oleksy was deputy chairman of the SLD parliamentary club; from June 2003 he was deputy chairman of the SLD, head of the parliamentary European commission, and a Polish delegate to the European Union convention; in early 2004 he was briefly minister of interior, and in April 2004 he became speaker of the parliament. (IS)

Sources: Mołdawa; *Biała Księga: Akta śledztwa prowadzonego przez Prokuraturę Warszawskiego Okręgu Wojskowego w Warszawie w sprawie wniosków Ministra Spraw Wewnętrznych z dnia 19.12.1995 r. i 16.01.1996 r.* (Warsaw, 1996); Janusz A. Majcherek, *Pierwsza dekada III Rzeczypospolitej* (Warsaw, 1999); Antoni Dudek, *Pierwsze lata III Rzeczyspospolitej 1989–2001* (Kraków, 2002).

OLSZEWSKI Jan (20 August 1930, Warsaw), Polish lawyer and politician. During the Nazi occupation Olszewski was active in the underground scouting movement, the Gray Ranks (Szare Szeregi). In 1953 he graduated in law from the University of Warsaw. Later he worked in the Ministry of Justice (1953–54) and in the Institute of Legal Sciences of the Polish Academy of Sciences (1954–56). Editor of the weekly *Po Prostu* (1956–57), in 1956–62 Olszewski was a member of the Crooked Circle Club, which included young intellectuals critical of Stalinism, and he was a member of its board (1958–61). In 1962–68 and after 1970 Olszewski worked as a defense counsel in the political trials of **Jacek Kuroń** and **Karol Modzelewski** (1965), Melchior Wańkowicz (1965), Janusz Szpotański (1967), and the organization Movement (1971). From 1968 to 1970 his legal license was suspended. Along with **Jan Józef Lipski**, Olszewski organized help for the politically oppressed and their families. In 1975–76 he took part in protests against amendments to the constitution, signing the "Letter of 59." Counsel for the defense in the trials of workers participating in the June 1976 protests and participant in the Committee for the Defense of Workers (Komitet Obrony Robotników [KOR]) and the Committee of Social Self-Defense–KOR, Olszewski belonged to the leadership of the secret Polish Association for Independence (Polskie Porozumienie Niepodległościowe [PPN]) of **Zdzisław Najder**.

In 1980 Olszewski co-authored the statutes of Solidarity, and, with **Wiesław Chrzanowski**, he represented the union during the registration process. An adviser to the Solidarity National Coordination Commission and later to its National Commission and a member of the Program Council of the Solidarity Center for Social and Professional Studies, Olszewski advocated a moderate line, which drew him close to the Solidarity advisers connected with the Catholic Church. He called himself a Socialist-independent, and he was connected with **Antoni Macierewicz's** periodical *Głos*. After the introduction of martial law in December 1981 Olszewski defended Solidarity activists, and in 1984–85 he was the spokesman for the family of Reverend **Jerzy Popiełuszko** during the trial of the priest's murderers in Toruń. An adviser to the underground organization Solidarity, from 1988 Olszewski belonged to the Civic Committee of the Chairman of Solidarity. He took part in the Round Table Talks, but he was critical of the April 1989 agreement. Olszewski gradually became a critic of the Civic Parliamentary Club and of **Lech Wałęsa**, whom he had supported in the presidential elections of 1990. In December 1990 Olszewski was given the mission to form a government, but he failed. In 1990–92 he belonged to the Center Alliance (Porozumienie Centrum [PC]), and from 1991 to 1993 he was an MP on its behalf.

After the elections of October 1991, from 5 December 1991 to 5 June 1992 Olszewski was prime minister. His gov-ernment, based on a minority center-right coalition, entered into conflict with President Wałęsa over the control of the army and the substance of the Polish-Russian treaty. The coalition collapsed when Minister of Interior Macierewicz started lustration. In 1992 Olszewski was excluded from the PC and formed the Movement for the Republic Party. He was the chairman of the new party, which advocated a radical de-Communization and lustration and presented the Round Table Talks as a plot to maintain Communist structures of power. In the elections of 1993 Olszewski lost, and his movement split in two. Olszewski drew closer to the new Solidarity leadership and co-authored its civic draft of the constitution. In 1995 Olszewski ran in the presidential elections, winning 7 percent of the vote. In November 1995 he formed the Movement for the Reconstruction of Poland (Ruch Odbudowy Polski [ROP]) and became its chairman. The ROP made references to the national tradition and anti-communism, and it called privatization a plunder of the national economy by domestic and foreign profiteers. Olszewski advocated the entry of Poland into NATO, but he was against a rapid integration into the European Union. In the elections of September 1997 the ROP gained 5.6 percent of the vote, and Olszewski won a seat. He ran in the presidential elections of 2000, but in view of his low ranking he withdrew before the first round, appealing to his supporters to vote for **Marian Krzaklewski**. In the parliamentary elections of September 2001 Olszewski won a seat on behalf of the League of Polish Families, but he belonged to the ROP club. (AF)

Sources: Andrzej Friszke, *Opozycja polityczna w PRL 1945–1980* (London, 1994); Jan Skórzyński, *Ugoda i rewolucja: Władza i opozycja 1985–1989* (Warsaw, 1995); Zdzisław Najder, *Jaka Polska? Co i komu doradzałem* (Warsaw, n.d.); *Opozycja w PRL: Słownik biograficzny 1956–89* (Warsaw, 2000); Antoni Dudek, *Pierwsze lata III Rzeczpospolitej 1989–2001* (Kraków, 2002); www.sejm.gov.pl.

OLSZOWSKI Stefan (28 August 1931, Toruń), Polish Communist activist. Born into a teacher's family, Olszowski graduated in Polish studies from the University of Łódź. From the late 1940s he was active in Communist youth organizations. In 1949–50 he commanded the Polish Scouting Association in Włocławek, from 1952 to 1954 he chaired the Łódź Association of Polish Students (Zrzeszenie Studentów Polskich [ZSP]), and in 1953–55 he was a member of the Łódź Presidium of the Union of Polish Youth. In 1956 Olszowski represented Poland at the International Student Union in Prague, where he began to make contacts with Soviet functionaries. In 1956–60 he chaired the ZSP Main Council and was a member of the Secretariat of the Central Committee (CC) of the Union of

Socialist Youth. From 1952 a member of the Polish United Workers' Party (Polska Zjednoczona Partia Robotnicza [PUWP]), in the 1960s Olszowski quickly advanced in the party apparatus. In 1960–63 he was secretary of the PUWP Provincial Committee in Poznań.

In 1963 Olszowski became head of the Press Office of the PUWP CC. He became allied with **Mieczysław Moczar** and played an important role as the instigator of the anti-Semitic campaign of 1967–68, in March 1968 in particular. From June 1964 Olszowski was a member of the PUWP CC, and at the Fifth PUWP Congress in November 1968 he entered the CC Secretariat. From 1969 to 1980 he was an MP. In December 1970 he played an active role in the toppling of **Władysław Gomułka**. After Moczar's fall in the summer of 1971 Olszowski parted ways with him. He resigned from the CC Secretariat, but at the Sixth PUWP Congress in December 1971 he was promoted to the CC Politburo and he became foreign minister. In this capacity he became **Edward Gierek**'s right-hand man in the policy of opening Poland to Western credits. Olszowski accompanied Gierek on his numerous trips—for example, to France and Germany. In December 1975 he returned to the CC Secretariat, but he gave up his position as foreign minister. Aware of the approaching economic disaster and the end of Gierek's rule, in February 1980 Olszowski left the Secretariat and Politburo, becoming ambassador to East Germany.

After the summer strikes and accords of August 1980, during a shuffling of the top party leaders, Olszowski returned to the CC Secretariat and Politburo, taking over the leadership of the hard-liners' faction, which strove for a crackdown on Solidarity and the democratic opposition. Despite his tactical declarations on the necessity to reach agreements with workers, Olszowski belonged to a special task force that analyzed the efficacy of the use of force against the workers. Within the CC apparatus Olszowski controlled the media, education, and culture. He supported the most dogmatic and pro-Muscovite tendencies in the Communist Party, among them the weekly *Rzeczywistość*. He also supervised youth organizations. Olszowski's role in the Bydgoszcz crisis of March 1981 remains unclear, but it is clear that during the campaign before the Ninth Extraordinary PUWP Congress in the spring of 1981 he presented a confrontational line, not only in relation to Solidarity, but also toward the party leadership of **Stanisław Kania**. During the congress in July 1981 he remained in the highest party organs, since he was perceived by the Kremlin as a potential alternative to Kania. During the period of martial law Olszowski belonged to the inner circle of decision-makers, although in July 1982 he left the CC Secretariat. In November 1985 he also left the Politburo; his departure was interpreted as a weakening of the extreme

dogmatic stance of General **Wojciech Jaruzelski** in connection with the murder of Reverend **Jerzy Popiełuszko** and the Toruń trial of his security service assassins. In July 1986 Olszowski was dropped from the PUWP CC, and at the end of the 1980s he left for the United States; this raises the question of the political price he paid for the American consent to settle near New York. (PK/WR).

Sources: Mołdawa; Jerzy Holzer, *"Solidarność"* (Warsaw, 1983); Jerzy Eisler, *Marzec 1968* (Warsaw, 1991); Andrzej Albert [Wojciech Roszkowski], *Najnowsza historia Polski 1918–1980*, vol. 2 (Warsaw, 1995); Włodzimierz Janowski and Aleksander Kochański, *Informator o strukturze i obsadzie personalnej centralnego aparatu PZPR 1948–1990* (Warsaw, 2000); Jerzy Eisler, *Grudzień 1970* (Warsaw, 2000); Dariusz Stola, *Kampania antysyjonistyczna w Polsce 1967–1968* (Warsaw, 2000); Andrzej Paczkowski, *Droga do "mniejszego zła"* (Kraków, 2002).

OLSZYNA-WILCZYŃSKI Józef [originally Wilczyński] (27 November 1890, Kraków–22 September 1939, Sopoćkinie), Polish general. The son of a bricklayer, Olszyna-Wilczyński graduated from a gymnasium in Kraków and started studies in the Department of Civil Engineering at Lwów (Lviv) Polytechnic College. In 1912–13 he served in the Austro-Hungarian Army, graduated from a school for reserve officers, and joined the Polish Riflemen Squads. After the outbreak of World War I, he entered the Polish Legions and commanded a company and later a battalion. In July 1917 Olszyna-Wilczyński refused to swear loyalty to the Austrian emperor, was forced to join the Austrian Army, and was sent to the Italian front and later to the Ukraine. He organized a cell of the Polish Military Organization, and in November 1918 he led his battalion into the Polish Army in-the-making. Olszyna-Wilczyński took part in the Polish-Ukrainian war in East Galicia. Taken prisoner of war, he was liberated by Polish troops in Buczacz (Buchach); from 1920 he commanded an infantry brigade. After the seizure of Kiev by Polish and Ukrainian troops in May 1920, Olszyna-Wilczyński became the town commander and was promoted to the rank of colonel. Until the end of the Polish-Soviet war he fought in Volhynia. In 1921–23 he served as head of engineering in the command of Corps District V in Kraków and later as commander of a brigade in the Border Protection Corps (Korpus Ochrony Pogranicza). In 1927 Olszyna-Wilczyński was promoted to the rank of general and appointed commander of the Tenth Infantry Division in Łódź. In January 1938 he was appointed commander of Corps District III in Grodno. During the September 1939 campaign he commanded the operation group Grodno, which organized the defense of the town and the Suwałki region. Captured by Soviet soldiers at the Lithuanian border, Olszyna-Wilczyński was shot dead by them. (WR)

Sources: *PSB*, vol. 24; Tadeusz Kryska-Karski and Stanisław Żurakowski, *Generałowie Polski niepodległej* (London, 1976).

OMAN Ivan (10 September 1929, Zminec, near Škofja Loka), Slovene Peasant Party politician. In 1943 Oman graduated from primary school. For most of his life he worked as a farmer, but thanks to his innate curiosity and talent, he gained considerable knowledge. In the 1980s he repeatedly criticized Yugoslav economic policies at the local self-government meetings in Škofja Loka, gaining authority among the local peasants. In 1989 Oman was co-founder of the Slovene Union of Farmers (Slovenske Kmečke Zveze), a trade organization that later turned into a political party. In the elections of April 1990 Oman became a member of the Presidium of the Slovene republican assembly, and after Slovenia gained independence, in the free elections of December 1992 he won a seat in the assembly. For some time he chaired the Slovenian People's Party (Slovenska Ljudska Stranka), but he left it as a result of conflicts in the leadership. He then joined Slovenian Christian Democracy (Slovenska Krščanska Demokracija [SKD]). A practicing Catholic, Oman is an authority on **Janez Evangelist Krek**. (WR)

Sources: *Enciklopedia Slovenije*, vol. 8 (Ljubljana, 1994); Leopoldina Plut-Progelj and Carole Rogel, *Historical Dictionary of Slovenia* (Lanham, Md., 1996).

OMELIANOVYCH-PAVLENKO Mykhailo (8 December 1878, Tiflis [Tbilisi]–29 May 1952, Paris), commander-in-chief of the Ukrainian Army. During the Russo-Japanese War of 1904–5 Omelianovych-Pavlenko commanded a company. In 1910 he graduated from the general staff school. During World War I he served as commander of a regiment, chief of staff of a corps, and commander of a cadet training school in Odessa. After the February 1917 revolution, he became the commander of a Ukrainian brigade in Yekaterinoslav (Dniepropetrovsk) and later the commander of the Third Riflemen's Division in Poltava. From December 1918 to June 1919 he served as commander of the army of the Western Ukrainian National Republic (Zakhidno-Ukrayins'ka Narodna Republika [ZUNR]). After its defeat in the war against Poland, Omelianovych-Pavlenko went over to the army of the Ukrainian National Republic (Ukrayins'ka Narodna Republika [UNR]) and served as commander of the UNR Zaporozhyan Corps. From December 1919 to November 1920 he served as commander of the UNR army. After the victory of the Bolsheviks, Omelianovych-Pavlenko settled in Prague and became the chairman of the Union of Ukrainian Organizations of War Veterans. After World War II, he served as minister of defense (1945–48) of the UNR government-in-exile and was promoted to general. His publications include *Ukraiinsko-polska viina 1918–1919 rr.* (The Ukrainian-Polish war of 1918–1919; 1929), *Zymovyi pokhid* (Winter campaign; 1934), and two volumes of memoirs published in 1933 and 1935. Omelianovych-Pavlenko's brother Ivan (1881–1962) served as commander of a cavalry division during the Polish-Ukrainian war. (WR)

Sources: *Encyclopedia of Ukraine*, vol. 3 (Toronto, 1993); Matthew Stachiv and Jaroslav Sztendera, eds., *Western Ukraine at the Turning Point of Europe's History, 1918–1923*, vols. 1–2 (New York, 1971); Maciej Kozłowski, *Między Zbruczem i Sanem: Walki o Lwów i Galicję Wschodnią 1918–1919* (Kraków, 1990); Orest Subtelny, *Ukraine: A History* (Toronto, 2000).

ONYSZKIEWICZ Janusz (18 December 1937, Lwów [Lviv]), Polish politician. In 1960 Onyszkiewicz graduated in mathematics from the University of Warsaw (UW), and in 1967 he received a Ph.D. there. He worked as an assistant professor at the UW Department of Mathematics, and in 1976–79 he lectured at the University of Leeds. Later he also taught at other Western universities. A keen mountaineer and speleologist, Onyszkiewicz took part in many expeditions. He was the first to climb Gasherbrum III (26,027 feet) in the Himalayas. Onyszkiewicz took part in the March 1968 student protests at the UW. Active in the democratic opposition of the late 1970s, in 1980–81 he was a member of the Presidium of the Solidarity Region of Mazowsze and also its spokesman. From April to October 1981 he was a spokesman for Solidarity's National Coordination Commission and later a member of the Presidium of its National Commission. During the period of martial law Onyszkiewicz was interned, and in 1983 he was arrested. Amnestied but frequently harassed by the political police, he collaborated with underground Solidarity structures. From 1986 he was a spokesman for the Provisional Coordination Commission and later the National Executive Commission. Onyszkiewicz took part in talks with many Western politicians who came to Poland. In 1988–90 he was a member of the Civic Committee of the Chairman of Solidarity, and in early 1989 he took part in the Round Table Talks. From June 1989 he was an MP on behalf of the Civic Parliamentary Club and later of the Democratic Union and the Union of Freedom. In 1990–92 Onyszkiewicz was deputy minister and from July 1992 to September 1993 minister of national defense in the government of **Hanna Suchocka**. He was minister of national defense again in the government of **Jerzy Buzek** from October 1997 to June 2000. In this role he contributed to the Polish entry into NATO in March 1999. Married to the grand-daughter of **Józef Piłsudski**,

Onyszkiewicz authored several works in mathematics. In July 2004 he was elected deputy speaker of the European Parliament. (AF)

Sources: *Nasi w Sejmie i Senacie* (Warsaw, 1990); Jan Skórzyński, *Ugoda i rewolucja: Władza i opozycja 1985–1989* (Warsaw, 1995); *Opozycja w PRL: Słownik biograficzny 1956–89* (Warsaw, 2000); Antoni Dudek, *Pierwsze lata III Rzeczpospolitej 1989–2001* (Kraków, 2002).

OPLETAL Jan (31 December 1915, Lhota, near Náklo–11 November 1939, Prague), Czech medical student. Born into the family of a forester, in 1934 Opletal graduated from high school in Litovel. After doing his military service, he successfully passed his exams and was admitted to the Medical School of Charles University in Prague. He was a member and then vice-chairman of the student self-government in the dormitories. On 28 October 1939—the anniversary of independence—Opletal took part in a demonstration held in the center of Prague against the Nazi occupiers. At the intersection of Žitná and Mezibranská Streets, he was shot in the stomach by a German policeman. Taken to a clinic, he died two weeks later. His funeral, on 15 November 1939, turned into another demonstration, which became a pretext for the Nazis to close down Czech universities two days later. Several student leaders were executed by a firing squad, and 1,200 students were sent to concentration camps. Opletal became a symbol of Czech resistance to occupation, both Nazi and Communist. Fifty years after his death, on 17 November 1989, Prague students, with the permission of the authorities, organized a mourning march to commemorate his sacrifice. This march turned into an anti-Communist demonstration that was dispersed by the police. This became the proverbial snowball that set off an avalanche toward the Velvet Revolution, which brought down the Communist regime in Czechoslovakia within a month. (PU)

Sources: *ČBS*; Jerzy Tomaszewski, *Czechosłowacja* (Warsaw, 1997); *Kdo byl kdo v našich dějinach ve 20. stoleti*, vol. 2 (Prague, 1998).

ORBÁN Viktor (31 May 1963, Alcsúton, near Székesfehérvár), Hungarian politician. Born into a poor Calvinist peasant family, in 1981 Orbán graduated from Blanka Teleki High School in Székesfehérvár. After serving in the army in 1981–82, he enrolled in the Department of Law of Eötvös University in Budapest. In the spring of 1983 Orbán co-founded the College of Legal and Social Sciences in Budapest (later the Bibó Collegium), designed according to the pre–1939 pattern of exclusive colleges for poor but especially talented youth. In 1986 he started

an uncensored quarterly, *Századvég*, which published articles contesting communism. On 30 March 1988 Orbán was co-founder of the Alliance of Young Democrats (Fiatal Demokraták Szövetsége [FIDESZ]; as of 1995, the Hungarian Civic Party [FIDESZ]), and in October 1988 he was elected its chairman. Orbán's master's thesis on self-government was based on the Polish Solidarity experience. During the ceremonial funeral of **Imre Nagy** and his aides in Budapest on 16 June 1989, Orbán made the most radical speech, demanding the withdrawal of Soviet troops from Hungary. In the fall of 1989 he took part in the Hungarian Round Table, but he refused to sign the final accord with the Communists because he thought it too compromising.

After the formation of the first freely emerged government of **József Antall** in May 1990, Orbán and FIDESZ stayed in the opposition; for instance, they criticized the government projects of land restitution to the former owners. In September 1992 Orbán became deputy chairman of the Liberal International. In 1992 he and his party were at the peak of their popularity, but when they refused to join the Democratic Charter (Demokratikus Charta) of the opposition parties (including the post-Communists), which claimed that democracy was in danger, Orbán and FIDESZ lost in the rankings. Orbán barely made it into the parliament in the elections of May 1994. In 1994–98 he chaired the parliamentary commission for European integration. At the same time he planned the transformation of FIDESZ from a liberal into a liberal-conservative party and a unification of the whole non-nationalist right under his leadership. After victorious parliamentary elections, on 6 July 1998 Orbán became prime minister. During his term talks were finalized on Hungary's access to the European Union, while the economy recovered and the negative demographic tendencies of the late twentieth century were reversed. Orbán spoke in defense of the Hungarian minorities in Romanian and Slovakia, creating some tensions in relations with these countries. In the parliamentary elections of April 2002 the FIDESZ won the largest number of votes (49 percent), but it was too little to form a government. The post-Communists joined with the Alliance of Free Democrats, and Orbán became the leader of the opposition. (MS)

Sources: László Kéri, *Orbán Viktor* (Budapest, 1994); P. Kende, *Viktor* (Budapest, 2002); *Rzeczpospolita*, 22 April 2002; *Eastern Europe and the Commonwealth of Independent States 1999* (London, 1999); www.kancellaria.gov.hu.

ORDASS Lajos [originally Wolf] (6 February 1901, Torzsa [now in Yugoslavia]–14 August 1978, Budapest), Hungarian Lutheran bishop. Ordass was the son of a teacher. After graduating from high school, he studied theology in Budapest, Wittenberg, and Sopron. In 1924 he took holy orders. At the end of the 1920s he went on a scholarly journey to Sweden and later worked as a military chaplain. In 1931 he became the pastor of the Protestant community in Cegléd. In 1937 he was appointed dean of the superintendency and in 1939 chairman of the consistory for the region of Bánya. In 1941 Ordass went to Budapest, where he became pastor of a congregation in one of the districts of the capital. In his articles he called for the revival of the Lutheran Church and paid much attention to social issues. He sharply criticized National Socialism. After the Germans invaded Hungary in March 1944, Ordass changed his German name. He helped to save Jews during the time of their persecutions. In August 1945 Ordass was elected bishop of the superintendency of the Lutheran Church in Bánya. Under Communist rule Ordass defended the independence of his church and stood for freedom of religion. As he opposed the nationalization of church-owned schools, he was placed under house arrest at the end of August 1948. In September 1948, along with other secular Lutheran bishops, Ordass was arrested on trumped-up charges and sentenced to two years' imprisonment. He was released in May 1950. In April 1950, on the basis of a decree by the state authorities, the ecclesiastic disciplinary court deprived Ordass of his post as bishop. On 5 October 1956 the sentence he had received in 1948 was quashed; therefore, on 31 October 1956 he assumed the office of bishop of the South Region of the Church. In June 1958 Ordass was again removed from his office. In 1957 he was elected first vice-chairman of the Lutheran World Federation, and in 1963 he became an honorary member of its executive committee. He was granted honorary doctorates from universities in Allentown, Pennsylvania, and Reykjavik, Iceland. He was a symbol of courageous resistance to Communist religious persecution. In 1990 Ordass was rehabilitated in legal terms and in 1991 according to ecclesiastic law. (JT)

Sources: *Magyar Életrajzi Lexikon* (Budapest, 1994); *A magyar forradalom és szabadságharc enciklopédiája* (Budapest, 1999).

ÖRKÉNY István (5 April 1912, Budapest–24 June 1979, Budapest), Hungarian writer. The son of a pharmacist, Örkény studied chemistry but graduated in pharmacy from Budapest University in 1934. He published his first novellas in the 1930s; his first volume of short stories, *Tengertánc* (Ocean dance), appeared in 1941. In 1941 Örkény received a diploma in chemical engineering from the Technical University in Budapest. In 1942 he was inducted into the labor service units and sent to the eastern front. Taken prisoner by the Soviets in 1943, he did not return to Budapest until 1946. Örkény's experiences of 1946–47 became the subjects of one drama and two novels. Örkény worked in a theater, and in 1954 he also got a job in a publishing house specializing in belles lettres books. At the beginning of the 1950s he briefly identified with communism, complying with the canons of Socialist realism, but as early as 1952 he was attacked as the author of *Lila tinta* (Lilac ink). From 1955 to 1956 Örkény took part in actions organized by writers (mainly party members) who protested the dismissal of **Imre Nagy** as prime minister. In September 1956 he joined the leadership of the Association of Hungarian Writers (AHW).

After the outbreak of the 1956 revolution, Örkény condemned the propaganda role of Hungarian Radio, using words that would become proverbial: "We lied by night; we lied by day; we lied on all wavelengths." On 10 November 1956 Örkény was refused political asylum at the Polish Embassy in Budapest. At the beginning of December in Budapest, as a member and translator for an AHW delegation, Örkény met the ambassador of India, Krishna Menon, whom the AHW wanted to ask to be a mediator between the Soviet Union and Hungary. In September 1957, along with five associates, Örkény signed a self-critical open letter about his work before and during the revolution. Despite this, in 1957 a ban was placed on the publication of his works, and he worked as a pharmacist until 1963. From the mid-1960s onwards his works were published and staged again. Örkény's writing is characterized by a grotesque style. In 1966 he published his first "one-minute short stories"—prose miniatures—often translated into foreign languages; with these he started a new literary genre. Örkény's most famous works are *Macskajáték* (1963; *Catsplay: A tragicomedy in two acts*, 1976) and *Tóték* (1967; *The Toth Family*, 1982). The novel *Pisti a vérzivatarban* (Pisti in a bloodbath; 1973) was also very popular. Örkény's memoirs, *Noteszlapok 1956-ból* (Pages from the diary of 1956; 1991), were published posthumously. (JT)

Sources: *A magyar forradalom és szabadságharc enciklopédiája*, CD-ROM (Budapest, 1999); *Ki kicsoda 2000* (Budapest, 2001); *Magyar Nagylexikon*, vol. 14 (Budapest, 2002); Peter Müller, *A groteszk dramaturgiája* (Budapest, 1990); *Örkény István emlékkönyv* (Budapest, 1995); István B. Szabó, *Örkény* (Budapest, 1997).

ORZECHOWSKI Marian (24 October 1931, Radom), Polish Communist activist. Orzechowski studied history at the university in Leningrad. From 1952 he was a member of the Polish United Workers' Party (Polska Zjednoczona Partia Robotnicza [PUWP]). From 1955 he worked at the

University of Wrocław. In 1969–72 he chaired its Institute of Political Science, from 1971 he was a professor, and in 1971–75 he was rector of the university. He published on the Marxist theory of the workers' movement in Poland. In July 1981 Orzechowski joined the PUWP Central Committee (CC). Thought dogmatic and close to the hardliner faction of **Tadeusz Grabski**, from October 1981 to November 1983 he was CC secretary and, in 1982–83, secretary general of the Provisional National Council of the Patriotic Movement of National Reconstruction (Patriotyczny Ruch Odrodzenia Narodowego [PRON]), a Communist-controlled imitation of national agreement. Until 1984 Orzechowski was the PRON secretary general and until 1987 a member of its Presidium. From November 1983 to July 1986 he was a deputy member and then, until January 1990, a member of the CC Politburo. In 1984–86 he was rector of the Academy of Social Sciences of the PUWP CC in Warsaw. From November 1985 to June 1988 he was minister of foreign affairs, trying to reactivate foreign relations after Poland's years of isolation during the period of martial law. From June 1988 he was CC secretary again. Turning pragmatic in the late 1980s, Orzechowski had a considerable influence on the ideological modification of PUWP activities. In the elections of June 1989 he won a seat in the parliament. Believed to be a rival of **Mieczysław Rakowski** in the succession to General **Wojciech Jaruzelski**, who gave up the party leadership after being elected president, Orzechowski lost and left the CC Secretariat in July 1989. He became head of the PUWP parliamentary club, and after the party was dissolved in January 1990, he continued as head of the parliamentary club of the Democratic Left until the fall of 1991. Later Orzechowski retired from politics. (PK)

Sources: *Mołdawa; Kto jest kim w Polsce? Informator biograficzny* (Warsaw, 1984); Jan Skórzyński, *Ugoda i rewolucja: Władza i opozycja 1985–1989* (Warsaw, 1995); Włodzimierz Janowski and Aleksander Kochański, *Informator o strukturze i obsadzie personalnej centralnego aparatu PZPR 1948–1990* (Warsaw, 2000).

OSADCHUK Bohdan (1 August 1920, Kołomyja [Kolomyia]), Ukrainian Sovietologist. The son of an activist of the Communist Party of Western Ukraine, Osadchuk studied at the University of Berlin (1941–45) and then at the Free Ukrainian University (FUU). From 1958 he lectured on East European history at the Freie Universität in Berlin, where he became a professor and director of the Institute of East European Studies in 1978. He also lectured at the FUU and was the dean of the Department of Law and Social Studies (1983–85) and deputy rector. For several decades Osadchuk wrote for the leading Ukrainian periodicals, such as *Ukraiinski Visti*, and for German language papers, such as *Die Zürcher Zeitung* and *Der Tagesspiegel*, commenting on Soviet developments. Thought to be one of the leading authorities on the Soviet system and on Soviet Ukraine in particular, Osadchuk maintained good relations with Polish émigré journalists and politicians, and he regularly wrote for the Paris monthly *Kultura*. In 1985 he became a member of the Taras Shevchenko Research Society. After the fall of Communist rule in Poland and after the Ukrainian declaration of independence, Osadchuk frequently visited both countries, encouraging Polish-Ukrainian reconciliation. Osadchuk authored several works, including *Die Entwicklung der Kommunistischen Parteien Ostmitteleuropas* (The development of the Communist parties of East Central Europe; 1962) and *Ukraiina, Polshcha, svit: Vybrany reportazhi ta statti*; Ukraine, Poland, the world: Selected reports and works; 2001). Osadchuk also co-edited *Der Sowjet-Kommunismus* (Soviet communism; 1964). (WR)

Sources: *Encyclopedia of Ukraine*, vol. 3 (Toronto, 1993); Ann Lencyk Pawliczko, *Ukraine and Ukrainians throughout the World* (Toronto, 1994); "Ukraiński Giedroyć," *Rzeczpospolita*, 28 October 2002.

OSADCHYI Mykhailo (22 March 1936, Kurmany, near Sumy–5 July 1994, Lviv), Ukrainian writer and dissident. Born into a family of kolkhoz farm workers, in 1958 Osadchyi graduated in journalism from Lviv University. In 1962 he became a member of the Communist Party of Ukraine (CPU) and worked as a journalist in Lviv television, press consultant to the Lviv committee of the CPU, and editor of a university newspaper. In 1965 he began lecturing in the Department of Journalism of Lviv University. A member of the Association of Ukrainian Journalists, Osadchyi earned a doctorate in 1965. He wrote critical pieces and poems, but the entire printing of the first collection of his poems, *Misiachne pole* (Moon field; 1965), was destroyed. Arrested for "anti-Soviet agitation and propaganda" in August 1965, Osadchyi was sentenced to two years in a labor camp. He served his sentence in Mordovia. After his release, he could get only a blue-collar job at an institution for the deaf. Osadchyi wrote two novels: *Geniy smikhu, abo zustrich iz vozhdem* (Genius of laughter, or a meeting with the chief), about Ostap Vyshnya, a Ukrainian journalist from the 1920s, and the autobiographical *Bilmo* (Cataract), which was devoted to his experiences in a labor camp. The latter was published in the underground press (1971) and in the West (1976) and brought him international fame. Arrested again in January 1972, in September 1972 Osadchyi was sentenced to seven years in a labor camp and three years in exile. He again served his labor camp term in Sosnovka in Mordovia and his exile term in the village of Milva in the Komi Autonomous SSR. After returning to Lviv, Osadchyi did various blue-collar jobs. In November 1987 he was co-founder of the Ukrainian Association of the Independent Creative Intelligentsia, and in 1988 he edited the underground periodical *Katedra*. Osadchyi was beaten by unknown assailants and repeatedly threatened with a new trial. In 1991 he received a postdoctoral degree from the Ukrainian Free University in Munich, and in 1993 he became an associate professor in the Department of Journalism of Lviv University. An honorary member of the Swiss branch of the PEN Club, Osadchyi also published two collections of poems: *Quos ego* (1979) and *Skytskyi oltar* (Scythian altar; 1990). (TS)

Sources: *Encyclopedia of Ukraine*, vol. 3 (Toronto, 1993); Ludmila Alekseieva, *Istoriia inakomysliia v SSSR* (Vilnius and Moscow, 1992); Heorhiy Kasianov, *Nezhodni: Ukraiinska intelihentsiia v rusi oporu 1960–80 rokiv* (Kiev, 1995); Anatoliy Rusnachenko, *Natsionalno-vyzvolnyi rukh v Ukraïni* (Kiev, 1998).

OSÓBKA-MORAWSKI Edward, pseudonyms "Janusz" and "Tadeusz Wróblewski" (5 October 1909, Bliżyn, Kielce region–9 January 1997, Warsaw), Polish political activist. Osóbka-Morawski studied at the Free Polish University in Warsaw and at Warsaw University, but he did not complete his studies in law there. He worked in the municipal administration and in the cooperative movement. In 1928 he joined the Polish Socialist Party (Polska Partia Socjalistyczna [PPS]). During the Nazi occupation he was an activist in a secret leftist organization called the Polish Socialists (Polscy Socjaliści). In 1943 he helped to found the Workers' Party of Polish Socialists (Robotnicza Partia Polskich Socjalistów [RPPS]). In January 1944 he became chairman of the RPPS. He supported close cooperation with the Communist Polish Workers' Party (Polska Partia Robotnicza [PPR]). A prewar acquaintance of **Bolesław Bierut**, on 1 January 1944 Osóbka-Morawski joined the National Home Council (Krajowa Rada Narodowa [KRN]), becoming Bierut's deputy. In March 1944 he was head of a KRN delegation to Moscow, where, thanks to the support of **Wanda Wasilewska**, he gained Stalin's acceptance and was appointed chairman of the Polish Committee of National Liberation (Polski Komitet Wyzwolenia Narodowego [PKWN]), which was established on 21 July 1944 in Moscow. On 27 July Osóbka-Morawski signed an agreement on a new Polish-Soviet border, ceding the Polish eastern territories to the Soviet Union; it was a precondition for the PKWN's being allowed to go to Poland. At the end of July Osóbka-Morawski arrived in Lublin, assuming power as head of the Polish executive

authorities endorsed by the Soviet Union and head of the ministry of foreign affairs. Although he was completely obedient to the Kremlin and to the Polish Communists, during talks with Stalin he attempted to persuade Stalin to leave Lwów (Lviv) within Polish territory, and he defended Poland's right to keep a part of the Białowieża Forest and Stettin (Szczecin).

As some of the RPPS activists opposed subordination to the Communists, in September 1944 Osóbka-Morawski effected a split within this party and established a new PPS under the tutelage of the PPR. From September 1944 to December 1948 he served as a member of the Chief Council and the Central Executive Committee of the PPS and a member of the PPS Political Commission. On 31 December 1944 he became prime minister of the Provisional Government, which was initially recognized only by the Soviet Union, but in the spring of 1945 it was also recognized by Yugoslavia, Czechoslovakia, and France. In this role Osóbka-Morawski endorsed the first stage of the Sovietization process of Poland, at a time when the Red Army was marching into Poland's territory.

Under agreements reached by the Big Three, on 28 June 1945 the Provisional Government of National Unity (Tymczasowy Rząd Jedności Narodowej [TRJN]) was established, and Osóbka-Morawski became its prime minister. During the so-called people's referendum in June 1946 and in the rigged elections to the Assembly on 19 January 1947, he helped to consolidate the new political system. From 1947 to 1952 he was an MP. He hoped for an independent role in governing Poland, but after democratic opposition had been suppressed, he was no longer useful to the Kremlin or to the Polish Communists. In the new government, established in February 1947, Osóbka-Morawski was offered the minor portfolio of minister of public administration. As he called for the independence of the PPS, he was removed from influence at a time when the PPS was being absorbed by the PPR. After the establishment of the (Communist) Polish United Workers' Party (Polska Zjednoczona Partia Robotnicza [PUWP]) in December 1948, he was dismissed from his ministerial position. He became director of the Central Board of Health Resorts, which he held until 1968. From 1956 to 1970 Osóbka-Morawski again was a member of the PUWP, but his attempt to enter parliament on the ticket of the National Unity Front ended in failure. In 1968 he was forced to take early retirement. After 1989 he unsuccessfully tried to reenter politics and undertook to establish a revived PPS. In 1990 he became chairman of the marginal Provisional Central Executive Committee of the PPS. Osóbka-Morawski was the author of the memoirs *Trudne drogi* (Difficult ways; 1992). (WD/WR)

Sources: Mołdawa; Marek Łatyński, *Nie paść na kolana: Szkice o opozycji lat czterdziestych* (Warsaw, 1987); Krystyna Kersten, *Narodziny systemu władzy: Polska 1943–1948* (Poznań, 1990); *Polska-ZSRR: Struktury podległości. Dokumenty WKP(b), 1944–1948* (Warsaw, 1995); Eleonora Syzdek and Bolesław Syzdek, *Cena władzy zależnej* (Warsaw, 2001).

OSTAPENKO Serhiy (1881, Volhynia–1937?), Ukrainian economist and politician. After graduating from a cadet training school in Kiev in 1909, Ostapenko studied and worked at an institute of commerce in Kiev. In his youth he joined the Socialist Revolutionary Party, but he took part in the events of 1917–20 as a nonparty economist. In 1917 he became a member of the Ukrainian Central Rada (Council). In January and February 1918 he took part in the German-Ukrainian negotiations in Brest-Litovsk. During the rule of Hetman **Pavlo Skoropadskyi**, Ostapenko was a member of a delegation that negotiated peace terms with Soviet Russia. He served as minister of trade and industry in the government of **Volodymyr Chekhivsky** (December 1918–February 1919), which was the first government of the Ukrainian National Republic (Ukrayinska Narodna Republika [UNR]) after the overthrow of the hetman. Ostapenko was a member of a delegation that conducted negotiations on military aid for the Ukraine with the commanders of the French expeditionary corps in Odessa. In order to finalize these negotiations, the UNR authorities decided to dismiss representatives of Socialist parties from the government, believing they were not credible to the French. On 13 February 1919, after Chekhivsky and the president of the UNR Directory, **Volodymyr Vynnychenko**, resigned, Ostapenko became prime minister of a government supported by the republican right wing—that is, the Ukrainian Party of Socialists-Federalists, the Ukrainian Party of Pro-Independence Socialists, and the People's Republicans. The Bolshevik victories over the UNR Army and the French decision to limit aid to the Ukraine undermined the position of the UNR government. Ostapenko's government lost the support of the workers' soviets. Pogroms of Jews, in which UNR troops took part, broke out throughout the country. As a result of the withdrawal of the French troops and opposition from the Socialist parties, Ostapenko's government collapsed on 9 April 1919. After the Bolshevik victory, he remained in the Ukraine. In 1921 he was sentenced for being a member of the Party of Socialist Revolutionaries, but he was soon released. Ostapenko taught statistics and demography at the universities in Kamyanets Podilskyi and Kharkiv. He published articles in *Chervonyi shliakh* and other periodicals. In 1937 Ostapenko was arrested and executed by a firing squad. Ostapenko left a number of publications in the field of foreign trade in agricultural products and wrote many textbooks, including *Ekonomichna heohrafiia Ukraiiny* (Economic geography of Ukraine; 1919) and *Politychna ekonomiia* (Political economy; 1920). (TS)

Sources: *Encyclopedia of Ukraine*, vol. 3 (Toronto, 1993); *Dovidnyk z istorii Ukraiiny*, vol. 2 (Kiev, 1995); Paul R. Magocsi, *A History of Ukraine* (Seattle, 1996); Orest Subtelny, *Ukraine: A History* (Toronto, 2000); Stanisław Kulczycki, ed., *Uriady Ukraiiny u XX st.* (Kiev, 2001).

OSUSKÝ Štefan (31 March 1889, Brezová pod Bradom–27 September 1973, Washington, D.C.), Slovak lawyer, journalist, diplomat, and politician. In 1906 Osuský emigrated to the United States, where, after graduating from high school, he studied philosophy, theology, law, and the natural sciences at the University of Chicago. In 1915 he began working as an attorney. Osuský supported the pro-independence movement of the Czechs and Slovaks and favored the idea of establishing Czechoslovakia. In 1916 he became vice-president of the Slovak League in the United States and established contacts with **Tomáš Garrigue Masaryk**, **Edvard Beneš**, and **Milan Štefánik**. From 1917 to 1918 Osuský directed a Czechoslovak press agency in Geneva. Along with Štefánik, he helped to organize the Czechoslovak Legions in Italy. In October 1918 he became the first ambassador of the independent Czechoslovak Republic to London.

In the interwar period Osuský played an active role in shaping Czechoslovak foreign policy. In 1919, as secretary general of the Czechoslovak delegation, he attended the Paris Peace Conference. He also had much influence on the provisions of the 1920 Treaty of Trianon with Hungary, and he signed treaties with Bulgaria and Turkey. From 1921 to 1940 Osuský was ambassador to France, and from 1920 to 1930 he was also a representative at the League of Nations. At that time he represented the interests of Czechoslovakia, Greece, Yugoslavia, Poland, and Romania in the Reparation Commission of the League of Nations. From 1922 to 1936 he served as chairman of the Control Commission of the League of Nations. In the early 1920s he also played an important role in the establishment of the Little Entente (Czechoslovakia, Yugoslavia, and Romania). Initially a supporter of "Czechoslovakism" and a critic of the Slovak drive for autonomy, Osuský gradually began to promote the cause of equal rights for the Czechs and the Slovaks within the state, which led to conflicts with President Beneš. After the Slovak Republic was established under the tutelage of the Third Reich, Osuský refused to hand over the Czechoslovak Embassy building in Paris and began to organize anti-Nazi resistance in France. Initially Osuský was Beneš's main rival for the role of leader of the Czechoslovak resistance in exile.

From 1939 to 1940 he was a member of the Czechoslovak National Committee in Paris, and from 1940 to 1942 he was minister of the Czechoslovak provisional government and a member of the Czechoslovak State Council in London. However, he criticized Beneš's policy, and their relationship deteriorated further. As a result, Osuský lost all his positions in the Czechoslovak government-in-exile. When the war ended, he did not return to Czechoslovakia but went to the United States, where, after the February 1948 Communist coup in Czechoslovakia, he cooperated with the new political émigrés, including **Josef Lettrich**, in the Council of Free Czechoslovakia. Osuský wrote many political works, including a biography of Štefánik and Masaryk, *Reparace* (Reparations; 1935); *Pravda vítazí*; Victorious truth; 1942); and *Úloha Československa w Európe* (Czechoslovakia's task in Europe; 1955). (PU)

Sources: *ČBS; Biographisches Lexikon*, vol. 3; *Kdo byl kdo v našich dejinách ve 20. století*, vol. 2 (Prague, 1998); *Politická elita meziválečného Československa 1918–1938: Kdo byl kdo za první republiky* (Prague, 1998); Slavomír Michalek, *Diplomat Štefan Osuský, 1889–1973* (Bratislava, 1999).

OTČENÁŠEK Karel (13 April 1920, Český Mezeřic, near Opočno), Czech bishop. Otčenášek graduated from the archiepiscopal high school in Prague and left for Rome to study theology. He graduated from the Lateran University, and in March 1945 he was ordained. After the war he returned to Czechoslovakia and started working as a minister in the parishes of Tynec nad Labou, Horni Rovne, near Pardubice, Žamberk, and Vrchlabi. From 1949 he was deputy director of the theological seminary in Hradec Králove, and on 30 April 1950 he was secretly consecrated bishop by the bishop of Hradec Králove, Mořic Picha. Otčenášek also became apostolic administrator of this diocese. The Communist authorities did not recognize these decisions and did not allow him to act. For the "illegal" consecration he was interned in Želiva Monastery in 1951. In 1953 he was imprisoned in Pardubice and soon sentenced to thirteen years in prison. Amnestied in 1963, he could find work only as a blue-collar laborer in a dairy. Thanks to the efforts by Pope John XXIII, in 1965 Otčenášek was allowed to work as a minister in a countryside parish in Northern Bohemia, but he was constantly harassed and subjected to eavesdropping by the political police. During the Prague Spring in 1968 he was rehabilitated and allowed to work in his archdiocese. In 1973 he was forced to leave Hradec Králove again. He settled in Usti nad Labou, where he was a parish administrator. He kept in touch with the underground Catholic Church and the democratic opposition. In 1987 Otčenášek was an adviser to Cardinal

Frántišek Tomašek, who worked out a ten-year program of "spiritual renaisssance of the Fatherland" that contributed to the renewal of Czech Catholicism on the eve of the Velvet Revolution in the fall of 1989. Otčenášek returned to Hradec Králove on 21 December 1989 after the fall of Communist rule. His ceremonial ingress took place in the Hradec Králove cathedral on 27 February 1990. In the Czech Episcopate he presided over the Iustitia et Pax Commission. To honor his uncompromising behavior during the Communist rule, in March 1995 Charles University in Prague awarded him the Golden Medal of Memory. In April 1997 Otčenášek welcomed Pope **John Paul II** in Hradec Králove. In July 1998 the Pope accepted his retirement, and in September 1998 he appointed Otčenášek titular archbishop. (AGr)

Sources: Vaclav Vaško, *Neumlčená: Kronika katolické Cirkve v Českolovensku po druhe světove válce*, vol. 2 (Prague, 1990); Tadeusz Fitych, *Kościół milczenia dzisiaj: Wypowiedzi księży biskupów Czech i Moraw w pięć lat po odzyskaniu niepodległości* (Prague and Nowa Ruda, 1995); *Annuario Pontifici, 2002*; Polish Catholic Information Agency News, 26 April 1997 and 24 September 1998.

OTTLIK Géza (9 May 1912, Budapest–9 October 1990, Budapest), Hungarian writer. His father, a clerk in the Ministry of Interior, died when Ottlik was a child. Ottlik had a modest childhood and was educated at cadet training schools. After graduating from the Department of Mathematics and Physics of Budapest University, he began working for the daily *Magyar Hirlap*, editing the bridge column. During World War II he served in the anti-aircraft forces. In 1945 he began working for Hungarian radio as a playwright and literary editor. In 1945–57 he served as secretary of the Hungarian PEN Club. Ottlik had made his literary debut as a student. During the war his first novels were published: *Hamisjátekosok* (False players; 1941) and *Hajnali Háztetők* (Roofs at dawn; 1944). An opponent of Socialist realism, in the late 1940s and early 1950s Ottlik was sidetracked as a writer and earned his living by doing translations. He rose to fame as the author of *Iskola a határon* (1959; *School at the Frontier*, 1966), which is one of the most frequently translated Hungarian novels. In it, he depicted his experiences in cadet schools and analyzed such concepts as patriotism, group solidarity, and individual autonomy. Another famous novel of his, *Buda* (1993), also takes place in a military school community. Ottlik's interests in bridge led him to publish *Kalandos hajózás a bridz ismeretlen vizein* (Adventurous sailing over the uncharted waters of bridge; 1979), which is one of the most popular books on this game in the world. (MS)

Sources: *Mały słownik pisarzy węgierskich* (Warsaw, 1977); Balázs Lengyel, *Ami volt: Van, Ottlik Géza köszöntése* (Budapest, 1986); Mihály Szegedy-Maszák, *Ottlik Géza* (Budapest, 1994); *Ottlik emlékkönyv* (Budapest, 1996).

OZGA-MICHALSKI Józef (8 March 1919, Bieliny, near Kielce–10 February 2002, Warsaw), Polish Communist peasant activist and writer. In 1939 Ozga-Michalski graduated from a high school in Kielce. In 1936 he joined the Union of Rural Youth of the Republic of Poland called Wici (Związek Młodzieży Wiejskiej Rzeczypospolitej Polskiej–Wici [ZMW RP–Wici]). During the Nazi occupation he co-founded the Peasant Party–People's Will (Stronnictwo Ludowe–Wola Ludu [SL–People's Will]) in the region of Kielce. He also cooperated with the (Communist) People's Army and with Soviet partisans. He was a deputy to the National Home Council (Krajowa Rada Narodowa [KRN]). After the Red Army entered Poland in the summer of 1944, Ozga-Michalski became secretary of the Provincial National Council in the Sandomierz bridgehead area. In September 1944 he joined the Provisional Main Board of the Peasant Party (Stronnictwo Ludowe [SL]), established by the activists of the SL–People's Will and subordinated to the Communists.

From 1945 to 1947 Ozga-Michalski served as chairman of the Provincial National Council in Kielce and vice-chairman of the SL Provincial Board, and from December 1946 to April 1947 he was chairman of the Wici National Democratization Committee, which sought to subordinate the organization to the Communists through a "unification" of the Polish youth movement. In July 1948 Ozga-Michalski became deputy chairman of the Main Board of the Union of Polish Youth (Związek Młodzieży Polskiej [ZMP]), taking an active part in the Stalinization of Poland. After his party merged with the remnants of the Polish Peasant Party (Polskie Stronnictwo Ludowe [PSL]) in November 1949, he became a member of the Supreme Council and the Chief Committee of the United Peasant Party (Zjednoczone Stronnictwo Ludowe [ZSL]). From December 1956 to December 1980 Ozga-Michalski was deputy chairman of the ZSL Chief Committee. From 1944 to 1952 he was chairman of the Main Board of the Union of Peasant Mutual Aid Associations, and from 1959 to 1962 he was chairman of the Central Union of Agricultural Associations. From 1947 to 1989 he was an MP, from 1952 to 1956 he was deputy speaker of the parliament, and from March 1972 to March 1976 he was deputy chairman of the Council of State. He was also a leading activist of the Society of Atheists and Freethinkers. At a session of the parliament in April 1968 Ozga-Michalski particularly viciously attacked members of the Catholic parliamentary group called Znak. Ozga-Michalski made his literary debut in 1937, and the following year he published the volume of novels *Łysica gwarzy: Godki Świętokrzyskie* (Łysica's stories: Legends from the Holy Cross Mountains). After the war Ozga-Michalski published many collections of stories and poems, including *Oberek świętokrzyski* (Oberek of the Holy Cross Mountains; 1945), *Lutnia wiejska* (Village lute; 1954), and *Sowizdrzał świętokrzyski* (A Picaro of the Holy Cross Mountains; 1972). (WD)

Sources: Mołdawa; *Słownik biograficzny działaczy ruchu ludowego* (Warsaw, 1989); Jerzy Eisler, *Marzec 1968* (Warsaw, 1991).

P

PACEPA Ion Mihai (28 October 1928, Bucharest), head of Romanian Communist intelligence. After graduating in chemistry from Bucharest Polytechnic University in 1951, Pacepa started working in special services. In 1956–64 he worked in intelligence in (among other places) West Germany. In 1959 he became head of technical intelligence, and in 1961, head of foreign intelligence. From 1971 Pacepa was head of the Foreign Information Directorate (Direcţia de Informaţii Externe) and deputy minister of interior with the rank of general. He developed scholarly intelligence and "operations of influence." He was one of the most trusted aides of **Nicolae Ceauşescu** and was his personal friend. At the top of his career in July 1978, during a trip to Germany, Pacepa fled to the United States, where he received political asylum and protection. During a three-year interrogation he supplied the American services with a lot of valuable information on the functioning of the Ceauşescu regime and the Soviet system. Pacepa's move not only shocked Ceauşescu and caused an extensive purge in the party and state apparatus, but also destroyed the Romanian foreign espionage network. In August 1978 Pacepa was sentenced to death in absentia. Romanian agents made numerous efforts to kill him. In 1985 in France Pacepa published an open letter to his daughter, Dana, who stayed in Romania and was not allowed to emigrate. In 1987 in the United States he published his memoirs, *Red Horizons*, in which he disclosed the criminal operations and hypocrisy of the Ceauşescu regime. After the fall of Ceauşescu, most of Pacepa's information was confirmed. In view of a great deal of continuity of power, Pacepa was not welcome in Romania. It was only on 7 June 1999 that his death sentence was annulled. (ASK)

Sources: *Keesing's Archive*, 1978; Mihai Pelin, "Scripta manent," *Lumea*, 2002, no. 9.

PACHA Augustin (26 November 1870, Maritzfeld [Mǎureni], Banat–4 November 1954, Timişoara), Roman Catholic bishop of Timişoara. The son of a German shoemaker from Banat, Pacha graduated from high school in Szeged, and then he studied theology in Temesvár [now Timişoara]. In 1893 he was ordained and later worked in various parishes in the Transylvanian countryside. In 1900 he became secretary to the bishop of Csanad, and in 1912, diocesan chancellor. After World War I, when Banat was incorporated into Romania, in 1923 Pacha was appointed apostolic administrator of the Romanian part of the Csanad diocese. On 16 October he was consecrated bishop of a newly established Timişoara diocese. While in the Kingdom of Hungary Roman Catholicism was a privileged religion, in Romania it became a religion of the Hungarian and German minority, exposed to Romanization policies of the Bucharest government. On 11 June 1929 Romania and the Holy See signed a concordat that improved conditions for the Catholic ministry. In his pastoral work, Pacha enjoyed the support of the German and Hungarian Episcopates, but it provided grounds for Romanian accusations that he had external ties. After the Nazi takeover in Germany and during growing pressure from the Third Reich on Romania in the late 1930s, Pacha's cooperation with the German Church was even more troublesome, but he tried to maintain independence from political pressures.

After the postwar Communist takeover Pacha's position grew even more complicated. The Communists sought every pretext to eliminate all religious institutions. In Pacha's case this was his connection with Romanian Germans. Pacha became the permanent target of hate campaigns in which he was accused of a "hatred of democracy." On the basis of a decree of September 1948 the number of Roman Catholic dioceses was reduced to two, and Pacha was removed from Timişoara. In June 1950 the eighty-year-old bishop was arrested and accused of espionage. Under brutal pressure he confessed to having been active in favor of Germany and to having taken part in an alleged "Vatican plot" since 1923. On 17 September 1951 he was sentenced to eighteen years in prison. Among other places, he worked on the construction of the Danube–Black Sea Canal. As a result he lost his sight. In 1954 Pacha was released and died soon thereafter. (WR)

Sources: *Biographisches Lexikon*, vol. 3; Nikolaus Engelmann, *Hirte seines Volkes: Aus dem Leben und Wirken des Temesvarer Bischofs Dr. Theol. H. C. Augustin Pacha* (Munich, 1955); Alexander Cretzianu, *Captive Romania* (New York, 1956); Kaspar Hügel, *Das Banater deutsche Schulwesen in Rumänien von 1918 bis 1944* (Munich, 1968); Robert L. Wolff, *The Balkans in Our Times* (New York, 1974).

PADEREWSKI Ignacy Jan (18 November 1860, Kuryłówka, Podolia–29 June 1941, New York), Polish pianist, composer, and politician. At the age of twelve Paderewski entered the Warsaw Music Institute. After completing his studies there, he taught music at the Warsaw conservatory. In 1880–81 and 1883–84 he continued music studies at the Royal Music Academy in Berlin, where he met many outstanding virtuosos of the period, such as Richard Strauss, Anton Rubinstein, and Pablo de Sarasate. These contacts, as well as the influence of Helena Modrzejewska, whom he met in Zakopane in 1884, induced him to begin a piano career. After his first successful performance in Kraków in October 1884, Paderewski gathered enough funds to go to Vienna, where he studied under the direction of Teodor Leszetycki. In 1885 he achieved his first success in Vienna. Then he played in Warsaw, Vienna, Strasbourg, Paris, London, and Berlin. His fame as a virtuoso spread after a very successful concert tour of the United States in 1891–92. Within 130 days Paderewski gave 107 concerts, including 32 in New York. This paved the way for his success in Europe, and he was acclaimed as one of the greatest virtuosos of the epoch. In the next decade Paderewski gave many concerts in Europe, North and South America, Australia, and South Africa. When in 1898 he came to Warsaw, the reception in his honor in the Town Hall changed into a patriotic demonstration.

Among Paderewski's earlier compositions, the *Minuet Op. 17* of 1887 gained the greatest popularity. At that time he also composed his major works, including *Sonata for Violin and Piano* (1880), *Piano Concerto in A minor* (1888), *Polish Fantasy for Piano and Orchestra* (1893), and the opera *Manru* (1900). In his later period Paderewski created many piano compositions, including the *Sonata in S minor, Variation and Fugue* (1903) and the monumental *Symphony in H minor, Polonia*, which was performed for the first time at the Warsaw Philharmonic in 1905.

Paderewski was deeply involved in patriotic activities, both at home and abroad. As a famous artist, he could influence public opinion in many countries and draw attention to the Polish cause. He himself donated lavishly to national causes and to charity. During his first visit to the United States he contributed to the construction of a monument of Tadeusz Kościuszko in Chicago. In 1910 he founded the Grunwald Monument in Kraków to commemorate the 500th anniversary of the battle of Grunwald. The unveiling ceremony for the monument drew great crowds and changed into a patriotic demonstration. After the outbreak of World War I, along with **Henryk Sienkiewicz**, Paderewski founded the Committee for Assistance to War Victims in the Swiss town of Vevey and the Polish Relief Fund in London. Paderewski represented views close to those of National Democracy and supported its initiatives, which aimed at the revival of Polish statehood with the help of the Entente. From 1917 Paderewski was a representative of the Polish National Committee in the United States, and he propagated among Polish Americans the notion of the formation of a Polish army. As a personal friend of President Woodrow Wilson, he had influence upon the formulation of the thirteenth point (which con-

cerned Poland) of Wilson's famous Fourteen Points speech of 8 January 1918.

At the end of 1918 Paderewski came to Poland. His arrival in Poznań on 26 December 1918 created enthusiasm and then indirectly, as a result of German provocation, gave rise to the Greater Poland Uprising. Trying to arrange a compromise between the pro-independence left and National Democracy, the provisional chief of state, **Józef Piłsudski**, appointed Paderewski head of the government. Between 16 January and 9 December 1919 Paderewski served as premier and minister of foreign affairs. He managed to mitigate internal tensions and to gain recognition for the Polish government abroad. He also represented Poland at the Paris Peace Conference and signed the Treaty of Versailles on behalf of the Republic of Poland. In 1920–21 Paderewski was Polish delegate to the League of Nations. Facing the opposition's criticism of Polish foreign policy and having concluded (partly under the influence of his wife Helen) that his efforts toward the revival of statehood had been disregarded, Paderewski withdrew from political life. After the coup of May 1926 he began to increasingly oppose the new system of government. In 1936 he was one of the main instigators of the Morges Front, which aimed at counteracting authoritarianism in Poland. The name of the organization came from Paderewski's residence in Switzerland.

During World War II Paderewski accepted the chairmanship of the National Council in exile and repeatedly spoke in support of the revival of an independent Poland. Paderewski left his memoirs, the first volume of which was published in New York in 1939 and in Poland in 1961. (WR)

Sources: Eugene Kusielewicz, "Wilson and the Polish Cause," *Polish Review*, 1956, vol. 1; Charles Philips, *Paderewski: The Story of a Modern Immortal* (New York, 1934); Jan Kucharzewski, *Ignacy Jan Paderewski* (New York, 1940); Władysław Kędra, *Ignacy Paderewski* (Warsaw, 1948); Henryk Opieński, *Ignacy Jan Paderewski* (Warsaw, 1960); Ignacy Jan Paderewski, *Pamiętniki*, compiled by Mary Lawton (Warsaw, 1961); Z. Sywak, *Ignacy Paderewski: Prime Minister of Poland, 16 January to 9 December 1919* (Stanford, 1977); Marek M. Drozdowski, *Ignacy Jan Paderewski: Zarys biografii politycznej* (Warsaw, 1979).

PÄHN August (20 January 1904, Märdi–4 June 1963, Tartu), Estonian clergyman. After completing theological studies at the university in Dorpat (Tartu), Pähn worked as a pastor in Koeru. In 1941 he took up a post at the cathedral in Tallinn. At that time the Estonian Evangelical Lutheran Church (EELC) lacked a continuity of leadership because Bishop **Johan Kõpp**, who had headed the EELC before World War II, had gone into exile, and Kõpp's legal successor, Anton Eilart, had to go into hiding. Thus, in February 1945 the EELC Episcopal Council elected a provisional consistory and appointed Pähn acting bishop. The members of the Episcopal Council had to sign a declaration of loyalty to the Communist authorities and to dismiss pastors who were living abroad. In July 1945 the government appointed a plenipotentiary for religious affairs, and he was given broad prerogatives concerning the rights and duties of clergymen and the building of new churches. All of this led to the increasing vassalage of the EELC, which Pähn failed to resist. Recently discovered materials indicate that he collaborated with the NKVD. A new system of dividing and registering Lutheran congregations was introduced, the administration was given a wide scope to interfere in the Church's domestic affairs, and at the same time the influence of the faithful on the religious life of congregations became much more limited. People willing to serve the Communists were promoted within the EELC structures. Pastors and laymen suspected of views hostile to the Communists were arrested. On the day before the mass deportations of 1949, the EELC was already effectively paralyzed, and six out of seven consistory members collaborated with security services on a regular basis. Nonetheless, for reasons not exactly clear, the authorities began to distrust Pähn. On 2 February 1949 he was replaced as acting bishop by **Jaan Kiivit**, and on 12 April 1949 he was arrested and deported to Siberia, where he was held until 1956. After returning to Estonia, Pähn took charge of the parish of Võnnu, where he worked until the end of his life. (AG)

Sources: "Religion in Estonia," www.okupatsioon.ee/english/ overviews/index.html; page of the Estonian Evangelical Lutheran Church, www.eelk.ee/~eelk109/kogudus.htm; page of the Estonian Evangelical Lutheran Church Charles XI Parish in Tallinn, www. ngonet.ee/kaarli/vaimulikud.html; www.eelk.ee/elulood; www.hot. ee/rauge/bettai/pet13.htm.

PAISI Vodica [originally Pashko] (June 1881, Vodice, near Kolonje–4 March 1966, Tirana), Albanian Orthodox bishop. Paisi studied at a Greek school in his home village and then in Kavalli (Greece). In 1910 he was ordained. At this time he got in touch with the Albanian pro-independence activists. Arrested by the Turks in 1912, Paisi was tortured and held in prison in Përmeti. After his release he returned to pastoral work, and in 1920 he became archimandrite and deputy ordinary bishop of Kolonje (Ersekë). Working with **Fan Noli**, Paisi belonged to a group of clergy who prepared a proclamation of the autocephaly of the Albanian Orthodox Church. In October 1940 Paisi was arrested by the Italian occupation authorities. After a short imprisonment in Korça and Tirana, he was interned in Bari, Italy, where he remained until 1941. After his release and return to Albania, Paisi became involved in the resistance movement in the Kolonje region, where in November 1914 he was elected to the local structure of the Front of National Liberation (FNL). Paisi actively supported the Communist guerrillas, and in July 1943 he was elected to the Chief Council of the FNL. In July 1948 he gained the position of ordinary bishop of Korça, thanks to the support of the Communists. He initiated close cooperation with the Russian Orthodox Church.

Under pressure from the Communists, on 28 August 1949 the Holy Synod elected Paisi archbishop and head of the Autocephalous Albanian Orthodox Church. The hitherto head of the church, Kristofor Kissi, opposed this decision as contrary to Church statutes, but the Communists interned him. At a congress of Orthodox laypeople and clergy in February 1950 Paisi insisted that the Albanian Orthodox Church had never had such amenable conditions for development. Paisi was also active in war veteran circles. His support for the Communist authorities gave the Albanian Orthodox Church a privileged place among other denominations, minimizing Communist attacks on the Orthodox community. Until his death Paisi enjoyed the trust of both the believers and the state, but his policies failed to stop the Communists from declaring Albania the first fully atheistic state in 1967. (TC)

Sources: Family archives of Lefter Thanasi (grandson of Vodica Paisi); Stavro Skendi, *Albania* (New York, 1956); Tadeusz Czekalski, *Zarys dziejów chrześcijaństwa albańskiego w latach 1912–1993* (Kraków, 1996); Tasi Blushi, Qetesor Kaltanji, and Lluka Pashko, "Figurë e nderuar dheimëmedhetar shquar," *Kushtrim Brezash*, 5 February 1999; Kristofor Beduli, ed., *Dhimiter Beduli*, (Tirana, 1999)

PAJDAK Antoni (7 December 1894, Biskupice, near Wieliczka–20 March 1988, Warsaw), Polish Socialist politician. The son of a miner, while still in school, Pajdak joined the Riflemen's Association. In 1914 he graduated from the Nowodworski Gymnasium in Kraków. In August 1914 he set out as a sergeant with the cadre company of **Józef Piłsudski**. Later, he followed the battle trail of the First Brigade of the Polish Legions, taking part, for example, in the battles of Krzywopłoty, Łowczówek, Kostiuchnówka, and the Stochód (Stokhid) River. In the fall of 1914 Pajdak was detached to work in the Polish Military Organization in the Lublin region. Arrested by the Austrians, he ended up on the Italian front in the ranks of the Austrian Army. After the end of the war Pajdak took up law studies at the Jagiellonian University in Kraków, and he completed his studies in 1922. He worked in the district administrations in Radomsko, Konin, and Słupca. In 1928 he became a *starost* (local representative of the authorities) of Radomsko. In 1931 he returned to Kraków, where he completed his training as an attorney and ran a law practice. In May 1939 he was named deputy mayor of Kraków, but the German aggression of September 1939 prevented him from assuming this post. During the September 1939 campaign Pajdak was assigned to the provincial police headquarters with the rank of major.

In October 1939 Pajdak returned from the front to Kraków and began underground activities in the Polish Socialist Party–Freedom–Equality–Independence (Polska Partia Socjalistyczna–Wolność–Równość–Niepodległość [PPS–WRN]). He also joined a Socialist military unit called the People's Guard (Gwardia Ludowa; not to be confused with the Communist People's Guard), and as commanding officer of the Militia of the PPS–WRN, the security branch of the party, Pajdak became a member of the High Command of the People's Guard. On behalf of the PPS–WRN, in 1943 Pajdak was appointed deputy delegate of the Polish Government-in-Exile for the Homeland and minister of the Polish government in London. He left for Warsaw, where he was active under the pseudonym "Traugutt." In the Delegation (Delegatura), Pajdak was responsible for transportation and social welfare. He participated in the Warsaw Uprising, and after its collapse he left the capital, along with the civil population, to continue his activities near Warsaw. On 27 March 1945 Pajdak was arrested by the Soviets, along with fifteen other leaders of underground Poland. Taken to Lubyanka Prison in Moscow and subjected to severe interrogations, Pajdak was excluded from the June 1945 Trial of the Sixteen. Between July and November 1945 he was held in Butyrki Prison and then sentenced in a secret trial to five years. After leaving the prison, in 1950 he was deported to Siberia for an unlimited period. He lived in the Arbansky region of Krasnoyarsk, where he worked as a woodcutter.

Pajdak returned to Poland in August 1955 and started working in law chambers. The legend of his underground work, his imprisonment in the USSR, his truly Socialist and patriotic convictions, his religiousness, and his great kindness to people won him immense authority in independent social circles. Thus, although he was advanced in years, after the events of 1976 in Radom, Pajdak became a member of the Committee for the Defense of Workers (Komitet Obrony Robotników [KOR]). In March 1981 he was severely beaten by an "unknown perpetrator." After recovering, he joined Solidarity and was a member of the Social Committee for the celebrations of the twenty-fifth anniversary of the June 1956 events in Poznań. Pajdak was decorated with (among other awards) the Golden Cross of Merit, the Order Pro Fide et Patriae, and the Home Army Cross. (WR)

Sources: Kunert, vol. 3; Andrzej Wernic, "Minister Antoni Pajdak 1894–1988," *Ład*, 8 May 1988; *Proces szesnastu: Dokumenty NKWD* (Warsaw, 1995).

PAKSAS Rolandas (10 June 1956, Telšiai), Lithuanian politician. Paksas studied at the Polytechnic College in Vilnius and at the Civil Aviation Academy in Leningrad. In 1979–85 he worked at a design office and as a pilot of an acrobatic aviation squad. He was a Soviet and Lithuanian champion in air acrobatics. Later he chaired the Vilnius Air Club, and in 1990–91 he was head of the air section of the National Volunteer Defense. From 1992 to 1997 Paksas chaired a building company, Restako. In March 1997 he was elected to the City Council of Vilnius, and in April 1997 he became mayor of Vilnius. He managed to reconstruct the historical center of the city, which added to his popularity. A member of the Homeland Union–Lithuanian Conservatives (Tėvynės Sąjunga–Lietuvos Konservatoriai), from 18 May to 27 October 1999 Paksas was prime minister, enjoying strong support in the parliament. Trying to meet popular expectations, he resigned in protest against the sale of a state oil concern to the American Williams group; the sale had been promoted by President **Valdas Adamkus**.

Before the parliamentary elections of October 2000, aware of the declining ratings of the conservatives, Paksas left his party and took the lead of the Lithuanian Liberal Union (Lietuvos Liberalų Sąjunga), which gained 17.3 percent of the vote and thirty-four mandates, becoming the third largest parliamentary faction. On 26 October 2000 he became prime minister of a minority cabinet, based on a coalition of liberals and the Socialist-Liberal New Union. Paksas also cooperated with the Lithuanian Poles' Electoral Action. He accelerated talks on Lithuania's entry into NATO and the European Union, but he failed to prevent the collapse of the coalition on account of differing attitudes on the privatization of the power sector. Paksas was accused of overly close links with Russian business and on 20 June 2001 he resigned. In 2002 he became head of the Lithuanian Liberal Democratic Party (Lietuvos Liberaldemokratų Partija). In the campaign before the presidential elections of December 2002, Paksas used radical populist rhetoric and advanced to the second round, in which he won 54.9 percent of the vote and defeated Adamkus. In the spring of 2003 Paksas supported Lithuania's entry into the European Union in a referendum that confirmed this decision. In November 2003 it was disclosed that Paksas's closest aides had cooperated with the Russian mafia, but Paksas stated he had nothing to do with that. Nevertheless, impeachment procedures were started, and they ended up in his recall from office on 6 June 2004. (WR)

Sources: *Europa Środkowo-Wschodnia 1999* (Warsaw, 2001); Bugajski; *Rzeczpospolita*, 5 and 6 January 2003; *New York Times*, 7 June 2004; www.rulers.org; www.electionworld.org/lithuania.htm; www.lrs.lt/n/rinkimai/20001008/kandvl.htm-151755.htm#autobio.

PALACH Jan (11 August 1948, Všetaty–19 January 1969, Prague), Czech student. Between 1967 and 1968 Palach was a student at the Higher Economic School, and from 1968, in the Department of Philosophy of Charles University in Prague. On 16 January 1969 in protest against the August 1968 Soviet invasion and against the Soviet occupation, Palach set himself on fire at Venceslas Square in Prague. Seriously burned, he was taken to a plastic surgery clinic, where he died. His funeral on 25 January 1969 became a nationwide demonstration against the occupiers and their Czech adherents. Buried at Olšany Cemetery in Prague, Palach was secretly exhumed in 1973, his body was cremated, and the urn with the ashes was carried to the cemetery in Všetaty. On 25 February 1969 another student, Jan Zajic, followed Palach's example in an attempt to protest the lack of social response to Palach's death. Both graves became places of pilgrimage and antigovernment demonstrations. On the twentieth anniversary of Palach's burning himself to death, Prague became the scene of mass anti-Communist demonstrations, brutally suppressed by the police. These were the first heralds of the Velvet Revolution, which ten months later overthrew the Communist regime in Czechoslovakia. In 1990 Palach's ashes were again placed at Olšany, and on 19 January 2000 a monument commemorating his death was unveiled at Venceslas Square. (PU)

Sources: *ČBS*; *Kdo byl kdo v našich dějinách ve 20. stoleti*, vol. 2 (Prague, 1998); Jiři Lederer, *Jan Palach* (Prague, 1990).

PALECKIS Justas (22 January 1899, Telšiai–21 February 1980, Vilnius), Lithuanian Communist activist. Paleckis spent his childhood in Riga, where he later studied journalism and also worked as a teacher. He published his first articles in the Latvian Communist newspaper, and in 1921–23 he wrote for the Lithuanian leftist press. In 1925 Paleckis founded the periodical *Naujas Žodis*, which came out in Riga for two years and in Kaunas until 1933. After the formation of a Socialist-populist government, in 1926 Paleckis became the head of the Lithuanian News Agency ELTA and held the post until May 1927. After a visit to the USSR in 1933, Paleckis published *SSSR musu akimis* (The USSR in our eyes), in which he rather critically described Soviet life. Nonetheless, he intensified his cooperation with the Lithuanian Communist underground. In 1937 he also attempted to organize an overt People's Front.

After the establishment of Soviet garrisons in October 1939, Paleckis's attitude induced the Lithuanian authorities to put him under detention. On 17 June 1940 the Kremlin deputy, Vladimir Dekanozov, appointed Paleckis the head of the so-called people's government and then the acting president of Lithuania. Paleckis presented himself unofficially as a rather moderate politician who could prevent further arrests. Following instructions from the Kremlin, on 6 July Paleckis issued a decree changing the electoral law so that only the Communist Party could propose candidates. On 14–15 July 1940 he staged the "elections" for the new People's Assembly, and then he arranged the incorporation of Lithuania into the USSR as a Soviet republic. After that on 25 August 1940 Paleckis assumed the post of president of the Supreme Council of the Lithuanian SSR. After the German invasion in June 1941 Paleckis fled to Moscow, only to resume his former post in the summer of 1944. While holding this post until 1967, he endorsed two great waves of deportations of Lithuanians far inside the USSR, in 1944 and 1949. In 1952 Paleckis became a deputy member of the CC of the CPSU. In 1966–70 he was also the president of the Council of Nationalities of the USSR and headed many Soviet delegations to conferences of the Interparliamentary Union. These aimed at the validation of the incorporation of Lithuania into the USSR. Paleckis published many articles praising the Soviet government in Lithuania; these were collected in, for example, *V dvukh mirakh* (In two worlds; 1974), and the memoirs *Driejuose pasauliuose: Atsiminimai* (1983). (WR)

Sources: *EL*, vol. 4; *The Annual Obituary* 1980; Bronis J. Kaslas, ed., *The USSR-German Aggression against Lithuania* (New York, 1973); Romuald J. Misiunas and Rein Taagepera, *The Baltic States: Years of Dependence, 1940–1980* (Berkeley, 1983).

PÁLFFY György [originally Oesterreicher] (16 September 1909, Temesvár [Timişoara]–24 October 1949, Budapest), Hungarian officer. Before World War I Pálffy's family moved from Transylvania to Budapest, where his father worked as a bank clerk. After graduating from high school, Pálffy did his military service. In 1932 he graduated from the Ludovika Military Academy, Budapest, and served in the army. After one year of training in Italy, he graduated from the General Staff Military Academy in Budapest (1938). In 1939 he left the army because of his anti-German views and the Jewish origin of his wife. During World War II he worked in a steelworks. In 1942 he became a member of the illegal Hungarian Communist Party (HCP). On the party's orders, in 1943 Pálffy also joined the Independent Smallholders' Party (ISP) and conducted anti-war agitation among the ISP members. In the autumn of 1944 he was appointed commander of the HCP Military Commission.

In December 1944 Pálffy joined the effort to establish an army of the Provisional National Government in Debrecen. In March 1945 he became commander of the Military Policy Department (counterintelligence) in the Ministry of National Defense. He was responsible for hunting down war criminals, but in practice he was more involved in imposing HCP control over the army and eliminating rivals to the Communists from public life. In the latter endeavor Pálffy competed with the political police, led by **Gábor Péter**. In 1945 Pálffy was promoted to colonel and in 1946 to brigadier general. In 1946 he became commander of the border guard and secretary of the HCP Military Commission. In 1947 he was promoted to major general and inspector general of the Hungarian Army. In February 1948 in Moscow Pálffy negotiated a Hungarian-Soviet agreement of friendship and mutual assistance. In June 1948 he became a member of the Central Committee (CC) of the Hungarian Workers' Party (HWP). At the end of 1948 Pálffy was appointed deputy minister of national defense and chief of training. On 5 July 1949 he was arrested at the instigation of **Mihály Farkas**, the minister of defense. Pálffy's case was linked with that of **László Rajk**, but Pálffy was tried separately, sentenced to death, and executed. On 6 October 1956 he was reburied, along with Rajk and other co-defendants who had been executed at the same time. Partially vindicated in 1955, Pálffy was fully rehabilitated in September 1963. (JT)

Sources: *Magyarország 1944–1956*, CD-ROM (Budapest, 2001); *Magyar Nagylexikon*, vol. 14 (Budapest, 2002); Béla Szász, *Volunteers for the Gallows: Anatomy of a Show Trial* (New York, 1972); Bennet Kovrig, *Communism in Hungary from Kun to Kádár* (Stanford, 1979).

PALIIV Dmytro (17 May 1896, Perevozets, near Kalush, Galicia–19 or 20 July 1944, Brody, Galicia), Ukrainian political and military leader. Born into the family of a Uniate clergyman, during World War I Paliiv was an officer in the Ukrainian Sich Riflemen. He co-organized the Ukrainian Military Committee and helped to prepare the Ukrainian Uprising in Lemberg (Lwów, Lviv) in November 1918. He served in the Ukrainian Galician Army (UGA) as an adjutant to General Miron Tarnavskyi. Paliiv was against reaching an agreement with Anton Denikin or transforming the UGA into the Red Galician Army. A founding member of the clandestine Ukrainian Military Organization (Ukraiinska Viyskova Orhanizatsiya [UVO]), Paliiv belonged to the UVO Supreme Command from 1921 to 1926. He served as a member of the UVO

probably until 1931. He opposed subordinating the UVO to the Organization of Ukrainian Nationalists (OUN). Paliiv was one of the founding members of the Ukrainian Party of National Work (UPNW) and co-edited its periodical, *Zahrava*. From 1923 to 1926 Paliiv was an editor of *Novyi Chas*. He supported the 1925 merger of the UPNW with the Ukrainian People's Labor Party into the Ukrainian National Democratic Alliance (Ukraiinske Natsionalno-Demokratychne Obyednannya [UNDO]), and in the same year he became a member of the Central Committee of the UNDO. Paliiv was an MP in the Assembly of the Republic of Poland from 1928 to 1930. Arrested on 10 September 1930, he was held in various prisons, including the Brześć (Brest) prison, until 6 July 1933. Paliiv opposed the OUN's use of terrorism in the political struggle and especially the involvement of youth in such actions. Nevertheless, he served as liaison officer between the UNDO and **Yevhen Konovalets** until July 1933, when he was expelled from the UNDO. A supporter of so-called constructive Fascist work, on 1 November 1933 Paliiv established the Front of National Unity (Front Natsionalnoy Yednosty). He edited the periodicals *Batkivshschyna* (1934–39) and *Ukraiinski visty* (1935–39). After the outbreak of World War II in 1939, Paliiv went to the German-occupied Krynica. One of the most devoted founding members of the SS Galician Division, Paliiv served as officer of this division. He was killed in the Battle of Brody. (GM)

Sources: *Encyclopedia of Ukraine*, vol. 4 (Toronto, 1993); *Kto był kim w Drugiej Rzeczpospolitej* (Warsaw, 1994); *Encyklopedia historii Drugiej Rzeczypospolitej* (Warsaw, 1999); Ryszard Torzecki, *Kwestia ukraińska w Polsce w latach 1923–1929* (Kraków, 1989); Andriy Bolianovskyi, *Dyviziia "Halychyna": Istoriia* (Lviv, 2000); Orest Subtelny, *Ukraine: A History* (Toronto, 2000).

PÁLINKÁS Antal [originally Pallavicini] (30 July 1922, Budapest–10 December 1957, Budapest), victim of the 1956 Hungarian Revolution. Pálinkás was born into an aristocratic family. After passing his high school final exams, he worked as a laborer from 1940. He later studied at the Ludovika Military Academy in Budapest and served in the army. After the Germans occupied Hungary in March 1944, Pálinkás joined the anti-Nazi resistance movement and helped to establish the Hungarian Front. Sent to the Soviet Union at the end of 1944, he served as the commander of a battalion in a division of soldiers who volunteered to serve with the Russians, and later he became the commander of a field hospital in an NKVD camp in Nikolayev. After returning to Hungary in 1946, Pálinkás was vetted and returned to the army. In 1947 he joined the Hungarian Communist Party, and in June 1948, the Hungarian Workers' Party (HWP). In 1948 Pálinkás was decorated with the Order of Hungarian Freedom for his services during World War II. In 1951 he became chief of staff of an armored regiment in the town of Aszód. It was then that he changed his name to Pálinkás, which sounded less aristocratic. In 1955 he became chief of staff of a regiment in the town of Rétság.

In October 1956 Pálinkás was elected chairman of the Revolutionary Military Council of the regiment and supplied weapons and ammunition to local units of the National Guard. On 31 October, on the orders of his superiors, he escorted Cardinal **József Mindszenty**, who had been held under house arrest near Rétság, to the archbishop's palace on Castle Hill in Buda. Upon the second Soviet invasion, on 4 November, on the orders of the regiment commander, Pálinkás raised an alarm. Men who had done military service were given weapons and ammunition. However, on the orders of the Ministry of National Defense, the arms were laid down without a struggle in front of Soviet units. At the beginning of January 1957 Pálinkás left the army on his own request, and in February he was arrested. By linking his aristocratic descent, which Pálinkás had rejected in his youth, with the fact that he had been randomly assigned to escort Cardinal Mindszenty, the authorities tried to falsely prove that the revolution was a counterrevolution organized mainly by former landowners and clerical reactionaries. On 16 September 1957 the court of first instance sentenced Pálinkás to life imprisonment, but on 11 November of that year the Supreme Court changed this sentence to death. One month later Pálinkás was executed. (JT)

Sources: *A magyar forradalom és szabadságharc enciklopédiája*, CD-ROM (Budapest, 1999); *Magyar Nagylexikon*, vol. 14 (Budapest, 2002); György Litván, ed., *Rewolucja węgierska 1956 roku* (Warsaw, 1996).

PANA Gheorghe (9 April 1927, Gherghiţa), Romanian Communist activist. During his studies in economics in Bucharest, in 1944 Pana joined the Union of Communist Youth, and in 1947, the Romanian Communist Party (RCP). In 1958–65 he was secretary of the RCP Committee in Bucharest, and from 1959 he also headed its Department of Propaganda. From December 1966 to 1968 he was first secretary of the RCP Provincial Committee in Braşov, and then until 1969, chairman of the local National Council. In 1969–75 Pana was a member of the Council of State. A deputy to the National Assembly and a member of the Standing Politburo of the RCP Executive Committee from 1969, in 1969–75 he was also Central Committee (CC) secretary. In 1969–77 Pana was responsible for the CC Department of Organization and Personnel. From April 1970 he was a member of the Defense Council, and from July 1971 he dealt with socioeconomic forecasting. In 1976–79 he headed the national trade union organization, and from January 1977 he was chairman of the Council for Social and Economic Organizations. In 1978 Pana was minister of labor, and from 1979 to 1985 he was mayor of Bucharest and first secretary of the RCP Bucharest Regional Committee. Until 1987 Pana headed the RCP CC Department of Consumer Industry and Purchasing of Farm Products. In 1987 he was appointed chairman of the Committee for People's Councils. After the fall of the **Nicolae Ceauşescu** regime Pana retired from politics. (PC)

Sources: Juliusz Stroynowski, ed., *Who's Who in the Socialist Countries of Europe* (Munich, London, and Paris, 1978); *International Year Book and Statesmen's Who's Who* (London, 1990).

PANIĆ Milan (20 December 1929, Belgrade), Yugoslav politician of Serb nationality. As a teenager, Panić served in the Communist guerrillas. In the early 1950s he became a well-known cyclist, and in 1955 he fled to the West. In 1956 he went to the United States, where he graduated from college, received American citizenship, and established the International Chemical and Nuclear Pharmaceuticals Company (ICN). In the late 1980s, thanks to the support of **Slobodan Milošević**, Panić gained control over the Yugoslav pharmaceutical company Galenika. In early July 1992 he came to Yugoslavia with a peace mission. Taking this as an opportunity in his international game, Milošević agreed to appoint Panić prime minister of the Yugoslav government on 14 July 1992. Panić surprised Milošević by criticizing aggressive Serbian operations in Bosnia-Herzegovina, which he called an independent state. He appealed for an end to these operations, calling ethnic cleansing "shameful" and dismissing extreme nationalists from the government. In the presidential elections Panić gained the support of a group of independent citizens. In the first round, on 20 December 1992 he gained 34 percent of the vote, but in the second round he lost to Milošević. At the end of December 1992, Panić lost a no-confidence vote in the parliament, and on 9 February 1993 he resigned. He returned to the United States and continued to run ICN. (WR)

Sources: *Lenard J. Cohen, Serpent in the Bosom: The Rise and Fall of Slobodan Milosevic* (Boulder, Colo., 1995); Laura Silber and Allan Little, *The Death of Yugoslavia* (London, 1995); Željan E. Šuster, *Historical Dictionary of the Federal Republic of Yugoslavia* (Lanham, Md., 1999); Bugajski; www.rulers.org.

PANUFNIK Andrzej (24 September 1914, Warsaw–27 October 1991, Twickenham, Greater London), Polish composer and conductor. From 1932 to 1936 Panufnik studied at the Warsaw Conservatory, from which he graduated as a student of composition under Kazimierz Sikorski. From 1937 to 1938 he studied conducting at the Vienna Academy. He then completed his studies in Paris (1938–39). During World War II Panufnik was in occupied Poland. In 1945 he became the conductor of the Kraków Philharmonic, and in 1946, director of the Warsaw Philharmonic. At an early age Panufnik achieved creative maturity and gained the recognition of music critics—for example, for his *Sinfonia rustica* (1948). From 1947 Panufnik performed in Germany, France, England, and the Soviet Union. During the heyday of Socialist realism, however, Polish Communist officials began criticizing the style and content of his works; therefore, in 1954 Panufnik decided to remain in the West. As a result, he became the target of vicious propaganda attacks and was subsequently totally blacklisted by censors in the Polish People's Republic. Panufnik settled in England, where in 1957 he became musical director of the City of Birmingham Symphony Orchestra. In 1963 his *Sinfonia sacra* won first prize at the International Composers' Competition in Monaco; consequently, his works were more and more often performed in Great Britain and the United States. In stylistic terms, Panufnik's music was based on intellectual constructions. He used carefully planned symmetric schemata and characteristic "note cells," but his music is nevertheless not void of romantic warmth and emotional elements. Although his were not programmatic compositions, religious and patriotic inspiration played an important role. Such was the character of his greatest works, including *Piano Concerto* (1962), *Katyń Epitaph* (1969), *Universal Prayer* (1969), *Sinfonia mistica* (1977), *Sinfonia votiva* (1981), *Harmony* (1987), and *Sinfonia di speranca* (1987). Panufnik's works were not performed in Poland until 1977. In 1987 he published his autobiography, *Composing Myself*. In 1990 he visited Poland for the first time in thirty-six years. In January 1991 Panufnik received a British knighthood. (WR)

Sources: *Britannica Book of the Year 1992* (Chicago, 1993); Tadeusz Kaczyński, *Andrzej Panufnik i jego muzyka* (Warsaw, 1994); Bernard Jacobson, *A Polish Renaissance* (London, 1996); *Leksykon kultury polskiej poza krajem od roku 1939* (Lublin, 2000).

PAPÁNEK Ján (24 October 1896, Brezová pod Bradlom, Senica district–30 November 1991, New York), Slovak journalist and diplomat. During World War I Papánek served in the Austro-Hungarian Army and was taken prisoner by the Italians in 1916. He soon enlisted in the Czechoslovak Legions in Italy, where he also worked as an editor of the newspaper *V boj*. From 1919 to 1923 he studied international law and political science at the Sorbonne, Paris, and afterwards he entered the diplomatic service. Papánek worked in the Ministry of Foreign Affairs in Prague and served on diplomatic missions in Budapest and Washington. He was a close associate of **Edvard Beneš**, whom he supported in his conflict with **Milan Hodža**. From 1935 to 1938 Papánek was a consul in Pittsburgh, Pennsylvania. He firmly opposed the partition of Czechoslovakia and the establishment of a separate Slovak state. During World War II Panánek was head of the Czechoslovak information office in the United States and one of the leaders of the émigré community linked with President Beneš. In April 1945 Papánek was secretary of the Czechoslovak delegation to an international conference in San Francisco at which the United Nations was established. He helped to draft the Charter of the United Nations and was one of its fourteen co-authors and signatories. From 1946 to 1948 Papánek was a delegate to the United Nations and took an active part in UN work. During the Communist coup in February 1948 he submitted a protest to the UN secretary general against Soviet interference in Czechoslovakia's domestic affairs. Soon he was recalled as ambassador by the new Communist government, but he refused to accept this recall and remained in exile. From 1948 to 1986 Papánek was chairman of the American Fund for Czechoslovak Refugees (Americký Fond pre Československých Utečencov), and in 1949 he helped to establish the Council of Free Czechoslovakia (Rada Svobodného Československa). Papánek was also an active member of other émigré organizations and published in their newspapers and periodicals. (PU)

Sources: *ČBS*; *Evanjelici v dejinách slovenskéj kultúry*, vol. 1, (Liptovský Mikuláš, 1997); Slavomír Michálek, *Ján Papánek: Politik, diplomat, humanista* (Bratislava, 1996); Halina Breňová, *Vzpomínky a dokumenty* (Prague, 1994); Halina Breňová, *Život pro jine* (Prague, 1995); http://www.vazka.sk/SOURCESs/Info/papanek_en.html.

PARHON Constantin (28 October 1874, Câmpulung, Argeş County–9 August 1969, Bucharest), Romanian doctor, endocrinologist, biologist, and political activist. Parhon attended high school in Focşani, Buzău, and Ploieşti. In 1893–1900 he studied medicine in Bucharest. In 1900 he earned the title of doctor of medicine. Parhon initially practiced as a neurologist and then as a psychiatrist. In 1909 he co-authored *Secreţiile interne* (Internal secretions), the first book on endocrinology ever written. From 1913 to 1933 Parhon was a professor at the Neuropsychiatric Department of the University of Iaşi Medical School. He simultaneously was an active member, and from 1915 to 1916 the president, of the Doctors' and

Naturalists' Society in Iaşi. He subsequently founded the Neurology, Psychiatry, Physiology, and Endocrinology Society. In 1913 he demonstrated the role of hormonal pathologies in psychosis. Parhon was also active in political life. In 1918 he was one of the founders of the leftist Workers' Party (Partidul Muncitor), which merged with the leftist Peasant Party (Partidul Ţărănesc), led by **Ion Mihalache**, in 1919. In 1933 Parhon moved to Bucharest, where he worked as a university lecturer at the Medical School from 1930 to 1940 and subsequently became director of the Institute of Nervous, Mental, and Hormonal Diseases. In 1928 he became a member of the Romanian Academy of Sciences and served as its honorary president from 1948 to 1969.

After World War II, Parhon supported the new authorities and joined the Romanian Communist Party (Partidul Comunist Român). From April 1948 to June 1952 he served as president of the Presidium of the Grand National Assembly (parliament). In 1947 he became a member of the Soviet Academy of Sciences. From 1949 to 1957 he was the director of the Institute of Endocrinology, and from 1952 to 1957 he was also the director of the Institute of Geriatrics. Parhon conducted research on the influence of hormonal activity on the normal and pathological functioning of the organism and on mental functions. The author of numerous works on the aging of the organism and the chances of extending human life, he was a member of many international scientific societies. Parhon's publications include *Les sécrétions internes au point de vue morphologique, chimique, physiologique, pathologique, et thérapeutique* (Internal secretions from the morphological, chemical, pathological, and therapeutic point of view, 3 vols.; 1923–33; co-author); *Psihozele afective* (Affective psychoses; 1925); and *Biologia vârstelor: Cercetări clinice şi experimentale* (The biology of old age: Clinical and experimental research; 1955). (LW)

Sources: *Wielka Encyklopedia Powszechna PWN*, vol. 8 (Warsaw, 1966); Constanţa Parhon-Stefanescu, *Constantin Parhon* (Bucharest, 1982); Dorina N. Rusu, *Membrii Academiei Române 1866–1999* (Bucharest, 1999); Ion Alexandrescu, Ion Bulei, Ion Mamina, and Ioan Scurtu, *Enciclopedia de istorie României* (Bucharest, 2000); www.dumitrescu.com/science.

PÄRT Arvo (11 September 1935, Paide), Estonian composer and conductor. Pärt was studying at a secondary music school in Tallinn when he was drafted into the Soviet Army in 1955. He played in a military band. Later he graduated, and in 1957–63 he studied under Heino Eller. From 1958 to 1967 Pärt was head of the music section of Estonian Radio. In 1962 he won an all-Soviet contest for young composers with the cantata *Meie*

Aed (Our garden) and the oratory *Mailmaa Samm* (The march of light). Creating Western-style music based on atonality and the so-called serial technique, Pärt evoked strong responses, from the esteem of experts (first prize in an all-Soviet contest for young composers in 1969 and an award from the Estonian SSR in 1978) to political attacks and censorship (for example, his *Credo* of 1969 was banned). Despite Moscow's accusations of "mysticism," Pärt's *Perpetuum mobile* was well received at the Warsaw Autumn Festival in 1964. Unconducive living and working conditions in the USSR made Pärt go abroad. In 1980 he went with his family to Vienna, and in 1981 he settled in Berlin.

Pärt is the best known Estonian composer. His works have been frequently performed by the Hillard Ensemble and the Chamber Choir of the Estonian Philharmonic, as well as by leading conductors and violinists. Pärt's chief publisher was Universal Editions in Vienna, and from 1984 he worked with ECM Records. Pärt won several Estonian and international awards, including the German Johann Gottfried von Herder Prize in 2000. He composed three symphonies (I, *Polyphonic*, 1964; II, 1966; III, 1971); two sonatas, *Mirror in Mirror*, for violin and piano (1958–59); the *Obituary* (1960); *Collage B-A-C-H*, for a symphony orchestra (1964); *Pro et contra*, a concerto for cello and symphony orchestra (1966); *Trivium* (1976); *Tabula rasa*, a concerto for two violins (1977); *Cantus*, in memory of Benjamin Britten, for string orchestra (1977); *De profundis* (1977–80); *Annum per annum*, for organ (1980); *Te Deum* (1984); *Festina lente* (1988); *Magnificat* (1989); *Miserere* (1990); *Silounans song* (1991); *Litany* (1994); *I Am a True Wine* (1996); *Penitential canon*, for mixed choir (1996); *Missa sylabica*, for choir and organ (1996); and *Como anhela la vine*, for soprano and symphonic orchestra (1999). Pärt also composed film music. (AG)

Sources: *Eesti Entsuklopeedia*, vol. 14 (Tallinn, 2000); Paul Hillier, *Arvo Pärt* (Oxford, 1997); "Famous Estonians," http://spunk. mfa.ee/eng/famous/Part.htm; www.musicolog.com/part.asp.

PÁRTAY Tivadar (6 September 1908, Dombóvár–8 August 1999, Balatonszárszó), Hungarian politician. Pártay was the son of a railway worker. After graduating from a teacher training college in Miskolc (1929), he worked as a teacher and organist in the town of Arnót. He also ran his own farm. In 1932 he joined the Independent Smallholders' Party (ISP). In 1933 he became secretary of an ISP organization in Upper Hungary, and in 1939 he became one of its national leaders. From 1938 to 1943 Pártay worked as a journalist for the newspapers *Független Magyarság* and *Miskolci Holnap* in Miskolc. In 1938–41 he served in the army in the territories of Transcarpathian Ruthenia and northern Transylvania, which had been returned to Hungary. In September 1943 Pártay organized an anti-war demonstration in Miskolc. Because of this, he was sent to the eastern front, from which he returned in February 1944. In 1945 he was again elected chairman of the ISP in Upper Hungary. In September 1946 he became one of the senior leaders of the ISP, and from 1945 to 1948 he served as a member of parliament. In March 1945 Pártay became owner and editor of *Miskolci Hírlap*, and in September 1946, co-owner and editor-in-charge of the Budapest newspaper *A Reggel*. From 1945 to 1946 Pártay was head of the ISP organizational department. In March 1947 he left the party as a result of a conflict with Prime Minister **Ferenc Nagy**. In May 1947, after the Communists had forced Nagy to go into exile, Pártay returned to the ISP, but he soon came into conflict with its leaders, who were increasingly dependent on the Communists. Arrested in February 1949, Pártay was imprisoned in Kistarcsa and then in a forced labor camp in Recsk (1950–53). After his release, he worked as a blue-collar laborer. During the 1956 revolution Pártay helped to reorganize the ISP, and on 30 October 1956, he became its deputy secretary general. Arrested in May 1957, he was released in July 1958, and no legal proceedings were instituted against him. Pártay later worked in transport companies. He retired in 1973. In 1988 he took an active part in reviving the ISP. He was elected chairman of the party in November 1988 and its honorary chairman in 1989. In 1988 he was also one of the founders of the Historical Compensation Committee. In 1989–91 he was the editor-in-chief of *Kis Újság*, an ISP newspaper. In June 1991 Pártay left the ISP in protest against its demagogic political line. Pártay's memoirs, *Veszélyes évszázad* (Dangerous century), were published in 1997. (JT)

Sources: *A magyar forradalom és szabadságharc enciklopédiája*, CD-ROM (Budapest, 1999); *Magyar Nagylexikon*, vol. 14 (Budapest, 2002).

PÂRVULESCU Constantin (1895, Oltenia–11 July 1992, Bucharest?), Romanian Communist activist. Pârvulescu was connected wit the revolutionary movement from 1917, when he deserted from the Romanian Army and joined the Red Army. In 1921 he co-founded the Socialist Communist Party of Romania, which in 1922 took the name of the Communist Party of Romania (Partidul Comunist din România [PCR]). After it was made illegal in 1924, Pârvulescu was active in the underground. From 1929 he was a member of the PCR Central Committee (CC), and for a brief time in 1930 he was its general secretary. In 1934 Pârvulescu was arrested and put in jail. After a few years he managed to escape, and shortly before 1939 he

got to the Soviet Union. In 1942 he married an NKVD agent, Ana Toma. In early April 1944 Pârvulescu was sent to Romania, along with **Emil Bodnaraş** and **Iosif Rangheţ**, and the three of them ran the party until the coup of 23 August 1944. In 1945–61 Pârvulescu headed the Central Control Commission of the party (in 1948–65, the Romanian Workers' Communist Party). In 1948–49 and 1953–61 he was speaker of the parliament, and in 1955–60 he was a member of the CC Politburo. At the end of 1961, as a result of the power struggle in the party leadership, Pârvulescu was dismissed from all positions and disappeared from public sight. At a CC meeting he was criticized for "ideological deviation" and for his links with **Iosif Chişinevschi** and **Miron Constantinescu**. In 1989 Pârvulescu briefly returned to political life, signing the "Letter of 6"—written by former high-ranking Communist officials and criticizing **Nicolae Ceauşescu** for violating human rights. (LW)

Sources: Ion Raţiu, *Contemporary Romania* (Richmond, 1975); Klaus-Detlev Grothusen, ed., *Rumänien* (Göttingen, 1977); Ghiţă Ionescu, *Comunismul în România* (Bucharest, 1994); Dennis Deletant, *Communist Terror in Romania: Gheorghiu-Dej and the Police State, 1948–1965* (New York, 1999); Ion Alexandrescu, Ion Bulei, Ion Mamina, and Ioan Scurtu, *Enciclopedia de istorie României* (Bucharest, 2000).

PAŠIĆ Nikola (31 December 1845, Zaječar–10 December 1926, Belgrade), Serb politician, prime minister of Serbia and prime minister of the Kingdom of Serbs, Croats, and Slovenes. Pašić studied in Belgrade and then graduated from the Zurich Polytechnic in 1872. In 1878 he was elected to parliament, and as leader of the opposition, he resisted the authoritarian monarchy of Milan Obrenović. Pašić's aim was to establish a parliamentary democracy. He was one the founders of the Radical Party (1881). When a popular uprising against the government, organized by the Radicals in 1883, led to persecutions, Pašić fled to Bulgaria. He returned to Serbia after Milan's abdication in favor of his son, Alexander (1889), and he became president of the parliament. Pašić was also twice elected mayor of Belgrade. He served as prime minister for the first time from February 1891 to August 1892. Appointed minister plenipotentiary of Serbia to St. Petersburg in 1893, he returned to Serbia the following year. In 1899 there was an unsuccessful attempt on Alexander's life, and charges were brought against members of the Radical Party. Pašić was sentenced to death but was granted amnesty and left the country. After the coup d'état of 1903 and the restoration of the Karadjordjević dynasty, Pašić returned to Serbia and became one of its most important political figures.

As prime minister and minister of foreign affairs

(10 December 1904–28 May 1905, 29 April 1906–20 July 1907, and 24 October 1909–4 July 1911), Pašić broke away from the pro-Viennese policy of Obrenović and strengthened relations with Russia and France. In 1906–1911 he showed great skill in a trade war against Austria-Hungary. In 1911 his most powerful political rival, **Milovan Milovanović**, became prime minister. After his sudden death, on 12 September 1912 Pašić again became premier and minister of foreign affairs. Under his government Serbia was victorious in the two Balkan Wars.

After the assassination of Archduke Francis Ferdinand in Sarajevo on 28 June 1914, Pašić tried to avoid war against Austria-Hungary, as Serbia was militarily and economically exhausted after the Balkan Wars. His government accepted the humiliating ultimatum issued by the Viennese government with the exception of one point concerning the inquiry into the assassination being conducted by the Austrian authorities in Serbia. Nevertheless, on 28 July 1914 Austria-Hungary declared war on Serbia. After the defeat of the Serbian forces as a result of the Austro-Hungarian, Bulgarian, and German offensive, which began in October 1915, Pašić's government withdrew to Corfu (winter 1915). During World War I Pašić was prime minister of the government-in-exile. As an advocate of the concept of a Greater Serbia, he did not agree to the formation of a federal Yugoslavia in which Slovenes, Croats, and Serbs would be autonomous and equal. After the collapse of the ruling coalition in 1917, Pašić became the head of a government formed by the Radicals alone. His position was further weakened after the fall of the tsarist regime in Russia in 1917. Pašić took part in negotiations with the Yugoslav Committee in London (which also had claims as a government in exile), which resulted in the Corfu Declaration (20 July 1917). According to the declaration, the common aim of both political centers in exile would be the unification of Serbs, Croats, and Slovenes into one kingdom under the rule of the Karadjordjević dynasty.

On 1 December 1918 the Kingdom of Serbs, Croats, and Slovenes was formed. Pašić, with **Ante Trumbić**, a Croat, and **Ivan Žolger**, a Slovene, represented the new state at the Paris Peace Conference in 1919. After assuming the premiership on 1 January 1921, Pašić co-established the Vidovdan Constitution, which was passed on 28 June 1921. On 28 July 1924 he stepped down, but on 6 November 1924 he resumed the duties of prime minister. In February 1925 Pašić dissolved parliament and brought drastic measures against the opposition, including the imprisonment of **Stjepan Radić** and the delegalization of his Croat Peasant Party. However, after the elections an agreement was reached between Pašić and Radić, the latter becoming minister of education in Pašić's government, but the attempt at cooperation was not successful. Pašić would not withdraw his support for a Greater Serbia and his centralist concept, and he ignored the requests of Croats and Slovenes to create a federation based on the equality of the nations. On 8 April 1926 Pašić resigned and died soon afterwards. (AO)

Sources: *Biographisches Lexikon*, vol. 3; Carlo Sforza, *Fifty Years of War and Diplomacy in the Balkans: Pashich and the Union of the Yugoslavs* (New York, 1940); Charles Jelavich, "Nikola S. Pašić: Greater Serbia or Jugoslavia?" *Journal of Central European Affairs*, 1951–52; Alex N. Dragnich, *Serbia, Nikola Pašić, and Yugoslavia* (New Brunswick, N.J., 1974); Wacław Felczak and Tadeusz Wasilewski, *Historia Jugosławii* (Wrocław, 1985); Mark Biondich, *Stjepan Radić, the Croat Peasant Party, and the Politics of Mass Mobilization, 1904–1928* (Toronto, 2000).

PASKAI László (8 May 1927, Szeged), primate of Hungary. Paskai graduated from a Piarist high school in Szeged. In 1949 he took vows in the Franciscan order, and in 1951 he was ordained. In 1952–55 he was an assistant to the bishop of Szeged, and then he taught philosophy at the theological seminary there. In 1965–69 he worked as minister at the Central Theological Seminary (CTS) in Budapest, and he taught philosophy at Elte University there. In 1973–78 he was CTS rector. On 31 March 1978 Paskai was appointed bishop of Veszprém; on 5 April 1982, archbishop of Kalocsa-Kesckemét; and on 3 March 1987, archbishop of Esztergom and primate of Hungary. On 28 June 1988 he became a cardinal. In 1986–90 he chaired the Conference of the Hungarian Episcopate. After he turned seventy-five years of age, on 7 December 2002, Paskai retired. As primate of Hungary, Paskai continued the policies of compromise of his predecessor, **László Lékai**. After the fall of Communist rule, he prevented Church involvement in public life, even in moral debates. Until 1999 Paskai objected to a synod aimed at clearing the past accounts of many priests, at internal reforms in the Hungarian Catholic Church, and at the strengthening of the Church's position in its relations with the state. (AH)

Sources: József Török, *A magyar egyház évezrede* (Budapest, 2000); *Ki kicsoda* (Budapest, 2001); *In virtute spiritus: A Szent István Akadémia emlékkönyve Paskai László bíboros tiszteletére* (Budapest, 2003); www.catholic-hierarchy.org.

PASTUKHOV Kristio (15 October 1874, Sevlievo–25 August 1949, Sliven), Bulgarian Social Democratic politician. In 1895 Pastukhov completed law studies in Sofia, between 1897 and 1898 he specialized in Germany, and then he practiced at the bar. From 1903 he belonged to the Bulgarian Social Democratic Workers' Party, and from the beginning he sided with the moderate majority faction of the party. From 1909 he was a member of the Central Committee (CC) of the party. From 1911 Pastukhov was an MP, and in 1911–34 he was the editor of the journal *Narod*. Between May and October 1919 he was minister of interior. In the interwar period he gradually moved toward the leadership of the Social Democratic party. In the 1930s Pastukhov opposed a rapprochement between Bulgaria and Germany. In February 1935 he appealed in an open letter to Tsar **Boris III** for the restoration of the Turnovo Constitution; because of this he was temporarily interned on St. Anastasia Island. Pastukhov was a co-organizer of a democratic agreement of five parties, called the Petorka (The Five), which in May 1936 demanded that the tsar restore democracy. He supported cooperation with the Western democracies, for which he was sharply attacked by the Communists, especially in 1939–40. In February 1941, along with the leaders of the opposition, Pastukhov submitted a letter to the tsar demanding the neutrality of Bulgaria. He refused to join the Fatherland Front, which was formed in the summer of 1942, because he thought it was too dependent on the USSR. In the summer of 1943 Tsar Boris III considered entrusting Pastukhov with the task of forming a government that was to announce Bulgaria's neutrality. After the sudden death of Boris, Pastukhov was one of the signatories of an appeal for the establishment of the Grand National Assembly and the withdrawal of Bulgaria from the war. He intended to join the government of **Konstantin Muraviov**, but the leaders of the party dissuaded him from that step. On 7 August 1944, along with twelve other leaders of the opposition, Pastukhov signed a declaration demanding a fundamental change in Bulgarian policy: withdrawal from the alliance with the Axis powers and rapprochement with the Allies.

After the coup of 9 September 1944 in Sofia, Pastukhov courageously defended the independence of Social Democracy and opposed the Communist dictatorship. On 25 January 1945 he was expelled from the leadership and from the ranks of the Social Democrats by the pro-Communist faction. From June 1945 Pastukhov worked toward the creation of a Social Democratic party that would be independent of the Communists. From 1945 to 1946 Pastukhov was the editor of the journal *Svoboden Narod*. On 22 February 1946, he published an article in it asking, "Why Do You Tempt Me, You Hypocrites?" It was the reason for his arrest four days later. In June 1946 Pastukhov was sentenced to five years of prison for "anti-people activities." In prison, he was strangled by a criminal. Pastukhov was the author of several works, including *Koi e iskal voinata?* (Who sought war? 1913); *Desetgodishninata na ruskata revolutsiia: Borbata me-*

zhdu Stalin i Trotsky (The tenth anniversary of the Russian Revolution: The fight between Stalin and Trotsky; 1928); *Demokratsiia i diktatura* (Democracy and dictatorship; 1929); and *Petiletka i protsesi* (The five-year plan and the trials; 1931). (JJ/WR)

Sources: *Kratka bulgarska entsiklopediya*, vol. 4; M. L. Miller, *Jerzy Jackowicz, Partie opozycyjne w Bułgarii 1944–1948* (Warsaw, 1997); Tasho Tashev, *Ministrite na Bulgariya 1897–1999* (Sofia, 1999).

PATEK Stanisław (1 May 1866, Rusinów, near Kozienice–22 August 1944, Warsaw), Polish diplomat. After graduating from high school in Radom, Patek studied law at Warsaw University, graduating in 1889. He subsequently did a legal internship, and in 1894 he became an attorney in Warsaw. He was the defense counsel in many political trials. During the 1905 revolution Patek established ties with the Polish Socialist Party (Polska Partia Socjalistyczna [PPS]) and with **Józef Piłsudski**, whom he sheltered in his flat. In April 1905 Patek signed a memorandum calling for autonomy for the Kingdom of Poland. In February 1908 he was arrested on charges of maintaining contacts with revolutionary groups. After his release, Patek was disbarred (May 1911), which led to protests by Russian liberal lawyers. They published *Delo prisiazhnago paverennago Patka* (The case of Defense Counsel Patek; 1911), which documented his case. Patek became chairman of the Mutual Credit Company (Towarzystwo Wzajemnego Kredytu) in Warsaw. After the outbreak of World War I, he went to Kraków, where he attended sessions of the Supreme National Committee (Naczelny Komitet Narodowy). He subsequently went westward and used his Masonic contacts to present Piłsudski's political goals to prominent Entente politicians, including Georges Clemenceau, and British diplomats. After returning to Warsaw, Patek established contacts with Russian Constitutional Democratic politicians. After the Germans seized Warsaw in 1915, Patek joined the Civic Guard. Briefly detained, in July 1916 he became a member of the City Council, and from September 1917 until the end of November 1918 he was chairman of the criminal department of the Court of Appeals. Patek was a member of the Le Rénovateur Masonic lodge, which was linked with the Grand East lodge in Paris; as a representative of the latter he helped to organize Polish Masonic lodges, including Zmartwychwstanie (Resurrection) and Kopernik.

After Poland regained its independence, Patek became a judge of the Supreme Court, but as early as December 1918 he went to France, where, as a representative of Piłsudski, he joined the Polish National Committee (Komitet Narodowy Polski [KNP]). Patek was supposed to become Poland's representative to Czechoslovakia, but he did not take up that appointment because he was too busy working with the KNP and the Polish delegation to the Paris Peace Conference. In November 1919, as a result of his efforts and the support of Clemenceau, the Supreme Council of the Entente rejected a decision concerning East Galicia that was unfavorable to Poland. In December 1919 Patek became minister of foreign affairs in the government of **Leopold Skulski**, and he strictly followed Piłsudski's policies. After this cabinet resigned in June 1920, Patek entered the army. He attended the Spa Conference and later took part in the battles of the First Light Cavalry Regiment. From 1921 to 1925 Patek was an envoy of the Republic of Poland to Japan. After the coup of May 1926, Piłsudski appointed him envoy to the Soviet Union. Patek enjoyed the respect of some Soviet government officials who remembered his courageous defense of revolutionaries. He brought about a certain degree of détente in Polish-Soviet relations: on behalf of Poland, he signed the Litvinov Protocol on 9 February 1929 and the Soviet-Polish Non-Aggression Pact on 25 July 1932. In January 1933 Patek became ambassador to the United States and an envoy to Cuba. In April 1936 he was recalled because of illness. Soon afterwards Patek was appointed to the Senate by President **Ignacy Mościcki**. Patek published *Ze wspomnień obrońcy* (From the memoirs of a defense attorney). During the Nazi occupation Patek continued writing his memoirs, but they were destroyed during the Warsaw Uprising. Patek was killed in a bomb explosion during the 1944 fighting in Warsaw's Old Town. His illegitimate son, Aleksander Sonie, was a Soviet diplomat. (WR)

Sources: *PSB*, vol. 25; Stanisław Łoza, *Czy wiesz kto to jest* (Warsaw, 1937); Tytus Komarnicki, *Rebirth of the Polish Republic* (London, 1957); Władysław Pobóg-Malinowski, *Najnowsza historia polityczna Polski*, vol. 2 (London, 1967); Jerzy Holzer and Jan Molenda, *Polska w pierwszej wojnie światowej* (Warsaw, 1973); Marian Leczyk, *Polityka II Rzeczypospolitej wobec ZRR w latach 1925–1934* (Warsaw, 1976); Ludwik Hass, *Masoneria polska XX wieku* (Warsaw, 1996).

PATOČKA Jan (1 June 1907, Trutnov, near Semily–13 March 1977, Prague), Czech philosopher. After passing his high school final exams in Prague (1925), Patočka began studies in philosophy and Romance and Slavic languages at Charles University in Prague. In 1928–29 he studied at the Sorbonne in Paris, where he met Edmund Husserl for the first time. After receiving a Ph.D. in 1931, Patočka continued his studies in Berlin and Freiburg, where he worked with Husserl and Martin Heidegger. From then on, phenomenology became the foundation of Patočka's philosophy. In 1936 he received the postdoc-

toral degree from the Department of Philology, Charles University. Until 1944 Patočka taught at a Prague high school. After World War II, he worked as a lecturer at the universities in Prague and Brno. In 1950 he was banned from teaching for political reasons. Until 1954 he worked at the Tomáš Garrigue Masaryk Institute, and after its closure he began working at the Jan Ámos Komenský Pedagogical Institute, where he was responsible for editing the works by Komenský. Patočka was also engaged in editorial work from 1956 to 1968, when he worked in the editorial department of the Institute of Philosophy of the Czechoslovak Academy of Sciences. In 1968 he was appointed professor of philosophy and was allowed to resume teaching in Prague and Brno. He was often invited to lecture at many European academic centers and was granted an honorary doctorate by the University of Aachen. Retired for political reasons in 1971, Patočka was banned from giving public speeches. He was an active lecturer of the secret "flying university," which attracted informal groups of academic youth.

Patočka drew on the thought of Komenský, Masaryk, and Husserl. He emphasized the need to anchor the moral dimension of the human being in an epoch that negated this dimension. In *Prirozený svet jako filozofický problém* (The natural world as a philosophical problem; 1936) he depicted and analyzed the "natural world," seeking its metaphysical foundations. Patočka defended the right of an individual to perceive himself as free despite a totalitarian system. He wrote studies, articles, and literary and philosophical essays. He made major contributions to the development of Czech philosophical thought in the twentieth century. He also analyzed Czech national consciousness in *Dve studie o Masarykovi* (Two studies on Masaryk; 1977), *Náš národní program* (Our national program; 1990), and *Co jsou Češi?* (Who are the Czechs? 1992). Patočka spiritually inspired the opposition in Czechoslovakia. He understood the activities of the opposition as the efforts of a community of "awakened" people who strove to conquer lawlessness and establish a society that would recognize human rights and give its citizens a chance for proper moral development. In 1976 Patočka joined protests against the harassment of the rock group Plastic People of the Universe. In January 1977 he was a co-founder and one of the first three spokesmen (along with **Václav Havel** and **Jiři Hajek**) for Charter 77. Patočka died as a result of exhausting secret police interrogations that lasted many days. His funeral turned into an anti-Communist demonstration. Patočka's publications also include *Aristoteles: Jeho předchouci a dedicové* (Aristotle: His forerunners and his heirs; 1964); *Kacířské eseje o filozofii dějin* (1975; *Heretical Essays* *in the Philosophy of History*, 1996); and *Negativní platonismus* (Negative Platonism; 1990). In 1997 Patočka's multi-volume *Sebrané spisy* (Collected works) began to be published. (AGr)

Sources: *Kdo byl kdo w našich dějinách ve 20. stoleti* (Prague, 1994); *Slovnik českých filozofů* (Brno, 1998; including a full bibliography of his works); *Studien zur Philosophie von Jan Patocka* (Freiburg, 1985); Miroslav Bednár, *České myslení* (Prague, 1996); Ivan Blecha, *Jan Patočka* (Olomouc, 1997); Halina Janaszek-Ivaničkova, ed., *Literatury zachodniosłowiańskie czasu przełomu 1890–1990*, vol. 2 (Katowice, 1999); Edward F. Findlay, *Caring for the Soul in a Postmodern Age: Politics and Phenomenology in the Thought of Jan Patocka* (Albany, N.Y., 2002); www.totalita.cz.

PĂTRĂŞCANU Lucreţiu (4 November 1900, Iaşi–17 April 1954, Bucharest), Romanian Communist activist. The son of a well-known writer, after completing law studies in Bucharest (1922), Pătrăşcanu studied in France and Germany, earning a doctorate in law and economics from Leipzig University for a dissertation on Romanian agrarian reform. In 1921 he joined the Communist Party of Romania (CPR) and acted as defense counsel in the trials of Communist activists. In 1931 he was elected to the parliament on the ticket of a crypto-Communist bloc of workers and peasants whose mandates were invalidated. At the Second CPR Congress in 1932 Pătrăşcanu was elected to its Central Committee (CC). At that time he called for cooperation with democratic and peasant parties in the spirit of a popular front, yet he did not question the territorial program of the Comintern, which called for incorporating Bessarabia into the USSR and separating Transylvania and Dobrudja from Romania. From 1933 to 1934 Pătrăşcanu was a representative of the CPR in the Comintern. After returning to Romania, he worked in the propaganda apparatus in Iaşi. From 1924 to 1941 he was arrested six times.

From 1943 to 1944 Pătrăşcanu was under house arrest in Poiana Ţapului, near Sinaia, but he was kept informed about plans to withdraw Romania from an alliance with Germany by Colonel Octava Ulea, the master of ceremonies at the royal court. In April 1944 Pătrăşcanu entered into close cooperation with **Titel Petrescu**, leader of the Social Democrats, and he even planned to establish a united workers' front. On 20 June 1944, on behalf of the Communist Party, Pătrăşcanu signed an agreement with the liberals, the Peasant Party, and the Social Democrats. This agreement, known as the National Democratic Bloc (NDB), was supported by King **Michael**. The NDB wanted Romania to switch to the Allied side and planned to overthrow Marshal **Ion Antonescu** in case he objected. Pătrăşcanu took part in the final preparations for a coup. On 23 August 1944 he became minister of justice in the coalition government established by General **Constantin Sănătescu** after the overthrow of Antonescu's regime, and he held this post in subsequent cabinets.

On 29 July 1944 Pătrăşcanu became head of the Romanian delegation to cease-fire negotiations with the Soviet Union in Moscow. He became known as a tough negotiator, speaking more on behalf of the new coalition government than on behalf of the Romanian Communist Party (RCP, as the party was renamed in 1943), a position that the Kremlin did not like. The overthrow of Antonescu and Romania's switch to the Allied side had interfered with Stalin's plans to destroy Antonescu's regime by Red Army forces and to treat Romania as a Third Reich satellite and a subjugated country. Pătrăşcanu confirmed his independent position in an interview for the Soviet news agency TASS in December 1944, when he criticized the RCP leadership for overthrowing the government of General Sănătescu, who, according to Pătrăşcanu, was more agreeable to the Communists than the new prime minister, General **Nicolae Rădescu**. In June 1945 Pătrăşcanu spoke at a rally in Cluj and attacked those who had spread rumors that the Romanian administration in Transylvania was only provisional. Actually, such rumors had been started by the Kremlin, which wanted to hold the Romanians in check by keeping them uncertain over the fate of this region. At the party's national conference in October 1945 Pătrăşcanu joined the RCP CC but failed to enter the Politburo. As head of the ministry of justice, he purged the judiciary by filling key posts with simpletons obedient to the RCP. He also endorsed court trials, not only against representatives of Antonescu's regime, but also against leaders of democratic parties. In that way he precipitated his tragic end.

Neither Stalin nor the RCP leadership, headed by **Gheorghe Gheorghiu-Dej**, liked Pătrăşcanu's genuine popularity and his intellectual manners. From 1946 he was the target of increasing criticism. In February 1947 he nonetheless attended the Paris Peace Conference, which led to a peace treaty with Romania. On 22 February 1948, at the "unification" congress of the Communist Party and the Socialist Party, Pătrăşcanu was frontally attacked by **Teohari Georgescu**, the minister of interior; **Vasile Luca**, a member of the Politburo; and others for "yielding to bourgeois influences." The CC Plenum openly denounced his tactic of making alliances with peasant parties and his policy of "nationalism," and soon "Titoism" was added to these accusations. Detained under house arrest on Lake Snagov, near Bucharest, on 28 April, Pătrăşcanu was formally arrested on 24 August. From January 1949 he was brutally interrogated by security officers, who were ordered by Gheorghiu-Dej to force Pătrăşcanu to admit to working with King Michael's security services. Although some of Pătrăşcanu's co-workers testified against him under torture, he himself did not admit to the charges. In September 1952, the fall of the Ana Pauker-Luca faction, which had opposed executing Pătrăşcanu, sealed his fate. Chief Investigating Officer **Mişu Dulgheru** was arrested for delays in conducting the investigation, and the case was taken over by Aleksandr Sakharovsky, the MGB adviser to the Romanian Ministry of Interior. In January 1954 a Romanian Workers' Party delegation headed by **Miron Constantinescu** presented charges against Pătrăşcanu to Soviet Prime Minister Georgy Malenkov and was given permission to execute him. During the trial Pătrăşcanu was falsely accused of spying for the United States and Great Britain, knowingly maintaining informers of the royal security services in the party leadership, and even of cooperating with Antonescu's regime against the RCP and the Soviet Union. Pătrăşcanu did not admit to these charges. After one week of "trial," the RCP Politburo decided to close his case. He was sentenced to death on 14 April 1954. He refused to ask for a pardon and was soon afterwards executed. At an RCP CC Plenum in April 1968 **Nicolae Ceauşescu** brought about Pătrăşcanu's rehabilitation, which was part of Ceauşescu's attempt to gain full control over the party, in which people responsible for Pătrăşcanu's death were still playing a leading role. (WR)

Sources: Arthur Gould Lee, *Crown against Sickle: The Story of King Michael of Rumania* (London, 1953); Ghita Ionescu, *Communism in Romania, 1944–1962* (London, 1964); Andrzej Koryn, *Rumunia w polityce wielkich mocarstw 1944–1947* (Wrocław, 1983); *Principiul Bumerangului: Documente ale Procesului Lucreţiu Pătrăşcanutrial documents* (Bucharest, 1996); Dennis Deletant, *Communist Terror in Romania: Gheorghiu-Dej and the Police State, 1948–1965* (New York, 1999); I. E. Russu, *Lukretsyu Patrashkanu* (St. Petersburg, 2001).

PÄTS Konstantin (23 February 1874, Tahkuranna–18 January 1956, Burashevo, near Kalinin [Tver], USSR), Estonian politician. Born into a peasant family, after graduating from a high school in Pärnu, Päts studied law at the University of Dorpat (Tartu), earning the title of candidate of law in 1898. He served in the army for one year and then worked in the office of an influential attorney in Tallinn, **Jaan Poska**, in 1900–1. Influenced by leftist ideology, Päts treated national liberation and social reforms as equally important issues. He supported the democratic movement in Russia because he hoped to reduce the economic advantage of Germans in Estonia and wanted to implement social reforms that could win the support of Estonians for the idea of a national state. In 1901 Päts founded *Teataja*, a radical newspaper in

which he promoted his views and published articles by representatives of the Estonian elite, including **Eduard Vilde, Anton H. Taamsaare, Jaan Teemant,** and **Mihkel Martna**. In 1904 he became a member of the Tallinn City Council. During the 1905 revolution he was deputy mayor of Tallinn and one of the leaders of an Estonian revolutionary uprising in Tallinn. After the fall of the revolution, a court martial sentenced him to death in absentia. Päts fled Estonia and lived in exile in Switzerland and Finland from 1906 to 1909. In 1909 he gave himself up to the St. Petersburg court authorities, who mitigated his sentence to a nine-month imprisonment, which he served in Kresty Prison, St. Petersburg. He continued to publish his articles in *Peterburi Teataja*. After his release, he edited *Tallina Teataja* (1911–16).

From 1916 to 1917 Päts briefly served in the tsarist army. After the February 1917 revolution, he was instrumental in the establishment of Estonian statehood. He was elected chairman of the Estonian National Council (Maapäev [ENC]), an autonomous body within the framework of the Russian state, and on 12 October 1917 he became head of the Estonian Provisional Government (Ajutise Maavalitsus). After the ENC was abolished by the local Bolsheviks and German forces entered Estonia, the offices of the Estonian state went underground. In February 1918 Päts became chairman of the Estonian Salvation Committee (Eesti Päästmises Komitee [ESC]), and, along with **Jüri Vilms** and **Konstantin Konik**, he assumed full power. On 24 February 1918 the ESC issued a declaration of Estonian independence, and Päts became prime minister of the Provisional Government of the Republic of Estonia and minister of interior. Arrested by the Germans, Päts was sent to a detention camp in the Polish territories, where he was held for half a year. On 11 November 1918 he returned to Estonia and again assumed the post of prime minister.

Päts's term was a particularly difficult time in the war of independence, but he managed to control the situation, and Estonian troops forced the Bolsheviks out of the country. However, because of Päts opposition to revolutionary proposals to expropriate land from German owners without compensation, as suggested by the left wing, the Rural Union (Maaliit), under Päts's leadership, lost in the elections to the Constitutional Assembly in May 1919. Päts was forced to resign. He reorganized the Rural Union into the Farmers' Union (Pollumeeste Kogu [FU]), which ran in the November 1920 elections under the slogan of using the reforms to modernize the country. As a consequence Päts not only regained the public trust, but also won the support of many previously landless peasants to whom the left wing gave ownership of land. The FU—on the right side of the parliamentary political spectrum—enjoyed the stable support of some 20–40 percent of the voters. As a result, Päts served as *riigivanem* (equivalent to president and prime minister) of Estonia from 25 January 1921 to 21 November 1922, from 2 August 1923 to 26 March 1924, and from 12 February 1931 to 19 February 1932. The FU was part of most of the cabinets. Päts was also an influential businessman and served as chairman of the Estonian branch of Lloyd's and chairman of the board of the Estonian Chamber of Industry. The collapse of the agrarian bank, with which he was linked, became a public scandal.

Päts early on sought to strengthen the executive branch of government, and from 1926 onwards he repeatedly proposed relevant constitutional amendments. The beginning of his third term as *riigivanem* in February 1931 coincided with the Great Depression, increased social discontent, and a looming threat of a takeover of power by the extremely rightist Estonian League of War of Independence Veterans (Eesti Vabadussojalaste Liit [EVL]). A constitutional bill proposed by Päts in 1932 was rejected because of the opposition of the Socialists; therefore, Päts supported a proposal by the EVL that received the support of the majority of voters in an October 1933 referendum. On 21 October 1933 Päts established a new government, this time as an interim cabinet until a new constitution came into force. With the help of an ally, General **Johan Laidoner**, who wielded great influence in the army, on 12 March 1934 Päts staged a coup and then introduced an authoritarian regime. Political parties were disbanded, censorship was introduced, and the police were given greater powers. Päts's regime was politically based on the bureaucracy, the army, and the Fatherland League (Isamaaliit), established in 1935. In August 1937 the National Assembly adopted a new constitution, which came into force at the beginning of 1938. It gave great legislative powers to the president, the post Päts assumed on 24 April 1938. Economic prosperity in the second half of the 1930s strengthened public support for the regime, which interfered in the freedom of economic activities through the trade unions. The struggle against the opposition continued until 1939, but in comparison with other dictatorships of that time Päts's regime had a relatively mild character.

In late September 1939 Päts accepted a treaty that allowed for the de facto occupation of Estonia by the Soviet Union and for the establishment of Soviet military bases without real control by Estonian authorities. This treaty was a consequence of the Molotov-Ribbentrop Pact of 23 August 1939. In June 1940, after the Soviet Union had given a new ultimatum; new units of the Red Army had entered Estonia; and Moscow's delegate, Andrey Zhdanov,

had arrived in Tallinn, Päts appointed the government of **Johannes Vares**, which consisted of Communists or Communist adherents, thus sealing the end of Estonian independence. Following the so-called people's elections of July 1940, the results of which were falsified by the Communists, Päts was dismissed and a few days later deported to Siberia, where he died after the end of World War II.

Päts's role as one of the founding fathers and head of an independent Estonia and then his deportation made him a martyr for the national cause. The respect he enjoyed among the Estonian people increased when, in 1977, his letters from prison were published in the West. In these letters he exhorted the Estonians to keep up their resistance and hope. In 1990 thousands of Estonians gathered at a ceremony at which his remains were returned to Estonia on the day before Estonia regained independence. Meanwhile, in 1999, after ten years of searching in the Moscow archives, the Estonian historian Magnus Ilmjärv declared that in the 1920s Päts had regularly received $4,000 from Soviet security services, which allegedly took advantage of the collapse of the agricultural bank to induce Päts into cooperation by offering him cash to save him from financial troubles. The documents Ilmjärv published also indicated that until the end of the 1920s Päts was on the payroll as the director of the Estonian-Soviet Chamber of Commerce, whose losses were defrayed by the Kremlin. These revelations became the subject of heated polemics. Because of disagreements among historians, the key question–that is, the impact of Päts's possible cooperation with Soviet services on his policies—remains without a clear-cut answer. (AG)

Sources: *Eesti Vabariigi president Konstantin Päts* (Tallinn, 1938); Eduard Laaman, *Konstantin Päts: Politiika-ja riigimees* (Stockholm, 1949); *Estonia: Story of a Nation* (New York, 1974); Märt Raud, *Kaks suurt: Jaan Tõnisson, Konstantin Päts ja nende ajastu* (Tallinn, 1991); Andres Kasekamp, *The Radical Right in Interwar Estonia* (London, 1995); *Res Publica*, 11 September 1999; Mel Huang, "Historical Regicide," *Central European Review*, 27 September 1999; East European Constitutional Review, 1999, no. 4; Ulrike Plath and Karsten Brüggemann, "Vom Tanz mit des Teufels Großmutter: Die estnische Debatte um die Zusammenarbeit von Präsident Konstantin Päts mit der Sowjetunion," *Osteuropa*, 2000, no. 50; www.president.ee/eng/president.

PAUKER Ana [née Rabinsohn] (12 December 1893, Codăeşti–14 June 1960, Bucharest), Romanian Communist activist. Pauker was born into an Orthodox Jewish family, and her grandfather was a rabbi. She completed university studies and after that, from 1915 to 1921, belonged to a Social Democratic party. In 1921, along with her husband, **Marcel Pauker**, she joined the newly created

Communist Party of Romania (CPR). The next year, partly because of an intimate relationship with its leader, **Elek Köblös**, she became a member of the Central Committee of the party. Between 1928 and 1932 Pauker studied in the Comintern School in Moscow, while her husband was the leader of the party. She went as a Comintern agent to France (1931) and to other countries. In 1932, when Marcel Pauker was dismissed as the secretary general of the CPR, she became a member of the Secretariat of the Central Committee. Marcel Pauker was arrested in the USSR during the Great Purge, and his wife distanced herself from him and accused him of "Trotskyism." Soon afterwards Marcel Pauker was executed. On 14 July 1935 Ana Pauker was arrested by the Romanian authorities and on 5 June 1936 sentenced to ten years of prison in a trial that won her popularity. In 1940 she was exchanged for Romanian prisoners in the USSR and returned to Moscow. She was active in the Executive Committee of the Comintern and was a member until 1943. She spoke on radio broadcasts in Romanian and organized the Tudor Vladimirescu Division among Romanian captives in the USSR. At that time she opposed the establishment of treaties with King **Michael I** by the Communists and spoke in favor of an overthrow of the regime of Marshal **Ion Antonescu** directly by the Red Army.

In September 1944 Pauker, who played a major role in the Communist takeover of power, went to Bucharest. She belonged to both the Secretariat and the Politburo of the CC of the CPR. She directed the organizational affairs of the party; among other things, the party admitted thousands of former members of the Iron Guard, who were otherwise threatened with death. In February 1945 Pauker spoke in favor of a possibly swift overthrow of the government of General **Nicolae Radescu**. From November 1947, after the deposal of **Gheorghe Tătărescu**, she was the minister of foreign affairs, and in February 1948, the secretary of the CC for agriculture. In the latter role Pauker was responsible for forced collectivization, which began in March 1949 and during which thousands of peasants perished. Pauker attended conferences of the Communist Information Bureau (Cominform). From 1949 she was deputy prime minister. She took an active part in the deposal and conviction of **Lucrețiu Pătrășcanu** and in the personnel purges in the party at the end of the 1940s. However, during a mounting anti-Semitic campaign Pauker's situation became increasingly difficult. Her Jewish origins and her contacts with Communists who had fought in the International Brigades in Spain gradually turned against her. Stalin was already insisting on her deposal. Pauker was attacked, along with **Vasile Luca** and **Teohari Georgescu**, for hesitation about a monetary reform that would deprive people of their savings, and she was accused of disloyalty at a meeting of the Politburo on 26 May 1952. On 12 September 1952 Pauker was deposed from all her posts, which was a signal of a new purge in the party. Imprisoned in February 1953, Pauker remained for some time under house arrest, but she was released in February 1954 and was even given a job as an editor in the Editura Politică publishing house. The *New York Times* announced her death, but the Romanian press made no mention of it at all. (WR)

Sources: *New York Times*, 15 June 1960; Branko Lazich, ed. *Biographical Dictionary of the Comintern*, (Stanford, 1973); Ghita Ionescu, *Communism in Rumania, 1944–1962* (Oxford, 1964); Dennis Deletant, *Communist Terror in Romania: Gheorghiu-Dej and the Police State, 1948–1965* (New York, 1999); Robert Levy, *Ana Pauker: The Rise and Fall of a Jewish Communist* (Berkeley, 2000).

PAUKER Marcel (1901, Bucharest–16 August 1938, Moscow), Romanian Communist activist. Pauker came from an intellectual Jewish family. At first he was a trade union activist. After graduating from a Lutheran school and after obtaining a Ph.D. in law in Paris, he joined the Communist Party, which was being organized at that time. In June 1921 he married **Ana Rabinsohn (Pauker)**, who later played a leading role in postwar Romania. In November 1921 Pauker represented Romania at a congress of trade unions of the Balkan countries in Sofia. In 1922 he joined the CC of the Communist Party of Romania (CPR), being a favorite of **Khristian Rakovski**. As such, he had a strong influence on the activities of the party on behalf of the Communist International. Pauker attended the Fourth Congress of the Comintern in 1922. When in 1924 the CPR was declared illegal, Pauker left for the USSR. Under the pseudonyms "Popescu" and "Luximin," he worked in the head office of the Comintern, attending its subsequent congresses. At the end of the 1920s he took control of the party, appointing its ruling "directory," with himself as its head. In 1929 he arrived secretly in Romania but was arrested. Released under amnesty, for over two years he was active in the underground before returning to the USSR. In 1931, the Comintern appointed Alexandru Stefanski, who was a member of the Communist Party of Poland, to be head of the party for a short time. In 1932 Pauker was expelled from the leadership of the party for "Trotskyism." His wife also left him and denounced his views. Arrested during the Great Purge, Pauker was sentenced to death and executed. According to information obtained from Soviet archives by his daughter, Tatiana Brătescu, Pauker was executed by a firing squad at the rifle range of the NKVD in Butovo, near Moscow. (WR)

Sources: Lazitch; Ghita Ionescu, *Communism in Rumania, 1944–1962* (Oxford, 1964); Robert R. King, *History of the Romanian Communist Party* (Stanford, 1980); Florin Constantiniu, ed., *O ancheta stalinista 1937–1938: Lichidarea lui Marcel Pauker* (Bucharest, 1995); Dennis Deletant, *Communist Terror in Romania: Gheorghiu-Dej and the Police State*, *1948–1965* (New York, 1999).

PAUL Karadjordjević (also spelled Karageorgevic) (28 April 1893, St. Petersburg–15 September 1976, Paris), regent of Yugoslavia from 1934 to 1941. The son of Arsen Karadjordjević (who was the brother of **Peter I Karadjordjević**) and Andra Dimidova, Paul was the cousin of **Alexander I Karadjordjević**. Educated at Oxford, he spent most of his youth in England. Absent from the country during both Balkan Wars and during World War I, Paul mainly dealt with art, and he knew little about the political problems of Yugoslavia. After the death of King Alexander I, who was murdered in Marseilles in October 1934, Paul became a member of the Regency Council, which exercised power on behalf of Alexander's minor son, Peter II. Actually, however, Paul became regent. He followed the policies of his predecessor, but in the face of tensions in Croatia and as the international situation of Yugoslavia deteriorated, on 6 June 1939 he authorized an agreement that granted the Croats some autonomy within the framework of the unitary state. Aligned with the British conservatives, who hoped for an agreement with Hitler, Paul worked toward a rapprochement between Berlin and London, although in fact he yielded to the mounting pressure of Germany. During Paul's visit to Berchtesgaden on 4 March 1941, Hitler informed Paul about his plans to attack the USSR. Nonetheless, Paul did not agree to Yugoslavia's accession to the Tripartite Pact. Finally, however, under pressure from Germany, the government agreed to sign the accession to the anti-Comintern Pact, which took place on 26 March 1941. The next day a group of officers and politicians overthrew the regents' rule and proclaimed Peter king. This led to the German invasion, the partition of Yugoslavia, and the occupation of a great part of Yugoslav territory by the Third Reich. Paul left for Greece and then for Kenya and South Africa, giving up his political role. At the end of his life he lived in France. (WR)

Sources: *Biographisches Lexikon*, vol. 3; Jacob B. Hoptner, *Yugoslavia in Crisis, 1934–1941* (New York, 1962); R. L. Knejevitch, "Prince Paul, Hitler and Salonika," *International Affairs*, 1951, vol. 27, no. 1.

PAUĻUKS Jānis (24 November 1865, Lielsesavas, Courland–21 June 1937, Bauska), Latvian politician. In 1885 Pauļuks finished a *Realschule* in Mitava (Jelgava), and in 1892 he graduated from the Technical University in Riga. From 1892 to 1894 he was an engineer with the railroad board in Riga, and from 1894 to 1897, an engineer during the construction of the Yekaterinburg-Chelabinsk railroad line. In 1897–1905 Pauļuks held responsible posts during the construction of the Transbaikal Railroad and later in the Urals, Northern Caucasia, and Stavropol Province. From 1920 to 1921 he was held prisoner by the Soviet authorities. In February 1921 Pauļuks returned to Latvia and became an engineer in the Latvian Main Railroad Board in Riga. From January 1921 to December 1925 he served as minister of transportation, and from 25 January to 26 June 1923 he also held the post of prime minister. In 1926–27 Pauļuks was inspector general at the Ministry of Transportation and a member of the Railroad Construction Council. After retiring in 1927, he was a private entrepreneur. In 1934 Pauļuks was granted an honorary doctorate by the University of Latvia. (EJ)

Sources: *Latviešu konversācijas vārdnīca*, vol. 16 (Riga, 1937–38); Alfreds Bilmanis, *Latvia as an Independent State* (Washington, D.C., 1947); Piotr Łossowski, *Kraje bałtyckie na drodze od demokracji parlamentarnej do dyktatury (1918–1934)* (Wrocław, 1972); *Latvijas valsts un tās vīri* (Riga, 1999).

PAVEL Ota [originally Otto Popper] (2 July 1930, Prague–31 March 1973, Prague), Czech journalist and writer. Pavel was born into the family of a Jewish peddler. His childhood coincided with the time of Nazi persecutions, and his father and brother were sent to concentration camps. In 1947 Pavel finished a two-year school of commerce. In 1949 he became a radio sports commentator. In 1956 he left radio and began writing sports reports for newspapers. In 1960 he passed his high school final examinations at a high school for adults. From 1964 until the end of his life Pavel struggled with mental illness, which forced him to quit work and claim a disability benefit in 1966. Pavel's best sports books include *Dukla mezi mrakodrapy* (Dukla among the skyscrapers; 1964), *Plná bedna šampaňského* (A barrel full of champagne; 1967), and *Pohádka o Raškovi* (A fable about Raška; 1974). Full of lyricism, the stories based on his childhood experiences are Pavel's greatest literary achievement. He combined idyllic descriptions of nature and the village of Berounki with reminiscences of the war. These stories make up a cycle of memoirs; they are full of humor, irony, and philosophical reflections that praise the basic values of life. Pavel did not idealize life, but he did not take a tragic view of things either. These stories were collected in two volumes, *Smrt krásných srnců* (The death of a beautiful roe deer; 1971) and *Jak jsem potkal ryby* (1974; *How I Came to Know Fish*, 1991). In 1991 the full collection of Pavel's stories *Zlatí úhoři* (Golden eels) was published, which included pieces previously excluded by the censors.

Some of his prose has been adapted for film. Pavel's works have also been frequently adapted for the stage, turned into radio plays, and translated into many languages, including English. (PU)

Sources: ČBS; Kdo byl kdo v našich dějinach ve 20. stoleti, vol. 2 (Prague, 1998); Slovník českých spisovatelů od roku 1945, vol. 2 (Prague, 1998); Otakar Brůna and Jan Šimon Fiala, Slzy na stoncích trávy Oty Pavla (Prague, 1990); Věra Pavlová, Vzpomínání na Otu Pavla (Prague, 1993); Otakar Brůna, Potkat Otu Pavla (Třebíč, 2000).

PAVELIĆ Ante (14 July 1889, Bradina, Bosnia–28 December 1959, Madrid), lawyer and head of the Ustaša Croatian state during World War II. After completing his studies, Pavelić worked as an attorney in Zagreb, where he joined the rightist and anti-Semitic National Party (Čista Stranka Prava) of **Josip Frank**. Elected to the Croatian Assembly (Sabor), in May 1917 Pavelić supported the declaration of the Yugoslav Club in the Austrian Reichsrat (Council of the Realm), which advocated the unification of Croats, Serbs, and Slovenes under Habsburg rule. This meant his separation from Frank's party. On 5 October 1918 the National Council of Slovenes, Croats, and Serbs was established, and Pavelić became a member of its board. Following the creation of the Kingdom of Serbs, Croats, and Slovenes, especially after the proclamation of the constitution of June 1921, Pavelić increasingly criticized centralization and the Serbianization of the country's political system. He voiced his criticism in parliament, in which he sat from 1927 to 1929.

When King **Alexander Karadjordjević** assumed dictatorial powers in 1929, Pavelić fled to Italy, where, in cooperation with fighters of the Internal Macedonian Revolutionary Organization (IMRO) and under the protection of the Italian Fascist authorities, he organized the terrorist organization called Ustaša (Insurgent) in 1930. His organization recruited young Croatian chauvinists and prepared them for action against the representatives of Yugoslavia, particularly against the Serbs. Ustaša training centers were created in Italy and Hungary. In Vienna in 1931 Pavelić published the work *Aus den Kämpfe um den selbstständigen Staat Kroatien* (From the struggles for an independent Croatia). On 9 October 1934 Vlada Makedonski, a member of the IMRO, murdered King Alexander and the French minister of foreign affairs, Louis Barthou, in Marseilles. The French court sentenced Pavelić, as a co-organizer of the plot, to death in absentia, since the Italian authorities refused to extradite him.

When Hitler's army invaded Yugoslavia in April 1941, the Ustaše had many supporters among the Croats, and as a result, some Croatian units capitulated without a fight.

Upon his arrival in Zagreb on 10 April 1941, Pavelić proclaimed the creation of the Independent State of Croatia (NHD), which also comprised a part of Bosnia and Dalmatia. Despite his racist views, Pavelić presented himself as a Catholic. In order to prevent the deterioration of the position of Croatian Catholics but at the same time to avoid the recognition of the Ustaša state, on 18 May 1941 Pope Pius XII gave Pavelić an audience as a private person, not as the head of government. Italian king Victor Emanuel II passed the Croatian throne on to his relative, Prince Aimone di Spoleto, but Pavelić was the de facto head (*poglavnik*) of the state, and he began implementing a program of exterminating the Serb minority and the Jews. This program was based upon a decree of 10 April 1941 about protecting Aryan blood. On the basis of this decree, the Ustaša minister of interior, **Andrija Artuković**, issued, among other things, a law that forbade "Serbs, Jews, Gypsies, and dogs" to enter parks in Zagreb. On 4 June 1941 the Ustaše, along with the German occupying authorities, decided that over 200,000 Slovenes, who were considered "Alpine Croats," were to be displaced from territories incorporated into the Third Reich to the NHD, and a similar number of Serbs were sent from Bosnia to Serbia. In fact, about 30,000 Serbs were displaced and around 170,000 fled to German-occupied Serbia. Even more people fell victim to massacres carried out by the Ustaše, especially in Bosnia, where under the supervision of Governor Viktor Gutić several concentration camps were established, such as those in the towns of Glina, Sanski Most, Klinč, and Karlovac. The estimated number of victims of Pavelić's regime range from 200,000 to 600,000, mainly Serbs, Jews, and gypsies. Among others, part of the Serbian Orthodox Church hierarchy was murdered. The atrocities perpetrated by the Ustaše and their close collaboration with the Third Reich (Pavelić met with Hitler on several occasions) evoked opposition and protests not only from Serbs, but also from Croatian politicians who had ties with the government in-exile in London. The hierarchy of the Catholic Church opposed these evil acts, although some priests collaborated in the exterminations.

Pavelić published *Die kroatische Frage* (The Croatian question; 1941) and other works. A collection of his speeches and works appeared under the title *Putem hrvatskog državnog prava: Poglavnikovi govori, izjave i članci* (Following Croatian state law: Speeches, statements, and articles of the head of state; 1942). Pavelić's government finally collapsed in the spring of 1945, when the Germans withdrew from Croatia and Communist guerrillas captured Zagreb. Pavelić fled to Austria and then went into hiding in Italy and Argentina. In 1957 he escaped an assassination attempt and went to Paraguay.

He later settled in Spain. Pavelić did not answer for his crimes against humanity, and his supporters continued terrorist attacks on the embassies of Communist Yugoslavia. Pavelić himself wrote a book in which he warned against the threat of communism: *Strahote zabluda: Komunizam i boljševizam u Rusiji i svijetu* (The dangers of mistakes: Communism and Bolshevism in Russia and the world), published posthumously in 1974. (WR)

Sources: *Biographisches Lexikon,* vol. 3; Constantin Fotich, *The War We Lost: Yugoslavia's Tragedy and the Failure of the West* (New York, 1948); Bogdan Krizman, *Pavelić izmedju Hitlera i Mussolinija* (Zagreb, 1980); Tadeusz Wasilewski and Wacław Felczak, *Historia Jugosławii* (Wrocław, 1985); Bogdan Krizman, *Pavelić u bjekstru* (Zagreb, 1986); Ivan Muzić, *Pavelić i Stepinac* (Split, 1991).

PAVLE [originally Gojko Stojčević] (11 September 1914, Kućani, near Donji Mohaljac, Slavonia), Patriarch of the Serbian Orthodox Church (SOC). Pavle graduated from high school in Belgrade, and then he studied theology in Sarajevo and Belgrade. In 1944–55 he was a monk at the Rača Monastery. In 1948 he took his vows, and from 1950 he taught music and Old Slavonic at Sts. Cyril and Methodius Seminary in Prizren. In 1954 he took eternal vows, adopting the name Pavle. In 1955–57 he studied at the Department of Orthodox Theology of the University of Athens, Greece. He was particularly engaged in the study of the New Testament and liturgy, and he published a lot. In 1957 Pavle became archimandrite. On 29 May 1957 he was elected bishop of Raška-Prizren in Kosovo. He presided over a commission of the SOC Synod supervising the first full translation of the Bible into Serbian; it was published in 1984.

On 1 December 1990 Pavle was elected the SOC Patriarch to succeed German Djorić, who resigned owing to ill health. Already in the 1980s, Pavle had warned against the growing Albanian (meaning Muslim) pressure in Kosovo and the emigration of the Kosovo Serbs. He alerted the public and protested the Albanian violence and desecration of Orthodox churches. Beaten by a group of Albanians in 1989, Pavle was hospitalized. As a result, he supported Serb nationalists in their attempts to gain full control over the rebellious province. He spoke in favor of a peaceful solution to the conflict, and in 1995 he supported the Dayton agreement, for which he was attacked by the extreme nationalists from the Serbian Orthodox hierarchy, including Bishop Atanasije Jevtić, who demanded Pavle's resignation. Under pressure from most Serb bishops, Pavle accepted a more militant attitude toward the Kosovo Albanians. In 1999, after the NATO intervention in Kosovo, he appealed to the Serbs to stay in the province. After the Serbian presidential elections of 24 September 2000, he recognized the victory of **Vojislav Koštunica** and appealed for a peaceful transition of power. Pavle authored several works, including *Dieu voit tout: L'Église orthodoxe face au conflit yougoslave* (God knows all: The Orthodox Church in light of the Yugoslav conflict; 1995), *Kosovska iskušenja* (Kosovo temptations; 2002), and many articles in *Glasnik Srpske Patrijaršije.* (AO/WR)

Sources: www.serbianorthodoxchurch.com/pages/s/pavle/biography-en.html; www.oea.serbian-church.net/pavle.html; www.spc.org.yu/Eng/patriarc.html; www.politika.co.yu/2003/0112/01_23.htm; www.incommunion.org/pav1299.htm.

PAVLOV Asen (9 March 1898, Aleksandrovo, near Lovech–3 October 1977, Sofia), Bulgarian politician. In 1919 Pavlov joined the Bulgarian Agrarian National Union (Bulgarski Zemedelski Naroden Suyuz [BANU]). In 1923 he completed a pedagogical course in Leipzig and subsequently studied in Czechoslovakia, where in 1930 he graduated in agronomy from the Cooperative College in Prague. From 1924 to 1928 Pavlov served as secretary of the Bulgarian Peasant Student Union in Czechoslovakia, and subsequently he was secretary of the Bulgarian Section of the Green International until 1932. He also served as deputy chairman of an anti-Fascist student organization called Narstud and as secretary of the International Youth Agrarian Bureau. After returning to Bulgaria in 1932, Pavlov co-founded and became secretary (1932–33) of the **Aleksandur Stamboliyski** BANU (Pladne). From 1933 to 1934 he was a member of the leadership of the BANU (United), which was established with the merger of the Aleksandur Stamboliyski BANU and the BANU–Vrabcha 1. After the coup of May 1934, Pavlov was in opposition to the regime and supported the establishment of an anti-Fascist people's front. An executive member of the General Union of Bulgarian Agricultural Cooperatives (1939–44), Pavlov was arrested and placed in an internment camp because of his anti-government activities.

After the coup of 9 September 1944, Pavlov became a member of the BANU Standing Committee and served as minister of agriculture and state property in the government of **Kimon Georgiev** (September 1944–August 1945). Disappointed with the policies of the Communist-dominated government of the Fatherland Front (FF), he resigned and moved over to the opposition. Pavlov was one of the founders and leaders (August 1945–August 1947) of the opposition BANU, led by **Nikola Petkov.** He was also a deputy to the National Assembly (1945–46) and a deputy to the Grand National Assembly (1946–47). He edited *Narodno zemedelsko zname,* an opposition newspaper.

Shocked by Petkov's execution (September 1947) and under pressure from the police, Pavlov abandoned political activities. After the plenum of the Central Committee (CC) of the Bulgarian Communist Party in April 1956, at which the "personality cult" was denounced, he again joined the FF. From 1957 until the end of his life Pavlov was a member of the BANU Council and from 1962 to 1972 also of the BANU Standing Committee. Pavlov was a member of the FF National Council Bureau (from 1957), the secretary of the FF National Council (1963–72), and a deputy to the National Assembly (1958–77). (JJ)

Sources: *Entsiklopediya Bulgariya,* vol. 5 (Sofia, 1986); *Narodni predstaviteli w Shesto narodno subranie* (Sofia, 1974); Tasho Tashev, *Ministrite na Bulgariya 1879–1999: Entsiklopedichen Spravochnik* (Sofia, 1999); Angel Tsurakov, *Entsiklopediia. Pravitelstvata na Bulgariya: Khronologiia na politicheskiya zhivot 1879–2001* (Sofia, 2001).

PAVLOV Todor (14 February 1890, Štip–8 May 1977, Sofia), Bulgarian Communist activist and Marxist philosopher. Pavlov was born into a family of teachers in Macedonia. After completing pedagogical and philosophical studies in Sofia (1914), he began working as a teacher. In 1919 he joined the Bulgarian Communist Party (BCP), as a result of which he was dismissed from work in 1922. He was also active in the Bulgarian Communist Youth Union, editing its press organ, *Mladezh.* After the September 1923 Communist uprising was suppressed, Pavlov helped to found the legal Labor Party (Partiya na Truda), which was to serve as a facade behind which the Communists would continue their activities, but it was dissolved as early as 1924. In May 1924, at a conference called to settle accounts with the past and to find those responsible for the failure of the 1923 uprising, Pavlov was elected to the Central Committee (CC) of the illegal BCP. Arrested in connection with a terrorist attack in Sofia on Easter Sunday, 16 April 1925, he was put in prison, where he was held off and on until 1929.

After his release, Pavlov went to Moscow, where he taught dialectical materialism at the Institute of Red Professorship (1932–36) and at the Institute of Philosophy of the Communist Academy. In Moscow he published *Teoriia otrazheniia* (Reflection theory; 1936), in which he adapted the psychological theory of Ivan Pavlov to the needs of the Marxist-Leninist doctrine; as a result, Pavlov rose to the position of the leading party ideologue. After returning to Bulgaria in 1937, he led various BCP protests. In October 1939 he published an article praising the Soviet involvement in the partition of Poland. He later published a book in the same spirit. He advocated considering Macedonians as Bulgarians and called for the incorporation of

the Macedonian territory into a Communist Bulgaria; as a result, the Bulgarian Communists came into conflict with the Yugoslav Communists. After the war with Yugoslavia broke out in April 1941, Pavlov was interned and sent to the Gonda Voda concentration camp, near Asenovgrad, where he was held until 1943.

After the coup of 9 September 1944, along with **Venelin Ganev** and **Tsvetko Boboshevski**, Pavlov became a member of a new, three-man Regency Council, which was given custody of the minor heir to the throne, **Simeon II**; he held this position until September 1946, when the monarchy was abolished. In 1945 Pavlov became an editor of the Marxist periodical *Filosofska misŭl.* In 1944–49 he served as chairman of the Bulgarian-Soviet Friendship Society. He taught philosophy at Sofia University, and in 1947 he was elected its rector for one year. From 1947 to 1954 Pavlov was a member of the Presidium of the Grand National Assembly. In 1957 he joined the BCP CC, and from 1966 to 1976 he was a member of the BCP CC Politburo. In 1962 he became honorary president of the Bulgarian Academy of Sciences and the Association of Bulgarian Writers. Pavlov was the author of many works typical of dialectical materialism, including *Osnovni vŭprosi na estetikata* (Basic issues in esthetics; 1949) and *Ravnosmetka na edna idealisticheska reaktsionna filozofia* (The balance of an idealistic reactionary philosophy; 1953). (AG)

Sources: *Biographisches Lexikon,* vol. 3; *Entsiklopediya Bulgariya,* vol. 5 (Sofia, 1986); Iordan Zaimov and Liliana Velinova, *Todor Dimitrov Pavlov: Biobibliografiya* (Sofia, 1957); Joseph Rothschild, *The Communist Party of Bulgaria: Origins and Development, 1883–1936* (New York, 1959); Marshall Lee Miller, *Bulgaria during the Second World War* (Stanford, 1975).

PAVLYCHKO Dmytro (28 September 1929, Stopchativ, near Stanisławów [now Ivano-Frankovsk]), Ukrainian poet, translator, and politician. In 1953 Pavlychko graduated in philology from Lviv University, and later he was literary director of the Maksim Gorky Young Spectators' Theater in Lviv. In 1953–56 he studied Ukrainian literature at Lviv University. From 1955 to 1958 he was head of the poetry section of the Lviv periodical *Zhovten,* and from 1964 to 1966 he worked in the Oleksandr Dovzhenko Film Studios, where he wrote screenplays for the movies *Son* (Dream; 1965) and *Zakhar Berkut* (1970; based on a novel by Ivan Franko). In 1971–78 Pavlychko was editor-in-chief of the periodical *Vsesvit,* in which translations from foreign literatures were published. In 1966–90 he was secretary of the Association of Ukrainian Writers and the Association of Soviet Writers. Co-organizer and in 1989–90 chairman of the Taras Shevchenko Ukrainian Language Society, in 1989 Pavlychko co-initiated the establishment of the Ukrainian Popular Movement for Restructuring (Narodnyj Ruch Ukrajiny za Perebudowu [LRU], or Rukh) and he became a member of its Grand Council. From 1990 to 1994 Pavlychko was a member of the Supreme Council of the Ukrainian SSR, and from 1991, of Ukraine. He also chaired the parliamentary commission on foreign affairs. In 1990 he co-founded the Democratic Party of Ukraine (Demokratychna Partiya Ukraiiny). From 1995 to 1998 he was ambassador to Slovakia. In March 1998 he was reelected to the Supreme Council of Ukraine, and then, until 2001, he was ambassador to Poland, contributing to Polish-Ukrainian reconciliation. Pavlychko authored more than thirty collections of poems, including *Lubov i nenavist* (Love and hatred; 1953); *Hranoslov* (1968); *Tajemnitsa tvoho oblychia* (The secret of your face; 1979); and a collection of translations, *Svitovyi sonet: Antolohia* (Anthology of sonnets in world literature; 1983). (BB)

Sources: *Nowa encyklopedia powszechna PWN*, vol. 4 (Warsaw, 1996); *Pysmennyky Radianskoyi Ukraiiny* (Kiev, 1966); Khto ye khto v Ukraiini 2000 (Kiev, 2000); *Szevchenkivski laureaty: Encyklopedychnyj dovidnyk* (Kiev, 2001).

PAWLAK Waldemar (5 September 1959, Model), Polish political activist. In 1983 Pawlak graduated in machine engineering from the Warsaw Polytechnic, and later he ran a family farm of forty acres in the village of Kamionka. In 1985–90 he belonged to the (Communist satellite) United Peasant Party (UPP). From 1988 he was a member of its provincial committee in Płock and head of the Communal National Council in Pacyna. In June 1989 Pawlak was elected MP on behalf of the UPP. After the name of the party was changed to the Polish Peasant Party (Polskie Stronnictwo Ludowe [PSL]), from June 1990 Pawlak chaired its Main Executive Committee. From 1992 he was chairman of the Main Board of the Union of Volunteer Fire Brigades. In early June 1992, after the **Jan Olszewski** government resigned, President **Lech Wałęsa** appointed Pawlak prime minister, but his mission to form a government failed because of a lack of parliamentary support. After early parliamentary elections, on 26 October 1993 Pawlak became prime minister of a government based on the PSL and the post-Communists. This government failed to make use of the economic prosperity to continue structural reforms. At the same time, many representatives from the Communist regime returned to high positions. On 1 March 1995 President Wałęsa made Pawlak step down because of errors made in the preparation of the budget. Pawlak was the PSL candidate in the presidential elections of 1995, but he lost. He was elected an MP in 1991, 1993, 1997, and 2001. In 1991–93 and 1993–97 he presided over the PSL parliamentary club. After the

electoral defeat of 1997 Pawlak resigned as chairman of the PSL. From 2001 he was chairman of the Warsaw Commodity Exchange. (IS)

Sources: *Kto jest kim w Polsce* (Warsaw, 2001); Janusz A. Majcherek, *Pierwsza dekada III Rzeczypospolitej* (Warsaw, 1999); Antoni Dudek, *Pierwsze lata III Rzeczyspospolitej 1989–2001* (Kraków, 2002); Wojciech Roszkowski, *Historia Polski 1914–2001* (Warsaw, 2002).

PAZNYAK Zianon (24 April 1944, Subotniki), Belorussian dissident, politician, art historian, and archaeologist. After high school, from 1962 to 1964 Paznyak headed a country club in Khilevichi. From 1964 he worked in the Minsk Theater of Opera and Ballet and in the Belorussian State Historical and Touring Museum. In 1967 he graduated from the Belorussian Institute of Art and Theater in Minsk, and in 1972 he started working at the Institute of Art History, Ethnography, and Folklore of the Belorussian Academy of Sciences (BAS). Panyak worked to preserve the old Minsk architecture, criticizing the decisions of city authorities to demolish it. In 1975, under the pseudonym "Henryk Rakutowicz," Paznyak published an analysis in the uncensored press of the situation in Soviet Belorussia, sharply criticizing its authorities for erasing references to or records of the repressions of the 1930s. He accused the Soviets of the extermination of the Belorussian intelligentsia. In 1975 Paznyak was fired for participating in the Academic Center, an informal BAS group. In 1976 he was rehired, this time in the BAS Institute of History. He directed excavations in Minsk, Miadziel, Losk, and other places. Not allowed to defend his Ph.D. in the Belorussian SSR, he received a Ph.D. in Leningrad in 1981.

In 1988, with a group of scholars, Paznyak studied mass graves in the village of Kuropaty, near Minsk, where remains of NKVD victims were found. It was estimated that the NKVD had murdered about 250,000 people there. In June 1988 in the weekly *Literatura i Mastatstva* Paznyak published (with Yeuhen Shmyhalou) the article "Kuropaty: Doroha smerti" (Kuropaty: The way of death), which started a political breakthrough in Belorussia. In 1988 Paznyak co-founded a society commemorating the victims of Stalinism in Belorussia, Martyrs of Belorussia (Martyrolog Byalorusi) and the Belorussian Popular Front (Belaruski Narodni Front [BNF]). He was the BNF chairman from 1989 to 1999. He was also an MP to the Supreme Council of the Belorussian SSR (1990–91) and Belarus (1991–95), leading a group of opposition deputies in the council. Paznyak opposed the idea of a presidential republic, fearing it would lead to dictatorship. In 1994 he ran in the presidential elections but won only 13 percent of the vote. In the elections of 1995 the BNF lost, failing to win even one seat. Harassed by the political police of the **Alyaksandr Lukashenka** regime and fearing for his life, in 1996 Paznyak emigrated to the United States. From 1997 he published, in Warsaw, Poland, the periodical *Wiadomości białoruskie*. After the BNF split in 1999 Paznyak established the Christian Democratic BNF Party. In 1994 he published *Kurapaty*. (AS/SA)

Sources: A. Ulitsonak, *Inshadumtsy: Myslyaszcziye inachye* (Minsk, 1991); Jan Zaprudnik, *Belarus: At a Crossroads in History* (Boulder, Colo., 1993); *Demakratychnaya apazytsia Byalorusi 1956–1991: Davednik* (Minsk, 1999); *Byalorus: Encyklapedychny davednik* (Minsk, 1995); Siergiej Owsiannik and Jelena Striełkowa, *Władza i społeczeństwo: Białoruś 1991–1998* (Warsaw, 1998); Bugajski.

PEČIULONIS Motiejus (31 January 1888, Ranciškės, near Sejny–26 January 1960, Ilguva), Lithuanian officer, leader of anti-Soviet guerrillas. After three years of studies in mathematics at Petersburg University, Pečiulonis was drafted into the Russian Army in 1914. In 1916 he graduated from an artillery school and fought on the German and Austrian fronts. In 1919 he returned to Lithuania and joined the Lithuanian Army. In the war against the Bolsheviks and German-Russian troops of Pavel Bermondt-Avałov, he commanded an artillery battery. In 1922 Pečiulonis went to study in the Artillery School in Fontainebleau, France, and in 1925–26 he also studied at the Higher School of Artillery in Paris. In 1926 he was appointed head of artillery supplies for the Lithuanian Army, and in 1930, head of all supplies for the army. In 1936 Pečiulonis retired and worked in a trade company. He avoided deportation during the first Soviet occupation (1940–41), and in 1941–44 he was director of an oil mill in Vilnius. With the reentry of the Red Army into Lithuania in the summer of 1944, Pečiulonis retreated to the forests of Samogitia and organized anti-Soviet guerrilla units there. Captured in 1946, he was sent to the Vorkuta area, where he spent ten years in labor camps. In 1956 Pečiulonis was released and allowed to return to Lithuania but could not find any work and died in an invalid shelter. (WR)

Sources: *EL*, vol. 4; Constantine R. Jurgėla, *Lithuania: The Outpost of Freedom* (St. Petersburg, Fla., 1976).

PEČKAUSKAITĖ Marija, literary pseudonym "Šatrijos Ragana" (Witch of Šatrijos) (24 February 1878, Medingėnai, near Telshe [Telšiai, Telsze], Samogitia–24 June 1930, Židikai), Lithuanian writer. Born into the Pieczkowski family of Polish nobility, Pečkauskaitė had contacts with Lithuanians from her childhood. The education she received at home consolidated her religious outlook and sensitivity to the conditions of the common people. She wrote her first works in Polish, but under the influence of her friendship with **Povilas Višinskis** she opted for Lithuanian national identity. Although she shared Višinskis's patriotic enthusiasm, she did not accept his religious indifference, and after making her literary debut in the Lithuanian liberal periodical *Varpas*, she began to publish her subsequent works in periodicals that had a Catholic orientation, including *Tėvynės Sargas*. In 1905 Pečkauskaitė won a scholarship to Switzerland, where she studied pedagogy in Zurich and Fribourg. It was there that she met Friedrich Foerster, whose pedagogical theories had a crucial influence on her. From 1909 to 1914 she taught at a high school for girls in Marijampolė. She subsequently settled in Židikai in northeastern Lithuania, where, despite modest living conditions, she continued writing and was engaged in charity work. Her prose, which consists of short stories and longer novellas, shows social changes in Lithuanian rural life and the emergence of a stratum of independent peasants aware of their Lithuanian national identity. Pečkauskaitė gradually gave up longings for the aristocratic Polish-Lithuanian commonwealth of the past and came to accept the new social requirements: the development of the educational system and a modern economy. In a masterly way she portrayed children and young people growing up in new social and national conditions. Her best stories include "Irkos tragedija" (The tragedy of Irka) and "*Vincas* Stonis." A six-volume edition of her works appeared in 1928. Pečkauskaitė's most important pedagogical work, *Motina auklėtoja* (Mother as a pedagogue), was published in 1936. (WR)

Sources: *EL*, vol. 4; K. Čibiras, *Gyvenimo menininkė: Marija Pečkauskaite* (Marijampolė, 1937); Konstantinas Gulbinas, *Das pädagogische Lebenswerk der litauischen Dichterin Marija Pečkauskaite* (Munich, 1971).

PEIVE Jānis (3 August 1906, near Pskov–13 September 1976, Moscow), Soviet activist of Latvian descent. In 1929 Pwicw graduated from the Timiryazev Agricultural Academy in Moscow. From 1930 to 1940 he was a researcher and from 1940 to 1942 deputy director and then director of a chemistry and agricultural research institute in Moscow. In 1940 he earned a Ph.D. in agricultural sciences and became a member of the All-Union Communist Party (Bolsheviks). In 1944 Peive was sent to Latvia, which had again been seized by the Red Army, and he was appointed rector of the Agricultural Academy. He also served as director of the Institute of Agricultural Sciences of the Academy of Sciences of the Latvian SSR (1946–48), secretary of the Academy of Sciences (1946–51), and head of the Institute of Biology of the Academy of Sciences (1946–66). In

1951–59 Peive was president of the Academy of Sciences of the Latvian SSR. From 1959 to 1962 he was chairman of the Council of Ministers of the Latvian SSR, and from 1958 to 1966, chairman of the Council of Nationalities of the Supreme Soviet of the USSR. Peive's appointment to the latter post was meant to give an impression of greater professionalism of the Latvian SSR authorities, while giving the Kremlin full control over the Latvian republic. In 1963 Peive returned to Moscow, where he served as a member (1966–71) of the Central Committee (CC) of the CPSU and a member and secretary (1971–76) of the General Biology Department of the USSR Academy of Sciences. (EJ)

Sources: *Ian Voldemarovich Peive* (Moscow, 1954); *Latvijas PSR mazā enciklopēdija*, vol. 2 (Riga, 1969); *Latvijas padomju enciklopēdija*, vol. 7 (Riga, 1986); Romuald J. Misiunas and Rein Taagepera, *The Baltic States: Years of Dependence, 1940–1980* (Berkeley, 1983).

PEJANI Bedri (10 June 1885, Peje [Peč]–6 July 1946, Prizren), Albanian politician and journalist. Born into a Muslim intelligentsia family from Kosovo, Pejani completed studies at the Galatasaray Lycée in Istanbul and at Munich University. He published extensively in Turkish and later in Albanian papers and periodicals. In 1907 he conducted negotiations with the Macedonians for a joint anti-Turkish uprising, and in 1908 he took part in Young Turk demonstrations. Pejani became involved in efforts to standardize the Albanian language. In February 1910 he co-organized a congress of Albanian national activists in Monastir (now Bitola, Macedonia), and then he became engaged in promoting the Albanian cause in Europe. In September 1910 a Turkish military court in Prizren sentenced him to death in absentia for his conspiratorial work. As a representative of Peje, Pejani attended the sessions of the National Assembly in Vlorë (November 1912) and was a signatory of the Independence Declaration. During World War I he was involved in the establishment of Albanian schools. One of the founders of the Committee for the Defense of Kosovo in 1919, Pejani was the author of its program. He considered that the most important goal for the Kosovo Albanians was to prevent cooperation between Rome and Belgrade on the Albanian issue. Pejani represented Kosovo Albanians at the Paris Peace Conference. He was also in charge of *Populli*, a sociopolitical periodical published in Shkodër.

From 1921 to 1923 Pejani was a member of parliament. After the collapse of the 1924 revolution, he went to Geneva—at that time the headquarters of the Committee for the Defense of Kosovo—and there he wrote numerous articles, attacking **Ahmed Zogu** and other leaders for their alleged plans to liquidate the political elite of Kosovo. In 1927 Pejani initiated the establishment of the Kosovo Liberation Committee in exile. In the late 1920s he traveled throughout Europe. Influenced by what he had observed in Spain, Pejani established ties with the Communist-dominated Balkan Federation. A contributor to the periodical *Sazani*, he worked with, among others, **Ali Kelmendi**. He also worked with **Llazar Fundo** and Riza Cerova. In 1932 Pejani was imprisoned in Turkey. After his release, he returned to Albania in the mid-1930s. In August 1935 he was arrested for his participation in an anti-government rebellion in Fier. Release in 1937, he went to France. After the Italian aggression in April 1939, Pejani sent memoranda to the prime ministers of Western countries in which he appealed to them to prevent the partition of Albania. In May 1941 he returned to Kosovo. Interned on one of the Italian islands and later in Porto Romano, near Durrës, he was released on 13 September 1943, after the capitulation of Italy. Fearing that Yugoslav rule would be restored in the province, Pejani entered into collaboration with the Germans and joined the Albanian government structures established under German supervision. In June 1944 he became head of the Second League of Prizren. He was one of the founders of the Twenty-first Skanderbeg Mountain Division of the Waffen SS, which was an Albanian unit fighting alongside the Germans. In 1945 Pejani was captured by the Yugoslav police. On 21 February 1946 the People's Court for Prizren District sentenced him to death for his active collaboration with the occupiers. Pejani died in a prison hospital. (TC)

Sources: Hakif Bajrami, *Bedri Pejani: Nje jete e nje vdekje për Shqipëri etnike 1885–1946* (Prishtina, 1996); Bardhosh Gaçe, *Ata që shpallën Pavarësinë Kombëtare* (Tirana, 1997); Bernd J. Fischer, *Albania at War 1939–1945* (London, 1999).

PEŁCZYŃSKI Tadeusz, pseudonyms "Grzegorz," "Robak," "Wolf," and others (14 February 1895, Warsaw–3 January 1985, London), Polish general. Born into an intelligentsia family, Pełczyński graduated from high school and commenced medical studies in Kraków in 1911. A member of the Union of Polish Youth called Zet and of the Riflemen's Association, in 1914 he began serving in the Polish Legions. After the so-called oath of allegiance crisis, Pełczyński was interned in a camp at Beniaminów (1917). In November 1918 he joined the Polish Army, and in 1923 he graduated from the Military College in Warsaw. He was a member of a secret organization, Honor and Fatherland (Honor i Ojczyzna), which from 1921 to 1923 comprised the opponents of **Józef Piłsudski**. In 1924 Pełczyński began working for the Bureau of the Supreme Council of War, first as acting head (1927) and then head (1929–32) of the Second Department (Intelligence) of the General Staff. He again became head of the intelligence department in October 1935. In 1927–29 he edited *Przegląd Wojskowy*. He was a member of the Chief Council of the National Youth Organization Seniors' Union, the Union of Polish Democratic Youth, and the High Command of the Polish Legionnaires' Union. He took part in the work of the Prime Minister's Committee for Ethnic Affairs.

During the September 1939 campaign, Pełczyński fought behind the German lines. He later lived in Warsaw under a false name. From October 1939 he conducted underground activities, first as a member of the Service for the Victory of Poland (Służba Zwycięstwu Polsce [SZP]), then of the Union of Armed Struggle (Związek Walki Zbrojnej [ZWZ]), and finally of the Home Army (Armia Krajowa [AK]). In July 1940 he became commander of the ZWZ Lublin district, with headquarters in Warsaw. Discovered by the Gestapo, Pełczyński changed his pseudonyms and continued his underground work, serving as deputy chief of staff (1941–44) and subsequently as chief of staff of the High Command of the ZWZ. (The ZWZ was transformed into the AK in 1942.) On 10 September 1943 Pełczyński became the AK deputy commander-in-chief, and on 24 November of that year he was promoted to brigadier general. He personally led units of the Directorate of Sabotage (Kierownictwo Dywersji [Kedyw]). He fought in the Warsaw Uprising, and after its failure he was held in POW camps in Langwasser and Colditz. After his liberation, Pełczyński went to London. As head of the office of the commander-in-chief, General **Tadeusz Bór-Komorowski** (July–November 1945), and chairman (until 1947) of the AK Historical Commission of the General Staff in London, Pełczyński was actively involved in fostering research on the history of World War II, and he supported the cultivation of the AK traditions. He was a co-founder and activist of the Polish Underground Movement's Study Trust (Studium Polski Podziemnej) and served as its chairman from 1956 to 1969. Pełczyński was decorated with the Cross of Valor (three times) and with the Order of Virtuti Militari. (PK)

Sources: Kunert, vol. 2; Tadusz Kryska-Karski and Stefan Żurakowski, *Generałowie Polski Niepodległej* (London, 1976); Jan Ciechanowski, *Powstanie Warszawskie* (Warsaw, 1984); Marek Ney-Krwawicz, "Generał Tadeusz Pełczyński," *Przegląd Katolicki*, 1985, nos. 9–10; Halina Zakrzewska, "Wspomnienie o "Grzegorzu,"" *Więź*, 1986, no. 1.

PELŠE Arvīds (7 February 1899, Grīnvaldes, Courland–29 May 1983, Moscow), Soviet Communist activist of Latvian descent. Born into a peasant family, Pelše graduated from a communal school and started polytechnic studies in Riga. In 1915 he joined the Social Democratic Workers' Party (Bolsheviks) of Latvia, acting within the All-Russian Bolshevik party. From 1915 he acted in the Bolshevik underground in Vitebsk, Kharkiv, Petrograd, and Arkhangelsk. In 1917 he became a member of the Petrograd Soviet. From 1918 Pelše worked for the Cheka in Moscow, and in early 1919 he was sent to Latvia as a member of the People's Commissariat of Construction and Public Works. After the failure of the Bolshevik revolution in Latvia Pelše was political commissar in the Latvian Riflemen's Division. From 1920 he lectured in military schools in Kharkiv and Leningrad. In 1926–29 he was secretary of the party committee of the Baltic Fleet. From 1929 he studied at the Academy of Red Professorship in Moscow, and in 1933–37 he worked in the party apparatus in Kazakhstan. During the Great Purge, in 1937 Pelše was deposed from all posts, but from the fall of 1937 he was allowed to return to Moscow and to lecture there. In the summer of 1940 he came to Latvia and co-organized its incorporation into the USSR. In 1941 he was appointed secretary of the Central Committee (CC) of the Communist Party of Latvia (CPL) for propaganda and agitation. After the German invasion (June 1941) Pelše left for Russia, but he returned in the same role after the reincorporation of Latvia into the USSR in the spring of 1945. After the so-called national Communists were deposed in 1959, Pelše became the head of the CPL. In this capacity he intensified Russification policies. He ruthlessly persecuted all those who showed signs of intellectual or national independence. In 1966 Pelše was recalled to Moscow, where he was appointed a member of the Politburo and head of the Central Party Control Commission of the CC CPSU. An impenitent hard-liner, he belonged to the closest co-workers of Leonid Brezhnev. In 1979 Pelše's *Runu un rakstu izlase* (Selection of speeches and articles) was published in Latvia. (EJ)

Sources: *Latvijas PSR Mazā enciklopēdija*, vol. 2 (Riga, 1969); *Latvijas padomju enciklopēdija*, vol. 7 (Riga, 1986); Romuald J. Misiunas and Rein Taagepera, *The Baltic States: Years of Dependence, 1940–1980* (Berkeley, 1983); Juris Dreifelds, *Latvia in Transition* (Cambridge, 1996); Andrejs Plakans, *Historical Dictionary of Latvia* (Lanham, Md., 1997).

PENDERECKI Krzysztof (23 November 1933, Dębica), Polish composer, conductor, and pedagogue. Penderecki graduated from the State Higher Musical School (Państwowa Wyższa Szkoła Muzyczna [PWSM]) in Kraków in 1958. From 1958 he lectured at the PWSM, and in 1972 he became a professor at this school. Penderecki started his musical career with the vanguard works

Tren pamięci ofiar Hiroszimy (1960; *Threnody for the Victims of Hiroshima*), *Anaklasis* for strings and drums (written for the 1960 Donaueschigen Festival), and the *First String Quartet* (1960), in which he became known for an original style and enormous sound imagination. Penderecki gradually enriched his means of expression, reaching for rare kinds of works, such as *Pasja według św. Łukasza* (The Passion according to St. Luke; 1965) and the oratory *Dies irae* (1967), commemorating the victims of the Nazi concentration camp of Auschwitz. In 1969 Penderecki won world renown for the opera *Diabły z Loudun* (The devils of Loudun). In subsequent works, such as *Magnificat* (1974) and the opera *Raj utracony* (Paradise lost; 1978), he evolved toward the neo-Romanticism of Richard Wagner and Alexander Bruckner. Penderecki authored three symphonies; two cello concertos; concertos for violin and viola; the symphonic cycle *De natura sonoris I–III* (1966–70); and the operas *Czarna maska* (The black mask; 1986) and *Ubu król* (Ubu Rex; 1991). In his works he referred to the universal problems of human existence. Penderecki received a number of prestigious awards, including the German Johann Gottfried von Herder Preis (1977), the Artur Honegger Award (1979), the Jan Sibelius Award (1983), and the Grammy Award in 1988. He belongs among the most outstanding and the most often performed contemporary composers. In 1972–87 Penderecki was rector of the PWSM (renamed the Musical Academy [Akademia Muzyczna] in 1979) in Kraków. From the 1970s Penderecki was frequently a conductor in (among other places) Hamburg, Germany, and in 1987–90 he was artistic director of the Kraków Philharmonic. From 1973 to 1978 he lectured at Yale University. In 1980 he initiated a private music festival in his countryside residence in Lusławice. From 1994 Penderecki was a member of the Polish Academy of Arts and Sciences in Kraków. A presentation of his works was a part of the Kraków 2000 Festival. (WR)

Sources: *Kto jest kim w Polsce 1984* (Warsaw, 1984); Ludwik Erhardt, *Spotkania z Krzysztofem Pendereckim* (Kraków, 1975); Mieczysław Tomaszewski, *Krzysztof Penderecki i jego muzyka* (Kraków, 1994); Wolfram Schwinger, *Krzysztof Penderecki: Begegnungen, Lebensdatum, Werkomentäre* (Mainz, 1994); Mieczysław Tomaszewski, ed., *The Music of Krzysztof Penderecki*, (Kraków, 1995); Barbara Malecka-Contamin, *Krzysztof Penderecki: Style et matériaux* (Paris, 1997).

PERL Feliks (26 April 1871, Warsaw–15 April 1927, Warsaw), journalist and politician, one of the leading ideologues of Polish socialism. Perl was brought up in a merchant family of Polonized Jews with Orthodox traditions. After graduating from a Russian high school, he studied law at Warsaw University and at Bern University in Switzerland, where in 1896 he received a Ph.D. in philosophy for the dissertation "Marx und Sismondi." A member of the Proletariat Social Revolutionary Party, Perl attended the congress of the Polish Socialists (Paris, November 1892) at which the Union of Polish Socialists Abroad (Związek Zagraniczny Socjalistów Polskich [ZZSP]) was established. He became a member of the leadership (Centralizacja) of the ZZSP and held this position until December 1894. In 1898 Perl became active in the ZZSP section in Lemberg (Lwów, Lviv). After the ZZSP became incorporated into the Polish Socialist Party (Polska Partia Socjalistyczna [PPS]) in 1900, he became a member of the PPS Foreign Committee. In 1900–1901 Perl was in London. After returning home, he joined the underground publishing movement and was in charge of the clandestine printing house that published the journal *Robotnik*.

In 1902–4 Perl was a member of the PPS Central Workers' Committee. After a split within the PPS in November 1906, he joined the PPS–Revolutionary Faction. He was a co-author of the agrarian program of the PPS that was adopted at the Tenth Congress of the party in 1907. From 1908 onwards Perl increasingly opposed **Józef Piłsudski**, whom he accused of abandoning the Socialist aims of the PPS. In 1911 Perl was finally expelled from the PPS–Revolutionary Faction. In December 1912 he was a co-founder of the PPS–Opposition, which existed until 1914. He then again joined the PPS and was a member (1914–19) of its Central Audit Commission. In 1918 he again began to edit *Robotnik*. A co-author of the PPS program of 1920 and a proponent of a pro-independence socialism and parliamentarism, Perl was a member of the PPS Supreme Council and Central Executive Committee from April 1919 until the end of his life (except for the years 1920–21) and chairman of the PPS Central Executive Committee from 1924 to 1926. Owing to deteriorating health, he gradually became less and less active. He treated Piłsudski's plans for a coup with reserve. From 1919 to 1927 Perl was an MP and one of the leaders of the Union of Polish Socialist Deputies. Among Socialists, he was regarded as a representative of the "old" group and as one of its main ideologues. Perl's publications include *Kwestia polska w oświetleniu Socjaldemokracji Polskiej* (The Polish question as seen by the Polish Social Democratic movement; 1906), in which he advocated that the PPS should give priority to national tasks; *Dzieje ruchu socjalistycznego w zaborze rosyjskim* (The history of the Socialist movement in the Russian part of Poland; 1910); and *O bolszewizmie i bolszewikach* (About Bolshevism and the Bolsheviks; 1918), in which he sharply criticized the Communist revolution. (PK)

Sources: *PSB*, vol. 25; M. Śliwa, *Feliks Perl* (Warsaw, 1988); Michał Czajka and Marcin Kamler, *Leksykon Historii Polski* (Warsaw, 1995); Lidia Ciołkoszowa, *Spojrzenie wstecz* (Paris, 1995); *Słownik polityków polskich XX w.* (Poznań, 1998).

PEROUTKA Ferdinand (6 February 1895, Prague–20 April 1978, New York), Czech writer and political journalist. In 1914, after graduating from high school in Prague, Peroutka began working for the periodical *Čas*. From 1919 to 1924 he edited the daily *Tribuna*. From 1924 to 1939 he was in charge of the political and cultural periodical *Přítomnost*, and he was also a regular contributor to *Lidové noviny*. His was a lively and robust style, with a tendency toward irony, and he showed great perspicacity in his judgments. Peroutka generally supported the line of a political group called Hrad (Castle) and President **Tomáš Garrigue Masaryk**, and he was a member of the Friday Circle (Pátečníci), a group of intellectuals who met every Friday at the home of **Karel Čapek**, a close friend of Peroutka. Peroutka approached politics pragmatically, emphasizing the role of reason and experience and rejecting all manifestations of totalitarianism. He had close links to the Hrad group, but he often criticized the views of Masaryk and **Edvard Beneš**. During the interwar period Peroutka published several books, including *Jací jsme* (Who we are; 1924), an unfinished fundamental work on the beginnings of the Czechoslovak state; *Budování státu* (Building of the state, 5 vols.; 1933–38); and a collection of critical literary essays, *Osobnost, chaos, a zlozvyky* (Personality, chaos, and bad habits; 1939).

During World War II Peroutka was imprisoned in Nazi camps at Dachau and Buchenwald. He repeatedly rejected offers of collaboration from **Emanuel Moravec** and Karl H. Frank; for example, he refused the offer to edit *Přítomnost*, which they presented to him in 1943. After the war, Peroutka was the editor-in-chief of the daily *Svobodné noviny* (1945–48) and the periodical *Dnešek* (1946–48); the latter was a continuation of *Přítomnost*. In 1945–46 he was a National Socialist deputy in the Provisional National Assembly. Both in the parliament and in his press articles, Peroutka criticized the increasing totalitarian tendencies; as a result, he became the target of vicious Communist propaganda attacks. After the February 1948 coup and the Communist takeover, in April of that year Peroutka emigrated to England and in 1950 to the United States. From 1951 to 1955 he was a member of the Council of Free Czechoslovakia, and from 1951 to 1961 he was the director of the Czechoslovak section of Radio Free Europe, for which he wrote weekly political commentaries. After retiring in 1961, he continued his work with Radio Free Europe. Peroutka's postwar publications include *Byl Edvard Beneš vinen?* (Was Edvard Beneš guilty? 1949);

Demokratický manifest (Democratic manifesto; 1959); the dramas *Oblak a valčík* (A cloud and waltz; 1947) and "Šťastlivec Sulla" (Sulla the happy man; manuscript, 1947; its premiere in 1948 was called off for political reasons); and a historical fiction novel about the further life of Joan of Arc after she was miraculously saved, *Pozdější život Panny* (The later life of the maid; Toronto, 1980; Prague, 1991). Peroutka's memoirs from 1945–48 and from exile were published under the title *Ferdinand Peroutka: Deníky, dopisy, vzpomínky* (Ferdinand Peroutka: Diaries, letters, memoirs; 1995), and a selection of his radio speeches from the period between 1951 and 1977 was published as *Úděl svobody* (The fate of freedom; 1995). In 1991 Peroutka's ashes were returned to Prague. (PU)

Sources: *ČBS*; *Kdo byl kdo v našich dějinach ve 20. století*, vol. 2 (Prague, 1998); *Slovník českých spisovatelů od roku 1945*, vol. 2 (Prague, 1998); Halina Janaszek-Ivančikova, ed., *Literatury zachodniosłowiańskie czasu przełomów 1890–1990*, vol. 2, *Literatura czeska* (Katowice, 1999); *Politická elita meziválečného Československa 1918–1938: Kdo byl kdo za první republiky* (Prague, 1998); Jaroslav Strnad, ed., *Ferdinand Peroutka: Muž Přítomností* (Zurich, 1985); Milan Otahal, *Ferdinand Peroutka: Muž Přítomností* (Prague, 1992); Pavel Kosatik, *Ferdinand Peroutka* (Prague and Litomyšl, 2000).

PESHEV Dimitur (13 June 1894, Kyustendil–23 June 1975, Sofia), Bulgarian politician. The son of a lawyer, Peshev attended high school in Salonika and Kyustendil. From 1914 to 1919 he studied law at Sofia University. During World War I he fought on the southern front. He subsequently worked as a judge in Plovdiv and Sofia, and in 1932 he became a defense attorney. In November 1935 Peshev became minister of justice in the cabinet of **Georgi Kioseivanov** but was dismissed after half a year because he had appealed to Tsar **Boris III** to mitigate the sentence of **Damian Velchev**. From 1938 to 1940 Peshev was a member of parliament, and from 1940 to 1944 he was the parliament's deputy speaker. When in March 1943 a delegation from his native Kyustendil asked him for help to prevent a secretly prepared deportation of Jews from the newly incorporated territories and from the big cities, Peshev successfully intervened, organizing and collecting signatures in protest against the deportation of Jews. The government suspended the deportation orders, and then, as a result of further pressures, including those from the Orthodox Church, it called off the deportation action. Prime Minister **Bogdan Filov**, fearing the Germans, brought about Peshev's dismissal as deputy speaker of parliament. After the coup of 9 September 1944, Peshev was arrested and sentenced to a fifteen-year imprisonment. He avoided a death sentence only because of the intercession of an attorney of Jewish descent who emphasized Peshev's role in defending the Bulgarian Jews. Amnestied in October 1945 and released, Peshev lived in total isolation as one of five (out of a total of forty-seven) signatories of the "letter of Peshev" who had escaped death at the hands of the Communists. In the 1990s Peshev's merits were again remembered, and his words were cited: "Small nations cannot underestimate moral values because these are their only capital." (JW/WDj)

Sources: Frank Chary, *The Bulgarian Jews and the Final Solution* (Pittsburgh, 1972); Christo Boyadjieff, *Saving the Bulgarian Jews in World War II* (Ottawa, 1989); Michael Bar-Zoar, *Beyond Hitler's Grasp: The Heroic Rescue of Bulgaria's Jews* (N.p., 1989); Gabriele Nisim, *L'uomo che fermo Hitler: La storia di Dimitar Pesev che salvo gli ebrei di una nazione intera* (Mondadori, 1998).

PÉTÉR Gábor (14 May 1906, Újfehértó–23 January 1993, Budapest), Hungarian Communist activist. Pétér worked as a tailor's assistant, and in 1931 he joined the illegal Communist Party. He took part in the activities of the Red Aid in Hungary and worked in the trade unions. From January 1945 he was head of the Political Department of the General Headquarters of the Hungarian People's Militia in Budapest and then of the separate Office of State Protection. From 1948 he was head of the newly created Office of State Security (Államvédelmi Hatóság [ÁVH]), which had a few thousand permanent employees and around three hundred thousand part-time workers. Formally, the office was subordinated to the Ministry of Interior, but Pétér was subordinated only to **Mátyás Rákosi,** to whom he was obligated to report on his activities. Thus in fact it was Rákosi himself who headed the ÁVH. However, Pétér played a key role in preparing the show trials (for example, the trial of **László Rajk**) and in breaking the law; he was co-responsible for torture, murders without trial, executions, and sentencing of a few hundred political prisoners, including Communists, to long prison terms. At the end of 1952 Pétér was dismissed from his post and expelled from the party. On 3 January 1953 he was arrested as a scapegoat for all Stalinist crimes in Hungary. In 1954 the Military Supreme Court sentenced him to life imprisonment. In 1957 the Military Council of the Supreme Court revised this judgment, and sentenced him to fourteen years of prison. In January 1959 Pétér was released on pardon. Until his retirement he worked as a librarian. He died in his own flat in one of the urban blocks of flats in Budapest. From the time of his release until his death, no one called Pétér to further account for his crimes. (JT)

Sources: Miklós Molnár, *From Béla Kun to János Kádár: Seventy Years of Hungarian Communism* (New York, 1990); *A magyar forradalom és szabadságharc enciklopédiája*, CD-ROM (Budapest, 1999).

PETER I Karadjordjević (also spelled Karageorgevic) (11 July 1844, Belgrade–16 August 1921, Topčider), king of Serbia and king of the Kingdom of Serbs, Croats, and Slovenes. In 1858 Peter's father, Prince Alexander Karadjordjević, was forced to abdicate, and Peter lived with him in exile for forty-five years, at first in Hungary, then in France. He was educated mainly at military schools. In 1862 he entered a prestigious school in Saint-Cyr and continued his education at the Artillery School in Metz. In 1870, fighting on the side of the French in the war against the Germans, he was taken captive but managed to escape. In 1875 in Herzegovina Peter, under the pseudonym of Piotr Mrkonjić, commanded a group of Serb insurgents fighting against Turkish rule. In 1883 he became an honorary senator in Montenegro. The same year he married Zorka, the daughter of Prince Nicholas of Montenegro. Peter lived with his wife and children in Geneva. After a coup d'état organized by a group of officers and the assassination of the king of Serbia, Alexander Obrenović, on 29 May 1903 the army proclaimed Peter the new monarch. During his reign the parliamentary system developed in Serbia. Peter had the reputation of a liberal with no absolutist leanings. In foreign policy Serbia abandoned the pro-Viennese policy of Obrenović and hence improved its relations with Russia and France. On 24 June 1914 Peter named his son, Prince Alexander, regent. During World War I, after the defeat of the Serb forces by the Central Powers, Peter, who was severely ill, went to Corfu in the winter of 1915–16. At the end of the war he returned to Belgrade, and on 1 December 1918 he was proclaimed king of the Kingdom of Serbs, Croats, and Slovenes. (AO)

Sources: Wacław Felczak and Tadeusz Wasilewski, *Historia Jugosławii* (Wrocław, 1985); Emile Haumant, *La formation de la Yougoslavie (XV–XX siècles)* (Paris, 1930); *Enciklopedija Jugoslavije* (Zagreb, 1962).

PETER II Karadjordjević (also spelled Karageorgevic) (6 September 1923, Belgrade–5 November 1970, Los Angeles, California), king of Yugoslavia. Peter was the son of King **Alexander I** and Mary, the daughter of **Ferdinand,** king of Romania. After the death of Peter's father, who was assassinated in October 1934 in Marseilles, Peter formally succeeded to the throne. However, the regency was in the hands of a three-person council, headed by his father's cousin, Prince **Paul Karadjordjević.** Paul's conciliatory policy toward the Axis powers led to Yugoslavia's accession to the Tripartite Pact and in consequence to a coup that on 27 March 1941 overthrew the existing government. A group of officers and politicians headed by General **Dušan Simović** declared Peter of age and proclaimed him king.

The coup led to the German invasion, partition, and occupation of a great part of Yugoslavia. Peter received verbal support from Great Britain and the United States, whose governments called the German attack "barbarity" and a "vicious rape." Evacuated by the British Navy, in June 1941 Peter arrived in London, where he formed an émigré government. The Serb-dominated Yugoslav National Army of Colonel **Dragoljub (Draža) Mihailović** was the exponent of this government at home. In June 1942 Peter visited the United States, where he was warmly welcomed by President Franklin D. Roosevelt, who promised him diplomatic and military assistance.

Despite the fact that on 1 December 1942 Peter promulgated a declaration of equality for all citizens of Yugoslavia, the émigré government was undermined by political and ethnic conflicts between the Serbs and the Croats. This weakened the position of this government in the eyes of the Allies. Under Peter's pressure, the government accepted a programmatic declaration announcing the revival of the state along the principles of democracy and federation. On 28 June 1943 Peter announced this declaration in a speech to the nation on the BBC. In August 1943 the royal government lost its coalition nature after Peter appointed **Božidar Purić** its head. Although Peter sought material support for the Chetniks headed by Mihailović, Great Britain and the United States, suspecting the revival of Serb nationalism among the Chetniks, more and more clearly shifted their support to the Communist Partisans of **Josip Broz Tito**, as the Partisans more and more actively frustrated the German forces in Yugoslavia.

In October 1943 Peter arrived with his government in Cairo, preparing for his return to Yugoslavia. In November 1943 the Communists, who controlled large parts of the country and fought with the Chetniks, created their own government and denied Peter the right to return. At the end of November in Cairo, Peter talked with Roosevelt, who promised him help in reaching an agreement with the Communists. However, in Tehran at the beginning of December 1943, the Big Three decided to abandon the Balkan offensive, and this additionally weakened Peter's position and that of his government. As he was losing the support of the Allies, Peter attempted to bring about a compromise with the Communists. In June 1944 he appointed the more conciliatory **Ivan Šubašić** as head of a new cabinet. On 1 November 1944 Šubašić signed an agreement with Tito under which, in return for the Communist government's inclusion of several émigré politicians in the government and vague promises to observe human rights, Peter agreed not to return to Yugoslavia without the consent of "the people" and to recognize the Communist-dominated Anti-Fascist Council for the National Liberation of Yugoslavia (AVNOJ) as the provisional parliament. On 13 February 1945 Peter agreed to Šubašić's departure for Belgrade and at the same time appointed **Milan Grol** and Juraj Šutej as provisional regents. Since Tito did not agree to these appointments to the Regency Council, Peter withdrew them and appointed men who would be acceptable to the Communist leader: Srdjan Budislavljević, **Ante Mandić**, and Dušan Sernec. When the AVNOJ objected to the return of the king, Tito adopted its decision as the expression of "the will of the people." On 29 November 1945 the National Assembly, which was elected under great pressure from the Communists, finally abolished the monarchy. Peter, who was leaning toward federalism and democracy, and even toward tactical compromises with the Communists, got sidelined. After the war he lived mainly in France, and later he moved to the United States, where in 1967 he became an official at the Sterling Savings and Loan Association of California. By his marriage with Alexandra, the daughter of the Greek king, Peter left a son, Alexander. (WR)

Sources: *Biographisches Lexikon*, vol. 3; *The Times*, 6 November 1970; Constantin Fotich, *The War We Lost* (New York, 1948); *A King's Heritage: King Peter of Yugoslavia* (New York, 1954); Vlatko Macek, *In the Struggle for Freedom* (London, 1957); J. Jukic, *The Fall of Yugoslavia* (New York and London, 1974); Michał Jerzy Zacharias, *Jugosławia w polityce Wielkiej Brytanii 1940–1945* (Wrocław, 1985).

PETERLE Lojze (5 July 1948, Cužnja vas), Slovene politician. Peterle studied history, geography, and economics. He graduated in the latter two, and in 1975–86 he worked at the Slovene Institute of Town Planning. He belonged to the Catholic intelligentsia connected with the periodical *2000*. In 1989 he co-organized the Slovenian Christian Democrats (Slovenski Krščanski Demokrati [SCD]) and became its chairman. As a result of the electoral victory of the DEMOS coalition, which included the SCD, on 16 May 1990 Peterle became head of the republican government of Slovenia. Initially he favored a Slovene-Croat union within the Yugoslav federation, but the pressure from Serb nationalists under **Slobodan Milošević** made Peterle and other Slovene leaders seek a separate road to independence. On 2 July 1990 Peterle's government announced the sovereignty of the Slovene republic, and in a referendum on 23 December 1990 most Slovenes voted in favor of independence. When talks on a confederation of Yugoslav republics failed, on 25 June 1991 the Peterle government announced independence, and the next day it was followed by a similar announcement from the Croat government. The Serb-dominated Yugoslav federal army tried to prevent the secession of Slovenia, but fifty thousand of its territorial defense soldiers managed to defend the country.

After the consolidation of independence, the ruling DEMOS coalition was fractured. In April 1992 **Janez Drnovšek**, the leader of the Liberal Democracy of Slovenia (Liberalna Demokracija Slovenije [LDS]), which emerged from a former Communist youth organization, created a new majority coalition, so on 14 May 1992 Peterle resigned. As a result of the December 1992 elections the SCD, led by Peterle, became the second largest parliamentary faction and joined a new ruling coalition. From December 1992 to October 1994 Peterle was minister of foreign affairs in the government of Drnovšek. For some time he was deputy chairman of the European Association of Christian Democrats. He gave up his ministerial position when his party went into the opposition. In the elections of November 1996 the SCD did not do as well, and in April 2000 it merged with the Slovenian People's Party (Slovenska Ljudska Stranka [SLS]) to form the SCD-SLS. In the elections of October 2000 this party won 9.6 percent of the vote, and Peterle won a parliamentary seat for himself. In June 2004 Peterle was elected a member of the European Parliament. (WR)

Sources: *Enciklopedija Slovenija*, vol. 8 (Ljubljana, 1994); Leopoldina Plut-Progelj and Carole Rogel, *Historical Dictionary of Slovenia* (Lanham, Md., 1996); *Europa Środkowo-Wschodnia 1992–1995* (Warsaw, 1994–1997); Jill Benderly and Evan Kraft, eds., *Independent Slovenia: Origins, Movements, Prospects* (London, 1994); Bugajski.

PETERSS Jēkabs (Jakov) (3 December 1886, Briņķu, Courland–25 April 1938, Moscow), Soviet Communist activist of Latvian descent. In his youth Peterss was an active member of Social Democratic parties in Libau (Liepāja). In 1904 he joined the Social Democratic Workers' Party of Latvia. He fought in the 1905 revolution. Arrested in March 1907, he was tortured during interrogation, but in September 1908 he was released for lack of evidence of his guilt. From 1909 to 1917 Peters was in political exile in London, where he was active among Latvian Social Democrats and British Socialists. After the February 1917 revolution, he returned to Russia, where in the summer of that year he became a representative of the Latvian Social Democratic Party's Bolshevik wing to the Central Committee (CC) of the Bolshevik party. As a member of the Military Revolutionary Committee, Peterss took part in the attack on the Smolny Institute and arrested some members of the Provisional Government during the November 1917 coup in Petrograd. A member of the Central Executive Committee, he became a member of the Presidium of the All-Russian Extraordinary Commission for Combating Counterrevolution and Sabotage (Cheka) on 20 December 1917 and subsequently president of the Revolutionary Tribunal and a deputy to **Feliks Dzerzhinsky**, the head of the Cheka. In this role Peterss personally implemented the principle of revolutionary terror and murdered opponents of the revolution and rivals of the Bolsheviks. For example, he personally supervised the investigation of an assassination attempt on Lenin in August 1918. In 1919 he was commander of the Revolutionary War Council for the Petrograd region and later for the Kiev and Tula regions. In 1920 Peterss became Cheka plenipotentiary for the Northern Caucasus railroads and chairman of the Revolutionary War Committee in Rostov-on-Don. In 1920 he became a member of the Organizational Bureau of the CC of the party in Turkestan and subsequently a member of the Presidium and chairman of the Eastern Department of the political police, OGPU, in Moscow. In 1927 Peterss became a deputy member, and in 1930 a member, of the CC of the All-Union Communist Party (Bolsheviks). From 1924 to 1930 he worked in the People's Commissariat of Workers' and Peasants' Inspection of the Soviet Union. From 1930 to 1933 he was chairman of the Party Central Control Commission of the Moscow committee. In 1934 he became a member of the Party Central Control Commission of the All-Union Communist Party (Bolsheviks). Peterss was arrested and murdered during the Great Purge. The year 1942 is also given as the date of his death. (EJ)

Sources: *MERSH*, vol. 28; *Latvijas PSR mazā enciklopēdija*, vol. 2 (Riga, 1969); Robert Seth, *The Executioners: The Story of the Smersh* (New York, 1967); Andrew Ezergailis, *The 1917 Revolution in Latvia* (New York, 1974); J. Riekstiņš, *Jēkabs Peterss Ievērojams un ļoti uzticams darbinieks* (Riga, 1987); Aleksandr Solzhenitsyn, *Archipelag Gułag*, vols. 1–3 (Warsaw, 1990); Richard Pipes, *Rewolucja rosyjska* (Warsaw, 1994).

PETKOV Dimitur (21 October 1858, Bashkoy, Northern Dobrudja–26 February 1907, Sofia), Bulgarian politician, father of **Nikola Petkov** and **Petko Petkov**. Petkov fought in the Serbo-Turkish war in 1876 and in the Russo-Turkish war of 1877–78. He distinguished himself in the battles of Stara Zagora and Shipka Pass. On the Mountain of St. Nikola he was seriously wounded in the left hand, which had to be amputated. The Russian tsar, Alexander II, personally decorated Petkov with the Cross of Merit. After the liberation of Bulgaria, Petkov worked as a clerk in the Department of the Interior (1878–82). Initially he belonged to the Liberal Party; after a split in its ranks in 1883, he supported the extremely leftist faction represented by **Petko Karavelov**. Petkov opposed the coup of April 1881 and the system of plenary powers introduced by Prince Alexander I Battenberg; as a result, in 1882 he was sentenced to life imprisonment and placed in one of the mosques. Released in 1884, he edited the satirical-humorous newspaper *Svirka* (1883–85) and other periodicals, including *Narodno subranie* (1885) and *Nezavisimost* (1885).

After leaving the Liberal Party in 1886, Petkov joined the newly established National Liberal Party (NLP) and edited its press organ, *Svoboda*. After the government of Stefan Stambolov was established, Petkov became mayor of Sofia (1887–93) and brought about its transformation into a city with a European character. Petkov served as a deputy to the National Assembly in 1884–94 and 1899–1907 and as chairman of the Grand National Assembly in 1892–93. From 1893 to 1894 Petkov was minister of public housing, roads, and transport. After the death of Stambolov in 1895, Petkov, who was Stambolov's closest co-worker, became NLP head. From May 1903 to October 1906 Petkov was minister of interior and minister of public housing, roads, and transport in the government of Racho Petrov. On 22 October 1906 he was appointed prime minister and minister of interior, and he continued as minister of public housing, roads, and transport. Petkov followed a pro-Western policy, in particular seeking rapprochement with Germany and Austria-Hungary. In domestic policy he used terror against political opponents. For example, in January 1907 he ordered that Sofia University be closed for half a year after students had booed Prince **Ferdinand** before the National Theater in Sofia. Petkov was shot by a political opponent near Eagle Bridge in Sofia. (JJ)

Sources: *Entsiklopediya Bulgariya*, vol. 5 (Sofia, 1986); Evgeni Pavlov, *Dimitur Petkov* (Sofia, 1987); A. Pantev and B. Gavrilov, *100-te nay-vliyatelni bulgari v nashata istoriya* (Sofia, 1997); Tasho Tashev, *Ministrite na Bulgariya 1879–1999: Entsiklopedichen Spravochnik* (Sofia, 1999); Milen Kumanov and Tania Nikolova, *Politicheski partii, organizatsii i dvizheniia w Bulgariya i tekhnite lideri 1879–1999: Kratuk spravochnik* (Sofia, 1999); Angel Tsurakov, *Entsiklopediya. Pravitelstvata na Bulgariya: Khronologiya na politicheskiia zhivot 1879–2001* (Sofia, 2001).

PETKOV Nikola (21 July 1893, Sofia–23 September 1947, Sofia), Bulgarian politician. The son of **Dimitur Petkov** and brother of **Petko Petkov**, in 1922 Petkov completed law studies in Paris. He fought in the Balkan Wars (1912–13) and in World War I. Later he worked in the Ministry of Foreign Affairs and served as secretary at the legation in Paris. He was dismissed from this post after the coup of 6 June 1923, in which the government of **Aleksandur Stamboliyski** was overthrown. In 1923, under the influence of his brother, Petkov joined the Bulgarian Agrarian National Union (Bŭlgarski Zemedelski Naroden Sŭyuz [BANU]). Until 1929 he lived in France,

where he was active as a politician and journalist. Petkov worked with **Georgi "Gemeto" Dimitrov, Aleksandur Obbov**, and other politicians. He edited the periodical *Narodna vola*. In France he became a strong supporter of democracy. After returning to Bulgaria, Petkov took part in the shaping of the ideological direction of the BANU–Pladne and in the establishment of the Aleksandur Stamboliyski BANU. From 1931 to 1932 he edited the newspaper *Zemya*. He served as a member of the BANU Standing Committee and edited a BANU press organ, *Zemedelsko zname* (1932–33, 1944). After the coup of May 1934, Petkov was in opposition to the authoritarian rule. He became a member of the BANU–Vrabcha 1 and joined a nonparty alliance called Petorkata (Five), which sought to restore constitutional rule. Petkov maintained contacts with all factions of the peasant movement but established the closest ties with the faction led by "Gemeto" Dimitrov. Elected to the National Assembly in 1938, Petkov was deprived of his parliamentary immunity for his part in the drafting of an appeal to Tsar **Boris III** in which the authoritarian system of government was criticized. In December 1938 Petkov was interned in Ivaylovgrad. At the beginning of 1939 he unsuccessfully attempted to organize a "people's front" consisting of the BANU, the Zveno group, and the Communists.

During World War II Petkov was persecuted for his criticism of authoritarian rule, the pro-German policies of Boris III, and the governments that were obedient to the tsar. Sent to the concentration camp of Gonda Voda, near Asenovgrad (December 1940–June 1941), he worked on the construction of a road in the mountains, along with the Communists **Todor Pavlov, Anton Yugov**, and other prisoners. After his release, Petkov wrote an open letter to Tsar Boris in which he condemned the pro-German policy implemented by the tsar and the government, as well as the terror instigated against their political opponents. In the autumn of 1941 Petkov came to the conclusion that Bulgaria's peasant and workers' parties, including the Communist Party, should cooperate after the war. He maintained contacts with activists of the opposition parties and organized assistance for people who were persecuted, including the Communists. He co-founded the Fatherland Front (FF) and represented this party in the FF National Committee (August 1943). However, Petkov remained an opponent of military struggle, which was preferred by the Communists. Again interned in the Gonda Voda concentration camp, in early 1944 Petkov was deported to Svishtovo, where, along with twelve other opposition leaders, on 7 July 1944 he signed a petition to the regents and to the government demanding fundamental changes in foreign policy and calling for Bulgaria's withdrawal from the war on the side of Germany, rapprochement with the Soviet Union, and the establishment of a constitutional people's government. Petkov refused to join the government of **Konstantin Muraviev**.

Petkov took part in secret preparations for the takeover of power by the FF (9 September 1944). After the coup, he became minister without portfolio in the government of **Kimon Georgiev** (September 1944–July 1945). Petkov was a member of the Bulgarian delegation that signed an armistice treaty with the United States, Great Britain, and the Soviet Union in Moscow on 28 October 1944. From January to July 1945 he was the BANU secretary general, and from March to July 1945 he was a member of the FF National Committee. On 30 July 1945 Petkov left the government in protest against a limitation of the BANU's role in governing the country, and he founded an opposition party, the Bulgarian Agrarian National Union–Nikola Petkov (BANU–Nikola Petkov). He was an editor of the opposition newspaper *Narodno zemedelsko zname* (1945–47). From July 1945 to June 1947 he was the leader not only of the BANU, but also of the entire anti-Communist opposition. As deputy to the Grand National Assembly (1946–47), Petkov led the struggle against the Communist dictatorship and fought for the rule of law and respect for democratic principles.

On 28 May 1947 Minister of Interior Yugov informed Prime Minister **Georgi Dimitrov** that materials had been compiled that incriminated Petkov. On 5 June 1947 the Grand National Assembly deprived Petkov of his parliamentary immunity, and then he was arrested in the sessions hall. In a rigged political trial (5–16 August 1947) Petkov was sentenced to death by hanging for allegedly preparing a coup d'état. After his sentence was announced, Petkov sent letters to Prime Minister Dimitrov, President **Vasil Kolarov**, and the Soviet minister plenipotentiary, Stepan Kirsanov, asking for a pardon. These letters did not satisfy the Communist leaders because they could not be used as a basis to fully discredit Petkov, who, although admitting that his opposition activities had been erroneous, acted in a dignified way. Thus on 16 September 1947 the Supreme Court of Appeals rejected Petkov's plea for a pardon, and Kolarov did not used his right to grant mercy. The sentence was carried out. Petkov was buried in a cemetery in Sofia, and later his body was taken to an unknown place. On 15 January 1990 he was posthumously rehabilitated. In July 1993 in Sofia a bust of Petkov was unveiled, and in February 1998 the Bulgarian Supreme Court of Appeals quashed the sentence of 1947. Petkov's publications include *Aleksandur Stamboliyski: Lichnost i idei* (Aleksandur Stamboliyski: Personality and ideas; 1930). (JJ)

Sources: *Entsiklopediya Bulgariya*, vol. 5 (Sofia, 1986); J. F. Brown, *Bulgaria under Communist Rule* (New York, 1970); Marshall Lee Miller, *Bulgaria during the Second World War* (Stanford, 1975); Petur Semerdzhev, *Sudebniiat protses sreshtu Nikola D. Petkov prez 1947 g.* (Paris, 1987); Georgi Gunev, *Kum brega na svobodata ili za Nikola Petkov i negovoto vreme* (Sofia, 1992); Jerzy Jackowicz, *Partie opozycyjne w Bułgarii 1944–1948* (Warsaw, 1997); Raymond Detrez, *Historical Dictionary of Bulgaria* (Lanham, Md., 1997); Milen Kumanov and Tania Nikolova, *Politicheski partii, organizatsii i dvizheniia v Bulgariya i tekhnite lideri 1879–1999* (Sofia, 1999); Tasho Tashev, *Ministrite na Bulgariia 1879–1999: Entsiklopedichen Spravochnik* (Sofia, 1999); *Bulgarski durzhavnitsi i polititsi 1918–1947* (Sofia, 2000).

PETKOV Petko (4 May 1891, Sofia–14 June 1924, Sofia), Bulgarian politician and diplomat. Petkov was the son of **Dimitur Petkov**, a well-known national-liberal politician. In 1912 he graduated in law and political science from the Sorbonne, Paris. He subsequently volunteered to serve in the army and fought in the Balkan Wars (1912–13). Promoted to officer, he then fought in World War I. In 1920 he became secretary at the legation in Paris and was a member of the Bulgarian delegation to a conference in Genoa. In 1922 Petkov became head of the political department of the Ministry of Foreign Affairs, and later he was appointed secretary general of this ministry. He owed his promotion to his career in the Bulgarian Agrarian National Union (Bulgarski Zemedelski Naroden Sayuz [BANU]), led by **Aleksandur Stamboliyski**. Petkov was the BANU's main authority on constitutional issues. After the coup of 9 June 1923 and the overthrow of Stamboliyski's government, Petkov was briefly detained. In the elections of November 1923 he was elected to the National Assembly. At that time he published extensively in *Zashtita* and *Zemedelska Zashtita*. Petkov was a member of the BANU left wing, which called for the establishment of a common front with the Communists. Petkov was shot by his political opponents on a street in Sofia. His funeral in Sofia became an occasion for a demonstration by the left wing. (AG)

Sources: *Entsiklopediya Bulgariya*, vol. 2 (Sofia, 1981); *Suvremenna Bulgarska Entsiklopediya*, vol. 4a (Sofia, 1994); John D. Bell, *Peasants in Power: Alexander Stamboliski and the Bulgarian Agrarian National Union, 1899–1923* (Princeton, 1978); Zygmunt Hammerling, *Ruch ludowy w Polsce, Bułgarii i Czechoslowacji 1893–1930* (Warsaw, 1987).

PETKUS Viktoras (30 December 1929, Aleksandrai, near Raseiniai), Lithuanian activist of the democratic opposition. Petkus graduated from a technical high school. Arrested for the first time in 1947, he escaped from prison but was caught by the Soviet security forces in 1948 and sentenced to ten years of labor camp for taking part in a Catholic organization, Ateitis (Future), which opposed the incorporation of Lithuania into the USSR. Released in

1953, in 1954 Petkus started literary studies at the University of Vilnius. In 1957 he was expelled from the university and arrested again. In mid-July 1958 he was sentenced to eight years of labor camp for possessing illegal literature. He served in the Tayshet camps near Irkutsk, in Mordvinian camps, and in Vladimir Prison. Released in December 1965, Petkus restarted his studies in Lithuanian history and literature. Expelled from the university, he worked as a blue-collar laborer in a hospital. In December 1975 he was arrested in connection with the publication of the underground periodical, "Chronicle of the Catholic Church in Lithuania" and with protests against the trial of Sergey Kovalyov in Vilnius. After his release, in November 1976, along with **Tomas Venclova**, Reverend Karolis Garuckas, and Eitanas Finkelsteinas, Petkus organized the Lithuanian Helsinki Group. He was arrested again in August 1977 and sentenced to ten years in camp and five years in exile in July 1978. While in the camp, Petkus joined the Ukrainian Helsinki Group. In 1985 he was suggested as a candidate for the Nobel Peace Prize. After his release, in May 1988 Petkus returned to Lithuania, and, along with **Nijole Sadūnaitė** and Antanas Terleckas, he started the official activities of the League of Lithuanian Freedom (Lietuvos Laisves Lyga), an organization started secretly in the late 1970s. During the elections to the Lithuanian Supreme Council in February 1990, in which the Lithuanian Movement for Reconstruction (Sąjūdis) won, Petkus had doubts about the freedom of choice and about the Sąjūdis itself. He joined the Lithuanian Christian Democratic Party (Lietuvos Krikščionių Demokratų Partija [LKDP]). Happy with Latvia's regained freedom, Petkus was disappointed by the dominant role of the post-Communists and by the social problems during the transition. Petkus belonged to the LKDP Council and was an honorary chairman of the Lithuanian Association of Human Rights. (WR)

Sources: S. P. de Boer, E. J. Driessen, and H. L. Verhaar, eds., *Biographical Dictionary of Dissidents in the Soviet Union, 1956–1975* (The Hague and Boston, 1982); Rasa Mažeika, ed., *Violations of Human Rights in Soviet Occupied Lithuania* (Philadelphia, 1988); Anatol Lieven, *The Baltic Revolution* (New Haven, 1993); Romuald J. Misiunas and Rein Taagepera, *The Baltic States: Years of Dependence, 1940–1990* (Berkeley, 1993).

PETLURA Symon (10 May 1879, Poltava–25 May 1926, Paris), Ukrainian politician and commander-in-chief of the Ukrainian Army. Born into a lower-middle-class family with Cossack traditions, Petlura did not complete his education because of his political activities. In 1901 he was expelled from the Poltava Theological Seminary, where he was in his last year, and was forbidden to reenter the university. In 1900 he became active in the

Revolutionary Ukrainian Party (RUP), and in 1905 he joined the Ukrainian Social Democratic Workers' Party (USDWP), the successor of the RUP. He represented the party group that sought the establishment of an autonomous Ukrainian state within the framework of the future Russian federation. In 1908 Petlura joined the Society of Ukrainian Progressives. During World War I he was active in the Union of Zemstvos, an aid organization to the wounded and civilians. After the outbreak of the February Revolution of 1917, as a delegate of the Ukrainian Military Committee of the Western Front, Petlura attended the First Ukrainian Military Congress in May 1917 in Kiev. He became head of the General Military Committee, which was established by the Congress. The General Military Committee endeavored to establish Ukrainian military units within the framework of the Russian Army. Later, Petlura directed sessions of the Second Congress (June 1917) at which a resolution claiming autonomy for the Ukraine was passed. Subsequently he was appointed to the first Ukrainian government, the General Secretariat, as secretary for military affairs. His efforts led to the establishment of the rudiments of a national army in the form of the First and Second Corps. After the seizure of power by the Bolsheviks, Petlura expressed support for the independence of the Ukraine, and he favored a pro-French orientation. As a result, he fell into conflict with members of the Ukrainian Central Rada (Council) who chose a pro-German option, and consequently he lost his post in December 1917.

Commanding his own units at the beginning of February 1918, Petlura greatly contributed to the seizure of the Kiev Arsenal from the Red Army. Under the rule of the Germans and Hetman **Pavlo Skoropadskyi**, Petlura organized opposition activities, for which he was arrested (July–November 1918). Despite protests by President **Volodymyr Vynnychenko**, in November 1918, as chief ataman (i.e., commander-in-chief of the army), Petlura joined the staff that was preparing an anti-hetman coup. After the overthrow of the hetman on 14 December 1918, Petlura faced the very difficult task of imposing discipline in various military units. A wave of anti-Semitic pogroms was perpetrated by soldiers of various formations (including Bolshevik troops and Denikin's) throughout the Ukraine, but the responsibility for these acts was attributed to Petlura. Measures counteracting the anarchy had limited effect. On 11 February 1919 Petlura replaced Vynnychenko, who was inclined to negotiate with the Bolsheviks, as president of the Directorate. This step was taken to gain the French as allies, but it failed because the Entente powers supported General Anton Denikin and did not trust the Ukrainian National Republic (UNR) because of its Socialist character and because of the pogroms. After the capture of Kiev by the Bolsheviks in February 1919, Petlura concentrated his units in Vynnytsa and sought contacts with the newly formed Polish state. Poland's recognition of the UNR and military aid were offered only in exchange for acceding to the Polish claims to Eastern Galicia and Western Volhynia. The negotiations with Poland strained Petlura's relations with the government of the Western Ukrainian National Republic (WUNR) in Eastern Galicia, right after the formal unification of the WUNR with the UNR on 22 January 1919. As a result, the union of the two republics disintegrated.

The successes of the Russian Whites and then of the Bolsheviks, who in the winter of 1920 seized the Ukraine, forced Petlura to even closer cooperation with Poland, especially when his army lost its fighting value after guerrilla activities in the rear of the Denikin army (the so-called first winter march, November–December 1919). The final Treaty of Alliance with Poland was signed on 21 April 1920. Consequently, combined Polish and Ukrainian forces launched a successful offensive on Kiev, which was seized on 8 May 1920. Petlura entered the capital ceremoniously, but as a result of the Soviet counteroffensive on 11 June it was already occupied by the Red Army. Petlura's forces remained faithful to Poland during the further war against Bolshevik Russia, but Poland gave up the defense of Ukrainian interests at the final peace negotiations with the Bolsheviks (October 1920–March 1921). Launching an attack by his units, Petlura undertook one more desperate attempt to instigate an anti-Bolshevik uprising in the Ukraine in November 1920. After the failure of the uprising, Poland reduced its contribution to granting political asylum and modest material help for the UNR authorities. Petlura tried to sustain the UNR's activities in Tarnów and Warsaw, but political conflicts in the emigrant community, as well as the pressure from Soviet authorities on Poland, resulted in the loss of the official standing of the UNR.

Finally, Petlura decided to move the UNR's state center to Paris, where he arrived in the spring of 1924. His sudden death at the hands of Samuel Schwartzbard, a Jewish émigré from the Ukraine, put an end to his efforts to integrate the Ukrainian diaspora. The assassin justified his deed as an act of revenge for the deaths of tens of thousands of Jews who had fallen victims to the pogroms carried out by Petlura's soldiers. In the atmosphere created by the French media the court acknowledged the moral rights of the killer and acquitted him. Many scholars in exile allege that there was a link between Schwartzbard and Soviet special services, but the allegations have not been proved thus far. Two volumes of Petlura's *Statti, listi, dokumenti* (Speeches, letters, and documents) were published in New York in 1956 and 1979 and *Statti* (Speeches) in Kiev in 1993. (TS)

Sources: *Encyclopedia of Ukraine*, vol. 3 (Toronto, 1993); Wasyl Iwanis, *Simon Petljura: Prezident Ukrajini* (Toronto, 1952); Pavlo Shandruk, *Arms in Valor* (New York, 1959); Alain Desroches, *Le problème ukrainien et Simon Petlura* (Paris, 1962); W. Kosik, ed., *Simon Petlyura: Zbirnyk studiino-naukowoii konferencii w Parizhi (v 1976): Statti, zamitki, materiiali* (Monachium and Paris, 1980); *Simon Petlyura ta ioho rodina: Do 70-richchia ioho tragichnoii zahibeli: Dokumenti i materijali* (Kiev, 1996), Stanisław Stępień, "Symon Petlura: Życie i działalność," *Warszawskie Zeszyty Ukrainoznawcze*, vol. 3 (Warsaw, 1996); Antoni Serednicki, *Symon Petlura: Życie i działalność* (Warsaw, 1997); Jan Jacek Bruski, *Petlurowcy: Centrum państwowe Ukraińskiej Republiki Ludowej na wychodźstwie 1919–1924* (Kraków, 2000); Orest Subtelny, *Ukraine: A History* (Toronto, 2000).

PETRESCU Constantin (Titel) (17 July 1888, Craiova–September 1957, Sighet), Romanian lawyer and politician. Petrescu studied at the School of Law of Bucharest University from 1906 to 1910. In his youth he became an activist in the Social Democratic Party of Romania (Partidul Social-Democrat din România [PSDR]), which played an important role in Romanian political life. Petrescu's views were close to syndicalism. He was also active in the trade union movement. From 1927 to 1938 he served as secretary of the PSDR, which was disbanded in February 1938, like all political parties in Romania after King **Charles II** established a royal dictatorship. Later Petrescu participated in a plot against General **Ion Antonescu**. On 20 June 1944 he signed an agreement among the liberals, Peasant Party members, Social Democrats, and Communists, as a result of which the National Democratic Bloc was formed.

After the coup d'état of 23 August 1944, Petrescu became head of the PSDR. He reorganized this party and attempted to implement a political course that was independent of the Communists. From 23 August to 6 December 1944 he was minister without portfolio in the government of General **Constantin Sănătescu**. In February 1945 the PSDR supported the Communist-dominated government of **Petru Groza**. At the end of 1945 Petrescu still had a majority in the party leadership, but gradually the crypto-Communists and their supporters took over control of the PSDR. When on 10 March 1946, at a congress of Socialists, the majority of delegates supported the PSDR's participation in an electoral bloc with the Communists, Petrescu and a group of his supporters left the party and founded the Independent Social Democratic Party. In the rigged elections of November 1946 Petrescu's party did not obtain any seats in parliament. Petrescu opposed Communist domination, Soviet military occupation, and the terror perpetrated under Groza's rule. In May 1948, soon after the PSDR was forcibly merged with the Communist Party, Petrescu was arrested. In January 1952, after many years of investigation, he was sentenced to life imprisonment as a "traitor" and "enemy of the unity of the working class." In December 1954 the minister of interior, **Alexandru Drăghici**, offered Petrescu freedom in exchange for his writing an open letter supporting the regime. Petrescu demanded that several other imprisoned Socialists also be released. As the authorities promised to meet this demand, Petrescu wrote the letter, which was published in the newspaper *Scîntea* on 18 December 1955, but the promised releases did not take place. Petrescu died in a prison for political prisoners in Sighet. He was the author of *Socialismul în România 1835–6 septembrie 1940* (Socialism in Romania, 1835–6 September 1940; 1940). (FA/TD)

Sources: Emil Jurcă, *Istoria social democraţiei în România*, vols. 1–2 (Bucharest, 1993); Hugh Seton-Watson, *The East European Revolution* (London, 1950); Robert Lee Wolff, *The Balkans in Our Time* (Cambridge, Mass., 1956); Adrian Dimitriu, "Mentorul meu politic: Constantin Titel Petrescu," *Magazin Istoric*, 1993, no. 9; Florin Constantinu, *23 August 1944* (Bucharest, 1986); Dennis Deletant, *Communist Terror in Romania: Gheorghiu-Dej and the Police State, 1948–1965* (New York, 1999).

PETRESCU-COMNEN Nicolae (24 August 1881, Bucharest–17 October 1949, Rome), Romanian lawyer, journalist, and diplomat. Petrescu-Comnen studied law in Paris, earning a doctorate in 1905. From 1902 to 1916 he worked as an attorney and lecturer at the School of Law of the University of Bucharest. After the end of World War I, he entered the diplomatic service. In 1919 he was a member of the Romanian delegation to the Paris Peace Conference, where he dealt with the issue of Dobrudja. From 1922 to 1929 he represented Romania at successive conferences in Geneva, where he worked as a minister plenipotentiary at the League of Nations from 1923 to 1928. From 1928 to 1938 he also served in the same rank at embassies in Germany (1928–31, 1933–38) and the Holy See (1931–33). After the 1938 royal coup d'état, he served as minister of foreign affairs (March 1938–December 1938). During the Czechoslovak crisis Petrescu-Comnen took a neutral position, fearing that Soviet support for Czechoslovakia might lead to a war on Romanian territory. In October 1938, shortly after the Munich agreement, King **Charles II** and Petrescu-Comnen met with the Polish minister of foreign affairs, **Józef Beck**. Romania rejected Poland's proposal that Romania take part in the occupation of the Czechoslovak part of Subcarpathian Ruthenia. From 1939 to 1940 Petrescu-Comnen again represented Romania at the Holy See. On 15 October 1940 he was dismissed from the diplomatic service for a statement criticizing the Iron Guard and General **Ion**

Antonescu. From 1940 until the end of his life Petrescu-Comnen lived in exile in Italy. Petrescu-Comnen was the author of numerous works in the field of contemporary international politics, including the following: *La revendication de la nationalité roumaine* (1918); *The Roumanian Question in Transylvania and Hungary* (1920); *Anarchie, dictature ou organisation internationale* (1946); *Preludi del grande dramma* (A prelude to the great drama; 1947); *I Responsabili* (The responsible; 1949); and "Campania românească din 1919 din Ungaria. Amintiri şi documente inedite" (The Romanian campaign of 1919 in Hungary: Unpublished memoirs and documents, in *Revista Istorica*, nos. 5–6, 1992). (FA/TD)

Sources: *Regele Carol al. II-lea, Inseminării zilnice*, vol. 1 (Bucharest, 1995); Raoul Bossy, *Amintiri din Viaţa diplomatică*, vols. 1–2 (Bucharest, 1993–94); Ion Calafeteanu, *Români la Hitler* (Bucharest, 1999); Henryk Batowski, "Rumuńska podróż Becka w październiku 1938 r.," *Kwartalnik Historyczny*, 1958, no. 2.

PETRI György (22 December 1943, Budapest–16 July 2000, Budapest), Hungarian poet and journalist. After graduating from high school in 1962, Petri took various odd jobs, mainly in sanatoriums and psychotherapeutic centers. In 1966 he took up philosophical studies at the University of Budapest but failed to complete them. In 1971 he published his first volume of poetry, *Magyarázatok M. számára* (Explanations for M.), which reflected the slogans of the European "new left wing" of that time. The next collection, *Körülírt zuhanás* (Circumscribed Fall; 1974), included poems with a similar message, written from the perspective of somebody who was rejected and misunderstood by those around him. Because of his activities in the democratic opposition, from the mid–1970s on Petri could publish only in samizdat periodicals and abroad. His collection of politically committed poems, *Örökhétfő* (1981; *Eternal Monday*, 1999), was also published underground. Nihilistic and blasphemous poems were another characteristic strand in Petri's writing of that period. From 1981 to 1989 Petri edited *Beszélő*, the most important periodical of the democratic opposition in Hungary at that time. In 1989 he became a member of the editorial council of the literary periodical *Holmi*. He was a founding member of the Alliance of Free Democrats. In the poetry written in the 1990s, Petri remained faithful to his manner of poetic articulation, which included commentaries on political events. (MS)

Sources: Géza Fodor, *Petri György költészete* (Budapest, 1991); *Beszélgetések Petri Györggyel* (Budapest, 1994); Tibor Keresztury, *Petri György* (Budapest, 1998).

PETRONIJEVIĆ Branislav (25 March 1875, Sovljak kod Uba–4 March 1954, Belgrade), Serbian philosopher and paleontologist. After graduating from a gymnasium in Valjevo, Petronijević studied philosophy at the University of Leipzig, earning a doctorate in 1898. In the same year he became an associate professor at the Superior School (Velika Škola) in Belgrade, and in 1903 he became a professor there. When in 1905 the Velika Škola was transformed into the University of Belgrade, Petronijević became an associate professor and in 1919 a full professor. During World War I Petronijević was in London, where he conducted research in the natural sciences. In 1920 he became a full member of the Serbian Academy of Sciences. Petronijević's philosophy was a synthesis of classical English empiricism and German rationalism. In metaphysics he aimed at harmonizing the monism of Baruch Spinoza and the idealism of Gottfried Wilhelm Leibnitz. He presented the world as a set of points of being, quality, and will. He significantly contributed to the development of discontinuous geometry. Petronijević's main works are the following: *Der ontologische Beweis für das Dasein des Absoluten* (1897); *Prinzipien der Erkenntnislehre* (1900); *Prinzipien der Metaphysik* (2 vols.; 1904–11); *Die typische Geometrien und das Unendliche* (1907); and *Istorija moderne filozofije* (History of modern philosophy; 1922). In paleontology Petronijević became famous for his research on the archaeopteryx. (WR)

Sources: *Enciklopedija Jugoslavije*, vol. 6 (Zagreb, 1965); Željan E. Šuster, *Historical Dictionary of the Federal Republic of Yugoslavia* (Lanham, Md., 1999); Mihailo Djurić, *Filozofija u dijaspori: Petronijevićeva načela metafizike* (Novi Sad, 1989); Andrija B. Stojković, *Branislav Petronijević* (New Belgrade, 1989).

PETROVIĆ Rastko (16 May 1898, Belgrade–15 August 1949, Washington, D.C.), Serbian writer. Petrović's father was a clerk and his mother a painter. During World War I, as a seventeen-year-old high school student, Petrović took part in the heroic retreat of the Serbian Army over the Albanian mountains. He later completed law studies in France, where he established contacts with the artistic elite of that period, including Pablo Picasso, André Breton, and Paul Eluard. In 1923 Petrović began working in the Ministry of Foreign Affairs in Belgrade, from 1926 to 1928 he was at a diplomatic mission in Rome, and in 1935 he was sent to the United States, where he remained after the end of World War II. Petrović made his literary debut during World War I and became famous as the author of the novel *Burleska gospodina Peruna boga groma* (The burlesque of Lord Perun, the god of thunder; 1921) and the poetry volume *Otkrovenja* (Revelation; 1922). In these works Petrović expressed his joy with the richness of the world

and life, and he sought inspiration from Slavic traditions. Petrović was influenced by the psychoanalytic school, Serbian native folklore, and exotic cultures. In 1928 he traveled to Africa, which inspired him to write the travel book *Afrika* (Africa; 1930). An enthusiastic traveler, he also visited other Balkan countries, Spain, Italy, Turkey, and Libya. His travels to Spain resulted in the story "Ljudi govore" (People talk; 1931). Petrović's poetic ecstasy over travel resulted from his interest in the world and a sense of the world's unity. His concept of a full life included, in his interpretation, both happiness and success, as well as suffering. In the 1930s Petrović began writing *Dan šesti* (The sixth day; 1961), a vast novel that came out after his death. In 1964 his *Izabrana dela* (Selected works) were published. (WR)

Sources: *Enciklopedija Jugoslavije*, vol. 6 (Zagreb, 1965); Željan E. Šuster, *Historical Dictionary of the Federal Republic of Yugoslavia* (Lanham, Md., 1999); Milivoje Minivić, *Rečenica u proznim djelima Rastka Petrovića* (Sarajevo 1970); Jasmina Musabegović, *Rastko Petrović i njegovo djelo* (Belgrade, 1976); Radovan Popović, *Izabrani čovek ili život Rastka Petrovicia* (Belgrade, 1986); Radomir Baturan, *Otkrovenja Rastka Petrovića* (Belgrade, 1993).

PETRUSHEVYCH Yevhen (3 June 1863, Busko–20 August 1940, Berlin), Ukrainian lawyer and politician. Petrushevych was educated at a secondary school and the university in Lviv (Lwów). He was chairman of the Academic Fraternity. In 1896 he began working as a lawyer, first in Sokal and, in 1910, in Skole. From 1907 to 1918 he was a member of the Austrian parliament of the Sokal-Radechów-Brody constituency, and from 1910 to 1914 he was a member of the Galician Sejm (parliament). Petrushevych was deputy president of the Ukrainian Parliamentary Club in Lviv and, from 1910, deputy president of the Ukrainian Parliamentary Representation in Vienna. He represented the Ukrainian National Democratic Party and for many years was one of its leaders. An opponent of opportunism, he advocated that the Ukrainians should firmly claim theirs rights in a parliamentary way. As a result of his work, the Galician Sejm amended its statutes and passed a new electoral law that was more favorable to the Ukrainians (1914).

Named president of the Ukrainian Parliamentary Representation in Vienna in 1917, Petrushevych aimed at the establishment of a royal province with a Ukrainian administration. On 10 October 1918 he summoned the Ukrainian Constituent Assembly in Lviv; the objective was to decide the fate of the lands populated by the Ukrainians but belonging to Austria-Hungary. This assembly was transformed into the Ukrainian National Council (UNC), and Petrushevych became its head. The UNC proclaimed the establishment of a Western Ukrainian National Republic (WUNR). Petrushevych informed U.S. President Woodrow Wilson, about its creation on 26 October 1918. After the formal union of the WUNR and the Ukrainian National Republic (UNR) in January 1919, Petrushevych became a member of the UNR Directorate. On 9 June 1919 the Ukrainian Council named him dictator of the WUNR. Petrushevych was in favor of continuing the war against Poland and opposed seeking an agreement with Poland; because of his views he clashed with Symon Petlura.

After the final defeat of the Western Galician army in the war against Poland in November 1919, Petrushevych went to live in Vienna. There he formed a government-in-exile that attempted to influence international opinion and to secure favorable decisions for the Ukraine regarding Galicia. After the Council of Ambassadors decided to award sovereignty over Eastern Galicia to Poland, Petrushevych dissolved his government and went to Berlin, where he further endeavored to represent Ukrainian interests. When the Ukrainian parties that were active in Poland withdrew their support for Petrushevych's actions on the international scene, he continued his work in private. For some time he hoped for the support of the USSR against Poland, but he realized that this was in vain. Petrushevych spent the rest of his life in Berlin, where he died. (GM)

Sources: *Encyclopedia of Ukraine*, vol. 3 (Toronto, 1993); Matthew Stachiv and Jaroslav Sztendera, eds., *Western Ukraine at the Turning Point of Europe's History, 1918–1923*, vols. 1–2 (New York, 1971); Maciej Kozłowski, *Między Sanem i Zbruczem: Walki o Lwów i Galicję Wschodnią 1918–1919* (Kraków, 1990); Ryszard Torzecki, *Polacy i Ukraińcy: Sprawa ukraińska w czasie II wojny światowej na terenie II Rzeczypospolitej* (Warsaw, 1993); Paul R. Magocsi, *A History of Ukraine* (Seattle, 1996); Orest Subtelny, *Ukraine: A History* (Toronto, 2000).

PEYER Károly (9 May 1881, Városlöd–25 October 1956, New York), Hungarian Social Democratic politician. Born into a peasant family, Peyer worked as a smith in a factory. In 1905 he was elected to the executive board of the trade union of metalworkers, and in 1911 he was promoted to secretary general of the council of the Hungarian trade unions. At the end of 1918 Peyer, as a commissar of the republican government, issued a decree on the eight-hour workday. Although during the revolution of 1919 Peyer spoke against the Red Terror, he took part in a delegation of the Hungarian Soviet Republic (HSR) that ineffectively attempted to reach an agreement with Romania at the end of July 1919. After the fall of the HSR Peyer became interim minister of the interior and then minister of labor and social welfare. However, when Admiral **Miklós Horthy** consolidated his power, Peyer had to resign and even leave

for Vienna, as he feared anti-Socialist repressive measures. After his return to Hungary in 1921 Peyer signed an agreement with the government of **István Bethlen**. This agreement allowed the right wing of the Social Democrat party to continue its activities on condition that the party's left was excluded. Peyer became head of the Hungarian Social Democratic Party (Magyarországi Szociáldemokrata Párt [MSP]), and in 1922 he was elected to the parliament. He was an MP during the entire interwar period. He represented the MSP in the Socialist International and also worked in the International Labour Office in Geneva.

After the German invasion of Hungary in March 1944, Peyer was imprisoned and put in the Mauthausen camp. In his absence **Árpád Szakasits** linked the MSP to the Communists. Upon his return to Hungary in August 1945 Peyer was offered a diplomatic post abroad, but he preferred to stay in Hungary and fight for the identity of his party. He courageously acted against the Communist terror. Since the Communists knew that Peyer was popular among the working class, they prevented him from meeting with factory workers. In 1946 Peyer issued a memorandum demanding the reinstatement of the rule of law. During the 1947 elections the Communists tripped up Peyer's candidature on the Social Democratic lists; therefore he ran as an independent candidate and entered the parliament. In response, the Communists accused him of "plotting against the state" and "collaboration with American imperialism to overthrow democracy." Peyer was stripped of his parliamentary immunity, and a trap was set for him when he was offered a "no-strings-attached departure to the West" because it might have become a pretext for his arrest. Peyer escaped the security police and on 18 November 1947 crossed the border into Austria. He went to Switzerland and then to the United States, where in 1949 he joined the Hungarian National Council. Peyer died of a heart attack when he learned about the revolution in Hungary. (WR)

Sources: *New York Times*, 27 October 1956; *Fifth Interim Report of Hearings before the Subcommittee on Hungary of the House of Representatives Select Committee on Communist Aggression* (Washington, D.C., 1954); Ignác Romsics, *Hungary in the Twentieth Century* (Budapest, 1999).

PFEIFFER Zoltán (15 August 1900, Budapest–16 August 1981, New York), Hungarian lawyer and politician. After graduating in law, Pfeiffer worked as an attorney. In 1931 he joined the Independent Smallholders' Party (ISP). From 1943 he represented this party in a coalition of opposition parties. After the Germans occupied Hungary in March 1944, Pfeiffer went underground and joined the anti-Nazi military resistance movement. When in November 1945 the ISP won the elections, he became secretary of state for political affairs at the Ministry of Justice. At that time Pfeiffer collected and published documentation on the mass murder of opposition activists in Gyömrő, committed probably by Communists who were assisted by Soviet troops, as well as documentation on pogroms initiated by Communists in Kunmadaras and Miskolc. Marshal Kliment Voroshilov, head of the Allied Control Commission, demanded that Pfeiffer be dismissed from his position. This took place in December 1946.

In March 1947 Pfeiffer left the ISP. In July 1947, after the ISP had become debilitated as a result of its leaders having been arrested or forced to go into exile, Pfeiffer founded the Hungarian Independence Party (Magyar Függetlenségi Párt). Despite the terror and manipulations of the Communists, his party won forty-nine seats (13.4 percent), becoming the second largest opposition party in the parliament elected in August 1947. During the election campaign Pfeiffer was badly beaten by a bunch of Communist thugs. In September 1947 he attacked the Communists for their use of terror and electoral fraud. The Communists responded by producing false accusations, as a result of which Pfeiffer's party was deprived of all seats won in the elections. The Communists also wanted to deprive him of his parliamentary immunity and charge him with criminal offenses. Pfeiffer succeeded in getting his wife and little daughter out of Hungary, and with the help of the U.S. mission he also left the country (4 November 1947). Less than three weeks later, he was stripped of his Hungarian citizenship. Pfeiffer settled in New York, where he was one of the founders of the Hungarian National Council (HNC). As a member of the HNC Executive Committee, he sat in the Assembly of Captive European Nations (ACEN). Pfeiffer worked with the Hungarian editorial staff of Radio Free Europe and was in charge of a section in the periodical *Független Magyarország* (1950–60). (WR)

Sources: *The Annual Obituary*, 1981; *Fifth Interim Report of Hearings before the Subcommittee on Hungary of the House of Representatives Select Committee on Communist Aggression* (Washington, D.C., 1954).

PIASECKI Bolesław, pseudonym "Sablewski" (18 February 1915, Łódź–1 January 1979, Warsaw), Polish nationalist politician. Born into a family of clerks that traced its origins to the nobility, as a teenager Piasecki joined the youth organizations of the National Party (Stronnictwo Narodowe [SN]), and in 1931 he became an active member of the Great Poland Camp (Obóz Wielkiej Polski [OWP]). In 1934, while a law student at Warsaw University, Piasecki was one of the founders of the rightist National Radical Camp (Obóz Narodowo-Radykalny

[ONR]), established in opposition to the SN leadership, which was seen as too moderate by the nationalist youth. In 1934 Piasecki was briefly held in the isolation camp at Bereza Kartuska. He completed his studies in 1935. When the ONR was declared illegal, he became a leader of an extremely rightist faction of the ONR, the National Radical Movement (also called the ONR–Falanga). From 1935 to 1938 Piasecki edited the monthly *Ruch Młodych*. In 1937 he established contacts with the pro-*sanacja* Camp of National Unity (Obóz Zjednoczenia Narodowego [OZN]), but after a short period of cooperation these contacts were severed. Piasecki initiated actions aimed at intimidating leftist activists and Jewish organizations. The totalitarian and anti-Semitic program of ONR–Falanga was inspired by Italian fascism rather than Nazism, and Piasecki himself delivered evidence to the Polish authorities that one of his supporters, Stanisław Brochwicz, had collaborated with the Third Reich.

Piasecki fought in the September 1939 campaign. Arrested in December 1939 (Brochwicz was instrumental in his arrest), he was released in April 1940 thanks to the intercession of Luciana Frassati-Gawrońska, the wife of a former Polish envoy to Vienna, with Benito Mussolini. After his release, Piasecki went into hiding because a special German court had sentenced him to death. He was active in underground resistance organizations, including the National Confederation (Konfederacja Narodu [KN]), of which he became the commander in 1941. From 1943 to 1944 he commanded a battalion of the Cadre Strike Battalions, which became subordinated to the Home Army (Armia Krajowa [AK]) in August 1943. Piasecki fought in the battles of Vilnius in 1944. On 12 November 1944 he was arrested by the NKVD near Warsaw. As he realized the hopelessness of Poland's situation, he entered into negotiations with **Władysław Gomułka**, head of the Polish Workers' Party (Polska Partia Robotnicza [PPR]), other representatives of the new authorities, and General Ivan Serov from the NKGB. During theses negotiations Piasecki agreed to cooperate with the Polish Communists and with the Soviet Union; as a result, he was later accused of being involved in spying.

On 2 July 1945 Piasecki was released. In November of that year, with the permission of the Communists, he founded the weekly *Dziś i Jutro*. He brought together a group of national and Catholic activists (including **Jan Dobraczyński** and **Konstanty Łubieński**) who declared their willingness to cooperate closely with the Communists in building a Socialist state. The theory of a "dual outlook," combining communism and Catholicism, was also promoted. In 1949 Piasecki established the PAX Publishing Institute, the only publishing house that published Catholic books in Stalinist times. When the PAX Association, an organization that attracted Catholics supporting the new government system, was established (10 April 1952), Piasecki became its head and held this position until the end of his life. The PAX Association had franchises to run various businesses; in them, with the permission of the authorities, Piasecki employed many people who were in danger of being arrested. Owing to the political context and the views that Piasecki promoted, the Church hierarchs watched his activities with anxiety. On 8 September 1949 in a pastoral letter Cardinal **Stefan Wyszyński**, the Primate of Poland, condemned the weekly *Dziś i Jutro*, which was seen by the Church hierarchs as a kind of fifth column among Catholics. In November 1950 Piasecki appointed a Commission of Intellectuals and Catholic Activists, which to some extent weakened the effects of the work of the "patriot priests" who collaborated with the Ministry of Public Security against the Church hierarchs. In 1953, though, Piasecki supported the "February decree" issued by the authorities, took over *Tygodnik Powszechny*, and accepted the arrest of Primate Wyszyński. In 1955 Piasecki's book, *Zagadnienia istotne*, and the weekly *Dziś i jutro* were placed on the index of forbidden books of the Holy Office.

At the time of the dramatic political breakthrough in October 1956, Piasecki favored the neo-Stalinist Natolin faction (Natolińczycy). On 16 October 1956 in the PAX periodical *Słowo Powszechne* he published the article "Instynkt państwowy" (State instinct), in which he vaguely warned against party "liberals" and pointed to the possibility of using force in the defense of "raison d'état." Despite this, Gomułka decided not to dissolve the PAX Association after October 1956. In later years, though, Piasecki supported the faction led by **Mieczysław Moczar**. In January 1957 Piasecki's sixteen-year-old son, Bohdan, was kidnapped and murdered. The circumstances of this tragedy remain unclear. Although Piasecki's aspirations to co-govern Poland ended in failure, in the 1960s and 1970s he was a member of the government elite. From May 1965 until the end of his life he was an MP, and from 22 June 1971 to 1 January 1979, a member of the Council of State. (PK)

Sources: Mołdawa; Andrzej Micewski, *Współrządzić czy nie kłamać? PAX i Znak w Polsce 1945–1976* (Warsaw, 1981); Andrzej Micewski, *Kardynał Wyszyński: Prymas i mąż stanu* (Paris, 1982); Szymon Rudnicki, *Obóz Narodowo-Radykalny* (Warsaw, 1985); Antoni Dudek and Grzegorz Pytel, *Bolesław Piasecki: Próba biografii politycznej* (London, 1990); Andrzej Albert [Wojciech Roszkowski], *Najnowsza historia Polski 1914–1993*, vols. 1–2 (Warsaw, 1995); Antoni Dudek, *Państwo i Kościół w Polsce 1945–1970* (Kraków, 1995); *Słownik polityków polskich XX w.* (Poznań, 1998).

PIEKAŁKIEWICZ Jan, pseudonyms "Juliański," "Wernic," and "Wrocławski" (19 September 1892, Kursk–19 or 21 June 1943, Warsaw), Polish politician and statistician. Piekałkiewicz completed studies in a gymnasium in Petersburg and graduated from the department of economics of the local polytechnic in 1914. From 1915 he conducted statistical research in Russia; for example, he directed the census in the Fergana Valley. After his return to Poland in 1918 Piekałkiewicz ran a family farm in Woskrzenice, near Biała. In 1920 he volunteered for the army to fight against the Bolsheviks. He later worked in the Central Statistical Office (Główny Urząd Statystyczny [GUS]). From 1923 he lectured in statistics at the university in Lwów (Lviv). In 1924 he obtained a Ph.D. in economics and political science and became chair of the Department of Statistics at the School of Political Sciences in Warsaw. From 1927 he was a member of the Statistical Committee of the League of Nations, and from 1933, a staff member of the International Statistical Institute. Piekałkiewicz belonged to the editorial staffs of the periodicals *Statystyka Pracy* and *Kwartalnik Statystyczny* and the *Atlas Statystyczny Rzeczypospolitej Polskiej* (Statistical atlas of the Republic of Poland; 1930). Piekałkiewicz belonged to the Polish Peasant Party–Piast (Polskie Stronnictwo Ludowe–Piast); therefore in 1929 he lost his job in the GUS. From 1931 he was in the leadership of the Peasant Party (Stronnictwo Ludowe [SL]). At the end of 1939 he became active in the underground program committee of the peasant movement called Roch. On 5 August 1941 he was appointed a deputy delegate, and on 5 August 1942 he became a delegate, of the Polish Government-in-Exile for the Homeland. With his approval, Żegota, the Council for Aid to Jews, was founded, and representatives of the Delegation of the Government in Exile (Delegatura) started talks with the Communist representatives in February 1943. However, the negotiations failed. Arrested by the SS on 19 February 1943, Piekałkiewicz was tortured with particular brutality by the SS hauptscharführer, Walter Vossberg, at the Gestapo headquarters on Szucha Street. On 28 May 1943, in a state of extreme exhaustion, Piekałkiwicz was transported to Pawiak Prison, where he died in strict isolation, deprived of medical help. (WR)

Sources: *PSB*, vol. 26; Kunert, vol. 2; Stefan Korboński, *Polskie państwo podziemne* (Paris, 1985); Waldemar Grabowski, *Delegatura Rządu Rzeczypospolitej Polskiej na Kraj 1940–1945* (Warsaw, 1995).

PIERACKI Bronisław (28 May 1895, Gorlice–15 June 1934, Warsaw), Polish officer and politician. From 1913 Pieracki belonged to the Riflemen's Association. He graduated from a high school in Nowy Sącz, and in 1914 he registered in the Department of Philosophy of the Jagiellonian University in Kraków. After the outbreak of World War I he fought as commander of a company in the Polish Legions. As a result of the refusal of top Legion officers to swear loyalty to the Austrian emperor, in July 1917 Pieracki was inducted into the Austro-Hungarian Army. Relieved in the spring of 1918, he entered the Polish Military Organization and commanded its Nowy Sącz and Lwów (Lviv) districts. From November 1918 he served in the Polish Army and took part in the struggle for Lwów against the Ukrainians. In 1919–23 Pieracki worked at various posts in the Ministry of Military Affairs and at the Headquarters of the Commander-in-Chief. He also belonged to a secret military organization, Honor i Ojczyzna (Honor and Fatherland), organized by the followers of **Józef Piłsudski**. In 1924 Pieracki completed a course at the Higher Military Academy in Warsaw, was promoted to colonel, and worked in the staff of the Fourth Army Inspectorate (1924–28). He took part in the preparations for and execution of the May 1926 coup d'état and later belonged to the leaders of the Nonparty Bloc of Cooperation with the Government (Bezpartyjny Blok Współpracy z Rządem [BBWR]). On its behalf Pieracki was elected MP in March 1928 and became deputy head of the BBWR parliamentary club. In October 1928 he gave up his mandate and took over the post of second deputy chief of the General Staff. In April 1929 he became undersecretary for political affairs in the Ministry of Interior. From December 1930 to June 1931 he was minister without portfolio in the government of **Walery Sławek**, and then he became minister of interior. Pieracki favored firm actions against the political opposition but was thought to be an opponent of open violence and desired Polish-Ukrainian cooperation. On his initiative in March 1934 the government established a Committee for Nationality Problems. Pieracki was shot dead by a member of the Organization of Ukrainian Nationalists in Warsaw. He was posthumously appointed brigadier general. Three days after Pieracki's death the president decreed the creation of special isolation camps for members of extremist organizations. On these grounds the Bereza Kartuska camp was established. (JS)

Sources: *PSB*, vol. 26; *Kto był kim w Drugiej Rzeczypospolitej* (Warsaw, 1994); *Bronisław Pieracki: Generał brygady, minister spraw wewnętrznych, poseł na Sejm, żołnierz, mąż stanu, człowiek* (Warsaw, 1934); Władysław Żeleński, *Zabójstwo ministra Pierackiego* (Paris, 1973); Władysław T. Kulesza, *Koncepcje ideowo-polityczne obozu rządzącego w Polsce w latach 1926–1935* (Wrocław, 1985); Ryszard Torzecki, *Polacy i Ukraińcy* (Warsaw, 1993).

PIIP Ants (28 February 1884, Tuhalaane–1 October 1941, labor camp near Perm), Estonian lawyer, politician, and writer. In 1912 Piip completed his studies in a gymnasium in Kuressaare, in 1916 he graduated in law from the University of St. Petersburg, and then he lectured there and worked in the department for national minorities of the Russian Ministry of Interior. In July 1917 he became a member of the Provisional National Council (Maapaev), which served as the first legislative body of Estonia. In April 1918 he went with Eduard Virgo and **Kaarel Pusta** on a diplomatic mission to the Entente states. As a result of Piip's meeting with Lord Balfour, Great Britain recognized him as an informal diplomatic representative of Estonia and acknowledged the Estonian National Assembly as the body that was entitled to act on behalf of the new state. To some extent, it was thanks to Piip's political efforts that Great Britain granted Estonia material assistance and sent its fleet to aid the Estonians, who were fighting for independence against the Germans and the Bolsheviks. At the same time Piip served as adviser to the foreign minister. He attended the Paris Peace Conference and then conducted negotiations with the Bolsheviks that led to the signing of a peace treaty with them on 2 February 1920 in Tartu. Between 26 October 1920 and 25 January 1921 Piip was head of the government, and then he repeatedly served as foreign minister (1921–22, 1925–26, 1932, 1933, and 1939–40); in these years he also conducted lectures on international public law at Tartu University. In 1923–25 Piip was ambassador to the United States, and in 1932 he was a guest lecturer in California. As minister, he promoted the idea of a broad Baltic league.

Aligned from his youth with the radical movement, in parliament Piip represented the centrist Labor Party. In May 1933 he became a member of **Jaan Tõnisson**'s cabinet, the "last chance for democracy." After the fall of this cabinet and the introduction of the dictatorship of **Konstantin Päts**, Piip went into the opposition. In November 1936 he protested—along with, among others, **Juhan Kukk** and **Jaan Teemant**—the electoral abuses of the regime. In 1938 he protested the electoral procedure that allowed Päts's adherents to dominate the parliament. Piip sat on the Tartu City Council and was its head between 1935 and 1938. He opposed signing the treaty of "mutual assistance" with the USSR of 29 September 1939 (it allowed the Soviets to bring their troops into the territory of Estonia), and after replacing **Karl Selter** as foreign minister in October of that year, Piip tried to maintain the independence of his country by implementing a policy of strict neutrality. After the seizure of the country by the Red Army, along with other politicians in opposition to the Päts dictatorship, Piip tried to run in the "elections" to the People's Assembly on 14–15 July 1940. Arrested in August 1940, Piip was deported to the USSR and died in a labor camp in the Perm region. (AG)

Sources: *Eesti Entsüklopeedia*, vol. 7 (Tallinn, 1995); Evald Uustalu, *The History of the Estonian People* (London, 1953); Georg von Rauch, *Geschichten der Baltischen Staaten* (Stuttgart, 1970); Piotr Łossowski, *Kraje bałtyckie na drodze od demokracji parlamentarnej do dyktatury 1918–1934* (Wrocław, 1972); Tõnu Parming, *The Collapse of Liberal Democracy and the Rise of Authoritarianism in Estonia* (London, 1975); Matti Laur, Tõnis Lukas, Ain Mäesalu, Ago Pajur, and Tõnu Tannberg, *History of Estonia* (Tallinn, 2000).

PIJADE Moša (4 Januaray 1890, Belgrade–15 March 1957, Paris), Yugoslav Communist activist. Pijade came from a Sephardic Jewish family who at the beginning of the nineteenth century lived in Serbia. In 1906–9 he studied fine arts in Munich and Paris, but his journalistic and political interests prompted him to found the first trade union journal in Yugoslavia, *Slobodna Reč* (1919). In January 1920 Pijade joined the Socialist Workers' Party of Yugoslavia (Communists) (Socijalistička Radnička Partija Jugoslavije [Komunista])—which from June of that year was called the Communist Party of Yugoslavia (CPY)—and there he soon became one of the main party ideologists and organizers. After the delegalization of the party in 1921 and the arrest or emigration of its leaders, Pijade became interim head of the party. In June 1922 he spoke as "Milan Popovich" at the Fourth Conference of the Communist Balkan Federation in Sofia. From 1923 Pijade was a member of the Independent Workers' Party of Yugoslavia (Nezavisna Radnička Partija Jugoslavije), which was a new incarnation of the Communist Party. He supported a Yugoslav federation and cooperation with the Croatian irredentists. In 1925 Pijade was arrested and sentenced to fourteen years of prison, where his Communist convictions became stronger. At that time he met many future leaders of the party, in particular **Josip Broz Tito**. In Sremska Mitrovica Prison and Leopoglava Prison Pijade organized secret courses, and in 1930, along with Tito, he established the Prison Committee of the CPY. He also published the journal *Za bolševizaciju*.

After his release in April 1939 Pijade was active in the Communist underground in Serbia and Montenegro. After the German attack against Yugoslavia in April 1941, and especially after the German attack against the USSR in June 1941, along with **Milovan Djilas**, Pijade organized the Communist guerrillas in Montenegro, resorting to brutal methods of persuading peasants to join. From December 1941 Pijade worked in Tito's central headquarters. He was one of the founders of the Anti-Fascist Council for the National Liberation of Yugoslavia (Antifašističko Veće Narodnog Oslobodjenja Jugoslavije [AVNOJ]), and at the congress of the council in Jajce in November 1943 Pijade became the council's vice-president. He also founded the New Yugoslavia Press Agency, also called Tanjug.

After the end of the war Pijade sat on the Politburo of the CC of the party and served as vice-president of the parliament. He was a member of the Yugoslav delegation to the peace conference in Paris in 1947. At the time of the crisis in relations between Yugoslavia and the USSR, Pijade supported Tito's stance, although the denouncement of Tito by the Information Bureau of the Communist and Workers' Parties (Cominform) in June 1948 was for Pijade, as an orthodox Stalinist, a great shock. After severing ties with Moscow, he was the leading theoretician of the "Yugoslav road to socialism" and the country's neutrality. In 1950 Pijade published "About the Legend that the Yugoslav Uprising Owed Its Existence to Soviet Assistance." When a new model of Yugoslav communism began to form, Pijade held a fairly conservative position that increasingly differed from that of Djilas, who was leaning toward greater pluralism. After the expulsion of Djilas, on 28 January 1954 Pijade became president of the National Assembly, and he held the post until his sudden death from a heart attack during a diplomatic journey. Pijade's *Izbrani spisy* (Collected works; 1964) were published posthumously. (WR)

Sources: *Enciklopedija Jugoslavije*, vol. 6 (Zagreb, 1965); *Biographisches Lexikon*, vol. 3; Slobodan Nešović, *Moša Pijade i njegovo vreme* (Belgrade, 1968); Radoljub Čolaković, *Tamnoranje sa Mošom Pijade* (Belgrade, 1977).

PÍKA Heliodor (3 July 1897, Štítina–21 June 1949, Plzen), Czech general. In 1915 Píka graduated from a high school in Troppau (Opava, Czech Republic). Inducted into the Austro-Hungarian Army, he briefly fought on the Russian front in 1916. In July 1916 he was taken prisoner by the Russians at Berestechko (in the Ukraine). In October 1916 he volunteered to serve in a Czechoslovak military unit that was being formed in the Russian Army. He soon became an officer of the Czechoslovak Legions in Russia. In October 1917 Píka made his way via Murmansk to France, where he fought in the Czechoslovak units. In January 1919 he returned to his country and fought in Teschen Silesia and Slovakia. After the end of the war Píka advanced step by step through the military ranks and completed many military courses. In 1926–27 he studied at the Military College in Paris. After returning to Czechoslovakia, he worked in the General Staff. From 1932 to 1937 he served as military attaché in Romania. Back in his country, he worked in the State Defense Council (Rada Obrany Státu), where he was responsible for contacts with the states of the Little Entente, and subsequently he took part in secret negotiations on cooperation with Romania and Yugoslavia. After the Munich agreement of September 1938, he concentrated his efforts on saving Czechoslovak weapons and troops.

After the Protectorate of Bohemia and Moravia was established and the Nazi occupation began, Píka worked with a military organization called the Defense of the Nation (*Obrana Naroda*) and was sent by its command to the West, where he entered into cooperation with **Edvard Beneš**. After the outbreak of World War II, Beneš sent him on a mission to the Balkans. In late 1940 and early 1941 in Istanbul, Píka conducted negotiations on intelligence cooperation with Soviet representatives. From 1941 to 1945 he was head of a Czechoslovak military mission to the Soviet Union, where he followed the political line of the government-in-exile. Píka worked for the release of over ten thousand Czechoslovak citizens from Soviet camps and prisons, with the aim of inducting them into the newly formed Czechoslovak Army. In 1943 he was promoted to brigadier general and in 1945 to major general. As a professional, Píka won the recognition of Soviet military cadres. Deputy chief of the Czechoslovak General Staff from 1945 to 1948, Píka attended the 1946 Paris Peace Conference. Expelled from the army at the end of February 1948 and arrested in May 1948, he was accused of sabotaging the operations of the Czechoslovak Army in the Soviet Union on the orders of the British and of acting to the detriment of the Soviet Union and the Czechoslovak Republic. On 28 January 1949, although all the charges were rebutted by his defense counsel, Píka was sentenced to death by the Tribunal of State, appointed to adjudicate political cases. **Bedřich Reicin**, the chief of military intelligence, confessed that Píka was executed because "he had known too much about the Soviet intelligence services." The sentence was carried out in Plzen Prison. In 1968 Píka was fully rehabilitated, and in 1990 he was posthumously promoted to general of the army. (PU)

Sources: *ČBS*; *Biografický slovník Slezska a Severní Moravy*, vol. 1 (Opava and Ostrava, 1993); Rastislav Váhala, *Smrt generála* (Prague, 1992); Karel Richter, *Kdo byl generál Píka: Portrét cs. vojáka a diplomata* (Brno, 1997); *Czarna księga komunizmu* (Warsaw, 1999).

PILECKI Witold (13 May 1901, Olonets on Lake Ladoga–May 1948?, Warsaw), Polish pro-independence activist, victim of communism. In 1914 Pilecki became active in the pro-independence scouting movement. At the end of 1918 he volunteered to serve in the Polish Army, first in the Self-Defense of Lithuania and Belorussia, and in January 1919 he joined the Uhlan Regiment, led by the famous Polish major, Jerzy Dąmbrowski, "Łupaszka." After a short break, during which he resumed his education, Pilecki again served in the regiment led by "Łupaszka" from July 1920 to January 1921. In 1921 he finished a non-commissioned officer training school run by the

Union for National Security. From 1922 to 1924 Pilecki studied agriculture at Poznań University. He later administered his family estate of Sukurcze, near Lida (now in Belarus). During the September 1939 campaign Pilecki fought as a cavalry platoon commander. In November 1939, as a reserve second lieutenant, he helped to found the Polish Secret Army (Tajna Armia Polska). In September 1940 Pilecki became a voluntary prisoner of the Auschwitz concentration camp, with the aim of setting up an underground resistance network and reporting atrocities committed by the Germans. Under the false name of "Tadeusz Serafiński" (prisoner number 4859), he founded the Military Organization Union, which was part of the Union of Armed Struggle (Związek Walki Zbrojnej [ZWZ]) and in 1942 became part of the Home Army (Armia Krajowa [AK]). In April 1943 Pilecki escaped from Auschwitz in order to prepare a report about the situation in the camp for the intelligence department of the AK High Command. He later fought in the Warsaw Uprising as an AK soldier under the false name of Roman Jezierski. Taken prisoner after the collapse of the uprising, he was held in the *oflag* (officers' POW camp) at Lamsdorf (now Łambinowice, Poland) and at Murnau, Germany, until the end of the war. After his liberation in April 1945, Pilecki volunteered to serve in the Second Corps, led by General **Władysław Anders** in Italy. At the end of 1945 Pilecki returned to Poland. On 5 May 1947 he was arrested by the Communist State Security Office on charges of collecting intelligence for General Anders. Prime Minister **Józef Cyrankiewicz**, who was familiar with Pilecki's deeds, refused to intervene in his case. Sentenced to death on 15 March 1948, Pilecki was executed soon afterwards. His symbolic grave is in Ostrów Mazowiecki, and there is a tombstone by St. Stanislaus Church, Warsaw. Pilecki is cited as one of the most unusual fighters in the anti-Nazi resistance movements in Europe. (WR)

Sources: Kunert, vol. 2; Józef Garliński, *Oświęcim walczący* (London, 1974); Michael Foot, *Six Faces of Courage* (London, 1978); Krzysztof Dunin-Wąsowicz, *Ruch oporu w hitlerowskich obozach koncentracyjnych 1939–1945* (Warsaw, 1979); Wiesław Jan Wysocki, *Witold Pilecki "Serafiński"* (Warsaw, 2000).

PILINSZKY János (25 November 1921, Budapest–25 May 1981, Budapest), Hungarian writer and poet. Pilinszky graduated from a prestigious Piarist gymnasium in Budapest, where he began writing poems. He then studied law, literature, and art history at Budapest University but failed to complete his studies. From 1941 to 1944 he contributed to the literary periodical *Élet*. Mobilized in the fall of 1944, he spent the last months of the war in Germany, where he saw the horrors of war and met concentration camp prisoners—an experience that he would carry with him for the rest of his life. In 1946 Pilinszky published his first collection of strongly existentialist poems, *Trapéz és korlát* (Trapeze and parallel bars). From 1946 to 1948 he edited the literary quarterly *Újhold*, but as a writer he was more closely tied with the Catholic monthly *Vigilia*. Banned from publishing his works in 1949, Pilinszky wrote verse fairytales that were published in the anthology *Aranymadár* (Golden bird) in 1957. In 1956 he worked for a short time as a reviewer of manuscripts submitted to the Magvető publishing house. In 1957 he began editing the Catholic weekly *Új Ember*, in which most of his poems, literary reviews, and articles were published. Pilinszky rose to literary fame with the poetry volume *Harmadnapon* (On the third day; 1959), which initially was to be titled *Senkiföldjén* (In no-man's land), but that title was rejected by the censors. It was a poetic portrayal of war and human weaknesses, full of apocalyptic visions. Pilinszky's catastrophism, sparing with means of artistic expression, and his very personal confessions, as well as references to God and Catholicism, are to be found in *Requiem* (1963), his next poetry volume, which also included the text of a film novella. Recognized by the 1960s and 1970s as the greatest Hungarian Catholic writer of the twentieth century, Pilinszky frequently traveled abroad, with longer stays in Germany, France, and the United States. At that time his works began to be widely translated and published in the West. After the death of his sister Erika in 1975, Pilinszky stopped writing poems. (MS)

Sources: *Mały słownik pisarzy węgierskich* (Warsaw, 1977); Katalin Bogyay, ed., *The Annual Obituary 1981* (Budapest, 1990); Tibor Tüskés, *Pilinszky János* (Budapest, 1996); *"Merre hogyan?" Tanulmányok Pilinszkyról* (Budapest, 1997).

PIŁSUDSKI Józef (5 December 1867, Zułów [Zalavas, Lithuania]–12 May 1935, Warsaw), Polish politician and statesman. Born the fourth of twelve children in an impoverished family of landed gentry in the region of Wilno (Vilnius), Piłsudski was initially educated at home and then at a gymnasium in Wilno, graduating in 1885. He subsequently began studying medicine at Kharkov (Kharkiv), where he met the Russian Narodniks, and later became interested in socialism. After one year, though, he discontinued his studies. As a result of his indirect involvement with members of the secret revolutionary organization Narodna Vola, who plotted to assassinate Tsar Alexander III (the group included Lenin's brother, Aleksandr Ulyanov), Piłsudski was arrested, together with his brother Bronisław, in March 1887. Sentenced to five years in exile, he was sent to St. Petersburg and subsequently to Tyumen; from there he went on foot

to Irkutsk and finally to Kirensk on the Lena River. In 1889 he was allowed to move to the village of Tunka in the Sayan Mountains, Buryatia. In July 1892, after his release, Piłsudski returned to Wilno and established ties with the emerging Polish Socialist Party (Polska Partia Socjalistyczna [PPS]) and wrote for the London *Przedświt*. He supported the PPS pro-independence program and opposed the internationalists. In October 1893 he joined the PPS Workers' Committee (renamed the Central Workers' Committee in 1895), where he represented the Lithuanian section of this party. From 1894 to 1900 he edited the underground newspaper *Robotnik*. Piłsudski was not interested in ideology but in action, and he was the de facto leader of the pro-independence Socialist organization in the Polish territories. In July–August 1896 he secretly went to a PPS congress in London. After returning home, he continued editing *Robotnik*. Arrested in Łódź in February 1900, he was taken to the Warsaw Citadel. Helped by his friends, he managed to escape in May 1901, and he made his way to Galicia.

At that time Piłsudski began making plans to instigate an anti-Russian insurrection. In July 1904, during the Russo-Japanese War, he went to Tokyo and unsuccessfully sought assistance from the Japanese government. In Tokyo he met **Roman Dmowski**, who had come there with exactly the opposite goal. After the outbreak of the 1905 revolution, Piłsudski's plans for an insurrection were no longer acceptable to the so-called young Socialists, who sought an agreement with the Russian revolutionary parties. Piłsudski did not join the new Central Workers' Committee. He became head of the Conspiratorial Military Department, which was in charge of the PPS Military Organization. At the Ninth Congress of the PPS in November 1906, Piłsudski's program suffered a defeat, which led to a split within this party and the establishment of the PPS–Revolutionary Faction, whose main aim was an independent Poland. In 1909 Piłsudski entered the Central Workers' Committee of the PPS–Revolutionary Faction and strongly encouraged the formation of paramilitary organizations—the secret Union of Active Struggle (Związek Walki Czynnej [ZWC]) and the official Riflemen's Association—which were to become the nuclei of a future Polish army. In 1912 Piłsudski brought about the establishment of the Provisional Commission of Confederated Pro-Independence Parties. This commission appointed him commander-in-chief of all Polish armed forces. On the eve of World War I Piłsudski considered Russia the main enemy of an independent Poland, and he was willing to seek a road to independence as an ally of the Central Powers.

In August 1914 Piłsudski disseminated false information that a national government had been established in Warsaw; by doing so, he wanted to justify the action of the so-called cadre company, which on 6 August crossed the border of the Kingdom of Poland into Russia to start an anti-Russian insurrection there. This action failed, though, because people in the Kingdom of Poland did not believe it was possible to overthrow the Russian rule. This failure made Piłsudski dependent on the Supreme National Committee (Naczelny Komitet Narodowy), which assumed command over the Polish Legions that fought alongside the Austro-Hungarian Army. Piłsudski became commander of the First Regiment of the Legions (from 1915 on the First Brigade) and achieved several victories on the Russian front. In August 1914 he also established the secret Polish Military Organization (Polska Organizacja Wojskowa [POW]), which was to run intelligence and sabotage operations in the rear of the Russian Army. Following the Manifesto of the Emperors of Germany and Austria-Hungary (5 November 1916), which opened the bidding for Polish support in the ongoing war but failed to present an attractive enough political offer, Piłsudski was no longer determined to associate the Polish cause with the Central Powers. In July 1917 he refused to swear allegiance to the two emperors; as a result, he was imprisoned in Magdeburg, Germany. Although some legionnaires did swear allegiance to the Central Powers, Piłsudski's authority as a politician now also increased among the supporters of the Entente. When in the late summer of 1918 the balance of the war tipped in favor of the Entente, Piłsudski's tactics proved right.

On 10 November 1918, the day before the Germans signed the armistice on the western front, Piłsudski was released and went to Warsaw. There he found a Regency Council established by the Germans and the Austrians and certain faits accomplis of various politicians (including his associates), such as the Lublin-based Socialist-peasant Provisional Government of the Republic of Poland, headed by **Ignacy Daszyński**; the Polish Liquidation Commission (Polska Komisja Likwidacyjna) in Galicia; the Poznań-based Supreme People's Council (Naczelna Rada Ludowa), dominated by members of the National Democratic Party (Narodowa Demokracja [ND]); and, finally, the revolutionary Councils of Workers' Deputies (Soviets), emerging in various parts of the country. On 14 November the abdicating Regency Council handed over command over the nascent Polish Army to Piłsudski. A former Socialist and supporter of the Central Powers, after the victory of the Entente Piłsudski faced a growing revolutionary wave that, if it joined with the Russian Bolsheviks, might pose a threat to the newly won independence. Therefore, on 17 November he appointed a new

central government, headed by **Jędrzej Moraczewski**. On 22 November, together with Moraczewski, Piłsudski signed a decree on the establishment of the office of the provisional chief of state, and he himself assumed it. The National Democratic Party members recognized Piłsudski's authority, regarding him as a "savior" capable of leading Poland through the dangerous times of revolution; nevertheless, they sabotaged the government, which announced a radical program that included the nationalization of key industries and an agrarian reform but also called for parliamentary elections. After appeasing the leftist tendencies in the country, Piłsudski sought agreement with the right. He was rather lenient in dealing with the leaders of an unsuccessful rightist coup d'état in early January 1919, and in the middle of the month he entrusted **Ignacy Paderewski** with the mission of forming a new government representing more conservative groups and capable of winning international recognition for Poland.

After the parliamentary elections of late January 1919, Piłsudski put himself at the disposal of the Constituent Assembly, which on 26 February elected him chief of state and commander-in-chief in the ongoing war against the Bolsheviks and the Ukrainians in the eastern parts of the country. In his eastern policy Piłsudski envisioned a federation of states independent of Russia and aligned with Poland: Lithuania, Belorussia, and the Ukraine. However, he did not find political partners to pursue his concept. As a result of successful military operations on the eastern front, by the end of 1920 the Polish Army had defeated the Galician Ukrainian Army and repelled the Red Army from the majority of Belorussian territories; such operations did not facilitate an agreement among these nations. Efforts to win the cooperation of the Lithuanian leaders and attempts to provide military support for the pro-Polish politicians in Lithuania ended in failure. The government of the Ukrainian National Republic, headed by **Symon Petlura**, which had been forced by the Bolsheviks to retreat from Kiev, turned out to be the only government willing to be a partner to Poland. On 21 April 1920 Piłsudski signed a treaty on military cooperation with Petlura against the Bolsheviks. The terms of this treaty also determined (against the wishes of the Galician Ukrainians) the future border between Poland and the Ukraine along the Zbruch River. The capture of Kiev by Polish and Ukrainian forces at the beginning of May did not end the campaign because the Bolsheviks redeployed their forces and attacked in Belorussia, reaching the outskirts of Warsaw at the beginning of August. A Polish counteroffensive launched from the Wieprz River line and a victorious Battle of Warsaw (12–16 August) forced the Red Army to retreat eastwards. Piłsudski's military strategy in this war proved successful, but in political terms the war ended in fiasco for his federalist concepts because the terms of the Polish-Soviet Treaty of Riga (18 March 1921) were closer to the "incorporationist" approach of the National Democrats.

As a result of the efforts of Piłsudski's opponents, the constitution of 17 March 1921 gave little power to the president; therefore, Piłsudski refused to stand in the presidential elections. On 14 December 1922 he handed over his powers to **Gabriel Narutowicz**, the newly elected president. After the assassination of Narutowicz and the election of **Stanisław Wojciechowski** as president, Piłsudski served as chief of the General Staff of the Polish Army for a few months. He resigned from this post in May 1923 and retired to his house at Sulejówek, near Warsaw. He observed the political strife and the unstable governments and ever more strongly criticized "party favoritism" in public life. He was still enormously popular among the public and had the support of the part of the officer corps that had past ties to the POW and the Legions. In the autumn of 1925, after a series of political and financial crises, Piłsudski began preparing for a coup d'état. An appropriate moment came after the establishment of the second government of the center-right parliamentary majority of the so-called Chjeno-Piast coalition, which was unpopular with the public. Another argument in favor of a coup was Poland's deteriorating strategic position after the Locarno Treaty (October 1925) and the German-Soviet Treaty of Berlin (April 1926). On 12 May 1926 regiments faithful to Piłsudski marched on Warsaw, taking control of the capital after three days of fighting.

After the successful takeover, which had cost the lives of around three hundred people, Piłsudski did not dissolve the parliament, but with the support of the left wing and a small shift in the center of the parliamentary spectrum, he was elected president. He refused the presidency, though, and **Ignacy Mościcki** was elected instead; still, although formally in the shadow of Mościcki, it was Piłsudski who actually ruled the country. He held the post of prime minister on two occasions (from 2 October 1926 to 27 June 1928 and from 25 August to 4 December 1930), and he served as minister of military affairs and inspector general of the armed forces until the end of his life. Piłsudski's political camp pursued a program of cleansing Polish politics of party factionalism and corruption; it was known as *sanacja*, a name later extended to his ruling camp. From 1926 to 1930 Piłsudski's main goal was to reduce the powers of the legislative bodies, to diminish the influence of the parliamentary opposition, and to establish his own strong ruling party. He failed to realize his goals, though, because after the coup of May 1926 the

PPS and the leftist peasant parties went over to the opposition. The elections of 1928 did not give his Nonparty Bloc of Cooperation with the Government (Bezpartyjny Blok Współpracy z Rządem [BBWR]) a majority of seats; therefore, in 1930 the parliament was dissolved and the opposition leaders were arrested on embezzlement charges. The new elections, held under pressure from the administration, also failed to return the BBWR a majority sufficient to amend the constitution. Owing to deteriorating health, Piłsudski slightly withdrew from influencing current decisions, leaving them to his associates. He was mainly engaged in foreign policies. As Poland was increasingly threatened from the neighboring Soviet Union and Germany, Piłsudski sought to establish relations with these countries based on the principle of the balance of power—that is, the avoidance of alliances with one of these countries against the other. This policy resulted in a Polish-German non-aggression declaration (26 January 1934) and a Polish-Soviet non-aggression treaty (5 May 1934), but it put off the threat to Poland only for five years. Through manipulations of parliamentary procedures, the ruling *sanacja* managed to adopt a constitution that greatly increased presidential powers and weakened parliamentary democracy. In late April 1935 Piłsudski endorsed the text of the constitution, and two weeks later he died. Despite the political framework he had created, his supporters failed to appoint a successor to him and became divided. The *sanacja* government collapsed with the defeat of Poland in 1939.

Piłsudski was an exceptional figure and was well aware of his greatness. Few other Polish politicians had such faithful followers and enjoyed such respect—even a cult status—among the public. An assessment of his deeds, though, has always divided the Poles. What is emphasized is both Piłsudski's foresight (for example, his concept of a preventive war against Germany in 1933) and his mistrust of projects to modernize the army and his ignorance about economic affairs. Some stress his great role in the rebirth of an independent Poland and in the Polish-Soviet war, while others point to his anti-democratic rhetoric, the May 1926 coup, and his dictatorship that followed. However, nobody denies that he possessed great political foresight and strategic talent. (WR)

Sources: *PSB*, vol. 26; *Encyklopedia historii Drugiej Rzeczypospolitej* (Warsaw, 1999); Wacław Lipiński, *Wielki marszałek* (Warsaw, 1937); Joseph Rothschild, *Pilsudski's Coup d'Etat* (New York, 1966); M. K. Dziewanowski, *Joseph Pilsudski: A European Federalist, 1918–1922* (Stanford, 1969); Norman Davies, *White Eagle, Red Star: The Polish-Soviet War, 1919–20* (London, 1973); Andrzej Garlicki, *Przewrót majowy* (Warsaw, 1979); Andrzej Garlicki, *Od maja do Brześcia* (Warsaw, 1981); Wacław Jędrzejewicz, *Pilsudski: A Life for Poland* (New York, 1982); Władysław Pobóg-

Malinowski, *Najnowsza histria polityczna Polski*, vol. 2 (London, 1983); Aleksandra Piłsudska, *Wspomnienia* (London, 1985); Wacław Jędrzejewicz, *Kronika życia Józefa Piłsudskiego*, vols. 1–2 (London, 1986); Andrzej Garlicki, *Od Brześcia do maja* (Warsaw, 1986); Włodzimierz Suleja, *Józef Piłsudski* (Wrocław, 1995); Zbigniew Wójcik, *Józef Piłsudski 1867–1935* (Warsaw, 1999); Andrzej Nowak, *Polska i trzy Rosje: Studium polityki wschodniej Józefa Piłsudskiego (do kwietnia 1920)* (Kraków, 2001).

PIŃKOWSKI Józef (17 April 1929, Siedlce), Polish Communist activist. Born into a laborer's family, Pińkowski graduated from the Higher Economic School in Poznań and from the Main School of Planning and Statistics in Warsaw. From 1951 he belonged to the (Communist) Polish United Workers' Party (Polska Zjednoczona Partia Robotnicza [PUWP]), in 1952–56 he served in the army, and then he worked in the central administration. From October 1971 to February 1974 Pińkowski was deputy chairman of the Planning Commission, from December 1974 he was a member of the PUWP Central Committee (CC), and from February 1974 he was CC secretary. He was co-responsible for the disastrous investment policies of the **Edward Gierek** regime. On 24 August 1980 Pińkowski became a member of the CC Politburo and prime minister. He endorsed the August 1980 agreements with striking workers, but he failed to take control of the aggravating economic crisis and the worsening social mood. He did not even control the apparatus of coercion, whose operations frequently provoked Solidarity. During his visits to the Kremlin in late October and early December 1980, Pińkowski passively observed talks between Leonid Brezhnev and other Soviet leaders with the head of the PUWP, **Stanisław Kania**, and the minister of defense, General **Wojciech Jaruzelski**. On 11 February 1981 Pińkowski resigned from leading the government, and in April 1981 he left the CC Politburo. Until 1985 he was an MP, and then he disappeared from public sight. (WR)

Sources: Mołdawa; Jerzy Holzer, *"Solidarność"* (Warsaw, 1983); Andrzej Albert [Wojciech Roszkowski], *Najnowsza historia Polski 1914–1993*, vol. 2 (Warsaw, 1995).

PINTILIE Gheorghe [originally Pantelimon Bondarenko], nickname "Pantiuşa" (1898, the Ukraine–13 July 1985, Bucharest), Romanian security officer of Ukrainian descent. From 1917 to 1921 Pintilie was a soldier and a propagandist of the Red Army in the Ukraine. After undergoing GPU training (1923–24), he was a Kremlin liaison officer in the Communist underground movement in Romania, although he spoke very little Romanian. From 1936 to 1944 Pintilie was incarcerated in various prisons for his Communist activities and for spying for the Soviet Union; for example, he was held in a prison in Doftana,

and when this prison was destroyed in a November 1940 earthquake, he was transferred to Caransebeş. After the Red Army entered Romania in August 1944, Pintilie became head of the Political and Administrative Department of the Central Committee (CC) of the Romanian Communist Party (RCP). In 1945, by then under the name of Pintilie, he became head of the Directorate of the Security Police. He worked closely with Dmitri Fedichkin, the chief adviser of the Soviet political police, and with a group of agents led by Ivan Didenko (later Ioan Vadraşcu), Pyotr Goncharuk (Petre Gonceariuc), Boris Grünberg (**Alexandru Nicolschi**), and Misha Postansky (Vasile Posteuca). With their help, in a short time Pintilie filled key posts in the Directorate with Communists. Pintilie was a drunkard and a bully. In the summer of 1946, on the personal orders of **Gheorghe Gheorghiu-Dej**, Pintilie imprisoned and then bestially murdered **Ştefan Foriş**, the former head of the RCP. He subsequently ordered the killing of Foriş's mother. In December 1946 he became head of the Special Information Services (Serviciul Special de Informaţii [SIS]). Pintilie's wife, Ana Toma, a close associate of **Ana Pauker**, was a so-called Amazon (the Romanian nickname for female NKVD agents) and served as a personal secretary to Gheorghiu-Dej.

In June 1948 Pintilie became a member of the CC of the Romanian Workers' Party (RWP). In August 1948 he became head of the newly established General Direction of National Security (Direcţia Generală a Securităţii Poporului [DGSP]), known as Securitate, which was formally subordinated to the Ministry of the Interior but which actually had unlimited control of Romania. For example, the DGSP probably bugged all members of the party executive. The apparatus of the DGSP, which steadily expanded, maintained surveillance over the everyday life of Romanian citizens, as well as all mass events. Pintilie helped to prepare the case against **Lucreţiu Pătrăşcanu**. He was one of the main founders of the Romanian concentration camp system; for instance, he initiated the establishment of the General Directorate for the Construction of the Danube–Black Sea Canal. In April 1950 he drafted a memo on the basis of which people were sent to prison camps without trial. After Stalin's death, Pintilie led the "purging" of the DGSP apparatus, as a result of which some of the worst criminals were imprisoned or even executed. After Romania was admitted to the United Nations in December 1955, the authorities in Bucharest had to release political prisoners. On the orders of Gheorghiu-Dej this action was led by Pintilie, who released not only the victims, but also many of their torturers. After Gheorghiu-Dej's death and the succession of **Nicolae Ceauşescu** (March 1965), the latter attempted to gain control over the security apparatus by removing the minister of interior, **Alexandru Draghici**, from power. The dismissal of Draghici was followed by the expulsion of Pintilie from the CC at the Ninth Congress of the RCP in July 1965. During the rehabilitation process of Pătrăşcanu, Pintilie was in trouble. Although at a CC plenum in April 1968 he was attacked for (among other things) murdering Foriş, he was not brought to justice for his crimes, and in May 1971 Ceauşescu presented him and his wife with prestigious awards on the occasion of an anniversary marking the party's half-century. Pintilie was officially buried at the expense of the state. (FA/WR)

Sources: Vladimir Tismăneanu, *Arheologia terrori* (Bucharest, 1992); P. Ştefănescu, *Istoria Serviciilor Secrete Româneşti* (Bucharest, 1994); Dennis Deletant, *Communist Terror in Romania: Gheorghiu-Dej and the Police State, 1948–1965* (New York, 1999).

PINTILIE Ilie (3 November 1903, Ploieşti–10 November 1940, Doftana), Romanian Communist activist. After finishing primary school, Pinriliw worked on the railways. In his youth he became involved in the Communist movement and joined a Socialist party in 1919. Fascinated by the Bolshevik revolution, he joined the newly established Romanian Communist Party (RCP) in 1921. In the 1930s he was one of the leaders of the Union of Communist Youth and served as secretary of the Railway Workers' Trade Union. At that time he most probably worked for the Soviet NKVD. In 1931 he organized a railway workers' strike. A member of the RCP Central Committee (CC) from 1933 onwards, Pintilie supported the Stalinist line of the party, which called for the separation of Bessarabia, Transylvania, and Dobrudja from Romania. In 1933 he co-organized a strike in the Griviţa factory, as a result of which he was sentenced to several years' imprisonment in August of that year. Arrested again in September 1939, he was sentenced to ten years in prison. Pintilie was killed in an earthquake that destroyed the prison in Doftana. (FA/WR)

Sources: Şerban N. Ionescu, *Who Was Who in Twentieth Century Romania* (Boulder, Colo., 1994); Dennis Deletant, *Communist Terror in Romania: Gheorghiu-Dej and the Police State, 1948–1965* (New York, 1999).

PIPA Arshi (28 February 1920, Shkodër–20 July 1997, Washington, D.C.), Albanian writer, cultural activist, and political prisoner. Pipa started writing at the age of sixteen. Pipa graduated from a Jesuit college in Shkodër and in literature and philosophy in Florence, Italy. In 1941 he returned to Albania and taught philosophy in a high school in Tirana. In 1942 he received a Ph.D. in philosophy in Florence. In 1942–43 he taught in a high school in Shkodër, and in 1944 he returned to Tirana. Unwilling to deal with politics, at the end of 1944 he tried to gather an artistic

circle around the Tirana periodical *Kritika*. In 1945, along with Archbishop **Vincenc Prennushi**, Pipa established the League of Writers and Artists. At the beginning tolerated by the Communist authorities, the organization was later considered a cover for subversion and spying. After a series of lectures in which he criticized Communist cultural policies, Pipa was arrested. In 1945 he was sentenced to two years in prison for "hostile propaganda." Soon released, in 1947 he was arrested again and accused of links with the so-called group of deputies and of preparations for an anti-Communist uprising. All together Pipa spent ten years in prison in Burrell, Vlocisht, Durres, and Tirana.

Released in April 1956, Pipa went to Shkodër. He refused to work in a collective farm and unsuccessfully tried to find employment in a research institution in Tirana. Dressed as a peasant and furnished with false documents, Pipa left Albania in 1957. For a year he lived in Sarajevo, and then, thanks to the help of the Albanian diaspora, he left for Italy and the United States, where he lived until he died. He worked at Georgetown University, Columbia University, and the University of California at Berkeley, and from 1996 he lectured in Albanian literature at the University of Minnesota. In the 1980s Pipa frequently lectured on the Albanians in Kosovo. The peak of his activity came in the 1990s. Following the pattern established by **Fan Noli**, Pipa wanted to consolidate the Albanian diaspora in the United States and to establish a party that could also develop in Albania. The idea has not materialized owing to conflicts within the Albanian community in exile. In 1991–92 Pipa directed the Pan-Albanian Association VATRA in the United States and its organ *Dielli*. He moved the headquarters of the organization from Boston to New York. Pipa returned to Albania in 1992. His first collection of poetry, *Lundertare* (Sailors), was published in 1944. He published the memoirs *Libri i burgut* (A prison book; 1959); a poem, "Rusha" (1969); the important study *Albanian Stalinism: Ideo-Political Aspects* (1990); and a number of other works on Albanian literature and language. (TC)

Sources: Stavro Skendi, *Albania* (New York, 1956); Peter R. Prifti, *Socialist Albania since 1944: Domestic and Foreign Developments* (Cambridge, Mass., 1978); Uran Kalakulla, *Arshi Pipa: Njeriu dhe vepra* (Tirana, 1999).

PIRINSKI Georgi (10 September 1948, New York), Bulgarian Communist and post-Communist activist. Pirinski is the son of Georgi Pirinski (originally Georgi Zaykov, 1901–92), a member of the Communist Party of the United States who was sentenced in 1951 to ten years in prison for spying for the Soviets but was later extradited and deported to Bulgaria. In 1972 Pirinski graduated from the

Karl Marx Economic Institute in Sofia. During his studies, he joined the Bulgarian Communist Party (BCP). He was closely connected with **Andrey Lukanov**. Pirinski worked at the Ministry of Foreign Trade (1974–76) and the Ministry of Foreign Affairs (1980–88). Devoid of ideals and realizing that the fall of communism was imminent, in 1989 he joined the party reformers, and after the toppling of **Todor Zhivkov**, in November 1989 Pirinski became a member of the BCP Central Committee and deputy prime minister. From September 1990 he was deputy chairman of the (post-Communist) Bulgarian Socialist Party (Bulgarska Sotsialisticheska Partiya [BSP]). After the BSP lost the elections and after the Lukanov government failed, in December 1990 Pirinski was dismissed from the party leadership. A candidate for deputy prime minister for economic affairs in the government of **Dimitur Popov**, he was vetoed by the Union of Democratic Forces (UDF).

In 1990 Pirinski joined the Alliance for Social Democracy of Chavdar Kyuranov, remaining in opposition to both the UDF and the dogmatic wing of the BSP, which, under the leadership of **Zhan Videnov**, took control of the BSP. On the eve of the parliamentary elections of 1994, Pirinski reconciled with Videnov, and in January 1995 he became foreign minister in Videnov's cabinet. Pirinski made efforts to bring Bulgaria closer to the European Union but not to NATO. He advocated neutrality for Bulgaria, which made the opposition accuse him of treason. Seeing the fatal mistakes of the Videnov government, in 1996 Pirinski joined the faction of **Georgi Purvanov** and resigned as head of the Foreign Ministry. This move weakened Videnov's position and finally led to his resignation and later to his expulsion from the BSP leadership. Owing to a dramatic decline in the BSP's ratings and to inter-party struggles, in early 1997 Pirinski became a compromise BSP candidate in the presidential elections. However, the Constitutional Tribunal determined that it was impossible for him to run because he had been born abroad. Owing to his contacts among the post-Communists, Pirinski has remained one of the most influential BSP activists. In 2001 he became the party's deputy chairman. (AG)

Sources: *Koy koy e v Bulgariya* (Sofia, 1998); Raymond Detrez, *Historical Dictionary of Bulgaria* (Lanham, Md., 1997); www.online.bg/politics/who/names/P/georgi_pirinski.htm; www.b-info.com/places/Bulgaria/news/96–11/nov13.html.

PIROS László (10 May 1917, Újkígyós), Hungarian Communist activist. Born into a peasant family, after trade school Piros worked as a butcher. In 1939–41 he served in the Frontier Guard (FG) and later on the front. In 1943 he was taken prisoner of war at Voronezh. He was trained by the Soviets and fought with the Soviet guerrillas in eastern Poland. In January 1945 Piros returned to Hungary and joined the Hungarian Communist Party (HCP). In November 1945 he was elected to the parliament. From January 1946 to January 1950 he was a member of the Budapest Committee of the HCP, and from 1948, of the Hungarian Workers' Party (HWP). In 1948–49 Piros was a deputy member and then until October 1956 a member of the HWP Central Committee (CC). In 1949 he was deputy general secretary of the National Council of Trade Unions (NCTU), and in 1950–53 he was a deputy member of the CC Politburo. In 1950 Piros became commander of the FG with the rank of brigadier general and later general of division. The FG was a part of the Office of State Security (Államvédelmi Hatóság [AVH]). From January to June 1953 Piros was deputy head of the AVH and a member of the commission that conducted an investigation concerning its head, **Gábor Péter**, arrested for the "violation of law and order." Piros personally interrogated Péter. From July 1953 Piros was deputy minister and from July 1954 minister of interior. At a meeting of the HWP CC in April 1955, when **Imre Nagy** was expelled from the Politburo, Piros became a deputy member of the body again.

On 23 October 1956 Piros became a member of the CC Military Commission, but he left the Politburo. On 25 October he appealed to the insurgents to lay down their arms. The next day he was deposed as minister of interior, and on 28 October, along with **Ernő Gerő** and **András Hegedüs**, he left for the USSR. On 3 November Piros returned to Hungary and took part in a KGB operation in which a delegation of the Nagy government, headed by General **Pál Maléter**, was arrested in the Soviet headquarters in Tököl, near Budapest. Piros took part in commanding the second Soviet intervention. On **János Kádár**'s request, on 10 November Piros left for the USSR again. In May 1957 the parliament deprived him of his mandate, but in August 1958 he returned to Hungary. He became managing engineer at the meat processing factory in Szeged; in 1969 he became its director, and in 1977 he retired. For many years Piros was also chairman of the NCTU Provincial Council in Csongrád, and later he was a member of the Town Committee of the Hungarian Socialist Workers' Party in Szeged. (JT)

Sources: *A magyar forradalom és szabadságharc enciklopédiája*, CD-ROM (Budapest, 1999); *Magyar Nagylexikon*, vol. 14 (Budapest, 2002); Miklós Molnár, *From Béla Kun to János Kádár: Seventy Years of Hungarian Communism* (New York, 1990).

PITHART Petr (2 January 1941, Kladno), Czech lawyer and politician. Pithart's father was a lawyer, and his mother was a teacher. After high school in Kladno, in 1957–62 Pithart studied law at Charles University in Prague. In

1960 he joined the Communist Party of Czechoslovakia (CPC). From 1962 to 1970 Pithart was a lecturer at Charles University and a visiting scholar at Oxford University. In early 1968 he edited the reform-oriented periodical *Literarni noviny*, and he left the CPC. After the suppression of the Prague Spring and during the so-called normalization Pithart worked as a blue-collar laborer and later as a legal adviser. He was among the close aides of **Václav Havel**. He published in the uncensored press, and he organized unlicensed education. In January 1977 Pithart was one of the first signatories of Charter 77, for which he was harassed by the political police for years. Forced to work as a blue-collar laborer in the water supply system and as a gardener and watchman, he wrote for the uncensored and foreign press.

In December 1989 Pithart became head of the Coordination Center of the Civic Forum (Občanske Fórum). When the forum split in 1991, he became a member of the leadership of the Civic Movement (Občanské Hnuti). From 6 February 1990 to 23 June 1992 Pithart was prime minister of the Czech republic. He worked to maintain the Czechoslovak federal state. He was also a spokesman for Czech-German reconciliation and for cooperation within the Visegrad Group. He advocated close cooperation with Poland based on the normalization of the situation of the Polish minority in the Czech part of Teschen Silesia. After Pithart lost in the parliamentary elections of June 1992, he withdrew from politics and returned to scholarly work at the Central European University in Prague. After the split of Czechoslovakia, he returned to political activity in 1996, winning a seat in the Czech Senate on behalf of the Christian and Democratic Union–Czech People's Party (Kreštanska a Demokratická Unie–Česká Strana Lidová) and becoming the speaker of the Senate. In December 2002 Pithart was reelected to the Senate and continued as its speaker. In January 2003 he ran in the presidential elections. In the third round he failed to win the required majority. Pithart authored one of the best analyses of the Prague Spring: *Osmašesdesátý* (Sixty-eight; 1990); he also wrote *Obrana politiky* (The defense of politics; 1991), *Dějiny a politika* (History and politics; 1991), and *Po devataosmdesátem. Kdo jsme?* (After eighty-nine: Who are we? 1998). (AGr)

Sources: *ČBS*; *Kdo byl kdo w našich dějinách ve 20. stoleti* (Prague, 1994); *Europa Środkowo-Wschodnia 1992* (Warsaw, 1994); *Deset pražských dnů* (Prague, 1990); Jana Klusáková, *Nadoraz: O Havlovi, Klausovi, Mečiarovi a revolci, která pozírá své deti* (Prague, 1992); www.pithart.cz.

PITKA Johan (19 February 1872, Jalgsema near Võhmuta–September 1944, near Läänemaa), Estonian vice-admiral and politician. Pitka studied in schools of commerce in Käsmu, Kuressaare, and Paldiski, where in 1895 he passed his captain's exams and subsequently went on sea voyages as a captain. From 1904 to 1911 he was in exile in England. During World War I he joined the national revival movement. After the February 1917 revolution, along with **Konstantin Päts**, Pitka founded the Estonian Military Bureau. On 23 February 1918 he commanded the troops that forced the Bolsheviks out of Tallinn, thus enabling the proclamation of Estonian independence on the following day, before the Germans occupied Estonia. Pitka founded the Estonian Self-Defense Units (Omakaitse) and the Defense League (Kaitseliit). He co-founded the Estonian Navy, of which he became commander on 16 December 1918, when the Estonians took over their first ship, the *Lembit*, from the Germans. Although during the war of independence the Estonian Navy played a symbolic role, Pitka initiated the buildup of the country's naval forces and the organization of the defense of the Estonian waterfront against a possible Soviet landing. During the war he was in charge of the redeployment of small operations units to the rear of advancing Bolshevik troops. These units disorganized the Soviet operations. Promoted to vice-admiral but dismissed from the army on 28 November 1919, Pitka became involved in politics. Elected to the Constitutional Assembly (Asutav Kogu), he founded the Estonian Guardsmen's Union (EGU) in April 1920. The EGU sharply criticized the pathologies of political life and the policy of the Ministry of War, which they accused of a lack of interest in the fate of war veterans. Violations committed by EGU members led to the abolition of this organization. In 1923 Pitka founded the National Liberal Party (Rahvuslik-Vabameelne Partei [RVP]), but with no great success. As a result of conflicts with other RVP activists, he resigned and in 1924 emigrated to Canada.

In 1930 Pitka returned to Estonia and became the deputy chairman of the extreme rightist Estonian League of War of Independence Veterans (Eesti Vabadussojalaste Liit [EVL]). He was also a radical ideologue of the EVL. In 1932 he protested a decision of the EVL Congress that granted membership to people who were not veterans of the war of independence. Pitka left the EVL and joined the National Centrist Party of **Jaan Tõnisson**. After the coup d'état of 1934 Pitka accepted the Päts dictatorship. He chaired the Estonian Consumers' Union and the Foundation for the Defense of the Homeland. After the Soviet invasion in June 1940, Pitka avoided arrest by the NKVD and made his way to Finland. He organized the Estonian forces, which fought alongside the Finnish forces against the Soviet Union in Karelia (1939–40 and

1941–44). In December 1941 Pitka submitted a proposal to Finland for a Finnish-Estonian union that involved a common economic, military, and foreign policy with common central authorities and one head of state. The Finns rejected this proposal, though, because they did not want to complicate their relations with the Germans. In the spring of 1944 Pitka returned to Estonia. In September 1944 he attempted to organize the defense of Tallinn against the Red Army and to take over power in Estonia from the German authorities-in-occupation. He also joined the National Committee of the Estonian Republic, but his attempts to seize control failed. Soon afterwards Pitka was killed while commanding a ship that probably sank fighting against the Red Army. (AG)

Sources: *Eesti Entsuklopeedia*, vol. 14 (Tallinn, 2000); Jaan Soots, "Wojna Estonji o wyzwolenie 1918–1920," *Przegląd Wojskowy*, 1929, no. 20; Evald Uustalu, *The History of the Estonian People* (London, 1952); Andres Kasekamp, *The Radical Right in Interwar Estonia* (London, 2000); Tõnu Tannberg, Matti Laur, Tõnis Lukas, Ain Mäesalu, and Ago Pajur, *History of Estonia* (Tallinn, 2000); Jan Lewandowski, *Estonia* (Warsaw, 2001); www.hot.ee/vabadussoda/pitka.htm.

PIWOWARCZYK Jan (29 January 1889, Brzeźnica, near Wadowice–29 December 1959, Kraków), Polish Catholic priest, journalist, and social activist. The son of a peasant, in 1907 Piwowarczyk passed his high school final exams in Wadowice and later graduated from a seminary. In 1911 he took holy orders. From 1928 to 1933 he taught Catholic social teachings at the Department of Theology of the Jagiellonian University in Kraków. From 1922 to 1939 he was the editor of *Głos Narodu*. He was also an active member of the Polish Christian Democratic Party. From 1939 to 1944 Piwowarczyk was a lecturer and the rector of a seminary in Kraków. In 1941–42 he was imprisoned by the Germans. In March 1945 he assumed the editorship of the weekly *Tygodnik Powszechny*, founded on the initiative of Archbishop **Adam Sapieha**, the metropolitan of Kraków. Piwowarczyk was associated with this weekly until the end of his life, even after **Jerzy Turowicz** assumed its editorship in the fall of 1945. From 1945 to 1946 Piwowarczyk was a member of the Labor Party (Stronnictwo Pracy). From 1947 to 1957 he again lectured at the Department of Theology of the Jagiellonian University. In his articles and monographs Piwowarczyk analyzed and popularized the papal encyclicals and the principles of Catholic social life, and he also undertook polemics with Marxism. The two-volume *Katolicka etyka społeczna* (Catholic social ethics; 1963–65), published posthumously in London, is his most important work. His other publications include *Idea chrześcijańsko-społeczna w historycznym rozwoju* (The Christian social idea: Historical development; 1922); *Socjalizm i chrześcijaństwo* (Socialism and Christianity; 1924); *Korporacjonizm i jego problematyka* (Corporatism and its issues; 1936); and *Katolicyzm a reforma rolna* (Catholicism and agrarian reform; 1938). (WR)

Sources: *PSB*, vol. 26; "Ksiądz Jan Piwowarczyk: Pożegnanie," *Tygodnik Powszechny*, 1960, no. 2; *70 żywotów* (Kraków, 1977); Andrzej Micewski, *Współrządzić czy nie kłamać? PAX i Znak w Polsce 1945–1976* (Warsaw, 1981).

PLANINC Milka [née Malada] (21 November 1924, Split), Yugoslav Communist activist of Croatian nationality. Planinc graduated from a high school in Split, where in the fall of 1941 she took part in a protest against the introduction of Italian as a language of instruction. In 1941 she also joined the Communist Union of Yugoslav Youth, and in 1943, after the capitulation of Italy, a Communist guerrilla unit. After the war Planinc became a member of the Communist Party, which became the League of Communists of Yugoslavia (LCY) in 1952. From 1959 she was a member of the Central Committee (CC) of the League of Communists of Croatia (LCC), and in 1963 she became secretary (minister) of education and science of the Croatian republic. In 1967–71 Planinc was speaker of the Federal Assembly. During the Croatian Spring of 1971 she stated that the LCC "had lost its political orientation" and that Croatia was in danger of "counterrevolution." At a meeting in Karadjordjevo on 30 November 1971 she supported **Josip Broz Tito**, and at the Twenty-third Plenum of the LCC CC on 12–13 December 1971 she was elected head of the Croatian party. Planinc held this position until May 1982. She was responsible for "clearing" the party of "nationalists." On 16 May 1982 she became prime minister of the federal government. She made efforts to stop the deterioration of the economic situation (high inflation, foreign debt, and unemployment). She wanted to continue earlier policies, but under pressure from the International Monetary Fund (IMF) she was forced to introduce a plan of stabilization (July 1983) that failed. In return for debt conversion, in March 1984 the IMF demanded a liberalization of prices, the reconstruction of currency reserves, and the introduction of a free rate of exchange for the dinar. Planinc's government did not implement these steps, and Yugoslavia's debt grew to U.S.$22 billion. On 16 May 1986 Planinc resigned. In June 1986 she was not reelected to the LCY Presidium, and she withdrew from political life. (JD)

Sources: H. Šošić, *Slom hrvatskog komunističkog proljeća 1971* (Zagreb, 1997); John Lampe, *Yugoslavia as History* (Cambridge, 1996); www.terra.es/personal2/monolith/00women3.htm; www.rulers.org; www.guide2womenleaders.com.

PLAVŠIĆ Biljana (7 July 1930, Tuzla), Serb politician from Bosnia-Herzegovina. Plavšić graduated in biology, and for many years she lectured at the University of Sarajevo. As a Fulbright scholar, she also taught in the United States. She started her political career in the early 1990s as one of the closest aides of **Radovan Karadžić**, leader of the Serbian Democratic Party (Srpska Demokratska Stranska [SDS]). From November 1990 Plavšić was a member of the Presidium of Bosnia-Herzegovina. From January 1991 to April 1992 she chaired its Council for the Protection of Constitutional Order. On 12 May 1992 she was elected to the three-person Presidium of the Serb Republic in Bosnia-Herzegovina, chaired by Karadžić, and from November she belonged to the high command of the republic's armed forces. Plavšić strongly opposed the Cyrus Vance and David Owen peace plan of May 1993, and she criticized the Dayton agreement of 1995. In June 1996, under international pressure, Karadžić resigned from chairing the Serb Republic, and Plavšić took over. Unexpectedly, the "iron lady of the Balkans," known for her extreme nationalist views and her approval of ethnic cleansing, began to advocate peace and accepted the Dayton agreement. She criticized the SDS leaders, accusing them of corruption and profiteering from the war and from smuggling. She dismissed the commander of the Serb troops in Bosnia-Herzegovina, General **Ratko Mladić**, and she purged the police and the media. In July 1997 she dissolved the SDS-dominated parliament and formed a new party called the Serbian National Union. Plavšić's policies were supported by the Western countries, but in September 1998 she lost the presidential elections in the Serb Republic in Bosnia-Herzegovina and withdrew from political life. The International Tribunal for War Crimes in Former Yugoslavia in The Hague accused Plavšić of genocide and crimes against humanity. In January 2001 she gave herself up at the disposal of the tribunal. In October 2002 she pleaded guilty of crimes against humanity, and in February 2003 she was sentenced to eleven years in prison. (AO)

Sources: Laura Silber and Allan Little, *The Death of Yugoslavia* (London, 1995); Richard Holbrooke, *To End a War* (New York, 1998); David Owen, *Balkan Odyssey* (New York, 1995); Bugajski; "Skrucha czy pragmatyzm," *Rzeczpospolita*, 3 October 2002; International Criminal Tribunal for the Former Yugoslavia, www.un.org/icty/indictment; www.rulers. org.

PŁAŻYŃSKI Maciej (10 February 1958, Młynary), Polish politician. Płażyński graduated in law from the University of Gdańsk. From 1977 he was connected with the opposition Movement of Young Poland (Ruch Młodej Polski). In August 1980 he co-founded the Independent Student Union (Niezależne Zrzeszenie Studentów). In the fall of 1981 he led the occupation strike at the University of Gdańsk. From 1983 to 1990 he managed the Cooperative of Skyscrapers Services–Gdańsk, supporting underground Solidarity activities in Pomerania and other regions. In 1987 Płażyński was elected chairman of the Lech Bądkowski Memorial Club of Political Thought, attracting both conservative and liberal opposition circles in Gdańsk. In 1989 he co-organized the economic association Liberal Congress. From 1990 he belonged to the Republican Coalition and in 1992–93 to the Conservative Party. He was active in charity organizations serving the disabled in the Gdańsk region. From August 1990 to July 1996 Płażyński was the provincial governor (*wojewoda*) of Gdańsk, and from 1996 he was deputy chairman of Solidarity Electoral Action (Akcja Wyborcza Solidarność [AWS]) in the Gdańsk region. In the parliamentary elections of September 1997 he had the best results in Poland, gaining 125,000 votes. In 1997–2001 he was speaker of the Lower House. Seeing a decline in the AWS ratings, on 19 January 2001, along with Andrzej Olechowski and Donald Tusk, Płażyński formed the Civic Platform (Platforma Obywatelska [PO]). From September 2001 he was an MP on behalf of the PO. He also chaired the PO parliamentary club and the party itself. In late May 2003 Płażyński left the PO, trying to form a separate Christian Democratic movement, but to no great avail. (IS)

Sources: *Kto jest kim w Polsce* (Warsaw, 1993); Antoni Dudek, *Pierwsze lata III Rzeczyspospolitej 1989–2001* (Kraków, 2002); Wojciech Roszkowski, *Historia Polski 1914–2001* (Warsaw, 2002).

PLECHAVIČIUS Povilas (1 February 1890, Bukončiai–10 December 1973, Chicago), Lithuanian general and politician. After graduating from a cavalry school in Moscow (1914), Plechavičius served in the Russian Army during World War I. He was wounded three times. After the February 1917 revolution, he continued serving in the White Russian units in southern Russia. In 1918 he returned to Lithuania and organized the defense of the regions of Telšiai (Telsze) and Mažeikiai (Możejki) against the Red Army. In the Lithuanian Army Plechavičius was promoted to battalion commander and then continued his education abroad. In 1926 he graduated from the General Staff School in Prague. Almost immediately after returning to Lithuania, he joined in clandestine activities against the leftist government of **Mykolas Sleževičius**. On 17 December 1926 he commanded the units that removed Sleževičius from power, opening the way for the nationalist dictatorship of **Antanas Smetona**. From 1927 to 1929 Plechavičius served as chief of staff of the army, and then he retired. From 1929 to 1940 he lived on his farm in the Samogitia region. After the Red Army seized Lithuania in June 1940, he went to Germany. In 1944, when the Red Army was again marching into Lithuania, he received permission from the Nazi authorities to organize voluntary Lithuanian units of the Home Formation (Vietinė Rinktinė), which were to defend the country. Plechavičius gathered around thirty thousand volunteers. His units fought against the (Polish) Home Army and pacified Polish villages. When the German authorities demanded that his units be subordinated to the German command, Plechavičius refused. Arrested along with his staff on 15 May 1944, he was placed in the concentration camp in Salaspils, Latvia. His units were disarmed. Taken to Germany toward the end of World War II, he was held under guard until the fall of the Third Reich. In 1949 Plechavičius left for the United States, where he presided over Ramove, the Lithuanian War Veterans' Association. (WR)

Sources: *EL*, vol. 4; Petras Jurgela, *Gen. Povilas Plechavičius* (Brooklyn, N.Y., 1978); Piotr Łossowski, *Litwa* (Warsaw, 2001).

PLEČNIK Jože (Josef) (23 January 1872, Laibach [Ljubljana]–7 January 1957, Ljubljana), Slovene architect. Born into a joiner's family, Plečnik entered the School of Handicrafts in Graz in 1888. After the death of his father in 1892, he did not take over his father's workshop but left for Vienna. Because of his great talent, he was accepted by Otto Wagner into the Vienna Academy of Fine Arts, where he studied from 1895 to 1898. Plečnik continued to work with Wagner until 1901, and then he opened his own workshop. His most famous works include the monumental Art Nouveau house of the manufacturer Johann E. Zacherl, known as the Zacherl Palace (1903–5), in Vienna and the Church of the Holy Spirit (1910–13) in Vienna. In 1911 Plečnik went to Prague, where he taught at the School of Arts and Crafts. In 1921 he returned to Ljubljana and became a professor at the School of Technology of Ljubljana University. Plečnik had strong links to Prague, though, because President **Tomáš Garrigue Masaryk** commissioned him to renovate and rebuild the Hradčany Castle complex, which was being adapted to serve as the residence of the president of Czechoslovakia. From 1921 to 1930, following Plečnik's designs, many projects were completed there, including the renovation of courtyards and gardens and the revamping of Plečnik Hall (1927–30). The capital of Slovenia is sometimes referred to as "Plečnik's Ljubljana" because he greatly influenced the character of this city. From 1928 to 1929 he prepared the urban development plan for the city. Many buildings and facilities were constructed according to his designs, such as the Vzajemna Zavarovalnica

Insurance Company's headquarters (1928–30), the university library building (1936–41), and the cemetery in Žale (1938). In addition to architectural work, Plečnik also designed furniture, lamps, and liturgical objects (among other things). During World War II he continued his work but also taught students in his house. After the end of the war, he devoted himself to church art. In 1940 the Ljubljana authorities founded an award named after Plečnik, granted for outstanding achievement in the field of architecture. (AO)

Sources: *Enciklopedija Slovenije*, vol. 8 (Ljubljana, 1994); Damjan Prelovšek, *Josef Plečnik 1872–1957: Architectura Perennis* (Salzburg and Vienna, 1992); Kazimierz Kuśnierz and Zdzisława Tołłoczko, eds., *Szkice z historii architektury i urbanistyki* (Kraków, 1999); www.ijs.si/slo/ljubljana/plecnik.html.

PLOJHAR Josef (2 March 1902, České Budějovice–5 November 1981, Prague), Czechoslovak Communist activist of German descent, former Catholic priest. Plojhar finished a German gymnasium and later a theological seminary in České Budějovice. He was a member of Staffelstein, a union of young German Catholics. As early as the 1930s he helped to establish the Association of Friends of the Soviet Union. In March 1939 Plojhar was suspended from priestly duties for the first time. After the German forces occupied Czechoslovakia, he was arrested and sent to a Nazi camp: first to Buchenwald and later to Dachau. By the time of his liberation in 1945, Plojhar had become an avowed supporter of communism, although formally he belonged to the Czechoslovak People's Party (Československá Strana Lidová [ČSL]), led by Father **Jan Šramek**. Along with Alois Petr, Plojhar led a crypto-Communist "leftist" faction within the ČSL, and he served as deputy chairman of the party. After the Communist coup d'état of February 1948, during which he effectively took over control of the ČSL, Plojhar became minister of health. Suspended from priestly duties again, he was elected to parliament in May 1948. In December 1951 he became the formal head of the ČSL, and he worked closely with the Communists. He was too discredited, though, to direct a "national" Catholic Church, which the Communists wanted to establish. In 1957 Plojhar became chairman of the Czechoslovak-Soviet Friendship Society, and in 1960, a member of the presidium of the National Front. From 1961 to 1963, as a representative of the Prague government, he served as vice-president of the World Health Organization (WHO). During the Prague Spring Plojhar retired in April 1968, but in December 1969 he again became head of a communist-sponsored peasant party. In 1970 Plojhar was made deputy chairman of the Czechoslovak group of the Interparliamentary Union. (WR)

Sources: *ČBS*; *Who's Who in the Socialist Countries of Europe* (Munich, London, and Paris, 1989); Václav Vaško, *Neumlčená: Kronika katolické Cirkve v Československu po druhé svétové válce*, vol. 2. (Prague, 1990).

PLYUSHCH Leonid (26 April 1939, Naryn, Kyrgyz SSR), Ukrainian mathematician, journalist, and human rights activist. Plyushch is the son of a laborer who was killed during World War II. Later his family moved to Odessa, where he graduated from high school in 1959. In 1962 he graduated from the Department of Physics and Mathematics of the University of Kiev. He worked at the Institute of Cybernetics of the Academy of Sciences of the Ukrainian SSR. Active in the "'60s generation" (*shestidesiatniki*), Plyushch became a link between the Moscow and Kiev groups of human rights activists. Remaining a Marxist, he openly criticized the Soviet reality; he did so, for instance, in a letter to the CPSU Central Committee in 1964 and in publications in the uncensored press. Fired for taking part in protests against the imprisonment of Aleksandr Ginzburg, Plyushch published in the *Khronika tekushchykh sobytiy* and distributed the *Ukraiinskyi visnyk*. In 1969 he joined the Initiative Group of Human Rights Protection in the USSR. Arrested on 15 January 1972, in July 1973 Plyushch was sentenced to forced psychiatric treatment in Dnepropetrovsk. He was kept there until 1976. Among others, his release was demanded by the International Congress of Mathematics in Vancouver (1974) and Western Communist parties. In 1975 an uncensored book by T. Khodorovych, *Istoriya khvoroby Leonida Plyushcha* (History of Leonid Plyushchš disease), was published. In January 1976 Plyushch was forced to leave the USSR, and he settled in France, where he published *Na karnavali istorii* (Carnival of history; 1976). In 1977 he became foreign representative of the Ukrainian Helsinki Group and worked for the release of its members from Soviet prisons. Active in the study of culture and literature, Plyushch was accepted into the Taras Shevchenko Research Society and published a monograph, *Ekzod Tarasa Shevchenka. Navkolo "Moskalevoyi krynytsi"* (The exodus of Taras Shevchenko: On the "Moscow Spring"; 1986). Plyushch also authored articles on Taras Shevchenko, **Mykola Khvylovyi**, **Pavlo Tychyna**, **Vasyl Stus**, **Mykola Rudenko**, and other Ukrainian writers, as well as on the state of Ukrainian culture. (TS)

Sources: *Encyclopedia of Ukraine*, vol. 4 (Toronto, 1993); Heorhiy Kasyanov, *Nezhodni: Ukraiinska intelihentsiya v rusi oporu 1960–80 rokiv* (Kiev, 1995), Anatoliy Rusnachenko, *Natsionalno-vyzvolnyi rukh v Ukraiini* (Kiev, 1998), Ludmila Alekseyeva, *Istoriia inakomyslia v SSSR* (Vilnius and Moscow, 1992); *Khronika tekushchiki sobytiy* (New York, 1974, 1975, 1976; Amsterdam, 1979).

PÕDDER Ernst (10 February 1879, Aleksandri, near Võrumaa–24 June 1932, Tallinn), Estonian commander and politician. In 1900 Põdder graduated from a military school in Vilnius. Promoted to company commander for his brilliant work during the Russo-Japanese War (1904–5), he left the tsarist army with the rank of colonel. Appointed one of the commanders of the new army by the Estonian Provisional Government in July 1917, he assumed command of the first and the third regiments. After the Bolshevik revolution, when the first Estonian division—an embryo of the future army—was established, Põdder became commander of the first regiment in Haapsalu. When German forces entered Estonia in 1918, he went underground, becoming deputy chief of the Defense League (Kaitseliit). During the Estonian war of independence Põdder initially commanded internal defense. On 4 April 1919 he became commander of the third division, which he commanded in the battle against the German Landswehr; fighting alongside Latvian forces, he achieved victory near Cēsis (Wenden). After the war, Põdder served as commander of a division, first in Pärnu, and from 1921 in Tartu. He helped to suppress a Communist coup d'état in December 1924. From 1926 onwards Põdder sat on the Supreme Council of War and was a member of the command of the Defense League. He then established ties with the (Fascist-like) Estonian League of War of Independence Veterans (Eesti Vabadussojalaste Liit [EVL]). A popular leader and a charismatic orator, Põdder was one of the main EVL ideologues. From 1928 to 1931 he was head of the EVL organization in Tallinn and a member of the central EVL leadership. After a conflict between him and Admiral **Johan Pitka**, Põdder was instrumental in transforming the EVL from an organization that rallied veterans of the war of independence into a mass political party because he had initiated changes in the statutes of the EVL. The new statutes granted membership not only to veterans of the war of independence, but also to people who shared the EVL outlook. In 1931, after the Ministry of Defense issued a circular forbidding officers in active service to be members of political organizations, Põdder resigned all his positions in the EVL but kept his membership. The following year he died of gangrene. (AG)

Sources: *Eesti Entsuklopeedia*, vol. 14 (Tallinn, 2000); Piotr Łossowski, *Kraje bałtyckie na drodze od demokracji parlamentarnej do dyktatury (1918–1934)* (Wrocław, 1972); Tõnu Parming, *The Collapse of Liberal Democracy and the Rise of Authoritarianism in Estonia* (Beverly Hills, Calif., 1975); Andres Kasekamp, *The Radical Right in Interwar Estonia* (London, 2000); www.mod.gov.ee/english/history/defhistory.html.

POGÁNYI József (8 November 1886, Budapest–1938 or 1939, Soviet Union), Hungarian Communist activist.

A journalist and writer by profession, before World War I Pogányi belonged to the Social Democratic Party and edited its press organ, *Népszava*. In the fall of 1918, under the government of **Mihály Károlyi**, he became chairman of the Council of Soldiers' Deputies (soviet) in Budapest and was responsible for contacts with other soviets. In this capacity, Pogányi played a crucial role in radicalizing the army. In March 1919, under the Hungarian Soviet Republic (HSR), he was appointed commissar for defense. Forced to resign by a more radical group led by **Tibor Szamuely**, Pogányi became commissar for foreign affairs in April 1919 and commissar for education in August of that year. He also served as commander of the Second Division of the Hungarian Red Army. After the collapse of the HSR, Pogányi fled to Austria. In exile he was active in the Hungarian Communist Party. In 1922 he went to the Soviet Union. From 1922 to 1929, as a representative of the Communist International, he frequently traveled to the United States, where, under the name of "John Pepper," he organized and de facto led the Communist Party of the United States. In 1925 Pogányi became a member of the political commission of the Comintern Executive Committee and head of the Department for Agitation and Information of the Comintern Secretariat. In March 1926 he became a deputy member of the Comintern Secretariat. In 1928 he came under attack in the Secretariat for "erroneous views" on the evolution of the workers' movement in Western Europe and the United States. In 1929 Stalin also began criticizing him. Expelled from all his positions in the Comintern in November 1929, Pogányi began working on the State Planning Commission of the Soviet Union and became a member of its executive. Arrested by the NKVD in 1937, he was killed in the purges. Pogányi's work *Kultúra, álkultúra* (Culture, pseudo-culture) was published in Hungary in 1962. (WR)

Sources: Rudolf L. Tőkes, *Bela Kun and the Hungarian Soviet Republic* (New York, 1967); Lazitch; *Magyar életrajzi lexikon*, vol. 2 (Budapest, 1967).

POLAŃSKI Roman [originally Raymond Liebling] (18 July 1935, Paris), Polish film director of Jewish origin. As a child Polański survived the extermination of the Kraków ghetto by the Nazis. In 1959 he graduated from the Department of Film Direction at the State Higher School of Theater and Film in Łódź. Already in the early pieces that he directed during his studies—for instance, *Dwaj ludzie z szafą* (Two men and a wardrobe; 1957)—Polański showed a great talent, which was also to be seen in his first feature film, *Nóż w wodzie* (Knife in the water; 1962). He soon won world renown for works combining absurd, grotesque, and surrealist metaphors. Film awards at the

Berlin Film Festival for *Repulsion* (1965) and *Cul-de-sac* (1966) opened him the way to Hollywood. In 1968 he directed an innovative psychological horror movie with Satanist overtones, *Rosemary's Baby*, starring Mia Farrow, for which he received an Oscar. In 1969 he made headlines because of a personal tragedy when the Charles Manson sect killed Polański's pregnant wife, Sharon Tate. Polański's subsequent films, such as *Macbeth* (1971); *What?* (1972); *Chinatown* (1974), starring Jack Nicholson and Faye Dunaway and for which he received ten Oscar nominations; and *Tess* (1977) consolidated his position as one of the leading film directors. Polański also staged theater plays, such as *Amadeus*, by Peter Shaffer (1981). After he was sentenced for having sex with a teenager in the United States, Polański settled in France. In the 1980s and 1990s he was less creative but still active, directing *Pirates* (1986), *Frantic* (1987), and *Bitter Moon* (1992). In 2002 he directed *The Pianist*, based on the memoirs of a Polish Jewish pianist, Władysław Szpilman, who survived the extermination of the Warsaw Ghetto, the Warsaw Uprising of 1944, and the winter of 1944–45 in the deserted ruins of Warsaw. For this movie Polański received the Golden Palm at Cannes in 2002 and the Oscar in 2003. Polański also published an autobiography, *Roman* (1989). (WR)

Sources: Virginia Wright Wexman, *Roman Polanski* (Boston, 1985); John Parker, *Polanski* (London, 1993); G. Stachówna, *Roman Polański i jego filmy* (Łódź, 1994); Krzysztof Dybciak and Zdzisław Kudelski, eds., *Leksykon kultury polskiej poza krajem od roku 1939* (Lublin, 2000).

POLLUZHA Shaban (1871, Godanc near Drenicës–17 February 1945, Cikatovë), Albanian independence fighter from Kosovo. Polluzha came from a Muslim family with patriotic traditions, and his relatives fought in anti-Turkish uprisings. During World War I, along with the unit he had formed, Polluzha conducted operations in the territory between the Bulgarian and Austro-Hungarian occupation zones. In 1924 he was a member of a unit led by Azem Galica, and he covered its retreat to Albanian territory after Galica had been wounded. In April 1941, along with his family, Polluzha was imprisoned in Peje (Peč) because he opposed cooperation with the Italians. Released probably in 1943, he formed a self-defense unit that was to defend the Albanian people from the Serbian Chetniks. In 1944 Polluzha decided to join the struggle against the Germans. In December 1944 he became a commander of a brigade of Kosovo Albanians that had been formed in Drenicë to support the Seventh Albanian Brigade. After talks with **Fadil Hoxha**, this brigade was to follow the orders of the Yugoslav command and go north to liberate Vojvodina;

however, because of the pacification of Albanian villages these plans were abandoned. After the massacre of the Albanian people in the village of Skenderaj, Polluzha became the leader of an anti-Yugoslav uprising. The center of this uprising was in Drenicë. Polluzha gathered around two thousand separatists under his command, engaging at least three Yugoslav divisions. His units tried to avoid major clashes and limited their activities to actions carried out by small groups. Encircled by pacification units in February 1945, Polluzha was seriously wounded while trying to break out. He died of his wounds. (TC)

Sources: Muhamet Mjeku, *Lufta e Drenicës dhe Shaban Polluzha* (Prishtina, 1991); Lefter Nasi, *Ripushtimi i Kosovës (shtator 1944–korrik 1945)* (Tirana, 1994); Muhamet Shatri, *Kosova në luften e dyte botërore 1941–1945* (Tirana, 1997); Noel Malcolm, *Kosovo: A Short History* (New York, 1998).

POLTAROKAS Kazimieras (3 January 1875, Gailionys, near Šiauliai–3 January 1958, Vilnius), Lithuanian Catholic bishop. Poltarokas graduated from a theological seminary in Kaunas and subsequently studied at the Theological Academy in St. Petersburg, graduating in 1902. Ordained in the same year, he began his pastoral work in Liepāja (Libau) and later in Surviliškis (now in Lithuania). In 1911 he became a professor and in 1917 the deputy rector of the Kaunas seminary. He taught introductory theology, philosophy, and sociology. In 1918 he became canon at the Samogitian cathedral, and in 1922, a professor of pastoral theology at the university in Kaunas. In May 1926 Poltarokas was consecrated bishop of Panevėžys and took charge of the newly established diocese. As a result of his efforts, a Cathedral church was erected in Panevėžys, and fifteen churches and fourteen chapels were built in the diocese during the subsequent thirty-two years. After the Red Army seized Lithuania in June 1940, Soviet soldiers were stationed in his residence. Poltarokas was interrogated many times but avoided deportation in the spring of 1941 because he went into hiding. During the German occupation (1941–44) he protested the extermination of Jews and the deportation of Lithuanians to forced labor in Germany. After Lithuania was again incorporated into the Soviet Union, Poltarokas was the only bishop who officially performed his duties in his country. He also administered the archdiocese of Vilnius. His efforts to save the Catholic Church in the worst Stalinist period brought some results. He succeeded in raising the morale of the faithful, prepared many candidates for the priesthood, and, in 1955, consecrated two new bishops, Petras Maželis and **Julijonas Steponavičius**. Poltarokas is buried in the cathedral in Panevėžys. He authored many theological and sociological articles, as well as studies on the history of the church in Panevėžys and a biography of Saint Casimir. (WR)

Sources: *Encyklopedia Lituanica*, vol. 4; V. Balčiunas, "Sacerdos Magnus," *Aidai*, 1958, no. 4; "Kazimieras Poltarokas," *L. K. M. Suvažiavimo Darbai*, 1961, vol. 6; Irena Mikłaszewicz, *Polityka sowiecka wobec Kościoła katolickiego na Litwie 1944–1965* (Warsaw, 2001).

PONGRÁTZ Gergely (18 February 1932, Szamosújvár), leader in the 1956 Hungarian Revolution. Pongrátz's father was a lawyer and mayor of Szamosújvár in Transylvania. In 1945 his family moved to Hungary and ran a farm near Budapest. After graduating from an agricultural high school, Pongrátz worked as an agronomist and stock breeder. In 1956 he worked on a state farm in Henyelpuszta. On hearing the news about a demonstration on 24 October 1956, he went to Budapest and joined the insurgent group in Corvina Passage, the largest group during the 1956 revolution. Along with his three brothers, Pongrátz gained considerable authority in the group. In early November he took over command of the group from **László Iván-Kovács**. After 4 November he continued fighting against the prevailing Soviet forces for a couple of days, and at the end of November he escaped abroad. For more than thirty years the **János Kádár** regime labeled Pongrátz the "leading counterrevolutionist" that the regime had failed to capture and punish. In February 1957 Pongrátz went to the United States, where he worked in a New York railway car factory and then as a cleaner in Boston. In 1957–82 he was deputy chairman of the Hungarian Freedom Fighters Union in Chicago. In 1959–71 he lived in Madrid, Spain. Later he returned to the United States, where he worked as an insurance agent, and he managed a pig farm in Arizona. In 1991 Pongrátz returned to Hungary, where he was active in organizations of veterans of the 1956 revolution. His memoirs, *Corvin köz, 1956* (Corvina Pasage, 1956), were first published in Chicago in 1982 and then in Hungary after 1989 in several editions. (JT)

Sources: *A magyar forradalom és szabadságharc enciklopédiája*, CD-ROM (Budapest, 1999); Attila Szakolczay, *Az 1956-os forradalom és szabadságharc* (Budapest, 2001); György Litván, ed., *Rewolucja węgierska 1956 roku* (Warsaw, 1996).

PONIATOWSKI Juliusz (17 January 1886, St. Petersburg–17 November 1975, Warsaw), Polish economist and politician. Poniatowski came from a landed gentry family. He graduated from high school in Vilnius and from the School of Agriculture at the Jagiellonian University in Kraków (1906). In 1911–13 he studied at the School of Economic and Social Sciences of the Université Libre in

Brussels and at the School of Agriculture of the Technical University in Prague. A member of the Riflemen's Association, in 1914 Poniatowski joined the Polish Legions, where he met **Józef Piłsudski** and his supporters. In 1915 he became a member of the Polish Military Organization (Polska Organizacja Wojskowa [POW]). In the summer of 1917 he joined the so-called Convention of Organization A (Konwent Organizacji A), a secret leadership of the pro-independence camp, in which he represented a radical peasant faction. One of the founders of the Polish Peasant Party–Liberation (Polskie Stronnictwo Ludowe–Wyzwolenie [PSL–Liberation]) in 1915, Poniatowski became its deputy chairman in January 1918. As minister of agriculture in the Provisional People's Government of the Republic of Poland (Tymczasowy Rząd Ludowy Republiki Polskiej), headed by **Ignacy Daszyński**, Poniatowski called for the expropriation of great landed estates without compensation to their owners. He subsequently served as commissioner of the Ministry of Interior in the Polish territory formerly under Austrian rule. In April 1919 he became a member of the Constituent Assembly after another PSL–Liberation MP had resigned his parliamentary seat. Poniatowski again served as minister of agriculture from July 1920 to February 1921 in the coalition Government of National Defense, headed by **Wincenty Witos**.

Elected again to the Assembly on the ticket of the PSL–Liberation in 1922, Poniatowski became deputy speaker of the Lower Chamber. He criticized the government project of agrarian reform, challenging it with a radical proposal put forward by the PSL–Liberation, but the proposal was rejected. After the coup of May 1926 the paths of the PSL–Liberation and Piłsudski parted. Poniatowski, who supported Piłsudski, retired from politics. He returned to political life in June 1934, becoming minister of agriculture. He held his post in successive cabinets until 30 September 1939, when he resigned along with the government of **Felicjan Sławoj Składkowski**. Poniatowski accelerated the implementation of the 1925 agrarian reform and promoted policies of land consolidation and drainage and the canceling of small farm debts that had come as the result of the reform. Such small farms came to be colloquially called *poniatówki*.

Poniatowski's agrarian policy met with sharp criticism from the right wing of the ruling *sanacja* camp and the larger landowners, to whom his policies were economically unjustified. In September 1939, along with the government, Poniatowski was interned in Romania, but he fled from the internment and made his way to Palestine, where the Polish Army was stationed. He later lived in Paris, struggling with poverty and earning a living from occasional lectures and publications. At that time he pub-

lished *Cele i założenia reformy rolnej w dwudziestoleciu niepodległości* (Goals and principles of the agrarian reform during the twenty years of independence; 1951). In December 1957 Poniatowski returned to Poland and took up the chair of pedagogy at Warsaw Agricultural University. Shortly afterwards he retired. (WR)

Sources: *PSB*, vol. 27; Adam Próchnik, *Pierwsze piętnastolecie Polski niepodległej* (Warsaw, 1957); Witold Stankiewicz, *Konflikty społeczne na wsi polskiej 1918–1920* (Warsaw, 1963); Jerzy Holzer, *Mozaika polityczna Drugiej Rzeczypospolitej* (Warsaw, 1974).

PONIKOWSKI Antoni (29 May 1878, Siedlce–27 December 1949, Warsaw), Polish politician. After passing his high school finals examinations in Siedlce, Ponikowski studied at the Department of Mathematics and Physics of Warsaw University. In 1898 he began to study at the Department of Civil Engineering of the Technical Institute in Warsaw, graduating in 1903. While a student, Ponikowski joined the Polish Youth Union called Zet and became a member of the secret National League (Liga Narodowa). In 1903–5 he worked in hydrology and drainage offices in Warsaw and Kraków. In 1911 he severed his ties with the national political camp in protest against its pro-Russian sympathies. During World War I Ponikowski joined the political camp of activists who hoped for the victory of the Central Powers. In 1916 he became a professor at Warsaw Technical University. From December 1917 to early November 1918 Ponikowski served as minister of education in the government of the Regency Council, and from 17 February to 4 April 1918 he was its prime minister. From 1921 to 1924 he was rector of Warsaw Polytechnic. From 19 September 1921 to 6 June 1922 he was prime minister in two successive cabinets. At the same time he served as minister of religious affairs and public education. He also held the portfolio of culture and arts until February 1922, when this ministry was abolished. Ponikowski's government lacked a parliamentary majority but was tolerated by the left wing. The second of his cabinets collapsed as a result of the efforts of the head of state, **Józef Piłsudski**. From 1924 to 1927 Ponikowski served as chairman of the Main Board of the League of the Air Defense of the State. In November 1927 he became a member of the Chief Council of the Polish Christian Democratic Party. Elected an MP, he became head of the Christian Democratic parliamentary representation in 1930. In 1934 he left the Christian Democratic Party and drew close to the ruling *sanacja*. From 1939 to 1944, during the German occupation, Ponikowski was involved in underground engineering education. After the collapse of the Warsaw Uprising, he went to Kraków. In September 1945 Ponikowski returned to Warsaw and helped to reestablish the Warsaw Polytechnic. He then became head of the Land Surveying Department at this university and held this post until the end of his life. (WR)

Sources: *PSB*, vol. 26; *Prezydenci i premierzy Drugiej Rzeczypospolitej* (Wrocław, 1992); *Kto był kim w Drugiej Rzeczpospolitej* (Warsaw, 1994); *Dziesięciolecie Polski Odrodzonej 1918–1928* (Warsaw, 1928); Adam Próchnik, *Pierwsze piętnastolecie Polski niepodległej* (Warsaw, 1983); Władysław Pobóg-Malinowski, *Najnowsza historia polityczna Polski*, vol. 2 (London, 1983).

PONOMARENKO Panteleymon (9 August 1902, Belorechensk [Kuban]–18 January 1984, Moscow), Soviet Communist activist in Belorussia. Born into a peasant family, in 1918 Ponomarenko fought in the Red Army. In 1922 he began working in the Komsomol apparatus. In 1932 he graduated from an institute for railroad engineers in Moscow. From 1932 to 1936 he worked to obtain military qualifications and rose through the ranks of the Communist Party. In 1938 Stalin appointed him first secretary of the Central Committee (CC) of the Communist Party (Bolsheviks) of Belorussia. In the following year Ponomarenko also joined the CC of the All-Union Communist Party (Bolsheviks). After 17 September 1939 he supervised the establishment of the party apparatus and the operations of Soviet security services in the northern part of the Polish eastern territories, which had been occupied by the Red Army and incorporated into the Belorussian SSR. Among other things, Ponomarenko supervised the mass deportations of Polish citizens. In September 1942 he became head of the Central Staff of the Partisan Movement, whose operations were directed not only against the Germans, but also against Polish underground pro-independence fighters. From 1944 to 1948, as chairman of the Council of Ministers of the Belorussian SSR, Ponomarenko directed persecutions and the complete Sovietization of the republic. From 1953 to 1954 he was minister of culture of the Soviet Union, and from 1954 to 1955, the first secretary of the CC of the Communist Party of Kazakhstan. In 1955 Ponomarenko became the ambassador of the Soviet Union to Poland. During the Polish "thaw" he tried to control the course of events. He supported the hard-line Natolin faction, but in October 1956 he accepted Nikita Khrushchev's orders that **Władysław Gomułka** be recognized as leader of the (Communist) Polish United Workers' Party. After leaving Poland, Ponomarenko served as ambassador of the Soviet Union to India, Nepal, and the Netherlands. In 1965 he became a lecturer at the Institute of Social Sciences of the CPSU CC. He served as a member of the CPSU CC until 1961 and as deputy to the Supreme Soviet of the Soviet Union until 1958. He then retired from public life. Ponomarenko was the author of the propaganda works *Par-*

tizanskoe dvizhenie v Velikoi Otechestvennoi Voine (The partisan movement during the Great Patriotic War; 1943) and *Vsenarodnaia borba v tylu nemetsko-fashistskikh zakhvatchikov* (The all-national struggle behind the lines of the German Fascist occupiers; 1986). (EM)

Sources: *Belarus: Entsyklapedychny davednik* (Minsk, 1995); *"Zachodnia Białoruś" 17 IX 1939–22 VI 1941, Wydarzenia i losy ludzkie*, vol. 1(Warsaw, 1998); *Entsyklapedyia historyi Belarusi*, vol. 5 (Minsk, 1999); Mieczysław Juchniewicz, *Polacy w radzieckim ruchu partyzanckim 1941–1945* (Warsaw, 1975); Rainer Lindner, *Historiker und Herrschaft: Nationsbildung und Geschichtspolitik in Weissrussland im 19. und 20. Jahrhundert* (Munich, 1999).

POP DE BĂSEŞTI Gheorghe (1 August 1835, Băseşti, Maramures–7 February 1919, Cluj), Romanian economist and politician from Transylvania. Born into a peasant family, after graduating from high school in Baia Mare, Pop studied law in Arad (Oradea), receiving a diploma in 1855. He worked in the Austro-Hungarian administration and at the same time was active in pro-independence circles of Transylvanian Romanians. In 1880 he abandoned the idea of establishing a united Romanian party that could represent the Romanians to the authorities. When the Romanian National Party (Partidul Naţional Român [RNP]) was established at a conference in Sibiu in 1881, Pop became its vice-chairman. He belonged to the RNP radical wing, which demanded autonomy for the Transylvanian Romanians. He formulated such a program with Ioan Raţiu. Pop was a signatory to a memorandum from the Transylvanian Romanian activists to Emperor Francis Joseph in 1892; in it they called for autonomy for Transylvania. In 1895 Pop became chairman of the RNP. Repeatedly arrested for his activities, after his release Pop always resumed his work for the cause of autonomy for Transylvania, seeking support from Vienna rather than Budapest. From the beginning of the twentieth century onwards he increasingly called for a union of Transylvania and the Old Kingdom of Romania. This did not seem possible until the end of World War I, when the Habsburg empire collapsed and particular national groups reoriented their policies. On 1 December 1918, toward the end of his life, Pop became chairman of the National Assembly in Alba Iulia at which the union of Transylvania and the Old Kingdom of Romania was proclaimed. (FA/WR)

Sources: Ştefan Pascu and Miron Constantinescu, eds., *Unification of the Romanian State: The Union of Transylvania with Old Romania* (Bucharest, 1971); Ştefan Pascu, *A History of Transylvania* (Detroit, 1982); Jean Nouzille, *La Transylvanie: Terre de contacts et de conflits* (Strasbourg, 1993).

POPA Vasko (29 June 1922, Grebenac, Serbia–5 January 1991, Belgrade), Serbian poet. During World War II Popa fought with a partisan Communist group. He then studied in Vienna and Bucharest before completing his education at the University of Belgrade (1949). He took a job as an editor, and in 1953 he made his literary debut with the collection of poems *Kora* (Bark). Popa was noticed for a style that combined elements of modernism with Serbian folk tradition and differed from the Socialist realist canons that dominated East European literature at that time. Popa further developed his style in his later collections: *Nepočin-polje* (Field of no rest; 1956); *Sporedno nebo* (Secondary heaven; 1968); *Uspravna zemlja* (1972; *Earth Erect*, 1973); *Vuča so* (Wolf's salt; 1975); *Od zlata jabuka* (1958; *The Golden Apple*, 1980); and *Rez* (Cut; 1981). Popa's poetry, imbued with a grotesque sense of humor and numerous original metaphors, is a kind of serial treatise on the absurdity of being. He wrote in a succinct style, confronting the concrete with the abstract and frequently resorting to paradox. Popa's publications include an anthology of Serbian poetic humor, *Urnebesnik* (At the top of one's voice; 1960) and an anthology of Serbian poetic fantasy, *Ponočno sunce* (Sun at midnight; 1962). The English translations of his poetry include *Collected Poems, 1943–1976* (1978) and *Homage to the Lame Wolf: Selected Poems, 1956–1975* (1979). (WR)

Sources: *Mały słownik pisarzy zachodnio-słowiańskich i południowo-słowiańskich* (Warsaw, 1973); *Britannica Book of the Year 1992* (Chicago, 1993); *Nowa encyklopedia powszechna PWN*, vol. 5 (Warsaw, 1996); Anita Lekić, *The Quest for Roots; The Poetry of Vasko Popa* (New York, 1993); Miodrag Petrović, *Univerzum Vaska Pope* (Niš, 1995); Ronelle Alexander, *Struktura poezije Vaska Pope* (Belgrade, 1996).

POPESCU Dumitru Radu (19 August 1935, Păpuşa), Romanian writer and playwright. In 1953 Popescu graduated from high school in Oradea (Arad), where he made his literary debut in the daily *Crişana*, and in 1953–56 he studied medicine at the University of Cluj-Napoca. He did not graduate but continued philological studies there in 1956–61. From 1956 to 1969 Popescu worked for a literary journal, *Steaua*, where he published a number of short stories. His first novel was *Fuga* (Flight; 1958), and his first play was *Mama* (Mommy; 1960). Popescu's other works include *Dor* (Longing; 1966); *Ploaia albă* (White rain; 1971); *Vânătoarea regală* (Royal hunting; 1973); *O bere pentru calul meu* (A beer for my horse; 1974); *Împăratul Norilor* (The ruler of clouds; 1976); *Leul albastru* (Blue lion; 1981); and the trilogy *Viaţa şi opera lui Tiron B.* (The life and works of Tiron B.; 1980–82). In 1969–82 Popescu was editor-in-chief of the literary journal *Tribuna* and secretary of the Writers' Union in Cluj. In 1969–79 he was a deputy member, and in 1979–90 a member, of the

Central Committee of the Romanian Communist Party. A leading eulogist of the **Nicolae Ceauşescu** dictatorship, in 1980–90 Popescu headed the Association of Romanian Writers, and from 1982 he was editor-in-chief of the literary journal *Contemporanul*. In 1990 Popescu retired from public life, but in 1997 he became a member of the Romanian Academy of Sciences. (LW)

Sources: Ion Alexandrescu, Ion Bulei, Ion Mamina, and Ioan Scurtu, *Enciclopedia de istorie României* (Bucharest, 2000); Dorina N. Rusu, *Membrii Academiei Române 1866–1999* (Bucharest, 1999); romania-on-line.net.

POPIEL Karol (28 October 1887, Rzochów, near Mielec–6 June 1977, Rome), Polish politician. The son of a carpenter, after finishing high school in Tarnów, Popiel studied law at the University of Lemberg (Lwów, Lviv) in 1908–12. While a student, he joined the Union of Polish Youth called Zet and the National League (Liga Narodowa). He helped to establish the Polish Riflemen's Association and the Polish Military Treasury, and as an emissary of these organizations, he traveled to Poznań and Warsaw. After the outbreak of World War I, Popiel made his way from Galicia to Warsaw, where he became a member of the Chief Committee of the United Independence Parties in August 1915 and a member of the Central National Committee in December of that year. Until the end of November 1916 Popiel worked with the pro-independence left wing and subsequently established ties with General **Władysław Sikorski** and the Military Department of the Chief National Committee. In 1917 he worked in the Executive Department of the Provisional Council of State. In January 1918 he became head of the Personnel Department in the Ministry of Interior.

In January 1920 Popiel assumed the editorship of *Sprawa Robotnicza*, a periodical linked with the National Workers' Union (Narodowy Związek Robotniczy [NZR]). He devoted himself to organizational work in Pomerania, supporting the newly established National Workers' Party (Narodowa Partia Robotnicza [NPR]). For example, he edited *Głos Robotnika*, a press organ of the NPR in Pomerania. In the elections of November 1922 Popiel obtained a seat on the NPR ticket, and from February to May 1923 he was chairman of the NPR Chief Executive Committee. In October 1924 he became chairman of the NPR parliamentary representation, but in 1927 he resigned his seat in order to be able to testify in the case against General **Michał Żymierski**, who was accused of corruption. In September 1929 Popiel became chairman of the NPR Chief Executive Committee. He edited *Placówka*, an opposition weekly. At a congress of the center-left opposition (Centrolew) on 29 June 1930 in Kraków, Popiel submitted a declaration against the *sanacja* regime on behalf of the NPR. Again attacked by the pro-government press, he was arrested and imprisoned in the Brześć fortress in September 1930. Popiel was beaten in prison, and the prison authorities staged his fictitious execution, but thanks to the intervention of the Primate of Poland, Cardinal **August Hlond**, Popiel was released in December 1930. Inspired by **Wojciech Korfanty**, with whom he had talked while in prison in Brześć, Popiel began working for the unification of the NPR and the Christian Democratic Party, but he was unsuccessful. In 1936 he became involved in the establishment of the opposition Morges Front. In March 1937 he entered into negotiations on the unification of the Christian Democratic movement, which led to the establishment of a united Labor Party (Stronnictwo Pracy [SP]) on 10 October 1937. He served as the acting chairman of the SP Main Board because Korfanty, the nominal chairman of the party, was in exile.

In September 1939 Popiel went to France, where he served as chairman of the SP. He also became a member of a commission set up to investigate the causes of the September defeat of Poland. In June 1940 he left for England. During negotiations on the Polish-Soviet Treaty of July 1941, Popiel supported the political line of Prime Minister Sikorski. In September 1941 Popiel became minister without portfolio in Sikorski's government-in-exile. In late 1941 and early 1942 he conducted negotiations with the leaders of the Czechoslovak government-in-exile about a future federation. After the death of Sikorski, Popiel continued to serve as minister without portfolio, and from August 1943 to November 1944 he served as minister for the reconstruction of public administration in the government of **Stanisław Mikołajczyk**. In 1944 Popiel opted for an agreement with the Soviet Union, even at the price of recognizing the Curzon Line. On 25 July 1944 he attended a meeting of the Committee for Home Affairs at which a decision was made to authorize the delegate of the Polish Government-in-Exile for the Homeland, the head of the National Unity Council, and the commander-in-chief of the Home Army to start an uprising in Warsaw at a time of their choosing. After Mikołajczyk's resignation, Popiel did not join the government headed by **Tomasz Arciszewski**. Having accepted the Yalta agreements, Popiel returned to Poland on 6 July 1945. In November 1945 there was an apparent union of former SP activists at home and in exile with the Party of National Upsurge (Stronnictwo Zrywu Narodowego [SZN]), led by **Zygmunt Felczak** and **Feliks Widy-Wirski**, but the latter party worked closely with the Communists and wanted to assume control of the SP. Popiel saw that there was no chance

for a fair agreement with the SZN, so on 18 July 1946 the SP Main Board, led by Popiel, made a decision to suspend the party's activities. In March 1947 Popiel still tried to legalize the Christian Social Party, but after the Communist authorities thwarted all his efforts, Popiel legally left Poland on 26 October 1947.

In exile Popiel directed the SP groups operating abroad that had supported his attempts to continue his party's activities in Poland. In 1950 he became leader of the Polish National Democratic Committee, which consisted of the SP, the Democratic Party (Stronnictwo Demokratyczne [SD]), and the Polish Peasant Party (Polskie Stronnictwo Ludowe [PSL]), led by Mikołajczyk. Popiel helped to establish the Christian Democratic Union of Central Europe. In 1962 he settled in Rome. Popiel authored numerous significant memoirs, including *Na mogiłach przyjaciół* (On the graves of friends; 1966); *Od Brześcia do Polonii* (From Brześć to the Polish Diaspora; 1967); *Generał Sikorski w mojej pamięci* (General Sikorski in my memory; 1978); and *Wspomnienia polityczne* (Political memoirs; 1983). Toward the end of his life he intended to returned to Poland, but an illness thwarted his plans. After his death, Popiel's body was returned to Poland and buried in the Powązki Cemetery, Warsaw. (WR)

Sources: *PSB*, vol. 27; *Encyklopedia historii Drugiej Rzeczypospolitej* (Warsaw, 1999); *Karol Popiel w naszej pamięci* (London, 1978); Andrzej Micewski, *Współrządzić czy nie kłamać: Pax i Znak w Polsce 1945–1976* (Paris, 1978); Henryk Przybylski, *Chrześcijańska Demokracja i Narodowa Partia Pracy w latach 1926–1937* (Warsaw, 1980); Konstanty Turowski, "Dzieje Stronnictwa Pracy w latach 1945–1946," *Chrześcijanin w Świecie*, 1982, no. 1; Janusz Zabłocki, *Chrześcijańska Demokracja w kraju i na emigracji 1947–1970* (Lublin, 1999).

POPIEŁUSZKO Jerzy (23 September 1947, Okopy, near Białystok–19 October 1984, near Toruń), Polish Catholic priest, martyr of communism. Popiełuszko completed studies at a theological seminary in Warsaw in 1972. During his studies he was drafted by the army for two years. Ordained in 1972, he worked as a curate in parishes near Warsaw and in 1979–80 in the Academic Church of St. Ann in Warsaw. From the end of 1978 Popiełuszko ministered among medium-level medical personnel, and from October 1981 he was a diocesan priest employed in the health service; for example, he raised the issue of the defense of unborn children. In 1979 he organized medical services during the visit of Pope **John Paul II** to Poland. From May 1980 he was resident of the parish of St. Stanisław Kostka in the Żoliborz district of Warsaw. On 31 August 1980 Popiełuszko said the mass for striking workers in the Warsaw Steel Plant (Huta Warszawa). Then he became the chaplain of Solidarity in this plant and ministered among workers. He also developed an education program concerning the culture of secular life.

After 13 December 1981 Popiełuszko attended the trials of steelworkers and organized material assistance for the families of people dismissed from work. From April 1982 every last Sunday of the month Popiełuszko said the Mass for the Homeland. These masses drew crowds of thousands in Warsaw. In his elaborate homilies Popiełuszko compared Christian moral values to contemporary life in Poland; defended the right to a life in freedom and justice; and opposed violence, lawlessness, and abusive propaganda. He called on people to preserve spiritual freedom, live in truth, and fight for truth. He reminded them that Solidarity still existed, despite an official ban against it. He propagated the idea of "overcoming evil with goodness." During his masses he recited fragments of poetry and prose, reminding listeners of the continuity of national history and the persistence of trust in the liberation of the country. In 1983 Popiełuszko organized a pilgrimage of workers to the Jasna Góra Monastery in Częstochowa. Popiełuszko maintained wide contacts with the underground Solidarity and the democratic opposition. In September 1983 an inquiry was instituted against him. Popiełuszko was accused of the abuse of the freedom of conscience and religion. In December of the same year he was detained for forty-eight hours, his flat was searched, and he was interrogated. However, Popiełuszko did not stop his pastoral activities. He was attacked in the press—for example, by government spokesman **Jerzy Urban**. In July 1984 an indictment against Popiełuszko was filed in court, but in August of the same year he was amnestied. There were attempts to send him abroad to study in Rome, but he did not agree to that.

On 19 October 1984 Popiełuszko was kidnapped and later murdered by three functionaries of the security service (Służba Bezpieczeństwa). Crowds gathered waiting for news of his fate in the Church of St. Stanisław Kostka, and masses were said for him throughout the country. On 30 October his body was found, and his funeral on 3 November 1984 turned into a huge occasion. His grave by the Church of St. Stanisław Kostka became a place of religious worship and the destination of pilgrimages by Solidarity activists, and it was also visited by foreign statesmen. In 1987 John Paul II prayed by his grave. A collection of Popiełuszko's sermons was published posthumously; until 1990 it was only through the unofficial, underground press. His beatification process is under way. (AF)

Sources: Grażyna Sikorska, *Prawda warta życia* (London, 1985); Krystyna Daszkiewicz, *Uprowadzenie i morderstwo ks: Jerzego Popiełuszki* (Poznań, 1990); Tadeusz Fredro-Bielecki, *Zwycięstwo księdza Jerzego* (Warsaw, 1991); Waldemar Chrostowski, *Świadectwo* (Innsbruck, 1991).

POPOV Blagoy (22 November 1902, Dren–28 September 1968, Varna), Bulgarian Communist activist. In September 1923 Popov was sentenced to fifteen years in prison for his part in the preparations for a Communist coup. Released under amnesty in 1926, he went to the Soviet Union, where he received training at the Leninist School of the Comintern. After returning to Bulgaria, he led an illegal Communist youth wing and became a member of the Central Committee (CC) of the Bulgarian Communist Party (BCP). He then returned to Moscow and worked in the Balkan Secretariat of the Communist International. In 1931 Popov joined the BCP CC Politburo. In June 1932 a Bulgarian court sentenced him in absentia to twelve years' imprisonment. At the end of 1932 Popov went to Berlin, where he worked with the West European Bureau of the Comintern, led by **Georgi Dimitrov**. Arrested on 9 March 1933, Popov was tried along with Dimitrov in the Leipzig Trial on charges of setting fire to the Reichstag. Released for lack of evidence, he returned to Moscow, where he was greeted by Stalin. At the Seventh Congress of the Comintern in 1935, Popov became a member of the Comintern Executive Committee. Popov's marriage to Hertta, a daughter of the high-ranking Soviet official Otto Kuusinen, did not save him from falling out of favor. In 1936 he was forced to make a self-criticism and subsequently disappeared from the Comintern's bureaus. Popov was arrested and deported into the depths of the Soviet Union but survived the war. In 1954, after the death of Stalin, Popov was allowed to return to Bulgaria, where he worked at the Ministry of Foreign Affairs until his retirement. (WR)

Sources: Lazitch; *Entsiklopediya Bulgariya*, vol. 7 (Sofia, 1986).

POPOV Dimitur (26 June 1927, Kula), Bulgarian lawyer and politician. Popov graduated in law in 1950, and later he worked as a lecturer and legal adviser. In 1970 he became judge in a regional court in Sofia, but as a nonparty man, he could not advance to the presidency of his court until 1983. The fact that Popov had a long-term legal practice and was not a member of the Bulgarian Communist Party made him a perfect candidate for top state positions after 1989. In June 1990 he was elected secretary of the Central Electoral Commission, which prepared and supervised the first free elections (10 and 17 June 1990). In view of the problems that the (post-Communist) Bulgarian Socialist Party (BSP) faced in resolving economic issues, after the resignation of **Andrey Lukanov**, on 20 December 1990 Popov became prime minister of a government based on experts connected with the BSP, its satellite Bulgarian

National Agrarian Union, and those few members of the Union of Democratic Forces (UDF) that became economic ministers and started reforms. These reforms, the Bulgarian version of "shock therapy," soon led to a dramatic decline in the standard of living and to widespread protests by the post-Communists and trade unions connected with the former opposition. The Popov government managed to prepare a new constitution and get it passed through the parliament, and it began to replace personnel in the military and the police force. After the parliamentary elections, on 13 October 1991 Popov resigned. In 1992 he ran as a candidate for vice-president with Khristo Genchev, but they lost to **Zhelyu Zhelev** and **Blaga Dimitrovą**. Later Popov withdrew from politics and returned to his legal practice. (AG)

Sources: *Koy koy e v Bulgariya* (Sofia, 1998); Tasho Tashev, *Ministrite na Bulgariya 1879–1999: Enciklopedichen spravochnik* (Sofia, 1999); Jerzy Jackowicz, *Bułgaria od rządów komunistycznych do demokracji parlamentarnej 1988–1991* (Warsaw, 1992); Raymond Detrez, *Historical Dictionary of Bulgaria* (Lanham, Md., 1997); www.rolli-new.com/nes/firms/dimitarpopov.

POPOVIĆ Koča (14 March 1908, Belgrade–20 October 1992, Belgrade), Yugoslav Communist politician and diplomat. Popović came from a well-known Serbian family and was related to Milentije and Vladimir Popović, prominent intellectuals and politicians. He graduated from high school in Belgrade. He studied in Belgrade, Switzerland, and Paris, graduating in philosophy in 1932. In 1933 he joined the Communist Party, which was illegal at that time. In 1937–39 Popović fought in the Spanish Civil War as an officer in the International Brigades. After a short stay at a camp in France, he returned to Yugoslavia. He was arrested but was soon released with the help of his family. In the summer of 1941 he joined the Partisans led by **Josip Broz Tito**. Captured and imprisoned in the camp of Pecin in Albania, Popović escaped with the help of Albanian Communists. He was appointed commander of the First Proletarian Brigade, famous for its march through the Igman Mountains in severe frost during its retreat before the German offensive at the beginning of 1942. In 1943 Popović served as commander of the First Proletarian Division, and toward the end of the war he became commander of the Second Army. He was a member of the Anti-Fascist Council for the National Liberation of Yugoslavia (Antifašističko veće narodnog oslobođenja Jugoslavije [AVNOJ]).

After the end of World War II, from 1945 to 1953, Popović served as chief of the General Staff of the Yugoslav Army. From January 1953 to April 1965 he was minister of foreign affairs. He strictly adhered to Tito's policies, which were aimed at bringing Yugoslavia out of isolation, reaching a new agreement with the Soviet Union in 1955, and involving Yugoslavia in the Movement of Non-Aligned Nations. Popović frequently accompanied Tito in foreign travels. He was a member of the Central Committee (CC) of the League of Communists of Serbia until 1959 and a member of the CC of the League of Communists of Yugoslavia (LCY; until 1952 called the Communist Party of Yugoslavia) from 1948 to 1972. In 1966 Popović became vice-president of the Socialist Federal Republic of Yugoslavia, formally the second head of state. In the early 1970s he called for the liberalization of the system. When Tito refused to implement reforms and soften his authoritarian regime, Popović resigned (1972) and subsequently retired from politics. (AO)

Sources: *Enciklopedija Jugoslavije*, vol. 5 (Zagreb, 1965); *Yugoslavia* (New York, 1957); Jerzy Kozeński, *Agresja na Jugosławię* (Poznań, 1979); Wacław Felczak and Tadeusz Wasilewski, *Historia Jugosławii* (Wrocław, 1985); Wiesław Walkiewicz, *Jugosławia* (Warsaw, 2000); *Current Biography Yearbook* (New York, 1993); Željan E. Šuster, *Historical Dictionary of the Federal Republic of Yugoslavia* (Lanham, Md., 1999); www.mfa.gov.yu/history/ministri/kpopovic_e.htm.

POPOVICI Aurel C. (16 October 1863, Lugos, Hungary [now Lugoj, Romania]–9 February 1917, Geneva), Romanian journalist and philosopher. In 1885 Popovici began to study medicine and philosophy at the University of Vienna, but after three years he transferred to the University of Graz. In 1891 he became one of the leaders of the National Romanian Party (Partidul Naţional Român [RNP]) in Transylvania and an editor of *Tribuna*, one of the most influential newspapers. The theorist of law Rudolf von Ihering exerted a great influence on Popovici's views. In 1892 Popovici co-authored the pamphlet *Replica*, in which he accused the Hungarian government in Budapest of forced Magyarization and justified the struggle of Transylvanian Romanians for their rights. This pamphlet, translated into five languages and published all over Europe, marked the beginning of Popovici's explorations of the concept of a federalist and autonomous model of monarchy. As a result, he was sentenced to four years in prison. After his release, he was forced to go into exile in Austria and Italy. In 1894 he settled in Bucharest, where he taught German, wrote textbooks, and worked for several periodicals. In his political and philosophical works, Popovici emphasized the importance of the development of national consciousness and stressed the role of education in this process. He believed that the dualist Habsburg empire should be replaced by a federalist model; this would resolve ethnic issues and afford more effective protection against the expansion of Russia and Germany. Popovici expressed his views in the treatise *Die Vereinigten Staaten von Groß-Österreich* (1906), which greatly impressed Archduke Francis Joseph. From 1908 to 1909 Popovici edited *Semă nă torul*, and in the following year he wrote *Nationalism sau demokraţie* (Nationalism or democracy). Popovici combined nationalism and conservatism, aiming to maintain a balance between the historical rights of the Habsburgs and the preservation of national interests. In 1912 he moved to Vienna. After Romania entered World War I, Popovici moved to Geneva. (PC)

Sources: Kurt W. Treptow and Marcel Popa, *Historical Dictionary of Romania* (Lanham, Md., 1996); Keith Hitchins, *The Idea of Nation: The Romanians of Transylvania, 1681–1848* (Bucharest, 1988); Mathias Bernarth, *Habsburg und die Aufänge der Rumänischen Nationbildung* (Leiden, 1972).

POSKA Jaan (24 January 1866, Laiuse–7 March 1920, Tallinn), Estonian national activist, politician, lawyer, and diplomat. In 1890 Poska graduated in law from the University of Dorpat (Tartu) and then started a law practice. By the turn of the century he had accumulated a substantial fortune and had one of the most influential law practices in Tallinn. Poska was friends with many politicians—for example, **Konstantin Päts**. At Päts's instigation, in 1913 Poska became mayor of Tallinn; as a result, politicians from the Päts group gained considerable influence in the town and in the region. Owing to his personal contacts and his ability to mitigate conflicts, Poska proved to be an efficient administrator, and his regime also enjoyed the support of the local Germans and Russians. In consequence, after the outbreak of the February 1917 revolution the Provisional Government appointed him Estonian commissioner of the newly created province of Estonia. Poska held this post until the Bolshevik revolution. In the middle of November 1917 the Bolsheviks dismissed the Estonian Provisional National Council by force, and they seized the offices of the commissioner of the province.

After the proclamation of Estonia's independence on 24 February 1918 Poska became a member of the Provisional Government led by Päts and was foreign minister in this government until the Germans seized Estonia. In November 1918 the Provisional Government resumed power, and Poska became its head, substituting for Päts, who was absent. Poska's most important achievement was the negotiation of a peace treaty with the Weimar Republic in Riga (18 November 1918); in it the Germans relinquished all claims to Estonian lands. In December 1918 Poska headed the Estonian delegation to the Paris Peace Conference, where he unsuccessfully tried to obtain the de jure recognition of Estonia by the Allied powers. This failure was the reason Poska decided to modify Estonian foreign policy and negotiate a peace agreement with Soviet Russia and other neighboring countries. Until then, Estonian foreign policy had relied only on the Entente powers for the security of Estonia. Poska proposed to tighten ties with all Baltic states, which, in his concept, would form a common defense system. At the same time, Poska refused to grant assistance to White Russia until the de jure recognition of Estonia. Despite pressure from England and France, Poska, who headed the Estonian delegation, managed to bring about a peace treaty with the Bolsheviks on 2 February 1920. This treaty was his last achievement. However, after his death the idea of a Baltic league was repeatedly taken up by the Estonian diplomatic corps—for example, by Poska's friends **Ants Piip** and **Kaarel Pusta**—and it was one of the main guidelines of Estonian foreign policy between the wars. In 1921 Poska's report of the Paris Peace Conference was published as *Eesti iseseisvuse võitluses kõige põnevamal*. (AG)

Sources: *Eesti Entsuklopeedia*, vol. 14 (Tallinn, 2000); Evald Uustalu, *The History of the Estonian People* (London, 1952); A. Hanko, *Jaan Poska: Eesti diplomaatia suurvaim* (Tallinn, 1990); Toivo Raun, *Estonia and the Estonians* (Stanford, 1991); Eduard Laaman, *Jaan Poska: Eesti riigitegelase elukäik* (Tallinn, 1998).

POSTYSHEV Pavel, pseudonym "Ermak" (18 September 1887, Ivanovo-Voznesensk [now Ivanovo], Russia–26 February 1939, Kuibyshev [now Samara], Russia), Communist activist in the Ukraine. Born into a Russian working-class family, in 1904 Postyshev joined the Bolshevik party. During the 1905 revolution he joined a workers' council, and in the following year he became one of the leaders of the textile workers' trade union. Arrested in 1908, Postyshev was imprisoned in Siberia for four years. From 1914 to 1917 he was active in the Bolshevik party in Irkutsk. In March 1917 he became deputy chairman, and in August 1917 chairman, of the Irkutsk Soviet of Workers' and Soldiers' Deputies. In December 1917 he became a member of a local revolutionary tribunal. During the civil war Postyshev commanded the Red Army units fighting against troops led by Baron Ungern-Sternberg on the Amur River; alongside Vasiliy Blyukher, he defeated them in the battle of Volochayevka. In 1920 Postyshev became a member of the Far East Bureau of the Bolshevik party. In 1923 he was transferred to work in the party apparatus in the Ukraine. He was in charge of establishing the Communist Party (Bolshevik) of Ukraine (CP[B]U) in Kiev, and in 1926 he joined the CP(B)U CC Politburo. At that time Postyshev played a leading role in the annihilation of Trotskyites and Ukrainian nationalist Communists, as well as in campaigns for the industrialization and collectivization of agriculture in the region of Kharkov (Kharkiv).

In the summer of 1930 he was summoned to Moscow, where he became head of the Department for Agitation and Propaganda of the CC of the All-Union Communist Party (Bolsheviks).

Because of a decision by the CC of the All-Union Communist Party on 24 January 1933, Postyshev was again delegated to the Ukraine, where he became second secretary of the CP(B)U CC and head of a party organization in Kharkiv. Along with **Stanisław Kosior**, he played a key role in the purge of the intelligentsia and in the collectivization of Ukrainian agriculture. Postyshev was responsible for mass killings during the liquidation of the kulaks, expropriating and starving to death millions of Ukrainians. He launched a purge of the Ukrainian nationalist Communists. He personally pointed out "state and party enemies" in cultural circles, and they were later imprisoned and executed. He supervised the abolition of the Autocephalous Orthodox Church in Ukraine and the Russification of the apparatus of power in the Ukrainian SSR. As a result of his attacks, **Mykola Skrypnyk** committed suicide. Around one hundred thousand party members were executed during the purges of the CP(B)U apparatus from January 1933 to January 1934. Because of these actions, Postyshev became notorious as the "hangman of the Ukraine." In 1934–37 he simultaneously served as secretary and deputy member of the Politburo of the CC of the All-Union Communist Party. Because he had become too influential during the purges and had even built a kind of personality cult around himself in the Ukraine, Postyshev fell into disfavor with Stalin. Expelled from his posts in March 1937, he became head of a party committee in Kuibyshev. Arrested in January 1938, he was executed over a year later. Postyshev was rehabilitated after the Twenty-second Congress of the CPSU in 1961. (WR)

Sources: *MERSH*, vol. 29; *Encyclopedia of Ukraine*, vol. 4 (Toronto, 1993); W. E. D. Allen, *The Ukraine: A History* (Cambridge, 1940); Hryhory Kostiuk, *Stalinist Rule in the Ukraine* (New York, 1960); *Who Was Who in the USSR* (Metuchen, N.J., 1972); Orest Subtelny, *Ukraine: A History* (Toronto, 1988); Jeanne Vronskaya and Vladimir Chuguev, *Biographical Dictionary of the Former Soviet Union: Prominent People in All Fields from 1917 to the Present* (London, 1992); Andrzej Chojnowski, *Ukraina* (Warsaw, 1997); Jarosław Hrycak, *Historia Ukrainy 1772–1999* (Warsaw, 1999).

POTOČNJAK Franko (2 August 1862, Novi Vinodol–18 January 1932, Zagreb), Croatian ideologue and politician. Potočnjak received a law degree from the University of Zagreb. He worked in the courts but was dismissed for his anti-government activities. He began working in a private law office (1887–96) and later devoted himself to politics and journalism. Potočnjak's nationalist ideology was inspired by **Tomáš Garrigue Masaryk**. In Zagreb Potočnjak founded the newspaper *Hrvatska domovina*, a press organ of one of the wings of the Fatherland Party of Rights (Matica Stranka Prava). In the 1897 elections Potočnjak established a coalition with another Croatian nationalist group, the National Independent Party (Neodvisna Narodna Stranka). His coalition was successful, and Potočnjak was elected to the local parliament, but he was later expelled for social radicalism. He established ties with the Social Democrats and supporters of cooperation with Serbia. He was then one of the founders of the Croatian Party of Rights (Hrvatska Stranka Prava [HSP]). The HSP became part of the Croatian-Serbian Coalition (1905), which brought together all Croatian and Serbian opposition parties and which worked with Hungarian oppositionists. In 1908 conflicts arose in the Croatian-Serbian Coalition; as a result, Potočnjak withdrew from politics and resumed his work in a law office in Crikvenica. After the outbreak of World War I, he emigrated to Italy. He was active in the Yugoslav Committee (Jugoslavenski Odbor). In 1915 at a congress in Chicago, Potočnjak called for the uniting of the South Slavic nations of the Habsburg empire into a common state with the Serbian nation. In 1916 Potočnjak organized the Yugoslav Voluntary Legion in Odessa. He attended a conference in Corfu that led to the signing of the Corfu Declaration (20 July 1917), which announced the intention of founding a unified South Slavic state. Potočnjak supported the program outlined in this declaration. After the establishment of the Kingdom of Serbs, Croats, and Slovenes, King **Alexander** appointed Potočnjak vice-governor of Croatia. Disappointed with Serbian policies, Potočnjak retired from politics and devoted himself to writing his memoirs and on the recent history of Croatia. His publications include *Iz mojih političkih zapisaka* (From my political notes; 1914); *Iz emigracije* (From exile, 4 vols.; 1919–27); *Malo istine iz naše nedavne prošlosti* (Some truth about our recent past; 1921); *Gdje smo to mi i na čemu smo?* (Where are we and why? 1927); and *Rapalski ugovor* (The Treaty of Rapallo; 1922). (MC)

Sources: *Biographisches Lexikon*, vol. 3; *Enciklopedija Jugoslavije*, vol. 6 (Zagreb, 1965); Vasilije Krestic, "Idea of Genocide Matured in Austria-Hungary," www.suc.org/culture/library/genocide/k6.htm.

POTOPEANU Gheorghe (15 April 1889, Târgoviște–1966, Bucharest), Romanian general and politician. From 1908 to 1910 Potopeanu studied at the Artillery, Engineering, and Naval Military School in Bucharest. He fought in World War I. In 1917 he was promoted to major. In 1918 he supervised the withdrawal of German troops from Romania. From 1919 to 1921 he studied at the Military College in Paris. From 1929 to 1933 he was chief of the operational section of the General Staff. In 1933 he was promoted to colonel. From 1935 to 1938 he served as military attaché in France and Belgium. After returning to Romania, he became commander of the Fifth Artillery Brigade. In 1939 he was promoted to brigadier general. In 1940 he was chief of staff of the Second Army and head of a mixed Romanian-German commission supervising a population exchange between Romania and Bulgaria in connection with the territorial concessions granted to Bulgaria. From January to May 1941, after General **Ion Antonescu** had suppressed a rebellion by the Iron Guard, Potopeanu served as minister of economy in Antonescu's government. In June 1941, after the Third Reich invaded the Soviet Union, Potopeanu became commander of the First Frontier Division, which entered southern Bessarabia. From 1943 to 1944 he was commander of the Second and Seventh Army Corps, and from February to March 1944 he was head of the Romanian administration in Transnistria. After handing over the administration of Transnistria to the withdrawing German troops, Potopeanu, organized (among other things) the repatriation of the local Jews and Romanies.

In the summer of 1944 Potopeanu belonged to a group of officers who established cooperation with the opposition and wanted Romania to sever its alliance with the Third Reich and enter the war on the Allied side. After the coup d'état of 23 August 1944 and the overthrow of Antonescu, Potopeanu served as minister of economy and finance until October 1944, when he was arrested for "war crimes" and placed in a military prison in Bucharest. Released at the end of 1944 owing to a lack of evidence and the intercession of Prime Minister General **Constantin Sănătescu**, Potopeanu was placed under house arrest. In 1945 he was arrested for the second time but was released after a few months. In 1948 he was arrested again, accused of war crimes, and condemned to five years in prison. Arrested for the fourth time in 1957, he was sentenced to fifteen years in a harsh prison for "spying for foreign powers." Potopeanu was held successively in prisons in Jilava, Piteşti, Dej, and Gherla, from which he was released in 1963. (LW)

Sources: Vlad Georgescu, *Istoria Românilor de la origini pînă în zilele noastre* (Oakland, 1984); Andrzej Koryn, *Rumunia w polityce wielkich mocarstw 1944–1947* (Wrocław, 1984); Costin Scorpan, *Istoria României: Enciclopedie* (Bucharest, 1997); Aleksandru Duţu and Florica Dobre, *Drama generalilor români* (Bucharest, 1997); Ion Alexandrescu, Ion Bulei, Ion Mamina, and Iona Scurtu, *Enciclopedia de istorie României* (Bucharest, 2000).

POZDERAC Hamdija (15 January 1924, Cazin–6 April 1988, Sarajevo), Muslim Communist activist from Bosnia.

Pozderac studied philosophy at the University of Belgrade and attended the Higher Party School in Moscow. In 1943 he became a member of the Communist Party of Yugoslavia (CPY), which was renamed the League of Communists of Yugoslavia (LCY) in 1952. After the end of World War II, Pozderac was rose through the party ranks. He initially served as secretary of the local committee of the CPY in Bihać. He lectured in the Department of Political Science of the University of Sarajevo. He was a member of the Central Committee (CC) of the League of Communists of Bosnia and Herzegovina (LCBH) (1965–69, 1974–78, and from 1982 on), a member of the Executive Committee of the CC of the LCBH (1966–69), and a member of the Secretariat of the CC of the LCBH (1969–71). He belonged to the Presidium of the CC of the LCBH (1974–78) and served as president of the Assembly of the Socialist Republic of Bosnia and Herzegovina (1971–78) and chairman of the CC of the LCBH (1982–84). He sat on the LCY CC and on the LCY CC Presidium (1979–86). In May 1986 Pozderac became a member of the presidency of the Socialist Federal Republic of Yugoslavia (SFRY), and on 15 May 1987 he was appointed vice-president of the SFRY. Pozderac's career ended as a result of a great scandal linked to the embezzlement of funds by Agrokomerc, a company with which he had personal and family ties. In addition, the weekly *Nin* alleged that Pozderac's book, *Od istorijsko ka konkretnoj inicjativi* (From historical to concrete initiatives), was plagiarized. On 12 September 1987 Pozderac resigned. He was elected, though, to a commission that dealt with constitutional amendments. A few months later he died of a stroke. (AO)

Sources: *Who's Who in the Socialist Countries of Europe*, vol. 3 (Munich, London, and Paris, 1989); Miko Tripalo, *Hrvatsko proljeće* (Zagreb, 1989); Ante Čuvalo, *Historical Dictionary of Bosnia and Herzegovina* (Lanham, Md., 1997).

POZSGAY Imre (26 November 1933, Kóny), Hungarian Communist activist and post-Communist politician. In 1957 Pozsgay graduated from the Department of History and Marxism-Leninism at the Lenin Institute in Budapest. In 1950–56 he was a member of the Hungarian Workers' Party, and from 1956 to 1989, the Hungarian Socialist Workers' Party (HSWP). From 1957 he worked in the HSWP committee in Bács-Kiskun County. From 1965 he was head of its agitation and propaganda department, and from 1968, its secretary. From 1969 Pozsgay was active in Budapest, where he became head of the Department of the Press of the HSWP Central Committee (CC), and in 1971, deputy editor-in-chief of the party monthly, *Társadalmi Szemle*. From 1975 Pozsgay was deputy minister of culture, in

1976–80 minister of culture, and from 1980 to 1982 minister of culture and education. From 1980 he was a member of the HSWP CC. Pozsgay entered into conflict with deputy prime minister **György Aczél** and left the government to become general secretary of the National Council of the Patriotic Popular Front (PPF; 1982–88). Under Pozsgay's leadership the PPF became a forum for numerous initiatives, while he became a leader of the reform wing in the party. He established contacts with the so-called people's national opposition, especially with the poet **Sándor Csoóri**. In September 1987 Pozsgay took part in a meeting of the followers of this movement in Lakitelek, where the Hungarian Democratic Forum (HDF), the first independent party, came into being. A few weeks later Pozsgay gave the PPF organ, *Magyar Nemzet*, an interview about the meeting and the HDF program. In May 1988 Pozsgay was elected to the CC Politburo, and from June 1989 he was a member of its four-man Presidium, along with **Rezső Nyers**, **Miklós Németh**, and **Károly Grósz**. From June 1988 to May 1990 Pozsgay was minister of state. In January 1989 he called the 1956 revolution a "people's uprising" instead of the traditional "counterrevolution," thus breaking an ideological taboo.

In the summer of 1989 Pozsgay presided over the HSWP delegation to Hungarian round table talks. He was a co-founder of the Hungarian Socialist Party (HSP), which emerged from the dissolved HSWP in October 1989. From May to November 1990 Pozsgay was the HSP deputy chairman. He personified the attempts at an evolutionary transition from communism to democracy. In the fall of 1989 Pozsgay was the HSP candidate for president, but most of the parties, excluding the HSP, demanded that presidential elections be held after the parliamentary elections. In a referendum of November 1989 this postulate was supported by 50.1 percent of the votes, thus making Pozsgay's candidacy invalid. In 1983–94 Pozsgay was an MP, and from April to November 1990 he was head of the HSP parliamentary club. In November 1990 he left the HSP and formed the National Democratic Union, which ceased to exist in 1996. From 1997 he worked for the HDF. In the elections of 1994 and 1998 Pozsgay lost, and in 2002 he did not even run. From 1991 Pozsgay was a professor of political science at the University of Debrecen, and in 1995–2000, rector of St. Laszló University in Budapest. Pozsgay published the memoirs *Politikuspálya a pártállamban és a rendszerváltásban* (A political career in a party state and during the systemic transformation; 1993) and *Koronatanú és tettestárs* (Crown witness and participant; 1998). (JT)

Sources: *Ki kicsoda 2000* (Budapest, 2001); *Magyar Nagylexikon*, vol. 15 (Budapest, 2002); Timothy Garton Ash, *We the People* (Cambridge, 1990); Jacek Gorzkowski and Wojciech Morawski, *Jesień narodów* (Warsaw, 1991); Rudolf L. Tőkés, *Hungary's Negotiated Revolution: Economic Reforms, Social Change, and Political Succession, 1957–1990* (Cambridge, 1996); Bugajski.

PRCHALA Lev (23 March 1892, Ostrava–11 June 1963, Feldbach, Austria), Czech general. After graduating from a German high school in Frýdek, Prchala briefly studied law at the University of Vienna. However, he did not finish his studies; instead he joined the Austro-Hungarian Army and graduated from a military school in Trieste. From 1914 to 1916 Prchala served as an officer on the eastern front. Taken prisoner by the Russians, he soon enlisted in the Czechoslovak Legion in Russia; in it he held various command positions until 1920. He also served as Czechoslovak delegate to the command of the White Russian forces led by Admiral Aleksandr Kolchak. In 1921–23 Prchala studied at the Military College in Paris. After returning to Czechoslovakia, he commanded a mountain brigade in Ružomberok for two years and then a division in Užhorod (Uzhhorod) from 1925 to 1931. In 1925 he was promoted to brigadier general, in 1928 to major general, and in 1936 to general of the army. From 1931 to 1933 Prchala served as deputy chief of the General Staff in Prague. Later he served as district military commander in eastern Slovakia and Transcarpathian Ruthenia until 1939. In March 1939 he served for nine days as minister of interior, finance, and transport in the government of autonomous Subcarpathian Ruthenia. After 15 March 1939 he attempted to defend Subcarpathian Ruthenia from invading Hungarian troops, but in vain.

In May 1939, after the capitulation of Czechoslovakia, Prchala made his way to Poland, where he became commander of the Czechoslovak Legion, which was formally established by a decree of 3 September 1939 issued by President **Ignacy Mościcki**. After the failure of Poland in the September 1939 campaign, Prchala made his way via Romania to France and then to Great Britain. In exile he cooperated politically with conservative groups, aspiring to a leadership position among the Czechoslovak émigrés. An opponent of **Edvard Beneš** and his supporters, Prchala worked with **Štefan Osuský** and **Milan Hodža**. After the end of World War II, he remained in exile in London, where he founded the Czech National Council and became its chairman. He worked with Polish and Slovak emigrant groups, as well as with the circle of Wenzel Jaksch, a German Social Democrat. Prchala promoted the project of a Central European federation. In 1945 the Czechoslovak government stripped him of his rank of general of the army. (PU)

Sources: ČBS; *Kdo byl kdo v našich dějinach ve 20. stoleti*, vol. 2 (Prague, 1998); *Politická elita meziválečného Československa 1918–1938: Kdo byl kdo za prvni republiky* (Prague, 1998).

PREISS Jaroslav (8 December 1870, Přeštice–29 April 1946, Prague), Czech lawyer and economist. Preiss graduated in law from the Czech University in Prague. He briefly practiced as an attorney in České Budějovice. In 1900 he became active in the Young Czech Party and edited the economic column of *Národné listy*, a press organ of this party. In 1902 he became secretary of the Society of Czech Textile Industrialists. In 1904 he began working in Živnostenska Banka, the leading Czech bank, first as the editor of its weekly, *Finanční listy*, and then as head of an industrial and mortgage department. From 1910 to 1907 Preiss was deputy director general for contacts with Russia and the Polish territories. He subsequently served as director general of the bank until 1938 and then as chairman of its supervisory board. He transformed this bank into a corporate giant with a very strong position in the Czechoslovak economy. From 1908 to 1913 Preiss sat on the Czech Land Diet on the ticket of the Young Czech Party. He advocated economic cooperation among the Slavic nations, and in 1908 he even proposed the establishment of a Slavic bank. He also served as chairman of the Russian-Czech Club. He saw Russia as the main market for Czech heavy industry. During the war, as a member of a secret Czech political organization called Mafia (Maffie), Preiss actively worked for independence from the Habsburg monarchy. Between June and July 1916 he was imprisoned on a charge of high treason.

In October 1918 Preiss took part in Geneva negotiations between the pro-independence movements at home and in exile. From 1918 to 1920 he sat on the Revolutionary National Assembly on the slate of Czechoslovak National Democracy, in which he had been active throughout the interwar period. Initially he was designated for the post of first minister of finance, but eventually his friend Alois Rašin was given this position. However, Preiss still had great influence on financial policy. He helped Rašin to draft reform plans, including one for a monetary reform carried out in 1919, and he also supported Rašin's deflation policy. In 1918–30 Preiss was deputy chairman, and in 1930–39 chairman, of the Central Union of Czech Industrialists. Preiss's position began to weaken in the mid-1930s, when he opposed the devaluation of the Czech crown and drifted politically toward the radical right wing.

During the German occupation Preiss attempted to protect the Czech economy from the expansion of German monopolies; as a result, in 1942 he was punished with a high fine by a German court. Arrested in 1945 and accused of collaboration with the occupier, Preiss died two days after his release. Preiss was the author of numerous works in economics, including *Z tendencí hospodářského vývoje současna* (From the tendencies of present economic development; 1905); *Průmysl a banky* (Industry and the banks; 1912); and *O vývoji a úkolech československého průmyslu* (On the development and tasks of Czechoslovak industry; 1928). Preiss directed many cultural institutions, including the National Museum, which he also supported financially. He was an enthusiastic bibliophile; his library included around forty thousand volumes and was the second largest collection in the country, after the private library of President **Tomáš Garrigue Masaryk**. (PU)

Sources: ČBS; *Politická elita meziválečného Československa 1918–1938: Kdo byl kdo za prvni republiky* (Prague, 1998); *Kdo byl kdo v našich dějinach ve 20. stoleti, vol. 2* (Prague, 1998).

PRELOG Vladimir (23 July 1906, Sarajevo–7 January 1998, Zurich, Switzerland), Swiss chemist of Croatian descent. In 1915 Prelog's family moved from Sarajevo to Zagreb, where he attended high school. From 1924 to 1929 he studied chemistry at the Czech Institute of Technology, Prague, and subsequently worked in a laboratory in Prague. In 1935 he returned to Zagreb, where he taught organic chemistry at the University of Zagreb. He also initiated research into the chemistry of quinine and related compounds. Working in Zagreb, Prelog succeeded in carrying out the first synthesis of adamantane, a hydrocarbon with a rare alicyclic structure. In 1942, along with his wife, Prelog went to Switzerland on the invitation of **Leopold Ružička**, the co-winner (with Adolf Butenandt) of the 1939 Nobel Prize in Chemistry. Prelog began working in the Organic Chemistry Laboratory at the Swiss Federal Institute of Technology (Eidgenössische Technische Hochschule) in Zurich. In 1952 he obtained a professorship. After Ružička retired, Prelog succeeded him as head of the Organic Chemistry Laboratory (1957–65). In 1959 he received Swiss citizenship. In 1961 he was elected a foreign associate of the U.S. National Academy of Sciences, and in 1962 he became a member of the Royal Academy of Britain. Prelog focused his research primarily on the stereochemistry of organic molecules and reactions. Along with Robert Cahn and Sir Christopher Ingold, he developed a method for specifying the chirality of molecules (the so-called CIP system, from the names of Cahn-Ingold-Prelog). Along with John Warcup Cornforth, Prelog was awarded the 1975 Nobel Prize for Chemistry for his work on the stereochemistry of organic molecules and reactions. In 1976 Prelog retired. In 1986 he became an honorary member of the Croatian Academy of Sciences and Arts. In 1991, along with 109 other Nobel Prize winners, he signed an appeal for peace in Croatia. In 1991 in the United States he published his memoirs, *My 132 Semesters of Chemistry Studies*. (AO)

Sources: www.nobel.se/chemistry/laureates/1975/prelog-auto-bio.html; www.posta.hr/mareasp/index_e.asp?brmare=417; www.aps-pub.com/proceedings/mar00/Prelog.pdf.

PRENNUSHI Vinçenc (4 September 1885, Shkodër–19 March 1949, Durrës), Albanian Roman Catholic bishop, writer, poet, and translator. In his youth Prennushi fought in one of the anti-Turkish uprisings, and he was imprisoned for doing so. After his release he completed school in Shkodër and then studied philosophy and theology in Salzburg. In 1908 he joined the Franciscan order. At first Prennushi managed a monastic publishing house, and then he directed a school run by the order. From 1929 to 1935 he served as a Franciscan provincial. In 1936 he was elevated to the position of bishop of Sapa, and in 1940 he became archbishop of the diocese of Durrës-Tirana. After the death of the Primate of Albania, **Gaspër Thaçi**, in 1946 Prennushi took over his duties. He participated in talks with the Communist leadership on the status of the Catholic Church, refusing to sever ties with the Holy See or to agree to the total subordination of the Church to the authorities. Arrested in February 1947, Prennushi was sentenced to twenty years in prison by a military court in November 1947. The indictment was issued on the grounds that Prennushi had accepted material benefits from the Italians (a Fiat car, which he used in his pastoral work) and maintained contacts with British diplomats.

Prennushi served the sentence in Durrës, where he was tortured and forced to do hard manual labor. He died in a prison hospital. Prennushi wrote about twenty literary works; the most noted is a collection of lyrical poems, *Gjeth e lule* (Leaves and flowers; 1925). He translated (among other works) the classics of German Romanticism and the novel *Quo vadis*, by **Henryk Sienkiewicz**. Prennushi was also the author of many pastoral works, including a biography of St. Francis of Assisi and a ten-volume discussion of the principles of Catholic teaching. He was co-editor of the journals *Hylli i Drites* and *Zani i Shen Ndout*. He collected Albanian folk songs. He also published *Visari Komtar* (The national treasure; 1911) and *Nder lamije te demokracise se vertete* (About the advantages of true democracy; 1922). (TC)

Sources: Arshi Pipa, *Albanian Stalinism: Ideo-Political Aspects* (Boulder, Colo., 1990); Czekalski Tadeusz, *Zarys dziejów chrześcijaństwa albańskiego w latach 1912–1996* (Kraków, 1996); Mirdita Zef, *Krishtenizmi nder Shqiptare* (Prizren and Zagreb, 1998); Arshi Pipa, "Si vdiq Vinçenc Prendushi," *Hylli i Drites* 1997, nos. 3–4.

PREZAN Constantin (27 January 1861, Butimanu–27 August 1943, Schinetea), Romanian marshal. After finishing high school in Bucharest, Prezan graduated from the Infantry and Cavalry Officers' School and the Artillery and Engineering School there. He subsequently went to France, where he continued his education at a school for artillery and engineering officers in Fontainebleau. After returning to Romania, Prezan was promoted to lieutenant in 1880. He was known as a brilliant military engineer. From 1886 to 1900 Prezan taught fortifications at the Artillery and Engineering School. Appointed colonel in 1895, he worked in the General Staff and served as aide-de-camp to King **Ferdinand**. In 1910 he became commander of an infantry division. In 1913 he fought in the Second Balkan War. In 1914 he became commander of the Third Corps, and in 1915, commander of the Fourth Army.

When Romania entered World War I in 1916, Prezan was appointed commander of the North Army, which fought in Transylvania. At the end of 1916 he assumed command of an army group that fought against the Germans, who were attacking Bucharest. Forced to retreat with the remnants of his army to Moldavia in the same year, Prezan was promoted to general and appointed chief of the General Staff. In April 1917, along with Premier **Ion Brătianu**, Prezan made a visit to St. Petersburg, where he was assured that Romania would receive assistance during a counteroffensive that was planned for the summer. Although the Romanians achieved several victories during the summer, their situation did not improve because of the fall of Russia. In December 1917, in the face of a German victory in the east and the necessity of working out a cease-fire, King Ferdinand appointed Prezan to the post of commander-in-chief of the army, which he held until 1920. In the autumn of 1918, upon the collapse of the Central Powers, Prezan agreed with Premier Brătianu that Romania should reenter the war. In 1919 the Romanian Army, led by Prezan, entered Transylvania, Banat, and then Budapest, where it overthrew the Communist government of **Béla Kun**. These successes won the Romanian delegation a very advantageous position at the Paris Peace Conference and greatly helped Romania to enlarge its territory. In 1920 Prezan retired. He reentered politics in 1930, when, as a result of a government crisis, King **Charles II** returned to Romania and assumed the throne. Appointed marshal, Prezan was entrusted with the mission of forming a nonparty government, but he was unsuccessful. In the same year he withdrew from public life for good. He settled in Italy. Shortly before his death Prezan returned to Romania and settled on his Moldavian estate, where he died. (LW)

Sources: Holger H. Herwig and Neil M. Heyman, *Biographical Dictionary of World War I* (Westport, Conn., 1982); Vasile Alexandrescu, *Romania in World War I* (Bucharest, 1985); Glenn Torrey, *General Henri Bertholet and Romania, 1916–1919* (Boulder, Colo., 1987); Emile Turdeanu, *Modern Romania: The Achievement of National Unity, 1914–1920* (Los Angeles, 1988); Józef Darski, *Rumunia: Historia, współczesność, konflikty narodowe* (Warsaw, 1995); Dorina N. Rusu, *Membrii Academiei Române 1866–1999* (Bucharest, 1999); Ion Alexandrescu, Ion Bulei, Ion Mamina, and Ioan Scurtu, *Enciclopedia de istorie României* (Bucharest, 2000).

PREŽIHOV Voranc [originally Lovro Kuhar] (10 August 1893, Kotlje, near Ravne na Koroškem–18 February 1950, Maribor), Slovene Communist writer and political activist. Born into a peasant family in Carinthia, from 1899 to 1907 Preïhov attended school and subsequently worked as a servant and a carpenter. In 1911 he left his village and tried to get to America to escape poverty, but after a few months he returned home from Trieste. From 1912 to 1913 he continued his education at a cooperative school in Ljubljana. His first publications appeared at that time. In 1916, during World War I, Prežihov, who served in the Austro-Hungarian Army, deserted from the Tirolean front to the Italian side. Because of this, he was sentenced to death in absentia. Initially the Italians put him in prison, but in September 1918 they admitted him to the Yugoslav Legion. After the war, Prežihov returned to his native region and joined the Communist movement. On his initiative, a branch of the Socialist Workers' Party of Yugoslavia (Socijalistička Radnička Partija Jugoslavije [SRPJ]) was established in Guštanj, Carinthia, on 1 May 1920. The SRPJ was renamed the Communist Party of Yugoslavia (CPY) in June 1920. After the CPY was declared illegal in 1921, Prežihov continued his activities underground. When King **Alexander I** established a dictatorship in 1929 and increased measures against the Communist movement, Prežihov was sentenced in absentia to six years' imprisonment. Prežihov had already gone to Vienna, where he served as secretary of the Yugoslav branch of the International Organization for Aid to Revolutionaries. In December 1932 he became an editor of *Delo*, a newspaper of the Slovene and Italian Communists. On the orders of the CPY Prežihov traveled to Moscow and Paris. In 1934 he became a member of the CPY Central Committee (CC). Arrested in March 1936 in Prague and handed over to the Austrian authorities, he spent thirteen months in prison. In August 1937 he went to Paris, where he was charged

with various responsibilities, including the printing of CPY newspapers and sending Yugoslav volunteers to the civil war in Spain.

In 1939, against the will of **Josip Broz Tito**, Prežihov returned from Paris to Ljubljana. On the orders of **Edvard Kardelj**, he was isolated from the party. Arrested in January 1943, he was held by the Italians. Prežihov was imprisoned in Ljubljana, Begunje, Berlin, and the Sachsenhausen concentration camp; from there he was transferred to Mauthausen in February 1945. After the war, Prežihov returned to his native village of Prežih. In November 1945 he was elected to the Communist parliament of Yugoslavia. In November 1949 he settled in Maribor. After the war, he was the main representative of Socialist realism in Slovene literature. His most important works include the collection of stories *Samorastniki* (1940; *The Self-Sown*, 1983), addressing the issues of his native Carinthia; *Povesti* (Stories; 1925); *Doberdob* (1940); *Borba na tujih tleh* (Struggle on foreign land; 1946); *Solzice* (Lilies of the valley; 1949); *Kanjuh iz Zagate* (Kanjuh from Zagata; 1952); and *Ljubezen na odoru* (Love on a precipice; 1954). (AO)

Sources: *Enciklopedija Jugoslavije*, vol. 6 (Zagreb, 1965); *Enciklopedija Slovenije*, vol. 9 (Ljubljana, 1996); *Antologia noweli jugosłowiańskiej* (Warsaw, 1964); *Mały słownik pisarzy zachodnio-słowiańskich i południowo-słowiańskich* (Warsaw, 1973); J. Koruza, "Prežihov Voranc i ljudska tradicija," *Slavistična revija*, 1976, vol. 24; M. Messner, *Prežihov Voranc und die Bauern* (Klagenfurt, 1980).

PRIBIĆEVIĆ Adam (24 December 1880, Hrvatska Kostajnica–1957, Canada), Serbian politician. Pribićević was the brother of **Svetozar Pribićević** and **Valerijan Pribićević**. After graduating from a high school in Sremski Karlovci, he studied law in Zagreb. He began his political activities by joining the Independent Serbian Party (Srpska Samostalna Stranka [SSS]). He published articles in the periodicals *Srbobrana* and *Srpsko kolo*. A supporter of the social philosophy of **Tomáš Garrigue Masaryk**, Pribićević emphasized the role of peasants in the social development of Serbia. Along with a group of Serbian politicians from Croatia (including his brother Valerijan), Pribićević was arrested during a mounting conflict between the Croatian-Serbian Coalition and the Hungarian authorities. This conflict intensified with the annexation of Bosnia and Herzegovina by Austria-Hungary in 1908. Pribićević was sentenced to twelve years' imprisonment for allegedly maintaining secret contacts with the Serbian government, but in 1910 the sentence was quashed and he was released. He then worked on the editorial staff of *Srpsko kolo*. In 1913 in Belgrade Pribićević talked with the Serbian prime minister, **Nikola Pašić**, whom he forewarned about a compromise between the Croatian-Serbian Coalition and the Hungarian government. After the outbreak of World War I, Pribićević was inducted into the Austro-Hungarian Army and sent to the Galician front. After the war he lived in Belgrade and worked as an editor of the periodical *Narod*. In 1924 he settled in Kosovo, where he was active in the Independent Democratic Party (Samostalna Demokratska Stranka [SDS]), founded by his brother Svetozar. He also edited the periodical *Reč*. After the death of Svetozar, Pribićević was elected to parliament in 1936. In 1938 he became chairman of the SDS. After the fall of Yugoslavia in April 1941, he went into exile. (WR)

Sources: *Enciklopedija Jugoslavije*, vol. 6 (Zagreb, 1965); Hrvoje Matković, *Svetozar Pribićević i Samostalna demokratska stranka do šestojanuarske diktature* (Zagreb, 1972); Mark Biondich, *Stjepan Radić, the Croat Peasant Party, and the Politics of Mass Mobilization, 1904–1928* (Toronto, 2000).

PRIBIĆEVIĆ Svetozar (26 October 1875, Hrvatska Kostajnica–15 September 1936, Prague), Serbian politician born in Croatia, the brother of **Adam Pribićević** and **Valerijan Pribićević**. After graduating from a high school in Sremski Karlovci (1894), Pribićević studied mathematics and physics in Zagreb. While a student, he was active in the Serbian and Croatian Progressive Youth (Napredna Srpska i Hrvatska Omladina), which sought cooperation between Serbia and Croatia within the framework of the Habsburg empire. As chairman of the Serbian faction, Pribićević worked out the main program guidelines, which were published in the periodical *Narodna misao* in the article "Misao vodilja Srba i Hrvata" (Main thoughts of Serbs and Croats) in 1897. This article pointed to the ethnic unity of Serbs and Croats and consequently called for national integration as the main direction of political activities. After completing his studies, Pribićević worked as a teacher in a Serbian school in Pankrac and later in Karlovac. In 1902 he began editing the periodical *Novi Srborban*, a press organ of the Independent Serbian Party (Srpska Samostalna Stranka [SSS]). His work as head of this periodical played a role in the establishment of the Croatian-Serbian Coalition (12 December 1905), which consisted of the SSS and Croatian parties. Pribićević briefly succeeded **Frano Supilo** after the latter resigned as president of this coalition in 1910. Although Pribićević's policy toward Austria-Hungary was viewed as almost opportunistic by the radicals, after the outbreak of World War I he was interned, and it was not until 1917 that he was able to resume his political activities.

In October 1918, after returning to Zagreb, Pribićević was elected vice-president of the newly established National Council of Slovenes, Croats, and Serbs. On 29

October 1918 he announced the severance of state ties between Croatia and Austria-Hungary. On 24 November 1918 he brought about an agreement with the Kingdom of Serbia on the establishment of a state, but the details of its political system remained an open issue. This de facto determined the unitary character of the Kingdom of Serbs, Croats, and Slovenes (SHS), which caused strong protests by the supporters of **Stjepan Radić**. On 7 December 1918 Pribićević assumed the post of minister of interior in the first government of the SHS, and he held this post until February 1920. On 15 February 1919 the Democratic Union had been established at a meeting of political parties from the former Austria-Hungary. In 1920 the Democratic Union was transformed into the Serbian Democratic Party (Srpska Demokratska Stranka [SDS]). The SDS program called for the centralization of the state. Pribićević lost the elections for head of the SDS, mostly because of his limited knowledge of the Kingdom of Serbia and concern that he might be rejected by the people there, and **Ljubomir Davidović** became head of the party. Because of the centralism of its program and its goal of the integration of the state, the SDS opposed all decentralizing forces and resorted to strong repressive measures. In his capacity as minister of interior, Pribićević played a certain role in those measures, directing the main thrust of persecutions against the Croatian Republican Peasant Party led by Radić. Pribićević was also instrumental in the support the SDS gave to the National Radical Party in the struggle for a centralist model for the constitution of June 1921 (the so-called Vidovdan Constitution). With the passing of time the two parties increasingly drifted apart. While some of the SDS members, led by Davidović, were willing to mitigate the centralism of the state and seek cooperation with Radić, Pribićević insisted on an alliance with the National Radical Party, led by **Nikola Pašić**. As a result, on 26 March 1924 Pribićević left the SDS, and along with his supporters he joined the National Radical Party, establishing the National Bloc.

After 1918 Pribićević realized that his concept of Yugoslavism was different from the centralist system defined by the 1921 constitution. This system was dominated by the National Radical Party politicians, the supporters of Greater Serbian nationalism, and he felt that this was the main reason for the permanent crisis of the state. From May 1920 to December 1922, from March to July 1924, and from November 1924 to July 1925 Pribićević served as minister of education. In 1925 he severed his ties with the National Radical Party and established the Independent Democratic Party (Samostalna Demokratska Stranka). As a result of the increasing chaos in the state, Pribićević decided to reach a compromise, enter into cooperation with Radić, and establish the Peasant Democratic Coalition with the Croat Peasant Party on 11 November 1927. Pribićević insisted on the revision and then the repeal of the centralist constitution. After the assassination of Radić in 1928, Pribićević became leader of the opposition, and his views evolved from an uncritical support of the centralized and authoritarian state to the gradual recognition of the separate ethnic identity of the Croats and a greater support of federalism.

After King **Alexander I** proclaimed a dictatorship (6 January 1929) and outlawed all political opposition parties, Pribićević was arrested and sent to Brus in Serbia and then to a hospital in Belgrade, where he was interned. After the intervention of the president of Czechoslovakia, **Tomáš Garrigue Masaryk**, and also because Pribićević went on a hunger strike, in July 1931 he was allowed to go to Prague. Pribićević fully blamed King Alexander for the conflicts and social tensions in Yugoslavia, and he did not hesitate to paint the monarch's activities black—for instance, in *La dictature du roi Alexandre* (The dictatorship of King Alexander; 1933). Toward the end of his life Pribićević firmly supported a republican model for the future political system of Yugoslavia, based on a federation of its constituent nations. (AG)

Sources: Biographisches Lexikon, vol. 3; *Enciklopedija Jugoslavije*, vol. 6 (Zagreb, 1965); Milan Kostić, *Pribićević-Radić* (Zagreb, 1925); *Osteuropa-Handbuch: Jugoslawien* (Cologne and Graz, 1954); Hrvoje Matković, *Svetozar Pribićević i Samostalna demokratska stranka do šestojanuarske diktature* (Zagreb, 1972); Ljubo Boban, *Svetozar Pribićević u opoziciji 1928–1936* (Zagreb, 1973); Wacław Felczak and Tadeusz Wasilewski, *Historia Jugosławii* (Wrocław, 1985); Hrvoje Matković, *Svetozar Pribićević: Ideolog, stranecki roda, emigrant* (Zagreb, 1995); Mark Biondich, *Stjepan Radić, the Croat Peasant Party, and the Politics of Mass Mobilization, 1904–1928* (Toronto, 2000).

PRIBIĆEVIĆ Valerijan (21 March 1870, Hrvatska Dubica–July 1941, Split), Serbian politician. Pribićević was the brother of **Adam Pribićević** and **Svetozar Pribićević**. After graduating from a seminary in Sremski Karlovci, he entered the Theological Academy in Kiev and later studied philosophy in Leipzig and Vienna. After returning home, Pribićević, together with his brothers, was active in the Independent Serbian Party (Srpska Samostalna Stranka [SSS]) and in the Croatian-Serbian Coalition. Along with a group of Serbian politicians from Croatia (including his brother Adam), Pribićević was arrested during a mounting conflict between the Croatian-Serbian Coalition and the Hungarian authorities. This conflict intensified with the annexation of Bosnia and Herzegovina by Austria-Hungary in 1908. Pribićević was sentenced to twelve years' imprisonment for allegedly maintaining secret contacts with the Serbian government, but in 1910 the

sentence was quashed and he was released. He became an archimandrite of the Jazak monastery. In 1914 he was elected to the Croatian National Assembly on the ticket of the Croatian-Serbian Coalition. At the beginning of World War I he was interned. In 1917 he left the party and supported the May Declaration, which advocated that the Slavic nations of the Austro-Hungarian Empire be united into a common state but under Habsburg rule. In January 1918 Pribićević began editing *Glas Slovenaca, Hrvata i Srba*, promoting a program of uniting the Slavic nations under Habsburg rule and the Serbian nation into a common state. In the Kingdom of Serbs, Croats, and Slovenes, Pribićević served as a member of parliament on the ticket of the Democratic Union, which was transformed into the Serbian Democratic Party (Srpska Demokratska Stranka) in 1920. In 1924 he became active in the Independent Democratic Party (Samostalna Demokratska Stranka), founded by his brother Svetozar. (AO)

Sources: *Enciklopedija Jugoslavije*, vol. 6 (Zagreb, 1965); Hrvoje Matković, *Svetozar Pribićević i Samostalna demokratska stranka do šestojanuarske diktature* (Zagreb, 1972); Mark Biondich, *Stjepan Radić, the Croat Peasant Party, and the Politics of Mass Mobilization, 1904–1928* (Toronto, 2000).

PRÍDAVOK Peter (27 November 1902, Stankovany–15 February 1966, London), Slovak politician. Prídavok studied theology in Innsbruck and then classical and Slavic philology at Charles University in Prague from 1923 to 1925. In 1926–29 he was executive editor of the weekly *Rodobrana*, which promoted a radical program of Slovak autonomy. He also edited the daily *Slovák*, a press organ of Hlinka's Slovak People's Party (Hlinková Slovenská L'udová Strana [HSL'S]), until 1931. In the HSL'S, Prídavok was a member of the group led by **Karol Sidor**. From 1938 to 1939 Prídavok was head of a Slovak press agency and head of the press department of the Slovak government. After Slovak independence was declared on 14 March 1939, he emigrated to Poland and protested the pro-German policy of the government. Following the German aggression against Poland in September 1939, he went to Yugoslavia and then to France. In Paris, along with **Milan Hodža**, Prídavok established the Slovak National Council, which was in opposition to the Czechoslovak National Committee headed by **Edvard Beneš**. After Germany attacked France in 1940, Prídavok went to Great Britain. Briefly interned, in 1943 he organized the Slovak National Council in London. He worked with Sidor, the Slovak ambassador to the Vatican, and maintained close contacts with the Polish émigré community. He published articles in *The Catholic Herald* and other periodicals, criticizing the pro-Soviet policy of Beneš and protesting against the program to reestablish a unitary Czechoslovakia. He called for the establishment of a Central European federation, with Slovakia as a rightful member. In 1943 Prídavok became chairman and later vice-chairman of the Central European Federal Club in London. After the war, along with Sidor, he established the Slovak National Council Abroad in 1948. In 1952 Prídavok became a journalist and later the head of the Slovak section of the BBC. (MG)

Sources: *SBS*; František Vnuk, "Peter Prídavok," *Kalendár Jednota*, 1972; František Vnuk *Rebelianti a suplikanti (Slovenská otázka v ilegalite a exile 1944–1945)* (Lakewood, Ohio, 1989).

PRINCIP Gavrilo (25 July 1894, Gornji Obljaj, Bosnia–28 June 1918, Theresienstadt, Austria), Serbian revolutionary who assassinated Archduke Francis Ferdinand. The assassination of the archduke provided the pretext for Austria-Hungary to declare war on Serbia and thus precipitated World War I. Born into a Bosnian Serb peasant family, Princip attended a gymnasium in Belgrade but never graduated. In 1911, while a student, he joined a student group of the Serbo-Croat Progressive Organization, where he met **Ivo Andrić**, the future famous writer. Princip was also active in the Young Bosnia (Mlada Bosna) organization, which was a part of Omladina, a great revolutionary youth movement. Young Bosnia sought to destroy the Habsburg monarchy and to unite the South Slavic peoples into a federal nation under Serbian leadership. The organization resorted to acts of terror. In 1912 Princip joined a secret organization of Serbian nationalists, Union or Death (Ujedinjenje ili Smrt), known as the Black Hand (Crna Ruka), where he underwent terrorist training. When the government in Vienna declared a state of emergency in Bosnia and ordered army maneuvers announcing that the Archduke Francis Ferdinand would pay an official visit to Sarajevo, Young Bosnia, with the help of the Black Hand, began preparations for an assassination. On 28 June 1914 in Sarajevo, Nedeljko Čabrinović threw a bomb at the archduke's car, but his attempt failed. Soon Princip fired deadly shots at Francis Ferdinand and his wife Sophie, Duchess von Hohenberg (née Chotek). Princip was caught on the spot. On 28 October 1914 he was sentenced to twenty years' penal servitude, the maximum penalty allowed for a person under the age of twenty on the day of his crime. Princip died of tuberculosis in a prison hospital. In Yugoslavia he is regarded as a national hero. (AO)

Sources: *Biographisches Lexikon*, vol. 3; *Obtužnica i obrazloženije protiv Gavrila Principa i drugova radi atentata Njeg. C. i Kr. Visosti Prestolonasljednika Nadvojevode Franje Ferdinanda i Visoke Mu supruge* (Sarajevo, 1914); *Osuda Okružnog suda u Sarajevu po završenoj raspravi protiv Gavrila Principa i drugova radi atentata Njeg. C. i Kr. Visosti Prestolonasljednika Nadvojevode Franje Ferdinanda i Visoke Mu supruge* (Sarajevo, 1914); Dragoslav Ljubibratić, *Gavrilo Princip* (Belgrade, 1959); Vladimir Dedijer, *The Road to Sarajevo* (New York, 1966).

PRISHTINA Hasan bey (1873, Vučitern–14 August 1933, Salonika), Albanian independence activist from Kosovo. Prishtina graduated from a French lycée in Salonika and subsequently studied law in Istanbul. After completing his studies, he became a clerk in Skopje, where he established contacts with national organizations. In 1908–12 he served as an MP from Prishtina to the Young Turk parliament. He protested in parliament against the atrocities committed by Turkish troops in Kosovo. On 21–25 May 1912 Prishtina co-organized a meeting of tribal leaders in the region of Junik; at this meeting a decision was made to start an anti-Turkish uprising, and he became its de facto political leader. Along with **Bajram Curri**, **Isa Boletini**, and other leaders, Prishtina was a co-author of a memorandum of August 1912 to the Turkish authorities that demanded broad autonomy for the Albanians who lived in the four European *vilayets* (provinces). Prishtina called for close cooperation with the Macedonians in order to establish an autonomous Albanian-Macedonian state. In November 1912 Prishtina represented the district of Prishtina at the sessions of the National Assembly in Vlorë and was also a signatory of the independence declaration. From 15 March to 20 May 1914 he served as minister of post and telegraphs in the government of Prince Wilhelm von Wied.

After World War I, Prishtina became aligned with the Committee for the Defense of Kosovo and was its delegate to the Paris Peace Conference. He helped to organize a congress in Lushnjë (January 1920) at which a decision was made about the structure of the government. In 1921, in the first elections in independent Albania, Prishtina won a seat as a deputy from Dibra. Supported by some tribal leaders from the north, he staged a coup d'état, after which he served as prime minister of Albania for five days (7–12 December 1921). Prishtina was removed from power by troops faithful to **Ahmed Zogu**. During the 1924 revolution Prishtina fought against the Serbs in the north of the country and established ties with Macedonian separatists. After the failure of the revolution, he made his way via Hungary to Italy, then to Bulgaria, and finally to Greece, where he spent most of his time. After **Luigji Gurakuqi** was killed in March 1925, Prishtina came to the conclusion that Zogu must be physically removed. In 1926 he attended a meeting of Albanian political leaders in emigration in Zadar, where plans to overthrow Zogu's rule were discussed. The plans for a coup failed, as the neighboring countries did not support a takeover of power by the émigrés. Prishtina was one of the candidates who would have taken over power from Zogu. In 1928, following an unsuccessful attempt to assassinate Zogu in the Vienna Opera House, the authorities in Tirana sentenced Prishtina to death. He was also hunted down by Yugoslav agents. Prishtina was shot and killed in Cafe Astoria, Salonika, by Ibrahim Xhelo, who worked for Zogu. The assassin was captured and explained during his trial that while talking to Prishtina, he had learned that Prishtina was planning to assassinate the king. In 1977 Prishtina's ashes were transferred from Salonika to Albania. (TC)

Sources: *Fjalor Enciklopedik Shqiptar* (Tirana, 1985); *Biographisches Lexikon*, vol. 3; Stavro Skendi, *The Albanian National Awakening 1878–1912* (Princeton, 1967); *Akte të Rilindjes Kombëtare Shqiptare 1878–1912* (Tirana, 1978); Bernd J. Fischer, *King Zog and the Struggle for Stability in Albania* (Boulder, Colo., 1984); Miranda Vickers, *Albania: A Modern History* (London, 1995); Noel Malcolm, *Kosovo: A Short History* (New York, 1998); Fatos Baxhaku, "Hasan Prishtina: Përse u vrane," *Klan*, 1999 no. 36.

PRODANOVIĆ Jaša (23 April 1867, Čačak–1 May 1948, Belgrade), Serbian politician and writer. Prodanović attended high schools in Čačak and Belgrade. He subsequently studied at the School of Mathematics and Natural Sciences of the University of Belgrade until 1890. While a student, Prodanović established ties with the Socialist youth movement. He was one of the editors of the collected writings of Svetozar Marković, a pioneer of socialism in the Balkans. He also edited the youth periodicals *Srpska misao* and *Narodna misao*. In 1890 Prodanović became a high school teacher and went into journalism and literary criticism. In 1901 he joined the Independent Radical Party (Samostalna Radikalna Stranka [SRS]), a faction of the Radical Party. From 1902 to 1912 (on and off) he edited an SRS periodical, *Odjek*. In 1903 Prodanović became an MP in the Serbian parliament. From 1909 to 1911 he served as minister of the economy in the government of **Stojan Novaković** and was instrumental in the adoption of a 1911 law on workers' insurance.

In 1919 Prodanović left the SRS and was one of the founders of the Yugoslav Republican Democratic Party (Jugoslovenska Republikanska Demokratska Stranka [JRDS]), which called for the introduction of a republican federal system. In the elections of 28 November 1920 the JRDS obtained 0.8 percent of the vote and won three seats. Although his party had little electoral support, Prodanović was highly respected on the political scene. In the 1920s he sharply criticized the way the parliamentary system functioned. He opposed the authoritarian style of King **Alexander I** and criticized the constitution promulgated by the king on 3 September 1931. The JRDS supported the Zagreb Manifesto of November 1932, in which ab-

solutism, centralism, and unitarism were condemned. In March 1945, toward the end of World War II, Prodanović became deputy prime minister of the federal government established by **Josip Broz Tito** on 1 February 1946, and he held this post until the end of his life, endorsing the shift to totalitarian rule in Yugoslavia. Prodanović's major works include *Ustavni razvitak i ustavne borbe u Srbiji* (Constitutional development and the struggle for a constitution in Serbia; 1936) and *Istorija političkih stranaka i struja u Srbji* (The history of political parties in Serbia; 1947). Prodanović also edited anthologies of works by Jovan Ilić (1929), Svetislav Vulović (1932), and Jovan Jovanović Zmaj (1933–37), as well as the collection *Antologija narodne poezije* (Anthology of national poetry; 1938). (AO)

Sources: *Biographishes Lexikon*, vol. 3; *Enciklopedija Jugoslavije*, vol. 4 (Zagreb, 1965); *Spomenica Jaše Prodanovića* (Belgrade, 1958); Željan E. Šuster, *Historical Dictionary of the Federal Republic of Yugoslavia* (Lanham, Md., 1999).

PRODEV Stefan (15 September 1927, Sofia), Bulgarian Communist journalist and political activist. From 1943 Prodev belonged to the Communist Youth Union. After graduating from high school (1946), he worked on the newspaper *Trud* (1946–48), and he was editor of *Literaturne Noviny* (1962–64) and *Bulgarska Muzyka* (1965). From 1965 to 1979 Prodev was editor-in-chief of *Paralele* and later of the periodicals *Sofia* (1979–84) and *Narodna Kultura* (from 1984). He won a reputation as a reporter. Some of his articles were published in book form and were very popular because of his vivid style and his interest in authentic problems of the common folk. A member of the Bulgarian Communist Party (BCP), Prodev knew how to zigzag between the BCP Central Committee Department of Propaganda and popular expectations. This strengthened his reputation as an unorthodox Communist, while *Narodna Kultura* became known as an official but crypto-opposition periodical. In 1988 Prodev joined the Independent Discussion Club for the Support of Glasnost and Perestroika, but he left it under official pressure. He lost his position as head of *Narodna Kultura*, and this made him look like a victim of the regime. After the fall of **Todor Zhivkov** in November 1989, Prodev returned to his previous position, and in January 1990 he became chairman of the Association of Bulgarian Journalists. He also became editor-in-chief of *Duma*, the main organ of the (post-Communist) Bulgarian Socialist Party (BSP). Initially the paper published articles settling past accounts, but soon it began to combat the anti-Communist opposition. Prodev was a member of the BSP leadership in 1990–96 and was an MP on behalf of the party (1991–97).

In 1999 he sharply criticized NATO air raids on the new Yugoslavia and the opening of Bulgarian air space for these operations. In 1999 *Duma* went bankrupt. In 2001 Prodev published *Nepisani razkazi* (Unrecorded tales), in which he summed up the first ten years of systemic transformation from the post-Communist point of view. (AG)

Sources: *Entsiklopediya Bulgariya*, vol. 5 (Sofia, 1986); Raymond Detrez, *Historical Dictionary of Bulgaria* (Lanham, Md., 1997); www.online.bg/politics/who/names/P/stefan_prodev.htm; www.swp-berlin.org/biost/ana99/aa99_17.pdf; www.hri.org/news/balkans/omri/95–09–19.0mri.html; bulrefsite.entrewave.com/view/bulrefsite/s129p165.htm; www.rferl.org/newsline/1998/08/190898.asp; www.ceri-sciencespo.com/publica/etude/etude31.pdf.

PROHÁSZKA Ottokár (10 October 1858, Nyitra [Nitra, now in Slovakia]–2 April 1927, Budapest), Hungarian bishop. Prohászka's father was a Moravian officer, and his mother was a daughter of a German baker. It was only while a high school student that he learned to speak Hungarian. From 1875 to 1882 he studied at the Collegium Germanico-Hungaricum in Rome. In 1881 he took holy orders, and in 1884 he became a teacher of theology and superior of a theological seminary in Esztergom. In the last years of the nineteenth century, Prohászka was one of the initiators and leaders of the Christian social movement in Hungary. He promoted the notion of the social responsibility of Catholics and translated the papal encyclical *Rerum novarum* of Leo XIII into Hungarian. From the beginning of the twentieth century Prohászka was the main speaker at annual national Catholic meetings. In 1904 he became a professor of dogmatics at Budapest University. In 1909 he became a corresponding member, and in 1920 a full member, of the Hungarian Academy of Sciences.

On 11 December 1905 Prohászka was ordained bishop of Székesfehérvár. He considered his main tasks to be the conversion of agnostics; an internal reform of the Church; and a modernization in the presentation of Christian teaching. Prohászka initiated the establishment of several orphanages. In 1916 he proposed that war invalids receive farms as compensation. In November 1918 in a pastoral letter he welcomed the republican upheavals as a sign of the future independence of Hungary. Even in the Hungarian Soviet Republic (HSR) he tried to see some positive elements—for example, in the slogans about social equality. At the same time he condemned Communist terror, just as he had denounced the "White terror" against HSR activists after the fall of the HSR. In January 1920 Regent **Miklós Horthy** offered Prohászka the post of prime minister, but Prohászka rejected this offer. In the same year, however, he became a member of parliament (and served until 1922) and assumed the post

of chairman of the ruling Christian National Union. He opposed socialism, liberalism, and great capital. In the fall of 1921 Prohászka resigned as chairman of the party, giving his pastoral duties as the reason, but actually it was his disappointment with the social policies of the new governments, including failures to implement agrarian reform. He described Horthy's system as a "Christian line without Christianity and without Christians." Prohászka died of a cerebral stroke while preaching a sermon.

Prohászka's publications include the following: *Isten és a világ* (God and the world; 1890); *A keresztény bűnbánat és bűnbocsánat* (Christian repentance and absolution; 1894); *A diadalmas világnézet* (Triumphant outlook; 1903); and *Modern katolicizmus* (Modern Catholicism; 1907). In his theological works, such as *Elmélkedések az evangéliumról* (1908; *Meditations on the Gospels*, 1936) and *Dominus Jesus* (1903), Prohászka combined neo-Thomism with the philosophy of Henri Bergson, as a result of which he incurred criticism from the Church hierarchs. Prohászka's theological innovation and his pro-social attitude (for example, his appeal for giving away Church possessions) met with the resistance of the Hungarian Church's conservative dignitaries, who prevented his appointment as archbishop in 1910. In 1911 the Holy See placed three works by Prohászka, including *Modern katolicizmus*, on the list of forbidden books. In 1943 the Vatican refused to begin his beatification process. Nowadays Prohászka is considered a spiritual precursor of the Second Vatican Council. Prohászka's collected works were published in twenty-five volumes (1928–29). (JT)

Sources: *Magyar Életrajzi Lexikon*, vol. 2 (Budapest, 1969); *Nagy Képes Milleniumi Arcképcsarnok* (Budapest, 1999); *Magyar Nagylexikon*, vol. 15 (Budapest, 2002); *Biographisches Lexikon*, vol. 3; Ernő Némethy, *Prohászka Ottokar életrajza* (Budapest, 1928); Péter S. Szabó, *A szacellum rózsajá: Prohászka-esszék* (Solymár, 2000).

PROTIĆ Stojan (28 January 1857, Kruševac, Serbia–28 October 1923, Belgrade), Serbian politician. Protić attended high schools in Kruševac, Kragujevac, and Belgrade and subsequently studied history and philology at the University of Belgrade. He then trained in an office in Šabac and was a clerk at a high school in Svilajnac. In 1881 he left the civil service and became involved in the activities of the National Radical Party (NRP), led by **Nikola Pašić**. In 1884 Protić became editor of *Srbski odjek*, which, after being banned by the authorities, was published under the titles *Drugi odjek* and *Treći odjek*. Elected to the Skupština (parliament) in 1887, Protić helped to draft the 1888 constitution. He took part in defining the position of the NRP in the negotiations and influenced the content of the constitution. In the same year he was appointed secretary in the Ministry of Interior and later in the Ministry of Finance. After Pašić resigned from the government in 1892, Protić left the ministry and worked in the municipality of Belgrade. After an attempt on the life of Milan Obrenović in 1899, Protić received a prison sentence for lèse-majesté, which he allegedly had committed in one of his articles. Reprieved after around one year, he worked successively in the National Library, as a director of the state monopoly, and a commissioner of the National Bank.

After King **Alexander Obrenović** was murdered in 1903, Protić became head of the Ministry of Interior in the government of **Jovan Avakumović**. He continued as head of this ministry in the cabinets of **Sava Grujić** (October–December 1904) and the government of Pašić (December 1904–May 1905 and June 1906–July 1907). In July 1907, after the police brutally crushed student demonstrations and worker strikes, Protić was forced to resign. After the outbreak of the Balkan crisis following the annexation of Bosnia and Herzegovina by Austria-Hungary, he returned to the government of **Stojan Novaković**, becoming minister of finance in February 1909. As a result of Protić's personal engagement, negotiations with France ended in success, and Serbia received a credit of 150 million dinars for the development of a railroad system and the purchase of modern weapons. Protić held the post of minister of finance for three subsequent years, first in the government of Pašić (beginning in October 1909) and then in the government of **Milovan Milovanović** (July 1911–May 1912). In September 1912 Protić became minister of interior in another Pašić government and held this post until December 1914.

Protić played an important political role during World War I. He drafted Serbia's reply to an ultimatum it was given by Austria-Hungary on 23 July 1914. This ultimatum was a prelude to a declaration of war. In 1917 Protić again joined the government of Pašić, becoming successively head of the Ministry of Finance, the Ministry of War, and the Ministry of Foreign Affairs. After the end of the war, he formed the first government of the newly established Kingdom of Serbs, Croats, and Slovenes and served as its prime minister from 7 December 1918 to 16 August 1919. He was also one of the architects of a coalition of parties that assumed power in the state in the spring of 1920. Protić served as minister of justice in the cabinet of **Milenko Vesnić** (May 1920–January 1921). Unlike most of the Radical Party members and their leader, Pašić, who favored a more centralist and unitary concept of the state, Protić argued for moderate decentralization and even prepared his own draft of a constitution; on that basis he broke

with the NRP and established the Independent Radical Party (Nezavisna Radikalna Stranka). His party failed to obtain any votes in the 1923 and 1925 elections, though, and subsequently disappeared from the political scene.

Protić was also a distinguished journalist, particularly regarding ethnic issues of the South Slavic nations. His most famous works include the following: *O Makedoniji i Makedoncima* (About Macedonia and the Macedonians; 1888); *Hrvatske prilike i jedinstvo Srba i Hrvata* (Croatian relations and the unity of the Serbs and Croats; 1911); *Odlomci iz Ustava i narodne borbe u Srbiji* (An excerpt from the Constitution and the national struggle of the Serbs, 2 vols.; 1911–12); *Albanski problemi i Srbija i Austro-Ugarska* (The Albanian issue, Serbia and Austria-Hungary; 1913); and *The Aspirations of Bulgaria* (1915), translated into Serbian in the same year. (AG)

Sources: *Biographisches Lexikon*, vol. 3; *Enciklopedija Jugoslavije*, vol. 6 (Zagreb, 1965); Wayne S. Vucinich, *Serbia between East and West: The Events of 1903–1908* (New York, 1968); Olga Popović, *Stojan Protić i ustavno rešenje nacjonalnog pitanja u Kraljeviny SHS* (Belgrade, 1988); Mark Biondich, *Stjepan Radić, the Croat Peasant Party, and the Politics of Mass Mobilization, 1904–1928* (Toronto, 2000).

PROTOGEROV Aleksandur (28 February 1867, Ohrid–7 July 1928, Sofia), Macedonian revolutionary activist. In 1887 Protogerov began serving in the Bulgarian Army, and in 1893 he also joined the Internal Macedonian Revolutionary Organization (Vnatrešna Makedonska Revolucionerna Organizacija [IMRO]). He was a representative of the party's right wing, which was sympathetic toward Bulgaria. In 1903 Protogerov fought in the Ilinden Uprising. After its collapse, he returned to Bulgaria, where he was promoted to general. In the Balkan Wars and in World War I he headed an IMRO faction that supported Bulgaria's claims to Macedonia. In the spring of 1919, on behalf of the Executive Committee of the Macedonian Societies in Bulgaria, Protogerov (together with **Todor Aleksandrov**) sent a letter to the participants in the Paris Peace Conference requesting that an "entire and indivisible Macedonia" be incorporated into the Bulgarian "motherland." However, under the terms of the Treaty of Neuilly (27 November 1919), most of the Macedonian territory was ceded to the Kingdom of Serbs, Croats, and Slovenes. Arrested in November 1919 by the authorities of the Bulgarian Agrarian National Union (BANU), headed by **Aleksandur Stamboliyski**, Protogerov was accused of contributing to Bulgaria's defeat in the war. After escaping from prison, he went underground, and from 1920 to 1923, he organized terrorist units of the IMRO on both sides of the border, particularly in the region of

Petrich in Bulgarian Pirin Macedonia. These units were instrumental in the overthrow of Stamboliyski's regime and in his death in June 1923. Subsequently Protogerov supported the government of the Democratic Alliance, led by **Aleksandur Tsankov**. On behalf of his faction within the IMRO, on 6 May 1924 in Vienna, Protogerov (together with the IMRO left wing and the Communists) signed a manifesto that called for uniting Macedonia into one state and political unit within its natural and ethnic borders. As a result of factional strife, Protogerov soon withdrew from this declaration. After the assassination of Aleksandrov in August 1924, Protogerov became head of the right wing of the IMRO. As a result of bloody factional strife within the IMRO, he was assassinated on the orders of **Ivan "Vančo" Mihailov**. (WR)

Sources: *Entsiklopediya Bulgariya*, vol. 5 (Sofia, 1986); John D. Bell, *Peasants in Power: Alexander Stamboliski and the Bulgarian Agrarian National Union, 1899–1923* (Princeton, 1977); Duncan M. Perry, *The Politics of Terror: The Macedonian Liberation Movements, 1893–1903* (Durham, N.C., 1988); Vasyl Pundev, *Sled zlodeistvoto: Shest mesetsa ot ubiistvoto na Aleksandur Protogerov* (Sofia, 1990); *Za shto be ubit Aleksandur Protogerov* (Sofia, 1992); Raymond Detrez, *Historical Dictionary of Bulgaria* (Lanham, Md., 1997); Irena Stawowy-Kawka, *Historia Macedonii* (Wrocław, 2000).

PRUNSKIENE Kazimiera (26 February 1943, Vasiuliškė), Lithuanian Communist and post-Communist political activist. In 1965 Prunskiene graduated in economics from the University of Vilnius, where she later worked. In 1971 she received a Ph.D. in economics, and in 1986–88 she worked at the Ministry of Agriculture of the Lithuanian SSR. In 1988 she became director of the Institute of Economic Personnel Training. From 1980 to 1990 she belonged to the CPSU and was a member of the Central Committee (CC) of the Communist Party of Lithuania (CPL). Promoted to the CPL CC Politburo, Prunskiene was among the supporters of perestroika and (later) Lithuanian independence. In 1988–90 she was connected with the Lithuanian Movement for Perestroika, Sąjūdis. In 1989 Prunskiene became deputy prime minister of the Lithuanian SSR. In February 1990 she was elected to the Supreme Council of the Lithuanian SSR. After Lithuania declared independence on 11 March 1990, she was in the Lithuanian delegation that held talks in the Kremlin. From 17 March 1990 Prunskiene was prime minister. In May 1990 she visited the United States and then Great Britain, France, and Germany, trying to gain international recognition for Lithuania. While the conflict with the Kremlin was aggravating, Prunskiene was accused by the radicals of submission to Russian pressure. At the same time, the Sąjūdis leaders criticized her economic policies. Unreformed Communists openly accused her of

"separatism" and looked forward to Russian intervention. As a result of a conflict with the chairman of the Supreme Council, **Vytautas Landsbergis**, on 10 January 1991 Prunskiene was dismissed.

In 1992 Prunskiene created the Lithuania-Europe Institute, aimed at strengthening links between Lithuania and the West. Later she chaired the East and Central European Forum of Innovations, established her own firm, co-founded the Association of Lithuanian Women (ALW), and was active in international women's associations. Prunskiene published the memoirs *Leben für Litauen: Auf dem Weg in die Unabhängichkeit* (A life for Lithuania: On the road to independence; 1992). In 1992 the Lithuanian Supreme Court found Prunskiene guilty of conscious cooperation with the KGB, but the parliament did not suspend her immunity and she did not withdrew from public life. For several years Prunskiene unsuccessfully tried to clear herself of these accusations. In January 1995 the ALW turned into a political party called the New Democracy–Women's Party (Naujoji Demokratija–Moterų Partija [NDMP]). In 1996 Prunskiene was elected to the parliament, where she belonged to a faction of independents, and in 2000 she was elected on behalf of the NDMP. In December 2002 she ran in the presidential elections but lost. From 1996 Prunskiene has been a professor at the Vilnius Polytechnic College. Prunskiene has authored a number of works on economics and on Lithuanian socioeconomic transformation. (JH)

Sources: *Kas yra kas Lietuvoje 95/96* (Vilnius, 1996); Saulius Sužiedelis, *Historical Dictionary of Lithuania* (Lanham, Md., 1997); Alfred E. Senn, *Lithuania Awakening* (Berkeley, 1990); Grzegorz Błaszczyk, *Litwa współczesna* (Warsaw, 1992); Anatol Lieven, *The Baltic Revolution* (New Haven, 1993); V. Stanley Vardys and Judith B. Sedaitis, *Lithuania: The Rebel Nation* (Boulder, Colo., 1997); www.lrs.lt.

PRYSTOR Aleksander (2 January 1874, Wilno [Vilnius]–October 1941, Moscow), Polish politician. Prystor graduated from high school in Wilno, and in 1894 he entered Moscow University, earning a first degree in 1900. He subsequently studied medicine but never graduated. At that time Prystor was introduced to the Socialist movement and met **Józef Piłsudski** personally. From 1903 to 1904 he served in the tsarist army and then went to Switzerland, where he took part in military courses conducted by a Japanese officer; this training was linked to the plans of the Polish Socialists, who wanted to use the Russo-Japanese War to work toward Polish independence. In March 1905 Prystor became head of the conspiratorial-military department of the Polish Socialist Party (Polska Partia Socjalistyczna [PPS]). He organized the PPS Military Organization in Warsaw and took part in the 1905 revolution. During a split within the PPS Prystor supported the PPS–Revolutionary Faction. After the failure of the revolution, he went to Galicia. In September 1908 Prystor took part in an expropriation action at Bezdany (Bezdonys), Lithuania and then assumed command of the Kraków district of the Riflemen's Association. In February 1912 he went to Warsaw, where he was arrested soon afterwards. In January 1914, after almost two years of investigations, Prystor was sentenced to seven years. Imprisoned in Orel, he was released in March 1917, after the tsarist system was abolished. Prystor worked in the Polish Military Organization (Polska Organizacja Wojskowa [POW]), in the PPS Central Committee in Russia, and in the Liquidation Commission for the Affairs of the Kingdom of Poland (Komisja Likwidacyjna do Spraw Królestwa Polskiego). After the Bolshevik revolution, Prystor served as commander of the guard of the Polish Security Council in Petrograd and subsequently worked in the city board of Minsk. In May 1918 he went to Warsaw, where he began working in the administration of the Regency Council.

In November 1918 Prystor became a member of the POW High Command. On 10 November 1918 he welcomed Piłsudski, who had returned from Magdeburg Prison. Prystor became undersecretary of state in the Ministry of Labor and Social Welfare in the Provisional People's Government of the Republic of Poland (Tymczasowy Rząd Ludowy Republiki Polskiej), headed by **Ignacy Daszyński**, and he held this post in successive governments until June 1921. In July 1920 he began serving in the Polish Army. During the Polish-Soviet war Prystor commanded a company, and as Piłsudski's trusted liaison with General **Lucjan Żeligowski**, he played a key role in a "rebellion" of Żeligowski's troops, which seized the Wilno (Vilnius) region on 9 October 1920. Prystor subsequently served as adjutant general to Żeligowski and head of the civil chancellery of Central Lithuania. After Central Lithuania was incorporated into Poland, Prystor worked in the General Staff and headed the personnel department of the Bureau of the Supreme Council of War. Relegated in May 1925 to the Wilno Draft Board, he had little part in the preparations for the coup d'état that was planned for 1926, but shortly after May 1926, he returned to Warsaw, assuming a post in the office of the Minister of Military Affairs. In November 1926 Prystor became head of the personnel department of the Inspectorate General of the Armed Forces. He was sent by Piłsudski on many delicate missions. Highly appreciated by Piłsudski, Prystor was a member of the so-called group of colonels that played a leading role within the ruling camp. In April 1929 Prystor became minister of labor and social welfare. While holding this post, he ran afoul of the Socialists because he sought to

abolish the autonomy of the Health Care Funds. Although in March 1930 the government collapsed, **Walery Sławek**, who had established a new cabinet, did not dismiss Prystor, throwing down the gauntlet to the Assembly. In August 1930 Prystor was appointed minister of industry and trade, and in November 1930 he became an MP on the slate of the Nonparty Bloc of Cooperation with the Government (Bezpartyjny Blok Współpracy z Rządem [BBWR]).

On 27 May 1931 Prystor assumed the post of prime minister. In October 1932 his government put forward a program to combat the Great Depression, but there was a shortage of financial means for its realization because of the deflation policy. Because of personal rivalries among his closest associates, Prystor soon lost the trust of Piłsudski. On 9 May 1933 he resigned as prime minister, and thenceforth his political role diminished. After the constitution of April 1935 was proclaimed, Prystor was a member of a commission drafting an undemocratic electoral law. In the 1935 elections he won a senatorial seat. From 4 October 1935 to 13 September 1938 he was the Senate speaker. In the Senate elected in 1938, Prystor won a seat on the slate of the authoritarian Camp of National Unity (Obóz Zjednoczenia Narodowego [OZN]), a party established to prevent the disintegration of the ruling camp after the death of Piłsudski. He lost in the elections for Senate speaker, though, and thereafter he began to criticize government policies. After the Red Army entered the Wilno region in September 1939, Prystor illegally crossed the Lithuanian border and developed wide-ranging activities in Kaunas. After Lithuania was incorporated into the Soviet Union in July 1940, Prystor was arrested by the NKVD and imprisoned in Kaunas, whence he was moved to a Moscow prison, where he probably perished. (WR)

Sources: *PSB*, vol. 28; *Kto był kim w Drugiej Rzeczypospolitej* (Warsaw, 1994); *Encyklopedia historii* Drugiej Rzeczypospolitej (Warsaw, 1999); Janusz Jędrzejewicz, *W służbie idei* (London, 1972); Władysław T. Kulesza, *Koncepcje ideowo-polityczne obozu rządzącego w Polsce w latach 1926–1935* (Wrocław, 1985); Andrzej Chojnowski, *Piłsudczycy u władzy: Dzieje BBWR* (Wrocław, 1986); Jacek Piotrowski, *Aleksander Prystor* (Wrocław, 1994).

PUČNIK Jože (9 March 1932, Črešnjevec, near Slovenska Bistrica), Slovene sociologist and politician. Pučnik graduated from high school in Maribor and enrolled in philosophy at the University of Ljubljana. During his studies he was twice arrested for "disloyal" publications in the periodical *Revija 57*. In 1958 he was sentenced to nine years in prison, of which he served five (1958–63). After his release he published in the periodical *Perspektive*. Arrested again and sentenced in 1964, he was allowed to emigrate to Germany in 1966. Pučnik worked as a blue-collar laborer, and he studied, receiving a Ph.D. at the University of Hamburg in 1971. Then he lectured there and became a professor. In 1989 Pučnik returned home and became active in the democratic opposition as a member of the Slovenian Democratic Union (Slovenske Demokratične Zveze). In 1989–93 he chaired the Social Democratic Party of Slovenia (Socialdemokratska Stranka Slovenije). In April 1990 Pučnik became the DEMOS coalition's candidate for president. He got to the second round, where he gained 41 percent of the vote, but he lost to **Milan Kučan**. In 1991 Pučnik was active in favor of Slovene independence, demanding a referendum on this issue. He authored *Članki in spomini 1957–1985* (Articles and memoirs 1957–1985; 1986) and *Kultura, družba in tehnologija* (Culture, society, and technology; 1988). (WR)

Sources: *Enciklopedia Slovenije*, vol. 10 (Ljubljana, 1996); Janez Janša, *Die entstehung des slowenischjen Staates, 1988–1992* (Ljubljana, 1994); Leopoldina Plut-Progelj and Carole Rogel, *Historical Dictionary of Slovenia* (Lanham, Md., 1996); James Gow and Cathie Carmichael, *Slovenia and the Slovenes* (London, 2000).

PUGO Boriss (19 February 1937, Kalinin–21 August 1991, Moscow), Soviet activist of Latvian descent. Adopted by **Arvids Pelše** after he had been orphaned, Pugo graduated from the Riga Technical Institute in 1960. He became involved in politics while still a student. In 1960 he began working as an engineer and secretary of the Komsomol (Young Communist League) in the Electrical Equipment Works in Riga. From 1961 to 1963 he served as first secretary of a Komsomol committee in the Proletarskiy district in Riga. From 1963 to 1968 he worked in the Komsomol central apparatus in Moscow. From 1968 to 1970 he was head of the Department of Organizational Work of the Central Committee (CC) of the Communist Party of Latvia (CPL) and first secretary of the Komsomol of the Latvian SSR. From 1970 to 1977 Pugo was secretary of the CC of the Komsomol of the Soviet Union, inspector of the CC of the Communist Party of the Soviet Union (CPSU), and first secretary of a committee of the CPL in Riga. In 1976 he became a member of the CC of the CPL. Deputy head (1977–80) and subsequently head (1980–84) of the KGB of the Latvian SSR, Pugo was responsible for quashing the liberation aspirations of the Latvian people and for persecuting the opposition. In August 1984 he was appointed first secretary of the CC of the CPL, although like his predecessor, **Augusts Voss**, Pugo hardly spoke any Latvian. In 1986 he became a member of the CPSU CC. From 1988 to 1990 he served as chairman of the CPSU CC Party Control Committee. Initially Pugo was a supporter of Mikhail Gorbachev,

but then he became aligned with the party hard-liners. In December 1990 he was appointed minister of interior of the Soviet Union. Pugo was responsible for a bloody intervention by Soviet special troops in Vilnius (January 1991) and later fiercely defended this intervention on television. He was one of the main organizers of a putsch whose aim was to uphold the Soviet Union and the Soviet system. On 19 August 1991 Pugo became a member of the State Committee for the State of Emergency, which failed to gain power. After the putsch was suppressed, Pugo committed suicide. (EJ)

Sources: *Latvijas Padomju enciklopēdija*, vol. 8 (Riga, 1986); *A Biographical Directory of 100 Leading Soviet Officials* (Boulder, Colo., 1990); *Enciklopēdiskā vārdnīca*, vol. 2 (Riga, 1991); David Remnick, *Grobowiec Lenina* (Warsaw, 1997).

PUJĀTS Jānis (14 November 1930, Nautrēni, Letgalia), Latvian Catholic cardinal. Pujāts graduated from high school in Rēzekne in 1948. Later he studied at the theological seminary in Riga until it was closed by the Soviets in 1951. He continued his education with his parish priest. In 1952 he was allowed to take his final seminary examinations. Ordained in March 1951, Pujāts worked as a minister in various parishes of Letgalia (Preiļi, Zosna, Dukstigals, Rozentava, Bērži, Rudzāti, and Stirniene). In 1958–64 he was a vicar in Riga, from 1964 he was parish priest of Riga's St. Anthony Parish, and in 1966–79 he was vicar in Riga's St. Francis Parish. From 1966 Pujāts taught in the Riga seminary. Despite constant invigilation, in the 1970s he managed to organize an uncensored publication of the Catholic catechism. In 1979–84 Pujāts was general vicar and chancellor of curia, in 1981–84 he was also parish priest of St. James Parish in Riga, and from 1987 to 1991 he was a professor at the Riga theological seminary. On 8 May 1991 Pujāts was consecrated archbishop metropolitan of Riga, in February 1998 he was appointed cardinal *in pectore*, and from 21 February 2001 he was a member of the college of cardinals. (EJ)

Sources: J. Cakuls, *Latvijas Romas katoļu priesteri 1918–1995* (Riga, 1996); *Who's Who in Latvia* (Riga, 2000); www.aciprensa.com/cardinales/pujats.htm; www.catholic-hierarchy.org.

PULJIĆ Vinko (8 September 1945, Prijecani, near Banja Luka), Croatian Roman Catholic bishop in Bosnia. After graduating from a theological seminary, Puljić was ordained in June 1970. Later he worked in Croatian parishes in Bosnia. On 19 November 1990 he was consecrated archbishop of Upper Bosnia (Vrhbosna). During the war of 1992–95, despite the Bosnian Serb siege, Puljić stayed in Sarajevo. Encouraged to leave for the Croatian-occupied part of Bosnia, he refused, and in August 1993 he took part in a celebration of the anniversary of the independence of Bosnia-Herzegovina. Puljić constantly appealed for a termination of the war; for respect for human life, the family, and ethnic identity; and for a peaceful resolution to the conflicts in the former Yugoslavia. Nevertheless, his appeals remained in vain. On 26 November 1994 Pope John Paul II appointed Puljić a member of the College of Cardinals—its youngest member. After the war Puljić remained an advocate of reconciliation in a multi-ethnic Bosnia-Herzegovina. In January 1996 he met with the Orthodox metropolitan, Nicholas. Puljić was the host for John Paul II's visit to Sarajevo in April 1997. (WR)

Sources: *Annuario Pontificio, 1995*; Ante Čuvalo, *Historical Dictionary of Croatia* (Lanham, Md., 1997); Carl Bildt, *Peace Journey: The Struggle for Peace in Bosnia* (London, 1998); Norman Cigar, *Genocide in Bosnia* (College Station, Tex., 1995).

PURIĆ Božidar (19 February 1891, Belgrade–1977, Chicago), Serbian politician. After finishing secondary school in Belgrade, Purić graduated in law in Paris in 1912. He later fought in World War I. In 1918 in Paris he earned a Ph.D. for a dissertation on the *rebus sic stantibus* clause in international law. Purić subsequently served as secretary of the legation of the Kingdom of Serbs, Croats, and Slovenes in Washington, D.C. (1919), chargé d'affaires in Vladivostok (1919–20), consul in San Francisco (1920–22) and Chicago (1922–26), head of a political department of the Ministry of Foreign Affairs (1927–35), and envoy and minister plenipotentiary in Paris (1935–40). On 10 August 1943 Purić became prime minister and minister of foreign affairs of the Yugoslav government-in-exile, which was faithful to King **Peter II Karadjordjević**. In Purić's cabinet the post of minister of war was given to **Dragoljub (Draža) Mihailović**, leader of the Chetniks (guerrillas), who fought both the Nazis and the Communist-led Partisans of **Josip Broz Tito** in occupied Yugoslavia. In November 1943 the Anti-Fascist Council for the National Liberation of Yugoslavia (Antifašističko Veće Narodnog Oslobođenja Jugoslavije [AVNOJ]), established by Tito's supporters in 1942, proclaimed itself the highest authority, denying the government-in-exile the right to represent Yugoslavia. The British authorities insisted that Purić enter into an agreement with Tito, but Purić steadfastly refused. Finally, under pressure from Great Britain, King Peter agreed to appoint a new cabinet that was more willing to compromise. On 1 June 1944 Purić was dismissed, and **Ivan Šubašić** assumed the post of prime minister. After World War II, Purić remained in exile and lived in the United States. Purić authored several poetry collections: *Pesme o nama* (Poems about us; 1919) and *Ljubavne svečanosti* (Love festivities; 1920). In 1963 his *Biografija Bože Rankovića: Doprinos istoriji srpskog iseljeništva u Severnoj Americi* (The biography of Boа Ranković: The history of Serbian emigration in Northern America) was published in Munich. (AO)

Sources: Constantine Fotich, *The War We Lost* (New York, 1948); Vlatko Macek, *In the Struggle for Freedom* (London, 1957); Ferdo Čulinović, *Jugoslavija izmedju dva rata*, vols. 1–2 (Zagreb, 1971); Michał Jerzy Zacharias, *Jugosławia w polityce Wielkiej Brytanii 1940–1945* (Wrocław, 1985); www.mfa.gov.yu.history/Ministri/BPuric_e.html.

PURVANOV Georgi (28 June 1957, Sirishtik), Communist activist and post-Communist politician, president of Bulgaria. In 1981 Purvanov graduated in history from the University of Sofia and started working at the Institute of History of the Bulgarian Communist Party (BCP). In 1981 he joined the party. In 1989 he received a Ph.D. in the nineteenth-century history of Bulgaria. In 1989 Purvanov supported the reform wing of the BCP. In 1990 he was elected to the Executive Bureau of the BCP Congress, which abandoned the term "Communist" and changed the name of the party into the Bulgarian Socialist Party (Bulgarska Sotsialisticheska Partiya [BSP]). From 1992 Purvanov headed the BSP Center for Historical and Political Studies, supporting the evolution of the party toward Social Democracy. After the electoral victory of the BSP in December 1994 Purvanov became head of the parliamentary commission for national minorities. A decline of the BSP's ratings, owing to its faulty economic policy, led to sharp conflicts in the party leadership. In 1996 Purvanov became chief of staff of the BSP presidential candidate, Ivan Marazov, and after his defeat Purvanov replaced **Zhan Videnov** as the BSP leader.

In this role Purvanov proved to be quite efficient. He apologized for BSP policies and made attempts to consolidate leftist groups around his party. After the early elections of April 1997, which the BSP lost, Purvanov initially turned his party into a constructive opposition to the government of **Ivan Kostov**, which introduced necessary reforms. Under populist pressure, Purvanov began to criticize this government for all actual and alleged mistakes. At the same time, he tried to change the attitude of the post-Communists toward foreign policy. Although in 1999 Purvanov criticized the NATO air raids on Yugoslavia and the opening of Bulgarian air space to these operations, he managed to convince the majority of the BSP leadership that it should pursue future NATO membership for Bulgaria. He also supported Bulgaria's entry into the European Union. Purvanov's tactics brought results since in the local elections of the fall of 1999 the BSP candidates won about 25 percent of the vote. This showed that the BSP was restoring its position. At the end of 2000 a further increase in the BSP's ratings was prevented by the emergence of the National Movement Simeon II, which won the parliamentary elections in June 2001. Purvanov ran as the BSP presidential candidate. In the second round, on 18 November 2001 Purvanov defeated the acting president, **Petur Stoyanov**, winning 54.1 percent of the vote. On 22 January 2002 Purvanov assumed office, continuing the pro-NATO and pro-European Union policies. (AG)

Sources: www.cidob.org/bios/castellano/lideres/p-043.htm; www.hri.org/news/balkans/bta/96–10–28.bta.html; www.sofiaecho.com/government01.php; www.electionworld.org/bulgaria; www.president.bg.

PUŞCARIU Sextil (4 January 1877, Braşov–5 May 1948, Bran), Romanian linguist and philologist. After graduating from high school in Braşov, Puşcariu studied linguistics in Leipzig, where he received a Ph.D. in 1899. From 1899 to 1901 he studied in Paris and Vienna, where in 1904 he received the postdoctoral degree. In 1905 he conducted a seminar in the Romanian language at the university in Vienna. In 1906 he returned to Romania and began working at the university in Tschernowitz (Cernăuţi, Chernivtsi), where he was a professor of Romanian language and literature from 1908 to 1918. In 1913 Puşcariu published *Dicţionarul limbii române* (Dictionary of the Romanian language), which earned him membership in the Romanian Academy of Sciences in 1914. In 1918 Puşcariu was an editor of the periodical *Glasul Bucovinei*. After World War I he worked in the diplomatic service, holding a variety of positions, including that of Romania's delegate to the League of Nations. In 1919 he moved to Cluj, where he was a co-founder and then the first rector of a university. In 1920 in Cluj Puşcariu founded the Museum of Romanian Language, later known as the Academic Linguistic Institute, which existed until 1951. In 1923 he also co-founded the Romanian Ethnographic Society in Cluj. In 1924 he edited the periodical *Cultura*. From 1940 to 1944 he directed the Romanian Institute in Germany, and from 1942 to 1944 he worked at the university in Berlin. Puşcariu was politically aligned with the radical nationalist right wing. He was a supporter of the theory of linguistic structuralism. Puşcariu authored about four hundred works in the fields of the history of language, dialectology, Romance studies, phonetics, lexicography, and literary history and criticism, including the following: *Atlasul lingvistic român* (Romanian linguistic atlas) in ten volumes, of which only three were published in his lifetime: *Atlasul lingvistic al României* (The linguistic atlas of Romanians; 1929), *Hărţile graiului* (The map of dialects; 1933), and *Atlasul lingvistic român: Prospect* (Romanian linguistic atlas: Prospect; 1936). Puşcariu was also the author of *Istoria literaturii române: Epoca veche* (The history of Romanian literature: Ancient times; 1921) and *Limba română* (The Romanian language; 1940). He founded the periodical *Dacoromania*, eleven volumes of which appeared in 1920–48. In postwar Romania some of Puşcariu's works were banned from publication. (LW)

Sources: Dorina N. Rusu, *Membrii Academiei Române 1866–1999* (Bucharest, 1999); *Dicţionarul scriitorilor Români* (Bucharest, 2001); www.miscarea-legionara.org.

PÜSKI Sándor (4 February 1911, Békés), Hungarian publisher. Püski graduated in law from the University of Budapest in 1935. In 1938 in Budapest he opened a bookstore that sold copies of lectures for students. In 1939 he established the Magyar Élet (Hungarian Life) press, which contributed substantially to the success of the so-called peasant writers. During World War II Püski was active against the extreme right. When the Communists nationalized the presses (1950), he worked as a blue-collar laborer. Imprisoned on false accusations in 1962–63, in 1970 Püski left for the United States, where he again took up book selling. In 1975 he started his own press—this time called Püski Könyvkiadó (Püski Bookstore)—and it became one of the foundations of Hungarian pro-independence activities abroad. Püski was also active in supporting the democratic opposition in Hungary in the 1980s. In 1989 he returned to Hungary and moved his press there. From 1995 he was a member of the leadership of the World Association of Hungarians. Püski received many Hungarian and foreign awards for his contribution to the struggle for the freedom of the word. (MS)

Sources: Ágnes Petőváry, *A Magyar Élet könyvkiadóról* (Budapest, 1986); *Új magyar irodalmi lexikon* (Budapest, 2000).

PUSTA Kaarel Robert (29 February 1883, Narva–4 May 1964, Madrid), Estonian diplomat and politician. Pusta established ties with a radical movement in his youth. Arrested for taking part in anti-tsarist activities in 1903, he shared a prison cell with Mikhail Kalinin, who would become a famous Bolshevik leader. From 1904 on Pusta lived in England, France, and Switzerland. In 1904–6 he studied in Paris and Bern, where he maintained contacts with radical activists in Estonia and contributed to *Uudiseed*, a leftist periodical published by activists of the Estonian Social Democratic Workers' Party. After returning to his country in 1906, Pusta contributed to the daily *Virulane* (1906–8) and edited the newspaper *Paevaleht* (1910–14). Mobilized in 1915, Pusta worked in the civil administration of the tsarist army. In 1917, along with **Jaan Tõnisson**, **Ants Piip**, and Eduard Virgo, Pusta became a member of a diplomatic mission sent by the Estonian National Council (Maapäev) to the West to seek recognition for Estonia by Great Britain and France. Pusta was the first Estonian ambassador to France; he was simultaneously ambassador to Belgium. He stayed in that position from 1919 to 1933, except for an interval in late 1924 and early 1925, when he served as foreign minister. Pusta subsequently served as ambassador to Poland (1934–35) and Sweden, simultaneously accredited to Denmark and the Soviet Union (from 1935). Pusta's greatest successes included obtaining France's recognition of Estonia in 1922. After the authoritarian coup of **Konstantin Päts** in March 1934, the activists of the radically rightist Estonian League of War of Independence Veterans (Eesti Vabadussojalaste Liit [EVL]) mentioned Pusta as a potential candidate for a government they planned to create; consequently, in 1936 Pusta was recalled from his mission in Scandinavia and was arrested on his arrival in Estonia. Since he proved that he had not known about the EVL's plans of conspiracy, he was released, but the case had far-reaching political repercussions in Estonia and abroad. As compensation, Pusta was given the post of counselor at the embassy in Paris (1939). After the 1940 Soviet invasion, Pusta stayed abroad, where he strove to prove to the international community that the 1940 incorporation of Estonia by the Soviet Union was an illegal act.

One of the main architects of Estonia's foreign policy, Pusta (along with Piip and **Jaan Poska**) belonged to a group of firm supporters of the concept of a broad Baltic league, which would include Lithuania, Latvia, Estonia, the Scandinavian states, and Poland. Such a league, which was to protect Estonia from potential aggression from the Soviet Union, was not realized, but proposals for it were among the main guidelines for the Estonian diplomatic services until the end of the 1930s. Pusta's publications include *Problèmes de la Baltique* (Problems of the Baltic; 1934) and *The Soviet Union and the Baltic States* (1942). An ardent champion of European unity, Pusta devoted one of his main works to this idea: *L'idee de l'union européenne devant les gouvernements et de la Société des Nations* (The idea of a European union and the governments of the League of Nations; 1931). Pusta was an active member of the Pan-European movement. Shortly before his death he published his memoirs, *Saadiku päevik* (The diary of an ambassador), a major source for the study of twentieth-century Estonian history. (AG)

Sources: *Eesti Entsuklopeedia*, vol. 14 (Tallinn, 2000); Evald Uustalu, *The History of the Estonian People* (London, n.d.); www.sada.ee/show_cand.php; Jüri Poska, *Pro Baltica* (Stockholm, 1965); Piotr Łossowski, *Kraje bałtyckie na drodze od demokracji parlamentarnej do dyktatury (1918–1934)* (Wrocław, 1972); Tõnu Parming, *The Collapse of Liberal Democracy and the Rise of Authoritarianism in Estonia* (London, 1975); Andres Kasekamp, *The Radical Right in Interwar Estonia* (London, 2000).

PUSTOVOYTENKO Valeryi (23 February 1947, Adamivka, Mykolayiv region), Ukrainian post-Communist politician. Initially Pustovoytenko worked as a carpenter in Odessa. In 1966–68 he served in the army. In 1975 he graduated from the Institute of Engineering and Construction in Dniepropetrovsk, and later he worked as the main engineer in a local machine building enterprise. In 1984–86 he was its director. In 1989 Pustovoytenko became chairman of the Dniepropetrovsk City Council, in 1991 mayor of the city, and in 1992 chairman of the Union of Ukrainian Towns. From 1991 he was a member of the Supreme Council of Ukraine. After he followed **Leonid Kuchma** to Kiev, from April to September 1993 Pustovoytenko was head of Kuchma's Office of the Prime Minister. Pustovoytenko received a Ph.D. in technical sciences and became deputy chairman of the union of Ukrainian builders and deputy chairman of the Board of Directors of the Expobank in Kiev. From 16 July 1997 to 22 December 1999 Pustovoytenko was prime minister. He remained a representative of the members of the Dniepropetrovsk clan that stayed loyal to President Kuchma. Given Kuchma's support, Pustovoytenko stayed in office after the parliamentary elections of March 1998, in which the president's People's Democratic Party of Ukraine won only twenty-eight mandates. During Pustovoytenko's term in office, reforms were halted. Elected for a second term in November 1999, Kuchma tried to accelerate reforms, so he dismissed Pustovoytenko and turned the office of prime minister over to **Viktor Yushchenko**. From June 2000 to May 2002 Pustovoytenko was minister of transportation. From December 2000 he was presidential adviser and secretary of Kuchma's Political Council. He was also chairman of the Ukrainian Soccer Federation. (TS)

Sources: Bohdan Nahaylo, *The Ukrainian Resurgence* (Toronto, 1999); *Europa Środkowo-Wschodnia 1997–1998* (Warsaw, 2000).

PUTEK Józef (4 July 1892, Wadowice–10 May 1974, Chocznia, near Wadowice), Polish Peasant Party politician. While a law student at the Jagiellonian University in Kraków, Putek established an organization of students of peasant origins. In 1913 he co-founded the Polish Peasant Party–Left (Polskie Stronnictwo Ludowe–Lewica [PSL–Left]), and in 1914 he became a member of the PSL Chief Council. During World War I Putek was a delegate of the pro-Austrian Supreme National Committee (Naczelny Komitet Narodowy) to Wadowice County, and he subsequently served as political commissioner of the Military Committee of the Supreme National Committee. Elected to the Legislative Assembly in 1919, Putek served as secretary of its lower chamber and vice-chairman of the PSL–Left parliamentary representation; he was one of the speakers presenting the draft constitution. He advocated the implementation of an agrarian reform. In 1920 Putek received a Ph.D. in law and did a legal internship. In August 1922 he took the lead of the Peasant Left, which entered into an electoral alliance with the Polish Peasant Party–Liberation (Polskie Stronnictwo Ludowe–Wyzwolenie [PSL–Liberation]). From 1922 to 1930 Putek was an MP. After the PSL–Left merged with the PSL–Liberation, he became vice-chairman of its parliamentary representation. A member and vice-chairman of the Main Board of the PSL–Liberation from 1923 to 1930, Putek and his party supported the coup of May 1926, but as early as 1927 he went over to the opposition. Elected mayor of the municipality of Chocznia, in April 1928 Putek was excommunicated by Archbishop **Adam Sapieha** for his militant anti-clericalism. Arrested in September 1930, he was imprisoned in the Brześć fortress, along with a group of opposition leaders. Released on bail, he attended the 1931 unification congress of the Peasant Party (Stronnictwo Ludowe [SL]), at which he was elected a member of the Chief Council and the Chief Executive Committee. In January 1932 Putek was sentenced in a trial in Brześć to three years in prison. While in prison, he wrote historical books. He was released after ten months. In 1935 Putek became vice-chairman of the SL. Expelled from the party after he had refused to support the peasant strike of 1937, he established the pro-government Union of Polish Peasant Activists, and he was elected MP in 1938.

Arrested by the Germans in October 1939 and deported to the concentration camp in Auschwitz in June 1940, Putek was transferred to the Mauthausen camp in July 1942. After liberation, he joined the International Administrative Committee and served as chairman of the Polish Prisoners' Committee. In May 1945 he became vice-chairman of the Chief Council of the Union of Former Political Prisoners of Nazi Prisons and Concentration Camps, and in September 1945, vice-chairman of the Chief Executive Committee of the SL, after this party had been reestablished under the aegis of the Communists. In January 1946 Putek became chairman of the SL Chief Council. In December 1945 he became a member of the National Home Council (Krajowa Rada Narodowa [KRN]). From March 1946 to January 1948 he served as minister of post and telegraphs. In January

1947 he became an MP in the Legislative Assembly. Dismissed as chairman of the SL Chief Council in September 1948, one month later Putek was expelled from the party for his interwar activities. Arrested and placed in a Kraków prison in October 1950, he was deprived of his parliamentary seat one year after his arrest. Released in January 1952, he was imprisoned again in July 1952 and then released in January 1953. Rehabilitated in January 1956, he retired from politics and resumed his work as an attorney. Putek's publications include the following: *Konkordat czy rozdział Kościoła od państwa* (Concordat or the separation of Church and state; 1925); *Obywatelskie prawo zgromadzeń* (Citizens' right of assembly; 1932); *Mroki średniowiecza: Obyczaje, przesądy, fanatyzm i okrucieństwa w dawnej Polsce* (The darkness of the Middle Ages: Customs, superstitions, fanaticism, and excesses in ancient Poland; 1935); *Z dziejów wsi polskiej* (From the history of Polish peasants; 1946); *Sejm w Ciemnogrodzie* (The Assembly in a backwater; 1948); and *Miłościwe pany i krnąbrne chłopy włościany* (Merciful lords of the manor and defiant peasants; 1969). (JS)

Sources: *PSB*, vol. 29; Mołdawa; *Słownik biograficzny działaczy ruchu ludowego* (Warsaw, 1989); *Kto był kim w Drugiej Rzeczypospolitej* (Warsaw, 1994); Maria Mioduchowska, *Materiały do bibliografii historii ruchu ludowego w latach 1864–1974* (Warsaw, 1979); Stanisław Giza, *Kalendarz wydarzeń historii ruchu ludowego, 1895–1965* (Warsaw, 1967); Stanisław Lato, *Ruch ludowy a Centrolew* (Warsaw, 1965).

PUTNA Vitovt (24 April 1893, Matskantse, near Vilnius–11 July 1937, Moscow), Soviet commander of Lithuanian descent. The son of a peasant, Putna graduated from a school of commerce in Riga. He was active in the Bolshevik movement, as a result of which he was arrested in 1913. Inducted into the army in 1915, he served in the Semyonov Guard Regiment, and in 1917 he graduated from a cadet school. As a commander of a battalion, Putna was instrumental in the Bolshevization of the Twelfth Russian Army. In April 1918 he joined the Red Army, becoming head of the military commissariat of Vitebsk. He subsequently served as commissar of the Smolensk rifle division. In May 1919 Putna became commander of the Twenty-seventh Rifle Division during the war against Poland. In 1921 he was one of the commanders who led a force that crushed the Kronstadt rebels. In 1923 Putna finished a course for senior commanders and then commanded an infantry school in Moscow. From 1924 to 1927 he worked in the General Staff of the Red Army and subsequently served as Soviet military attaché in Japan, Finland, and Germany. In 1931–34 he commanded a corps, and then an army, in the Far East. From 1934 to 1936 Putna was the Soviet military attaché in London. One of the closest associates of Mikhail Tukhachevsky, at the beginning of 1937 Putna was recalled to Moscow, and, along with other top Red Army commanders, he was accused of taking part in a "Trotskyite conspiracy," spying, and other fictitious crimes. Sentenced to death in the trial of Tukhachevsky and his associates, Putna was executed in prison. (WR)

Sources: *MERSH*, vol. 30; *EL*, vol. 4; *Vytautas Putna* (Vilnius, 1962).

PUTNIK Radomir (12 January 1847, Kragujevac, Serbia–4 May 1917, Nice, France), Serbian field marshal. As an artillery officer, Putnik distinguished himself in the war against Turkey (1876–78). After completing his studies in Russia, he started working in the General Staff of the Serbian Army. In 1885 he fought in the Serbo-Bulgarian war. Promoted to colonel in 1889, he became deputy chief of the General Staff in 1890. In 1895 he was dismissed for his ties with the Radical Party, and he subsequently retired. In 1903, when **Peter I Karadjordjević** came to the throne, Putnik was promoted to general and chief of staff of the army. From 1904 to 1914 he served as minister of war three times and was responsible for the modernization of the Serbian Army. Putnik's reforms played a role in the Serbian victory over the Turks in the battle of Kumanovo (23–24 October 1912) during the First Balkan War. After this victory Putnik was promoted to field marshal. In 1913 the Serbian Army under his command defeated the Bulgarians in the Second Balkan War.

When World War I began, Putnik was undergoing treatment at the spa of Bad Gleichenberg, Austria. He was interned there but was allowed to return to Serbia after the intervention of Emperor Francis Joseph. Putnik resumed the post of chief of staff, although Prince Regent Alexander (the future King **Alexander I**) was the commander-in-chief of Serbia's armed forces. The first Austrian offensive met with strong resistance and ended in a Serbian victory at Cer Hills (August 1914). However, in September 1914 the Austrian forces managed to enter Belgrade. After receiving military equipment from the Entente, the Serbian Army launched a counteroffensive. Putnik defeated the enemy troops at the Kolubara River, the biggest battle fought by the Serbs during World War I. In December 1914 the Austrian forces were driven from Belgrade and soon afterwards from the entire Serbian territory. In October–November 1915, however, the Austro-Hungarian forces, supported by German and Bulgarian troops, launched a new attack and broke down Serbian resistance. Too ill to walk, on 15 November 1915 Putnik decided to evacuate the Serbian Army across Albania to the Adriatic coast. He had to be carried the entire distance in a sedan chair. Around two hundred thousand soldiers

and civilians perished during this winter retreat over the mountains of Albania. On 7 December 1915 Putnik reached the Albanian port of Scutari. He spent the last years of his life in Nice. (AO)

Sources: *Enciklopedija Jugoslavije*, vol. 6 (Zagreb, 1965); John Clinton Adams, *Flight in Winter* (Princeton, 1942); Holger H. Herwig and Neil M. Heyman, *Biographical Dictionary of World War I* (Westport, Conn., 1982); Wacław Felczak and Tadeusz Wasilewski, *Historia Jugosławii* (Wrocław, 1985).

PUTVINSKIS Vladas (24 September 1873, Riga–5 March 1929, Kaunas), Lithuanian national activist. Putvinskis came from a Polish noble family. His father, Rafał Putwiński, was a guerrilla leader during the January Insurrection in 1863, and his mother, Idalia (née Broel-Plater), supported the Polish insurgent struggle. Putvinskis studied agriculture at the University of Halle and then fisheries in Warsaw. In 1896 he began farming on the estates of his father in Šiauliai and Raseinai Counties. Putvinskis inherited both estates in 1904. In 1897 he married Emilija Gruzdytė, a cousin of Bishop Motiejus Valančius. Putvinskis did not speak Lithuanian until the beginning of the twentieth century. Interested in philosophy and fascinated with Hegel since his youth, Putvinskis worked out his own version of mystical social and national radicalism. He developed his estates to a high economic level, and under the influence of his wife and **Povilas Višinskis**, he learned Lithuanian and transformed his estates into important centers of the Lithuanian national movement, introducing democratic practices. Putvinskis soon came into conflict with the neighboring nobility of Polish national identity, as well as with the Russian authorities. Persecuted by the police, he even more strongly supported Lithuanian nationalism and ever more often used the Lithuanized version of his surname, Pūtvis. Arrested on two occasions (in 1906 and 1914), during World War I Putvinskis was deported to Russia. He returned to Poland in 1918 and firmly supported the Lithuanians in their conflict with Poland, which was regaining its independence. In August 1919 Putvinskis founded a paramilitary youth organization, the National Guard (Šaulių Sąjunga), and became its chairman and commander. He also edited its press organ, *Trimitas*. The nationalist program of the National Guard, supervised by the Ministry of Defense, was directed mainly against Poland and the Poles. In 1922 Putvinskis resigned his leadership of the National Guard and became a lecturer in fishery management at the Agricultural Academy in Dotnuva. In 1928 he resumed his post of chairman of the National Guard, and he held it until the end of his life. Selected writings by Putvinskis were edited and published by Aleksandras Mantautas in 1933. (WR)

Sources: *EL*, vol. 4; J. Matusas, *Šaulių Sąjunga istorija* (Kaunas, 1939); Aleksandras Marcinkevičius-Mantautas, *Gyvenimas ir parinktieji raštai Vladas Putvinskis-Pūtvis* (Chicago, 1973); Vaidievutis A. Mantautas, *Žmogus, idėja ir idėjos problema Vlado Pūtvio filosofije* (Rome, 1974).

PUŻAK Kazimierz (26 August 1883, Tarnopol [Ternopil]–30 April 1950, Rawicz), Polish Socialist politician. In 1899, while a student at a high school in Tarnopol, Pużak established a clandestine organization that, among other things, smuggled underground publications. He began to study at the School of Law and Political Skills of the University of Lemberg (Lwów, Lviv) but did not complete his studies. In 1904 he joined the Polish Socialist Party (Polska Partia Socjalistyczna [PPS]). During the 1905 revolution Pużak took part in military actions conducted by the PPS. After a split within the PPS, he became aligned with the PPS–Revolutionary Faction. Arrested in 1911 and sentenced to eight years of hard labor for his involvement in the PPS Military Organization, Pużak served his sentence in Warsaw, Petrograd, and Schlisselburg. Released during the February 1917 revolution, he joined the PPS Provisional Central Executive Committee and edited the periodical *Głos Robotnika i Żołnierza* in Russia. Pużak was active in the organizational work of the party and, among other things, helped the former soldiers of the Second Brigade of the Legions, led by General **Józef Haller**. In October 1918 Pużak returned to Poland. An MP from 1919 to 1935, he worked in parliamentary commissions and assiduously strove to strengthen the rights of tenants, improve the situation of prisoners, and obtain amnesties. From the PPS unification congress in April 1919 until September 1939 Pużak was a member of the Chief Council and the Central Executive Committee of the PPS, and from 1921 to 1939 he served as secretary general and treasurer of the party.

In September 1939 Pużak fought in the defense of Warsaw. After the defeat of Poland in the war against the Germans, he decided to stay in occupied Poland. In October 1939 he co-initiated the underground Polish Socialist Party under the slogan of "Freedom–Equality–Independence" (PPS–Wolność–Równość–Niezawisłość [PPS–WRN]) and became its secretary. Pużak helped to found the underground interparty Chief Political Council. In February 1940 he became a member of the Coordinating Political Committee (Polityczny Komitet Porozumiewawczy [PKP]) of the Union of Armed Struggle (Związek Walki Zbrojnej [ZWZ]). Elected chairman of the PKP, Pużak did not take part in its work from September 1941 to March 1943 because the PPS–WRN left the PKP, one of the reasons being the PPS–WRN's critical position concerning the Polish-Soviet Agreement of 30 July 1941. In January 1944 Pużak was elected chairman of the National Unity Council (Rada Jedności Narodowej [RJN]), a clandestine quasi-parliament that brought together the main Polish underground political parties and groups, and he served as chairman of its executive organ, the Chief Commission of the RJN. In March 1945 Pużak was treacherously arrested by the NKVD, when, along with the leaders of the Polish Underground State, he went to negotiate with General Ivan Serov. Tried in Moscow in the so-called Trial of the Sixteen, Pużak was sentenced to one and a half years in prison on trumped-up charges (21 June 1945). Released in November 1945, he returned to Poland but did not take part in politics. Arrested again in May 1947, Pużak was tried for maintaining contacts with political émigrés. In November 1948, in a trial against leaders of the PPS–WRN, Pużak was sentenced to ten years in prison. His sentence was later commuted to five years. Particularly persecuted in prison, he died of heart failure. Pużak's *Wspomnienia 1939–1945* (Memoirs 1939–45) were published posthumously in 1989. (PK)

Sources: *PSB*, vol. 29; Tadeusz and Witold Rzepeccy, *Sejm i Senat 1922–1927* (Poznań, 1923); *Słownik polityków polskich XX w.* (Poznań, 1998); Jerzy Lerski, "Wspomnienie o Bazylim," *Kultura*, 1951, no. 5; Stefan Korboński, *Polskie Państwo Podziemne* (Paris, 1975); Krystyna Kersten, *Narodziny systemu władzy* (Poznań, 1990); *The Trial of the Sixteen: Court Record of the Case of Organizers, Leaders, and Members of the Polish Underground in the Rear of the Red Army in the Territories of Poland, Lithuania, and Western Districts of Belorussia and Ukraine, Heard by the Military Board of the Supreme Court of the Soviet Union on 18–21 June 1945* (Rzeszów, 1991).

PYATAKOV Georgiy [originally Kievsky] (6 August 1890, Horodyshche, near Cherkasy–30 January 1937, Moscow), Communist activist in the Ukraine of Jewish descent. The son of a laborer, Pyatakov did studied at St. Petersburg University and in Western Europe. An anarchist and a member of the Bolshevik party from 1910, he was deported for his activities. In 1915–19 Pyatakov argued with Lenin over ethnic issues and took a position that was close to that of **Rosa Luxemburg**. After the February 1917 revolution, Pyatakov headed a Kiev-based Bolshevik committee, which he represented in the Ukrainian Central Rada (Council). Although an opponent of Ukrainian independence, he was a member of the so-called Small Rada of the Ukrainian Central Rada from August to November 1917. In September 1917 Pyatakov became chairman of the Kiev Soviet (council) of Workers' Deputies. He was one of the founders of the first Bolshevik Ukrainian government, which was established in Kiev in February 1918. One month later, when German troops seized the capital, Pyatakov represented the so-called Kiev group among the Bolsheviks in the Ukraine. He came to the conclusion that a proclamation of a separate Ukrainian state for the interim would help in the struggle against the German occupation and the government of Hetman **Pavlo Skoropadskyi**. Pyatakov's position was accepted by Lenin.

In April 1918 Pyatakov attended a party conference in Taganrog at which a decision was made on the establishment of the Communist Party (Bolsheviks) of Ukraine (CP[B]U), which, although a separate party, was linked with the All-Russian Communist Party (Bolsheviks). After the CP(B)U was founded at a congress in Moscow in July 1918, Pyatakov became head of its Organizational Bureau and secretary of its Central Committee (CC). In August 1918, along with **Mykola Skrypnyk** and **Volodymyr Zatonskyi**, Pyatakov attempted to instigate a peasant uprising in the Ukraine. After the failure of this attempt, he lost his power in the party to the so-called Yekaterinoslav group, whose members called for an even stricter subordination to Moscow. After the end of German rule in the Ukraine, Pyatakov became head of the Soviet Provisional Workers' and Peasants' Government of Ukraine on 20 November 1918. In this role he endorsed the offensive of Soviet troops against the army of the Ukrainian National Republic (UNR) and suppressed other revolutionary factions in the Ukraine, particularly the Borotbist faction. On 29 January 1919 he resigned his position.

After the Bolshevik government was established in the Ukraine, Pyatakov worked as the director of a mine in the Urals (1920) and as the director of the administration of mines in the Donbas (1921–23). He drafted the First Five-Year Plan (1926–30), which put particular emphasis on industrializing the Ukraine. In his so-called testament, Lenin cited Pyatakov as one of the two most talented people in the party (in addition to Nikolay Bukharin). Pyatakov was a member of the CC of the All-Russian Communist Party (Bolsheviks) from 1923 to 1927 (in 1925 the party changed its name to the All-Union Communist Party [Bolsheviks]) and also from 1930 to 1937. In 1923 he became deputy chairman of the Supreme Council of the National Economy. Linked with Leon Trotsky, Pyatakov was dismissed from his position and expelled from the party in 1927. After making a self-criticism in 1929, he was reinstated to his former position and readmitted to the party. He was also appointed head of the State Bank in Moscow. As deputy head of the Soviet Union's heavy industry, Pyatakov was responsible for (among other things) the implementation of the Second Five-Year Plan (1933–37). Arrested in the fall of 1936, he was sentenced to death in the trial of the so-called Trotskyite opposition in January 1937. Pyatakov confessed to working to separate the Ukraine from the Soviet Union. The sentence was carried out immediately. Pyatakov was posthumously rehabilitated in 1988. (TS)

Sources: *MERSH*, vol. 28; Alexander Orlov, *The Secret History of Stalin's Crimes* (New York, 1953); Taras Hunczak, ed., *The Ukraine, 1917–1921: A Study in Revolution* (Cambridge, 1977); Yuri Borys, *The Sovietization of Ukraine, 1917–1923: The Communist Doctrine and Practice of National Self-Determination* (Edmonton, 1980); James E. Mace, *Communism and the Dilemmas of National Liberation: National Communism in Soviet Ukraine, 1918–1933* (Cambridge, 1983).

PYNZENYK Viktor (15 April 1954, Smolohovytsi, Transcarpathian Ruthenia), Ukrainian economist and politician. The son of teachers, in 1975 Pynzenyk graduated in economics from the University of Lviv (UL). In 1979 he received a Ph.D. there. In 1989 he received his second degree in Moscow. At UL University, he advanced from assistant professor to professor (1990). In 1990–92 Pynzenyk was director of the UL Institute of Management. In 1991 he was elected to the Supreme Council of Ukraine and became deputy chairman of its commission for the national economy. In October 1992 he became deputy prime minister for economic reform in the government of **Leonid Kuchma**. Until March 1993 he was also minister of the national economy. Taking advantage of a six-month period of special powers given by the Supreme Council to the government, Pynzenyk tried to curb hyperinflation (2000 percent in 1992) by introducing privatization, abolishing subsidies and price controls, supporting the development of financial markets, and attracting foreign capital. Only some of these reforms were realized since Kuchma entered into conflict with President **Leonid Kravchuk** and resigned in September 1993.

Pynzenyk returned to the position of deputy prime minister for economic reform in 1994, when Kuchma took over as president. He stayed in office in the governments of **Vitaliy Masol** (July 1994–March 1995), **Yevhen Marchuk** (March 1995–May 1996), and **Pavlo Lazarenko** (May 1996–July 1997). Thanks to Pynzenyk's restrictive monetary policy, inflation went down to 0.1 percent per month in 1996, so in September 1996 he introduced a new currency, the hryvna. Having stabilized the currency, in the fall of 1996 Pynzenyk presented further reforms, including an increase in private investments, a reduction of budget expenditures (especially in the field of social policies), the introduction of a common VAT, a reduction of the tax progression, and a liquidation of export taxes. The resistance of the Supreme Council, dominated by post-Communists, to the tax reform caused Pynzenyk to resign in April 1997. In the parliamentary elections of March 1998 Pynzenyk ran on behalf of his own Reform and Order Party. Its program, which combined pro-market and pro-Western declarations with references to national traditions and Christian values, proved not attractive enough since it gained only 3.1 percent of the vote. (TS)

Sources: Marek Dąbrowski and Rafał Antczak, *Economic Transition in Russia, the Ukraine and Belarus in Comparative Perspective* (Warsaw, 1995); Marek Dąbrowski, *Inflatsionnye posledstviya devaluatsionnogo krizisa v Rossii i Ukraine: Pervye nablyudeniya* (Warsaw, 1999); Bohdan Nahaylo, *The Ukrainian Resurgence* (Toronto, 1999).

R

RAČAN Ivica (24 February 1944, Ebersbach, Germany), Croatian Communist activist and post-Communist politician. Račan graduated in law from the University of Zagreb in 1970, but from 1965 he worked at the Institute of Social Studies in Zagreb. From 1974 he was active in the apparatus of the League of Communists of Yugoslavia (LCY). In 1972–82 Račan was a member of the Presidium of the Central Committee (CC) of the League of Communists of Croatia (Savez Komunista Hrvatske [LCC]), and from 1982 to 1986 he was director of the party school, the Tito Memorial Political School, in Kumrovec. From 1986 Račan belonged to the Presidium of the LCY CC, and in 1989 he was elected chairman of the LCC CC. In January 1990 he led the Croatian delegation to the Fourteenth LCY Congress, during which Croatian and Slovene Communists confronted the party majority, led by the Serb leader, **Slobodan Milošević**, on the extension of republican autonomy. The Croatian and Slovene delegations left the congress; the move presaged the dissolution of the LCY. As the leader of the Croatian Communists, Račan agreed to the first free elections, and after electoral defeat in April 1990 he gave up power to the victorious Croatian Democratic Union of **Franjo Tudjman**.

Račan was the key engineer of the transformation of the LCC into the LCC–Party of Democratic Change and then into the Social Democratic Party of Croatia (Socialdemokratska Partija Hrvatske), which he chaired. From 1990 Račan was a member of the Croatian parliament, and in 1992–2000 he succeeded in making his party one of the two leading opposition parties, the other being the Social Liberals of **Dražen Budiša**. In 1998 Račan entered into a coalition with the Budiša party. The coalition won 47 percent of the mandates in the elections of 3 January 2000, and on 27 January Račan became prime minister of a government composed of post-Communists, Social Liberals, and four minor center groups. Račan's government radically reoriented economic and foreign policies. Račan agreed to the return of Serbian war refugees and to the handover of those suspected of war crimes to The Hague Tribunal for War Crimes in Former Yugoslavia. In October 2001 his government signed a treaty of association with the European Union. In the parliamentary elections of November 2003 Račan's center-left coalition lost, and on 23 December 2003 Račan gave up his post as prime minister. (AW)

Sources: *Europa Środkowo-Wschodnia 1991–1998* (Warsaw 1992–2000); *Tko je tko u Hrvatskoj* (Zagreb, 1993); Zoran Kusovac, "The Prospects for Change in Post-Tudjman Croatia," *East European Constitutional Review*, 2000, no. 2; Alex J. Bellamy, "Croatia after Tudjman: The 2000 Parliamentary and Presidential Elections," *Problems of Post-Communism*, 2001, no. 5; www.vlada.hr/racan-bio.html; www.sdp.hr.

RACIN Kosta, "Koco" [originally Solev] (22 December 1909, Veles–13 June 1943, Planina Lopušnik), Macedonian poet and writer. The son of a potter, Racin never completing high school. He joined the clandestine Communist Party. He wrote poetry and other works, and in 1939 he published *Beli Mugri* (White dawns) in Zagreb. The book was his most influential work and secured him a place in the pantheon of important twentieth-century Macedonian writers. Drawing deeply on Macedonian life, the book was proscribed but nevertheless circulated in Macedonia. For a time after the fall of Yugoslavia in April 1941, Racin worked on the railroad in Bulgaria. He fled back to Macedonia when he was wanted by the police. Arrested by the Bulgarian occupation authorities, he was eventually released and joined the Partisan movement of Josip Broz Tito. Racin was killed in battle. Believed to be very important for the creation of the Macedonian literary language, Racin authored several other books of poetry and three novels. One of them, *Afion* (Poppy), was in large part destroyed by the interwar Yugoslav police. (DP)

Sources: *Enciklopedija Jugoslavije*, vol. 7 (Zagreb, 1968); *Mały słownik pisarzy zachodnio-słowiańskich i południowo-słowiańskich* (Warsaw, 1973); Pero Korobar, *Racin* (Skopje, 1978); Valentina Georgieva and Sasha Konechni, *Historical Dictionary of the Republic of Macedonia* (Lanham, Md., 1998).

RACOVIȚĂ Mihail (7 March 1889, Bucharest–28 June 1954, Sighet), Romanian general. In 1906–7 Racoviță studied at the Military School of Artillery and Cavalry and from 1907 to 1909 in the Military Academy in Hannover (Germany). In 1918 he was responsible for the repatriation of Romanian prisoners of war from Germany. In 1928 he was promoted to colonel, in 1936 to brigadier general, and in 1940 to general of division. In 1941–42 Racoviță commanded a cavalry corps. In 1942 he was appointed general of the army corps and in 1943 commander of the Bucharest garrison; in 1943–44 he commanded armored troops. In 1944 he was commander of the Fourth Army. After the coup of 23 August 1944, which toppled Marshal **Ion Antonescu**, Racoviță became minister of defense in the government of General **Constantin Sănătescu**. He ordered the interrogations and, in October 1944, the arrests of Romanian generals. After he left his post in November 1944, Racoviță was general inspector of cavalry and chief inspector of the General Inspectorate of the Third Army. In 1946 he was appointed general of the army, and in 1946–47 he commanded the First Army. In September 1947 he retired. Arrested on 2 April 1950 for being the "general of a bourgeois army," on 5 July 1950 Racoviţă was moved to the Sighet prison. He was called an "element hostile to the present authorities and to the Soviet Union" and accused of supporting a "cavalry and caste spirit," of "political reactionism," of contacts with the anti-Communist opposition, and of war crimes because he defended officers taking part in the Iaşi pogrom. Racoviţă's trial continued until May 1952, when he was sentenced to hard labor for life. Racoviţă was tried in absentia, and he was not recorded in any penal institution, while the court "did not know his whereabouts." In fact he was kept in the Sighet prison until he died. (LW)

Sources: Vlad Georgescu, *Istoria Românilor de la origini pînă în zilele noastre* (Oakland, 1984); Costin Scorpan, *Istoria României: Enciclopedie* (Bucharest, 1997); Aleksandru Duţu and Florica Dobre, *Drama generalilor români* (Bucharest, 1997).

RACZKIEWICZ Władysław (28 January 1885, Kutaisi, Georgia–6 June 1947, Ruthin, Great Britain), Polish lawyer and politician, president-in-exile of the Polish Republic. Raczkiewicz was the son of a judge and the grandson of an insurgent who was subjected to property confiscation and deported to the Caucasus following the Polish January Uprising of 1863. Upon graduating from a classical high school in Tver, Raczkiewicz studied mathematics and law at the University of St. Petersburg. As a student, he joined the illegal Organization of Nationalist Youth and the Union of Polish Youth–Zet. Threatened with arrest, Raczkiewicz transferred to the Law School of the University of Dorpat (Tartu), where he graduated in May 1911. Following a year-long stint in the military, he was promoted to officer rank in 1912. Later he worked as a lawyer in Minsk in Belorussia. Raczkiewicz was mobilized in 1914. After the overthrow of the tsar in 1917, he began organizing Polish military units in Russia, becoming chairman of the board of the Union of Military Poles in Minsk. On 7 June 1917, during the First General Congress of Military Poles in Petrograd, he was elected chairman of the Supreme Polish Military Committee (Naczpol). Despite opposing the Bolsheviks, Raczkiewicz was against involving the Polish military units on the side of the Whites, and he supported the subordination of the First Polish Corps (formed in August 1917) to the Regency Council, a Polish provisional authority in Warsaw dependent on the Central Powers. In February 1918 Raczkiewicz became chairman of the clandestine Supreme Council of the Polish Armed Forces in Kiev and plenipotentiary of the Regency Council for Polish military formations in Russia. From 1917 to 1918 he served as a city councilman in Minsk and organized the Polish School Matrix there, as well as taking care of refugees and founding self-defense units.

In December 1918 Raczkiewicz took the helm of the military department of the Committee to Defend the Eastern Borderlands in Warsaw. In April 1919 he was assigned to the General Staff of the Polish Army. On 16 May 1919 he was appointed deputy general commissioner of the Eastern Lands. Upon the capture of Minsk by the Poles, Raczkiewicz became the supervisor of the Civilian Board of the District of Minsk. In April 1920 he was promoted to the rank of major in the artillery. Between July and September 1920, he led volunteer eastern Polish units in their fight for Wilno (Vilnius). Between December 1920 and June 1921 he served as delegate to the Lithuanian government in Vilnius. From June through September 1921 he was minister of interior in the government of **Wincenty Witos**. Then Raczkiewicz assumed the functions of governor (*wojewoda*) of Nowogródek Province (October 1921–August 1924), government delegate in Wilno (until June 1925), and once again minister of interior (from 5 May 1926).

After the coup d'état of May 1926, Raczkiewicz—as a follower of **Józef Piłsudski**—was considered a candidate for the presidency of the Polish Republic. However, he became the governor of Wilno Province (1926–30). In November 1930 he was elected to the Senate from the lists of the Nonparty Bloc of Cooperation with the Government; however, he failed to join this parliamentary club. On 9 December 1930 Raczkiewicz was elected speaker of the Senate. He focused mainly on a reform of the public administration. In August 1935 he became governor of Kraków Province, and in July 1936, provincial governor of Pomerania. Meanwhile, between October 1935 and May 1936, Raczkiewicz served as minister of interior. He supported the policy of cracking down on the anti-Polish organizations of the German minority. He belonged to the so-called Castle group, which sided with Poland's president, **Ignacy Mościcki**. Raczkiewicz held numerous public and pro-bono posts, including the chairmanship of the World Union of Poles Abroad.

Following the outbreak of World War II in September 1939, Raczkiewicz was charged by his government with organizing assistance among Polish Americans for occupied Poland. On 27 September 1939, he reached Paris, where he was tapped by President Mościcki to succeed him. In a radio address on 30 November 1939 Raczkiewicz declared that he would carry out the prerogatives of his office, as enshrined in the April 1935 constitution, jointly with his prime minister. In November 1939 Raczkiewicz nominated General **Władysław Sikorski** to the prime ministership, and in December 1939 he established the National Council, which was Poland's skeletal parliament-in-exile, led by **Ignacy Paderewski**. Raczkiewicz and Sikorski often clashed on various issues. On 18 July 1940, proclaiming the need to keep military and civilian functions separate, Raczkiewicz dismissed Sikorski and charged **August Zaleski** with the mission of assembling a new government, while allowing Sikorski to keep the post of commander-in-chief. Thanks to the mediation of General **Kazimierz Sosnkowski**, Sikorski retained the helm of the government. Another serious difference of opinion occurred when, on 30 July 1941, Sikorski signed, against Raczkiewicz's objections, a Polish-Soviet treaty. The altercation lasted several weeks and resulted in the resignation of three cabinet ministers. Ultimately, Raczkiewicz came to regard the treaty as a fait accompli. Following the death of Sikorski, on 14 July 1943, Raczkiewicz appointed **Stanisław Mikołajczyk** as his prime minister, and, in September 1943, General Sosnkowski as the commander-in-chief. In August 1944 he appointed the Socialist **Tomasz Arciszewski**, who had recently arrived from Poland, as his successor. Under pressure from the British, Raczkiewicz dismissed Sosnkowski, who opposed any compromise with the Soviets regarding Poland's Eastern Borderlands, and appointed General **Tadeusz Bór-Komorowski** as the commander-in-chief. After the failure of the Warsaw Uprising, General Komorowski was taken prisoner by the Germans, so some of the functions of the commander-in-chief were taken over by the president himself. On 29 November 1944 Raczkiewicz appointed Arciszewski to replace Mikołajczyk as prime minister. In July 1945 the Polish government-in-exile lost international recognition. In April 1947, despite earlier agreements, Raczkiewicz changed his mind about his successor, anointing Zaleski; this led to the implosion of the Polish political émigré community. Sick with leukemia, in March 1947 Raczkiewicz checked into a sanatorium in Ruthin in northern Wales, where he died. He was buried at the Cemetery of the Polish Airmen in Newark, England. (JS)

Sources: *PSB*, vol. 29; *Kto był kim w Drugiej Rzeczypospolitej* (Warsaw, 1994); Witold Babiński, "Prezydent Raczkiewicz. Wspomnienie," *Zeszyty Historyczne*, 1979, no. 47; Józef Garliński, *Polska w drugiej wojnie światowej* (London, 1982); Władysław Pobóg-Malinowski, *Najnowsza historia polityczna Polski 1864–1945*, vol. 3 (London, 1986); John Coutouvidis and Jaime Reynolds, *Poland, 1939–1947* (Leicester, 1986); Andrzej Albert [Wojciech Roszkowski], *Najnowsza historia Polski 1914–1993*, vol. 1 (Warsaw, 1995); Marian M. Drozdowski, *Władysław Raczkiewicz: Prezydent RP*, vols. 1–2 (Warsaw, 2003).

RACZYŃSKI Edward (19 December 1891, Zakopane–30 July 1993, London), Polish politician and diplomat.

Raczyński was born into an aristocratic family, the son of the owner of the estate of Rogalin in Wielkopolska. He studied at the university in Leipzig, the London School of Economics and Political Sciences, and the Jagiellonian University in Kraków, where he graduated with a doctorate in law. Following a short stint in the military, Raczyński was drafted into the diplomatic corps. He was the secretary of Poland's legations in Copenhagen (1920–22) and London (1922–24). Then he worked in the Ministry of Foreign Affairs in Warsaw as the supervisor of the Eastern Department and the Department of International Organizations. Between 1932 and 1934 he represented Poland at the League of Nations. He participated in the disarmament conference in Geneva. From November 1934 through July 1945 he served as ambassador to London. Raczyński was the co-author of the Polish-British mutual aid treaty of 25 August 1939. In September 1939 he energetically appealed for assistance to Poland, which was being overrun by the Nazis, but in vain. During the war he played an important role as a non-partisan diplomat who knew the British very well. As minister of state, Raczyński was the supervisor of the Ministry of Foreign Affairs in the government of General **Władysław Sikorski** (1941–43). He supported postwar Poland's federation with Czechoslovakia and negotiated the issue with President **Edvard Beneš** in London. After the outbreak of the uprising in Warsaw in August 1944, Raczyński endeavored to convince the British about the righteousness of the cause and the hostility of the USSR toward the Poles. He vainly urged the British government to increase arms drops for fighting in Warsaw and to dispatch a Polish paratrooper brigade to Poland's capital.

Following World War II Raczyński remained in Great Britain, participating actively in building the political institutions of the Polish émigré community and organizing assistance for refugees. He defended the Polish cause in numerous memoranda, letters, and press articles. He maintained permanent contacts with the British authorities who dealt with Polish matters. The (Communist) Provisional Government in Warsaw demanded that Raczyński be barred from diplomatic issues concerning Poland. After Great Britain recognized the Communist-controlled Provisional Government of National Unity in Warsaw in July 1945, London withdrew its recognition of Raczyński. He continued to be active in the European Movement and the Liberal International. Between 1954 and 1972 Raczyński was a member of the émigré Council of Three, fulfilling the duties of Poland's president-in-exile in opposition to **August Zaleski**. From 1979 to 1986, he was the president-in-exile of Poland. At that time, the dissident movement and Solidarity emerged in Poland;

they also suffered under martial law and witnessed a wave of political emigrations to the West. During his tenure, on 19 January 1986 Raczyński signed a joint declaration with the Council of Free Czechoslovakia concerning prospects for a future Central European federation. He also endeavored to maintain friendly relations with the Ukrainian émigré community (the Polish-Ukrainian declaration of 28 November 1978). He was a co-founder of the Fund to Assist the Homeland, which was intended to support the political opposition in Poland. Raczyński enjoyed a great deal of authority among Poles both at home and abroad. After resigning from office, although blind, he maintained an active interest in democratic transformation in Poland. Raczyński authored (among other works) *Polska polityka zagraniczna w czasie II wojny światowej* (Polish foreign policy during World War II; 1953); a diary, *W sojuszniczym Londynie* (In Allied London; 1960); and *Od Narcyza Kulikowskiego do Winstona Churchilla* (From Narcyz Kulikowski to Winston Churchill; 1976). (JS)

Sources: Jan Karski, *The Great Powers and Poland, 1919–1945* (Lanham, Md., 1985); *Edward Raczyński: Czas wielkich zmian* (Paris, 1990); *Prezydenci Polski* ed. Andrzej Ajnenkiel (Warsaw, 1991); *Encyklopedia Historii Polski: Dzieje polityczne*, vol. 2 (Warsaw, 1995); *Encyklopedia historii Drugiej Rzeczypospolitej* (Warsaw, 1999).

RĂDĂCEANU Lothar (19 May 1899, Rădăuţi, near Suceava–24 August 1955, Helsinki, Finland), Romanian Socialist and Communist activist. After finishing secondary school in Bucharest, Rădăceanu began to study in the Department of Literature and Philosophy of the University of Bucharest. In 1919 he joined the Social Democratic Party (Partidul Social-Democrat). After completing his studies, he earned a Ph.D. in philosophy from the University of Bucharest in 1925. In 1927 he became secretary of the newly established Romanian Social Democratic Party (Partidul Social-Democrat din România [PSDR]) and a member of its Executive Committee. After the PSDR was declared illegal in 1938, he directed its underground structures until 1944. From 1944 to 1948 Rădăceanu was secretary general of the PSDR, which co-formed several governments after the war. He represented the PSDR left wing, which brought about a split within the party in 1946 and a union with the Communists in February 1948. From November 1944 to February 1945 Rădăceanu occupied the post of minister of labor. In the successive governments of **Petru Groza**, he served as minister of labor (March 1945–October 1946) and minister of labor and social welfare (October 1946–August 1952). From January to April 1948 he simultaneously served as interim minister of national education. In February 1948 Rădăceanu became a member of the Politburo and secretary of the Central Committee of the Romanian Workers' Party (Partidul Muncitoresc Român). He held these two positions until 1952. Dismissed during the suppression of the group led by **Ana Pauker**, **Vasile Luca**, and **Teohari Georgescu,** Rădăceanu dealt with foreign policy in parliament, where he sat from 1946 on. In 1955, shortly before his death, he became a member of the Romanian Academy of Sciences. (LW)

Sources: Klaus-Detlev Grothusen, ed., *Rumänien* (Göttingen, 1977); Ghiţă Ionescu, *Comunismul în România* (Bucharest, 1994); Józef Darski, *Rumunia: Historia, współczesność, konflikty narodowe* (Warsaw, 1995); Dorina N. Rusu, *Membrii Academiei Române 1866–1999* (Bucharest, 1999); Ion Alexandrescu, Ion Bulei, Ion Mamina, and Ioan Scurtu, *Enciclopedia de istorie a României* (Bucharest, 2000).

RĂDESCU Nicolae (30 March 1874, Bucharest–16 May 1953, New York), general and prime minister of Romania. Rădescu was a commander on different fronts of World War I, and after the end of the war he served as a military attaché in London in the 1920s. In 1933 he resigned from the army to protest the dictatorial policies of King **Charles II**. Under the government of **Ion Antonescu**, Rădescu's patriotic attitude drew German attention, and he was interned at the Târgu-Jiu concentration camp, where he personally met some Communist activists. After the overthrow of Antonescu in August 1944 Rădescu was appointed chief of staff of the army, which was now on the side of the Allies. On 2 December 1944 King Michael V designated Rădescu prime minister and minister of interior of a coalition cabinet in which the Communists took part. Stalin, hoping that Rădescu would become a tool in his hands, accepted the composition of the government. However, Rădescu implemented his own policy and, counting upon the support of the Western Allies, tried to retain independence from the USSR. The Kremlin and the Romanian Communists controlled Moldavia and Transylvania, though, and they had at their disposal the powerful units of the Patriotic Guard of **Emil Bodnaraş**. When in January 1945 Rădescu attempted to dissolve them, he met effective resistance from them and counteraction from their Soviet protectors. On 24 February 1945 a demonstration in Bucharest was suppressed at which Rădescu openly accused the Communists of acting to the detriment of Romania and in the interests of the USSR. After that, on 3 March 1945 Rădescu was forced to resign by the special emissary of the Kremlin, Andrey Vyshinsky. Fearing arrest, in June 1946 Rădescu fled to Cyprus and then went to the United States, where he lived until his death. (WR)

Sources: Dinu C. Giurescu, *Romania's Communist Takeover: The Radescu Government* (Boulder, Colo., 1994); Andrzej Koryn, *Rumunia w polityce wielkich mocarstw 1944–1947* (Wrocław, 1983); Ghita Ionescu, *Communism in Rumania, 1944–1962* (London and New York, 1964); *New York Times*, 19 May 1953.

RADEV Simeon (19 January 1879, Resen, Macedonia–15 February 1967, Sofia), Bulgarian writer, historian, diplomat, and journalist. Radev graduated from a French lycée in Istanbul. In 1895 he became a member of the Internal Macedonian Revolutionary Organization (IMRO). While a law student in Geneva (1898–1902), he continued his activities in the IMRO; among other things, he was an editor of *Le Mouvement Macédonien* (1902). In 1901 Radev began his association with the periodical *Vecherna poshta*, first as its editor (1905) and later as its editor-in-chief (1907–9). He was a co-founder of the periodical *Hudozhnik* (1906–9) and the editor of the newspaper *Volya* (1912–13). In over 250 articles from that period Radev expressed the national aspirations of Bulgarians from Macedonia and criticized the Bulgarian foreign policy on this issue. From 1910 to 1911 he wrote his most famous work, the political chronicle *Stroitelite na sŭvremenna Bŭlgariia* (The builders of contemporary Bulgaria), in which he depicted the social atmosphere, political clashes, and images of politicians of the first decade of the free Bulgarian state (1878–87). Radev fought in the Balkan Wars and then worked in the diplomatic services, holding the post of minister plenipotentiary to Bucharest (1913–16), The Hague (1920–21), Istanbul (1923–25), Washington, D.C. (1925–33), London (1933–38), and Brussels (1938–40). Radev was the author of *La Macédonie et la renaissance bulgare au XIX siècle* (1918) and the co-author of *La question bulgare et les états balkaniques* (1919). These works, which served as encyclopedias on the Bulgarian national issue, did not prevent the adoption of decisions unfavorable to Bulgaria in the 1919 Neuilly peace negotiations. After returning to Bulgaria in 1940, Radev worked in the Ministry of Foreign Affairs. In 1944 he was dismissed by the new authorities. Under the Communist governments, he wrote a great number of historical works and memoirs, becoming a master of documentary prose. Most of Radev's literary output remains unpublished. (JW)

Sources: *Entsiklopediya Bulgariya*, vol. 6 (Sofia, 1996); *Aleksander Balabanov i Simeon Radev v spomenite na suvremennitsite si* (Sofia, 1986); Iordan Vasilev, *Patila i radosti* (Sofia, 2002).

RADIĆ Antun (11 June 1868, Trebarjevo Desno–10 February 1919, Zagreb), Croatian politician. The son of a poor, illiterate peasant and the brother of **Stjepan Radić**, Radić graduated from high school in Zagreb and in Slavic studies in Zagreb and Vienna. He worked as a teacher and journalist. In December 1899, along with his brother, he founded the periodical *Dom*, which played a signifcant role in the national awakening of the Croatian countryside. In 1896–1902 Radić was the editor of the six-volume *Zbornik na narodni život i običaje Južnih Slavena* (Collection on the national life and customs of the South Slavs), and from 1901 to 1909 he was secretary of the Croatian Matrix (Matica Hrvatska) and editor of the periodical *Glas*. In December 1904 Radić and his brother established the Croatian People's Peasant Party (Hrvatska Pučka Seljačka Stranka [CPPP]). Its program, mostly written by Radić, included a demand for universal suffrage, the parceling out of the landed estates of more than 300 hectares (750 acres), and the transformation of the Habsburg monarchy into a federation of nations. The party's ideology was based on class, anticlerical, populist, and republican foundations; it identified the national interest of the Croats with the interests of the peasantry, and it referred to Pan-Slavic ideas. Apart from its critical attitude toward the clergy, the emergence of the CPPP made it difficult to create a more conservative Croatian Catholic party. Thus the party was not welcomed by the Catholic hierarchy. In 1910 and 1911 Radić was a deputy to the Croat Assembly (Sabor), and from 1912 to 1914 he was editor-in-chief of *Dom*, which resumed publication and became the organ of the CPPP. During World War I Radić was less active owing to poor health, and he died prematurely. His numerous articles and proposals were published in 1936–39 in a nineteen-volume work, *Sabrana djela dra Antuna Radića* (Collected works of Dr. Antun Radić). (WR)

Sources: *Biographisches Lexikon*, vol. 4; *Enciklopedia Jugoslavije*, vol. 7 (Zagreb, 1968); Ljubica Vuković-Todorović, *Hrvatski seljački pokret braće Radića* (Belgrade, 1940); Zvonimir Kulundzić, *Ante Radić i klerikalci* (Zagreb, 1951); Mark Biondich, *Stjepan Radić, the Croat Peasant Party, and the Politics of Mass Mobilization, 1904–1928* (Toronto, 2000).

RADIĆ Stjepan (11 July 1871, Trebarjevo Desno–8 August 1928, Belgrade), Croatian politician. The son of a poor, illiterate peasant and the brother of **Antun Radić**, Radić struggled financially to obtain a primary education in Martinska Ves and a secondary education in Zagreb and Karlstadt. He started legal studies in Zagreb but was dismissed for anti-Hungarian actions. He continued his studies in Prague and Budapest and from 1895 again in Zagreb. In October 1895 Radić was arrested for taking part in a Croatian demonstration during which the Hungarian flag was burned. After his release he left for Russia and then again for Prague, where he joined the United Croatian and Serbian Youth (Ujedinjena Hrvatska i Srpska Omladina), organized under the patronage of **Tomáš Gar-**

rigue **Masaryk**. From 1899, along with his brother Antun, Radić edited the periodical *Dom*. He finally graduated in law in Paris. In 1902 he founded the periodical *Hrvatska Misao* in Zagreb, and on 5 December 1904, along with his brother, he initiated the Croatian People's Peasant Party (Hrvatska Pučka Seljačka Stranka [CPPP]). In view of a property requirement for voting rights, most Croatian peasants could not vote. Thus in the elections of 1908 and 1910 the party gained only a small percentage of the vote. Along with his brother, Radić developed a radical party ideology, based on class, anticlerical, populist, and republican foundations; it identified the national interest of the Croats with the interests of the peasantry, and it referred to Pan-Slavic ideas. Radić also published analyses of the international situation as seen from the Croatian point of view: *Savremena Evropa: Karakteristika evropskih država i naroda* (Contemporary Europe: Characteristics of European states and nations; 1905) and *Živo hrvatsko pravo na Bosnu i Hercegovinu* (Vital Croatian rights in Bosnia and Hercegovina; 1908).

During World War I Radić represented "Austro-Slavism," supporting the unification and autonomy of Habsburg Slavs, but in mid-1918 he turned toward an agreement with Serbia. On 5 October 1918 the CPPP took part in the founding congress of the National Council of Slovenes, Croats, and Serbs, and Radić was elected to its leadership. On 29 October 1918 the council broke away from the Kingdom of Hungary and the Austrian empire. After the formation of the Kingdom of Serbs, Croats, and Slovenes at the beginning of December 1918, the CPPP advocated a republican federation and opposed monarchy and Serb domination. In February 1919 Radić sent a memorandum to the Paris Peace Conference declaring the right of the Croats to self-determination; for this he was temporarily arrested. In the elections of 1920, his party ran as the Croatian Republican Peasant Party (Hrvatska Republikanska Seljačka Stranka [CRPP]), a title that was provocative to King **Alexander**, who was of Serb nationality. The CRPP won the majority of the Croatian votes but had no chance of gaining the majority in the all-national parliament in Belgrade. The passing of a centralist constitution on 28 June 1921 (Vidovdanski Ustav) was a new challenge for the Croats, so Radić and his party refused to take part in the parliamentary rule.

In the elections of March 1923 the CRPP ran again, winning the Croatian majority and becoming the second largest faction in the all-national parliament. Despite the creation of the Federalist Bloc in April 1923—which included the CRPP, the Slovene People's Party, and the Organization of Yugoslav Muslims—opponents of the centralist Serb governments lacked a majority to change

them. In June 1924 Radić went to Moscow and entered into cooperation with the Communist Peasant International (Krestintern). In July 1924 the Krestintern admitted the CRPP, and the Communist International changed its previous stance and condemned Serbian centralism, now supporting the dissolution of the Kingdom of Serbs, Croats, and Slovenes. Radić also visited Paris and London, seeking support for a separate Croatian republic. After returning home, on 12 October 1924 he made a passionate speech accusing the Serbian elite of an abuse of power. On 5 January 1925 Radić was arrested, along with key aides, and accused of treason and cooperation with the international Communist movement. His arrest caused unrest in Croatia. In the elections of February 1925 the CRPP won its largest electoral success to date. In view of the losses suffered by the Serbian nationalists, King Alexander and the Serbian leaders changed their policy. With these conciliatory gestures, Radić declared his recognition of the 1921 constitution and changed the name of his party into the Croatian Peasant Party (Hrvatska Seljačka Stranka [CPP]). In return for a break with the Krestintern and withdrawal of his party's republican ideology, Radić was released from house arrest. In November 1925 he even became minister of education in the government of **Nikola Pasić**. The compromise caused serious criticism of Radić within his party and the departure of most consistent federalists and republicans from the CPP. Moreover, the Serbs failed to reciprocate with concessions. When in April 1926 **Nikola Uzunović** formed a new cabinet, Radić stayed in it. He increasingly insisted on constitutional reform, but in vain.

In January 1927 Radić refused to join another Uzunović government and remained in the opposition. In the elections of September 1927, the CPP lost many votes, mainly in towns. On 10 November 1927, along with the Serbian Democrat **Svetozar Pribićević**, Radić formed the Peasant Democratic Coalition. Given the lack of a clear parliamentary majority, in February 1928 King Alexander proposed that Radić form a government, but the latter did not want to rule on the basis of a parliamentary minority. Radić's demands that the constitution be changed and that all territories inhabited by Croats be united into one administrative unit —demands that were backed by the threat that the Croats would otherwise cease paying taxes—infuriated Serb nationalists. The climax of the crisis came on 20 June 1928, when Radić fell victim to a shooting in the parliament. His nephew Pavle was shot dead; Radić himself was badly wounded by a Montenegrin nationalist, Puniša Racić, and he soon died in a hospital. The shootings caused a serious constitutional crisis and led to the royal dictatorship of King Alexander and the renaming of the state into Yugoslavia in 1929. Since 1991 many works by Radić have been published in independent Croatia, including *Hrvatski politički katehizam* (Croatian political catechism; 1995), *Izbrani politički govori* (Selected political speeches; 1995), and *Izbrani politički spisi* (Selected political writings; 1995). (WR)

Sources: *Biographisches Lexikon*, vol. 4; *Enciklopedia Jugoslavije*, vol. 7 (Zagreb, 1968); A. Verus, *Radic: Portret historijske ličnosti* (Zagreb, 1925); M. Marjanović, *Stjepan Radić* (Belgrade, 1937); R. G. Livingstone, "Stjepan Radic and the Croatian Peasant Party," Ph.D. diss., Harvard University, 1959; Stjepan Radić, *Korespondencija Stjepana Radića*, vols. 1–2 (Zagreb, 1972–73); Zvonimir Kulundžić, *Atentat na Stjepana Radića* (Zagreb, 1967); Ivan Mužić, *Stjepan Radić v Kraljevini Srba, Hrvata i Slovenaca* (Zagreb, 1988); Mark Biondich, *Stjepan Radić, the Croat Peasant Party, and the Politics of Mass Mobilization, 1904–1928* (Toronto, 2000).

RADKIEWICZ Stanisław (19 January 1903, Kosów Poleski–13 December 1987, Warsaw), Polish Communist activist. The son of a peasant, Radkiewicz completed high school and joined the Communist Party of Poland (Komunistyczna Partia Polski [KPP]) in 1925. Initially, he was a local activist. Later, he completed a Komintern course in Moscow and joined the KPP Central Committee (CC) apparatus. Radkiewicz was arrested and sentenced a few times for his Communist activities in Poland. From December 1937 to July 1938, during the purge of the Polish Communists in the USSR and the dissolution of their party by the Communist International, Radkiewicz was one of the five leaders heading the Provisional Leadership Board of the KPP in Poland. After September 1939 he found himself in eastern Poland under Soviet occupation. Like many other Polish Communists, he was relegated to a minor post. In June 1941 he was evacuated deep into the USSR. Radkiewicz co-organized the Kremlin-controlled Union of Polish Patriots. In April 1944 he was appointed to its Main Board and charged with maintaining contact with Poland. He was the secretary of the Central Bureau of Polish Communists, which was founded in Moscow in January 1944. He co-organized the Polish Committee of National Liberation (PKWN), and on 22 July 1944 he was appointed to head its Department of Public Security (and from 1 January 1945) the Ministry of Public Security. In August 1944 Radkiewicz was appointed to the CC and in December 1945 to the Politburo of the (Communist) Polish Workers' Party (as of December 1948, the Polish United Workers' Party [PUWP]). He was a member of the Home National Council (1944–47) and the parliament (1947–56).

Between 1944 and 1954 Radkiewicz belonged to the top Communist leadership of Poland. Because of his security post, he was personally responsible for the mass terror and criminal activities of the security apparatus. However, he seems to have been a zealous executor of the terror rather than the initiator of this particular policy line. Nonetheless, from its creation in February 1949, along with **Bolesław Bierut** and **Jakub Berman**, Radkiewicz supervised the Security Commission of the PUWP CC Secretariat. During the initial stage of the "thaw," in December 1954, a meeting of the central party activists forced the reorganization of the security apparatus, which the party leadership tried to scapegoat as solely responsible for the terror. Consequently, Radkiewicz was transferred to a lesser post and appointed minister for the state agricultural farms. Radkiewicz was purged from the Politburo in July 1955, from the government in April 1956, and ultimately from the party in May 1957. Unlike a few of his underlings, he was never tried for his Stalinist crimes. (AP)

Sources: Mołdawa; Stanisław Marat and Jacek Snopkiewicz, *Ludzie bezpieki* (Warsaw, 1990); Jerzy Poksiński, *"TUN," Tatar-Utnik-Nowicki: Represje wobec oficerów Wojska Polskiego* (Warsaw, 1992); Gennadia Borgyunov, ed., *Polska-ZSRR: Struktury podległości* (Warsaw 1995); Henryk Dominiczak, *Organy bezpieczeństwa PRL 1944–1990* (Warsaw, 1997).

RADNÓTI Miklós [originally Glatter] (5 May 1909, Budapest–6 or 10 November 1944, Abda, Hungary), Hungarian poet of Jewish descent. Radnóti's mother died in childbirth, and his father died when Radnóti was eleven, so he was brought up by his uncle, the owner of a textile factory in Reichenberg (now Liberec, Czech Republic), where Radnóti worked to learn the business. It was in Reichenberg that he learned about the Communist movement, which had a great influence on his views and early poems. Radnóti never became a member of the Communist Party, though, because its dogmatism antagonized him. In 1930 he began to study Hungarian and Romance languages and literatures at the University of Szeged, and in the same year he published his first volume of poetry, *Pogány köszöntő* (Pagan greeting). In 1931 Radnóti published the volume *Újmódi pásztorok éneke* (Song of modern shepherds), which brought him greater publicity, but because of it he was sentenced to eight days' arrest for "indecency and inciting religious hatred." In 1934, by then under the surname of Radnóti, he earned a doctorate in the humanities, and one year later he obtained teaching qualifications. Radnóti earned a living by giving private lessons and from author's royalties. Almost every year he published a new poetry volume, each rich and varied in formal construction, content, and mood. His poetry collections include *Válogatott versek* (Selected poems; 1940) and *Tajtékos ég* (1946; *Foamy Sky: The Major Poems of Miklós Radnóti*, 1992). His only prose piece, *Ikrek hava* (1940; *Under Gemini*, 1985), was his lyrical and intimate confession about the experiences of his childhood and youth. From 1940 to 1944, when he had problems getting his own writings published, Radnóti often did translations, mainly from French literature. Radnóti served in forced labor battalions three times. This experience was reflected in a series of eight eclogues and in *razglednice* (postcards)—poetic notes written during a death march to Germany from the evacuated forced labor camp in Bor, Serbia. These notes, full of faith in humanism, were found after the war, when Radnóti's body was exhumed. (MS)

Sources: *Magyar Életrajzi Lexikon*, vol. 2 (Budapest, 1969); Imre Bori, *Radnóti Miklós költészete* (Újvidék, 1965); *The Poetry of Miklós Radnóti* (New York, 1986); Bela Pomogats, ed. *Emlék és varázslat: Vallomások Radnótiról* (Budapest, 1984); *Pisarze świata: Słownik encyklopedyczny* (Warsaw, 1999).

RADOSLAVOV Vasil (15 July 1854, Lovech–21 October 1929, Berlin), Bulgarian politician. After finishing high school in Prague, Radoslavov studied law in Heidelberg, Germany, and subsequently returned to Bulgaria, where he took a job as a journalist and became involved in politics. He became aligned with the Liberal Party. In 1884 Radoslavov became minister of justice. From August 1886 to July 1887 he was in charge of the government and held the post of minister of interior. From January 1899 to the beginning of 1901 he served as minister of interior again. Radoslavov gained notoriety for corruption and the bloody suppression of peasant revolts. He was a supporter of Bulgaria's cooperation with the Central Powers. In July 1913, during the Second Balkan War, Radoslavov called upon Tsar **Ferdinand** to cease cooperating with Russia because he believed that good relations with Austria-Hungary and Turkey were more important for Bulgaria. Radoslavov's strategy struck a chord with Ferdinand, who appointed him prime minister (18 July 1913). In the elections of December 1913 the ruling coalition did not win a majority of seats, but the support of the tsar saved Radoslavov's government. In the elections of March 1914 Radoslavov's government gained the support of a parliamentary majority but only because Muslims from the territories seized during the Balkan Wars were allowed to vote. Although Bulgarian finances had until then been supported chiefly by France, Radoslavov convinced the National Assembly to accept a loan from Germany and Austria-Hungary (July 1917).

When World War I began, Radoslavov's government was ever more inclined to support the Central Powers, which, he hoped, might reward Bulgaria at the expense of Serbia—an ally of Russia and the Entente—by, for instance, sending supplies for Turkey via Bulgaria. Formally, though, he maintained neutrality, encouraging both sides to bid for Bulgarian support. When Berlin and Vienna directly proposed that Bulgaria should take over Macedonia, Tsar Ferdinand and Radoslavov decided to sign a treaty (September 1915) by which the Central Powers accepted the establishment of a Greater Bulgaria. In October 1915 the Bulgarian Army attacked Serbia and occupied Macedonia. The opposition recognized this success, but when in early 1916 Radoslavov sent Bulgarian troops against Romania, in the hope of gaining Dobrudja, signs of discontent began to increase, in both the parliamentary opposition and the general public. The increasing costs of war in 1916 and 1917 and the lack of new successes further undermined the position of the government. Radoslavov was openly criticized as a "hireling of Berlin." The peace treaty concluded between Romania and the Central Powers in May 1918 prevented Bulgaria from gaining Dobrudja. In June 1918 the tsar dismissed Radoslavov and entrusted the task of forming a new government to **Aleksandur Malinov**, who was known for his pro-Western sympathies. Radoslavov still insisted that Bulgaria continue taking part in the war on the side of the Central Powers. After the Salonika Offensive of September 1918 ended in the success of the Allied forces and led to Bulgaria's capitulation, Radoslavov fled to Berlin. Under the rule of **Aleksandur Stamboliyski** Radoslavov was sentenced in absentia to life imprisonment for leading Bulgaria into the war. After Stamboliyski's fall in 1923, though, many politicians who had worked for the tsar were granted amnesty. In June 1929 Radoslavov was also pardoned but was severely ill and did not live to return to his country. In 1923 his memoirs, *Bulgarien und die Weltkriese* (Bulgaria and the world crisis), were published in Germany. (WR)

Sources: *Entsiklopediya Bulgariya*, vol. 5 (Sofia, 1986); *Obvinitelen akt protiv bivshute ministri ot kabineta na Dr V.Radoslavov prez 1913–1918 godini* (Sofia, 1921); Joachim von Königslöw, *Ferdinand von Bulgarien* (Munich, 1970); Stephen Constant, *Foxy Ferdinand, 1861–1948: Tsar of Bulgaria* (London, 1979); Holger H. Herwig and Neil M. Heyman, *Biographical Dictionary of World War I* (Westport, Conn., 1982); Richard C. Hall, *Bulgaria's Road to the First World War* (Boulder, Colo., 1996).

RADOVIĆ Andrija (28 January 1872, Martinići–1947 Belgrade), Montenegrin politician. Radović graduated from high school in Cetije and then completed engineering studies in Italy. He worked in the government administration; his positions included that of the head of a department in the Ministry of Interior. A close associate of **Prince Nicholas**, Radović served as prime minister from 1 February to 17 April 1907. In this role, he launched an investigation into embezzlement perpetrated by the state financial administration; this indirectly damaged the reputation of the prince. Dismissed by Nicholas, Radović emigrated for a short time. During World War I he reconciled with Nicholas, and in December 1915 he became minister of finance and minister of foreign affairs. In April 1916 he resigned as minister of foreign affairs. After Montenegro's defeat in the war in 1916, together with Nicholas, Radović fled the country. From 12 May 1916 to 17 January 1917 he again served as prime minister, this time heading the government-in-exile in Paris. Radović changed his political orientation, though, and sought a union of Montenegro with Serbia. In March 1917 he became head of the Montenegro Committee. He edited the Geneva-based periodical *Ujedninjenje* (1917–18), in which he promoted a program of uniting the South Slavic nations. After the establishment of the Kingdom of Serbs, Croats, and Slovenes (SHS), Radović served as an MP on the ticket of the Serbian Democratic Party (Srpska Demokratska Stranka) and held the post of chairman of the National Bank in Belgrade. Radović's publications include (under the pen name of Montinegrinus) *Ujedinjenje Crne Gore sa Serbijom* (The unification of Montenegro with Serbia; 1917). (WR)

Sources: *Enciklopedija Jugoslavije*, vol. 7 (Zagreb, 1968); John D. Treadway, *The Falcon and the Eagle: Montenegro and Austria-Hungary, 1908–191* (West Lafayette, Ind., 1983); www.rulers.org; www.montenegro.org.au/crnogorske_vlade.html.

RADULESCU Gheorghe (5 September 1914, Bucharest), Romanian Communist activist. As a student in a trade school in Bucharest, Radulescu joined the Union of Communist Youth, and in 1933 he became a member of the Communist Party of Romania. According to some sources, as a lieutenant in the Romanian Army during World War II, Radulescu deserted with his unit and went over to the Soviet side. Upon his return to Romania in March 1944, he started working at the Ministry of the Economy. Soon he was noticed by **Gheorghe Gheorghiu-Dej**, and in September 1949 he was appointed deputy minister of foreign affairs. After the dismissal of **Ana Pauker** in June 1952, Radulescu was also dismissed and even briefly arrested. In November 1956 he returned as minister of domestic trade. In March 1957, when the ministries of domestic and foreign trade were merged, Radulescu became deputy minister and, in August 1959, minister of trade. When the two ministries were separated again in 1962, Radulescu became minister of foreign trade. In October 1963 he was appointed deputy prime minister. From 1957 he was director of the Institute of Economic Research; from April 1959 to April 1962 he was deputy chairman and then, until 1963, chairman of the Economic Committee of the UN Social and Economic Council. From 1960 he was a member of the Communist Party Central Committee, and from 1961 he was a member of parliament. In July 1965, during the Ninth Congress of the Romanian Communist Party, Radulescu became a member of the newly established Political Executive Committee (PEC). From 1963 to March 1975 he chaired the government Commission for Economic and Technical Cooperation. From August 1969 to January 1977 and then from 1986 he was a member of the PEC Standing Committee. From April 1979 he was deputy chairman of the Council of State. After the fall of the **Nicolae Ceauşescu** regime in December 1989 Radulescu retired from political life. (PC)

Sources: *International Year Book and Statesmen's Who's Who* (London, 1990); *Who's Who in the Socialist Countries in Europe* (Munich, London, and Paris, 1978).

RADULOVIĆ Marko (15 December 1866, Pazici, Danilovgrad–?), Montenegrin politician. Radulović finished a primary school run by a monastery in Zdrebanik and subsequently attended secondary school, initially in Belgrade and then in the town of Zaječar, Serbia. In 1892 he completed law studies in Belgrade and assumed the post of assistant minister of justice of Montenegro. In 1893 he became responsible for affairs related to the administration of the judiciary. In 1896 he was appointed president of the district court in Danilovgrad. From 1903 to 1905 he served as president of the regional court in Podgorica. In 1905 Prince **Nicholas** granted a constitution to Montenegro and convened the parliament. In the same year Radulović became an MP. On 11 November 1906 he was appointed prime minister and minister of foreign affairs. He carried out a reform of the state budget and introduced parliamentary elections by secret ballot. However, he failed to win recognition from Nicholas, who dismissed him on 19 January 1907, dissolved parliament, and resumed an autocratic style of government. In 1910 Radulović opened a law practice in Cetinje. In 1913 he became a member of the Supreme Court. From December 1915 to April 1916 he served as minister of justice and vice-minister of education. During World War I the Montenegrin Army was defeated by Austro-Hungarian troops (January 1916), and Radulović was interned in Hungary and in Lower Austria from 1916 to 1918. After the establishment of the Kingdom of Serbs, Croats, and Slovenes, Radulović became a member of the Radical Party in 1919 and worked as a private lawyer. In 1924 he was appointed president of the court in Podgorica. Radulović was elected senator in 1932 and 1935. (AO)

Sources: www.mfa.gov.yu/history/MinistiCG/MRadulovic_s.html; Jerzy Skowronek, Mieczysław Tanty, and Tadeusz Wasilewski, *Historia Słowian południowych i zachodnich* (Warsaw, 1988).

RADZIŅŠ Pēteris Voldemārs (2 May 1880, Lugažu, Livonia–8 October 1930, Riga), Latvian general. Radziņš finished a *Realschule* in Valk and in 1901 a Junkers' school in Vilnius (Wilno). He subsequently served as an officer in the infantry of the Russian Army. He took part in the Russo-Japanese War, where he commanded a company. In 1910 he graduated from the General Staff Academy. During World War I he held staff positions. In February 1916 he became chief of staff of a division, and in 1917 he became a colonel. Dismissed from service in March 1918, he joined the Ukrainian Army, led by Hetman **Pavlo Skoropadskyi**, and served as head of a department in the General Staff. On 27 December 1918 Radziņš became assistant to the chief of staff of the army of the Ukrainian National Republic (UNR). In October 1919 he made his way via Poland to Latvia. On 27 October 1919 he was appointed chief of staff of the commander-in-chief of the Latvian Army. He prepared a battle plan against the German-supported forces of Pavel Bermondt-Avalov and then against the Red Army. In December 1919, along with General **Janis Balodis**, the commander-in-chief, Radziņš signed an agreement on Polish-Latvian military cooperation for liberating the eastern part of Latvia (Latgalia). Radziņš was in favor of close cooperation with the Polish Army. In February 1920 he was promoted to general. In October 1920 he retired from the army. In 1928 he became director of academic courses for officers. Radziņš was buried in a military cemetery in Riga. He was the holder of many awards and distinctions, including the Polish Order of Virtuti Militari. (EJ)

Sources: *Latvijas darbinieku galerija* (Riga, 1928); E. Prieditis, "Pulkvedis Pēteris Radziņš," *Militārais Apskats*, 1995, no. 2; *Latvijas armijas augstākie virsnieki 1918–1940: Biogrāfiska vārdnīca* (Riga, 1998).

RADZIWIŁŁ Janusz (3 September 1880, Berlin–4 October 1967, Warsaw), prince–heir in tail of Ołyka, Polish conservative politician, and economic activist. Radziwiłł was descended from the Berlin line of the Radziwiłł house. Politically, he was closest to the traditions of the conservative Kraków Stańczycy. He studied law at Berlin University and at the Forestry College in Eberswalde, near Berlin. In 1914 he organized a relief effort for refugees from the Congress Kingdom of Poland; it was carried out by the gentry from the Eastern Borderland (Kresy). After the outbreak of the February 1917 revolution Radziwiłł became, for a short time, a member of the Workers' and Soldiers' Council in Równe. Despite this, during the revolution he was forced to flee to Kiev and then to St. Petersburg, Finland, and Sweden. At the beginning of 1918 Radziwiłł reached Warsaw via Berlin; there, according to **Stanisław Mackiewicz**, the Germans offered him the Lithuanian crown. In the government of the Regency Council, between April and October 1918, Radziwiłł headed the Department of Political Affairs and then the Department of State, which was the germ of the Ministry of Foreign Affairs. He had a reputation as an advocate of activist option, seeking support both in Germany and in Austria-Hungary. Radziwiłł tried to take advantage of the contradictions between these two states. He also aimed at establishing contacts with neutral countries. Radziwiłł was one of the politicians who prepared the proclamation of 7 October 1918, which announced the creation of an independent Poland, with access to the sea. After unsuccessful talks with **Józef Piłsudski** and with leftist parties on broadening the political platform of the government, in November 1918 Radziwiłł withdrew from the political scene.

In 1922, during a disarmament conference in Moscow, Radziwiłł represented the interests of Poland and also Romania, which did not have diplomatic relations with Soviet Russia. After the coup of May 1926 he returned to active politics. He was a candidate for minister of foreign affairs in the first government of **Kazimierz Bartel**. From 1928 to 1935 Radziwiłł was an Assembly deputy from the Piłsudski lists and presided over the parliamentary committee for foreign affairs. In 1935–39 he was a senator. In the 1930s he successfully expanded his family fortune and supported the conservative newspapers *Dzień Polski* and *Czas*. After Piłsudski's death, Radziwiłł's political importance diminished. He opposed the electoral law changes that were being introduced by the ruling *sanacja*, and he defended **Wincenty Witos**. In 1931–37 he was president of the National Right Party (Stronnictwo Prawicy Narodowej) and a member of the leadership of the Central Union of Polish Industry—that is, the so-called Lewiatan.

After the outbreak of World War II Radziwiłł was initially imprisoned by the Soviets in Ołyka, and between September and December 1939 he was interrogated in Moscow—even personally by Lavrenty Beria, who unsuccessfully tried to talk him into some form of cooperation. Like other members of the Radziwiłł family, he was released as a result of the intervention of the Italian ruling family. With the consent of the main political forces in Poland and abroad, Radziwiłł went to Berlin with a mission to personally present the situation on the Polish territories to Hermann Goering. However, this mission failed and was in part the reason that Hans Frank blocked Radziwiłł's bid for the presidency of the Main Welfare Council. During the Nazi occupation Radziwiłł and his son Edmund, farming in Nieborów, maintained contacts with the Polish Home Army. After the collapse of the Warsaw Uprising, Radziwiłł, along with his wife, was taken to Berlin for interrogations. In the fall of 1944 he returned to Nieborów, where he took in many refugees from Warsaw. In January 1945, along with his wife, his son Edmund, and a group of other Polish aristocrats, Radziwiłł was arrested by the NKVD and imprisoned in a camp in Krasnogorsk. His wife Anna (née Lubomirska) died there. Radziwiłł returned to Poland in 1947. He lived in Warsaw in a two-room flat, which was given to him in return for his confiscated goods, and he did not participate in public life. In 1959 he lived for some time in the West, where he held several public meetings. (PK)

Sources: *PSB*; Stanisław Mackiewicz-Cat, *Historia Polski od 11 listopada 1918 r. do 5 lipca 1945 r.* (London, n.d.); Krzysztof Jasiewicz, *Zagłada polskich kresów* (Warsaw, 1998); Michał Czajka and Marcin Kamler, *Leksykon historii Polski* (Warsaw, 1995); *Słownik polityków polskich XX w* (Poznań, 1998).

RAHAMÄGI Hugo Bernhard (2 June 1886, Kurtna–1 September 1941, Kirov, USSR), Estonian clergyman, politician, and social activist. In 1906–13 Rahamägi studied theology in Yuryev (now Tartu, Estonia). He was a member of the Estonian Student Union (Eesti Üliõpilaste Seltsi) and served as chairman of the Tartu Association of Male Evangelical Youth (Tartu Evangeelsete Noorte Meeste Seltsi). From 1914 to 1920 he worked in the parish of Kaarma (Saaremaa Island), serving as head of the local Estonian Evangelical Lutheran Church (EELC) for one year. In 1920 he became an associate professor at Tartu University, and from 1926 to 1934 he was professor and dean of the School of Theology at this university. From 1923 to 1931 Rahamägi worked as an assessor at the EELC consistory and a teacher. A well-regarded author of theological works and religious poems, he was awarded an honorary doctorate by Uppsala University in 1932. In the 1930s Rahamägi served as vice-chairman of the Estonian Writers' Union and a member of many social organizations. Chairman of the Temperance Brotherhood and founder of the Union of Nordic and Baltic Lutheran Churches, he was one of the leading activists of the Estonian Christian Democratic movement. He became a member of the first parliament. This parliament was dominated by the left wing, but owing to Rahamägi's efforts, the Evangelicals achieved success when proposals to remove religion from public schools were rejected in a 1923 referendum. The campaign over religious education led to great success for the Christian Democratic Party in the 1923 parliamentary elections, and Rahamägi rose to become one of the party leaders. Minister of education

in the government of **Friedrich Akel**, he maintained this position in the nonparty government of **Jüri Jaakson** (March 1924–December 1925), at a time of sharp political struggle against the left wing. At that period, as the assessor in the consistory, Rahamägi was one of the highest Church dignitaries.

On 19 June 1934 Rahamägi was elected bishop of the EELC. His election coincided with a coup d'état staged by **Konstantin Päts** and marked a new stage in the relations between the Church and the state. The EELC was generally opposed to democracy, while Päts, who fought against the radical right wing, needed support from the Church. Under these circumstances, both sides decided to reach a compromise. The EELC was officially recognized as a state institution, and clergymen were granted many privileges; in exchange, the Ministry of Internal Affairs was given the right to assign pastoral positions. Meanwhile, Rahamägi had an extramarital affair that led to a conflict in which theological elements were mixed with political ones. Owing to the scandal and a rift within the EELC, the government reacted sharply: Rahamägi was suspended as bishop. The consistory and the Council of the EELC were also suspended. The Ministry of Internal Affairs imposed a new administrator, who was in charge until the election of new authorities. Finally dismissed in 1939, Rahamägi was succeeded by **Johan Kõpp**. After the Red Army occupied Estonia, Rahamägi was arrested. Sentenced to death on 25 July 1941, he was subsequently murdered in prison. (AG)

Sources: *Eesti Entsuklopeedia*, vol. 14 (Tallinn, 2000); Andres Kasekamp, *The Radical Right in Interwar Estonia* (London, 2000); Web site of the EELC parish of Sts. Peter and Paul in Kaarma, Saaremaa, www.saaremaa.ee/kaarmakirik/opetajad.htm; EELC Web site, www.eelk.ee/1_reisil.html.

RAINIS Jānis [originally Jānis Pliekšāns] (11 September 1865, Dunavas, Courland–12 September 1929, Majori), Latvian poet. In 1879 Rainis graduated from a German school in Grīva, and in 1883 from a German high school in Riga. In 1888 he graduated from the School of Law of the University of St. Petersburg. He began writing poems as a high school student. In 1884 he translated *Boris Godunov*, the tragedy by Aleksandr Pushkin, into Latvian. From 1889 to 1891 Rainis worked in the Vilnius District Court. From 1891 to 1895 he edited the Riga newspaper *Dienas Lapa*, which was the center of a leftist poetic movement known as the New Current. Rainis wrote numerous articles on popular education and on the democratic development of society. His views were greatly influenced by the German Socialists. In 1895 Rainis began working as a notary public in Mitava (Jelgava), and in March

1897 he became an attorney in Panevėžys. That same year he married Elza Rozenberga (**Aspāzija**). Arrested in May 1897 for his involvement with New Current, he was imprisoned in Panevėžys, Liepāja, and Riga. While in prison, Rainis translated *Faust*, by Johann Wolfgang Goethe, into Latvian. In 1899, Rainis was banished to Slobodka, near Vyatka, where he continued writing; he also translated works by Henrik Ibsen, Gotthold E. Lessing, Heinrich Heine, and Pushkin. His own poems of that period expressed a premonition of a great social upheaval. For example, in his first volume of poetry, *Tālas noskaņas zilā vakarā* (Far-off reflections on a blue evening), natural phenomena allegorically reflected social problems.

In 1903 Rainis returned to Latvia. He took part in the 1905 revolution, which, he believed, was the beginning of the liberation of the Latvian nation from Russian rule. At that time he wrote poems and stage plays in which he used allegory to depict the national struggle against evil; one example was the drama *Uguns un nakts* (1946; *Fire and Night*, 1981). In December 1905, along with his wife Aspazija, Rainis, using an assumed name, went to Switzerland. He settled on Lake Lugano, where he wrote stage plays, poetry, and articles. At that time he called for close cooperation among Estonia, Latvia, and Lithuania within the framework of a federation. Elected chairman of the Latvian Committee in Switzerland in 1917, Rainis supported the cause of Latvian independence. In April 1920 he returned via Warsaw to Latvia and was enthusiastically welcomed by thousands of people. Elected deputy to the Constitutional Assembly, in 1922 he entered the Saeima (Parliament) on the ticket of the Social Democratic Workers' Party of Latvia. From 1920 to 1921 Rainis also served as director of Riga's Dailes Theater. From 1926 to 1928 he held the post of minister of education. He also wrote poems for children. Rainis was buried in Riga. His works were published in thirty volumes and his translations in four volumes. Rainis's works had a great influence on the national consciousness of the Latvian people. Under Soviet rule his works were initially banned from publication, but after 1956 they were more and more often republished. Rainis's monument in the center of Riga has been preserved. (EJ)

Sources: Antons Birkerts, *J. Rainis dzīvē un darbā* (Riga, 1930); Karlis Dziļleja, *Raiņa ģenealoģija* (Riga, 1932); Antons Birkerts, *J. Raiņa dzīve: Rainis J. Dzīve un darbi*, vol. 1 (Riga, 1937); Felikss Cielēns, *Rainis un Aspazija* (Vesterosa, 1955); Ēvalds Sokols, *Rainis* (Riga, 1962); Viktors Hausmanis, *Rainis un treātris* (Riga, 1965); Kārlis Freinbergs, *Kopā ar Raini* (Riga, 1974); Saulcerīte Viese, *Jaunais Rainis* (Riga, 1982); *Rainis laikabiedru atmiņās* (Riga, 1985); *Rainim 125* (Riga, 1990); Imants Ziedonis, *Mūžības temperaments* (Riga, 1991); Andrejs Plakans, *Historical Dictionary of Latvia* (Lanham, Md., 1997).

RAJK László (8 March 1909, Székelyudvarhely [now in Romania]–15 October 1949, Budapest), Hungarian Communist activist. Rajk's father was a Szekler shoemaker. Rajk attended secondary school in his home town and then in Budapest. From 1927 he studied Hungarian and French philology at Péter Pázmány University in Budapest. In 1928 he went to France. After his return in 1930 he joined the illegal Communist movement. From 1931 he was a member of the Communist Union of Young Workers and of the Hungarian Communist Party (HCP). He was repeatedly arrested, and as a result he could not continue his studies. From 1933 Rajk worked as a construction worker. He was one of the main organizers and initiators of a construction workers' strike in 1935, for which he was expelled from Hungary. In 1936, on the recommendation of the party, Rajk went to Prague and from there to Spain, where he took part in the civil war. He served as a political commissar of the Hungarian battalion in the International Brigade, and he was severely wounded in the fighting. In Spain Rajk was accused of Trotskyism, and only in 1941 did the Communist International clear him of the charges. After the fall of the Spanish Republic, Rajk was interned in France. In 1941 he returned to Hungary, where he was imprisoned. After his release in September 1944, he obtained false documents and became secretary of the CC of the HCP. He was also one of the leaders of the Hungarian National Independence Front, thus one of the main organizers of the resistance movement. In December 1944 Rajk was arrested by members of the Arrow Cross Party, who did not, however, find out his true role. Thus his brother Endre, a minister without portfolio in the government of the Arrow Cross Party, managed to save him from execution. Rajk was taken to a prison in Sopronkőhida and then to Germany; from there he returned to Hungary in May 1945.

In Hungary Rajk joined the executive organs of the HCP and the Provisional National Assembly. Between May and November 1945 he was secretary of the party's CC; until March 1946 he was deputy secretary general; in 1945–46 and 1948–49 he was a member of the Politburo, and until August 1948 he was minister of the interior. Rajk played a major role in the Communist takeover and in breaking up the structures of the civil society. Under the guise of prosecuting Fascist and reactionary groups, he dissolved or banned many religious, national, or other democratic institutions and organizations. He co-organized the first show trials. In 1947 he covered up electoral fraud in the form of the so-called blue cards. Thanks to these cards, the functionaries of the HCP cast several thousand—and according to some estimates, almost two hundred thousand—additional votes. Rajk ruthlessly eliminated real or alleged anti-Stalinist forces. He was one of the most consistent executors of "salami tactics." At the same time a competition for power intensified among Rajk, **Gábor Pétér**, and **Mihály Farkas**. **Mátyás Rákosi** also feared Rajk because of the popularity that he had gained among party members. Therefore in August 1948 Rajk was dismissed as minister of interior and was appointed to the less important post of minister of foreign affairs.

At the end of May 1949 Rajk was arrested on the basis of fabricated evidence. His trial in September of that year was given great publicity. For example, live reports of the trial proceedings were broadcast on the radio. In this and in other similar concurrent trials, a total of nearly one hundred sentences were passed, including more than twenty death sentences. One of the main aims of the so-called trial for Rajk was to launch a propaganda campaign against **Josip Broz Tito**. Rajk's group was charged with, for example, trying to provoke riots in the country and to liquidate Communist leaders. During interrogations the accused were repeatedly tortured and mentally terrorized. For example, Rajk's friend, **János Kádár**, tried to make Rajk take on the role of a Titoist traitor for the sake of the proletarian authorities. On 24 September 1949 the people's court, accusing Rajk of crimes against humanity and treason (spying), sentenced him to death. The trial became a model for similar trials in other countries of the Soviet bloc. Rajk was executed; his body was flooded with lime and buried by a suburban road. His wife was sentenced to many years in prison, and his infant son, was sent to a state educational institution. In March 1956 Rajk was rehabilitated. His ceremonial funeral, organized on 6 October 1956, changed into a demonstration against the Rákosi regime and became a prelude to the Hungarian Revolution. (JT)

Sources: *Magyar Életrajzi Lexikon*, vol. 2 (Budapest, 1969); Béla Szász, *Volunteers for the Gallows: Anatomy of a Show-Trial* (New York, 1972); *Rajk-dossié: Soltész István dokumentumválogatása* (Budapest, 1989); *A magyar forradalom és szabadságharc enciklopédiája*, CD-ROM (Budapest, 1999); Bennet Kovrig, *Communism in Hungary from Kun to Kádár* (Stanford, 1979).

RAK-MIKHAILOUSKI Shyman (14 April 1885, Maksimauka, near Molodechno–1937), Belorussian social activist and politician. In 1904 Rak-Mikhailouski graduated from a teacher training college in Molodechno. He took an active part in the revolutionary events of 1905–7 in Belorussia. From 1908 to 1912 he studied at the Pedagogical Institute in Feodosiya in the Crimea. Until 1914 he worked as a teacher in the Belorussian territories. Mobilized in 1914, he fought on the Romanian front. In 1917 Rak-Mikhailouski worked for the establishment of Belorussian

national organizations among soldiers, and he became head of the Belorussian Central Military Council, which tried to organize separate Belorussian military units. After returning from the front lines in 1917, Rak-Mikhailouski served as one of the leaders of the Belorussian Socialist Hromada. He helped to organize and then took part in the proceedings of the First All-Belorussian Congress in December 1917, and he became a member of the Council of the Belorussian National Republic (BNR). He served as head of the military department of the BNR Executive Committee. In 1918, as a representative of the BNR government, Rak-Mikhailouski organized the Belorussian educational system in the region of Minsk. In 1920, along with his family, he settled in Wilno (Vilnius), where he became a member of the Belorussian National Committee. From 1920 to 1922 he worked as a mathematics teacher at a Belorussian high school. At that time he prepared a math textbook in Belorussian for secondary schools. He also edited *Belaruskae slova*. In 1922 Rak-Mikhailouski became a member of the Polish parliament. Along with **Branislau Tarashkevich**, the chairman of the Belorussian parliamentary representation, he initially sought an agreement with Polish politicians on cultural autonomy for the Belorussians who were citizens of the Second Republic of Poland. In 1923, together with two other MPs, Rak-Mikhailouski established a parliamentary representation of the Belorussian Independent Socialists.

In the mid-1920s, when hopes for cultural autonomy failed, Rak-Mikhailouski declared himself a supporter of the integration of the Belorussian territories within the framework of the Belorussian SSR. In 1926 he joined the Communist Party of Western Belorussia and was one of the founders of the pro-Soviet Belorussian Peasants' and Workers' Hromada. Arrested in January 1927 and sentenced to twelve years' imprisonment by the Wilno District Court, Rak-Mikhailouski was handed over to the Soviet authorities as part of an exchange of political prisoners in 1931. He was freed in the USSR and became director of the Belorussian State Museum in Minsk. He was arrested in the USSR by the NKVD in 1933 and sentenced to ten years in labor camps on charges of Belorussian nationalism. Tried again in 1937, he was sentenced to death on the charge of spying for Poland, and then he was executed. According to another version, Rak-Mikhailouski died in a labor camp on the Solovets Islands. (EM)

Sources: *Belaruskaia Savetskaia Entsyklapedyia*, vol. 9 (Minsk, 1973); *Belarus: Entsyklapedychny davednik* (Minsk, 1995); Nicholas P. Vakar, *Belorussia: The Making of a Nation* (Cambridge, Mass., 1956); Aleksandra Bergman, *Sprawy białoruskie w II* Rzeczypospolitej (Warsaw, 1984); Vitaut Kipel and Zora Kipel, eds., *Byelorussian Statehood* (New York, 1988); *Kto był kim w Drugiej* Rzeczypospolitej (Warsaw, 1994).

RÁKOSI Mátyás (9 March 1892, Ada [now in Yugoslavia]–5 February 1971, Gorky, USSR), Hungarian Communist leader. Born into the family of a small shopkeeper of Jewish origin, Rákosi graduated from high school, and from 1910 he studied at the Academy of Eastern Commerce in Budapest, joining the Hungarian Social Democratic Party. In 1912 he obtained his diploma. Rákosi mastered six languages—an indication of his intellectual abilities. From 1912 to 1914 Rákosi trained in trading firms in Hamburg and London. At the beginning of 1915 he was sent to the eastern front. He was taken into Russian captivity, where he met the Bolsheviks. At the beginning of 1918 he escaped and returned to Hungary. He became a training officer in an infantry regiment that was stationed in Szabadka (now Subotica) in Voivodina. In December 1918 Rákosi was one of the founders of the Hungarian Communist Party (HCP). In March 1919, after the proclamation of the Hungarian Soviet Republic (HSR), he was appointed deputy people's commissar for commerce, and he also became a member of the Revolutionary Government Council. From April Rákosi was people's commissar and a member of the governing body of the People's Committee for Socialist Production and of the Supreme Council of the People's Economy. At the end of April he was appointed political commissar of the southern front, in June a member of the Central Revision Committee of the Government Council, and in July 1919 commander of the Hungarian Red Guards.

After the fall of the HSR in August 1919, Rákosi went to Vienna, where he was interned along with other Communist émigrés. In 1920 he was released; after a speech he gave on 1 May, he was expelled from Austria and prohibited to return. Rákosi left for Soviet Russia and joined the Executive Committee of the Communist International. In 1921 he became secretary of the Comintern. In December 1924 he was dispatched to Hungary. Following Comintern instructions, he formed the Hungarian Socialist Labor Party, which was a legal appendage of the delegalized HCP. At an HCP Congress in 1925 Rákosi was elected a member of the CC and was entrusted with managing the national secretariat. In September 1925 he was arrested in Hungary, along with the entire leadership, and was accused of instigating riots. In 1926 Rákosi was sentenced to eight and a half years in prison. Upon the expiration of his term, he was again brought to trial for his activities at the time of the HSR and was sentenced to life. In 1940, in exchange Moscow's returning the Honvéd banners of the 1848 revolution, Rákosi was allowed to go to the USSR. His two trials made Rákosi one of the most noted personages of the international Communist movement. Nonetheless, after his arrival in Moscow, disciplinary proceedings were conducted against him. These proceedings had already been initiated earlier because of his behavior during the investigation of his 1925 arrest. In 1942 Rákosi became the leading politician of the Hungarian Communist émigrés. At first he was the HCP representative in the Comintern and, after its official dissolution in 1943, a member and head of the Foreign Committee of the informal continuation of the Comintern. He was also one of the editors of Kossuth Radio in Moscow.

At the end of January 1945 the Soviet leadership dispatched Rákosi to Debrecen to reorganize the HCP. He assumed the post of general secretary of the party's CC. After the elections of November 1945 Rákosi was minister without portfolio; from February 1946 he was deputy prime minister; and after the elections of August 1947 he was again minister without portfolio. On 12 June 1948, at the founding congress of the Hungarian Workers' Party (HWP), Rákosi was elected the party's general secretary. On 14 August 1952 he became president of the Council of Ministers, combining, on the Soviet model, the highest party and state posts. From his return to Hungary, Rákosi was number one among the Communists. As early as 1945 his political rank and influence were greater than his formal positions would suggest. In May 1947, while serving as head of the government in the absence of Prime Minister **Ferenc Nagy**, Rákosi accused Nagy of a plot against the state and forced him to resign, blackmailing him that he would not allow his wife and son to leave the country. In the cabinet of **Lajos Dinnyés**, who was obedient to the Communists, Rákosi continued to hold the post of deputy prime minister. He succeeded in breaking up the opposition, and he was instrumental in the "victory" of the Communist bloc in the elections of 1947 and 1949.

As the HWP leader, after the Communist takeover Rákosi was the all-powerful head of the country, as well as the embodiment not only of the personality cult, but also of a Stalinist dictatorship in its Hungarian version. He was responsible for the collectivization of agriculture, the suppression of the Catholic Church and other religions, and purges in the party—under such guises as the fight against Titoism. From the very beginning Rákosi personally supervised the Office of State Security (Államvédelmi Hatóság [ÁVH]). Developing the Communist dictatorship, he tried to follow Stalin and the USSR pattern in every aspect, including the fact that in an almost Byzantine way he demanded to be worshipped as the best Hungarian pupil of Stalin.

After Stalin's death, when "collective leadership" prevailed in the Kremlin and Rákosi's protector, Vyacheslav Molotov, was struggling against his rivals, Rákosi lost full control over Hungary. At a meeting of the CC of the HWP in June 1953, according to Soviet directives, Rákosi was dismissed as prime minister. He resigned on 4 July 1953. During the tenure of his successor, **Imre Nagy**, Rákosi tried by all means to sabotage Nagy's attempts at correcting the system. From May 1954 Rákosi headed the committee dealing with the rehabilitation of show trial victims, but he worked to postpone resolutions on the rehabilitation of party members who had been illegally sentenced—for example, **Laszlo Rajk** and his associates, whose trials and executions Rákosi had supervised in 1949.

With the fall of Georgy Malenkov in the Kremlin, Rákosi's position strengthened again. In the spring of 1955, after persistent intrigues and with Soviet support, he caused the departure of Imre Nagy, but he could no longer control the growing ferment. After the Twentieth Congress of the CPSU even some of his former comrades in the Hungarian leadership turned against him. Rákosi tried unsuccessfully to shift the responsibility for political trials onto **Gábor Pétér** and **Mihály Farkas**. At the same time he tried to save his position by attacking the party opposition. At a CC plenum on 12 July 1956 Rákosi accused Nagy and his associates of a "plot" and demanded their arrest. This provoked a reaction from Moscow. Six days later, at a meeting of the CC, under pressure from Anastas Mikoyan, who arrived from the USSR, Rákosi was dismissed as first secretary in favor of **Ernő Gerő** and dropped from the Politburo. After this meeting, alleging illness, Rákosi went to the USSR for treatment. During the Hungarian Revolution he was in Moscow. On 5 November 1956 the Presidium of the CC of the CPSU made a decision to ultimately remove Rákosi from power, although he repeatedly wrote to the CC of the CPSU and to Khrushchev asking for their consent to his quick return to Hungary. The CPSU decision was a guarantee to **János Kádár** that he did not have to fear the return of Rákosi.

Until the end of his life Rákosi was under the illusion that the Hungarian nation was waiting for his return, whereas he was the most detested person in Hungary. In February 1957 the leadership of the Hungarian Socialist Workers' Party (HSWP) decided that Rákosi would not be allowed to return to Hungary for five years. The resolution of the HSWP was approved by the CC of the CPSU in April 1957. In June of that year Rákosi was removed from Moscow; along with his wife he was transferred to Krasnodar, then to the town of Tokmak in Kyrgyz SSR, and finally to the town of Gorky. At the beginning of November 1960 the Politburo of the HSWP suspended Rákosi's party membership, and in August 1962 it expelled him from the party as the main person responsible for the personality cult and for lawlessness. In April 1970 the CC of the HSWP considered allowing Rákosi to return to the

country if he agreed in writing not to return to politics, but Rákosi did not accept such a condition. Soon after his death, Rákosi's ashes were secretly brought to Hungary and buried at Farkasréti Cemetery in Budapest. In 1997 his memoirs, titled *Visszaemlékezések, 1940–1956* (Memoirs, 1940–1956) were published. (JT)

Sources: *Magyar Életrajzi Lexikon*, vol. 3 (Budapest, 1985); *Current Biography*, 1949, 1971; Bennet Kovrig, *Communism in Hungary from Kun to Kádár* (Stanford, 1979); János Botos et al., *Magyar hétköznapok: Rákosi Mátyás két emigrációja között, 1945–1956* (Budapest, 1988); Árpád Pünkösti, *Rákosi a hatalomért: 1945–1948* (Budapest, 1992); István Feitl, *A bukott Rákosi. Rákosi Mátyás 1956–1971 között: Tanulmány* (Budapest, 1993); Árpád Pünkösti, *Rákosi a csúcson, 1948–1953* (Budapest, 1996); *Nagy Képes Milleniumi Arcképcsarnok* (Budapest, 1999); *A magyar forradalom és szabadságharc enciklopédiája*, CD-ROM (Budapest, 1999).

RAKOVSKY Khristian, pseudonym "H. Insarov" (1 August 1873, Gradec, near Kotel, Dobrudja–11 September 1941), Bulgarian Communist activist in the Ukraine. The son of a rich landowner and merchant from Dobrudja, Rakovsky was a nephew of Georgi Sava Rakovski, a poet and revolutionary. Rakovsky attended a gymnasium in Kotel but was expelled for organizing a student strike. He later studied at Geneva University (1890–93). In 1897 in Montpellier, France, he earned a medical degree. In his thesis Rakovsky argued that all social pathologies were generated by capitalism. For a short time he also studied law at the University of Paris (1903–4). In 1897–1900 Rakovsky worked as a doctor in the Romanian Army. In his youth, Rakovsky was aligned with revolutionary organizations, supporting them with his family wealth. While in Geneva, he became involved in the Socialist movement. He joined the Russian Social Democratic Party and edited the periodical *Sotsialdemokrat*. Arrested and deported in 1893, Rakovsky established ties with revolutionary groups in Berlin. After he had been arrested and deported for the second time, he went to France. He joined the Bulgarian Social Democratic Workers' Party, which he represented at a congress of the Second International. Rakovsky was also active in Romanian, German, Swiss, Russian, and Ukrainian revolutionary organizations. He worked with Vladimir Lenin and Leon Trotsky, and he contributed to Russian revolutionary newspapers in exile, *Iskra* and *Pravda*.

From 1900 to 1903 Rakovsky was in Russia, where he was kept under surveillance by the tsarist police. He subsequently opened a medical practice in Paris. In 1904 he inherited his father's fortune and then settled in Constanța, where he worked as a doctor and lawyer. In March 1905 he revived the Socialist periodical *România Muncitoare*. He supported and initiated strikes and revolutionary riots in Romania. He conducted agitation among crew members of the Russian battleship *Potemkin* who had revolted and then sought refuge in Constanţa. Despite his advice, the Russian sailors refused to send their battleship to Russia to support the revolution. In 1907 the Romanian authorities banned Rakovsky from returning to Romania because of riots that had turned into a peasant revolution. He went to live in Germany and France. Rakovsky returned to Romania in 1910 but was arrested and expelled. He moved to Bulgaria, where he edited the periodical *Napred*. Amnestied in 1912, he undertook lawful activities in Romania. In 1914 Rakovsky protested against World War I. In September 1915 he attended the Zimmerwald Conference and subsequently continued revolutionary activities in Romania. Arrested by the Romanian authorities in August 1916, Rakovsky was released after the capitulation of Romania in May 1917. During the German counteroffensive he moved to Russia, where he worked with the Bolsheviks in Odessa and St. Petersburg. From August to December 1917, fearing arrest by the government of Aleksandr Kerensky, Rakovsky was in hiding in Sweden, and he did not take part in the Bolshevik coup.

In January 1918 Rakovsky officially joined the Bolshevik party and was coopted into its Central Committee (CC). Appointed head of the Cheka in the Ukraine, he also served as a member of the Executive Committee of the Communist International. From January 1919 to July 1923 Rakovsky held the post of chairman of the Council of People's Commissars (the government) of the Ukraine. An advocate of autonomy for the republics within the framework of the Soviet Union, Rakovsky clashed on this issue with Stalin. He was a member of the Soviet delegation to a conference in Genoa (1922). Subsequently, as the Soviet deputy commissar for foreign affairs, he held diplomatic posts in Great Britain (1923–25) and France (1925–27). In January 1928, as one of the leaders of the Trotskyite opposition, Rakovsky was removed from all his positions and banished to Central Asia. He was held in Astrakhan, then in Saratov, and later in Barnaul, increasingly harsh conditions. In 1934 Rakovsky publicly dissociated himself from Trotsky and his earlier views. He was allowed to return to Moscow and was reinstated in the party and given a post in the scientific institute of the Commissariat of Health. Arrested in the fall of 1937, Rakovsky was forced to admit to being a British and Japanese agent. In March 1938 he was sentenced to twenty years of hard labor. He was executed in prison after the Third Reich invaded the Soviet Union. Rakovsky was the author of numerous articles and brochures, including "Rossiya na istok" (Russian policy in the East;

1898), "France contemporaire" (1901), "La Roumanie des Boyars" (1909), and "Roumania and Bessarabia" (1925). (MC)

Sources: *Encyclopedia of Ukraine*, vol. 4 (Toronto, 1993); Francis Conte, *Un révolutionnaire-diplomate: Christian Rakovski, L'Union soviétique et l'Europe (1922–1941)* (Paris, 1978); Gus Fagan, "Biographical Introduction to Christian Rakovsky," *Selected Writings on Opposition in the USSR 1923–30* (London and New York, 1980); Francis Conte, *Christian Rakovski (1873–1941): A Political Biography* (Boulder, Colo., 1989); Robert Conquest, *The Great Terror: A Reassessment* (New York and Oxford, 1990); Jarosław Hrycak, *Historia Ukrainy 1772–1999* (Lublin, 2002); www.spartacus.schoolnet.co.uk/RUSrakovsky.htm; www.marxists.org/archive/rakovsky/.

RAKOWSKI Mieczysław (4 December 1926, Kowalewko), Polish Communist activist. Born into a peasant family, during World War II Rakowski worked as a blue-collar laborer in Poznań. In 1945–49 he served in the army. From 1946 he belonged to the (Communist) Polish Workers' Party, and from December 1948, to the Polish United Workers' Party (Polska Zjednoczona Partia Robotnicza [PUWP]). From 1949 Rakowski worked in the PUWP Central Committee (CC) apparatus, and in 1955–57, in the Department of Propaganda of the PUWP CC. In 1955 Rakowski graduated from the Institute of Social Sciences of the PUWP CC, and two years later he received a Ph.D. in history there. From 1957 to 1958 he was deputy editor-in-chief, and then (until 1982) editor-in-chief, of the weekly *Polityka*. Under his leadership it won great popularity and was recognized as a relatively open and modern periodical. In 1958–61 Rakowski chaired the Main Board of the Union of Polish Journalists. In 1968 he and his staff were attacked by the National Communists, but Rakowski managed to maintain his line. Making use of his position, he established numerous international contacts, particularly among German and Austrian Social Democrats. At the same time he advanced in the party ranks. In 1964 Rakowski became a deputy member, and in 1975 a member, of the PUWP CC. In 1972–89 he was a member of parliament. He enjoyed a reputation as a party "liberal," ready to participate in discussions and consider reforms.

In February 1981 General **Wojciech Jaruzelski** appointed Rakowski deputy prime minister. Rakowski served in this capacity until November 1985. After the introduction of martial law on 13 December 1981, Rakowski was among the closest aides of Jaruzelski, dealing with (among other things) the politically delicate issue of trade unions. In August 1983 Rakowski visited the Gdańsk Shipyard, where during a televised meeting he clashed with **Lech Wałęsa**. This was Wałęsa's first public appearance after the introduction of martial law. Rakowski's aggressive attitude was badly received by the workers. As deputy prime minister, Rakowski chaired the government Sociopolitical Committee and the Youth Committee. In 1985–88 he was deputy speaker of the parliament and chaired its Socioeconomic Commission. From 1987 he chaired the Society for the Support of Economic Initiatives. In December 1987 he became a member of the PUWP CC Politburo.

After a wave of summer strikes, on 27 September 1988 Rakowski became prime minister. Despite his efforts, he failed to attract to the government any representatives of the opposition, with whom he wanted to share responsibility for the economic crash. Rakowski slowed down preparations for the Round Table Talks with the opposition. His controversial decision to close down the Gdańsk Shipyard, the cradle of Solidarity—allegedly for economic reasons—was treated as a challenge by the opposition. Rakowski's government started to liberalize the economic system (the commercialization of state enterprises, freedom of economic activity, the liberalization of foreign exchange); this helped the party nomenklatura to appropriate state assets. During the Tenth Plenum of the PUWP CC in December 1988 and January 1989 Rakowski finally supported the idea of the Round Table Talks, held from February to April 1989. In the elections of 4 June 1989 Rakowski ran on the so-called national ballot, but he lost. In July 1989, when Jaruzelski was elected president, Rakowski became the PUWP CC first secretary and served in this capacity until the party was dissolved on 27 January 1990. He then joined the Social Democracy of the Polish Republic, which had emerged on the ruins of the PUWP. From 1990 Rakowski was editor-in-chief of the post-Communist monthly *Dziś*. Among other works, Rakowski published his memoirs, *Jak to się stało?* (How did this happen? 1991), and four volumes of diaries from 1967 to 1978 (1999–2002). (PK)

Sources: Mołdawa; *Słownik polityków polskich XX wieku* (Poznań, 1998); Antoni Czubiński, *Dzieje Najnowsze Polski 1944–1989* (Poznań, 1992); Jan Skórzyński, *Ugoda i rewolucja: Władza i opozycja 1985–89* (Warsaw, 1995); Włodzimierz Janowski and Aleksander Kochański, *Informator o strukturze i obsadzie personalnej centralnego aparatu PZPR 1948–1990* (Warsaw, 2000); Andrzej Paczkowski, *Droga do "mniejszego zła": Strategia i taktyka obozu władzy lipiec 1980-styczeń 1982* (Kraków, 2002).

RALEA Mihail (1 May 1896, Huşi–17 August 1964, Berlin), Romanian psychologist, literary critic, and leftist activist. In 1919 Ralea graduated from the School of Law and the Department of Literature of the University of Iaşi. From 1919 to 1923 he studied at the École Normale Supérieure in Paris, earning doctorates in philosophy and law. Both of his doctoral dissertations dealt with Com-

munist ideals, with which Ralea associated himself. After returning to Romania, Ralea worked at the University of Iaşi, initially as a lecturer in social pedagogy and then as a professor of psychology and esthetics. He published articles in the periodical *Viaţa româneasca*, which came out in Iaşi (until 1930) and subsequently in Budapest. From 1933 to 1940 Ralea was the editor-in-chief of *Viaţa româneasca*. This periodical condemned the cosmopolitanism of the elites and regarded the peasantry as the class that preserved the spirit of Romania. In 1938 Ralea became professor of esthetics at Bucharest University and later director of the Institute of Psychology in Bucharest. After King **Charles II** disbanded political parties, Ralea served as minister of labor (March 1938–July 1940). When General **Ion Antonescu** came to power and established a dictatorship, Ralea joined the underground resistance movement and worked with the Communists. In 1943 he founded the Socialist Peasant Party, which in the same year entered the Patriotic Anti-Nazi Front (Frontul Patriotic Antihitlerist), formed by the Communists and leftist parties. After Antonescu's government had been overthrown, the Socialist Peasant Party merged with the Communist Party. Ralea became minister of arts (March 1945–August 1946) and editor-in-chief (1944–46) of the revived *Viaţa româneasca*. In 1946 he was a member of the Romanian delegation to the Paris Peace Conference, and then he was appointed ambassador to the United States. In 1948 he became a member of the Romanian Academy of Sciences. He represented Romania in international organizations. Ralea's publications include *Problema inconştientului* (The problem of unconsciousness; 1925); *Psihologie şi viaţă* (Psychology and life; 1938); *Introducere în sociologie* (Introduction to sociology; 1944); and *Istoria psihologiei* (The history of psychology; 1955), as well as essays and memoirs. (LW)

Sources: Halina Mirska-Lasota, *Mały słownik pisarzy rumuńskich* (Warsaw, 1975); Andrzej Koryn, *Rumunia w polityce wielkich mocarstw 1944–1947* (Wrocław, 1984); Dorina N. Rusu, *Membrii Academiei Române 1866–1999* (Bucharest, 1999); Ion Alexandrescu, Ion Bulei, Ion Mamina, and Ioan Scurtu, *Enciclopedia de istorie României* (Bucharest, 2000).

RAMANAUSKAS Adolfas, pseudonym "Vanagas" (Hawk) (1918, United States–1957, Kaunas, Lithuania), leader of the Lithuanian anti-Soviet partisan movement. Ramanauskas was born into a family of Lithuanian émigrés in the United States who returned to Lithuania when he was three years old. He graduated from the Kaunas Military School, and in 1939 he also finished a pedagogical institute. During the first Soviet occupation (1940–41) Ramanauskas avoided deportation. From 1941 to 1944 he taught at a teacher training college in Alytus and was active in an anti-German pro-independence underground movement. When the Red Army again seized Lithuania in the summer of 1944, Ramanauskas became engaged in the partisan struggle. In 1945 he commanded a partisan group in Merkinė, and in 1948 he became commander of units in the region of Dainava, southern Lithuania. In 1949 he was appointed adjutant to the command of the partisan Movement of Lithuania's Struggle for Freedom (Lietuvos Laisvės Kovu Sąjudis), and in December 1951 he became its chairman and commander-in-chief, consolidating the central command center. However, the partisan struggle was ending, undermined by the collectivization of agriculture and the deportation of thousands of peasants. Seeing that the situation of the underground resistance was becoming hopeless, in 1952 Ramanauskas ordered that the partisans end the military struggle, return to civilian life, and take up passive resistance. Ramanauskas himself continued the underground struggle until 1956. Captured by Soviet special services, he was executed without trial. (WR)

Sources: *EL*, vol. 4; V. Ramojus, *Kritusieji už laisvę* (Chicago, 1954); Romuald J. Misiunas and Rein Taagepera, *The Baltic States: Years of Dependence, 1940–1980* (Berkeley, 1983).

RAMANAUSKAS Pranciskus (6 October 1893, Betygala, near Raseiniai, Samogitia–15 October 1959, Telšiai), Lithuanian bishop. After graduating from a seminary in Kaunas, Ramanauskas was ordained a priest in 1917. He served in the parishes of Raseiniai and Telšiai and later studied in Rome, earning a doctorate in theology in 1932. In the same year Ramanauskas became a professor of dogmatic theology and religious pedagogy at the theological seminary in Telšiai. He was also in charge of a diocesan synodal court and was responsible for church censorship. In 1934 Ramanauskas published *Tikybos pamokos praktikoje* (Religious teaching in practice). In 1940 he became rector of the Telšiai seminary. Ramanauskas avoided deportation during the first Soviet occupation (1940–41), and in 1944 he was consecrated auxiliary bishop of Telšiai. When the Red Army again occupied Lithuanian in the summer of 1944, Ramanauskas found it increasingly difficult to continue his pastoral duties. In 1946 he was arrested and exiled to Siberia. In 1956 he was allowed to return to Lithuania but was banned from exercising his pastoral ministry. He died soon after his return. (WR)

Sources: *EL*, vol. 4; Irena Mikłaszewicz, *Polityka sowiecka wobec Kościoła katolickiego na Litwie 1944*–1965 (Warsaw, 2001).

RANCĀNS Jāzeps (25 October 1886, Nautrēni, Latgalia–2 December 1969, Grand Rapids, Michigan), Latvian Catholic bishop. After finishing high school in Kronstadt (1905) and a seminary in St. Petersburg (1908), Rancāns studied at the St. Petersburg Theological Academy, from which he graduated in 1912. Ordained a priest in 1911, he worked as a parish priest, school chaplain, and teacher of Latvian at a seminary in St. Petersburg. He was a member of the Board of the Latvian Mutual Aid Society. In 1914, after the outbreak of war, Rancāns served as a military chaplain. From 1916 to 1918 he worked as a professor at the St. Petersburg Theological Academy and as deputy parish priest and deputy dean of St. Catherine parish in St. Petersburg. Rancāns was active in Latvian refugee organizations. In 1917 he attended a congress of Latvians in Rēzeknē, supporting the unification of all Latvian lands. From February 1918 to August 1920 he was a counselor to the diocese of Riga and a member of the Latvian National Council. In October 1919 the government appointed Rancāns as Latvia's special envoy to the Holy See, and he held this post until 1925. In August 1920 he also became the chancellor of the diocese of Riga and a professor and rector of a seminary in Riga. From 1922 to 1934 Rancāns was a member of parliament, briefly serving as its deputy speaker. In 1923 he was appointed suffragan bishop of Riga and papal prelate. In 1938 he became dean and professor of the School of Catholic Theology of the University of Latvia. Rancāns wrote many theological works. After the Red Army occupied Latvia in June 1940, Rancāns was dismissed from the university, as the School of Theology was abolished, but he avoided deportation. During the German occupation he worked as dean of the Theological School of Riga University from 1943 to 1944. In 1943 he joined the underground Central Council of Latvia, which strove for Latvian independence. Before the Red Army again occupied Latvia, Rancāns left for Germany (September 1944), where in 1945 he became chairman of the Central Council of Latvia. In 1951 he emigrated to the United States, where he supported efforts to maintain international recognition of the Latvian state and was engaged in extensive pastoral and charity work. (EJ)

Sources: *Latvijas darbinieku galerija* (Riga, 1927); *Latviešu konversācijas vārdnīca*, vol. 18 (Riga, 1937); *Es viņu pazīstu* (Riga, 1939); *Bīskaps Jāzeps Rancāns—dzīve un darbs* (Greensboro, N.C., 1973); J. Cakuls, *Latvijas Romas katoļu priesteri 1918–1995* (Riga, 1996); *Lacuaniai–70* H. Tichovska, ed., (Riga, 1999).

RANGHEȚ Iosif (1904, Transylvania–1 September 1952, Bucharest), Romanian Communist activist. Rangheț had only an elementary school education. In 1930 he joined the Communist Party of Romania (CPR), which had been active in the underground from 1924 on. In 1933–34 Rangheț served as secretary of a CPR organization in Cluj.

He subsequently headed CPR organizations in Banat and in the Jiu coal basin. He was one of the few Romanian Communists who avoided imprisonment in the second half of the 1930s, but he was in constant touch with the group led by **Gheorghe Gheorgiu-Dej** in the Caransebeş prison and in the Tîrgu-Jiu detention camp. In April 1944, along with **Emil Bodnaraş** and **Constantin Pârvulescu**, who had come from Moscow, Ranghet called for the takeover of power by the RCP and the elimination of the group led by **Stefan Foriş**. Until the coup of 23 August 1944, Ranghet (together with Bodnaraş and Pârvulescu) served as a member of a triumvirate that ruled the party, which was preparing to take over power with the help of the Red Army. In 1945 Ranghet formally became a member of the Central Committee (CC) of the Romanian Communist Party (RCP), serving simultaneously as head of the RCP CC Staff Training Department. At that time the RCP increased its membership from several thousand to several hundred thousand by recruiting (among others) former Iron Guard members, who now showed repentance for their past activities. From February 1948 until the end of his life Ranghet was a member of the Politburo of the CC of the Romanian Workers' Party, formed by incorporating the Romanian Social Democratic Party into the Communist Party. In August 1948 Ranghet was a member of a party commission that interrogated **Lucreţiu Pătrăşcanu** after the latter's arrest. (LW)

Sources: Klaus-Detlev Grothusen, ed., *Rumänien* (Göttingen, 1977); Ghiţă Ionescu, *Comunismul în România* (Bucharest, 1994); Józef Darski, *Rumunia: Historia, współczesność, konflikty narodowe* (Warsaw, 1995); Dennis Deletant, *Communist Terror in Romania: Gheorghiu-Dej and the Police State, 1948–1965* (New York, 1999); Ion Alexandrescu, Ion Bulei, Ion Mamina, and Ioan Scurtu, *Enciclopedia de istorie României* (Bucharest, 2000).

RANKOVIĆ Aleksandar (28 November 1909, Šumadija–19 August 1983, Dubrovnik), Yugoslav Communist activist. Born into a Serb peasant family, Ranković in his youth joined the Communist movement, which was illegal in the Kingdom of Serbs, Croats, and Slovenes. In 1928 he became secretary of the League of Young Communists of Serbia. Sentenced to six years of prison, after serving the sentence, Ranković resumed his conspiratorial activities, first against the Yugoslav government and, after June 1941, against the German occupiers. Under the alias "Marko," he served as aide-de-camp to **Josip Broz Tito**. Arrested and tortured by the Gestapo, Ranković did not give away any information and was not recognized. After being rescued from prison, he worked as the chief of Tito's intelligence, gathering information about collaborators. He was also a member of the General Staff of the National Liberation Army.

After the power takeover by the Communists, Ranković became head of the security forces, leading a massacre of the Ustashe in retaliation for the cruelties that they had committed during the war. He advocated the suppression of wide circles of Croatian Catholics under the pretext of hunting down war criminals. Ranković organized intelligence, counterintelligence, and the secret political police, developing forces that became the foundation of his special position in the Titoist system. In 1946 Ranković was appointed minister of interior and vice-president of the republic. After June 1948, when the Comintern denounced Tito, Ranković led the elimination of the supporters of the pro-Moscow line in the Yugoslav party. They were arrested and sent to a camp on the island of Beli Otok. In 1952 Ranković left the ministry but was promoted in the hierarchy of the party, which at that point took on the name of the League of Communists of Yugoslavia (LCY). Ranković criticized Soviet interference in the domestic affairs of Communist states. After a congress of the LCY in 1958 Ranković became head of the political-organizational secretariat of the Central Committee (CC) of the party. The secretariat strengthened the role of the party bureaucracy in the system. Ranković was an ardent but conservative follower of Tito's line, opposing the reform wing of **Edvard Kardelj**. At a plenum of the CC in July 1962 Tito backed Ranković, who therefore in 1963 became the secretary of the CC of the LCY. Meanwhile, reformers were beginning to dominate in the party apparatus.

In the spring of 1966 a conflict within the party intensified for ethnic reasons (among other things). Ranković was blamed for favoring the Serbs, especially in the political police, the UDB (Uprava Državne Bezbednosti), and for aiming at the centralization of the state at the expense of the Croats, Slovenes, and other nations. On 16 June 1966 the Executive Committee of the party voted to remove Ranković. At a plenum of the CC that was held in July 1966 on the island of Brioni, Ranković, Svetoslav Stefanović (the minister of interior), and other co-workers were accused of impeding reforms for direct democracy and of holding personal power that threatened the interests of the state. It was revealed that Ranković had tapped Tito's telephone and was collecting a private dossier on leading party and state functionaries. Ranković carried out a moderate self-criticism and in return was dismissed from all his posts but was spared a trial. After retiring, he did not hold any posts. (WR)

Sources: *Annual Obituary 1983*; Vladimir Dedijer, *Tito* (New York, 1953); Aleksander Ranković, *Izbrani govori i članci 1941–1951* (Belgrade, 1951); Vojin Lukić, *Sečancja i saznanja: Aleksander Ranković i Brionski plenum* (Titograd, 1989); Zoran Sekulić, *Pad i čutnja Aleksandra Rankovića* (Belgrade, 1989); Jovan Kesar, *Leka Aleksander Ranković* (Belgrade, 1990).

RAPACKI Adam (24 December 1909, Lwów [Lviv]–10 October 1970, Warsaw), Polish Communist activist and diplomat. Rapacki came from an intellectual family. In 1932 he graduated from the Warsaw School of Economics. From 1930 to 1934 he was active in the Union of Independent Socialist Youth, and in 1932–37, in the Socialist Workers' University Society. Rapacki took part in the September 1939 campaign, and then he spent the war years in German captivity. After his return to Poland, he joined the Polish Socialist Party (Polska Partia Socjalistyczna [PPS]), which was licensed by the Communists. Between 1946 and 1948 Rapacki was a member of the Chief Council and the Central Executive Committee (Centralny Komitet Wykonawczy [CKW]) of the PPS. Along with **Józef Cyrankiewicz**, he aimed at the unification of the PPS with the Communist Polish Workers' Party (Polska Partia Robotnicza [PPR]). In December 1948 Rapacki joined the Polish United Workers' Party (Polska Zjednoczona Partia Robotnicza [PUWP]). In 1948–68 Rapacki sat on the Central Committee (CC); between December 1948 and March 1954 he sat on the Politburo; from July 1956 he was a deputy member of the Politburo, and then he was again a full member. From 1947 Rapacki was an MP; in 1947–50 he was minister of navigation; from 1950 to 1956 he was minister for higher education; in 1956–68 he was minister of foreign affairs. On 2 October 1957, at the Twelfth Session of the UN General Assembly, Rapacki presented a plan to establish a denuclearized zone in Central Europe. This proposal became known as the Rapacki Plan. The plan was then developed further in a government memorandum in 1958. The nuclear-free zone was to include Poland, the German Federal Republic, the German Democratic Republic, and Czechoslovakia. Giving up nuclear weapons on these territories would involve the withdrawal of nuclear weapons and a ban on the production, storage, or installation of the equipment and devices used for their maintenance, as well as a ban on the use of nuclear or hydrogen weapons against any state in the zone. As all disarmament proposals by the Socialist states, this one was also inspired and closely coordinated with the USSR. Rapacki opposed the Communist anti-Semitic campaign in March 1968, and when it reached the Ministry of Foreign Affairs, he withdrew from diplomatic work and from political life in general. (JS)

Sources: Mołdawa; A. Albrecht, *Plan Rapackiego: Dokumenty i opinie* (Warsaw and Poznań, 1964); W. Nagórski and M. Tomala, eds., *"Plan Rapackiego": Dokumenty i materiały* (Warsaw, 1959); Longin Patuskiak, ed., *Rapacki Adam: Przemówienia, artykuły, wywiady, 1957–1968* (Warsaw 1982); Jerzy Eisler, *Marzec 1968* (Warsaw 1991).

RĂŞCANU Ioan (1874, Moldavia–25 February 1952, Sighet), Romanian general and politician. In 1891–96 Răşcanu studied at an officer training school. In 1903 he graduated from an officers' school of artillery and engineering. From 1907 to 1911 he served as military attaché to the embassy in Berlin. In 1916, after Romania entered World War I on the side of the Entente, Răşcanu was appointed colonel. In 1917 he took part in heavy battles against German troops at Mărăşeşti. The Romanian troops, supported by Russian forces, succeeded in stopping the German offensive at the Seret River. In the same year Răşcanu was promoted to general. In December 1917 he took part in the signing of the Truce of Focşani between Romania and the Central Powers. From September 1919 to December 1921, as a representative of the National Liberal Party (Partidul Naţional Liberal), Răşcanu served as minister of war. From January to June 1927 and from June 1931 to May 1932 he was minister for the affairs of Bessarabia and Bukovina, which had been incorporated into Romania in 1918. Răşcanu vigorously strove for the unification of the Romanian state, particularly for the integration of Bessarabia and Bukovina. At the end of the 1930s he retired. After World War II, when the Communists consolidated their power in Romania, Răşcanu was arrested, like many other Romanian generals, who were usually accused of treason and spying for Western countries. He died in prison. (LW)

Sources: Józef Darski, *Rumunia: Historia, współczesność, konflikty narodowe* (Warsaw, 1995); Costin Scorpan, *Istoria României: Enciclopedie* (Bucharest, 1997); Ion Alexandrescu, Ion Bulei, Ion Mamina, and Ioan Scurtu, *Enciclopedia de istorie României* (Bucharest, 2000).

RAŠTIKIS Stasys (3 September 1896, Kuršenai, near Šiauliai–2 May 1985, Los Angeles, California), Lithuanian general. During World War I Raštikis fought on the Lithuanian, Galician, and Romanian fronts. In 1917 he graduated from the Military Academy in Tiflis (now Tbilisi, Georgia). After the October Revolution, he returned to Lithuania and fought against the Bolsheviks. Wounded and taken prisoner in 1919, he was held in a camp near Tula and later in Moscow, but he returned to Lithuania in 1921 as part of an exchange of prisoners of war. Raštikis returned to the army and served in the infantry and later in the General Staff. In 1929 he completed law studies at the University of Kaunas, and in 1932 he graduated from the General Staff Academy in Berlin. From 1933 to 1934 Raštikis served as commander of a regiment, chief of staff of a division, and chief of Lithuania's General Staff. Promoted to general in 1935, he became minister of defense in 1938. In 1935–40 he served as commander-in-chief of the army. As part of a program to improve relations with Poland, Raštikis made a visit to Warsaw in May 1939. In October 1939 he took part in negotiations in Moscow, during which the Kremlin coerced Lithuania into agreeing to (among other things) the establishment of Soviet military bases in Lithuania. Raštikis was instrumental in the modernization of the Lithuanian army, trying to prevent its excessive politicization by the dictatorship of **Antanas Smetona**. The democratic forces hoped that Raštikis would stage a coup against Smetona, but he remained politically neutral. However, Smetona did not trust him, and in January 1940 Raštikis was dismissed.

In the face of increasing Soviet pressure, Smetona decided to reinstate Raštikis to power and on 14 June 1940 appointed him prime minister. However, the Kremlin did not recognize this decision and invaded Lithuania. Raštikis was able to avoid arrest and fled to Germany. After the Third Reich attacked the Soviet Union in June 1941, politicians who had survived the Soviet occupation proclaimed a provisional government in Vilnius, and Raštikis was appointed minister of defense. On 5 August 1941 this provisional government ceased to exist. Raštikis was offered the post of general adviser in the civil administration, but he rejected this offer and began working in the War Museum in Kaunas. Fearing the return of the Red Army, in 1944 Raštikis went to Germany and then to the United States in 1949. He taught Russian at Syracuse University (1951–52) and at the Institute of Foreign Languages in Monterey, California. He was the author of numerous articles in the field of military science and politics. In 1956–73 Raštikis published a three-volume memoir, *Kovose del Lietuvos* (Fighting for Lithuania). (WR)

Sources: *Encyclopedia Lituanica*, vol. 4; *New York Times*, 19 May 1949; Bronis J. Kaslas, ed., *The USSR-German Aggression against Lithuania* (New York, 1973); Saulius Sužedielis, *Historical Dictionary of Lithuania* (Lanham, Md., 1997); Henryk Wizner, *Litwa: Dzieje państwa I narodu* (Warsaw, 1999).

RATAJ Maciej (19 February 1884, Chłopy, East Galicia–21 June 1940, Palmiry, near Warsaw), Polish politician and Peasant Party activist. Rataj came from a poor peasant family, but he graduated in classical philology from the University of Lwów (Lviv) in 1908. After graduation he taught Latin, Greek, and introductory philosophy. Involved in the peasant movement from his student days, after the split in the Polish Peasant Party (PSL) in 1913, Rataj favored the Polish Peasant Party–Piast (Polskie Stronnictwo Ludowe–Piast), on whose behalf he took part in the All-Polish Congress of Peasant Intellectuals in June 1918. In January 1919 Rataj was elected to the Constituent Assembly and moved to Warsaw. He was vice-president

and then president of the Constitutional Commission. He was also active in the commissions for foreign affairs and education. He served as vice-president of the parliamentary club of the PSL–Piast, and until 1920 he sat on the State Defense Council, which was established during the Polish-Soviet war. Rataj became known as a diligent parliamentarian and a gifted speaker. He was leaning toward the concept of a federal, not an ethnic, state, and he considered Bolshevism the worst threat. He regarded Soviet Russia as simply a successor of tsarist Russia, and he wanted to form a federation with Lithuania, Belorussia, and the Ukraine against Soviet Russia. He thought that Warmia (Ermland) and Mazuria should be incorporated into Poland and that a plebiscite should be avoided.

From July 1920 to September 1921 Rataj served as minister of religious affairs and of public education. In this role, he carried out reforms that were to consolidate and spread education over the whole country and in particular to facilitate access to education in the countryside. Rataj also contributed to the development of higher education; for example, he granted a new charter to Poznań University and established the Academy of Technical Sciences. His work in the Ministry of Education won him general support, as well as the recognition of the political elite for his organizational skills. After the fall of the first cabinet of **Wincenty Witos**, Rataj resumed parliamentary work, and after the elections of 1922 he was elected as speaker of the Assembly (1 December 1922).

As speaker of the Assembly, Rataj performed the duties of Poland's president on two occasions: after the murder of **Gabriel Narutowicz** (16–22 December 1922) and immediately after the coup of May 1926 (15 May–1 June 1926). Following the murder of Narutowicz, Rataj immediately appointed General **Władysław Sikorski** as prime minister, and he declared a state of emergency in Warsaw. On 20 December 1922 **Stanisław Wojciechowski** became new president of Poland, and Rataj handed over his duties to him. After resuming his parliamentary duties, Rataj helped pass many important laws; his main success was the adoption of an agrarian reform by the Assembly in 1925. In May 1926 Rataj unsuccesfully tried to persuade Witos not to accept the post of prime minister, as he feared an open conflict with **Józef Piłsudski**. When Wojciechowski resigned as a result of Piłsudski's coup d'état, Rataj again served as interim head of state until the National Assembly sanctioned the coup, electing Piłsudski (who refused to assume the office), and then a few days later **Ignacy Mościcki**, as president. In the elections of March 1928 the PSL–Piast suffered a defeat, and Rataj was elected to the Assembly only from the national lists. The paths of Rataj, who was leaning toward the left, and Witos, who was growing increasingly rightist, were gradually diverging. Despite that, Rataj inspired the unification of the peasant parties and assumed the leadership of the Peasant Party (Stronnictwo Ludowe [SL]), which was formed from the merger of the peasant parties in 1931. In 1930 Rataj did not enter the Assembly, but for a short time he took Witos's place in it from 1934 to 1935.

On 1 September 1939, along with **Kazimierz Bagiński** and some Socialists, Rataj suggested the creation of a government of national consent, but the proposal was rejected by the *sanacja* regime. Rataj was a co-initiator and the SL member of the Chief Political Council (Główna Rada Polityczna), which was the political base of the Service for the Victory of Poland (Służba Zwycięstwu Polsce). On 20 November 1939 Rataj was arrested by the Gestapo. Released on 14 February 1940, he resumed his underground work and established the Central Leadership of the Peasant Movement—that is, the underground leadership of the SL. Re-arrested by the Gestapo on 24 March 1940, Rataj was executed in a mass execution in the Kampinos Forest near Warsaw. After the war his body was exhumed and buried at the cemetery in Palmiry. In 1965 Rataj's *Pamiętniki 1918–1927* (Diary 1918–1927) was published. (PU)

Sources: *PSB*, vol. 30; *Przywódcy ruchu ludowego* (Warsaw, 1968); Jerzy Holzer, *Mozaika polityczna Drugiej Rzeczpospolitej* (Warsaw, 1974); Zygmunt Hemmerling, *Maciej Rataj* (Warsaw, 1975); *Maciej Rataj we wspomnieniach współczesnych* (Warsaw, 1984); *Historia sejmu polskiego*, vol. 2, part 2 (Warsaw, 1989); Arkadiusz Kołodziejczyk, *Maciej Rataj 1884–1940* (Warsaw, 1991); *Kto był kim w Drugiej Rzeczypospolitej* (Warsaw, 1994); Ludwik Malinowski, *Politycy II Rzeczypospolitej*, vol. 1 (Toruń, 1995); *Encyklopedia Historii Drugiej Rzeczypospolitej* (Warsaw, 1999).

RATAJSKI Cyryl, pseudonyms: "Górski," "Wartski," and "Wrzos" (3 March 1875, Zalesie Wielkie, near Gostyń–19 October 1942, Warsaw), Polish politician. Upon graduating from a high school in Poznań, Ratajski studied law at the University of Berlin. Afterwards he worked as a court clerk in Torgau, Germany. In 1905 he passed an exam for judges and opened his own law firm in Raciborz. During the Poznań Uprising, in January 1919, Ratajski became an envoy of the Supreme Popular Council to the Polish National Committee in Paris. Between 1919 and 1922 Ratajski worked as the head supervisor of a chemical factory owned by his father-in-law, Roman May. In April 1922 he was elected mayor of Poznań, a post he held with a short interruption until April 1934. Meanwhile, between November 1924 and June 1925 he served as minister of internal affairs. In 1929 he co-organized the General Domestic Exibition in Poznań. In recognition for his contributions to the development of the city, Ratajski was awarded honorary citizenship of Poznań in 1934. Politically, Ratajski was close to the Christian Democrats. In October 1937, he joined the newly founded Labor Party (Stronnictwo Pracy [SP]) and the Front Morges, which opposed the ruling *sanacja*. In May 1938 Ratajski was elected provincial chairman of the SP for Poznania. In March 1939 he headed a delegation of scholars and democratic activists who pleaded fruitlessly with President Ignacy Mościcki for an amnesty for political prisoners and for a government of national unity.

During the September campaign of 1939, after the Polish authorities had abandoned Poznań, Ratajski again became mayor on 5 September. A week later he was forced to surrender the city to the Germans. When the Nazis demanded that he assemble a list of hostages, Ratajski submitted only one name: his own. Soon he joined the underground. Ratajski was arrested and imprisoned at Fort VII and later deported to Nazi-occupied central Poland, the so-called General Government. From the fall of 1940 Ratajski lived in Warsaw under the assumed name of "Celestyn Radwański." As a compromise candidate accepted by both the Polish right and the Socialists, Ratajski was nominated by the London-based prime minister, General **Władysław Sikorski**, to be the government delegate for the homeland on 3 December 1940. Ratajski enlarged both the central and provincial administrations of the Polish Underground State. In April 1942 he nominated **Stefan Korboński** to be his plenipotentiary for civilian struggle. In the spring 1942 Ratajski fell seriously ill. During the summer, unable to continue his work, he delegated his duties to **Jan Piekałkiewicz** and soon tendered his resignation to General Sikorski; the latter accepted it on 5 August 1942. He died undetected by the Germans. Ratajski was the author of *Mowy 1922–1928* (Speeches, 1922–1928; 1929); *Mowy 1929–1933* (Speeches, 1929–1933; 1934), and "Moje wspomnienia" (My recollections, *Polonia*, 20 August 1939). (WR)

Sources: *PSB*, vol. 30; Kunert, vol. 2; Karol Popiel, *Na mogiłach przyjaciół* (London, 1966); Stefan Korboński, *Polskie Państwo Podziemne* (Paris, 1975); Waldemar Grabowski, *Delegatura Rządu Rzeczypospolitej Polskiej na Kraj 1940–1945* (Warsaw, 1995).

RAŢIU Ion (6 June 1917, Turda–16 January 2000, London), Romanian politician. Raţiu attended high school in Turda and Cluj. Then he studied law at the University of Cluj, graduating in 1938. As a student, he became involved with the National Peasant Party (Partidul Naţional Ţărănesc) of **Iuliu Maniu**. From 1938 to 1940 Raţiu worked in a law firm, and in 1940 he secured a job at the Ministry of Foreign Afffairs, leaving for the Romanian Embassy in London. Following Romania's alliance with

Hitler and the abdication of King **Charles II** in 1940, Raţiu resigned in protest and asked for political asylum in Great Britain. He began contributing to the British press on Romanian affairs and working for the BBC. In 1940 he enrolled at Cambridge University to study economics, earning a doctorate in 1943. While at Cambridge, Raţiu founded the Union of Romanian Students in Great Britain. He was also deputy chairman of the International Student Council and a member of the Executive Committee of the World Council of Youth and the Executive Committee of the Movement of Free Rumanians, which opposed the Nazi German–Romanian alliance and supported democracy and a pro-Western orientation for Romania.

After the war, as instructed by Maniu, Raţiu remained in Great Britain to lobby for democracy in Romania. From 1946 to 1947 he attended the peace conference in Paris as a correspondent of the American press agency International News Service. Until 1957 he was a press and radio journalist focusing on Romanian and East European affairs at the BBC, the Voice of America, and Radio Free Europe. From 1951 to 1957 Raţiu also worked for a maritime transport company and later founded a similar company, which brought him substantial wealth. In 1955 Raţiu launched a weekly, *Free Romanian Press*, which was the best Western source for information about Romania. He became one of the most prominent émigré opponents of the Communist system in Romania. From 1957 to 1984 Raţiu led the International Federation of Free Journalists. He published *Policy for the West* (1957) and *Contemporary Romania* (1975). Meanwhile, in 1960 he co-founded Amnesty International. Objecting to the visit of **Nicolae Ceauşescu** to Great Britain in 1978, Raţiu chained himself to the fence of the Ritz Hotel. In 1984 he co-founded and chaired the Union of Free Romanians (Uniunea Românilor Liberi), which advocated an independent and democratic Romania. In 1958 he launched the daily *Românul Liber* (Free Romanian). In 1989 agents of the Securitate attempted to assassinate Raţiu, but he was forewarned by Scotland Yard and survived.

At the beginning of 1990, a month after the overthrow of Ceauşescu, Raţiu returned to Romania and became deputy chairman of the restored Christian Democratic National Peasant Party (Partidul Naţional Ţărănesc-Creştin Democrat [CDNPP]). He and his party opposed the government dominated by the Communists of the National Salvation Front. Between 1990 and 1992, as well as from 1992 to 1996, Raţiu served as a senator. In 1990 he entered the presidential elections, gaining 4.3 percent of the vote. At that time he founded a right-wing daily, *Cotidianul*. Opposed by the post-Communists, Raţiu nonetheless continued as deputy chairman of the CDNPP

after 1996, and he remained until his death a member of the International PEN Club. (LW)

Sources: Józef Darski, *Rumunia: Historia, współczesność, konflikty narodowe* (Warsaw, 1995); Tom Gallagher, *Romania after Ceausescu* (Edinburgh, 1995); Ion Alexandrescu, Ion Bulei, Ion Mamina, and Ioan Scurtu, *Enciclopedia de istorie României* (Bucharest, 2000); David Phinnemore, *Post-Communist Romania* (Polgrave, 2001); www.tripod.com; www.rulers.org.

RAUCH Pavle (20 February 1865, Zagreb–29 November 1933, Martijanec, near Varaždin), Croatian politician. Rauch completed law studies. As a supporter of a union with Hungary, he became a member of the Croatian Sabor (National Assembly). When the Hungarians increased their oppression of the Croats, causing protests from the Croatian-Serbian Coalition, Rauch was appointed *ban* (governor) of Croatia by the authorities in Budapest (January 1908). In spite of Rauch's policy of intimidating the opposition, in the 1908 elections to the Sabor the Croatian-Serbian Coalition won a decisive victory, gaining fifty-seven out eighty-eight seats. Rauch postponed calling the Sabor and introduced absolutist rule. Politicians of the Croatian-Serbian Coalition were accused of contacts with the Serbian government. **Adam** and **Valerijan Pribićević**, the leaders of the Independent Serbian Party (Srpska Samostalna Stranka [SSS]), were arrested. In January 1909 there were fifty-eight Serbian leaders in prisons, awaiting trial. In an effort to discredit the Croatian-Serbian Coalition, Austro-Hungarian authorities provided the Austrian historian Heinrich Friedjung with documents alleging that the politicians of this coalition were secretly cooperating with the government of Serbia. In March 1909 Friedjung published these documents, and the politicians who had been accused sued him. At trial it was proved that the documents were forgeries, and Friedjung was discredited as a historian. In 1910, under the pressure of European public opinion, the Hungarian authorities dismissed Rauch as *ban*. Thereafter, Rauch did not play any political role. (AO)

Sources: *Biographishes Lexikon*, vol. 4; *Enciklopedija Jugoslavije*, vol. 7 (Zagreb, 1968); Wacław Felczak and Tadeusz Wasilewski, *Historia Jugosławii* (Wrocław, 1985); Mark Biondich, *Stjepan Radić, the Croat Peasant Party, and the Politics of Mass Mobilization, 1904–1928* (Toronto, 2000).

RAVASZ László (29 September 1882, Bánffyhunyad [now Huedin, Romania]–6 August 1975, Budapest), Hungarian Evangelical bishop. In September 1900 Ravasz began to study at the Theological Academy of the Evangelical Reformed Church in Kolozsvár (Cluj) and at the Humanities Department there. From 1903 to 1905 he was a pastor's assistant in Kolozsvár and a bishop's secretary. For one year he studied at the university in Berlin. In 1906 he worked as a pastor's assistant in Bánffyhunyad. Ravasz earned a Ph.D. from the University of Kolozsvár and lectured at the Theological Academy there. From 1907 to 1921 he worked as a pastor in Budapest. He also edited the periodical *Protestáns Szemle* in 1914–18 and the periodical *Út* in 1915–18. Ravasz founded the periodicals *Református élet* and *Magyar Kálvinizmus*. In 1920 he became bishop of the Evangelical Reformed Church for the region of Dunamellék. Ravasz was a member (1925–49) and vice-chairman (1937–40) of the Hungarian Academy of Sciences. From 1927 to 1944 he was a member of the upper chamber of parliament. Under Communist pressure Ravasz resigned as bishop in 1948 and retired in 1953. His daughter Boriska married **István Bibó**, an outstanding sociologist, in 1940. During the 1956 revolution Ravasz returned to public life. On 31 October he became head of the Hungarian Evangelical Reformed Church. On 1 November, after an appeal by Cardinal **József Mindszenty**, the Primate of Hungary, Ravasz also made a speech on the radio. He also took part in the so-called Evangelical Revival Movement. From early November 1956 to April 1957 he was an assistant preacher in the Calvinist church on Kalvin Square in Budapest. Later Ravasz was again forced to withdraw from public life. In 1960 he published his memoirs, *Emlékezéseim* (My memoirs). In 1989 Ravasz was posthumously reinstated as a member of the Hungarian Academy of Sciences. His numerous theological works were published in twelve volumes in 1993. (JT)

Sources: *Magyar Életrajzi Lexikon*, vol. 3 (Budapest, 1985); *Ószövetségi magyarázatok: Zsoltárok könyve* (Budapest, 1993); *A magyar forradalom és szabadságharc enciklopédiája* (Budapest, 1999).

RAŽNJATOVIĆ Željko, known as Arkan (17 April 1952, Brežice, Slovenia–15 January 2000, Belgrade), head of a Serbian paramilitary force, indicted for war crimes during the war in the former Yugoslavia. While still a teenager, Ražnjatović became involved in criminal activities (bank robberies, thefts) in West European countries. He managed to escape from jail several times. In 1986 he returned to Belgrade, where he opened a bakery. He established ties with the Crvena Zvezda (Red Star) football team. In October 1990 he created a nationalist paramilitary organization known as Arkan's Tigers. This force became infamous around the world for atrocities committed in the area of Vukovar in eastern Croatia. Around two thousand Croats were killed there in November 1991, following three months of siege. In 1992 Ražnjatović became active in Bosnia, particularly in the towns of Bijeljina and Zvornik. Arkan's Tigers are accused of "ethnic cleansing," rape, and the murder of Croats and Muslims. In 1992 Ražnjatović briefly served as an independent MP for Kosovo in the Serbian parliament. He became leader of the Serbian Unity Party, which was against independence for Bosnia-Herzegovina and called for its union with Serbia. In 1993 Ražnjatović was put on the list of war crime suspects wanted by the International Criminal Tribunal for Former Yugoslavia in The Hague. In March 1999 he was officially indicted for crimes against humanity and war crimes. Ražnjatović was regarded as one of the closest associates of **Slobodan Milošević**. During the 1999 NATO intervention in Kosovo, he was frequently in the media at home and abroad, and he condemned the NATO air raids. He often appeared in public with his wife, the popular Serbian singer Svetlana "Ceca" Veličković. Ražnjatović was gunned down in the lobby of the Intercontinental Hotel in Belgrade. Speculation then arose as to whether his death was a political or a gangland killing. (AO)

Sources: International Criminal Tribunal for the Former Yugoslavia, www.un.org/icty/indictment; Laura Silber and Allan Little, *The Death of Yugoslavia*, (London, 1995); Tom Gjelten, *Sarajevo Daily* (New York, 1995); Warren Zimmermann, *Origins of a Catastrophe* (New York and Toronto, 1996); *Conflict in the Former Yugoslavia: An Encyclopedia* (Denver, 1998).

RÁZUS Martin (18 October 1888, Vrbica–8 August 1937, Brezno), Slovak writer and politician, Lutheran pastor. Rázus attended schools in his native Vrbica and in Liptovský Sv. Mikuláš, Banská Bystrica, and Kežmarok. He subsequently studied Protestant theology at the University of Bratislava (1907–11) and Edinburgh University (1911–12). His stay in Scotland increased his religiousness and national consciousness. After returning home, Rázus became a Lutheran pastor and then parish priest in Pribylina (1913–20), Moravské Lieskové (1921–30), and Brezno (1930–37). Active in politics since his student days, his views evolved from supporting a union of Czechs and Slovaks to supporting the struggle for Slovak autonomy. During World War I Rázus was an opponent of the Austro-Hungarian monarchy and maintained contacts with Czech politicians. After the war, he supported the Czechoslovak state, but he soon lost trust in his Czech partners as "Prague-centrism," Czechoslovakism, and a lack of autonomy for Slovakia became facts. In 1922 Rázus became a member and the main ideologue of the Slovak National Party (SNP). In 1925 he led an unsuccessful electoral campaign for his party, and the SNP failed to enter parliament.

In 1929 Rázus became chairman of the SNP and entered into an electoral alliance with the National Democratic Party in Slovakia. He became an MP on a joint ticket for these parties but soon left their parliamentary group. Rázus served as an MP until the end of his life, frequently defending the social and cultural interests of Slovakia. He also called on all Slovak MPs to establish a common front, but to no effect. In 1932 Rázus entered into cooperation with Hlinka's Slovak People's Party (Hlinková Slovenská L'udová Strana [HSL'S]). As a result he became more radical in his views. In the 1935 elections the HSL'S and SNP candidates ran on a joint ticket. However, after the elections the coalition broke up because the HSL'S failed to keep its promise of a fair share of seats, and the SNP received only one. Also, conflicts on religious grounds increased between Catholics from the HSL'S and Protestants from the SNP. Criticized within his party, Rázus suffered greatly because of this failure. He then became seriously ill and died two years after the elections.

Rázus was also one of the greatest Slovak poets. In his works he included war motifs—these can be found, for instance, in the collections *Z tichych a búrnych chvíl'* (From quiet and stormy moments; 1917) and *To je vojna!* (That's war! 1919)—as well as social and national themes, as in the volumes *Kameň na medzi* (Milestone; 1925), *Šípy duše* (Arrows of the soul; 1929), and *Cestou* (Journey; 1935). In *Stretnutie* (Encounter; 1937)—an important poetry volume written shortly before his death—Rázus was critical of his political activities. He also wrote a number of novels and the autobiographical pieces *Maroško* (1932) and *Maroško študuje* (1933). (PU)

Sources: *ČBS*; *SBS*, vol. 5; *Kto bol kto za I. ČSR* (Bratislava, 1993); *Kdo byl kdo v našich dějinach ve 20. stoleti*, vol. 2 (Prague, 1998); Joseph A. Mikus, *Slovakia: A Political History, 1918–1950* (Milwaukee, 1963); *Mały słownik pisarzy zachodnio-słowiańskich i południowo-słowiańskich* (Warsaw, 1973); Dušan Kováč, *Dejiny Slovenska* (Bratislava, 1998); Rudolf Chmel, ed., *Kwestia slowacka w XX wieku* (Gliwice, 2002).

REBET Lev, pseudonyms "Klishch" and "Star" (3 March 1912, Stryi–12 October 1957, Munich), Ukrainian lawyer and nationalist politician. Because of his underground activities, Rebet was imprisoned by the Polish authorities. In 1934–38 he served as head (*providnyk*) of the Organization of Ukrainian Nationalists (OUN) in Poland, reconstructing the network of the organization destroyed by the arrests in 1933–34. After the split of the OUN into two factions, Rebet, as a supporter of **Stepan Bandera**, became a member of the leadership of the OUN-B. He became deputy prime minister in the **Yaroslav Stetsko** government, which was created by the supporters of Bandera in 1941. Arrested by the Gestapo on 15 September 1941, Rebet was a prisoner in the concentration camp in Auschwitz until the fall of 1944. From 1945 he was in exile in Munich.

In March 1945 at the so-called Vienna congress, where the Foreign Units (Zakordonni Chastyny [ZCh]) of the OUN (the name of the OUN-B in exile) were created, Rebet proposed Bandera as leader of the organization. Soon, however, he backed pro-democratic changes in the OUN, according to the resolutions of the Third Congress of 1943. As a result and since Bandera questioned the authority of the Ukrainian Supreme Liberation Council (USLC) to represent the national movement, Rebet parted with Bandera. In December 1946 Bandera dismissed him as chief justice of the ZCh of the OUN. Along with Zinovy Matla, Rebet created a new faction of the OUN, the so-called agents, joined by, for example, **Mykola Lebed**, Myroslav Prokop, Ivan Hryniokh, and Rebet's wife, Daria, who was an emissary of the commander of the UPA, **Roman Shukhevych**. In 1950 Rebet became a member of the foreign representation of the USLC. He was a respected publicist and theoretician of the movement and also a scholar. Rebet became an assistant professor (1952) and professor (1954) of law at the Ukrainian Free University in Munich. He co-edited the journals *Ukraiins'ka Trybuna* and *Chas i suchasna Ukraiina*. He edited the weekly *Ukraiinskyi Samoistiinyk*. He published *Svitla i tiny OUN* (The splendors and miseries of the OUN; 1954), *Formovanie natsii* (Formation of the nation; 1951), and *Teoriia natsii* (Theory of the nation; 1956). Rebet was murdered by a KGB agent, Bohdan Stashevs'kyi, who also killed Bandera two years later. (GM)

Sources: *Encyclopedia of Ukraine*, vol. 4 (Toronto, 1993); Petro Mirchuk, *Narys istorii OUN 1920–1939* (Munich, London, and New York, 1968); Władysław Żeleński, "Zabójstwo ministra Pierackiego," *Zeszyty Historyczne*, 1973, no. 25; Alexander J. Motyl, *The Turn to the Right: The Ideological Origins and Development of Ukrainian Nationalism, 1919–1929* (Boulder, Colo., 1980); Ryszard Torzecki, *Polacy i Ukraińcy: Sprawa ukraińska w czasie II wojny światowej na terenie Ii Rzeczpospolitej* (Warsaw, 1993).

REI August (22 March 1886, Kabala, near Pilistvere–29 March 1963, Stockholm), lawyer, leader of Estonian Social Democracy. Rei took part in the revolution of 1905. After graduating in law from Petersburg University in 1911, he became aligned with the Social Democratic Party. In November 1918 he became minister of labor in the government of **Konstantin Päts**. He supported radical social reforms that would prevent a Bolshevik revolution in Estonia. Rei became a member of the Constituent Assembly as a representative of Social Democracy; he was elected president of the parliament and directed its work in the most difficult period of the war for independence. Next he was an MP from the first to the fifth terms of the parliament and president of Social Democracy. Between 4 December 1928 and 9 July 1929 Rei served as the prime minister and president (*riigivanen*) of Estonia, and in 1932–33 he served as minister of foreign affairs. After the implementation of an authoritarian constitution, which was ratified in a general referendum, in February 1934 Rei decided to become a candidate in the presidential elections. During a fierce campaign before the elections the leader of the agrarian forces, Prime Minister Päts, put down coup attempts by the extreme right and assumed dictatorial powers. Joining the ruling coalition, Rei actually gave his support to Päts. For some time he was a deputy minister for foreign affairs, and from February 1938 to June 1940 he was ambassador to the USSR. On 16 June 1940 Rei received an ultimatum from the Kremlin, which demanded that Estonia form a government "friendly" to the USSR. Before Rei was able to take any steps, the Red Army invaded Estonia and put an end to its independence. When on 19 June 1940 Andriei Zhdanov came to Tallinn, Päts wanted to appoint a new government with Rei as its head, but Zhdanov did not agree. Rei survived the Soviet and German occupations, and when they were over, he took part in the work of the Estonian National Committee (Eesti Vabariigi Rahvuskomiteega), which was preparing to take over power.

On 18 September 1944, shortly before the return of the Red Army, Rei became minister of foreign affairs in the provisional government of **Otto Tief**. When Estonia was again occupied by the Soviets, Rei managed to get to Sweden, where he remained until his death. From 1945 he headed the Estonian National Committee, which was active in Stockholm. Rei published several works propagating the idea of the independence of the Baltic states—for example, *Have the Baltic Nations Voluntarily Renounced Their Freedom?* (1944), *Have the Small Nations a Right to Freedom and Independence?* (1946), *Nazi-Soviet Conspiracy and the Baltic States* (1948), and *The Drama of the Baltic Peoples* (published posthumously in 1970). (WR)

Sources: *Eesti Entsuoklopeedia*, vol. 6 (Tallinn, 1974); P. Wieselgren, "Minu kirjavahetusest August Reiga," *Teataja*, 18 May and 1 June 1963; J. Pihlak, "Riigivanem August Rei mälestuseks," *Sakala*, 23 March 1991; A. Pajur, *August Rei, Eesti ajalugu elulugudes* (Tallinn, 1997); www.sada.ee/php/query.

REICH Leon (11 July 1879, Drohobycz [Drohobich]–1 December 1929, Lwów [Lemberg, Lviv]), Zionist lawyer and politician in Poland. Reich came from a wealthy merchant family of Orthodox Jews. After graduating from a high school in Sambor, he entered the law school at the University of Lemberg (Lviv), where he received his doctorate. Then he studied at the School of Political Sciences in Paris. As a student, Reich became active in the Zionist movement and was coopted to the Central Committee of the Zionist Organization. In 1905 he participated in a Zionist congress in Basel, and afterwards he took part in all subsequent congresses. Reich published in the Zionist weekly *Wschód*. He visited Palestine in 1918. In 1913 he became a member of the Executive Committee of the World Zionist Organization. During World War I Reich served in the military courts of the Austro-Hungarian Army. In November 1918 he was temporarily interned by the Polish authorities at Baranów for suspicion of collaboration with the Ukrainians. He was released after the intervention of the Zionist Organization, backed by the British government. During the Paris Peace Conference Reich served as deputy chairman of the Committee of the Jewish Delegations (Comité des Délégations Juives). At its behest he edited *Les droits nationaux des Juifs en Europe Orientale* (The national rights of the Jews in Eastern Europe; 1919). In 1922 Reich published, in Polish, his recollections about the conference: *Żydowska delegacja pokojowa w Paryżu* (The Jewish peace delegation in Paris). In 1920 Reich became chairman of the Zionist Organization of Eastern Galicia, and in 1922 he was elected to the Polish parliament from the lists of the United National Jewish Parties. As chairman of the Jewish Club, Reich negotiated a Polish-Jewish agreement in 1925 that granted the Polish government the support of Jewish deputies in exchange for certain rights for the Jewish minority. When the agreement collapsed, Reich quit his post. Following the coup d'état of May 1926, Reich advocated accommodation with the *sanacja* government. In 1927 he published the Zionist *Dziennik Warszawski*. In 1928 he was once again elected to the Parliament to represent the National Jewish Union. He also practiced law in Lwów. In 1934, Reich's ashes were taken to Tel Aviv. (WR)

Sources: *PSB*, vol. 21; *Encyclopedia Judaica*, vol. 14 (Jerusalem, 1971); *Kto był kim w Drugiej Rzeczypospolitej* (Warsaw, 1994); *Encyklopedia historii Drugiej Rzeczypospolitej* (Warsaw, 1999).

REICIN Bedřich (29 September 1911, Pilsen [now Plzeň, Czech Republic]–3 December 1952, Prague), Czech officer and Communist activist. In the 1930s Reicin was an activist in a Communist youth organization and a sports editor for *Rudé Právo*. Imprisoned by the Gestapo in March 1939, he was released after a few months. In 1940 he went to the Soviet Union, where he worked in the Czechoslovak section of Moscow Radio and worked with the leadership of the Communist Party of Czechoslovakia abroad. In 1942 Reicin served in the Czechoslovak military units in the Soviet Union. From 1944 to 1945 he was chief of counterintelligence of the First Czechoslovak Army.

As head of military intelligence (1945–48), Reicin was in charge of the Communist infiltration of the army. After a coup in February 1948, he initiated and then conducted purges in the army. He was also responsible for many court sanctioned crimes (such as government approved executions), and he developed a reputation of widespread ill fame. The most widely known case was that of General **Heliodor Píka**, a war hero who was sentenced in 1948 and executed in 1949 because, according to Reicin, "Píka knew too much about the Soviet intelligence services." From 1948 to 1951 Reicin served as deputy defense minister for personnel affairs. In 1948 he became brigadier general and in 1950 major general. Arrested in February 1951 as a result of a political struggle with **Alexej Čepička**, Reicin was sentenced to death in the trial of **Rudolf Slanský** and his associates in November 1952. Reicin was hanged in Pankrac Prison, Prague. (PU)

Sources: *ČBS*; *Kdo byl kdo v našich dějinach ve 20. stoleti*, vol. 1 (Prague, 1998).

REIFF Ryszard, pseudonym "Jacek" (4 July 1923, Warsaw), Polish politician. Born into a white-collar family, Reiff graduated from Warsaw University. During the Nazi occupation, from 1941 he was active in the extreme rightist Confederation of the Nation (Konfederacja Narodu) and its armed units, the Cadre Shock Battalions (Uderzeniowe Bataliony Kadrowe), which were subordinated to the Home Army in 1944. At the end of 1944 Reiff was captured by the NKVD and imprisoned in the Diagilev camp, but he fled and returned to Poland in 1946. He worked as a journalist for the *Dziś i Jutro* group, and then, as a close associate of **Bolesław Piasecki**, he became editor-in-chief of the daily *Słowo Powszechne* and leading organizational activist of the association PAX. From May 1965 to May 1969 Reiff was a member of parliament, supporting the policies of **Władysław Gomułka**. In 1976–79 he was deputy chairman of the PAX Main Board, and after the death of Piasecki, from 14 January 1979 he was chairman. Reiff supported the policies of **Edward Gierek**. In March 1980 he was reelected to the parliament and chaired its PAX club. During the sixteen months of the Solidarity self-containing revolution, Reiff attempted to transform the PAX into a Christian Democratic party and called for an agreement between the Communists and Solidarity. On 12 February 1981 Reiff became a member of the Council of State. On the night of 12–13 December 1981 he was the only member of the council who protested against martial law and declined to sign a relevant resolution. During martial law, Reiff's opponents within the PAX, led by Zenon Komender and supporting the party line, man-

aged to oust Reiff in January 1982. In May 1982 he was also dropped from the Council of State. From February to April 1989 Reiff took part in the Round Table Talks, and on 4 June 1989 he was elected to the senate on behalf of the Civic Committee of the Chairman of Solidarity, **Lech Wałęsa**. Reiff chaired the senate Commission for Emigration and Poles Abroad. From 1989 he chaired the Union of Former Siberian Exiles (Związek Sybiraków). Among other works, Reiff published *Czas Solidarności* (The time of solidarity, 1988; uncensored edition) and *Wybór jutra, czyli reforma socjalizmu czy reforma w socjalizmie* (The choice for tomorrow: Reform of socialism or reform within socialism; 1988). (PK)

Sources: Mołdawa; Antoni Czubiński, *Dzieje Najnowsze Polski 1944–1989* (Poznań, 1992); Andrzej Albert [Wojciech Roszkowski], *Najnowsza historia Polski 1914–1993*, vol. 2 (Warsaw, 1995); Jan Skórzyński, *Ugoda i rewolucja: Władza i opozycja 1985–1989* (Warsaw, 1995).

REINYS Mečislovas (5 February 1884, Daugailiai–8 November 1953, Vladimir), archbishop of Vilnius (Wilno), victim of communism. After graduating from a seminary in Vilnius in 1905, Reinys studied at the St. Petersburg Theological Academy from 1905 to 1909. Ordained in July 1907, he continued his studies at the University of Louvain, Belgium, earning a doctorate in philosophy in 1912. He subsequently studied biology at the same university and apologetics at the University of Strasbourg. Afterwards, Reinys returned to Lithuania, where in 1916 he became a professor at a seminary in Vilnius. Throughout this time he worked for the cause of Lithuanian independence. After the Bolsheviks seized Vilnius at the beginning of 1919, Reinys was briefly detained. When Polish forces recaptured the Vilnius region in October 1920, he continued to defend Lithuania's right to the city. Arrested by the Polish authorities of Central Lithuania and forced to go to the territories of the Lithuanian Republic, Reinys settled in Kaunas. He taught theology and philosophy at the newly established university and held the chair of psychology there. In 1925–26, as a representative of the Christian Democratic Party, Reinys served as minister of foreign affairs. In this role he helped to regulate Lithuania's relations with the Holy See and to establish a Lithuanian province of the Catholic Church, with its capital in Kaunas. On 5 April 1926 Reinys was consecrated bishop-coadjutor of Vilkaviškis. He was also a co-founder of the Lithuanian Academy of Arts and Sciences and strove for the establishment of a Catholic university, which the government of **Antanas Smetona** would not permit.

During the Soviet occupation Reinys avoided arrest, and on 9 July 1940 he was appointed titular and auxiliary archbishop of the archdiocese of Vilnius. After the Germans arrested Archbishop **Romuald Jałbrzykowski**, Reinys was assigned as administrator of the archdiocese of Vilnius, with the right of succession. In 1945, when the Soviet authorities prevented Archbishop Jałbrzykowski from returning to Vilnius—which was part of the Lithuanian Soviet Socialist Republic at that time—Reinys continued his pastoral duties, but under increasingly difficult conditions. In 1947 he was arrested and accused of supporting the Lithuanian pro-independence underground. Sentenced to ten years' imprisonment, Reinys served his sentence in the Vladimir prison, where he died. Reinys was the author of numerous articles in the field of theology and psychology. "Rasizmo problema" (Problems of racism; 1939) is his most significant work. (WR)

Sources: *EL*, vol. 4; G. Starke, "Arkivyskupas M. Reinys S.S.R. kaléjme," *Draugas* (Chicago) 7 June 1958; S. Matulis, "Arkivyskupas Mečislovas Reinys," *L.K.M.A. Suvažiavimo Darbai*, vol. 4 (Rome, 1961); V. Pavalkis, "Arkivyskupas Mečislovas Reinys Vilniuje 1940–1947," *Aidai* (Brooklyn), 1974, no. 2; Irena Mikłaszewicz, *Polityka sowiecka wobec Kościoła katolickiego na Litwie 1944–1965* (Warsaw, 2001).

RETINGER Józef (17 April 1888, Kraków–12 June 1960, London), Polish politician. Retinger came from a family of Galician intelligentsia with aristocratic connections. He graduated from a high school in Kraków, studied at the Academia Nobili Ecclesiastici in Rome, and received a Ph.D. in literature from the Sorbonne in Paris in 1908. He specialized in French Romanticism and published two monographs on the topic. The sponsorship of Count Władysław Zamoyski facilitated Retinger's contacts in France's intellectual world and in postgraduate studies at the Ecole des Science Politiques (1908–9), as well as in Munich, Florence, and at the London School of Economics and Political Science (1909–11). Following his return to Kraków, Retinger joined the local avant garde and published the journal *Miesięcznik Literacki i Artystyczny*. Soon, however, he returned to England and began dabbling in politics. Initially, Retinger supported an anti-German orientation, exposing the Prussian persecution of the Poles. He worked at the time with **Ignacy Paderewski** and Joseph Conrad.

The outbreak of World War I caught Retinger in Galicia. He left immediately for Switzerland and France. He used informal contacts with the French Foreign Ministry to influence Polish affairs. He wrote profusely, arguing for the need to restore Poland's independence. Retinger maintained contact with all Polish political orientations at home and abroad, although he eschewed joining any. He was considered to be an expert on Polish affairs, and some suspected him of being a Freemason and an agent of British intelligence. In May 1918 Retinger was expelled from France to Spain. Thanks to the financial assistance of Conrad, he left for Latin America. He participated in the Mexican revolution, advising President Plutarco Elias Calles. Retinger described his adventures and reflections in *The Social Movements in Mexico* (1925). In the mid-1920s Retinger returned to Great Britain. He worked closely with the Labour Party and maintained links to Polish Socialists. He worked to improve Polish-Soviet and Polish-British relations. At the same time, he represented a number of British companies in Poland. In 1931 Retinger participated in negotiations with Berber rebels in Morocco. He kept in touch with some in the Polish-American diaspora. After the coup d'état of May 1926 of **Józef Piłsudski**, Retinger supported the center-left opposition. He also renewed his friendships among the artistic and literary figures in Poland, in particular in the milieu of the liberal *Wiadomości Literackie*, becoming its London correspondent. On the eve of war he worked closely with the anti-Pilsudskite Front Morges.

Following the outbreak of World War II, Retinger became a permanent adviser to Prime Minister General **Władysław Sikorski**. On the initiative of the British (specifically Ambassador Stafford Cripps and Foreign Secretary Anthony Eden) and in accord with his own beliefs, Retinger worked to improve Poland's relations with the USSR. He supported Sikorski's plans for a federation in East Central Europe. Retinger accompanied the prime minister on foreign trips and negotiations with Allied leaders. Between 30 July and 4 September 1941 he was the main Polish diplomat accredited with the Kremlin, conducting a policy of appeasement toward Stalin. After the death of General Sikorski in July 1943, Retinger formally quit his posts with the Polish government. However, on 4 April 1944 he was parachuted as a political courier over Nazi-occupied Poland. He held talks with the leaders of the Polish underground, including the government delegate, **Jan Stanisław Jankowski**. The leadership of the Polish military underground objected to Retinger's presence. Subsequently, he left Poland, along with the Socialist **Tomasz Arciszewski**, on 26 July 1944. A supporter of granting recognition to the Communist-dominated Provisional Government of National Unity, Retinger visited Poland thrice with the British charitable relief (1945–46). Later, he distanced himself from Polish affairs and concentrated on the issue of European unity. During a congress at The Hague (7–11 May 1948), Retinger co-initiated the foundation of the European Parliament. He also co-founded the so-called Bildenberg Group (1952) and participated in its work. Retinger authored many works, including *Polacy w* *cywilizacjach świata do końca wieku XIX* (Poles in world civilizations through the nineteenth century; 1937) and *Memoirs of an Eminence Grise* (1972). (MC)

Sources: *PSB*, vol. 31; Olgierd Terlecki, *Barwne życie szarej eminencji* (Kraków, 1981); Olgierd Terlecki, *Kuzynek diabła* (Kraków, 1988); Jan Pomian, *Józef Retinger: Życie i pamiętniki szarej eminencji* (Warsaw, 1990); Paweł Maria Lisiewicz, *Bezimienni: Z dziejów wywiadu Armii Krajowej* (Warsaw, 1987); "50th Anniversary of ELEC (1946–1996): In Remembrance of Jozef Retinger," *European League for Economic Cooperation* (June 1996); Thierry Grosbois, "L'action de Jozef Retinger en faveur de l'idée européenne 1940–46," *Revue européenne d'histoire*, 1999, vol. 6, no 6.

REVAI József (12 October 1898, Budapest–4 August 1959, Budapest), Hungarian Communist activist. Revai was born into a Jewish middle-class family. During World War I he worked at a bank and belonged to the Social Democratic Party. In 1917 Revai created his own anarchist-socialist group, and in 1919 he was one of the co-founders of the Hungarian Communist Party (HCP). At the time of the Hungarian Soviet Republic (HSR) Revai worked for the journal *Vörös Újság* and was among the intellectual leaders of the extreme left. After the fall of the HSR in August 1919, Revai fled to Austria. Later he also lived in Germany, France, Czechoslovakia, and the USSR. At a meeting of the CC of the HCP in June 1926 Revai became a member of that body. He was linked to the faction of **Jenö Landler** and was known in the Communist underground as "Kemény." During secret visits to Hungary Revai maintained contacts with the Communist circles. In an atmosphere of growing distrust and personal squabbles, which were the result of Stalin's machinations, at the Sixth Comintern Congress in 1929, Revai attacked **Béla Kun**. When the latter ordered the GPU to arrest the supporters of Landler's faction on charges of Trotskyism, Revai counterattacked effectively. After his arrival in Hungary in December 1930, Revai was arrested. Released, he went to the USSR, where in 1934 he started work in the Comintern. At the beginning of 1936, when the purge of the Hungarian Communists in the USSR began, Revai became responsible for the affairs of the HCP in the Comintern, which probably was related to his role in the purge.

During World War II Revai directed the Kosuth Moscow Radio and took part in a special program for Communist indoctrination of Hungarian POWs in the USSR. In 1944 he became a member of an interim parliament organized by the Communists and of a provisional Presidential Council. In 1945 Revai became minister of culture in the coalition government of **Zoltán Tildy**. He played a major role in the overthrow of democracy in Hungary. Between 1945 and 1950 Revai was the editor-in-chief of *Szabad Nép*, the organ of the CC of the HCP. He was a member of the party's Politburo and represented it at the founding congress of the Cominform in Szklarska Poręba in September 1947. In 1949–53 Revai was minister of culture and the dictator of Hungarian intellectual life. He supervised, for example, an introductory program to Socialist realism. After Stalin's death in 1953 Revai lost his post in the government and in the Politburo; his dismissal was the result of a clash with **Mátyás Rákosi**. After the fall of Rákosi in July 1956, Revai returned to the party leadership. At the end of October 1956, during the Budapest uprising, he went to the USSR. He returned at the beginning of 1957 and joined in the political pacification led by **János Kádár**, although during a party conference in June 1957 he criticized Kádár from a super-Stalinist position—for example, for the dissolution of the Hungarian Workers' Party. As a result, Revai was expelled from the party. (MS/WR)

Sources: Lazitch; Erik Molnár, "Révai József történetszemléletéröl," *Kritika*, 1966, no. 7; Rudolf L. Tőkes, *Bela Kun and the Hungarian Soviet Republic* (New York, 1967); Károly Urbán, "Politikus pályák," *Társadalmi Szemle*, 1983, no. 1; László Péter, *Szegedi örökség* (Budapest, 1983); György Borsányi, *The Life of a Communist Revolutionary: Bela Kun* (Boulder, Colo., 1993).

REYMONT Władysław Stanisław [originally Rejment] (7 May 1867, Kobiele Wielkie, near Radomsko–5 December 1925, Warsaw), Polish writer. The son of a village organist, from 1880 Reymont lived in Warsaw, where from 1880 to 1884 he was a tailor's apprentice and then a journeyman. He probably completed only three grades of a school of trade school. In 1884–87 he acted, under the pseudonym "Urbański," with traveling troupes of actors. In 1888 he started working at the Warsaw-Vienna Railway; at that time he also changed his name. Around 1890 Reymont established contacts with spiritualist circles in Częstochowa, which had some influence on his creative activity. He was also a lay brother in the Pauline order at Jasna Góra in Częstochowa. In 1891 Reymont became associated with the Dramatic Society in Piotrków and also performed at an amateur theater in Skierniewice. In 1892 he made his debut as a journalist in the Warsaw *Głos*. In 1893 he moved to Warsaw, where he became involved in journalism and other literary activities, paying much attention to the problems of social injustice. In 1895–97 he traveled a lot throughout Europe (for example, Berlin, Brussels, Paris, Rome, and London).

In 1896 Reymont lived in Łódź, where he collected material for his novel *Ziemia obiecana* (The promised land; 1899), which depicted the birth of capitalism on the Polish territories. In 1902 he began to work on his novel *Chłopi* (The peasants; 1904–9), which was recognized as an epic masterpiece that presented a picture of peasant life in accordance with the rhythms of nature. The novel, completed in 1909, was enhanced with modernistic descriptions of nature. During World War I Reymont took part in the work of patriotic social and civic committees. In 1917 he received the award of the Polish Academy of Arts and Sciences for *Chłopi*. He also became president of the Committee of the Warsaw Fund of Prudence and Assistance for Writers and Journalists (the predecessor of the Writers' and Journalists' Association, of which he also was president later). In 1919 and 1920 Reymont visited the Polish community in the United States.

In 1920 Reymont settled in Kołaczkowo, near Września. He was interested in film; he co-founded one of the first cinematographic cooperatives in Poland. In 1924 Reymont received the Nobel Prize in literature. This consolidated his fame and made *Chłopi*, translated into other languages as well, almost a symbol of Polish peasant culture. Reymont was a member of the Polish Peasant Party–Piast (Polskie Stronnictwo Ludowe–Piast). He was buried in Powązki Cemetery in Warsaw, and his heart was laid in the pillar of Holy Cross Church in Warsaw. Reymont is considered one of the main representatives of the realistic trend in the prose of Young Poland. In his works, we find a combination of expressive realism with naturalistic descriptions of nature and elements of impressionism, as well as symbolism and the romantic atmosphere typical of modernism. His other most important works include the novels *Komediantka* (The comedienne; 1896); *Fermenty* (Ferments; 1897); and *Rok 1794* (The year 1794; 1913–18), a historical trilogy composed of three novels: *Ostatni Sejm Rzeczypospolitej* (The last Assembly of the Republic of Poland), *Nil desperadum*, and *Insurekcja* (The insurrection). (JS)

Sources: *Literatura polska: Przewodnik encyklopedyczny*, vol. 2 (Warsaw, 1985); Barbara Kocówna, *Reymont: Z dziejów recepcji twórczości* (Warsaw, 1975); Józef Rurawski, *Władysław Reymont* (Warsaw, 1977); Stefan Lichański, *Władysław Stanisław Reymont* (Warsaw, 1984).

RIBAR Ivan (21 January 1881, Vukmanić [Kordun]–2 February 1968, Belgrade), Yugoslav politician. After graduating from a high school in Karlovac, Ribar studied law at the universities in Vienna, Prague, and Zagreb, earning a Ph.D. in 1904. He subsequently ran a law practice. He began his political career by taking part in opposition protests against the regime of Ban **Károlyi Khuen-Hédérváry** (who was in office until 1903). Ribar's views were influenced by contacts with the leading opposition politicians in Austria-Hungary: **Tomáš Garrigue Masaryk**, **Frano Supilo**, Josip Juraj Strossmayer, and **Jovan Skerlić**, as well as members of the organizations Omladina and Sokol. In 1904 Ribar was one of the founders of the Croatian Progressive Party (Hrvatska Napredna Stranka), which later merged with two smaller parties and assumed the name of the Croatian United Independent Party (Hrvatska Ujedinjena Samostalna Stranka). In 1905 this party joined the Croatian-Serbian Coalition. In 1913, supported by the left wing of the party, Ribar was elected to the Provincial Parliament in Zagreb. At that time he also served as an MP in the Croatian-Hungarian parliament in Budapest.

When World War I broke out, Ribar was inducted into the Austro-Hungarian Army. In 1917 he returned home and became chairman of the local people's council in Djakovo. In October 1918 he was elected to the Executive Committee of the National Council of Slovenes, Croats, and Serbs in Zagreb. With the growing disintegration of Austria-Hungary, he called for tightening Austria-Hungary's cooperation with the Kingdom of Serbia. In March 1919 Ribar became vice-chairman of the Provisional National Assembly of the newly established Kingdom of Serbs, Croats, and Slovenes (SHS). A supporter of the idea of Yugoslavism, he was one of the founders of the Serbian Democratic Party (Srpska Demokratska Stranka [SDS]) and then served as a deputy to its leader, **Ljubomir Davidović**. From December 1920 to October 1922 Ribar presided over the sessions of the Constitutional Assembly. However, his ideas were rejected by Serbian politicians of the older generation who wanted the former Kingdom of Serbia to play a dominant role in the newly established state. Thus Ribar joined those who called for a coalition between the SDS and the Croatian Peasant Party, led by **Stjepan Radić**. In 1927 Ribar also supported the SDS's joining an opposition bloc formed around the Croatian Peasant Party and the Independent Democratic Party. As a result of the dictatorship of King **Alexander I** (1929–34), Ribar became disenchanted with centralism and began to support a federal model of the state. In the 1930s, as leader of the SDS left wing, Ribar drifted toward communism and established contacts with leaders of the Communist Party of Yugoslavia (CPY). He ever more often defended CPY leaders in court trials. Ribar's involvement with Communists led to a sharp conflict between him and activists of non-Communist parties. His name was taken off the SDS electoral register, and in the elections of December 1938 he failed to win a parliamentary seat.

After the German invasion in April 1941, Ribar returned to Belgrade and entered into secret negotiations with **Josip Broz Tito** on the establishment of a liberation movement. He simultaneously maintained contacts with opposition politicians that he had established earlier. In the summer of 1942 Ribar went to the territories liberated by Tito's Partisans and joined the CPY. Along with **Moša Pijade**, Ivan Milutinović, Veselin Masleša, and Ribar's son Ivan-Lola Ribar, Ribar conducted negotiations on the establishment of the Anti-Fascist Council for the National Liberation of Yugoslavia (Antifašističko Veće Narodnog Oslobođenja Jugoslavije [AVNOJ]). At the first session of AVNOJ, Ribar was elected chairman of the AVNOJ Executive Committee. In 1944 on the island of Vis, Ribar was Tito's adviser in negotiations conducted with **Ivan Šubašić**, the prime minister of the Yugoslav government-in-exile. In October 1944 Ribar became chairman of the Provisional People's Assembly, and in November 1945, chairman of the Constitutional Assembly of Yugoslavia. After a new state constitution was adopted on 30 January 1946, Ribar served as chairman of the parliament until 1953 and as deputy until 1963. A participant in and a close observer of key events in the twentieth-century history of Yugoslavia, he left volumes of memoirs, including *Hrvatsko-srpski odnosi u prošlosti* (Croatian-Serbian relations in the past; 1939); *Politički zapisi* (Political notes, 4 vols.; 1948–52); *Uspomene iz NOB-e* (Memoirs from the people's liberation struggle; 1961); and *Stara Jugoslavija i komunizam* (Old Yugoslavia and communism; 1968). (AG)

Sources: *Biographisches Lexikon*, vol. 4; *Enciklopedija Jugoslavije*, vol. 7 (Zagreb, 1968); Kosta Milutinović, *Dr. Ivan Ribar* (Sisak, 1968); Stevo Reljić and Đuro Mihaljčić, *Dr. Ivan Ribar i sinovi* (Zagreb, 1975); Michał J. Zacharias, *Jugosławia w polityce Wielkiej Brytanii 1940–1945* (Wrocław, 1987).

RIBIČIĆ Ciril (30 June 1947, Ljubljana), Slovene Communist activist and lawyer. The son of a Communist activist, **Mitja Ribičić**, in 1970 Ribičić graduated in law, and in 1978 he received a Ph.D. in law at the University of Ljubljana, where he then taught constitutional law and where he became a professor in 1988. In 1982–84 Ribičić chaired the Sociopolitical Assembly of the Slovene republican parliament. In December 1989 he took the lead of the League of Communists of Slovenia (LCS), whose delegation left the Fourteenth Extraordinary Congress of the League of Communists of Yugoslavia in early 1990 in protest against the centralist policies of the Serb Communists. Soon the LCS was transformed into the Party of Democratic Reform (Stranka Demokratskih Reform [SDR]), which lost the elections of April 1990 and joined the opposition. Before the next elections the POD entered a coalition called the United List of Social Democrats (Združena Lista Socjalnih Demokrativ [ULSD]), which co-ruled from May 1992 to January 1993. Ribičić chaired the POD until 1993, when it entered the ULSD. He sat in the parliament on behalf of the ULSD until 2000. In December 2000 he was supported by President **Milan Kučan**

and elected a member of the Constitutional Tribunal. Ribičić authored a number of works, including *Ustavno pravo SFR Jugoslavije* (The constitutional law of the Socialist Federal Republic of Yugoslavia; 1978 [co-author Miha Ribarić]), *Ustavnopravni vidiki osamosvajanja Slovenije* (Constitutional aspects of Slovene independence; 1992), and *Rad sem jih imel* (I liked them; 1993). In early 2000 Ribičić appeared before The Hague International Tribunal for War Crimes in Former Yugoslavia as an expert on the constitutional system of the Croatian Herzeg-Bosnia Republic in Bosnia-Herzegovina, which he described in *Geneza jedne zablude* (The origins of an error; 2000). In 2000 he published *Podoba parlamentarnega desetletja* (The image of a parliamentary decade). (AO)

Sources: *Enciklopedija Slovenije*, vol. 10 (Ljubljana, 1996); Bugajski; www.us-rs.si/about/compossi.htm.

RIBIČIĆ Mitja (19 May 1919, Trieste), Slovene Communist activist. In 1938 Ribičić enrolled in legal studies at the University of Ljubljana. During World War II he fought with the Communist guerrillas and was active in the Communist Party of Slovenia. He graduated from a military academy in Moscow. Upon his return home, he worked in the department of defense of the Slovene republic (1945–46) and then in the republic's department of interior (1947–51). Ribičić was responsible for the repression of opponents of communism and, after June 1948, of followers of the Cominform. In 1952 he became a public prosecutor of the Slovene republic. In 1953–58 he was deputy secretary and then secretary (minister) of interior of the Slovene Socialist Republic. Ribičić was a member of the executive council of the republican assembly (1959–63), and from 1974 he sat in the parliament of the Socialist Federal Republic of Yugoslavia (SFRY). From 1964 he was secretary of the regional committee of the League of Communists of Slovenia (LCS) in Ljubljana, and in 1965 he joined the Executive Committee of the LCS Central Committee. In 1968–69 he was a member of the Executive Committee of the CC of the League of Communists of Yugoslavia (LCY). As chairman of the Federal Executive Council (government), Ribičić headed the federal government in Belgrade from June 1969 to August 1971. Later he was a member of the SFRY Presidium (June 1971–May 1974) and its deputy chairman (August 1973–May 1974). Ribičić was chairman of the Socialist Union of the Working People of Slovenia, its councils for publication, and its relations with religious communities (1974–82). He was a member of the LCY CC (June 1982–April 1986) and of its Presidium (June 1982–April 1986), and from June 1982 to June 1983 he headed the LCY CC. Ribicić authored *Glasna premišljanja* (Reflections aloud; 1983), *Iskanja* (Inquiries; 1995), and other works. His son, **Ciril Ribičić**, is also a Communist and post-Communist activist. (AO)

Sources: Juliusz Stroynowski, ed., *Who's Who in the Socialist Countries of Europe* (Munich, London, and Paris, 1989); *Enciklopedija Slovenije*, vol. 10 (Ljubljana, 1996).

RIES István (14 November 1885, Küngös–15 September 1950, Vác), Hungarian Communist activist. Ries was the son of an agrarian leaseholder. After the premature death of his father, his mother moved with her children to Budapest. Ries graduated from the School of Law and Political Science of the Hungarian Royal Academy. In 1912, after passing his exams, he opened a law practice. During World War Ries he fought on the front lines and was taken prisoner by the Russians. He returned to Hungary in the summer of 1918. Under the Hungarian Soviet Republic (HSR) in 1919 Ries worked as a clerk in the propaganda department of the People's Commissariat of Education. He also joined the Hungarian Red Army. Following the fall of the HSR, Ries fled to Vienna for a few months. After returning to Hungary, he continued to run his law practice. He was a defense counsel in the trials of HSR people's commissars. In 1924 Ries joined the Hungarian Social Democratic Party (HSDP). He wrote articles for the HSDP press organs, *Népszava* and *Szocializmus*. He was a member of the executive of the Socialist Association of Lawyers and the HSDP National Bureau for the Defense of Workers' Rights. In the 1930s Ries served as chairman of the HSDP organization in the eighth district of Budapest. From 1933 to 1935 and then from 1939 onwards he was a member of the HSDP national executive. In 1943 he also took part in the work of the five-member Presidium of the HSDP. When the Germans occupied Hungary in March 1944, he had to go into hiding.

In August 1945 Ries was elected to the HSDP Politburo. In April 1945 he became an MP, and in late July 1945, minister of justice. After the elections of August 1947, Ries resigned his position in protest against Communist electoral fraud. Other HSDP government officials also resigned. Along with these officials, Ries returned to the government after a "ministers' strike." In 1948 he also held the post of chairman of the Association of Hungarian Lawyers and of the Hungarian Football Association. Before the "unification" of workers' parties in June 1948, Ries served as deputy secretary general of the HSDP. He subsequently became a member of the Central Committee of the Hungarian Workers' Party (HWP). During his term as minister, a Soviet-style constitution was drafted and came into force in 1949. On 8 July 1950, along with thousands of former Social Democrats, Ries was arrested on false charges but was not dismissed as minister until nine days later. The Communists planned to convict Ries in the trial of **Árpád Szakasits**, but Ries died of injuries sustained during vicious interrogations in a prison in Vác. His wife, also arrested in 1950, was released after four years. In June 1956 Ries was rehabilitated. (JT)

Sources: Ferenc Nagy, *The Struggle behind the Iron Curtain* (New York, 1948); Imre Kovacs, ed., *Facts About Hungary: The Fight for Freedom* (New York, 1966); *Magyar Életrajzi Lexikon*, vol. 2 (Budapest, 1969); *A magyar forradalom és szabadságharc enciklopédiája* (Budapest, 1999).

RIPKA Hubert (26 July 1895, Kobeřice, Moravia–7 January 1958, London), Czech historian and politician. After graduating in history and receiving a Ph.D. at Prague University, Ripka lectured on international relations at this university, and he was a political journalist, editing *Lidové Noviny*. He was a member of the Czechoslovak Nationalist Socialist Party of **Tomáš Garrigue Masaryk**. After Hitler came to power, Ripka repeatedly warned against Hitler's aggressive plans regarding Czechoslovakia. After German forces entered Prague on 15 March 1939, Ripka left for Paris, then for London, where he joined the Czechoslovak National Committee, and in July 1940 he became deputy foreign minister of the government-in-exile. Ripka enjoyed the special trust of President **Edvard Beneš**, who saw him as his successor. Ripka supported Beneš's policy toward the USSR, but gradually he became increasingly disillusioned with its effects. He returned to Czechoslovakia as foreign trade minister of the Košice government, which was established by Beneš on 4 April 1945. Ripka wanted to maintain close economic relations with the West, and he supported the adoption of the Marshall Plan by Czechoslovakia, but at the beginning of July 1947, along with the minister of foreign affairs, **Jan Masaryk**, Ripka was called to Moscow and was forced by Vyacheslav Molotov to reject the plan.

At the beginning of 1948 Ripka was aware that the Communists wanted to use the trade unions and security forces, which they controlled, to change the political system. Since protests had no effect, on 20 February Ripka and other non-Communist ministers of **Klement Gottwald**'s cabinet agreed to resign in a body, to enable President Beneš to change the government. However, Gottwald, who was supported by the Kremlin's special envoy, Valeriy Zorin, resorted to mass demonstrations, which were inspired by the Communists, and on 25 February he forced the president to reconstruct the cabinet through a replacement of the ministers who had resigned. Threatened with arrest, Ripka was forced to escape from the country and went to France, while the Communist "security police" arrested two of his co-workers. From France he went to London, where he lived after the war as one of the leaders of the political émigrés. Ripka was an advocate of a broader federation of the states of Central and Eastern Europe as a counterbalance to the USSR and Germany. Among other works, Ripka published *Munich: Before and After* (1939); *S Východem i Západem* (With the East and the West; 1944); *Československo ve světovém hospodářství* (Czechoslovakia in the world economy; 1945); *ČSR v nové Evropé* (Czechoslovakia in the new Europe; 1945); *Czechoslovakia Enslaved* (1950); and *Federation of East Central Europe* (1955). (WR)

Sources: *Politická elita meziválečného Československa 1918–1938: Kdo byl kdo za první republiky* (Prague, 1998); *Kdo byl kdo v našich dějinach ve 20. stoleti*, vol. 2 (Prague, 1998); *The Times*, 8 January 1958; Karel Kaplan, *The Short March: The Communist Takeover in Czechoslovakia, 1945–1948* (London, 1987).

RODE Gunārs (8 September 1934, Riga), Latvian dissident. In 1945–46 Rode took part in an underground anti-Communist school movement, the Green Partisans (Zaļie Partizāņi), near Vecpiebalga in the Cēsis county of Semigalia. In 1953–56 he studied at the State University of Latvia and from 1956 at the Polytechnic Institute in Riga. In 1958 he was expelled from this school for pro-independence activities; he then worked as a trolley driver in Riga. In May 1962 Rode was arrested for disseminating "anti-Soviet" literature and for "agitation." In December 1962 he was sentenced, along with a group of other Latvian dissidents, to fifteen years in a labor camp. Rode was sent to Mordvinian camps, where he took part in many protests by prisoners. In 1966–68, 1970–73, and 1975–77 Rode was held in Vladimir Prison. Released in 1977, he worked as a blue-collar laborer in Riga. He married a Swede with Latvian roots, Ieva Strauberga, so in May 1978 he was allowed to emigrate to Sweden. For some time Rode worked in the Stockholm office of the Union of Free Latvians of the World (Pasaules Brīvo Latviešu Apvienība). He wrote articles for the Latvian émigré press and lectured in Latvian centers in the United States and Canada. As a leading Latvian dissident, Rode was received by the Baltic Department of the U.S. Department of State. After Latvia regained its independence, Rode published in nationalist periodicals in Latvia. (EJ)

Sources: S. P. de Boer, E. J. Driessen, and H. L. Verhaar, eds., *Biographical Dictionary of Dissidents in the Soviet Union, 1956–1975* (The Hague and Boston, 1982); *Latvju enciklopēdija*, vol. 4 (Rockville, 1990).

ROKOSSOVSKY Konstantin (21 December 1896, Velikiye Luki–3 August 1968, Moscow), marshal of the USSR

and of Poland. Rokossovsky's origins and childhood are unclear. According to one version, he was the son of a Polish railway clerk in Russia; another version notes that he was brought up in Warsaw; still another presents him as an orphan of Polish origins. Perhaps all these versions contain some elements of truth. In 1914 Rokossovsky volunteered for the Russian Army, and in 1917 he joined the Red Guards. In 1919 he joined the Bolshevik party. In 1920 he fought in the Red Army against Poland. In 1926 he graduated from the Cavalry School, and in 1929 he completed courses for commanders at the Frunze Military Academy. Rokossovsky subsequently commanded a brigade, then a division, and later a cavalry corps. Imprisoned during the Great Purge of the army in 1937, he was sent to a forced labor camp in the Far East. In 1940 he was released and resumed command of a cavalry corps. At the end of 1941 he fought in the battle of Moscow. Later he commanded armies in Bryansk, on the Don River, and in the battles at Stalingrad and Kursk.

In mid-1943 Rokossovsky assumed command of the first Belorussian front, and in 1944 he commanded the second Belorussian front, which occupied Poland. In June 1944 he was promoted to the rank of marshal. As commander of the second Belorussian front, Rokossovsky followed Stalin's orders to stop the offensive on Warsaw when the uprising broke out there on 1 August 1944. Rokossovsky's deputy, General Yakov Yedunov, who was in charge of the counterespionage Smiersh; Lavrenty Tsanava, a special plenipotentiary for security to the command of the second division; and General Ivan Serov were instrumental in dismantling the Polish independence underground and subsequently in the arrests of its activists. Rokossovsky reached Berlin as the commander of the front, and he led the victory parade on Red Square in Moscow in May 1945.

One of the outstanding Soviet military commanders, after the end of the war in Europe, Rokossovsky assumed command of the Group of Soviet Troops, with headquarters in Legnica; these troops occupied Poland. In fact, Rokossovsky became the military governor of Poland. On 5 November 1949 **Bolesław Bierut** named Rokossovsky marshal of Poland and defense minister. Although this violated Communist Party statutes, the party made him a member of the Central Committee (CC), and in May 1950, a member of the Politburo of the CC of the Polish United Workers' Party (Polska Zjednoczona Partia Robotnicza [PUWP]). Soon after Rokossovsky's appointment, other officers of the Soviet Army took over top command posts in the Polish Army. From November 1952 to November 1956 Rokossovsky was deputy prime minister. In 1951 he was decorated with the Order of Builders of the People's

Poland. Because of his position, Rokossovsky bore special responsibility for the crimes perpetrated by the Chief Board of the Polish Army Information Service, which reported directly to him.

At the Eighth Plenum of the PUWP CC in October 1956 Rokossovsky formally lost an election to the Politburo. On 24 October the new Politburo decided to ask the Soviet authorities to recall him, and after consent was granted, on 10 November he was dismissed as minister. Rokossovsky received official acknowledgments and an annuity in the amount of the salary he had been paid to date. Rokossovsky left for the USSR with a few dozen Soviet commanders. In the Soviet Union he was nominated deputy defense minister. Between 1957 and 1959 he headed the Transcaucasian Military District, and from 1961 until his death he was a deputy member of the Soviet party's Central Committee and a deputy to the USSR Supreme Soviet. Rokossovsky was decorated with seven Orders of Lenin. His publications include *Vilikaia pobeda na Volge* (The great victory on the Volge; 1965) and his memoirs, *Soldatskii dolg* (The soldier's debt; 1968). Rokossovsky was buried under the Kremlin Wall. (WR)

Sources: *MERSH*, vol. 31; Mołdawa; V. Kardashov, *Rokossowskyi* (Moscow, 1973); Adam Ciołkosz, *Walka o prawdę: Wybór artykułów 1940–1983* (London, 1978); Władysław Pobóg-Malinowski, *Najnowsza historia polityczna Polski*, vol. 3 (London, 1986); Jerzy Poksiński, *"TUN" Tatar-Utnik-Nowicki* (Warsaw, 1992); Edward Jan Nalepa, *Oficerowie Armii Radzieckiej w Wojsku Polskim 1943–1968* (Warsaw, 1995); Krzysztof Persak, "Kreski Rokossowskiego," *Polityka*, 19 October 1996.

ROMAN Petre (22 July 1946, Bucharest), Romanian post-Communist politician. The son of Valter Roman (Ernst Neulander), a colonel in the Soviet NKVD and one of the founders of the Romanian political police (Securitate), in 1959–63 Roman studied at the Higher School of Information; from 1963 to 1968 he studied at the Department of Power Engineering of the Polytechnic Institute in Bucharest, where he then worked as a teacher. In 1971 he left for France, where he obtained an M.A. degree. Until 1974 Roman pursued doctoral studies at the University of Toulouse, France, working for Mihai Caraman, head of the Romanian spy ring in France. Upon returning to Romania, he taught at the Bucharest Polytechnic Institute. In 1985 he held the chair of hydraulics, and in 1990 he became a full professor. Roman started his political career at the end of December 1989, when, after the toppling and execution of **Nicolae Ceauşescu**, he joined **Ion Iliescu** and the founders of the National Salvation Front (Frontul Salvării Naţionale [NSF]). Roman became a member of the Provisional Council of National Unity (Consiliul Provizoriu de Uniune Naţionala), and on 26 December

1989, prime minister of a provisional government. In the parliamentary elections of May 1990 Roman won a mandate and remained in office until 1 October 1991, when he was forced to step down by striking miners from the Jiu mining region. Leaders of the Jiu strike were suspected of connections with President Iliescu, who had entered into conflict with Roman over leadership and over the rate at which economic liberalization was unfolding (Roman favored an acceleration).

After a split in the NSF, in 1992–93 Roman remained its chairman. In 1993 the NSF merged with the small Democratic Party (Partidul Democrat [DP]) and adopted its name. Roman remained its chairman until May 2001. In 1993–96 he was accredited at the NATO Assembly. In 1995 the DP merged with the Romanian Social Democratic Party into the Social Democratic Union (Uniunea Social Democrata [SDU]). After the parliamentary elections of November 1996, Roman became a senator and speaker of the senate. Before the presidential elections of November 1996 he withdrew his candidature and called for support of the rightist candidate, **Emil Constantinescu**. After leaving the SDU, in 1997–99 Roman remained a senator on behalf of the DP. From 1997 to 1998 he chaired the Parliamentary Assembly of Economic Cooperation of the Black Sea Countries. From December 1999 to December 2000 he was foreign minister. Elected again to the senate in November 2000, in the presidential elections held at the same time, Roman won 3 percent of the vote. He authored several books and articles in hydrology and power engineering. (LW)

Sources: Andrei Codrescu, *The Hole in the Flag* (New York, 1991); Daniel N. Nelson, ed., *Romania after Tyranny* (Boulder, Colo., 1992); Józef Darski, *Rumunia: Historia, współczesność, konflikty narodowe* (Warsaw, 1995); *Personalităţi politice, publice* (Bucharest, 1994); Tom Gallagher, *Romania after Ceausescu* (Edinburgh, 1995); Ion Alexandrescu, Ion Bulei, Ion Mamina, and Ioan Scurtu, *Enciclopedia de istorie României* (Bucharest, 2000).

ROMAN Štefan (17 April 1921, Vel'ký Ruskov–23 March 1988, Toronto), Slovak entrepreneur and émigré activist. Born into a Uniate peasant family, Roman emigrated to Canada in 1937. During World War II he served in the Canadian Army and subsequently worked as a blue-collar laborer. In 1945 he started his own mining company. In the early 1950s Roman bought land in the Elliot Lake area, Ontario, and founded Denison Mines, which soon became the owner of the world's largest uranium mines. Roman successfully developed his industrial and financial empire, which included Roman Corporation, Lake Ontario Cement, and the Crown Life Insurance Company. Richard Nixon, the future president of the United States, was his financial adviser. Roman's business success allowed him to sponsor many cultural initiatives of the Slovak émigré community. These included the establishment of the Slovak Institute (Slovenský Ústav) in Rome and the Slovak Uniate diocese in Canada. In 1963 Roman presided over a committee for celebrations in honor of Ss. Cyril and Methodius in Rome. In 1964 he became a lay observer at the second Vatican Council. He was instrumental in uniting Slovak émigré organizations. In 1970, on his initiative, the Slovak World Congress (Svetový Kongres Slovákov [SKS]) was founded in New York. The SKS called for independence for Slovakia. Roman served as president of the SKS until the end of his life. (MG)

Sources: *SBS*; *Who's Who in America*, vol. 2 (Chicago, 1980–81); *Štefan Roman: človek v rozdelenom svete* (Cambridge, Ont., 1981); Jozef Špetko, *Slovenská politická emigrácia v 20. storočí* (Prague, 1994).

ROMANCHUK Yuliyan (24 February 1842, Krylos, near Halych, Galicia–22 April 1932, Lwów [Lemberg, Lviv]), Ukrainian politician and social activist. The son of a teacher, Romanchuk completed philological studies at the University of Lemberg. He subsequently taught at a German high school (1863–68) and at the Ukrainian Academic Gymnasium (1868–1900) in Lemberg. Devoted to the development of Ukrainian education, Romanchuk served as an MP in the Galician Assembly (1883–95), becoming chairman of the Ukrainian parliamentary group in 1889. In this role, in November 1890 he reached a Ukrainian-Polish political agreement with Kazimierz Badeni, the governor of Galicia. However, in 1894 Romanchuk joined forces with the opposition, accusing the Poles of having violated the terms of this agreement. Romanchuk served as an MP (1891–97 and 1901–18) in the parliament of the Austro-Hungarian monarchy, chairman of the Ukrainian parliamentary representation (1901–10 and 1916–17), and deputy speaker of the Austrian parliament (from 1910 on).

On 26 December 1899 Romanchuk brought about the establishment of the moderately rightist Ukrainian National Democratic Party and then served as its leader until 1907. He was engaged in the struggle for the Ukrainization of the University of Lemberg. He condemned the assassination of Governor Andrzej Potocki in 1908. During World War I Romanchuk chaired the Ukrainian Assistance Committee and the Ukrainian Cultural Council in Vienna. As a member of the National Council of the Western Ukrainian National Republic (Zakhidno-Ukraiiinska *Narodna* Republika [ZUNR]) and the oldest Ukrainian politician, Romanchuk administered the oath to members of the ZUNR government on 10 November 1918. After

the Council of Ambassadors recognized Poland's right to Eastern Galicia in March 1923, Romanchuk administered the Ukrainians' oath of allegiance to their national state on St. George Square in Lwów. Romanchuk co-founded and was the chairman (1896–1906) of the Prosvita Society. He was also a founding member and a full member of the Shevchenko Scientific Society (NTSh); the founder of the Ridna Shkola Society; and the founder, honorary member, and chairman (1912–15) of Uchytels'ka Hromada (Teachers' Society). Romanchuk founded and edited the periodical *Bat'kivshschyna* (1879–87) and contributed to the Lemberg daily *Dilo*, to the Vienna-based monthly *Ruthenische Revue* (1903–5), and to *Ukrainische Rundschau* (1905–14). He was the publisher, editor, and interpreter of works by Taras Shevchenko. He initiated and then edited *Ruska pysmennist*, a series of classics of Ukrainian literature. He also edited one of the first Ukrainian textbooks for schools in Galicia. Like Mykhailo Drahomanov, **Ivan Franko**, and **Mykhailo Hrushevskyi**, Romanchuk was one of the first Ukrainian politicians to maintain contacts with representatives of the Ukrainian movement in both parts of the Ukraine long before 1914. (TS)

Sources: *Encyclopedia of Ukraine*, vol. 4 (Toronto, 1993); Czesław Partacz, *Od Badeniego do Potockiego: Stosunki polsko-ukraińskie w Galicji w latach 1888–1908* (Toruń, 1960); *Ihor Deichakivskyi, Iuliian Romanchuk: Pedahoh, hromadskyi diyach, polityk* (Ivano-Frankivsk, 1999).

ROMASZEWSKI Zbigniew (2 January 1940, Warsaw), Polish dissident and politician. Romaszewski graduated in physics from Warsaw University in 1964, and until 1983 he worked at the Institute of Physics of the Polish Academy of Sciences, where he received a Ph.D. in 1980. In 1975–76 he took part in protests against the amendment of the constitution, and from September 1976 he worked with the Committee for the Defense of Workers. Along with his wife, Zofia, Romaszewski led the assistance for those who had been repressed during the Radom riots. From September 1977 he belonged to the KOR Self-Defense Committee, gathering information about violations of the law by the Communist police and courts and assisting those persecuted. In 1979 Romaszewski co-organized the Helsinki Commission, which put together "Raport madrycki" (The Madrid report; 1980) on the respect for human rights in Poland. From September 1980 Romaszewski headed the Intervention and Legal Commission of the Mazowsze Region of Solidarity. In 1981 he was a member of the Regional Board Presidium and a delegate to the First Solidarity Congress in Gdańsk, where he was elected to the union's National Commission.

After the introduction of martial law on 13 December

1981, Romaszewski was active in the Solidarity underground as a member of its Mazowsze Regional Executive Committee and Inter-Factory Workers' Committee (Międzyzakładowy Komitet Robotniczy Solidarności). He also organized the underground Solidarity radio broadcasts. In 1982 Romaszewski was arrested and sentenced to four and a half years in prison. Amnestied in 1984, in 1986–89 he headed the Solidarity Intervention and Legal Commission. From 1987 he belonged to the National Executive Commission, and in 1988 he co-organized an unofficial international human rights conference in Kraków. From late 1988 Romaszewski belonged to the Civic Committee of the Chairman of Solidarity. A participant in the Round Table Talks, in June 1989 Romaszewski was elected to the senate and chaired its Commission of Human Rights and Legality. During the so-called war at the top, Romaszewski sided with **Lech Wałęsa**, and in 1991 he joined the Presidium of the Civic Committee. In 1991 Romaszewski was reelected to the senate on behalf of Solidarity. From May to June 1992 he chaired the Committee for Radio and Television. From 1996 he was a member of the Movement for the Reconstruction of Poland (Ruch Odbudowy Polski [ROP]). From 1997 to 2001 Romaszewski sat on the senate on behalf of the ROP, and from 2001, on behalf of the Bloc Senate 2001. (AF)

Sources: *Nasi w Sejmie i Senacie* (Warsaw, 1990); Jerzy Holzer and Krzysztof Leski, *"Solidarność" w podziemiu* (Łódź, 1990); Jan Skórzyński, *Ugoda i rewolucja: Władza i opozycja 1985–1989* (Warsaw, 1995); Antoni Dudek, *Pierwsze lata III Rzeczpospolitej 1989–2001* (Kraków, 2002); Zdzisław Najder, *Jaka Polska? Co i komu doradzałem* (Warsaw, n.d.).

ROMER Tadeusz (6 December 1894, Antonosz, near Kaunas–23 March 1978, Montreal, Canada), Polish diplomat. Born into a landed noble family, after graduating from a Kraków high school in 1913, Romer studied in Lausanne, Switzerland, where he completed a law degree in 1917. From his early youth he was involved with the nationalist movement. During World War I he was the editorial secretary of the *Grande Encyclopédie Polonaise* and secretary of the Committee to Aid War Victims in Poland. In 1917, Romer became the personal assistant of **Roman Dmowski** and the Polish National Committee. In 1919 he became the first secretary of the Polish legation in Paris. From 1921 to 1927, he held various posts at the Ministry of Foreign Affairs in Warsaw, including that of director of the political department and deputy chief of the political cabinet. In 1928 Romer joined the staff of the Polish Embassy in Italy. Between 1935 and 1937 he served as envoy to Portugal. Despite his links to the National Democrats and because of his personal and professional attributes, Romer was appointed envoy (in 1937) and then ambassador (in 1938) to Japan. After the German invasion of Poland in 1939, Romer organized assistance for the Poles and conducted an information campaign concerning Nazi atrocities in Poland. His efforts resulted in the friendly neutrality of Japan, despite its status as an ally of the Third Reich. The Polish Embassy in Tokyo was closed only when Japan joined the war in December 1941.

At that time, Romer was evacuated to South Africa, where he was tapped by the Polish government-in-exile to become ambassador to the USSR. He traveled through Cairo and Tehran to reach Kuibyshev in October 1942. After two months he reported personally to the Polish government in London about the steady deterioration of Polish-Soviet relations because of the Kremlin's intransigence. After returning to his post in February 1943, Romer conducted negotiations with Stalin and Molotov. However, the breaking off of diplomatic relations by the USSR in April 1943 forced him to close the embassy. After leaving the USSR, Romer was stationed in Cairo as the commissar for Polish Affairs in the Middle East. Following the death of General **Władysław Sikorski**, Romer joined the government of **Stanisław Mikołajczyk** as the minister of foreign affairs. He strove to restore diplomatic relations with the USSR. In July 1944, along with **Stanisław Grabski** and Mikołajczyk, Romer traveled to Moscow. However, talks with Stalin failed. After his next visit to the USSR in October 1944 and yet another failure of negotiations, Romer tendered his resignation, as did the entire government. The great stress of his work resulted in a heart attack. In 1945 Romer was active in Polish émigré organizations in Great Britain, and in 1948 he moved to Canada, where he became a lecturer in Latin studies at McGill University. (AG)

Sources: *Kto był kim w Drugiej Rzeczypospolite* (Warsaw, 1994); Józef Garliński, *Polska w drugiej wojnie światowej* (London, 1982); Jan Karski, *The Great Powers and Poland, 1919–1945: From Versailles to Yalta* (Lanham, Md., 1985); Władysław Pobóg-Malinowski, *Najnowsza historia polityczna Polski*, vol. 3 (London, 1986); Andrzej Albert [Wojciech Roszkowski], *Najnowsza historia Polski 1914–1993*, vol. 1 (Warsaw, 1995).

ROMZHA Fedor (14 April 1911, Velikiy Bychkiv, Transcarpathian Ruthenia–1 November 1947, Mukachevo). Greek Catholic bishop. Romzha studied philosophy (1930–33) and theology (1933–37) in Rome, obtaining a bachelor's degree. After taking holy orders, in 1938 he began working as a parish priest in Berezovo in Transcarpathian Ruthenia. At the beginning of 1939 he became a professor of philosophy at a theological seminary in Uzhhorod. He performed his duties without any major obstacles under the Hungarian government (1939–44). Shortly before the arrival of the Red Army, on 24 September 1944 Romzha was ordained bishop of Mukachevo. After the invasion of the Red Army and the incorporation of Transcarpathia into the Ukrainian SSR, Romzha defended religious freedom for the nation and its right to self-determination. As a result, he incurred the wrath of the Soviet authorities. After the official abolishment of the Greek Catholic Church and its incorporation into the Orthodox Church in March 1946, in May of that year Romzha received a special emissary of the Orthodox Church; despite threats and accusations of collaboration with the Hungarians, he refused to submit to the decisions on incorporation. The current head of the party in the Ukraine, **Nikita Khrushchev**, informed Stalin that Romzha posed a "threat" to the Soviet authorities. In May 1947 Romzha sent an emissary to Moscow with a letter protesting the arrests of priests and the takeover of the Uniate Churches by the Orthodox Church. In answer, the Soviet authorities approved the plan of incorporating the Greek Catholic Church of Transcarpathian Ruthenia into the Orthodox Church; they had supported a similar plan in Eastern Galicia. On 27 October 1947 Romzha was severely injured in a car accident caused by a special group from the Soviet Ministry of State Security (MGB). The assailants took him to a hospital, where he was poisoned by Soviet special services; this was done with Khrushchev's approval. On 27 June 2001 Pope **John Paul II** beatified Romzha at a solemn Holy Mass in Lviv. (WR)

Sources: *Encyclopedia of Ukraine*, vol. 4 (Toronto, 1993); Yaroslav Lialka et al., eds., *Litopys neskorennoi Ukrainy: Dokumenty, materialy, spohady* (Lviv, 1993); László Puskás, *Romzsa Tódor püspök élete és halála* (Budapest, 1998); Bohdan R. Bociurkiw, *The Ukrainian Greek-Catholic Church and the Soviet State (1939–1950)* (Edmonton, 1996); Paweł Sudopłatow, *Wspomnienia niewygodnego świadka* (Warsaw, 1999); *Osservatore Romano* (weekly edition in English), 2001, nos. 25 and 27.

RÓNAI Sándor (6 October 1892, Miskolc–28 September 1965, Budapest), Hungarian Social Democratic and Communist activist. The son of an agrarian worker, after finishing primary school, Rónai worked as a mason's apprentice. In 1910 he joined the Hungarian Social Democratic Party (HSDP). In 1918 he served as head of a local organization of his trade union. In 1919, under the Hungarian Soviet Republic (HSR), he was a member of a workers' council in Miskolc. In 1922 he was elected secretary of a trade union and party organization in Miskolc. In 1936 he became an HSDP secretary in Northern Hungary. In April 1941 Rónai was sent to a penal colony for his political activities. In the spring of 1944 he was interned in Nagykanizsa; he returned from there to Miskolc at the end of 1944. In

January 1945 he was again elected secretary of an HSDP regional organization. Shortly afterwards he became the editor-in-chief of *Felvidéki Népszava*, an HSDP press organ in Northern Hungary. From July to November 1945 Rónai was minister for supplies. After the parliamentary elections of November 1945, he became minister of trade and cooperatives and held this post until June 1949. He subsequently served as minister of foreign trade until May 1950. One of the top leaders of the HSDP from 1947 onwards, Rónai supported the "unification" of workers' parties under Communist leadership in June 1948. In that year he became a member of the Central Committee (CC) of the Hungarian Workers' Party (HWP). From June 1948 to June 1953 he was a member of the HWP Politburo. Chairman of the Presiding Council (May 1950–August 1952) and subsequently the parliament speaker (until 1963), Rónai was the only leading Social Democratic activist who not only avoided arrest in the first half of the 1950s, but also held a prominent party and government post. In July 1956 he became a deputy member of the HWP Politburo and a member of the Presiding Council. He held the latter post until the end of his life. From 4 November 1956 to February 1957 Rónai was minister of trade in the government of **János Kádár**, and in November 1956 he became a member of the government's Economic Commission. From November 1956 until the end of his life he served as a member of the CC and the Politburo of the Hungarian Socialist Workers' Party. In 1963 he retired. In 1960–65 Rónai served as chairman of the Hungarian-Soviet Friendship Society. (JT)

Sources: *Magyar Életrajzi Lexikon*, vol. 2 (Budapest, 1969); *A magyar forradalom és szabadságharc enciklopédiája*, CD-ROM (Budapest, 1999); Bennet Kovrig, *Communism in Hungary from Kun to Kádár* (Stanford, 1979); Miklós Molnár, *From Béla Kun to János Kádár: Seventy Years of Hungarian Communism* (New York, 1990).

RONIKIER Adam (1 November 1881, Warsaw–4 September 1952, Orchard Lake, Michigan), Polish conservative activist. In 1905 Ronikier graduated from the Department of Architecture at Riga Polytechnic University, where he was a member of the Arconia student fraternity. In October 1915 in Warsaw he took the lead of the (conservative) National Party (not to be confused with the National Democratic outfit of the same name), which cooperated with the Germans. Simultaneously, Ronikier pursued charity work in the Main Welfare Council (Rada Główna Opiekuńcza [RGO]), becoming its chairman in October 1916. He supported Poland's eastward expansion in exchange for ceding most of its western territories. After the nation regained its independence, Ronikier was ostracized for his Germanophilism. Seriously crippled in an accident, he was unable to fight in the Polish-Soviet war. Between 1922 and 1939 he unsuccessfully attempted to return to politics several times in the ranks of conservative and center-right outfits. After the fall of Warsaw in September 1939, Ronikier devoted himself once again to charity work, informally reassembling the RGO on 22 February 1940. On 22 May 1940 the Nazi authorities of the General Government legalized the RGO and confirmed Ronikier as its deputy chairman. Ronikier worked closely with the Catholic Church, assisting the civilian population. He intervened numerous times with the Germans in the defense of Poles. He also worked with Jewish Social Self-Aid (JSSA) and officially objected to the Germans for their persecution of the Jews. Ronikier sheltered the chairman of the JSSA, Michał Weichert, and worked with the Polish underground Council to Aid Jews (Żegota). On 25 October 1943 Ronikier was fired from the RGO by the Germans for insubordination, and on 26 January 1944 he was arrested by the Gestapo. Released in March 1944, he was nonetheless accused by the underground of appeasing the occupiers, and he was ostracized. During the Warsaw Uprising Ronikier devoted himself to assisting the civilian population. In October 1944, terrified of the imminent Soviet occupation, he decided to commence open collaboration with the Germans. He founded the Bureau of Political Studies and called on the Poles to desist fighting against the Third Reich. In January 1945, under the blows of the Red Army offensive, Ronikier escaped to the West with the retreating Germans. After the war he reached Italy, where he found shelter with General **Władysław Anders**. Ostracized by the Polish government-in-exile in London, in 1948 Ronikier emigrated to the United States, where he died shortly after. His *Pamiętniki* (Memoirs) were published in 2000. (MC)

Sources: *PSB*, vol. 32; *1879–1979 Arkonia: Księga Pamiątkowa* (London, 1981); Bohdan Kroll, *Rada Główna Opiekuńcza, 1939–1945* (Warsaw, 1985).

ROP Anton (27 December 1960, Ljubljana), Slovene politician. Rop graduated in economics from the University of Ljubljana, and in 1984–93 he worked at the Slovene Institute of Macroeconomic Analysis and Development. As deputy director of this institute and government adviser, in 1992 Rop dealt with privatization and new economic legislation. From 1993 he was undersecretary of state in the Ministry of Economic Relations and Development, where he was responsible for privatization and regional development. In 1996–2000 he was minister of labor, family, and social affairs, dealing with pension reforms and tightening pension requirements in view of demographic changes and budget shortages. Rop co-authored a law on social security in 1999 that entered into force in 2000. He became deputy chairman of Liberal Democracy of Slovenia (Liberalna Demokracija Slovenije [LDS]) and won a mandate on its behalf in the parliamentary elections of October 2000. In December 2000 Rop became minister of finance in the government of **Janez Drnovšek**. When on 1 December 2002 the latter won the presidency and resigned from heading the government, the outgoing president, **Milan Kučan**, appointed Rop prime minister. Rop was confirmed by the parliament on 19 December 2000. His government was based on a coalition of the LDS, the United List of Social Democrats, the Slovenian National Party, and the Democratic Party of Pensioners. As prime minister, Rop finalized talks on Slovenia's entry into NATO and the European Union. (AO)

Sources: www.sigov.si/pv; www.fact-index.com.

ROPP Edward (2 December 1851, Liksin, near Dünaburg [Daugavpils]–25 July 1939, Poznań), Roman Catholic bishop. Ropp came from a Polonized German family of Courland. In 1874 he graduated in law from the University of St. Petersburg. Next, he worked at the Russian Ministry of Justice. In 1879 he quit his job and moved to the family estate of Nishcha, near Vitebsk. In 1884 Ropp enrolled at a Catholic seminary, and in 1886 he was ordained. He completed theological studies in Innsbruck, and in 1889 he became a parson in Libau (Liepaja). On 16 November 1902 Ropp was consecrated bishop, and on 9 November 1903 he was appointed ordinary bishop of Vilnius. Ropp reformed the administration of his diocese. Although he supported the Polish community in the area, he ordered that religious instruction be provided in the native tongues of the inhabitants. In 1906 he took over the publishing of *Kurier Litewski*, and he co-founded the Constitutional Catholic Party of Lithuania and White Ruthenia, which was based upon social Catholic rules. Ropp was elected to the First State Duma and joined the Club of the Autonomists. Because of an anti-Jewish pogrom in Białystok in June 1906, Ropp issued an appeal calling for calm, denouncing violence, and pointing out that the events had been triggered by provocation. Ropp's social and political activities caused the Russian authorities to demand that the Holy See transfer him to a different diocese. Because he refused a transfer, Ropp was recalled to St. Petersburg and banned from returning to Vilnius. Between 1907 and 1917 he remained at Nishcha.

Following the February 1917 revolution, Ropp returned to Vilnius and carried on with his pastoral duties. After the Bolshevik revolution, at the beginning of November 1917, he joined the Polish Security Council in Petrograd, becoming its chairman. On 25 July 1917 Ropp was appointed metropolitan of the Mogilev archdiocese, which was the world's largest in terms of territory, for it encompassed the entire area of Russia. On 19 November 1917 Ropp was enthroned in Petrograd. In December 1917, reacting to peasant attacks on manor houses and the murder of landed nobles, Ropp called for peace and constraint. On 29 April 1919 he was placed under house arrest by the Bolsheviks. However, because of the intervention of the Polish authorities and papal diplomats, he was soon released on condition that he leave for Poland. Initially, Ropp settled in Warsaw. His attempts to return to Mogilev came to naught. Nonetheless, he refused to believe in the permanence of the Bolshevik regime and remained ready to continue with his duties. Between 1921 and 1922 Ropp headed the Committee to Aid Victims of Hunger in Russia. He also founded the Missionary Society (1922) and the Marian Institute (1924). In 1927 he was honored with the title of assistant to the papal throne. In the interwar period in Poland Ropp was a symbol of the Bolshevik repression against the Catholic Church. In 1932 he was in a car accident, which put an end to his public activities. He spent his last years in Poznań. In 1993 Ropp's remains were reburied at the Białystok cathedral. (WR)

Sources: *PSB*, vol. 32; Ks. Walerian Meysztowicz, *Gawędy o czasach i ludziach* (London, 1983); Czesław Brzoza and Kamil Stepan, *Posłowie polscy w parlamencie rosyjskim 1906–1917* (Warsaw, 2001).

RÕUK Theodor (14 December 1891, Viljandi–21 June 1940, Tallinn), Estonian politician, officer, and lawyer. In 1911 Rõuk finished a seminary in Riga. After graduating in law from Warsaw University in 1915, he studied at the Vladimir Military College in Petrograd and served in the Russian Army. After the February 1917 revolution, he served in an Estonian regiment. In 1918 he was assigned to organize civil defense, serving as the commander for Tallinn. Rõuk was a public prosecutor (1920–22) and chairman (1923–24) of the People's Assembly of Tallinn–Haapsalu. In March 1924 he became minister of interior. In this role he was instrumental in suppressing an attempted Communist coup d'état on 1 December 1924. In January 1925, as minister of interior, Rõuk was given broad powers under a law enacted to protect the government. He replaced several existing services with a uniformed police force that was subordinated to the Ministry of Interior, and he brought about the establishment of a police school. Following the Communist coup in December 1924, Rõuk reestablished the Estonian Defense League (Eesti Kaitseliit), a voluntary civilian auxiliary unit under the leadership of

the head of the Ministry of Interior. After the resignation of the government in November 1925, Rõuk worked as a sworn attorney-at-law in Tallinn.

A long-time friend of **Konstantin Päts** and an acquaintance of **Artur Sirk**, who had began his law career in Rõuk's office, Rõuk decided to reenter politics at the end of the 1920s. He was one of the main founders of the Estonian League of War of Independence Veterans (Eesti Vabadussõjalaste Liit [EVL]). Along with Sirk, Rõuk developed a Fascist ideology for the EVL movement, along the lines of the Italian and German models. At the second EVL congress in March 1931 Rõuk demanded that the constitution be amended in this spirit. In the autumn of 1933, on Sirk's orders, Rõuk conducted secret negotiations with the aim of winning Päts over to the EVL side and subsequently of putting forward Päts's candidacy as a representative of the radical right wing and the Farmers' Union. However, these negotiations ended in failure. In March 1934, after the coup d'état staged by Päts, Rõuk was briefly detained. He avoided imprisonment but was forced to withdraw from politics. In 1938–40 he served as chairman of the Association for Border Defense. After the Red Army occupied Estonia, Rõuk committed suicide. (AG)

Sources: *Eesti Entsuklopeedia*, vol. 14 (Tallinn, 2000); Piotr Łossowski, *Kraje bałtyckie na drodze od demokracji parlamentarnej do dyktatury (1918–1934)* (Wrocław, 1972); Andres Kasekamp, *The Radical Right in Interwar Estonia* (London, 2000); www.sisemin. gov.ee/eng/inimesed/theodorrouk.html; www.sisemin.gov.ee/eng/ministeerium/index.html.

ROWECKI Stefan Paweł, pseudonyms "Grot," "Grabica," "Rakoń," and "Kalina" (25 December 1895, Piotrków Trybunalski–August 1944, Sachsenhausen), Polish general and military theoretician. While still in school, in 1911 Rowecki joined a secret scouting organization. In 1913 he became a member of the Polish Riflemen's Association. Between 1914 and 1917 he was in the Polish Legions, where he served as an officer and platoon commander in the First and then the Fifth Infantry Regiment of the First Brigade. As a result of the oath crisis (**Józef Piłsudski** and his followers refused to swear loyalty to the Austro-Hungarian and German emperors. Piłsudski was interned in Magdeburg and his followers in various other places) Rowecki was interned in Beniaminów. In 1918 he served in the Polish Military Force, where he was (among other things) an instructor at the Officers' Infantry School in Ostrów Mazowiecka. Then he served in the Polish Army. Rowecki participated in the Polish-Soviet war (1919–20 as (among other things) head of counterintelligence of the southeastern front and head of the Shock Group of General **Edward Rydz-Śmigły**. In 1921–26 Rowecki was an officer of the Bureau of the Strict Council of War and deputy head of the Military-Scientific Publishing Institute (1923–26). From 1926 to 1930 he worked as an officer of the inspectorate of the army of General Józef Rybak. Rowecki was the founder and until 1933 the editor of *Przegląd Wojskowy*. From 1930 to 1935 he commanded the Fifty-fifth Infantry Regiment in Leszno, in 1935–38 he was a brigade commander of the Podole Border Guard Corps in Czortków, and in 1938–39 he commanded the Second Infantry Division of the Legions in Kielce. In June 1939 Rowecki was charged with organizing the Warsaw Armored Motorized Brigade. He commanded this brigade in September 1939. He fought his last battle on 18–20 September near Tomaszów Lubelski.

Immediately after the end of the fighting Rowecki became involved in underground work. In October 1939 he was appointed deputy commander-in-chief and chief of staff of the Service for the Victory of Poland (Służba Zwycięstwu Polski [SZP]). From January 1940 he was commander of the Warsaw District of the Union of Armed Struggle (Związek Walki Zbrojnej [ZWZ]), and then he was commander of the entire Polish territory under German occupation. On 30 June 1940 Rowecki was appointed commander-in-chief of the ZWZ and commander of the armed forces in the Homeland. He helped to establish the post of Delegate of the Polish Government-in-Exile for the Homeland (Delegat Rządu RP na Kraj). He put forward this proposal to General Władysław Sikorski in 1940. At the end of 1941 Rowecki created an underground intelligence organization called Wachlarz. His efforts led to the consolidation of the majority of underground military organizations into a uniform underground army that in 1942 assumed the name Home Army (Armia Krajowa [AK]). Rowecki expanded the AK, restructured it, and improved its command system. He monitored the preparations for a general uprising that was to begin in the final stages of the war. He opposed cooperation with the Communist Polish Workers' Party (Polska Partia Robotnicza [PPR]). In July 1942 Rowecki obtained permission to conduct a limited armed struggle. On 30 June 1943 he was arrested by the Germans in Warsaw, taken to the Gestapo headquarters in Berlin, and then interned in the camp of Sachsenhausen, where he was executed after the outbreak of the Warsaw Uprising. Rowecki's most important publications include a pioneering manual of the urban guerrillas, *Walki uliczne* (Street fighting; 1928); *Propaganda jako środek walki* (Propaganda as a means of struggle; 1932); and *Wspomnienia i notatki autobiograficzne* (Memoirs and autobiographical notes; 1988). (JS)

Sources: Kunert, vol. 1; Tomasz Szarota, *Stefan Rowecki "Grot,"* (Warsaw, 1983); Tadeusz Żenczykowski, *Generał Grot u kresu walki* (London, 1983); Andrzej Chmielarz and Andrzej Krzysztof Kunert, *Spiska 14: Aresztowanie generała "Grota"–Stefana Roweckiego* (Warsaw, 1983); Cezary Leżański, *Bez buławy: Generała "Grota" żołnierski los* (Warsaw, 1988); *Stefan Rowecki w relacjach* Stefan Rowecki *"Grot" w relacjach i w pamieci zbiorowej,* (eds.) Andrzej Krzysztof Kunert and Tomasz Szarota, eds., (Warsaw, 2003); Marek Ney-Krwawicz, *Komendanci Armii Krajowej* (Warsaw, 1992); Grzegorz Gołębiewski, *Zanim zostałem "Grotem": Służba Stefana Roweckiego w wojsku II Rzeczypospolitej do 1939 r.* (Toruń, 1997).

RÓŻAŃSKI Józef (13 July 1907, Warsaw–21 August 1981, Warsaw), functionary of the Communist security apparatus in Poland. Różański was the son of Abram Goldberg, who wrote for *Hajnt*, and the half-brother of **Jerzy Borejsza**. After completing high school in 1925, he studied law at the University of Warsaw, where he graduated in 1929. The following year, when working as a court clerk, Różański joined the Communist Party of Poland. In 1936 he became a member of the Warsaw bar. Following the outbreak of World War II, he fled to Soviet-occupied eastern Poland, where in 1940 he joined the Political Department of the NKVD. After the Nazi attack on the Soviet Union, Różański left for Samarkand, and in February 1944 he volunteered to serve in the Third Romuald Traugutt Pomeranian Infantry Division; where in Samarkand he graduated from a school for political officers. In September 1944, Różański commenced work with the security department of the (Communist) Polish Committee of National Liberation (PKWN). In January 1945 he joined the Polish Workers' Party (Polska Partia Robotnicza [PPR]). Simultaneously, he served as a department head at the Ministry of Public Security (Ministerstwo Bezpieczeństwa Publicznego [MBP]). On 1 July 1947 Różański was promoted to the directorship of the MBP Investigative Department and became infamous for his interrogation techniques, which included physical and psychological torture. Released from his security job in March 1954 and having reached the rank of colonel, Różański was decorated with the Chevalier's Cross of the Rebirth of Poland. He then began to work at the State Publishing Institute. During the apparent purge of the security apparatus during the so-called thaw, Różański was arrested on 8 November 1954, and on 23 December 1955 he was sentenced to five years in jail for torturing prisoners, although the torture had, in fact, been unofficially condoned by the Communist authorities. In July 1956 the Supreme Court ordered the General Prosecutor's Office to expand its investigation, which then also came to include Różański's superiors: Colonel Anatol Fejgin and General Roman Romkowski. On 11 November 1957 the Provincial Court in Warsaw sentenced Różański to fifteen years in prison. In October 1958 the Supreme Court overturned the sentence, lowering the penalty to fourteen years. In October 1964 the Council of State applied a clemency clause to his case, releasing Różański from jail. Afterward, Różański worked at the State Mint, isolating himself from the outside world. (WR)

Sources: Stanisław Marat and Jacek Snopkiewicz, *Ludzie bezpieki* (Warsaw, 1990); Barbara Fijałkowska, *Różański i Borejsza: Przyczynek do dziejów stalinizmu w Polsce* (Olsztyn, 1995); Zdzisław Uniszewski, "Józef Różański," *Karta*, 2000, no. 31.

ROŽMAN Gregorij (9 March 1883, Dolinčiče [now Dolintschach], Austria–16 November 1959, Cleveland, Ohio), Slovene Roman Catholic bishop. Born into a peasant family in Carinthia, after finishing secondary school, Rožman studied theology in Klagenfurt, graduating in 1907. In 1912 in Vienna he earned a doctorate. After taking holy orders, he worked in various parishes in Slovenia and lectured at the Theological School of Ljubljana University. In 1929 he became coadjutor to Bishop **Anton Jeglič**. After Jeglič retired in 1930, Rožman was consecrated bishop of Ljubljana. In the 1930s he organized many important celebrations, including a ceremony to commemorate the 1900th anniversary of the death of Christ (1933), the Second Eucharistic Congress of Yugoslavia (1935), and the Sixth International Congress of Christ the King. Rožman supported the conservative clerical faction of the Slovene People's Party (Slovenska Ljudska Stranka [SLS]) and Catholic Action, and he advocated the political involvement of Catholics. After the fall of Yugoslavia in April 1941, Rožman tried to maintain good relations with the Italian authorities-in-occupation. He was strongly opposed to the Communist Partisans and supported the Home Guard (*domobranci*). Fearing arrest by the Communists, toward the end of the war Rožman went to Austria and then to the United States, where he became active among the Slovene émigré community in Ohio. In 1946 a Yugoslav Communist court sentenced Rožman in absentia to eighteen years' imprisonment. (WR)

Sources: *Slovenski biografski leksikon*, vol. 9 (Ljubljana, 1960); *Enciklopedija Slovenije*, vol. 10 (Ljubljana, 1996); Leopoldina Plut-Progelj and Carole Rogel, *Historical Dictionary of Slovenia* (Lanham, Md., 1996).

ROZWADOWSKI Tadeusz (20 May 1866, Babino, near Kałusz [Kalush]–18 October 1928, Warsaw), Polish general. In 1880 Rozwadowski enrolled in a military high school run by the Habsburg army. In 1883 he commenced studies at the Military Technical Academy in Vienna. Upon graduation, he received an officer's commission. Then he attended the School of the General Staff in Vienna, which he completed in 1891 with the rank of lieutenant. Rozwadowski was a staff aide-de-camp in a cavalry brigade in Marburg and Budapest. In 1895 he was dispatched as a military attaché to Bucharest. In 1908 he was promoted to colonel, and in 1913, to general. Meanwhile, in 1912 he took over command of the Twelfth Artillery Brigade in Kraków. During World War I, from August 1914, Rozwadowski commanded a brigade, fighting with it in the Battle of Gorlice, and then he led a division on the Russian front. He worked with the Polish pro-independence movement. In March 1916 Rozwadowski was dismissed from active duty for political reasons. He was offered a number of prominent posts in the Austro-Hungarian power structure (governor of Galicia, commander of the Polish Legions, governor of the Austro-Hungarian zone of occupation in Lublin), but he turned them down as contrary to his political beliefs.

On 28 October 1918 the Regency Council appointed Rozwadowski chief of the General Staff of the Polish Army in the making. On 10 November 1918 Rozwadowski declared himself subordinate to **Józef Piłsudski**, who had just returned from prison in Magdeburg. On 20 November Rozwadowski was appointed chief-in-command of the East Army and of the Polish-Ukrainian front in Eastern Galicia. In March 1919 he became chief of the Polish Military Mission in France with the Supreme Allied Command. He participated in the Paris Peace Conference, and then he traveled on diplomatic missions to Bucharest, London, and Rome. In June 1919 Rozwadowski was promoted to three-star general. Between 22 July 1920 and 1 April 1921 he served as chief of the General Staff of the Polish Army. He was a member of the Council for the Defense of the State and a commander in the defense of Warsaw against the Bolsheviks. He co-authored and co-executed a counterattack from the Wieprz River in August 1920. He also supervised operations in the south of Poland, eastern Little Poland, and Volhynia. In April 1921 Rozwadowski was promoted to four-star general. Between April 1921 and November 1922 he served as inspector of the Second Army, based in Warsaw, and he was a member of the Main Military Council. He became a permanent member of the Highest Military Advisory Commission of the Supreme Commander in April 1921 and inspector general of cavalry in November 1921. During the coup d'état of May 1926, Rozwadowski led the pro-government military forces and supervised the defense of Warsaw as its military governor. After the fighting ended, Rozwadowski was arrested and imprisoned at Antokol Prison in Wilno. In April 1927 he was dismissed from active duty. He moved to Lwów (Lviv), where he wrote studies about the defense of Poland and memoirs about World War I. Rozwadowski was buried at the Cemetery of the Defenders of Lwów in Łyczaków. (JS)

Sources: *PSB*, vol. 32; T. Kryska-Karski and S. Żurakowski, *Generałowie Polski Niepodległej* (London, 1976); *Encyklopedia historii Drugiej Rzeczypospolitej* (Warsaw, 1999); Kornel Krzeczunowicz, *Wspomnienia o generale Tadeuszu Rozwadowskim* (London, 1983); Stanisław Rozwadowski, ed., *Tadeusz Jordan Rozwadowski: Generał broni* (Katowice, 1993); Piotr Stawecki, *Słownik biograficzny generałów Wojska Polskiego, 1918–1939* (Warsaw, 1994); Tadeusz Kmiecik, *Generał Tadeusz Jordan Rozwadowski (1866–1928): Pierwszy szef Sztabu Generalnego Odrodzonego Wojska Polskiego* (Warsaw, 1998).

RUBIK Ernő (13 July 1944, Budapest), Hungarian inventor. Rubik's father was an inventor and the holder of several patents. In 1967 Rubik graduated from the Budapest Polytechnic, and in 1971, from the Department of Interior Design at the Higher School of Artistic Design, where he also taught and became a professor in 1987. In 1968–75 Rubik worked as a designer in state design offices. In 1975 he invented the so-called Rubik's Cube, which made him famous all over the world. In 1980–81 Rubik's Cube was recognized as the toy of the year in many countries. Even world championships in this game were organized. Rubik's other toys were also successful—for example, the magic serpent (1977) and the magic squares (1985)—but none became as popular as the cube. While Hungary was still under Communist rule, in 1982 Rubik established two foundations for innovation and scholarship, and in 1983 he established his own firm, the Rubik Studio. In 1988 he founded the International Rubik Foundation. In 1990–96 Rubik chaired the Hungarian Engineering Academy, and from 1996 he was its honorary chairman. In 1996 he also received an honorary doctorate from the Budapest Polytechnic. Rubik was awarded several Hungarian orders and authored many works, including *A bűvös kocka* (The magic cube; 1981), *Bűvös négyzetek* (The magic squares), and *Rubik's Cubic Compendium* (1987). (JT)

Sources: *Ki kicsoda 2000* (Budapest, 2001); *Magyar Nagylexikon*, vol. 15 (Budapest, 2002).

RUBIKS Alfreds (24 September 1935, Daugavpils), Latvian Communist activist of Polish descent. In 1957–61 Rubiks worked as a blue-collar laborer in an electrical appliance factory in Riga. From 1959 he belonged to the Communist Party of Latvia (CPL). In 1961 he graduated from Riga Polytechnic Institute. From 1962 to 1968 he was secretary of the Riga committee of the Komsomol, and in 1968–69 he was secretary of the Latvian republican Komsomol Central Committee (CC). From 1969 the deputy head of a department of the CPL CC and from 1976 to 1982 the first secretary of a party committee in a Riga district, in 1980 Rubiks graduated from the Higher Party School in Leningrad. From 1980 Rubiks was a deputy to the Supreme Council of the Latvian SSR; from 1981 he was a member of the CPL CC; in 1982–84 he was minister of industry of the Latvian SSR; and from 1985 he was chairman of the Council of People's Deputies of Riga. During perestroika Rubiks was one of the leaders of the conservatives, defending the Soviet system. At the Fifteenth CPL Congress, on 7 April 1990, when the party split into "nationalist" Communists (who founded the Independent CPL) and orthodox supporters of the Soviet system, Rubiks became first secretary of the latter's CPL CC. In August 1991 he actively supported the Moscow putsch, leading activities of the State Committee for Emergencies in Latvia. When the putsch was suppressed, on 21 August 1991, Rubiks was arrested and tried for anti-state activities, but he proved that he was defending Soviet statehood. After the emergence of independent Latvia, it was proved that Rubiks had acted against the existing power, and he was sentenced to eight years in prison in July 1995. Released in 1998, Rubiks took the lead of the Latvian Socialist Party (Latvijas Sociālistiskā Partija), which mostly included the Russian-speaking inhabitants of Latvia. Since owing to his sentence Rubiks could not run for the parliament, he kept on attempting to draw Latvia closer to Russia and advocating that Latvian citizenship be granted to all the Russian inhabitants of the country. (EJ)

Sources: *Latvijas Padomju enciklopēdija*, vol. 8 (Riga, 1986); *Who Is Who in Latvia?* (Riga, 1999); Andrejs Plakans, *The Latvians: A Short History* (Stanford, 1995).

RUBINSTEIN Arthur (28 January 1886, Łódź–20 December 1982, Geneva, Swizerland), Polish pianist of Jewish descent. Rubinstein came from a poor family. Thanks to the financial sponsorship of Emil Młynarski, who appreciated the phenomenal talent of the boy, Rubinstein studied piano with Heinrich Bartsch and music theory with Max Bruch in Berlin from 1897 to 1899. For a spell, he was also a student of **Ignacy Paderewski**. Rubinstein's debut took place in Potsdam in 1898 with Wolfgang Amadeus Mozart's *Concerto No. 23 in A Major*. An incredible memory and natural technique constantly refined by practice made Rubinstein, for almost eighty years, one of the world's leading interpreters of many composers, from Johann Sebastian Bach through the Romantics (including Ludwig van Beethoven, Johannes Brahms, and Robert Schumann) through the composers of contemporary music, of which Rubinstein was an enthusiast. He played Maurice Ravel, Igor Stravinsky, and Sergei Prokofiev. He also performed the works of Polish composers, including **Karol Szymanowski**. Rubinstein's performances of Frédéric Chopin, truly historical in scope, were all recorded. Despite his constant travels and changes of domicile, Rubinstein often stressed his ties to Poland. During the founding conference of the United Nations in San Francisco in April 1945, he played the Polish national anthem, "Mazurek Dąbrowskiego," to mark Poland's membership in the organization, notwithstanding the absence of the Polish government, which was no longer recognized by the Allies. Rubinstein gave many concerts in Poland after the war, even after an anti-Semitic campaign by the Communist authorities in 1967 and 1968. He published his memoirs as *My Young Years* (1973) and *My Many Years* (1980). Rubinstein was decorated with the order of Polonia Restituta. (WR)

Sources: *New Encyclopedia Britannica: Micropedia*, vol. 10 (Chicago, 1990); H. C. Schonberg, *The Great Pianist* (London, 1964); Henryk Sztompka, *Artur Rubinstein* (Kraków, 1966); Bruno Tosi, *Artur Rubinstein: Una vita nella musica*ed. (Venice, 1986); Harvey Sachs, *Rubinstein: A Life* (New York, 1995); Krzysztof Dybciak and Zdzisław Kudelski, eds., *Leksykon kultury polskiej poza krajem od roku 1939* (Lublin, 2000).

RUDENKO Mykola (19 December 1920, Yurivka, near Lugansk–1 April 2004, Kiev), Ukrainian writer and dissident. Initially Rudenko was a regular Soviet author and cultural activist. In 1947–50 he worked as editor of the periodical of the Union of Ukrainian Writers (UUW), *Dnipro*, and was secretary of the UUW party organization. Rudenko published ten collections of poems and other Socialist realist works. From the early 1970s he began to support dissident activities, for which he was expelled from the party in 1974 and from the UUW in 1975. In November 1976 he took the lead of the Ukrainian Helsinki Group. In February 1977 he was arrested for "anti-Soviet agitation," and in July 1977 he was sentenced to seven years of labor camp and five years of forced settlement. Rudenko served his term in a camp near Perm and in the Mordvinian Autonomous SSR. Later he was forced to settle in the Altai Krai (Siberia). Ten of Rudenko's works were smuggled from the camp and exile to the West, including the play *Khrest* (The cross; 1977); the Pantheist reflections *Ekonomichny monolohy* (Economic monologues; 1978); the collection of poems *Za hratamy* (Beyond bars; 1980); the play *Na dni morskomu* (At the bottom of the sea; 1981); and the novel *Orlova balka* (Eagle's gorge; 1982). In 1987 Rudenko was allowed to leave for the West with his wife. They lived in the United States until 1990, when they returned to the Ukraine. (WR)

Sources: *Encyclopedia of Ukraine*, vol. 4 (Toronto, 1993); *Index on Censorship*, 1988, no. 5.

RUDNYTSKA Milena (15 July 1892, Zborów [Zboriv]–29 March 1976, Munich), Ukrainian social and political activist. Rudnytska's was a well-known Ukrainian Galician family; she was the sister of **Ivan Rudnytsky** and the mother of **Ivan Lysiak-Rudnytskyi**, a leading Ukrainian émigré historian. After graduating from a classical gymnasium in Lemberg (Lwów, Lviv) in 1910, Rudnytska studied at the University of Lemberg and at the University of Vienna from 1910 to 1917, earning a Ph.D. for a dissertation on the mathematical foundations of Renaissance esthetics. In the 1920s she lectured at a gymnasium and at a teacher training college in Lwów. A member of the Ukrainian National Democratic Alliance (Ukraiiinske Natsionalno-Demokratychne Obyednannya [UNDO]), Rudnytska served as an UNDO MP in the Polish Assembly from 1928 to 1935. In 1928–34, as a delegate of the Ukrainian Parliamentary Representation to the League of Nations in Geneva, she defended the rights of the Ukrainian people, particularly during the 1930 pacification of Western Ukraine and during the Great Famine of 1932–33 in the Soviet Ukraine. From 1936 to 1939 Rudnytska belonged to the Presidium of the Ukrainian Coordination Committee (Ukraiinskyi Koordynatsyinyi Komitet) in Lwów. From 1919 she was active in the Ukrainian women's movement. From 1928 to 1939 she was president of the Union of Ukrainian Women (Soyuz Ukraiinok) in Lwów. In 1934 she became president of the World Union of Ukrainian Women. She also headed a women's political organization called Druzhyna Kniahyni Olhy (Duchess Olga's Army). In 1935–39 she edited the women's semi-monthly *Zhinka*.

After the Red Army occupied Galicia in September 1939, Rudnytska secretly made her way to the German-occupied part of Poland, known as the General Guvernment, and settled in Kraków; from there she moved to Berlin and then to Prague. After World War II, she co-founded and was director of the Ukrainian Relief Committee (Ukraiinskyi Dopomohovyi Komitet) until April 1950. In 1948–50 Rudnytska served as a representative of the Ukrainian National Council (Ukraiiinska Natsionalna Rada)—a kind of Ukrainian parliament in exile in Switzerland. In 1951 she went to the United States but soon returned to Europe and settled in Munich. Rudnytska's publications include *Ukraiinska diisnist i zavdannia zhinky* (The Ukrainian reality and the tasks of women; 1934); *Don Bosko: Liudyna, pedahoh, sviatyi* (Don Bosco: Man, pedagogue, saint; 1963); a biography of Yosyf Slipyi, *Nevydymi styhmaty* (The invisible stigmata; 1970); and the collection *Zakhidnia Ukraiina pid bolshevykamy* (Western Ukraine under Bolshevik rule; 1944). Rudnytska's husband, Pavlo Lysiak (1887–1948), served as a UNDO member of parliament in the Second Republic of Poland. (BB)

Sources: *Encyclopedia of Ukraine*, vol. 4 (Toronto, 1993); *Entsyklopediia Ukraiinoznavstva*, vol. 7 (Lviv, 1997); *Dovidnyk z istorii Ukraiiny* (Kiev, 2001); *Kto był kim w Drugiej Rzeczypospolitej* (Warsaw, 1994); Milena Rudnytska, *Statti, Lysty, Dokumenty* (Lviv, 1998).

RUDNYTSKYI Ivan, pseudonym "Kedryn" (22 April 1896, Chodorów [Khodoriv]–4 March 1995, New Jersey), Ukrainian journalist and political activist. Rudnytskyi came from a well-known Ukrainian Galician family; he was the brother of **Milena Rudnytska** and the uncle of **Ivan Lysiak-Rudnytskyi**, a leading Ukrainian émigré historian. Rudnytskyi attended gymnasiums in Brzeżany (Berezhany) and Lemberg (Lwów, Lviv). In 1915 he joined the Austrian Army, and in 1916 he was taken prisoner by the Russians. During the February 1917 revolution Rudnytskyi went to Kiev, where he worked for Ukrainian state institutions. As a soldier of the army of the Ukrainian National Republic (Ukraiinska Narodna Republika [UNR]), he fought for Ukrainian independence. In 1920 Rudnytskyi went into exile. In 1920–21 he edited the periodical *Vola*. After graduating in history from the University of Vienna (1922), he returned to Lwów, where he became engaged in journalistic work. In the same year, thanks to the recommendation of **Yevhen Konovalets**, he joined the editorial staff of *Dilo*, a leading Ukrainian newspaper published in Poland. From 1925 to 1931 Rudnytskyi was the Polish Assembly correspondent for *Dilo*, and he also served as press secretary of the Ukrainian Parliamentary Representation (Ukraiinska Parlamentska Reprezentatsiya). Rudnytskyi was a long-time secretary of the Writers' and Journalists' Association in Lwów. In the 1920s and 1930s he was an activist of the Ukrainian National Democratic Alliance (Ukraiinske Natsionalno-Demokratychne Obyednannya [UNDO]). As a UNDO representative, he maintained contacts with the UNR government-in-exile, with the Ukrainian Military Organization (Ukraiinska Viyskova Orhanizatsiya [UVO]), and with the Organization of Ukrainian Nationalists (Orhanizatsiya Ukraiinskykh Natsionalistiv [OUN]).

Shortly before the Red Army occupied Lwów in 1939, Rudnytskyi went to Kraków, where he worked in the General Gouvernment press agency. In 1944 he moved to Austria, and in 1949 he emigrated to the United States. From 1953 to 1973 he worked on the editorial staff of *Svoboda*, the largest Ukrainian-language newspaper in America. He took an active part in the Ukrainian émigré community, holding a variety of positions, including that of president of the Presidium of the Ukrainian National Council (Ukraiinska Natsionalna Rada), which served as a Ukrainian parliament in exile; as a member of the UNDO Central Committee in exile; as president of the Ukrain-ian Journalists' Union of America; as vice-president of the Shevchenko Scientific Society (NTSh) in America; and as co-editor (from 1961 on) of *Visti Kombatanta*, a press organ of the Union of Former Ukrainian Soldiers in America. Rudnytskyi authored *Beresteiskyi myr: Spomyny ta materiialy* (The Beresteczko peace: Memoirs and materials; 1928); *Prychyny upadku Polshi* (Causes of Poland's fall; 1940); *Paraleli z istorii Ukraiiny* (Parallels from the history of Ukraine; 1971); and the memoirs *Zhyttia—podii—liudy* (Life—events—people; 1976). (BB)

Sources: *Encyclopedia of Ukraine*, vol. 4 (Toronto, 1993); *Entsyklopediia Ukraiinoznavstva*, vol. 3 (Lviv, 1994); *Dovidnyk z istorii Ukraiiny* (Kiev, 2001); *Ukraiinska zhurnalistyka v imenakh* (Lviv, 1997); Ivan Kedryn, *Zhyttia—podii—liudy: Spomyny i komentari* (New York, 1976).

RUDNYTSKYI Stepan (15 December 1877, Tarnopol [now Ternopil, Ukraine]–3 November 1937, Solovets Islands), Ukrainian geographer. Rudnytskyi studied at Lemberg (Lwów, Lviv) and Vienna, graduating in 1901, and subsequently he taught at a gymnasium in Tarnopol and lectured at the University of Lemberg. In 1901 he became a member of the Shevchenko Scientific Society (NTSh). During World War I Rudnytskyi lived in Vienna and was active in the Union for the Liberation of Ukraine. At that time he wrote his first, pioneering work, *Ukraina: Land und Volk* (Ukraine: Land and people; 1916). After the war, Rudnytskyi served as a consultant to the government of the Western Ukrainian National Republic (Zakhidno-Ukraiinska Narodna Republika [ZUNR]) and later as a consultant to the ZUNR government-in-exile. Rudnytskyi was one of the main founders of, and then a lecturer in, the Ukrainian Free University in Vienna and Prague. His publications from that period include *Osnovy zemleznannia Ukraiiny* (Foundations of Ukrainian pedology, 2 vols.; 1924–26). Rudnytskyi was a leading authority in Ukrainian geography and a pioneer of research into the geomorphology and geology of the Ukraine. He authored *Osnovy morfolohii i heologii Pidkarpatskoi Rusy* (Foundations of geomorphology and geology of Transcarpathian Ruthenia, 2 vols.; 1925–27) and several dozen articles on the methodology and history of geography. In 1926 Rudnytskyi accepted an invitation from the authorities of the Ukrainian SSR to lecture at the Institute for People's Education in Kharkiv. He also became head of the Geography Department of the Ukrainian Academy of Sciences. Arrested in 1933 and dismissed from work for promoting "Fascist geography," he was deported to a labor camp on the White Sea coast, where he was executed. (WR)

Sources: *Encyclopedia of Ukraine*, vol. 4 (Toronto, 1993); Paul Robert Magocsi, *A History of Ukraine* (Seattle, 1996).

RUGOVA Ibrahim (2 December 1944, Cerrcë–21 January 2006, Prishtina) Albanian writer and politician from Kosovo. Rugova was the son of a peasant shopkeeper. When he was a few months old, his father and grandfather were shot by the Communist guerrillas of **Josip Broz Tito**. Rugova graduated from high school in Peja (Peć) and (in 1971) in philosophy from the University of Prishtina. He continued his studies at the Ecole Pratique des Hautes Études in Paris (1976–77), and in 1984 he received a Ph.D. at the University of Prishtina. He belonged to the League of Communists of Yugoslavia. For about twenty years Rugova worked at the Institute of Albanian Studies in Prishtina, dealing with literature. Among other works, he published the following: *Prekje lirike* (Lyrical touch; 1971); *Bibliografia e kritikës letrare shqipe* (Bibliography of Albanian literary critics; 1976); *Kah teoria* (Evolution of theory; 1978); *Kritika letrare* (Literary critics; 1979 [with Sabri Hamiti]); *Strategjia e kuptimit* (Strategies of understanding; 1980); *Kahe dhe premisa të kritikës shqiptare 1504–1983* (Lines and conditions of Albanian critics 1504–1983; 1985); *Refuzimi estetik* (Aestethic negation; 1987); *Pavarësia dhe demokracia* (Independence and democracy; 1991); and *La question du Kosovo* (The Kosovo Question; 1994). From 1996 Rugova was a corresponding member of the Kosovo Academy of Arts and Sciences; in 1996 he received an honorary doctorate from the University of Paris, and in 1998 he received the Sakharov Prize of the European Parliament.

In 1988 Rugova was elected chairman of the Union of Kosovo Writers, remaining in opposition to the policies of **Slobodan Milošević**. When Kosovo was deprived of autonomy in 1989, Rugova favored peaceful methods in the struggle for Albanian rights, taking the lead of the Democratic League of Kosovo (Lidhja Demokratike e Kosovës [DLK]), founded in December 1989. In the elections of 1992 and 1998 Rugova was elected president of the Republic of Kosovo. Its independence was proclaimed in 1991, but it was recognized only by Albania. Rugova contributed substantially to the formation of unofficial state structures in Kosovo and a network of Albanian schools there. His opposition to violence made him a lot of critics, who created the Kosovo Liberation Army to undertake an armed struggle. Their activities were intensified when the 1995 Dayton Agreement ignored the Kosovo question. On 18 March 1999 Rugova signed the Paris Peace Plan for Kosovo. When the Serbs rejected this plan, NATO intervention started against the Federal Republic of Yugoslavia (March–June 1999). In April 1999 Rugova met with Milošević and Serbian president **Milan Milutinović** and appealed for an end to the NATO military operation, which was contrary to the usual Kosovo demands for Western intervention. In May 1999 Rugova recanted this appeal. Contrary to the expectations that this spelled the end of his political career, Rugova remained very popular. In the elections of 18 November 2001 his DLK won 47 out of 120 mandates. Although the deputies rejected his candidature for president in three rounds of voting, on 4 March 2002 the major factions came to an agreement, and Rugova was elected president of Kosovo. While in office he died of lung cancer. (AO)

Sources: Ibrahim Rugova, Marie-Françoise Allain, and Xavier Galmiche, *La question du Kosovo* (Paris, 1994); Jean-Yves Carlen, *Ibrahim Rugova: La frele colosse du Kosovo* (Paris, 1999); Bugajski; www.kosova.com; www.rulers.org.

RULEWSKI Jan (18 April 1944, Bydgoszcz), Polish trade union activist and politician. Rulewski studied at the Military Technical Academy in Warsaw. In 1965 he refused to take part in the "elections" to the national council and parliament; for this he was placed in a psychiatric ward and expelled from the school. He tried to flee Communist Poland, for which he was sentenced to five years in prison. Released after four years, Rulewski studied extramurally at the Higher Engineering School in Bydgoszcz, and in 1980 he graduated in mechanics there. In 1970–80 he worked as a designer in the Romet bicycle factory in Bydgoszcz. Elected chairman of the official trade unions, in August 1980 Rulewski organized a strike in Romet. Temporarily arrested, from 7 September 1980 he chaired the Inter-Factory Strike Committee, and from 17 September, the Inter-Factory Founding Committee of Solidarity in Bydgoszcz. From February 1981 Rulewski belonged to the Provisional Presidium of the Solidarity National Coordination Commission. Thought the leader of the radical faction of the union, on 19 March 1981 Rulewski was badly beaten by the police during a session of the Provincial National Council in Bydgoszcz, where he was invited to represent Solidarity. This still unexplained incident led to a serious crisis, eased by the government-Solidarity agreement of 31 March. During the First Solidarity Congress in September 1981 Rulewski ran for the union's chairmanship but lost to **Lech Wałęsa**.

When martial law was introduced on 13 December 1981, Rulewski was interned and later arrested on account of alleged attempts to topple the political system. Held in Strzebielinek, Białołęka, and the Rakowiecka Street Prison in Warsaw, he refused release on the conditions offered by the authorities (abandonment of Solidarity activities or emigration). Amnestied in July 1984, Rulewski returned to his job at Romet. In 1985 he was fired, and in 1985–90 he worked as a cab driver. Active in the Solidarity underground, Rulewski was critical of Wałęsa's policies. In

1987–89 Rulewski belonged to the Working Group of the Solidarity National Commission (along with, for example, Andrzej Słowik and **Andrzej Gwiazda**), calling for a convention of the National Commission elected in 1981. In November 1988 he founded the Provisional Board of Solidarity's Bydgoszcz Region. Rulewski criticized the new union structures created by Wałęsa and the Round Table Talks. From 1989 he chaired the Solidarity Regional Executive Committee, appealing for the reunification of the union; from 1990 to 1993 he belonged to its National Commission, and in 1991–93 he was deputy chairman of Solidarity. In 1991–2001 Rulewski was a member of parliament, and from 1991 to 1993, deputy head of the Solidarity Parliamentary Caucus. When the Solidarity MPs recalled the **Hanna Suchocka** government in June 1993, Rulewski left the union and joined the Democratic Union. From 1993 to 1997 Rulewski was an MP on behalf of the Union of Freedom and later as an independent. (PK)

Sources: *Słownik polityków polskich XX w.* (Poznań, 1998); Jerzy Holzer, *"Solidarność"* (Warsaw, 1983); Teresa Torańska, *My* (Warsaw, 1994); Janusz A. Majcherek, *Pierwsza dekada III Rzeczpospolitej 1989–1999* (Warsaw, 1999); *Opozycja w PRL: Słownik biograficzny 1956–1989*, vol. 1 (Warsaw, 2000).

RUML Jan (5 March 1953, Prague), Czech politician. After graduating from high school in 1972, Ruml could not find a white-collar job because of the opposition activities of his father, so until the late 1980s he worked as a stoker and lumberjack. In 1977 he signed Charter 77, and from 1979 he belonged to the Committee for the Defense of the Unjustly Prosecuted (Výbor na Obranu Nespravedlivě Stíhaných [VONS]). In 1981–82 Ruml was imprisoned without a trial. In the 1980s he edited several periodicals in the uncensored press and co-founded *Lidove noviny*; from November 1989 he headed the Independent Press Center; from February to April 1990 he was editor-in-chief of the weekly *Respekt*; and in 1990 he was a spokesman for Charter 77. After the "Velvet Revolution," from April 1990 Ruml was deputy minister of interior, and from May to June 1990 he was head of the Office for Protection of the Constitution and Democracy. In the spring of 1992 he joined the Civic Democratic Party (Občanská Demokratická Strana [ODS]) of **Václav Klaus**, and on its behalf he won a seat in the Chamber of the People of the Federal Assembly (June–December 1992). From July 1992 to November 1997 Ruml was minister of interior of the Czech Republic. In 1996–98 he was a member of parliament. When it turned out that the ODS had received illegal financing, Ruml criticized Prime Minister Klaus and demanded his resignation. In December 1997 Ruml became the leader of an ODS faction demanding a de-parture from the previous political style. When he failed to take over the party leadership, Ruml and his followers left the ODS and founded the Union of Freedom (Unie Svobody [US]), and Ruml became its chairman on 22 February 1998. In the early elections of June 1998 the US won 8.6 percent of the vote and stayed in the opposition. In November 1998 Ruml won a seat in the senate, and in December 2000 he became its deputy speaker. In February 1999 he was reelected the US chairman, but he was the only key politician who responded to the appeals of "Thank You, But Leave," addressed publicly to the new Czech leadership. In November 1999 Ruml resigned his position. (PU)

Sources: *ČBS*; www.janruml.cz/; wtd.vlada.cz/scripts/detail. php?id=576.

RUPEL Dimitrij (7 April 1946, Ljubljana), Slovene politician. In 1970 Rupel graduated in sociology from the University of Ljubljana. In 1976 he received a Ph.D. in sociology from Brandeis University in Waltham, Massachusetts. Rupel lectured at Queen's University in Canada (1977–78), the New School for Social Research in New York (1985), and Cleveland State University (1989). In the 1980s Rupel co-founded the periodical *Nova revija*, in which in 1987 he published the "Slovene National Program." In January 1989 he took the lead of the Slovenian Democratic Alliance (Slovenska Demokratična Zveza [SDZ]), the first opposition party that joined the Democratic Opposition of Slovenia (DEMOS). Rupel became the DEMOS deputy chairman. Along with some of his party members, he finally joined Liberal Democracy of Slovenia (Liberalna Demokracija Slovenije [LDS]). From April 1990 to February 1992 Rupel was minister of foreign affairs. During his term Slovenia gained independence (June 1991) and international recognition, and it also joined the Central European Initiative. Afterwards Rupel taught at the University of Ljubljana. In the elections of December 1992 he won a seat in the parliament. In December 1994 he became mayor of Ljubljana, and from 1997 he was ambassador to the United States. In February 2000 he became foreign minister again, but owing to the resignation of Prime Minister **Janez Drnovšek** in June 2000, Rupel lost this position. In October 2000 Rupel won a parliamentary seat again, and in December 2000 he regained the portfolio of foreign affairs in another cabinet of Drnovšek, continuing his efforts to gain entry for Slovenia into NATO and the European Union in the government of **Anton Rop**. Soon after Rupel managed to achieve this goal in May 2004, in July 2004 he was replaced as foreign minister. Rupel authored several publications, including *Svobodne besede* (Free word; 1976);

Maks (1983); *Povabljeni pozabljeni* (The invited forgotten; 1985); *Slovenski intelektualci* (Slovenian intellectuals; 1989); and the memoirs *Skrivnost države* (State secrets; 1992) and *Odčarana Slovenija* (Disenchanted Slovenia; 1993). (AO)

Sources: *Europa Środkowa i Wschodnia 1992* (Warsaw, 1994); Leopoldina Plut-Progelj and Carole Rogel, *Historical Dictionary of Slovenia* (Lanham, Md., 1996); www.sigov.si/mzz/eng/index.html.

RUPNIK Leon (11 August 1880, Lokve, Nova Gorica–4 September 1946, Ljubljana), Slovene general and politician. Rupnik began his military career in the Austro-Hungarian Army. In 1907 he completed military studies in Vienna. Assigned to the General Staff in 1911, he was promoted to captain in 1913. During World War I he initially fought in Mostar, eastern Bosnia, on the Italian front, and in 1916 he was sent to the Russian front. In 1918 he became commander of the staff in the town of Boka Kotorska. In 1919 he began serving in the army of the Kingdom of Serbs, Croats, and Slovenes. In 1937 he was promoted to major general. He was responsible for the construction of the defense line (the so-called Rupnik Line) near the border with Italy. After the Yugoslav forces were defeated in the war against the Third Reich in April 1941, Rupnik went to Ljubljana. An avowed anti-Communist, he collaborated with the Italian occupier in the struggle against the Communist Liberation Front. In September 1941 Liberation Front members organized an unsuccessful attempt on his life. On 2 June 1942 the Italian authorities appointed Rupnik governor of Ljubljana. In 1943, after the German troops seized Ljubljana, Rupnik became head of the local government of the Province of Ljubljana. He was a co-founder of the Home Guard (*domobranci*), also known as the White Guard, a Slovene nationalist and anti-Communist military organization. Rupnik initially served as head of this organization, but the Germans forbade him to maintain any formal links with it. It was not until September 1944 that the German authorities conferred on him the title of general inspector of the Home Guard, but his powers were very limited. On 3 May 1945 Rupnik proclaimed a separate Slovene state, which existed only two days. With the defeat of the Axis powers in the war, Rupnik, along with his family, went to Carinthia, Austria. Until January 1946 he lived in an Italian refugee camp, but the American-English forces handed him over to the Yugoslav authorities. On 30 August 1946 the military court sentenced him to death by firing squad. The sentence was carried out. (AO)

Sources: *Slovenski biografski leksikon*, vol. 3 (Ljubljana, 1960–71); *Enciklopedija Slovenije*, vol. 10 (Ljubljana, 1996); Dusan Željeznov, *Rupnikov proces* (Ljubljana, 1980); Wacław Felczak and Tadeusz Wasilewski, *Historia Jugosławii* (Wrocław, 1985); Aleksandar Vojinović, *Leon Rupnik* (Zagreb, 1988); Leopoldina Plut-Pregelj and Carole Rogel, *Historical Dictionary of Slovenia* (Lanham, Md., 1996).

RUSEV Rusi (27 November 1887, Khabrovo–2 February 1945, Sofia), Bulgarian general. In 1909 Rusev graduated from a military school in Sofia. He later fought in the Balkan Wars (1912–13) and in World War I as an artillery officer. Despite his skills, he was promoted slowly. For a long time Rusev stayed away from politics. After the coup d'état of 19 May 1934 and the takeover of power by **Boris III**, Rusev was appointed army inspector for weaponry, and he held this post from 1936 to 1942. In 1940 he was promoted to lieutenant general. Rusev entered politics during the regimes of **Dobri Bozhilov** and **Ivan Bagrianov**, when he served as head of the Ministry of Defense from September 1943 to September 1944. Although during the war the Bulgarian government made attempts to reach an agreement with the Allies, it also implemented harsh domestic policies and used the army to suppress the Communist partisans. Because of his position, Rusev was an official who was particularly hated by the Communists. Arrested after the coup of 9 September 1944 and brought before the court, Rusev was sentenced to death, and, along with other members of the prewar Bulgarian elite, he was executed by firing squad. (AG)

Sources: *Entsiklopediya Bulgariya*, vol. 5 (Sofia, 1986); Jerzy Jackowicz, *Partie opozycyjne w Bułgarii 1944–1948* (Warsaw, 1997).

RUSTEMI Avni (26 September 1895, Libokhove–20 April 1924, Tirana), Albanian politician. Rustemi was a teacher by profession. In 1918 he organized the youth against the Italian invaders in Vlorë, and then he went to France, where he studied at the Sorbonne. On 13 June 1920 Rustemi carried out the successful assassination of Essad Pasa Toptani, who, based in Paris, had led the secessionists from Dürres. From June to November 1920 Rustemi was kept prisoner by the French authorities. Released, he returned to Albania and was active in the people's radical movement. Between 1922 and 1924 Rustemi was one of the leaders of Bashkimi (Union), which had a radical-democratic program. In December 1923 he was elected to a parliament that was dominated by conservative forces. In an atmosphere of chaos and fratricidal in-fighting following an injury to Prime Minister **Ahmed Zogu** and the murder of two American tourists, Rustemi, as one of the main opponents of the prime minister, was murdered by factions connected with Zogu. Rustemi's funeral on 1 May 1924 turned into a demonstration by radical Albanian youth against such a political outrage. This demonstration induced a group of parliamentary democratic oppositionists to appeal to the people to disregard the new conservative parliament of Shefqet Vërlaci and, as a result, it contributed to the uprising of May 1924. (WR)

Sources: *Biographisches Lexikon*, vol. 4; L. Dilo, *Avni Rustemi* (Tirana, 1960); John Swire, *Albania: The Rise of a Kingdom* (New York, 1971); Stefanaq Pollo and Arben Puto, *The History of Albania from Its Origins to the Present Day* (London, 1981); Jerzy Hauziński and Jan Leśny, *Historia Albanii* (Wrocław, 1992).

RUSU Alexandru (22 November 1884, Şăulia–9 May 1963, Gherla), Romanian Greek Catholic bishop. Rusu graduated from high school in Blaj. Between 1903 and 1910 he studied theology at the University of Budapest and then in Bucharest. He received a Ph.D. in theology in 1910 and entered the priesthood. Soon Rusu was appointed a professor of the Department of Dogmatic Theology at the Theological Academy in Blaj. On 30 January 1931 he was consecrated bishop by the metropolitan, **Vasiliu Suciu**. Rusu took over the bishoprics of Maramureş and moved to Baia-Mare. In 1946 the Metropolitan Synod elected him metropolitan of the Blaj diocese. However, the Communists refused to recognize the election, as the persecution of the Uniate Church was well under way at the time. Rusu openly opposed the liquidation of the Uniate Church and its absorption into the Romanian Orthodox Church. As a result, he was arrested on 28 October 1948. Rusu and five remaining Romanian Greek Catholic bishops were isolated at the Dragoslavele Monastery (the summer residence of the Orthodox patriarchs of Romania that was turned into a prison by the Communists). At the beginning of 1949 they were transferred to another prison monastery at Căldăruşani and then, in 1950, to the prison at Sighet Marmaţiei. Rusu spent five years there without a trial; he was brutally beaten. In 1955, he was released with two other Uniate bishops who had remained alive: **Iuliu Hossu** and **Ioan Bălan**. However, they were immediately placed under house arrest at the Curtea de Argeş Monastery, which soon became a famous place of pilgrimage and a resilient religious center. In 1956, Rusu co-authored a memorandum to the Communist government demanding the restoration of the Uniate Church. The appeal was signed by a great many people, causing apprehension among the authorities. As a result, the bishops were transferred to the monastery at Ciorogârla, and then they were separated. Rusu was placed in the monastery of Cocoş. He was subsequently accused before a military tribunal in Cluj for allegedly

receiving an envoy from the Vatican. In 1957, despite his advanced age, Rusu was sentenced to twenty-five years of hard labor for "provocation and treason." Imprisoned at Gherla, he was kept for six years under inhuman conditions in an unheated cell. Until the very end, Rusu offered his priestly services to fellow prisoners. Rusu was buried at the prison cemetery. His beatification process is currently under way. (LW)

Sources: Józef Darski, *Rumunia: Historia, współczesność, konflikty narodowe* (Warsaw, 1995); Paul Caravia, Virgiliu Constantinescu, and Flori Stănescu, *The Imprisoned Church of Romania, 1944–1989* (Bucharest, 1999); Dennis Deletant, *Communist Terror in Romania* (New York, 1999); www.bru.ro.

RÜÜTEL Arnold (10 May 1928, Saarema), Estonian Communist activist and post-Communist politician. Rüütel graduated from a higher agricultural school, and then he worked as head of the agricultural department of the regional administration in Saarema. In 1957 he became director of an experimental center of the Estonian Institute of Animal Breeding and Veterinary Medicine, and in 1963–69 he headed a model kolkhoz in Tartu. In 1964 he received a Ph.D. from the Department of Agriculture of the Estonian Agricultural Academy, and in 1969 he became the academy's rector. From 1964 Rüütel belonged to the Communist Party of Estonia (CPE), and in 1971 he joined its Central Committee (CC). His career coincided with the dogmatic rule of **Karl Vaino** and the Russification policy of the latter. In 1977–79 Rüütel was CPE CC secretary for agriculture and deputy prime minister of the Estonian SSR, and from 1983 he was chairman of the Supreme Council of the Estonian SSR; he lacked any inclinations toward reform.

From 1985 Rüütel zigzagged between the dogmatic faction of Vaino and the pragmatic faction of **Edgar Savisaar**. He gradually evolved toward becoming a supporter of perestroika. On 16 November 1988 he took part in the preparation and adoption of the declaration of Estonia's sovereignty within the reformed USSR. Since the Soviet Supreme Council found the declaration invalid, Rüütel gained a reputation as a supporter of Estonia's independence. Under his leadership the Estonian Supreme Council adopted a law forcing the republican administration to learn Estonian. The traditional national holiday of 24 February and the prewar flag were restored. Modest economic reforms were also started. The Kremlin showed little resistance, expecting that a reformed Estonia would be more determined to stay within the USSR. However, the idea of independence gained momentum, and Rüütel's activities as chairman of the Estonian Supreme Council became increasingly more popular. In the elections to the Supreme Council held in 1990 Rüütel ran on behalf of Free Estonia (Vaba Eesti), representing the so-called national Communists. Although they failed (12 out of 105 mandates), their coalition with the Popular Front, in opposition to the more radical spokesmen of independence and Communist hard-liners, made it possible for Rüütel to remain chairman of the Estonian Supreme Council. Under the pressure of events, the council leaned toward the idea of the restitution of independence. Rüütel took part in preparing the declaration of the state status of Estonia, in which the incorporation of the country by the USSR was found to be illegal. At the same time Rüütel left the CPE.

On 19 April 1990 Rüütel and Savisaar met with Mikhail Gorbachev in Moscow, and the two sides could not agree about signing a new union agreement. In May 1990, at a meeting of the heads of the supreme councils of Estonia, Latvia, and Lithuania, Rüütel initiated the Council of Baltic States. During a failed hard-liner putsch in Estonia, Rüütel was a member of the three-man Extraordinary Council of Defense. In January 1991 he went to Moscow, where Gorbachev assured him that military measures would not be used in Estonia. Rüütel became a member of the Constitutional Assembly, and after the Moscow putsch he supported the restitution of Estonian independence on 20 August 1991. As a result of his support for independence, in the first presidential elections of October 1992 he won 43 percent of the vote, but in the end his Communist past prevented him from winning the presidency.

Rüütel became a member of the Tallinn City Council and set out to develop a political base in the shape of the Estonian Rural People's Party (Eesti Maarahva Erakond [ERPP]), founded in 1994. Because of the social costs of transformation, as well as corruption scandals among the new power elite, the center-left parties won the elections of March 1995. Heading the ERPP, Rüütel entered into a coalition with the Coalition Party, won a record number of votes, and became deputy speaker of the parliament. Nevertheless, in September 1996 he lost the presidential election again, this time to **Lennart Meri**. The defeat of the ERPP in the elections of March 1999 looked like the end of Rüütel's career, and he was moved to the position of honorary leader of his party. However, conflicts among the rightist candidates and renewed social support for the left made Rüütel's presidential campaign a success, and he won the presidency on 21 September 2001. His election was a surprise, and many observers feared he would change the priorities of Estonian foreign policy, but he continued with the pro-Western line. Far from the enthusiasm of his predecessors, Rüütel supported Estonia's entry into NATO and the European Union in May 2004. (AG)

Sources: *Eesti Entsuklopeedia*, vol. 8 (Tallinn, 1995); Kristian Gerner and Stefan Hedlund, *The Baltic States and the End of the Soviet Empire* (London and New York, 1993); Anatol Lieven, *The Baltic Revolution* (New Haven, 1993); Rein Taagepera, *Estonia: Return to Independence* (Boulder, Colo., 1993); www.president. ee/eng/president_arnoldryytel; www.balticsww.com/ruutel.htm.

RUŽIČKA Leopold (Lavoslav) (13 September 1887, Vukovar–26 September 1976, Mammern, Zurich, Switzerland), Swiss chemist of Croatian descent. The son of a cooper, Ružička finished a primary school and then high school in Osijek. In 1906 he began to study chemistry at the Technical University of Karlsruhe, Germany. After completing his studies, he became an assistant to Professor Hermann Staudinger. With Staudinger, in 1912 Ružička left for Switzerland, where he began working at the Federal Institute of Technology (Eidgenössische Technische Hochschule [ETH]) in Zurich. In 1917 he acquired Swiss citizenship. In 1918 he received a postdoctoral degree and became a lecturer at the ETH. In 1921 he began to lecture at the University of Zurich. In 1923 he became a professor. Ružička did research on civetone and muscone, the odoriferous components of civet and musk. He discovered that the molecules of muscone and civetone contain rings of fifteen and seventeen carbon atoms respectively. Before this discovery, the existence of such rings had been considered impossible. In 1925–26 Ružička worked in Geneva. In October 1926 he became a professor of organic chemistry at the University of Utrecht in the Netherlands. Three years later he returned to Switzerland to work at the ETH, where he had better conditions for research. Ružička was the first to succeed in synthesizing the male sex hormones androsterone and testosterone (1934–35). In 1939, along with the German biochemist Adolf Butenandt, Ružička was awarded the Nobel Prize in Chemistry for his work on polymethylenes and higher terpenes. Because of the outbreak of World War II, Ružička received the prize in Zurich, instead of Stockholm, on 16 January 1940. In 1941 he invited **Vladimir Prelog** from Zagreb to work with him. Ružička was the founder of the Swiss-Yugoslav Society. He then turned to biochemistry and published "Biogenetic isoprene rule." At the age of seventy, Ružička retired and was succeeded as head of the Organic Chemistry Laboratory by Prelog, a future Nobel Prize winner. In Switzerland the Ružička Award was established for outstanding chemists. In 1977 a museum in Ružička's honor was opened in Vukovar, but it was seriously damaged during the war in 1991. (AO)

Sources: Wulf von Bonin, Erich Bagge, and Robert Herrlinger, *Laureaci Nagrody Nobla: Chemia, fizyka, matematyka* (Warsaw, 1969); www.nobel.se/chemistry/laureates/1939/ ruzicka-bio.html; www.posta.hr/markeasp/index_e.asp?brmarke=416.

RYBARSKI Roman (3 July 1887, Zator–March 1942, Auschwitz), Polish economist and politician. Rybarski came from a burgher family. After graduating from a high school in Rzeszów in 1898, he studied law, economics, and economic history at the Jagiellonian University (UJ) in Kraków. While at the university, Rybarski served as a personal assistant to Julian Dunajewski and was active in nationalist youth organizations. In 1910 Rybarski joined the National League and passed his doctoral exams in law at the UJ. Between 1911 and 1912 he studied in London and Oxford, and he traveled around the United States and Italy. Upon his return to Kraków, he worked as assistant professor at the School of Political Sciences. After he completed his postgraduate degree, based on his work *Badania podmiotu ekonomii społecznej* (The study of the subject of social economy; 1912), Rybarski became an assistant professor at the UJ in March 1913. In 1914 he published *Wartość wymienna jako miara bogactwa* (The Exchange Value as a Measure of Wealth), where he combined the theories of the Vienna school of psychology with the German historical school. During World War I he published the periodical *Rok Polski*, where he opposed linking the Polish cause with the Central Powers.

In March 1919 Rybarski was an economic expert of the Polish delegation to the Paris Peace Conference and represented Poland on its Commission of Reparations and Finances. In October 1919 he was appointed undersecretary of state in the Ministry of the Former Prussian Partition. Between February 1920 and August 1921 he served as undersecretary of state at the Ministry of Treasury. In 1922 he published *Marka polska i złoty polski* (The Polish mark and the Polish zloty) and *Wartość, kapitał i dochód* (Value, capital, and income). From 1924 Rybarski was a full professor at the Warsaw Polytechnic, and in 1924 he was hired by the University of Warsaw (UW), where he headed the Department of Treasury until 1939. Rybarski's most important theoretical works include the three-volume *System ekonomii politycznej* (The system of political economy), comprised of *Rozwój życia gospodarczego i idei gospodarczych* (The development of economic life and ideas; 1924), *Teoria gospodarstwa społecznego* (A theory of social economy; 1930), and *Psychologia społeczno-gospodarcza* (Socioeconomic psychology; 1939). According to Rybarski, the development of capitalism brought about a gradual increase in prosperity, despite its cyclical crises, which were caused by the disproportion between the growth of capital and consumption. Among the motives spurring economic activity, he noticed not only rational factors, but also emotional ones, including national traditions and religion. Rybarski supported the development of small and medium-size enterprises and

economic entities as the basis for Poland's economy. The primacy of the nation over the freedom of the individual constituted the main thesis of his *Naród, jednostka, i klasa* (Nation, individual, and class; 1926). However, in economic policy he attempted to reconcile economic freedom with limited state interventionism. He grappled with that in *Przyszłość gospodarcza Polski* (The economic future of Poland; 1933) and *Podstawy narodowego programu gospodarczego* (The foundations of the national economic program; 1934). He also wrote on the economic history of Poland. From 1926 Rybarski was a member of the leadership of the Camp of Great Poland, and in 1928 he joined the Main Board of the National Party (Stronnictwo Narodowe [SN]). From 1928 to 1930 and from 1930 to 1935 he was an MP on behalf of the SN. Contrary to the young activists in the party, Rybarski spoke in favor of parliamentary democracy and the rule of law. From 1937 he was the dean of the UW Law School. He was also a member of the Polish Academy of Arts and Sciences and the Warsaw Scientific Society. During the Nazi occupation Rybarski initiated the underground UW Law School. He continued his research and also remained active in the clandestine SN. Rybarski was arrested by the Nazis in May 1941 and shipped off to Auschwitz, where he died. (WR)

Sources: *PSB*, vol. 33; *Kto był kim w Drugiej Rzeczypospolitej* (Warsaw, 1994); Roman Wapiński, *Narodowa Demokracja 1893–1939* (Wrocław, 1980); *Krakowscy twórcy polskiej myśli ekonomicznej* (Kraków, 1987); Krzysztof Kawalec, *Narodowa Demokracja wobec faszyzmu 1922–1939* (Warsaw, 1989).

RYBICKI Józef (18 December 1901, Kołomyja [Kolomyia]–9 May 1986, Warsaw), Polish pro-independence activist. Rybicki came from an intelligentsia family. He studied at high schools in Brzeżany, Lwów (Lviv), Wadowice, and again Lwów. In July 1920, along with his entire high school class, Rybicki volunteered for the Polish Army to defend Poland from the Soviet invasion. He suffered a serious wound on his shoulder, which left him crippled for life. In May 1924 he was therefore released from the military. After graduating from high school in 1921, Rybicki enrolled at a university but had to interrupt his studies to convalesce in Switzerland and Italy. In 1927 he graduated from the Department of Humanities of Stefan Batory University in Wilno (Vilnius), becoming a lecturer there. In 1930 he successfully defended his Ph.D. in classical philology. In 1931 he commenced teaching at a high school in Wilno. Between 1934 and 1937 he served as the headmaster of a high school in Nowogródek (Novahrudak) and between 1938 and 1939 in Tomaszów Lubelski.

In September 1939 Rybicki attempted to volunteer for the Polish Army, but instead he was forced to hide from the Soviets, who had just invaded Poland. In the fall of 1939 he joined the Secret Military Organization (Tajna Organizacja Wojskowa [TOW]) in the Lublin and Kielce areas. In 1940, he arrived in Warsaw. In 1941 he became TOW deputy commander, and after its absorption into the Home Army (Armia Krajowa [AK]), he was appointed deputy commander of the Directorate of Diversion (Kedyw) of the Warsaw District of the AK. In November 1943 Rybicki took over the command of the Warsaw Kedyw. He distinguished himself during the Warsaw Uprising of 1944. After the collapse of the insurrection, Rybicki found himself in the Nazi filtration camp in Pruszków. Then he fled from a prison transport to Germany. Afterwards, for a time he commanded the remnants of the Kedyw of the AK High Command.

After the formation of the clandestine anti-Communist Office of the Delegate of the Armed Forces (Delegatura Sił Zbrojnych [DSZ]) in April 1945, Rybicki was appointed to head its Warsaw district. In August 1945 he became commander of the DSZ Central Area. Before the DSZ was dissolved, Rybicki issued an order, on 6 August 1945, to stop fratricidal fighting, thus forbidding revenge actions against the Communists. At the beginning of September 1945, Rybicki was one of the five founders of the secret Union for Freedom and Independence (Wolność i Niezawisłość [WiN]), and he became the chairman of its Central Area. Following the arrest of the WiN leadership by the Communist secret police, Rybicki served briefly as acting chairman of the Main Board of the organization in November 1945. He was arrested on 22 December 1945 and sentenced to ten years in jail in February 1947. He was released in 1954. Rybicki settled in Milanówek, near Warsaw, and worked as an editor of encyclopedias and dictionaries. At the same time, he was actively involved in the sobriety movement. From May 1963 he served as a member of the Main Board of the Social Anti-Alcohol Committee. In January 1967 he became deputy to the organization's secretary general. Rybicki published a great many articles and booklets on anti-alcohol activism. He was a member of the Committee of Poland's Episcopate for Sobriety and of the Team of Experts of the Council of Ministers to Struggle against Alcoholism. Following the worker riots in Radom and Ursus in June 1976, Rybicki joined the endeavor to assist the victims, and in September he became a founding member of the Committee for the Defense of Workers (Komitet Obrony Robotników [KOR]). Later, he participated in the Committee of Social Self-Defense–KOR until its self-dissolution in September 1981. Rybicki remained a moral authority for the dissident milieu. (WR)

Sources: Kunert, vol. 3; J. Jurkszus-Tomaszewska, "Józef Rybicki," *Zeszyty Historyczne*, vol. 78; Jan Józef Lipski, *KOR* (Warsaw, 1983); L. Kindlein, "Śp. Józef Rybicki," *Dziennik Polski i Dziennik Żołnierza* (London), 29 May 1986; *Opozycja w PRL: Słownik biograficzny 1956–89*, vol. 1 (Warsaw, 2000).

RYCHETSKÝ Pavel (17 August 1943, Prague), Czech lawyer and politician. In 1966 Rychetský graduated in law from Charles University in Prague, where he later worked in a municipal court and at the Department of Civic Law of Charles University. From 1966 he belonged to the Communist Party of Czechoslovakia, but owing to the Warsaw Pact invasion of August 1968 and the "normalization" policies that followed, in 1969 he left the party. In 1970 Rychetský was forced to leave the university and worked in an advertising agency. From 1974 to 1989 he was a lawyer at a housing cooperative. In the 1970s and 1980s he took part in opposition activities. From 1975 to 1989 he published in such émigré periodicals as *Svědectvi* (of **Pavel Tigrid**) and *Listy* (of Jiří Pelikan). In 1977 Rychetský was one of the initiators and first signatories of Charter 77, and from 1987 he also wrote for the uncensored *Lidové noviny*. In November 1989 he co-founded the Civic Forum (Občanské Fórum [OF]) and took part in negotiations with the authorities. A leading author of the draft constitution of Czechoslovakia, presented by the OF in December 1989, from January to July 1990 Rychetský was prosecutor general of the Czech republic, and after the first free elections of June 1990 he became deputy prime minister of the federal government and chairman of the government legislative council. He remained in these positions until the elections of June 1992. After the OF split in the spring of 1991, Rychetský became deputy chairman of the center-left Civic Movement (Občanské Hnutí). From 1993 he was a member of the Presidium of Free Democrats (Svobodní Demokrati), and in 1995 he joined the Czech Social Democratic Party (Česká Strana Socialně Demokratická [ČSSD]). In November 1996 Rychetský was elected senator and became chairman of the senate legal and constitutional commission. From July 1998 he was deputy prime minister and head of the government legislative council in the government of **Miloš Zeman**. He also chaired councils for research and development, gypsy culture, and the national minorities. From October 2000 to February 2001 Rychetský was minister of justice. After the elections of June 2002 and the formation of a center-left coalition, he remained deputy prime minister and minister of justice. (PU)

Sources: *ČBS*; *Českoslovenští politici: 1918–1991* (Prague, 1991); Jan Rychlík, *Rozpad Československa: Česko-slovenské vztahy 1989–1992* (Bratislava, 2002); Eric Stein, *Czecho/Slovakia: Ethnic Conflict, Constitutional Fissure, Negotiated Breakup* (Ann Arbor, 1997); wtd.vlada.cz/scripts/detail.php?id=2340; www.cssd.cz/vismo/index.asp?tz=4&id_org=422010&id_u=6463.

RYDZ-ŚMIGŁY Edward [originally Rydz] (11 March 1886, Brzeżany–2 December 1941, Warsaw), Polish military leader, marshal of Poland. Rydz-Śmigły lost his parents as a child, and he grew up under tough conditions. In 1905 he graduated from a high school in Brzeżany. He enrolled at the Academy of Fine Arts in Kraków, which he finished, after briefly dropping out, in 1913. Between 1905 and 1907 he studied art history and philosophy at the Jagiellonian University in Kraków, and in 1907 he studied painting in Munich, Nuremberg, and Vienna. He was a member of the Socialist organization Promień (Ray) and the independent Odrodzenie (Rebirth). In fall 1908 Rydz-Śmigły was elected deputy chief organizer of the secret Union of Active Struggle in Brzeżany. He assumed a pseudonym: "Śmigły" (the Swift One). Between 1910 and 1911 he served in the Austro-Hungarian Army. In 1912 he graduated first in his class from the officers' school of the Riflemen's Association (Związek Strzelecki [ZS]). He was appointed commander of the introductory and intermediate levels of the school and ZS deputy chairman in Kraków. In 1913 he became commander of the Lwów (Lvov) district of the ZS. From March to August 1914 he was editor of the monthly *Strzelec*, which was published there. At that time he became one of the closest associates of **Józef Piłsudski**.

At the beginning of World War I Rydz-Śmigły was released from service in the Austro-Hungarian Army. In August 1914 he joined a riflemen's unit in Chęciny. As the commander of the third cadre battalion, he participated in operations conducted by Piłsudski along the Vistula. In October he was promoted to major, and in December he took over the command of the First Infantry Regiment of the Polish Legions in Nowy Sącz. He fought with his regiment near the Nida River. In June 1915 he was promoted to lieutenant colonel, and in September he became the second in command of the First Brigade of the Legions in Volhynia. In February 1914 he was coopted to the Council of Colonels, which demanded the removal of Austrian officers from the Legions and proclaiming them a Polish army. In May 1916 he was promoted to full colonel. Following the so-called oath crisis in July 1917, Rydz-Śmigły was suspended from regimental command and dismissed from the Legions. Before his internment, Piłsudski ordered him to take over the Supreme Command of the Polish Military Organization (Polska Organizacja Wojskowa [POW]), a secret body fighting for Poland's independence. Rydz-Śmigły also founded a clandestine entity in Kraków: the Convent. He rejected the war ministry portfolio that was offered to him by the Regency Council, and on 1 November 1918 he issued a call for the mobilization of the POW to eliminate the Austrian occupation.

In the government of **Ignacy Daszyński**, which was formed in Lublin on the night of 6 November 1918, Rydz-Śmigły accepted, in place of Piłsudski, the war ministry portfolio, and he was duly appointed brigadier general and supreme commander of all Polish forces. On 10 November he officially ordered the POW to commence disarming the troops of the Central Powers, an operation that had already been unofficially under way for some time. At Piłsudski's request, the government that Rydz-Śmigły was serving dissolved itself. However, Piłsudski confirmed the promotion of Rydz-Śmigły to brigadier general on 21 November 1918. Meanwhile, on 16 November he took over the command of the General District in Lublin, and on 7 December, of the General District in Warsaw. During the Polish-Ukrainian war Rydz-Śmigły was ordered to lead the tactical group Kowel in February 1919. He also commanded the First Legion Infantry Division during the Wilno (Vilnius) operation. In May he commanded the operational group Wilno-Święciany, which took Minsk. From 11 November 1919 he led the army group fighting on the Lithuanian-Belorussian front, and on 30 December he headed the operational group Zima (Winter), consisting of Polish and Lithuanian troops, which captured Dünaburg (Daugavpils) from the Bolsheviks. In April 1920 Rydz-Śmigły was promoted to three-star general. On 5 May he was put in command of the Third Army, which two days later captured Kiev. During the Polish retreat, he commanded the southeastern front and then the central front. On 18 August he took over the Second Army, which he led to capture Grodno.

After the conclusion of hostilities, in May 1921 Rydz-Śmigły was appointed army inspector in Wilno. Between 1922 and 1926 he organized and trained troops. With permission from Piłsudski, from fall 1921 to summer 1923, he belonged to a secret military organization, Honor and Fatherland, founded by General **Władysław Sikorski**. In November and December 1925 Rydz-Śmigły sojourned in France to learn about the organization of its armed forces. He backed Piłsudski in May 1926, sending a part of the Wilno army garrison to Warsaw. In October 1926 he became army inspector with the General Inspectorate of the Armed Forces. From April 1926 he served as Piłsudski's deputy for operations in the east. Between 1929 and 1931 he sponsored the secret organization White Eagle, of which Piłsudski disapproved. Following Piłsudski's death, he was appointed general inspector of the armed forces on 13 May 1935.

From mid-1935, Rydz-Śmigły became actively involved in politics. In a memorandum issued by Prime Minister **Felicjan Sławoj Składkowski** on 13 July 1936—at the urging of President **Ignacy Mościcki**—Rydz-Śmigły was proclaimed to be the second most important official of the Polish state. On 10 November 1936 he became a four-star general and, almost immediately after, a marshal of Poland. Supporting authoritarian rule, Rydz-Śmigły quarreled with Mościcki and his Castle group of supporters. The marshal's political machine emerged in 1937 as the quasi-totalitarian Front of National Unification. As far as foreign policy was concerned, Rydz-Śmigły considered an alliance with France to be crucial. He undertook a six-year plan to modernize the armed forces, and he embarked on designing a new defense doctrine. He strove to curtail the involvement of generals in the state administration and politics. Aware of the danger of Nazi German aggression, in March 1939 he ordered the secret mobilization of two military districts and an acceleration of defense preparations for Poland. He refused publicly to back down before Nazi threats and Soviet demands, which Stalin advanced in the course of his negotiations with Great Britain and France, so as to allow the Red Army to cross Polish territory.

When Germany attacked Poland on 1 September 1939, Rydz-Śmigły became the commander-in-chief and was nominated by the president as his successor. He ordered parts of the army to break through to Romania and Hungary. Faced with the Soviet invasion on 17 September 1939, he decided to undertake defensive measures against the Red Army as the last resort. On the night of 17 September Rydz-Śmigły crossed the border into Romania. He was criticized for abandoning the units that were still fighting. He was interned in the village of Dragoslavele. On 7 November he finally resigned as the commander-in-chief. During his sojourn in Romania, Rydz-Śmigły wrote an account of the September campaign; it was first published in 1941 in Hungary and then in Poland. In the fall of 1940 Rydz-Śmigły decided to return home. On 10 December 1940 he illegally crossed the Romanian-Hungarian border. In the summer of 1941 in Hungary he wrote a report, "Could Poland Have Avoided the War?" Then he co-founded the secret organization Camp of Fighting Poland. At the end of October 1941 he reached Nazi-occupied Warsaw. He was, however, refused membership in Poland's mainstream underground. Rydz-Śmigły died of a heart attack and was buried secretly at the Powązki Cemetery in Warsaw as "Adam Zawisza." (JS)

Sources: *PSB*, vol. 33; Kazimierz Cepnik, *Edward Śmigły-Rydz, generalny inspektor Sił Zbrojnych: Zarys życia i działalności* (Warsaw, 1936); Maciej Gruszczyński, *Gen. Edward Rydz-Śmigły, Generalny Inspektor Sił Zbrojnych: Szkic życiorysu* (Warsaw, 1936); Roman Zawada, *Opowieść żołnierska o generale Śmigłym* (Warsaw, 1936); Tomasz Nałęcz, *Polska Organizacja Wojskowa 1914–1918* (Warsaw, 1984); *Marszałek Edward Śmigły-Rydz, 1886–1986* (London, 1986); Ryszard Mirowicz, *Edward Rydz-*

Śmigły: Działalność wojskowa i polityczna (Warsaw, 1988); Cezary Leżeński, *Kwatera 139: Opowieść o marszałku Rydzu-Śmigłym*, 2 vols. (Lublin, 1989).

RYLSKYI Maksym (19 March 1895, Kiev–24 July 1964, Kiev), Ukrainian poet, translator, and community activist. Rylskyi's father Tadey, a well-known Ukrainian ethnographer and community activist, was of Polish descent. In 1915 Rylskyi began to study at Kiev University, initially at the School of Medicine, transferring to the School of History and Philology in 1918, but he never graduated. From 1919 until the autumn of 1923 he worked as the headmaster of a school in the village of Romanivka. From 1923 to 1929 he taught Ukrainian language and literature at schools in Kiev, and subsequently he devoted himself to writing only. In 1943–46 Rylskyi served as president of the Ukrainian Writers' Union (Spilka Pysmennykiv Ukraiiny). From 1944 until the end of his life he was director of the Institute of Art Studies, Folklore, and Ethnography of the Academy of Sciences of the Ukrainian Soviet Socialist Republic (SSR); the institute is now named after him. In 1943 Rylskyi became a member of the Academy of Sciences of the Ukrainian SSR, and in 1958, a member of the Academy of Sciences of the Soviet Union. From 1957 until the end of his life he worked as editor-in-chief of the periodical *Narodna tvorchist ta etnohrafiia*, and he was an informal patron of the so-called generation of the sixties (*shestidesiatniki*).

Rylskyi made his literary debut in 1907, and in 1910 he published his first poetry collection, *Na bilykh ostrovakh* (On the white islands). His later collections of poems include *Pid osinnimy zoriami* (Beneath the autumn stars; 1918) and *Synia dalechin* (The blue distance; 1922) and the poems "Tsarivna" (Tsarevna; 1917) and "Na uzlissi" (On the edge of a forest; 1917). In the 1920s Rylskyi was drawn to the literary group of neoclassicists. At that time he wrote new poetry collections, including *Kriz buriu i snih* (Through storm and snow; 1925); *De skhodiasia dorohy* (Where the roads meet; 1929); and *Homin i vidhomin* (The resonance and the echo; 1929). Accused of being a member of an underground terrorist organization and arrested in March 1931, Rylskyi was released after six months. Owing to his stay in prison and a mounting campaign against "Ukrainian bourgeois nationalism," he began to affirm the Soviet reality. In the 1930s he published new poetry collections, including *Kiiv* (Kiev; 1935); *Ukraiina* (Ukraine; 1938); and *Zbir vynohradu* (The harvest of grapes; 1940). After the outbreak of the German-Soviet war, patriotic elements began to increasingly appear in his poetry. In November 1941 Rylskyi wrote the famous collection *Slovo pro ridnu matir* (A song about my mother), expressing his faith in the indomitability of the nation and his belief that victory was certain. Some of Rylskyi's postwar poetry collections—including *Virnist* (Fidelity; 1946); *Chasha druzhby* (The cup of friendship; 1946); and *Ranok nashoy Vitchyzny* (The morning of our homeland; 1953)—were banned from publication because they allegedly included "bourgeois nationalist distortions." Rylskyi authored over thirty collections of poems. His greatest translation achievements include *Pan Tadeusz*, by Adam Mickiewicz; *Evgeniy Onegin*, by Aleksandr Pushkin; *Cyrano de Bergerac*, by Edmond Rostand; and *King Lear*, by William Shakespeare. (BB)

Sources: *Encyclopedia of Ukraine*, vol. 4 (Toronto, 1993); *Pisarze świata: Słownik Encyklopedyczny* (Warsaw, 1995); *Dovidnyk z istorii Ukraiiny* (Kiev, 2001); Stepan Krizhanivskyi, *Maksym Rylskyi* (Kiev, 1960); H. Donets and M. Nahnybida, *Niezabutniy Maksym Rylskyi: Spohady*ed (Kiev, 1968); Kateryna Skokan, *M. T. Rylskyi: Bibliohrafichnyi Pokazchyk 1907–1965* (Kiev, 1970); Leonid Novychenko, *Poetycznyi svit Maksyma Rylskoho (1910–1941)* (Kiev, 1980).

RZEPECKI Jan, pseudonyms "Prezes" and "Ożóg" (29 September 1899, Warsaw–28 April 1983, Warsaw), Polish officer, historian, and social activist. While in high school, Rzepecki joined a secret scouting troop in 1912. From May 1914 he belonged to the Riflemen's Association. From August 1914 to July 1917 he served in the infantry of the Polish Legions. After the oath crisis in July 1917, Rzepecki was admitted to the German-mandated Polish Armed Forces, and in November 1918 he began to serve in the Polish Army. He fought in the Polish-Bolshevik war. In April 1921 he completed a course for company and battalion commanders at the Center for Infantry Training in Rembertów, and in August 1921 he completed a similar course in France. From 1921 to 1922 Rzepecki studied law at the University of Warsaw. Between 1923 and 1924 he was enrolled at the School of Political Sciences in Warsaw, and from 1922 through 1924, at the Higher Military School in Warsaw. From October 1924 he lectured in tactics and war history at the Infantry Officers' School in Warsaw. Along with the military students, Rzepecki fought on the government's side during the coup d'état of 1926. His duties including protecting Poland's president, **Stanisław Wojciechowski**. After the coup, Rzepecki was expelled from the school and transferred to the staff of the command of the Second Corps District in Lublin. In November 1926 he was appointed chief of staff of the brigade of the Border Defense Corps in Czortków. From May 1928 he lectured on tactics at the Center for Infantry Training in Rembertów, and from October 1934, at the Higher Military School in Warsaw. In March 1939 he became a staff officer of the Kraków Army.

Rzepecki participated in the September campaign of 1939. Upon reaching Warsaw on 1 October 1939, he joined the underground. He was appointed chief of staff of the City of Warsaw District Command of the Service for the Victory of Poland and, later, the Union of Armed Struggle (Związek Walki Zbrojnej [ZWZ]). In July 1940 he was promoted to full colonel. From October 1940 to October 1944 Rzepecki served as chief of the Bureau of Information and Propaganda of the ZWZ High Command and then of the Home Army (Armia Krajowa [AK]). From 1941 to 1942 he edited the monthly *Insurekcja*. He was a member of the Directorate of the Underground Struggle and the Nationalities Council with the Office of the Government Delegate. However, he refused to participate in the Social Anti-Communist Committee. Of leftist sympathies, Rzepecki volunteered to join the underground Polish Socialist party Freedom, Equality, Independence in the summer of 1940. During the Warsaw Uprising of 1944, he was active in the staff of the commander of the AK Warsaw District and the AK High Command. After the failure of the uprising, Rzepecki was interned in the Łambinowice and Dobiegniewo POW camps. Upon his release, in March 1945 he was appointed deputy chief and chief of staff of the last AK commander in chief, General **Leopold Okulicki**. Following the arrest of General Okulicki by the NKVD in March 1945, Rzepecki commanded the underground Nie (No) organization. On 30 April 1945 he was appointed to serve as the chief of the Office of the Delegate of the Armed Forces for the Homeland. On 6 August 1945 he ordered it dissolved.

Between September and November 1945, Rzepecki was chairman of the Main Executive Committee of the Freedom and Independence Union. He was arrested on 5 November 1945. Believing the false guarantees of the Communists, he decided to reveal the names and whereabouts of his underlings, which expedited their capture by the secret police. In February 1947 he was sentenced to eight years in jail, but Communist president **Bolesław Bierut** granted him clemency on his first day in office. Rzepecki was employed as deputy director of the Military-Scientific Publishing Institute and later as chief of the Department of Studies of the Academy of the General Staff of the Communist-led army. In January 1949 he was arrested once again and imprisoned for five years. Freed in December 1954, he remained unemployed for almost a year. From 1955 to 1969, Rzepecki worked at the Institute of History of the Polish Academy of Sciences in Warsaw. In 1964 he received a Ph.D. in history. After 1956 he became active in public life; among other things, he published an open letter "To my colleagues from the Home Army," which called for participation in elections and a political renewal of the nation. Rzepecki belonged to the leadership of the (Communist-led) Union of the Fighters for Freedom and Democracy but also to the dissident Crooked Circle Club. Rzepecki authored a great many publications concerning the history of the Polish Underground State and military history, including the following: *Taktyka* (Tactics; 1932); *Wspomnienia i przyczynki historyczne* (Recollections and historical anecdotes; 1956); *Rodowód wojska Drugiej Rzeczypospolitej* (The origins of the army in the Second Republic; 1959); *Sprawa Legionu Wschodniego 1914 roku* (The case of the Eastern Legion in 1914; 1966); and *Rok 1945. Wspomnienia i dokumenty* (1945: Recollections and documents; 1983). (JS)

Sources: *PSB*, vol. 34; Kunert, vol. 1; Krystyna Kersten, *Narodziny systemu władzy: Polska 1943–1948* (Poznań, 1990); Stanisław Kluz, *W potrzasku dziejowym: WIN na Szlaku AK* (Warsaw, 1989); *Koniec polskiego państwa podziemnego* (Łódź, 1987); Marek Łatyński, *Nie paść na kolana: Szkice o opozycji lat czterdziestych* (London, 1985); Marek Ney-Krwawicz, *Komendanci Armii Krajowej* (Warsaw, 1992).

RZYMOWSKI Wincenty (19 July 1883, Kuczbork, near Mława–30 April 1950, Warsaw), Polish politician and lawyer. Rzymowski came from an intelligentsia family. He studied law in Lausanne, Geneva, and Odessa. He belonged to the milieu of left-radical intellectuals. In 1907 Rzymowski co-organized the Congress of Free Thinkers and joined the Polish Progressive Union. In the 1920s he was the editor-in-chief of *Kurier Poranny* and the weekly *Epoka*. He contributed to many periodicals, including *Prawda, Robotnik, Wiadomości Literackie,* and *Oblicza Dnia.* He was a prolific anti-clerical author. From 1923 to 1927 Rzymowski served as a press clerk at the Polish Embassy in Italy. Between 1933 and 1937 he belonged to the Polish Academy of Literature but was forced to resigned because of charges of plagia-

rism. Although he supported the ruling *sanacja*, after 1935 he drew closer to the Communists, participating in some of the activities of the International Organization to Aid Revolutionaries. From 1937 Rzymowski became active in the Democratic Club. In 1938 he belonged to the program commission of the Democratic Party (Stronnictwo Demokratyczne [SD]). In February 1939 he was coopted to its board. During World War II Rzymowski lived in Krzemieniec and published in the Soviet press. After the return of the Red Army in spring 1944, he collaborated with the Communist-led Union of Polish Patriots in Moscow. In July 1944 he joined the Home National Council and soon became the supervisor of the Department for Culture and Art of the Polish Committee of National Liberation (Polski Komitet Wyzwolenia Narodowego [PKWN]). From August to September 1944 Rzymowski represented the PKWN with the Soviet government. From September 1944 he served as chairman of the SD Main Board. In May 1945 he became minister of foreign affairs of the Provisional Government and continued in this function until February 1947. He completely followed the Communist line. In November 1945 Rzymowski became chairman of the SD Central Committee. As a result of the falsified elections of January 1947, he became an MP representing the SD in the Constitutional Parliament. He was also coopted as minister without portfolio to the government of **Józef Cyrankiewicz**. He also headed the Parliamentary Club of the SD. (WR)

Sources: *PSB*, vol. 34; Mołdawa; *Encyklopedia historii Drugiej Rzeczpospolitej* (Warsaw, 1999); *Stronnictwo Demokratyczne w Polsce Ludowej: Wybór dokumentów 1944–1968* (Warsaw, 1968); Józef Kowalski, *Komunistyczna Partia Polski 1935–1938* (Warsaw, 1975); Andrzej Paczkowski, *Prasa polska w latach 1918–1939* (Warsaw, 1980); Marek Łatyński, *Nie paść na kolana: Szkice o opozycji lat czterdziestych* (Warsaw, 1987).

S

SADOVEANU Mihail (5 November 1880, Paşcani–19 October 1961, Bucharest), Romanian writer. In 1892–97 Sadoveanu studied at a high school in Fălticeni and later in Iaşi. In 1897 he made his literary debut in a satirical periodical, *Dracu*. From 1898 he contributed to Bucharest periodicals such as *Convorbiri literare, Pagini literare*, and *Viaţa nouă*. In 1900 Sadoveanu started legal studies at Bucharest University but failed to complete them. In 1902 he served in the army. In 1903 he moved to Bucharest again, and until 1906 he worked for a conservative peasant literary weekly, *Sămănatorul*. In 1904 Sadoveanu published the short stories "Povestiri" (Tales), "Şoimii" (Falcons), and "Dureri înăbuşite" (Muffled pains), and in 1905, "Crîşma lui Moş Precu" (Grandpa Precu's inn); in these he presented the life of the Moldavian countryside and small towns, as well as Romanian culture and history. In 1906–16 Sadoveanu worked with the periodical *Viaţa românească*, promoting peasantry as the sole bearer of the Romanian national spirit and stigmatizing the cosmopolitism of the Romanian elites. Further collections of short stories—including *Floare ofilită* (Fading flower; 1906) and *Însemnările lui Neculai Manea* (Notes by Neculai Manea; 1908)—strengthened his literary reputation. In 1907 he received a literary award from the Romanian Academy of Arts and Sciences.

In 1907–8 Sadoveanu was an inspector of countryside community centers in Moldavia. This experience served as a source for his novel *Oameni şi locuri* (People and places; 1908). From 1908 he chaired the Association of Romanian Writers (ARW), and in 1910–19 he was the director of the National Theater in Iaşi. In 1915 he published his first historical novel, *Neamul Şoimăreştilor* (The falcon tribe). Mobilized during World War I, in 1916–18 Sadoveanu founded and edited a military daily, *România*. He presented his wartime experience in two volumes of memoirs, published as *Strada Lăpuşneanu* (Lăpuşneanu Street; 1921). In 1919 in Iaşi, Sadoveanu founded the weekly *Însemnări literare*, referring to *Viaţa românească*. When the latter was resumed in 1920, Sadoveanu entered into a working arrangement with the periodical. At that time he published (among other works) *Frunze înfurtună* (Leaves in the storm; 1920) and *Cocostârcul albastru* (Blue cock; 1921). In 1923 he became a member of the Romanian Academy of Arts and Sciences. He described peasant protests against exploitation in the novels *Venea o moară pe Şiret* (There was a mill on the Şiret River;

1923), *Hanu-Ancuţei* (Hanu's inn; 1928) and *Baltagul* (The perished; 1930). He expressed his fascination with Romanian nature in *Nopţile de Sînzene* (St. John's nights; 1934) and presented a legendary Romanian past in the trilogy *Fraţii Jderi* (The Jderi brothers; 1935–42). From 1936 Sadoveanu lived in Bucharest, editing the dailies *Adevărul* and *Dimineaţa*. He opposed the Iron Guard, which burned his books at the end of the 1930s. In 1938 he received an honorary doctorate from Iaşi University. After World War II Sadoveanu wrote in the spirit of Socialist realism—for instance, the novels *Mitrea Cocor* (1949) and *Nada florilor* (Island of flowers; 1950)—supporting the Communists and becoming their leading writer. From 1949 to 1961 he chaired the ARW. In the 1950s Sadoveanu was vice-president of the Great National Assembly and president of the National Committee of Peace Defenders. He authored about one hundred books. (LW)

Sources: Halina Mirska-Lasota, *Mały słownik pisarzy rumuńskich* (Warsaw, 1975); Juliusz Demel, *Historia Rumunii* (Wrocław, 1986); Dorina N. Rusu, *Membrii Academiei Române 1866–1999* (Bucharest, 1999); Ion Alexandrescu, Ion Bulei, Ion Mamina, and Ioan Scurtu, *Enciclopedia de istorie României* (Bucharest, 2000).

SADOWSKI Zdzisław (10 February 1925, Warsaw), Polish economist and politician. Sadowski studied at the Main School of Commerce and worked there as an assistant to Professor **Edward Lipiński**. In 1951 he graduated in economics from Warsaw University (Uniwersytet Warszawski [UW]), and from 1953 he worked there, receiving doctorate and postdoctoral degrees. In 1965–70 Sadowski lectured at the University of Accra (Ghana), and in 1970–72 he was deputy director of the Center for Planning, Development, Forecasting, and Economic Policy of the UN Secretariat in New York. From 1973 to 1981 he worked at the Institute of Planning in Warsaw; in 1980–81 he was its deputy director. In 1980 Sadowski became a professor at the UW. He did not belong to the Communist Party, yet in October 1981 he became undersecretary of state in the Office of the Council of Ministers and deputy plenipotentiary of the government for economic reform. Sadowski continued in the government during the period of martial law. From 1985 he was deputy chairman and from 1987 chairman of the Consultative Economic Council. In 1986–87 he belonged to the Socioeconomic Council of the parliament, and from 1986 to 1989, to the Consultative Council of the Chairman of the Council of State. From April 1987 to October 1988 Sadowski was deputy prime minister responsible for economic policy and chairman of the government Planning Commission. He introduced the concept of the "second stage of economic reform," which proved to be a mere propaganda action. In the fall of 1987 a referendum was held in order to gain social acceptance for austerity measures, but the referendum failed. In February 1988 serious price increases were the final blow to the fiction of the "second stage of reform." Sadowski took part in the Round Table Talks on behalf of the government (February–April 1989). From 1985 he was chairman of the Polish Economic Association. (PK)

Sources: Mołdawa; *Kto jest kto w Polsce* (Warsaw, 1993); Andrzej Albert [Wojciech Roszkowski], *Najnowsza historia Polski 1914–1993*, vol. 2 (Warsaw, 1995); Jan Skórzyński, *Ugoda i rewolucja: Władza i opozycja 1985–1989* (Warsaw, 1995); *Polska 1986–1989: Koniec systemu* (Warsaw, 2002).

SADŪNAITĖ Nijolė (21 July 1938, Kaunas), Lithuanian nun and dissident. The daughter of a teacher, in 1955 Sadūnaitė graduated from a high school in Anykščiai. Because of anti-religious discrimination, she could not study medicine, so she became a professional nurse. In 1958 she joined the Order of the Immaculate Holy Virgin Mary. She took care of the sick, including a long-term Gulag prisoner, Reverend Petras Rauda. In 1970 Sadūnaitė organized legal aid for Reverend Antanas Šeškevičius, who was accused of teaching the catechism to children. From 1972 she worked with the underground *Chronicle of the Catholic Church In Lithuania*. On 27 August 1974 Sadūnaitė was arrested while working on the next issue of the *Chronicle*. In June 1975 she was tried in deep secrecy, the only witness being her brother Jonas. Sadūnaitė turned her plea into an accusation that the Communist system violated the conscience. She was sentenced to three years in prison and three years of forced exile. She served her term in Dubravlag in Mordvinia. In September 1977 Sadūnaitė was exiled to Boguchani in the Krasnoyarsk region of Siberia. As a result of camp conditions she suffered a heart attack. As the news of her trial and imprisonment leaked out to the West and as her own account was published there as *No Greater Love: The Trial of a Christian in Soviet Occupied Lithuania* (1975), she received parcels with food and medicine, which she passed on to other political prisoners in the camps of Yakutia and Magadan.

Released in July 1980, Sadūnaitė returned to Lithuania and continued her work with the *Chronicle*. In 1982–87 she lived in hiding. In June 1983 she organized the signing of protests against the imprisonment of Fathers **Alfonsas Svarinskas** and **Sigitas Tamkevičius**. In this connection the KGB repressed Sadūnaitė's sister-in-law, and her brother was placed in a psychiatric ward. In 1986 her *Pamiętnik* (Diary) was published in Polish in Paris. In April 1987 Sadūnaitė was temporarily arrested and threatened with death. Despite this, in August 1987 she co-organized

a demonstration commemorating the anniversary of the Moltov–Ribbentrop pact of 1939. She joined the League for a Free Lithuania (Lietuvos Laisves Lyga), which started official activities. KGB agents deported Sadūnaitė to Belorussia, where they threatened her with execution for thirty hours. In May 1988 she met with President Ronald Reagan, who visited Moscow. In June 1988 she was left out of the Initiative Group of the Lithuanian Movement for Perestroika (Sąjūdis) and remained in the shadows of Lithuanian politics. In August 1988 Sadūnaitė took part in a hunger strike on Gediminas Square in Vilnius, organized to demand the release of the last political prisoners from the Baltic republics. After Lithuania regained its independence in 1991, Sadūnaitė began to work with the Vilnius branch of Caritas, a Catholic charity organization reactivated in Lithuania for the first time in fifty years. In 1992 her *Radiance from the Gulag* was published in the United States. In August 1998 Sadūnaitė was awarded the Order of the White Knight. (WR)

Sources: S. P. de Boer, E. J. Driessen, and H. L. Verhaar, eds., *Biographical Dictionary of Dissidents in the Soviet Union, 1956–1975* (The Hague and Boston, 1982); Michael Bourdeaux, *Land of Crosses: The Struggle for Religious Freedom in Lithuania, 1939–1978* (Devon, 1979); www.pfm.pl/u235/back/183229/navi/183392; www.theatlantic.com/issues/94jul/pope.htm; www.karta.org.pl/WspolneMiejsce.asp.

SAKUZOV Yanko (24 September 1860, Shumen–2 February 1941, Sofia), Bulgarian politician. In 1878 Sakuzov moved to Russia. He initially attended a high school in Nikolayev, and then, along with **Dimitur Blagoev**, he studied at a theological seminary in Odessa. In 1880 he left the seminary and went to Germany. He studied the natural sciences, philosophy, and history at the universities in Jena, Leipzig, and Thuringia (1881–83) and then biology in London (1883–84) and literature and literary criticism in Paris (1884). After returning to Bulgaria, Sakuzov taught biology, history, and literature at a school in Shumen. In 1885 he fought as a volunteer in the Serbo-Bulgarian war. In 1886 he opposed the coup and the dethronement of Prince Alexander Battenberg. In 1887–90 Sakuzov was deputy prosecutor in Shumen. He edited *Den*, one of the first Bulgarian Socialist periodicals, initially in Shumen (1891–92) and then in Sofia (until 1896). Sakuzov was one of the founders of the Bulgarian Social Democratic Party (BSDP). After a split in the movement in 1892, he joined the Bulgarian Social Democratic Union, which merged with the BSDP to form the Bulgarian Social Democratic Workers' Party (BSDWP) two years later. From 1894 Sakuzov was one of the top-ranking party leaders. After a split in the BSDWP at the Tenth Congress in 1903, he became the leader of a BSDWP faction known as the Broad Socialists. He edited the BSDWP periodical *Obshto delo* (1900–5) and organized a trade union movement. In 1917 he attended an international Socialist conference in Stockholm.

From 1906 to 1908 Sakuzov was active in the opposition Patriotic Bloc. He supported the proclamation of full independence for Bulgaria in 1908 but protested the strengthening of royal power. He opposed Bulgaria's entering World War I on the side of the Central Powers. It was only toward the end of the war that he agreed to assume the portfolio of minister of trade, industry, and labor in the governments of **Aleksandur Malinov** and **Teodor Teodorov** (October 1918–October 1919). Sakuzov was a member of the Bulgarian delegation to the Paris Peace Conference in 1919, a deputy to the National Assembly (1893–96, 1902–3, 1911–23, and 1923–34), and a deputy to the Grand National Assembly in 1911. He edited the newspapers *Drugar* (1893–94), *Rabotnicheska borba* (1903–8), and *Narod* (1911–34), as well as the periodicals *Obshtestvena misul* (1909), *Suvremenna misul* (1910–14, 1919–20), and *Sotsialdemokrat* (1920–28). After the coup of May 1934 Sakuzov retired from active politics. As his last political act, he signed a letter of protest against the parliament's enacting a law on the protection of the nation in 1940. Sakuzov's publications include *Cezarizum ili demokratsia* (Caesarism or democracy; 1905); *Inteligentsiiata i neinata rola v obshtestvoto* (The intelligentsia and its role in society; 1906); *Bulgarite v svoiata istorii* (The Bulgarians in history; 1922, 3d ed.); and *Protiv monarkhiiata: V zashtita na republikata* (Against Monarchy: In defense of the republic; 1946). (JJ)

Sources: *Entsiklopediya Bulgariya*, vol. 6 (Sofia, 1988); Georgi Dimitrov, *Suchineniia*, vol. 15 (Sofia, 1989); T. Dobrev, "Ianko Sakuzov," *Novo Vreme*, 1990, no. 1; Dimo Dimov, *Dimitur Blagoev i Ianko Sakuzov v Shumen* (Shumen, 1994); Tasho Tashev, *Ministrite na Bulgariya 1879–1999: Entsiklopedichen spravochnik* (Sofia, 1999); Milen Kumanov and Tania Nikolova, *Politicheski partii, organizatsii i dvizheniia v Bulgariia i tekhnite lideri 1879–1999: Kratuk spravochnik* (Sofia, 1999); *Bulgarski durzhavnitsi i polititsi 1918–1947* (Sofia, 2000); Angel Tsurakov, *Entsiklopediya Pravitelstvata na Bulgariya: Khronologiia na politicheskiya zhivot 1879–2001* (Sofia, 2001).

ŠALKAUSKIS Stasys (4 May 1886, Ariogala–4 December 1941, Šiauliai), Lithuanian philosopher. Šalkauskis graduated in philosophy and law from Moscow University in 1911. During World War I he continued his studies in Fribourg, Switzerland, where he received a Ph.D. for a dissertation on Vladimir Soloviev. In 1922 Šalkauskis started teaching in the Department of Theology and Philosophy of Vytautas Magnus University in Kaunas, and in 1939 he became the university's rector. Removed after the Soviet invasion and after the incorporation of Lithuania into the USSR in 1940, he died soon after Lithuania was occupied by Nazi Germany. Šalkauskis was the most prominent representative of Lithuanian Christian philosophy. Connected with the Roman Catholic movement Ateitis (Future), he opposed the nationalist regime of **Antanas Smetona**. He thought that Lithuanian culture was a unique combination of the traditions of Eastern and Western Europe. His thinking stemmed from the works of St. Thomas Acquinas but was also closely connected with contemporary Catholic thought. Šalkauskis defended democracy and moral values as the foundations of national life. He played a serious role in the shaping of the Lithuanian intelligentsia. Among other works Šalkauskis authored the following: *Bendrosios mokslinio darbo metodikos pradai* (Foundations of the general methodology of science; 1926); *Kultūros filosofijos metmenys* (Outline of the philosophy of culture; 1926); *Tautybė, patriotizmas ir lietuvių tautos pašaukimas* (Nationality, patriotism, and the destiny of the Lithuanian nation; 1928); *Visuomeninis auklėjimas* (Social education; 1932); *Lietuvių tauta ir jos ugdymas* (The Lithuanian nation and its development; 1933); and *Tiesos kelias* (The path of truth; 1938). Šalkauskis's works, banned under Soviet rule, became very popular after Lithuania regained its independence in 1991. (WR)

Sources: *EL*, vol. V; Saulius Sužiedelis, *Historical Dictionary of Lithuania* (Lanham, Md., 1997); Juozas Eretas, *Stasys Šalkauskis* (Brooklyn, N.Y., 1960); Julija Šalkauskiene, *I idealu aukštumas. Atsiminimai apie prof. Stasi Šalkauskis* (Vilnius, 1998).

ŠÁMAL Přemysl (4 October 1867, Prague–9 March 1941, Berlin), Czech lawyer and politician. Šámal received a law degree from the Czech University in Prague, and he subsequently worked as an attorney (1898–1919). He was vice-chairman of the Central School Organization (Ústřední Matica Školská) from 1902 to 1922 and a member of the Prague City Council from 1908 to 1911. Before World War I he was active in the Czech Progressive Party (the so-called realists) and was a close associate of **Tomáš Garrigue Masaryk**. During the war Šámal was one of the leaders of the Czech pro-independence movement. In March 1917 he helped to establish a secret Czech political organization called Mafia. From September 1915 onwards he was one of the Mafia leaders, serving as head of its information network. Šámal coordinated the activities of all unofficial organizations in the Czech territories and was responsible for contacts with the émigré community and with all major Czech politicians. Toward the end of the war he sought to unify all political forces around the idea of Czechoslovak independence. In July 1918 Šámal became a member of the Czechoslovak National Committee (Národní Výbor). In October of that year, as a representative of the Mafia, he took part in Geneva negotiations between representatives of the pro-independence movement at home and abroad.

In 1918–20 Šámal sat on the Revolutionary National Assembly, and from November 1918 to June 1919 he served as mayor of Prague, elected with the support of all major political forces. From 1919 to 1938 he held various positions, including that of head of President Masaryk's chancellery. Šámal was one of Masaryk's closest associates. He played a major role in shaping the president's policies and organized the work of the chancellery. When Masaryk resigned as president, **Edvard Beneš** asked Šámal to remain in his post, so as to symbolize the continuity of the chancellery's work. Šámal resigned as head of the chancellery when **Emil Hácha** became president of Czechoslovakia (30 November 1938), after the Pact of Munich (September 1938). At the beginning of World War II Šámal was in charge of the Political Center (Politické Ústředí), an underground pro-independence organization. He also organized help for the families of prisoners. Arrested by the Gestapo in January 1940, Šámal was sent to a prison in Berlin, where he died. (PU)

Sources: *ČBS*; *Politická elita meziválečného Československa 1918–1938: Kdo byl kdo za první republiky* (Prague, 1998); *Kdo byl kdo v našich dějinách ve 20. stoleti*, vol. 2 (Prague, 1998); Milada Paulová, *Dějiny Maffie*, vols. 1–2 (Prague, 1938); Eduard Beneš, *My War Memoirs* (Boston and New York, 1928).

SĂNĂTESCU Constantin (14 January 1885, Craiova–8 November 1947, Bucharest), Romanian general and politician. Sănătescu completed his military studies at the Military Academy in Bucharest in 1907 and at the War College in 1919–20. With the rank of major, he fought in World War I. He was promoted to general in 1935. Sănătescu was commander of the Fourth Army Corps in 1941–43 and of the Royal Guard between March 1943 and August 1944. During World War II he commanded the Romanian forces against the USSR in Bessarabia (June–July 1941), at Odessa (August–October 1941), and on the Don River (1942). He was decorated with the orders of the Star of Romania (1941) and Michael the Brave (1944) and with the German Iron Cross (1942).

Sănătescu did not participate in the political life of Romania until the coup of 23 August 1944, of which he was one of the main organizers. In June 1944 he took part in a meeting of opposition representatives, including Communists, the army, and the royal court. The participants at the meeting decided that Marshal **Ion Antonescu** should be dismissed. During the coup Sănătescu contributed to the arrest of Antonescu,

and from 23 August 1944 he was prime minister. His cabinet, called the "government of national unity," included (among others) **Iuliu Maniu** and **Constantin Brătianu**. Under pressure from the Soviet president of the Allied Control Commission, on 4 November 1944 King **Michael** appointed a reformed **Sănătescu** cabinet, in which Sănătescu also became minister of war. The second government of Sănătescu was also of a coalition nature, and most departments were still in the hands of democratic politicians. As a representative of Romania, Sănătescu participated in talks with a Soviet delegation headed by Minister of Foreign Affairs Andrey Vyshinsky, and he tried to prevent the vassalization of the country. After the establishment of the government of General **Nicolae Radescu**, between December 1944 and June 1945 Sănătescu served as chief of the general staff. He worked with King Michael and with the democratic parties, mainly the National Peasant Party and the National Liberal Party. Sănătescu was dismissed from his posts after the creation of the government of **Petru Groza** in June 1945. In 1995 his *Jurnal (1944–1947)* (Diary [1944–1947]) was published in Romania. (FA/TD)

Sources: Andrzej Koryn, *Rumunia w polityce wielkich mocarstw 1944–1947* (Wrocław, 1983); Stephen Fischer-Galati, *Twentieth Century Rumania* (New York, 1991); Józef Darski, *Rumunia: Historia, współczesność, konflikty narodowe* (Warsaw, 1995); N. Baciu, *Agonia României 1944–1948* (Bucharest, 1992); M. Ciobanu, *Convorbiri cu Regele Mihai*, vols. 1–2 (Bucharest, 1991–92); A. Duțu, F. Dobre, and L. Loghin, *Armata româna în al: Doilea război mondial (1941–1945)* (Bucharest, 1999).

SANDANSKI Yane (18 May 1872, Vlahi, near Melnik–22 April 1915, Pirin Planina), Macedonian revolutionary. With a primary school education, Sandanski entered the military; following his discharge, he held various jobs. He became an insurgent in Macedonia and was wounded in 1897. Becoming a leader of the Internal Macedonian Revolutionary Organization (Vnatrešna Makedonska Revolucionerna Organizacija [IMRO]), he masterminded the well-publicized abduction of the American missionary Ellen Stone and her Albanian companion, Katerina Tsilka, in eastern Macedonia in 1901. Sandanski and his compatriots captured the women to extort ransom from the United States for their release. The IMRO eventually received a sizable amount, which was used to purchase weapons. Sandanski was a strong proponent of the liberation of Macedonia from the Ottomans and of noncooperation with the Supreme Macedonian Committee (Vyrchoven Makedonski Komitet), based in Sofia. He led his guerrilla band in an ill-fated uprising in Ilinden in 1903, following which he took over the leadership of the anti-supremist, left-wing faction of the organization. Sandanski was behind the murder of two opponents, **Boris**

Sarafov and Ivan Garvanov, in 1907. He embraced the 1908 Young Turk Revolution, with the hope that it would bring equality for all peoples within the Ottoman Empire and political autonomy for Macedonia. He was soon disappointed. Sandanski took up arms on the side of Bulgaria during the Balkan Wars (1912–13). He was assassinated in 1915 by agents of his archenemy **Todor Aleksandrov,** who favored the annexation of Macedonia to Bulgaria. As the leader of the IMRO Federalists, Sandanski stood for the autonomy of Macedonia. (DP)

Sources: Ellen M. Stone, "Six Months among Brigands," *McClure's Magazine,* May–October 1902; Liubomir Miletich, ed., *Materiiali za istoriiata na Makedonskoto osvoboditelno dvizhenie,* vol. 7, *Dvizhenieto otsam Vardara i borbata s vurhovisti: Po spomeni na Yane Sandanski, Hristo Cherno Peev, Sava Mihailov Hr. Kuslev, Ivan Anastasov-Gurcheto, Petur Hr. Iurukov i Nikola Pushkarov* (Sofia, 1928); Duncan M. Perry, *The Politics of Terror: The Macedonian Liberation Movements, 1873–1903* (Durham, N.C., 1988); Mercia MacDermott, *For Freedom and Perfection: The Life of Yané Sandansky* (London and Nyack, N.Y., 1988); Laura Beth Sherman, *Fires on the Mountain* (Boulder, Colo., 1980).

SANGHELI Andrei (20 June 1944, Grinautsy), post-Communist Moldavian politician. Sangheli graduated from the Agricultural Institute in Kishinev. From 1967 he belonged to the CPSU. He started his professional career as the director of a sovkhoz and secretary of the party committee in Kamenka. In 1979–80 he was deputy chairman of the Sovkhoz Council of the Moldavian SSR, and until 1986 he was chairman of the regional executive committee and first secretary of the party committee in Dondyushany. Later he worked as head of the Industrial and Agricultural Committee of the Council of Ministers of the Moldavian SSR. In 1989 Sangheli became deputy prime minister of the republic and minister of agriculture in the government of **Valeriu Muravschi,** which, after the failure of the Moscow putsch in August 1991 and given the approval of President **Mircea Snegur,** proclaimed Moldavian independence. In November 1991 Sangheli and Snegur were among the founders of the Agrarian Democratic Party of Moldova (Partidul Democrat Agrar din Moldova [ADPM]), whose base was the economic nomenklatura, mostly former sovkhoz directors. In view of growing ethnic tensions in Transnistria and the Gagauz lands and owing to fears of the national minorities that the new country would merge with Romania, Snegur decided to form a multi-ethnic cabinet of "national accord," and he placed Sangheli at the head of it on 1 July 1992. Sangheli assured the Moldovans that Moldova would not unite with Romania. In the elections of February 1994 the ADPM won 56 out of 104 mandates, and Sangheli remained prime minister. In a referendum of March 1994 about 95 percent

of those who voted were in favor of independence and against unification with Romania. In the new constitution, passed in July 1994, permanent neutrality was adopted, along with special autonomous status for Transnistria and the Gagauz lands. The official language was called Moldavian and not Romanian. Before the presidential elections of November 1996 Snegur distanced himself from the Sangheli government, which had lost popularity because of economic decline. On 2 December 1996, the day after Snegur's defeat, Sangheli resigned but stayed in office until the end of January 1997, when a new cabinet was formed by Ion Ciubuc. Later Sangheli worked in agro-business. (WR)

Sources: *Europa Środkowo-Wschodnia 1993–1996* (Warsaw, 1995–98); *The Europa World Year Book 2000* (London, 2000); Bugajski; *The International Who's Who 2002* (London, 2002).

SAPIEHA Adam Stefan (14 May 1867, Krasiczyn–23 July 1951, Kraków), prince, Polish cardinal, archbishop of Kraków. Born into an aristocratic family with staunch patriotic traditions, Sapieha attended the Fourth High School in Lvov and later studied law at the University of Vienna and the Jagiellonian University in Kraków, as well as theology in Innsbruck (1890–94). He was ordained on 1 October 1893. After a brief sojurn as a vicar in Buchacz, he left for Rome to continue his studies. In 1896 Sapieha received his doctorate in law at the Papal Ecclesiastical Academy (Lateranum). He also studied diplomacy at the Ecclesiastical Academy for the Nobility. In 1897–1901 Sapieha served as the deputy president of the Catholic Seminary in Lvov. He traveled extensively, including trips to the Balkans and the United States. Between 1906 and 1911 Sapieha served at the Vatican as a papal chamberlain. An expert on Russia and Polish Catholic Church affairs, he solidified his position at the Roman Curia, including the Secretariat of the State, influencing the Vatican's personnel policy. He coordinated the move by the Polish bishops in Galicia to oppose the official policy of Russification in the Khmelnytski district. He also co-founded the Polish press bureau in Rome.

In November 1911, Sapieha was consecrated and appointed bishop of Kraków, and his ingress took place on 3 March 1912. He was also a deputy to the Parliament of the Land (Sejm Krajowy) in Galicia. Appreciating the necessity to elevate the intellectual level of the clergy, Sapieha co-founded the Scientific Catholic Institute in Kraków. Before the outbreak of the World War I, he was involved with the Central National Committee (Centralny Komitet Narodowy) in Galicia. During the war he devoted himself to charity and humanitarian work. He headed the Princes' and Bishops' Committee for Aid to War Victims

(Książęco-Biskupi Komitet Pomocy dla Dotkniętych Klęską Wojny). Following the war, Sapieha devoted himself to the Polish cause in Upper Silesia. This caused conflict with the papal nuncio, Achille Ratti, the future Pope Pius XI. From 1922 to 1923 Sapieha was a senator of the center-right Christian Union for National Unity.

On 28 October 1925, the Pope bestowed metropolitan status upon Kraków, and on 14 December 1925 he nominated Sapieha as the first archbishop metropolitan. Sapieha's ingress took place on 17 January 1926. Initially an opponent of a concordat between Poland and the Vatican, Sapieha then changed his mind and worked strenuously to hammer it out. He was further involved in political conflicts of the time. In 1930 he sided with the politicians of the so-called Center-Left (Centrolew) who were imprisoned by the *sanacja* government. In 1937 he ordered that the remains of **Józef Piłsudski** be moved from St. Leonard's Crypt to the Tower of Silver Bells of Wawel Castle in Kraków, a move that triggered a crisis in Church-state affairs. Also in 1937 Sapieha backed Front Morges, a centrist political initiative against the *sanacja*. Although an opponent of the Socialist leadership, he defended striking workers. In 1939, he vainly appealed to the Pope twice to relieve him of his post because of poor health. In May 1939 he withdrew his appeal because of the specter of war looming large on the horizon. During the German occupation Sapieha remained in Kraków and demanded the same of his ecclesiastical underlings. Following the departure from Poland of Cardinal **August Hlond**, Sapieha fulfilled the duties of the head of the Catholic Church in Poland. He was greatly respected. His attitude toward the occupiers was intrepid and dignified. He personally intervened numerous times concerning various matters before the Nazi governor general of occupied central Poland, Hans Frank. The archbishop initiated and supported underground theological studies. He assisted Polish slave laborers shipped off to the Reich. He actively participated in rescue operations of Jews. He stayed in touch with the Holy See, informing the Pope about the situation in Poland. He also maintained contact with the Polish underground and headed the Civic Committee of Assistance (Obywatelski Komitet Pomocy), and he reactivated the Main Welfare Council (Rada Główna Opiekuńcza).

After the war, Sapieha directed the Episcopate of Poland until the return of Primate Hlond in July 1945 and then again following Hlond's death (October 1948) until the ascent of Archbishop **Stefan Wyszyński**. On 18 February 1946, during the first secret consistory following the war, Sapieha received a cardinal's hat. He was involved in revitalizing and reorganizing the Catholic Church in Poland, including many of its subsidiary organizations. On 25 August 1945, he established the Home Center of Charity, Caritas. He supported the beatification processes of Queen Jadwiga, **Albert Chmielowski**, and Rafał Kalinowski. In March 1945 the cardinal founded *Tygodnik Powszechny*, and he intervened numerous times with the Communist regime regarding its violation of civic rights and Church rights. (PK)

Sources: *PSB*; Ks. Jerzy Wolny., ed., *Księga Sapieżyńska*, vols. 1–2 (Kraków, 1982–86); S. Stępień, ed., *Kardynał Adam Stefan Sapieha: Środowisko rodzinne, życie i dzieło* (Przemyśl, 1995); Michał Czajka and Marcin Kamler, *Leksykon historii Polski* (Warsaw, 1995); J. Czajkowski, *Kardynał Adam Stefan Sapieha* (Wrocław, 1997).

SARAFOV Boris (12 July 1872, Libiahovo, Nevrokop region–28 November 1907, Sofia), Macedonian revolutionary. Sarafov was the son of Petro Sarafov and brother of Kristo Sarafov, Macedonian freedom fighters. He completed military training at the Sofia Military Academy, a classmate of **Georgi Delchev**. He was commissioned a lieutenant in the Bulgarian Army and led an ill-fated foray against Ottoman forces in the Melnik region of Macedonia in 1895. A flamboyant personality, Sarafov was, by most accounts, an opportunist and adventurer who in 1896 proposed that the Internal Macedonian Revolutionary Organization (IMRO) "abduct" him while he was traveling on a Russian passport. IMRO activists could hold him for ransom and generate revenue for their cause. Sarafov also suggested kidnapping the Serbian king to raise money and allegedly offered to raise a contingent of men to fight as mercenaries in the Spanish-American War on the side of the United States. In 1899, with the support of IMRO leaders who hoped he would be friendly to their cause, Sarafov was elected president of the Supreme Macedonia Committee. Quixotic and non-consultative, he nevertheless aided IMRO by providing arms and raising money for its efforts. Sarafov was jailed on murder charges involving the death of a Macedonian-born vlach. He was acquitted but not before the leadership of the Supreme Macedonia Committee had passed on to Colonel Ivan Tsonchev. At the Smilevo Congress in 1903, Sarafov was selected to be a member of the three-man IMRO general staff for a forthcoming uprising at Ilinden. The revolt failed, and Sarafov returned to Bulgaria, where he remained active in Macedonian affairs until his assassination by a protégé of **Yane Sandanski**. (DP)

Sources: *Entsiklopediya Bulgariya*, vol. 6 (Sofia, 1988); Liubomir Miletich, ed., *Materiiali za istoriiata na Makedonskoto osvoboditelno dvizhenie*, vol. 5, *Spomeni na Damian Gruev, Boris Sarafov, Ivan Garvanov* (Sofia, 1927); Duncan M. Perry, *The Poli-*

tics of Terror: The Macedonian Liberation Movements, 1873–1903 (Durham, N.C., 1988); Mercia MacDermott, *For Freedom and Perfection: The Life of Yané Sandansky* (London and Nyack, N.Y., 1988); Valentina Georgieva and Sasha Konechni, *Historical Dictionary of the Republic of Macedonia* (Lanham, Md., 1998).

SÄRE Karl (2 July 1903, Yuryev [now Tartu, Estonia]–1943?), Estonian Communist activist. In 1921 Säre went to the Soviet Union, where he studied briefly at Leningrad University. He became affiliated with the Communist Party of Estonia (CPE) in 1927. From 1933 to 1934 he studied at a school of the Communist International in Moscow, and from 1925 to 1927 he worked in the Soviet Embassy in China. After the CPE, which was illegal in Estonia, was dissolved by a decision of the Comintern, the Estonian party units were to contact only the leadership of the party in Copenhagen. The authorities in Moscow assigned Säre as head of the purged and reorganized party. In 1933, on the initiative of Johannes Meerits, the de facto leader of the CPE, Säre took up the post in Denmark. In 1935 one of the experienced agents, Johannes Eltermann, was arrested by the Estonian police. After Eltermann's release, Säre and Meerits ordered him to Copenhagen, where they murdered him. During the Great Purge Säre lived in the United States, where he conducted unsuccessful activities among the Estonian émigré community. After the Estonian government declared an amnesty in 1938, he returned to Tallinn.

After the Soviet invasion of Estonia in June 1940, Säre became first secretary of the CPE Central Committee and the main associate of Andrey Zhdanov. He expelled alleged and genuine opponents from the party. It is believed that it was Säre who recommended to Zhdanov that **Johannes Vares** become prime minister of the pro-Soviet government and proposed that the request for the incorporation of Estonia into the Soviet Union should come from the government without any overt participation of the Communists. During the Soviet occupation of 1940–41 Säre was responsible for the confiscation of private property, the persecution of political opponents, enforced atheization and collectivization, and the deportation of around ten thousand Estonians. He headed the state "troika"—the main organ that laid down directives for lower-level "troikas," which made concrete decisions on who was to be declared dangerous to the regime and consequently deported to Siberia.

After Germany occupied Estonia, Säre was arrested (3 September 1941) and sent to Sachsenhausen. There are suspicions that he agreed to collaborate with the Gestapo and that his testimony was instrumental in the arrests of many Communists in hiding, left behind by Moscow to organize sabotage behind the front lines. The wave of arrests of Communist activists contributed to the breakup of the Communist structures, and in 1944 there were virtually no pro-Soviet forces left in Estonia. In early 1941 and late 1942, hoping that he would be allowed to leave for Denmark, Säre admitted to having killed Eltermann. During a trial in Copenhagen Säre pleaded guilty. He was handed over to the Gestapo, who probably killed him. His trial, which was given wide publicity by Nazi propaganda, revealed the terrorist character of the Comintern and to some extent diminished Soviet influence in Denmark. As a result, Säre's name disappeared from all Soviet history textbooks, and it was only after 1991 that he became the subject of more thorough research. (AG)

Sources: *Eesti Entsuklopeedia*, vol. 14 (Tallinn, 2000); Erik Norgaard, *Mändene fra Estland* (Copenhagen, 1990); Endel Krepp, *Mass Deportations of Populations from the Soviet Occupied Baltic States* (Stockholm, 1981); Romuald J. Misiunas and Rein Taagepera, *The Baltic States: The Years of Dependence, 1940–1970* (Berkeley, 1993); Jan Lewandowski, *Estonia* (Warsaw, 2001).

ŠARINIĆ Hrvoje (17 February 1935, Sušak), Croatian politician. After graduating in engineering studies in Zagreb, Šarinić left for France. For many years he worked there constructing nuclear power plants. On behalf of French companies he also dealt with such projects in South Africa. In 1980–84 Šarinić represented the French nuclear industry in Zagreb, and in 1990 he became head of the chancellery of President **Franjo Tudjman**. On 8 September 1992 Šarinić became prime minister, succeeding **Franjo Gregurić**. At that time Croatia was struggling with the consequences of the dissolution of Yugoslavia. The budget was imbalanced due to military spending, and inflation was growing. Šarinić headed the government until 29 March 1993. He belonged to the Croatian Democratic Union (Hrvatska Demokratska Zajednica [HDZ]) from its beginnings, and he remained an adviser to Tudjman and head of the Office of National Security (Ured za Nacionalnu Sigurnost). Rated among the closest aides of Tudjman, Šarinić went on several delicate missions—for instance, he went to talks with **Slobodan Milošević**. Šarinić played an important role in negotiating peace in the former Yugoslavia. The process ended with the Dayton Agreement of 1995. In 1996 Šarinić regained the position of head of the president's chancellery. His relationship with Tudjman worsened in the fall of 1998, when Šarinić publicly accused the president's adviser, Ivica Pasalić, of an abuse of the secret services and media for political games and when he demanded an explanation of the "Dubrovačka Banka affair." In October 1998 Šarinić resigned from all his positions and left the HDZ. In 1999 he published his memoirs, *Svi moji tajni pregovori* *sa Slobodanem Miloševićem* (All my secret talks with Slobodan Milošević). After the HDZ lost the elections, in April 2000 Šarinić joined the Croatian Democratic Center (Hrvatski Demokratski Centar). (AO)

Sources: *Hrvatski Leksikon*, vol. 2 (Zagreb, 1997); *Europa Środkowo-Wschodnia 1993–1998* (Warsaw, 1995–2000); Bugajski.

SARKOTIČ VON LOVČEN Stefan (4 October 1858, Sinac, Croatia–16 October 1939, Vienna), general, commander of the Austro-Hungarian Army in the Balkans. Sarkotič was born into the family of a Catholic officer of Croatian descent. Like his father, he chose a military career. In 1879 he graduated from the Maria Theresa Military Academy. In 1882–84 he studied at another military academy. He published a monograph on Russian military science, *Das russische Kriegstheater: Strategische und geographische Studie* (The Russian war theater: Strategic and geographic studies; 1894). He briefly served in a provincial garrison and helped to suppress a rebellion in southern Dalmatia (1882). He then served in the General Staff and was promoted to major (1896), colonel (1901), and general (1907). Because of his friendship with Archduke Eugen, Sarkotič had connections with officials in the emperor's court. In 1912 he was appointed commander of the Fourth Military District, with its headquarters in Agram (Zagreb). At the beginning of World War I Sarkotič assumed command of the Forty-second Croatian Division but then developed dysentery and was taken to a hospital in September 1914. He handed over command to General Oskar Potiorek; it saved Sarkotič from being held responsible for an ignominious defeat of the army during the first stage of the war against Serbia. Although he had not recovered completely, on 22 December 1914 Sarkotič was appointed commander-in-chief of the Habsburg forces in Dalmatia and Bosnia-Herzegovina. Within a year he restored discipline in the army after the defeat, and then he launched an offensive. In January 1916 his troops occupied Montenegro. He personally took part in the assault on fortified positions at Lovčen. For his success in this operation, Sarkotič was granted the title of baron by the new emperor, Charles. In July 1916 he was offered the post of commander of the eastern front, but he refused owing to ill health. In December 1917 in the Imperial Council in Vienna Sarkotič sharply protested plans to divide the army into an Austrian and a Hungarian part, according to ethnic and geographic criteria. He was also against e plans to unite the Southern Slav parts of the empire into a separate kingdom. He believed that such a union should be a part of the Kingdom of Hungary within the empire. After the collapse of the Austro-Hungarian monarchy,

Sarkotič was interned in Wagram but was soon released. He returned to Vienna, where he lived until the end of his life. Sarkotič authored *Der Banjaluka Prozess* (The Banjaluka trial), a two-volume monograph that was published in 1933. (MC)

Sources: Holger H. Herwig and Neil M. Heyman, *Biographical Dictionary of World War I* (Westport, Conn., 1982); Ernest Bauer, *Der letzte Paladin des Reiches: Generaloberst Stefan Freiherr Sarkotic von Lovcen* (Graz, 1988); Scott W. Lackey, *The Rebirth of the Habsburg Army: Friedrich Beck and the Rise of the General Staff* (Westport, Conn., 1995).

SAUL Bruno (8 January 1932, Narva), Estonian Communist activist. In 1956 Saul graduated in electronics from the Polytechnic Institute in Leningrad (now St. Petersburg), and in 1973 he graduated from the Higher Party School of the Central Committee (CC) of the CPSU. In 1977 he received a Ph.D. in economics. His marriage to a Russian and his good contacts in Moscow facilitated his career. A member of the Communist Party of Estonia (CPE) from 1960, in 1961–63 Saul was chief engineer of the Estonian Radio Committee; from 1963 to 1964 he chaired this committee; in 1964–66 he was chief engineer of the Estonian Ministry of Communications; and from 1969 to 1975 he was Estonian minister of communications. From 1975 Saul was deputy prime minister of the Estonian SSR, and in 1984 he became chairman of the Estonian Council of Ministers and joined the Supreme Soviet of the USSR. He took over these posts at a time when Russification policies in the Estonian republic were becoming less oppressive, but Saul generally failed to meet the expectations for reform. In 1987, when a crisis occurred connected with plans to construct a phosphate mine that could devastate one-third of the Estonian territory, Saul stopped the project in order to appease social discontent, but otherwise his policies were inconsistent. On 2 February 1988 riot police were ordered to brutally suppress a demonstration in Tartu, but on 24 February 1988 another demonstration met with no violent reaction from the authorities. On the other hand, a day after **Karl Vaino** was dismissed as first secretary of the CPE CC, in June 1988 Saul ordered housing cooperatives to offer preferential treatment to people coming from Russia. When the party press released information about this decision (*Edasi*, 26 August 1988), a scandal broke out. Saul supported the new CPE first secretary, **Vaino Väljas**, but he still cooperated with the dogmatic faction in the Kremlin. On 16 November 1988, when the Estonian Supreme Council adopted an independence declaration, Saul resigned. In 1990 he left the CPE and started a his own business venture, the Union of Small Investors (Väikeinvestorite Ühendus). (AG)

Sources: *Eesti Entsuklopeedia*, vol. 14 (Tallinn, 2000); Rein Taagepera, *Estonia: Return to Independence* (Boulder, Colo., 1993); Jan Lewandowski, *Estonia* (Warsaw, 2001); http://hot.ee/investors/news.htm.

SAVISAAR Edgar (31 May 1950, Harjumaal Harkus), Estonian Communist activist and post-Communist politician. In 1973 Savisaar graduated in history from the University of Tartu. During his studies he was active in the Comsomol. In 1976–79 he continued with doctoral studies at the Academy of Sciences of the Estonian SSR, and in 1981 he defended a Ph.D. dissertation on "global issues in Socialist philosophy." From 1982 Savisaar belonged to the Communist Party of Estonia (CPE). He started his political career as head of the planning commission in the City Council of Tallin (1980–85), and in 1985–88 he headed a department in the Planning Commission of the Estonian SSR. In 1987, along with other Comsomol leaders, including **Siim Kallas**, Savisaar worked out and published in the party organ, *Edasi*, a program for the "economic sovereignty" of the Estonian republic based on market reform and the Estonian budget and currency. The article—whose authors demanded the introduction of real perestroika into the republic, which was ruled by old-style dogmatists—brought Savisaar significant popularity and became a prelude to the substitution of those dogmatists by Comsomol pragmatists. It also began the appropriation of state assets by the party nomenklatura. Savisaar was one of the pioneers of this action, establishing the consulting firm Mainor. Along with **Marju Lauristin**, Savisaar founded the Popular Front of Estonia (Eesti Rahvarinne [ER]).

The creation of the ER was welcomed by a part of the CPE leadership. Initially the movement's goal was to support perestroika and to strengthen Estonia's sovereignty within a renewed Soviet Union. Savisaar developed a campaign for constitutional change; it succeeded on 16 November 1988, when the Supreme Soviet of the Estonian SSR adopted a declaration of Estonian sovereignty within the USSR. As head of the Planning Commission, Savisaar supported economic reform, but under the pressure of civic committees demanding the restitution of prewar independence, Savisaar developed the idea of the "Third Republic," to be ruled by the reformed Communist elite. In January 1990 he left the CPE, and in February 1990 he was elected to the Estonian Congress, organized by the non-Communist opposition. This is why in the elections to the Estonian Supreme Soviet of March 1990 Savisaar received the support of the congress, while his alliance with national Communists brought him the portfolio of prime minister of the Estonia SSR on 3 April 1990. From May 1990 the country was called the Republic of Estonia.

Savisaar's government began economic reforms. The restitution of landed property was started, a three-year tax exemption was passed, and an oil terminal was begun to make Estonia independent from Russian supplies. On 19 April 1990 Savisaar and the chairman of the Estonian Supreme Council, **Arnold Rüütel**, met with Mikhail Gorbachev in Moscow, and despite Soviet pressures, they declined to sign a new union agreement. The idea of a Third Republic proved to be unacceptable for both Gorbachev and the Estonian society. Nevertheless, Savisaar remained very popular as long as a Soviet intervention seemed likely. His authoritarian style and attempts to limit the freedom of speech damaged his ratings. Although he supported the restitution of Estonian independence on 20 August 1991, he was increasingly perceived as a check to further steps toward liberalization. Fearing for the country's economic safety, Savisaar defended trade links with Russia. He signed a September 1991 law allowing the KGB to withdraw archives to Russia and allowing KGB agents to stay in Estonia. The economic collapse in Estonia in 1991 additionally eroded his popularity. At the end of his rule Savisaar was mostly supported by Supreme Council deputies from the Soviet Army, perceived as the occupying force. Since Savisaar opposed an annulment of their mandates, he was increasingly criticized and resigned on 30 January 1992.

After his resignation, Savisaar took the lead of the ER-based (Populist) Estonian Center Party (Eesti Keskerond [EK]). He criticized liberal reforms and center-right governments of 1992–94 and 1999–2002. From 1991 Savisaar was an MP, and in 1992–95 he was speaker of the parliament. As a result of the March 1995 elections Savisaar entered into a coalition with the Estonian Coalition Party, and he entered the **Tiit Vähi** government as minister of interior and deputy prime minister. This coalition lasted until October 1995, when it turned out that Savisaar, as minister of interior, had eavesdropped on President **Lennart Meri** and other key politicians. The government stepped down, and the EK went into the opposition. From 1996 to 1999 Savisaar chaired the City Council of Tallinn, defending the privileges of social groups most affected by market reforms. His anti-government rhetoric and his plans to abolish the flat tax in favor of a progressive tax made Savisaar popular again. In the elections of March 1999 the EK emerged as the strongest parliamentary faction. A center-right coalition made it impossible for the EK to form a government. In January 2002 the EK entered the Kallas government, but Savisaar stayed out of it. (AG)

Sources: *Eesti Entsuklopeedia*, vol. 8 (Tallinn, 1995); Kristian Gerner and Stefan Hedlund, *The Baltic States and the End of the Soviet Empire* (London and New York, 1993); Anatol Lieven, *The*

Baltic Revolution (New Haven, 1993); Rein Taagepera, *Estonia: Return to Independence* (Boulder, Colo., 1993); *Eastern Europe and the Commonwealth of Independent States, 1999* (London, 1999); Tõnu Tannberg, Matti Laur, Tõnis Lukas, Ain Mäesalu, and Ago Pajur, *History of Estonia* (Tallinn, 2000); Bugajski; www.riikogu.ee/parlament.html; www.rulers.org.

SAVOV Dimitur (5 September 1897, Vratsa–18 August 1951, Belene), Bulgarian financier and politician. In 1919–44 Savov was a member of many supervisory boards of banks and corporations. He served as vice-chairman (1927–43) and then chairman of the Sofia Chamber of Commerce and Industry. He also held the post of chairman of the Bulgarian committee at the International Chamber of Commerce in Paris and sat on the board of this chamber. Savov was a deputy (1938–39) to the National Assembly and chairman (1940–41) of the Bulgarian-Yugoslav Chamber of Commerce. From early June to early September 1944 he served as minister of finance in the government of **Ivan Bagrianov** and attempted to loosen economic ties with the Third Reich. Shortly after the Communist coup of 9 September 1944, Savov was arrested. In January 1945 the leaders of the Bulgarian Communist Party ordered that he be sentenced to life imprisonment. Although he had suffered two heart attacks, in 1951 he was taken to a concentration camp, where he died. (WR)

Sources: Jerzy Jackowicz, *Partie opozycyjne w Bułgarii 1944–1948* (Warsaw, 1997); Tasho Tashev, *Ministrite na Bulgariya 1879–1999: Entsiklopedichen Spravochnik* (Sofia, 1999).

SAVOV Stefan (8 January 1924, Sofia–8 January 2000, Sofia), Bulgarian politician. For many years after World War II Savov was persecuted by the Communist authorities, deported to prison camps, and displaced. For example, he was a political prisoner in a labor camp in Belene, along with his father, Dimitur. For fifteen years Savov was forced to work as a bricklayer in the construction industry. Despite the persecutions, he graduated in law from Sofia University and worked as a recognized translator, mainly of Spanish literature. Savov was president of the Association of Hispanists and a member of the Presidium of the Union of Translators in Bulgaria. After the fall of the Communist system, he actively joined the political life. From 1990 he was a member of the National Executive Council of the Union of Democratic Forces (UDF), and from 15 December 1990 he served as president of the Democratic Party. In 1990–91 Savov was an MP and co-president of the UDF Parliamentary Group. On 14 May 1991, along with thirty-eight other deputies of the UDF, he left the parliament to protest plans for a new constitution, which was being prepared by the parliament, dominated by the Bulgarian Socialist Party (former Communists). Two

days before the passing of the constitution in July 1991, Savov intensified his protest by going on a hunger strike. Between October 1991 and December 1994 Savov was an MP again and president of the Parliamentary Group of the Democratic Party. Between 4 November 1991 and 24 September 1992 he was the speaker of the parliament. His resignation of this post was a result of a clash within the coalition of the UDF and the Turkish Movement for Rights and Freedoms of **Ahmed Dogan**. In 1993 Savov served as president of the UDF Parliamentary Group. In 1995–97 he was an MP on behalf of the People's Union (a coalition of the Bulgarian Agrarian National Union and the Democratic Party), co-president of the Parliamentary Group of the People's Union, and a member of the parliamentary Committee on Foreign Policy. Savov also held these parliamentary posts in the next term of the parliament. (JJ)

Sources: *Koy koy e v Bulgariya* (Sofia, 1998).

SCHAFF Adam (10 March 1913, Lwów [Lviv]), Polish Marxist philosopher and Communist activist. In 1935 Schaff graduated from Lwów University and in 1936 from the Ecole des Sciences Politiques et Economiques in Paris. In 1932–36 he belonged to the Communist Union of Polish Youth and from 1936 to 1938 to the Communist Party of Poland (Komunistyczna Partia Polski). During World War II Schaff lived in the USSR and worked at the Institute of Philosophy of the Soviet Academy of Sciences in Moscow. In 1941 he received a Ph.D. and in 1945 a second degree in Marxist philosophy. In 1944 Schaff joined the Polish Workers' Party (Polska Partia Robotnicza [PPR]). Upon his return to Poland in 1946, he published *Wstęp do teorii marksizmu* (Introduction to Marxist theory), and in 1945–47 he lectured in political doctrines at the university in Łódź. At the same time, he worked at the party school of the PPR Central Committee (CC). A member of the Polish United Workers' Party (Polska Zjednoczona Partia Robotnicza [PUWP]) and a professor at Warsaw University from 1948, in 1950–57 Schaff headed the Institute of Social Sciences (later the Institute of Formation of Scientific Personnel) of the PUWP CC. At that time he promoted the Stalinist version of Marxism, sharply attacking non-Marxist philosophers.

In 1954 Schaff was appointed full professor. In 1956–68 he was director of the Institute of Philosophy and Sociology of the Polish Academy of Sciences, and in 1959 he became a member of the PUWP CC. In the early 1960s Schaff silently protected the Crooked Circle Club, which united opposition intellectuals, but his role in the dissolution of the club in February 1962 remains unclear. In

1965 his book *Marksizm a jednostka ludzka* (*Marxism and the Human Individual*, 1970) raised controversy among Marxists and Communist leaders. After the student protests of March 1968, Schaff was sharply criticized (by, among others, the followers of **Mieczysław Moczar**) for alleged revisionism, and he was finally dismissed from the PUWP CC and Warsaw University. Schaff later dealt with Marxist semantics, ethics, nationalism, and capitalism. In 1969–72 he lectured in philosophy at the University of Vienna, and until 1988 he was an honorary professor there. In his book *Die kommunistische Bewegung am Scheideweg* (1982; *Ruch komunistyczny na rozdrożu*, 1983) Schaff prophesied a fundamental crash of capitalism within twenty years. During martial law in Poland Schaff tried to help the General **Wojciech Jaruzelski** regime out of international isolation. Schaff published about three hundred articles and about twenty books, including *Język i poznanie* (1964; *Language and Cognition*, 1973); *Entefremdung als soziales Phänomenon* (Callousness as a social phenomenon; 1977); and *Perspektywy współczesnego socjalizmu* (Prospects of contemporary socialism; 1988). He received honorary doctorates from many universities (including the University of Michigan and the Sorbonne in Paris). In 1993 Schaff published his memoirs, *Pora na spowiedź* (Time for a confession). (PK)

Sources: *Kto jest kim w Polsce* (Warsaw, 1993); Stanisław Jedynak and Lech Zdybel, eds., *Etyka w Polsce: Słownik pisarzy* (Wrocław, 1986); Stanisław Borzym, *Filozofia polska 1900–1950* (Wrocław, 1991); Krzysztof Lesiakowski, *Mieczysław Moczar "Mietek": Biografia polityczna* (Warsaw, 1998); Andrzej Albert [Wojciech Roszkowski], *Najnowsza historia Polski 1914–1993*, vol. 2 (Warsaw, 1995).

SCHELINGOVÁ Zdenka Cecilia (24 December 1916, Krivá, Orava–31 July 1955, Trnava), Czech nun and political prisoner. Born the tenth child of a large peasant family and brought up in a religious atmosphere, after graduating from a medical school and completing her novitiate, in January 1943 Schelingová took her final vows in the Congregation of the Sisters of Charity of the Holy Cross and was given the religious name of Zdenka. She worked as a laboratory technician at a state-owned hospital in Bratislava. When in 1950 the persecution of the Church in Slovakia intensified, Schelingová helped the persecuted clergymen. In February 1952 she helped one of the arrested priests to escape from a closed hospital ward. She also helped in the preparations for the escape of six priests imprisoned in Bratislava. However, this turned out to be a provocation organized by the Communist security services. Arrested on 29 February 1952, Schelingová was interrogated and tortured for a long time, but she did not give anyone away. Sentenced to twelve years' imprisonment for "high treason" on 17 June 1952, she served her sentence in the harshest prisons in Rimavská Sobota, Pardubice, Brno, and Prague. She endured this persecution with great dignity, bringing help to other inmates and demonstrating her faithfulness to the Gospel in the most difficult circumstances. Schelingová fell ill at the beginning of her imprisonment, and then her health quickly deteriorated. On 16 April 1955, when she was dying, the authorities decided to release her from prison conditionally. Terminally ill, she died soon afterwards in Trnava. Initially buried in Trnava, she was later reburied at the Podunajské Biskupice Cemetery. On 14 September 2003 in Bratislava Schelingová was beatified by Pope John Paul II. (AGr)

Sources: Anton Habovštiak, *Za mrakami je moje milované Slnko* (Bratislava, 2003); Bartek Dobroch, "Uśmiech zza krat," *Tygodnik Powszechny*, 21 September 2003; www.papez.info.

SCHILLER Leon (14 March 1887, Kraków–25 March 1954, Warsaw), Polish theater director and theoretician. Schiller's debut as a stage director took place at the Popular Theater while he was still in high school. His singing debut occurred at the Little Green Baloon (Zielony Balonik) cabaret in 1905. In 1906 Schiller started to study philosophy at the Jagiellonian University in Kraków, but he dropped out to travel between 1908 and 1911. Following his return to Kraków, he enrolled at the Trade Academy, and after graduating in 1912, he entered the family business. Later, in 1916 and 1917, Schiller studied composition and music theory in Vienna. Afterward he moved to Warsaw, where he directed his first play (1917) and wrote his first script (1919). Between 1917 and 1939, Schiller worked with Warsaw, Łódź, and Lwów (Lviv) theaters. He was active in the Union of Artists of Polish Scenes (Związek Artystów Scen Polskich). During the Polish-Bolshevik war, Schiller worked for the Main Propaganda Committee, but later he moved to the extreme left. Schiller's staging of avant garde plays stirred controversy. *Die Dreigroschenopera*, by Bertoldt Brecht, ignited a political scandal in 1929, as did *Cjankali* (Cyanide), by Friedrich Wolf, in 1930. However, his staging of *Dziady* (Forefather's Eve), by Adam Mickiewicz, was considered a theatrical masterpiece. From 1928 Schiller worked with Polish Radio. In 1933 he founded the Department of Directing at the State Institute of Theatrical Arts, where he taught.

During the Nazi occupation, from October 1939, Schiller conducted underground classes at the institute. He joined a boycott of German-controlled theaters, and he supported himself by performing in Warsaw cafes and participating in the Conspiratorial Theater Council. Schiller was arrested in March 1941 and sent to the Auschwitz concentration camp. He participated in underground work there, staging clandestine music concerts. He was released in May 1941. During the Warsaw Uprising in 1944 Schiller led the theater brigade of the Home Army. Following the capitulation of the uprising, he was interned at the Oflag in Murnau. Freed in April 1945 and appointed head of the traveling theater of the Free Polish First Armored Division, in December 1945 Schiller returned to Warsaw. Supported by the new regime, he joined the (Communist) Polish Workers' Party (Polska Partia Robotnicza). Schiller was a parliamentary deputy (1947–52) and a delegate to the December 1948 Congress at which the Communists merged with the Socialists; he was also a delegate to the Second Congress of the Polish United Workers' Party in 1954. From 1946 to 1949, Schiller worked as director and supervisor of the Polish Army Theater in Łódź, as well as president of the local State Higher Theatrical School. In 1949–50, he headed the Polish Theater in Warsaw. From 1947 he was a member of the Executive Committee of the International Theatrical Institute of the UNESCO. In 1950 he became president of the Association of Polish Theater and Film Artists (Stowarzyszenia Polskich Artystów Teatru i Filmu). In 1951 became head of the Theatrical Section of the State Institute of Arts of the Polish Academy of Sciences. Between 1947 and 1949 he served as editor-in-chief of the monthly *Teatr*, and in 1952 he founded and commenced editing *Pamiętnik Teatralny*.

Schiller's artistic output is evident in three strands of theater: the monumental theater (among others, the *Nie-Boska komedia* [Un-divine comedy], by Zygmunt Krasiński; *Kordian*, by Juliusz Słowacki; and *The Tempest*, by William Shakespeare); the politically involved leftist modern theater; and musical theater (among others, various plays scripted by Schiller; *Pastorałka* [A shepard's song; 1931]; and *Kram z piosenkami* [A market stall with songs; 1945]). Schiller also directed ballets (among others, *Harnasie* [Montagnard outlaws], by Karol Szymanowski), composed film music, and co-staged and art directed the movie *Halka* (1937); he also authored a multitude of articles, essays, and recollections published in collections such as *Teatr ogromny* (Humongous theater; 1961), *Na progu nowego teatru, 1908–1924* (At the threshold of a new theater, 1908–1924; 1978), *Droga przez teatr, 1924–1939* (The road through theater, 1924–1939; 1983), *Theatrum militans* (1987), and *Rozmowy z Leonem Schillerem: Wywiady i autowywiady* (Conversations with Leon Schiller: Interviews and self-interviews; 1995). (JS)

Sources: *PSB*, vol. 35; *Encyklopedia historii Drugiej Rzeczypospolitej* (Warsaw, 1999); Edward Csató, *Leon Schiller* (Warsaw, 1968); Lidia Kuchtówna and Barbara Lasocka, eds., *Leon Schiller: W stulecie urodzin, 1887–1987* (Warsaw, 1990); *Ostatni romantyk sceny polskiej: Wspomnienia o Leonie Schillerze* (Kraków, 1990); Henryk Izydor Rogacki, *Leon Schiller: Zzłowiek i teatr* (Łódź, 1995).

SCHMÖGNEROVÁ Brigita (17 November 1947, Bratislava), Slovak economist and political activist. In 1971 Schmönerová graduated from the Higher Economic School in Bratislava, and later she worked there in the Department of Mathematical Economics. In 1976 she also graduated in mathematical statistics from Bratislava University. She worked as a fellow at the Center of Economic Planning in Athens, Greece (1976), and at Georgetown University in Washington, D.C. (1979). In the 1980s she worked at the Institute of Economics of the Slovak Academy of Sciences as head of its Department of Macroeconomics. Schmögnerová started her political career after the Velvet Revolution of 1989. In 1990–92 she was an expert in the Ministry of Industry of the Slovak Republic, and after Slovakia became an independent state in 1993, she was economic adviser to the president. After the fall of the **Vladimír Mečiar** government, from March to November 1994 Schmögnerová was deputy prime minister for the economy in the cabinet of **Jozef Moravčik**. In the early parliamentary elections of September–October 1994 Schmögnerová won a seat on behalf of the Party of the Democratic Left (Strana Demokratickej L'avice [PDL]) and joined the commission of finance, budget, and currency. In 1995 she was elected PLD chairman. Schmögnerová belonged to the right wing of the PLD, close to **Peter Weiss**. In the late 1990s her group gradually lost to the party left. In 1998 Schmögnerová ran in the presidential elections, but to no avail. After the parliamentary elections of September 1998 she became minister of finance in the government of **Mikulaš Dzurinda**. She undertook necessary reforms in the banking sector and in the tax system, stabilizing the economic situation. In 2000 she received the Finance Minister of the Year award from Euromoney Institutional Investor PLC. Schmögnerová resigned in January 2002 owing to growing discrepancies within the PLD, and along with Weiss and Erika Kvapilova she left the party. On 28 February 2002 Schmögnerová was appointed executive secretary of the UN Economic Commission for Europe. (PU)

Sources: Ján Liďák, Viera Koganová, and Dušan Leška, *Politické strany a hnutia na Slovensku po roku 1989* (Bratislava, 1999); www.home.sk/www/slovpolitika/schmognerova.htm; www.referaty.sk/?referat=1445; www.unece.org/press/pr2002/02gen03e.htm.

SCHULZ Bruno (12 July 1892, Drohobycz–19 November 1942, Drohobycz), Polish writer. Schulz came from an urban, middle-class, Polish-speaking Jewish family of

Judaic faith. After graduating from high school in 1910, he studied architecture in Lwów (Lviv) and painting at the Viennese Academy of Fine Arts. From 1924 to 1941 he worked as an art teacher at various schools in Drohobycz. In the mid-1920s he began writing short stories. His first known piece, "Noc lipcowa" (A July night), dates 1928. In 1933 Schulz published a collection of short stories, *Sklepy Cynamonowe* (Cinnamon shops), written as addenda to letters to his friend, the poetess Deborah Vogel. The collection made a splash in Lwów and Warsaw literary circles. Subsequently, Zofia Nałkowska introduced Schulz to the literary group Suburb (Przedmieście). In 1937 Schulz published his second volume of short stories, *Sanatorium pod klepsydrą* (*Sanatorium under the Sign of the Hourglass*, 1979), which included some of his earlier work. During the Nazi occupation, Schulz was forced into the Drohobycz ghetto, where he was shot on the street by a Gestapo officer. Schulz wrote poetic prose relegating the developing story to a secondary position, thus contributing to an original and fantastic transformation of reality. of a small Galician town into more general and symbolic images. He also left behind numerous drawings. Some of his pictures and stories were lost. His works of literary criticism, reviews, and about a hundred letters of high artistic value were saved. In the 1990s frescoes were discovered at his house in Drohobycz. They were illegally removed to Israel, which caused a media scandal. Schulz's creativity sprang from an expressionism that drew on an indefinable subconscious. His stories stress the importance of the symbolism of dreams, often with erotic subtexts. Already highly esteemed before World War II, Schulz was also discovered in the West because of the translation of his works into English, German, French, and other languages. His *Collected Works* were published in London in 1998. (WR)

Sources: *Literatura polska: Przewodnik encyklopedyczny*, vol. 2 (Warsaw, 1985); Jerzy Ficowski, *Regiony wielkiej herezji: Szkice o życiu i twórczości Bruno Schulza* (Kraków, 1967); Artur Sandauer, *Rzeczywistość zdegradowana: Rzecz o Bruno Schulzu* (Kraków, 1973); Russell E. Brown, *Myths and Relatives: Seven Essays on Bruno Schulz* (Munich, 1991); Czeslaw Z. Prokopczyk, ed., *Bruno Schulz: New Documents and New Interpretations* (New York, 1999); Wiesław Budzyński, *Schulz pod kluczem* (Warsaw, 2001).

SCHUSTER Rudolf (4 January 1934, Košice), Slovak post-Communist politician. Schuster graduated in construction engineering from the Bratislava Polytechnic in 1959, and in 1960–62 he worked as an assistant at the Institute of Water Engineering and Hydraulics of the Slovak Academy of Sciences. Later he worked in the Košice iron mill, reaching the position of assistant technical director. In 1964–90 Schuster belonged to the Communist Party of Czechoslovakia. From 1974 he was deputy chairman of the City National Committee in Košice; from 1983 to 1986 he was mayor of Košice; and in 1986–89 he was chairman of the East Slovak Provincial National Committee. After the Velvet Revolution, on 30 November 1989 Schuster was appointed chairman of the Slovak National Council, and he held this position until 30 June 1990. From 1990 to 1992 he was ambassador to Canada. Upon returning home, Schuster briefly worked in the Ministry of Foreign Affairs in Prague; after the formation of independent Slovakia, from 1994 he was mayor of Košice again.

In 1998 Schuster co-founded and became chairman of the Party of Civic Understanding (Strana Občianskeho Porozumenia [SOP]), a leftist, pro-Western group opposing the rule of **Vladimír Mečiar**. In the elections of September 1998 his party won 8 percent of the vote and thirteen mandates, including one for himself. In December 1998 Schuster was reelected mayor of Košice, where he enjoyed high ratings. After the establishment of an anti-Mečiar coalition, Schuster stayed out of the government, demanding that the coalition put forward his candidacy for president. The new coalition— which included the SOP, the Slovak Democratic Coalition (Slovenská Demokratická Koalicie [SDK]), the Party of Hungarian Coalition (Magyar Koalíció Pártja, Strana Maďarskej Koalíció [SMK]), and the Party of the Democratic Left (Strana Demokratickej L'avice [PDL'])—amended the constitution to allow for direct presidential elections. Despite his Communist past, Schuster became a candidate of the whole coalition and defeated Mečiar in the second round, winning 57 percent of the vote. Schuster was sworn into office on 15 June 1999. Using the consolidation of the nation as a pretext, Schuster undertook several controversial steps that showed his links to a Communist past and his leftist leanings. He quickly entered into conflict with rightist groups, especially when, during a serious illness in the summer of 2000, he accused the government of wanting to take over his position. After his term ended in June 2004, it was disclosed that Schuster had been a secret collaborator with Communist services. (PU)

Sources: *Slovensko 1996: Súhrnná správa o stave spoločnosti* (Bratislava, 1997); *Slovensko 1997: Súhrnná správa o stave spoločnosti* (Bratislava, 1998); *Slovensko 1998–1999: Súhrnná správa o stave spoločnosti* (Bratislava, 1999); *Slovensko 2000: Súhrnná správa o stave spoločnosti* (Bratislava, 2000); www.kosice.sk/gov/primsk.htm; www.president.sk.

SEIFERT Jaroslav (23 September 1901, Prague–10 January 1986, Prague), Czech poet. Born into a working-class family, Seifert attended high school but failed to finish and began to work as a journalist. In the 1920s he joined the Communist Party of Czechoslovakia (CPC) and contributed to the Communist press and to avant-garde periodicals. In 1929, along with other leftist writers, Seifert signed a protest against the appointment of **Klement Gottwald** as head of the CPC; as a result, he was expelled from the party. In the 1930s he joined the Social Democratic Party and became an editor of *Právo lidu*. (During the Nazi occupation it was called *Národní práce*.) From 1945 to 1949 Seifert contributed to the daily *Práca*, and from 1946 to 1948 he edited the periodical *Kytice*. In 1946 he was elected a full member of the Czech Academy of Sciences and Arts. In the 1950s he came under attack from the supporters of Socialist realism, because of both his poetry and his views. Nevertheless, he received the Klement Gottwald State Prize (1955 and 1968) and was awarded the title of National Artist of Czechoslovakia (1966). During the Prague Spring Seifert became involved in public work, becoming chairman of the Union of Czech Writers in 1969. He held this post until 1970, when the union was dissolved by the authorities. He later retired from public life but maintained contacts with the cultural and political opposition and was one of the first signatories of Charter 77. In 1984 Seifert became the first Czech to win the Nobel Prize for Literature.

In 1921 Seifert published his first book of poetry, *Město v slzách* (City in tears). He was initially faithful to the principles of an avant-garde group called Devětsil, which promoted proletarian literature and social revolution. However, in his second volume of poetry, *Samá láska* (Nothing but love; 1923), he embraced pure poetry, and his third volume, *Na vlnách TSF* (On wireless waves; 1925), was the culmination of that tendency. His later collections—*Slavík zpíva špatně* (The nightingale sings poorly; 1926), *Jablko z klína* (An apple from the lap; 1933), and *Ruce Venušiny* (The hands of Venus; 1936)—were imbued with reflections and mediations on the passing of the world, commendations of the small gifts of life, and reminiscences of his childhood, and they also expressed national feelings. The poetic form also changed: numerous metaphors disappeared, while classical stanzaic forms and melodiousness became dominant. Seifert was faithful to this style in his subsequent volumes—*Zhasněte světla* (Turn off the lights; 1938), *Vějíř Boženy Němcové* (Božena Němcová's fan; 1940), and *Kamenný most* (The stone bridge; 1944). In the 1950s Seifert published two volumes of memoir lyrics. He was subsequently silenced for many years. Stalinist critics brutally attacked his poetry, stating that his works were pessimistic and did not conform to the tenets of Socialist realism. The final, most mature period of Seifert's writing lasted from the late 1960s to the beginning of the 1980s. At that time he published *Koncert na ostrově* (Concert on the island; 1965); *Halleyova kometa* (Halley's Comet; 1967); *Odlévání zvonů* (1967; *The Casting of Bells*, 1983); *Morový sloup* (1981; *The Plague Column*, 1979); *Býti básníkem* (To be a poet; 1983), and other volumes. Seifert's works increasingly contained confessions, memories, and motifs of death. He ever more often depicted contradictions of life and relativism. Seifert also wrote the collection of memoirs *Všechny krásy světa* (All the beauties of the world; Cologne, 1981; full Czech edition, 1993). (PU)

Sources: ČBS; *Kdo byl kdo v našich dějinach ve 20. stoleti*, vol. 2 (Prague, 1998); *Slovník českých spisovatelů od roku 1945*, vol. 2 (Prague, 1998); Halina Janaszek-Ivančikova, ed., *Literatury zachodniosłowiańskie czasu przełomów 1890–1990*, vol. 2, *Literatura czeska* (Katowice, 1999); Zdeněk Pešat, *Jaroslav Seifert* (Prague, 1991); *Le prix Nobel en 1984* (Stockholm, 1985).

SELTER Karl (24 June 1898, Kapu–31 January 1958, Geneva), Estonian politician, diplomat, and business activist. Selter studied at Tartu University, initially medicine (1919–21) and then law, graduating in 1925. Until 1933 he worked in the national defense and justice departments and also ran a law practice. From October 1933 to May 1938 he served as minister of the economy. At that time the situation of Estonia improved for several reasons: an upturn in the economy, the successful policies implemented by Selter's predecessors, and the policy of state intervention pursued by Selter. The economic development was stimulated by the tax policy; by the state's support of production (at the end of the 1930s nearly 25 percent of Estonia's output was produced by state companies); and by Estonia's gaining of new markets (for example, in Germany) for its agricultural products.

In 1937 Selter became a deputy to the National Assembly, and in May 1938 he was appointed minister of foreign affairs. The problems he encountered were definitely impossible to solve in a way that would allow Estonia to survive as an independent state. Selter rejected Soviet proposed guarantees of independence for Estonia, put forward on the eve of the outbreak of the war in 1939, but then the defeat of Poland in September 1939 caused a dramatic change in Estonia's international situation. In May 1939 Selter attempted to base Estonia's security on the Third Reich and signed an Estonian-German non-aggression pact; however, these efforts proved unsuccessful because Hitler did not intend to get involved in defending the independence of Estonia. On 28 September 1939 Selter signed a treaty of mutual assistance with the Soviet government. This treaty—imposed on Estonia by the Kremlin—in fact meant the subordination of Estonia to the USSR, and it led to the collapse of the government of **Kaarel Eenpalu** and to Selter's resignation (12 October of that year). Selter was sent to Geneva, where he was appointed Estonia's ambassador to the League of Nations. This appointment saved his life because other members of the last prewar government of Estonia were murdered by the NKVD. During the occupation of Estonia by the Soviet Union and later by Nazi Germany, Selter maintained loose contacts with other Estonian diplomats. In 1946 he left Geneva, when he learned that the Western powers did not recognize his diplomatic status. After the war, Selter served as an informal representative of Estonia to the government of West Germany. (AG)

Sources: *Eesti Enstuklopeedia* vol. 14 (Tallinn, 2000); Matti Laur, Tõnis Lukas, Ain Mäesalu, Ago Pajur, and Tõnu Tannberg, *History of Estonia* (Tallinn, 2000); Web site of the Ministry of Finance of Estonia, www.fin.ee/pages.php/011805; M. Vahur, "The Baltic States and the League of Nations 1940–1946: A Test Case for British Diplomacy," www.tellur.ru/~historia/archive/06-01/made.htm.

SEMERDZHIEV Atanas (21 May 1924, Lydzhene [now a quarter of Virshets]), Bulgarian Communist activist. In 1939 Semerdzhiev joined the Workers' Youth Union and in 1943 the Bulgarian Workers' Party, a legal cover for the Bulgarian Communist Party (BCP). From April 1942 he was a guerrilla fighter; from November 1943 he commanded a guerrilla detachment, Brat'a Krystnitsi (Godbrothers); and from July 1944 he commanded a detachment (and later brigade), Chepinets. After the coup of 9 September 1944 Semerdzhiev fought against the Germans. He graduated from high school in Pazardzhik in 1945 and returned to the army. He graduated from a military course in Sofia (1946), from the Mikhail Frunze Military Academy in Moscow (1950), and from the Kliment Voroshilov Academy of the Soviet General Staff (1960). From 1962 Semerdzhiev was chief of the General Staff of the Bulgarian People's Army, and in 1966–89 he was deputy minister of national defense. In 1962–66 he was a deputy member and then, until 1990, a member of the Central Committee of the BCP. From December 1989 to August 1990 he was minister of interior in the governments of **Georgi Atanasov** and **Andrey Lukanov**, and then he was vice-president (1 August 1990–22 January 1992). In July 1991 Semerdzhiev retired with the rank of general-colonel. After the BCP was transformed into the Bulgarian Socialist Party, he became a member of its Supreme Board (February–September 1990). A deputy to the National Assembly (1966–90) and to the Great National Assembly (June–August 1990), Semerdzhiev authored (among other works) *I wsichki tse biakha obrekli: Spomeni* (And everyone took an oath: Memoirs; 1985),

Lato '90: Pozharyt (Summer of 1990: The fire; 1996), and *Prezhivianoto ne podlezhi na obzhalvane* (What we survived cannot be a matter of an appeal; 1999). (JJ)

Sources: *Entsiklopediya Bulgariya*, vol. 6 (Sofia, 1988); *Narodni predstawiteli na Deweto narodno sybranie* (Sofia, 1987); *Trudovata slava na Bulgariya* (Sofia, 1987); Tasho Tashev, *Ministrite na Bulgariya 1879–1999: Enciklopedichen spravochnik* (Sofia, 1999); Angel Tsurakov, *Enciklopedia. Pravitelstvata na Bylgariya: Chronologia na politicheskiya zhivot 1879–2001* (Sofia, 2001).

SENDOV Blagovest (8 February 1932, Asenovgrad), Bulgarian politician and mathematician. The son of a rich businessman, Sendov had great difficulties enrolling in higher education, but he graduated in mathematics from Sofia University (SU) in 1956. Later he chose a scholarly career. In 1964 he received a Ph.D. and three years later the second degree in mathematics at the Steklov Institute of Mathematics in Moscow. From 1974 he was a corresponding member and from 1981 a full member of the Bulgarian Academy of Sciences (BAS). In 1960–61 Sendov completed a specialization in numerical methods at Moscow University; in 1968 he did so in computer science in London. In 1956–58 he lectured in mathematics at SU; he was an assistant professor from 1958 to 1963, an associate professor from 1968, and a full professor from 1968. In 1967–70 he was chair of numerical methods and deputy director of the Institute of Mathematics at the BAS Computing Center. From 1970 to 1973 he was dean of the SU Department of Mathematics, and in 1973–79 he was the rector of SU. From 1980 he was deputy chairman and in 1988–91 he was chairman of the BAS. From 1991 to 1993 he headed the BAS Center of Informatics and Computer Technology, and later he worked there. In 1976–89 Sendov chaired the Committee for Science of the Council of Ministers and was the only MP not belonging to the Communist Party. In 1990 he refused to run, but from 1991 he sat in parliament again. In 1995–97 he was its speaker. In 1992 he ran for the presidency but lost. Sendov authored more than thirty textbooks and about two hundred scholarly works. (JJ)

Sources: *Entsiklopediya Bulgariya*, vol. 6 (Sofia, 1988); *Koy koy e v Bulgariya* (Sofia, 1988); Raymond Detrez, *Historical Dictionary of Bulgaria* (Lanham, Md., 1997).

ŠEPER Franjo (2 October 1905, Djakovo–30 December 1981, Rome), Croatian cardinal. The son of a tailor, Šeper finished high school in Zagreb and then studied in Rome, graduating from the Pontifical Gregorian University. In October 1930 he was ordained, and then he returned to Yugoslavia. In 1934 he became secretary to the coadjutor archbishop , and in 1937, secretary to **Alojzije Stepinac**, the diocesan bishop of Zagreb. After the fall and dismemberment of Yugoslavia in April 1941, Šeper helped Stjepinac to implement a complicated policy toward the Ustasha regime—among other things through the ostensible conversions of Serbs and Jews, who were persecuted by this regime, to Catholicism. When the Communists gained full power after World War II, the Catholic Church in Croatia was severely persecuted. In September 1946, following the arrest and trial of Archbishop Stjepinac, Šeper was sent to a parish in the provinces, and it was not until 1954 that he was allowed to return to Zagreb. On 21 September 1954 he was consecrated. In that very year he was also appointed coadjutor archbishop of Zagreb. After the death of Stjepinac in February 1960, Pope John XXIII appointed Šeper as a diocesan bishop. Taking advantage of the fact that the state had softened its atheistic stance and by using his negotiating talents, Šeper gradually rebuilt the Catholic organizations and the religious press. He also helped to reestablish diplomatic relations between the government of **Josip Broz Tito** and the Holy See. Šeper attended the Second Vatican Council. On 22 February 1965 Pope Paul VI elevated him to cardinal and in 1968 appointed him prefect of the Congregation for the Doctrine of the Faith. In this latter role, Šeper proved to be a defender of the traditional position of the Church on doctrinal issues. In 1978 he lifted the ban on the cult of the Divine Mercy, based on the visions of Sister **Faustyna Kowalska**. Šeper retired a few months before his death. (WR)

Sources: *The Annual Obituary*, 1981; *Annuario Pontificio* 1980; Duro Pukeand Vlaimir Stankovic, ed., *Šeper: Grada za životopis* (Zagreb, 1982); Vinko Nikolic, ed., *Stjepinac mu je ime: Zbornik uspomena, svjedočanstava i dokumenata*, vols. 1–2 (Zagreb, 1991); Stefan Ljubica, *Stepinac i Židovi* (Zagreb, 1998).

SERÉDI Jusztinián [originally György Szapucsek] (23 April 1884, Deáki [now in Slovakia]–29 March 1945, Esztergom), primate of Hungary. Serédi was born the tenth of eleven children into the family of a Slovak industrialist. In 1901, after completing six grades of a Catholic gymnasium in Pozsony (now Bratislava, Slovakia), he entered the Benedictine order in Pannonhalma, where he received the monastic name of Jusztinián. He graduated in theology from the University of St. Anselm, Rome. After earning a doctorate, he returned to Pannonhalma, where in July 1908 he was ordained a presbyter. In the fall of that year, though, he returned to Rome and became an associate of a canon law codification committee and a lecturer in canon law at the University of St. Anselm. In 1918 he became a military chaplain in Esztergom. After World War I, he again went to Rome. Serédi served as a procurator general of the Hungarian Benedictine order,

a canon law counselor to the Hungarian legation in the Vatican, and a representative of the Hungarian dioceses at the Holy See. The nine-volume *Codicis Juris Canonici Fontes* (Sources of the new code of canon law) was the work of his life. In recognition of his achievements in the field of canon law, Oxford University awarded him an honorary doctorate in 1936.

On 30 November 1927 Pope Pius XI appointed Serédi archbishop of Esztergom, despite the fact that the Hungarian government had proposed Lajos Szmrecsányi, archbishop of Eger, as a candidate for that post. In December 1927 the Pope elevated Serédi to cardinal; thus he became head of the Hungarian Catholic Church. In 1928 he was elected director of the Hungarian Academy of Sciences, and in 1934 he became an honorary member of this academy. As a member of the upper house of parliament, in 1935 Serédi presented a bill on the abolition of obligatory civil marriages—in other words, on the recognition by the state of marriages celebrated by the Church. Serédi followed the position of Pope Pius XII on all issues concerning the extreme right wing. He defended constitutional law and protested against racism. When the Germans occupied Hungary in March 1944, he stood up in defense of the Jewish people, particularly Catholics of Jewish descent. After the Arrow Cross Party (led by **Ferenc Szálasi**) came to power in October 1944, Serédi, regarding Szálasi's government as illegal, refused to attend the swearing-in ceremony. (JT)

Sources: *Magyar Életrajzi Lexikon*, vol. 2 (Budapest, 1969); *Serédi Jusztinian, hercegprimás, feljegyzései, 1941–1944* (Budapest, 1990); György Tarczai, *Az Árpádház szentjei: Serédi Jusztinian előszaval* (Budapest, 1994); *A magyar forradalom és szabadságharc enciklopédiája* (Budapest, 1999).

ŠEŠELJ Vojislav (10 November 1954, Sarajevo), nationalist Serb politician. Šešelj went to primary and secondary school in Sarajevo. At the age of seventeen he joined the League of Communists of Yugoslavia (LCY). Within two and a half years he graduated in law from Sarajevo University. At twenty-five he received a Ph.D. in political science, becoming the youngest Ph.D. recipient in Yugoslavia. In 1981 he was expelled from the LCY for his criticism of the Yugoslav system. In 1984 he was arrested and then sentenced to eight years in prison. He served in the Sarajevo and Zenica prisons, but only for twenty-two months. After his release he lived in Belgrade, where he became friends with **Vuk Drašković**. Šešelj was active in the St. Sava Society, which was transformed into an extreme nationalist party called the Renewal of the Serbian Nation. On 14 March 1990 Šešelj and Drašković founded the Serbian Renewal Movement (Srpski Pokret Obnove

[SPO]), chaired by Drašković, but just two weeks after it was founded, Šešelj left it to form the Serbian Radical Party (Srpska Radikalna Stranka [SRS]). In 1991 he was elected to the Serbian parliament from Rakovica. At the end of 1992 the SRS became one of the leading political powers in Serbia. Šešelj advocated a Greater Serbia, attracting attention by his shocking and offensive statements (for example, he encouraged "killing Croatians with rusty spoons" and threatened to blow up a Slovene nuclear power plant). In December 1994 he was sentenced to thirty years of house arrest for his conduct in the Serbian parliament. In 1993 he criticized **Slobodan Milošević** for supporting the Vance and Owen peace plan for Bosnia-Herzegovina and for closing the border between the new Yugoslavia and the self-proclaimed Bosnian Serbian Republic. In 1994 Šešelj had to dissolve the paramilitary Chetnik Movement, formed in 1991 and accused of war crimes in Croatia and Bosnia-Herzegovina. When Milošević accepted the Dayton Agreement, Šešelj called him a traitor. In March 1998 the SRS entered into a coalition with Milošević's Socialist Party of Serbia. As a result, on 24 March 1998 Šešelj became deputy prime minister of Serbia. He supported Milošević during the NATO air raids on Yugoslavia.

Šešelj ran for president of Serbia several times. In September 1997 he defeated **Zoran Lilić**, but because of a low turnout, the election was not recognized as valid. In December 1997 Šešelj lost to **Milan Milutinović**. Supported by Milošević (then already in prison in The Hague), in September 2002 Šešelj came in third, but the results were again found invalid. In February 2003 he went to The Hague, where he voluntarily appeared before the International Tribunal for War Crimes in Former Yugoslavia, pleading not guilty to "extermination, murder, torture, and forced ethnic cleansing." Šešelj authored several works, including *Disidentski spomenar* (A dissident's diary; 1991) and *Sumrak iluzija* (The end of illusions; 1991). (AO)

Sources: *Europa Środkowo-Wschodnia 1993–1999* (Warsaw, 1995–2001); David Owen, *Balkan Odyssey* (New York, 1995); Warren Zimmermann, *Origins of a Catastrophe* (New York and Toronto, 1996); Bugajski; www.balkans.eu.org; www.mirhouse.com/ce-review/anastasijevic1.pdf.

SEYDA Marian (7 July 1879, Poznań–17 May 1967, Buenos Aires, Argentina), Polish politician. Seyda was the brother of Władysław Seyda (1863–1939), who was also a National Democratic politician. In 1900, Seyda joined the National League (Liga Narodowa). He was one of its leaders in the Prussian partition, representing that territory in the Central Committee of the league. In 1906 he became

the founding editor of *Kurier Poznański*. He advocated firm Polish resistance to German rule. During World War I Seyda became active abroad. In 1915–17 he served as secretary general and political director of the Central Press Agency in Lausanne, Switzerland; the agency was tied to the Polish National Committee (Komitet Narodowy Polski [KNP]) in Paris. From 1917 through 1918 he served on the KNP. In 1919, after Poland regained its independence, he served as an expert with the Polish delegation to the Paris Peace Conference. From 1919 to 1927, Seyda was an MP representing the Popular National Union (Związek Ludowo-Narodowy). He was also appointed foreign minister in the government of **Wincenty Witos** (May–October 1923). In 1928 and 1930, he was elected to the Senate from the National Democratic lists. By the end of the 1930s his influence in the National Party (Stronnictwo Narodowe [SN]) had waned because of the radicalization of the younger generation of nationalist activists, while Seyda was considered a part of the liberal part of the movement, the so-called "old group."

During World War II, Seyda was active in exile in France and England. He represented the SN in the National Council, which was a multiparty advisory body for the president and government of the Polish Republic in exile. From October 1939 to June 1940, he served as minister without portfolio; from January 1942, as minister of justice; and from November 1944, as minister for peace congress affairs in the governments of General **Władysław Sikorski** and (after July 1943) **Stanisław Mikołajczyk**. During the crisis triggered by the signing of a Polish-Soviet treaty by General Sikorski in July 1941, Seyda initially resigned from his post. However, in October 1941, at the general's insistence, he returned to the government. Since his party objected to his return, he was duly expelled from the SN. As a cabinet member, Seyda opposed further concessions to Stalin. In particular, he objected to Soviet claims against Poland's Eastern Borderlands. He argued that Stalin's aim was to enslave Poland completely and not to compromise. After the war, Seyda emigrated to Argentina. He was active in émigré circles and published in the nationalist press. In the early 1950s, along with Tytus Komarnicki, he attempted to coordinate the activities of the émigré nationalists in the United States. Seyda authored (among other works) *Territoires polonais sous la domination prusienne* (Polish territories under Prussian occupation; 1918) and two volumes of memoirs, *Polska na przełomie dziejów* (Poland at the breaking point of history; 1927–31). (MC/WR)

Sources: *Kto był kim w Drugiej Rzeczypospolitej* (Warsaw, 1994); *Encyklopedia historii Drugiej Rzeczypospolitej* (Warsaw, 1999); Stanisław Kozicki, *Historia Ligi Narodowej* (London, 1964);

Andrzej Friszke, *O kształt niepodległej* (Warsaw, 1989); Krzysztof Kawalec, *Roman Dmowski* (Warsaw, 1996); Zdzisław Zakrzewski, "Środowsko SN na emigracji."

SHANDRUK Pavlo (28 February 1889, Borsuky, Kremenets County–15 February 1979, Trenton, New Jersey), Ukrainian general. A graduate of the Prince A. Bezborodko Institute (1911) and the Alexander Military School in Moscow (1913), Shandruk fought in the Russian Army and was promoted to staff captain. In 1917 he joined the army of the Ukrainian National Republic, becoming commander of a brigade with the rank of lieutenant general in April 1920. After the Bolsheviks occupied Kiev, Shandruk settled in Poland at the end of 1920. He edited the historical periodical *Tabor* and worked with the Military Historical Bureau and the Military-Scientific Publishing Institute. He co-authored *Polska Encyklopedia Wojskowa* (Polish military encyclopedia; 1934). A contract officer in the Polish Army, Shandruk served in the Twenty-sixth Infantry Division with the rank of major from 1936 onwards. He fought in the Polish September campaign of 1939 against Germany. He distinguished himself in the battles of the Twenty-ninth Infantry Brigade. He was wounded and taken prisoner but was released thanks to the intervention of **Andriy Livytskyi**. Arrested by the Gestapo, Shandruk was released after he promised to collaborate with the Roland Battalion, which fought alongside the Wehrmacht against the Red Army in the summer of 1941. After one month, Shandruk retired and took a job in a cinema house in Skierniewice, Poland. In November 1944 Livytskyi brought Shandruk to Berlin, where he was to co-organize the Ukrainian Army. In 1945 Shandruk became chairman of the Ukrainian National Committee and commander-in-chief of the Ukrainian National Army. He saved many former soldiers of the SS Halychyna Division from arrest by the Soviet authorities. In 1949 he emigrated to the United States. Shandruk published his memoirs, *Arms in Valor* (1959). (WR)

Sources: *Encyclopedia of Ukraine*, vol. 5 (Toronto, 1993); Ryszard Torzecki, *Polacy i Ukraińcy: Sprawa ukraińska w czasie II wojny światowej na terenie II Rzeczypospolitej* (Warsaw, 1993); Jarosław Hrycak, *Historia Ukrainy 1772–1999* (Lublin, 2002).

SHANTYR Fabiyan (4 February 1887, Kapyl, near Slutsk–spring of 1920), Belorussian writer, journalist, and politician. Born into the family of a bricklayer, Shantyr entered politics during the 1905 revolution, when he took part in demonstrations, as a result of which he spent two years in prison in Slutsk. He began writing in 1909, publishing articles in the periodical *Nasha Niva*. He authored the sentimental-romantic stories "Zakhar, Noch" (Night),

"Smerts ubohaha" (Death of a poor man), "Pad shum lesu, Sviaty Bozha" (O Holy God), "U vialiki dzen" (On a great day), "Da dumak" (For reflection), "Sanet" (Sonnet), and "U chas baratsby" (In the time of struggle). In his journalism Shantyr paid particular attention to the role of education in the development of the nation and the shaping of Belorussian national identity. Mobilized into the Russian Army in 1914, Shantyr fought in the defense of a hospital in Bobruysk. He was active in the Belorussian Committee for Aid to War Victims and in a society called Belorussian Cottage. In March 1917 he attended the First Congress of Belorussian Parties and Organizations, becoming a member of the Belorussian National Committee, which served as the executive organ of this congress. He was the leader of the leftist faction of the Belorussian Socialist Hromada and attended the First All-Belorussian Congress in December 1917. In 1918 Shantyr chose the pro-Soviet orientation. In January 1919 he became commissar in the Bolshevik-established Provisional Revolutionary Workers' and Peasants' Government of the Belorussian SSR. After the fall of this government, he joined the Editorial Commission of the Central Committee of the Communist Party (Bolshevik) of Belorussia and worked as editor of the newspaper *Savetskaya Belarus*. As commissar for nationality affairs of the Belorussian SSR, Shantyr protested the exploitation of national feelings by the Bolsheviks. In February 1920 Shantyr was mobilized into the Red Army. A few months later he was accused of nationalism and counterrevolutionary activities, sentenced to death, and executed. His wife, Ludwika Siwicka (pseudonym "Zośka Wieras"), was a well-known writer. (EM)

Sources: *Belarus: Entsyklapedychny davednik* (Minsk, 1995); *Bielaruskiya pismienniki: Biabibliahrafichny Slounik*, vol. 6 (Minsk, 1996); Vitaut Kipel and Zora Kipel, eds., *Byelorussian Statehood* (New York, 1988); H. Głogowska, *Białoruś 1914–1929: Kultura pod presją polityki* (Białystok, 1996).

SHAPOVAL Mykyta (8 June 1882, Sriblianka, Yekaterinoslav Province–25 February 1932, Řevnice, near Prague, Czechoslovakia), Ukrainian political scientist, sociologist, and poet. Shapoval was born into a peasant family. His brother Mykola was a general in the army of the Ukrainian National Republic (UNR) and then a leader of the Ukrainian émigré community in France. Shapoval graduated from a forestry school in Novyi Glukhov, near Kharkov (Kharkiv), in 1900. In 1901 he joined the Ukrainian Revolutionary Party. From 1903 to 1906 he attended an infantry officer training school in Chuguyev, Russia. Expelled from the army for his revolutionary activities in 1906, he was held in the Warsaw Citadel for eight months. From 1908 to 1909 Shapoval studied at the university in Kharkov but never graduated. In 1909–14 in Kiev he co-edited *Ukrayinska khata*, a periodical that served as a tribune for the upcoming revolution. He also published the poetry collections *Sny viry* (Dreams of faith; 1908) and *Samotnist* (Loneliness; 1910). In 1917, along with **Mykhailo Hrushevskyi**, Shapoval co-established the Ukrainian Party of Socialist Revolutionaries (UPSR). He represented this party in the Ukrainian Central Council (Rada) and in the so-called Small Rada, the executive organ of the Central Rada. After the Third Universal Declaration of the Ukrainian Central Rada was issued in November 1917, Shapoval became a member of the General Secretariat (Ukrainian government), in which he was responsible for the departments of post and telegraphs. In January 1918 he co-edited the Ukrainian Central Rada's Fourth Universal, which declared the UNR independent from Russia. In late 1918 and early 1919 Shapoval also served as a member of the All-Russian Assembly and the Ukrainian Constituent Assembly. He was in opposition to the government of Hetman **Pavlo Skoropadskyi**. In November and December 1918 he was involved with the Ukrainian National Union, which led an anti-hetman uprising.

From December 1918 to February 1919, as minister of agriculture in the government of **Volodymir Chekhivskyi** Shapoval drafted decrees on agricultural reform. These decrees, issued on 7–8 January 1919, were a Socialist Revolutionary (SR) alternative to the Bolshevik program. However, Shapoval's program was not implemented because of Bolshevik attacks and also because the government sought support from the Entente states; therefore, Shapoval left Ukraine. Shapoval believed that there was a need for a world revolution led by the Socialist Revolutionaries, and in the spring of 1919 he agitated in favor of such a revolution in Eastern Galicia. Expelled from there, he went to the Hungarian Soviet Republic (HSR). In October 1919, after the collapse of the HSR, he arrived in Prague, where he spent the rest of his life. In the autumn of 1920 Shapoval established the so-called foreign committee of the UPSR, and until the end of his life he was an indisputable leader of the SR circles in the émigré community, especially after his rival Hrushevskyi returned to Ukraine in 1924. In 1922–28 Shapoval edited *Nova Ukrayina*, a party monthly in which he attempted to theoretically justify the need for an SR revolution. He foresaw revolutionary cooperation among the different nationalities of Russia against Bolshevik rule. In 1927, along with Russian, Belorussian, and Armenian Socialists, Shapoval co-established the Socialist League of the New East. In the 1920s he worked closely with Czechoslovak authorities, which helped Ukrainian émigrés. From 1921 to 1925 Shapoval presided over the Ukrainian Civic Committee. He was in fierce conflict with representatives of the pro-Petlura part of the émigré community, which had a dominant position in the Ukrainian Free University. Shapoval devoted his polemic work *Lakhomania* (1929) to the pro-Polish attitude of this group. In 1924 Shapoval founded the Ukrainian Sociological Institute, a center for sociological studies that was an alternative to the Ukrainian Free University. Shapoval's publications include the following: *Revoliutsiynyi sotsializm na Ukraiini* (Revolutionary socialism in Ukraine; 1921); *Svitova revoliutsiya: Rosiya i Ukraiina* (World revolution: Russia and Ukraine; 1921); *Problema demokratii u T. G. Masaryka* (T. G. Masaryk and the problem of democracy; 1925); *Stara i nova Ukraiina* (The old and the new Ukraine; 1925); *Natsionalna sprava na Skhodi Ievropy* (National issues in Eastern Europe; 1928); *Zahalna sotsiolohiia* (General sociology; 1929); *Systema suspilnykh nauk i sotsiohrafiia* (Social sciences and sociography; 1931); *Sotsiohrafiia Ukraiiny* (Sociography of Ukraine; 1933); and *Sotsiolohiia ukraiinskoho vidrodzhennia* (Sociology of the Ukrainian renaissance; 1936). (TS)

Sources: *Encyclopedia of Ukraine*, vol. 4 (Toronto, 1993); Nadiia Myronets, "M. IU. Shapoval pro natsionalne vidrodzhennia ta derzhavnist," *Politolohichni chytannia*, 1993, no. 2; Borys Homzyn, *Mykyta Shapoval: Ukraiinskyi hromadskyi diyach* (Lwów, 1932); S. Narizhnyi, *Ukraiinska emihratsiia* (Prague, 1942).

SHARAYEVSKYI Nestor (1865, near Chyhyryn–29 October 1929, Kiev), archbishop of the Ukrainian Autocephalous Orthodox Church. Sharayevskyi graduated from the Kiev Theological Academy in 1890 and was ordained into the priesthood in 1891. He subsequently taught law at a gymnasium in Vinnytsia. In 1917 he was appointed a delegate of the clergy to the Ukrainian Central Council (Rada). At that time, along with Archbishop **Vasyl Lypkivskyi**, Sharayevskyi organized the All-Ukrainian Orthodox Church Council and began to lay the foundations of the Ukrainian Autocephalous Orthodox Church. After the Bolsheviks captured Kiev, Sharayevskyi was appointed archbishop and deputy to the metropolitan of Kiev in 1921. He also served as a member of the Presidium of the All-Ukrainian Orthodox Church Council and chairman of its commission for the translation of liturgical texts into Ukrainian. Although he was persecuted in various ways by the Bolshevik authorities in the 1920s, Sharayevskyi was the only hierarch of the autocephalous Orthodox Church in the Ukraine to die a natural death. (WR)

Sources: *Encyclopedia of Ukraine*, vol. 4 (Toronto, 1993); Metropolit Vasyl Lypkivsky, *Vidrodzhennia tserkvy v Ukraiini, 1917–1930* (Toronto, 1959).

SHARETSKY Syamyon (23 September 1936, Lavrushevo, near Nowogródek [now Navahrudak]), Belorussian politician. After graduating from the Belorussian Agricultural Academy in 1959, Sharetsky became chairman of a collective farm (kolkhoz). In 1970 he graduated from the Higher Party School of the Central Committee of the Communist Party of Belorussia, and subsequently he became head of the school's Department of Economics and Organization of Agricultural Production. In 1984 he received a Ph.D. in economics, and in 1989 he became a professor. From 1984 to 1993 Sharetsky was chairman of a collective farm in the region of Valozhyn. In 1993 he was appointed adviser to **Vyacheslav Kebich**, prime minister of the Republic of Belarus, and in 1994 he became chairman of the Agrarian Party, which was to support Kebich in the presidential elections. In 1995 Sharetsky was elected deputy to the Supreme Soviet, and on 10 January 1996 he became speaker of the parliament. President **Alyaksandr Lukashenka**'s attempt to subordinate the Supreme Soviet led to a sharp dispute over the delimitation of authority between the legislative and executive branches. In April and May 1996 the crisis came to a head, but despite street demonstrations, Lukashenka managed to control the situation. When in the summer of 1996 Lukashenka proposed a referendum on constitutional changes, the opposition organized new demonstrations, and Sharetsky issued a statement declaring Lukashenka's step as the beginning of dictatorship. The Supreme Soviet approved a plan to abolish the office of president, but Lukashenka rallied the support of the police and military, as well as manipulating the crowds. Thanks to the mediation of the Russian prime minister, Viktor Chernomyrdin, a meeting between Sharetsky and Lukashenka on 21 November 1996 brought an apparent compromise, whereby an agreement was reached for a referendum and a decision was made to convene a Constitutional Assembly composed in equal parts of representatives of the Supreme Soviet and presidential appointees. This compromise was in fact a victory for Lukashenka. The referendum, held at the end of November, allowed Lukashenka to introduce a new constitution, as a result of which Sharetsky was de facto sidelined. Although Sharetsky still held the post of speaker of the Supreme Soviet, this body was not recognized by Lukashenka, who, under the terms of the new constitution, was able to establish his own parliament. On 21 July 1999 the deputies to the Soviet, who remained faithful to the 1994 constitution, proclaimed Sharetsky acting president of Belarus. Fearing for his safety, Sharetsky fled to Lithuania and thence to the United States in 2000. (EM)

Sources: *Kto est kto v Respublike Belarus* (Minsk, 1999); *Kto jest kim w Białorusi* (Białystok, 2000); David R. Marples, *Belarus: A Denationalized Nation* (Amsterdam, 1999).

SHCHERBYTSKYI Volodymyr (17 February 1918, Verkhnodniprovsk, Yekaterinoslav [now Dniepropetrovsk] region–16 February 1990, Kiev), Soviet Communist activist of Ukrainian descent. In 1941 Shcherbytskyi graduated from the Mechanical Department of the Dniepropetrovsk Chemical Technology Institute. During World War II he studied at the Chemical Troops Academy and served in the army near Moscow and in the Caucasus. Demobilized, he worked in a coking and chemical plant, becoming secretary of the Communist Party committee in 1946. Rising steadily through the party ranks, Shcherbytskyi became first secretary (1955–57) of the Dniepropetrovsk District Committee of the Communist Party of Ukraine (Komunistychna Partiya Ukrayiny [CPU]). In 1955 he became deputy to the Supreme Soviet of the Ukrainian SSR; in 1958, deputy to the Supreme Soviet of the Soviet Union; and in 1972, a member of the presidia of these Soviets. In 1957 Shcherbytskyi became a member of the Presidium of the Central Committee (CC) of the CPU and secretary of the CPU CC. From 1961 to 1963 he served as prime minister of the Ukrainian SSR and deputy member of the Presidium of the CC of the CPSU. Shcherbytskyi was dismissed from these positions by **Nikita Khrushchev** after he had opposed Khrushchev's idea to divide party committees into industrial and rural ones. From 1963 to 1965 Shcherbytskyi served as first secretary of the Dniepropetrovsk District Party Committee.

After Khrushchev was removed from power, Shcherbytskyi—owing to his good relations with Leonid Brezhnev—again became prime minister of the Ukrainian SSR (1965), and then he was named a member of the CPU CC Politburo (1966) and a member of the CPSU CC Politburo (1971). A member of the so-called Dniepropetrovsk clan, which played a decisive role in the Soviet Union during Brezhnev's rule, Shcherbytskyi was instrumental in the removal of **Petro Shelest** as first secretary of the CPU CC, and in May 1972 he replaced Shelest in that position. Shcherbytskyi is blamed for purging the party and government apparatus of people who supported a policy line relatively autonomous from Moscow. He endorsed the brutal repression of dissidents and intensified the Russification of Ukraine. On his initiative, Russian was used at official conferences and meetings. After the death of Yuri Andropov in February 1984, Shcherbytskyi supported Konstantin Chernenko's candidacy for head of the CPSU. After the nuclear power station accident at Chernobyl on 26 April 1986, Shcherbytskyi concealed from the Ukrainian people the true extent of the catastrophe; as a result, he exposed millions of people to unnecessary radiation. During perestroika he attempted to halt democratization processes in Ukraine. Shcherbytskyi retired in September 1989, shortly after a meeting of the People's Movement of Ukraine for Reconstruction, the first legal mass opposition organization. (BB)

Sources: *Encyclopedia of Ukraine*, vol. 4 (Toronto, 1993); *Entsyklopediya Ukraiinoznavstva*, vol. 10 (Lviv, 2000); *Dovidnyk z istorii Ukraiiny* (Kiev, 2001); Vitaliy Vrublevskyi, *Vladimir Shcherbitskyi, pravda i vymysly— Zapiski pomoshchnika: Vospominaniia, dokumenty, slukhi, legendy, fakty* (Kiev, 1993); Bohdan Nahaylo, *Ukrainian Resurgence* (Toronto, 1999).

SHEHU Mehmet (10 January 1913, Çorrush, Mallakastër–17 December 1981, Tirana), Albanian Communist politician. The son of a Muslim clergyman, Shehu graduated from the American Vocational School in Tirana in 1932. He also attended a military school in Naples but was expelled for anti-Fascist activities. He returned to Albania and enrolled in the officer training school in Tirana, from which he graduated with the rank of lieutenant. In 1936 he went to Spain, where he took part in the civil war, fighting in the Garibaldi International Brigade. After several weeks he became a commander of its Fourth Battalion. In 1937 Shehu joined the Communist Party of Spain. After the war he was interned in France (1939–42). In August 1942 he was transported to Tirana, where he was confined in a local detention house for a short time. After his release Shehu joined the Communist partisans and became a member of the party leadership in the region of Vlorë. In 1943 he was appointed commander of the First Partisan Brigade, and in November 1944 he became a major general. From September 1945 to August 1946 Shehu was in Moscow, where he graduated from the Kliment Voroshilov Military Academy. After his return to Albania, he was appointed chief of the General Staff of the Albanian Army. In February 1948, as a supporter of **Enver Hoxha**, Shehu was temporarily removed from the post of chief of staff and from the CC of the Albanian Labor Party (ALP). Between February and June 1948 he remained under the close surveillance of security authorities. After the conflict between Stalin and **Josip Broz Tito** and following the dismissal of **Koci Xoxe** (a supporter of integration of Albania with Yugoslavia), Shehu was appointed minister of interior. Soon afterwards, he also became deputy prime minister, a member of the ALP CC Politburo, and secretary of the ALP CC. From 20 July 1954 until his death Shehu was prime minister, and from 1974 to 1980 he also served as minister of national defense.

The closest co-worker of Hoxha, Shehu co-founded and co-implemented the most extreme line of the party, both on the international level and at home. He took an active part in all repressive actions and purges, which regularly swept the Albanian party. He became famous for saying that he had only one answer for people who did not support the leadership of the party: "A fist in the face and a bullet to the head." Shehu applied this rule in practice. In 1950, for example, he shot dead an activist who had criticized the Kremlin at a meeting of the CC. After Albania's split with Beijing, Shehu wanted to slightly normalize relations with Western Europe. Perhaps this was the reason for a conflict that ensued between him and Hoxha. On 18 December 1981 the Albanian news agency announced that Shehu had "committed suicide." In fact, the previous day he had been shot dead at a meeting of the top leadership of the party. Shehu's name was soon removed from official publications, and his family was persecuted. (WR)

Sources: Mehmet Shehu, *Vepra të zgjedhura* (Tirana, 1981); *The Annual Obituary*, (New York, 1981); Enver Hoxha, *So Stalinym: Vospominaniia* (Tirana, 1979); Arshi Pipa, *Albanian Stalinism: Ideo-Political Aspects* (Boulder, Colo., 1990); Miranda Vickers, *The Albanians: A Modern History* (London, 1995); James S. O'Donnell (James Salibur), *A Coming of Age: Albania under Enver Hoxha* (Boulder, Colo., 1999).

SHELEST Petro (14 February 1908, Andriyivka, Kharkov [Kharkiv] Province–22 January 1996, Moscow), Soviet Communist activist of Ukrainian descent. In 1923 Shelest took a job as a workman on the railways. In 1927 he went to a party school and became head of a Komsomol regional committee. In 1928 he joined the Communist Party (Bolshevik) of Ukraine (Komunistychna Partiya (Bilshovykiv) Ukraiiny [CP(B)U]). Shelest was sent to study at Artem Communist University in Kharkov and then the Engineering and Economics Institute in Kharkov. From 1932 to 1936 he worked for a metallurgical conglomerate in Mariupol. After doing his military service (1935–37), he worked in Kharkov's Hammer and Sickle factory. In 1940 Shelest became secretary of the Kharkov municipal party committee for defense industries. During the German-Soviet war he worked as head of the defense industry department of the Chelyabinsk district party committee. He later held a variety of positions, including those of instructor at the Central Committee (CC) of the All-Union Communist Party (Bolsheviks), head of party organizations in the factories of Saratov, and deputy secretary of the Saratov district party committee for defense production. From 1948 to 1954 Shelest worked as a plant director in Leningrad and Kiev. In 1954 he became second secretary of the Kiev municipal party committee and a member of the CC of the Communist Party of Ukraine (Komunistychna Partiya Ukraiiny [CPU]);

in February 1957 he became first secretary of the Kiev district party committee; in August 1962, secretary of the CC; and in December 1962, head of the CPU CC Bureau for Industry and Construction.

A protégé of **Nikita Khrushchev** and Nikolay Podgorny, Shelest rose to the position of first secretary of the CPU CC in July 1963, and then he was elected a member of the Presidium of the Ukrainian Supreme Soviet. In October 1964, along with Podgorny, Shelest played an important role in removing Khrushchev from power. In 1966 he became a member of the CPSU CC Politburo, and then he was elected to the Presidium of the Supreme Soviet of the Soviet Union and to the CPU CC Politburo. In the mid-1960s Shelest started the persecution of Ukrainian dissidents. Fearing that the influence of the Prague Spring might filter into Ukraine, he supported the Soviet intervention in Czechoslovakia in 1968. At the same time, considering mainly the interests of the Ukrainian party elites, he pressed for greater autonomy (mainly economic) for Ukraine as a union republic. In the field of culture, Shelest pursued policies that supported a limited Ukrainization. In his book *Ukraiino Nasha Radianska* (Our Soviet Ukraine; 1970), he referred to Cossack war traditions; as a result, he was attacked by his opponents for displaying "Ukrainian bourgeois nationalism." This book was sent to a paper mill, and Shelest was sharply criticized in Moscow. On 10 May 1972 Shelest was removed as first secretary of the CPU CC "owing to his transfer to another position," that of deputy prime minister of the Soviet Union. He was also expelled from the Presidium of the Supreme Soviet of the USSR and from the Presidium of the Supreme Soviet of the Ukrainian SSR. In April 1973 Shelest was expelled from the CPSU CC Politburo for "health reasons" and forced to retire. He also lost his post in the Soviet government. From 1974 to 1985 Shelest worked as a director of a research and production design bureau at an aviation works near Moscow. In 1995, after a dozen or so years of silence, he published his memoirs, *Da ne sudimy budete: Dnevnikovye zapisi, vospominaniia chlena Politbiuro TsK KPSS* (You will not be judged: Daily notes and memoirs of a member of the CPSU CC Politburo). In 1996 the urn with Shelest's ashes was brought to Ukraine and buried in one of Kiev's cemeteries. (BB)

Sources: *Encyclopedia of Ukraine*, vol. 4 (Toronto, 1993); *Za shcho usunuly Shelesta?* (Munich, 1973); *Dovidnyk z istorii Ukraiiny* (Kiev, 1999); *Entsyklopediya Ukraiioznavstva* (Lviv, 2000); *Malyi Slovnyk Istorii Ukraiiny* (Kiev, 1997); Andrzej Chojnowski, *Ukraina* (Warsaw, 1997); Bohdan Nahaylo, *The Ukrainian Resurgence* (Toronto, 1999); Paul R. Magocsi, *A History of Ukraine* (Seattle, 1996); Orest Subtelny, *Ukraine: A History* (Toronto, 2000); Jarosław Hrycak, *Historia Ukrainy 1772–1999* (Lublin, 2000).

SHEPTYTSKYI Andriy [original name Roman] (29 July 1865, Przyłbice [Prylbychi], near Jaworów [Yavoriv]–1 November 1944, Lviv), Ukrainian clergyman and national activist, metropolitan of the Ukrainian Greek Catholic Church. Born into a Ruthenian aristocratic family that had become Polonized in the eighteenth century, Sheptytskyi was the grandson of the dramatist Aleksander Fredro and the brother of **Stanisław Szeptycki**, a general in the Polish Army. After graduating from St. Anna Gymnasium in Kraków in 1883, Sheptytskyi served in the army for some time but was discharged for health reasons. He subsequently studied law at the universities in Kraków and Breslau (now Wrocław, Poland). In 1887 he traveled to Russia and Ukraine. In 1888 he earned a doctorate in law, and then he entered the monastery of the Order of Saint Basil in Dobromil (Dobromyl) and took the monastic name of Andriy. Sheptytskyi took holy orders in 1892 in Przemyśl. From 1892 to 1896 he was master of novices in Dobromil, and in 1896 he became hegumen (superior) of St. Onuphrius Monastery in Lemberg (Lviv, Lwów). In 1899 Pope Leo XIII named Sheptytskyi bishop of Stanisławów (now Ivano-Frankivsk, Ukraine) and in 1900 elevated him to the position of metropolitan of the Ukrainian Greek Catholic Church. He was ceremoniously installed in office on 17 January 1901.

From the beginning of his time in office Sheptytskyi was devoted to Ukrainian national life. In 1901 he supported the secession of Ukrainian students from the University of Lemberg; in 1902 he called for the establishment of a Ukrainian gymnasium in Stanisławów; and in 1903 he founded the People's Infirmary, which became transformed into a modern hospital in 1930–38. In 1905 Sheptytskyi founded a church museum. Thanks to his financial support, a building was bought for the art school of Oleksyi Novakivskyi, one of the greatest Ukrainian painters in the first half of the twentieth century. He sponsored scholarships for Ukrainian artists, enabling them to study at the best European universities. Sheptytskyi served as an MP in the Galician Provincial Diet (1901–14) and was a member of the Austrian House of Lords (1903–14). In 1906 he headed a delegation that presented demands to Emperor Francis Joseph that the Ukrainian people be given rights equal to those of other nations in the empire. In 1910 at a session of the House of Lords of the parliament in Vienna Sheptytskyi called for the establishment of a Ukrainian university in Lemberg. In the same year he initiated the establishment of the Land Bank (Zemelnyi Bank) in Lemberg. Thanks to his financial support, a seminary was built in Lemberg and the library of the Stanisławów chapter was founded. In 1901 Sheptytskyi established the St. Theodore the Studite monastic order, and in 1913 he invited the Redemptorist order to Galicia. Sheptytskyi was also greatly involved in ecumenical work. In 1907 and 1912 he made two visits to Russia. He founded the Russian Catholic Church of the Eastern Rite and created the vicariate apostolic for Eastern Rite Catholics in Bosnia. As a result of his efforts, the Pope appointed a bishop for the Uniates in the United States (1907) and Canada (1912). In 1907 and 1909 Sheptytskyi presided over the First and Second Ecumenical Congresses in Velehrad. In 1910 he attended the Eucharistic Congress in Montreal. He established a new eastern branch of the Benedictine order in Belgium.

After the Russian Army seized Galicia, Sheptytskyi was arrested on 18 September 1914 and then deported, first to Kiev and then into the depths of Russia. He was released after the February 1917 revolution. In March in Petrograd he convoked a synod of the Russian Catholic Church of the Eastern Rite and appointed Reverend Leonid Fyodorov exarch for the Catholics of the Byzantine rite in Russia. During his stay in Kiev Sheptytskyi appointed Reverend Mykhailo Tsehelskyi exarch for the Catholics of the Byzantine rite in Ukraine. In September 1917 Sheptytskyi returned to Lemberg, where he became a member of the Ukrainian National Council of the Western Ukrainian National Republic (Ukraiinska Natsionalna Rada Zakhidno-Ukraiinskoy Narodnoy Respubliki [ZUNR]) in October 1918. During the Polish-Ukrainian war (1918–19) Sheptytskyi was interned by the Polish authorities. In December 1920 he went to Rome and thence to visit the Ukrainian communities in North and South America. After returning to Poland in 1923, he was interned in Poznań. Thanks to the intervention of Pope Pius XI and after Sheptytskyi had declared loyalty to the Polish state, he was released. He returned to Lwów. On his initiative the Lwów Greek Catholic Academy (Lvivska Hreko-Katolytska Akademiia) was founded in 1928, the Theological Scholarly Society (Bohoslovske Naukove Tovarystvo) in 1929, and the Ukrainian Catholic Institute for Church Unification (Ukraiinskyi Katolytskyi Instytut Tserkovnoho Zyednannya) in 1939. In 1930 Sheptytskyi condemned Polish reprisals in connection with a pacification campaign against Ukrainian villages in Eastern Galicia. In 1933, along with other bishops, he issued an address condemning the Soviet government for orchestrating an artificial famine in the Ukrainian SSR. In 1938 he issued a letter protesting the persecution of the Orthodox population in Volhynia and the Chełm region and condemning the destruction of Orthodox churches. He supported the work of the Ukrainian National Democratic Alliance and abandoned the idea of establishing an independent Ukrainian state.

After the Red Army seized Galicia in September 1939, Sheptytskyi secretly consecrated **Josyf Slipyi**, the rector of a seminary, as his successor. In October 1939 he appointed exarchs for the Catholics of the Byzantine rite in Volhynia and the Pripet Marshes and also in Russia and Siberia. After the outbreak of the German-Soviet war in 1941, Sheptytskyi issued a proclamation greeting the German units. However, he soon realized his error, and in a letter to Pope Pius XII he described the German rule as "evil, almost devilish." Sheptytskyi supported the establishment of a government and the restoration of Ukrainian statehood by the Bandera faction of the Organization of Ukrainian Nationalists (OUN), but he dissociated himself from organizations that collaborated with the Germans. In 1941 he became head of the Ukrainian National Council (Ukraiinska Natsionalna Rada), and in 1944, head of the All-Ukrainian National Council (Vseukraiinska Natsionalna Rada). In 1943 Sheptytskyi appointed chaplains for pastoral ministry in the SS Galizien Division. In a letter to Heinrich Himmler, Sheptytskyi protested the extermination of the Jewish population. He himself provided shelter to Jewish people and exhorted Greek Catholic monasteries to do the same. In November 1942 Sheptytskyi issued the pastoral letter "Ne Ubyi" (Thou shalt not kill), in which he threatened excommunication to those who organized or committed the crime of killing. Sheptytskyi was one of the initiators of Polish-Ukrainian talks (1943–44), but they were unsuccessful. Sheptytskyi died in the archbishop's palace and was buried in the crypt of St. George's Cathedral in Lviv. (BB)

Sources: *Encyclopedia of Ukraine*, vol. 4 (Toronto, 1993); *Dovidnyk z istorii Ukraiiny* (Kiev, 1999); Volodymyr Doroshenko, *Velykyi Mytropolyt: Pamiati Mytrop. A. Sheptytskoho; spohady i narysy* (Yorkton, Saskatchewan 1958); Cyril Korolevsky, *Métropolite André Szeptyckyj, 1865–1944* (Rome, 1964); Ryszard Torzecki, "Metropolita Andrzej Szeptycki," *Znak*, 1988, no. 9; Paul R. Magocsi, ed., *Morality and Reality: The Life and Time of Andrei Sheptytskyj* (Edmonton, 1989); Andrzej A. Zieba, ed., *Metropolita Andrzej Szeptycki: Studia i materiały,* (Kraków, 1994); Tadeusza Stegnera, ed., *Metropolita Andrzej Szeptycki: Materiały z sesji naukowej pod,* (Gdańsk, 1995); Orest Ia. Krasivskyi, *Za ukraiinsku derzhavu i tserkvu: Hromadska ta suspilno-politychna diialnist Mytropolyta Andreia Sheptytskoho v 1918–1923 rr.* (Lviv, 1995); Jaroslav Moskalyk, *Kontseptsiia Tserkvy Mytropolyta Andreia Sheptytskoho* (Lviv, 1997).

SHEPTYTSKYI Kliment [original name Kazimierz] (17 November 1869, Przyłbice [Prylbychi], near Jaworów [Yavoriv]–1 May 1951, Vladimir, Russia), archimandrite of the Ukrainian Greek Catholic Church, martyr for the faith. Born into a well-known aristocratic family, Sheptytskyi was the younger brother of Archbishop **Andriy Sheptytskyi** and General **Stanisław Szeptycki**. He gave up a promising secular career and in 1911 entered the monastery of St. Theodore the Studite. He completed his theological studies in Innsbruck. In August 1915 he was ordained a Catholic priest of the Eastern rite. During the interwar period Sheptytskyi served as hegumen (superior) of the Studite monastery. On 9 October 1939 his brother Andriy named him a Uniate exarch for Ruthenia and Siberia. When the Soviet authorities were withdrawing from Lviv in June 1941, Sheptytskyi barely escaped execution by the NKVD. In 1944 he was elevated to archimandrite (head of a monastery). During the Nazi occupation he provided shelter to the Jewish people, including the son of the chief rabbi of Lviv. In December 1944, after the death of his brother Andriy, Sheptytskyi headed a delegation of the Ukrainian Greek Catholic Church sent by Archbishop **Josyf Slipyi** to Moscow, where the delegation presented a letter to Stalin and the Soviet authorities. In this letter, the archbishop expressed gratitude for the liberation of Ukraine from German occupation and conveyed hopes for good relations between the Uniate Church and the Soviet state. After the arrest of nearly all Ukrainian Greek Catholic bishops in April 1945, Sheptytskyi and some sixty other priests signed a protest letter to the Soviet government. In March 1946 the Kremlin abolished the Ukrainian Greek Catholic Church and allowed the Orthodox Church to take over its churches. More and more of Sheptytskyi's co-workers were arrested. Sheptytskyi became the de facto leader of all the priests and monks who had not yet been arrested. In January 1946 he was forcibly deported to the monastery in Univ. Arrested by the NKVD on 5 June 1947, he was sentenced to eight years in a forced labor camp. He died in the Vladimir prison. The year 1958 is also given as the date of his death. On 27 June 2001 Pope John Paul II beatified Sheptytskyi at a solemn Holy Mass in Lviv. (WR)

Sources: Lesia Krychuk, "Kazymyr Sheptytskyi: Malodoslidzhena zasluzhena postat v zhytti UKTs," *Tserkovnyi visnyk* (Chicago), 17 December 1995; Bohdan R. Bociurkiw, *The Ukrainian Greek-Catholic Church and the Soviet State (1939–1950)* (Edmonton, 1996); *Osservatore Romano* (weekly edition in English), 2001, nos. 25 and 27.

SHISHMANOV Dimitur (19 November 1889, Sofia–2 February 1945, Sofia), Bulgarian politician, diplomat, playwright, and journalist. Shishmanov was the son of **Ivan Shishmanov**; his mother, Lidia, was the daughter of the Ukrainian historian Mykhailo Drahomanov. In 1913 Shishmanov completed law studies in Geneva. From 1914 to 1919 he served in the intelligence service. In 1919 he entered the diplomatic service. He initially represented Bulgaria in international organizations, as a result of which he had an opportunity to travel extensively and tour Europe. This experience is reflected in his literary works,

including the novel *Buntovnik* (Rebel; 1912) and the drama *Koshmar* (Nightmare; 1927). Shishmanov was a department head in the Ministry of Foreign Affairs (1932–35), Bulgaria's envoy to Athens (1935–40), and chief secretary of the Ministry of Foreign Affairs (March 1940–October 1943). From October 1943 to June 1944 he served as minister of foreign affairs. His time in office coincided with the death of Tsar **Boris III**. Despite an imminent breakthrough in war operations, the Ministry of Foreign Affairs under his leadership worked sluggishly, and some of its key decisions were made without his knowledge. Bulgaria was seen by Western countries as an ally of the Axis powers. Negotiations led by Bulgarian representatives in Turkey in late 1943 and early 1944 made it clear to England and the United States that Bulgaria was not going to unilaterally withdraw from the war without the Allies' guarantees of military assistance. The position of the government in Sofia on giving up territories gained by Bulgaria with Germany's consent after 1941 was also ambiguous. After the coup of 9 September 1944 and the occupation of Bulgaria by the Red Army, Shishmanov was arrested. He was initially sent to the Soviet Union, but in December 1944 he was handed over to Bulgaria, brought before the court, and, along with other members of the prewar Bulgarian elite, executed by firing squad. Shishmanov's *Pisma do men samiya* (Letters to myself) were published in 1995. (AG)

Sources: Peter Tunkur, *International Directory of Foreign Ministers* (Munich, Paris, London, and New York, 1989); *Entsiklopediya Bulgariya*, vol. 7 (Sofia, 1996); Marshall Lee Miller, *Bulgaria during the Second World War* (Stanford, 1975); Jerzy Jackowicz, *Partie opozycyjne w Bułgarii 1944–1948* (Warsaw, 1997).

SHISHMANOV Ivan (22 June 1862, Svishtov–23 June 1928, Oslo, Norway), Bulgarian ethnographer, philologist, and diplomat. After graduating from a pedagogical school in Vienna, Shishmanov studied philosophy and philology in Jena, Geneva, and Leipzig (1888). He fought as a volunteer in the war against Serbia in 1885. After returning to Bulgaria, he co-founded the Bulgarian Higher School (the future Sofia University), where he taught general history. From 1889 to 1894 Shishmanov worked in the Ministry of National Education. As minister of education (May 1903–March 1907), he greatly contributed to the establishment of the National Theater, state music and art schools, and the Museum of Ethnography. Head of the Department of History and Comparative Literature at Sofia University and dean of the History Department, Shishmanov served as minister plenipotentiary to Ukraine (1918–19) and president of the Bulgarian PEN Club (from 1926). Shishmanov's publications include *Znachenie i* *zadachi na nashata etnografiia* (The role and tasks of our ethnography; 1888) and the famous conversations with **Ivan Vazov**, published in the volume *Ivan Vazov: Spomeni i dokumenty* (Ivan Vazov: Recollections and documents; 1930). Three volumes of Shishmanov's literary output were published in 1965–71. (JW)

Sources: *Entsiklopediya Bulgariya*, vol. 7 (Sofia, 1996).

SHLLAKU Bernardin (23 June 1875, Shkodër–9 November 1956, Tirana), Albanian Catholic bishop. In 1890 Shllaku joined the Franciscan order. He graduated in theology in Graz. In 1898 he was ordained a priest. Shllaku initially worked in Shkodër and then became a parish priest in Kastrati (1899). From 1906 onwards he gave classes at the Franciscan College in Shkodër. In 1909 he took charge of the parish of Vuksan-Lekaj. One year later he was consecrated bishop and appointed auxiliary bishop of the diocese of Pulati. From 1921 on he headed this diocese. After the death of Archbishop **Gasper Thaçi** and the arrest of Archbishop **Vinçenc Prennushi** in February 1947, Shllaku became the ordinary of the archdiocese of Shkodër. He also became the head of the Catholic Church in Albania. In 1949 Shllaku headed an Episcopate delegation in negotiations with the Communist authorities on the legal status of the Church in the state. **Mehmet Shehu**, who represented the government, accused Shllaku of hindering the negotiations through his tenacity in opposing the creation of a national church and the severing of ties with the Holy See. On 30 July 1951 the negotiations ended in a compromise, under which contacts with the papacy were to be reduced to a minimum. In practice, the Communist authorities did not respect this negotiated compromise and made it public despite the previous agreements. The crisis in the Albanian Church, stemming from the reluctance to reach a compromise, worked against Shllaku, who was blamed for excessive concessions. At the same time, under mounting pressure from the authorities, he was forced to undertake activities showing the Church's support for the new political situation. For example, in January 1954 he signed an appeal urging the faithful to take part in the elections and vote for the Democratic Front candidates. Despite these concessions, the Church and the faithful continued to be a target of attacks by the Communists. (TC)

Sources: Ajet Shahiu, "Shteti komunist dhe Kisha Katolike," in *Krishtërimi nder Shqiptare: Simpoziumi Nderkombëtar* (Shkodër, 2000); Gjush Sheldija, *Kryepeshkvia metropolitane e Shkodrës e dioqezat sufragane: Shenime historike* (Shkodër, 1957–58).

SHUKHEVYCH Roman, pseudonyms "Dzvin," "Shchuka," "Tur," "R. Lozovskyi," and "Taras Chuprynka" (17 July 1907, Krakowiec [Krakovets]–5 March 1950, Bilohorshcha, near Lviv), leader of Ukrainian nationalists. The son of a judge, Shukhevych attended high school in Lwów (Lviv), and in 1926 he began to study at the technical universities of the free city of Gdańsk (Danzig) and Lwów. In 1923 he joined the clandestine Ukrainian Military Organization (Ukraiinska Viyskova Orhanizatsiya [UVO]), which sought to establish an independent Ukrainian state in Eastern Galicia. In 1926 he took part in the assassination of the Polish superintendent of schools in Lwów. From 1928 to 1929 Shukhevych did his military service in the Polish Army. In 1934 he completed architectural studies at Lwów. By then, he was already one of the leaders of the UVO and the Organization of Ukrainian Nationalists (OUN), founded in 1929. He led many attacks on the Polish administration in Eastern Galicia and was responsible for the assassination of the Soviet consul in Lwów— a retaliatory measure for the famine in the Ukrainian SSR caused by the Soviet authorities. Imprisoned at Bereza Kartuska for his part in the preparations for the assassination of Minister **Bronisław Pieracki**, Shukhevych was sentenced to four years in prison in June 1934 but was released under an amnesty at the beginning of 1937. In 1938 Shukhevych went abroad and met **Yevhen Konovalets**, head of the OUN, who was assassinated shortly afterwards by a Soviet agent. In Subcarpathian Ruthenia from 1938 to 1939, Shukhevych was one of the main founders of the Carpathian Sich.

After the defeat of Poland in September 1939, Shukhevych served as an OUN liaison officer in Kraków and cooperated with the Ukrainian military underground movement in the Soviet-occupied territories of Eastern Galicia. Counting on Nazi support to gain independence for Ukraine, Shukhevych joined the Ukrainian Nachtigall Battalion in April 1941. After the outbreak of the German-Soviet war in June 1941, he became commander of the OUN units in Eastern Galicia, which had been incorporated into the General Government. Shukhevych helped to draft the declaration of Ukrainian independence of 30 June 1941. When in October 1941 the Nachtigall and Roland battalions were merged into the Schutzmannschaftbataillon, Shukhevych became deputy commander of the latter, with the rank of captain. However, this battalion was disbanded and its officers were arrested. Shukhevych managed to escape. Since **Stepan Bandera** and **Yaroslav Stetsko** were imprisoned in a Nazi concentration camp, Shukhevych became head of the OUN–Bandera faction (OUN–B) on 25 August 1943, and in November of that year he was appointed supreme commander of the Ukrainian Insurgent Army (UPA), which served as the military force of the OUN. When the Ukrainian Supreme Liberation Council (Ukraiinska Holovna Vyzvolna Rada) was established on the OUN–B's initiative, Shukhevych became chairman of its General Secretariat on 15 July 1944. He was responsible for the killings of the Polish civilian population committed by Ukrainian units in Eastern Galicia and Volhynia. The UPA's activities were directed against the Polish Home Army and the Nazi German administration, but they also involved ethnic cleansing aimed at removing the Polish population from Eastern Galicia.

When the Red Army started entering Eastern Galicia in the spring of 1944, Shukhevych's insurgent forces took up the struggle against the Soviet troops. At that time Shukhevych used the pseudonym of "General Taras Chuprynka." The UPA's guerrilla struggle against Red Army units and political police in the territories incorporated into the Ukrainian SSR—as well as against the Czechoslovak Army, the new Polish Army, and the Communist State Security Office in Poland—continued for several years after the end of World War II and caused heavy losses among the civilian population of Eastern Galicia, Transcarpathia, and southeastern Poland. Encircled with his staff by forces of the Soviet Ministry of Internal Affairs near Lviv, Shukhevych was killed during combat. In August 1948 the MVD arrested and deported his widow and fifteen-year-old son to Siberia, only because they were his family. His son, Yuriy, was incarcerated in prisons and Soviet forced labor camps for over thirty years. Polish people mainly associate Shukhevych with the killings of the Polish civilian population, while in the memory of many Ukrainians he is a hero who fought for Ukraine's independence. Shukhevych was the patron of the Anti-Bolshevik Bloc of Nations (ABN), which he founded in November 1943 near Zhytomyr and which was active in the United States for many years after the war. (WR)

Sources: *Encyclopedia of Ukraine*, vol. 4 (Toronto, 1993); *The Ukrainian Insurgent Army in a Fight for Freedom* (New York, 1954); John A. Armstrong, *Ukrainian Nationalism, 1939–1945* (New York, 1955); Yaroslav Bilinsky, *The Second Soviet Republic: The Ukraine after World War II* (New Brunswick, N.J., 1964); Ryszard Torzecki, *Polacy i Ukraińcy: Sprawa ukraińska w czasie II wojny światowej na terenie II Rzeczypospolitej* (Warsaw, 1993); Petro Mirchuk, *Roman Shukhevych* (New York, 1970); *Ukrainian Review*, 1985, nos. 1 and 2; *ABN Correspondence*, 1985, no. 5; Roman Drozd, *Ukraińska Powstańcza Armia. Dokumenty-struktury* (Warsaw, 1998); Orest Subtelny, *Ukraine: A History* (Toronto, 2000).

SHULHYN Oleksandr (30 July 1889, Sokhvyne, Poltava Province–4 March 1960, Paris), Ukrainian social activist, politician, historian, and journalist. The son of a historian and politician, from 1908 Shulhyn studied the natural sciences at St. Petersburg University but transferred to its Department of History and Philology in 1910. After graduating in 1915, he took up research work at this university. He also taught at pedagogical schools and high schools in St. Petersburg. An active member of Ukrainian associations in St. Petersburg, he initiated the establishment of the Union of Ukrainian Student Associations. After the February 1917 revolution, Shulhyn went to Kiev, where he joined the Ukrainian Democratic Radical Party (Ukraiinska Radykalno-Demokratychna Partiya). In April 1917 he became a member of the Union of Ukrainian Autonomist Federalists (Soyuz Ukraiinskykh Avtonomistiv-Federalistiv), and in September 1917 he became a member of the Central Committee (CC) of the Ukrainian Party of Socialist Federalists (Ukraiinska Partiya Sotsialistiv-Federalistiv). He was also a member of the Society of Ukrainian Progressives. A delegate to the Ukrainian Central Rada (Council), he was elected to its executive organ, the so-called Little Rada, in July 1917. From July 1917 to January 1918 Shulhyn was secretary general for the national minorities (later for international affairs). Through his efforts, the Ukrainian National Republic (UNR) was officially recognized by France and Great Britain. In September 1917 in Kiev he organized the Congress of Captive Nations of Russia. In January and February 1918 he took part in negotiations with the Central Powers at Brest-Litovsk. Under the rule of Hetman **Pavlo Skoropadskyi**, Shulhyn was head of a political commission of the Ukrainian delegation to the peace negotiations with Soviet Russia. In July 1918 he became Ukrainian ambassador to Bulgaria. In 1919 he was in the Ukrainian delegation to the Paris Peace Conference. In 1920 he headed the UNR delegation to the First Assembly of the League of Nations in Geneva. In 1921 he headed the UNR extraordinary diplomatic mission in Paris.

From 1923 to 1927 Shulhyn was a professor at the Ukrainian Free University and at the Ukrainian Pedagogical Institute in Prague. He served as minister of foreign affairs (1926–36, 1939–40, 1945–46) of the UNR government-in-exile. From 1929 to 1939 he served as head of the Ukrainian Supreme Council in Exile (Holovna Ukraiinska Emihratsiyna Rada), and from 1939 to 1940 he was head of the UNR government-in-exile. Shulhyn co-founded and headed the Ukrainian Academic Society in Paris (1946–60). In 1952 he co-initiated the International Free Academy of Sciences in Paris and served as its vice-president until 1960. From 1952 onwards Shulhyn was vice-president of the Taras Shevchenko Scientific Society (Naukove Tovarystvo im. Tarasa Shevchenka [NTSh]) in Europe. In his scholarly work Shulhyn dealt with modern history. His publications include the following: *Uvahy do rozvytku ranishnoho kapitalizmu* (Remarks on the development of early capitalism; 1930); *Les origines de l'esprit national moderne et J.-J. Rousseau* (1938); and *Istoriia ta zhyttia* (History and life; 1957). He also wrote works on the history of the Ukrainian national liberation movement: *Polityka* (Politics; 1918); *L'Ukraine et le cauchemar rouge: Les massacres en Ukraine* (1927); *Derzhavnist chy Haidamachchyna?* (Statehood of Haidamaka Uprisings? 1931); *Bez terytorii: Ideolohiia ta chyn uriadu UNR na chuzhyni* (Without a territory: Ideology and activities of the UNR Government-in-Exile; 1934); and *L'Ukraine contre Moscou 1917* (1935). (BB)

Sources: *Encyclopedia of Ukraine*, vol. 4 (Toronto, 1993); V. Verstiuk and T. Ostashko, *Diiachi Ukraiinskoy Tsentralnoy Rady: Bibliohrafichnyi dovidnyk* (Kiev, 1998); *Dovidnyk z istorii Ukraiiny* (Kiev, 1999); *Entsyklopediya Ukraiinoznavstva* (Lviv, 2000); *Zbirnyk na poshanu Oleksandra Shulhyna* (N.p., 1969).

SHUMSKYI Oleksandr (2 December 1890, Borova Rudnya, near Kiev–18 September 1946, on the way from Saratov to Kiev), Ukrainian Communist activist. Shumskyi joined the Ukrainian Social Democratic Union in 1908 and the Ukrainian Party of Socialist Revolutionaries (Ukraiinska Partiya Sotsialistiv-Revolyutsioneriv [UPSR]) in the autumn of 1917. He was a member of the Central Council (Rada). In January 1918 Shumskyi conspired with the Bolsheviks to stage a coup, with the aim of establishing a Soviet system in Ukraine. A member of the pro-Bolshevik leftist faction of the UPSR, he was among those who effected a split in the party in May 1918; the split led to the establishment of the UPSR–Borotbists (the name was derived from the title of the periodical *Borotba* [Struggle]). In the spring of 1919 the UPSR–Borotbists supported **Georgy Pyatakov**'s Soviet government of Ukraine. The Borotbists accused the Bolsheviks of ignoring the national cause and called for the establishment of parliamentary democracy. The Borotbists expressed their views in a memorandum submitted by Shumskyi to the authorities of the Communist International (Comintern) in August 1919; in it they criticized the policy of the Communist Party (Bolshevik) of Ukraine (CP[B]U). Although the Comintern did not accept their views, it needed the Borotbists, who had a strong following among the peasants. When in 1920 the Borotbists were invited to voluntarily join the CP(B)U, the majority accepted the offer. Among them was Shumskyi, who soon became a member of the Central Committee (CC) of the party. Shumskyi belonged to a CP(B)U faction that insisted on the party's independence from the Russian Communists and advocated that the CP(B)U maintain contact with the Russians through the Comintern. In 1919 Shumskyi was appointed people's commissar of education in the Soviet government of Ukraine. In 1920 he was made people's

commissar of internal affairs. In 1921 he became the ambassador of the Ukrainian SSR to Poland.

After returning to Ukraine, Shumskyi edited the monthly *Chervonyi shliakh* from 1923 to 1926 and directed the CP(B)U CC Department of Agitation and Propaganda from 1923 to 1925. In September 1924 he again became people's commissar of education and actively implemented Ukrainization policies. In October 1925, in a conversation with Stalin, Shumskyi demanded that **Lazar Kaganovich** be dismissed as the CP(B)U CC general secretary. He urged that, in line with the Ukrainization policy, Kaganovich be replaced by a Ukrainian, **Vlas Chubar**. As a result of Shumskyi's conflict with Kaganovich, in a 1926 letter to the CP(B)U CC Politburo, Stalin accused Shumskyi of inciting anti-Russian sentiments in Ukraine. Shumskyi's policy was labeled a "deviation." In June 1926, after a smear campaign had been launched against him at a plenum of the CP(B)U CC, Shumskyi made a self-criticism. Dismissed as commissar of education and relieved of all his party posts (February 1927), he was transferred to Moscow, where he became president of the All-Soviet Board of the Trade Union of the Educational Sector. Accusations of "Shumskyism" caused serious consequences not only for the CP(B)U; even greater persecutions were launched against the Communist Party of Western Ukraine (Komunistychna Partiya Zakhidnoyi Ukraiiny [KPZU]), operating in Poland; a majority of its leaders had supported Shumskyi, and as a result they soon became the victims of purges.

In 1933 Shumskyi was arrested on a fabricated charge of being a member of the Ukrainian Military Organization (Ukraiinska Viyskova Orhanizatsiya [UVO]), which, according to the OGPU (political police), was allegedly preparing an anti-Soviet uprising. Sentenced to ten years of labor camp, Shumskyi was incarcerated on the Solovets Islands from 1933 to 1935. He repeatedly wrote to the party leaders and to Stalin himself, asking for a review of his case. In December 1935 a decision was made to commute his sentence from labor camp to forced settlement in Krasnoyarsk. After this decision, Shumskyi went on a hunger strike, demanding a complete rehabilitation. Seriously ill, in 1937 he was arrested again, this time in connection with the case of the Borotbists. In 1939 the case was discontinued owing to his illness. After the end of his term (1943), Shumskyi remained in Krasnoyarsk because of his serious condition. In 1946 he made an unsuccessful suicide attempt. In the same year, while on the way from Saratov to Kiev, he was murdered on the personal orders of Stalin and Kaganovich. However, there are also other accounts of Shumskyi's death. Shumskyi's publications include *Stara i nova Ukraiina* (The old and the new Ukraine; 1923); *Politychna sytuatsiia v skhidnoyi Halychyni* (Political situation in Eastern Galicia; 1924); and *Ideolohichna borotba v ukrainskomu kulturnomu protsesi* (Ideological struggle in the Ukrainian cultural process; 1927). (BB/TS)

Sources: *Encyclopedia of Ukraine*, vol. 4 (Toronto, 1993); *Entsyklopediya Ukraiinoznavstva*, vol. 10 (Lviv, 2000); *Dovidnyk z istorii Ukraiiny* (Kiev, 2001); Ivan Maistrenko, *Borotbism: A Chapter in the History of Ukrainian Communism* (New York, 1954); Roman Solchanyk, "The Communist Party of Western Ukraine," Ph.D. diss., University of Michigan, 1973; Janusz Radziejowski, *Komunistyczna Partia Zachodniej Ukrainy 1919–1929: Węzłowe problemy ideologiczne* (Kraków, 1976); James Mace, *Communism and the Dilemmas of National Liberation: National Communism in Soviet Ukraine, 1918–1933* (Cambridge, 1983); Iurii Shapoval, *Lyudyna i systema* (Kiev, 1994).

SHUSHKEVICH Stanislav (15 December 1934, Minsk), Belorussian politician and nuclear physicist. Shushkevich is the son of Stanislav Shushkevich, a Belorussian writer, poet, and journalist who spent twenty years in Soviet forced labor camps and in exile. His mother, Alena, was also persecuted by the authorities. Shushkevich graduated from the Belorussian State University (BSU) in 1956 and completed postgraduate studies in 1959. In 1959 he began working at the Institute of Physics of the Belorussian Academy of Sciences (BAS). In 1967 he joined the CPSU. In 1969 he became head of a department for the civilian use of nuclear energy at the BSU. In 1973 he became a professor and in 1988 the deputy rector of the BSU. After the nuclear power station accident at Chernobyl in April 1986, Shushkevich criticized the authorities for withholding information on the consequences of the catastrophe. He became a member of a commission to investigate the effects of the disaster. This commission was established by a decision of the BAS and the Central Committee of the Communist Party of Belorussia. The task of the commission was to calm the public, but Shushkevich disseminated information about the true extent of the contamination of the Belorussian territory; for that reason he was removed from the commission. In the summer of 1986, along with his colleagues from the department of nuclear physics, Shushkevich set up a station where people could measure the contamination of foodstuffs. This station enjoyed great popularity, but the first secretary of the party committee in Minsk described it as "anti-state."

In the 1989 elections Shushkevich was elected to the Supreme Soviet of the Soviet Union. He became a member of the Interregional Group and worked with, among others, Andrei Sakharov, Boris Yeltsin, and Galina Starovoytova. Shushkevich called for an inquiry into the suppression of demonstrations in Tbilisi in April 1989. On 4 March 1990 he was elected a deputy to the Communist-dominated Belorussian Supreme Soviet. On 24 March 1990 at a conference of the Democratic Platform, consisting of twenty-three deputies of the Belorussian SSR and twenty-one councillors of the Minsk Council, Shushkevich called for cooperation with pragmatic Communist deputies. In June 1990 Shushkevich left the CPSU. On 27 July 1990 he was one of the initiators of the declaration of independence of Belarus. From 1990 to 1991 he was first deputy speaker of the Supreme Soviet of the Republic of Belarus, and on 17 September 1991 he became speaker.

On 8 December 1991, along with Boris Yeltsin, the president of Russia, and Leonid Kravchuk, the president of Ukraine, Shushkevich signed an agreement on the establishment of the Commonwealth of Independent States (CIS). The agreement provided for the dissolution of the Soviet Union. In May 1992 in Tashkent, a Belarusian delegation headed by Shushkevich refused to sign three treaties within the framework of the CIS: on collective security, chemical weapons, and common border protection. In March 1993 Shushkevich protested against the CIS Treaty on Collective Security, which had been ratified by the Belarusian parliament. After he had put forward a proposal that a referendum be held to decide on Belarus's membership in a new military alliance with Russia, Shushkevich was more and more often attacked by the Communists. His proposal did not gain the support of a parliamentary majority. On 1 July 1993, in a vote of no confidence in Shushkevich, only eight more votes were needed to dismiss him as speaker of the parliament. In July 1993 Shushkevich went to the United States, where he met with President Bill Clinton. In January 1994 Clinton paid a return visit to Belarus, the first CIS country he visited. In November 1993 **Alyaksandr Lukashenka** groundlessly accused Shushkevich of embezzlement. On 26 January 1994 Shushkevich was dismissed by a majority of votes.

In June 1994 Shushkevich ran in the presidential elections in Belarus but received only 10 percent of the vote, mainly in the big cities. In 1994 he became director of the Center for Political and Economic Studies at the European Humanities University in Minsk. In May 1995 he was elected to the parliament. Shushkevich was one of the initiators of a procedure to dismiss Lukashenka as president of Belarus (November 1996). Shushkevich refused to recognize the results of Lukashenka's referendum of 24 November 1996 and did not become a member of his pseudo-parliament. In February 1998, at the founding congress of the Belarusian Social Democratic Party–Hramada, Shushkevich was elected its chairman. In May 1999, in reaction to a violation of the constitution by Lukashenka, Shushkevich (along with members of his party) helped to organize opposition presidential elections. Shushkevich also took part in the proceedings of international organizations, including the Organization for Security and Cooperation in Europe, which dealt with international security and human rights. Shushkevich published several research works on the foundations of radioelectronics. (AS/SA)

Sources: *Belarus: Entsyklapedychny davednik* (Minsk, 1995); Jan Zaprudnik, *Belarus: At a Crossroads in History* (Boulder, Colo., 1993); Eberhard Schneider, *Drei GUS-Führer: Portraits von Jelzin, Krawtschuk und Schuschkewitsch* (Cologne, 1993); Liudmila Klaskouskaia and Aliaksandr Klaskouski, *Stanislau Shushkevich: Putsiavina liosu* (Minsk, 1994); Siergiej Owsiannik and Jełena Striełkowa, *Władza a społeczeństwo: Białoruś 1991–1998* (Warsaw, 1998); *Tsentrum Karta, Arkhiu nainoushae gistoryi, Demakratychnaia apazytsyia Belarusi 1956–1991: Davednik* (Minsk, 1999).

SICHYNSKYI Myroslav (11 October 1887, Czernichowce, near Zbaraż [now Chernykhivtsi]–16 February 1979, Westland, Michigan), Ukrainian nationalist activist. Sichynskyi's father was a Uniate parish priest and an MP in the Provincial Diet. Sichynskyi attended high school in Kołomyja (Kolomyya) in 1897–1900 and in Przemyśl in 1900–1904. Involved in the activities of secret youth groups, he was punished with a fine and expelled from school for taking part in a demonstration. He passed his high school final examinations as an extramural student. In 1905 Sichynskyi began to study in Vienna, and one year later he transferred to the University of Lemberg (Lwów, Lviv). He became a member of the Academic Hromada (Akademichna Hromada), a student organization in Lemberg, and a member of the Ukrainian Social Democratic Workers' Party. He joined a student campaign aimed at gaining permission for the Ukrainization of the university. In January 1907, as part of a protest against the decision of the university authorities to ban the use of Ukrainian for the academic year 1906–7, Sichynskyi, along with a group of Ukrainian students, destroyed lecture halls and assaulted a Polish lecturer. Arrested by the police, the participants of the protest went on a hunger strike in prison; the strike received a lot of publicity across Europe and influenced the court's decision to release the students. In retaliation for the police brutality toward peasants during the election campaign for the Provincial Diet in 1907–8, particularly after the death of one of the peasants, Sichynskyi made a decision to radicalize the methods of struggle. He blamed Count Andrzej Potocki, the governor of Galicia, for the situation of the Ukrainian people. Potocki opposed the Ukrainization of the university and sought to consolidate old-Ruthenian political parties, which were competitive with the Ukrainian parties.

On 12 April 1908 in Lemberg, Sichynskyi assassinated Count Potocki and subsequently offered no resistance when arrested. He was sentenced to death, and the sentence was upheld on appeal. At the suggestion of the new governor, **Michał Bobrzyński**, and, according to some sources, Count Potocki's widow, Krystyna Potocka, the emperor, reprieved Sichynskyi and commuted his death sentence to twenty years in prison. The assassination led to a sharp deterioration in Polish-Ukrainian relations in Galicia. Most Ukrainian politicians justified Sichynskyi's deed, and Sichynskyi himself became a symbol of heroism for the Ukrainian youth. On 10 November 1911, with the help of funds raised in Galicia and abroad, Sichynskyi succeeded in escaping from prison in Stanisławów (now Ivano-Frankivsk) and went to Berlin and then to Sweden. After the outbreak of World War I, Sichynskyi worked for the Ukrainian cause in the United States, where he led the Social Democratic movement among the émigré community. Despite protests by Polish politicians, he was granted an audience with U.S. President Woodrow Wilson, and then he submitted a letter to Wilson protesting the possible award of Eastern Galicia to Poland. During the interwar period Sichynskyi kept the American press informed about the situation of Ukraine and attempted to cause a reaction in the U.S. State Department on the issue of the pacification of Galicia in 1930. In 1940 Sichynskyi became one of the leaders of the Ukrainian Congress Committee of America, an organization that brought together Ukrainian pro-Allied émigré groups. After World War II, at the invitation of the Soviet government, Sichynskyi visited Ukraine, including Lviv, on several occasions. Until the end of his life Sichynskyi believed in the rightness of his act of 1908. (TS)

Sources: *PSB*, vol. 36; Józef Buszko, "Kryzys polityczny 1908 roku w Galicji," in *Księga pamiątkowa ku czci Konstantego Grzybowskiego* (Kraków, 1971); M. Demkovych-Dobrianskyi, *Pototskyi i Bobzhynskyi: Tsisarski namisnyky Halychyny, 1903–1913* (Rome, 1987).

SIDOR Karol (16 July 1901, Ružomberok–20 October 1953, Montreal), Slovak politician and writer. A close relative of Father **Andrej Hlinka**, after Hlinka's imprisonment in 1919, Sidor organized a protest strike at a Piarist gymnasium in Ružomberok, as a result of which he was expelled from school. In 1920 he began to study law, initially in Prague, later transferring to Bratislava, but he never graduated. Sidor was a co-founder and then editor of the Catholic literary monthly *Vatra* (1919–25). While a student, he became active in the Slovak autonomist movement, which increasingly sharply protested the centralist policies of the Prague government and the official doctrine, which stated that there was one Czechoslovak nation. From 1920 Sidor was editor and then editor-in-chief (1931–38) of the daily *Slovák*, a press organ of the Slovak People's Party, renamed Hlinka's Slovak People's Party (Hlinkova Slovenská Ľudová Strana [HSL'S]) in 1925. Sidor gradually became one of the closest associates of Hlinka. Sidor's articles were frequently censored, and in November 1932 he was sentenced to seven weeks in prison for publishing a critical letter from Hlinka in *Slovák*. As a result, Sidor, who was already seen as the leader of the young, progressive faction within the HSL'S, became even more popular.

From 1935 to 1939 Sidor sat in the parliament in Prague, where he strove for the implementation of the ethnic and religious demands of the HSL'S. He described his efforts in support of Slovak autonomy in the work *Slovenská politka na pôde pražského snemu 1918–1938* (Slovak policy in the parliament in Prague; 1943). He also participated in a parliamentary committee for foreign affairs. In the National Assembly, Sidor frequently attacked the policies of President **Edvard Beneš**. He maintained that instead of hoping for an alliance with remote France, Czechoslovakia should turn to Poland, which might protect the Slovaks from Czech centralism. He thought that a Polish-Czech-Slovak alliance would guarantee the security of the region. He expressed his Polonophilia in numerous press articles, as well as in the monograph *Cestou po Poľsku* (Traveling over Poland; 1927). On 28 September 1938, during the Munich crisis, Sidor and Father **Jozef Tiso** submitted a declaration to the Polish ambassador in Prague in which they proposed that Slovakia form a union with Poland in the case that Czechoslovak statehood was abolished.

After the death of Hlinka (August 1938), Sidor lost the race for the position of the HSL'S leader to Tiso, who became head of the Slovak government that was established after Slovakia gained autonomy in October 1938. On 1 December 1938 Sidor became a member of the central government headed by **Rudolf Beran**. As deputy prime minister, Sidor represented Slovak interests in this government. On 18 December 1938 he became an MP in the parliament in Bratislava and chief of the paramilitary Hlinka Guard (Hlinkova Garda [HG]). However, Sidor's political position and that of his supporters deteriorated after Poland occupied some territory in the north of Slovakia, including Javořina (Jaworzyna), in November 1938. Politicians with a pro-German orientation became increasingly influential in the HSL'S. On the night of 9–10 March 1939 the Czechoslovak authorities ordered the army onto the streets in Slovakia and dismissed the government of Tiso, whom they accused of separatism. Sidor became head of a new Slovak government. He re-

fused to proclaim Slovak independence, which the German emissaries demanded from him on 12 March 1939. After Hitler gave an ultimatum to Father Tiso, Sidor resigned his position. As a result, on 14 March 1939 the Slovak parliament proclaimed independence. Sidor briefly held the portfolio of minister of interior in the new government, but the Germans did not accept his political stance. Dismissed under pressure from Berlin, he assumed the post of Slovakia's ambassador to the Holy See in June 1939 and held this post until the end of World War II. Sidor described his diplomatic work in the memoirs *Šes_ rokov vo Vatikáne* (Six years in the Vatican; 1947).

In 1945 Sidor remained in exile. Granted political asylum, he organized assistance for Slovak refugees in Rome. In 1947 a Czechoslovak court sentenced him in absentia to twenty years' imprisonment. In October 1948 Sidor became president of the Slovak National Council Abroad (Slovenská Národná Rada v Zahraničí [SNRvZ]), whose program promoted the establishment of an independent Slovakia within the framework of a Central European bloc of nations. In 1950 Sidor moved to Canada. He was the leader of the Slovak émigré community in North America until the end of his life. His memoirs from March 1939 were published posthumously as *Moje poznámky k historickým dňom* (My comments on historical days; 1971) and *Takto vznikol slovenský štát* (How the Slovak state was established; 1991). (MG/PU)

Sources: *SBS*; *Biographisches Lexikon*, vol. 4; *Kto bol kto za I. ČSR* (Bratislava, 1993); *Politická elita meziválečného Československa 1918–1938: Kdo byl Kdo* (Prague, 1998); Jozef Paučo, *Karol Sidor: Politik, novinár, spisovateľ* (Middletown, Conn., 1962); Pavol Čarnogurský, "Deklarácia o únii Slovenska s Poľskom z 28.9.1938," *Historický časopis*, 1968; Jozef Kapala, *Spod Rohačov po Vatikan* (Galt, Ont., 1972); *Karol Sidor 1901–1953: Zborník zo seminára o Karolovi Sidorovi v Ružomberku 16.10. 1998* (Žilina, 2001).

SIDZIKAUSKAS Vaclovas (10 April 1893, Siaudine–2 December 1973, New York), Lithuanian Peasant Party politician, diplomat, and leader in exile. Sidzikauskas studied law in Moscow, Bern, and Kaunas. During World War I he was one of the organizers of the populist National Democratic Freedom League called Santara. In 1925 the league transformed itself into the Lithuanian Peasant Party. Between the wars Sidzikauskas was Lithuanian envoy to Switzerland, Germany, Austria, and Great Britain. While in London, he signed on behalf of Lithuania the "London convention" (5 July 1933), which defined the notion of aggression. Fearing arrest by the Soviets, in June 1940 Sidzikauskas left for Germany but was captured there by the Gestapo. Imprisoned in the camps in Soldau and Auschwitz, he was released in 1944 and was held under house arrest in Berlin. At the end of the war Sidzikauskas co-organized the Supreme Committee for the Liberation of Lithuania in Germany. In April 1947 he was elected president of this committee, which in 1950 moved to New York. He held the post until his death. In 1959 Sidzikauskas served as vice-president, and in 1960 as president, of the Assembly of Captive European Nations in New York. He repeatedly protested the incorporation of the Baltic states by the USSR, deportations, and the economic exploitation of these states by the Kremlin. (WR)

Sources: *EL*, vol. 5.

SIENKIEWICZ Henryk, pen name "Litwos" (5 May 1846, Wola Okrzejska, Podlasie–15 November 1916, Vevey, Switzerland), Polish novelist. Sienkiewicz came from an impoverished noble landowning family that settled in Warsaw. From 1866 to 1871, he studied at the Main School and at the Russian university in Warsaw, but he failed to graduate. From 1872 he contributed to the press. He contributed to the bi-monthly *Niwa*, which he co-owned, and to *Słowo* (1882–87). From 1876 to 1878 Sienkiewicz traveled in the United States, and from 1879, because of his wife's illness, took extended annual trips to Western Europe. Sienkiewicz's first works conformed with positivistic realism —for example, *Szkice węglem* (1880; *Charcoal Sketches*, 1990) and *Janko Muzykant* (1880; *Yanko the Musician*, 1893)—and put him in the spotlight with critics and readers. However, he became truly famous because of his trilogy: *Ogniem i mieczem* (1883–84; *With Fire and Sword*, 1890), *Potop* (1885; *The Deluge*, 1891), and *Pan Wołodyjowski* (1888; *Pan Michael*, 1905). The trilogy depicts the crisis of the Polish Noble Commonwealth of the seventeenth century and the attempts to overcome it. Sienkiewicz's literary heroes became extremely popular, and some of their utterances became colloquialisms in Polish. Following the death of his wife, Sienkiewicz traveled to Istanbul, Athens, Naples, Rome, Spain, and East Africa. The expeditions inspired him to write *Listy z podróży do Ameryki* (Letters from travels to America; 1876–78) and *Listy z Afryki* (Letters from Africa; 1891–92). Sienkiewicz frequently visited the resort town of Zakopane in southern Poland He was a devout Catholic, and a novel depicting the life of the first Christians, *Quo Vadis* (1896), brought him international fame and the Nobel Prize in literature in 1905. Sienkiewicz's psychological novel *Bez dogmatu* (1889–90; *Without Dogma*, 1893) aroused great interest, particularly abroad, and *Rodzina Połanieckich* (The Połaniecki family; 1895) did the same among Polish readers.

In 1900 Sienkiewicz published his next historical bestseller, *Krzyżacy* (*The Knights of the Cross*, 1900),

and in 1911 he published a popular novel for children, *W pustyni i w puszczy* (*In Desert and Wilderness*, 1912). In his works, he managed to combine a lively and flexible style of expression, largely realistic psychological portraits, and a patriotic message. His traditionalism caused a torrent of criticism from the adherents of modernism, who advocated social progress. Most notably, **Stanisław Brzozowski** accused Sienkiewicz of conservatism and of fostering indifference to the suffering of the lower classes. Despite the fact that most of his literary output came at the end of the nineteenth century, Sienkiewicz exerted an enormous amount of influence on many subsequent generations of Poles, who often yearned for patriotic prose "to fortify the heart," as Sienkiewicz himself put it. Aside from writing, Sienkiewicz supported the development of Polish culture. Among other things, he co-organized the Mianowski Fund for scholars and artists (Kasa im. Mianowskiego) and the self-help Fund of Prudence for Writers and Journalists. In 1900 Sienkiewicz celebrated a jubilee of his literary works, where he was recognized as the most popular Polish writer. To commemorate his achievement, the jubilee committee awarded him a small landed estate, Oblęgorek, near Kielce, where Sienkiewicz often spent his summers. During the revolution of 1905–7, Sienkiewicz demanded autonomy for the Polish Kingdom and appealed to the Poles to unite to achieve independence. However, he criticized the radicalism of the leaders of the revolution—for example, in his political novel *Wiry* (The guilts; 1910). Sienkiewicz was in Oblęgorek when World War I broke out, but he quickly left his estate and traveled through Kraków and Vienna to Switzerland. At Vevey, along with Antoni Osuchowski and **Ignacy Paderewski**, Sienkiewicz organized the General Committee to Aid War Victims in Poland, sending money, medicine, and food to his war-devastated country. (WR)

Sources: *Literatura polska: Przewodnik encyklopedyczny*, vol. 2 (Warsaw, 1985); Stanisław Brzozowski, *Henryk Sienkiewicz i jego stanowisko w literaturze współczesnej* (Warsaw, 1903); Julian Krzyżanowski, *Henryk Sienkiewicz: Kalendarz życia i twórczości* (Warsaw, 1956); Waclaw Lednicki, *Henryk Sienkiewicz: A Retrospective Synthesis* (The Hague, 1960); Julian Krzyżanowski, *Henryk Sienkiewicz: Żywot i sprawy* (Warsaw, 1976); Tadeusz Bujnicki, *Sienkiewicz i historia* (Warsaw, 1981).

SIERPIŃSKI Wacław (14 March 1882, Warsaw–21 October 1969, Warsaw), Polish mathematician. After high school Sierpiński studied at the Physical-Mathematical Department of Warsaw University (1900–4). He graduated with a gold medal for a thesis on numerical theory. In 1906 he received a Ph.D. at the Jagiellonian University in Kraków; in 1908 he became an associate professor (*docent*) and in 1910 a full professor at the university in

Lwów (Lviv). Interned during World War I by the Russian authorities, Sierpiński spent three years in Vyatka and Moscow, where he taught in Polish high schools. After his return to Poland, he resumed lecturing at Lwów University, and in 1919 he was appointed professor at Warsaw University. In 1920 Sierpiński co-founded the periodical *Fundamenta Mathematica*, which won international renown. He was also a co-founder of the Warsaw school of mathematics. He mostly dealt with the theory of great numbers, topology, and the theory of real functions. Sierpiński published (among other works) *Hypothèse du continu* (1934), *Introduction to General Typology* (1934), and *Elementary Theory of Numbers* (1964). In 1958–69 he was editor-in-chief of the only periodical in the world dealing with numerical theory, *Acta Arithmetica*. From 1917 he was a member of the Polish Academy of Arts and Sciences; from 1952 he was a member of the Polish Academy of Sciences (Polska Akademia Nauk [PAN]); and in 1931–51 he chaired the Warsaw Scientific Society. From 1952 to 1957 he was deputy chairman of the PAN. Sierpiński held honorary doctorates from universities in Amsterdam, Bordeaux, Lwów, Moscow, Paris, Prague, Sofia, and Tartu. (WR)

Sources: Andrzej Schinzel, *Wacław Sierpiński* (Warsaw, 1976); Krzysztof Kwasniewski and Lech Trzeciakowski, ed., *Polacy w historii i kulturze krajów Europy Zachodniej* (Poznań, 1981).

ŠIK Ota (11 September 1919, Plzen–22 August 2004, St. Gallen, Switzerland), Czech economist and Communist activist. One of the main founders of Czech Marxist economics, Šik dealt with issues concerning a planned economy and Socialist commodity relations. He joined the Communist Party of Czechoslovakia (CPC) in 1940. Between 1941 and 1945 he was imprisoned in a concentration camp. From 1953 he was a professor at the Higher School of Economics in Prague; in the 1960s he worked at the Czechoslovak Academy of Sciences in Prague. In 1958 he became a candidate member of the Central Committee of the CPC, and in 1962, a full member. From 1964 Šik directed work on the reform of the principles governing national economic policy and was the author of the basic premises of the reform. He attempted to combine the primary objectives of a centrally planned economy with elements of a market economy. From 1968 to 1969 Šik belonged to the Government Economic Council, and from 8 April 1968 to 3 September 1968 he was the deputy prime minister in the cabinet of **Oldřich Černik**, responsible for economic reform. As a supporter of the reformist movement after the Prague Spring, Šik was among those who were forced to withdraw from political life. In 1969 he emigrated to Switzerland. Between 1970 and 1989 he was a professor at the universities of St. Gallen and Zurich. In 1983 he was granted Swiss citizenship. After the Velvet Revolution in 1989, Šik returned for a short time to Czechoslovakia, where he became a member of the Council of Consultants of President **Václav Havel**. However, having no real influence upon economic decisions, Šik returned to Switzerland; from there he critically observed the transformations in the country. Šik authored (among other works) the following: *Plán a trh za socalismu* (Planning and market in socialism; 1967); *Třetí česta* (The third way; 1972); *For a Human Economic Democracy* (1985); and *Wirtschaftssysteme* (Economic systems; 1987), as well as the memoirs *Prager Frühlingserwachen* (The Prague Spring awakening; 1988). (PU)

Sources: *ČBS*; *Kdo był kdo v našich dějinách ve 20. stoleti*, vol. 2 (Prague, 1998); René Höltschi, *Bausteine für Alternativen: Ota Sik's Dritter Weg in ein Wirtschaftsssytem der Bachmoderne* (Grüsch, 1985); Zdeněk Mlynář, *Nightfrost in Prague: The End of Humane Socialism* (New York, 1980).

SIKORSKI Władysław Eugeniusz, pseudonyms "Władek" and "Orliński" (20 May 1881, Tuszów Narodowy, near Mielec–4 July 1943, Gibraltar), Polish general and politician. While still in high school, Sikorski joined secret self-education organizations and the Society of People's Schools (Towarzystwo Szkoły Ludowej). In 1902 he enrolled in the Department of Roads and Bridges of the Lemberg (Lwów, Lviv) Polytechnic. He joined the Union of Polish Youth (Związek Młodzieży Polskiej), which was tied to the National League and later to the Union for the Rebirth of the Polish Nation (Związek Odrodzenia Narodu Polskiego), which worked with the Polish Socialist Party. In 1904 Sikorski was drafted into the Austrian Army for a year and dismissed with the rank of second lieutenant of reserves. He lectured on military tactics in secret Polish organizations that sought independence. In 1908, he co-organized the Union for Active Struggle (Związek Walki Czynnej), and he joined its Main Council. After earning a diploma in hydraulic engineering, Sikorski worked in the Department of Water Works in Lwów. In 1910 he founded a chapter of the Riflemen's Association (Związek Strzelecki) there. In 1912 he advocated the creation of the Polish Rifle Federation. Sikorski was active in the Polish Progressive Party (Polskie Stronnictwo Postępowe), which demanded voting rights for women and the secularization of the schools. In November 1912, he co-founded the Provisional Commission of Confederated Independentist Parties (Komisai Tymczasowa Skonfederowanych Stronnictw Niepodległościowych), which supported Austria-Hungary. Working with **Józef Piłsudski**, Sikorski became the commission's clerk for military affairs and then controller of its Military Department in Lesser Poland and the Kingdom of Poland.

Following the outbreak of World War I, Piłsudski appointed Sikorski as the commissar plenipotentiary of the National Government for Galicia, then a member of the Chief National Committee (Naczelny Komitet Narodowy), and later chief of its Military Department. Gradually, however, Sikorski became critical of Piłsudski's endeavor to form the Polish Legions and his policy of searching for allies. In contrast to Piłsudski's pro-German orientation, Sikorski preferred an Austro-Hungarian alliance. In October 1914, Sikorski organized the School for Officer Cadets in Kraków, which he commanded. In December 1914 he carried out recruitment for the Legions in the Kingdom of Poland. In August 1916, following the transformation of the Polish Legions into the Polish Auxiliary Corps (Polski Korpus Posiłkowy), he commanded the Third Infantry Regiment. Following the act of 5 November 1916, by which the German and Austro-Hungarian emperors promised to create the Kingdom of Poland, Sikorski participated in the creation of the Polish Armed Forces (Polska Siła Zbrojna). During the oath crisis of July 1917, Sikorski stayed in service and took over the command of the Staff Headquarters of the Reserve of the Polish Auxiliary Corps in Bolechów. For cooperating with General **Józef Haller** (in the breakthrough of the Second Polish Brigade at Rarańcza and its escape to the Russian side) and for refusing to acknowledge the validity of the Treaty of Brest (9 March 1918), Sikorski was interned at a POW camp in Hungary (February–May 1918). Upon his return to Lwów, he clandestinely organized Polish military cadres.

At the beginning of November 1918, Sikorski was appointed by the Regency Council to be the chief of staff of the Command for Eastern Galicia and Silesia. He then joined the newly formed Polish Army (Wojsko Polskie). He participated in organizing the defense of Przemyśl and later became chief quartermaster in the newly formed Command–East. In January 1919 Sikorski led an operational group and in March 1919 an infantry division in the defense of Lwów. In August 1919, he took command of the Polesie Group and the Ninth Infantry Division, organizing the Polish lines of defense among the Styr and Słucz Rivers. In April 1920, Sikorski was promoted to brigadier general. During the Kiev offensive he reached the Dnieper River. In August 1920 he was put in command of the Fifth Army, fighting near the Wkra River, and he contributed significantly to the Polish victory in the Battle of Warsaw. Then he became commander of the Third Army (fighting in Volhynia and Polesia) and later of the new Third Army, which fought in the Vilnius area. In February 1921, he was promoted to major general.

In April 1921, Sikorski became chief of the General Staff of the Polish Army. He devoted much attention to the defense of the state from outside aggression; he thus advocated the parity of treatment of Germany and Russia and the need to preserve the European status quo as the foundation of Poland's foreign policy. He supported close links with France. Although he was accused of vanity, his superior leadership and organizational skills were appreciated. On Sikorski's initiative, Honor and Fatherland (Honor and Ojczyzna) was established at the end of 1921 or the beginning of 1922. It was a secret organization of military officers who opposed Piłsudski. Following the assassination of President **Gabriel Narutowicz**, Sikorski became prime minister and minister of interior on 16 December 1922. He managed to calm the nation, and in March 1923, at the Conference of Ambassadors, he achieved recognition for Poland's eastern borders. After the fall of his government (26 May 1923), Sikorski traveled in France for a few months. Upon his return, from November 1923 to February 1924, he served as chief inspector of the infantry. On 17 February 1924, he became minister for military affairs in the government of **Władysław Grabski**. Sikorski initiated changes in military law, prepared the initial plans for operations and mobilization, organized first maneuvers, and fostered an increase in the defensive potential of the nation. He also initiated the formation of the Borderlands Defense Corps (Korpus Ochrony Pogranicza) to protect Poland's eastern border. Sikorski published prodigiously and maintained numerous political contacts. He distanced himself even further from Piłsudski, who considered Sikorski his rival. In December 1925, Sikorski became the commander of the Lwów Army Corps. During the coup d'état of May 1926, he remained neutral.

In March 1928, Sikorski was dismissed and transferred to the direct jurisdiction of the minister of military affairs. He then devoted himself to studying defense matters and international affairs. He spent a lot of time in France. He correctly foresaw the future of warfare in Europe, stressing the primacy of tanks. From 1928 Sikorski strengthened his links with French politicians and with **Wincenty Witos** and **Ignacy Paderewski**. In 1936, he co-organized a concord of liberal-democratic forces in the so-called Front Morges. In 1937, he participated in the foundation of the (Christian Democratic) Labor Party (Stronnictwo Pracy). In March 1939, he returned to Poland. On 24 August 1939, he reported to Marshal **Edward Rydz-Śmigły** to secure an active commission in the army, but he was turned down.

On 18 September 1939 Sikorski crossed over to Romania and then left for France. On 28 September in Paris he was appointed the chief-in-command of Polish military units in France; on 30 September he became prime minister and minister for military affairs of the Polish government-in-exile, and on 7 November he was proclaimed the commander-in-chief and the chief inspector of the Polish Armed Forces. His position was strengthened following an announcement by President **Władysław Raczkiewicz**, who declared that he would carry out his duties only in strict cooperation with the prime minister. On 13 November 1939, to continue the struggle at home, Sikorski substituted the secret Service for the Victory of Poland (Służba Zwycięstwu Polski) with the Union for Armed Struggle (Związek Walki Zbrojnej), which in February 1942 was redesignated the Home Army (Armia Krajowa). He also created the office of the Home Government Delegate (Delegat Rządu na Kraj).

After the fall of France in June 1940, Sikorski carried out the evacuation of the government and military to Great Britain. He backed the idea of a close political union with Czechoslovakia. He endeavored to secure the support of the United States for the idea of a central European federation. In December 1940, Sikorski was promoted to general of the army. On 30 July 1941, he concluded a pact in Moscow normalizing Soviet-Polish relations. Its result was "an amnesty" for Polish citizens deported and imprisoned in the USSR, as well as the creation of a Polish army there. Until June 1942, in an effort to maintain proper relations with Stalin, Sikorski opposed the total evacuation of the Polish army from the Soviet Union. The opposition accused Sikorski of betraying the national interest. Sikorski strove to secure just and equal relations with the USSR, while insisting on the reconstruction of an independent Poland with its eastern borders in tact. Sikorski's government found itself in a precariously difficult situation following the discovery of mass graves of Polish officers at Katyn in April 1943. When the Polish government asked the International Red Cross to investigate the matter, the Kremlin broke diplomatic relations with the Poles. On his way back to London following the inspection of Polish military units in the Middle East, Sikorski perished tragically in an air crash. The circumstances of his death still remain murky. The most plausible speculation is that the general was assassinated by the Soviet secret services. Sikorski was buried at the cemetery for airmen at Newark, Great Britain. On 17 September 1993, his ashes were buried at the cathedral on Wawel Hill in Kraków. In London, the Polish Institute and a museum bearing his name were created. Sikorski was the author of many works, including the following: *O polską politykę państwową* (For a Polish state policy; 1923); *Nad Wisłą i*

Wkrą. Studium z polsko-rosyjskiej wojny 1920 roku (By the Vistula and Wkra: A study of the Polish-Russian war of 1920; 1928); *Polska i Francja w przeszłości i w dobie obecnej* (Poland and France in the past and in contemporary times; 1931); and *Przyszła wojna, jej możliwości i charakter oraz związane z nią zagadnienia obrony kraju* (1934; *Modern Warfare*, 1943). (JS)

Sources: *PSB*, vol. 37; Karol Popiel, *Generał Sikorski w mojej pamięci* (London, 1978); Olgierd Terlecki, *Generał Sikorski* (Kraków, 1981); Roman Wapiński, *Władysław Sikorski* (Warsaw, 1982); Józef Garliński, *Poland in the Second World War* (New York, 1985); Walentyna Korpalska, *Władysław Eugeniusz Sikorski: Biografia polityczna* (Wrocław, 1988); Tadeusz Panecki, *Generał broni Władysław Eugeniusz Sikorski (1881–1943)* (Warsaw, 1993); Piotr Stawecki, *Słownik biograficzny generałów Wojska Polskiego, 1918–1939* (Warsaw, 1994); Marian Kukiel, *Generał Sikorski: Żołnierz i mąż stanu Polski Walczącej* (London, 1995); Roman Horyń, *Generał Sikorski w świetle dokumentów* (Warsaw, 1996).

SILAJDŽIĆ Haris (1 September 1945, Breza, near Sarajevo), Muslim politician from Bosnia. In 1971 Silajdžić graduated in Arab and Islamic studies from Benghazi University in Libya. For more than a year he continued with doctoral studies in the United States, studying the U.S.-Albanian relationship. In 1980 he received a Ph.D. Upon his return home he lectured at the University of Priština. For several years he also worked in Libya. A member of the Muslim Supreme Board in Sarajevo, in 1990 Silajdžić joined the electoral campaign of **Alija Izetbegović**, who ran for the presidency of the Presidium of the (Yugoslav) Republic of Bosnia and Herzegovina. After Izetbegović won, Silajdžić became minister of foreign affairs (December 1990–October 1993) and then prime minister (25 October 1993–30 January 1996) of the country, which proclaimed independence in 1992. During the war in Bosnia-Herzegovina, Silajdžić appealed to the international community for intervention that would prevent the ethnic cleansing of Bosnian Muslims and demanded a lifting of the international ban on arms supplies to Bosnia-Herzegovina. He took part in negotiating the Dayton Agreement of 1995, which terminated the war. From 31 May 1994 to 31 January 1996 Silajdžić was prime minister of the Muslim-Croat Federation within Bosnia-Herzegovina. He resigned from his position and from chairing the Party of Democratic Action to establish his own Party for Bosnia and Herzegovina (Stranka za Bosnu i Hercegovinu). In September 1996 he ran for president of Bosnia-Herzegovina, but he lost to Izetbegović. From 3 January 1997 to 6 April 2000 Silajdžić co-ran the government of Bosnia-Herzegovina, rotating every week with Boro Bosić (until 3 February 1999) and later with Svetozar Mihajlović. Among other works, Silajdžić authored *Za Bosnu i Hercegovinu: Izbor* *iz dokumentacije Harisa Silajdžića* (For Bosnia-Herze-govina: Selections from Haris Silaidžić's Documentation; 1998) and *Na putu ka modernoj državi* (On the road to a modern statehood; 2000). (AO)

Sources: David Owen, *Balkan Odyssey* (New York, San Diego, and London, 1995); Laura Silber and Allan Little, *The Death of Yugoslavia* (London, 1995); Warren Zimmermann, *Origins of a Catastrophe* (New York and Toronto, 1996); Richard Holbrooke, *To End a War* (New York, 1998); Ante Čuvalo, *Historical Dictionary of Bosnia and Herzegovina* (Lanham, Md., 1997); Bugajski; www.rulers.org.

SIŁA-NOWICKI Władysław (22 June 1913, Warsaw–25 February 1994, Warsaw), Polish lawyer and political activist. In 1935 Siła-Nowicki graduated in law from Warsaw University. A participant in the September 1939 campaign, from 1941 he was active in the Union of Armed Struggle and the Home Army as a member of an underground Catholic organization, Unia. In 1943 he joined the underground Labor Party (Stronnictwo Pracy [SP]). He took part in the Warsaw Uprising and was decorated with the Cross of Valor. From 1945 to 1946 Siła-Nowicki served as vice-president of the SP Provincial Board in Lublin. He was also in the underground organization Freedom and Independence (Wolność i Niezawisłość [WiN]), initially as head of propaganda and, in 1946, as commander of the Lublin Town District. He was also deputy inspector and, from November 1946 inspector, of the Lublin WiN. After the amnesty of 22 February 1947 Siła-Nowicki entered into talks with the Communist security services to allow forest detachments to come out of hiding. Arrested on 16 September 1947 and sentenced to death, he had his sentence commuted to life imprisonment after the intervention of his aunt, who was the sister of **Feliks Dzerzhinsky**. On 1 December 1956 he was released and acquitted.

From 1959 Siła-Nowicki worked as a lawyer. He pleaded the cases of former Home Army soldiers, priests, and Jehovah's Witnesses, as well as the case of a conspiracy called Ruch (1971). In 1968 and 1969 his right to practice law was suspended. Siła-Nowicki was legal adviser to the Polish Episcopate. In 1961 he became a member of the Club of Catholic Intellectuals (Klub Inteligencji Katolickiej [KIK]) in Warsaw. In 1968 he stated that members of the parliamentary group Znak should resign in protest against the invasion of Czechoslovakia. From 1975 to 1976 Siła-Nowicki participated in a protest action against amendments to the constitution, and he was a signatory of the "Letter of 59." After the events of June 1976 he was an attorney in the trials of the participants in these events, and he was a close co-worker of the Committee for the Defense of Workers (Komitet Obrony Robotników [KOR]). In

1980 he co-authored the statute of the Independent Self-Governing Trade Union Solidarity (NSZZ Solidarność). He subsequently was an expert on Solidarity's National Coordination Commission (Krajowa Komisja Porozumiewawcza) and one of the advisers to **Lech Wałęsa**. During talks with the government Siła-Nowicki supported a moderate line. During martial law he was a lawyer in political trials, but in 1983 he was superannuated. In 1986 he became a member of the Consultative Council to the President of the State Council, General **Wojciech Jaruzelski**. Siła-Nowicki took part as an adviser in the strikes of 1988, and he tried to initiate talks between the strikers and General **Czesław Kiszczak**.

Siła-Nowicki was at odds with Solidarity leaders over their tactics and took part in the Round Table Talks in 1989 as an independent politician invited by the government. Critical about the adopted agreement, he worked with the so-called Solidarity Working Group (Grupa Robocza Solidarności), which was in opposition to the leadership of the union. In the elections of June 1989 Siła-Nowicki ran against **Jacek Kuroń** but lost. In 1989–92 he served as president of the board of the Christian Democratic Labor Party and later as its honorary president. In 1992 Siła-Nowicki was elected a judge of the Tribunal of State. (AF)

Sources: *Opozycja w PRL: Słownik biograficzny 1956–89* (Warsaw 2000); Aniela Steinsbergowa, *Widziane z ławy obrończej* (Paris, 1977); Andrzej Friszke, *Opozycja polityczna w PRL 1945–1980* (London, 1994); Janusz Zabłocki, *Chrześcijańska demokracja w kraju i na emigracji 1947–1970* (Lublin, 1999).

SIMA Horia (3 June 1906, Mândra, Transylvania–25 May 1993, Augsburg, Germany), Romanian Fascist politician. In 1926 Sima began to study at the School of Literature and Philosophy at Bucharest University. In 1927 he joined the mystical nationalist Legion of the Archangel Michael (Legiunea Arhangelul Mihail), also called the Legion or Legionary Movement. It later became known as the Iron Guard (Gărdia de Fier). Sima was a student of **Nae Ionescu**, one of the main ideologues of the Legion. After graduating in 1932, Sima became a teacher of Romanian in Caransebeş, Banat. In 1935 **Corneliu Codreanu-Zelea**, the leader of the Iron Guard, appointed Sima head of the Ninth District of the Legion in Banat. After King **Charles II** established a dictatorship and then ordered the arrest of Codreanu, as well as hundreds of other Legionnaires, in the spring of 1938, Sima became leader of the Iron Guard. He quickly restructured the organization, which went underground and began to assassinate its political opponents. In December 1938, after Codreanu and a dozen or so Legion leaders were killed on the orders of the king, Sima fled to Germany, which supported and financed his movement. From August to October 1939 Sima secretly lived in Romania, where he tried to consolidate his leadership, and then returned to Berlin. In May 1940 he again crossed the Romanian border but was arrested. Because Sima and the Iron Guard enjoyed the support of Germany and King Charles' position was weak, in June 1940, in an attempt to gain the support of the Iron Guard, Charles invited the Legionnaires to join the new government. Sima assumed the portfolio of minister of education, but a few days later, in July 1940, he resigned this post owing to the opposition of the majority of the Legionnaires.

In early September 1940, following an unsuccessful attempt by the Iron Guard to take over power, Charles II appointed General **Ion Antonescu**, who held moderate pro-German views, as prime minister. On Hitler's request, Antonescu formed a government in alliance with the Iron Guard. Romania was proclaimed a "National Legionary State." Sima was appointed deputy prime minister. His Legionnaires pursued a campaign of political assassinations and conducted pogroms of Jews. In January 1941 the Legionnaires instigated fighting in Bucharest, and Sima resigned as deputy prime minister. He demanded that Antonescu be dismissed, claiming the post of prime minister for himself. The Romanian Army, which was faithful to Antonescu, suppressed the Iron Guard and, by 23 January of that year, was in control of the situation. Hitler lent his support to Antonescu because he needed the Romanian Army for a planned attack against the Soviet Union. Sima and his closest associates took refuge in the Third Reich. They served as an alternative for Hitler in the case of Antonescu's disobedience. Sima was interned in Sachsenhausen and other camps. After the coup d'état of 23 August 1944 and the overthrow of Antonescu, Sima was taken to Vienna, where he became head of a puppet Romanian government. In February 1945, in the face of the collapse of Germany, his government was moved to Alt-Aussee, as it had no chance of operating in Romanian territory. After the end of World War II, Sima made his way, via France and Italy, to Argentina and thence to Spain, where he lived safely until the end of his life. In 1946 in Communist Romania he was sentenced to death in absentia. In 1949 he apologized to the Romanian political émigrés for his anti-royalist attitude in 1944. Sima lectured at a university in Barcelona. He also published papers on Fascist and Iron Guard doctrines, as well as on Romanian history and the history of the Legionary Movement. (LW)

Sources: Andrzej Koryn, *Rumunia w polityce wielkich mocarstw 1944–1947* (Wrocław, 1983); Józef Darski, *Rumunia: Historia, współczesność, konflikty narodowe* (Warsaw, 1995); Vlad Georgescu, *Istoria Românilor de la origini pînă în zilele noastre* (Oakland, 1984); Ion Alexandrescu, Ion Bulei, Ion Mamina, and Ioan Scurtu, *Enciclopedia de istorie României* (Bucharest, 2000); *Dictionar Enciclopedic*, vol. 3 (Bucharest, 1999); Krzysztof Dach and Tadeusz Dubicki, *Żelazny Legion Michała Archanioła* (Warsaw, 1996); Philip Rees, *Biographical Dictionary of the Extreme Right since 1890* (New York, 1990); www.miscarea-legionara.org.

ŠIMEČKA Milan (7 April 1930, Nový Bohumín–24 September 1990, Prague), Czech political scientist, essayist, and literary critic active in Slovakia. From 1949 to 1953 Šimečka studied Czech and Russian literature at Masaryk University in Brno and then worked as a teacher of Czech in Kroměříž for one year. In 1954 he went to Bratislava and became an assistant at the department of Marxism-Leninism at the university there. In 1957 he transferred to the School of Musical Arts, where he did research on the history of social utopias. At that time he published two books devoted to this issue: *Sociálne utópie a utopisti* (Social utopias and utopians; 1963) and *Kríza utopizmu* (The crisis of utopianism; 1968). The latter was also his dissertation for the postdoctoral degree. In 1967–68, as a scholarship holder, Šimečka lectured at the Institute of European History. During the Prague Spring he repeatedly expressed critical assessments of the situation in the country. During the so-called normalization period he was expelled from the Communist Party of Czechoslovakia and was subsequently banned from publishing his works. Dismissed from the university, he worked as a blue-collar laborer.

In Bratislava Šimečka was one of the few active opponents of the "normalization" policy. Along with Miroslav Kusý, he organized samizdat publishing operations, and in 1977 he signed Charter 77. His book *Obnovení pořádku: Příspěvek k typologii reálného socialismu* (The restoration of order: The normalization of Czechoslovakia, 1969–1976; Cologne, 1979; with a preface by **Zdenek Mlynar**, 1984) was an émigré publication and is an account of the Communist regime's "normalization" policy and its negative influence on the society. Arrested in 1981, Šimečka was kept in prison for over one year, although he had not been convicted. After his release, he earned his living as a writer. In 1984 he wrote the essay "Náš soudruh Winston Smith" (Our comrade Winston Smith), influenced by George Orwell's *1984*. The year 1985 saw the publication of *Kruhová obrana* (The full resistance), a collection of columns by Šimečka that were a defense against the repressive atmosphere of "normalization." Owing to his prison experience, Šimečka became convinced that socialism was impossible to reform and that a leadership change would not be sufficient since a change of the system was necessary. He expounded his views most fully in his last book, *Koniec nehybnosti* (The end of idleness;

1989). After the Velvet Revolution, Šimečka consistently refused to accept any academic or political positions, and it was only after a personal request by **Václav Havel** in 1990 that he agreed to become chairman of a council of presidential advisers. (PU)

Sources: *ČBS*; Vilém Prečan, "Velké a malé dějiny Milana Šimečky," *Slovenské pohľady*, 1992, no. 1; *Kdo byl kdo v našich dějinách ve 20. století*, vol. 2 (Prague, 1998); *Slovník českých filozofů* (Brno, 1998).

SIMEON II Saxe-Coburg-Gotha [or Sakskoburggotski] (16 June 1937, Sofia), tsar (1943–46) and prime minister of Bulgaria. The son of Tsar **Boris III** and Tsarina Joanna (formerly Princess Giovanna, the daughter of Italian king Victor Emmanuel III), Simeon was only six years old when his father died; therefore, a three-man Regency Council was established to rule Bulgaria on behalf of the minor heir to the throne; it consisted of **Bogdan Filov**, General **Nikola Mikhov**, and Simeon's uncle, **Kiril**. After the Communists seized power, their rigged referendum of 8 October 1946 abolished the monarchy, and Simeon and his mother and sister went into exile in Egypt, where his grandfather, the dethroned king of Italy, also lived. Simeon attended Victoria College in Alexandria. In 1951 the royal family was granted asylum in Spain, and Simeon entered the Lycée Français in Madrid. In 1959 he graduated from the Valley Forge Military Academy in the United States, where he was known as "Cadet Rylski." In 1962 he married the Spanish aristocrat Margarita Gomez-Acebo y Cejuela, with whom he had four sons and one daughter. For many years Simeon pursued a successful business career. He never formally abdicated.

Shortly after the collapse of the Communist regime in Bulgaria (November 1989), some politicians, including **Stefan Savov**, **Konstantin Trenchev**, and **Filip Dimitrov**, called for the restoration of the monarchy and for the reinstatement of Simeon to the throne, but at that time the idea did not gain the support of the majority of Bulgarians. In January 1990 Simeon announced that he was ready to return to Bulgaria, not as tsar but as a person who might be useful to his country owing to his experience and contacts. It is believed that he was greatly influenced in this decision by King Juan Carlos, who had been instrumental in Spain's transition from Francoism to democracy. For a long time, a referendum on the restoration of the monarchy was considered, but after a republican constitution was adopted in June 1991, such a restoration was no longer on the agenda. In 1993 the issue was raised again in a public debate, but no conclusion was reached. In May 1996 Simeon and his wife visited Bulgaria, where he was very warmly welcomed.

In 1998 the Constitutional Court ordered restitution to the royal family of its property in Bulgaria.

After less than four years in power, the popularity of the Union of Democratic Forces (UDF) and Prime Minister **Ivan Kostov** dropped drastically as a result of only a slow improvement in the economic situation. Simeon returned to Bulgaria (6 April 2001) and founded the National Movement Simeon II (Natsionalno Dvizhenie Simeon Vtori). He promised an improvement in the economic situation of the poorest and a restoration of law and order, as well as a general continuation of privatization and the pro-Western foreign policy. In his election campaign, he won the support of people disappointed by the rule of the UDF and the post-Communists. In the elections of 17 June 2001 the National Movement Simeon II scored unexpected success, receiving 42.7 percent of the vote and 120 out of 240 seats. One week later, Simeon became head of a government formed in coalition with the Turkish Movement for Rights and Freedoms. Simeon is the first former European monarch of the twentieth century to have returned to power in his former country. Because progress in the implementation of the election promises was rather slow, the popularity of his government soon diminished, but Simeon succeeded in maintaining relative domestic stability, and he intensified efforts to secure Bulgaria's admission into NATO and the European Union. (WR)

Sources: Raymond Detrez, *Historical Dictionary of Bulgaria* (Lanham, Md. 1997); George Knupffer, *King Simeon II of Bulgaria* (London, 1969); *Nogov Tsarsko Velichestvo Simeon Kniaz Turnovski, Bulgarski Prestolonaslednik* (La Mesa, Calif., 1983); Stanko Mikhailov, *Tsar Simeon II* (Sofia, 2001); Bugajski; Ramón Pérez-Maura, *El rey posible: Simeon de Bulgaria* (Barcelona, 2002); www.government.bg.

SIMONE André [originally Otto Katz] (27 May 1895 or 1900, Prague–3 September 1952, Prague), Communist activist mainly associated with Czechoslovakia. The son of a Jewish textile industrialist, in his youth Simone was friends with **Franz Kafka**. Thanks to his family's financial support, he published several of Kafka's plays, but they were unsuccessful. In 1922 Simone joined the Communist Party of Germany (CPG) and took charge of a radical leftist publishing house. In 1928 he began to work with Soviet intelligence. In 1932–33 he lived in the Soviet Union and then went to France, where he took the pseudonym of André Simone and became the right-hand man of Willy Münzenberg, head of propaganda and disinformation of the Communist International and a former leader of the CPG. Simone co-founded the International Committee for Aid to Victims of Nazi Fascism, which organized the "Leipzig counter-trial" in London.

After the Molotov-Ribbentrop Pact was signed in August 1939, Münzenberg criticized Stalin, and in October 1940 Simone allegedly took part in the execution of Münzenberg. Subsequently, as a German political refugee, he made his way via Portugal to the United States, where he organized the Soviet intelligence network. He then had to escape from the FBI to Mexico and subsequently returned to the Soviet Union. When the Red Army marched into Czechoslovakia in 1945, Simone became head of NKVD headquarters in Prague. In 1946 he joined the Communist Party of Czechoslovakia (CPC). After the coup of February 1948, he became chief of Czechoslovak intelligence, although officially he was the press director in the Ministry of Foreign Affairs. There are suspicions that Simone was instrumental in the alleged suicide of **Jan Masaryk**. In 1951 Simone became entangled in the case of Noel Field, which had been prepared by the services of the Soviet Union and other Communist bloc countries. As part of the purge of the apparatus of power in Czechoslovakia, Simone was accused of being involved in an "anti-state conspiracy center" and in a "Zionist plot." On 27 November 1952, after a one-week trial, he was sentenced to death and then executed, along with **Rudolf Slánský** and nine other defendants. In 1963 Simone was posthumously reinstated to membership in the CPC. (WR)

Sources: Eugen Loebl, *Stalinism in Prague: The Loebl Story* (New York, 1969); Jiři Pelikán, *The Czechoslovak Political Trials, 1950–1954* (Stanford, 1971); R. Seth, *Encyclopedia of Espionage* (Aylesbury, 1972); Roger Faligot and Remi Kauffer, *Służby specjalne: Historia wywiadu i kontrwywiadu na świecie* (Warsaw, 1998).

SIMOVIĆ Dušan (9 November 1882, Kagujevac–26 August 1962, Belgrade), Serbian general and politician. In 1900 Simović graduated from a military academy. He took part in the Balkan Wars (1912–13) and subsequently fought in World War I as the chief of staff of a division. Between world wars Simović held several military positions, including that of commander of the second divisional district. Until the fall of 1940 he served as chief of staff of the army, and then he became commander-in-chief of the Yugoslav air force. Simović authored the textbooks—for example, *Taktika vazduhoplovstva* (Air force tactics; 1928) and *Savremene ratne doktrine* (Modern military doctrines; 1939). After the outbreak of World War II, from 1939 onwards Simović helped in the intensive development of the military forces. He had a critical attitude toward Yugoslavia's rapprochement with the Axis countries. The British and American diplomats supported his stance, particularly as Simović promised them that Yugoslavia would fight against Italy and Germany. Simović hoped for

British aid to Yugoslavia and believed that Great Britain, supported by the United States, would defeat Germany.

After Prince Regent Paul and Prime Minister **Dragiša Cvetković** signed the protocol on Yugoslavia's accession to the Tripartite Pact in Vienna (25 March 1941), a military coup d'état was staged in Belgrade on the night of 26–27 March 1941. As a result of this coup, Prince **Peter** ascended to the throne and Simović became head of the government. In order to alleviate the tensions between the Serbs and Croats, Simović invited **Vladko Maček**, leader of the Croatian Peasant Party, to join his government. In Belgrade, people demonstrated their support for the coup. Initially Simović tried to proceed with caution and declared that there would be no major changes in Yugoslavia's policy, but the German reaction to the coup was definitely hostile. Seeking foreign support, Simović and Minister of Foreign Affairs **Momčilo Ninčić** entered into negotiations with John Dill, the British chief of staff. On the night of 5–6 April Simović also signed a treaty of friendship and non-aggression with the Soviet Union. However, his efforts did not prevent the invasion of Yugoslavia by the Third Reich, which took place on 6 April. Simović became chief of the general staff of the Yugoslav army, which was soon defeated. On 14 April 1941 Simović resigned his command, and, along with the government, he went into exile in Great Britain. He sought to obtain British aid for the underground army led by General **Dragoljub (Draža) Mihailović** in occupied Yugoslavia, but the British help was relatively small. The Kremlin, which supported the Communist Partisans led by **Josip Broz Tito**, had an even more negative attitude toward Simović's government. On 12 January 1942 Simović resigned as prime minister of the government-in-exile. In February 1944, when the Communists were in control of a substantial part of Yugoslavia, Simović saw that it was necessary to reach a compromise with Tito, and in May 1945 he returned to Yugoslavia. However, he did not play any political role. (WR)

Sources: *Biographisches Lexikon*, vol. 4; Constantin Fotitch, *The War We Lost* (New York, 1948); Peter II, King of Yugoslavia, *A King's Heritage* (New York, 1954); Vlatko Maček, *In the Struggle for Freedom* (London, 1957); Jacob B. Hoptner, *Yugoslavia in Crisis, 1934–41* (New York, 1962); Ferdo Čulinović, *Jugoslavija izmedju dva rata*, vols. 1–2 (Zagreb, 1971); Michał Jerzy Zacharias, *Jugosławia w polityce Wielkiej Brytanii 1940–1945* (Wrocław, 1985).

SINGER Isaac (Icchok) Bashevis, pseudonyms "Icchok Warszawski" and "D. Segał" (14 July 1907, Leoncin, near Radzymin–24 July 1991, Miami, Florida), Jewish writer from Poland. Singer was the son of an unofficial rabbi of the poor. Raised in Warsaw (1908–17) and Biłgoraj

(1917–22), he worked as an editor for *Literarisze Bleter* and a translator into Yiddish of the works of Erich Maria Remarque, Thomas Mann, and Stefan Zweig. The award-winning short story "Ojf der elter" (Old age) was his literary debut in 1925. From the early 1930s Singer worked with the Warsaw monthly *Globus*. In 1933, he published the novel *Szatan w Goraju* (Satan in Goraj), considered one of his most important works.

In 1935 Singer emigrated to the United States. He worked for the New York daily *Forverts*, writing literary criticisms, editorials, short stories, and serialized novels, including *Der zindiker Moshiekh* (Moses the Sinner; 1935–36); *Familie Mushkat* (The Mushkat family; 1945); *Gimpl tan* (Gimpal the idiot; 1950); *Oseh ha-nifla'ot mi-Lublin* (The magician from Lublin; 1960); *Der knecht* (The slave; 1962); *Der Hojf* (The court; 1967); *Der man fun chalojmes* (A dreamer; 1970–71); *Sonim* (Enemies; 1972); *Der baal tszuve* (Penitent; 1974); and *Shosha* (1978). Some of Singer's short story collections were translated simultaneously into English—for example, *Short Friday* (1965) and *Death of Methuselah and Other Stories* (1988). Singer focused on the philosophical and religious problems of the Orthodox and assimilated Jews. His works contain autobiographical elements and reveal his links to Poland. In some of his novels—*Der kenig fun di felder* (The king of fields; 1988), for example—he drew a broad historical background of Jewish life in Poland. The author of several hundred stories and novels gradually translated into English, Singer was recognized by critics for the art of narration in his novellas. In 1978 he was awarded the Nobel Prize for literature. In postwar Poland Singer was completely glossed over in silence until 1978, when he became a best-selling author recalling the joint Polish-Jewish heritage. (WR)

Sources: *Encyclopedia Britannica*, vol. 10 (Chicago, 1948); *Britannica Book of the Year 1992*; *Nowa encyklopedia powszechna PWN*, vol. 5 (Warsaw, 1996); Irving Malin, *Isaac Bashevis Singer* (New York, 1972); Edward Alexander, *Isaac Bashevis Singer* (Boston, 1980); Lawrence S. Friedman, *Understanding Isaac Bashevis Singer* (Columbia, S.C., 1988); Chome Shmeruk, *Historia literatury jidysz* (Warsaw, 1992); Frances Gibbons Vargas, *Transgression and Self-Punishment in Isaac Bashevis Singer* (New York, 1995).

SINISHTA Gjon (1929, Montenegro–1995, San Francisco), Albanian politician and cultural activist. Sinishta studied at the Jesuit Collegium Xaverianum in Shkodër. In 1946 he was briefly arrested with a group of students, and a year later he entered the novitiate in Shkodër. In view of an anti-church campaign by the Communists he discontinued the novitiate and left Albania. He moved to Yugoslavia, where he worked as a journalist for the Albanian-language press. After military service, Sinishta worked for Radio Prishtina and the Albanian periodical *Rilindja*. In September 1956 he was arrested and sentenced to five years in prison for allegedly spying for the United States and for anti-Communist propaganda. After leaving prison in 1961, Sinishta worked as a bookkeeper in Zagreb and Ljubljana. Harassed by the police and frequently arrested, in 1964 he illegally left for Austria and then for Italy. For more than a year he worked at the Jesuit Center for Social Studies in Milan. In 1965 he went to the United States, where he worked in a Detroit factory. He graduated from Saint Coral University, and in 1967 he created an Albanian Catholic Information Center. Owing to Sinishta's initiative, the Albanian Catholic Bulletin was founded in Santa Clara, California, in 1980, and it moved to San Francisco in 1994. The bulletin recorded the persecutions of Albanian Catholics. Sinishta also co-founded the Daniel Dajani Institute in San Francisco, which dealt with studies in Albanian Catholicism. Sinishta was a devoted collector of testimonies of anti-religious persecution. In 1992 he returned to Albania. After his death Sinishta was buried in Rrmajt Cemetery in Shkodër. His book, Sacrifice for Albania; The Fulfilled Promise: A Documentary Account of Religious Persecution in Albania (1976), was the first monograph on the martyrdom of the Albanian clergy. (TC)

Sources: Matish Shestani, *Te njohim Gjon Sinishtes* (Tirana, 1997).

SIRK Artur (25 September 1900, Järvamaal–2 August 1937, Echternach, Luxembourg), leader of Estonian Fascists. Sirk was born into a peasant family. He fought as a volunteer in the war of 1918–19. He subsequently completed law studies. From 1920 to 1926 he served in the army and worked for some time as a military court secretary. In 1926 he began practicing as an attorney. Brilliant and energetic, he had great political ambitions. He initially became a member of the New Settlers' Party and later joined the League of Veterans of the Struggle for Freedom (Vabadussõjalaste Keskliit), which was transformed into the Estonian League of War of Independence Veterans (Eesti Vabadussojalaste Liit [EVL]) in 1924. In October 1926, at the First Congress of this organization, Sirk became its deputy chairman. Along with **Theodor Rõuk**, he developed the EVL's Fascist ideology, along the lines of the Italian and German models. In March 1931, at the Second Congress of the EVL, Sirk announced the rebuilding of the country according to the principles of the EVL movement. He became head of the EVL, which he transformed into a right-wing political party. EVL propaganda gained popularity because it built on the veteran origins of the EVL movement and took advantage of the impoverishment of society during the Great Depression. The EVL movement became a paramilitary organization founded on a leadership model, with frequent parades and a fondness for uniforms and ranks.

As early as 1931 Sirk called for a constitutional reform that would bring about the end of the system of parliamentary democracy. The EVL movement no longer resorted to rhetoric against the German minority because it cooperated with and was supported by the Nazis. The Deutsch-Baltische Partei, led by Victor zur Muehlen-Eigstfer, openly supported the EVL. After winning 33 percent support in a referendum of June 1933, the EVL proposed its own draft for a constitution and demanded a referendum on its adoption. On 11 August 1933 the government of **Jaan Tõnisson** declared a state of emergency and banned the EVL's activities. In a referendum of 14–16 October 1933 the draft constitution promoted by the EVL received 419,000 votes (56.4 percent). Sirk organized large demonstrations under Fascist slogans. In the January 1934 elections the EVL won the majority in all major cities, including Tallinn, Tartu, Pärnu, and Viljandi. In response **Konstantin Päts** staged a coup d'état, declaring a state of emergency on 12 March 1934 and assuming dictatorial powers with the help of part of the army. Sirk and other EVL leaders were arrested. On 11 November 1934 Sirk managed to escape from prison. He went to Finland; from there he directed a national conspiracy that plotted a coup. However, in 1935 the plot was discovered by the police; therefore, Sirk remained in exile. He went to live in Luxembourg. He died two days after falling out of a window on the first floor of a hotel. Sirk's death was generally believed to be a suicide, but there was also speculation that it was a political murder. (WR)

Sources: Kaarel Pusta, *Saadiku päevik*, vol. 1 (Geislingen, 1964); William Tomingas, *Vaikiv ajustu Eestis* (New York, 1961); Piotr Łossowski, *Kraje bałtyckie na drodze od demokracji parlamentarnej do dyktatury (1918–1934)* (Wrocław, 1972); Tõnu Parming, *The Collapse of Liberal Democracy and the Rise of Authoritarianism in Estonia* (Beverly Hills, Calif., 1975); Philip Rees, *Biographical Dictionary of the Extreme Right since 1890* (New York, 1990); Andres Kasekamp, *The Radical Right in Interwar Estonia* (London, 2000).

ŠIROKÝ Viliam (31 May 1902, Bratislava–6 October 1971, Prague), Czechoslovak Communist activist. The son of a Slovak laborer of Hungarian descent, after finishing elementary school, Široký worked on the railways and joined the Social Democratic Party. In 1921 he was one of the founders of the Communist Party of Czechoslovakia (CPC). He subsequently worked in the party apparatus in Prague and Bratislava. As secretary of an organization of the Slovak Communists, Široký attended the Sixth Congress of the Communist International in Moscow (1928). In 1929 he became a member of the Central Committee (CC), in 1931 a member of the Politburo, and in 1935 a member of the Secretariat of the CC of the CPC. In 1935 Široký spoke at the Seventh Congress of the Comintern and became a deputy member of the Comintern Executive Committee. In 1935 he also became an MP in the Prague parliament. After the Pact of Munich of September 1938, Široký left for Paris, from where he went to Moscow in March 1940. Like other Slovak Communist leaders, until the end of 1943 he believed that after the war Slovakia should become a Soviet republic. In 1941 Široký returned to Slovakia to organize the Communist underground resistance, but he was arrested and sentenced to fourteen years' imprisonment. In February 1945 he escaped and, with the help of Communist partisans, made his way to Moscow. Široký took part in negotiations that resulted in the establishment of a Czechoslovak government in Košice (April 1945). He assumed the post of deputy prime minister and held this post until 1950. From August 1945 onwards he also served as first secretary of the CP of Slovakia, and he was among the leaders of the Presidium of the CPC CC that led the coup d'état in February 1948. In June 1948, along with **Rudolf Slánský**, Široký represented the CPC at a conference of the Information Bureau of the Communist and Workers' Parties (Cominform) at which **Josip Broz Tito** and the Yugoslav party were denounced. In September 1948 at a meeting of the CC of the CP of Slovakia, Široký delivered a speech in which he gave a signal to attack "bourgeois nationalism" within the party. Later he led the purges and persecutions of Slovak activists accused of "Titoism." Co-responsible for the decision to persecute participants of the Slovak National Uprising, he supervised these persecutions.

In March 1950 Široký was appointed prime minister, and in January 1951 he became a member of the CC "political secretariat," which was in charge of the security apparatus. In December 1952 Široký exercised political supervision over the trial of Slánský and his associates, which ended in eleven death sentences. After the death of Stalin and **Klement Gottwald** in 1953, Široký, as the right-hand man of **Antonín Novotný**, was largely responsible for the continuation of the persecutions and the slowing down of de-Stalinization in Czechoslovakia. In the late 1950s and early 1960s, when Slovak Communist activists were being released from prison, Široký had to assume an increasingly defensive position. Although **Rudolf Barák**, who had been co-responsible for the political trials but now supported the rehabilitation of wrongly accused politicians, was removed from power in 1962, Široký was unable to save his position. In June 1963 a special commission of the CC of the CP of Slovakia recommended changes in the leadership of the party. A bad economic situation was another argument in favor of these changes. In September of that year Široký lost both of his posts. In May 1968, during the Prague Spring, he was suspended as a party member for co-organizing the political trials and purges, but in May 1971 he was reinstated to full membership of the CPC. Široký was never brought to justice for his complicity in the crimes of the Stalinist period. (WR)

Sources: *ČBS*; Lazitch; *The Times*, 7 October 1971; Edward Taborsky, *Communism in Czechoslovakia, 1948–1960* (Princeton, 1961); Jiři Pelikán, *The Czechoslovak Political Trials, 1950–1954* (Stanford, 1971).

SIWICKI Florian (10 January 1925, Łuck [Lutsk]), Polish Communist general. The son of a non-commissioned officer of the Polish Army, after the Red Army occupied the Eastern Borderlands of interwar Poland, in 1940 Siwicki was deported with his family deep into the USSR. In early 1943 he was drafted into the Red Army. On his request he was transferred to the Polish Army, created under the command of General **Zygmunt Berling**, and he was sent to an officer training course at the Ryazan School of Infantry. Siwicki graduated from this school in December 1943. Later he commanded a detachment of cadets of the Tadeusz Kościuszko Infantry Officers' School. At the end of World War II and soon thereafter Siwicki took part in combating the Polish pro-independence underground in Poland. From December 1948 he belonged to the (Communist) Polish United Workers' Party (Polska Zjednoczona Partia Robotnicza [PUWP]). In the early 1950s he left for the USSR, where he graduated from the Academy of the Soviet General Staff in 1956. In 1961–63 Siwicki was military attaché in China. In 1962 he was promoted to brigadier general. From April 1968 he commanded the Silesian Military District, and in this capacity he commanded Polish troops during the Warsaw Pact invasion of Czechoslovakia in August 1968. In October 1968 Siwicki was promoted to general of division, and in 1974, to general of arms. From May 1971 he was deputy chief and from January 1973 chief of the General Staff and deputy minister of national defense. Siwicki owed his rapid career rise to General **Wojciech Jaruzelski**. In December 1975 Siwicki became a member of the PUWP Central Committee (CC), and in October 1981, a deputy member of the PUWP CC Politburo. He belonged to a close circle of those who engineered the period of martial law, leading a team that planned it from October 1980; later he belonged to the non-constitutional

Military Council of National Salvation (Wojskowa Rada Ocalenia Narodowego), which functioned as the governing body during martial law. In November 1983 Siwicki was appointed minister of national defense, and in July 1986 he joined the PUWP CC Politburo as a full member. After the formation of the **Tadeusz Mazowiecki** government in September 1989, Siwicki remained in office, not really understanding the nature and depth of the change. As late as 1990 he pointed to the alleged NATO danger to Poland and to the necessity of Soviet guarantees. Dismissed in July 1990, Siwicki retired. (WR)

Sources: Mołdawa; Leopold Labedz, ed., *Poland under Jaruzelski* (New York, 1984); Lech Kowalski, "Dunaj 68: Wejście generałów," *Karta*, 1991, no. 6; Stanisław Dronicz, *Wojsko i politycy* (Warsaw, 2001); Lech Kowalski, *Generał ze skazą* (Warsaw, 2001).

ŠĶĒLE Andris (16 January 1958, Aluksne), Latvian politician and businessman. In 1981 Šķēle graduated from the Latvian Agricultural Academy, specializing in engineering. In 1981–90 he worked in managerial positions at the Latvian Research Institute, dealing with the mechanization and electrification of agriculture. From 1990 to 1993 he was first deputy minister of agriculture of the Latvian SSR and (from 1991) of independent Latvia. In August 1993 he became minister of agriculture. In 1994–95 Šķēle was a successful businessman, chairing several food processing companies (for example, AveLat) and serving as a consultant to the Latvian Privatization Agency. After parliamentary elections, on 21 December 1995, still a nonparty person, Šķēle became prime minister of a center-right coalition government. He continued with market reforms, overcoming several political problems. In May 1996 he dismissed Deputy Prime Minister Alberīs Kauls. In July 1996, as a result of the presidential election won by **Guntis Ulmanis**, the ruling coalition faced new problems. When in October 1996 Šķēle dismissed another deputy prime minister, Ziedonis Čevers, he was accused of dictatorial aspirations. Since Ulmanis questioned his choice for minister of finance, on 20 January 1997 Šķēle resigned. The conflict ended in victory for Šķēle, when on 27 February 1997 he formed another government; however, in connection with accusations of his having taken part in financial scandals, on 28 July 1997 Šķēle resigned. In 1998 he co-founded and chaired the center-right People's Party (Tautas Partija [PL]), which won 24 percent of the mandates in the elections of October 1998. As a result of another coalition agreement among the PL, the (Liberal) Latvian Way, and the National Conservatives, on 16 July 1999 Šķēle formed another center-right government. Involved in the struggle for privatization of the largest state enterprises, on 12 April 2000 Šķēle was forced to resign. Šķēle's governments played an important role in preparing Latvia for integration into NATO and the European Union. As a result Šķēle has also become one of the richest Latvians. (JH)

Sources: *Who's Who in Latvia* (Riga, 1996); *Europa Book of the Year 2000* (London, 2002) *1*; Bugajski; "Liga kapitału," *Wprost*, 25 June 2000; www.mk.gov.lv; www.rulers.org; www.terra.es/persona12.

SKERLIĆ Jovan (8 August 1877, Belgrade–15 May 1914, Belgrade), Serbian critic and literary historian. Skerlić studied in Belgrade and Lausanne, where he earned a doctorate. He subsequently taught at a high school and worked as an associate professor and full professor at the Superior School (Velika Škola), which became the University of Belgrade in 1905. A politician from the Radical Party, which ruled in Serbia from 1903 onwards, Skerlić brie fly leaned toward socialism. In 1905–7 he edited *Srpski književni glasnik*, the leading Serbian literary periodical. He founded the Association of Serbian Writers (Udruženje Književnika Srbije) and the Serbian Literary Association (Srpska Književna Zadruga). He was the author of the monographs *Jakov Ignjatović* (1904); *Omladina i njena književnost* (Omladina and its literature; 1906); *Srpska književnost u XVIII veku* (Serbian literature in the eighteenth century; 1909); and *Svetozar Marković: Njegov život, rad i ideje* (Svetozar Marković: His life, work, and ideas; 1910). Skerlić's most important work, *Istorija nove srpske književnosti* (The history of modern Serbian literature; 1914), presented the development of contemporary Serbian literature as a process similar to the trends prevailing in Europe. Six volumes of his critical articles were published during his lifetime. Skerlić worked for the establishment of Yugoslavia and was the spiritual leader of the so-called revolutionary youth. **Gavrilo Princip**, a member of Young Bosnia (an organization within Omladina, a great revolutionary youth movement that spread across all the South Slavic countries at the beginning of the twentieth century), carried a wreath at Skerlić's funeral. (AO)

Sources: *Enciklopedija Jugoslavije*, vol. 7 (Zagreb, 1968); Željan E. Šuster, *Historical Dictionary of the Federal Republic of Yugoslavia* (Lanham, Md., 1999); *Mały słownik pisarzy zachodnio-słowiańskich i południowo-słowiańskich* (Warsaw, 1973).

SKIRMUNT Konstanty (30 July 1866, Mołodów, Polesia–24 July 1949, Warsaw), Polish diplomat. Skirmunt came from the landed nobility. After graduating from a law school in St. Petersburg, he worked as an attorney and a manager of his family estate. He belonged to the "realist" group, which sought to achieve the moderate political aim of modernizing the autocratic system in Russia. In 1907, Skirmunt, along with other politicians connected with the periodical *Kurier Litewski* (Lithuanian courier), co-founded the Home Party of Lithuania and Ruthenia (Stronnictwo Krajowe Litwy i Rusi). The party invoked the historical legacy of the Grand Duchy of Lithuania. Royalist loyalism and fear of social radicalism prompted Skirmunt to seek ties with the Party of Real Politics (Stronnictwo Polityki Realnej). Between 1907 and 1917 he was a deputy to the Russian State Duma. In 1916 he left for the West, where he joined an effort to convince the Entente powers to embrace the cause of Poland's independence. In the summer of 1917 he participated in the foundation of the Polish National Committee (Komitet Narodowy Polski) and represented it in Italy, including the Vatican.

In independent Poland, between 1919 and 1921, Skirmunt was envoy to Italy, and from June 1921 to June 1922 he served as minister of foreign affairs in the governments of **Wincenty Witos** and **Antoni Ponikowski**. He endeavored to improve the image of Poland in the West, to achieve the recognition of its borders by the Entente powers, and to improve its relations with neighboring states. In November 1921, Skirmunt signed a Polish-Czechoslovak agreement for cooperation. However, the German-Soviet Rapallo Pact of April 1922 jeopardized his mission. Between 1923 and 1924 Skirmunt represented Poland in the League of Nations. From 1922 to 1929 he served as its envoy to Great Britain and then as the Polish ambassador to London until 1934. Later, Skirmunt withdrew from active political life, objecting to the policies of **Józef Beck**. In September 1939 some of his family was murdered when the Red Army invaded Polesia in eastern Poland. Skirmunt settled in Warsaw, where he died destitute after the war. His unpublished memoirs are deposited in the manuscript collection of the library of the Catholic University of Lublin. (WR)

Sources: *Kto był kim w Drugiej Rzeczypospolitej* (Warsaw, 1994); *Encyklopedia historii Drugiej Rzeczypospolitej* (Warsaw, 1999); Andrzej Ajnenkiel, *Od rządów ludowych do przewrotu majowego* (Warsaw, 1978); Czesław Brzoza and Kamil Stepan, *Posłowie polscy w parlamencie rosyjskim 1906–1917* (Warsaw, 2001).

ŠKIRPA Kazys (18 February 1895, Nemajūnai, near Biržai–18 August 1979, Washington, D.C.), Lithuanian officer and politician. Born into a peasant family, in 1916 Škirpa was inducted into the Russian Army. After graduating from the Military Academy in Peterhof, he was sent to Siberia. In the autumn of 1917 he returned to Petrograd (St. Petersburg), where he formed Lithuanian units that supported Lithuanian independence. In 1918 he joined the newly formed Lithuanian Army and took part in its front-line operations, serving as commander of a regiment. In 1920 Škirpa was elected to the Legislative Assembly on the Populist ticket. After graduating from the Military School in Kaunas, he went to study at the Belgian Military Academy in Brussels, graduating in 1925. After returning to his country, Škirpa became head of the Second Department (Intelligence) of the General Staff, but he had to resign this position after the nationalist coup d'état of December 1926. He then began working in the diplomatic service, initially as a clerk in the consular section at the legation in Berlin (1927–30) and then as a military attaché in Germany. In 1937 Škirpa became Lithuania's representative to the League of Nations. After Lithuania was presented with the Polish ultimatum of March 1938, he was sent as a special envoy to Warsaw and established diplomatic relations between Poland and Lithuania. He subsequently became minister to Poland and then to Berlin.

Škirpa supported a pro-German orientation. After Lithuania was occupied by the Red Army and in 1940 incorporated into the Soviet Union, he helped to establish the Front of Lithuanian Activists. Following the German invasion of the Soviet Union, Lithuanian pro-independence forces began to form a provisional government, and on 23 June 1941 Škirpa was to assume the post of prime minister of this government. However, knowing his pro-independence ambitions, the Third Reich authorities did not allow him to go to Lithuania. He was placed under house arrest in southern Germany. When in 1944 he renewed his demands for the establishment of an independent government in Lithuania, he was taken to a concentration camp in Bad Godesberg. After the end of World War II, he went to France. In 1946 he moved to Ireland, where he taught Russian at the University of Dublin. In 1949 he emigrated to the United States and worked at the Library of Congress, Washington, D.C. In 1965 he retired. In 1975 Škirpa published his memoirs, depicting his activities in Germany, *Sukilimas Lietuvos suverenumui atstatyti* (The uprising for Lithuanian independence). (WR)

Sources: *EL*, vol. 5; Saulius Sužiedelis, *Historical Dictionary of Lithuania* (Lanham, Md., 1997); *Washington Post*, 21 August 1979; Algirdas Budreckis, *The Lithuanian National Revolt of 1941* (Boston, 1968).

SKŁADKOWSKI Felicjan Sławoj (9 June 1885, Gąbin, near Gostynin–31 August 1962, London), Polish general, politician, and physician. After graduating from high school in Kielce in 1904, Składkowski enrolled at the Medical School of the University of Warsaw. Simultaneously, he became active in the struggle for independence through the Polish Socialist Party (in its Revolutionary Faction from 1906). In November 1904, he was imprisoned at the Pawiak jail for participating in a demonstration in Warsaw. Expelled from the medical school, he was deported to Kielce and put under police supervision. To avoid a trial, he left for Kraków, where he completed his medical studies in 1911, specializing in surgery. Składkowski interned at the Surgical Clinic of the Jagiellonian University and later supervised a surgical clinic in Sosnowiec. In August 1914 he joined the Polish Legions, which had been created as an auxiliary force for the Austro-Hungarian Army. He served as a physician until their dissolution. Following the oath crisis, he was interned in Beniaminów. Released in August 1918, he worked as a doctor at a coal mine.

In November 1918, Składkowski participated in disarming German soldiers and Communist Red Guards in the Zagłębie Dąbrowskie area. He briefly served as the military commander of the Army Command in Dąbrowa Górnicza and, from February 1919, as its staff and political officer. In 1919 and 1920, he participated in the Polish-Soviet war as the chief military surgeon of various units. From 1921 to 1923 he was appointed inspector of the medical units of the Polish Army. In 1924 he graduated from the Ecole Supérieure de Guerre. Appointed head of the Medical Department of the Ministry of Military Affairs, Składkowski was promoted to brigadier general. During the coup d'état of May 1926, he sided actively with **Józef Piłsudski**. Following the latter's victory, Składkowski was assigned the post of government commissioner of the City of Warsaw. In August 1926, he was shifted to the reserves, and between October 1926 and December 1929 he served as minister of interior, as well as extraordinary commissioner for the struggle against contagious diseases. Składkowski concentrated on the reform of the administrative apparatus and improving the nation's level of hygiene. At that time, Poland's wits jokingly began referring to public toilets as "sławojki." Składkowski loyally carried out all of Piłsudski's directives. He personally participated in forcibly ejecting protesting Communist deputies on the first day of the inaugurations for the newly elected parliament in March 1928. In January 1930, Składkowski became a deputy to the first vice-minister of military affairs and the chief of the army administration. In June 1930, he was once again appointed minister of interior. He personally signed orders to arrest many MPs following the dissolution of parliament in September 1930. From 1930 to 1939, he held a seat in the parliament, and in 1931 he was reappointed deputy minister of military affairs and chief of the army administration. In March 1936, he was promoted to major general.

On 15 May 1936, Składkowski became prime minister

and minister of interior. However, his power was secondary to that of the ruling triumvirate of **Ignacy Mościcki**, **Edward Rydz-Śmigły**, and **Józef Beck**. Therefore he concentrated on matters of administration and hygiene. Składkowski became the longest-sitting prime minister of interwar Poland. In September 1939, along with his government, he left Warsaw for Romania, where he was interned. On 30 September 1939, he resigned. Eventually, through Bulgaria and Turkey, he reached the Polish Army units in Palestine in January 1941. His attempt to join the medical corps was rejected. Składkowski testified several times before a commission investigating the causes of the fall of Poland in 1939. He arrived in Great Britain in 1947, and after being processed in the camps of the Polish Retraining and Resettlement Corps, he settled in London. Składkowski published *Moja służba w brygadzie: Pamiętnik polowy* (My service in the brigade: A field memoir; 1932–33); *Strzępy meldunków* (The shreds of reports; 1936); and *Nie ostatnie słowo oskarżonego: Wspomnienia i artykuły* (Not the last word of the accused: Memoirs and articles; 1964). In 1990 Składkowski's ashes were reinterred in Powązki Cemetery in Warsaw. (JS)

Sources: *PSB*, vol. 38; Piotr Stawecki, *Słownik biograficzny generałów Wojska Polskiego 1918–1939* (Warsaw, 1994); *Kto był kim w Drugiej Rzeczypospolitej* (Warsaw, 1994); Bernard Singer, *Od Witosa do Sławka* (Paris, 1962); *Gabinety II Rzeczypospolitej* (Szczecin and Poznań, 1991); *Prezydenci i premierzy Drugiej Rzeczypospolitej* (Wrocław, 1992); Arkadiusz Adamczyk, *Generał dywizji Sławoj Felicjan Składkowski (1885–1962): Zarys biografii politycznej* (Toruń, 2001).

SKŁODOWSKA-CURIE Maria (7 November 1867, Warsaw–4 July 1934, Sancellemoz, France), Polish and French scientist, Nobel Prize winner. Skłodowska-Curie came from a family of impoverished landed nobility. Her parents worked as teachers. She had seven siblings. Because of an imperial ban on admitting women to the University of Warsaw, she was unable to study in Russian Poland. Since she lacked the means to study abroad, she became a teacher, while also taking classes at the underground "Flying University." However, in 1891, Skłodowska-Curie enrolled at the Sorbonne. She passed her physics and math exams in 1894 with the highest scores, and a year later she married the French physicist Pierre Curie. His respect for her scientific abilities allowed her to continue her research. Consequently, in 1898, Skłodowska-Curie discovered the chemical element called polon (to commemorate Poland), and, in the following year, radium. Working under hazardous conditions, including exposure to radioactivity (whose lethal qualities were quite unknown at the time) caused the deterioration of the Curie couple's health. However, the derivation of radium in 1903 brought them international fame, especially since medical experiments showed that radioactivity was a useful tool to fight cancer. Refusing to deny radium to the sick, who turned to the Curies to obtain the element for medical reasons, the couple continued to produce radium for free. They failed to patent their discovery because they believed that their discovery should serve humanity. However, the hazardous nature of the production of radium had already become apparent to the couple.

In 1903, Skłodowska-Curie successfully defended her doctoral dissertation at the Sorbonne, the first woman to do so there. In the very same year, along with her husband and the French physicist Antoine Henri Becquerel, she was awarded the Nobel Prize in physics. Their success led the French government to endow a chair of general physics at the Sorbonne. While Pierre held the chair, Skłodowska-Curie was his deputy. Following her husband's death in a traffic accident in 1906, she took over the chair, becoming the first female lecturer at the Sorbonne. Her further scientific success notwithstanding, Skłodowska-Curie was not elected to the French Academy of Sciences—solely because she was a woman. In 1911 she was awarded a Nobel Prize in chemistry, which solidified her position as the world's leading scientist. Meanwhile, the tabloids accused her of a love affair with the young physicist Paul Langevin and of plagiarizing his work. She denied the allegations, but the scandal press whipped up a nationalist frenzy, with demands to strip her of the chair and even to expel her from France. Skłodowska-Curie left Paris briefly but did not move to Poland, despite the encouragement of such people as **Henryk Sienkiewicz**. In 1912, she was appointed head of the Radium Institute in Paris. In time, at the institute, she supervised the work of her daughter and her husband, Frédéric Jolliot, who eventually won the Nobel Prize as well. During World War I Skłodowska-Curie organized radiological services for military hospitals, trained their personnel, and rescued thousands of wounded servicemen. Hospital emergency vehicles based upon her specifications and widely used in France were dubbed *les petites Curie* (Little Curies). In the 1920s, Skłodowska-Curie often visited Poland and contributed to the establishment of the Radium Institute in Warsaw (1932). She successfully raised funds in the United States for scientific work. She died of leukemia. She was buried at her husband's family cemetery in Sceaux. After World War II Skłodowska-Curie's ashes were transferred to the Panthéon in Paris. (AG)

Sources: *Polacy w historii i kulturze krajów Europy Zachodniej* (Poznań, 1981); Eve Curie, *Madame Curie* (Garden City, N.J., 1937); Henry John Hayward, *A Torchbearer of Science: The Life of Marie Curie* (Auckland, 1940); Paul Ulrich, *Maria Curie: Die Be-*

gründerin eines neuen Zeitalters (Stuttgart, 1948); Eleanor Doorly, *The Radium Woman: A Life of Marie Curie* (New York, 1954); Keith Brandt, *Marie Curie: Brave Scientist* (Mahwah, N.J., 1983); Jacek Stefański, "Maria Skłodowska-Curie," in *Wybitni Polacy XIX wieku* (Kraków, 1998); Beverley Birch, *Marie Curie: Courageous Pioneer in the Study of Radioactivity* (Woodbridge, Conn., 2000).

SKOROPADSKYI Pavlo (15 May 1873, Wiesbaden, Germany–26 April 1945, Metten, Germany), hetman of Ukraine. Skoropadskyi was descended from an old Cossack family and inherited the Trostyanets estate in the Poltava region in Ukraine. After finishing high school in Starodub, he graduated from the Page Corps in 1893. He subsequently served in the tsar's Horse Guards. During the 1904–5 Russo-Japanese War, Skoropadskyi was aide-de-camp to Tsar Nicholas II. In 1906 he was promoted to colonel, and in 1912 he became general and commander of a cavalry regiment in the tsar's Horse Guards. During World War I Skoropadskyi commanded the First Division of the Horse Guards, the Thirty-fourth Army Corps, and from August to December 1917—after the February 1917 revolution—he commanded the First Ukrainian Corps. Along with **Symon Petlura**, Skoropadskyi organized the army of the Ukrainian Central Rada (Council). In October 1917, at the All-Ukrainian Congress of the Free Cossacks in Chyhyryn, Skoropadskyi was elected commander-in-chief of this army. In November 1917 the units he commanded, about sixty thousand strong, seized control of the Zhmerynka-Shepetovka railway line and then disarmed pro-Bolshevik military forces advancing into the Ukraine from the Romanian front.

Skoropadskyi disagreed with the radical program of the Rada, particularly on the issue of agricultural reform; therefore, he established a conservative opposition known as the Ukrainian National Hromada. His plans to overthrow the Rada were also supported by the Union of Landowners. When Austrian and German troops seized Ukraine at the beginning of 1918, Skoropadskyi, helped by conservative officers, removed the Rada government, and, on 29 April 1918 in Kiev he was named hetman of Ukraine. The Rada, along with its land committees, was dissolved; the administration was changed; and all laws passed by the Rada were abrogated. "Ukrainian State" was adopted as the name of the nation, and its system was a combination of dictatorship and republic. Skoropadskyi received support from the Russian Constitutional Democratic Party and even from monarchists. He was also supported by Ukrainian landowners, rich peasants, entrepreneurs, and merchants. Still, he was a tool in the hands of the occupation authorities, the Central Powers. For some time Skoropadskyi managed to control the social situation and end peasant riots wherein peasants had plundered manor houses and murdered the owners. He created a semblance of independence of Ukraine, and as a result of his efforts, Ukraine's independence was recognized by Germany, Austria-Hungary, Turkey, Bulgaria, and Romania. However, the Central Powers restricted the development of the Ukrainian Army, thus undermining Skoropadskyi's position. Moreover, Skoropadskyi attempted to restore the pre-revolutionary social order and surrounded himself with Russian officials. In May 1918 the leftist opposition to the hetman's government united into the Ukrainian National Union. In the summer of that year peasant rebellions and riots began to increase, and assassination attempts on prominent Austrians and Germans became more frequent.

When Austria-Hungary collapsed in the fall of 1918, Skoropadskyi made attempts to reach an agreement with the opposition, but his November 1918 address announcing his intention to enter into a federation with a future non-Bolshevik Russia only worsened the situation. When on 11 November 1918 the armistice was signed on the Western front, radical peasant riots increased. Abandoned by the best military units, including the Sich Riflemen, Skoropadskyi followed the German Army, which withdrew from Kiev on 14 December 1918. Kiev was later invaded by the troops of the Directory (a government established by the Rada) under the leadership of Petlura. Skoropadskyi went to live in Wannsee, near Berlin. He became one of the most prominent figures of the Ukrainian émigré community. He rallied national conservative groups around himself, including groups led by **Vyacheslav Lypynskyi**. Skoropadskyi led the Ukrainian Agrarian National Union, as well as the Ukrainian "hetmanite" organizations in the United States and Canada. In 1923 he gave his support to Adolf Hitler. Aligned with conservative Junker groups, Skoropadskyi brought about the establishment of the Ukrainian Scientific Institute and the Ukrainian Hromada in 1926. After Hitler came to power, Skoropadskyi maintained contacts with Nazi authorities. These contacts ended after the Third Reich and the Soviet Union signed the Molotov-Ribbentrop Pact on 23 August 1939; therefore, when Germany occupied Ukraine in June 1941, Skoropadskyi did not play any role in the occupation government. Skoropadskyi died as the result of an Allied bombing raid. (WR)

Sources: *MERSH*, vol. 35; *Encyclopedia of Ukraine*, vol. 4 (Toronto, 1993); T. Hunczak, ed., *The Ukraine 1917–1921: A Study in Revolution* (Cambridge, Mass., 1977); Jean Pélissier, *La tragédie ukrainienne* (Paris, 1988); Myron Korolyshyn, ed., *Za vsenatsionalnu iednist: U 110-richchia narodzhennia Hetmana Pavla: U 65-richchia vidnovlennia hetmanstva 1980 r.* (Toronto, 1983); V. P. Fediuk, *Ukraiina v 1918 godu: Getman P. P. Skoropadskyi: Uchebnoe posobie* (Yaroslavl, 1993); Oles Bilodid and Volodymyr Panchenko, *Pavlo Skoropadskyi i Ukraiina* (Kiev, 1997).

SKRYPNYK Mykola (25 January 1872, Yasnovatoie, near Donetsk–7 July 1933, Kiev), Ukrainian Communist activist. Skrypnyk was born into the family of a railroad worker. In 1897 he joined the Russian Social Democratic Workers' Party (RSDWP). He was one of the main party agitators in the early stages of the party's development. He traveled a lot throughout Russia, the Ukraine, and Siberia, establishing party units. He was arrested fifteen times and deported seven times. In 1900 Skrypnyk enrolled at the St. Petersburg Technological Institute. After a split in the party in 1903, Skrypnyk supported the Bolsheviks. In 1905 he was a delegate to the Third Congress of the RSDWP(B) in London. During the revolution of 1905 he was secretary of the St. Petersburg committee of the party. After the suppression of the revolution, Skrypnyk very often traveled abroad, getting in touch with the party leadership in exile (for example, with Lenin). He also secretly organized party units in, for example, Yaroslavl, Moscow, and the Urals. In 1908 Skrypnyk was sentenced to five years of exile in the Yakutsk guberniya (province). In 1913 he returned to St. Petersburg and edited *Pravda*. In July 1914 he was imprisoned again and was held in the Tambov guberniya. After the February 1917 revolution Skrypnyk was released. He went back to the capital, where he organized Bolshevik factory committees. He represented them at the First, and Second All-Russian Congresses of Soviets of Workers' and Soldiers' Deputies. In 1917 he became a deputy member of the CC of the Bolshevik party.

During the Russian Revolution in October 1917 Skrypnyk was a member of the Military Revolutionary Committee, which headed the coup. At the end of 1917 Lenin dispatched him to the Ukraine, where he was to consolidate the Bolshevik organization and to safeguard links between the Ukraine and Russia in the new system of government. In December 1917, as commissar of labor, Skrypnyk joined the government of the Ukrainian Soviet Socialist Republic in Kharkiv, and in March 1918 he became head of the government and commissar of foreign affairs of the republic. On his motion, the Second All-Ukrainian Congress of Soviets formally declared Ukraine independent; the aim of this decision was to make the Bolsheviks credible in their struggle against the Ukrainian national authorities supported by the Germans and Austrians. In April 1918 Skrypnyk's efforts led to the creation of a seemingly separate party, the Communist Party (Bolshevik) of Ukraine (CP[B]U). However, after the Germans removed the Bolsheviks from the Ukraine, the founding congress of the party had to be held in Moscow. In March 1919 Skrypnyk represented the Ukraine at the founding congress of the Communist International.

After the Bolshevik authorities were set up in Kiev

and the Riga peace treaty was concluded with Poland in 1921, Skrypnyk served as commissar of interior of the Ukrainian SSR, and in 1922–27 he was commissar of justice and public prosecutor general. From 1927 to 1933 he was commissar of education. At the Twelfth Congress in 1923 he became a member of the CC of the All-Russian Bolshevik party. At that time he expressed criticism of "Great Russian chauvinism" and of the policy of Russification of the Ukraine, particularly in the Red Army. On his motion, the autonomous CP(B)U was preserved within the framework of the All-Russian Communist Party (Bolsheviks). At that time Skrypnyk maintained particularly close contacts with the Communist Party of Poland and the Communist Party of Western Ukraine (which was an autonomous part of the former), attempting to convert the Ukrainians on the Polish side of the border to communism. In 1927 he joined the Politburo of the CC of the All-Union Communist Party (Bolsheviks), and in 1928 he became a member of the Executive Committee of the Comintern. Skrypnyk was an advocate of Ukrainization of the government apparatus in the Ukrainian SSR, but he also supported Stalin in his struggle for power. He was a peculiar combination of Ukrainian patriot and Communist doctrinaire. In 1929 Skrypnyk himself brought Communists into the Ukrainian Academy of Sciences, and they soon launched an attack against Ukrainian culture. With the implementation of collectivization, initiated in 1930, Skrypnyk's role ended; during the purge of Ukrainian functionaries, Stalinist attacks against Skrypnyk intensified. His defense before the Politburo of the CC of the CP(B)U was rejected; therefore, anticipating arrest, he committed suicide. In 1974 Skrypnyk's *Statti i promovy z natsionalnoho pitaniia* (Writings and speeches on the national question) were published in Munich. (WR)

Sources: *MERSH,* vol. 35; *Encyclopedia of Ukraine*, vol. 4 (Toronto, 1993); George S. N. Luckyj, *Literary Politics in the Soviet Ukraine, 1917–1934* (New York, 1956); Panas Fedenko, "Mykola Skrypnyk: His National Policy, Conviction and Rehabilitation," *Ukrainian Review*, 1957, no. 5; Jurij Babko, *Soldat partii* (Kiev, 1962); Yurii Babko and I. Bilokobylskyi, *Mykola Oleksiiovych Skrypnyk* (Kiev, 1967); Ivan Koshelivec, *Mykola Skrypnyk* (Munich, 1972); Yurii Borys, *The Sovietization of Ukraine, 1917–1923* (Toronto, 1982).

SKRŻYŃSKI Aleksander (19 March 1882, Zagórzany, near Gorlice–25 September 1931, Ostrów Wielkopolska), Polish politician, diplomat, and lawyer. Born into a landowner's family, Skrzyński studied law in Vienna (1900–1904) and Kraków (1904–5), and in 1906 he received a Ph.D. in law. In 1908 he started working in the Lwów (Lemberg) administration, and in 1909 he was sent as an attaché to the Austro-Hungarian Embassy in the

Vatican. Appointed chamberlain to the court of Emperor Francis Joseph in 1912, Skrzyński went to the embassy in The Hague and then to those in Berlin, Paris, Washington, D.C., and Stuttgart. After the outbreak of World War I he joined the army. As a political conservative, at the end of the war Skrzyński joined the Party of the National Right. After its dissolution in November 1918, he was one of the vice-presidents of the Party for the Construction of a United Poland and later a member of the Supreme Board of the Party of Constitutional Work.

After the restoration of Polish statehood, Skrzyński started working in the Foreign Ministry. In 1919–22 he was Polish ambassador to Bucharest, where in March 1921 he managed to finalize the signing of a Polish-Romanian treaty of mutual aid. From December 1922 to May 1923 he was minister of foreign affairs in the government of General **Władysław Sikorski**. He contributed to the recognition of Poland's eastern border by the Council of Ambassadors (15 March 1923). Skrzyński's project to establish a Ukrainian university in Poland was opposed by the National Democracy. From April 1924 to December 1925 Skrzyński was Poland's permanent delegate to the League of Nations and one of its vice-presidents. In December 1924 he was again appointed minister of foreign affairs, this time in the government of **Władysław Grabski**. Skrzyński improved relations with Czechoslovakia by signing an arbitration treaty, a trade agreement, and an agreement on the treatment of national minorities in both countries in April 1925. He also improved Polish relations with the Baltic nations. In February 1925 he signed a concordat with the Holy See. Skrzyński failed to achieve better terms for Poland in the Locarno treaties of 16 October 1925. As a result, the eastern borders of Germany gained weaker guarantees than the western German borders, which worsened Poland's security.

Under growing inflation, on 20 November 1925 Skrzyński became prime minister of a wide parliamentary coalition, ranging from the Socialists to the National Democrats. He also continued as foreign minister. His attempts to stabilize the economy failed, as the Socialists refused to support proposals for a balanced budget that involved tax increases and a reduction of employment in the state sector. After the Socialists left the government coalition, on 20 April 1926 Skrzyński submitted his resignation, but President **Stanisław Wojciechowski**, who wanted him to complete his work on the budget, did not accept the resignation. Nevertheless, because of strikes and demonstrations, on 5 May 1926 Skrzyński resigned and withdrew from political life. He gave lectures and wrote articles, defending his foreign policy and promoting the League of Nations. Skrzyński was killed in a motor

car crash. Among other works he authored the following: *Poland and Peace* (1923; Polish edition: *Polska a pokój*, 1924); *Polska a protokół w sprawie pokojowego rozwiązywania sporów międzynarodowych* (Poland and the protocol on the peaceful resolution of international conflicts; 1924); and *Liga Narodów jako punkt centralny polityki zagranicznej* (The League of Nations as a center of foreign policy; 1929). (JS)

Sources: *PSB*, vol. 38; *Kto był kim w Drugiej Rzeczypospolitej* (Warsaw, 1994); Bernard Singer, *Od Witosa do Sławka* (Paris, 1962); Stanisław Mackiewicz, *Historia Polski od 11 listopada 1918 do 17 września 1939* (London, 1985); Wojciech Morawski, *Polityka gospodarcza rządu Aleksandra Skrzyńskiego* (Warsaw, 1990); *Gabinety II Rzeczypospolitej* (Szczecin and Poznań, 1991); Janusz Pajewski ed., *Ministrowie spraw zagranicznych II Rzeczypospolitej* (Szczecin, 1992); *Prezydenci i premierzy Drugiej Rzeczypospolitej* (Wrocław, 1992).

SKUBISZEWSKI Krzysztof (8 October 1926 Poznań), Polish lawyer and diplomat. Skubiszewski graduated from Poznań University in 1949, from the University of Nancy in 1957, and from Harvard University in 1958. In 1948–73 he worked at the university in Poznań; from 1973 he was a professor at the Institute of Legal Studies of the Polish Academy of Sciences, specializing in international law. A member of many international scientific associations, from 1989 Skubiszewski was a member of the Polish Academy of Sciences. From 1980 he belonged to Solidarity; between 1981 and 1984 he belonged to the Social Council of the Primate of Poland; and between 1984 and 1989 he was a member of the Coordination Committee of the Poland–Federal Republic of Germany Forum. In 1986–89 Skubiszewski belonged to the Consultative Council of the Chairman of the Council of State. In 1989 he co-founded a political club called Law and Freedom (Ład i Wolność).

From September 1989 to October 1993 Skubiszewski was the minister of foreign affairs in the governments of **Tadeusz Mazowiecki, Jan Krzysztof Bielecki, Jan Olszewski**, and **Hanna Suchocka**. He carried out a gradual replacement of the diplomatic personnel. In 1990 he succeeded in securing a place for Poland at a conference with united Germany at which the inviolability of the border on the Oder and Neisse line was confirmed (the Two Plus Four Agreement Treaty). In 1990 Skubiszewski signed a treaty on the recognition of the existing border, and in 1991 he signed a good neighbor treaty with united Germany. From 1990 Skubiszewski sought rapprochement among Poland, Czechoslovakia, and Hungary, and this led to the formation of the Visegrad Group. He initiated the integration of Poland into the West European structures. Skubiszewski's achievements included the following: an economic cooperation agreement with the EEC and unofficial talks on Poland's association with the European Communities (1989); an official motion to start negotiations on the association agreement (1990); admittance of Poland to the Council of Europe (26 November 1991); ratification of the Treaty on European Union by the Polish parliament and ratification of the Association Agreement between Poland and the European Communities by the European Parliament (1992). From 1989 to 1991 Skubiszewski led a transformation of the relations between Poland and the USSR, from Poland's position of dependency to a position of sovereignty, at the same time retaining good-neighbor relations. He took part in negotiations on the withdrawal of Soviet troops (and then of Russian troops) from Poland. The cost to Poland of recognizing that Polish-Russian relations had priority in its foreign policy was a policy of caution toward the aspirations for independence of Lithuania, Ukraine, Latvia, and Estonia. During and after the disintegration of the USSR in 1991 Skubiszewski pursued a policy of positive relations with Russia (a treaty of 22 May 1992); Ukraine (recognition of its independence in 1991, a treaty in 1992); Belorussia (a treaty in 1992); and Lithuania (a declaration of cooperation in 1992, a negotiated treaty signed in 1994). In 1993 Skubiszewski prepared and signed a concordat with the Holy See. Skubiszewski authored many scholarly publications on international law, and many of his works appeared in foreign languages. In Polish he published (among other works) *Zachodnia granica Polski* (The western border of Poland) and *Zachodnia granica w świetle traktatów* (The western border in light of the treaties). (AF)

Sources: Jan Skórzyński, *Ugoda i rewolucja: Władza i opozycja 1985–1989* (Warsaw, 1995); Antoni Dudek, *Pierwsze lata III Rzeczpospolitej 1989–1995* (Kraków, 1997); Wojciech Roszkowski, *Historia Polski 1914–2000* (Warsaw, 2001); *Dziesięciolecie Polski Niepodległej 1989–1999* Waldemar Kuczynski (Warsaw, 2001).

SKUČAS Kazys (3 March 1894, Mauručiai, near Marijampolė–June 1941, Moscow), Lithuanian general. Skučas was born into a peasant family. After graduating from a teacher training school in Veiveriai (1912), he worked as a teacher. He later enrolled as a student at the Pedagogical Institute in St. Petersburg. Inducted into the Russian Army in 1915, he graduated from a military school and was subsequently sent to the Romanian front. After returning to Lithuania in 1918, Skučas volunteered to serve in the newly formed Lithuanian Army, and he was then promoted to commander of a division. He later worked as director for personnel development at the Military School in Kaunas. From 1934 to 1938 Skučas served as a military attaché in the Soviet Union. After returning to his country, he became head of the Military School in Kaunas. At the beginning of 1939 he was promoted to general, and in March of that year he became minister of interior in the government of General **Jonas Černius**. Skučas continued in this post in the cabinet of **Antanas Merkys**, at a time of growing pressure from the Kremlin and increasing Soviet provocations. Skučas tried to counteract such pressures; therefore, in an ultimatum of 14 June 1940 the Kremlin demanded, among other things, that he be dismissed as minister of interior. After the Red Army occupied Lithuania, Skučas was almost immediately arrested and taken to Moscow, where he was executed. (WR)

Sources: *EL*, vol. 5; Bronis J. Kaslas, ed., *The USSR-German Aggression against Lithuania* (New York, 1973); Georg von Rauch, *The Baltic States: The Years of Independence, 1917–1940* (London, Berkeley, and Los Angeles, 1974.)

SKUJENIEKS Margers (23 June 1886, Riga–12 July 1941, Moscow), Latvian statistician and Social Democratic politician. From 1903 Skujenieks belonged to the Social Democratic Party and worked with the Menshevik faction. In 1904 he was held under arrest for seven months for taking part in a demonstration. He was active in the revolution of 1905 and then emigrated to London as he was threatened with Russian prison. In 1907 Skujenieks returned to Russia and graduated from the Moscow Institute of Trade. Between 1912 and 1915 he edited a newspaper in Libava (Liepaja) and later served as secretary of the Russian Labor Office in Moscow. In 1916 Skujenieks returned to Riga, where he headed a statistical office for Baltic refugees. In November 1918 he was elected vice-president of the Latvian National Council. From March 1919 he represented Latvia at the Paris Peace Conference. From the fall of 1919 he was director of the State Statistical Office. He was an MP to the Constituent Assembly and to the parliament of the republic. He presided over a parliamentary committee on the preparation of a Latvian constitution, which was passed on 15 February 1922. Skujenieks belonged to the right wing of Social Democracy. In June 1921 he became head of the faction of the so-called minimalists within the party. Skujenieks was the author of statistical studies and of a monograph, *Latvija 1918–1928 gados* (Latvia in the years 1918–1928), which was published for the tenth anniversary of Latvian independence. At the beginning of 1931 Skujenieks left Social Democracy, forming the Union of Progressives. From 19 March 1926 to 23 January 1928 and from 6 December 1931 to 23 March 1933 he was prime minister. During his first term, on 9 March 1927 he signed the Latvian-Soviet Treaty of Non-Aggression, which he renewed on 5 February 1932. Skujenieks became increasingly disillusioned with parliamentary democracy, and after the coup of **Kārlis Ulmanis** he declared his support for the nonparty government that was formed by Ulmanis. In May 1934 Skujenieks became deputy prime minister in this government. He held the post until 1936. After the invasion of Latvia by the Red Army in 1940, Skujenieks was arrested and deported to Russia. He was held in prison in (among other places) Moscow, where he was shot dead. (WR/EJ)

Sources: Janis Rutkis, ed., *Latvia: Country and People* (Stockholm, 1967); *Latviju Enciklopedija* (Riga, 1936).

SKULBASZEWSKI Antoni (29 January 1915, Peregonomka, Kiev region), Soviet security officer in Poland. The son of a carpenter of Polish descent, from 1935 Skulbaszewski served in the Red Army, and in 1936–37 he took part in NKVD officer training in Kiev. At this time he joined the Bolshevik party. In 1939–40 he took part in the Soviet-Finnish war, and from 1941 he fought against Germany on the southern front and in Moscow. In 1943 Skulbaszewski graduated from the Department of Engineering of the Institute of Drainage and Agricultural Mechanization in Tashkent. In May 1943 he was sent to the Polish Army, formed in the USSR under Soviet control. Skulbaszewski became investigating officer in the field prosecutor's office of the First Infantry Division, military prosecutor of the Second Infantry Division (April–September 1944), deputy prosecutor of the First Army (until April 1945), prosecutor of the Second Army (until June 1945), and (from August 1945) deputy supreme military prosecutor. He held this last position until October 1948, when he became supreme military prosecutor. In May 1946 Skulbaszewski was promoted to colonel. From 1 August 1950 he was deputy chief of the ill-famed Main Information Administration (Główny Zarząd Informacji) of the Ministry of National Defense, which was headed by Colonel Dmitry Voznesensky. Working in close cooperation with the Soviet organs and with the Polish Communist Party leadership, Skulbaszewski was responsible for the system of cruel reprisals. He personally supervised the interrogation of many Polish officers falsely accused of espionage; almost two dozen of these officers were executed. In 1954 Skulbaszewski was dismissed and left for the USSR. He lived in Kiev and worked in the Soviet security apparatus. (WR)

Sources: Central Military Archive in Warsaw, File 497/58/7960; Stanisław Marat and Jacek Snopkiewicz, *Ludzie bezpieki* (Warsaw, 1990); Jerzy Poksiński, *TUN, Tatar-Utnik-Nowicki: Represje wobec oficerów Wojska Polskiego w latach 1949–1956* (Warsaw, 1992); Jerzy Poksiński, *"My sędziowie nie od Boga..."* (Warsaw, 1996); Krzysztof Szwagrzyk, *Zbrodnie w majestacie prawa 1944–1955* (Warsaw, 2000).

SKULSKI Leopold (15 November 1877, Zamość–after 1939, USSR), Polish politician. Skulski studied pharmacy at Warsaw University and chemistry in Karlsruhe, where he graduated as an engineer. Later he was the owner of a drugstore in Łódź. In 1906 he chaired a committee for aid to the children of striking workers in Łódź. Probably in 1916 he entered the National League (Liga Narodowa). In 1916–19 Skulski was mayor of Łódź. In January 1919 he was elected to the Constituent Assembly from the lists of National Democracy, but he left its club to establish a Christian Social party, the National People's Union (Narodowe Zjednoczenie Ludowe [NZL]). After the fall of the **Ignacy Paderewski** government, on 13 December 1919 Skulski became prime minister. Apart from social problems such as unemployment and shortages of primary goods, Skulski struggled with the problems of preparing a budget, with growing inflation, and with a prolonged military conflict in the east. Contrary to the stance of National Democracy, he accepted the federation plans of **Józef Piłsudski** and his Ukrainian campaign of April 1920. Along with the economic problems, this became the reason for Skulski's resignation on 9 June 1920. From July 1920 to June 1921 he was minister of interior in the coalition Government of National Defense of **Wincenty Witos**. In June 1922 he refused to try to create a new government. In the parliamentary elections of November 1922 Skulski's party did not enter a nationalist coalition. After an election defeat, Skulski merged the NZL with the Polish Peasant Party–Piast. Elected vice-president of Piast, he refused to take over this position. In 1925 Skulski became a member of the Tribunal of State. In the 1930s he approached the Piłsudski *sanacja* bloc, and in 1937 he joined the pro-government Camp of National Unity. After the Red Army invaded Poland in September 1939, Skulski was arrested by the NKVD and sent deep into the Soviet interior, where he perished under unknown circumstances. (WR)

Sources: Adam Próchnik, *Pierwsze piętnastolecie Polski niepodległej* (Warsaw, 1983); *Prezydenci i premierzy Drugiej Rzeczypospolitej* (Wrocław, 1992); *Kto był kim w Drugiej Rzeczypospolitej* (Warsaw, 1994).

ŠKULTÉTY Jozef (25 November 1853, Potok–19 January 1948, Martin), Slovak linguist and social activist. Škultéty graduated from a teacher training college in Budapest. In 1881 he began working as an editor of the newspaper *Národnie noviny*, which became a platform for the Slovak national movement. In 1890–1916 he edited the literary monthly *Slovenské pohľady*. Škultéty was a member of the conservative leadership of the Slovak National Party in Turčiansky Svätý Martin (now Martin).

He represented the view that the Slovak nation had a separate national identity, and he criticized representatives of the young intelligentsia, such as **Vavro Šrobár** and **Milan Hodža**, who called for close cooperation with the Czechs. Until 1917 Škultéty represented a Russophile orientation. He was repeatedly arrested by the Hungarian authorities for his journalism. His post-Romantic literary output was largely unsuccessful. From 1882 on Škultéty was active as an editor and pioneered Slovak academic editing. He edited works by Slovak poets and compiled the first anthology of Slovak poetry, *Veniec slovenských národných piesní* (Garland of Slovak national poems; 1897), which was repeatedly reissued. An advocate of realism, Škultéty believed that art was a weapon in the struggle for preserving Slovak national consciousness. He greatly contributed to the field of linguistics. At the beginning of 1919, Škultéty was an expert for Slovak affairs at the Paris Peace Conference. During the interwar period he opposed the idea of "Czechoslovakism." In the work *Stodvadsat'pät'rokov zo slovenského života* (One hundred and twenty-five years of Slovak national life; 1920) he expounded his ideas on national history and argued against Hodža's views. When the Slovak cultural organization Slovenská Matica was revived in 1919, Škultéty was appointed its administrator. In 1921 he became a professor of Slovak language and literature at Comenius University, Bratislava. He was awarded an honorary doctorate by Charles University in Prague. In 1920 Škultéty became a member of the Czech Academy of Science and Art and in 1929 a corresponding member of the Polish Academy of Arts and Sciences. (MG)

Sources: *SBS*; Pavol Vongrej, "Nestor národnej kultúry," *Slovenské pohľady*, 1983, no. 11; Anna Holla, ed., *Jozef Škultéty* (Martin, 1983); *Literatury zachodniosłowiańskie czasu przełomów 1890–1990*, vol. 1 (Katowice, 1994).

SKVIRECKAS Juozapas (18 September 1873, Rimkūnkai, Panevėžys County–3 December 1959, Zams, Austria), first archbishop and metropolitan of Kaunas. Skvireckas studied theology at the Kaunas Seminary (1892–96) and then at the Theological Academy in St. Petersburg, graduating in 1900. Ordained a priest on 24 June 1899 in Kaunas, he began to teach exegesis, catechism, and Latin at the Kaunas Seminary in 1901. In 1911 he became canon and in 1914 prelate of the Samogitian diocese. During World War I the Russians forced him to leave Kaunas. Skvireckas went to Smolensk and Tula, where he helped organize aid for Latvian refugees who were wounded or ill. After the end of the war, he returned to Lithuania, where in 1919 he became vicar general of the Samogitian diocese, with the title of auxiliary bishop. In 1926, when a separate church province was established in Lithuania, he was elected archbishop and metropolitan of Kaunas. In 1931 Pope Pius XI honored him with the title of assistant to the papal throne. Skvireckas served as the highest dignitary in the Lithuanian Church at a time of conflict with the political authorities. He had many opponents, particularly after the nationalists took over power in 1926 and Lithuania severed ties with the Vatican. However, his obstinacy and patience led to the stabilization of relations between the state and the Church. In the 1930s, despite frictions with the Holy See, the Church played a very important role in Lithuanian social life. In 1922 Skvireckas became a professor of biblical studies at the School of Theology and Philosophy of the University of Kaunas and professor of theology at the Kaunas Seminary. He co-founded the Lithuanian Catholic Academy of Sciences. As a result of his efforts, a new headquarters of the archdiocese was built, and the cathedral in Kaunas was renovated.

From 1940 to 1944, during the Soviet and then the German occupations, Skvireckas defended the persecuted and tried to bring relief to the suffering; for instance, he issued an appeal to the bishops in the United States, requesting help for people who were deported to Siberia. When the Red Army reoccupied Lithuania in the summer of 1944, Skvireckas left Lithuania. From 1945 he lived in the convent of the Congregation of the Sisters of St. Vincent á Paulo in Zams, Tyrol, Austria. Skvireckas left a great literary output. The translation of the Bible into Lithuanian—with his own commentary—is his greatest achievement. Skvireckas began this translation in 1900 and finished it in 1935; in the meantime (in 1922 and 1936) two editions of the New Testament were published for use by the faithful. The entire Old Testament, translated into Lithuanian by Skvireckas, was published in 1955–58. Skvireckas also authored a biography of St. Pius X (1904), St. Paul (1907), and Bishop Merkelis Giedraitis (1908). (AG)

Sources: *EL*, vol. 5; V. Padolskis, "Arkivyskupas Juozapas Skvireckas: Šventojo Rašto vertėjas," *Aidai* (Brooklyn), 1953, no. 6; L. Tulaba, "Nei trigesimo della morte di S.R. Mons. Giuseppe Skvireckas," *L'Osservatore Romano*, 1960, no. 9.

ŠKVORECKÝ Josef (27 September 1924, Náchod), Czech writer, translator, and publisher. After graduating from high school in Náchod (1943), Škvorecký worked as a blue-collar laborer. In 1945–49 he studied medicine and then English and philosophy at Charles University in Prague. After graduation he worked as a teacher and served in the army. In 1953–55 and 1959–63 he was an editor for the State Literary Press, where he translated English prose and wrote articles in this field. In 1956–58 he edited the periodical *Světová literatura*. From 1963 Škvorecký mainly began to write. After the suppression of the Prague Spring, in 1969 he emigrated to Canada, where he taught at the University of Toronto. In 1975 he became a professor there. In 1971, along with his wife, he founded the 68 Publishers Press, which published Czech and Slovak works banned by Communist censorship at home. In 1978 the Communist authorities deprived Škvorecký of his Czechoslovak citizenship. After the Velvet Revolution, in 1990 he returned to Czechoslovakia.

Škvorecký made his literary debut with the novel *Zbabělci* (1958; *Cowards*, 1980), in which he presented the fall of the Czech middle class and the advance of the Red Army with its barbarian culture. Its main hero, Danny Smiřický, the author's alter ego, also appeared in other works by Škvorecký. *Zbabělci* could only appear in Czechoslovakia because of a political struggle between Stalinists and reformers in the Communist Party. When the book was out, it was strongly attacked and the authorities decided to requisition its circulation, but in vain, since it was sold out. Nevertheless, Škvorecký had to leave the *Světova literatura* editorial board. He touched on a similar topic in the book *Konec nylonového věku* (The end of the nylon century; 1967), in which he said farewell to the burgher world and prophesied the advance of a Communist world ruled by opportunists. In 1964 he published a volume on the Holocaust in the Protectorate of Bohemia and Moravia: *Sedmiramený svícen* (The menorah). Škvorecký continued to present the Communist reality when he went abroad—for instance, in the novels *Tankový prapor* (Battalion of tanks; 1971) and *Mirákl* (Miracle; 1972), in which he presented the prosecution of the Catholic Church under Stalinism; *Příběh inženýra lidských duší* (The case of the engineer of human souls; 1977); and the play *Ze života české společnosti* (From the life of Czech society; 1980). In a grotesque way Škvorecký described the functioning of the Communist state, stressing the links between Czech culture and the West and the alien nature of the eastern despotism. He also wrote popular stories and biographies (for example, the biographies of Antonín Dvořák: *Scherzo capriccioso* [1984] and *Dvorak in Love* [1988]); essays; an autobiography, *Příběh neúspěšného tenorsaxofonisty* (The case of an unfortunate tenor sax player; 1994); and a book on the 68 Publishers, *Samožerbuch* (An album for myself; 1977). (PU)

Sources: *ČBS*; *Kdo byl kdo v našich dějinach ve 20. stoleti*, vol. 2 (Prague, 1998); *Slovník českých spisovatelů od roku 1945*, vol. 2 (Prague, 1998); Jana Kalish, *Josef Škvorecký* (Toronto, 1986); Andrzej Jagodziński, *Banici: Rozmowy z czeskimi pisarzami emigracyjnymi* (Kraków, 1988); Ilja Matouš, *Bibliografie Josefa Škvoreckého* (Prague, 1990); Paul Trensky, *The Fiction of Josef Škvorecký* (New York and London, 1991); Milan Jungmann, *O Josefu Škvoreckým* (Prague, 1993).

SLACHTA Margit (18 September 1884, Kassa [now Košice, Slovakia]–6 January 1974, Buffalo, New York), Hungarian nun and social worker. Slachta's Polish ancestors were landowners in Slovakia. She was the second of six daughters. When her father and some members of the family emigrated to the United States, Slachta remained in Hungary, and in 1906 she was certified as a German and French teacher. While a student, she was greatly influenced by a lecture on the protection of female workers and on patronage. In November 1908 she joined the Social Mission Society, an organization founded by Edith Farkas, and became a leading representative of the Christian social movement in defense of women. Slachta traveled throughout the country giving lectures; she conducted community research, collected donations, and opened a school. Unlike Church authorities, she wanted to solve social problems through practical work, not only through charity. In October 1918 Slachta founded the Union of Catholic Women, whose program combined Christian, national, and social principles. She initiated nursing education in Budapest. In 1920 she was the first woman to be elected to the Hungarian parliament.

In May 1923 Slachta founded the Sisters of Social Service. During World War II, counteracting Nazi propaganda, she organized presentations and lectures designed to propagate Christian values. She criticized anti-Jewish laws and protested against them to the authorities. In November 1940, on behalf of the Union of Catholic Women, Slachta acted in defense of the Jewish people, who were being used as slave laborers, and in the winter of 1941 she protested their deportation. When in February 1943 Slovakia announced that it was going to get rid of all Jews, Slachta met with Pope Pius XII and appealed for his intercession. From the spring of 1944 on, she provided shelter to persecuted people in the convent of her society. In 1945 Slachta was reelected to the parliament, where she dealt with law and order. She believed law and order could be guaranteed by maintaining the monarchy; therefore, she rejected the republican system. She sought to reestablish diplomatic relations with the Vatican. She was devoted to protecting the rights of Hungarian people living abroad. She was also engaged in defending the rights of other small nations and in protecting family life and national morality.

After the Sovietization of Hungary, Slachta's work became increasingly difficult. A speech she gave on 28 October 1947 was labeled detrimental to the interests of the state, and she was excluded from parliamentary sessions for sixty days. Her last speech in parliament, delivered on 16 June 1948, was rudely interrupted by Communist MPs. In this speech she protested a bill to nationalize church-owned schools. After this bill was passed, Communist MPs sang the national anthem. Slachta continued to sit while they sang; as a result, the disciplinary commission deprived her of her parliamentary immunity. Fearing arrest, in January 1949 Slachta went into hiding in the convent of the Dominican Sisters. In June 1949, along with her sister, she went to Austria and then to the United States. While in exile, she submitted a memorandum to U.S. President Harry Truman and to American bishops, trying to draw their attention to the situation of citizens of Communist countries. She collected signatures in protest against the imprisonment of Cardinal **József Mindszenty**, the Primate of Hungary. She also helped refugees after the 1956 revolution. Slachta died in the convent of the Sisters of Social Service. In 1985 Israel honored her with the title "Righteous among Nations," and a tree was planted in her memory at the Yad Vashem garden. In May 1995 Slachta was posthumously awarded the Order for Courage of the Hungarian Republic. (JT)

Sources: Ilona Mona, *Slachta Margit* (Budapest, 1997); *A magyar forradalom és szabadságharc enciklopédiája* (Budapest, 1999).

SLADKEVIČIUS Vincentas (20 August 1920, Guronys, near Kaišiadorys–28 May 2000, Kaunas), Primate of Lithuania. Born the fifth child of a poor peasant family, after graduating from high school in Kaunas, Sladkevičius studied at the Kaunas Seminary. Ordained in 1944, he worked in the parishes of Kietaviškés and Kuktiškés, taught religion at a high school in Merkiné, and became parish priest at Inturké in 1948. From 1952 to 1958 Sladkevičius taught dogmatic theology and biblical exegesis and worked as rector of the Kaunas Seminary, the only theological seminary in Soviet Lithuania. In this role, he was under constant pressure from the Soviet political police, who wanted to recruit informers among the clergy. In 1958, without permission from the Soviet authorities, **Teofilis Matulionis**, the bishop of Kaišiadorys, appointed Sladkevičius auxiliary bishop of the diocese of Kaišiadorys. The Holy See granted Sladkevičius the authority of an apostolic administrator with episcopal powers. The KGB responded with repressive measures. Sladkevičius was forced to leave the diocese of Kaišiadorys and was dismissed from the Kaunas Seminary. He was forced to settle in the village of Nemunello Radviliškis. From 1963 to 1982 he was de facto under house arrest. Despite these difficulties, he courageously continued his pastoral work. It was only in 1982 that the Soviet authorities allowed him to return to Kaišiadorys and to assume the position of apostolic administrator of the diocese of Kaišiadorys.

After the start of perestroika, the Lithuanian people could more firmly demand their rights. As the Soviet Union's policies became more flexible, on 29 May 1988 Pope **John Paul II** elevated Sladkevičius to the College of Cardinals and named him president of the Lithuanian Episcopal Conference. Sladkevičius was the second Lithuanian to become a cardinal. He vigorously set about rebuilding Church structures. At that time 686 priests were working in Lithuania. On 23 October 1988 Sladkevičius celebrated the first mass in Vilnius Cathedral in forty years. He was subsequently named archbishop of Kaunas by the Pope. On 16 February 1989, on the anniversary of the prewar Lithuanian independence day, Sladkevičius celebrated a solemn mass in his cathedral. The majority of the members of the Lithuanian Seimas (parliament) attended this mass. Sladkevičius spoke on the square in front of the Military Museum, where, in the presence of one hundred thousand people, the restored prewar Freedom Monument was rededicated. Sladkevičius tried to avoid direct entanglements in political strife, but he explicitly supported Lithuanian aspirations for independence. At the end of November 1990 he met with a delegation of the Central Committee of the Communist Party of Lithuania to negotiate the role of the Church in the ongoing transformations. As a result of these transformations, Lithuania finally regained its independence in 1991. In 1996 Sladkevičius retired. Until the end of his life he enjoyed great respect among the Lithuanian people, regardless of their religious beliefs. (WR)

Sources: *EL*, vol. 5; Saulius Sužiedelis, *Historical Dictionary of Lithuania* (Lanham, Md., 1997); Alfred E. Senn, *Lithuania Awakening* (Berkeley, 1990); V. Stanley Vardys and Judith B. Sedaitis, *Lithuania: The Rebel Nation* (Boulder, Colo., 1997); Vytautas Landsbergis, *Lithuania Independent Again* (Cardiff, 2000); Irena Mikłaszewicz, *Polityka sowiecka wobec Kościoła katolickiego na Litwie 1944–1965* (Warsaw, 2001).

SLÁNSKÝ Rudolf [originally Salzman] (31 July 1901, Nezvěstice, near Plzeň–3 December 1952, Prague), Czechoslovak Communist activist. Born into a lower-middle-class Jewish family, after graduating from high school, Slánský briefly served as a member of the Czechoslovak Social Democratic Party, but in 1921 he joined the newly established Communist Party of Czechoslovakia (CPC). He worked in the party apparatus in Prague and edited the party press organ, *Rudé Právo*. He subsequently served as regional party secretary in Moravská Ostrava (1926–28) and Prague (1929–30). In 1928 Slánský attended the Sixth Congress of the Communist International. In the following year, thanks to the support of **Klement Gottwald**, he became a member of the Central Committee (CC) and the Politburo of the CPC. In 1930 he was also made secretary of the CC. In 1935 he spoke at the Seventh Congress of the Comintern in Moscow. In December 1938, after the Pact of Munich, Slánský fled to the Soviet Union, where he worked in the central apparatus of the Comintern and edited the Czech broadcasts of Moscow Radio. In 1944 he went to the headquarters of Soviet Partisans near Kiev, where he prepared himself for a return to his country. As a result of an agreement with the government-in-exile, Gottwald aspired to assume governmental positions, so Slánský took the post of secretary general of the party CC (early 1945). In September 1947 he was head of the Czechoslovak delegation to the founding congress of the Communist Information Bureau (Cominform) at Szklarska Poręba, Poland, and in June 1948 he headed the Czechoslovak delegation to a Cominform conference at which **Josip Broz Tito** was denounced. After the Communist coup of February 1948, Slánský, together with Gottwald, was in charge of the accelerated Sovietization of Czechoslovakia, and he supervised the brutal persecutions of non-Communist politicians and the Catholic Church. He also called for a purge of the army.

At the end of the 1940s Slánský was the second most powerful person in the regime, and his name day was celebrated with Stalinist pomp. In 1949 he co-initiated a purge of the party, justifying it as a struggle against "Titoism." He pressed the security apparatus for greater effectiveness in hunting down and eliminating hidden "enemies," and in November 1949, along with Gottwald, Slánský requested that the Soviet leadership send a greater number of functionaries to help. In 1950 Slánský instigated the expulsion from the party leadership and then the imprisonment of **Vladimír Clementis**, **Gustav Husák**, and hundreds of other activists. In the spring of 1951 he suggested that the situation necessitated finding a Czech counterpart to **László Rajk**—that is, an "enemy" among top-ranking Communist Party officials.

Meanwhile, testimonies extorted through the torture of those arrested indicated that it was Slánský himself who headed a network of "spies" linked to the case of Noel Field. A case against Field was being prepared by the services of the Soviet Union and other Soviet bloc countries. In June 1951 the leadership of the Czech secret police and Soviet advisers reinforced the suspicions regarding Slánský by introducing a campaign of combating "Jewish bourgeois nationalism." In July the Czechoslovak minister of defense, **Alexej Čepička**, was sent by Gottwald to the Kremlin, where he attended sessions of the Politburo of the CC of the Communist Party of the Soviet Union at which it was decided that the accusations against Slánský were insufficiently proven, but it was stated that Slánský had made too many political errors and therefore could not continue as secretary general of the party. At the end of July 1951 Slánský

received the country's most prestigious award, the Order of Klement Gottwald. However, at a CC plenum in September he became the target of sharp attacks, and although he had made a self-criticism, he was removed from his position and became a vice-premier. On 11 November Anastas Mikoyan brought a special letter from Stalin to Gottwald, demanding the arrest of Slánský. On 26 November 1951 Slánský was expelled from all his positions and then imprisoned. The CC of the CPC accepted this decision without protest. Slánský was accused not only of espionage and "treason," but also of "Zionism." Under torture he confessed to all the absurd charges that had been prepared against him. Along with ten other activists (including Clementis), Slánský was sentenced to death in a show trial (20–27 November 1952) and executed soon afterwards. In 1963, during the belated and limited de-Stalinization in Czechoslovakia, Slánský was posthumously exonerated of the criminal charges of treason and espionage for which he had been condemned, but he was not cleared of "political errors." (WR)

Sources: *ČBS*; Lazitch; *Enciklopedia Slovenska*, vol. 5 (Bratislava, 1980); *Kdo byl kdo v našich dějinách ve 20. století*, vol. 2 (Prague, 1998); *Českoslovenští politici: 1918–1991* (Prague, 1991); Josef Korbel, *The Communist Subversion of Czechoslovakia, 1938–1948* (Princeton, 1959); Edward Taborsky, *Communism in Czechoslovakia, 1948–1960* (Princeton, 1961); Josefa Slánská, *Report on My Husband* (London, 1969); Jiří Pelikán, *The Czechoslovak Political Trials, 1950–1954* (Stanford, 1971).

SLAVEYKOV Pencho (27 April 1866, Tryavna, Bulgaria–28 May 1912, Como Brunate, Italy), Bulgarian poet. Slaveykov's father, Petko Slaveykov (1827–95), was also a poet. From 1892 to 1898 Slaveykov studied philosophy in Leipzig, where he became interested in the works of Friedrich Nietzsche and other German philosophers. After returning to Bulgaria, he contributed to Krustyo Krustev's periodical, *Misul*. He also worked as a teacher, theater director, and librarian. Slaveykov was an ideologue of the so-called young modernists with neo-Romantic leanings. He also advocated the "Europeanization" of Bulgarian culture and was influenced by Western symbolism and expressionism. Slaveykov won acclaim as the author of lyrical and contemplative-philosophical poems in the collections *Sun za shtastie* (The dream of happiness; 1907) and *Na Ostrova na Blazhenite* (Isle of the Blessed; 1910). He is also famous for his unfinished epic poem, *Kurvava Pesen* (Song of blood; written 1911–12; published 1913), which describes the Bulgarian uprising of April 1876 and reflects on the role of national myths. Because of this poem Slaveykov was nominated for the Nobel Prize in literature. Because he satirized the authorities in his poems, Slaveykov lost his job in 1911, and in the following year he went to Italy, where he died. (WR)

Sources: Svetoslava Slaveikova, *Pencho Slaveikov: Biografícheski ocherk* (Sofia, 1955); *Pencho Slaveikov* (Sofia, 1967); Teresa Dąbek-Wirgowa, *Penczo Sławejkow, Tradycjonalizm i nowatorstwo* (Wrocław, 1973); Hilde Fai, *Pencho Slaveikov i nemskata literature* (Sofia, 1981); Raymond Detrez, *Historical Dictionary of Bulgaria* (Lanham, Md., 1997).

SLAVICI Ioan [originally Sârbu] (18 January 1848, Şiria, near Arad–17 August 1925, Panciu), Romanian writer and political activist. After graduating from high school in his native Transylvania, Slavici studied in Budapest and Vienna, where in 1869 he met the poet Mihai Eminescu, who exerted a great influence on his writing. In the same year Slavici began to write for the daily *Comvorbiri Literare*. After receiving a teaching position in Bucharest, he began to work with Eminescu, becoming a member of the editorial staff of *Timpul*, a newspaper of the Conservative Party. In 1881 Slavici made his literary debut with the collection *Nuvele din popor* (Folk stories), which included one of his most famous works, "Moara cu noroc" (The mill of luck and plenty, 1994). In 1884 Slavici went to Sibiu, Transylvania, where he became an editor of *Tribuna*, a Romanian national radical daily, and joined the Central Committee of the Romanian National Party (Partidul Naţional Român [RNP]), the leading political party of the Transylvanian Romanians. He was subsequently arrested and spent one year in an Austro-Hungarian prison for instigating a rebellion against the authorities. In 1890 Slavici returned to Bucharest. In 1894 the literary daily *Vatra*, for which he worked from 1894 to 1896, began the publication of *Mara*, one of his most famous novels, which was published in book form in 1906. As was typical of nineteenth-century East European writers, Slavici sought inspiration in folklore and the everyday life of Transylvanians. In 1904 he joined the editorial staff of *Ziua*, a pro-German newspaper in Bucharest. During World War I he favored the Central Powers. After the Germans occupied Bucharest, he became an editor of the daily *Bucharest Gazette*. In 1919, after the end of World War I, he was sentenced to five years' imprisonment for acting to the detriment of the country during the war. Although after one year he was released, this sentence destroyed his reputation. Slavici died in poverty and disfavor. (PC)

Sources: Marcea Pompiliu, *Ioan Slavici* (Bucharest, 1965); Dimitrie Vatamaniuc, *Ioan Slavici: Opera literaria* (Bucharest, 1970); Ian Dodu Balan, *Ioan Slavici* (Bucharest, 1985); Kurt W. Treptow and Marcel Popa, *Historical Dictionary of Romania* (Lanham, Md., 1996); *Pisarze świata: Słownik encyklopedyczny* (Warsaw, 1999).

SLÁVIK Juraj (28 January 1890, Dobrá Niva, Austria-Hungary [now in Slovakia]–20 May 1969, Washington, D.C.), Slovak politician, diplomat, and journalist. Born into the family of a Lutheran pastor, Slávik studied law in Budapest, Berlin, and Paris. From 1912 to 1913 and from 1921 to 1923 he edited *Prúdy*, a literary periodical that served as a platform for the young Slovak intelligentsia who called for close cooperation with the Czechs. At the end of 1918 Slávik became secretary of the Slovak National Council in Bratislava and helped to organize the Czechoslovak administration. After the invasion by the Hungarian Red Army in 1919, he was appointed government commissar for the affairs of eastern Slovakia. In 1920 he became government delegate to the international plebiscite commission in Spiš and Orava. From 1918 to 1920 and from 1929 to 1935 Slávik sat in the parliament in Prague. He was a member of the leadership of the Agrarian Party in Slovakia and held various executive positions in many community organizations; for example, he was vice-president of the Sokol Organization, president of the Czechoslovak Officers' Union, and president of the Aero Club of Czechoslovakia. In 1926 Slávik became minister of agriculture and head of the department of unification. From December 1929 to October 1932 he was minister of interior. In 1936 he became ambassador to Warsaw and held this post until the dismemberment of Czechoslovakia in March 1939. In exile Slávik worked closely with **Edvard Beneš** and helped to establish the Czechoslovak National Committee in Paris. In the fall of 1939 he represented the Czechoslovak National Committee before the Polish government in Angers. From 1940 to 1945 Slávik served as minister of interior in the London-based Czechoslovak government-in-exile, and he took part in Polish-Czechoslovak negotiations on the establishment of a federation. In 1946 he became ambassador to the United States. After the Communist coup of February 1948, Slávik resigned from this position and became active in various émigré organizations. In 1949 he was one of the founders of the Council of Free Czechoslovakia (Rada Svobodného Československa). Slávik's publications include *Zapredané Slovensko* (Betrayed Slovakia; 1939); *Peace Treaties and Central Europe* (1941); *Masaryk a Slovensko* (Masaryk and Slovakia; 1960); and the memoirs *Moja pamät': živá kniha* (My memory: A living book; 1955). (MG)

Sources: *SBS*; *ČBS*; *Kdo byl kdo v našich dějinách ve 20. století* (Prague, 1998); Jozef Špetko, *Líšky kontra ježe: Slovenská politická emigrácia 1948–1989* (Bratislava, 2002).

SLAVOV Atanas (25 July 1930, Sliven), Bulgarian poet and writer. Slavov graduated in English studies from Sofia University, and then he worked there as a lecturer in the history of Bulgarian literature and art. His early poems were sharply criticized by **Todor Zhivkov** himself. In 1975 Slavov was allowed to go on a Bulgarian Academy of Sciences scholarship to the United States, where he stayed to do research and publish poetry and memoirs. In 1978–79 he wrote and in 1986 he published his memoirs, *With the Precision of Bats*; they are one of the best records of the political and intellectual atmosphere in Bulgaria in the 1960s and 1970s. Slavov's other best-known work is *The "Thaw" in Bulgarian Literature* (1981), a combination of memoirs, history of literature, and literary criticism illustrating cultural life under communism. Slavov has also published *Stikhotvoreniya: Pornografska poema* (Poetry: A pornographic poem; 1980), as well as science fiction and additional memoirs, either in Bulgarian or in English. He also authored *Traditional Bulgarian Cookbook* (1998). (WR)

Sources: Raymond Detrez, *Historical Dictionary of Bulgaria* (Lanham, Md., 1997).

SŁAWEK Walery, pseudonym "Gustaw" (2 November 1879, Strutynka, Podolia–3 April 1939, Warsaw), Polish politician. Sławek came from an impoverished noble family and graduated from a gymnasium in Niemirów; then he was a student at the Kronenberg College of Commerce in Warsaw until 1899, and thereafter he worked in banking. From 1900 he belonged to the Polish Socialist Party (Polska Partia Socjalistyczna [PPS]), and he was involved in its underground activities in Łódź and Warsaw. In June 1902 Sławek joined the Central Workers' Committee of the PPS. At that time he became acquainted with **Józef Piłsudski**; this had a decisive influence on his career. In March 1903 Sławek was arrested, but nine months later he escaped from prison at Sieradz, avoiding deportation. In 1904 he started working on creating the Fighting Squads of the PPS (Organizacja Bojowa PPS), and the following year, along with **Aleksander Prystor**, he became head of the Fighting Squads' Underground Military Department. In September 1905 Sławek was rearrested, but in November he was released for lack of evidence. From 1906 he was in the PPS–Revolutionary Faction. On 9 June 1906 Sławek was severely injured in the explosion of a bomb that he was planting under a mail train in Milanówek. After this attempt he was arrested but again was not convicted as he maintained that the explosion came from an accidentally found parcel. The bomb failure, the serious injuries, and the death of his great love, Wanda (the stepdaughter of Piłsudski) caused a severe depression and a drop in Sławek's activities. He did not participate in any undertakings until a successful action at Bezdany in September 1908. Sławek was active in the Union of Active Struggle (Związek Walki Czynnej), and from 1912 he was secretary of the Polish Military Treasury and became

a member of the Provisional Committee of Confederated Pro-Independence Parties.

After the outbreak of World War I Sławek joined the staff of the First Brigade of the Polish Legions. On 1 August 1914 he became head of the Intelligence Bureau of the High Command of the Riflemen's Association, and in 1915 he took over the post of head of the Intelligence Bureau of the First Brigade. Sławek became the most trusted confidant of Piłsudski, who entrusted him with various responsible missions. In 1915 he became a member of the Chief Command of the Polish Military Organization (Polska Organizacja Wojskowa) and the Central National Committee (Centralny Komitet Narodowy), the representation of pro-independence parties that aimed at the reconstruction of the state with the assistance of the central states. Sławek's extensive conspiratorial activities led to his arrest by the Germans on 14 July 1917.

Released from the Modlin fortress on 12 November 1918, from 1 January 1919 Sławek headed the political section of the Second Department of the General Staff (Intelligence) and took part in a complicated Polish-Lithuanian game that ended in an unsuccessful pro-Polish coup d'état in Kaunas (Kovno). The coup led to a further increase in tensions between the two countries. During the Polish-Soviet war Sławek was dispatched to the High Command of **Symon Petlura.** He served there as a liaison officer between the Ukrainian leader and Piłsudski. After the end of the war Sławek completed a one-year course at the Military College, and then he went into the reserves. In 1924 he started a consolidation of Piłsudski adherents. He became (among other things) president of the Main Board of the Association of Polish Legionnaires, and he founded the Confederation of Working People. In the coup of May 1926 Sławek played a political rather than a military role. From then on he was one of the leaders of the *sanacja* regime and a member of the "group of colonels." In 1927 Sławek formed a political representation for the Piłsudski camp, the Nonparty Bloc of Cooperation with the Government (Bezpartyjny Blok Współpracy z Rządem [BBWR]), and after the elections in 1928 he became head of the party. Sławek firmly struggled against both the opposition and the liberals of the *sanacja* regime. He was an advocate of a considerable consolidation of the presidential powers, a reduction of "party favoritism," and the introduction of an elitist government system. From 1928 Sławek worked on changing the constitution. Between 29 March and 23 August 1930 Sławek held the post of prime minister for the first time. He was followed by Piłsudski himself, who suppressed the opposition by imprisoning its activists in the fortress of Brześć. Sławek took part in this, and he became much tougher toward the opponents of the *sanacja* regime, reducing the number of liberals on the BBWR electoral lists in the early elections of 1930. On 4 December 1930 he again became prime minister and held the post until 26 May 1931, when he resigned, largely owing to an economic crisis. Sławek had considerable influence on the new constitution, passed on 23 April 1930, as he drew up its first ten articles, which were referred to as the "constitutional Decalog." Between 28 March and 12 October 1935 he served as prime minister for the third time.

Piłsudski was planning for Sławek to take over the post of president but did not leave an explicit order on the issue. Thus, after Piłsudski's death in May 1935, Sławek recognized the authority of **Ignacy Mościcki**, counting on succeeding him after the forthcoming elections. Gradually removed from power, Sławek made several political errors; for example, he dissolved the BBWR on 30 October 1935. In place of the BBWR, he planned to establish a General Organization of Society, a kind of a mono-party. However, he failed to win the support of *sanacja* hard-liners, who were oriented toward General **Edward Rydz-Śmigły**, and he was even less successful among the liberals of the *sanacja* regime. On 24 May 1936 Sławek was dismissed as president of the Association of Polish Legionnaires, and soon he also lost his post as president of the Józef Piłsudski Institute of Modern History. In 1928–38 Sławek was an MP, and between June and September 1938 he was the speaker of the Assembly. However, after the dissolution of the parliament, as a result of a particularly aggressive negative campaign, Sławek lost in the subsequent parliamentary election of 1938. Suffering from depression and feeling political defeat, Sławek committed suicide. (PU)

Sources: *PSB*, vol. 38; Piotr Stawecki, *Następcy Komendanta* (Warsaw, 1969); Andrzej Chojnowski, *Piłsudczycy u władzy: Dzieje BBWR* (Wrocław, 1986); Jerzy Marek Nowakowski, *Walery Sławek (1879–1939): Zarys biografii politycznej* (Warsaw, 1988); *Kto był kim w Drugiej Rzeczypospolitej* (Warsaw, 1994); Ludwik Malinowski, *Politycy II Rzeczypospolitej*, vol. 2 (Toruń, 1995); *Encyklopedia historii Drugiej Rzeczypospolitej* (Warsaw, 1999).

ŠLECHTA Emanuel (19 December 1895, Kuttenberg [now Kutná Hora, the Czech Republic]–17 March 1960, Prague), Czech engineer, economist, and political activist. A mechanical engineer by profession, Šlechta was involved in the organization of the production and transportation industries. From 1923 to 1926 he was in the United States. In 1935 he became an associate professor and in 1945 a full professor at the Technical University of Prague. Šlechta's publications include the following: *Hospodárná velikost sériové výroby* (The economic scale of mass production; 1927); *Americký industrialismus* (American industrialism;

1928); *Organisace průmyslových podniků* (The organization of industrial enterprises; 1935); and *Plynulá a přerušovaná výroba* (Steady and intermittent production; 1938). Between world wars Šlechta was active in the National Socialist Party, and, from 1938 to 1939, in the National Unity Party (Strana Národní Jednoty). In 1939–45 Šlechta was imprisoned in the Buchenwald concentration camp. After the war, from 1948 onwards, he served as chairman of the board of Živnobanka and was a member of the leadership of the National Socialist Party. Šlechta worked closely with the Communists. In February 1948 he supported the Communist coup and joined a special committee of the National Front whose aim it was to "purge the public arena of reactionaries and enemies of the people's democratic system." Šlechta helped to establish the Communist-controlled Czechoslovak Socialist Party (Československá Strana Socialistická) and became its chairman. From 1948 he sat on the National Assembly and held the post of minister of technology. In 1950 he became minister of construction, and in 1956, minister and chairman of the National Construction Committee. In March 1960 Šlechta and his wife committed suicide for political reasons. (PU)

Sources: *ČBS*; *Českoslovenští politici: 1918–1991* (Prague, 1991).

SLEŽEVIČIUS Adolfas (2 February 1948, near Šiauliai), Lithuanian post-Communist politician. Sleževičius graduated in economics, and owing to his membership in the Communist Party, he quickly advanced professionally. In 1977–81 he was deputy minister of the meat and dairy industry of the Lithuanian SSR. From 1983 to 1989 he worked in the Central Committee (CC) of the Communist Party of Lithuania. In 1990–91 he was deputy minister of agriculture. In 1991 he became head of a Lithuanian-Norwegian joint venture company and then chairman of the Association of Lithuanian Dairy Producers. After the (post-Communist) Lithuanian Democratic Labor Party (Lietuvos Demokratinė Darbo Partija [LDLP]) won the October 1992 elections, Sleževičius became an MP on its behalf. When the LDLP leader, **Algirdas Brazauskas**, became president, Sleževičius took the lead of the party, and on 10 March 1993 he became prime minister. In the fall of 1995 he became involved in a financial scandal, since a few days before some banks were closed, he withdrew his deposits from them. Accused of corruption, he refused to step down, as President Brazauskas demanded. He did not resign until he was voted out of power by the parliament on 8 February 1996. Sleževičius is one of the richest people in Lithuania, with extensive business connections in Russia and the Caucasus. (WR)

Sources: Saulius Sužiedelis, *Historical Dictionary of Lithuania* (Lanham, Md., 1997); Richard J. Krickus, *Showdown: The Lithuanian Rebellion and the Breakup of the Soviet Empire* (Washington, D.C., 1997); "Liga kapitału," *Wprost*, 25 June 2000.

SLEŽEVIČIUS Mykolas (21 February 1882, Drembliai, near Raseiniai–11 December 1939, Kaunas), Lithuanian politician. From 1902 to 1907 Sleževičius studied law at the university in Odessa. He subsequently returned to Lithuania and joined the Lithuanian Democratic Party. He also edited the periodicals of this party, *Lietuvos Žinios* and *Lietuvos Ūkininkas*. During World War I he was active in the Lithuanian Central Relief Committee in Petrograd. After the February 1917 revolution, he joined a group of Socialists-Populists. At a stormy conference of Lithuanian delegates in Petrograd (late May and early June 1917), Sleževičius put forward a resolution demanding Lithuanian independence. As the supporter of a more moderate approach to social issues, he was expelled from the Lithuanian Socialist People's Party. Along with his supporters, Sleževičius founded the Lithuanian Socialist People's Democratic Party (Lietuvos Socialistų Liaudininkų Demokratų Partija [LSLDP]) in Voronezh in November 1917. In 1918 he was briefly detained by the Bolsheviks in Voronezh. After his release, he helped Lithuanian refugees to return home.

After returning to Lithuania, Sleževičius became head of the second government of the republic on 26 December 1918. Because of the Bolshevik offensive, this government had to move from Vilnius (Wilno) to Kaunas. In mid-February Sleževičius's government imposed martial law. After a short interval in March 1919, Sleževičius again served as head of the government and head of the ministry of foreign affairs from 12 April to 6 October 1919. He engaged the Lithuanians in the defense of their country against the Bolsheviks and against the forces of Pavel Bermondt-Avalov. He also suppressed a coup attempt in Kaunas. This attempt had been organized by the Polish Military Organization in August 1919. In the elections of April 1920 Sleževičius won a seat on the LSLDP slate. As a result of his efforts, the LSLDP and the Peasant Populist Party, led by Kazys Grinius, merged to form the Lithuanian Peasant Populist Party (Lietuvos Valstiečių Liaudininkų Sąjunga [LVLS]) at the end of 1922. From 1920 to 1926 Sleževičius headed a parliamentary commission for foreign affairs, but he was in the opposition after the elections of May 1923. On 15 June 1926, after the LVLS and the Social Democratic Party won the elections, he again became head of a center-left government, serving simultaneously as minister of foreign affairs and minister of justice. The new government lifted martial law, declared an amnesty, developed social legislation, improved the situation of the national minorities, and (on 28 September) concluded a non-aggression pact with the Soviet Union. The opposition did not approve of these policies and accused the leftist government of the "Polonization" and "Bolshevization" of Lithuania. On 17 December 1926, along with President **Kazys Grinius**, Sleževičius was removed from power in a nationalist coup d'état led by **Antanas Smetona**. During the period of the nationalist dictatorship, Sleževičius was a member of the municipal government of Kaunas and an activist in the Lithuanian Law Association, and he practiced law. He was also the leader of the LVLS, but he did not have a chance to play any active political role. (WR)

Sources: *EL*, vol. 5; Saulius Sužiedelis, *Historical Dictionary of Lithuania* (Lanham, Md., 1997); Antanas Rūkas, ed., *Mykolas Sleževičius* (Chicago, 1954); Alfonsas Eidintas and Vytautas Žalys, *Lithuania in European Politics: The Years of the First Republic, 1918–1940* (New York, 1997); Wojciech Roszkowski, "Litewskie partie chłopskie (1905–1970)," in Krzysztof Jasiewicz, ed., *Europa Nieprowincjonalna* (Warsaw, 1999).

SLEZYUK Ivan (14 January 1896, Żywaczów, near Stanisławów, Austria-Hungary [now Zhyvachiv, near Ivano-Frankivsk, Ukraine]–2 December 1973, Ivano-Frankivsk), Uniate bishop. After graduating from a seminary in 1923, Slezyuk was ordained a priest. He then worked in various parishes in Eastern Galicia. Anticipating his own arrest by the Communists, Bishop **Hryhory Khomyshyn** appointed Slezyuk coadjutor with the right of succession in April 1945. However, soon after Khomyshyn and the majority of Ukrainian Uniate bishops were arrested, Slezyuk was also imprisoned on 2 June 1945. Sentenced to ten years of forced labor, he served his sentence in forced labor camps in Vorkuta. In 1950 he was transferred to a forced labor camp in the Mordvinian ASSR. Released on 15 November 1954, he returned to Ivano-Frankivsk and continued his underground pastoral work. On 27 November 1957, shortly before his death, Bishop **Ivan Latyshevskyi** ordained Slezyuk a bishop. In 1962 Slezyuk was arrested again and sentenced to five years in a particularly harsh forced labor camp. Released on 30 November 1968, he had to report regularly to the KGB. On 27 June 2001 Pope **John Paul II** beatified him at a solemn Holy Mass in Lviv. (WR)

Sources: Bohdan R. Bociurkiw, *The Ukrainian Greek-Catholic Church and the Soviet State (1939–1950)* (Edmonton, 1996); *Osservatore Romano* (weekly edition in English), 2001, nos. 25 and 27.

SLIPYI Josyf [originally Kobernytskyi-Dychkovskyi] (17 February 1892, Zazdrist, near Trembowla [now Terebovlya]–7 September 1984, Rome), Patriarch of the Ukrainian Greek Catholic Church, cardinal. After graduating from a seminary in Lemberg (Lwów, Lviv), Slipyi studied theology at Innsbruck, Austria, from 1912 to 1914, earning a doctorate in 1918 and the postdoctoral degree in 1920. He was ordained by Archbishop **Andriy Sheptytskyi** in 1917. From 1920 to 1922 Slipyi continued his studies at the Pontifical Gregorian University in Rome, where he received another postdoctoral degree. In 1922 he became a professor of dogmatic theology at a seminary in Lwów, and in 1925 he was appointed rector of this seminary. It was then that Slipyi for the first time came into conflict with Reverend **Havryl Kostelnyk**, a lecturer at this seminary, and with those who wanted the Uniate Church to break its ties with Rome. Slipyi was a co-founder and then an editor of the quarterly *Bohoslovya*. In 1928 he became the rector of the Greek Catholic Theological Academy. In 1935 he became the canon of St. George's Cathedral in Lwów and archdean of the archeparchy of Lwów. After the Red Army occupied Lwów, Pope Pius XII appointed Slipyi bishop-coadjutor, with the right of succession in Lviv (25 November 1939), and exarch of the Ukrainian territory to the east of the Zbruch River (9 October). On 22 December 1939 Slipyi was secretly consecrated archbishop and coadjutor to Metropolitan Sheptytskyi.

On 1 November 1944, after the reoccupation of Eastern Galicia by the Red Army and the death of Sheptytskyi, Slipyi became metropolitan of Halych and archbishop of Lviv. Right from the start he realized the intentions of the Soviet authorities, as pressure was put on him by Serhiy Danylenko, a colonel of the NKGB (the People's Commissariat for State Security) who served as a "representative of the Soviet Ukrainian government for religious affairs." On 23 November 1944 Slipyi sent a pastoral letter expressing gratitude to the Red Army for liberating the Ukraine and conveying the hope of a "better future" for the Ukrainian people. In this letter he assumed a neutral attitude to the ongoing battles between the Ukrainian Insurgent Army (UPA) and the Soviet troops, and he only expressed the hope that the bloodshed would end soon. In December 1944, in an attempt to establish relations between the Ukrainian Uniate Church and the authorities of the Soviet Union, Slipyi sent a delegation headed by Reverend **Kliment Sheptytskyi** to Moscow, where the members of the delegation presented a letter to Stalin and the Soviet authorities. In this letter, Slipyi expressed gratitude for the liberation of the Ukraine from German occupation and conveyed the hope that "minor problems" encountered by the Church in the new reality would be overcome in the spirit of respect for the autonomy of the Church and the state. The members of the delegation were received by the state authorities and by Patriarch Alexey and were also invited to the headquarters of the General Staff of the Red Army, where they were informed that the attitude of the Soviet authorities to the Uniate Church would depend on the attitude of this church to the UPA.

Slipyi appealed to the UPA and the Soviet authorities for a cease-fire. In a pastoral letter of 28 March 1945 he called for an end to the hostilities and for resolving the conflict through peaceful negotiations. Because the UPA continued its resistance to the Red Army and the Soviet authorities wanted to abolish the Ukrainian Greek Catholic Church anyway, on 11 April 1945 Slipyi was arrested, along with a group of other hierarchs of this church. St. George's Cathedral was searched by the NKGB. On 3 June 1946 the Soviets sentenced Slipyi to eight years in a forced labor camp for "treason," although he had never been a Soviet citizen. Slipyi was initially imprisoned in Novosibirsk, and then he was held in forced labor camps in Mariinsk and Boymy, the Kemerovo region. He later served his sentence in Inta, in the Pechora River basin, and in Dubrovlag. In the meantime, the Uniate Church was incorporated into the Orthodox Church in March 1946 by decision of a spurious "council" (Sobor) under the leadership of Father Kostelnyk in Lviv. After the end of Slipyi's term, the Soviet authorities demanded that he recognize the decision of that "council" and the supremacy of the Orthodox patriarch of Moscow. Since Slipyi refused to comply with this demand, he was additionally sentenced to indefinite exile in the Krasnoyarsk region in 1953, and in 1957 he was condemned to a further eight years in a forced labor camp. He was held in a camp in Mordvinia. Despite an official campaign of hatred against Slipyi and the Uniate Church and the persecution he suffered personally, Slipyi courageously stood for the independence of his church from the Orthodox Church and defended its union with Rome.

After a long effort by the Holy See, with the personal involvement by Pope John XXIII, Slipyi was released on 9 February 1963 and was allowed to go to Rome. He attended the Second Vatican Council, at which he urged that the Ukrainian Greek Catholic Church be raised to the status of a patriarchate. However, the eastern policy of Pope John XXIII was based on avoiding friction with the Kremlin, so the implementation of Slipyi's proposal was delayed. In December 1963 Slipyi was recognized as head of the Ukrainian Greek Catholic Church and a member of the Congregation for Eastern Churches. On 22 February 1965 he was solemnly proclaimed cardinal, and in 1975 Pope Paul VI finally consented to recognize Slipyi as patriarch of the Ukrainian Greek Catholic Church. In 1976 Slipyi made a missionary visit to Canada and the United States, where he was enthusiastically greeted by the Ukrainian émigré community. He was received by U.S. President

Gerald Ford in the White House. Slipyi was awarded many honorary doctorates, including those from the University of Ottawa, the University of Chicago, and the Catholic University of America in Washington, D.C. Slipyi strove for a spiritual and intellectual revival of the Ukrainian Greek Catholic Church. He founded a Uniate parish in Rome and reestablished the Studite monastic community, for which he gained the monastery of Castel Gandolfo. In 1963–84 he was in charge of efforts to found a Ukrainian Catholic university in Rome, and he revived the Ukrainian Academic Theological Society and its periodical, *Bohoslovya*. He also published many scholarly works. Slipyi specialized in the theology of the Holy Trinity. His manuscripts on the sacraments were smuggled from the Soviet Union and were published in three volumes in Canada in 1953–60. Slipyi also wrote on the Union of Brest-Litovsk and on the influence of St. Thomas Aquinas in the Ukraine. All together, thirteen volumes of his works were published from 1968 to 1984. His *Spomyny* (Memoirs), written in 1963–64, are kept in the Vatican's Archivum Patriarchalis S. Sophiae. Slipyi was an honorary member of the Shevchenko Scientific Society (NTSh) and a member of the Papal Academy of St. Thomas. Toward the end of Slipyi's life, the Ukrainian Greek Catholic Church received strong support through the work of Pope **John Paul II**, who convened a synod of this church in Rome in March 1980. This synod, the first in fifty-one years, was also attended by fifteen bishops from all over the world. Pope John Paul II also established the Ukrainian Catholic University in Rome. According to Slipyi's last wishes, his remains were reburied in the crypt of St. George's Cathedral in Lviv; this took place during a solemn ceremony on 28 August 1992. Slipyi's beatification process is under way. (WR)

Sources: *Encyclopedia of Ukraine*, vol. 4 (Toronto, 1993); P. Bilaniuk, "The Father of Modern Ecumenism: Patriarch Joseph Cardinal Slipy (1892–1984)," *Bohoslovia*, 1984, no. 48; *Intrepido Pastori: Naukovyi zbirnyk na chest blazhennishoho Patriiarkha Iosyfa v soroklittia vstuplennia na halytskyi prestil* (Rome, 1984); Ivan Hrynokh, "Vvedennia do tvoriv kard: Iosyfa, Verkhovnoho Arkhyiepyskopa," *Suchasnist* (1988); Jaroslav Pelikan, *Confessor between East and West: A Portrait of Ukrainian Cardinal Josyf Slipyj* (Grand Rapids, Mich., 1990); Bohdan R. Bociurkiw, *The Ukrainian Greek-Catholic Church and the Soviet State (1939–1950)* (Edmonton, 1996).

ŚLIUPAS Jonas (23 February 1861, Rakandžiai, near Šiauliai–6 November 1944, Berlin), Lithuanian doctor and politician. From 1880 to 1883 Šliupas studied at the Universities of Moscow and St. Petersburg and then in Geneva for a short time. He worked with the Polish Social Revolutionary Party Proletariat in 1882–83. In 1883 in Geneva he wrote the brochure *Išganymas vargdienio* (The salvation of a pauper; 1886), in which he expressed a belief that in the future Lithuania would be an independent national state. From 1883 to 1884 Šliupas edited the monthly *Aušra*, in which he presented liberal-positivist and anti-religious views. He maintained that the Catholic Church was an instrument of the Polonization of Lithuania and that Christianity immensely harmed the Lithuanian nation. Because of his views, he came into conflict with the Church hierarchs and the Lithuanian clergy. In 1884 Šliupas submitted a memorandum to Josif Hurko, the governor-general of Warsaw, in which he called for the lifting of a ban on printing in Lithuanian using the Latin alphabet. In exchange, Šliupas offered cooperation against the Poles, who allegedly Polonized and "corrupted" the Lithuanian people. However, his efforts were unsuccessful, and Šliupas left for the United States. He received a medical degree from the University of Maryland Medical School in 1891, and then he began practicing as a doctor in Scranton, Shenandoah, and other mining districts of Pennsylvania. He also edited the periodicals *Unija* (1884–85), *Apšvieta* (1892–93), and *Laisvoji Mintis* (1910–15). Despite his radical materialist views, Šliupas worked with Catholic priests who were devoted to the Lithuanian national cause. During World War I he actively promoted the cause of Lithuania's independence in various circles in America.

After Lithuania regained its independence, Šliupas returned to his country in 1921. He taught the history of medicine at the University of Kaunas and worked for the secularization of Lithuanian society. He openly criticized the dictatorship of **Antanas Smetona**, as a result of which he came into conflict with the political authorities and with the Church hierarchs. In 1933 he was elected mayor of the seaside resort of Palanga. He survived the Soviet occupation (1940–41), and toward the end of World War II he went to Germany, where he died. Šliupas authored *Lietuvių tauta senovėje ir šianden* (The Lithuanian nation in the past and present, 2 vols.; 1904–5) and *Essays on the Past, Present and Future of Lithuania* (1918). He also wrote atheist and anti-church satires, including *Tikyba ar mokslas* (Religion or science; 1895). (WR)

Sources: *EL*, vol. 5; Saulius Sužiedelis, *Historical Dictionary of Lithuania* (Lanham, Md., 1997); Jerzy Ochmański, *Litewski ruch narodowo-kulturalny w XIX wieku* (Białystok, 1965); Alfred E. Senn, *Jonas Basanavičius: The Patriarch of the Lithuanian National Renaissance* (Newtonville, Mass., 1980); Grażina Pranckietyte, *Jono Šliupo filosofine kūryta* (Vilnius, 1993); Juozas Jakštas, *Dr. Jonas Šliupas* (Šiauliai, 1996).

ŚLIWIŃSKI Artur (17 August 1877, Ruszki, near Kutno–16 January 1953, Warsaw), Polish politician.

Śliwiński graduated from a high school in Warsaw and studied at a trade academy in Leipzig. In 1902 he joined the Polish Socialist Party (Polska Partia Socjalistyczna [PPS]), and in 1906 in Kraków he became editor-in-chief of *Trybuna*, which was the local organ of the PPS–Revolutionary Faction. In August 1914, following the orders of **Józef Piłsudski**, Śliwiński unsuccessfully attempted to create a national government. Then he founded the Polish National Organization (Polska Organizacja Narodowa), which joined the Main National Committee (Naczelny Komitet Narodowy). In December 1915, Śliwiński became the chairman of the Central National Committee (Centralny Komitet Narodowy), which was the political superstructure of the clandestine Polish Military Organization (Polska Organizacja Wojskowa [POW]). In March 1917 he became the leader of the Party of National Independence (Stronnictwo Niezawisłości Narodowej), which was tied to the PPR–Revolutionary Faction, and in July he became secretary of the Provisional Council of State, a Polish political body created in Warsaw with German acquiescence. Between 1917 and 1918, Śliwiński served as deputy chairman of the City Council in Warsaw and from 1919 through 1922 as deputy mayor of the Polish capital. On 28 June 1922 Piłsudski entrusted him with creating a government, but Śliwiński failed to rally the necessary parliamentary support and quit his mission on July 7. Later Śliwiński worked as general director of Urban Theaters, chairman of the Polish Radio Company, and (between 1932 and 1939) director of the Polish Communal Bank. From 1935 through 1938, he sat in the Senate. During the German occupation, between 1939 and 1941, he served as chairman of the Warsaw Committee for Social Self-Assistance. Śliwiński penned several works on military history and Poland's struggle for independence. (WR)

Sources: *Kto był kim w Drugiej Rzeczypospolitej* (Warsaw, 1994); *Encyklopedia historii Drugiej Rzeczypospolitej* (Warsaw, 1999); Władysław Pobóg-Malinowski, *Najnowsza historia polityczna Polski*, vol. 2 (London, 1983).

SŁONIMSKI Antoni (15 October 1895, Warsaw–4 July 1976, Warsaw), Polish poet. Słonimski came from an assimilated Jewish family with an old intellectual pedigree. He was the son of the prominent physician Stanisław Słonimski, grandson of the mathematician Zelig Słonimski, and great-grandson of Abraham Stern, who was a member of the Warsaw Scientific Society. Słonimski studied at the Academy of Fine Arts in Warsaw and then in Munich. The year 1913 witnessed his poetic debut. Between 1917 and 1919 Słonimski worked with the periodical *Pro arte et studio*, and in 1920 he co-founded the Skamander poetry group. Słonimski's most important interwar collections of poetry include *Sonety* (Sonnets; 1918); *Harmonia* (Harmony; 1919); *Godzina poezji* (The hour of poetry; 1923); *Z dalekiej podróży* (From a distant journey; 1926); and *Okno bez krat* (A window with no bars; 1935). His poetry combined elements of expressionism and Romanticism with secular and liberal ideology. Between 1924 and 1939 Słonimski collaborated with the weekly *Wiadomości Literackie*. He edited its theatrical reviews section and regularly wrote its "Kronika tygodniowa" (Weekly chronicle), lashing out at stupidity and prejudice. Along with **Julian Tuwim**, Słonimski was a representative of the interwar surrealistic humor school, represented in (for example) the collection *W oparach absurdu* (In the fumes of the absurd; 1958). During World War II Słonimski was in Paris (1939–40) and then in London, where, between 1942 and 1946, he edited the journal *Nowa Polska*, which accepted the Yalta accords. In 1945 he published *Wiek klęski* (The age of defeat). Between 1946 and 1948, he headed the Literature Section of the UNESCO, and in 1948 he participated in the Congress of Intellectuals in the Defense of Peace in Wrocław; this was a propaganda spectacle organized by the Communists. Later Słonimski headed the Institute of Polish Culture in London, and in 1951 he returned permanently to Poland. In 1955, he was awarded the First Class State Award for his poetic output. During the "thaw" he supported the liberalization of the Communist system. Between 1956 and 1959 he served as chairman of the Main Board of the Association of Polish Writers. He became increasingly disillusioned with the anti-intellectual attitude of the regime of **Władysław Gomułka**. In 1964, Słonimski co-signed the "Letter of 34" dissenting intellectuals. He attracted a circle of young Marxist revisionist intellectuals and became a leader among the leftist and liberal opposition. **Adam Michnik** was his personal assistant. A rationalist and a skeptic, Słonimski spoke for the secular intelligentsia and was a master of scathing humor. From 1971 he collaborated with the Catholic weekly *Tygodnik Powszechny*. In 1975, Słonimski published *Alfabet wspomnień* (The alphabet of memoirs). (WR)

Sources: *Literatura polska: Przewodnik encyklopedyczny*, vol. 2 (Warsaw, 1985); Stanisław Barańczak, "Poezja Słonimskiego," *Twórczość*, 1974, no. 6; Artur Hutnikiewicz, "Słonimski," *Więź*, 1977, no. 2; A. Kowalczykowa, *Słonimski* (Warsaw, 1977); *Poeci czterech pokoleń* (Warsaw, 1977).

SMAL-STOTSKYI Roman (8 January 1893, Czernowitz [now Chernivtsi, Ukraine]–27 April 1969, Washington, D.C.), Ukrainian scholar and politician. Smal-Stotskyi's father, Stepan Smal-Stotskyi (1859–1938), was a noted philologist and educational activist. Smal-Stotskyi studied in Vienna, Leipzig, and Munich, earning a Ph.D. in philology in 1914. During World War I he was a representative in Munich of the Union for the Liberation of Ukraine. In 1918 he became a representative in Berlin of the Western Ukrainian National Republic, and from 1919 to 1923 he served as an adviser and minister plenipotentiary of the Ukrainian National Republic (Ukraiinska Narodna Republika [UNR]) to Berlin. Smal-Stotskyi taught comparative Slavic linguistics at the Ukrainian Free University in Prague (1923–26), and, from 1924 to 1925, he worked as a professor at Cambridge and served as an informal UNR representative to Great Britain. From 1926 to 1939 he was a professor at Warsaw University, and he also served as deputy minister and then minister of foreign affairs, minister of culture, and deputy prime minister of the UNR government-in-exile. In 1929–39 Smal-Stotskyi held the post of secretary of the Ukrainian Scientific Institute in Warsaw, and in 1934 he became a member of the Shevchenko Scientific Society (NTSh). He edited the periodical *Pratsy* and the series *Studii do ukraiinskoy hramatyki* (Studies on Ukrainian grammar, 7 vols.; 1926–29). He was also engaged in the Promethean movement, which sought to liberate various nations from Soviet occupation and which was discreetly supported by the Polish authorities.

During World War II, Smal-Stotskyi was held under house arrest in Prague by the Germans. Toward the end of the war, with the help of the Polish National Armed Forces (Narodowe Siły Zbrojne [NSZ]), he avoided arrest by the NKVD and went to Germany and subsequently to the United States in 1947. Smal-Stotskyi taught the history of Central and Eastern Europe at Marquette University in Milwaukee, Wisconsin. In 1951 he became president of the American branch of the NTSh, and in 1955, a member of the Ukrainian Congress Committee of America (UCCA). Smal-Stotskyi authored many works that are vital to Ukrainian linguistics and literary studies and to Ukrainian history, including *Narys slovotvoru prykmetnykiv ukraiinskoy movy* (An outline of Ukrainian adjectival word formation; 1925); *Ukraiinska mova v sovetskiy Ukraiini* (The Ukrainian language in the Soviet Ukraine; 1936); *The Nationality Problem of the Soviet Union and Russian Communist Imperialism* (1952); and *The Captive Nations: Nationalism of the Non-Russian Nations in the Soviet Union* (1960). (WR)

Sources: *Ukraine: A Concise Encyclopedia*, vols. 1–2 (Toronto, 1963–71); *Encyclopedia of Ukraine*, vol. 4 (Toronto, 1993); John A. Armstrong, *Ukrainian Nationalism* (Littleton, Colo., 1980); Iwo Werschler, *Z dziejów obozu belwederskiego: Tadeusz Hołówko-życie i działalność* (Warsaw, 1984); Ryszard Torzecki, *Kwestia ukraińska w Polsce 1923–1929* (Kraków, 1989).

ŠMERAL Bohumír (25 October 1880, Třebíč–8 May 1941, Moscow), Czech Social Democratic and Communist politician. Born into a family of teachers, after graduating from high school in Třebíč, Šmeral studied law at the universities in Prague, Berlin, and London, graduating in 1904. In his student years, he joined Slávia, a nationally oriented and pro-Slavic student movement. He founded its Marxist group. From 1899 to 1900 he edited *Studentský sborník*. While a student, he also began contributing to *Právo lidu*, a Social Democratic newspaper. He became an editor of this newspaper in 1904, and from 1907 to 1917 he was its editor-in-chief. An active member of the Czech Social Democratic Party, Šmeral joined the ČSSD Executive Committee in 1909. In 1911 he became an MP in the parliament in Vienna. He soon became the leading Social Democratic politician in Bohemia. In 1916–17 he was head of the party and vice-president of the Czech representation in the Austro-Hungarian parliament. An adherent of the internationalist line in the workers' movement and of the view that the world war was imperialist in character, Šmeral did not support the Entente or the Central Powers. He also did not establish contacts with the Czech politicians in exile or with the members of a Czech secret political organization called Mafia. Under pressure from members of the opposition within the party who represented the national wing of the party (including **Gustáv Habrman**), Šmeral resigned his positions in August 1917.

After Czechoslovakia was created, Šmeral refused to accept a ministerial position and rejected membership in the Revolutionary National Assembly. He went to Switzerland, where he worked as a correspondent for *Právo lidu*. After a visit to Russia and a meeting with Lenin, he returned to Czechoslovakia as a supporter of the Social Democratic Party's accession to the Communist International. A split occurred within the party and within the trade unions over strategic goals and current tactics. As a result of Šmeral's activities, two factions emerged within the Social Democratic Party. Šmeral took the lead of the faction that sought to establish a Communist party. After the Communist Party of Czechoslovakia (CPC) was founded, he became its first chairman. He headed the CPC from 1920 to 1925. He served as a Communist member of parliament (1920–29) and senator (1935–38). He was also active in the Comintern, serving as a member of the Presidium of the Comintern Executive Committee (in 1924 and from 1927 to 1931). In the early 1930s Šmeral founded the Union of Friends of the Soviet Union and became the editor-in-chief of its press organ, *Svět sovětů*. In 1934 he again became active in the Comintern, traveling around Europe as its envoy. In November 1938 Šmeral went to

Moscow, where he entered into cooperation with **Klement Gottwald**. (PU)

Sources: *ČBS*; *Kto bol kto za I. ČSR* (Bratislava, 1993); *Kdo byl kdo za první republiky* (Prague, 1998); Bernard Wheaton, *Radical Socialism in Czechoslovakia: Bohumir Šmeral, the Czech Road to Socialism and the Origins of the Czechoslovak Communist Party, 1917–1921* (Boulder, Colo., 1986).

SMETONA Antanas (10 August 1874, Užulėnis, near Vilkomir [now Ukmergė, Lithuania]–9 January 1944, Cleveland, Ohio), Lithuanian lawyer and politician. Smetona was the son of a poor peasant. After finishing primary school in Taujenai, he studied at a high school in Palanga. Along with **Jonas Jablonskis,** Vincas Kudirka, and others, he was a member of pro-independence student groups. In the autumn of 1896 Smetona organized a student demonstration against the obligation to attend the Orthodox Church; as a result, he was expelled from school. He passed his secondary school examinations in St. Petersburg, and then he began to study law at the university there. He served as chairman of the Lithuanian Student Organization and became involved in distributing Lithuanian publications banned by the Russian authorities. Arrested in 1899, he was released after two weeks. He resumed his studies, graduating in 1902, and then he began working at the Land Bank in Vilnius (Wilno). Smetona joined the Lithuanian Democratic Party (LDP) and rose quickly through the party ranks. After the ban was lifted on printing in Lithuanian using the Latin alphabet, he became editor of the daily *Vilniaus Žinios* in 1904. In 1905–6 he also edited the weekly *Liteuvos Ūkininkas*. In December 1905, during sessions of the Lithuanian Diet, he was elected to its five-member presidium. In 1907 Smetona left the LDP, and, along with Reverend **Juozas Tumas-Vaižgantas,** he founded the triweekly *Viltis*, in which he propagated Lithuanian national ideas. Although Smetona was a firm opponent of Marxism, his outlook on the world was too liberal for the spiritual directors of this triweekly. In 1913 Smetona left *Viltis* and rallied his supporters around the periodical *Vairas*, which he published in 1914–15. In this periodical he called for the national unity of the Lithuanian people.

After the outbreak of World War I, Smetona became deputy chairman of the Lithuanian Central Relief Committee in Vilnius (November 1914). After the Germans occupied Vilnius in 1915, he did not leave the city. He was in charge of political activities in Vilnius and continued his work in the Lithuanian Learned Society. In the summer of 1916 Smetona appealed to the German authorities for permission to establish an independent Lithuanian state. In September 1917 he began publishing the periodical *Lietuvos Aides*, in which he outlined plans for such a state. When on 18 September 1917 the Germans agreed to the establishment of the Lithuanian Council (Lietuvos Taryba), Smetona was elected its president. The German occupation authorities were inclined to recognize the independence of Lithuania on condition that Lithuania remained allied with Germany. Smetona wanted to agree to this compromise, but the majority of the members of the Lithuanian Council were against it; therefore, he resigned. However, he soon again became president of this council, which proclaimed Lithuania's unconditional independence on 16 February 1918. It remained a paper proclamation only, until the Germans had to accept their defeat in war. On 11 November 1918 the State Council (as the Lithuanian Council was renamed) established the first government of Lithuania under **Augustinas Voldemaras**.

In late 1918 and early 1919 Smetona was in Berlin, where he worked for the smooth withdrawal of German troops from Lithuania. He also visited the Scandinavian countries, where he solicited economic and political aid. After returning home, he was elected the first president of Lithuania under the provisional constitution of the state (4 April 1919). Within a year the foundations of the administration and the army were created, and elections to the Constitutional Assembly were called. After these elections, Smetona resigned as president of the state on 19 June 1920 because of the poor electoral showing of the nationalists. He handed over his office to **Aleksandras Stulginskis**, the parliament speaker. In the parliamentary elections in 1922 and 1923 Smetona and his National Progress Party (Tautos Pažanga [NPP]) failed to obtain a seat; this failure resulted from the NPP's moderate views on agricultural reform. In 1923 Smetona became the government commissioner for Klaipėda (German: Memel), but because of his disagreements with Prime Minister **Ernestas Galvanauskas**, he resigned this post and resumed his scholarly and editorial work. He briefly taught philosophy, ethics, and rhetoric at Vytautas Magnus University in Kaunas. He also translated the classics of Greek philosophy, including Plato. In the periodicals *Lietuvos balsas* and *Vairas*, he sharply criticized the parliamentary system of government; as a result, he constantly came into conflict with the authorities. In the elections of May 1926 Smetona was elected to the parliament, along with two other members of his party, which had been renamed the Union of Lithuanian Nationalists (Tautininkų Sąjunga [ULN]) in 1924.

On 17 December 1926 Smetona's supporters, backed by the Christian Democrats and a part of the army led by Major **Povilas Plechavičius**, removed the center-left government of **Mykolas Sleževičius** from power. As a result of a boycott by the parties that had until then been in power, only forty out of eighty-five MPs took part in the presidential election, and Smetona became president again. After another clash with the parliament, Smetona dissolved the chamber on 12 April 1927. When new elections were not held within the deadline defined by the constitution, the Christian Democrats and their allies from the Lithuanian Farmers' Union left the ruling coalition. On 15 May 1928 the ULN pushed through constitutional amendments that gave sweeping powers to Smetona as president. Smetona consolidated his position in the ruling camp by dismissing Prime Minister Voldemaras, who tried to compete with him for power, on 19 September 1929. Smetona then appointed his brother-in-law, **Juozas Tūbelis**, to this post. Opposition parties admittedly existed in the system of government established by Smetona, but they had no influence on the way the country was governed. Power was in the hands of the activists of the ULN, the army, and the state bureaucracy. A paramilitary organization called Iron Wolf was established in order to suppress the opposition. Smetona was worshipped as the Leader of the Nation (Tautos Vadas). He was reelected president in 1931 and 1938. A new constitution was adopted that extended the powers of the president and his administration and introduced an authoritarian system. However, in the face of threats to Lithuania in 1939, Smetona succeeded in bringing some of the opposition members into the government. In foreign policy he favored the Western and Scandinavian countries and represented an intransigent attitude toward Poland, which was accused of the unlawful annexation of the Vilnius (Wilno) region. Smetona and his government refused to enter into relations with Poland until March 1938, when bilateral relations between the two countries were reestablished as a result of a Polish ultimatum.

In September 1939 Smetona decided to remain neutral in the face of the German and Soviet invasions of Poland, but in October 1939 he accepted the Soviet offer of the Vilnius region, which had been seized by the Soviets. In return he accepted a Kremlin ultimatum, and on 10 October 1939 he agreed to the presence of Soviet troops in Lithuania. However, that did not prevent another ultimatum by the Soviet Union and the invasion of Lithuania by the Red Army on 15 June 1940. Smetona's suggestion that the country offer armed resistance against the Soviet troops was not accepted by the majority of the government; therefore, on the same day Smetona handed over his office to Prime Minister **Antanas Merkys** and then crossed over the German border. Subsequently, along with his family, Smetona made his way, via Switzerland, to the United States, where he arrived at the beginning of 1941. In the United States he campaigned for the restoration of Lithuanian independence and disseminated information about the unlawful political steps and genocidal policies of the Soviet Union. Smetona perished in a fire at his son's house.

Smetona left a vast written legacy. Four volumes of his articles and speeches from 1907–18, edited by him, were published in 1930–31: *Vienybės gairėmis* (Toward unity); *Šviesos takais* (Following the paths of light); *Atgimstant* (In a time of revival); and *Lietuvių santykiai su lenkais* (Polish-Lithuanian relations). A collection of his speeches from 1927–34, when he served as president, was published under the title *Pasakyta Parašyta* (Speeches and statements; 1935). A second volume, covering the period 1935–40, was compiled and edited under the same title and was published in the United States in 1974. Smetona's style was regarded as a model of linguistic clarity and accuracy. (WR)

Sources: *EL*, vol. 5; Saulius Sužiedelis, *Historical Dictionary of Lithuania* (Lanham, Md., 1997); Alfred E. Senn, *The Emergence of Modern Lithuania* (New York, 1959); A. Merkelis, *Antanas Smetona: Jo visuomeninė, kultūrinė ir politinė veikla* (New York, 1964); Leonas Sabiliūnas, *Lithuania in Crisis: Nationalism to Communism* (Bloomington, 1972); Bronis J. Kaslas, ed., *The USSR-German Aggression against Lithuania* (New York, 1973); Algirdas Banevicius, *111 Lietuvos valstybes 1918–1940 politikos veikeju* (Vilnius, 1991); David M. Crowe, *The Baltic States and the Great Powers: Foreign Relations, 1938–1940* (Boulder, Colo., 1993); Liudas Truska, Algimantas Lileikis, Gediminas Ilgunas, and Rimgaudas Gelezevicius, *Lietuvos prezidentai* (Vilnius, 1995).

ŠMIDKE Karol (21 January 1897, Ostrava–15 December 1952, Bratislava), Slovak Communist activist of Czech origin. A mining carpenter by trade, Šmidke joined the Communist Party of Czechoslovakia (CPC) in 1921. From 1930 he belonged to the Slovak party leadership, and in 1930–31 he was organization secretary of the Central Committee (CC) of the Communist Party of Slovakia (CPS). From 1935 to 1938 Šmidke was an MP, and in 1939 he left for the Soviet Union, where he worked in the Moscow office of the CPC. He returned to Slovakia in 1943 to establish an underground CPS leadership along with **Gustav Husák** and **Laco Novomeský**. Šmidke was co-author of the "Christmas accord" between the Communists and non-Communist resistance fighters. He also took part in the creation of the Slovak National Council (SNC) and in preparations for the Slovak National Uprising. Šmidke commanded the general staff of the guerrilla movement, and during the uprising he, along with **Vavro Šrobár**, co-chaired the SNC. In 1944–45 Šmidke was president and then (from 1945 to 1950) vice-president of the CPS. In 1945 he was briefly a member of the Presidium of the CC of the CPC and was vice-president of the party. From 1949 to 1951 he was a member of the

CC of the CPC; from 1946 to 1948 he was vice-president and then (until 1950) president of the SNC. From 1945 Šmidke was an MP. As a "one of Husák's men," in 1950 he was accused of "Slovak bourgeois nationalism." After an extensive self-criticism Šmidke left the political scene but avoided arrest. He worked as the director of the Tesla Factory in Bratislava. In 1963 Šmidke was posthumously rehabilitated. (PU)

Sources: *ČBS*; *SBS*, vol. 5; *Kdo byl kdo v našich dějinach ve 20. stoleti*, vol. 2 (Prague, 1998); Jan Pešek, *Štátna bezpečnost na Slovensku 1948–1953* (Bratislava, 1999).

SMIRNOV Igor (1941, Petropavlovsk Kamchatski), Russian separatist politician in Moldavia. In 1959 Smirnov moved from Kamchatka to Zaporozhye in the Ukrainian SSR to study in the Institute of Machine Construction. In 1959–87 he worked as an engineer, shopkeeper, and director of a machine factory in Zaporozhye. From 1963 he belonged to the Communist Party. In 1987 he went to the Moldavian SSR and joined the Union of Directors, an organization of Russian nomenklatura established to preserve the USSR. In 1988 Smirnov was co-founder of another conservative organization, Unitatea (Unity). In 1989–91 he headed the trade union United Council of Labor Collectives (UCLC), the leading force in the pro-Russian Interfront, created in 1989. As the result of strikes, the UCLC took over control of the administration in Transnistria, a part of Moldova dominated by Russians and Russian-speaking Ukrainians. After a referendum in 1990 this region proclaimed sovereignty, and Smirnov was elected chairman of its Supreme Council.

After the dissolution of the Soviet Union in December 1991, Transnistria proclaimed independence. Facing hostility from Moldova, Smirnov considered a merger of the region with the Ukraine. The Moldovan secret service kidnapped Smirnov in Kiev but soon released him. Smirnov proclaimed himself president of the Transnistrian Republic of Moldova, which was not recognized by any country. As a result military operations began between Moldova and the new republic, whose separate status was defended by the Fourteenth Russian Army, stationed In Transnistria. In 1992 the Moldovan parliament deprived Smirnov of a mandate that he had held since 1990. In 1992–96 Smirnov rejected proposals for Transnistrian autonomy within Moldova, negotiated with the help of Russia, and in 1995 he demanded the federalization of Moldova and the recognition of his republic. In 1996 Smirnov was re-elected president of Transnistria and continued to oppose the withdrawal of Russian troops from his region. In 2001 he was reelected again; there was widespread election fraud. In November 2003 a Russian-sponsored peace plan for the region was rejected by Moldova after Moldovan demonstrations against it; the deal would have permitted Russian troops to remain until 2020. (LW)

Sources: Józef Darski, *Rumunia: Historia, współczesność, konflikty narodowe* (Warsaw, 1995); *Europa Środkowo-Wschodnia 1994–1995* (Warsaw, 1997); Tod Lindberg, "Turmoil in Transnistria, a Black Hole of the Black Sea Region," *Washington Times*, 6 January 2004; Bugajski; www.nupi.no; www.rulers.org; www.osw.waw.pl.

SMODLAKA Josip (9 November 1869, Imotski–31 May 1956, Split), Croatian politician from Dalmatia. Smodlaka graduated in law in Zagreb and Graz, and then he worked as a lawyer in Imotski and Split. From 1897 he belonged to the Party of Law (Stranka Prava), and in 1901 he was elected to the regional parliament of Dalmatia. Along with **Ante Trumbić** and **Frano Supilo**, Smodlaka instigated the political movement for autonomy in the Croatian province (*banovina*), and in 1903 he announced a "new political course," consisting of sharpening the struggle against the Habsburg authorities. In 1905 Smodlaka established the periodical *Sloboda* and the Croatian Democratic Party (Hrvatska Demokratska Stranka), whose program combined national and social goals. He defended the rights of the peasants and acted against colonate-church estates (which was an ancient form or land lease that gave tenants very limited rights) and usury in the countryside. After the passing of the Rijeka Resolution in October 1905 Smodlaka acted in favor of a Serbo-Croat rapprochement. In 1910 he was elected to the parliament in Vienna on behalf of the Split constituency.

At the end of World War I Smodlaka supported the unification of Habsburg Slavs and belonged to the Dalmatian delegation that joined in the proclamation of the Kingdom of Serbs, Croats, and Slovenes (SHS) on 1 December 1918. In the provisional parliament Smodlaka sat as an independent deputy. He was a member of the SHS delegation to the Paris Peace Conference. During a constitutional debate in which spokesmen for Serbian centralism clashed with federalists, Smodlaka followed a middle-of-the road course. After the passing of the centralist constitution in June 1921, he tried to mitigate its pro-Serbian interpretation and organized a congress of public activists in Zagreb in September 1922. Later Smodlaka worked in the diplomatic service as an envoy to the Holy See, Berlin, and Madrid. Nevertheless, the Serbianization of the royal administration under the dictatorship of King **Alexander Karadjordjević** was contrary to Smodlaka's federalist inclinations. From 1936 he again advocated a reform of the Yugoslav state into a federation of four parts: Serbia, Croatia, Slovenia, and a "dinar" region. After the Serbo-Croat agreement of August 1939, at the end of 1939 Smodlaka was appointed senator. The collapse of Yugoslavia in April 1941 undermined his trust in the established institutions of this state. During the Ustasha regime Smodlaka went underground and started to work with the guerrillas of **Josip Broz Tito**. He joined the Anti-Fascist Council for the National Liberation of Yugoslavia, and in March 1945 he became minister without portfolio in the Tito government. He also represented the new Yugoslav authorities with the allied command in Rome. Later, owing to ailing health, Smodlaka withdrew from politics. (WR)

Sources: *Enciklopedija Jugoslavije*, vol. 7 (Zagreb, 1968); Marko Kostrenčić, ed., *Zapisi dra Josipa Smodlake* (Zagreb, 1972); Alex N. Dragnich, *The First Yugoslavia* (Stanford, 1983); Ivan Mužić, *Stjepan Radić u Kraljevini Srba, Hrvata i Slovenaca* (Zagreb, 1988); Franko Mirošević, *Počelo je 1918 . . . Južna Dalmacija 1918–1929* (Zagreb, 1992); Franjo Tudjman, *Hrvatska u monarhističkoj Jugoslaviji, 1918–1941*, vols. 1–2 (Zagreb, 1993).

SMOLICH Arkadź (29 November 1891, Batsevichi–17 June 1938?), Belorussian economist, cartographer, and politician. The son of a countryside Orthodox priest, in 1916 Smolich graduated from the Novoalexandriyskiy Institute of Agriculture and Forestry. From 1910 he belonged to the Belorussian Socialist Hromada, and in 1917 he joined the closed circle of the party leadership. He also edited the party periodical, *Hramada*. In March 1917 Smolich co-organized the First Congress of Belorussian Parties and Organizations in Minsk and was elected to the Belorussian National Committee. After the Bolshevik revolution, in December 1917 Smolich took part in the First All-Belorussian Congress and joined the Secretariat of the Belorussian People's Republic (BPR). He participated in the creation of its state apparatus. From 1919 Smolich was vice-president of the BPR Council and secretary of education in the first BPR government. In 1919–22 he lived in Wilno (Vilnius) and was co-founder of the Association of Belorussian Schools. In 1922 he left for Minsk, where he became president of the Central Belorussian Bureau. From 1925 he was deputy director of the Institute of Belorussian Culture, and from 1929 he was a member of the Presidium of the Academy of Sciences of the Belorussian SSR. At the same time he lectured at the Belorussian State University. In 1927 Smolich was appointed professor. He taught economics and geography and authored a textbook on Belorussian geography. In 1930 Smolich was arrested and sentenced to long-term imprisonment for his activities in a nonexistent organization, the Union of Liberation of Belorussia. In 1939 Smolich was tried again, sentenced to death, and executed by firing squad. (EM)

Sources: *Bielarus: Encyklapedychny davednik* (Minsk, 1995); Vitaut Kipel and Zora Kipel, eds., *Byelorussian Statehood* (New York, 1988); H. Głogowska, *Białoruś 1914–1929: Kultura pod presją polityki* (Białystok, 1996).

SMORAWIŃSKI Mieczysław (25 December 1893, Kalisz–April 1940, Katyn), Polish general. After completing chemistry studies in Lemberg (Lwów, Lviv), Smorawiński joined independence activities in Galicia. During World War I he served in the Polish Legions, and in 1917 he joined the Polish Auxiliary Corps (Polski Korpus Posiłkowy). At the end of 1918 he entered the Polish Army with the rank of major. In February 1919 Smorawiński took command of the Eighth Infantry Regiment, and during the Polish-Soviet war he was in command of the Fourth Infantry Brigade. In March 1927 he assumed command of the Sixth Infantry Division, and in January 1928 he was promoted to general. In October 1932 Smorawiński became deputy commander of the Corps Area in Grodno (Corps Area HQ III) and in October 1934 of the Corps Area in Lublin (Corps Area HQ II). In September 1939 he led the defense of the Lublin region. When the Red Army entered this territory, Smorawiński ordered his subordinates to offer no resistance but to disperse and try to get to the West, where, he hoped, the Polish Army would be rebuilt. Taken captive by the Red Army, Smorawiński was put in a transition camp in Talitsa. Later, he was transported to the prison camp in Kozelsk. In April 1940 he was deported to the Katyn Forest, and, along with others, he was executed without trial by order of the Politburo of the CC of the All-Russian Communist Party (Bolsheviks). The execution was carried out by a special unit of the NKVD. In April 1943 Smorawiński's body was found among the victims murdered in Katyn. (WR)

Sources: Henryk Żelewski, *Dzieje bojowe 8 PP Leg. w walkach obronnych 1939 r.* (Lublin, 1984); Tadeusz Kryska-Karski and Stanisław Żurakowski, *Generałowie Polski Niepodległej* (Warsaw, 1991).

SMRKOVSKÝ Josef (26 February 1911, Velenka, Nymburk district–15 January 1974, Prague), Czech Communist activist. A baker by trade, Smrkovský was active in the Communist trade unions and youth organizations in the 1930s. In 1933 he joined the Communist Party of Czechoslovakia (CPC). After finishing a party school in the Soviet Union (1937), Smrkovský became CPC secretary in Brno. During World War II he was active in the Communist underground. From 29 April to 11 May 1945 he held the post of deputy chairman (in fact served as chairman) of the Czech National Council, and he was one of the leaders of the Prague Uprising, for which he was criticized by the Soviets, as well as by the CPC leadership. Smrkovský subsequently briefly served as chairman of the Provincial National Committee (Zemský Národní Výbor) in Bohemia but was dismissed under Soviet pressure. From 1945 to 1948 he was chairman of the National Land Fund and then served as deputy minister of agriculture and general director of state-owned farms for two years. Smrkovský played an important role during the Communist coup of February 1948, serving as one of the organizers and then as deputy chief of the General Staff of the People's Militias. From 1945 to 1951 Smrkovský was a member of the Presidium of the CPC Central Committee (CC). From 1946 to 1951 he was a deputy to the National Assembly. Arrested in 1951, Smrkovský was dismissed from his positions and sentenced to life imprisonment for taking part in an alleged "plot" led by **Rudolf Slanský**. Released in 1955, he served as chairman of the Pavlovice agricultural cooperative until 1963. Rehabilitated in 1963, he served as deputy minister of people's control for two years. From 1965 to 1967 he was minister-chairman of the Central Board of Water Management, and from 1967 to 1968 he was minister of forest and water management.

In the second half of the 1960s Smrkovský was one of the main representatives of the pro-reform faction within the CPC. He was instrumental in the overthrow of **Antonín Novotný**, and his January 1968 address was an important impulse for the Prague Spring. From 1966 to 1969 Smrkovský was a member of the CPC CC, and from March 1968 to April 1969 he was a member of the CC Presidium. He was a deputy to the National Assembly (1964–69) and a deputy to the Federal Assembly (until December 1969). He served as chairman of the National Assembly (April 1968–January 1969) and chairman of the People's Chamber of the Federal Assembly (until October 1969). A very popular speaker during the Prague Spring, Smrkovský strongly protested the invasion of Czechoslovakia by Warsaw Pact troops. On 23 August 1968, along with a group of party and government leaders (including **Alexander Dubček**, **Oldřich Černík**, and **František Kriegel**), Smrkovský was taken to Moscow, where he took part in negotiations with Soviet leaders on the situation in Czechoslovakia. He was one of the signatories of the "Moscow Protocol," which sanctioned the invasion and announced the so-called normalization. As a result of this "normalization" policy, Smrkovský was dismissed from his all positions in late 1969 and expelled from the party in 1970. (PU)

Sources: ČBS; Českoslovenští politici: 1918–1991 (Prague, 1991); Kdo byl kdo v našich dějinách ve 20. století, vol. 2 (Prague, 1998); Gordon H. Skilling, Czechoslovakia's Interrupted Revolution (Princeton, 1976); Vladimir V. Kusin, From Dubcek to Charter 77: A Study of "Normalization" in Czechoslovakia, 1968–1978 (New York, 1978); Alexander Dubcek, Hope Dies Last (New York, 1993).

SNEGUR Mircea (17 January 1940, Trifăneşti, near Soroki), Moldavian post-Communist politician. In 1961 Snegur graduated from the Agronomic Institute in Kishinev (Chişinău), and later he worked in the administration of a state farm. In 1964 he joined the Communist Party of Moldavia (Partidul Comunist din Moldova [CPM]), a part of the CPSU, and remained a member until 1990. In 1967–71 Snegur was the director of a state farm, and from 1971 to 1978 he was chief of administration in the Ministry of Agriculture of the Moldavian SSR. From 1978 to 1981 he was general director of the Selektsya Research and Production Society in Kishinev, and in 1981–85 he was first secretary of the regional CPM committee in Edineţ. In 1985 he was promoted to secretary of the CPM Central Committee (CC) and soon became second CC secretary, responsible for ideology. In 1989–90 Snegur chaired the Supreme Council of the Moldavian SSR. At this time he spoke in favor of Moldavian sovereignty but also supported a new union agreement to change the system of the USSR along the lines of the perestroika policy of Mikhail Gorbachev.

On 23 June 1990 the Supreme Council of the Moldavian SSR proclaimed the state sovereignty of the republic. Soon the republican parliament introduced the presidential system and elected Snegur as president of the republic on 3 September 1990. Snegur opposed the idea of a merger with Romania, favored by the government of **Valeriu Muravschi**. In view of pro-Russian separatism in Transnistria and the Gagauz territory in 1991, Snegur delayed the formation of a Moldavian army and asked for help from Soviet Ministry of Interior troops, which, nevertheless, supported the separatists. As a result of the failure of the Moscow putsch in August 1991, Snegur supported the full independence of Moldova, which was proclaimed by the parliament on 27 August 1991. At the same time he introduced Moldova to the Commonwealth of Independent States (CIS). On 8 December 1991 Snegur was elected president of Moldova and held this office until 15 January 1997. From 1994 Snegur distanced himself from the CIS, but he also opposed unification with Romania. In 1995 he entered into conflict with the pro-Russian and Populist parliamentary majority of the Agrarian Democratic Party of Moldova (Partidul Democrat Agrar din Moldova), and he turned to the right. He simultaneously drew his supporters to the Moldovan Party of Renewal and Accord (Partidul Renaşterii şi Conşlierii din Moldova [MPRA]). Despite these efforts, on 1 December 1996 Snegur lost the presidential election to **Petru Lucinschi**. In 1998–2001 Snegur was an MP on behalf of the Democratic Convention of Moldova (Convenţia Democrata din Moldova), a coalition co-founded with the pro-Romanian Christian

Democrats. In the parliamentary elections of 25 February 2001 the MPRA failed to cross the threshold and stayed out of the parliament. (LW)

Sources: *Dictionar Enciclopedic*, vol. 4 (Bucharest, 2001); *Longman Biographical Dictionary of Decision-Makers in Russia and the Successor States* (London, 1993); Józef Darski, *Rumunia: Historia, współczesność, konflikty narodowe* (Warsaw, 1995); Bugajski; www.cidob.org; www.nupi.no.

SNIEČKUS Antanas (7 January 1903, Bubleliai, near Šakiai–22 January 1974, Druskininkai), prominent Lithuanian Communist activist. Sniečkus came from a wealthy peasant family. During World War I, he was in Russia, where he attended a secondary school in Voronezh. After the February 1917 revolution he joined the Bolshevik party and took part in propaganda activities. After returning to Lithuania, he worked as a telephone clerk in southern Lithuania from 1919 to 1921. He repeatedly went to Minsk and Moscow illegally, bringing back instructions and propaganda literature for Lithuanian Communists. Arrested during a demonstration in Alytus in 1921 and released on parole before trial, Sniečkus fled to Russia, where he underwent organizational training. In 1926 he returned to Lithuania and became secretary of the Central Committee of the Lithuanian Communist Party. In 1931 he was sentenced to fifteen years in prison, and in 1933 he was exchanged, along with other Lithuanian Communists, for Bishop **Teofilis Matulionis** and priests released from Soviet labor camps. Almost immediately Sniečkus returned to Lithuania and, under an alias, worked in the Communist underground. In 1938 he became leader of the Communist Party of Lithuania as the first secretary of its Central Committee. In 1940 he was temporarily arrested, but after the entry of the Red Army in June he was named head of the special "security department." On 7 July 1940 Sniečkus ordered the abolishment of non-Communist parties, and he subsequently supervised the arrests and deportation of the Lithuanian political and intellectual elite. In the spring of 1941 he prepared and organized another deportation of around thirty thousand Lithuanians to Siberia. Among the deported was his sister and other members of the family.

After the German invasion in June 1941 Sniečkus fled far into the Russian interior, but in 1942 he returned to Lithuania as chief of the Soviet guerrillas who fought against the Germans and the Polish Home Army. When the Red Army returned to Lithuania in the summer of 1944, Sniečkus resumed the leadership of the party. He supervised two great waves of deportations of Lithuanians into the Soviet interior, in 1944 and 1949, and the ruthless suppression of the anti-Communist guerrillas.

Sniečkus's mother, brothers, and sisters, fearing for their lives, fled to the West. When in 1947 he invited his mother to return, she refused, cursing the day she gave birth to the "traitor destroying his own nation." After the collectivization of agriculture in 1949 and the deportations had ended, Sniečkus implemented a policy of Sovietization of the national culture, and he suppressed the Catholic Church. After Stalin's death, he accepted a short respite of terror, though in a strictly limited framework. Sniečkus denounced Lavrenty Beria but delayed the popularization of **Nikita Khrushchev**'s policy of the Twentieth CPSU Congress, and in 1957 he opposed "decentralization tendencies" and began a campaign against the more independent creators of culture, fearing that the Lithuanization of the party apparatus might endanger his position. After Khrushchev's fall in 1964, Sniečkus continued his policies, but at the end of the 1960s he slowed their course since he noticed that under Leonid Brezhnev the Kremlin favored a stabilization of the party apparatus. Sniečkus's faithful service to the Kremlin, from Stalin to Brezhnev, and his close ties with Mikhail Suslov, the *éminence grise* of the Kremlin, allowed him to remain in his post the longest of any of the leaders of the republican parties. The party and government machinery in Lithuania was an efficient mechanism of his personal power. (WR)

Sources: *EL*, vol. 5; Testimony by Juozas Sniečkus before the House of Representatives Select Committee to Investigate Incorporation of the Baltic States into the U.S.S.R., First Interim Report, 83rd Congress, 1st Session (Washington, D.C., 1954); T. Zhenklis, "Proshchaias z Antanasom Sniechkusom," *Kontinent*, 1977, vol. 14; Romuald J. Misiunas and Rein Taagepera, *The Baltic States: Years of Dependence, 1940–1980* (Berkeley, 1983).

SOKOL Ján (9 October 1933, Jacovce, Topoľčany district, Slovakia), Slovak archbishop. After graduating from high school in Topoľčany, Sokol entered the Higher Theological Seminary in Bratislava. In June 1957 he was ordained to the priesthood by Bishop Ambróz Lazík. Sokol served as a priest in the parishes of Šurany (1957–58), Levice (1958–60), and Bratislava (1960–68). From 1968 to 1970 he served as prefect of a seminary in Bratislava. After the suppression of the Prague Spring, when repressive measures against the Catholic Church were reintroduced as part of the so-called normalization, Sokol was dismissed from his position. In the 1970s he held a variety of positions, including that of dean in the town of Sereď, and he was a member of Pacem in terris, a movement of the Catholic clergy established on the initiative of the authorities. When in 1982 the Holy See forbade priests to be members of political organizations, Sokol left this movement. In the 1980s he was not active in the underground church but was regarded as a priest faithful to the Holy See. As a result, before his death, Archbishop Juliuš Gábriš, the metropolitan of Trnava, appointed Sokol as his successor.

On 14 November 1987, in spite of pressure from the authorities, which suggested another candidate, six archdiocesan consultors elected Sokol administrator of the archdiocese, and this election was soon approved by Pope **John Paul II**. However, the religious affairs authorities in Trnava notified Sokol that they did not recognize his election. After long negotiations between the Czechoslovak government and the Vatican concerning succession in the archdiocese of Trnava, in April 1988 the authorities agreed to accept Sokol's appointment to the position of apostolic administrator of Trnava. Sokol was consecrated bishop on 12 June 1988 in the cathedral in Trnava. On 26 July 1989 he was named archbishop and metropolitan of Trnava and primate of the Slovak province of the Church. He received the pallium, a symbol of the archbishop's authority, from John Paul II on 22 April 1990, at a ceremony in Bratislava, during the Pope's visit to Czechoslovakia. After 1990 Sokol was among those who called for the establishment of an independent Slovak state. On 31 March 1995 John Paul II reorganized Church structures in Slovakia. The Trnava archdiocese was renamed the Bratislava-Trnava archdiocese, with the archbishop's seat in Trnava, and Sokol was named metropolitan of Bratislava-Trnava. The vice-chairman of the Slovak Bishops' Conference from August 2000 on, Sokol took part in negotiations to prepare an agreement between Slovakia and the Holy See. (AGr)

Sources: *Annuario Pontificio, 2000*; Anton Hlinka, *Sila slabych a slabost silnych: Cirkev na Slovensku w rokoch 1945–89* (Bratislava, 1990); Andrzej Grajewski, *Kompleks Judasza. Kościół zraniony: Chrześcijanie w Europie Środkowo-Wschodniej między oporem a kolaboracją* (Poznań, 1999); Oficjalna stranka katolickiej Cirkvi: www.rcc.sk; www.catholic-hierarchy.org.

SOLARZ Ignacy, pseudonym "Chrzestny" (28 December 1891, Ołpiny, near Jasło–8? January 1940, Jarosław), Polish Populist leader, pedagogue, and pundit. Solarz came from a peasant family. In 1912 he graduated from high school in Jasło, and he was drafted into the Austro-Hungarian Army the following year. During World War I he fought in the Carpathian Mountains. Wounded in 1916, he was discharged. Between 1916 and 1921 Solarz studied agriculture at the Jagiellonian University in Kraków. He joined the Polish Peasant Party–Piast and became involved in its educational activities. In 1920 he volunteered to fight in the Polish-Soviet war. A year later, Solarz worked as an instructor for the Lesser Polish Agricultural Society and as a lecturer at the Agricultural School in Sąsiadowice. In

1922 he was awarded an agricultural internship in Denmark. Solarz was the founder and director and a lecturer in the Rural Popular University in Szyce, near Kraków (1924–31). In 1924 Solarz became a member of the Central Union of Rural Youth (Centralny Związek Młodzieży Wiejskiej), joining its board in 1925 and serving as its deputy chairman between 1926 and 1928. Also in 1928, Solarz co-founded the Union of Rural Youth of the Polish Republic–Beacon's Fire (Związku Młodzieży Wiejskiej Rzeczypospolitej Polskiej–Wici). In 1939, he was elected to its Main Board. Between 1932 and 1939, Solarz served as the director of and lecturer in the Władysław Orkan Memorial Rural University, which he founded in Gać Przeworska. In addition, he was a village cooperative activist. Among other things, Solarz founded Poland's first health cooperative in Markowa, near Łańcut. An advocate of agrarianism, Solarz published prolifically, mostly in the periodicals *Siew, Wici, Młoda Myśl Ludowa*, and *Zielony Sztandar*. In January 1940 Solarz was arrested by the Gestapo and murdered soon after. His place of burial is unknown, but a symbolic grave was built in the forest of Palmiry, near Warsaw. (JS)

Sources: *Wielka Encyklopedia Powszechna PWN*, vol. 10 (Warsaw, 1967); *Słownik biograficzny działaczy ruchu ludowego* (Warsaw, 1989); Lucjan Turos, *Patrzeć szeroko i daleko . . . Dziedzictwo pedagogiczne Ignacego Solarza* (Warsaw, 1983); Lucjan Turos, *Uniwersytet Ludowy Ignacego Solarza i jego wychowankowie* (Warsaw, 1970); Zofia Mierzwińska-Szybka, ed., *Wspomnienie o Ignacym Solarzu "Chrzestnym"* (Warsaw, 1983).

SÓLYOM László [originally Schick] (17 December 1908, Muraszombat [now in Slovenia]–19 August 1950, Budapest), Hungarian officer, victim of communism. Sólyom's father was a government official but died early, and Sólyom's mother brought up two sons on her own. Sólyom initially finished a military secondary school, and in 1931 he graduated from the Ludovika Military Academy, Budapest, and served in the army. While a student, he Magyarized his surname to Sólyom. In 1934 he did a one-year training course in France. In 1938 he graduated from the Military Academy of the General Staff in Budapest. After Hungary increased its cooperation with the Third Reich and declared war on the Soviet Union in June 1941, Sólyom left the army because of his Jewish origins. Along with his friend **György Pálffy**, he worked in a factory. In 1942, together with Pálffy, he became a member of the illegal Hungarian Communist Party (HCP), and in 1943, on the orders of the HCP, he also joined the Independent Smallholders' Party (ISP). After Germany occupied Hungary in March 1944, Sólyom went underground. As a member of the HCP Military Committee and the Hungarian National Insurrection and Liberation Committee, he organized military resistance groups. In November 1944 he was arrested by the leaders of the Arrow Cross Party, but he managed to escape.

At the beginning of 1945 Sólyom was appointed commander of the militia of liberated Budapest. Formally, he was to restore public order and attempt to bring war criminals to justice. In fact, though, the objective was also to take control of the ISP and to strengthen the power of the HCP. As a result of conflicts in connection with the displacement of the German population, Sólyom asked for a transfer to the army. In May 1946 he was promoted to brigadier general and assigned to the Ministry of National Defense. He was later promoted to major general, and in December 1948 he became chief of the General Staff of the Hungarian People's Army. In 1947–50 Sólyom also taught military history at an officers' military academy. Arrested in May 1950, Sólyom was sentenced to death in a rigged trial and executed shortly afterwards. In 1956 he was partially rehabilitated. On 13 October 1956, one week after the solemn reburial of **László Rajk** and his associates, a ceremonial reburial of Sólyom and four other generals executed along with him took place. (JT)

Sources: *Magyar Életrajzi Lexikon*, vol. 2 (Budapest, 1969); *Magyarország 1944–1956*, CD-ROM (Budapest, 2001); Béla Szász, *Volunteers for the Gallows: Anatomy of a Show Trial* (New York, 1972); Bennet Kovrig, *Communism in Hungary from Kun to Kádár* (Stanford, 1979).

SOOTS Jaan (12 March 1880, Helme–6 February 1942, Solikamsk, Molotov [now Perm], Russia), Estonian general and politician. In 1900 Soots volunteered to serve in the tsarist army. In 1904 he graduated from a military school in Vilnius, and then he fought in the Russo-Japanese War (1904–5). From 1910 to 1913 he studied at the Nikolayev Military Academy in St. Petersburg. During World War I he served in the Russian general staff and was promoted to lieutenant colonel. In 1917 Soots returned to Estonia, where he organized the staff of the newly established First Estonian Division, becoming its chief in December 1918. During the Estonian war of independence (1918–20) Soots served as chief of the General Staff of the Estonian Army. He also attended the Tartu peace conference that ended the war against the Bolsheviks. After the war, Soots became aligned with the Farmers' Union (FU), led by **Konstantin Päts**. Elected to parliament on the FU ticket, he served as a member of parliament for its first four terms. From 1921 to 1927, except for a brief interval in 1924, Soots held the post of minister of war. He protected the interests of the army, paying particular attention to land allocations for military men and war veterans. Under his ministry,

the first academic military school in the Baltic states was established in 1921. Soots was one of the supporters of a military convention with Poland. He believed that close relations between Poland and Estonia would safeguard the independence of Estonia against Soviet aggression. However, Soots's personnel policy aroused controversy. As a prewar tsarist officer, he appreciated people with a professional military background; therefore, he mostly hired graduates of military schools, as well as former tsarist officers who came to Estonia only after 1920 and who had not fought in the Estonian war of independence. Some of the officers he employed had served in the White armies or even in the Red Army in 1917–20. Soots's policies sparked protests among war veterans who had fought for independence but were not commissioned officers. As a result, the popularity of the Estonian League of War of Independence Veterans (Eesti Vabadussojalaste Liit [EVL]) greatly increased in the first half of the 1920s.

In 1933 Soots was appointed to a parliamentary constitutional commission as an FU representative. After the coup d'état staged by Päts (12 March 1934), Soots was proposed as a candidate for the position of speaker of the new parliament, but his candidacy was rejected. Although he was a supporter of Päts and **Johan Laidoner**, after the coup Soots's political position weakened. From 1934 to 1939 he was a member of the Tartu City Council, serving as its chairman from 1938 to 1939. He was also a member of the Estonian Union of Entrepreneurs, a member of the Union for the Defense of the Republic (Riigikaitse Nõukogu), and the chairman of the Historical Committee of the Estonian War of Independence. After the Red Army occupied Estonia, Soots was arrested on 20 September 1940 and deported to a forced labor camp in Molotov Province, where he perished. (AG)

Sources: *Eesti Entsuklopeedia*, vol. 14 (Tallinn, 2000); Tõnu Tannberg, Matti Laur, Tõnis Lukas, Ain Mäesalu, and Ago Pajur, *History of Estonia* (Tallinn, 2000); Andres Kasekamp, *The Radical Right in Interwar Estonia* (London, 2000); Web site of the Republic of Estonia Ministry of Defense, http://www.mod.gov.ee/english/history/defhistory.html; Web site of the Museum of Occupations, http://www.okupatsioon.ee/english/lists/index.html.

SOROS George (György) (12 August 1930, Budapest, Hungary), American financier, Hungarian of Jewish descent. Soros is the son of Tivadar Soros (Theodor Schwarz), a well-known attorney and Esperantist. After Nazi troops occupied Hungary (March 1944), Soros, along with his family, went into hiding in Budapest until Soviet troops entered Hungary in February 1945. He realized that the Sovietization of Hungary was inevitable and emigrated to Great Britain in 1947. In 1952 he graduated from the London School of Economics. In 1956 he moved to the United States. He initially worked as a broker and analyst at a stock exchange firm, and in 1969 he founded the Quantum Fund N.V., considered for years to be one of the most effective investment funds in the world. It became part of the Quantum Group of Funds, managed by Soros Fund Management, owned by Soros. In 1994 Soros also established Global Power Investments. Using mathematical analyses, he speculated on the stock market and earned billions of dollars. In 1983 he founded the Soros Foundation, which started operating in Hungary one year later. Its activities (such as the awarding of scholarships to young and gifted Hungarians to study at the best West European and American universities and the financing of publications) contributed to the peaceful transformation of the political system in Hungary after 1989.

After 1983 Soros's foundations were established in many other countries. At the end of the twentieth century they operated in more than twenty-five countries (in Central and Eastern Europe, South Africa, and Haiti). Dedicated to the modernization of education, culture, and the economy, they supported the building of infrastructures and institutions of an "open society." In establishing them, Soros was motivated by his experiences during the Holocaust and the Communist regime. By 2010 Soros intends to withdraw his foundations from the Central European countries which by then will have become members of the European Union, as he believes that the mission of these foundations will then be over. In 1990 Soros also founded the Central European University, based in Budapest and Warsaw, offering studies in the fields of history, economics, political science, art history, and the social sciences. Soros's publications include *Alchemy of Finance* (1987), *Opening the Soviet System* (1990), *Underwriting Democracy* (1991), *The Crisis of Global Capitalism* (1998), *George Soros on Globalization* (2002), and *The Age of Fallibility* (2006). Soros has been awarded honorary doctorates from the New School for Social Research in New York (1980), and in 1991 from Oxford University, Yale University, and the School of Economics in Budapest. He has also received many other honors, including the Laurea Honoris Causa from the University of Bologna (1995) and the Hannah Arendt Prize (1999). (JT)

Sources: *Ki kicsoda 2000* (Budapest, 2001); *Magyar Nagylexikon*, vol. 16 (Budapest, 2003).

SOSABOWSKI Stanisław (8 May 1892, Stanisławów [Ivano-Frankivsk]–25 September 1967, London), Polish general. Sosabowski studied at the Trade Academy in Kraków. Starting in 1909, he joined various pro-independence organizations and organized the scouting movement. Between 1911 and 1914, he belonged to the Union of Active Struggle (Związek Walki Czynnej) and the Polish Riflemen's Association (Polskie Drużyny Strzeleckie). Drafted into the Austro-Hungarian Army, following the outbreak of World War I, Sosabowski fought on the eastern front. He was active in the clandestine Polish Military Organization (Polska Organizacja Wojskowa). In November 1918, he joined the Polish Army. In 1923 he graduated from the Higher Military Academy in Warsaw. Until May 1927, he worked at the Fourth Department of the General Staff. Later he was appointed to a succession of leadership positions. From 1929 to 1937, Sosabowski held a chair at the Higher Military Academy. He published on education and character formation in the army. In 1937, he was appointed the regimental infantry commander of the Polish Legions and in 1939 of the Children of Warsaw infantry regiment, which he led in the defense of the Polish capital in September 1939. Sosabowski escaped captivity and joined the underground Service for the Victory of Poland. He was the first military emissary sent out to General **Władysław Sikorski** in Paris. In 1940 Sosabowski was appointed to lead the Polish First and then Fourth Division in France.

After the fall of France and the evacuation of the Polish units to Great Britain, on 23 September 1941, Sosabowski became the organizer and commander of the First Independent Parachute Brigade, the first paratrooper unit of the Polish Army. In June 1944, he was promoted to brigadier general. The British high command took over the brigade and sent it to participate in the invasion on the western front. In September 1944 the brigade participated in a failed Allied air assault near Arnhem and Driel in Holland (the so-called Operation Market-Garden), and in October 1944 it covered the Allied retreat near the Mosse River. In December 1944, for criticizing the Allied leadership, Sosabowski was recalled as the commander of the brigade. Until 1948, he served as the inspector of stage and guard units in the Polish Corps for Training and Placement, which was formed by the British to accommodate former soldiers of the Polish Armed Forces in the West. Following his discharge, Sosabowski worked as a blue-collar laborer at a factory in London. In 1946, the Communists stripped him of his Polish citizenship. Sosabowski authored, among other works, *Wychowanie żołnierza obywatela* (The upbringing of a citizen-soldier; 1931); *Najkrótszą drogą* (The closest route; 1957); and *Droga wiodła ugorem* (The road led through fallow land; 1967). Sosabowski's ashes were interred in Powązki Cemetery in Warsaw. (JS)

Sources: Tadeusz Kryska-Karski and Stanisław Żurakowski, *Generałowie Polski Niepodległej* (London, 1976); Zbigniew Mierzwiński, *Generałowie II Rzeczypospolitej* (Warsaw, 1990);

Juliusz L. Englert and Krzysztof Barbarski, *Generał Stanisław Sosabowski: Dowódca 1 Samodzielnej Brygady Spadochronowej* (London, 1996); Henryk Piotr Kosk, *Generalicja polska: Popularny słownik biograficzny*, vol. 2 (Pruszków, 2001).

SOSIURA Volodymyr (6 January 1898, Debaltsevo, near Yekaterinoslav–8 January 1965, Kiev), Ukrainian poet. Born into a working-class family, Sosiura began working at a very young age; among other things, we was a miner in the Donbas. In 1918 he took part in an uprising against the Germans, and then he fought in the army of the Ukrainian National Republic (UNR). In 1920 he became a supporter of the Bolsheviks and joined the All-Russian Communist Party (Bolsheviks). He studied at a university (1922–23) and at the Institute of Public Education (1923–25) in Kharkov (Kharkiv). Sosiura made his literary debut in 1921, and his collection *Chervona zyma* (Red winter; 1922) was accepted as a model of revolutionary poetry. His poem about the Paris Commune, "1871 rik" (Eighteen seventy-one; 1923), as well as the collections *Misto* (City; 1924) and *Snihy* (Snows; 1925), were dominated by motifs of the revolution. In the 1920s Sosiura was a member of the literary groups Pluh and Hart and the Free Academy of Proletarian Literature (Vilna Akademiya Proletarskoy Literatury [VAPLITE]). He became one of the leading figures of the Ukrainian cultural revival. However, in his writing, he did not strictly follow the orders of the Soviet authorities. He became famous not only for his talent in rendering the atmosphere of war, the pathos of the revolution, and the building of a new political system, but also for the subtlety of his love poems and the lyricism of his descriptions of nature. There was also despair, sadness, and loneliness in his poems—for example, in the collections *Zoloti shuliky* (Golden hawks; 1927) and *Koly zatsvitut akatsii* (When acacias bloom; 1928). The situation of the Ukrainian intelligentsia of that period, torn between Communist and nationalist ideas, was depicted in the poem "Dva Volodky" (Two Volodkos; 1930) and in the collection *Sertse* (Heart; 1931), which were banned by the authorities shortly after their publication.

Stalinist persecutions and the Great Famine in the Ukraine in the 1930s brought Sosiura to the verge of a nervous breakdown. However, his writing did not change. He remained the only author of lyrical love poetry in the Ukrainian SSR. He published *Chervoni troiandy* (Red roses; 1932); *Liubliu* (1939; I love; 1939); and *Zhuravli pryletily* (The cranes have returned; 1940). In 1940 he also published the autobiographical poem "Chervonoh-vardiyets" (Red Guard). From 1942 to 1944 Sosiura was a war correspondent and published the collections *Pid hul kryvavyi* (In bloody tumult; 1942) and *V hodyny hnivu* (In the hour of anger; 1944). In 1948 he received a Stalin Prize, and in 1949 he published the collection *Zelenyi svit* (Green world). In 1951 Sosiura was sharply attacked for "nationalist deviation," allegedly expressed in the poem "Liubit Ukraiinu" (Love your Ukraine; 1944), and from then on he was in disgrace until Stalin's death. In the last years of his life Sosiura published, among other works, the collections *Soloviyni dali* (Nightingale distances; 1957); *Tak nikhto ne kokhav* (No one has ever loved so; 1960); and *Osinni melodii* (Autumn melodies; 1964). Sosiura's collected works were published in the Soviet Union in 1929–30 (3 vols.), 1957–58 (3 vols.), and 1970–72 (10 vols.). (TS)

Sources: *Encyclopedia of Ukraine*, vol. 4 (Toronto, 1993); M. Dolengo, *Tvorchist V. Sosiury* (Kharkiv, 1931); Ilia Stebun, *Volodymyr Sosiura* (Kiev, 1948); O. Kudin, *Volodymyr Sosiura* (Kiev, 1959); I. Radchenko, *Volodymyr Sosiura: Literaturno-krytychnyi narys* (Kiev, 1967); Volodymir Morenets, *Volodymyr Sosiura: Narys zhyttia i tvorchosti* (Kiev, 1990).

SOSNKOWSKI Kazimierz (19 November 1885, Warsaw–11 October 1969, Arundel, Canada), Polish general and politician. Sosnkowski came from an intelligentsia family. Upon graduation from a Petersburg high school, he studied at the Warsaw Polytechnic and then, from 1907, at the Lwów (Lviv) Polytechnic. He joined the Polish Socialist Party (Polska Partia Socjalistyczna [PPS]) in 1905. Later he enrolled in its Fighting Organization (Organizacja Bojowa) and served as its Warsaw District and then its Dąbrowa Basin commander. In 1908, Sosnkowski was a co-founder of the Union for Active Struggle and (in 1910) of the Riflemen's Association, for which he was appointed deputy commander and chief of staff under **Józef Piłsudski**. As the closest collaborator of Piłsudski, Sosnkowski was assigned to be the deputy commander and chief of staff of the First Brigade of the Polish Legions. Promoted to colonel, Sosnkowski took over the brigade's command in August 1916, only to be relieved of it by the Austrians in September. In April 1917, he became the deputy chief of the Military Department of the Provisional State Council, which was created under the German occupation of the Kingdom of Poland. In July 1917, Sosnkowski joined Piłsudski in refusing to swear the oath of allegiance to the emperors of Germany and Austria-Hungary and was therefore imprisoned with him in Gdańsk and Magdeburg.

Upon his return to Warsaw on 10 November 1918, Sosnkowski assumed the command of the Polish Army, which was then forming in the Warsaw region. In March 1919, he was appointed deputy minister for military affairs, and in June he was promoted to general of division. In May 1920, he commanded the Reserve Army. In August he became minister for military affairs, a post he held until May 1923 and then again, in the cabinet of **Władysław Grabski**, from December 1923 through February 1924. In April 1925, Sosnkowski commanded the army Corps District VII Poznań. On 13 May 1926, reacting to the coup d'état of Marshal Piłsudski, Sosnkowski unsuccessfully attempted to commit suicide. This prompted the marshal to exclude him from his most intimate circle. Following five months of hospital recuperation, Sosnkowski returned to active service as the inspector of the army. In November 1936, he was promoted to general of the army.

During the September campaign of 1939, Sosnkowski commanded the southern front. At the beginning of October he broke through to Hungary and later to France. On 12 October 1939, President **Władysław Raczkiewicz** nominated Sosnkowski as his successor and as minister of state. In General **Władysław Sikorski**'s government Sosnkowski was minister without portfolio; chairman of the Committee of the Council of Ministers for the Homeland; chairman of the Political Committee of the Council of Ministers; and commander-in-chief of the Union of Armed Struggle (Związek Walki Zbrojnej [ZWZ]), the principal underground organization in occupied Poland. In the summer of 1940, Sosnkowski resigned as head of the ZWZ, and in July 1941 he quit all his posts, save that of successor to the president, to protest the conditions of a Polish-Soviet agreement (the Sikorski-Mayski Agreement). Following the death of Sikorski, Sosnkowski assumed the post of supreme commander of the Polish Armed Forces on 8 July 1943. Since he firmly opposed concessions to Stalin, the Soviets pressured the British government to have him removed. Sosnkowski believed that following the entry of the Red Army into Poland, the scenario of the 1939–41 Soviet occupation would repeat itself: Poland would be subjugated to the Communists. Therefore, he argued that a compromise with Stalin would only expedite the Sovietization of the Polish nation. Because he openly criticized the conduct of Great Britain toward the Warsaw Uprising, at the insistence of the British, he was dismissed as the supreme commander and successor to the president.

In November 1944, Sosnkowski left for Canada, where he lived in Arundel, near Montreal. After World War II, he became one of the leading political authorities of the Polish émigré community. U.S. President Dwight Eisenhower received Sosnkowski at the end of 1952 and reaffirmed his support for the liberation of Poland from the Soviet yoke. However, the presidential declaration remained an empty promise. Shortly after, at the invitation of the exiled Polish president, **August Zaleski**, Sosnkowski visited London, where he attempted to unite the émigré community. On 14 March 1954, his persistence led to the signing of the Unification Act, but when Sosnkowski appeared before President Zaleski to be appointed his successor, the latter prevaricated and refused to consider the matter until the lapse of his next term. Disappointed, Sosnkowski returned to Canada and withdrew from active politics. (WR)

Sources: *Kto był kim w Drugiej Rzeczypospolitej* (Warsaw, 1994); *Encyklopedia historii Drugiej Rzeczypospolitej* (Warsaw, 1999); Wacław Jędrzejewicz, *Józef Piłsudski: Życiorys* (London, 1982); Władysław Pobóg-Malinowski, *Najnowsza historia polityczna Polski*, vol. 2 (London, 1983) and vol. 3 (London, 1986); *Generał Kazimierz Sosnkowski: W stulecie urodzin* (London, 1986); Andrzej Albert [Wojciech Roszkowski], *Najnowsza historia Polski 1914–1993*, vols. 1–2 (Warsaw, 1995).

SOUKUP František (22 August 1871, Kamenná Lhota, near Kutná Hora–11 November 1940, Prague), Czech journalist and Social Democratic politician. Soukup became interested in politics in his last year of high school in Kolín, joining a progressive student movement. After graduating from high school in 1890, he began to study law at the Czech University in Prague. He continued with political activities in the youth movement Omladina; as a result, he was expelled from the university in 1892. He continued to study law at the German university in Prague and in Graz. In 1896, after a split in the Czech Progressive Party, Soukup became a member of the Czechoslovak Social Democratic Workers' Party (Českoslovanská Sociálně Demokratická Strana Dělnická). One year later he co-founded the periodical *Právo lidu* and became its commentator on the sessions of the parliament in Vienna. Soukup advocated universal suffrage and was active among the Socialist youth. He maintained extensive contacts with Social Democrats abroad. From 1904 to 1938 he was a Czech representative in the Second International. After universal suffrage was instituted in 1907, Soukup served as an MP in the parliament in Vienna until 1911 and then from 1913 to 1918.

During World War I, Soukup worked with the national independence movement. He belonged to a group that established a Czech secret committee, later called the Mafia. Imprisoned for two months in 1915, Soukup was kept under surveillance after his release, and it was not until September 1917 that he resumed contacts with the Mafia. Under his influence, the Czech Social Democrats took an anti-Habsburg stance. A member of the Czechoslovak National Committee from July 1918, Soukup was active as its secretary and authored most of its statements. On 28 October 1918 Soukup was one of five politicians who proclaimed Czechoslovakia's independence, the so-called statesmen of 28 October (*muži 28. října*). Two weeks later he became a deputy to the Provisional National Assembly and the first minister of justice. He held this position until

July 1919, and in 1920 he was elected a senator. He served as deputy speaker (1920–29) and speaker (1929–39) of the upper chamber of the Czechoslovak parliament. He was also active in the international arena, and in 1931 he became a member of the leadership of the Socialist International. Soukup was deeply shocked by the Pact of Munich. He wrote a sharp protest to the International; then, on his initiative, the Czechoslovak Democratic Party left this organization. On 31 December 1938 the last edition of *Právo lidu* that Soukup edited was published. In 1939 Soukup was twice arrested and detained by the Gestapo. His publications include the vast work *28 říjen 1918* (28 October 1918; 1928); *T. G. Masaryk* (1930); and *Revoluce práce* (Revolution of labor; 1938). (PU)

Sources: *ČBS*; *Kto bol kto za I. ČSR* (Bratislava, 1993); Libor Vukoupil, *Slovník českých dějin* (Brno, 2000); *Politická elita meziválečného Československa 1918–1938: Kdo byl kdo za prvni republiky* (Prague, 1998); *Kdo byl kdo v našich dějinach ve 20. stoleti*, vol. 2 (Prague, 1998).

SPAHIU Bedri (1906, Gjirokastër, Albania–1999, Tirana), Albanian Communist activist. Born into a Bektashi family, Spahiu finished high school in Shkodër and graduated from an artillery school in Tirana. He was expelled from the army for being a member of a subversive group, and from 1932 to 1935 he was imprisoned. After his release, he worked as a representative of a commercial company in Gjirokastër. After the Italian invasion of Albania in 1939, Spahiu joined the Albanian Fascist Party and was a member until 1940. He then helped to found the Communist Party of Albania (CPA) and was one of its top leaders from its foundation. During the war Spahiu organized the structures of the CPA in the south of the country. In July 1943 he became a member of the General Staff of the Communist National Liberation Army. In 1944 he was head of an Albanian delegation that was sent to Bari to request Allied help. After the war, Spahiu was a prosecutor in the biggest show trials, including that of **Koçi Xoxe**. A member of parliament for the Gjirokastër district, Spahiu became a member of the presidium of the parliament in 1948, and from 1953 to 1956 he was deputy speaker of the parliament. He headed the Ministry of Reconstruction (October 1944–March 1946) and the Ministry of Education (April 1952–July 1954) and served as one of the deputy prime ministers (April 1952–August 1953). He also held the post of chairman of the Soviet-Albanian Friendship Society.

Expelled from the Politburo of the Albanian Labor Party in June 1955, Spahiu worked at a company in Elbasan for almost two years. In 1956 he was interned in Kanine, near Vlorë. Spahiu's fall was caused by a conflict with

Enver Hoxha over state control of special services and his positive attitude toward a reestablishment of relations with Yugoslavia during the thaw between Moscow and Belgrade. Initially Spahiu was sentenced to ten years in prison, and then his sentence was extended. Fearing for his life, he regularly sent letters to the state authorities demanding that he be given a private cell. In 1971 he was one of the first prisoners of the new Benca Penitentiary, near Tepelenë. Spahiu was released toward the end of 1990. In 1991 in the periodical *Republika*, he critically reviewed his past in the article "Bedri Spahiu revizionon Bedri Spahiu" (Bedri Spahiu critically reviews Bedri Spahiu). One year later Spahiu was accused in the press of the massacre of a National Front (Balli Kombëtar) unit in Gerhot in September 1943 and of maintaining contacts with Italian officers during the struggle against the non-Communist resistance movement. (TC)

Sources: Raymond Hutchings, *Historical Dictionary of Albania* (Lanham, Md., 1996); Agim Musta, *Mandelët e Shqipërise* (Tirana, n.d.); David Smiley, *Albanian Assignment* (London, 1984); Klaus-Detlev Grothusen, ed., *Albanien* (Göttingen, 1993).

SPAHO Mehmed (13 March 1883, Sarajevo–29 June 1939, Belgrade), Muslim politician from Bosnia and Herzegovina. Spaho finished primary and secondary school in Sarajevo and then studied in Vienna. With a doctorate in law, he began working in a law office in Sarajevo (1908). He subsequently served as secretary of the Chamber of Commerce and Crafts of Bosnia and Herzegovina until 1918. Before World War I Spaho joined the Independent Muslim Party (Muslimanska Samostalna Stranka). In 1921 he became chairman of the Yugoslav Muslim Organization (Jugoslavenska Muslimanska Organizacija), which had been founded in 1919. Spaho became an indisputable leader of the Muslims in the Kingdom of Serbs, Croats, and Slovenes (SHS). Like Slovene politicians, he generally favored a federal model of the state, but for tactical reasons, he often formed coalitions with centralist Serbian parties. From December 1918 to February 1919 Spaho was minister of forestry and mining; from March to December 1922 he was minister of trade and industry; from July to September 1925 he was minister of finance; and from April 1927 to January 1929 he was again minister of trade and industry. After King **Alexander I Karadjordjević** established a royal dictatorship in 1929, Spaho joined the opposition to the Serbian government. In November 1932 he supported the so-called Zagreb Manifesto announced by **Vladko Maček**, in which absolutism, centralism, and unitarism were condemned. As a result, Spaho was briefly detained.

In the summer of 1936 Spaho joined the Yugoslav

Radical Union Party (Jugoslovenska Radikalna Zajednica), a new political party founded by Prime Minister **Milan Stojadinović** that won a substantial majority in the Skupština (parliament). Spaho entered the government of Stojadinović. He also remained in the cabinet of **Dragiša Cvetković** (from February 1939), but shortly after this cabinet was constituted, Spaho died suddenly in unexplained circumstances. Spaho had contributed to the success of negotiations that led to the signing of the Sporazum (Agreement) between the Serbs and the Croats after his death, in August 1939. The aim of Spaho's political efforts was to maintain an integral and autonomous Bosnia and Herzegovina within Yugoslavia that would not become dependent on the Serbs or the Croats. Spaho authored a monograph on Gazi Husrev Bey. He also published extensively in the periodicals *Behar, Novi Behar, Pravda*, and *Nova Evropa*. (AO)

Sources: *Biographishes Lexikon*, vol. 4; *Enciklopedija Jugoslavije*, vol. 7 (Zagreb, 1968); Alija Nametak, "Uspomnene na dra Mehmeda Spahu," *Novi Behar*, 1939, no. 1/6; Muhadem Hadžijakić, *Od tradicije do identiteta: Geneza nacionalnog pitanja bosanskih Muslimana* (Sarajevo, 1974); Alex N. Dragnich, *The First Yugoslavia* (Stanford, 1983).

SPEKKE Arnolds (14 June 1887, Vecmuižas, Courland–27 July 1972, Washington, D.C.), Latvian diplomat and historian. In 1906–7 Spekke studied mechanics at the Riga Polytechnic and from 1908 Romance philology at Moscow University. He graduated from the latter in 1915 and then taught German and ancient languages in several high schools and at the Institute of Archaeology in Moscow. In 1918 he returned to Latvia. He worked as a teacher and schoolmaster, and from 1919 to 1933 he lectured in Romance philology at the University of Riga. From 1922 Spekke was a professor; in 1925–27 he was dean of the Department of Philology and Philosophy; and from 1927 to 1929 he was deputy rector of this university. In 1930 he received a Ph.D. in philology. From October 1933 Spekke was Latvian ambassador to Italy and later to Greece, Bulgaria, and Albania, while residing in Italy. After the Soviet invasion of Latvia and the incorporation of the country into the USSR, in August 1940 Spekke was dismissed. He stayed in Milan and later in Rome, where he worked as a teacher and translator. In 1944–45 Spekke worked with the Polish periodical *Orzeł Biały*. From April 1954 he was Latvian chargé d'affaires and general consul in the United States. After the death of **Kārlis Zariņš**, in May 1963 Spekke took over the entire Latvian diplomatic service in exile. In October 1970 he retired. Spekke received many honors, including the Polish order of Polonia Restituta, and he authored many important works on the history of Latvia, including the following: *History of Latvia: An Outline* (1951); *Some Problems of Baltic-Slavic Relations in Prehistoric and Early Historic Times* (1962); and *Balts and Slavs in Their Early Relations* (1965), as well as the memoirs *Mani studiju gadi Maskavā. Pašportreti* (My years of study in Moscow: Self-portraits; 1965), *Atmiņu brīži* (Moments of Memory;1967), and *Kā Itālijā sabruka fašisms: Personīgās atmiņas* (The fall of fascism in Italy: Personal account; 1967). (EJ)

Sources: *Latvijas darbinieku galerija* (Riga, 1928); *Es viņu pazīstu* (Riga, 1939); *Arnolds Spekke—70-gadnieks* (Stockholm, 1957); E. Andersons, "Dr. Arnolds Spekke," *Jaunā Gaita*, 1973, no. 92; Adolf Blodnieks, *The Undefeated Nation* (New York, 1960).

ŠPIDLA Vladimír (22 April 1951, Prague), Czech politician. In 1976 Špidla graduated in history and archaeology from the School of Arts of Charles University in Prague. He subsequently worked in Jindřichův Hradec, taking up a variety of jobs, both white collar (such as archaeologist) and blue collar (such as dairy worker). In 1990 he became a clerk at a district office in Jindřichův Hradec, and from 1991 to 1996 he was director of the local job center there. In 1990 in South Bohemia, Špidla was one of the initiators of the revival of Czechoslovak Social Democracy (Československá Sociální Demokracie; later renamed the Czech Social Democratic Party: Česká Strana Sociálně Demokratická [ČSSD]), and he became chairman of the local party committee. In 1992 he joined the ČSSD leadership and soon became a trusted associate of **Miloš Zeman**. In June 1996 Špidla became a member of parliament and chairman of the parliamentary committee for social policy and health care. In 1997 he became vice-chairman of the ČSSD. After early elections in June 1998 and the victory of the Social Democrats, Špidla became first deputy prime minister and minister of labor and social affairs in Zeman's government. After Zeman announced his plans to retire from politics following the next elections and decided not to seek reelection as party leader, Špidla was elected chairman of the ČSSD at a party congress in April 2001. He then announced that the line of the party would be shifted to the left. After the elections of June 2002, which again brought victory to the Social Democrats, Špidla became head of a government formed in coalition with the Freedom Union–Democratic Union (Unie Svobody–Demokratická Unie [US–DEU]) and the Christian Democratic Union–Czechoslovak People's Party (Křest'anská a Demokratická Unie–Československá Strana Lidová [KDU–ČSL]). He served as prime minister of the Czech Republic from 15 July 2002 to 1 July 2004. In the fall of 2002 Špidla came into sharp conflict with Zeman, who played a peculiar game around the presidential elections. This led to a deep conflict within the ČSSD and the electoral defeat of all the Social Democratic candidates. In June 2003 Špidla led his country to a referendum in which the Czech people voted for accession to the European Union. (PU)

Sources: *ČBS*; Alexandr Mitrofanov, *Za fasádou lidového domu: Česka socialní demokracie 1989–1998: Lidé a události* (Prague, 1998); www.vladimirspidla.cz; www.vlada.cz/1250/vlada/vlada_clenove.htm; www.cssd.cz.

ŠPILJAK Mika (28 November 1916, Odra, near Sisak, Croatia), Croatian Communist activist. After finishing primary school, Špiljak worked as a shoemaker and was active in the trade union movement. In 1935 he became a member of the League of Yugoslav Communist Youth, and in 1938, a member of the Communist Party of Yugoslavia (CPY) in Croatia. In June 1941 he joined the Partisans led by **Josip Broz Tito**. During World War II Špiljak was promoted to secretary of the district committee of the Communist Party of Croatia (CPC). He became a member of the Central Committee (CC) of the CPC in February 1944. From 1945 onwards he served as secretary of the Zagreb City Committee of the party. From 1948 to 1950 Špiljak was chairman of the Zagreb City Council, and in 1951 he became a member of the Politburo of the CC of the League of Communists of Croatia (LCC). He was head of the government of the Croatian republic (1963–67), prime minister of the federal government of Yugoslavia (16 May 1967–18 May 1969), and chairman of the federal trade union board (1969–78). Špiljak was an unswerving follower of Tito's political line. After the death of Tito, as part of the rotating leadership of the state, Špiljak served as chairman of the state presidency from 15 May 1983 to 15 May 1984. In his capacity as formal head of state, in February 1984 he made a visit to the United States, where he was received by President Ronald Reagan, who appreciated Yugoslavia's neutral policy during a new stage of the Cold War. In February of that year Špiljak opened the Olympic Winter Games in Sarajevo. From May 1984 to May 1986 he served as chairman of the LCC. Špiljak was forced to resign as result of his conflict with **Stipe Šuvar**. (JD/WR)

Sources: *Enciklopedija Jugoslavije*, vol. 8 (Zagreb, 1971).

SPIRU Nako (4 January 1918, Durrës–20 November 1947, Tirana), Albanian Communist activist. The son of a Durrës tobacco factory owner, after finishing a school of commerce in Corfu, Spiru studied political economy at Turin University. Along with **Enver Hoxha** (among others), he belonged to a Communist group called Puna (Work) in Korçë and helped to found the Communist Party of Albania (CPA) in November 1941. Spiru was an organizational secretary of a youth group within the CPA, and, after the death of Qemal Stafa, he became the leader of this group. Spiru wrote popular articles for the underground press. Initially he was regarded as the right-hand man of Hoxha, who noticed Spiru's brilliance and organizational talent, as well as his penchant for scheming. In November 1944 at a plenum of the CPA Central Committee (CC) in Berat, Spiru changed tactics. Backed by Yugoslavia, Spiru (together with **Sejfulla Malëshova** and **Koçi Xoxe**) attacked Hoxha, forcing him to make a self-criticism. In 1945 Spiru married **Liri Belishova**, a high-ranking party activist. From 1946 to 1947 Spiru held the ministry of the economy and headed the State Committee for Economic Planning. He was regarded as being in favor of cooperation with the Soviet Union. In 1945–46 Spiru made visits to Moscow in various capacities, including that of representative of the executive of the Albanian-Soviet Friendship Society. Spiru was against the pro-Yugoslav faction led by Xoxe and rejected Belgrade's proposals that Albanian industrial plants be closed down and Albania be treated as a raw material base. Spiru invited Soviet advisers, trying to organize assistance for Albania. As political strife within the party grew, Spiru began to be accused of collaboration with the occupier because during the Italian occupation his family allegedly had befriended a major in the Italian Army and invited him to their home. Attacked by Xoxe for his anti-Yugoslav stance and deprived of Hoxha's support, Spiru allegedly committed suicide. Belishova maintained that Spiru was murdered on Hoxha's orders. (TC)

Sources: *Bashkimi*, 18 November 1945; *Fjalor Enciklopedik Shqiptar* (Tirana, 1985); Arshi Pipa, *Albanian Stalinism: Ideo-Political Aspects* (Boulder, Colo., 1990); Lefter Nasi, "Aspekte nga jeta dhe veprimtaria e Nako Spirut ne vitet 1943–1947," *Studime Historike*, 1998, nos. 1–2.

SPRINGOVICS Antonijs (31 October 1876, Rezekne–1 October 1958, Riga), archbishop of Riga, primate of Latvia. In 1893 Springovics graduated from a municipal school in Rēzekne and in 1897 from a theological seminary in St. Petersburg. He worked as a priest in parishes and schools near Orel and Pinsk and from 1905 in Liksne in Latvia. In 1917 Springovics was appointed general curate to **Edward Ropp**, the archbishop of Mogilev (now Mahilyow). After the visit of papal nuncio Achille Ratti (later Pius XI) to Riga, Springovics was appointed bishop of Riga and was ordained on 22 March 1920. At the same time he became the primate of independent Latvia. After signing a concordat with Latvia in 1922, Pius XI raised Riga to the rank of archbishopric, and Springovics was appointed archbishop on 25 October 1923. Springovics advocated moderation in the Latviazation of the Catholic Church in Latvia and opposed the removal of Polish priests. In 1934 in order to negotiate a *modus vivendi* with the new government, which favored the Protestants, Springovics met with **Kārlis Ulmanis**, who had assumed dictatorial powers in Latvia. The government did not always comply with established rules, but the Latvian Church emerged unscathed from a confrontation with the Peasant-Nationalist regime of Ulmanis. During World War II Springovics avoided Soviet and German deportation. In 1947 the Communist authorities arrested his auxiliary bishop, Kazimirs Dulbinskis. Springovics was allowed to stay, but he was given very little freedom to continue his pastoral activities. (WR/EJ)

Sources: *The Catholic Church in Latvia under the Bolshevik Torture* (New York, 1950); Janis Rutkis, ed., *Latvia: Country and People* (Stockholm, 1967).

SPYCHALSKI Marian (6 December 1906, Łódź–7 June 1980, Warsaw), Polish Communist activist. Spychalski was adopted into a working-class family. In 1931 he graduated from the Warsaw Polytechnic and joined the Communist Party of Poland. In 1935 he was appointed supervisor in the department of urban development with the city administration in Warsaw. In 1937 he took the Grand Prix in an urban development competition in Paris. During World War II Spychalski was in the underground, joining the Polish Workers' Party (Polska Partia Robotnicza [PPR]) in 1942. He was a co-founder and, between January and August 1942, chief of staff of the People's Guard. He worked closely with **Władysław Gomułka**. In December 1943 Spychalski became a member of the Home National Council (Krajowa Rada Narodowa [KRN]). In early 1944, he was appointed chief of the information department of the General Staff of the People's Army (Armia Ludowa [AL]). Between March and June 1944, as a member of the KRN delegation, Spychalski traveled to Moscow. Upon his return, he served for a few months as chief of the Supreme Staff of the Polish (Communist) Army. From September 1944 through March 1945, he worked as the mayor of Warsaw and chairman of its National Council. Between 1944 and 1948, Spychalski was a member of the PPR Central Committee (CC); in May 1945 he was elevated to its Politburo; and in December 1948 he automatically entered the CC and the Politburo of the Polish United Workers' Party (Polska Zjednoczona Partia Robotnicza [PUWP]). From March through April 1949, Spychalski served as deputy minister of national defense and deputy commander-in-chief for political-educational affairs of the (Communist) Polish Army. In

1945, he was promoted to brigadier general. In 1947, he became an MP. In June 1948, during a CC plenum, he was psychologically coerced to criticize Gomułka. In April 1949 he was appointed minister for reconstruction and later for construction. In November 1949 Spychalski was dismissed from all of his official posts; afterwards, he worked as an architect in Wrocław. Arrested in May 1950 (despite his parliamentary immunity, which was not officially revoked until 1951) and charged with assisting the infiltration of the army by counterrevolutionary agents, Spychalski was imprisoned and tortured until his release in March 1956.

Rehabilitated in July 1956, Spychalski returned to the post of deputy minister of national defense and became chief of the Main Political Board of the Polish Army in October 1956. During the Eighth Plenum of the party, he was restored as a member, and during the third congress of the PUWP in March 1959, he was again coopted to the Politburo. Between November 1956 and April 1968, Spychalski served as minister of national defense. He restored to the military many commanders formerly associated with the underground AL. From 1957 to 1972, Spychalski was an MP again. In 1963, he was promoted to the rank of marshal of Poland. He displayed a passive attitude toward the anti-Semitic purge in the military at the beginning of the 1960s, notwithstanding that it undermined his own position in the army. At the end of Gomułka's reign, Spychalski was attacked by the so-called partisan group of **Mieczysław Moczar**. Following the March 1968 events, he was dismissed from the Ministry of National Defense, and in April 1968 he was appointed chairman of the Council of State and of the All-Polish Committee of the Front of National Unity. Spychalski actively participated in the December 1970 events; he was involved on the anti-crisis staff. Spychalski's political career ended with the fall of Gomułka. At the end of 1970 and the beginning of 1971, he was relieved of all his posts. (PK)

Sources: Mołdawa; *Słownik polityków polskich XX wieku* (Poznań, 1998); Michael Checinski, *Poland: Communism, Nationalism, Anti-Semitism* (New York, 1982); Krzysztof Lesiakowski, *Mieczysław Moczar: Biografia polityczna* (Warsaw, 1998); Włodzimierz Janowski and Aleksander Kochański, *Informator o strukturze i obsadzie personalnej centralnego aparatu PZPR 1948–1990* (Warsaw, 2000); Jerzy Eisler, *Grudzień 1970* (Warsaw, 2000).

ŠRAMEK Jan (12 August 1870, Grygov, near Olomouc–22 April 1956, Prague), Czech Catholic priest and Christian Democratic leader. In 1892 Šramek graduated from a theological seminary in Olomouc and was ordained a priest. From 1902 he lectured on theology at a seminary in Brno. In 1924 he received a Ph.D. in philosophy. He was elected an MP in 1906, and in 1913 he became head of the National Council (Zemski Vybor) in Moravia. After the creation of Czechoslovakia, between September 1921 and October 1922 Šramek was minister of railways in the government of **Edvard Beneš**. In 1922 he was elected president of the unified Czechoslovak People's Party (Československá Strana Lidová [ČSL]), whose program was based upon the principles of the encyclical *Rerum Novarum* of Pope Leo XIII. Šramek was one of the organizers of the Czech Catholic trade unions. Although initially he had a good relationship with Reverend **Andrej Hlinka**, the leader of the Slovak Catholics, from the early 1920s there was a growing conflict between them: Šramek supported the administrative autonomy of Slovakia within the framework of a unitary state, while Hlinka sought constitutional equality for both parts of the state. In October 1922 Šramek became minister of health in the government of **Antonín Švehla**, and later he headed the departments of post and social welfare in this cabinet. In 1926 he became deputy prime minister, and when in February 1929 Švehla resigned after a heart attack, Šramek temporarily took over the duties of head of government. In the elections of October 1929 the ČSL lost many votes; therefore Šramek left the government. In 1930 he published *Životni data, dokumenty, vzpomínky, úvahy* (Biography, documents, memoirs, thoughts).

During the Munich crisis of 1938 Šramek counted on Soviet support and opposed capitulation. After the Munich agreement was signed, he went to France and then to England, where in December 1939 he co-founded the Czechoslovak National Committee. Since he proved to be an efficient mediator between the supporters of Beneš and the adherents of **Milan Hodža**, Šramek soon became head of the committee. He transformed this body into a provisional government-in-exile that on 21 July 1940 was recognized by Great Britain. As prime minister, Šramek supported plans to create a Polish-Czechoslovak federation; these plans were crowned with a preliminary agreement with the Polish government of **Władysław Sikorski**. Later, however, Šramek favored the policy of President Beneš, who, on 12 December 1943, signed a treaty of friendship and mutual assistance with the USSR and subsequently an agreement with the Czechoslovak Communists. These treaties formed the basis of the coalition government of **Zdenek Fierlinger**, established in March 1945. The ČSL joined this government.

After his return to Czechoslovakia, Šramek became deputy prime minister in both governments of Fierlinger (April 1945–July 1946). He protested the ceding of the Subcarpathian Ukraine to the USSR. In the elections of May 1946 Šramek obtained a parliamentary seat, although his party had lost its former influence, even in the Moravian countryside, where it had been the strongest party. Šramek remained in the government of **Klement Gottwald** as deputy prime minister, but because of old age and illness, he was less and less active. Although at the time of the crisis in January–February 1948 Šramek acted cautiously and in a conciliatory way, believing that too harsh a reaction to the Communist actions might only cause the situation to deteriorate, on 20 February, along with other non-Communist ministers, he resigned in protest against the corrupt practices of the Communists in the Ministry of Interior and against the growing terror. This gave Gottwald a chance to illegally replace the vacancies with Communist ministers and to seize full power. Fearing arrest, Šramek attempted to leave the country but was arrested and imprisoned by the police. He spent the rest of his life in prison and under house arrest in a monastery, where he died. (WR)

Sources: *ČBS*; *Enciklopedia Slovenska*, vol. 5 (Bratislava, 1980); V. S. Mamatey and R. Luža, *A History of the Czechoslovak Republic 1918–1948* (Princeton, 1973); Karel Kaplan, *The Short March: The Communist Takeover in Czechoslovakia, 1945–1948* (London, 1981); Miloš Trapl, *Political Catholicism and the Czechoslovak People's Party in Czechoslovakia, 1918–1938* (Boulder, Colo., 1995).

ŠROBÁR Vavro (9 August 1867, Lisková, Slovakia–6 December 1950, Olomouc), Slovak politician, journalist, and doctor. Born into a Catholic peasant family, in 1886 Šrobár was expelled from a Hungarian high school in Banská Bystrica for spreading "Pan-Slavic propaganda." He graduated from high school in Přerov, Moravia. From 1888 to 1898 he studied medicine in Prague, where he became a leading activist of the Slovak academic youth and maintained contacts with **Tomáš Garrigue Masaryk**. After returning to Slovakia, Šrobár worked as a doctor in Ružomberok. He was one of the ideologues of the young Slovak intelligentsia centered around the liberal monthly *Hlas*. He strongly criticized the conservative center (the so-called Martin center) of the national movement, led by **Svetozár Hurban-Vajanský**. Šrobár himself remained under the influence of positivist ideas, Pan-Slavism, evolutionism, and Darwinism. In the spirit of Masaryk, he encouraged education among peasants and the upgrading of the economic standards of the country. He called for the democratization of political and cultural life, advocated close cooperation with the Czechs, and promoted the idea of a "single Czechoslovak nation." Because of his activities, Šrobár was imprisoned in Ružomberok (1906) and Szeged (1907–8).

During World War I Šrobár worked with Czech activists. He drafted a resolution in which the participants in the 1918 May Day gathering in Liptovský Sv. Mikuláš demanded the right to self-determination for the nations of Austria-Hungary. It was the first such Slovak document, and émigré politicians could use it for propaganda in the international forum. In October 1918 Šrobár joined the leadership of the Czechoslovak National Committee in Prague. After the establishment of the Czechoslovak state (28 October 1918), he ardently implemented the policy of centralization. From 4 to 14 November 1918 Šrobár served as prime minister of the Slovak provisional government. He subsequently became minister plenipotentiary for the administration of Slovakia. He organized the Czechoslovak administration, which consolidated its power after the invasion by the Hungarian Red Army was repulsed and the ephemeral Slovak Soviet Republic was abolished in mid-1919. Šrobár resorted to dictatorial methods of governing, as a result of which he was criticized not only by the members of the Slovak People's Party (led by Father **Andrej Hlinka**), but also by the Social Democrats, including **Ivan Dérer**, who replaced Šrobár as minister plenipotentiary in April 1920. In the interwar period Šrobár was one of the leaders of the Agrarian Party in Slovakia. He sat in the parliament from 1918 to 1935 (from 1925 as a senator). He also lectured at Comenius University Medical School in Bratislava, where he was given a professorship in 1935. He sharply opposed Hlinka's party and demands for Slovak autonomy. Šrobár's publications include the memoirs *Pamäti z vojny a väzenia* (War and prison memoirs; 1922); *Oslobodené Slovensko* (The liberation of Slovakia; 1928); and *Z môjho života* (From my life; 1946).

During World War II Šrobár organized an underground group in Slovakia. This group recognized the Czechoslovak government-in-exile led by **Edvard Beneš**. After the outbreak of the Slovak National Uprising, Šrobár, together with the Communist **Karol Šmidke**, took the helm of the Slovak National Council (Slovenská Národná Rada [SNR]). He also became honorary chairman of the Democratic Party (Demokratická Strana). As a member of the SNR delegation, in March 1945 Šrobár took part in negotiations in Moscow on the establishment of a new Czechoslovak government, and he assumed the post of minister of finance in this government. Before the elections in 1946 Šrobár helped to found the Party of Freedom (Strana Slobody), which, however, failed to enter parliament. He represented this party in the leadership of the National Front. After the Communist coup in February 1948, Šrobár assumed the portfolio of minister of unification. (MG)

Sources: *SBS*; *Biographisches Lexikon*, vol. 4; *Kdo byl kdo v našich dějinách ve 20. století* (Prague, 1998); *Kto bol kto za I. ČSR* (Bratislava, 1993); *Šrobárov zborník k sedemdesiatym narodeninám* (Bratislava, 1938); Włodzimierz Wincławski, *Lud, naród, socjologia: Studium o genezie socjologii słowackiej* (Toruń, 1991); *Politické strany na Slovensku 1860–1989*ed. Lubomír Lipták (Bratislava, 1992); Marián Hronský, *The Struggle for Slovakia and the Treaty of Trianon* (Bratislava, 2001).

SRŠKIĆ Milan (3 March 1880, Belgrade, Serbia–12 April 1937, Belgrade), Serbian politician from Bosnia. Srškić completed law studies in Vienna, where he also earned a doctorate. He actively worked for the autonomy of religious schools in Bosnia and Herzegovina, contributing to the periodicals *Srpske riječi* in Sarajevo and *Die Zeit* in Vienna. In 1910 he was elected to the Sabor (Assembly) of Bosnia and Herzegovina. At the beginning of World War I Srškić was in Russia; from there he returned to his country toward the end of the war. In 1918 he was a member of the Yugoslav Committee (Jugoslovenski Odbor), a member of the provisional executive of Bosnia and Herzegovina, and a deputy to the Constitutional Assembly. He was elected to parliament in 1923, 1925, 1927, and 1931. In 1923 Srškić became minister of forestry and mining in the government of **Nikola Pašić**. He also headed the ministry of interior (1924 and 1932) and the ministry of justice (1926–27, 1929–31). A member of the Serbian Radical Party and a staunch supporter of the monarchy, Srškić was one of the main executors of the dictatorial policy of King **Alexander Karadjordjević** in Bosnia and Herzegovina after 1929. From 13 July 1932 to 27 January 1934 Srškić served as prime minister. He left the Serbian Radical Party and was one of the founders of the authoritarian ruling Yugoslav National Party (Jugoslovenska Nacionalna Stranka). (WR)

Sources: *Enciklopedija Jugoslavije*, vol. 8 (Zagreb, 1971); www.beotel.yu/~ninic/srpskopit.html.

STAMBOLIĆ Ivan (5 November 1936, Brezova, near Ivanjica–25 August 2000, Novi Sad), Serbian Communist activist. Stambolić was born into a family with Communist traditions. Working in a factory, he also studied law at the University of Belgrade, where he met **Slobodan Milošević**, who was to become his closest friend and protégé. Stambolić was the best man at the wedding of Milošević and Mira Marković. After completing his studies, Stambolić entered politics, encouraged by his uncle, **Petar Stambolić**, who was a close associate of **Josip Broz Tito**. Stambolić became the director of the state company Tehnogas and held this post until 1973, when he was promoted to chairman of the Belgrade Chamber of Commerce, and Milošević was appointed his successor. Later Stambolić served as prime minister of Serbia. In April 1984 he resigned as chairman of the Belgrade City Committee of the League of Communists of Serbia (LCS) in favor of Milošević. Stambolić became head of the Central Committee (CC) of the LCS. In 1986 he became chairman of the presidency (president) of the Socialist Republic of Serbia. He lent his support to Milošević's election to the position of head of the LCS, although some warned him against doing so. In April 1987 Stambolić made a big mistake when he did not personally go to Kosovo but instead sent Milošević, who fueled nationalist feelings, presenting himself as a defender of the Serbs against the Albanians. Milošević also exploited the conflict in Kosovo for his political games, accusing Stambolić of incompetence. On 23–24 September 1987 at the Eighth Plenum of the LCS CC—broadcast live on television—Milošević effected the dismissal of Dragiša Pavlović, who was supported by Stambolić. This was Stambolić's political defeat, and it was sealed with his forced resignation as president on 14 December 1987.

In November 1987 Stambolić became the director of the Yugoslav Bank for International Economic Cooperation and held this post until 1997. In April 1995, after a few years of silence, he gave an interview in Sarajevo. A collection of Slobodan Inić's interviews with Stambolić, titled *Put u bespuce* (Road to nowhere), was published in the same year. In this book, Stambolić presented his views on the events of the 1980s and on the end of his political career. Stambolić did not intend to reenter politics or to run in the presidential elections, yet he severely criticized Milošević. On 25 August 2000, a few weeks before the presidential elections, Stambolić did not return from the park in which he jogged every day. His remains were found in March 2003. According to the findings of the investigation that followed, Stambolić had been abducted by officers of the now disbanded Special Operations Unit, killed near Novi Sad, and buried in a lime pit. (AO)

Sources: Laura Silber and Allan Little, *The Death of Yugoslavia* (London, 1995); www.rferl.org/newsline.

STAMBOLIĆ Petar (12 May 1912, Brezova, Serbia), Yugoslav Communist activist, ethnic Serb. Stambolić attended high school in the village of Brezova and then in Ivanjica and Čačak. In 1932 he began to study at the School of Agriculture of the University of Belgrade. He became a member of the League of Yugoslav Communist Youth in 1933 and a member of the Communist Party of Yugoslavia (CPY) in 1935. In December 1941 he joined the General Staff of **Josip Broz Tito**'s Partisans in Serbia, and at the beginning of 1944 he became commander of the General Staff. At the second session of the Anti-Fascist Council for the National Liberation of Yugoslavia in November 1943

Stambolić was elected to its presidium. After World War II, he was a member of the party leadership in the Serbian republic and at the federal level. He was a member of the Central Committee (CC) of the Communist Party of Serbia (CPS) from 1945 to 1952 and then a member of the CC of the League of Communists of Serbia (LCS) from 1952 to 1969. Stambolić served as a member of the CC Politburo of the CPS (1945–52), secretary of the CPS CC (1948–52), and secretary of the LCS CC (1952–57). From January to November 1968 he headed the LCS CC. He was a member of the CPY CC (1949–52) and the CC of the League of Communists of Yugoslavia (LCY) (1952–69 and 1974–86). He was a member of the LCY CC Executive Committee (1954–66) and chairman of the LCY CC Ideological Committee (1958–63). He sat on the Presidium of the LCY CC (1966–69 and 1974–81) and the Presidium of the LCY (1969–74 and 1978–86). Stambolić served as deputy prime minister and minister of finance in the government of the Serbian republic (1945–47) and minister of agriculture in the federal government (1947–48). He was prime minister of Serbia (1948–53), speaker of the Serbian parliament (1953–57), and speaker of the federal parliament (1957–63). A close associate of Tito, Stambolić served as prime minister of Yugoslavia from 29 June 1963 to 16 May 1967. He was a member of the presidency of the Socialist Federal Republic of Yugoslavia (May 1974–May 1985), its vice-chairman (1974–75 and 1981–82), and its chairman (May 1982–May 1983). (AO)

Sources: *Who's Who in the Socialist Countries of Europe* (Munich, London, and Paris, 1989); *Enciklopedija Jugoslavije* (Zagreb, 1975); Slobodan Stanković, *The End of the Tito Era: Yugoslavia's Dilemmas* (Stanford, 1981).

STAMBOLIYSKI Aleksandur (1 March 1879, Slavovitsa–14 June 1923, near Pazardzhik), Bulgarian Peasant Party leader. After attending agricultural colleges in Sadovo and Pleven, Stamboliyski studied agriculture in Halle, Germany. In 1899 he attended the founding congress of the Bulgarian Agrarian National Union (Bulgarski Zemedelski Naroden Suyuz [BANU]). After returning to Bulgaria, he turned to politics. On 10 November 1904, at the Sixth BANU Congress in Varna, Stamboliyski was elected chairman of the BANU and appointed editor-in-chief of *Zemedelsko zname*, a party newspaper. In his essay "Politicheski partii ili suslovni organizatsii?" (Political parties or state organizations?), Stamboliyski laid down the ideological foundations of the Bulgarian agrarian movement. Considering cities as sources of evil, he praised the peasant virtues and promoted the idea of cooperatives, as he believed that cooperatives would modernize farming in traditional peasant communities, upgrade living standards in rural areas, and help create a more egalitarian society. Stamboliyski's ideology exerted a strong influence on the peasant movement both in Bulgaria and abroad—for example, in Bohemia and Croatia. In 1911 the BANU, led by Stamboliyski, protested the new constitution, which consolidated the tsar's rule.

During World War I Stamboliyski sharply protested Bulgaria's involvement on the side of the Central Powers; as a result, he was sentenced to life imprisonment in 1916. After the outbreak of a military rebellion in Radomir, he was released and sent there to restore order among the mutinous troops. Instead, Stamboliyski joined in the proclamation of the Republic of Radomir and became its president on 27 September 1918. After this rebellion was suppressed, he went underground for some time, but as early as October 1918 he became minister of public works in the government of **Teodor Teodorov**.

After the parliamentary elections in August 1919, on 2 October 1919 Stamboliyski assumed the post of prime minister of a coalition government formed by the BANU, the liberals, and the nationalists. On 17 November he represented Bulgaria at the signing of the Treaty of Neuilly. After an unsuccessful general strike organized by the Communists, he dissolved parliament and called new elections on 28 March 1920. His party was five seats short of being able to establish an independent government; therefore, a dozen or so seats of other parties were declared invalid, and on 20 May Stamboliyski formed a new government based only on the BANU. In May 1921 the parliament, dominated by his supporters, enacted an agricultural reform that limited land ownership to thirty hectares (seventy-five acres). Land owned by monasteries was also confiscated. Many leading opposition politicians (even those who, like **Aleksandur Malinov**, had opposed the policies of Tsar **Ferdinand**) were arrested under the pretext of being responsible for Bulgaria's defeat in war. Hoping for concessions, Stamboliyski tried to improve relations with the victorious Entente states. To that end, in the fall of 1920 he went on a three-month tour of Europe, visiting France, Great Britain, Italy, Switzerland, Poland, and other countries. In late 1920 Bulgaria was admitted into the League of Nations. However, Stamboliyski failed to get the Entente to fulfill its promise that Bulgaria would gain the Thracian coast of the Aegean Sea. His efforts to improve relations with the Kingdom of Serbs, Croats, and Slovenes resulted in the Treaty of Niš (23 March 1923), under the terms of which Stamboliyski promised to combat the Macedonian independence movement. The opposition called this treaty treason, and the Internal Macedonian Revolutionary Organization (IMRO) undertook military action against the government. Pressured by the young

Tsar **Boris III**, traditional parties, and particularly the IMRO, as well as by the Communists (whose power had grown), and faced with discontent among his own supporters, Stamboliyski—with the help of his guards—increasingly resorted to dictatorial methods of government. As a result, he won the parliamentary elections of 23 April 1923, when the BANU obtained 53 percent of the votes and 85 percent of the seats. However, this electoral success did not prevent Stamboliyski's fall. On 9 June 1923 the secret National Alliance (Naroden Sgovor) and the Military League, led by **Damian Velchev**, supported by a part of the army, overthrew Stamboliyski's government. Stamboliyski himself was captured by Military League soldiers and IMRO members in the vicinity of the village of Golak, near Pazardzhik, and he was brutally murdered. (WR)

Sources: *Entsiklopediya Bulgariya*, vol. 6 (Sofia, 1988); *Biographisches Lexikon*, vol. 4; John D. Bell, *Peasants in Power: Alexander Stamboliski and the Bulgarian Agrarian National Union, 1899–1923* (Princeton, 1977); Heinz Gollwitzer, ed., *Europaeische Bauernparteien im 20. Jahrhundert* (Stuttgart and New York, 1977); Khristo Khristov, *Alexander Stamboliski: His Life, Ideas, and Work* (Sofia, 1981); Zygmunt Hemmerling, *Ruch ludowy w Polsce, Bułgarii i Czechosłowacji 1893–1930* (Warsaw, 1987); *Ubietsut na Aleksandur Stamboliiski govori* (Veliko Turnovo, 1991); Ivanka Mavrodieva-Georgieva, *Aleksandur Stamboliiski* (Sofia, 1993); Raymond Detrez, *Historical Dictionary of Bulgaria* (Lanham, Md., 1997); Vulo Ivanov, *Aleksandur Stamboliiski: Zvezda na politicheskiya nebosvod na Bulgariya* (Sofia, 1997).

STANCHEV Kiril (14 December 1895, Kyustendil, Bulgaria–11 April 1968), Bulgarian military man. Stanchev graduated from a military school in Sofia (1915) and then fought in World War I. He was subsequently the commander of regiment and lecturer at a military school in Sofia. As one of the founders and leaders of an underground organization of military men holding leftist views, Stanchev was dismissed from the army after the monarchist coup of 1934. Arrested in 1935, he was sentenced to death in 1936, but his sentence was commuted to life imprisonment. In 1940 he was released under amnesty. Stanchev began to study law at Sofia University. At that time he established contacts with the Communists and was one of the main organizers of the coup of 9 September 1944 in Sofia. He became a member of a delegation that conducted talks with the leadership of the Soviet Second Ukrainian Front. From 1944 to 1945 Stanchev commanded the Second Bulgarian Army. Although he had ties with the Communists, the opposition regarded him as rather neutral politically and even considered him a close associate of **Damian Velchev**, the minister of war. When in September 1945 **Nikola Petkov** called for the dismissal of the government of **Kimon Georgiev**, he suggested that Stanchev assume the ministry of war in the future cabinet. This was enough for the Communists to treat Stanchev as an enemy. At the end of July 1946 he was dismissed as commander of the Second Army and arrested for allegedly leading an organization called the Military Union (Voenen Suyuz). Subjected to torture, Stanchev confessed to being a leader of this organization, which had allegedly sought to overthrow the government. However, Stanchev incriminated neither his superior, Velchev, nor Petkov, disappointing those who had trumped up this trial. The Stanchev case led to a conflict in the Politburo of the Communist Party. Although some Communist activists (for example, **Traycho Kostov**) demanded a death sentence for Stanchev, finally—under pressure from **Georgi Dimitrov**—Stanchev was sentenced to life imprisonment in October 1947. He served eighteen years of this sentence. Released in 1965, Stanchev died three years later. (AG)

Sources: *Entsiklopediya Bulgariya*, vol. 6 (Sofia, 1982); Jerzy Jackowicz, *Partie opozycyjne w Bułgarii 1944–1948* (Warsaw, 1997).

STANCULESCU Victor Atanasie (10 May 1928, Tecuci), Romanian Communist activist and general. After graduating from an officer training school and a military college, Stanculescu gradually rose through the army ranks. In the 1970s he worked in the Ministry of National Defense, and from 1981 to 1986 he served as deputy minister. He subsequently served as first deputy minister of defense until December 1989. On 17 December 1989 Stanculescu was responsible for the suppression of protests in Timişoara; the suppression gave rise to a revolution and the overthrow of **Nicolae Ceauşescu**. From December 1989 to February 1990 Stanculescu was minister of defense. He subsequently served as minister of defense in the government of **Petre Roman** until May 1991. At that time he supervised the reconstruction of the security apparatus. In 1991 he was promoted to the highest rank of general. From May to September 1991 Stanculescu was minister of industry, and in 1993 he became director of a credit bank. From 1992 to 1994 he was a delegate of the London-based Balli Group, and he subsequently served as senior adviser to the director of Group London PLC until 1997. In 1995 he became vice-president of Robank. In 1995 the American Biographical Institute awarded him a prize for outstanding professional achievements, and the International Biographical Center in Cambridge named him man of the year. In May 2000 Stanculescu was sentenced in absentia to fifteen years' imprisonment because he was found co-responsible for the death of 72 people and the wounding of 253 people who had protested in Timişoara in December 1989. In May 2000 Romania

asked Interpol for help in finding Stanculescu and bringing about his extradition. (PC)

Sources: *Who's Who in the World 2000* (New Providence, 2000); Mark Almond, *The Rise and Fall of Nicolae and Elena Ceauşescu* (London, 1992); Daniel N. Nelson, ed., *Romania after Tyranny* (Boulder, Colo., 1992).

STANKIEWICZ Adam (24 December 1891, Arlyanyaty,, near Ashmyany–29 November 1949, near Irkutsk, Siberia), Catholic priest, Belorussian religious activist, politician, and historian. Stankiewicz's brother, Jan Stankiewicz (1891–1976), was a philologist, an MP in the Assembly of the Republic of Poland (1928–30), and a Belorussian activist in exile. In 1914 Stankiewicz graduated from the Catholic Seminary in Wilno (Vilnius) and in 1918 from the Catholic Theological Academy in Petrograd. In 1911 he began to be involved in public life, founding a Belorussian club at the seminary in Wilno. This club was officially recognized by the rector. In 1917 Stankiewicz helped to found the Belorussian Christian Democratic Union (Khrystsiianskaia Dèmakratychnaia Zluchnasts [KhDZ]) in Petrograd, and he attended the First Congress of Belorussian Parties and Organizations in Minsk in March of that year. Stankiewicz became a member of the Council of the Belorussian People's Republic. In 1919 he returned to Wilno, where he revived the periodical *Krynitsa* in Belorussian. This periodical was addressed to the Catholic community. He also worked as a religion teacher at a Belorussian high school in Wilno and edited the periodical *Khrystsiianskaia Dumka*. From 1922 to 1927 Stankiewicz was an MP in the Assembly of the Republic of Poland. He was a member of the successor to the KhDZ, the Belorussian Christian Democratic Alliance, renamed Belorussian Christian Democracy in 1926 and the Belorussian People's Union in 1935. After the Parliamentary Group of the Belorussian Peasants' and Workers' Hromada was established (1925), Stankiewicz founded a parliamentary faction of the Belorussian Peasant Union. From 1924 to 1926 he was the chairman of the Belorussian School Society, and subsequently he became the director of the Belorussian Institute of Economy and Culture.

After Poland was defeated and the Vilnius region was seized by Lithuania (1939), Stankiewicz became the chairman of the Belorussian Center in Lithuania. During the German occupation he continued to publish *Krynitsa*, but he refused to collaborate with the Nazi authorities. He supported anti-Nazi efforts and tried to help the Jewish people. Arrested by the NKVD in 1944, Stankiewicz was sentenced to twenty-five years in Soviet forced labor camps in 1949, and he perished in Siberia. Stankiewicz authored many books on the history of Belorussia, among them the following: *Rodnaia mova u sviatyniakh* (The mother tongue in the churches; 1929); *Kastus Kalinouski* (1933); *Muzhytskaia Prauda i idėia nezalezhnastsi Belarusi* ("Muzhytskaia Prauda" and the idea of Belorussian independence; 1933); *Da historyi belaruskaha palitychnaha vyzvalennia* (On the history of Belorussian political liberation; 1935); *Belaruski khrystsiianski rukh* (The Belorussian Christian movement; 1939); and *Khrystsiianstva i belaruski narod* (Christianity and the Belorussian nation; 1940). (EM)

Sources: *Belarus: Entsyklapedychny davednik* (Minsk, 1995); W. Jarmołkowicz, "Białoruska Chrześcijańska Demokracja," *Więź,* 1986, nos. 11–12; Vitaut Kipel and Zora Kipel, eds., *Byelorussian Statehood* (New York, 1988); Jan Zaprudnik, *Historical Dictionary of Belarus* (Lanham, Md., 1998).

STANKOVIĆ Borislav (31 March 1875, Vranje, Serbia–21 October 1927, Belgrade), Serbian writer. Stanković lived in poverty from childhood. Orphaned at an early age, he was brought up by his illiterate grandmother Zlata, whose character he immortalized in his later works. After finishing primary school, he attended high school in Niš, graduating in 1896. He subsequently enrolled as a student in the Department of Economics and Politics of the Superior School in Belgrade, but he never graduated. Stanković made his literary debut in 1898. One year later he published the first collection of his stories, *Iz starog ivandjelja* (From the old gospel). From 1897 to 1900 Stanković worked at a printing house, then in the Ministry of Education, the Ministry of Foreign Affairs (from 1901 on), and the Ministry of Finance in Belgrade (1903–12). Stanković wrote most of his works in 1900–12, when he published, among other works, the drama *Koštana* (1902) and the novel *Nečista krv* (Tainted blood; 1910). In 1913 he began working in the Ministry of Education. During World War I Stanković was interned in Bosnia. After the war he resumed his former post, but he ceased writing and lived in isolation. In his works, Stanković depicted the traditional Balkan society: a circle of a peculiar fatalism and biological motivation. In a masterly way he portrayed merchants, peasants, beggars, and women, depicting people who had had been shaped during many centuries of foreign rule. Stanković enriched the Serbian language with borrowings from rural dialects, full of archaisms and influences from other Balkan languages. After his death, eight volumes of his *Sabrana dela* (Collected works; 1928–30) were published. They included the unfinished dramas *Tašana* (1910) and *Jovča* (1910), as well as the war memoirs *Pod okupacijom* (Under occupation; 1922). (WR)

Sources: *Enciklopedija Jugoslavije*, vol. 7 (Zagreb, 1968); *Mały słownik pisarzy zachodnio-słowiańskich i południowo-słowiańskich* (Warsaw, 1973).

STANOVNIK Janez (4 August 1922, Ljubljana), Yugoslav Communist activist, ethnic Slovene. In March 1941, while at the University of Ljubljana, Stanovnik became a member of the Committee of the Liberation Front ,and, along with Christian Socialists, he opposed the pro-German policy of the government. He joined the Partisans led by **Josip Broz Tito** during World War II. After the war, he earned a doctorate and became director of the Institute of International Politics and Economics in Belgrade (1956–62). He also served as head of Tito's office; a minister in the federal government of **Mika Špiljak** (1967); a co-worker in the UN Organization for Economic Cooperation and Development in Geneva; and UN Economic Commission for Europe (ECE) executive secretary (1968–82). In 1982 Stanovnik became a professor at the Department of Economics of the University of Ljubljana. As chairman of the presidency (president) of the Slovene Republic (May 1988–May 1990), Stanovnik received representatives of the Human Rights Defense Committee; this was seen as a gesture of support from Slovene political leaders for **Janez Janša**'s adherents, who had been arrested as a result of their conflict with the army. At the same time Stanovnik advocated that the Slovene republic remain part of Yugoslavia, and he publicly stated (for example, in April 1989) that separating from Yugoslavia would be a suicidal step for Slovenia. He also did not resign his membership in the League of Communists of Slovenia–Party of Democratic Renewal. Stanovnik received the Golden Honorary Medal of Freedom of the Republic of Slovenia (2002). His publications include *Gospodarski razvoj Jugoslavije v luči svetovnega gospodarskega razvoja* (Economic development of Yugoslavia in the light of world economic development; 1958); *Mednarodni gospodarski sistem: Od dominacije k enakopravnosti* (The international economic system: From domination to equal rights; 1982); and *Svet v dolgovih in mednarodni monetarni sklad* (The world in debt and the International Monetary Fund; 1985). (JD)

Sources: *Enciklopedija Slovenija*, vol. 12 (Ljubljana, 1998); Drago Bajt, *Slovenski kdo je kdo* (Ljubljana, 1999).

STAPIŃSKI Jan (21 December 1867, Jabłonica Polska–17 February 1946, Krosno), Polish Peasant Party politician. In 1889 Stapiński graduated from a Jasło high school. He then studied law for a year at the University of Lemberg (Lwów, Lviv). In the 1890s, he worked for the Concordia Insurance Company, but he also published prolifically in the press and periodicals put out by the populist leaders Reverend Stanisław Stojałowski and Maria and Bolesław Wysłouch. Stapiński was one of the pioneers of the populist movement in Galicia. In 1895, he co-founded the Peasant Party (Stronnictwo Ludowe), and in 1905 he joined the Polish Peasant Party (Polskie Stronnictwo Ludowe [PSL]). Between 1902 and 1934, he published and contributed to *Przyjaciel Ludu* (A friend of the people). From 1898 to 1900 and 1907 to 1918, he was a deputy to the Austrian Council of State and to the Galician National Parliament (Sejm Krajowy) (1901–8). In 1908 Stapiński was elected chairman of the PSL. After a split in the party, he headed the PSL–Left. During the parliamentary elections of 1919 Stapiński represented his party in the Constitutional Assembly. After the PSL–Left joined the dissidents from the PSL–Piast, Stapiński became a deputy chairman of a new group, the Peasant Union (Związek Chłopski), which soon united with the politicians who split from the PSL–Liberation (PSL–Wyzwolenie) to form the Peasant Party (Stronnictwo Chłopskie [SCh]). Stapiński continued on as a deputy chairman of the SCh. However, in 1928 he was expelled from the party for having too close links with the followers of **Józef Piłsudski**. Subsequently, he was elected to the parliament from the Nonparty Block of Cooperation with the Government (Bezpartyjny Blok Współpracy z Rządem [BBWR]) list. Stapiński officially joined the BBWR in 1930, but disillusioned with the *sanacja* government, he left active political life and devoted himself to his farm in Klimkówka, near Gorlice. During the Nazi occupation he was hiding in Lesser Poland. Stapiński authored *Pamiętnik* (Memoirs), published posthumously in 1959. (WR)

Sources: *Kto był kim w Drugiej Rzeczpospolitej* (Warsaw, 1994); *Encyklopedia historii Drugiej Rzeczypospolitej* (Warsaw, 1999); Krzysztof Dunin-Wąsowicz, *Jan Stapiński: Trybun ruchu ludowego* (Warsaw, 1969); Władysław Pobóg-Malinowski, *Najnowsza historia polityczna Polski*, vols. 1–2 (London, 1984–86).

STAROSOLSKYI Volodymyr (8 January 1878, Jarosław–25 February 1942, Mariinsk, Western Siberia), Ukrainian theorist of law, lawyer, sociologist, and politician. Born into a Galician family of lawyers, Starosolskyi graduated from high school in Kraków and subsequently studied in Lemberg (Lviv, Lwów), Kraków, Vienna, and Prague. After earning a Ph.D. in Prague in 1909, he continued his studies in Heidelberg, Germany. Starosolskyi was active in the Ukrainian student movement. In 1900 in Lemberg he helped to establish Young Ukraine, a radical student organization that strove for the Ukrainization of the University of Lemberg. He also edited the press organ of this organization. In 1902 he co-organized the so-called secession of Ukrainian students, who temporarily transferred to study at universities in Austria, Bohemia, and Germany in protest against the mainly Polish authorities of the University of Lemberg. Starosolskyi was a member

of a foreign committee of the Ukrainian Radical Party and then a member of the leadership of the Ukrainian Social Democratic Workers' Party (Ukraiinska Sotsial-Demokraticheskaya Rabochaya Partiya [USDRP]) in Galicia. In the 1920s, during a stay in Czechoslovakia, he belonged to the USDRP leadership in exile.

In 1907 Starosolskyi opened a law practice in Lemberg. In 1908 he was the defense counsel in the trial of **Myroslav Sichynskyi**, who had assassinated Count Andrzej Potocki, the governor of Galicia. In 1914 Starosolskyi opened a law practice in Gródek Jagielloński (now Horodok, Ukraine). One of the founders of a Ukrainian paramilitary organization called the Sich Riflemen, Starosolskyi was the organization's chairman from 1913. After the outbreak of World War I, Starosolskyi became a member of the Ukrainian Chief Council and a member of the military command of the Ukrainian Sich Riflemen. As a member of the Military Committee, he took part in preparations for the takeover of power in Lemberg on 1 November 1918 and for the establishment of the Western Ukrainian National Republic (Zakhidno-Ukraiinska Narodna Republika [ZUNR]). In the fall of 1919, after the ZUNR united with the Ukrainian National Republic (Ukraiinska Narodna Republika [UNR]), Starosolskyi worked as vice-minister of foreign affairs in the government of **Isaak Mazepa**. In 1920–27 Starosolskyi lived in Vienna and Prague. He continued his party work in the USDRP, as well as his scholarly work as associate professor and lecturer at the Ukrainian Free University, the Ukrainian Sociological University, and the Ukrainian Academy of Economics. In 1928 he returned to Lwów. He resumed his law practice and defended representatives of the young generation of various Ukrainian organizations, from Communists to members of the Organization of Ukrainian Nationalists (OUN). Starosolskyi attempted to create a programmatic and moral alternative to integral nationalism, which was increasingly popular among the Galician youth. He began to criticize the ideology of **Dmytro Dontsov**, yet he was opposed to the concept of a dictatorship of the proletariat. In the autumn of 1939, after the Red Army occupied Lwów, Starosolskyi became a professor at the university there. Arrested the following year, he was sentenced to ten years' imprisonment. He was subsequently deported to Mariinsk in Western Siberia and perished there.

Starosolskyi published *Das Majoritätsprinzip* (The principle of primogeniture; 1916); *Metodolohichna problema v nautsi pro derzhavu* (The problem of methodology in the science of the state; 1925); and *Do pytannia pro formy derzhavy* (On the issue of the state system; 1925). He also authored the books *Teoriia natsii* (Theory of the nation; 1921) and *Derzhava i politychne pravo* (The state and the political law, 2 vols.; 1924). In the former he presented the nation as a phase in the development of forms of human life and justified the right to national self-determination, which was to fulfill itself as both national and social liberation (democracy, abolition of class, and universal will). In the latter he foresaw that all European nations would be formed into separate states and then federalized in order to reduce absolute sovereignty and to create an efficient system to defend the rights of individuals. (TS)

Sources: *Encyclopedia of Ukraine*, vol. 5 (Toronto, 1993); Ryszard Torzecki, *Kwestia ukraińska w Polsce w latach 1923–29* (Kraków, 1989); Ulyana Starosolska, ed., *Volodymyr Starosolskyi, 1878–1942* (New York, 1991).

STARZYŃSKI Stefan (19 August 1893, Warsaw–19 March 1944? Germany), Polish politician, entrepreneur, and pundit. In 1914, Starzyński graduated from the August Zieliński Higher Courses in Trade. Then he studied law at the University of Warsaw and completed an officer training school. In 1910, he had joined the Union of Progressive-Independentist Youth (Związek Młodzieży Postępowo-Niepodległościowej). In 1913 and 1914, he served on its Central Committee in the Kingdom of Poland. In 1912 Starzyński became involved with the Union of Active Struggle and the Riflemen's Association in Warsaw. He was arrested several times by the Russian authorities. Between 1914 and 1917, he served as an officer with the First Brigade of the Polish Legions. After the oath crisis in July 1917, Starzyński was interned in Beniaminów; he then joined the clandestine Polish Military Organization. In 1918, he volunteered for the Polish Army, fighting on the Ukrainian front. In 1919, he was assigned to the High Command, and in 1921 he was dismissed from the army as a captain of the reserves. Between 1921 and 1924 Starzyński served as general secretary of the Polish delegation in the Joint Polish-Soviet Reevacuation and Special Commission in Moscow. He was an active supporter of Piłsudski. Starzyński was promoted to director of a department at the Ministry of the Treasury, and in September 1929 he was handed a vice-ministerial portfolio at the ministry. Between 1930 and 1933, he served as an MP on behalf of the Nonparty Bloc of Cooperation with the Government (Bezpartyjny Blok Współpracy z Rządem [BBWR]). In 1931 he commenced teaching at the Main Trade School in Warsaw. In 1933, he was appointed deputy chairman of the Bank of the National Economy (Bank Gospodarstwa Krajowego [BGK]) and commissar of the National Loan. He was known for his support of economic statism and state interventionism in the economy.

From 1933 through 1934, Starzyński chaired the BBWR in Warsaw, and between 1934 and 1939 he was the commissary mayor of Warsaw. In 1937, he initiated a four-year plan to develop and modernize the capital. The plan was dubbed "The capital presents its front to the Vistula River." In 1937, Starzyński became an activist of the pro-government Camp of National Unity (Obóz Zjednoczenia Narodowego [OZN]) as the chairman of its Warsaw section, and in 1938 he was elected to the Senate from the OZN lists. In September 1939, he was appointed civilian commissioner with the Command of the Defense of Warsaw. Starzyński rendered civilian assistance to the military; in practice this translated into a mass mobilization of the Polish society to fight. Thus, a legend was born of Starzyński as the leader of the fighting capital. Starzyński participated in the conceptualization and establishment of the Polish Underground State. Following the capitulation of Warsaw, he was arrested by the Germans and imprisoned in Pawiak Prison on 27 October 1939. In December 1939 he was transferred (most likely) to Berlin. According to some sources, Starzyński was sent to Dachau; according to others, he was sent to the potassium mine at Baelberge. The circumstances and the precise date of his death remain unknown. His symbolic grave is at Powązki Cemetery in Warsaw. Starzyński authored numerous economic works, including *Rola państwa w życiu gospodarczym* (The role of the state in economic life; 1927) and *Myśl państwowa w życiu gospodarczym* (Etatist thought in economic life; 1928). (JS)

Sources: *Kto był kim w Drugiej Rzeczypospolitej* (Warsaw, 1994); *Encyklopedia historii Polski: Dzieje polityczne*, vol. 2 (Warsaw, 1995); Marian Marek Drozdowski, *Stefan Starzyński prezydent Warszawy* (Warsaw, 1980); *Wspomnienia o Stefanie Starzyńskim* (Warsaw, 1982); Julian Kulski, *Stefan Starzyński w mojej pamięci* (Warsaw, 1990); Marian Marek Drozdowski, Juliusz L. Englert, and Hanna Szwankowska, *Stefan Starzyński: "Chciałem by Warszawa była wielka"* (Warsaw, 1994); Anna Kardaszewicz, *Stefan* Starzyński (Warsaw, 2000).

STAYNOV Petko (19 May 1890, Kazanluk–24 July 1972, Sofia), Bulgarian lawyer and politician. After finishing high school in Stara Zagora (1908), Staynov studied law and administration in Grenoble and Paris, graduating in 1911. From 1911 to 1912 he continued his studies in Leipzig. He fought as an officer in the Balkan Wars (1912–13). In 1914 he earned a Ph.D. in economic and political sciences from the University of Paris. From 1919 to 1920 Staynov headed the Office for the Press in Bulgaria. In 1923 he began working at Sofia University, first as an associate professor (1937–47) and then as full professor and dean of the Department of Administrative Law (1947–63). He also lectured at the Free University (1925–39). In 1935 Staynov became a corresponding member and in 1942 a full member of the Bulgarian Academy of Sciences. From May 1930 to June 1931 Staynov served as minister of railways, post, and telegraph. He was a minister to Belgium (1934) and France (1934–35). In 1934 he became a member of the International Institute of Public Law, and in 1935, a member of the International Institute of Constitutional and Political History. In December 1941 Staynov protested in parliament against Bulgaria's declaration of war on the United States and Great Britain. He also signed a protest against the deportation of Bulgarian Jews in 1943. He called for a change in Bulgarian foreign policy: Bulgaria should cease to side with Germany in the war; there should be rapprochement with the Soviet Union and the establishment of a government that would observe the constitutional rules. Along with twelve other opposition politicians, Staynov signed an appeal to the regents on these issues (7 August 1944). Staynov served as deputy to the National Assembly from 1923 to 1946 and then, under Communist rule, from 1950 to 1972.

After the coup of 9 September 1944, Staynov served as minister of foreign and religious affairs until March 1946. He was a member of the Bulgarian delegation to the armistice negotiations between Bulgaria and the Soviet Union, the United States, and Great Britain in Moscow on 28 October 1944. He also took part in negotiations on the establishment of a federation of South Slavic nations (1944). In 1949 Staynov became a member of the National Council of the Fatherland Front and a member of the National Council for the Defense of Peace in Bulgaria. From 1949 to 1959 he served as secretary of the Department of Legal and Economic Sciences of the Bulgarian Academy of Sciences. Staynov's publications include *Administratsiia i pravosudie v Germaniya* (Administration and the judiciary in Germany; 1923); *Administrativno pravosudie* (Administrative judiciary; 1936–37); *Administrativno pravo* (Administrative law; 1945); *Voenno administrativno pravo* (Military administrative law; 1946); and *Razdelnostta na vlastta i konstitutsiiata* (The separation of powers and the constitution; 1946). (JJ)

Sources: *Entsiklopediya Bulgariya*, vol. 6 (Sofia, 1988); *100 godini na BAN*, vol. 1 (Sofia, 1969); *Belezhiti Bulgari*, vol. 7 (Sofia, 1982); Tasho Tashev, *Ministrite na Bulgariya 1879–1999: Entsiklopedichen Spravochnik* (Sofia, 1999); Angel Tsurakov, *Entsiklopediya. Pravitelstvata na Bulgariya: Khronologiya na politicheskiia zhivot 1879–2001* (Sofia, 2001).

STECKI Jan (22 March 1871, Siedliska, near Lubartów–30 June 1954, Bełżyce), Polish conservative politician. The son of an estate manager, Stecki graduated from high school in 1889 and then studied medicine at Warsaw University and participated in the Association of Polish Youth–Zet. Arrested temporarily in 1891, in 1893 he joined the National League (Liga Narodowa) but was also a member of the Workers' Committee of the Polish Socialist Party for a while. After getting married in 1900, Stecki managed the Łańcuchów estate and participated in the Lublin Agricultural Association. In 1906 he was elected to the First State Duma and worked in its Agricultural Commission. Elected again to the Second State Duma, he prepared a proposal of autonomy for the Kingdom of Poland. After the outbreak of World War I Stecki supported the Entente, but in December 1917 he became minister of interior in the **Jan Kucharzewski** government of the Regency Council. In protest against the Treaty of Brest-Litovsk, in March 1918 Stecki resigned but continued to serve in the same capacity in the next cabinet, that of Jan Kanty Steczkowski, from April to October 1918.

After Poland regained independence, Stecki was on the Board of Directors of the Association of Landowners (Związek Ziemian [ZZ]); from June 1919 he was its chairman, and in September 1919 he became chairman of the Supreme Council of Landowners' Organizations. Stecki protested the expropriation of large estates without compensation, a ruling passed by the Constituent Assembly in July 1919. During the Polish-Soviet war, in July 1920 he initiated a ZZ resolution offering estate mortgages for the defense of Poland. In the elections of 1922 Stecki was elected MP on behalf of National Democracy, but after the party reached a compromise on land reform with the Peasant Party–Piast (the Lanckorona Pact of May 1923), he moved to the Christian National Agricultural Party. After the May 1926 coup d'état Stecki supported **Józef Piłsudski**, and in 1930 he was elected senator on behalf of the Nonparty Bloc of Cooperation with the Government. When in 1933 it was disclosed that Stecki had obtained a loan from ZZ funds, he became a target of sharp criticism and gave up the ZZ chairmanship and his senatorial seat. He continued to publish articles. During World War II and the Nazi occupation Stecki lived in Łańcuchów. After the war, the estate was confiscated as part of the Communist land reform. Stecki moved to Lublin, where he worked in the provincial administration. He authored a lot of articles, pamphlets, and other works, mainly on land reform, among them the following: "W obronie prawdy" (In the defense of truth; 1928); "Wartość i ceny ziemi" (The value and price of land; 1937); and "Zagadnienie rozwoju gospodarczego wsi polskiej" (The question of economic development of the Polish countryside; 1938). (WR)

Sources: Czesław Brzoza and Kamil Stepan, *Posłowie polscy w parlamencie rosyjskim 1906–1917* (Warsaw, 2001); Włodzimierz Mich, *Jan Stecki (1871–1954): Portret polityka ziemiańskiego* (Lublin, 1990); Wojciech Roszkowski, "Wielcy właściciele ziemscy jako grupa nacisku w Drugiej Rzeczypospolitej," in *Społeczeństwo polskie XVIII i XIX wieku*, vol. 9 (Warsaw, 1991).

STEFAN [original name Stoyan Popgeorgiev] (19 September 1878, Shiroka Luka, near Devin–14 May 1957 Banja, near Karlovo), exarch of the Bulgarian Orthodox Church. Stefan attended a rural elementary school in Shiroka Luka and then went to a high school in Oriakhovo. In 1899 he finished a theological seminary in Samokov, and in 1904 he graduated from the Kiev Theological Academy. While a student, Stefan embraced Russophile and Pan-Slavic views. Before going to Russia, he worked as a village teacher. After completing his studies, he taught at a high school in Plovdiv and at a seminary in Istanbul. He also served as secretary to Josif I, the Bulgarian exarch. Ordained on 16 October 1910, he took the monastic name of Stefan. In 1911 he was named archimandrite. After World War I, Stefan studied at the University of Freiburg, earning a Ph.D. in 1919 for a dissertation on the Bogomil heresy. After returning to Bulgaria, he rose through the ranks of the Orthodox Church. In 1921 he was ordained titular bishop of Martianopolis, and on 29 March 1922 he was elected the metropolitan of Sofia. De facto, Stefan became the most important clergyman in Bulgaria. De jure, the election of the exarch was postponed because of the domestic situation in Bulgaria and because of a conflict within the Orthodox Church over the extent of the jurisdiction of the exarchate of Bulgaria. Furthermore, Stefan was in opposition to Tsar **Boris III**. After the royal dictatorship was established in 1935, Stefan founded an Orthodox Church committee for peace and cooperation in the Balkans, which was seen as an expression of support for the opposition. He also took part in ecumenical work, using his contacts with Old Catholics and Anglicans. During World War I Stefan protested the persecution of the Jewish people and of the Orthodox Church and the Orthodox faithful in Serbia.

On 21 January 1945 Stefan was officially appointed exarch of Bulgaria. The Communists tried to exploit his prestige, and Stefan believed that it was necessary to cooperate with Stalin and the Bulgarian Communists in order to gain concessions for the Orthodox Church. As early as February 1945 he went to Moscow and took part in negotiations with the hierarchs of the Russian Orthodox Church. He strove to end the conflict between the Russian and Bulgarian churches, which went back to 1872. He was given consent by the hierarchs of the Moscow patriarchate to transform the exarchate of Bulgaria into an autocephalous church. In return, Stefan fully supported the policies of Stalin and the Communists. On 8 September 1946, along with all members of the Bulgarian Holy

Synod, Stefan called for the abolishment of the monarchy and the establishment of a republic. In 1947 he officially blessed the establishment of the Information Bureau of the Communist and Workers' Parties, and in July 1948 at the General Synod of Orthodox Churches in Moscow he praised the Kremlin's activities aimed at uniting the Slavic nations. Despite his servility, Stefan became the victim of triumphant totalitarianism. Abducted by the Communists on 8 September 1948, he was forced to move to the village of Banja, near Karlovo, where he was held under house arrest until the end of his life. In 2001 the Yad Vashem Institute honored Stefan posthumously with the title of "Righteous among Nations." (MC)

Sources: *Biographisches Lexikon*, vol. 4; Mikhail Arnaudov, *Zhivot i deinost na ekzarkh Iosif* (Sofia, 1965); Khristo Bruzitsov, *Ekzarkh Iosif I* (Sofia, 1973); Djoko Slijepčević, *Die Bulgarische orthodoxe Kirche, 1944–1956* (Munich, 1957); Totiu Totev and Kina Vachkova, eds., *Bog i tsar v bulgarskata istoriya* (Plovdiv, 1996); Bojidar B. Andonov, *Der Religionsunterricht in Bulgarien: Geschichte, Gegenwart und Zukunft religiöser Bildung in der orthodoxen Kirche Bulgariens* (Essen, 2000).

ŠTEFÁNEK Anton (15 April 1887, Vel'ké Leváre, Slovakia–29 April 1964, Žiar nad Hronom, Slovakia), Slovak sociologist and politician. In 1898 Štefánek began to study in Vienna, but he discontinued his studies owing to financial difficulties. He belonged to a circle of the young Slovak intelligentsia centered around the liberal monthly *Hlas*. Inspired by **Tomáš G. Masaryk**, Štefánek promoted education among the peasants, the economic development of provincial Slovakia, and the democratization of public life. He called for close cooperation with the Czechs and criticized the activists of the nationalist movement. In *Hlas*, he promoted modern philosophy and rationalism and opposed (among others) the neo-Thomist **František Jehlička**. In 1906 Štefánek began working in Budapest. He initially edited the periodical *Slovenský týždenník* and then the periodical *Slovenský obzor* from 1907 to 1908. In 1908 he became editor of *L'udové noviny*. In 1910 he went back to Budapest and became the editor-in-chief of the newspaper *Slovenský denník*. During World I Štefánek worked on the editorial staff of the Prague-based periodical *Národní listy*. He also maintained contacts with the activists of the so-called Mafia, a Czech secret political organization, and in October 1918 he joined the Czechoslovak National Committee. Štefánek helped to organize the Slovak school system. He was one of the Slovak leaders of the Agrarian Party, on whose ticket he won a parliamentary seat, which he held from 1918 to 1920. In 1924 Štefánek completed his studies, earning a Ph.D. from the Department of Philosophy of Komenský University, Bratislava. In 1924 he began working in the

Ministry of Education. From February to December 1929 he served as minister. In that year he again became an MP, and in 1935, a senator.

Štefánek was one of the leading promoters of the idea of the "Czechoslovak" nation. He discussed Masaryk's influence on the process of shaping Slovak thought in the book *Masaryk a Slovensko* (Masaryk and Slovakia; 1931), and he described the concept of Czechoslovak unity in the works *Slovenská a československá otázka* (The Slovak and the Czechoslovak question; 1922); *Československo a autonómia* (Czechoslovakia and autonomy; 1923); and *Československý problém* (The Czechoslovak issue; 1924). Štefánek was a pioneer of Slovak sociology. From 1937 he held the Chair of Applied Sociology at Bratislava University. He dealt with the phenomenon of the nation and nationalism and with the sociology of rural communities. He emphasized the importance of empirical methods. A Czechophile, Štefánek was briefly interned after the Slovak state was established in March 1939. However, he was later allowed to continue his scholarly work. In 1942 he became a full professor and a member of the newly established Slovak Academy of Sciences and Arts. The work *Základy sociografie na Slovensku* (Basics of sociography of Slovakia; 1945) is a synthesis of his research. In 1945 Štefánek became rector of Bratislava University, but then his position gradually weakened. After the Communist coup, he was forced to retire in April 1949. In 1950 the Chair of Sociology was abolished for political reasons. (MG)

Sources: *SBS*; *ČSB*; Włodzimierz Wincławski, *Lud, naród, socjologia: Studium o genezie socjologii słowackiej* (Toruń, 1991); Marek Junek, "Pražská léta Antona Štefánka (1915–1918)," *Československá historická ročenka*, 2000.

ŞTEFĂNESCU-DELÁVRANCEA Barbu (5 April 1858, Bucharest–11 May 1918, Iaşi), Romanian writer, journalist, and politician. In 1882 Ştefănescu-Delávrancea graduated from medical and legal studies at the University of Bucharest. In 1884 he joined the Social Democratic movement, and from 1890 he belonged to the Conservative Party. From 1892 to 1914 he was an MP, and in 1899–1901 and 1906–8 he was mayor of Bucharest. Ştefănscu-Delávrancea was minister of public works in a conservative government (1910–12) and minister of industry in a liberal government (1917–18). In 1917–18 he actively supported the alliance with the Entente, and he was a declared adversary of Hungary. During the stay of Romanian authorities in Iaşi, he strongly advocated the unification of all Romanian territories and a continuation of the struggle against the Central Powers until final victory. Ştefănescu-Delávrancea made his journalistic debut with a series of patriotic articles in *România libera* during the struggle for independence in 1877. In 1884–1918 he published in many periodicals, among them *Epoca, Familia Românul, Revista nouă, Democraţia, Convorbiri literare, România, Placăra,* and *România libera.* He also published *Guvern, prefecţi şi deputaţi* (Government, prefects, and MPs; 1890); *Chestiunea naţionala* (The national question; 1897); and *A doua conştiinţa* (Double consciousness; 1922). Ştefănescu-Delávrancea is well known for having written plays on national questions and short stories presenting the life of the common people. He was on friendly terms with the wife of King Charles I, Queen Elisabeth, known under the pen name of Carmen Sylva. (FA/TD)

Sources: Cella Delavrancea, *Dintr-un secol de viaţa* (Bucharest, 1987).

ŠTEFÁNIK Milan Rastislav (21 July 1880, Košariská, near Myjava, Slovakia–4 May 1919, Bratislava), Slovak politician. Born the sixth of twelve children into the family of a poor Lutheran pastor, Štefánik finished a rural elementary school and then a gymnasium in Szarvas. From 1897 to 1904 he studied philosophy in Zurich and then astronomy at Charles University in Prague, earning a Ph.D. in astronomy in 1904. He subsequently went to France, where he was in charge of research at the astronomical observatory at Meudon. Štefánik conducted astronomy observations all over the world: Spain, England, Germany, Russia, the United States, North Africa, Brazil, Australia, the Fiji Islands, and New Zealand. On 28 April 1911 he observed a solar eclipse in Tahiti. In 1912 Štefánik received French citizenship, and in 1914 he was made a Knight of the Legion of Honor. When World War I broke out, Štefánik volunteered to serve in the French air force. In 1915 he started efforts to establish separate Czechoslovak units under the auspices of the French Army. In November 1915 he was wounded in an air crash in Albania. After recovering, he was encouraged by **Vavro Šrobár** to enter into cooperation with **Tomáš G. Masaryk** and **Edvard Beneš**. Their cooperation resulted in the establishment of the Czechoslovak National Council in France. Štefánik became vice-president of this council. Thanks to his great skills, he was promoted in the French Army. In 1916 he became a captain, in 1917 a major, and in 1918 a colonel and then a general. From 1916 to 1917 Štefánik traveled to Italy, Romania, and Russia with the mission of ensuring that Czech and Slovak prisoners of war were given special status. In the autumn of 1917 he visited the United States, where he recruited Slovak volunteers to fight in France. After the Czechoslovak Legion was formed in Russia,

Štefánik received permission to establish a Czechoslovak army in France (16 November 1917) and in Italy (May 1918). In April 1918 in Rome he co-organized the Congress of Captive Nations of Austria-Hungary.

When Štefánik learned, during a visit to Japan, that Beneš and Masaryk had put his name to the Independence Declaration of 18 October 1918, he asked them for an explanation regarding the vaguely formulated statements concerning Slovakia's status in the future union, but he did not receive a clear answer. As a result, he lost his post as minister of war in the provisional Czechoslovak government. In late 1918 and early 1919 Štefánik visited the Siberian headquarters of the Czechoslovak Legion. A firm opponent of the Bolsheviks, he anxiously observed that his position toward them had weakened and that cooperation with Admiral Aleksandr Kolchak was getting complicated. In January 1919 Štefánik went back to Paris and then to Italy, from where he flew to his country. His plane crashed while attempting to land. The causes of the accident remain unexplained. The Slovaks suspected that Štefánik's plane had been shot down either by mistake or on the orders of Czech leaders, who had allegedly wanted to get rid of a dynamic and troublesome partner. The legend of Štefánik, which developed after his tragic death, did not help to solve the mystery, particularly as the traces of his work and death were allegedly covered up, both during the interwar period and after World War II. (WR)

Sources: *ČBS*; *Encyklopedia Slovenska*, vol. 5 (Bratislava, 1980); *Biographisches Lexikon*, vol. 4; Štefan Osuský, Bohdan Pavlů, and Josef Bartůšek, eds., *Štefanik*, vols. 1–2 (Prague and Bratislava, 1938); Konštantin Čulen, *Zločin vo fundamente: Svadectvo o Štefanikovej smrti* (Winnipeg, 1955); Joseph A. Mikus, *Slovakia: A Political History 1918–1950* (Milwaukee, 1963); Milan S. Ďurica, "Milan R. Štefanik and His Tragic Death in the Light of Italian Military Documents," *Slovak Studies*, 1970, no. 10; Jozef Ihnat et. al., *General Milan Štefanik*ed. (New York, 1981); Dušan Kovač, *Dejiny Slovenska* (Prague, 1998).

STEFANYK Vasyl (14 May 1871, Rusów, near Śniatyń [now Rusov, near Snyatyn, Ukraine]–7 December 1936, Rusów, Poland) Ukrainian writer and politician from Galicia. Stefanyk was born into a rich peasant family. Expelled from a high school in Kołomyja (Kolomyia) for belonging to a secret self-education group, he moved to Drohobych. Stefanyk made his literary debut in *Narod*, a Lemberg (Lviv, Lwów) periodical edited by **Ivan Franko**. In 1892 Stefanyk began to study at the Jagiellonian University Medical School in Kraków, where he met many outstanding members of the Young Poland movement, including Władysław Orkan and Stanisław Przybyszewski. The lifestyle of Kraków's bohemia and the works of

leading Western modernist writers influenced Stefanyk, whose letters of that period are deeply introspective and of a poetic nature. Some of these letters were published in the periodical *Literaturno-Naukovy Vistnyk* in 1898 and then in the collections *Synia knyzhechka* (Blue book; 1899); *Kaminnyi khrest* (1900; *The Stone Cross*, 1971); *Doroha* (The road; 1901); and *Moie slovo* (My word; 1905). Stefanyk also published short-story collections. In these works the influence of Polish modernism can be found. Stefanyk's stay in Kiev and Poltava in 1903 resulted in contacts with **Mykhailo Kotsiubynskyi** and **Lesya Ukrainka**. Later, Stefanyk lived in the countryside, in Steców (Pokutia region, now in Ukraine) and in Rusov.

From 1901 to 1916 Stefanyk ran his farm and was involved in politics. In 1908–18 he sat in the Austrian parliament in Vienna as a representative of the Ukrainian Radical Party (URP). Influenced by the bloody events of World War I in Galicia, Stefanyk decided to resume writing. In 1916 he wrote the collection *Zemlia* (The land) which was published 1926). In November 1918 he became vice-president of the National Council of the Western Ukrainian National Republic (Zakhidno-Ukraiinska Narodna Republika [ZUNR]), and in January 1919 in Kiev he represented the ZUNR during the signing of the Act of Unification between the ZUNR and the Ukrainian National Republic (Ukraiinska Narodna Republika [UNR]). After the fall of the ZUNR, Stefanyk remained in Poland. In 1922 he became chairman of a URP county organization. The Soviet authorities granted him a pension, which he accepted from 1928 until 1933, when information about the Great Famine in Ukraine was revealed. Complete editions of Stefanyk's literary output were published in 1927 in the Ukrainian SSR, in 1933 in Lwów (Lviv), in 1948 in Ratisbon, and in 1964 again in the Ukrainian SSR. Stefanyk was a master of the short story. He depicted human life as an arena of suffering, acts of pure fate, and tragedy. His attachment to Pokutia manifested itself not only as the place of origin of his characters, but also in the dialect of his prose. Stefanyk's stories were translated into French (1975) and English (1971, 1988). The library of the National Academy of Sciences of Ukraine (formerly the Ossolineum Library) in Lviv has been named after him. (TS)

Sources: *Encyclopedia of Ukraine*, vol. 5 (Toronto, 1993); Stepan Kryzhanivskyi, *Vasyl Stefanyk: Krytyko-biohrafichnyi narys* (Kiev, 1946); Toma Kobzei, *Velykyi rizbar ukrainskykh selianskykh dush* (Toronto, 1966); Luke Lutsiv, *Vasyl Stefanyk: Spivets ukrainskoy zemli* (New York, 1971); Danylo Struk, *A Study of Vasyl Stefanyk: The Pain at the Heart of Existence* (Littleton, Colo., 1973); Elżbieta Wiśniewska, *Wasyl Stefanyk w obliczu Młodej Polski* (Wrocław, 1986); Olena Hnidan, *Vasyl Stefanyk: Zhyttia i tvorchist* (Kiev, 1991).

STEINHAUS Hugo (14 January 1887, Jasło–25 February 1972, Wrocław), Polish mathematician. Upon graduating from high school in Jasło, in 1906 Steinhaus commenced mathematical and philosophical studies at the University of Lemberg (Lwów, Lviv). Next, he transferred to Göttingen, where he defended his doctoral dissertation in mathematics in 1911. During World War I Steinhaus fought in the Polish Legions as an artillery officer. In 1916 he returned to the University of Lwów, received his advanced doctoral degree the following year, and was appointed full professor in 1920. Steinhaus taught at the University of Lwów until 1941. In the course of his early academic career, he met **Stefan Banach**, and together they arrived at many important mathematical discoveries. Along with their collaborators, dubbed the "Lwów mathematical school," they developed a new branch of mathematics: functional analysis. Among their greatest achievements was the "Banach-Steinhaus proof." In 1929, both scholars founded the *Studia Mathematica*, a multilingual periodical that was soon recognized as one of the most important in its field. In 1937, along with Stefan Kaczmarz, Steinhaus worked out the theory of orthogonal ranks, which was published in the United States after World War II. During the Nazi occupation, Steinhaus went into hiding because of his Jewish origins. He supported himself by clandestine teaching. In November 1945 he moved to Wrocław (Breslau), where he taught at the local university until his retirement. Steinhaus was a member of the Polish Academy of Arts and Sciences and, from 1952, of the Polish Academy of Sciences. After the war, he became interested in applying mathematics to cartography and statistical quality control, as well as in game theory. Steinhaus published about 250 original scholarly works. His *Kalejdoskop matematyczny* (Mathematical kaleidoscope; 1938) was translated into ten languages. Many of Steinhaus's students, including one of the founders of American atomic science, Stanisław Ulam, became internationally known. In 1992 Steinhaus's *Wspomnienia i zapiski* (Memoirs and notes) were published posthumously. (WR)

Sources: E. Marczewski, "Hugo Steinhaus," *Nauka Polska*, 1967, vol. 15; *The International Who Is Who 1970–71* (London, 1971); *Polacy w historii i kulturze krajów Europy Zachodniej* (Poznań, 1981).

STELMACHOWSKI Andrzej (28 January 1925, Poznań), Polish lawyer and politician. During World War II Stelmachowski was a soldier in the Home Army (Armia Krajowa). He received a law degree from Poznań University in 1947 and earned a doctorate there in 1950. He began working at Warsaw University, becoming an associate professor in 1962 and a full professor in 1973. From 1962

to 1969 he worked at Wrocław University, and in 1970 he also took up a position at the Warsaw Academy of Catholic Theology. In August 1980 Stelmachowski became an adviser to the Inter-Factory Strike Committee in Gdańsk. From 1980 to 1981 he was an expert at the Center for Social and Labor Initiatives of Solidarity. In 1981 he became an adviser to the Independent Self-Governing Trade Union of Independent Farmers–Solidarity. In 1975 he became a member of the Primate's Council for the Construction of Churches. Stelmachowski was a co-founder and chairman (1982–85) of the Organizational Committee of the Church Foundation for Polish Agriculture, but it failed to achieve its goals because of opposition from the Communist authorities. Stelmachowski works with the Polish Episcopate. In 1972 he became a member of the Club of the Catholic Intelligentsia (Klub Inteligencji Katolickiej) in Warsaw and served as its chairman from 1987 to 1990. In December 1988 he joined the Civic Committee of the Chairman of Solidarity. During the summer strikes of 1988 Stelmachowski played a great role in bringing about the first negotiations between **Lech Wałęsa** and General **Czesław Kiszczak**. One of the initiators of the Round Table negotiations, Stelmachowski was involved in their plenary and working sessions. From 1989 to 1991 Stelmachowski served as a senator of the Civic Parliamentary Caucus (Obywatelski Klub Parlamentarny [OKP]) and as senate speaker. From December 1991 to June 1992 he was minister of national education in the government of **Jan Olszewski**. In 1990 he co-founded and then became chairman of the Polish Community Association (Stowarzyszenie Wspólnota Polska). (AF)

Sources: *Nasi w Sejmie i Senacie* (Warsaw, 1990); Jan Skórzyński, *Ugoda i rewolucja: Władza i opozycja 1985–1989* (Warsaw, 1995); Antoni Dudek, *Pierwsze lata III Rzeczpospolitej 1989–1995* (Kraków, 1997); Janusz A. Majcherek, *Pierwsza dekada III Rzeczpospolitej 1989–1999* (Warsaw, 1999).

STEPINAC Alojzije (8 May 1898, Brezani, near Krašic–10 February 1960, Brezani, near Krašic), cardinal and primate of Croatia. Stepinac was the fifth of eight children born into a peasant family. During World War I he was inducted into the army and fought on the Italian front. After being taken captive, he joined the Yugoslav Legion, which was formed of Croatian and Slovenian prisoners of war alongside the coalition army. Fighting on the front lines near Salonika, Stepinac attained the rank of lieutenant; he received the Order of the Star of Karadjordjević after the war. In 1919 he began studying at the School of Agriculture at the Academy of Economics in Zagreb. However, in 1924 he decided to become a priest. He took up studies at the Gregorian University in

Rome and received a Ph.D. in philosophy in 1927 and in theology in 1931. He was ordained on 26 October 1930. After his return to Yugoslavia Stepinac began work as a diocesan priest, and then he served in the Zagreb curia. Because of his piety and energy, the archbishop of Zagreb, Antun Bauer, saw him as his successor. In May 1934 Pius XI appointed Stepinac titular archbishop of Nicopolis and coadjutor with the right of succession to the archdiocese of Zagreb. Stepinac became the youngest archbishop of the Catholic Church at that time. In a short period he visited half of the parishes in the archdiocese and initiated annual pilgrimages to Marija Bistrica.

After his predecessor's death on 7 December 1937, Stepinac assumed the post of archbishop ordinary of Zagreb. He supported a unified Yugoslavia but one based upon a federation of autonomous nations, not a centralized autocratic state dominated by Serbs, as was Yugoslavia at that time. Seeing growing tensions between the Croatian National Party and the government in Belgrade; the terrorist activities of the Ustashe-in-exile of **Ante Pavelić**; and radical tendencies among the Catholic youth of the Križari (Crusaders) movement, Stepinac strenuously sought a Serb-Croat agreement and contributed to its signing in April 1939. The agreement stipulated autonomy for Croatia within the framework of Yugoslavia. From 1939 to 1941 Stepinac took care of Czech, Polish, and Jewish refugees from German-occupied countries and organized a special committee of Caritas in Zagreb, thereby attracting the attention of the Nazis.

When in June 1941 the Germans conquered Yugoslavia and the created a puppet Croatian state under Pavelić, Stepinac continued his activities in dramatically difficult circumstances—all the more so because Pavelić professed his attachment to Catholicism, and part of the clergy favored him. In a special pastoral letter of 28 April 1941 Stepinac regarded the formation of the Croatian state as "the creation of God's hand" and welcomed it by singing a *Te Deum* in the Zagreb cathedral. However, he repeatedly asked the Ustasha authorities, and Pavelić personally, to stop the massacre of Serbs and Jews. The authorities demanded declarations of nationalism and arrested many moderate Croatian politicians. In November 1941, following the instructions of the Holy See, the Croatian bishops founded a committee for re-Catholicization and thus made it more difficult for the Ustashe to exterminate minorities. In May 1942 Stepinac refused to accept the methods adopted by the government. He then gave priests confidential instructions to admit Serbs and Jews into the Catholic Church, assuming that they may leave it after the war. Although many priests supported the regime, Pavelić was "disappointed" with the attitude of bishops,

especially with the position of Stepinac. The archbishop publicly stated that "we have always stressed in public life the principles of God's eternal laws, regardless of whether they related to Croats, Serbs, Jews, gypsies, Catholics, Muslims, the Orthodox, or anyone else." In October 1943 the Ustashe temporarily put Stepinac under house arrest and waged propaganda attacks against him.

After the liberation of Yugoslavia by the Communist partisans of **Josip Broz Tito**, Stepinac decided to remain in the country, despite the arrests and persecutions of the clergy. After the murder of the Franciscans from the monastery in Široki Brijeg, on 24 March 1945 Stepinac issued a pastoral letter defending the Croatian nation. Arrested in May 1945 Stepinac but was released. Stepinac met with Tito and spoke in defense of the constitution and human rights. He also rejected Tito's proposal of creating a national Catholic Church. On 20 September 1945 Stepinac published a pastoral letter in which he criticized the hatred contained in the Communist doctrine. As a result, the Titoist authorities launched a massive propaganda attack. In November 1945 Stepinac was assaulted and stoned by Tito's partisans in uniform. In a series of press attacks Stepinac was presented as an adherent of Pavelić and the Nazis. Various false statements were produced. In 1946 the Communists organized a series of trials of priests, who testified under torture that the archbishop had collaborated with the occupying power. Arrested on 18 September 1946 and accused of collaboration and support of the cruelties of the Ustashe, on 11 October 1946 Stepinac was sentenced in a fake trial to sixteen years of forced labor. Before the announcement of his sentence, Stepinac gave a speech that has passed into history as the "Stepinac's defense." As Tito's government was generally recognized, the trial did not evoke protests in the international arena, and Stepinac's heroism was not known.

In December 1951 Stepinac was released from prison in Lepoglava and put under house arrest in his native village of Krašic. On 29 November 1952 Pope Pius XII named him cardinal, which led Tito to break off diplomatic relations with the Holly See. Stepinac continued to refuse to leave his country, and until his death he remained an opponent of the anti-religious policy of the Communists. Stepinac died in his native village, exhausted by a blood disease. There is some suspicion that he was poisoned. In 1985, the prosecutor in his case, Jakov Blažević, admitted publicly that the charges against Stepinac had been trumped up. In 1992 the authorities of independent Croatia rehabilitated the cardinal. On 3 October 1998 Pope John Paul II beatified him during a ceremony in Marija Bistrica. After his death some of his writings and documents were published: *Stepinac govori: Život i rad, te zbirka govora,*

*propovijedi, pisama i okružnica velikog hrvatskog ro-
doljuba i mučenika dra Alojzija Stepinca* (Stepinac speaks:
The life, work, and collection of speeches, sermons, letters,
and circulars of the great patriot and martyr, Dr. Alojzije
Stepinac; 1967) and *Alojzije Stepinac: Propovijedi, govori,
poruke 1941–1946* (Alojzije Stepinac: Sermons, speeches,
1941–1946; 1996). (WR)

Sources: *Current Biography*, 1953, 1960; Anthony Henry
O'Brien, *Archbishop Stepinac: The Man and His Case* (Westminster,
Md., 1947); Richard Patee, *The Case of Cardinal Aloysius Stepinac*
(Milwaukee, 1953); Ernst Bauer, *Aloisius Kardinal Stepinac: Ein
Leben fuer Wahrheit, Recht und Gerechtigkeit* (Vienna, 1974);
Bohdan Cywiński, *Ogniem próbowane*, vol. 1 (Rome, 1982); M.
Landercy, *Kardinal Alojzije Stepinac* (Dakovački Selci, 1989);
Vinko Nikolić, ed., *Stepinac mu je ime: Zbornik uspomena,
svjedočanstava i dokumenata*, vols. 1–2 (Zagreb, 1991); Stefan
Ljubica, *Stepinac i Židovi* (Zagreb, 1998); www.dalmatia.net/
croatia/religion/stepinac.htm.

STEPONAVIČIUS Julijonas (18 October 1911,
Gervečiai–18 June 1991, Vilnius), Lithuanian archbishop
of Vilnius. Steponavičius graduated in theology from
Wilno (Vilnius) University and was ordained in June 1936.
In 1936–39 he worked as a school chaplain in Grodno
and then as a parish priest in Palūše, Daugėliškis, and
Adutiškis. On 11 September 1955 he was consecrated auxiliary bishop of Panevėžys. Two years later the Holy See
appointed him apostolic administrator of the Panevėžys
and Vilnius dioceses with the right of a resident bishop. He
took over these posts after the death of the ordinary bishop,
Kazimieras Paltarokas, in 1958. In 1961 Steponavičius
was arrested by the Soviet authorities and deported to the
village of Žagarė, situated outside these dioceses. Kept
under house arrest for years, he could not perform his
duties, but for Lithuanian Catholics he remained a symbol
of their martyrdom under Soviet power. After **Algirdas
Brazauskas** became the new head of the Communist
Party of Lithuania in October 1988 and after he turned
the Vilnius cathedral over to the Catholics, in December
1988 Steponavičius was allowed to return to the capital.
He visited Rome and was received by Pope John Paul II,
and on 5 February 1989 he solemnly took over the duties
of the archbishop of Vilnius. (WR)

Sources: *EL*, vol. 5; *Annuario Pontificio*, 1991; *Acta Apostalicae
Sedis*, 1991, no. 7; V. Stanley Vardys and Judith B. Sedaitis, *Lithu-
ania: The Rebel Nation* (Boulder, Colo., 1997); Irena Mikłaszewicz,
Polityka sowiecka wobec Kościoła katolickiego na Litwie 1944–1965
(Warsaw, 2001).

STERE Constantin (13 June 1865, Khorodishte,
Bessarabia–26 June 1936, Bucov, Romania), Romanian
politician, journalist, and writer. The son of a landowner
of Greek descent, Stere graduated from high school in
Kishinev, where, as early as 1881, he met members of the
Russian organization Narodna Vola (People's Will). As
a member of youth groups, he organized self-education
meetings in Kishinev and Odessa. These meetings were
suppressed by the Russian police. In 1886 Stere was
sentenced to three years in exile in Tobolsk. In March
1889 he co-organized a prisoners' revolt; as a result, he
was condemned to a further three years. While in exile
in the Krasnoyarsk region, Stere met, among others,
Vladimir Lenin and **Józef Piłsudski**. In 1892 he escaped
to Romania. In the following year he began to study at
the School of Law of the University of Iaşi, graduating
in 1897. In 1893 he began publishing articles in the periodical *Evenimentul literar*, and later he co-edited *Viaţa
Româneasca*, one of the most important Romanian literary periodicals. In 1898 Stere joined the National Liberal
Party, and as its nominee was deputy mayor of Iaşi from
1898 to 1899. At the end of the nineteenth century Stere
became involved in the movement against the Russian occupation of Bessarabia and helped Romanian youth from
Bessarabia to study in Romania. In 1901 he won a seat
as a deputy to the Romanian parliament and was given
a professorship in law at the University of Iaşi, where
he later served as rector. He also designed a program of
social reforms based on the development of schools and
agricultural cooperatives. After the 1905 revolution in
Russia, Stere—supported by radical liberals from his
party—attempted to establish a political representation
of peasants and warned against tensions in rural areas;
such tensions led to a bloody revolt in Moldavia in 1907.
Influenced by Social Democratic concepts of revolution, Stere worked out a program for the non-capitalist
development of rural areas through the support of small
farms and agricultural cooperatives and through a greater
involvement of peasants in political life. Stere put this
program forward in the work *Social-democratism sau
poporanism?* (Social democracy or populism? 1908). In
February 1914 he submitted to the government of **Ion
I.C. Brațianu** a program of universal suffrage and the
parceling out of large estates.

During World War I Stere represented a pro-German
orientation. He presented arguments in favor of this position in *Marele razboi şi politica României* (The great war
and Romanian policy; 1918). Stere remained in German-
occupied Bucharest and published the German-spon-
sored periodical *Lumina*, which was strongly involved in
combating the influences of the Romanian government,
at that time based in Iaşi. In this periodical Stere also attacked the royal family and the army. These attacks were
prompted by Romania's alliance with tsarist Russia. In
March 1918 Stere approved the unification of Bessarabia

with Romania, announced by the pro-German government of **Alexandru Marghiloman**. In the last stages of the war Stere joined the Bessarabian National Council (Sfatul Ţării) and supported the union of Bessarabia and the Old Kingdom of Romania, thus avoiding accusations of collaboration with the defeated Central Powers. After the end of the war, Stere established ties with the Peasant Party, led by **Ion Mihalache**, and later with the National Peasant Party (Partidul Naţional Ţărănesc [NPP]), led by Mihalache and **Iuliu Maniu**. Stere contributed to the merger of Mihalache's and Maniu's parties into the NPP in 1926. He also organized the NPP structures in the Bessarabian territory. Stere was one of the main theorists of Romanian peasant socialism (*ţărănismul*). As a result of his conflict with NPP leaders who came from Transylvania and represented a more moderate political program, Stere left this party and in 1931 founded the Radical Peasant Party (Partidul Radical-Ţărănesc), but it was of little importance. Stere wrote the vast autobiographical novel *In preajma revoluţiei* (In the revolutionary circle, 8 vols.; 1935–38). (FA/TD/WR)

Sources: *Biographisches Lexikon*, vol. 4; Pamfil Şeicaru, *Un siguratec: C. Stere* (Madrid, 1956); R. W. Seton-Watson, *A History of the Roumanians* (London, 1963); Zigu Ornea, *Viaţa lui Constantin Stere*, vols. 1–2 (Bucharest, 1991); Keith Hitchins, *Rumania 1866–1947* (Oxford, 1994).

STERNIUK Volodymyr (12 February 1907, Pustomyty, near Lemberg [Lviv, Lwów]–29 September 1997, Lviv), bishop of the Ukrainian Greek Catholic Church. Sterniuk studied philosophy and theology in Belgium, where he joined the Redemptorist order in 1927. Ordained into the priesthood in 1931, he completed theological studies in 1932 and then returned to Galicia to do his pastoral work in the dioceses of Tarnopol (Ternopil) and Stanisławów (now Ivano-Frankivsk). When the Soviet authorities abolished the Ukrainian Greek Catholic Church in 1946, Sterniuk refused to recognize the decision to incorporate its structures into the Orthodox Church. As a result, he was arrested. After five years in exile in Yertsevo in Siberia, he returned to Pustomyty, where he worked at various odd jobs, including that of night watchman, all the while continuing his pastoral work in the underground Uniate Church. In 1967 Archbishop **Vasyl Velychkovskyi** secretly consecrated him bishop. In 1972 Metropolitan **Josyf Slipyi** appointed Sterniuk *locum tenens* (acting archbishop) of Lviv and Halych. Sterniuk held this position until August 1989, when the Soviet authorities agreed to the relegalization of the Ukrainian Greek Catholic Church. In 1989–91 Sterniuk led negotiations with the political authorities and the hierarchs of the Russian Orthodox Church concerning the return of church property and institutions abolished after 1946. In 1991 Sterniuk handed over his duties to Metropolitan **Myroslav Lubachivskyi**. (WR)

Sources: *Encyclopedia of Ukraine*, vol. 5 (Toronto, 1993); Jaroslav Pelikan, *Confessor between East and West: A Portrait of Ukrainian Cardinal Josyf Slipyj* (Grand Rapids, Mich., 1990); www.rulers.org.

STETSKO Yaroslav, pseudonyms "Z. Karbovych" and others (16 January 1912, Tarnopol [Ternopil]–5 July 1986, Munich, Germany), Ukrainian politician and journalist. Born into the family of a Uniate clergyman, Stetsko studied at the Universities of Kraków and Lwów (Lviv), where he joined the underground Ukrainian Nationalist Youth, the Ukrainian Military Organization, and the Organization of Ukrainian Nationalists (OUN). He was aligned with the so-called youth group within the OUN. In 1932 Stetsko became a member of the OUN leadership (Provid), responsible for ideology and propaganda. Repeatedly arrested, Stetsko was sentenced to five years' imprisonment in 1936 but was released under an amnesty in 1937 and then emigrated. While abroad, Stetsko worked with **Roman Shukhevych** and with the "youth groups" at home. He helped to organize a convention of the OUN in Rome, although he did not accept its resolutions. After the defeat of Poland in 1939, Stetsko worked with **Stepan Bandera**. He helped to found the Bandera faction of the OUN (OUN-B) and was a member of the leadership of the OUN-B. He also organized the OUN Mobile Units (Pokhidni Grupy) and the Ukrainian National Committee. On 30 June 1941, after the Germans occupied Lviv, Stetsko issued a proclamation of the restoration of Ukrainian statehood and announced the establishment of a government, of which he became prime minister. On 12 July 1941 Stetsko was arrested and taken to Berlin. Since he refused to annul the proclamation of Ukrainian statehood, he was incarcerated (along with Bandera) in the Zellenbau block of the Sachsenhausen concentration camp. He was released in the fall of 1944.

After the end of World War II, Stetsko settled in Munich. In the late 1940s he emigrated to the United States. After the Foreign Units of the OUN (Zakordonnyye Chastyny OUN [ZCh OUN]) were established, Stetsko (together with Bandera) joined the ZCh OUN Leadership Bureau. Stetsko became the leader of the OUN in the United States. From 1946 until the end of his life he was head of the Anti-Bolshevik Bloc of Nations. After the death of Bandera, Stetsko became the leader (*providnyk*) of the ZCh OUN. From 1967 onwards he served on the executive board of the World Anti-Communist League, and in 1969 he became head of the OUN-B. Stetsko wrote *Trydtsiatoho chervnia 1941* (June 30, 1941; 1967), an account of the attempts to establish a Ukrainian government in 1941. Stetsko authored numerous ideological and propaganda brochures. He was against the democratization of the OUN and was known for his dogmatism. Stetsko's works *Ukraiinska vyzvolna kontsepsiia* (The Ukrainian liberation concept; 1987) and *Ukraine and the Subjugated Nations* (1989) were published posthumously. (GM)

Sources: *Encyclopedia of Ukraine*, vol. 5 (Toronto, 1993); *Entsyklopediya Ukraiinoznavstva*, vol. 8 (Lviv, 2000); Ryszard Torzecki, *Polacy i Ukraińcy: Sprawa ukraińska w czasie II wojny światowej na terenie II Rzeczypospolitej* (Warsaw, 1993); Paul R. Magocsi, *A History of Ukraine* (Seattle, 1996); Orest Subtelny, *Ukraine: A History* (Toronto, 2000).

ŞTIRBEI Barbu (4 November 1872, Bucharest–25 March 1946, Bucharest), Romanian prince and politician. Ştirbei was descended from the Wallachian family of *hospodars* (rulers) and was closely connected with the royal court; between 1913 and 1919 he was an administrator of royal domains. He was closely connected with King **Ferdinand I** (1914–27) and his wife, Queen Maria. He was friends with **Ioan I. C. Brătianu**, prime minister in 1922–26 and 1926–27. Politically neutral, during King Ferdinand's grave illness Ştirbei served as prime minister (4–21 June 1927). Earlier, he was co-author of the Dynastic Act of 4 January 1926, which excluded the heir to the throne, Charles, from the succession. When, despite this act, Charles succeeded to the throne in 1930, Ştirbei left for France and Great Britain. From then on he represented a pro-British orientation. King **Michael**, Marshal **Antonescu**, and **Iuliu Maniu** appointed Ştirbei a secret negotiator in talks with the Allies in Cairo in the spring of 1944. Ultimately, the results of the talks were unfavorable to Romania. Ştirbei was an adviser to King Michael during the coup of 23 August 1944, and then he was a member of a Romanian delegation that on 12 September 1944 was successful in negotiating a cease-fire. He also advised King Michael at the time of the king's conflict with the government of **Petru Groza** and during the "royal strike." Ştirbei also supported the main opposition parties—that is, the Liberals and the Peasants. (FA/TD)

Sources: Andrzej Koryn, *Rumunia w polityce wielkich mocarstw 1944–1945* (Wrocław, 1983); *Maria, Regina României, Inseminaări zilnice*, vol. 1 (Bucharest, 1996); *Maria, Regina României, Povestea vieţii mele* (Iaşi 1990–91); Guy Gauthier, *Missy: Reine de Roumanie* (Paris, 1995).

STOICA Chivu (8 August 1908, Buzau–18 February 1975, Bucharest), Romanian Communist activist. After finishing primary school, Stoica worked on the railroads.

In 1929 he joined the Union of Communist Youth and in 1931 the Communist Party of Romania (Partidul Comunist din România). In 1933, along with **Gheorghe Gheorghiu-Dej**, Stoica was one of the leaders of a strike in the Griviţa factory in Bucharest. Arrested in the same year, he was sentenced to fifteen years' imprisonment for Communist activities. In April 1944 Stoica attended a prisoners' meeting led by Gheorghiu-Dej; at the meeting they decided to take over control of the party, which in 1943 had changed its name to the Romanian Communist Party (Partidul Comunist Român [RCP]). Stoica was released in August 1944, after the Red Army entered Romania. In 1945 he became a member of the Central Committee (CC) of the RCP. He was a deputy member (1948–52) and a member (1952–68) of the CC Politburo, and in 1967 he became secretary of the CC of the Romanian Workers' Party (Partidul Muncitoresc Român [RWP]; again renamed the Romanian Communist Party in 1965). Stoica served as minister of industry (April 1948–November 1949), then minister of metallurgical and chemical industries (until May 1952) and minister of metallurgical and engineering industries (October 1953–October 1955). He was deputy chairman of the Council of Ministers (March 1950–August 1954) and then first deputy prime minister (until October 1955). After the Twentieth Congress of the CPSU, Stoica opposed de-Stalinization, supporting Gheorghiu-Dej. From 2 October 1955 to 21 March 1961 Stoica served as prime minister. After Gheorghiu-Dej's death and **Nicolae Ceauşescu**'s coming to power, Stoica served as chairman of the Council of State from 24 March 1965 to 9 December 1967. In 1968 he was stripped of all his positions as a result of Ceauşescu's purge of the party leaders closely linked with Gheorghiu-Dej. Stoica returned to public life after the new leadership consolidated its power. In 1974 he assumed the minor post of chairman of the Central Party Board. (LW)

Sources: *Who's Who in the World, 1971–1972* (Chicago, 1972); Klaus-Detlev Grothusen, ed., *Rumänien* (Göttingen, 1977); Ghiţă Ionescu, *Comunismul în România* (Bucharest, 1994); Józef Darski, *Rumunia: Historia, współczesność, konflikty narodowe* (Warsaw, 1995); Dennis Deletant, *Communist Terror in Romania: Gheorghiu-Dej and the Police State, 1948–1965* (New York, 1999); Ion Alexandrescu, Ion Bulei, Ion Mamina, and Ioan Scurtu, *Enciclopedia de istorie României* (Bucharest, 2000).

STOICHKOV Grigor (2 February 1926, Gorna Malina), Bulgarian Communist activist. During World War II Stoichkov joined the Communist Partisans. After the war, he gradually rose through the ranks of the party and the state administration. He served as minister of transportation (1969–73), minister of public works and architecture (1973–84), and minister of public works and urbanization

(1984–86). He was deputy prime minister from 1976 to 1989 and a deputy member of the Politburo of the Central Committee of the Bulgarian Communist Party from 1984. As head of a natural disasters commission, Stoichkov was responsible for withholding information from the Bulgarian public about the true extent and consequences of the catastrophe at the Chernobyl nuclear power station in April 1986. The true information was given only to the top-ranking regime officials, who were thus able to protect their families from radiation. After the fall of **Todor Zhivkov** in November 1989, Stoichkov was accused of causing a threat to public health. Forced to resign his party and governmental positions in December 1989, he was brought to trial in April 1991 and was sentenced to three years in prison in December 1991. In June 1992 his sentence was commuted to two years. (WR)

Sources: *Entsiklopediya Bulgariya*, vol. 6 (Sofia, 1988); Raymond Detrez, *Historical Dictionary of Bulgaria* (Lanham, Md., 1997); Tasho Tashev, *Ministrite na Bulgariya 1879–1999: Entsiklopedichen Spravochnik* (Sofia, 1999)

STOJADINOVIĆ Milan (23 July 1888, Čačak–October 1961, Buenos Aires), Yugoslav politician of Serb nationality. Stojadinović graduated from the University of Belgrade, and then he studied in England, France, and Germany. From 1914 he worked in the Serbian Ministry of Finance. In 1920–22 he lectured on economics at the University of Belgrade and was active in the Radical Party. In December 1922 he became finance minister, and, except for one interruption, he held the post until April 1926. Stojadinović was elected to parliament in 1923, 1925, and 1927, and he was (among other things) president of the parliament's finance committee. He edited *Samouprava*, a periodical of strong nationalist tendencies.

After the elections of May 1935 Prince Paul, whose wife was friends with Stojadinović's, appointed Stojadinović prime minister. In this capacity Stojadinović, who was regarded as an outstanding political personality, implemented a strong-arm policy toward the opposition and supported a gradual rapprochement with the Axis countries, particularly on the economic plane. In 1936 Stojadinović escaped an attempt on his life. In April 1937 he signed a non-aggression treaty with Italy. The treaty guaranteed the existing borders and recognized Italian rights in Albania, but it also stipulated the withdrawal of Italian support for the Croatian separatists of **Ante Pavelić**. Although Stojadinović attempted to implement the policy of "equal distance" toward the Axis countries and the Western democracies, in practice between 1937 and 1938 he expressed himself in favor of Germany and Italy. Therefore he remained indifferent to the annexation of Austria and

to the partition of Czechoslovakia, Yugoslavia's ally in the Little Entente. He believed that good relations with the Third Reich might guarantee the security of Yugoslavia. When the parliament ratified, under his influence, a concordat with the Holy See, the Orthodox Patriarchate of Serbia excommunicated all those who had voted in favor of the motion, including Stojadinović. Stojadinović himself removed all the opponents of this decision from the government party. With street demonstrations and under pressure from the Orthodox Church, the Senate did not support the act, and Stojadinović lost the political battle. He was also against a compromise between the Serbs and Croats. After the elections of December 1938, when the opposition gained 45 percent of the vote and did not support very far-reaching cooperation with Berlin, Stojadinović's position was weakened. During a visit of the Italian minister of foreign affairs, Galeazzo Ciano, in January 1939 Stojadinović showed too much ambition toward leadership; therefore Regent Paul brought about his removal in February 1939. During a coup in March 1941 Stojadinović was interned, and then he was delivered to the British authorities, which held him in Mauritius until 1948. Later he was allowed to go to South Africa and then to Argentina, where he published the periodical *La Economista*. Stojadinović's memoirs, *Ni rat ni pakt: Jugoslavija izmedju dva rata* (Neither war nor compromise: Yugoslavia between two wars), were published posthumously in 1963 in Buenos Aires. (WR)

Sources: *The Times*, 27 October 1961; *Biographisches Lexikon*, vol. 4; *Tri godine vlade g. D-r. Milana M. Stojadinovica* (Belgrade, 1938); Jacob B. Hoptner, *Yugoslavia in Crisis, 1934–1941* (New York, 1962); Todor Stojkov, *Vlada Milana Stojadinovica (1935–1937)* (Belgrade, 1985).

STOJAN Antonín Cyril (22 May 1851, Beňov u Přerova–29 September 1923, Olomouc), Czech archbishop and politician. Born into a large, poor family, thanks to the financial help of his uncle, Stojan graduated from high school in Kroměříž (1872) and then entered a metropolitan seminary in Olomouc. He took holy orders in July 1876. While a student at the seminary, he became interested in the work of the Slavic Apostles and made pilgrimages to Velehrad, a Cistercian abbey in Moravia where, according to legend, Saint Methodius was buried. Stojan worked in the town of Příbor, where he succeeded in (among other things) organizing a gymnasium in Svébohov in 1887–88 and then a gymnasium in Dražovice in the diocese of Brno by 1908. At that time Stojan earned a doctorate from the Higher Seminary in Olomouc. He believed that the work of Saints Cyril and Methodius was common to all Slavic nations and that it should be a foundation for their spiritual, cultural, and national revival, as well as for their return to a union with Rome. In 1892 Stojan founded the Saints Cyril and Methodius Mission, which promoted the idea of Christian unity among the Slavic nations, first in Bohemia, later in Slovakia, and after 1918 also in the Kingdom of Serbs, Croats, and Slovenes, as well as among the Czech and Slovak émigrés in the United States. The mission organized three international union congresses in Velehrad (1907, 1909, and 1911) and then three other international conferences (1914, 1921, and 1922); these resulted in the establishment of the international Velehrad Academy (Akademie Velehradská) and the scholarly periodical *Acta Academiae Velehradensis*.

Stojan was also active in Svatý Hostýn, the largest Marian sanctuary in Moravia, around which he developed a mass pilgrimage movement. He established the Center of Svatý Hostýn, whose numerous units were active in Bohemia and Moravia. He initiated fund raising for the construction of a Jesuit monastery, which was erected in Hostýn in 1885. In March 1897 Stojan obtained a seat in the Austrian parliament in Vienna on the ticket of the National Catholic Party. He again became an MP in Vienna in 1901, 1907, and 1911. From 1900 to 1907 he also served as an MP in the Moravian Provincial Diet in Brno. In the autumn of 1918, at the time when the Czechoslovak Republic was being created, Stojan took part in many rallies and demonstrations. He supported the establishment of a common state of Czechs and Slovaks and promoted this idea among Slovak Catholic activists. Stojan initiated the establishment of the Czechoslovak People's Party (Československá Strana Lidová [ČSL]), which was a joint political representation of Czech and Slovak Catholics. In October 1918 Stojan was a member of the National Council in Olomouc. In November 1918 he joined the National Assembly in Prague. In April 1920 he obtained a senatorial seat on the ČSL ticket and held this seat until the end of his life. A gifted speaker, Stojan enjoyed general respect. As an MP, he was particularly devoted to the development of the educational system and, after 1918, to the normalization of relations between the Church and the state. He also strove for the establishment of a scholarship system for youth from poor families.

In September 1920 Stojan was elected vicar capitular of the archdiocese of Olomouc and became provisional head of the archdiocese. On 10 March 1921 Pope Benedict XV appointed him metropolitan of Olomouc. On 3 April 1921 Stojan was consecrated bishop. He continued to promote the idea of the revival of Czech Catholicism in the spirit of Cyril and Methodius—for example, through retreats that he conducted in Velehrad. As tens of thousands of people attended these retreats, they can be said to have shaped the Czech intelligentsia at the turn of the nineteenth and twentieth centuries. On 25 July 1923 Stojan had a stroke that left him partially paralyzed. Soon afterwards he died. He was buried in the royal chapel in Velehrad. His beatification process began in July 1965 and was completed on the diocesan level in October 1985. Stojan was the author of many popular and scholarly articles. (AGr)

Sources: *Kdo byl kdo v našich dějinách ve 20. století* (Prague, 1994); Ludvik Nemec, *Antonin Cyril Stojan, Apostle of Church Unity: Human and Spiritual Profile* (New Rochelle, N.Y., 1983); Vojtěch Tkadlčik, *Antonin Cyril Stojan w. Bohemia sancta: Živopisy českých světců a přatel Božich* (Prague, 1989); Zdenek Libosvar, *Arcibiskup Stojan: Život a dilo* (Brno, 1995); Josef Vašica, *Eseje a studie ze starši české literatury* (Opava and Šenov u Ostravy, 2001).

STOJANOVIĆ Ljubomir (6 August 1860, Užice, Serbia–3 June 1930, Prague), Serbian politician, historian, and philologist. After graduating from high school in Belgrade, Stojanović studied at the Department of History and Philosophy of the Superior School (Velika Škola) in Belgrade, graduating in 1883. He later studied in Vienna, St. Petersburg, Berlin, and Leipzig. In 1888 he began working as a teacher at a high school in Belgrade. In 1891 he became an associate professor and in 1893 a full professor at the Superior School. In 1892–1905 Stojanović served as chairman of the Serbian Literary Association (Srpska Književna Zadruga). In 1897 he entered politics, becoming a member of the Radical Party (Radikalna Stranka), which was in opposition to the government at that time. After the Radical Party merged with the Progressive Party in 1901 and became reconciled with the absolutism of King **Alexander Obrenović**, Stojanović (together with a group of younger activists of the Radical Party) left the party in 1902 and founded the Independent Radical Party (Samostalna Radikalna Stranka [SRS]). Stojanović became vice-chairman and then chairman (1904–12) of the SRS. After King Alexander was assassinated in 1903, the SRS joined the government of **Jovan Avakumović**, and Stojanović held the post of minister of education from June to October 1903. After the parliamentary elections, Stojanović continued to hold this post in the government of **Sava Grujić** until January 1904. On 25 May 1905 Stojanović became head of the government, serving simultaneously as minister of interior. He resigned on 7 March 1906, when Grujić again became prime minister. Stojanović briefly held the portfolio of minister of education, resigning in April of that year. He again assumed the portfolio of education in the government of **Stojan Novaković** (February–October 1909). Because of a disagreement with other SRS leaders, in 1912 Stojanović left the SRS and retired from public life. In 1913 he became secretary of the Serbian Academy of Sciences.

After World War I, Stojanović (along with, among others, **Jaša Prodanović**) was a co-founder of the Yugoslav Republican Democratic Party (Jugoslovenska Republikanska Demokratska Stranka [JRDS]), which called for the introduction of a republican and federal system. Stojanović was a member of the party leadership until 1923, when he resigned in protest against a law that forbade public officials to comment on the political system of the state. Stojanović authored a great number of articles and books on the political system and history of Serbia and on the Serbian language, including the following: *Državna uprava u demokratiji* (State government in a democratic system; 1911); *O državnim činovnicima* (On state officials; 1911); *Nekoliko misli o našem novom državnom uredjenju* (Some reflections on our new state political system; 1919); and *Republikanski pogledi na nekoliko savremenih pitanja* (Republican views on some contemporary issues; 1920). Stojanović also wrote the biographies *Život i rad Vuka St. Karadžića* (The life and work of Vuk S. Karadžić; 1924) and *Stari srpski letopisi i rodoslovi* (Old Serbian, chronicles and genealogies; 1927). (WR)

Sources: *Enciklopedija Jugoslavije*, vol. 8 (Zagreb, 1971); Ljubomir Stojanović, "Autobiografija sa bibliografijom," *Srpski kniževni glasnik*, 1930, nos. 6–7; Michael Petrovic, *A History of Modern Serbia, 1804–1918*, vol. 2 (New York, 1976).

ŠTOLL Ladislav (26 June 1902, Jablonec on Nisou–6 January 1981, Prague), Czech Communist activist, literary critic, and journalist. After graduating from high school, Štoll worked as a bank clerk. In 1926 he joined the Communist Party of Czechoslovakia, and in 1929 he began working for its press organs. Between 1934 and 1937 he lectured in Moscow, from where he returned as an avowed Stalinist. In 1946 he became a professor and later the rector of the Higher Party Political and Social School. In the late 1940s and early 1950s, Štoll became the official literary critic, and he recognized Socialist realism only. He became known as a dogmatic Marxist and became a symbol of Stalinism in culture. He was also associated with the vulgarization of literary criticism. The term "Štollism" became a part of colloquial speech and was used in combination with the Soviet word *zhdanovshchina*. From 1952 on, Štoll held high posts in the government and in cultural institutions. He served as minister of higher education, minister of education, and minister of culture. From 1962 to 1968 and after 1972, he was director of the Institute of Czech and World Literature in the Czechoslovak Academy of Sciences. Štoll performed all the scientific and academic functions although he did not have higher education qualifications. (PU)

Sources: *ČBS*; *Kdo byl kdo v našich dejinách ve 20. století*, vol. 2 (Prague, 1998); Jaroslava Hertova, *Ladislav Štoll* (Prague, 1986).

STOLOJAN Theodor (24 October 1943, Târgovişte), Romanian politician. Stolojan graduated with a bachelor's degree from the Bucharest Academy of Economic Studies in 1966. He worked at the Ministry of Food Industry (1966–72) and was a lecturer at the Bucharest Academy of Economic Studies (1974–80 and 1990–91). He held a variety of positions in the Ministry of Finance, including that of inspector general at the Department of State Revenue (1988–89). After the collapse of **Nicolae Ceauşescu**'s regime, Stolojan served as vice-minister (December 1989–June 1990) and minister of finance (June 1990–April 1991). From 1 October 1991 to 19 November 1992 Stolojan served as prime minister of a coalition government supported mainly by the post-Communists and the Christian Democratic National Peasants' Party. He failed to halt an economic crisis or curb inflation. From 1992 to 1999 Stolojan worked at the World Bank. In August 2000 he joined the National Liberal Party (Partidul Naţional Liberal [NLP]), on whose ticket he ran for the presidency of Romania in November 2000, but he came in third, with 11.8 percent of the vote. In August 2002 Stolojan became chairman of the NLP. (AB)

Sources: *The International Who's Who 2002* (London, 2002); Stan Stoica, *România: O istorie cronologică 1989–2002* (Bucharest, 2002); *Enciclopedia de istorie a României* (Bucharest, 2002); http://romania-on-line.net/whoswho/StolojanTheodor.htm.

STOMMA Stanisław (18 January 1908, Szacuny [now in Lithuania]), Polish lawyer, politician, and journalist. In 1932 Stomma received a law degree from Stefan Batory University, and in 1937 he earned a Ph.D. there. He was awarded a postdoctoral degree by the Jagiellonian University in Kraków, where he worked until 1950. From 1953 to 1978 Stomma was an associate professor and a full professor there. Before World War II, Stomma was a member of the Association of Catholic Academic Youth called Odrodzenie (Revival). In 1946 he became an editor of the monthly *Znak*. Stomma authored, among other works, the famous article "Maksymalne i minimalne tendencje społeczne katolików" (Maximal and minimal social tendencies of Catholics; 1946), in which he called for the intellectual strengthening of Polish Catholicism instead of a struggle against the Communists over the form of the political system in Poland. From 1945 to 1953 and then again after 1956 Stomma was a member of the editorial staff and one of the leading journalists of the weekly *Tygodnik Powszechny*.

In October 1956 Stomma co-founded the All-Polish

Club of Progressive Catholic Intelligentsia. In 1957 he joined the Club of the Catholic Intelligentsia (Klub Inteligencji Katolickiej [KIK]) in Warsaw and served as its vice-chairman from 1958 to 1962. He was also active in the Kraków KIK, which he headed between 1958 and 1964. Stomma was an MP in the Polish Assembly from 1957 to 1976. Stomma created the concept of neo-positivism, which recognized the necessity of respecting the political and geopolitical realities of the Polish People's Republic without accepting Marxism-Leninism. This concept of realism was a starting point for a demand for the gradual evolution of the system through the extension of the rule of law, civil rights, rights of the Church and the faithful, and the rationalization of the economy. This program was pursued in the Assembly by members of the Znak Parliamentary Caucus, for which Stomma served as president from 1957 to 1976. In 1958 Stomma initiated a dialogue with Germany with the aim of overcoming hostilities and subsequently reaching a normalization of relations based on the recognition of the border on the Oder and Neisse lines. In 1968 Stomma was co-author of a parliamentary question submitted by Znak members to the prime minister concerning persecutions of protesting students. In 1976 Stomma was the only MP who did not vote in support of amendments to the constitution, as a result of which he lost his parliamentary seat. From 1981 to 1985 he chaired the Primate's Social Council. From 1984 to 1989 he was chairman of the Club of Political Thought called Dziekania, which brought together various groups of the Catholic intelligentsia. From 1988 to 1990 Stomma was a member of the Civic Committee of the Chairman of Solidarity. In 1989 he took part in the Round Table negotiations. In 1989 he became a senator. Stomma was a member of the Civic Parliamentary Caucus and then the Democratic Union Caucus. Stomma authored works in the field of penal law and books of commentaries: *Myśli o polityce i kulturze* (Thoughts about politics and culture; 1960); *Czy fatalizm wrogości: O stosunkach polsko-niemieckich 1871–1933* (The fatalism of animosity: Polish-German relations 1871–1933; 1980); and the memoirs *Pościg za nadzieją* (Chasing hope; 1991). (AF)

Sources: Andrzej Micewski, *Współrządzić czy nie kłamać?* (Paris, 1978); Peter Raina, *Political Opposition in Poland, 1954–1977* (London, 1978); *Nasi w Sejmie i Senacie* (Warsaw, 1990); Jan Skórzyński, *Ugoda i rewolucja: Władza i opozycja 1985–1989* (Warsaw, 1995); Wolfgang Pailer, *Stanisław Stomma* (Bonn, 1995).

STOYANOV Khristo (25 January 1892, Oriakhovo–5 March 1970, Shumen), Bulgarian Peasant Party activist. In 1914 Stoyanov graduated in law from Sofia University. In 1910 he founded a student group whose members represented views close to those of the Bulgarian Agrarian National Union (BANU). Stoyanov published in the periodicals *Vertokeshchnik* (1909–12) and *Selski Glas*. He fought as an officer in the Balkan Wars (1912–13) and in World War I. After 1918, he ran a law practice and was active in the Shumen region. Stoyanov served as minister of foreign affairs (March–June 1922) and minister of interior (March–June 1923) in the government of **Aleksandur Stamboliyski**. After the coup of 9 June 1923, Stoyanov was arrested but escaped from prison and emigrated to Yugoslavia. While in exile, he called for a common front with the Bulgarian Communist Party (BCP). After returning to Bulgaria, Stoyanov attended the unification conference of the BANU–Vrabcha 1 and the BANU–Aleksandur Stamboliyski in 1933, and he became head of a BANU district party organization in Shumen. During tsarist rule Stoyanov was arrested several times. After 1944, he was active in the BANU led by **Nikola Petkov**. Stoyanov had a rather compromising attitude toward the Communists but failed to create a program that would be acceptable both to the Communists and to the independent peasant party. Arrested in 1947, Stoyanov was sent to the Belene concentration camp, which he left as a completely broken man. (AG)

Sources: *Entsiklopediya Bulgariya*, vol. 6 (Sofia, 1988); Zygmunt Hemmerling, *Ruch ludowy w Polsce, Bułgarii i Czechosłowacji 1893–1930* (Warsaw, 1987); Jerzy Jackowicz, *Partie opozycyjne w Bułgarii 1944–1948* (Warsaw, 1997).

STOYANOV Petko (30 November 1879, Oryakhovo–7 December 1973, Sofia), Bulgarian lawyer, economist, and politician. In 1902 Stoyanov completed law studies in St. Petersburg and subsequently specialized in finance and economics in Munich (1902–3). From 1905 to 1909 he was a prosecutor and a member of the Sofia District Court. In 1923 he was the prosecutor in a trial against the ministers of the government of **Vasil Radoslavov** (1913–18). In 1909 Stoyanov became an associate professor. From 1916 to 1947 he worked as a professor of finance at Sofia University. He also served as the dean (1915–16 and 1935–36) of the School of Law of Sofia University. Stoyanov was one of the founders, a professor (from 1929), and deputy director (1923–47) of the Balkan Middle East Institute of Political Sciences, which was renamed the Free University in 1924. Stoyanov was elected a corresponding member (1923) and then served as a full member (1935–49) of the Bulgarian Academy of Sciences. He also served as secretary (1938–44) of the Philosophical and Social Department of the Bulgarian Academy of Sciences, chairman (1926–44) of the Bulgarian–Turkish

Society, and editor-in-chief (1929–38) of the periodical *Stopanska misul*. Initially Stoyanov was a leading activist of the Radical Democratic Party, but he left it in 1927 and joined the Democratic Party. He also served as a deputy to the National Assembly (1919–23, 1931–39). During World War II Stoyanov was in opposition to the pro-German government. He criticized the parliament's enactment of a law on the protection of the nation and protested the deportation of Bulgarian Jews. In 1942 he joined the Communist-dominated Fatherland Front.

After the coup of 9 September 1944, Stoyanov became minister of finance in the cabinet of **Kimon Georgiev** and held this position until 17 August 1945. He was also a member of the Bulgarian delegation that signed an armistice between Bulgaria and the Soviet Union, Great Britain, and the United States in Moscow on 28 October 1944. In March 1945 Stoyanov unsuccessfully tried to revive the Radical Party. After leaving the government, he boycotted the elections to the National Assembly in 1945 and then joined the opposition Bulgarian Agrarian National Union (BANU), led by **Nikola Petkov**. On 11 June 1947 Stoyanov was stripped of his parliamentary seat for his anti-government speeches at the Sixth Grand National Assembly. In 1949 he was deprived of membership in the Bulgarian Academy of Sciences and sent to the Belene concentration camp. Released after a few years, he remained in retirement. He was rehabilitated posthumously in March 1990. Stoyanov's publications include *Osnovni nachala na finansovata nauka* (Basic principles of the science of finance; 1933); *Biudzhetut na suvremennata durzhava* (The budget of a modern state; 1938); and *Danuchno pravo* (Tax law; 1943). (JJ)

Sources: *Entsiklopediya Bulgariya*, vol. 6 (Sofia, 1988); Georgi Dimitrov, *Suchineniya*, vol. 8 (Sofia, 1985); Tasho Tashev, *Ministrite na Bulgariya 1879–1999: Entsiklopedichen Spravochnik* (Sofia, 1999); Angel Tsurakov, *Entsiklopediya. Pravitelstvata na Bulgariya: Khronologiya na politicheskiia zhivot 1879–2001* (Sofia, 2001).

STOYANOV Petur (25 May 1952, Plovdiv), politician and lawyer, president of Bulgaria. After receiving a law degree from Sofia University in 1972, Stoyanov worked as an attorney in Plovdiv until 1992. In 1989 he became a member of the Club for the Support of Glasnost and Perestroika and a member of the coalition Union of Democratic Forces (Sayuz na Demokratichnite Sili [UDF]). Stoyanov was a spokesman for the UDF in Plovdiv (1990–92), deputy minister of justice in the government of **Filip Dimitrov** (1992–93), vice-chairman of the National Club for Democracy (1993), chairman of the UDF Legal Council (1993–94), deputy to the National Assembly (1994–97),

vice-chairman of the UDF parliamentary group, and vice-chairman of the UDF coalition responsible for domestic policy (1995–96). He was a UDF candidate in the presidential primary elections on 1 June 1996. In the presidential elections held on 26 October and 3 November 1996, Stoyanov defeated the post-Communist candidate Ivan Marazov, and on 19 January 1997 he assumed the office of president. The beginning of his term coincided with a political and economic crisis in the country. Stoyanov mediated in negotiations among political forces concerning the conclusion of an agreement about early parliamentary elections and measures to overcome the crisis. He dissolved the parliament, established an interim administration under Stefan Sofiyanski consisting of UDF politicians (12 February–21 May 1997), and called elections to the National Assembly, which brought victory to the UDF. Having brought the economic crisis under control, Stoyanov sought closer relations with and then admission to NATO and the European Union. This goal became more immediate after Bulgaria supported NATO air raids on Yugoslavia in the spring of 1999. In the next presidential elections Stoyanov reached the second round and then lost to the post-Communist candidate, **Georgi Parvanov**, on 18 November 2001. (JJ)

Sources: *Koy koy e v Bulgariya* (Sofia, 1998); *Europa Środkowo-Wschodnia 1996–1997/97* (Warsaw, 1998–2000); Evgeniia Kalinova and Iskra Baeva, *Bulgarskite prekhodi 1944–1999* (Sofia, 2000).

STRANDMANN Otto August (30 November 1875, Vadli, near Undla–5 February 1941, Kadrina), Estonian politician. Strandmann attended high school in Tallinn and St. Petersburg and then passed his final examinations at an Estonian high school in Tallinn. He subsequently worked in the Tallinn branch of the Russian State Bank for some time and later studied law at the University of St. Petersburg (1899–1901) and at Dorpat (later Tartu) University (1901–3). After graduating, Strandmann ran a law practice in Narva and Tallinn. He had to begin earning a living at a young age. In his youth he also established ties with the radical movement led by **Konstantin Päts,** and worked on the editorial staff of *Teataja*, the leading press organ of the Estonian left. From 1904 to 1905 Strandmann sat on the Tallinn City Council as a member of the first-ever Socialist group to be elected to this council. After the defeat of the Russian revolution of 1905, Strandmann had to emigrate. From 1905 to 1909 he lived in Switzerland and other West European countries and then returned to Tallinn, where he again ran a law practice. Shortly before the February 1917 revolution, he became prosecutor of the Tallinn District Court. After the fall of tsarism in February 1917, Strandmann was quickly promoted within the structures of the newly established Estonian state. In 1917–18 he served as chairman of the Estonian Provincial Assembly (Eesti Maanõukogu). From 1918 to 1919 he was successively minister of justice and minister of agriculture in the Provisional Government. During the German occupation of Estonia, Strandmann was arrested in 1918. After the German forces were driven out of Estonia, he became a member of the Constituent Assembly (Asutav Kogu).

From 9 May to 18 November 1919 Strandmann held the post of prime minister, and from 1920 to 1921 he served as minister of war. As leader of the Estonian Labor Party (Eesti Tööerakond), Strandmann won the largest number of seats in the first parliament and became its speaker. He was also elected head of state (riigivanem). He greatly contributed to the passing of bills introducing agricultural reforms in a much more radical form than those adopted in other Central European countries. The Estonian reforms did not provide for any compensations, and not only land, but also live stock was expropriated. In this way the influence of the German landed gentry in Estonia was destroyed, and tensions in the countryside were eased because the granting of land ownership to leaseholders was accompanied by the granting of land to landless peasants. As minister of finance (1924), Strandmann was the driving force behind the reforms, which were based on cutting public expenditure, restricting credit, reducing imports, and promoting exports, while abandoning the subsidization of industry and recognizing agriculture as the main lever for the development of the national economy. However, these reforms did not prevent a drop in the popularity of the Labor Party, which suffered splits and a steady decline in public support from one election to the next. Still, Strandmann managed to win a seat in each of the five successive terms of parliament. He also became minister of foreign affairs and minister of finance. From 1927 to 1929 he was ambassador to Poland. This appointment reflected Estonia's efforts to achieve a rapprochement with Poland because Strandmann held unequivocally pro-Polish personal sympathies. From 9 July 1929 to 12 February 1931 Strandmann served as head of state and continued a pro-Polish line in foreign policy. In 1933 he became ambassador to Paris, Belgium, and the Vatican. He served as ambassador until November 1939. After the Red Army occupied Estonia in June 1940, Strandmann avoided arrest for some time. In 1941 he committed suicide when NKVD officers came to arrest him. (AG)

Sources: Evald Uustalu, The History of the Estonian People (London, 1952); Piotr Łossowski, Stosunki polsko–estońskie 1918–1939 (Gdańsk, 1992); Matti Laur, Tõnis Lukas, Ain Mäesalu, Ago Pajur, and Tõnu Tannberg, History of Estonia (Tallinn, 2000); Web site of the president of Estonia, www.president.ee/eng/riigipead/OttoStrandman.html; Web site of Riigikogu, www.riigikogu.ee/history.html.

STRÁNSKÝ Jaroslav (15 January 1884, Brünn [Brno]–13 August 1973, London), Czech lawyer, journalist, and politician. In 1907 Stránský received a law degree from the Czech University in Prague. Before World War I he wrote commentaries on the domestic policies of the Habsburg monarchy, mainly for Lidové noviny, a periodical published by his father, Adolf Stránský. At that time Stránský was also active in the People's Progressive Party in Moravia (Pokroková Strana Lidu na Moravě). In 1918, along with the whole party, Stránský joined the Czechoslovak National Democratic Party (Československá Národní Demokracie) and became one of its leaders. In March 1921 he resigned his parliamentary seat in protest against the policy of the Prague center. Shortly afterwards, along with Karel Engliš, Stránský established an opposition "Moravian wing" in the Czechoslovak National Democratic Party. In 1925 the conflict reached its apogee, and Stránský, together with a group of Moravian activists, left the party and founded the National Labor Party (Národní Strana Práce [NSP]). After a failure in the parliamentary elections, the NSP joined the Czechoslovak National Socialist Party (Československá Strana Národně Socialistická) in 1929. From 1918 to 1921 and from 1929 to 1938 Stránský sat in the National Assembly. From 1929 to 1938 he also served as deputy chairman of the foreign affairs committee of the Chamber of Deputies. In 1925 he became the owner of the František Borový publishing house, and he also succeeded his father as the publisher and editor-in-chief of Lidové noviny. In his journalism Stránský protested against fascism and corruption and attacked particular politicians, including Jiří Stříbrný. In 1921 he became an associate professor and in 1934 a full professor of criminal law. From 1945 to 1948 he was full professor at Masaryk University in Brno.

In 1938 Stránský was a member of the Committee for the Defense of the Republic (Výbor na Obranu Republiky) and protested Czechoslovakia's capitulation to Munich. On 16 December 1938 he resigned his parliamentary seat, and in 1939 he went into exile in Great Britain. From 1941 to 1945 Stránský served as minister of justice of the Czechoslovak government-in-exile. Like President Edvard Beneš, he harbored the illusion that after the war it would be possible to establish relations with the Soviet Union while maintaining democracy. In March 1945 Stránský took part in Moscow negotiations that resulted in the formation of a coalition government with the Communists. After the war, Stránský was a member of the Presidium of the National Socialist Party and a deputy to the National Assembly. He also served as minister of justice in the government of Zdenek Fierlinger (April 1945–May 1946), and then he became deputy prime minister. From May

1946 to February 1948 he served as minister of education in the cabinet of **Klement Gottwald**. A firm critic of the Communists, Stránský repeatedly protested against Communist practices. On 20 February 1948, along with other ministers representing democratic parties, he resigned his position. After the Communist coup d'état, Stránský, along with his family, emigrated to Great Britain in March 1948. He worked with Czechoslovak émigré organizations there; for example, he helped to found the Czechoslovak section of the BBC and broadcast on Radio Free Europe under the pseudonym of Jan Zedník. (PU)

Sources: *ČBS*; *Českoslovenští politici: 1918–1991* (Prague, 1991); *Politická elita meziválečného Československa 1918–1938: Kdo byl kdo za první republiky* (Prague, 1998); *Kdo byl kdo v našich dějinách ve 20. století*, vol. 2 (Prague, 1998); Karel Kaplan, *The Short March: The Communist Takeover in Czechoslovakia, 1945–1948* (London, 1987).

STRÁSKÝ Jan (24 December 1940, Plzeň), Czech economist and politician. From 1963 to 1970 Stráský studied at a school of commerce in Plzeň and pursued philosophical and political economy studies at Charles University, Prague. From 1958 to 1990 he worked for the Czechoslovak central bank, initially in the town of Blovice, near Plzeň, and then at the head office in Prague. In 1964 Stráský became a member of the Communist Party of Czechoslovakia (CPC). During the so-called normalization he left the party in 1969 and was then expelled from it in 1970. In the 1970s and 1980s Stráský was active in the dissident movement, in the Democratic Initiative and elsewhere. From 1990 to 1991 he was a deputy director of Komerční Banka and an adviser to the prime minister of the Czech Republic. In the spring of 1991 he was a co-founder of the Civic Democratic Party (Občanská Demokratická Strana [ODS]), which was established from the remnants of the Civic Forum (Občanské Fórum [OF]). From May 1991 to July 1992 he served as deputy prime minister of the Czech government and chairman of its Economic Council.

From 1 July to 31 December 1992 Stráský was the last prime minister of the federal government of Czechoslovakia, simultaneously acting as minister of foreign trade. After **Václav Havel** resigned as president of the federation, Stráský became acting president on 20 July 1992. His government was formed as a result of an agreement between the strongest parties—the ODS in the Czech Republic and the Movement for Democratic Slovakia in Slovakia—and its mission was to supervise the peaceful dissolution of the federation of the republics. From June to December 1992 Stráský also served as a deputy to the Czech National Council. In November 1992 he became vice-chairman of the ODS and held this position until December 1997. After the dissolution of Czechoslovakia, he sat in the Czech parliament from January 1993 to June 1998. From January 1993 to October 1995 Stráský was minister of transportation and subsequently served as minister of health in successive cabinets of **Václav Klaus** until early January 1998. After the outbreak of a scandal linked to the illegal financing of the ODS in November 1997, which led to the breakup of the ruling coalition and the collapse of Klaus's government, Stráský, together with some of the party activists, left the ODS and founded the Freedom Union (Unie Svobody) in December 1997. In 1998 Stráský retired, and in January 2001 he became head of the Provincial Office of South Bohemia Province. (PU)

Sources: *ČBS*; *Kdo byl kdo v našich dějinách ve 20. století*, vol. 2 (Prague, 1998); Petr Štěpánek, *Jan Stráský: Prezident na půl úvazku* (Prague, 1993); Jan Rychlík, *Rozpad Československa: Česko-slovenské vztahy 1989–1992* (Bratislava, 2002); Eric Stein, *Czecho/Slovakia: Ethnic Conflict, Constitutional Fissure, Negotiated Breakup* (Ann Arbor, 1997); http://zdrav.cz/kdojekdo/ministri/strasky_j.htm; http://wtd.vlada.cz/scripts/detail.php?id=554.

STŘÍBRNÝ Jiří (14 January 1880, Rokycany–21 January 1955, Valdice), Czech journalist and political activist. At the beginning of the twentieth century Stříbrný wrote articles for Socialist and nationalist newspapers. In 1911 he became editor of *České slovo*. From 1911 to 1918 he served as a National Socialist MP in the parliament in Vienna. During World War I he initially served in the Austro-Hungarian Army, but in 1917 he joined the anti-Habsburg resistance movement, and in 1918 he joined the Czechoslovak National Committee, which on 28 October 1918 passed a bill on the establishment of the Czechoslovak state. Stříbrný signed this bill on behalf of the National Socialists. He was deputy to the National Assembly from 1918 to 1928 and from 1929 to 1935. In 1920–26 he was deputy chairman of the Czechoslovak National Socialist Party (called the Czech National Socialist Party from 1897 to 1918 and the Czechoslovak Socialist Party from 1918 to 1926). Stříbrný was minister of post and telegraphs (until 1919), minister of railways (1919–20 and 1922–25), and minister of national defense (1925–26). From 1924 to 1925 he also served as deputy prime minister, and from 1920 to 1926 he was a National Socialist representative in the Pětka (Five) inter-party agreement.

Stříbrný's political career collapsed in 1926, when, following an electoral failure the year before, an open struggle for power broke out among the party members. As a result of his conflicts with President **Edvard Beneš** and chairman of the party **Václav Klofáč**, Stříbrný—who increasingly drifted toward the right—was expelled from the party at its congress in September 1926. In the same year he established the Tempo press company, which published *Polední list* and *Expres*. They soon became press organs of his new political enterprises. In 1927 Stříbrný founded the pro-Fascist Party of Slavic National Socialists, transformed in 1930 into the extreme nationalist National League, which won three parliamentary seats and one senatorial seat in the elections. At that time cooperation was established with the National Fascist Community, led by General **Radola Gajda**. In 1935 the National League merged with the Czechoslovak National Democratic Party, led by **Karel Kramář**, and with the National Front, led by František Mareš, to form the National Union, and Stříbrný became its vice-chairman. In 1937 the National League left this coalition and at the end of 1938 joined the Party of National Unity (Strana Národní Jednoty), led by **Rudolf Beran**. This party drew on authoritarian concepts. During World War II Stříbrný retired from public life and refused to take part in the Nazi propaganda campaign. Nevertheless, he was imprisoned in 1945 and sentenced to life imprisonment in 1947 for "crimes against the republic." He died in prison. Stříbrný wrote the polemical book *TGM a 28. říjen* (Tomaš G. Masaryk and 28 October; 1938). He was also the author of extensive political memoirs, which he wrote in prison. (PU)

Sources: *ČBS*; Philip Rees, ed., *Biographical Dictionary of the Extreme Right since 1890* (New York, 1990); *Českoslovenští politici: 1918–1991* (Prague, 1991); *Kto bol kto za I. ČSR* (Bratislava, 1993); *Politická elita meziválečného Československa 1918–1938: Kdo byl kdo za prvni republiky* (Prague, 1998); Libor Vykoupil, *Slovník českých dějin* (Brno, 2000); F. G. Campbell, *Confrontation in Central Europe* (Chicago, 1975).

STROKACH Timofey (19 February 1903, Bialotserkevka, Primorsky krai, Russia–15 August 1963, Kiev), Soviet political and military activist in the Ukraine. From 1919 to 1922 Strokach fought with the Communist partisans in the Far East. A Red Army soldier from 1923 onwards, he served (among other places) in the border guards. He joined the Bolshevik party in his youth. At the Fourteenth Congress of the Russian Communist Party (Bolsheviks) in December 1925 Strokach joined its Central Committee (CC). In 1941–46 he was deputy people's commissar of interior of the Ukrainian SSR. At the beginning of the German-Soviet war in 1941 he commanded the "destructive battalions" (*istrebitelnye bataleny*) and partisan units. Strokach was co-responsible for the decision to murder prisoners held in Lviv prisons before the Germans entered the town. From June 1942 to 1945 he headed the Ukrainian Staff of the Partisan Movement in the territories occupied by the Third Reich. He commanded units that organized sabotage against the Germans and fought against the Ukrainian and Polish pro-independence partisans. These units often incited hostilities between the Poles and the Ukrainians. In 1944 Strokach became lieutenant general. As minister of interior of the Ukrainian SSR (1946–56), he was responsible for the bloody suppression of units of the Ukrainian Insurgent Army. From 1956 to 1957 Strokach served as deputy minister of interior of the Soviet Union and head of the Main Board of Border Guards and the Interior Army of the Ministry for Internal Affairs of the Soviet Union. He was a deputy to the Supreme Soviet of the USSR and to the Supreme Soviet of the Ukrainian SSR. After the Twentieth Congress of the CPSU Strokach left the CC. He authored the memoirs *Nash pozyvnoi—svoboda* (Our call—freedom; 1975). (GM)

Sources: *Ukrainskaya sovetskaia entsiklopediia*, vol. 10 (Kiev, 1984); Yaroslav Bilinsky, *The Second Soviet Republic: The Ukraine after World War II* (New Brunswick, N.J., 1964); Mieczysław Juchniewicz, *Polacy w radzieckim ruchu partyzanckim 1941–1945* (Warsaw, 1975); Piotr Kołakowski, *NKWD i GRU na ziemiach polskich 1939–1945* (Warsaw, 2002).

STROKATA-KARAVANSKA Nina (31 January 1926, Odessa), Ukrainian dissident. During her studies at the Medical Institute in Odessa, Strokata-Karavanska married the poet **Svyatoslav Karavanskyi**, sentenced to twenty-five years for independentist activity in 1945. After graduation (1947) she worked as a microbiologist. After her husband was released during the second "thaw" of Nikita Khrushchev in 1962, she worked with him, but in 1965 he was arrested again. For her endeavors for his release she was harassed by the KGB. In May 1971 Strokata-Karavanska was arrested, and a year later she was sentenced to four years of labor camp. She was detained in the camp for women in the Mordvinian Autonomous SSR, where she participated in protest actions and hunger strikes. Thanks to information about her passed to the West, in 1974 she became a member of the American Society for Microbiology. After her release in December 1975 Strokata-Karavanska was banned from returning to the Ukraine and forced to settle in Tarusa, near Kaluga, where she was kept under police surveillance and persecuted. In November 1976 she joined the founders of the Ukrainian Helsinki Group and continued her protests. In November 1979 she was forced, along with her released husband, to leave the USSR. They went to the United States, where she was active in the support of human rights in the Ukraine. Strokata-Karavanska edited the volume *Ukrainian Women in the Soviet Union: Documented Persecution* (1980); she authored the memoirs *A Family*

Torn Apart (1981) and several short essays on Ukrainian women political prisoners. (WR)

Sources: *Encyclopedia of Ukraine*, vol. 5 (Toronto, 1993); S. P. de Boer, E. J. Driessen, and H. L. Verhaar, eds., *Biographical Dictionary of Dissidents in the Soviet Union* (The Hague, 1982).

STROŃSKI Stanisław (18 August 1882, Nisko–20 October 1955, London), Polish politician. Stroński graduated with a degree in Romance philology, and from 1909 he lectured at the Jagiellonian University in Kraków. In 1904, he joined the National Democratic Party and in the following year the National League. However, in 1908 he left the party in protest of its pro-Russian line. He then founded the newspaper *Rzeczpospolita*. Between 1913 and 1914 Stroński was a deputy to the Galician Home Parliament. After the outbreak of the war in 1914, he was interned by the Austro-Hungarian authorities as an enemy of the Central Powers. Released in 1917, he was active in the National Committee of Poland (Komitet Narodowy Polski), editing its main organ, *L'Indépendence Polonaise*, which also served as the voice of the Polish delegation to the Paris Peace Conference. Between 1922 and 1924, Stroński edited *Rzeczpospolita* and then, until 1928, the newspaper *Warszawianka*. He launched strident journalistic attacks against **Józef Piłsudski** and his policies. From 1927 to 1939 Stroński was a professor at the Catholic University of Lublin. In 1922, he was elected to the parliament as a Christian Democrat, but following the coup d'état of 1926, he returned to the nationalist movement. In 1928 he was coopted to the Grand Council of the Camp of Great Poland. In 1928 and 1930 he was elected to the parliament from the National Party (Stronnictwo Narodowe [SN]) lists. Stroński was a determined critic of the *sanacja* regime. At the end of the 1930s, he advocated collaboration between the SN and the (Christian Democratic) Front Morges. After the fall of Poland, in October 1939 Stroński became deputy prime minister and minister for information and documentation in the government of General **Władysław Sikorski**. He left the government following the general's death in July 1943. Stroński was a member of a commission to establish culpability in the September 1939 defeat of Poland. In July 1941, he supported a treaty with the Soviet Union. After the war, he remained in Great Britain, where he taught at the Polish University in Exile from 1950. Stroński authored many works of punditry, including the collection *Pierwsze lat dziesięć 1918–1928* (The first ten years, 1918–1928; 1928). (WR)

Sources: *Kto był kim w Drugiej Rzeczpospolitej* (Warsaw, 1994); *Encyklopedia historii Drugiej Rzeczypospolitej* (Warsaw, 1999); *Stanisław Stroński w 50-lecie pracy pisarskiej* (Tunbridge Wells, UK, 1954); Roman Wapiński, *Narodowa Demokracja 1893–1939* (Wrocław, 1980); Janusz Faryś, *Stanisław Stroński: Biografia polityczna do 1939 roku* (Szczecin, 1990).

ŠTROUGAL Lubomír (19 October 1924, Veselí nad Lužnicí, Tábor district), Czech Communist activist. In 1945 Štrougal took up law studies at Charles University in Prague, graduating in 1949. In 1948 he began working in the apparatus of the Communist Party of Czechoslovakia (CPC). From 1957 to 1959 he was secretary general of the CPC committee in České Budějovice, and in 1958 he became a member of the party Central Committee (CC). Štrougal served as minister of agriculture, forests, and water management from March 1959 to June 1961 and minister of interior from June 1961 to April 1965. In 1963 he became a member of a commission of the CPC CC whose task was to finish the process of rehabilitating party members. Štrougal served as secretary of the CPC CC (April 1965–April 1968), deputy prime minister (April–December 1968), and chairman of the Economic Council (1968–69). In August 1968, after Prime Minister **Oldřich Černík** had been taken to Moscow, Štrougal substituted for him for several days. At that time he refused to join the "workers' and peasants' government" formed by **Alois Indra**. In November 1968 Štrougal was elected a member of the Presidium and reelected secretary of the CPC CC responsible for party work in the Czech territory. From 1960 to 1969 he was a deputy to the National Assembly. After the federalization of the country, he served as deputy to the People's Chamber of the Federal Assembly until 1989.

In August 1968 Štrougal initially reacted negatively to the invasion of Czechoslovakia by Warsaw Pact troops, but he soon joined the pro-Moscow bloc. However, he represented a pragmatic rather than an ideological line. On 28 January 1970 he became prime minister and endorsed the so-called normalization policy. He was one of the top figures in **Gustav Husák**'s regime. After **Miloš Jakeš** took over as leader of the CPC in December 1987, Štrougal insisted that economic reforms be undertaken; as a result, he came into conflict with Jakeš and resigned as prime minister on 12 October 1988. Štrougal was also expelled from the CPC Presidium. In November 1989 he was one of the candidates for the post of secretary general of the party, but after **Karel Urbánek** was appointed to this post, Štrougal, who also lost his parliamentary seat owing to the reconstruction of parliament, retired from politics in December 1989. In February 1990 he was expelled from the CPC. In 2000 the Office for the Documentation and Investigation of the Crimes of Communism accused Štrougal of an abuse of power and of preventing the punishment of security officers who had committed crimes at the time when he was serving as minister of interior. Štrougal's trial began in December 2001, but in February 2002 the Prague City Court cleared him of charges. (PU)

Sources: *ČBS; Who's Who in the Socialist Countries of Europe*, vol. 3 (Munich, London, and Paris, 1989); *Českoslovenští politici: 1918–1991* (Prague, 1991); *Kdo byl kdo v našich dějinách ve 20. století*, vol. 2 (Prague, 1998); Gordon H. Skilling, *Czechoslovakia's Interrupted Revolution* (Princeton, 1976); Vladimir V. Kusin, *From Dubcek to Charter 77: A Study of "Normalization" in Czechoslovakia, 1968–1978* (New York, 1978); http://wtd.vlada.cz/scripts/detail.php?id=447.

STRZELECKI Ryszard (31 January 1907, Warsaw–10 January 1988, Warsaw), Polish Communist activist. Before World War II Strzelecki was a blue-collar laborer. In 1942, he joined the (Communist) Polish Workers' Party (Polska Partia Robotnicza [PPR]), the People's Guard, and then the People's Army. Between 1945 and 1948, he was an alternate member of the PPR Central Committee (CC). He was appointed deputy head of the Organizational Department of the PPR Provincial Committee in Katowice, and between 1945 and 1946 he served as its second secretary. From December 1945, Strzelecki was a deputy to the Home National Council (Krajowa Rada Narodowa [KRN]) and then to the parliament (1947–56). Between 1946 and 1948, he served as the first secretary of the PPR Provincial Committee in Kraków. After the creation of the (Communist) Polish United Workers' Party (Polska Zjednoczona Partia Robotnicza [PUWP]), from December 1948 Strzelecki was a member of its CC and first secretary of its Provincial Committee in Katowice. From 1950 to 1951 he worked as deputy minister of transportation; between September 1951 and April 1957, as minister for railroads; and as minister of transportation until February 1960. A hard-liner, Strzelecki belonged to the orthodox Stalinist Natolin group and later to the faction of **Mieczysław Moczar**. In January 1960, he was appointed secretary of the PUWP CC, and in November 1964 he became a full member of its Politburo. His advancement came on the heels of the purge of party liberals by first secretary **Władysław Gomułka**. Strzelecki was responsible for the Main Political Administration of the Polish Army and for the CC Administrative Department. From 1968 he was responsible for inter-party collaboration, trade unions, national councils, and the CC Organizational and General Departments. He became an increasingly close aide to Gomułka, and he belonged to the top leadership of the party. From 1961 Strzelecki was a member of the Council of State, and between 1961 and 1972 he served as an MP. During worker unrest on the Baltic Sea coast in December 1970, Strzelecki supported Gomułka's decision to fire on the demonstrators. Along with the first secretary and his top aides, Strzelecki was expelled from the Secretariat and the Politburo (20 December 1970), the CC (December 1971), and the Council of State (March 1972). A party commission to establish culpability for the unrest of 1970 judged Strzelecki to be co-responsible for the crisis, but he suffered no other consequences. (PK)

Sources: Mołdawa; Krzysztof Lesiakowski, *Mieczysław Moczar: Biografia polityczna* (Warsaw, 1998); Włodzimierz Janowski and Aleksander Kochański, *Informator o strukturze i obsadzie personalnej centralnego aparatu PZPR 1948–1990* (Warsaw, 2000); Jerzy Eisler, *Grudzień 1970* (Warsaw, 2000).

STRZEMBOSZ Adam (11 September 1930, Warsaw), Polish lawyer and politician. Strzembosz studied at the Jagiellonian University in Kraków and then at Warsaw University. After 1956 he was involved in efforts to revive the Polish scouting movement. When he saw that scouting had again come under Communist control, he left the Polish Scouting Association in 1958. Although he had a degree in international law, Strzembosz could not enter the diplomatic service because he was not a member of the Communist Party. After graduating, he worked in the Social Insurance Institution (Zakład Ubezpieczeń Społecznych) and in the Ministry of Labor and Social Welfare. After doing a legal internship, Strzembosz began working as a judge at a court for juveniles in 1961. After receiving the postdoctoral degree, he became an associate professor (*docent*) at the Institute for Judicial Law Studies in 1974. Because of his activities in support of Solidarity, Strzembosz lost his job at the court and at the institute after the introduction of martial law in December 1981. He found employment as a lecturer at the Catholic University of Lublin. A participant in the Round Table negotiations, Strzembosz served as deputy minister of justice in the government of **Tadeusz Mazowiecki** from September 1989 to June 1990 and subsequently became first president of the Supreme Court and chairman of the State Judiciary Council. He opposed a radical verification process for judges, as he believed in the self-purification of the judiciary, but he also advocated lustration and partial de-communization. Strzembosz was a candidate in the 1995 presidential elections but was unsuccessful and withdrew before election day. In October 1998, on his last day in office, Strzembosz appointed Bogusław Nizieński as public interest commissioner, opening the way for lustration procedures. After retiring in 1999, Strzembosz resumed teaching at the Catholic University of Lublin. (AG)

Sources: Mołdawa; Wojciech Borek and Andrzej Urbański, *Strzembosz portret rodzinny* (Kraków, 1995); Antoni Dudek, *Pierwsze lata III Rzeczypospolitej 1989–2001* (Kraków, 2002).

STUČKA Pēteris (26 July 1865, Koknese, Livonia–25 January 1932, Moscow), Soviet activist of Latvian descent. Born into a peasant family, in 1888 Stučka graduated from the School of Law of St. Petersburg University. While a student, he was drawn to socialism. In the 1890s he was one of the leaders of a national Marxist movement called Jaunā strāva (New Current). He edited its periodical, *Dienas Lapa*, from 1888 to 1891 and from 1895 to 1897. In 1895 Stučka became active in the Social Democratic movement. Arrested and sentenced to exile in 1897, he served his sentence in Vitebsk, Slobodsk, and Vyatka. Released in 1903, he co-founded the Social Democratic Workers' Party of Latvia in 1904. An active member of the Bolshevik faction, he was involved in the work of a party organization in St. Petersburg from 1907 on; for example, he contributed to the newspaper *Pravda*. He also served as deputy to the second State Duma and as party delegate to the Stuttgart Congress of the Second International in 1908. In February 1917 Stučka was elected to the Executive Committee of the St. Petersburg Soviet of Workers' and Peasants' Deputies. In the summer of 1917 he organized the base for a Bolshevik coup in Riga, and in October 1917 he became chairman of the Military Investigation Committee of the Petrograd Military and Revolutionary Committee.

After the Bolshevik coup of November 1917, Stučka served as acting people's commissar of justice, subsequently becoming deputy people's commissar of justice. He was also a member of the board of the Commissariat of Foreign Affairs and a delegate to the peace negotiations with the Central Powers in Brest-Litovsk. In March 1918 Stučka joined the Central Committee (CC) of the All-Russian Communist Party (Bolsheviks) and was appointed people's commissar of justice. He co-authored the constitution of the Russian Federal Soviet Socialist Republic (RSFSR), which deprived former great landowners and entrepreneurs of the protection of the law. He also co-authored decrees issued by Lenin that extended Bolshevik law to territories beyond Bolshevik control. Stučka led the attempts to establish Bolshevik rule in Latvia. He subsequently left the office of head of the Commissariat of Justice to become head of the government of Soviet Latvia on 14 December 1918. After Riga was occupied by the Red Army, Stučka held his office there until May 1919, when the Red Army withdrew from Riga and his government left for Russia. Stučka's unpopular agrarian policy was one of the factors that undermined his government in Riga. In October 1919 Stučka became a member of the Council of People's Commissars' select committee to counteract profiteering; in May 1920 he became a member of the CC of the Bolshevik party; and in March 1921 he

became a deputy people's commissar of justice. In 1923 he was made chairman of the Supreme Court of the RSFSR, and he also became a professor and head of a department at Moscow University. In 1927 Stučka co-authored the new civil code. A Marxist theorist of law and an editor of the periodical *Revoliutsiia prava*, he was a co-founder of the Institute of Soviet Law in Moscow in 1931 and then served as the first director of this institute. Stučka (was also one of the leaders of the Communist Party of Latvia, a member of its Foreign Office, and a representative of this party to the Communist International. During the Soviet rule in Latvia (1940–41 and 1945–91) Stučka belonged to Latvia's Communist pantheon. A town built in the late 1960s was named after him. After Latvia regained independence, the name of this town was changed, and Stučka's statue in front of the presidential palace in Riga was removed. Stučka's publications include *Kurs sovetskogo grazhdanskogo prava* (Outline of Soviet Civil Law) 3 vols.; 1927–31. (EJ)

Sources: *MERSH*, vol. 53; *Latvijas PSR Mazā enciklopēdija*, vol. 3 (Riga, 1970); *Latvijas padomju enciklopēdija*, vol. 9 (Riga, 1987); *Stučka P. rakstu izlase*, vols. 1–7 (Riga, 1976–84); P. Dauge, *P. Stučkas dzīve un darbs* (Riga, 1958); Andris Plotnieks, *Petr Stuchka i istoki sovetskoĭ pravovoĭ mysli* (Riga, 1970); Kārlis Gērķis and Imants Kirtovskis, *Pētera Stučkas ekonomiskie uzskati* (Riga, 1977); Andrejs Plekans, *Historical Dictionary of Latvia* (Lanham, Md., 1997).

STUDNICKI Władysław (3 November 1867, Dünaburg [Daugavpils]–10 January 1953, London), Polish politician and pundit. As a young man, Studnicki was a working-class activist. Between 1888 and 1889 he was a member of the Second Proletariat. From 1890 through 1896 he was exiled to Siberia. In 1897 he joined the Polish Socialist Party. Then he became involved with the Peasant Party and National Democracy. In 1905 he moved to Warsaw and broke away from the nationalists. In 1912 he participated in a congress of independentist activists in Zakopane, when the clandestine military treasury was established. After the Germans occupied Warsaw, in 1916 Studnicki co-founded and led the Club of Polish Statists (Klub Państwowców Polskich), which backed the Central Powers. He advocated collaboration with Germany, postulated the abandonment of the Polish Western lands, and spoke in favor of extending Poland's eastern borders to the Dvina and Berezina Rivers. Between 1917 and 1918 he served on the Provisional Council of State and the State Council of the Kingdom of Poland.

Following World War I, Studnicki worked as the supervisor of the statistical office of the Central Board for the Eastern Territories (Centralny Zarząd Ziem Wschodnich), adviser at the Ministry of Industry and Trade, and an official at the Ministry of Foreign Affairs. From 1930, he was also a lecturer at the newly founded Research Institute of Eastern Europe (Instytut Naukowo Badawczy Europy Wschodniej) in Vilnius. Following the death of **Józef Piłsudski**, Studnicki repeatedly clashed with his successors. He published political, economic, and historical articles in various periodicals, including the monarchist *Słowo*. Studnicki's brand of conservatism favored a strong but lawful state. He criticized communism stridently and strongly supported cooperation with the Third Reich. After the outbreak of World War II, Studnicki proposed to the Germans that he form a collaborationist government. However, because he objected to the Nazi terror, he was arrested and imprisoned, first in Warsaw and then, in 1941, in Berlin. After the war, Studnicki emigrated to Great Britain. He wrote numerous works, including the following: *Od socjalizmu do nacjonalizmu* (From socialism to nationalism; 1904); *Wskazania polityczne irredentysty polskiego* (Political directives of a Polish irridentist; 1913); *Szkice polityczne z zakresu polityki międzynarodowej* (Political sketches from the field of international politics; 1917); *Ludzie, idee i czyny* (People, ideas, and deeds; n.d.); *Sprawa polska* (The Polish question; 1919); *Z przeżyć i walk* (From experience and struggles; 1928); and *System polityczny Europy a Polska* (The European political system and Poland; 1935). (JS)

Sources: *Wielka Encyklopedia Powszechna*, vol. 11 (Warsaw, 1968); *Encyklopedia historii Polski: Dzieje polityczne*, vol. 1 (Warsaw, 1995); Janusz Pajewski, *Odbudowa państwa polskiego, 1914–1918* (Warsaw, 1985); Stanisław Mackiewicz-Cat, *Historia Polski od 11 listopada 1918 do 17 września 1939 r.* (Warsaw, 1989); Jacek Gzella, *Myśl polityczna Władysława Studnickiego na tle koncepcji konserwatystów polskich (1918–1939)* (Toruń, 1993).

STUDYNSKYI Kyrylo (4 October 1868, Kamianka, near Tarnopol [Ternopil]–1941, place unknown), Ukrainian literary scholar and social activist. Born into the family of a clergyman, Studynskyi attended high schools in Tarnopol and Lemberg (Lviv, Lwów) from 1878 to 1887. He subsequently studied theology in Lemberg (1887–89) and theology and Slavic philology in Vienna (1889–94), earning a Ph.D. in philosophy. In 1893 Studynskyi became an MP in the parliament in Vienna. In 1896 he received the postdoctoral degree from the Jagiellonian University in Kraków. In 1897–99 he taught Ukrainian literature at the Jagiellonian University and worked in Kraków high schools. It was not until 1900 that Studynskyi was given a professorship at the University of Lemberg; until then the appointment had been blocked by the university authorities. In 1899 he became a full member of the Taras Shevchenko Scientific Society (NTSh). One of the leaders of the Ukrainian Social Christian Party, Studynski edited its press organ, *Ruslan*, from 1897. As a member (1905–14) of the National School Council of Galicia, he strove for the development of a system of education with Ukrainian as the language of instruction. He worked in the Prosvita Educational Society and in a teachers' union called Uchytelska Hromada (serving as its president from 1916 to 1920). At the beginning of the 1920s Studynskyi served as president of a Galician unit of the Relief Committee for Starving Ukrainians and as president of the Ukrainian Fund for War Widows and Orphans. In late 1918 the authorities of the Western Ukrainian National Republic (Zakhidno-Ukraiinska Narodna Republika [ZUNR]) appointed him commissioner for the University of Lemberg for the duration of the war against Poland. Since he refused to declare loyalty to Poland, Studynskyi was interned in the Baranów and Dąbie camps from 1919 to 1920.

After Poland defeated the ZUNR forces, Studynskyi was not allowed to work at the University of Lwów and worked for the NTSh. In 1923–32 he was the president of the NTSh, an academic institution that served as a substitute for a Ukrainian university in Poland. From 1921 to 1922 Studynskyi was also president of the Ukrainian National Council. In 1924 he supported the return of the historian **Mykhailo Hrushevskyi** to the Ukrainian SSR, and thanks to his friendship with Hrushevskyi, Studynskyi succeeded in establishing cooperation between the NTSh and the All-Ukrainian Academy of Sciences (VUAN) in Kiev. In 1927–29 Studynskyi visited Kharkov (Kharkiv) on several occasions. Thanks to him, the NTSh received occasional financial support from the Soviet authorities. In September 1929 he organized a visit to Lwów by **Mykola Skrypnyk**, the minister of education of the Ukrainian SSR. Studynskyi frequently spoke favorably about the prospects of developing Ukrainian science under Soviet rule. This political commitment—as well as Studynskyi's conflict with **Serhiy Yefremov**, a writer sentenced in the "trial" of the Union for the Liberation of Ukraine in the Ukrainian SSR in 1930 and regarded as a national hero in Galicia—led to Studynskyi's being insulted by members of the Organization of Ukrainian Nationalists (OUN) and sharply criticized for his activities by the press. Studynskyi was even accused of being a Soviet agent; as a result, at the beginning of 1932, he resigned as president of the NTSh. At the same time, as the Ukrainization policy in the Soviet Union came to an end, in October 1933 Studynski was also deprived of a VUAN academic title, which he had held from 1924, and he was then accused of being a Polish agent.

The Soviet authorities again needed Studynskyi after 17 September 1939. On 26–28 October 1939 he presided over sessions of the People's Assembly of Western Ukraine in Lviv at which a resolution was passed to incorporate Western Ukraine into the Ukrainian SSR. In March 1940 Studynskyi was elected deputy to the Supreme Soviet of the Soviet Union. In 1939 his professorship was reinstated, and he was appointed deputy rector of the University of Lviv. Studynski used his position to help the persecuted. On 24 June 1941 he was forcibly evacuated into the depths of the Soviet Union and perished under unknown circumstances. Studynskyi published over five hundred scholarly works on the history of literature and on Ukrainian culture. (TS)

Sources: *Encyclopedia of Ukraine*, vol. 5 (Toronto, 1993); O. S. Rublov and Iu. A. Cherchenko, *Stalinshchyna i dolia zakhidnoukrainskoy intelihentsii* (Kiev, 1994); O. Haiova, ed., *U pivstolitnikh zmahanniakh: Vybrani lysty do Kyryla Studynskoho 1891–1941* (Kiev, 1993).

STULGINSKIS Aleksandras (26 February 1885, Kutaliai, near Taurage–22 September 1969, Vytenai, near Kaunas), Lithuanian Christian Democratic politician. The sixteenth child of an agricultural tenant, Stulginskis completed a gymnasium in Libava (Liepaja), and studied theology in a diocesan seminary in Kaunas and at the university in Innsbruck. In 1913 he graduated from the Agricultural Institute in Halle and then worked as an agronomist in Alytus. During World War I he was active in Vilnius (Wilno), where he organized courses for teachers and published the periodical *Ukininkas*. He also belonged to the Lithuanian Relief Committee for War Victims. Stulginskis ran a twenty-five-acre farm near Vilnius. He became aligned with Christian Democracy and from 1917 headed this party in the region of Vilnius and was the secretary of its central committee. Elected to the Council of Lithuania (Taryba), Stulginskis signed the Lithuanian declaration of independence of 16 February 1918. He spoke against placing Wilhelm von Urach on the Lithuanian throne. In 1918 Stulginskis presided over a Christian Democratic conference in Vilnius that adopted a rather moderate program for the party, whose spokesman he was. Elected to the Lithuanian Constituent Assembly (Seimas), in 1920 Stulginskis, along with fifteen other Christian Democratic MPs, founded the Lithuanian Farmers' Union (Lietuvos Ukininku Sajunga) and became its leader. In 1920–22 he also served as chairman of the Constituent Assembly of Lithuania.

On 21 December 1922 Stulginskis was elected the second president of Lithuania and remained in office until May 1926. Under his presidency Lithuania established diplomatic relations with Western countries, joined the League of Nations, and seized the region of Klaipeda.

Economic relations also became stabilized. Stulginskis represented a conservative-national trend in the peasant movement, one that was reluctant to make major overtures toward Poland. This trend was closely tied with Christian Democracy. Stulginskis belonged to a narrow circle of six leaders heading a bloc of three Christian Democratic parties: Christian Democracy proper, the Farmers' Union, and the workers' Labor Federation. In March 1923 Stulginskis dissolved the parliament and called new elections in which Christian Democracy won an absolute majority. Although this bloc lost power in the elections of 1926, Stulginskis remained an MP. After the coup of 17 December 1926 he was the chairman of the Constituent Assembly until its dissolution by the nationalists of **Antanas Smetona** on 12 April 1927.

Stulginskis rejected a proposal by the nationalists that he enter the government, and he withdrew to his farm in Jokubovas, near Kretinga. In 1925–30 he directed the Lithuanian scouting movement. In 1938 he took part in a world congress of Lithuanians in Kaunas and gave a speech in which he stressed the importance of democracy for small countries. After the Soviet invasion Stulginskis was arrested by the NKVD in July 1940 and was deported to a camp in the Siberian region of Krasnoyarsk. He worked in very harsh conditions in a sawmill. In 1952 he received an additional sentence of twenty-five years of forced labor camp. Released in 1954, he joined his wife Ona (neé Matulaitite), who had been sent to the Komi ASSR. In 1956 the Soviet authorities allowed them to return to Lithuania, where Stulginskis worked until his death as a gardener. His only daughter, Aldona Juozeviciene, graduated in medicine in Kaunas, evaded arrest in 1940, and left for the West in 1944. Stulginskis's *Atsiminimai* (Memoirs) were published in Chicago in 1980. (WR)

Sources: *EL*, vol. 5; Mykolas Krupavicius, "Aleksandras Stulginskis," *Aidai* (Brooklyn, N.Y.) 1965, no. 2; Algirdas Banevicius, *111 Lietuvos valstybes 1918–1940 politikos veikeju* (Vilnius, 1991); Liudas Truska, Algimantas Lileikis, Gediminas Ilgunas, and Rimgaudas Gelezevicius, *Lietuvos prezidentai* (Vilnius, 1995); Alfonsas Eidintas and Vytautas Žalys, *Lithuania in European Politics: The Years of the First Republic, 1918–1940* (New York, 1997); www.ktl.mii.lt/prezidentai.

STURDZA Dimitrie Alexandru Prince (10 March 1833, Miclăuşeni, Moldavia–8 October 1914, Bucharest), Romanian historian and politician. Sturdza was descended from a family of *hospodars* (rulers) of Moldavia whose surname was also written Sturza or Stourza. From 1851 to 1855 he studied law and history at the University of Bonn. He began his political career in 1857, becoming secretary of the Divan ad hoc of Moldavia, a commission that prepared the groundwork for the unification of

Wallachia and Moldavia. Devoted to the unification idea, Sturdza initially worked with Alexandru I. Cuza, the prince of Romania from 1859. In 1860, though, he joined the opposition to Cuza. Sturdza organized a coup d'état (23 February 1866), as a result of which Cuza was forced to abdicate and Prince Karl of Hohenzollern-Sigmaringen (the future King **Charles I**) became prince of Romania. Sturdza played an important political role in Romania for the next ten years, until 1876–77, when he came into conflict with Charles. Although Sturdza had studied in Germany, unlike **Petru P. Carp** or **Titu Maiorescu**, he had a pro-French and anti-Hungarian stance. In 1875 Sturdza founded the National Liberal Party (Partidul National Liberal), in which he played a decisive role, serving as its chairman from 1892 to 1911. He also held a number of governmental positions, including those of prime minister (1895–96, 1897–99, 1901–2, and 1907–8); minister of public works (1866–67, 1876–77, and 1902–3); minister of finance (1870–71, 1877, 1878–80, 1881, and 1902); minister of foreign affairs (1882–85, 1895–96, 1897–99, 1901–2, and 1907–8); minister of interior (1896); minister of war (1901–2 and 1902–4); and minister of education (1885–88). When in charge of the government, Sturdza contributed to the balancing of the budget through a savings policy from 27 February 1901 to 4 January 1906. Appointed prime minister for the fourth time (25 March 1907), he faced the task of suppressing a peasant revolt in Moldavia. He entrusted the post of minister of war to General **Alexandru Avarescu**, who put down this revolt at the cost of ten thousand lives. On 9 January 1909 Sturdza resigned owing to ill health. Shortly before his death, in order to for the country to attain social peace, he called for the expropriation of some landed estates.

A member (from 1871) and secretary (1871–92) of the Romanian Academy, Sturdza generously supported it with his own funds. Sturdza's publications include *Memoriu asupra portretelor domnitorilor români* (Bibliography of portraits of Romanian rulers; 1874); *Partidul National Liberal de la 1876 pînă la 1878* (The National Liberal Party from 1876 to 1878; 1888); *Europa, Rusia şi România* (Europe, Russia, and Romania; 1890); *Acte şi documente relative la istoria renascerei României* (Acts and documents on the Romanian historic revival, editor, vol. 11; 1889–1909); *Chestiunea naţională* (The national issue; 1894); *Documente privitoare la istoria românilor* (Documents on Romanian history, editor, vols. 5–6; 1894–95); *Carol I, Roi de Roumanie* (Charles I, king of Romania; 2 vols.; 1899–1904); and *Serbare la împlinirea vîrştei de 70 ani, 25 februarie 1903* (My seventieth birthday, 25 February 1903; 1903). (FA/TD)

Sources: *Biographisches Lexikon*, vol. 4; *Prinos lui D. A. Sturdza la împlinirea celor şapte zeci de ani* (Bucharest, 1903); R. W. Seton-Watson, *A History of the Roumanians* (London, 1963); Ion Bulei, *Lumea româniasca la 1900* (Bucharest, 1987); Ion Bulei, *Atuna când veacul se năştea* (Bucharest, 1990); Dumitru Vitcu, *Diplomats of the Union* (Bucharest, 1989); *Enciclopedia istoriografiei româneşti* (Bucharest, 1978); Keith Hitchins, *Rumania, 1866–1947* (Oxford, 1994).

STUS Vasyl (8 January 1938, Rakhnivka, near Vinnytsya–4 September 1985, Perm), Ukrainian poet and democratic activist. In 1964 Stus graduated in pedagogy at Donetsk, and then he studied and worked at the Taras Shevchenko Institute of Literature in Kiev, publishing poems and articles in the official press. From 1965 Stus increasingly opposed the persecutions of Ukrainian intellectuals by the KGB. Expelled from the institute, he worked on a subway construction site in Kiev. In April 1968 Stus signed a letter of 139 dissidents to Leonid Brezhnev protesting the trials of young Ukrainian artists. From then on he published his poems and political texts in samizdat publications only. He published, for example, the poetry volumes *Zymovi dereva* (Winter trees; 1968) and *Veselyi tsmintar* (Happy cemetery; 1970). Stus took part in most protests against Soviet persecutions in the Ukraine. On 12 January 1972 he was arrested and sentenced to five years of labor camp and three years of exile. Stus was imprisoned (among other places) in Camp No. 35 in Perm. After his release from labor camp, Stus was beaten up by KGB functionaries following his publication of an open letter, "Ya obviniayu" (I accuse), in which he accused the police of persecuting the Ukrainian people. In 1980 he was sentenced again, this time to ten years of labor camp, for his participation in the Moscow Helsinki Group. He openly supported the Polish Solidarity movement. Stus died in Camp No. 36 near Perm. (WR)

Sources: S. P. de Boer, E. J. Driessen, and H. L. Verhaar, eds., *Biographical Dictionary of Dissidents in the Soviet Union* (The Hague, 1982); *Svoboda* (Jersey City, N.J.), 7 September 1985.

STYPUŁKOWSKI Zbigniew (26 March 1904, Warsaw–30 March 1979, London), Polish politician. In 1925 Stypułkowski graduated in law from Warsaw University and joined the National Popular Union (Związek Ludowo-Narodowy [ZLN]). In 1930 he became the youngest MP in the Assembly during its third term. In September 1939 he participated in the war against the Germans. Stypułkowski was seized by the Soviets and was held in a temporary camp in Talitsa in the Urals. Exchanged on the basis of a German-Soviet agreement, in the spring of 1940 he arrived in Warsaw, where he organized the Polish military underground. He presided over the political committee of the

National Armed Forces (Narodowe Siły Zbrojne [NSZ]), which was initially against unification with the Home Army (Armia Krajowa [AK]). Appreciating the organizational development of the AK and realizing its political necessity, Stypułkowski brought about the incorporation of part of the NSZ into the AK in March 1944. Stypułkowski was one of sixteen leaders of Underground Poland who were treacherously arrested by the NKVD in March 1945. Taken to Moscow and interrogated in Lubyanka Prison, during the Trial of the Sixteen Stypułkowski delivered a now famous plea for his case. On 21 June 1945 he was sentenced to four months' imprisonment, although he was the only defendant who refused to plead guilty. Stypułkowski returned to Warsaw, and in November 1945 he managed to get to London. He played an important role in the political life of Polish émigrés there. In London, he represented the National Party (Stronnictwo Narodowe) in the Political Council, and in 1959–70 he was its representative in Washington, D.C. Stypułkowski published well-known memoirs about the Trial of the Sixteen: *Zaproszenie do Moskwy* (Invitation to Moscow; with a preface by H. R. Trevor-Roper, 1962; 1977). (WR)

Sources: *Britannica Book of the Year 1980* (Chicago, 1981); Jan Żaryn, "Stronnictwo Narodowe na emigracji," in Andrzej Friszke, ed., *Warszawa nad Tamizą* (Warsaw, 1994); *Proces szesnastu: Dokumenty NKWD* (Warsaw, 1995).

ŠUBAŠIĆ Ivan (27 May 1892, Vukova Gorica, near Karlovac, Croatia–22 March 1955, Zagreb), Croatian politician, prime minister of the Yugoslav government-in-exile. Šubašić began to study theology but in 1914 discontinued his studies because he was inducted into the Austro-Hungarian Army. He was sent to the Serbian front. Sentenced to death for desertion but pardoned, he later fought on the Italian front and in Galicia. After World War I, Šubašić completed law studies and worked as an attorney. One of the leading activists of the Croatian Peasant Party, Šubašić was elected to parliament on the ticket of this party in 1938. After an agreement between the Serbs and Croats was signed on 26 August 1939, he became the governor (*ban*) of the newly established Croatian province (*banovina*). After the coup d'état of March 1941 and the German invasion of Yugoslavia, Šubašić left for England. He called for the unity of Yugoslavia and condemned the killings of the Jewish and Serbian people by the Ustashe, led by **Ante Pavelić**. In 1942, though, Šubašić also became critical of the Chetniks, led by Colonel **Dragoljub (Draža) Mihailović**. His criticism undermined the unity of the Yugoslav émigré community in the face of claims by the Communists, led by **Josip Broz Tito**.

On 1 June 1944 King **Peter II** appointed Šubašić prime minister of a government that was to reach an agreement with the Communists. On 1 November 1944 Šubašić entered into an agreement with Tito, under the terms of which—in exchange for promises of democratic freedoms, free elections, and the admission of several émigré politicians into the coalition government—he agreed to recognize the Communist-dominated Anti-Fascist Council for the National Liberation of Yugoslavia (AVNOJ) as a provisional parliament and to accept Tito as head of the new government. Šubašić made King Peter recognize this compromise. In March 1945 Šubašić became minister of foreign affairs in Tito's cabinet. He then made far-reaching concessions to the Communists and condemned the activities of Mihailović. However, Šubašić's compromises did not help. He was totally unable to pursue a policy independent from the Communists and was even refused permission to go to a conference of ministers of foreign affairs in London. Under these circumstances, he resigned his governmental position on 8 October 1945 and retired from politics. (WR)

Sources: *Biographisches Lexikon*, vol. 4; *Enciklopedija Jugoslavije* vol. 5; Constantine Fotich, *The War We Lost* (New York, 1948); Vlatko Macek, *In the Struggle for Freedom* (London, 1957); Ferdo Čulinović, *Jugoslavija izmedju dva rata*, vols. 1–2 (Zagreb, 1971); *Draža Mihailović Memorial Edition* (Chicago, 1975); Michał Jerzy Zacharias, *Jugosławia w polityce Wielkiej Brytanii 1940–1945* (Wrocław, 1985).

SUBEV Khristofor (3 May 1946, Gabrovo), Bulgarian monk and politician. Subev studied nuclear physics, and after graduating, he worked as a teacher. In 1980 he joined a religious order and began to study theology at the Theological Academy in Sofia. He was one of the founders of the Committee for Religious Rights, Freedom of Conscience, and Spiritual Values. Subev came into conflict with the patriarchate of the Bulgarian Orthodox Church, supported by the Holy Synod, which blocked the registration of this committee. In April 1989 Subev was arrested and sentenced to eighty days in prison for "disseminating false information." After his release, he founded the Salvation (Spasenie) Christian Union, and, as its leader, he joined the Union of Democratic Forces (UDF) in 1990. Promoted to vice-president of the UDF National Coordinating Committee, Subev held this position until June 1992. In October 1991 he also became a deputy to the National Assembly on the UDF ticket. At that time he maintained close contacts with **Konstantin Trenchev**, leader of the Podkrepa trade union. From January to March 1990 Subev took part in round table talks, the results of which he did not accept, as he believed excessive concessions had been made to the Communists. He demanded that the forty years of Communist rule be immediately investigated and evaluated, and he also called for lustration and de-communization. Subev's conflict with the authorities of the Bulgarian Orthodox Church also intensified. His demands for the immediate resignation of Patriarch Maxim (whose opponents maintained that he had not been elected in conformity with canon law or church tradition) and for the election of a new head of the Orthodox Church led to a split in the Orthodox Church in Bulgaria. In mid-1992 a group of hierarchs elected Bishop Pimen as the new patriarch, while the rest remained faithful to Maxim. On 26 June 1992 Subev was elevated to bishop of Makariopol, and one month later he was excommunicated by Maxim. The split in the Orthodox Church coincided with a conflict within the party. The post-Communists supported Maxim, while the UDF supported Pimen. Subev is often accused of mixing religion with politics and of an authoritarian style of governing the institutions that are under his authority. (AG)

Sources: Jerzy Jackowicz, *Bułgaria od rządów komunistycznych do demokracji parlamentarnej 1988–1991* (Warsaw, 1992); Raymond Detrez, *Historical Dictionary of Bulgaria* (Lanham, Md., 1997); www.mediacenterbg.org/library/GeorgiKapriev.doc;www.columbia. edu/~lc116/papers/1992_fall_of_the_dimitrov_government.htm.

SUCHOCKA Hanna (3 April 1946, Pleszew), Polish politician. In 1968 Suchocka graduated from the School of Law of Adam Mickiewicz University in Poznań. She began lecturing there in 1972, earning a Ph.D. in 1975. A specialist in constitutional law, in 1969 Suchocka joined the Democratic Party (Stronnictwo Demokratyczne [SD]). From 1980 to 1985 she was an MP in the Assembly. A member and expert in Solidarity from 1980, in 1982 Suchocka voted against the decree imposing martial law in Poland and outlawing Solidarity and against repressive penal laws; as a result, she was suspended as an SD member. She then began lecturing at the Catholic University of Lublin. In 1984 she left the SD in protest against a proposal for a new electoral law. In the elections of 4 June 1989 she obtained a seat as a representative of the opposition and joined the Civic Parliamentary Caucus (Obywatelski Klub Parlamentarny [OKP]). Suchocka was a member of the Presidium of the OKP, a member (from 1991 on) of the Democratic Union (Unia Demokratyczna [UD]), vice-chairman of the Assembly Legislative Committee, and deputy chairman of the Constitutional Committee (1991–93). In 1992 she served as vice-president of the Parliamentary Assembly of the Council of Europe and head of the Polish delegation to the Council of Europe.

From 10 July 1992 to 25 October 1993 Suchocka was prime minister. Her government was based on a center-right coalition formed with (among others) the Christian National Union (Zjednoczenie Chrześcijańsko-Narodowe), Christian Democratic parties, Solidarity, the UD, and the Liberal Democratic Congress (Kongres Liberalno-Demokratyczny). Faced with economic difficulties and the social effects of systemic transformation and beset by protest actions by post-Communist trade union activists and activists of the Self-Defense (Samoobrona) Party (who, for example, set up road blocks all over the country), Suchocka's government was also attacked by the post-Communists in the Assembly. Trying to maintain correct relations with President **Lech Wałęsa**, Suchocka fell afoul of Wałęsa's opponents, who organized spectacular street demonstrations against him. Trying to prevent the destabilization of the country, Suchocka tolerated the surveillance of anti-Wałęsa groups by the secret services. Because the leaders of Solidarity wanted to exploit social dissatisfaction for their own purposes, in May 1993 Solidarity MPs called for a vote of no confidence in Suchocka's government; she lost it by one vote and had to resign. President Wałęsa dissolved the parliament and called new elections, which were held in September 1993 and brought defeat to the post-Solidarity parties. Suchocka won a seat on the UD ticket. In 1994 she became a member of the Presidium of the National Council of the Freedom Union (Unia Wolności), on whose ticket she was reelected as an MP in September 1997. In 1994 Suchocka was elected to the Council of the Pontifical Academy of Social Sciences at the Vatican. Suchocka has authored numerous scholarly works on the organization of the state political system, law and order, and human rights. In 2001 Suchocka became the Polish ambassador to the Holy See. (AF)

Sources: *Nasi w Sejmie i Senacie* (Warsaw, 1990); Janusz A. Majcherek, *Pierwsza dekada III Rzeczpospolitej 1989–1999* (Warsaw, 1999); *Opozycja w PRL: Słownik biograficzny 1956–89* (Warsaw, 2000); Antoni Dudek, *Pierwsze lata III Rzeczpospolitej 1989–2001* (Kraków, 2002).

SUCIU Ioan (4 December 1907, Blaj–27 June 1953, Sighet Marmaţiei), Romanian Greek Catholic bishop. The son of a Greek Catholic priest, Suciu graduated from high school in Blaj. In 1925, along with his friend **Liviu Chinezu**, he left for Rome, where he studied theology. In 1930, he successfully defended his doctoral dissertation in theology, and in 1931 he was ordained. Suciu returned to Blaj, where he taught religion at a high school for boys and at the local theological academy. He focused on young people in particular; hence his nickname, "the Shepard of the Youth." In the slums of Blaj, Suciu also ministered to the gypsy children. In 1940, he was named auxiliary bishop of Oradea (Arad) under Bishop **Valeriu Frenţiu**, thus becoming the titular bishop of Moglena-Slatina in Bulgaria. Following the expulsion of Frenţiu, when Oradea was reincorporated into Hungary (1940), Suciu substituted for him in the diocese. In 1947, upon Frenţiu's return, Suciu was named the apostolic administrator of the Alba-Iulia and Fargaş archdioceses. In June 1947, as Communist repression against the Church intensified, Suciu issued a pastoral letter calling on believers to resist. Suciu's fearless attitude toward the regime was constant; for example, in December 1947, he delivered a sermon in Bucharest calling communism the ideology of satan. In September 1948, the Communists stripped Suciu of his bishop's post. On 28 October, along with all other Greek Catholic bishops in Romania, Suciu was arrested and imprisoned in the Dragoslavele Monastery. At the beginning of 1949, the bishops were transferred to the Căldăruşani Monastery, which had been turned into a prison. In May 1950, Suciu was brought to the Ministry of Internal Affairs in Bucharest for interrogation. In September he was sent to the Sighet Marmaţiei Prison. Accused of links to the anti-Communist guerrilla movement in the mountains of Transylvania, after three years of imprisonment under inhuman conditions, Suciu fell seriously ill and died. He never faced a trial and was never sentenced. The process of his beatification in the Greek Catholic Church is under way. (LW)

Sources: Józef Darski, *Rumunia: Historia, współczesność, konflikty narodowe* (Warsaw, 1995); Paul Caravia, Virgiliu Constantinescu, and Flori Stănescu, *The Imprisoned Church of Romania, 1944–1989* (Bucharest, 1999); Dennis Deletant, *Communist Terror in Romania: Gheorghiu-Dej and the Police State, 1948–1965* (New York, 1999); www.bru.ro.

SULYOK Dezső (28 March 1897, Simaházapuszta–18 May 1965, New York), Hungarian politician. The son of a miller, Sulyok was orphaned at the age of nine and was brought up by an uncle. After high school he was inducted into the army and served on the Italian and Russian fronts from 1916 to 1918. After returning to Hungary, Sulyok completed a course for police officers. Under the Hungarian Soviet Republic (HSR), he was responsible for public security in the town of Pápa in 1919. After the fall of the HSR, Sulyok became commander of a police unit. In February 1920 he left the army and began to study law at Budapest University. After earning a doctorate and passing the bar, he opened a law office in Pápa in 1924. He joined the ruling Party of Unity and served as a member of its presidium from 1926 to 1931. Because this party did not support his candidacy before the parliamentary elections in 1931, Sulyok retired from politics. In 1935 he ran in the elections as an independent candidate and won a seat

in parliament from Pápa, outstripping even the official candidate of the ruling party. In 1937 Sulyok joined the opposition Independent Smallholders' Party (ISP). In 1938 he raised a parliamentary question on the Jewish descent of Prime Minister **Béla Imrédy**, who insisted on passing anti-Jewish laws. As a result, Imrédy resigned. However, in the spring of 1939 Sulyok voted against the second anti-Jewish law.

From January 1942 to June 1943 Sulyok served on the Russian front. In 1943 he became co-chairman of the ISP civic platform. He helped to draft an anti-war memorandum that was presented to Prime Minister **Miklós Kállay**. Arrested and interned in Nagykanizsa in April 1944, Sulyok was released after two months, thanks to the intervention of **József Mindszenty**, the bishop of Veszprém. After the Arrow Cross Party came to power in October 1944, Sulyok had to go into hiding. From April to September 1945 he served as mayor and commander of the police in Pápa. He was elected to the ISP National Executive Committee in August 1945, a deputy to the Provisional National Assembly in June 1945, and a deputy to the National Assembly in November 1945. In November 1945 Sulyok was a prosecutor in Imrédy's trial. After **Zoltán Tildy** was elected president, Sulyok was one of the candidates for the office of prime minister, but the leftist parties opposed his candidacy. The Communists hated his legally accurate parliamentary questions. On the demand of the Leftist Bloc (Communists and Social Democrats), Sulyok and nineteen other MPs were expelled from the ISP on 12 March 1946. A few days later Sulyok co-founded the Hungarian Freedom Party (Magyar Szabadság Párt [MSP]). He became its chairman and the editor-in-chief of its press organ, *Holnap*. After the Communists modified the electoral law in 1947, Sulyok was prevented from running in the upcoming elections. In July 1947 he disbanded the MSP and resigned his parliamentary seat.

Fearing arrest, on 14 August 1947 Sulyok fled from Hungary. On 7 October 1947 he was stripped of his Hungarian citizenship. He settled in the United States, where he served as a member of the Executive Committee of the Hungarian National Committee from 1949 to 1950. He left this committee because of a conflict with **Ferenc Nagy** and **Béla Varga**, whom he accused of conducting a conciliatory policy toward the Communists. In 1948–50 Sulyok was the editor of the newspaper *Amerikai Magyar Népszava* and the author of many publications issued through émigré publishing houses. His memoirs, *Zwei Nächte ohne Tag* (Two nights without a day), were published in Switzerland in 1948, and in 1954 they came out in Hungarian in New York. After 1956 Sulyok founded the independent Hungarian October 23rd Movement, which did not play any major role. (JT)

Sources: *Magyar Életrajzi Lexikon*, vol. 2 (Budapest, 1969); *A magyar forradalom és szabadságharc enciklopédiája* (Budapest, 1999); Ferenc Nagy, *The Struggle behind the Iron Curtain* (New York, 1948).

SUPILO Frano (30 November 1870, Cavtat–25 September 1917, London), Croatian politician. Supilo graduated from an agricultural school in Gruž, and in the 1890s he edited the periodical *Crvena Hrvatska*. From 1899 he lived in Rijeka, where he edited the journal *Novi List*. In a few years he transformed this bilingual Italian-Croatian journal into an influential political organ. Along with **Ante Trumbić**, Supilo belonged to the ideologists of the Croatian Party of Rights (Hrvatska Stranka Prava) in Dalmatia. He defended the interests of Croats and Serbs in Austria-Hungary. He was one of the drafters of the Rijeka Resolution, adopted on 3 October 1905 by Croatian politicians; in it they expressed themselves in favor of Hungarians who were aiming at full independence and against the domination of Austria. The resolution received the support of the Serbs who were living in the Habsburg monarchy on condition that the status of Croatia-Slavonia would be changed; democratization of the electoral law would be introduced; and freedom of the press, freedom of speech, and freedom of association would be respected. The resolution initiated the creation of the Croatian-Serbian Coalition, which, under the leadership of Supilo, won the elections to the Sabor (Assembly) in May 1906. In 1909, after the Austrian historian Heinrich Friedjung published documents alleging that the politicians of the coalition had secretly collaborated with the Belgrade government, the Croats sued Friedjung, and the results of the ensuing trial brought discredit to the author of the accusation. Disappointed with cooperation with the Hungarians, Supilo withdrew from the leadership of the coalition and also from its ranks.

During World War I Supilo worked for Yugoslav unity, and he sought the recognition of the Serbian-Croatian-Slovenian alliance by the Entente states. Along with Trumbić and **Ivan Meštrović**, he co-founded the Yugoslav Committee (Jugoslavenski Odbor) in exile, which began its activities in December 1914. Supilo consistently expressed himself in favor of the unification of Serbs and Croats based on the principle of federation. In April 1916 he gave up his work in the committee after the rejection of his proposal to adopt a constitution before unification. Supilo was one of the signatories of the Declaration of Corfu (20 July 1917), whereby the South Slavic peoples would form a single kingdom. He did not live to see the implementation of this idea. After Supilo's premature death, collections of his texts were published: "Korespondencija Frana Supila iz perioda 1891–1914" (Letters of Frano Supilo from the period 1891–1914, *Archivski Vestnik*, 1963, no. 7); *Pisma i memorandumi Frana Supila 1914–1917* (Letters and memoranda of Frano Supilo 1914–1917; 1967); and *Politički spisi* (Political writings; 1970). (AO)

Sources: *Biographisches Lexikon*, vol. 4; Josip Horvat, *Frano Supilo* (Belgrade, 1961); Dragovan Šepić, *Supilo diplomat* (Zagreb, 1961); Wacław Felczak and Tadeusz Wasilewski, *Historia Jugosławii* (Wrocław, 1985).

SUSHKO Roman (1894, Remeniv, near Lemberg [Lwów, Lviv]–12 January 1944, Lviv), Ukrainian political and military activist. A lieutenant in the Ukrainian Sich Riflemen during World War I, Sushko fought in many battles, including those of Makivka and Lysonia. In 1916–17 he was held prisoner of war by the Russians. In 1918 he was a co-founder and colonel of the Sich Riflemen in Kiev, and then he became commander of a Sich Riflemen division. A colonel in the Ukrainian Galician army, Sushko was interned in Poland in 1919. In 1920 he became commander of the Sixteenth Brigade of the Sich Riflemen's Division, which fought against the Bolsheviks. In 1921 he commanded the Second Brigade during the Second Winter Campaign, led by **Yuriy Tyutyunnyk**. Co-founder of the Ukrainian Military Organization and its home commander from 1927 to 1930, Sushko was repeatedly arrested by the Polish authorities. He was one of the founders of the Organization of Ukrainian Nationalists (Orhanizatsiya Ukrayinskykh Natsionalistiv [OUN]) and worked in its military staff. Sushko was also editor of the periodical *Surma*. In the early 1930s he emigrated to Vienna. In September 1939 Sushko became commander of the Legion of Ukrainian Nationalists, which was formed under the aegis of the German. He led this legion to Stryi, but after the Soviet Union attacked Poland, the Germans dissolved it, and its soldiers were incorporated into auxiliary police units. At the end of 1939 Sushko settled in Kraków, where he was the leader (*providnyk*) of the OUN in the part of Poland known as the General Government. After an internal split within the OUN in 1940, Sushko remained loyal to **Andriy Melnyk**. Sushko developed the network of the OUN–Melnyk faction. From the summer of 1941 onwards Sushko lived in Lviv, where he was probably killed by activists of the OUN–Bandera faction. Sushko authored memoirs on the battle of Bazar and on his service in the Ukrainian Sich Riflemen. He also wrote the book *Khto vbyv polkovnyka Otmarshteina?* (Who killed Colonel Otmarshtein? 1933). (GM)

Sources: *Encyclopedia of Ukraine*, vol. 5 (Toronto, 1993); *Entsyklopediya Ukraiinoznavstva*, vol. 8 (Lviv, 2000); Ryszard Torzecki, *Polacy i Ukraińcy: Sprawa ukraińska w czasie II wojny światowej na terenie II Rzeczypospolitej* (Warsaw, 1993).

ŠUŠTAR Alojzij (14 September 1920, Grmada, near Trebnje), Slovene Catholic archbishop. Born into a peasant family, after graduating from high school at the Ljubljana Curia, Šuštar was sent to study theology in Rome in 1940. He took holy orders in October 1946. After earning a doctorate, he was sent to Switzerland, where he worked as an assistant to the parish priest in St. Moritz and taught philosophy and theology at a high school in Schwyz. He subsequently became a professor of moral theology and rector of a seminary in Chur. From 1971 to 1976 Šuštar served as a curate and as a secretary of the Council of European Episcopal Conferences. In 1977 he returned to Slovenia (then part of Yugoslavia), where he became a leading figure of the Catholic Church and the spiritual leader of the society. On 13 April 1980 he was consecrated archbishop of Ljubljana. He also became chancellor of the School of Theology in Ljubljana and president of the Conference of Slovene Bishops. Šuštar patiently strove for the return of the faithful to public life. Thanks to his moderate views and charming personality, he was able to attract many people to the Catholic Church who had previously stayed away from it. Šuštar played a major role in the revival of Slovene Christian Democracy, and in 1991 he was instrumental in bringing a moral dimension to Slovene efforts to regain independence. He also contributed to the recognition of the Slovene state by the Holy See. In August 1992 Šuštar requested that the government return church property that had been nationalized by the Communist regime after World War II. In March 1997 he retired. (WR)

Sources: Leopoldina Plut-Progelj and Carole Rogel, *Historical Dictionary of Slovenia* (Lanham, Md., 1996); *Annuario Pontificio 1997*; www.catholic-hierarchy.org; www.rkc.si/eng/info/struct5.html.

ŠUŠTERŠIČ Ivan (29 May 1863, Ribnica–7 October 1925, Ljubljana), Slovene politician. Šušteršič studied law in Vienna from 1881 to 1885 and earned a doctorate in 1889. He subsequently worked as an attorney in Laibach (Ljubljana). In 1890 he helped to found the Catholic Political Society in Laibach. Elected to the parliament in Vienna in 1896 and 1897, he resigned his parliamentary seat in 1898. He again served as a member of parliament from 1900 to 1918. He was also a deputy to the provincial assembly of Krajina (1901–18). An active member of the Catholic National Party (Katoliška Narodna Stranka), Šušteršič was the de facto leader of this party from 1899 onwards, becoming its formal head in October 1902. In 1905 the Catholic National Party was renamed the Slovene People's Party (Slovenska Ljudska Stranka [SLS]). Šušteršič served as chairman of the SLS until November

1917. The SLS was composed of representatives of two different social orientations: the right-wing orientation, led by Šušteršič and supported by the higher-ranking clergy, and the Christian social orientation, led by **Janez Krek** and supported by peasants, the lower middle class, and the intelligentsia. In the elections to the provincial assembly of Krajina in 1908, the SLS won a sweeping majority, which strengthened Šušteršič's position on the political scene. He called for uniting the South Slavic nations within the framework of the Habsburg empire. Cooperation with the Croats on this unification issue resulted in the establishment of Croat and Slovene parliamentary representation in Vienna under Šušteršič's leadership. Because of his different attitude to the First Balkan War against Turkey, Šušteršič came into conflict with the majority of this representation at the end of 1912. In 1914 he resigned as chairman of the parliamentary representation and was replaced by **Anton Korošec**.

When, after the assassination of Archduke Francis Ferdinand in Sarajevo, Austria-Hungary declared war on Serbia on 28 July 1914, the SLS, led by Šušteršič, took a firm position against Serbia. The party's attitude met with many critical voices. However, Šušteršič's policies as governor of Krajina (January 1912–October 1918) enjoyed social support because he had successfully opposed the demands of the army that threatened the economy of the region. In 1917 Šušteršič was one of the founders of the Yugoslav Club and helped to draft the so-called May Declaration, which advocated that Slovenes, Croats, and Serbs be united into a common state within the Habsburg empire. Contrary to more and more politicians, Šušteršič did not demand independence for the South Slavic nations. After the war, Šušteršič went to Vienna and then to Switzerland. He tried to persuade the Vatican to put pressure on Italy to limit its territorial demands at the Paris Peace Conference. In the book *Moj odgovor* (My answer; 1922) Šušteršič criticized clericalism and stated that SLS links with Church hierarchs were harmful both to the multi-religious state and to the Church. After the establishment of the Kingdom of Serbs, Croats, and Slovenes, Šušteršič played a marginal role in politics. From February 1923 he edited the newspaper *Ljudski dnevnik*. In the parliamentary elections of 18 March 1923 the National People's Party (Narodna Ljudska Stranka) under his leadership obtained only 0.4 percent of the vote in the Slovene constituencies. In April 1923 Šušteršič again began working as an attorney. (AO)

Sources: *Slovenski bijografski leksikon*, vol. 11 (Ljubljana, 1971); *Enciklopedija Jugoslavije*, vol. 8 (Zagreb, 1971); *Enciklopedija Slovenije*, vol. 11 (Ljubljana, 1998); Leopoldina Plut-Pregelj and Carole Rogel, *Historical Dictionary of Slovenia* (Lanham, Md.,

1996); Fran Erjavec, *Zgodovina katoliškego gibanja na Slovenskem* (Ljubljana, 1928); Carole Rogel, *The Slovenes and Yugoslavism, 1890–1914* (Boulder, Colo., 1977); Wacław Felczak and Tadeusz Wasilewski, *Historia Jugosławii* (Wrocław, 1985).

SÜTŐ András (17 June 1927, Cămăraşu [Pusztakamarás], Transylvania), Hungarian writer. Sütő graduated from Bethlen College, Aiud (Nagyenyed) in 1945. After World War II, he initially worked as a reporter and then as an editor of the Hungarian-language periodicals in Romania. An editor (from 1958) and then editor-in-chief (1971–89) of the literary periodical *Új Élet*, Sütő became one of the leading figures in the cultural life of Hungarians in Romania. In his writing, he eulogized the countryside and rural landscapes. Sütő won international recognition as the author of *Anyám könnyű álmot ígér* (Mother promised me a light sleep; 1970), a novel combining a plot set in a rural environment with universal sociological observations. In the novel *Engedjétek hozzám jönni a szavakat* (Let the words come to me; 1977) Sütő raised the issue of the responsibility of the grandfather generation for the outlook on life and national consciousness of grandchildren. The theme of Hungarian ethnicity in Transylvania grew stronger in Sütő's subsequent novels and essays—including *Advent a Hargitán* (Advent in Hargita; 1985)—which were published from 1981 to 1989 outside Romania. In his dramas Sütő referred to characters and events from the folk mythology of the Transylvanian Szeklers and reflected on the position of the individual in confrontation with totalitarianism. (MS)

Sources: Zoltan Bertha, *Sütő András* ed. (Pozsony, 1995); *Új magyar irodalmi lexikon* (Budapest, 2000).

ŠUVAR Stipe (17 February 1936, Zagvozd–29 June 2004, Zagreb), Croatian sociologist and Communist activist. Šuvar graduated in sociology (1960) and earned a doctorate in this field. From 1963 to 1972 he worked as an editor of the periodical *Naše teme*. He also rose through the ranks of the League of Communists of Croatia (LCC). In 1972 he became a member of the LCC Central Committee (CC). From 1974 to 1982 Šuvar served as minister of education and culture of the Croatian republic. He was the author of an unsuccessful reform of the educational system—called the *šuvarica* after him—that was introduced in 1977–78 and resulted in an even greater politicization of teaching based on Marxism. After the death of **Josip Broz Tito**, Šuvar tried to continue Tito's ideological legacy. On his initiative, an ideological conference was held in October 1983 in Zagreb that revealed—against Šuvar's intentions—that the Titoist version of Marxism was already defunct. Closely linked to the Yugoslav army, Šuvar

sabotaged reforms, and as late as May 1987 he called for a struggle against "bourgeois laws" and the recognition of the superiority of "class interests." The LCC's pro-reform faction, led by **Ivica Račan**, decided to rid the party of Šuvar by promoting him to the post of rotating chairman of the Presidium of the League of Communists of Yugoslavia (LCY). Šuvar held this post from 30 June 1988 to 17 May 1989. In October 1988 he called a conference of the LCY Presidium at which a purge was conducted involving the expulsion of one-third of the 165-member CC and 5 members of the 23-member Presidium of the party. Šuvar was also Croatia's representative in the collective state presidency from 1989 to 1990 and its vice-chairman until 15 May 1991. After the breakup of the Yugoslav federation and the establishment of an independent Croatia, Šuvar retired from politics. He taught sociology and philosophy at the University of Zagreb. In 1997 he chaired the Returning Home Citizens' Committee and founded the Socialist Workers' Party of Croatia (Socijalistička Radnička Partija Hrvatske), but this party was of minor importance. Šuvar's publications include *Klasno i nacionalno u suvremenom socijalizmu* (Class and nation in modern socialism; 1970); *Politika i kultura* (Politics and culture; 1980); *Samoupravljanje i alternative* (Self-government and alternatives; 1983); and *Sociologija sela* (Rural sociology, 2 vols.; 1988). (JD/WR)

Sources: *Tko je tko u Hrvatskoj* (Zagreb, 1993); www.moljac. hr/biografije/suvar.htm.

ŠVĀBE Arveds (25 May 1888, Lielstraupē–20 August 1959, Stockholm), Latvian historian and politician. From 1911 to 1915 Švābe studied the natural sciences, history, and law at Moscow University. In 1921–25 he completed studies in law and history at the university in Riga. He subsequently worked as a researcher at the university in Riga, as well as in Germany, Sweden, Poland, Austria, and Italy. His research resulted in, among other things, the work *Agrarian History of Latvia* (1928). In 1932 Švābe earned a Ph.D., and in 1936 he became a professor at the university in Riga. In 1927–40 he edited *Latviesu konversācijas vardnica*, a twenty-volume Latvian dictionary. After Latvia was incorporated into the Soviet Union in 1940, Švābe avoided deportation. In 1944 he fled from the Red Army to Sweden. In 1947 he became head of the Latvian National Committee in Germany. He later taught history at the University of Stockholm. In 1950 in Stockholm he began editing *Latviju enciklopēdiju*, an encyclopedia in the Latvian language. In 1950–55 Švābe published three volumes of this work. He also authored a history of Latvia in English, *The Story of Latvia* (1950). (WR)

Sources: Edgars Andersons et. al., eds., *Cross-Road Country Latvia* eds., (Waverly, Iowa, 1953); Andrejs Plakans, *Historical Dictionary of Latvia* (Lanham, Md., 1997).

SVARINSKAS Alfonsas (21 January 1925, Vatslavovo [now in Belarus]), Lithuanian priest and activist of the democratic opposition. In 1942 Svarinskas entered the Kaunas Seminary. After the Red Army again seized Lithuania, he was arrested in December 1946 and then sentenced to ten years in a forced labor camp and five years in exile for his pro-independence activities. In 1954, while in a forced labor camp in Abez in the Komi ASSR, Svarinskas was ordained into the priesthood by Bishop **Pranciskus Ramanauskas**. Released in 1956, he returned to Lithuania, where he exercised his pastoral ministry in the parish of Vidukle. Arrested again in April 1959, he was sentenced by the Supreme Court of the Lithuanian SSR to six years in a forced labor camp for "anti-Soviet activities." He served his sentence in Mordvinia. Released in 1964, Svarinskas worked as a curate in the parish of Igliauka in Lithuania. In November 1979 he co-founded the Catholic Committee for the Defense of Rights of Believers, for which he was arrested in January 1983. In May 1983 he was tried, together with Father **Sigitas Tamkevicius**, and he was sentenced to seven years in a forced labor camp and three years in exile. In June 1983 around forty-seven thousand Lithuanians signed a petition for the release of both priests. In February 1987 Svarinskas was brought to the KGB headquarters in Vilnius, but after refusing to plead guilty, he was sent back to the labor camp in Perm. Soviet television then broadcast a diatribe on his activities. Released in July 1988, Svarinskas became chancellor of the archdiocesan curia in Kaunas in 1990. After Lithuania regained independence, he became head of the Lithuanian branch of Catholic Action. With the consent of Archbishop **Vincentas Sladkevicius**, as a sign of appreciation for the Church's efforts to uphold Lithuanian national traditions, in September 1991 Svarinskas became a member of the Supreme Soviet of the Lithuanian SSR, and his election was supported by the Lithuanian Movement for Restructuring (Sajudis). Svarinskas sat on the Supreme Soviet until the elections of October 1992 and was an advocate for the nationalist and conservative members of the clergy, who regarded the achievements of the Second Vatican Council with mistrust and were wary of all forms of liberalism. (WR)

Sources: S. P. de Boer, E. J. Driessen, and H. L. Verhaar, eds., *Biographical Dictionary of Dissidents in the Soviet Union, 1956–1975* (The Hague and Boston, 1982); Rasa Mažeika, ed., *Violations of Human Rights in Soviet Occupied Lithuania* (Philadelphia, 1988).

ŠVEHLA Antonín (15 April 1873, Hostivař, near Prague–12 December 1933, Hostivař), Czech Peasant Party politician. Švehla was born into a family of farmers. His father was the village headman (*starosta*) of Hostivař. Švehla finished three grades of high school in Prague and one grade of a German high school in Česká Lípa. He subsequently attended an agricultural vocational school. He then continued to study on his own and was particularly interested in politics and agriculture. From 1899 onwards Švehla ran his father's farm. He began his public activities in 1893, founding the gymnastic society Sokol (Hawk). At the turn of the twentieth century Švehla became involved in the work of the newly established Czech Agrarian Party (Česká strana Agrární), co-founded by his father. In 1902 he became vice-chairman of the Czech Farmers' Society (Sdružení Českých Zemědělců). He was seriously involved in the development of the party's press organs. In 1901 Švehla became a member of the leadership and in 1903 the chairman of the Agricultural Press and Publishing Cooperative. In 1906 he succeeded in founding the press organs of the Czech Agrarian Party—the daily *Venkov* and the weekly *Cep*. In 1908 Švehla refused to run in elections to the parliament in Vienna, as he believed that he could do more in his country. He became an MP in the Czech Land Diet and chairman of the agrarian parliamentary representation. In 1909 he became chairman of the Czech Agrarian Party and in 1912 chairman of the Czech Club in the Land Diet. From this position he protested the dissolution of the Diet and its replacement by a commission appointed by the authorities in Vienna (the so-called *anenské patenty* of 26 July 1913).

According to Švehla, the Agrarian Party was to be a middle-of-the-road party, between the leftist Socialist parties and the right-wing conservatives. It was to become a mass movement with which the entire rural community, not only the great landowners, could identify. According to him, the nation consisted primarily of two equally important large social groups, the workers and the peasants, and the latter should be as well organized as the former. Švehla believed that the agrarian movement was part of the all-national movement, whose aim was to fight for the Czech nation's historical right to statehood. From the beginning of World War I Švehla held an anti-Habsburg position and made efforts to unite Czech parties on issues concerning the legal status of the Bohemian lands. In 1916 he was one of the founders of the National Committee (Národní Výbor) and the Czech Union (Český Svaz) in the parliament in Vienna. After the arrest of **Karel Kramář**, Švehla became the leader of the Czech political representation, and he organized many political actions. Toward the end of the war Švehla started preparing for a takeover of power by Czech political forces and was involved in the building of an independent state, paying much attention to economic and social issues, as he realized there was the danger of a social revolution. In July 1918 Švehla became vice-president of the National Committee, which he reorganized in order to take over power. He was one of the leaders of the coup of 28 October 1918 and one of the founders of an independent Czechoslovakia. Along with **Alois Rašin**, **František Soukup**, **Vavro Šrobár**, and **Jiří Stříbrný**, Švehla signed a manifesto establishing the Czechoslovak state.

From 1918 Švehla sat in the National Assembly, and he held the post of minister of interior in the first Czechoslovak government (November 1918–July 1919). He tried to avert party conflicts and believed that a coalition that would strengthen and develop the young state's structures was more important than party interests. Švehla initiated the establishment of the Pětka (The Five), an informal decision-making organ that consisted of the leaders of the main political forces. In 1919 he became head of the Agrarian Party, which then took on the name of the Republican Party of the Czechoslovak Rural Community (Republikánská Strana Československého Venkova), and in 1925 it was renamed the Republican Party of Peasants and Smallholders (Republikánská Strana Zemědělského a Malorolnického Lidu). On 8 October 1922 Švehla became prime minister of an "all-national" broad coalition government (made up of the Agrarians, Peasant Party members, National Democrats, National Socialists, and Social Democrats). After the elections of November 1925 the center of gravity in parliament moved to the right. Švehla's new cabinet, based on a similar coalition but without the National Democrats and Social Democrats, was established on 9 December of that year but was short-lived. On 12 October 1926, after a short interlude of **Jan Černý**'s cabinet of civil servants, Švehla again became head of a coalition government, known as the "government of the gentlemen's coalition." This coalition included the National Democrats, Agrarians, Populists, tradesmen, German parties, and members of Hlinka's Slovak People's Party, led by Father **Andrej Hlinka**. Švehla's government was a time of stabilization and prosperity. Švehla paid much attention to the strengthening of the country and the development of democracy. He also cared greatly for economic development. He completed the implementation of agricultural reforms under which great landed estates were parceled out and medium-size farms received aid. Švehla was a close associate of President **Tomáš Garrigue Masaryk**, whom he supported in the 1927 elections, refusing to run against Masaryk. Owing to ill health, on 1 February 1929 Švehla resigned his position and then retired from public life. (PU)

Sources: *ČBS*; *Kto bol kto za I. ČSR* (Bratislava, 1993); *Politická elita meziválečného Československa 1918–1938: Kdo byl kdo za první republiky* (Prague, 1998); Robert J. Kerner, ed., *Czechoslovakia: Twenty Years of Independence* (Berkeley, 1940); *The Times*, 14 October 1953; S. Harrison Thomson, *Czechoslovakia in European History* (Princeton, 1953); Anthony Palecek, "Antonin Svehla: Czech Peasant Statesman," *Slavic Review*, 1962, no. 4; Vladimir Dostál, *Antonín Švehla: Profil československého státnika* (New York, 1989); Josef Hanzal, *Antonín Švehla k. 120. výroči narozeni a 60. výroči úmrti* (Prague, 1993); Daniel E. Miller, *Forging Political Compromise: Antonín Švehla and the Czechoslovak Agrarian Party* (Pittsburgh, 1999).

ŠVERMA Jan (23 March 1901, Mnichovo Hradiště, Mladá Boleslav County–10 November 1944, Mt. Chabenec, Lower Tatra Mountains), Czech Communist activist and journalist. The son of a lawyer, Šverma studied medicine and law at Charles University in Prague, but he failed to graduate owing to his extensive journalistic and political activities. In 1921 he joined the Communist Party of Czechoslovakia (CPC) and became active in the Communist Youth Union. He also edited the party daily, *Rudé Právo*. In 1926–28 Šverma studied at the Lenin School in Moscow. After his return to Czechoslovakia, at the Fifth CPC Congress in February 1929 he became a member of the Central Committee (CC) and Politburo of the party. Šverma supported the "Bolshevization" of the CPC and worked closely with **Klement Gottwald**. He was also active in the Communist trade unions. From August 1930 he was a member of the Executive Bureau of the Red Trade Union International (Profintern). In September 1932 Šverma took part in the Twelfth Plenum of the Executive Committee of the Communist International (Comintern). Šverma's position grew more important when Gottwald and **Václav Kopecký** left for Moscow in 1934 in order to avoid arrest. At the Seventh Congress of the Comintern Šverma was elected a deputy member of its Executive Committee.

In 1935 Šverma was elected an MP. According to Comintern instructions, he advocated the creation of a wide anti-Fascist front. As a result he supported **Edvard Beneš** for president, persuading other Communist deputies to follow suit. This step was not welcomed by the Kremlin or by Gottwald because they thought it too independent. Thus at the next Comintern Congress at the beginning of 1936 Šverma had to submit a self-criticism. In 1936–38 Šverma was editor-in-chief of *Rudé Právo*. After the Pact of Munich of September 1938, he voted against **Emil Hácha** in the presidential elections. Soon he left for Moscow, where he was active in the CPC leadership abroad. In 1939–40 Šverma was head of the foreign section of the CPC in Paris and edited the periodical *Světovy rozhled*. After the defeat of France in July 1940, he returned to Moscow, where apart from working in the party leadership he edited Czech and Slovak broadcasts on Moscow Radio and the periodical *Československé listy*. From 1941 Šverma was in the Panslavic Committee. During the Slovak National Uprising he was sent to Slovakia as a delegate of the CPC leadership abroad. During the retreat with the partisans Šverma died of exhaustion. (PU)

Sources: *ČBS*; Lazitch; *Politická elita meziválečného Československenska 1918–1938: Kdo byl kdo za prvni republiky* (Prague, 1998); *Kdo byl kdo v našich dějinach ve 20. stoleti*, vol. 1 (Prague, 1998); *SBS*, vol. 5; Jan Suchl, *Novinář Jan Šverma* (Prague, 1981); Vera Holá, *Jan Šverma* (Prague, 1985).

ŠVERMOVÁ Marie [née Švábová] (17 August 1902, Trnovany–14 February 1992, Prague), Czech Communist activist, wife of **Jan Šverma**. Švermová belonged to the group that initiated the Communist Party of Czechoslovakia (CPC) after a split in the Social Democratic movement, and she was a CPC member from its beginnings in 1921. In 1929–38 she was a member of the Central Committee (CC) of the CPC, and during World War II she worked in Moscow. After she returned to Czechoslovakia, in 1945–51 she belonged to the CC Presidium; until 1949 she was head of the Organization Department of the CC, and from 1949 to 1951 she was deputy secretary general of the CPC. Švermová actively supported the Stalinization of Czechoslovakia. In February 1951 she was deprived of all her positions and arrested. After a fake trial, on 28 January 1954 she was sentenced to life imprisonment. Soon the sentence was reduced to ten years, and in 1956 she was released. In 1963 Švermová was rehabilitated by the court and by the party authorities. In April 1963 she was accepted back into the party. During the Prague Spring she supported reforms, and in 1977 she signed Charter 77. (PU)

Sources: *ČBS*; Jiři Pelikán, *The Czechoslovak Political Trials, 1950–1954* (Stanford, 1971); Karel Kaplan, *K politickým procesům v Československu 1948–54: Dokumentace komise ÚV KSČ pro rehabilitaci 1968* (Prague, 1994).

SVERSTYUK Yevhen (13 December 1928, Silce [now Siltse], Volhynia), Ukrainian literary critic, dissident, and religious activist. From 1947 to 1952 Sverstyuk studied at the Department of Logic and Psychology of Lviv University and then worked as a teacher of Ukrainian. From 1953 to 1956 he pursued postgraduate studies at the Psychological Research Institute of the Ministry of Education of the Ukrainian SSR. From 1956 to 1959 he taught Ukrainian literature at the Poltava Pedagogical Institute. From 1959 to 1960 he worked at the Institute of Psychology. Sverstyuk was head of the prose section

of the monthly *Vitchyzna* (1961–62), a research worker at the Department of the Psychology of Education at the Psychological Research Institute (1962–65), and secretary of the editorial staff of the periodical *Ukraiinskyi botanichnyi zhurnal* (1965–72). In the 1960s he was often dismissed from work for political reasons. Arrested in January 1972, Sverstyuk was sentenced to seven years in a forced labor camp and five years in exile for preparing and distributing samizdat publications. In 1983 he returned to Kiev, where he worked as a carpenter until 1988, when he became editor-in-chief of the religious weekly *Nasha vira*, which was published under the aegis of the Ukrainian Autocephalous Orthodox Church. Sverstyuk has authored numerous essays; articles in the field of literary studies, psychology, and religious studies; and several books, the most important of which are *Sobor u ryshtovanni* (A cathedral in scaffolding; 1970); *Pidpilni eseyi* (Clandestine essays; 1976); *Eseyi* (Essays; 1976); *Bludni syny Ukraiiny* (Prodigal sons of Ukraine; 1993); *Shevchenko i chas* (Shevchenko and time; 1996); and *Na sviati nadiyi* (At the celebration of hope; 1999). (BB)

Sources: *Encyclopedia of Ukraine*, vol. 5 (Toronto, 1993); *Khto ie khto v Ukraiini 2000* (Kiev, 2000); Bogumiła Berdychowska and Ola Hnatiuk, ed., *Bunt pokolenia: Rozmowy z intelektualistami ukraińskimi* (Lublin, 2000).

SVITLYCHNYI Ivan (20 September 1929, Polovynkyne, Luhansk district–25 October 1992, Kiev), Ukrainian dissident, literary critic, and poet. Born into a family of kolkhoz farm workers, Svitlychni finished high school in Starobelsk in 1947 and graduated in philology from the university in Kharkiv in 1952. He subsequently was a postgraduate student and, from 1957 to 1963, assistant professor at the Institute of Literature of the Academy of Sciences of the Ukrainian SSR. Forced to leave his job, Svitlychnyi worked at the Institute of Philosophy from 1963 to 1964. After 1965 he did not have a permanent job and published his articles under pseudonyms. Known for his non-conformist attitude, Svitlychnyi was involved in most of the independent cultural initiatives of the 1960s and 1970s. He became a great moral authority among "the generation of the sixties" (*shestidesiatniki*). He played a major role in the establishment of relations between the intelligentsias of Kiev and Lviv and also in the establishment of contacts with the Ukrainian diaspora in the West. In 1962–63 he helped to found the Club of Young Artists. On 30 August 1965 Svitlychnyi was arrested for "anti-Soviet propaganda and agitation," but after a few months he was released as "socially safe." From 1966 to 1971 he published extensively in the underground periodicals. Arrested again in January 1972, Svitlychnyi was sentenced to seven years in forced labor camps and five years in exile in April 1973. He served his sentence in labor camps near Perm. He was often additionally punished for taking part in protest actions and hunger strikes. In June 1978 Svitlychnyi was exiled to Ust-Kan in Altai. In August 1981 he suffered a stroke, which left him an invalid. Released in January 1983, he was no longer able to continue his opposition work. Svitlychnyi was a member of the International PEN Club from 1978 on, and in 1990 he became a member of the Association of Ukrainian Writers. In 1989 he received the Vasyl Stus Award, and in 1994 he was posthumously awarded the Taras Shevchenko Prize. Svitlychnyi wrote poetry and also translated from Slavic languages and French. His publications include the volumes *Hratovani sonety* (Sonnets behind bars; 1977); *Sertse dlia kul i dlia rym* (A heart for bullets and rhymes; 1991); and *U mene—tilky slovo* (I only have the word; 1994). A posthumous edition of his poems and a volume of memoirs, *Dobrookyi: Spohady pro Ivana Svitlychnoho* (The man with kind eyes: Memoirs of Ivan Svitlychnyi; 1998), were edited by his wife, Leonida, and his sister Nadia. His wife—a pillar of strength to the family—nursed him during his illness while he was in exile in Altai. His sister Nadia, an activist in the dissident movement, had been imprisoned in forced labor camps from 1973 to 1976, and in 1978 she settled in the United States. (TS)

Sources: *Encyclopedia of Ukraine*, vol. 5 (Toronto, 1993); Kharkiv Human Rights Defense Group; Heorhiy Kasyanov, *Nezhodni: Ukraiinska intelihentsiia v rusi oporu 1960–80-kh rokiv* (Kiev, 1995); Anatoliy Rusnachenko, *Natsionalno-vyzvolnyi rukh v Ukraiini* (Kiev, 1998).

SVOBODA Ludvik (25 November 1895, Hroznatín–20 September 1979, Prague), Czech general, president of the Czechoslovak Socialist Republic. During World War I Svoboda fought in the Czechoslovak Legion in Russia, taking part in the battles of Zborów and Bachmače (among others). He returned to Czechoslovakia in 1920, and from 1922 he served as an officer of the Czechoslovak Army. He held a number of military posts—for example, he was deputy commander of a battalion in Uzhhorod, a lecturer in the Hungarian language at the military academy in Hraníce, and deputy commander and then commander of a battalion in Kroměřiži; after the mobilization in 1938 he became commander of an infantry regiment. At the beginning of the German occupation Svoboda was active in the organization called Defense of the Nation. In June 1939 he moved to Poland, where, under the command of General **Lev Prchala**, he began to form the Czechoslovak Legion in Bronowice, near Kraków. The legion was for-

mally established by a decree issued by President **Ignacy Mościcki** on 3 September 1939. On 18 September 1939 Svoboda moved, along with his units, to the territories that had been seized by the USSR, but he was interned and held in the Soviet Union until June 1941. After the German attack against the USSR Svoboda became commander of the first independent Czechoslovak battalion; in 1943 he became commander of the first independent Czechoslovak brigade; and in 1944 he became commander of the First Czechoslovak Army in the USSR. He quickly rose through the ranks of the army as well: in 1943 he became brigadier general, in April 1945 major general, and in August 1945 general of the army.

Svoboda returned to Czechoslovakia in April 1945, assuming the post of nonparty minister of national defense in the first Czechoslovak postwar cabinet, the so-called Košice Government. He also held the post in **Klement Gottwald**'s government, established in July 1945. During the Communist coup in February 1948 Svoboda proclaimed s the neutrality of the army, a move favorable to the Communists. At the time of the government crisis Svoboda did not resign; rather he collaborated with the Communists. He accepted the coup and soon joined the Communist Party. Since the Kremlin did not trust him and also because he did not conduct a sufficiently efficient purge of the army, in April 1950 Svoboda was replaced as minister of national defense by **Alexej Čepička**. Svoboda assumed the post of deputy prime minister and president of the national committee for physical education and sports. At the end of 1951 he was deprived of all his posts, and in 1952 he was arrested for a short time. After his release Svoboda worked as an accountant at a cooperative farm. In 1954 he returned to political life, becoming a member of the Presidium of the National Assembly. From 1955 to 1958 he was head of the Klement Gottwald Military Academy in Hraníce, and later he headed the Military History Institute in Prague.

During the Prague Spring, after the resignation of **Antonín Novotný**, on 30 March 1968 Svoboda was elected president of Czechoslovakia, enjoying the confidence of the first secretary of the Central Committee (CC) of the CPSU, Leonid Brezhnev. However, after the invasion by the Warsaw Pact troops, Svoboda refused, after some hesitation, to appoint a "revolutionary government of workers and peasants." Also, during talks with the Soviet leadership between 23 and 26 August 1968 in Moscow, Svoboda was successful in securing the participation in the negotiations of party leaders and reformers headed by **Alexander Dubček**, who had been interned during the Soviet invasion. In talks with interned members of the leadership of the Communist Party of Czechoslovakia (CPC), Svoboda insisted that they sign the "Moscow Protocol," which annulled the previous decisions of the leadership and in fact announced the "normalization" of Czechoslovakia. After his return to Prague Svoboda began to trim and slow down the "normalization," but at the same time he supported it. As early as 31 August 1968 he was coopted, along with **Gustav Husák**, to the CC of the CPC, in place of the reformers Čestimír Císař and **František Kriegel**. In 1969 Svoboda backed Husák, and he had a significant role in Husák's taking over the post of first secretary of the CC of the CPC from Dubček. Thereafter, he passively watched the purges in the party, in the state apparatus, and in the culture. From April 1974 Svoboda effectively was not serving as president owing to ill health, but he refused to resign. On 25 May 1975 he was recalled as president. The direct reason was the fact that he had been diagnosed—by Soviet specialists from the notorious Serbsky Institute of Forensic Psychiatry—as suffering from "arteriosclerosis dementia." Svoboda was the author of the memoirs *Z Buzuluku do Prahy* (From Buzuluk to Prague; 1960) and *Cestami života* (On the paths of life; 1971). (PU)

Sources: *ČBS*; *Kdo byl kdo v našich dějinách ve 20. století*, vol. 2 (Prague, 1998); *Českoslovenští politici: 1918–1991* (Prague, 1991); Teodor Fis, *Mein Kommandeur, General Svoboda: Vom Ural zum Hradschin* (Vienna, 1969); V. Kožnar, *Ludvík Svoboda* (Prague, 1975); Gordon H. Skilling, *Czechoslovakia's Interrupted Revolution* (Princeton, 1976); Vladimir V. Kusin, *From Dubcek to Charter 77: A Study of "Normalization" in Czechoslovakia, 1968–1978* (New York, 1978); V. Kadlec, *Podivné konce našich prezidentu* (Hradec Kralove, 1991); Andrzej Garlicki and Andrzej Paczkowski, eds., *Zaciskanie pętli: Tajne dokumenty dotyczące Czechosłowacji 1968 r.* (Warsaw, 1995).

SWIANIEWICZ Stanisław (7 November 1899, Dünaburg [Daugavpils]–22 May 1997, London), Polish economist and lawyer. After graduating from high school in Orel, Russia, Swianiewicz studied law in Moscow and Wilno (Vilnius). Then he studied economics in Paris, Breslau (Wrocław), and Vienna. In 1917, he joined the secret Polish Military Organization, and from 1919 to 1921 he served in the Polish Army, including the period during the Polish-Soviet war. After his dismissal from the army, Swianiewicz commenced working at Stefan Bathory University in Wilno. Initially, he was a graduate assistant, but after receiving first his doctorate and then an advanced postgraduate degree, he became an associate professor. He also lectured at the School of Political Sciences and supervised the Department of Economic Studies at the Research Institute of Eastern Europe in Wilno. A member of the Econometric Society and many Polish scholarly associations, Swianiewicz was considered a leading authority on totalitarian economies. Among other works, he published *Lenin jako ekonomista* (1930; Lenin as an economist; 1930); *Problemy sowieckiej polityki gospodarczej* (Problems of Soviet economic policy; 1934); and *Polityka gospodarcza hitlerowskich Niemiec* (The economic policy of Hitler's Germany; 1938).

Mobilized in September 1939, Swianiewicz fought against the Nazis, including in the battle of Tomaszów Lubelski. Captured by the Soviets near Lwów (Lviv), he was transported to a POW camp in Kozielsk. On 19 April 1940, along with a group of other Polish officer prisoners, Swianiewicz was taken to the Gnezdovo railroad station, where he was separated from the others. He observed them being escorted from their cattle cars onto special buses. They were driven by the NKVD into a forest, and after a while, the buses returned empty. Swianiewicz was transferred first to the Lubyanka Prison and then to the Butyrki Prison in Moscow. He survived a brutal interrogation. He was accused of espionage against the Soviet Union, and in February 1941 he was sentenced to eight years in the camps. In August 1941, Swianiewicz was excluded from the Soviet "amnesty" for Polish prisoners, and he remained in the Ust-Vim camp until April 1942. He was freed following the persistent efforts of the Polish Embassy in Kuibyshev. After his release, Swianiewicz confirmed the claims that he was the only eye witness to the operation connected to the Katyn forest massacre. His story contradicted the official Soviet version that it was the Germans who were guilty. Protected to the utmost by Polish diplomats, Swianiewicz managed to leave for Iran, thus narrowly escaping an attempt by the NKVD to rearrest him. He then supervised the Bureau for Studies in Palestine. In 1944, Swianiewicz took over the eastern department at the Ministry of Peace Congress Preparations of the Polish government-in-exile in London. After the war, he returned to academia. He headed the Department of Economics and Trade at the Polish University College. Then he studied rural overpopulation in Eastern Europe and Asia at the University of Manchester. Between 1956 and 1958, Swianiewicz worked in Indonesia as a UNESCO expert. After returning to the United Kingdom, he lectured at the London School of Economics. In 1963, he took over the chair of economics and statistics at the University of Halifax in Canada. In 1965 he published *Forced Labour and Economic Development*. In 1973 Swianiewicz retired, and in 1977 he published his memoirs, *W cieniu Katynia* (In the shadow of Katyn), where he described in detail his experiences in the USSR. (WR)

Sources: Stanisław Łoza, *Czy wiesz kto to jest*, vol. 1 (Warsaw, 1938); Stanisław Swianiewicz, *W cieniu Katynia* (Paris, 1977); *Kultura*, 1997, no. 6.

ŚWIĄTEK Kazimierz [Belorussian: Svyontak] (21 October 1914, Valga, Estonia), cardinal of the Roman Catholic Church in Belorussia. Świątek was born into a Polish noble family. His father was killed in the Polish-Soviet war in 1920. In 1939 Świątek graduated from the Higher Theological Seminary in Pińsk. In April 1939 he was ordained a priest. He started his ministry in Prużany in the summer of 1939, but in the fall of that year, after the Soviet invasion of Poland, he was arrested by the NKVD, taken to Brest Prison, and hardly escaped death. Released after the German seizure of the town in June 1941, Świątek returned to his ministry in Prużany. In 1944 he was arrested again by the Soviet organs and sentenced to ten years of a labor camp. He served in the Vorkuta camps, where he secretly ministered among the prisoners. After his release in 1953 Świątek became a parish priest in the Pinsk cathedral. He continued his ministry despite constant harassment by the Soviet authorities. On 21 May 1991 Świątek was appointed archbishop of Minsk-Mogilev and administrator of the Pinsk diocese. On 26 November 1994 Pope **John Paul II** elevated him to the rank of cardinal. In his pastoral work Świątek dealt with the organization of church work and tried to avoid involvement in the current political struggles. Świątek enjoys enormous popularity among the Poles in Belorussia, although he avoids the identification of Roman Catholicism with the Polish culture. He supports Belorussian national revival, using the Belorussian language in public. (EM)

Sources: *Kto jest kto w Respublike Belarus* (Minsk, 1999); Jan Zaprudnik, *Belarus: At a Crossroads of History* (Boulder, Colo., 1993); A. Hlyabovich, "Kastsiol u niavoli," *Spadchyna*, 1994, nos. 1–2; Jan Zaprudnik, *Historical Dictionary of Belarus* (Lanham, Md., 1998); *Annuario Ponitificio*, 2001; Marek A. Koprowski, "Może uchodzić za symbol," *Gość Niedzielny*, 15 September 2002.

ŚWIĄTKOWSKI Henryk (2 April 1896, Dzierzążnia, near Płońsk–2 March 1970, Warsaw), Polish Communist activist. Born into a teacher's family, in 1920 Świątkowski graduated from the Law School of the University of Warsaw. In 1923 he joined the Polish Socialist Party. Between May 1931 and February 1934, he sat on its Supreme Council, and from 1928 through 1935, he represented it in the parliament. Świątkowski was a political trial lawyer in Zamość and Warsaw, defending Communists (among others). In 1940 and 1941 he was imprisoned in Pawiak Prison in Warsaw and in the Auschwitz concentration camp. After his release, he joined the leftist underground. In May 1944 Świątkowski became a member of the Supreme Council of the Workers' Party of Polish Socialists (Rada Naczelna Robotniczej Partii Polskich Socjalistów), which collaborated with the Communists. One of the leaders of the Communist-approved Polish Socialist Party (PPS), between February and June 1945 Świątkowski chaired its Supreme Council, and in July he was coopted as a member of the PPS Central Executive Committee. He strove to achieve its unification with the (Communist) Polish Workers' Party by purging the ranks of the PPS of non-conformist activists. In April 1945 Świątkowski was appointed deputy minister and in May 1945 minister of justice in the Provisional Government. In 1947, he became a professor at the University of Warsaw, presenting the idea that law was "the will of the ruling class." Świątkowski fulfilled his ministerial functions in the Provisional Government of National Unity and in succeeding governments that were fully controlled by the Communists. In December 1948, he became a member of the Central Committee of the (Communist) Polish United Workers' Party (Polska Zjednoczona Partia Robotnicza). From December 1948 to 1950 he also served on its Politburo and in the Secretariat. As minister of justice, Świątkowski rubber-stamped the crimes of Stalinism in Poland. He was relieved of his portfolio in April 1956 during the "thaw." He not only was not punished for his role in the Stalinization of the judiciary, but in 1957 he was also appointed dean of the Law School at the University of Warsaw. Świątkowski retired in 1961. (WR).

Sources: Mołdawa; Marek Łatyński, *Nie paść na kolana: Szkice o opozycji lat czterdziestych* (Warsaw, 1987); Andrzej Werblan, *Stalinizm w Polsce* (Warsaw, 1993).

ŚWIERCZEWSKI Karol, pseudonym "Walter" (10 February 1897, Warsaw–28 March 1947, near Baligród, Poland), Soviet general of Polish descent. The details of Świerczewski's descent, childhood, and youth are uncertain. According to the official biography, he was born into the family of a Polish skilled laborer in Warsaw. He had five siblings. He finished four grades of primary school, where he learned Russian. He worked as an apprentice in the workshops of the Gwiździński plant and then in the Gerlach factory. After his father's death in 1912, he became the main breadwinner in the family. In 1915 the withdrawing Russian troops evacuated the Gerlach factory and some of its employees, including Świerczewski and his family. They were sent to Kazan and then to Moscow, where he got a job in the Pravodnik cable factory.

After the Bolshevik revolution, Świerczewski joined the Red Guards (December 1917) and then the Bolshevik party (November 1918). As a soldier of the 123rd Rifle Regiment, he fought against the White Russian forces. In the summer of 1920 he took part in the Bolshevik invasion of Poland. Wounded two times, he spent several months in a hospital. Assigned to the Red Communard

School in March 1921, he taught infantry tactics. He was also promoted to battalion commander, later becoming a political commissar. As part of their training, in 1921 he and his students helped to beat the insurgent troops led by Sergey Antonov in Tambov Province. Later Świerczewski studied at the Frunze Military Academy. After graduating, he was successively promoted to chief of staff of a cavalry regiment in the Kiev Military District, deputy chief of the Seventh Department of the staff of the Belorussian Military District, and chief of the Fourth Department of the Board of the Red Army General Staff. He simultaneously served as deputy chief of one of the departments of the Soviet military intelligence directorate (Glavnoe Razvedyvatelnoe Upravlenie [GRU]). In December 1936 Świerczewski was sent, with the rank of general, to Spain, where he commanded the Fourteenth International Brigade on the southern front, and in February 1936 he became commander of Division A on the Madrid front. He later commanded the Thirty-fifth and then the Forty-fifth Divisions. He distinguished himself during the Saragossa offensive and the retreat on the Aragon front. Apart from fighting against Franco's forces, Świerczewski energetically conducted purges in the ranks of the international volunteers and executed prisoners of war as well as his own men. However, he was a very popular commander with the Stalinists. In May 1938 he was called back to the Soviet Union, where he became a lecturer at the Frunze Military Academy.

After the Third Reich attacked the Soviet Union in June 1941, Świerczewski commanded the 248th Rifle Division, and when it was defeated, he became commander of the Forty-third Reserve Rifle Brigade. Evacuated to the Siberian Military District, he reestablished the Kiev Officers' School there and became its commander. In August 1943 he was assigned, as deputy commander, to the First Corps of the Polish Military Forces, established with Stalin's approval. Świerczewski was also appointed deputy commander of the Polish Army in the Soviet Union and coopted to the Central Office of Polish Communists. He then commanded the Second Polish Army (August–October 1944) and the Third Army (October–December 1944). In January 1945 he again became commander of the Second Army. He also rose through the ranks of the Communist political structures in Poland. A deputy to the National Home Council (Krajowa Rada Narodowa [KRN]) and a member of the Central Committee of the (Communist) Polish Workers' Party (Polska Partia Robotnicza [PPR]), he closely adhered to Stalin's political directives—for example, by refusing clemency to former Home Army soldiers who were sentenced to death. The Second Polish Army under his command was part of the First Belorussian Front. Świerczewski distinguished himself in the battles of the Neisse River and Bautzen. When World War II ended, he was a lieutenant general.

In the summer of 1945 Świerczewski became chief inspector for military settlement and commander of the Poznań Military District. He was in charge of deporting the German population and settling demobilized Polish soldiers in place of the Germans. In February 1946 he was appointed deputy minister of national defense. In the following months he traveled abroad, conducting agitation among the Polish diaspora in Canada, the United States, and Mexico. After returning to Poland, he became an MP in the Polish Legislative Assembly as a result of the rigged parliamentary elections of 19 January 1947. At that time he was in charge of deporting the Ukrainian population from the territories of southeastern Poland (Operation Vistula). In March 1947, while on an inspection trip to the units he commanded, Świerczewski was killed in an ambush set up by the Ukrainian Insurgent Army (UPA). (JK/MC)

Sources: *MERSH*, vol. 38; Saturnina L. Wadecka, *Generał Karol Świerczewski "Walter" 1897–1947* (Warsaw, 1976); "Ten co się kulom nie kłaniał," *Gazeta Wyborcza*, 8 November 1990; A. K. Sverchevskaia, *Soldat trekh armii: Karol Sverchevskiy: Rasskaz ob ottse* (Moscow, 1993); Marek Jan Chodakiewicz, *Zagrabiona pamięć: Wojna w Hiszpanii, 1936–1939* (Warsaw, 1997); Antoni Czubiński, *Polska i Polacy po II wojnie światowej* (Poznań, 1998); Ronald Radosh, Mary R. Habeck, and Grigory Sevostianov, eds., *Spain Betrayed: The Soviet Union and the Spanish Civil War* (New Haven and London, 2001); "Lieutenant General Karol Swierczewski," www.geocities.com/byron_b86/swierczewski.html.

ŚWIERZYŃSKI Józef (19 April 1868, Wolnice, near Sandomierz–12 February 1948, Sandomierz), Polish doctor and politician. Born on the estate of his parents, Władysław and Helena (née Konarska), Świerzyński completed a gymnasium in Radom, and in 1887 he enrolled at the School of Medicine of Warsaw University, from which he graduated in 1893. During his studies he was active in secret associations of the pro-independence youth. After gaining a diploma, Świerzyński specialized in internal medicine at the university clinics in Berlin and Giessen. After his return to Poland he worked in a Warsaw hospital, and in 1897 he moved to Jeleniowo, to the estates inherited by his wife in the Świętokrzyskie Mountains. Świerzyński developed educational and social activities there, treating poor country folk for free. The recognition he gained as a result, as well as his joining the National League, led to his election to the State Duma as an MP for his constituency in 1905. Later he was also a member of the Second and Fourth Duma, from which he withdrew in 1915. In 1907 Świerzyński and his family moved from Jeleniowo to Szydłowice, near Sandomierz, where he bought an estate. During World War I he was active in the Relief Committee organized by Bishop **Adam Sapieha**. In 1917, as the representative of National Democracy, Świerzyński was elected to the Council of State of the Kingdom of Poland. On 23 October 1918 he was appointed head of its new government. Świerzyński sought the resignation of the Regency Council and the creation of a national government. On 3 November he made an attempt in that direction, but he did not get the support of the left or of the peasant parties; therefore he resigned. Between 1919 and 1921 Świerzyński participated in the preparation of the constitution. Later he withdrew entirely from political life and held only the post of chairman of the Polish Educational Society. In 1924, in recognition of his work, he was given the Commander's Cross of the Order of Polonia Restituta. Świerzyński lived and farmed in Szydłowice. At the end of 1939 he established contacts with the Polish underground, which was beginning to form, but because of his ill health his help was limited to financial support. In August 1944 the front line ran through Szydłowice, so Świerzyński and his family had to hide in the cellar. He and his family then went to Sandomierz. As a result of the agricultural reform of the Polish Committee of National Liberation, Świerzyński's land was expropriated, and he died in very difficult material circumstances. (WR)

Sources: J. Szmurło, "Wspomnienia pośmiertne," *Polski Tygodnik Lekarski*, 1948, nos. 29–30; Czesław Brzoza and Kamil Stepan, *Posłowie polscy w parlamencie rosyjskim 1906–1917* (Warsaw, 2001).

ŚWIĘTOCHOWSKI Aleksander, pseudonyms "Poseł Prawdy," "Oremus," and others (18 January 1849, Stoczek Łukowski–25 April 1938, Gołotczyzna), Polish pundit and writer. The son of a teacher, Świętochowski graduated from high school in Lublin, and in 1866 he enrolled at the Main School in Warsaw. However, because the school was closed down by the Russian government, his studies were interrupted. In 1870 Świętochowski commenced publishing in *Przegląd Tygodniowy*, advocating the idea of Positivism. He rejected the Romantic tradition and championed "work at the foundations" (*praca u podstaw*), which was to raise the nation up from backwardness. He unequivocally supported the emancipation of women. In 1874, Świętochowski left for the University of Leipzig, where the following year he successfully defended his doctoral dissertation in psychology. He also wrote novels, novellas, and plays. His play *Ojciec Makary* (Father Makary; 1876) caused a scandal (among other things, it was accused of propagating moral anarchy) and ruined his chances of securing a professorship in Galicia. In 1880, Świętochowski founded his own paper, *Prawda*. It became

one of the most influential organs of Polish Positivism. Among other pieces, in it he published his famous column, "Liberum Veto." His rejection of the insurgent tradition made him vulnerable to accusations of collaboration with the partitioning powers, even though he never advocated collaboration.

In the 1890s, Świętochowski was much less active. In 1902, he briefly flirted with the Polish Socialist Party. However, during the revolution of 1905, he advocated liberal democratic solutions, founding and leading the Progressive Democratic Union (Związek Postępowo-Demokratyczny). His links to the Socialists were further weakened because of a serious conflict with **Józef Piłsudski**, whom Świętochowski considered a terrorist until his dying day. Disappointed in politics, he returned to charity and social work. In 1906, he founded the Society for Polish Culture to fight illiteracy and to propagate the national culture. He sponsored the foundation of an all-female school in Gołotczyzna. Later, a school for boys was also founded. After the outbreak of World War I, Świętochowski sided with the Entente. When Poland regained its independence, he rejoined the political fray, vigorously fighting against Piłsudski, working with the National Democrats, and publishing in their *Gazeta Warszawska*. He attacked the national minorities (his aphorism was, "Just because vermin feast on an eagle, they won't grow wings"); he enthusiastically embraced right-wing nationalist Eligiusz Niewiadomski, the assassin of Poland's President **Gabriel Narutowicz**. Świętochowski broke off many old friendships because of his ideological evolution, his disillusionment with democracy, and a certain degree of support for an authoritarian government. However, he firmly criticized Piłsudski's coup d'état in May 1926. He wrote for the opposition press, mainly Christian Democratic papers. Świętochowski published the political pamphlet *Geneaologia teraźniejszości* (The genealogy of the present; 1936) and also the highly valued monograph *Historia chłopów polskich* (The history of Polish peasants, 2 vols.; 1925–28). (AG)

Sources: *Literatura polska: Przewodnik encyklopedyczny*, vol. 2 (Warsaw, 1985); S. Sadler, *Ze studiów na Świętochowskim* (Warsaw, 1957); Jerzy Rudzki, *Aleksander Świetochowski i pozytywizm warszawski* (Warsaw, 1968); Maria Brykalska, *Aleksander Świętochowski: Biografia* (Warsaw, 1987).

ŚWITALSKI Kazimierz (4 March 1886, Sanok–28 December 1962, Warsaw), Polish politician. Świtalski graduated from the University of Lwów (Lviv), where he also received a Ph.D. in philosophy. He was a member of the Union of Active Struggle and the Riflemen's Association. During World War I, from 1914 he served in the Polish Legions, fighting in the Austro-Hungarian Army, and in 1918 he joined the secret Polish Military Organization (Polska Organizacja Wojskowa [POW]). In December 1918, Świtalski became a political adjutant in the General Aide de Camp Office of the Head of State. He was one of the most trusted associates of **Józef Piłsudski**. From March 1919 to December 1921, Świtalski was his political aide and personal assistant, and between July and October 1920 he worked as secretary of the Council of State Defense. Afterwards, he published in the monthly *Droga*. In February 1925, he was dismissed from the army at his own request and participated in the preparations for Piłsudski's coup d'état.

Following the coup of May 1926, in June Świtalski was appointed deputy chief of the Civilian Chancellery of the President of the Polish Republic, fulfilling the function of liaison between Piłsudski and President **Ignacy Mościcki**. Between October 1926 and June 1928, he was director of the Political Department of the Ministry of Interior, organizing the parliamentary elections of 1928. Świtalski belonged to the so-called group of colonels, who supported strong-arm rule by the *sanacja* regime. Between June 1928 and April 1929 Świtalski was minister for religious confessions and public education, and from 14 April until 7 December 1929 he served as prime minister. His premiership coincided with the Great Depression. In 1930, Świtalski directed the *sanacja* campaign in the parliamentary elections and was responsible for abuses in the electoral process. Between 1930 and 1935, he was an MP on behalf of the Nonparty Bloc of Cooperation with the Government. From 1933 through 1935, he was the speaker of the Lower House (Sejm). Świtalski was co-author of the April Constitution and the Electoral Law of 1935, which stripped the political parties of the right to propose candidates for parliamentary deputies. Between 1935 and 1938, the president of Poland appointed him senator and deputy speaker of the Senate. However, his career was already on the wane at that time. Between 1935 and 1936 Świtalski served as the governor of Kraków Province. He co-founded the Józef Piłsudski Institute and became its deputy chairman. Between 1939 and 1945 he was in a German POW camp, Oflag Woldenberg. After the war, in 1945, Świtalski returned to Poland. He was imprisoned by the Communists between 1948 and 1956 but was rehabilitated after his release. Świtalski authored *Diariusz 1919–1935* (Diary 1919–1935; 1992). (JS)

Sources: *Kto był kim w Drugiej Rzeczypospolitej* (Warsaw, 1994); *Encyklopedia historii Polski: Dzieje polityczne*, vol. 2 (Warsaw, 1995); Marian Marek Drozdowski, *Sprawy i ludzie II Rzeczypospolitej: Szkice i polemiki* (Kraków, 1979); Władysław T. Kulesza, *Koncepcje ideowo-polityczne obozu rządzącego w Polsce w latach 1926–1935* (Wrocław, 1985); Wacław Jędrzejewicz, *Kronika życia Józefa Piłsudskiego* (London, 1986); Marian Leczyk, ed., *Sprawa brzeska* (Warsaw, 1987).

SYMONENKO Petro (1 August 1952, Stalino [now Donetsk]), Ukrainian Communist and post-Communist activist. From 1969 to 1974 Symonenko studied at the Donetsk Polytechnic Institute, graduating as a mining electromechanical engineer. He was a designer at an institute of the Dondniprovuglemash Works in Donetsk from 1974 to 1975 and an instructor and department head at the Donetsk City Committee of the Komsomol from 1975 to 1977. Symonenko was second secretary of the Donetsk City Committee of the Komsomol (1977–80), secretary of the Donetsk district committee of the Komsomol (1980–82), and secretary of the Komsomol Central Committee (1982–88). From January 1988 to September 1989 he was secretary of the City Committee of the Communist Party of Ukraine (Komunistychna Partiya Ukraiiny [CPU]) in Zhdanov (now Mariupol). From 1989 to 1990 he served as secretary for ideology. In 1990 he became second secretary of the Donetsk Regional Committee of the CPU. From December 1991 to December 1993 Symonenko was deputy director of the Ukrvuglemash corporation. In 1993 he became first secretary of the Donetsk Regional Committee of the CPU, and on 19 June 1993, at a CPU congress, he was elected first secretary of the CPU CC. He became a deputy to the Supreme Council of Ukraine in 1994 and leader of the CPU parliamentary faction in 1998. In 1999 Symonenko was a CPU candidate for president of Ukraine. In the first round of the presidential elections he came in second, and in the runoff he obtained 37.8 percent of the vote and was defeated by **Leonid Kuchma**. In 2002 Symonenko joined the radical anti-presidential opposition formed by Yulia Tymoshenko and the Socialist Party leader, **Oleksandr Moroz**. He also supported **Viktor Yushchenko** in the presidential elections of 2004. (BB)

Sources: Bohdan Nahaylo, *The Ukrainian Resurgence* (Toronto, 1999); *Khto ie khto v Ukraiini 2000* (Kiev, 2000); Bugajski; *Europa Środkowo-Wschodnia 1999* (Warsaw, 2001).

SYROVÝ Jan (24 January 1888, Třebíč–17 October 1970, Prague), Czech general and politician. After finishing a building school in Brno (1907), Syrový worked in various construction companies in Bohemia and, from 1912, in Russia and Warsaw. After the outbreak of World War I, he joined a Czech military unit in the tsarist army in Kiev; he fought in it from October 1914, initially as an ordinary soldier and then as an officer. In 1917 Syrový joined the Czechoslovak Legion, and, as a company commander, he distinguished himself in the battle of Zborów (Zboriv) in Galicia, in which he lost his right eye. Promoted to brigadier general in 1918, Syrový assumed command of Allied forces in the area of the Legion's operations but was then replaced by French general Pierre Janin, whereupon he was appointed commander of the Legion. Syrový served as commander of the Legion during the fighting in the Urals and Siberia and supervised its evacuation to Czechoslovakia in 1920. From 1920 to 1924 he was commander of the Bohemian military district. He subsequently served as deputy chief and, from 1 January 1926 to 1 December 1933, as chief of the General Staff of the army. Syrový was the first Czechoslovak citizen to hold this post (previously held by representatives of the French military mission). He then served as inspector general of the Czechoslovak military forces for five years. Syrový became major general in 1923 and general of the army in 1926. He greatly contributed to the development of the army, cultivated the Legion's traditions, and helped to develop the military doctrine of the state.

From March to October 1926 and from September 1938 to April 1939 Syrový served as minister of national defense in successive cabinets, and in two of them—the last pre-Munich cabinet and the first post-Munich one (22 September–1 December 1938)—he also served as prime minister. As head of the government, Syrový initially announced the mobilization of the army, but under pressure from the Western powers and when General **Heliodor Píka** had determined that the Western powers were unwilling to help in the case of an outbreak of war with Germany, Syrový was forced to accept the Pact of Munich of 30 September 1938. After President **Edvard Beneš** resigned, Syrový served as president from 5 October to 30 November 1938. After the Nazi occupation began, Syrový retired from public life and moved to the countryside, where he was kept under surveillance by the Gestapo. Nevertheless, in 1945 he was accused of collaboration with the occupiers. In 1947 the People's Tribunal found him guilty of failure to have ordered the destruction of military equipment and failure to preserve the dignity of a Legionnaire after 15 March 1939. Sentenced to twenty years' imprisonment, Syrový was released under an amnesty in 1960. Until his retirement in 1964 he worked as a night watchman. (PU)

Sources: ČBS; Libor Vykoupil, *Slovník českých dějin* (Brno, 2000); *Českoslovenští politici: 1918–1991* (Prague, 1991); *Politická elita meziválečného Československa 1918–1938: Kdo byl kdo za prvni republiky* (Prague, 1998); *Kto bol kto za I. ČSR* (Bratislava, 1993); J. Skácal, *S generálem Syrovým na Sibiři* (Prague, 1923).

SZABÓ Dezső (10 June 1879, Kolozsvár [now Cluj-Napoca], Transylvania–5 or 13 January 1945, Budapest), Hungarian writer and journalist. Born into a Transylvanian Calvinist noble family with strong patriotic traditions, Szabó graduated from the Humanities Department of Budapest University as a member of the Eötvös Collegium, an elite school for particularly gifted youth. After graduation, he worked as a gymnasium teacher and was also engaged in committed journalism. He initially contributed to the periodicals *Nyugat* and *Huszadik Század*. His views were based on Christianity and on his belief in the superiority of folk culture over cosmopolitan urban culture and his hostile attitude toward capitalism and individualism, as well as on racial determinism, which led to anti-Semitic opinions. Supported by great erudition and literary talent, these views gave rise to many heated polemics and press attacks, winning him great popularity. One of the precursors of expressionism in Hungary, Szabó was also the founder of the so-called allegorical novella and one of the more acclaimed Hungarian naturalist prose writers. His most popular work, *Az elsodort falu* (The village that was swept away; 1919)—a novel about life in the Hungarian provinces—is interpreted as praise for the rule of Regent **Miklós Horthy**. In the 1930s, though, in his articles and in the periodicals he founded and edited (*Kritikai Füzetek, Ludas Mátyás Füzetek*), Szabó was aligned with those who protested against Horthy's social conservatism. At that time Szabó expounded his views in a series of eighty essays, each about one hundred pages long, published under the title *Ludas Mátyás Füzetek* (The essays of Matthias Goose) in 1934–42. A selection from this collection was also published under the title *Egész látóhatár* (The whole horizon; 1939). In the 1940s Szabó became an outspoken critic of fascism and Nazism, and he greatly contributed to the dispelling of illusions about Hungary's alliance with Nazi Germany. Seriously ill, Szabó died in solitude during the siege of Budapest by the Red Army. Until the end of the 1960s his name and works seldom appeared in print in Hungary, and when they did, it was in a negative context. (MS)

Sources: Gyula Gombos, *Szabó Dezső* (Munich, 1966); István Király, "Az ellentmondások írója," *Alföld*, 1986; Gáspár Gróh, "A látóhatár egésze," *Hitel*, 1992; Steven Bela Vardy, *Historical Dictionary of Hungary* (Lanham, Md., 1997).

SZABÓ István Nagyatádi (from the town of Nagyatád) (17 September 1863, Erdőcsokonya–1 November 1924, Erdőcsokonya), Hungarian Peasant Party politician. The son of a smallholder, Szabó finished six grades of an elementary school and three grades of supplementary school but then had to give up education owing to financial difficulties. After military service in Budapest (1884–87), he returned to the countryside, where he ran a small farm.

He worked hard, and by the outbreak of World War I he had enough savings to enlarge his farm. From 1889 to 1904 Szabó worked as a judge in his home town. In 1904 he became a member of the local government of Somogy County. In January 1908 he helped to establish the Association of Smallholders of Somogy County and then became its head. A few weeks later he also became a member of the leadership of the Smallholders' Union in Hungary. In that year he also won a parliamentary seat, which he held until the end of his life. Dissatisfied with the policies of the ruling '48 and Independence, in 1909 Szabó co-organized a peasant congress in Nagyatád, where the '48 and Independence National Farmers' Party (48-as és Függetlenségi Országos Gazdapart) was established, and he became its chairman. The program of this party included a demand to expropriate some of the large landed estates.

Fearing that the so-called historical Greater Hungary might disintegrate, Szabó passively observed the revolution of 31 October 1918, and it was not until ten days later that he joined the Hungarian National Council. In November his party was renamed the National Smallholders' Party. The program of the party included a radical agricultural reform and the introduction of universal suffrage and the secret ballot. In January 1919 Szabó became minister for agricultural reform and, one month later, minister of the economy in Dénes Berinkey's government, established after Count **Mihály Károlyi** was elected president. After the Hungarian Soviet Republic (HSR) was established, Szabó returned to the countryside. After the fall of the HSR, he briefly served as minister of agriculture in the government of **István Friedrich** (August 1919). He protested against the "White Terror" and plans to impose a military dictatorship; as a result, he was detained in September but was soon released on the orders of **Miklós Horthy**. Two months later Szabó's party merged with another agrarian party into the Smallholders' and Agrarian Laborers' Party (Országos Kisgazda és Földműves Párt [OKFP]), led by Szabó. Szabó served as minister for supplies (November 1919–August 1920) and minister of agriculture (August 1920–December 1921 and June 1922–October 1924) in the governments of Count **Pál Teleki** and Count **István Bethlen**. From December 1920 to June 1921 he also served as minister for smallholders' affairs.

On the orders of Prime Minister Teleki, Szabó drafted a proposal for agricultural reform that was enacted in November 1920 by the parliament in a form changed for the benefit of large estate owners. Szabó attempted to implement this law—which was linked to his name—but had to make numerous compromises and concessions. In the 1920s, under this law over 400,000 peasants gained on average 2.38 cadastral acres (2.47 acres to one hectare), and over 250,000 peasants received a building plot. In February 1922 Bethlen, along with his supporters, joined the OKFP and then transformed and expanded it as Unity Party (Egységes Párt), which, as the strongest parliamentary force, was the ruling party for over ten years. Szabó formally continued as its leader but actually had no influence in this new party. At the beginning of 1924 Bethlen attempted to force Szabó to resign, accusing him of involvement in a corruption scandal. Although the court was unable to prove anything against Szabó, in October 1924 Szabó resigned and returned to his native village, where he suffered a stroke and died. (JT)

Sources: *Magyar Életrajzi Lexikon*, vol. 2 (Budapest, 1969); *Nagy Képes Milleniumi Arcképcsarnok* (Budapest, 1999); *Die ungarische Agrarreform* (Budapest, 1921); C. A. Macartney, *Hungary and Her Successors* (London, 1937); C. A. Macartney, *October Fifteenth: A History of Modern Hungary, 1920–1945* (Edinburgh, 1961); Joseph Held, ed., *The Modernization of Agriculture: Rural Transformation in Hungary, 1848–1975* (Boulder, Colo., 1980); Ignác Romsics, *Hungary in the Twentieth Century* (Budapest, 1999).

SZABÓ János (17 November 1897, Zaruzsény [now in Romania]–19 January 1957, Budapest), one of the leaders of the Hungarian Revolution of 1956. Born into a poor peasant family from Transylvania, Szabó completed two grades of secondary school and then trained as a locksmith. From 1914 to 1918 he fought in the Austro-Hungarian Army. Under the Hungarian Soviet Republic (March–August 1919), Szabó served as a company commander in the Hungarian Red Army. After Transylvania was incorporated into Romania, he worked as a railwayman there. In 1944 Szabó moved to Hungary and worked as a chauffeur at the Ministry of Agriculture. From 1946 onwards he made a living doing odd jobs. In 1945 he joined the Hungarian Communist Party (HCP), and in 1948–49 he belonged to the Hungarian Workers' Party (HWP). In 1949 Szabó was sentenced to three months' imprisonment for trying to illegally cross the border. Arrested again in 1953 and charged with espionage, he was released after nine months in jail. On 26 October 1956 Szabó joined the insurgents from Széna Square in Budapest and soon became their leader. His group was repeatedly dispersed by Soviet attacks, but each time it resumed fighting. In late October his group moved its headquarters to the barracks of the State Security Authority (Államvédelmi Hatóság [ÁVH]), which had been dissolved by then. Between two Soviet interventions (30 October–4 November) the members of the group led by "Uncle Szabó" (as he was called) kept order and controlled communications. They also searched the homes of security officers and HWP functionaries, many of whom were arrested. Having surrendered Széna Square, his group continued fighting in the outskirts of Budapest. On 19 November Szabó was arrested. He was initially interrogated by KGB officers. On 14 January 1957 the Supreme Court sentenced Szabó, together with **József Dudás**, to death without the right of appeal on charges of leading a conspiracy against "the people's government." Szabó was executed five days later. (JT)

Sources: *A magyar forradalom és szabadságharc enciklopédiája*, CD-ROM (Budapest, 1999); Attila Szakolczay, *Az 1956-os forradalom és szabadságharc* (Budapest, 2001); György Litván, ed., *Rewolucja węgierska 1956 roku* (Warsaw, 1996).

SZAKASITS Árpád (6 December 1888, Budapest–3 May 1965, Budapest), Hungarian Socialist politician who cooperated with the Communists. Born into a very poor family, Szakasits began working as a carpenter and stonemason at the age of thirteen. He became active in the trade union movement before World War I. In 1919, under the Hungarian Soviet Republic, he took part in the plundering of bourgeois houses, as a result of which he was arrested by the Horthy authorities and spent almost one year in prison. Between the two wars Szakasits was a member of the Hungarian Social Democratic Party (Magyarországi Szociáldemokrata Párt [MSP]). In November 1938 he became the MSP secretary general, and from 1939 to 1944 he was the editor-in-chief of its press organ, *Népszava*. From 1941 on Szakasits increasingly sharply protested against the policy of **Miklós Horthy**. As a result of his close relations with the Communists, Szakasits was removed from the leadership of the MSP in June 1942. At the end of 1944, taking advantage of the fact that the MSP leader, **Károly Peyer**, had been imprisoned by the Germans, Szakasits took over the leadership of the MSP with the help of a group of his pro-Communist supporters.

From 1945 to 1948 Szakasits served as minister of state. At the beginning of 1945 he again became secretary general of the MSP and followed a policy of close cooperation with the Communists. He prevented Peyer from regaining the leadership of the party and effected the dismissal of Ágoston Valentiny, the MSP minister of justice who conducted an investigation on crimes committed by the political police. Szakasits also led a campaign against the ruling Independent Smallholders' Party (ISP). In reward, after President **Zoltán Tildy** was forced to resign, Szakasits was made president of Hungary (3 August 1948), and when a Communist constitution came into force, he became chairman of the Presiding Council of the Hungarian People's Republic (August 1949). In June 1948, at the "unification" congress of the two parties of

workers, Szakasits was elected chairman of the newly established Hungarian Workers' Party (Magyar Dolgozók Pártja [MDP]), but he actually did not have any power. The party purge machinery crushed him as well: imprisoned on 24 April 1950, Szakasits was dismissed from his position two weeks later and sentenced to life imprisonment in November 1950. Released in March 1956, Szakasits was rehabilitated four months later, but he was too discredited to play any role in the 1956 revolution. Under the government of **János Kádár** Szakasits served as an MP (from 1958), chairman of the Association of Hungarian Journalists, and deputy chairman and chairman (from 1963) of the Hungarian Peace Council. From 1959 until the end of his life Szakasits was a member of the Central Committee (CC) of the (Communist) Hungarian Socialist Workers' Party, and from 1959 to 1963 he served as chairman of the World Union of Hungarians. (WR)

Sources: *Obituaries from The Times* (Reading, 1975); Ferenc Nagy, *The Struggle behind the Iron Curtain* (New York, 1948); *Szakasits Árpád Válogatott eszédei és írásai* (Budapest, 1966); Ignác Romsics, *Hungary in the Twentieth Century* (Budapest, 1999).

SZÁLASI Ferenc (6 January 1897, Kassa [now Košice, Slovakia]–12 March 1946, Budapest), Hungarian leader of the extreme right-wing nationalists. Szálasi's father was a Transylvanian Armenian by the name of Salosján, and his mother came from a mixed Slovak-Hungarian family. After graduating from the Military Academy in Wiener Neustadt (1915), Szálasi was promoted to lieutenant and fought on the Italian front until 1918. In 1924 he graduated from another military academy. From 1925 on he held various positions in the General Staff in Budapest. In 1930 he joined the Hungarian Life League, a secret organization with a racist program. Promoted to major in 1932, Szálasi began to work in counterintelligence in 1933. In the work "Cél és Követelesék" (Goals and demands; 1933) Szálasi presented his own ideological system, known as Hungarism, which combined extreme populism, nationalism, and anti-Semitism. Like in Nazism, a special role was to be played by the leader, who was best aware of the problems plaguing the nation. Banned from conducting political activities in the army, Szálasi was allowed to retire from the army in 1935. He then founded the Party of National Will (Nemzet Akaratának Pártja), but it was disbanded in April 1937 and Szálasi was sentenced to three months' imprisonment for subversive activities. In March 1938, after his release, he brought about a unification of the extremely rightist groups into the Hungarian National Socialist Party–Hungarist Movement (Magyar Nemzeti Szocialista Párt–Hungarista Mozgalom) and served as its leader. This party gained popularity as a result of its propaganda of territorial revisionism; slogans of radical agricultural reform; and calls for combating Bolshevism, liberalism, plutocracy, and the Jews.

Arrested again in the spring of 1938, Szálasi was sentenced to three years in prison for anti-state activities. In February 1939 his party was declared illegal, but with German financial and political support it was soon revived as the Arrow Cross Party–Hungarist Movement (Nyilaskeresztes Párt–Hungarista Mozgalom); it obtained over one million votes and 12.5 percent of the seats in the elections of May 1939. In 1940 Szálasi was released from prison under an amnesty declared on the occasion of the Second Vienna Award of August 1940, when Hungary regained Northern Transylvania. In the autumn of 1943 the Germans increased their pressure on Regent **Miklós Horthy** because of the increasingly uncertain stance of Hungary as their ally. A day after Horthy failed in an attempt to extricate Hungary from the war (15 October 1944), Szálasi—with the help of German occupation troops—took over power, and Horthy was forced to make him prime minister. On 3 November, as a self-appointed "head of the nation" (*nemzetvezető*), Szálasi combined the powers of head of state and prime minister. His main aim was to continue the war, as he believed in the victory of the Third Reich. He ordered a general mobilization, and the state machine introduced unlimited terror. Many thousands of Jews were killed or deported to extermination camps. Deserters from the front lines and people of anti-Nazi views were imprisoned and executed. As the Red Army approached, Szálasi and his government moved to western Hungary, and at the end of March 1945 he fled to Germany. Captured by U.S. troops on 5 May, Szálasi was returned to Hungary five months later. Brought before the People's Tribunal in Budapest, he was tried for war crimes, sentenced to death on 1 March 1946, and executed. *Szálasi naplója* (Szálasi's diary) was published in Budapest in 1978. (JT)

Sources: *Biographisches Lexikon*, vol. 4; *Magyar Életrajzi Lexikon*, vol. 2 (Budapest, 1969); *Nagy Képes Milleniumi Arcképcsarnok* (Budapest, 1999); *Magyarország 1944–1956*, CD-ROM (Budapest, 2001); C. A. Macartney, *October Fifteenth: A History of Modern Hungary*, vols. 1–2 (Edinburgh, 1957–61); M. Lacko, *Arrow Cross Men, 1935–1944* (Budapest, 1969); Nicholas Nagy-Talavera, *The Green Shirts and the Others* (Stanford, 1970); Elek Karsai and Laszlo Karsai, *A Szálasi-per* (Budapest, 1988); Philip Rees, *Biographical Dictionary of the Extreme Right since 1890* (New York, 1990); Béla Vinceller, *Szálasi hat hónapja* (Budapest, 1996); Steven Bela Vardy, *Historical Dictionary of Hungary* (Lanham, Md., 1997); Ignác Romsics, *Hungary in the Twentieth Century* (Budapest, 1999).

SZAMUELY Tibor (27 December 1890, Nyíregyháza–2 August 1919, Austria), Hungarian Communist activist.

Szamuely came from a Jewish merchant family. He became involved in the worker movement in his youth. After going to Budapest, he worked as deputy editor of a minor anti-clerical periodical, and in 1913 he joined the editorial staff of the Socialist newspaper *Népszava*. At that time he drafted an anti-church pasquinade about a "Country of the Virgin Mary under the Yoke of Priests." Inducted into the army in 1914, Szamuely was taken prisoner by the Russians. In captivity he consolidated his revolutionary views. In January 1918, after his release, he arrived in Moscow, where he met **Béla Kun**. Together they edited Bolshevik papers in Hungarian and campaigned among former Hungarian prisoners of war for a world revolution on the side of Lenin. A political commissar in an international battalion in Moscow, Szamuely often traveled to Switzerland on the orders of the Bolshevik authorities. After a meeting with Lenin in late 1918, Szamuely hatched a plan to seize power in Hungary, and in January 1919 he went to Budapest.

Arrested on suspicion of having committed killings in Russia but then released, from February to March 1919 Szamuely de facto headed the Hungarian Communist Party (HCP), most of whose members were in prison. After an agreement between the Social Democrats and President **Mihály Károlyi** was reached in late March 1919, these Communists were released, and a radical left-wing government was established. Szamuely became deputy commissar for military affairs and commissar for trade and education of the Hungarian Soviet Republic (HSR). He was a member of the radical, terrorist wing of the HSR authorities and served as a liaison officer between these authorities and Lenin. In April 1919 Szamuely was appointed political officer of the Budapest military district. In this role he was responsible for the killings and lynchings of "counterrevolutionaries" and "enemies of the people." He personally led many such actions. In May Szamuely flew to Moscow; from there he brought Lenin's appeal to the Hungarian proletariat. In June 1919 he also briefly served as commissar for production of the short-lived Slovak Soviet Republic. Szamuely's zealotry led to the unleashing of terror, which ended with the fall of the HSR. Szamuely fled Budapest, crossed the Austrian border, and then was killed in unclear circumstances, probably in an encounter with the soldiers of **Miklós Horthy**. (WR)

Sources: Lazitch; *133 Tage ungarischer Bolschewismus, die Herrschaft Bela Kuns und Tibor Szamuellys, die blutigen Ereignisse in Ungarn* (Leipzig, 1920); Rudolf L. Tőkes, *Bela Kun and the Hungarian Soviet Republic* (New York, 1967); Sándorné Gábor, *Szamuely Tibor* (Budapest, 1974); Miklós Zalka, *Szamuely* (Budapest, 1979); György Borsányi, *The Life of a Communist Revolutionary, Bela Kun* (Boulder, Colo., 1993).

SZÁNTÓ Zoltán (17 December 1893, Nagykanizsa–26 March 1977, Budapest), Hungarian Communist activist. The son of a butcher, Szántó graduated from a school of commerce. In 1914, after completing officer training, he was sent to the Galician front. Taken prisoner by the Russians in May 1916, he became involved in the Russian revolutionary movement. After returning to his country, Szántó helped to establish the Hungarian Communist Party (HCP) in November 1918. Under the Hungarian Soviet Republic (HSR) Szántó held a variety of positions, including those of regiment commander in the Hungarian Red Army and political commissar of a division. In the summer of 1919, after the fall of the HSR, Szántó fled to Vienna, where he became a deputy member of the HCP Central Committee (CC) in the spring of 1926. After returning to Hungary, he was arrested in January 1927 and sentenced to eight and a half years in prison. Released in 1935, Szántó emigrated to Moscow, where he worked in the secretariat of the Communist International, and in 1938 he became HCP representative on the Comintern Executive Committee. During World War II he edited Hungarian-language broadcasts for Moscow Radio. In 1944 he became editor-in-chief of the Hungarian Kossuth Radio in Moscow.

After returning to Hungary in June 1945, Szántó became secretary of an HCP committee in northwestern Hungary and a member of parliament (1945–47). He served as ambassador to Belgrade and Tirana (1947–49) and then Paris (until 1954). In May 1945, on behalf of Prime Minister **Imre Nagy**, Szántó organized the Information Office of the Council of Ministers in Budapest and then became its chairman. He also joined the CC of the Hungarian Workers' Party (Magyar Dolgozók Pártja [HWP]). After the fall of Nagy in the spring of 1955, Szántó became ambassador to Warsaw. In late July 1956 he returned to Hungary. At a late-night CC meeting on 23 October 1956 he was elected a member of the HWP Politburo. He soon joined an even more important executive committee of the party. On 30 October on his initiative the Hungarian Socialist Workers' Party (Magyar Szocialista Munkáspárt [HSWP]) was established. The following day Szántó became a member of the seven-member committee of the HSWP. Along with **György Lukács**, he was against Hungary's withdrawal from the Warsaw Pact. On 4 November Szántó was granted asylum in the Yugoslav Embassy in Budapest. On 18 November, like Lukács, he left the embassy building and was arrested by the Russians. On 23 November, together with other members of Nagy's group, Szántó was interned in Romania. He almost immediately dissociated himself from this group, and during the investigations he testified against Nagy and

his associates. After returning to Hungary in the autumn of 1958, Szántó retired. (JT)

Sources: *Magyar Életrajzi Lexikon*, vol. 3 (Budapest, 1981); *A magyar forradalom és szabadságharc enciklopédiája*, CD-ROM (Budapest, 1999); William Shawcross, *Crime and Compromise: Janos Kadar and the Politics of Hungary since Revolution* (New York, 1974); Bennet Kovrig, *Communism in Hungary from Kun to Kádár* (Stanford, 1979); Miklós Molnár, *From Béla Kun to János Kádár: Seventy Years of Hungarian Communism* (New York, 1990).

SZÁSZ Béla (9 July 1910, Szombathely–25 June 1999, Norfolk, England), Hungarian politician. In 1928 Szász began to study at the Department of Economics of the Technical University of Budapest. He later studied Hungarian and French philology and art history at Péter Pázmány Royal Hungarian University in Budapest. In 1930 he began to study at the Sorbonne. While a student, Szász joined the illegal Communist movement and contributed to the periodicals *Virradat* and *Kortárs*. In 1932 the Horthy authorities sentenced Szász to a three-month imprisonment. In 1937 he emigrated to France, where he worked as an assistant to Jean Renoir. He shot films and wrote articles for newspapers. In 1939 he edited *Üzenet*, a Paris-based periodical of Hungarian writers. From 1939 to 1946 Szász lived in Argentina. He worked as a laborer to make ends meet and was a keen photographer. In 1941 he became secretary general of the South American Movement of Free Hungarians and the editor-in-chief of the newspapers *Szabad Magyar Értesítő* and *Új Világ*. After returning to Hungary in 1946, Szász worked as editor of the periodicals *Képes Hét* and *Jövendő*. In 1948 he began working at the Ministry of Foreign Affairs, and in 1949 he was transferred to the Ministry of Agriculture, where he headed a press department.

On 24 May 1949 Szász was arrested on a false charge of spying in connection with the case of **László Rajk**. Despite being tortured, Szász did not plead guilty. Sentenced to ten years' imprisonment in 1950, he was released on 1 September 1954, and then he was rehabilitated. Szász worked as a reviewer of manuscripts submitted to various publishing houses. On 6 October 1956, at the funeral of Rajk and his associates, Szász delivered a funeral speech on behalf of the surviving co-defendants. In 1957 he emigrated again. He initially lived in Vienna and then settled in England. From 1959 to 1963 Szász participated in the work of the Imre Nagy Institute in Brussels. The year 1963 saw the publication of his famous memoirs, *Minden kényszer nélkül: Egy műper története (Volunteers for the Gallows: Anatomy of a Show-Trial*, 1971). This book is still the most credible chronicle of lawlessness surrounding the Rajk trial. It was translated into many languages, but it was not until 1989 that it could be legally published in

Hungary. In 1965 Szász became a commentator for the Hungarian section of the BBC. In 1991 he was honored with the Ius Humana prize, and in 1994 he was awarded the Imre Nagy Commemorative Plaque. (JT)

Sources: *A magyar forradalom és szabadságharc enciklopédiája* (Budapest, 1999).

SZEKFŰ Gyula (23 May 1883, Székesfehérvár–29 June 1955, Budapest), Hungarian historian. In 1904 Szekfű became a history and Latin teacher at the elite Eötvös Collegium and at Budapest University. After earning a Ph.D., he worked at the Hungarian National Museum, and then he began working at the State Archives (1908) and at the Imperial Court Archives in Vienna (1909). In 1916 Szekfű became a visiting lecturer at the university in Budapest. In 1925 he took up the Chair of the Recent History of Hungary there and founded a new school of thought. In 1927 Szekfű founded and, until 1938 edited, the liberal-conservative cultural periodical *Magyar Szemle*, which was highly regarded by the Hungarian intellectual elite. During World War II Szekfű actively opposed Hungary's involvement on the side of the Third Reich. After Germany occupied Hungary in March 1944, he went underground. In 1945 he entered the diplomatic service. He served as ambassador to Moscow until 1948. He became an MP (1953) and a member of the Presiding Council (1954). In 1925 he became a corresponding member and in 1941 a full member of the Hungarian Academy of Sciences.

Szekfű left a very strong mark on twentieth-century Hungarian historiography. He was an opponent of the "laws of history" and emphasized the role of a creative spirit in history. However, he was against a romantic-national understanding of Hungarian history and adhered to the principles of the verification of sources, rational argumentation, and scientific proof. His work *Három nemzedék* (Three generations; 1920) provided historical legitimization for the takeover of power by **Miklós Horthy** after the fall of the Hungarian Soviet Republic; still, Szekfű was less critical of the role of the Habsburgs in Hungarian history than other authors. Szekfű played a major role in raising the nineteenth-century poet Sándor Petőfi to the position of the greatest figure in Hungarian history. From the 1930s on Szekfű openly criticized fascism from the conservative and Christian points of view. He presented a pessimistic vision of social evolution in *Három nemzedék és ami utána következik* (Three generations and what comes next; 1934). Although Marxists sharply criticized him, Szekfű was the only eminent prewar Hungarian historian who neither emigrated nor was imprisoned after the Communists came to power. Communist historiography accepted many of his views on Hungarian history and its heroes. Among Szekfű's other major works are the following: *Petőfi centenárium* (The one hundredth birthday of Petőfi; 1924); *A magyar állam életrajza* (Curriculum vitae of the Hungarian state; 1917); *Magyar történet* (Hungarian history, 8 vols.; 1929–33 [co-authored with Bálint Hóman]); *Állam és nemzet* (State and nation; 1942); *Valahol utat vesztettünk* (We lost our way somewhere; 1942–43); and *Az öreg Kossuth* (The old Kossuth; 1952). (MS)

Sources: *Biographisches Lexikon*, vol. 4; Sándor Pethő, *Szekfű Gyula történetírása* (Budapest, 1933); László Németh, *Szekfű Gyula* (Budapest, 1940); Ferenc Glatz, *Történetíró és politika* (Budapest, 1980); Irene Raab Epstein, *Szekfű Gyula: A Study in the Political Basis of Hungarian Historiography* (New York, 1987); Ferenc Glatz, *Nemzeti kultúra—kultúrált nemzet* (Budapest, 1988); Steven Bela Vardy, *Historical Dictionary of Hungary* (Lanham, Md., 1997).

SZÉLL Kálmán (8 June 1843, Gasztony–16 August 1915, Rátót), Hungarian politician. Born into a lesser gentry family, Széll received a law degree from Budapest University. In 1861 he passed an official exam and two years later earned a Ph.D. In 1867 he became deputy head of Vas County. In the same year he married. His wife—a daughter of Mihály Vörösmarty, the finest Hungarian Romantic poet—had been brought up by Ferenc Deák, one of the greatest nineteenth-century Hungarian politicians and the co-author of the Compromise (Ausgleich) of 1867, by which the Dual Monarchy of Austria-Hungary was established. Elected to the parliament on the slate of the ruling party in 1868, Széll served as an MP until 1911. From 1875 to 1878 he was minister of finance. He then became the managing director and chairman of the Mortgage Bank, which under his management became one of the most important banks in Hungary. On his Rátót estate, he created a model farm, famous for cattle breeding. On 26 February 1899 Széll became prime minister of Hungary. At the beginning of 1903, as a result of his efforts, an agreement on the restoration of economic union between Austria and Hungary, necessary for the maintenance of the monarchy, was signed with the Austrian prime minister, Ernst von Körber (hence it is also known as the Széll-Körber Compact). When Francis Joseph, emperor of Austria and king of Hungary, soon insisted on an increase in military spending and on the recruitment of Hungarians into a common army, the parliamentary opposition reacted by stonewalling and demanding that first Hungarian be introduced as the language of military service and in the commands of military units stationed in Hungary. As a result of this parliamentary obstruction, on 27 June 1903 the government collapsed. In 1905 Széll left the Liberal Party (Szabadelvű Párt), which lost the elections after having been in power for thirty years. He then went over to the Constitutional Party (Alkotmánypárt), which was a part of the "national coalition" that ruled the country from 1906 to 1910. Széll became chairman of the Constitutional Party and held this post until 1910. He later refused to take part in governing the state and devoted himself to business. (JT)

Sources: *Magyar Életrajzi Lexikon*, vol. 2 (Budapest, 1969); *Nagy Képes Milleniumi Arcképcsarnok* (Budapest, 1999); *Biographisches Lexikon*, vol. 4; Paul Ignotus, *Hungary* (London, 1972); *Magyarország történeti kronológiája*, vol. 3 (Budapest, 1983); Steven Bela Vardy, *Historical Dictionary of Hungary* (Lanham, Md., 1997).

SZENT-GYÖRGYI Albert (16 September 1893, Budapest–22 October 1986, Woods Hole, Massachusetts), Hungarian biochemist, winner of the 1937 Nobel Prize for physiology or medicine, representative of the fourth generation of scholars in the family. While a student at the University of Budapest (1911–17), Szent-Györgyi became interested in morphology, conducting independent research on tissue samples in the family's Lenhossék Institute. After earning a medical degree, he underwent further training and conducted research at the Universities of Bratislava, Prague, Berlin, Leiden, Groningen, and Oxford, earning a Ph.D. in 1927. In 1928 Szent-Györgyi identified vitamin C as ascorbic acid, which he isolated from paprika, and in 1933 he established its chemical structure. From 1931 to 1945 he was a professor at the University of Szeged. Using his scholarly authority and international connections, Szent-Györgyi joined the diplomatic efforts of **Miklós Kállay**'s government to extricate Hungary from World War II. In 1943 he traveled to Turkey to negotiate with the representatives of the Western powers, but these negotiations were only a qualified success, partly as a result of a restrained response from the Allies and partly because of a failure to keep this mission secret from the Germans. From 1945 to 1947 Szent-Györgyi taught at the University of Budapest. He also served as vice-president of the Hungarian Academy of Sciences (until 1948). In 1947 he left for the United States, where he became a recognized authority in the biochemistry of muscles and the mechanisms of cell respiration. From the mid-1960s onwards he occasionally visited Hungary for scholarly purposes. From the mid-1970s on his works began to be published in Hungary again. After his death, the Medical University in Szeged was named after him. Szent-Györgyi's most important works include *Muscular Contraction* (1947), *Az élet jellege* (The essence of life; 1975), and *Introduction to a Submolecular Biology* (1960). (MS)

Sources: *Nowa encyklopedia powszechna PWN*, vol. 6 (Warsaw, 1996); Ferenc Nagy, *Szent-Györgyi Albert és a magyar Nobeldíjasok* (Budapest, 1993); Tibor Szabó, *Szent-Györgyi Albert and Szeged* (Szeged, 1993); Endre Czeizel, *Szent-Györgyi Albert* (Budapest, 1997); Steven Bela Vardy, *Historical Dictionary of Hungary* (Lanham, Md., 1997).

SZEPTYCKI Stanisław (3 November 1867, Przyłbice, near Jaworów–9 October 1950, Korczyn), Polish general. Szeptycki came from an aristocratic family. He was the brother of **Andriy Sheptytskyi**, the Greek Catholic archbishop metropolitan of Lviv (Lwów). He graduated from high School in Kraków, the Military Technical Academy in Vienna (1888), the Higher Cavalry School (1892), and the School of the General Staff (1896). Gradually advancing in the Austro-Hungarian Army, Szeptycki first became chief of staff of an infantry brigade and then, in 1904, military attaché in Russia as an observer at the Russian-Japanese front. Upon his return in 1906, he was appointed chief of staff of a cavalry division and, in 1912, military attaché to Italy. During World War I Szeptycki served on the Supreme Command and then became chief of staff of the Second Corps. At the end of 1915 he was transferred to lead the Thirtieth Artillery Brigade. On 16 July 1916 he was appointed commander-in-chief of the Third Brigade of the Polish Legions, on 1 August deputy commander of the Legions, and on 21 November commander of the Legions. Because of their differences regarding the Central Powers, Szeptycki clashed with **Józef Piłsudski**. Whereas Szeptycki was loyal to the Austro-Hungarian leadership, Piłsudski played a complex political game. Between April 1917 and February 1918, Szeptycki served as the Austro-Hungarian governor general in Lublin. He quit his post to protest the Treaty of Brest-Litovsk between the Central Powers and the Bolsheviks. The treaty limited the territory of the Kingdom of Poland, severing the Chełm (Kholm) area from it. Subsequently, Szeptycki was transferred to the Italian front.

At the end of October 1918, Szeptycki arrived in Warsaw, where he was appointed by the Regency Council to become the inspector general of the Polish Army in the making. When, upon his release from Magdeburg Prison Piłsudski appeared in Warsaw, Szeptycki handed him the reins of command over the Polish Army, and he became chief of the General Staff. At the beginning of 1919, Szeptycki nipped a rightist coup in the bud in Warsaw. On 7 February 1919, he tendered his resignation, protesting the Piłsudskite "political intrigues" aimed against him. He took over the command of the Lithuanian-Belorussian Division and, as of April 1919, the Lithuanian-Belorussian front in the struggle against the Bolsheviks. In June 1919, Szeptycki was promoted to the rank of major general. In

July 1920 he led the Fourth Army. During the retreat of the Polish troops, a serious clash occurred between Szeptycki and Piłsudski over the command of the military. Following the peace treaty of Riga with Soviet Russia, in March 1921 Szeptycki became the army inspector in Kraków, and in 1922 he led the Polish units to Upper Silesia, which was awarded to Poland by the Council of Ambassadors. Between June and December 1923 he was minister of military affairs with the center-right government of **Wincenty Witos**, but afterward he returned to his post as the army inspector in Kraków. After the coup d'état of May 1926, Szeptycki resigned his commission and was shifted to the inactive reserves, completely withdrawing from public life. (WR)

Sources: *Kto był kim w Drugiej Rzeczypospolitej* (Warsaw, 1994); *Encyklopedia historii Drugiej Rzeczypospolitej* (Warsaw, 1999); Tadeusz Kryska-Karski and Stanisław Żurakowski, *Generałowie Polski Niepodległej* (London, 1976); Norman Davies, *White Eagle, Red Star: The Polish-Soviet War, 1919–20* (London, 1972); Andrzej Nowak, *Polska i trzy Rosje: Studium o polityce wschodniej Józefa Piłsudskiego (do kwietnia 1920 roku)* (Kraków, 2001).

SZIGETHY Attila (10 March 1912, Kapuvár–12 August 1957, Győr), one of the leaders of the Hungarian Revolution of 1956. After completing secondary school, Szigethy became a notary. In the mid-1930s he sympathized with the peasant movement, and in 1939 he joined the National Peasant Party (Nemzeti Parasztpárt [NPP]). In 1943 he attended a meeting in Balatonszárszó at which representatives of various orientations (from Catholics and peasants to Communists) condemned Nazism and the regime of **Miklós Horthy**. After Germany occupied Hungary (March 1944) and the Arrow Cross Party came to power (October 1944), Szigethy sheltered people who were being persecuted, including **István Dobi**. In 1944 he joined the activities of the Peace Party, which served as a cover for the Communist Party. A local leader of the NPP after the war and a member of parliament from 1947 to 1957, Szigethy was obedient to the Communists. From 1950 to 1954 he was vice-president of the National Council of Győr-Sopron County. In late 1954, as a supporter of the reforms of Prime Minister **Imre Nagy**, Szigethy was dismissed from his position and appointed director of a state farm in Győr-Sopron County.

On 26 October 1956 Szigethy was elected president of the newly established Provisional National Council in Győr. During the revolution he tried to maintain order and prevent bloodshed in this city. On 28 October he demanded that Nagy abolish the Office of State Security (Állam-védelmi Hatóság [ÁVH]), call multiparty parliamentary elections, and enter into negotiations on the withdrawal of

Soviet troops from Hungary. On 30 October, by mobilizing the employees of Győr's big factories and soldiers of local units of the Hungarian Army, Szigethy successfully thwarted an attempted putsch against Nagy's government. On that day the Transdanubian National Council was established, and on the following day Szigethy was elected its chairman. Some leaders, including **József Dudás**, wanted to turn this council into a counter-government to Nagy's cabinet, but Szigethy rejected this idea. On 2 November he headed the council's delegation at negotiations with Nagy in Budapest. After an agreement was reached, Szigethy called on Győr's workers to cooperate. After the second Soviet intervention (4 November), Szigethy went into hiding for a few days, but then he returned to Győr and tried to prevent the arrests of local leaders of the revolution. After the uprising was suppressed, **János Kádár** attempted to win Szigethy over and offered him the post of government commissioner or minister, but Szigethy rejected this offer. In February 1957 Szigethy went with an official delegation of the Patriotic People's Front to Bulgaria. Arrested on 3 May 1957, he was deprived of his parliamentary seat six days later. Before his trial began, Szigethy committed suicide after several unsuccessful attempts. (JT)

Sources: *A magyar forradalom és szabadságharc enciklopédiája*, CD-ROM (Budapest, 1999); Attila Szakolczay, *Az 1956-os forradalom és szabadságharc* (Budapest, 2001); Tibor Méray, *Thirteen Days That Shook the Kremlin* (New York, 1959); Paul E. Zinner, *Revolution in Hungary* (New York, 1962); György Litván, ed., *Rewolucja węgierska 1956 roku* (Warsaw, 1996).

SZILÁGYI József (24 April 1917, Debrecen–24 April 1958, Budapest), Hungarian Communist activist, one of the leaders of the Hungarian Revolution of 1956. Szilágyi graduated from a high school run by the Evangelical Reformed Church, and in 1939 in Debrecen he received a diploma in law. In 1937, while a student, he joined the leftist March Front, and in 1938 he became a member of the Communist Party, which was illegal at that time. Arrested in the spring of 1940, Szilágyi was sentenced to three years' imprisonment for trying to overthrow the system. Released in March 1944, he remained in hiding until the end of World War II. After the war, he became the chief of police in Debrecen and later organized the national command of the police. From 1947 to 1948 Szilágyi served as head of the Security and Army Department of the Central Committee (CC) of the Hungarian Communist Party (HCP) and then of the Hungarian Workers' Party (Magyar Dolgozók Pártja [HWP]). In 1949 Szilágyi questioned the credibility of the trial of **László Rajk** and his associates; as a result, he was removed from his position, and from

1950 he worked as head of a department in a company that sold agricultural products. In July 1953 he became a co-worker of Prime Minister **Imre Nagy**. After Nagy was forced out of office, Szilágyi was expelled from the HWP at the beginning of 1956.

On 13 October 1956 Szilágyi spoke on behalf of his friends and brothers-in-arms at the ceremonial funeral of officers who had been the victims of the regime of **Mátyás Rákosi**. On 22 October he spoke at a rally held by students of Budapest Technical University; at the rally a decision was made to demonstrate in solidarity with the Poles. During the first days of the revolution Szilágyi worked with **Sándor Kopácsi** in the Budapest Department of the Ministry of Interior, and he negotiated with delegations of the insurgents, trying to limit the number of victims. Szilágyi was one of the aides of Prime Minister Nagy who convinced him to change political direction (27 October). He subsequently organized and headed Nagy's secretariat. On 4 November Szilágyi found refuge in the Yugoslav Embassy, and on 22 November, along with other members of the Nagy group, he was interned in Romania. On 27 March 1957 he was brought back to Budapest. During the investigation Szilágyi refused to answer questions, as he believed the proceedings were illegal, and he went on a hunger strike. Because of this, his case was excluded from the trial of the Nagy group. On 22 April 1958 the Supreme Court sentenced Szilágyi to death without the right of appeal on charges of leading a conspiracy against "the government of the people." Szilágyi was executed two days later. Information about his execution was not announced to the public until June 1958, when a communiqué was issued about the trial and execution of Nagy and his associates, together with whom Szilágyi was ceremonially reburied in June 1989 in Budapest. (JT)

Sources: *A magyar forradalom és szabadságharc enciklopédiája*, CD-ROM (Budapest, 1999); Attila Szakolczay, *Az 1956-os forradalom és szabadságharc* (Budapest, 2001); Ferenc A. Vali, *Rift and Revolt in Hungary* (Cambridge, Mass., 1961); Paul E. Zinner, *Revolution in Hungary* (New York, 1962); Paul Ignotus, *Hungary* (London, 1972); György Litván, ed., *Rewolucja węgierska 1956 roku* (Warsaw, 1996).

SZLACHCIC Franciszek (5 February 1920, Byczyna, near Chorzów–4 November 1990, Warsaw), Polish Communist activist. As a young man, Szlachcic worked at the Jaworzno coal mine as a porter. During World War II, he joined the secret (Communist) People's Guard and then the People's Army. In 1943, he became a member of the Polish Workers' Party. After 1945 he worked in the Communist police, in both the uniformed Civic Militia and the plain clothes' Security Office. Among other functions, Szlachcic headed the Provincial Office of Public Security

in Olsztyn. In 1953 he graduated from the Party School of the Central Committee (CC) of the Polish United Workers' Party (Polska Zjednoczona Partia Robotnicza [PUWP]), in 1956 from the Higher Military School in Moscow, and in 1960 from the Coal Mining–Steel Works Academy in Kraków. At the time, Szlachcic was a close aide of **Mieczysław Moczar**. From May 1962 to February 1971, Szlachcic served as deputy minister of interior. In 1963, he was promoted to brigadier general of the Civic Militia. In 1964 he became a deputy member of the PUWP CC, maintaining close contact with the representatives of the Soviet secret services. During the spring of 1968, he directed the police pacifications of student demonstrations. In November 1968, he became a full member of the PUWP CC. In December 1970, he played a significant role in the ousting of **Władysław Gomułka** and his replacement by **Edward Gierek**. During the struggle between Moczar and Gierek, Szlachcic supported the latter, and in 1971 he was coopted to the top leadership. He supported the policy of openness toward the West and became a patron of some of the conformists among the intelligentsia. In December 1971 Szlachcic became secretary and member of the Politburo. He supervised the militia and the secret police. Between February and December 1971 he served as minister of interior, and from 1972 through 1974, he sat on the Council of State. By the beginning of 1974, Szlachcic had become the most serious rival to Gierek, and he became the target of attacks of the supporters of the first secretary. In May 1974 Szlachcic became deputy prime minister, but in the following month he was dismissed from the CC Secretariat and the Council of State. In December 1975 he was expelled from the Politburo and the PUWP CC. He became head of the Polish Committee of Norms and Measures (from 1979, the Polish Committee of Norms, Measures, and Quality), keeping his post until 1985. Szlachcic published *Gorzki smak władzy: Wspomnienia* (A bitter taste of power: Memoirs; 1990). (PK)

Sources: Mołdawa; *Słownik polityków polskich XX wieku* (Poznań, 1998); Witalij Pawłow, *Generał Pawłow: Byłem rezydentem KGB w Polsce* (Warsaw, 1994); Janusz Rolicki, *Edward Gierek: Przerwana dekada* (Warsaw, 1990); Krzysztof Lesiakowski, *Mieczysław Moczar: Biografia polityczna* (Warsaw, 1998); Włodzimierz Janowski and Aleksander Kochański, *Informator o strukturze i obsadzie personalnej centralnego aparatu PZPR 1948–1990* (Warsaw, 2000).

SZŐCS Géza (21 August 195,3 Târgu-Mureş [Marosvásárhely], Transylvania), Hungarian poet and politician from Transylvania. Szőcs graduated in Hungarian and Russian languages and literatures from Babeş-Bolyai University in Cluj. In 1974 he became an editor of and contributor to leading Hungarian-language periodicals in Romania. In 1980 he became editor of the samizdat periodical *Ellenpontok*, as a result of which he was persecuted. In 1986 Szőcs emigrated to Switzerland, where he worked with Hungarian and Romanian pro-independence communities and for Radio Free Europe. From 1989 to 1990 Szőcs was director of the Budapest section of Radio Free Europe. In 1990 he returned to Romania, where he became senator and secretary general of the Democratic Alliance of Hungarians in Romania (DAHR), the largest Hungarian minority organization in Romania. Szőcs later served as vice-chairman of the DAHR and was a member of its radical wing. In 1992 he became director of the Transylvanian Press, Book, and Information Publishing House. Since 1974 Szőcs has been publishing poems in which he often draws on fairy tale and surrealistic motifs for inspiration. He has authored the following poetry volumes: *Te mentél át a vízen?* (Did you walk on water? 1975); *Kilátótorony és környéke* (The observation tower and the surrounding area; 1977); *Ki cserélte el a népet?* (Who has exchanged our nation? 1996); and *Passió* (Passion; 1999). (MS)

Sources: Éva Blénesi, *Géza Szőcs* (Pozsony, 2000); *Új magyar irodalmi lexikon* (Budapest, 2000); Bugajski.

SZTÓJAY Döme [originally Stojaković] (5 January 1883, Versec [now Vršac, Serbia]–22 August 1946, Budapest), Hungarian general, war criminal. Born into a Serbian family in Temes County (now Timiş, Romania), in 1902 Sztójay graduated from a cadet school in Pécs and then continued military studies in Budapest. After doing his military service in various units, he studied at the Military Academy in Vienna (1907–10). In 1910 he was assigned to staff work. During World War I, until 1917 he was in the staff that commanded units in Bosnia and Herzegovina and in Dalmatia. He subsequently served as commander of the Twenty-first Mountain Brigade and head of the Balkan group in the intelligence department of the army high command. After the victory of the Hungarian republican revolution in October 1918, Sztójay became head of the intelligence, counterintelligence, and records department of the Ministry of Military Affairs. Under the Hungarian Soviet Republic (HSR) in 1919 he served as chief of intelligence and counterintelligence of the Hungarian Red Army. After the collapse of the HSR, he again became chief of intelligence in the Ministry of Military Affairs, and then, in November 1919, he was appointed chief of an intelligence group of the command of the National Army led by **Miklós Horthy**. From July 1920 to 1925 Sztójay was chief of the department of intelligence and counterintelligence. In 1925 he became military attaché with the rank of colonel of the general staff at the legation in Berlin.

In 1933 Sztójay became general. In December 1935 he was appointed ambassador to Berlin. Representing Hungary in the Third Reich, he was fully convinced that it was most beneficial for Hungary's interests to establish as close relations with Nazi Germany as possible. After Nazi troops occupied Hungary (22 March 1944), the Germans demanded that Sztójay be appointed prime minister, as well as minister of foreign affairs. As head of the government, Sztójay subordinated Hungary to the Germans. The opposition parties were disbanded; total press censorship was imposed; the Jews were first confined to ghettos, and then deportations to concentration camps began. The number of Hungarian soldiers fighting on the front increased to three hundred thousand. It was not until late June 1944 that Horthy stood up against Sztójay, banning further deportations of the Budapest Jews. On 29 August 1944, after Romania switched to the Allied side, Horthy dismissed Sztójay, who withdrew from public life. After Horthy resigned as regent and the Arrow Cross Party took over power, Sztójay did not accept any positions, yet in November 1944 he was promoted to lieutenant general in retirement. At the beginning of 1945 he fled to Germany, where he was arrested by the Americans in May 1945 and handed over to Hungary in October 1945. The People's Tribunal declared Sztójay a war criminal because of the directives he had issued as prime minister and on 22 March 1946 sentenced him to death by firing squad. The sentence was upheld by the appellate court and carried out in a prison in Budapest. (JT)

Sources: *Magyar Életrajzi Lexikon*, vol. 2 (Budapest, 1969); *Biographisches Lexikon*, vol. 4; Miklos Horthy, *Memoirs* (New York, 1954); *A magyar forradalom és szabadságharc enciklopédiája* (Budapest, 1999).

SZWALBE Stanisław (3 June 1898, Warsaw–17 September 1996, Warsaw), Polish Socialist and cooperative activist. Szwalbe came from an intelligentsia family and graduated from the University of Warsaw. Between 1917 and 1922 he was a member of the Polish Socialist Party (Polska Partia Socjalistyczna [PPS]). He was active in cooperative organizations, including the Union of Workers' Cooperative Societies (1919–25), the Społem (Togetherness) Union of Consumer Cooperatives, the Warsaw Building Cooperative (which he founded in 1922), and the Social Building Undertaking. Szwalbe belonged to the Society of the Workers' University (1928–39) and the Workers' Society of the Friends of Children (1928–39). Between 1927 and 1930, he lectured at the Free Polish Academy in Warsaw, and from 1928 through 1936 he sat on the board of the Institute of Social Economy.

During World War II, Szwalbe became a leader of the Workers' Party of Polish Socialists (Robotnicza Partia Polskich Socjalistów [RPPS]), working closely with the Communists. In May 1944, he became chairman of the RPPS Supreme Council and in February 1945 deputy chairman of the Central Executive Committee of the Communist-sponsored PPS. On 1 January 1944 Szwalbe joined the Communist-led Home National Council (Krajowa Rada Narodowa [KRN]). In May 1945, he was appointed its deputy chairman. In June 1945, he participated in a KRN delegation to Moscow for negotiations over the composition of the Provisional Government of National Unity. Szwalbe approved of the tactics of the Kremlin and the (Communist) Polish Workers' Party (PPR). Between July 1945 and September 1945, he chaired the PPS Supreme Council. Following the falsified elections of January 1947, Szwalbe became an MP and was appointed deputy speaker of the Assembly. During the "unification of the workers' movement"—which meant the absorption of the PPS by the Communists—Szwalbe developed some doubts in 1948, but eventually he supported the unification tactics of the PPR. Between December 1948 and March 1954, Szwalbe was a member of the Central Committee (CC) of the Polish United Workers' Party (Polska Zjednoczona Partia Robotnicza [PUWP]), and he also participated in its Central Revisory Commission. Purged from the leadership during the second party congress in 1954, Szwalbe remained in the leadership of the cooperative institutions. From 1949 to 1953 he chaired the Supervisory Council of Społem, and between 1953 and 1955 he chaired the Council of the Central Union of Labor Cooperatives. In 1957 he became deputy chairman of the Supreme Cooperative Council and a year later a deputy chairman of the Cooperative Research Institute. Szwalbe published *Wspomnienia i komentarze* (Recollections and comments; 1996). (JS)

Sources: Mołdawa; *Wielka Encyklopedia Powszechna*, vol. 11 (Warsaw, 1968); Krystyna Kersten, *Narodziny systemu władzy: Polska 1943–1948* (Poznań, 1990); Andrzej Albert [Wojciech Roszkowski], *Najnowsza historia Polski 1914–1993*, vol. 2 (Warsaw, 1995).

SZYDLAK Jan (24 November 1925, Siemianowice), Polish Communist activist. Szydlak finished a secondary school. He joined the Polish Workers' Party (Polska Partia Robotnicza [PPR]) in 1945 and the Polish United Workers' Party (Polska Zjednoczona Partia Robotnicza [PUWP]) in December 1948. He was an active member of the Union of Fighting Youth and the Union of Polish Youth operating in Silesia, Kielce, Szczecin, and other areas. In 1951 Szydlak finished the Party School of the Central Committee (CC) of the PUWP and began his party career in Silesia. He headed the Propaganda Department of the PUWP Provincial Committee in Katowice (1951–52) and served as its secretary (1952–54). For two years he served as secretary of the Main Board of the Union of Polish Youth, and then he was again secretary of the PUWP Provincial Committee in Katowice from 1957 to 1960. He was a deputy member (1954–64) and then a member of the PUWP CC. He also served as first secretary of the PUWP Provincial Committee in Poznań (1960–68) and as an MP in the Assembly (1961–80). In 1968 Szydlak took part in a propaganda campaign against intellectuals and students who were on strike. He became secretary of the CC and a deputy member of the PUWP CC Politburo in November 1968 and a member of the PUWP CC Politburo in December 1970. One of the closest associates of **Edward Gierek**, Szydlak was in charge of (among other things) economic policy and ideology. In 1973 and in 1976 he was considered as a candidate for prime minister. In 1971 Szydlak headed a special party commission to investigate the circumstances of the 1970 strikes on the Baltic Coast, but the commission formulated only superficial conclusions. Szydlak was secretary of the All-Polish Committee of the National Unity Front (1970–72) and chairman of the Main Board of the Polish-Soviet Friendship Society (1974–80). In November 1977 Szydlak left the PUWP CC Secretariat. From December 1976 to February 1980 he served as deputy prime minister and subsequently held the post of chairman of the Central Council of Trade Unions (Centralna Rada Związków Zawodowych) for several months. Szydlak left the Politburo in August 1980 and the CC in October 1980. (PK)

Sources: Mołdawa; Krzysztof Lesiakowski, *Mieczysław Moczar: Biografia polityczna* (Warsaw, 1998); Włodzimierz Janowski and Aleksander Kochański, *Informator o strukturze i obsadzie personalnej centralnego aparatu PZPR 1948–1990* (Warsaw, 2000); Antoni Czubiński, *Dzieje Najnowsze Polski 1944–1989* (Poznań, 1992).

SZYMANOWSKI Karol (6 October 1882, Tymoszówka, Ukraine–29 March 1937, Lausanne, Switzerland), Polish composer. In 1889, Szymanowski began to take piano lessons with his father and then in the music academy of Gustav Neuhaus in Yelizavetgrad. He graduated from high school in 1900. Between 1901 and 1905, he studied composing with Zygmunt Noskowski and Marek Zawirski in Warsaw. In 1905 he co-founded the Partnership of Young Composers. Later dubbed "Young Poland," the partnership organized concerts and published musical works. Szymanowski's *C-minor Piano Sonata* received an award at a Chopin competition in Lemberg (Lwów, Lviv) in 1910. Szymanowski traveled abroad quite a bit, and he gave concerts in Germany, Italy, Austria, Algeria, France, and Great Britain. In 1914 he returned to his home estate of Tymoszówka, where he spent the war. Because of the anarchy and peasant attacks on manor houses in the Ukraine, Szymanowski sought shelter in Yelizavetgrad, and in 1919 he moved to Warsaw. Between 1920 and 1921, he and the famous violinist Paweł Kochański traveled to the United States twice. In 1922 Szymanowski began visiting Zakopane as he became interested in Polish high-landers' music. From 1927 to 1929 Szymanowski served as director of the Warsaw Conservatory and between 1930 and 1932 as president of the Higher Music Academy in Warsaw. In 1930 he received an honorary doctorate in philosophy from the Jagiellonian University in Kraków. In 1935 he was awarded the State Music Prize. Despite tubercular bouts, Szymanowski performed in many European countries, including France, Belgium, Holland, Italy, Yugoslavia, Bulgaria, Germany, Denmark, Sweden, Norway, and the Soviet Union. Szymanowski died of tuberculosis at a sanatorium in Lausanne and was buried in the Crypt of the Distinguished at the Church of the Pauline Fathers on Skałka in Kraków. Szymanowski was an honorary member of the Czech Academy of Arts and Sciences, the Royal Academy of St. Cecilia in Rome, the Royal Music Academy in Belgrade, and the International Society of Contemporary Music.

Szymanowski's artistic output can be divided into three periods: early (until 1914), middle (Impressionistic), and late (dubbed "national"). The early period was characterized by the influences of Frédéric Chopin, Alexander Skryabin, Richard Wagner, Max Reger, and Richard Strauss. In this period Szymanowski created the variations for piano, *First Symphony* (1917), *Second Symphony* (1910), many chants (for example, *The Love Chants of Hafisa*; 1911), and the opera *Hagith* (1913). After a trip to Italy and a sojourn in Paris and London in 1914, Szymanowski fell under the influence of Impressionism. During World War I he wrote the *Demeter* cantata; a piece for piano, *Metopy*; a piece for violin, *Myths* (1915); the *First Violin Concerto* (1916); the *Third Symphony* (1916); and the *Third Piano Sonata* (1917). After the war, Szymanowski's compositions also reflect Eastern influences (*The Chants of the Mad Muezin*, 1918; the ballet *Mandragora*, 1920; chants to the lyrics of Rabindranath Tagore), as well as the influence of Claude Debussy and Maurice Ravel (*Nocturne and Tarantella* and the opera *King Roger*; 1926). After 1924, the dominant element in his works was Polish Kurpie and Podhale folklore, as well as Polish Renaissance music (*Mazurkas for the piano*, 1926; *The Kurpie Chants*, 1929; *Stabat Mater*, 1926; *Fourth Symphony*, 1932; *Second Violin Concerto*, 1932; the ballet *Harnasie* [Highland bandits], 1933).

Considered the greatest Polish composer of the first half of the twentieth century, Szymanowski achieved European fame thanks to the richness of his style and individualism, which absorbed the various eclectic influences of his times but always in his own, easily detectable, personal way. Szymanowski expounded his artistic credo in the novel *Efebos* (1918). His treatise *Wychowawcza rola muzyki w społeczeństwie* (The educational role of music in the society; 1925) still remains valuable. Posthumously, the following works of Szymanowski were published: *Pisma muzyczne* (Musical writings; 1984), *Pisma literackie* (Literary writings; 1994), and four volumes of *Korespondecja* (Correspondence; 2002). (JS)

Sources: *Mała encyklopedia muzyki* (Warsaw, 1960); Teresa Chylińska, *Szymanowski i jego muzyka* (Warsaw, 1980); Jerzy Waldorff, *Serce w płomieniach: Opowieść o Karolu Szymanowskim* (Warsaw, 1980); Krystyna Dąbrowska, *Karol z Atmy* (Warsaw, 1982); Maciej Pinkwart, *Zakopiańskim szlakiem Karola Szymanowskiego* (Warsaw, 1988); Teresa Chylińska, *Karol Szymanowski: His Life and Works* (Los Angeles, 1993); Alistair Wightman, *Karol Szymanowski: His Life and Work* (Ashgate, 1999); Kornel Michałowski, *Karol Szymanowski: Bibliografia, 1967–1991, Dyskografia, 1981–1991* (Kraków, 1993).

SZYMBORSKA Wisława (2 July 1923, Bnin [now a part of the town of Kórnik]), Polish poet. Between 1945 and 1948 Szymborska studied Polish literature and sociology at the Jagiellonian University in Kraków. She made her debut as a poet in 1945. Her first volume of poetry, *Dlatego żyjemy* (That's why we are alive), of a didactic and propagandist character, was published in 1952, and her second collection of poems, *Pytania zadawane sobie* (Questions put to myself), appeared in 1954. Initially deeply involved in the Communist reality, Szymborska was on the editorial staff of the weekly *Życie Literackie* from 1952 to 1966, contributing a regular book review column titled "Lektury nadobowiązkowe" (Nonrequired reading) from 1968 to 1981. A collection of these columns was published in 1973 under the same title. From the mid-1950s on, Szymborska gradually abandoned references to modern politics and switched to a personal lyric poetry written in an intellectual and moralizing style. She published further volumes of verse: *Wołanie do Yeti* (Calling out to Yeti; 1957); *Sól* (Salt; 1962); *Sto pociech* (No end of fun; 1967); *Wszelki wypadek* (Could have; 1972); and *Wielka liczba* (A large number; 1976). In her poems Szymborska reflected on the existential condition of man and on human attitudes to the passing of time. She presented individuals as beings subjected to the unchanging laws of biology, defenseless and misguided in their hopes and plans and at risk of being alienated and misunderstood. The following collections contain poems noteworthy for their refined simplicity, slightly ironic detachment, precise metaphors, and originality of language jokes: *Ludzie na moście* (1986; *People on a Bridge*, 1990); *Koniec i początek* (The end and the beginning; 1993); *Widok z ziarnkiem piasku: 102 wiersze* (1996; *View with a Grain of Sand*, 1995); and *Chwila* (2002; *Chwila/Moment*, 2003). Translated into many languages, Szymborska's poems have also won recognition abroad. She has been honored with numerous awards, including the Goethe Prize (1991) and the Herder Prize (1995). In 1996 Szymborska received the Nobel Prize for literature, which won her wide international recognition. Szymborksa has been a member of the Polish Academy of Arts and Sciences since 1995. (WR)

Sources: *Literatura polska XX wieku: Przewodnik encyklopedyczny*, vol. 2 (Warsaw, 2000); *Teksty Drugie*, 1991, no. 4; Małgorzata Baranowska, *Wisława Szymborska: Nobel 96 for Literature* (Warsaw, 1996); Anna Legeżyńska, *Wisława Szymborska* (Poznań, 1996); Tadeusz Nyczek, *22 x Szymborska* (Poznań, 1997); Wojciech Ligęza, *O poezji Wisławy Szymborskiej* (Kraków, 2001).

SZYR Eugeniusz [originally Gershon] (15 April 1915, Łodygowice, near Żywiec–15 January 2000, Warsaw), Polish Communist activist. Szyr came from a Jewish working-class family. He graduated from high school, and from his youth he was involved with the extreme left, finally joining the Communist Party of Poland in 1934. In 1936, Szyr left for France, where he enrolled in the French Communist Party. From 1937 to 1938, he fought in the Spanish Civil War as a deputy commander of the Thirteenth Jarosław Dąbrowski International Brigade. In March 1939 he was interned in France and Algeria. In 1943, he went to the USSR, where he was assigned to the Union of Polish Patriots and (between 1944 and 1945) to the political apparatus of the Polish Army under Soviet control as chief of the General Organization Department of the Main Political Administration. After his return to Poland, Szyr joined the (Communist) Polish Workers' Party (Polska Partia Robotnicza [PPR]). In April 1947, he was appointed a deputy member of the Central Committee (CC) of the PPR, and between December 1948 and July 1981 he was a member of the CC of the Polish United Workers' Party (Polska Zjednoczona Partia Robotnicza [PUWP]). From June 1964 through November 1968 Szyr was a member of the Politburo of the PUWP CC. Between 1945 and 1946 Szyr worked as director of the Economic Department of the Ministry of Industry; between March 1947 and April 1949 he was deputy minister of industry and trade; and between April 1949 and March 1954 he was deputy chairman of the State Commission for Economic Planning and later the chairman of the commission until July 1956. Szyr worked closely with the Stalinist economic dictator, **Hilary Minc**. In particular, from 1947 to 1949, he was the secretary of the Economic Committee of the Council of Ministers, playing an important role in the Stalinization of Poland's economy ("the battle for trade" and the etatization of the cooperative movement). From July to October 1956 he was minister for construction.

As a hard-liner, after the events of 1956, Szyr remained in the shadows for a while, only to return to the pinnacle of power once again. Between 27 October 1959 and 28 March 1972 he was deputy prime minister for economic affairs. His ascent is considered the halting point of the post-October 1956 economic reforms. Between June 1963 and December 1968 Szyr chaired the Committee for Science and Technology. After the March events of 1968, during the anti-Semitic campaign, Szyr was attacked by Communists of the younger generation, but he managed to stay in the government and the party CC because of the support of **Władysław Gomułka**. Between March 1972 and March 1976 he chaired the State Council for Raw Material Economics, and between March 1976 and October 1981, he served as minister of raw material economics. Szyr was a deputy to the Communist parliament in 1952–56, 1961–69, and 1972–76. (PK)

Sources: Mołdawa; Henryk Różański, *Śladem wspomnień i dokumentów (1943–1948)* (Warsaw, 1987); Michał Czajka and Marcin Kamler, *Leksykon Historii Polski* (Warsaw, 1995); Dariusz Stola, *Kampania antysyjonistyczna w Polsce 1967–1968* (Warsaw, 2000).

T

TAMÁSI Áron (20 September 1897, Farkaslaka [now in Romania]–26 May 1966, Budapest), Hungarian writer and politician. Tamási was born into a Szekler peasant family. Called up for the army in 1916, he took his high school final examinations a year later. In 1918 Tamási fought on the Italian front, where he distinguished himself in the battle of the Piave River. In fall 1918 he failed to return to his unit after a holiday and stayed in Transylvania, taken over by Romania. In 1922 Tamási graduated in law from the Higher School of Economics in Cluj and then worked as a bank clerk. In 1923–25 he lived in the United States, where he also worked at a bank. After his return in 1926, Tamási became a journalist for the Hungarian newspaper *Újság*, and he began to publish his works. His most famous work is the *Ábel* trilogy (1932–34) about the fortunes of a Hungarian boy living in a rural environment in a Romania-ruled Transylvania after 1919, then in Romania proper, and then in the United States. A part of this trilogy was translated into English as *Abel Alone* (1966). In 1934 Tamási became an editor of the literary journal *Válasz* in Cluj. In 1935, along with other writers, he supported the idea of the New Intellectual Front, and in 1937 he co-organized a meeting in Tîrgu Mureş where the problems of Transylvanian Hungarians were given a critical presentation.

In 1944 Tamási moved to Budapest. In 1945–47 he was a member of parliament representing the National Peasant Party (NPP), and from 1943 to 1949 he was a corresponding member of the Hungarian Academy of Sciences. In the first half of the 1950s he was ignored; after 1953 his works were published again. In 1954 Tamási became a member of the National Council of the Patriotic People's Front, reorganized by Prime Minister **Imre Nagy**. In September 1956 he was elected co-chairman of the Hungarian Writers' Association (HWA). Tamási was among the first writers to take sides with the revolution, reading his "Hungarian Sigh" on the air on 26 October 1956, a piece that was later also published in the form of leaflets. On 31 October Tamási became a member of the leadership of the renewed NPP, and, along with **István Bibó** and others, he formulated its program. On 28 December 1956, at a general meeting of the HWA he read a statement he had authored in which Hungarian writers took sides with the suppressed revolution. A year later, however, Tamási publicly distanced himself from the revolution, and in 1959 he became a founding member of the HWA that was established on "new foundations." From 1963 Tamási was a member of the leadership of the Hungarian Peace Council. (JT)

Sources: *Magyar Életrajzi Lexikon*, vol. 2 (Budapest, 1969); *A magyar forradalom és szabadságharc enciklopédiája*, CD-ROM (Budapest, 1999); William Shawcross, *Crime and Compromise: Janos Kadar and the Politics of Hungary since Revolution* (New York, 1974).

TAMKEVIČIUS Sigitas (7 November 1938, Gudoniai), archbishop of Kaunas. In 1955 Tamkevičius entered the Kaunas Seminary. He was in his third year when he was inducted into the Red Army, where the Communists made efforts to persuade him to abandon his priestly vocation. Discharged from military service in 1960, he returned to the seminary. The KGB unsuccessfully tried to recruit him as an informer, threatening him with expulsion from the seminary. After graduating from the seminary, Tamkevičius was ordained into the priesthood in April 1962 and joined the Jesuit order. He worked in the parishes of Prienai and Vilkaviškis, where he was constantly persecuted by the police because he taught religion to children and preached patriotic sermons. In 1969 he was banned from exercising his pastoral ministry, which he continued underground. In 1970 the KGB allowed him to return to the parish of Kybartai. In 1972 Tamkevičius became one of the leaders of a group that published the underground *Chronicle of the Catholic Church of Lithuania*. In November 1979 he was a co-founder of the Catholic Committee for the Defense of Rights of Believers. In the spring of 1983, along with Father **Alfonsas Svarinskas**, Tamkevičius was arrested. In December 1983 he was sentenced to six years of forced labor camp and three years in exile. Around forty-seven thousand Lithuanians signed a petition for the release of both priests in June 1993. At the beginning of 1987 Tamkevičius was brought from the labor camp in Perm to KGB headquarters in Vilnius. After he refused to plead guilty, he was again sent to the labor camp. Released in 1988, he returned to Lithuania and became rector of the Kaunas Seminary. On 8 May 1991 he was consecrated bishop. On 4 May 1996 he was appointed archbishop of Kaunas, and on 19 November of that year he became president of the Conference of Lithuanian Bishops. (WR)

Sources: S. P. de Boer, E. J. Driessen, and H. L. Verhaar, eds., *Biographical Dictionary of Dissidents in the Soviet Union, 1956–1975* (The Hague and Boston, 1982); *ABN Correspondence*, 1984, no. 2; Rasa Mažeika, ed., *Violations of Human Rights in Soviet Occupied Lithuania* (Philadelphia, 1988); *Annuario Pontificio*, 2001.

TAMMSAARE Anton H. [originally Anton Hansen] (30 January 1878, Vetepere, near Albu–1 March 1940, Tallinn), Estonian writer. Tammsaare came from a peasant family. With the help of his family and taking up various jobs, he graduated from high school (1903) and then became involved in the **Konstanin Päts** group and had articles published in the radical paper *Teataja*. After several years Tammsaare managed to save enough money to take up legal studies in Dorpat (Tartu), but tuberculosis forced him to stop in 1911. As a student, Tammsaare was involved in a radical group, Noor Eesti. He went to the Caucasus to improve his health, but after a year returned to Estonia for good. He spent the next six years on his brother's farm in the Kohtla-Järve region. After Estonia gained independence, Tammsaare moved to Tallinn, where he lived with his family until the end of his life. At the beginning, he was involved in political activities, but in the twenty-year period between wars he became entirely devoted to literature, remaining, however, an attentive and critical observer of the Estonian reality in the 1920s and 1930s.

Tammsaare's first works were strongly influenced by the classic writers of Estonian realism, chiefly **August Kitzberg** and **Eduard Vilde**, with whom he used to work at *Teataja*. The revolution of 1905 strongly affected his works. Characteristic of pieces written in this period were psychological portraits of characters such as *Kaks paari ja üksainus* (Two couples and an only daughter; 1902) and *Vanad ja noored* (The old and the young; 1903). As a student, Tammsaare touched upon the emancipation of women in the novel *Üle piiri* (Abroad; 1910). The peak of his literary career was in the independence period. In 1921 he published the drama *Juudit* and in 1922 a novel, *Kõrboja peremees* (The master of Kõrboja farm), one of the best Estonian psychological novels, and the five-part novel *Tõde ja õigus* (Truth and justice; 1928–33) is one of the most important achievements of Estonian literature. In addition to autobiographical themes and descriptions of authentic events from the country's history, in this novel Tammsaare depicted the fortunes of several Estonian generations involved in the revolutionary changes of the nineteenth century. Up to a point, the novel's main character is an alter ego for the author; disgusted by materialism and hypocrisy, the character decides to leave town after many years spent there, moves back to the village where he was born, and regains his calm and spiritual balance. As time went by, Tammsaare became more and more critical of the injustice of the social system, writing *Elu ja armastus* (Life and love; 1934), *Ma armastasin sakslast* (I loved a German girl; 1935), and *Põrgupõhja uus Vanapagan* (Misadventure of the new satan; 1939). In the 1930s he also went in for criticizing dictatorial regimes. For example, in the drama *Kuningal on külm* (The king is cold; 1936) Tammsaare clearly alludes to Päts's dictator-

ship. Tammsaare's synthesis of various styles and literary forms in his works is considered one of the main strengths of his writing. Tammsaare enjoyed tremendous authority among his compatriots when he was still alive; with time this appreciation turned into a cult of the writer, for whom a monument was erected in his native Albu while he was still alive. In 1958, in Tammsaare's former home, the authorities of the Estonian SSR arranged a museum dedicated to his writings. Tammsaare's *Miniatures* were published in English in 1977. (AG)

Sources: *Eesti Entsuklopeedia*, vol. 14 (Tallinn, 2000); Endel Nirk, "Anton Hansen Tammsaare," www.einst.ee/literary/spring97/04ahtamm.htm; *Kto iest kto w kulture Estonii: izobrazytelnyie iskustva: literatura, teatr, muzika, kino* (Tallinn, 1996); www.kirjasto.sci.fi/tammsaar.htm.

TAMOŠAITIS Antanas (18 August 1894, Smukučiai, near Raseiniai–July 1940, Kaunas), Lithuanian lawyer and politician, victim of communism. After graduating from a theological seminary in Kaunas in 1915, Tamošaitis taught in a high school, and from 1919 he worked as a school inspector in Zarasai County. In 1920 he was elected to the Constituent Assembly on behalf of the Populists and worked on the parliamentary commission for education. In 1922–25 Tamošaitis studied law at Kaunas University and (from 1925 to 1928) in Vienna and Paris. In 1928 he received a Ph.D. in law at Kaunas University on the basis of a dissertation on the German historical school in economic theory. From 1930 to 1939 Tamošaitis lectured in law at the same university and worked as a lawyer. In 1939 he represented Lithuania before The Hague Tribunal of Justice. In the last government of independent Lithuania, chaired by **Antanas Merkys** (September 1939–June 1940), Tamošaitis was minister of justice. He authored many articles on law and translated the Code of Hammurabi into Lithuanian. After the Red Army invaded Lithuania, on 12 July 1940 Tamošaitis was arrested by the NKVD and then tortured to death in the Kaunas prison. (WR)

Sources: *EL*, vol. 5; Alfonsas Eidintas and Vytautas Žalys, *Lithuania in European Politics: The Years of the First Republic, 1918–1940* (New York, 1997).

TANCHEV Petur (12 July 1920, Gledka, near Chaskov–21 July 1992, Sofia), Bulgarian peasant activist. In 1935 Tanchev joined the Bulgarian Agrarian Youth Union (BAYU), and in 1945 he became a member of the Bulgarian Agrarian National Union (BANU). In 1941 he graduated in law from the University of Sofia. During his studies he was a leader of the illegal Peasant Youth Association affiliated with BANU and named after **Alexandur Stamboliyski**. In 1942 Tanchev was arrested for anti-state activities and then detained in Chaskov, where he participated in preparations for the 9 September 1944 coup. After the Fatherland Front took power, Tanchev became secretary of the Central Committee of the Democratic Youth Union (1944–46). In 1944–47 he was also chairman of the BAYU. In 1948–57 Tanchev was vice-secretary for organizational affairs of the Communist satellite BANU Chief Committee, and from 1951 he was a committee member. From 1957 to 1974 he was secretary of the BANU Chief Committee, and then until December 1989 he was its first secretary. From March 1962 to March 1966 he was minister of justice and then deputy prime minister in the government of **Todor Zhivkov** (12 March 1966–9 July 1971) and first deputy prime minister in the government of **Stanko Todorov** (9 July 1971–1 November 1974). A member of the National Assembly from 1950 to 1990, in 1958–61 Tanchev was its deputy speaker. In 1971–89 Tanchev was first deputy chairman of the State Council, fully supporting the Communist regime. Tanchev authored publications on the building of a "developed Socialist society" and on BANU "cooperation" with the Bulgarian Communist Party. (JJ)

Sources: *Entsiklopediya Bulgariya*, vol. 6 (Sofia, 1988); Raymond Detrez, *Historical Dictionary of Bulgaria* (Lanham, Md., 1997); *Narodni predstaviteli ot Deveto narodno sybranie* (Sofia, 1987); Tasho Tashev, *Ministrite na Bylgariya 1879–1999: Entsiklopedichen spravochnik* (Sofia, 1999).

TÁNCZOS Gábor (2 April 1928, Budapest–6 December 1979, Budapest), Hungarian Communist activist, one of the leaders of the 1956 revolution. Tánczos was the son of a paint salesman. During World War II he worked as a nurse in a concentration camp hospital. In 1945 he joined the Hungarian Communist Party (HCP), and in 1946 he became HCP secretary in Baj County. After graduating from high school, Tánczos was sent to Budapest, where he became vice-secretary general of the Communist-dominated Hungarian National Student Association. In 1948 he took up philosophical studies in the Department of Humanities of Budapest University and was active in various youth organizations. In 1953 Tánczos graduated and became an assistant professor in the Department of Philosophy of this university. At the beginning of 1955 he was elected chairman of the Petőfi Circle (then the Petőfi Club), whose program he formulated in the spirit of Prime Minister **Imre Nagy**'s reformist policy. After Nagy's removal, during one of the most memorable meetings of the circle in June 1956, the Hungarian press was openly criticized. Despite party attacks, Tánczos refused to do a self-criticism; therefore the Central Committee of the party passed a resolution that banned the club.

On 23 October 1956 Tánczos participated in a student demonstration criticizing the inconsistencies of **Ernő Gerő**'s policy and demanding that Nagy be brought back to power. Tánczos took part in establishing the Revolutionary Council of the Hungarian Intelligentsia; after the uprising was suppressed, this group turned out to be one of the most significant organizations offering passive resistance to the new authorities led by **János Kádár**. On 4 November, Tánczos, along with his wife, joined Nagy's group, asking for asylum in the Yugoslav Embassy. Along with others, Tánczos was abducted on 23 November and kept in detention in Romania. In March 1957 he was taken back to Hungary and sentenced by the Supreme Court to fifteen years in prison on 19 August 1958 in a trial accompanying that of Nagy. In spring 1963 Tánczos was released on a pardon. He then taught in an evening high school and worked in the National Pedagogical Institute. At the end of his life he focused on the fate of the poor, gypsies, and Hungarians living in neighboring countries. In 1979 Tánczos signed a declaration of the emerging Hungarian opposition that expressed solidarity with imprisoned members of the Charter 77 human rights defense movement in Czechoslovakia. Tánczos committed suicide in a fit of depression. In 1990 his remains were moved to the quarters of the executed heroes of the 1956 Hungarian Revolution. (JT)

Sources: *Tánczos Gábor emlékkönyv* (Budapest, 1997); *A magyar forradalom és szabadságharc enciklopédiája*, CD-ROM (Budapest, 1999); György Litván, ed., *Rewolucja węgierska 1956 roku* (Warsaw, 1996).

TARAND Andres (11 January 1940, Tallinn), Estonian politician and ecologist. In 1963 Tarand graduated in geography from Tartu University. From 1963 to 1965 he served in the Soviet Army and subsequently began working in the Tallinn Botanical Gardens, becoming the director at the end of the 1980s. From 1968 to 1970 Tarand took part in the Fourteenth Soviet Antarctic Expedition. In 1973 he earned a doctorate. In 1980, after police had brutally dispersed student demonstrations, Tarand (along with forty other intellectuals) sent a protest letter to the editorial staff of *Pravda*, in which discrimination against the Estonian language was also condemned. In 1987 Tarand became involved in the activities of the Green Movement (Roheline Likumine), which was founded during protests against the construction of a phosphorite mine that might have caused an ecological catastrophe. Initially Tarand was against the Green Movement's involvement in politics. He took part in the work of the People's Front. Elected to the Supreme Soviet of the Estonian SSR in 1990, Tarand became chairman of its Environmental Protection Committee. In September 1992, in the first free parliamentary elections, he was elected deputy and became minister of environmental protection (October 1992–November 1994).

On 8 November 1994 Tarand became prime minister following the resignation of the center-right cabinet led by **Mart Laar**, which was discredited by scandals only four months before the new elections. Tarand's cabinet was accepted, to a large extent, owing to the tolerance of the post-Communists. Both Tarand and the opposition regarded it as a provisional cabinet. Still, because he had not been involved in the rivalries among political parties in the 1992–94 period, Tarand enjoyed great popularity, and his government continued free-market reforms. Before the elections of March 1995 Tarand became the leader of the Moderates (Mõõdukad), which saved them from losing all seats in the parliamentary elections. However, the Moderates suffered a defeat in relative terms; therefore, on 17 April 1995 Tarand resigned as head of the government. In the March 1999 elections the Moderates obtained 15 percent of the vote, partly as a result of cooperation with the People's Party. In May 1999 the two parties merged into the People's Party Moderates (Rahvaerakond Mõõdukad). After the elections, Tarand was not invited to join the new center-right government led by Mart Laar. He became chairman of the parliamentary commission for foreign affairs. After the left wing of the People's Moderates suffered a defeat in the local elections in the autumn of 1999—while the right wing of the party, led by **Toomas Hendrik Ilves**, was quite successful—Tarand's influence diminished, and in 2001 he lost the leadership of the party to Ilves. The official reason for Tarand's resignation was that he was to run in the presidential elections of October 2001; however, he lost these elections. Tarand is one of the most famous Estonian intellectuals. A member of the ecological board of GLOBE, a non-governmental organization, he has authored over one hundred works in the field of climatology and urban environmental protection. In June 2004 Tarand was elected to the European Parliament. (AG)

Sources: Eastern Europe and the Commonwealth of Independent States, 1999 (London, 1999); *Eesti Entsuklopeedia*, vol. 14 (Tallinn, 2000); Mel Huang, "Right-Wing Socialists," *Central European Review*, 1999, no. 37; Web site of Józef Darski, republika.pl/darski1/kraje/estonia/chronb.htm; republika.pl/darski1/kraje/estonia/niepo.htm; republika.pl/darski1/kraje/estonia/pol.htm; Andres Tarand's CV, www.estemb.be/English/Estonia/polsystem/Andres%20Tarand.htm.

TARASHKIEVICH Branislau (20 January 1892, Maciuliszki, Lithuania–29 November 1938, USSR), Belorussian politician and linguist. Tarashkievich came from a Catholic peasant family. While a student at the gymnasium in Wilno (Vilnius), he belonged to Polish pro-independence groups. He completed his secondary education in 1911 and historical and philological studies at the university in Petrograd in 1916. From 1911 Tarashkievich was a member of the Belorussian Socialist Hromada (Belaruskaia Satsialistychnaia Hramada) and from October 1917 a mber of its Central Committee (CC). Between 1918 and 1920 he was one of the leaders of Belorussian Social Democracy. In 1918 Tarashkievich published a Belorussian grammar for the schools, and from 1918 to 1920 he lectured at the Pedagogical Institute in Minsk, laying the foundations of the modern national consciousness of the Belorussian people. At the beginning of 1919 Tarashkievich was temporarily arrested by the Soviets. From 1919 to 1920 he supported the federation plans of **Józef Piłsudski**, and in 1919–23 he belonged to the Polish Prawda (Truth) Freemason Lodge. In 1920 Tarashkievich became head of the Department of Belorussian Schools under the Polish administration and head of the Provisional Governing Committee of Central Lithuania, but without the support of the Belorussian National Committee in Wilno. In 1921–22 he was headmaster of the Vilnius Belorussian Gymnasium and one of the leaders of the Society of Belorussian Schools.

In 1922 Tarashkievich was elected to the Polish Assembly, where he headed the Belorussian Parliamentary Club. In most of his thirty-four Assembly speeches he protested the limits on Belorussian education and the restrictions on the social and national freedoms of the Belorussians living in the Eastern Borderland (Kresy) of the Second Republic of Poland. Tarashkievich campaigned for autonomy for these territories. Until 1925 he was involved in undertakings that were supposed to ensure the realization of Belorussian national interests within the framework of Polish democracy, particularly in the field of education. Seeing the fruitlessness of his endeavors, Tarashkievich became associated with communism, recognizing the USSR as an ally in the Belorussian national revival, especially since the Belorussian SSR enjoyed considerable freedom in the arena of national culture at that time. From 1925 he was president of the Belorussian Peasants' and Workers' Hromada (Belaruskaia Sialanska-Pratsounaia Hramada), which favored the creation of an independent Belorussian people's state. At that time the Hromada controlled most important Belorussian organizations and institutions in Poland. From 1925 Tarashkievich was also a member of the Communist Party of Western Belorussia. The Hromada became a hundred-thousand-member organization that threatened the Polish rule in the Eastern Borderland.

On 14 January 1927 Tarashkievich was arrested by the Polish authorities in Wilno. At a trial of Hromada leaders in Wilno he was sentenced to a twelve-year imprisonment for his activities against the Polish state. At the same time he was admitted in absentia as member of the Belorussian Academy of Sciences. In August 1929 Tarashkievich's sentence was commuted to six years. On 28 April 1930 he was released by decree of the president of the Republic of Poland, but he was arrested again in Tczew in February 1931. On 29 November 1931 the District Court in Wilno sentenced Tarashkievich to an eight-year imprisonment for his Communist activities. While in prison, Tarashkievich translated the *Iliad*, by Homer, and *Pan Tadeusz* (Master Thaddeus), by Adam Mickiewicz, into Belorussian. On 7 September 1933 Tarashkievich left for the USSR as a result of an exchange of political prisoners between Poland and the Soviet Union. As the Soviet authorities forbade him to stay in the Belorussian SSR, from 1933 Tarashkievich worked at the International Agriculture Institute in Moscow. Within the Great Purge, on 6 May 1937 Tarashkievich was arrested and accused of spying for Poland. Over a year later he was executed by firing squad. He was "rehabilitated" in 1957. In 1991 a collection of Tarashkievich's writings, under the title *Vybranaia krytyka, publitsystyka, pereklady* (Selected criticisms, political journalism, and translations), was published in Minsk. (AS/SA)

Sources: MERSH, vol. 38; *Belarus: Entsyklapedychny daviednik* (Minsk, 1995); *Encyklopedia historii Drugiej Rzeczypospolitej* (Warsaw 1999); N. P. Vakar, *Belorussia: The Making of a Nation* (Cambridge, Mass., 1956); Aleksandra Bergman, *Rzecz o Bronislawie Taraszkiewiczu* (Warsaw, 1977); Lis Arseni Siarheevich, *Branislau Tarashkevich* (Minsk, 1966); Jan Zaprudnik, *Historical Dictionary of Belarus* (Lanham, Md., 1998); A. I. Valahanovich and U. M. Mihniuk, *Spovedz u nadzei zastatstsa zyvym: Autabiiahrafiia Branislava Tarashkevicha* (Minsk, 1999).

TARTO Enn (25 September 1938, Tartu), Estonian politician. At the beginning of the 1960s Tarto joined the Estonian National League (Eesti Rahvuslaste Liit), an underground organization founded in a forced labor camp; its program drew on the ideology of the prewar extreme right. Arrested many times by the KGB for his opposition activities, Tarto was imprisoned in 1956–60, 1962–67, and 1983–88, all together spending fourteen years in prisons and forced labor camps. Between his second and third terms, Tarto studied literature and Estonian philology (1969–71), but after graduating, he could get a job only as a laborer. Tarto was the main founder of the Estonian democratic opposition. In 1979, along with forty-five other dissidents from the Baltic republics, he signed the so-called Baltic Appeal, which described Estonia as an occupied nation and declared the Molotov-Ribbentrop Pact null and void. Tarto was a signatory of many public statements, including one in support of Polish Solidar-

ity. Imprisoned in 1983, he maintained contacts with dissidents in Estonia. As a result, in 1987 he could support the Estonian Group for Publication of the Molotov-Ribbentrop Pact, which the dissidents founded. Tarto was the last Estonian political prisoner to be released from the camp in 1988.

In 1989 Tarto founded the Conservative Party, which did not work with the Estonian National Independence Party (Eesti Rahvusliku Sóltumatuse Partei [ERSP]), led by two other prominent dissidents, Lagle Parek and **Tunne Kelam**. This discord resulted in a rivalry between Tarto and Kelam, particularly after the elections to the Congress of Estonia, of which Tarto became deputy speaker. When Kelam, helped by the national Communists, attempted to overthrow Prime Minister **Edgar Savisaar** in 1990, Tarto unsuccessfully tried to exploit the failure of this attempt to oust Kelam as speaker of the Congress. In the 1992 parliamentary elections, Tarto ran on the ticket of the center-right Fatherland (Isamaa) party. When support for the government drastically eroded as a result of economic reforms and corruption scandals, he began to compete with Prime Minister **Mart Laar** for leadership of the Fatherland. Tarto lost this competition. The decline in the government's popularity, the halting of lustration and de-communization, wrong privatization decisions, and what Tarto considered an excessively conciliatory policy toward Russia influenced his decision to resign as a member of the Fatherland in 1994. He founded the Right-Wingers' Club, which became the Republican and Conservative People's Party (Vavariiklaste ja Konservativne Rahvaerakond). Elected to parliament in 1995, Tarto unsuccessfully tried to form a coalition with the post-nomenklatura Estonian Coalition Party. In 1998 he joined the Estonian People's Party (Eesti Rahvaerakond), led by **Toomas Hendrik Ilves**; it later merged with the Moderates to form the People's Party Moderates (Rahvaerakond Mõõdukad). Tarto enjoys considerable popularity among the Estonians. In the 1999 local elections in Tartu, where the People's Moderates suffered a defeat, he was the only representative of the party elected to the City Council. He is also chairman of the Council of the Human Rights Institute and a member of the leadership of the Estonian Defense League. (AG)

Sources: *Eesti Entsuklopeedia*, vol. 14 (Tallinn, 2000); Rein Taagepera, *Estonia: Return to Independence* (Boulder, Colo., 1993); Jan Lewandowski, *Estonia* (Warsaw, 2001); http://www.riigikogu.ee/parliament.html; http://republika.pl/darski1/kraje/estonia/chronb.htm.

TASHKO Koço (1899, Alexandria–1984, Thumana, near Krujë), Albanian Communist activist. Tashko came from a wealthy merchant family. He graduated from an Arabic-language school in Cairo and then studied in Beirut and Triffin (United States); subsequently, he graduated from Harvard University. In the United States as of 1915, Tashko became involved in the activities of the Albanian minority. His father's friendly ties with **Fan Noli** enabled him to work at the *Dielli* periodical and the Aresimi association. In 1922–25 Tashko worked at the Albanian consulate in New York. After the 1924 revolution he returned to Albania and went to live in Korçe. He became involved in a Communist youth group in Korçe, and he was a close associate of **Ali Kelmendi**. In 1936 Tashko and Kelmendi went to Moscow, where Tashko worked for the Balkan section of the Comintern. On its order, Tashko returned to Albania in 1937. The directives he brought with him were accepted by the Puna (Work) group in Korçe but rejected by groups in Shkodër and Tirana.

After the Italian invasion of Albania in 1939, the Korçe group was the most active but confined itself to organizing street demonstrations. Tashko co-founded a joint central committee with the Shkodër Communists; this became possible because in January 1939 most Shkodër group members were arrested. As a co-founder of the Communist Party of Albania (CPA), Tashko was one of the few people who new the basics of Marxist theory. During the wartime occupation he used the pseudonym "Skender Dine." Tashko was secretary of the Council of the Anti-Fascist National Liberation Front, set up in May 1944 at a congress in Përmeti as a temporary legislative organ. From March 1946 until February 1947 he was a diplomat in Moscow, supporting strict cooperation between Albania and the USSR. From 1948 he was a member of the Central Committee of the Albanian Party of Labor and chairman of its Central Commission of Party Control. Probably involved in a Moscow-inspired conspiracy against **Enver Hoxha**, Tashko was dismissed in June 1956, and in September 1960 he was arrested as a supporter of continued cooperation with the USSR rather than the Hoxha-chosen China. Incarcerated without a formal trial, in 1971 Tashko was put into a newly built prison in Benca, near Tepelena. During the last years of his life he was detained in Thumana. (TC)

Sources: *Fjalor Enciklopedik* (Tirana, 2001); *Bashkimi*, 24 October 1945; William E. Griffith, *Albania and the Sino-Soviet Rift* (Cambridge, Mass., 1963); David Smiley, *Albanian Assignment* (London, 1984).

TĂTĂRĂSCU Gheorghe (22 December 1886, Craiova–28 August 1957, Bucharest), Romanian lawyer and politician. Tătărăscu studied law in Paris in 1905–9 and received his Ph.D. in law there in 1912, defending a dissertation on the Romanian electoral system. In the 1920s he was undersecretary of state in the Ministry of Interior. In 1924 he was responsible for the bloody pacification of the village of Tatar Bunar in Bessarabia, where local peasants were accused of favoring the Communists. A member of the National Liberal Party (NLP), in December 1930 Tătărăscu was appointed its secretary general. From November 1933 to January 1934 he was minister of trade and industry. After the assassination of Prime Minister **Ion G. Duca** by an Iron Guard raiding party (29 December 1933), despite the objections of the party he led, on 5 January 1934 Tătărăscu accepted the offer of King **Charles II** and assumed the post of prime minister. He also remained minister of trade and industry and headed the ministries of war, defense industry, and interior. The protection that his government provided to domestic industry, writing off agricultural debts and promoting the state-owned sector, contributed to an economic improvement. At the same time, Tătărăscu governed by decree, maintained a state of emergency, and imposed censorship. In the wake of the autocratic government policy, a conflict escalated between Tătărăscu and the NLP chairman, **Constantinu Brațianu**, as a result of which Tătărăscu resigned from the party's leadership. He was prime minister until 28 December 1937. After the royal coup in February 1938, Tătărăscu supported the introduction of an anti-parliamentarian power system and assumed the position of foreign minister in the Government of National Unity of Patriarch **Miron Cristea**. On 30 March 1938 Tătărăscu became a member of the Crown Council, and between December 1938 and September 1939 he was ambassador to Paris. After the assassination of **Armand Călinescu** by the Iron Guard, Tătărăscu again became prime minister on 24 November 1939 and kept this post until 4 July 1940, when—as a result of a Soviet ultimatum—Romania had to give up Bessarabia and Northern Bukovina.

After General **Ion Antonescu** took power, Tătărăscu joined the opposition, supporting its attempts to get Romania out of its alliance with Germany. After the 23 August 1944 coup he joined the National Democratic Bloc. In October 1944 his liberal faction joined a coalition with the Communists, and on 6 March 1945 Tătărăscu was appointed deputy prime minister and foreign minister in the cabinet of **Petru Groza**. Because his biography included anti-Communist activities, Tătărăscu acted not only out of opportunism, but also out of fear. In the November 1946 elections his party formed a coalition bloc with the Communists. In charge of diplomacy, Tătărăscu chaired the Romanian delegation to the Paris Peace Conference (1946–47), and in February 1947 he signed the peace treaty. He hoped for financial assistance from the West, and he wrote a special memorandum on this issue, the theses of which were incompatible with the Communists' stance. When **Ana Pauker** accused him of treason and collaboration with the West in November 1947, Tătărăscu was dismissed and soon incarcerated in Sighet Prison. Broken by torture, he testified in the **Lucreţiu Pătrăşcanu** trial. In 1955 he was released. Tătărăscu's works include, among others, *Relele organice ale armatei noastre* (The natural perimeters of our army; 1913); *Pe drumul anarhiei* (On the way to anarchy; 1920); *Internaţionala III şi Basarabia* (The Third International and Bessarabia; 1925); *Besarabie et Moscou* (Bessarabia and Moscow; 1926) and *Măriturii pentru istorie* (Historical merits; 1996). (FA/TD).

Sources: *Biographisches Lexikon*, vol. 4; Hugh Seton-Watson, *The East European Revolution* (London, 1950); Robert Lee Wolff, *The Balkans in Our Time* (Cambridge, Mass., 1956); Ion Enescu, *Politica externa a României în perioada 1944–1947* (Bucharest, 1979); Dov. B. Lungu, *Romania and the Great Powers, 1933–1940* (Durham, N.C., 1989); Ioan Chiper, Florin Constantiniu, and Adrian Pop, *Sovietizarea României: Percepţii anglo-americane (1944–1947)* (Bucharest, 1997); Mircea Ciobanu, *Convorbiri cu Regele Mihai I al României* (Bucharest, 1991).

TATARKA Dominik (14 March 1913, Drienové–10 May 1989, Bratislava), Slovak writer. After high school in Trenčín, Tatarka graduated from Charles University in Prague in Slovak and Romance philology in 1938. Subsequently he spent a year studying at the Sorbonne in Paris. In 1939–44 Tatarka taught French in high schools in Žilin and Martin. In 1944 he took part in the Slovak National Uprising and joined the Communist Party of Slovakia (CPS). After the war he worked as a journalist for (among other publications) the journals *Pravda* and *Literárný život*. In 1949–51 Tatarka was secretary of the Association of Czechoslovak Writers and then a screenwriter for Czechoslovak Film. In 1969 he received the title of Artist of Merit, but his objections to the Warsaw Pact aggression and the so-called normalization led to repression against him. In October 1969 Tatarka turned in his CPS membership card. Constantly under surveillance, in 1970–71 he worked as a blue-collar laborer. He was deprived of the opportunity to earn money in any other way and was banned from traveling and publishing. In 1977 Tatarka signed Charter 77.

Tatarka made his literary debut in 1942 with a collection of short stories, *V úzkosti hľadania* (In the unrest of the search), and in 1944 he published a novel, *Panna zázračnica* (Miss Miracle-Maker), in which he showed a fascination with surrealism and existentialism. After the war, Tatarka took to political literature and Socialist realism, publishing, among other works, the novel *Farská republika* (The republic of shavelings; 1948), a satire on

the Slovak Republic at wartime, and then two "production" novels. Soon after that, however, he cracked down on communism in *Démon súhlasu* (Demon of agreement, 1956; published as a book in 1963); in subsequent novels—*Rozhovory bez konca* (Unending conversations; 1959) and *Prútené kreslá* (Wicker armchairs; 1963)—Tatarka reflected philosophically on love as the basis of the meaning of life. In the 1970s and 1980s he had his works published illegally, out of the reach of censors, as well as abroad. He presented the totalitarian reality of Czechoslovakia and memories from his own life. Tatarka's most important work from that period is a prose trilogy: *Listy do večnosti* (Letters to eternity; 1988), *Sám proti noci* (Alone against the night; 1984), and *Písačky* (Writings; 1984); it included autobiographical themes permeated with eroticism and showed an expressive picture of life in a "normalized" Czechoslovakia. Abroad Tatarka also published the draft *V ne-čase* (In evil-time; 1986) and a tape-recorded tale, *Navrávačky* (Blabbing; 1988). Tatarka authored screenplays, received many prestigious awards, and also translated works by French writers. In 1990 in Stockholm the Dominik Tatarka Award was established. (PU)

Sources: *SBS*; Milan Ferko, ed., *Sto slávnych Slovákov* (Martin, 1995); *Reprezentačný biografický lexikón Slovenska* (Martin, 1999); Bernard Noël, *La recontre avec Tatarka* (Le Roeulx, 1986); Dagmar Perstická and Lea Přerostová, *Dominik Tatarka a ti druzí* (Brno, 1991); *Dominik Tatarka* (Prešov, 1991); Halina Janaszek-Ivančikova, ed., *Literatury zachodniosłowiańskie czasu przełomów 1890–1990*, vol. 1, *Literatura łużycka i słowacka* (Katowice, 1994); Zdeněk Eis, *Dominik Tatarka: Mezi domovem, Prahou a Paříží: vyprávění o zrodu spisovatele* (Prague, 2001); *Slovenská literatúra*, 1993, no. 2.

TAVČAR Ivan (28 August 1851, Poljanie, near Škofjo Loko–19 February 1923, Ljubljana), Slovene politician, pundit, and lawyer. Tavčar came from a poor peasant family with many children. In 1875 he graduated in law from Vienna University. After almost a ten-year apprenticeship he opened his own legal practice in Ljubljana (1884). From his youth he showed literary interests. Tavčar owed the style and spirit of his first pieces to the influence of Christian Friedrich Grabbe; in these he used the convention of romantic lyricism to express native Slovenian subject matter. After 1871 Tavčar became interested in the theories of the theologian Anton Mahnič; these gave his nationalism a Catholic and anti-German character. Tavčar advocated autonomy for Slovenia. Also in this period he became close to **Ivan Hribar**. Together they established the periodical *Slovan*, and then in 1894 they assumed leadership of the National Liberal Party, renamed in 1905 the National Progressive Party. This party advocated radical views and opposed both the conciliatory liberals, who ruled Kraina with Habsburg consent, and the clerical conservatives. In addition to autonomy, Tavčar and Hribar advocated pan-Slavism and promoted the Yugoslav idea. The formula they developed turned out to be effective. Tavčar himself was a long-term councilor of Ljubljana (1884–1921) and its vice-mayor (1909–10) and mayor (1911–21). He sat in the local parliament of Kraina (1889–1918) and the Austrian Council of State in Vienna (1901–6). In addition to his political work, Tavčar was a businessman. Together with Hribar in 1900 he co-founded the first Slovenian bank, which he later directed (1916–23). After World War I he supported the creation of the Kingdom of Serbs, Croats, and Slovenes, but because of his deteriorating health he did not play a major political role. In his works Tavčar idealized the Slovene peasants. He authored (among other works) a cycle of twelve novels, *Med gorami* (Among the mountains; 1876–88), and dozens of other pieces, the most famous of which are *Izza kongresa* (After the congress; 1905–8); *Cvetje v jeseni* (Autumn flowers; 1917); and *Višoška kronika* (The Višoška chronicle; 1919). Tavčar's *Zbrano delo* (Complete works) was published in Ljubljana in eight volumes (1951–59). (MC)

Sources: *Biographisches Lexikon*, vol. 4; *Enciklopedija Jugoslavije*, vol. 8 (Zagreb, 1971); Marja Borsnik, *Ivan Tavcar: Leposlovni ustvarjalec* (Maribor, 1973); *Mały słownik pisarzy zachodnio-słowiańskich i południowo-słowiańskich* (Warsaw, 1973); Carole Rogel, *The Slovenes and Yugoslavism, 1890–1914* (Boulder, Colo., 1977); Francek Bohanec, *Ivan Tavčar* (Ljubljana, 1985); Irena Gantar Godina, "Novoslovanska Ideja in Slovenci," *Zgodovinski Casopis*, 1989, no. 4; Leopoldina Plut-Pregelj and Carole Rogel, *Historical Dictionary of Slovenia* (Lanham, Md., 1996).

TEEMANT Jaan (12 September 1872, Vigala–after 1941, USSR), Estonian politician. Teemant graduated in law from Petersburg University, and then he worked as an attorney in Tallinn. During the 1905 revolution he was, together with **Konstanin Päts**, one of the leaders of the "Tallinn radicals," a socially radical group close to the Russian Socialist Revolutionaries that advocated a radical program for combating the tsarist system: a boycott of government institutions, tax collection, and military service, as well as arming the peasants and expropriating the major landed estate owners. When the police shot sixty people in Tallinn after a series of demonstrations on 16 October 1905, tensions dramatically increased. On 10–12 December the All-Estonian Meeting of People's Delegates gathered in Tallinn; during the meeting two tactics clashed: those of the moderates and those of the radicals. Teemant, representing the radical wing, was elected chairman of the meeting, defeating the moderate **Jaan Tõnisson**. The radicals demanded that the tsarist system be overthrown and a revolutionary local self-government be established;

the moderates favored constitutional changes. When on 10 December 1905 martial law was imposed in Tallinn and Harjumaa, Teemant, in danger of arrest, had to flee the country, where he was later sentenced to death in absentia. After the martial law had been lifted, Teemant returned to Estonia, where he was sentenced to one and a half years in prison and to forced settlement near Archangel.

Released after the February 1917 revolution, Teemant joined the then established Farmers' Party (Põllumeeste Kogu [FP]), led by Päts. In the National Council (Maapäev) elections held on 7 and 8 July 1917 this party won the most votes, and Päts became prime minister of the Provisional National Government, which proclaimed the independence of Estonia on 24 February 1918. In 1918–19 Teemant was attorney general of Estonia, and then he was an MP in the second, third, and fourth terms. From 15 December 1925 to 22 June 1926 he was head of state (*riigivanem*) for the first time, heading a coalition government consisting of the FP, liberals, New Settlers, Christian nationalists, and National Liberals. After parliamentary elections Teemant assumed this function again, this time leading a government without the (liberal) Estonian Labor Party but with nationalists and large landowners. This cabinet was reconstructed in February 1927 and lasted under his leadership until 9 December 1927. After the FP and the New Settlers merged into the Agrarian Union (AU), on 19 February 1932 Teemant returned to the position of prime minister of a government supported by the AU and Tõnisson's National Center Party. This cabinet lasted until 20 June 1932, when new elections were held. When in office, Teemant signed an Estonian-Soviet non-aggression treaty on 5 May 1932. In the same year he received an honorary doctorate from Tartu University.

During the Great Depression Teemant and Päts went separate ways for good. Whereas Päts decided to reach for dictatorial powers, Teemant supported democracy and became an opposition member after Päts's coup d'état of 1934. Teemant signed a memorandum protesting the dictatorship; it was also signed by three other *riigivanem*: Tõnisson, **Ants Piip**, and **Juhan Kukk**; it was published on 5 November 1936 in the Finnish daily *Helsingin Sanomat*. After the Molotov-Ribbentrop Pact had been signed, the Baltic Germans were evacuated, and Teemant became the Estonian proxy in a fund managing the real estate of the displaced. When the Red Army entered Estonia, putting an end to its independence, Teemant was arrested by the NKVD on 23 July 1940. Sentenced to ten years in prison in 1941, Teemant died in unknown circumstances. (WR)

Sources: *Eest Biografiline Leksikon*, vol. 1 (Tartu, 1926–29); Evald Uustalu, ed., *Eesti Vabariik, 1918–1940: Ülevaade sõnas ja pildis* (Lund, 1968); Piotr Łossowski, *Kraje bałtyckie na drodze od demokracji parlamentarnej do dyktatury 1918–1934* (Wrocław, 1972); Georg von Rauch, *The Baltic States, The Years of Independence: Estonia, Latvia, Lithuania, 1917–1940* (Berkeley, 1974); Tönu Parming, *The Collapse of Liberal Democracy and the Rise of Authoritarianism in Estonia* (Beverly Hills, Calif., 1975); Ü. Pärn, "Jaan Teemant," *Vooremaa*, 17 March 1990; A. Pajur, *Jaan Teemant: Eesti ajalugu elulugudes* (Tallinn, 1997).

TEJCHMA Józef (14 July 1927, Markowa, Rzeszów Province), Polish Communist activist. Born into a peasant family, after graduating from high school in Łańcut, Tejchma received a Master's degree from the Higher School of Social Sciences at the Central Committee (CC) of the Polish United Workers' Party (Polska Zjednoczona Partia Robotnicza [PUWP]) in 1958. He began his career as a youth activist in the Union of Rural Youth of the Republic of Poland called Wici (Związek Młodzieży Wiejskiej Rzeczypospolitej Polskiej–Wici [ZMW RP–Wici]). He then served as an instructor at the Main Board of the Union of Polish Youth (Związek Młodzieży Polskiej [ZMP]) (1948–51), representative of the ZMP Main Board at the construction site of Nowa Huta (1951–54), deputy head of the Organizational Department of the ZMP (1954–55), and chairman of the Main Board of the Rural Youth Union (Związek Młodzieży Wiejskiej [ZMW]) (February 1957–July 1963). In 1952 Tejchma joined the PUWP. In March 1959 he became a deputy member, and in June 1964 a member, of the PUWP CC. From November 1963 to June 1964 he headed the CC Agricultural Department. From June 1964 to March 1972 he served as the CC secretary, and in November 1968 he became a member of the CC Politburo. Tejchma enjoyed the trust of **Władysław Gomułka**, first secretary of the PUWP CC, and was among his close associates, but in December 1970 he was among those who brought about the removal of Gomułka.

In March 1972 Tejchma resigned as the CC secretary to become deputy prime minister, and from February 1974 to January 1978 he also served as minister of culture. He was regarded as a representative of a moderate wing within the party leadership and a someone who tolerated a certain relaxation of the ideological straitjacket imposed on the culture. For example, with Tejchma's permission, **Andrzej Wajda** could make the film *Człowiek z marmuru* (Man of marble). In February 1979 Tejchma resigned as deputy prime minister, and he headed the ministry of education until April 1980. At the Eighth Congress of the PUWP in February 1980 Tejchma was not elected to the CC Politburo. From May to October 1980 he was ambassador to Switzerland. He then returned to Poland and again served as minister of culture and arts until October 1982. He subsequently worked in the Ministry of Foreign Affairs, and from 1984 to 1988 he was ambassador to Greece. An MP in the Assembly (1958–80), Tejchma served as chairman of the PUWP Parliamentary Caucus from 1970 to 1972. He was secretary of the All-Polish Committee of the National Unity Front from June 1971 to January 1972 and its vice-president from July 1971 to July 1983. Tejchma published his memoirs, *Pożegnanie z władzą* (Farewell to power; 1996). (PK/WR)

Sources: Mołdawa; Antoni Czubiński, *Dzieje najnowsze Polski 1944–1989* (Poznań, 1992); Andrzej Albert [Wojciech Roszkowski], *Najnowsza historia Polski 1918–1980*, vol. 2 (Warsaw, 1995); Włodzimierz Janowski and Aleksander Kochański, *Informator o strukturze i obsadzie personalnej centralnego aparatu PZPR 1948–1990* (Warsaw, 2000); Jerzy Eisler, *Grudzień 1970* (Warsaw, 2000).

TELEKI Pál (1 November 1879, Budapest–3 April 1941, Budapest), Hungarian politician and geographer, count. Born into an aristocratic family from Transylvania, after graduating from college, Teleki received a Ph.D. in 1903 and began lecturing in geography at Budapest University. From 1913 he was a corresponding member and from 1922 a full member of the Hungarian Academy of Sciences. From 1909 to 1913 he was director of the Institute of Geography, and in 1910–23 he was secretary general and deputy chairman of the Hungarian Geographical Association. Before World War I Teleki made a number of research trips in Europe, North Africa, and America. During World War I he briefly served on the southern front. In 1919 Teleki became a professor. As a politician, Teleki realized the paramount importance of social issues; however, he represented conservative and anti-Semitic views. In 1917 he presided over the Hungarian Association of Population Growth and Racial Hygiene Policy, in 1917–18 he was president of the All-National Veterans' Care Office, and in 1918–19 he was chairman of the Hungarian Territorial Defense League. In 1905–10, 1915–18, 1920–21, 1922–26, and 1938–41 Teleki was an MP, and from 1927 to 1938 he was a member of the upper house.

When in Switzerland in March 1919, Teleki learned about the establishment of the Hungarian Soviet Republic (HSR). He went to Vienna, where he joined the Anti-Bolshevik Committee, set up in April 1919 by Count **István Bethlen**. In June of the same year, as a close associate of Admiral **Miklós Horthy**, Teleki became foreign minister of the counter-government established in Szeged. After the fall of the Austro-Hungarian monarchy Teleki used his scientific knowledge to defend Hungarian territorial integrity. Under his leadership an ethnographic map of Hungary was produced at the beginning of 1919. In 1920 Teleki was a member of the Hungarian delegation participating in peace talks in Paris. From April 1920

Teleki was foreign minister, and from 19 July 1920 to 14 April 1921 he was prime minister; at the same time, until September 1921, he was head of diplomacy. As prime minister, Teleki had to ratify the peace treaty that he himself signed (among others) in Trianon on 4 June 1920. Teleki opposed armed groups that used white terror against active HSR participants. On his orders, the minister of agriculture, **István Nagyatádi Szabó**, worked out a blueprint for an agrarian reform. Teleki's name is also associated with the numerus clauses, passed in September 1920, which discriminated against Jews at universities. In foreign policy Teleki represented a pro-French orientation. During the first attempt of Charles IV Habsburg to regain the Hungarian throne (March–April 1921), Teleki was supportive of him; therefore, he stepped down after the move became a fiasco.

In the 1920s and 1930s Teleki was mainly occupied with research and advocacy of the Hungarian policy of territorial revision. In 1924 he founded the Hungarian Sociographical Institute and in 1926 the Institute of Political Sciences. He was also the main founder and leader of Hungarian scouting. Teleki was chairman of the Christian National Party. He also founded the Hungarian Revisionist League. Teleki hoped that German support would help achieve Hungarian revisionist goals, but he very quickly recognized the dangers from Hitler's Third Reich, and he tried to confine its influence in Hungary. In 1932–36 Teleki was chairman of the Stipend Council, in 1936–37 he was chairman of the National Education Council, and from 1936 he chaired the board of Hungarian Institutes acting abroad. Teleki organized international conferences and personally invited outstanding people to Hungary to win their support for Hungarian revisionism. At Regent Horthy's request, in May 1938 Teleki accepted the religion and national education portfolio in the government of **Béla Imrédy**. After the latter's resignation, Teleki assumed leadership of the government on 16 February 1939.

Under Teleki's rule in March 1939, following the fall of Czechoslovakia, Transcarpathian Ruthenia was reincorporated into Hungary, whereby the Polish-Hungarian border was restored, and in August 1940, as a result of the second Vienna Award, Northern Transylvania was incorporated. On 24 February Hungary joined the anti-Comintern Pact. In May 1940 a second bill was passed that limited the rights of the Jews, and a third one was prepared. In September 1939 Teleki maintained neutrality regarding the Polish-German War. With Horthy's consent, he refused to permit German Army units to cross Hungary on their way to the battlefield in Poland. As a friend of the Poles, with Horthy's acceptance, Teleki opened the Polish-Hungarian border to them and then looked after Polish refugees. He advocated a policy of so-called military neutrality. He vigorously opposed the extreme right and had a number of Arrow Cross activists detained or arrested. Teleki had to give in, however, on the issues of Hungarian-German economic agreements and the right of the Volksbund to act in Hungary. Teleki believed the Germans and their allies would lose the war, and he did everything he could to keep his country neutral and not take part in the war on the side of the Third Reich at any price at all. The purpose of the Hungarian-Yugoslav friendship treaty Teleki signed in December 1940 was to create a gap in the German ring surrounding Hungary. After the anti-German coup in Belgrade on 27 March 1941 his policy crumbled into ruins. Teleki came to the conclusion that if Hungary joined the German-Italian invasion of Yugoslavia, a British declaration of war on Hungary would become unavoidable. Not willing to participate in a future national disaster for his country, Teleki committed suicide after Regent Horthy expressed willingness to take part in the attack on Yugoslavia. This symbolic step earned him great respect in international opinion. Teleki authored a number of scientific works, among them the following: *Atlasz a japán szigetek cartográphiájának történetéhez* (Historical atlas of Japanese cartography; 1909); *Amerika gazdasági földrajza* (Economic geography of America; 1922); *Általános gazdasági földrajz* (General economic geography; 1927); as well as a documentary propaganda piece, *The Evolution of Hungary and Its Place in European History* (1923). (JT)

Sources: *Biographisches Lexikon*, vol. 4; Steven Bela Vardy, *Historical Dictionary of Hungary* (Lanham, Md., 1997); *Magyar Életrajzi Lexikon*, vol. 2 (Budapest, 1969); *Nagy Képes Milleniumi Arcképcsarnok* (Budapest, 1999); *Magyarország 1944–1956*, CD-ROM (Budapest, 2001); C. A. Macartney, *October Fifteenth: A History of Modern Hungary*, vols. 1–2 (Edinburgh, 1957–61); Lorant Tilkovszky, *Pál Teleki (1879–1941): A Biographical Sketch* (Budapest, 1974); Ignác Romsics, *Hungary in the Twentieth Century*, (Budapest, 1999); Anton Czettler, *Pál Graf Teleki und die Aussenpolitik Ungarns 1939–1941* (Munich, 1996); Károlyi Vigh, *Ismeretlen fejezetek Teleki Pál eléleből* (Budapest, 2001).

TELIHA Olena [née Shovheniva or Shovhenova] (21 July 1907, St. Petersburg–21 February 1942, Babi Yar, near Kiev), Ukrainian poet, journalist, and political activist. In 1922 Teliha emigrated with her parents to Czechoslovakia, where in 1924 she began to study philology at the Pedagogical Institute in Prague. Involved with the Ukrainian student community, she embraced Ukrainian national ideals. After marrying Mykhailo Teliha, she moved to Warsaw, where she taught at a Ukrainian school. In 1932 Teliha began contributing to *Vistnyk*, a periodical published in Lwów (Lviv). In Kraków from 1939 to

1941, she headed the literary-artistic society Zarevo and worked in the cultural sector of the Organization of Ukrainian Nationalists (OUN). After a split in the OUN, she supported the OUN–Melnyk faction (OUN–M), led by **Andriy Melnyk**. With the outbreak of the German-Soviet war in 1941 Teliha moved to Lviv and then, with a group of OUN supporters, to Kiev, where she became head of the Ukrainian Writers' Union and editor of the weekly *Lytavry*. After the Nazi regime closed down *Lytavry*'s parent newspaper, *Ukraiinske Slovo*, and replaced it with *Nove Ukraiinske Slovo*, Teliha refused to cooperate. Arrested by the Gestapo on 9 February 1942, about a week later, along with a group of other Ukrainian nationalists, Teliha was executed by a firing squad in Babi Yar. After the war, her poems were published in separate collections: *Dusha na storozhi* (The soul on guard; 1946); *Prapory dukha* (The banners of the spirit; 1947); and *Olena Teliha: Zbirnyk* (Olena Teliha: Collection; 1977). Teliha's poems also appeared in English as *Boundaries of Flame: A Complete Collection of Poetry* (1977). (GM)

Sources: *Encyclopedia of Ukraine*, vol. 5 (Toronto, 1993); *Entsyklopediya Ukraiinoznavstva*, vol. 8 (Lviv, 2000); Ievhen Onatskyi, *Tvorche zhyttia i heroiska smert Oleny Telihy* (Buenos Aires, 1949); Dmytro Dontsov, *Poetka vohnennykh mezh—Olena Teliha* (N.p., 1953); Bohdan Chervak, *Olena Teliha: Zhyttia i tvorchist* (Kiev, 1997).

TEOCTIST [originally Toader Arapaşu] (7 February 1915, Tocileni–30 July, 2007, Bucharest), Patriarch of the Romanian Orthodox Church (ROC). After primary school in Tocileni (1927), Teoctist attended a seminary at the Vorona Monastery, Botoşani County (1928–31). He joined an order in 1931. He attended a seminary at Neamţ Monastery and then a seminary at Cernica Monastery (1932–40). In 1935 he took his monastic vows at Bistriţa-Neamţ Monastery, receiving the name of Teoctist. A hierodeacon from 1937, from 1940 to 1945 Teoctist studied theology at the University of Bucharest and also worked at the local archbishopric office and then as a deacon in the Patriarchal Cathedral. In 1945 he was transferred to the metropolitan cathedral in Iaşi, and was ordained a hieromonk. In 1946 Teoctist was elevated to archimandrite. From 1948 to 1950 he served as vicar of the archdiocese of Iaşi. In 1948, on the initiative of the Communist authorities and Metropolitan **Justinian**, Teoctist unsuccessfully tried to persuade the Romanian Uniate bishops imprisoned by the Communist authorities at the monastery of Dragoslavele to join the Orthodox Church. In 1950, on Justinian's recommendation, the Holy Synod of the ROC elected him assistant bishop to the patriarch. From 1950 to 1954 Teoctist was rector of the Theological Institute of Bucharest, secretary of the Holy Synod of the

ROC, and vicar of the archdiocese of Bucharest. In 1962 he became bishop of Arad. In 1963 the Congress of the Romanian Orthodox Bishops in America appointed him bishop of Detroit, but he was refused an entry visa to the United States and Canada and did not assume this position. In 1973 he became archbishop of Craiova.

After the death of Patriarch Justinian in 1977, Teoctist became archbishop of Iaşi and metropolitan of Moldavia and Suceava, becoming de facto head of the ROC. He did not protest when in 1977 the Communist authorities ordered the destruction of the historic Orthodox church in Enei in Bucharest, as well as may other places of religious worship in Romania. From 1980 to 1982 Teoctist served as *locum tenens* in the absence of the archbishop of Sibiu and metropolitan of Transylvania. On 10 November 1986 he became metropolitan of Muntenia and Dobrogea and Patriarch of the ROC. Throughout the Communist regime Teoctist accepted the complete subordination of the ROC to the Communist authorities. On 17 December 1989 he supported the repressive measures introduced by **Nicolae Ceauşescu** against protesters in Timişoara, and on 21 December he supported the imposition of a state of emergency. After the overthrow of Ceauşescu on 22 December 1989 and the outbreak of unrest in Romania, Teoctist, fearing for his life, was in hiding in one of the monasteries for several weeks. In 1991 he called for a boycott of the Catholic Church as long as the office of Pope was held by John Paul II, who insisted, among other things, on the return of property seized by the ROC from the Uniate Church. At the beginning of the 1990s Teoctist admitted he had made mistakes during the Communist era. He initiated a rapprochement with the Catholic Church and established contacts with the Pope, who visited Romania in 1999. In 1999 Teoctist became an honorary member of the Romanian Academy of Sciences. In October 2002 he made a visit to the Vatican, where he issued a joint ecumenical statement with Pope John Paul II. (LW)

Sources: *Dictionar Enciclopedic*, vol. 4 (Bucharest, 2001); Ion Raţiu, *Contemporary Romania* (Richmond, 1975); Slivestru Prunduş and Clemente Plaianu, *Catolicism şi ortodoxie românească: Scurt istoric al Bisericii Române Unite* (Cluj and Napoca, 1994); Józef Darski, *Rumunia: Historia, współczesność, konflikty narodowe* (Warsaw, 1995); Paul Caravia, Virgiliu Constantinescu, and Flori Stănescu, *The Imprisoned Church of Romania, 1944–1989* (Bucharest, 1999); Dennis Deletant, *Communist Terror in Romania* (New York, 1999); uk.geocites.com; romania-on-line.net/whoswho/PFTeoctist.htm; www.petersnet.net/browse/4513.htm.

TEODOROIU Ecaterina [originally Cătalina Toderoiu] (14 January 1894, Vădeni, near Tîrgu Jiu–22 August 1917, near Muncelu), Romanian national heroine. After Romania had entered World War I in 1916, Teodoroiu voluntarily joined the Romanian Army. From October 1916, she took part in the defense of German-besieged Tîrgu Jiu. Subsequently, she took part in regular battles with the Germans, which earned her a promotion to second lieutenant. In November 1916 she was taken prisoner by the Germans but escaped several days later. In the same month she was wounded in action and was sent to a hospital as a result. In March 1917 she received a medal for valor and was made a lieutenant. Teodoroiu was killed in battle at Muncelu, leading a charge of her troops. Her life and the way she died resulted in her postwar popularity as a national heroine, inspiring Romanian artists to create patriotic pieces of art about her. In the early 1920s, one of the first Romanian-made motion pictures was titled *Ecaterina Teodoroiu*. (AB/LW)

Sources: Ion Mocioi, *Ecaterina Teodoroiu, eroina poporului Român* (Craiova, 1981); Costin Scorpan, *Istoria Romaniei: Enciclopedie* (Bucharest, 1997).

TEODOROV Teodor (27 March 1859, Elena–5 August 1924, Borovets), Bulgarian politician. In 1880 Teodorov finished high school in the Russian town of Nikolayev. In 1883 he received a law degree from New Russia University in Odessa. After returning to Bulgaria, he worked as a deputy public prosecutor in the Sofia District Court and as a judge in Ruse. After receiving a Ph.D. in law from Paris University in 1886, he assumed the post of public prosecutor in the Sofia District Court. He was also a judge of the Appeals Court and a defense attorney. In 1896 Teodorov became a member of the National Party and soon became one of its leaders. He served as minister of justice (February 1896–March 1897), minister of finance (August 1897–January 1899 and March 1911–July 1913), minister of foreign and religious affairs (October–November 1918), and prime minister and minister of foreign affairs (28 November 1918–6 October 1919). In 1919 Teodorov headed the Bulgarian delegation to the Paris Peace Conference.

From 1919 to 1923 Teodorov was a firm opponent of the government of the Bulgarian Agrarian National Union (BANU), led by **Aleksandur Stamboliyski**. In November 1920, after the National Party merged with the Progressive Liberal Party into the United National Progressive Party (UNPP), Teodorov became the leader of the UNPP. He joined the Constitutional Bloc, which was established in the summer of 1922 and which consisted of the Democratic Party, the Radical Democratic Party, and the UNPP. Teodorov attended an anti-government congress of the Constitutional Bloc in Turnovo (15 September 1922), as a result of which he was arrested and imprisoned in Shumen. In 1923 he was to stand trial as one of those who had brought about the first "national catastrophe" in Bulgaria

in 1913, but his trial was prevented by the coup of 9 June 1923. After the BANU government was overthrown, Teodorov and his party joined the Democratic Alliance. Teodorov served as deputy to the National Assembly (1894–99 and 1901–24), deputy to the Grand National Assembly (1911), and president of the Eighth National Assembly (1894–96). (JJ)

Sources: *Entsiklopediya Bulgariya*, vol. 6 (Sofia, 1988); *Sbornik v pamet na Teodor Iv. Teodorov* (Sofia, 1925); Milen Kumanov and Tania Nikolova, *Politicheski partii, organizatsii i dvizheniia v Bulgariya i tekhnite lideri 1879–1999: Kratuk spravochnik* (Sofia, 1999); Tasho Tashev, *Ministrite na Bulgariia 1879–1999: Entsiklopedichen Spravochnik* (Sofia, 1999); Angel Tsurakov, *Entsiklopediya. Pravitelstvata na Bulgariya: Khronologiya na politicheskiya zhivot 1879–2001* (Sofia, 2001).

TERELYA Yosyp (27 October 1943, Transcarpathia), Ukrainian dissident. After completing courses at a building school, Terelya worked as a blue-collar laborer. Arrested for the first time in 1962 and sentenced to a four-year imprisonment for "disloyalty," he managed to escape from prison twice. From 1965 to 1966 he was in hiding in Transcarpathia. Captured in March 1966 and sentenced to seven years in a forced labor camp, he served his sentence in a camp in Ladychyn; in prisons in Vinnytsya, Kirovohrad, and Vladimir; and in the camps of the Mordvinian ASSR. After another attempt to escape, Terelya was transferred to Vladimir in September 1969. He was imprisoned in a psychiatric hospital in Dniepropetrovsk and Berehovo in Transcarpathia and then at the Serbian Institute in Moscow. In 1970 he went on a hunger strike in the psychiatric "hospital" in Sychevka. In 1976 Terelya wrote an open letter to Yury Andropov, head of the KGB, protesting his imprisonment and the inhumane conditions in this hospital. The letter was published in the West as "Notes from a Madhouse" (1977). Released in 1977, Terelya was soon imprisoned again and spent the next four years in prisons and psychiatric hospitals. A practicing Uniate, after his release in 1982 Terelya established the Initiative Group for the Defense of the Rights of Believers and of the Church in Transcarpathian Ukraine. His brother Boris, who was in hiding for a year and a half after he had blown up a section of the pipeline near Uzhhorod, was killed in a clash with the KGB in June 1982. Arrested at the end of 1982, Terelya was sentenced to one year in a forced labor camp for "parasitism." Released in December 1983, he joined the work of the Central Committee of Ukrainian Catholics. In 1984 he renounced his Soviet citizenship and began publishing *The Chronicle of the Catholic Church in Ukraine*. Arrested in February 1985, two months later Terelya sent an open letter from prison to **Lech Wałęsa**, expressing his appreciation for Polish workers' leaders and for the Polish Episcopate. On 20 August 1985 in Uzhhorod Terelya was sentenced again, this time to seven years in a forced labor camp and five years in exile. He was released in the spring of 1987, on the wave of perestroika. Along with his family, Terelya was allowed to go to Canada, where he edited the periodical *Khrest*. (WR)

Sources: *Encyclopedia of Ukraine*, vol. 5 (Toronto, 1993); *Bibliographical Dictionary of Dissidents in the Soviet Union, 1956–1975* (The Hague, 1982); *ABN Correspondence*, 1985, nos. 3–4.

THAÇI Gasper (23 January 1889, Shkodër–26 May 1946, Shkodër), Albanian Roman Catholic bishop. Thaçi graduated from a theological seminary in Shkodër and then studied in Italy. Ordained in January 1911, he worked as a parish priest in Nenshat Dajç and Qelez in the diocese of Sappa. In 1930 he was moved to Shkodër, where he took over the local parish. Owing to the ailing health of the ordinary archbishop of Shkodër, Lazer Mjedja, Thaçi often replaced him in his duties. On 19 March 1936 Thaçi was appointed the ordinary archbishop of Shkodër and at the same time the primate of Albania. In 1939–43 Thaçi distanced himself from the Italian occupation authorities. After the war, despite Communist pressure, he refused to break with the Holy See. Thaçi died because of long-time diabetes. He was initially buried in the Shkodër Cathedral, but in 1967 his remains were removed from there in the course of a new wave of antireligious repressions following the proclamation of Albania as the first atheist state in the world. (TC)

Sources: Tadeusz Czekalski, *Zarys dziejów chrześcijaństwa albańskiego w latach 1912–1993* (Kraków, 1996); Didier Rance, *Albanie: Ils ont voulu tuer Dieu; La persécution contre l'Église catholique (1944–1991)* (Paris, 1996); Gjush Sheldija, *Kryepeshkvia metropolitane e Shkodrës e dioqezat sufragane (Shenime historike)* (Shkodër, 1957–58).

THAÇI Hashim (24 April 1968, Burojë [Broja], Drenica region, Kosovo), Albanian politician from Kosovo. Thaçi studied history at the University of Prishtina. From 1989 to 1991 he took part in protests against the abolition of Kosovo's autonomy. In 1993 he organized military resistance of the Kosovo Albanians and joined the Kosovo Liberation Army (Ushtria Çlirimtare e Kosovës [KLA]). For a few years he worked at the Institute of History in Tirana and then went to Switzerland and Austria. In 1996 in the Federal Republic of Yugoslavia (FRY), Thaçi was sentenced in absentia to ten years' imprisonment for his activities in the KLA. He called for independence for Kosovo, where he returned in 1998. On behalf of the KLA, he became a member of the Albanian delegation that held negotiations with the Serbs in Rambouillet,

near Paris. He initially opposed the agreement proposed by the mediators but finally accepted it. After the Serbs rejected this agreement, NATO began bombing the FRY. After the bombings ended in June 1999, the KLA fighters were enthusiastically greeted as heroes and victors, and Thaçi gained wide support among the Kosovo Albanians. Despite protests by **Ibrahim Rugova**, Thaçi became prime minister of the provisional government of Kosovo.

The provisional government's attempts to assert its authority in Kosovo and Thaçi's style of governing caused protests from the UN mission. Thaçi also quickly lost public support. The KLA was suspected of having links with organized crime and using brutal methods against its opponents. The KLA was to be demilitarized by September 1999, and then it was transformed into the Kosovo Protection Corps, operating under the auspices of the United Nations. In November 1999 Thaçi founded the Democratic Party of Kosovo (Partia Demokratike e Kosovës [PDK]). On 15 December 1999 UN representatives and the Kosovo Albanians' leaders, including Rugova and Thaçi, concluded an agreement, under the terms of which, among other things, the provisional government headed by Thaçi was abolished. The Joint Interim Administrative Structure was established, which was to function until the elections. Thaçi's position weakened because of his conflict with Ramush Haradinaj, the former KLA commander who founded his own party, the Alliance for the Future of Kosovo, in April 2000. In the local elections held in Kosovo on 18 October 2000, the PDK won some 27 percent of the votes, losing to Rugova's party, the Democratic League of Kosovo, which obtained 58 percent of the votes. In the parliamentary elections of 18 November 2001 the PDK obtained 25.5 percent of the votes, which allowed it to block the election of Rugova as president of Kosovo for several months. Finally, though, in March 2002 a compromise was reached, and the PDK was allowed to name its candidate for prime minister. However, owing to Rugova's -unwillingness to accept Thaçi, the post of prime minister was given to Bajram Rexhepi. (AO)

Sources: Bugajski; *Europa Środkowo-Wschodnia 1999* (Warsaw, 2001); www.rferl.org; www.state.gov/www/regions/eur/rpt%5F99 05%5Fethnic%5Fksvo%5Ftoc.html.

THALER Zoran (21 January 1962, Kranj), Slovene diplomat. In 1986 Thaler completed studies in political science and international relations at the University of Ljubljana. After the elections of April 1990, he became a member of parliament. In May 1990 he was appointed vice-minister of foreign affairs in the government of **Lojze Peterle**. Thaler was a member of the Liberal Democratic Party, renamed Liberal Democracy of Slovenia (Liberalna

Demokracija Slovenije [LDS]) in March 1994, and on its ticket he was elected to parliament in December 1992. In 1993 he became chairman of the parliamentary committee for international relations. In January 1995 he became minister of foreign affairs. At that time the efforts of the diplomatic service were primarily aimed at integrating Slovenia with the European Union (EU) and NATO, and this required improving relations with Italy. In March 1995 Italy withdrew its objections to an association agreement with the EU that Slovenia sought. The agreement was finally signed in June 1996. However, the opposition, as well as the MPs of the co-ruling Slovene Christian Democratic Party, were dissatisfied with Thaler's policy and passed a vote of no confidence against him in May 1996. In July 1996 he resigned his position. Thaler again became minister of foreign affairs in the new government of **Janez Drnovšek**, which was established in February 1997. Following a decision made in Madrid on 8 July 1997 to admit only Poland, the Czech Republic, and Hungary into NATO, Thaler was increasingly criticized in Slovenia. The mood improved when on 15 July 1997 the European Commission recognized Slovenia as one of the applicant states that was to start negotiations for admission to the European Union. Nevertheless, Thaler resigned at the end of July 1997. (AO)

Sources: "Noty biograficzne," *Redakcja Dokumentacji Prasowej PAP*, August 1997; *Europa Środkowo-Wschodnia 1995–1998* (Warsaw, 1997–2000); *Europa World Year Book 2000* (London, 2000).

THON Ozjasz Jehoshua (13 February 1870, Lemberg [Lwów, Lviv]–11 November 1936, Kraków), Zionist activist in Poland. Thon graduated in philosophy and sociology from Berlin University and from a rabbinical school in Berlin. It was then that he met Teodor Herzl, co-organized the first Zionist congress in Basel, and published *Zur geschichtsphilosophischen Begründungen des Zionismus* (1897). From 1897, Thon was a rabbi in Kraków. He co-founded the Zionist movement and numerous Jewish organizations in Galicia. For many years, he led the Zionist Organization of Western Galicia and Silesia. He founded the Ezra Library, the Solidarity Association, and *Nowy Dziennik*, the first Jewish daily published in Polish. Thon published (among other works) the monographs *Herbert Spencer* (1910) and *Teodor Herzl* (1914). In 1919, he represented the Galician Jews in the Comité des Délégations Juives during the Paris Peace Conference. Thon was a member of the Executive Committee of the World Zionist Organization. He represented the Kraków Zionists in the first Polish Assembly (1919–22) and was reelected for subsequent terms. In 1935, as a result of the debilitation

of Zionist organizations, Thon failed to keep his seat for another term. He propagated the study of Hebrew, founded a number of Tarbut schools in Poland, and co-organized the Judaic Institute in Warsaw. Thon's memoirs were published in the *Pirkei Galizyah* collection (1957), and some of his parliament speeches are in *Sejm redes 1919–1922* (1923). The Israeli town of Beth Jehoshua bears his name as a tribute to his memory. (WR)

Sources: Nella Rost Hollander, *Jehoshua Thon: Preacher, Thinker, Politician* (Montevideo, 1966); *Encyclopedia Judaica*, vol. 15 (Jerusalem, 1971); *Kto był kim w Drugiej Rzeczpospolitej* (Warsaw, 1994).

THUGUTT Stanisław (30 July 1873, Łęczyca–15 June 1941, Stockholm), Polish politician and cooperative activist. Thugutt came from a well-educated family; his father was a doctor. He graduated from Wojciech Górski High School in Warsaw and took business courses in Łódz. From his youth he worked in various private companies in the (Russian-controlled) Polish Kingdom and eventually came to live in Warsaw, where he was appointed literary manager for the weekly *Ziemia*. In 1915–16, when he was a soldier in the Polish Legions, Thugutt voiced radical social and anti-Russian opinions, and he edited the *Biuletyn* periodical of the Central National Committee. The Germans blocked Thugutt's candidature for the Provisional State Council, established by the Austro-Hungarian and German occupying authorities. In 1918, he was imprisoned in the Modlin and Warsaw Citadel prisons. Thugutt was minister of interior in **Ignacy Daszyński**'s Provisional People's Government of the Republic of Poland, established on 7 November 1918, and he kept this position until January 1919 in the government of **Jędrzej Moraczewski**. During the right-wing coup d'état attempt of 4–5 January 1919 he was briefly arrested.

As a prominent member of the Masonic Great National Lodge, Thugutt was considered very influential in the first period of the Second Republic. In 1919, he was coopted into the Polish National Committee in Paris as a delegate of the head of state, **Józef Piłsudski**. During the Polish-Soviet war he volunteered to fight on the front. In 1917–24 he was a member of the Polish Peasant Party–Liberation (Polskie Stronictwo Ludowe–Wyzwolenie [PSL–Liberation]), and from 1921 to 1924 he was chairman of its Main Board. In November 1922 Thugutt was elected MP and subsequently was appointed leader of the PSL–Liberation parliamentary fraction. He put forward **Gabriel Narutowicz** as candidate for president. After the fall of the **Wincenty Witos** government in 1923, President **Stanisław Wojciechowski** entrusted Thugutt with forming a new government; the attempt ended in failure because of the resistance of the center-right parties. In July 1924, Thugutt was offered the portfolio of foreign affairs in the government of **Władysław Grabski**. After encountering objections from his party colleagues, Thugutt left the PSL–Liberation parliamentary fraction. Eventually he became deputy prime minister in charge of nationality affairs (November 1924–May 1925). As radical views were becoming increasingly dominant in the PSL–Liberation, in April 1925 Thugutt left the party, along with **Kazimierz Bartel**, and joined the Labor Club, supporting Piłsudski. He did not support the May 1926 coup, though. Critical of the *sanacja* policies, Thugutt was one of the leaders of the Centrolew, an opposition bloc of leftist and centrist parties. Thugutt was a leading cooperative activist; for example, he chaired the Association of Cooperativists (1932–39) and the Cooperative Research Institute (1931–39). He was a member of the State Tribunal and chairman of the Parliamentary Speaker's Court in the case of **Wojciech Korfanty**. From 1931, Thugutt belonged to the Peasant Party, and during 1935–38 he was chairman of its Supreme Council. After the outbreak of World War II, General **Władysław Sikorski** called Thugutt to England, but he never reached his destination as he died on his way there. (PK)

Sources: *Słownik Polityków Polskich XX w* (Poznań, 1998); Władysław Pobóg-Malinowski, *Najnowsza historia polityczna Polski 1864–1945*, vol. 2 (London, 1983); Andrzej Ajnenkiel, *Od rządów ludowych do przewrotu majowego* (Warsaw, 1978); *Kto był kim w Drugiej Rzeczypospolitej* (Warsaw, 1994); Włodzimierz Suleja, *Józef Piłsudski* (Wrocław, 1995); Ludwik Hass, *Masoneria polska XX wieku* (Warsaw, 1996).

TIEF Otto (14 August 1889, Uuskula Rapla–5 March 1976, Ahja), Estonian politician and lawyer. In 1910–16 Tief studied law at St. Petersburg University, where he belonged to Rotalia, an Estonian academic corporation. During the Estonian war of independence Tief commanded the elite battalion of the Academic Legion (Vabadus Sõjas Kalevlaste Maleva), serving the Estonian Supreme War Committee (Eesti Sojaväelaste Ülemkomiteessee). After the war, Tief graduated in law from Tartu University, and from 1923 to 1926 he worked as a legal counselor in the Ministry of Justice. At the same time, he was a leader of the New Settlers Association (Asunike Koondis [SA]) which, founded in 1923, represented the farmers endowed with land after land reforms. Tief was also elected to the parliament on behalf of the SA. From July 1926 to March 1927, he was minister of labor and social affairs, and from March to December 1927, he was minister of justice in the government of **Jaan Teemant**. Afterwards, he was registered as a chartered attorney and opened his own legal practice. From 1928, Tief worked as a counselor at

the Agricultural Bank. He was later elected to the parliament, but he did not play an important role in politics until wartime.

In the summer of 1944 Tief assumed the leadership of the National Committee of the Estonian Republic (Eesti Vabariigi Rahvuskomitee), set up a few months earlier and made up of politicians of various parties. The committee aimed at establishing contacts with the Western Allies and getting Estonia out of the war, as well as keeping it independent from the USSR. Its plans fell flat. On 18 September 1944, the acting Estonian president, **Jüri Uluots**, appointed a government of the Estonian Republic with Tief as prime minister. Tief's cabinet declared independence. However, it failed when it attempted to organize its own armed forces, independent of the Germans, and to capture power in Tallinn. On 21 September, Tief's government and acting president Uluots decided to leave Estonia and move their headquarters to Sweden. During the evacuation, on 10 October 1944, Tief was arrested, as were most of his ministers; subsequently he was brought before the Soviet Supreme Military Court, which sentenced him to ten years in labor camp. Tief was kept in camps in Siberia and Kazakhstan. In 1956, he was released and returned to Estonia, but two years later, he was arrested again and sent to work in the Ukraine. From 1965, Tief lived in Ainazis in Latvia. A few days before his death he was allowed to return to Estonia but was ordered to settle far from Tallin, in Ahja, near Tartu. (AG)

Sources: *Eesti Entsuklopeedia*, vol. 14 (Tallinn, 2000); Mati Laur, Tõnis Lukas, Ain Mäesalu, Ago Pajur, and Tõnu Tannberg, *History of Estonia* (Tallinn, 2000); www.rotalia.ee/ajalugu.html; www.riik.ee/primeminister/p/tieftol.htm; www.iur.ut.ee/Juridica/Abstracts/1998/n-4/abs10.htm; www.okupatsioon.ee/kaastood/vab/Vabkon06.htm.

TIGRID Pavel [originally Pavel Schönfeld] (27 October 1917, Prague–31 August 2003, Prague), Czech journalist and politician. Before World War II Tigrid studied law at Charles University in Prague. In March 1939 he emigrated to England, where he worked as a journalist for the Czechoslovak section of the BBC and edited the periodicals *Kulturní zápisník* (in Czech and Slovak) and *Review 42* (in English). In June 1945 Tigrid returned to Prague and worked briefly in the Ministry of Foreign Affairs and later for the press organs of the Czechoslovak People's Party (Československá Strana Lidová [ČSL]). From 1945 to 1948 he was a commentator for the periodicals *Lidová demokracie* and *Ozbory*, and from 1946 to 1948 he was editor-in-chief of the weekly *Vývoj*. In his articles Tigrid criticized the developments in Czechoslovakia; as a result, he came into conflict with the Communists.

During the Communist coup of February 1948 Tigrid was in West Germany, where he stayed. In Frankfurt, he founded the Committee for Aid to Czechoslovak Refugees. From 1951 to 1952 he was the program director of the Czechoslovak section of Radio Free Europe. In November 1952 Tigrid resigned this post and left for the United States, where he made a living as a waiter. He also studied at Columbia University. In 1956 he founded the quarterly *Svědectví*—the most important periodical of the Czech émigré community initially published in the United States—and until 1990 was its editor-in-chief. In 1960 Tigrid left for Paris, where he lived for the next thirty years and continued publishing *Svědectví*. In 1966 the court in Prague sentenced him in absentia to fourteen years' imprisonment. One of the main spokespersons for the Czechoslovak political émigré community, Tigrid actively promoted the Czechoslovak opposition and dissident movement in the West. In *Svědectví*, various factions of the opposition movement could freely exchange their views: both writers like **Václav Havel** and **Milan Kundera** and party reformers like **Zdeněk Mlynář** published articles there. The periodical played a very important role after the Prague Spring, during the apathy of the "normalization" period in Czechoslovakia, when it published critical commentaries on the situation in the country, as well as many documents from the interwar and Stalinist periods. At that time Tigrid also strove for a dialogue between émigrés who had gone into exile in 1948 and in 1968.

In 1990 Tigrid returned to Czechoslovakia. He initially served as a member of the Council of Consultants to President Havel, and from 1991 to 1992 he was an adviser to Havel. In 1992 the last issue of *Svědectví* was published. From January 1994 to June 1996 Tigrid served as minister of culture, appointed on the recommendation of the Christian Democratic Union–Czechoslovak People's Party (Křest'anská a Demokratická Unie–Československá Strana Lidová [KDU–ČSL]). In 1996 Tigrid unsuccessfully ran in the elections to the Senate on the KDU–ČSL ticket. From March 1997 until the end of 1998 he served as the president's adviser on Czech-German relations. The author of a great number of articles, Tigrid also wrote several plays and books, devoted mainly to the analysis of the Communist system; these include *Ozbrojený mír* (Armed peace; 1948); *Marx na Hradčanech* (Marx in Hradčany; 1960); *Politická emigrace v atomovém věku* (Political refugees in the age of the atom; 1968; 1974; 1990); *Le printemps de Prague* (1968); *La chute irrésistible d'Alexandre Dubcek* (1969); and a fictionalized history of Czechoslovakia, *Kapesní průvodce inteligentní ženy po vlastním osudu* (An intelligent woman's pocket guide to her own fate; 1988). (PU)

Sources: *ČBS*; *Kdo byl kdo v našich dějinách ve 20. století*, vol. 2 (Prague, 1998); *Slovník českých spisovatelů od roku 1945*, vol. 2 (Prague, 1998); František Knopp, *Česká literatura v exilu 1948–89: Bibliografie* (Prague, 1996); Halina Janaszek-Ivančikova, ed., *Literatury zachodniosłowiańskie czasu przełomów 1890–1990*, vol. 2, *Literatura czeska* (Katowice, 1999).

TILDY Zoltán (18 November 1889, Losonc [now Slovakia]–3 August 1961, Budapest), Hungarian Peasant Party politician. Tildy's father was a *comitat* (county) official. After graduating from the Theological Academy of the Evangelical-Reformed Church in Pápa, Tildy spent one year on scholarship at the Assemble College in Belfast, Ireland. After returning to Hungary, between 1921 and 1929 he served as pastor in the town of Szenna and later in Tahitótfalu. He edited the only national daily of the Hungarian Calvinists, *Keresztény család*, and the journals *Téli újság*, *Református lelkipásztor*, and *Magyarföld*. Between 1928 and 1932 Tildy was director-pastor of the Hungarian Tract Society, and later, until 1946, he was pastor of the Protestant church in Szeghalom. Already in 1917 Tildy had joined the National Independence Party. From 1922 he was a member of the Unity Party, which was founded to support the consolidation program of Prime Minister **Istvan Bethlen**. The main aim of the program was to improve the tragic economic and social situation of Hungary after the war and revolution.

In 1929–30 Tildy co-organized the Independent Smallholders' Party (Független Kisgazdapárt [ISP]), and he became its executive vice-president. From 1936 he was an MP, representing the district of Szeghalom, and from 1939 he represented the district of Békés. From January 1940 Tildy was plenipotentiary executive president of the party. From 1942 he advocated the establishment of an alliance with the workers' parties, and he tried to persuade Regent **Miklós Horthy** to quickly withdraw from the war. After the Germans entered Hungary in March 1944, Tildy continued his activities in the underground. On 11 October 1944 he talked with Horthy, who finally agreed to a peace agreement to win over the approaching Red Army. However, it did not prevent a coup staged by the Arrow Cross Party. From November 1944 Tildy was leader of the ISP and head of the editorial staff of the political weekly *Független Kisgazdapárt*.

In November 1945 the ISP won the elections, gaining 57 percent of the vote. The party declared its support for parliamentary democracy, respect of property rights and civic liberties, and a foreign policy based on an alliance with the Western Allies. After the elections, on 15 November 1945, Tildy became prime minister, and on 11 February 1946, after a proclamation of the republican system, he was elected the first president of the Hungarian

Republic. From the end of 1946, when the Communists intensified their arrests of "plotters" in the ISP, Tildy was more and more indecisive, especially because his family got involved in obscure interests. When in May 1947 the Communists demanded the resignation of Prime Minister **Ferenc Nagy**, Tildy accepted the change of government and agreed to call new elections at the end of August; in these the fractious ISP suffered defeat. Still serving as president, Tildy continued to authorize the participation of the ISP in the government, as well as the purge, which led to the subordination of the party to the Communists.

Despite these moves, Tildy failed to save his post. When his son-in-law, Viktor Csornoky, was accused of corruption and treason, on 30 June 1948 the Communists forced Tildy to resign. Between August 1948 and May 1956 Tildy was held under house arrest in Budapest. On 27 October 1956 he became minister without portfolio and in practice deputy prime minister in the government of **Imre Nagy**. During the Hungarian Revolution, Tildy was involved mainly in developing contacts with peasant organizations and with churches. In his radio speeches, Tildy came out in support of a multiparty system, national independence, and freedom. He also called for the reorganization of the ISP. On 4 November Tildy left the parliament building through the cordon of Soviet soldiers surrounding the building. Soon after, he was arrested, and on 15 June 1958, in the trial of Imre Nagy and associates, Tildy was sentenced to six years by the People's Judicial Council of the Supreme Court. In April 1959, owing to his advanced age, and in fact because of illness, Tildy was released under an individual amnesty. Until his death he lived in seclusion. (JT)

Sources: *Magyar Életrajzi Lexikon*, vol. 2 (Budapest, 1969); *Biographisches Lexikon*, vol. 4; Ferenc Nagy, *The Struggle behind the Iron Curtain* (New York, 1948); *New York Times*, 4 August 1961; Imre Kovacs, ed., *Facts about Hungary* (New York, 1966); Károly Vigh, *Tildy Zoltán életútja* (Békéscsaba, 1991); Erzsébet Rácz, *Feljegyzések a vihar kapujában: Emlékezés Tildy Zoltánra* (Budapest, 1995); *A magyar forradalom és szabadságharc enciklopédiája*, CD-ROM (Budapest, 1999).

TIMOSHENKO Semyon (18 February 1895, Furmanka, near Odessa–31 March 1970, Moscow), Soviet marshal of Ukrainian descent. The son of a peasant, during World War I Timoshenko served in the tsarist army, but in October 1917 he joined the Bolshevik units, which were transformed into the Red Army in early 1918. In 1919 Timoshenko joined the Bolshevik party, as a result of which he quickly rose through the ranks. He commanded a cavalry brigade that in 1919 became part of the Cavalry Army led by Semyon Budenny. In the summer of 1920 Timoshenko fought against Polish forces in Kiev and then against the forces led by General Pyotr Wrangel and **Nestor Makhno**. Timoshenko completed military courses (1922) and courses for commanders at the Lenin Military and Political Academy (1930). From 1933 to 1935 he was deputy commander of the Belorussian Military District, and from 1935 to 1937 he was commander of the Kiev Military District. He then assumed command of the Military District in the Northern Caucasus and Kharkiv (1937) and command of the Military District in Kiev (1938). In the spring of 1938 Timoshenko was accused of being an "enemy of the people," but he was saved by **Nikita Khrushchev**, the new first secretary of the Central Committee (CC) of the Communist Party (Bolshevik) of Ukraine (CP[B]U).

In 1939 Timoshenko joined the CC of the All-Union Communist Party (Bolsheviks). As a commander of the Ukrainian Front, he led the invasion of Poland on 17 September 1939. Although he announced that the Red Army was marching into Poland to offer its assistance against Germany, the Soviets treated the captured members of the Polish armed forces as prisoners of war, and Polish officers were arrested and handed over to the NKVD, which massacred them in 1940. In January 1940 during the Soviet-Finnish war Timoshenko was placed in command of the Red Army's operations but failed to force the Finns to capitulate. In May 1940 he was appointed marshal and then commissar for defense of the Soviet Union. In July 1940 he barely escaped an assassination attempt by activists of the Polish pro-independence underground. After Germany invaded the Soviet Union in June 1941, Timoshenko became commander of the Western and Southwestern Fronts and consequently assumed the position of deputy commissar for defense. He commanded the Stalingrad Front (1942) and the Northwestern Front (1943), and then he was appointed the Soviet Supreme Command representative for coordinating army movements, mainly in the Balkans. After World War II, Timoshenko served as commander of the Military District in the Urals (1945–49) and then in Belorussia (1949–60). From 1949 to 1960 he was a member of the CC and of the Politburo of the Communist Party of Belorussia. In 1952 he became a deputy member of the CC of the Communist Party of the Soviet Union (CPSU). After retiring in 1960, Timoshenko chaired the State Committee for War Veterans. (WR)

Sources: *MERSH*, vol. 39; *Prominent Personalities in the USSR* (Metuchen, N.J., 1968); *Encyclopedia of Ukraine*, vol. 5 (Toronto, 1994); Walter Mehring, *Timoshenko: Marshal of the Red Army* (New York, 1942); Seweryn Bialer, *Stalin and His Generals* (New York, 1969); David R. Marples, *Stalinism in Ukraine in the 1940s* (London, 1992).

TISCHNER Józef (12 March 1931, Stary Sącz–28 June 2000, Kraków), Polish priest and philosopher. Tischner came from a highlander family and spent his childhood in Łopuszna. After graduating from high school in Nowy Targ, for a year he studied law, and in 1950–55 he studied theology at the Jagiellonian University in Kraków. Ordained in 1955, Tischner continued philosophical studies at the Catholic Theology Academy (CTA) in Warsaw and, from 1957 to 1959, at the Philosophical-Historical Department of the Jagiellonian University. He was tutored by Roman Ingarden. In 1963, Tischner received a Ph.D. on the basis of his dissertation "Ja transcendentalne w filozofii Edmunda Husserla" (The transcendental me in Edmund Husserl's philosophy; 1963). In 1968, Tischner received a scholarship and spent a year at the University of Louvain, Belgium. His stay there resulted in the dissertation "Studia z teorii świadomości" (Studies in the theory of consciousness), which earned him a postdoctoral degree at the CTA in 1974. In the 1970s, Tischner became increasingly influential in Poland's intellectual life. While sticking to the phenomenological tradition, he headed for the philosophy of drama and the metaphysics of good, taking his own path, different from that of Husserl. In an article titled "Schyłek chrześcijaństwa tomistycznego" (The decline of Thomist Christianity; 1970), he called into question the philosophical primacy of Thomism on the grounds that it rendered faith ideological and concealed the Revelation. From that point there was not a significant debate in the Polish Church in which Tischner did not take part; many of them he initiated himself. His most important texts from that period are found in the books *Świat ludzkiej nadziei* (The world of human hope; 1975) and *Myślenie według wartości* (Thinking by the values; 1982). At the end of the 1970s, Tischner also took issue with Marxism in the book *Polski kształt dialogu* (The Polish shape of dialogue; 1979).

The year 1980 marked the beginning of Tischner's public activity. His October 1980 sermon at Wawel Castle in Kraków during a mass for Solidarity leaders ("Solidarity means carrying one another's burdens"; "The deepest solidarity is that of consciences") initiated a series of texts published in *Tygodnik Powszechny*. Later, those texts were published as a collection titled *Etyka Solidarności* (The ethics of solidarity; 1981); in them Tischner reflected on the ethical dimensions of contemporary events. Since then he was generally regarded as the chaplain of Solidarity. The sermon he preached at the First Congress of Solidarity became part of its official documents. In a homily that Pope **John Paul II** preached at Zaspa in Gdańsk in 1987, he cited Tischner's texts as the ones that best rendered the truth about Solidarity. Accepting the duty of the chaplain

of the Association of the Tatra Highlanders in 1980, Tischner set out to "crystallize the highlander idea." He organized annual masses at Mt. Turbacz and supported the development of the highlander culture. Owing to his initiative, the Tatra farmers gained the opportunity to study in Austria; they also received help with equipment. The literary aftermath of Tischner's support for the highlanders was the sermons he preached in the local highland dialect and the book *Historia filozofii po góralsku* (History of philosophy the highlander way; 1997).

After 1989, Tischner supported the Poles in their endeavors to build a new social, political, and—first and foremost—ethical order. He wrote articles for *Tygodnik Powszechny*; these were collected and published in books such as *Nieszczęsny dar wolności* (The unfortunate gift of freedom; 1993), *W krainie schorowanej wyobraźni* (In the land of morbid imagination; 1997), and *Ksiądz na manowcach* (A stray priest; 1999). Tischner also continued purely philosophical activities. The works in which he presented his own original philosophy include *Filozofia dramatu* (The philosophy of drama; 1990) and *Spór o istnienie człowieka* (The debate over the existence of man; 1998). From 1982, Tischner was dean of the Philosophical Department of the Papal Theological Academy in Kraków several times. When he was elected rector, he refused to accept the position on the grounds that it would be incompatible with his priestly duties. For many years, Tischner was president of the Institute for Human Sciences in Vienna. He received a number of awards. In 1999, he was decorated with the Polish Order of the White Eagle. The last years of his life were marked with a struggle with cancer of the larynx. In this period, Tischner's literary output intensified even further. His writings touched upon the profoundest religious experiences: the relation of freedom and grace, as well as mercy. In a telegram sent after Tischner's death, John Paul II wrote, "He was a man of the Church, always careful not to lose sight of man when defending the truth." (ZS)

Sources: Teresa Szczerbińska and Beata Zalewska, *Bibliografia publikacji ks. Józefa Tischnera 1955–1994* (Kraków, 1995); Jarosław Gowin, *Kościół w czasach wolności 1989–1999* (Kraków, 1999); Józef Kwapiszewski, *Filozofia ks. Józefa Tischnera jako źródło dialogu* (Słupsk, 1999); Wojciech Bonowicz, *Tischner* (Kraków, 2001).

TISO Jozef (13 October 1887, Bytča–18 April 1947, Bratislava), priest, president of Slovakia. Born into a large family of farmers, after completing a Catholic school (where he studied in Slovak, Hungarian, and German), Tiso attended a gymnasium in Žilina. Then he began theological studies in Nitra and in a Hungarian seminary,

Pazmaneum, in Vienna. He was ordained in 1910 in Vienna. Tiso began his pastoral work in 1910 in the Slovak village of Osčadnice and then in Rajca, combining pastoral work with social engagement. Tiso created cultural-educational associations and people's banks through the parish. In 1913 he went to the parish in Bánovce-nad-Bebravou and was involved in pastoral work there until 1945. After the outbreak of World War I Tiso became the chaplain of a Slovak regiment from Trenčín. However, he was soon taken seriously ill and was moved to Nitra, where he worked at a local theological seminary, lecturing in moral and pastoral theology. From 1920 to 1923 Tiso was a secretary to Bishop **Karel Kmetko** in Nitra. In 1924 he became a parish priest in Bánovce-nad-Bebravou.

From his youth Tiso remained under the influence of Reverend **Andrej Hlinka**, acting in favor of the national emancipation of the Slovaks. He sought equality for the Slovak language in pastoral work and religious instruction. He spoke against the use of Church structures for the Magyarization of Slovak Catholics. From the mid-1920s Tiso was a member of the leadership of Rev. Hlinka's party, the Slovak People's Party (Slovenská L'udova Strana [SL'S]). Between 1925 and 1939 he was an MP to the National Assembly, a president of the parliamentary club, and vice-president of the SL'S. In 1927–28, when the Prague government encouraged Slovak autonomists to co-rule, Tiso held the post of minister of education and physical culture. In the parliament he supported Slovak autonomy within the framework of a common state with the Czechs. He was critical of Prague centralism, which, according to him, led to economic difficulties and mass unemployment in Slovakia. At first Tiso put his hopes in President **Edvard Beneš**, who had pledged to respect the program of Slovak autonomy. When Beneš failed to keep his promise, Tiso increasingly sharply criticized the president of Czechoslovakia.

After the Pact of Munich and the First Vienna Award, when Transcarpathian Ruthenia was ceded to Hungary and Slovakia gained autonomy within Czechoslovakia (19 November 1938), Tiso became prime minister of the autonomous Slovak government. On the night of 9–10 March 1939 the president of Czechoslovakia, **Emil Hácha**, dismissed the autonomous Slovak government, and the army assumed power in Slovakia. For a short time Tiso found himself under house arrest. Despite pressure from adherents of the Third Reich, Tiso hesitated to ask Hitler for political support. He thought the situation was not ripe enough to proclaim an independent state. On 13 March 1939 Tiso was summoned to Berlin, where Hitler informed him that the liquidation of Czechoslovakia had been determined. Tiso was only to agree to the proclamation of

independence of Slovakia. Otherwise Hitler threatened to allow the occupation of Slovakia by Hungarian troops. Under these circumstances Tiso accepted the proclamation of independence of Slovakia. He refused, though, to announce the declaration of sovereignty on Berlin radio, stating that this was in the area of competence of the Slovak parliament. However, he accepted a telegram prepared by the Germans that stated that Hitler would guarantee the independence of Slovakia. On 14 March 1939, at a meeting of the Slovak parliament, the sovereignty of Slovakia was unanimously announced, and the creation of an independent state was proclaimed.

From 14 March to 28 October 1939 Tiso was prime minister, and then until early April 1945 he was president of Slovakia. The government he headed swerved between authoritarianism and a Slovak version of fascism, supported by, among others, Prime Minister **Béla Tuka**. Tiso tried to organize the sociopolitical life of Slovakia on the authoritarian model, although the parliament still functioned. During the war Slovakia was completely subordinated to the Third Reich, in both foreign and domestic policy; extreme forces, represented by paramilitary units, the Hlinka Guard, gradually began to come into prominence. At first, because of favorable circumstances stemming from the war, the Slovak economy flourished. However, after 1943 the negative effects of the dependence on Germany became more obvious and led to an increase of opposition to Tiso's rule. Severe repressive measures were taken against the opposition, mainly the Communists, but also against the representatives of other parties. Tiso was responsible for the involvement of the Slovak Army in the aggression against Poland in September 1939, for the declaration of war against Great Britain and the United States, and for the participation of the Slovak military in an attack on the USSR in June 1941. At home he allowed the Fascist circles, rallied around **Alexander Mach** and Tuka, to carry out the so-called Aryanization—that is, nationalization—of Jewish property and to introduce the so-called Jewish code on 9 September 1941. The code outlawed Slovak citizens of Jewish nationality. From March 1942 many of them were deported and killed in Nazi death camps. Over all, around seventy thousand Slovak Jews perished. As a result of the intervention of the Holy See in 1943, Tiso forbade the further deportation of Jews.

After the outbreak of the Slovak National Uprising in August 1944, Tiso sided with the Nazi army, supporting the bloody pacification it carried out. He thought that the uprising was instigated only by Communists sent from Moscow and that it threatened the independence of the state. He did not attempt to negotiate with the military leaders of the uprising. In October 1944, at a victory parade in Banska Bystrica, Tiso personally decorated the commanders of the Germans units. In the struggle against the partisans the Operational Units of the Hlinka Guard supported the Germans. In the autumn of 1944 Tiso's rule was mainly based upon the backing of German garrisons. The apparatus of violence—especially the Hlinka Guard, led by a Germanophile, Otomar Kubala, and the Headquarters of State Security—functioned until the end of the war. On 3 April 1945 Tiso fled to Austria and took refuge in a Benedictine monastery, Kremsmünsteri, where the American Army interned him in June. Tiso was delivered to Czechoslovak authorities in September 1945. On 2 December 1945 a public trial of top Slovak leaders, including Tiso, began in Bratislava. Tiso was sentenced to death, and President Beneš rejected his plea for pardon. At an extraordinary meeting on 16 April 1947, the Czechoslovak government led by Prime Minister **Klement Gottwald** decided to confirm the death sentence, despite the votes of ministers from the Czechoslovak People's Party and the Slovak Democratic Party. As a result Tiso was hanged.

After Slovakia's proclamation of independence in 1992 a discussion on Tiso's role in the recent history of Slovakia was launched. It was emphasized that although personally Tiso was often an opponent of radical activities in the domestic arena and tried to prevent the involvement of greater numbers of Slovak forces in the war on the side of the Third Reich, he bore responsibility for the policy of loyalty to Hitler. Despite the endeavors of Slovak nationalists, Tiso was not officially rehabilitated. (AGr)

Sources: Konštantin Čulen, *Po Svätoplukovi druhá naša hlava: Život dr. Jozefa Tisu* (Radošina, 1992); Henryk Batowski, *Zdrada monachijska: Sprawa Czechosłowacji i dyplomacja europejska w roku 1938* (Poznań, 1973); Jerzy Kozeński, *Czechosłowacka jesień 1938* (Poznań, 1989); *Kdo byl kdo v našich dějinách ve 20 století* (Prague, 1994); Ivan Kamenec, *Slovenský Stát 1939–1945* (Prague, 1992); Ewa Orlof, *Dyplomacja polska wobec sprawy słowackiej w latach 1938–1939* (Kraków, 1980); Ferdinand Beer, *Słowacja na przełomie: Powstanie słowackie 1944* (Warsaw, 1969); Václav Vaško, *Neumlčena, Kronika katolické Cirkvé v Československu po druhé světové válce* (Prague, 1990); Miloslav Moulis, *Akcja "Märzwirbel"* (Warsaw, 1983); *Dějiny zemi koruny české: Od nástupu osvícenstvi po naši dobu*, vol. 2 (Prague, 1993).

TISZA István (22 April 1861, Geszt–31 October 1918, Budapest), Hungarian politician. Tisza was a son of Count Kálmán Tisza, a leading nineteenth-century Hungarian politician, co-founder of the ruling Liberal Party (Szabadelvú Párt [LP]). When he was only fourteen years old, Tisza passed his high school final exams and took up legal and economic studies in Budapest and then in Berlin and Heidelberg, where he graduated. In 1881, he received a Ph.D. in political science in Budapest. Tisza belonged to the Evangelical Reformed Church. For five years he ran a family estate, and then he was elected MP as an LP representative in 1886. In 1897, Tisza received, from Emperor Francis Joseph, the title of count that had belonged to his uncle Lajos Tisza. Like his father, Tisza was a staunch advocate of the 1867 compromise. He held the view that only in alliance with Austria and within the monarchy could Hungary maintain the status of a power and—under the leadership of the native aristocracy and nobility—maintain its territorial integrity because it was a country that had so many national minorities. Tisza believed in law and order and a constitutional system as long as they strengthened rather than weakened the Hungarian state. He was against expanding voting rights on the grounds that such a move would jeopardize Hungarian supremacy in the state. A supporter of dualism, Tisza was determined to prevent the opposition from taking power since the opposition was against the 1867 compromise. Therefore, he tacitly supported voting abuse that prevented the opposition from winning elections.

On 3 November 1903, Tisza became prime minister. The task he considered crucial was to overcome the parliamentary obstruction of the opposition, which did not want to let a bill pass that would increase the number of recruits called up for the joint Austro-Hungarian Army. Tisza was not willing to accept compromise solutions; he rejected all proposals to transform the monarchial structure. His rigid stance made the parliamentary chambers look more and more often like a battlefield (fights, damaged equipment, and the like). In addition, Tisza ruthlessly combated workers' and agrarian-Socialist movements. In April 1904 he did not hesitate to order a violent crackdown on a strike of railroaders. He ordered the police to open fire on Romanian peasants who participated in a demonstration in the village of Élesd, leading to thirty-three deaths. In November 1904 he pushed for a modification of parliamentary regulations that resulted in the breakup of the LP, its defeat in the parliamentary elections, and Tisza's resignation from the government on 18 June 1905.

After a government had been established by a national coalition in 1906, Tisza withdrew from the political scene. After the fall of the coalition in 1910, he returned, setting up the National Labor Party (Nemzeti Munkapárt [NLP]) and winning the parliamentary elections. The NLP gained an absolute parliamentary majority. On 22 May 1912, Tisza became speaker of the parliament. Because of the Balkan Wars, he accelerated the draft for increased numbers of recruits; the following day this move resulted in a series of strikes and a huge, bloodily suppressed demonstration of workers (the so-called bloody Thursday). Five days later, there was an unsuccessful bomb attempt to kill him. In

June, Tisza pushed for a bill to increase the joint army and had opposition parliamentarians forcibly removed if they protested it. One of them made a failed attempt on Tisza's life and then committed suicide. Tisza removed all obstructions; on his orders, the police did not let opposition MPs into the parliament building for two months.

On 10 June 1913, Tisza became prime minister again. Immediately after the assassination of the heir to the throne, Francis Ferdinand, and his wife in Sarajevo, he was against declaring war on Serbia as he considered the monarchy not to be sufficiently prepared for it. He was also afraid lest Russia join the war. Three weeks later, he changed his mind, mobilizing society both in the parliament and outside of it. Convinced that all forces must be concentrated on the war, he was even more against proposals for political reforms. After the death of Francis Joseph in 1916, his successor, Charles IV, refused to support Tisza and his rigid policies, contrary to his predecessor. Therefore, on 15 June 1917 Tisza resigned. Since his party had a parliamentary majority, he was able to torpedo the reformist initiatives of his successor, **Sándor Wekerle**. To set a personal example, in summer 1917 Tisza went to the front lines for over two months as the commander of a cavalry regiment. When he returned to Budapest, a third unsuccessful attempt on his life was made. Dislike for him turned into hatred as the situation at the front deteriorated. In fall 1918, as the personification of a war already lost and of a dual state that was falling apart, Tisza was the most hated politician in Hungary. On the last day of October, he was shot dead by an eight-soldier unit in his own house. The perpetrators were never caught. (JT)

Sources: *Magyar Életrajzi Lexikon*, vol. 2 (Budapest, 1969); *Nagy Képes Milleniumi Arcképcsarnok* (Budapest, 1999); *Biographische Lexikon*, vol. 4; Nicholas Horthy, *Memoirs* (Paris, 1954); Michael Karolyi, *Faith without Illusion* (London, 1959); Paul Ignotus, *Hungary* (London, 1972); *Magyarország történeti kronológiája*, vol. 3 (Budapest, 1983); Steven Bela Vardy, *Historical Dictionary of Hungary* (Lanham, Md., 1997); Ignac Romsics, *Hungary in the Twentieth Century* (Budapest, 1999).

TITO Josip [originally Broz] (7 May 1892, Kumrovec–4 May 1980, Ljubljana), Yugoslav Communist leader. Tito was the seventh of fifteen children born into a Catholic peasant family on the borders of Croatia and Slovenia. From early youth he worked as a locksmith, crisscrossing his homeland, as well as Czechoslovakia and Germany. In 1910 he joined the Croatian Social Democratic Party. From 1913 he served in the Austro-Hungarian Army. In 1915 he was taken captive by the Russians. He stayed in the Ural Mountains and then worked as a mechanic in the Volga region and in Siberia. Released after the February 1917 revolution, he went to Petrograd, where he was active in the preparations for the Bolshevik coup.

Arrested by the authorities of the Provisional Government and sent again to Siberia, he took part in the revolution as a member of the Red Guard in Omsk and then in Kazakhstan.

In 1920 Tito returned to Yugoslavia as a Bolshevik activist. After the outlawing of the Communist Party, he was arrested twice, in 1923 and 1927. At that time he officially served as the secretary general of the metalworkers' trade union. In April 1927 Tito illegally joined the party committee in Zagreb, and in 1928, as a supporter of Stalin in his fight against Trotsky, he became a deputy member of the Politburo of the party. Arrested again in 1929, he spent five years in prison, where he met (among others) **Moša Pijade**, the leading ideologist of the party. After his release, Tito resumed his conspiratorial work, traveling, for example, to Paris, Vienna, and Prague. For a year he worked in Moscow in the Balkan unit of the Comintern. Although he was known there as "Comrade Walter," it was then he assumed another of his pseudonyms, Tito, as his surname. In the spring of 1936 he became an organizational secretary of the Central Committee of the Communist Party of Yugoslavia (CPY). As a loyal Stalinist, he avoided the massacre among the Yugoslav Communists during the great purge of 1937–38; according to some reports, he was an accomplice to it. In 1937 the Comintern designated him as the provisional secretary general of the party. Tito then promoted his supporters—among others, **Milovan Djilas**, **Aleksander Ranković**, and **Edvard Kardelj**. He also mobilized Yugoslav volunteers to fight on the side of the Spanish Republic. In October 1940 a secret CPY conference accepted Tito as the head of the party. The Communists remained passive when the Yugoslav government signed the anti-Comintern Pact. They also did not take action after Hitler's invasion of Yugoslavia in June 1941, as Berlin was still Moscow's ally.

Only after Hitler's invasion of the USSR did Tito, heading a Communist faction of the anti-German guerrillas in occupied Yugoslavia, issue a call to arms. He issued a general declaration, "Death to fascism; freedom to the people," which gained him support especially in the countryside. His partisans controlled a sizable mountainous part of the country. For a long time the general headquarters of the movement remained in Serbian Užice. There the Communists created a revolutionary government for the freed areas, excluding from this government the partisans of Colonel **Dragoljub (Draža) Mihailović**—that is, the Chetniks, linked with the government-in-exile of King Peter in London. Tito's partisans received Soviet aid, though in amounts suitable for the tactics of Stalin, who was apprehensive that excessively swift Communist successes might complicate his game with the Western Allies. In November 1941 the Germans attacked Užice. Tito's partisan army, involved at the same time in struggles against the Croatian Ustashe and the Chetniks, suffered great losses.

After the fall of the "Užice Republic" the movement centered in Bosnia and Montenegro, where Tito quickly rebuilt his troops. In November 1942 he established the Anti-Fascist Council for the National Liberation of Yugoslavia (Antifašističko Vijeće Narodnog Oslobodjenja Jugoslavije [AVNOJ]), which proclaimed the program of a federal people's republic. Tito became the head of its provisional government, gaining the title of marshal. Despite further losses in the battles at the Neretva and Sutjeska Rivers against the Germans, the Italians, and the Ustashe at the beginning of 1943, Tito's guerrillas continued to revive because their tactics and AVNOJ's program appealed to the peasants more than the strategy of the Chetniks, who were gathering strength and weapons for a decisive attack at the time of the Allies' offensive. After the capitulation of Italy in September 1943 Tito's troops of around fifty thousand partisans became considerably reinforced with weapons and equipment seized from the Italians. In May 1944 the German offensive in Bosnia again threatened the partisans, and Tito himself barely avoided being captured in his headquarters in Drvar. The Allies' backing for the government-in-exile and the Chetniks was diminishing; therefore from mid-1944 Tito's supporters liberated the country from the Germans and also eliminated the Chetniks. In September 1944 Tito met with Stalin and behaved as though he were his partner rather than his subordinate, which made the Soviet dictator suspicious.

Under pressure from the Allies, on 1 November 1944 Tito made an agreement with the London government-in-exile of **Ivan Šubašić**. In return for including several ministers-in-exile in the provisional government led by Tito, Šubašić would recognize AVNOJ as a provisional parliament and guarantee that King Peter would not return home without the approbation of the "Yugoslav masses." The Big Three accepted the agreement in Yalta. On 6 March 1945 Tito became the head of the provisional government, in which Šubašić assumed the portfolio for foreign affairs. Tito's supporters immediately broke the agreement, deposing the king, changing the name of the state, and establishing Communist legislation. When the ministers-in-exile resigned in protest, the Communists increased the terror. The Communist political police arrested not only Serb collaborators and Croatian Ustashe, but thousands of innocent people as well. Particular repression fell upon Slovene and Croatian Catholics.

In November 1945 the Communists organized an election. According to the announced results, 90.6 percent of the vote supposedly went to the Communist lists. In March 1946 Mihailović was captured. After a fabricated trial he was sentenced to death and executed in July 1946. In a show trial the Communists also sentenced the primate of Croatia, Archbishop **Alojzije Stepinac**, to sixteen years of hard labor. With considerable influence upon the part of society to which the socially radical and federal program of the Communists was a counterpoint to the unstable and Serb-dominated Yugoslavia, Tito imposed a brutal Stalinist dictatorship upon the country. Although in Yugoslavia tensions appeared between Tito's administration and Soviet advisers who interfered in domestic matters, in Moscow Tito was at first treated as one of the prominent leaders of the Communist movement. Tito actively supported the Greek Communist guerrillas. In 1947 he belonged to the promoters and founders of the Communist Information Bureau (Cominform). At the same time, he aimed at the unification of Yugoslavia, Albania, and Bulgaria into a Balkan federation. The project won the support of the leader of the Bulgarian Communists, **Georgi Dimitrov**, but provoked objections from Stalin, who summoned Tito and Dimitrov to Moscow. Dimitrov went, but Tito sent only his delegates. The delegates agreed to consult on Yugoslavia's foreign policy with the Kremlin, but Tito rejected this agreement. In response the USSR withdrew its military advisers in March 1948. Tito's conciliatory letter expressing regret and a willingness to cooperate closely was met with Stalin's fundamental criticism of Tito, who replied that he was willing to invite the leaders of the USSR for ideological talks but reserved the right of self-determination in regard to national aims. Stalin rejected this standpoint as "arrogant" and "anti-party."

In June 1948 the conflict was revealed in a Cominform statement that denounced the ideology and policy of the Yugoslav leaders. Soon, in Moscow's propaganda, "Tito-ism" became an enemy as terrible as "imperialism," and Tito himself was described as a "watchdog of imperialism." Yugoslavia, isolated from the West, found itself in a vacuum. Tito took control of the situation within the party by purging it of around one hundred thousand members suspected of disloyalty. Around fifteen thousand supporters of the Cominform were imprisoned in a concentration camp at Beli Otok, and several leading Stalinists were murdered. At first Tito attempted to outdo the USSR in Communist orthodoxy, but a collapse of the economy forced him to change course. In 1950 the collectivization of the countryside was abandoned, and the supervision of industry was decentralized with the introduction of the self-management system of ownership. In return for Yugoslavia's sealing off of the border between Yugoslavia and Greece—which definitely undermined the position of the Greek Communists—the United States granted Yugoslavia $1 billion in economic aid. The new constitution of

June 1953 strengthened the federal character of the state. At the same time, Tito suppressed the supporters of further reforms by removing their leading spokesman, Džilas, and sentencing him to a long prison term.

After Stalin's death the Soviet collective leadership began to seek a reconciliation with Yugoslavia, and in May 1955 **Nikita Khrushchev** came to Belgrade with a conciliatory mission. Soviet-Yugoslav relations improved thereafter, but Tito remained fully independent in foreign policy. In 1956 he condemned the Soviet invasion of Hungary, although he agreed to deliver **Imre Nagy**, who took refuge in the Yugoslav Embassy. In 1968 Tito criticized the Warsaw Pact invasion of Czechoslovakia. However, he avoided antagonizing the Kremlin, and in 1971 he and Leonid Brezhnev signed a treaty of mutual non-interference in domestic matters. In 1979 Tito protested the Soviet invasion of Afghanistan. Tito was one of the founders and leaders of the movement of non-aligned states. In 1961 a conference of the movement was held in Belgrade. Tito visited numerous countries in Africa, Asia, and Latin America, including Cuba, where he tried to persuade Fidel Castro to assume a more independent position from the USSR. Tito visited the United States four times and also maintained good relations with India and China. In domestic policy he held the government apparatus in an iron grip but opened Yugoslavia to Western tourists and allowed the Yugoslavs to travel abroad to earn money. Income from tourism and foreign assistance supported the Yugoslav balance of payments. In 1966 Tito eliminated the influence of **Aleksander Ranković** and his political police and based his power upon the party and the state bureaucracy. In 1971 he suppressed national ferment in the Croatian party. In 1974 he became Yugoslavia's president for life. At first Tito was a man of modest material needs, but as the years went by, he surrounded himself with increasing luxury. Apart from a residence on Brioni Island, he owned seventeen palaces, as well as hunting grounds, and his vanity and fondness for splendor became an open secret. Tito was married three times, the last time to Jovanka Budisavljević. His funeral in 1980 was an unprecedented gathering of world political leaders. After Tito's death the state he created began to disintegrate. (WR)

Sources: *Enciklopedija Jugoslavije*, vol. 7 (Zagreb, 1968); Adam Ulam, *Titoism and the Cominform* (Cambridge, Mass., 1952); Vladimir Dedijer, *Tito* (New York, 1953); Roger Swearingen, ed., *Leaders of the Communist World* (New York, 1971); *Annual Obituary*, 1980; Milovan Djilas, *Tito: The Story from Inside* (New York, 1980); Michał Jerzy Zacharias, *Jugosławia w polityce Wielkiej Brytanii 1940–1945* (Wrocław, 1985).

TITULESCU Nicolae (4 March 1882, Craiova–17 March 1941, Cannes), Romanian politician. After graduation from college, Titulescu obtained a Ph.D. in legal sciences from a university in Paris in 1905. The same year he began scholarly work at the university in Iași. He started his political career in February 1908, joining the Conservative Democratic Party of **Dumitru (Take) Ionescu**. In 1912 Titulescu became an MP. From August 1913 he took part in the committee for the affairs of Southern Dobruja during the Bucharest peace conference. After Romania entered World War I, Titulescu became a member of the government for the first time, assuming the portfolio of minister of finance in the cabinet of **Ion Brătianu** and then in the cabinet of Ionescu. After the capitulation of Romania, Titulescu left for Paris to continue actions in favor of his country. He was one of the delegates to the Paris Peace Conference. From July 1920 he was minister of finance in the governments of **Alexandru Averescu** and Ionescu, implementing a tax reform. On 16 December 1921 Titulescu became envoy to Great Britain and held the post, with a year's break, until October 1932. At the same time, from 1 April 1924, he served as the permanent representative to the League of Nations. From 1925 Titulescu participated in the works of the International Diplomatic Academy in Paris, of which he became vice-president.

In July 1927 Titulescu assumed the post of minister of foreign affairs for the first time in the government of Ion Brătianu, and he held the post until August 1928. Between 1930 and 1931 he presided over the debates of the Eleventh and Twelfth Sessions of the League of Nations Assembly. Moreover, on 16 October 1930 he became a member of the Permanent Court of Arbitration in The Hague. Between October 1932 and August 1936, after his return from a post in London, Titulescu again served as minister of foreign affairs in the governments of **Ion Duca** and **Gheorghe Tătărescu**. At that time he enjoyed an almost autonomous position in the government. Titulescu's diplomatic achievements include the transformation of the Little Entente from a strictly military alliance into a political and economic alliance (30 May–1 June 1933), the normalization of Romania's relations with the USSR (9 July 1934), and the creation of the Balkan Entente (9 February 1934). The second term of his ministry coincided with a deterioration of relations with Italy and Poland. Titulescu sharply opposed Italian aggression against Ethiopia in 1935. He was also one of the most ardent advocates of imposing severe economic sanctions on Italy. Problems in the relations with Poland resulted from Titulescu's attempts to sign a treaty of mutual assistance with the USSR. These moves met with protests in Romania as well. As a result of international pressure and domestic opposition, which rallied around King **Charles II** and was supported by the Polish ambassador, on 29 August 1936 Titulescu was removed from the government under the pretext of its reconstruction. As minister, Titulescu was considered an outstanding politician and a leading opponent of fascism and territorial revisionism. After his dismissal from the government Titulescu never returned to politics. He went to Switzerland and then to France, where he remained from 1937 until his death. Some of Titulescu's works, including *Documente diplomatice* (Diplomatic documents; 1967), were issued in Romania under Communist rule, while others were issued in the 1990s. Titulescu's *Documente confidentiale* (Confidential documents) were published in 1992 and *Romania's Foreign Policy* in 1994. (FA/TD)

Sources: *Biographisches Lexicon*, vol. 4; *Politics and Political Parties in Roumania* (London, 1936); Şerban N. Ionescu, *Who Was Who in Twentieth Century Romania* (Boulder, Colo., 1994); Józef Beck, "Polska polityka zagraniczna 1926–1932," in Anna M. Cienciała, ed. (Paris, 1990); I. Grecescu, *Nicolae Titulescu: Gindire şi actiune* (Bucharest, 1980); *Marii figuri ale diplomaţiei româneşti, Nicolae Titulescu* (Bucharest, 1982); Ion M. Oprea, *Nicolae Titulescu* (Bucharest, 1966); Ion M. Oprea, *Titulescu's Diplomatic Activity* (Bucharest, 1968); *Probleme de politică externă a României* (Bucharest, 1977).

TKACHOU Mikhas (10 March 1942, Mstsislau, Belorussian SSR–31 October 1992, Minsk), Belorussian historian and politician. In 1964 Tkachou graduated from the Department of History of the Belorussian State University in Minsk. He began working at the Institute of History of the Academy of Sciences of the Belorussian SSR in 1968 and at the Institute of History of Hrodna University in 1978. Tkachou earned a doctorate in history in 1987 and became a professor in 1989. His research focused particularly on defense architecture in Belorussia in the thirteenth–eighteenth centuries. He wrote the books *Zamki Belorussii* (The castles of Belorussia; 1987), *Zamki i liudzi* (Castles and people; 1991), and *Pakhodnia* (Torch; 1994). From 1989 Tkachou was one of the leaders of the Belorussian democratic opposition. A co-founder of the Belorussian People's Front, he became its vice-chairman in June 1989. In 1991 he founded the Belorussian Social Democratic Hromada and became its first chairman. From 1989 to 1992 he was responsible for the history section of the Belorussian Encyclopedia publishing house. In 1992 he became the editor-in-chief of this publishing house. Tkachou died suddenly of coronary heart disease. (EM)

Sources: *Belarus: Entsyklapedychny davednik* (Minsk, 1995); Jan Zaprudnik, *Belarus: At a Crossroads of History* (Boulder, Colo., 1993).

TODEA Alexandru (5 June 1912, Teleac–21 May 2002, Tîrgu Mures), Romanian Greek Catholic cardinal. Todea came from Transylvania. After theological studies in Rome, he took holy orders in March 1939. In 1940 in Rome, he received a Ph.D. in theology. He worked in Transylvanian parishes, also teaching Latin and Italian. After World War II, when the Communists began to eliminate the Greek Catholic Church, Todea was arrested and released five times in 1946. In 1948, Greek Catholic bishops and priests were faced with the dilemma of either joining the Orthodox Church or risking most severe punishments. Todea was one of the priests who chose strict obedience to the Pope. After another incarceration in 1948, he escaped arrest and went into hiding. On 19 November 1950, Bishop Joseph Schubert secretly consecrated him bishop; subsequently, Todea assumed the duties of archbishop in the towns of Făgăraş and Alba Iulia. Caught by the political police in January 1951, after long and brutal interrogations in the prisons in Tîrgu Mures, Bucharest, Jilava, and Uranus, Todea was sentenced to hard labor for life in December 1952. He was kept in a number of prisons—for example, in Sighet; in Râmnicu Sărat from 1955; in Piteşti from 1957; and in Gherla from 1962. Todea was released in 1964, when the new party leader, **Nicolae Ceauşescu**, announced an amnesty for political prisoners. Todea settled in Reghin, where he clandestinely performed his duties as bishop in spite of constant persecutions and obstacles from the authorities. During a secret meeting of Romanian Greek Catholic Church leaders in 1986, Todea was elected chairman of the episcopate and received the title of metropolitan. After the fall of the Ceauşescu regime in December 1989, the Greek Catholic Church was formally recognized. In 1990, Pope **John Paul II** recognized Todea as the leader of Romanian Greek Catholics and appointed him cardinal on 28 June 1991. In 1992 Todea suffered a stroke but did not formally retire until July 1994. (WR)

Sources: *Annuario Pontificio*, 1999; Dennis Deletant, *Communist Terror in Romania: Gheorghiu-Dej and the Police State, 1948–1965* (New York, 1999); *Washington Post*, 24 May 2002.

TODOROV Stanko (10 December 1920, Klenovik [now Kolosh], near Radomir–17 December 1996, Sofia), Bulgarian Communist activist. In 1936 Todorov became a member of the Working Class Youth Union and in 1943 a member of the (Communist) Bulgarian Workers' Party. While doing his military service, he co-founded illegal Communist groups. After these activities were discovered, Todorov fled the barracks and went into hiding. In 1943 he was sentenced to death in absentia. Todorov was a member of the staff of partisan groups in Sofia. Seriously wounded during a skirmish with the police, he was captured but managed to escape from prison during the Allied bombing of Sofia in March 1944. After the coup of 9 September 1944, Todorov initially worked in the district committee of the Working Class Youth Union (until 1947) and then served as secretary of the Central Committee (CC) of the People's Youth Union (until 1949). He subsequently rose through the ranks of the Communist Party. Todorov served successively as secretary of the district committee of the Bulgarian Communist Party (BCP) in Sofia (1950), first secretary of the BCP district committee in Burgas (1950–52), head of the CC Agricultural Department (1952), and member of the BCP CC (1954–90). One of the top leaders of the party from 1957 to 1988, he served as CC secretary (1957–59 and 1966–71) and deputy member (1959–61) and member of the BCP CC Politburo (1961–88).

Todorov also held top governmental positions. He served as minister of agriculture in the governments of **Vulko Chervenkov** and **Anton Yugov** (September 1952–February 1957); minister of agriculture and forestry in Yugov's cabinet (February–July 1957); deputy prime minister (25 December 1959–20 November 1962); Bulgaria's permanent representative to the Council for Mutual Economic Assistance (CMEA; also known as Comecon) (1960–65); chairman of the State Planning Committee (25 December 1959–27 September 1962); deputy prime minister in the cabinet of **Todor Zhivkov** (27 November 1962–22 November 1966); and prime minister (9 July 1971–18 June 1981). A deputy to the second through ninth National Assemblies (1954–90) and to the Seventh Grand National Assembly (1990), Todorov served as parliamentary speaker from 1981 to 1990. In 1989 he was appointed to the parliamentary commission for drafting constitutional amendments. Todorov was a close associate of Zhivkov for many years. It was not until the late 1980s that their relationship deteriorated, and Todorov was dismissed from the party leadership because of the role of his wife, Sonia Bakish, in the establishment of the Citizens' Committee for the Protection of Ruse on 3 March 1988. On 10 November 1989 Todorov was instrumental in removing Zhivkov from power. After the BCP was transformed into the Bulgarian Socialist Party (BSP), Todorov was elected a member of the BSP Supreme Council, but he was not reelected at the BSP congress in September 1990. In October 1990 he resigned his parliamentary seat and retired from public life. Todorov's publications include *Usilni godini: Izbrani proizvedeniya 1949–1979* (Intensive years: Selected works; 1980) and *Do vurkhovete na vlastta* (Rising to the top; 1995). (JJ)

Sources: *Entsiklopediya Bulgariya,* vol. 7 (Sofia, 1996); Raymond Detrez, *Historical Dictionary of Bulgaria* (Lanham, Md., 1997); *Trudovata slava na Bulgariya* (Sofia, 1987); *Narodni predstaviteli na Deveto narodno subranie* (Sofia, 1987); Tasho Tashev, *Ministrite na Bulgariya 1879–1999: Entsiklopedichen Spravochnik* (Sofia, 1999); Evgeniia Kalinova and Iskra Baeva, *Bulgarskite prekhodi, 1944–1999* (Sofia, 2000); Angel Tsurakov, *Entsiklopediya. Pravitelstvata na Bulgariya: Khronologiya na politicheskiya zhivot 1879–2001* (Sofia, 2001).

TOKARSKI Julian (25 December 1903, Czersk–15 August 1977, Warsaw), Polish Communist activist. The son of a laborer, after finishing primary school, Tokarski worked as a turner. In 1921 he joined the Communist Workers' Party of Poland (Komunistyczna Partia Robotniczej Polski [KPRP]). In 1927–29 Tokarski was a member of the Central Committee (CC) and CC secretary of the Union of Communist Youth. In 1929 he left for the USSR, where he underwent Comintern training, and he joined the All-Union Communist Party (Bolsheviks). During World War II, Tokarski was active in the Central Bureau of Polish Communists, and in 1943 he became a political officer of the Polish Army, which was formed in the USSR at that time. In 1944 he became deputy commander of the First Armored Corps for political and educational affairs, and in 1945 he was appointed to a similar post in the Internal Security Corps (Korpus Bezpieczeństwa Wewnętrznego [KBW]). Tokarski subsequently joined the apparatus of the Polish Workers' Party (Polska Partia Robotnicza [PPR]). From September 1947 to December 1948 he was first secretary of the Provincial Committee of the PPR in Warsaw Province. He subsequently became secretary and later first secretary of the Warsaw City Committee of the Polish United Workers' Party (Polska Zjednoczona Partia Robotnicza [PUWP]) in Warsaw. In 1950 for a short time Tokarski headed the Cadres Department of the party's Central Committee. From October 1950 to February 1952 he served as minister of heavy industry and until April 1955 as minister of machine industry; in July 1956 he became minister of motor industry. As a representative of the Stalinist wing of the party, Tokarski was dismissed in October 1956. However, in April 1959, when the former Natolin faction (Natolińczycy) began to consolidate its position, Tokarski again became deputy head of the CC Economic Department, and in October 1959 he was appointed deputy prime minister. In December 1965 he resigned from this post, but he continued to serve as a member of the State Council. In June 1969 he retired. Tokarski was an uneducated dogmatist and a faithful follower of the Stalinist "iron-hand" policy. (WR)

Sources: Mołdawa; Włodzimierz Janowski and Aleksander Kochański, *Informator o strukturze i obsadzie personalnej centralnego aparatu PZPR 1948–1990* (Warsaw, 2000).

TŐKÉS László (1 April 1952, Cluj-Napoca [Kolozsvár, Klausenburg], Transylvania), bishop of the Hungarian Evangelical Reformed Church in Transylvania. Tőkés is the son of a pastor. After graduating from high school, he studied theology at the Protestant Institute of Theology in Cluj, earning a degree in 1975. He then began working as an assistant pastor in Braşov (Brassó). Subjected to compulsory assimilation during **Nicolae Ceauşescu**'s dictatorship and deprived of their schools and cultural institutions, the Hungarians in Romania sought refuge in the church. From the beginning of his work, Tőkés was pestered by the political police (Securitate), who, by resorting to bribery, blackmail, and threats, tried to persuade him to inform on his colleagues and his parishioners. From 1977 to 1984 Tőkés served as pastor in Dej [Dés]. At that time he published an article in *Ellenpontok* (the first underground periodical in Romania) on the fate of the local Hungarian community and a vast work on the situation of his church, most of whose bishops collaborated with the Securitate. In 1984 Tőkés was dismissed and was unemployed for over two years. His father, Dr. István Tőkés, who had served as deputy bishop, was also dismissed from his position.

In 1986 Tőkés organized a sit-in strike in protest against the abuses in the Church and against restrictions on the freedom of religion. He became famous abroad, and since the Ceauşescu regime did not want to spoil Romania's image in the international arena, Tőkés was appointed assistant pastor (1986) and soon afterwards pastor in Timişoara (Temesvár). For his criticism of the situation of his church and protests against the destruction of Hungarian villages in Romania, from 1988 he was systematically persecuted. At the beginning of 1989 church and state authorities filed a lawsuit against Tőkés and banned him from giving sermons. In agreement with the authorities, the bishop who supervised Tőkés ordered that Tőkés be moved to a remote province. Tőkés refused to obey this order. In April 1989 his parishioners stood up in his defense. In the summer of that year, *Panorama*, a program on Hungarian Television, presented an interview with Tőkés that focused on the destruction of Hungarian villages by Romanian authorities and exposed the Communists' anti-religious policies. In the autumn of 1989 Tőkés was de facto under house arrest. As a result of the local bishop's efforts, a municipal court ordered his eviction from his church flat, which gave rise to a uprising in Timişoara. On 15 December the parishioners gathered around the church and Tőkés's flat to prevent his eviction. In the following days other people joined the protesters, standing up against military units sent to dispel the demonstrators. The events in Timişoara triggered off social unrest in Bucharest one week later, eventually leading to the fall of Ceauşescu.

In 1990 Tőkés was a member of the Provisional Council of the National Salvation Front. In March 1990 he became bishop of the Evangelical Reformed Superintendency for the district of Királyhágómellék, with its seat in Oradea (Nagyvárad). He also became co-chairman of the Synod of the Evangelical Reformed Church in Romania. Elected honorary chairman of the Democratic Union of Hungarians in Romania, Tőkés represents its radical wing. In 1992 he became a member of the Honorary European Senate and a member of the Order of the Knights of St. John. In 1999 he was elected president of the World Federation of Hungarian Calvinists. Tőkés has received many Hungarian and foreign awards and distinctions, including the Grand Cross of the Order of Merit of the Hungarian Republic in 1999. He has been awarded honorary doctorates by the Reformed Theological Academy of Debrecen (1990), Regent University, Virginia Beach, United States (1991), and Hope College, Michigan, United States (1991). (JT)

Sources: Andrei Codrescu, *The Hole in the Flag* (New York, 1991); Daniel N. Nelson, ed., *Romania after Tyranny* (Boulder, Colo., 1992); József Darski, *Rumunia: Historia, współczesność, konflikty narodowe* (Warsaw, 1994); Valéria Fazekas, *Tőkés püspök kálváriája* (Budapest, 2000); *Ki kicsoda 2000* (Budapest, 2001); Steven Bela Vardy, *Historical Dictionary of Hungary* (Lanham, Md., 1997).

TOMANOVIĆ Lazar (1845, Lepetane, Boka Kotorska, Montenegro–November 1932?), Montenegrin politician. Born into a peasant family, Tomanović attended secondary schools in Zadar and Novi Sad and then studied law in Budapest and Graz, where he earned a doctorate. While a student, he became a member of the United Serbian Youth. After returning to Montenegro, Tomanović served as secretary of the Senate and president of the Supreme Court, and he held numerous ministerial positions. He contributed to the Cetinje-based periodicals *Nova Zeta* (1889–92), *Grlica* (1889–97), and *Glas Crnogorca* (1891–1903). From 17 April 1907 to 19 June 1912 Tomanović served as prime minister of Montenegro. He worked closely with Prince Nicholas (the future King **Nicholas**). Planning a complicated game for influence in the Albanian territories and for Montenegro's participation in the Balkan Wars, the king removed Tomanović from power. Tomanović's publications include the memoirs *Iz moga ministrovanja* (My years as minister; 1921). (WR)

Sources: *Enciklopedija Jugoslavije*, vol. 8 (Zagreb, 1971); *Povodom aneksije Bosne i Hercegovine* (Cetinje, 1909); John D. Treadway, *The Falcon and the Eagle: Montenegro and Austria-Hungary, 1908–1914* (West Lafayette, Ind., 1983); www.rulers.org.

TOMÁŠEK František (30 June 1899, Studénka–4 August 1992, Prague), cardinal, Czech primate. Tomášek was born into the large family of a teacher. In 1918, he graduated from the Slavonic High School in Olomouc and then took up studies in the Theological Department at Olomouc University. His spiritual formation was greatly affected by the Olomouc metropolitan, Archbishop **Antonin Stojan**, who consecrated Tomášek in July 1922. In 1927–34, Tomášek worked as a catechist in the town of Kelči u Hranic in Moravia. In 1934, he became a lecturer in the Theological Department at Olomouc University, and in 1947 he was appointed a professor at this university. In the 1930s and 1940s, Tomášek published thirty-one books and papers on pedagogy and catechization. Some of his books, like *Katechismus* and *Pedagogy*, were reissued a number of times. Tomášek worked at the university until 1950, except during the period of German occupation. Pope Pius XII appointed Tomášek auxiliary bishop of the Olomouc archdiocese. On 14 October 1949 he was secretly ordained bishop by the Olomouc archbishop, Josef Matoch. Tomášek was not allowed to fulfill his duties, however, and he was soon incarcerated in a concentration camp for priests in Želiv. He was kept there from 23 July 1951 until 28 May 1954. After his release Tomášek began performing his priestly duties under the strict control of the authorities in the town of Moravske Huzové, near Olomouc. On 18 February 1965, Pope Paul VI appointed him apostolic administrator of the Prague archdiocese. Earlier, the Prague metropolitan, Cardinal **Josef Beran**, who had been kept in detention for many years, agreed to leave Prague in return for his freedom. Cardinal Beran accepted this compromise since it meant that the Prague metropolitan province could have a legally acting bishop.

Tomášek participated in the Second Vatican Council, where he was on committees that worked on developing ecumenical bonds with the Orthodox Church. In 1968, he was one of the initiators of the lay and clerical organization called Council Renovation Endeavor, aimed at replacing the Communist-founded movement of "patriot-priests." As others, Tomášek had to remain silent after the Warsaw Pact invasion of Czechoslovakia in 1968. However, as the authorities intensified their persecutions of the Church, he supported the so-called underground church, with which he was in constant touch. On 24 May 1976, Pope Paul VI appointed Tomášek cardinal *in pectore*—that is, without publicly announcing his name—and on 30 December 1977 he was consecrated archbishop of Prague.

Tomášek remained in close contact with Pope **John Paul II**, who knew well the realities of church life in Czechoslovakia. The change in the so-called Eastern policy of the Vatican enabled Tomášek to conduct a more independent policy toward the authorities in the 1980s. Initially, he hesitated and made some concessions, such as signing the so-called anti-Charter, a document inspired by the authorities and condemning the signatories of Charter 77. However, at the beginning of the 1980s Tomášek established contact with representatives of the democratic opposition. He initiated the Great Novena and the Decade of Spiritual Renovation of the Nation before the 1,000th anniversary of the martyr's death of Saint Adalbert (Vojtech). Many times he stood up for the violated rights and freedoms of citizens, becoming one of the greatest moral authorities in the country. In 1988, in a special pastoral letter Tomášek supported the appeal of Moravian Catholics (led by Augustin Navrátil), who collected signatures for a thirty-one-point petition to the authorities that demanded that religious freedoms and the separation of church and state be respected. By the end of 1988, around six hundred thousand people had signed the petition, which was subsequently submitted to President **Gustav Husák**. Tomášek also stood up for the Slovak Catholics who had been imprisoned after a demonstration in Bratislava in March 1988. In 1989, he repeatedly urged the authorities to take up a dialogue with the society.

When on 17 November 1989 in Prague an independent demonstration was suppressed—which was the beginning of the Velvet Revolution—Tomášek was in the Vatican, where the canonization of Agnes of Prague, a Czech princess, was being celebrated on his initiative. On 21 November 1989, immediately after his return home, Tomášek issued an extensive statement in which he presented a severe criticism of the forty years of communism in Czechoslovakia and of the current situation in the country. The statement met with an enthusiastic reception from two hundred thousand demonstrators gathered in a Prague park. On 25 November, Tomášek supervised a celebration in which the relics of St. Agnes were brought to Prague, and he expressed the support of the Church for democratization. He urged his compatriots to combine courage with prudence and to renounce violence. The celebration, broadcast by state television, evoked a lively response in the society. After **Václav Havel** assumed the presidency, Tomášek supported his efforts to build a democratic society. He supported the president's appeal for an agreement between the Czech and German nations. Together with Havel, he issued an invitation to Pope John Paul II, who paid a visit to Czechoslovakia in April 1990. Legal regulations passed soon after that visit provided a solution to the most urgent needs of the Catholic Church. Preparations were made for new nominations of bishops; also, laws that restricted the public activity of the Church were repealed, and measures were taken with the aim of returning some confiscated Church property. During his pilgrimage to the

Czech Republic, **John Paul II** said that Tomášek's attitude toward recent injustices "was one of the most vocal expressions of the solidarity of the Church with the persecuted, of solidarity with the people." Tomášek put a lot of effort in endeavors to maintain the Czechoslovakian federation. He repeatedly appealed to Czech and Slovak politicians to be reasonable and moderate and to put the problems of the entire country before their particular interests. The last letter Tomášek submitted to the state authorities was an appeal to maintain the federal state. On 27 March 1991, John Paul II accepted Tomášek's resignation as metropolitan of Prague, handed in because he was of retirement age and in ailing health. Tomášek held honorary doctorates from Charles University in Prague and the University of the Most Sacred Heart of Jesus in Milan, Italy. (AGr)

Sources: *ČBS;* Jan Hartmann et al. *Kardinál Tomášekeds.,* (Prague, 1994); Václav Vaško, *Neumlčená: Kronika katolické Cirkve v Československu po druhé světové válce,* vol. 2. (Prague, 1990); Hansjakob Stehle, *Tajna dyplomacja Watykanu: Papiestwo wobec komunizmu (1917–1991)* (Warsaw, 1993).

TOMAŠIĆ Nikola (13 January 1864, Zagreb–29 May 1918, Treščerovec, near Ozlja), conservative Croatian politician. Tomašić graduated in law in Zagreb. In 1890–91, he was an undersecretary in the Ministry for Croatian Affairs in Budapest. From 1892 he was a professor of economics at Zagreb University. In 1892 Tomašić was also elected a member of the Croatian National Parliament as a representative of the National Party (Narodna Stranka), and he remained an MP until 1906. He was closely associated with the governor (*ban*) of Croatia, **Károly Khuen-Héderváry**. When the latter became prime minister of Hungary in 1903, Tomašić was appointed minister for Croatian affairs and chairman of the National Party. After the Croatian-Serb Coalition had been formed in December 1905, the National Party's position became weaker, especially after the coalition won the 1908 elections. After Khuen-Héderváry had again become prime minister of Hungary, at the beginning of 1910 Tomašić was appointed *ban* of Croatia. He did not manage to mitigate the conflict between the Hungarian authorities and the Croats and Serbs, whose aspirations were increasing, and he left his position in January 1912. (WR)

Sources: *Enciklopedija Jugoslavije,* vol. 8 (Zagreb, 1971); Mark Biondich, *Stjepan Radić, the Croat Peasant Party, and the Politics of Mass Mobilization, 1904–1928* (Toronto, 2000).

TOMAŽIĆ Ivan Jožef (1 August 1876, Miklavž, near Ormož–26 February 1949, Maribor), Slovene Catholic bishop. Tomažić graduated from a theological school in Maribor and was ordained in 1898. In 1906 he received a Ph.D. in theology in Innsbruck. He served as secretary to the bishop of Maribor and taught Church history in a theological school. In 1928 Tomažić was appointed auxiliary bishop and in 1933 ordinary bishop of Maribor. He issued a declaration encouraging the Church and priests to stay above interparty struggles; for it he was criticized by clerical politicians. Tomažić developed Catholic Action, Virgin Mary congregations, the Bishop Anton Slomšek Memorial Brotherhood of Cyril and Methodius, and other educational and religious institutions. In 1934 he headed the Eucharistic Synod of Bishops, and in 1936, special celebrations in memory of Bishop Slomšek. Thanks to his endeavors, a new seminary for priests was built in Maribor, as was a Higher Theological School (transformed into agricultural schools by the Communists after the war). During World War II Tomažić advocated "Non ego, sed Deus" (Not me, but God) and protested the German occupation policies. Owing to his uncompromising position, he faced numerous problems in the administration of his diocese of five hundred thousand believers. After the war the Communist authorities ignored Tomažić because his wartime position did not fit the official image of the collaboration of the Catholic clergy. (AO)

Sources: Leopoldina Plut-Pregelj and Carole Rogel, *Historical Dictionary of Slovenia* (Lanham, Md., 1996); *Enciklopedija Slovenije,* vol. 13 (Ljubljana, 1999).

TOMKO Jozef (11 March 1924, Udavské), Slovak cardinal. Tomko commenced his theological studies at a seminary in Bratislava. In 1945 he was sent to study in Rome, where he graduated from the Pontifical Lateran University in 1949. Later he received doctorates in theology, canon law, and the social sciences. Tomko was ordained in March 1949. He taught at the Pro Deo University (1950–55) and at the Pontifical Gregorian University in Rome (1970–78). For fifteen years he served as vice-rector and then became rector of the Nepomucenum Pontifical College for clerical students from Bohemia, Moravia, and Slovakia. In 1962 Tomko became a member of the Congregation for the Doctrine of the Faith. In 1966 he joined in the preparations for the first Synod of Bishops. In December 1974 he became undersecretary of the Congregation for Bishops. On 12 July 1979 he was elected titular archbishop. On 15 September 1979 he was consecrated bishop by Pope **John Paul II**; this move was seen as support for the persecuted Catholic Church in Slovakia. Tomko incorporated Slovakia's national emblem into his bishop's coat of arms. From 1980 to 1983 Tomko took part in preparations for two ordinary synods, and in 1980 and 1985 he also helped to prepare two extraordinary synods. On 12 July 1979 he became secretary general of the Synod of Bishops. He represented the Holy See at international conferences and ecumenical meetings, including the Conference of the Latin American Episcopate in Puebla, Mexico (1979), and Rio de Janeiro (1980) and the World Council of Churches in Geneva.

On 25 May 1985 Tomko was appointed cardinal, the first Slovak member of the college of cardinals in the twentieth century. From May 1985 to May 2001 he was prefect of the Congregation for the Evangelization of Peoples and grand chancellor of the Pontifical Urban University. Tomko's missionary work extended to all continents other than Europe and North America. He made fifteen visits to Africa, Asia, Latin America, Australia, and Oceania. He contributed to the establishment of 182 new dioceses and ordained 60 bishops. He authored many scholarly works on topics including mixed marriage, modern Christianity, and the role of Ss. Cyril and Methodius in Slovak history. He also wrote his memoirs, *Na misijných cestách* (On missionary paths; 1989). Tomko was awarded many honorary doctorates, including those from the Academy of Catholic Theology in Warsaw and universities in the United States and Taiwan.

Tomko was also involved in Slovak issues. He initiated the establishment of the Institute of SS. Cyril and Methodius in Rome for Slovak candidates for the priesthood. He helped to draft the papal constitution "Praescriptionum sacrosancti" of 30 December 1977, which ended the period of provisional Church administration existing in Slovakia since 1918. Slovakia became an independent ecclesiastical province, with its seat in Trnava. Tomko also maintained contacts with the Slovak diaspora in Western Europe and the United States. In 1968, for the first time since 1945, Tomko was able to go to his homeland. Later he was not allowed to visit his country for many years. It was not until the second half of the 1980s that he was allowed to visit his homeland again. In the 1990s Tomko went to Slovakia several times. In 1991, speaking before the Slovak National Council, he called for the revival of social life and emphasized that the weakest social groups should be protected during the systemic transformation. In March 1995 Tomko was awarded an honorary doctorate by Komenský University in Bratislava. (AGr)

Sources: *Annuario Pontificio*, 2000; www.vatican; www. petersvoice.org; www. referaty.sk; www.bratislava.sk; www. nieuwsbronnen.com.katholirke.

TOMOV Aleksandur (27 April 1954, Sofia), Bulgarian economist and post-Communist activist. Tomov studied at the University of the National and World Economy in Sofia and subsequently completed political economy studies in Leningrad (now St. Petersburg) in 1978 and pursued specialization studies in Great Britain and the Soviet Union. From 1979 to 1983 he was an assistant professor at the Economic Institute in Sofia and from 1984 to 1988 a lecturer at Sofia University, where he earned a Ph.D. and then the postdoctoral degree in 1988. In 1985–89 Tomov was an adviser to Prime Minister **Georgi Atanasov**. On 10 November 1989, as leader of the Movement for Democratic Socialism (Dvizhenie za Demokratichen Sotsializum [DEMOS]) within the Bulgarian Communist Party (BCP), Tomov was involved in the removal of **Todor Zhivkov** and his team from power. At the Fourteenth Congress of the BCP (30 January–2 February 1990), Tomov joined the leadership of the party. After the BCP was transformed into the Bulgarian Socialist Party (BSP), he was elected a member and coordinating secretary of the BSP Supreme Council and vice-chairman of the BSP Presidium. From 20 December 1990 to 8 November 1991 Tomov served as a deputy prime minister, representing the BSP in the coalition government of **Dimitur Popov**.

In 1992 Tomov was appointed head of the shadow cabinet of the BSP, but he gradually departed from the line of the new party leadership with **Zhan Videnov** at the helm. In 1993 in parliament Tomov founded the Citizens' Union for the Republic (Grazhdansko Obedinenie za Republikata), and in July 1993 he finally left the BSP and established the Democratic Alternative for the Republic (Demokratichna Alternativa za Republikata), which did not pass the threshold of 4 percent of the vote in the elections to the National Assembly in December 1994. In October 1996 Tomov unsuccessfully ran in the presidential elections. In the following year he took the helm of the Bulgarian Euroleft (Bulgarska Evrolevitsa [BEL]), a new center-left party that won seats in parliament in the elections of April 1997 and then supported **Ivan Kostov**'s government, joining the so-called pro-reform majority. In 1998 opposition to the government increased among BEL members; as a result, in the local elections of October 1999 the BEL formed a coalition with other opposition parties. Tomov was a deputy to the Grand National Assembly (1990–91) and to the National Assembly (1991–94 and 1997–2001), a member of the World Future Society, director of the East-West Institute in New York, and the founder and general director of the Center for Twenty-first Century Strategic Research. Tomov's publications include *Sotsializum i samoupravlenie* (Socialism and self-government; 1989); *Firmenata organizatsiia i strategicheskite strukturni promeni v ikonomikata* (Corporate organization and strategic structural problems in the economy; 1989); and *Chetvurtata tsivilizatsiia* (The fourth civilization; 1998). (JJ)

Sources: *Koy koy e v Bulgariya* (Sofia, 1998); *Duma*, 25 February 1998; Tasho Tashev, *Ministrite na Bulgariya 1879–1999: Entsiklopedichen Spravochnik* (Sofia, 1999); Evgeniya Kalinova and Iskra Baeva, *Bulgarskite prekhodi, 1944–1999* (Sofia, 2000); Bugajski; Angel Tsurakov, *Entsiklopediya. Pravitelstvata na Bulgariya: Khronologiya na politicheskiya zhivot 1879–2001* (Sofia, 2001).

TÕNISSON Aleksander (17 April 1875, Härjanurme [Herjanorm], Livonia–30 June 1941, Tallinn), Estonian general. Tõnisson served in the tsarist army from 1896 onwards, initially as a volunteer. In 1899 he graduated from a military school in Vilnius. In 1904–5 he fought in the Russo-Japanese War. In 1909 he became a battalion commander in Riga. As a soldier of this battalion he fought in World War I. After the February 1917 revolution, Tõnisson formed the first Estonian military units. He subsequently commanded the First Estonian Regiment, which captured Riga, and fought in the region of Haapsalu and Muhumaa. Arrested after the Bolshevik revolution for refusing to comply with an order, Tõnisson was sentenced to death but managed to escape. He returned to Estonia, where he helped to establish the Estonian Army. On 17 December 1917 he became commander of an infantry brigade and deputy commander of the first Estonian division. On 25 March 1918 he was one of the first three officers promoted to major general. Unable to oppose the German invasion, Tõnisson made his way to Finland, but after the German capitulation, he returned to Estonia and assumed command of the Virumaa front. In late December 1918 and early January 1919 he succeeded in halting the offensive of the Bolshevik troops, which at a critical moment got as close as thirty kilometers from Tallinn. In November and December 1919, in the final stages of the war against the Bolsheviks, Tõnisson commanded the defense of Narva. He succeeded in keeping the town in Estonian hands, which influenced the course of ongoing negotiations in Tartu, which ended in a cease-fire in January 1920.

From July to October 1920 Tõnisson served as minister of war in the government of **Jaan Tõnisson**. In 1927–33 he served as president of the Central Union of Officers of the Republic. He also published extensively but was not involved in active politics. From May to October 1933 Tõnisson again served as minister of war in the government of **Konstantin Päts** and was a permanent member of the board of the Defense Ministry. After the coup staged by Päts in 1934, Tõnisson was forced to retire. Gradually, though, he came to accept the dictatorship. He served as president of the Tartu City Council from 1934 to 1939 and president of the Tallinn City Council from 1939 to 1940. In 1937 he became a member of the National Assembly. He also served as a member of the pro-government Fatherland League (Isamaaliit) and a member of the sixth parliament

(1938–40). After the Red Army occupied Estonia in June 1940, Tõnisson was arrested and then murdered in a prison in Tallinn. (AG)

Sources: *Eesti Entsuklopeedia*, vol. 14 (Tallinn, 2000); Jaan Soots, "Wojna Estonji o Wyzwolenie 1918–1920," *Przegląd Wojskowy*, 1929, no. 20; www.okupatsioon.ee/english/photos/index.html.

TÕNISSON Jaan (22 December 1868, Viljandi–after 1940, USSR), Estonian lawyer and politician. Tõnisson came from a wealthy peasant family. After graduating in law, from 1896 he published a liberal national periodical, *Postimees*, in Dorpat (Tartu) for over thirty years. He also became the owner of the periodical. Tõnisson promoted national awareness among the Estonian peasants, which was opposed to German influence. He supported mass education and the principles of the cooperative movement. He stressed the necessity of forming an ethical foundation for Estonian independence. He was a friend of **Tomáš Garrigue Masaryk**. In 1898 Tõnisson became the leader of the Union of Farmers in Tartu, which propagated modern methods of farming in the country. He initiated annual agricultural exhibitions. From 1899 to 1905 he organized several national conferences on agricultural issues. In 1898 he contributed to the establishment of the first Estonian agricultural cooperative. During the revolution of 1905 Tõnisson created the Progressive Peasant Party and was a co-organizer of the National Assembly in Tartu on 27 November 1905. At that time he advocated a moderate plan for the autonomy of Estonia within the framework of the Russian empire, and he supported the tsarist program of reforms. Therefore he was not persecuted after the revolution and sat in subsequent State Dumas.

In 1906 Tõnisson organized the first Estonian gymnasium. In 1915 he founded the Baltic North Committee, which sought to establish cooperation between Estonia and the Scandinavian countries. In March 1917 he became leader of the Estonian autonomists, who brought about the creation of the Estonian National Council (Maapäev). Tõnisson was an advocate of a northern union with Lithuania, Latvia, and the Scandinavian countries. On 25 August 1917 he launched a campaign for the full independence of Estonia. As a delegate of the Maapäev, in London Tõnisson received the support of Great Britain, whose armed forces cooperated with the Estonian Army in the liberation of the country from the Germans and then in the defense against the Bolsheviks.

In independent Estonia Tõnisson headed the national-liberal Estonian Democratic Party (Eesti Demokraatlik Erakond) and then the Estonian People's Party (Eesti Rahvaerakond [EPP]). He was an MP representing these parties in the Constituent Assembly and in subsequent parliaments. From 18 November 1919 to 28 July 1920 Tõnisson was prime minister. On 2 February 1920 he signed a peace treaty with Soviet Russia that recognized the full independence of Estonia. Tõnisson again became the head of government between 9 December 1927 and 13 November 1928. In 1930–32 he was minister of foreign affairs. On 18 May 1933 he became prime minister for the third time. Then Tõnisson implemented the devaluation of the Estonian kroon, which revived exports in the long run but provisionally intensified economic problems; these increased the popularity of the Fascist-like Estonian League of War of Independence Veterans (Eesti Vabadussojalaste Liit [EVL]) and the protests of the Socialists. On 11 August 1933 Tõnisson's government introduced a state of emergency. The results of a referendum of 14–16 October 1933, in which the majority of society backed anti-democratic changes in the constitution, were the final blow for Tõnisson. Submitting his resignation, he lifted the state of emergency, but this failed to prevent the EVL from taking advantage of the democratic rules of the game. The majority of the press, mainly agrarians and Fascists, greeted the resignation of Tõnisson's government, as well as his rescinding of the state of emergency, with derision.

After the assumption of power by **Konstantin Päts** in 1934, Tõnisson, as a supporter of parliamentary democracy, found himself in the opposition. However, he welcomed the reinstatement of the state of emergency and the delegalization of the EVL. The EPP disintegrated and then was dissolved by Päts. Tõnisson returned to Tartu. He was the chair of the department of sociology at the local university and of the Estonian-Swedish Society. On several occasions he protested the authoritarian rules; for example, he signed a memorial of the democratic opposition that was published in Finland in November 1936. In 1938 Tõnisson regained his seat in parliament and was one of seventeen opposition MPs in the eighty-member parliament. Along with three former prime ministers—**Juhan Kukk, Ants Piip**, and **Jaan Teemant**—Tõnisson protested the electoral abuse. After the Red Army entered Estonia in June 1940, Tõnisson proposed his candidacy in the "elections" to the People's Assembly from a list that was independent of the Communists but was annulled by the Russians. He was soon arrested by the NKVD and deported far inside Russia, and his further fate was unknown. (WR)

Sources: *Eesti Biografiline Leksikon*, vol. 1 (Tartu, 1926); Hans Kruus, *Jaan Tõnisson Eesti kodanluse juhina* (Tartu, 1921); *Jaan Tõnisson töös ja võitluses: Koguteos tema seitsmekümnenda sünnipäeva puhul* (Tartu, 1938); Evald Uustalu, *The History of the Estonian People* (London, n.d.); *Jaan Tõnisson* (Stockholm, 1960); Karl Eerne, *Jaan Tõnisson* (New York, 1965); Georg von Rauch, *The Baltic States: The Years of Independence—Estonia, Latvia, Lithuania, 1917–1940* (Berkeley, 1974); Piotr Łossowski, *Kraje bałtyckie na drodze od demokracji parlamentarnej do dyktatury 1918–1934* (Wrocław, 1972); Märt Raud, Kaks Suurt, and Jaan Tõnisson, *Konstantin Päts ja nende ajastu* (Tallinn, 1991); *Eesti välispoliitikas 1917–1920: Dokumente ja materiale* (Tallinn, 1993).

TOOME Indrek (19 September 1943, Tallinn), Estonian Communist activist. In 1968 Toome graduated in electronic engineering from the Technical University in Tallinn and joined the Communist Party of the Soviet Union (CPSU). From 1972 to 1978 he was first secretary of the Central Committee (CC) of the Estonian Komsomol, and from 1978 to 1984 he was first secretary of the Tallinn Committee of the Communist Party of Estonia (CPE). In 1972 he became a member of the Supreme Soviet of the Estonian SSR. From 1984 to 1987 he was deputy chairman of the Council of Ministers of the Estonian SSR. A typical apparatchik, Toome initially ignored the policy of perestroika and maneuvered between a dogmatic group led by **Karl Vaino**, then first secretary of the CC of the CPE, and his own Komsomol colleagues, led by **Edgar Savisaar**. Toome's appointment as CC secretary for ideology was a prelude to the dismissal of Vaino. This did not mean the introduction of more liberal policies toward the pro-independence opposition. When on 24 February 1988—the anniversary of the prewar Estonian independence day (until then proscribed)—the opposition organized a demonstration, Toome, feeling that the former ruling clique's time was coming to an end, demonstrated some flexibility by organizing an alternative rally.

On 1 April 1988 Toome announced the beginning of perestroika in the Estonian SSR and encouraged support for it. When **Vaino Väljas** came to power, Toome became one of the symbols of cooperation that the CPE established with the Popular Front in the summer of 1988. The Popular Front, whose leaders included Savisaar, called for sovereignty for the Estonian SSR within the Soviet Union. As part of the cooperation efforts, attempts were made to remove the former associates of Vaino from power and to thwart the anti-Communist opposition's efforts to restore the full independence of the state. After the Supreme Soviet of the Estonian SSR adopted a declaration of sovereignty of the republic within the Soviet Union on 16 November 1988, Toome resigned as secretary of the CC to become prime minister of the republic. Although still a supporter of a reorganized Soviet Union, he took steps to make his country economically independent from Moscow. He founded the Free Estonia (Vaba Eesti) bloc, but it obtained only 12 seats out of 105 in the elections to the Supreme Soviet of the republic. The new parliament was under pressure from the right-wing-dominated Congress, which strove for the restitution of Estonian independence and the restoration of the status quo in 1940. This led to a drop in popularity of a new treaty with the Soviet Union, under which Estonia was to remain part of the USSR. Toome, who supported this treaty, also became less popular. On 30 March 1990 he resigned. Under his leadership Free Estonia evolved toward economic liberalism, and Toome came into conflict with Savisaar, the new prime minister.

In the autumn of 1990 Toome became a supporter of the restitution of independence and even began to accuse Savisaar of attempts to transform Estonia—formally independent—into a satellite of the newly emerging Russia. In the spring of 1990, on behalf of the Supreme Soviet of the Estonian SSR, Toome conducted unsuccessful negotiations with the Soviet deputy prime minister. After Estonia regained its independence, Toome retired from politics to become a businessman. Since 1992 he has been the development director of a construction company, SRV Kinnisvara AS. Toome's name has appeared several times in the media in connection with corruption scandals involving representatives of central and local governments. In 1994 he was even detained on charges of corruption but was released for lack of evidence, and he resumed his work for the company. (AG)

Sources: *Eesti Entsuklopeedia*, vol. 14 (Tallinn, 2000); Anatol Lieven, *The Baltic Revolution* (New Haven, 1993); Rein Taagepera, *Estonia: Return to Independence* (Boulder, Colo., 1993); Mel Huang, "All Important News from Estonia, Latvia, and Lithuania," *Central European Review*, 1999, no. 12; Jan Lewandowski, *Estonia* (Warsaw, 2002).

TOPULLI Çerçiz (1880, Gjirokastër–17 July 1915, Fushë e Shtoit), Albanian pro-independence activist. Topulli began his patriotic activities in a secret association called Për Lirinë e Shqipërisë, which operated in Gjirokastër. In 1906 he assumed command of a military unit that operated in the south of the country, in the region of Korçë-Gjirokastër. He became famous after his unit assassinated the commander of the Turkish gendarmerie in Gjirokastër in March 1908. In January 1907 Topulli wrote the manifesto "Nga malet e Shqipërise" (From the Albanian mountains), which was addressed to the Albanian nation and published in the periodical *Shpresa e Shqipërisë*. In this manifesto, he called for the separation of the Albanian territories from the Ottoman Empire and the establishment of an independent state through a national uprising. The Young Turk revolution of 1908 changed the character of his activities. Topulli became involved in the establishment of Albanian political clubs, as well as schools with Albanian as the language of instruction. After a declaration

of independence was proclaimed on 28 November 1912, Topulli joined the government security units led by **Ismail Kemali**. After the outbreak of World War I, he moved to Shkodër. When Montenegrin troops seized Shkodër, Topulli was arrested on 15 July 1915. King Nicholas's order that Topulli be released failed to arrive in time. Along with a group of other Albanians, Topulli was sentenced by a military court to death as a rebel and then executed by a firing squad. In 1937 his mortal remains were buried in Gjirokastër. (TC)

Sources: *Akte të Rilindjes Kombëtare Shqiptare 1878–1912* (Tirana, 1978); *Fjalori Enciklopedik Shqiptar* (Tirana, 1985); Sejfi Vllamasi, *Ballafaqime politike në Shqipëri (1897–1942)* (Tirana, 1995).

TOSHEV Andrey (4 April 1867, Stara Zagora–10 October 1944, Sofia), Bulgarian politician and biologist. In 1885 Toshev graduated from high school in Edirne (Adrianople) and then worked as a teacher in Salonika, Stara Zagora, and Varna (1890–95). After completing studies in the natural sciences in Geneva and Brussels (1891), he taught at high schools in Salonika, Stara Zagora, and Varna and at the Military School in Sofia (1892–1903). In 1903–5 Toshev was Bulgaria's trade representative to Monastir (now Bitola, Macedonia), and then he served as diplomatic representative to Montenegro (1905–6), Greece (1906–8), Serbia (1908–13), Turkey (1913–14), Switzerland (1915–16), the Austro-Hungarian Empire (1917–18), and Austria (until 1920). Toshev was a member of the Bulgarian delegation during the signing of the peace treaty in Constantinople (now Istanbul) in 1913. From 21 April to 23 November 1935 Toshev served as Bulgarian prime minister, helping to consolidate the monarchial system in Bulgaria. He was also an accomplished scholar. In 1898 he became a corresponding member, and in 1900 a full member, of the Bulgarian Literary Society, which was later transformed into the Bulgarian Academy of Sciences. Toshev headed the Department of Natural Sciences and Medicine of the Bulgarian Literary Society from 1901 to 1903 and the Department of Natural Sciences and Mathematics of the Bulgarian Academy of Sciences from 1929 to 1930. Toshev's publications include *Ranni spomeni 1873–1879* (Early memoirs 1873–1879; 1890); *Balkanski voini* (The Balkan Wars, 2 vols.; 1929–31); *Surbsko-bulgarskata razpra* (The Bulgarian-Serbian dispute; 1932); *Stranitsi iz minaloto na surbsko-bulgarskite otnosheniya* (Pages from the past of Serbo-Bulgarian relations; 1941); and *Bulgariya i neinite susiedi* (Bulgaria and its neighbors; 1943). (JJ)

Sources: *Entsiklopediya Bulgariya*, vol. 7 (Sofia, 1996); *Iubileen sbornik Andrei Toshev* (Sofia, 1942); *100 godini na BAN*, vol. 1

(Sofia, 1969); Tasho Tashev, *Ministrite na Bulgariya 1879–1999: Entsiklopedichen Spravochnik* (Sofia, 1999); Angel Tsurakov, *Entsiklopediya. Pravitelstvata na Bulgariya: Khronologiya na politicheskiya zhivot 1879–2001* (Sofia, 2001).

TOŠOVSKÝ Josef (28 September 1950, Náchod), Czech economist and politician. Upon graduating in foreign trade from the Prague School of Economics in 1973, Tošovský was employed in the State Bank of Czechoslovakia, where he worked his way up the ladder to become an adviser to the president of the bank. In 1977 he underwent further training in Great Britain, and in 1980, in France. From 1984 to 1985 he worked at the London branch of Źivnostenská Banka, becoming deputy director of this branch in 1989. Tošovský was a member of the Communist Party of Czechoslovakia from 1976 to 1989. In December 1989 he was appointed president of the State Bank of Czechoslovakia, which under his leadership was transformed into an independent central bank. After the breakup of Czechoslovakia, he was appointed governor of the Czech National Bank on 20 January 1993, and he successfully carried out the separation of the Czech and Slovak korunas. Tošovský achieved considerable success in stabilizing the Czech currency, curbing inflation, and establishing the internal convertibility of the Czech koruna. For his achievements he has been honored with numerous awards, including the title of Central Banker of the Year 1993. During the economic slump in the Czech Republic (1996–97), Tošovský defended the stability of the Czech koruna and came into conflict with Prime Minister **Václav Klaus** on several occasions. After the collapse of Klaus's government and in the face of difficulties in forming a new ruling coalition, at the end of 1997 President **Václav Havel** entrusted Tošovský with the task of forming a cabinet that was to consist partly of civil servants and that was to rule the country until early elections in June 1998. From 2 January to 7 July 1998 Tošovský served as prime minister. Since he had no parliamentary base, his role was reduced to administering the state. After the end of his mission, Tošovský again became governor of the Czech National Bank on 22 July 1998, but on 30 November 2000 he resigned to become chairman of the Financial Stability Institute of the Bank for International Settlements in Basel. (PU)

Sources: *Kdo byl kdo v našich dějinách ve 20. století*, vol. 2 (Prague, 1998); *ČBS*; Oldřich Dědek et al., *Ekonomické aspekty zániku Československa* (Prague, 1997); http://wtd.vlada.cz/scripts/detail.php?id=458.

TÓTH Ilona (23 October 1932, Árpádföld–26 June 1957, Budapest), Hungarian doctor, victim of communism. In 1951 Tóth passed her secondary school final examinations at a school where she had served as secretary of the Working Youth Union. In the same year she entered medical school. In October 1956 she trained in internal medicine at the hospital on Szövetség Street in Budapest. On 23 October, along with her colleagues, Tóth took part in a demonstration, and two days later she was assigned to work at the hospital on Sándor Péterffy Street, where she joined the Voluntary Ambulance Service. On 1 November she became acting head of an auxiliary hospital unit. After the end of fighting, Tóth joined the political resistance movement, helping to draft and distribute leaflets and to print the illegal periodical *Élünk*. On 20 November she was arrested and accused of killing an unidentified man, probably a security agent. Tóth was tried along with two writers, **Gyula Obersovszky** and József Gáli. The show trial was intended to prove an alleged plot by two "counterrevolutionary" groups: writers and insurgents. On 8 April 1957 the court of first instance sentenced Tóth to death. On 20 June 1957 the Supreme Court upheld the sentence, accusing her in addition of being involved in anti-state opposition and a plot against "the government of the people." As a result of international protests, Obersovszky's and Gáli's death sentences were commuted, but Tóth was executed. (JT)

Sources: *A magyar forradalom és szabadságharc enciklopédiája*, CD-ROM (Budapest, 1999); György Litván, ed., *Rewolucja węgierska 1956 roku* (Warsaw, 1996); Attila Szakolczay, *Az 1956-os forradalom és szabadságharc* (Budapest, 2001).

TRAJKOVSKI Boris (25 June 1956, Strumica, Macedonia–26 February 2004, near Stolac, Bosnia-Herzegovina), Macedonian politician. Trajkovski earned a law degree at Ss. Cyril and Methodius University in Skopje in 1980. Specializing in commercial and employment law, he was head of the legal department at the Slobodna construction company in Skopje until 1997. That year Trajkovski became mayor of the Kisela Voda municipality in Skopje. He was chairman of the Foreign Relations Commission of the Internal Macedonian Revolutionary Organization–Democratic Party for Macedonian National Unity (Vnatrešno-Makedonska Revolucionerna Organizacija–Demokratska Partija za Makedonsko Edinstvo [IMRO–DPMNU]). When the party won the parliamentary elections in fall 1998, Trajkovski became deputy minister of foreign affairs. As a moderate member of the nationalist IMRO–DPMNU, he ran for president of the republic in November 1999. He reached the second round behind a Social Democrat, Tito Petkovski, who tried to take advantage of anti-Albanian fears. In contrast, the nationalist Trajkovski stressed economic problems and proved victorious in the second round. Since his inauguration on 15 December 1999 Trajkovski has been active on the international level, trying to strengthen the position of Macedonia and to improve relations with neighboring countries. A Methodist in an overwhelmingly Eastern Orthodox land whose Albanian population is Muslim, Trajkovski was a voice of moderation, a fact evidenced during the Albanian insurgency of 2001, when he was able to counterbalance the saber rattling of the right-wing **Ljubčo Georgievski** government. In May 2001 Trajkovski issued a settlement plan including a partial amnesty for the Albanian guerrillas, extensive linguistic rights, educational reform, and the inclusion of greater numbers of Albanians in state institutions. The plan led to the Ohrid Agreement, signed in August 2001, and it eased the ethnic tensions in Macedonia. Trajkovski perished in an airplane crash. (DP)

Sources: Bugajski; www.rulers.org; www.president.gov.mk/eng/pretsedatel.htm.

TRĄMPCZYŃSKI Wojciech (8 February 1860, Dębłowo, near Gniezno–2 September 1953, Poznań), Polish politician. After graduating from high school, Trąmpczyński studied law at the University of Breslau (Wrocław) and was an activist in the Slavic Literary Society. In 1886, after receiving a degree, he settled in Posen (Poznań), where he ran a law and notary practice. Trąmpczyński was the defense counsel in the political trials of Polish pro-independence activists in the German courts. From 1901 to 1902 he was a member of the Poznań City Council, chairman of its Polish Circle (Koło Polskie), and president of the Law Committee. From 1905 to 1912 he was the director of Bazar, a company that rendered great services to the Polish cause. From 1910 to 1918 he was an MP in the Prussian parliament, and from 1913 to 1919 he chaired the Polish Circle there. In 1912 Trąmpczyński was elected to the Reichstag. An outstanding speaker, he became famous for his criticism of the anti-Polish policy of the German authorities in the Prussian partition of Poland. He protested the land expropriations and the abolition of Polish as the language of instruction in the schools. During World War I Trąmpczyński criticized the economic war policy of the Reich. From 1912 on he worked with the National Democratic Party (Narodowa Demokracja [ND]). During World War I he was a member of the secret Interparty Civic Committee and later a member of the underground and pro-coalition Central Civic Committee in Posen.

In November 1918 Trąmpczyński took part in negotiations on the establishment of a central government in Warsaw and in negotiations with the Prussian government in Berlin. He became a member of the Supreme People's Council (Naczelna Rada Ludowa), on behalf of which he served as chief president of the province and regency of Poznań from 4 January 1919 until the time when Greater Poland (Wielkopolska) was incorporated into the Republic of Poland. In January 1919 Trąmpczyński was elected to the Legislative Assembly on the ND ticket. After the Assembly was constituted in February of that year, he became its speaker. He organized the Assembly Chancellery, the Speaker's Guard, and the Speaker's Court. In the summer of 1920, during the Bolshevik offensive, Trąmpczyński became a member of the State Defense Council. He also chaired the Central Plebiscite Committee, the Committee for Aid to Repatriates, and the Committee for Aid to Soldiers in Poland. In the November 1922 elections he was elected senator on the ND ticket. In December 1922 he became speaker of the senate and organized its work. Reelected to the Assembly in 1928 and 1930, Trąmpczyński was a member of the presidium of the parliamentary National Caucus and a member of the Political Committee of the National Party (Stronnictwo Narodowe [SN]) and of the Great Poland Camp (Obóz Wielkiej Polski [OWP]). A critic of the *sanacja* government system, Trąmpczyński gave extensive testimony in defense of the MPs tried in the Brześć trial. In the late 1930s he drifted to the opposition groups of the so-called Morges Front. After the German invasion of Poland, the Nazi authorities forced Trąmpczyński to move from Poznań to Warsaw in 1940. After the Warsaw Uprising of 1944, he settled in Milanówek. In the spring of 1945 he returned to Poznań. Before the January 1947 elections, Trąmpczyński attempted to establish a Catholic party in Poznań, but the Communist authorities thwarted his efforts. (WR)

Sources: *Kto był kim w Drugiej Rzeczypospolitej* (Warsaw, 1994); *Encyklopedia historii Drugiej Rzeczypospolitej* (Warsaw, 1999); Andrzej Ajnenkiel, *Od rządów ludowych do przewrotu majowego* (Warsaw, 1978); Roman Wapiński, *Narodowa Demokracja 1893–1939* (Wrocław, 1980); Adam Próchnik, *Pierwsze piętnastolecie Polski niepodległej* (Warsaw, 1983); Zygmunt Kaczmarek, *Wojciech Trąmpczyński (1860–1953)* (Poznań, 1993).

TRAYKOV Georgi (2 April 1898, Vurbeni [Ksino Nero, now in Greece]–14 January 1975, Sofia), Bulgarian Peasant Party activist. Traykov's family had fought for the liberation of Bulgarians in Aegean Macedonia and then settled in Varna. In 1919 Traykov became a member of the Bulgarian Agrarian National Union (BANU). He co-founded the Bulgarian Agrarian Youth Union (BAYU) in 1922 and organized a peasant armed struggle in the Varna district after the overthrow of **Aleksandur Stamboliyski**'s government in June 1923. Arrested after the failure of the 1923 Communist uprising but released under an amnesty in 1924, Traykov became secretary of the central leadership of the BAYU and editor of the newspaper *Mladezhko zname*, a BAYU press organ. An active leader of the BANU in the Varna district, Traykov sought rapprochement between the BANU and the Bulgarian Communist Party (BCP) after the coup of May 1934. In 1943 he became a member, and later the chairman, of the underground District Committee of the Fatherland Front (FF) in Varna.

After the coup of 9 September 1944, Traykov helped to establish the Communist-dominated FF government in Varna. In May 1945 he became chairman of its Executive Council. He also served as secretary (1945–48) and chairman (1972–75) of the FF National Council. After the Communists broke down the BANU; arrested its independent leaders; and sentenced its chairman, **Nikola Petkov**, to death and then executed him, Traykov was elected BANU secretary at the Twenty-seventh BANU Congress in December 1947 and chairman of the BANU Supreme Committee in 1974. In October 1948 the BANU Supreme Council under his leadership accepted the leading role of the BCP. In return for his total submissiveness to the Communists, Traykov was appointed to top governmental positions. He served as minister of agriculture and state property (November 1946–December 1947), deputy prime minister (December 1947–April 1956), minister of agriculture and forestry (December 1947–December 1948), minister of agriculture (December 1948–January 1950), first deputy prime minister (until April 1964), and chairman of the Council for Agricultural Affairs (November 1962–March 1966). Traykov accepted the total collectivization of agriculture and the brutal suppression of peasants who resisted collectivization. From 1971 to 1974 he served as first vice-president of the Council of State. He served as deputy to the National Assembly (1945–46, 1950–75) and the Grand National Assembly (1946–49). From 1971 to 1972 he served as chairman of the Sixth National Assembly. Traykov's publications include *Izbrani proizvedeniya 1944–1973* (Selected works 1944–1973; 1980) and *Izbrani suchineniya* (Selected works, 2 vols.; 1985). (JJ)

Sources: *Entsiklopediya Bulgariya*, vol. 7 (Sofia, 1996); *Narodni predstaviteli v Shesto narodno subranie* (Sofia, 1974); Milen Kumanov and Tania Nikolova, *Politicheski partii, organizatsii i dvizheniya v Bulgariya i tekhnite lideri 1879–1999: Kratuk spravochnik* (Sofia, 1999); Tasho Tashev, *Ministrite na Bulgariya 1879–1999: Entsiklopedichen Spravochnik* (Sofia, 1999); Evgeniya Kalinova and Iskra Baeva, *Bulgarskite prekhodi, 1944–1999* (Sofia, 2000); Angel Tsurakov, *Entsiklopediya. Pravitelstvata na Bulgariya: Khronologiya na politicheskiya zhivot 1879–2001* (Sofia, 2001).

TRČKA Dominik Metod (6 July 1886, Frýdlant nad Ostravicí, Moravia–23 March 1959, Leopoldov, Slovakia), Czech monk and missionary, martyr of the Catholic Church. In 1903 Trčka entered the Congregation of the Most Holy Redeemer (Redemptorists) in Červenka, and after one year he took his first monastic vows. After graduating from a seminary in Obořiště, he took holy orders in 1910. He worked in Bohemia and Moravia. In 1919 he joined the Redemptorists of the Eastern rite and began his missionary work among the Uniate faithful in Lwów (Lviv), and in 1920 he moved to Stanisławów (now Ivano-Frankivsk, Ukraine). At the end of 1921 Trčka began working in eastern Slovakia. He served as the superior of the monastery in Stropkov and then in Michalovce. From March 1945 on he headed the newly established Uniate Redemptorist Vice-Province. After the Uniate Church in Czechoslovakia was formally abolished, Trčka continued his work in union with the Holy See. In 1950 he was interned in Podolinec. Two years later he was accused of collaboration with Bishop **Pavel Gojdič** and spying for the Vatican, and he was then sentenced to twelve years' imprisonment. Trčka died in prison of pneumonia. In 1990 he was formally rehabilitated. On 4 November 2001 he was beatified by Pope **John Paul II**. (MG)

Sources: *Lexikón katolíckych kňazských osobností Slovenska* (Bratislava, 2000); J. Babjak and P. Kušnír, *Zostali verní I, Osudy greckokatolíckych kňazov* (Košíce, 1997).

TRENCHEV Konstantin (8 February 1955, Stara Zagora), Bulgarian trade union activist. In 1970 Trenchev graduated from high school in Algeria, where he lived with his parents. After returning to Bulgaria, he graduated in medicine and began working in the emergency ambulance service in Stara Zagora. In February 1989 he founded the Podkrepa Labor Confederation, the first independent trade union in Bulgaria. This trade union, consisting of only two hundred members in 1989, grew to five hundred thousand members two years later. Trenchev was initially imprisoned for his trade union activities but was released on the day before the overthrow of **Todor Zhivkov**'s regime in November 1989. In 1990 Podkrepa did not join the Union of Democratic Forces (UDF), maintaining the status of an observer, because, according to Trenchev, Podkrepa did not seek power. Trenchev was critical of the Round Table agreements (January-March 1990 and similar to the Polish one), which, he believed, left too much power to the Communists. The radical activities of Podkrepa and its leader intensified after the June 1990 parliamentary elections. Among other things, Trenchev stirred up riots that ended up in the vandalization of the Sofia headquarters of the post-Communist Bulgarian Socialist Party (BSP). When the government of **Andrey Lukanov** launched market reforms, Trenchev organized street protests, hurling vulgar insults at the prime minister and calling for the deportation of BSP members to Siberia.

At the end of 1990 Trenchev supported the UDF's efforts to take over power from the BSP, and by organizing a general strike in which almost one million people took part, he was instrumental in forcing the resignation of Lukanov. At that time, the press published information on Trenchev's cooperation with the security services during Zhivkov's dictatorship. In January 1991 Trenchev signed an agreement with **Dimitur Popov**'s government; in it Trenchev promised to stop strike actions during the first months of "shock therapy," but he failed to keep his promise. Trenchev's role as a constant protester has won him the position of indisputable leader of Podkrepa, which still has over two hundred thousand members. He has combined his trade union activities with an ostentatious devotion to the Orthodox Church and an active engagement in conflicts within the Orthodox Church after the 1992 split. Trenchev has always been seen as a supporter of the restoration of the monarchy, and as early as 1993 he sought to invite Simeon II to Bulgaria. (AG)

Sources: Jerzy Jackowicz, *Bułgaria od rządów komunistycznych do demokracji parlamentarnej 1988–1991* (Warsaw, 1997); Raymond Detrez, *Historical Dictionary of Bulgaria* (Lanham, Md., 1997); http://www.online.bg/politics/who/names/T/konstantin_trenchev.htm.

TREPPER Leopold (23 February 1904, Nowy Targ–19 January 1982, Jerusalem), head of Die Rote Kapelle, the Soviet intelligence network in Germany. The son of a Jewish shopkeeper from Galicia, after World War I Trepper joined Hashomer Hatzair, a Zionist revolutionary organization. Wanted by the police for his participation in the Kraków events of 1923, he left for Palestine. In 1925 he joined the Communist Party. Expelled by the British, in 1929 Trepper landed in France, where he worked for the Communist press. In 1932 he arrived in the USSR, where, at the Julian Marchlewski University in Moscow, he completed studies that he had begun at the Jagiellonian University in Kraków. Then he graduated from a special school of the Soviet intelligence service. In March 1939 Trepper installed himself as head of the GRU in Brussels. In one year, he became the USSR's most important source of intelligence information in Western Europe. After the German invasion of the USSR in June 1941, Trepper already headed seven intelligence networks in the countries occupied by the Third Reich. He transmitted around 1,500 radio messages during the war. In December 1942 Trepper was arrested by the Gestapo. Trepper knew that the GRU had a second intelligence network, so to save his life, he testified extensively on Die Rote Kapelle. Treated

considerably well and used as a decoy, Trepper escaped in July 1943 and remained in hiding until the liberation of France, maintaining contact with Moscow. In May 1945 he was called to Moscow, arrested, and sentenced to nine years of labor camp. After his release in 1954 Trepper managed to leave for the Polish People's Republic. He settled in Warsaw, becoming head of the Cultural Society of Jews in Poland. During the Communist anti-Semitic campaign in 1967 Trepper's family managed to leave for Israel, while he was not allowed to go on the grounds of *raison d'état*. In the West, mass protests against this stance of the Polish People's Republic were organized; therefore in November 1973 the **Edward Gierek** administration finally allowed him to leave. In Israel, Trepper wrote his memoirs, *The Great Game* (1977). (WR)

Sources: G. Perreault, *The Red Orchestra* (New York, 1969); *Annual Obituary*, 1982.

TRIFUNOVIĆ Miloš (Miša) (30 October 1871, Užice, Serbia–19 February 1957, Belgrade), Serbian politician. Trifunović graduated from high school in his native Užice. In 1894 he completed philosophical studies in Belgrade and then worked as a teacher at a high school in Užice. In 1903 he was elected to parliament, in which he sat for many years, serving as its secretary for several periods. A member and one of the leaders of the Serbian Radical Party, Trifunović later became first deputy to the party leader, Aca Stanojević. He contributed to the newspapers *Samouprava* and *Odjek* and to the periodicals *Srpski književni glasnik* and *Novi život*. For many years Trifunović was a member of the cabinet, serving as minister of education and religious affairs (June 1917–November 1918), minister of education (February–May 1920, December 1922–May 1923, April 1926–February 1927, March 1941–June 1943), minister of public works (March–July 1924), and minister for religious affairs (November 1924–April 1926). During World War II, when Germany occupied Belgrade in April 1941, King **Peter II** and the government initially took refuge in Jerusalem, and from there moved to London. In October 1941 Trifunović went to North America as a member of a Yugoslav delegation that sought American and Canadian support for the independence and territorial integrity of Yugoslavia. On 6 June 1943 he became prime minister and minister of interior of the Yugoslav government-in-exile. In the face of Italy's capitulation, in July 1943 Trifunović's government approached Great Britain, the Soviet Union, and the United States with a proposal to establish an army of about one hundred thousand. This army was to consist of Yugoslav citizens, as well as Yugoslav prisoners of war in Italy.

However, this plan was rejected by the Great Powers. On 10 August 1943 Trifunović's government was dismissed. After the war, Trifunović returned to Yugoslavia but did not play any political role. (AO)

Sources: *Enciklopedija Jugoslavije*, vol. 8 (Zagreb, 1971); Michał Jerzy Zacharias, *Jugosławia w polityce Wielkiej Brytanii 1940–1945* (Wrocław, 1985); www.mfa.gov.yu/history/Ministri/MTrifunovic_s.html.

TRIPALO Mika (16 November 1926, Sinj, Croatia), Croatian Communist activist. At the age of fifteen Tripalo joined the Partisans led by **Josip Broz Tito**, and in 1943 he became a member of the Communist Party of Yugoslavia. During World War II he was active in Communist youth organizations. He served as secretary of the League of Yugoslav Communist Youth (Savez Komunističke Omladine Jugoslavije [SKOJ]) in Kotor and Knin. After 1945 Tripalo graduated from high school in Sinj and subsequently completed law studies in Belgrade. In 1950 he graduated from the Djuro Djakovič Political School. From 1947 to 1953 he served as secretary and chairman of the Croatian organization of People's Youth (Narodna Omladina). From 1953 to 1955 he was chairman of the Central Committee (CC) of the League of Yugoslav Students (Savez Studenata Jugoslavije). From 1955 to 1962 he was secretary of the CC of the federal organization of People's Youth. In 1962 Tripalo was promoted to secretary of a district party committee in Zagreb. He became a member of the CC of the League of Communists of Yugoslavia (LCY) in 1958, a member of the LCY CC Executive Committee in 1963, and secretary of the LCY CC Executive Committee in 1966. At the Ninth Congress of the LCY in 1969 he was elected to the Presidium of the LCY CC.

Tripalo was in favor of greater ideological openness. From the late 1960s, he supported Croatian efforts to increase the cultural autonomy of the Yugoslav republics and nations. An advocate of greater independence for Croatia, he worked with **Savka Dapčević-Kučar**, the leader of the Croatian party. As a result of their efforts, at the Tenth Plenum of the CC of the Communist Party of Croatia (CPC) in January 1970, conservatives and supporters of centralism were expelled from the leadership of the party. The dogmatists counterattacked, exaggerating the threat of the growing nationalist mood in Croatia. The "Croatian Spring" was halted at the Seventeenth Session of the Presidium of the LCY CC, which was held on Brioni Island at the end of April 1971. In mid-May several supporters of liberalization were expelled from the CC of the CPC. Tito himself came to Croatia to support the conservatives. This led to even stronger opposition from the most radical Croatian activists, who called for "state sovereignty" for the republic. On 22 November 1971 students went on strike in Zagreb. At a meeting of the Croatian party leaders with Tito in Karadjordjevo on 30 November, Tripalo defended the views of the leadership of the CPC. He emphasized, among other things, that Croatia did not have equal access to loans from the International Monetary Fund or from the Soviet Union. On the following day, at the Twenty-first Session of the Presidium of the LCY CC, Tito admitted that the economic claims of the Croatian leadership were justified, but he stressed that it was a "class" rather than a "national" issue and that a loosening of the unity of the party and the state must be prevented. Under pressure from the central leadership of the LCY, on 8 December Tripalo resigned all his positions, and the following day Dapčević-Kučar did the same. They were accused of national factional work. As a result of a purge that was launched in late 1971 and early 1972, 740 people were expelled from the party, and around 400 people resigned their party positions. For many years Tripalo was sidelined in public life. After 1991, he joined the leadership of the Croatian People's Party (Hrvatska Narodna Stranka). Tripalo's publications include *Hrvatsko proljeće* (Croatian Spring; 1989). (WR)

Sources: *Enciklopedija Jugoslavije*, vol. 8 (Zagreb, 1971); Milovan Baletić, ed., *Ljudi iz 1971: Prekinuta šutnja* (Zagreb, 1990); Ante Čuvalo, *The Croatian National Movement, 1966–1972* (Boulder, Colo., 1990).

TROCHTA Štěpán (26 March 1905, Francova Lhota, Vsetín district, Moravia–6 April 1974, Litoměřice), Czech cardinal. Born into a family of smallholders, Trochta's father died in Trochta's childhood. Trochta studied in a seminary run by the Salesians in Turin, where he took holy orders in June 1932. After returning to Czechoslovakia, he briefly worked in a Salesian parish in Moravia and then in a Salesian institute in Prague. In the 1930s Trochta established Salesian institutions to care for youth, as well as workshops and sports clubs in the poorest districts of Prague. He was also a member of the leadership of Junák, a Catholic scouting organization. From the beginning of the Nazi occupation, Trochta maintained contacts with the Czech resistance movement. His patriotic sermons, preached in Holy Cross Church in Prague, enjoyed great popularity. Arrested in 1940, Trochta was released after some time. In May 1942, following the assassination of Reinhard Heydrich, the governor of the Protectorate of Bohemia and Moravia, Trochta was arrested again and sent to the concentration camp in Terezín and then to Mauthausen, where, among other things, he worked in a quarry. He was finally imprisoned in Dachau, where he remained until the end of the war.

After returning to Czechoslovakia in 1945, Trochta resumed his pastoral work in a Salesian parish in Prague. On 27 September 1947 he was appointed bishop in Litoměřice, where the Communist authorities had forced the resignation of Bishop Alois Weber, an anti-Fascist but a German. Trochta was consecrated bishop on 16 November 1947 in Prague. In assuming his position, he emphasized that he was going to minister to all Catholics, regardless of their nationality. He also rejected the notion of the collective responsibility of the German people. Trochta defended the independence of the Church; for example, he prevented the so-called patriot priests, loyal to the Communist government, from taking control of the theological seminary. From June 1949 onwards Trochta was interned in his own residence, and the government of the diocese was handed over to a vicar capitular who was dependent on the Communist authorities. On 10 January 1953 Trochta was arrested. After a brutal interrogation, he was sentenced to twenty-five years in prison in a show trial in 1954.

Released under an amnesty in 1960, Trochta was banned from exercising his pastoral ministry. He began working as a bricklayer. As a result of hard physical work, he had a heart attack in 1962. From then on he lived in Church-run charity houses, including one in Radvanov, where he met Archbishop **Josef Beran** in 1965. Rehabilitated during the Prague Spring, Trochta again became the bishop of Litoměřice on 1 September 1968. On 5 March 1973 Pope Paul VI appointed him cardinal. At the time of increasing persecution of the Church, during the so-called normalization, Trochta attempted to defend the freedom of the Church. He was one of the key figures in the underground church in Bohemia. He secretly ordained many underground priests, who did their pastoral work without the permission of the Communist authorities. Seriously ill after an eye operation, Trochta died a few hours after an interrogation in the office for religious affairs. His funeral liturgy was celebrated by Cardinal Karol Wojtyła, the metropolitan of Kraków, but the authorities banned him from delivering a funeral speech. (AGr)

Sources: *ČBS*; Frantz Hummer, *Bischőfe für Untergrund* (Munich, 1981); Bohdan Cywiński, *I was prześladować będą* (Lublin and Rome, 1990); Václav Vaško, *Neumlčená: Kronika Katolicke Cirkve v Československu po druhé světové válce* (Prague, 1990); Karel Kaplan, *Stát a Cirkev v Československu 1948–1953* (Brno, 1993); Hansjakob Stehle, *Tajna dyplomacja Watykanu: Papiestwo wobec komunizmu (1917–1991)* (Warsaw, 1993); Agostino Casaroli, *Pamiętniki—męczeństwo cierpliwości: Stolica Święta i kraje komunistyczne (1963–1989)* (Warsaw, 2001); Jaroslav Novosad, *Štěpan Trochta: Svědek "T"* (Prague, 2001).

TRUMBIĆ Ante (17 May 1864, Split–17 November 1938, Zagreb), Croatian politician. Trumbić studied law in Zagreb, Vienna, and Graz, earning a doctorate in 1890. He subsequently worked as a lawyer in Split. He was elected to the Dalmatian Diet in 1895 and to the Austrian parliament (Reichsrat) in Vienna in 1897. Elected mayor of Split in 1905, Trumbić played a great role in drafting the Rijeka Resolution, adopted by Croatian politicians on 3 October 1905; in it they protested Austrian domination and supported the Hungarians, who sought full independence. The adoption of this resolution was supported by the Serbs and led to the establishment of the Croatian-Serbian Coalition, which was successful in the elections of May 1906. Trumbić strove for the unification of the South Slavic nations outside Austria-Hungary. From 1914 to 1918 he was in exile. He unsuccessfully attempted to dissuade the Entente states from making territorial concessions to Italy at the expense of the South Slavic nations; these concessions were sealed in the secret Treaty of London in 1915. From 1915 to 1918 Trumbić served as president of the Yugoslav Committee, whose position in the international arena was undermined by the fact that the Serbian government refused to recognize it as a legitimate representation of Slovenes, Croats, and Serbs. After the National Council of Slovenes, Croats, and Serbs was constituted in October 1918, Trumbić was appointed its official plenipotentiary.

While negotiating with the Serbian government of **Nikola Pašić**, Trumbić failed to break the resistance against a federal model for a future state, under which all the nationalities would be afforded equal rights. Trumbić was one of the signatories of the Declaration of Corfu (20 July 1917), which called for the creation of a common kingdom of Serbs, Croats, and Slovenes under the rule of the Karadjordjević dynasty. He also conducted negotiations with the Italian deputy, Andrea Torre, on the revision of the 1915 Treaty of London, leading to the signing of an agreement on 7 March 1918. This was an important step toward overcoming Italy's reluctance to the establishment of a Yugoslav state. In April 1918 in Rome Trumbić headed the Yugoslav delegation to a congress of all nationalities of Austria-Hungary except the Germans and Hungarians. In October 1918 he negotiated the establishment of a state with Prime Minister Pašić and **Anton Korošec**, the representative of the National Council in Zagreb. These negotiations resulted in the Geneva Declaration of 9 November 1918. In December 1918, after the creation of the Kingdom of Serbs, Croats, and Slovenes under the rule of the Karadjordjević dynasty, Trumbić became minister of foreign affairs in its first government and held this post until November 1920. He was one of the delegates to the Paris Peace Conference, where he showed great diplomatic skills. Trumbić had the final word in border negotiations with the Italians, although he was not fully content with the Treaty of Rapallo between Italy and the Kingdom of Serbs, Croats, and Slovenes (12 November 1920).

In domestic policy, Trumbić opposed plans to establish a centralist state and proposed a federal model. His relations with **Stjepan Radić** were not good. When Radić began to work with Pašić, Trumbić established a competition group, the Croatian Federal Peasant Party, in 1926, but it failed to gain much influence. After the tragic death of Radić in 1928, Trumbić began to work with the Croatian Peasant Party (CPP), which he joined formally in 1931. He firmly opposed the dictatorship of King **Alexander I**. Trumbić supported the adoption of the so-called Zagreb Manifesto, passed by the Croatian opposition in November 1932, in which absolutism, centralism, and unitarism were condemned. After CPC chairman **Vladko Maček** was sentenced to three years' imprisonment, Trumbić became an interim leader of the party. Until the end of his life Trumbić was in opposition to the authorities in Belgrade. His memoirs, *Iz mojih političkih uspomena* (From my political memoirs), were published in 1936. (AO)

Sources: *Biographisches Lexikon*, vol. 4; *Enciklopedija Jugoslavije*, vol. 8 (Zagreb, 1971); Werner Markert, *Jugoslawien* (Cologne, 1954); Ante Smith-Pavelic, *Dr Ante Trumbić: Problemi hrvatsko-srpskih odnosa* (Munich, 1959); Ljubo Boban, "Prilozi za biografiju Ante Trumbića u vrijeme šestojanuarskova režima (1929–1935)," *Historijski Zbornik*, 1968–69, vols. 21–22; Holger H. Herwig and Neil M. Heyman, *Biographical Dictionary of World War I* (Westport, Conn., 1982); Wacław Felczak and Tadeusz Wasilewski, *Historia Jugosławii* (Wrocław, 1985); Ivo Petrinović, *Ante Trumbić: Politička shvaćanja i djelovanje* (Zagreb, 1986); *Život i djelo Ante Trumbicia: Prilozi sa znanstvenog skupa* (Zagreb, 1991).

TRUSAU Aleh (7 August 1954, Mstsislau, Belorussian SSR), Belarusian historian and politician. In 1976 Trusau graduated from the Department of History of the Belarusian State University. In 1981 he earned a doctorate in history. From 1976 to 1991 he worked at the Belarusian Architectural Preservation and Restoration Institute. He studied Belarusian architecture of the eleventh through seventeenth centuries and organized its restoration. From 1990 to 1995 Trusau was a deputy to the Belarusian Supreme Soviet. He served as deputy chairman of the Commission for Education, Culture, and Preservation of the Historical Heritage. Since 1989 he has been linked with the democratic opposition. Trusau was one of the top leaders of the Rebirth Belarusian Popular Front. A co-founder of the Belarusian Social Democratic Hromada, Trusau served as its chairman from 1992 to 1995. In 1999 he became chairman of the Belarusian Language Society. Trusau works at the Belarusian University of Culture. (EM)

Sources: *Narodnyia deputaty Respubliki Belarus: Dvanatstsatae sklikannie* (Minsk, 1992); *Kto jest kim w Białorusi* (Białystok, 2000).

TSANKOV Aleksandur (29 June 1879, Oryakhovo–17 July 1959, Buenos Aires, Argentina), Bulgarian politician. After graduating from high school in Ruse in 1900, Tsankov studied law at the University of Sofia and then law and economics in Munich, Breslau (Wrocław), and Berlin. He started his political career in the Social Democratic Party but left it in 1907. After graduation, he returned to Bulgaria. He worked in a bank and from 1911 at the University of Sofia. From 1916 Tsankov was an associate professor, then a full professor, and in 1919–20, rector. In 1916 he published *Voynata na narodite* (War of nations). After the war he was in opposition to the **Aleksandur Stamboliyski** dictatorship. In 1922 Tsankov co-founded and became leader of the secret National Alliance (Naroden Sgowor). Along with the secret Military League of **Damyan Velchev** and with the support of part of the army, on 9 June 1923 Tsankov overthrew the Stamboliyski regime and took the lead of a new government based on the Democratic Alliance which included the National Alliance and radical, democratic and populist parties formerly in opposition to the Stamolyiski regime . In September 1923 he baffled an attempted Communist coup, outlawed the Communist Party of Bulgaria, and stabilized the political situation by a brutal repression of the supporters of the Populist and Communist dictatorships. For this reason the extreme left called him a "bloody professor." On 4 June 1926 Tsankov resigned in favor of **Andrey Lyapchev**, and he assumed the position of speaker of the National Assembly.

In May 1930 Tsankov became minister of education, but, increasingly disappointed with democracy, he broke with the Democratic Alliance, and in 1932 he created the National Social Movement (Narodno Sotsyalno Dvizhenye [NSM]), whose program was modeled on Italian fascism. In 1931 Tsankov published the textbook *Politicheska ikonomia* (Political economy). Thanks to a split in the military faction Zveno and in the Military League, the NSM began to gain followers, and Tsankov planned to introduce authoritarian power. In reaction to these plans, on 19 May 1934 the Zveno leaders toppled the democratic government of **Nikola Mushanov** and assumed dictatorial power themselves. The foreign policy of the new government of **Kimon Georgiev**, as well as Georgiev's republican rhetoric, caused Tsar **Boris III** to remove this government in January 1935. Although Tsankov had followers among the tsar's supporters, Boris was reluctant to build on new rightist movements, and he preferred a bureaucracy and a part of the army as the foundation for his royal dictatorship. Tsankov was even temporarily interned. During World War II he was in moderate opposition to the tsarist rule, but he declared support for the pro-German policies. In 1942 Tsankov published *Trite stopanski sistemi* (Three economic systems), in which he analyzed capitalism, communism, and the Nazi economy, rating the last the highest. When on 9 September 1944 the pro-German government collapsed as a result of a leftist coup, Tsankov left for Vienna, where under German shelter he founded a Bulgarian government-in-exile. After the fall of the Third Reich, Tsankov stayed in Austria. A Communist court sentenced him to death in absentia, and in 1949 the occupation authorities forced him to emigrate to Argentina, where he died. In 1998 Tsankov's *Bylgariya v burno vreme: Spomeni* (Bulgaria in stormy times: Memoirs) was published in Bulgaria. (WR)

Sources: *Biographisches Lexikon*, vol. 1; *Entsiklopediya Bulgariya*, vol. 7 (Sofia, 1986); Raymond Detrez, *Historical Dictionary of Bulgaria* (Lanham, Md., 1997); *Almanakh na Sofiyskiya Universitet 1888–1928* (Sofia, 1929); Todor Vyalkov, *Politicheski zhivot u nas: Statii i belezhki*, vol. 5 (Sofia, 1930); L. A. D. Dellin, ed., *Bulgaria* (New York, 1957); Marshall Lee Miller, *Bulgaria during the Second World War* (Stanford, 1975); Tasho Tashev, *Ministrite na Bulgariya 1879–1999: Entsiklopedichen spravochnik* (Sofia, 1999).

TSANKOV Georgi [originally Veselinov] (26 March 1913, Kytina, near Sofia–21 November 1990, Sofia), Bulgarian Communist activist. After joining the Bulgarian Communist Party (BCP) in 1932, Tsankov was active in the trade union movement until 1938 and then in the district committee and the municipal committee of the BCP in Sofia. After the coup of 9 September 1944 he became secretary of the BCP Municipal Committee in Sofia and a member of the National Council of the Fatherland Front. Then until 1948 he was secretary general of the Central Committee (CC) of the General Trade Union of Workers in Bulgaria. Thanks to the support of **Vulko Chervenkov**, who surrounded himself with national activists who were younger but totally obedient to Stalinist orthodoxy, in 1948 Tsankov became a member of the CC and then BCP CC secretary for organizational affairs. From January 1951 to March 1962 he served as minister of interior. In 1954 Tsankov joined the Politburo, becoming one of the most powerful men in Bulgaria. He was in charge of the entire persecution apparatus. He was responsible for political terror, forceful suppression of the resistance to collectivization, concentration camps, and the system of mass surveillance of citizens. In July 1956, along with **Anton Yugov** and other senior officials of the interior and military ministries, Tsankov was in Moscow, where they met with Anastas Mikoyan and Mikhail Suslov to discuss ways of preventing the system's erosion from the "thaw." After

Tsankov's subsequent visit to the Kremlin at the end of 1959, a system of "teams," modeled on those of the Soviet Union, was introduced in Bulgaria. These "teams"—that is, voluntary workers' brigades—fought against trivial offenses and also controlled factory workforces.

From 1946 Tsankov was a deputy to the parliament, and from 1947 to 1949, a member of the Presidium of the Grand National Assembly. On 17 March 1962 he was appointed deputy prime minister; the appointment in fact only seemed to be a promotion because Tsankov simultaneously lost his influence in the security apparatus. In this way, **Todor Zhivkov** undermined the independence of this apparatus, since the new minister, General Diko Dikov, came from the army. After consultations in Moscow, in a speech at the Eighth Congress of the BCP on 5 November 1962, Zhivkov demanded that Tsankov be dismissed from all his posts and from the CC. On 20 November 1962 Tsankov ceased to be deputy prime minister. In this move Yugov and former party leader Chervenkov were expelled as well, under the guise of eliminating the remnants of the "personality cult"; however, the move in fact greatly consolidated Zhivkov's control over the entire government apparatus in Bulgaria. In 1964 Tsankov was dismissed from his parliamentary post, and after that he sank into obscurity. He was never brought to justice for his activities. (JJ/WR)

Sources: J. F. Brown, *Bulgaria under Communist Rule* (New York, 1970); Tasho V. Tashev, *Ministrite na Bulgariya 1879–1999* (Sofia, 1999).

TSELEVYCH Volodymyr (21 April 1891, Lemberg [Lviv, Lwów]–1944, Saratov), Ukrainian politician and lawyer. Tselevych graduated from high school and then from the Department of Law of the University of Lviv, where he later he worked as a judge and journalist. In 1918–21 he was secretary of the Ukrainian Citizens' Committee (Horożańśkyj Komitet), representing the interests of the Ukrainian population after the army of the Western Ukrainian National Republic was dislodged by the Polish Army. In July 1925 Tselevych was co-founder and from 1928 secretary general of the Ukrainian National Democratic Union (Ukraińsko Nacionalno-Demokratyczno Objednanije [UNDO]). During the May coup of 1926 he was dismissed as judge and temporarily arrested. In 1928–30 Tselevych was an MP on behalf of the UNDO and deputy chairman of the Ukrainian parliamentary club. In 1930 he was arrested again and put in the Brest Fortress prison. His case was separated from those of the Polish MPs and then discontinued. In 1932–35 Tselevych was editor of the Lviv weekly *Svoboda*, and from 1932 to 1937 he was the UNDO secretary general. In 1935 he was the co-author of an agreement between the UNDO and the Polish government. As a result, in 1935–39 he was an MP again. After the Red Army entered eastern Poland in September 1939, Tselevych was arrested by the NKVD and imprisoned in Brest, Moscow, and Saratov, where he died. (WR)

Sources: *Encyclopedia of Ukraine*, vol. 1 (Toronto, 1984); *Kto był kim w Drugiej Rzeczypospolitej* (Warsaw, 1994); *Posłowie . . . ; Encyklopedia historii Drugiej Rzeczypospolitej* (Warsaw, 1999); *Wielka encyklopedia PWN*, vol. 5 (Warsaw, 2001).

TSVIKEVICH Aleksandr (1888, Brest-Litovsk–30 December 1937, Minsk), Belorussian philosopher, historian, and politician. In 1912 Tsvikevich graduated from the University of St. Petersburg. In 1917 in Moscow he founded the Belorussian People's Hromada, a party that rallied refugees from Belorussia. Opposed to an agreement with the Poles, Tsvikevich actively participated in the creation of the Belorussian People's Republic (BPR). After its proclamation at the beginning of 1918, he was a delegate of the BPR to the peace negotiations in Brest-Litovsk, and then he was minister of foreign affairs in the BPR government. Then Tsvikevich went into exile in Czechoslovakia, where from 1923 he served as prime minister of the BPR. At a conference of Belorussian émigré circles in Berlin in the fall of 1925, Tsvikevich advocated the recognition of the Belorussian SSR government as the only representation of the Belorussian nation. Tsvikevich resigned his post and returned to Minsk at the end of 1925. At first he worked in the People's Commissariat of Finance of the Belorussian SSR, and then he served as secretary at the Institute of Belorussian Culture. From 1929 he was a professor of history at the Belorussian SSR Academy of Sciences. Tsvikevich mainly did research on the history of political thought in Belorussia and on Belorussian national consciousness. In November 1930, along with a few hundred other intellectuals, Tsvikevich was accused of being a member of the Belorussian Liberation Union, an anti-Soviet conspiratorial organization that actually did not exist. Convicted and deported to Siberia, he was executed by firing squad. Tsvikevich was the author of several scholarly works, which are still topical today—for example, *Belarus: Palitychny narys* (Belarus: A political outline; 1919); *Adradzhennie na Belarusi i Polshcha* (Revival of Belarus and Poland; 1921); and *Zapadno-russizm* (Western Russophilia; 1929). (EM)

Sources: *Akhviary balshavizmu* (Białystok, 1944); Nicholas P. Vakar, *Belorussia: The Making of a Nation* (Cambridge, Mass., 1956); *Byelorussian Times*, 7 December 1976; Vitaut Kipel and Zora Kipel, eds., *Byelorussian Statehood* (New York, 1988); *Bielarus: Entsyklapeidychny daviednik* (Minsk, 1995).

TŪBELIS Juozas (18 April 1882, Ilgalaukiai, Rokiškis County–30 September 1939, Kaunas), Lithuanian agronomist, social activist, and politician. In his youth Tūbelis was aligned with the radical movement. In 1908 he graduated from the Technical University of Riga. While a student, he took part in the work of Lithuanian nationalist organizations, serving as publisher and editor-in-chief of *Lietuvos Ukininkas*, *Viltis*, and *Rygos Garsas*. After graduating, Tūbelis worked as a teacher and journalist. Inducted into the tsarist army in 1915, he was assigned to work in the War Commissariat. As a result of his efforts, the Lithuanian Relief Committee received 100,000 rubles, which made it possible to offer substantial aid to war refugees. Tūbelis's frequent official visits to Russia enabled him to contact and financially support Lithuanian colonies scattered throughout Russian territory. He also worked in commissions that prepared Lithuanian textbooks.

In the first government of independent Lithuania, established on 11 November 1918, Tūbelis assumed the portfolio of minister of agriculture. In subsequent cabinets he served as minister of education (1919) and again minister of agriculture (1919–20). After the end of the armed struggle for Lithuania's independence, Tūbelis retired from active politics and became involved in business, where he was very successful, co-founding trade and production companies, mainly in the field of agricultural processing (Maistas, Pienocentras, and Lietukis), as well as the Lithuanian Regional Electric Power Station Company. These enterprises were important for the economy of the newly established state. One of the major entrepreneurs in Lithuania, Tūbelis was a member of the Chamber of Agriculture and the Chamber of Commerce and Industry. After **Antanas Smetona** came to power in 1926, Tūbelis returned to active politics. He owed his meteoric career and rise to top governmental positions not only to his excellent professional qualifications, but also to the fact that he was Smetona's brother-in-law. In 1927 Tūbelis assumed the portfolio of minister of finance. After **Augustinas Voldemaras** was dismissed as prime minister, Tūbelis became head of the government on 23 September 1929. In 1931 he became head of the Union of Lithuanian Nationalists (Tautininkų Sąjunga), becoming the second most important politician in Lithuania after Smetona. In 1935, as a result of a peasant strike, Tūbelis changed the composition of the cabinet. He continued as prime minister until 28 March 1938 and simultaneously almost uninterruptedly served as minister of finance. In 1929 he also briefly held the ministry of foreign affairs, and in 1938 he additionally served as minister of agriculture. Tūbelis proved to be an efficient administrator and deserves credit for relatively quickly pulling Lithuania out of the economic crisis of the 1930s and putting the economy on a steady growth track. He founded his policy on a strong currency, sharp financial discipline, and limitations on foreign debt and imports. However, the state coordinated activities supporting exports, particularly those of agricultural produce. Under Tūbelis's government the cooperative movement also developed. The litas was one of the most stable European currencies, and Lithuania successfully developed until the end of the 1930s. The crisis of March 1938, linked to the Polish-imposed establishment of diplomatic relations, led to the collapse of his cabinet, and Tūbelis became head of the Central Bank. (AG)

Sources: *EL*, vol. 5; Saulius Sužiedėlis, *Historical Dictionary of Lithuania* (Lanham, Md., 1997); Owen J. C. Norem, *Timeless Lithuania* (Chicago, 1943); Alfonsas Eidintas and Vytautas Žalys, *Lithuania in European Politics: The Years of the First Republic, 1918–1940* (New York, 1997).

TUDJMAN Franjo (14 May 1922, Veliko Trogovišće–10 December 1999, Zagreb), president of Croatia. Tudjman was born in a village in the Croatian Zagorje. His father, Stjepan, was a well-known political activist during the interwar period and a member of the leadership of the Croatian Peasant Party (Hrvatska Seljačka Stranka). Tudjman graduated from high school in Zagreb. In 1941 he deserted from the Croatian Army and joined the anti-Fascist guerrillas of **Josip Broz Tito**. He served in the Radić Brothers Brigade and later on the staff of the Tenth Partisan Corps, which operated in the southwest regions of Croatia. After the war Tudjman continued his career in the army; for example, he was an officer of the General Staff of the Yugoslav People's Army. In 1957 he graduated from the Military Academy in Belgrade, and in 1961 he was promoted to major general. He was the youngest general in the Yugoslav Army at that time. As a result of a conflict with Tito, Tudjman retired from military service and returned to Zagreb. In 1962 he became director of the Institute of the History of the Workers' Movement in Croatia and held the post for six years. At that time he was the editor-in-chief of the periodical *Putovi revolucije*. He also lectured on recent history in the Department of Philosophical Sciences of Zagreb University. In 1965 Tudjman defended his postdoctoral dissertation, "Uzroci krize monarhističke Jugoslavije od ujedinjenja 1918 do sloma 1941" (The sources of crisis of monarchist Yugoslavia from the unification in 1918 to the collapse in 1941). He also worked as an editor of the *Military Encyclopedia*, the *Encyclopedia of Yugoslavia*, and many other scholarly publications. Tudjman attended scholarly congresses and symposia in many European countries and the United States; among other things, he conducted a series of lec-

tures on supremacy and coexistence in the nuclear era at Harvard University.

In 1967 Tudjman was accused of "Croatian nationalism" and was expelled from the League of Communists of Yugoslavia. From 1970 he worked in Croatian cultural and educational associations; for example, he was one of the leaders Croatian Matrix. He belonged to the Association of Croatian Publishers and Booksellers and to the Union of Croatian Writers. At that time Tudjman wrote a considerable part of his over 150 publications on military doctrine, recent history, politics, law, and international relations. Among other things, he came to the conclusion that for propaganda purposes Tito's regime had exaggerated the crimes committed by the Ustashe in the Jasenovac concentration camp. This was considered a manifestation of Croatian nationalism. As a result, Tudjman was accused of anti-Yugoslav activities during the so-called Croatian Spring of 1971, when Croatian party reformers put forward a proposal for the reform of the self-government system that also included increased autonomy for the union republics. In 1972 Tudjman was sentenced to two years of prison on the charge of propagating separatism. After his release from prison, he devoted himself to writing. Among other works, he published *Nacionalno pitanje u suvremenoj Evropi* (The national movement in contemporary Europe) and *Velike ideje i mali narodi* (Great ideas and small nations), reflecting on the right of self-determination of nations in the light of international law and to the Croatian question in the twentieth century.

Soon after Tito's death, in 1982, Tudjman was arrested again and sentenced to three years in the severe Lepoglava Prison because of interviews that had appeared on German television and French radio in which he postulated the introduction of democracy and political pluralism. For many Croats he became a leader struggling for national sovereignty. In 1983, owing to illness, Tudjman was temporarily released from prison, but after a few months he had to return. Finally he was released in 1984. In 1987 he obtained a passport and left for Canada and the United States, where he met with Croatian emigrants. Tudjman wanted to eliminate the old divisions between the Ustashe and the partisans. Modifying history, he whitewashed the crimes of both sides. Soon he was a recognized leader of the entire Croatian emigration, which financially supported his activities to rebuild a sovereign Croatian state. Later he also traveled throughout Europe, seeking support from the international community for this idea.

In June 1988 Tudjman founded the Croatian Democratic Union (Hrvatska Demokratska Zajednica [HDZ]), which favored the independence of Croatia. In June 1990 he was elected the leader of the HDZ. In April

1990 the HDZ won the first free elections since 1945 to the Croatian parliament (Sabor). In May 1990 the Sabor appointed Tudjman president; this was the beginning of Croatia's secession in June 1991. Tudjman was reelected president of Croatia by popular vote in July 1992, when he gained 57 percent of the vote. In 1991 he also assumed the post of commander-in-chief of the army. In the war against the Serbs (1991–95) Tudjman had the support of a definite majority of the nation. After initial failures in the struggles for Krajina and Slavonia in the summer and autumn of 1991, Tudjman succeeded in building an efficient and modern army. In May 1995 Croatian units regained Western Slavonia, and in August 1995 they seized Krajina, causing an exodus of nearly one million Serbian refugees. After the outbreak of conflict in Bosnia and Herzegovina, Tudjman initially supported forces aiming at the creation of an autonomous Croatian republic in Herzegovina with its capital in Mostar, and then he formed an alliance with Muslim forces against the Serbs. Along with **Alija Izetbegović**, the president of Bosnia and Herzegovina, and **Slobodan Milošević**, the president of Serbia, Tudjman took part in peace negotiations in Dayton, Ohio, where on 21 November 1995 the Dayton Agreement, which ended the war in Bosnia, was signed. In the general elections of 1997 Tudjman was elected president of Croatia for the third time. The same year, as a result of international mediation, he regained Baranja, the last part of Croatia that still remained under Serbian occupation. He also committed himself to respecting the rights of the Serbian minority. Tudjman was accused of having created a corruption-generating system with one predominant party and of not seeking a reckoning for the crimes committed by the Ustashe. At the time of his rule the HDZ was victorious in all the elections, and its majority in the parliament gave it unlimited legislative freedom. Legal guarantees of human rights and freedom of the press were violated. The return of Serbian refugees to Krajina was not secured. At the same time, Tudjman did counteract the activities of the other smaller parties with more parties with more clearly fascist and expansionist programs, which unanimously turned to Fascist ideology and spread propaganda for creating a "racially pure Croatia." Tudjman received many national and international awards, including that of Catarina de Medici. He was also doctor *honoris causa* of the university in Seville. After Tudjman's death, his cult ended, and the HDZ lost the elections. (AGr)

Sources: *Bałkański węzeł* (Kraków, 1999); *Kroatien zwischen Krieg und Selbstandigkeit* (Zagreb, 1991); Ilija Marinković, *Wojna w Jugosławii: Dlaczego* (Warsaw, 1991); Tadeusz Olszański, *Mój brat cię zabije: O wojnie w Jugosławii* (Warsaw, 1995); Andelko Milardović, *Requiem za Jugoslaviju (Komentarii i dnevnici 1989–1992)* (Zagreb, 1992); "Dr. Franjo Tudjman. Historian and Statesman. Republic of Croatia," Office of the President, www.urpr.hr; *Franjo, Tudjman: Father of Croatia*; BBC News.

TUDOR Corneliu Vadim (28 November 1949, Bucharest), Romanian nationalist politician. Tudor graduated from high school in Bucharest in 1967. In the same year he began to study philosophy at the University of Bucharest. After graduating in 1971, he worked as a journalist for the periodical *România Liberă-Magazin*. In 1975 he underwent training at the Reserve Officers' School in Bucharest, where he began working with the political police, Securitate. In the same year he became an editor at the Romanian Press Agency (Agentia Româna de Presa; Agerpress). From 1978 to 1979 Tudor studied history in Vienna. From 1979 until the collapse of **Nicolae Ceaușescu**'s regime in December 1989, he worked as an editor at Agerpress and served as Ceaușescu's eulogist and "court poet" and remained very close to the Romanian dictator and his family. In 1990 Tudor became the owner of a press group and began to publish nationalist and populist periodicals, *România Mare* and *Politică*. In 1991 he co-founded the Great Romania Party (Partidul România Mare [PRM]), a nationalist and anti-Semitic party of which he became the leader. The PRM brought together former Communist ideologues and former Securitate members who began to draw on peculiarly understood Christian and national values and opposed privatization and market reforms. In 1992 Tudor became a senator on the PRM ticket, and until 1995 he worked closely in parliament with the ruling post-Communist Party of Social Democracy in Romania (Partidul Democrației Sociale din România [PSDR]). From 1996 to 2000 Tudor again served as a senator, and his party strengthened its position in the parliament. In the parliamentary elections of 26 November 2000 Tudor became a senator for the third time, and the PRM came in second, with 19.5 percent of the vote. In the first round of the presidential elections, held on the same day, Tudor obtained 28.3 percent of the vote and went on to the second round, in which he obtained 33.2 percent of the vote, losing to **Ion Iliescu**. Tudor's party remained in opposition to the ruling PDSR and to President Iliescu. Tudor has published a dozen or so volumes of poetry and has written several plays. (LW)

Sources: Józef Darski, *Rumunia: Historia, współczesność, konflikty narodowe* (Warsaw, 1995); *Europa Środkowo-Wschodnia 1994–1995* (Warsaw, 1997); Tom Gallagher, *Romania after Ceaușescu* (Edinburgh, 1995); Duncan Light and Daniel Phinnemore, *Post–Communist Romania* (London, 2001); www.nordest.ro; www.romare.ro; www.time.com; www.idgr.de; www.electionworld.org.

TUKA Vojtech (Béla in Hungarian) (4 July 1880, Piarg [now Štiavnické Bane]–20 August 1946, Bratislava), Slovak lawyer and politician. Tuka was born in a Magyarized Slovak family. Until the age of forty he considered himself a Hungarian. He completed law studies in Budapest, Berlin, and Paris. He could speak several languages but knew Slovak poorly. In 1907–14 Tuka lectured on law in Transylvania and in the Department of Law of the University of Budapest. Then he became chair of the Department of the Philosophy of Law at the Hungarian Elizabethan University in Bratislava. Tuka maintained that during World War I his Slovak national consciousness matured. Some researchers think that joining the Slovak nationalists was just a part of Tuka's work as an agent for the Hungarian special services, which wanted to infiltrate the Slovak irredentist movement. Reverend **Andrej Hlinka** accepted Tuka into the leadership of the Slovak People's Party (Slovenská L'udova Straná [SL'S]) so as to gain votes and financial support from the Hungarian minority. As early as 1921, on the personal orders of Reverend Hlinka, Tuka developed a plan for the autonomy of Slovakia. At that time he also became editor-in-chief of the periodical *Slovák*, an organ of the SL'S. From the beginning of the 1920s Tuka favored Italian fascism, and in 1923 he established ties with a Munich unit of the Nazi movement. From 1923 to 1929 Tuka was the leader of a paramilitary organization called Rodobrana, which became the Hlinka Guard (Hlinkova Garda) in 1938. In 1925 he was elected to the Czechoslovak National Assembly.

At the beginning of 1928 Tuka wrote his famous text, "Vacuum iuris," for *Slovák*. In it, he proved that the Czechoslovak agreement on a common state—the so-called declaration of St. Martin—contained a secret addendum that stated that the agreement was valid for ten years only. Thus, he reasoned, a new state agreement was necessary, and it had to be signed by 30 September 1928; otherwise that "loophole" (*vacuum iuris*) would take effect. According to Tuka, the legal situation required that the Slovaks decide once again whether they wanted a common state with the Czechs. In 1929 Tuka was arrested and in September 1929 sentenced to fifteen years of prison for attacks against the territorial integrity of Czechoslovakia and for espionage for Hungary. Because of Tuka's trial, Reverend Hlinka had to rescind the policy of normalizing relations with Prague. After eight years of prison, in July 1937 Tuka was pardoned by President **Edvard Beneš**. Although Tuka was banned from returning to Slovakia, he appeared there nonetheless, instigating anti-Czechoslovak demonstrations. After his release from prison he was still active in the SL'S and attempted to establish close ties with the German Nazis. In 1937 Tuka prepared a plan for autonomy that in June 1938 was passed as an official SL'S program. The plan, designed on the model of the Austro-Hungarian political system, envisioned the creation of a Czechoslovak unionist republic consisting of two parts: the Czech and the Slovak. Tuka maintained close relations with the leadership of the Third Reich, attempting to push through the leadership of the SL'S a decision to proclaim the independence of the Slovak state.

In January 1939, along with **Alexander Mach, Ferdinand Ďurčansky**, and the leaders of the Deutsche Partei (the party of the German national minority in Slovakia), Tuka founded the German-Slovak Society, which became an important lobby in favor of the pro-German policy of Slovakia. On 12 February 1939, along with **Franz Karamsin**, the leader of the German minority in Slovakia, Tuka was received by Hitler in Berlin. Tuka arbitrarily declared, "I place the fate of my nation in your hands, my Führer; my nation expects full liberation with your help." He was assured then that the Third Reich would support an independent Slovakia. In March 1939, along with Ďurčansky, Tuka appealed to Hermann Göring for his support in the creation of a Slovak state. From 14 March 1939 Tuka was deputy prime minister, minister of interior, and vice-president of the SL'S.

On 27 October 1939, against the will of President **Josef Tiso**, who, however, yielded to Berlin's demands, Tuka became prime minister of Slovakia. Later Tuka prepared a coup against Tiso, whom he accused of a lack of radicalism and too little support for the policy of the Third Reich. In 1940 Tuka was forced by Tiso to go on sick leave. However, after a meeting of a Slovak delegation with Hitler in Salzburg in June 1940, Tuka resumed his post of prime minister. At the same time, he became minister of foreign affairs and served as the rector of the university in Bratislava. After his return from Salzburg, Tuka announced that he intended to "finish the national revolution"—that is, complete the total fascization of Slovakia. At the beginning of 1941 he proclaimed a fourteen-point program that became the political platform of the extreme rightist forces in the SL'S.

Without informing President Tiso, on 22 June 1941 Tuka announced in the parliament that Slovakia had declared war against the USSR and the Western Allies. A few months later he personally prepared anti-Jewish laws that he announced on 9 September 1941 without the knowledge of the other members of the cabinet or Tiso. These were a Slovak version of the Nuremberg Laws; they initiated the Aryanization process of the Slovak economy and social life. Along with Mach, the minister of interior, Tuka organized the deportation of Jews beginning in March 1942. From about ninety thousand Slovak Jews, over fifty-seven thousand were deported to the concentration camps in German-occupied Poland and Germany, and only eight hundred of them survived. The deportations were stopped in the autumn of 1942, after Tiso's intervention, when it turned out that instead of labor camps the Jews had been deported to places of extermination. Tuka was dismissed as prime minister in September 1944, when the Slovak National Uprising broke out. In 1945 he fled to Austria, where he was captured by the Americans and extradited on the request of the Slovak public prosecutor's office. On 29 September 1945 a plane arrived in Bratislava with Tiso, Tuka, and other Slovak activists who were considered war criminals. As the result of a trial before the National Tribunal in Bratislava, Tuka was sentenced to death and executed. (AGr)

Sources: Henryk Batowski, *Zdrada monachijska: Sprawa Czechosłowacji i dyplomacja europejska w roku 1938* (Poznań, 1973); *Kdo byl kdo v našich dějinách ve 20 století* (Prague, 1994); Ivan Kamenec, *Slovenský Stát 1939–1945* (Prague, 1992); *Słowacja na przełomie: Powstanie słowackie 1944* (Warsaw, 1969); Miloslav Moulis, *Akcja "Märzwirbel"* (Warsaw, 1983); Ivan Rada et al., *Dějiny zemi koruny české: Od nástupu osvícenstvi po naši dob*ued, vol. 2 (Prague, 1993); Konštantin Čulen, *Po Svätoplukovi druhá naša hlava: (Život dr. Jozefa Tisu)* (Radošina, 1992).

TUMAS-VAIŽGANTAS Juozas (8 September 1869. Maleišiai, Rokiškis County–29 April 1933, Kaunas), Lithuanian priest, writer, and politician. Tumas-Vaižgantas was born into a peasant family. While a student at a high school in Dvinsk (now Daugavpils, Latvia), he developed an interest in literature and writing. After graduating from the Kaunas Seminary, Tumas-Vaižgantas was ordained a priest in 1893. Because he showed his patriotic feelings, he was constantly transferred from one parish to another. From 1896 to 1902 he edited the periodical *Tėvynės Sargas*, which was printed in Eastern Prussia and smuggled into the Russian territories inhabited by the Lithuanians. Tumas-Vaižgantas's brother was sentenced to five years in exile in Siberia for distributing this periodical. Church authorities subsequently banned Tumas-Vaižgantas from his editorial and publishing activities without the bishop's permission. During the 1905 revolution Tumas-Vaižgantas attended the Grand Lithuanian Assembly in Vilnius as a representative of Christian Democratic groups. In 1907 he joined the editorial staff of the periodical *Viltis*, where he met **Antanas Smetona** and Juozas Kubilius. In 1911 he went to the United States, where he raised funds to support an educational society. After returning to his country, he wrote his impressions in *Ten gera, kur mūsų nėra* (The grass is always greener on the other side; 1912), calling on his compatriots not to leave their homeland in search of an easier life abroad. In 1914 Tumas-Vaižgantas

began to edit the periodical *Rygos Garsas*, and in 1915 he became a member of the Lithuanian Central Relief Committee in Petrograd. In June 1917 he attended the Lithuanian Conference in Petrograd and wholeheartedly supported the demands for Lithuanian independence. In 1920 he returned to Kaunas, where he edited periodicals representing nationalist views: *Tauta, Trimitas,* and *Mūsų Senovė*. From 1920 to 1932 he was rector of the Church of the Assumption of the Blessed Virgin Mary in Kaunas, and from 1922 to 1929 he taught Lithuanian literature at the University of Kaunas.

Tumas-Vaižgantas was a very prolific author. He started his literary life by publishing small pieces under the pen name of Juozapas iš Popšutės and then took on the pseudonym "Vaižgantas," which he subsequently added to his surname. His writings awoke patriotic feelings but also dislike of Poles and other nations. His most popular works include the stories *Karo vaizdai* (War sketches; 1915) and the novels *Pragiedruliai* (Rays of hope; 1918), which described life in Samogitia at the end of the nineteenth century; *Dėdės ir dėdienės* (Uncles and aunts; 1920); *Išgana* (The degenerate; 1929); *and Žemaičių Robinzonas* (Samogitian Robinson; 1932), in which he combined elements of reportage, descriptions of customs, psychology, allegory, and poetic fiction. (WR)

Sources: *EL*, vol. 5; A. Merkelis, *Juozas Tumas-Vaižgantas* (Kaunas, 1934); J. Ambrazevičius, *Vaižgantas* (Kaunas, 1936); A. Vaitiekūniene, *Vaižgantas* (Vilnius, 1959).

TUPURKOVSKI Vasil (8 April 1951, Skopje), Macedonian Communist and post-Communist politician. Tupurkovski graduated from the School of Law of Ss. Cyril and Methodius University in Skopje (1972) and from the University of Michigan Law School (1973). In 1976 he earned a Ph.D. in international public law from Ss. Cyril and Methodius University in Skopje. From 1974 to 1976 Tupurkovski was an assistant professor at the School of Law of this university, becoming an associate professor in 1976 and a full professor in 1983. He served as the chairman of the League of Yugoslav Communist Youth (Savez Komunističke Omladine Jugoslavije [SKOJ]) from 1979 to 1980, a member of the Presidium of the League of Communists of Yugoslavia (LCY) from 1986 to 1989, and a member of the collective presidency of Yugoslavia from 1988 to 1992. Until 1990 Tupurkovski called for maintaining the Yugoslav federation. He was also a sports activist: in 1992 he became president of the Macedonian Olympics Committee, and until 2000 he served as president of the Association of the Balkan National Olympics Committees.

In 1995 Tupurkovski was a special envoy of President

Kiro Gligorov to the United States, where he spoke against the policy of equal distance toward all of Macedonia's neighbors. In 1998 he founded the Democratic Alternative (Demokratska Alternativa [DA]), a political party that brought together former Communists who had links with Belgrade. In alliance with the Internal Macedonian Revolutionary Organization–Democratic Party for Macedonian National Unity (Vnatrešna-Makedonska Revolucionerna Organizacija–Demokratska Partija za Makedonsko Nacionalno Edintsvo [IMRO–DPMNU]), the DA won twelve seats in the 1998 elections, and eight of its members became ministers in the government of **Ljubčo Georgijevski**. From November 1998 to December 1999 Tupurkovski served as director of the Agency for Reconstruction and Development. On 27 December 1999 he became first deputy prime minister. In December 2000 he resigned his position and withdrew the DA from the government, accusing the prime minister of a failure to introduce reforms and of violating the rules of democracy. Tupurkovski ran in the 1999 presidential elections as the leader of the DA. He did not gain the support of the IMRO–DPMNU, though, and in the first round obtained 16.1 percent of the vote, losing to **Boris Trajkovski**, a candidate supported by the IMRO–DPMNU. In July 2000 Tupurkovski became minister without portfolio in the government of national unity. In the 2002 parliamentary elections the DA failed to enter parliament. Tupurkovski is a member of the International Law Association. He has written works on UN peace missions, a textbook on international public law (1984), and historical books, including *Istorija na Makedonija od drevnina do smrtta na Aleksandar Makedonski* (History of Macedonia from earliest times until the death of Alexander the Great; 1993) and *Istorija na Makedonija od smrtta na Aleksandar Makedonski do makedonsko-rimskite vojni* (History of Macedonia from the death of Alexander the Great to the Macedonian-Roman wars; 1994). (JD)

Sources: Valentina Georgieva and Sasha Konechni, *Historical Dictionary of the Republic of Macedonia* (Lanham, Md., 1998); Duncan Perry, "Macedonia's Quest for Security and Stability," *Current History*, 2000, no. 3; Irena Stawowy-Kawka, *Historia Macedonii* (Wrocław, 2000); Bugajski; www.sinf.gov.mk/Prez-Elec/Biografii/vtbiografijaen.htm.

TUROWICZ Jerzy (10 December 1912, Kraków–27 January 1999, Kraków), Polish journalist and politician. After graduating from high school, Turowicz studied at the Department of Machine Construction of the Technical University in Lwów (Lviv) from 1930 to 1934 and at the Department of Philosophy of the Jagiellonian University from 1934 to 1939. From 1930 onward he was active in the Association of Catholic Academic Youth known as Odrodzenie (Revival), an organization that shaped the youth in the spirit of open Catholicism. In 1939 Turowicz became the editor-in-chief of the Kraków-based daily *Głos narodu*. During the Nazi occupation he lived in Kraków, which always remained his hometown.

At the beginning of 1945 Turowicz helped to establish the weekly *Tygodnik Powszechny*, initiated by Archbishop **Adam Sapieha**, the metropolitan of Kraków. After a few months of editing the weekly, Turowicz became its editor-in-chief, and in June 1946 he also became the co-editor of the monthly *Znak*. In *Tygodnik Powszechny* Turowicz brought together the most eminent Catholic writers and journalists, including Father **Jan Piwowarczyk**, **Paweł Jasienica**, **Stefan Kisielewski**, and **Stanisław Stomma**. While avoiding a direct involvement in politics, the weekly strove to defend values threatened by communism and promoted not only Catholicism, but also a culture based on Christianity yet open to dialogue with all social and political movements. In March 1953, when the editorial staff led by Turowicz refused to print a panegyric on Stalin after the dictator's death, the authorities of the Polish People's Republic suspended the publication of *Tygodnik Powszechny*, while the pro-regime PAX Association began to publish an identically titled periodical under the editorship of **Jan Dobraczyński**. Turowicz lost his job and was forced to rely on occasional translations and the support of his friends.

After October 1956, the new authorities of the Polish United Workers' Party (Polska Zjednoczona Partia Robotnicza [PUWP]), led by **Władysław Gomułka**, agreed to permit the revival of *Tygodnik Powszechny* under Turowicz's editorship. At that time the line of the weekly was often described as "political neo-positivism." Turowicz was a commentator at the sessions of the Second Vatican Council and promoted its teachings. This led to tensions between the editorial staff and the Church hierarchs, who, led by Cardinal **Stefan Wyszyński**, the primate of Poland, were more cautious in promoting post-conciliar renewal among the faithful, fearing the erosion of Polish Catholicism as a result of some kind of "progressivism." In March 1964 Turowicz signed the "Letter of 34" in defense of the freedom of culture, in retaliation for which the Communist authorities reduced the circulation of *Tygodnik Powszechny*. In January 1966 at a meeting of the All-Polish Committee of the National Unity Front Turowicz defended an address issued by the Polish bishops to the German bishops and denounced by the Communist authorities; his stance prompted a fierce attack against him by Gomułka. After March 1968, Turowicz invited poets and writers persecuted by the regime (also those with an anti-clerical past, such as **Antoni Słonimski**) to publish in *Tygodnik Powszechny*. This facilitated cooperation among various groups opposing communism. In January 1976, together with activists linked to the parliamentary group called Znak, Turowicz signed a letter to the Assembly Constitutional Committee in protest against proposed amendments to the constitution. In the second half of the 1970s *Tygodnik Powszechny* became a forum for authors associated with the Workers' Defense Committee (Komitet Obrony Robotników [KOR]), who published under pen names. In October 1978 the weekly solemnly celebrated the election of Cardinal Karol Wojtyła as Pope **John Paul II**.

In 1980 Turowicz and *Tygodnik Powszechny* helped to establish the Independent Self-Governing Trade Union–Solidarity (Niezależny Samorządny Związek Zawodowy–Solidarność). After martial law was imposed, the weekly was suspended for six months. Reestablished, it continued to serve as a platform for opposition groups calling for social dialogue and—with the increase in economic stagnation and social apathy—for political changes. In the 1980s Turowicz was a member of the Episcopal Subcommittee for Dialogue with Judaism and a member of the Primate's Social Council. On 10 October 1986, along with **Lech Wałęsa**, **Tadeusz Mazowiecki**, and **Bronisław Geremek**, Turowicz signed a statement calling for a new political climate in Poland, to be established by meeting people's expectations. On 31 May 1987, on the eve of another visit by Pope John Paul II to Poland, Turowicz signed a statement that set out the basic goals of the opposition, including trade union and political pluralism. On 18 December 1988 Turowicz became a member of the Civic Committee of Lech Wałęsa. He also took part in the Round Table negotiations on the side of the opposition.

After Mazowiecki's government was formed in September 1989, Turowicz and his weekly supported economic and political reforms. In the spring of 1990 Turowicz supported Mazowiecki, who ran against Wałęsa in the presidential elections. Turowicz co-founded Civic Movement–Democratic Action (Ruch Obywatelski–Akcja Demokratyczna), which criticized Wałęsa for dictatorial leanings and methods. In the 1990s Turowicz promoted a model of liberal Catholicism in his weekly, often critical of the Church hierarchs; his position caused protests by other Catholic groups. On the fiftieth anniversary of *Tygodnik Powszechny*, Pope John Paul II summed up its achievements in a special letter to Turowicz, emphasizing the great accomplishments of the weekly and its editor-in-chief but expressing regret over the lack of understanding of the Church's place in the reemerging Polish democracy. (WR)

Sources: *Opozycja w PRL: Słownik biograficzny 1956–89* (Warsaw, 2000); Andrzej Micewski, *Współrządzić czy nie kłamać? PAX i "Znak" w Polsce 1945–1976* (Paris, 1978); Andrzej Friszke, *Opozycja polityczna w PRL 1945–1980* (London, 1994); Tadeusz Kraśko, *Wierność* (Poznań, 1995).

TUSAR Vlastimil (18 October 1880, Prague–22 March 1924, Berlin), Czech Social Democratic politician. Tusar completed a two-year trade school. In 1903–8 he was a journalist, and between 1908 and 1911, editor-in-chief of a Brno publication, *Rovnosti*, which under his direction became a daily newspaper. Between 1911 and 1918 Tusar was an MP in the Vienna parliament. After the outbreak of World War I, he initially supported the pro-Habsburg policy of the leadership of Czech Social Democracy. Later, however, at an international meeting of trade union activists in Switzerland in September 1917 he changed his orientation, establishing a cooperative relationship with the Czech independence movement. At the end of the war Tusar led negotiations with the Austrian authorities. On 27 October 1918 he gave a signal from Vienna for **Alois Rašin**, one of the leaders of the independence movement linked with a conspiratorial political organization called Maffie (Mafia), to take over power. In 1918–21 Tusar was an MP in the Czechoslovak parliament, and from 1918 to 1919 he represented Czechoslovakia in negotiations in Vienna on the delimitation of the Austrian-Czechoslovak border; in these he gained considerable success owing to his personal acquaintance with many Austrian politicians. From 8 July 1919 Tusar was prime minister of subsequent cabinets of the "red and green coalition," with a membership of Socialist nationalists, landowners, and some Slovak politicians. Under pressure from the radical left in the party, Tusar, as a representative of the right wing of Social Democracy, resigned on 15 September 1920. From 1921 Tusar was Czechoslovak representative in Berlin, where he strove for the normalization of Czechoslovak-German relations. (PU)

Sources: *ČBS*; *Kto bol kto za I. CSR* (Bratislava, 1993); *Kdo byl kdo v našich dějinách ve 20. století*, vol. 2 (Prague, 1998).

TUWIM Julian (13 September 1894, Łódź–27 December 1953, Zakopane), Polish poet of Jewish descent. After graduating from high school in Łódź, Tuwin studied law and philosophy at Warsaw University (1916–18). He made his literary debut in 1913. From 1916 to 1919 he contributed to the student periodical *Pro arte et studio*. He co-founded the literary cabaret Pod Picadorem (1918) and the Skamander group of experimental poets (1920), and he worked with Warsaw cabarets. Tuwim was literary director of the Qui pro Quo cabaret from 1919 to 1932 and the Cyrulik Warszawski (Barber of Warsaw) cabaret from 1935 to 1939. In 1924 Tuwim became a staff writer for the weekly *Wiadomości Literackie* and was on the staffs of the satirical periodicals *Cyrulik Warszawski* (1926–33) and *Szpilki* (1936–39). In 1939, after the outbreak of World War II, Tuwim emigrated via Romania to France. After the fall of France, he went to Portugal, then to Brazil, and finally to the United States, settling in New York, where he lived for five years. In 1939–41 Tuwim contributed to the weekly *Wiadomości Polskie, Polityczne i Kulturalne* and (in 1942–46) to *Nowa Polska*, a London-based leftist weekly edited by **Antoni Słonimski**. During the war Tuwim wrote "Kwiaty Polskie" (Polish flowers; 1949), an epic lyrical poem that drew on the Romantic tradition; in it Tuwim combined patriotic and religious elements with reflections on the causes of the 1939 defeat of Poland. Tuwim called for an agreement between Poland and the Soviet Union, thereby alienating the Polish political émigré community; in 1946 he returned to Poland. From 1947 to 1950 Tuwim worked as an artistic director of the Nowy Theater in Warsaw and wrote pieces that affirmed the Communist reality.

Tuwim was one of the leading and most popular twentieth-century Polish poets. He drew on the experience of Russian Futurism and German Expressionism. He introduced everyday themes into poetry and often used colloquial language. His first poems, in which he broke away from the decadent style of the Young Poland movement, include the volumes *Czyhanie na Boga* (Lying in wait for God; 1918); *Sokrates tańczący* (1920; *The Dancing Socrates and Other Poems*, 1968); *Siódma jesień* (The seventh autumn; 1922); and *Wierszy tom czwarty* (Poems, volume 4; 1923). Tuwim gradually drifted toward classicism in the volumes *Rzecz czarnoleska* (The Czarnolas speech; 1929); *Biblia cygańska* (The gypsy Bible; 1933); and *Treść gorejąca* (The burning content; 1936). In his later works, Tuwim became involved in social issues, expressing pacifist, liberal, and anti-nationalist views; examples are the collection of satires *Jarmark rymów* (Rhyme fair; 1934) and the satirical poem "Bal w Operze" (Ball at the Opera House; 1936; full edition, 1946). Tuwim collected folklore and historical tidbits, which he then published as (among others works) *Czary i czarty polskie* (Polish magic and demons; 1923); *Wypisy czarnoksięskie* (Magic excerpts; 1923); *Polski słownik pijacki* (Polish drunkard's dictionary; 1935); *Antologia bachiczna* (Bacchanalian anthology; 1935); *Cztery wieki fraszki polskiej* (Four centuries of Polish epigrams; 1937); *Cicer cum caule, czyli Groch z kapustą* (Mishmash, 3 vols.; 1958–63); *Pegaz dęba, czyli panopticum poetyckie* (Poetic collection of curiosities; 1950); and *Księga wi-*

erszy polskich XIX w. (The book of nineteenth–century Polish poems, 3 vols.; 1954). Tuwim translated Russian literature and was the editor of many anthologies, songs, cabaret monologues, and children's pieces, including *Lokomotywa* (1938; *Locomotive*, 1939). Tuwim's *Dzieła* (Works, 5 vols.; 1955–64); *Wiersze wybrane* (Selected poems; 1969); *Wiersze zebrane* (Collected poems, 2 vols.; 1975); and *Pisma zebrane* (Collected writings, 6 vols.; 1986–93) were published posthumously. (JS)

Sources: *Literatura polska: Przewodnik encyklopedyczny*, vol. 2 (Warsaw, 1985); Michał Głowiński, *Poetyka Tuwima a polska tradycja literacka* (Warsaw, 1962); Artur Sandauer, *Poeci trzech pokoleń* (Warsaw, 1962); Jadwiga Sawicka, *Julian Tuwim* (Warsaw, 1986); Anna Węgrzyniakowa, *Dialektyka językowej organizacji tekstu w poezji Tuwima* (Katowice, 1987); Tomasz Stępień, *Kabaret Juliana Tuwima* (Katowice, 1989); Ryszard Löw, *Hebrajska obecność Juliana Tuwima: Szkice literackie* (Łódź, 1996).

TYCHYNA Pavlo (27 January 1891, Pisky, Chernihiv region–16 September 1967, Kiev), Ukrainian poet. Tychyna initially studied at home and then went to a local school. He made his debut as a poet in 1906. From 1907 to 1913 he studied at a seminary and from 1913 to 1917 at the Institute of Commerce in Kiev. At that time he contributed to the periodical *Svitlo* and the newspaper *Rada* and worked for the Ukrainian theater of Mykola Sadovsky. Tychyna welcomed the national revival movement after the February 1917 revolution, as evidenced by the 1917 poem "Zolotyi homin" (Golden hubbub). In 1918 he published his first poetry collection, *Soniashni kliarnety* (Solar clarinets). His next collections—*Pluh* (The plow; 1920); *V kosmichnomu orkestri* (In the cosmic orchestra; 1921); *Skovoroda: Uryvky z symfonii* (Skorovoda: Symphony fragments; 1923); and *Viter z Ukraiiny* (The wind from Ukraine; 1924; dedicated to **Mykola Khvylovyi**)—consolidated Tychyna's position as one of the most innovative Ukrainian poets.

In 1923 Tychyna moved to Kiev, where he worked for the periodical *Chervonyi shliakh*. Initially he belonged to the literary group Hart, and in 1927 he became a member of the Free Academy of Proletarian Literature (Vilna Akademiia Proletarskoy Literatury [VAPLITE]), which consisted of twenty-two writers led by Khvylovyi, who was regarded as the leading representative of national communism in Ukraine. Tychyna's membership in the VAPLITE became a pretext to accuse him of Ukrainian "bourgeois nationalism." As a result of these accusations, Tychyna ceased publishing for some time. In 1929 he became a member of the Academy of Sciences of the Ukrainian SSR, and in 1938, a deputy to the Supreme Soviet of the Ukrainian SSR and to the Supreme Soviet of the Soviet Union. From 1936 to 1939 and from 1941 to 1943

Tychyna served as director of the Institute of Literature of the Academy of Sciences of the Ukrainian SSR. At that time he wrote several poetry volumes, including *Chernihiv* (1931); *Partiia vede* (The party is our guide; 1934); and *Stal i nizhnist* (Steel and tenderness; 1941), already written in the style of Socialist realism. Tychyna's work became a paragon of the subordination of Ukrainian literature to Stalinism. During the German-Soviet war Tychyna was evacuated to Bashkiria, where he wrote the moving poem "Pokhoron druha" (Funeral of a friend; 1942). In 1943–48 Tychyna served as minister of education of the Ukrainian SSR. From 1953 to 1959 he was chairman of the Supreme Soviet of the Ukrainian SSR. In the 1950s and 1960s Tychyna wrote several poetry collections, all in the spirit of Socialist realism and apologias for the Communist system. (BB)

Sources: *Encyclopedia of Ukraine*, vol. 5 (Toronto, 1993); *Entsyklopediia Ukraiinoznavstva*, vol. 9 (Lviv, 2000); *Dovidnyk z istorii Ukraiiny* (Kiev, 2001); Leonid Novychenko, *Poeziia i revoliutsiia; tvorchist P. Tychyny v pershi pisliazhovtnevi roky* (Kiev, 1968); Stanislav Telniuk, *Molodyi ia, molodyi: Poetychnyi svit Pavla Tychyny (1906–1925)* (Kiev, 1990); Vasyl Stus, "Fenomen doby," in Vasyl Stus, *Tvory u chotyrokh tomakh, shesty knyhakh*, vol. 4 (Lviv, 1994).

TYKHYI Oleksy (27 January 1927, YIzhivka, Stalino [now Donetsk] Province–6 May 1984, Perm), Ukrainian human rights activist. Tykhyi studied at the Agricultural Institute in Zaporizhzhya and at the Institute of Transport Engineering in Dniepropetrovsk. He later graduated in philosophy from Moscow University and then worked as a teacher in the region of Zaporizhzhya and Stalino. Arrested in mid-January 1957 on charges that included the criticism of Soviet schools and writing a letter to the Central Committee (CC) of the CPSU in protest against the Soviet invasion of Hungary, Tykhyi was sentenced to seven years in a forced labor camp in May 1958. He served his sentence in Mordvinia. Released in 1964, he worked as a laborer. Tykhyi became involved in distributing samizdat publications and published articles on the disappearance of the Ukrainian language and culture in the Donbas region. In June 1976 during a search of Tykhyi's home the police confiscated his collection of quotations from famous Ukrainians, *Mova narodu* (Speech of the people).

In February 1977 Tykhyi was arrested again for "anti-Soviet agitation," but the real reason was the fact that he had co-founded the Ukrainian Helsinki Group in November 1976. He was tried together with **Mykola Rudenko**. In July 1976 Tykhyi was found to be a recidivist and sentenced to ten years in a forced labor camp and five years in exile. He was sent to Sosnovka in Mordvinia.

He took part in protests, and in the spring of 1978 he was on a hunger strike for fifty-two days. In the summer of 1978 Tykhyi and Vasyl Romaniuk (the future bishop **Volodymyr**) wrote the work *Istorychna dolia Ukraiiny* (Historical fate of Ukraine), in which they sharply criticized Soviet ethnic policy in Ukraine from the point of view of the UN Universal Declaration of Human Rights. They called for using Soviet constitutional provisions for the defense of the national rights of the Ukrainian people. In April 1979, while on a hunger strike, Tykhyi suffered internal hemorrhaging. He was blackmailed with threats that the results of an operation might depend on whether or not he denounced and gave up his opposition activities, but he refused. The operation was done in such a careless way that the doctor could be suspected of ill will. Despite his serious condition, Tykhyi was often put in solitary confinement. In March 1980 he was transferred to the village of Kuchino, near Perm, and punished in a similar way, but he did not give up his protests. In 1982 and 1984 Tykhyi twice underwent operations in a prison hospital in Vsekhsvyatka. He died in a prison hospital in Perm. In November 1989 Tykhyi's remains were brought to Kiev and reburied in Baykovo Cemetery. (TS)

Sources: *Encyclopedia of Ukraine*, vol. 5 (Toronto, 1993); Kharkiv Human Rights Protection Group and Heorhiy Kasianov, *Nezhdoni: Ukraiinska intelihentsiia v rusi oporu 1960–80 rokiv* (Kiev, 1995); Anatoliy Rusnachenko, *Natsionalno-vyzvolnyi rukh v Ukraiini* (Kiev, 1998); Ludmila Alekseeva, *Istoriia inakomysliia v SSSR* (Vilnius and Moscow, 1992); Zakordonne Predstavnytstvo Ukraiinskoy Helsinskoy Hrupy, *Visnyk represii w Ukraiini* (New York, 1984).

TYUTYUNNYK Yuriy (20 April 1891, Budyshcha, near Chernigov [Chernihiv]–1929, Moscow), Ukrainian officer and politician. In 1917 Tyutyunnyk organized Ukrainian military units in Simferopol and Zvenyhorodka. He was a member of the Ukrainian Central Rada (Council) and president of the Kiev Revolutionary Committee, which was preparing an uprising against the government of Hetman **Pavlo Skoropadskyi**. In February 1919 Tyutyunnyk became chief of staff of **Matviy Hryhoryiv**'s guerrilla group, which operated in the southern Ukraine. After getting across the Bolshevik front, Tyutyunnyk made his way to the army of the Ukrainian National Republic (UNR) and became commander of the Kiev group in the Kiev offensive in August 1919. During the winter campaign of 1919–20 he commanded the Kiev division and served as deputy commander of the UNR army, with the rank of brigadier general. After the Riga Peace Treaty was signed, Tyutyunnyk organized new military units (known as the Ukrainian Insurgent Army) in Lviv (Lwów) to fight against the Bolsheviks. In early November 1921 three military units led by Tyutyunnyk, about 1,500 strong, made their way to the Bolshevik-controlled Ukrainian territory to the east of the Zbruch River. However, Tyutyunnyk failed to rally wider circles of the Ukrainian public to join the struggle, and after the defeat at Bazar, where the Bolsheviks murdered their prisoners of war, he returned to the territories of the Second Republic of Poland. Taking advantage of an amnesty, Tyutyunnyk became formally reconciled with the Bolsheviks and went to the Ukrainian SSR in 1923. He lectured at the Red Officers' School in Kharkiv and wrote screenplays. Arrested by the political police (OGPU) in the late 1920s, Tyutyunnyk was executed as a Polish spy. His memoirs were published in the periodicals *Literaturno-naukovyi visnyk* and *Zahrava*, and his political and military sketches in various publications; these sketches include "Zymovyi pokhid 1919–1920" (Winter campaign of 1919–1920; 1923) and "Z Poliakamy proty Ukraiiny" (With the Poles against Ukraine; 1924). (WR)

Sources: *Encyclopedia of Ukraine*, vol. 5 (Toronto, 1993); Sergiusz Mikulicz, *Prometeizm w polityce II Rzeczypospolitej* (Warsaw, 1971).

U

UDOVENKO Hennadiy (22 June 1931, Kryvy Rih), Ukrainian diplomat and politician. Udovenko graduated from the Foreign Relations Department of Kiev University in 1954. He continued his studies at the Institute of Economics and Agriculture. In 1955–58 he was head of a kolkhoz near Kiev. From 1959 he was first secretary of the Communist Party committee and head of the departments of economic organization and personnel in the Foreign Ministry of the Ukrainian SSR. From 1965 to 1971 Udovenko worked in the UN Secretariat in Geneva, and from 1977 to 1980 he was head of the department of conference services in the UN headquarters in New York. From 1980 to 1985 he was deputy minister of foreign affairs of the Ukrainian SSR, and from 1985 to 1992 he was the republic's representative to the United Nations. In July 1985 Udovenko presided over the UN Security Council. From 1989 to 1991 he was vice-president of the UN Social and Economic Council, and in 1991, vice-president of the Forty-sixth UN General Assembly Session. In 1997 he presided over its Fifty-second Session. From 1992 to 1994 Udovenko was ambassador of independent Ukraine to Poland, and in August 1994 he became Ukrainian foreign minister. In this capacity he helped to resolve basic problems between Ukraine and Russia (for example, the division of the Black Sea Fleet and the determination of the status of Crimea), and he consolidated the pro-Western orientation of Ukraine. For instance, he did not object to Poland's entry into NATO. In 1996–98 Udovenko was also a member of the security council of the Ukrainian president.

In March 1998 Udovenko won a seat on the Supreme Council on the lists of the National Movement of Ukraine (Narodny Rukh Ukrainy [NMU]), so he resigned from his position as foreign minister in April 1998. At the time of a split in the NMU in February 1999, Udovenko supported its chairman, **Vyacheslav Chornovil**. When the latter was killed in a car crash in March 1999, Udovenko became head of the party and its parliamentary caucus. However, Yuri Kostenko's faction, which had caused the split, did not recognize Udovenko. Udovenko and Kostenko ran separately in the presidential elections of November 1999, when Udovenko gained 1.2 percent of the vote. In January 2000 two different parties registered from what had been the NMU; the Udovenko faction kept the original name. In connection with the hijacking and death of the journalist Grigory Gongadze in 2001, Udovenko supported actions against President **Leonid Kuchma**, who was accused of involvement in the affair. In early 2002 both former NMU factions joined the election coalition Our Ukraine (Nasha Ukraina) of **Viktor Yushchenko**. In the April 2002 elections Udovenko won a seat on behalf of this coalition. Udovenko has demanded a resumption of the investigation into the death of Chornovil. (TS)

Sources: Bohdan Nahaylo, *The Ukrainian Resurgence* (Toronto, 1999); www.rulers.org.

UDRŽAL František (3 January 1866, Dolní Roveň–24 April 1938, Prague), Czech politician. In 1886 Udržal graduated from a higher agricultural school in Tábor and then went to Germany for training. He did his military service in Budapest, attaining officer rank, and from 1894 he ran his own estate in Dolní Roveň. Udržal joined entered political life in the 1890s. At first he was active in the Young Czech Party, but in 1906 he joined the Agrarian Party, which was programmatically closer to him. He soon became one of the party leaders, co-author of its political program, and a co-worker of **Milan Hodža**. Between 1897 and 1918 Udržal was a member of the Viennese parliament. In the first decade of the twentieth century he began to work with **Antonín Švehla**. Udržal was one of the founders of the Czech Association of Deputies and became its chairman. From 1917 to 1918 he was the first vice-chairman of the Chamber of Deputies. During World War I he mainly resided in Vienna but maintained contacts with the Czech independence movement, providing it with information.

After the creation of the Czechoslovak state, between 1918 and 1935 Udržal was an MP and, until 1937, a senator. In 1921–25 and 1926–29 he held the post of minister of national defense in the cabinets of **Edvard Beneš** and Švehla, and he developed the armed forces of the young state. Udržal focused mainly on supplying the army with military equipment and on reinforcing its personnel with proven soldiers. He also nurtured good relations with the allies of Czechoslovakia, especially with France, where he went on an official mission in 1925 and gained confirmation of a Czechoslovak-French alliance. On 1 February 1929 Udržal became prime minister, taking over the post after the withdrawal of his party colleague, Švehla, from political life. Udržal retained his post after the parliamentary elections in the fall of 1929, which were won by the Agrarians, and after the formation of a broad coalition of all parties that rejected fascism and communism. At that time Udržal was also the chairman of the parliamentary club of his party. As head of government, he had to face the serious worldwide economic crisis of the Great Depression. Udržal's health was also weakened by intraparty struggles with **Jan Malypetr**, so he resigned as prime minister on 29 October 1932. He left the political scene because of ill health in December 1937. In the last months of his life Udržal supported the work of the first Czech mutual insurance company in Prague. (PU)

Sources: *ČBS*; *Kdo byl kdo v našich dějinách ve 20. století*, vol. 2 (Prague, 1998); *SBS*; *Kto bol kto za I. ČSR* (Bratislava, 1993).

UHDE Milan (28 July 1936, Brno), Czech writer and politician. Uhde graduated in philosophy from Brno University in 1958. In 1958–70 he edited the monthly *Host do domu* and lectured at the Music Academy in Brno. From 1971 to 1989 he remained jobless because of political repression. Uhde published under pseudonyms in samizdat publications and abroad. He was a signatory of Charter 77; from 1988 he edited *Lidove noviny*, and in 1989–90 he was editor-in-chief of Atlantis Press, which he founded along with his wife. After the Velvet Revolution, from June 1990 to June 1992 Uhde was minister of culture of the Czech Republic. In 1991 Uhde co-founded the Civic Democratic Party (Občanská Demokratická Strana [ODS]) and was one of its leaders. From June to December 1992 he was an MP and speaker of the Czech National Council; from January 1993 to June 1998 he was an MP, and from January 1993 to June 1996 he was speaker of the parliament of the independent Czech Republic. When scandal concerning ODS financing broke out and when the **Václav Klaus** government stepped down in January 1998, Uhde left the party and joined the newly established Union of Freedom (Unie Svobody). Disappointed with its program, he soon left the political arena.

Uhde is one of the creators of the Czech theater of the absurd. A rationalist criticizing historical myths and clichés, he wrote allegorical stories full of sad humor. His plays and radio plays have been translated into many languages, among them French and German. Uhde made his literary debut in 1952 publishing short poems; in 1962 he published the volume *Lidé z přízemí* (People from the ground floor). In the 1960s he published the allegorical and satirical plays *Král Vávra* (King Vavra; 1965) and *Děvka z města Théby* (A girl from Thebes; 1967); numerous radio plays; and the short stories "Hrách na stěnu" (Wasting one's breath; 1964) and "Záhadná věž v B." (A mysterious tower in B.; 1967). Uhde made critical allusions to the Communist system and social relations in Czechoslovakia. In his later dramas—such as *Hra na holuba* (Playing a dove; 1974) and *Zvěstování aneb Bedřichu: Jsi anděl* (Annunciation or Bedřich: You're an angel; 1986)—Uhde stigmatized the empty rituals confining human freedom. He also wrote song lyrics and puppet theater plays, and he collaborated with the Brno theaters Divadlo X and Divadlo na Provázku. Uhde also authored the screenplay for the movie *Šach-mat Vaše Vysosti* (Checkmate, Your Highness; 1969). Uhde's columns from the 1990s were published in the volume *Česká republiko, dobrý den* (Good morning, Czech Republic; 1995). (PU)

Sources: *ČBS*; *Kdo byl kdo v našich dějinach ve 20. stoleti*, vol. 2 (Prague, 1998); *Slovník českých spisovatelů od roku 1945*, vol. 2 (Prague, 1998); Halina Janaszek-Ivančikova, ed., *Literatury zachodniosłowiańskie czasu przełomów 1890–1990*, vol. 2, *Literatura czeska* (Katowice, 1999).

UKRAINKA Lesya [originally Larysa Kosach-Kvitka] (25 February 1871, Zvyahel–1 August 1913, Surami, Georgia), Ukrainian poet, playwright, translator, and literary critic. Ukrainka was the daughter of the well-known Ukrainian writer and social activist Olena Pchilka, the sister of Mikhailo Drahomanov, a veteran Ukrainian Socialist. She was on friendly terms with such outstanding personalities of Ukraninian culture as **Olha Kobylyanska**, **Ivan Franko**, **Vasyl Stefanyk**, and **Mikhajlo Hrushevsky**. Because Ukrainka had bone tuberculosis, she studied at home, attaining a vast education in the humanities. She spoke many languages, including Russian, French, German, English, Italian, Greek, Polish, Bulgarian, and Latin. She traveled to Germany, Austria-Hungary, and Italy for health reasons, but these journeys also expanded her cultural horizons. Ukrainka translated the works of Homer, Adam Mickiewicz, Victor Hugo, Heinrich Heine, George Byron, and others. In 1890 she wrote a textbook for her sister: *Starodavnya istoriya skhidnykh narodiv* (Ancient history of the eastern nations; 1918). Ukrainka made her debut as a poet in 1884 in the Lviv periodical *Zorya*. It was then that she took the pen name of Lesya Ukrainka. In 1885 in Lviv she published (with her brother Mikhailo) a volume of translations from Nikolay Gogol. Her world outlook was largely shaped by her yearly stay at her Uncle Drahomanov's in Sofia.

In 1896 Ukrainka criticized the French poets who gave a warm welcome to Tsar Nicholas II when he visited France. In her protest she called Russia a "prison of nations." In the mid-1880s Ukrainka's family moved to Kiev, where she joined a poetry group, the Pleiad. The first collection of Ukrainka's original works, *Na krilyakh pisen* (On the wings of songs), appeared in Lviv in 1893. It was also there that she published her second volume, *Dumy i mriyi* (Thoughts and dreams; 1899). The third collection, *Widhuky* (Echoes), was published in Chernyovtsi in 1902. Ukrainka's first play was *Blakytna Troyanda* (Blue rose), written in 1896 and presenting the life of the Ukrainian intelligentsia. A special place in her work is taken by dramatic poems dealing with the Babylonian bondage of the Israelis: "Na ruinakh" (On the ruins; 1903); "Vavylonskyi polon" (Babylonian bondage; 1903); and "V domu roboty—v krayini nevoli" (In the house of labor—in the country of bondage; 1906). In these works Ukrainka developed analogies between the Babylonian bondage and the fate of the Ukrainians in the Russian empire. In the drama *Kassandra* (1907) Ukrainka's vision of a ruined Troy became a metaphor for an enslaved Ukraine. In the drama *V katakombakh* (In the catacombs; 1905) she sharply criticized the passivity and amicability of the Ukrainian intelligentsia. In the drama *Rufin i Pristsilla* (1908) she contrasted the brutal force of Rome with a magnificent Christian woman. Her drama *Boyaryn'a* (Princess; 1910) also includes strong anti-Russian elements. Ukrainka's other outstanding works include the dramas *Kaminnyi hospodar* (Landlord of stone; 1912) and *Lisova pisnya* (Song of the forest; 1911). In 1907 Ukrainka was temporarily arrested, and at the end of her life she was often living under police surveillance because of her contacts with Russian Marxists. She also spent much time in Egypt and the Caucasus for health reasons.

Ukrainka was one of the leading Ukrainian poets at the turn of the twentieth century. Her lyrics increasingly engaged with social and political affairs. She advocated bravery and a national struggle. She greatly modernized the poetic form of Ukrainian drama but also wrote prose. Ukrainka contributed to a number of Ukrainian periodicals, such as *Literaturno—naukowyi visnyk, Nova hromada, Narod, Dzvin,* and *Ridnyi kray.* (BB)

Sources: *Encyclopedia of Ukraine*, vol. 5 (Toronto, 1993); *Pisarze świata: Słownik encyklopedyczny* (Warsaw, 1995); *Dowidnyk z istoriji Ukrajiny* (Kiev, 2001); Mikhailo Dray-Khmara, *Lesya Ukrainka: Zhyttia i tvorchist* (Kiev, 1926); Petro Odarchenko, *Lesya Ukrainka i M. P. Drahomanov* (New York, 1954); Oleh Babyshkin, *Dramaturhia Lesi Ukrainky* (Kiev, 1964); Constantin Bida, *Lesya Ukrainka: Life and Work* (Toronto, 1968); Anatol Kostenko, *Lesia Ukrainka* (Kiev, 1971).

ULASAU Aleksandr (16 August 1874, Wilejka–June 1941, Minsk), Belorussian editor and politician of Russian descent. Ulasau graduated from a theological seminary in Pinsk, and in 1899–1905 he studied at the Polytechnic Institute in Riga. At the end of 1904 he was a co-founder of the Belorussian Socialist Hromada, and in 1907–14 he was editor of the periodical *Nasha Niva.* From 1912 to 1915 Ulasau edited the periodicals *Sakha* (for the countryside) and *Luchynka* (for children). In 1918 he became a member of the Council of the Belorussian People's Republic. In 1919 he initiated the resumption of Nasha Khatka, a Belorussian editing association in Wilno (Vilnius). In 1922–27 Ulasau was a Polish senator. He also

acted in the Association for Belorussian Education and published in the Wilno press. In September 1939 Ulasau was arrested by the NKVD and sentenced to five years' imprisonment. According to information obtained by his family, he was shot by the NKVD during the evacuation of the Minsk prisons. (EM)

Sources: *Bielarus: Encyklapiedychny davednik* (Minsk, 1995); Aleksandra Bergman, *Sprawy białoruskie w II Rzeczypospolitej* (Warsaw, 1984); Vitaut Kipel and Zora Kipel, eds., *Byelorussian Statehood* (New York, 1988).

ULASHCHYK Mikola (14 February 1906, Vitskaushchyna–14 November 1986, Minsk), Belorussian historian and archaeologist. Ulashchyk graduated in history from the Belorussian University in Minsk in 1929. In 1930–55 he was arrested three times and spent the next ten years in and out of prison for "anti-Soviet" activities. Ulashchyk taught at Moscow University (1948–49) and in high schools. From 1955 he was employed at the Academy of Sciences of the USSR, dealing with the earliest history of Belorussia and Lithuania, as well as with the implementation of the tsarist agrarian reform of 1861 in the western provinces of the Russian empire. Ulashchyk's major works include the following: *Ocherki po arkheografii i istochnikovedeniiu istorii Belorussii feodalnogo perioda* (Studies in archeography and knowledge of sources for a history of feudal Belorussia; 1973); *Vvedenie v izuchenie belorussko-litovskogo letopisaniia* (Introduction to studies in Lithuanian and Belorussian chronicle writing; 1985); and *Byla takaya vyoska* (There was once a village like this; 1989). (EM)

Sources: *Bielarus: Encyklapiedychny davednik* (Minsk, 1995); Jan Zaprudnik, *Historical Dictionary of Belarus* (Lanham, Md., 1998).

ULMANIS Guntis (13 September 1939, Riga), Latvian politician. The grandson of **Kārlis Ulmanis**, during mass Soviet repressions, on 14 June 1941 Ulmanis was deported with his family to the Krasnoyarsk district in Siberia. In 1946 the family was allowed to return to Latvia, but because of a ban on settlements in Riga, they moved to Kuldīga and, in 1949, to Jūrmala. In 1963 Ulmanis was allowed to graduate from the Department of Economics of the Latvian State University in Riga. In 1963–65 he served in the Soviet Army, and later he worked as an economist in the construction industry and in the Riga town administration. At the same time, he started lecturing at Riga University. From 1965 to 1989 Ulmanis belonged to the Communist Party of the Soviet Union. In 1971 he became director of the Riga administration of social services. After Latvia regained its independence (1991), Ulmanis joined the Latvian Agrarian Union (Latvijas Zemnieku Savien-iba) in 1992. In June 1993 he was elected to the parliament (Saeima). After three rounds of voting, on 7 July 1993 Ulmanis was elected president; this had a symbolic meaning, considering his family connections. As president, Ulmanis supported market reforms and Latvian efforts to integrate with West European structures. Nevertheless, in July 1994 he refused to sign radical legislation on citizenship and naturalization. On 18 June 1996 he was reelected for a second term, during which he continued his former foreign policy. In January 1997 Ulmanis criticized the personnel decisions of Prime Minister **Andris Šķēle**, which led to the resignation of the whole cabinet. After the termination of his second term on 8 July 1999, Ulmanis retired. He authored, among other works, *No tevis jau neprasa daudz* (I do not expect much from you; 1995) and *Put' prezidenta* (The president's way; 1996). (EJ)

Sources: *Mans prezidenta laiks* (Riga, 1999); *Who Is Who in Latvia 1996: Biographical Dictionary* (Riga, 1996); Juris Dreifelds, *Latvia in Transition* (Cambridge, 1996); Andrejs Plakans, *Historical Dictionary of Latvia* (Lanham, Md., 1997); *Eastern Europe and the Commonwealth of Independent States, 1999* (London, 1999); Bugajski.

ULMANIS Kārlis (4 September 1877, Bērzes, Courland–20 September 1942, Krasnovodsk), Agrarian politician, president of Latvia. Born into a peasant family, in 1896 Ulmanis graduated from high school in Jelgava and in 1897 from a dairy economics school in East Prussia. In 1902–3 he studied agriculture at the Higher Technical School in Zurich, Switzerland, and from 1903 to 1905 he studied at the Agricultural Institute in Leipzig. Ulmanis worked as an agronomist, social worker, and editor of the periodical *Lauksaimnieks* in Livonia. During the Russian revolution of 1905 he demanded that Latvian be used in the schools; for this he was arrested in September 1905. Imprisoned in Pskov, after his release in May 1906 Ulmanis worked on his brother's farm. Avoiding another arrest, Ulmanis left to go abroad. In 1906–7 he taught at an agricultural school in Saxony, and in 1907 he arrived in the United States. In 1909 he graduated from the Department of Agriculture of the University of Nebraska, and then he lectured there. Ulmanis returned to Latvia in 1913, taking up a job as an agronomist in an agricultural society in Valmiera and Riga. During World War I Ulmanis supported Latvian organizations of war refugees. In 1914–15 he edited the periodical *Zeme*. From April to September 1917 he was a member of the Livonian Land Council and its deputy governor. In April 1917 he co-founded and became one of the leaders of the Latvian Agrarian Union (Latviešu Zamnieku Sanienība [LAU]). He also edited agricultural periodicals.

From the beginning of 1918 Ulmanis worked for Latvian independence within the multiparty Democratic Bloc and then within the Provisional Latvian National Council (PLNC) in Riga.

On 18 November 1918, when the PLNC proclaimed the independence of Latvia, Ulmanis became head of its provisional government. On the same day his cabinet issued a declaration of the political principles of the new state, including territorial integrity and parliamentary democracy. Apart from serving as prime minister, Ulmanis was minister of agriculture (November–December 1918), minister of supplies (November 1918–December 1919), and minister of war (October 1919–June 1920). In view of the domination of German troops and Bolshevik proclamations of a Latvian Soviet Republic, on 7 December 1918 Ulmanis agreed to let the Germans organize the defense of Latvia in return for the recognition of its sovereignty in internal affairs. On 3 January 1919 Bolshevik troops, helped by Red Latvian Riflemen, captured Riga. Ulmanis and his government left for Liepaja, from where they controlled only a small area, but thanks to desertions of the Latvian Riflemen, the concentration of Estonian troops in the north, and German volunteers in the middle of Latvia, they survived. At the beginning of February 1919 General Rüdiger von Goltz came to Liepaja to take over command of a German corps. He prevented recruitments to the Latvian Army and wanted to make Latvia a stepping stone for his plans to restore the German empire, which would include the Baltic area. The Germans established a puppet government with **Andrievs Niedra** at the head, but their attempt to topple Ulmanis failed since he found refuge on a Latvian vessel under British protection. The Latvian Army, supported by the Estonians and the Entente, managed to recapture Riga on 23 May 1919. On 8 July the Ulmanis government returned to Riga and took diplomatic steps aimed at the international recognition of Latvia. During a battle with the White Russian army of Pavel Bermondt-Avalov in October 1919, Ulmanis was lightly wounded. At the end of November 1919 the German attack was forced back, and soon the whole of Latvian territory was under the control of the Ulmanis government. On 11 August 1920 Ulmanis concluded a treaty of non-aggression with Soviet Russia that recognized Latvian independence. In May 1920 the Latvian Constituent Assembly was convened; on 1 June it passed a provisional constitution, and on 22 December 1919, a land reform that strengthened the social foundations of the new state. Ulmanis remained prime minister until 18 June 1921.

In subsequent parliaments Ulmanis was the leader of the second largest faction of the LAU and frequently held ministerial posts. From 24 December 1925 to 6 May 1926 he was prime minister; from May to December 1926 he was foreign minister; and from 27 March to 5 December 1931 he was prime minister again. Ulmanis blocked changes in the electoral system, which caused strong fragmentation in the parliament. Later some thought that Ulmanis had already considered taking dictatorial powers. On 17 March 1934 Ulmanis became prime minister again, striving to combat an economic depression and the threat of a coup by the extreme right. On 15 May 1934, with the help of a relatively numerous LAU paramilitary organization, Ulmanis introduced a state of emergency, arrested leaders of the left and extreme right, and dissolved the parliament and all political parties, including the LAU. He then ruled with the help of a "national unity" government, based on politicians from the LAU and other parties, the bureaucracy, and the military. On 11 June 1936 Ulmanis also took over the duties of the president. He never changed the constitution, which he had promised to do. The economic and political system was based on corporations or "chambers." The State Economic Council was created, composed of four economic chambers (industry and trade, handicrafts, agriculture, and labor), while the State Cultural Council included two chambers (literature and arts and the free professions). As dictator, Ulmanis developed a personal cult around himself. He thought that the peasantry was the principal stratum of society, and he identified it with the national interest. He was an advocate of agrarianism and saw medium-size family farms as the driving force of the national economy. Among other works, Ulmanis published *Sabēdriskē raksti un runas* (Writings and public speeches; 1935); *Runas un raksti 1899–1918* (Speeches and writings 1899–1918; 1939); and *Dzives filozofija* (Philosophy of life; 1940).

After the signing of a forced agreement with the USSR in October 1939, when Ulmanis had to accept the introduction of Soviet military bases and twenty thousand Red Army soldiers, Ulmanis stayed in power. On 15 June 1940 the Kremlin sent another ultimatum, which Ulmanis also accepted. This did not prevent a full-scale Soviet invasion the next day. Apart from Red Army units, a special Soviet envoy, Andrey Vyshinsky, came to Riga to supervise the takeover of power. Ulmanis became a hostage of the invaders and agreed to legislative changes allowing for new elections. On 19 June he was forced to step down, and a new government was formed by **Augusts Kirhenšteins**. Ulmanis intended to leave for Switzerland, which the Soviets promised him he could do, but on 22 July he was forced to take a train to Moscow, from where he was transferred to a special NKVD-controlled apartment in Voroshilovsk (now Stavropol). On 4 July 1941 Ulmanis was arrested and, owing to the approaching front, he was soon moved to Ordzhonikidze, Baku, and

then to Krasnovodsk in Turkmenistan, where he died in prison. He was buried in a common grave, and his body was never identified. Ulmanis's *Klausaities vestures solos* (Listening to the footsteps of history; 1968) and *Redzu jaunu dzienu nakam* (New prospects for the future; 1992) were published posthumously. (EJ/WR)

Sources: *Encyclopedia Europa*, vol. 11; Alfreds Bilmanis, *Latvia as an Independent State* (Washington, D.C., 1947); Arnolds Spekke, *History of Latvia* (Stockholm, 1951); *Kārlis Ulmanis 75 gads* (Briva Zeme, 1952); Edgars Andersons, ed., *Cross Road Country: Latvia* (Waverly, Iowa, 1953); Mikelis Valters, *Mana sarakste ar Kārli Ulmani un Vilhelmu Munteru Latvijas tragiskajos gadas* (Stockholm, 1957); Piotr Łossowski, *Kraje bałtyckie na drodze od demokracji parlamentarnej do dyktatury (1918–1934)* (Wrocław, 1972); Adolfs Šilde, *Latvijas Vēsture* (Stockholm, 1976); Žanis Unams, ed., *Kārlis Ulmanis: 4.9.1877–4.9.1977: Tautai un valstij veltits mužs* (East Lansing, Mich., 1977); David M. Crowe, *The Baltic States and the Great Powers: Foreign Relations, 1938–1940* (Boulder, Colo., 1993); Andrejs Plakans, *Historical Dictionary of Latvia* (Lanham, Md., 1997).

ULUOTS Jüri (13 January 1890, Kirbla–9 January 1945, Stockholm), Estonian lawyer and politician. After high school Uluots studied law at the University of St. Petersburg, graduating in 1915. Later he continued his studies in Rome and practiced as a judge in Haapsalu (1918–19). In 1919 Uluots was elected to the Estonian Constituent Assembly and then to the parliaments of subsequent terms on behalf of the Farmers' Union (Põllumeestekogude) of **Konstantin Päts**. At the same time he lectured in Roman law at the University of Tartu. In 1925 Uluots became an associate professor and in 1927 a full professor at this university. In 1924–31 and 1942–44 he was dean of the Department of Law and from 1931 to 1934 deputy rector of this university. During the constitutional crisis Uluots was elected head of the parliamentary commission for the amendment of the constitution. He presented the results of the commission's work on 18 March 1932, but they proved disappointing to the Union of Veterans of the War of Independence (Eesti Vabadussõjalaste Liit [EVL]), which strove for a totalitarian political system. After the fall of the **Karl Eenpalu** government in October 1932, Uluots failed to create another cabinet. After the coup and introduction of a state of emergency by Päts in March 1934, Uluots was moderately critical of these steps, so he was seen as a candidate for opposition leader. But in February 1935 he agreed to head the Fatherland League (Isamaaliit), a new pro-government party created after the dissolution of all previous parties. He also became one of the key ideologues of the new authoritarian system.

At the end of September 1939, when the Kremlin sent an ultimatum to Tallinn demanding the introduction of Soviet bases in Estonia, as well as exterritorial roads and a change of government, Uluots became a member of the Estonian delegation negotiating in Moscow. On 28 September 1939 the Estonian government agreed to the Kremlin's conditions, and on 12 October 1939 Uluots became the new prime minister. He tried to widen the political foundation of his cabinet, but only **Ants Piip** of the Center Party agreed to head the Foreign Ministry. Uluots attempted to attract the fractured EVL, but he failed. His government tried at all costs to avoid further Soviet demands and closed its eyes to the use of Soviet bases in Estonia for air raids against Finland (November 1939–March 1940). In the face of the Soviet invasion of mid-June 1940 Uluots resigned and avoided arrest and deportation.

After the German invasion of the USSR in June 1941, a local Estonian administration emerged spontaneously. At the beginning of July 1941 Uluots convened a political council in Tartu consisting of politicians who had avoided Soviet deportation, but no formal government was announced. On 29 July he sent a memorandum to the German authorities suggesting the creation of an Estonian government and army to cooperate with the Germans against the Soviet Union. Instead, on 21 December 1941 the Germans established a Land Administration Office (Landerverwaltung; Omavalitsus) headed by an EVL member, **Hjalmar Mäe**. The Germans offered Uluots the presidency of this office, but in view of its limited powers, he refused. On 1 February 1944 Mäe called all Estonians born between 1904 and 1923 to arms against the approaching Red Army. Uluots supported this appeal in a special radio speech, counting on the delay of German capitulation until the Western powers defeat the Third Reich on the western front. These calculations failed. By September 1944 all of Estonian territory was in Soviet hands again. At the end the German occupation Uluots, as the last prime minister of independent Estonia and thus the legal substitute for the absent President Päts, appointed **Otto Tief** as prime minister. In view of the Soviet takeover, Uluots left for Sweden, where he soon died. Uluots authored (among other works) the following: *Eestima õiguse ajalugu* (History of law in Estonia, 2 vols.; 1930); *Grundzüge der Agrargeschichte Estlands* (Outline of the agrarian history of Estonia; 1935); and *Die Verträge der Esten mit den Fremden im XIII Jahrhundert* (Estonian agreements with foreigners in the thirteenth century; 1938). (WR)

Sources: *Prof. Jüri Uluotsa mälestusraamat* (Stockholm, 1945); Evald Uustalu, "The National Committee of the Estonian Republic," *Journal of Baltic Studies*, 1976, no. 3; P. Järvelaid, and T. Põder, "Esimene Tartu Ülikooli eesti rahvusest eesti õigusajaloo õppejõud Jüri Uluots (1890–1945)," in *70 aastat Eesti ülikooli* (Tartu, 1989); H. Walter, "Jüri Uluots, 1890–1945," *Looming*, 1990, no. 1; Mart Laar, "Jüri Uluots aastal 1944," *Looming*, 1990, no. 4; Andres Kasekamp, *The Radical Right in Interwar Estonia* (London, 2000).

UNDER Marie (27 March 1883, Tallinn–25 March 1980, Stockholm), Estonian writer. The daughter of a German teacher, in 1891–1900 Under studied in a private German school where she mastered German, French, and Russian. Apart from those languages, she was fluent in Esonian and Finnish. Under wrote her first poems in German at the age of thirteen. Forced to make her living early, she worked as a bookseller. At seventeen she met the writer Eduard Vilde, who drew her into the radical group of Konstanin Päts and his newspaper, *Teataja*, and she worked on its editorial staff. In 1902 Under married a bookkeeper, Karl Hacker, a Germanized Estonian, with whom she had two daughters. Then for four year she lived in Kuchino, near Moscow.

Under's talent developed slowly. Ants Laikmaa, an Estonian painter with whom she had a love affair, convinced her to write in Estonian. From 1906 she maintained a literary salon in Tallinn. A new love affair with the poet Artur Adson became another incentive to write. Under's divorce proceedings with Hacker dragged on for years, providing reasons for spicy gossip. In 1924 Under married Adson. In 1917 she published her first volume, *Sonetid* (Sonets), and the following year another, *Eelõitseng* (Early maturing), which included mostly love poetry influenced by Impressionism. Estonian independence also influenced her views and style. Brought up in the German tradition in the center of the so-called Siuru Group, Under began to promote Expressionism and Futurism. In 1920 she published a collection of translations from contemporary German poetry and then two volumes of her own in which she adopted new German patterns: *Verivalla* (Bloodletting; 1921) and *Pärisosa* (Legacy; 1923). This change in style corresponded with Under's assault on bourgeois values in a widely publicized volume, *Sinine Puri* (Blue sail; 1918), where, apart from a criticism of social relations, she developed erotic poetry. In the course of time Under's writing showed a growing disillusionment with life and human nature, and she drew attention to the conflict between the individual and society, as well as between good and evil. In the volume *Õnnevarjutus* (Ellipse of happiness; 1929), Under used folk motifs, which greatly influenced poets making their debuts in the 1930s.

In 1922 Under was among the co-founders of the Association of Estonian Writers; from 1932 she was an honorary member of the Estonian Literary Society, and in 1937 she was accepted into the PEN Club in London. She survived the first Soviet occupation (1940–41), and after the German invasion she published a volume, *Jõulutervitus* (New Year's greetings; 1941), in which she praised the heroism of the Estonians. In view of a second Soviet occupation, Under decided to emigrate to Sweden, where she worked as an archivist in the Theater Museum in Stockholm. In 1954 Under published *Sädemed tuhas* (Sparks in ashes), and in 1963, *Ääremail* (Borderland), in which she dealt with uprooting and homelessness in a universal sense. Fluent in six languages, Under was among the key translators of world literature into Estonian. For instance, she translated works by Friedrich Schiller, Johann Wolfgang Goethe, Boris Pasternak, and Pär Lagerkvist. Under spent her last years in a hospital. Totally banned in Soviet Estonia, after 1955 some of Under's works were published there, and in 1963 the authorities of the Estonian SSR even sent her birthday greetings. (AG)

Sources: Helmi Rajamaa, *Marie Under inimesena* (Stockholm, 1983); Piret Lotmant, "Censorship during the Occupation of Estonia," www.okupatsioon.ee/english/overviews/index.html; www.einst.ee/literary/autumn2000/11_under.htm; www.kirjasto.sci.fi/under.htm; www.ilmamaa.ee/Raamatud/RISTIKIV/roommure.html; mapage.noos.fr/estonie/Under.html.

URBAN Jerzy (3 August 1933, Łódź), Polish journalist and editor. Born into a journalist's family, after World War II Urban studied at Warsaw University but did not graduate. During his studies he belonged to the Stalinist Polish Youth Association (Związek Młodzieży Polskiej). In 1955–57 Urban contributed to the weekly *Po prostu*, criticizing social pathologies. From 1961 he worked for the weekly *Polityka* but was fired for his independent views in 1963. Thanks to good contacts with party leaders responsible for the press, Urban got a job on the weekly *Życie Gospodarcze* and published in popular papers such as *Kulisy* and *Ekspres Wieczorny* under the pseudonym "Jerzy Kibic." His articles were stylized as ironic court coverage and presented social relations in a critical light. In 1980 Urban spoke decidedly against Solidarity. Thanks to the support of Deputy Prime Minister **Mieczysław Rakowski**, in August 1981 Urban became a government spokesman. His role on the team of General **Wojciech Jaruzelski** was more important than his formal position, since he became a key adviser and the co-author of many of Jaruzelski's pronouncements. As an unscrupulous and cynical propagandist, at his press conferences of the 1980s Urban was as clever as he was deceitful in slandering leaders of the democratic opposition and the Catholic Church. In a series of aggressive articles published under the pseudonym "Jan Rem" in the weekly *Tu i Teraz* in 1984, Urban contributed to the hostile campaign that preceded the murder of Reverend **Jerzy Popiełuszko** by three officers of the security service (Służba Bezpieczeństwa [SB]). In 1987–88 Urban co-authored special analyses, submitted to Jaruzelski, in which he presented a strategy of retreat from communism without the Communists' giving up

power. From April 1989 he was head of the Committee for Radio and Television and minister without portfolio. In the elections of June 1989 he lost.

After leaving the government in August 1989, Urban published a couple of scandalous best sellers. Taking advantage of the freedom of the press, in 1990 he founded the weekly *Nie*, in which he addressed those affected by "transformation neurosis," using extremely vulgar language and disregarding all values. Urban gained fame and fortune taunting the public with visions of a denominational state ruled by the Catholic clergy. He aggressively attacked post-Solidarity governments, contributing to the electoral success of the post-Communist Democratic Left Alliance (Sojusz Lewicy Demokratycznej [SLD]) in September 1993. Attempts to curb the abusive style and lies of *Nie* were usually fruitless. For instance, in 1996 court proceedings concluded that Urban's disclosure of state secrets could not justify depriving him of the right to practice journalism. Although he lost some trials, Urban won (for example) a case against Ryszard Bender, who had called him the "Goebbels of martial law." *Nie* became the foundation of Urban's personal wealth. Urban belongs to the business elite, supplementing profits from *Nie* with revenues from the pornographic industry, in which he has become a magnate. In 1990 Urban joined the post-Communist Social Democracy of the Polish Republic and (in 1999) the SLD, but his contacts with the party leadership have cooled since 2001, when he began to criticize the post-Communist government of **Leszek Miller**. Urban's testimony before a special parliamentary commission to investigate a corruption case against Lew Rywin in March 2003 threw new light on the functioning of the post-Communist oligarchy. (AG)

Sources: Mołdawa; *Kto jest kim w Polsce* (Warsaw, 2001); Jan Skórzyński, *Ugoda i rewolucja: Władza i opozycja 1985–1989* (Warsaw, 1995); Antoni Dudek, *Pierwsze lata III Rzeczypospolitej 1989–2001* (Kraków, 2002); nie.com.pl; www.zrodlo.krakow.pl/archiwum/2001/42/09.html; polskaludowa.com/biografie/Urban.

URBÁNEK Karel (22 March 1941, Bojkovice, near Uherské Hradiště), Czech Communist activist. In 1962–69 Urbánek worked as a train dispatcher, and in 1970–72 he was head of the Bojkovice railway station. From 1973 he was active in the South Moravian district committee of the Communist Party of Czechoslovakia (CPC) in Brno. In 1982 he became secretary and in 1984 first secretary of the CPC town committee in Brno. In 1986 he became a member of the CPC Central Committee. From 1988 to 1989 Urbánek was a member of CPC CC Presidium and chairman of a special committee for party work. After the first week of the Velvet Revolution, on 24 November

1989, he became CPC secretary general, replacing **Miloš Jakeš**. Because of the fall of the Communist regime, he held this position only until 21 December 1989. Until the first free elections of June 1990 Urbánek was chairman of the CPC Central Control Commission, but after the elections he left the public scene entirely. (PU)

Sources: *ČBS*; *Kdo byl kdo v našich dějinach ve 20. stoleti*, vol. 2 (Prague, 1998).

URBŠYS Juozas (29 February 1896, Šateikiai, near Kėdainiai–2 May 1991, Kaunas), Lithuanian officer, diplomat, and politician. During World War I Urbšys worked in the Central Lithuanian Relief Committee in Moscow (1915–16). In 1917 he graduated from a Russian military school, and he served in the tsarist army. After his return to Lithuania in 1918, Urbšys volunteered for the Lithuanian Army and took part in the war of independence as an officer of the general staff. He ended his military career as a captain in 1922, and he started to work in the diplomatic service. Urbšys was sent to Berlin (1922–27) and Paris (1927–33). Simultaneously he published a major work on the incorporation of the Vilnius (Wilno) region into Poland, *Medžiaga Vilniaus ginčo diplomatinei istorjai* (Materials in the history of the diplomatic conflict on the Vilnius issue; 1932). In 1933–34 Urbšys headed the diplomatic mission to Riga and worked in the Foreign Ministry, first as head of the Political Department (1934–36), then as secretary general (1936–38), and finally, from December 1938, as minister of foreign affairs.

As the head of diplomacy, Urbšys struggled with problems beyond the powers of Lithuania, while increasing pressure from mighty neighbors was putting an end to independence. On 22 February 1939 Urbšys had to sign an agreement with the Third Reich ceding the Klaipeda region to it. Despite desperate attempts, Urbšys could not prevent the Soviet occupation and incorporation of Lithuania into the USSR. Under Soviet pressure, in agreement with President **Antanas Smetona**, Urbšys made the decision to annex the Vilnius region, offered by the Soviets after their invasion of Poland, in exchange for consent to the entry of Soviet garrisons into Lithuania (agreement of 10 October 1939). Expecting a Soviet invasion, on 30 May 1940, Urbšys instructed Lithuanian diplomatic missions abroad that in such a case the envoy to Italy, **Stasys Lazoraitis**, would be responsible for Lithuanian foreign policy. On 14 June 1940 Urbšys was called to Moscow to discuss another Soviet ultimatum. Although he failed to prevent the Soviet invasion the next day, he stubbornly defended the Lithuanian standpoint. Therefore, on 16 June he was arrested and deported with his family deep into

Russia. Urbšys lived there for sixteen years. In 1956 he was allowed to return to Vilnius, where until his death he worked as a translator of French literature. Among other works, he translated those of Gustave Flaubert, Molière, and Romain Roland. In 1988 the publication of Urbšys's memoirs on the tragic years 1939–40 became a political sensation. At the end of Soviet rule Urbšys became a symbol of the continuity of Lithuanian aspirations for independence and a remainder of the violence of which Lithuania was a victim. (AG)

Sources: *EL*, vol. 5; *New York Times*, 2 May 1991; P. Mačiulis, *Trys ultimatumai* (Brooklyn, 1962); V. Stanley Vardys, ed., *Lithuania under the Soviets* (New York, 1965); Leonas Sabiliūnas, *Lithuania in Crisis: Nationalism to Communism* (Bloomington, 1972); Bronis J. Kaslas, ed., *The USSR-German Aggression against Lithuania* (New York, 1973); David M. Crowe, *The Baltic States and the Great Powers: Foreign Relations, 1938–1940* (Boulder, Colo., 1993); Saulius Sužiedelis, *Historical Dictionary of Lithuania* (Lanham, Md., 1997).

URSÍNY Ján (11 October 1896, Rakša, near Martin, Slovakia–8 January 1972, Slovakia), Slovak Peasant Party politician. After graduating from a farm school in Šlapanice in Moravia, Ursíny returned to farm in his native village. He was also active in agricultural organizations. Between 1935 and 1938 he sat in parliament as a representative of the Slovak Democratic Party (SDP). In September 1938 he signed an agreement in Zlín by which many SDP activists joined the party of Reverend **Andrej Hlinka**. Under the rule of Reverend **Josef Tiso**, Ursíny moved to the opposition, along with the group of **Josef Lettrich**. Between 1939 and 1942 Ursíny was held prisoner by the Germans. After his release he established contacts with the left and the Communists, and he joined the conspiratorial Slovak National Council, which was preparing an uprising against the Germans in the summer of 1944. After the collapse of the uprising, Ursíny was a member of a delegation that in October 1944 reached an agreement with the government of **Edvard Beneš** on the composition of a coalition government. After his return to Slovakia via Moscow, Ursíny worked in this government's delegation for the affairs of the territories occupied by the Red Army and in the Presidium of the Board of Commissioners, which served as the provisional Slovak government. In March 1945 Ursíny assumed the post of deputy prime minister in the governments of **Zdenek Fierlinger** and **Klement Gottwald**. In the elections of May 1946 Ursíny entered parliament, and his party won the elections in Slovakia, becoming the fourth largest parliamentary faction. During preparations to take over full power at the end of September 1947, the Communist-dominated security organs arrested Ursíny's secretary, Otto Obuch, who was accused of organizing an "anti-state plot," which implicated Ursíny. On 30 October 1947 Ursíny resigned his post, and after the Communist coup of February 1948 he was arrested. In April 1948 he was sentenced to seven years' imprisonment on the basis of false evidence. Released in 1953, Ursíny returned to his farm work, and from then on he did not play any political role. (WR)

Sources: *Enciklopedia Slovenska* (Bratislava, 1980), vol. 4; Karel Kaplan, *The Short March: The Communist Takeover in Czechoslovakia, 1945–1948* (London, 1981); Milan Churaň et al., *Kdo byl kdo v našich dějinach ve 20. stoleti* (Prague, 1994).

URSU Gheorghe (1 July 1926, Soroca, Bessarabia–17 November 1985, Bucharest), Romanian dissident, victim of communism. During World War II, along with his family, Ursu moved to Galaţi, where he graduated from high school in 1945. In July 1944 he joined a Communist youth organization. In 1950 he graduated from the Bucharest Polytechnic College. In 1943–85 Ursu kept a diary in which he not only registered events, but also recorded his comments, increasingly critical of the tyrannical Communist regime. Ursu worked in the Institute of Construction Design in Bucharest. In the 1970s he kept sending letters to the organ of the Romanian Communist Party, *Scînteia*, and the periodical *Contemporanul*; these letters stigmatized official anti-Semitism, demagoguery, and abuse of power. In 1977 two of these letters were broadcast by Radio Free Europe (RFE). In January 1985 the security police, Securitate, searched Ursu's apartment and confiscated his diary and other materials. In August 1985 Ursu was severely criticized at a special gathering of his institute; on 21 September he was arrested, accused of having founded a "reactionary" organization, collaboration with the RFE, and illegal possession of U.S.$16. Among those who defended him abroad were U.S. congressmen. After almost two months of brutal interrogation Ursu was murdered in Calea Rahovei Prison. The case received extensive coverage in the Western media. Ursu's *Europa mea* (My Europe; 1991) was published posthumously. (WR)

Sources: "Cazul Gheorghe Ursu," Dvadsat dva, 27 April 1990; *Merea călătorie: Viata si moartea inginerelui Gheorghe Ursu* (Bucharest, 1998); Radoslav Doru, "Gheorghe Ursu" (Karta Center in Warsaw); gh-ursu.ong.ro/life.htm.

UZUNOVIĆ Nikola (3 May 1873, Niš–20 September 1954, Belgrade), Serb politician. Born into a merchant's family, Uzunović graduated in law from Belgrade University. Then he worked as a judge, mayor of his hometown of Niš, and governor of southern Serbia. In 1905 he was elected an MP on behalf of the Serbian Radical Party (SRP), and he belonged to its leadership. When the Kingdom of Serbs, Croats, and Slovenes came into being in 1918, Uzunović was one of the Serb leaders that advocated the centralist option. The parliamentary crisis of the kingdom and the growth of importance of the SRP helped Uzunović's career. From March 1921 to April 1926 he was minister of land reform, then minister of public works, post, and telegraph. From 8 April 1926 to 17 April 1927 Uzunović was prime minister. At the same time he headed a centrist faction of the SRP closely associated with King **Alexander I**. After the royal coup of January 1929 and the proclamation of a dictatorship, Uzunović was minister without portfolio in the government of General **Petar Živković** (January 1929–January 1932). When the king granted a new constitution, introducing the appearance of parliamentary rule, in September 1931 Uzunović became head of one of the government parties, the Yugoslav Radical Peasant Democracy, which became the Yugoslav National Party (Jugoslovenska Nacionalna Stranka [YNP]) in 1933. Uzunović was close to the royal court but still in the shadow of General Živković. After the latter's resignation, from 17 January to 22 December 1934 Uzunović was prime minister again. The assassination of King Alexander (October 1934) and a relatively moderate policy introduced by Prince **Paul Karadjordjević** and the new prime minister, **Milan Stojadinović**, deprived Uzunović and the YNP leadership of influence on Yugoslav politics. (AW)

Sources: *Who's Who in Central and East Europe* (Zurich, 1937); *Biographisches Lexikon*, vol. 4; Ferdo Čulinović, *Jugoslavija izmedju dva rata*, vols. 1–2 (Zagreb, 1961); Todor Stojkov, *Opozicija u vreme šestojanuarske diktature 1929–1935* (Belgrade, 1969); Wacław Felczak and Tadeusz Wasilewski, *Historia Jugosławii* (Wrocław, 1985).

V

VACAROIU Nicolae (24 October 1943, Tighina, Bessarabia [now Moldova]), Romanian politician. In 1964 Vacaroiu graduated from the Academy of Economic Studies in Bucharest. From 1986 to 1989 he served as deputy chairman of the State Planning Commission. A close associate of **Ion Iliescu**, Vacaroiu was active in the post-Communist National Salvation Front, representing a conservative approach to market reforms and reluctance toward rapprochement with the West. On 13 November 1992 Vacaroiu became the prime minister of a government based on a coalition of the Democratic National Salvation Front (Frontul Democrat al Salvării Naţionale), the Romanian National Unity Party, the nationalist Great Romania Party (Partidul România Mare [PRM]), and the Socialist Party of Labor. His government pursued a policy of deterring transformations and rapprochement with **Vladimír Mečiar**'s Slovakia and **Slobodan Milošević**'s new Yugoslavia. At the end of 1992 Vacaroiu came into conflict with the Transylvanian Hungarians, who sought autonomy, but at the beginning of 1993 he managed to get the situation under control. In February 1993 Romania signed an association agreement with the European Union (EU), but the government made little effort to accelerate accession negotiations with the EU. In 1993 demonstrations by the Jiu Valley coal miners almost brought about the collapse of Vacaroiu's government. Despite his conservative views, under Vacaroiu's rule the Bank of Romania limited the issue of the lei and in April 1994 freed its exchange rate. The structural transformations proved too weak to put Romania on the road to development. As a result of growing economic stagnation and social discontent, the post-Communists lost the elections of November 1996. Consequently, Vacaroiu resigned on 12 December 1996. In the new parliament, he became deputy speaker of the Senate, representing the post-Communist opposition. After the electoral success of the post-Communist Party of Social Democracy in Romania (Partidul Democraţiei Sociale din România [PDSR]), Vacaroiu became speaker of the Senate and vice-chairman of the PDSR on 20 December 2000. (FA/WR)

Sources: *Europa Środkowo-Wschodnia 1993–1996* (Warsaw, 1995–98); Józef Darski, *Rumunia: Historia, współczesność, konflikty narodowe* (Warsaw, 1995); *Europa Środkowo-Wschodnia, 1992 i 1993* (Warsaw, 1994 and 1995); Tom Gallagher, *Romania after Ceauşescu* (Edinburgh, 1995); Duncan Light and Daniel Phinnemore, *Post-Communist Romania* (London, 2001).

VĀCIETIS Jukums (23 November 1873, Lutriņi, Courland–28 July 1938, USSR), Soviet military man of Latvian descent. Vācietis graduated from high school in Kuldīga in 1891, from the Military Academy in Vilna (Wilno, Vilnius) in 1895, and from the Academy of the General Staff in Petersburg in 1909. He served as an infantry officer. At the beginning of World War I Vācietis was wounded, and in 1915 he became commander of the Zemgale Latvian Riflemen's battalion (as of 1916, a regiment), which fought on the Latvian front in 1915–17. From 1916 Vācietis was a colonel, decorated with the Golden Sword of St. George for bravery. After the Bolshevik revolution, in November 1917 soldiers elected Vācietis commander of the Second Latvian Riflemen's Brigade. In December 1917 he was made corps commander, temporarily of the Twelfth Army, and later he was head of the operations department of the Revolutionary General Staff. In January and February 1918 Vācietis led the disarmament of the Polish First Corps of General **Józef Dowbór-Muśnicki**. In April 1918 he was appointed commander of the Latvian Riflemen's Division and led a bloody suppression of a rebellion of Social Revolutionaries in Moscow. Then he was appointed commander-in-chief of the Eastern Front. From September 1918 to July 1919 Vācietis was commander-in-chief of the armed forces of the Russian Soviet Federative Socialist Republic, and from January to March 1919 he was commander-in-chief of the Latvian Soviet Army. After a conflict with the top Bolshevik command, in July 1919 Vācietis was dismissed and temporarily arrested. The Bolshevik authorities did not agree to his return to Latvia, where he had sent his family. From 1922 Vācietis was a senior lecturer, professor, and head of the Department of Military History at the Military Academy of the Red Army in Moscow. He authored (among other works) *Latviešu strēlnieku vēsturiskā nozīme* (The historical importance of the Latvian Riflemen, 2 vols.; 1922–24), arguing that Red Latvian riflemen had fought for Latvian independence against monarchists. Vācietis was murdered during the Great Purge. (EJ)

Sources: *Latvijas PSR mazā enciklopēdija*, vol. 3 (Riga, 1970); *Latvijas padomju enciklopēdija*, vol. 10 (Riga, 1987); Valdis Bērziņš and Jānis Ruberts, *Pirmais virspavēlnieks* (Riga, 1973); *Jukums Vācietis: Pers. lit. Rādītājs* (Riga, 1973); Valdis Bērziņš, *Es iešu pirmais* (Riga, 1984); Andrejs Plekans, *Historical Dictionary of Latvia* (Lanham, Md., 1997).

VACULÍK Ludvík (23 July 1926, Brumov, Zlin district), Czech writer and journalist. In 1941–46 Vaculík worked in the Bata shoe factory in Zlin and Zruči-nad-Sázavou. At the same time he studied at a trade high school. In 1950 he graduated in journalism from the Higher Political and Social School in Prague. In 1948–51 Vaculík worked as a tutor in boarding schools. From 1953 to 1957 he was an editor for Rudé Právo Press, and in 1959–65 he edited radio broadcasts for youngsters. From the mid-1960s Vaculík was increasingly outspoken in criticizing Communist cultural policies, publishing a lot in the periodicals *Literární listy* and *Literární noviny*, whose editor he was from 1965. Vaculík became widely known for a critical speech at the Fourth Congress of Czechoslovak Writers in June 1957, in which he said that for twenty years no social problems had been solved in Czechoslovakia, and for the manifesto "Dva tisíce slov" (Two thousand words), published in June 1968 in *Literární listy*. Vaculík was the co-author of the manifesto; in it the Communist totalitarian system was critically analyzed. The authorities pronounced the manifesto counter-revolutionary, and Vaculík was banned from publishing. During the so-called normalization, Vaculík was one of the leading representatives of the democratic opposition, and he published in the uncensored press and abroad. In 1973 he became director of the Petlice underground press, which had published about four hundred books by 1989. In 1977 Vaculík was one of the first signatories of Charter 77. After the Velvet Revolution of 1989, he returned to journalism, mainly to *Lidové noviny*, where he critically assessed contemporary issues. He was, for instance, the first to touch upon the taboo subject of the split of Czechoslovakia.

As a writer, Vaculík made his debut in 1963 with the novel *Rušný dům* (A living house), in which, based on his experiences as a tutor in boarding schools, he described the moral decline among youngsters and the hypocrisy of the Communist system. His next novel, *Sekyra* (The axe), brought him even wider renown. In it he critically analyzed real socialism. In the novels *Morčata* (The Guinea pigs; 1977) and *Český snář* (Czech dreambook; 1983), Vaculík introduced an atmosphere of the absurd. In the latter, he ironically presented the Czech intelligentsia under totalitarianism. The book was based on the author's memories of 1971–80, when he was constantly under the surveillance of the security services. Vaculík's memories of childhood and his student years were included in *Milí spolužáci* (My dear school friends; 1995), while those of 1969–72 were in *Nepaměti* (A non-memoir; 1998). Vaculík also published a collection of essays, *Jaro je tady* (Spring is here; 1987); *Srpnový rok* (The August year; 1990); and *Stará dáma se baví* (The old lady has fun; 1991). (PU)

Sources: *Kdo byl kdo v našich dějinach ve 20. stoleti*, vol. 2 (Prague, 1998); *Slovník českých spisovatelů od roku 1945*, vol. 2 (Prague, 1998); *Who's Who in the Socialist Countries of Europe*, vol. 3 (Munich, London, and Paris, 1989); Gordon H. Skilling, *Czechoslovakia's Interrupted Revolution* (Princeton, N.J., 1976); Vilém Precan, ed., *Charta 77 (1977–1989), Od morální k demokratické revoluci: Dokumentace* (Bratislava, 1990).

VAGNORIUS Gediminas (10 June 1957, Plungė), Lithuanian politician. In 1980 Vagnorius graduated as an engineer-economist from the Vilnius Engineering Construction Institute (now the Vilnius Gediminas Technical University [VGTU]). From 1980 to 1987 he worked as a teacher at the VGTU. Elected a member of the broad leadership of the Lithuanian Movement for Restructuring (Sąjūdis) in 1988, Vagnorius was a close associate of its leader, **Vytautas Landsbergis**. In March 1990 Vagnorius became a member of the Presidium of the Lithuanian Supreme Council. After Soviet special forces occupied the Lithuanian television broadcast center in Vilnius and Prime Minister **Kazimiera Prunskiene** was forced to resign, Vagnorius became head of the government on 13 January 1991. His situation was very difficult. Attacked by Prunskiene, who accused his government of being unconstitutional, and criticized by the extreme nationalists, Vagnorius was in charge of the difficult task of making the Lithuanian economy independent from Russia, dismantling the system of kolkhozes (collective farms), and replacing the ruble by the Lithuanian currency. Although the reforms he implemented were partially successful, a sudden decrease in the standard of living in Lithuania led to a drop in popularity of Sąjūdis and of Vagnorius himself. Moreover, the failure of a project to print new litas banknotes—for which the government had awarded a contract to an irresponsible American firm—led to a conflict between Vagnorius and the Bank of Lithuania. Vagnorius resigned on 22 July 1992, and his party lost the elections of October 1992 and went over to the opposition. However, Vagnorius won a seat. In 1992–96 he was one of the leaders of the Homeland Union–Conservatives of Lithuania (Tėvynės Sąjunga–Lietuvos Konservatoriai [TS–LK]), the largest opposition party in parliament. On 28 November 1996, after the TS–LK won the new parliamentary elections, Vagnorius became head of a government formed in coalition with the Christian Democrats. As long as **Algirdas Brazauskas** served as president, Vagnorius had to make compromises, as their views often clashed. Vagnorius's cooperation with the next president, **Valdas Adamkus**, was much easier. In November 1997 Vagnorius's government rejected the offer of Russian unilateral guarantees for Lithuania's independence and emphasized Lithuania's aspirations to join NATO. Vagnorius served as prime minister until 3 May 1999. In the elections of 2000 he won a seat on the ticket of the moderate Conservatives. (WR)

Sources: Saulius Sužiedelis, *Historical Dictionary of Lithuania* (Lanham, Md., 1997); Alfred E. Senn, *Lithuania Awakening* (Berkeley, 1990); Grzegorz Błaszczyk, *Litwa współczesna* (Warsaw, 1992); Anatol Lieven, *The Baltic Revolution* (New Haven, 1993); V. Stanley Vardys and Judith B. Sedaitis, *Lithuania: The Rebel Nation* (Boulder, Colo., 1997); www.rulers.com; www.lrs.lt.

VÄHI Tiit (10 January 1947, Kaagjärve), Estonian politician and businessman. Vähi graduated in mechanical engineering from the Technical University of Tallinn (1970). Employed at a transport base in Valga (1972), he rose to become its director (1976–89). A member of the Communist Party of Estonia (CPE), Vähi served as minister of transport of the Estonian SSR in the government of **Indrek Toome** in 1989 and then in the government of **Edgar Savisaar** from 1990 to 1992. Vähi sought cooperation with the Nordic countries. He was also successful in transferring control of Estonia's transportation to authorities within the republic and making them independent from the central administration in Moscow. Having realized that the role of the CPE was coming to an end, Vähi resigned his party membership in 1989 and was one of the founders of the Estonian Coalition Party (Eesti Koonderakond [ECP]) in December 1991. The ECP—founded after a split in the post-Communist Free Estonia (Vaba Eesti) group—represented the industrial management apparatus, which, in the new circumstances, wanted to introduce a free market economy.

After the collapse of Savisaar's government on 30 January 1992, Vähi became prime minister of a government that was composed of members of Free Estonia and the ECP but was also supported by the anti-Communist camp. The new ruling team was seen as a barrier against Savisaar, who was being accused of dictatorial leanings. Vähi's government was an interim one, meant to remain in power until the first free parliamentary elections were called in October 1992. Vähi unsuccessfully strove for the withdrawal of the Russian Army from Estonia. Fearing the Russian factor, he did not insist on the return of the Estonian SSR's KGB archives, which had been removed to Moscow. He also did not launch lustration and favored close economic cooperation with Russia and a strong position for Russia in Estonia's economy. However, Vähi replaced the Russian ruble with the Estonian kroon, curbed galloping inflation, and founded a privatization agency. Vähi resigned on 21 October 1992. He did not run in the parliamentary elections of October 1992, as he chose the prestigious post of mayor of Tallinn (1993–95), which gave him control over nearly one-third of Estonia's population and the biggest foreign investment center. Although he did not sit in parliament, Vähi took over the leadership of the ECP in 1993.

As a result of social discontent caused by "shock therapy" and numerous scandals with which the center-right wing was entangled, Vähi and his electoral bloc (the ECP and the People's Union) won the 1995 parliamentary elections, and on 17 April 1995 Vähi again became prime minister. After his election, economic transformations slowed down because Vähi was in favor of maintaining large subsidies, particularly for agriculture, and expanding welfare policies. His cabinet was based on a coalition with the Center Party, led by Savisaar, but when in October 1995 it was revealed that Savisaar, while serving as minister of interior, had bugged other politicians, this coalition broke up. Vähi changed partners by inviting the liberal Reform Party, led by **Siim Kallas**, to join the government. However, program differences between the partners and then the presidential elections led to the breakup of this coalition as well. In December 1996 Vähi formed a minority government, which he headed only until 17 March 1997, when he was forced to resign as the result of a corruption scandal: the media revealed that as mayor of Tallinn, Vähi had allotted flats to his acquaintances and family members, bypassing legal procedures. Vähi resigned as leader of the ECP and as MP. In 1998 he became one of the directors of the metal-producing Silmet Group. (AG)

Sources: *Eastern Europe and the Commonwealth of Independent States 1999* (London, 1999); *Eesti Entsuklopeedia*, vol. 14 (Tallinn, 2000); Bugajski; www.stars.coe.fr/Magazine/te0197/profiles1.htm; www.helsinki-hs.net/today/161299-01.html.

VAIDA-VOEVOD Alexandru (27 February 1873, Alparét [now Bobâlna], Transylvania–25 May 1950, Bucharest), Romanian politician. After graduating from high school in Kronstadt, Vaida-Voevod studied medicine at the university in Vienna. He completed his studies in 1894. While still a student, he joined the Romanian national movement; in 1896 in Vienna, at a meeting of members of this movement, he for the first time publicly accused Hungary of violating the rights of the Romanian population in Transylvania. In the same year Vaida-Voevod became a member of the Romanian National Party (Partidul Naţional Român [RNP]) in Transylvania. An MP (1906–7) in the Hungarian parliament on the RNP ticket, Vaida-Voevod strove for the implementation of agricultural reform, the introduction of universal suffrage, and the right of women to study at universities, but above all he protested the forced Magyarization of schools in Transylvania. Because of his activities, in 1907 he was expelled from parliament, but in 1910 he was reelected as an MP. From 1914 to 1918, the Hungarian authorities forced Vaida-Voevod into exile in Vienna and Switzerland. At that time he leaned toward the concept of restructuring Austria-Hungary in a federalist spirit; this notion was supplemented by a Daco-Romanian idea of uniting all Romanian lands under Habsburg rule, which would de facto mean the end of the Old Kingdom of Romania. In this spirit Vaida-Voevod worked with the Slovak politician **Milan Hodža** and Archduke Francis

Ferdinand. The defeat of the Central Powers and the collapse of Austria-Hungary determined the fate of the other Romanian territories. The Romanian National Central Council, established in Transylvania in October 1918, pursued a policy of *faits accomplis*. On 18 October 1918 in the Hungarian parliament Vaida-Voevod announced the separation of Transylvanian Romanians from Hungary. Vaida-Voevod was also a member of the National Assembly in Alba Iulia, which voted for the unification of Transylvania and Banat with the Old Kingdom of Romania (1 December 1918).

From 1918 to 1920 Vaida-Voevod was a member of the Transylvanian Governing Council, led by **Iuliu Maniu**; in 1919 the council passed decrees on agricultural reform and the Romanization of the University of Kolozsvár (Cluj). Vaida-Voevod served as head of the department of foreign affairs in this council. From December 1918 to December 1919 he also held the post of minister for Transylvanian affairs. From 9 December 1919 to 19 March 1920 Vaida-Voevod was premier and foreign minister. He also was a member of the Romanian delegation to the Paris Peace Conference (1919). As prime minister, Vaida-Voevod signed the peace treaty with Austria at Saint-Germain-en-Laye (10 December 1919). From 1919 to 1920 he served as speaker of the Chamber of Deputies of the Romanian parliament.

Vaida-Voevod was a member of the Transylvanian National Romanian Party until 1926, when he helped to found the united National Peasant Party (Partidul Naţional ţărănesc [NPP]). In 1933 he briefly served as chairman of the NPP. He also held the posts of minister of interior (November 1928–October 1930), minister of foreign affairs (June–October 1932), and minister of trade and industry (June–November 1933). As an NPP nominee, Vaida-Voevod twice held the post of prime minister: from 6 July to 20 October 1932 and from 14 January to 14 November 1933. In 1935, however, Vaida-Voevod severed his ties with the NPP and drifted toward a position close to the nationalist right wing. From 12 May 1935 to 10 February 1938 he headed the Romanian Front, an organization with a nationalist and anti-Semitic tinge but little political influence. A supporter of the coup staged by **Charles II** (10 February 1938), Vaida-Voevod became an adviser to the king and minister of state in the National Unity government led by Patriarch **Miron Cristea**. Vaida-Voevod again held the post of minister of state in early June and late July 1940, during a crisis brought about by a Soviet ultimatum demanding the cession of Bessarabia. After Charles II abdicated, Vaida-Voevod retired from politics. Vaida-Voevod's publications include *Chestia Banatului* (The question of Banat; 1924); *Problema frontierilor românești* (The problems of Romanian borders; 1926); and *Memorii* (Memoirs, 3 vols.; 1993–95). (FA/TD)

Sources: *Biographisches Lexikon*, vol. 4; R. W. Seton-Watson, *A History of the Roumanians* (London, 1963); Florea Nedelcu, *Viaţa politică din România în preajma instaurării dictaturii regale* (Cluj, 1973); Keith Hitchins, ed., *The Nationality Problem in Austria-Hungary: The Reports of Alexander Vaida to Archduke Franz Ferdinand's Chancellery* (Leiden, 1974); Ştefan Pascu, *A History of Transylvania* (Detroit, 1982); Liviu Maior, *Alexandru Vaida Voievod între Belvedere și Versailles* (Cluj and Napoca, 1993); Liviu Maior, ed., *History of Transylvania* (Budapest, 1994).

VAINO Karl (1923, Tomsk, Russia), Estonian Communist activist. Born and brought up in the Soviet Union, Vaino was almost totally Russified despite his Estonian descent. He initially used the name Kiril Voinov. He did not live in Estonia until 1947, when he went there on Moscow's orders, with other Communist activists, to assume key positions in the Estonian SSR, replacing local Communists who had lost the trust of Stalin. Despite many years spent in Estonia after the war, Vaino learned very little Estonian. A particularly servile activist, he was quickly promoted. He became a member of the Central Committee (CC) of the Communist Party of Estonia (CPE) in 1948 and a member of the Politburo in 1954. In 1960 he was promoted to the position of CC secretary for industry and held this position for the next eighteen years. In 1978, owing to the intensification of the Russification policy in all the territories of the Soviet Union, Moscow dismissed **Johannes Käbin** as head of the CPE and assigned the task of Russifying the Estonian SSR to Vaino. This appointment met with opposition within the party because Käbin wanted **Vaino Väjlas** to succeed him. After coming to power, Vaino expelled the more moderate leaders from the party. At that time he became a member the CC of the CPSU, and he held that post until 1989.

As early as December 1978 the Politburo of the CC of the CPE passed a secret resolution "on the further improvement of the teaching of and access to the Russian language," as a result of which the Russification policy intensified. Russian was officially recognized as the language of "international communication," and according to party guidelines, only a "bilingual" person was trustworthy. Russian became compulsory as early as kindergarten, and in 1980 the number of hours taught in Russian at universities and colleges was increased. In response to protests against the appointment of Elsa Grechkina to the position of minister of education in the autumn of 1980—the protests broke out among students and intellectuals (the famous "Letter of 40," signed by **Jaan Kaplinski**, **Marju Lauristin**, and others)—Vaino launched repressive measures, including expulsions from the university, printing bans, and the like. However, mass public support and publicity on the issue in the world media forced the party to stop its offensive. After the system of food distribution in the Estonian SSR was made part of the Soviet Union-wide system of food supply, the standard of living in the Estonian SSR deteriorated. The crisis also affected industry. During Vaino's regime relations between Estonians and immigrants, who increasingly flooded into Estonia, worsened. The state of the natural environment also deteriorated. In 1979 Imre Arakas tried to assassinate Vaino.

The beginning of perestroika did not herald changes in Estonia. Vaino regarded the program launched by Mikhail Gorbachev as harmful and believed that it would cause opposition from CPSU dogmatists, who would expel Gorbachev, and Moscow's policy would then fall back into the same old rut. Initially, Moscow did not intend to introduce any changes in Estonia. In 1986, after information leaked to the public about plans to construct new phosphorite mines that might cause an ecological catastrophe, an open public rebellion broke out; as a result, after a series of protests in the spring of 1987, the government had to abandon these plans. The issue became a turning point in the history of the democratic opposition in Estonia, giving an impetus to the institutionalization of anti-Communist activities, which intensified in the second half of 1987 and the beginning of 1988. The brutal suppression of student demonstrations in Tartu acted as a catalyst for the activities of the opposition, which put forward demands for Vaino's dismissal. These demands gained mass support in the first half of 1988. Meanwhile, in the Politburo and the CPE CC a fierce struggle was going on between supporters and opponents of the reforms. Vaino consistently refused to meet the demands of the opposition. Finally Moscow forced his dismissal, fearing that the actions of the Popular Front might spontaneously turn into political activities over which the party might lose control or that they might even turn into a grassroots revolution. In June 1988 Vaino tried to manipulate the election of delegates to a CPSU conference. When the Popular Front called a demonstration in defense of free elections, he allegedly asked for military assistance. On 16 June 1988, the day before the demonstration, Vaino was dismissed from his position, with Gorbachev's consent, and he went to Moscow. (AG)

Sources: *Eesti Entsuklopeedia*, vol. 14 (Tallinn 2000); Romuald J. Misunas and Rein Taagepera, *The Baltic States: The Years of Dependence, 1940–1970* (Berkeley, 1993); Tõnu Tannberg, Matti Laur, Tõnis Lukas, Ain Mäesalu, and Ago Pajur, *History of Estonia* (Tallinn, 2000); Jan Lewandowski, *Estonia* (Warsaw, 2001); Väino Sirk, "The Soviet Educational System in Estonia 1940–1991," http://www.okupatsioon.ee/english/overviews/index.html.

VAITOIANU Artur (14 April 1864, Ismail, Bessarabia–1956, Bucharest), Romanian general and politician. In 1886 Vaitoianu graduated from the Military Academy in Bucharest, where he lectured from 1897. By 1915 he had been promoted to general. During World War I Vaitoianu commanded an army corps during the battles of Giurgiu, Olteniţa, and Râmnicu Sărat in 1916. Closely connected with the National Liberal Party (NLP) of **Ion I.C. Bratianu**, from 1916 Vaitoianu served on various political missions. From 1917 he was Romanian representative in Bessarabia, and after it was proclaimed a part of the Old Kingdom in April 1918, he was its representative to the Romanian government. The minister of interior from October to late November 1918, Vaitoianu was then minister of military affairs until September 1919. In this capacity he took part in the Paris Peace Conference and organized the Romanian occupation of Hungary (August–September 1919). From 27 September 1919 Vaitoianu was prime minister and minister of interior; despite Entente orders, he was reluctant to withdraw troops from the territory that was to be incorporated into Hungary. Vaitoianu resigned on 1 December 1919, and his successor, **Alexandru Vaida-Voevod**, gave in to pressure from the Entente. From January 1922 to October 1923 Vaitoianu was again minister of interior, and then, until March 1926, minister of transportation. In the 1930s he sided with the dissidents from the NLP led by **Gheorghe Bratianu**. From February to late March 1938 Vaitoianu was minister of state without portfolio in the so-called government of national unity, which actually initiated the royal dictatorship of King **Charles II**. In 1938–40 Vaitoianu was a member of the Crown Council, called by the king. After World War II he was arrested by the Communists and sentenced to long-term imprisonment in 1950. Vaitoianu died soon after his release. His brother, Alexandru Vaitoianu (1866–1939), was also a general. (FA/WR)

Sources: *Politics and Political Parties in Roumania* (London, 1936); R. W. Seton-Watson, *A History of the Roumanians* (London, 1963); Şerban N. Ionescu, *Who Was Who in Twentieth Century Romania* (Boulder, Colo., 1994); Keith Hitchins, *Rumania 1866–1947* (Oxford, 1994).

VAIVODS Julijans (18 August 1895, Vārkava, Latgale–24 May 1990, Riga), Latvian cardinal. After graduating from high school in Preiļi, in 1913–18 Vaivods studied at a Catholic theological seminary in St. Petersburg (Petrograd). Ordained in April 1918, in view of the closing of the Theological Academy by the Bolsheviks, Vaivods gave up further studies and returned to Latvia. In 1918–25 he worked as a vicar and school chaplain in Aglona, Rēzekne, and Daugavpils. From 1925 he was parish priest in Ciecere, Saldus, Vaiņode, Alsunga, Dviete, and Ventspils in Courland. In July 1938 Vaivods was appointed parish priest and chancellor of the newly created diocese in Liepāja, and in April 1940 he was appointed vicar general of the Liepāja bishopric. In 1938–40 he studied at the Department of Catholic Theology at the University of Latvia in Riga. Vaivods avoided arrest during the Soviet occupation of 1940–41. During the German occupation he was dean of the Courland decanate.

After Bishop Antons Urbšis left for Germany, from October 1944 to July 1947 Vaivods performed the duties of the bishop of Liepāja and then returned to the position of vicar general. In January 1958 he was arrested for dissemination of "anti-Soviet" publications and sentenced to two years of labor camp in Mordovia. In 1960 Vaivods came back to Latvia, but since the authorities did not agree to his return to Liepāja, he worked as a parish priest in Vainode. In 1961–62 he was parish priest of St. James Cathedral in Riga and then vicar general of the Riga metropolis. On 18 November 1964 in Polish Częstochowa Vaivods was consecrated bishop and appointed apostolic administrator of the Riga archbishopric and the Liepāja bishopric. In 1965 Pope Paul VI appointed him a member of the commission of canon law, and on 2 February 1983 Pope John Paul II appointed him a cardinal. Vaivods became the first cardinal on the territory of the Soviet Union. He was buried in the Aglona basilica. His works—*Krīstigās baznīcas vēsture senajā Livonijā* (History of the Catholic Church in Old Livonia; 1994) and *Baznīcas vēsture Kurzemē XIX un XX gadsimtos* (History of the Catholic Church in Courland in the nineteenth and twentieth centuries; 1994)—were published only posthumously. (EJ)

Sources: H. Trūps, *Kardināls Julijans Vaivods. J. Septiņi mēneši Liepājas cietoksnī (1944. gada 9. oktobris–1945. gada 9. maijs)* (Riga, 1990); J. Cakuls, *Latvijas Romas katoļu priesteri 1918–1995* (Riga, 1996); www.catholic-hierarchy.org.

VALENTIĆ Nikica (24 November 1950, Gospić, Croatia), Croatian politician. Valentić studied law at the University of Zagreb. He was the editor-in-chief of the periodical *Pravnik*, and from 1978 to 1983 he served as director of housing cooperatives. He subsequently worked as an attorney (1983–90) and the director of the INA petrochemical works (1990–93). A member of the Croatian Democratic Union (Hrvatska Demokratska Zajednica [HDZ]), Valentić was promoted to the post of its deputy chairman. After the 1992 elections, he became a member of parliament. On 29 March 1993 Valentić assumed the post of prime minister, replacing **Hrvoje Šarinić**. Under his government, Croatia's economic situation significantly improved. After an anti-inflation package was introduced in October 1993, inflation—which in 1993 had soared to 1,600 percent—dropped to 95 percent in 1994 and about 4 percent in 1995. In May 1994 a new currency was introduced, the kuna. It was the name of the currency used at the time of the independent state of Croatia during World War II. In 1994 a decline in national income was halted, and as a result of the reform of the tax system, the budget was balanced. Exports increased; as a result, Croatia's trade balance was positive. In 1994 also the Privatization Ministry was established. Valentić resigned as prime minister on 4 November 1995. In 1996 he became involved in private business, but he retained his membership in the HDZ. Before the elections to the lower chamber of parliament on 3 January 2000, the HDZ proposed him as its candidate for prime minister. After its electoral failure, the HDZ went over to the opposition. Following a split within the HDZ, Valentić has been a supporter of the Croatian Democratic Center (Hrvatski Demokratski Centar [HDC]) since April 2000. (AO)

Sources: *Hrvatski Leksikon*, vol. 2 (Zagreb, 1997); *Europa Środkowo-Wschodnia 1993–95* (Warsaw, 1995–97); Bugajski.

VALEŠ Václav (7 April 1922, Smečno, Kladno district), Czech economist and political activist. Valeš graduated from a school of commerce in Slaný (1941) and from the School of Chemical Technology in Pardubice (1966). During World War II he was active in the resistance movement and was imprisoned by the Germans in the concentration camp in Terezín from 1941 to 1942. After the war, Valeš worked for ten years in the chemical plants in Záluží, near Most, and was promoted to deputy director. In 1956 he became deputy minister of the chemical industry, and from 1965 to 1968 he served as minister of the chemical industry department. From April to December 1968 Valeš was minister of foreign trade. From January to September 1969 he served as deputy prime minister and head of the Economic Council of the Czechoslovak government. A firm supporter of reforms, Valeš helped to prepare economic transformations. In the fall of 1969 he was dismissed from his governmental position, and one year later he was expelled from the Communist Party of Czechoslovakia. For ten years Valeš worked as a researcher in Prague. Arrested on trumped-up charges in 1980, he was held in prison until 1982. After his release from prison, Valeš retired. He returned to public life after the victory of the Velvet Revolution. From January to April 1990 he was an adviser to the prime minister, and subsequently he served as deputy prime minister of Czechoslovakia, chairman of the Economic Council, and vice-president of the State Defense Council until September 1991. After lustration accusations were made against him, Valeš resigned and then retired from public life. (PU)

Sources: *ČBS*; *Českoslovenští politici: 1918–1991* (Prague, 1991).

VÄLJAS Vaino (28 March 1931, Kulakula, Hiiumaa), Estonian Communist activist. The son of a fisherman, Väljas graduated in history from Tartu University in 1955. He began his party career in 1949, becoming head of the Propaganda and Agitation Department of the Central Committee (CC) of the Communist Party of Estonia (CPE) on his native island of Hiiumaa. While a student, Väljas was secretary of the Komsomol at the university (1951–52) and in Tartu (1953–55) and then served as first secretary of the CC of the Estonian Komsomol (1955–61). In 1952 he also joined the CPSU. He became a deputy member of the Politburo of the CC of the CPE in 1956, first secretary of the Tallinn city committee of the CPE in 1961, and a member of the Politburo of the CC of the CPE in 1964. In 1971 Väljas joined the top-ranking leadership of the party, becoming the CC secretary for ideology. In 1973 he earned a Ph.D. in history. Owing to his rapid career rise, in the mid-1970s Väljas began to be considered as a potential candidate to succeed **Johannes Käbin**, the head of the party. Väljas, who enjoyed the support of Käbin, was not acceptable to Moscow, however. The Kremlin leaders believed that Väljas would not be an efficient executor of the Russification policy in Estonia, and in 1978 the post of secretary general of the CPE was given to the completely Russified dogmatist **Karl Vaino**. With Vaino's team coming to power Väljas's career collapsed. In 1980 he was removed from the CPE leadership and sent into political exile, becoming the ambassador of the Soviet Union to Venezuela (1980–86) and Nicaragua (1986–88).

The policy pursued by Vaino led to the deterioration of the situation in Estonia. Because Vaino opposed perestroika, the government in Moscow decided to introduce personnel changes in the CPE leadership. On 16 June 1988 Väljas became the first secretary of the party CC. One of his first decisions was to support the Popular Front's efforts for equal rights for Estonia within the framework of a planned new treaty with the Soviet Union. Väljas played a key role in the drafting of the Sovereignty Declaration of 16 November 1988. Under his rule the CPE shook off the dominance of the CPSU and consequently regained the trust of nearly one-third of the people of Estonia. Perceiving a threat from the opponents of the reforms, the Estonians regarded Väljas as the defender of the interests of the Estonian SSR. However, the guidelines that in 1988 might have been seen as radical and on which his program was based proved too cautious in the following year for the increasingly bold anti-Communist opposition. As a result, CPE structures began to disintegrate beginning in December 1989. Väljas tried to keep up with the changes, evolving toward national communism and greater independence from the CPSU, but these efforts did not prevent mass resignations from the party in 1989–91; these led to the marginalization of his role. Finally, in 1991 Väljas changed the name of the remnants of the CPE to the Estonian Democratic Labor Party (Eesti Demokraatlik Tööpartei), but the party was of minor importance and failed to win even 2 percent of the vote in the elections of 1995 and 1999. (AG)

Sources: *Eesti Entsuklopeedia* vol. 14 (Tallinn, 2000); *Eesti Entsuklopeedia Kirjastus* (Tallinn, 2000); Aleksander Rahr, ed., *A Biographical Directory of 100 Leading Soviet Officials* (Boulder, Colo., 1990); Rein Taagepera, *Estonia: Return to Independence* (Boulder, Colo., 1993); Tõnu Tannberg, Matti Laur, Tõnis Lukas, Ain Mäesalu, and Ago Pajur, *History of Estonia* (Tallinn, 2000).

VALOSHYN Pavel (10 July 1891, Harkawicze, near Sokółka [now in Poland]–3 November 1937, Leningrad?), Belorussian social and political activist. Valoshyn finished six grades of a science-oriented high school. From 1908 to 1912 he worked as a telephone operator at the post office in Krynki (now in Poland). In 1912 he began serving in the Russian Army. During World War I he was taken prisoner by the Germans. At the end of 1917, searching for his family, Valoshyn went to Yekaterinoslav (Dniepropetrovsk, Ukraine), where he briefly worked as a policeman. During the Civil War in Russia Valoshyn first served in the White Russian Army, led by General Anton Denikin, and later he became a soldier in the Red Army. After the war, Valoshyn worked on the railways for one year, and in 1922 he returned to Harkawicze. He completed a Polish-language course and got a job as a telecommunications installer. Valoshyn soon joined the Belorussian Social Democratic Party, and in 1923 he became an MP in the Polish Assembly and a member of the Belorussian parliamentary representation, in which he was one of the most radical MPs. He demanded that the colonization of the Belorussian-populated territories be stopped and that the authorities approve the use of Belorussian as the language of instruction in the schools. Taking advantage of his parliamentary immunity, Valoshyn organized rallies during Orthodox Church fairs and at local markets. In 1925 he cofounded the Belorussian Peasants' and Workers' Hromada, and then he became a member of its Central Committee and represented it in the Assembly. Valoshyn organized the Hromada's district meetings in the region of Białystok, but they were usually dispersed by the police. A member of the Communist Party of Western Belorussia from December 1926 onwards, Valoshyn was arrested in February 1927, along with other Hromada leaders. In February 1927 he was sentenced to twelve years' imprisonment.

In 1932, as part of an exchange of political prisoners, Valoshyn was handed over to the Soviet authorities. For one year he was used in agitation work: he talked about the harsh situation of the working class in Poland. He later worked as deputy director of the Belorussian State Library in Minsk. In 1933 Valoshyn was arrested for being a member of a non-existent organization, the Belorussian National Center, which, according to the NKVD, was scheming to overthrow the Soviet government. In 1934 Valoshyn was sentenced to ten years in a forced labor camp on the Solovets Islands. In October 1937 he was tried again, and the court of the Leningrad NKVD sentenced him to death for spying for Poland. Valoshyn was subsequently executed by a firing squad. (EM)

Sources: *Entsyklapiedyia historyi Bielarusi*, vol. 2 (Minsk, 1994); *Encyklopedia historii Drugiej Rzeczypospolitej* (Warsaw, 1999); Nicholas P. Vakar, *Belorussia: The Making of a Nation* (Cambridge, Mass., 1956); Aleksandra Bergman, *Sprawy białoruskie w II Rzeczypospolitej* (Warsaw, 1984).

VALTERS Miķelis (7 May 1874, Liepaya [Libau, Liepāja]–27 March 1968, France), Latvian diplomat and politician. Born into a working-class family, Valters finished school in Liepaya. Early on he became involved in the patriotic and literary movement known as the New Current. Arrested in 1897, he was held in prison for fifteen months. Fearing he might be exiled far inside Russia, Valters fled to Switzerland in 1899. He studied at the University of Bern and then received a law degree from the University of Zurich. In 1905 Valters returned to Latvia. During the 1905 revolution he was the leading activist of the Union of Latvian Social Democrats and was the first to put forward a program of struggle for independence, which was contrary to the position of the influential Social Democratic Workers' Party of Latvia. Valters believed that Latvia should fight against Russia and hoped for the disintegration of Russia. After the failure of the 1905 revolution, Valters was forced to emigrate to Finland and then to Germany, Switzerland, and England. From 1909 to 1910 he studied at the Sorbonne. In 1914 he published the theoretical treatise *Mūsu tautības jautājums* (The question of our nationality). In May 1917 Valters returned to Latvia and was one of the founders and theorists of the newly established Peasant Union. From November 1918 to August 1919 Valters served as minister of home affairs in the first government of **Kārlis Ulmanis**. On 16 April 1919, during the German coup, Valters was briefly detained in Liepāja. Valters was an envoy to Italy (1920–24) and France (1924–25), consul general in Königsberg, Germany (now Kaliningrad, Russia) (1925–34), and envoy to Poland (1934–37) and Belgium (1937–40). After the German Army invaded Belgium, Valters moved to Switzerland and then to France, where he lived until the end of his life. Valters's publications include *Lettland* (Latvia; 1923), *Baltengedanken und Baltenpolitik* (1926), *Das Verbrechen gegen die baltischen Staaten* (1962), and collections of poems and memoirs. (EJ)

Sources: J. Lapiņš, "Miķeļa Valtera dzīve un darbi," *Piesaule*, 1930, no. 10; Žanis Unāms, *Laiku atspulgā* (Oldenburg, 1953); Mikelis Valters, *Atmiņas un domas: Trimdas rakstnieki* (Kemptene, 1947); Žanis Unāms, "Pie Latvijas šūpuļa," *Laiks*, 6 May 1959; E. Andersons, "Dr. Miķelis Valters," *Jaunā Gaita*, 1968, no. 69; Miķelis Valters, *Atmiņas un sapņi* (Stockholm, 1969); Ā. Šilde, "Miris vientuļais cīnītājs," *Laiks*, 3 April 1968; Andrejs Plakans, *Historical Dictionary of Latvia* (Lanham, Md., 1997).

VANAGS Jānis (25 May 1958, Liepāja), archbishop of the Evangelical Lutheran Church of Latvia (ELCL). Vanags passed his high school final examinations in Liepāja. He subsequently graduated from the Department of Chemistry of the Latvian State University in 1982 and from a seminary in 1985. In 1982–85 Vanags worked as a chemistry teacher at a high school in Riga. Ordained a pastor in 1985, he served in St. John Lutheran Church in Saldus until 1993. Because under Soviet rule the Latvians had become largely atheistic, at the time of the revival of Latvian statehood Vanags actively helped to strengthen moral and religious values, particularly among the youth, by founding the Latvian Christian Movement for Rebirth and Renewal. In 1993 he was elected archbishop of the ELCL. An adviser to the Ministry of Justice and the founder of the Lutheran Academy in Riga, Vanags has received prestigious national awards, and in 1997 he was awarded an honorary doctorate by Concordia University, Fort Wayne, in the United States. Vanags actively opposes the ordination of women into the Lutheran Church. (EJ)

Sources: *Who Is Who in Latvia* (Riga, 2000); www.kwasizabantu.com/Ministers_conference/2001/vanags_cv_eng.htm.

VAPTSAROV Nikola (24 November 1909, Bansko–23 July 1943, Sofia), Bulgarian poet and Communist activist of Macedonian descent. Vaptsarov studied at the Varna Polytechnic College, and from 1933 he worked as an engineer, specializing in shipbuilding. In 1934 he joined the illegal Bulgarian Communist Party. He was also a co-founder of the Macedonian Literary Circle in Sofia (1938). In 1941 Vaptsarov was active in the military section of the BCP, responsible for sabotage, in which he took part. Arrested in March 1942, he was sentenced to death and executed. Postwar Bulgarian Communist authorities launched a cult of Vaptsarov as an activist and revolutionary poet, and his collection *Motorni pesni* (Motor songs; 1940), close to the style of Vladimir Mayakovski, was presented as a model of "proletarian" literature. Vaptsarov was also widely published in other Soviet bloc countries. (WR)

Sources: *Entsyklopediya Bulgariya*, vol. 1 (Sofia, 1978); *Mały słownik pisarzy zachodnio-słowiańskich i południowo-słowiańskich* (Warsaw, 1973); Raymond Detrez, *Historical Dictionary of Bulgaria* (Lanham, Md., 1997).

VARES Johannes, pen name "Barbarus" (12 January 1890, Heimtali–29 November 1946, Tallinn), Estonian poet and politician. In 1917 Vares graduated from the Medical School of Kiev University. At that time he was a member of the Siuru poetry group (named after a mythical bird). From 1920 to 1939 he worked as a doctor in Pärnu and then in Tallinn. He also wrote poems and published successive volumes of poetry. In 1918 Vares published the first volume, *Fata Morgana*, followed by *Inimene ja sfinks* (Man and the Sphinx; 1919) and *Katastroofid* (1920; Disasters; 1920). Sensuous poems gradually gave way to more philosophical and allegorical poems, as seen in the collections *Geomeetriline inimene* (Geometric man; 1924); *Multiplitseerit inimene* (Multiplied man; 1927); *Tulipunkt* (Focus; 1934); *Memento* (1936); and *Üle läve* (Over the threshold; 1939). His poetry reflected his philosophy of pessimism.

In his circles Vares was known for his leftist views, but he was not involved in overt political activities. After the Red Army invaded Estonia in mid-June 1940, the special envoy of the Kremlin, Andrey Zhdanov, demanded that President **Konstantin Päts** appointed Vares as prime minister. After some delay and a display of military might by the Soviets, Päts yielded to this demand, and on 22 June 1940 Vares became the head of government. The composition of his cabinet, including the appointment of history professor **Hans Kruus** as deputy prime minister, was decided by Zhdanov. Vares reportedly initially strove to attain a status for Estonia similar to that of Mongolia—that is, that of an external satellite. However, he then yielded to the Soviets without major qualms and on 22 July 1940 put forward a motion that Estonia be incorporated into the Soviet Union. After the Estonian SSR was established in August 1940, Vares became chairman of its Supreme Soviet. His government conducted purges in the state and local government administrations and disbanded most social organizations and political parties, except for the Communist Party of Estonia. Vares endorsed three waves of deportations of Estonians far into the Soviet Union, during which thousands of Estonians lost their lives. After German troops occupied Estonia in June and July 1941, Vares went to the Soviet Union. In 1944 he published his last collection of propaganda poems, *Rindeteedel* (Way to the front). At the beginning of 1945 Vares returned to

Estonia and resumed the post of chairman of the Supreme Soviet of the Estonian SSR. He also served as a member of the Politburo of the Central Committee of the Estonian party. In November 1946 Vares allegedly committed suicide, but there are suspicions that his death was staged by the Soviet security services. (WR)

Sources: Hendrik Adamson, *Väike luuleraamat* (Tallinn, 1965); R. Hinrikus, *J. Barbaruse ja L. Toomi kirjavahetusested* (Tallinn, 1984); Toivo Raun, *Estonia and the Estonians* (Stanford, 1991); Rein Taagepera, *Estonia: Return to Independence* (Boulder, Colo., 1993); Jan Lewandowski, *Estonia* (Warsaw, 2001); http://www.sada.ee.

VARGA Béla (18 February 1903, Börcs–13 October 1995, Budapest), Hungarian priest and politician. Varga was born into a peasant family. As a student of a Benedictine gymnasium in Györ, in 1921 he joined insurgents who wanted to capture the town of Sopron, which was initially granted to Austria under a peace treaty. The action took place before a referendum that decided in favor of Hungary and, as a result, Sopron and its surrounding area went to Hungary. In 1921 Varga participated in Charles IV Habsburg's attempt to return to the Hungarian throne. After graduating from high school in 1922, Varga completed studies in the Roman Catholic Theological College in Veszprém, and in 1926 he was ordained. Varga served as curate in Somlóvásárhely and in Várpalota, and from 1929 he was a presbyter in Balatonboglár. He was friends with a well-known politician and landowner, **Gaston Gaál**, who was head of a local organization of the Independent Smallholders' Party (ISP). In 1931 Varga joined the ISP; from 1937 he was its deputy president, and in 1943 he served as president of its civic platform. In 1939 Varga entered parliament, where he voted against the new anti-Jewish law. The same year he was elected to a committee that was appointed by the Episcopate and aimed at supporting Catholics of Jewish origin.

After the German attack against Poland in 1939, at the request of Prime Minister **Pál Teleki**, Varga very actively participated in relief efforts for Polish refugees, maintaining contacts with Edmund Fietowicz, a representative of the Polish government to Hungary. In Balatonboglár, Varga established a Polish gymnasium, at that time the largest Polish secondary school in Europe; in it around eight hundred students had passed final examinations (*matura*) by 1944. He also helped French and Jewish refugees. Risking his life, Varga helped Polish couriers who went from Poland to London via Hungary. Varga was the first in Hungary to publish the results of an International Red Cross committee investigation that proved that the Katyń Forrest Massacre had been committed by NKVD units.

Varga rescued the son of future Polish prime minister **Stanisław Mikołajczyk** from the Gestapo. In 1943 Varga signed an ISP anti-war memorandum addressed to Prime Minister **Miklós Kállay**, and he also took part in a famous anti-war meeting in Balatonszárszó. Varga supported a parliamentary alliance with the Social Democrats. After the seizure of Hungary by Germany in March 1944, Varga went into hiding at a monastery in the countryside and later in Budapest. At the beginning of 1945 he was arrested by the Soviet authorities, and he accidentally escaped execution at the hands of the NKVD.

From February 1945 Varga was president of the ISP in Budapest, and from August he was deputy president of the party and a member of its Political Bureau. From April 1945 he was a deputy to the Provisional National Assembly. In the parliamentary elections of November 1945 Varga defeated the head of the Communist Party, **Mátyás Rákosi**, in his constituency. From February 1946 Varga was president of the National Assembly. After **Ferenc Nagy** was forced to resign as prime minister in May 1947, on 1 June Varga went to the West, fearing arrest by the Communists. The same month he was deprived of his Hungarian citizenship. He settled in New York and became a clergyman for the Congregation of Sisters of God's Love, which consisted mainly of Hungarian nuns. In 1949 Varga formed the Hungarian National Committee and became its president. In 1955 he was appointed a prelate of the Pope. Varga co-created the Hungarian section of Radio Free Europe. Within the framework of the Green International he worked closely with Mikołajczyk, and he received a high decoration from the Polish government-in-exile. During the uprising of 1956 Varga warned the Security Council of the UN about the Soviet invasion, but the Western powers did not recognize his right to represent Hungary. From 1960 Varga headed the Hungarian Committee in exile, which also included some leaders of the uprising. In May 1990, trying to emphasize the continuity of Hungarian democratic traditions, Varga took part in the inaugural session of the Hungarian parliament, elected in free elections. In 1991 he returned to Hungary. His house became a place of pilgrimage for Poles. Varga published *Genocide by Deportation* (1951). (JT)

Sources: *Time*, 8 February 1960; Tibor Szy, ed. *Hungarians in America* (New York, 1966); György Haas, "A menekültek patrónusa, Varga Béla," *Vigilia*, 1993, no. 3; *Ki kicsoda 1994* (Budapest, 1994); Károly Kapronczay, "Szabad és független Magyarországról álmodtunk," *Valóság*, 1995, no. 12.

VARNAVA [originally Petar Rosić] (29 August 1880, Pljevlja, Montenegro–24 July 1937, Belgrade), Patriarch of Serbia. The son of an agricultural laborer, after finishing primary school in Pljevlja, Varnava studied at a teacher training college and at a seminary in Prizren until 1898–99. In 1900 he received a scholarship funded by the Russian Orthodox Church, and from 1900 to 1905 he studied at the St. Petersburg Theological Academy, where, among other things, he attended lectures by the writer and philosopher Dmitry Merezhkovsky. In 1905 Varnava joined a religious order. In the same year he was named hierodeacon and then hieromonach. From 1905 to 1910 he worked as a clergyman in Istanbul, where he taught at a local Serbian school and contributed to the local newspaper, *Carigradski glasnik*. During a visit by the king of Serbia, **Peter I Karadjordjević**, to Patriarch Joachim III, Varnava was elevated to bishop and appointed head of the newly created eparchy of Debar-Veles, with its seat in Kičevo. Varnava's successes in establishing the Serbian Church conflicted with the interests of the Bulgarian exarchate. In 1917 he again went to Russia to seek support for a struggling Serbia and to conduct propaganda efforts. During the February 1917 revolution Varnava was in Petrograd. In November 1920 he was granted the bishopric of Skopje, which was under the jurisdiction of the patriarchate in Belgrade. His work played a great role in the revival of spiritual life in Macedonia.

Varnava's elevation to the patriarch of Serbia on 12 April 1930 occurred under complicated circumstances. A conflict with the Yugoslav government over the ratification of a concordat with the Vatican, which Varnava firmly opposed, ended in the 1937 excommunication of Prime Minister **Milan Stojadinović** and all the deputies to the Skupština (parliament) who had voted for the adoption of the concordat. This conflict further escalated when the prime minister expelled all opponents of the concordat from the ruling party and Varnava suddenly died. The public suspected that his death had been arranged by government agents, who were even suspected of poisoning Varnava. Under the circumstances Stojadinović abandoned plans to resume the debate on the matter; consequently, the status of the Catholic Church in Yugoslavia remained unregulated. Under Varnava's patriarchate a modern school of theology was established in Belgrade, and new rules for the spiritual and intellectual formation of clergymen were introduced. Religious and theological journalism flourished. Varnava introduced innovative methods of pastoral work, such as parish missions and the military ordinariate. He improved relations with other Orthodox Churches, particularly those in Romania and Bulgaria (the 1934 Declaration of Rila and the 1936 Declaration of Ohrid). He also supported the Russian Orthodox Church in exile, which settled in Sremski Karlovci, Yugoslavia, and continued its work there. Negotiations with the Slovenes were successful, so the Orthodox community could return to Ljubljana. Under Varnava's patriarchate many new churches were built, and an icon-painting school was found in Rakovica. (AG)

Sources: *Biographisches Lexikon*, vol. 4; *Threskeutike kai ethike enkyklopaideia*, vol. 3 (Athens, 1963); Djoko Slijepčević, *Istorija srpske pravoslavne crkve*, vol. 2 (Munich, 1966); Milan Mladenović, ed. *Memoari patrijarha srpskog Gavrila* (Paris, 1974); Wacław Felczak and Tadeusz Wasilewski, *Historia Jugosławii* (Wrocław, 1985).

VARONKA Yazep (17 April 1891, Sokółka County–4 June 1952, Chicago), Belorussian political activist and journalist. From 1909 to 1914 Varonka studied at the university in St. Petersburg. At the beginning of 1917 he joined the Belorussian Socialist Hromada, and from June 1917 he was a member of its Central Committee. He simultaneously headed the Belorussian Relief Committee for War Victims. At a meeting of the Great Belorussian Council, which was created from the Central Council of the Belorussian Parties and Organizations, in October 1917 Varonka pressed for autonomy for Belorussia. He co-initiated the First All-Belorussian Congress in December 1917 and was president of the Executive Committee (EC) of the Council of the Congress and head of the council's Foreign Department. Between February and July 1918 Varonka chaired the People's Secretariat of Belorussia, which was appointed by the EC, and he co-initiated the proclamation of the Belorussian People's Republic in March 1918. Varonka was editor-in-chief of the newspaper *Belaruskaia ziamla* and the periodical *Varta*. From the end of 1918 he oriented himself toward the Lithuanian Taryba (Council), seeing it as an ally in the struggle for Belorussian statehood. Varonka considered Poland and Russia as opponents of Belorussia's independence. From December 1918 to October 1920 Varonka was minister for Belorussian affairs in the government of Lithuania. He was also leader of the Belorussian Party of Socialists-Federalists. From November 1922 he served as president of the Belorussian Hromada in Kaunas. Varonka was the author of *Belorusskii vopros k momentu Versalskoi mirnoi konferentsii: Istor-politicheski ocherk* (The Belorussian question at the Versailles Conference: Historical and political outline; 1919) and *Bialoruski rukh ad 1917 da 1920 hodu: Karotki ahlad* (The Belorussian movement between 1917 and 1920: A short review; 1920). Varonka also wrote many historical and political essays, in which he described the development of the Belorussian national movement during World War I, as well as during the Bolshevik revolution, and he analyzed the current political situation. In 1923 Varonka left for the United States and

settled in Chicago. In the United States, he was one of the founders of the Belorussian movement in exile and headed the Belorussian-American Association. (AS/SA)

Sources: *Belarus: Entsyklapedychny daviednik* (Minsk, 1995).

VAS Zoltán (30 March 1903, Budapest–13 August 1983, Budapest), Hungarian Communist activist. While a gymnasium student, Vas joined the Communist Party. In 1919, under the Hungarian Soviet Republic, he was a party agitator. Arrested in 1921, he was subsequently handed over to Soviet Russia as part of an exchange of prisoners of war. Vas returned to Hungary in 1924, becoming secretary of an illegal Communist youth union. Arrested one year later, he was sentenced to sixteen years' imprisonment, but in 1940 he was exchanged (along with **Mátyás Rákosi**) for Hungarian flags taken by the Russian Army during the Springtime of Nations. He then went to the Soviet Union. Vas came back to Hungary in 1944 as one of the founders and leaders of the new political system. In 1945 he served as commissar for supplies for Budapest, and he became mayor of Budapest. From 1946 to 1949 Vas was secretary of the Supreme Economic Council. He then held the post of president of the State Planning Office (until 1953). From 1945 to 1956 he was a member of the Central Committee (CC) of the Hungarian Communist Party (HCP) and later a member of the Hungarian Workers' Party (HWP). From 1948 to 1953 he was a deputy member and then a full member of the HWP CC Politburo.

After the death of Stalin in 1953, Vas was dismissed from his prominent party and governmental positions and was appointed director of a group of coal mining enterprises based in Komló. In 1954 he returned to Budapest to become head of the secretariat of the Council of Ministers, and then he took the post of deputy minister of trade. During the 1956 revolution, Vas was one of the closest associates of **Imre Nagy**, responsible for supplies in Nagy's government. After Soviet troops occupied Budapest, Vas took refuge in the Yugoslav Embassy. Given guarantees of personal safety, he left the embassy building, but the Soviet Union reneged on the guarantees, and in December 1956 Vas and other members of Nagy's group were deported to Romania, where they were interned. Unlike the others, though, Vas was not brought to trial and was not convicted. In August 1958 he returned to Hungary, where he was forced to retire. He then devoted himself to writing historical works and memoirs. Vas published two volumes of memoirs: *Viszontagságos életem* (My stormy life; 1979) and *Akkori önmagamról* (About myself at that time; 1982). A third volume, which included an interesting account of the struggle for power in the Communist ranks after World War II, was not allowed to be published. It was published in fragments from the end of the 1980s onwards and caused quite a sensation, increasing the democratic and pro-independence tendencies among Hungarians. It was published as *Betiltott könyveim* (My banned book) in 1990. (MS)

Sources: *Magyarország 1944–1956*, CD-ROM (Budapest, 2001); Ferenc Nagy, *The Struggle behind the Iron Curtain* (New York, 1948); László Zöldi, "Az emlékezések ködei," *Napjaink*, 1981, no. 9; Klaus-Deytlev Grothusen, ed., *Ungarn* (Göttingen, 1987); Judit Ember, *Menedék jog–1956: A Nagy Imre-csoport elrablása* (Budapest, 1989).

VÁSÁRHELYI Miklós (9 October 1917, Fiume [Rijeka]–31 July 2001, Budapest), Hungarian Communist activist, one of the leaders of the 1956 revolution. Born into a middle-class family, from 1936 to 1937 Vásárhelyi studied law at a university in Rome, where he became interested in Fascist ideas. From 1939 to 1942 he continued his law studies in Debrecen. In 1938 he joined the illegal Hungarian Communist Party (HCP). During World War II he was called into the labor service and worked at a munitions factory. In 1944 he joined the military resistance movement. In 1945 Vásárhelyi began working for *Szabad Nép*, the central press organ of the HCP. From 1951 he was an editor of the periodical *Művelt Nép* and the editor-in-chief of the periodical *Hungary-Vengriya* (1952–54); from May 1954 he was deputy head of the Information Office of the Council of Ministers. One of the closest associates of Prime Minister **Imre Nagy**, Vásárhelyi was dismissed from his position after Nagy was removed from office in April 1955. In May 1955 Vásárhelyi was given a party reprimand because he had demanded an explanation regarding Hungarian-Yugoslav relations and a review of the sentences passed in the trial of **László Rajk**. In October 1955 Vásárhelyi was a signatory of a memorandum presented to the Central Committee of the Hungarian Workers' Party (HWP) by writers protesting the tightening of party controls over culture. Because of this, he was expelled from the HWP in December 1955.

On 1 November 1956, during the revolution, Vásárhelyi became head of the press bureau of Nagy's government. On 23 November, along with other members of Nagy's group, he was interned in Romania. On 10 April 1957 Vásárhelyi was brought back to Hungary, and on 15 June 1958, in the trial of Nagy and his associates, he was sentenced to five years' imprisonment by the Supreme Court. Released in April 1960 under an amnesty, Vásárhelyi began working as a lecturer in 1961 and then as a supplies officer. From 1972 to 1990 he was a researcher at the Institute of Literary Studies of the Hungarian Academy of Sciences. He concentrated on the history of the press. In 1979 Vásárhelyi signed a declaration of the newly established Hungarian opposition expressing solidarity with the imprisoned members of Charter 77, a Czechoslovak human rights defense movement. From 1984 until the end of his life he served as a personal representative of **George Soros** in the Soros Foundation in Hungary. He was also president of this foundation. In 1985 Vásárhelyi co-organized the only meeting of all opposition movements in Monor. He was a founding member (1988) and president (until 1992) of the Committee for Historical Justice, which set itself the task of bringing about a ceremonial reburial of Nagy, his associates, and all victims of the 1956 revolution. On 16 June 1989 Vásárhelyi spoke at the solemn funeral for Nagy and his associates. From 1988 to 1989 he co-founded the liberal Alliance of Free Democrats (AFD), and in 1990 he became a member of its National Council. From 1990 to 1994 Vásárhelyi served as a member of parliament on the AFD ticket. (JT)

Sources: *A magyar forradalom és szabadságharc enciklopédiája*, CD-ROM (Budapest, 1999); *Ki kicsoda 2000* (Budapest, 2001); Paul Ignotus, *Hungary* (London, 1972); György Litván, ed., *Rewolucja węgierska 1956 roku* (Warsaw, 1996).

VASILE Radu (10 October 1942, Sibiu), Romanian politician. In 1967 Vasile graduated with a bachelor's degree from the Department of History of the University of Bucharest. From 1967 to 1969 he worked at the Village Museum in Bucharest, and from 1969 to 1972 he was a researcher at the Nicolae Iorga Institute of History of the Romanian Academy of Sciences. Vasile continued his career at the Bucharest Academy of Economic Studies. In 1993 he became a professor. A member of the Christian Democratic National Peasants' Party (Partidul Naţional Ţărănesc Creştin Democrat [CDNPP]) since 1990, Vasile served as its spokesman for economic reforms, deputy chairman (1990–92), and secretary general (1996–98). In 1996 he became a senator and served as deputy speaker of the Senate from 1996 to 1998. From 1997 to 1998 Vasile represented the Romanian parliament in the Council of Europe. On 17 April 1998 he became prime minister. Under his government, economic stagnation in Romania continued, and the social crisis culminated in a protest march on Bucharest by the Jiu Valley coal miners (January 1999), with clashes with the police along the way. Because the opposition parties supported the miners' protest (known as the *mineriada*), President **Emil Constantinescu** and Vasile entered into negotiations with the miners, and Vasile signed a negotiated agreement with the miners' leader, Miron Cozma, at the Cozia Monastery. When the miners broke this agreement, the government used force. Cozma was arrested and sentenced to eighteen years' imprisonment, and the next *mineriada* was suppressed with repressive measures. Social unrest continued, and in March 1999 Vasile suffered a heart attack. Finally, on 17 December 1999 he resigned as a result of conflicts within the ruling coalition, formed by the PNȚCD and the Democratic Party, led by **Petru Roman**. In February 2000 Vasile went over to the Romanian National Party (Partidul Național Român). In the elections of November 2000 he won a senatorial seat on the ticket of the Democratic Party (Partidul Democrat). (AB)

Sources: Stan Stoica, *România: O istorie cronologică 1989–2002* (Bucharest, 2002); *Enciclopedia de istorie a României*, (Bucharest, 2002); Bugajski; romania-on-line.net/whoswho/VasileRadu.htm.

VASILYEV Yordan (26 September 1935, Radomir), Bulgarian literary scholar, writer, and politician. Vasilyev is the son of a rich doctor persecuted by the Communist regime after World War II. In 1948 his family was forced to move to Troyan, where Vasilyev graduated from a gymnasium. He studied Bulgarian philology at Sofia University. Expelled in his fourth year for political reasons, he finally graduated in 1959. Vasilyev worked as a literary critic for the periodicals *Septemvri* (1966–67), *Literaturna misul* (1969–75), and *Letopisy* (1989–90). He was dismissed from work several times, among other reasons for contacts with Bulgarian activists of the interwar period. These contacts shaped Vasilyev's independent attitude as a researcher and as a person. In 1967 he married the poet **Blaga Dimitrova**. Their shared literary interests subsequently led to opposition work. Dismissed from the editorial staff of the periodical *Literaturna misul*, Vasilyev found employment at the Institute of Literature of the Bulgarian Academy of Sciences (BAS), where he was a member of a team dealing with periodicals; as a result, he gained an encyclopedic knowledge of Bulgarian history, literature, and public life. Vasilyev earned a doctorate in 1988 and became an associate professor at the BAS in 1990. In November 1988 he co-founded the dissident Club for the Support of Glasnost and Perestroika. In the spring of 1989, along with Dimitrova, Vasilyev stood up in defense of the Bulgarian Turks, who were being forced to emigrate. Vasilyev was repeatedly arrested by the security services for statements he gave to the foreign media. At the end of 1989 he became active in the Union of Democratic Forces (UDF). He co-founded *Demokratsiia*, the first independent newspaper, and served as its editor-in-chief from 1990 to 1991. In the 1990 elections to the National Assembly Vasilyev defeated General **Dobri Dzhurov**. In May 1991 he took part in a hunger strike in protest against the adoption of a new constitution. In the next parliament, Vasilyev served as chairman of a committee for national security, and in this capacity he visited NATO headquarters in Brussels in 1991. Vasilyev was chairman of the BAS General Assembly from 1991 to 1995 and a member of the BAS Executive Council from 1996 to 1998. Vasilyev's publications include books about Ivan Khadzhiiski (1988) and Khristo Radevski (1993) and the memoirs *Patila i radosti* (Miseries and joys; 2002). (WDj)

Sources: *Koy koy e v bulgarskata kultura* (Sofia, 1998).

VASYLENKO Mykola (14 February 1866, Esman, Chernihiv region–3 October 1935, Kiev?), Ukrainian lawyer and politician. From 1885 to 1890 Vasylenko studied medicine, history, and philology at the university in Dorpat (Yuryev, Tartu). He subsequently taught at a gymnasium in Kiev, worked in the Russian Ministry of Interior (1902–5), and edited the periodical *Kievskiye otkliki*. In 1907 he was arrested for "disloyalty." After his release, Vasylenko took up legal studies, which he completed in 1907 in Odessa. He worked as an attorney and was active in the Russian Constitutional Democratic Party. After the February 1917 revolution, Vasylenko briefly served as deputy minister of education in Petrograd. In January 1918 he became a member of the board of the Ukrainian Supreme Court. He then served as prime minister and minister of education in the government of Hetman **Pavlo Skoropadskyi**. In August 1918 he also became speaker of the senate. Vasylenko contributed to the foundation of Ukrainian state universities in Kiev and Kamenets-Podolsky (Kamyanets Podilskyi), the Ukrainian Academy of Sciences (UAS), and the National Library. After the overthrow of the hetman's government, Vasylenko retired from politics and devoted himself to science. After the Bolshevik government was established (1920), he was elected president of the UAS but was not approved by the Bolsheviks. He was allowed to head the UAS Socioeconomic Department. In 1924 Vasylenko was arrested and sentenced to ten years' imprisonment but was released under an amnesty. In 1929 he was dismissed from all his positions in the UAS. A ban was placed on the publication of his works, and then Vasylenko was arrested again. He probably perished in prison. Vasylenko edited *Materialy dlia istorii ekonomicheskogo, iuridicheskogo i obshchestvennogo byta staroy Malorossii* (Materials on the history of the economic, legal, and social life of Old Little Russia, 3 vols.; 1901–8); many volumes of source documents for the study of Ukrainian law during the time of the Republic of Poland; *Ocherki po istorii Zapadnoy Rusi i Ukrainy* (Studies in the history of Western Rus and Ukraine; 1916); and

Materialy do istorii ukraiinskoho prava (Source documents for the study of Ukrainian law; 1929). (WR)

Sources: Volodymyr Kubijovyč, ed., *Ukraine: A Concise Encyclopedia*, vols. 1–2 (Toronto, 1971); *Encyclopedia of Ukraine*, vol. 5 (Toronto, 1993).

VASYLKO Mykola (21 March 1868, Czernowitz, Austria-Hungary [Cernăuţi, Chernivtsi]–2 August 1924, Bad Reichenhall, Germany), Ukrainian politician from Bukovina. A landowner and a descendant of Bukovinian nobles, Vasylko studied at the Theresianum in Vienna. Later he served as mayor of Łukawiec, near Wyżnica (now Lukavets, near Vyzhnytsya), and later he was elected to the local Bukovinian diet. From 1898 to 1918 he was an MP in the parliament in Vienna and deputy chairman of the Ukrainian parliamentary representation. Vasylko was granted the title of baron. He often defended the rights of the Ukrainians from Bukovina. Along with the leaders of Bukovinian Romanians, Jews, and Armenians, he extracted many concessions from the Austrian authorities. As a result of his efforts, an unpopular governor of the province was dismissed in 1903, and then a Ukrainian high school was founded in Vyzhnytsya. Vasylko was one of the founders of the Hutsul Bukovinian Battalion, a volunteer unit that fought alongside the Austro-Hungarian Army from 1915 to 1916. He was one of the supporters of the so-called Austro-Ukrainian solution, hoping that if the Central Powers won the war, it would be possible to unite Eastern Galicia, Bukovina, Volhynia, and Podolia into an autonomous state within the Habsburg empire. After the outbreak of World War I, Vasylko co-founded the General Ukrainian Council (Zahalna Ukraiinska Rada) in Lemberg (Lwów, Lviv) in August 1914. He also organized assistance to war refugees and the victims of military operations. He took part in the negotiations that led to the signature of the Treaty of Brest-Litovsk between Bolshevik Russia and the Central Powers (March 1918). He served as a representative of the Western Ukrainian National Republic in Austria (1918–19) and in Switzerland and Germany (1919–24). Vasylko published *Posolska diyatilnist v Derzhavniy Radi i Kraievym Soymi v rokakh 1901–3* (Parliamentary work in the Council of State and the Provincial Parliament from 1901 to 1903; 1904). (WR)

Sources: Volodymyr Kubijovyč, ed., *Ukraine: A Concise Encyclopedia*, vols. 1–2 (Toronto, 1971); *Encyclopedia of Ukraine*, vol. 5 (Toronto, 1993).

VAZOV Ivan (27 June 1850, Sopot, Bulgaria–22 September 1921, Sofia), Bulgarian writer, poet, and political activist. Born into the family of a rich trader, Vazov studied in a school of commerce. He made his debut as a writer in 1870. In the 1870s he became involved in the national liberation movement among the Bulgarian émigrés in Romania. He took part in the 1876 uprising. After the outbreak of the Russo-Turkish war in 1877, Vazov returned to Bulgaria with the Russian Army. After Bulgaria gained autonomy in 1878, he held various administrative positions in the Principality of Bulgaria and served as a deputy to the Provincial Assembly of Eastern Rumelia. When Stefan Stambolov assumed power in 1886, following the unification of Bulgaria with Eastern Rumelia, Vazov, a confirmed Russophile, thought it best to leave Bulgaria. He found refuge in Istanbul and then in Odessa, where he devoted himself to literary work. In 1889 he returned to Bulgaria and settled in Sofia. After Stambolov's fall in 1894, Vazov twice served as a deputy to the National Assembly (in 1894 and 1896). From 1897 to 1899 he served as minister of culture and education and then retired from public life but continued writing. The celebration of fifty years of his work as a writer in 1920 turned into a national demonstration.

Vazov was a prolific poet, short story writer, novelist, and playwright. He introduced the achievements of modern European style into Bulgarian literature, but his artistic design, requiring that literature be realistic and national in character, to some extent set him apart from the European modernists. Vazov's best novels and short stories deal with the Bulgarian nation's struggle for liberation from the Turkish yoke at the end of the nineteenth century and combine elements of realism with patriotic romanticism. Vazov's work was regarded as a continuation of the work of Khristo Botev. Vazov's most famous novel, the two-volume *Pod igoto* (1889–90; *Under the Yoke*, 1894), describes the 1876 uprising, and the novel *Nemili—nedragi* (Unloved and unwanted; 1881) portrays the life of Bulgarian émigrés. Vazov also published many other historical novels, including *Kazalarskata Tsaritsa* (The empress of Kazalar; 1903) and *Ivan Aleksandur* (Ivan Alexander; 1907); several poetry collections, including *Izbavlenie* (Salvation; 1878), *Polia i gori* (Fields and mountains; 1884); and *Lulaka mi zamirisa* (I smelled lilac; 1919); the drama *Kum propast* (Toward the abyss; 1910); as well as collections of stories. Vazov's writing has become part of the canon of twentieth-century Bulgarian literature. (WR)

Sources: *Entsiklopediya Bulgariya*, vol. 1 (Sofia, 1978); Milena Tsaneva, *Ivan Vazov v Plovdiv* (Sofia, 1966); E. Możejko, *Iwan Wazow* (Warsaw, 1967); Iliia Boiadzhiev, *Iz zhivota i tvorchestvo na Ivan Vazov* (Sofia, 1968); *Mały słownik pisarzy zachodnio-słowiańskich i południowo-słowiańskich* (Warsaw, 1973); Raymond Detrez, *Historical Dictionary of Bulgaria* (Lanham, Md., 1997).

VEIMER Arnold (20 June 1903, Nehatu–3 March 1977, Tallinn), Estonian Communist activist. Born into the family of an agricultural laborer, Veimer became involved in revolutionary activities in his youth, and in 1922 he joined the Communist Party. After his participatiin an attempted Communist coup d'état in Tallinn (December 1924), Veimer was sentenced to life imprisonment. Released under an amnesty in 1938, he again became involved in party activities. After the Soviet invasion in June 1940, Veimer began a meteoric career. After the "elections" of July 1940, he became a deputy to the People's Assembly, which was then transformed into the Supreme Council of the Estonian SSR. In August 1940 Veimer became the people's commissar of light industry, and at the beginning of 1941 he joined the Central Committee (CC) of the Communist Party (Bolshevik) of Estonia (CP[B]E). He also received a diploma from the Department of Economics of Tartu University. After the Germans occupied Estonia, Veimer was evacuated to the Soviet Union. In 1944, after Estonia was again occupied by Soviet troops, he returned to Tallinn. He became chairman of the Council of People's Commissars of the Estonian SSR, which was transformed into the Council of Ministers of the Estonian SSR in 1946. In March 1951, as part of a purge campaign, Veimer was replaced by **Aleksei Müürisepp**, who was totally Russified. Veimer became director of the Economics and Law Institute of the Academy of Sciences of the Estonian SSR. As a result of the Khrushchev's "thaw," Veimer was appointed chairman of the People's Economic Council of the Supreme Soviet of the Estonian SSR (1957–65) and then deputy prime minister of the republic (1955–68). He was also reinstated to membership in the CC of the Communist Party of Estonia (1958–76) and the Supreme Soviet of the Estonian SSR (1958–77). Throughout this time Veimer pursued an academic career, becoming a member of the Academy of Sciences of the Estonian SSR in 1967 and serving as its chairman from 1968 to 1973. However, he merely wrote clichéd papers on economic problems of the Estonian SSR. (AG)

Sources: *Bolshaia Sovetskaia Entsiklopediia*, vol. 4 (Moscow, 1971); *Eesti Entsuklopeedia*, vol. 14 (Tallinn, 2000).

VELCHEV Damian (20 February 1883, Gabrovo–25 January 1954, France), Bulgarian general and politician. In 1903 Velchev graduated from a military school in Sofia. He served in the Bulgarian Army during both Balkan Wars and in World War I. After the end of World War I Velchev was one of the leading organizers, in addition to **Kimon Georgiev**, of the secret Military League (1919), the secret nationalist Officers' League, and the political group called Zveno (Link), for which he was expelled from the army in February 1921. In June 1923 Velchev was one of the main organizers of the coup that overthrew the dictatorial rule of **Aleksandur Stamboliyski**. From 1923 he was deputy commander and from 1927 commander of the Military Academy in Sofia. In 1928 he was again expelled from the army because of his conflict with the war minister, General Ivan Vylkov. In 1929 Velchev initiated the reestablishment of the Military League, which had been dissolved after the coup. From 1928 he studied at Sofia University, and in 1932 he graduated in law. At the beginning of the 1930s Velchev was head of the League of Reserve Army Officers. He returned to active politics in 1933, and he played a key role in preparing and staging a military coup in May 1934. The coup overthrew the democratic government of **Nikola Mushanov** and established a military cabinet. Velchev refused to become prime minister, so the post was assumed by Georgiev. The government abolished all political parties, imposed censorship, and took action against the Internal Macedonian Revolutionary Organization (IMRO). As the result of a counteroffensive by royalist forces, the dictatorship of Tsar **Boris III** was established. In July 1935 Velchev left for Yugoslavia, where he directed activities against Tsar Boris. When in October 1935 Velchev attempted to return to the country, he was arrested at the border, tried, and on 22 February 1936 sentenced to death. His sentence was commuted to life imprisonment. In 1940 he was released under an amnesty.

During World War II Velchev began to associate with the Communists, deluding himself into believing that an agreement with the USSR would allow Bulgaria to become independent from Germany and to preserve its sovereignty at the same time. He supported the participation of the Zveno group in the Fatherland Front, formed in the summer of 1942 with the Communists, Peasant Party members from the group called Pladne, and the Socialist left. Velchev played a key role in organizing the Sofia coup of 9 September 1944. The coup toppled the government of **Konstantin Muraviev**. In the new cabinet, headed by Georgiev, Velchev became minister of defense. After some hesitation he condoned the bloody purge of the army command and accepted the subjection of the army to the control of Soviet political commissars; he also condoned sending Bulgarian soldiers to the front in Austria and Hungary. In May 1945 Velchev was promoted to colonel general (the highest general rank in Bulgaria). After the end of the war he appointed General Ivan Kinov, a Bulgarian with Soviet citizenship, as head of staff. Velchev also had to sanction another purge of around three thousand Bulgarian officers and to approve the replacement of those officers by two thousand Soviet officers. However, as the Bulgarian Communists steadily consolidated their position, from 1945 Velchev became their main target.

The Communists tortured his personal secretary to death, trying to extort testimony against Velchev from him. As Velchev opposed further army purges, which were conducted by the Communist security minister Anton Yugov, in September 1946 the Communists sent him to a diplomatic post in Switzerland. Fearing for his life, on 25 October 1947 Velchev refused to return to Bulgaria. As a result, he was deprived of his Bulgarian citizenship. He spent the rest of his life in exile in France. (JJ/WR)

Sources: *Kratka bulgarska entsiklopediya*, vol. 1 (Sofia); *Biographisches Lexikon*, vol. 4; Dimo Kazasov, *Burni godine 1918–1944* (Sofia, 1949); L. A. D. Dellin, ed., *Bulgaria* (New York, 1957); Marshall Lee Miller, *Bulgaria during the Second World War* (Stanford, 1975); Jerzy Jackowicz, *Partie opozycyjne w Bułgarii 1944–1948* (Warsaw 1997); Tasho Tashev, *Ministrite na Bulgariya 1897–1999* (Sofia, 1999).

VELYCHKOVSKYI Vasyl (1 June 1903, Stanisławów [now Ivano-Frankovsk, Ukraine]–30 June 1973, Canada), bishop of the underground Greek Catholic Church in the Ukraine. After graduating from a theological seminary in Lwów (Lviv), in 1925, Velychkovskyi took vows in the Redemptorist Order, and in October 1925 he was ordained a priest. Between 1929 and 1935 he worked in different parishes in Volhynia. Then he was hegumen (prior) of the Redemptorists in Stanisławów. During World War II Velychkovskyi worked in Kam'yanets Podilskyy and Ternopil (Tarnopol), where he also served as hegumen. Arrested by the MVD (Ministry for Internal Affairs) on 11 April 1945, he was interrogated in a Kiev prison for more than three years. Sentenced to death, Velychkovskyi awaited execution for over three months. His sentence was commuted to ten years of labor camp. From 1949 Velychkovskyi was held in in Kirov, Vorkuta, and other labor camps, where he conducted pastoral work among the prisoners. Released in 1955, Velychkovskyi returned to Lviv, where he continued his work in the underground Greek Catholic Church. Secretly designated a bishop in 1959, he was formally ordained by Metropolitan **Josif Slipyi** in 1963. During the Czechoslovak Prague Spring Velychkovskyi officially served as a Uniate bishop. Arrested again on 2 January 1969 and sentenced to three years' imprisonment in March 1970, he was held in prison in Kommunarsk in the Donbas. Released in 1972, he was forcibly displaced to his family in Yugoslavia. From Yugoslavia he went via Rome to Canada, where he worked among the Ukrainian émigrés until his death. On 27 June 2001 Pope **John Paul II** beatified Velychkovskyi at a solemn Holy Mass in Lviv. (WR)

Sources: *Encyclopedia of Ukraine*, vol. 4 (Toronto, 1993); *Martirolohia ukrain's'kikh tserkov u chetyriokh tomakh*, vol. 2 (Toronto); *Vasyl Vsevolod Velychkovs'kyi: Iepiskop-ispovidnik* (Yorkton, 1975); Bohdan R. Botsiurkiv, *The Ukrainian Greek-Catholic Church and the Soviet State (1939–1950)* (Edmonton, 1996); *Osservatore Romano* (weekly edition in English), 2001, nos. 25 and 27.

VENCLOVA Tomaš (11 September 1937, Klaipeda [Memel]), Lithuanian poet. Venclova is the son of Antanas Venclova, a leftist writer who accepted the post of minister of education offered by the Soviets in 1940 and after World War II served as president of the Union of Lithuanian Writers. In 1960 Venclova graduated in Lithuanian language and literature from Vilnius University, where in 1966 he began to teach applied linguistics and the history of Western literature. At that time he translated the works of (among others) T. S. Eliot, James Joyce, and Boris Pasternak into Lithuanian. He also published his own pieces in various periodicals. In 1972 Venclova published his first collection of poems, *Kalbos ženklas* (Sign of speech), astonishing in its originality and with a combination of traditional form, great imagination, and rich metaphors. Despite his father's position, Venclova more and more openly criticized the Communist system, and in May 1975 he wrote a letter to the Central Committee of the Communist Party of Lithuania stating that the Communist ideology was alien to him, that it had caused much harm to Lithuania, and that to accept it would be hypocritical of him. In November 1976 he co-founded the Lithuanian Helsinki Group, which monitored Soviet violations of human rights in Lithuania. In 1977 he was allowed to emigrate from Lithuania.

When Venclova went to the United States, he was invited to give lectures in literature at the University of California, Berkeley. Meanwhile, he was stripped of his Soviet citizenship. In 1980 he became professor of Russian literature at Yale University. He published little, but every piece he wrote was enthusiastically received by critics. His style, marked by an ironic wit and a distanced perspective toward reality, won him critical recognition and the artistic friendship of eminent East European writers, including **Czesław Miłosz** and Joseph Brodsky. Venclova was one of few Lithuanian dissidents who maintained friendly contacts with Poles. He often translated works by Polish writers, including Miłosz and Stanisław Barańczak. In December 1981 Venclova signed a protest by Western intellectuals against the imposition of martial law in Poland. Venclova's most famous works include poems from the collection *Winter Dialogue* (1987) and the essays *Forms of Hope* (1989). A retrospective collection of his poems was published in Lithuania in 1992. In 1996 in the United States Venclova published the study *Aleksander Wat: Life and Art of an Iconoclast*. In 1999 he was awarded the Lithuanian Order of the Cross of Vytis.

He has been a contributor to the Polish quarterly *Zeszyty Literackie* and a member of its editorial staff. Venclova has recently settled in Kraków, Poland. (WR)

Sources: *EL*, vol. 6; Romuald J. Misiunas and Rein Taagepera, *The Baltic States: Years of Dependence, 1940–1980* (Berkeley, 1983); Leonidas Donskis, *Identity and Freedom: Mapping Nationalism and Social Criticism in the Twentieth Century* (London, 2002).

VERDEŢ Ilie (10 May 1925, Comăneşti, Bacău County–20 March 2001, Bucharest), Romanian Communist activist. Verdeţ's mother, Regina Manescu, was the sister of **Nicolae Ceauşescu**. Verdeţ finished several grades of primary school and then worked as a miner. In 1945 he joined the Romanian Communist Party (Partidul Comunist Român [RCP]). From 1945 to 1948 he studied economics at the University of Bucharest. After graduating, he moved to Banat, where, from 1948 to 1954, he worked in the apparatus of the Romanian Workers' Party (Partidul Muncitoresc Român [RWP]; established in 1948). In 1954 Verdeţ became head of a department in the RWP Central Committee (CC); from 1954 to 1965 he was first secretary of the RWP in Hunedoara, and from 1960 to 1989 he served as a member of the RWP CC (which was again renamed the Romanian Communist Party [RCP] in 1965). From 1961 to 1989 Verdeţ was a member of parliament. After Ceauşescu came to power in 1965, Verdeţ became one of the top leaders of the RCP. He was a deputy member of the CC Executive Committee from 1965 to 1966 and a full member from 1966 to 1986. He held the posts of deputy prime minister (March 1965–January 1967) and first deputy prime minister (December 1967–January 1969, March 1974, March 1978–March 1979). He was a member of the Standing Presidium of the RCP CC (1966–74 and 1984–86), secretary of the CC (1974–78 and 1982–85), and a member of the RCP Executive Committee Politburo (1977–86). In addition, in 1974–78 and 1982–89 he served as chairman of the Central Council of Workers' Control over the Economy and Social Activities. From 1978 to 1979 he again served as first deputy prime minister and also held the post of chairman of the State Planning Committee. From 29 March 1979 to 21 May 1982 Verdeţ was deputy prime minister. In this capacity, he was a pliable tool of Ceauşescu. From October 1985 to September 1987 he served as minister of mining. On 22 December 1989, during the turmoil after the overthrow of Ceauşescu, Verdeţ unsuccessfully attempted to form a new government, but the initiators of the coup took over control. In November 1990 Verdeţ established the populist Socialist Labor Party (Partidul Socialist al Muncii [PSM]), and in 1991 he became its chairman. In the elections of 1992 the PSM won 3 percent of the votes and thirteen seats but was later marginalized; therefore, in 2000 Verdeţ resigned as its leader and retired from public life. (LW)

Sources: Klaus-Detlev Grothusen, ed., *Südosteuropa-Handbuch: Rumänien* (Göttingen, 1977); Mark Almond, *The Rise and Fall of Nicolae and Elena Ceauşescu* (London, 1992); József Darski, *Rumunia: Historia, współczesność, konflikty narodowe* (Warsaw, 1995); Ion Alexandrescu, Ion Bulei, Ion Mamina, and Ioan Scurtu, *Enciclopedia de istorie României* (Bucharest, 2000); *Personalităţi politice, publice* (Bucharest, 1996); *International Who's Who 2000* (London, 2000).

VERES Péter (6 January 1897, Balmazújváros–16 April 1970, Budapest), Hungarian writer and politician. Veres's mother was a servant. After finishing four grades of primary school, he worked as a swineherd, servant, and railroad worker. In 1914 he joined the Agrarian-Socialist movement and continued his education on his own. From 1917 to 1918 Veres fought on the Italian front. In 1919, under the Hungarian Soviet Republic (HSR), he was a member of a commission for parceling out land and a member of the community directorate in Balmazújváros. Interned by the Romanian troops in Braşov (Brassó), Veres returned to Hungary in 1921. A court in Debrecen sentenced him to one year in prison for his activities under the HSR. In 1922 Veres founded a village committee of the Hungarian Social Democratic Party (HSDP) in Balmazújváros, as well as the National Trade Union of Agrarian Workers. Veres made his literary debut with the book *Az Alföld parasztsága* (Peasants of the Great Hungarian Plain; 1936), whereby he joined the so-called peasant writers' movement. He contributed to the leftist and peasant periodicals *Válasz*, *Gondolat*, and *Kelet Népe*, defending the rights of poor peasants and calling for a solution to the agrarian issue. In 1937 Veres was one of the founders of the March Front. In 1939 he co-founded the National Peasant Party (Nemzeti Parasztpárt [NPP]) and became a member of its leadership. In 1941 he wrote *Falusi krónika* (Rural chronicle). In 1943 in Balatonszárszó Veres attended a meeting of representatives of various opposition movements, from Catholic to Communist; at the meeting he pointed out that it was necessary to choose a leftist path after World War II. During the war Veres was inducted into the labor service units. After the Germans occupied Hungary in March 1944, he went into hiding.

Elected to parliament on the NPP ticket in November 1945, Veres served as an MP until the end of his life. From 1945 to 1947 he was president of the National Council for Land Property Regulation and played an active role in implementing the agricultural reform of March 1945. From 1945 onwards he supported the party's full cooperation with the Communists. Veres served as minister of construction and public works (March–September

1947) and minister of national defense (until September 1948). At the end of 1948 he was dismissed because he propagated the notion of the superiority of peasant farming; still, in 1949 he became a member of the leadership of the National Council of the Patriotic People's Front, and from 1954 to January 1957 he served as president of the Association of Hungarian Writers (AHW). Veres was the author of the trilogy *Három nemzedék* (Three generations; 1950–57), a novel of peasant life in the first half of the twentieth century. In 1953 he became a supporter of **Imre Nagy**.

On 23 October 1956 Veres read an AHW statement at a student demonstration in front of the statue of General József Bem in Budapest. During the first days of fighting, the Corvin Lane insurgents wanted Veres to become prime minister. On 31 October he became a member of the leadership of the reorganized NPP. As late as 28 December 1956 he chaired a general AHW meeting at which those present supported the revolution. He refused to join the Writers' Council, whose aim was to support the government of **János Kádár**. Veres was interrogated several times, and officials of the Ministry of Interior insisted on his arrest. Veres was a co-founder of the reorganized AHW, established on "new foundations" in 1959. He was a very popular author, and his works were translated into seventeen languages. In the 1960s the authorities exploited Veres's popularity; therefore, he received many prizes and awards. (JT)

Sources: *Biographisches Lexikon*, vol. 4; *Magyar Életrajzi Lexikon*, vol. 3 (Budapest, 1985); *Nagy Képes Milleniumi Arcképcsarnok* (Budapest, 1999); *Magyarország 1944–1956*, CD-ROM (Budapest, 2001); Zoltán Szabó, "Veres Péter 1897–1970," *Új Látóhatár*, 1970, no. 13 (21); *Mały słownik pisarzy węgierskich* (Warsaw, 1977); Hans-Detlev Grothusen, ed., *Ungarn* (Göttingen, 1987); Steven Bela Vardy, *Historical Dictionary of Hungary* (Lanham, Md., 1997).

VERHUN Petro (18 November 1890, Gródek Jagielloński [now Horodok], near Lemberg [Lwów, Lviv]–7 February 1957, Angarskiy, Krasnoyarsk region, Soviet Union), Uniate priest, martyr for the faith. After graduating from a seminary, Verhun was ordained into the priesthood by Archbishop **Andriy Sheptytskyi** in October 1927 and sent to Germany to minister to Ukrainian Catholics living there. Later he was appointed apostolic visitator to Germany. On 15 June 1945, after the Soviet Army captured Berlin, Verhun was arrested by the Soviet security services and taken to Kiev. On 3 June 1946 he was sentenced to eight years in a labor camp, although he had never been a Soviet citizen. Verhun served his sentence in extremely harsh conditions in the camps of Boymy and Inta, all the while continuing his pastoral work. After his release, he

was forced to settle in Siberia. The Soviet authorities consistently denied him the right to return to Germany, although Verhun had German citizenship. He died in exile in the Krasnoyarsk region. On 27 June 2001 Pope **John Paul II** beatified Verhun at a solemn Holy Mass in Lviv. (WR)

Sources: *Osservatore Romano* (weekly edition in English), 2001, nos. 25 and 27.

VERNADSKYI Volodymyr (12 March 1863, St. Petersburg, Russia–6 January 1945, Moscow), Ukrainian natural scientist and mineralogist, one of the pioneers of geochemistry, biogeochemistry, and the science of the noosphere and the biosphere. In 1885 Vernadskyi graduated from the Department of Physics and Mathematics of St. Petersburg University. From 1888 to 1890 he studied abroad. He subsequently taught at Moscow University (1890–1911; a professor from 1897). He then gave up his university post in protest against the reactionary education policies of the tsar's government. In 1911 Vernadskyi organized the first expedition in search of radioactive ores. In 1912 he became a full member of the Russian Academy of Sciences, and in 1914, director of the Geological and Mineralogical Museum of the Academy of Sciences in St. Petersburg. From June 1917 onwards Vernadskyi lived in Ukraine. In June 1918, at the behest of **Mykola Vasylenko**, the minister of education in the government of Hetman **Pavlo Skoropadskyi**, Vernadskyi became head of a commission for drafting a parliamentary bill on the Ukrainian Academy of Sciences (Ukraiinska Akademiya Nauk [UAN]). In mid-November 1918 the project was endorsed by Skoropadskyi. Vernadskyi served as the first president of the UAN from 1918 to 1919.

From 1920 to 1921 Vernadskyi was a professor at the university in Simferopol. In 1922 he founded the Radium Institute in Petrograd. From 1923 to 1926 he lectured at Charles University, Prague, and at the Sorbonne in Paris, where he worked with (among others) **Maria Skłodowska-Curie**. In 1926 Vernadskyi became a member of the Czechoslovak Academy of Sciences, and in 1928, a member of the French Academy of Sciences. He served as a professor at the London School of Slavonic Studies. From 1928 on he directed the Radium Institute of the Soviet Academy of Sciences. In the 1930s Vernadskyi conducted research on heavy water and began the construction of the first Soviet cyclotron. In 1939, along with his co-workers, he established a commission on isotopes. Vernadskyi's research focused on the physicochemical processes involved in the formation of minerals, including radioactive ones. Vernadskyi is particularly famous for his theory of the structure of aluminosilicates. In his honor one mineral was named vernadite. The National Library of Ukraine was also named after him. Vernadskyi authored nearly four hundred scientific works, including the following: *Opyt opisatelnoy mineralogii* (The experience of descriptive mineralogy, 2 vols.; 1908–22); *Istoriia mineralov zemnoy kory* (The history of minerals of the earth's crust; 1923–36); *La géochimie* (Geochemistry; 1924); *La biosphère* (1929; *The Biosphere*, 1986); *Ocherki geokhimii* (Studies in geochemistry; 1924); and *Biokhimicheskie ocherki* (Biochemical studies; 1922–32, 1940). (BB)

Sources: *Encyclopedia of Ukraine*, vol. 5 (Toronto, 1993); *Entsyklopediya Ukraiinoznavstva*, vol. 1 (Lviv, 1993); *Dovidnyk z istoriï* (Kiev, 2001); *Vydatni diyachi Ukraiiny mynulykh stolit* (Kiev, 2001); Rudolf Balandin, *Vladimir Vernadskyi* (Moscow, 1982); Nikolai Shcherbak, *Vladimir Ivanovich Vernadskyi* (Kiev, 1988); Kendall E. Bailes, *Science and Russian Culture in an Age of Revolution: V. I. Vernadsky and His Scientific School, 1863–1945* (Bloomington, 1990).

VESELICA Marko (9 January 1936, Glavice, near Sinj, Croatia), Croatian politician. Veselica completed studies in economics at the University of Zagreb, earning a Ph.D. in economic theory. From 1967 to 1971 he worked as an associate professor at the Department of Economics of the University of Zagreb. A member of the board of Matica Hrvatska (a Croatian cultural and publishing organization), Veselica was one of the leaders of the Croatian Spring, at which time he served as an MP in the federal parliament in Belgrade. During the suppression of "Croatian nationalism," Veselica was expelled from the League of Communists of Croatia on 23 July 1971, arrested on 11 January 1972, and soon afterwards sentenced to seven years' imprisonment and four years' ban on public activities for "activities against the nation and the state." Named by Amnesty International as the "prisoner of the year" in 1976 and "prisoner of the world" for November in 1977, Veselica was released in December 1977. In 1981, after giving an interview to the German magazine *Der Spiegel*, in which he described the Croatian question as "the fatal disease of Yugoslavia," Veselica was accused of "falsely presenting the Yugoslav reality" and sentenced to eleven years' imprisonment and four years' ban on public activities.

Released in 1988, Veselica (along with **Franjo Tudjman**) founded the Croatian Democratic Union (Hrvatska Demokratska Zajednica [HDZ]) in 1989, but after a conflict over leadership Veselica seceded from the HDZ, and on 4 November 1989 he established the Croatian Democratic Party (CDP), which won thirteen seats in parliament in the 1990 elections. In 1992 the CDP won no seats in the Sabor (Legislature), and in December it merged with the Croatian Christian Democratic Party to form the Croatian Christian Democratic Union (Hrvatska Kršćansko-Demokratska Unija [CCDU]), of which Veselica served as president from 1992 to 2001. In the 1999 elections the CCDU formed a bloc with the radical Croatian Party of Rights, led by Anto Djapić, and jointly won five seats. In 1990 and 2002 Veselica was elected president of the Croatian Association of Political Prisoners (Hrvatsko Društvo Političkih Zatvorenika). He served as an MP from 1995 to 1999. He is also a member of the board of the Trade Unions of Croatia and vice-president of the Dr. Ivo Pilar Croatian Geopolitical Association. Veselica is against the agreement with the International Criminal Tribunal for the Former Yugoslavia (ICTY) in The Hague, as he believes that war criminals should be tried in Croatia. According to Veselica, Croatia should adopt from the West only "what is needed." He is against building an open civil society and in favor of a national and agricultural character for Croatia. Veselica authored *Zov savjesti iz hrvatskog Sibira: S vjerom u Hrvatsku* (The call of conscience from the Croatian Siberia: With faith in Croatia; 1990). (JD)

Sources: *Interview with Marko Veselica* (London, 1980); Dubravka Drača, *Hrvatski feniks* (Zagreb, 1992); Nikole Muslima, *Dr. Marko Veselica: Zatvorenik savjesti planete* (Zagreb, 1993); Bugajski.

VESNIĆ Milenko (13 February 1863, Dunište, Sandžak, Serbia–15 February 1921, Paris), Serbian politician. Vesnić studied law in Berlin, Munich, and Leipzig. In 1891 he began working in the Serbian Ministry of Foreign Affairs and briefly served as secretary at a legation in Istanbul. After leaving the diplomatic service, he edited the periodical *Pravnik*. From 1892 onwards Vesnić taught international law at the School of Law of Belgrade University. From 1893 to 1894 he served as minister of education and subsequently resumed the post of professor of law at Belgrade University. Following the publication of a letter in the Paris periodical *Les Temps* in 1899, Vesnić was arrested and sentenced to prison. Pardoned the following year, he returned to the diplomatic service after 1903, serving as an envoy to Istanbul, Paris, and Rome. In 1906 Vesnić briefly served as minister of justice in the government of **Nikola Pašić**. In the first half of 1919 Vesnić was a delegate of the Kingdom of Serbs, Croats, and Slovenes (SHS) to the Paris Peace Conference. At a session of the Supreme Council of the Paris Peace Conference in February 1919 he put forward a demand that not only Montenegro, Bosnia, Dalmatia, Slovenia, Bačka, and Banat be incorporated into the SHS, but also south Styria and parts of Carinthia, Trieste, and Gorizia. However, these additional demands were rejected. From 16 May 1920 to 1 January 1921

Vesnić served as prime minister. He signed an agreement with Italy on the demarcation of a final border between it and SHS, succeeded in quelling a dangerous wave of strikes, and called parliamentary elections. Vesnić died suddenly. (WR)

Sources: *Enciklopedija Jugoslavije*, vol. 8 (Zagreb, 1971); Seton-Watson Collection, School of Slavonic and East European Studies (University College of London); Wiesław Walkiewicz, *Jugosławia* (Warsaw, 2000).

VIDENOV Zhan (22 February 1959, Plovdiv), post-Communist Bulgarian politician. Videnov graduated from the English Language High School in Plovdiv and from the Moscow State Institute of International Relations in 1985. From 1985 to 1986 he worked in the Biotekhnika and Avtoelektronika factories in Plovdiv. From 1986 to 1989 he was a member of the Dimitrov Communist Youth League. From 1989 to 1990 he again worked at Avtoelektronika. After the Bulgarian Communist Party (BCP) was transformed into the Bulgarian Socialist Party (BSP) on 3 April 1990, Videnov was elected a member of its Supreme Council. From 1991 to 1997 he was a member of the Presidium, and from 16 December 1991 onwards, chairman of the Presidium of the BSP Supreme Council and a deputy to the National Assembly, reelected for successive terms. From 25 January 1995 to 23 December 1996 Videnov served as prime minister, and in this capacity he represented the interests of the party nomenklatura and impeded systemic transformations. His government pursued a pro-Russian and anti-Western policy that led to the breakdown of supplies to the consumer market. His government was brought down by a deepening economic and sociopolitical crisis in Bulgaria. On 24 December 1996 Videnov resigned as leader of the BSP. (JJ)

Sources: *Koy koy e v Bulgariya* (Sofia, 1998).

VIEST Rudolf (24 September 1890, Revúca [now in Slovakia]–spring of 1945, Flossenbürg, Germany?), Slovak general. In 1909 Viest graduated from an industrial school in Budapest, where he subsequently worked for a construction company. In 1914 he was taken prisoner of war by the Russians. He then enlisted as a volunteer in the Serbian Army. In 1916, as a soldier of this army, he fought in Dobruja and was wounded. He subsequently served as an officer in the Czechoslovak Legions in Russia and fought against the Bolsheviks in Siberia. In 1920 Viest made his way, via Japan, Canada, and the United States, to Czechoslovakia, where he graduated from the Military College in Prague. From 1922 to 1923 he served as deputy military attaché in Budapest and then became chief of staff

of the Second Infantry Division in Plzeň. From 1925 to 1929 Viest was a military attaché in Poland. After returning to his country, he commanded a regiment in Trnava and served as chief of staff of the district command in Bratislava. He later became commander of the seventh and sixth military corps. In 1933 he was promoted to brigadier general. In 1938 Viest became a major general, the only Slovak in pre-Munich Czechoslovakia to do so.

Viest was a member of the Czechoslovak delegation at the First Vienna Arbitration in 1938. After the award was made, he became a member of the Slovak-Hungarian delimitation commission, which demarcated new borders between Slovakia and Hungary. On 14 March 1939, just after independence was proclaimed by the Slovak parliament, Viest signed a memorandum in protest against this proclamation and in support of a common Czechoslovak state. In 1939 Viest briefly served as inspector general of the Slovak Army and maintained contacts with the newly formed resistance movement at home and abroad. In August 1939 he emigrated to France, where he served as commander of the First Division of the Czechoslovak Army (January–June 1940), and he was also a member of the Czechoslovak National Committee. In 1940 Viest became an adviser to the president-in-exile of Czechoslovakia. From 1940 on he worked in the defense ministry of the government-in-exile, and in 1944 he briefly served as defense minister. In 1940, by a decision of the president of the Slovak Republic, Viest was stripped of his rank of major general, and two years later he was sentenced to death in absentia. In August 1944 in Moscow Viest took part in negotiations of the London-based Czechoslovak government-in-exile. After the outbreak of the Slovak National Uprising, he made his way from Moscow to Slovakia, and on 7 October 1944, in difficult circumstances, he replaced **Ján Golian** as commander of the First Czechoslovak Army. On 27 October 1944 Viest issued his last order, calling for the continuation of fighting in the mountains after the collapse of the uprising. On 3 November 1944, Viest (together with Golian) was captured by the Germans in Pohronský Bukovec and then deported to Germany. Tried in Berlin, Viest was condemned to death. The circumstances of his death are unknown; most probably he was executed in the Flossenbürg concentration camp. In 1945 Viest was posthumously promoted to four-star general. (PU)

Sources: *ČBS*; *SBS*, vol. 6; Libor Vykoupil, *Slovník českých dějin* (Brno, 2000); *Českoslovenští politici: 1918–1991* (Prague, 1991); *Politická elita meziválečného Československa 1918–1938: Kdo byl kdo za první republiky* (Prague, 1998); *Reprezentačný biografický lexikón Slovenska* (Martin, 1999); Joseph S. Rouček, *Slavonic Encyclopaedia* (New York, 1949); Miroslav Kropilak and

Jozef Jablonický, *Malý slovník Slovenského národného povstania* (Bratislava, 1964); Ján Čajak, *Po stopách generála Viesta* (Bratislava, 1947).

VIKE-FREIBERGA Vaira (1 December 1937, Riga), psychology professor, president of Latvia. After World War II, Vike-Freiberga lived with her parents in a refugee camp in Germany, from where the family emigrated to Canada. She graduated from the University of Toronto and then earned a Ph.D. from McGill University in Montreal. From 1965 to 1998 Vike-Freiberga worked as a psychology professor at the University of Montreal. She held many prestigious scholarly positions, including president of the Canadian Psychological Association, deputy chairperson of the Science Council of Canada, and president of the Académie des Lettres et des Sciences Humaines of the Royal Society of Canada. Vike-Freiberga's numerous scholarly publications include *Latvian Sun-songs* (1988; co-authored by her husband, Imants Freibergs, professor of computer science at the University of Quebec in Montreal) and *Linguistics and Poetics of Latvian Folk Songs* (1989). She has also written several dozen articles. Vike-Freiberga is a prominent specialist in the field of Latvian folklore. Increasingly active in the public life of a revived Latvia in the 1990s, Vike-Freiberga was appointed director of the Latvian Institute in Riga in the autumn of 1998. On 17 June 1999 the parliament chose Vike-Freiberga for president by a slim majority, comprised of the People's Party, the Social Democrats, and the Fatherland and Freedom Party; on 8 July of that year she assumed the office of president. She was reelected as president on 20 June 2003. As the head of state, Vike-Freiberga kept the country's foreign policy on a Western-oriented course, in which Latvia's bid to join NATO and the European Union was a priority, and she supported Latvia's economic transformation. After the parliament passed a new language bill that limited the use of languages other than Latvian (December 1999), Vike-Freiberga refused to sign it and returned it to the parliament to be revised according to EU standards. In September 2000 she was awarded an honorary doctorate by the University of Latvia in Riga. Vike-Freiberga managed to lead Latvia into NATO and the European Union in 2004. (WR)

Sources: *Europa Środkowo-Wschodnia 1999* (Warsaw, 2001); Ausma Cimdina, *Brīvības vārdā* (Riga, 2001); Bugajski; www.president.lv/index.php.

VILDE Eduard (4 March 1865, Pudivere–26 December 1933, Tallinn), Estonian writer, playwright, and politician. In 1882 Vilde graduated from a German high school. From 1883 to 1886 he worked on the editorial staff of *Virulase*

in Dorpat (Tartu, Yuryev), and from 1887 to 1888, on the editorial staff of *Postimees* in Tallinn and then in Riga (1889–90), where he contributed to *Zeitung fuer Stadt und Land*, and in Berlin (1890–92), where he became acquainted with socialism and French Impressionism. Both these movements played a crucial role in shaping Vilde as a writer and politician. In 1893 he returned to Estonia and worked for *Postimees* in Yuryev (1893–96). From 1897 to 1898 he was the editor-in-chief of the Narva-based newspaper *Virmalist*. From 1898 to 1901 he worked as a journalist for *Eesti Postimees* in Tallinn. In 1901–4 he was one of the leading editors of the newspaper *Teataja*, which was founded and published by Konstantin Päts. In 1904–5 Vilde also contributed to the Yuryev-based *Uudiseed*. He took an active part in the 1905 revolution, and, after its failure he emigrated to Switzerland and then to Finland, where he published the satirical newspaper *Kaak*. From 1906 to 1917 Vilde lived in various countries of Europe and in the United States. After the outbreak of the February 1917 revolution, Vilde returned to Estonia, where he again was a journalist and did freelance work for the Estonia Theater. From 1919 to 1920 he was the head of the Copenhagen-based propaganda bureau of the Estonian National Council (Maapäev), and subsequently he became Estonia's envoy to Berlin. In 1920 he resigned and spent the next three years in Germany. He returned to Estonia in 1923. In 1928 he became an honorary member of the Finnish Writers' Union. In 1929 he was granted an honorary doctorate by the Department of Philosophy of Tartu University.

Vilde is considered the first Estonian professional writer and the first representative of realism in Estonian literature. His first stories were targeted at a mass audience and are characterized by humor, sharp language, and a strong plot. Vilde's total output consists of thirty-three volumes. Among others things, his success resulted from his unique worldly refinement and his wide contacts. A true European, Vilde transplanted fashionable ideas of socialism and realism into art on an Estonian background. He condemned social inequities that led to the difficult financial and spiritual situation of workers and peasants. He addressed these issues in such books as the novel *Külmale maale* (To the frozen land; 1896) and the three-volume saga *Mahtra soda* (The Mahtra war; 1902). The latter was based on documents and accounts that Vilde had collected concerning a 1858 peasant uprising against the German landed gentry. *Kui Anija mehed Tallinnas käisid* (When the Anija men went to Tallinn; 1903) and the trilogy *Prohvet Maltsvet* (The Prophet Maltsvet; 1905–8) address similar issues. Vilde also dealt with the emancipation of women. His last novel, *Mäeküla piimamees* (Milkman from Mäeküla), is a critique of social conditions in which a German baron could buy a poor peasant's consent to seduce his wife. Vilde also wrote plays, but they were less successful. (AG)

Sources: *Kto yest kto v kulture Estonii: Izobrazitelnye iskusstva—literatura, teatr, muzyka, kino* (Tallinn, 1996); *Eesti Entsuklopeedia*, vol. 14 (Tallinn, 2000); Toomas Haug, "Eduard Vilde," *Estonian Literary Magazine*, 1999, no. 8; "Noos et Bayardweb," mapage.noos.fr/estonie/Vilde.html.

VILFAN Josip (30 August 1878, Trieste–8 March 1955, Belgrade), Slovene politician. In 1901 Vilfan completed law studies in Vienna. He initially worked in a law office in Trieste and then in the office of the renowned Croatian politician Matko Laginja in Pola (Pula). In 1904 Vilfan returned to Trieste, where in 1909 he opened his own law office and ran it until 1928. He entered the political scene in 1906, when he became secretary of Edinost (Unity), a society founded in 1874 for the defense of the rights of Slovenes living in Trieste and the neighboring area. Vilfan held this position until 1909. From 1910 until the dissolution of Edinost in 1928, he served as its chairman. Vilfan accused the Italian administration of irregularities in conducting a census in the Trieste area and was instrumental in bringing about a revision of the census in 1910. Its results showed that nearly fifty-seven thousand people used Slovene in everyday speech. In 1909 and 1913 Vilfan was elected to the Trieste City Council.

Vilfan defended the principle of equal rights for all nations. With the collapse of the Habsburg empire, he unsuccessfully strove for the incorporation of Trieste into the Kingdom of Serbs, Croats, and Slovenes and emphasized that the rights of the Italian minority must be respected. Elected to the parliament in Rome on two occasions, in 1921 and 1924, Vilfan defended the rights of the Slovene and Croatian minorities and protested against Fascist tendencies. On his initiative a congress on national minorities in Europe was held in Geneva. Vilfan presided over the congress and ran its permanent office. As a result of his efforts, the issue of the protection of minority rights in Europe became widely known, but although it gained international recognition, the Fascist authorities did not approve of it and outlawed Edinost. After a meeting with Benito Mussolini in 1928, Vilfan left Italy and went to Yugoslavia and thence to Vienna, where he ran an office of the congress of national minorities in Europe until 1939. In 1939, in the face of the imminent outbreak of World War II, Vilfan moved to Belgrade. From 1945 to 1947 he was a member of the Institute of International Affairs of the Ministry of Foreign Affairs of Yugoslavia. He also took part in the preparations for the Paris Peace Conference, where Yugoslavia signed the peace treaty with Italy in 1947. (AO)

Sources: *Enciklopedija Slovenije*, vol. 14 (Ljubljana, 2000); *Biographishes Lexikon*, vol. 4; Egon Pelikan, *Josip Vilfan v parlamentu: Discorsi parlamentari dell'on Josip Vilfan* (Trieste, 1997).

VILMS Jüri (13 March 1889, Arkma, near Viljandi–13 April 1918, Helsinki, Finland), Estonian lawyer, journalist, and politician. In 1911 Vilms completed law studies in Yuryev (now Tartu, Estonia) and then ran a law practice in Tallinn until 1917. He began his political career in 1917. He published articles in *Päevaleht* and was one of the founders of the Estonian Social Radical Party, later transformed into the Estonian Labor Party. Despite his young age and lack of political experience, Vilms quickly rose to a prominent position in the Estonian National Council (Maapäev). On 19 February 1918, along with **Konstantin Päts** and **Konstantin Konik**, Vilms joined the three-man Estonian Salvation Committee (Eesti Päästmises Komitee [ESC]), which was given extraordinary powers by the Estonian National Council. Shortly before the German occupation of Estonia, Vilms co-signed the declaration of Estonian independence (24 February 1918). He became deputy prime minister and minister of justice in the provisional government of the new state led by Päts. The declaration of Estonian independence was passed during the struggle between the Germans and the Bolsheviks for supremacy over Estonia. Both stated that the declaration was illegal and treated those who had initiated it as rebels. Vilms attempted to escape to Finland, but after crossing the frozen Gulf of Finland on foot, he was caught by the Germans and executed by a firing squad. In 1920 his ashes were returned to Estonia and buried in Pilistverre. Because of the circumstances of his death and his young age, Vilms was often cited as an archetype of the national hero and a martyr in the struggle for independence. **Jaan Kross** devoted a novel to Vilms, and Vilms appeared as a character in several films. (AG)

Sources: *Eesti Entsuklopeedia*, vol. 14 (Tallinn, 2000); August Tammann, *Jüri Vilms elulugu ja tegerus* (Tallinn, 1923); Evald Uustalu, *The History of the Estonian People* (London, 1952); Andres Pärl, *Jüri Vilms: Eesti iseseivuse märter* (Tallinn, 1990); Hando Runnel, ed. *Jüri Vilms mälestustes* (Tartu, 1998); Tõnu Tannberg, Matti Laur, Tõnis Lukas, Ain Mäesalu, and Ago Pajur, *History of Estonia* (Tallinn, 2000).

VIŠINSKIS Povilas (29 June 1875, Ušnėnai, near Šiauliai–26 June 1906, Berlin), Lithuanian editor and literary critic. After graduating from high school in Šiauliai in 1894, Višinskis began to study the natural sciences at St. Petersburg University, but he contracted tuberculosis and had to discontinue his studies. While still a student, he began researching Lithuanian folklore. From 1899 to 1906 he edited the periodical *Varpas* and co-edited the daily *Vilniaus žinios*. At that time he published extensively. In 1901 Višinskis expressed support for a "free and independent Lithuania, liberated from foreign and domestic despots." He was a co-founder of the Lithuanian Democratic Party. He also rendered great services to Lithuanian literature, promoting many new talented writers, such as **Julija Žymantienė-Žemaitė**, Jonas Biliūnas, and Jonas Krikščiūnas-Jovaras. In 1900 Višinskis deliberately let the authorities sentence him to a fine and one day in jail for publishing a poster printed in Lithuanian using the "Latin-Polish alphabet." Since his lawyer stated that the poster had been printed in the "Latin-Lithuanian" alphabet, in 1903 an appeal was granted and Višinskis was released because it was proved that the sentence had been based on a non-exiseant regulation. By reducing to absurdity the tsar's ban on printing in Lithuanian using the Latin alphabet, Višinskis contributed to the abolition of this ban by the Russian authorities in May 1904. Under his influence, some Poles, including Władysław Putwiński (**Vladas Putvinskis**) and Maria Pieczkowska (**Marija Pečkauskaitė**), changed their national identity, becoming Lithuanian nationalists. Višinskis died prematurely of tuberculosis. His collected writings, *Raštai*, were published in 1964. (WR)

Sources: *EL*, vol. 6; Julius Būtėnas, *Povilas Višinskis* (Kaunas, 1936); Constantine R. Jurgėla, *Lithuania: The Outpost of Freedom* (St. Petersburg, Fla., 1976); Adolfas Sprindis, *Povilas Višinskis* (Vilnius, 1978).

VISOIANU Constantin (4 February 1897, Urlaţi–2 January 1994, New York), Romanian politician. In 1919 Visoianu completed philosophical and legal studies in Paris. In 1920 he earned a Ph.D. in law from the Sorbonne. From 1927 to 1929 and from 1932 to 1936 he was a close associate of the minister of foreign affairs, **Nicolae Titulescu**. Visoianu was secretary of the Arbitration Commission in Paris (1926–29) and an expert on the Romanian delegation to the League of Nations (1929–31). He subsequently served as Romania's representative in the General Secretariat of the League of Nations (until 1933). Visoianu was an envoy to the Netherlands (1933–35) and to Poland (1935–36). After Titulescu was forced to resign from the Ministry of Foreign Affairs in August 1936, Visoianu was dismissed from the diplomatic service. Aligned with the Liberal Party and the National Peasant Party, he was in opposition to the governments of King **Charles II** and Marshal **Ion Antonescu**. In April 1944, together with Prince **Barbu Ştirbei**, Visoianu agreed to undertake a diplomatic mission whose aim was to switch Romania to the Allied side. Cease-fire negotiations in Cairo ended in failure as a result of opposition from the Kremlin.

Visoianu took part in preparations for the overthrow of Marshal Antonescu's regime. After the coup d'état of 23 August 1944, Visoianu became minister of foreign affairs in the government of General **Constantin Sănătescu** and held this post in the cabinet of General **Nicolae Rădescu** until Rădescu's fall on 28 February 1945. Visoianu signed the truce with the Allies in Moscow (September 1944). After leaving the government, he sharply criticized brutal Soviet interference in Romania's domestic affairs. Fearing arrest, Visoianu fled Romania in October 1946. For some time he stayed in Switzerland and then settled in the United States, where he co-founded the Romanian National Committee (RNC) in 1947. In the same year the Communist authorities sentenced him in absentia to life imprisonment. From 15 November 1950 to 15 September 1975 Visoianu served as chairman of the RNC. He took an active part in the work of the Assembly of Captive European Nations (ACEN). He repeatedly protested the Soviet occupation of Romania, the abuses committed by the Communist regime in Romania, and the Soviet invasions of Hungary (1956) and Czechoslovakia (1968). Visoianu later resigned his position and disbanded the RNC because of the Western countries' support for the seemingly independent foreign policy of **Nicolae Ceauşescu**'s regime. Visoianu authored *Misiunile mele* (My missions; 1997). (FA/WR)

Sources: Ghita Ionescu, *Communism in Rumania 1944–1962* (London and New York, 1964); Şerban N. Ionescu, *Who Was Who in Twentieth Century Romania* (Boulder, Colo., 1994); Dinu C. Giurescu, *Romania's Communist Takeover: The Radescu Government* (Boulder, Colo., 1994); Ioan Chiper, Florin Constantinescu, and Vitali Varatec, eds., *Misiunele lui A. I. Vişinschi în Romania: Din istoria relaţiilor romano-sovietice, 1944–1946; Documente secrete* (Bucharest, 1997).

VITKAUSKAS Vincas (4 October 1890, Uzhbale, Volkovysk district–3 March 1965, Vilnius), Lithuanian general. Between 1914 and 1916 Vitkauskas studied mathematics at the university in Moscow. In 1916 he was called up into the army, with which he was linked until his death. Vitkauskas graduated from a military academy and completed a sharpshooters' course. After the outbreak of the war for the independence of Lithuania, he volunteered for the newly formed Lithuanian Army. He fought against the White Russians and against Poland. After the end of the warfare he was decorated with the Cross of St. Vytautas with Swords. In 1924–40 Vitkauskas worked on the general staff and was an instructor in an infantry school. Between 1926 and 1927 he commanded the Seventh Infantry Regiment and then returned to his work on the staff. In

1935 he rose to the rank of brigadier general; in 1939 was promoted to general of division, and in 1940 he assumed the post of commander-in-chief of the Lithuanian Army. When on 15 June 1940 a Soviet ultimatum was submitted to Lithuania, Vitkauskas objected to the use of the army to stop the Soviet aggression. He argued that the Lithuanian Army had no chance in a clash with the Red Army. Two days later Vitkauskas assumed the post of minister of national defense in the so-called people's government. After the annexation of the country by the USSR, Vitkauskas actively helped to incorporate the Lithuanian Army, as the Twenty-ninth Territorial Corps, into the Red Army. After the outbreak of the German-Soviet war on 22 June 1941, Vitkauskas fled to Moscow, where he lectured at the Higher Military Academy, combining the post of lecturer with a seat on the Supreme Council of the USSR. After 1945 he returned to Lithuania and continued lecturing on military subjects at the University of Kaunas. Between 1946 and 1954 Vitkauskas was a deputy to the Supreme Council of the Lithuanian SSR. (AG)

Sources: *EL*, vol. 6; Bronis J. Kaslas, ed., *The USSR-German Aggression against Lithuania* (New York, 1973); Henryk Wisner, Litwa (Warsaw, 1999).

VITOVSKYI Dmytro (8 November 1887, Meducha [Medukha], near Stanisławów [Ivano-Frankivsk]–8 July 1919, near Ratibor [now Racibórz in Poland]), Ukrainian officer and politician. Vitovskyi studied at the university in Lemberg (Lviv, Lwów). He was the founder of and an activist in Ukrainian educational and paramilitary organizations in Stanisławów. During World War I Vitovskyi served in the Ukrainian Sich Riflemen as a company commander with the rank of captain. On 19 October 1918 **Yevhen Petrushevych** became head of the Ukrainian National Rada (Council), which proclaimed the establishment of an independent state, and Vitovskyi became head of the Military Commissariat of the Rada. On 31 October he ordered that the main strategic points of Lemberg be captured, and on 1 November he became the commander of the Ukrainian units that seized power in this city after the Austrians withdrew. For the next five days, Vitovskyi served as the first commander of the Ukrainian Galician Army. He then became minister of defense of the Western Ukrainian National Republic and held this position until mid-February 1919. On 1 January 1919 he was promoted to colonel. From February to April of that year Vitovskyi took part in the Paris Peace Conference as a delegate of the Ukrainian National Rada. On 8 May 1919, during a hearing before the Commission of the Paris Peace Conference, he presented a proposal for establishing the Polish-Ukrainian border on the San River. Since the Entente tried to exploit Poland's involvement in the war against the Bolsheviks, it evidently delayed recognizing the Ukrainian demands. Vitovskyi signed a statement condemning the Allies' inability to halt the Polish offensive. On his way back from Paris, Vitovskyi was killed in an air crash in Silesia. (WR)

Sources: *Ukraine: A Concise Encyclopedia* (Toronto, 1971); *Encyclopedia of Ukraine*, vol. 5 (Toronto, 1993); Myron Zaklynskyi, *Dmytro Vitovskyi: Hromadskyi diyach, striletskyi ideoloh, vozhd Lystopadovoho zryvu* (New York, 1967); Matthew Stachiw and Jaroslaw Sztendera, *Western Ukraine at the Turning Point of Europe's History, 1918–1923*, vols. 1–2 (New York, 1971); Maciej Kozłowski, *Między Sanem i Zbruczem: Walki o Lwów i Galicje Wschodnią 1918–1919* (Kraków, 1990); Orest Subtelny, *Ukraine: A History* (Toronto, 2000).

VLAD Iulian (23 February 1931, Gogoşiţa), Romanian officer of the Communist political police. At the end of the 1950s Vlad served as a captain in the personnel administration of the political police, Securitate. He quickly rose through the ranks, becoming a major general in 1977. From May 1977 to December 1989 Vlad served as secretary of state in the Ministry of Interior; in April 1983 he became deputy minister of interior, in August 1984 colonel general (highest ranking general in Bulgaria), and in November 1987 head of the Securitate. Vlad led the forcible suppression of the strike of the Jiu Valley coal miners in August 1977 and the workers' demonstrations in Braşov in November 1987. He personally beat participants who were interrogated about the demonstrations in Braşov. After the overthrow of **Nicolae Ceauşescu**, Vlad was arrested on 26 December 1989. Initially he was tried for "taking part in genocide," for which life imprisonment was the maximum penalty, but later the classification of the crime was changed to "supporting genocide," for which ten years' imprisonment was the maximum penalty. On 22 July 1991 Vlad was sentenced to nine years' imprisonment. During his trial he was accused of various kinds of wrongdoing, including "abuses during detention" of over a thousand demonstrators in December 1989 and the persecution and discrediting of some Romanian intellectuals, including Dorin Tudoran, a poet and literary critic who had been forced to emigrate in July 1985. Vlad was also accused of tolerating corruption in customs houses, illegally bugging state officials, persecuting the Transcendental Meditation sect, detaining oppositionists as a preventive measure, and working closely with **Elena Ceauşescu**, particularly in tightening passport regulations and persecuting opposition activists, including the signatories of the so-called Letter of Six, former top-ranking Communist officials. Conditionally released owing to ill health on 30 December 1993, Vlad subsequently retired from public life. (AB)

Sources: Marius Oprea, *Banalitatea răului: O istorie a Securității în documente (1949–1989)* (Iaşi, 2002); Doina Jela, *Lexiconul negru: Unelte ale represiunii comuniste* (Bucharest, 2001).

VLAHOV Dimitar (8 November 1878, Kukuš [now Kilkís, Greece]–7 April 1953, Belgrade), Macedonian revolutionary and Communist activist. Vlahov studied chemistry in Germany and Switzerland. In 1903 he began working as a teacher in Salonika. He was a member of the Central Committee of the Internal Macedonian Revolutionary Organization (IMRO). After the Ilinden Uprising (1903), he was briefly detained. A supporter of autonomy for Macedonia within the framework of the Ottoman Empire, Vlahov was elected to the Young Turk parliament in Istanbul after the revolution of 1908. During World War I Vlahov commanded Bulgarian military districts in Vardar Macedonia and Kosovo. Subsequently, he was sent to Istanbul, Kiev, and Odessa as an envoy of the Bulgarian Army Directorate for Economic Affairs and Planning. After the war, as Bulgaria's consul and commercial attaché in Vienna, Vlahov attempted to negotiate an agreement between rival IMRO factions and the Communist International. When this agreement was rejected in 1924 by its two main signatories, **Todor Aleksandrov** and **Aleksandŭr Protogerov**, Vlahov lost his post in Bulgaria's diplomatic service. He remained in Austria as a political émigré and was active as a Comintern delegate to the Balkans. At the end of the 1920s Vlahov headed the District Committee of the IMRO of United Pirin Macedonia in Sofia, but because of his close relations with the Communists, he was forced to leave Bulgaria. After spending some time in Berlin and Paris, Vlahov went to the Soviet Union in 1935. He managed to escape with his life during the Great Purge only because of the intercession of **Georgi Dimitrov**. Meanwhile, Bulgaria's court sentenced him to death in absentia in 1936. From 1941 onwards, as a Comintern representative again, Vlahov was active in the Balkans, mainly in Greece. On 23 November 1943 he was appointed vice-president of the Anti-Fascist Council for the National Liberation of Yugoslavia (AVNOJ), a quasi-parliament of Communist Partisans led by **Josip Broz Tito**. In October 1944 Vlahov returned to Vardar Macedonia and joined the Communist Party of Yugoslavia. At that time he supported the concept of a Great Macedonia, which would include the Vardar part in the west, the Pirin part in the east, and the Aegean part in the south; as a result, he came into conflict with those—a majority in Skopje—who called for incorporating Vardar Macedonia into Yugoslavia. In 1946 Vlahov was appointed deputy speaker of the federal parliament in Belgrade and lost his political importance. His *Memoari* (Memoirs) were published in 1970. (WR)

Sources: *Enciklopedija Jugoslavije*, vol. 8 (Zagreb, 1971); Gustav Vlahov, *Spomeni na tatko mi* (N.p., 1968); Gorgija Nadoski, *VMRO (Obedinata) i žurnalistickata dejnost na Dimitar Vlahov* (Skopje, 1987); Richard Frucht, ed., *Encyclopedia of Eastern Europe* (New York and London, 2000); Irena Stawowy-Kawka, *Historia Macedonii* (Wrocław, 2000).

VLK Miloslav (17 May 1932, Lišnice), cardinal, metropolitan of Prague, Czech primate. After graduating from high school in České Budějovice, Vlk did two years of military service. He subsequently studied history and archival studies at Charles University in Prague and then worked as an archivist in Třeboň, Jindřichův Hradec, and České Budějovice. It was not until 1964 that Vlk began to study theology at a seminary in Litoměřice. On 23 June 1968 he was ordained a priest and appointed secretary to Bishop Josef Hlouch of České Budějovice. Under pressure from the political authorities, in 1971 Vlk was transferred to the small parish of Rožmitál-pod-Třemšínem. In 1978 the Communist authorities revoked his license to exercise a priestly ministry. Vlk went to Prague, where he earned a living as a window cleaner for eight years. In 1986 he had to abandon this work for health reasons, and he took a job as an archivist at a bank. Throughout that time, Vlk maintained contacts with underground church circles and with democratic opposition activists. In January 1989 the authorities allowed him to resume his pastoral ministry for a "trial period."

Shortly after the Velvet Revolution, Vlk was elected (14 February 1990) and then consecrated (31 March) bishop of České Budějovice. On 27 March 1991 he became archbishop of Prague and primate of the Czech Catholic Church. Like other Czech bishops, Vlk called for maintaining the federal state shared with Slovakia. Vlk's time in office was marked by negotiations that settled relations between the Church and the state in the Czech Republic and talks concerning the return of church property seized by the Communist authorities after 1945. Vlk repeatedly spoke out in defense of people who found themselves on the margins of society in the new economic circumstances. He strove for a Czech-German reconciliation. He supported the lustration law. He called on all clergymen who in conscience felt guilty of collaborating with the Communist secret police to give an account to their bishops, but he emphasized that the Church did not come to terms with its past through lustration but through penance and reconciliation. In 1933 Vlk was elected president of the Council of European Episcopal Conferences. On 26 November 1994 Pope **John Paul II** elevated him to cardinal. In 2000 Vlk ceased to serve as president of the Czech Bishops' Conference but continued as president of the Czech Episcopate's Council for the Media. Vlk is one of the leaders of Focolare, an international religious movement. (AGr)

Sources: *Kdo byl kdo v našich dějinách ve 20. století* (Prague, 1994); Tadeusz Fitych, *Kościół milczenia dzisiaj: Wypowiedzi księży biskupów Czech i Moraw w pięć lat po odzyskaniu niepodległości* (Prague and Nowa Ruda, 1995); Andrzej Grajewski, *Kompleks Judasza: Kościół zraniony. Chrześcijanie w Europie Środkowo-Wschodniej między oporem a kolaboracją* (Poznań, 1999); Catholic Information Agency news bulletin, 27 March 2001; www.catholic-hierarchy.org.

VOITEC Ştefan (19 June 1900, Corabia–4 December 1984, Bucharest), Romanian Communist activist. In 1918 Voitec joined the Social Democratic Workers' Party of Romania (Partidul Social-Democrat al Muncitorilor din România), which was renamed the Socialist Party (Partidul Socialist) in the same year. In 1924 Voitec graduated from the Bucharest Polytechnic and the University of Bucharest. He subsequently worked as a teacher at Sfântul Iosif Gymnasium in Bucharest. From 1925 to 1927 he was the editor of the radical leftist daily *Socialismul*. He also contributed to many Socialist and Communist newspapers, including *Libertatea*, *Lumea nouă*, and *Proletarul*. In 1928 Voitec was one of the founders of the Socialist Workers' Party of Romania (Partidul Socialist al Muncitorilor din România), whose aim was to conduct a social revolution and which demanded that Romania officially recognize the Soviet Union. In 1938 this party joined the Social Democratic Party of Romania (Partidul Social-Democrat din România [PSDR]).

In 1944 Voitec was active in the United Workers' Front, formed by Communists and Socialists. The positions of Voitec and some other PSDR members evolved, approaching those of the Romanian Communist Party (RCP). After **Ion Antonescu**'s government was overthrown and Soviet troops entered Romania, the RCP took over power. From 1944 to 1947 Voitec was minister of national education. From 1945 to 1946 he briefly served as minister of justice and was responsible for the Sovietization of the judicial system. In 1948 the pro-Communist groups of the PSDR merged with the RCP to form the Romanian Workers' Party (Partidul Muncitoresc Român [RWP]). Voitec served as deputy to the Grand National Assembly (from 1946 onwards) and deputy prime minister (1948–52 and 1957–61). From 1955 to 1956 he was a member of the Central Committee (CC), deputy member of the RWP Politburo, and minister of domestic trade. From 1957 to 1959 he was minister of the consumer goods industry. Voitec held the post of deputy chairman of the Council of State from 1961 to 1965 and from 1974 to 1984. In 1961–74 he was speaker of the parliament, and in 1965–84 he was a member of the RCP CC Executive Committee. The vice-chairman of the National Council of the Socialist Unity Front (1974–84), Voitec was a close associate of **Nicolae Ceauşescu**. (LW)

Sources: *Who's Who in the Socialist Countries of Europe* (Munich, London, and Paris, 1989); Józef Darski, *Rumunia: Historia, współczesność, konflikty narodowe* (Warsaw, 1995); Dorina N. Rusu, *Membrii Academiei Române 1866–1999* (Bucharest, 1999); Ion Alexandrescu, Ion Bulei, Ion Mamina, and Ioan Scurtu, *Enciclopedia de istorie a României* (Bucharest, 2000).

VOJTAŠŠÁK Ján (14 November 1877, Zákamenné, Dolný Kubín County [now in Slovakia]–4 August 1965, Řičany, Bohemia), bishop of Spiš, Slovak political prisoner. Born into a large peasant family, after graduating from high school in Ružomberok, Vojtaššák entered a seminary in Spišská Kapitula in 1895. It was then that he met Father **Andrej Hlinka**, who shaped his national consciousness and social views. In July 1901 Vojtaššák was ordained into the priesthood and then worked as a curate in the parishes of Orava and Spiš. An active supporter of the Slovak national movement, he protested the Magyarization of Slovak-populated parishes. In 1908 Vojtaššák co-founded, and then edited the periodical *Svätá Rodina*. In 1910 he became the parish priest of Veličná, where he developed Catholic organizations and organized assistance for the victims of World War I. He supported Hlinka's efforts to separate Slovakia from Hungary and to establish a common state with the Czechs. On 30 October 1918 in Turčiansky Sv. Martin Vojtaššák signed the declaration of the Slovak nation. He later worked for the establishment of an independent Church hierarchy in Slovakia and for its separation from the archdiocese of Esztergom.

On 13 November 1920 Vojtaššák was appointed bishop of Spiš. On 13 February 1921 in Nitra, he was consecrated bishop, along with two other Slovak clergymen, **Karol Kmeťko** and Marián Blaha. They were the first Slovaks to be elevated to bishop. Vojtaššák initiated the organization of a synod of the Spiš diocese in 1924, contributed to the establishment of a new seminary, and developed charity services, as well as a network of Catholic schools. In 1939 he supported the establishment of the Slovak state. From 1940 to 1943, with the consent of the Holy See, he served as a member of the Council of State, a collective supervisory body with limited powers, and he protested the policies of the executive authorities. In 1943, having learned that Slovak Jews were being deported to Nazi extermination camps, Vojtaššák issued a protest to the Slovak authorities, as a result of which the deportations were stopped. He called for the establishment of a special committee to explain the real fate of the deported Jews. When the Communist-inspired uprising broke out in August 1944 and there were numerous killings and cases of violence, the victims of which included Catholic priests, Vojtaššák exhorted the clergy to stay in Slovakia and help those affected. Arrested in May 1945, he was held in a prison in Bratislava for seven months, although no charges were formally brought against him. Released in November 1945, he publicly protested the policies aimed at abolishing Catholic schools and limiting the rights of the faithful. In 1949 he threatened to excommunicate priests who adhered to the so-called peaceful clergy movement. Interned in his own residence on 3 June 1950, Vojtaššák was taken to a prison in Prague in October 1950. In January 1951, along with Bishop **Michal Buzalka** and the Uniate bishop **Pavel Gojdič**, Vojtaššák was accused of high treason in a show trial in Bratislava. In February 1951 he was sentenced to twenty-four years' imprisonment. He was imprisoned in Valdice, Leopoldov, and Ilava. In 1956 he was allowed to settle in a nursing home in Děčín, but after a few months he was again imprisoned. On his eightieth birthday, Vojtaššák received a congratulatory telegram from Pope Pius XII. The prison authorities persecuted Vojtaššák, assigning him to cells he had to share with criminals who tormented the ailing old man morally and physically. Released in September 1963, Vojtaššák was not allowed to return to Slovakia and had to settle in a nursing home near Prague. He was buried in Zákamenné. His funeral turned into a huge silent demonstration of Slovak Catholics. In 1977 his memoirs were published in Canada: *Životopis Jána Vojtaššáka, biskupa spišského* (Biography of Ján Vojtaššák, bishop of Spiš). (AGr)

Sources: *Biographisches Lexikon*, vol. 3; *Kdo byl kdo v našich dějinách ve 20. století.* (Prague, 1994); Jozef Mikuš, *The Three Slovak Bishops* (Passaic, N.J., 1953); Vincent Tatranský, *Biskup Jána Vojtaššak* (Cleveland, 1977); František Mikloško, *Nebudete ich moct rozvratit: Z osudov katolickej Cirkvi na Slovensku v rokoch 1943–89* (Bratislava, 1991); Viktor Trstenský, *Sila wiery, sila pravdy: Život a dielo najdostojnejšieho otca biskupa Jána Vojtaššaka, mučenika Cirkvi a naroda* (Bratislava, 2000); Norbert Kmet', *Postavenie Cirkvi na Slovensku 1948–1951* (Bratislava, 2000).

VOLAJ Gjergji (21 September 1904, Shirokë, near Scutari [now Shkodër]–3 February 1947, Shkodër), Albanian Catholic bishop, victim of communism. Volaj attended St. Francis Xavier College in Shkodër and then studied theology in Padua from 1926 to 1930. Ordained a priest in Shkodër Cathedral (June 1930), he worked in the parish of Mali i Jushit, near Shkrel (Malesia e Madhe). In 1936 he was transferred to Shkrel, where he worked until 1940. On 26 June 1940 Volaj was consecrated bishop and appointed head of the diocese of Sappa. At that time he was the youngest Catholic bishop in the world. His seat was in Zadrimë. In 1944, despite his protests, Communist resistance units plundered the curia's buildings in Zadrimë. On 25 June 1946, during celebrations honoring the Virgin Mary, the patroness of Shkodër, Volaj gave his last homily to the faithful. Defending the rights of Albanian Catholics, he accused the Communist authorities of running a smear campaign. Arrested in 1947, after a short trial Volaj was executed by a firing squad in the Rozafat cinema in Shkodër. The reasons cited for the sentence included the fact that Volaj was a bishop of the Catholic Church. The place of his burial is not known. (TC)

Sources: *Martirizimi i Kishës Katolike Shqiptare (1944–1990)* (Shkodër, 1993); Ndoc Dom Nogaj, *Kisha Katolike Shqiptare 1944 nëntor 1990: Humbje dhe fitore* (Shkodër, 1999); Didier Rance, *Albanie: Ils ont voulu tuer Dieu; La persécution contre l'Église catholique (1944–1991)* (Paris, 1996); Robert Royal, *Catholic Martyrs of the Twentieth Century* (New York, 2000).

VOLDEMARAS Augustinas (4 April 1883, Dysna, near Święciany [Švenčionys]–16 December 1942, Moscow), Lithuanian politician. Voldemaras studied philology and history at St. Petersburg University. After graduating in history (1910), he worked as a lecturer. From 1914 to 1915 he studied in Italy and Sweden and then returned to Russia and obtained a professorship at the university in Perm. In 1916 Voldemaras joined the nationalist National Progress Party (Tautos Pažanga [NPP]), led by **Antanas Smetona**; it called for Lithuania's independence. In September 1917 Voldemaras was Lithuania's delegate to a Kiev conference of nationalities living in Russia; there he was appointed Lithuania's representative to the Ukrainian Central Rada. As an adviser to the Ukrainian delegation, Voldemaras also took part in the peace negotiations between the Bolsheviks and the Central Powers in Brest-Litovsk. In the summer of 1918 Voldemaras returned to Lithuania and was coopted into the Lithuanian Council (Lietuvos Taryba). On 11 November 1918 the Lithuanian Council appointed him prime minister of the first government of independent Lithuania. He also assumed the portfolio of foreign affairs. On 23 November Voldemaras signed an order on the organization of the Lithuanian Army. In December he went to Paris, seeking recognition for Lithuania and asking for the official admission of the Lithuanian delegation to the Peace Conference at Versailles. During his absence, a new cabinet was installed in Lithuania, although Voldemaras kept his post as foreign minister. After the elections to the Constituent Assembly in May 1920, Voldemaras resigned as prime minister. He worked as a lecturer, teaching academic pedagogical courses in Kaunas. When in February 1922 Vytautas Magnus University was established in Kaunas, Voldemaras became its dean of the School of Social Sciences. He also edited the periodical *Tėvynės*

Balsas, in which he sharply criticized the government's policies. Because of this, in 1923 he was expelled from Kaunas and transferred to Varniai, but the following year he returned to the university. In the 1926 elections Voldemaras won a seat on the ticket of the Union of Lithuanian Nationalists (Tautininkų Sąjunga [ULN]).

On 17 December 1926, the Nationalists, supported by Christian Democratic politicians and a part of the army, removed the center-left government of **Mykolas Sleževičius** from power. President **Kazys Grinius** resigned, entrusting the mission of forming a new government to Voldemaras. Smetona became the new president. Voldemaras's government was based on a coalition of Nationalists, Christian Democrats, and the Lithuanian Peasant Union. On 12 April 1927 the parliament passed a vote of no confidence in Voldemaras's government. In response, Smetona dissolved the parliament. Moreover, as Smetona and Voldemaras were reluctant to call new elections, the former allies of the Nationalists withdrew their support for the government. Still, Voldemaras stayed in power because he had the support of the administration and a segment of the army. He strove to improve Lithuania's relations with other countries. In the autumn of 1927 in Geneva he negotiated with **Józef Piłsudski**, convincing him that Lithuania did not want a war with Poland. On 29 January 1928 Voldemaras signed a border agreement with Germany and then a trade agreement with Italy. On 6 May 1929 three leftist students staged an attempt on Voldemaras's life, killing his assistant. Voldemaras became more involved in Iron Wolf (Geležnis Vilkas), a semi-secret paramilitary extreme nationalist organization. Fearing that Voldemaras wanted to stage a coup, Smetona dismissed him as prime minister on 19 September 1929 and then had him deported to Plateliai and later to Zarasai. After a group of officers indeed tried to overthrow Smetona's regime in June 1934, Voldemaras was sentenced to twelve years' imprisonment. In 1938 he was released under an amnesty but was forced to leave Lithuania. In 1939 Voldemaras attempted to return from France, where he lived, but he was arrested and expelled from Lithuania. Shortly after the Soviet invasion of Lithuania in June 1940, Voldemaras again returned to his country, but he was arrested by the Soviet authorities and sent to Ordzhonikidze in the Caucasus. When the Germans approached that region in 1942, Voldemaras was transferred to a prison in Moscow, where he died.

Voldemaras was regarded as a ruthless and extremely ambitious politician who sought dictatorial power. He left a considerable literary output. His doctoral dissertation on agrarian reforms under Emperor Hadrian was published in 1910. In his other historical works, he presented the Lithuanian point of view in the history of the Jagiellonian

state. In the 1920s and 1930s Voldemaras published only political studies, such as *Les relations russo-polono-lithuaniennes* (1920) and *La Lithuanie et ses problèmes: Lithuanie et Allemagne* (1933). In 1976 a collection of his writings was published by Morkus Šimkus in Chicago. (WR)

Sources: *EL*, vol. 6; Saulius Sužiedelis, *Historical Dictionary of Lithuania* (Lanham, Md., 1997); Alfred E. Senn, *The Emergence of Modern Lithuania* (New York, 1959); Leonas Sabiliūnas, *Lithuania in Crisis: Nationalism to Communism* (Bloomington, 1972); Bronis J. Kaslas, ed., *The USSR-German Aggression against Lithuania* (New York, 1973); Alfred E. Senn, "Augustinas Voldemaras in France, 1938–1940," *Journal of Baltic Studies*, 1979, vol. 10, no. 3; Algirdas Banevicius, *111 Lietuvos valstybes 1918–1940 politikos veikeju* (Vilnius, 1991); Henryk Wizner, *Litwa: Dzieje państwa i narodu* (Warsaw, 1999).

VOLOBUYEV Mykhailo (24 January 1900, Nikolayev [Mykolayiv], near Kherson–1932, Soviet Union), Ukrainian economist of Russian descent. Volobuyev taught at the Technical High School of the National Economy in Kharkov (Kharkiv). In 1928 in *Bilshovyk Ukraïny* he published "Do problemy Ukraiinskoy ekonomiky" (On the problem of the Ukrainian economy), in which he stated that the Russian empire had not been a single economic system and that the Ukrainian economy should be examined separately from Russia because of its different development. Volobuyev defended Ukraine's right to control its economic resources. He also pointed out Russian chauvinism in its economic exploitation of Ukraine. Volobuyev's views became very popular in Ukraine, but the Communist authorities sharply attacked him, accusing him of being a "bourgeois nationalist" and an enemy of Soviet rule. Volobuyev was forced to recant his views in the periodical *Kommunist*, and in 1930 in *Bilshovyk Ukraiiny*, in a second article, he condemned the "economic platform of nationalism." Nevertheless, Volobuyev was soon arrested and perished in the Gulag. All supporters of his views were also persecuted. (WR)

Sources: *Encyclopedia of Ukraine*, vol. 5 (Toronto, 1993); Hryhory Kostiuk, *Stalinist Rule in the Ukraine* (New York, 1960).

VOLODYMYR [originally Vasyl Romanyuk] (9 December 1925, ?–14 July 1995, Kiev), metropolitan of the Ukrainian Autocephalous Orthodox Church (UAOC). After the Red Army entered Eastern Galicia in 1944, Volodymyr was arrested by the NKVD and sent to a Soviet forced labor camp for his pro-independence work. From 1944 to 1953 he was imprisoned in Soviet forced labor camps in the Urals and in Kolyma. Freed from the camps, he was forced to remain in internal exile. In 1959 Volodymyr was allowed to return to Ukraine, and he was formally rehabilitated. He commenced correspondence studies at the Moscow Theological Seminary. Ordained in 1964, he began his pastoral ministry in Kosmach, near Kosiv in Pokutia. Arrested in 1972, Volodymyr was sentenced to seven years in a special-regime forced labor camp. He served his sentence in the camps of the Mordvinian ASSR. In 1975 he went on a hunger strike, and in February 1979 he joined the Ukrainian Helsinki Group. As punishment for that, upon his release from labor camp, Volodymyr was forced to settle in the Yakutian ASSR. Released in 1981, it was not until 1984 that he was able to resume his pastoral ministry in the parish of Pistyn. As Communist rule weakened in Ukraine, Volodymyr was consecrated bishop of Bila Tserkva and took on the name of Volodymyr in 1990. After the death of Archbishop **Mstyslav Skrypnyk**, Volodymyr became the Kiev metropolitan of the revived UAOC in October 1993. The year 1980 saw the publication of Volodymyr's *A Voice in the Wilderness*, a collection of letters, appeals, and essays concerning his imprisonment. (WR)

Sources: *Encyclopedia of Ukraine*, vol. 4 (Toronto, 1993); Maksym Sahaydak, *Ethnocide of Ukrainians in the USSR* (Baltimore, 1976); Anatoliy Kalosha, "Kiivskiy patriarkhat: Neprostyi shliakh do ednosti," *Holos Ukraiiny*, 31 July 1993; Stephen K. Batalden, *Seeking God: The Recovery of Religious Identity in Orthodox Russia, Ukraine, and Georgia* (De Kalb, Ill., 1993).

VOLOSHYN Avhustyn (17 March 1874, Kelechin, Subcarpathian Rus–11 July 1945, Moscow), Ukrainian Greek Catholic priest, leader of Subcarpathian Ruthenia. In 1892 Voloshyn entered a seminary in Uzhhorod, and after completing studies there, he studied in Budapest. He was ordained a Greek Catholic priest and worked in a parish in Uzhhorod. In 1900 he gained a diploma to teach mathematics and physics. From 1917 to 1938 Voloshyn headed a teachers' training school in Uzhhorod. He edited textbooks and literary works. Voloshyn's publications include *O pismiennom yazyke podkarpatskikh Rusinov* (The literary language of Subcarpathian Rusyns; 1921) and *Azbuka karpato-ruskoho i tserkovno-slavyanskoho chtennya* (Outline of Subcarpathian Rusyn and Old Church Slavonic literature; 1924). Voloshyn was a prominent Ukrainian politician in Subcarpathian Ruthenia, which constituted a part of Czechoslovakia in 1918–38. Between 1919 and 1925 he was an MP in Prague. He also gained the title of papal chamberlain. After the Munich treaty of September 1938 Voloshyn became a leader of circles that saw a chance to create an independent Subcarpathian state supported by Nazi Germany. Under pressure from the Third Reich, Subcarpathia received autonomy within the framework of Czechoslovakia, and on 8 October 1938 Voloshyn became

head of the government of the country. On 14 March 1939, at the same time the independence of Slovakia was announced, Voloshyn proclaimed the independence of Subcarpathian Ruthenia and became the president of the new state. When it turned out that on 11 March Germany had already agreed to the incorporation of Subcarpathia into Hungary and Hungarian forces invaded the territory, Voloshyn went to Prague (which was occupied at that time by the Germans) to continue pedagogical work. He became dean and later rector of the Ukrainian university in Prague. In April 1944 Voloshyn contributed to the unification of groups led by Hetman **Pavlo Skoropadskyi** and **Andriy Melnyk** and independent factions that remained outside the Ukrainian Supreme Liberation Council into a council advisory to Archbishop **Andriy Sheptytskyi**. Arrested in Prague by the Soviet security organs, Voloshyn was sent to Lefortovo Prison in Moscow and soon executed there. His *Spomyny* (Memoirs) were published in exile in 1959. (WR)

Sources: *Encyclopedia of Ukraine*, vol. 5 (Toronto, 1993); *Martirologia ukraińskich cerkow u czetirioch tomach*, vol. 2 (Toronto, 1985); Vincent Shandor, *Carpatho-Ukraine in the Twentieth Century* (Cambridge, Mass., 1997).

VORONIN Vladimir (25 May 1941, Corjova, near Kishinev [now Chişinău]), post-Communist Moldovan politician, ethnic Russian. After graduating from a technical high school in Kishinev in 1961, Voronin became the manager of a bakery. From 1966 to 1971 he was director of a similar enterprise in Dubasari and subsequently worked in Moscow's Institute of Food Industry and was active in the district committee of the Communist Party of Moldavia (Partidul Comunist din Moldova [CPM]) in Dubasari and in the CPM regional committee in Ungheni. From 1980 to 1990 Voronin served as deputy to the Supreme Soviet of the Moldavian SSR. In 1983 he became a member of the Academy of Social Sciences of the Central Committee (CC) of the CPSU, a member of the CPSU CC, and head of the CC organizational department. Voronin was first secretary of the district party committee in Bender from 1985 to 1989 and minister of internal affairs (with the rank of general) of the Moldavian SSR from 1989 to 1990. Because he was an opponent of the policy of perestroika and since the CPM lost influence after the parliamentary elections in which the opposition took part, Voronin went to Moscow in 1990; there he worked as a lawyer in the Police Academy of the Ministry of Internal Affairs of the Russian Federation from 1991 to 1993.

In 1993 Voronin served as co-chairman of the organizing committee of a new Communist Party of Moldova (the CPM had been declared illegal in 1991), and in 1994 he became first secretary of the party. Although the Communists and Voronin did not openly question the independence of Moldova, they called for Moldova's close cooperation with the Commonwealth of Independent States (CIS) and for the introduction of Russian as an official language, and they distanced themselves from Romania and the Western countries. Voronin was against privatization, particularly against the privatization of land, and he supported state protectionism. In the 1996 presidential elections, Voronin obtained 10.2 percent of the votes, and in the second round he supported **Petru Lucinschi**, who became president. In 1997, following a split within the CPM, the party changed its name to the Party of Communists of the Republic of Moldova (Partidul Comuniştilor din Republica Moldova [PCRM]), and Voronin became its chairman. In the 1998 parliamentary elections the PCRM won 40 out of 101 seats, and Voronin became head of the largest parliamentary caucus. In order to enlarge its political base, in 1999 the PCRM partially accepted the existence of a market economy and a multiparty system. However, Voronin still opposed the privatization of land and the main branches of industry. He was also against Moldova's having ties with Romania, Western countries, and such organizations as NATO, the European Union, and the International Monetary Fund.

In 2000, in the face of a conflict between the parliament and President Lucinschi, the PCRM entered into an agreement with center and right-wing parties and succeeded in limiting the president's powers. However, the PCRM failed to elect a new head of state. As part of his struggle against the parliament, Lucinschi called early parliamentary elections, which were held in February 2001 and gave a sweeping victory to the PCRM (71 out of 101 seats). The new parliament elected Voronin as president of Moldova. He assumed the office on 7 April 2001. After his election, Voronin withdrew plans to integrate Moldova into the CIS. However, he did not seek a rapprochement with the West and saw Russia as Moldova's main partner. He also did not insist on the withdrawal of Russian troops from the separatist Transnistria. In 2001 Voronin ceased negotiations with this region concerning its possible unification with Moldova, thus justifying the presence of the Russian troops. At the beginning of 2002 the government established de facto by Voronin introduced Russian as an obligatory subject in schools. (LW)

Sources: Józef Darski, *Rumunia: Historia, współczesność, konflikty narodowe* (Warsaw, 1995); Bugajski; www.cidob.org; www.moldova.md; www.osw.waw.pl.

VOSS Augusts (30 October 1916, Saltykovo, near Tobolsk, Siberia–10 February 1994, Moscow), Latvian Communist activist. Born into a family of Latvian settlers in Siberia, Voss completed teacher training courses and then worked as a teacher at schools in Tyumen Province (1933–36). In 1939 he graduated from the Department of Physics and Mathematics of the State Teachers' Institute in Tyumen and worked as a high school teacher in Armizonskoye. Mobilized into the Red Army in 1940, Voss completed a course for political commanders in 1941 and became a member of the All-Union Communist Party (Bolsheviks) in 1942. During the German-Soviet war he took part in the defense of Moscow, serving in the anti-aircraft units and later becoming deputy commander for political affairs in the Forty-third Latvian Division. Seriously wounded in January 1943, after recovery Voss returned to work as a headmaster of a high school in Vikulovo. In 1945 he went back to Latvia and started working in the apparatus of the Central Committee (CC) of the Communist Party of Latvia (CPL). In 1948 he graduated from the Higher Party School in Moscow and then worked as a secretary of the organizational committee of the CPL at the Latvian State University. In 1953 Voss became a lecturer in economic sciences at the Academy of Social Sciences of the CC of the Communist Party of the Soviet Union (CPSU). He was head of the Department of Culture and Science of the CPL CC (1953–54), a member of the CPL CC (from 1954 onwards), and a deputy to the Supreme Soviet of the Latvian SSR (1955–85). From 1954 to 1960 Voss served as head of the Organizational Department, and from 1960 to 1966, as secretary of the CC of the CPL. In 1966 he became first secretary of the CPL CC and in 1971 a member of the CPSU CC (until 1990). Voss intensified the Russification efforts started by his predecessors. He spoke very little Latvian; therefore, he tried to persuade the party and state apparatus to use Russian, which, according to him, was "the language of Socialist culture." Voss followed a policy of blind loyalty to Moscow and developed a program of industrialization in Latvia that stimulated an influx of Russian labor from the Soviet Union and the Russification of the society. In August 1984 Voss left the leadership of the CPL to assume the post of chairman of the Council of Nationalities of the Supreme Soviet of the Soviet Union and held this post until 1989. Voss authored *Pēc Ļeņina novēlējumiem* (Lenin's behests; 1968). (EJ)

Sources: *Latvijas PSR Mazā enciklopēdija*, vol. 3 (Riga, 1970); *Latvijas Padomju enciklopēdija*, vol. 10 (Riga, 1987); Romuald J. Misiunas and Rein Taagepera, *The Baltic States: Years of Dependence, 1940–1990* (Berkeley, 1990); A. Bērziņa, "Miris Augusts Voss," *Diena*, 12 February 1994; Juris Dreifelds, *Latvia in Transition* (Cambridge, 1995); I. Lipa, "Augusta Vosa brāļa stāsts," *Vakara Ziņas*, 6 August 2001.

VRHOVEC Josip (9 February 1926, Zagreb), Yugoslav Communist activist. In 1943 Vrhovec joined the Partisans led by **Josip Broz Tito**, and in 1944 he became a member of the Communist Party of Yugoslavia (CPY). In 1951 he completed economic studies in Belgrade. From 1952 to 1969 Vrhovec was the editor-in-chief of the daily *Vjesnik* and the weekly *Vjesnik u srijedu*, and he worked as a correspondent in the United States. In January 1970 he became member of the Executive Committee of the Central Committee (CC) of the League of Communists of Croatia (LCC). Vrhovec started to advance through the political ranks after the so-called Croatian Spring, when Tito conducted a purge of the LCC in 1971. From December 1971 to April 1974 Vrhovec served as secretary of the LCC CC Executive Committee. He was a member of the Presidium of the CC of the League of Communists of Yugoslavia (LCY) (May 1974–June 1978, May 1983–May 1984) and chairman of its Committee for Ideological and Theoretical Affairs (May 1974–June 1978). Vrhovec served as federal secretary for foreign affairs (that is, foreign minister) (May 1978–May 1982), chairman of the Presidium of the LCC CC (May 1983–May 1984), and a member of the presidency of the Socialist Federal Republic of Yugoslavia (14 May 1984–15 May 1989). (AO)

Sources: *Who's Who in the Socialist Countries of Europe*, vol. 3 (Munich, London, and Paris, 1989); www.mfa.gov.ju/history/ministri/jvrhovec_e.html.

VUIA Traian (17 August 1872, Surducul Mic [now Vuia Traian]–2 September 1950, Bucharest), Romanian attorney and pioneer of aviation. In 1892 Vuia enrolled in the School of Mechanics of the Technical University of Budapest. After one year, because of financial difficulties, he transferred to the School of Law of Budapest University, where he was able to continue his studies and work at the same time. In May 1901 Vuia earned a Ph.D. in law and then settled in Lugoj, where he designed his first flying machine. Owing to financial constraints, in July 1902 he decided to go to Paris—which was then considered the center of aeronautics—hoping to find someone interested in financing his project. In mid-February 1903 Vuia sent his project proposal to the Paris Academy of Sciences, which rejected it, stating that a heavier-than-air mechanical machine could not possibly fly. Despite many financial difficulties, Vuia did not give up. In the autumn of 1904 he began building an engine of his own invention. In the same year he received a patent for his invention in Great Britain. This aircraft, called the Traian Vuia 1, was completed in December 1905, and on 18 March 1906 it took off and flew a dozen or so meters at Montesson, near Paris. Vuia soon built new prototype machines, the Vuia 1-bis and Vuia 2. Between 1918 and 1922 he also constructed two helicopters. At the Paris Peace Conference in 1919 Vuia supported the Romanian cause in the international arena. In 1925 he designed a steam generator. During the interwar period Vuia continued his research in the field of aeronautics. During World War II he served as chairman of the Romanian National Front in France. In May 1946 he became an honorary member of the Romanian Academy (*Academia Română*). The name of Vuia's native village has been changed in his honor to Traian Vuia. (PC)

Sources: Elie Carafoli, *A Pioneer of World Aviation: Traian Vuia* (Bucharest, 1956); Constantin C. Gheorghiu, *Romanian Inventions and Priorities in Aviation* (Bucharest, 1979); Ion N. Iacovachi, *Traian Vuia: Viata și opera* (Bucharest, 1988).

VUJOVIĆ Radomir (8 September 1895, Požarevac–1938? Soviet Union), Communist activist of Serbian descent. In 1911 Vujović joined a Socialist group at school. During World War I he studied in France, where he was active among Serbian students and radical French left-wing groups. In November 1919, under the pseudonym "Wolf," Vujović attended the founding congress of the Communist Youth International (CYI), a section of the Communist International. He traveled through Western Europe establishing CYI units in Switzerland, Austria, and Germany. At the Second CYI Congress in Moscow (1921), Vujović was elected to its executive committee and became one of its two secretaries. He was a CYI representative accredited to the Comintern. In April 1922 Vujović was a member of a Comintern delegation to a meeting with representatives of other factions of the workers' movement in Berlin. After Willy Münzenberg left in 1923, Vujović became secretary general of the CYI. At the Fifth Congress of the Comintern Vujović became a member of the Executive Committee and the Presidium of the Comintern. He supported the faction led by Leon Trotsky; therefore, after Stalin's offensive, Vujović's position weakened. In May 1927 he was expelled from the Comintern's leadership and then from the party. Arrested in the summer of 1927, Vujović was held in prison for nearly five years. Released in 1932, he went to the Soviet Union. Arrested after Sergey Kirov's assassination in December 1934, Vujović was exiled to Verkhneuralsk and executed, most probably in 1938. (WR)

Sources: Lazitch; *Enciklopedija Jugoslavije*, vol. 8 (Zagreb, 1971); Radoljub Čolaković, *Kazivanja o jednom pokoljenju* (Zagreb, 1964); Radoljub Čolaković, *Sečanja i sustreti* (Zagreb, 1959).

VUKIČEVIĆ Velimir (11 July 1871, Oparić, Serbia–27 November 1930, Belgrade), Serbian politician. Vukičević finished a gymnasium and then graduated from the Superior School (Velika Škola) in Belgrade (1893). He subsequently worked as a teacher at high schools in Škol and Belgrade. From 1902 to 1904 he was a school inspector in the town of Smederovo and later a lecturer at a teacher training college in Jagodina and a teacher at a high school in Pirot. Elected to the parliament on the ticket of the Serbian Radical Party, Vukićević served as minister of public works (1921–22), minister of post and telegraph (1924), and minister of education (1925). He later became president of the Belgrade stock exchange. On 17 April 1927 Vukičević became prime minister of a government based on the centralist radicals and the Serbian Democratic Party (Srpska Demokratska Stranka [SDS]). The position of his government weakened when the Croatian Peasant Party, led by **Stjepan Radić**, lost public support. However, Vukičević succeeded in securing the cooperation of the Slovene People's Party instead. The parliamentary elections of July 1927 strengthened the centralist forces and their allies. In February 1928 Vukičević's cabinet remained in power despite a split in the SDS, but protests by the opposition increased, particularly after the Peasant Democratic Coalition demanded a reorganization of the state along federalist lines and rights for the other nationalities equal to those of the Serbs. Parliamentary debates were more and more heated, with outbreaks of fisticuffs and police interventions. Unable to achieve its goals in parliament, the Peasant Democratic Coalition staged street demonstrations. Difficult relations with Italy added to the government's problems. Its concessive attitude caused sharp criticism by the opposition; in answer, government circles launched a press campaign against Radić. On 20 June 1928 a radical deputy fired shots during a heated parliamentary debate, killing two and wounding three opposition deputies, including Radić, who died of his wounds. In the face of the crisis that followed, Vukičević resigned as prime minister on 7 July 1928. (WR)

Sources: *Enciklopedija Jugoslavije*, vol. 8 (Zagreb, 1971); Zvonimir Kulundžić, *Atentat na Stjepana Radića* (Zagreb, 1967); Jerzy Skowronek, Mieczysław Tanty, and Tadeusz Wasilewski, *Historia Słowian południowych i zachodnich* (Warsaw, 1988); Mark Biondich, *Stjepan Radić, the Croat Peasant Party, and the Politics of Mass Mobilization, 1904–1928* (Toronto, 2000).

VUKMANOVIĆ Svetozar, pseudonym "Tempo" (3 August 1912, Podgor, Montenegro–7 December 2000, Reževići), Yugoslav Communist activist. After graduating from high school in Cetinje, Vukmanović studied law in Belgrade. He became an activist in the League of Yugoslav Communist Youth (Savez Komunističke Omladine Jugoslavije [SKOJ]) in 1932 and a member of the Communist Party of Yugoslavia (CPY) in 1933. Arrested several times for his political activities, in October 1940 Vukmanović was elected to the CPY Central Committee (CC), where he used the pseudonym "Tempo." On 26 September 1941 he became commander of the General Staff of **Josip Broz Tito**'s Partisans in Bosnia and Herzegovina. In February 1943, as a delegate of the CPY CC and the General Staff, Vukmanović went to Macedonia, where he strengthened the Communist organization promoting the Yugoslav cause: he established a new CC of the Communist Party of Macedonia and the General Staff of the Partisans in Macedonia, who launched successful military operations. On 20 June 1943, Vukmanović, representing Yugoslavia, and **Enver Hoxha**, representing Albania, signed a draft agreement on the establishment of a permanent General Staff of the National Liberation Army of the Balkans by August 1943. Vukmanović also discussed this idea in Greece but failed to gain support. As a result of the negative attitude of the Bulgarian Communists, Tito abandoned the idea of establishing the staff in September 1943. However, Vukmanović gained the consent of the Communist Party of Greece for Macedonians to establish separate military units within the Greek People's National-Liberation Army in August 1943.

In March 1945 Vukmanović became deputy minister of national defense, and in 1948, minister of mining. He served as president of the Council for Industry, and from 1953 on he headed the Economic Council, advising the Federal Executive Council. From 1952 to 1958 Vukmanović was vice-president of the Federal Executive Council, and from 1958 to 1967 he was head of the Central Council of Yugoslav Trade Unions. He became a member of the Executive Committee of the CC of the League of Communists of Yugoslavia (LCY) in 1952 and secretary of the CC in 1958. From October 1966 on Vukmanović sat on the LCY CC Presidium. Vukmanović's publications include the following: *O narodnoj revoluciji u Grčkoj* (1950; *How and Why the People's Liberation Struggle of Greece Met with Defeat*, 1985); *Ekonomski problemi Jugoslavije* (Yugoslavia's economic problems; 1954); *Aktuelni problemi medžunarodnog sindikalnog pokreta* (1962; *Topical Problems of the International Trade Union Movement*, 1962); *Problemi razvoja i unapredženja socijalističke poljoprivrede: Izabrani govori i članci* (Problems of the development and promotion of Socialist agriculture: Selected speeches and articles; 1967); *Revolucija koja teče* (Revolution in progress; 1971); *Borba za Balkan* (1981; *Struggle for the Balkans*, 1990); *Pisma iz Reževića* (Letters from Reževići; 1983); and *Zašto se i kako raspala Jugoslavija* (Why and how Yugoslavia disintegrated; 1994). (AO)

Sources: *Enciklopedija Jugoslavije*, vol. 8 (Zagreb, 1971); *Wielka encyklopedia powszechna PWN*, vol. 12 (Warsaw, 1969); Valentina Georgieva and Sasha Konechni, *Historical Dictionary of the Republic of Macedonia* (Lanham, Md., 1998); Stephen E. Palmer, Jr. and Robert R. King, *Yugoslav Communism and the Macedonian Question* (Hamden, Conn., 1971); Stoyan Pribichevich, *Macedonia, Its People and History* (University Park, Pa., and London, 1982); Irena Stawowy-Kawka, *Historia Macedonii* (Wrocław, 2000).

VUKOTIĆ Janko (18 February 1866, Čevo, Montenegro–4 February 1927, Belgrade), Montenegrin and Yugoslav military commander. In 1886 Vukotić graduated from the Military Academy in Modena, Italy. He subsequently served in the Montenegrin Army and was promoted to brigadier in 1902. After the Montenegrin Army was reorganized in 1910, Vukotić assumed command of the First Division. During the First Balkan War he commanded the eastern front, and in mid-November 1912 the units he led besieged Shkodër. In 1914 Vukotić was appointed chief of staff of the army and commander of the northern front. When the Austro-Hungarian troops launched a southward offensive at the end of October 1915, the army resisted for three months but then surrendered. Vukotić was put in charge of the evacuation of the government from Cetinje. On 12 January 1916 he became commander-in-chief of the army, but the following day the capital was forced to surrender. For a few days he continued to command the retreat. After the capitulation, Vukotić was held prisoner for the rest of the war. When the Kingdom of Serbs, Croats, and Slovenes was established after the end of World War I, Vukotić served in its army (from 1919 on). In 1926 he was promoted to general. (WR)

Sources: *Enciklopedija Jugoslavije*, vol. 8 (Zagreb, 1971); John D. Treadway, *The Falcon and the Eagle: Montenegro and Austria-Hungary, 1908–1914* (West Lafayette, Ind., 1983).

VULKOV Ivan (19 January 1875, Kazanluk–20 April 1962, Stara Zagora), Bulgarian general and politician. In 1896 Vulkov graduated from the Military School in Sofia and then served in the arsenal, in the artillery, and in other units. In 1909 he graduated in land surveying from the General Staff Academy in St. Petersburg. Vulkov fought in the Balkan Wars (1912–13) as chief of staff of the troops that laid siege to Adrianople (Edirne). From 1913 to 1915 he worked as a lecturer at the Military School in Sofia. After Bulgaria joined World War I on the side of the Central Powers, Vulkov held a variety of military positions, including those of commander of an infantry regiment and chief of staff of an infantry division. From 1919 to 1923 he was the director of the Cartographic Institute. Co-founder (1919) and then chairman of the Military League, Vulkov took part in the military coup of 9 June 1923. After accepting the portfolio of minister of war in the government of **Aleksandur Tsankov** in June

1923, Vulkov suppressed the Communist uprising of September 1923. After an assassination attempt on the life of Tsar **Boris III** in Sveta Nedelya Cathedral in Sofia (April 1925), Vulkov unleashed a reign of terror. In January 1926 he became minister of war in the government of **Andrei Liapchev** and strove to subordinate the Military League to the tsar. When his efforts failed, he tried to replace the Military League with the State Military League (1928). In July 1923 Vulkov became major general, in March 1925 lieutenant general, and in May 1928 colonel general (highest rank of general in Bulgaria). In January 1929 he retired. He subsequently served as minister plenipotentiary to Italy until 1934 and then retired from politics. In 1954 the Communists sentenced Vulkov to death for "activities against the people." Because of his advanced age, the sentence was commuted to life imprisonment. Vulkov died in prison. His publications include *Voenna topografiia* (Military topography; 1911) and *Iztochniiat sektor pri blokadata i atakata na Odrinskata krepost 1912–1913 g.* (The eastern sector during the blockade and attack on the Adrianople Fortress in 1912–1913; 1913). Vulkov edited the periodicals *Godishnik na Geografskia institut pri Ministerstvoto na voinata* (1922–29) and *Bŭlgarska voenna misul* (1943). (JJ)

Sources: *Entsiklopediya Bulgariya*, vol. 1 (Sofia, 1978); R. Rumenin, *Ofitserskiyat korpus v Bulgariya 1879–1944*, vol. 1 (Sofia, 1996); A. Gurkov, *General-polkovnik Ivan Vulkov* (Sofia, 1997); Tasho Tashev, *Ministrite na Bulgariya 1879–1999: Entsiklopedichen Spravochnik* (Sofia, 1999); Angel Tsurakov, *Entsiklopediya. Pravitelstvata na Bulgariya: Khronologiya na politicheskiya zhivot 1879–2001* (Sofia, 2001).

VYDŪNAS Vilius [originally Storasta] (22 March 1868, near Heydekrug, Prussia [now Šilutė, Lithuania]–20 February 1953, Detmold, West Germany), Lithuanian writer and philosopher. After graduating from a teacher training college in Ragnit, East Prussia (now Neman, Kaliningrad district, Russia), Vydūnas taught French and English at a high school in Tilsit (now Sovetsk, Russia) until 1912. While a student at the Universities of Leipzig and Berlin, he mastered Sanskrit and developed a lifelong interest in Indian philosophy. From 1917 to 1919 Vydūnas taught Lithuanian language and literature at Berlin University. He was the most prominent representative of the Lithuanian community in East Prussia during the interwar period. He strove to develop the Lithuanian culture in the so-called Lithuania Minor and criticized the German policy of Germanization—for example, in the work *Sieben Hundert Jahre deutsch-litauischer Beziehungen* (1932), for which he was persecuted by the Nazis. In 1935 the Lithuanian cultural institutions that he supported were disbanded. Vydūnas himself was arrested in 1938. Vydūnas's writings to a great extent drew on Oriental religious philosophy, fashionable during the interwar period. He was a proponent of the doctrines of pantheism and reincarnation. He also promoted an idealistic vision of the medieval pagan culture of Lithuania. Vydūnas's most important works are the dramas *Prabočių šešėliai* (Shadows of ancestors; 1908), *Amžina ugnis* (The eternal fire; 1912), and *Pasaulio gaisras* (The world on fire; 1928). (WR)

Sources: *EL*, vol. 6; Saulius Sužiedelis, *Historical Dictionary of Lithuania* (Lanham, Md., 1997); Vincas Mykolaitis, *Vydūno dramaturgija* (Kaunas, 1935); Aleksandras Merkelis, ed., *Vydūnas* (Detmold, 1948); Vacys Bagdonavičius, *Filosofiniai Vydūno humanizmo pagrindai* (Vilnius, 1987); Androné B. Willeke, "Vudūnas' Dramas: A Ritual of National Salvation," *Journal of Baltic Studies*, 1990, no. 4; Bernardas Aleknavičius, *Vydūnas* (Vilnius, 1999).

VYNNYCHENKO Volodymir (7 August 1880, near Kherson–6 March 1951, Mougins, France), Ukrainian writer and politician. In 1901, during his studies at Kiev University, Vynnychenko joined the Revolutionary Ukrainian Party, which in 1905 was transformed into the Ukrainian Social Democratic Party (USDP). From 1907 he was a member of its Central Committee. In his first literary works—*Holota* (Rascaldom; 1905) and *Kto voron?* (Who's a crow? 1906)—Vynnychenko depicted the life of the provincial populace, its misery and suffering. Later on he often reached for a means of expression that would show the brutality of social relations. Vynnychenko spent 1907–14 in exile, mainly in France. At that time he wrote many works presenting the experience of the revolution of 1905: the dramas *Velykyi molokh* (1907; *The Great Moloch*, 1907), *Brekhnia* (The lie; 1910), and *Chornaya pantera i bilyi medvid* (The black panther and the white bear; 1911); the novel *Chestnist z soboiu* (Honesty to oneself; 1911); and the ironic *Zapyśky kyrpatoho Mefistofelia* (Notes by Mefisto; 1917). After his return to the Ukraine he joined in the independence activities of the Ukrainian Social Democrats.

In April 1917 Vynnychenko was among the chief founders of the Ukrainian Central Rada (Council). He also assumed the post of its vice-president. In May 1917 he was a member of a Rada delegation to Petrograd that demanded autonomy for the Ukraine and recognition of its provisional government by Russia. After the Russian Provisional Government rejected these demands, on 23 June 1917 Vynnychenko wrote the First Universal of the Rada, proclaiming the independence of the Ukraine. Five days later he became the head of the General Secretariat, which functioned as a provisional executive government, and also headed the Secretariat of Home Affairs. On 11 July 1917 Vynnychenko met with a delegate of the Russian Provisional Government, Alexander Kerenski, who de facto recognized the Secretariat as the Ukrainian government. On 20 November 1917 Vynnychenko signed the Third Universal of the Rada, in which the Ukrainian National Republic (UNR) was proclaimed. Despite the laudable democratic principles and individual freedoms declared by the authorities of the republic, its territory continued to be the scene of peasant attacks on mansions and of Jewish pogroms. The Fourth Universal of the Rada (24 January 1918), after which the UNR was recognized by the Central Powers, also failed to put an end to the atrocities. Nor did it avert the Bolshevik offensive in the northeast of the country. Since Vynnychenko's political line—which relied upon radical revolutionary agitation and at the same time sought an agreement with the Bolsheviks—failed, at the end of January 1918 Vynnychenko resigned from the Secretariat. During the occupation of the Ukraine by the Central Powers Vynnychenko mediated between the representatives of the Rada and Hetman **Pavlo Skoropadskyi**. On 14 November 1918 Vynnychenko became the head of the Directorate. Under pressure from the Bolshevik offensive, the Directorate had to move to Vynnytsa, where, after another failure to reach an agreement with the Bolsheviks, on 13 February 1919 Vynnychenko resigned from his post and went into exile. There he wrote his three-volume memoirs, *Vidrodzhennya Ukrainy* (The revival of the Ukraine), describing the struggle for the independence of the country; they were published in Canada in 1985.

After the Bolsheviks created the Ukrainian Soviet Socialist Republic in January 1920, Vynnychenko accepted the concept of cooperation with Soviet Russia on the basis of the Bolshevik declaration of 6 November 1919 on the sovereignty of the Ukraine. He returned to the Ukraine and discussed joining the USSR government and the Politburo of the Ukrainian Communist Party (Bolshevik). Vynnychenko was appointed vice-president of the Council of People's Commissars of the USSR, but he did not join the party. Disappointed with the lack of possibilities for independent activities and prospects of sovereignty for a Communist Ukraine, Vynnychenko went into exile again. In 1926 in Lviv (Lwów) he published *Povrot na Ukrainu* (Return to the Ukraine), in which he explained his decision of cooperation with the Bolsheviks. Between 1922 and 1928 Vynnychenko published the *Nova Ukraina* journal in Prague. After that he left for France, where he mainly wrote. In 1928 he published *Soniachna mashyna* (Sunny machine), and in 1949, *Nova zapovid* (New prophecy), in which he outlined Utopian solutions to world conflicts. Other works were published after his death—for example, the novel *Slovo za toboiu, Staline* (Funeral speech for

Stalin; 1971) and *Krasa i syla* (Beauty and power; 1988). After 1991 many of Vynnychenko's works were reprinted in the Ukraine. (WR)

Sources: *Ukraine: A Concise Encyclopedia*, vol. 2 (Toronto, 1963); *Kleine Slavische Biographie* (Wiesbaden, 1958); Volodymir Vynnychenko, *Schchodennyk*, vols. 1–2 (Edmonton, 1980–83); Andrzej Chojnowski, *Ukraina* (Warsaw, 1997); Volodymir Panchenko, *Budynok z khymerami: Tvorchist Volodymira Vynnychenki 1900–1920 r.r. u evropeiskomu literaturnomu kontekstu* (Kirovgrad, 1998).

VYSHYVANYI Vasyl [originally Habsburg-Lothringen Wilhelm] (10 February 1895, Pula, Croatia–after 1949, Soviet Union), Austrian duke, son of Archduke Karl Stephan of Saybusch, Galicia, Austria-Hungary (now Żywiec, Poland). In February 1918 Vyshyvanyi commanded the Austrian troops, including the Ukrainian Sich Riflemen, that entered southern Ukraine. After the Treaty of Brest-Litovsk was signed in February 1918, he supported the cause of Ukrainian independence. In May 1918 he announced—to the indignation of the Galician Poles—that Emperor Charles was ready to divide Galicia between the Poles and the Ukrainians. Because Vyshyvanyi was sympathetic toward the cause of Ukrainian independence, some conservative circles in Ukraine wanted him to become the ruler of Ukraine. In the autumn of 1918 he transferred his headquarters from Zaporizhzhya to Bukovina. In 1919 he served as colonel in the army of the Ukrainian National Republic (UNR) and an adviser to Ataman (commander-in-chief) **Symon Petlura**. Disinherited from the Saybusch estates, Vyshyvanyi lived in Austria during the interwar period. In August 1947 he was arrested by order of the Soviet Ministry of Internal Affairs (MVD) in Vienna and deported to the Soviet Union, where he either perished in prison (1949 or 1951) or died soon after being released in 1956. (WR)

Sources: *Encyclopedia of Ukraine*, vol. 2 (Toronto, 1988); Nykyfor Hirniak, *Polk. Vasyl Vyshyvanyi* (N.p., 1956); Pavlo Shandruk, *Arms of Valor* (New York, 1959); Maciej Kozłowski, *Między Sanem i Zbruczem* (Kraków, 1990); Tadeusz Andrzej Olszański, *Historia Ukrainy XX w.* (Warsaw, n.d.)

VYTVYTSKYI Stepan (13 March 1884, Uhorniki [Uhornyky], Galicia–19 October 1965, New York), Ukrainian politician. Vytvytskyi graduated in law and then earned a doctorate. While a student, he was the leader of the Academic Hromada in Lemberg (Lviv, Lwów) and the Sich Society in Vienna. After graduating, he opened a law practice in Drohobych. He was active in various Ukrainian community organizations. From 1915 to 1918 Vytvytskyi was an editor of the periodicals *Dilo* and *Svoboda*. In 1918 he became the secretary of the Ukrainian National Council of the Western Ukrainian National Republic (Ukraiinska Natsionalna Rada Zakhidno-Ukraiiinskoy Narodnoy Respubliki [ZUNR]). On 22 January 1919 in Kiev Vytvytskyi took part in the ceremony of uniting the ZUNR and the Ukrainian National Republic (Ukraiinska Narodna Republika [UNR]). He subsequently represented Ukraine in negotiations with the Entente states. In late 1919 Vytvytskyi served as deputy chairman of the UNR Directorate delegation to Warsaw, but then he resigned this post in protest against the position of the Ukrainian government during the negotiations. After the fall of the UNR, Vytvytskyi left for Austria and headed the Ministry of Foreign Affairs of **Yevhen Petrushevych**'s Ukrainian government-in-exile in Vienna. From 1921 to 1923 Vytvytskyi headed the Ukrainian missions in Paris and London. After returning to Poland, he worked as a lawyer. He also served as chairman of the local board of the Prosvita Society in Drohobych and belonged to almost every Ukrainian organization in this city. At that time Vytvytskyi represented a more conciliatory attitude toward Poland. In 1928 he became a deputy senator on the ticket of the Ukrainian National Democratic Alliance (Ukraiinske Natsionalno-Demokratychne Obyednannya [UNDO]), and in 1932 he joined the UNDO Central Committee. In 1938 he became deputy chairman of the UNDO. From 1935 to 1939 Vytvytskyi served as a member of the Polish parliament. After World War II, he lived in Germany, where he co-founded the Ukrainian National Council and served as its vice-president and minister of foreign affairs. Vytvytskyi subsequently moved to the United States, where in 1954 he became president of the UNR government-in-exile. (WR)

Sources: *Encyclopedia of Ukraine*, vol. 5 (Toronto, 1993); *Kto był kim w Drugiej Rzeczypospolitej* (Warsaw, 1994).

W

WAJDA Andrzej (6 March 1926, Suwałki), Polish film and theater director. During World War II Wajda worked on the railways and attended secret educational classes. He received a degree in painting from Kraków's Academy of Fine Arts in 1949 and in film directing from the State Film School in Łódź in 1953. Wajda made his debut as a film director with the film *Pokolenie* (Generation) in 1955 and as a theater director at the Wybrzeże Theater in Gdańsk in 1959. One of the main founders of the Polish school of cinematography in the 1950s, Wajda directed such films as *Kanał* (Canal; 1957) and *Popiół i diament* (Ashes and diamonds; 1958). He later often drew upon the time of war for inspiration—for example, in the films *Krajobraz po bitwie* (Landscape after battle; 1970), *Korczak* (1990), *Pierścionek z orłem w koronie* (The ring with a crowned eagle; 1992), and *Wielki tydzień* (Holy Week; 1995). Wajda is also famous for screen adaptations of Polish literary classics, including *Popioły* (Ashes; 1965), based on a novel by Stefan Żeromski; *Brzezina* (Birch grove; 1970) and the Oscar-nominated *Panny z Wilka* (Lasses from Wilko; 1979), based on the prose works of **Jarosław Iwaszkiewicz**; *Wesele* (The wedding; 1973), based on a drama by **Stanisław Wyspiański**; the Oscar-nominated *Ziemia obiecana* (The promised land; 1975), based on a novel by **Władysław Reymont**; and *Pan Tadeusz* (Master Thaddeus; 1998), based on the epic poem by Adam Mickiewicz. Wajda's films presenting the Communist experience include *Człowiek z marmuru* (Man of marble; 1977), *Bez znieczulenia* (Without anesthesia/Rough treatment; 1978), and *Człowiek z żelaza* (Man of iron; 1981). In such films as *Wszystko na sprzedaż* (Everything for sale; 1969), *Polowanie na muchy* (Hunting flies; 1969), and *Panna Nikt* (Miss Nobody; 1996) Wajda dealt with contemporary social issues. Some of his films were made in cooperation with foreign producers; for example, *Danton* (1983) was made in France. His films often gave rise to heated political and ideological disputes.

Wajda has worked with many theaters, both in Poland (including Kraków's Old Theater and Warsaw's Atheneum and Powszechny Theaters) and abroad (including Berlin's Schaubühne Theater, Moscow's Sovremennik Theater, Tokyo's Benisan Theater, and New Haven's Yale Repertory Theater). His most important theater productions include Wyspiański's *Noc listopadowa* (November night; 1974); Stanisława Przybyszewska's *Sprawa Dantona* (The Danton affair; 1975); *Z biegiem lat, z biegiem dni . . .* (As years go

by, as days go by . . . ; 1978); *Zbrodnia i kara* (Crime and punishment; 1984), based on Fyodor Dostoevsky's novel; and William Shakespeare's *Hamlet* (1989). Wajda also worked with Polish Television to make the series *Ziemia obiecana* (1975) and *Z biegiem lat, z biegiem dni . . .* (1980).

Wajda was artistic director of Film Unit X (1972–83) and president of the Polish Filmmakers' Association (1978–83). In 1982 he became an honorary member of the British Academy of Film and Television Arts (BAFTA) and then a member of the European Film Academy and the Union of European Theaters. In 1988 he joined the Civic Committee of the Chairman of Solidarity, where he chaired a subcommittee for culture and the media. Wajda served as senator (1989–91) and chairman of the Polish President's Council for Culture (1992–94). He became a member of the Polish Academy of Arts and Sciences in 1994 and a member of the French Académie des Beaux-Arts in 1997. In 1987 he received the Kyoto Prize, which allowed him to initiate the establishment of the Manggha Center of Japanese Art and Technology in Kraków (1994). Wajda is the holder of many film awards, including the most prestigious ones: the Grand Prix at the Cannes International Film Festival (1981), the French César Award (1982), the Felix Award (1990), the Silver Bear Award in Berlin (1996), the Golden Lion in Venice (1998), and an Honorary Oscar for Lifetime Achievement (2000). Wajda has received numerous honorary doctorates, as well as the highest state distinctions of Japan, France, and Germany. In 2000 he received the prestigious Grand Award of the Culture Foundation. Wajda critically drew on national tradition but also sought inspiration from universal values. As a result, his films have appealed to audiences throughout the world. By using poetic metaphors and expressive symbolism, he raised contemporary moral issues. Wajda has authored autobiographical books, including *Powtórka z całości* (Revision of the whole; 1986); *Wajda mówi o sobie: Wywiady i teksty* (Wajda talks about himself: Interviews and texts; 1991); *Podwójne spojrzenie* (Double insight; 1998); *O polityce, sztuce, o sobie* (On politics, art, and himself; 2000); and *Kino i reszta świata* (The cinema and the rest of the world; 2000). (JS)

Sources: Tadeusz Miczka, *Inspiracje plastyczne w twórczości filmowej i telewizyjnej Andrzeja Wajdy* (Katowice, 1987); *International Dictionary of Films and Filmmakers*, vol. 2 (Chicago and London, 1991); Maciej Karpiński, *Teatr Andrzeja Wajdy* (Warsaw, 1991); Wanda Wertenstein, *Zespół filmowy "X"* (Warsaw, 1991); Geoffrey Nowell-Smith, *The Oxford History of World Cinema* (Oxford, 1996); Ewelina Nurczyńska-Fidelska, *Polska klasyka literacka według Andrzeja Wajdy* (Katowice, 1998); Wiesław Kot, *Dzieje filmu polskiego* (Poznań, 1999); www.wajda.pl.

WAŁĘSA Lech (29 September 1943, Popowo, Bydgoszcz Province), Polish worker, social activist, and politician.

In 1961 Wałęsa graduated from a vocational school for agricultural machinery technicians in Lipno. In 1967 he began working as an electrician in the Gdańsk Shipyard (then called the Lenin Shipyard). He took part in the workers' protests in December 1970 and was elected to the strike committee. Arrested and interrogated, he made some commitments to the secret police but did not fulfill them later. Released four days after the fall of **Władysław Gomułka**'s regime, Wałęsa was active in the trade unions, holding a variety of positions, including that of trade union safety inspector. In February 1976 at a trade union meeting Wałęsa criticized the situation in Poland, and as a result he lost his job. After several months, he managed to get a job as an electrician at ZREMB Repair and Construction Works. In June 1978 he began to work with the underground Founding Committee of the Free Trade Unions of Pomerania. In July 1978 he was twice arrested by the secret police, and in December he was fined for taking part in a demonstration commemorating the victims of the December 1970 events, and he was again dismissed from his job. In 1979 Wałęsa became one of the editors of *Robotnik Wybrzeża*, a periodical of the Free Trade Unions. He was one of the signatories of the Charter of Workers' Rights and a co-organizer of an anniversary demonstration on 18 December 1979 at which he delivered a speech to several thousand people announcing that within a year a monument to the victims of the December 1970 events would be erected. In January 1980 Wałęsa was a member of an unofficial workers' committee whose aim was to defend workers dismissed from Elektromontaż, a large Polish electrical construction firm where he had been working since May 1979. In February 1980 he lost his job again for taking part in protest actions.

On 14 August 1980, after the outbreak of a strike in the Gdańsk Shipyard, Wałęsa climbed over the shipyard fence and joined the workers at a rally inside. Elected head of the Strike Committee, Wałęsa became head of the Inter-Factory Strike Committee (Międzyzakładowy Komitet Strajkowy [MKS]) on 16 August. He led the strike, proving himself to be a charismatic leader with excellent skills in communicating with mass audiences. Wałęsa led the negotiations with Deputy Prime Minister **Mieczysław Jagielski**. He approached **Tadeusz Mazowiecki** and **Bronisław Geremek** with a proposal to establish a committee of experts to advise the MKS. This committee supported Wałęsa during the negotiations with the government delegation. On 31 August Wałęsa signed the August Agreement. He became chairman of the Inter-Factory Founding Committee of Independent Self-Governing Trade Unions in Gdańsk. On 17 September 1980, at a congress of representatives of the new trade unions, a national federation

of unions was established under the name of the Independent Self-Governing Trade Union–Solidarity (Niezależny Samorządny Związek Zawodowy "Solidarność"). Wałęsa became chairman of its National Coordinating Commission (Krajowa Komisja Porozumiewawcza), the supreme executive body of the union.

Wałęsa won great popularity as the leader and icon of Solidarity. He had a great ability to sense the mood of crowds at big rallies and easily established excellent rapport with his audience. He emphasized his Catholicism and was in constant touch with Church authorities. He advocated a moderate strategy and tried to avoid an all-out confrontation with the Communist authorities. However, he always agreed to local confrontations when he sensed a determination to undertake them; in all cases, though, he strove for an agreement that would end the conflict and widen the scope of freedom. In March 1981, following the Bydgoszcz conflict, Wałęsa opposed a general strike. In his day-to-day work and during negotiations with the authorities, especially during particularly dramatic conflicts, Wałęsa was supported and advised only by a handful of his close associates and experts. This caused criticism from various groups and circles within Solidarity, which accused him of dictatorial leanings. On 2 October 1981, at the First Congress of Solidarity in Gdańsk, Wałęsa was elected chairman of the union by 55 percent of the votes.

On 13 December 1981 Wałęsa was interned. He was detained in Chylice, near Warsaw, then in Otwock, and in May 1982 he was transferred to Arłamów in the Bieszczady Mountains. He refused to capitulate or to condemn the participants in the civil resistance movement. Released on 14 November 1982, Wałęsa was subsequently treated as a "private person." In 1983 he was again employed as a worker in the Gdańsk Shipyard. He did not go underground but maintained regular contacts with Solidarity activists and advisers, Church authorities, and foreign politicians and journalists. He appealed to the authorities of the Polish People's Republic to restore trade union pluralism. Pope John Paul II granted him special audiences during his pilgrimages to his homeland in 1983 and 1987. In 1983 Wałęsa received the Nobel Prize for Peace. After the amnesty of 1986, Wałęsa established the Provisional Council of Solidarity, transformed into the National Executive Commission in 1987. In May 1988 he joined the strike in the Gdańsk Shipyard, and in August 1988, during another strike, he supported the demand for the legalization of Solidarity. However, Wałęsa accepted an offer to negotiate with the authorities, and on 31 August he met with General **Czesław Kiszczak**; the meeting marked the beginning of a process of negotiations that ultimately led to the Round Table Talks. On 30 November 1988 Wałęsa took part in a televised debate with Alfred Miodowicz, leader of the state-sponsored All-Polish Alliance of Trade Unions. This debate was widely seen as Solidarity's triumphant return to the official political arena. In December 1988 Wałęsa visited France, where he was received with honors befitting a head of state.

On 18 December 1988 the Civic Committee of the Chairman of Solidarity was constituted. It was composed of the most famous Solidarity activists, as well as experts and organizations that cooperated with Solidarity. On 6 February 1989 Wałęsa took part in the inaugural sessions of the Round Table Talks. He subsequently participated in major decisions that prepared the ground for the agreement of 5 April 1989. Wałęsa did not run in the elections of 4 April 1989, but his photographs with each Solidarity candidate—printed in the form of a poster—were a basic element of the victorious electoral campaign. In August 1989 Wałęsa called for an agreement in the coalition of the Civic Parliamentary Club (Obywatelski Klub Parlamentarny [OKP], consisting of Solidarity MPs and senators), the United Peasant Party (Zjednoczone Stronnictwo Ludowe), and the Democratic Party (Stronnictwo Demokratyczne). He proposed Mazowiecki as a candidate for prime minister. In the fall of 1989 Wałęsa made visits to several West European countries and the United States. On 15 November he spoke in the U.S. Congress, where his speech was received with an ovation. At the end of 1989 Wałęsa began to propose initiatives that were in the government's powers; for example, he demanded the withdrawal of Soviet troops from Poland (January 1990). He also criticized the government for its slowness in reforming the country. At the Second Congress of Solidarity (19–25 April 1990) Wałęsa was reelected its chairman. He announced his intention to run for the office of president of the Republic of Poland.

In the spring of 1990 Wałęsa confronted the government group within the Solidarity camp, declaring the so-called "war at the top." He had the support of those Solidarity circles that had lost direct influence on the government and on the OKP leadership, as well as of many local Solidarity activists. As a result of Wałęsa's efforts, the membership of the Civic Committee of the Chairman of Solidarity was expanded, and a new group of leaders took over the initiative within the committee; consequently, the adherents of Mazowiecki's government left the OKP on 24 June 1990. In his electoral campaign Wałęsa criticized the government and called for accelerated political transformations, decommunization, general ownership reforms ("100 million [zloty] for every citizen"), and a return to grass-roots social activity. Wałęsa obtained 40 percent of the votes in the first

round of the elections and 74 percent of the votes in the second round (9 December 1990).

On 22 December 1990 Wałęsa was sworn in as president of the Republic of Poland. However, he never tried to deliver on his election promises. He established a cabinet, led by **Jan Krzysztof Bielecki**, that continued the economic reforms started by **Leszek Balcerowicz** (who kept the post of deputy prime minister). Activists of the Center Alliance (Porozumienie Centrum) took charge of the President's Chancellery, but after a conflict with Wałęsa, they resigned on 1 November 1991. Wałęsa dissolved the parliament elected in June 1989 and called free parliamentary elections on 27 October 1991. In the new Assembly, he appointed a cabinet headed by **Jan Olszewski**, on the motion of a center-right coalition, but his relations with Olszewski were bad. On 4 June 1992, after a scrutiny action by Minister **Antoni Macierewicz** (who produced a list of alleged Communist collaborators with Wałęsa on it), Wałęsa supported the dismissal of the government. He assigned the post of prime minister to **Waldemar Pawlak**, leader of the Polish Peasant Party (Polskie Stronnictwo Ludowe [PSL]). In the face of difficulties in forming the government, Wałęsa supported a coalition of Solidarity parties and a cabinet with **Hanna Suchocka** at the helm (July 1992). After the Assembly passed a vote of no confidence in the government on 28 May 1993, Wałęsa dissolved the parliament and called early elections. These elections, held on 19 September 1993, were based on a new electoral statute. Its results brought defeat to post-Solidarity parties and success to the (post-Communist) Alliance of the Democratic Left (Sojusz Lewicy Demokratycznej [SLD]).

Wałęsa was forced to enter into cooperation with the SLD–PSL coalition, but he maintained the constitutional right to veto Assembly resolutions and continued to have a say in the appointment of the ministers of foreign affairs, interior, and national defense. He often came into conflict with the SLD–PSL coalition and with Prime Ministers Pawlak and **Józef Oleksy**. Wałęsa's personnel policy was characterized by instability; he tried to justify it with theoretical arguments (for example, the so-called bumper theory, according to which some politicians are needed to front unpopular reforms and should be replaced once they lose the public trust). Wałęsa increasingly relied on the support and advice of his former chauffeur, Mieczysław Wachowski, who was suspected of links with the former Communist security services but was nevertheless promoted to a ministerial position in the President's Chancellery. Wałęsa tried to maintain special relations with top-ranking military officers. He supported the concept of stretching the law to find solutions that would suit him, particularly for personal advantage. This approach came to be known as the "falandization of the law" (from the surname of Minister Lech Falandysz, Wałęsa's main legal adviser). Between 1990 and 1995 Wałęsa lost the support of successive groups of the intelligentsia and the post-Solidarity parties. He also lost his former ability to establish rapport with the masses, and he withdrew from public meetings. In the 1995 presidential elections Wałęsa obtained 33 percent of the votes in the first round and 48 percent in the second round, losing to **Aleksander Kwaśniewski**, leader of the SLD. After losing the elections, Wałęsa established the Christian Democratic Party of the Third Republic of Poland (Chrześcijańska Demokracja III Rzeczypospolitej Polskiej), but this party failed to enter the Assembly in the 1997 elections. The Lustration Court cleared Wałęsa of charges of working with the former secret police; therefore, he ran in the 2000 presidential elections, but he gained barely over 1 percent of the vote. Wałęsa authored the memoirs *Droga nadziei* (1990; *Way of Hope*, 1987) and *Droga do wolności* (1991; *The Struggle and the Triumph: An Autobiography*, 1992). Wałęsa often gave lectures and public speeches in various countries. (AF)

Sources: *Lech Wałęsa* with an introduction by Bronislaw Geremek (Gdańsk, 1990); Jarosław Kurski, *Wódz* (Warsaw, 1993); Caroline Lazo, *Lech Wałęsa* (New York, 1993); Paweł Rabiej and Inga Rosińska, *Kim pan jest, panie Wachowski?* (Warsaw, 1993); Roger Boyes, *The Naked President: A Political Life of Lech Walesa* (London, 1994); Jan Skórzyński, *Ugoda i rewolucja: Władza i opozycja 1985–1989* (Warsaw, 1995); Antoni Dudek, *Pierwsze lata III Rzeczpospolitej 1989–1995* (Kraków, 1997); Janusz A. Majcherek, *Pierwsza dekada III Rzeczpospolitej 1989–1999* (Warsaw, 1999).

WARSKI Adolf [originally Warszawski] (20 April 1868, Warsaw–1937?, Soviet Union), Polish Communist activist of Jewish descent. Warski finished six grades of high school. He established ties with the revolutionary movement in his youth, becoming a member of the International Social Revolutionary Party Proletariat, and he co-founded the Polish Workers' Union (Związek Robotników Polskich [ZRP]) in 1889. After the tsarist police broke up the ZRP, Warski went into exile in France and Germany (1892), serving as one of the main leaders of the Social Democracy of the Kingdom of Poland (Socjaldemokracja Królestwa Polskiego [SDKP]), renamed the Social Democracy of the Kingdom of Poland and Lithuania (Socjaldemokracja Królestwa Polskiego i Litwy [SDKPiL]) in 1900. A close associate of **Rosa Luxemburg**, Warski was one of the leading ideologues of the revolutionary left, which opposed the reconstruction of the Polish state and called for close cooperation with Russia as part of a world revolution. From 1905 to 1907 Warski organized strikes in the Kingdom of Poland. After the failure of the revolution of 1905, he made his way back to Germany, where he was interned during World War I.

In the fall of 1918 Warski returned to Warsaw. He co-founded the Soviets of Workers' Delegates and the Communist Workers' Party of Poland (Komunistyczna Partia Robotnicza Polski [KPRP]; renamed the Communist Party of Poland, Komunistyczna Partia Polski [KPP], in 1925). Warski was a member of the Central Committee (CC) (1919–24, 1925–29) and a member of the Politburo of the CC of the party (1928–29). As one of the party leaders, he supported Soviet Russia during the Polish-Soviet war in 1920. After the Treaty of Riga (March 1921), Warski consistently supported the Russian Bolshevik Revolution and maintained close contacts with the Soviet Embassy in Warsaw. However, he was instrumental in the party's adoption of a modified program on national and agrarian issues. In 1923 Warski supported the faction led by Leon Trotsky in Trotsky's struggle against Stalin; this led to a conflict within the KPP after the death of Lenin in 1924. As a result, Warski and the activists of the so-called majority faction were expelled from the leadership in July 1924. Warski kept his post as editor-in-chief of *Nowy Przegląd*, a theoretical periodical of the party. He and the KPP initially supported the coup staged by **Józef Piłsudski** in May 1926; however, as the pickets organized by the KPP were soon dispersed by the police, the Communists went over to the opposition. In 1926 Warski became a member of parliament by taking over Stefan Królikowski's seat. He headed the Communist faction from 1928 on. As Communist activities were against the law and the causes Warski promoted were detrimental to the interests of the state, on 13 March 1929 the Polish Assembly stripped him of his parliamentary immunity and made a decision to hand him over to court authorities. On the party's orders, in April 1929 Warski resigned his parliamentary seat and secretly made his way to the Soviet Union. Accused of "rightist deviation," he was suspended as a KPP member in the same year. Arrested during the great purges in June 1937, Warski disappeared without trace. He was rehabilitated after the Twentieth CPSU Congress in 1956. In 1958 Warski's two-volume *Wybór pism i przemówień* (Selected writings and speeches) was published. (WR)

Sources: *Kto był kim w II Rzeczpospolitej* (Warsaw, 1994); M. K. Dziewanowski, *The Communist Party of Poland* (Cambridge, Mass., 1959); Feliks Tych, *PPS-Lewica 1914–1918* (Warsaw, 1960); *Tragedia KPP* (Warsaw, 1989).

WASILEWSKA Wanda (21 January 1905, Kraków–29 July 1964, Kiev), Polish Communist activist and writer. Wasilewska's father, the eminent pro-independence Socialist politician **Leon Wasilewski**, did not devote much attention to her. In 1923 Wasilewska became a member of the Union of Independent Socialist Youth and established ties with the Communists. In 1927 she graduated in Polish philology from the Jagiellonian University in Kraków and began working as a teacher. She also edited *Płomyk* and *Płomyczek*, periodicals for children. She was active in the Workers' University Society. In 1925 Wasilewska began working with the International Organization for Aid to Revolutionaries. From 1934 to 1937 she was a member of the Chief Council of the Polish Socialist Party (Polska Partia Socjalistyczna [PPS]). She was active in the Polish Teachers' Association, in which the extreme left wing gained much influence, and in the League for the Defense of Human and Civic Rights. In 1936, on her initiative, a special issue of *Płomyk* came out in which the Soviet Union was glorified. Wasilewska co-founded the Congress of Culture Workers in Lwów (Lviv) in 1936 and co-organized a teachers' strike in 1937. Also in 1937 she began to contribute to *Dziennik Popularny*, a periodical that was linked to the Communist Party of Poland (Komunistyczna Partia Polski [KPP]) and supported a united leftist front. Wasilewska also published articles in both legal and illegal leftist papers and periodicals, including *Łamy*, *Oblicze dnia*, *Po prostu*, and *Robotnik*. Until 1939 she formally continued as a member of the PPS, although she followed the Kremlin's political line.

During the September 1939 campaign, Wasilewska went to Lwów and became involved in active political and social work under the Soviet occupation. At that time she published propaganda pasquinades on interwar Poland. She was made president of the local branch of the Union of Polish Writers. At the end of 1939 Wasilewska attempted to establish contacts with prewar PPS activists in Warsaw, but her efforts were unsuccessful because at the time of collaboration between the NKVD and the Gestapo she was seen in the company of German officers. As a Soviet citizen, Wasilewska was elected to the Supreme Soviet of the Soviet Union in 1940. In 1941 she joined the All-Union Communist Party (Bolsheviks) and worked on the Main Political Board of the Red Army. From 1941 to 1943 she edited *Nowe Widnokręgi*, a periodical of the Communist left wing in the Soviet Union, and then the periodical *Wolna Polska*. Wasilewska had close relations with Stalin and initially advocated that Poland enter the state structures of the Soviet Union. At Stalin's instigation, she became president of the Main Board of the Union of Polish Patriots (Związek Patriotów Polskich [ZPP]) in June 1943 and in this capacity closely followed Stalin's guidelines. Wasilewska was the main founder of the Tadeusz Kościuszko First Division. On 15 July 1943 in Sielce

on the Oka River she gave a fiery speech to Polish soldiers who were going to the front. In 1944 Wasilewska became a member of the Central Bureau of Polish Communists in the Soviet Union. She completely accepted Stalin's policy toward Poland, and in the summer of 1944 she was a founding member of the Polish Committee of National Liberation (Polski Komitet Wyzwolenia Narodowego [PKWN]), a Kremlin-dependent political structure that competed with the government-in-exile of the Republic of Poland. Wasilewska recommended PKWN members to Stalin. She was formally appointed vice-president of the PKWN and a member of the National Home Council (Krajowa Rada Narodowa [KRN]) but de facto did not exercise the powers of these positions. In the fall of 1944 Wasilewska took part in unsuccessful negotiations at the Kremlin conducted by **Stanisław Mikołajczyk**, the prime minister of the London-based Polish government-in-exile, with PKWN representatives on the establishment of a common government.

After the war, Wasilewska remained in the Soviet Union, where she married for the third time, this time becoming the wife of the Ukrainian writer **Oleksander Korniychuk**, and she settled in Kiev. She served as a deputy to the Supreme Soviet of the Soviet Union until 1964. In 1956 she became a member of the World Peace Council. Wasilewska was a leading representative of the propagandist revolutionary and Socialist realist movement in Polish literature. Her most important works include: *Oblicza dnia* (Colors of the day; 1934); *Ojczyzna* (Fatherland; 1935); *Ziemia w jarzmie* (Land under the yoke; 1938); *Płomień na bagnach* (Flame in the marshes; 1940); *Tęcza* (Rainbow; 1945); *Rzeki płoną* (Rivers on fire; 1952); and *Że padliście w boju* (That you fell in battle; 1958). In 1943 Wasilewska received a Stalin Prize for literature. Her collected writings were published in four volumes in Warsaw (1955–56), based on a similar six-volume Moscow edition. Before her death, Wasilewska recorded her memoirs in Warsaw. They were published in *Archiwum Ruchu Robotniczego* (Archives of the Workers' Movement) in 1982. (WD/WR)

Sources: Mołdawa; *Literatura polska XX wieku: Przewodnik encyklopedyczny*, vol. 2 (Warsaw, 2000); Stefan Korboński, *W imieniu Rzeczypospolitej* (Paris, 1954); Helena Zatorska, *Wanda Wasilewska* (Warsaw, 1976); Eleonora Syzdek, *Działalność Wandy Wasilewskiej w latach drugiej wojny światowej* (Warsaw, 1981); Władysław Pobóg-Malinowski, *Najnowsza historia polityczna Polski*, vol. 3 (London, 1986); Zbigniew S. Siemaszko, *W sowieckim osaczeniu* (London, 1991).

WASILEWSKI Leon, pseudonyms "Leon Płochocki" and "Osarz" (24 August 1870, St. Petersburg–10 December 1936, Warsaw), Polish politician, diplomat, and historian; father of **Wanda Wasilewska**. Wasilewski graduated from high school in St. Petersburg and then completed his studies in Lemberg (Lwów, Lviv) and Prague. While a student, he joined the National League (Liga Narodowa) and served as a member from 1893 to 1894. He dealt with ethnic issues relating to the Ukrainians and the Czechs. After graduation, Wasilewski went to Switzerland, where he joined the Union of Polish Socialists Abroad (Związek Zagraniczny Socjalistów Polskich [ZZSP]) in 1896. Elected to the ZZSP leadership at a congress of the ZZSP in 1897, he became one of the leaders of the Polish Socialist Party (PPS). He then took up the post of editor of *Przedświt* and moved along with this periodical to Kraków in 1903. During the 1905 revolution Wasilewski was briefly active in the Kingdom of Poland. After a split in the Polish Socialist movement in 1906, he was a leading activist of the PPS–Revolutionary Faction and a member of its Central Workers' Committee (along with **Józef Piłsudski** and **Walery Sławek**). He also edited *Robotnik.* A secretary of the Commission of Confederated Independence Parties from 1912 onwards, Wasilewski was one of the closest co-workers of Piłsudski during World War I. He was active in the Polish National Organization (Polska Organizacja Narodowa) (1914), the Supreme National Committee (Naczelny Komitet Narodowy) (1914–17), the Central National Committee (Centralny Komitet Narodowy) (1917), the Convention of Organization A (Konwent Organizacji A, a top secret group that operated during the time when Piłsudski was interned), and the Polish Military Organization (Polska Organizacja Wojskowa).

After Poland regained its independence, Wasilewski served as minister of foreign affairs in the government of **Jędrzej Moraczewski** from November 1918 to January 1919. He then went to Paris, where he represented Piłsudski, the chief of state, on the Polish National Committee (Komitet Narodowy Polski) until April 1919. He subsequently worked with the Polish delegation to the Paris Peace Conference. After returning to Poland, Wasilewski dealt with Poland's relations with the Baltic states and Ukraine. From August 1919 to January 1920 he was in charge of a campaign aimed at establishing a government in Lithuania that would be favorably inclined toward Poland. In the autumn of 1920 he joined the Polish delegation to peace negotiations with Soviet Russia, and in March 1921 he was a signatory of the Riga Peace Treaty. Wasilewski supported the "Promethean" program, which called for independence for the Kremlin-dominated nations of the Soviet Union. In 1928 he became a member of the PPS Chief Board and its vice-president in 1931. Wasilewski was a member of the moderate wing of the party. In 1924 he became president of the Institute for Research in the Modern History of Poland; in 1929 an editor of its press organ, *Niepodległość*; and in 1931 president of the Institute for Ethnic Affairs. He was a member of the editorial committee of Piłsudski's *Pisma—Mowy—Rozkazy* (Writings, speeches, orders). An expert on ethnic issues in Central and Eastern Europe, Wasilewski authored the following (among other works): *Narodowości Austro-Węgier* (The nations of Austria-Hungary; 1907); *Kwestia żydowska na ziemiach dawnej Rzeczypospolitej* (The Jewish question in the lands of the former Republic of Poland; 1913); *Śląsk polski* (Polish Silesia; 1915); *Polityka narodowościowa Rosji* (Russia's ethnic policy; 1916); *Rosja wobec Polaków w dobie konstytucyjnej* (Russian attitudes toward the Poles during the constitutional period; 1916); *Kresy Wschodnie* (The Polish Eastern Territories; 1916); *Ukraińska sprawa narodowa w jej rozwoju historycznym* (The historical development of the Ukrainian national issue; 1925); *Zarys dziejów PPS* (An outline of the history of the PPS; 1925); *Sprawy narodowościowe w teorii i życiu* (Ethnic issues in theory and practice; 1929); *Skład narodowościowy państw europejskich* (The ethnic composition of European states; 1933); *Kwestia ukraińska jako zagadnienie międzynarodowe* (The Ukrainian question as an international issue; 1934); and *Józef Piłsudski jakim go znałem* (Józef Piłsudski as I knew him; 1935). (WD)

Sources: *Kto był kim w Drugiej Rzeczypospolitej* (Warsaw, 1994); *Nowa encyklopedia powszechna PWN*, vol. 6 (Warsaw, 1996); Władysław Pobóg-Malinowski, *Najnowsza historia polityczna Polski*, vol. 2 (London, 1983); Barbara Stoczewska, *Litwa, Białoruś i Ukraina w myśli politycznej Leona Wasilewskiego* (Kraków, 1998); Andrzej Nowak, *Polska i trzy Rosje: Studium polityki wschodniej Józefa Piłsudskiego (do kwietnia 1920 roku)* (Kraków, 2001).

WASIUTYŃSKI Wojciech (8 September 1910, Warsaw–19 August 1994, Rye, New York), Polish journalist and politician. Wasiutyński completed high school in Warsaw and graduated from the School of Law of Warsaw University in 1932. In 1936 he received a Ph.D. in the history of Polish law. During his studies he began writing for the national democratic press, and after graduating, Wasiutyński was one of the founders of the Radical Nationalist Camp (Obóz Narodowo-Radykalny [ONR]) which had elements of a totalitarian regime. He co-authored the ONR program declaration of September 1934 and the ONR Falangist program of 1937. He also presented his views in the book *Naród rządzący* (The ruling nation; 1934). In September 1939, along with a wave of refugees from Warsaw, Wasiutyński found himself in the Eastern Borderlands (Kresy), and then via Hungary he managed to get to France. There he was active in the National Party (Stronnictwo Narodowe [SN]). After the collapse of France Wasiutyński was threatened with arrest; therefore he left for Great Britain in September 1942. He served in the Tenth Dragoon Regiment in Scotland and then was assigned to the diplomatic service. From September 1944 he was again in active service and worked in the press section of the First Armored Division. After the demobilization Wasiutyński settled in London. Between 1948 and 1957 he was an editor of *Myśl Polska* and wrote for other emigrant magazines. He also worked with Radio Free Europe (RFE), the Polish Section of the BBC, and the Voice of America. In 1957 Wasiutyński was elected president of the Association of Polish Journalists in London. However, he resigned this post in 1958 because he assumed the post of deputy, and then director, of the Polish section of the RFE in New York. Wasiutyński moved to the United States, where he edited *Nowy Dziennik* and also wrote for the London *Wiadomości*. From 1958 until his death Wasiutyński was president of the Roman Dmowski Institute in New York. In postwar works Wasiutyński rejected totalitarian views and considerably broadened his political perspective. He published, for example, *Tysiąc lat polityki polskiej* (A thousand years of Polish policy; 1946); *Millenium—tysiąclecie Polski chrześcijańskiej, 996–1966* (The millennium of Christianity in Poland, 996–1966; 1964); and an analysis of the history of the nationalist movement, *Czwarte pokolenie* (The fourth generation; 1982). He also wrote for the underground press in Poland. Wasiutyński exerted an ideological influence upon the Young Poland Movement in Poland. (WR)

Sources: Szymon Rudnicki, *Obóz Narodowo-Radykalny* (Warsaw, 1985); Jan Żaryn, "Stronnictwo Narodowe na emigracji," in Andrzej Friszke, ed., *Warszawa nad Tamizą* (Warsaw, 1994); Krzysztof Kawalec, "System polityczny Wojciecha Wasiutyńskiego," in Andrzej Friszke, ed., *Myśl polityczna na wygnaniu* (Warsaw, 1995).

WEISS Peter (7 July 1952, Bratislava), post-Communist Slovak politician. In 1975 Weiss completed his studies in philosophy at the university in Bratislava. From 1975 to 1989 he worked at the Marx-Lenin Institute of the Central Committee (CC) of the Communist Party of Slovakia (CPS), where he did research on Slovak society. In December 1989 he joined the CC of the CPS and the CC of the Communist Party of Czechoslovakia (CPC). In January 1990 he became president of the Executive Committee of the CC of the CPS. After the Velvet Revolution, Weiss was a representative of the younger, undiscredited Communist activists, quickly becoming one of the top party leaders. In June 1990 he became a deputy to the Slovak National

Council, and in October, at a congress of the CPS in Prešov, he was elected the party's leader. Weiss insisted that the party dissociate itself from its disgraceful past and called for its transformation into a Western-style Social Democratic party. In order to make this transformation credible, in January 1991 the party changed its name to the Party of the Democratic Left (Strana Demokratickej L'avice [SDL]), and in December 1991 a decision was made that the SDL leave the confederation with the Czech Communists, who had failed to undertake any internal reforms. These changes brought results: in the elections of June 1992 the SDL received almost 15 percent of the vote, becoming the second most influential party in Slovakia, and Weiss was elected deputy speaker of the Slovak parliament. In the elections of September and October 1994 the SDL achieved unsatisfactory results, which undermined Weiss's position. On 28 April 1996 at a congress in Nitra, Weiss lost the position of party chairman to Jozef Migaš. Weiss became SDL vice-chairman responsible for foreign policy and held this post until August 2000. From October 1998 to September 2002 Weiss served as chairman of a parliamentary committee for foreign affairs. However, he was losing influence in the SDL, which under Migaš's leadership increasingly drifted toward the left. In January 2002, along with (among others) **Brigita Schmögnerova**, Weiss left the SDL and founded the Social Democratic Alternative (Sociálnodemokratická Alternatíva [SDA]) on 20 February 2002. At the founding congress of the SDA on 13 April 2002 Weiss was elected its deputy chairman. In the elections of September 2002 the SDA received only 1.8 percent of the vote and failed to enter parliament; therefore, taking responsibility for this failure, Weiss resigned. (PU)

Sources: *ČBS*; Ján Liďák, Viera Koganová, and Dušan Leška, *Politické strany a hnutia na Slovensku po roku 1989* (Bratislava, 1999); www.sdalternativa.sk/opweiss.asp.

WEKERLE Sándor (14 November 1848, Mór–26 August 1921, Budapest), Hungarian politician. Born into a German family that had settled in Hungary, Wekerle graduated in law from Budapest University. In 1870 he became an official in the Ministry of Finance, in 1878 head of a department, and in 1882 ministerial adviser. In 1886 Wekerle became secretary of state and actually directed the finances of the state. From 1889 to 1895 Wekerle served as minister of finance, becoming the leading financial expert of the Habsburg monarchy. He reorganized the tax system and the financial accounts of Austria-Hungary, and he drafted bills on consumption taxes on sugar and alcohol, excise duties on tobacco, and the commutation of royalties and the conversion of national debts. In November 1892 Wekerle became prime minister and simultaneously held the portfolio of minister of finance.

The first Hungarian prime minister with a middle-class background, he established a balanced budget and made a switch to the gold standard. He also drafted legislation on the separation of church and state. With some effort, Wekerle pushed through bills introducing vital statistical records and obligatory civil marriages. In exchange for Emperor Francis Joseph's signature endorsing these bills, Wekerle offered to resign, which he did on 1 January 1895.

From 1896 to 1906 Wekerle was president of the Administrative Court and later also held the post of director of the National Casino. In 1905 the Liberal Party, which had ruled the country for thirty years, lost the elections to the opposition "national coalition," which drew on the tradition of the 1848–49 Hungarian Revolution and criticized the agreement of 1867 that gave Hungary autonomy in internal affairs. After more than a year of tension, Francis Joseph agreed that the "national coalition" could establish a government, on condition that the coalition would not change the foundations of the dualist state. This condition was accepted. On 8 April 1906 Wekerle—a politician faithful to the idea of the agreement of 1867—became head of this coalition government. He also served as minister of finance. Among other things, Wekerle planned to reform the tax system, but because he had to make numerous concessions since he did not have a sufficient political base (although he had joined the co-ruling Constitutional Party), only some of the reforms he had planned were implemented. Wekerle resigned on 17 January 1910. He became prime minister for the third time on 20 August 1917, becoming head of a minority government and trying to prevent the collapse of the monarchy. His plans to extend voting rights and grant broad autonomy to national minorities within the framework of the Hungarian kingdom ended in failure. On 31 October 1918, three days after Wekerle's resignation, a republican government led by Count **Mihály Károlyi** was established. Under the Hungarian Soviet Republic, Wekerle was held under arrest as a hostage. From the autumn of 1919 onwards he was involved only in business. Wekerle served as a member of parliament four times (1887–96, 1906–10, 1917–18, and 1920–21), always representing the party then in power. He was elected a corresponding member (1914) and then a full member (1918) of the Hungarian Academy of Sciences. He was a member of the Freemasons. (JT)

Sources: *Magyar Életrajzi Lexikon*, vol. 2 (Budapest, 1969); *Nagy Képes Milleniumi Arcképcsarnok* (Budapest, 1999); Oszkar Jaszi, *Revolution and Counterrevolution in Hungary* (London, 1924); Holger H. Herwig and Neil M. Heyman, *Biographical Dictionary of World War I* (Westport, Conn., 1982); Géza Andreas von Geyr, *Sándor Wekerle, 1848–1921: Die politische Biographie eines Staatsmannes der Donaumonarchie* (Munich, 1993); Steven Bela Vardy, *Historical Dictionary of Hungary* (Lanham, Md., 1997).

WEÖRES Sándor (22 June 1913, Szombathely–22 January 1989, Budapest), Hungarian poet and writer. Born into a wealthy family with landed gentry and military traditions, Weöres received a thorough education in his youth, studying aesthetics, history, law, and philosophy (he earned a Ph.D. in 1939). In 1928 he made his literary debut with the short story "Egyszer régen" (Once) and with poems published in the daily *Hír* and in papers and periodicals for youth. In 1932 Weöres published his poems in *Nyugat*, the leading Hungarian literary periodical of the time. He soon became one of its main contributors. Weöres published his first collection of poems, *Hideg van* (Cold), in 1934. In 1941 he founded and co-edited the Pécs-based periodical *Sorsunk*. After the end of World War II, Weöres moved to Budapest. An opponent of Socialist realism, he found it increasingly difficult to find a job and to publish his works. From 1949 on he published only translations that he did, as well as poems for children, which, because of their remarkable content and unique melody, were a part of the school canon for several generations of Hungarians. At the end of 1956 Weöres published *A hallgatás tornya* (The tower of silence), a collection of poems he had written over a period of thirty years; following this, he was again unable to publish anything until the mid-1960s. In 1970 Weöres received the Kossuth Prize, the nation's highest award for artists. Apart from poems and translations from many languages, Weöres also tried his hand at writing dramas: *Színjátékok* (Dramas; 1983). He won the widest acclaim for the poetic novel *Psyché* (Psyche; 1972), the history of a poetess' life written in nineteenth-century language. This novel was adapted for the stage many times and for the screen in 1979. Weöres's poems are characterized by a great richness of content, form, and language. The range of his inspiration is impressive, from antique cultures to African mythology and Chinese poetry. He was a master in the use of parable and allusion. He saw the absurdity of the world around him and the increasing mechanisms of self-destruction of man and man-made civilization. English-language translations of Weöres's poetry include *Selected Poems* (1970), *If All the World Were a Blackbird: Poems* (1985), and *Eternal Moment: Selected Poems* (1988). (MS)

Sources: "Weöres Sándor tanulmányok," *Magyar Műhely* (Paris), 1964, nos. 7–8; *Emlékkönyv Weöres Sándor hetvenedik születésnapjára* (Pécs, 1983); Matyas Domokos, ed. *Magyar Orpheus: Weöres Sándor emlékére* ed. (Budapest, 1990); "Lator László bevezetője a Petőfi Irodalmi Múzeum: Weöres kiállításának megnyitóján," *Élet és Irodalom*, 1993, no. 44.

WERBLAN Andrzej (30 October 1924, Tarnopol [now Ternopil, Ukraine]), Polish Communist activist and historian. Werblan was born into a family of teachers. In September 1939 he found himself in the Soviet territories. Exiled to Siberia, he joined the Polish Army in the Soviet Union in 1943. He remained in the army until 1947 and then joined the Polish Socialist Party (Polska Partia Socjalistyczna [PPS]). In April 1948 Werblan became a member of the PPS Chief Council and first secretary of the PPS Provincial Committee in Białystok. In December 1948 he joined the Polish United Workers' Party (Polska Zjednoczona Partia Robotnicza [PUWP]). From 1952 to 1955 he studied history at Warsaw University, graduating in 1954, and at the Institute of Social Sciences of the PUWP CC, earning a doctorate from Adam Mickiewicz University in Poznań. Werblan simultaneously rose through the party ranks: he became a deputy member of the CC in 1948 and then served as a member of the PUWP CC from 1956 to 1981. In 1952–56 he was an MP in the Assembly. He headed the CC Propaganda and Agitation Department (beginning in 1956), the CC Propaganda and Press Department (1956–57), the CC Propaganda Department (1957–60), and the PUWP CC Education Department (1960–71). Regarded as an ally of **Mieczysław Moczar**, Werblan played a certain role in the anti-intelligentsia and anti-Semitic witch hunt of March 1968. He was an MP in the Assembly for the second time from 1961 to 1985, serving as deputy speaker from 1971 to 1982. The editor-in-chief of *Nowe Drogi* from 1972 to 1974, Werblan was seen as one of the leading party ideologues. He was a member of the CC Secretariat (December 1971–February 1974), secretary of the PUWP CC (until December 1980), and director of the PUWP CC Institute for Fundamental Issues in Marxism-Leninism (until 1981). In 1974 Werblan became an associate professor of political science at the University of Silesia. In 1975 he became a member of the Assembly committee for drafting amendments to the constitution of the Polish People's Republic; these amendments formalized the alliance between the Polish People's Republic and the Soviet Union, as well as the leading role of the PUWP. Werblan was a member of the PUWP CC Politburo (February–December 1980) and chairman of the PUWP Parliamentary Caucus in the Assembly (April–December 1980). After 1981 he increasingly dissociated himself from the party line and leaned toward its liberal faction. From 1981 to 1983 Werblan was a member of the Presidium of the All-Polish Committee of the National Unity Front. Werblan's numerous publications include *Władysław Gomułka, sekretarz generalny PPR* (**Władysław Gomułka**, the secretary general of the PPR; 1988). Werblan edited and prepared for printing Gomułka's *Pamiętniki* (Memoirs; 1994). (PK)

Sources: Mołdawa; Włodzimierz Janowski and Aleksander Kochański, *Informator o strukturze i obsadzie personalnej centralnego aparatu PZPR 1948–1990* (Warsaw, 2000); Krzysztof Lesiakowski, *Mieczysław Moczar* (Warsaw, 1998); Andrzej Paczkowski, *Droga do "mniejszego zła": Strategia i taktyka obozu władzy lipiec 1980–styczeń 1982* (Kraków, 2002).

WIDY-WIRSKI Feliks (11 July 1907, Lwów [Lviv]–15 January 1982, Warsaw), Polish politician. After high school in Brodnica, Widy-Wirski completed medical studies at Poznań University in 1931. From 1932 he practiced as a gynecologist and was known for performing illegal abortions. He belonged to a pro-government faction of the National Workers' Party–Left (Narodowa Partia Robotnicza–Lewica) and to the radical Association of Polish Democratic Youth (Związek Polskiej Młodzieży Demokratycznej). Widy-Wirski was close to the radical left; for instance, he wrote approvingly of Lenin. Wounded in the September 1939 campaign, Widy-Wirski was taken prisoner of war, but he was released in 1940. He went to Warsaw and joined the underground activities of the radical group Zryw (Upsurge), transformed into the Party of National Upsurge. In November 1944 the party proclaimed itself in favor of the Polish Committee of National Liberation (Polski Komitet Wyzwolenia Narodowego), and Widy-Wirski was included in the National Home Council (Krajowa Rada Narodowa). At the beginning of 1945 Widy-Wirski became a member of the Communist Polish Workers' Party. On its behalf, along with **Zygmunt Felczak**, he reconstructed the prewar Christian Democratic Labor Party (Stronnictwo Pracy [SP]) and became its vice-president in July 1945. When the real SP leaders began to return to their official activities, they had to accept a fifty-fifty parity in the party leadership with the Upsurge activists. In July 1946, when the real Christian Democratic leaders gave up their membership in the party, which was actually controlled by the Communists, and unsuccessfully tried to form a separate party, Widy-Wirski became SP chairman. At the same time, he was provincial governor (*wojewoda*) in Poznań and deputy minister of information (from September 1946 to April 1947). Widy-Wirski became an MP after the falsified parliamentary elections of January 1947. Later he was deputy minister of culture and deputy minister of navigation. After the dissolution of the SP, some of its leaders joined the satellite Democratic Party, and Widy-Wirski joined its leadership. Since he was closely connected to **Władysław Gomułka**, on 2 November 1952 Widy-Wirski was arrested. Interrogated as a witness during preparations for Gomułka's trial and released in December 1954, Widy-Wirski was later deputy minister of health and a professor at the Polish Academy of Sciences. In 1956 he was accepted into the Polish United

Workers' Party (Polska Zjednoczona Partia Robotnicza). A delegate to its Third and Fourth Congresses and an MP from 1957 to 1965, Widy-Wirski was a member of the leadership of the Association of Fighters for Freedom and Democracy (Związek Bojowników o Wolność i Demokrację). (WR)

Sources: Kunert, vol. 2; Mołdawa; Mirosław Piotrowski, *Służba idei czy serwilizm? Zygmunt Felczak i Feliks Widy-Wirski w najnowszych dziejach Polski* (Lublin, 1994).

WIED Wilhelm von (26 March 1876, Neuwied–18 April 1945, Predeal, Romania), prince of Albania. The son of Adolf Maximilian Karl Wied and Princess Mary of the Netherlands, Wied was also related to the Romanian ruling family of Hohenzollern-Siegmaringen. He served as an officer in the German Army. In July 1913, at a Conference of Ambassadors in London, under pressure from the Central Powers, Wied was elected prince of Albania. His rank as an officer and the fact that as a Protestant he did not identify himself with any of the major religious groups in Albania won Wied respect among the Albanian people. In February 1914 a delegation of Albanians headed by **Essad Pasha Toptani** came to the castle of Neuwied, where he lived, and invited him to accept the Albanian crown. In March 1914 Wied arrived in Albania along with his wife and a group of advisers. He established his residence in Dürres, which was designated as the capital of the country. Despite his official title of *mbret* (king), the Albanian people more often called him *princ* (prince). As the situation of the country was unstable, Wied's power was limited to a small part of the territory that was granted to Albania. His prestige among the Albanian people diminished significantly after he took refuge in a ship during an attack by the Muslim rebels on Dürres. Wied left Albania on 3 September 1914 because of the outbreak of World War I. However, he promised to return as soon as the international situation became stable. During the war Wied fought on the eastern front as a captain in the German Army. In January 1920 the congress in Lushnje, which defined the new political system of Albania, deprived him of the throne. Only the Italian diplomatic service worked for his return to the throne, at the price of maintaining Italian influence in Albania. After World War I, Wied and his family lived in the Tyrol and Munich and, from 1925, on the Romanian estate of his wife, Princess Sofia Waldenberg. In interviews, Wied repeatedly asserted that he was ready to return to the Albanian throne. (TC)

Sources: *Biographisches Lexikon*, vol. 4; Constantine Chekrezi, *Albania: Past and Present* (New York, 1919); Ekrem bey Vlora, *Lebenserinnerungen*, vols. 1–2 (Munich, 1968–73); Jerzy Hauziński and Jan Leśny, *Historia Albanii* (Wrocław, 1992).

WIELOWIEYSKI Andrzej (16 December 1927, Warsaw), Polish journalist and politician. During the German occupation in World War II, Wielowieyski served as a soldier of the Home Army. After the war, he was a member of the Union of Rural Youth of the Republic of Poland called Wici (Związek Młodzieży Wiejskiej Rzeczypospolitej Polskiej–Wici [ZMW RP–Wici]). After receiving a law degree from the Jagiellonian University in 1947, Wielowieyski worked as a clerk. In 1961 he joined the editorial staff of the monthly *Więź*. He served as a member (from 1957), vice-chairman (1965–72), and secretary (1972–81 and 1984–89) of the Club of the Catholic Intelligentsia (Klub Inteligencji Katolickiej) in Warsaw. He was elected to the leadership of Pax Romana, the International Catholic Movement for Intellectual and Cultural Affairs. In 1978 Wielowieyski co-founded the "Experience and Future" seminar series and co-authored "Raport o stanie Rzeczypospolitej i drogach wiodących do jej naprawy" (Report on the condition of the Republic of Poland and ways to improve it), which included a description of the crisis in Poland and proposals for reforms that would not undermine the foundations of the political system of the Polish People's Republic. Wielowieyski subsequently co-authored further "Experience and Future" reports. In August 1980 he was an expert-adviser to the Inter-Factory Strike Committee in the Gdańsk Shipyard. He subsequently became an adviser to the National Coordinating Commission (Krajowa Komisja Porozumiewawcza) of Solidarity and headed its Center for Social and Labor Initiatives. From 1981 to 1985 Wielowieyski was a member of the Primate's Social Council and a journalist for church periodicals, including *Królowa Apostołów* and *Gość Niedzielny*. From 1983 on he was one of the advisers to Solidarity (which had been declared illegal during martial law in Poland). Wielowieyski played an important role in getting negotiations started between Solidarity and the Communist authorities in 1988. In December 1988 he became a member of the Citizens' Committee of the Chairman of Solidarity. From February to April 1989 he took part in the Round Table Talks. In 1989–91 Wielowieyski served as deputy speaker of the Senate. In 1991 he became an MP in the Assembly. He was also a member of the Citizens' Parliamentary Caucus. He joined the Democratic Union (Unia Demokratyczna) in 1991 and subsequently was a member of the Freedom Union (Unii Wolności) from 1994 to 2001. In 1992–93 Wielowieyski was vice-chairman of the Polish delegation to the Parliamentary Assembly of the Council of Europe. He authored many works devoted to socioeconomic issues and to Catholic sexual ethics and education, including *Przed nami małżeństwo* (Preparing for marriage; 1974). (AF)

Sources: *Nasi w Sejmie i Senacie* (Warsaw, 1990); Jan Skórzyński, *Ugoda i rewolucja: Władza i opozycja 1985–1989* (Warsaw, 1995); Janusz A. Majcherek, *Pierwsza dekada III Rzeczpospolitej 1989–1999* (Warsaw, 1999); *Opozycja w PRL: Słownik biograficzny 1956–89* (Warsaw, 2000); Antoni Dudek, *Pierwsze lata III Rzeczpospolitej 1989–2001* (Kraków, 2002).

WIERZBICKI Andrzej (7 June 1877, Warsaw–11 February 1961, Warsaw), Polish engieneer, businessman, and politician. Wierzbicki graduated from the Technological Institute in Petersburg. From 1910 he belonged to the National League, and from 1912 he was director of the Association of Industrialists of the Kingdom of Poland. During World War I Wierzbicki was a member of the Central Civic Committee, the Main Charity Council (Rada Główna Opiekuńcza), and the Inter-Party Circle connected with National Democracy. In 1916–17 he was a member of the Provisional Council of State (Tymczasowa Rada Stanu). In 1917–18 he was one of the leaders of the Society for Economic Independence, a political representation of Polish big business. In November 1918 Wierzbicki became minister of industry and trade in the government of **Józef Świerzyński**. In 1919 he joined the National Committee of Poland and headed the Polish economic delegation to the Paris Peace Conference. On his return to Poland in 1919 Wierzbicki was co-founder of the Central Association of Polish Industry, Mining, Trade, and Finance, called the Lewiatan for short. In the following years he played a key role in the association as its general director and, from 1932, chairman of the board. Wierzbicki was a member of the boards of many enterprises and banks, including Bank Handlowy w Warszawie S.A. (1918–20 and 1928–49) and the Bank of Poland (1928–32), as well as of government advisory bodies. In 1919–28 he was an MP on behalf of National Democracy and, in 1935–38, on behalf of the ruling *Sanacja*. In September 1939 Wierzbicki joined the Committee for the Defense of Warsaw. During the Nazi occupation he was imprisoned in Pawiak Prison in Warsaw and Montelupi Prison in Kraków. After the war he retired. Among other works, Wierzbicki authored *Idea i taktyka gospodarcza* (Economic ideas and practice; 1928), *Program gospodarczy Lewiatana* (The economic program of the Lewiatan; 1933), and *W terenie i z trybuny* (On the premises and from the tribunal; 1936), as well as the memoirs *Pamiętniki i dokumenty* (Memoirs and documents; 1957) and *Żywy Lewiatan* (Lewiatan alive; 2001). (WR)

Sources: *Kto był kim w Drugiej Rzeczypospolitej* (Warsaw, 1994); *Encyklopedia historii Drugiej Rzeczpospolitej* (Warsaw, 1999); Jan Kofman, *Lewiatan a podstawowe zagadnienia ekonomiczno-polityczne Drugiej Rzeczypospolitej* (Warsaw, 1986).

WITASZEWSKI Kazimierz (1 April 1906, Warsaw?–22 February 1992, Warsaw), Polish Communist activist. Born into a working-class family, Witaszewski was a textile worker. A trade union activist, he was imprisoned at Bereza Kartuska for his activities in the Communist Party of Poland (Komunistyczna Partia Polski [KPP]). During World War II he found himself in the Soviet Union. A political officer in the Polish Army in the Soviet Union (1943–44), Witaszewski was one of the Kremlin's most trusted co-workers. In 1944 he joined the (Communist) Polish Workers' Party (Polska Partia Robotnicza [PPR]) and briefly served as head of the Trade Union Department of the PPR Central Committee (CC). He subsequently became mayor of the city of Łódź. In 1944 Witaszewski became a deputy to the National Home Council (Krajowa Rada Narodowa [KRN]), and until 1956 he served as an MP in the Legislative Assembly and the Assembly. He was secretary general of the Provisional Central Commission of Trade Unions (1944–45) and then chairman of the Central Commission of Trade Unions (November 1945–November 1948). From 1948 to 1949 he was deputy minister of labor and social policy. Witaszewski joined the Polish United Workers' Party (Polska Zjednoczona Partia Robotnicza [PUWP]) in December 1948 and was a member of the PUWP CC from 1948 to 1968. He served as first secretary of the PUWP Provincial Committee in Wrocław (1949–51) and head of the PUWP CC Personnel Department (1951–52). From 1952 to 1956 he was deputy minister of national defense, head of the Main Political Board of the Polish Army, and one of the closest co-workers of Marshal **Konstantin Rokossovsky**. Witaszewski was aligned with the dogmatic Natolin faction (Natolińczycy), and in the spring of 1956 he was against the dissemination of Nikita Khrushchev's secret report, which exposed Stalin's crimes. A supporter of hard-line policies, Witaszewski was called "General Bludgeon," an allusion to his preference for brutal methods of solving conflicts. As a result of the "thaw" in 1956, he lost his post and served as a military attaché in Prague from 1957 to 1959.

As part of his struggle against the liberal faction in the PUWP, **Władysław Gomułka** appealed for support from members of the Natolin faction, including Witaszewski, whom he appointed head of the Main Political Board of the Polish Army in 1959. From 1960 to 1968 Witaszewski headed the crucial Administrative Department of the PUWP CC. He was in charge of (among other things) controlling government and personnel affairs in the special services and the army, as a result of which he held a particularly strong position in the power structure. He was personally involved in actions against the Catholic Church—for example, trying to prevent the construction of a church in Nowa Huta in 1960 and in sabotaging the 1966 celebrations of the Millennium of Christianity in Poland. From 1968 to 1971 Witaszewski was a member of the PUWP Central Audit Commission. (PK)

Sources: Mołdawa; *Trybuna*, 27 March 1992; *Polska-ZSRR: Struktury podległości* (Warsaw, 1995); Henryk Dominiczak, *Organy bezpieczeństwa PRL 1944–1990* (Warsaw, 1997); Krzysztof Lesiakowski, *Mieczysław Moczar "Mietek": Biografia polityczna* (Warsaw, 1998); Włodzimierz Janowski and Aleksander Kochański, *Informator o strukturze i obsadzie personalnej centralnego aparatu PZPR 1948–1990* (Warsaw, 2000).

WITKIEWICZ Stanisław Ignacy, pseudonym "Witkacy" (24 February 1885, Warsaw–18 September 1939, Jeziory [Ozery], Volhynia), Polish painter, playwright, and art theoretician. Witkiewicz's father, Stanisław Witkiewicz, was a writer, painter, literary critic, and leading thinker of the Young Poland movement. Brought up in an atmosphere of artistic freedom, already in his childhood Witkiewicz showed great abilities combined with an unbridled imagination. From 1904 to 1910 he studied at the Academy of Fine Arts, under, among others, Józef Mehoffer. He traveled extensively in Germany, Italy, and France, exploring modern tendencies in art. In 1914 he went to Australia as an illustrator for an anthropological expedition led by **Bronisław Malinowski**. At the end of World War I, as an officer in the tsarist guard regiment, Witkiewicz witnessed the Bolshevik revolution—a traumatic experience that left a distinctive stamp on his work and ultimately on his life. In 1918 he settled in Zakopane, where he painted and wrote and was a founding member of a group called Formiści Polscy (Polish Formists). Witkiewicz was an exponent and theoretician of the "pure form" theory, which ignored existing cultural content and values. He included the concepts of "pure form" in a number of his studies, including *Nowe formy w malarstwie i wynikające stąd nieporozumienia* (New forms in painting and the resulting misunderstandings; 1919); *Szkice estetyczne* (Esthetic sketches; 1922); and *Teatr: Wstęp do teorii Czystej Formy w teatrze* (Theater: An introduction to the pure form theory in theater; 1923). From 1925 to 1927 Witkiewicz ran the experimental Formist Theater in Zakopane, and in 1926 in Warsaw he opened a commercial "portrait studio," where he painted—often under the influence of drugs—original, expressionist portraits of various people. He also wrote many plays, but they were seldom staged during the interwar period because they included shocking scenes and dialogue. Witkiewicz's theatrical works include *Tumor Mózgowicz* (Tumor brainowich; 1921); *Kurka wodna* (The water hen; 1922); *W małym dworku* (1923; *Country House*, 1997); *Jan Maciej Karol Wścieklica* (1925); and *Mątwa* (The cuttlefish; 1933), as well as *Szewcy* (Shoemakers; premiere in 1957), *Matka* (1964; *The Mother and Other Unsavory Plays: Including the Shoemakers and They*, 1993), and *Oni* (They; 1966), which were not staged during his lifetime. Witkiewicz also published fantasy and grotesque novels, including *622 upadki Bunga czyli demoniczna kobieta* (1910; *The 622 Downfalls of Bungo or the Demonic Woman*, 2000); *Pożegnanie jesieni* (Farewell to autumn; 1927); and *Nienasycenie* (1930; *Insatiability: A Novel in Two Parts*, 1977). He wrote *Pojęcia i twierdzenia implikowane przez pojęcie istnienia* (Concepts and theses entailed by the concept of existence; 1935), a philosophical treatise in which he outlined the system of biological monadism.

Witkiewicz's works are characterized by a great freedom of composition, macabre humor, and the surrealistic grotesque. In his works he depicted the disintegration of traditional society and its values. Highly regarded by some and considered a scandalmonger and amateur by others, Witkiewicz was a member of the artistic avant garde of interwar Poland. He became subject to recurrent fits of depression and committed suicide upon hearing of the Soviet invasion of Poland. His dramas became very famous in the 1960s, when they began to be staged in Western Europe and soon thereafter throughout the world. At first considered a pioneer and then a classic writer of twentieth-century absurdist literature, Witkiewicz earned his place in the pantheon of world literature, and his works were translated into many languages. In 1970–74 a three-volume edition of his *Pisma zebrane* (Collected writings) was published in Kraków. His *Seven Plays* were published in English in 2004. (WR)

Sources: K. Kwasniewski and L. Trzeciakowski, eds. *Polacy w historii i kulturze krajów Europy Zachodniej* (Poznań, 1981); *Literatura polska: Przewodnik encyklopedyczny*, vol. 2 (Warsaw, 1985); T. Kotarbinski and J. Plomienski eds. *Stanisław Ignacy Witkiewicz: Człowiek i twórca*, eds., (Warsaw, 1957); Jan Błoński, *Stanisław Ignacy Witkiewicz jako dramaturg* (Kraków, 1973); *S. I. Witkiewicz: Génie de la Pologne* (Lausanne, 1981); Daniel Gerould, *Witkacy: Stanislaw Ignacy Witkiewicz as an Imaginative Writer* (Seattle, 1981).

WITOS Wincenty (22 January 1874, Wierzchosławice, near Tarnów–31 December 1945, Kraków), Polish Peasant Party politician. Witos's father was a smallholder and sometimes worked as a woodcutter. Witos was a very gifted child, but because of poverty he finished only a rural elementary school, and then he ran a farm. In 1891 he took part in the electoral campaign for **Jakub Bojko**, a Galician peasant leader. From 1895 to 1899 he served in the Austrian Army and then joined the Polish Peasant Party (Polskie Stronnictwo Ludowe [PSL]). In 1903 Witos was elected to the PSL Chief Council, and then he became the mayor of the municipality of Wierzchosławice. In 1908 he became an MP in the Galician Provincial Diet in Lemberg (Lwów, Lviv) and in 1911 an MP in the Austrian parliament in Vienna. In December 1913 Witos was one of the initiators of a split in the PSL, and then he supported the Polish Peasant Party–Piast (PSL–Piast). In February 1914 he became deputy chairman of the PSL–Piast, and after the outbreak of World War I, he joined the Supreme National Committee (Naczelny Komitet Narodowy [NKN]), on which he served as vice-president of its western section in Kraków. Witos did not actively support Austria-Hungary, adopting a wait-and-see attitude and then demanding full independence for Poland. From 1917 to 1918 he was a member of the National League (Liga Narodowa). He co-initiated a resolution presented by the Polish Circle (Koło Polskie) in the Austrian parliament on 28 May 1917 that demanded independence for Poland and defended Poland's right to access to the sea. After the Austrian Army was disarmed, Witos became head of the Polish Liquidation Commission (Polska Komisja Likwidacyjna [PKL]) in Kraków on 28 October 1918. He did not join the Lublin-based Provisional People's Government of the Republic of Poland (Tymczasowy Rząd Ludowy Republiki Polskiej), headed by **Ignacy Daszyński**, as he believed that this government did not reflect the real political power structure in Poland and that its program was too radical. At the end of 1918, though, Witos subordinated the PKL to the central government, headed by **Jędrzej Moraczewski**, in Warsaw.

In the Second Republic of Poland, Witos initially played a key political role. He was chairman of the Main Board of the PSL–Piast (1918–31) and chairman of the party's parliamentary representation (1919–27 and 1930–31). Elected to the Legislative Assembly in January 1919, he was a candidate of the left for the chamber's speaker. In December 1919, as a result of an agreement reached by the PSL–Piast with the Polish Peasant Party–Liberation (PSL–Wyzwolenie) and the National Peasant Union (Narodowe Zjednoczenie Ludowe), the centrist cabinet of **Leopold Skulski** was established. Witos headed the Assembly's Agrarian Commission and played an important role in the adoption of an agricultural reform bill in July 1919 and a bill on the implementation of the agricultural reform in July 1920. In the face of the Bolshevik offensive on Warsaw, Witos became head of the coalition Government of National Defense on 24 July 1920. His appeal to the peasants helped to consolidate them around the cause of independence. After the Soviet threat was gone, the constitution of March 1921 was adopted, and the division of Upper Silesia between Poland and Germany was decided, Witos resigned as prime minister on 13 September 1921

because of the breakup of the ruling coalition. In November 1922 **Józef Piłsudski** proposed Witos as president of the Republic of Poland, but owing to objections from the PSL–Liberation, the candidacy was not officially put forward. In the spring of 1923 Witos was a co-author and signatory of the so-called Pact of Lanckorona, which led to the establishment of a coalition formed by the National Democrats, the Christian Democrats, and the PSL–Piast. These groups reached a compromise on the agricultural reform, and a cabinet headed by Witos and backed by a parliamentary majority was established. Witos served as prime minister from 28 May to 14 December 1923, but he failed to halt inflation, which turned into hyperinflation and a social crisis. During riots in Lesser Poland (Małopolska) in the autumn of 1923, the government used force, as a result of which several people were killed or wounded. On 10 May 1926 Witos again became prime minister of a center-right majority government (the so-called Chjeno-Piast coalition), but he failed to counter a growing wave of criticism or to prevent Piłsudski from staging a military coup d'état that overthrew the government.

After the coup of May 1926, Witos returned to his family farm at Wierzchosławice. He firmly criticized the new form of government. He succeeded in rebuilding the influence of the PSL–Piast among the peasants. In 1929 he was one of the founders of the so-called Centrolew, a center-left coalition of opposition parties. Witos organized and took part in many rallies against the *sanacja* regime. On 29 June 1930 he co-founded the Congress for the Defense of People's Rights and Freedoms in Kraków. On 10 September, along with other Centrolew leaders, Witos was arrested and imprisoned in the Brześć fortress. In November 1930 he was released on bail, but soon the authorities removed him from all the public and business positions he still held and dismissed him as mayor of Wierzchosławice. In 1931 Witos took part in the unification of the PSL–Piast, the PSL–Liberation, and the Party of Peasants (Stronnictwo Chłopskie [SCh]) into the Peasant Party (Stronnictwo Ludowe [SL]), and he became the chairman of the SL Chief Council. Witos was tried in the Brześć (Brest) trial (1931–32) and was sentenced to one and a half years' imprisonment. In September 1933, after the sentence became final and binding, Witos left for Czechoslovakia, from where he exerted a great influence on the opposition activities against the *sanacja* regime. For example, in 1936 he co-founded the opposition Morges Front, and in 1937 he advocated a general peasant strike. At that time, his views evolved toward the left; these were expressed in (among other things) his support for an agricultural reform without compensation to landowners. However, Witos was against the participation of Communists in the "people's front." After Nazi troops occupied Prague, the Gestapo searched for Witos as it wanted to win his cooperation; therefore he secretly returned to Poland on 30 March 1939. Briefly detained, Witos was released after a few weeks. An unquestionable authority among the peasants and a symbol of peasant resistance to the ruling camp, Witos became chairman of the SL on 17 May 1939. In the face of a threat to Poland, he called for unity among the Poles. At a rally at Mościska he said, among other things, that the peasants should serve their country regardless of its government.

Arrested by the Germans in September 1939, Witos firmly refused to take part in the establishment of a collaborationist government. He was imprisoned in Rzeszów and Berlin and then held under house arrest in Zakopane and Wierzchosławice. Toward the end of the occupation Witos went into hiding. The Germans imprisoned his daughter Julia in a concentration camp, but Witos did not yield to Nazi demands and did not agree to any compromise. After Soviet troops entered Lesser Poland in early 1945, the new authorities tried to persuade Witos to join the "national unity" government under the Communist aegis. At the end of March 1945 Witos was forcibly brought to Warsaw and then to Brześć. He was offered the position of prime minister of the "national unity" government, but he rejected it, explaining that he would need permission from the PSL leadership (headed by **Stanisław Mikołajczyk**) to assume this post. Released from house arrest after one week, Witos returned home severely ill and wrote an appeal to peasants that was a kind of political testament; in it he warned against promoting people with no dignity or conscience to important positions. He supported the PSL headed by Mikołajczyk and became its honorary chairman, despite the fact that his health further deteriorated. From his deathbed in a hospital in Kraków, Witos sent his last appeal; in it he recognized that it was necessary to regulate relations with the Soviet Union but on an equal rights basis. Witos's funeral in Wierzchosławice turned into a great demonstration of peasant support for the PSL. Witos authored *Moje wspomnienia* (My memoirs, 3 vols.; 1964–65), an important source for the history of prewar Poland, and *Moja tułaczka* (My wanderings; 1967). (WR)

Sources: *Encyklopedia historii Drugiej Rzeczypospolitej* (Warsaw, 1999); Antoni Gurnicz and Stanisław Lato, "Wincenty Witos," in *Przywódcy ruchu ludowego* (Warsaw, 1968); Andrzej Zakrzewski, *Wincenty Witos: Chłopski polityk i mąż stanu* (Warsaw, 1978); Andrzej Ajnenkiel, *Od rządów ludowych do przewrotu majowego* (Warsaw, 1978); Andrzej Albert [Wojciech Roszkowski], "Wincenty Witos," *PPN*, 1981, no. 49; Franciszek Ziejka, ed., *O Wincentym Witosie* (Warsaw, 1983); Jan Borkowski, ed., *O Wincentym Witosie: Relacje i wspomnienia* (Warsaw, 1984); Marian Leczyk, ed., *Sprawa brzeska* (Warsaw, 1987); Andrzej Paczkowski, "Wincenty Witos, premier rządu polskiego 24 VIII 1920–13 IX 1921, 28 V–14 XII 1923, 10 V–14 V 1926," in Andrzej Chojnowski and Piotr Wróbel, eds., *Prezydenci i premierzy Drugiej Rzeczypospolitej* (Wrocław, 1992).

WOJCIECHOWSKI Stanisław (15 March 1869, Kalisz– 9 April 1953, Gołąbki, near Warsaw), Polish cooperative and political activist, president of Poland. After graduating from high school in Kalisz in 1888, Wojciechowski studied physics, mathematics, and the natural sciences at Warsaw University. He began his political activities in a secret group of Kalisz youth, and in 1890 he joined the Union of Polish Youth called Zet (Związek Młodzieży Polskiej–Zet). Two years later he joined the leadership of this organization. After being arrested twice by Russian authorities in 1891–92, Wojciechowski emigrated to Switzerland; from there he went to France. In France, he attended the Paris Congress, at which he was elected a member of the leadership of the newly formed Union of Polish Socialists Abroad (Związek Zagraniczny Socjalistów Polskich). Because of his Socialist activities, Wojciechowski was ordered to leave France and went to London. In 1893 he attended the founding congress of the Polish Socialist Party (Polska Partia Socjalistyczna [PPS]) in Wilno (Vilnius), at which he met **Józef Piłsudski**. An able organizer and conspirator, Wojciechowski repeatedly traveled to Poland illegally. Between 1895 and 1905 he belonged to the top leadership of the PPS and was a coeditor, publisher, and distributor of the newspaper *Robotnik*. In 1905, after a split in the PPS, Wojciechowski left the party and became involved in the cooperative movement. A year later he returned permanently to Warsaw, where he became director of the Confederation of Cooperative Associations, editor of the periodical *Społem*, and co-founder of the Cooperative Society (Towarzystwo Kooperatystów), pioneering the Polish cooperative movement in the Russian sector of partitioned Poland.

After the outbreak of World War I Wojciechowski decided that Germany posed the greatest threat to Poland. He became active in the Central Civic Committee (Centralny Komitet Obywatelski) and in the Polish National Committee (Komitet Narodowy Polski) in Warsaw. When the Germans captured Warsaw in 1915, Wojciechowski left for Russia, where he developed economic programs for the benefit of Poles in Russia. After the fall of tsarism, in August 1917 Wojciechowski was elected president of the Council of the Polish Interparty Union in Moscow (Rada Polskiego Zjednoczenia Międzypartyjnego), which was linked with the Polish National Committee in Paris, and he became involved in forming the Polish Army in Russia. In June 1918 he returned to Warsaw, where he again became engaged in the cooperative movement, organizing a congress of members of cooperative societies in November 1918. In January 1919 Wojciechowski became minister of interior in the government of **Ignacy Paderewski**. In his political activities, Wojciechowski put special emphasis on security, organizing the state police. He remained minister of interior in the cabinet of **Leopold Skulski** and held the post until June 1920. After leaving his ministerial post, Wojciechowski was active in the national savings committee, and he lectured at the Warsaw College of Commerce (Wyższa Szkoła Handlowa). In 1921 he joined the Polish Peasant Party–Piast (Polskie Stronnictwo Ludowe–Piast [PSL–Piast]) and became editor of *Wola Ludu*. In November 1922 Wojciechowski unsuccessfully ran in the elections to the Senate from the Piast lists. On 9 December 1922 the PSL–Piast nominated Wojciechowski as candidate for president, but he lost on the fourth ballot. After the assassination of President **Gabriel Narutowicz**, Wojciechowski was nominated again, and on 20 December 1922 he was elected president of the Republic of Poland.

The beginning of Wojciechowski's presidency coincided with a time of great economic problems that led to the escalation of social conflicts. After the fall of the cabinet of **Wincenty Witos**, when it turned out that it was impossible to form a coalition government with the support of a parliamentary majority, in December 1923 Wojciechowski designated **Władysław Grabski** prime minister of a "cabinet of experts." He consistently supported this government, helping it carry out its reform tasks. After the fall of the Grabski cabinet in November 1925, Wojciechowski appointed **Aleksander Skrzyński** as prime minister. When the increasingly tense political situation led to the fall of this cabinet as well, Wojciechowski reluctantly charged Witos with the task of forming a new government of a parliamentary majority. On 12 May 1926 Wojciechowski came out against Piłsudski, who was marching on Warsaw at the head of his faithful regiments. Wojciechowski held the now famous talks with Piłsudski on the Poniatowski Bridge, rejecting Piłsudski's conditions. During three successive days of fighting Wojciechowski refused to mediate. After the capture of Warsaw by Piłsudski, Wojciechowski, having withdrawn to Wilanów, decided to end the fighting. At midnight on 14–15 May 1926 he handed in his resignation as president to the speaker of the Assembly, **Maciej Rataj**, and he retired from political life. Between 1926 and 1939 Wojciechowski was professor at Warsaw Agricultural University (Szkoła Główna Gospodarstwa Wiejskiego), and in 1928–29 he was director of the Cooperative Research Institute. During the Nazi occupation Wojciechowski lived in Warsaw. After the war he settled in Gołąbki, near Warsaw. (PU)

Sources: Andrzej Ajnenkiel, ed., *Prezydenci Polski* (Warsaw, 1991); Pawluczuk Zdzisław, *Konspirator i prezydent: Rzecz o Stanisławie Wojciechowskim* (Lublin, 1993); *Kto był kim w Drugiej Rzeczypospolitej* (Warsaw, 1994); Ludwik Malinowski, *Politycy II Rzeczypospolitej*, vol. 1 (Toruń, 1995); *Słownik polityków polskich XX w.* (Poznań, 1998); *Encyklopedia Historii Drugiej Rzeczypospolitej* (Warsaw, 1999).

WRZASZCZYK Tadeusz (12 September 1932, Stradom), Polish Communist activist. Born into a working-class family, Wrzaszczyk graduated from Warsaw Technical University in 1954 and subsequently worked at the Radio Works in Warsaw. In 1956 he joined the Polish United Workers' Party (Polska Zjednoczona Partia Robotnicza [PUWP]), thanks to which he was promoted to chief engineer of the Żerań Car Factory in 1962 and to managing director of the Automotive Industry Union in 1965. Wrzaszczyk became minister of the engineering industry in December 1970 and a member of the PUWP CC in December 1971. Thanks to his close relations with Prime Minister **Piotr Jaroszewicz**, he became deputy prime minister and chairman of the Planning Committee of the Council of Ministers in October 1975 and an MP in the Assembly in March 1976. Wrzaszczyk endorsed the disastrous continuation of the economic policy launched in the early 1970s, which was based on an excessive increase in capital investments and consumption combined with an uncoordinated and irrational use of funds. This policy led to the breakdown of supplies to the consumer market in 1976 and a collapse of capital investments and national income in 1979. Dismissed in August 1980 and forced to resign his parliamentary seat four months later, Wrzaszczyk was expelled from the party in April 1981. In February 1984 the Assembly brought him to constitutional accountability before the Tribunal of State, but the case was discontinued under an amnesty in July 1984. (WR)

Sources: Mołdawa; Zbigniew Błażyński, *Towarzysze zeznają. Z tajnych archiwów Komitetu Centralnego* (London, 1987).

WYCECH Czesław (20 July 1899, Wilczogęby, near Węgrów–26 May 1977, Warsaw), Polish Peasant Party activist. Born into a peasant family, Wycech graduated from a teacher training college (1918) and from the State Teachers' Institute (1926). In 1919 he began working as a teacher in elementary schools. He joined the Polish Peasant Party–Liberation (Polskie Stronnictwo Ludowe–Wyzwolenie [PSL–Liberation]) in 1918. An activist of the Lublin Union of Peasant Youth, Wycech joined the Peasant Party (Stronnictwo Ludowe [SL]) in 1931. From 1921 he was mostly active in the Polish Teachers' Association (Związek Nauczycielstwa Polskiego [ZNP]), initially in its local units (in Węgrów) and at the regional level (in Lublin). Wycech was aligned with the Society of Democratic Education known as Nowe Tory (New Way), a leftist faction of the ZNP. During World War II, as one of the founders of the Underground Teachers' Organization and director of the Education and Culture Department of the underground Delegation of the Polish Government-in-Exile for the Homeland, Wycech was one of the main founders of an extensive underground teaching network. He was also active in the underground Peasant Party called Roch (Stronnictwo Ludowe–Roch [SL–Roch]). In April 1945 Wycech became chairman of the ZNP. In June 1945, after the coalition Provisional Government of National Unity (Tymczasowy Rząd Jedności Narodowej [TRJN]) was established, he assumed the post of minister of education, becoming one of the three representatives of the Polish Peasant Party (Polskie Stronnictwo Ludowe [PSL]) in the government. He also joined the National Home Council (Krajowa Rada Narodowa [KRN]). In July 1945 Wycech became a member of the PSL Provisional Chief Executive Committee. After the PSL congress in January 1946, he became a member of the Chief Council and the Chief Executive Committee of the PSL.

Wycech was in favor of concessions to the (Communist) Polish Workers' Party (Polska Partia Robotnicza [PPR]). In March 1947, following elections rigged by the Communists, he was expelled from the PSL for causing a split within the party. He then founded the ephemeral Polish Peasant Party–Left (Polskie Stronnictwo Ludowe–Lewica [PSL–Left]). After **Stanisław Mikołajczyk** fled Poland in October 1947, Wycech became deputy chairman of the PSL Chief Executive Committee and was one of the leaders responsible for subordinating the PSL to the PPR. After the Communist-controlled United Peasant Party (Zjednoczone Stronnictwo Ludowe [ZSL]) was established in 1949, Wycech was one of the top leaders of this Communist satellite. From 1962 to 1971 he was chairman of the ZSL Chief Committee. For a long time he served as an MP in the Assembly (1947–72) and was its speaker (1957–71), which was in conformity with the custom according to which this post was given to a peasant party representative. Wycech authored several books on historical subjects, mainly on the so-called peasant issue in the nineteenth century, including *Powstanie chłopskie 1846: Jakub Szela* (The peasant uprising of 1846: Jakub Szela; 1955) and *Społeczna gospodarka rolna w polskiej myśli politycznej* (Social agricultural economy in Polish political thought; 1963). In 1956 Wycech co-founded the Institute of the History of the Peasant Movement. (AP)

Sources: *Słownik biograficzny działaczy ruchu ludowego* (Warsaw, 1989); *Encyklopedia Historii Polski: Dzieje polityczne*, vol. 2 (Warsaw, 1995); *Encyklopedia historii Drugiej Rzeczypospolitej* (Warsaw, 1999); Roman Buczek, *Stronnictwo Ludowe w latach 1939–1945* (London, 1975); Krystyna Kersten, *Narodziny systemu władzy: Polska 1943–1948* (Poznań, 1990); Stanisław Łach, *Polskie Stronnictwo Ludowe w latach 1945–1947* (Gdańsk, 1995).

WYSPIAŃSKI Stanisław (15 January 1869, Kraków–28 November 1907, Kraków), Polish poet, dramatist, and painter. The son of a sculptor, in 1884–85 and 1887–95 Wyspiański studied at the Kraków's School of Fine Arts under (among others) Jan Matejko. From 1890 to 1894 he was in Paris, where he was greatly impressed by the work of Paul Gauguin and the Nabis and by Japanese wood engraving. From 1898 to 1905 Wyspiański worked as a stage designer and stage manager in Kraków's theaters, and from 1902 on he also lectured as a docent in the Academy of Fine Arts. In 1897 he became a member of the Sztuka (Art) Society of Polish Artists, and in 1902, a member of the Polish Applied Art Society. In his artistic works, Wyspiański mostly used pastels, painting numerous portraits of children, girls, and women, as well as landscapes—for example, *Chochoły na Plantach* (Straw men in Planty Park; 1898–99). Wyspiański designed and in part created the polychromes and stained glass windows in the Franciscan church in Kraków (1897–1905) and reformed the art of book illustration along art nouveau lines. Wyspiański was a pioneer in modern theater stage design and was the first to stage Adam Mickiewicz's drama *Dziady* (Forefather's Eve) in 1901.

Wyspiański was the leading Polish turn-of-the-century dramatist. Metaphysical themes and antique inspirations prevail in his early works, such as *Meleager* (1899; *Meleager*, 1933) and *Protesilas i Laodamia* (Protesilas and Laodamia; 1899). In *Warszawianka* (The girl from Warsaw; 1898) he combined these themes with Polish history, specifically the events of the Polish Uprising of November 1830. In his later dramas, including *Wesele* (1901; *The Wedding*, 1990); *Wyzwolenie* (Liberation; 1903); *Bolesław Śmiały* (1903); *Noc listopadowa* (November night; 1904); *Akropolis* (Acropolis; 1904); and *Zygmunt August* (Sigismund Augustus; 1907), Wyspiański addressed key issues in the philosophy of history and Polish politics. *Wesele*—based on the real wedding of the poet Lucjan Rydel to Jadwiga Mikołajczyk, a peasant girl from the village of Bronowice—is often described as the greatest Polish drama of the twentieth century. The wedding party, at which peasants and "refined" guests from the city met, served to show contemporary social relations and to present a symbolic vision of Poland's history. The mocking confrontation between the romantic myth and the immaturity of Polish society, which made it impossible to realize this myth, is an important message of this drama. Many lines and symbols from *Wesele* (such as the Straw Man, a character in the drama, or the saying, "Boor, you had the horn of gold" [pertaining to Poland's decline, brought about by the arrogance and shortsightedness of its elites]) became deeply rooted in the twentieth-century imagination and everyday speech of the Poles. In *Wyzwolenie* Wyspiański contrasted the myths that originated in Polish Messianism with a program of liberating Poland as a "normal" European country. Wyspiański had a hunch that there was a chance for the realization of such a program, but he died prematurely and did not live to see it. (WR)

Sources: *Literatura polska: Przewodnik encyklopedyczny*, vol. 2 (Warsaw, 1985); Tymon Terlecki, *Stanislaw Wyspianski* (Boston, 1983); Zdzisław Kępiński, *Stanisław Wyspiański* (Warsaw, 1984); Alicja Okońska, *Stanisław Wyspiański* (Warsaw, 1991).

WYSZYŃSKI Stefan (3 August 1901, Zuzela, near Ostrów Mazowiecka–28 May 1981, Warsaw), cardinal, Primate of Poland. Wyszyński graduated from a theological seminary in Włocławek and was ordained in 1924. He studied sociology and economics at the Catholic University of Lublin, where in 1929 he defended his Ph.D. in canon law. Then he traveled to Western Europe to become acquainted with the development of social Catholicism. Wyszyński was a curate in Przedecz and Włocławek, a lecturer in social economics at a theological seminary, and editor-in-chief of *Ateneum Kapłańskie* from 1932 to 1939. He was active in the Christian Trade Unions, directed the Christian Workers' University, and organized the Catholic Union of Working Youth. From 1937 he was a member of the Social Council of the Primate of Poland. By 1939 Wyszyński was the author of over one hundred publications devoted to (among other things) Christian social science. He emphasized the theological character of the social teachings of the Church. He dealt with working-class issues, was involved in the upbringing of youth, and popularized the ideas of Catholic Action. He criticized the ideological background and practices of communism.

In October 1939 Wyszyński escaped arrest by the Gestapo and went into hiding. From 1940, at the request of Rev. Władysław Korniłowicz, he looked after blind children from Laski who had been rehoused on the estates of Kozłówka. From June 1942 he served as chaplain at the Institute for the Blind in Laski, near Warsaw. He delivered secret lectures and remained in contact with the underground. During the Warsaw Uprising Wyszyński was chaplain of the Military District of Żoliborz-Kampinos and of the insurgent hospital in Laski. In 1945 he returned to Włocławek, organized the theological seminary there, and

was its rector. On 4 March 1946 Wyszyński was appointed bishop of Lublin by Pope Pius XII and was consecrated on 12 May at Jasna Góra in Częstochowa. After the death of Cardinal **August Hlond** on 12 November 1948, the Pope named him archbishop metropolitan of Gniezno and Warsaw, thereby the Primate of Poland and the president of the Conference of the Polish Episcopate. Wyszyński's ingress into Gniezno Cathedral took place on 2 February 1949 and into Warsaw Cathedral on 6 February 1949.

Wyszyński assumed his office at a time of increasing Stalinization in Poland and an intensified struggle against the Church and religion. The signs of the times were the imprisonment of the primates of Hungary (1948) and the Czech Republic (1949). In Poland the authorities began to organize the movement of "priests-patriots" and to reduce Church ownership. Wyszyński strove to maintain the independence of the Church from the government, to delay and reduce the atheistic attacks, and to the retain the possibility of ministry. On 14 April 1950 he signed an agreement with the government in which the Episcopate declared its loyalty to the state authorities and its readiness to counteract anti-state manifestations, while the government promised to retain religious instruction in the schools and to ensure the functioning of the Catholic schools, press, and publishing houses and the organization of the ministry and religious pilgrimages and processions.

The authorities frequently violated the concluded agreement. In 1951 Bishop **Czesław Kaczmarek** was arrested, and apostolic administrators of the dioceses in the Western Territories were removed. Priests imposed by the authorities took their places. Wyszyński granted them jurisdiction in order to avoid a schism. In 1952 the authorities removed religion from the schools, liquidated junior theological seminaries, and removed the bishops of Katowice and Kraków from their dioceses. The primate, who was appointed cardinal on 12 January 1953, was not allowed to go to Rome. On 9 February 1953 a decree was passed by which the authorities usurped the right to have the final word on appointments to Church offices; the Conference of the Episcopate, on Wyszyński's motion, sent a letter to the government on 8 May 1953 in which the Church refused to submit to the decree (*non possumus*). On 25 September 1953 Wyszyński was arrested and put in Rywałd Prison, then in under house arrest in Stoczek, near Lidzbark Warmiński, then in Prudnik Śląski (from October 1954), and then in Komańcza (from October 1955). It was there that he wrote the text of the Jasna Góra Vows, a program preparing the nation for the Millennium of Christianity in Poland.

One of the most frequently repeated demands during the "thaw" of 1956 was for Wyszyński's release. After the

October 1956 breakthrough and **Władysław Gomułka**'s assumption of the post of first secretary of the CC of the PUWP on 28 October 1956, Wyszyński was released and reinstated in his functions. Wyszyński moderated the mood of agitation, fearing that a social outbreak might provoke a Soviet intervention in Poland as had occurred in Hungary. He concluded the so-called Small Agreement with the government (8 December 1953), which annulled the decree of 9 February 1953—that is, it reinstated religious instruction in the schools, allowed for religious assistance to the sick and to prisoners, allowed displaced nuns to return, and allowed for the appointment of new bishops in the Western Territories by the Pope. In January 1957 the Episcopate called on people to vote in Assembly elections; the primate himself also voted. This was significant support for Gomułka's new team. In May 1957 Wyszyński left for Rome, where he received a cardinal's hat.

From the fall of 1957 relations between Wyszyński and the Communist authorities were full of conflict. The authorities saw the strong position of the Church in society and the immense popularity of the primate as factors limiting their monopoly of power. They reacted with extreme hostility to the Millennium program of Wyszyńsi, who on 20 June 1957 announced the peregrination of the picture of the Holy Mother of Częstochowa to all parishes, and this was combined with the Jasna Góra Vows of the Nation. In 1958 the Primate's Institute in Jasna Góra was searched, and religion began to be removed from the schools. From 1959 the Church was harassed with high taxes, the drafting of clergymen into the army, and attempts at subordinating theological seminaries to secular jurisdiction. However, the authorities did not violate the bishops' right of assigning Church posts. Wyszyński entered into numerous mediations and talks with Gomułka, but to no greater effect. He set up thousands of ministry centers in special parish centers that were independent of government control.

The most important method of counteracting atheism was the program of the Great Novena of the Millennium. Wyszyński saw the strength of the Church and religion in traditional faith and the customs attached to it. He developed a theology of the nation, pointing to the relationship between the Polish nation and Catholicism. He also strongly emphasized the cult of the Holy Mother. At the Second Vatican Council Wyszyński was regarded as a moderate conservative. He wanted to raise the intellectual standard of the clergy, and the Catholic University of Lublin was under his patronage. However, he found it hard to accept criticism and distrusted new theological trends from the West. He saw them as a threat leading to the disintegration of faith and of the Church. He advocated a cautious introduction of the Vatican Council resolutions in Poland. He did not trust the political organizations of secular Catholics—that is, Pax and the Christian Social Association—but he stayed in touch with the Znak movement and with the Catholic parliamentary group Znak. Despite their differences and periodical tensions, until 1976 Wyszyński encouraged Znak members to participate in the Assembly and to defend the Catholic postulates.

In December 1965 Wyszyński co-authored the letter from the Polish bishops addressed to the German bishops in which the words "We forgive and we ask for forgiveness" were included. As a result, he became the object of violent attacks by Communist propaganda. In 1966, in an atmosphere of sharp confrontation with the authorities, Wyszyński celebrated the Millennium of Christianity in Poland. During the social conflicts of 1968 and 1970 he remained cautious and decided to issue conciliatory statements and to appeal to the authorities to desist from repressive measures.

After **Edward Gierek** came to power, Wyszyński assumed a positive attitude toward offers of partial normalization, although this did not mean a return to the resolutions of the Small Agreement of 1956. The position of the Church in the 1970s became stabilized as a result of the following: granting the Church the right of ownership of churches, buildings, and land used in the Western Territories (1971); the establishment of new dioceses in the Western Territories by the Vatican (1972); the establishment of diplomatic relations between the Polish People's Republic and the Holy See (1974); and the government's ceasing to attempt to control ministry centers and theological seminaries and relative freedom for the development of the Catholic youth movement (Oases, festivals of religious songs). Wyszyński repeatedly criticized materialism and atheism, especially in school instruction, as well as discrimination against the faithful in their access to public posts. He insisted on a recognition of the legal status of the Church and on its access to the mass media. Wyszyński presented his proposal for a social order—clearly different from the official one—in *Kazania Świętokrzeskie* (Świętokrzyskie sermons; 1974) and in an Episcopate protest against amendments to the constitution (1975–76).

At a time of mounting economic and social crisis in 1976–80, Wyszyński was an authority recognized by all social forces. In 1976 the authorities expressed a wish that he remain in office, although he was over seventy-five. Centers of emerging opposition recognized him as the highest national moral authority. In the face of mounting tensions Wyszyński maintained the position of a moderator—for example, he requested that the authorities desist from the use of repressive measures after June 1976, lent cautious support for the actions of the Committee for the Defense of Workers (KOR), opposed the persecutions of those who had been previously convicted or had a disobedient civil attitude, and gave people who could not participate in official cultural life an opportunity to lecture in the churches and parish rooms. His prestige in Polish society, as well as abroad, increased even more after the election of Cardinal Karol Wojtyła to the Holy See on 16 October 1978 and after Pope **John Paul II** visited his homeland in June 1979.

In August 1980 Wyszyński feared bloodshed or even a Soviet intervention. On 26 August he preached a sermon —part of which was shown on television for the first time—appealing to strikers for moderation and maturity; this was seen by many as a lack of clear support for far-reaching political claims. The next day Wyszyński partly revised his stance: the Chief Episcopate Council supported the workers' rights to organize into independent trade unions. Wyszyński established friendly relations with Solidarity, guiding its leaders toward moderation and caution. He appointed Ryszard Kukułowicz his representative and adviser to Solidarity. He appealed to the authorities to respect civil rights, revive social life, and continue dialogue. In February 1981 he was deeply involved in supporting the claims for the legalization of Rural Solidarity. Wyszyński died after a long, serious illness. In 1989 his beatification process began. Wyszyński was the author of many books and collections of sermons, including the following: *Nauczanie społeczne 1946–1981* (Social teachings 1946–1981; 1982); *Wielka Nowenna Tysiąclecia* (The Great Millennium Novenna; 1962); *Z rozważań nad kulturą ojczystą* (Reflections on national culture; 1979); and the diary *Zapiski więzienne* (*Freedom within: The Prison Notes of Stefan Cardinal Wyszyński,* 1983). (AF)

Sources: *Stefan Kardynał Wyszyński: Biografia w fotografiach* (Orchard Lake, MI, 1969); Andrzej Micewski, *Współrządzić czy nie kłamać? PAX i "Znak" w Polsce 1945–1976* (Paris, 1978); Peter Raina, *Stefan Kardynał Wyszyński Prymas Polski,* vols. 1–3 (London, 1979–88); Andrzej Micewski, *Kardynał Wyszyński: Prymas i mąż stanu* (Paris, 1982); Antoni Dudek, *Państwo i Kościół w Polsce 1945–1970* (Kraków, 1995).

X

XHAFERI Arben (24 January 1948, Tetovo), Macedonian politician. Xhaferi holds a degree in philosophy from the University of Belgrade and has for many years worked for Kosovo radio and television in Prishtina. Initially a member of the Party for Democratic Prosperity (Partija za Demokratski Prosperitet/Partia ë Prosperiteti Demokratike [PDP]), Xhaferi was elected to the parliament (Sobranie) of the Republic of Macedonia in 1994. He and his followers then spilt, forming the PDP–Sh (PDP–Albanian). Xhaferi's objective has been the recognition of the ethnic Albanians in Macedonia as a constituent people, with representation in the government and state infrastructure comparable to the size of the Albanian population. In 1997 Xhaferi's group and the People's Democratic Party merged into the Democratic Party of Albanians (Demokratska Partija na Albancite/Partia Demokratike Sqiptare [DPA]). Outspoken in his demands, Xhaferi has been accused of complicity with the Albanian insurgents of the Kosovo Liberation Army, which fought in Macedonia in 2001. Xhaferi's party is especially popular in rural areas. Nevertheless, it failed in the September 2002 elections. (DP)

Sources: Duncan Perry, "Republic of Macedonia: On the Road to Stability or Destruction?" *Transition*, 25 August 1995; Duncan Perry, "Macedonia's Quest for Security and Stability," *Current History*, March 2000; Duncan Perry, "Macedonia: Melting Pot or Meltdown?" *Current History*, November 2001; Valentina Georgieva and Sasha Konechni, *Historical Dictionary of the Republic of Macedonia* (Lanham, Md., 1998).

XOXE Koçi (1 May 1911, Negovan, near Flórina, Ottoman Empire [now in Greece]–11 June 1949, Tirana), Albanian Communist activist. Xoxe was born into an Orthodox family from the Gorani ethnic group, which spoke a language closely related to Macedonian. He finished only elementary school and then began working as a sheet-metal worker in Korçë, where in 1933 he established a trade union organization called Puna (Work). Arrested for the first time in 1938, Xoxe was imprisoned in Muhur, near Peshkopi. Along with **Enver Hoxha**, Xoxe was one of the founders of the Communist Party of Albania (CPA) in 1941. He held a variety of leadership positions in the party. He was a member of the Central Committee (CC) (1941–48), a member of the Politburo (1943–48), and the organizational secretary of the CC (1943–48). From 1944 to 1946 he served as vice-chairman of the Anti-Fascist Council of the National Liberation Front, later the Communist-dominated Democratic Front. Elected to parliament in 1945, Xoxe served as vice-president of its presidium. In January 1945, with the rank of lieutenant general, he presided over the Special People's Tribunal in Tirana, established for "trying war criminals and enemies of the people." This tribunal was responsible for many judicial crimes. From March 1946 to October 1948 Xoxe held the portfolio of minister of interior and served as one of the deputy prime ministers. He also controlled the State Audit Commission. He was one of the main founders and then served as the first head of the People's Defense Department (Divizioni i Mbrojtjes së Popullit), a political police established in May 1945 and later transformed into the State Security Armed Forces (Arma e Sigurimit të Shtetit), commonly known as Sigurimi. Xoxe, who had little education, hated the intelligentsia, even among party members. One of the most influential but also one of the cruelest leaders of the CPA, he was called "the butcher" by some and "the party tank" by others.

Xoxe, who had personal ties with **Aleksander Ranković**, head of the Yugoslav security apparatus, owed his position in the CPA to Belgrade's support. He represented a pro-Yugoslav line in the Albanian leadership, ruthlessly eliminating all signs of discontent with such a policy. Among his victims were **Sejfulla Malëshova**, **Nako Spiru**, and **Liri Belishova**. The factional strife within the Albanian party was fueled by Stalin, who—in his attempts to undermine **Josip Broz Tito**'s position—gave his support both to the pro-Yugoslav faction led by Xoxe and to Hoxha, secretary general of the CPA. At the beginning of 1948 Xoxe had strengthened his position to such an extent that he could attack Hoxha, who had to justify his policies at the Eighth Plenum of the CPA CC in late February and early March. This plenum supported the idea of close cooperation between the Albanian and Yugoslav parties and armies, and a union between them was not ruled out.

After the Information Bureau of the Communist and Workers' Parties (Cominform) severed its ties with Yugoslavia in June 1948, the roles changed. Xoxe made a visit to southern Albania, explaining the reasons for the current situation and personally attacking Tito. Nevertheless, on 3 October Xoxe was transferred from the ministry of interior to the ministry of industry, and on 7 November he was attacked by the press as a "Trotskyite." Arrested on 2 December 1948, Xoxe was tried along with a group of his associates. **Bedri Spahiu**, another leader of the CPA, was the chief prosecutor. During Xoxe's trial, demonstrations were staged in Tirana, the participants demanding the death sentence for Xoxe. On 10 June 1949 Xoxe was found guilty of Trotskyism and Titoism and sentenced to death. His last words before the execution were, "I am not guilty. Long live the party, the republic, the Soviet Union, and Stalin. Blame for sentencing me to death falls on Bedri Spahiu." After Xoxe's death a propaganda campaign tried to convince the public that he had been responsible for all the abuses of the security apparatus. Moscow's efforts to rehabilitate Xoxe in the second half of the 1950s led to the deterioration of relations between Tirana and Moscow. (TC)

Sources: *Bashkimi,* 14 November 1945; Milovan Džilas, *Rozmowy ze Stalinem* (Paris, 1962); William E. Griffith, *Albania and the Sino-Soviet Rift* (Cambridge, Mass., 1963); Arshi Pipa, *Albanian Stalinism: Ideo-Political Aspects* (Boulder, Colo., 1990); Jerzy Hauziński, *Historia Albanii* (Wrocław, 1992); Klaus-Detlev Grothusen, ed., *Albanien* (Göttingen, 1993); Pjeter Pepa, *Dosja e diktaturës* (Tirana, 1995); *Marrëdhëniet shqiptaro-jugosllave 1945–1948: Dokumente* (Tirana, 1996).

Y

YANOVSKYI Yuryi [also spelled Ianovskyi Iurii] (14 August 1902, Mayerove–25 February 1954, Kiev), Ukrainian writer. Between 1922 and 1923 Yanovskyi studied at the Kiev Polytechnic Institute. From 1925 to 1926 he was an artistic editor at the Odessa film studios. In 1927 he moved to Kharkiv and in 1939 to Kiev. In 1922 he made his debut writing in Russian, and in 1924 he began to write in Ukrainian. In 1927 Yanovskyi published the collection of poems *Prekrasna Ut* (Most beautiful Ut), but he won the widest acclaim as the author of romantic novels and novellas, including *Maister korablia* (Shipmaster; 1928) and *Chotyry shabli* (Four swords; 1930), a novel that was banned from distribution; in it Yanovskyi depicted the social upheavals of 1917–19 as a spontaneous uprising of the Ukrainian peasants. In a later novel, *Vershnyky* (Riders; 1935), which was also devoted to the revolution, Yanovskyi moved away from a romantic style and formal literary avant garde experiments of the 1920s. Because of its language, composition, and richness of metaphors, the novel remains a classic of Ukrainian Soviet literature, and it was translated into several foreign languages. During World War II Yanovskyi was a war correspondent and editor of the periodical *Ukrainska literatura,* and in 1945 he covered the Nuremberg trials for the Soviet press. In 1947 he published the novel *Zhivaya voda* (Living water), devoted to the reawakening of social life in the Ukraine after the Nazi occupation. Attacked for propounding nationalism in it, Yanovskyi was forced to rewrite this novel and to republish it in a definitely weaker version, under the title *Myr* (Peace; 1956). In November 1951 the Plenum of the CC of the Ukrainian party denounced a number of works by Ukrainian writers, including two stories by Yanovskyi. However, he did not abandon his artistic ambitions and went on to write the play *Doch prokuratora* (The prosecutor's daughter; 1953), which raised the problem of the moral responsibility of parents for the behavior of their children. Yanovskyi's works were reissued in the Ukraine several times—for example, as *Zbirka tvoriv* (Collected works, 4 vols.; 1931–32) and *Tvory* (Works, 5 vols.; 1958–59). (TS)

Sources: O. Klimnik, *Iurii Ianovs'kyi* (Moscow, 1962); *Istoriia ukrainskoi literatury XX stolittia u dvokh knigakh* (Kiev, 1998).

YARESHCHENKO Oleksander (12 September 1890, near Poltava–1938, Far East of the USSR), archbishop of the Ukrainian Autocephalous Orthodox Church. Yareshchenko graduated from the Moscow Theological Academy, earning a Ph.D. in theology, and from the Railroad Institute in St. Petersburg. In 1920–21 he was director of the railroads in the Poltava region. After the occupation of the Ukraine by the Bolsheviks, Metropolitan **Vasyl Lypkivskyi** ordained Yareshchenko as bishop of Poltava (27 October 1921). Yareshchenko worked in Lubny, where between 1921 and 1923 he established fifty parishes of the Ukrainian Autocephalous Orthodox Church. In 1923 he was appointed archbishop of Kharkiv, vice-president of the Council of the All-Ukrainian Orthodox Church, and a member of the doctrinal commission of this council. A gifted preacher and a courageous critic of the Soviet system, Yareshchenko was one of the first hierarchs of the Ukrainian Autocephalous Orthodox Church arrested by the GPU in 1926. He was held in prisons in Moscow and Tashkent. Released in 1934, Yareshchenko went to Kursk, but soon after that he was imprisoned again and deported to camps in the Far East. The exact circumstances of his death are not known. (WR)

Sources: *Encyclopedia of Ukraine,* Vol. 5 (Toronto, 1993); Vasyl Lipkivs'kyi, *Vidrozhdzheniia Tserkvi v Ukraini 1917–1930* (Toronto, 1959).

YAVOROV Peyo [originally Kracholov] (1 January 1878, Chirpan–16 October 1914, Sofia), Bulgarian poet. The son of a merchant, already in high school in Plovdiv Yavorov showed literary talent. After graduating, he worked at the Chirpan post office. In 1898 he started publishing in the Modernist periodical *Misul,* using the pen name "Yavorov" (invented by **Pencho Slaveykov**) from 1899. In 1903 Yavorov took part in the Illinden Uprising; after its failure he went to Sofia, where he worked in the National Library from 1904. In 1906 he spent a year in France, and in 1909–14 he was literary director of the National Theater in Sofia. With his personal experience and the influence of contemporary artistic trends, the patriotic and social elements present in Yavorov's earlier collection, *Stikhotvorenya* (Poems; 1901), gave way to hopelessness and despair, apparent in the volumes *Bezsynitsi* (Sleepless nights; 1907) and *Podir senkite na oblatsite* (Over the shadows of clouds; 1910), in which his sense of solitude was combined with a sense of the inevitability of suffering and death. Yavorov's works were full of eroticism. The female was for him the personification of a contradiction between the sublime and the demonic. His well-known love affairs with his sister Mina and Lora Karavelova were realizations of the literary fashion of his time and the inspirations for his modernist erotic poetry. Yavorov remembered his struggles in Macedonia in *Haydushki kopnenya* (Hayduk longings; 1909). At the end of his life he wrote the dramas *W polite na Vitosha* (At the foot of Mount Vitosha; 1911) and *Kogato grym udari* (When the thunder strikes; 1912). Yavorov's personal life was tragic. His marriage to Karavelova ended in her suicide after a year. Yavorov attempted suicide himself but failed. As a result, he lost his sight. Accused of Karavelova's death, he finally shot himself. In 1934–36 Yavorov's *Sybrani suchinenya* (Collected works, 5 vols.) were published. (WR)

Sources: *Mały słownik pisarzy zachodnio-słowiańskich i południowo-słowiańskich* (Warsaw, 1973); Raymond Detrez, *Historical Dictionary of Bulgaria* (Lanham, Md., 1997); Pencho Danchev, *Yavorov, Tvorcheski put: Poetika* (Sofia, 1978); Nikola Gaydarov, *Zhiteyskata drama na Yavorov* (Sofia, 1979); Mina Todorova, *Intimi i predsmurtni izpovedi* (Plovdiv, 1991); Georgi Raychevski, ed. *Dve dushi: Spomeni za Yavorov*ed (Chirpan, 1993).

YAVORSKYI Matviy (15 November 1885, Korchmin, near Sokal–3 November 1937, Solovets Islands), Ukrainian Marxist historian, victim of communism. In 1910 Yavorskyi graduated in law from the university in Lemberg (Lviv, Lwów), and in 1912 he earned a Ph.D. in political science. During World War I he was an officer in the Austrian Army and later fought in the Ukrainian Galician Army (UGA). After the Ukrainian defeat in the war against Poland, Yavorskyi prepared the transfer of part of the UGA to the Bolshevik side. In April 1920 in Kiev he joined the Communist Party (Bolshevik) of Ukraine (CP[B]U). In 1924–27 Yavorskyi was in charge of the Administration of Scientific Institutions (Uprnauka) in the Commissariat of Education of the Ukrainian SSR. He headed the historical department of the Ukrainian Institute of Marxism-Leninism (VUAMLIN) and subsequently became director of this institute. He lectured on Ukrainian history at institutions of higher education in Kharkiv. In the 1920s Yavorskyi formulated a new, Marxist interpretation of Ukrainian history consistent with the paradigm of the Russian historian Mikhail Pokrovsky. Yavorskyi presented this interpretation in the works *Narys istorii Ukrainy* (An outline of Ukrainian history, 2 vols.; 1923–24); *Korotka istoriia Ukrainy* (Short history of Ukraine; 1927); and *Istoriia Ukrainy v styslomu narysi* (A detailed account of Ukrainian history, 3 vols.; 1928–29). Although Yavorskyi analyzed history from the point of view of the development of Marxist productive forces, on the basis of his findings the Russian and Ukrainian historical processes could be separated, and Russia's backwardness in comparison with the Ukraine up until the beginning of the twentieth century could be demonstrated. In the 1920s, at the time of Ukrainization, Yavorskyi's theory was embraced by the Soviet leaders, who adhered to so-called national commu-

nism, and it was used in the ideological struggle against non-Marxist national historiographies, represented in the works of, among others, **Mykhailo Hrushevskyi**.

In 1929 Yavorskyi became a full member of the All-Ukrainian Academy of Sciences (VUAN) and was in charge of its first department of history and philosophy. In that year, however, as result of a Stalinist campaign against "nationalist deviation" in the Ukraine, Yavorskyi was officially denounced and dismissed from the VUAMLIN. In February 1930 he was expelled from the party and from the VUAN. Arrested in March 1931 and sentenced to six years' imprisonment in February 1932, Yavorskyi was exiled to the Solovets Islands. Although during his trial he cooperated with the investigators, while serving the sentence, he openly spoke out against the Stalinist administration of justice. On 9 October 1937 the NKVD "troika" found Yavorskyi guilty of conducting "nationalist" activities, and he was executed by a firing squad, along with a group of other prisoners from the Western Ukraine, among them **Mykhailo Lozynskyi**. Yavorskyi's works include *Narysy z istorii revoliutsiinoi borotby na Ukraini* (Essays in the history of revolutionary struggle in the Ukraine, 2 vols.; 1927–28) and *Ukraina v epokhu kapitalizmu* (Ukraine in the epoch of capitalism, 3 vols.; 1924–25), as well as numerous articles on methodological subjects. (TS)

Sources: *Encyclopedia of Ukraine,* vol. 5 (Toronto, 1993); Hryhory Kostiuk, *Stalinist Rule in the Ukraine* (New York, 1960); James Mace, *Communism and the Dilemmas of National Liberation: National Communism in Soviet Ukraine, 1918–1933* (Cambridge, 1983); O. Rublov and Iu. Cherchenko, *Stalinshchyna i dola zakhidnoukrainskoi intelihentsii 20–50-ti roky XX st.* (Kiev, 1994); Heorhii Kasianov, "Akademik M. I. Iavorskyi: Dola vchenoho," *Ukrainskyi istorychnyi zhurnal,* 1990, no. 8.

YČAS Martynas (13 November 1885, Šimpeliškiai, near Biržai–5 April 1941, Rio de Janeiro), Lithuanian lawyer and politician. Born into a Protestant family, after passing his high school graduation examinations, Yčas studied law at the university in Tomsk, Siberia, receiving a degree in 1911. He subsequently worked as an attorney in Kaunas. Elected a deputy to the fourth Russian State Duma in 1912, Yčas was a member of a faction of the Russian Constitutional Democratic Party. He put forward a proposal for a statute of autonomy for Lithuania. From 1912 to 1914 Yčas edited the periodical *Vairas* in Kaunas. After the outbreak of World War I, he became chairman of the Lithuanian Central Relief Committee. Before the front line approached, Yčas moved to the interior of Russia, where he continued to carry on the committee's work, among other things using funds provided by an organization established by Grand Duchess Tatyana, the daughter of Tsar Nicholas II. Yčas became vice-chairman of this organization, which helped him to obtain permission to establish two Lithuanian schools in Voronezh. From 1915 to 1918 he edited the weekly *Lietuvių Balsas* in Petrograd. He also worked for the promotion of the Lithuanian cause abroad. Yčas made visits to Sweden, Switzerland, and the United States, where he sought the support of the Lithuanian émigré community for Lithuania's independence. He briefly served as minister of education in the first Provisional Government after the February 1917 revolution. Arrested after the Bolshevik revolution, he escaped from prison and returned to Lithuania.

In August 1918 Yčas was coopted into the Lithuanian Council (Taryba). In the first Lithuanian government, established on 11 November 1918, he assumed the portfolio of minister of trade and industry, and in the subsequent cabinets he served as minister of finance. He then secured loans from Germany, Great Britain, and the United States. In 1919 Yčas was a member of the Lithuanian delegation to the Paris Peace Conference, at which Lithuania failed to gain the status of a full participant. In 1921 he was a member of an arbitration commission that demarcated the border between Lithuania and Latvia. He was instrumental in the establishment of the Bank of Lithuania and in the introduction of the Lithuanian currency, the litas. Yčas organized many enterprises, including the Nemunas foundry, the Ringuva oil mill, and a textile factory in Panevėžys. He was also a co-founder of the Lithuanian merchant navy. He was repeatedly elected head of the synod of the Evangelical Reformed Church. As a result of his efforts, the Department of Protestant Theology was established at the university in Kaunas. Yčas published his memoirs, *Nepriklausomybės keliais* (Toward independence, 3 vols.; 1935–36). In 1940 he went to Portugal and thence to Brazil, where he died. His brother, Jonas Yčas (1880–1931), a historian and politician, served as minister of education (1918–19) and worked as a professor at the university in Kaunas. (WR)

Sources: *EL*, vol. 6; J. Mikelėnas, "Dr Martynas Yčas," *Žiburiai*, 1947, no. 31; Alfred E. Senn, *The Emergence of Modern Lithuania* (New York, 1959); Constantine R. Jurgela, *Lithuania: The Outpost of Freedom* (St. Petersburg, Fla., 1976).

YEFREMOV Serhiy (6 October 1876, Palchik, Kiev region–1937 or 1939, Vladimir?), Ukrainian literary critic and historian, victim of Stalinist persecution. Yefremov was born into a clergyman's family and graduated from theological seminaries in Human and Kiev and from the Law School of Kiev University. He wrote for the *Hromadska dumka*, *Rada*, *Literaturno-Naukovyi Visnyk*, and *Zapysky Naukohovo Tovarystva imieni Shevchenka* periodicals. From the beginning of the 1890s Yefremov belonged to the Kiev Narodniks. He was active in the Old Hromada and its editorial initiative, *Vik* (The century, 1895–1918), contributing to the edition of many works of Ukrainian literature. Yefremov co-founded successive political groups that developed from this society: the All-Ukrainian Nonparty Democratic Organization in 1897 and the Ukrainian Democratic Radical Party (1904–5), which advocated the transformation of Russia into a federation of equal nations, the nationalization of the manufacturing industry, and an agrarian reform without compensation to landowners. In 1908 Yefremov joined the Society of Ukrainian Progressives, the group that led the initiatives of the main current of the Ukrainian movement under the Russian government until 1917.

In March 1917 Yefremov became a member of the Ukrainian Central Rada (Council) (UCR) and served as a deputy to President **Mykhailo Hrushevskyi**. However, their political paths diverged, and Yefremov chose the centrist direction. He co-established the Ukrainian Party of Socialists-Federalists in 1917. As its representative, he became a member of the so-called Small Rada and took part in negotiations with the Provisional Government in Petrograd on the status of the Ukraine in a future Russian state. He also served as secretary for national minorities in the government of the General Secretariat of the UCR. Yefremov did not leave Kiev after the fall of the UCR in February 1918 and continued to work with representatives of the independent Ukraine orientation, the Directorate of **Symon Petlura**, until the failure of the Ukrainian question on the international scene in 1923.

Despite Bolshevik attempts to win him over, Yefremov did not assume any political functions in the Ukrainian Soviet Socialist Republic and concentrated only upon literary theory and scholarly endeavors. His consistent stance got him the title of "the conscience of the Ukraine." In the 1920s Yefremov was president of the Ukrainian Academy of Sciences. In 1924, as a result of the Ukrainization policy of the party, a group of scholars and politicians of the Narodnik orientation, with Hrushevskyi as leader, returned from exile. The scholarly work of non-Communist scholars became easier then, though it was not free from the personal conflicts between Yefremov and Hrushevskyi, the two most prominent humanists and Narodniks in the Ukraine of that time. With the increase in Stalinist terror, the USSR security forces prepared the so-called trial of the Union for the Liberation of Ukraine in order to get rid of the non-Bolshevik intelligentsia. Arrested on 2 July 1928, along with a group of co-workers, Yefremov was accused of preparing an armed uprising aimed at the rebuilding of a "bourgeois" Ukraine. Most historians incline toward the opinion that this organization did not exist and that all of the evidence against it was false. Yefremov rejected Stalin's offer of a pardon, addressed personally to him, at the cost of lending his writing talents to the services of the regime. On 19 April 1930 Yefremov received a death sentence, changed later to ten years of prison. He served the sentence in Yaroslav and (from 1937) in Vladimir, where he probably perished.

Yefremov left many monographs on Ukrainian writers of the nineteenth century, including *Spivets borotby i kontrastiv* (Songster of struggle and contrasts; 1913); *Shevchenko* (1914); *M. Kotsiubynskyi* (1922); *Nechuy-Levytskyi, Karpenko-Kary* (1924); and *Panas Mirny* (1928). Yefremov owes his place in the history of Ukrainian culture above all to the two-volume *Istoriia ukrainskoho pysmenstva* (History of Ukrainian literature; 1910). Aside from the works of Hrushevskyi, this work contained one of the last studies of the nineteenth-century Ukrainian Narodnik movement. Like the Russian Narodniks, Yefremov perceived the historical process as an arena of progress created by sovereign human decisions. He credited the Ukrainian nation with persevering in the fight for freedom and concentrated his attention upon its means of expression: the national language and literature. (TS)

Sources: *Encyclopedia of Ukraine*, vol. 5, (Toronto, 1993); W. Kubijowycz, ed., *Entsyklopedia ukraiinoznavstva*, vol. 2 (Lviv, 1993); "Do stolettia narodzhennya Serhiya Yefremova," *Suchasnist*, 1976, no. 10; Georgi Kasyanov, *Ukraiska intelihentsia 1920–30-ch rokiv: Sotsialny portret ta istorychna dolya* (Kiev, 1992).

YERMACHENKA Ivan (13 May 1894, Kopychovka, near Borisov–25 February 1970, South River, New Jersey), Belorussian politician. Yermachenka graduated in electrical engineering in Moscow. Mobilized into the Russian Army in 1914, he was taken prisoner of war by the Germans but managed to escape. He fought as a colonel on the side of the Whites during the civil war in Russia. Aide-de-camp to General Pyotr Wrangel, in 1920, along with a remnant of Wrangel's army, Yermachenka escaped to Istanbul. He founded the Belorussian Committee in Turkey, where in 1921 he became ambassador of the Belorussian People's Republic (BPR) and consul general in the Balkans. In 1922 Yermachenka moved to Kaunas and was appointed deputy minister for foreign affairs in the BPR émigré government. In 1923 he settled in Prague, where he studied medicine at Charles University and later had his own medical practice. He was also involved in the work of Belorussian émigré organizations. In August 1939, along with **Vasil Zakharka**, president of the BPR Council, Yermachenka conducted talks with representatives of the Ministry of Foreign Affairs of the Third Reich concerning cooperation between Belorussia and Nazi Germany in the case of a German-Soviet conflict. From October 1941 Yermachenka lived in German-occupied Minsk. He became head of the Belorussian People's Mutual Aid Association, which was to serve as a government of the Belorussian state allied with Germany. In April 1943 he was forced by the Nazi security services to resign from his position for exceeding his powers, and he had to go to Prague. In May 1945 Yermachenka went to western Germany and in 1948 to the United States, where he had a medical practice, was active among Belorussian émigré circles, and published in the émigré press. (EM)

Sources: *Belaruskaia Dumka* (South River, N.J.), 1969–70, nos. 12–13; *The 40th Anniversary of the Proclamation of the Independent Byelorussian Republic* (New York, 1958); Vitaut Kipel and Zora Kipel, eds., *Byelorussian Statehood* (New York, 1988); Jerzy Turonek, *Wacław Iwanowski i odrodzenie Białorusi* (Warsaw, 1992); Larysa Heniush, *Spovedz'* (Minsk, 1993); *Entsyklapiedyia historyi Bielarusi*, vol. 3 (Minsk, 1996).

YERMALOVICH Mikalai (29 April 1921, Malyia Navasiolki, near Minsk–4 March 2000, Minsk), Belorussian historian and literary scholar. After graduating from the Pedagogical Institute in Minsk (1947), Yermalovich worked as a lecturer in Belorussian literature at the Teachers' Institute in Molodechno (1948–55). From 1957 onwards he concentrated on the earliest history of Belorussia, publishing many articles on the political history of the Polotsk Principality and the Novogrudok Duchy. Yermalovich was the originator of the theory that ethnically the Belorussian population was composed largely of Slavicized Balts. According to his theory, ancient Lithuania was located between Novogrudok and Minsk. The Novogrudok Duchy, the first form of Lithuanian statehood, dating back to the eleventh century, was supposed to have been inhabited by a Christianized population representing the Russo-Byzantine culture. Yermalovich presented his theory in three books: *Starazhytnaia Belarus: Polatski i novaharodski periyady* (Ancient Belarus: The Polotsk and Novogrudok Period; 1990); *Pa sladakh adnaho mita* (Following the traces of one myth; 1991); and *Starazhytnaia Belarus: Vilenski periyad* (Ancient Belarus: The Vilnius period; 1993). Yermalovich's thesis challenged the findings of Russian and Lithuanian historiography, which postulated the subjugation of the Belorussian territory by the Balts in the thirteenth and fourteenth centuries, and it gave rise to a stormy discussion among Belorussian, Russian, and Lithuanian historians. At that time, Yermalovich's books were the most sought-after literature in Belarus. (EM)

Sources: Jan Zaprudnik, *Belarus: At a Crossroads in History* (Boulder, Colo., 1993); *Bielaruskiya pismienniki (1917–1990): Davednik* (Minsk, 1994); *Kto est' kto v Respublike Belarus* (Minsk, 1999).

YEZAVITAU Kanstantsin (17 November 1893, Dvinsk–23 May 1946, Minsk), Belorussian politician, journalist, and historian. In 1913 Yezavitau joined the Belorussian Socialist Hromada. In 1916 he graduated from the Teachers' Institute in Vitebsk and the Pavlov Military Academy in St. Petersburg, and then he was sent to the northern front. After the February 1917 revolution, Yezavitau organized the Congress of the Belorussian Veterans of the Northern Front, and in November he became deputy president of the Belorussian Central Military Council. He was arrested by the Bolsheviks for taking part in the work of the First All-Belorussian Congress, but in February 1918 he managed to escape from prison. After the Red Army left Minsk, Yezavitau became commander of the Minsk garrison. He took part in preparations for the declaration of independence of the Belorussian People's Republic (BPR) on 25 March 1918. Yezavitau served as secretary for military affairs with the rank of colonel in the BPR Council, organizing Belorussian units. According to the decision of the Belorussian Council in Vilnius (Wilno), in December 1918 he was appointed commissioner of Białystok and commander of an infantry regiment in Grodno. He initiated publication of the newspaper *Bats'kaushchina*. In the summer of 1919 the BPR Council appointed Yezavitau head of a military mission to the Lithuanian government and later head of a military mission to Latvia and Estonia. Under Yezavitau's mediation, the corps of **Stanislau Bulak-Balakhovich** subordinated itself to the BPR Council. In May 1920 the BPR Council promoted Yezavitau to major general.

After the signing of the Treaty of Riga between Poland and Soviet Russia (March 1921), Yezavitau settled in Latvia and took Latvian citizenship. He was involved in organizing cultural and educational activities among the local Belorussians and worked as an inspector of Belorussian schools for the Latvian Ministry of Education. He founded several publishing houses, and he published extensively. He compiled a considerable collection of books, worked on a Belorussian biographical dictionary, and compiled an archive of the Belorussian liberation movement. In 1924 Yezavitau was arrested on charges of scheming to sever the southern districts of Latvia from the country and bring them under Belorussian rule. Released for a lack of evidence after nearly one year of imprisonment, Yezavitau was later arrested on two occasions. After the annexation of Latvia by the USSR in 1940, Yezavitau worked as a teacher and cultural instructor for the board of the Trade Union of Education Workers of the Latvian

SSR. In August 1941, during the German occupation, he became president of the Belorussian Central Committee in Riga. He was mainly involved in organizing Belorussian education in Latvia. In June 1944 he attended the Second All-Belorussian Congress in Minsk. He became a member of the Belorussian Central Council and the chief inspector of the Belorussian Army. In August 1944 he went from Riga to Germany, where in April 1945 he was arrested by the Soviet intelligence services. He was taken to Moscow and later to Minsk. Yezavitau died in prison while his case was being investigated. Tuberculosis was given as the official cause of death. (EM)

Sources: *Entsyklapiedyia historyi Bielarusi*, vol. 3 (Minsk, 1996); *Belarus: Entsyklapedychny davednik* (Minsk, 1995); A. Khatskevich, "Heneral Yezavitau: Zdradnik, tsi ahient KDB?" *Zviazda*, 19 August 1992; S. Paniznik, "Kanstantsin Ezavitau (1893–1946)," *Rodnae Slovo*, 1993, no. 11; U. Mikhniuk and I. Paulau, "Kanstantsin Ezavitau: Materyialy da biiahrafii," *Malados'ts'*, 1995, no. 1.

YORDANOV Aleksandur (13 February 1952, Varna), Bulgarian politician, literary critic, and journalist. Yordanov graduated in Bulgarian philology from the Higher Pedagogical Institute in Shumen. In 1986 he received a Ph.D. at the Institute of Literature of the Bulgarian Academy of Sciences (BAS) and started working there. In 1990–91 Yordanov was deputy to the Grand National Assembly on behalf of the Union of Democratic Forces (Sayuz na Demokratichnite Sili [UDF]) and spokesman of the UDF parliamentary club. On 14 May 1991, along with thirty other UDF deputies, he left the Assembly in protest against the draft constitution. From October 1991 to December 1994 Yordanov was a UDF deputy again, presiding over its parliamentary club and over the foreign affairs commission of the Assembly. From November 1992 to December 1994 he was speaker of the parliament. From 1990 to 1992 he was editor-in-chief of the newspaper *Vek*. In 1991–97 Yordanov was deputy chairman of the Radical Democratic Party, and from 1997 he was its chairman. From 1991 he was also deputy head of the UDF National Coordination Council for mediation and for contact with the daily *Demokratsia*. In 1998 Yordanov became ambassador to Poland. He authored several books and more than two hundred articles, including *Lichnosti i idei* (Personalities and ideas; 1986); *V siankata na dumite* (In the shadow of words; 1989); *Svoechuzhdiyat modernizym* (Familiar-alien modernism, 1993); and *Nadezhdata sreshtu bezvremeto* (Hope against inactivity; 1993). (JJ)

Sources: *Koy koy e v Bulgariya* (Sofia, 1998); Jerzy Jackowicz, *Bułgaria od rządów komunistycznych do demokracji parlamentarnej 1988–1991* (Warsaw, 1992); Raymond Detrez, *Historical Dictionary of Bulgaria* (Lanham, Md., 1997).

YOSIF I [originally Lazar Yovchev] (5 May 1840, Kalofer–20 June 1915, Sofia), exarch of Bulgaria. Yosif graduated from the French Catholic high school in Istanbul and later in philosophy (1864–67) and law (1867–70) from the Sorbonne in Paris. After returning home, he joined in the struggle for the independence of the Bulgarian Orthodox Church from the patriarch of Constantinople. He edited the periodicals *Chytalishte* and *Makedonia*. Ordained in 1872, Yosif worked as secretary for Exarch Antim I, and from 1876 he was metropolitan of Lovech. After the outbreak of the Russo-Turkish War of 1877, the Turkish government expelled Antim, and Yosif acted on his behalf. He retained the headquarters of the exarchate in Istanbul, taking care of the Bulgarians under the Turkish yoke in Macedonia and Eastern Thrace; in view of the revision of the San Stefano Peace Treaty and the loss of these territories by Bulgaria under the terms of the Berlin Treaty of 1878, Yosif's actions were politically significant. Despite Turkish obstacles, Yosif managed to appoint Bulgarian bishops in Skopje and Ohrid and to establish a network of Bulgarian schools. Thanks to his endeavors, until World War I, about 1,300 schools were established, including high schools and seminaries. In 1893–1912 a Bulgarian theological seminary functioned in Istanbul. Yosif mediated between the sultan and the prince of Bulgaria. After the defeat of Bulgaria in the Second Balkan War in 1913, Yosif decided to return to Bulgaria, but the Bulgarian authorities were not eager to move the seat of the exarchy, hoping for the recovery of Macedonia and Eastern Thrace. In 1994 Yosif's *Pisma i dokladi* (Writings and lectures) were published. (JW/WDj)

Sources: *Entsiklopediya Bulgariya*, vol. 3 (Sofia, 1978); Mikhail Arnaudov, *Ekzarch Yosif i bulgarskata kulturna borba sled syzdavaneto na Ekzarkhiyata (1870–1915)* (Sofia, 1940).

YUGOV Anton (15 August 1904, Karasuli, Macedonia–8 July 1991, Sofia), Bulgarian Communist activist. After World War I, Yugov's family settled in Bulgaria, where he started working in a cigarette factory in Plovdiv in 1919. In 1920 he became active in the trade union movement, and in 1922 he joined a Macedonian leftist organization in Bulgaria. In September 1923 he took part in an unsuccessful Communist uprising in Sofia, although he had joined the Bulgarian Communist Party (BCP) only in 1928. In 1934 Yugov was sent to Moscow for fifteen months; there he underwent training at the Leninist School of the Comintern. After his return to Bulgaria in February 1936, he quickly rose through the party ranks. In 1937 he joined the Politburo of the BCP CC. The BCP was officially active under the name of the Bulgarian Workers' Party, and Yugov was in charge of its trade union department. In 1941, after the occupation of Macedonia by the Bulgarian Army, he supervised the takeover of control over the Macedonian Communists. Arrested in 1942, he escaped from prison and continued party work in the underground.

After the coup of 9 September 1944, Yugov was appointed minister of interior. He organized the People's Militia, and with the help of Soviet advisers, he set up a security apparatus that used cruel terror against all opponents of the system. Yugov was particularly known for his brutality. In 1944–46 over 2,100 Bulgarian political activists were executed. Yugov was directly responsible for staging the trials of prominent politicians of tsarist Bulgaria: 162 people were tried in these trials; 96 of them were sentenced to death and executed by firing squad on 1 and 2 February 1946. In July 1949 Yugov became deputy prime minister. As a Communist who had lived in Bulgaria during the war, Yugov was attacked by **Vulko Chervenkov** during the trial of **Traicho Kostov** in 1949. By August 1949 Yugov had already ceased to be minister of interior, and he also left the Politburo. In January 1950 he ceased to be deputy prime minister, but he managed to keep the post of minister of industry. After making a self-criticism, Yugov managed to save his position. In September 1951 he regained his place in the Politburo, and in August 1952 he was again appointed deputy prime minister. In May 1953 he was sent to Plovdiv, where he brutally crushed a strike in the tobacco industry. At the same time, as a "victim" of the Stalinist regime, he supported the release of Kostov's former adherents from prison, which gave him leverage against Chervenkov. After the Sixth Congress of the BCP in March 1954, Yugov was already one of the top party leaders. At that time, following the Soviet example, he helped to introduce "collective leadership." It meant that Chervenkov, who until then had been his rival, remained prime minister but had to yield his post as party leader to **Todor Zhivkov**.

Yugov was a member of the Bulgarian delegation to the Twentieth Congress of the CPSU in Moscow in February 1956. At a crucial plenum of the CC of the BCP on 2–6 April 1956 a decision was made to remove Chervenkov from the premiership, and on 17 April Yugov was appointed in his place. At that time he played an important role in suppressing the "thaw" tendencies in Bulgarian society and in restoring relations with the Yugoslav party. At the end of the 1950s competition between Yugov and Zhivkov increased. This competition manifested itself in economic policy and in relations with China. While Zhivkov supported the acceleration of industrialization and supported the Kremlin against Beijing, Yugov was more skeptical about the acceleration of capital formation and more cautious about policy toward China. Through a series of government reshuffles, in 1959 Zhivkov managed to weaken Yugov's position. During **Nikita Khrushchev**'s visit to Bulgaria in May 1962, Zhivkov gained support against his rival. Khrushchev publicly backed Zhivkov. After consultations in Moscow, on 4 November of that year the CC plenum decided to remove Yugov from the CC and recommended that he be dismissed as prime minister. The following day, in a speech at the Eighth Congress of the BCP, Zhivkov announced these decisions. Subsequent speakers directed accusations against Yugov, charging him with "anti-party" activities, opposition to economic policy, "dishonesty and arrogance," abuses of power, and the persecution of party activists in the Stalinist years. One of the speakers even accused Yugov of responsibility for the Kostov trial. With Yugov's dismissal, Zhivkov finally consolidated his power over the party. In June 1964 Yugov was also deprived of his parliamentary seat. For many years he remained in the shadows, although he was never held responsible for his activities. After Zhivkov's resignation in November 1989, Yugov was in the limelight again: he received the most prestigious order of the Bulgarian People's Republic. In January 1990, in a decision by the Politburo of the BCP, Yugov was "rehabilitated" as a "victim" of Zhivkov. (WR)

Sources: *Entsiklopediya Bulgariya*, vol. 7 (Sofia, 1996); Jerzy Tomaszewski, *Bułgaria 1944–1971* (Warsaw, 1989); J. F. Brown, *Bulgaria under Communist Rule* (New York, 1970); Raymond Detrez, *Historical Dictionary of Bulgaria* (Lanham, Md., 1997); Tasho Tashev, *Ministrite na Bulgariya 1879–1999: Entsiklopedichen spravochnik* (Sofia, 1999).

YUKHNOVSKYI Ihor (1 September 1925, Kniahynyn, near Równe [Rivne]), Ukrainian scholar and politician. Born into an intelligentsia family, Yukhnovskyi took part in World War II. In 1951 he graduated in physics from the University of Kiev. In 1954 he defended a Ph.D. dissertation and became an associate professor there. In 1959–69 Yukhnovskyi was the chair of theoretical physics at this university, and in 1965 he received a postdoctoral degree there. In 1969–90 Yukhnovskyi directed the Department of Statistical Physics at the Institute of Theoretical Physics of the Academy of Sciences of the Ukraine in Lviv. From 1990 he directed the Institute of the Physics of Condensed Systems of the National Academy of Sciences of the Ukraine (NASU). In 1990–98 he was a member of the NASU Presidium and chairman of the West Ukrainian NASU Research Center. Yukhnovskyi authored more than four hundred articles. From 1956 to 1990 he was a member of the Communist Party, and in 1964–66 he was a deputy of the Lviv City Council. In 1990 Yukhnovskyi was elected

to the Supreme Council of the Ukrainian SSR and was suggested by former dissidents as a candidate for deputy speaker of parliament. Although the Communist majority prevented his election, from this time Yukhnovskyi became an informal leader of the pro-independence opposition (the so-called National Council). After the failure of the Moscow putsch, on 24 August 1991 Yukhnovskyi moved to proclaim the independence of the Ukraine and to confirm this act by a popular referendum. In the presidential elections of 1 December 1991 Yukhnovskyi won only 1.7 percent of the vote. From October 1992 to March 1993 he was deputy prime minister in the government of **Leonid Kuchma**. Yukhnovskyi took part in a commission preparing the constitution of June 1996. From 1998 to 2002 he was an MP on behalf of the Popular Movement of the Ukraine, and from 2002, of the Our Ukraine bloc of **Viktor Yushchenko**. A member of many advisory government bodies, Yukhnovskyi was also chairman of the Derzhavnist (Statehood) Research Society and the Ukrainian Veterans' Union. (TS)

Sources: Radzisława Gortat, *Ukraińskie wybory* (Warsaw, 1998); Bohdan Nahaylo, *The Ukrainian Resurgence* (Toronto, 1999); oracle2.rada.gov.ua.

YURYNETS Volodymyr (1891, Olesko, near Busko, Galicia–4 October 1937, USSR), Ukrainian Marxist philosopher, publicist, and art critic. After graduating from a gymnasium in Lemberg (Lviv, Lwów), Yurynets studied at the university in Lemberg. In 1910 he began to study in Vienna, where, among other things, he attended lectures by Sigmund Freud. Yurynets continued studies in philosophy, mathematics, and physics in Berlin and Paris. He learned ten foreign languages. During World War I Yurynets was taken prisoner by the Russians. In 1920 he joined the Red Army, where he served as a political commissar, edited front-line newspapers, and fought against Poland. In 1920 he was also admitted to the Communist Party (Bolshevik) of Ukraine (CP[B]U), and in 1924 he graduated from the Institute of Red Professorship in Moscow. Yurynets lectured at the Communist University of Eastern Nations, Moscow University, and other universities. In 1925 he took the chair of sociology at the Ukrainian Institute of Marxism-Leninism in Kharkiv, and he began working in the editorial offices of *Bilshovyk Ukrainy* (1926–34) and *Prapor marksyzmu* (1927–33), the organs of the CP(B)U, and in the editorial office of the literary periodical *Chervonyi Shliakh*. Yurynets published works in dialectics and historical materialism, the history of philosophy and the philosophy of history, sociology, aesthetics, physics, and criticism of Western philosophy and Ukrainian nationalism. While a student in Moscow, he began to study Edmund Husserl's phenomenology, and later he studied Democritus, Immanuel Kant, and Freud. Although in 1929 Yurynets was elected a member of the Ukrainian Academy of Sciences, an increasing number of his works were being banned from distribution. Such was the fate of the following books: *Pavlo Tychyna: Sproba krytychnoi analizy* (Pavlo Tychyna: An attempt at critical analysis; 1928); *Filosofichno-sotsiolohichni narysy* (Philosophical and sociological sketches; 1930); and the textbook *Diialektychnyi materiializm* (Dialectical materialism; 1932). Yurynets was accused of yielding to the influences of neo-Kantianism, neo-Hegelianism, and "bourgeois nationalism," and in 1933 he was expelled from the party. Arrested in July 1937, Yurynets was sentenced to death and executed by firing squad. (TS)

Sources: *Encyclopedia of Ukraine*, vol. 5 (Toronto, 1993); Iuriy Lavrynienko, *Rozstriliane vidrodzhennia* (Munich, 1959); V. Gorskyi, *Istoriia ukraiinskoi filosofii* (Kiev, 1997); I. Ogorodnyk and V. Ogorodnyk, *Istoriia filosofskoi dumky v Ukraiini* (Kiev, 1999).

YUSHCHENKO Viktor (23 February 1954, Khoruzhivka, Sumy district), Ukrainian economist and politician. In 1975 Yushchenko graduated from the Ternopil Institute of Economics and Finance, and in 1984, from the Ukrainian Institute of Economics and Agricultural Management. He worked as a bookkeeper in a kolkhoz in the Ivano-Frankivsk region. In 1976–85 Yushchenko worked in the State Bank in Ulyanivka (Sumy district). From 1985 he was deputy director of the agricultural credit department of the State Bank of the Ukrainian SSR in Kiev; in 1987 he became head of the department of economic planning in the Agroprom Bank, and in 1990–92 he was deputy director of this bank. After the transformation of this bank into Bank Ukraina in 1992, Yushchenko was its first deputy director. From January 1993 to January 2000 he was chairman of the National Bank of Ukraine. Yushchenko became known as an advocate of economic reforms and enjoyed the support of President **Leonid Kuchma**. As a Ukrainian representative in international financial institutions (the International Monetary Fund and the European Bank for Reconstruction and Development), Yushchenko contributed to Ukraine's receiving stabilization loans, which made it possible to introduce the Ukrainian currency (hryvna) in 1996. Later he continued his efforts to defend the rate of exchange of the hryvna, a task that was particularly difficult during the financial crisis in Russia in August 1998. Yushchenko was also a member of many government economic, security, and cultural councils and committees.

After his reelection in November 1999, President Kuchma entrusted Yushchenko with the position of prime minister. On 22 December 1999 his government was approved by the Supreme Council by an overwhelming majority of 296 mandates to 12. During Yushchenko's term, the functioning of the government apparatus was improved, while the Ukrainian economy managed to gain more trust among international financial institutions, mostly thanks to a restrictive monetary policy, a liberalization of land sales, and a restructuring of the fuel and power industries. For the first time since independence the gross national product started growing. Liquidating the brokerage of private companies in gas trade operations with Russia, Yushchenko managed to improve the budget situation and, in consequence, to restore the regular payment of wages in the public sector. He gained enormous popularity, which jeopardized the position of President Kuchma. The fall of Yushchenko's government on 29 May 2001 did not damage his ratings. He had to resign under pressure from former Communists and opposition oligarchs. In the elections of March 2002 the center-right bloc Our Ukraine, created by Yushchenko, ran in opposition to President Kuchma and gained 23.6 percent of the vote. Yushchenko won a seat for himself and remained the most popular Ukrainian politician. During the presidential campaign of 2004 he won widespread support, promising a cleanup in public life. In the second round of the election, on 21 November 2004 Yushchenko was declared a loser to the pro-Russian candidate, Viktor Yanukovych. There were obvious traces of election fraud, so this result caused huge demonstrations in support of Yushchenko (the so-called Orange Revolution). A serious constitutional crisis was resolved through international mediation, and on 26 December 2004 Yushchenko won the rerun second round, gaining 52 percent of the vote. On 23 January 2005 he was sworn in as the new president. (TS)

Sources: Oksana Slipushko, *Viktor Yushchenko: Bankir i polityk* (Kiev, 2000); Bugajski; www.rulers.org; www.electionworld.org.

Z

ŻABIŃSKI Andrzej (28 May 1938, Katowice–17 March 1988, Katowice), Polish Communist activist. Żabiński graduated from the Higher School of Social Sciences of the Polish United Workers' Party (PUWP) Central Committee and from Warsaw University. He joined the PUWP in 1956 and started his party career in 1960. He was, among other things, head of the Main Board of the Socialist Youth Association (1967–72) and first secretary of provincial PUWP committees in Opole (1972–80) and Katowice (1980–82). From 1968 to July 1981 Żabiński was a member of the PUWP CC; from August 1980 he was a deputy member of the CC Politburo, and from September 1980 to July 1981 he was a full member. In 1965–85 Żabiński was an MP, and from 1980 to 1982 he was head of the parliamentary commission of national defense. One of the younger party leaders, he advocated a hard line in dealing with Solidarity and the democratic opposition. Żabiński enjoyed the trust of Moscow and was a pretender to the highest ranks in leadership in the case that **Stanisław Kania** was removed as first secretary of the PUWP. After the introduction of martial law Żabiński advocated a radical line, including the dissolution of the PUWP and the creation of a new, "truly Communist" party. Therefore he was removed from the party leadership by General **Wojciech Jaruzelski** and sent as a councillor to the embassy in Budapest (1982–87). (AP)

Sources: Mołdawa; Jerzy Holzer, *"Solidarność"* (Warsaw, 1983); Timothy Garton Ash, *Polish Revolution: "Solidarity"* (London, 1983); Andrzej Paczkowski, *Droga do "mniejszegi zła": Strategia i taktyka obozu władzy lipiec 1980-styczeń 1982* (Kraków, 2002).

ZABŁOCKI Janusz (18 February 1926, Grodzisk Mazowiecki), Polish politician. During World War II Zabłocki was a member of the Gray Ranks (Szare Szeregi), an underground scouting organization, and a soldier in the Home Army (Armia Krajowa). In 1949 he received a law degree from the Jagiellonian University in Kraków. A member of the PAX association from 1950, Zabłocki contributed to its periodicals, *Dziś i Jutro*, *Słowo Powszechne*, and *Tygodnik Powszechny*. During the "thaw" in 1955 he left the PAX association in protest against the support given by its head, **Bolesław Piasecki**, to the dogmatic Natolin faction within the Polish United Workers' Party (PUWP). In 1956 Zabłocki co-founded the National Club of Progressive Catholic Intelligentsia and the Club of the Catholic Intelligentsia in Warsaw. At that time he began to work for the monthly *Więź*, and in 1963–65 he was its correspondent at the Second Vatican Council. Zabłocki was also the founder of the Center of Documentation and Social Studies in Warsaw, which published the monthly *Chrześcijanin w świecie* from 1969 on. From 1965 to 1985 Zabłocki was an MP in the Assembly. At the end of the 1960s he became a supporter of the PUWP faction led by **Mieczysław Moczar**, and after Moczar's fall he hoped that the continuing members of this faction, led by **Franciszek Szlachcic**, would offer lay Catholics a chance to expand their political activities. In 1976 Zabłocki established a separate Polish Club of Catholic Intelligentsia in Warsaw. In 1981 he founded the Polish Catholic Social Union, but it failed to gain the support of wider circles of the Catholic opposition. Zabłocki's presence in the Assembly during martial law in Poland did not help to enhance his credibility among Polish Catholics. In 1986 Zabłocki became a member of a consultative council to the president of the Council of State. In 1988 he was elected chairman of the Christian Democratic Club of Political Thought. After the 1989 Round Table negotiations the club was transformed into the Labor Party, but it failed to play the role of a revived Christian Democratic party. Zabłocki's publications include *Kościół i świat współczesny* (The Church and the modern world; 1967); *Na polskim skrzyżowaniu dróg* (At the Polish crossroads; 1972); *Tożsamość i siły narodu* (The identity and the power of the nation; 1978); *Chrześcijańska demokracja w kraju i na emigracji 1947–1970* (Christian Democracy in Poland and in exile 1947–1970; 1999); and *Prymas Stefan Wyszyński* (Primate Stefan Wyszyński; 2002). (WR)

Sources: *Kto jest kim w Polsce* (Warsaw, 2001); Andrzej Micewski, *Współrządzić czy nie kłamać: PAX i Znak w Polsce 1945–1976* (Warsaw, 1981); Andrzej Friszke, *Opozycja polityczna w PRL 1945–1980* (London, 1994).

ZAHRADNÍČEK Ján (17 January 1905, Mastník, Třebíč district–7 October 1960, Uhřínov, Žďár-nad-Sázavou district), Czech poet and translator. From 1926 to 1930 Zahradníček studied philosophy at Charles University in Prague, but he never graduated, devoting himself to poetry and journalism. From 1940 to 1948 he edited the Catholic periodical *Akord* in Brno, and from 1945 to 1949 he was an editor at the Brněnské Tiskárny publishing house. A leading Czech Catholic poet, Zahradníček was initially influenced by symbolism. His first collections of poems—*Pokušení smrti* (Tempting death; 1930), *Návrat* (Return; 1931), and *Jeřáby* (Cranes; 1933)—were imbued with religious symbolism and motifs. Contrary to the trends of that period, in the second half of the 1930s

Zahradníček expressed delight in life and faith in the future, publishing the collections *Žíznivé léto* (Thirsty summer; 1935) and *Pozdravení slunci* (Greetings to the sun; 1937). In his two postwar collections, *Stará země* (Old earth; 1946) and *Svatý Václav* (Saint Wenceslas; 1946), he critically reviewed the realities of war from a Christian standpoint.

Zahradníček did not accept the Sovietization of Czechoslovakia. In *La Saletta* (1947), the last volume published during his lifetime, he stressed that only the Christian faith could prevent a world catastrophe. His next collection, *Znamení moci* (Sign of power; 1950), was banned from printing, and it was not published until 1990. One of the leading representatives of Czech Catholic culture, Zahradníček was arrested in June 1951. After a rigged trial of the "Green International," he was sentenced to thirteen years' imprisonment in July 1952. Amnestied in 1960, he was posthumously rehabilitated in 1968. Poems that Zahradníček wrote in prison were published in the volumes *Čtyři léta* (Four summers; 1969) and *Dům strach* (House fear; 1981). The prison poetry reflects Zahradníček's suffering and experiences as a prisoner, but it also shows a strength coming from his Christian faith. Zahradníček authored the collection of essays *Oslice Balaamova* (Balaam's ass; 1940). He also translated poems by Rainer Maria Rilke and Friedrich Hölderlin, as well as Thomas Mann's prose. Together with Otto Babler Zahradníček translated Dante's *The Divine Comedy*. (PU)

Sources: *ČBS*; *Kdo byl kdo v našich dějinách ve 20. století*, vol. 2 (Prague, 1998); *Slovník českých spisovatelů od roku 1945*, vol. 2 (Prague, 1998); Halina Janaszek-Ivančikova, ed., *Literatury zachodniosłowiańskie czasu przełomów 1890–1990*, vol. 2, *Literatura czeska* (Katowice, 1999); Zdeněk Kalista, *Vzpomínání na Jana Zahradníčka* (Munich, 1988).

ZAKHARKA Vasil (1 April 1877, Dobroseltsy, near Volkovysk–14 March 1943, Prague), Belorussian politician. Born into a poor peasant family, Zakharka was orphaned at the age of sixteen. From 1895 to 1898 he worked as a teacher in schools run by the Orthodox Church, supporting his brother and sister. Inducted into the army in 1898, he began a military career that lasted until 1917. After the February 1917 revolution, Zakharka was the main founder of Belorussian military units in the territory of Belorussia. In the summer of 1917 he initiated the organization of a congress of Belorussian soldiers' delegates, which elected him secretary of the Belorussian Central Military Council (22 October 1917). At that time Zakharka was one of the leaders of the Belorussian Socialist Hromada. At the First All-Belorussian Congress in December 1917 he was elected to its council. In Febru-

ary 1918 Zakharka became one of the top leaders of the People's Secretariat of Belorussia, which was appointed by the Executive Committee of the All-Belorussian Congress and recognized by Germany as a representation of the Belorussian people. After the independence of the Belorussian National Republic (BNR) was proclaimed in March 1918, Zakharka held various ministerial and diplomatic posts in the BNR. After the Polish-Soviet Treaty of Riga was signed in March 1921, he co-initiated the organization of the First Belorussian National and Political Conference, held in Prague in September 1921, where the situation of Belorussia was recognized as the country's occupation by its two neighboring states. Zakharka served as minister of finance in the Kaunas-based BNR's government-in-exile. At the Second Belorussian Conference (in Berlin, October 1925), Zakharka was one of the few émigré politicians to refuse to recognize the government of the Belorussian SSR as a representation of the Belorussian nation. Zakharka did not return to his country and lived in exile in Prague. After the death of **Pyotr Kracheuski,** Zakharka became chairman of the BNR Council in exile (March 1928). He defended the cause of a free Belorussia. For example, he wrote protests to the League of Nations against the persecution of the Belorussian people. In 1941 Zakharka declined to collaborate with the Germans and refused to pass the symbols of power of the BNR to politicians who did so. (EM)

Sources: *Entsyklapiedyia historyi Bielarusi*, vol. 2 (Minsk, 1994); Vitaut Kipel and Zora Kipel, eds., *Byelorussian Statehood* (New York, 1988); H. Hlahoŭskaya, "Vasil Zahharka: Druhi Prezydent BRL," *Spadchyna*, 1994, no. 1; Jan Zaprudnik, *Historical Dictionary of Belarus* (Lanham, Md., 1998).

ZALESKI August (30 September 1883, Warsaw–7 April 1972, London), Polish diplomat, politician, and historian. Zaleski completed university studies in London and then began working in the library and museum of the Krasiński Entail in Warsaw. During World War I he was responsible for propaganda for the Supreme National Committee (Naczelny Komitet Narodowy [NKN]) from 1915 to 1917, and then he worked as head of a section in the State Department of the Kingdom of Poland. In 1918 Zaleski became head of the Polish mission in Switzerland, in May 1919 Polish delegate to Greece, and in July 1920 envoy to Athens. In January 1921 he began working in the Political Department of the Ministry of Foreign Affairs in Warsaw. In April 1922 he became an envoy to Italy. In February 1926 he returned to the headquarters of the Ministry of Foreign Affairs and began preparing for a new mission in Japan. However, after the coup of May 1926, Zaleski accepted **Józef Piłsudski**'s offer to join the new government. He became head of a department (15 May 1926) and minister of foreign affairs (25 May). He tried to secure a permanent seat for Poland in the League of Nations Council. In 1927 Poland obtained a "semi-permanent" seat in the council, and Zaleski became Poland's representative there. On behalf of Poland, Zaleski signed the Briand-Kellogg Pact on the peaceful settlement of international disputes (27 August 1928), the Litvinov Protocol (9 February 1929), and the Soviet-Polish Non-Aggression Pact (25 July 1932). In November 1932 Zaleski left the diplomatic service and handed over his position to **Józef Beck**. He served as senator on the ticket of the Nonparty Bloc of Cooperation with the Government (Bezpartyjny Blok Współpracy z Rządem [BBWR]) from 1935 to 1938 and chairman of the Supervisory Board of the Commercial Bank (Bank Handlowy) in Warsaw from 1935 to 1939.

After the defeat of Poland in September 1939, Zaleski served as minister of foreign affairs in the government of General **Władysław Sikorski** from October 1939 to July 1941. An opponent of the agreement with the Soviet Union, he resigned after the Polish-Soviet Treaty of 30 July 1941 was signed. From 1943 to 1945 Zaleski served as head of the Civil Chancellery of **Władysław Raczkiewicz**, president of the Republic of Poland. After the war, he remained in exile. Since Raczkiewicz picked him as his successor, after Raczkiewicz's death, Zaleski became president on 9 June 1947. His role as president was diminished because of a conflict with the Polish Socialist Party in exile, whose leader, **Tomasz Arciszewski**, had been originally designated by Raczkiewicz as the next president. Zaleski assumed that if Poland became independent from the Soviet Union, its security would depend on the establishment of a broader Central European union, to include Ukraine, Belorussia, and the Baltic states. After unification negotiations among the various Polish political émigré groups ended in failure in 1954, the majority of these groups refused to recognize Zaleski as president and subordinated themselves to the Provisional National Unity Council and its collective leadership, the Council of the Three. Although the group of Zaleski's supporters continued to diminish, Zaleski formally held the post of president of the Republic of Poland in exile until the end of his life. (JS/WR)

Sources: *Kto był kim w Drugiej Rzeczypospolitej* (Warsaw, 1994); Marian Leczyk, *Polityka II Rzeczypospolitej wobec ZSRR w latach 1925–1934* (Warsaw, 1976); Piotr Wandycz, *August Zaleski: Minister spraw zagranicznych RP 1926–1932 w świetle wspomnień i dokumentów* (Paris, 1980); Rafał Habielski, "Kryzysy prezydenckie 1947 i 1954 roku," in *Warszawa nad Tamizą* (Warsaw, 1994); Piotr Wandycz, *Z Piłsudskim i Sikorskim: August Zaleski minister spraw zagranicznych w latach 1926–1932 i 1939–1941* (Warsaw, 1999).

ZAMBROWSKI Roman (15 July 1909, Warsaw–19 August 1977, Warsaw), Polish Communist activist. Born into a lower-middle-class Jewish family, Zambrowski was a teacher by profession. In 1928 he joined the Communist Party of Poland (Komunistyczna Partia Polski [KPP]). From 1930 to 1938 he was a member and secretary of the Central Committee (CC) of the Communist Union of Polish Youth and represented this union in the Communist Youth International. Zambrowski graduated from the Higher Party School in Moscow. In Poland he was imprisoned several times, including a term in the camp at Bereza Kartuska (1938–39). In September 1939 he found himself in the Soviet territories, where he worked as a teacher (until 1943) and was active in the Central Office of Polish Communists. From the spring of 1943, Zambrowski took part in the formation of Polish military units under Soviet command. As head of the Political and Educational Board of the First Polish Army (March–September 1944), he cooperated with the Soviet security services. After Soviet troops entered Polish territories, Zambrowski became a member of the CC of the Polish Workers' Party (Polska Partia Robotnicza [PPR]) in August 1944 and subsequently served as head of the PPR CC Organizational Department. He became secretary of the CC in April 1945 and a member of its Politburo in May 1945. Coopted into the National Home Council (Krajowa Rada Narodowa [KRN]), Zambrowski joined its presidium in May 1945. He soon became one of the top-ranking members of the party leadership, where he represented Stalinist orthodoxy. From November 1945 to December 1954 he also served as chairman of the Select Committee to Counteract Embezzlement and Economic Sabotage. The committee had the power to send people to forced labor camps without court procedures. Zambrowski was thus one of those directly responsible for the Stalinist terror. In the summer of 1948 he actively supported a campaign against the "rightist-nationalist deviation" of **Władysław Gomułka**.

After the (Communist) Polish United Workers' Party (Polska Zjednoczona Partia Robotnicza [PUWP]) was established in December 1948, Zambrowski became one of its leaders, joining the PUWP CC and its Secretariat and Organizational Bureau. From February 1947 to November 1952 he served as deputy speaker of the Legislative Assembly, first as a representative of the PPR and then of the PUWP. From February 1947 to May 1955 Zambrowski was also a member of the Council of State. His position in the party leadership weakened during the anti-Semitic campaign in the Soviet bloc at the beginning of the 1950s. In February 1954 Zambrowski became chairman of the Committee for Administrative Subdivisions, and in March of that year, at the Second PUWP Congress, he left the Secretariat of the CC. From April 1955 to October 1956 he served as minister of state audits. During the "thaw" Zambrowski abandoned the Stalinist line. At the time of factional strife in 1955–56, he was one of the leaders of the Puławska faction (Puławianie), which called for the democratization of relations within the party and some liberalization of public life. After the death of **Bolesław Bierut**, Zambrowski was a candidate to succeed him. However, **Nikita Khrushchev**, who came to the Sixth Plenum of the PUWP CC on 20 March 1956, was against the appointment of a person of Jewish descent and sealed the election of **Edward Ochab** as first secretary of the PUWP CC. At the Eighth Plenum of the CC in October of that year, Zambrowski again became a member of the Secretariat and played the role of the patron of party "liberals" in the leadership. As the new party leadership (headed by Gomułka) intensified a campaign against revisionism, Zambrowski's position weakened. At the ideological Thirteenth Plenum of the PUWP CC (4–6 July 1963) he was dropped from the Secretariat and the Politburo and was appointed vice-president of the Supreme Chamber of Control. Zambrowski was the target of official propaganda attacks during the anti-Semitic campaign in the second half of 1967, and particularly in March 1968. **Mieczysław Moczar**'s supporters groundlessly accused him of instigating the student movement. In April 1968 Zambrowski was expelled from the party, dismissed from the Supreme Chamber of Control, and forced to retire. His son, Antoni, became an activist of the democratic opposition. Zambrowski wrote *Dziennik* (Diary), issued by the underground publisher of the quarterly *Krytyka* in 1980. (WR)

Sources: Mołdawa; Konrad Syrop, *Spring in October: The Story of the Polish Revolution of 1956* (New York, 1957); Jan Nowak, *Wojna w eterze* (London, 1985); John Coutouvidis and Jaime Reynolds, *Poland 1939–1947* (Leicester, 1986); Jan Nowak, *Polska z oddali* (London, 1988); Jerzy Eisler, *Marzec 1968* (Warsaw, 1991); Krzysztof Lesiakowski, *Mieczysław Moczar "Mietek": Biografia polityczna* (Warsaw, 1998); Dariusz Stola, *Kampania antysyjonistyczna w Polsce 1967–1968* (Warsaw, 2000).

ZAMENHOF Ludwik (15 December 1859, Białystok–14 April 1917, Warsaw), Polish philologist of Jewish descent, creator of the artificial language of Esperanto. Zamenhof studied medicine and became an ophthalmologist. Influenced by his father, he was interested in languages from childhood. He attempted to write a Yiddish grammar but failed to complete it. In 1878 Zamenhof established the foundations of an artificial international language based on only nine hundred main words and sixteen rules of grammar. He published this work in 1887 as *Lingvo In-ternacia* (International language) under the pseudonym of Dr. Esperanto. Initially disregarded, the language attracted followers and gained the name of Esperanto. In the course of time its vocabulary was expanded to one hundred thousand words. Zamenhof translated many German literary works and the Bible into Esperanto, trying to prove that despite its simplicity, Esperanto could be used to express complicated material. An anthology of these translations was published as *Fundamenta Krestomatio* (1904). In 1905 the first international Esperanto Congress was held, and in 1908 the Universal Esperanto Association was created. In his political views Zamenhof was close to the Zionist movement. Monuments were erected to Zamenhof in Wasaw (1928) and Białystok (1934). (WR)

Sources: *Encyclopedia Judaica*, vol. 16 (Jerusalem, 1971); Edmond Privat, *The Life of Zamenhof* (London, 1931); Maria Ziółkowska, *Doktor Esperanto* (Warsaw, 1959); Marjorie Boulton, *Zamenhof: Creator of Esperanto* (London, 1960); K. Kwasniewski and L. Trzeciakowski, eds., *Polacy w historii i kulturze krajów Europy Zachodniej* (Poznań, 1981).

ZAMFIRESCU Duiliu (30 October 1858, Plăineşti [Dumbrăveni], Moldavia–3 June 1922, Agapia), Romanian writer and diplomat. Zamfirescu attended high school in Focşani from 1869 to 1873 and in Bucharest from 1874 to 1876. After receiving a law degree from Bucharest University in 1880, he worked as a judge in Hîrşova and then as a prosecutor in Tîrgovişte. In 1880 Zamfirescu made his debut as a poet in the periodical *Literatorul*. In 1881 he moved to Bucharest, where, under the pseudonym of "Don Padil," he edited the daily *România liberă*. He published articles in the conservative periodical *Convorbiri literare* from 1883 to 1885, and in 1883 he joined the Junimea (Youth) Literary Society, which represented the idealistic trend and aestheticism in art. In 1888 Zamfirescu began his diplomatic and political career. He served as attaché and secretary at the Romanian Embassy in Rome (until 1892), Athens (1893), and Brussels (until 1906). He also represented Romania in the Danube Commission. During World War I Zamfirescu lived in Odessa and then in Iaşi, where in 1918 he edited the daily *Îndreptarea* and the periodical *Îndreptarea literară*. In 1918 he joined the conservative People's Party (Partidul Poporului), led by General **Alexandru Averescu**. On the ticket of this party, Zamfirescu was an MP and speaker of the lower chamber of parliament from 1920 to 1922 and also briefly served as minister of foreign affairs in 1920.

At the same time Zamfirescu was active on the literary scene, the author of lyric poems, short stories, novels, and plays. In 1883 he published his first volume of poems, *Fără titul* (Without a title). Altogether, he published several poetry volumes, written in a romantic and later in a neoclassical style: *Alte orizonturi* (Other horizons; 1894); *Imnuri păgîne* (1897; Pagan hymns; 1897); and *Pe Marea Negră* (On the Black Sea; 1919). In 1888 Zamfirescu made his debut as the author of short stories, which were written in the spirit of realism. He published *Novele* (Short stories), *Novele romane* (Roman short stories; 1896), and *Furfanţo* (1911), whose main characters were often people from the lower strata of society. In 1884 Zamfirescu published his first novel, *În faţa vieţii* (In the face of life). He gained the greatest acclaim for the five-part series *Comăneşteni* (The Comăneşteanu family), which consisted of *Viaţa la ţară* (Life in the countryside; 1898), *Tănase Scatiu* (1900), *În război* (At war; 1902), *Îndreptări* (Improvements; 1908), and *Anna sau ceace nu se poate* (Anna, or what cannot be; 1910). From a conservative point of view, using the example of one family, Zamfirescu depicted social transformations in Romania, particularly the end of the era of boyar families and the upward social mobility of those who leased their land and were hated by the peasants. Zamfirescu also wrote several theater dramas: *O amică* (Girlfriend; 1912), *Lumină nouă* (New light; 1912), and *Voichiţa* (1914). He also translated works by Giosuè Carducci, Théophile Gautier, Victor Hugo, and Giacomo Leopardi. (LW)

Sources: *Wielka Encyklopedia Powszechna PWN*, vol. 12 (Warsaw, 1969); Halina Mirska-Lasota, *Mały słownik pisarzy rumuńskich* (Warsaw, 1975); Juliusz Demel, *Historia Rumunii* (Wrocław, 1986); Şerban N. Ionescu, *Who Was Who in Twentieth Century Romania* (Boulder, Colo., 1994); Dorina N. Rusu, *Membrii Academiei Române 1866–1999* (Bucharest, 1999); Ion Alexandrescu, Ion Bulei, Ion Mamina, and Ioan Scurtu, *Enciclopedia de istorie României* (Bucharest, 2000).

ZAMOYSKI Maurycy Klemens (30 July 1871, Warsaw–5 May 1939, Warsaw), Polish aristocrat, politician, entrepreneur, and philanthropist. Zamoyski received a primary education at home and then finished high school in Leszno. He studied at the university in Stuttgart, where he moved in artistic circles, making friends with Wojciech Kossak, Józef Chełmoński, and other painters. After returning from Stuttgart, Zamoyski administered his entail, which he had inherited from his father, Tomasz. In 1898 he became engaged in social and charity work; among other things, he provided funds for the construction of the Zachęta Gallery of Fine Arts in Warsaw, the National Philharmonic, monuments to Frédéric Chopin and Adam Mickiewicz, the Polish Educational Society, and other social and national purposes. He also sponsored historical publishing houses, as well as poorhouses and hospitals for the poor. Linked with **Henryk Sienkiewicz** and others, Zamoyski was one of the founders of the Central Agricultural Society in 1903 and then served as its chairman. Despite his monarchist and conservative views, Zamoyski worked with **Roman Dmowski**, the National Democratic leader, from 1901 onwards. Zamoyski sponsored the newspaper *Wiadomości Codzienne*, which was published by the nationalists and targeted at Polish peasants. He also funded several other periodicals published by the National Democratic Party, which he joined in 1905. In November 1904 Zamoyski co-organized a great patriotic demonstration in Warsaw, and in 1905 he took part in mass religious processions and ceremonies marking the return to the Catholic Church of the Uniates of the Zamość region, whom the tsarist authorities had forced to join the Orthodox Church. In the elections of March 1906 Zamoyski was elected to the first State Duma on the ticket of the National Democratic Party. He continued the policy of loyalty to Russia, in return for which Poland gained concessions in education and the economy.

After the outbreak of World War I, Zamoyski (along with Dmowski and other leading politicians of the National Democratic Party) joined the Polish National Committee (Komitet Narodowy Polski [KNP]) in November 1914. Zamoyski represented the loyalist wing of the KNP. After emigrating to the West in January 1916, Zamoyski revised his attitude toward Russia: he became an advocate of full independence for Poland with an orientation toward the Entente states. Along with Dmowski, Sienkiewicz, Erazm Piltz, and **Ignacy Paderewski**, Zamoyski was the main spokesman of the Polish cause in the West. He provided substantial funds to support the political, diplomatic, and propaganda work of Polish centers, particularly the KNP in France, England, and Switzerland. He also sponsored military and charity activities. In March 1918 he helped to form the Polish Army in France under the command of General **Józef Haller**. Zamoyski attended the Paris Peace Conference. In May 1919 he was appointed the first envoy of the Second Republic of Poland to France. As a result of his persistent pressure on the French authorities and public opinion, France agreed to grant military assistance to Poland during the Polish-Soviet war. As collateral for French loans to Poland, Zamoyski pledged his Zamość entail.

Zamoyski lived off and on in France until 1924. He reluctantly agreed to run as a right-wing candidate in the Polish presidential elections. In successive election rounds in the National Assembly he obtained the majority of votes, but in the final round on 9 December 1922 he lost to **Gabriel Narutowicz**, a left-wing candidate. Two years later Zamoyski accepted an appointment as minister of foreign affairs in the government of **Władysław Grabski** (January–July 1924). Zamoyski always advocated a Polish-French alliance. He also strove for the establishment of a Polish-Lithuanian union and called for close cooperation with the Baltic states. After resigning, Zamoyski retired from active politics. He served as chairman of the Supreme Council of Landowner Organizations (1925–37) and dealt with the affairs of the Zamoyski family and the administration of his entail. Because of huge debts, which he had incurred to further the national cause, and owing to bad administration, his entail fell into financial trouble and was partly parceled out at the end of the 1930s. After Zamoyski's death, the entail was inherited by his eldest son, Jan. (MC)

Sources: Robert Jarocki, *Ostatni ordynat: Z Janem Zamoyskim spotkania i rozmowy* (Warsaw, 1990); Jan Zamoyski, *Powrót na mapę: Polski Komitet Narodowy w Paryżu 1914–1919* (Warsaw, 1991); Teresa Zielińska, *Poczet polskich rodów arystokratycznych* (Warsaw, 1997); Joanna Janicka, *Maurycy hrabia Zamoyski: Zarys losów życiowych i politycznych oraz wgląd w struktury gospodarcze ordynacji* (Lublin, 2000); Czesław Brzoza and Kamil Stepan, *Posłowie polscy w parlamencie rosyjskim 1906–1917* (Warsaw, 2001).

ZANUSSI Krzysztof (17 June 1939, Warsaw), Polish film director. Zanussi studied in the Department of Physics of Warsaw University and in the Department of Philosophy of the Jagiellonian University in Kraków, and in 1966 he graduated from the State Theater and Film School of Łódź. He made his debut with a short film in 1958, but *Struktura kryształu* (The structure of crystals; 1969) was the first film that attracted greater attention to him. Subsequent films—particularly *Za ścianą* (Behind the wall; 1971); *Życie rodzinne* (Family life; 1972); *Iluminacja* (Illumination; 1973); *Bilans kwartalny* (The quarterly balance; 1975); the highly acclaimed *Barwy ochronne* (Camouflage; 1976); and *Kontrakt* (The contract; 1980)—established Zanussi's position as the creator of the "cinema of moral anxiety," which developed in the 1970s in an atmosphere of opposition to **Edward Gierek**'s rule. Pope **John Paul II** gave Zanussi his permission to film his biography, *Z dalekiego kraju* (From a far country; 1980). Zanussi received the Jury Prize for his film *Constans* (The constant factor) at the Cannes International Film Festival in 1980 and a Special Jury Award for *Imperative* at the Venice International Film Festival in 1982. During martial law in Poland Zanussi mainly worked abroad, making such films as *Le pouvoir du Mal-Paradigme* (1983), *Rok spokojnego słońca* (The year of the quiet sun; 1984), and *Wherever You Are* (1987). In 1990 he made *Życie za życie* (Life for life), about the martyr's death of St. Maksymilian Kolbe, and in 1995, *Cwał* (In full gallop), a semi-autobiographical film about the Stalinist years. Zanussi's films touch upon fundamental existential issues and human attitudes toward danger and death, and they provoke deep moral reflection. Zanussi has worked with major film studios and theaters in Great Britain, Italy, Germany, and Switzerland. From 1971 to 1983 he served as vice-chairman of the Union of Polish Filmmakers. In 1992 he became a professor at the University of Silesia, and in 1997, a member of the Papal Academy of Art and Literature. He has authored the memoirs *Pora umierać* (Time to die; 1997) and a collection of essays, *Między jarmarkiem i salonem* (Between a fair and a salon; 1999). (WR)

Sources: *Kto jest kim w Polsce* (Warsaw, 2001); *International Dictionary of Films and Filmmakers*, vol. 2 (Chicago and London, 1991); David W. Paul, ed., *Politics, Art and Commitment in the East European Cinema* (New York, 1983); Michel Esteve, *Krzysztof Zanussi* (Paris, 1987).

ZÁPOTOCKÝ Antonín (19 December 1884, Zákolany, near Kladno–13 November 1957, Prague), Communist president of Czechoslovakia. The son of a tailor, Zápotocký was a member of Socialist organizations from his youth, and from 1902 he belonged to the Social Democratic Party. Arrested in 1905 for his participation in an illegal demonstration, after his release he headed the party unit in Kladno. During World War I Zápotocký served in the Austrian Army in Italy, Serbia, and Romania. At the end of 1918 he returned to political activity. Arrested for his participation in organizing strikes, he spent two and a half years in prison, where he acquired revolutionary beliefs. In September 1921 Zápotocký was one of the founders of the Communist Party of Czechoslovakia (CPC) and was in charge of organizing the party in Prague. From 1922 he was secretary of the Central Committee (CC) of the CPC. In 1924 he was elected a deputy member of the Executive Committee of the Communist International. Between 1925 and 1938 Zápotocký sat in parliament. In February 1929 at the Fifth Congress of the party Zápotocký, along with other adherents of Stalin, again joined the Secretariat of the CC, and he became a member of the Politburo. Between 1929 and 1939 he headed the Communist Trade Unions.

After the capture of Prague by the Germans in March 1939, Zápotocký was put in a concentration camp, first in Sachsenhausen and then in Oranienburg. Released in April 1945 by the Soviet troops, he returned to Prague and assumed the leadership of the trade unions, which became important tools in the hands of the Communists in their struggle for power. Zápotocký played a very important role during the coup of February 1948, as he mobilized the "will of the working masses" against democracy. At a trade union congress on 22 February 1948 Zápotocký gave a speech calling for revolution. After the February coup Zápotocký became deputy prime minister, and between

15 June 1948 and 21 March 1953 he was prime minister. As the right hand of **Klement Gottwald**, he supervised a purge that affected all non-Communist political forces in the country. He was responsible for the Stalinist mass terror and for political show trials. He played an important role in the case of **Rudolph Slánský**, charging Slánský and his comrades with false evidence. After Gottwald's death, in March 1953 Zápotocký became president of Czechoslovakia, sharing power with the new secretary general of the party, **Antonín Novotný**, and with Prime Minister **Viliam Široký**. Zápotocký was a guest at the Twentieth Congress of the CPSU. However, he contributed to an effective inhibition of the "thaw" in Czechoslovakia in 1956. A selection of Zápotocký's publications, titled *Antonín Zápotocký: Výbor z díla* (Antonín Zápotocký: Selection of works, 3 vols.), appeared in 1984. (WR)

Sources: *ČBS*; *The Times* 14 November 1957; Lazitch; Edward Taborsky, *Communism in Czechoslovakia, 1948–1960* (Princeton, 1961); Eugen Loebl, *Stalinism in Prague* (New York, 1969); Ludmila Šumberova, *Antonín Zápotocký* (Prague, 1984); Milena Beránková, *Novinař a publicista Antonín Zápotocký* (Brno, 1984).

ZAREMBA Zygmunt (28 April 1895, Piotrków Trybunalski–5 October 1967, Sceaux, near Paris), Polish Socialist politician and journalist. In 1912 Zaremba joined the underground Polish Socialist Party (Polska Partia Socjalistyczna [PPS]). In 1915 he began law studies in Kharkiv. In 1917 he organized the Polish Socialist Union (Zjednoczenie Socjalistyczne Polskie) in the Ukraine, which included various movements of Polish Socialists. In 1918 Zaremba returned to Poland. In September 1918 he joined the PPS Central Workers' Committee and later the PPS Central Executive Committee (Centralny Komitet Wykonawczy), where he sat until 1945. An MP in 1922–35, Zaremba was a representative of the PPS left wing, but he opposed cooperation with the Communists. He organized workers' self-government and propaganda activities, edited party periodicals, and authored many articles and brochures. After the coup of May 1926, Zaremba advocated firm opposition to the government. During the Great Depression, he supported a program to implement the struggle for socialism, which he interpreted in a way similar to the Austro-Marxists. He advocated cooperation with the parties of the national minorities and called for a coalition against authoritarianism in Poland and against fascism abroad. Zaremba wanted to establish such a coalition with parties of the democratic intelligentsia and the peasant left. From 1933 to 1939 he created and ran the consortium Group of Periodicals of the PPS, which published a daily, two weeklies, and two monthlies, with a total circulation of over one hundred thousand. He was active in the struggle against anti-Semitism.

In September 1939 Zaremba fought in the defense of Warsaw. He subsequently co-organized the underground Polish Socialist Party–Freedom-Equality-Independence (PPS–Wolność-Równość-Niepodległość [PPS–WRN]) and was a member of the top leadership of the party. He was in charge of the party's publishing houses, and he edited the underground biweekly *WRN* (1940–44). Zaremba was in favor of creating parliamentary democracy after the war but called for the establishment of a multi-sector economy and the socialization of large industries. He expounded his views in *Demokracja społeczna* (Social democracy), which was published in the underground in 1944. Zaremba worked closely with General **Stefan Grot-Rowecki**, the commander of the Union of Armed Struggle of the Home Army. In 1944 he joined the Council of National Unity (Rada Jedności Narodowej). He took part in the Warsaw Uprising and was editor of the daily *Robotnik*. After the failure of the uprising, Zaremba was active in the underground leadership, which was linked with the Polish government in London. He was against cooperation with the Communists and was alert to the imperialistic plans of the USSR regarding Poland. Zaremba remained in the underground after the Red Army marched into Poland. In the fall of 1945 he worked for establishing the Social Democratic Party in Poland as an alternative to the "revived" PPS, which was under Communist control. As the plan failed and as he was unable to undertake legal publishing activities, he secretly left Poland in March 1946.

Zaremba settled in France, taking part in the activities of the PPS in exile. In 1948–57 and 1959–67 he was president of the Central Council (Rada Centralna) of the PPS. Between 1949 and 1956 he represented the PPS in the interparty bodies of Polish émigrés. In 1948 he organized the International Socialist Bureau, which rallied Socialists from countries beyond the Iron Curtain. In 1949 he became general secretary of the Socialist Union of Central and Eastern Europe, which he represented in the Socialist International from 1950 on. From 1946 to 1959 Zaremba edited the monthly *Światło*. In 1948–56 he worked with the Polish sections of the Voice of America and Radio Free Europe. After 1956 he hoped for transformations toward political pluralism in the Communist movement, for an increase in an independent workers' movements, and for a chance for the PPS to carry on direct activities in Poland. Zaremba tried to promote such changes in his political journalism and in his books, including *Narodziny klasy rządzącej w ZSRR* (The birth of the ruling class in the USSR; 1958) and *Przemiany w światowym ruchu komunistycznym* (Transformations in the world Communist movement; 1965). Zaremba also wrote diaries of his youth and memoirs of the occupation period. (AF)

Sources: O. Blatonowa and A. Friszke, eds., *Zygmunt Zaremba, Listy 1946–1967* (Warsaw, 2000); A. Jaeschke, *Myśl społeczno-polityczna Zygmunta Zaremby w latach 1916–1967* (Kraków, 1992); A. Siwik, *PPS na emigracji w latach 1945–1956* (Kraków, 1998); Andrzej Friszke, Paweł Machcewicz, and Rafał Habielski, *Druga wielka emigracja 1945–1990*, vols. 1–3 (Warsaw, 1999).

ZARIŅŠ Kārlis Reinholds (4 December 1879, Ipiķu, Livonia–29 April 1963, London), Latvian diplomat and politician. After graduating from a rural school in 1899, Zariņš went to St. Petersburg, where he completed courses in bookkeeping and foreign languages. During World War I he was active in organizations for aid to Latvian refugees. From 1917 to 1918 he was a member of the Latvian Provisional National Council. He returned to Latvia in September 1918. In December 1918 Zariņš became a member of the Latvian National Council. In January 1919 he attended the Paris Peace Conference as an attaché of the Latvian delegation. From April to September 1919 he served as chargé d'affaires in Stockholm and subsequently headed a diplomatic mission in Poland. In October 1919 he became diplomatic representative to Helsinki (becoming a minister in 1921). In 1923 he was also appointed an envoy to Sweden, Norway, and Denmark, residing in Helsinki. From 1925 to 1930 Zariņš was an envoy to Sweden, Denmark, and Norway, residing in Stockholm. He subsequently served as envoy to Estonia until 1933. From March 1931 to March 1933 he also held the post of minister of foreign affairs. In mid-1933 Zariņš was appointed envoy extraordinary and minister plenipotentiary to Great Britain and consul general in London. On 17 May 1940 Zariņš received special authority to head the diplomatic service and represent the state in case the government was unable to exercise its authority. After Latvia was seized by the Red Army and then incorporated into the Soviet Union, the Communist authorities recalled Zariņš in August 1940, but he continued to work in London in accordance with the powers granted to him. He headed the entire diplomatic and consular service of the Latvian state in exile until the end of his life, vigorously promoting the cause of Latvia's independence in the West. Zariņš's publications include *Par Latvijas tapšanu: Īsas atmiņas* (On the emergence of Latvia: Short Memoirs; 1945). (EJ)

Sources: Arturs Bērziņš, *Kārlis Zariņš dzīvē un darbā* (London, 1959); "Sūtnis Kārlis Zariņš pēdējā gaitā," *Londonas Avīze*, 10 May 1963; A. Liepa, "Politisko konjunktūru viļņos," *Lauku Avīze*, 15 March 1991; J. Andrups, *Lielbritānijas latviešu vēsture: Latvijas sūtniecība Londonā: Kārlis Zariņš* (London, 1995); J. Lauga, "Latvijas diplomāts Kārlis Zariņš," *Atmoda*, 23 December 1992; Andrejs Plakans, *Historical Dictionary of Latvia* (Lanham, Md., 1997).

ŽARNOV Andrej [originally František Šubík] (19 November 1903, Kuklov–16 March 1982, Poughkeepsie, New York), Slovak poet, translator, and doctor. Žarnov graduated in medical studies from the University of Bratislava. In 1931–45 he was director of the university's Institute of Pathology; from 1940 he was a professor. From November 1938 he was a member of Hlinka's Slovak People's Party (Hlinková Slovenská Ľudová Strana [HSĽS]) and the Hlinka Guard (Hlinkova garda [HG]). After the proclamation of Slovak independence in March 1939, Žarnov managed the department of health services of the HG High Command, and from 1942, the Department of Health of the Ministry of Interior. He was also a member of the Council of State. In April 1943 Žarnov joined an international commission created by the Nazis to investigate the circumstances of the Katyn Forest massacre of Polish officers by the NKVD. After his return to Slovakia, Žarnov delivered a lecture, "Pravda o Katyńskom Lese" (Truth about the Katyn Forest), whose text was widely distributed. In March 1945 Žarnov fled to Bavaria but was delivered to the new Czechoslovak authorities and tried by the National Court in Bratislava. Among other things, he was accused of taking the part of Slovak authorities and "slandering" the USSR. In December 1947 Žarnov repented and was released. The release was also based on the testimonies of many doctors who owed him their lives during the wartime persecutions. In fear of another arrest, in 1952 Žarnov fled with his family to Austria and then went to the United States, where he worked as a pathologist. He belonged to the College of American Pathologists and the American Medical Association. He was also active in Slovak émigré organizations; for example, he presided over the Association of Slovak Writers and Artists.

Žarnov's first volume of poems, *Stráž pri Morave* (Guard on the Morava River; 1925), confiscated by the censors, was a manifesto of the young Slovak Catholic intelligentsia. His patriotic works gained popularity among autonomists, who criticized the centralist policies of the Czechoslovak authorities. Of highest renown are Žarnov's lyrics from the volumes *Štít* (The shield; 1940) and *Mŕtvy* (The dead; 1941). In exile Žarnov published *Preosievač piesku* (Sand sifter; 1978), which was a manifestation of his longing for his homeland and a protest against the Warsaw Pact intervention in Czechoslovakia. Žarnov was also known as a translator of classical Polish and English poetry. Among other translations Žarnov published the collection *U poľských básnikov* (At the Polish poets; 1937). (MG)

Sources: Jozef Chreňo, *Malý slovník slovenského štátu: 1938–1945* (Bratislava, 1965); Joseph G. Cincik, *One Hundred Famous Slovak Men* (Cambridge, Ont., 1984); Augustín Maťovčik et al.,

Reprezentačný biografický lexikón Slovenska (Martin, 1999); *Slovník slovenských spisovateľov* (Prague, 1999); Ján Sedlák, *Básnicky profil Andreja Žarnova* (Bratislava, 1943); *Biele miesta v slovenskej literatúre* (Bratislava, 1991); Slovenský Národný Archív Bratislava, *Národný súd*, sygn. Tnľud 5/46.

ZARUSKI Mariusz (31 January 1867, Dumanovo, Podolia–April 1941, Kherson, Soviet Union [now in Ukraine]), Polish general, sailor, mountaineer, and writer. Zaruski was a member of the Sokół (Falcon) Gymnastics Society and the National League (Liga Narodowa). In 1894, because of his patriotic activities, he was sentenced to exile in Arkhangelsk, where he finished a naval school. He subsequently made many arctic voyages, also as a merchant navy captain. Upon his return (1901) to Poland, Zaruski settled in Zakopane. In 1906 he graduated from the Academy of Fine Arts in Kraków. He was one of the pioneers of skiing and mountaineering in Poland. He made numerous first ascents of summits in the Tatras, and in 1909 he established the Tatra Mountains Voluntary Rescue Service, which he headed until 1926. In 1912 Zaruski joined the Riflemen's Association. In August 1914 he became commander of the Zakopane Company in the Uhlan Regiment of the Polish Legions, and from July to November 1917 he served as commander of the entire regiment. In November 1918 he joined the Polish Army. From February 1919 to July 1920 he commanded an Uhlan regiment. In the spring of 1919 he distinguished himself during the Polish campaign leading to the takeover of Wilno (Vilnius). Zaruski served as adjutant general to the head of state, **Józef Piłsudski**, until 1922 and as adjutant general to President **Stanisław Wojciechowski** from 1923 to 1926. In 1924 Zaruski was promoted to general. In April 1926 he retired and devoted himself to social work. He was a member of the Council of the Marine and River League, a member of the Maritime and Colonial League (from 1930 on), commodore of the Yacht Club of Poland, president of the National Fleet Committee (1926–32), and captain of the scouting yacht *Zawisza Czarny* (1934–39), on which several generations of Polish sailors were educated. Arrested by the NKVD in Lwów (Lviv) in October 1939, Zaruski died of cholera in prison. As a sailor and mountaineer, he became a legend for the interwar generation of Polish youth, whose imaginations he excited through his numerous publications on sailing, mountaineering, and equestrianism and through his memoirs, *Na morzach dalekich* (On the high seas; 1920), *Na bezdrożach tatrzańskich* (Off the beaten track in the Tatras; 1923), and *Wśród wichrów fal* (Among whirlwinds of waves; 1935). Zaruski also wrote poems, some of which were published as *Sonety morskie; Sonety północne* (Sea sonnets; northern sonnets; 1902). (WR)

Sources: *Wielka encyklopedia powszechna*, vol. 12 (Warsaw, 1969); *Encyklopedia historii Drugiej Rzeczypospolitej* (Warsaw, 1999); Tadeusz Kryska-Karski and Stanisław Żurakowski, *Generałowie Polski Niepodległej* (London, 1976); Henryka Stępień, *Mariusz Zaruski: Opowieść biograficzna* (Warsaw, 1997).

ZARYTSKYI Oleksy (1913, Bicze, near Brzeżany [now Berezhany]–30 October 1963, Dolinka, near Karaganda, Kazakhstan), Greek Catholic missionary to Siberia, martyr for the faith. The son of a deacon, Zarytskyi entered a seminary in 1931. Ordained into the priesthood in 1936, he worked as a chaplain in the archdiocese of Lwów (Lviv). After the Soviet authorities abolished the Ukrainian Greek Catholic Church in 1946, Zarytskyi did not abandon his pastoral ministry. In 1948 he was arrested and sentenced to ten years' imprisonment. After his release from a forced labor camp, he was forced to settle in Kazakhstan, where he began a pastoral ministry in Karaganda. In 1957 he traveled to the Krasnoyarsk region to meet with Archbishop **Josyf Slipyi**, who was imprisoned there. Slipyi appointed Zarytskyi apostolic administrator of Kazakhstan and Siberia. Arrested again, Zarytskyi was sentenced to three years' imprisonment. After an early release, he was constantly threatened with arrest. Zarytskyi left Karaganda, and in the following years he made numerous missionary visits to various places, including Kuibyshev (now Samara, Russia), Perm Province, Orenburg, Aktyubinsk (now Aqtobe, Kazakhstan), Kokchetav (now Kokshetau, Kazakhstan), and Tselinograd (now Astana, Kazakhstan). After the KGB discovered his missionary work in 1960 in Orsk, near Orenburg, Zarytskyi traveled without a permanent address, also visiting Tajikistan. Arrested in mid-May 1962 in Karaganda, he was sentenced to two years in a forced labor camp. Zarytskyi died in a forced labor camp near Karaganda. On 27 June 2001 Pope **John Paul II** beatified him at a solemn Holy Mass in Lviv. (WR)

Sources: Ks. Władysław Bukowiński, "Ks. Aleksy Żarecki," *Dziennik Polski*, 19 November 1980; *Osservatore Romano* (weekly edition in English), 2001, nos. 25 and 27.

ZATONSKYI Volodymyr (8 August 1888, Lisets [Lysets], Podolia–29 July 1938, Kiev), Ukrainian Communist activist. In 1912 Zatonskyi graduated from Kiev University and then taught at the Kiev Polytechnic Institute. In early 1917 he joined the Bolshevik party, and in May 1917 he became a member of the presidium of the party's Kiev committee and a member of the Kiev soviet. After the Bolshevik revolution in Petrograd, Zatonskyi became head of a revolutionary committee in Kiev and prepared a takeover of power. From December 1917 to April 1918 he served as commissar of education in the first Bolshevik government of Ukraine; in January 1918, as a plenipotentiary of this government, he was sent to Moscow. After Austrian and German troops occupied central Ukraine, Zatonskyi also headed the Bolshevik Central Executive Committee of Ukraine from late March to mid-April. At a conference in Taganrog in April 1918, Zatonskyi was instrumental in establishing the Communist Party (Bolshevik) of Ukraine (CP[B]U) and became a member of its Central Committee (CC) and its Organizational Bureau. In November 1918 he became a commissar in the Provisional Workers' and Peasants' Government of Ukraine. He supported the idea of a Russian-Ukrainian federation. From July to September 1920, during the invasion of Poland by the Red Army, Zatonskyi also headed the Galician Revolutionary Committee (Galrevkom) in Tarnopol (Ternopil). He endorsed the Bolshevik terror in the occupied territories.

After the Bolsheviks consolidated their rule in Ukraine, Zatonskyi became a commissar of education in the Council of People's Commissars of the Ukrainian SSR in December 1920. From 1923 to 1924 he was a deputy member and in 1924 he became a member of the Politburo of the CP(B)U CC. From 1921 to 1922 he headed the All-Ukrainian Union of Consumer Cooperatives. From 1922 to 1923 he again served as head of the republic's commissariat of education. From 1924 to 1925 he also briefly served as political commissar of the Ukrainian Military District. In 1926 he became editor of the periodical *Chervonyi shliakh* and then became vice-chairman of the republic's Council of People's Commissars. As the director of the Institute of Soviet Construction (1927–33) and head of the governmental Engineering and Chemical Committee (1928–34), Zatonskyi took part in the preparation and implementation of the First Five-Year Plan, as a result of which, because of the government's policy, millions of Ukrainian people starved to death. In 1933 Zatonskyi again assumed the position of commissar of education, and in 1934 he became a deputy member of the CP(B)U CC in Moscow. Although he was an obedient executor of the current party line, Zatonskyi generally cautiously supported the Ukrainian character of the republic's authorities. In 1926 Zatonskyi published a book on the national issue in Ukraine. In 1929 his memoirs from the revolutionary period appeared. A selection of his speeches was published in 1935. During the Great Purge Zatonskyi was arrested (along with his wife) in November 1937. He was subsequently secretly tried and executed. (WR)

Sources: *MERSH*, vol. 45; *Encyclopedia of Ukraine*, vol. 5 (Toronto, 1993); Hryhory Kostiuk, *Stalinist Rule in the Ukraine* (New York, 1960); Robert S. Sullivant, *Soviet Politics and the Ukraine, 1917–1957* (New York and London, 1962); Jurij Borys, *The Sovietization of Ukraine, 1917–1923* (Toronto, 1982).

ZAWADZKI Aleksander (16 December 1899, Dąbrowa Górnicza, Silesia–7 August 1964, Warsaw), Polish Communist activist. Born into a working-class family, Zawadzki was a miner and steelworker in his youth. In 1918 he volunteered to serve in the Polish Army. He fought against the Ukrainians in Lwów (Lviv) and elsewhere in Eastern Galicia and was decorated with the Cross of Valor for his service during the Polish-Soviet war in 1920. Demobilized in 1921, Zawadzki joined the Union of Communist Youth. In 1923 he became a professional activist in the apparatus of the Communist Workers' Party of Poland (Komunistyczna Partia Robotnicza Polski [KPRP]), which in 1925 changed its name to the Communist Party of Poland (Komunistyczna Partia Polski [KPP]). In 1924 Zawadzki underwent training in a special party school in Moscow and then conducted party work in the Dąbrowa Górnicza mining district and Belorussia. Arrested for the first time in 1925, he was released in 1932. He was later convicted twice on charges that included subversive activities in the army (he served as head of the Central Military Department of the Central Committee [CC] of the KPP). Released from the prison in Brześć (Brest) on the Bug River after the Red Army invaded Poland in September 1939, Zawadzki worked in Soviet trade unions and the administration in Western Belorussia. After Nazi Germany attacked the Soviet Union in June 1941, he was evacuated to the Stalingrad area and then to the Novosibirsk region, where he worked in labor battalions and in a mine.

Zawadzki resumed his party work after joining the Tadeusz Kościuszko Division in September 1943. He was quickly promoted, in part owing to the support of General **Karol Świerczewski** and **Alfred Lampe**. In December 1943 he was appointed deputy commander of the corps for political and educational affairs. Zawadzki's promotion was intended to prevent General **Zygmunt Berling** from pursuing independent policies in the army. From January to July 1944 Zawadzki served as chairman of the Central Office of Polish Communists in the Soviet Union, and in April 1944 he became a colonel and briefly served as a member of the Main Board of the Union of Polish Patriots (Związek Patriotów Polskich [ZPP]). For a short time he served as chief of the Polish Partisan Staff, which was incorporated into the Polish Army. Promoted to brigadier general in July 1944, Zawadzlo became a member of the Politburo of the Polish Workers' Party (Polska Partia Robotnicza [PPR]) in August 1944. In January 1945 he was assigned to work in Upper Silesia. Appointed governor of Silesia and Dąbrowa Province in February 1945, Zawadzki implemented a program of social and economic transformation there. He opposed the interwar movement for an autonomous status for the Silesian province and called for a radical solution to the ethnic issue in Upper Silesia. As early as January 1945 he issued a ban on the use of German and ordered that all German traces be removed. His plan, according to which all Germans were to be expelled from Upper Silesia, were in accord with international plans, adopted during the conference of the Big Three in Potsdam.

Zawadzki realized that apart from the Silesians who declared either German or Polish nationality, Upper Silesia was inhabited by many people with indifferent national views, and he tried to implement a Polonization policy toward them. In February 1945 Zawadzki was promoted to major general. Following **Jerzy Ziętek**'s advice, he tried to include the tradition of Silesian anti-German uprisings (1919–21) into the new reality, emphasizing that these were "people's uprisings." Zawadzki used prewar cadres to establish the administration and to rebuild industry in Upper Silesia and the Dąbrowa Górnicza mining district. In December 1948, at the congress that established the (Communist) Polish United Workers' Party (Polska Zjednoczona Partia Robotnicza [PUWP]), Zawadzki called for confrontation with the Catholic Church. In December 1948 he became a member and secretary of the PUWP CC and Politburo and the PUWP CC Organizational Bureau. From January to June 1949 Zawadzki served as deputy prime minister, then president of the Central Council of Trade Unions (Centralna Rada Związków [CRZZ]), and from April 1950 to November 1952 he was again deputy prime minister. During factional strife in 1948–49, Zawadzki supported the group led by **Bolesław Bierut** against **Władysław Gomułka**. On 20 November 1952 he became president of the Council of State and held this position until the end of his life. Zawadzki was co-responsible for mass repressions, the policy of the collectivization of agriculture, and the crushing of the opposition during the Stalinist period. In 1956 he supported the dogmatic Natolin faction in the PUWP, but he nevertheless kept all his positions during the Seventh Plenum of the PUWP CC in October of that year. From August to November 1956 and from January 1958 until the end of his life Zawadzki served as president of the All-Polish Committee of the National Unity Front. He was a deputy to the National Home Council (Krajowa Rada Narodowa) and an MP in the Assembly. Before his death, Zawadzki returned to the Catholic Church with the help of a friar who, disguised as a doctor, visited him while he was in a government clinic. (AGr)

Sources: Mołdawa; *Śląski Słownik Biograficzny*, vol. 1 (Katowice, 1977); Henryk Rechowicz, *Aleksander Zawadzki: Życie i działalność* (Katowice, 1969); Jan Nowak, *Wojna w eterze* (London, 1985); Piotr Madajczyk, *Przyłączenie Śląska Opolskiego do Polski 1945–1948* (Warsaw, 1996); Włodzimierz Janowski and Aleksander Kochański, *Informator o strukturze i obsadzie personalnej centralnego aparatu PZPR 1948–1990* (Warsaw, 2000); *Śląsk w myśli politycznej i działalności Polaków i Niemców w XX wieku* (Opole, 2001).

ZAWADZKI Tadeusz, pseudonyms "Tadeusz Zieliński" and "Zośka" (24 January 1921, Warsaw,–21 August 1943, Sieczychy, near Wyszków), legendary commander of the military resistance during the German occupation of Poland. Zawadzki's father was a chemist and the rector of Warsaw Polytechnic. Zawadzki graduated from Warsaw's Stefan Batory Gymnasium in the spring of 1939. In the autumn of 1933 he joined the scouts, becoming a scoutmaster in January 1939. From the beginning of the German occupation in the fall of 1939, Zawadzki took part in small sabotage operations—for example, he painted the anchor sign of Fighting Poland on walls. In March 1941, along with his unit, Zawadzki joined the Gray Ranks, an underground successor of the prewar Polish Scouting Association, and he became head of the Mokotów scout troop. After completing an underground training course, Zawadzki was promoted to cadet corporal in January 1943. Because he had many duties in the underground resistance movement, he discontinued his studies at the underground Warsaw Polytechnic. He took part in many military resistance operations, and on 26 March 1943 he commanded the most famous one: near the Arsenal in Warsaw, Zawadzki and his men freed prisoners who were being transported from Pawiak Prison (among them were two friends of Zawadzki's, the resistance fighters Jan Bytnar [Rudy] and Aleksander Dawidowski [Alek]). He also commanded a prisoner rescue operation near Celestynów (May 1943). Zawadzki was killed during an attack on a Grenzschutz watchtower near Wyszków. Zawadzki was regarded as an exceptional leader and a person of high moral virtue. He was a model of heroism and devotion to the cause of Poland's independence for generations of youth. A scout battalion of the Home Army (Armia Krajowa) was named "Zośka" after one of Zawadzki's pseudonyms. (WR)

Sources: Kunert, vol. 2; Aleksander Kamiński, *Kamienie na szaniec* (Warsaw, 1943); Tomasz Strzembosz, *Oddziały szturmowe konspiracyjnej Warszawy 1939–1944* (Warsaw, 1979); Stanisław Broniewski, *Całym życiem* (Warsaw, 1982); Stanisław Broniewski, *Akcja pod Arsenałem* (Warsaw, 1983); Tomasz Strzembosz, *Bohaterowie "Kamieni na szaniec" w świetle dokumentów* (Warsaw, 1996).

ZAWIEYSKI Jerzy [originally Henryk Nowicki] (2 October 1902, Radogoszcz–18 June 1969, Warsaw), Polish Catholic writer and social activist. From 1923 to 1926

Zawieyski studied at a drama school in Kraków, and then he performed at the Reduta Theater. He spent 1929–32 in France, working as a theater instructor among Polish emigrants. After his return to Poland, he performed at the Atheneum Theater, and he was active in the Institute of Folk Theaters. Zawieyski was closely tied with the peasant movement, especially with the Union of Rural Youth of the Republic of Poland–Wici (Związek Młodzieży Wiejskiej RP–Wici). Brought up as a Catholic and prepared to enter a religious order, Zawieyski had lost faith in his youth, but later he repeatedly returned to the faith and finally experienced a religious conversion in 1942. From then on his entire creative work and social activities were religiously motivated. Zawieyski advocated that Catholicism be open to people who doubted and remained outside the Church, as well as to atheists. He stigmatized the ties of Catholicism with nationalism. He was strongly influenced by French Catholic thought. During the war, Zawieyski established close ties with Reverend **Stefan Wyszyński**, the future primate of Poland. He corresponded with him during Wyszyński's imprisonment. For many years he was associated with the weekly *Tygodnik Powszechny*.

In 1945–49 and 1956–62 Zawieyski was vice-president of the Polish Writers' Association (Związek Literatów Polskich [ZLP]). At a Szczecin congress of the ZLP in 1949, he was one of the few to come out against Socialist realism, which was being promoted by the authorities. At that time Zawieyski stopped publishing and was destitute. In 1956 he was a co-founder and president of the All-Polish Club of Progressive Catholic Intellectuals, and from 1957 to 1969, he was president of the Club of Catholic Intellectuals (Klub Inteligencji Katolickiej [KIK]) in Warsaw. He was an MP (1957–69) and a member of the Catholic Parliamentary Group Znak (Koło Posłów Katolickich Znak). Between 1957 and 1968 Zawieyski was a member of the State Council, and in 1958–69, a member of the Presidium of the All-Polish Committee of the National Unity Front. After 1956 he held high posts in the Polish People's Republic, a fact that signified a partial normalization in relations between the state and the Church. Zawieyski repeatedly tried to mediate during conflicts between state and Church authorities and he appealed to both sides for moderation. He was in permanent contact with Primate Wyszyński and in frequent touch with **Władysław Gomułka**. Critical of the program of the Great Novena of the Millennium—especially of the form it took—he was reluctant to endorse great religious demonstrations. However, for the sake of the primate, he avoided public statements on this subject. An advocate of the renewal of the Church initiated by Pope John XXIII and the Second Vatican Council, Zawieyski sought a swift implementation of the council's resolutions in Poland. He was the first lay Catholic from a Communist country received by the Pope in private audience (1962). With the consent of Primate Wyszyński, Zawieyski mediated in the establishment of diplomatic relations between the Polish People's Republic and the Holy See in 1964, but in vain.

In March 1968 Zawieyski co-authored an interpellation of the Catholic Parliamentary Group Znak in defending youth who were beaten by the police during student demonstrations. Because of this, he was personally attacked in the Assembly and through Communist propaganda. On 10 April 1968 in the Assembly he delivered a speech in which he rejected the attacks and slander against Catholic MPs and supported the point of the interpellation. As a result, Zawieyski was dismissed as a member of the State Council, and in 1969 he was removed from the list of candidates to the Assembly. Zawieyski was president of the Society of Friends of the Catholic University of Lublin. Zawieyski wrote such novels as *Droga do domu* (The way home; 1946) and *Konrad nie chce zejść ze sceny* (Konrad does not want to leave the stage; 1966); the stories *Romans z ojczyzną* (Romance with the homeland; 1963); and the drama *Dyktator Faust* (Dictator Faust; 1934). Zawieyski was also the author of essays, including *Droga katechumena* (The way of a catechumen); the film script *Prawdziwy koniec wielkiej wojny* (The real end of the Great War; 1957); and diaries, of which only the fragments were published. (AF)

Sources: *Literatura polska: Przewodnik encyklopedyczny*, vol. 2 (Warsaw 1985); Andrzej Micewski, *Współrządzić czy nie kłamać? PAX i "Znak" w Polsce 1945–1976* (Paris, 1978); Antoni Dudek, *Państwo i Kościół w Polsce 1945–1970* (Kraków, 1995).

ZDZIECHOWSKI Jerzy (27 August 1880, Rozdół [Rozdil], Podolia–25 April 1975, Kraków), Polish politician and economist. From 1916 Zdziechowski was one of the leading National Democratic activists. From 1917 to 1918 he belonged to the Council of the Polish Inter-Party Union, which represented pro-Russian rightist parties that called for independence for Poland. Zdziechowski was involved in organizing an unsuccessful coup d'état on 4–5 January 1919 aimed at overthrowing the government of **Jędrzej Moraczewski**, but he was not punished for it. From 1922 to 1927 Zdziechowski was an MP on the ticket of the National Popular Union (Związek Ludowo-Narodowy [ZLN]), the largest political party in Poland. From November 1925 to May 1926 he served as minister of the treasury in the cabinets of **Aleksander Skrzyński** and **Wincenty Witos**. Zdziechowski's policy led to the stabilization of the Polish złoty. In April 1926 he proposed an economic program that included tax increases (except for the property tax) and monopoly charges, as well as layoffs in the railroad sector. The Polish Socialist Party (Polska Partia Socjalistyczna [PPS]), which opposed this program, withdrew its ministers from Skrzyński's cabinet and brought about its collapse. Zdziechowski subsequently served as an activist and deputy chairman of the Lewiatan, the short name for the Union of Polish Industry, Trade, and Finance. He was one of the MPs who were in opposition to the *sanacja* regime. After Zdziechowski had demanded budget cuts in the Ministry of Interior, he was beaten in his apartment by unknown assailants on 1 October 1926. From 1926 to 1933 he was a member of the leadership of the Camp of Great Poland (Obóz Wielkiej Polski [OWP]) and worked closely with **Roman Dmowski**. Zdziechowski authored numerous works in the field of financial policy, and in 1937 he published the study *Mit złotej waluty* (The myth of gold currency).

From September 1939 Zdziechowski lived in exile in France and then in London. He was aligned with the Polish underground movement linked to the National Party (Stronnictwo Narodowe). In January 1946 he became head of the Paris-based Polish Committee of Wartime Émigrés. From December 1949 to 1954 he was chairman of the Executive Department of the Political Council, which he joined as a nonparty politician. He was a member of the Polish delegation in the Eastern Europe Section of the European Movement. Along with Mieczysław Thugutt, he represented the Political Council in negotiations led by General **Kazimierz Sosnkowski** on the unification of major émigré political centers. The main negotiations were held in July 1953 but were unsuccessful. In 1954 Zdziechowski became a member of the Provisional National Unity Council, which did not accept **August Zaleski** as president of the Republic of Poland in exile. After the October 1956 watershed in Poland, Zdziechowski called for some form of agreement with the Soviet Union in exchange for broader political freedoms in Poland and permanent endorsement of the Oder-Neisse border. He publicly addressed this issue in numerous press articles. He also spoke about it at a meeting of the Provisional National Unity Council in London in November 1956. As a result, he was attacked by many émigré politicians. From 1959 on Zdziechowski lived in Paris, where he co-edited *Horyzonty*. He returned to Poland in 1966. Zdziechowski's publications include *Skarb i pieniądz* (Treasury and money; 1955). (PK)

Sources: Wojciech Morawski, *Polityka gospodarcza rządu Aleksandra Skrzyńskiego* (Warsaw, 1990); Andrzej Albert [Wojciech Roszkowski], *Najnowsza Historia Polski 1914–1993*, vols. 1–2 (Warsaw, 1995); Andrzej Friszke, *Życie polityczne emigracji* (Warsaw, 1999); Paweł Machcewicz, *Emigracja w polityce międzynarodowej* (Warsaw, 1999); Rafał Habielski, *Życie społeczne i kulturalne emigracji* (Warsaw, 1999).

ZDZIECHOWSKI Marian (30 April 1861, Novosyelki [Navasyolki], Minsk region–5 October 1938, Wilno [Vilnius]), Polish literary historian, philosopher, and journalist. Zdziechowski was descended from a landed gentry family. In 1883 he received a degree in comparative linguistics from the university in Dorpat (Tartu), where he was influenced by Russian thinkers, including Nikolay Berdyayev and Leo Tolstoy. He subsequently studied in Graz, Zagreb, and Geneva. In 1894 he received the postdoctoral degree from the Jagiellonian University in Kraków. In 1899 he became a professor of world literature there. In 1902 he became a member of the Polish Academy of Arts and Sciences. On his initiative, the Slavic Club in Kraków was established and the periodical *Świat Słowiańszczyzny* (1905–14) was founded. Zdziechowski propagated knowledge about other Slavic countries in Poland. After Poland regained its independence, he moved to Wilno, where he held the chair of general literature at Stefan Batory University from 1919 to 1931. He served as rector (1925–27) and honorary professor (from 1938 onwards) of this university. After the coup of May 1926, **Józef Piłsudski** proposed Zdziechowski as a candidate for president of the Republic of Poland, but Zdziechowski refused to run for that office. Zdziechowski's research mainly involved comparative studies of the cultures of the Slavic nations, as well as studies on sociopolitical systems and social philosophy. He believed that his contemporary civilization was in a crisis stemming from extreme rationalism, an uncritical cult of science and progress, and atheistic humanism. He called for moral revival based on Christian values. A liberal conservative in his political views, Zdziechowski opposed socialism and communism, as well as nationalism and fascism, in which he saw signs of the disintegration of European culture. Zdziechowski left a vast literary legacy, including the following: *Mesjaniści i słowianofile* (Messianists and Slavophiles; 1888); *Europa Zachodnia* (Western Europe; 1894); *Czechy, Rosja i Polska* (Bohemia, Russia, and Poland; 1897); *Pestis perniciosissima: Rzecz o współczesnych kierunkach myśli katolickiej* (Pestis perniciosissima: Modern trends in Catholic thought; 1905); and *Pesymizm, romantyzm a podstawy chrześcijaństwa* (Pessimism, romanticism, and the foundations of Christianity, 2 vols.; 1914). Some of Zdziechowsi's observations—for example, those included in the collection of sketches *W obliczu końca* (Facing the end; 1937) or *Widmo przyszłości* (The specter of the future; 1938)—proved to be accurate prophecies. (MC/WR)

Sources: *Literatura polska: Przewodnik encyklopedyczny*, vol. 2 (Warsaw, 1985); Wojciech Karpiński, "Marian Zdziechowski," *Znak*, 1973, no. 3; Jan Skoczyński, *Pesymizm filozoficzny Mariana Zdziechowskiego* (Wrocław, 1983); Jan Krasicki, *Eschatologia* *i mesjanizm: Studium światopoglądu Mariana Zdzechowskiego* (Wrocław, 1994); Ewa N. Wesołowska, *Działać przed katastrofą: O poglądach społecznych i politycznych Mariana Zdziechowskiego* (Toruń, 1994).

ŻELEŃSKI Tadeusz, pseudonym "Boy" (21 December 1874, Warsaw–3 or 4 July 1941, Lwów [Lviv]), Polish literary critic, writer, and translator. Żeleński was the son of the composer Władysław Żeleński and cousin of the poet Kazimierz Przerwa-Tetmajer. After graduating from a gymnasium in Kraków, he studied medicine at the Jagiellonian University (1892–1900). From 1901 to 1906 he practiced as a doctor. Żeleński was aligned with Kraków's bohemian circles, and from 1906 onwards he co-authored programs for the Zielony Balonik (Little Green Balloon) cabaret. Mobilized into the Austrian Army in 1915, Żeleński served as a railway doctor until the end of World War I. The author of numerous translations of French literature, he was awarded the Palms of the French Academy in 1914 and the Knight's Cross of the Legion of Honor in 1922. In 1922 Żeleński settled in Warsaw, where, among other things, he contributed to *Wiadomości Literackie, Kurier Poranny,* and *Ilustrowany Kurier Codzienny.* From 1923 to 1924 he was literary director of the Polish Theater. In 1933 he became a member of the Polish Academy of Literature. In 1939 he moved to Lwów, where he was given the chair of the history of French literature at the university. He also contributed to Communist periodicals. After Nazi troops occupied Lwów, he was arrested and executed by a firing squad.

An opponent of traditional moral standards and attitudes and an advocate of the secularization of culture, Żeleński ridiculed clericalism, prudery, and bourgeois conservatism, as well as the decadent posturing of bohemian artists. He wrote popular satirical cabaret pieces that were collected between 1908 and 1917 into eleven publications, of which *Słówka* (Little words; 1913) became the most famous. Żeleński's publications include *Studia i szkice z literatury francuskiej* (Studies and sketches in French literature; 1920); *Mózg i płeć* (Brain and gender; 3 vols.; 1926–28); *Molier* (Molière; 1924); and *Balzak* (Balzac; 1934). A highly regarded theater critic, Żeleński wrote columns published in the collection *Flirt z Melpomeną* (A flirtation with Melpomene; vols. 1–10, 1920–32; vols. 11–17, 1933–39). Żeleński engaged in campaigns concerning birth control and sex education by writing such works as *Dziewice konsystorskie* (Consistorial virgins; 1929); *Piekło kobiet* (Women's hell; 1930); and *Nasi okupanci* (Our occupiers; 1932). He called for the demythologizing of the lives of the luminaries of Polish literature, publishing such pieces as "Ludzie żywi" (Living people; 1929) and "Brązownicy" (Gilders; 1930). Żeleński

authored the memoirs *Plotki . . . plotki . . .* (Rumors . . . rumors . . . ; 1927) and *Znaszli ten kraj?* (Do you know this country? 1931). Żeleński's posthumous publications include *Pisma* (Writings, 28 vols.; 1956–75); *Listy* (Letters; 1972); *Reflektorem w mrok* (Floodlight into the darkness; 1978); and *O literaturze niemoralnej* (Immoral literature; 1990). (JS)

Sources: *Literatura polska: Przewodnik encyklopedyczny,* vol. 2 (Warsaw, 1985); Andrzej Stawar, *Tadeusz Żeleński (Boy)* (Warsaw, 1958); Roman Zimand, *Trzy studia o Boyu* (Warsaw, 1961); Wojciech Natanson, *Boy-Żeleński: Opowieść biograficzna* (Warsaw, 1983); Andrzej Z. Makowiecki, *Tadeusz Żeleński (Boy)* (Warsaw, 1987); *Boy we Lwowie, 1939–1941* (Warsaw, 1992); Barbara Winklowa, *Nad Wisłą i nad Sekwaną: Biografia Tadeusza Boya-Żeleńskiego* (Warsaw, 1998); Henryk Markiewicz, *Boy-Żeleński* (Wrocław, 2001).

ŻELIGOWSKI Lucjan (7 October 1865, Oszmiana–9 July 1947, London), Polish general. The son of a participant in the January 1863 Insurrection, in 1885 Żeligowski joined the Russian Army. In 1888 he graduated from an officer training school in Riga. He took part in the Russo-Japanese War of 1904–5. During World War I he initially fought in the ranks of the Polish Rifle Brigade along with the Russian Army, and in 1917 he took command of a brigade in the First Polish Corps in Russia. In August 1918 Żeligowski began organizing Polish soldiers in Kuban. As head of the Fourth Rifle Division, he managed to get from Kuban to Poland via Odessa and Bessarabia in May 1919. In 1920 he commanded the Operational Group in the region of Minsk. At the beginning of October 1920, in agreement with representatives of the Polish government, Żeligowski simulated a rebellion of the Lithuanian-Belorussian Division, which was subordinate to him. Although on 7 October 1920 the Polish command signed the Suwałki Agreement about the demarcation line, which left Wilno (Vilnius) on the Lithuanian side, two days later Żeligowski's units entered Vilnius and proclaimed the creation of Central Lithuania. Żeligowski named himself commander-in-chief of the military forces of Central Lithuania. The Polish authorities formally dissociated themselves from this action, but in fact the Polish head of state, **Józef Piłsudski**, was well aware of it. Moreover, Poland provided military protection for the captured territories. At the end of 1921 Żeligowski handed over power to the Provisional Civil Administration, which in January 1922 held elections for the Vilnius Assembly. The Assembly in turn voted for the incorporation of Central Lithuania into Poland. Despite the fact that the majority of the population of the disputed territory felt Polish, because of the Vilnius action the Lithuanians began to perceive Żeligowski as a symbol of Polish disloyalty.

From 1921 to 1925 Żeligowski was an army inspector. In July 1923 he was promoted to lieutenant general, and between November 1925 and May 1926 he served as minister for military affairs in the cabinet of **Aleksander Skrzyński**. He appointed adherents of Piłsudski to higher military posts, which made it easier for him to prepare a coup d'état. After the collapse of Skrzyński's government, Żeligowski again assumed the post of army inspector, and after the coup of May 1926, he became head of the Liquidation Committee, whose task was to calm the situation in the army. In August 1927 Żeligowski retired. In 1928 he became president of a chapter of the Order of Polonia Restituta, and in 1929, a member of the Tribunal of State. Żeligowski returned to political life in 1935, becoming an MP representing the Nonparty Bloc of Cooperation with the Government in the Assembly. Until December 1937 he headed the Assembly's Military Committee, but he resigned as a result of a disagreement with the group of Marshal **Edward Rydz-Śmigły**. In September 1939 he managed to get to the West, where he was a member of the National Council of the Republic of Poland (Rada Narodowa RP) in London; the group was active under the auspices of the Polish government-in-exile. After the war, Żeligowski settled in London. After he died, his body was transported and buried in Poland. General Stanisław Tatar transported 350 kilograms of gold from the National Defense Fund in the plane that flew Żeligowski's body to Poland. Żeligowski authored the memoirs *Wojna w roku 1920: Wspomnienia i rozważania* (The war in 1920: Memoirs and reflections; 1930). (PU)

Sources: *Kto był kim w Drugiej Rzeczypospolitej* (Warsaw, 1994); *Encyklopedia historii Drugiej Rzeczypospolitej* (Warsaw, 1999); *Słownik polityków polskich XX w.* (Poznań, 1998); Grzegorz Łukomski and Bogusław Polak, *W obronie Wilna, Grodna i Mińska: Front Litewsko-Białoruski wojny polsko-bolszewickiej 1918–1920* (Koszalin and Warsaw, 1994); Piotr Stawecki, *Słownik biograficzny generałów Wojska Polskiego, 1918–1939* (Warsaw, 1994).

ŻEMAITIS Jonas, pseudonym "Vytautas" (1909 Palanga, Russian Empire [now in Lithuania]–26 November 1954, Moscow), leader of the Lithuanian anti-Communist partisan movement. During the interwar period Żemaitis studied at the military academy at Saint-Cyr, near Paris and was promoted to captain of the general staff. After the Soviet Union occupied Lithuania in 1940, he was inducted into the Red Army, but he managed to leave it when Germany invaded Lithuania in June 1941. During the Nazi occupation (1941–44) Żemaitis was active in the underground National Guard (Šaulių Sąjunga). After the Red Army again seized Lithuania in the summer of 1944, Żemaitis continued his underground struggle, trying to

centralize various partisan forces. In 1948 he became commander of a partisan force in the Kęstutis region in Western Lithuania, which comprised the territory from Kaunas to Klaipėda. In 1949 he became head of the Movement of Lithuania's Struggle for Freedom (Lietuvos Laisvės Kovų Sąjudis) and commander-in-chief of its military forces. Despite difficulties linked to the collectivization of agriculture and mass deportations of peasants, who until then had supported the partisans, from late 1951 on Żemaitis directed most partisan activities in the territory of the republic, maintaining contacts with the outside world. Because of illness, in December 1951 he had to withdraw from active struggle. He spent a year and a half in hiding in the Šimkaičiai forests. On 23 May 1953, along with his wife, Żemaitis was captured by the Soviet security services and taken to Moscow, where he was interrogated by Lavrenty Beria. After he refused to cooperate, he was sentenced to death and executed. (WR)

Sources: *EL*, vol. 6; V. Ramojus, *Kritusieji už laisvę* (Chicago, 1954); J. Daumantas, *Fighters for Freedom: Lithuanian Partisans in Soviet Russia* (New York, 1975); Piotr Łossowski, *Litwa* (Warsaw, 2001).

ZEMAN Miloš (28 September 1944, Kolín), Czech economist and politician. In 1969 Zeman graduated from the Prague School of Economics. During the Prague Spring he became a member of the Communist Party of Czechoslovakia (CPC). He also declared his intention of joining the Social Democratic Party, which was undergoing renewal in July 1968, but after the invasion by Warsaw Pact troops, the party was not registered. In 1970 Zeman was expelled from the CPC after he had criticized the so-called normalization. From 1971 to 1984 he worked for Sportpropag, a sports organization, from which he was dismissed for critical remarks on the state of Czechoslovak society. He worked at the Institute of Management Improvement, but in 1989 he was dismissed again. From 1990 to 1993 Zeman was a researcher at the Forecasting Institute of the Czechoslovak Academy of Sciences. In the 1970s and 1980s he contributed to underground publications. During the Velvet Revolution he helped to establish the Civic Forum (Občanské Fórum [OF]), and in the spring of 1990 he was one of the main authors of its economic program. Coopted into the reconstructed parliament in January 1990, Zeman sat in the Chamber of Nations of the Federal Assembly. Reelected to parliament in the first free elections in June 1990, he served as chairman of the parliamentary committee for planning and budget until June 1992. After the breakup of the OF, Zeman became a member of the Civic Movement. In April 1992 he joined the Czechoslovak Social Democratic Party, which was soon renamed the Czech Social Democratic Party (Česká Strana Sociálně Demokratická [ČSSD]), and he became chairman of the ČSSD Prague branch. A deputy to the People's Chamber of the Federal Assembly (June–December 1992), Zeman called for maintaining a federation with Slovakia. Elected chairman of the ČSSD in February 1993, he was reelected at the party congresses in 1995, 1997, and 1999. In April 2001 Zeman resigned his position in favor of **Vladimír Špidla**.

Zeman was in opposition to the liberal government of the Civic Democratic Party (Občanská Demokratická Strana [ODS]) led by **Václav Klaus**. Zeman particularly sharply criticized the "coupon privatization" and promoted a "social market economy" based on small and medium-size enterprises. This brought him electoral success in 1996, when the Social Democrats won over 30 percent of the seats, and the ruling coalition lost its majority in parliament. As a result of a political compromise with the ODS, Zeman became speaker of the lower chamber of the Czech parliament, in exchange for which the Social Democrats agreed that the ruling coalition would stay in power. After the collapse of Klaus' government, Zeman succeeded in persuading his party to support **Josef Tošovský**'s cabinet of civil servants in January 1998. Zeman served as speaker of the Chamber of Deputies until the early elections in June 1998, when the Social Democrats defeated the ODS, and, as a result of another "opposition agreement" with their main rival, on 17 July 1998 they formed a minority government headed by Zeman. In exchange for the ODS tolerating a Social Democratic government, members of the party were appointed as speakers of both chambers of parliament, and the ODS retained substantial influence on major decisions. During Zeman's four-year term in office, the country overcame the economic crisis: inflation was curbed and unemployment was kept at a low level. Zeman accelerated negotiations with the European Union, revitalized cooperation with the Visegrád Group, and led the Czech Republic into NATO, despite his party's previously skeptical attitude toward Czech membership. However, Zeman did not succeed in resolving the problems in Czech-German relations (stemming from the deportation of the Sudeten Germans after World War II) or a conflict with Austria over the construction of the Temelín nuclear power plant. While serving as head of the government, Zeman became known for his controversial statements. Thanks to the genuine successes of his government, the Social Democrats—now led by Špidla—won the next elections in June 2002. Zeman, who had resigned as party leader the year before, refused to accept any position in the new government and held to his decision to retire from

politics. In the autumn of 2002 Zeman entered the race for president of the Czech Republic. Despite his definite victory in the party primaries, Zeman did not take part in the first, unsuccessful, attempt to elect the head of state. His game led to conflicts within the ČSSD, as a result of which, during the second presidential elections, instead of achieving brilliant success and returning to the limelight as a savior, Zeman suffered a defeat in the first round. (PU)

Sources: ČBS; *Kdo byl kdo v našich dějinách ve 20. století*, vol. 2 (Prague, 1998); Alexandr Mitrofanov, *Za fasádou lidového domu: Èeska sociální demokracie 1989–1998: Lidé a události* (Prague, 1998); Jan Bauer, *Miloš Zeman: Zpověĭ bývalého prognostika* (Prague, 1995); http://www.cssd.cz; http://www.psp.cz; http://www.vlada.cz/1250/vlada/vlada_historie.htm.

ZEMGALS Gustavs (12 August 1871, Džūkstes, Courland–6 January 1939, Riga), president of Latvia. Born into a family of craftsmen, Zemgals finished high school in Riga and then graduated from the School of Law of Moscow University. He subsequently worked as an attorney. While still a student, Zemgals entered politics, joining a Socialist movement called Jaunā Strāva. Inducted into the army as a reserve officer during the Russo-Japanese War of 1904–5, Zemgals fought in battles in the Far East. During the 1905–7 revolution he helped to found the Latvian Democratic Party and edited its newspaper. As mayor of Riga, Zemgals joined the Radical Democratic Party of Latvia. During the German occupation he was active in the Latvian Democratic Bloc. On 17 November 1918 he was elected second deputy chairman of the Latvian Provisional National Council (LPNC). On the following day, in the absence of the chairman, Zemgals chaired a session at which he read the proclamation of Latvia's independence. In December 1918 he was also elected chairman of the Riga Municipal Duma. During the German coup in Liepāja (Libau), Zemgals was in charge of the LPNC's work. In July 1919 he was again elected mayor of Riga and deputy chairman of the LPNC. From 1921 to 1923 he served as minister of war. In 1922 he was elected to parliament on the ticket of the Democratic Center Party. After the death of **Janis Čakste**, Zemgals became the new president of Latvia on 8 April 1927. At the end of his term (8 April 1930), he refused to run for a second term. He subsequently worked as an attorney in Riga until the end of his life. In 1931 Zemgals was reelected to parliament. In 1933 he became president of the Baltic Union. After his death, Zemgals was buried in Riga. (EJ)

Sources: Paul Kroders, ed. *Latvijas darbinieku galerija* (Riga, 1928); *Latvijas vadošie darbinieki* (Riga, 1935); *Es viņu pazīstu* (Riga, 1939); Adolfs Šilde, *Latvijas Vēsture* (Stockholm, 1976); Andrejs Plakans, *Historical Dictionary of Latvia* (Lanham, Md., 1997).

ZENKL Petr (13 June 1884, Tábor–3 November 1975, Raleigh, North Carolina), Czech politician and social activist. After graduating from the Department of Philosophy of the Czech University in Prague, Zenkl taught Czech in high schools in Prague from 1906 to 1918. He also authored Czech textbooks. He was active in the National Socialist Party (from 1913) and in the local government (from 1911). From 1919 to 1922 he served as head of the Karlín district of Prague. From 1918 to 1926 he worked in the Ministry of Social Welfare. He subsequently served as head of the Central Social Welfare Fund until 1939. In 1923 Zenkl became a member of the Prague City Council. From 1937 to 1939 he served as mayor of Prague. He played a major role in the drafting and implementation of many welfare and community projects and was active in many social welfare institutions. In 1932 he initiated a program of public works for the unemployed. As mayor of Prague, Zenkl was instrumental in reforming the entire social welfare system of the city. He briefly served as minister without portfolio (October–November 1938), and then he became minister of social welfare, health, and physical education in **Jan Syrový's** cabinet of civil servants.

Throughout World War II Zenkl was imprisoned in the Nazi concentration camps of Dachau and Buchenwald. From 1945 to 1948 he served as chairman of the Czechoslovak National Socialist Party, which joined the National Front of Czechs and Slovaks. At that time Zenkl was also a member of the National Assembly, and from 1945 to 1946 he again served as mayor of Prague and head of the Central Social Welfare Fund. Zenkl subsequently became one of the deputies to Prime Minister **Klement Gottwald**, and in this capacity he became one of the main representatives of the newly formed anti-Communist front. On 20 February 1948, during the Communist coup, Zenkl (along with eleven other ministers) announced to President **Edvard Beneš** that he was resigning from his position in protest against the activities of the Communists, who sought to take over full control of the state, and against the undemocratic methods they employed. In August 1948 Zenkl emigrated to West Germany, from where he made his way, via London, to the United States. In the United States he served as the leader of the National Socialists in exile until the end of his life. In 1949 he also became chairman of the Council of Free Czechoslovakia. Zenkl published a number of books, including *Masarykova Československá republika* (Masaryk's Czechoslovak Republic; 1955); *Masaryk and the Idea of European and World Federation* (1955); *The Communist Seizure of Power and the Press 1945–48* (1962); and *A History of the Czechoslovak Republic, 1918–1948* (1973). (PU)

Sources: *ČBS*; Karel Kaplan, *The Short March: The Communist Takeover in Czechoslovakia, 1945–1948* (London, 1981); *Českoslovenští politici: 1918–1991* (Prague, 1991); Jozka Pejskar, *Pražský primátor* (Prague, 1993); *Národ ho potřeboval* (Prague, 1994); *Politická elita meziválečného Československa 1918–1938: Kdo byl kdo za první republiky* (Prague, 1998); Libor Vukoupil, *Slovník českých dějin* (Brno, 2000).

ŻEROMSKI Stefan, pseudonyms "Maurycy Zych" and "Józef Katerla" (14 October 1864, Strawczyn, near Kielce–20 November 1925, Warsaw), Polish writer and journalist. Żeromski came from an impoverished noble family of patriotic traditions. After completing his education at a Kielce high school (1874–86), he began to study at the Veterinary College in Warsaw, but in 1888 he gave up his studies for lack of money. At that time he took part in the activities of secret organizations—for example, the Union of Polish Youth (Związek Młodzieży Polskiej). From 1888 to 1891 Żeromski worked as a resident tutor in noble houses in the Kielce region, Mazovia, Podlasie, and Nałęczów. In 1892 he left for Switzerland, where he worked as an assistant librarian in the Polish National Museum in Rapperswil. During his four-year stay in Switzerland Żeromski acquainted himself with archival materials on the history of Polish nineteenth-century emigration and established contacts with Socialist politicians. From 1897 to 1903 he worked at the Zamoyski Library in Warsaw. He was linked with the Polish Socialist Party (Polska Partia Socjalistyczna [PPS]) and with the periodical *Głos*. As his financial situation improved significantly after 1904, he was able to devote himself exclusively to literary work.

In 1905 Żeromski settled in Nałęczów, where he initiated the establishment of the People's University. Forced to leave the Russian sector of partitioned Poland, in 1908 he moved to Galicia; in 1909 left for Paris, and in 1913 he settled in Zakopane. Żeromski was linked with the independence movement. After the outbreak of World War I, he enlisted in the Polish Legions, but shortly thereafter, because of his negative assessment regarding the policy of the Central Powers, he moved away from the camp of **Józef Piłsudski**. In the fall of 1918, as president of the so-called Republic of Zakopane, Żeromski participated in the formation of the Polish state authority in Podhale. In 1919 he moved to Warsaw. He was an initiator of the project to establish an academy of literature, a co-founder and president of the Polish Writers' Union in 1920, and founder of the Guardians of Polish Writing and the Polish PEN club in 1924. In 1920 he co-organized the Society of Friends of Pomerania. Żeromski took part in a plebiscite action in Warmia (Ermland) and Mazuria. He was also a war correspondent during the Polish-Soviet war. He immortalized this war—for example, in his famous short story, "Na parafii w Wyszkowie" (At the presbytery in Wyszków). In recognition of his merits, in 1924 he received a flat at the Royal Castle in Warsaw.

Żeromski began his literary career writing stories and novels, the first collection of which appeared in 1895. In his writing he raised issues of social injustice, cultural backwardness, and the struggle for justice and progress. Independence issues were also very important in his works. Apart from allusions to social, patriotic, and moral issues, Żeromski wrote impressionistic descriptions of nature and wove in lyrical romantic threads. He combined epic narration with elements of political journalism and erudite reflection. He voiced opinions on all vital social issues and often raised morally sensitive issues. His writing style was full of expression and naturalism. In 1924 Żeromski was a candidate for the Nobel Prize in literature. However, he did not receive it, it is believed, because of the negative reception of his novel *Wiatr od morza* (Wind from the sea; 1922) in Germany. In 1925 Żeromski was the first winner of the national literary award in Poland. Żeromski's most important works include *Syzyfowe prace* (Sisyphean labors; 1897); *Ludzie bezdomni* (Homeless people, 2 vols.; 1900); *Popioły* (4 vols., 1904; *Ashes*, 1928); *Wierna rzeka* (1912; *Faithful River*, 1943); the scandalous *Dzieje grzechu* (The story of sin, 2 vols.; 1908); and *Przedwiośnie* (Springtime; 1925). In *Przedwiośnie*, Żeromski included many critical remarks on the Polish reality in the first years of independence. (JS)

Sources: *Literatura polska: Przewodnik encyklopedyczny*, vol. 2 (Warsaw, 1985); Stanisław Kasztelowicz and Stanisław Eile, *Stefan Żeromski: Kalendarz życia i twórczości* (Kraków, 1961); Wacław Borowy, *O Żeromskim: Rozprawy i szkice* (Warsaw, 1964); Z. Jerzy Adamczyk, ed., *Żeromski: Z dziejów recepcji twórczości 1895–1964* (Warsaw, 1975); J. Z. Jakubowski, *Stefan Żeromski* (Warsaw, 1975); H. Markiewicz, *W kręgu Żeromskiego* (Warsaw, 1977); Z. Golinksi, ed., *Stefan Żeromski—w pięćdziesiątą rocznicę śmierci: Studia i szkice* (Warsaw, 1977); Artur Hutnikiewicz, *Żeromski* (Warsaw, 1987).

ZEROV Mykola (26 April 1890, Zinkiv, Poltava Province–9 October 1937, Solovets Islands), Ukrainian poet and literary historian. Zerov studied philology at the university in Kiev. From 1917 to 1920 he edited the literary periodical *Knyhar*. From 1918 to 1935 he taught the history of Ukrainian literature at Kiev's Institute of Architecture, at a cooperative technical high school, and at Kiev's Institute of People's Education. From 1930 to 1933 he also taught translation theory at the Ukrainian Institute of Language Education. Arrested by the NKVD in April 1935 and falsely accused of spying and directing a "nationalist and terrorist" group, Zerov was sentenced to ten years in Soviet forced labor camps on the Solovets Islands in January 1936. On 9 October 1937, while he was in a camp, the sentence was changed to the death penalty, and Zerov was immediately executed by a firing squad. In his work, as both a poet and a translator, Zerov was influenced by the ideas of neoclassicism and the Parnassian school. The sonnet was his favorite poetic form. Zerov translated many works by classical Roman poets, works by contemporary French authors, and some works by Adam Mickiewicz and Juliusz Słowacki. Zerov's publications include the translation collections *Antolohiia rymskoy poezii* (Anthology of Roman poetry; 1920) and *Kamena* (1924), as well as the critical works *Nove ukraiinske pysmenstvo* (New Ukrainian literature; 1924); *Do dzherel* (To the sources; 1926); and *Vid Kulisha do Vynnychenka* (From Kulish to Vynnychenko; 1928). Zerov's poetry collections *Sonnetarium* (1948), *Catalepton* (1952), and *Corollarium* (1958) were published posthumously. Zerov was formally rehabilitated in 1958. His selected works were published in 1966. The most complete selection of his works appeared in two volumes in 1990. (WR)

Sources: *Encyclopedia of Ukraine*, vol. 5 (Toronto, 1993); Hryhory Kostiuk, *Stalinist Rule in the Ukraine* (New York, 1960).

ZHECHEV Toncho (6 July 1929, Divyadovo, near Shumen–22 February 2000, Sofia), Bulgarian writer. Zhechev graduated from high school in Shumen and from the Law School of Sofia University, and then he received a Ph.D. in Moscow. He worked for the periodical *Septemwri*, from which he was fired for "deviation from the party line" in 1967. Zhechev got a job in the Institute of Bulgarian Literature of the Bulgarian Academy of Sciences (IBL BAS), and from 1974 to 1983 he was its director. Among other things, he dealt with historical changes in the Bulgarian national consciousness and the history of the Bulgarian Orthodox Church. In 1975 Zhechev published *Byłgarskijat Welikden ili Strastite Byłgarski* (Bulgarian Resurrection Day or Bulgarian passions), in which he showed the efficacy of nonviolent tactics in the struggle of the Bulgarian Orthodox Church for independence from the Constantinople patriarchate. As director of the IBL BAS, Zhechev defended scholars attacked by the authorities. He published about seven hundred scholarly works and was recognized in Cambridge's "Men of Achievement." After 1989 Zhechev again edited *Septemwri*, changing its title to *Letopisy*. A keen supporter of Bulgaria's integration with Western security structures, Zhechev also worked to invite Pope John Paul II to Bulgaria, a visit that materialized after his death in May 2002. (WDj)

Sources: *Koy koy e v bulgarskata kultura* (Varna, 1998); Wanda Smochowska-Petrowa, "Literaturniyat institut bez nebe," *Literaturna misyl,* 1997, no 3; Yordan Vasiliev, *Patila i radosti* (Sofia, 2002).

ZHEKOV Nikola (25 December 1864, Sliven–6 October 1949, Füssen, Germany), Bulgarian general. Zhekov came from a poor family and worked as a shoemaker's apprentice. Later he graduated from high school and from the Military Academy in Sofia. In 1885 he fought in the war against Serbia. Then he studied in Italy, and after returning to Bulgaria, he was commander of a regiment and a division. During the Balkan Wars (1912–13) Zhekov was chief of staff of the Second Army. From August to October 1915 he was minister of war in the government of **Vasil Radoslavov**. He led the preparations for Bulgaria's entry into war on the side of the Central Powers. When it happened, on 11 October 1915, Zhekov became commander-in-chief of the Bulgarian Army. At the end of 1915 the Bulgarian troops broke through the Serbian defenses and entered Macedonia. Zhekov's demands that the Allied bases in eastern Greece be taken before they became the stepping stones for an Allied counteroffensive were ignored by the German command. In August and September 1916 the Bulgarian Army took the Aegean coast near Kavalla, but the Germans moved some of the Bulgarian troops to the Romanian front. In view of Bulgaria's exhausted economic resources, in the fall of 1917 some of the opposition politicians wanted to attract Zhekov to the idea of a separate peace with the Entente, but he gave them away to the authorities. After the fall of the Radoslavov government in June 1918, Zhekov left for Germany. Meanwhile the Bulgarian army was scattered, and the new government had to accept harsh conditions under the armistice, hardly escaping a bloody revolution. In 1923 Zhekov returned to Bulgaria and tried to defend his wartime position. He was sentenced to a long imprisonment but released after three years owing to an amnesty. In the 1930s Zhekov led a group of extreme pro-German politicians and officers. He hoped to take over power with the help of the Third Reich. In the summer of 1940 he was invited by the Germans to France to visit the battlefields of the Wehrmacht victories. Zhekov received a German pension, but Hitler was reluctant to use him as a tool against Tsar **Boris III**. After World War II Zhekov stayed in Germany and died there. (WR)

Sources: Ivan Stoichev, *Stroiteli i boini vozhdovie na bylgarskata voiska* (Sofia, 1941); Alan W. Palmer, *The Gardeners of Salonika* (New York, 1965); John D. Bell, *Peasants in Power: Alexander Stamboliski and the Bulgarian Agrarian National Union, 1899–1923* (Princeton, 1977); Holger H. Herwig and Neil M. Heyman, *Biographical Dictionary of World War I* (Westport, Conn., 1982); Richard C. Hall, *Bulgaria's Road to the First World War* (Boulder, Colo., 1996).

ZHELEV Zhelyu (3 January 1935, Veselinovo, near Shumen), philosopher, sociologist, politician, and president of Bulgaria. In 1958 Zhelev graduated in philosophy from Sofia University and subsequently worked on a doctoral dissertation on the philosophical definitions of matter in the modern natural sciences. Since he dared to criticize Lenin's theory of matter, Zhelev was not allowed to defend his dissertation, lost his job at the university, and in 1965 was expelled from the Bulgarian Communist Party, which he had joined in 1961. Unable to get a job for political reasons, Zhelev moved to the countryside, where he devoted himself to scholarly work and to writing books. It was then that he wrote his most famous book, *Fashizmut* (Fascism), which was a critical analysis of totalitarian systems, with obvious allusions to Stalinism. Banned from publication by the Communist regime, the book was circulated in manuscript form among Bulgarian intellectuals for many years. In 1982 it finally appeared in print, but the authorities did not allow it to be sold, and after a few days it was withdrawn from the bookstores. In 1974 Zhelev earned a Ph.D. in philosophy for a dissertation on the modal categories of dialectics. From 1975 he was a researcher at the Cultural Research Institute in Sofia, where he headed the Culture and Personality Department between 1977 and 1982. In 1988 he received the postdoctoral degree for a dissertation on the theory of personality.

Zhelev was one of the founders and organizers of the opposition movement in Bulgaria. On 3 November 1988 he co-founded the Club for Support of Glasnost and Perestroika. After the fall of the totalitarian regime of **Todor Zhivkov** on 10 November 1989, Zhelev co-founded and then became the leader (that is, president of the National Executive Council) of the Union of Democratic Forces (Sayuz na Demokratichnite Sili [UDF]). The UDF, established on 7 December 1989, was a coalition initially formed of nine, and later a dozen or so, Bulgarian opposition parties and organizations. Zhelev headed a delegation of the anti-Communist opposition in the Round Table talks (16 January–15 May 1990), during which the conditions of Bulgaria's transition to a democratic system were agreed upon, including the date of the first free parliamentary elections, which were to be held on 10 and 17 June 1990. In these elections Zhelev was elected to the Grand National Assembly. After the UDF's failure in the elections to the Grand National Assembly, which brought success to the Bulgarian Socialist Party (formerly the Bulgarian Communist Party), the slogan "Your prime minister, our president" appeared among the Bulgarian opposition. On 1 August 1990 the parliament elected Zhelev as the first non-Communist president of Bulgaria. Reelected in January 1992, this time in a general election, Zhelev served until 3 November 1996. During his term in office, he took a moderate line, and, in consequence, he lost the support of part of his electorate, especially the extreme right wing and the anti-Communists. As a result of an anti-presidential campaign, the Bulgarian vice-president, **Blaga Dimitrova**, resigned. There also occurred incidents involving the burning of copies of Zhelev's book on fascism. In November 1996 Zhelev withdrew from the presidential race after he had lost in the primary elections held by the UDF to **Petar Stoyanov**, who then became president.

Zhelev published many books and scholarly articles, including the following: *Samodeinoto izkustvo v usloviiata na NRB* (Amateurish art in the People's Republic of Bulgaria; 1976); *Fizicheskata kultura i sportut v urbaniziranoto obshtestvo* (Physical culture and sports in urbanized society; 1978); *Modalnite kategorii* (Modal categories; 1979); *Fashizmut* (Fascism; 1982), which was translated into English, French, Russian, Esperanto, Romanian, Macedonian, and other languages; *Chovekut i negovite lichnosti* (Man and his personalities; 1992); and *Relatsionna teoriia za lichnostta* (A relational theory of personality; 1993). (JJ)

Sources: *Koy koy e v Bulgariya* (Sofia, 1998); Tasho Tashev, *Ministrite na Bulgariya 1879–1999: Entsiklopedichen spravochnik* (Sofia, 1999); Jerzy Jackowicz, *Bułgaria od rządów komunistycznych do demokracji parlamentarnej 1988–1991* (Warsaw, 1992); Raymond Detrez, *Historical Dictionary of Bulgaria* (Lanham, Md., 1997); "Filozof, opozycjonista, prezydent. Wywiad Adama Michnika z Żeliu Żelewem," *Gazeta Wyborcza*, 18–19 August 1990.

ZHIVKOV Todor (7 September 1911, Pravets, near Sofia–9 August 1998, Sofia), Bulgarian Communist leader. Zhivkov came from a poor peasant family. Because of his father's illness, at fourteen he had to start working in a brickyard. In a high school in Okhranie (1926–29) he was introduced to Marxist ideology. Forced to leave the high school for financial reasons, Zhivkov took up work in a printing house in Sofia, at the same time learning printing at a night school, from which he graduated in 1932. In 1930 he joined the Bulgarian Communist Youth League, and in 1932, the Bulgarian Communist Party (BCP). In 1932–41 Zhivkov was a member and secretary of regional committees of the BCP in Sofia. As a "suspicious element," from 1936 to 1937 he did substitute military service building roads. For his Communist activities he was arrested and tortured. After completing his military service, Zhivkov married Dr. Mara Maleeva, with whom he had two children, **Ludmila Zhivkova** and Vladimir. Later both children held high party and state posts. After the German aggression against the USSR in 1941, Zhivkov, as the secretary of the third Sofia district of the BCP, organized

protests against sending Bulgarian troops to the eastern front and against deporting Jews to concentration camps. From 1942 Zhivkov was a member of the Sofia District Committee of the BCP and was responsible for the partisan movement outside the capital. At the end of 1943 he was sent as the plenipotentiary of the District Committee of the BCP to Botevgrad, where he headed the Communist guerrilla movement in the region. Under his leadership the first Sofia partisan brigade, called Chavdar, was created (April 1944); it was commanded by **Dobri Dzhurov**, later the minister of national defense.

During the coup of 9 September 1944 Zhivkov commanded the operational staff of the insurgent forces in Sofia and the vicinity. After the seizure of power by the Communists the operational staff became the staff of the People's Militia in Sofia and was active under Zhivkov's political leadership until November 1944. From then on Zhivkov quickly rose in the ranks. At the end of 1944 he became secretary of the Sofia Regional Committee of the BCP and was responsible for organizational affairs. At the Eighth Plenum of the Central Committee (CC) in 1945 he was elected a deputy member of the CC, and at the Fifth Congress of the BCP in December 1948 he became a member of the CC. From 1945 Zhivkov was a deputy to eleven consecutive parliaments. In 1948–49 he served as the first secretary of the Sofia City Committee of the BCP, and from 1950 he was the first secretary of the Sofia Regional Committee. In January 1950 he was elected secretary for agitation and propaganda of the CC, and then he was also appointed a deputy member of the Politburo of the CC of the BCP. In July 1951 he became a full member of the Politburo of the CC, joining the top leadership of the party. From 1953 he directed the works of the Secretariat of the CC of the BCP. At the Sixth Congress of the BCP in 1954 Zhivkov was elected the first secretary of the CC of the BCP. He held the post until November 1989 (from 1981 as secretary general). In addition, from November 1962 to June 1971 he was prime minister, and then until November 1989 he was the president of the State Council.

At first Zhivkov did not have full power in the party or in the state. **Vulko Chervenkov** still remained the most powerful person in the BCP, directing the work of the Politburo in 1954–56. Zhivkov became the leader of the BCP only after a criticism of the cult of personality at the Twentieth Congress of the CPSU and at the April Plenum of the CC of the BCP in 1956. At that time Chervenkov was dismissed as secretary general of the BCP and as prime minister. In consequence Zhivkov assumed the leadership of the Politburo and became an indisputable leader of the BCP. The election of **Anton Yugov** as prime minister caused the emergence of a de facto second center of power, but it was eliminated in 1962 after Zhivkov's assumption of the post of prime minister.

The April 1956 Plenum of the BCP led to a certain liberalization of political life but did not change the essence of the system; the principles of "democratic centralism" and the leading role of the Communist Party were retained. Zhivkov was partially responsible for the persecution of the opposition in the 1940s and 1950s, and he bore full responsibility for the domestic and foreign policy of Bulgaria between 1962 and 1989, especially for the absolute subordination of the country to the Soviet Union. (In 1963 he even planned for the incorporation of Bulgaria into the USSR.) Zhivkov was also entirely responsible for the participation of Bulgaria in the invasion of Czechoslovakia in 1968, for the persecution of political opponents, and for the so-called revival process, based upon the forced assimilation of the Roma, Pomak, and Turkish populations in Bulgaria. This policy led to the emigration of around 320,000 Bulgarian citizens of Turkish origin to Turkey in 1989.

In the fall of 1989 Zhivkov was removed from power. On 10 November he resigned as secretary general of the CC of the BCP, and on 17 November the National Assembly dismissed him as president of the State Council. Between 11 and 13 December of the same year, the Plenum of the CC of the BCP expelled him from the party for "serious infringements of basic party and moral principles, deep deformations in the party and in society, and major errors in the social and economic development of the country." Along with Zhivkov, many others were expelled from the party, among them his son, Vladimir. In 1990 Zhivkov was arrested, and on 18 January 1994, he was sentenced to seven years of prison for the embezzlement of state funds (giving away flats, cars, and money in the amount of $24 million). Zhivkov served the sentence under house arrest in the villa of his granddaughter near Sofia. On 9 February 1996 the Criminal Chamber of the Supreme Court quashed the sentence of 1994, acquitting Zhivkov of the charges of the misappropriation of public funds. Inquiries against Zhivkov were also conducted in three other cases (an embezzlement case of the Moscow fund, assistance to Communist parties and to developing countries, and the forced assimilation of Turks). However, none of the cases resulted in a trial. In 1997 Zhivkov published *Memoari* (Memoirs), in which he defended his political line and critically evaluated Mikhail Gorbachev and the Bulgarian politicians who assumed power in 1989. From then Zhivkov's popularity in Bulgarian society grew steadily. Zhivkov intended to return to political life, joining the Bulgarian Socialist Party in March 1998, but a few months later he died. (JJ)

Sources: *Entsiklopediya Bulgariya*, vol. 1 (Sofia, 1981); *Koy koy e v Bulgariya* (Sofia, 1998); Todor Zhivkov, *Sreshtu niakoi lyzhi* (Sofia, 1993); Niko Yakhiel, *Todor Zhivkov i lichnata vlast: Spomeni, dokumenti, analizi* (Sofia, 1997).

ZHIVKOVA Ludmila (26 July 1942, Sofia–21 July 1981, Sofia), Bulgarian Communist activist, daughter of **Todor Zhivkov**. In 1965 Zhivkova graduated in history from Sofia University. From 1974 to 1981 she worked at the Institute of Balkan Studies of the Bulgarian Academy of Sciences. In the late 1960s and early 1970s she studied at Oxford, where she worked on her doctoral dissertation, "Anglo-turskite otnosheniia, 1933–1939" (1971; *Anglo-Turkish Relations, 1933–1939*, 1976). She received a Ph.D. in 1971. Zhivkova's later works, including *Kazanlushkata grobnitsa* (1974; *Tomb in Kazanluk*, 1975), were devoted to archaeological discoveries in Bulgaria and to the chapels of Tsar Ivan Aleksandur. She also held prominent party and government positions. She served as deputy chairperson (1971–75) and chairperson (1975–81) of the Committee for Culture and Art, and in 1980 she became head of the Department for Science, Culture, and Art of the Central Committee of the Bulgarian Communist Party (BCP). Zhivkova surrounded herself mostly with party activists who sought foreign contacts, and her strong position as the daughter of the head of the BCP allowed for more open criticism of the pathologies of life in Communist Bulgaria. Her work helped to promote Bulgarian culture abroad. Given a modicum of tolerance, Bulgaria became more open to Western cultural trends and ideas, even though Bulgarian Communist officials did not approve. Many Bulgarian artists and writers for the first time in their lives had an opportunity to travel to the West. Zhivkova was interested in Eastern philosophy; she was a vegetarian and practiced yoga. In her research, she stressed the role of the Thracians and the Proto-Bulgarians in the formation of the Bulgarian nation, and she reduced the importance of the Slavic element to more modest proportions. The Russians did not like that, seeing it as a revival of nationalism. Zhivkova's views on the origins of her nation were reflected in the celebrations of the 1,300th anniversary of the foundation of the Bulgarian state organized by the authorities in late 1981. Zhivkova did not live to see them. The circumstances of her death have not been explained. According to one version, she was murdered by KGB agents, and according to another, she committed suicide. Zhivkova became the object of a kind of cult, and the People's Palace of Culture, built on her initiative in Sofia, was named after her. (AG)

Sources: Raymond Detrez, *Historical Dictionary of Bulgaria* (Lanham, Md., 1997); Tasho Tashev, *Ministrite na Bulgariya 1879–*

1999: *Entsiklopedichen Spravochnik* (Sofia, 1999); Stoyan Mihailov, ed., *Think of Me as Fire: A Book about Lyudmila Zhivkova* (Sofia, 1985); *Lyudmila Zhivkova: Her Many Worlds* (Oxford 1986).

ZHURBA Halyna [originally Halina Dąbrowska] (29 December 1888, Teplyk, near Haysyn, Podolia–9 April 1979, Philadelphia, Pennsylvania), Ukrainian writer. The daughter of a Polish noble and a Polonized Ukrainian mother, Zhurba absorbed the rural Ukrainian culture in her childhood. She published her first collection of stories, *Z zhyttia* (From life), in Odessa in 1909. She then contributed several stories to the journal *Ukraiinska khata*. In 1912 the tsarist censors confiscated an issue of this journal because it published her story "Koniaka" (The horse). From 1917 to 1919 Zhurba edited the daily *Nova Rada* in Kiev. In 1919 she published her second collection of short stories, *Pokhid zhyttia* (The march of life). In 1920 she fled Bolshevik rule to a Polish transition camp in Tarnów and then settled in Zdołbunów (Zdolbuniv), where she lived with her husband, Andriy Nyvynskyi, an activist of the Ukrainian Socialist Radical Party. Zhurba later lived in Lwów and Warsaw. In the 1920s she published her works in Poland, Czechoslovakia, and the Ukrainian Soviet Socialist Republic. Her most famous novels—*Zori svit zapovidaiut* (The dawn heralds sunrise; 1933) and *Revolutsiia ide* (The revolution is coming, 2 vols., 1937–38)—were published in Lwów (Lviv). During the Nazi occupation Zhurba's sensational novel *Doktor Kachioni* (1943) was published in Kraków. Before the arrival of the Red Army, Zhurba went to Germany. In 1950 she settled in the United States, where she published an autobiographical account of her childhood, *Dalekyi svit* (A distant world; 1955). (WR)

Sources: *Encyclopedia of Ukraine*, vol. 5 (Toronto, 1993).

ZHYLUNOVICH Zhmitser, pseudonym "Tsishka Gartny" (4 November 1887, Kopyl, near Minsk–11 April 1937, Mogilev, Russia [now Mahyliou in Belarus]), Belorussian writer and Communist activist. In 1904 Zhylunovich became a member of the Social Democratic Party. He took part in the revolution of 1905–7. In the spring of 1905 he graduated from a two-year high school in Kopyl, and in 1906 he started working as a tanner. In 1908 he began to write for the periodical *Nasha Niva*. During his stay in St. Petersburg in 1913 Zhylunovich established close ties with the Bolshevik *Pravda* editors. He again went to St. Petersburg, where he worked in the Volcano factory. In 1913 the Zahlanie Sontsa i u Nashaie Vakontsa (The sun will shine into our window also) publishing house issued the first collection of Zhylunovich's poems, *Pesni* (Songs), written in Belorussian using the Latin alphabet. In March 1917 Zhylunovich entered the Belorussian National Committee, and in June of the same year he became president of the Belorussian Socialist Hromada. On 14 February 1918 he became a member of the Belorussian National Commissariat of the Government of the RSFSR in Moscow as secretary of the commissariat and as the editor of its press organ, *Dzannitsa*.

In October 1918 Zhylunovich became a member of the Russian Bolshevik party. On 1 January 1919, on the party's recommendation, he became president of the Provisional Revolutionary Government of Workers and Peasants of the Belorussian Soviet Socialist Republic. In this capacity he sought an agreement with the government of the Belorussian People's Republic, which opposed the plans of the Bolshevik "internationalists." At the beginning of February Zhylunovich and his comrades were temporarily arrested, and then he was mobilized into the Red Army, in which he fought against the troops of General Anton Denikin. Zhylunovich served as political commissar in the Fourteenth Army and on the Western Front Staff. In 1920 he joined the Central Executive Committee of the Belorussian SSR. In 1922 he published a collection of poems, *Piesni pratsy i zmahannia* (Songs of work and struggle). In 1923 the plenum of the party Central Committee decided to award him the title of "National Poet," but this decision was not implemented. A deputy member of the CC of the Belorussian party in 1927–29, Zhylunovich became a professor at the Belorussian Academy of Sciences in 1928. He was also a member of the Institute of Belorussian Culture, editor-in-chief of the newspaper *Savietskaia Belarus* and the periodical *Polymia*, head of the Belorussian State Publishing House, deputy minister of education of the Belorussian SSR, and president as well as a member of the council of the Belorussian Society for Cultural Relations with Foreign Countries. Zhylunovich published a collection of his critical articles, *Uzhorki i niziny* (Hills and plains; 1928); a collection of prose, *Homan Zarnits* (1932); and a novel, *Pierahudy* (1935).

During the suppression of national freedom in Soviet Belorussia, on 16 January 1931 Zhylunovich was expelled from the party, and in March he was sentenced to ten years of labor camp on trumped-up charges of creating the "counterrevolutionary" Belorussian Liberation Union. He was temporarily released but was rearrested on 15 November 1936. Tortured during interrogations, on 7 April 1937 Zhylunovich was taken to a mental hospital in Mogilev, where, according to an official version, he died of gangrene. In fact, he was probably murdered by the NKVD. In 1988 Zhylunovich was rehabilitated. In 1967 his *Vershy* (Poems) were published, and 1978 saw the publication of *Nasutrach sontsu: Vybranyia apaviadanni*

(To meet the sun: Selected novels). In 1987–93 four volumes of Zhylunovich's *Zbior tvorau* (Collected works) were published. (AS/SA)

Sources: *Bielarus: Entsyklapedychny davednik* (Minsk, 1995); A. M. Klachko, *Tsishka Hartny* (Minsk, 1961); H. D. Zhylunovich and S. K. Aleksandrovich, eds., *Uspaminy pra Cishku Hartnaha* (Minsk, 1984); Vitaut Kipel and Zora Kipel, eds., *Byelorussian Statehood* (New York, 1988); Ernest Yalugin, *Bez epitafii: Dokumentalnaia apoviests* (Minsk, 1989); Jerzy Turonek, *Wacław Iwanowski i odrodzenie Białorusi* (Warsaw, 1992); Jan Zaprudnik, *Historical Dictionary of Belarus* (Lanham, Md., 1998).

ZIEJA Jan (1 March 1897, Osse, near Sandomierz–19 October 1991, Warsaw), Polish Catholic priest. Zieja completed a theological seminary in Sandomierz and was ordained in 1919. He studied theology at Warsaw University and in Rome but did not complete his studies. From 1912 Zieja was in the secret scouting and the illegal peasant movements, and he belonged to the National Peasant Union. In 1920 he was a chaplain in the Polish Army. In 1928–32 he was a parish priest of Łohiczyn parish in Polesie, a lecturer at the theological seminary in Pińsk, head of the diocesan Catholic Action, an organizer of charity work, and spokesman for practical ecumenism in relations with the Orthodox faithful and the Jews. After completion of Judaic studies at Warsaw University, Zieja reassumed his priestly activities in Polesie. He was linked with the Peasant Youth Union–Wici of the Republic of Poland. In September 1939 he was a chaplain in the Polish Army and then a chaplain for (among other groups) the underground Gray Ranks (Szare Szeregi) scouting units. Zieja participated in actions to save the Jews. During the Warsaw Uprising he was chaplain of the Baszta regiment. At the end of 1944 Zieja voluntarily went to Germany in order to offer moral support to the Poles who had been deported there for forced labor. From 1945 to 1949 he was a priest in Słupsk, where he organized (among other things) the House for Mother and Child and a people's university. After returning to Warsaw in 1949, from 1950 Zieja was rector of the church of the Visitant Order. In 1953 after a sermon that was a reaction to the arrest of Primate **Stefan Wyszyński**, the authorities demanded Zieja's removal from Warsaw. Between 1955 and 1959 Zieja was again rector of the Visitant church. He gained great popularity for his courage, rectitude, and literal interpretation of Christ's teachings. In 1960 Zieja's health declined; in 1963 he was released from diocesan service and became occupied with writing. In 1976 Zieja was a co-founder of the Committee for the Defense of Workers (Komitet Obrony Robotników [KOR]). (AF)

Sources: Andrzej Friszke, *Opozycja polityczna w PRL 1945–1980* (London, 1994).

ZIELENIEC Josef (28 April 1946, Moscow), Czech economist and politician of Polish descent. A graduate of the Prague School of Economics, from 1973 to 1986 Zieleniec was employed at the Research Institute for Machine Building Technology and Economics in Prague, where he worked on the application of mathematical methods in economics. From 1986 to 1990 he was a researcher at the Institute of Economics of the Czechoslovak Academy of Sciences, and then for two years he directed the Center for Economic Research and Graduate Education (CERGE) at Charles University, Prague, where he was appointed associate professor in 1991. At the beginning of the economic transformation of Czechoslovakia, Zieleniec headed a team that prepared the study *Československo na rozcestí: Zpráva o stavu národního hospodářství a možnostech jeho nápravy* (Czechoslovakia at a crossroads: Report on the state of the national economy and chances for its improvement; 1990). A co-founder of the Civic Democratic Party (Občanská Demokratická Strana [ODS]) in April 1991, Zieleniec co-authored its program and served as its deputy chairman from November 1991 to October 1997. After the elections of June 1992, Zieleniec became minister of international relations of the Czech Republic. When the breakup of Czechoslovakia proved unavoidable, he played an important role in the negotiation of terms for the dissolution of the federation.

After the independent Czech Republic was established, Zieleniec became its minister of foreign affairs in the government of **Václav Klaus** in January 1993 and continued to hold this position after the elections of June 1996, when he also assumed the post of deputy prime minister. In June 1996 he also became an MP. Zieleniec pursued a pro-Western foreign policy and played a major role in the process of Czech-German reconciliation. Beginning in 1996 he increasingly opposed the political line and the governing style of Klaus. As a result of friction within his party, Zieleniec resigned his parliamentary seat in August 1997, and at the end of October 1997 he gave up all his governmental and party positions. Shortly after the exposure of a corruption scandal in the ODS, Zieleniec left the party in January 1998. In the spring of 2000 he ran in the elections to the Senate as an independent candidate supported by a center-right coalition of four smaller parties that were against the "opposition agreement" between the two strongest parties, the ODS and the Czech Social Democratic Party. Zieleniec won the elections in the first round, obtaining over 50 percent of the vote. He is a member of the Senate Committee on Foreign Affairs, Defense, and Security. Zieleniec published *Přemýšlení o svete* (Reflections on the world, 1998; co-authored by Libuše Koubská). From July 2004 Zieleniec has been a member of the European Parliament. (PU)

Sources: ČBS; *Kdo je kdo v České Republice na přelomu 20. století* (Prague, 1998); www.zieleniec.cz; wtd.vlada. cz/scripts.

ZIEMBIŃSKI Wojciech (22 March 1925, Gniew–13 January 2001, Warsaw), Polish social and political activist. During the Nazi occupation Ziembiński was active in the pro-independence underground movement. Arrested in July 1942, he was imprisoned in a camp in Karlsruhe and then sent to forced labor in the Rhineland. After World War II, he served in the Polish Armed Forces in the West. In 1947 he returned to Poland. Ziembiński studied law at Nicolaus Copernicus University in Toruń and at Warsaw University. Later he worked as an editor and journalist in the Czytelnik Publishing House, from which he was expelled in 1953 for refusing to commemorate the death of Stalin. He later worked in the Legal Publishing House and on the editorial staffs of *Nasza Ojczyzna* and *Lekkoatletyka*, where he was transferred for disciplinary reasons in 1968 for refusing to sign an anti-Zionist manifesto. Ziembiński was a member of the Crooked Circle Club (1955–62), an independent discussion club. He was also active in the Club of the Catholic Intelligentsia (Klub Inteligencji Katolickiej) in Warsaw. Ziembiński brought together pro-independence supporters, establishing a political opposition salon in Warsaw. He was arrested and imprisoned several times (for example, in 1971 and 1979) for organizing demonstrations in Warsaw to mark the Polish Independence Day, 11 November. In the 1970s Ziembiński became secretary of the informal Committee of Senior Officers of the Polish Army, whose members included prewar officers of the Polish Army. In 1975 he signed the "Letter of 59" in protest against proposed amendments to the constitution. From 23 September 1976 to 29 September 1977 he served on the Committee for the Defense of Workers (Komitet Obrony Robotników [KOR]), of which he was one of the founding members. One of the leaders of its right wing, Ziembiński left the KOR, along with Andrzej Czuma and others. On 25 March 1977 he joined the Movement for the Defense of Human and Civil Rights (Ruch Obrony Praw Człowieka i Obywatela [ROPCiO]) and was a member of its presidium. He published articles in underground periodicals and edited the monthly *Opinia*. In 1979 Ziembiński became head of the Committee for National Self-Determination. He edited *Rzeczpospolita*, an underground periodical that frequently discussed Poland's eastern policy and other issues. Ziembiński urged successive U.S. presidents to help improve Poland's international situation, citing the obligations of the United States as Poland's World War II ally.

From 1980 to 1981 Ziembiński worked for the defense of political prisoners. Arrested in 1982, during martial law in Poland, Ziembiński was held in prison for seven months. In 1983 he became the leader of the Congress of National Solidarity, which became the Party of Loyalty to Poland (Stronnictwo Wierności Rzeczypospolitej) in 1989. He edited the periodicals of these parties, *Solidarność Narodu* and *Polska Jutra*. In June 1988 Ziembiński traveled to Paris for medical treatment and used the occasion to initiate the establishment of the Congress of East Central Europe. In 1989 he opposed the Round Table compromise. From 1995 to 1997 Ziembiński belonged to the right-wing Movement for the Reconstruction of Poland (Ruch Odbudowy Polski). He was a member of the Józef Piłsudski Institute in New York. He was a co-founder and then chairman of the council of the Foundation for the Fallen and Murdered in the East. As a result of his efforts, a monument to the Victims of Soviet Aggression of 17 September 1939 was unveiled in Warsaw in 1995. From 1991 Ziembiński was active in the Katyń Foundation (he was chairman of its council from 1993 to 2000). In 1995 he was one of the founders of the Poland-Chechnya Committee. (PK)

Sources: Kazimierz Groblewski, "I to był cały Wojtek," *Rzeczpospolita*, 19 January 2001; Andrzej Friszke, *Opozycja polityczna w PRL 1945–1980* (London, 1994); *Opozycja w PRL: Słownik biograficzny 1956–1989*, vol. 1 (Warsaw, 2000).

ZIĘTEK Jerzy (10 June 1901, Petersdorf [now Szobiszowice], near Gliwice–20 November 1985, Zabrze), Polish activist in Upper Silesia. Born into the large family of a railway engine driver, Ziętek attended high school in Gleiwitz (Gliwice) but was expelled before his final exams for his activity in a Polish patriotic organization called Filareci. After 1918 he was active in the Polish Plebiscite Commissariat for Gleiwitz County, and he fought in the Third Silesian Uprising (1921). After the division of Upper Silesia, Ziętek, fearing German persecution, moved to Poland. He worked in the local government administration in Tarnowskie Góry. In May 1926 he supported the coup staged by **Józef Piłsudski**. In 1929 he was appointed administrator of the municipality of Radzionków. In 1930 Ziętek became an MP on the Silesian ticket of the Nonparty Bloc of Cooperation with the Government (Bezpartyjny Blok Współpracy z Rządem [BBWR]). In the summer of 1939 he headed the civil defense of the municipality and tried to eliminate German saboteurs. In September 1939 he went to Lwów (Lviv); the move saved his life because the Gestapo had placed his name on a list of Poles to be executed. In June 1940 the NKVD deported Ziętek to a forced labor camp in Rybinsk and then to one in the Caucasus. Released to join an army formed by the (Communist) Union of Polish Patriots (Związek Patriotów Polskich) in June 1943, Ziętek served in the Second Infantry Division as an officer for educational and political affairs. In January 1945 he participated in the liberation of Warsaw.

In early 1945 Ziętek joined the Upper Silesia Operational Group, which, under the command of General **Aleksander Zawadzki**, was establishing the government apparatus in the Dąbrowa Górnicza mining district and in the territories of the former Silesian province. In March 1945 Ziętek became provincial vice-governor of Silesia and Dąbrowa Górnicza Province. He was given relatively much independence in administering the province and tried to use local cadres to reestablish the economy and administration. He opposed the plundering of the Red Army and pleaded on behalf of Silesian miners who had been deported to the Soviet Union in the spring of 1945. Ziętek played a major role in resolving the issue of the so-called Volkliste (started in October 1939, a list of ethnic Germans living in Nazi-occupied Poland; as of 1941 the list comprised four categories of people with varying degrees of loyalty to the Third Reich). As a result of Ziętek's efforts, no punishment was to be administered to people in the third and fourth categories, nor to many people in the second category. Ziętek initiated many programs for the regional development of Upper Silesia. In 1952 he supervised the expulsion of Silesian bishops from Katowice. As a result of his efforts, the Cathedral Chapter elected a vicar capitular obedient to the authorities. From 1957 to 1975 Ziętek was an MP. In 1963 he became a member of the Council of State, and in 1964, the president of the Presidium of the Provincial National Council and a member of the Executive of the Provincial Committee of the (Communist) Polish United Workers' Party (Polska Zjednoczona Partia Robotnicza [PUWP]) in Katowice. Ziętek initiated a number of environmental projects, including the construction of a water reservoir in Goczałkowice and a green belt around the Upper Silesian Industrial District, as well as the construction of recreational centers and hospitals for miners. He campaigned for the granting of war veterans' rights to Silesian uprising fighters. After 1970 Ziętek was frequently in conflict with **Zdzisław Grudzień**, the first secretary of the PUWP Provincial Committee in Katowice, who represented the Communists of the Dąbrowa Górnicza area. From 1973 to 1975 Ziętek served as provincial governor of Katowice, and in April 1980 he became deputy chairman of the Council of State. (AGr)

Sources: Mołdawa; *Śląski Słownik Biograficzny*, vol. 1 (Katowice, 1999); Andrzej Topol, *Jerzy Ziętek 1901–1985, generał, wojewoda, mąż stanu* (Katowice, 1986); *Śląsk w myśli politycznej i działalności Polaków i Niemców w XX wieku* (Opole, 2001); Jan Walczak, *Generał Jerzy Ziętek, Wojewoda katowicki: Biografia Ślązaka 1901–1985* (Katowice, 2002).

ŽIVKOVIĆ Petar (23 January 1879, Negotin, Serbia–1947 Paris, France), Serbian general and politician.

Živković graduated from the Military Academy in Belgrade. He was actively involved in staging the coup of May 1903, in which King **Alexander Obrenović** was assassinated. After the coup, King **Peter I Karadjordjević** ascended the throne. In response to the establishment of Ujedinjenje ili Smrt (Union or Death, also known as the Black Hand), a secret organization led by Colonel **Dragutin "Apis" Dimitrijević**, Živković co-founded and headed the so-called White Hand, a group of officers with close ties to the royal court. During World War I Živković commanded a regiment, and in 1917 he became commander of the royal guard. He was one of the organizers of the so-called Salonika Trial, in which Dimitrijević was sentenced to death and then executed in June 1917. Živković played an active role in expelling Black Hand members from the army of the Kingdom of Serbs, Croats, and Slovenes. In 1923 he was promoted to major general. When, following a prolonged crisis of the state, King **Alexander I Karadjordjević** assumed dictatorial power, he appointed Živković prime minister and minister of interior on 6 January 1929. Promoted to four-star general in 1930, Živković was the main executor of the king's policy. He supervised the 1931 parliamentary elections, in which all candidates ran on one ticket approved by the government. After resigning as prime minister on 3 April 1932, Živković served as minister of military affairs in the cabinets of **Nikola Uzunović**, **Bogoljub Jevtić**, and **Milan Stojadinović** (January 1934–February 1939). In 1936 Živković founded the Yugoslav National Organization (Jugoslovenska Nacionalna Organizacija), but it did not become a mass government party. After the German invasion of Yugoslavia in April 1941, Živković emigrated to Great Britain, where he served as minister without portfolio in the government of **Miloš Trifunović** (June–August 1943). A firm opponent of communism, Živković supported the activities of Colonel **Dragoljub (Draža) Mihailović** and his guerrillas in occupied Yugoslavia. In July 1946 Živković was sentenced to death in absentia in the trial of Mihailović. (WR)

Sources: *Enciklopedija Jugoslavije*, vol. 8 (Zagreb, 1971); Željan E. Šuster, *Historical Dictionary of the Federal Republic of Yugoslavia* (Lanham, Md., 1999); Richard Frucht, ed., *Encyclopedia of Eastern Europe* (New York and London, 2000).

ZLENKO Anatoly (2 June 1938, near Kiev), Ukrainian diplomat. After finishing school, Zlenko worked in the coal mining industry in the town of Kadiyivka. From 1962 to 1967 he studied at the university in Kiev and then entered the diplomatic service of the Ukrainian SSR, fully controlled by the Kremlin. In 1967 he became second secretary in the Department of International Organizations of the Ministry of Foreign Affairs of the Ukrainian SSR. In March 1973 he became a staff member of the UNESCO Secretariat in Paris. In 1979 he was appointed counselor in the Department of International Organizations of the Ukrainian Ministry of Foreign Affairs, and in 1983, permanent representative of the Ukrainian SSR to the UNESCO. In April 1987 he was appointed deputy minister of foreign affairs and in July 1990 minister of foreign affairs of the Ukrainian SSR. After Ukraine regained its independence in 1991, Zlenko reorganized its diplomatic service and established diplomatic relations with most countries of the world. He played an important role in negotiations with Russia on borders; the division of the Black Sea Fleet; and the Soviet nuclear arsenal, which was kept by Russia in exchange for American and Russian security guarantees and American economic assistance to Ukraine. After leaving the Ministry of Foreign Affairs, Zlenko served as the permanent representative of Ukraine to the United Nations (October 1994–September 1997). He subsequently became ambassador of Ukraine to Portugal. From October 2000 to September 2003 Zlenko was minister of foreign affairs of Ukraine and a member of the President's Council for the National Security and Defense of Ukraine. (WR)

Sources: *Europa Środkowo-Wschodnia 1992–1994/95* (Warsaw, 1994–97); Bohdan Nahaylo, *The Ukrainian Resurgence* (Toronto, 1999); www.kmu.gov.ua/menu/main_uryad_engl.htm.

ZNANIECKI Florian (15 January 1882, Świątniki, near Włocławek–23 March 1958, Urbana-Champaign, Illinois), Polish sociologist and philosopher. The son of an estate administrator, Znaniecki was expelled from Warsaw University for taking part in a protest against the restriction of academic freedoms by the Russian authorities. In 1904 he went to Switzerland. He studied in Geneva, Zurich, and Paris and also worked as a librarian at the Polish Museum in Rapperswil. In 1910 he received his postdoctoral degree from the Jagiellonian University. In 1911 Znaniecki published *Myśl i rzeczywistość* (Thought and reality), and in 1912, *Humanizm i poznanie* (Humanism and cognition), in which, influenced by Henri Bergson, Wilhelm Dilthey, and American pragmatism, Znaniecki developed his own humanist theory. In 1914 he went to the United States on the invitation of William I. Thomas. From 1917 to 1919 he taught at the University of Chicago. In 1919 he published *Cultural Reality* in Chicago, which was the crowning achievement of the philosophy of culturalism. In collaboration with Thomas, Znaniecki co-authored the five-volume *The Polish Peasant in Europe and America* (1918–20), in which the personal documents, letters, and diaries of émigrés were used in an innovative way.

Znaniecki returned to Poland in 1920, by then a world-famous scholar, and took up the chair of Sociology and the Philosophy of Culture at Poznań University. He founded the Polish Sociological Institute (1922) and the periodical *Przegląd Socjologiczny* (1930). He expounded on the foundations of his theory of humanist sociology in *Wstęp do socjologii* (Introduction to sociology; 1922). In *The Laws of Social Psychology* (1925) Znaniecki described regularities in changes in attitudes and values. In his pioneering work, *Socjologia wychowania* (Sociology of education, 2 vols.; 1928–30), Znaniecki described relations between the social system and personality. From 1931 to 1933 he lectured at Columbia University and conducted research on the sociology of education. After returning to Poland, he published a book based on these lectures, *Ludzie teraźniejsi i cywilizacja przyszłości* (Contemporary people and the civilization of the future; 1934). His two subsequent works, *The Method of Sociology* (1934) and *Social Action* (1936), included a criticism of the positivist methodology in sociology and an analysis of social activities based on qualitative studies taking into consideration the so-called humanist factor. In the summer of 1939 Znaniecki resumed lecturing at Columbia University. The outbreak of World War II prevented his return to Poland. From 1940 he worked at the University of Illinois at Urbana-Champaign, where he published *The Social Role of the Men of Knowledge* (1940), *Modern Nationalities* (1952), *Cultural Sciences* (1952), and other books. Znaniecki did not return to Poland because he did not accept the Communist regime imposed on the country after 1944. In recognition of his scholarly position and his influence on American sociology, Znaniecki was elected president of the American Sociological Society in 1952. His work *Social Relations and Social Roles* was published posthumously in 1965. (WR)

Sources: *International Encyclopedia of the Social Sciences*, vol. 16 (London, 1968); Theodore Abel, "Florian Znaniecki 1882–1958," *American Sociological Review*, 1958, vol. 23; *Florian Znaniecki i jego rola w socjologii* (Poznań, 1975); Jerzy Szacki, *Znaniecki* (Warsaw, 1986); Krzysztof Dybciak and Zdzisław Kudelski, eds., *Leksykon kultury polskiej poza krajem od roku 1939* (Lublin, 2000).

ZOG I [originally Ahmed Zogu] (8 October 1895, Burgayet, Mati–9 April 1961, Paris), king of Albania. Zog was born the son of Xhemal Pasha, head of Zogolli, one of the most powerful Albanian clans. Zog completed a lycée and the Turkish Officers' Academy in Istanbul. During World War I he served in the Austrian Army as *colonel honoris causa*. In 1920 he became the commander-in-chief of the Albanian Army, and in 1921 he became minister of interior. In November 1921 Zog was commissioned to suppress an insurrection in the north of the country. His armed forces were composed of volunteers who were linked to his clan. His units became the foundation of a gendarmerie and the base of his political power. Declaring himself a supporter of the People's Party, Zog at the same time maintained contacts with leaders of the opposition party, the conservative Progressive Party. After a series of government changes, on 14 December 1921 Zog entered Tirana with his armed units and forced the resignation of the government and the General Council. He appointed Xhafer Ypi the new prime minister. Zog himself remained minister of interior. The opposition was concentrated in the National Assembly, where Bishop **Fan Noli**, Stevro Vinjay, and **Luigj Gurakuqi** were especially influential. On 22 March 1922 units of Zog's opponents gained control of the capital but withdrew under pressure from the Western powers.

After the parliament passed the provisional statutes of the state in September 1922, Zog became prime minister, and this intensified the conflict. Now the opposition also demanded the removal of the relics of feudalism from the countryside, dominated by the great landowners. In the elections of December 1923 Zog's adherents won the majority of the vote, but they did not manage to control the disastrous economic situation. On 23 February 1924 Zog was injured in an assassination attempt by a high school student. Since the parliament was dominated by conservative lords, Zog bestowed the premiership on Shefket Vërlaci. Provocations and treacherous assassinations committed on the government's orders inflamed the populist opposition to an insurrection, which in May 1924 spread throughout Tirana. The government fled to Greece and Zog to the Kingdom of Serbs, Croats, and Slovenes. On 16 June 1924 the reformers established a cabinet headed by Noli. Before this government had a chance to implement a reform program, Zog returned with his armed forces from Yugoslavia. After a two-week struggle, on 24 December 1924 he entered the capital and established a dictatorship.

On 6 January 1925 Zog became head of the government and divided the country into ten military zones supervised by clan leaders (*bayraktar*). Having prepared a reform of the system, on 25 January Zog summoned the Constituent Assembly, which proclaimed a republic and passed a preliminary constitution, on the basis of which on 1 February Zog became president. On 2 March the Assembly passed a new constitution, which declared the state to be a parliamentary republic. However, the president nominated one-third of the MPs and senators, while women, the clergy, and military men became disenfranchised. Zog's power was based upon the commanders-in-chief and clan leaders, especially the great landowners from the south. Zog organized a rally of their representatives

in Tirana, where on 25 June 1925 they took an oath of loyalty (*besa*) in exchange for an acknowledgment of their privileges. Zog's position depended on the strength and loyalty of the gendarmerie, trained by the British general Joselyn Percy. At the same time Zog brutally suppressed the opposition. Most probably on his orders Gurakuqi was murdered in Bari in March 1925 and **Bayram bey Curri** a month later; Zog's brother-in-law, Ceno bey Kryeziu, was killed in Prague in November 1927. Zog also forced Vërlaci to emigrate.

In June 1928 Zog dissolved the Assembly and called an election. The voting on 17 August 1928 was carried out under the supervision of the army and the police. The new assembly proclaimed Albania a monarchy, and on 1 September 1928 it pronounced Zog the king of Albania. He assumed the title of Zog I. In a proclamation of 5 December 1928 Zog presented himself to the nation as a king-reformer and announced the modernization of the country and its adoption of European standards. In 1929 a civil code came into force and, in 1930, a criminal code. In May 1930 a limited agrarian reform, designed by an Italian expert, Giovanni Lorenzoni, began to be implemented. However, it did not change much in the disproportionate structure of land ownership. Little changed as well with regard to literacy and economic development. Under strict royal rule Albania enjoyed political stability, although opposition was suppressed and reforms were only half measures. In foreign policy Zog sided with Fascist Italy. In 1925 he obtained a loan there, and a year later he signed an Albanian-Italian treaty of friendship and security. In 1927 a twenty-year treaty of mutual aid subordinated the country to Italy. Benito Mussolini made Albania his bridgehead to the Balkans, controlling Albanian finances and the army. Italian influence led to some economic developments in the region of Tirana and Durrës, where the Italians built a port. As king, Zog attempted to exert his authority over the Albanians in Greece and Yugoslavia, which aroused tensions there. In 1938 Zog married a Hungarian princess, Geraldine Apponyi. From this marriage a successor to the throne, his son **Leka**, was born.

On 7 April 1939 Mussolini ordered the invasion of Albania and the dissolution of Albania's status as a formally independent state. Victor Emmanuel III assumed the throne of Albania, and Zog fled with his family across the mountains to Greece; then, via Romania, Poland, Latvia, and Sweden, he arrived in Great Britain. After the war Zog could not return home, where the influence of his supporters had diminished and the Communists had taken power. He formally abdicated on 2 January 1946. Zog later lived for some time in England and then moved to Cannes, France. (WR)

Sources: *Biographisches Lexikon*, vol. 4; Bernd Jürgen Fischer, *King Zog and the Struggle for Stability in Albania* (Boulder, Colo., 1984); Mirash Ivanaj, *24 orët e fundit të mbretërisë së Zogut: Ditar* (Tirana, 1997); Jerzy Hauziński and Jan Leśny, *Historia Albanii* (Wrocław, 1992); *Obituaries from The Times 1961–1970* (Reading, 1975).

ZÖLD Sándor (19 May 1913, Nagyvárad [now Oradea, Romania]–20 April 1951, Budapest), Hungarian Communist activist. Zöld's father was a shoemaker and bricklayer. After the 1920 Peace Treaty of Trianon, Zöld's family moved to Hungary. After passing his high school final examinations, Zöld enrolled at the Debrecen University Medical School, from which he received a degree in 1939. In 1932, when Zöld was beginning his studies, **Gyula Kállai** persuaded him to join the illegal Communist Party. Zöld was also active in legally operating youth organizations. In 1933 he was elected secretary of the István Tisza Circle, which brought together students of Bihar County. In 1937 in Debrecen, on behalf of the Academic Circle, Zöld signed a declaration on joining the March Front, initiated by the so-called peasant writers. In 1942 Zöld became a doctor at a hospital in Berettyóújfalu. After the Arrow Cross Party seized power in October 1944, he went underground for some time.

After the Red Army entered Hungary, Zöld was appointed governor of Bihar County on 18 November 1944. From December 1944 until the end of his life he served as a member of parliament. From 3 December 1944 to 15 July 1945 he was secretary of state for political affairs in the Ministry of Interior in the Provisional National Government. In March 1945 he became head of the administration and economics department of the Central Committee (CC) of the Hungarian Communist Party (HCP). In November 1946 he was transferred to Szeged, where he became secretary of the municipal party committee. At the founding congress of the Hungarian Workers' Party (HWP) in June 1948, Zöld was elected a deputy member of its CC. In September 1949 he became a member of the CC, and in May 1950 he also joined the Politburo. On 30 October 1948 Zöld returned to the Ministry of Interior, becoming secretary of state for administrative affairs. After the resignation of **János Kádár**, Zöld was appointed minister of interior in late June 1950. In this role, he was responsible for the continuation of the police terror in Hungary. On 19 April 1951, at a meeting of the HWP CC Politburo, the head of the party, **Mátyás Rákosi**, sharply criticized the functioning of the ministry and condemned Zöld for maintaining friendly contacts with the Communists who had been imprisoned for participating in the March Front. According to official information, Zöld shot and killed his two children, his wife, and his mother, before committing suicide. Probably he did not want to share the fate of **László Rajk** and Kádár, his immediate predecessors. On the day of his death Zöld was dismissed as minister of interior and expelled from the party. On 1 June 1957 his ashes were solemnly reburied at the Kerepesi Cemetery in Budapest. However, the circumstances of his death have not been fully explained to this day. (JT)

Sources: *Magyar Életrajzi Lexikon*, vol. 2 (Budapest, 1969); Bennet Kovrig, *Communism in Hungary from Kun to Kádár* (Stanford, 1979); *A magyar forradalom és szabadságharc enciklopédiája* (Budapest, 1999).

ŽOLGER Ivan (22 October 1867, Devina–16 May 1925, Lassnitzhöhe, Austria), Slovene lawyer and politician. Žolger studied law in Graz and Paris, earning a degree in 1895. In 1900 he received the postdoctoral degree from the University of Vienna. For many years he worked in the Austrian state administration, initially in the town of Pettau (now Ptuj, Slovenia), then in Graz, and from 1902 onwards in the central government administration in Vienna. In 1917 Žolger was granted a noble title. In July 1918 he became minister without portfolio responsible for preparing a constitutional reform of the monarchy. On 27 October 1918, in the face of Austria-Hungary's defeat in World War I, Žolger resigned. After returning to Slovenia, he became chairman of a commission that presented a draft provisional constitution for the Kingdom of Serbs, Croats, and Slovenes (SHS). This draft was adopted in November 1918. Along with the Croat **Ante Trumbić** and the Serb **Nikola Pašić**, Žolger represented the SHS at the Paris Peace Conference in 1919. He was also a representative of the SHS at the First Assembly of the League of Nations in Geneva (1920), and he sat on the Permanent Arbitration Tribunal in The Hague. In 1918 Žolger became a professor at the University of Vienna, and in 1919, a professor at the School of Law of the University of Ljubljana. Žolger's publications include *Oesterreichisches Verordnungsrecht* (Austrian administrative law; 1898); *Der Hofstaat des Hauses Österreich* (The Court State of the Austrian house; 1917); *Les Slovenes* (The Slovenes; 1919); and *Kršitev mednarodne obveznosti in njena pravna posledica* (The violation of international commitments and its legal consequences; 1921–22). (AO)

Sources: *Enciklopedija Slovenije*, vol. 15 (Ljubljana, 2001); Carole Rogel, *The Slovenes and Yugoslavism, 1890–1914* (Boulder, Colo., 1977).

ŻÓŁKIEWSKI Stefan (9 December 1911, Warsaw–4 January 1991, Warsaw), Polish Communist activist and literary critic. Born into an intelligentsia family, after graduating from Warsaw University in 1934, Żółkiewski worked as a high school teacher. During the Nazi occupation he was involved in underground teaching. He favored Marxism and the extreme left wing, and in 1942 he joined the Polish Workers' Party (Polska Partia Robotnicza [PPR]). From 1945 to 1948 Żółkiewski was the editor-in-chief of the periodical *Kuźnica*, which promoted a radical Marxist vision of Polish culture. He became a deputy member of the Central Committee (CC) of the PPR in December 1945 and head of the CC Department of Education and Culture in December 1947. From December 1948 to March 1954 he was a deputy member and then a full member of the CC of the (Communist) Polish United Workers' Party (Polska Zjednoczona Partia Robotnicza [PUWP]), and he became head of the CC Department of Culture. He was also an associate professor at Warsaw University. After earning a doctorate in 1952, Żółkiewski became a professor at Warsaw University in 1954, and he was the founder and director of the Institute of Literary Studies of the Polish Academy of Sciences. In 1950 he published *Stare i nowe literaturoznawstwo* (Old and new literary studies), which was an exposition of the Stalinist understanding of literature. From 1953 to 1955 Żółkiewski served as academic secretary of the Polish Academy of Sciences and was in charge of party control over this institution. From April 1955 to June 1956 he was head of the PUWP CC Department of Culture and Science. Politically close to the Puławska faction (Puławianie), Żółkiewski advocated a political thaw and a revision of Communist dogma. He expressed his views in *Kultura i polityka* (Culture and politics; 1958); *Perspektywy literatury XX wieku* (Prospects of twentieth-century literature; 1960); *Zagadnienia stylu* (Issues of style; 1965), and other works. From April 1956 to June 1959 Żółkiewski served as minister of higher education. From March 1957 to June 1958 he was editor-in-chief of *Polityka* and then editor-in-chief of *Nowa Kultura* and *Kultura i Społeczeństwo*. From 1960 to 1968 he was secretary of the first Department of Social Sciences of the Polish Academy of Sciences. In March 1968 Żółkiewski stood up in the defense of persecuted students at Warsaw University; as a result, he was dismissed from his position in the Polish Academy of Sciences. Attacked by the propaganda apparatus, he was expelled from the CC at the Thirteenth Plenum of the CC in November 1968. He then retired from politics. However, he continued writing and published scholarly treatises, including *Kultura literacka 1918–1932* (Literary culture 1918–1932; 1973); *Kultura, socjologia, semiotyka literacka* (Literary culture, sociology, and semiotics; 1979); and *Cetno i licho* (Trick or treat; 1983). Żółkiewski trained many cultural researchers and literary critics. (WR)

Sources: Mołdawa; *Nowa encyklopedia powszechna PWN*, vol. 6 (Warsaw, 1996); Jerzy Eisler, *Marzec 1968* (Warsaw, 1991).

ZSEDÉNYI Béla (5 April 1894, Aknasugatag [now Ocna Şugatag, Romania]–8 February 1955, Budapest), Hungarian politician, victim of communism. Zsedényi's father was a mining engineer. Zsedényi attended a state gymnasium in Nagyszeben (now Sibiu, Romania) and then a Protestant gymnasium in Máramarossziget (now Sighetu Marmaţiei, Romania). He studied at a Protestant law academy in Máramarossziget but received a degree from Budapest University. During World War I Zsedényi served on the Italian front. After the collapse of the Austro-Hungarian Empire, he became secretary of the municipality of Komárom (now Komarno, Slovakia), situated on the left bank of the Danube River, but he was interned by the Czechoslovak authorities. In 1924 Zsedényi moved to Hungary. In 1925 he became a lecturer at a Protestant law academy in Miskolc, and in 1928 he passed examinations to become an attorney and a judge. After receiving the postdoctoral degree from the University of Pécs, Zsedényi was appointed a full professor in September 1928. He authored many publications on the theory of law and state law. He served as a member of the synod and as the municipal secretary of the superintendency of the Evangelical Reformed Church. In 1929, as a member of the leadership of the minor Independent Democratic Party, Zsedényi was elected to the Miskolc municipal government on a joint ticket with the Hungarian Social Democratic Party. For a short time he shifted to the right wing, supporting **Gyula Gömbös** and editing the ruling party newspaper, *Felsőmagyarország*, and then he again joined the liberal opposition. In 1939 Zsedényi took over the editorship of *Felsőmagyarországi Reggeli Hírlap*, which was regarded as an opposition periodical. In January 1944 he retired and opened his own law practice in Budapest. During the German occupation in 1944 he was in hiding. On 17 October 1944 the members of the Arrow Cross Party interned him in Szilvásvárad, from where he escaped after a few weeks.

In December 1944 Zsedényi became a member of the Provisional National Assembly in Debrecen. As a result of an agreement among political parties, he was elected president of the Provisional National Assembly on 21 December. From 26 January to 7 December 1945 he also served as president of the assembly's provisional presiding committee, the National Supreme Council. In November 1945 Zsedényi was elected to the National Assembly. In 1947 he co-founded the Hungarian Independence Party, led by **Zoltan Pfeiffer**, which was in opposition to the Communists. In the elections in August 1947, Zsedényi was elected to parliament for the third time. On 20 November 1947, like many of his party colleagues, he was illegally deprived of his parliamentary seat. He then resumed working as an attorney. Arrested on trumped-up charges on 24 May 1950, Zsedényi was sentenced to life imprisonment on 10 November of that year. He died in the main prison in Budapest and was secretly buried. In 1963 his trial was repeated, and he was acquitted, but the Communists failed to inform his family about it. It was not until 6 July 1989 that Zsedényi was officially rehabilitated. After his remains were identified, he was solemnly reburied in December 1990. (JT)

Sources: *Magyar Életrajzi Lexikon*, vol. 3 (Budapest, 1985); *A magyar forradalom és szabadságharc enciklopédiája* (Budapest, 1999).

ZUCKERMAN Yitzhak [also spelled Yitzhak Cukierman], pseudonym "Antek" (1917, Vilnius–17 June 1981, Lohamei Hagetaot, Israel), activist of the Jewish Zionist left in Poland. Born into a family of merchants and craftsmen, Zuckerman graduated from Tarbut Hebrew High School in Vilnius. From his youth he was linked with the Zionist movement of the Dror-Hehalutz, a youth organization of the Jewish Social Democratic Workers' Party–Poale Zion. From 1936 he worked in the Dror head office in Warsaw, and in 1938 he became secretary general of this organization.

From the fall of 1939 Zuckerman organized the underground of the Zionist left in the Warsaw Ghetto, representing an anti-German, anti-British, and pro-Soviet stance. Ideologically close to communism, he was in conflict with the Orthodox Jewish leadership, and to some extent he was also in disagreement with Zionists-Revisionists. Zuckerman was one of the first Jewish leaders to call for armed resistance to the Germans, but his arguments were rejected at a meeting of Zionist underground groups in March 1942. However, during the mass deportations of Jews to extermination camps in the summer of 1942, his views gained support. The Jewish left—mainly the Poale Zion and the Bund—reached an agreement and created the Jewish Fighting Organization (Żydowska Organizacja Bojowa [ŻOB]; also known as the Jewish Defense Organization). Zuckerman became one of the three deputy commanders of the ŻOB leader, **Mordecai Anielewicz**. He was also active in the Jewish National Committee (Żydowski Komitet Narodowy [ŻKN]), which affiliated leftist and Zionist currents. On behalf of the ŻKN, Zuckerman negotiated with various groups of the Polish underground. He also obtained material and training assistance from the Home Army (Armia Krajowa [AK]) and the Communist People's Guard. On his own, Zuckerman also organized

black-market purchases of arms, which he smuggled into the Warsaw Ghetto. He alerted the Polish underground to the situation in the Warsaw Ghetto and appealed for an increase in the supply of weapons for Jewish fighters, for more propaganda, and for increased Allied bombings. Zuckerman's interventions intensified especially during the Warsaw Ghetto Uprising (19 April–16 May 1943). When the fighting began, Zuckerman was outside the ghetto. At the end of the uprising he returned to the ghetto, and then he led seventy-five ŻOB fighters through the sewers to the territory outside the ghetto. With the help of the Communists, Zuckerman managed to get the whole group to the forests near Wyszków. After a short stay with the forest partisans, he returned to Warsaw. He remained in hiding, cooperating with the Polish Żegota (Council for Aid to Jews) and providing rescue services. He also provided documents and funds to the Jews in hiding.

After the Red Army entered Poland and the Communists seized power, Zuckerman continued his activities among the Zionist left. With numerous contacts among the Communists, he managed to organize semi-legal transportation for tens of thousands of Jews from Poland to the West. Some Jewish refugees went to Palestine, where in 1947 Zuckerman arrived as well. He fought in Israel's war for independence and was one of the founders of the Kibbutz Lohamei Hagetoat (Ghetto Fighters). Zuckerman was a prosecution witness in the 1961 trial of Adolf Eichmann in Jerusalem. Zuckerman wrote his memoirs, *A Surplus of Memory: Chronicle of the Warsaw Ghetto Uprising* (1993). (MC)

Sources: *Annual Obituary*, 1981; Zivia Lubetkin, *In the Days of Destruction and Revolt* (Tel Aviv, 1981); Hanna Krall, *Shielding the Flame: Intimate Conversations with Marek Edelman* (New York, 1986); *The Warsaw Ghetto: The 45th Anniversary of the Warsaw Uprising* (Warsaw, 1988); Michael R. Marrus, "Ghetto Fighter: Yitzhak Zuckerman and the Jewish Underground in Warsaw," *American Scholar*, 1995, vol. 64; Marek Jan Chodakiewicz, *Żydzi i Polacy, 1918–1955: Współistnienie, Zagłada, Komunizm* (Warsaw, 2000); Kazik (Simcha Rotem), *Memoirs of a Warsaw Ghetto Fighter: The Past Within Me* (New Haven, 2001).

ŽUJOVIĆ Sreten (24 June 1899, Mala Vrbica, Serbia–1976, Belgrade), Serbian Communist activist. Žujović was a high school student in Belgrade when World War I broke out. He followed the Serbian Army to France, where he became a soldier and fought on the western front. He returned to Belgrade in 1921 and joined the Communist Party of Yugoslavia (CPY) in 1924. He worked in a bank and was active in the trade union movement. Arrested for his illegal Communist activities, Žujović was sentenced to half a year in prison in March 1930. After his release, he went to the Soviet Union, where he attended the Leninist

School of the Comintern. In December 1934, at the Fourth Conference of the CPY, Žujović became a member of its Central Committee (CC). In 1935 he settled in Vienna, where the CPY had its headquarters. In 1936 he became a member of the CPY CC Politburo. In the second half of 1937 the head of the CPY, **Milan Gorkić**, was summoned to Moscow and was soon murdered there. **Josip Broz Tito** became the acting head of the CPY, and Žujović was expelled from its leadership. He returned to Yugoslavia, where, using the pseudonym of "Crni," he became involved in underground work. From 1939 to 1940 he served as a party instructor in Serbia and Macedonia, and at the Fifth Conference of the CPY in October 1940 he again joined its CC. On 4 July 1941, after Germany attacked the Soviet Union, the CPY leadership decided to take up the struggle against Yugoslavia's occupiers. Žujović became commander of the Partisan forces in Serbia. Wounded in November 1941, after recovering, he resumed working at the headquarters of the Partisan movement led by Tito. In November 1942 Žujović became minister of transport in the provisional government headed by Tito. At that time he was also promoted to general.

In March 1945 Žujović became minister of finance in Tito's government. In April 1945 he was a member of the Yugoslav delegation to the founding conference of the United Nations in San Francisco. He was one of the top leaders of the CPY until May 1948, when he called for concessions to Stalin in the latter's conflict with Tito. Stripped of all his positions, Žujović was arrested and spent over two years in prison, although he had not been convicted. He was accused of being a "slanderer," an "enemy of the party and the nation," and even a "henchman of the Ustashe." After making an extensive self-criticism and condemning Stalin and the Cominform in November 1950, he was released. Žujović worked in an economic research institute and in the administration of the daily *Borba* until his retirement. (WR)

Sources: Lazitch; *Enciklopedija Jugoslavije*, vol. 8 (Zagreb, 1971); Adam B. Ulam, *Tito and the Cominform* (Westport, Conn., 1952); Vladimir Dedijer, *The Battle Stalin Lost: Memoirs of Yugoslavia, 1948–1958* (New York, 1970); Stephen Clissold, ed., *Yugoslavia and the Soviet Union, 1939–1973* (London, 1975); Željan E. Šuster, *Historical Dictionary of the Federal Republic of Yugoslavia* (Lanham, Md., 1999).

ŻUKAUSKAS Silvestras (31 December 1860, Poškiečiai-Dovainiškiai, Šiauliai County–26 November 1937, Wilno [Vilnius]), Lithuanian general. Žukauskas began his military career in the tsarist army. After graduating from the Military College in Vilnius (1887), he was stationed in Vilnius and then in Kaunas. He fought in the Russo-Japanese War of 1904–5. At the beginning of World War I he served as the commander of a regiment. He fought in the battle of the Dubysa River and in the regions of Šiauliai, Radviliškis, and Biržai. Žukauskas was awarded the Golden Sword for his bravery in the defense of Šiauliai. In 1915 he was appointed commander of a brigade and promoted to major general. In 1917 he became commander of a division. After the establishment of an independent Lithuanian state, he returned to Vilnius, but because of illness, he did not assume the post of minister of national defense, which he had been promised.

After his recovery, Žukauskas was appointed chief of staff on 26 April 1919 and commander of the Lithuanian Army on 7 May. As commander of the military forces, he led the counteroffensive of May and August 1919 that drove the Red Army out of Lithuania (the action was facilitated by the fact that the Polish Army had previously captured Vilnius). After an unsuccessful coup attempt by the Polish Military Organization in Kaunas on 28–29 August 1919, Žukauskas's position weakened because one of his closest associates was arrested and because Žukauskas himself was accused of pro-Polish sympathies. On 7 October 1919 he resigned as commander and then acted as an observer with General Albert Niessel's mission, which supervised the withdrawal of Pavel Bermondt-Avalov's army from Lithuania. Because of the increasingly low morale and discipline in the Lithuanian military forces, Žukauskas was again appointed commander-in-chief of the army (February 1920), and in a relatively short time he restored order and discipline. As part of the reorganization of the government and the military forces, introduced by a resolution of the Constitutional Assembly, Žukauskas was appointed army inspector on 14 June 1920, and on 6 October 1920 he again became commander of the army. He failed to halt the offensive led by General **Lucjan Żeligowski**, who seized Vilnius. However, Žukauskas succeeded in stabilizing the front on the Musninkų-Širvintos-Giedraičiai-Dubingiai line. On 7 March 1921 he was again appointed commander-in-chief of the army, but in May 1921 he resigned. He again held this post from May 1923 to January 1928, and then he retired. Žukauskas was awarded the Vytautas Cross and numerous foreign medals and decorations. (AG)

Sources: *EL*, vol. 6; Alfred E. Senn, *The Emergence of Modern Lithuania* (New York, 1959); Alfred E. Senn, *The Great Powers, Lithuania, and the Wilna Question 1920–1928* (Leiden, 1966).

ŻUŁAWSKI Zygmunt (31 July 1880, Młynne, near Limanowa–4 September 1949, Kraków), Polish politician. In 1903 Żuławski graduated from the Department of Natural Sciences of the Jagiellonian University in Kraków. In 1895 he established ties with the Socialist movement. While a student, Żuławski was involved in the activities of the Polish Socialist Party (Polska Partia Socjalistyczna [PPS]) in Tarnów and Borysław. He was an activist in the student organizations Zjednoczenie (Union) (1899–1900) and Ruch (Movement) (1901–3). From 1900 to 1919 Żuławski was a member of the leadership of the Polish Socialist Democratic Party of Galicia and Silesia. He was also active in the trade union movement. From 1905 on he served as head of the Provincial Trade Union Secretariat for Galicia and as a member of the Austrian national trade union leadership. In 1908 he became head of the Health Care Fund in Kraków. From 1907 to 1914 he edited *Związkowiec*, a press organ of the National Commission of Trade Unions. During World War I he served in the Austrian Army. In 1918 Żuławski was a member of the Polish Liquidation Commission (Polska Komisja Likwidacyjna), as a representative of which he served as head of Chrzanów County. One of the most prominent trade union activists in the Second Republic of Poland, Żuławski strove to unite the Galician trade unions with trade union organizations from other regions of Poland. A member of the Central Commission of Class Trade Unions, the largest national organization of trade unions, Żuławski served as its secretary general from 1922 to 1939. He was also one of the top leaders of the PPS: a member of the PPS Central Executive Committee from 1920 to 1937 and chairman of the PPS Chief Council from 1937 to 1939. He was a member of the governing body of the International Labor Organization. From 1919 to 1935 Żuławski was an MP in the Assembly on the PPS ticket. In 1926 he opposed **Józef Piłsudski** and later was one of the leading opposition MPs. He was one of the leaders of the so-called Centrolew, a center-left coalition of parties in opposition to the *sanacja* regime.

After the defeat of Poland in September 1939, Żuławski went underground. He served as chairman of the Polish Socialist Party–Freedom-Equality-Independence (PPS–Wolność-Równość-Niepodległość [PPS–WRN]) in Kraków and took part in the work of the Coordinating Political Committee (Polityczny Komitet Porozumiewawczy) there. In June 1945 in Moscow he attended a conference on the establishment of the Provisional Government of National Unity (Tymczasowy Rząd Jedności Narodowej [TRJN]); the conference ended on 21 June, when an agreement was signed on coopting new members into the Presidium of the National Home Council (Krajowa Rada Narodowa [KRN]) and expanding the membership of the Provisional Government by including, among others, **Stanisław Mikołajczyk**. At the end of June 1945, as one

of the leaders of the underground PPS–WRN, Żuławski (together with **Zygmunt Zaremba**) entered into the negotiations on merging his party with the so-called licensed PPS (i.e., permitted by the Communist authorities). As the Polish Workers' Party (Polska Partia Robotnicza [PPR]) and the PPS faction approved by the Communists refused to treat the PPS–WRN on an equal-rights basis, Żuławski (along with other activists) established the Organizational Committee of the Polish Social Democratic Party. As a result of protests by the KRN and threats by the Communists, he agreed that PPS–WRN activists could join the PPS individually, hoping to outnumber opponents in the PPS. In January 1946 Żuławski was coopted into the PPS Chief Council, but in August 1946 he resigned. In January 1947 he was elected to the Legislative Assembly. In parliament, he defended the idea of socialism and condemned the abuse of power by the Communists. He declared his willingness to cooperate with the Soviet Union but on an equal-rights basis. After his speech of 20 June 1947, in which he demanded increased spending on social welfare at the expense of funds for security and the army and sharply criticized the government, Żuławski was not allowed to speak again, and his speech was censored in the stenographic record of the Assembly session. (PK)

Sources: *Kto był kim w Drugiej Rzeczpospolitej* (Warsaw, 1994); Stefan Korboński, *W imieniu Rzeczypospolitej* (Paris, 1954); Stanisław Mikołajczyk, *Gwałt na Polsce* (Warsaw, 1983); Marek Łatyński, *Nie paść na kolana* (Warsaw, 1987); Krystyna Kersten, *Narodziny systemu władzy: Polska 1943–1948* (Poznań, 1990); "My tu żyjemy jak w obozie warownym," *Listy PPS-WRN Warszawa-Londyn 1940–1945* (London, 1992).

ZULFIKARPAŠIĆ Adil-beg (23 December 1921, Foča), Muslim politician from Bosnia. Zulfikarpašić was born into the family of Husein-beg Zulfikarpašić-Čengić, the largest private forest owner in Yugoslavia, whose house was the meeting place of the Muslim elite. Zulfikarpašić became a member of the League of Yugoslav Communist Youth (Savez Komunističke Omladine Jugoslavije [SKOJ]) in 1936 and a member of the Communist Party of Yugoslavia (CPY) in 1939. He finished a school of commerce in Sarajevo and went to university, but in 1941 he discontinued his studies and joined the Partisans, led by **Josip Broz Tito**. He served at the Partisan headquarters in Bosnia. Arrested in 1942 in Sarajevo, Zulfikarpašić was sentenced to death by the Ustasha regime but was pardoned owing to interventions, and his sentence was commuted to twenty years' imprisonment. He escaped from a prison in Zagreb, and by the end of World War II he was a lieutenant colonel. In 1945 Zulfikarpašić was an assistant to the minister of trade of the Republic of Bosnia and Herzegovina, administering property abandoned after the war. Outraged by the persecutions unleashed by the new authorities and by their misuse of funds, he fled to Trieste in February 1946, from where he moved to Austria. He studied political science and law in Graz, Vienna, and Freiburg. After graduating in 1954, he worked as a journalist in Switzerland for an émigré periodical of the Croatian Peasant Party. Following an intervention by the Yugoslav authorities, the police banned him from writing and publishing. Zulfikarpašić began to work for an insurance company. He subsequently founded his own company, Adeks Import-Export, and then another one, Stamaco, which he managed until 1987.

In 1960 in Munich Zulfikarpašić co-founded and then served as chairman of the Liberal Democratic Union of Muslim Bosniaks (Liberalni Demokratski Savez Bošnjaka-Muslimana), which called for cooperation with the Serbs and the Croats in Bosnia. He founded the émigré periodical *Bosanski pogledi* and was its editor-in-chief from 1960 to 1967. He was an activist in the Democratic Alternative (Demokratska Alternativa), a party founded by Yugoslav émigrés in London in 1963 that advocated that Yugoslavia should be maintained as a confederation. In June 1988 Zulfikarpašić established the Bosnian Institute in Zurich, which promoted the culture, literature, language, and history of the Muslims of Bosnia and Herzegovina.

In November 1988 Zulfikarpašić met **Alija Izetbegović** in Zurich. In 1990 he returned to Bosnia, and on 26 May 1990 he became deputy chairman of the (Muslim) Party of Democratic Action (Stranka Demokratske Akcije [SDA]), which he supported financially. Zulfikarpašić was a member of the SDA's liberal wing. He believed that the Muslims in Bosnia and Herzegovina should be referred to as Bosniaks. In September 1990 the liberal wing members left the SDA, and in October Zulfikarpašić became head of the Muslim Bosniak Organization (Muslimanska Bosnjacka Organizacija [MBO]). This split was caused by a conflict with the extreme wing, led by Izetbegović. Zulfikarpašić accused Izetbegović of subjecting the SDA to clerical influence and of dictatorial inclinations and also criticized him for refusing to expel Salem Šabić, the SDA deputy chairman who had collaborated with the Communist secret police. In July 1991 Zulfikarpašić initiated an agreement with the Serbs, the so-called Belgrade Initiative, under the terms of which Bosnia and Herzegovina was to remain part of Yugoslavia. This agreement was never implemented because of opposition by Izetbegović and the SDA. In the elections of 1990 the MBO won two seats in the parliamentary elections. On 24 May 2001 Zulfikarpašić founded and endowed the Bosnian Institute in Sarajevo, which promoted Bosnian culture. Zulfikarpašić's publications include *Zbirka radova* (Collection of speeches;

1971); *Bosanski pogledi* (Bosnian views; 1984); *Bosanski Muslimani* (Bosnian Muslims; 1986), *Povratak u Bosnu* (Return to Bosnia; 1990); and *Članci i intervjui povodom 70-godisnjice* (Articles and interviews on the occasion of my seventieth year; 1991). (JD)

Sources: Ivo Banac, ed., *The Bosniak: Adil Zuflikarpašić in Dialogue with Milovan Džilas and Nadežda Gace* (London, 1996); Ante Čuvalo, *Historical Dictionary of Bosnia and Herzegovina* (Lanham, Md., 1997); Bugajski.

ŽUPANČIČ Oton (23 January 1878, Weinitz [now Vinica, Slovenia]–11 June 1949, Ljubljana), Slovene poet. Župančič was born into a middle-class family. After graduating from high school in Ljubljana, he studied geography and history in Vienna (1896–1900). In 1899 he published the volume of poems *Čaša opojnosti* (Ecstasy cup), which reveals the influence of the French symbolists and the Viennese modernists. In 1900 he did his military service in Graz and then worked as a teacher. In 1904 he published the volume *Čez plan* (Across the fields). In 1905 he went to France and Germany, where he worked as a tutor. In 1908 he published *Samogovori* (Monologues), which is regarded as one of his best poetry volumes. In 1910 Župančič settled in Ljubljana, where he managed a theater from 1910 to 1912 and subsequently worked in the City Archives. From 1914 to 1917 he edited the literary periodicals *Slovan* and *Ljublanski zvon*. In 1915 he published *Ciciban* and *Sto ugank* (A hundred puzzles), children's books that became very popular with young readers. The year 1919 saw the publication of *Mlada pota* (Young paths), a selection of poems written between 1897 and 1915. In 1920 the poetry volume *V zarje Vidove* (Toward St. Vitus's auroras) appeared. By then regarded as one of the greatest Slovene poets, Župančič became director of the Slovene National Theater the same year. He translated many literary classics, including William Shakespeare and Molière. In 1924 he published *Veronika Deseniška* (Veronica of Desenice), a drama styled on Shakespearean tragedies that stirred up controversy. In 1934 he published *Med ostrnicami* (Among thistles), a series of poems showing the influence of Charles Baudelaire. In 1939 Župančič was elected to the Slovene Academy of Sciences and Arts. In 1943, during World War II, he became a member of the plenum led by the Communist-dominated Yugoslav National Liberation Front. In 1945 he published the volume *Zimzelen pod snegom* (A periwinkle under the snow), which included a call for struggle against the occupier: "Veš, poet, svoj dolg?" (Do you know your duty, poet?). After the war, Župančič became a member of the Slovene National Assembly. In 1948 he was awarded an honorary doctorate from the University of Ljubljana. (AO)

Sources: *Enciklopedija Slovenije,* vol. 15 (Ljubljana, 2001); Marja Boršnik, *Oton Županèiè* (Belgrade, 1962); *Mały słownik pisarzy zachodnio-słowiańskich i południowo-słowiańskich* (Warsaw, 1973); Joza Mahnić, *Oton Županèiè: Ustvarjanje, razvoj, recepcija* (Ljubljana, 1998).

ŻYCIŃSKI Józef (1 September 1948, Stara Wieś, near Piotrków Trybunalski), metropolitan archbishop of Lublin, philosopher, and journalist. Życiński was born in the countryside into a socially mixed family. His father worked on the railways. Życiński studied at a seminary in Kraków (1966–72). He took holy orders in May 1972. He worked as a parish curate and then as an assistant dean, associate dean (1982–85), and dean (1988–91) of the Department of Philosophy of the Pontifical Academy of Theology in Kraków, where he earned a doctoral degree in theology in 1976. In 1978 he earned a Ph.D. in philosophy from the Academy of Catholic Theology in Warsaw. He also studied at the Catholic University in Washington, D.C., and at the Catholic University of Louvain, Belgium. In 1980 Życiński received the postdoctoral degree in the philosophy of science. In 1988 he became a full professor of philosophy at the Pontifical Academy of Theology in Kraków. He also holds the chair of Relations between Science and Faith at the Department of Philosophy of the Catholic University of Lublin. Życiński is a member of numerous learned societies in Poland and abroad, including the Evolutionary and Theoretical Biology Committee of the Polish Academy of Sciences, the European Academy of Sciences and Arts in Salzburg, and the Russian Academy of Natural Sciences in Moscow. He has authored dozens of scholarly works in the field of theology, philosophy, and philosophy of science, including the following: *Wszechświat i filozofia* (The universe and philosophy; 1980; co-authored by Michał Heller); *Język i metoda* (Language and method; 1983); *Teizm i filozofia analityczna* (Theism and analytic philosophy, 2 vols.; 1985–86); *W kręgu nauki i wiary* (Between religion and science; 1989); and *Bóg Abrahama i Whiteheada* (The God of Abraham and Whitehead; 1992). In the 1980s Życiński contributed to periodicals in the uncensored press, including the political quarterly *Krytyka.* His *Pisma z kraju Ubu* (Letters from the land of Ubu; 1988), in which he described a state controlled by the secret police, were published in this quarterly's *Biblioteka* series.

On 29 June 1990 Życiński became bishop ordinary of the diocese of Tarnów, and on 14 June 1997, metropolitan archbishop of Lublin. He is, among other things, a member of the Pontifical Council for Culture and a member of the Vatican Congregation for Catholic Education. He is head of the Polish Episcopate's Council for Lay Apostolate and a member of several councils and commissions of the Polish Episcopate, including the Joint Commission of the Polish Episcopate and Government. He is chairman of the Program Council of the Catholic Information Agency. He has always opposed the formal engagement of clergymen in politics, but at the same time he has advocated that the Church should take a stand on important public issues and also that it should disclose its finances. He has called for an investigation and explanation of the crimes of the Communist regime in Poland. At the beginning of the 1990s he strongly protested attempts to legalize abortion in Poland, but at the same time he was against punishing women who had resorted to abortion. As the bishop of the diocese of Tarnów, Życiński was very active in the Polish-Ukrainian (Lemko) dialogue in the territory of this diocese. He returned the Greek Catholic churches to the Lemko community, and in a pastoral letter he condemned Operation Vistula (through which the Ukrainian population from the territories of southeastern Poland was deported in 1947). Życiński has publicly condemned the immoral practices of people who exercised power. He has also protested the abuse of religion, as well as religious intolerance and xenophobia. As a result, he is often attacked by ultra-conservative groups. Życiński has written many essays and columns that generalize the experiences of system transformation. They have been collected in (among other places) the volumes *Na Zachód od domu niewoli* (West of the house of slavery; 1997); *Ziarno samotności* (The seed of loneliness; 1997); and *Bruderszaft z Kainem* (Making friends with Cain; 1998). (PK)

Sources: *Nowa encyklopedia powszechna PWN,* vol. 6 (Warsaw, 1996); Ks. Wiesław Niewęgłowski, *Nowe Przymierze Kościoła i środowisk twórczych* (Warsaw, 1997); Grzegorz Polak, *Kto jest kim w Kościele?* (Warsaw, 1999); Jarosław Gowin, *Kościół w czasach wolności 1989–1999* (Kraków, 1999).

ZYGELBOIM Shmul Mordechai, pseudonym "Artur" (1895–11 May 1943, London), Jewish Socialist activist in Poland. Zygelboim came from a poor urban family and was one of thirteen siblings. He studied in a heder and on his own. He was a glover by trade. Before World War I Zygelboim joined the Universal Jewish Workers' Association Bund and was active in the Russian partition and later in Poland. From the mid-1920s Zygelboim wrote political articles, and in the 1930s he belonged to the Central Committee of the Bund. In September 1939 he fought in the defense of Warsaw, co-organizing workers' battalions, including about six thousand Jewish soldiers, many Bund members. After the capture of Warsaw by the Germans, Zygelboim was arrested on 28 September and held hostage, along with other well-known politicians—for example, **Stefan Starzyński**. After his release, he co-organized underground Bund activities. In December 1939 Zygelboim left the General Government on a false passport. Arrested at the Belgian border, he was released thanks to the intervention of the head of the Belgian Socialist Party, Henri Spaak, and continued his trip to Brussels, where he informed the international community about the Nazi persecution of Jews in occupied Poland.

After the capitulation of Belgium in 1940 Zygelboim left for France and in September 1940 for the United States. In New York he worked as a glover and continued his Bund activities. The party recommended him to the National Council of Poland in London. Thus in March 1942 Zygelboim moved to England. He studied secret reports from Poland and was one of the few who realized the mass nature of the massacre of Jews. He warned the West and attempted to influence the Allied governments to counteract the massacre, but in vain. Zygelboim also criticized the Polish government-in-exile for its ineffectiveness in helping the Jews. The Holocaust affected Zygelboim personally because the Germans killed his first wife and son. His second wife and other children also perished. Psychically broken by the news from Poland and by the hopelessness of the situation, after the failure of the Warsaw Ghetto Uprising Zygelboim committed suicide. In a farewell letter he explained the move as a protest against the indifference of the Western governments to the tragedy of the Jews and the insufficient response of the Polish government-in-exile. (MC)

Sources: Zofia Lewin and Władysław Bartoszewski, eds., *Righteous among Nations* (London, 1969); Aviva Ravel, *Faithful unto Death: The Story of Arthur Zygielbaum* (Montreal, 1980); *Encyclopedia of the Holocaust*, vol. 4 (New York, 1990); Dariusz Stola, *Nadzieja i Zagłada: Ignacy Schwarzbart—żydowski przedstawiciel w Radzie Narodowej RP (1940–1945)* (Warsaw, 1995); Rudi Assuntino and Włodek Goldkorn, *Strażnik: Marek Edelman opowiada* (Kraków, 1999); www.davka.org/what/shoa/lasttestame ntszmulzygelboj.html.

ŻYMANTIENĖ Julija [née Beniuszewicz], pseudonym "Žemaitė" (31 May 1845, Bukantė, Samogitia region–7 December 1921, Marijampolė), Lithuanian writer. Born into a Polish lesser gentry family in Samogitia, Žymantienė was educated at home. Against the wishes of her parents, she maintained lively contacts with Lithuanian youth and with the language of the local peasants. In 1865 she married Laurynas Žymantas, a participant in the 1863 uprising, and lived with him in poverty, isolated from the Polish community. The financial situation of the couple and their children improved slightly after they had moved to the village of Ušnėnai, where Žymantienė met Povilas Višinskis. Under the influence of Višinskis, she became interested in Lithu-

anian literature and wrote her first stories in Lithuanian, including "Rudens vakaras" (Autumn winter; 1895) and "Piršlybos" (Matchmakers; 1895). Višinskis suggested that she should use the pseudonym "Žemaitė" (Samogitian woman). Žymantienė's works became classics of Lithuanian realist literature, conspicuously depicting the backwardness and ignorance of the peasants and the injustices of rural life. In her prose, Žymantienė presented the Polish nobility as an alien group that demoralized the peasants. She also described the difficult social situation of women. In 1912 Žymantienė moved to Vilnius, where she contributed to *Lietuvos Žinios* from 1913 to 1915. After Germany occupied Lithuania, she went to Petrograd and in 1916 to the United States, where she raised funds for Lithuanian war victims. In 1917 she joined the Social Democratic Party. Despite her socially radical and anti-clerical views, Žymantienė opposed Bolshevism. "Marti" (Daughter-in-law) is the best known of her stories. Shortly before her death, Žymantienė returned to Lithuania. A four-volume edition of her stories was published in 1924–31. (WR)

Sources: *EL*, vol. 6; Saulius Sužiedelis, *Historical Dictionary of Lithuania* (Lanham, Md., 1997); Julius Būtenas, *Žemaitė* (Kaunas, 1938).

ŻYMIERSKI Michał [originally Łyżwiński], pseudonym "Rola" (4 September 1890, Kraków–15 October 1989, Warsaw), Polish general. After graduating from high school, Żymierski began to study law at the Jagiellonian University in Kraków in 1910. He then joined a secret organization called Armia Polska (Polish Army) and did one year of military service in Tyrol. During World War I Żymierski served in the Polish Legions as commander of a battalion and later as commander of an infantry regiment. At that time he was regarded as one of the more courageous officers, and in 1915 he briefly headed the secret Polish Military Organization (Polska Organizacja Wojskowa [POW]). In November 1918 he joined the Polish Army. During the Polish-Soviet war Żymierski served as commander of a brigade and then commander of the Second Infantry Division. From 1921 to 1923 he studied at the Ecole Supérieure de Guerre (War College) in Paris and underwent training in the French General Staff. Promoted to general in 1924, Żymierski became deputy chief of the army administration for weaponry in the Ministry of Military Affairs. During the coup of May 1926 he supported the government. After the coup, he was accused of accepting a bribe for buying gas masks from a French supplier, and he was sentenced to several years in prison. In 1931 Żymierski went to France, where he began working with the Communist movement and, in 1932, with the Soviet intelligence services. Records exist of his earnings from that period. Records have been found that show that he was paid by the soviets for information on Polish officers. In 1938 he returned to Poland and unsuccessfully tried to return to military service.

During the Nazi occupation Żymierski maintained contacts with a Communist group called Hammer and Sickle. In August 1943 he became military adviser to the People's Guard (Gwardia Ludowa [GL]). He took part in the inaugural session of the National Home Council (Krajowa Rada Narodowa [KRN]) on New Year's Eve of 1943–44, and then he was appointed commander-in-chief of the People's Army (Armia Ludowa). As a prewar general, Żymierski was politically attractive to the Communists, but he did not enjoy the trust of the leaders of the Polish Workers' Party (Polska Partia Robotnicza [PPR]). Promoted to lieutenant general in July 1944, Żymierski was a member of a KRN delegation to negotiations held in Moscow with the Soviet government and the Soviet-controlled Union of Polish Patriots (Związek Patriotów Polskich [ZPP]). Żymierski was appointed head of the national defense department of the Polish Committee of National Liberation (Polski Komitet Wyzwolenia Narodowego [PKWN]) and commander-in-chief of the new Polish Army. During the Warsaw Uprising he declared that he would move on the capital and, after liberating it, punish those who had started the uprising. Appointed minister of defense in the provisional government, Żymierski held this post in the Provisional Government of National Unity (Tymczasowy Rząd Jedności Narodowej [TRJN]; June 1945–February 1947) and in the government headed by **Józef Cyrankiewicz**. On 3 May 1945, by a decision of the KRN, he was made marshal of Poland.

A secret member of the PPR, Żymierski was a puppet in the hands of the Communists and of Soviet advisers and officers, after the end of the war as well. His presence gave credibility to the Communist authorities, and during his numerous inspections of military units, he confirmed soldiers' beliefs that they were serving Poland. After the end of World War II, he was awarded the Order of Victory by the Soviet Union and the Legion of Merit by the United States. As minister of defense, Żymierski complied with all the orders of the PPR and (after December 1948) the Polish United Workers' Party (Polska Zjednoczona Partia Robotnicza [PUWP]). For example, he endorsed the persecution of the Polish pro-independence underground, tolerated the criminal activities of the Main Information Board, and approved almost all death sentences against prewar officers of the Polish Army. Although he loyally followed the directives of the Communists and the Kremlin, at the end of the 1940s Żymierski was no longer needed. On 6 November 1949 he was dismissed "on his own request" to make place for Soviet marshal **Konstantin Rokossovsky**, who became minister of defense. Żymierski was still a member of the Council of State, but after the arrest of **Władysław Gomułka**'s associates, including **Marian Spychalski**, dark clouds began to gather over Żymierski at the beginning of the 1950s. After the intelligence services arrested his brother, Stanisław, in late November 1952, an investigation was also instituted against Żymierski. He was dismissed from the Council of State. On 14 March 1953 he was arrested and accused of collaborating with French intelligence. After more than two years of interrogation, he was released on 19 August 1955. In April 1956 the investigation was discontinued. In December 1956 Żymierski was appointed vice-president of the National Bank of Poland. In December 1967 he retired. Often referred to as the patron of the "People's" Polish Army, Żymierski continued to be invited to celebrations organized by the (Communist) Association of Fighters for Freedom and Democracy (Związek Bojowników o Wolność i Demokrację) in the 1970s and 1980s. At the Ninth Extraordinary PUWP Congress in July 1981 Żymierski became a member of the CC and held this position until July 1986, the oldest member of this body ever. (WR)

Sources: Mołdawa; Jerzy Poksiński, *Tatar-Utnik-Nowicki: Represje wobec oficerów Wojska Polskiego w latach 1949–1956* (Warsaw, 1992); Edward Jan Nalepa, *Oficerowie Armii Radzieckiej w Wojsku Polskim 1943–1968* (Warsaw, 1995); Andrzej Albert [Wojciech Roszkowski], *Najnowsza historia Polski 1914–1993*, vol. 2 (Warsaw, 1995); Stanisław Dronicz, *Wojsko i politycy* (Warsaw, 2001).

List of Entries by Country

Albania

Alia Ramiz
Alizoti Fejzi bey
Arbnori Pjetër
Bajraktari Muharrem
Balluku Beqir
Banushi Ireneo Ilia
Belishova Liri
Berisha Sali Ram
Boletini Isa
Bumçi Luigji
Çarçani Adil
Çoba Ernesto M.
Curri Bajram bej
Dani Riza
Delvina Suleyman Pasha
Deva Xhafer
Evangjeli Pandeli
Ekrem bey Vlorë
Essad Pasha Toptani
Evangjeli Pandeli
Fishta Gjergj
Frashëri Mehdi
Frashëri Midhat
Fundo Llazar
Galica Shote
Gega Liri
Germenji Themistokli
Gjini Frano
Gurakuqi Luigji
Hajdari Azem
Hoxha Enver
Hoxha Nexhmije
Jakova Tuk
Kadare Ismail
Kapo Hysni
Këlcyra Ali bey
Kelmendi Ali
Kemali Ismail Vlorë bey
Kokalari Musine
Koliqi Ernest

Koliqi Mikel
Konitza Faik
Kotta Kostaq Koço
Kruja Mustafa Merlika
Kupi Abas
Leka I
Libohova Myfit bey
Malëshova Sejfulla
Martaneshi Baba Faja
Meidani Rexhep
Meksi Aleksander Gabriel
Migjeni (Gjergji Millosh)
Mitrovica Rexhep bey
Moisiu Spiro
Mother Teresa of Calcutta (Bojaxhiu Anjeze Gonxhe)
Nano Fatos
Negovani Kristo
Noli Fan
Nosi Lef
Paisi Vodica
Pejani Bedri
Pipa Arshi
Polluzha Shaban
Prennushi Vinçenc
Prishtina Hasan bey
Rustemi Avni
Shehu Mehmet
Shllaku Bernardin
Sinishta Gjon
Spahiu Bedri
Spiru Nako
Tashko Koço
Thaçi Gasper
Thaçi Hashim
Topulli Çerçiz
Volaj Gjergji
Wied Wilhelm von
Xoxe Koçi
Zog I (Ahmed Zogu)

Belarus

Abetsedarsky Laurentsi
Abramchik Mikalay
Abrantowicz Fabian
Adamovich Ales
Adamovich Anton
Adamovich Yazep
Akinchits Fabiyan
Aksyonau Aleksandr
Aleksiyevich Svyatlana
Alsheuski Anatol
Antanovich Ivan
Antonchik Siarhey
Arekhva Mikalay
Arlou Uladzimir
Arsenneva Natalya
Astrouski Radaslau
Bahdankevich Stanislau
Bahdanovich Maxim
Balitsky Anton
Baradulin Ryhor
Biadula Zmitrok
Bieniashevich Uladzimir
Bulak-Balakhovich Stanislau
Bykau Vasil
Cherviakou Alyaksandr
Chyhir Mikhail
Dounar-Zapolski Mitrafan
Dvarchanin Ihnat
Dzemyantsiey Mikalay
Dziamidau Mikalay
Hadleuski Vintsuk
Halubok Uladzimir
Hanchar Viktar
Haretski Maksim
Haretski Radzim
Harun Ales (Aleksandar Prushynski)
Haurylik Yazep
Heniush Larysa
Hryb Miechyslau
Ihnatouski Usevalad
Ivanouski Vatslau
Janowicz Sokrat

Karatkevich Uladzimir
Karpenka Henadz
Kazlouski Pavel
Kebich Vyacheslau
Khadyka Yuriy
Kolas Yakub (Kanstantsin Mitskevich)
Krecheuski Pyotr
Kukabaka Mihas
Kupala Yanka (Ivan Lutsevich)
Kushal Frantsishak
Lastouski Vaclau
Losik Yazep
Lukashenka Alyaksandr
Lutskevich Anton
Lutskevich Ivan
Masherau Pyotr
Matskevich Uladzimir
Mazurau Kiryl
Nekrashevich Stsiapan
Paznyak Zianon
Ponomarenko Panteleymon
Rak-Mihailouski Shyman
Shantyr Fabiyan
Sharetsky Syamyon
Shushkevich Stanislav
Smolich Arkadź
Stankiewicz Adam
Świątek Kazimierz
Tarashkievich Branislau
Tkachou Mikhas
Trusau Aleh
Tsvikevich Aleksandr
Ulasau Aleksandr
Ulashchyk Mikola
Valoshyn Pavel
Varonka Yazep
Yermachenka Ivan
Yermalovich Mikalai
Yezavitau Kanstantsin
Zakharka Vasil
Zhylunovich Zhmitser (Tsishka Gartny)

Bulgaria

Aleksandrov Todor
Atanasov Georgi
Atanasov Nedylko
Bagrianov Ivan
Balabanov Aleksandur
Beron Petyr
Berov Luben
Blagoyev Dimiter
Boboshevski Tsvetko
Boris III
Bosilkov Evgeni
Bozhilov Dobri
Bumbarov Boris
Burov Atanas
Chervenkov Vulko
Cheshmedzhiev Grigor
Damianov Georgi
Danev Stoyan
Daskalov Rayko
Delchev Georgi Nikolov
Dertliev Petyr
Dimitriev Radko
Dimitrov Filip
Dimitrov Georgi ("Gemeto")
Dimitrov Georgi (Mikhailov)
Dimitrova Blaga
Dogan Ahmed
Draganov Pyrvan
Dragoycheva Tsola
Drenchev Milan
Dynov Petur
Dzhurov Dobri
Fadenchecht Yosif
Ferdinand I
Filipov Georgi (Grisha)
Filov Bogdan
Gabrovski Petar
Ganev Dimitur
Ganev Stoyan
Ganev Venelin
Ganovski Sava
Georgiev Kimon
Geshov Ivan
Gichev Dimitur
Girginov Aleksandur
Gruev Damian

Hadzhiyski Ivan
Ivanov Tsveti
Kabakchiev Khristo
Kalfov Khristo
Karavelov Petko
Kazasov Dimo
Kioseivanov Georgi
Kiril (Prince of Preslav)
Kiryl (Konstantin Konstantinov)
Kolarov Vasil
Konstantinova Elka
Kostov Ivan
Kostov Traycho
Kosturkov Stoyan
Kozovski Ferdinand
Lilov Aleksandur
Ludzhev Dimitur
Lukanov Andrey
Lukanov Karlo
Lukov Khristo
Lulchev Kosta
Lyapchev Andrei
Madzharov Mikhail
Malinov Aleksandur
Markov Georgi
Mihailov Ivan (Vanćo)
Mikhalchev Dimitur
Mikhov Nikola
Minev Iliya
Misirkov Krste
Mladenov Petur
Moser Anastasya
Moshanov Stoycho
Muraviev Konstantin
Mushanov Nikola
Neychev Mincho
Neykov Dimitur
Obbov Aleksandur
Pastukhov Kristio
Pavlov Asen
Pavlov Todor
Peshev Dimitur
Petkov Dimitur
Petkov Nikola
Petkov Petko
Pirinski Georgi

Popov Blagoy
Popov Dimitur
Prodev Stefan
Protogerov Aleksandur
Purvanov Georgi
Radev Simeon
Radoslavov Vasil
Rusev Rusi
Sakuzov Yanko
Sandanski Yane
Sarafov Boris
Savov Dimitur
Savov Stefan
Semerdzhiev Atanas
Sendov Blagovest
Shishmanov Dimitur
Shishmanov Ivan
Simeon II
Slaveykov Pencho
Slavov Atanas
Stamboliyski Aleksandur
Stanchev Kiril
Staynov Petko
Stefan (Stoyan Popgeorgiev)
Stoichkov Grigor
Stoyanov Khristo
Stoyanov Petko

Stoyanov Petur
Subev Khristofor
Tanchev Petur
Teodorov Teodor
Todorov Stanko
Tomov Aleksandur
Toshev Andrey
Traykov Georgi
Trenchev Konstantin
Tsankov Aleksandur
Tsankov Georgi
Vaptsarov Nikola
Vasilyev Yordan
Vazov Ivan
Velchev Damian
Videnov Zhan
Vulkov Ivan
Yavorov Peyo
Yordanov Aleksandur
Yosif I (Lazar Yovchev)
Yugov Anton
Zhechev Toncho
Zhekov Nikola
Zhelev Zhelyu
Zhivkov Todor
Zhivkova Ludmila

Czech and Slovak

Adamec Ladislav
Bacilek Karel
Barák Rudolf
Bat'a Tomáš
Battěk Rudolf
Bechyně Rudolf
Beneš Edvard
Beran Josef
Beran Rudolf
Bienert Richard
Bil'ak Vasil
Blaho Pavel
Březina Otokar
Budaj Ján
Bugár Béla
Buzalka Michal
Čalfa Marián
Čapek Karel
Čarnogurský Ján
Čarnogurský Pavol
Čatloš Ferdinand
Čepička Alexej
Černík Oldřich
Černý Jan
Černý Václav
Chňoupek Bohuslav
Chvalkovský František
Chytilová Věra
Čič Milan
Clementis Vladimir
Colotka Peter
Csáky Pal
Czernin Ottokar
David Josef
Dérér Ivan
Dienstbier Jiří
Dlouhý Vladimír
Dobrovský Luboš
Dolanský Jaromír
Drtina Prokop
Dubček Alexander
Dula Matúš
Duray Miklós
Ďurčanský Ferdinand
Dzurinda Mikulaš
Eliaš Alois
Engliš Karel
Erban Evžen

Feierabend Ladislav
Fierlinger Zdenek
Forman Miloš
Gajda Radola (Rudolf Geidl)
Gál Fedor
Gašparovič Ivan
Geminder Bedřich
Gojdič Pavel
Golian Ján
Gottwald Klement
Habrman Gustáv
Hácha Emil
Hájek Jiří
Hampl Antonín
Hašek Jaroslav
Havel Václav
Havelka Jiři
Hendrych Jiří
Henlein Konrad
Heyrovský Jaroslav
Hlinka Andrej
Hodža Milan
Hopko Wasyl
Horakova Milada
Hrabal Bohumil
Hronský Jozef (Cíger)
Hrozný Bedřich
Hurban Vajanský Svetozár
Husák Gustav
Hviezdoslav Pavol (Országh)
Indra Alois
Ingr Jan Sergej
Ivanka Milan
Jakeš Miloš
Jakubisko Juraj
Janáček Leoš
Janoušek Karel
Jehlička František
Jičinský Zdeněk
Juriga Ferdinand
Kafka Franz
Kalvoda Jan
Karmasin Franz
Karvaš Imrich
Kašpar Karel
Kavan Jan
Klaus Václav
Klofač Václav

Trochta Štěpán
Tuka Vojtech (Béla)
Tusar Vlastimil
Udržal František
Uhde Milan
Urbánek Karel
Ursíny Ján
Vaculík Ludvík
Valeš Václav
Viest Rudolf

Vlk Miloslav
Vojtaššák Ján
Weiss Peter
Zahradníček Jan
Zápotocký Antonín
Žarnov Andrej
Zeman Miloš
Zenkl Petr
Zieleniec Josef

Estonia

Akel Fredrich Karl
Allik Hendrik
Alliksaar Artur
Andresen Nigol
Anvelt Jaan
Birk Aadu
Eenpalu Kaarel
Ilves Toomas Hendrik
Jaakson Ernst
Jaakson Jüri
Jakobson August
Käbin Johannes
Kallas Siim
Kapliński Jaan
Karotamm Nikolai
Kelam Tunne
Kiivit Jaan
Kingisepp Viktor
Kitzberg August
Klauson Valter
Konik Konstantin
Kõpp Johan
Kross Jaan
Kruus Hans
Kukk Juhan
Kukk Jüri
Kuperjanov Julius
Laar Mart
Laidoner Johan
Larka Andres
Lauristin Johannes
Lauristin Marju
Mäe Hjalmar
Martna Mikhel
Meri Lennart
Müürisepp Aleksei
Niklus Mart-Olav

Pähn August
Pärt Arvo
Päts Konstantin
Piip Ants
Pitka Johan
Põdder Ernst
Poska Jaan
Pusta Kaarel Robert
Rahamägi Hugo
Rei August
Rõuk Theodor
Rüütel Arnold
Säre Karl
Saul Bruno
Savisaar Edgar
Selter Karl
Sirk Artur
Soots Jaan
Strandmann Otto
Tammsaare Anton H.
Tarand Andres
Tarto Enn
Teemant Jaan
Tief Otto
Tõnisson Aleksander
Tõnisson Jaan
Toome Indrek
Uluots Jüri
Under Marie
Vähi Tiit
Vaino Karl
Väljas Vaino
Vares Johannes
Veimer Arnold
Vilde Eduard
Vilms Jüri

Hungary

Áchim András
Aczél György
Ady Endre
Alapy Gyula
Andrássy Gyula, Jr.
Angyal István
Antall József, Jr.
Antall József, Sr.
Apor Vilmos
Apponyi Albert
Apró Antal (Klein)
Babits Mihály
Bajcsy-Zsilinszky Endre
Balogh István
Bánffy Dezső
Barankovics István
Bárdossy László
Bartók Béla
Bata István
Benke Valéria
Berecz János
Bethlen István
Bibó István
Biszku Béla
Bőhm Vilmos
Brusznyai Árpád
Csernoch János
Csoóri Sándor
Csurka István
Czapik Gyula
Czinege Lajos
Darányi Kálmán
Darvas József
Demény Pál
Déry Tibor
Dinnyés Lajos
Dobi István
Donáth Ferenc
Dudás József
Eckhardt Tibor
Erdei Ferenc
Esterházy János
Faludy György
Farkas Mihály
Fazekas György
Fejérváry Géza

Fock Jenő
Friedrich István
Gaál Gaszton
Garami Ernő
Garbai Sándor
Gáspár Sándor
Gerő Ernő
Gimes Miklós
Gömbös Gyula
Göncz Árpád
Grősz József
Grósz Károly
Hamvas Béla
Haraszti Sándor
Háy Gyula
Hegedüs András
Herczeg Ferenc
Hóman Bálint
Horn Gyula
Horthy Miklós
Horváth Márton
Huszár Károly (Schorn)
Ignotus Pál
Illyés Gyula
Imrédy Béla
Iván-Kovács László
Jancsó Miklós
Jánosi Ferenc
Jaross Andor
Jászi Oszkár
József Attila
Kádár János
Kállai Gyula
Kállay Miklós
Károlyi Gyula
Károlyi Mihály
Kassák Lajos
Keresztes-Fischer Ferenc
Kertész Imre
Kéthly Anna
Khuen-Héderváry Károlyi
Király Béla
Kis János
Kiss János
Klebelsberg Kunó
Kodály Zoltán

Konrád György
Kopácsi Sándor
Kornai János
Korvin Otto
Kós Károly
Kosztolányi Dezső
Kovács Béla
Kovács Imre
Kővágó József
Krassó György
Kun Béla
Landler Jenő
Lázár György
Lékai László
Losonczy Géza
Lukács György
Mádl Ferenc
Makovecz Imre
Maléter Pál
Mansfeld Péter
Márai Sándor
Marosán György
Márton Áron
Medgyessy Péter
Mező Imre
Miklós Dálnoki Béla
Mindszenty József
Molnár Ferenc
Móricz Zsigmond
Münnich Ferenc
Nagy Ferenc
Nagy Imre
Németh László
Németh Miklós
Nickelsburg László
Nyers Rezső
Obersovszky Gyula
Orbán Viktor
Ordass Lajos
Örkény István
Ottlik Géza
Pálffy György
Pálinkás Antal (Pallavicini)
Pártay Tivadar
Paskai László
Pétér Gábor
Petri György
Peyer Károly
Pfeiffer Zoltán
Pilinszky János

Piros László
Pogányi József
Pongrátz Gergely
Pozsgay Imre
Prohászka Ottokár
Püski Sándor
Radnóti Miklós
Rajk László
Rákosi Mátyás
Ravasz László
Revai József
Ries István
Rónai Sándor
Rubik Ernő
Serédi Jusztinián
Slachta Margit
Sólyom László
Soros George (György)
Sulyok Dezső
Sütő András
Szabó Dezső
Szabó István Nagyatádi
Szabó János
Szakasits Árpád
Szálasi Ferenc
Szamuely Tibor
Szántó Zoltán
Szász Béla
Szekfű Gyula
Széll Kálmán
Szent-Györgyi Albert
Szigethy Attila
Szilágyi József
Szőcs Géza
Sztójay Döme
Tamási Áron
Tánczos Gábor
Teleki Pál
Tildy Zoltán
Tisza István
Tőkés László
Tóth Ilona
Varga Béla
Vas Zoltán
Vásárhelyi Miklós
Veres Péter
Wekerle Sándor
Weöres Sándor
Zöld Sándor
Zsedényi Béla

Latvia

Aspāzija (Elza Rozenberga Pliekšāne)
Astra Gunārs
Balodis Janis
Bangerskis Rūdolfs
Barons Krišjānis
Belševica Vizma
Berķis Krišjānis
Berklavs Eduārds
Bērziņš Alfreds
Bērziņš Jānis
Bīlmanis Alfreds
Birkavs Valdis
Blaumanis Rūdolfs
Bļodnieks Ādolfs
Briedis Fridrihs
Čakste Jānis
Celmiņš Gustavs Adolfs
Celmiņš Hugo
Dankers Oskars
Eglītis Andrejs
Ēķis Ludvigs
Feldmanis Jūlijs
Godmanis Ivars
Goppers Karlis
Gorbunovs Anatolijs
Grīnbergs Teodors
Grīns Aleksandrs Jēkabs
Kalnbērzinš Jānis
Kalniņš Bruno
Kalniņš Pauls
Ķeniņš Atis
Kirchenšteins Augusts
Kruminš Janis
Kviesis Alberts
Lācis Mārtiņš

Lacis Vilis
Latkovskis Vikentijs
Māsēns Vilis
Medenis Janis
Meierovics Sigfrids
Munters Vilhelms
Niedra Andrievs
Pauļuks Jānis
Peive Jānis
Pelše Arvīds
Peterss Jēkabs (Jakov)
Pugo Boriss
Pujāts Jānis
Radziņš Pēteris Voldemārs
Rainis (Jānis Pliekšāne)
Rancāns Jāzeps
Rode Gunārs
Rubiks Alfreds
Šķēle Andris
Skujenieks Margers
Spekke Arnolds
Springovics Antonijs
Stučka Pēteris
Švābe Arveds
Ulmanis Guntis
Ulmanis Kārlis
Vācietis Jukums
Vaivods Julijans
Valters Miķelis
Vanags Jānis
Vike-Freiberga Vaira
Voss Augusts
Zariņš Kārlis
Zemgals Gustavs

Lithuania

Adamkus Valdas
Aleksa Jonas
Aleksa-Angarietis Zigmas
Ambrazevičius-Brazaitis Juozas
Bačkis Audrys
Barkauskas Antanas
Basanavičius Jonas
Bielinis Jurgis
Biržiška Mykolas
Bistras Leonas
Bizauskas Kazimieras
Borisevičius Vincentas
Brazauskas Algirdas Mykolas
Černius Jonas
Čiurlionis Mikolajus
Galvanauskas Ernestas
Garmus Antanas
Gedvilas Mečislovas
Gira Liudas
Grinius Kazys
Griškevičius Petras
Guzevičius-Gudaitis Aleksandras
Jablonskis Jonas
Kairys Steponas
Kalanta Romas
Kapsukas-Mickevičius Vincas
Karevičius Pranciskus
Kreve-Mickevičius Vincas
Krupavičius Mykolas
Kubiliūnas Petras
Kubilius Andrius
Landsbergis Vytautas
Leonas Petras
Lozoraitis Stasys
Lukša Juozas
Maironis-Mačiulis Jonas
Matulaitis-Matulevičius Jurgis
Matulionis Teofilis
Merkys Antanas
Mironas Vladas
Paksas Rolandas
Paleckis Justas

Pečiulonis Motiejus
Pečkauskaitė Marija
Petkus Viktoras
Plechavičius Povilas
Poltarokas Kazimieras
Prunskiene Kazimiera
Putna Vitovt
Putvinskis Vladas
Ramanauskas Adolfas (Vanagas)
Ramanauskas Pranciskus
Raštikis Stasys
Reinys Mečislovas
Sadūnaitė Nijolė
Šalkauskis Stasys
Sidzikauskas Vaclovas
Škirpa Kazys
Skučas Kazys
Skvireckas Juozapas
Sladkevičius Vincentas
Sleževičius Adolfas
Sleževičius Mykolas
Šliupas Jonas
Smetona Antanas
Sniečkus Antanas
Steponavičius Julijonas
Stulginskis Aleksandras
Svarinskas Alfonsas
Tamkevičius Sigitas
Tamošaitis Antanas
Tūbelis Juozas
Tumas-Vaižgantas Juozas
Urbšys Juozas
Vagnorius Gediminas
Venclova Tomaš
Višinskis Povilas
Vitkauskas Vincas
Voldemaras Augustinas
Vydūnas Vilius
Yčas Martynas
Žemaitis Jonas
Žukauskas Silvestras
Žymantienė Julija (Žemaitė)

Poland

Estreicher Stanisław
Falter Alfred
Felczak Zygmunt
Fieldorf Emil August
Finder Paweł
Fiszbach Tadeusz
Frasyniuk Władysław
Gałczyński Konstantin Ildefons
Gawlina Józef
Geremek Bronisław
Giedroyć Jerzy
Gierek Edward
Giertych Jędrzej
Gieysztor Aleksander
Głąbiński Stanisław
Glemp Józef
Gliwic Hipolit
Gocłowski Tadeusz
Gombrowicz Witold
Gomułka Władysław
Górecki Henryk Mikołaj
Górecki Roman
Goździk Lechosław
Grabski Stanisław
Grabski Tadeusz
Grabski Władysław
Grażyński Michał
Gronkiewicz-Waltz Hanna
Groszkowski Janusz
Grotowski Jerzy
Grudzień Zdzisław
Grünbaum Icchak
Grydzewski Mieczysław
Grześkowiak Alicja
Gucwa Stanisław
Gwiazda Andrzej
Halecki Oskar
Hall Aleksander
Haller Józef
Haller Stanisław
Herbert Zbigniew
Herling-Grudziński Gustaw
Hlond August
Hołówko Tadeusz
Horwitz-Walecki Maksymilian
Ignar Stefan
Iwaszkiewicz Jarosław
Jabłoński Henryk
Jagielski Mieczysław
Jałbrzykowski Romuald
Jankowski Jan Stanisław

Jaroszewicz Piotr
Jaruzelski Wojciech
Jasienica Paweł (Lech Beynar)
Jasiukowicz Stanisław
Jaszczuk Bolesław
Jaworowski Rajmund
Jaworski Marian
Jędrychowski Stefan
Jędrzejewicz Janusz
Jędrzejewicz Wacław
Jodko-Narkiewicz Witold
John Paul II (Karol Wojtyła)
Józewski Henryk
Jóźwiak Franciszek
Jurczyk Marian
Kaczmarek Czesław
Kaczorowski Ryszard
Kaczyński Jarosław
Kaczyński Lech
Kaczyński Zygmunt
Kajka Michał
Kąkol Kazimierz
Kakowski Aleksander
Kalecki Michał
Kamiński Aleksander
Kania Stanisław
Kantor Tadeusz
Kapuściński Ryszard
Karaszewicz-Tokarzewski Michał
Karpiński Stanisław
Karski Jan
Kasprzycki Tadeusz
Kępa Józef
Kiernik Władysław
Kieślowski Krzysztof
Kilar Wojciech
Kiniorski Marian
Kisielewski Stefan
Kiszczak Czesław
Kleeberg Franciszek
Klepacz Michał
Kliszko Zenon
Koc Adam
Kociołek Stanisław
Kołakowski Leszek
Kolbe Maksymilian Maria
Kołodziejski Henryk
Kominek Bolesław
Komorowski Tadeusz
Kopański Stanisław
Korboński Stefan

Korczak Janusz
Korfanty Wojciech
Korniłowicz Władysław
Kościałkowski-Zyndram Marian
Koszutska Maria
Kot Stanisław
Kotański Marek
Kowalczyk Stanisław
Kowalska Mary Faustyna
Kowalski Władysław
Kozal Michał
Kozicki Stanisław
Kozłowski Leon
Kruczek Władysław
Krzaklewski Marian
Krzyżanowski Adam
Krzyżanowski Aleksander
Kubina Teodor Filip
Kucharzewski Jan
Kukiel Marian
Kukliński Ryszard
Kuroń Jacek
Kutrzeba Stanisław
Kutrzeba Tadeusz
Kwapiński Jan
Kwasiborski Józef
Kwaśniewski Aleksander
Kwiatkowski Eugeniusz
Lampe Alfred
Lange Oskar
Lechowicz Włodzimierz
Lednicki Aleksander
Lednicki Wacław
Lem Stanisław
Leszczyński-Leński Julian
Liberman Herman
Limanowski Bolesław
Lipiński Edward
Lipiński Wacław
Lipski Jan Józef
Lipski Józef
Loga-Sowiński Ignacy
Łubieński Konstanty
Lubomirski Zdzisław
Łukaszewicz Jerzy
Lutosławski Kazimierz
Lutosławski Wincenty
Lutosławski Witold
Luxemburg Rosa
Macierewicz Antoni
Mackiewicz Józef

Mackiewicz Stanisław
Maczek Stanisław
Makowski Wacław
Malinowski Bronisław
Malinowski Roman
Marchlewski Julian
Matuszewski Ignacy
Matuszewski Stefan
Matwin Władysław
Mazowiecki Tadeusz
Mazur Franciszek
Messner Zbigniew
Micewski Andrzej
Michnik Adam
Miedziński Bogusław
Mieroszewski Juliusz
Mierzwa Stanisław
Mikołajczyk Stanisław
Milczanowski Andrzej
Milewski Mirosław
Miłkowski Stanisław
Miller Leszek
Miłosz Czesław
Minc Hilary
Młynarski Feliks
Moczar Mieczysław
Moczarski Kazimierz
Moczulski Leszek
Modzelewski Karol
Moraczewski Jędrzej Edward
Morawski Jerzy
Mościcki Ignacy
Mosdorf Jan
Mrożek Sławomir
Najder Zdzisław
Narutowicz Gabriel
Niećko Józef
Niedziałkowski Mieczysław
Niepokólczycki Franciszek
Niesiołowski Stefan
Nowak Zenon
Nowak-Jeziorański Jan
Nowotko Marceli
Ochab Edward
Okulicki Leopold
Olechowski Andrzej
Oleksy Józef
Olszewski Jan
Olszowski Stefan
Olszyna-Wilczyński Józef
Onyszkiewicz Janusz

Orzechowski Marian
Osóbka-Morawski Edward
Ozga-Michalski Józef
Paderewski Ignacy Jan
Pajdak Antoni
Panufnik Andrzej
Patek Stanisław
Pawlak Waldemar
Pełczyński Tadeusz
Penderecki Krzysztof
Perl Feliks
Piasecki Bolesław
Piekałkiewicz Jan
Pieracki Bronisław
Pilecki Witold
Piłsudski Józef
Pińkowski Józef
Piwowarczyk Jan
Płażyński Maciej
Polański Roman
Poniatowski Juliusz
Ponikowski Antoni
Popiel Karol
Popiełuszko Jerzy
Prystor Aleksander
Putek Józef
Pużak Kazimierz
Raczkiewicz Władysław
Raczyński Edward
Radkiewicz Stanisław
Radziwiłł Janusz
Rakowski Mieczysław
Rapacki Adam
Rataj Maciej
Ratajski Cyryl
Reich Leon
Reiff Ryszard
Retinger Józef
Reymont Władysław Stanisław
Rokossovsky Konstantin
Romaszewski Zbigniew
Romer Tadeusz
Ronikier Adam
Ropp Edward
Rowecki Stefan (Grot)
Różański Józef
Rozwadowski Tadeusz
Rubinstein Artur
Rulewski Jan
Rybarski Roman
Rybicki Józef

Rydz-Śmigły Edward
Rzepecki Jan
Rzymowski Wincenty
Sadowski Zdzisław
Sapieha Adam Stefan
Schaff Adam
Schiller Leon
Schulz Bruno
Seyda Marian
Sienkiewicz Henryk
Sierpiński Wacław
Sikorski Władysław
Siła-Nowicki Władysław
Singer Isaac (Icchok) Bashevis
Siwicki Florian
Skirmunt Konstanty
Składkowski Felicjan Sławoj
Skłodowska-Curie Maria
Skrzyński Aleksander
Skubiszewski Krzysztof
Skulbaszewski Antoni
Skulski Leopold
Sławek Walery
Śliwiński Artur
Słonimski Antoni
Smorawiński Mieczysław
Solarz Ignacy
Sosabowski Stanisław
Sosnkowski Kazimierz
Spychalski Marian
Stapiński Jan
Starzyński Stefan
Stecki Jan
Steinhaus Hugo
Stelmachowski Andrzej
Stomma Stanisław
Stroński Stanisław
Strzelecki Ryszard
Strzembosz Adam
Studnicki Władysław
Stypułkowski Zbigniew
Suchocka Hanna
Swianiewicz Stanisław
Świątkowski Henryk
Świerczewski Karol
Świerzyński Józef
Świętochowski Aleksander
Świtalski Kazimierz
Szeptycki Stanisław
Szlachcic Franciszek
Szwalbe Stanisław

Szydlak Jan
Szymanowski Karol
Szymborska Wisława
Szyr Eugeniusz
Tejchma Józef
Thon Ozjasz Jehoshua
Thugutt Stanisław
Tischner Józef
Tokarski Julian
Trąmpczyński Wojciech
Trepper Leopold
Turowicz Jerzy
Tuwim Julian
Urban Jerzy
Wajda Andrzej
Wałęsa Lech
Warski Adolf (originally Warszawski)
Wasilewska Wanda
Wasilewski Leon
Wasiutyński Wojciech
Werblan Andrzej
Widy-Wirski Feliks
Wielowieyski Andrzej
Wierzbicki Andrzej
Witaszewski Kazimierz
Witkiewicz Stanisław (Witkacy)
Witos Wincenty
Wojciechowski Stanisław
Wojtyła Karol. See **John Paul II**
Wrzaszczyk Tadeusz

Wycech Czesław
Wyspiański Stanisław
Wyszyński Stefan
Żabiński Andrzej
Zabłocki Janusz
Zaleski August
Zambrowski Roman
Zamenhof Ludwik
Zamoyski Maurycy
Zanussi Krzysztof
Zaremba Zygmunt
Zaruski Mariusz
Zawadzki Aleksander
Zawadzki Tadeusz (Zośka)
Zawieyski Jerzy
Zdziechowski Jerzy
Zdziechowski Marian
Żeleński Tadeusz (Boy)
Żeligowski Lucjan
Żeromski Stefan
Zieja Jan
Ziembiński Wojciech
Ziętek Jerzy
Znaniecki Florian
Żółkiewski Stefan
Zuckerman Yitzhak
Żuławski Zygmunt
Życiński Józef
Zygelboim Shmul
Żymierski Michał (Rola)

Romania and Moldova

Luca Vasile
Lucaciu Vasile
Luchian Ştefan
Lucinschi Petru
Lupescu Magda Elena
Mădgearu Virgil
Măgureanu Virgil
Maiorescu Titu Liviu
Mănescu Corneliu
Mănescu Manea
Maniu Iuliu
Manoilescu Mihail
Manolescu Nicolae
Marghiloman Alexandru
Maurer Ion
Michael I
Mihalache Ion
Mironescu Gheorghe G.
Mocsony-Stârcea Ion
Moruzov Mihail
Muravschi Valeriu
Năstase Adrian
Nicolschi Alexandru
Noica Constantin
Pacepa Ion Mihai
Pacha Augustin
Pana Gheorghe
Parhon Constantin
Pârvulescu Constantin
Pătrăşcanu Lucreţiu
Pauker Ana
Pauker Marcel
Petrescu Constantin (Titel)
Petrescu-Comnen Nicolae
Pintilie Gheorghe
Pintilie Ilie
Pop de Băseşti Gheorghe
Popescu Dumitru Radu
Popovici Aurel C.
Potopeanu Gheorghe
Prezan Constantin
Puşcariu Sextil
Racoviţă Mihail

Rădăceanu Lothar
Rădescu Nicolae
Radulescu Gheorghe
Ralea Mihail
Rangheţ Iosif
Răşcanu Ioan
Raţiu Ion
Roman Petre
Rusu Alexandru
Sadoveanu Mihail
Sănătescu Constantin
Sangheli Andrei
Sima Horia
Slavici Ioan
Smirnov Igor
Snegur Mircea
Stanculescu Victor Atanasie
Ştefănescu-Delavrancea Barbu
Stere Constantin
Ştirbei Barbu
Stoica Chivu
Stolojan Theodor
Sturdza Dimitrie
Suciu Ioan
Tătărăscu Gheorghe
Teoctist (Toader Arapaşu)
Teodoroiu Ecaterina
Titulescu Nicolae
Todea Alexandru
Tudor Corneliu Vadim
Ursu Gheorghe
Vacaroiu Nicolae
Vaida-Voevod Alexandru
Vaitoianu Artur
Vasile Radu
Verdeţ Ilie
Visoianu Constantin
Vlad Iulian
Voitec Ştefan
Voronin Vladimir
Vuia Traian
Zamfirescu Duiliu

Ukraine

Antonov-Ovseyenko Volodymyr
Bachynskyi Lev
Bachynskyi Yulian
Badzio Yuriy
Bandera Stepan
Bazhan Mykola
Begma Vasyl
Berdnyk Oleksandr
Blakytnyi Vasyl
Bondarchuk Serhiy
Boretsky Mykola
Borovets Taras (Bulba)
Buchko Ivan
Budka Mykyta
Charnetskyi Mykola
Chekhivsky Volodymir
Chornovil Viacheslav
Chubar Vlas
Chykalenko Yevhen
Chyzhevskyi Dmytro
Dionisius (Konstantin Valedinsky)
Dontsov Dmytro
Doroshenko Dmytro
Doroshenko Volodymyr
Dovzhenko Oleksandr
Drach Ivan
Dzhemilev Mustafa
Dzyuba Ivan
Fedak Stepan
Fedorchuk Vitalyi
Fedoryk Yosafat Yosif
Fedun Petro (Petro Poltava)
Feshchenko-Chopivskyi Ivan
Filaret (Mykhailo Denisenko)
Fokin Vitold
Franko Ivan
Goldelman Salomon
Hel Ivan
Hermaize Josyf
Holubovych Vsevolod
Honchar Oles
Horbovyi Volodymir
Horyn Bohdan
Horyn Mykhailo
Hrechukha Mykhailo
Hrinchenko Borys
Hrushevskyi Mykhailo
Hryhorenko Petro
Hryhoriiv Matvii Nykyfor

Huzar Lubomyr
Ivashko Volodymyr
Kaganovich Lazar
Kalchenko Nikifor
Kalynets Ihor
Kandyba Ivan
Kandyba Oleh
Karavanskyi Svyatoslav
Khira Oleksandr
Khmara Stepan
Khomyshyn Hryhoriy
Khrushchev Nikita
Khvylovy Mykola
Kistiakovskyi Bohdan
Kobylyanska Olha
Kondratiuk Yuriy
Konovalets Yevhen
Korniychuk Oleksander
Koshelivets Ivan
Kosior Stanislav
Kostelnyk Havryil
Kostenko Lina
Kotsiubynskyi Mykhailo
Kotsiubynskyi Yuri
Kotsylovskyi Iosyf
Kovalyk Zinoviy
Kovpak Sydor
Kravchuk Leonid
Krilyk Osyp (Vasylkiv)
Krushelnytskyi Anton
Krymskyi Ahatanhel
Krypyakevych Ivan
Kubiyovych Volodymyr
Kuchma Leonid
Kulish Mykola
Kurbas Les
Kyrychenko Oleksiy
Lakota Hryhoriy
Latyshevskyi Ivan
Lazarenko Pavlo
Lebed Dmytro
Lebed Mykola
Levytskyi Borys
Levytskyi Dmytro
Levytskyi Kost
Livytskyi Andriy
Livytskyi Mykola
Lototskyi Oleksandr
Lozynskyi Mykhailo

Lubachivskyi Myroslav
Lukyanenko Lev
Lypa Yuriy
Lypkivskyi Vasyl Ivan
Lypynskyi Vyacheslav
Lysiak-Rudnytskyi Ivan
Lyubchenko Panas
Makhno Nestor
Malanchuk Valentyn
Malaniuk Yevhen
Manuilskyi Dmytro
Marchenko Valery
Marchuk Yevhen
Masol Vitaliy
Mazepa Izaak
Melnyk Andriy
Mikhnovskyi Mykola
Mitrynga Ivan
Moroz Oleksandr
Moroz Valentyn
Mstyslav (Stepan Skrypnyk)
Mudryi Vasyl
Nazaruk Osyp
Ohiyenko Ivan (Ilarion)
Omelianovych-Pavlenko Mykhailo
Osadchuk Bohdan
Osadchyi Mykhailo
Ostapenko Serhiy
Paliiv Dmytro
Pavlychko Dmytro
Petlura Symon
Petrushevych Yevhen
Plyushch Leonid
Postyshev Pavel
Pustovoytenko Valeriy
Pyatakov Georgiy
Pynzenyk Viktor
Rakovsky Khristian
Rebet Lev
Romanchuk Yuliyan
Romzha Fedor
Rudenko Mykola
Rudnytska Milena
Rudnytskyi Ivan (Kedryn)
Rudnytskyi Stepan
Rylskyi Maksym
Shandruk Pavlo
Shapoval Mykyta
Sharayevskyi Nestor
Shcherbytskyi Volodymyr
Shelest Petro
Sheptytskyi Andriy
Sheptytski Kliment
Shukhevych Roman
Shulhyn Oleksandr

Shumskyi Oleksandr
Sichynskyi Myroslav
Skoropadskyi Pavlo
Skrypnyk Mykola
Slezyuk Ivan
Slipyi Josyf
Smal-Stotskyi Roman
Sosiura Volodymyr
Starosolskyi Volodymyr
Stefanyk Vasyl
Sterniuk Volodymyr
Stetsko Yaroslav
Strokach Timofey
Strokata-Karavanska Nina
Studynskyi Kyrylo
Stus Vasyl
Sushko Roman
Sverstyuk Yevhen
Svitlychny Ivan
Symonenko Petro
Teliha Olena
Terelya Yosyp
Timoshenko Semyon
Tselevych Volodymir
Tychyna Pavlo
Tykhyi Oleksy
Tyutyunnyk Yuriy
Udovenko Hennadiy
Ukrainka Lesya
Vasylenko Mykola
Vasylko Mykola
Velychkovskyi Vasyl
Verhun Petro
Vernadskyi Volodymyr
Vitovskyi Dmytro
Volobuyev Mykhailo
Volodymyr (Vasyl Romanyuk)
Voloshyn Avhustyn
Vynnychenko Volodymir
Vyshyvanyi Vasyl (Hapsburg-
    Lothringen Wilhelm)
Vytvytskyi Stepan
Yanovskyi Yury
Yareshchenko Oleksander
Yavorskyi Matviy
Yefremov Serhiy
Yukhnovskyi Ihor
Yurynets Volodymyr
Yushchenko Viktor
Zarytskyi Oleksy
Zatonskyi Volodymyr
Zerov Mykola
Zhurba Halyna
Zlenko Anatoly

Yugoslavia and Its Successor States

Abdić Fikret
Alexander I Karadjordjević
Alexander Obrenović
Alijagić Alija
Aliti Abdurahman
Andov Stojan
Andrić Ivo
Artuković Andrija
Avakumović Jovan
Babić Milan
Bakarić Vladimir
Balantić France
Bašagić-Redžepasić Safetbeg
Bebler Aleš
Bijedić Džemal
Boban Mate
Bozanić Josif
Bučar France
Budak Mile
Budiša Dražen
Bulatović Momir
Bulić Frane
Cankar Ivan
Cincar-Marković Aleksandar
Ćolaković Radoljub
Ćosić Dobrica
Crnjanski Miloš
Crvenkovski Branko
Cuvaj Slavko
Cvetković Dragiša
Cvijić Džuro
Dabčević-Kučar Savka
Davidović Ljubomir
Dimitrije (Pavlović)
Dimitrijević Dragutin (Apis)
Dizdarević Raif
Djaković Djuro
Djilas Milovan
Djindić Zoran
Djukanović Milo
Djuranović Veselin
Drašković Vuk
Drljević Sekula
Drnovšek Janez
Džabić Ali Fehmi
Ehrlich Lambert

Filipović Filip
Frank Josip
Frlec Boris
Ganić Ejup
Gavrilo (Djordje Dožić)
Gavrilović Mihajlo
Georgievski Ljubcho
Gligorov Kiro
Gorkic Milan
Gotovac Vlado
Granić Mate
Grol Milan
Grujić Sava
Hasani Sinan
Hebrang Andrija
Hribar Ivan
Izetbegović Alija
Jakopić Rihard
Janša Janez
Jeftić Bogoljub
Jeglič Anton Bonaventura
Jelavić Ante
Jovanović Dragoljub
Jovanović Slobodan
Jovanović Vladislav
Jovanović Živadin
Kapetanović Izudin
Karadžić Radovan
Kardelj Edvard
Kavčić Stane
Kidrič Boris
Kiš Danilo
Kljusev Nikola
Kocbek Edvard
Kolishevski Lazar
Koneski Blazhe
Kontić Radoje
Korošec Antun
Koštunica Vojislav
Kraigher Sergej
Krajišnik Momčilo
Krek Janez Evangelist
Krek Miha
Krleža Miroslav
Kučan Milan
Kuharić Franjo

Stepinac Alojzije
Stojadinović Milan
Stojanović Ljubomir
Šubašić Ivan
Supilo Franjo
Šuštar Alojzij
Šušteršić Ivan
Šuvar Stipe
Tavčar Ivan
Thaçi Hashim
Thaler Zoran
Tito Josip Broz
Tomanović Lazar
Tomašić Nikola
Tomažić Ivan Jožef
Trajkovski Boris
Trifunovic Miloš (Miša)
Tripalo Mika
Trumbić Ante
Tudjman Franjo

Tupurkovski Vasil
Uzunović Nikola
Valentić Nikica
Varnava (Petar Rosić)
Veselica Marko
Vesnić Milenko
Vilfan Josip
Vlahov Dimitar
Vrhovec Josip
Vujović Radomir
Vukičević Velimir
Vukmanović Svetozar (Tempo)
Vukotić Janko
Xhaferi Arben
Živković Petar
Žolger Ivan
Žujović Sreten
Zulfikarpašić Adil-beg
Župančič Oton